SAXON®
ALGEBRA 2

Teacher's Edition

www.SaxonPublishers.com
800-531-5015

ISBN 13: 978-1-6027-7304-2
ISBN 10: 1-6027-7304-1

Printed in the United States of America

3 4 5 6 7 8 0868 15 14 13 12 11 10 09

Algebra 2 Content Overview

Saxon Secondary Mathematics

Saxon Secondary Mathematics Provides the Time to Learn, Process, and Master

Saxon Math's approach of distributed instruction, practice, and assessment gets results for today's standards, where mastery learning is required of all students. This approach makes the difference in helping high school students master the standards—with an understanding that lasts a lifetime—and is supported by research studies on effective teaching strategies.

Distributed Units of Instruction

Mastery of standards happens at different rates for different students.

Saxon's distributed approach breaks apart traditional units and then distributes and integrates the concepts across the year. This creates a learning curve that provides the time most students need to master every part of every standard. With this structure, no skills or concepts get dropped and students retain what they have learned well beyond the test.

The instruction of related concepts in Saxon is carefully distributed throughout each course.

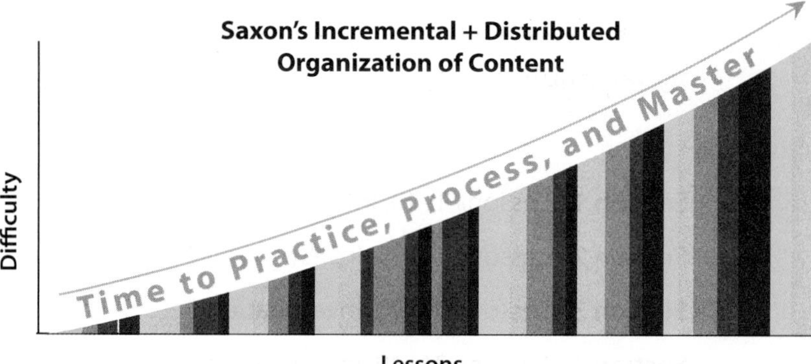

The traditional chapter approach allows only a few weeks for student mastery of concepts

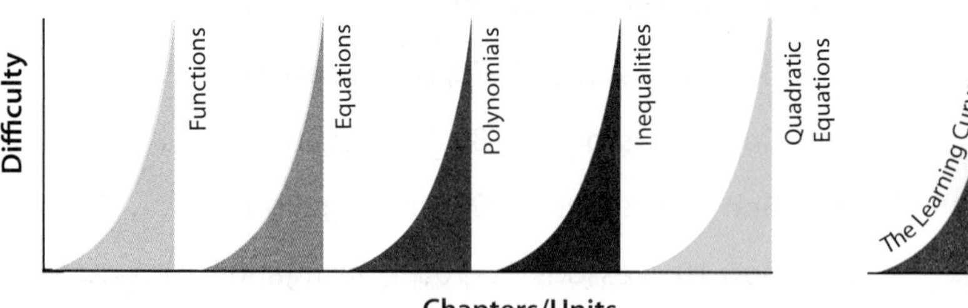

Research shows that there is value in a teaching method that uses small, easily digestible chunks of information within its lessons (Ausubel, 1969; Brophy & Everston, 1976). Studies by Rosenshine and Stevens (1986) and Brophy and Everston (1976) demonstrated the importance of using incremental steps when teaching new information.

Saxon's instructional approach to teaching mathematics is supported by Gagne's (1962, 1965) cumulative-learning theory and Anderson's (1983) ACT theory. Foundational research has also shown that distributed instruction results in greater student achievement (English, Wellburn, & Killian, 1934) and leads to a higher level of recall (Glenberg, 1979; Hintzman, 1974) than does massed instruction.

Continual Practice

Review over time promotes long-term retention.

Students attain a depth of understanding on a particular concept by practicing it over time and in a variety of ways. Saxon Math provides that depth with its continual practice. Every day Saxon students practice not only the day's concept but also concepts and skills from previous lessons.

Saxon's continual practice provides cumulative review throughout the year.

- Skills and concepts are kept alive and reinforced through daily practice.
- Math connections are strengthened and made meaningful.
- Practice sets are rich and varied—just like state assessments and in real life.

The Saxon pedagogy of continual, distributed practice ensures that concepts are committed to students' long-term memory.

Research studies have shown that students, who are taught with a mathematics curriculum using continual practice and review, demonstrate greater math achievement and skill acquisition than do students who are taught with a massed approach (Good & Grouws, 1979; Hardesty, 1986; MacDonald, 1984; Mayfield & Chase, 2002; Ornstein, 1990; Usnick, 1991).

Long-term retention is best served if assignments about a particular skill are spread out in time, rather than concentrated within a short interval (Suydam, 1984). Additional studies have concluded that spaced (distributed) practice results in higher performance than massed practice (Dhaliwal, 1987).

Frequent, Cumulative Assessment

Progress is evaluated throughout the year.

Frequent, cumulative assessments are an integral part of Saxon Math, giving students the opportunity to demonstrate and communicate what they know and can do. Regular evaluation of skills helps teachers pinpoint areas where students may need further practice or reteaching before moving on to new concepts.

The consistently-placed assessments in Saxon Math are cumulative. This approach leads to greater understanding because students reflect on past concepts and make connections across all math strands. With a regular, cumulative method for testing and tracking student mastery, Saxon helps all students achieve the goal of long-term retention.

Research has indicated that well-designed classroom testing programs that are routine rather than an interruption (National Council of Teachers of Mathematics [NCTM], 2000) have a positive impact on later student achievement (Dempster, 1991). Dempster found that higher levels of achievement occur when testing is frequent and cumulative rather than infrequent or related only to content covered since the last test.

According to Fuchs (1995), cumulative assessment that is frequent and distributed has been found to be effective by a number of studies which show that students who are assessed frequently have higher test scores than do students who are assessed infrequently (Blair, 2000; Peckham & Roe, 1977; Rohm, Sparzo, & Bennett, 1986).

A History of Measurable Results

For more than 25 years, both classroom results and scientific research have shown *Saxon Math* to be effective. Saxon's approach to teaching mathematics has been found to be consistently successful for students of varying ability levels and socioeconomic backgrounds.

In addition, *Saxon Math* has been extensively field-tested to guarantee its grade-level appropriateness and effectiveness of explicit instruction.

Clopton, McKeown, McKeown, and Clopton (1999) concluded that

" the Saxon program has many high-quality features of presentation including clear statements of the lesson objectives, daily structure, [and] clear and explicit instructional materials."

Statistical analysis revealed that the average gain over the year was significantly higher for the Saxon group than the group using the traditional approach, despite the fact that the Saxon group began the year at a disadvantage.

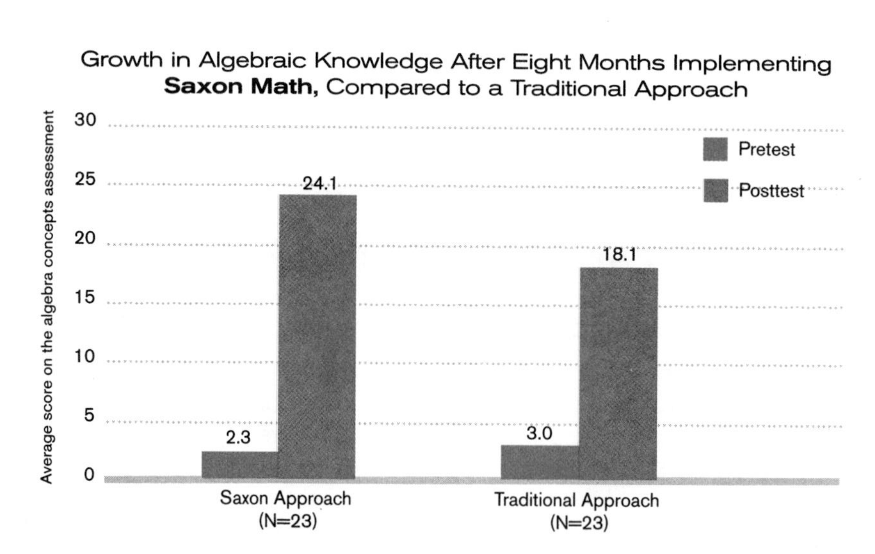

Gain from pretest to posttest was significantly higher for the Saxon approach at the 95% confidence interval. A post-hoc effect size was calculated from the existing data to be d=0.82.

Program Efficacy Studies

Effectiveness of *Saxon Math* on the Achievement of High School Students' Math Performance

A quasi-experimental study by McBee (1982) also demonstrated the effects of the *Saxon Algebra 1* textbook in Oklahoma City Public Schools during one school year.

Data analysis showed that the Saxon group significantly outperformed the group using a traditional chapter text on 11 of the 21 subsections. A deeper analysis of the test scores showed that the Saxon students scored significantly higher than the other students at all ability levels (low, medium, and high).

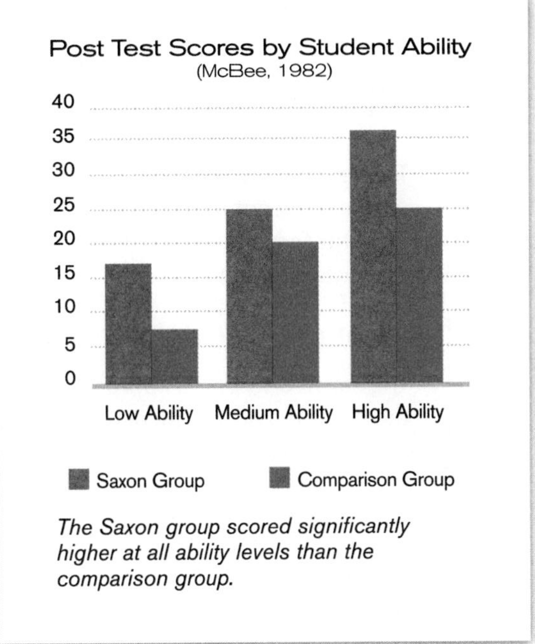

The Saxon group scored significantly higher at all ability levels than the comparison group.

Impact of *Saxon Math* on College Preparation

In a comparison-group study, Sanders (1997) investigated the differences in the math achievement of students preparing for college using *Saxon Math* and the math achievement of those using textbooks with more traditional methods of math instruction. In Georgia, 120 high school juniors from two schools participated in this comparison study. There were 81 students who used various textbooks and 39 students who used a Saxon textbook. At the end of the school year, these students were given the Georgia High School Graduation Tests which contained four math subsections.

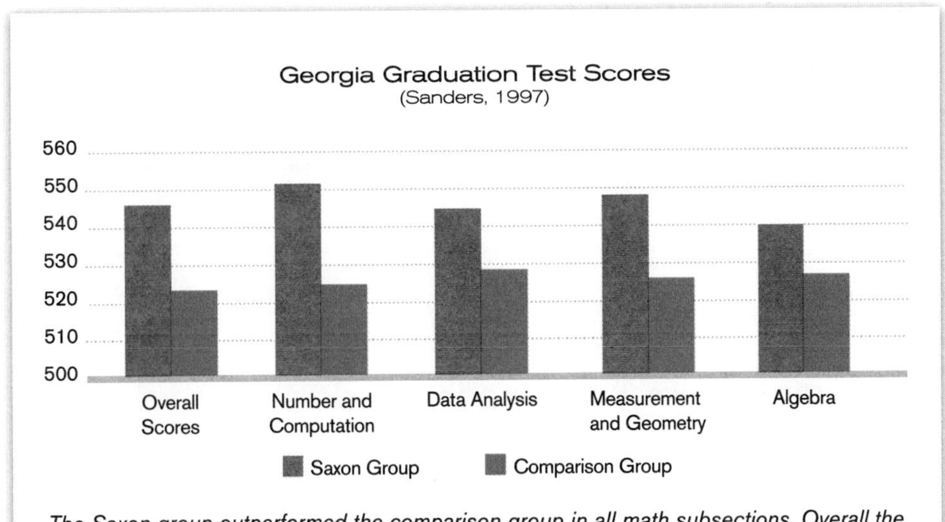

The Saxon group outperformed the comparison group in all math subsections. Overall the Saxon group scored higher than the non-Saxon group.

A comparison of the mean scores of both groups showed that the Saxon group scored significantly higher in all four math subsections of the graduation tests.

It is important to note that these research designs are among the most appropriate methods used to measure the effects of a curriculum on educational outcomes such as student performance (*What Works Clearinghouse*, 2003).

Consistent Lesson Structure That Enhances Mastery

A Three-Part Lesson Plan

This regular format allows students to become comfortable with the lessons and to know what to expect each day. By not including colorful distracting photographs, *Saxon Math* with its predictable format lets students focus solely on the mathematics. The color and vibrancy of mathematics comes from the students' learning.

Recommended Daily Pacing

The Saxon distributed approach is unique in that the focus of the day is mainly on the rich depth of content in the distributed Practice problems.

In a typical 60-min class period, it is suggested that you spend about half of the class period having the students complete the Practice problems. This allows you to have meaningful math conversations with students as they work out the problems.

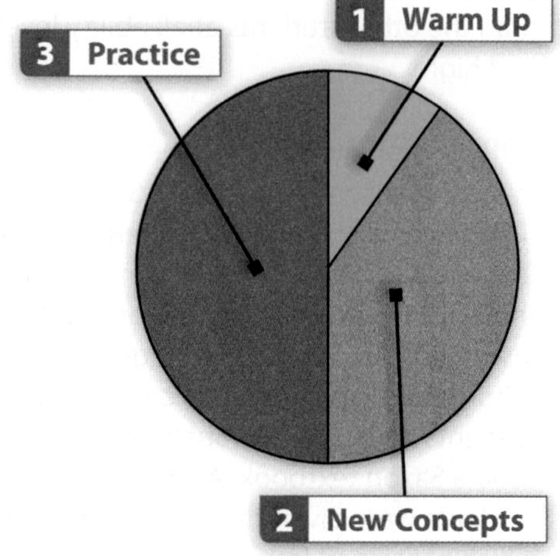

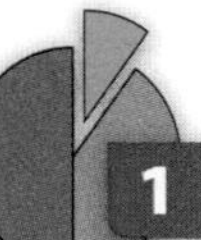

1 Warm Up Prevention through Built-In Intervention

The **Warm Up** at the beginning of every lesson provides practice of those prerequisite skills, concepts, and vocabulary needed to be successful in that day's lesson.

Lesson reference numbers with each problem show where students can go back to get additional help.

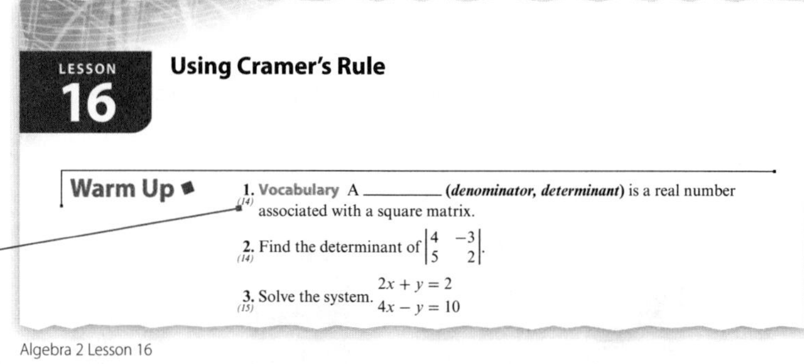

LESSON 16 **Using Cramer's Rule**

Warm Up

1. (14) **Vocabulary** A ________ (*denominator, determinant*) is a real number associated with a square matrix.
2. (14) Find the determinant of $\begin{vmatrix} 4 & -3 \\ 5 & 2 \end{vmatrix}$.
3. (15) Solve the system. $\begin{aligned} 2x + y &= 2 \\ 4x - y &= 10 \end{aligned}$

Algebra 2 Lesson 16

2 New Concepts with Lesson Practice Increase Student Knowledge

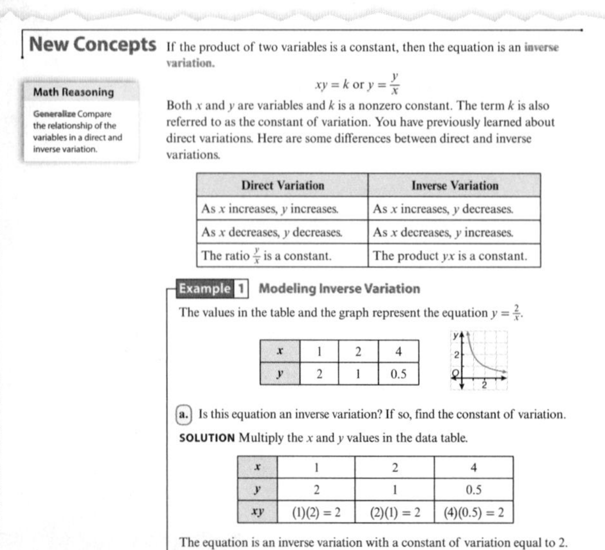

New Concepts If the product of two variables is a constant, then the equation is an **inverse variation**.

$$xy = k \text{ or } y = \frac{k}{x}$$

Math Reasoning

Generalize Compare the relationship of the variables in a direct and inverse variation.

Both x and y are variables and k is a nonzero constant. The term k is also referred to as the constant of variation. You have previously learned about direct variations. Here are some differences between direct and inverse variations.

Direct Variation	Inverse Variation
As x increases, y increases.	As x increases, y decreases.
As x decreases, y decreases.	As x decreases, y increases.
The ratio $\frac{y}{x}$ is a constant.	The product yx is a constant.

Example 1 Modeling Inverse Variation

The values in the table and the graph represent the equation $y = \frac{2}{x}$.

x	1	2	4
y	2	1	0.5

a. Is this equation an inverse variation? If so, find the constant of variation.

SOLUTION Multiply the x and y values in the data table.

x	1	2	4
y	2	1	0.5
xy	$(1)(2) = 2$	$(2)(1) = 2$	$(4)(0.5) = 2$

The equation is an inverse variation with a constant of variation equal to 2.

Each day the **New Concepts** introduces a new topic through clear explanations and Examples that build in-depth understanding and use a variety of methods and real-world applications.

Thinking and reasoning questions, reading math tips, math language notes, cautions, hints, graphing calculator tips—all help students understand how and why the math works.

Algebra 2 Lesson 12

Hint

Since $f(x) = |x + 4| = |x - (-4)|$, the h value is negative, not positive.

Exploration Transforming $f(x) = |x|$

Use a table of values to graph each of the following equations.

a. $f(x) = -|x|$ **b.** $f(x) = \frac{1}{2}|x|$ **c.** $f(x) = |x - 4|$

d. $f(x) = |x + 4|$ **e.** $f(x) = |x| - 4$ **f.** $f(x) = |x| + 4$

The graph of the absolute value function $y = a|x - h| + k$ can be used to model the transformations of the graph of the parent function $f(x) = |x|$.

g. Use the graphs of the functions to describe the effect of h and k on the graph of the parent function.

h. How is the shape and orientation of the graph determined?

i. Can the equation $y = a|x - h| + k$ be used to determine the vertex, or turning point, of the graph?

Algebra 2 Lesson 17

Through the in-lesson **Explorations,** students go into greater depth with the mathematics by investigating math concepts using manipulatives, patterns, simulations, and discovery.

Students work the **Lesson Practice** in class to see how well they understand today's new skills and concepts.

Lesson Practice

a. (Ex 1) Multiply using the FOIL method. $(a + 7)(a - 4)$

b. (Ex 1) Multiply using the FOIL method. $(4x + 5)(3x - 2)$

c. (Ex 2) Multiply $(a + 9)(2a^2 - 6a + 5)$.

d. (Ex 3) Multiply $(r + 3)(r - 6)(r + 2)$ in two different ways using the Associative Property of Equality.

e. (Ex 4) Multiply $(4y + 3)^2$.

f. (Ex 4) Multiply $(7a + 3b)(7a - 3b)$.

g. (Ex 4) Multiply $(5q + 4r)^2$.

h. (Ex 5) The food court at the Galleria Mall forms a rectangle with eateries on all sides. The length of the food court can be expressed as $(x - 15)$ yards. The width of the food court can be expressed as $(x - 12)$ yards. Write a polynomial to express the area of the food court at the Galleria Mall.

Algebra 2 Lesson 19

3 Practice Distributed and Integrated

The distributed **Practice** provides students with a depth of understanding. Because students practice the same topic over several lessons, they have "time to learn" the concept and have multiple opportunities to show that they understand.

The integrated nature of the **Practice** allows students to maintain and build on concepts and skills previously taught. By practicing problems from many lessons every day, students see how math concepts connect to each other and to the real world.

To help students build their mathematical language, *Saxon Math* provides continual exposure to and review of math vocabulary.

The distributed and mixed practice is unpredictable and therefore challenging. It mirrors the format of state tests.

17. (8) **Chemistry** A formula requires that 20 kilograms (kg) of carbon be used to produce 160 kg of a compound. How many kilograms of other components are needed to make 640 kg of the compound?

Justify Determine if these statements are a tautology, a contradiction, or neither. Justify your answer by constructing truth tables.

18. (Inv. 1) $\neg p \rightarrow q$ **19.** (Inv. 1) $\neg p \vee q$

20. (10) **Consumer** Nerissa's car can travel between 380 and 410 miles on a full tank of gas. She filled her gas tank and drove 45 miles. How many miles m can she drive without running out of gas?

21. (3) **Astronomy** The speed of light is about 3×10^8 meters/second. If Saturn's distance from Earth is about 1.321×10^{12} meters, about how many seconds would it take light to reach Saturn from Earth? Round the answer to the nearest second.

22. (3) **Earth Science** The garter snake is a small snake that is typically no more than 6×10^{-4} km in length. About how many garter snakes would it take to equal the circumference of the earth at the equator, if its circumference measures about 4.0076×10^4 km? Write the answer in scientific notation rounded to the nearest ten thousandth.

Analyze Determine if the expressions are polynomials. If the expression is a polynomial, rewrite it in standard form. If the expression is not a polynomial, explain why.

***23.** (11) $5x^2 + 3x^4 + 2$

***24.** (11) $\sqrt{3x + 5x^3}$

Classify the polynomial expressions by their degree and by the number of terms.

***25.** (11) $7x^3 + 3x^2 + 5x$ ***26.** (11) $x^1 + 5x^0$

Simplify the expression.

***27.** (11) $(7x^3 + 3x^2 + 5x) - (3x^3 + x)$

28. (4) **Multiple Choice** Choose a letter that represents a set of x- and y-values that makes the equation $y = \frac{1}{2}x + 4$ true.

A $x = 2, y = 4$ **B** $x = 6, y = 6$

C $x = 4, y = 6$ **D** $x = 4, y = 8$

Graphing Calculator Multiply the matrices. Check using a graphing calculator.

***29.** (9) $\begin{bmatrix} 2 & -3 & 4 \\ 5 & 8 & -1 \\ 7 & 0 & 9 \end{bmatrix} \cdot \begin{bmatrix} -4 & 7 \\ 0 & 1 \\ 3 & 6 \end{bmatrix}$

***30.** (9) $\begin{bmatrix} 4 & -1 \\ 6 & -2 \end{bmatrix} \cdot \begin{bmatrix} -1 & \frac{1}{2} & 0 \\ -2 & 4 & -3 \end{bmatrix}$

76 *Saxon Algebra 2*

Algebra 2 Lesson 11

Students get a **test prep** experience every day!

Differentiated Instruction: Built-in support for all students

Lesson Structure *Saxon Math* provides a predictable routine that enables all learners to be successful. By focusing on the mathematics and not the "fluff" seen in other math texts, *Saxon Math* makes higher-level mathematical thinking accessible for every student.

For All Learners

***Saxon Math* provides additional support that can be valuable to all types of learners.**

In the student text, there are **Hints** for extra help and **Cautions** to prevent common errors.

Explorations and **Labs** in the student edition allow students to investigate mathematics in more depth through manipulatives, technology, patterning, and other methods.

Alternate Method and **Manipulative Use** show different ways to solve the same problem.

Error Alerts in the teacher's edition offer additional ways that teachers can help students avoid common misunderstandings.

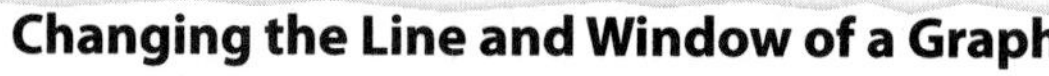

Changing the Line and Window of a Graph

Graphing Calculator Lab (Use with Lessons 17 and 39)

Adjusting the Viewing Window

The viewing window of the graphing calculator can be adjusted to best display a graph.

1. Graph the function $y = |2x - 3| + 1$.

2. Center the window on the vertex.

Hint

If you choose to expand a row or column that has a zero, it makes your calculations easier.

NDOW
in=-8.5
ax=11.5
cl=1
in=-9
ax=11
cl=1
es=1

ALTERNATE METHOD FOR EXAMPLES 3 AND 4

Polynomials can be added and subtracted vertically. Tell students to line up like terms vertically and perform the indicated operation.

Adding Polynomials:

$$\begin{array}{r} 2x^3 - 3x^2 + x - 5 \\ + \quad - x^2 \quad\quad + 5 \\ \hline 2x^3 - 4x^2 + x \quad\quad \end{array}$$

Subtracting Polynomials:

$$\begin{array}{r} 5x^3 - 3x^2 \quad\quad \\ -(2x^3 - x^2 \quad + 4) \\ \hline 3x^3 - 2x^2 \quad - 4 \end{array}$$

Samples from Algebra 2

English Learners

English learners will find structures in *Saxon Math* to help them acquire mathematical understanding and language. Visual models, activities and labs, math conversations, and language prompts all help students in their daily learning.

The **English Learners tips** focus on language acquisition, not on reteaching or simplifying the math. These tips are based on a proven approach with these steps:

- Define and Hear
- Model and Connect
- Discuss and Explain
- Apply and Use

The **Multilingual Glossary** provides math vocabulary and definitions in 13 languages: Armenian, Arabic, Cantonese, English, Hmong, Khmer, Korean, Punjabi, Russian, Spanish, Tagalog, Urdu, and Vietnamese.

The **English Learners Handbook** offers professional development and practical classroom tips on teaching mathematics to English learners.

The **Glossary** in the student textbook provides a Spanish translation of each math term and definition.

ENGLISH LEARNERS

For example 2, explain the meaning of the word intercept. Say:

"The word intercept means to interrupt progress. In math, the word intercept is a point where the graph crosses a coordinate axis."

Graph the line $x + y = 4$ on the board. Make sure the graph shows the x and y intercepts clearly. Point to the x-intercept and say:

"The line has an intercept at $x = 4$."

Have students identify the point where the line intercepts the y-axis answering with the sentence: "The y-intercept of the line is at $y = \ldots$." 4

Samples from Algebra 2

Struggling Learners

Saxon Math includes a number of support features to help various categories of struggling learners.

The daily **Warm Up** exercises help students with prerequisite skills needed in order to be successful.

The **Skills Bank** in the student textbook offers instruction and practice on prerequisite skills.

Prerequisite Skills Intervention gives students more instruction and practice on prerequisite skills.

The **Reteaching Masters** provide intervention pages of instruction and stepped-out practice for the new concepts in every lesson.

Inclusion tips help teachers to accommodate special needs in the classroom.

Adaptations for Saxon Math provides complete and parallel support for special needs students.
See pp. T12–T13 for details.

INCLUSION

Suggest that students use different color pens or pencils to circle, underline, or mark the like terms in polynomials. Then tell students to combine the terms by color.

INCLUSION

Draw a coordinate grid on the board. Then have students demonstrate how the domain restrictions– *reals, integers, whole numbers, positive integers,* and *negative integers*– affect functions added or subtracted geometrically on the coordinate grid.

Samples from Algebra 2

Advanced Learners

Saxon Math provides advanced learners with many opportunities for expanding their concept development.

A **Challenge** problem is provided for every lesson.

Challenge and Enrichment Masters offer more in-depth extensions of the content.

The **Extend the Example, Extend the Problem,** and **Extend the Exploration** suggestions in the teacher's edition provide even more ways to engage the advanced learner.

CHALLENGE

A quadrilateral has coordinates (3, 3), (4, 0), (0, −1) and (−3, 1). Use what you know about finding the area of triangles to find the area of the quadrilateral. 15.5 sq units

Problem 13
Extend the problem
"What is the actual percent decrease?" 33.3%

CHALLENGE

Have students measure the classroom and use the information in Problem 18 to determine the number of pennies that would fit in the classroom.

Samples from Algebra 2

Adaptations for *Saxon Math:* Complete and Parallel Support for Special Populations

The flexible curriculum design of Adaptations for *Saxon Math* can be integrated into inclusion classrooms, pullout programs, or self-contained resource classrooms, ensuring that special needs students keep pace with the core curriculum.

Saxon Math Core Program

SAXON ALGEBRA 1

SAXON GEOMETRY

SAXON ALGEBRA 2

Practice Distributed and Integrated

***1.** (21) **Safety** For every 4 feet a ladder rises, the base of a ladder should be placed 1 foot away from the bottom of a building. If the base of a ladder is 7 feet from the bottom of a building, find the height the ladder rises up the building?

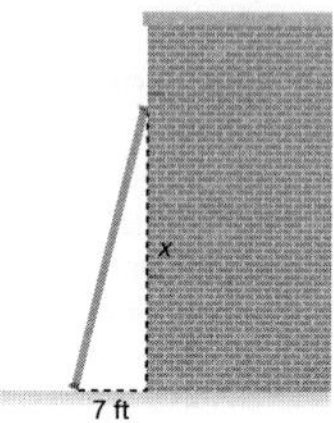

2. (2) What is a term of an algebraic expression?

***3.** (21) **Write** Explain how to use inverse operations to solve $\frac{2}{3}x = 8$.

***4.** (19) **Physics** In physics equations, a change in a quantity is represented by the delta symbol, Δ. A change in velocity, Δv, is calculated using the equation $\Delta v = v_f - v_i$, where v_i is the initial velocity and v_f is the final velocity. If a cart has an initial velocity of 5 miles per second and experiences a change in velocity of 2 miles per second, what is the final velocity of the cart?

5. (20) Graph the ordered pair $(-2, 6)$ on a coordinate plane.

6. (31) **Geometry** The length of a rectangular picture frame is 3 times the width.
a. Draw a picture of the picture frame and label the dimensions.
b. Write an expression for the area of the frame.

7. (20) Complete the table for $y = 2x + 7$.

x	-5	1	4
y			

***8.** (21) Solve $\frac{x}{3} = 5$.

***9.** (21) **Multiple-Choice** Which step can you use first to solve $-\frac{x}{9} = -52$?
A Multiply both sides by 9.
B Multiply both sides by -9.
C Divide both sides by -52.
D Divide both sides by 52.

***10.** (19) **Estimate** Alan makes $1 for each snow cone he sells. Alan calculates his profit by subtracting the daily cost of $195 to run the stand from the total number of snow cones he sells each day. How many snow cones does Alan need to sell to make a profit of $200 a day?

124 *Saxon Algebra 1*

Support for Learning Disabilities

The unique design organizes exercises in ways that allow success for students with learning disabilities, such as:

- Visual-motor integration
- Number reversal in reading
- Distractibility or lack of focus
- Verbal explanation
- Math anxiety
- Receptive language
- Spatial organization
- Number reversal in reading and copy work

Adapted Practice Problems and Assessments

The carefully structured layout of the Practice pages helps special needs students focus on mastering the concept, rather than figuring out the directions.

Saxon Math Adapted Pages

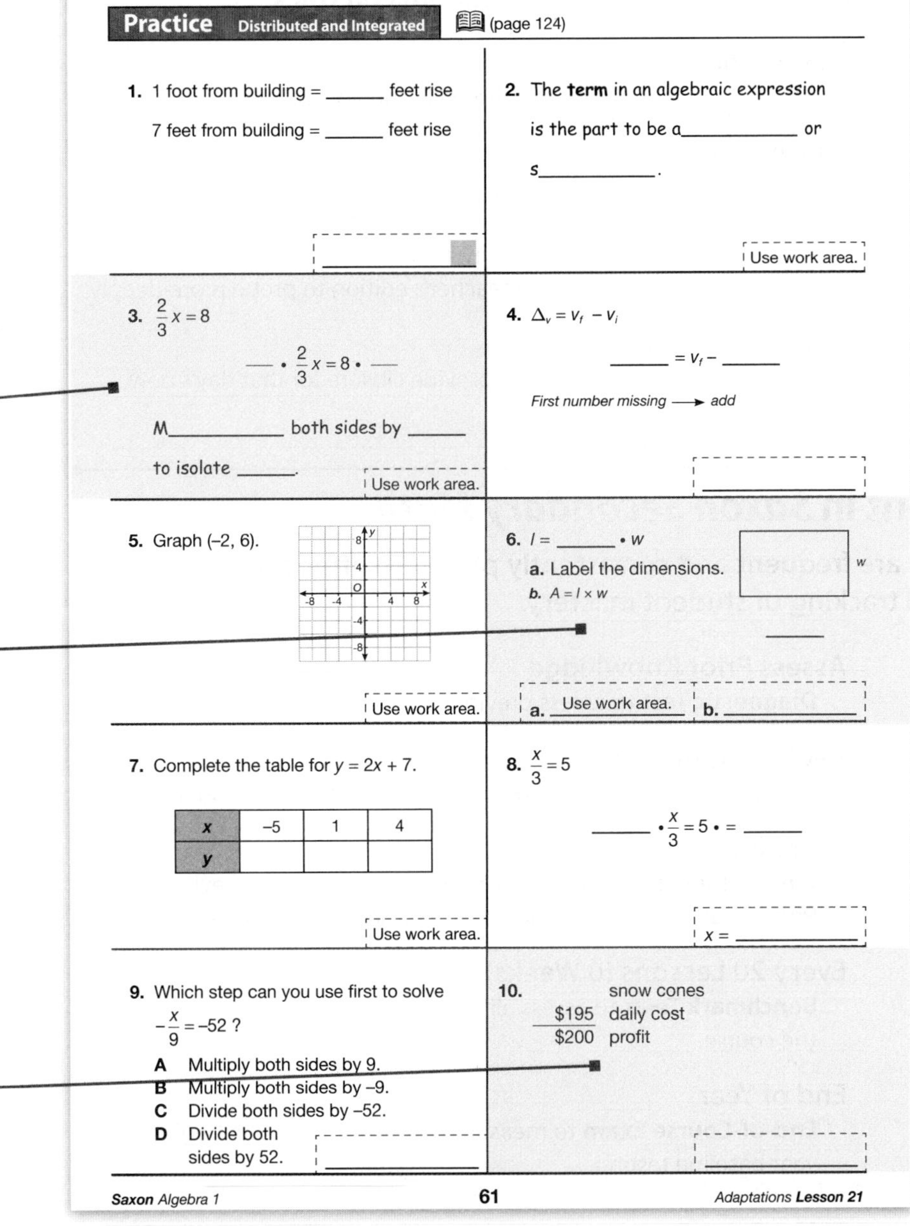

Practice Distributed and Integrated (page 124)

1. 1 foot from building = ______ feet rise
   7 feet from building = ______ feet rise

2. The **term** in an algebraic expression is the part to be a__________ or s__________.
   Use work area.

3. $\frac{2}{3}x = 8$
   $\_\_\_ \cdot \frac{2}{3}x = 8 \cdot \_\_\_$
   M__________ both sides by ______ to isolate ______.
   Use work area.

4. $\Delta_v = v_f - v_i$
   ______ $= v_f -$ ______
   First number missing ⟶ add

5. Graph (–2, 6).
   Use work area.

6. $l =$ ______ $\cdot w$
   a. Label the dimensions.
   b. $A = l \times w$
   a. Use work area. b. ______

7. Complete the table for $y = 2x + 7$.

x	–5	1	4
y			

Use work area.

8. $\frac{x}{3} = 5$
   $\_\_\_ \cdot \frac{x}{3} = 5 \cdot = \_\_\_$
   $x =$ ______

9. Which step can you use first to solve $-\frac{x}{9} = -52$?
   A Multiply both sides by 9.
   B Multiply both sides by –9.
   C Divide both sides by –52.
   D Divide both sides by 52.

10. snow cones
    \$195 daily cost
    \$200 profit

Saxon Algebra 1 61 *Adaptations* **Lesson 21**

Adaptations for *Saxon Algebra 1, Geometry,* and *Algebra 2*

This unique program is available in these easy-to-use components:

- **Classroom Package**
  Teaching Guide, Student Reference Guide, CD of all adapted pages
- **Student Workbook**
  consumable workbook of all adapted practice pages
- **Assessment Masters**
  blackline masters of all adapted tests
- **Student Reference Guide**
  for each individual student

Ongoing Assessment and Intervention

Assessments can be categorized in two ways, both of which are valuable and necessary in helping students succeed in mathematics.

Formative Assessment in *Saxon Secondary Math*

The instructional design of *Saxon Math* effectively helps you to identify immediately any learning gaps and to provide successful intervention to keep students on track.

Formative Assessment
• *Purpose:* Improvement
• Assess continuously **during** teaching to influence learning.
• Use for **immediate feedback** to intervene, if necessary, on a particular concept.

Before the Lesson

Warm Up to check prerequisite skills and vocabulary

During the Lesson

Reasoning questions to clarify students' thinking
Lesson Practice to assess today's New Concepts
Practice problems to check previously-taught content
Math Conversations in the teacher's edition to probe more deeply

After the Lesson

Check for understanding to provide closure for that day's new concept

Summative Assessment in *Saxon Secondary Math*

The assessments in *Saxon Math* are frequent and consistently placed to offer a regular method of ongoing testing and tracking of student mastery.

Summative Assessment
• *Purpose:* Accountability
• Assess periodically **after** teaching to gather evidence of learning.
• Use to **judge** learning, usually in the form of a grade or score.

Assess Prior Knowledge

Diagnostic Test to assess previous year's content

Beginning of Year

Baseline Test to benchmark knowledge of this year's course material

Every Five Lessons

Cumulative Test to check mastery of concepts from previous lessons
Performance Task a theme-based, rubric-scored assessment

Every 20 Lessons (6 Weeks)

Benchmark Tests to assess all concepts and skills up to that point in the course

End of Year

End-of-Course Exam to measure progress against the beginning-of-year baseline testing

Intervention Support

Use these resources to intervene when students are not showing progress on formative assessments or are scoring below 80% on summative assessments.

- Prerequisite Skills Intervention
- Skills Bank
- Reteaching Masters
- Scaffolding questions in teacher's edition
- Worked-out Examples in student text
- Additional Examples in teacher's edition
- Test and Practice Generator

Components

Resources for Teaching

turn page

Technology
- Student Edition eBook
- Teacher's Edition eBook
- Resources and Planner CD
- Instructional Presentations CD
- Online support

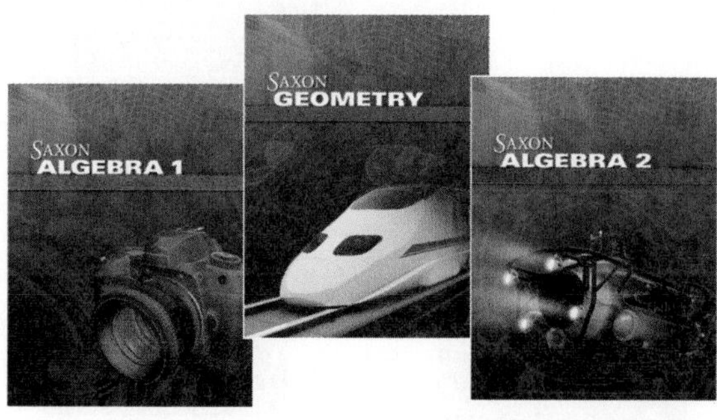

Student Edition

Teacher's Edition

Instructional Masters
teaching tools and recording forms

Technology Lab Masters
activities for graphing calculator and geometry software

Warm Up and Teaching Transparencies
teaching tools and student edition Warm Up

Solutions Manual
full solutions to all problems in student text

Resources for Practice and Assessment

turn page

Technology
- Examview™ Test and Practice Generator
- Online support

Student Edition Practice Workbook
all Practice problems; no need to carry the textbook home

Course Assessments
diagnostic, baseline, cumulative, benchmark tests, and performance tasks

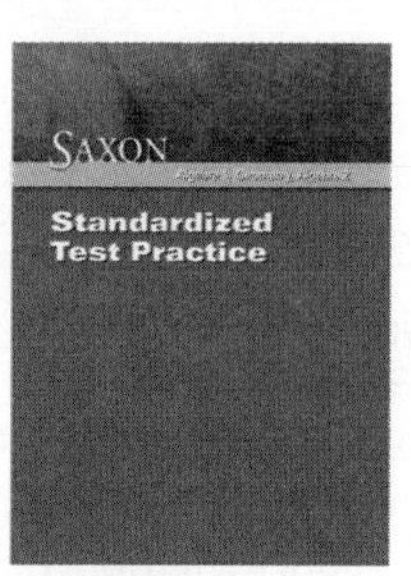

Standardized Test Practice
diagnostic test, standards practice, sample tests

College Entrance Exam Practice
practice tests for PSAT, SAT, ACT

Components

For description of additional print components, turn back one page.

Resources for Differentiated Instruction

Reteaching Masters
one for every lesson and investigation

Challenge and Enrichment Masters
every challenge problem from TE plus additional enrichment sheets

Prerequisite Skills Intervention
pre-course skills and remediation

Adaptations for Saxon Math
A parallel program for special populations
(See pages T12–T13.)

Multilingual Glossary
terms and definitions in 13 languages

English Learners Handbook
guidance for modifying instruction for English learners; background on specific language issues

Technology

Student Edition eBook
complete student text on CD

Teacher's Edition eBook
complete teacher's edition on CD

Resources and Planner CD
electronic pacing calendar with standards, plus PDF resources

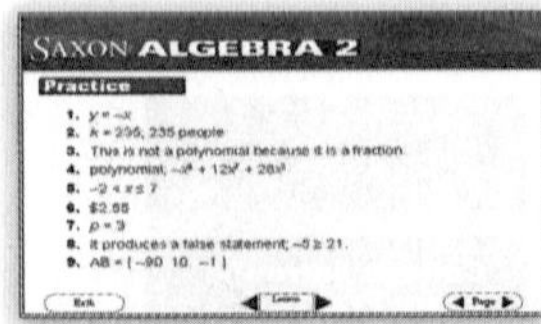

Instructional Presentations CD
Interactivities that model and demonstrate key concepts to engage students and enhance learning. These are correlated to program lessons.

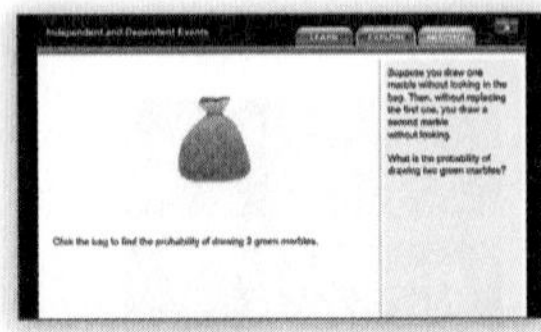

Online Support
Interactivities, graphing calculator tutorials and labs, multilingual glossary, math tools, homework help www.SaxonMathResources.com

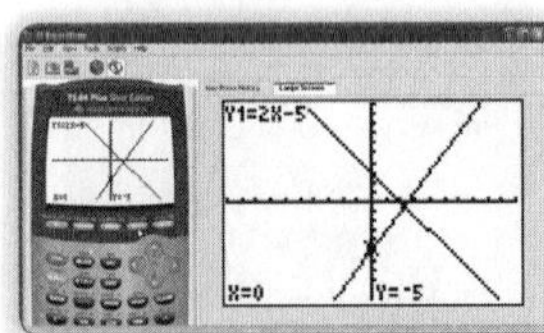

Texas Instruments (TI) Resources CD
keystroke tutorials, TI graphing calculator activities, TI application guides

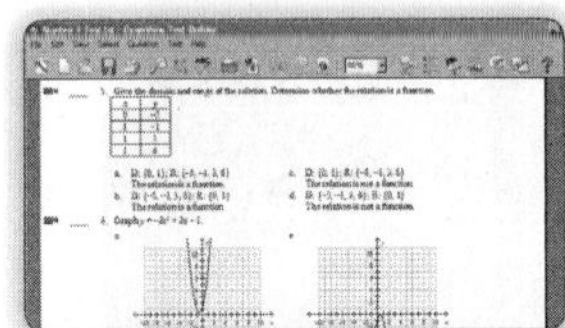

Test and Practice Generator—Examview™
LAN, web, or print based customizable testing with dynamic items; track student progress with reports

Table of Contents

Section 1: Lessons 1-10, Investigation 1

DISTRIBUTED STRANDS

- Number Sense and Foundations of Algebra
- Linear Functions
- Matrices
- Polynomials and Polynomial Functions
- Rational and Radical Functions
- Linear Systems
- Probability and Statistics
- Quadratic Functions
- Trigonometry
- Exponential and Logarithmic Functions
- Conic Sections
- Sequences, Series, and Logic

TABLE OF CONTENTS

Section 2: Lessons 11-20, Investigation 2

Section 3: Lessons 21-30, Investigation 3

DISTRIBUTED STRANDS

- Number Sense and Foundations of Algebra
- Linear Functions
- Matrices
- Polynomials and Polynomial Functions
- Rational and Radical Functions
- Linear Systems
- Probability and Statistics
- Quadratic Functions
- Trigonometry
- Exponential and Logarithmic Functions
- Conic Sections
- Sequences, Series, and Logic

Section 4: Lessons 31-40, Investigation 4

Section 5: Lessons 41-50, Investigation 5

DISTRIBUTED STRANDS

- Number Sense and Foundations of Algebra
- Linear Functions
- Matrices
- Polynomials and Polynomial Functions
- Rational and Radical Functions
- Linear Systems
- Probability and Statistics
- Quadratic Functions
- Trigonometry
- Exponential and Logarithmic Functions
- Conic Sections
- Sequences, Series, and Logic

TABLE OF CONTENTS

Section 6: Lessons 51-60, Investigation 6

Section 7: Lessons 61-70, Investigation 7

DISTRIBUTED STRANDS

- Number Sense and Foundations of Algebra
- Linear Functions
- Matrices
- Polynomials and Polynomial Functions
- Rational and Radical Functions
- Linear Systems
- Probability and Statistics
- Quadratic Functions
- Trigonometry
- Exponential and Logarithmic Functions
- Conic Sections
- Sequences, Series, and Logic

TABLE OF CONTENTS

Section 8: Lessons 71-80, Investigation 8

Section 9: Lessons 81-90, Investigation 9

DISTRIBUTED STRANDS

- Number Sense and Foundations of Algebra
- Linear Functions
- Matrices
- Polynomials and Polynomial Functions
- Rational and Radical Functions
- Linear Systems
- Probability and Statistics
- Quadratic Functions
- Trigonometry
- Exponential and Logarithmic Functions
- Conic Sections
- Sequences, Series, and Logic

Section 10: Lessons 91-100, Investigation 10

Section 11: Lessons 101-110, Investigation 11

DISTRIBUTED STRANDS

- Number Sense and Foundations of Algebra
- Linear Functions
- Matrices
- Polynomials and Polynomial Functions
- Rational and Radical Functions
- Linear Systems
- Probability and Statistics
- Quadratic Functions
- Trigonometry
- Exponential and Logarithmic Functions
- Conic Sections
- Sequences, Series, and Logic

TABLE OF CONTENTS

Section 12: Lessons 111-119, Investigation 12

Content By Strand

LESSON	
NUMBER SENSE AND FOUNDATIONS OF ALGEBRA	
1	Using Properties of Real Numbers
2	Evaluating Expressions and Combining Like Terms
3	Using Rules of Exponents
6	Finding Percent of Change
10	Solving and Graphing Inequalities
18	Calculating with Units of Measure
LINEAR FUNCTIONS	
LAB 1	Graphing a Function and Building a Table
4	Identifying Functions and Using Function Notation
7	Solving Linear Equations
8	Finding Direct Variation
LAB 3	Calculating Points on a Graph
13	Graphing Linear Equations I
LAB 4	Setting the Viewing Window and Using Different Line Tools
17	Solving Equations and Inequalities with Absolute Value
20	Performing Operations with Functions
22	Analyzing Continuous, Discontinuous, and Discrete Functions
26	Writing the Equation of a Line
34	Graphing Linear Equations II
36	Using Parallel and Perpendicular Lines
39	Graphing Linear Inequalities in Two Variables
LAB 8	Applying Linear and Median Regression
45	Finding the Line of Best Fit
50	Finding Inverses of Relations and Functions
53	Performing Composition of Functions
79	Understanding Piecewise Functions
INV 9	Understanding Step Functions
MATRICES	
LAB 2	Storing and Recalling Data in a Matrix
5	Using Matrices to Organize Data and to Solve Problems
9	Multiplying Matrices
14	Finding Determinants
16	Using Cramer's Rule
32	Solving Linear Systems with Matrix Inverses
INV 4	Understanding Cryptography

LESSON	
99	Using Vectors
104	Finding Transformations

SEQUENCES, SERIES, AND LOGIC

INV 1	Logic and Truth Tables
INV 8	Finding the Area Under a Curve
92	Finding Arithmetic Sequences
97	Finding Geometric Sequences
105	Finding Arithmetic Series
113	Using Geometric Series
INV 12	Using Mathematical Induction

POLYNOMIALS AND POLYNOMIAL FUNCTIONS

11	Understanding Polynomials
19	Multiplying Polynomials
23	Factoring Polynomials
38	Dividing Polynomials Using Long Division
51	Using Synthetic Division
61	Understanding Advanced Factoring
66	Solving Polynomial Equations
76	Finding Polynomial Roots I
85	Finding Polynomial Roots II
95	Factoring Higher-Order Polynomials
101	Making Graphs of Polynomial Functions
106	Using the Fundamental Theorem of Algebra
111	Transforming Polynomial Functions

RATIONAL AND RADICAL FUNCTIONS

12	Solving Inverse Variation Problems
28	Simplifying Rational Expressions
31	Multiplying and Dividing Rational Expressions
37	Adding and Subtracting Rational Expressions
40	Simplifying Radical Expressions
44	Rationalizing Denominators
48	Understanding Complex Fractions
59	Using Fractional Exponents
70	Solving Radical Equations I
75	Graphing Radical Functions
84	Solving Rational Equations
88	Solving Abstract Equations
94	Solving Rational Inequalities
100	Graphing Rational Functions I
107	Graphing Rational Functions II

LESSON	
	LINEAR SYSTEMS
15	Solving Systems of Equations by Graphing
INV 2	Solving Parametric Equations
21	Solving Systems of Equations Using the Substitution Method
24	Solving Systems of Equations Using the Elimination Method
29	Solving Systems of Equations in Three Variables
INV 3	Graphing Three Linear Equations in Three Variables
43	Solving Systems of Linear Inequalities
54	Using Linear Programming
	PROBABILITY AND STATISTICS
LAB 5	Entering a List of Data and Using the Stat Plot Feature
LAB 6	Using the 1-Variable and 2-Variable Statistic Features
25	Finding Measures of Central Tendency and Dispersion
33	Applying Counting Principles
LAB 7	Calculating Permutations and Combinations
42	Finding Permutations and Combinations
49	Using the Binomial Theorem
INV 5	Finding the Binomial Distribution
55	Finding Probability
60	Distinguishing Between Mutually Exclusive and Independent Events
68	Finding Conditional Probability
INV 7	Collecting Data
LAB 11	Calculating Confidence Intervals
73	Using Sampling
LAB 12	Calculating Normal Distribution Areas and Z-Scores
80	Finding the Normal Distribution
LAB 14	Determining Regression Models
116	Finding Best Fit Models
118	Recognizing Misleading Data
	QUADRATIC FUNCTIONS
27	Connecting the Parabola with the Quadratic Function
30	Applying Transformations to the Parabola and Determining the Minimum or Maximum
35	Solving Quadratic Equations I
58	Completing the Square
INV 6	Deriving the Quadratic Formula
62	Using Complex Numbers
65	Using the Quadratic Formula
69	Simplifying Complex Expressions
74	Finding the Discriminant
78	Solving Quadratic Equations II
83	Writing Quadratic Equations from Roots

LESSON	
89	Solving Quadratic Inequalities
	TRIGONOMETRY
41	Using Pythagorean Theorem and Distance Formula
46	Understanding Trigonometric Functions and their Reciprocals
LAB 9	Changing Modes and Using the Trigonometry Keys along with their Inverses
52	Using Two Special Right Triangles
56	Finding Angles of Rotation
63	Understanding the Unit Circle and Radian Measures
67	Finding Inverse Trigonometric Functions
71	Using the Law of Sines
77	Using the Law of Cosines
82	Graphing Sine and Cosine Functions
86	Translating Sine and Cosine Functions
90	Graphing the Tangent Function
96	Using Polar Coordinates
INV 10	Graphing Polar Models
103	Graphing Reciprocal Trigonometric Functions
108	Using Fundamental Trigonometric Identities
INV 11	Using De Moivre's Theorem
112	Using Sum and Difference Identities
115	Finding Double-Angle and Half-Angle Identities
119	Solving Trigonometric Equations
	EXPONENTIAL AND LOGARITHMIC FUNCTIONS
47	Graphing Exponential Functions
57	Finding Exponential Growth and Decay
LAB 10	Using the Log Keys
64	Using Logarithms
72	Using the Properties of Logarithms
81	Using Natural Logarithms
87	Evaluating Logarithmic Expressions
93	Solving Exponential Equations and Inequalities
102	Solving Logarithmic Equations and Inequalities
110	Graphing Logarithmic Functions
	CONIC SECTIONS
LAB 13	Graphing Circles and Polar Equations
91	Making Graphs and Solving Equations of Circles
98	Making Graphs and Using Equations of Ellipses
109	Making Graphs and Using Equations of Hyperbolas
114	Identifying Conic Sections
117	Solving Systems of Nonlinear Equations

Pacing Guide

Pacing for the Year

The guide below will help you decide how to pace your instruction across the school year and how much time you have left in your schedule for other instructional or assessment options. For example, Benchmark Tests can be administered after every 20 lessons in order to check student progress. You can also assign Reteaching Masters or Challenge and Enrichment Masters to help struggling or advanced students.

Pacing Suggestions

The suggestions below for pacing each Section in a 45-minute class include one Lesson per day, one Investigation per day, and cumulative testing on two days. *See pages T8–T9 for more about the daily lesson structure.*

The suggestions on the next page will help you to sequence the instruction, practice, and assessment within a 90-minute block schedule.

Page A in each Section Overview gives day-by-day pacing for the lessons within that Section.

Section	Core Material to Cover	45-Minute Class	90-Minute Block *
1	Lessons 1–10; Investigation 1; Cumulative Test 1	12 days	6 days
2	Lessons 11–20; Investigation 2; Cumulative Tests 2, 3	13 days	7 days
3	Lessons 21–30; Investigation 3; Cumulative Tests 4, 5	13 days	6 days
4	Lessons 31–40; Investigation 4; Cumulative Tests 6, 7	13 days	7 days
5	Lessons 41–50; Investigation 5; Cumulative Tests 8, 9	13 days	6 days
6	Lessons 51–60; Investigation 6; Cumulative Tests 10, 11	13 days	7 days
7	Lessons 61–70; Investigation 7; Cumulative Tests 12, 13	13 days	6 days
8	Lessons 71–80; Investigation 8; Cumulative Tests 14, 15	13 days	7 days
9	Lessons 81–90; Investigation 9; Cumulative Tests 16, 17	13 days	6 days
10	Lessons 91–100; Investigation 10; Cumulative Tests 18, 19	13 days	7 days
11	Lessons 101–110; Investigation 11; Cumulative Tests 20, 21	13 days	6 days
12	Lessons 111–119; Investigation 12; Cumulative Tests 22, 23	13 days	7 days
	TOTAL	**155 days**	**78 days**

*** For block scheduling, the pace is consistent. However, on some days, the suggested pacing calls for teaching an Investigation and the following lesson, which is in the next section.**

You can use the Resources and Planner CD to map out your yearly schedule. The software can create a personalized schedule based on your school's calendar. If unexpected school cancellations or other events occur, you can easily use the pacing calendar in the software to produce a revised schedule.

Daily Pacing for Block Scheduling

For block class periods of 90 minutes, you should expect to (1) teach two lessons per class or (2) teach one lesson and give a Cumulative Test. Sometimes the lesson might be an Investigation so you may need to adjust your pacing accordingly. The charts below give just one suggestion on how to sequence your class instruction for each part of the class period.

Suggested Class Sequence for Non-Test Days

Two Lessons
Project the Warm Up from the first lesson. Have students work the problems as they enter the classroom.
Go over homework from the day before.
Instruct the New Concept from the first lesson.
Have students work the Lesson Practice from the first lesson. Also have students work the problems for the first lesson that are in the Practice. These problems are indicated by the lesson's number in the student text. If students have trouble sitting for the entire 90 minutes, you may want to have them work in groups or at the board.
Project the Warm Up from the second lesson.
Instruct the New Concept from the second lesson.
Have students work the Lesson Practice from the second lesson. Check their work while they are completing the problems.
Assign the remaining Practice problems from the first lesson and the Practice problems from the second lesson. Have students work some problems in class and complete the rest for homework.

One Lesson, One Investigation
Project the Warm Up from the lesson. Have students work the problems as they enter the classroom.
Go over homework from the day before.
Engage the students by working the Investigation in small groups or as a whole-class discussion activity.
Instruct the New Concept from the lesson.
Have students work the Lesson Practice from the lesson. Check their work while they are completing the problems.
Assign the Investigation Practice problems and the Practice problems from the lesson. With the remaining time, have students begin work on the problems in class. Assign the rest as homework.

Suggested Class Sequence for Test Days

Cumulative Test, One Lesson
Have students take the Cumulative Test.
Project the Warm Up from the new lesson. Have students work the problems.
Go over homework from the day before.
Instruct the New Concept from the new lesson.
Have students work the Lesson Practice from the new lesson. Check their work while they are completing the problems.
Assign the Practice problems from the new lesson. Have students work some problems in class and complete the rest for homework. You can also assign the Performance Task, either as class work or homework.

Cumulative Test, One Investigation
Have students take the Cumulative Test.
Go over homework from the day before.
Engage the students by working the Investigation in small groups or as a whole-class discussion activity.
Assign the Investigation Practice problems. Have students begin work in class and complete the rest for homework. You can also assign the Performance Task, either as class work or homework.

Teaching Over Two Years

Sometimes Algebra 1 and Geometry are taught over two years. The pace is much slower and more time can be spent to explain concepts and to check thoroughly each homework Practice set. You can use additional program resources to adjust the pacing or to cover particular topics in more depth. Here is one suggested plan for each of the two years.

Year 1
Lessons 1–60
Investigations 1–6
Use Benchmark Test 3 after lesson 60 as the end-of-course exam for the first half of the book.

Year 2
Lessons 61–120
Investigations 7–12
Use the End-of-Course Exam to assess student progress on the entire course.

Lesson Planner

Lesson	New Concepts
1	Using Properties of Real Numbers
2	Evaluating Expressions and Combining Like Terms
3	Using Rules of Exponents
LAB 1	*Graphing Calculator Lab:* Graphing a Function and Building a Table
4	Identifying Functions and Using Function Notation
LAB 2	*Graphing Calculator Lab:* Storing and Recalling Data in a Matrix
5	Using Matrices to Organize Data and to Solve Problems
6	Finding Percent of Change
7	Solving Linear Equations
8	Finding Direct Variation
9	Multiplying Matrices
10	Solving and Graphing Inequalities
	Cumulative Test 1, Performance Task 1
INV 1	Investigation: Logic and Truth Tables

Resources for Teaching

- Student Edition
- Teacher's Edition
- Student Edition eBook
- Teacher's Edition eBook
- Resources and Planner CD
- Solutions Manual
- Instructional Masters
- Technology Lab Masters
- Warm Up and Teaching Transparencies
- Instructional Presentations CD
- Online activities and tools
- Online homework help
- Online connection: **www.SaxonMathResources.com**

Resources for Practice and Assessment

- Student Edition Practice Workbook
- Course Assessments
- Standardized Test Practice
- College Entrance Exam Practice
- ExamView™ Test and Practice Generator CD

Resources for Differentiated Instruction

- Reteaching Masters
- Challenge and Enrichment Masters
- Prerequisite Skills Intervention
- Adaptations for Saxon Algebra 2
- Multilingual Glossary
- English Learners Handbook
- TI Resources

Pacing Guide

Resources and Planner CD for lesson planning support

45-Minute Class

Day 1	Day 2	Day 3	Day 4	Day 5	Day 6
Lesson 1	Lesson 2	Lesson 3	Lab 1 Lesson 4	Lab 2 Lesson 5	Lesson 6
Day 7	**Day 8**	**Day 9**	**Day 10**	**Day 11**	**Day 12**
Lesson 7	Lesson 8	Lesson 9	Lesson 10	Cumulative Test 1	Investigation 1

Block: 90-Minute Class

Day 1	Day 2	Day 3	Day 4	Day 5	Day 6
Lesson 1 Lesson 2	Lesson 3 Lab 1 Lesson 4	Lab 2 Lesson 5 Lesson 6	Lesson 7 Lesson 8	Lesson 9 Lesson 10	Cumulative Test 1 Investigation 1

** For suggestions on how to implement Saxon Math in a block schedule, see the Pacing section at the beginning of the Teacher's Edition.*

Differentiated Instruction

Below Level		Advanced Learners	
Warm Up	SE pp. 2, 8, 13, 21, 29, 36, 42, 48, 54, 61	Challenge	TE pp. 7, 11, 15, 17, 25, 32, 40, 46, 52, 59, 67
Skills Bank	SE pp. 862–885	Extend the Example	TE pp. 3, 4, 8, 23, 30, 38, 44, 50, 56, 63, 70
Reteaching Masters	Lessons 1–10, Investigation 1	Extend the Problem	TE pp. 6, 7, 12, 17, 18, 25, 26, 34, 35, 40, 47, 52, 58, 60, 67
Warm Up Transparencies	Lessons 1–10	Challenge and Enrichment Masters	C1–C10 E3, E7
Prerequisite Skills Intervention	Skills 1–4, 7–9, 11, 14, 16, 43–49, 51–52, 55–60, 68–71, 74, 78–80		
English Learners		**Special Needs**	
EL Tips	TE pp. 6, 10, 14, 24, 30, 37, 45, 49, 58, 62, 70	Inclusion Tips	TE pp. 5, 11, 16, 22, 33, 39, 44, 51, 56, 63, 66
Multilingual Glossary	Booklet and Online	Adaptations for Saxon Algebra 2	Lessons 1–10; Cumulative Test 1
English Learners Handbook			
For All Learners			
Exploration	SE pp. 42	Alternate Method	TE pp. 3, 4, 9, 23, 31, 38, 43, 50, 55, 57, 64, 65
Caution	SE pp. 2, 9, 21, 31 54	Online Tools	
Hints	SE pp. 3, 8, 10, 15, 36, 43, 48, 49, 55, 57, 62		
Error Alert	TE pp. 5, 8, 9, 13, 15, 16, 18, 19, 24, 26, 27, 30, 33, 36, 37, 38, 43, 44, 45, 50, 51, 54, 55, 64, 69		

SE = Student Edition; TE = Teacher's Edition

Math Vocabulary

Lesson	New Vocabulary		Maintained	EL Tip in TE
1	integers irrational numbers rational numbers	real numbers whole numbers	negative	additive inverse associative property commutative property multiplicative inverse
2	algebraic expression constant term evaluated like terms terms of an algebraic expression variable		coefficient	variable
3	exponent negative exponent	scientific notation		exponent power
4	dependent variable domain function function notation	independent variable range relation vertical line test	coordinate	independent independent variable
5	additive inverse matrix address dimensions of a matrix element matrix	matrix addition matrix equation scalar zero matrix	inverse	matrix
6	percent of change		percent	decrease increase
7	equation solution of an equation		commutative property	equation solution
8	constant of variation direct variation		constant	constant of variation
9	main diagonal (of a matrix) multiplicative identity matrix	product matrix square matrix	element	column row element sum product
10	inequality		equation	inequality
INV 1	conjunction disjunction			bi-directional contrapositive converse logic operators logical implication

SECTION OVERVIEW 1

Math Highlights

Enduring Understandings – The "Big Picture"

After completing Section 1, students will understand:

- How to use the properties of real numbers and the rules of exponents.
- How to find percent increase and decrease and how to solve and graph compound inequalities.
- How to identify functions, solve linear equations, and find direct variation.
- How to use matrices and multiply matrices.
- How to use truth tables.

Essential Questions

- How do functions and equations relate to each other?
- What is the nature of equality and how is it represented through mathematical symbols?
- Why do we use matrices?

Math Content Strands

Number Sense and Foundations of Algebra

- Lesson 1 — Using Properties of Real Numbers
- Lesson 2 — Evaluating Expressions and Combining Like Terms
- Lesson 3 — Using Rules of Exponents
- Lesson 6 — Finding Percent of Change
- Lesson 10 — Solving and Graphing Inequalities

Linear Functions

- Lab 1 — Graphing a Function and Building a Table
- Lesson 4 — Identifying Functions and Using Function Notation
- Lesson 7 — Solving Linear Equations
- Lesson 8 — Finding Direct Variation

Matrices

- Lesson 5 — Using Matrices to Organize Data and to Solve Problems
- Lesson 9 — Multiplying Matrices

Sequences, Series, and Logic

- Inv. 1 — Logic and Truth Tables

Connections in Practice Problems

	Lessons
Coordinate Geometry	3, 6, 9
Geometry	1, 2, 3, 4, 5, 6, 7, 8, 9, 10
Measurement	2
Probability	4
Statistics	1, 8, 10

Math Processes

Reasoning and Communication

	Lessons
• Analyze	1, 3, 4, 5, 6, 8, 10
• Connect	5
• Error analysis	1, 2, 3, 4, 5, 6, 7, 8, 9, 10
• Estimate	5, 6, 7, 10
• Formulate	5, 7
• Generalize	4, 7, Inv. 1
• Justify	1, 3, 4, 5, 7, Inv. 1
• Math reasoning	3, 5, 10
• Model	5
• Multiple choice	1, 2, 3, 4, 5, 6, 7, 8, 9, 10
• Multi-step	1, 2, 3, 4, 5, 6, 7, 8, 9, 10, Inv. 1
• Predict	10
• Verify	1, 2, 3, 4, 5, 6, 7, 8, 9, 10, Inv. 1
• Write	1, 2, 3, 4, 5, 6, 8, 9, 10
• Graphing Calculator	1, 2, 3, 4, 5, 6, 7, 8, 9, 10

Connections

In Examples: Astronomy, Biology, Chemistry, Consumer math, Distances, Finance, Marked up price, Metalworking, Population, Sales price, Transportation

In Practice problems: Amusement parks, Astronomy, Baseball, Biology, Bowling, Budgets, Bulk foods, Coffee, Consumer, Currency, Diving, Earth, Economics, Education, Exports, Football, Geography, Golf, Interest rates, Hawaii, Hybrids, Marketing, Museums, Nutrition, Planets, Population, Precipitation, Property management, Sales tax, Scores, Solar system, Speed of sound, Sports, Skyscrapers, Volcanoes

Content Trace

Lesson	Warm Up: Prerequisite Skills	New Concepts	Where Practiced	Where Assessed	Looking Forward
1	Skills Bank	Using Properties of Real Numbers	Lessons 1, 2, 3, 4, 5, 6, 7, 8, 9, 10, 12, 13, 14, 21, 22, 25, 26, 95, 96, 100	Cumulative Tests 1, 2, 3, 4, 5, 8	Lessons 2, 3, 6, 10
2	Skills Bank 1	Evaluating Expressions and Combining Like Terms	Lessons 2, 3, 4, 5, 6, 7, 8, 10, 11, 12, 13, 23, 98	Cumulative Tests 1, 2, 3, 5, 6, 12	Lessons 3, 7, 11
3	Skills Bank	Using Rules of Exponents	Lessons 3, 4, 5, 6, 7, 8, 9, 10, 11, 12, 17, 19, 22, 28, 34, 98, 99	Cumulative Tests 1, 2, 3, 4, 6, 7, 11, 17	Lessons 11, 19, 28, 70
4	Skills Bank 2	Identifying Functions and Using Function Notation	Lessons 4, 5, 6, 7, 8, 9, 10, 15, 16, 23, 30	Cumulative Tests 1, 2, 3, 4, 5	Lessons 22, 47, 50, 53
5	Skills Bank 1, 2	Using Matrices to Organize Data and to Solve Problems	Lessons 5–10, 12, 14, 101, 102, 109	Cumulative Tests 1, 2, 3, 4, 6, 9, 18, 20	Lessons 14, 16, 32, 99, 104
6	Skills Bank	Finding Percent of Change	Lessons 6, 7, 8, 9, 10, 11, 12, 13, 14, 15, 16, 20, 22, 28	Cumulative Test 2, 3, 4, 11, 15	Lessons 10, 18
7	1, 2	Solving Linear Equations	Lessons 7, 8, 9, 10, 11, 12, 13, 15, 16, 17, 20, 21, 22, 23, 25, 27, 32, 34, 35, 53	Cumulative Test 2, 3, 4, 5, 6, 10, 14, 20	Lessons 10, 13, 17
8	Skills Bank 2	Finding Direct Variation	Lessons 8, 9, 10, 11, 12, 14, 15, 17, 18, 19, 21, 22, 23, 25	Cumulative Test 2, 3, 4, 6, 8, 13	Lessons 12, 13, 34
9	1, 5, 7	Multiplying Matrices	Lessons 9, 10, 11, 12, 13, 14, 15, 16, 17, 18, 21, 22, 23, 24, 25, 26, 27, 31	Cumulative Test 2, 3, 4, 5, 7, 12, 16, 21	Lessons 14, 16, 32
10	Skills Bank 7	Solving and Graphing Inequalities	Lessons 10, 11, 12, 13, 14, 15, 16, 17, 21, 22, 23, 24, 25, 26, 29, 31, 32, 33, 35, 96	Cumulative Test 2, 3	Lessons 17, 39, 43
INV 1	N/A	Logic and Truth Tables	Lessons 11, 12, 41, 65	Cumulative Test 5	N/A

SECTION OVERVIEW 1

Ongoing Assessment

	Type	Feature	Intervention *
BEFORE instruction	Assess Prior Knowledge	• Diagnostic Test	• Prerequisite Skills Intervention
BEFORE the lesson	Formative	• Warm Up	• Skills Bank • Reteaching Masters
DURING the lesson	Formative	• Lesson Practice • Math Conversations with the Practice problems	• Additional Examples in TE • Test and Practice Generator (for additional practice sheets)
AFTER the lesson	Formative	• Check for Understanding (closure)	• Scaffolding Questions in TE
AFTER 5 lessons	Summative	After Lesson 10 • Cumulative Test 1 • Performance Task 1	• Reteaching Masters • Test and Practice Generator (for additional tests and practice)
AFTER 20 lessons	Summative	• Benchmark Tests	• Reteaching Masters • Test and Practice Generator (for additional tests and practice)

* for students not showing progress during the formative stages or scoring below 80% on the summative assessments

Evidence of Learning – What Students Should Know

Because the Saxon philosophy is to provide students with sufficient time to learn and practice each concept, a lesson's topic will not be tested until at least five lessons after the topic is introduced.

On the Cumulative Tests that are given during this section of ten lessons, students should be able to demonstrate the following competencies:

- Use properties of real numbers.
- Simplify and evaluate algebraic expressions.
- Understand the rules of exponents.
- Identify functions and use function notation.
- Use matrices to organize data and to solve problems.

ExamView™ Test and Practice Generator CD

The Test and Practice Generator is an easy-to-use benchmark and assessment tool that creates unlimited practice and tests in multiple formats and allows you to customize questions or create new ones. A variety of reports are available to track student progress toward mastery of the standards throughout the year.

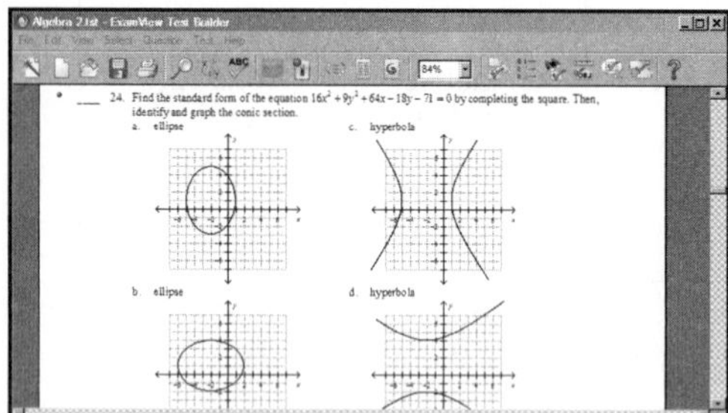

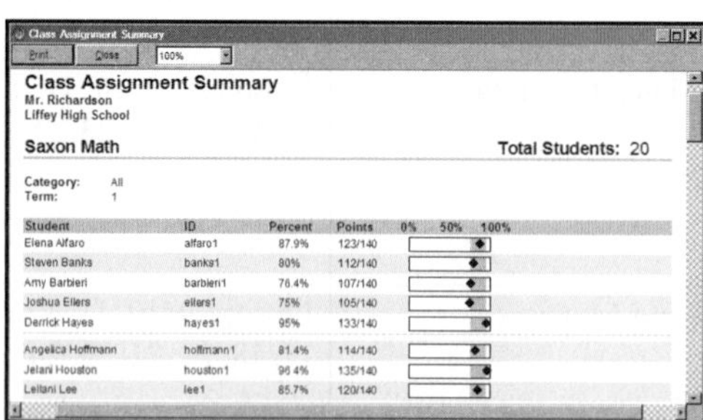

Assessment Resources

Resources for Diagnosing and Assessing

- **Student Edition**
  - Warm Up
  - Lesson Practice
- **Teacher's Edition**
  - Math Conversations with the Practice problems
  - Check for Understanding (closure)
- **Course Assessments**
  - Cumulative Tests
  - Performance Tasks
  - Benchmark Tests
- **Prerequisite Skills Intervention**
  - Diagnostic Test

Resources for Intervention

- **Student Edition**
  - Skills Bank
- **Teacher's Edition**
  - Additional Examples
- **Prerequisite Skills Intervention**
  - Skill worksheets
- **Reteaching Masters**
  - Lesson instruction and practice sheets
- **ExamView™ Test and Practice Generator CD**
  - Lesson practice problems
  - Additional tests

Resources for Test Prep

- **Student Edition Practice**
  - Multiple-choice problems
  - Multiple-step and writing problems
  - Daily cumulative practice
- **Standardized Test Practice**
- **College Entrance Exam Practice**
- **Test and Practice Generator CD using ExamView™**

Cumulative Tests

The assessments in Saxon Math are frequent and consistently placed after every five lessons to offer a regular method of ongoing testing. These cumulative assessments check mastery of concepts from previous lessons.

Performance Tasks

The Performance Tasks can be used in conjunction with the Cumulative Tests and are scored using a rubric.

After Lesson 10

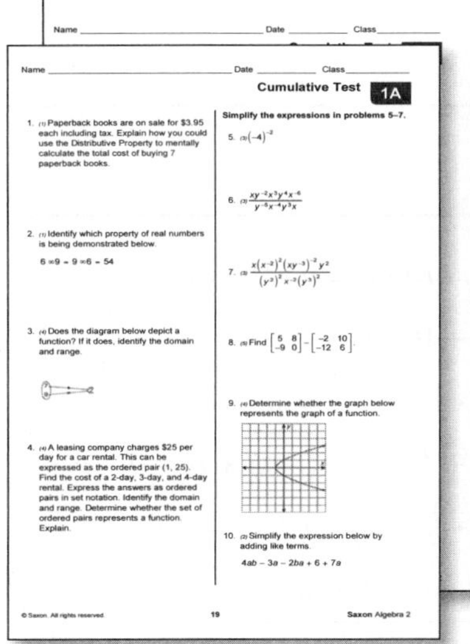

Name ______________________ Date __________ Class __________

Cumulative Test 1A

1. (1) Paperback books are on sale for $3.95 each including tax. Explain how you could use the Distributive Property to mentally calculate the total cost of buying 7 paperback books.

2. (1) Identify which property of real numbers is being demonstrated below.

   $6 \times 9 = 9 \times 6 = 54$

3. (4) Does the diagram below depict a function? If it does, identify the domain and range.

4. (4) A leasing company charges $25 per day for a car rental. This can be expressed as the ordered pair (1, 25). Find the cost of a 2-day, 3-day, and 4-day rental. Express the answers as ordered pairs in set notation. Identify the domain and range. Determine whether the set of ordered pairs represents a function. Explain.

Simplify the expressions in problems 5–7.

5. (3) $(-4)^{-2}$

6. (3) $\frac{xy^{-2}x^3y^4x^{-6}}{y^{-5}x^{-4}y^3x}$

7. (3) $\frac{x(x^{-2})^2(xy^{-3})^{-2}y^2}{(y^2)^2x^{-3}(y^3)^2}$

8. (5) Find $\begin{bmatrix} 5 & 8 \\ -9 & 0 \end{bmatrix} - \begin{bmatrix} -2 & 10 \\ -12 & 6 \end{bmatrix}$.

9. (4) Determine whether the graph below represents the graph of a function.

10. (2) Simplify the expression below by adding like terms.

    $4ab - 3a - 2ba + 6 + 7a$

 19 Saxon Algebra 2

For use with Performance Tasks

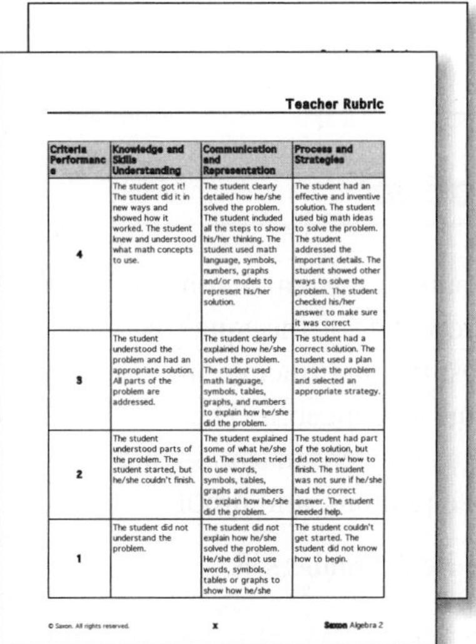

Teacher Rubric

Criteria Performance	Knowledge and Skills Understanding	Communication and Representation	Process and Strategies
4	The student got it! The student did it in new ways and showed how it worked. The student knew and understood what math concepts to use.	The student clearly detailed how he/she solved the problem. The student included all the steps to show his/her thinking. The student used math language, symbols, numbers, graphs and/or models to represent his/her solution.	The student had an effective and inventive solution. The student used big math ideas to solve the problem. The student addressed the important details. The student showed other ways to solve the problem. The student checked his/her answer to make sure it was correct
3	The student understood the problem and had an appropriate solution. All parts of the problem are addressed.	The student clearly explained how he/she solved the problem. The student used math language, symbols, tables, graphs, and numbers to explain how he/she did the problem.	The student had a correct solution. The student used a plan to solve the problem and selected an appropriate strategy.
2	The student understood parts of the problem. The student started, but he/she couldn't finish.	The student explained some of what he/she did. The student tried to use words, symbols, tables, graphs and numbers to explain how he/she did the problem.	The student had part of the solution, but did not know how to finish. The student was not sure if he/she had the correct answer. The student needed help.
1	The student did not understand the problem.	The student did not explain how he/she solved the problem. He/she did not use words, symbols, tables or graphs to show how he/she	The student couldn't get started. The student did not know how to begin.

 x Saxon Algebra 2

LESSON 1

1 Warm Up

Remind students that sets of numbers can be specified by listing the elements or describing the properties. The set of negative numbers could be described as $N = \{\text{all numbers } x, \text{ such that } x < 0\}$.

2 New Concepts

In this lesson, students learn to classify numbers according to which subset(s) of the real numbers they belong to. They also identify and apply the real number properties.

Remind students that a number is rational if and only if it can be represented by a ratio.

Example 1

Students classify numbers by membership in subsets of the real numbers.

Additional Example 1

Identify the subsets of real numbers of which each number is a member.

a. -16 real, rational, integer

b. 32 real, rational, integer, whole, natural

c. $-\sqrt{20}$ real, irrational

LESSON RESOURCES

Student Edition Practice Workbook 1
Reteaching Master 1
Adaptations Master 1
Challenge and Enrichment Master C1

LESSON 1

Using Properties of Real Numbers

Warm Up

Start off each lesson by practicing prerequisite skills and math vocabulary that will make you more successful with today's new concept.

1. **Vocabulary** A number whose value is less than 0 is called a ______ number. negative (SB)
2. Add $12 + (-12)$. 0 (SB)
3. Multiply $\frac{2}{3} \cdot \frac{3}{2}$. 1 (SB)
4. Subtract $10 - 9.85$. 0.15 (SB)

New Concepts

A set is a collection of objects. If all of the objects in one set are also members of a second set, then the first set is a subset of the second. The real numbers are a set of numbers consisting of several subsets of numbers. The **real numbers** consist of the **rational numbers** and the **irrational numbers.** The rational numbers include the natural numbers $\{1, 2, 3, \ldots\}$, the **whole numbers** $\{0, 1, 2, 3, \ldots\}$, and the **integers** $\{\ldots, -3, -2, -1, 0, 1, 2, 3, \ldots\}$.

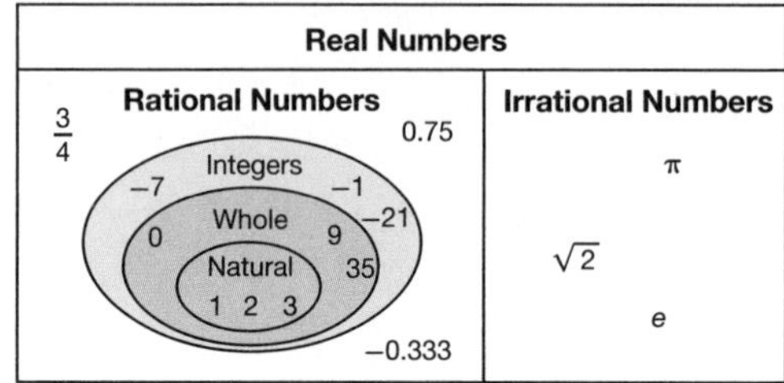

Rational numbers can be written as quotients of integers. Rational numbers can also be written as decimals that terminate or repeat. Irrational numbers cannot be written in any of these ways. Pi and many roots of real numbers are common examples of irrational numbers.

Caution

The negative integers are not considered whole numbers even though they do not contain fractions.

Example 1 Classifying Real Numbers

Identify the subsets of real numbers of which each number is a member.

a. -5

SOLUTION -5 is a real number, a rational number, and an integer.

b. 25

SOLUTION 25 is a real number, a rational number, an integer, a whole number, and a natural number.

c. $-\sqrt{5}$

SOLUTION $-\sqrt{5}$ is a real number and an irrational number.

Online Connection
www.SaxonMathResources.com

MATH BACKGROUND

The eleven field axioms of the real numbers, together with the properties of the equality relation and the substitution principle, are the foundation for most of algebra. The axioms are used to justify steps in simplifying expressions, solving equations, and proof.

Field Axioms of the Real Numbers $\Re$

If $a, b, c \in \Re$, then:

1. $a + b \in \Re$
2. $a \cdot b \in \Re$
3. $(a + b) + c = a + (b + c)$
4. $(a \cdot b) \cdot c = a \cdot (b \cdot c)$
5. $a + 0 = 0 + a = a$
6. $a \cdot 1 = 1 \cdot a = a$
7. $a + (-a) = (-a) + a = 0$
8. $a \cdot \frac{1}{a} = \frac{1}{a} \cdot a = 1 \ (a \neq 0)$
9. $a + b = b + a$
10. $a \cdot b = b \cdot a$
11. $a \cdot (b + c) = (a \cdot b) + (a \cdot c)$

There are a number of properties that can be used when adding and multiplying real numbers.

Properties of Addition and Multiplication

Let a, b, and c be real numbers.

Property	Addition	Multiplication
Closure	$a + b$ is a real number	ab is a real number
Commutative	$a + b = b + a$	$ab = ba$
Associative	$(a + b) + c = a + (b + c)$	$(ab)c = a(bc)$

The following property involves both addition and multiplication.

Distributive $a(b + c) = ab + ac$

Example 2 Identifying Properties of Real Numbers

Identify which property of real numbers is being demonstrated.

a. $3 \cdot 8 = 8 \cdot 3 = 24$

SOLUTION Commutative Property of Multiplication

b. $5(7 + 11) = 5 \cdot 7 + 5 \cdot 11 = 35 + 55 = 90$

SOLUTION Distributive Property

c. $(12 + 20) + 30 = 12 + (20 + 30) = 12 + 50 = 62$

SOLUTION Associative Property of Addition

Example 3 Using the Properties of Real Numbers

Simplify each expression. Identify which property you used for each step.

a. $12 + 4 + 18 + 56$

SOLUTION

$12 + 4 + 18 + 56$

$= 12 + 18 + 4 + 56$ Commutative Property of Addition

$= (12 + 18) + (4 + 56)$ Associative Property of Addition

$= 30 + 60$ Add.

$= 90$ Add.

b. $5(23)$

SOLUTION

$5(23)$

$= 5(20 + 3)$

$= (5 \cdot 20) + (5 \cdot 3)$ Distributive Property

$= 100 + 15$ Multiply.

$= 115$ Add.

Hint

The Distributive Property makes multiplying easier by breaking down a number into numbers where mental math can be used.

ALTERNATE METHOD FOR EXAMPLE 2

Some students may have trouble understanding the multi-step examples of the properties in which more than one equal sign is used in a line. Presenting each step on a separate line may clarify which property is being used.

Commutative Property

$3 \cdot 8 = 8 \cdot 3$

$= 24$

Distributive Property

$5(7 + 11) = 5 \cdot 7 + 5 \cdot 11$

$= 35 + 55$

$= 90$

Associative Property

$(12 + 20) + 30 = 12 + (20 + 30)$

$= 12 + 50$

$= 62$

Example 2

Students identify examples of the real number properties.

Additional Example 2

Identify which property of real numbers is being demonstrated.

a. $23 + 10 = 10 + 23 = 33$
Commutative, Addition

b. $\left(\frac{1}{4} \cdot \frac{1}{3}\right) + \left(\frac{1}{4} \cdot \frac{2}{5}\right) = \frac{1}{4}\left(\frac{1}{3} + \frac{2}{5}\right)$ Distributive

c. $-3[7 \cdot (-5)] = (-3 \cdot 7) \cdot (-5)$
Associative, Multiplication

Extend the Example

Ask students if the real number properties can be proven by giving specific examples. Sample: No. Giving an example does not prove a statement for an entire set of numbers.

Example 3

Students use real number properties to simplify numerical expressions. The examples illustrate how the properties can facilitate the use of mental math.

Additional Example 3

Simplify each expression. Identify which property you used for each step.

a. $2.5 + 4.3 + 8.5 + 1.7$
$2.5 + 8.5 + 4.3 + 1.7$: Commutative, Addition; $(2.5 + 8.5) + (4.3 + 1.7)$: Associative, Addition; $11 + 6$: Add; 17: Add.

b. $24\left(5\frac{3}{4}\right)$ $(24 \cdot 5) + \left(24 \cdot \frac{3}{4}\right)$: Distributive; $120 + 18$: Multiply; 138: Add.

Extend the Example

Use the Distributive Property to justify the fact that $3x + 5x$ is equal to $8x$. Sample: $3x + 5x = (3 + 5)x$. $(3 + 5)x = 8x$. Therefore, $3x + 5x = 8x$.

Example 4

Students write the additive and multiplicative inverses of given numbers or expressions.

Additional Example 4

a. Find the additive inverse of $3 - d$. $-(3 - d) = -3 + d$

b. Find the multiplicative inverse of $\frac{2}{y+5}$. $\frac{y+5}{2}$

Error Alert When finding the reciprocal, remind students to first write the given number as a fraction. For example, the reciprocal of 0.26 is usually written as $\frac{100}{26}$ rather than $\frac{1}{0.26}$.

Extend the Example

Have students find the reciprocals of the repeating decimals $0.6\overline{6}$, $0.7\overline{7}$, $0.08\overline{3}$, and $0.3\overline{63}$. If they need a hint, tell them that the denominators of the equivalent fractions are 3, 9, 11, and 12. $\frac{3}{2}$, $\frac{9}{7}$, 12, $\frac{11}{4}$

Example 5

Students use real number properties to simplify calculations in practical applications.

Additional Example 5

Sharona uses $1\frac{1}{3}$ lb of grapes to make one jar of grape jelly. She is making 12 jars as gifts for friends. Use the Distributive Property to mentally calculate the number of pounds of grapes she needs. Sample: $12 \cdot 1\frac{1}{3} = (12 \cdot 1) + \left(12 \cdot \frac{1}{3}\right) = 12 + 4 = 16$; She needs 16 lb.

Problem b

Scaffolding Refer students back to the diagram at the beginning of the lesson. Tell them to choose from the sets in the diagram.

More Properties of Addition and Multiplication		
Property	**Addition**	**Multiplication**
Identity	$a + 0 = a, 0 + a = a$	$a \cdot 1 = a, 1 \cdot a = a$
Inverse	$a + (-a) = 0$	$a \cdot \frac{1}{a} = 1, a \neq 0$

Math Language

The **additive inverse** of a number is sometimes called the opposite of the number.

Example 4 Finding Inverses of Real Numbers

a. Find the additive inverse of $-7a$.

SOLUTION The additive inverse of $-7a$ is $7a$ since $-7a + 7a = 0$.

b. Find the multiplicative inverse of $\frac{5n}{12p}$.

SOLUTION The multiplicative inverse is the reciprocal of $\frac{5n}{12p}$ which is $\frac{12p}{5n}$.

$$\frac{5n}{12p} \cdot \frac{12p}{5n} = 1$$

Example 5 Application: Finance

DVDs are on sale at Tech World for \$11.95 each including tax. Use the Distributive Property to mentally calculate the total cost of buying 5 DVDs.

SOLUTION Think of \$11.95 as \$12.00 – \$0.05.

Write an expression for the cost of 5 DVDs.

$5(12 - 0.05)$

$= 5(12) - 5(0.05)$ Use the Distributive Property.

$= 60 - 0.25$ Multiply.

$= 59.75$ Subtract.

The total cost of 5 DVDs is \$59.75.

Lesson Practice

a. Identify the subsets of real numbers of which $\sqrt{3}$ is a member. *(Ex 1)* real numbers and irrational numbers

b. Identify the subsets of real numbers of which $-\frac{2}{3}$ is a member. *(Ex 1)* real numbers and rational numbers

c. Identify the subsets of real numbers of which 1 is a member. *(Ex 1)* real numbers, rational numbers, integers, whole numbers, and natural numbers

d. Identify which property of real numbers is being demonstrated. *(Ex 2)* Distributive Property

$$-2(5 + 9) = -2 \cdot 5 + (-2) \cdot 9 = -10 - 18 = -28$$

e. Identify which property of real numbers is being demonstrated. *(Ex 2)* Associative Property of Multiplication

$$(12 \cdot 6) \cdot 2 = 12 \cdot (6 \cdot 2) = 12 \cdot 12 = 144$$

f. Identify which property of real numbers is being demonstrated. *(Ex 2)*

$$3 + 21 = 21 + 3 = 24$$ Commutative Property of Addition

g. Simplify the expression $(43 + 21) + 9$. Identify which property you used for each step. *(Ex 3)*

g. $43 + (21 + 9)$ Associative Property of Addition
$= 43 + 30$ Add.
$= 73$ Add.

ALTERNATE METHOD FOR EXAMPLE 4

For a visual representation of a number and its additive and multiplicative inverses, have students use a graphing calculator to graph $y = -x$ and $y = \frac{1}{x}$. Ask "On the first graph, how are x and y related?" Sum is always 0.

Explain that x and y are additive inverses because their sum is equal to 0. Repeat to introduce multiplicative inverses.

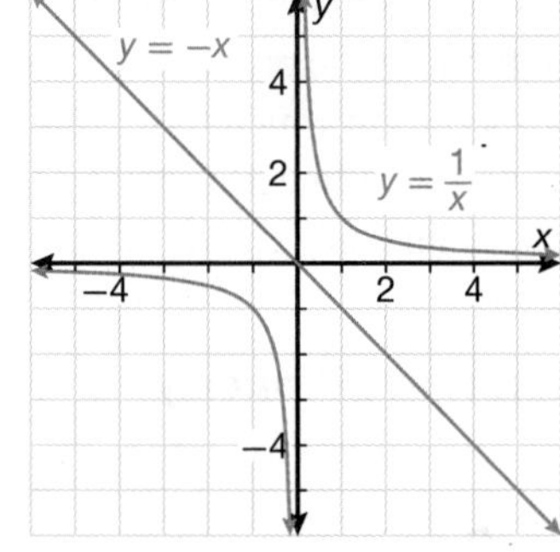

h. (16 • 4) • 4 — Commutative Property of Multiplication
16 • (4 • 4) — Associative Property of Multiplication
16 • 16 — Multiply.
256 — Multiply.

h. (Ex 3) Simplify the expression (4 • 16) • 4. Identify which property you used for each step.

i. (Ex 4) Find the additive inverse of $\frac{3q}{2}$. $-\frac{3q}{2}$

j. (Ex 4) Find the multiplicative inverse of −4. $-\frac{1}{4}$

k. (Ex 5) Lucinda drove four hours from her house to a family reunion. Her average speed was 55 mph. Use the Distributive Property to mentally calculate the distance between Lucinda's house and the reunion.
220 miles

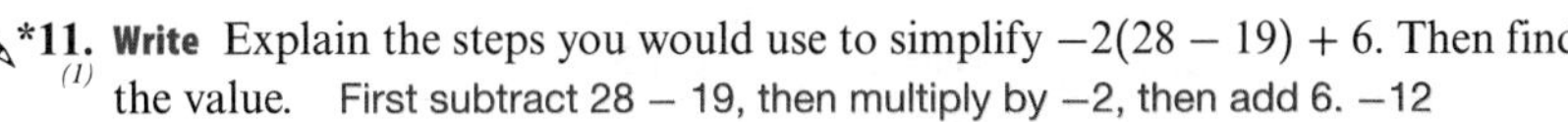

Practice Distributed and Integrated

Simplify each expression.

1. (SB) −3 − 6 + 1 −8

2. (SB) −4 + 6 − 8 = −6

Simplify each expression using the properties of real numbers.

***3.** (1) −2[(5 − 7 − 2) − (−2 − 7) − 2] −6

***4.** (1) 4[3 − (−2)] + 5(−2 + 1) 15

Simplify each expression.

5. (SB) 14.6 − 9.03 5.57

6. (SB) 39.75 + 49.2 88.95

Order the given numbers from least to greatest.

7. (SB) 2.1, 2.3, 2.09 2.09, 2.1, 2.3

8. (SB) $\frac{3}{5}, \frac{4}{7}, \frac{1}{2}$ $\frac{1}{2}, \frac{4}{7}, \frac{3}{5}$

Find the distance traveled given the rate and time below.

9. (SB) rate = 40 miles per hour, time = $3\frac{1}{2}$ hours 140 miles

10. (SB) rate = 55 miles per hour, time = 0.5 hours 27.5 miles

***11.** (1) **Write** Explain the steps you would use to simplify −2(28 − 19) + 6. Then find the value. First subtract 28 − 19, then multiply by −2, then add 6. −12

***12.** (1) **Justify** Simplify 2 • 3 • 6. Justify your answer by identifying which property you used for each step. Possible answer: 2(3 • 6), Associative Property of Multiplication; 2(18), Multiply; 36, Multiply.

13. (SB) **Geography** The following graph represents the elevations of mountains located in the United States.

Which mountain has the lowest elevation? Mount Hood

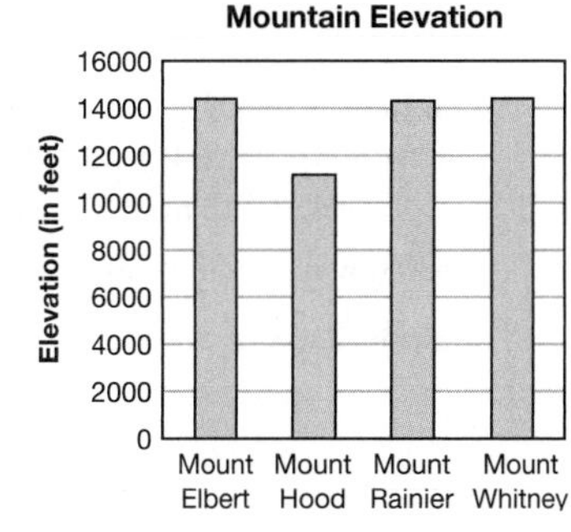

INCLUSION

Some students may have difficulty remembering the difference between the commutative and associative properties. Since these are learned together, it is often the case that students confuse them. Use everyday, non-mathematical meanings of the related verbs to help students remember the distinction between these adjectives.

associate to join a group, or to spend time with members of a group. *You can associate with school friends or family members.*

commute to interchange; to travel back and forth over the same route. When you commute to work, you go one way in the morning. Then at the end of the day you go the other way.

Problem i

Error Alert Watch for students who automatically write a reciprocal when they see a fraction. Remind them to read carefully to find out which type of inverse is asked for.

Problem k

Students will need to use the distance formula $d = st$, where s is the speed in miles per hour and t is the time in hours.

Check for Understanding

The questions below help assess the concepts taught in this lesson.

1. **"What is the difference between a set and a subset?"** A set and a subset are collections of objects, but a subset is a set contained with another set.
2. **"Can a number be both rational and irrational? Explain."** No. A rational number can be expressed as a fraction, $\frac{a}{b}$ where $b \neq 0$, an irrational number cannot be expressed as a fraction.

3 Practice

Math Conversations

Discussions to strengthen understanding

Problem 8

Students can use the least common denominator 70 or order the decimal equivalents.

Problem 11

Error Alert
Check that students do not get (−56 − 38) for −2(28 − 19). The correct product is (−56 + 38). The product of two negative numbers is positive.

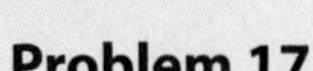

Problem 17

Guide the students by asking them the following questions.

"Write a ratio in fraction form for the pages Suzy can read in four minutes." $\frac{12}{4}$

"Write a ratio for the pages she can read in 1 minute. Use x for the number of pages." $\frac{x}{1}$

"Write a proportion you can solve to find x." $\frac{12}{4} = \frac{x}{1}$

Problem 18

Extend the Problem

Show that two real number properties are used in this statement.

$(25 + 87) + 175 =$
$87 + (25 + 175)$

Sample: $(25 + 87) + 175 = (87 + 25) + 175$ because of the commutative property; then $(87 + 25) + 175 = 87 + (25 + 175)$ because of the associative property.

14. (SB) **Sports** A football field is 120 yards long and 160 feet wide. What is the area in square yards? 6400 square yards

***15.** (1) **Verify** Simplify the expression $(6 \cdot 5) \cdot 2$ using only one property of real numbers. Identify the property that you used. Verify your result using two properties of real numbers.

***16.** (1) **Multiple Choice** Identify the subset of real numbers of which 7 is not a member. A

A irrational number **B** integer
C whole number **D** real number

17. (SB) **Multi-Step** Suzy can read 12 pages in four minutes. Jonas can read 9 pages in three minutes.

a. Find the number of pages Suzy and Jonas can read per minute.

b. Compare the rates. Suzy and Jonas read at the same rate.

***18.** (1) **Multiple Choice** Identify which property or properties of real numbers are being demonstrated. D

$$27 \cdot 3 = (20 \cdot 3) + (7 \cdot 3) = 60 + 21 = 81$$

A Commutative Property of Addition

B Associative Property of Addition

C Both A and B

D Distributive Property

19. (SB) **Sports** The specified circumference of an official professional baseball is from 9 to 9.25 inches.

a. Find the approximate radius of the smallest official baseball. 1.43 inches

b. Find the approximate surface area of the smallest official baseball. 25.68 square inches

***20.** (1) **Statistics** The table below shows the number of homeruns hit by a softball player over a three-year period. Use properties of real numbers to mentally calculate the average annual homeruns that she hit during this period. 11 homeruns

	Year 1	Year 2	Year 3
Homeruns	6	13	14

***21.** (1) **Interest Rates** The average credit card annual interest rate is around 19%. Use the Distributive Property to mentally calculate the amount of interest paid annually on a \$500 balance.

22. (SB) **Biology** Some large species of bamboo plants can grow at a rate of 1 meter per day.

a. If a 2-meter tall bamboo plant grows at this rate, how tall will it be after 2 weeks? 16 m

b. How long will it take for the bamboo plant to reach a height of 50 meters? 48 days

15. $(6 \cdot 5) \cdot 2 = 6 \cdot (5 \cdot 2) = 6 \cdot 10 = 60$, Associative Property of Multiplication; $(6 \cdot 5) \cdot 2 = (5 \cdot 6) \cdot 2 = 5 \cdot (6 \cdot 2) = 5 \cdot 12 = 60$, Commutative Property of Multiplication and Associative Property of Multiplication

17a. Suzy: $\frac{3 \text{ pages}}{1 \text{ minute}}$; Jonas: $\frac{3 \text{ pages}}{1 \text{ minute}}$.

21. Think of 19% as $0.20 - 0.01$. Write an expression for the annual interest: $500(0.20 - 0.01)$. Use the Distributive Property: $500(0.20) - 500(0.01)$. Multiply: $100 - 5$. Subtract: 95. The annual interest is \$95.

ENGLISH LEARNERS

This lesson presents a great deal of mathematical terminology. Point out to students that they already know many of these ideas, but they may have learned them by easier terms in earlier grades.

Illustrate informal terms by making a two-column chart. Have students copy the chart and add a third column in which they write an example for each term.

Term	Also Called
additive inverse	opposite
multiplicative inverse	reciprocal
commutative property	order property
associative property	grouping property

*23. **Geometry** The base of a triangle equals $\frac{1}{m}$ and the height equals m. The area of the triangle can be calculated as shown below. Which properties of real numbers are demonstrated? Inverse Property of Multiplication, Identity Property of Multiplication
(1)

$$A = \frac{1}{2}(bh) = \frac{1}{2}\left(\frac{1}{m} \cdot m\right) = \frac{1}{2} \cdot 1 = \frac{1}{2}$$

24. Carlos measures an angle x. He then finds that the complement of the angle is 35°.
(SB)

a. What is the measure of angle x? 55°

b. What is the supplement of angle x? 125°

*25. **Error Analysis** Explain the error in the statement that follows and correct the statement. "−7 is a real number, a rational number, and a whole number."
(1)

25. Negative integers are not considered whole numbers. The statement should be "−7 is a real number, a rational number, and an integer."

26. **Estimate** The chart below shows the total amount of hybrid vehicles sold by a manufacturer over a 4-year time span. Round to the nearest ten-thousand to estimate:
(SB)

a. the total number of hybrid vehicles sold from 2003 to 2006. 590,000

b. the sales increase from 2003 to 2006. 200,000

Year	2003	2004	2005	2006
Cars Sold	47,525	83,153	209,711	246,642

*27. **Graphing Calculator** Use the Distributive Property to mentally calculate 12(18). Check using a graphing calculator. 216
(1)

28. **Error Analysis** Two students calculated the total cost for 3 CDs. Each CD cost $14.95. Which student has the correct answer? Explain the other student's error.
(SB)
Student B is correct. Student A did not distribute the 3 to the second term.

Student A	Student B
3(15 − 0.05) 3(15) − (0.05) 45 − 0.05 44.95	3(15 − 0.05) 3(15) − 3(0.05) 45 − 0.15 44.85

29. A cube has a side length of 5 centimeters.
(SB)

a. Find the surface area of the cube. 150 cm^2

b. Find the volume of the cube. 125 cm^3

30. **Analyze** John asked 100 people to choose their favorite pet.
(SB)

Use the chart to determine how many people chose dogs as their favorite pet. 44 people chose dogs as their favorite pet.

Favorite Pet

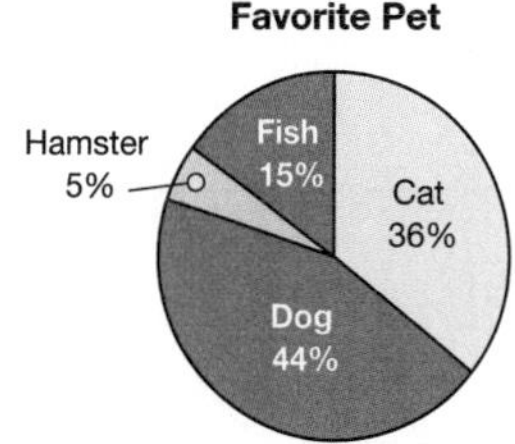

Problem 23

Have students sketch some triangles with different values of m in inches. Have them find each area. They will find that the area is always $\frac{1}{2}$ in.^{2}

Extend the Problem

The height and base of a parallelogram are reciprocals. If the dimensions are given in centimeters, what is the area of the parallelogram? 1 cm^2

Problem 24

Remind students that the sum of two complementary angles must be 90°. The sum of supplementary angles is 180°.

Problem 25

Extend the Problem

A whole number a is rational because it can be written as the ratio $\frac{a}{1}$. When is a rational number also a whole number?
Sample: when numerator and denominator are positive, and the numerator is a multiple of the denominator

Problem 29

If students cannot find the surface area, remind them that a cube has 6 square faces. If possible, hold up a cube as a model. The surface area is the sum of the areas of these 6 surfaces. So, students should square the side length, then multiply by 6.

CHALLENGE

An operation ⊙ is defined over the set of whole numbers. For each problem, decide (1) if the whole numbers are closed under ⊙, (2) if the operation ⊙ is commutative, and (3) if the operation ⊙ is associative.

a. $a \odot b = 2a + b$ closed, not commutative, not associative

b. $a \odot b = a - b$ not closed, not commutative, not associative

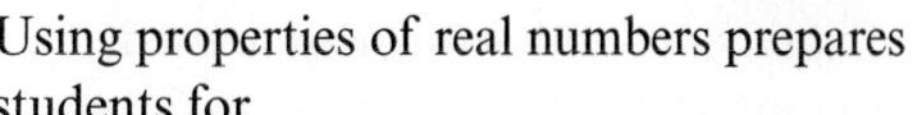

LOOKING FORWARD

Using properties of real numbers prepares students for

- **Lesson 2** Evaluating Expressions and Combining Like Terms
- **Lesson 3** Using Rules of Exponents
- **Lesson 6** Finding Percent of Change
- **Lesson 10** Solving and Graphing Inequalities

1 Warm Up

Remind students to perform division before the addition and subtraction in problem 3.

2 New Concepts

In this lesson, students learn to evaluate expressions and combine like terms.

Example 1

Remind students that an exponent of a variable indicates the variable must be multiplied that many times. So x^2 means x times x.

Error Alert Students may accidentally omit negative signs when evaluating. Show the following example:

If $x = -5$, then $x^2 = (-5)^2 = 25$.

Extend the Example

Have students evaluate the expression in part **a** if $x = -\frac{1}{2}$ and $y = -\frac{1}{4}$. $\frac{3}{16}$

Additional Example 1

Evaluate each expression if $x = -3$ and $y = -1$.

a. $3x^2 - y^2$ 26

b. $-xy + x^2y^2$ 6

LESSON RESOURCES

Student Edition Practice Workbook 2
Reteaching Master 2
Adaptations Master 2
Challenge and Enrichment Masters C2

LESSON 2

Evaluating Expressions and Combining Like Terms

Warm Up

1. (SB) **Vocabulary** In the term $3xy$, 3 is the ________. coefficient
2. (1) True or False: $23 + 2(4) = 5(6) + 7$. False
3. (SB) Simplify: $8 + 12 \div 4 - 5$. 6

New Concepts

An **algebraic expression** can contain letters that represent unspecified numbers. These letters are called **variables.** The value of the algebraic expression $x + 4$ depends on the number you use as a replacement for x. If you replace x with -32, the expression will have a value of -28.

$$x + 4$$
$$(-32) + 4 = -28$$

When you replace the variables in an expression with selected numbers and simplify using the order of operations, you have **evaluated** the expression.

Order of Operations
1. Parentheses and grouping symbols
2. Exponents
3. Multiply and divide from left to right
4. Add and subtract from left to right

Hint

Subtracting a number is the same as adding its opposite.

Example 1 Evaluating Expressions with Exponents

Evaluate each expression if $x = -2$ and $y = -4$.

a. $x^2y - y$

SOLUTION

$x^2y - y$

$= (-2)^2(-4) - (-4)$ Replace x with -2 and y with -4.

$= (+4)(-4) - (-4)$ Perform operations with exponents.

$= -16 - (-4)$ Multiply.

$= -16 + 4 = -12$ Subtract.

b. $2xy + 3y^2$

SOLUTION

$2xy + 3y^2$

$= 2(-2)(-4) + 3(-4)^2$ Replace x with -2 and y with -4.

$= 2(-2)(-4) + 3(16)$ Perform operations with exponents.

$= 16 + 48 = 64$ Multiply and add.

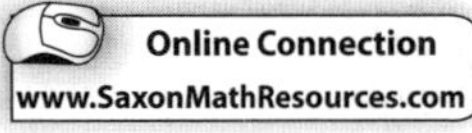

MATH BACKGROUND

Expressions with variables are used to represent ever changing situations. Variables are used when a value changes or is unknown. For example, the perimeter of a rectangle is found by adding twice the length to twice the width, which can be expressed as $2l + 2w$. Once the dimensions of the rectangle are known, the values can be substituted in the expression to find the perimeter. In this way, the same formula can be used for every rectangle.

Variables are especially useful when working with computers. A program can include a variable expression, prompting the user to input the value of the variable. For example, if a company offers a \$20 discount on items sold online, the program may include the expression $x - 20$ where x is equal to the total cost of your order before the discount.

Example 2 **Evaluating Expressions with Parentheses**

Evaluate each expression if $a = -2$ and $b = 4$.

a. $a(-b - a) - ab$

SOLUTION

$a(-b - a) - ab$

$= -2[-(4) - (-2)] - (-2)(4)$	Replace a with -2 and b with 4.
$= -2(-2) - (-2)(4)$	Perform operations inside parentheses.
$= 4 - (-8)$	Multiply.
$= 4 + 8$	Subtract.
$= 12$	

b. $ab - a + \frac{a + b}{2}$

SOLUTION

$ab - a + \frac{a + b}{2}$

$= (-2)(4) - (-2) + \frac{(-2) + 4}{2}$	Replace a with -2 and b with 4.
$= (-2)(4) - (-2) + \frac{2}{2}$	Perform operations inside parentheses.
$= (-8) - (-2) + 1$	Divide.
$= -8 + 2 + 1$	Add and subtract.
$= -5$	

Example 3 **Using a Calculator to Evaluate Expressions**

Caution

When using your calculator to square negative numbers you need to use parentheses. $(-3)^2 = 9$, but $-3^2 = -9$.

Use a calculator to evaluate $3mp + 2p^2$ if $m = 6$ and $p = -3$.

SOLUTION Replace m with 6 and p with -3.

$$3(6)(-3) + 2(-3)^2$$

Enter this expression into the calculator as shown.

```
3(6)(-3)+2(-3)²
```

Press ENTER to find the answer is -36.

Example 2

Tell students the brackets shown in the solution are a grouping symbol and should be treated in the same manner as parentheses. If parentheses are required inside of other parentheses, brackets are often used in place of the outer parentheses.

Additional Example 2

Evaluate each expression if $a = 5$ and $b = -3$.

a. $ab^2 - (a - b)$ 37

b. $\frac{a^2b + 3}{-2}$ 36

Example 3

Point out that not all calculators evaluate expressions in the same way. Be sure students are familiar with the calculator they will be using.

Error Alert Students are often confused by the number of parentheses in the calculator entry. Explain that parentheses come in pairs so that each open parenthesis "("must have a matching closing parenthesis ")".

Additional Example 3

Use a calculator to evaluate each expression if $m = 4$ and $p = -2$.

a. $5p^2(6m + p)$ 440

b. $m^2p^2 - (m - p)$ 58

ALTERNATE METHOD FOR EXAMPLE 3

If students prefer, have them enter the expression in the calculator in parts, writing down each value as they work.

$$mp = (6)(-3) = -18$$

$$3mp = 3(-18) = -54$$

$$p^2 = (-3)^2 = 9$$

$$2p^2 = 2(9) = 18$$

Then students can use the calculator to finish the problem. The screen shot might look like this:

```
3*(−18)+2*(9)
                −36
```

or

```
−54+18
                −36
```

Example 4

Remind students that because $-6yx$ is subtracted, they must bring the subtraction sign with the term when moving it.

Additional Example 4

Simplify the expression by adding like terms.

$7mp + 8 - 2m + 5pm - 3$
$12mp - 2m + 5$

Example 5

Point out that area will always result in units squared.

Additional Example 5

Use the diagram in the example to answer the following questions.

List the areas of the smallest three sheets of metal. What is the sum of these three sheets?
$2x$ square units, $4x$ square units, $6x$ square units; Total of the three sheets is $12x$ square units.

What is the difference between the area of the larger sheet and the sum of the areas of the three smaller sheets?
$3x$ square units

TEACHER TIP

Ask students to give examples of terms that are like terms and terms that are not like terms. Begin by discussing that variables x and y are not like terms. Continue the discussion by looking at the terms x and x^2. If students believe these are like terms, use examples with numbers. Ask "Are 5 and 25 the same term?" Show them that if $x = 5$, then x and x^2 are not like terms.

The **terms of an algebraic expression** are separated by addition and subtraction symbols. **Like terms** have the same variable raised to the same power. **Constant terms** are like terms that always have the same value.

Like terms

$$5x^2 + 4 - 8xy + 3x^2 - 1$$

Constant terms

Add like terms by adding the coefficients of the terms, as shown in the following examples.

Example 4 Simplifying Expressions

Simplify the expression by adding like terms.

$$3xy - 2x + 4 - 6yx + 3x$$

Hint

The order of the variables that a term is composed of doesn't change its value (*xyz* equals *zyx*).

SOLUTION Rearrange the expression so that the like terms are next to each other. Then add like terms.

$3xy - 2x + 4 - 6yx + 3x$
$= 3xy - 6yx - 2x + 3x + 4$
$= -3xy + x + 4$

Example 5 Application: Metalworking

A metal worker is using the four sheets of metal shown below with their dimensions. What is the total area of the four sheets?

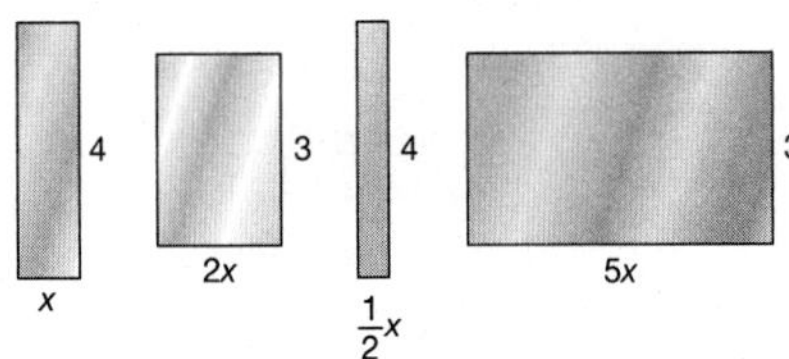

SOLUTION

First find the individual areas.

$$4 \cdot x = 4x \text{ square units}$$
$$3 \cdot 2x = 6x \text{ square units}$$
$$4 \cdot \frac{1}{2}x = 2x \text{ square units}$$
$$3 \cdot 5x = 15x \text{ square units}$$

Now add to find the total area.

$$4x + 6x + 2x + 15x = 27x \text{ square units}$$

ENGLISH LEARNERS

Define **variable** as a letter used to represent a number. Explain that to vary means to change. Therefore, a variable is a letter that can have different values.

Use the word to describe other occurrences that change values. Examples include the outside temperature, the amount of money earned at a job, or the amount of homework required each night.

Help students make the connection by providing different values for variables using the same expression. For example, have students evaluate the expression $x^2 + 4x$ for $x = -3, 0,$ and 1.

Lesson Practice

a. Evaluate $2x - 5x^2y$ if $x = 3$ and $y = -2$. 96
(Ex 1)

b. Evaluate $4xy^2 + x^2$ if $x = -3$ and $y = -1$. −3
(Ex 1)

c. Evaluate $\frac{2(a + b) + 4}{4} - a$ if $a = -4$ and $b = 6$. 6
(Ex 2)

d. Evaluate $-3ab - b(4 - a)$ if $a = -2$ and $b = 7$. 0
(Ex 2)

e. Use a calculator to evaluate $p(-p + 1) - m$ if $m = 5$ and $p = -3$. −17
(Ex 3)

f. Simplify the expression by adding like terms.
(Ex 4)

$-xy + 9 - 7x - 9xy + 7$ $-10xy - 7x + 16$

g. At the local drugstore, notebooks cost $7x$ dollars, pens cost $2x$ dollars, folders cost $3x$ dollars, and highlighters cost $4x$ dollars. Trent bought 1 notebook, 2 pens, 3 folders, and 1 highlighter. What was the total cost?
(Ex 5)
$24x$ dollars

Practice Distributed and Integrated

Find the volume of the rectangular prisms with the given dimensions.

1. $l = 2$ inches, $w = 4$ inches, $h = 9$ inches 72 in^3
(SB)

2. $l = 0.5$ cm, $w = 1.2$ cm, $h = 6$ cm 3.6 cm^3
(SB)

3. (Golf) Tiger Woods obtained an average score of 68 during the four rounds of golf at the PGA Championship in 2007. Use the Distributive Property to mentally calculate his total score for the four rounds of golf. 272
(1)

***4.** (Amusement Parks) An amusement park in Atlanta, Georgia offers a child's ticket for \$29.99 and an adult ticket for \$39.99.
(2)

a. Round individual ticket prices to the nearest dollar and write an expression for the total ticket cost for a family with A adults and C children. $40A + 30C$

b. Which would pay more, a family with one adult and four children, or a family with three adults and one child? Explain. $40(1) + 30(4) = \$160$ or $40(3) + 30(1) = \$150$. The family with one adult and four children would pay more.

Evaluate each expression for the given values of x and y.

***5.** $x - xy^2 - xy$ if $x = -2$ and $y = -3$
(2) 10

***6.** $(x - y) - x(-y)$ if $x = -5$ and $y = 3$
(2) −23

***7.** $x^2(x - xy)$ if $x = -2$ and $y = 3$ 16
(2)

***8.** $x^2 - y(x - y)$ if $x = -\frac{1}{2}$ and $y = \frac{1}{4}$
(2) $\frac{7}{16}$

***9.** $xy(1 - y)$ if $x = \frac{1}{5}$ and $y = -10$ −22
(2)

***10.** $xy - (x^2 - y)$ if $x = -\frac{1}{3}$ and $y = \frac{1}{2}$
(2) $\frac{2}{9}$

Identify the subsets of real numbers of which each number is a member.

11. $\sqrt{8}$ irrational; real
(1)

12. -3 integer; rational; real
(1)

13. $\frac{2}{3}$ rational; real
(1)

INCLUSION

To help with evaluating expressions, have students write the expression in large print on the board or piece of paper. Then write the values of the variables on post-it notes or other smaller pieces of paper. Have students place the value of the variable over the expression to see how the values will be substituted.

For example, $4m^2 - 3m$ with $m = -2$ will look like the following:

$$4m^2 - 3m$$

$$4 -2^2 - 3 -2$$

CHALLENGE

Variables can represent decimals, fractions, or even other expressions.

What is $x^2 + x$ if $x = m + 2$?
$m^2 + 5m + 6$

Lesson Practice

Problem c

Scaffolding Point out to students that the fraction bar acts as a grouping symbol to separate the numerator and the denominator.

Check for Understanding

The questions below help assess the concepts taught in this lesson.

1. **"Explain the difference between $(-x)^2$ and $-x^2$. Give an example."** Sample: The expression $(-x)^2$ means $(-x)(-x)$ while $-x^2$ means $-(x)(x)$. So if $x = 7$, then $(-x)^2 = (-7)^2 = 49$ and $-(7)^2 = -49$.

2. **"A student states that the simplified form of $3x^2 + x + 4x$ is equal to $8x^4$. Explain the mistakes the student is making. What is the correct simplified expression?"** Sample: The student thought that x^2 and x could be combined. Also the student thought that $x + x$ would be x^2. The correct simplified expression is $3x^2 + 5x$.

3 Practice

Math Conversations

Discussions to strengthen understanding

Problem 4

Guide the students by asking them the following questions.

"Write an expression for the total cost of the family with A adults and C children." $40A + 30C$

"How much would it cost if 1 adult and 4 children bought tickets?" \$160

"How much would it cost if 3 adults and 1 child bought tickets?" \$150

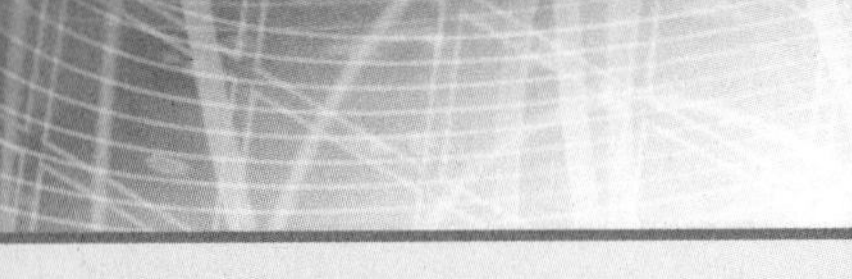

Problem 16
Extend the Problem

"How high was the football after 1 second?" 32 feet

"After how many seconds will the football first reach the ground?" 3 seconds

Problem 21

Error Alert Students selecting C as the answer forgot the negative when substituting $y = -2$. Encourage students to write out the problem when evaluating to be sure each step is correct.

Problem 23
Extend the Problem

"What is the perimeter of each rectangle?" $2c + 4d$; $18 - 2c$

"What is the combined perimeter of the rectangles?" $4d + 18$

Problem 24

Tell students that to prove a statement false, they need only find one example that makes the statement false. Point out that zero makes the statement true but that other numbers must be checked.

Problem 26

Remind students that a multiplicative inverse of a number is the reciprocal of that number.

***14.** (2) **Budgets** Van budgets $12 a day for groceries for weekdays and $15 a day for weekends. Write an expression in simplest form to show his grocery budget for w weeks. $90w$

***15.** (2) **Multi-Step** For the expression $2qr(3 + r)$

a. evaluate if $q = 2$ and $r = -1$. -8

b. explain how the result would be affected if q was doubled. The result would double.

c. show this is true by evaluating the expression if $q = 4$ and $r = -1$. -16

***16.** (2) **Sports** A football is kicked from ground level. The height h in feet of the ball after t seconds can be modeled by the expression $-16t^2 + 48t$. Find the height of the ball after 2 seconds. 32 feet

Measurement **Find the measure of the complementary angle given the measures of the angles below.**

17. (SB) 35° 55° **18.** (SB) 68° 22° **19.** (SB) 5° 85° **20.** (SB) 89° 1°

***21.** (2) **Multiple Choice** Evaluate $4x^2 + 7y$ if $x = 3$ and $y = -2$. D

A 10 **B** 41 **C** 50 **D** 22

22. (1) **Error Analysis** Two students multiplied $-13 \cdot 18$ using the Distributive Property. Which student is correct? Find and explain the other student's error.

22. Student A is correct. Student B did not distribute the negative sign when multiplying -13 by 2.

Student A	Student B
$-13 \cdot 18 = -13(20 - 2)$	$-13 \cdot 18 = -13(20 - 2)$
$= -13(20) + 13(2)$	$= -13(20) - 13(2)$
$= -260 + 26$	$= -260 - 26$
$= -234$	$= -286$

***23.** (2) **Geometry** A rectangle has length c and width $2d$. Another rectangle has length 4 and width $(5 - c)$. Write a simplified expression of their combined area. $2cd - 4c + 20$

***24.** (2) **Verify** Is $a^2 + b^2 = (a + b)^2$? Support your answer with an example. No. Sample: $2^2 + 3^2 = 13$ and $(2 + 3)^2 = 25$

***25.** (2) **Consumer** A local sandwich shop has $6 lunches, and you receive a $5 discount on the tenth lunch. Calculate your total cost for ten lunches at this shop. $6(10) - 5 = \$55$

26. (1) **Write** Does zero have a multiplicative inverse? Explain your answer. No. Division by zero is undefined.

***27.** (2) **Graphing Calculator** Use a calculator to evaluate the expression $fg^2 - (2f - g^2)$ if $f = 1$ and $g = -2$. Then, verify the answer by simplifying and solving. $(1)(-2)^2 - (2(1) - (-2)^2) = (1)(4) - (2 - 4) = 4 - (-2) = 6$

Simplify by combining like terms.

***28.** (2) $5ab + 7a - 3ab + 4b$ $2ab + 7a + 4b$

***29.** (2) $y - 9x^2y + 4 + 3x^2y + 12$ $-6x^2y + y + 16$

***30.** (2) $2(x + 3) - x$ $x + 6$

LOOKING FORWARD 

Evaluating expressions and combining like terms prepares students for

- **Lesson 3** Using Rules of Exponents
- **Lesson 7** Solving Linear Equations
- **Lesson 11** Understanding Polynomials

LESSON 3

Using Rules of Exponents

Warm Up

1. **Vocabulary** In the expression 3^2, 2 is the ________. exponent (SB)

2. True or False: $5^4 = 5 + 5 + 5 + 5$. False (SB)

3. Evaluate $n \cdot n \cdot n \cdot n$ for $n = -3$. 81 (SB)

New Concepts

In an expression such as x^n the **exponent** tells the number of times that the base is a factor. So 2^3 is defined as 2 times 2 times 2. Two to the negative third power is defined as 1 over 2 to the third power.

$$2^{-3} = \frac{1}{2^3}$$

Reading Math

In the expression 5^4, 5 is the base and 4 is the exponent. The expression is read "5 raised to the 4th power."

The formal definition of **negative exponents** is as follows:

Definition of x^{-n}
If n is any real number and x is any real number that is not zero, $x^{-n} = \frac{1}{x^n}$.

This definition says that when an exponential expression is written in reciprocal form, the sign of the exponent must be changed. If the exponent is negative, it is positive in reciprocal form; and if it is positive, it is negative in reciprocal form.

Example 1 Simplifying Negative Exponents

Simplify.

a. $\frac{1}{3^{-2}}$

b. 3^{-3}

SOLUTION

a. $\frac{1}{3^{-2}} = 3^2 = 9$

b. $3^{-3} = \frac{1}{3^3} = \frac{1}{27}$

c. -3^{-2}

d. $(-3)^{-2}$

SOLUTION

c. $-3^{-2} = -\frac{1}{3^2} = -\frac{1}{9}$

d. $(-3)^{-2} = \frac{1}{(-3)^2} = \frac{1}{9}$

e. $-(-3)^{-3}$

SOLUTION

e. $-(-3)^{-3} = -\frac{1}{(-3)^3} = -\frac{1}{-27} = -\left(-\frac{1}{27}\right) = \frac{1}{27}$

Online Connection
www.SaxonMathResources.com

LESSON 3

1 Warm Up

Remind students that exponents indicate multiplication in problem 2.

2 New Concepts

In this lesson, students learn about exponents, including negative exponents, the product rule and the power rule.

Example 1

Tell students to pay close attention to parentheses as they will indicate what part of the term is raised to the power and what part is not.

Error Alert Students might think that 3^{-2} can be simplified to -3^2. Explain that the negative in an exponent simply changes the position of the term from numerator to denominator or denominator to numerator.

Additional Example 1

Simplify.

a. $\frac{1}{5^{-2}}$ 25

b. 5^{-2} $\frac{1}{25}$

c. -5^{-2} $-\frac{1}{25}$

d. $(-5)^{-2}$ $\frac{1}{25}$

e. $-(-5)^{-2}$ $-\frac{1}{25}$

MATH BACKGROUND

Exponents arose out of the need to condense expressions. Consequently, rather than writing $(x)(x)(x)(x)(x)$, we need to write only x^5. Because this exponential is a condensed expression, we have rules for combining these terms. Most importantly, the base must always be the same. If the base is the same, we can add, subtract, or multiply the exponents to simplify expressions.

This short-hand method for writing multiplication also allows us to write very large or very small numbers using a smaller expression called scientific notation. This notation is a method of writing a number as the product of a number greater than or equal to 1 but less than 10 and a power of 10.

LESSON RESOURCES

Student Edition Practice Workbook 3
Reteaching Master 3
Adaptations Master 3
Challenge and Enrichment Masters C3, E3
Technology Lab Master 3

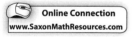

Example 2

Remind students that if no exponent is shown, the exponent is 1.

Additional Example 2

Simplify.

a. $y^{-4}y^2x^2yx^{-3}y^{-2}x^{-5}$ $\frac{1}{x^6y^3}$

b. $\frac{x^{-3}xy^2x^{-1}yx^5}{y^{-7}x^3y^4}$ $\frac{y^6}{x}$

TEACHER TIP

Although students may understand that exponents indicate the number of times a quantity is multiplied by itself, the concept of negative exponents may be difficult to grasp. Explain that a negative exponent can be thought of as an indication of where the exponential should be placed.

Two rules for exponents are the product rule and the power rule. These rules simplify operations with bases.

The product of powers whose bases are the same can be found by writing each power as repeated multiplication. $x^2 \cdot x^3$ means $x \cdot x$ times $x \cdot x \cdot x$ which equals x^5. The exponents may be added to obtain the same result: $x^2 \cdot x^3 = x^{2+3} = x^5$. This demonstrates the product rule for exponents.

Math Reasoning

Connect Apply the definition of negative exponents to explain why the product theorem states that $x \neq 0$.

If 0 is raised to a negative power, then 0 will be in the denominator of a fraction. Division by 0 is undefined.

Product Rule for Exponents
If m, n, and x are real numbers and $x \neq 0$, $x^m \cdot x^n = x^{m+n}$.

Example 2 Simplifying Expressions Using the Product Rule

Simplify.

a. $x^2yx^{-5}y^{-4}x^5x$

SOLUTION

Simplify by adding the exponents of like bases.

$$x^2yx^{-5}y^{-4}x^5x$$
$$= x^2x^{-5}x^5xyy^{-4}$$
$$= x^{2+(-5)+5+1}y^{1+(-4)}$$
$$= x^3y^{-3}$$

x^3y^{-3} may also be written with positive exponents as $\frac{x^3}{y^3}$.

b. $\frac{yy^{-3}x^4y^5x^{-10}}{y^{-6}x^{-3}y^{10}x^2}$

SOLUTION

Step 1: Simplify the numerator and denominator by adding the exponents of like bases.

Step 2: Apply the definition of x^{-n}.

Step 3: Repeat step 1.

$$\frac{yy^{-3}x^4y^5x^{-10}}{y^{-6}x^{-3}y^{10}x^2} = \frac{x^{4+(-10)}y^{1+(-3)+5}}{x^{(-3)+2}y^{(-6)+10}} = \frac{x^{-6}y^3}{x^{-1}y^4} = x^{-6} \cdot x^1 \cdot y^3 \cdot y^{-4} = x^{-5}y^{-1} \text{ or } \frac{1}{x^5y}$$

Math Reasoning

Analyze In Example 2 the definition of x^{-n} is used to simplify each expression. What mathematical operation would have the same result? Explain.

Subtraction; If the bases are the same in the numerator and denominator, subtracting the exponents will have the same result. For example, $\frac{x^{-6}}{x^{-1}} = x^{-6-(-1)}$ $= x^{-6+1} = x^{-5} = \frac{1}{x^5}$.

The product rule can be used to expand $(x^2)^3$ as

$$(x^2)^3 = x^2x^2x^2 = x^{2+2+2} = x^6$$

This demonstrates the power rule for exponents.

Power Rule for Exponents
If m, n, and x are real numbers, $(x^m)^n = x^{m \cdot n}$.

This rule extends to any number of exponential factors, so that

$$(x^ay^bz^c\ldots)^n = x^{an}y^{bn}z^{cn}\ldots.$$

ENGLISH LEARNERS

Several phrases in this lesson can be used interchangeably. Write x^3 on the board and tell the students it can be said as:

- x to the power of 3
- x to the 3rd power
- x has an exponent of 3

Explain that all 3 phrases show that the base is x, while the **power** or **exponent** is 3. Each phrase means $(x)(x)(x)$.

Be sure to rephrase when asking questions to be sure students understand all three ways of stating the same expression. You might ask "What is the power of y?" and "What is the exponent of y?" so students can use and understand both phrases.

Example 3 Simplifying Using the Power Rule of Exponents

Simplify.

a. $\dfrac{x(x^{-3})^2y(xy^{-2})^{-3}}{(x^2)^3y^{-3}(x^2)^3}$

SOLUTION

Use the power rule in both the numerator and denominator, then simplify the expressions using the product rule.

$$\frac{x(x^{-3})^2y(xy^{-2})^{-3}}{(x^2)^3y^{-3}(x^2)^3} = \frac{xx^{-6}yx^{-3}y^6}{x^6y^{-3}x^6} = \frac{x^{-8}y^7}{x^{12}y^{-3}} = x^{-20}y^{10} = \frac{y^{10}}{x^{20}}.$$

b. $\dfrac{(x^a)^b(y^a)^{b+2}}{x^{-a}}$

SOLUTION

$$\frac{(x^a)^b(y^a)^{b+2}}{x^{-a}} = \frac{x^{ab}y^{ab+2a}}{x^{-a}} = x^{ab}x^a y^{ab+2a} = x^{ab+a}y^{ab+2a}$$

Scientific notation is a method of writing a number as the product of a number greater than or equal to 1 but less than 10 and a power of 10. Multiplying a number by a positive integral power of 10 moves the decimal point to the right. Multiplying a number by a negative integral power of 10 moves the decimal point to the left.

Number	The decimal moves	Scientific Notation
412.36	Two places left	4.1236×10^2
0.041236	Two places right	4.1236×10^{-2}

Writing very large or small numbers in scientific notation can be helpful. Rules of exponents can be used to simplify expressions written in scientific notation.

Hint

The Commutative and Associative Properties of Multiplication allow you to move the numbers and to group them to make calculations easier.

Example 4 Simplifying Expressions in Scientific Notation

Simplify $\dfrac{(0.0003 \times 10^{-6})(4000)}{(0.006 \times 10^{15})(2000 \times 10^4)}$.

SOLUTION

Begin by writing all four numbers in scientific notation. Then multiply and divide.

$$\frac{(3 \times 10^{-4} \times 10^{-6})(4 \times 10^3)}{(6 \times 10^{-3} \times 10^{15})(2.0 \times 10^3 \times 10^4)} = \frac{(3 \times 10^{-10})(4 \times 10^3)}{(6 \times 10^{12})(2 \times 10^7)}$$

$$= \frac{3 \cdot 4}{6 \cdot 2} \times \frac{10^{-7}}{10^{19}} = 1 \times 10^{-7+(-19)} = 1 \times 10^{-26}$$

CHALLENGE

Simplify the following. Write with all positive exponents.

$$\frac{\dfrac{(4)(2^3)(3^{-5})^{-4}}{(2^3)(3^{-1})}}{(4^2)}$$

$\dfrac{3^{21}}{4}$

Example 3

Encourage students to write out all steps when simplifying the expressions so that errors might be spotted easily.

Error Alert Students may begin to divide terms in the numerator by terms in the denominator as their first step. Remind students of the order of operations and tell them to use the rules of exponents first before dividing.

Additional Example 3

Simplify.

a. $\dfrac{(xy^3)^2x^{-4}(x^{-2}y)^{-3}}{(xy)^3y^{-4}x}$ y^4

b. $\dfrac{x^{a+3}(xy^{-2})^b}{(xy)^{-a}}$ $x^{2a+b+3}y^{-2b+a}$

Example 4

Remind students they can add and subtract exponents only when the bases are the same.

Additional Example 4

Simplify.

$$\frac{(4.2 \times 10^{-7})(0.0028)}{2400(1.6 \times 10^{-10})}$$

3.0625×10^{-3}

Example 5

Point out that using the rules of exponents, $\frac{10^8}{10^8} = 10^{8-8} = 10^0 = 1$.

Additional Example 5

The maximum distance of the earth from the sun is 152,000,000,000 meters. How many seconds does it take light to reach the earth from the sun? Give answer to the nearest hundredth. 506.67 seconds

Lesson Practice

Scaffolding Have students convert all numbers to scientific notation. Then have them rewrite the expression so all terms with base 10 are together. Finally, use the rules of exponents to simplify.

Error Alert Students attempting to input the entire expression in a calculator will often get an incorrect answer due to misplacement of parentheses.

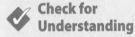

Check for Understanding

The question below helps assess the concepts taught in this lesson.

"A student states that a negative exponent means the exponential must be in the denominator. Is this correct? Explain." Sample: No. If the exponent is negative in the denominator, it will be positive in the numerator. If the exponent is negative in the numerator, it will be positive in the denominator.

Example 5 **Astronomy**

The speed of light is 3×10^8 meters/second. If the moon is 3.844×10^8 meters from the earth, how many seconds does it take light to reach the moon from the earth? Give the answer to the nearest hundredth.

SOLUTION Divide the moon's distance from the earth by the speed of light.

$$\frac{3.844 \times 10^8}{3 \times 10^8} = \frac{3.844}{3} \times \frac{10^8}{10^8} = \frac{3.844}{3} \approx 1.28 \text{ seconds}$$

It takes light about 1.28 seconds to reach the moon from the earth.

Lesson Practice

Simplify.
(Ex 1)

a. $\frac{1}{2^{-3}}$ 8 **b.** 2^{-4} $\frac{1}{16}$ **c.** -2^{-2} $-\frac{1}{4}$ **d.** $(-2)^{-3}$ $-\frac{1}{8}$

e. (Ex 1) $-(-2)^{-4}$ $-\frac{1}{16}$

f. (Ex 2) $x^9y^{-1}x^{-2}y^3y^{-7}$ x^7y^{-5}

g. (Ex 2) $\frac{xx^6y^8x^{-11}y^{-3}}{x^{-5}yy^2x^{-4}}$ x^5y^2

h. (Ex 3) $\frac{(y^2)^{-3}x^4(xy^{-2})^{-2}}{xy^4}$ $\frac{x}{y^6}$

i. (Ex 3) $\frac{(x^b)^{a-1}(xy^{-a})^{-b}}{y^{-1}}$ $x^{ab-2b}y^{ab+1}$

j. (Ex 4) $\frac{(0.004)(600 \times 10^9)}{(30000 \times 10^{-12})(0.0001 \times 10^3)}$ 8×10^{17}

k. (Ex 5) The United States population is approximately 2.99×10^8. In one year, the United States produced 4.78×10^{11} pounds of garbage. Approximately how much garbage did the average American produce that year?
1.60×10^3 pounds

Practice Distributed and Integrated

Evaluate each expression for the given values of *a* and *b*.

1. (2) $-b^2 - b(a - b^2)$ if $a = 4$ and $b = -3$ −24

2. (2) $a^2 - b^3(a - b)$ if $a = -2$ and $b = -3$ 31

State the properties illustrated below.

3. (1) $a + b + c = b + a + c$ Commutative Property

4. (1) $a(b + c) = ab + ac$ Distributive Property

Use the rules of exponents to simplify the expressions below.

***5.** (3) $\frac{(2x^2)^{-3}(xy^0)^{-2}}{2xx^0x^1xxy^2}$ $\frac{1}{16x^{12}y^2}$

***6.** (3) $\frac{a^0bc^0(a^{-1}b^{-1})^2}{ab(ab^0)abc}$ $\frac{1}{a^5b^3c}$

***7.** (3) $\frac{(2x^2y^3)^{-3}y}{(4xy)^{-2}(x^{-2}y)^3y}$ $\frac{2x^2}{y^{10}}$

***8.** (3) $\frac{xx^{-2}y(x^{-3})^2xy^0}{(2xy)^{-2}x^2(y^{-3})^2}$ $\frac{4y^9}{x^6}$

9. (SB) What is the area of a circle with radius 3 meters? Give your answer in terms of π. 9π m²

INCLUSION

Encourage students to write out the terms when exponents are raised to a power to help them visualize the power rule.

For example, to simplify $(x^{-3})^2x(y^4)^3$, students can write $(x^{-3})(x^{-3})x(y^4)(y^4)(y^4)$. Simplifying using the product rule, we have $x^{-5}y^{12}$.

10. Angles a and b are vertical angles. If angle b measures 74°, what is the measure of angle a? 74°
(SB)

*11. **Write** In 2002, the average height of a 10-year old girl was 1.4×10^{-3} km. Approximately 3×10^7 10-year old girls lying head-to-toe would equal the circumference of the earth at the equator. Explain how you could use properties of real numbers to mentally estimate the circumference.
(3)
See Additional Answers.

12. **Consumer** Your dinner total at your favorite restaurant is \$18.
(1)

a. Use the Distributive Property to mentally calculate 10% of your dinner bill. See Additional Answers.

b. Explain how the result in part **a** would be helpful to mentally calculate a 15% tip. A 15% tip equals a 10% tip plus one-half of the 10% tip. So, a 15% tip equals \$1.80 + \$0.90 = \$2.70.

13. **Error Analysis** A student is asked to simplify an expression and identify which property was used for each step. His answer is shown below. Identify and explain the error(s). The first step should be labeled "Distributive Property." The second step should be labeled "Multiply."
(1)

$(8 + 4) \cdot 9$	
$(8 \cdot 9) + (4 \cdot 9)$	Associative Property of Addition
$72 + 36$	Distributive Property
108	Add.

14. a. Evaluate the expression $1 - (3x^2 - 2y)$ if $x = 2$ and $y = 3$. −5
(2)

b. Explain how the result would be affected if y was doubled. The result would increase by $2y$.

c. Show that this is true by evaluating the expression if $x = 2$ and $y = 6$. 1

15. **Nutrition** The U.S. recommended daily amount of calcium for most adults is 1000 mg per day. Milana's breakfast consists of cereal that contains 33 mg calcium in $\frac{1}{4}$-cup and milk that contains 75 mg calcium per $\frac{1}{4}$-cup. Calculate the total amount of calcium in milligrams in Milana's breakfast of $\frac{3}{4}$-cup cereal with $\frac{1}{2}$-cup milk. $3(33) + 2(75) = 99 + 150 = 249$ mg
(2)

16. **Justify** A square drawn on a coordinate grid has adjacent vertices at points $(u, 1)$ and $(5u, 1)$. Another square has adjacent vertices at points $(2u, 1)$ and $(4u, 1)$. Write a simplified expression of their combined area. Explain how you obtained your answer. See Additional Answers.
(2)

 **17.** **Coordinate Geometry** A figure on a coordinate graph is translated 2 units to the right and 5 units up. Its new coordinates can be written with the expressions $(x + 2, y + 5)$. A point is translated to (19, 19), what are the coordinates of the original point? (17, 14)
(2)

18. **Verify** Evaluate the expression $3g - 2f + fg^2 - 5g + 4fg^2 + 6f$ if $f = 1$ and $g = -1$ by inserting the variable values into the expression as written. Verify your answer by simplifying the expression first, then inserting the variable values. See Additional Answers.
(2)

*19. **Multiple Choice** Simplify $\frac{y^{-3}xy^2x^{-4}x^5}{x^3y^{-1}}$. A
(3)

A $\frac{1}{x}$ B $\frac{1}{x^2y^5}$ C $\frac{x^5}{y^2}$ D $\frac{x^3}{y}$

CHALLENGE

Simplify the following. Write with all positive exponents.

$$\frac{\frac{a^3bab^{-5}b^4a^{-2}}{a^3b^{-1}}}{a^{-2}b^4b^{-2}}$$ $\frac{b^3}{a^3}$

3 Practice

Math Conversations

Discussions to strengthen understanding

Problem 16

Guide the students by asking them the following questions.

"If a line is drawn through coordinates $(u, 1)$ and $(5u, 1)$, is this line horizontal or vertical? Explain." The y-coordinates are the same, therefore the line is horizontal.

"What is the length of this line? Explain." The length of the line is $5u - u = 4u$.

"What is the area of this square?" $16u^2$

"What is the length of the line drawn through $(2u, 1)$ and $(4u, 1)$? Explain." The length of the line is $4u - 2u = 2u$.

"What is the area of this square?" $4u^2$

"What is the combined area of the squares?" $20u^2$

Problem 21

Extend the Problem

What is the correct simplification of the expression $\frac{2^3(2^{-2})^3}{2(2^2 + 2)}$? $\frac{1}{96}$

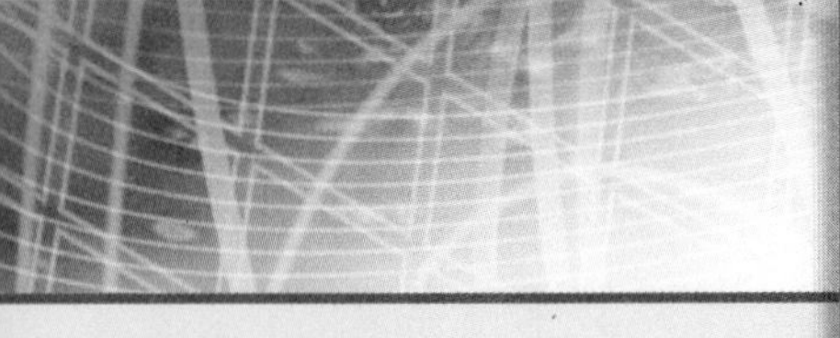

Problem 22

Error Alert Students might subtract the numbers in this problem, thinking that height and depth are opposites. Tell students to draw a picture and label the dimensions to help them see that 4200 must be added to 590 to find the depth of the sea floor.

Problem 23

Guide the students by asking them the following questions.

"What is the formula for volume?" $l \times w \times h$

"What is meant by the surface area?" This is $l \times w$.

"What is the volume of the Atlantic Ocean?" 3.24×10^{17} m^3

"What is twice the volume of the Atlantic Ocean?" 6.38×10^{17} m^3

"Use the dimensions in the problem to find the volume of the Pacific Ocean. Explain." The Pacific Ocean has a surface area of 1.66×10^{14} m^2 and a depth of 3.93×10^3 m. The volume is 6.5238×10^{17} m^3.

"Does the Pacific Ocean have twice the volume of the Atlantic? Explain." Yes. Twice the volume of the Atlantic is 6.38×10^{17} m^3 and the Pacific is 6.5238×10^{17} m^3.

Problem 25

Tell students to simplify the volume and the area before trying to find height.

Problem 26

Extend the Problem

"How many free videos will Rita receive if she rents 12 videos from Store 1?" 1

"How much will it cost for Rita to rent 12 videos at Store 1?" \$55

"How many free videos will Rita receive if she rents 12 videos from Store 2?" 3

"How much will it cost for Rita to rent 12 videos at Store 2?" \$63

20. *(SB)* **Write** Why is $1^{10000000} = 1$? See Additional Answers.

***21.** *(3)* **Error Analysis** Two students incorrectly simplified the expression $\frac{2^3(2^{-2})^3}{2(2^2+2)}$. Their steps are shown below. Explain the error of each student.
See Additional Answers.

Student A	Student B
$\frac{2^3(2^{-2})^3}{2(2^2+2)} = \frac{2^3(2^{-6})}{2(4+2)}$	$\frac{2^3(2^{-2})^3}{2(2^2+2)} = \frac{2^3(2^{-6})}{2(2^3)}$
$= \frac{2^{-3}}{12} = \frac{1}{12(-2)^3} = -\frac{1}{96}$	$= \frac{2^{-3}}{2^4} = \frac{1}{2^7} = \frac{1}{128}$

22. *(SB)* **Volcanos** Vailulu'u is an underwater volcano in the Pacific Ocean. The volcano has a height of about 4,200 m off the sea floor. If the top of the volcano is at a depth of 590 m below sea level, what is the depth of the sea floor in this area? 4790 m

***23.** *(3)* **Verify** The Atlantic Ocean is 3.93×10^3 m deep and has 8.24×10^{13} m^2 of surface area. Calculate the total volume of the Atlantic Ocean. Write your answer in scientific notation. Verify your answer if you know that the Pacific Ocean has approximately two times the volume and approximately the same depth of the Atlantic Ocean, and a surface area of about 1.66×10^{14} m^2.
See Additional Answers.

24. *(SB)* **Geography** The Danube River is Europe's second longest river. It flows through 9 countries and has a length of 1,770 miles. About how many feet long is the Danube? 9,345,600 ft

***25.** *(3)* **Geometry** A box has a volume of $\frac{x^3y^2x^{-2}}{y^{-3}x^2y}$. The area resulting from length times width is $\frac{x^{-2}y^3x^{-1}}{y^{-4}x^{-2}y^2}$. Find an expression for the height of the box. See Additional Answers.

26. *(2)* **Analyze** Rita can choose to rent movies from one of two movie stores. The first store charges \$5 per movie, and she can rent her 8th movie for free. The second store charges \$7 per movie, and she can rent her 4th movie for free. Rita assumes that the second shop has a better deal because she must only rent 3 movies before receiving a free movie rental. Explain why she should not make this assumption.

26. 8 movies at the first store will cost \$35. 8 movies at the second store will cost \$42. She must consider that the second store charges more for each movie rental.

***27.** *(3)* **Graphing Calculator** Simplify $\frac{2^{-3}}{8^{-2}}$. Use a calculator to check your answer. 8

28. *(2)* **Error Analysis** The EPA lists the greenest hybrid car as getting 61 miles per gallon on the highway and 50 miles per gallon in the city. Assuming the fuel tank holds 15 gallons of gas, one owner decided to calculate the total miles that he could drive one tank of gas if 4 gallons were used in the city. Explain and correct his error.

$$61(4) + 50(15 - 4) = 244 + 75 - 200 = 119 \text{ miles}$$

He multiplied the highway fuel efficiency by the city mileage. $61(15 - 4) + 50(4) = 871$ miles

29. *(1)* **Analyze** Identify which property of real numbers is being demonstrated. Explain why this property might be helpful in solving this problem without a calculator.
See Additional Answers.

$$(9 \cdot 3) \cdot 3 = 9 \cdot (3 \cdot 3) = 9 \cdot 9 = 81$$

***30.** *(2)* **Multi-Step** Shane spent \$2.24 on breakfast and x dollars on lunch.

a. Write an expression for the amount of money Shane spent on breakfast and lunch. $\$2.24 + x$

b. If Shane spent \$5.97 on lunch, how much money did he spend in all? $\$2.24 + \$5.97 = \$8.21$

LOOKING FORWARD

Using exponents prepares students for

- **Lesson 11** Understanding Polynomials
- **Lesson 19** Multiplying Polynomials
- **Lesson 28** Simplifying Rational Expressions
- **Lesson 70** Solving Radical Equations

LAB
1

Graphing a Function and Building a Table

Graphing Calculator Lab (*Use with Lesson 4*)

A graphing calculator can be used to analyze functions. The calculator can be used to graph the function as well as build tables of data. Use the graphing calculator to graph the line $y = 2x + 7$.

Graphing a Function in the Standard Window

1. Enter the equation $y = 2x + 7$.

Open the Y= equation editor by pressing Y=.

Enter the equation in the first row next to \Y1= by pressing 2 X,T,θ,n + 7.

2. Graph the line.

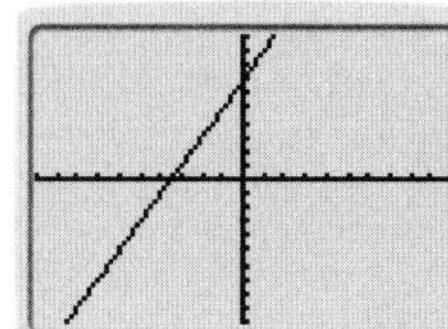

Press GRAPH, and the line will be displayed on a coordinate plane. If the graph does not appear identical to the screen to the right, press ZOOM and select **[6: ZStandard]**.

Tracing a Line to Find Points

1. Trace the Line.

Press TRACE. A blinking cursor will appear on the graph as well as an x-and y-value displayed at the bottom of the screen. The values at the bottom are the coordinates of the cursor.

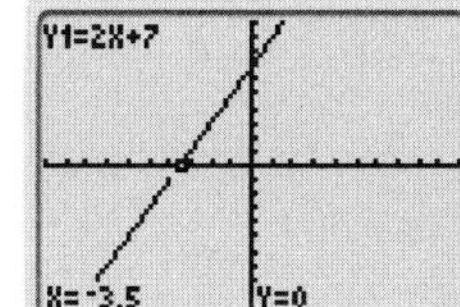

By pressing the arrow buttons ◀ ▶, you can move the cursor along the line to find the x-and y-intercepts.

2. Find the x-and y-intercepts.

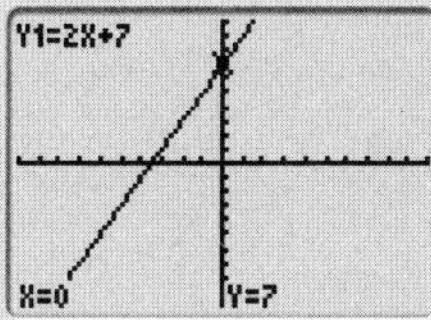

Use the coordinates displayed at the bottom to find the place where $y = 0$ (x-intercept) and $x = 0$ (y-intercept). While in the TRACE feature, you can also move the cursor by entering the x-value of the coordinate you are looking for and pressing ENTER.

Online Connection
www.SaxonMathResources.com

LAB
1

Materials

• graphing calculator

Discuss

In this lab, students will use the graphing calculator to graph and trace a line. Points on the line will be investigated by using the trace and table features.

Define **Trace, x- and y-intercepts, TBlStart** and **Δ Tbl.**

Graphing a Function in the Standard Window

Remind students that they should be in function mode (MODE **[FUNC]**) when graphing a function.

Tracing a Line to Find Points

Students will discover that moving the cursor off the screen will not affect the tracing command.

Error Alert

When entering the x-value, stay within the window of values. The calculator error ERR: INVALID will occur if a value is chosen beyond the window interval.

Building a Table From a Function

Indicate that the table of values include values beyond the specified window.

Lab Practice C

What values of **[TblStart=]** and **[Δ Tbl=]** would you use to create a table beginning with 8 and containing multiples of 4?
TblStart=8; Δ Tbl=4

TEACHER TIP

For Lab Practice **c** and **d**, use **[TblStart=]** and **[Δ Tbl=]** to create the specified table.

TEACHER TIP

If students are struggling to remember the calculator steps, have them write down their keystrokes as they complete each problem.

Building a Table From a Function

The calculator can also produce a table of values for an equation. Generate a table of values for the equation $y = 2x + 7$, graphed above.

1. Display a table.

Press 2nd GRAPH to open the **[TABLE]** feature. The x-values will be displayed in the first column, and the corresponding y-values will be in the second column. These points correspond to points on the graph of the line. Use the arrow keys to scroll through the data.

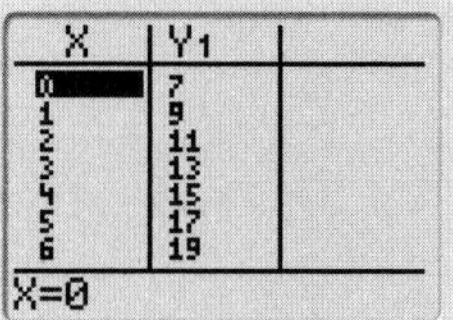

2. Adjust the table.

Press 2nd WINDOW to open the **[TBLSET]** menu. The line [**TblStart=**] allows you to change the first x-value listed in the table, or where you want the table to start. The line [Δ **Tbl=**] defines the change between each subsequent x-value in the table. To change the table in the [**TBLSET**] menu, press 8 ENTER after [**TblStart=**] and press 2 ENTER after [Δ **Tbl=**]. Press 2nd GRAPH to reopen the table feature. The table's x-values will now be the even numbers between 8 and 20. The arrow keys can still be used to scroll through the table's data.

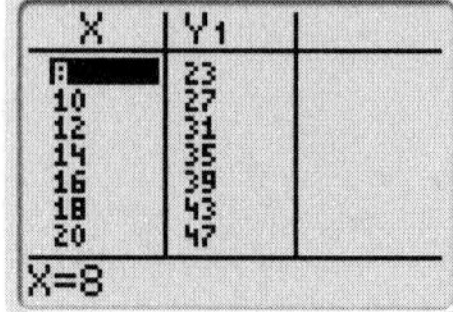

Lab Practice

a. Use the graphing calculator to graph the line $y = -5x + 3$.

b. Use the graphing calculator to find the x-and y-intercepts of $y = -2x + 4$. x-intercept (2, 0) y-intercept (0, 4)

c. Use the graphing calculator to create a table of the odd numbers between 1 and 13, for the equation $y = -3x + 8$.

d. Use the graphing calculator to fill in the table for the graph of $y = 4x - 6$.

x	y
0	−6
0.5	−4
1	−2
1.5	0
2	2

a.

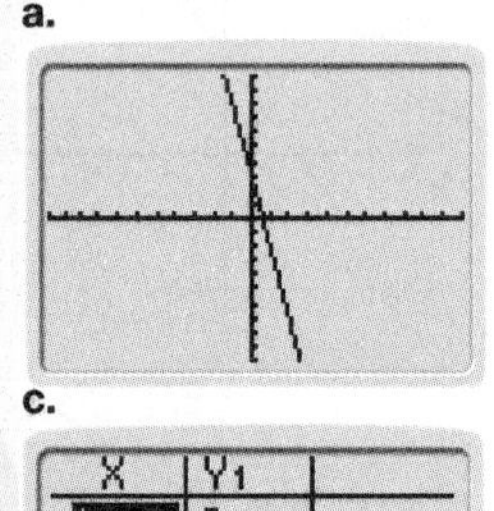

c.

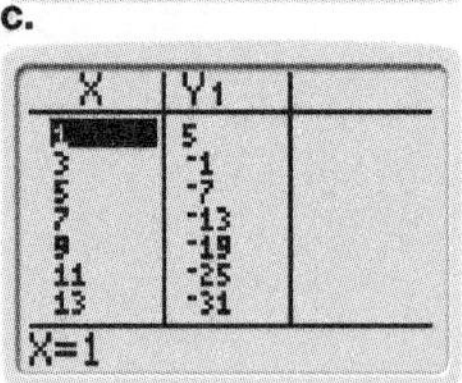

LESSON 4 Identifying Functions and Using Function Notation

Warm Up

1. (SB) **Vocabulary** A number used to locate a point on a graph is called a
   a. coordinate. **b.** integer. **c.** line. a
2. (2) Evaluate $5x^3 - 3x$ for $x = 2$. 34
3. (SB) List the x-coordinates from the ordered pairs: (−2, 4), (0, 7), (2, 10).
   −2, 0, 2

New Concepts

A **relation** is a pairing of input and output values.

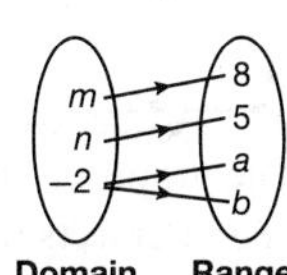

The **domain** contains the input values: m, n, and −2. The **range of a function or relation** contains the output values: 8, 5, a, and b.

The input value, normally x, is the **independent variable.** The output, normally y, is called the **dependent variable.**

Caution

In a function, the y values may repeat. The x values may not.

A **function** is a mapping between two sets that associates with each element of the first set, the domain, a unique (one and only one) element of the second set, the range.

x	y
−5	4
−2	2
1	0
0	−2

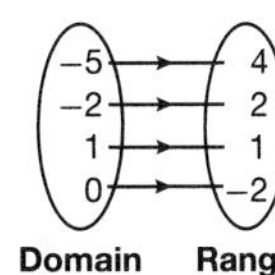

Example 1 Identifying Functions, Domain, and Range

Which of the following depict functions? Identify the domain and the range.

a.

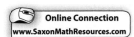

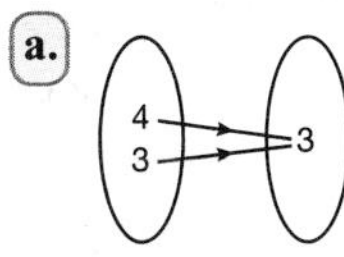

SOLUTION Function.
Domain: 4, 3; Range: 3

b.

x	y
7	3
5	3
5	4

SOLUTION Not a function.
Domain: 5, 7; Range: 3, 4

Math Reasoning

Formulate Give three ordered pairs for the function in Example 1b.

See student work.
(7, 3), (5, 3), (5, 4)

Online Connection
www.SaxonMathResources.com

MATH BACKGROUND

When a number is paired with another number, we have a relation. But some relations have a unique pairing where the element of the first set is paired with one and only one element of the second set. In this case, the relation is also a function. We can determine if a relation is a function by looking at the domain and range or by using the vertical line test.

Function notation is simply a different way of writing how to evaluate a function. Instead of saying "Evaluate $y = 3 + x$ for $x = -2$" we say "$f(-2) = 3 + x$". These equations mean exactly the same thing. Function notation is useful when we are dealing with more than one function. Note that calculators often list the functions as y_1, y_2, y_3, etc. With function notation we can list them as $f(x)$, $g(x)$, $h(x)$, etc.

LESSON 4

1 Warm Up

For problem 3, remind students the x-coordinate is listed first in an ordered pair.

2 New Concepts

In this lesson, students learn to identify functions by inspecting the domain and range and by using the vertical line test. Students will also be using function notation to evaluate functions.

Example 1

Tell students that the mapping in part **a** can also be represented by the ordered pairs (4, 3) and (3, 3).

Additional Example 1

Which of the following depict functions? Identify the domain and range.

a.

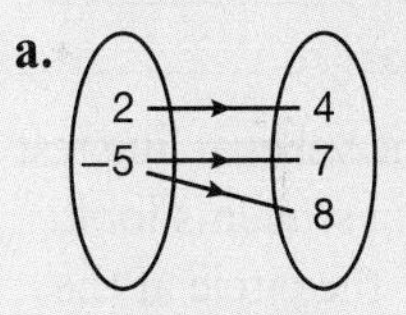

not a function;
D: 2, −5
R: 4, 7, 8

b.

x	y
4	5
4	7
−3	9
0	12

not a function;
D: 4, −3, 0
R: 5, 7, 9, 12

LESSON RESOURCES

Student Edition Practice Workbook 4
Reteaching Master 4
Adaptations Master 4
Challenge and Enrichment Master C4

Example 2

Tell students that the vertical line test encourages a visualization of a function.

Additional Example 2

Determine if each graph represents the graph of a function.

a.

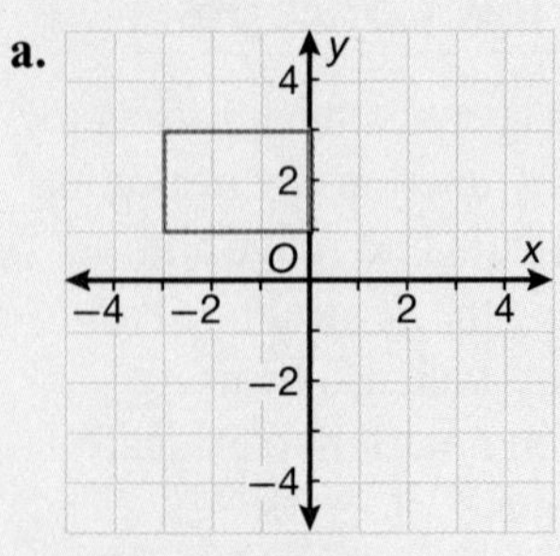

not a function

b.

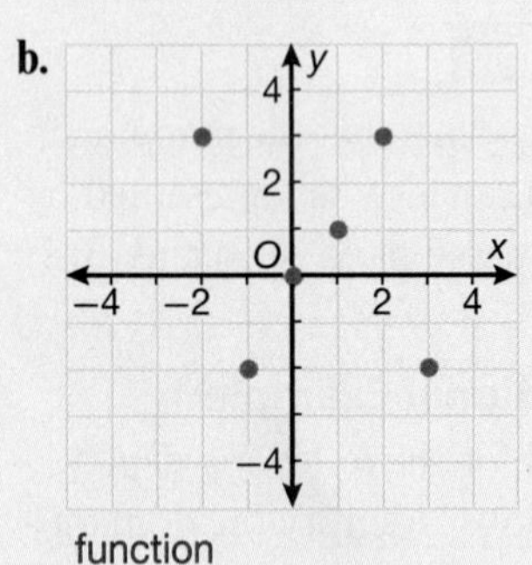

function

TEACHER TIP

Discuss how the vertical line test works by having students look at the graph of the circle at the top of the page. Then ask them to look at where the vertical line touches two points on the graph. Write this sentence on the board and have students fill in the blanks. **For the *x*-value of ______, I have *y*-values of ______ or ______.** Then show students how this *x*-value would be represented in a mapping, as ordered pairs, or in a table.

For example, students might write: For the *x*-value of 0, I have *y*-values of 3 or −3. The ordered pairs are (0, 3) and (0, −3).

When a relation is represented with a graph, the **vertical line test** is used to determine if the relation is a function.

> A graph on the coordinate plane represents the graph of a function provided that any vertical line intersects the graph no more than once.
>
> 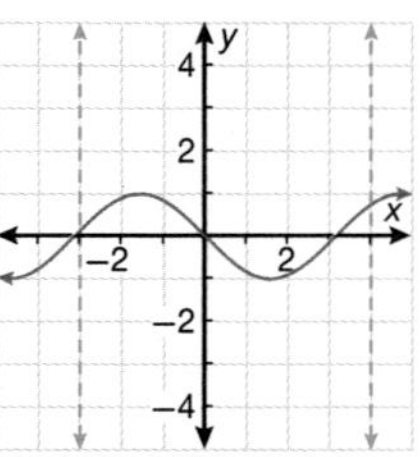
>
> **Graph of a Function**
>
> 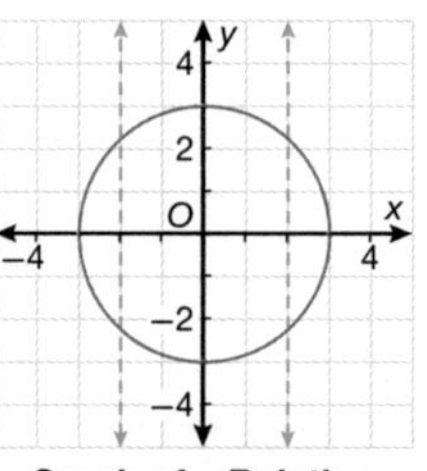
>
> **Graph of a Relation but Not a Function**

Math Reasoning

Model Draw a line that does not pass the vertical line test.

See student work. Only a vertical line does not pass the vertical line test.

The graph on the left represents the graph of a function since any vertical line intersects the graph no more than once. The graph on the right is not the graph of a function as there are vertical lines that intersect the graph at more than one point.

Example 2 Using the Vertical Line Test

Determine if each graph represent the graph of a function.

a.

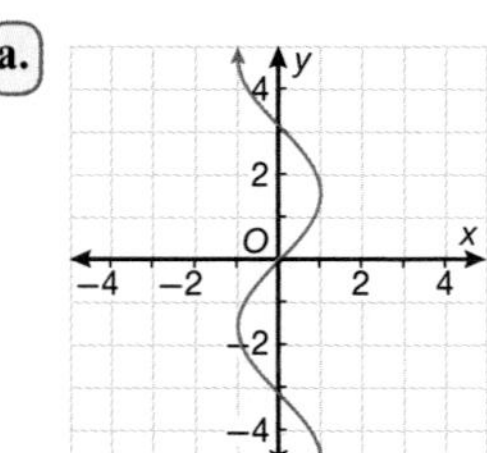

SOLUTION Not a function. The graph does not pass the vertical line test. A vertical line can be drawn so that it intersects the graph at more than one point. For example, the *y*-axis is such a line.

b.

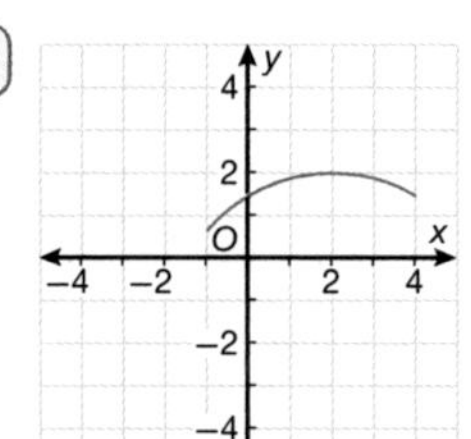

SOLUTION Function. Every vertical line drawn intersects the graph no more than once.

c.

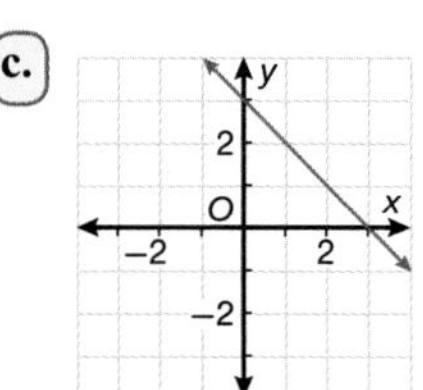

SOLUTION Function. Every vertical line drawn intersects the graph no more than once.

INCLUSION

Provide students with a ruler to help them use the vertical line test. Have students place the ruler vertically over the graph. Then have them count the number of places that the graph touches the ruler. If the graph touches only once, the graph is a function. If the graph touches more than once, it is not a function.

In mathematics it is sometimes necessary to work with more than one equation at a time. If given the two equations

$$y = x + 2 \text{ and } y = x - 5$$

to evaluate for $x = 2$, it may be confusing to know which equation to evaluate. **Function notation** uses parentheses and letters to distinguish between equations.

$$f(x) = x + 2 \text{ and } g(x) = x - 5$$

Reading Math

The equation on the left is read "*f* of *x* equals *x* plus 2" and the equation on the right "*g* of *x* equals *x* minus 5."

The notation $g(2) = (x) - 5$ means to find the value of the g equation when $x = 2$.

$g(2) = (x) - 5$

$g(2) = (2) - 5$ Replace x with 2.

$g(2) = -3$ Simplify.

Since the answer is -3 when x equals 2, the answer is read "g of 2 equals -3."

Math Reasoning

Verify Have students use a graphing calculator to check the solution.

Example 3 Using Function Notation to Evaluate Functions

If $h(x) = 4x - 3$ and $p(x) = x^2 - 3x$, find $p(-3)$.

SOLUTION Substitute -3 for x in $p(x)$ not $h(x)$.

$p(-3) = (-3)^2 - 3(-3)$ Replace x with -3.

$p(-3) = 9 + 9$ Simplify.

$p(-3) = 18$ Simplify.

$p(x)$ is 18 when x is -3.

Example 4 Consumer Math

a. A company charges \$0.25 per minute for a cell phone call. This can be expressed as the ordered pair (1, 0.25). Find the cost of a 2-minute, 3-minute, and 4-minute call. Express the answers as ordered pairs in set notation. Identify the domain and range. Determine if the set of ordered pairs represents a function. Explain.

SOLUTION {(2, 0.5), (3, 0.75), (4, 1)} Domain: 2, 3, 4. Range: 0.5, 0.75, 1. The set of ordered pairs represents a function since for every value of x there is exactly one y value.

b. Suppose that the same company charges \$1.00 for any call up to and including 4 minutes in length. Find the cost of a 2-minute, 3-minute, and 4-minute call. Express the answers as ordered pairs in set notation. Identify the domain and range. Determine if the set of ordered pairs represents a function. Explain.

SOLUTION {(2, 1), (3, 1), (4, 1)} Domain: 2, 3, 4. Range: 1. The set of ordered pairs represents a function since for every value of x there is exactly one y value.

ALTERNATE METHOD FOR EXAMPLE 4

Students can also graph the ordered pairs and then use the vertical line test to determine if the graph represents a function.

a.

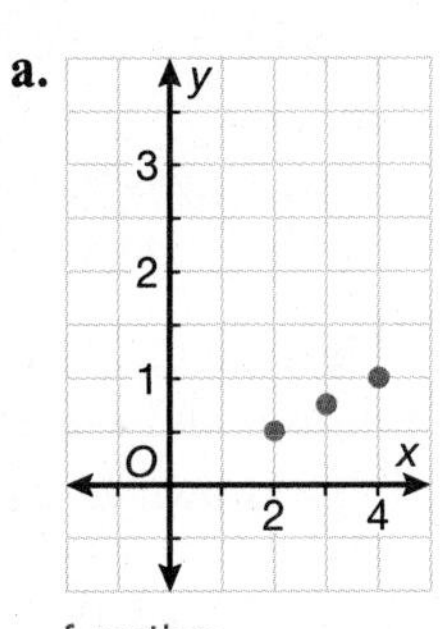

function

b.

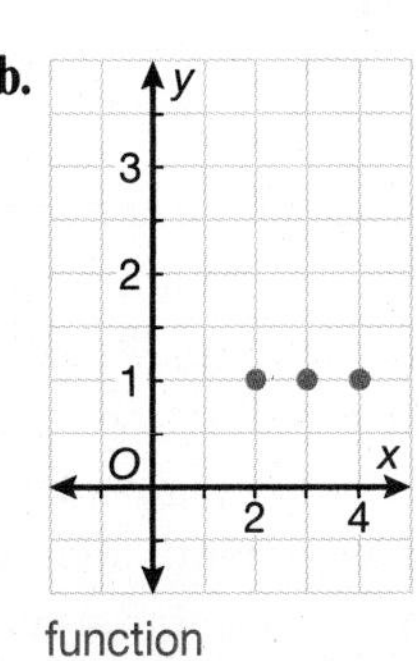

function

Example 3

Relate to Lesson 2 by telling students that finding $p(-3)$ is the same as evaluting $y = x^2 - 3x$ when $x = -3$.

Additional Example 3

If $h(x) = -5x^2 + 2$ and $p(x) = \frac{x}{2} - 3x$, find $h(-2)$. -18

Example 4

Remind students that the domain and range can have a different number of elements.

Additional Example 4

For each situation below, find the cost of a 2-minute, 3-minute, and 4-minute call. Express the answers as ordered pairs in set notation. Identify the domain and range. Determine if the set of ordered pairs represents a function.

a. The company charges \$0.25 per minute for up to 3 minutes and then \$0.10 for every minute thereafter. {(2, 0.5), (3, 0.75), (4, 0.85)}; D: {2, 3, 4}, R: {0.5, 0.75, 0.85}; This is a function because for every value of x there is exactly one y value.

b. The company charges \$0.25 per minute for Plan A and \$0.50 per minute for Plan B. {(2, 0.5), (2, 1), (3, 0.75), (3, 1.50), (4, 1.00), (4, 2.00)}; D: {2, 3, 4}, R: {0.50, 1.00, 0.75, 1.50, 2.00}; This is not a function because there are two different values for each x.

Extend the Example

"What is a real life example where the cost for something is NOT a function? Explain."

Airline tickets; For example, a ticket could cost \$99 or \$225. Tickets purchased at different times cost different amounts but they are for the same trip.

Lesson Practice

Problem b

Error Alert Students having difficulty determining functions from mappings can be encouraged to write the ordered pairs. The mapping in problem **b** results in the ordered pairs (m, p) and (n, p). Point out that the y-values repeat but the x-values do not. Therefore, this is a function.

Problem h

Scaffolding Have students make a table to show the price for each number of shirts purchased. From the table, students can write ordered pairs, identify the domain and range, and state whether the set is a function.

Check for Understanding

The questions below help assess the concepts taught in this lesson.

1. **"How does the vertical line test relate to determining a function from ordered pairs?"** A vertical line runs along all the values of y for a given x-value. If the graph intersects this line twice, then the x-value has two possible values for y. As ordered pairs, this means the same x would be repeated twice with two different values of y.

2. **"What is function notation? Why is it used?"** Function notation is when $f(x)$ or $g(x)$ is used instead of y in a function equation. It is used when there are many different functions so we can tell them apart.

Lesson Practice

Which of the following depict functions? Identify the domain and the range. (Ex 1)

a.

x	3	6	2	3
y	9	7	5	4

not a function; Domain: 2, 3, 6; Range: 4, 5, 7, 9

b. 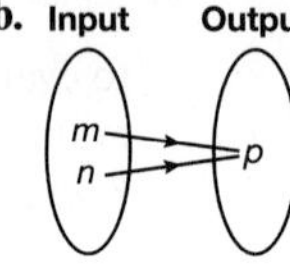

function; Domain: m, n; Range: p

Determine if the graph represents a function. (Ex 2)

c. function

d. not a function

e. 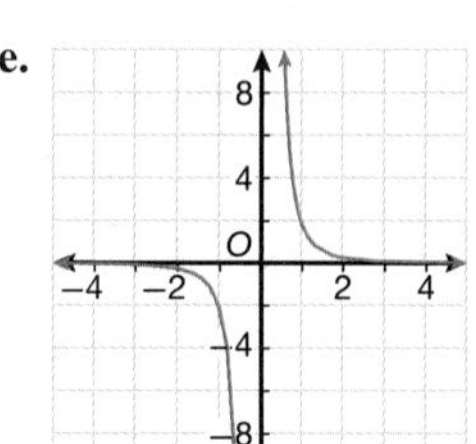

function

f. If $a(x) = 9 + 6x$ and $v(x) = 9x + 3x^2$, find $v(2)$. (Ex 3) 30

g. If you buy one ticket to a local baseball game, the cost is \$25. This can be expressed as the ordered pair (1, 25). There is a one-day special if you buy one ticket at regular price, each additional ticket is \$20. Find the total cost if you buy 2, 3, and 4 tickets. Express the answers as ordered pairs in set notation. Identify the domain and range. Determine if the set of ordered pairs represents a function. Explain. (Ex 4)

g. {(2, 45), (3, 65), (4, 85)}; Domain: 2, 3, 4; Range: 45, 65, 85; The set of ordered pairs represents a function since for every value of x there is exactly one y value.

h. If you buy one t-shirt from your favorite store, the cost is \$15.50. This can be expressed as the ordered pair (1, 15.5). The store is having a buy-one-get-one-free sale on t-shirts. For each t-shirt that you purchase at regular price you get the next one free. Find the total cost if you buy 2, 3, 4, 5, and 6 t-shirts. Express the answers as ordered pairs in set notation. Identify the domain and range. Determine if the set of ordered pairs represents a function. Explain. (Ex 4)

h. {(2, 15.5), (3, 31), (4, 31), (5, 46.5), (6, 46.5)}; Domain: 2, 3, 4, 5, 6; Range: 15.5, 31, 46.5; The set of ordered pairs represents a function since for every value of x there is exactly one y value.

Practice Distributed and Integrated

Find the additive inverse for each of the following.

1. $-3p$ (1) $3p$

2. 50 (1) -50

Evaluate each expression for the given values of m and n.

3. $2m - 4n(3m - 4)$ if $m = 1$ and $n = -3$ (2) -10

ENGLISH LEARNERS

Define **independent** as something that is not controlled or determined by anything else. Something that is dependent is controlled by something else.

Discuss the meaning by relating the words to other phrases or ideas. A country can be independent of another country. A business can work independently and not be told by another business how to operate. One employee might be independent and another might have a boss telling the employee how to operate.

In mathematics, a variable is said to be independent if it does not depend on another variable for its value. In the equation $y = x + 3$, y depends on the value of x. So y is the dependent variable and x is the **independent variable**.

Dependent variables are also known as output and range. Independent variables are also known as input and domain.

4. (2) $-m^3 + mn^2(n - m)$ if $m = -2$ and $n = -3$ 26

Use the rules of exponents to simplify the expressions below.

5. (3) $\frac{(m^3n^{-1})^{-4}}{(3mn)^{-2}}$ $\frac{9n^6}{m^{10}}$

6. (3) $\frac{-a^3(a^3b^{-2})^3}{ab(ab)^{-4}}$ $-\frac{a^{15}}{b^3}$

Identify whether each of the following represent a function. If so, state the domain and range.

*7. (4) $y^2 = x$ Not a function

*8. (4) $y = 3x^2 - 2$ Function. Domain: All real numbers. Range, $y \geq -2$

9. (3) **Error Analysis** Two students simplified $\frac{x^{-2}(y^2)^3}{y(x^{-1})^2}$. Their steps are shown below. Who is correct? Explain the error in the other student's work.

Student A	Student B
$\frac{x^{-2}(y^2)^3}{y(x^{-1})^2} = \frac{x^{-2}y^6}{yx^{-2}} = y^5$	$\frac{x^{-2}(y^2)^3}{y(x^{-1})^2} = \frac{x^{-2}y^5}{yx} = \frac{y^4}{x^3}$

9. Student A is correct. Student B added the exponents shown in power form instead of multiplying them.

10. (SB) What is the radius of a circle with circumference 16π feet? 8 feet

*11. (4) Use the table to answer the following questions.

a. What is the domain? 2, 3, 5, 7

b. What is the range? 4, 7, 9, 11

c. Does this data represent a function? Explain.
No; A value of 2 for x gives two possible y values.

x	y
2	9
5	7
3	4
2	11
7	7

*12. (4) **Multiple Choice** Which set of x- and y-values makes the equation $y = 3x^2 + 4$ true? B

A $x = 1, y = 10$ B $x = 3, y = 31$ C $x = 5, y = 229$ D $x = 2, y = 24$

13. (1) **Write** Alyson saves $75 each month. Use the distributive property to mentally calculate the amount of money that she will save in 12 months. Explain.

13. Sample: Think of 12 months as 10 months +2 months. Write an expression for the savings in 12 months: 75(10 + 2). Use the distributive property: 75(10) + 75(2). Multiply: 750 + 150. Add: 900. The amount saved will be $900.

*14. (4) **Geometry** Explain whether the relationship from a circle's radius to its area is a function. Yes; A radius from the domain would be associated with only one area. The relation from radius to area of a circle is a function.

15. (3) (**Hawaii**) Mauna Kea in Hawaii is about 1.02×10^4 meters from its base to its peak. The speed of light is about 3×10^8 meters/second. About how many seconds would it take light to reach the base from the peak? Write your answers in scientific notation. 3.40×10^{-5} sec

16. (2) **Verify** Evaluate the expression $ab + 3b - a - 5ab + 2b$ if $a = -3$ and $b = 2$ by inserting the variable values into the expression as written. Verify your answer by simplifying the expression first, then inserting the variable values. 37

17. (3) **Multiple Choice** Simplify $\frac{a^3b^{-2}c^{-3}b^6c^{-1}a^{-1}}{b^2c^4b^{-1}a^{-5}}$. C

A $\frac{b^5c^8}{a^3}$ B a^3b^5 C $\frac{a^7b^3}{c^8}$ D $\frac{b^6}{a^2c}$

CHALLENGE

If $f(x) = x + 2$ and $g(x) = 3x^2$, what is $f(g(x))$ and $g(f(x))$?
$f(g(x)) = 3x^2 + 2$; $g(f(x)) = 3x^2 + 12x + 12$

3 Practice

Math Conversations

Discussions to strengthen understanding

Problem 5

Point out that students can rewrite the fraction as $\frac{(3mn)^2}{(m^3n^{-1})^4}$ before using the power rule.

Problem 7

Extend the Problem

What are values for x and y that show that $y^2 = x$ is not a function?
$x = 4$ and $y = 2$ or -2

Problem 14

Suggest that students create a table where x is the radius for different circles and y is the area.

Problem 16

Guide the students by asking them the following questions.

"What is the value of $uv + 8v - u - 4uv + 7u$ if $u = -1$ and $v = -1$? Do NOT simplify the expression first. Show your work."
$(-1)(-1) + 8(-1) - (-1) - 4(-1)(-1) + 7(-1) = 1 - 8 + 1 - 4 - 7 = -17$

"What is the simplified form of $uv + 8v - u - 4uv + 7u$?"
$-3uv + 6u + 8v$

"Evaluate the simplified expression if $u = -1$ and $v = -1$. Show your work."
$-3(-1)(-1) + 6(-1) + 8(-1) = -3 + (-6) + (-8) = -17$

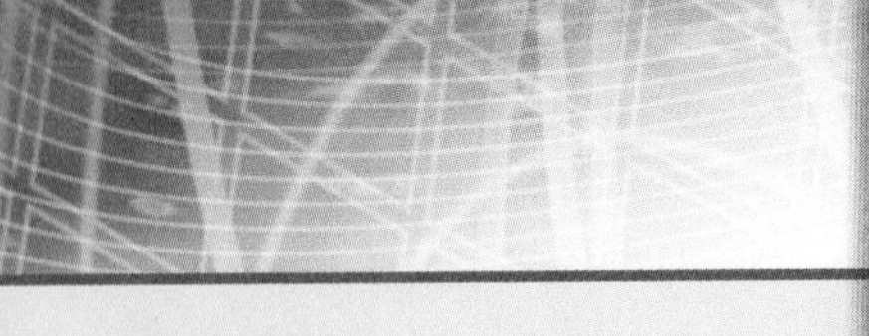

Problem 19

Extend the Problem

"How many printers will the sales representative have sold in an 8 hour day if she sells 15 computers and makes $662?"

7 printers

"Is it possible for the sales person to make exactly $120 in an 8 hour day? Explain."

Sample: No. If the sales representative makes $9 per hour, then her salary will be $72 for an 8 hour day. Then she has $48 (120 − 72 = 48) she can make for the computers and printers she sells. If she makes $20 for every printer and $30 for every computer, there is no way to get a total of $48 from these sales.

Problem 22

Tell students that one of the functions represents the discounted price and one represents the amount of the discount. Remind students to read the question carefully to determine which function is being asked for.

Problem 24

Tell students to convert the centimeters to meters before multiplying to determine the volume.

Problem 25

Error Alert Students might interpret function notation as multiplication, reading $f(x)$ as "f times x". Explain that they must take the term in context to realize it is only a name for $y = 3x^2 + x$.

18. (1) **Baseball** The table shows the number of homeruns hit by Ryan Howard of the Philadelphia Phillies over a three-year period. Which property of real numbers would be useful to mentally calculate as quickly as possible the total homeruns that he hit over this period? Explain.

	2004	2005	2006
Homeruns	2	22	58

18. Commutative Property. Adding the numbers in order would result in $2 + 22 + 58 = 24 + 58$, which is more difficult to mentally add than $2 + 58 + 22 = 60 + 22$.

19. (2) **Multi-Step** A computer sales representative makes a base salary of $9/hr. She can also earn an additional $30 for every computer that she sells and $20 for every printer that she sells.

a. Write an expression to represent the total amount the representative will make in an 8-hour day. $9(8) + 30c + 20p = 72 + 30c + 20p$

b. How much will she make if she sells 10 computers and 4 printers in an 8-hour day? $72 + 30(10) + 20(4) = 72 + 300 + 80 = \$452$

20. (1) **Generalize** The product of a number and its multiplicative inverse is one. What is the product of a number and its additive inverse? The opposite of the square of the number.

21. (2) **Hybrids** The EPA lists the greenest hybrid car as getting 61 miles per gallon on the highway and 50 miles per gallon in the city. Write and simplify an expression for the total number of miles the car will travel if the fuel tank holds 15 gallons of gas. Sample: Let h be the number of gallons used on the highway. Then $15 - h$ is the remaining number of gallons used in the city. $61(h) + 50(15 - h) = 61h + 750 - 50h = 11h + 750$

***22.** (4) **Error Analysis** PC Haven sells computers at a 15% discount on the original price plus a $200 rebate. Which function correctly represents the final price of a computer at PC Haven? Explain the error. $f(r)$ is correct. $g(r)$ calculates the total discount from the regular price.

$f(r) = 0.85r - 200$ $\quad g(r) = 0.15r + 200$

***23.** (4) **Analyze** What values of a and b would make the relation not a function? Explain your reasoning.

x	2	3	a
y	5	b	8

23. If a is 2, then the relation is not a function because 2 would go to 5 and 8. If a is 3, then the relation is not a function unless b is 8 and this is the only case where the value of b matters.

24. (3) **Precipitation** New York City gets an average of 1.14×10^2 cm of rainfall each year. The area of New York City is 8.02×10^8 m². Calculate the average annual volume in cubic meters of precipitation in New York City. Write your answer in scientific notation. 9.14×10^8 m³

For the function $f(x) = 3x^2 + x$, evaluate:

***25.** (4) $f(-1)$ 2 ***26.** (4) $f(0)$ 0 ***27.** (4) $f\left(\frac{3}{2}\right)$ $\frac{33}{4}$

***28.** (4) **Justify** Simplify the expression, $-36 + (36 + 17)$, using properties of real numbers. Justify your answer by identifying which property you used for each step. See Additional Answers.

***29.** (4) **Graphing Calculator** For the function $f(x) = x^2$, use a calculator to find $f(-2.8)$ and $f(2.8)$. Did you use the same key strokes to evaluate both? Explain.

29. $f(-2.8) = f(2.8) = 7.84$; Sample: no; To evaluate $f(-2.8)$ you have to use parenthesis to square −2.8. For $f(2.8)$ you don't need parenthesis because it's positive.

30. (3) **Probability** In a year, lightning strikes one person out of every 2.8×10^5 people. Calculate the number of people in the United States that will likely be struck by lightning this year if the population is 2.8×10^8. Write your answer in standard notation. 1000 people

LOOKING FORWARD

Identifying functions and using function notation prepares students for

- **Lesson 22** Analyzing Discrete and Continuous Functions
- **Lesson 47** Graphing Exponential Functions
- **Lesson 50** Finding Inverses of Relations and Functions
- **Lesson 53** Performing Compositions of Functions

LAB
2

Storing and Recalling Data in a Matrix

Graphing Calculator Lab (*Use with Lessons 5, 9, and 14*)

A graphing calculator can be used to work with matrices. Use the graphing calculator to store and manipulate data in 2×2 matrices.

Storing Data in a Matrix

1. Input the matrix $A = \begin{bmatrix} 1 & 2 \\ 3 & 4 \end{bmatrix}$.

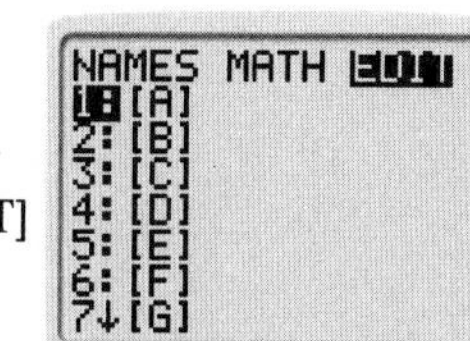

a. Press 2nd x^{-1} to get to the matrix menu. Use the arrow button ▶ to highlight **[EDIT]** and select [**1:** [A]] to open matrix A.

b. The calculator will prompt you for the dimensions of the matrix you want to create. Enter the number of rows in the matrix and press ENTER, and then enter the number of columns and press ENTER.

c. Input each element of the matrix as prompted by the calculator and press ENTER after each.

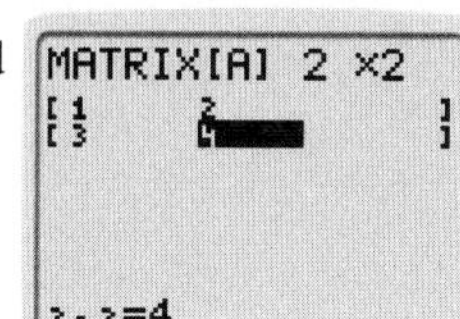

Graphing Calculator

To start with a blank home screen press 2nd MODE CLEAR.

2. Input the matrix $B = \begin{bmatrix} 5 & 0 \\ -2 & 1 \end{bmatrix}$.

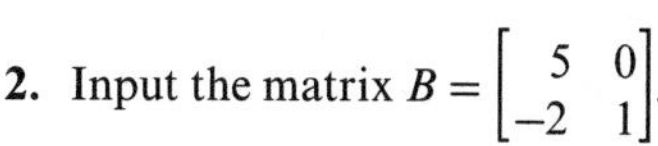

Press 2nd x^{-1} to return to the matrix menu. Use the arrow button ▶ to highlight **[EDIT]** and use ▼ to select [**2:** [B]] to open matrix B. Repeat the same process for inputting matrix B.

Recalling Matrices to Use in Calculations

1. Calculate $A \times B$.

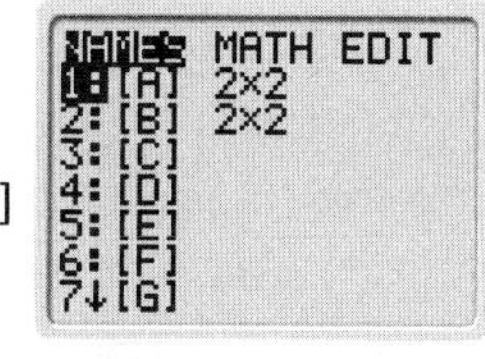

From the home screen, press 2nd x^{-1} to open the matrix menu and while the **[NAMES]** heading is still highlighted select [**1:** [A]] and press ENTER. Press ×, and then 2nd x^{-1} to return to the **[NAMES]** menu and use ▼ to select [**2:** [B]] and press ENTER. Press ENTER again to calculate.

2. Find the inverse of matrix A.

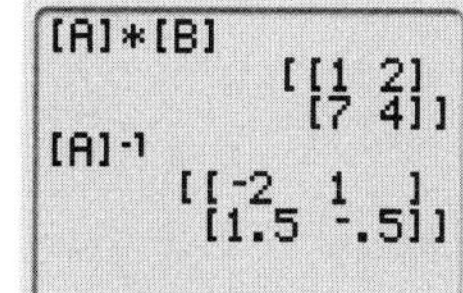

Press 2nd x^{-1} to open the matrix menu and while the **[NAMES]** menu is still highlighted use ▼ to select [**1:** [A]] and press ENTER. Press x^{-1}, and then press ENTER.

Online Connection
www.SaxonMathResources.com

LAB
2

Materials
- graphing calculator

Discuss
In this lab, students will store data in a matrix. The matrix functions explored are multiplication, matrix inversion, determinant, and Reduced Row-Echelon Form.

Define matrix, inverse, determinant, and Reduced-Row-Echelon Form.

Storing Data in a Matrix
There are limits to the number of rows and columns that a student can input. Consult your calculator textbook to determine the greatest matrix dimensions that your calculator will accept. Our examples will stay within the limits of the calculator.

Error Alert
Matrix multiplication is only defined when the inner dimensions of the matrix factors are identical. Students will see **ERR: DIM MISMATCH** if they try to multiply two matrices with unequal inner dimensions.

Error Alert
Only square matrices have inverses. **ERR: INVALID DIM** will be shown if students try to calculate an inverse of a non-square matrix.

Recalling Matrices to Use in Calculations

Remind students that a determinant is a value.

Reducing a Matrix into Reduced-Row-Echelon Form

Tell students to use the arrow keys to examine the data of a large matrix.

Reduced-Row-Echelon Form of a matrix can be used to solve large systems of equations by hand or by computer.

Practice Problem a

Do the matrices have the same inner dimensions?

Practice Problem b

TEACHER TIP

B^{-1} means the inverse of B.

3. Find the determinant of matrix A.

Press 2nd x^{-1} and press ▶ to highlight the [MATH] menu, use ▼ to select [**1: det(**]. Press ENTER. Press 2nd x^{-1} to return to the matrix menu and select [**1: [A]**] and press ENTER. Press ENTER. The determinant of A = –2.

Reducing a Matrix into Reduced-Row-Echelon Form

1. Enter the system of equations into the calculator as an augmented matrix.

Use the method shown on the previous page to input a 3 × 4 matrix,

$$C = \begin{bmatrix} 3 & -2 & -3 & 5 \\ -1 & 4 & 5 & 7 \\ 2 & 5 & -1 & 0 \end{bmatrix}.$$

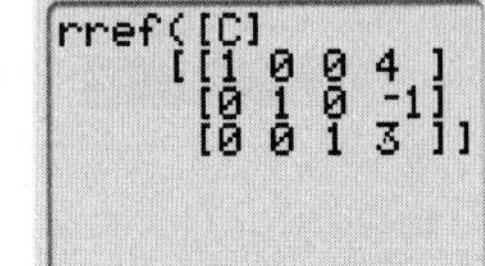

2. Reducing a matrix to echelon form.

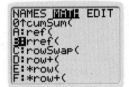

Within the home screen, press 2nd x^{-1} and press ▶ to highlight the [**MATH**] menu, then use ▼ to select [**B: rref(**] and press ENTER. Press 2nd x^{-1} to return to the matrix menu and use ▼ to select [**3: [C]**]. Press ENTER. The row reduced matrix will be displayed.

```
rref([C]
 [[1 0 0 4 ]
  [0 1 0 -1]
  [0 0 1 3 ]]
```

Lab Practice

a. Use the graphing calculator to input matrices $A = \begin{bmatrix} -2 & 0 \\ 7 & 3 \end{bmatrix}$ and $B = \begin{bmatrix} 1 & -5 \\ -3 & 0 \end{bmatrix}$ and calculate $A \times B$. $A \times B = \begin{bmatrix} -2 & 10 \\ -2 & -35 \end{bmatrix}$

b. Use the graphing calculator to calculate B^{-1}. $B^{-1} = \begin{bmatrix} 0 & -\frac{1}{3} \\ -\frac{1}{5} & -\frac{1}{15} \end{bmatrix}$

c. Use the graphing calculator to find the determinant of matrix A. –6

d. Use the graphing calculator to find the reduced-row-echelon form of the matrix, $C = \begin{bmatrix} -2 & -10 & 9 & 1 \\ 1 & 7 & -5 & -6 \\ 5 & 10 & 13 & 7 \end{bmatrix}$. $C = \begin{bmatrix} 1 & 0 & 0 & 10 \\ 0 & 1 & 0 & -3 \\ 0 & 0 & 1 & -1 \end{bmatrix}$

LESSON 5

Using Matrices to Organize Data and to Solve Problems

Warm Up

1. (1) **Vocabulary** The Additive Inverse Property states that $a + (-a) = 0$.
2. (SB) Add $16.5 - (-24.8)$. 41.3
3. (SB) Solve $4 - 3y = 16$. -4
4. (1) True or False: By the Commutative Property: $j - k = k - j$. False
5. (2) Simplify $-4(x + 1) + 3(2x - 7)$. $(2x - 25)$

New Concepts

A **matrix** is a rectangular array of numbers. The number of rows and columns in a matrix gives the **dimensions of a matrix.** A matrix with r rows and c columns is called an $r \times c$, r by c, matrix. Look at the matrices shown below. Matrix A is a 3×2 matrix and B is a 4×1 matrix.

> **Reading Math**
>
> Matrix A can be written as $A_{3\times2}$ to show both its name and dimensions.

$$A = \begin{bmatrix} -1 & 0 \\ 4 & -5 \\ 3 & 7 \end{bmatrix} \qquad B = \begin{bmatrix} 3 \\ -6 \\ 2 \\ 11 \end{bmatrix}$$

Each number in the matrix is an **element** and has a unique address which tells its location in the matrix. The **address** of an element is formed by the lowercase letter of the matrix name, followed by its row number and column number, in subscripts. Therefore, the element located at a_{12} is 0 and the element at b_{31} is 2.

Matrices can be used to store data that would otherwise be presented in a table. This can make it easier to perform calculations on the data, such as **Matrix Addition.**

Matrix Addition
To add two matrices, A and B, of the same dimensions, add each element in the first matrix to the element that is in the same location in the second matrix. $$\begin{bmatrix} a_{11} & a_{12} \\ a_{21} & a_{22} \end{bmatrix} + \begin{bmatrix} b_{11} & b_{12} \\ b_{21} & b_{22} \end{bmatrix} = \begin{bmatrix} a_{11} + b_{11} & a_{12} + b_{12} \\ a_{21} + b_{21} & a_{22} + b_{22} \end{bmatrix}$$

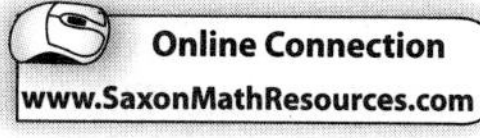

The Commutative Property holds true for Matrix Addition. That is, $A + B$ gives the same matrix as $B + A$.

MATH BACKGROUND

Students have worked with data stored in tables and are familiar with rows and columns of information. Data stored in matrices mirror data stored in tables but without the column and row labels. Finding the address of an element in a matrix is analogous to finding the row and column of a value in a table.

The additive properties of real numbers, including the commutative, associative, inverse, and identity properties hold for matrices.

It is important for students to understand that a zero matrix is different than the real number 0. For example the operation $0 + \begin{bmatrix} a & b \\ c & d \end{bmatrix}$ is undefined. The zero matrix is the additive identity matrix.

LESSON 5

1 Warm Up

Ask students what properties are used to simplify the expression in Problem 5. The Distributive Property and the Commutative Property of Addition

2 New Concepts

In this lesson, students are introduced to matrices and some of the basic operations with matrices including addition, subtraction, and scalar multiplication. Students also learn how to use a matrix to organize data that would otherwise be stored in a table.

Explain that **matrices** are named using uppercase letters such as A and B. **Elements** of A are named using the lowercase letter a with subscripts indicating their positions in the array. Put several matrices of different dimensions on the board and have students find the dimensions and reference different elements of each matrix by their addresses.

Reinforce that matrix addition and subtraction are only defined for matrices that have the same dimensions.

LESSON RESOURCES

Student Edition Practice Workbook 5
Reteaching Master 5
Adaptations Master 5
Challenge and Enrichment Master C5

Example 1

This example shows students how to store tabular data in matrices. Point out that the tables have the same number of rows and columns.

Error Alert Students may be confused by the column headings which are numeric, thinking they represent data in the table. Have students identify the actual data in the tables and the number of rows and columns used by the data.

Extend the Example

Ask students to explain what the elements in $M + F$ represent.

$M + F$ represents the sum of male and female students, respectively, participating in each sports category by grade level.

Additional Example 1

Use the data in the tables to create two matrices, one for DVD rentals at the Center City Store, C and one for the North County Store, N. Then find $C + N$.

Center City Store

	January	February
Comedy	1,250	1,340
Drama	1,893	2,455
Other	2,388	3,674

North County Store

	January	February
Comedy	985	1,020
Drama	1,987	1,765
Other	1,582	2,001

$$C = \begin{bmatrix} 1{,}250 & 1{,}340 \\ 1{,}893 & 2{,}455 \\ 2{,}388 & 3{,}674 \end{bmatrix}$$

$$N = \begin{bmatrix} 985 & 1{,}020 \\ 1{,}987 & 1{,}765 \\ 1{,}582 & 2{,}001 \end{bmatrix}$$

$$C + N = \begin{bmatrix} 2{,}235 & 2{,}360 \\ 3{,}880 & 4{,}220 \\ 3{,}970 & 5{,}675 \end{bmatrix}$$

Example 1 **Creating and Adding Matrices**

Create two matrices, one for male students, M, and one for female students, F. Then find $M + F$.

Male Students

	9th	10th	11th	12th
JV Sports	82	54	8	0
Varsity Sports	44	62	71	124
No Sports	50	93	85	43

Female Students

	9th	10th	11th	12th
JV Sports	91	46	39	5
Varsity Sports	22	45	112	137
No Sports	86	95	30	66

SOLUTION Enter the data in the order shown in the table.

$$M = \begin{bmatrix} 82 & 54 & 8 & 0 \\ 44 & 62 & 71 & 124 \\ 50 & 93 & 85 & 43 \end{bmatrix} \qquad F = \begin{bmatrix} 91 & 46 & 39 & 5 \\ 22 & 45 & 112 & 137 \\ 86 & 95 & 30 & 66 \end{bmatrix}$$

$$M + F = \begin{bmatrix} 173 & 100 & 47 & 5 \\ 66 & 107 & 183 & 261 \\ 136 & 188 & 115 & 109 \end{bmatrix}$$

Math Reasoning

Connect The zero matrix is the additive identity matrix. Explain.

Any matrix, plus the zero matrix, results in the original matrix.

A matrix in which every element is zero is a **zero matrix.** A zero matrix is formed when a matrix is added to its additive inverse matrix. The elements in an **additive inverse matrix** are the opposite of every element in the original matrix. Here, $-A$ is the additive inverse of A.

$$A = \begin{bmatrix} 4 & -15 \\ 9 & -1 \end{bmatrix} \qquad -A = \begin{bmatrix} -4 & 15 \\ -9 & 1 \end{bmatrix} \qquad A + (-A) = \begin{bmatrix} 0 & 0 \\ 0 & 0 \end{bmatrix}$$

Matrix Subtraction

To subtract two matrices of the same dimensions, $A - B$, take the opposite, or additive inverse, of B and add it to A.

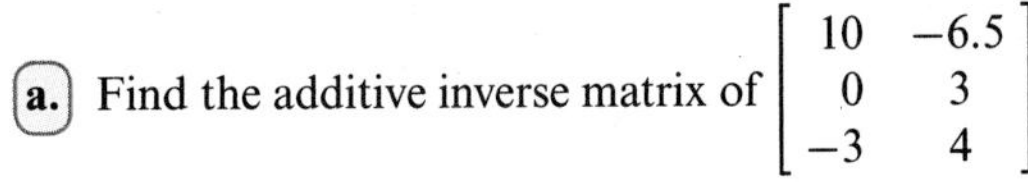

$$\begin{bmatrix} a_{11} & a_{12} \\ a_{21} & a_{22} \end{bmatrix} - \begin{bmatrix} b_{11} & b_{12} \\ b_{21} & b_{22} \end{bmatrix} = \begin{bmatrix} a_{11} + (-b_{11}) & a_{12} + (-b_{12}) \\ a_{21} + (-b_{21}) & a_{22} + (-b_{22}) \end{bmatrix}$$

Example 2 **Using the Additive Inverse and Subtracting Matrices**

a. Find the additive inverse matrix of $\begin{bmatrix} 10 & -6.5 \\ 0 & 3 \\ -3 & 4 \end{bmatrix}$.

SOLUTION Make a matrix so that every element is the opposite. The additive inverse matrix is

$$(-)\begin{bmatrix} 10 & -6.5 \\ 0 & 3 \\ -3 & 4 \end{bmatrix} = \begin{bmatrix} (-)10 & (-)-6.5 \\ (-)0 & (-)3 \\ (-)-3 & (-)4 \end{bmatrix} = \begin{bmatrix} -10 & 6.5 \\ 0 & -3 \\ 3 & -4 \end{bmatrix}.$$

ENGLISH LEARNERS

The word **matrix** may be new or unclear for some students. Say:

"A matrix is a rectangular array of numbers."

Discuss the plural of matrix. The plurals of some words ending in "x," such as box and fox, are found by adding "es." Other words like matrix drop the "x" and add "ces" to the end.

Have students use the words matrix and matrices in sentences such as "Matrix A has 2 rows and 3 columns." and "Matrices A and B contain 3 rows and 2 columns."

Ask students to think of other words ending in "x" and discuss the plurals of those words.

Caution

To subtract 2 matrices, A–B, by adding the opposite, be sure to take the opposite of each element in B.

(b.) Find $\begin{bmatrix} 3 & 16 \\ -23 & 0 \end{bmatrix} - \begin{bmatrix} -1 & 9 \\ -18 & 14 \end{bmatrix}$.

SOLUTION Subtract by adding the opposite.

$$\begin{bmatrix} 3 & 16 \\ -23 & 0 \end{bmatrix} - \begin{bmatrix} -1 & 9 \\ -18 & 14 \end{bmatrix} = \begin{bmatrix} 3 & 16 \\ -23 & 0 \end{bmatrix} + \begin{bmatrix} 1 & -9 \\ 18 & -14 \end{bmatrix}$$

$$= \begin{bmatrix} 3+1 & 16+(-9) \\ -23+18 & 0+(-14) \end{bmatrix} = \begin{bmatrix} 4 & 7 \\ -5 & -14 \end{bmatrix}$$

In a **matrix equation,** an entire matrix can be a variable. To solve a matrix equation, begin by isolating the variable using inverse operations.

Example 3 Solving a Matrix Equation

Solve for X: $\begin{bmatrix} 3 & 7 \\ 9 & 1 \end{bmatrix} + X = \begin{bmatrix} 5 & 9 \\ 2 & -6 \end{bmatrix}$.

SOLUTION Subtract $\begin{bmatrix} 3 & 7 \\ 9 & 1 \end{bmatrix}$ from both sides of the equation.

$$\begin{bmatrix} 3 & 7 \\ 9 & 1 \end{bmatrix} + X = \begin{bmatrix} 5 & 9 \\ 2 & -6 \end{bmatrix}$$

$$\begin{bmatrix} 3 & 7 \\ 9 & 1 \end{bmatrix} - \begin{bmatrix} 3 & 7 \\ 9 & 1 \end{bmatrix} + X = \begin{bmatrix} 5 & 9 \\ 2 & -6 \end{bmatrix} - \begin{bmatrix} 3 & 7 \\ 9 & 1 \end{bmatrix}$$

$$X = \begin{bmatrix} 2 & 2 \\ -7 & -7 \end{bmatrix}$$

Variables may also appear as elements of a matrix or within elements of a matrix.

Example 4 Solving for Variables in Matrices

Solve for a, b, c, and d: $\begin{bmatrix} a+12 & 2b \\ 23 & d \end{bmatrix} = \begin{bmatrix} 18 & -14 \\ a+c & 3 \end{bmatrix}$.

SOLUTION Equal matrices have equal elements in matching locations. Therefore, $a + 12 = 18$ and $a = 6$. Also, $2b = -14$, so $b = -7$. Continuing to match elements, $23 = a + c$, and after substituting 6 for a, $23 = 6 + c$, and $c = 17$. Last, $d = 3$.

A **scalar** is a constant by which a matrix is multiplied. Scalar multiplication is analogous to repeated matrix addition.

Scalar Multiplication
To multiply matrix A by scalar n, multiply every element of A by n.
$n\begin{bmatrix} a_{11} & a_{12} \\ a_{21} & a_{22} \end{bmatrix} = \begin{bmatrix} n \cdot a_{11} & n \cdot a_{12} \\ n \cdot a_{21} & n \cdot a_{22} \end{bmatrix}$

ALTERNATE METHOD FOR EXAMPLE 3

When solving the matrix equation, students may want to use addition instead of subtraction:

$$\begin{bmatrix} 3 & 7 \\ 9 & 1 \end{bmatrix} + X = \begin{bmatrix} 5 & 9 \\ 2 & -6 \end{bmatrix}$$

$$\begin{bmatrix} 3 & 7 \\ 9 & 1 \end{bmatrix} - \begin{bmatrix} 3 & 7 \\ 9 & 1 \end{bmatrix} + X = \begin{bmatrix} 5 & 9 \\ 2 & -6 \end{bmatrix} - \begin{bmatrix} 3 & 7 \\ 9 & 1 \end{bmatrix}$$

$$X = \begin{bmatrix} 5 & 9 \\ 2 & -6 \end{bmatrix} + \begin{bmatrix} -3 & -7 \\ -9 & -1 \end{bmatrix}$$

$$X = \begin{bmatrix} 2 & 2 \\ -7 & -7 \end{bmatrix}$$

Example 2

In this example, students are taught how to find the additive inverse matrix of a matrix and how to use it to subtract matrices.

Additional Example 2

a. Find the additive inverse matrix of

$$\begin{bmatrix} 0 & 4.5 & -5 & 21 \\ 1 & -1 & 12 & 2.5 \end{bmatrix}.$$

$$\begin{bmatrix} 0 & -4.5 & 5 & -21 \\ -1 & 1 & -12 & -2.5 \end{bmatrix}$$

b. Find $\begin{bmatrix} 2.3 & -9 & 1 \\ 0 & -45 & 17 \\ -8 & 7.2 & -15 \end{bmatrix} - \begin{bmatrix} 4.3 & 0 & 25 \\ -6 & 10.5 & 10 \\ -14 & 6 & 30 \end{bmatrix}$.

$$\begin{bmatrix} -2 & -9 & -24 \\ 6 & -55.5 & 7 \\ 6 & 1.2 & -45 \end{bmatrix}$$

Example 3

Students learn how to solve a matrix equation where the unknown is a matrix.

Explain that subtracting a matrix from both sides of the equation produces a zero matrix on the left side, not the real number 0.

Additional Example 3

Solve for X: $\begin{bmatrix} 12 \\ -3 \end{bmatrix} + X = \begin{bmatrix} -7 \\ 0 \end{bmatrix}$.

$X = \begin{bmatrix} -19 \\ 3 \end{bmatrix}$

Example 4

Scalar multiplication is similar to the Distributive Property.

Additional Example 4

Solve for a, b, c, and d:

$$\begin{bmatrix} a+1 & 14 \\ c & d \end{bmatrix} = \begin{bmatrix} 5 & b \\ b-2 & \frac{1}{2}ab \end{bmatrix}$$

$a = 4$; $b = 14$; $c = 12$; $d = 28$

Example 5

Be certain students understand that the entries in the resulting matrix represent dollar amounts.

Additional Example 5

The tables show the cost of items at a clothing store. The store is having a sale and you can choose from one of two different deals. The Deal 1 table shows the price per item if you buy three or more of an item. The Deal 2 table shows the regular price of an item. If you choose Deal 2 you get 25% off of every item you purchase. Create matrices A and B and find $3A - 3(0.75)B$ which represents the differences in cost for buying 3 items. Which deal is better for which items?

Deal 1

	Women's	Men's
Pants	\$25.00	\$20.00
Shirts	\$19.50	\$15.50

Deal 2

	Women's	Men's
Pants	\$30	\$28
Shirts	\$24	\$20

Sample: $3A - 3(0.75)B = \begin{bmatrix} 7.50 & -3 \\ 4.50 & 1.50 \end{bmatrix}$

It is a better deal to choose the 25% discount on every item except men's pants.

Lesson Practice

Problem a

Scaffolding Ask, **"What are the dimensions of matrix W?"** 2×3 **"of matrix E?"** 2×3 **"of matrix $W + E$?"** 2×3

After students complete the problem ask, **"What is the value of element two one?"** 5 **"What does the element represent?"** The total number of small jackets in inventory for both stores.

Math Reasoning

Analyze Why are we finding $0.75B$ and not $0.25B$? What extra step would we need to take if we did find $0.25B$?

Because 100% of the fee is reduced by 25%, leaving 75%. If we found 25%, we would have to subtract those values from B.

Example 5 Application: Transportation

The tables show proposed fees for a new toll road. No one is happy with either plan. Some believe the fees in Plan A should be doubled; others believe that Plan B is appropriate if the fees are reduced by 25%. Create matrices A and B and find $2A - 0.75B$ to discuss differences in costs between these two ideas.

Plan A

	Class 1	Class 2	Class 3
Exit 1	\$1.25	\$1.75	\$2.00
Exit 2	\$2.50	\$3.00	\$3.50

Plan B

	Class 1	Class 2	Class 3
Exit 1	\$3.00	\$4.60	\$5.80
Exit 2	\$4.00	\$6.20	\$8.00

SOLUTION

$$2A = \begin{bmatrix} 2(1.25) & 2(1.75) & 2(2.00) \\ 2(2.50) & 2(3.00) & 2(3.50) \end{bmatrix} = \begin{bmatrix} 2.50 & 3.50 & 4.00 \\ 5.00 & 6.00 & 7.00 \end{bmatrix}$$

$$0.75B = \begin{bmatrix} 0.75(3.00) & 0.75(4.60) & 0.75(5.80) \\ 0.75(4.00) & 0.75(6.20) & 0.75(8.00) \end{bmatrix} = \begin{bmatrix} 2.25 & 3.45 & 4.35 \\ 3.00 & 4.65 & 6.00 \end{bmatrix}$$

$$2A - 0.75B = \begin{bmatrix} 2.50 & 3.50 & 4.00 \\ 5.00 & 6.00 & 7.00 \end{bmatrix} - \begin{bmatrix} 2.25 & 3.45 & 4.35 \\ 3.00 & 4.65 & 6.00 \end{bmatrix}$$

$$= \begin{bmatrix} 0.25 & 0.05 & -0.35 \\ 2.00 & 1.35 & 1.00 \end{bmatrix}$$

Differences range from a nickel to \$2.00. In all but one situation, doubling Plan A is more expensive than reducing Plan B.

Lesson Practice

a. (Ex 1) Use the data in the tables to create two matrices, one for the West-Side store, W, and one for the East-Side store, E. Then find $W + E$.

West-Side Store

	Small	Medium	Large
Vests	13	4	8
Jackets	1	6	2

East-Side Store

	Small	Medium	Large
Vests	0	11	3
Jackets	4	2	5

a. $W = \begin{bmatrix} 13 & 4 & 8 \\ 1 & 6 & 2 \end{bmatrix}$ $E = \begin{bmatrix} 0 & 11 & 3 \\ 4 & 2 & 5 \end{bmatrix}$ $W + E = \begin{bmatrix} 13 & 15 & 11 \\ 5 & 8 & 7 \end{bmatrix}$

b. (Ex 1) Find the additive inverse matrix of $\begin{bmatrix} 1 \\ -1 \\ 5 \end{bmatrix}$. $\begin{bmatrix} -1 \\ 1 \\ -5 \end{bmatrix}$

CHALLENGE

Solve for a, b, c, and d:

$$\begin{bmatrix} 8 & d - c \\ a - 2b & 3d + c \end{bmatrix} = \begin{bmatrix} a + b & 15 \\ -10 & 9 \end{bmatrix}$$

$a = 2$; $b = 6$; $c = -9$; $d = 6$

c. Find $\begin{bmatrix} -1 & 0 \\ 6 & -8 \\ 5 & 3 \end{bmatrix} - \begin{bmatrix} 2 & -4 \\ 2 & -1 \\ 5 & -3 \end{bmatrix}$. $\begin{bmatrix} -3 & 4 \\ 4 & -7 \\ 0 & 6 \end{bmatrix}$
(Ex 2)

d. Solve for Y: $Y - \begin{bmatrix} 2 & -4 \\ -4 & 8 \end{bmatrix} = \begin{bmatrix} 6 & 5 \\ -10 & 2 \end{bmatrix}$. $\begin{bmatrix} 8 & 1 \\ -14 & 10 \end{bmatrix}$
(Ex 3)

e. $x = 25, y = 7, z = -5$

e. Solve for x, y, and z: $\begin{bmatrix} 10 & x & 1 \\ 20 & -5 & x - y \end{bmatrix} = \begin{bmatrix} 10 & 25 & 1 \\ x + z & z & 18 \end{bmatrix}$.
(Ex 4)

f. $0.80A - 0.70B = \begin{bmatrix} 0 \\ 0.10 \\ 0.50 \\ 0.20 \end{bmatrix}$, differences range from \$0 to \$0.50. Theater A is more expensive than Theater B for all ticket categories next Saturday.

f. The tables show the cost of tickets at two competing theaters. Next Saturday, all categories of tickets at both theaters will be on sale. Theater A will sell their tickets at a discount of 20% of the original price and Theater B will sell theirs at 30% of the original price. Find the matrix that represents the difference of the sale prices and discuss the differences in price.
(Ex 5)

Theater A

Ticket Category	Cost
Child 0–3	Free
Child 4–14	\$4.50
Adult 15–65	\$8.50
Senior Citizen 66+	\$5.50

Theater B

Ticket Category	Cost
Child 0–3	Free
Child 4–14	\$5.00
Adult 15–65	\$9.00
Senior Citizen 66+	\$6.00

Practice Distributed and Integrated

Find the multiplicative inverse for each of the following.

1. $-\frac{2}{3}$ $-\frac{3}{2}$
(1)

2. 6 $\frac{1}{6}$
(1)

3. Evaluate $x^2y(x + 3y)$ for $x = 0$ and $y = -6$. 0
(2)

4. Simplify: $4x^2(x^{-2}y^{-4})^{-1}$ $4x^4y^4$
(3)

5. Determine whether the graph represents a function. Explain. No; a vertical line can be drawn that passes through the graph more than once.
(4)

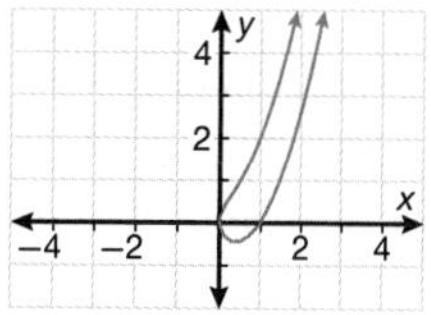

Graphing Calculator **Simplify the following matrices. Check using a graphing calculator.**

***6.** $4\begin{bmatrix} 2 & 1 \\ -6 & 3.5 \end{bmatrix} - 3\begin{bmatrix} 0 & 0.4 \\ 8 & -2 \end{bmatrix}$
(5)

***7.** $\frac{1}{4}\begin{bmatrix} 2 & 4 \\ 6 & 8 \end{bmatrix} + \begin{bmatrix} -2 & 1 \\ -\frac{1}{2} & 5 \end{bmatrix}$ $\begin{bmatrix} -1\frac{1}{2} & 2 \\ 1 & 7 \end{bmatrix}$
(5)

6. $\begin{bmatrix} 8 & 2.8 \\ -48 & 20 \end{bmatrix}$

Find the area of each triangle.

8. $h = 2$ cm, $b = 10$ cm 10 cm²
(SB)

9. $h = \frac{1}{3}$ feet, $b = 18$ feet 3 ft²
(SB)

INCLUSION

When solving for variables in a matrix, have students write statements equating corresponding elements in the matrices. Then have them work with the system of equations to find the value of each variable. For instance, for Example 4, students should write and solve the equations:

$$a + 12 = 18 \qquad 2b = -14$$

$$23 = a + c \qquad d = 3$$

Problem c

Suggest that students find the additive inverse of $\begin{bmatrix} 2 & -4 \\ 2 & -1 \\ 5 & -3 \end{bmatrix}$ and rewrite the problem as an addition problem.

Problem d

Error Alert Remind students that Y is a matrix. Ask, **"What are the dimensions of matrix Y?"** 2 × 2

Check for Understanding

The questions below help assess the concepts taught in this lesson.

1. **"How are matrices different than tables? How are they the same?"** Sample: Tables and matrices both have rows and columns of information. Matrices do not have row and column headers, or titles.

2. **"Explain how adding and subtracting matrices is similar to and different from adding and subtracting whole numbers."** Sample: When you add or subtract matrices, you must add or subtract each individual element in the matrix instead of a single value. The properties of real numbers hold for matrices.

3 Practice

Math Conversations

Discussions to strengthen understanding

Problems 1 and 2

Error Alert Since the lesson discussed additive inverses of matrices, students may erroneously find the additive inverse of each number instead of the multiplicative inverse.

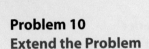

Problem 10

Extend the Problem

Have students draw the parallel lines and transversal and find the measures of the remaining angles formed by the intersections.

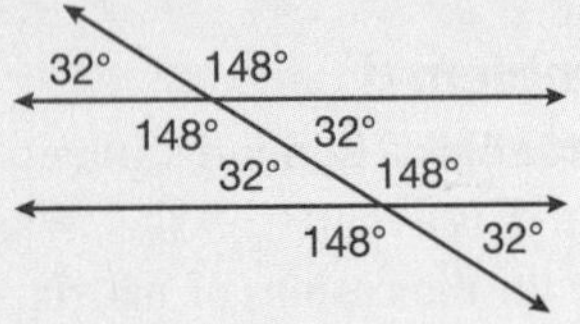

Problem 12a

Error Alert

Remind students one counterexample can prove a statement false, but one example does not prove it true.

10. (SB) Angles x and y are alternate interior angles formed by a transversal and 2 parallel lines. What is the measure of x if y measures 32°? 32°

11. (1) **Golf** Tiger Woods obtained an average score of 72 during the four rounds of golf at the Player's Championship in 2007. Explain how you can use the distributive property to mentally calculate his total score for the four rounds of golf.

12. (1) **Multi-Step** Classify each statement as sometimes, always, or never true. Use properties of real numbers to support your answer.

a. $a \cdot \left(-\frac{1}{b}\right) = b \cdot \left(-\frac{1}{a}\right)$ sometimes true; Sample: true example: $3 \cdot \left(-\frac{1}{3}\right) = 3 \cdot \left(-\frac{1}{3}\right)$; false example: $4 \cdot \left(-\frac{1}{3}\right) \neq 3 \cdot \left(-\frac{1}{4}\right)$, (true only when $a = b$.)

b. if a and b are rational numbers, then $a + b$ is a real number.

13. (2) **Museums** The Bob Bullock Texas State History Museum offers student tickets for 3 dollars to view the exhibits. Tickets to view the IMAX theatre cost 5 dollars. The table below shows expressions for the number of students that visited the exhibits and theater over a 2-day period. Write an expression for the total cost of student tickets to view the exhibits during the 2 days. $3(9v + 7v) = 48v$

Number of Students

	Exhibits	IMAX Theater
Day 1	$9v$	$7v$
Day 2	$7v$	$6v$

14. (3) **Solar System** The average distance between Jupiter and the Sun is approximately 7.786×10^{11} m.

a. Estimate the distance in kilometers that Jupiter travels around the Sun in one rotation. Write your answer in scientific notation. Round to the nearest hundredth. 4.89×10^9 km

b. Estimate the average speed at which Jupiter rotates around the Sun in km/s. Jupiter makes one rotation in 4,333 Earth days. 13.1 km/s

15. (4) Tell whether the given ordered pairs satisfy a function.

$$\{(2, 5), (2, 4), (2, 3), (2, 2), (2, 1)\}$$ no

***16.** (5) **Geometry** The matrix $R = \begin{pmatrix} 3 & 3.5 \\ 4 & 4.5 \end{pmatrix}$ shows the radii of four circles.

a. Write the matrix operation that gives the related circumferences.

b. Is there an addition or scalar-multiplication matrix operation that could show the related areas of the circles? Explain. See Additional Answers.

17. (4) **Precipitation** The mass of a large raindrop is equivalent to 1×10^{22} water molecules. The mass of a snowflake is equivalent to 1×10^{20} water molecules. Write a function to represent the mass of a raindrop in terms of the mass of a snowflake. $r = 100s$.

***18.** (5) **Error Analysis** Find and explain the error the student made below. Matrices that are of different dimensions cannot be added.

$$\begin{bmatrix} 14 \\ 0 \\ 7 \end{bmatrix} + [23 \quad -8 \quad -6] = [37 \quad -8 \quad 1]$$

11. Sample: Think of 72 as 70 + 2. Write an expression for the total score during the four rounds: 4(70 + 2). Use the distributive property: 4(70) + 4(2). Multiply: 280 + 8. Add: 288. His total score was 288.

12b. always true; Rational numbers are a subset of real numbers, so, if a and b are rational numbers, then they are real numbers. Therefore, by the Closure Property of Addition, $a + b$ is a real number.

***19.** (4) **Write** Explain why the vertical line test works. See Additional Answers.

20. (SB) The length of the side of a square is given by the expression $2x + 5$. Use the Distributive Property to write an expression for the perimeter of the square. $8x + 20$

***21.** (5) **Estimate** Estimate $4.8P$ given that $P = \begin{bmatrix} 2\frac{2}{3} & \pi \\ -\frac{1}{8} & 0.4\overline{5} \end{bmatrix}$. Sample: $\begin{bmatrix} 15 & 15 \\ -\frac{5}{8} & 2.5 \end{bmatrix}$

22. (2) **Multiple Choice** Evaluate $x(xy + 2y^2)$ if $x = 4$ and $y = -1$. C

A -24 B -12 C -8 D -2

***23.** (5) **a.** Create matrix A such that $a_{11} = 4$, $a_{12} = 6$, $a_{21} = 0$, and $a_{22} = -1$. $\begin{bmatrix} 4 & 6 \\ 0 & -1 \end{bmatrix}$

b. What is the additive inverse of A? $\begin{bmatrix} -4 & -6 \\ 0 & 1 \end{bmatrix}$

24. (1) **Error Analysis** Explain the error in the statement that follows and correct the statement. "$\sqrt{48}$ is a real number and a rational number." $\sqrt{48}$ can be written as $4\sqrt{3}$ and $\sqrt{3}$ is not a rational number.

25. (2) **Verify** Evaluate the expression $uv + 8v - u - 4uv + 7u$ if $u = -1$ and $v = -1$ by inserting the variable values into the expression as written. Verify your answer by simplifying the expression first, then inserting the variable values. -17

***26.** (4) $f(x) = x + 2$. Find $f(16)$. 18

***27.** (4) **Formulate** Write a function that represents the data set $(-4, 9)$, $(0, 1)$, $(1, -1)$, $(3, -5)$, $(4, -7)$. $f(x) = -2x + 1$

28. (4) **Model** One day the value of one US dollar was equivalent to 0.49 British pounds. On the same day, one US dollar was equivalent to 115.84 Japanese yen. Write a function to represent the value of yen in pounds. $f(y) = \frac{0.49y}{115.84}$

***29.** (5) **Justify** Does the Commutative Property hold true for Matrix Subtraction? Justify your answer. No; Sample: $\begin{bmatrix} 3 & 5 \\ 9 & 0 \end{bmatrix} - \begin{bmatrix} 1 & 0 \\ 2 & 6 \end{bmatrix} = \begin{bmatrix} 2 & 5 \\ 7 & -6 \end{bmatrix}$ but $\begin{bmatrix} 1 & 0 \\ 2 & 6 \end{bmatrix} - \begin{bmatrix} 3 & 5 \\ 9 & 0 \end{bmatrix} = \begin{bmatrix} -2 & -5 \\ -7 & 6 \end{bmatrix}$.

30. (3) **Skyscrapers** One cubic foot of pennies contains approximately 4.9×10^4 pennies. If the Sears Tower in Chicago were filled with pennies, it would hold about 2.6×10^{12} pennies. What is the approximate volume of the Sears Tower? Write your answer in scientific notation rounded to the nearest tenth. 5.3×10^7 cubic feet

Problem 19

Extend the Problem

Explain one-to-one functions. Help students formulate the horizontal test and how, once it has been established that a relationship is a function, they can use the horizontal test to determine whether the function is one-to-one.

Problem 23

Extend the Problem

Given the conditions for problem 23, have students formulate a 3×3 matrix and find its additive inverse.

LOOKING FORWARD

Using matrices to organize data and to solve problems prepares students for:

- **Lesson 14** Finding Determinants
- **Lesson 16** Using Cramer's Rule
- **Lesson 32** Solving Linear Systems with Matrix Inverses
- **Lesson 99** Using Vectors
- **Lesson 104** Finding Transformations

LESSON 6

1 Warm Up

Remind students that "of" means "times" in Problems 2 and 5.

2 New Concepts

In this lesson, students learn to find the percent of change between two numbers.

Discuss the formula for percent change and the definitions of **percent increase** and **percent decrease.**

Example 1b

Remind students that percents can be greater than 100%.

Error Alert Watch for students who forget to add the percent sign after moving the decimal point. Discuss with students the difference between the numbers 3.5 and 3.5%. Ask students which value is greater. 3.5

Additional Example 1

a. Change 0.12 to a percent. 12%

b. Change 8 to a percent. 800%

c. Change $\frac{4}{5}$ to a percent. 80%

d. Change $\frac{22}{8}$ to a percent. 275%

LESSON RESOURCES

Student Edition Practice Workbook 6
Reteaching Master 6
Adaptations Masters 6
Challenge and Enrichment Masters C6

LESSON 6

Finding Percent of Change

Warm Up

1. **Vocabulary** Percent means per ______ (hundred/thousand). hundred
(SB)

2. Find 30% of 40. 12
(SB)

3. Write $\frac{5}{8}$ as a decimal. 0.625
(SB)

4. Write 25% as a fraction. $\frac{1}{4}$
(SB)

5. Find 20% of 60. 12
(SB)

New Concepts

Any fraction or decimal can be written as a percent.

To write a decimal as a percent, multiply the decimal by 100.

To write a fraction as a percent, divide the numerator by the denominator to get a decimal, and then multiply the decimal by 100.

Hint

To multiply a number by 100, move the decimal point two places to the right.

Example 1 Changing Fractions and Decimals to Percents

a. Change 0.035 to a percent.

SOLUTION $0.035 \times 100 = 3.5$, so $0.035 = 3.5\%$.

b. Change 4 to a percent.

SOLUTION $4 \times 100 = 400$, so $4 = 400\%$.

c. Change $\frac{1}{8}$ to a percent.

SOLUTION $1 \div 8 = 0.125 = 12.5\%$

d. Change $\frac{12}{5}$ to a percent.

SOLUTION $12 \div 5 = 2.4 = 240\%$

The **percent of change** is the increase or decrease given as a percent of the original amount.

$$\text{percent of change} = \frac{\text{amount of increase or decrease}}{\text{original amount}}$$

When the new amount is greater than the original amount, the change is a percent increase. When the new amount is less than the original amount, the change is a percent decrease.

MATH BACKGROUND

Markup is a term used in marketing and business. The term implies a percent of increase over the price paid for an item.

Markups are dependent on the amount of profit desired from a sale. If a company wants to sell items at an x% markup from the wholesale price, they can use the formula:

marked up price = wholesale cost + markup

to find the marked up price.

Consumers may also want to calculate the markup they are paying for items. To do so, they can find the wholesale price of the item they are purchasing and solve the equation for markup:

markup = marked up price − wholesale cost

Example 2 Finding the Percent Change

Calculate the percent change and tell if the change is a percent increase or percent decrease.

a. from 120 to 168

SOLUTION Use the formula.

$$\text{percent change} = \frac{\text{amount of increase}}{\text{original amount}}$$ The change is an increase.

$$= \frac{48}{120}$$ 168 − 120 = 48

$$= 0.4 = 40\%$$

The percent change is a 40% increase.

b. from 6 to 5.1

SOLUTION Use the formula.

$$\text{percent change} = \frac{\text{amount of decrease}}{\text{original amount}}$$ The change is a decrease.

$$= \frac{0.9}{6}$$ 6 − 5.1 = 0.9

$$= 0.15 = 15\%$$

The percent change is a 15% decrease.

Example 3 Determining the New Amount

Math Language

In Example 3a, the **percent decrease** is 70% and the **amount of decrease** is 40.6.

a. What is the new amount when 58 is decreased by 70%?

SOLUTION Find the amount of decrease.

70% of 58

0.7 × 58 Write the percent as a decimal and multiply.

40.6

Subtract the amount of decrease from the original amount to find the new amount: 58 − 40.6 = 17.4.

b. What is the new amount when 620 is increased by 350%?

SOLUTION Find the amount of increase.

350% of 620

3.5 × 620 Write the percent as a decimal and multiply.

2170

Add the amount of increase to the original amount to find the new amount: 620 + 2170 = 2790.

When an item in a store is on sale, the new price reflects a discount. The amount of discount is the difference between the old and new price and the percent of discount is a percent decrease.

Example 2

Discuss with students how to determine if the percent change is a percent increase or a percent decrease. If the new value is greater than the original value it is a percent increase. If the old value is greater than the new value it is a percent decrease.

Error Alert Students may find the amount of increase or decrease and add a percent sign to that value. Remind students that finding the percent change is a three-step process. First, find the amount of change. Second, divide that value by the original amount. Third, write the quotient as a percent.

Additional Example 2

Calculate the percent change and tell if the change is a percent increase or a percent decrease.

a. from 18 to 72 300% increase

b. from 240 to 60 75% decrease

Example 3

Show students that the formula

$$\text{percent change} = \frac{\text{amount of change}}{\text{original amount}}$$

is being used to solve the examples.

Solve the formula for amount of change:

percent change × original amount = amount of change

Additional Example 3

a. What is the new amount when 125 is decreased by 15%? 106.25

b. What is the new amount when 48 is increased by 175%? 132

ENGLISH LEARNERS

The words increase and decrease sound and look very similar. Say:

"Decrease means to reduce or make smaller."

"Increase means to enlarge or make bigger."

Discuss the meaning of the prefix "de" with students. The prefix "de" means "down," "away from," or "reversing."

Ask students to think of other words starting with "de" where the prefix has the same meaning as in the word decrease, and discuss the meanings of those words. Some possible words include decelerate, deduce, deemphasize, and deficit.

Then ask students to think of other "in"/"de" pairs of words and discuss their meanings. Some possible pairs include inductive/deductive, incline/decline, infer/defer, and infect/defect.

Example 4

Error Alert Students may think that the sale price is found by multiplying the original price by the discount percentage. Remind students that value is the discount amount, or the amount that needs to be subtracted from the original price.

Additional Example 4

A digital camera that regularly costs $128 is being offered at a 25% discount. Find the sale price of the camera. $96

Example 5

Extend the Example

Suppose the store owner buys 150 candles from the candle maker and sells all 150 candles. How much profit did the store owner make from the sale of the candles? $1,890

Additional Example 5

A grocer buys watermelons from a farmer for 1.34 each and sells them at a 250% markup. What is the cost of a watermelon at the grocer's store? $4.69

On the other hand, when the price of an item increases, the increase is a markup and the percent change is a percent increase. A markup can refer to an increase in the retail price of an item, or it can refer to the amount by which the wholesale cost of the item is increased.

sale price = original price − discount

marked up price = original price (or wholesale cost) + markup

Example 4 Determining a Sale Price

A hiking backpack that regularly costs $98 is being offered at a 15% discount. Find the sale price of the backpack.

SOLUTION

1. Understand The sale price is the original price, $98, minus the discount, which is 15% of $98.

2. Plan Translate the sentence into algebra.

> **Math Language**
>
> When translating from words to algebra, **is** changes to = and **of** changes to ×.

sale price is original price − discount

sale price is 98 − 15% of 98

$$s = 98 - 0.15(98)$$

3. Solve $s = 98 - 14.7$

$s = 83.3$

The sale price is $83.30.

4. Check Find the percent decrease: $\frac{98 - 83.3}{98} = \frac{14.7}{98} = 0.15 = 15\%$.

Example 5 Determining a Marked Up Price

A store owner buys candles from a local candle maker at $3.15 each and sells them at a 400% markup. How much does the store owner sell each candle for?

SOLUTION

1. Understand The marked up price is the wholesale cost, $3.15, plus the markup, which is 400% of $3.15.

2. Plan Translate the sentence into algebra.

marked up price is wholesale cost + markup

marked up price is 3.15 + 400% of 3.15

$$m = 3.15 + 4(3.15)$$

3. Solve $m = 3.15 + 12.6$

$m = 15.75$

The store owner sells each candle for $15.75.

4. Check Find the percent increase: $\frac{15.75 - 3.15}{3.15} = \frac{12.6}{3.15} = 4 = 400\%$.

ALTERNATE METHOD FOR EXAMPLE 4

A discount of 15% means the discounted price will be 100 − 15 = 85% of the original price. The problem can then be solved by multiplying the original price by 85%.

$$98 \times 0.85 = 83.30$$

Lesson Practice

a. (1) Change 1.65 to a percent. 165%

b. (1) Change 0.2 to a percent. 20%

c. (1) Change $\frac{7}{4}$ to a percent. 175%

d. (1) Change $\frac{3}{5}$ to a percent. 60%

Calculate the percent change and tell if the change is a percent increase or percent decrease.

e. (2) from 10 to 11 10% increase

f. (2) from \$50 to \$12 76% decrease

g. (3) What is the new amount when 700 is increased by 3%? 721

h. (3) What is the new amount when 6.2 is decreased by 90%? 0.62

i. (4) Ethan receives a 10% employee discount on any item in the store. How much will he pay for a printer that costs \$230? \$207

j. (5) The price of a baseball card is marked up by 45%. What is the new price of the card if the price before the markup was \$60? \$87

Practice Distributed and Integrated

Determine whether the following numbers are rational numbers.

1. (1) $\sqrt{225}$ Rational

2. (1) π Not rational

3. (2) Evaluate $\frac{xy(x^2)}{2x}$ for $x = -1$ and $y = 4$. 2

4 (3) Simplify $x^5y(2x^{-5}y^4)^3$. $\frac{8y^{13}}{x^{10}}$

5. (5) **Graphing Calculator** Find $\begin{bmatrix} 1 & 5 \\ 2 & -3.2 \end{bmatrix} + 2\begin{bmatrix} 1 & 0 \\ -1 & 4 \end{bmatrix}$. Check using the calculator. $\begin{bmatrix} 3 & 5 \\ 0 & 4.8 \end{bmatrix}$

6. (SB) What solid figure is described by the net? Rectangular prism

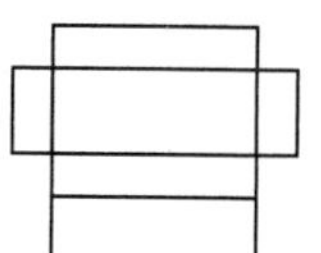

Find the percent change.

***7.** (6) from 3 to 4.5 50%

***8.** (6) from 0.8 to 2.74 242.5%

Identify whether each of the following represent a function. If so, state the domain and range.

9. (4) $y^2 = x + 1$ Not a function

10. (4) $y = x^2 - 2$ Function. Domain: All real numbers. Range, $y \geq -2$

INCLUSION

Have students use separate formulas for percent increase and decrease.

$$\text{percent increase} = \frac{\text{new amount} - \text{original amount}}{\text{original amount}}$$

$$\text{percent decrease} = \frac{\text{original amount} - \text{new amount}}{\text{original amount}}$$

Lesson Practice

Problems a and b

Scaffolding Ask, **"When you are changing a decimal to a percent, which way do you move the decimal point?"** to the right

Problems c and d

Remind students that changing a fraction to a percent is a two-step process. 1. Write the fraction as a decimal. 2. Change the decimal to a percent.

Check for Understanding

The questions below help assess the concepts taught in this lesson.

1. **"Explain how to find the new amount when a number is increased by a percent."** Sample: Multiply the percent times the original amount to find the amount of increase. Then add the amount of increase to the original amount.

2. **"Explain the difference between a discount and a markup."** Sample: A discount is a percent decrease. You subtract the discount amount from the regular price of an item. A markup is a percent increase. You add the markup amount to the wholesale cost of an item.

3 Practice

Math Conversations

Discussion to strengthen understanding

Problem 1

Error Alert

Students may assume $\sqrt{225}$ is irrational because of its radical sign. Remind students that some numbers, such as 225, are perfect squares.

Problem 14

Extend the Problem

Have students find the cost of a 20-minute call $4.30 and a 30-minute call. $6.30 Have them make a conjecture about the cost of a 50 minute call and use the function to see if their conjecture is correct. $10.30

Problem 17

Extend the Problem

Ask students to analyze the data in the difference matrix. Ask, **"What does element two three represent?"** During Meet 2, twenty-one more 3rd place medals were won this year than last year.

11. **Error Analysis** Two students are asked to simplify an expression and identify which property was used for each step. Their answers are shown below. Identify which student has an error in the procedure and correct the error. Simplify $(4 + 2) \cdot 10$. (1)

11. Student A made an error. The first step should be labeled "Distributive Property". The second step should be labeled "Multiply".

Student A	
$(4 \cdot 10) + (2 \cdot 10)$	Associative Property
$40 + 20$	Distributive Property
60	Add.

Student B	
$6 \cdot 10$	Add
60	Multiply

*12. A student bought a $3.20 notebook for 30% off and a $78 calculator for 10% off. (6)

a. How much did the student spend? $72.44

b. **Verify** Show that it is not correct to add the prices of the items and then take 40% off their total. 40% off $81.20 is $48.72.

13. **Multiple Choice** Evaluate $-x^2 + 6y$ if $x = 2$ and $y = 0$. B (2)

A -10 B -4 C 4 D 10

14. Ty uses the function $g(x) = 0.5 + 0.2(x - 1)$ to calculate the cost in dollars of using a calling card to make a long distance call lasting x minutes. The variable x must be a natural number. Determine the cost of a 10-minute call. $2.30 (4)

*15. **Population** The population of Indiana in 1990 was reported to be 5,544,159 and in 2000 was reported to be 6,080,485. Find the percent increase. Round to the nearest hundredth of a percent. 9.67% (6)

16. **Multiple Choice** Identify the subset of real numbers of which -5 is not a member. C (1)

A integer B real number C whole number D rational number

17. **Sports** The table shows results from the first three track meets last year and this year. (5)

Last Year

	1st	2nd	3rd
Meet 1	27	33	51
Meet 2	29	42	41
Meet 3	25	29	60

This Year

	1st	2nd	3rd
Meet 1	18	45	47
Meet 2	34	33	62
Meet 3	35	31	54

a. Create a matrix for each year.

b. Use matrix subtraction to subtract last year's matrix from this year's matrix.

18. **Multi-Step** a. Evaluate the expression $-5vw(-2 + w)$ if $v = 3$ and $w = -4$. -360 (2)

b. Explain how the result would be affected if v was tripled. The result would triple.

c. Show that this is true by evaluating the expression if $v = 9$ and $w = -4$. -1080

*19. **Analyze** What is the percent decrease when the original amount is 75 and the new amount is 0? Explain. The percent decrease is 100% because the amount of decrease is 75, and 75 divided by 75 equals 1, or 100%. (6)

17.a. $\begin{bmatrix} 27 & 33 & 51 \\ 29 & 42 & 41 \\ 25 & 29 & 60 \end{bmatrix} \begin{bmatrix} 18 & 45 & 47 \\ 34 & 33 & 62 \\ 35 & 31 & 54 \end{bmatrix}$; b. $\begin{bmatrix} -9 & 12 & -4 \\ 5 & -9 & 21 \\ 10 & 2 & -6 \end{bmatrix}$

CHALLENGE

The sale price of a DVD is $28.79. The discount was 10%. What was the original price of the DVD? $31.99

20. **Planets** The speed of light is about 3×10^8 meters/second.
(2)
a. About how many seconds would it take light to reach Pluto from the Sun at their minimum distance apart of about 4.437×10^{12} meters? 14,790 sec

b. About how many seconds would it take light to reach Pluto from the Sun at their maximum distance apart of about 7.376×10^{12} meters? Round your answers to the nearest second. 24,587 sec

*21. **Write** Compare and contrast markups and discounts.
(6)

*22. **Geometry** Every side of a 2 by 7 rectangle is tripled to form a new rectangle. By what percent did the area of the rectangle increase? 800%
(6)

23. **Verify** Simplify the expression $(2 + 3) + 1$ using only one property of real numbers. Identify the property that you used. Verify your result using two properties of real numbers.
(1)

24. **Currency** On the first day of 2007, the value of one US dollar was equivalent to 119 Japanese yen. On the same day, one euro was equivalent to 157 Japanese yen.
(4)
a. Write a function to represent the value of US dollars in euros. $d = \frac{157e}{119}$

b. What is the value of the function for an input of 5 rounded to the nearest cent, and what does it represent? $d = \frac{157(5)}{119} = 6.60$; on that day, 5 euros was equivalent to \$6.60 US.

*25. Evaluate $a^2b^3 - (5a - b^2)$ if $a = 1$ and $b = 3$. 31
(2)

26. For the expression $\frac{-4x}{7}$
(1)
a. find the additive inverse. $\frac{4x}{7}$

b. find the multiplicative inverse. $-\frac{7}{4x}$

27. **Coordinate Geometry** The coordinates of points in the coordinate plane can be written in matrices where the x-coordinates are listed in the first row and the corresponding y-coordinates are listed in the second row. b. The triangle was translated four units right and two units up.
(5)

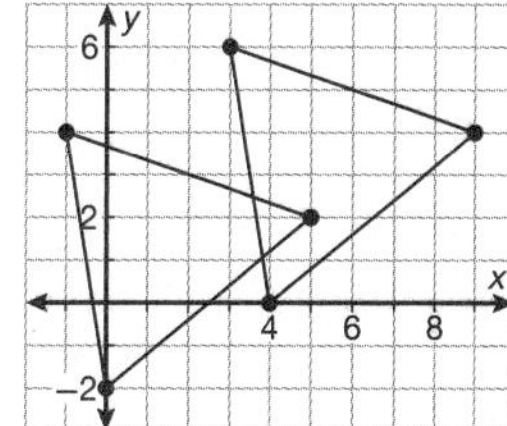

a. Graph $A = \begin{bmatrix} -1 & 0 & 5 \\ 4 & -2 & 2 \end{bmatrix}$.

b. Graph $A + B$ where $B = \begin{bmatrix} 4 & 4 & 4 \\ 2 & 2 & 2 \end{bmatrix}$. What happened?

*28. Find the additive inverse matrix of $\begin{bmatrix} 2 \\ 4 \\ -5 \end{bmatrix}$. $\begin{bmatrix} -2 \\ -4 \\ 5 \end{bmatrix}$
(5)

29. **Estimate** One cubic foot of pennies contains approximately 4.9×10^4 pennies. The Giants Stadium in New Jersey has an approximate volume of 6.45×10^7 cubic feet. About how many pennies would fit in the Giants Stadium? Approximately 3.2×10^{12} pennies
(3)

30. **Write** Explain how Scalar Multiplication is similar to the Distributive Property and how it is different.
(5)

21. Sample: Markups and discounts are both percent changes; a markup is a percent increase and a discount is a percent decrease. They can both be used to find the new price of an item. A discount is subtracted from the old price and a markup is added to the old price.

23. $(2 + 3) + 1 =$
$2 + (3 + 1) =$
$2 + 4 = 6$
Associative Property of Addition;
$(2 + 3) + 1 =$
$(3 + 2) + 1 =$
$3 + (2 + 1) =$
$3 + 3 = 6$,
Commutative Property of Addition & Associative Property of Addition

30. Sample: In both, you multiply a group of objects by one outside object. In the Distributive Property, the factor that everything is multiplied by can be a constant or a variable expression; in Scalar Multiplication, that factor is a constant.

LOOKING FORWARD

Using matrices to organize data and to solve problems prepares students for:

- **Lesson 10** Solving and Graphing Inequalities
- **Lesson 18** Calculating with Units of Measure

Problem 21

Remind students the relationship between "increase" and "decrease" and the words "markup" and "discount." Ask students to determine which two terms imply a quantity larger than the original and which two terms imply a quantity smaller than the original. Increase and markup imply larger quantities while discount and decrease imply smaller quantities.

Problem 28

Students may need to be reminded that an additive inverse is the number which, added to the quantity given, equals zero. Given the quantity a, the additive inverse is $-a$, since $a + (-a) = 0$.

LESSON 7

1 Warm Up

In problem 2, remind students that the Distributive Property states that $5(x - 3) = 5 \cdot x - 5 \cdot 3$.

2 New Concepts

In this lesson, students review how to solve linear equations. A **linear equation** is one that can be simplified to the form $ax + b = 0$ (where a and b are constants and $a \neq 0$). Point out that in a linear equation, the variable is raised to the first power.

Throughout the lesson, emphasize ideas of balance and equality. To solve an equation, students will perform operations to isolate x. Constantly remind them that any operation done to one side of the equation must be done to the other side in order to maintain the balance. Also point out that when the same operation is performed on both sides of an equation, the result is an equivalent equation.

LESSON 7

Solving Linear Equations

Warm Up

1. **Vocabulary** $x + 3 = 3 + x$ demonstrates the ________ Property of Addition. (1) Commutative

2. Simplify $5(x - 3)$. (1) $5x - 15$

3. Simplify $3x + 4y - 8x - 4y$. (2) $-5x$

New Concepts

An **equation** is a statement which indicates that two expressions are equal.

$2 + 3 = 5$ $x = 3$ $5a - 12 = 13$ are all examples of equations.

You can use algebra tiles to help you solve equations.

Math Language

A **solution set of an equation** is the set of values that makes an equation true.

Exploration Solving Equations Using Algebra Tiles

Use algebra tiles to model and solve $2x + 3 = 7$.

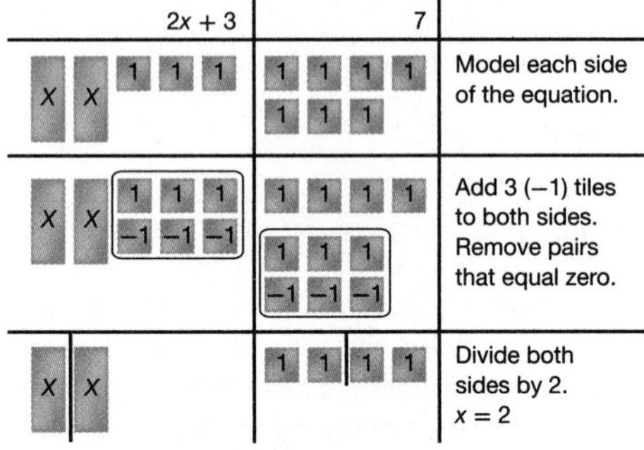

Use algebra tiles to model and solve $3x + 1 = 10$.

A number is a **solution of an equation** in one variable if substituting the number for the variable results in a true statement. An equation can be solved using the properties of equality to transform the equation into an equivalent equation.

Math Reasoning

Write Why is there a restriction of $c \neq 0$ in the Multiplication and Division Properties?

For the Multiplication Property, if $c = 0$, then the product is zero whether $a = b$ or not. For the Division Property, division by zero is undefined so c cannot equal zero.

Properties of Equality		
Addition Property of Equality	Add the same number to both sides.	If $a = b$ then $a + c = b + c$.
Subtraction Property of Equality	Subtract the same number from both sides.	If $a = b$ then $a - c = b - c$.
Multiplication Property of Equality	Multiply both sides by the same number.	If $a = b$ then $ac = bc$.
Division Property of Equality	Divide both sides by the same number.	If $a = b$ and $c \neq 0$ then $a \div c = b \div c$.

LESSON RESOURCES

Student Edition Practice Workbook 7
Reteaching Master 7
Adaptations Master 7
Challenge and Enrichment Masters C7, E7

MATH BACKGROUND

Previous lessons have prepared students for solving equations in one variable. A solution to a linear equation in one variable is any number which, when substituted for the variable, makes the equation true.

The procedures learned in this lesson will be further explained and used when solving systems of linear equations and inequalities as well as non-linear systems.

There are many applications of systems of equations. Systems of linear equations can be used to represent real situations in various fields including botany. For example, the growth of a plant may be observed in two different mediums. The height of the plants can be expressed as a function with respect to the days in two different equations that make up the system.

Example 1 Solving Equations with a Variable on One Side

> **Hint**
>
> Use the Addition or Subtraction Property of Equality to solve before the Multiplication or Division property.

Solve $-5x + 12 = -23$.

SOLUTION

$$\begin{aligned} -5x + 12 &= -23 \\ -12 &= -12 \quad \text{Subtract 12 from both sides.} \\ -5x \quad &= -35 \\ \frac{-5x}{-5} &= \frac{-35}{-5} \quad \text{Divide both sides by } -5. \\ x &= 7 \end{aligned}$$

Check Check 7 in the original equation.

$$\begin{aligned} -5x + 12 &= -23 \\ -5(7) + 12 &\stackrel{?}{=} -23 \\ -5(7) + 12 &\stackrel{?}{=} -23 \\ -35 + 12 &\stackrel{?}{=} -23 \\ -23 &= -23 \quad ✓ \end{aligned}$$

Equations can be transformed using the properties of equality on terms with variables. Variable terms can be added to or subtracted from both sides of an equation.

Example 2 Solving Equations with Variables on Both Sides

Solve $2n - 3 = 6n + 25$.

SOLUTION

$$\begin{aligned} 2n - 3 &= 6n + 25 \\ +3 \quad &\quad +3 \quad \text{Add 3 to both sides.} \\ 2n \quad &= 6n + 28 \\ -6n \quad &= -6n \quad \text{Subtract } 6n \text{ from both sides.} \\ \frac{-4n}{-4} &= \frac{28}{-4} \quad \text{Divide both sides by 4.} \\ n &= -7 \end{aligned}$$

Check $2(-7) - 3 \stackrel{?}{=} 6(-7) + 25$

$$\begin{aligned} -14 - 3 &\stackrel{?}{=} -42 + 25 \\ -17 &= -17 \quad ✓ \end{aligned}$$

ALTERNATE METHOD FOR EXAMPLE 2

Show students that the order in which the Properties of Equality are applied and the selection of which terms to eliminate from a certain side does not affect the solution. Emphasize that there is a unique solution to a linear equation, and that any justifiable method should lead to that solution.

Contrast the following solution process with the one shown:

$$\begin{aligned} 2n - 3 &= 6n + 25 \\ -25 &= \quad - 25 \\ 2n - 28 &= 6n \\ -2n \quad &= -2n \\ \frac{-28}{4} &= \frac{4n}{4} \\ -7 &= n \end{aligned}$$

Example 1

Tell students to isolate the variable term $(-5x)$ on the left side using the Subtraction Property of Equality. Then, eliminate the coefficient of x (-5) using the Division Property of Equality.

Be sure students understand the symbol "$\stackrel{?}{=}$" used in checking the solution. Notice that the question mark disappears when it has been shown that the equation is true.

Additional Example 1

Solve $3x - 9 = -15$.
$x = -2$

TEACHER TIP

Be sure students understand that the vertical format used to show the addition or subtraction of a term from both sides of an equation could also be written horizontally. For example,

$$\begin{aligned} -5x + 12 &= -23 \\ -12 &= -12 \end{aligned}$$

could also be written as

$-5x + 12 - \mathbf{12} = -23 - \mathbf{12}$

Some students might prefer to use the latter method of recording their work.

Example 2

Error Alert Students sometimes try to accelerate the solution process by performing two operations at once. In this example, they might try to add 3 to both sides and subtract $6n$ in a single step. Encourage them to combine constants first, then combine like variable terms.

Additional Example 2

Solve $2b + 7 = 4b - 9$.
$x = 8$

Example 3

Remind students to simplify within each side of the equation before using Properties of Equality.

Additional Example 3

Solve $4(t + 6) + 2t = 7(t + 3)$.

$t = 3$

Example 4

Error Alert Students might forget to multiply each term on each side by 6. In particular, they may forget to distribute to the whole-number term (4). Remind them that the entirety of each side must be multiplied by 6. Since the left side is a binomial, 6 is distributed to each of 2 terms.

Additional Example 4

Solve $\frac{1}{4}x + \frac{1}{2} = -\frac{3}{4}x - 4$.

$x = -\frac{9}{2}$

Extend the Example

Have students use substitution to check the solution $x = -3$. Remind them that they must check the solution in the original equation.

$$\frac{1}{2}x + 4 = -\frac{2}{3}x + \frac{1}{2}$$

$$\frac{1}{2}(-3) + 4 = -\frac{2}{3}(-3) + \frac{1}{2}$$

$$-\frac{3}{2} + 4 = 2 + \frac{1}{2}$$

$$-\frac{3}{2} + \frac{8}{2} = \frac{4}{2} + \frac{1}{2}$$

$$\frac{5}{2} = \frac{5}{2}$$

TEACHER TIP

Emphasize that the equation could be solved in fraction form. However, eliminating the fractions by multiplying through by a common denominator eliminates the need to operate with fractions.

Example 3 **Solving Equations Using the Distributive Property**

Solve $12(r + 3) = 2(r + 5) - 3r$.

SOLUTION

$12(r + 3) = 2(r + 5) - 3r$	
$12r + 36 = 2r + 10 - 3r$	Distribute.
$12r + 36 = -r + 10$	Combine like terms.
$\underline{\quad -36 = \quad -36}$	Subtract 36.
$12r = -r - 26$	
$\underline{+r = +r}$	Add r.
$13r = -26$	
$\frac{13r}{13} = \frac{-26}{13}$	Divide by 13.
$r = -2$	

Check $12(r + 3) = 2(r + 5) - 3r$

$$12(-2 + 3) \stackrel{?}{=} 2(-2 + 5) - 3(-2)$$

$$12(1) \stackrel{?}{=} 2(3) - (-6)$$

$$12 \stackrel{?}{=} 6 - (-6)$$

$$12 = 12 \checkmark$$

Example 4 **Solving Equations with Fractions**

Solve $\frac{1}{2}x + 4 = -\frac{2}{3}x + \frac{1}{2}$.

SOLUTION

$\frac{1}{2}x + 4 = -\frac{2}{3}x + \frac{1}{2}$	
$6\left(\frac{1}{2}x + 4\right) = 6\left(-\frac{2}{3}x + \frac{1}{2}\right)$	Multiply both sides by 6.
$3x + 24 = -4x + 3$	
$\underline{\quad -24 \quad\quad -24}$	Subtract 24.
$3x = -4x - 21$	
$\underline{+4x = +4x}$	Add $4x$.
$7x = -21$	
$\frac{7x}{7} = \frac{-21}{7}$	Divide by 7.
$x = -3$	

Math Reasoning

Generalize For any equation containing fractions how do you eliminate the fractions?

Multiply by the least common multiple of the denominators.

INCLUSION

An equation for which the solution takes more than a few steps might be daunting for some students. Work with students to make a list of the steps needed to solve the equations in this lesson. For example:

1. Use the Distributive Property.
2. Multiply by a common denominator to eliminate fractions.
3. Combine like terms within each side.
4. Use the Addition or Subtraction Property of Equality to eliminate the constant from one side.
5. Use the Addition or Subtraction Property of Equality to eliminate the variable term from the other side.
6. Use the Multiplication or Division Property of Equality to make the coefficient of the variable term 1.
7. Check your answer using substitution.

Example 5 Application: Population

> **Math Reasoning**
>
> **Estimate** Work the problem by estimating the populations to the nearest thousands first.

According to the 2000 census, the three smallest states in the United States by population are North Dakota, Vermont, and Wyoming. The total population of these three states is 1,774,779. If Vermont has a population of 623,908 and North Dakota has a population of 635,867, write and solve an equation to determine the population of Wyoming.

SOLUTION Let x equal the population of Wyoming.

$$\begin{aligned} x + 623{,}908 + 635{,}867 &= 1{,}774{,}779 \\ x + 1{,}259{,}775 &= 1{,}774{,}779 \\ -1{,}259{,}775 &= -1{,}259{,}775 \\ \hline x &= 515{,}004 \end{aligned}$$

The population of Wyoming is 515,004 people.

Check $515{,}004 + 623{,}908 + 635{,}867 = 1{,}774{,}779$ ✓

Lesson Practice

Solve.

a. $8t - 21 = 11$ $t = 4$
(Ex 1)

b. $5r - 12 = -4r - 30$ $r = -2$
(Ex 2)

c. $6(y - 5) + 4y = 5(y + 2)$ $y = 8$
(Ex 3)

d. $-\frac{3}{4}s - 3 = \frac{1}{3}s + \frac{1}{4}$ $s = -3$
(Ex 4)

e. Aaron is traveling 955 miles from Phoenix, AZ to Jackson, WY. He leaves Phoenix, driving 410 miles before stopping for gas in Cortez, Co. He makes one last stop in Rock Springs, WY before traveling the final 180 miles to Jackson. Write and solve an equation to find the number of miles between Cortez and Rock Springs. $410 + d + 180 = 955$; $d = 365$ miles
(Ex 5)

Practice Distributed and Integrated

Find the measure of the angles that are supplementary to the angles given.

1. 65° 115°
(SB)

2. 138° 42°
(SB)

3. Evaluate $3xy^3 + x - y$ for $x = -2$ and $y = -2$. 48
(2)

***4.** **Graphing Calculator** Find $\frac{3}{4}\begin{bmatrix} 8 & -4 \\ 2 & 0 \end{bmatrix} - \begin{bmatrix} 1 & -6 \\ -7 & -2 \end{bmatrix}$. Check using a graphing calculator. $\begin{bmatrix} 5 & 3 \\ 8\frac{1}{2} & 2 \end{bmatrix}$
(5)

Find the area of each rectangle given the dimensions below.

5. $l = 2$ inches, $w = 1.3$ inches 2.6 in.^{2}
(SB)

6. $l = 4$ cm, $w = 3$ cm 12 cm^2
(SB)

7. Find the percent change from 5 to 6.1. 22%
(6)

ENGLISH LEARNERS

Explain the meaning of the word **equation.** Say:

"An equation is a statement which indicates that two quantities are equal. An equation always contains an equals sign."

Show students a mix of equations and expressions and ask them to identify the equations. Show them how a simple equation like $2 + 2 = 4$ shows that the quantities $2 + 2$ and 4 are equal.

Also explain the meaning of the word **solution.** Say:

"Solution means two things. It can mean the set of steps you take to solve an equation. It can also mean the answer itself."

Example 5

Error Alert Students might just subtract. Encourage students to model the situation algebraically, so that they are prepared to solve word problems they cannot do without algebra.

Additional Example 5

The Ironman Triathlon is held every year in Hawaii. The race covers a total distance of 140.6 miles. If the swim is 2.4 miles long and the bike route is 112 miles long, how long is the run? The run is 26.2 miles.

Lesson Practice

Problem b

Suggest that students add $4r$ to each side so that the variable term has a positive coefficient.

Problem d

Remind students that they must multiply each term on each side by the LCD, 12.

Check for Understanding

The questions below help assess the concepts taught in this lesson.

1. **"What are the steps for solving linear equations?"** Simplify each side. Move variables to one side and constants to the other. Make the coefficient 1. Check.
2. **"Explain how to solve an equation that has fractions."** Find the LCM of all the denominators of the fractions. Multiply each side of the equation by that number, distributing to each term on each side. Then, simplify and solve.

Lesson 7 45

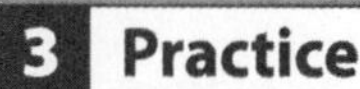

3 Practice

Math Conversations

Discussion to strengthen understanding

Problem 11

Some students might prefer to change 6.5×10^2 to 650 before multiplying by 5.

Problem 12

Error Alert

Students might fail to see how properties of real numbers are used to simplify the expression. Guide them to see that their natural inclination to multiply 3 and $\frac{1}{3}$ first shows the Commutative, Associative, and Multiplicative Inverse Properties.

Problem 14

Guide the students by asking them the following questions.

"What is the price of the \$85 pair of shoes after the 40% discount?" \$51

"What is the price of the \$68 pair of shoes after the 15% discount?" \$57.80

Compare prices. Which is less? \$51 **How much less?** \$6.80

Problem 17

Tell students that there are two ways to find the answer. They can solve the equation and compare their answer to the one given. Or, they can substitute the given value for x and determine whether it yields a true equation.

Problem 18

Remind students of the Vertical Line Test for functions. Since a circle can never pass the Vertical Line Test, a circle does not represent a function.

Solve each equation.

***8.** (7) $3(x + 2) = 2x - 1$ $x = -7$

***9.** (7) $\frac{1}{2}x + 8 = 24$ $x = 32$

10. (4) Use the table to answer the following questions.

x	0	1	2	3
y	9	7	5	3

a. What is the domain? 0, 1, 2, 3

b. What is the range? 9, 7, 5, 3

c. Does this data represent a function? Explain. This is a function because each domain value has exactly one range value.

11. (3) (**Astronomy**) Saturn's smallest moon, Tethys, has a diameter of about 6.5×10^2 miles. The diameter of Jupiter's largest moon, Ganymede, is 5 times that of Tethys. Determine the diameter of Ganymede. Write your answer in standard form. about 3250 miles

12. (1) **Justify** Simplify the expression using properties of real numbers. Justify your answer by identifying which property you used for each step.

$$3 \cdot 5 \cdot \frac{1}{3}$$

13. (4) (**Diving**) The pressure on a diver is given by $P(d) = \frac{1}{33}d + 1$ where the pressure is in atmospheres and d is the diver's depth in feet. What is the approximate pressure of the diver at 50 feet under water? about 2.5 atm

14. (6) Which is less expensive: an \$85 pair of shoes with a 40% discount or a \$68 pair of shoes with a 15% discount? How much less expensive is it? \$85 with 40% discount; \$6.80 less

***15.** (7) Sandra's brother is 6 years older than her, her sister is 2 years younger than her, and her mother is 3 times her age. Her brother, sister, and mother's combined age is 64.

a. Write an equation to solve for Sandra's age. $(s + 6) + (s - 2) + (3s) = 64$

b. Solve your equation. $s = 12$

16. (3) (**Speed of Sound**) Mauna Kea in Hawaii is about 1.02×10^4 meters from its base to its peak. Assume that the speed of sound is about 3.44×10^2 meters/second. Use this information to solve the following questions. Write your answers in scientific notation.

a. About how many seconds would it take sound to reach the base from the peak? Round your answer to the nearest second. 30 sec

b. Approximately 5.96×10^3 meters of Mauna Kea is below sea level. About how many seconds would it take sound to reach sea level from the peak? 12 sec

***17.** (7) **Verify** Is $x = \frac{1}{14}$ the solution to the equation $9x - \frac{2}{7} = 8x + \frac{11}{14}$?

18. (4) **Coordinate Geometry** Explain whether a circle drawn on a coordinate grid represents a function.

12. $3 \cdot \frac{1}{3} \cdot 5$ Commutative Property of Multiplication;
$\left(3 \cdot \frac{1}{3}\right) \cdot 5$ Associative Property of Multiplication;
$1 \cdot 5$ Multiplicative Inverse;
5 Identity Property of Multiplication

17. No;
$9\left(\frac{1}{14}\right) - \frac{2}{7} = 8\left(\frac{1}{14}\right) + \frac{11}{14}$
$\frac{9}{14} - \frac{2}{7} = \frac{8}{14} + \frac{11}{14}$
$\frac{5}{14} \neq \frac{19}{14}$

18. No; At a given value of x, two y-values will result – a point along the top of the circle and a point along the bottom of the circle.

CHALLENGE

Have students use a strategy similar to the one in Example 4 to solve the problem shown here. Show them how to eliminate decimals by multiplying through by a power of 10.

$$1.5(x + 7) = 1.9x + 9.7$$

$$\begin{aligned} 10[1.5(x + 7)] &= 10[1.9x + 9.7] \\ 15(x + 7) &= 19x + 97 \\ 15x + 105 &= 19x + 97 \\ -4x &= -8 \\ x &= 2 \end{aligned}$$

19. (Economics) The median income for US females with a doctorate degree rose from $40,172 in 1990 to $60,733 in 2000. The median income for US males with a doctorate degree rose from $54,626 to in 1990 to $78,092 in 2000. Which group had the greater percent increase? How much greater? (Round to the nearest percent.) US females, by about 8%
(6)

20. **Error Analysis** Find and explain the error the student made below.
(5)

$$6\begin{bmatrix} 2 & 5 \\ 9 & -2 \end{bmatrix} = \begin{bmatrix} 8 & 11 \\ 15 & 4 \end{bmatrix}$$ Instead of multiplying each element by 6, the student added 6 to each element.

21. Given that $A = \begin{bmatrix} 4 & 5 & -6 \\ -9 & 0 & 3 \\ 8 & 2 & -1 \end{bmatrix}$ and $B = \begin{bmatrix} 1 & 7 \\ 8 & -14 \\ 5 & -9 \end{bmatrix}$, what is $a_{13} + b_{21}$? 2
(5)

*22. **Error Analysis** A student said that a change from 15 to 30 is a 50% increase because 15 is 50% of 30. Explain the error in the student's thinking.
(6)

*23. (Coffee) On Sunday a coffee shop sold 115 lb of coffee. The amount of regular coffee sold was 5 lb more than the amount of decaffeinated coffee sold. There were twice as many pounds of flavored coffee sold than there was regular coffee sold.
(7)

a. Write an equation to solve for the amount of regular coffee sold. $(r - 5) + r + 2r = 115$

b. Solve the equation from part a. $r = 30$ lb

*24. **Multiple Choice** What is the discount when a $14 shirt is on sale for 20% off? A
(6)

A $2.80 B $7.00 C $11.20 D $16.80

25. **Multiple Choice** Evaluate $-5x^2 + 2y$ if $x = 1$ and $y = -1$. A
(2)

A −7 B −3 C 3 D 7

26. **Formulate** Write a function that represents the data set (−19, −12), (−12, −5), (−5, 2), (2, 9), (9, 16). $f(x) = x + 7$
(4)

27. **Verify** Show how to check that 28 increased by 80% is 50.4.
(6)

22. The percent change is the amount of change as a percent of the original number, not as a percent of the new number. Since the amount of change is 15, and 15 divided by 15 is 1, the percent change is 100%.

27. Subtract to find the difference between the two amounts: 50.4 − 28 = 22.4. Divide the result by the original amount: 22.4 divided by 28 equals 0.8, which is 80%.

*28. **Geometry** Janice wants to find the value of y for the triangle shown. The perimeter of the triangle is $8y$. Write and solve an equation to find the value of y. $9 + 8 + 3y - 2 = 8y, y = 3$
(7)

9
3y − 2
8

29. **Multi-Step** **a.** Evaluate the expression $6st(6 + t)$ if $s = 6$ and $t = -2$. −288
(2)

b. Explain how the result would be affected if s was doubled. The result would double.

c. Show that this is true by evaluating the expression if $s = 12$ and $t = -2$. −576

*30. (Sales Tax) The state sales tax for Colorado, Louisiana, and Nevada total to 13.4%. The sales tax in Colorado is 1.1% less than that of Louisiana and 3.6% less than that of Nevada. Find the state sales tax rate for Colorado. 2.9%
(7)

LOOKING FORWARD

Solving linear equations prepares students for the following lessons:

- **Lesson 10** Solving and Graphing Inequalities
- **Lesson 13** Graphing Linear Equations I
- **Lesson 17** Solving Equations and Inequalities with Absolute Value

Problem 21

"What is meant by a_{13}? The element in Matrix A that lies in the first row and third column.

"What is a_{13}? −6

"What is b_{21}? 8

Problem 23

Extend the Problem

Have students use their answers to find the amounts of decaffeinated and flavored coffees. decaffeinated coffee: 25 lb; flavored coffee: 60 lb What if Monday showed a 20% increase in the amounts of each type of coffee? How much coffee would be sold on Monday? regular: 36 lb; decaffeinated: 30 lb; flavored: 72 lb

Problem 26

Point out that as the value of x increases, the value of y increases. Ask students to consider how much greater each y-value is than its corresponding x-value.

Problem 28

Remind students that the perimeter of a polygon can be found by adding the lengths of its sides.

Problem 30

Extend the Problem

Have students find the total price for the purchase of a television in Colorado if the television is normally priced at $250 but is on sale for 15% off. Tell them to round their answers up to the next penny. $218.67

LESSON 8

1 Warm Up

Remind students that a constant is a number. Show them that in an equation like $y = 3x$, 3 is a constant.

2 New Concepts

In this lesson, students learn how to write and use **direct variation** equations.

Discuss the definition of a direct variation relationship. Point out that when direct variation equations are written in the form $A = kB$, A and B will be replaced by situation-specific variables, while k will be replaced by a constant.

Example 1

Students write a direct variation equation, solve for k, then use the value of k to find unknown information.

Additional Example 1

The number of teaspoons varies directly as the number of tablespoons. If using 12 teaspoons is the same as using 4 tablespoons, how many tablespoons would be needed in a recipe calling for 6 teaspoons? 2

LESSON RESOURCES

Student Edition Practice Workbook 8
Reteaching Master 8
Adaptations Master 8
Challenge and Enrichment Masters C8

LESSON 8

Finding Direct Variation

Warm Up

1. **Vocabulary** The value of a _________ (***constant, variable***) never changes. constant
(2)

2. Solve: $42 = 6k$ $k = 7$
(SB)

3. Solve: $\frac{3}{x} = \frac{4}{12}$ $x = 9$
(SB)

New Concepts

When the statement of a problem says that A ***varies directly as*** B or that A ***is directly proportional to*** B, the equation

$$A = kB$$

is implied. This relationship is called **direct variation.** The constant k in the equation is called the **constant of variation.** The following are examples of direct variation.

Statement	Implied Equation
The circumference of a circle varies directly as the radius.	$C = kR$
The resistance is directly proportional to the length.	$R = kL$
The water produced varied directly as the amount of hydrogen burned.	$W = kH_B$

Example 1 Solving a Direct Variation Problem

The number of seconds varies directly as the number of minutes. When 120 seconds have passed, 2 minutes have passed. If 300 seconds have passed, how many minutes have passed?

Hint

Choosing appropriate variable names helps avoid confusion when substituting values.

SOLUTION

$S = kM$ Write a direct variation.

$(120) = k(2)$ Substitute the given values.

$k = 60$ Solve for k.

$S = 60M$ Replace k with its value.

$(300) = 60M$ Substitute for S.

$\frac{300}{60} = \frac{60M}{60}$ Divide.

$M = 5$ minutes

Example 2 Solving with a Fractional Constant

Distance traveled is directly proportional to the time spent traveling. A motorized scooter can travel 10 kilometers in 30 minutes. How far can this scooter travel in 45 minutes?

MATH BACKGROUND

In Lesson 2, students saw that in a function, the value of one variable depends on the value of one or more other variables. A **direct variation** is one type of function. In a direction variation, the equation $A = kB$ shows that the value of A can be found by multiplying the value of B by a constant k. Another way to write the relationship is $\frac{A}{B} = k$, which shows that the ratio of A and B is always equal to the constant k.

Students have studied proportions in previous courses, and should find similarities between direct variation and proportions. Since $\frac{A}{B} = k$ for any set of values A and B, the proportion $\frac{A_1}{B_1} = \frac{A_2}{B_2}$ can be written and used to find unknown values. For this reason, when A varies directly as B, we can also say *A is directly proportional to B.*

SOLUTION

$D = kT$	Write a direct variation.
$10 = k(30)$	Substitute the given values.
$k = \frac{1}{3}$	Solve for k.
$D = \frac{1}{3}T$	Replace k with its value.
$D = \frac{1}{3}(45)$	Substitute for T.
$D = 15$	Multiply.

It can travel 15 kilometers in 45 minutes.

Hint

The cross products of a proportion are equal. For $\frac{A_1}{A_2} = \frac{B_1}{B_2}$, $A_1 \cdot B_2 = B_1 \cdot A_2$.

There is another way to work direct variation problems. In addition to the equation discussed above, the statement A ***varies directly as*** B also implies the proportion.

$$\frac{A_1}{A_2} = \frac{B_1}{B_2}$$

Example 3 Direct Variation as a Ratio

a. Cost varies directly as the number purchased. If 12 items can be purchased for $78, how much would 42 items cost?

SOLUTION

$\frac{C_1}{C_2} = \frac{N_1}{N_2}$	Write a proportion.
$\frac{78}{C_2} = \frac{12}{42}$	Substitute the given values.
$78 \cdot 42 = 12C_2$	Cross multiply.
$\frac{78 \cdot 42}{12} = \frac{12C_2}{12}$	Divide both sides by 12.
$273 = C_2$	

42 items would cost $273.

b. The number of railroad ties used in a section of track is directly proportional to the length of the section. If 15 ties are used in a 30 foot section of track, how many ties are used in a 50 foot section?

SOLUTION Write the equation and substitute the given values.

$$\frac{T_1}{T_2} = \frac{L_1}{L_2} \rightarrow \frac{(15)}{T_2} = \frac{(30)}{(50)}$$

Cross multiply and solve.

$$15 \cdot 50 = 30T_2 \rightarrow \frac{15 \cdot 50}{30} = \frac{30T_2}{30} \rightarrow T_2 = 25 \text{ ties}$$

ENGLISH LEARNERS

Review the term **constant of variation.**

The term constant of variation might be confusing because it uses seemingly contradictory words. Remind students that the constant of variation is a constant (a number) that defines how one quantity varies in relation to another.

Show students a direct variation equation like $S = 60M$ and point out that S varies according to this rule. Show them that S and M vary, while 60 is constant.

Work with students to apply verbal descriptions to variation equations. For example, the number of seconds is 60 times the number of minutes.

Example 2

Additional Example 2

When an item of clothing is on sale with a percent discount, the sale price varies directly as the original price. If a shirt normally priced at $30 is on sale for $21, what is the sale price (under the same discount structure) of a shirt normally priced at $40? $28

TEACHER TIP

Point out that if A varies directly as B, then B varies directly as A, and the values of k in the two associated direct variation equations are reciprocals. Tell students that variation equations can be written in either of two ways; however, point out that the relationship is best represented by a variation equation when the dependent variable equals the product of the constant of variation and the independent variable. In these examples, point out that distance depends on time and volume depends on temperature, not vice versa.

Example 3

Students solve direct variation problem using proportions.

Additional Example 3

a. The perimeter of a square varies directly as the length of one side. If the perimeter is 20 when the side is 5, what is the perimeter when the side is 9? 36

b. The number of pages printed by a laser printer is directly proportional to the time the job takes. If the printer can print 21 pages in 2 minutes, how many pages can it print in 5 minutes? 52.5 pages

Example 4

Error Alert Students might think that they can find the missing value in the table by finding the difference in the given values for volume and adding it to 236 mL. Point out that since the temperatures do not increase by a constant amount, the volumes will not increase by a constant amount. (Contrast this with the values given in Lesson Practice e.)

Additional Example 2

The speed (in m/s) of an object falling from rest in a vacuum is directly proportional to the time (in sec) it has been falling. The table shows the speed of an object after two falling times.

Speed	19.6	39.2	x
Time	2	4	7

a. Find x. 68.6

b. Plot the three ordered pairs on a graph and draw the line that connects the three points.

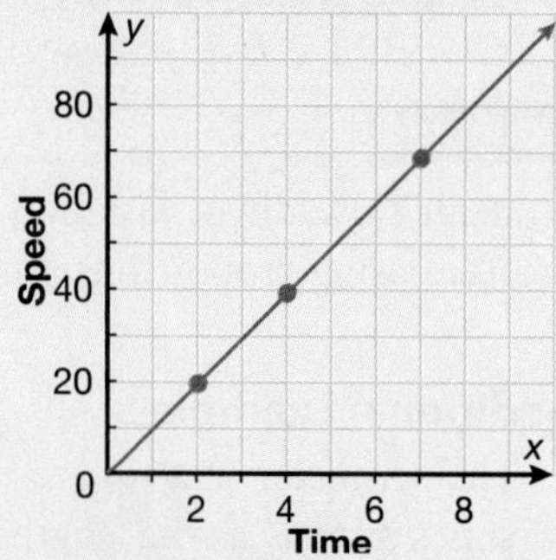

c. Use the equation to predict the speed of the object after falling 10 seconds. 98 m/s

Extend the Example

For Part a, have students use the other volume/temperature pair to verify the constant of variation.

(224) = K (280)

$K = \frac{4}{5}$

For Part c, have them use the graph to predict what volume the gas would have at 255 K. Then, have them use the variation equation to check the accuracy of their predictions. 204

Math Language

A **kelvin** (K) is a unit for measuring temperature. Temperature in kelvins is equal to temperature in degrees Celsius plus 273.15.

Example 4 Application: Chemistry

The volume of a certain gas varies directly as its temperature in kelvins. The table below shows the volume of this gas at two temperatures.

Volume	224 mL	236 mL	?
Temperature	280 K	295 K	315 K

a. Find the volume of the gas at the third temperature in the table.

SOLUTION The implied equation is $V = kT$. Use either of the two given volume/temperature pairs to find the constant of variation.

$$(236) = k(295)$$

$$k = \frac{4}{5}$$

So the equation that represents the relationship between the volume and temperature of this gas is

$$V = \frac{4}{5}T$$

Substitute the temperature that corresponds to the unknown volume to find V.

$$V = \frac{4}{5}(315)$$

$$V = 252 \text{ mL}$$

b. Plot the three volume/temperature pairs on a graph and draw the line that connects the three points.

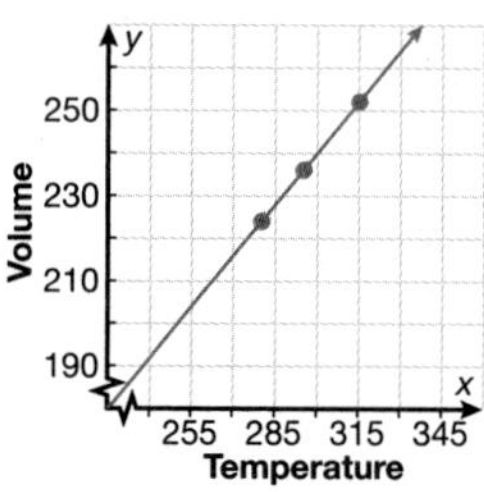

This is a visual representation of the equation $V = \frac{4}{5}T$. Like the equation, this graph also represents the relationship between the volume and temperature of this gas.

c. **Predict** Use the equation to predict what volume the gas would have at 400 K.

$$V = \frac{4}{5}(400)$$

$$V = 320 \text{ mL}$$

ALTERNATE METHOD FOR EXAMPLE 4

Reinforce the idea that the ratio of volume to temperature is constant by adding a third row to the table.

Volume	224 mL	236 mL	?
Temperature	280 K	295 K	315 K
$\frac{V}{T}$	$\frac{4}{5}$	$\frac{4}{5}$	$\frac{4}{5}$

To find the missing value (v), write and solve a proportion:

$$\frac{v}{315} = \frac{4}{5}$$

$$5v = 1260$$

$$v = 252$$

Lesson Practice

a. The number of inches varies directly with the number of feet. If a board measures 36 inches, it measures 3 feet. If a board measures 60 inches, how many feet does it measure? 5 feet
(Ex 1)

b. The number of cups varies directly with the number of fluid ounces. In 5 cups, there are 40 fluid ounces. How many cups are there in 64 fluid ounces? 8 cups
(Ex 2)

c. The cost of gas varies directly with the number of gallons purchased. If 10 gallons can be purchased for $25, how much would 15 gallons cost? $37.50
(Ex 3)

d. The amount of dirt needed to cover a garden varies directly with the area of the garden. If 2 bags of dirt are needed to cover a garden with an area of 54 square feet, how many bags are needed to cover a garden with an area of 135 square feet? 5 bags
(Ex 3)

e. The volume of a certain pipe varies directly with its length. The table below shows the volume of the pipe at two lengths.
(Ex 4)

Volume	30 gallons	45 gallons	?
Length	20 feet	30 feet	40 feet

Find the volume of the pipe at the third length in the table. 60 gallons

f.

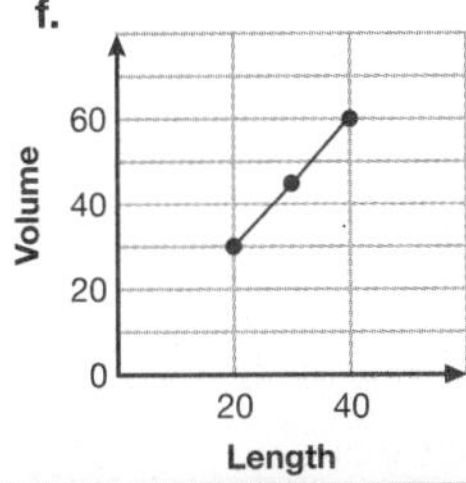

f. Plot the three volume/length pairs on a graph and draw the line that connects the three points.
(Ex 4)

g. Write the equation that represents the relationship between volume and length, and use it to predict the volume of the pipe at a length of 100 feet. $V = \frac{3}{2}L$; $V = 150$ gallons
(Ex 4)

Practice Distributed and Integrated

1. Simplify the expression using the properties of real numbers.
(1)

$$(-7 + 3) - |-2 + 9| - 2[1 - (-5)] \quad -23$$

2. Simplify $\frac{3x}{y} - 7x^2x^{-1}y^{-1} + 2y^2y^{-1}x^{-1}$.
(2)
$2yx^{-1} - 4xy^{-1}$

3. Simplify $\frac{xy^2}{x^0x^{-3}}\left(\frac{xy^{-2}}{x(y^2)^0} - \frac{3y^{-2}}{x^4}\right)$.
(3)
$x^4 - 3$

4. Find the approximate area of a circle with radius 1.5 inches. 7.07 in.^{2}
(SB)

5. Find the percent change from 10 to 12.8. 28%
(6)

Solve each equation.

***6.** $15(4 - 5b) = 16(4 - 6b) + 10$
(7)
$b = \frac{2}{3}$

***7.** $-2(2x - 3) - 2^3 - 3 = -x - (-4)$
(7)
$x = -3$

For the following problems, *x* varies directly with *y*. Find the constant of variation.

***8.** $x = 12, y = 3$ 4
(8)

***9.** $x = 4, y = 16$ $\frac{1}{4}$
(8)

10. Simplify the expression $5x^2 - 2(x - 3x^2)$. $11x^2 - 2x$
(2)

INCLUSION

Help auditory learners recognize the relationship between the two variables in these variation equations by reading equations like $V = \frac{4}{5}T$ in Example 4 using words like *the volume is always equal to four-fifths of the temperature.* Show the statement is true by having them verify that each volume number in the table is four-fifths the corresponding volume number. After solving Part c, students can use the verbal description of the relationship to check their final answer.

Lesson Practice

Problem a

Scaffolding Tell students to write the variation equation for the given board, solve for *k*, then use *k* to write the variation equation for the board of unknown length.

Problem f

Error Alert Students might be unsure which variable belongs on which axis of the graph. Remind them that volume depends on length, so length (the independent variable) should go along the horizontal axis.

Check for Understanding

The questions below help assess the concepts taught in this lesson.

1. **"How do you know whether a set of ordered pairs represents a direct variation?"** If each pair can be written in the form $A = kB$, where *k* is the same for each ordered pair, then the set is a direct variation.

2. **"What does the constant of variation tell us?"** It tells us the factor that relates one variable to the other. One variable × the constant of variation = the other variable.

3 Practice

Math Conversations

Discussions to strengthen understanding

Problem 2

Students should first simplify each addend by eliminating negative exponents. Then, they should find like terms and add.

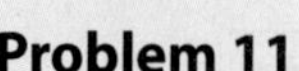

Problem 11
Remind students that they can find 0.19×600 by finding $(0.10 \times 600) + (0.09 \times 600)$.

Problem 14
Extend the Problem
What if 5 cups of peanut butter are used? How much sugar is called for? $3\frac{3}{4}$ cups

Problem 15
Remind students that one way to estimate is to round each number to its greatest place value. This method leads to an estimate of 7×10^{-2}, or 0.70 in.
A better estimate is found when the factor 13.9 is rounded to a number closer to its actual value. For example, $7 \times 10^{-2} \times 14$, or 0.98 in.

Problem 18
Extend the Problem
Have students check their answers by finding the value of each element in the matrices using their values for x, y, and z.

$$\begin{bmatrix} 1 & 5^2 \\ 12+4 & \frac{12}{2} \end{bmatrix} \stackrel{?}{=} \begin{bmatrix} -1+2 & 25 \\ 16 & 5+1 \end{bmatrix}$$

$$\begin{bmatrix} 1 & 25 \\ 16 & 6 \end{bmatrix} = \begin{bmatrix} 1 & 25 \\ 16 & 6 \end{bmatrix}$$

***11.** (1) **Graphing Calculator** The average credit card annual interest rate is around 19%. Use the distributive property to mentally calculate the amount of interest paid annually on a \$600 balance. Use a graphing calculator to verify your answer. \$114

12. (6) **Multi-Step** Admission to the museum is \$12. Students receive a 15% discount.
a. How much is the discount? \$1.80
b. How much do students pay? \$10.20

13. (5) **Education** The table shows the number of men and women who attended a university and if they were attending on a full or part-time basis.

University Enrollment

	2000		2005	
	Men	Women	Men	Women
Full-time	315	484	511	562
Part-time	631	709	826	914

a. Create a matrix to show the number of men attending the university in both years. $\begin{bmatrix} 315 & 511 \\ 631 & 826 \end{bmatrix}$
b. Create another matrix to show the number of women attending the university in a way that it could be added to the matrix in part a. $\begin{bmatrix} 484 & 562 \\ 709 & 914 \end{bmatrix}$
c. Add the matrices. $\begin{bmatrix} 799 & 1073 \\ 1340 & 1740 \end{bmatrix}$

***14.** (8) **Multiple Choice** In a peanut butter cookie recipe, the amount of sugar used varies directly with the amount of peanut butter used. For 2 c of peanut butter, $1\frac{1}{2}$ c of sugar is needed. Circle the letter that best represents the constant of variation. C

A 1 **B** $\frac{1}{4}$ **C** $\frac{3}{4}$ **D** 2

15. (3) **Analyze** A quarter is about 6.89×10^{-2} inches thick. A quarter has a diameter that is about 13.9 times its thickness. Estimate the diameter of a quarter in inches. Write your answer in scientific notation. Explain whether you think the magnitude of your answer seems reasonable. 9.8×10^{-1} inches; Yes, 10^{-1} indicates that the answer is in tenths of an inch. Nine tenths of an inch is a reasonable diameter for a quarter.

16. (6) **Statistics** The first time a teacher tested her students, the scores were 75, 82, 93, 81, 64, 78, and 80. The second time she tested them, the scores were 65, 72, 100, 83, 68, 55, and 40. What was the percent change in the average score from the first to the second testing? Round to the nearest whole percent. 13% decrease

***17.** (8) **Bowling** The number of pounds varies directly with the number of ounces. A bowling ball that weighs 12 pounds weighs 192 ounces. What is the constant of variation? Find the weight, in pounds, of a bowling ball that weighs 240 ounces. $\frac{1}{16}$; 15 pounds

18. (5) **Multi-Step** Solve for x, y, and z: $\begin{bmatrix} 1 & x^2 \\ y+4 & \frac{y}{2} \end{bmatrix} = \begin{bmatrix} z+2 & 25 \\ 16 & x+1 \end{bmatrix}$. $x = 5, y = 12, z = -1$

CHALLENGE

On a certain stretch of roadway, the distance (in feet) that a car needs in order to come to a stop when the brakes are applied at a given speed is directly proportional to the square of the speed (in mph).

a. Write the direction variation equation. $d = ks^2$

b. When a car is traveling at 60 mph, it requires 225 feet in order to come to a stop. What is the value of k? $k = \frac{1}{16}$

c. If it takes a car 50 feet to come to a stop, how fast was the car going? about 28 mph

d. A car traveling at 47 mph brakes to avoid a traffic cone 140 feet in the distance. Will the car be able to stop before striking the traffic cone? Explain how you know. Yes. It will take the car 138 feet to come to a stop.

*19. **Geometry** The area of a triangle varies directly with the product of the base and height of the triangle. If the area of a triangle is 6 cm^2 then the product of the base and height is 12 cm^2, find the area of a triangle whose product of base and height is 27 cm^2. (8) 13.5 cm^2

20. **Consumer** A ticket service marks up prices on concerts and other events by 150%. Use a scalar product to find the marked up prices. (5)

Concert Ticket Prices

Day	Floor	Balcony
Friday	$60	$35
Saturday	$80	$45

20. **Ticket Service Prices**

Day	Floor	Balcony
Friday	$150	$87.50
Saturday	$200	$112.50

*21. **Verify** Is $x = 2$ the solution to the equation $-10x + 6 = 4x + 34$? (7)

21. No; $-10(2) + 6 = 4(2) + 34$
$-20 + 6 = 8 + 34$
$-14 \neq 42$

22. Solve the equation $6x + 3 - 8x = 13$. (7) $x = -5$

23. **Marketing** If you buy one quarter page ad, the cost is $400 per week. This can be expressed as the ordered pair (1, 400). There is a special if you buy one ad at the regular price, each additional week is $300. Find the total cost if you buy 2, 3, and 4 ads. Express the answer as ordered pairs in set notation. (4) {(2,700), (3,1000), (4,1300)}

24. **Write** Does $(x^2)^3 = (x^3)^2$? Explain. (3) Yes, because of the Commutative property of Multiplication they are both equal to x^6.

25. **Analyze** When will a percent change equal 0%? Give an example. (6) When there is no change in the old and new amounts, possible answer: from 25 to 25.

*26. **Verify** The volume of a sphere varies directly with the cube of the radius. The table shows the volume and radius of three different spheres. Verify the constant of variation is 4.189. (8)

Volume	Radius
2,144.768 in^3	8 in.
20,580.557 in^3	17 in.
65,453.125 in^3	25 in.

26. $4.189 \times 8^3 = 2{,}144.768$; $4.189 \times 17^3 = 20{,}580.557$; $4.189 \times 25^3 = 65{,}453.125$; The constant of variation is 4.189.

27. **Multiple Choice** What are the dimensions of matrix $C = [9\ 1\ 7\ 0]$? (5) **B**

A 1×3 **B** 1×4 **C** 3×1 **D** 4×1

*28. **Exports** The total exports of goods and services, in millions of dollars, for the U.S. in 2004, 2005, and 2006 was 3,886,023. The exports in 2005 were 125,820 more than in 2004 and 162,633 less than in 2006. What were the exports in millions of dollars in 2005? (7) 1,283,070

29. If $a(x) = 12 + 9x$ and $v(x) = 5x + 2x^2$, find $v(4)$. (4) 52

30. **Error Analysis** Explain the error in the statement that follows and correct the statement. "3 is an irrational number and an integer." (1) 3 is a rational number, as it can be written as a fraction $\frac{3}{1}$

Problem 19

Be sure students understand that if the area varies directly as the product of the base and height, then the equation $A = kbh$ describes the direct variation.

Problem 24

Guide the students by asking them the following questions.

"What does $(x^2)^3$ mean?" $x^2 \cdot x^2 \cdot x^2$

"How can you write that in expanded form?"
$(x \cdot x) \cdot (x \cdot x) \cdot (x \cdot x)$

"How can you write that in exponent form?" x^6

"What does $(x^3)^2$ mean?" $x^3 \cdot x^3$

"How can you write that in expanded form?"
$(x \cdot x \cdot x) \cdot (x \cdot x \cdot x)$

"How can you write that in exponent form?" x^6

Problem 26

Error Alert

Students might forget to cube the radius when finding the ratio. Have them re-read the description of the direct variation relationship, underlining the variables (volume; cube of radius).

Problem 28

Suggest that students assign 2005 to be the unknown value, since the values for 2004 and 2006 are described in terms of the value for 2005.

LOOKING FORWARD 

Writing and solving direct variation equations prepares students for

- **Lesson 12** Solving Inverse Variation Problems
- **Lesson 13** Graphing Linear Equations I
- **Lesson 34** Graphing Linear Equations II

LESSON 9

1 Warm Up

For Problem 3, remind students that the dimensions of a matrix are $m \times n$, where m is the number of rows and n is the number of columns.

2 New Concepts

In this lesson, students learn to multiply matrices. Unlike with real numbers, there will be instances in which two matrices can not be multiplied together.

Example 1

Error Alert Students might look at the wrong numbers when determining whether a matrix product is defined. Have them cover the "outside" dimensions, then check whether the visible "inside" dimensions are the same.

Additional Example 1

Determine if the product of the matrices is defined. If so, give the dimensions of the product matrix.

a. Matrix A: 2×4
Matrix B: 4×2 yes; 2×2

b. Matrix A: 3×2
Matrix B: 3×2 no

c. Matrix A: 3×2
Matrix B: 2×5 yes; 3×5

LESSON RESOURCES

Student Edition Practice Workbook 9
Reteaching Masters 9
Adaptations Masters 9
Challenge and Enrichment Master C9
Technology Master 9

LESSON 9

Multiplying Matrices

Warm Up

1. (7) **Vocabulary** The individual symbols in a matrix are the ________ of the matrix. elements

2. (1) Simplify $2(-5) + 2(6) + (-1)(-5) + (-1)(6) + 3(-5) + 3(-6)$. -32

3. (5) Give the dimensions of matrix $A = [-2 \quad 3 \quad 0 \quad -1]$. 1×4

New Concepts

A matrix A can be multiplied by another matrix B if the number of columns of matrix A is the same as the number of rows of matrix B. The "inside" numbers, that is the last number of the dimensions of matrix A and the first number of the dimensions of matrix B, must be the same.

Dimensions of Matrix A				Dimensions of Matrix B			
Row	×	Column		Row	×	Column	
3	×	(2)	Yes	(2)	×	2	Multiplication possible.
2	×	(4)	No	(2)	×	4	Multiplication not possible.

The product of two matrices is a matrix whose dimensions are determined by the two "outside" numbers.

Caution

Pay attention to the order in which matrices are multiplied. To find the product AB, keep matrix A on the left and matrix B on the right.

Dimensions of Matrix A				Dimensions of Matrix B			
(3)	×	2	times	2	×	(2)	→ a 3 × 2 matrix
(2)	×	5	times	5	×	(3)	→ a 2 × 3 matrix

When two matrices can be multiplied, the product is said to be defined. The matrix that results is called a **product matrix.**

Example 1 Using Dimensions of Matrices

Determine if the product of the matrices is defined. If so, give the dimensions of the product matrix.

a. Matrix A: 4×3, Matrix B: 3×2

SOLUTION

Yes, the "inside" numbers are equal. The number of columns of A = the number of rows of B. AB is a 4×2 matrix.

b. Matrix A: 3×1, Matrix B: 2×1

SOLUTION

No, the "inside" numbers are not equal. The number of columns of $A \neq$ the number of rows of B.

MATH BACKGROUND

With real numbers, multiplication is defined as repeated addition. So, $5 \times 4 = 5 + 5 + 5 + 5$. Five is used as an addend 4 times. In Lesson 5, students saw that scalar multiplication of matrices can be interpreted the same way. For example,

$$2 \cdot \begin{pmatrix} 3 & 5 \\ 2 & 7 \end{pmatrix} = \begin{pmatrix} 3 & 5 \\ 2 & 7 \end{pmatrix} + \begin{pmatrix} 3 & 5 \\ 2 & 7 \end{pmatrix}$$

$$= \begin{pmatrix} 2 \cdot 3 & 2 \cdot 5 \\ 2 \cdot 2 & 2 \cdot 7 \end{pmatrix} = \begin{pmatrix} 6 & 10 \\ 4 & 14 \end{pmatrix}$$

In this lesson, students will see that addition and multiplication of matrices are not related quite so simply. Instead, multiplying matrices consists of finding sums of products of specified elements.

Multiplication of matrices is one example of a way in which matrix operations are not analogous to real number operations. However, matrices do behave in certain ways like real numbers. For example, addition of matrices is commutative and associative.

(c.) Matrix A: 1×5, Matrix B: 5×1

SOLUTION

Yes, the "inside" numbers are equal. AB is a 1×1 matrix.

Matrix Multiplication
Any element in a particular row and column of the product matrix is the sum of the product of the corresponding elements in the corresponding row and column of the matrices being multiplied.

$$\underset{A}{\begin{bmatrix} a & b \\ c & d \end{bmatrix}} \bullet \underset{B}{\begin{bmatrix} e & f \\ g & h \end{bmatrix}} = \underset{AB}{\begin{bmatrix} ae + bg & af + bh \\ ce + dg & cf + dh \end{bmatrix}}$$

The row one elements of matrix A are multiplied by the corresponding column one elements of matrix B. Then these products are added to find the corresponding element in the product matrix AB. Continue this pattern row by column to find all of the elements in the product matrix.

Example 2 Multiplying Matrices

Hint

Find the dimensions of the product matrix before multiplying the matrices.

(a.) Find AB if $A = \begin{bmatrix} 2 & -3 \\ 3 & 1 \\ 4 & 5 \end{bmatrix}$ and $B = \begin{bmatrix} 1 & 2 \\ 4 & -5 \end{bmatrix}$

SOLUTION

Since matrix A is a 3×2 matrix and matrix B is a 2×2, the number of columns of $A =$ the number of rows of B. The product AB is defined.

$$AB = \begin{bmatrix} 2 \cdot 1 + (-3) \cdot 4 & 2 \cdot 2 + (-3) \cdot (-5) \\ 3 \cdot 1 + 1 \cdot 4 & 3 \cdot 2 + 1 \cdot (-5) \\ 4 \cdot 1 + 5 \cdot 4 & 4 \cdot 2 + 5 \cdot (-5) \end{bmatrix} = \begin{bmatrix} -10 & 19 \\ 7 & 1 \\ 24 & -17 \end{bmatrix}$$

(b.) Find BA if $A = [-3 \quad 0 \quad 4]$ and $B = \begin{bmatrix} 2 \\ -5 \\ 1 \end{bmatrix}$

SOLUTION

Since matrix B is a 3×1 matrix and matrix A is a 1×3, the number of columns of $B =$ the number of rows of A. The product BA is defined.

$$BA = \begin{bmatrix} 2 \cdot (-3) & 2 \cdot 0 & 2 \cdot 4 \\ (-5) \cdot (-3) & (-5) \cdot 0 & (-5) \cdot 4 \\ 1 \cdot (-3) & 1 \cdot 0 & 1 \cdot 4 \end{bmatrix} = \begin{bmatrix} -6 & 0 & 8 \\ 15 & 0 & -20 \\ -3 & 0 & 4 \end{bmatrix}$$

ALTERNATE METHOD FOR EXAMPLE 2

Use this method to find AB:

Use graph paper to draw a product matrix with the correct dimensions. Place A to the left of the product matrix, and B above it, so that rows and columns line up. Students can find each element of the product matrix by looking to the left and above to find the correct numbers to multiply and add.

$$\begin{matrix} & \begin{bmatrix} 1 & 2 \\ 4 & -5 \end{bmatrix} \\ \begin{bmatrix} 2 & -3 \\ 3 & 1 \\ 4 & 5 \end{bmatrix} & \begin{bmatrix} \square & \square \\ \square & \square \\ \square & \square \end{bmatrix} \end{matrix}$$

TEACHER TIP

When multiplying matrices, point out the position of the element you are finding in the product matrix. Say, "I'm finding the element in the *first row* and *second column* of the product matrix. I'll look at the *first row* of the first factor matrix and the *second column* of the second factor matrix."

Example 2

Error Alert Students often do the arithmetic incorrectly when one or more element in a factor matrix is negative. Suggest that they take the time to write out the expressions (like $2 \cdot 1 + (-3) \cdot 4$), and then simplify.

Additional Example 2

a. Find AB.

$A = \begin{bmatrix} 2 & 4 & 2 \\ 1 & -5 & 1 \\ 3 & 0 & 2 \end{bmatrix}$ $B = \begin{bmatrix} 3 & 2 \\ -1 & 4 \\ 0 & 2 \end{bmatrix}$

$AB = \begin{bmatrix} 2 & 24 \\ 8 & -16 \\ 9 & 10 \end{bmatrix}$

b. Find BA.

$A = [-3 \quad 2 \quad 6 \quad 4]$ $B = \begin{bmatrix} 5 \\ 0 \\ -1 \\ 3 \end{bmatrix}$

$BA = \begin{bmatrix} -15 & 10 & 30 & 20 \\ 0 & 0 & 0 & 0 \\ 3 & -2 & -6 & -4 \\ -9 & 6 & 18 & 12 \end{bmatrix}$

c. Determine if $(AB)C = A(BC)$

$A = \begin{bmatrix} 3 & 1 \\ 2 & 3 \end{bmatrix}$ $B = \begin{bmatrix} -1 & 0 \\ 1 & 2 \end{bmatrix}$

$C = \begin{bmatrix} 2 & 1 \\ 3 & 1 \end{bmatrix}$

$(AB)C = \begin{bmatrix} 2 & 0 \\ 20 & 7 \end{bmatrix}$

$A(BC) = \begin{bmatrix} 2 & 0 \\ 20 & 7 \end{bmatrix}$

$(AB)C = A(BC)$

c. Determine if $AB = BA$. $A = \begin{bmatrix} -1 & 0 \\ 3 & -2 \end{bmatrix}$ and $B = \begin{bmatrix} 5 & -3 \\ 0 & 1 \end{bmatrix}$

SOLUTION

$$AB = \begin{bmatrix} -1 & 0 \\ 3 & -2 \end{bmatrix} \begin{bmatrix} 5 & -3 \\ 0 & 1 \end{bmatrix} = \begin{bmatrix} -5 & 3 \\ 15 & -11 \end{bmatrix}$$

$$BA = \begin{bmatrix} 5 & -3 \\ 0 & 1 \end{bmatrix} \begin{bmatrix} -1 & 0 \\ 3 & -2 \end{bmatrix} = \begin{bmatrix} -14 & 6 \\ 3 & -2 \end{bmatrix}$$

$$\begin{bmatrix} -5 & 3 \\ 15 & 11 \end{bmatrix} \neq \begin{bmatrix} -14 & 6 \\ 3 & -2 \end{bmatrix}$$

$$AB \neq BA$$

Refer to page 27 to check the answers using a graphing calculator.

The multiplication of real numbers is a commutative operation because either number can be first: $ab = ba$. This property does not hold for matrix multiplication.

A **square matrix** is a matrix with the same number of rows and columns. It has a **main diagonal** of elements from the top left hand corner to the bottom right hand corner of the matrix. The **multiplicative identity matrix,** called I, is a square matrix in which all of the elements are zero except the main diagonal. All of the elements in the main diagonal are ones.

$$I = \begin{bmatrix} 1 & 0 \\ 0 & 1 \end{bmatrix} \text{ is a } 2 \times 2 \text{ multiplicative identity matrix.}$$

The product of any matrix A and the multiplicative identity matrix I is matrix A.

$$AI = IA = A$$

Example 3 Working with Multiplicative Identity Matrices

Find AI. $A = \begin{bmatrix} 4 & 3 & -1 \\ 6 & -2 & -3 \\ -5 & 1 & 0 \end{bmatrix}$ and $I = \begin{bmatrix} 1 & 0 & 0 \\ 0 & 1 & 0 \\ 0 & 0 & 1 \end{bmatrix}$

SOLUTION

$$\begin{bmatrix} 4 & 3 & -1 \\ 6 & -2 & -3 \\ -5 & 1 & 0 \end{bmatrix} \begin{bmatrix} 1 & 0 & 0 \\ 0 & 1 & 0 \\ 0 & 0 & 1 \end{bmatrix}$$

$$= \begin{bmatrix} 4 \cdot 1 + 3 \cdot 0 + (-1)0 & 4 \cdot 0 + 3 \cdot 1 + (-1) \cdot 0 & 4 \cdot 0 + 3 \cdot 0 + (-1) \cdot 1 \\ 6 \cdot 1 + (-2) \cdot 0 + (-3) \cdot 0 & 6 \cdot 0 + (-2) \cdot 1 + (-3) \cdot 0 & 6 \cdot 0 + (-2) \cdot 0 + (-3) \cdot 1 \\ (-5) \cdot 1 + 1 \cdot 0 + 0 \cdot 0 & (-5) \cdot 0 + 1 \cdot 1 + 0 \cdot 0 & (-5) \cdot 0 + 1 \cdot 0 + 0 \cdot 1 \end{bmatrix}$$

$$= \begin{bmatrix} 4 & 3 & -1 \\ 6 & -2 & -3 \\ -5 & 1 & 0 \end{bmatrix}$$

Math Reasoning

Verify In Example 3, show that $AI = IA$.

Check student work.

TEACHER TIP

When reviewing $AI = IA = A$, point out that this statement shows one of the ways in which matrix properties are analogous to real number properties. Remind students that Identity Properties for real numbers state that $a \times 1 = a$ and $a + 0 = a$ for any real number a. Stress that not all properties of real numbers apply to matrices. For example, matrix multiplication is not commutative, as seen in Example 2c.

Example 3

In this example, students find the product of a 3×3 matrix A and a 3×3 identity matrix. The product is a 3×3 matrix identical to A.

Additional Example 3

Find AI.

$$A = \begin{bmatrix} 4 & -2 & 1 \\ 2 & 6 & -3 \end{bmatrix}$$

$$I = \begin{bmatrix} 1 & 0 & 0 \\ 0 & 1 & 0 \\ 0 & 0 & 1 \end{bmatrix}$$

$$AI = \begin{bmatrix} 4 & -2 & 1 \\ 2 & 6 & -3 \end{bmatrix}$$

Extend the Example

Ask students to determine the identity matrix for the following matrices. Remind students that every identity matrix is a square matrix.

a. $\begin{bmatrix} 3 & 0 & -4 \\ 6 & 1 & 2 \end{bmatrix}$ $I = \begin{bmatrix} 1 & 0 & 0 \\ 0 & 1 & 0 \\ 0 & 0 & 1 \end{bmatrix}$

b. $\begin{bmatrix} 2 & 1 \\ -4 & 3 \end{bmatrix}$ $I = \begin{bmatrix} 1 & 0 \\ 0 & 1 \end{bmatrix}$

c. $[3 \quad -5 \quad 4]$ $I = [1]$

d. $[2 \quad 5 \quad -6 \quad -2 \quad 4]$

$$I = \begin{bmatrix} 1 & 0 & 0 & 0 & 0 \\ 0 & 1 & 0 & 0 & 0 \\ 0 & 0 & 1 & 0 & 0 \\ 0 & 0 & 0 & 1 & 0 \\ 0 & 0 & 0 & 0 & 1 \end{bmatrix}$$

INCLUSION

If students have trouble keeping track of which elements to multiply when multiplying matrices and/or where to place elements in the product matrix, have them cover up the irrelevant rows and columns with strips of paper or correction tape, leaving only the relevant elements exposed. If tape is placed on the product matrix in the same rows and columns as in the factor matrices, the correct location in the product matrix will be exposed.

$$\begin{bmatrix} 3 & 1 & -3 \\ 4 & 2 & 6 \\ 2 & -1 & 3 \end{bmatrix} \begin{bmatrix} 4 & -2 & 3 \\ 2 & -1 & 0 \\ 1 & 0 & 5 \end{bmatrix} = \begin{bmatrix} \square & \square & \square \\ \square & \square & \square \\ \square & \square & \square \end{bmatrix}$$

Example 4 Consumer Math Application

John, My-Lieng, and Rochelle are purchasing supplies for a camping trip. Use matrix multiplication to find the amount each spent on supplies.

Camping Gear

	Day pack(s)	Tent	Sleeping bag(s)
John	1	1	3
My-Lieng	1	1	2
Rochelle	2	0	1

Cost of Gear

Day pack	\$16
Tent	\$50
Sleeping bag	\$85

Hint

To multiply $A \times B$, multiply rows of A with columns of B.

SOLUTION

$$\begin{bmatrix} 1 & 1 & 3 \\ 1 & 1 & 2 \\ 2 & 0 & 1 \end{bmatrix} \begin{bmatrix} 16 \\ 50 \\ 85 \end{bmatrix} = \begin{bmatrix} 1 \cdot 16 + 1 \cdot 50 + 3 \cdot 85 \\ 1 \cdot 16 + 1 \cdot 50 + 2 \cdot 85 \\ 2 \cdot 16 + 0 \cdot 50 + 1 \cdot 85 \end{bmatrix} = \begin{bmatrix} 321 \\ 236 \\ 117 \end{bmatrix}$$

John spent \$321, My-Lieng spent \$236, and Rochelle spent \$117 on camping gear.

Refer to page 27 to check the answer using a graphing calculator.

Lesson Practice

a. (Ex 1) Determine if the product of matrices A and B is defined. If so, give the dimensions of the product matrix. Yes; AB is a 5×4 matrix.

Matrix A: 5×1, Matrix B: 1×4

b. (Ex 1) Determine if the product of matrices A and B is defined. If so, give the dimensions of the product matrix. No; AB is undefined.

Matrix A: 4×7, Matrix B: 4×7

c. (Ex 2) Determine if the product of matrices A and B is defined. If so, give the dimensions of the product matrix. Yes; AB is a 3×3 matrix.

Matrix A: 3×9, Matrix B: 9×3

d. (Ex 2) Find AB if $A = \begin{bmatrix} 4 & 2 \\ 1 & 6 \\ 3 & 9 \end{bmatrix}$ and $B = \begin{bmatrix} 0 & 3 \\ 5 & 8 \end{bmatrix}$. $AB = \begin{bmatrix} 10 & 28 \\ 30 & 51 \\ 45 & 81 \end{bmatrix}$

e. (Ex 3) Find BA if $A = [4 \quad -2 \quad 10]$ and $B = \begin{bmatrix} -1 \\ 3 \\ -6 \end{bmatrix}$. $BA = \begin{bmatrix} -4 & 2 & -10 \\ 12 & -6 & 30 \\ -24 & 12 & -60 \end{bmatrix}$

f. (Ex 3) Determine if $AB = BA$. $A = \begin{bmatrix} 4 & -2 \\ 2 & 0 \end{bmatrix}$ $B = \begin{bmatrix} 1 & 0 \\ 4 & -2 \end{bmatrix}$. $AB \neq BA$

g. (Ex 4) Find AI. $A = \begin{bmatrix} -1 & 4 & 2 \\ 0 & 5 & -3 \\ 1 & -2 & 10 \end{bmatrix}$ and $I = \begin{bmatrix} 1 & 0 & 0 \\ 0 & 1 & 0 \\ 0 & 0 & 1 \end{bmatrix}$. $AI = \begin{bmatrix} -1 & 4 & 2 \\ 0 & 5 & -3 \\ 1 & -2 & 10 \end{bmatrix}$

ALTERNATE METHOD FOR EXAMPLE 4

Provide a real-life interpretation of matrix multiplication by showing students how the factor matrices relate to the product matrix in the given situation. Point out that the first factor matrix has rows that show the 3 campers and columns that show the 3 types of gear. It is a 3×3 matrix. Using a practical, verbal interpretation of the matrices, we can think of the matrix as a "camper name" × "gear-type" matrix. Similarly, the second matrix is a "gear-type" × "cost" matrix. Since the "inside" designations are the same ("gear type"), the product of the matrices is defined. The product is a "camper name" × "cost" matrix.

Example 4

Students often find matrix multiplication strange. Use the Example to show students why matrix multiplication is done the way it is. Show them how, for each person, each type of gear is multiplied by its price, then the subtotals are added to get the final cost.

Additional Example 4

The tables show the number of each type of dessert ordered from each of 4 waiters and the time to prepare each one. Use matrix multiplication to find the total amount of time each server spent preparing desserts.

Server	Milkshake	Hot Fudge	Banana Split	Ice Cream Sandwich
Jen	2	1	2	0
Brent	3	3	2	0
Ted	2	2	3	1
Oscar	1	0	1	0

Preparation Time (min)

Milkshake	4
Hot Fudge Sundae	1
Banana Split	3
Ice Cream Sandwich	2

$$\begin{bmatrix} 2 & 1 & 2 & 0 \\ 3 & 3 & 2 & 0 \\ 2 & 2 & 3 & 1 \\ 1 & 0 & 1 & 0 \end{bmatrix} \begin{bmatrix} 4 \\ 1 \\ 3 \\ 2 \end{bmatrix} = \begin{bmatrix} 15 \\ 21 \\ 21 \\ 7 \end{bmatrix}$$

Jen: 15 min; Brent: 21 min; Ted: 21 min; Oscar: 7 min

Lesson Practice

Problem e

Make sure students recognize that they are asked to find BA, not AB.

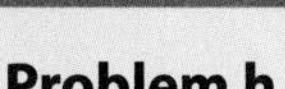

Problem h

Scaffolding Have students write matrices to represent the tables. Ask them to verify that the product is defined. Have them use matrix multiplication, then interpret the product matrix for the given situation.

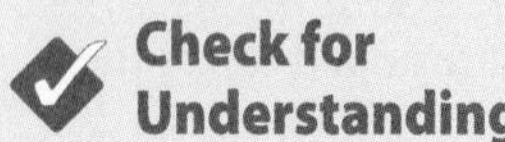

Check for Understanding

The questions below help assess the concepts taught in this lesson.

1. **"How do you find the element in the second row and second column of a product matrix?"** Multiply corresponding elements from the second row of A and the second column of B, then add the products.
2. **"How do you know whether the product of two given matrices is defined?"** Check the dimensions. If the inside dimensions are equal, the product is defined.
3. **"What are the dimensions of the product matrix?"** They are defined by the outside dimensions.

3 Practice

Math Conversations

Discussion to strengthen understanding

Problem 6

Remind students to use scalar multiplication first, then add.

Problem 7

Extend the Problem

Have students use the value of k to find m when n is 7. 28

Problem 12

Error Alert

Students might select the wrong numbers as dividend and divisor. Remind them to divide the area of Earth by the area of New York.

---

h. $\begin{bmatrix} 1 & 2 & 1 \\ 2 & 0 & 1 \\ 1 & 2 & 2 \end{bmatrix}\begin{bmatrix} 3 \\ 2 \\ 1 \end{bmatrix} = \begin{bmatrix} 8 \\ 7 \\ 9 \end{bmatrix}$

h. (Ex 5) Alana, Maurice, and Jon are each ordering lunch. Use matrix multiplication to find the amount each spends on lunch.

Lunch

	Sandwich	Side order	Drink
Alana	1	2	1
Maurice	2	0	1
Jon	1	2	2

Cost of Lunch

Sandwich	\$3
Side order	\$2
Drink	\$1

Alana spent \$8, Maurice spent \$7, and Jon spent \$9.

Practice Distributed and Integrated

Write each decimal as a fraction in lowest terms.

1. (SB) 0.24 $\frac{6}{25}$ **2.** (SB) 0.82 $\frac{41}{50}$ **3.** (SB) 0.32 $\frac{8}{25}$

4. (SB) What is the measure of an interior angle of a regular pentagon? 108°

5. (4) Determine whether $y^2 = 8x$ is a function. If so, state the domain and range. Not a function.

6. (5) Find the sum: $2\begin{bmatrix} 1 & 0 \\ 0 & 1 \end{bmatrix} + \begin{bmatrix} -3 & -2 \\ -4 & 0 \end{bmatrix}$ $\begin{bmatrix} -1 & -2 \\ -4 & 2 \end{bmatrix}$

***7.** (8) If m varies directly with n, and $m = 8$ when $n = 2$, what is the value of the constant of variation? 4

Graphing Calculator **Find each product. Check using the graphing calculator.**

***8.** (9) $\begin{bmatrix} 2 & -1 \\ 3 & 0 \\ 1 & 4 \end{bmatrix} \times \begin{bmatrix} 1 & 1 & -3 \\ 6 & -5 & 0 \end{bmatrix}$ ***9.** (9) $\begin{bmatrix} -1 & -1 & -1 \\ 2 & 5 & 3 \\ -5 & 4 & -2 \end{bmatrix} \times \begin{bmatrix} 0 \\ 1 \\ 0 \end{bmatrix}$ $\begin{bmatrix} -1 \\ 5 \\ 4 \end{bmatrix}$

8. $\begin{bmatrix} -4 & 7 & -6 \\ 3 & 3 & -9 \\ 25 & -19 & -3 \end{bmatrix}$

10. (5) **Verify** Use the matrices A and B below to verify that $A + B = B + A$.

$$A = \begin{bmatrix} -3 & 7 \\ 12 & -1 \end{bmatrix} \quad B = \begin{bmatrix} 9 & 17 \\ 3 & -1 \end{bmatrix} \quad A + B = B + A = \begin{bmatrix} 6 & 24 \\ 15 & -2 \end{bmatrix}$$

11. (1) **Baseball** The table shows the number of home runs hit by Orlando Hernandez of the New York Yankees over a three-year period. Which property of real numbers would be useful to mentally calculate as quickly as possible the total home runs that he hit over this period? Explain.

	2004	2005	2006
Home Runs	9	18	22

11. Associative Property. Adding the numbers in order would result in $(9 + 18) + 22 = 27 + 22$, which is more difficult to mentally add than $9 + (18 + 22) = 40 + 9$.

12. (3) **Earth** The surface area of the land on Earth is approximately 1.488×10^{14} m^2. The state of New York has a surface area of approximately 1.272×10^{11} m^2. Approximately how many times could the state of New York fit on the land of the Earth? Write your answer in scientific notation. approximately 1.170×10^3 times

ENGLISH LEARNERS

Review the terms row, column, element, product, and sum.

Explain how to find each element in a product matrix, pointing to rows, columns, elements, products, and sums as you use the words.

Quiz students by giving directions like *find the product of the element in the first row and second column of A and the element in the second row and third column of B.*

Have students talk through an example of matrix multiplication, using correct vocabulary to explain each step.

*13. **Multiple Choice** Circle the letter that best represents the product matrix AB. B
(9)

$$A = \begin{bmatrix} -3 & 1 & -1 \\ -4 & 6 & 2 \\ -1 & -1 & 4 \end{bmatrix} \quad B = \begin{bmatrix} -7 & 0 & 1 \\ -8 & -2 & -1 \\ 0 & 3 & -3 \end{bmatrix}$$

a. $\begin{bmatrix} 20 & -8 & 11 \\ 33 & -19 & 0 \\ -9 & 21 & -6 \end{bmatrix}$ **b.** $\begin{bmatrix} 13 & -5 & -1 \\ -20 & -6 & -16 \\ 15 & 14 & -12 \end{bmatrix}$

c. $\begin{bmatrix} 21 & 0 & -1 \\ 32 & -12 & -2 \\ 0 & -3 & -12 \end{bmatrix}$ **d.** $\begin{bmatrix} -10 & 1 & 0 \\ -12 & 4 & 1 \\ -1 & 2 & 1 \end{bmatrix}$

14. Sample: $J = \begin{bmatrix} 34{,}950 & 7800 & 12{,}300 \\ 6400 & 2100 & 970 \end{bmatrix}$, $T = \begin{bmatrix} 28{,}900 & 10{,}450 & 11{,}950 \\ 7200 & 3600 & 4860 \end{bmatrix}$

14. **Scores** Create matrices to represent the following: Juan's high scores on three arcade games in one year are 34,950, 7800, and 12,300. His low scores on the same games are 6400, 2100, and 970. Tatia's high scores on the same games are 28,900, 10,450, and 11,950. Her low scores are 7200, 3600, and 4860.
(5)

15. **Write** Is $a^{-1} < 1$, for all $a > 1$? Explain why or why not. Yes, when a^{-1}, than it is the same as $\frac{1}{a}$ and if $a > 1$ than $\frac{1}{a}$ is always a fraction less than 1.
(3)

16. **Population** The population of Alaska in 1990 was reported to be 550,043 and in 2000 was reported to be 626,932. Find the percent increase. Round to the nearest hundredth of a percent. 13.98%
(6)

17. **Property Management** The table shows the cost of renting three different apartment styles in an apartment complex.
(5)

	Monthly Rental Cost
One bedroom	\$650
Two bedrooms	\$890
Three bedrooms	\$940

a. Convert the table into a 3 × 1 matrix.

b. All rents at an apartment complex will be increased by 10%. What scalar can be used to make a matrix with the updated prices? Create this matrix.

17. a. $\begin{bmatrix} 650 \\ 890 \\ 940 \end{bmatrix}$ b. 1.1; $\begin{bmatrix} 715 \\ 979 \\ 1034 \end{bmatrix}$

18. **Verify** Verify that $D = \begin{bmatrix} -14 & -6 \\ -6 & -1 \end{bmatrix}$ if $\begin{bmatrix} 1 & -6 \\ -6 & 4 \end{bmatrix} = D + \begin{bmatrix} 15 & 0 \\ 0 & 5 \end{bmatrix}$.
(5)

18. $\begin{bmatrix} -14 & -6 \\ -6 & -1 \end{bmatrix} + \begin{bmatrix} 15 & 0 \\ 0 & 5 \end{bmatrix} = \begin{bmatrix} -14 + 15 = 1 & -6 + 0 = -6 \\ -6 + 0 = -6 & -1 + 5 = 4 \end{bmatrix}$

19. Identify which property of real numbers is being demonstrated.
(1)

$5(2 + 9) = 5 \cdot 2 + 5 \cdot 9$ Distributive Property

*20. **Planets** The weight of an object on Saturn varies directly with the weight of that object on Earth. An object that weighs 2 kg on Earth, weighs 1.86 kg on Saturn. Find the weight of an object on Saturn that weighs 85 kg on Earth. 79.05 kg
(8)

21. **Error Analysis** Two students were asked to determine which of the following sets of ordered pairs are functions. Set 1: (9, 4), (7, 9), (8, 2) and Set 2: (3, −1), (4, −1), (7, 9). Their answers are below. What is the correct answer? Explain the error(s).
(4)

Britan's Answer: Set 2 because the 9's are paired with different values.

Sara's Answer: Set 1 because the −1's are paired with different values. See Additional Answers.

Problem 13

Students can find the answer simply by finding the element in the first row and first column of the product matrix, then comparing it to the answer choices. They should verify their answer by finding at least one more element in the product matrix.

Problem 14

Guide students to see that for each player, there are two score classifications (high and low) and three different games. So, each player's matrix will be either 2 × 3 or 3 × 2.

Problem 15

Error Alert

Students often think that a^{-1} means the same as $a \cdot -1$. Remind them of the definition of negative exponents $\left(a^{-n} = \frac{1}{a^n}\right)$.

Problem 20

Guide students with the following conversation:

"What equation defines the direct variation?" $s = ke$

"Write an equation with values for s and e." $1.86 = k \cdot 2$

"Solve for k." $k = 0.93$

"Write and solve an equation you can use to find the unknown value of s." $s = 0.93 \cdot 85$; $s = 79.05$

CHALLENGE

Have students explore whether the Distributive Property applies to matrices as well. Have them make up matrices to test each property, then share and generalize their results:

a. Left-Distributive:

Is $A(B + C) = AB + AC$? yes

b. Right-Distributive:

Is $(B + C)A = BA + CA$? yes

Problem 27

Guide the students by asking them the following questions.

"What are the denominators?" 4 and 5

"What is the least common multiple of 4 and 5?" 20

"Multiply each side by 20. What is the resulting equation?" $15x - 4x = 55$

Problem 29

Extend the Problem

Have students graph the original triangle and the transformed triangle. Have them describe the transformation in words.

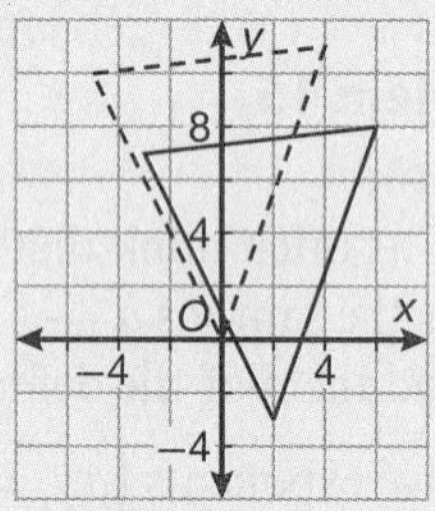

The transformation moves the triangle 3 units up and 2 units to the left.

22. *(6)* **Economics** In 2002, San Jose, California topped the list for the US metropolitan areas with the highest average annual salaries with an average salary of \$76,252. Find the approximate average annual salary in 2001 if the percent change from 2001 to 2002 was a percent increase of about 15.6%. About \$64,357

23. *(1)* Classify each statement as sometimes, always, or never true. Give examples to support your answer.

a. $a \cdot \left(\frac{1}{b}\right) = b \cdot \left(\frac{1}{a}\right)$

b. if a and b are irrational numbers, then $a \cdot b$ is an irrational number.

23.a. sometimes true; true example: $5 \cdot \left(\frac{1}{5}\right) = 5 \cdot \left(\frac{1}{5}\right)$, if $a = b$ and they are not equal to 0, the statement is true; false example: $5 \cdot \left(\frac{1}{6}\right) = 6 \cdot \left(\frac{1}{5}\right)$, if $a \neq b$ and they are not equal to 0, the statement is never true.

23.b. sometimes true. If $a = b$ and they are irrational numbers, they sometimes equal a rational number. For example: $\sqrt{2} \cdot \sqrt{2} = 2$. However, if $a = b = \pi$, $\pi \cdot \pi = \pi^2$, which is still irrational.

***24.** *(9)* **Geometry** Create a matrix representing the three triangles below.

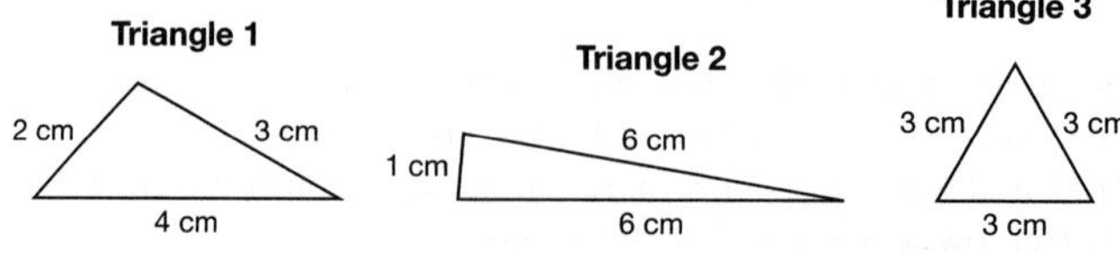

Use matrix multiplication to double side 1 (left), triple side 2 (bottom) and half side 3 (right) of each triangle and find the new perimeter of each triangle. Which new triangle has the greatest perimeter? See Additional Answers.

25. *(6)* **Multi-Step** A mechanic bought a part for \$4.25 and marked the price up by 200% to sell to a customer. How much did the customer pay for the part? How much would the customer have paid if she had used a 5% off coupon? \$12.75; \$12.11

Solve for *x*.

26. *(7)* $3x - 5 = 2 - 4x$ 1 ***27.** *(7)* $\frac{3}{4}x - \frac{1}{5}x = 2\frac{3}{4}$ 5 **28.** *(7)* $5x - 2 = 7 + 2x$ 3

29. *(5)* **Coordinate Geometry** The coordinates for a triangle are $A\ (-3, 7)$, $B\ (6, 8)$, and $C\ (2, -3)$.

a. Write the coordinates as a matrix such that row one is x-values, row two is y-values, and each column is a coordinate. $\begin{bmatrix} -3 & 6 & 2 \\ 7 & 8 & -3 \end{bmatrix}$

b. Add the transformation matrix $\begin{bmatrix} -2 & -2 & -2 \\ 3 & 3 & 3 \end{bmatrix}$. $\begin{bmatrix} -5 & 4 & 0 \\ 10 & 11 & 0 \end{bmatrix}$

c. What are the coordinates of the transformation? $A\ (-5, 10)$, $B\ (4, 11)$, $C\ (0, 0)$

***30.** *(8)* Juanita is conducting an experiment where the temperature of a liquid varies directly with time. Her observations are recorded in the table below.

Temperature	80 degrees	120 degrees	? degrees
Time	120 seconds	180 seconds	240 seconds

a. Using the values in the table, identify the constant of variation. $k = \frac{3}{2}$

b. Find the missing temperature in the table. 160 degrees

c. Determine an accurate prediction for the temperature of the liquid after 360 seconds. 240 degrees

LOOKING FORWARD 

Studying multiplication of matrices prepares students for the following lessons

- **Lesson 14** Finding Determinants
- **Lesson 16** Using Cramer's Rule
- **Lesson 32** Solving Linear Systems with Matrix Inverses

LESSON 10

Solving and Graphing Inequalities

Warm Up

1. (7) **Vocabulary** A mathematical statement comparing quantities that are equal is called an ________. equation

2. (7) For what value of x is the sentence $3x - 4 = -12$ true? $-\frac{8}{3}$

3. (7) True or False: -5 is a solution to the equation $-x - 2 = -3$. False

4. (SB) Compare 0.25 and $\frac{1}{4}$. Use <, >, or =. =

5. (SB) Compare 6.5 and 6.38. Use <, >, or =. >

New Concepts

An **inequality** is a mathematical statement comparing quantities that are not equal. There are four inequality symbols:

$<$	less than	$>$	greater than
$\leq$	less than or equal to	$\geq$	greater than or equal to

Solving an inequality is similar to solving an equation. All the values that satisfy the original inequality make up the solution set. The properties used to solve inequalities are similar to those used when solving equations.

Math Reasoning

Analyze Why does the inequality symbol change direction when multiplying or dividing by a negative number?

The symbol is reversed because we are multiplying by –1, which gives us the opposite of the original numbers. For example, 3 < 12 is a true inequality. If we multiply each of the numbers by –1, then we would have –3 < –12, which is incorrect.

Properties of Inequalities

The following properties hold true for real numbers a, b, and c.
Addition and Subtraction Properties for Inequalities
If $a < b$ then $a + c < b + c$ and $a - c < b - c$.
Multiplication and Division Properties for Inequalities
If $c < 0$ and $a < b$, then $ac > bc$ and $\frac{a}{c} > \frac{b}{c}$.
If $c > 0$ and $a < b$, then $ac < bc$ and $\frac{a}{c} < \frac{b}{c}$.
Transitive Property for Inequalities
If $a < b$ and $b < c$, then $a < c$.
Note: All the properties above hold true for the inequality symbols $\leq$, $\geq$, and $>$.

The solution of an inequality can be graphed on a number line. Look at the graphs below.

$x > 1$
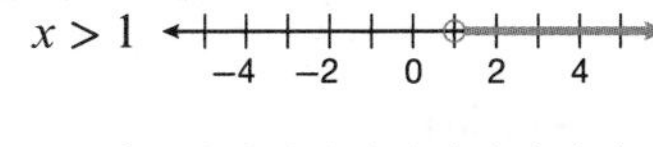

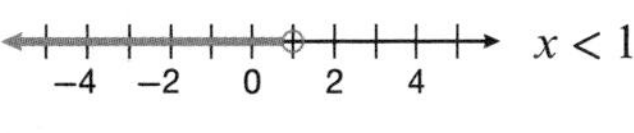
$x < 1$

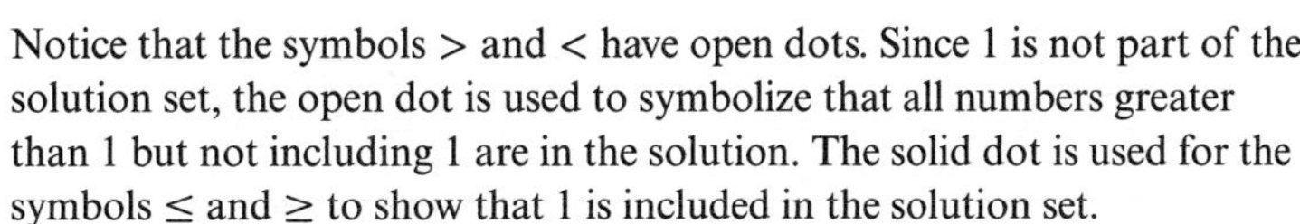
$x \geq 1$

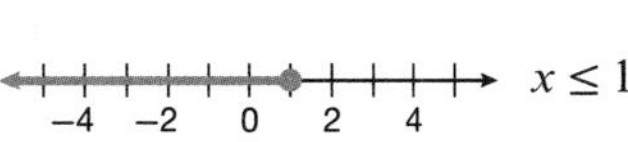
$x \leq 1$

Notice that the symbols > and < have open dots. Since 1 is not part of the solution set, the open dot is used to symbolize that all numbers greater than 1 but not including 1 are in the solution. The solid dot is used for the symbols $\leq$ and $\geq$ to show that 1 is included in the solution set.

Online Connection www.SaxonMathResources.com

LESSON 10

1 Warm Up

For Problem 3, remind students that -5 is a solution if the equation is true when -5 is substituted for x.

2 New Concepts

In this lesson, students solve and graph **inequalities.**

Discuss the definition of inequality and compare and contrast it to the definition of an equation (shown in Warm Up Problem 1). Point out that a linear equation in one variable, like $3x - 4 = 12$ has one solution, while a corresponding inequality ($3x - 4 < 12$) has an infinite number of solutions, because any value of x that makes $3x - 4$ less than 12 is a solution.

MATH BACKGROUND

In Lesson 7, students used the Properties of Equality to solve equations. These properties state that when identical operations are performed on both sides of an equation, the result is a related true equation. In this lesson, they are introduced to Properties of Inequality, which state that the same properties hold for inequalities, with one exception. When both sides of an inequality are multiplied or divided by the same negative number, the result is a related true inequality, but the direction of the inequality changes.

Previously, students might have used a number line to graph a single number. To do this, a point (dot) is drawn on the number line at the given number. When the infinite solutions to an inequality are graphed, the many points (dots) become densely packed, with too many to draw, and a ray is used to show the infinite number of solutions. The arrow at the end of the ray show that the solutions continue infinitely in one direction of the number line.

LESSON RESOURCES

Student Edition Practice Workbook 10
Reteaching Master 10
Adaptations Masters 10
Challenge and Enrichment Master C10

Example 1

Point out that the open circle indicates that the number 1 is not included in the solution set.

Additional Example 1

Solve each inequality and graph the solution set.

a. $m - 4 \geq 6$ $m \geq 10$

0 2 4 6 8 10 12 14

b. $3(t - 4) > -6$ $t > 2$

−4 −2 0 2 4

TEACHER TIP

Show students that if they have correctly solved an inequality and written the solution with the variable on the left side, the direction in which the inequality symbol points is the same as the direction the arrowhead points on the graph of the solution. For example, if the solution is $x < 7$, both the inequality symbol and the arrowhead on the ray point to the left:

Hint

< or >	open circle
≤ or ≥	closed circle

Example 1 Solving Inequalities Using Properties

Solve each inequality and graph the solution set.

a. $t + 6 < 7$

SOLUTION Solve the inequality.

$t + 6 - 6 < 7 - 6$	Subtraction Property of Equality
$t < 1$	Simplify.

Graph the solution set.

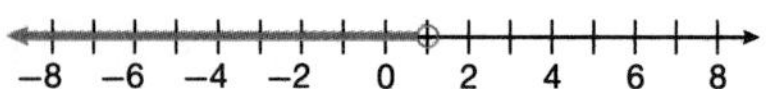

The arrow drawn shows that all values less than 1 are included in the solution set.

The solution is all values of t less than 1.

Check your solution. To check the solution, substitute 1 in the inequality and a number less than 1 to verify that it is included in the solution set.

Let $t = 1$	Let $t = -2$
$(1) + 6 \overset{?}{<} 7$	$(-2) + 6 \overset{?}{<} 7$
$7 \not< 7$	$4 < 7$ ✓
1 is not in the solution set.	−2 is in the solution set.

b. $-2(4 + b) \leq 4$

SOLUTION

Solve the inequality.

$-2(4 + b) \leq 4$	
$-8 - 2b \leq 4$	Distributive Property
$-8 + 8 - 2b \leq 4 + 8$	Addition Property of Equality
$-2b \leq 12$	Simplify.
$\frac{-2b}{-2} \geq \frac{12}{-2}$	Division Property
$b \geq -6$	Simplify.

Graph the solution set.

Check your solution.

Let $b = -6$	Let $b = 0$
$-2(4 + (-6)) \leq 4$	$-2(4 + (0)) \leq 4$
$4 \leq 4$ ✓	$-8 \leq 4$ ✓
−6 is in the solution set.	0 is in the solution set.

ENGLISH LEARNERS

Break the word **inequality** down into its components. Tell students that the prefix "in" means "not" and that "equality" means "being equal."

Discuss the meaning of inequality with students. Show them that inequality means not an equality or not an equation. Remind them that an equation shows that two expressions are equal, while an inequality shows that two expressions are not equal.

Show students several statements and ask them to identify each one as an expression (e.g. $2x$), an equation (e.g. $4x = 16$), or an inequality (e.g. $3x > 9$).

Study the prefix "in" by showing students the following words: independent means not dependent; incapable means not capable; invalid means not valid. Study the word equality by discussing related words: equation, equal, equals, equalize, equally.

Example 2 Solving Inequalities that are Always True or Always False

Solve each inequality.

a. $-2(x + 3) < -2x + 1$

SOLUTION Solve the inequality.

$-2(x + 3) < -2x + 1$	
$-2x - 6 < -2x + 1$	Distributive Property
$-2x + 2x - 6 < -2x + 2x + 1$	Addition Property of Inequality
$-6 < 1$	

Notice that the inequality will always be true, as -6 is always less than 1. Any value of x will make the inequality true. The solution is all real numbers.

The graph includes all values of x.

Math Reasoning

Verify Check your answer by substituting different values for x. The resulting inequality will always be $-6 < 13$.

b. $4b < 3 + 4(b - 1)$

Solve the inequality.

$4b < 3 + 4(b - 1)$	
$4b < 3 + 4b - 4$	Distributive Property
$4b - 4b < 3 + 4b - 4b - 4$	Subtraction Property of Inequality
$0 < 3 - 4$	Simplify.
$0 < -1$	

This solution is always false since 0 will never be less than -1. There are no values of x that will make this statement true.

A compound inequality is composed of two inequalities combined with the word *and* or *or*. Examples of compound inequalities include:

a. $-5 < -2$ and $x + 4 > 1$

b. $y > y - 4$ or $2y < y + 5$

c. $2 \leq 3x + 2 < 14$

In example **a,** the solution set includes the *intersection* of the solutions of the two inequalities given.

In example **b,** the solution set will be the *union* of the solutions to each of the inequalities given.

In example **c,** the *and* is not written, but understood. This inequality can also be written as two inequalities: $2 \leq 3x + 2$ and $3x + 2 < 14$. The solution set is the *intersection* of the solutions to each of the inequalities that compose the compound inequality.

A compound inequality such as $-2 < x < 6$ can be read as "-2 is less than x, which is less than 6."

Example 2

This example shows students that there are some inequalities that are always true or always false, despite the fact that the equations contain variables. For those that are always true, the solution is all real numbers. For those that are always false, there is no solution; no value of the variable makes the inequality true.

Additional Example 2

Solve each inequality.

a. $3x - 3 < 2(x + 4) + x$

$-3 < 8$; all real numbers

b. $4m + 3 \leq 5 + 4(m - 3)$

$3 \leq -7$; no solution

Extend the Example

Have students graph the solutions.

a.

b.

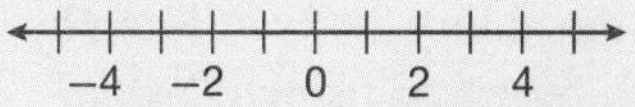

INCLUSION

Students might have trouble distinguishing between *and* and *or*. Provide a variety of examples to reinforce the difference.

For *and,* say, "Name a number that is less than 7 *and* greater than 4. What is the number?" Show them how their answer (e.g. 5) is *at the same time* less than 7 and greater than 4.

For *or,* say, "Name a number that is greater than 5 *or* less than 3." Show that how their answer (e.g. 8) only needs to satisfy *one* of the verbal inequalities to be correct.

Example 3

Error Alert Students might set up compound inequalities using the format $a < x < b$ incorrectly. Tell them that in this form, the inequality signs must face the same direction. If the symbols $<$ or $\leq$ are used, a must be less than b.

Additional Example 3

Solve each compound inequality and graph the solution set.

a. $2x + 1 > 9$ and $2x + 1 < 15$

$4 < x < 7$

b. $3n \geq 24$ or $4 + 2n \leq 12$

$n \geq 8$ or $n \leq 4$

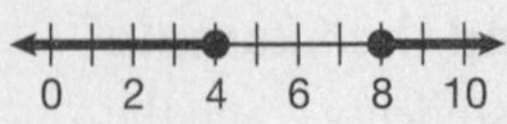

TEACHER TIP

Tell students that the compound inequality $2 \leq x \leq 5$ can be interpreted using the word *between*. This inequality shows that x is between 2 and 5, inclusive of the endpoints. This interpretation corresponds to the graph, in which all the points *between* 2 and 5 (and 2 and 5 themselves) are plotted.

Example 3 **Solving and Graphing a Compound Inequality**

Solve each compound inequality and graph the solution set.

a. $4x - 10 \geq -2$ *and* $4x - 10 \leq 10$

SOLUTION There are two methods for solving a compound inequality involving *and.*

Method 1: Solve each inequality separately.

$$4x - 10 \geq -2 \qquad 4x - 10 \leq 10$$
$$4x \geq 8 \qquad 4x \leq 20$$
$$x \geq 2 \qquad x \leq 5$$

Write the solution as a compound inequality: $2 \leq x \leq 5$.

Method 2: Write the inequalities as a compound inequality and apply the properties for solving inequalities.

$$-2 \leq 4x - 10 \leq 10$$
$$-2 + 10 \leq 4x - 10 + 10 \leq 10 + 10$$
$$8 \leq 4x \leq 20$$
$$2 \leq x \leq 5$$

Reading Math

The compound inequality $2 \leq x \leq 5$ may also be written as $\{x| 2 \leq x \leq 5\}$.

The graph of the solution set of this inequality includes all values of x such that $2 \leq x \leq 5$.

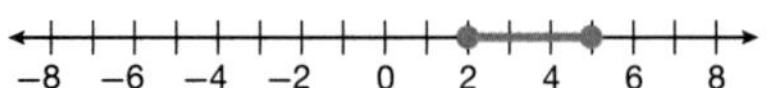

b. Solve and graph the compound inequality.

$$2x + 1 < 3 \text{ or } 3x - 6 > 6$$

SOLUTION The compound inequality includes two inequalities. Solve each inequality separately.

$$2x + 1 < 3 \qquad 3x - 6 > 6$$
$$2x < 2 \qquad 3x > 12$$
$$x < 1 \qquad x > 4$$

Reading Math

The compound inequality $x < 1$ or $x > 4$ may be written as $\{x| x < 1 \text{ or } x > 4\}$.

The graph of the solution is the set of all values of x such that $x < 1$ *or* $x > 4$.

Notice that the inequality includes all values greater than 4, not including four, and all values less than 1, not including 1. Any values between 1 and 4, inclusive, are not solutions to the compound inequality.

ALTERNATE METHOD

Have students use different colored highlighters to graph the two inequalities used to find the solution set to a compound inequality. When they graph an "and" inequality, have them graph one inequality in yellow and the other in blue. Any overlapping sections will be green; this area of the number line shows the solution.

When they graph an "or" inequality, have them use a pink highlighter. Any number on the number line for which there is pink ink is a solution to the "or" inequality.

For "and"

For "or"

Example 4 Application: Distances

Claire and Deanna are soccer players. In the off-season they practice together at an indoor complex. Claire lives 12 miles from the complex and Deanna lives 18 miles from the complex. Write an inequality to represent the possible distances between their homes.

SOLUTION To solve this problem, there are three things to consider:

1. The girls may live in the same direction, or along the same path, from the complex.

Look at the picture below. The distance between Deanna's and Claire's homes is exactly 6 miles if they live in the same direction, or along the same path, from the complex.

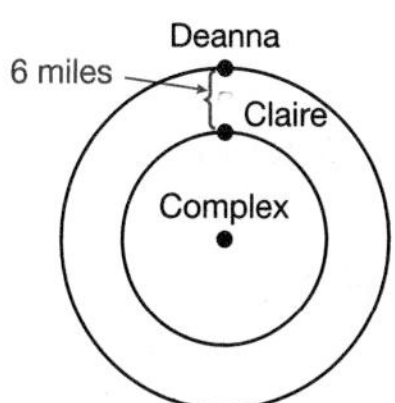

2. The girls may live in opposite directions from the complex.

The illustration shows the distance if Claire and Deanna live in opposite directions from the complex. The distance between Claire's home and the complex is 12 miles and the distance from Deanna's home to the complex is 18 miles, so $12 + 18 = 30$ miles.

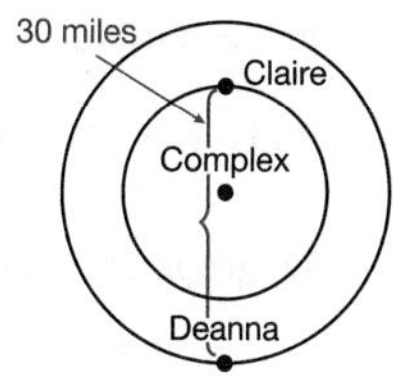

3. The girls may live in directions other than those described above.

The illustration shows one possible scenario where Deanna and Claire live in directions that are not directly opposite or along the same path as the complex.

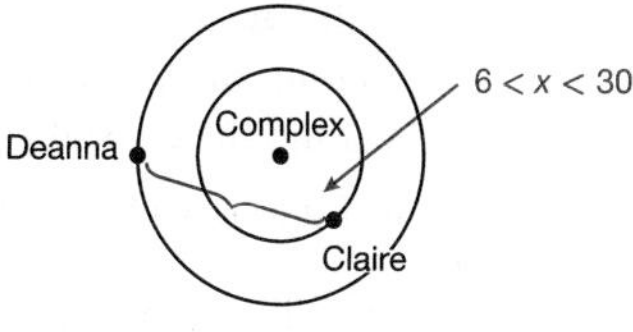

Hint

Because three points describe a triangle, we can use the **Triangle Inequality Theorem** to solve.

The largest distance will happen when Deanna and Claire live in directly opposite directions. The shortest distance will happen when they live along the same path as the complex. Based on this information, the distance between the girl's houses may be written as $6 \leq x \leq 30$.

Lesson Practice

Solve each inequality and graph the solution set when possible.

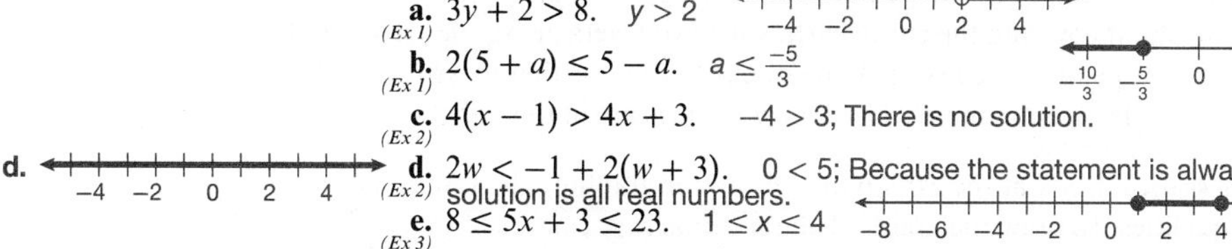

a. (Ex 1) $3y + 2 > 8$. $y > 2$

b. (Ex 1) $2(5 + a) \leq 5 - a$. $a \leq \frac{-5}{3}$

c. (Ex 2) $4(x - 1) > 4x + 3$. $-4 > 3$; There is no solution.

d. (Ex 2) $2w < -1 + 2(w + 3)$. $0 < 5$; Because the statement is always true, the solution is all real numbers.

e. (Ex 3) $8 \leq 5x + 3 \leq 23$. $1 \leq x \leq 4$

f. (Ex 4) David kicked his soccer ball 6 feet from a tree. Alannah kicked her soccer ball 10 feet from the same tree. Write an inequality to determine the distance David's ball is from Alannah's ball. $4 \leq x \leq 16$

ALTERNATE METHOD FOR EXAMPLE 4

Show the possibilities for the distances between the girls' houses using these one-dimensional sketches:

Farthest-case scenario:

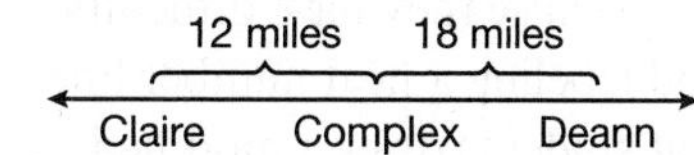

Closest-case scenario:

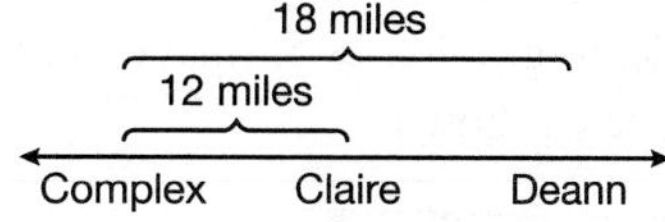

Example 4

Additional Example 3

A poll shows that 78% of voters plan to participate in a local election. The margin of error for the poll is ±3.5%. Write a compound inequality to represent the possible actual number of voters who plan to participate. $74.5\% \leq x \leq 81.5\%$

Lesson Practice

Problem e

Scaffolding Walk students through the solution. First, have them subtract 3 from all three "sides" of the inequality. Then, have them divide all three "sides" by 5.

Check for Understanding

The questions below help assess the concepts taught in this lesson.

1. **"Explain how to solve an inequality."** You solve an inequality just like you solve an equation. Add, subtract, multiply, and divide both sides by whatever you need in order to isolate the variable. When you divide or multiply both sides by a negative number, the direction of the inequality switches.

2. **"How are the graphs of solutions of equations different from the graphs of the solutions of inequalities?"** For an equation, the graph is a point. For an inequality, the graph is a set of points making up a line segment, a ray, or a line.

3 Practice

Math Conversations

Discussions to strengthen understanding

Problem 2

Remind students that a relation is a function if each x value produces exactly one y value.

Problem 10

Remind students to work from the inside out. They should first distribute, then simplify inside brackets. Finally, they can distribute 4 into the expression inside brackets.

Problem 11

Guide students through finding each element of the product matrix using questioning like this:

"How do you determine the element in the first row and first column?" Multiply 1×-1 and 0×3, then add the products.

"What is $1 \times -1 + 0 \times 3$?" -1

Problem 13

Error Alert

Students sometimes do percent change problems incorrectly because they identify the original and ending amounts incorrectly. Remind them to use estimation to check their answers. For example, 265 to 318 shows an increase. Ten percent of 265 is about 30; 20% is about 60. Since $265 + 30 = 295$ and $295 + 60 = 325$, they can estimate the percent increase to be about 20%.

Practice Distributed and Integrated

1. (SB) What solid figure is described by the net shown? Square pyramid

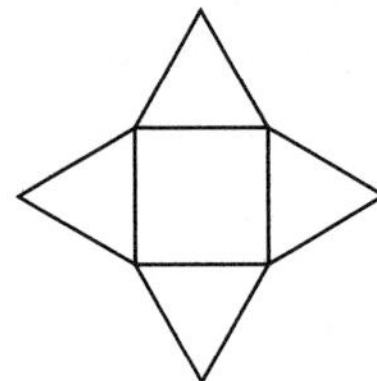

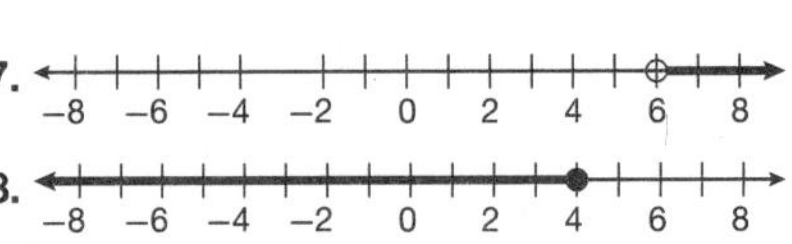

2. (4) Determine whether $y = -2x^2$ is a function. If so, state the domain and range. Function. Domain: all real numbers; Range: $y \leq 0$.

Simplify.

3. (3) $\dfrac{(2x^{-2}y^0)^{-2}yx^{-2}}{xxxy^2(y^{-2})^2}$ $\quad \frac{y^3}{4x}$

4. (3) $\dfrac{(m^2n^{-5})^{-2}m(n^0)^2}{(m^2n^{-2})^{-3}m^2}$ $\quad mn^4$

Solve each equation.

5. (7) $0.003x + 0.02x - 0.03 = 0.177$ $\quad x = 9$

6. (7) $4\frac{1}{3}x - \frac{1}{2} = 3\frac{2}{5}$ $\quad x = \frac{9}{10}$

Solve and graph each inequality.

***7.** (10) $3(x - 4) > 6$ $\quad x > 6$

***8.** (10) $2x + 3 \geq 4x - 5$ $\quad x \leq 4$

9. (8) **Multi-Step** The amount of water added to a dry mortar mix varies directly with the amount of dry mortar. 100 lb of dry mortar requires 11.25 pt of water.

a. Find the constant of variation for the dry mortar mix. 0.1125

b. Find how many pints of water are needed for 240 lb of dry mortar mix. 27 pints

10. (2) Simplify $4[3(x + 9) + 2]$. $\quad 12x + 116$

Graphing Calculator **Find each product. Check using the graphing calculator.**

***11.** (9) $\begin{bmatrix} 1 & 0 \\ 0 & 1 \end{bmatrix} \times \begin{bmatrix} -1 & 2 \\ 3 & -2 \end{bmatrix}$ $\quad \begin{bmatrix} -1 & 2 \\ 3 & -2 \end{bmatrix}$

***12.** (9) $\begin{bmatrix} 0 & -1 \\ -1 & 0 \end{bmatrix} \times \begin{bmatrix} 4 & -1 \\ -2 & -6 \end{bmatrix}$ $\quad \begin{bmatrix} 2 & 6 \\ -4 & 1 \end{bmatrix}$

Find each percent change. Tell whether it is a percent increase or decrease.

13. (6) 265 to 318 $\quad$ 20% increase

14. (6) 17 to 14.45 $\quad$ 15% decrease

15. (3) **Estimate** One cubic foot of pennies contains approximately 4.9×10^4 pennies. Think about covering the entire earth with two layers of pennies. The total number of pennies needed could be stacked in a cube that measures 2.73×10^4 ft on each side. Approximately how many pennies are in this cube? Approximately 1.0×10^{18} pennies

***16.** (10) **Error Analysis** Look at the explanation given for graphing the solution of two inequalities. To draw the graph of the solution $x \leq 2$ or $x > 5$ you draw a number line. Draw an open circle around the point 2 and a line through all the values less than 2. Next draw an open circle around the point 5 and a line through all values greater than 5. Is this explanation correct? The explanation is not correct. The $\leq$ tells you to draw a closed circle instead of an open circle.

INCLUSION

Students might have trouble graphing inequalities because they have difficulty creating and labeling a neat number line. Suggest that students draw a modified number line in which only 0 and the endpoint(s) of the solution set are labeled. For example, to graph $x > 5$, then can draw a number line as shown.

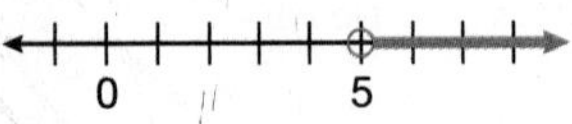

17. (4) **Currency** On the first day of 2007, the value of one US dollar was equivalent to 0.76 euro. On the same day, one US dollar was equivalent to 1.22 Swiss francs.

a. Write a function to represent the value of francs in euros.

b. What is the value of the function for an input of 5 rounded to the nearest euro, and what does it represent?

c. How can you tell from the given data that your answer makes sense?

See Additional Answers.

18. (6) **a.** Which is the greater percent change: from 50 to 60 or from 60 to 50? from 50 to 60

b. Analyze How can the answer to part **a** be found without actually finding the percents? See Additional Answers.

19. (7) **Error Analysis** Find and explain the error in solving the equation below. Correct the error and solve:

The solution is incorrect because from the first line to the second line 14 should be added to both sides and $-9 + 14 = 5$ not -23. The correct answer is $x = -1$.

$$7x - 14 = -9 + 12x$$
$$7x = -23 + 12x$$
$$-5x = -23$$
$$x = \frac{23}{5}$$

 **20.** (1) **Geometry** The length of a rectangle equals $x + 4$ and the width equals 5 inches. The perimeter of the rectangle can be calculated as shown below. Which properties of real numbers are demonstrated?

$$P = 2(x + 4) + 2(5) = 2(x + 4 + 5) = 2(x + 9) = 2x + 18.$$

Distributive Property, Associative Property

21. (7) **Statistics** The mean for the list of numbers below is 11.8. Use the formula for mean to create a linear equation to solve for the missing data point. $11 + \frac{1}{5}x = 11.8; x = 4$

12, 15, 8, ?, 20

22. (8) **Predict** The weight of an object on Neptune varies directly with the weight of that object on Earth. An object that weighs 5 g on Earth, weighs 6 g on Neptune. Without doing any calculations, predict the weight of an object on Neptune that weighs 10 g on Earth. Explain your prediction. Possible response: 12 g; Since 10 g on Earth is twice 5 g on Earth, then twice 6 g is 12 g.

23. (3) In 2002, the average height of a 15-year old boy was 1.737×10^3 mm. About how many 15-year old boys lying head-to-toe would it take to equal the circumference of the earth at the equator, if its circumference measures about 4.0076×10^4 km? Write the answer in scientific notation rounded to the nearest ten thousandth. about 2.307×10^7 boys

***24.** (8) **Verify** The circumference of a circle varies directly with the radius. The table below shows the circumference and radius of three different circles. Verify that the constant of variation is 6.283. The constant of variation is $\frac{C}{r}$. Each of the circles has a constant of variation of 6.283.

Circumference	Radius
12.566 cm	2 cm
94.245 cm	15 cm
232.471 cm	37 cm

Problem 17a

Be sure students understand that their function should show how to find euros, given Swiss francs.

Problem 19

If students have difficulty finding the mistake, have them copy and solve the equation on a separate sheet of paper. Then they can compare their work to the solution shown.

Problem 21

Error Alert

Students might write the equation $\frac{x + 55}{4} = 11.8$, dividing the sum of the numbers by 4 instead of 5. Show them that they are finding the average of 5 numbers (one of which is unknown), not 4.

Problem 23

Before they divide, say, **"The dividend and divisor must be in the same units before you divide. What common unit can you use?"** meters

Problem 24

Extend the Problem

"Write a direct variation equation to show the relationship." $C = 6.283r$

"Use the equation to find the radius of a circle for which the circumference is 20 feet." about 3.183 feet

CHALLENGE

Have students explore other solution types with the following inequalities:

Solve.

a. $x + 2 < 6$ or $x + 1 > -1$
$x < 4$ or $x > -2$
solution: all real numbers

b. $4x < 12$ and $3x + 3 > 30$
$x < 3$ and $x > 9$
solution: no solution

c. $-x + 2 < 7$ or $2x + 2 > 2$
$x > -5$ or $x > 0$
solution: $x > -5$

d. $3x + 5 < 14$ and $-5x + 12 > -13$
$x < 3$ and $x < 5$
solution: $x < 3$

Problem 26

"A budget is a maximum amount. What must be less than \$300?" The total cost of the meals prepared

"What expression represents the total cost of x meals at \$2.25 each?" $2.25x$

"What inequality represents the situation?" $2.25x \leq \$300$ **"Solve the equation."** $x \leq 133.33$

"How can you interpret the decimal?" Only a whole number of meals can be prepared, so we must round either up to 134 or down to 133. Since 134 is not in the solution set, the solution is $x \leq 133$.

Problem 29

Remind students that the position of the factors is important when multiplying matrices. To find AB, they should place A on the left; to find BA, they should place B on the left.

***25.** (9) **Football** The first table below show the scoring plays made in three games by the Philadelphia Eagles. The second table shows the point value of each play. Use matrix multiplication to find out in which game the team scored the most points. Use your graphing calculator to verify your answer.

Plays Made

Game	Touchdown	Field Goal	Extra Point
# 4	4	1	4
# 9	3	2	3
# 12	5	0	5

Point Value

Touchdown	6
Field Goal	3
Extra Point	1

25. $\begin{bmatrix} 4 & 1 & 4 \\ 3 & 2 & 3 \\ 5 & 0 & 5 \end{bmatrix} \begin{bmatrix} 6 \\ 3 \\ 1 \end{bmatrix} = \begin{bmatrix} 31 \\ 27 \\ 35 \end{bmatrix}$; The most points were scored in game # 12.

***26.** (10) **Multiple Choice** A school is holding an International dinner as a fundraiser to raise money for a local charity. The budget for the food is \$300. It will cost \$2.25 to prepare the food and beverages for one meal. Which inequality represents the number of meals that can be prepared? C

A $x \leq 134$ **B** $x \geq 134$ **C** $x \leq 133$ **D** $x \geq 133$

27. (5) **Bulk Foods** The table shows the cost of three sizes of bottles of water.

Cost of Water Bottles

16 oz	24 oz	32 oz
\$0.75	\$1.20	\$1.60

27.a. $[0.75 \quad 1.20 \quad 1.60]$ or $\begin{bmatrix} 0.75 \\ 1.20 \\ 1.60 \end{bmatrix}$;

a. Create two different matrices with different dimensions for the table.

b. Choose one of the matrices in part **a** and multiply it by a scalar to show the cost of purchasing 200 bottles of each size. $[150 \quad 240 \quad 320]$

c. When a total of 500 bottles or more are purchased, a discount of 5% off each bottle is given. Use scalar multiplication to show the cost of each bottle when 500 or more of each size are purchased.
$0.95[0.75 \quad 1.20 \quad 1.60] = [0.7125 \quad 1.14 \quad 1.52]$

28. (6) **Multiple Choice** What is the percent change from 35 to 31.5? A

A 10% **B** 90% **C** 100% **D** 900%

***29.** (9) $A = \begin{bmatrix} 6 & -3 \\ 1 & 4 \end{bmatrix}$ and $B = \begin{bmatrix} 0 & 4 \\ -2 & 6 \end{bmatrix}$.

a. Find AB. **b.** Find BA. **c.** Is $AB = BA$?

a. $\begin{bmatrix} 6 & 6 \\ -8 & 28 \end{bmatrix}$ b. $\begin{bmatrix} 4 & 16 \\ -6 & 30 \end{bmatrix}$ c. No, $\begin{bmatrix} 6 & 6 \\ -8 & 28 \end{bmatrix} \neq \begin{bmatrix} 4 & 16 \\ -6 & 30 \end{bmatrix}$.

***30.** (9) **Write** If the number of columns of matrix A is not the same as the number of rows of matrix B, explain why the product AB is not defined. In order for two matrices to be multiplied there needs to be a one-to-one correspondence between the number of columns in matrix A with the number of rows in matrix B.

LOOKING FORWARD

Solving and graphing inequalities prepares students for the following lessons:

- **Lesson 17** Solving Equations and Inequalities with Absolute Value
- **Lesson 39** Graphing Linear Inequalities in Two Variables
- **Lesson 43** Solving Systems of Linear Inequalities

68 *Saxon Algebra 2*

INVESTIGATION 1

Logic and Truth Tables

Biology Field biologists are constantly discovering new organisms. One of their tasks is to classify any new organism based on existing taxonomies. For example, biologists know that all organisms with feathers are birds. So if they encounter a new organism with feathers, it can be classified as a bird.

Let p be the statement "an organism has feathers" and q be the statement "it is a bird." The logic statement "If an organism has feathers, then it is a bird" can be written in symbolic form as $p \rightarrow q$, "p implies q." This is an example of logical implication.

You can use a truth table to determine the conditions under which $p \rightarrow q$ is true. The statement $p \rightarrow q$ is false only when p is true and q is false.

1. **Generalize** Complete the truth table for $p \rightarrow q$.

p	q	$p \rightarrow q$
T	T	T
T	F	F
F	T	T
F	F	T

Math Reasoning

Formulate Suppose a logic statement includes n different statements p_1 to p_n. How many total entries would there be in the truth table? 2^n

The converse of $p \rightarrow q$ is $q \rightarrow p$. The statement $q \rightarrow p$ is false only when q is true and p is false.

2. The statement "If an organism is an eagle, then it eats fish." is true. Write the converse. Is it true? Explain. If an organism eats fish, then it is an eagle.; No, people eat fish, but they are not eagles.
3. **Justify** If $p \rightarrow q$ is true, is $q \rightarrow p$ also true? Construct a truth table to justify your answer. See Additional Answers.

The negation of p is written $\neg p$, read "not p." If p is true, then $\neg p$ is false. The contrapositive of $p \rightarrow q$ is $\neg q \rightarrow \neg p$.

4. **Justify** If $p \rightarrow q$ is true, is the <u>contrapositive</u> also true? Construct a truth table to justify your answer. See Additional Answers.

Some logic statements are *always* true. Such a statement is known as a tautology. Take the statement,

"An organism is either <u>a bird</u> OR <u>not a bird</u>"
1 2

Let p be statement 1 and $\neg p$ be statement 2. The logic statement above becomes $p \vee \neg p$. The symbol $\vee$ is "or." An "or" statement, also called a **disjunction,** is true as long as *at least* one of the statements is true.

Online Connection
www.SaxonMathResources.com

INVESTIGATION 1

Materials

- Pencil, paper

Discuss

In this investigation, logic statements are defined and evaluated using truth tables. The logic operators implication, negation, disjunction, conjunction, and bi-directional are used to translate and evaluate arguments.

Define implication, negation, disjunction, conjunction, bi-directional, converse, contrapositive, tautology, contradiction, and truth table.

TEACHER TIP

In the statement, "If an organism has feathers, it is a bird", "an organism has feathers" is the hypothesis and "it is a bird" is the conclusion.

Error Alert Examine the truth table $p \rightarrow q$. The only case when $p \rightarrow q$ is false is when the hypothesis is true and the conclusion is false. Therefore, "an organism has feathers" is true but "it is a bird" is false, means that p does not imply q.

MATH BACKGROUND

The study of logic is the study of systems of conditional statements that can be evaluated as true or false. The fundamental concept of logic is the argument, or a set of statements consisting of premises and one conclusion in which the premises support the conclusion. Our goal is to determine if an argument is valid through the use of logical operators and the truth table. Logical arguments play a key role in philosophy and many of the logical constructions that we study today can be credited to the Greek philosopher Aristotle (384-322 B.C.).

INVESTIGATION RESOURCES

Reteaching Master
Investigation 1

TEACHER TIP

The OR statement defined is called the inclusive OR. The exclusive OR (XOR) is defined differently. The XOR is true when one of the statements is true, but false otherwise.

p	q	p XOR q
T	T	F
T	F	T
F	T	T
F	F	F

Problem 8

Circle the phrase after "If" and after "then." Assign each phrase to a variable.

Write the converse and contrapositive of the statement before evaluating.

Teacher Tip

Logical operators have an order of precedence like mathematical operators. The table below shows the order from top to bottom. Expressions are evaluated from left to right.

( )	( )
×	¬
÷	∧
+	∨
−	→
	↔

Problem 9

Extend the Problem

Write a logic statement for "If a bird is an eagle or hawk, then it eats meat and drinks water."

Let p = bird is an eagle, q = bird is a hawk and r = it eats meat. s = drinks water

$(p \vee q) \rightarrow (r \wedge s)$

---

5. Create a truth table for the logic statement $p \vee \neg p$ to show that it is a tautology.

5. In all cases the statement $p \vee \neg p$ is true.

p	$\neg p$	$p \vee \neg p$
T	F	T
F	T	T

On the other hand, a logical contradiction is a statement that is always false. Take the statement,

"An organism is both <u>a bird</u> AND <u>not a bird</u>"
1 2

Let p be statement 1 and $\neg p$ be statement 2. The logic statement above becomes $p \wedge \neg p$. The symbol $\wedge$ is "and." An "and" statement, also called a **conjunction**, is true when *both* statements are true.

6. Create a truth table for the logic statement $p \wedge \neg p$ to show that it is a contradiction.

6. In all cases the statement $p \wedge \neg p$ is false.

p	$\neg p$	$p \wedge \neg p$
T	F	F
F	T	F

Although the converse of any statement isn't always true, there are cases when it is. For example, since *all* birds have feathers and all animals that have feathers are birds, the following statement and its converse are true.

$p \rightarrow q$	$q \rightarrow p$
"If <u>an organism has feathers</u>, <u>it is a bird</u>."	"If <u>an organism is a bird</u>, <u>then it has feathers</u>."

A logic statement whose converse is true is bi-directional and is written this way, $p \leftrightarrow q$, "p is true if and only if q is true."

7. Construct the truth table for $p \leftrightarrow q$.

7.

p	q	$p \leftrightarrow q$
T	T	T
T	F	F
F	T	F
F	F	T

Math Reasoning

Generalize Describe the conjunction of a tautology and a contradiction. Describe the disjunction.

a contradiction; a tautology

8. **Multi-Step** All birds have feathers, but only those that fly have flight feathers. Consider the following statement, "If an organism has flight feathers, then it can fly."
   a. Write a logic statement.
   b. Is the converse of the statement true? Explain.
   c. Is the contrapositive true? Explain.
   d. Is it correct to conclude $q \leftrightarrow p$? Explain.

8a. Let p = an organism has flight feathers and q = it can fly. The logic statement is $p \rightarrow q$.

8b. No. There are flying organisms that aren't birds. For example, bats.

8c. Yes. Any organism that cannot fly doesn't have flight feathers.

d. No. Since the converse isn't true, the statement is not bi-directional.

9. **Multi-Step** All birds have contour feathers, but only birds that fly have flight feathers. So, consider the following statement, "If a bird has contour feathers AND has flight feathers, then it can fly."
   a. Write a logic statement.
   b. Create a truth table.
   c. Is the statement a tautology, a contradiction, or neither? Neither

9a. Let p = has contour feathers, q = has flight feathers, and r = it can fly. The logic statement is $(p \wedge q) \rightarrow r$.

9b.

p	q	r	$(p \wedge q) \rightarrow r$
T	T	T	T
T	T	F	F
T	F	T	T
T	F	F	T
F	T	T	T
F	F	T	T
F	T	F	T
F	F	F	T

10. Consider the following statement, "If an organism has contour feathers OR flight feathers, then it is a bird."
   a. Write a logic statement.
   b. Create a truth table.
   c. Is the statement a tautology, a contradiction, or neither? Neither

10a. Let p = has contour feathers, q = has flight feathers, and r = it is a bird. The logic statement is $(p \vee q) \rightarrow r$.

10b. See Additional Answers.

ENGLISH LEARNERS

Write a short phrase to define each logic operator. Students should repeat these phrases each time they complete a truth table.

¬ change value; ∧ true when both are true; ∨ true when one or both are true; → true, false gives false; ↔ true when both have same value

Provide students with a list of logic statements. Students should identify **logic operators** as well as the **logical implication**, **converse**, **contrapositive**, and **bi-directional**.

Some logic statements can appear different but have the same truth table. In such a case the statements are said to be logically equivalent.

11. **Verify** Show that the logic statements $p \rightarrow q$ and $\neg p \vee q$ are logically equivalent. Check students' work.

Investigation Practice

a. Create the truth table for $\neg p \rightarrow \neg q$.

1. If $\neg p \rightarrow \neg q$ is true, what can you conclude about $q \rightarrow p$? The statement is also true.
2. Why? It is the contrapositive of the original statement

b. Identify if each statement is a tautology, a contradiction, or neither.

1. $(\neg p \wedge \text{p}) \rightarrow \neg q$ Neither.
2. $(\neg p \wedge p) \rightarrow p$ Tautology
3. $(\neg p \wedge p) \rightarrow (\neg q \wedge q)$ Tautology

c. Determine if each set of statements is logically equivalent.

1. $(\neg p \wedge p) \rightarrow (\neg q \wedge q)$ and $(\neg p \vee p) \rightarrow (\neg q \vee q)$ Equivalent
2. $(p \wedge q) \rightarrow r$ and $r \rightarrow (p \wedge q)$ Not equivalent

TEACHER TIP

Another way to show that two statements are logically equivalent is to connect them with the bi-directional. If $p \rightarrow q \leftrightarrow \neg p \vee q$ is a tautology, then the statements $p \rightarrow q$ are $\neg p \vee q$ are logically equivalent.

Investigation Practice

Math Conversations

Discussions to strengthen understanding

Problem a

p is equivalent to $\neg\neg p$. Remember that logical implication and the contrapositive have the same truth value.

Problem b

Use order of precedence to evaluate: parentheses, negation, and conjunction. Logical implication should be the final operator.

Problem c

Evaluate separately to see if the truth tables are identical or use the bi-directional and determine if the statement is a tautology.

LOOKING FORWARD

Understanding logic and truth tables prepares students for

- **Investigation 12** Using Mathematical Induction

Lesson Planner

Lesson	New Concepts
11	Understanding Polynomials
12	Solving Inverse Variation Problems
LAB 3	*Graphing Calculator:* Calculating Points on a Graph
13	Graphing Linear Equations I
14	Finding Determinants
15	Solving Systems of Equations by Graphing
	Cumulative Test 2, Performance Task 2
16	Using Cramer's Rule
LAB 4	*Graphing Calculator:* Changing the Line and Window of a Graph
17	Solving Equations and Inequalities with Absolute Value
18	Calculating with Units of Measure
19	Multiplying Polynomials
20	Performing Operations with Functions
	Cumulative Test 3, Performance Task 3, Benchmark Test 1
INV 2	*Investigation:* Solving Parametric Equations

Resources for Teaching

- Student Edition
- Teacher's Edition
- Student Edition eBook
- Teacher's Edition eBook
- Resources and Planner CD
- Solutions Manual
- Instructional Masters
- Technology Lab Masters
- Warm Up and Teaching Transparencies
- Instructional Presentations CD
- Online activities and tools
- Online homework help
- Online connection: **www.SaxonMathResources.com**

Resources for Practice and Assessment

- Student Edition Practice Workbook
- Course Assessments
- Standardized Test Practice
- College Entrance Exam Practice
- ExamView™ Test and Practice Generator CD

Resources for Differentiated Instruction

- Reteaching Masters
- Challenge and Enrichment Masters
- Prerequisite Skills Intervention
- Adaptations for Saxon Algebra 2
- Multilingual Glossary
- English Learners Handbook
- TI Resources

Pacing Guide

Resources and Planner CD for lesson planning support

45-Minute Class

Day 1	Day 2	Day 3	Day 4	Day 5	Day 6
Lesson 11	Lesson 12	Lab 3 Lesson 13	Lesson 14	Lesson 15	Cumulative Test 2
Day 7	**Day 8**	**Day 9**	**Day 10**	**Day 11**	**Day 12**
Lesson 16	Lab 4 Lesson 17	Lesson 18	Lesson 19	Lesson 20	Cumulative Test 3

Block: 90-Minute Class

Day 1	Day 2	Day 3	Day 4	Day 5	Day 6
Lesson 11 Lesson 12	Lab 3 Lesson 13 Lesson 14	Lesson 15 Cumulative Test 2	Lesson 16 Lab 4 Lesson 17	Lesson 18 Lesson 19	Lesson 20 Cumulative Test 3
Day 7					
Investigation 2 Lesson 21					

** For suggestions on how to implement Saxon Math in a block schedule, see the Pacing section at the beginning of the Teacher's Edition.*

Differentiated Instruction

Below Level		Advanced Learners	
Warm Up	SE pp. 72, 77, 86, 93, 100, 116, 124, 129, 136	Challenge	TE pp. 75, 81, 91, 97, 105, 112, 122, 128, 135, 141
Skills Bank	SE pp. 862–885	Extend the Example	TE pp. 74, 79, 80, 89, 94, 95, 102, 108, 109, 115, 125, 131
Reteaching Masters	Lessons 11–20, Investigation 2	Extend the Problem	TE pp. 76, 82, 83, 91, 92, 97, 98, 104, 110, 121, 123, 127, 135, 141
Warm Up Transparencies	Lessons 11–20	Challenge and Enrichment Masters	Challenge C11–C20 Enrichment E11, E19
Prerequisite Skills Intervention	18–21, 54, 61–66, 75		

English Learners		Special Needs	
EL Tips	TE pp. 74, 80, 87, 94, 101, 108, 110, 120, 127, 132, 137, 145	Inclusion Tips	TE pp. 76, 79, 80, 90, 95, 102, 109, 117, 125, 131, 139
Multilingual Glossary	Booklet and Online	Adaptations for Saxon Algebra 2	Lessons 11–20; Cumulative Test 2, 3
English Learners Handbook			
Online multilingual glossary			

For All Learners			
Exploration	SE pp. 120	Alternate Method	TE pp. 73, 78, 88, 96, 111, 118, 119, 126, 130, 133, 138, 140
Caution	SE pp. 78, 87, 89, 93, 108, 131	Online Tools	
Hints	SE pp. 73, 86, 89, 94, 100, 117, 120, 143		
Error Alert	TE pp. 73, 76, 78, 81, 84, 87, 88, 90, 94, 95, 96, 101, 105, 108, 109, 110, 112, 117, 119, 120, 127, 131, 135, 137, 140, 143, 144		

SE = Student Edition; TE = Teacher's Edition

Math Vocabulary

Lesson	New Vocabulary		Maintained	EL Tip in TE
11	binomial degree of a monomial degree of a polynomial leading coefficient monomial polynomial	polynomial function standard form trinomial	constant term term variable	binomial monomial trinomial
12	inverse variation joint variation		constant	direct variation inverse variation joint variation
13	intercepts slope slope-intercept form	*x*-intercept *y*-intercept	vertical	intercept
14	determinant	minor	matrix	minor
15	consistent system dependent system inconsistent system independent system	intersect linear system system of equations	slope	consistent
16	coefficient matrix	Cramer's rule	determinant	coefficient euro
17	absolute value absolute value function extraneous solutions	parent function transformations vertex	conjunction	extraneous
18	accuracy conversion factor	precision significant digits	equivalent	unit
19			coefficient	foil
20			function	algebraically geometrically numerically
INV 2	parameter	parametric equations		parameter

SECTION OVERVIEW 2

Math Highlights

Enduring Understandings – The "Big Picture"

After completing Section 2, students will understand:

- How to solve inverse variation problems.
- How to graph linear equations and systems of equations.
- How to solve equations and inequalities with absolute value.
- How to find determinants.
- How to multiply polynomials.

Essential Questions

- How can you use Cramer's rule to solve equations?
- How do you choose an appropriate conversion factor?
- What is a function?

Math Content Strands

Linear Functions

• Lab 3	Calculating Points on a Graph
• Lesson 13	Graphing Linear Equations I
• Lab 4	Changing the Line and Window of a Graph
• Lesson 17	Solving Equations and Inequalities with Absolute Value
• Lesson 20	Performing Operations with Functions

Linear Systems

• Lesson 15	Solving Systems of Equations by Graphing
• Investigation 2	Solving Parametric Equations

Matrices

• Lesson 14	Finding Determinants
• Lesson 16	Using Cramer's Rule

Number Sense and Foundations of Algebra

• Lesson 18	Calculating with Units of Measure

Polynomials and Polynomial Functions

• Lesson 11	Understanding Polynomials
• Lesson 19	Multiplying Polynomials

Rational and Radical Functions

• Lesson 12	Solving Inverse Variation Problems

Connections in Practice Problems

	Lessons
Geometry	11, 12, 13, 14, 15, 16, 17, 18, 19, 20
Measurement	14, 15, 16
Data Analysis	12, 19

Math Processes

Reasoning and Communication

	Lessons
• Analyze	11, 12, 13, 18, 19
• Connect	12, 14, 19
• Error analysis	11, 13, 14, 15, 16, 17, 18, 19, 20
• Estimate	11, 12, 13, 16
• Explain	16, 17, 18, 19
• Formulate	11, 12, 13, 14, 15, 18, 19, 20, Inv. 2
• Generalize	12, 15, 16, 17, 19, 20, Inv. 2
• Justify	11, 12, 13, 20
• Math reasoning	15, 16, 17, 18, 20
• Model	14, 16, Inv. 2
• Multiple choice	11, 12, 13, 14, 15, 16, 17, 18, 19, 20
• Multiple representations	19, 20
• Multi-step	11, 12, 13, 14, 15, 16, 17, 18, 19, 20
• Predict	12, 18, Inv. 2
• Verify	13, 14, 15, 17, 18, 19, 20
• Write	15, 16, 19, 20, Inv. 2
• Graphing Calculator	11, 12, 13, 14, 15, 16, 17, 18, 19, 20, Inv. 2

Connections

In Examples: Business, Chemistry, Consumer math, Geography, Geometry, Railroads, Revenue from sales of electricity, Science, Sports

In Practice problems: Aquarium design, Architecture, Astronomy, Baseball, Basketball, Bird flight, Business, Chemical elements, Chemical mixture, Chemistry, Civil engineering, Citrus production, Construction, Construction engineering, Consumer, Demography, Earth science, Exterior design, Geography, Landscaping, Meteorology, Packaging technology, Physics, Population, Scoring, Simple interest, Solar system, Space travel, Spending and saving, Sports, Temperature, Transportation, Travel, Woodworking

Content Trace

Lesson	Warm Up: Prerequisite Skills	New Concepts	Where Practiced	Where Assessed	Looking Forward
11	Lessons 1, 2, 4, 6	Understanding Polynomials	Lessons 11, 12, 13, 14, 15, 16, 17, 18, 19, 20, 21, 22, 23, 24, 25, 27, 28, 30, 31, 32, 35, 42, 50, 103, 108, 112	Cumulative Tests 3, 4, 5, 6, 7, 10, 15, 19	Lessons 19, 23
12	Lessons 5, 7, 8	Solving Inverse Variation Problems	Lessons 12, 13, 14, 15, 17, 18, 19, 20, 21, 22, 27, 31, 32, 35, 36, 38, 58, 101, 103	Cumulative Tests 3, 4, 5, 6, 9	Lessons 18, 100
13	Skills Bank, Lessons 2, 4	Graphing Linear Equations I	Lessons 13, 14, 15, 16, 17, 18, 19, 21, 22, 23, 24, 25, 26, 27, 28, 29, 31, 32, 34, 37, 47, 61	Cumulative Tests 3, 4, 5, 8, 11, 16	Lessons 15, 26, 29, 34, 36, 39, 43, 45
14	Lessons 5, 7, 9	Finding Determinants	Lessons 14, 15, 16,17, 18, 20, 21, 22, 24, 25, 26, 27, 29, 30, 31, 32, 36, 37, 38, 110	Cumulative Tests 3, 4, 5, 7, 8, 13, 23	Lessons 16, 32, 99, 104
15	Lessons 2, 13	Solving Systems of Equations by Graphing	Lessons 15, 16, 17, 18, 19, 20, 28, 30, 31, 32, 34, 37, 47, 48	Cumulative Tests 3, 4, 5, 7, 14	Lessons 21, 24, 29, 43
16	Lesson 14	Using Cramer's Rule	Lessons 16, 17, 18, 20, 21, 22, 23, 26, 28, 29, 32, 37, 38, 39, 43, 46, 47	Cumulative Tests 4, 5, 7, 9, 12, 17	Lesson 29, Inv. 3
17	Lesson 10	Solving Equations and Inequalities with Absolute Value	Lessons 17, 18, 19, 20, 21, 22, 23, 24, 25, 26, 27, 28, 29, 30, 31, 32, 37, 47, 49, 50, 77, 108	Cumulative Tests 4, 5, 8, 11	Lessons 22, 69
18	Skills Bank, Lesson 3	Calculating with Units of Measure	Lessons 18, 19, 20, 23, 24, 25, 26, 27, 28, 29, 30, 31, 33, 35, 42, 48, 105, 112	Cumulative Tests 4, 5, 6, 7, 9, 13	Lessons 33, 113
19	Lessons 1, 2, 3, 11	Multiplying Polynomials	Lessons 19, 20, 21, 26, 27, 28, 29, 30, 31, 32, 33, 34, 37, 43, 45, 47, 50, 63	Cumulative Tests 4, 5, 6, 8, 10, 13, 18	Lessons 23, 31
20	Lessons 4, 7	Performing Operations with Functions	Lessons 20, 21, 22, 23, 24, 25, 26, 27, 28, 29, 30, 31, 32, 33, 35, 37, 39, 40, 41, 43, 46, 48, 50, 79	Cumulative Tests 4, 5, 9, 15	Lessons 24, 31, 37
INV 2	N/A	Solving Parametric Equations	Lessons 22, 26, 33, 36, 48	Cumulative Test 6	N/A

Ongoing Assessment

	Type	Feature	Intervention *
BEFORE instruction	Assess Prior Knowledge	• Diagnostic Test	• Prerequisite Skills Intervention
BEFORE the lesson	Formative	• Warm Up	• Skills Bank • Reteaching Masters
DURING the lesson	Formative	• Lesson Practice • Math Conversations with the Practice problems	• Additional Examples in TE • Test and Practice Generator (for additional practice sheets)
AFTER the lesson	Formative	• Check for Understanding (closure)	• Scaffolding Questions in TE
AFTER 5 lessons	Summative	After Lesson 15 • Cumulative Test 2 • Performance Task 2 After Lesson 20 • Cumulative Test 3 • Performance Task 3	• Reteaching Masters • Test and Practice Generator (for additional tests and practice)
AFTER 20 lessons	Summative	• Benchmark Tests	• Reteaching Masters • Test and Practice Generator (for additional tests and practice)

* for students not showing progress during the formative stages or scoring below 80% on the summative assessments

Evidence of Learning – What Students Should Know

Because the Saxon philosophy is to provide students with sufficient time to learn and practice each concept, a lesson's topic will not be tested until at least five lessons after the topic is introduced.

On the Cumulative Tests that are given during this section of ten lessons, students should be able to demonstrate the following competencies:

- Use properties of real numbers.
- Simplify and evaluate algebraic expressions.
- Understand the rules of exponents.
- Identify functions and use function notation.
- Use matrices to organize data and to solve problems.

ExamView™ Test and Practice Generator CD

The Test and Practice Generator is an easy-to-use benchmark and assessment tool that creates unlimited practice and tests in multiple formats and allows you to customize questions or create new ones. A variety of reports are available to track student progress toward mastery of the standards throughout the year.

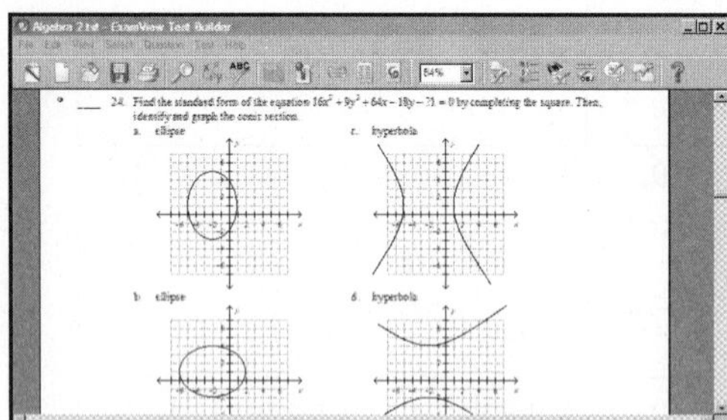

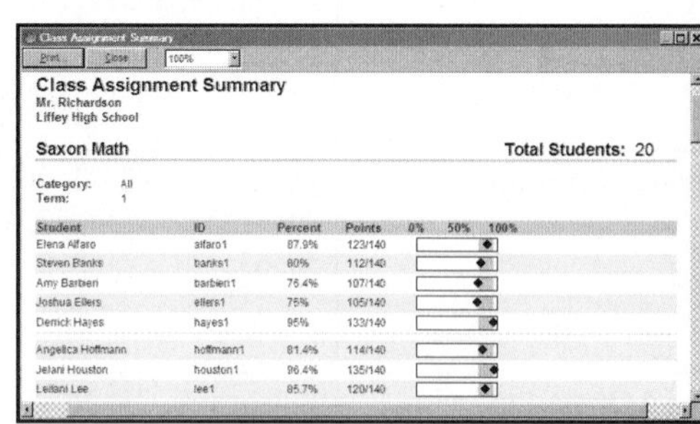

Assessment Resources

Resources for Diagnosing and Assessing

- **Student Edition**
  - Warm Up
  - Lesson Practice
- **Teacher's Edition**
  - Math Conversations with the Practice problems
  - Check for Understanding (closure)
- **Course Assessments**
  - Cumulative Tests
  - Performance Tasks
  - Benchmark Tests
- **Prerequisite Skills Intervention**
  - Diagnostic Test

Resources for Intervention

- **Student Edition**
  - Skills Bank
- **Teacher's Edition**
  - Additional Examples
- **Prerequisite Skills Intervention**
  - Skill worksheets
- **Reteaching Masters**
  - Lesson instruction and practice sheets
- **ExamView™ Test and Practice Generator CD**
  - Lesson practice problems
  - Additional tests

Resources for Test Prep

- **Student Edition Practice**
  - Multiple-choice problems
  - Multiple-step and writing problems
  - Daily cumulative practice
- **Standardized Test Practice**
- **College Entrance Exam Practice**
- **Test and Practice Generator CD using ExamView™**

SECTION OVERVIEW 2

Cumulative Tests

The assessments in Saxon Math are frequent and consistently placed after every five lessons to offer a regular method of ongoing testing. These cumulative assessments check mastery of concepts from previous lessons.

Performance Tasks

The Performance Tasks can be used in conjunction with the Cumulative Tests and are scored using a rubric.

After Lesson 15

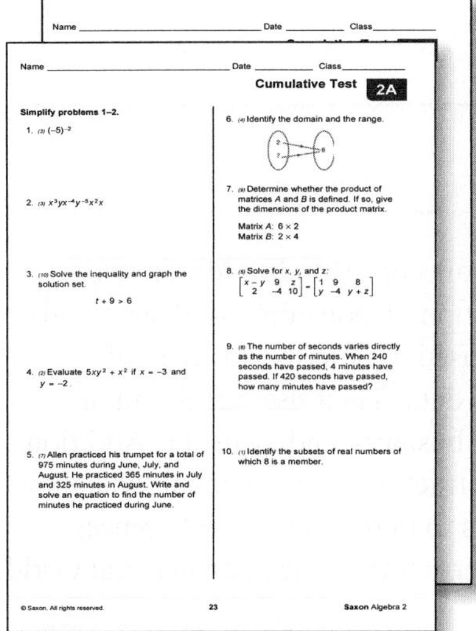

Name ____________ Date ______ Class ______

Cumulative Test 2A

Simplify problems 1–2.

1. (3) $(-5)^{-2}$
2. (3) $x^3yx^{-4}y^{-5}x^2x$
3. (10) Solve the inequality and graph the solution set.
   $t + 9 > 6$
4. (2) Evaluate $5xy^2 + x^2$ if $x = -3$ and $y = -2$.
5. (7) Allen practiced his trumpet for a total of 975 minutes during June, July, and August. He practiced 365 minutes in July and 325 minutes in August. Write and solve an equation to find the number of minutes he practiced during June.
6. (4) Identify the domain and the range.
7. (9) Determine whether the product of matrices A and B is defined. If so, give the dimensions of the product matrix.
   Matrix A: 6×2
   Matrix B: 2×4
8. (5) Solve for x, y, and z:
   $\begin{bmatrix} x-y & 9 & z \\ 2 & -4 & 10 \end{bmatrix} = \begin{bmatrix} 1 & 9 & 8 \\ y & -4 & y+z \end{bmatrix}$
9. (8) The number of seconds varies directly as the number of minutes. When 240 seconds have passed, 4 minutes have passed. If 420 seconds have passed, how many minutes have passed?
10. (1) Identify the subsets of real numbers of which 8 is a member.

© Saxon. All rights reserved. 23 Saxon Algebra 2

After Lesson 20

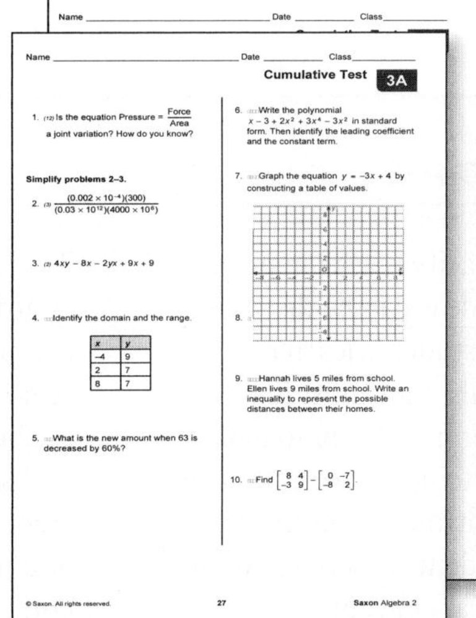

Name ____________ Date ______ Class ______

Cumulative Test 3A

1. (12) Is the equation Pressure = $\frac{\text{Force}}{\text{Area}}$ a joint variation? How do you know?

Simplify problems 2–3.

2. (3) $\frac{(0.002 \times 10^{-4})(300)}{(0.03 \times 10^{12})(4000 \times 10^{6})}$
3. (2) $4xy - 8x - 2yx + 9x + 9$
4. Identify the domain and the range.

x	y
–4	9
2	7
8	7

5. What is the new amount when 63 is decreased by 60%?
6. Write the polynomial $x - 3 + 2x^2 + 3x^4 - 3x^2$ in standard form. Then identify the leading coefficient and the constant term.
7. Graph the equation $y = -3x + 4$ by constructing a table of values.
8.
9. Hannah lives 5 miles from school. Ellen lives 9 miles from school. Write an inequality to represent the possible distances between their homes.
10. Find $\begin{bmatrix} 8 & 4 \\ -3 & 9 \end{bmatrix} - \begin{bmatrix} 0 & -7 \\ -8 & 2 \end{bmatrix}$.

© Saxon. All rights reserved. 27 Saxon Algebra 2

For use with Performance Tasks

Teacher Rubric

Criteria Performance	Knowledge and Skills Understanding	Communication and Representation	Process and Strategies
4	The student got it! The student did it in new ways and showed how it worked. The student knew and understood what math concepts to use.	The student clearly detailed how he/she solved the problem. The student included all the steps to show his/her thinking. The student used math language, symbols, numbers, graphs and/or models to represent his/her solution.	The student had an effective and inventive solution. The student used big math ideas to solve the problem. The student addressed the important details. The student showed other ways to solve the problem. The student checked his/her answer to make sure it was correct
3	The student understood the problem and had an appropriate solution. All parts of the problem are addressed.	The student clearly explained how he/she solved the problem. The student used math language, symbols, tables, graphs, and numbers to explain how he/she did the problem.	The student had a correct solution. The student used a plan to solve the problem and selected an appropriate strategy.
2	The student understood parts of the problem. The student started, but he/she couldn't finish.	The student explained some of what he/she did. The student tried to use words, symbols, tables, graphs and numbers to explain how he/she did the problem.	The student had part of the solution, but did not know how to finish. The student was not sure if he/she had the correct answer. The student needed help.
1	The student did not understand the problem.	The student did not explain how he/she solved the problem. He/she did not use words, symbols, tables or graphs to show how he/she	The student couldn't get started. The student did not know how to begin.

© Saxon. All rights reserved. x Saxon Algebra 2

LESSON 11

1 Warm Up

Remind students to distribute −5 when multiplying on problem 2.

2 New Concepts

In this lesson, students learn to classify, add, and subtract polynomials.

Discuss the definition of **monomial, polynomial, degree of a monomial** and **degree of a polynomial.** Explain that polynomials can often be simplified by addition or subtraction.

Example 1

Remind students that in Lesson 2 they learned to combine like terms.

Additional Example 1

Write the polynomial $5 - 2y + 2y^3 - 5 + 4y^3$ in standard form. Then identify the leading coefficient and the constant term.
$6y^3 - 2y$; 6; 0

LESSON 11

Understanding Polynomials

Warm Up

1. **Vocabulary** A variable is a letter that is used to represent a number. (2)
2. Distribute. $-5(6x - 2)$ $-30x + 10$ (1)
3. Collect like terms. $6 + 3x - 5x + 4y + 17 - 2y$ $-2x + 2y + 23$ (2)
4. Let $g(x) = 2x + 7$ and $f(x) = x - 5$. Find $f(g(x))$. $f(g(x)) = 2x + 2$ (6)
5. True/False The function $f(x) = 3x^2 + 4$ is linear.   false (4)

New Concepts

A **monomial** is a number, a variable, or the product of a number and one or more variables with whole-number exponents. A **polynomial** is a monomial or sum of monomials. The terms of a polynomial are its monomials. The **degree of a monomial** is the sum of the exponents of its variable factors. The **degree of a polynomial** is the degree of its monomial with the greatest degree.

Math Language

The suffix *nomial* means a name or a term.

The monomial $5ab^3$ has degree 4.

$$5a^1b^3 \leftarrow 1 + 3 = 4$$

The polynomial $-xy^3 - 3x^2y^2 + x^2y^3$ has degree 5.

$$-x^1y^3 - 3x^2y^2 + x^2y^3 \leftarrow 2 + 3 = 5$$

A one-variable polynomial is in **standard form** when all like terms have been combined and its terms are in descending order by degree.

The polynomial $-x^4 + x^3 - 3x + 2$ is in standard form.

$$-x^4 + x^3 - 3x^1 + 2x^0 \leftarrow \text{4, 3, 1, 0 are in descending order.}$$

A **polynomial function** is a function of the form

$$f(x) = a_nx^n + a_{n-1}x^{n-1} + \ldots + a_1x + a_0,$$

where n is a nonnegative integer and the coefficients $a_n, \ldots, a_0$ are real numbers. The **leading coefficient** is a_n, the **constant term** is a_0, and the degree is n.

Example 1 Writing a Polynomial in Standard Form

Write the polynomial $x - 5 + 4x^2 + 2x^5 - x^2$ in standard form. Then identify the leading coefficient and the constant term.

SOLUTION

$x - 5 + 4x^2 + 2x^5 - x^2 = 2x^5 + 4x^2 - x^2 + x - 5$ Write terms in descending order by degree. Then combine like terms.
$= 2x^5 + 3x^2 + x - 5$

The leading coefficient is 2 and the constant term is −5.

Online Connection
www.SaxonMathResources.com

LESSON RESOURCES

Student Edition Practice Workbook 11
Reteaching Master 11
Adaptations Master 11
Challenge and Enrichment Masters C11, E11

MATH BACKGROUND

It is important to clarify math language so that mathematical ideas can be discussed. For example, when students learn a rule to multiply binomials, they must first understand the meaning of a binomial so they know when to apply the rule. The vocabulary words introduced in this lesson are used to help students describe, explain, and use mathematical concepts.

These concepts include addition and subtraction of polynomials. Polynomials can be used to describe a variety of real-life data. Their uses are found in science, business, and medicine. Addition and subtraction of polynomials will allow students to find totals and differences and interpret their meaning in a real world context.

Polynomials can be classified by degree and by number of terms. Some examples are given below.

Hint

The prefix *quart-* indicates 4, as in *quarter* and *quartet*. The prefix *quint-* indicates 5, as in *quintuplets*.

Polynomial	Degree	Classification by Degree	Number of Terms	Classification by Number of Terms
-4	0	constant	1	monomial
$x + 2$	1	linear	2	binomial
$x^2 + x - 6$	2	quadratic	3	trinomial
x^3	3	cubic	1	monomial
$-3x^4 + 2x^3 - x^2$	4	quartic	3	trinomial
$x^5 - 4x^2$	5	quintic	2	binomial

Example 2 Classifying Polynomials

Classify each polynomial by degree and by number of terms.

a. $x^2 - 9$

SOLUTION The degree is 2, so it is quadratic. It has 2 terms, so it is a binomial.

b. $x^3 + x - 2x^3 - \frac{1}{2}x^5$

SOLUTION Combine like terms and write in descending order by degree to write the polynomial in standard form.

$$x^3 + x - 2x^3 - \frac{1}{2}x^5 = -\frac{1}{2}x^5 - x^3 + x$$

The degree is 5, so it is quintic. The standard form has 3 terms, so it is a trinomial.

Example 3 Adding Polynomials

Add: $(2x^3 - 3x^2 + x - 5) + (5 - x^2)$.

SOLUTION To add polynomials, combine like terms.

$$(2x^3 - 3x^2 + x - 5) + (5 - x^2) = 2x^3 - 3x^2 + x - 5 + 5 - x^2$$
$$= 2x^3 - 3x^2 - x^2 + x - 5 + 5$$
$$= 2x^3 - 4x^2 + x$$

Example 4 Subtracting Polynomials

Subtract: $(5x^3 - 3x^2) - (2x^3 - x^2 + 4)$.

SOLUTION To subtract a polynomial, add the opposite of each term.

$$(5x^3 - 3x^2) - (2x^3 - x^2 + 4) = 5x^3 - 3x^2 - 2x^3 + x^2 - 4$$
$$= 5x^3 - 2x^3 - 3x^2 + x^2 - 4$$
$$= 3x^3 - 2x^2 - 4$$

ALTERNATE METHOD FOR EXAMPLES 3 AND 4

Polynomials can be added and subtracted vertically. Tell students to line up like terms vertically and perform the indicated operation.

Adding Polynomials:

$$\begin{array}{r} 2x^3 - 3x^2 + x - 5 \\ + \quad - x^2 \quad + 5 \\ \hline 2x^3 - 4x^2 + x \end{array}$$

Subtracting Polynomials:

$$\begin{array}{r} 5x^3 - 3x^2 \quad\quad \\ -(2x^3 - x^2 \quad + 4) \\ \hline 3x^3 - 2x^2 \quad - 4 \end{array}$$

Example 2

Tell students that a constant is a number that is called a coefficient when it is multiplied by a variable. Point out that a constant can also be a term.

Additional Example 2

Classify each polynomial by degree and by number of terms.

a. $x^3 + 4x^2 - 3$
cubic trinomial

b. $m^4 + 0.5m + 3m^4$
quartic binomial

Example 3

Remind students that in order to add terms, the terms must have the same variable with the same exponent.

Additional Example 3

Add $(3x^2 + 7 + x) + (10x^3 + 2 + x^2 - x)$.
$10x^3 + 4x^2 + 9$

Example 4

Error Alert Students often forget to add the opposite of each term in the parentheses. Point out that the parentheses indicate the entire polynomial is subtracted, therefore the opposite of each term must be found. Show the following example:

$(a + b) - (c - d)$
$= a + b - c + d$

Additional Example 4

Subtract:

$(4m^2 - 3m + 2) - (m^3 - 2m + 5)$
$-m^3 + 4m^2 - m - 3$

Example 5

Additional Example 5

The profits of two manufacturing plants are modeled as $-0.03x^2 + 25x - 1500$ and $-0.02x^2 + 21x - 1700$. Write a polynomial expression that represents the difference of the profits.
$-0.01x^2 + 4x + 200$

Extend the Example

Have students determine the total revenue for the commercial and industrial sectors.
$f(x) = 1.07x^2 + 2.42x + 129.15$

Have students find the difference in the total for the commercial and industrial sector revenues versus the revenue of the residential sector.
$f(x) = 0.32x^2 + 0.69x + 29.83$

Lesson Practice

Problem e

Scaffolding Before combining terms, have students rewrite the expression without parentheses. Be sure students find the opposite of each term in the second polynomial.

Check for Understanding

The questions below help assess the concepts taught in this lesson.

1. **"Explain how to classify the polynomial $5x^3 - 1$."** This polynomial can be classified by the highest degree and the number of terms. The highest degree is 3, so it is a cubic. There are 2 terms, so it is a binomial.
2. **"What are the similarities when adding and subtracting polynomials? What are the differences?"** When adding and subtracting polynomials you must combine like terms. When subtracting polynomials you must add the opposite term of the second polynomial.

Example 5 **Application: Revenue from Sales of Electricity**

Revenue (in billions of dollars) from retail sales of electricity in the U.S. for the years 2000 through 2005, is modeled by these polynomial functions. The variable x represents the number of years since 2000.

Residential $R = 0.75x^2 + 1.73x + 99.32$

Commercial $C = 0.44x^2 + 3.91x + 79.26$

Industrial $I = 0.63x^2 - 1.49x + 49.89$

Write a model for total revenue from sales in all three sectors combined.

SOLUTION

1. **Understand** Sales in each sector is modeled by a polynomial function.
2. **Plan** To find a model for all three sectors combined, add the polynomials.
3. **Solve**
$$\begin{array}{r} 0.75x^2 + 1.73x + 99.32 \\ 0.44x^2 + 3.91x + 79.26 \\ +\ 0.63x^2 - 1.49x + 49.89 \\ \hline 1.82x^2 + 4.15x + 228.47 \end{array}$$
$f(x) = 1.82x^2 + 4.15x + 228.47$ is a model for all three sectors combined.
4. **Check** The answer makes sense because the polynomial $1.82x^2 + 4.15x + 228.47$ is the sum of the three given polynomials.

Math Reasoning

Estimate Use the model in Step **3** to estimate the revenue for the year 2002.

about 244 billion dollars

Lesson Practice

a. Write the polynomial $3x - 1 + 4x^4 + x$ in standard form. Then identify the leading coefficient and the constant term. *(Ex 1)* $4x^4 + 4x - 1$; 4; -1

b. Classify $-x^3$ by degree and by number of terms. *(Ex 2)* cubic monomial

c. Classify $x^2 + 40x + 10 - 9x^2 - 1$ by degree and by number of terms. *(Ex 2)* $x^2 + 40x + 10 - 9x^2 - 1 = -8x^2 + 40x + 9$; quadratic trinomial

d. Add: $(2x^2 - 3x^5) + (2x^5 - x^2 + 1)$. *(Ex 3)* $-x^5 + x^2 + 1$

e. Subtract: $(1 - x - x^3) - (x^3 + 2x^2 - x)$. *(Ex 4)* $-2x^3 - 2x^2 + 1$

f. The average retail price (in cents per kilowatt hour) of electricity for the years 2000 through 2005, is modeled by these polynomial functions. The variable x represents the number of years since 2000. *(Ex 5)*

Residential $R = 0.041x^2 + 0.009x + 8.334$ (highest price)

Commercial $C = 0.013x^2 + 0.137x + 7.555$

Industrial $I = 0.028x^2 + 0.037x + 4.756$ (lowest price)

What polynomial function is a model that describes how much higher the average retail price was in the residential sector than in the industrial sector? $f(x) = 0.013x^2 - 0.028x + 3.578$

ENGLISH LEARNERS

To help students understand the meaning of **monomial, binomial,** and **trinomial,** define the prefixes of each and show how it is used with different words.

mono = one; bi = two; tri: = three

Each prefix represents a number. Any word with the prefix mono indicates there is only one item. A word with the prefix bi indicates two items and a word with the prefix tri indicates three items.

Other words: monologue: a speech by one person; monoplane: a plane with one wing; bicycle: a vehicle with 2 wheels; bilingual: a person speaking two languages; triangle: a figure with 3 angles; triceratops: a dinosaur with 3 horns; tricycle: a vehicle with 3 wheels; trilogy: a set of 3 related books.

monomial: has 1 term. Example: $3x$
binomial: has 2 terms. Example $3x + 5$
trinomial: has 3 terms. Example $2x^2 + x - 2$

Practice Distributed and Integrated

*1. (7) **Geography** The table shows the relationship of the annual estimated population for three cities in the year 2005. The population in Oklahoma City, Oklahoma, is represented by the variable x.

a. Formulate Write a linear equation to approximate the population in Oklahoma City in 2005. $x + 5.354x + 0.683x = 3{,}736{,}275$

b. Estimate Find the approximate population in Oklahoma City in 2005. Round to the nearest hundred. 530,900

2005 City Population

City	Population
Oklahoma City	x
Chicago	$5.354x$
Arlington	$0.683x$
Total of 3 cities	3,736,275

2. (7) **Multi-Step** Twice a number is decreased by 9, and then multiplied by 4. The result is 8 less than 10 times the number. What is the number? −14

Simplify the expressions.

3. (3) $x^6(2x^2)$ $2x^8$

4. (3) $2(2x^2)^6$ $128x^{12}$

5. (3) $\frac{x^2}{2x^6}$ $\frac{1}{2}x^{-4}$

6. (7) **Geometry** Let x represent the first angle in a triangle. The second angle is twice the measure of the first. The third angle is triple the measure of the first. Write and solve a linear equation to find the measures of all three angles. $x + 2x + 3x = 180$; 30°, 60°, 90°

Solve the inequalities.

*7. (10) $-7 \leq -2x + 3 < 9$ $-3 < x \leq 5$

*8. (10) $\frac{3}{2}x + 2 < \frac{1}{2}x + 5$ $x < 3$

Evaluate.

9. (2) $(a - b) - a(-b)$ if $a = -5$ and $b = 3$ −23

10. (2) $(a - x)(x - a)$ if $a = -2$ and $x = 4$ −36

11. (2) $a^2 - y^3(a - y^2)y$ if $a = -2$ and $y = -3$ 895

Write each fraction or decimal as a percent.

12. (6) 0.05 5%

13. (6) $\frac{3}{10}$ 30%

14. (6) $\frac{4}{5}$ 80%

15. (6) 0.37 37%

*16. (8) **Error Analysis** Two scientists solved the following problem:

Sulfur is mixed with other chemicals to make sulfuric acid. If it takes 16 tons of sulfur to make 49 tons of sulfuric acid, how many tons of other constituents are needed to make 294 tons of acid? (Hint: Sulfuric acid is the total.) Which scientist solved the problem using the correct steps? Explain your reasoning.

Scientist A	Scientist B
$\frac{16}{49} = \frac{x}{294}$	$\frac{33}{49} = \frac{x}{294}$
$(16)(294) = 49x$	$(33)(294) = 49x$
$x = 96$ tons	$x = 198$ tons

16. Scientist B. The amount of other constituents is $49 - 16 = 33$ tons. The ratio is set up as $\frac{\text{amount of other constituents}}{\text{total amount of acid}}$.

INCLUSION

Suggest that students use different color pens or pencils to circle, underline, or mark the like terms in polynomials. Then tell students to combine the terms by color.

3 Practice

Math Conversations

Discussions to strengthen understanding.

Problem 2

Guide the students by asking them the following questions.

"How can you write twice a number?" $2x$

"How can you decrease this first term by 9?" $2x - 9$

"How can you write this expression multiplied by 4?" $4(2x - 9)$

"How can you write 8 less than 10 times a number?" $10x - 8$

"What is the equation you must solve?" $4(2x - 9) = 10x - 8$

"What is the value of x?" −14

Problem 16

"How many tons of sulfur are needed to make 49 tons of sulfuric acid?" 16

"How many tons of other constituents are needed to make 49 tons of sulfuric acid?" 33

"What is the ratio for other constituents to the 49 tons of sulfuric acid?" $\frac{33}{49}$

"Which scientist is correct?" Scientist B

TEACHER TIP

Review with students the definition of like terms. Use examples to show that x^2y and xy^2 are not like terms because the exponents are not with the correct variables. Have students think of terms and then state whether they are like terms or not.

Problem 21

Extend the Problem

"Neptune's distance from Earth is about 4.3×10^{12} meters. How many *more* seconds does it take light to reach Neptune than it takes light to reach Saturn from Earth? Round the answer to the nearest second." 9,930 seconds

Problem 22

Error Alert When dividing these expressions, students might subtract the exponents of 10 and divide the first terms, yielding an answer of 0.66793×10^8. Remind students that scientific notation requires the first term to be between 1 and 10. The correct answer is 6.6793×10^7.

Problem 26

Remind students that anything raised to the zero power has a value of 1. Thus, $5x^0 = 5(1) = 5$.

Problem 28

Point out that both **C** and **D** have 4 as the x-value. Tell students to substitute $x = 4$ first to either eliminate **C** and **D** or determine that the answer is **C** or **D**.

17. (8) **Chemistry** A formula requires that 20 kilograms (kg) of carbon be used to produce 160 kg of a compound. How many kilograms of other components are needed to make 640 kg of the compound? 560 kg

Justify **Determine if these statements are a tautology, a contradiction, or neither. Justify your answer by constructing truth tables.**

18. (Inv. 1) $\neg p \rightarrow q$ neither

19. (Inv. 1) $\neg p \vee q$ neither

18. neither;

p	q	$\neg p \rightarrow q$
T	T	T
T	F	T
F	T	T
F	F	F

19. neither;

p	q	$\neg p \vee q$
T	T	T
T	F	F
F	T	T
F	F	T

20. (10) **Consumer** Nerissa's car can travel between 380 and 410 miles on a full tank of gas. She filled her gas tank and drove 45 miles. How many more miles, m, can she drive without running out of gas? $335 \leq m \leq 365$

21. (3) **Astronomy** The speed of light is about 3×10^8 meters/second. If Saturn's distance from Earth is about 1.321×10^{12} meters, about how many seconds would it take light to reach Saturn from Earth? Round the answer to the nearest second. 4403 seconds

22. (3) **Earth Science** The garter snake is a small snake that is typically no more than 6×10^{-4} km in length. About how many garter snakes would it take to equal the circumference of the earth at the equator, if its circumference measures about 4.0076×10^4 km? Write the answer in scientific notation rounded to the nearest ten thousandth. 6.6793×10^7 snakes

Analyze **Determine if the expressions are polynomials. If the expression is a polynomial, rewrite it in standard form. If the expression is not a polynomial, explain why.**

***23.** (11) $5x^2 + 3x^4 + 2$ polynomial; $3x^4 + 5x^2 + 2$

***24.** (11) $\sqrt{3x + 5x^3}$ This is not a polynomial because of the radical.

Classify the polynomial expressions by their degree and by the number of terms.

***25.** (11) $7x^3 + 3x^2 + 5x$ cubic trinomial

***26.** (11) $x^1 + 5x^0$ linear binomial

Simplify the expression.

***27.** (11) $(7x^3 + 3x^2 + 5x) - (3x^3 + x)$ $(4x^3 + 3x^2 + 4x)$

28. (4) **Multiple Choice** Choose a letter that represents a set of x- and y-values that makes the equation $y = \frac{1}{2}x + 4$ true. **C**

A $x = 2,\ y = 4$
B $x = 6,\ y = 6$
C $x = 4,\ y = 6$
D $x = 4,\ y = 8$

Graphing Calculator **Multiply the matrices. Check using a graphing calculator.**

***29.** (9) $\begin{bmatrix} 2 & -3 & 4 \\ 5 & 8 & -1 \\ 7 & 0 & 9 \end{bmatrix} \cdot \begin{bmatrix} -4 & 7 \\ 0 & 1 \\ 3 & 6 \end{bmatrix}$ $\begin{bmatrix} 4 & 35 \\ -23 & 37 \\ -1 & 103 \end{bmatrix}$

***30.** (9) $\begin{bmatrix} 4 & -1 \\ 6 & -2 \end{bmatrix} \cdot \begin{bmatrix} -1 & \frac{1}{2} & 0 \\ -2 & 4 & -3 \end{bmatrix}$ $\begin{bmatrix} -2 & -2 & 3 \\ -2 & -5 & 6 \end{bmatrix}$

CHALLENGE

Add and subtract as indicated:

$4x^2 - 2x + 3 - [x^2 + 2 - (x + 2)]$
$3x^2 - x + 3$

LOOKING FORWARD

Understanding polynomials prepares students for

- **Lesson 19** Multiplying Polynomials
- **Lesson 23** Factoring Polynomials

Solving Inverse Variation Problems

Warm Up

1. **Vocabulary** Of the terms x, z, and 3, only the number 3 is a ________.
(8) constant

2. Is $(3, -3)$ a solution to the equation $3x - 7y = 15$? no
(7)

3. Graph $5x + 4y = 20$.
(5)

New Concepts

If the product of two variables is a constant, then the equation is an **inverse variation.**

$$xy = k \text{ or } y = \frac{k}{x}$$

Math Reasoning

Generalize Compare the relationship of the variables in a direct and inverse variation.

In an inverse variation, the product of the variables equals a constant. In a direct variation, the quotient of the variables equals a constant.

Both x and y are variables and k is a nonzero constant. The term k is also referred to as the constant of variation. You have previously learned about direct variations. Here are some differences between direct and inverse variations.

Direct Variation	Inverse Variation
As x increases, y increases.	As x increases, y decreases.
As x decreases, y decreases.	As x decreases, y increases.
The ratio $\frac{y}{x}$ is a constant.	The product yx is a constant.

3.
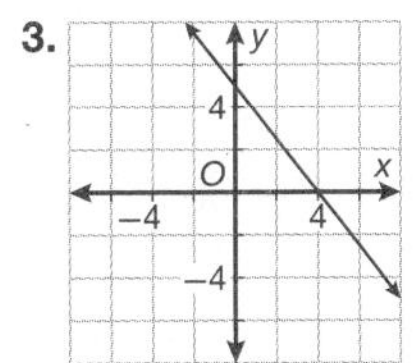

Example 1 Modeling Inverse Variation

The values in the table and the graph represent the equation $y = \frac{2}{x}$.

x	1	2	4
y	2	1	0.5

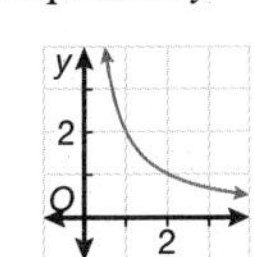

a. Is this equation an inverse variation? If so, find the constant of variation.

SOLUTION Multiply the x and y values in the data table.

x	1	2	4
y	2	1	0.5
xy	$(1)(2) = 2$	$(2)(1) = 2$	$(4)(0.5) = 2$

The equation is an inverse variation with a constant of variation equal to 2.

b. **Predict** What will the y value be when the x value is 8?

SOLUTION The product of x and y will be 2.

$$8y = 2$$

$$y = \frac{1}{4}$$

Online Connection
www.SaxonMathResources.com

MATH BACKGROUND

Students have a great deal of experience with direct variation equations, since linear equations of the form $y = ax$ represent direct variation relationships. In these equations, the ratio $\frac{y}{x}$ is as the slope of the line, and is constant for all ordered pairs on the line.

In inverse variation relationships, a different relationship between the variables exists. In an inverse variation, the product of the variables remains constant. So, inverse variation relationships can occur when two variables are multiplied and must have a constant product. For example, since the area of a rectangle is found by multiplying length and width, an inverse variation exists between these variables when the area is fixed. If the area must stay constant, increasing the length necessitates decreasing the width. As another example, if a chorus has only 30 minutes to perform, as the number of songs they sing increases, the length of each song must decrease.

1 Warm Up

In problem 3, suggest that students find and plot the intercepts to graph the line.

2 New Concepts

In this lesson, students solve problems involving inverse and joint variation. Variation problems represent one way in which the variables in an equation depend on each other.

Tell students that in an **inverse variation,** two variables have a constant product. Contrast this with direct variation, where two variables have a constant quotient. In a **joint variation,** one variable varies directly with the product of two or more other variables.

Additional Example 1

The data shown in the table represents the equation $y = \frac{8}{x}$.

x	1	2	4
y	8	4	2

a. Is this equation an inverse variation? If so, find the constant of variation. yes; 8

b. What will the y value be when the x value is 16? $y = \frac{1}{2}$

LESSON RESOURCES

Student Edition Practice Workbook 12
Reteaching Master 12
Adaptations Master 12
Challenge and Enrichment Master C12

Example 2

Error Alert Students sometimes test only the first few ordered pairs to see whether the products equal the same constant. Remind them that they must test every pair.

Additional Example 2

a. Determine if the data set shown represents an inverse variation. If so, find the constant of variation and the equation.

x	2	3	4	5
y	6	4	3	2.4

Inverse variation; the constant of variation is 12, so $y = \frac{12}{x}$.

b. Determine if this data set represents a direct or an inverse variation. If so, find the constant of variation and the equation.

x	3	4	5	6
y	6	8	10	12

Direct variation; the constant of variation is 2, so $y = 2x$.

Given a set of coordinates, it is possible to determine if they represent an inverse variation. By finding the constant of variation, it is possible to find the equation for the inverse variation.

Example 2 Testing for an Inverse Variation

a. Determine if the data set shown represents an inverse variation. If so, find the constant of variation and the equation.

x	1	2	3	4
y	3	1.5	1	0.75

SOLUTION Multiply the x and y coordinates to see if the products equal the same constant.

x	1	2	3	4
y	3	1.5	1	0.75
xy	$(1)(3) = 3$	$(2)(1.5) = 3$	$(3)(1) = 3$	$(4)(0.75) = 3$

Yes, each product is equal to 3, which is the constant of variation for the inverse variation $y = \frac{3}{x}$.

b. Determine if this data set represents a direct or an inverse variation. If so, find the constant of variation and the equation.

x	1	2	3	4
y	25	10	3	1

SOLUTION

Step 1: Before performing any calculations with the data, look at the basic relationship between x and y.

As x increases, does the value of y decrease? Yes. This could be an inverse variation and is definitely not a direct variation.

Step 2: Multiply the x and y coordinates to see if the products equal the same constant.

x	1	2	3	4
y	25	10	3	1
xy	25	20	9	4

The product xy is not the same from one set of coordinates to another, so the data set is not an inverse variation.

Caution

Check carefully to make sure that each product of the variables equals the same constant.

Reading Math

The expression $\frac{z}{xy} = k$ is read "z varies jointly as x and y." This means that z varies directly as the product of x and y.

A **joint variation** involves three variables, one of which depends on changes in the other two variables. A joint variation can be written as shown below.

$$\frac{z}{xy} = k$$

The variables are x, y, and z, and k is the nonzero constant of variation.

ALTERNATE METHOD FOR EXAMPLE 1

Have students graph the equation $y = \frac{2}{x}$ on a graphing calculator. Have them use the TRACE feature to verify that the ordered pairs in the table lie on the curve. For Part b, have students verify the results in the example by using the TRACE feature to find the value of y when x is 8. As an extension, have students use algebraic methods to determine other ordered pairs in the variation, then verify their results using the graphing calculator.

Example 3 Joint Variation

a. The force (F) on an object of mass m that causes it to move with acceleration a can be found using the equation $F = ma$. Is this an example of a joint variation? Explain.

SOLUTION In the equation shown, there are three variables, F, m, and a. The equation can be rewritten as $\frac{F}{ma} = 1$.

Since 1 is a constant, the equation $F = ma$ is a joint variation.

b. The kinetic energy (KE) of a moving object is based on its mass (m) and the square of its velocity (v^2). Use the data set below to see if this is a joint variation.

KE	2	9	24	50
m	1	2	3	4
v^2	4	9	16	25

SOLUTION Calculate the ratio $\frac{KE}{mv^2}$ for each set of data points to see if they equal a constant value.

KE	2	9	24	50
m	1	2	3	4
v^2	4	9	16	25
$\frac{KE}{mv^2}$	$\frac{1}{2}$	$\frac{1}{2}$	$\frac{1}{2}$	$\frac{1}{2}$

In each case the ratio is the same value: $\frac{1}{2}$. So this is a joint variation.

c. In an electric circuit, the electric power (P) is the product of the square of the current (I) and the electrical resistance (R). Write an equation that represents this relationship. Is it a joint variation?

SOLUTION The equation can be written as $P = I^2R$.

It is a joint variation with a constant of variation equal to 1.

Many real-world phenomena can be explained through direct, inverse, or joint variation. To determine which, if any, variation applies, look for the constant of variation.

Example 4 Determining the Type of Variation

a. Two objects of different masses experience a gravitational force of attraction. Isaac Newton found that this force is proportional to the product of the two masses. What kind of variation is this? Write the equation.

SOLUTION Define the variables m_1 and m_2 to represent the masses, and let F_g be the gravitational force of attraction. If F_g is proportional to the product of m_1 and m_2, then the equation can be written as $F_g = km_1m_2$.

Since there are two variables for mass, this represents a joint variation.

INCLUSION

Students might have trouble translating from a verbal description of a variation to equation form. Scaffold the problems by providing them with words and equations for generic variations. For example, the phrases x varies directly with y and x is proportional to y are written as $y = kx$ or $\frac{y}{x} = k$. The phrases *y varies inversely with x* and *x is inversely proportional to y* are written $xy = k$ or $y = \frac{k}{x}$.

Have students highlight key words and phrases (e.g. "is inversely proportional to") that indicate the type of variation. Then have them look for the verbal descriptions of the variables (which should lie before and after the phrase) that have the highlighted relationship. Then they can use the scaffolding to help them decide how to write the equation.

Example 3

Students with experience in physics might be familiar with these formulas in other forms. For example, $F = ma$ and $KE = \frac{mv^2}{2}$.

Extend the Example

For Example 3b, ask students to find the kinetic energy (KE) of a moving object if $m = 5$ and $v = 10$. $KE = 250$

Additional Example 3

a. Is the equation $d = rt$ an example of a joint variation? Explain. Yes. The equation can be rewritten as $\frac{d}{rt} = 1$ and 1 is a constant.

b. Does the data table below represent a joint variation?

x	4	16	36	64
y	1	2	3	4
t	2	4	6	8

yes

c. Does the equation $V = As^2$ represent a joint variation? yes

TEACHER TIP

Emphasize that in a joint variation one variable varies directly as a second variable *and* directly as a third variable. In the joint variation $\frac{P}{I^2R} = 1$, P varies directly with the I^2 and also with R.

Example 4

Students are given facts about the relationships between variables, and must determine the type of variation.

Additional Example 4

a. The area of a triangle is given by $A = \frac{1}{2}bh$, where b is the base and h is the height. What kind of variation is this? joint variation

Additional Example 4

b. The total cost of x number of shirts at $20 is an example of what kind of variation? Write the equation.
direct variation $T = 20x$

c. Give an example of an equation that is both a joint and an inverse variation.
Sample: $L = p\frac{d}{b}$

Extend the Example

The distance between Earth and the sun is 1.5×10^{11} m. The mass of Earth is 5.98×10^{24} kg, and the mass of the sun is 1.99×10^{30} kg. Use these facts and the given value for g to determine the gravitational force of attraction between Earth and the sun. about 3.53×10^{22}

Lesson Practice

Problem c

Scaffolding Have students test whether each product of x and y is equal to the same constant. Then, have them write the equation in the form $xy = k$. Finally, have them solve for y to write the equation.

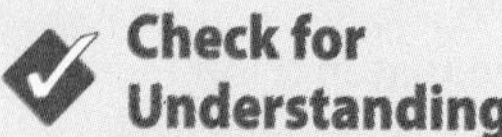

Check for Understanding

The question below helps assess the concepts taught in this lesson.

"Given a set of ordered pairs, how can you determine whether it shows a direct variation, an indirect variation, or neither?"
Find the product of each x and y pair. If all the products are the same constant, it's an inverse variation. Find the quotient of y and x for each pair. If all the quotients are the same constant, it's a direct variation.

b. Newton also found that the gravitational force of attraction, F_g, is inversely proportional to the square of the distance between the two masses. What kind of variation is this? Write the equation.

SOLUTION

Step 1: Define the variable d to represent the distance between the two masses.

Step 2: If F_g is inversely proportional to d^2, then the equation can be written as $F_g = \frac{k'}{d^2}$.

(The constant of variation k' is used to distinguish it from the constant of variation, k, in part **a.**) This equation represents an inverse variation with constant of variation k'.

c. Newton's Universal Law of Gravitation shows that the gravitational force of attraction is both a joint variation and an inverse variation. Use the results from parts **a** and **b** to show how this equation is derived.

SOLUTION

Step 1: Define the constant of variation g.

Step 2: F_g is inversely proportional to d^2 and directly proportional to m_1m_2. So the combined equation can be written as $F_g = g\frac{m_1m_2}{d^2}$.

This is Newton's Universal Law of Gravitation and is made up of both an inverse and a joint variation. The accepted numerical value for g is approximately 6.67×10^{-11}.

Math Reasoning

Connect Use your understanding of scientific notation to judge how strong the force of gravitation is.

Because the value of g includes a factor of 10^{-11}, gravitation is a very weak force.

Lesson Practice

a. (Ex 1) Look at the data set below. How can you tell if it represents an inverse variation? Multiply each xy pair to see if they equal the same constant, k.

x	1	2	3	4
y	4	2	$1\frac{1}{3}$	1

b. (Ex 1) Is $k = 3.5$ the constant of variation for this data set? Explain. No; The inverse variation in the data set has constant of variation $k = 1.5$.

x	3	4	5	6
y	0.5	0.375	0.3	0.25

c. (Ex 2) Determine if this data set is an inverse variation. If so, find the constant of variation and the equation.

x	$-\frac{1}{2}$	3	5	9
y	$-\frac{1}{2}$	$\frac{1}{12}$	$\frac{1}{20}$	$\frac{1}{36}$

c. The constant of variation is $k = \frac{1}{4}$, and the equation is $y = \frac{1}{4x}$.

ENGLISH LEARNERS

To help students distinguish among **direct, inverse,** and **joint variation,** discuss the meanings of the three words.

Direct means straightforward. Terms like direct quote and direct route indicate uncomplicated exactness. In a direct variation, one variable does what the other one does. If x increases, y increases.

Inverse means opposite. Remind students of inverse operations, like addition and subtraction. One operation is the opposite of the other. Likewise, in an inverse operation, one variable does the opposite of what the other does. If x increases, y decreases.

Joint means together. Two people might own a joint bank account. Countries work together to make joint declarations. In each case, two or more entities work together.

In a joint variation, both direct and inverse variations work together to determine one constant of variation.

d. This is a direct variation; The constant of variation is $k = 4.5$, and the equation is $y = 4.5x$.

d. (Ex 2) Determine the kind of variation represented by this data. Find the constant of variation and the equation for the data.

x	−2	8	10	20
y	−9	36	45	90

e. (Ex 2) Determine whether this is a direct or an inverse variation. If so, find the constant of variation and the equation. This is neither a direct nor an inverse variation.

x	1	2	3	4
y	2	6	8	10

f. Yes; Voltage is dependent on two variables, current and resistance, and the ratio of voltage and current × resistance is a constant.

f. (Ex 3) Is the equation $V = CR$, where V is voltage, C is current, and R is resistance, a joint variation? How do you know?

g. This is an inverse variation that can be written as $S = \frac{k}{P}$.

g. (Ex 3) **Economics** In economics, the graph of the *supply curve* has this behavior: As the supply (S) item decreases, the price (P) for the item increases. Likewise, when the supply of the item increases, the price decreases. The product of P and S is a constant. Name the type of variation that describes this economic phenomenon and write a generic equation.

h. (Ex 3) The potential energy (PE) of an object of mass m depends on the height (h) of the mass above Earth's surface. Use the data set at right to see if this is a joint variation. If so, find the constant of variation and the equation.
Yes; This is a joint variation, with constant of variation 9.8; The equation is $PE = 9.8mh$.

PE	m	h
196	2	10
588	3	20
1176	4	30
1960	5	40

i. This is an inverse variation that can be written as $I = \frac{k}{d^2}$, where k is the constant of variation.

i. (Ex 4) The intensity (I) of light is inversely proportional to the distance (d) from the light squared. Write an equation for this phenomenon.

j. This is a joint variation that can be written as $F_e = kq_1q_2$, where k is the constant of variation.

j. (Ex 4) Two electrically charged objects have a charge of q_1 and q_2. The electric force (F_e) between the two charges is directly proportional to the product of the two charges. Write an equation for this phenomenon.

k. (Ex 4) Coulomb's Law states that the electric force (F_e) between two objects of charge q_1 and q_2 is directly proportional to the product of the charges and inversely proportional to the square of the distance (d) between the charges. Write an equation for this phenomenon. $F_e = k\frac{q_1q_2}{d^2}$, where k is the constant of variation.

CHALLENGE

Under a given tension, the amount of stretch in a wire varies directly as the wire's length and inversely as the square of its diameter. A wire that is 3 m long and 2.0 mm in diameter stretches 1.0125 mm.

a. What is k, the constant of variation? 1.35

b. How much will a wire that is 4 meters long stretch if its diameter is 1.2 mm? (Note: assume both wires experience the same amount of tension.) 3.75 mm

Problem f

Error Alert Students might fail to recognize that there is a "hidden" factor of 1 on the right side of the equation $V = C \times R$. Remind them that the Identity Property of Multiplication states that $C \times R = 1 \times C \times R$.

Problem k

Scaffolding Remind them that d^2 goes in the denominator because it is inversely proportional to F, while q_1q_2 goes in the numerator because it is directly proportional to F. Point out that F is *directly* across from q_1q_2, whereas d^2 is in the *opposite* position from F: q_1q_2 is in the numerator, d^2 is in the denominator.

3 Practice

Math Conversations

Discussion to strengthen understandings.

Problem 4

Remind students that the sum of the angle measures in any triangle is 180°.

Problem 7

Guide students by asking the following questions:

"What are the three variables?" Numbers of runners (r), bicyclists (b), and walkers (w).

"In the given information, what is the product of b and w?" 20

"What is r?" 100

"Since r varies jointly as b and w, $r = kbw$. What is k?" 5

"If $r = kbw$ and we know $k = 5$, $r = 20$, and $w = 2$, what is b?" 2

Problem 14

Error Alert

A common error when evaluating this kind of expression is to "lose" negative signs. Suggest that students take a moment to simplify the expression to $-p^2 - pa + p^3$ before evaluating. Then, they can substitute values for a and p, using parentheses where necessary, and evaluate.

Problems 15 & 16

Extend the Problem

Have students graph the solutions on a number line.

Practice Distributed and Integrated

Analyze **Determine if each expression is a polynomial. If the expression is a polynomial, write it in standard form. If the expression is not a polynomial, explain why not.**

*1. (11) $\dfrac{3x + 7x^2}{10x^5}$ This is not a polynomial because it is a fraction.

*2. (11) $28x^2 - x^9 + 12x^7$ polynomial; $-x^9 + 12x^7 + 28x^2$

*3. (8) **Data Analysis** Two scientists solved the following problem:

It takes 900 kg of acetylene to make 2400 kg of a compound. How many kilograms of other components will be required to make 3600 kg of the compound? Which scientist solved the problem using the correct steps? Explain your reasoning. Scientist A; Scientist B found the amount of acetylene required.

Scientist A	Scientist B
$\dfrac{1500}{2400} = \dfrac{x}{3600}$	$\dfrac{900}{2400} = \dfrac{x}{3600}$
$\dfrac{5}{8} = \dfrac{x}{3600}$	$\dfrac{3}{8} = \dfrac{x}{3600}$
$8x = 5(3600)$	$8x = 3(3600)$
$x = 2250$ kg	$x = 1350$ kg

*4. (7) **Geometry** An isosceles triangle has two angles that each measure $x°$. The third angle is 1.75 times the measure of either angle. Write and solve a linear equation to find the measure of each angle. $2x + 1.75x = 180$; 48°, 48°, 84°

Determine the constant k, then solve the problem.

*5. (12) The number of revolutions per minute (RPM) varies inversely as the number of teeth in the gear. If 40 teeth result in 120 RPM, what would the RPM be if the gear had 30 teeth? $k = 4800$; 160 RPM

*6. (12) The number of students in every class varies directly with the number of basketballs. For one class there are 8 students and 2 basketballs. If in another class there are 7 basketballs, how many students are in this class? $k = 4$; 28 students

*7. (12) The number of runners varies jointly as bicyclists and walkers. If 100 runners went with 4 bicyclists and 5 walkers, how many bicyclists would go with 20 runners and 2 walkers? $k = 5$; 2 bicyclists

Simplify the expressions.

8. (3) $5x^7(3^3xy^2)$ $135x^8y^2$

9. (3) $\left(\dfrac{5xy^3}{2x^3y^2z^{-4}}\right)^2$ $\dfrac{25y^2z^8}{4x^4}$

10. (3) $\dfrac{2^{-2}}{x^{-6}}$ $\frac{1}{4}x^6$

11. (3) **Earth Science** The typical length of a green frog is about 5 to 10 cm. If a green frog is about 7.5×10^{-5} km, about how many green frogs would it take to equal the diameter of the Earth? The diameter is about 1.2753×10^4 km. Round the answer to the nearest ten thousandth. 1.7004×10^8 frogs

Evaluate.

12. (1) $-8 - 3^2 - (-2)^2 - 3(-2) + 2$ -13

13. (1) $-\{-[-5(-3 + 2) 7]\}$ 35

14. (2) $-p^2 - p(a - p^2)$ if $a = 4$ and $p = -3$ -24

Solve the inequalities.

15. (10) $-9 \le 2x - 5 < 9$ $-2 \le x < 7$

16. (10) $-\frac{1}{2}x + 7 \ge 15$ $x \le -16$

City	Population
Albuquerque	$0.151x$
Madison	$0.336x$
Phoenix	x
Total of 3 cities	2,185,816

2005 City Population

*17. (7) **Geography** The table shows the relationship of the annual estimated population for three cities in the year 2005. The population in Phoenix, Arizona, is represented by the variable x.

a. **Formulate** Write a linear equation to approximate the population in Phoenix in 2005. $x + 0.336x + 0.151x = 2{,}185{,}816$

b. **Estimate** Find the approximate population of Phoenix in 2005. Round to the nearest thousand. 1,470,000

18. (7) **Multi-Step** The number of ducks on the pond tripled when the new flock landed. Then, 11 more ducks came. The resulting number of ducks was 13 less than 4 times the original number. How many ducks were there to begin with? 24

Write each fraction or decimal as a percent.

19. (6) 1.3 130% 20. (6) $\frac{5}{8}$ 62.5% 21. (6) $\frac{13}{20}$ 65% 22. (6) 0.4 40%

23. (8) **Chemistry** A formula required that 500 kilograms (kg) of sulfur be used to produce 3000 kg of a compound. How many kilograms of other materials are needed to make 6000 kg of the new compound? 5000 kg

24. (4) **Multiple Choice** Which set of x- and y-values would make the equation $y = \frac{3}{4}x - 1$ true? B

A $x = 8, y = -5$ **B** $x = -8, y = -7$

C $x = 4, y = -2$ **D** $x = -8, y = 7$

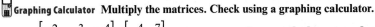

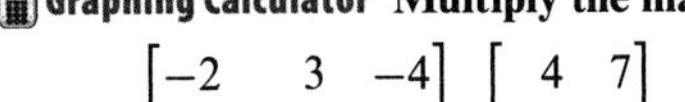
Graphing Calculator **Multiply the matrices. Check using a graphing calculator.**

*25. (9) $\begin{bmatrix} -2 & 3 & -4 \\ 0 & -3 & -1 \\ 5 & 0 & 2 \end{bmatrix} \cdot \begin{bmatrix} 4 & 7 \\ -6 & 1 \\ 3 & 6 \end{bmatrix}$ *26. (9) $\begin{bmatrix} -2 & -1 \\ 6 & 4 \end{bmatrix} \cdot \begin{bmatrix} -1 & 0 & 1 \\ 0 & 1 & 0 \end{bmatrix}$

25. $\begin{bmatrix} -38 & -35 \\ 15 & -9 \\ 26 & 47 \end{bmatrix}$

26. $\begin{bmatrix} 2 & -1 & -2 \\ -6 & 4 & 6 \end{bmatrix}$

27. (3) **Astronomy** The speed of light is about 3×10^8 meters/second. If Saturn is about 1.35×10^{12} meters from the sun, how many seconds would it take light to reach Saturn from the Sun? Round the answer to the nearest hundredth of a second. 4500 s

Justify **Determine if these statements are a tautology, a contradiction, or neither. Justify your answer by constructing truth tables.**

28. (Inv. 1) $(p \wedge q) \rightarrow \neg p$ 29. (Inv. 1) $(p \vee q) \vee q$

30. (5) **Justify** Does the Commutative Property hold true for matrix subtraction? Justify your answer.

No; Sample: $\begin{bmatrix} 3 & 5 \\ 9 & 0 \end{bmatrix} - \begin{bmatrix} 1 & 0 \\ 2 & 6 \end{bmatrix} = \begin{bmatrix} 2 & 5 \\ 7 & -6 \end{bmatrix}$ but $\begin{bmatrix} 1 & 0 \\ 2 & 6 \end{bmatrix} - \begin{bmatrix} 3 & 5 \\ 9 & 0 \end{bmatrix} = \begin{bmatrix} -2 & -5 \\ -7 & 6 \end{bmatrix}$.

28. neither;

p	q	$(p \wedge q)$	$(p \wedge q) \rightarrow \neg p$
T	T	T	F
T	F	F	T
F	T	F	T
F	F	F	T

29. neither;

p	q	$(p \vee q)$	$(p \vee q) \vee q$
T	T	T	T
T	F	T	T
F	T	T	T
F	F	F	F

Problem 17

Extend the Problem

Have students find the populations of Albuquerque and Madison. Have them find the percent of the total population that is represented by each city.

Problem 23

Suggest that students use reasoning and mental math to solve. If 3000 kg of compound contains 500 kg of sulfur, the compound is $\frac{1}{6}$ sulfur and $\frac{5}{6}$ other materials. So, 6000 kg of the new compound is $\frac{5}{6}$ other materials. $\frac{5}{6}$ of $6000 = 5000$.

Problem 27

Remind students to use the formula $d = rt$. Since the problem asks them to find time, they might choose to think of the formula in another form, $t = \frac{d}{r}$. Remind them that to divide numbers in scientific notation, they can divide the decimal numbers first, then divide the powers of 10. The quotient is the product of those quotients.

Problem 30

Remind students that the Commutative Property is sometimes called the Order Property, and states that the order in which numbers appear in an operation expression does not affect the answer. For example, $7 + 3 = 3 + 7$.

LOOKING FORWARD

Solving problems with inverse variation prepares students for

- **Lesson 18** Calculating with Units of Measure
- **Lesson 100** Graphing Rational Functions I

LAB

3

Materials

- graphing calculator

Discuss

In this lab, students will explore the calculator menu functions value, zero, minimum, maximum and intercept.

Define zero, minimum and maximum of quadratic functions, and intersection point of a system of equations.

Calculating *y*-Values and Roots

Moving the cursor to the approximate location of the zero is important because more complex functions have more than one zero.

Error Alert When determining a zero of the function, the cursor must cross the *x*-axis. **ERR: NO SIGN CHNG** will be shown indicating no sign change if the axis is not crossed.

Calculating Minimums and Maximums

Determining the minimum or maximum of a parabola means to locate its vertex.

LAB

3

Calculating Points on a Graph

Graphing Calculator Lab (Use with Lessons 13, 15, and 30)

Calculating *y*-Values and Roots

A graphing calculator can be used to calculate *y*-values and zeros of equations. Use the equation $y = 2x - 4$ and find the *y*-values for $x = 3.7$ and $x = 0$. Then find the zero.

Graphing Calculator Tip

For help with graphing equations, see the graphing calculator keystrokes on page 19.

1. Enter the equation into the [Y=] editor.
2. Graph the equation.
3. Calculate the *y*-values.

   Press [2nd] [TRACE] to open the CALC menu, and select **1: value.** Enter the *x*-value and press [ENTER]. The *x*- and *y*-values will be displayed at the bottom of the screen and highlighted on the graph.

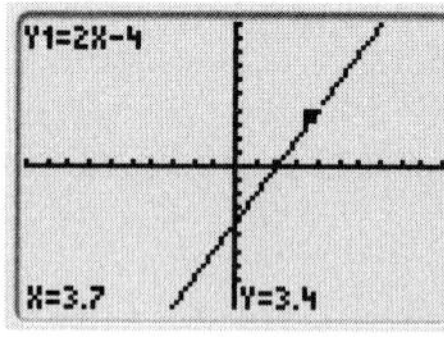

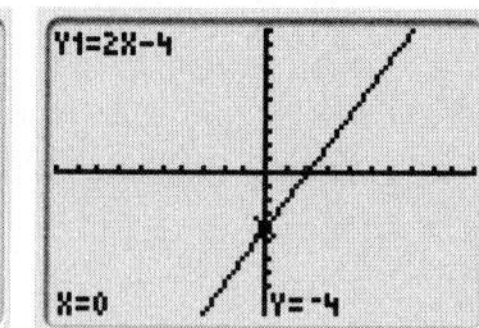

4. Calculate the zero.

   Press [2nd] [TRACE] and select **2: zero.** Use the arrow keys [◄] [▲] [▼] [►] to move the cursor to the left of the zero and press [ENTER]. Move the cursor to the right of the zero and press [ENTER]. Move the cursor to the approximate location of the zero and press [ENTER]. The zero will be displayed at the bottom of the screen and highlighted on the graph.

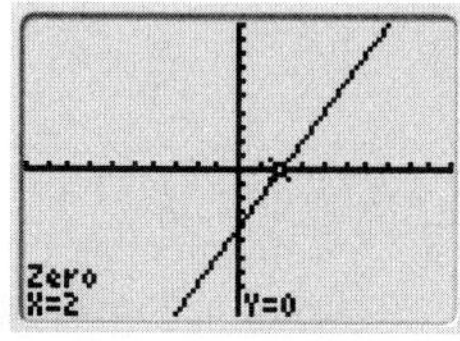

Calculating Minimums and Maximums

A graphing calculator can be used to find minimums and maximums.

Find the minimum of $y = x^2 + 3x - 4$.

1. Enter the equation into the [Y=] editor.
2. Graph the equation.
3. Calculate the minimum.

Press 2nd TRACE and select **3: minimum.** Use the arrow keys ◀ ▲ ▼ ▶ to move the cursor to the left of the minimum and press ENTER. Move the cursor to the right of the minimum and press ENTER. Move the cursor to the approximate location of the minimum and press ENTER. The minimum will be displayed at the bottom of the screen and highlighted on the graph.

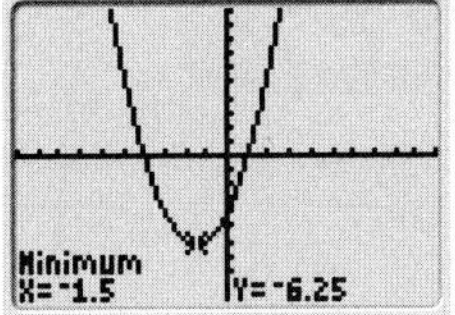

4. Calculate the maximum.

   The same process can be repeated to find the maximum of a parabola like $y = -x^2 + 3x - 4$. Simply select **4: maximum** from the CALC menu and repeat the same steps.

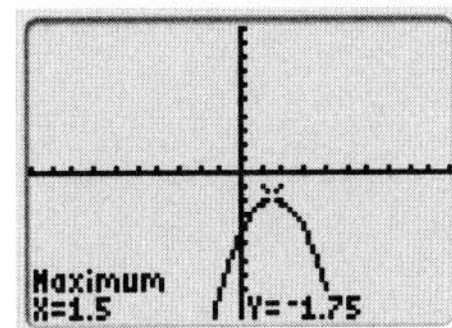

Calculating an Intersection Point

A graphing calculator can be used to find the intersection of two lines. Find the intersection of $y = x - 5$ and $y = -3x + 7$.

1. Enter the equations into the Y= editor.
2. Graph the equations.
3. Press 2nd TRACE and select **5: intersect.** Press ENTER to select the first line, and then ENTER to select the second line. Use the arrow keys ◀ ▲ ▼ ▶ to move the cursor to the approximate location of the intersection and press ENTER. The solution is displayed as a decimal at the bottom of the screen.

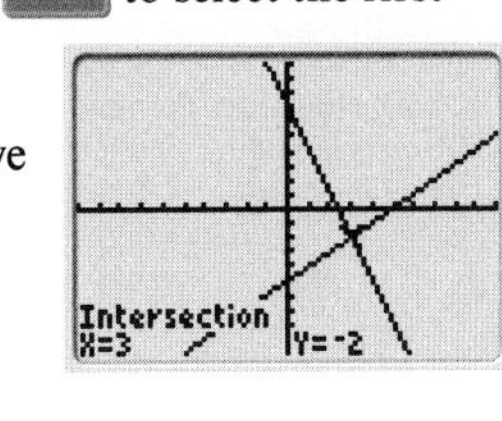

Graphing Calculator Practice

a. Use a graphing calculator to find the zero of $y = -17x + 51$. $x = 3$

b. Use a graphing calculator to find the maximum of the parabola $y = -x^2 - 4x + 5$. (−2, 9)

c. Use a graphing calculator to find the intersection of $y = -x + 2$ and $y = -5x - 1$. (−.75, 2.75)

a.

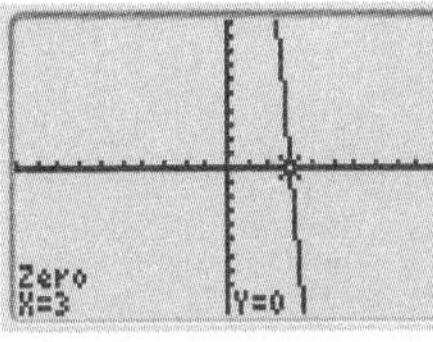

b.

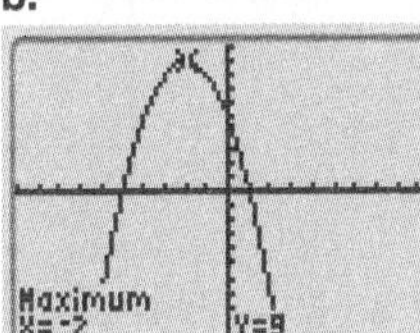

c.

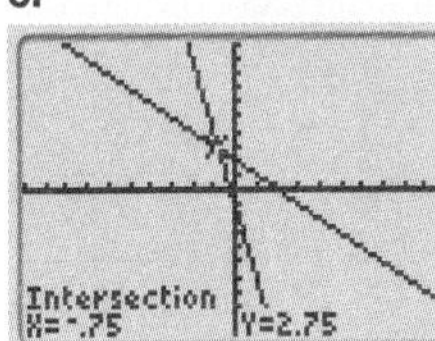

Moving the cursor to the left and right of the vertex defines the interval where the vertex is located. Find the maximum only on a parabola opening downward and find the minimum only on a parabola opening upward.

Calculating an Intersection Point

After the first line is selected the cursor automatically jumps to the second line.

It is possible to find the intersection point without moving the cursor. Pressing ENTER three times will find the intersection of two lines.

Practice Problems

TEACHER TIP

Use the CALCULATE menu for all of the problems.

Determining the zero of a function means finding x when $y = 0$.

LESSON 13

Graphing Linear Equations I

Warm Up

1. **Vocabulary** The vertical line test is used to determine if a graph is that of a function. (4)

2. Subtract $-8 - (-6)$. -2 (SB)

3. Evaluate $-5x + 3y$ for $x = -2$ and $y = -3$. 1 (2)

New Concepts

An equation such as $y = 2x - 3$ is a linear equation in two variables. An ordered pair (x, y) is a solution to an equation in two variables if substituting the values of both x and y into the equation produces a true statement. For example, $(4, 5)$ is a solution to $y = 2x - 3$ since $5 = 2(4) - 3$. The graph of an equation in two variables is the set of all points (x, y) that are solutions to the equation.

Graphing Equations in Two Variables

Step 1: Construct a table of values. Choose a reasonable value for x and solve the equation for y. Repeat this step several times.

Step 2: Plot the points represented by the solutions to the equation.

Step 3: Connect the points to form a line. Extend the line and draw arrowheads on the ends to indicate that the line extends to infinity.

Math Reasoning

Verify Have students use a graphing calculator to check the y values.

Example 1 Graphing a Linear Equation Using a Solution Table

Graph the equation $y = -2x + 1$.

SOLUTION

Construct a table of values.

x	-2	-1	0	1	2
y	5	3	1	-1	-3

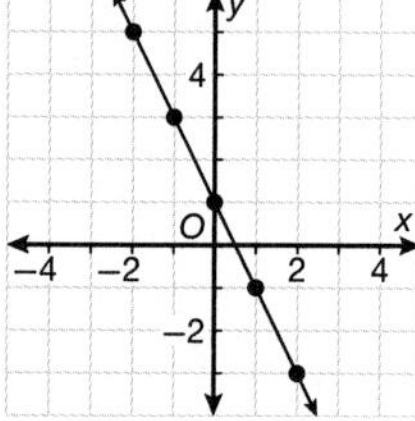

Plot and connect the points. The points should form a line.

The points where the graph intersects the axes on the coordinate plane are called the **intercepts**. The point where the graph intersects the x-axis is called the **x-intercept**, and the point where the graph intersects the y-axis is called the **y-intercept**.

Online Connection
www.SaxonMathResources.com

LESSON 13

1 Warm Up

Remind students that a horizontal line is a function.

2 New Concepts

In this lesson, students learn to solve linear equations in two variables by graphing.

Explain that a linear equation in two variables has an infinite number of solutions. The graph of a linear equation is a line on the coordinate plane and each point which lies on the line is a solution to the equation.

Example 1

This example shows students one way to graph a linear equation by using a solution table.

Additional Example 1

Graph the equation $y = 3x - 2$.

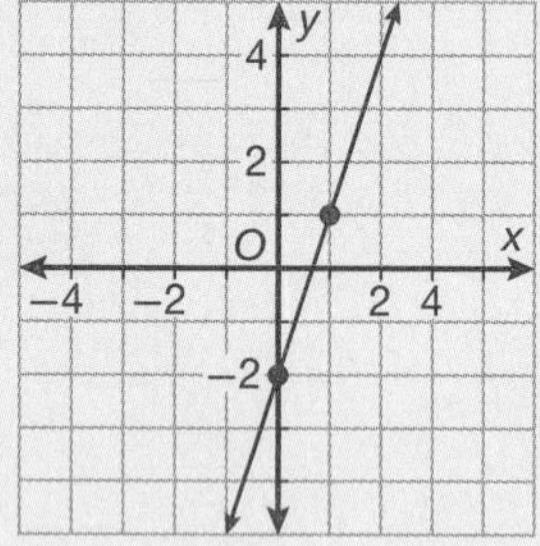

LESSON RESOURCES

Student Edition Practice Workbook 13
Reteaching Master 13
Adaptations Master 13
Challenge and Enrichment Master C13

MATH BACKGROUND

There are different kinds of equations that have results which can be graphed.

An equation in one variable has one solution and can be graphed on a number line. The graph can also be displayed on a coordinate plane. For an equation such as $x = 2$, the graph of the solution is a vertical line, showing that the value of x doesn't change for any value of y. The graph of an equation such as $y = 2$ is a horizontal line, showing that any change in the value of x does not affect the value of y.

A linear equation shows the relationship between two variables. If the slope is positive, the value of x increases as the value of y increases. If the slope is negative, the value of x decreases as the value of y increases.

86 Saxon Algebra 2

Graphing a Linear Equation Using Intercepts	
Find the x-intercept.	Let $y = 0$. Solve the equation for x.
Find the y-intercept.	Let $x = 0$. Solve the equation for y.
Plot and connect the intercepts.	
Extend the line and add arrowheads to the ends.	

Example 2 Graphing a Linear Equation Using Intercepts

Graph $3x - 2y = 6$ using the intercepts.

SOLUTION

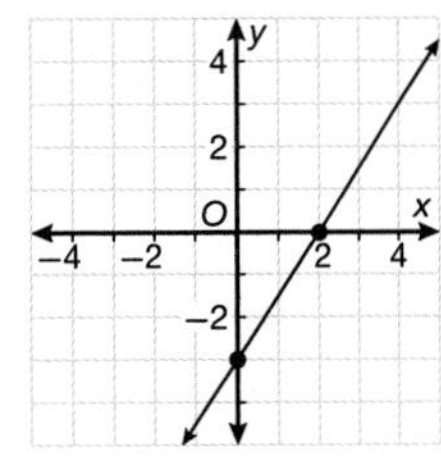

Let $y = 0$. Solve for x.

$$3x - 2(0) = 6$$
$$\frac{3x}{3} = \frac{6}{3}$$
$$x = 2$$

Let $x = 0$. Solve for y.

$$3(0) - 2y = 6$$
$$\frac{-2y}{-2} = \frac{6}{-2}$$
$$y = -3$$

Plot and connect points $(2, 0)$ and $(0, -3)$. Extend the line through the points and draw arrows on the ends of the line.

Caution

When finding the x intercept, do not make x equal 0. Make $y = 0$ then solve for x.

Slope of a Line

The slope of a line is the ratio of the vertical change (rise) to the horizontal change (run).

If (x_1, y_1) and (x_2, y_2) are the coordinates of any two points on the same line, the slope m of that line is calculated using the formula:

$$m = \frac{y_2 - y_1}{x_2 - x_1} = \frac{rise}{run}$$

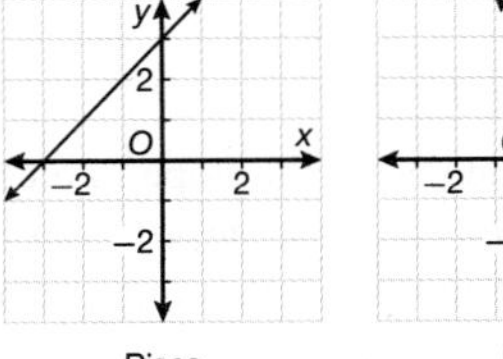

Rises

Falls

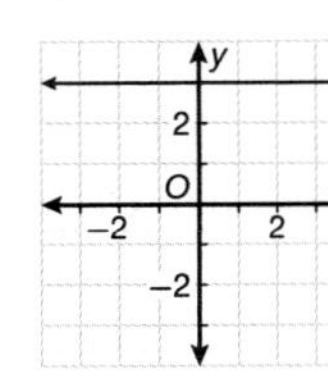

Horizontal

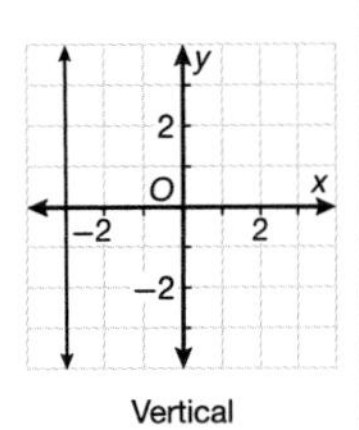

Vertical

Example 2

In this example, students graph the equation of a line using its x- and y-intercepts.

Error Alert Students may set $x = 0$ when finding the x-intercepts and $y = 0$ when finding the y-intercept. Graph a point on each axis such as $(1, 0)$ and $(0, 3)$. Lead students to understand that when a line intersects the x-axis its y-coordinate is 0, and when it intersects the y-axis its x-coordinate is 0.

Additional Example 2

Graph $4x + 5y = 20$ using the intercepts.

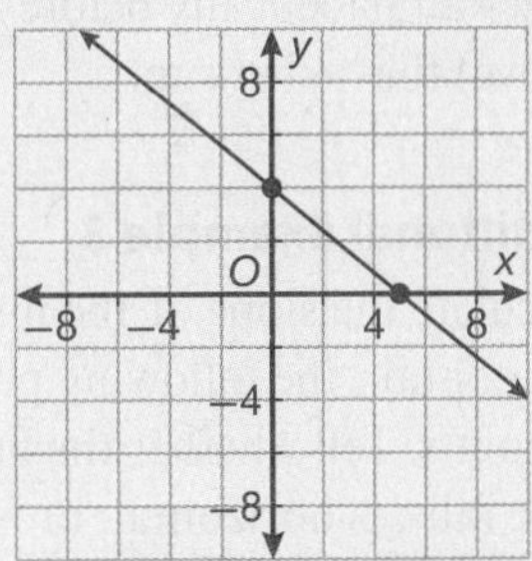

ENGLISH LEARNERS

For example 2, explain the meaning of the word intercept. Say:

"The word intercept means to interrupt progress. In math, the word intercept is a point where the graph crosses a coordinate axis."

Graph the line $x + y = 4$ on the board. Make sure the graph shows the x and y intercepts clearly. Point to the x-intercept and say:

"The line has an intercept at $x = 4$."

Have students identify the point where the line intercepts the y-axis answering with the sentence: "The y-intercept of the line is at $y = \ldots$." 4

Example 3

In this example, students learn to use the slope of a line to classify the line as rising, falling, horizontal, or vertical.

Error Alert Watch for students who think that a fraction with a zero in the denominator is equal to zero. Remind students that a vertical line has no slope, not zero slope.

TEACHER TIP

Students might incorrectly use the slope formula as $\frac{run}{rise}$. To help them remember that rise is in the numerator of the ratio, tell students that the "i" in rise, comes alphabetically before (above) the "u" in run.

Additional Example 3

Calculate the slope of the lines that contain the following pairs of points. Tell whether the line rises, falls, is horizontal, or is vertical.

a. (4, 5), (0, 3) $\frac{1}{2}$, rises

b. (0, −3), (7, −3) 0, horizontal

c. (3, 8), (3, −2) undefined, vertical

d. (2, 3), (−5, 4) $-\frac{1}{7}$, falls

Example 3 Classifying Lines Using Slope

Calculate the slope of the lines that contain the following pairs of points. Tell whether the line rises, falls, is horizontal, or is vertical.

a. (−2, 3), (−1, 5)

SOLUTION

$m = \frac{5-3}{-1-(-2)} = \frac{2}{1} = 2$ Because m is positive, the line rises.

Math Reasoning

Verify If the order of the coordinates in the slope equation were reversed, would the value of the slope change?

b. (−4, −1), (2, −1)

SOLUTION

$m = \frac{-1-(-1)}{2-(-4)} = \frac{0}{6} = 0$ Because $m = 0$, the line is horizontal.

c. (6, −2), (6, −3)

SOLUTION

$m = \frac{-3-(-2)}{6-6} = \frac{-1}{0}$ Because m is undefined, the line is vertical.

d. (3, 7), (−1, 10)

SOLUTION

$m = \frac{10-7}{-1-3} = \frac{3}{-4}$ Because m is negative, the line falls.

The Slope-Intercept Form of a Linear Equation

A linear equation written in the form $y = mx + b$ is written in **slope-intercept form,** where m is the slope of the line and b is the y-intercept.

In the equation $y = -\frac{2}{3}x + 4$, the slope is $-\frac{2}{3}$ and the y-intercept is 4.

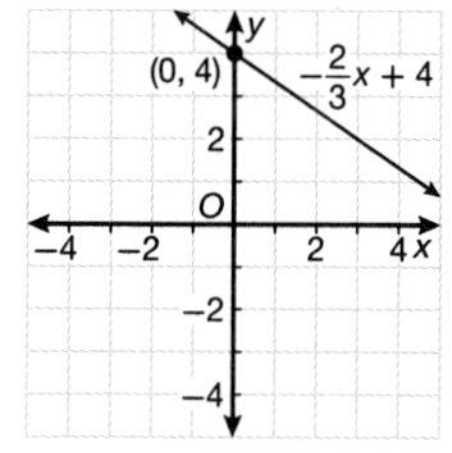

A line can be graphed using the slope-intercept form by plotting the y-intercept first, then using the slope to move to and plot another point. The slope is like a set of directions that indicate how many units to move and in which direction.

Moving from Point to Point Using the Slope			
Positive slope	$\frac{up}{right}$	or	$\frac{down}{left}$
Negative slope	$\frac{up}{left}$	or	$\frac{down}{right}$

ALTERNATE METHOD FOR EXAMPLE 3

Students can graph each pair of points and draw a line connecting the two points to determine whether the line rises, falls, is horizontal, or is vertical.

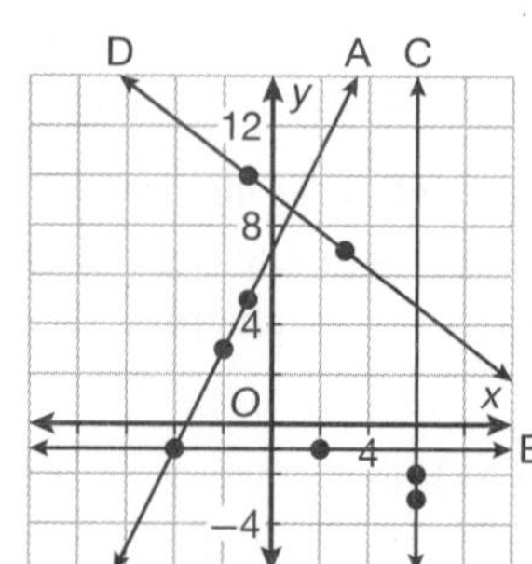

Example 4 Graphing a Line in Slope-Intercept Form

Identify the slope and y-intercept of the line with the given equation. Graph the line.

a. $y = -\frac{1}{2}x + 3$

SOLUTION

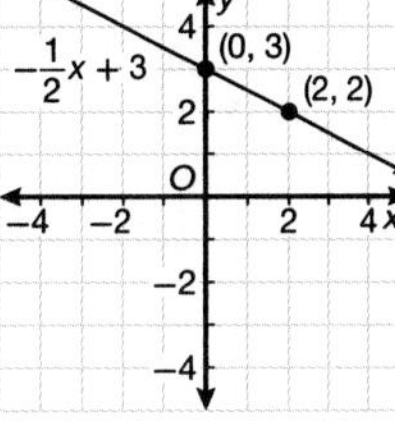

The equation is in the form $y = mx + b$. The slope of the line is $-\frac{1}{2}$ and the y-intercept is 3.

Plot the y-intercept (0, 3).

From (0, 3), move down 1 and 2 to the right to plot another point at (2, 2). Draw a line through (0, 3) and (2, 2).

b. $3x - 2y = 6$

SOLUTION

Rewrite the equation in slope-intercept form by solving for y.

$3x - 2y = 6$ Subtract $3x$ from both sides.

$\underline{-3x \quad = -3x}$

$\frac{-2y}{-2} = \frac{-3x + 6}{-2}$ Divide each term by −2.

$y = \frac{3}{2}x - 3$ The line has a slope of $\frac{3}{2}$ and a y-intercept of −3.

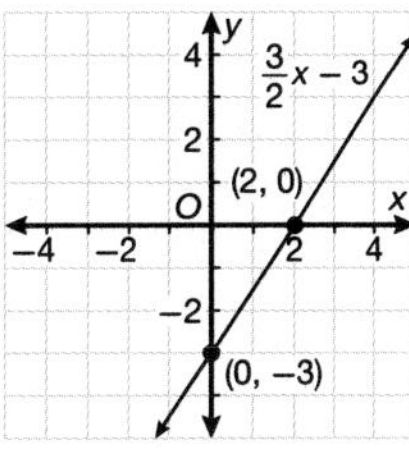

Plot the y-intercept (0, −3).

From (0, −3), move up 3 and 2 to the right to plot another point at (2, 0). Draw a line through (0, −3) and (2, 0).

Caution

When dividing by a coefficient to isolate y, divide every term in the equation, not just the term with x.

Example 5 Application: Railroads

A section of the Lookout Mountain Incline Railway in Tennessee has a vertical change of 1 mile upward for every 1.37 miles it moves along horizontally. What is the slope of the railroad for this section?

SOLUTION

The slope of the railroad can be calculated using $m = \frac{\text{rise}}{\text{run}}$.

The rise = 1 mi and the run = 1.37 mi.

The slope $= \frac{1 \text{ mi}}{1.37 \text{ mi}}$

$= \frac{1}{1.37}$

$= 0.73$.

Hint

Notice that the units must be the same when you are finding the slope so that they cancel out.

Example 4

In this example, students are given equations in slope-intercept form (Example 4a) and standard form (Example 4b) and use the slope and y-intercept to graph the line.

Additional Example 4

Identify the slope and y-intercept of the line with the given equation. Graph the line.

a. $y = -x - 3$ $m = -1$, y-intercept = −3

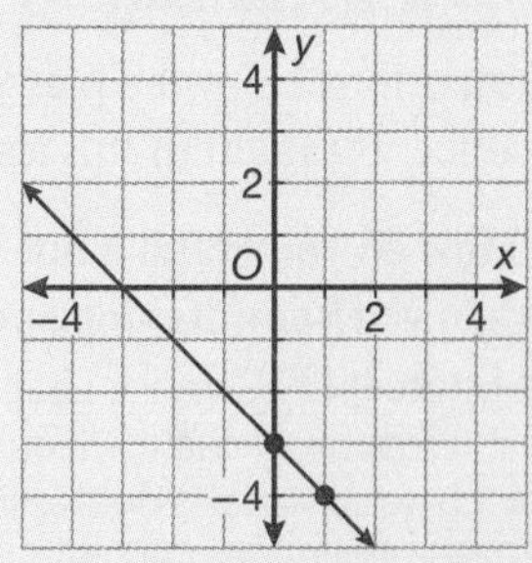

b. $-5x + 2y = 10$ $m = \frac{5}{2}$, y-intercept = 5

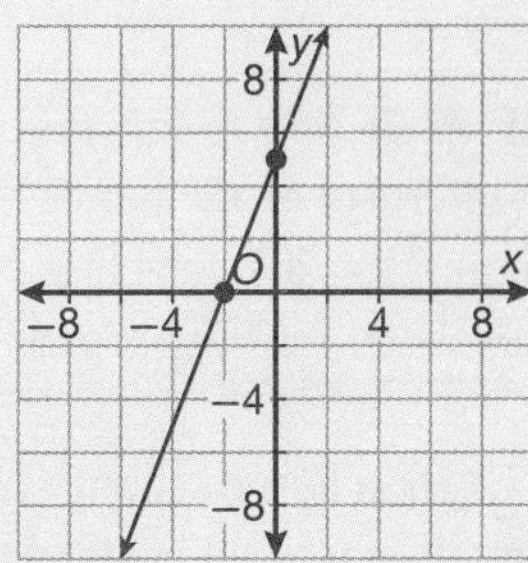

Example 5

Extend the Example

Have students use the value of the slope to check that this section of the railway rises. The slope is positive, so the section rises.

Additional Example 5

A ramp has a vertical change of 5.5 inches for every 10 inches of length. What is the slope of the ramp? 0.55

Lesson Practice

Problems c–e

Scaffolding Suggest that students label the values for x_1, x_2, y_1, and y_2 above each ordered pair.

Error Alert Errors in sign are common when finding slope. Encourage students to write each step when finding slope using the slope formula. They should only use mental math when checking their answers.

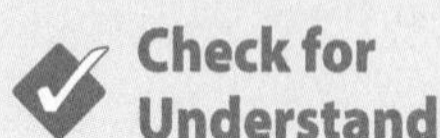

Check for Understanding

The questions below help assess the concepts taught in this lesson.

1. **"How do you graph a line when you know its slope and y-intercept?"** Sample: Graph the y-intercept and use the slope to plot a second point on the line. Start at the y-intercept and move up or down (depending on the sign of the rise), then move left or right (depending on the sign of the run).
2. **"Explain how to find the x-intercept of the line $6x + 2y = 8$."** Sample: Substitute 0 into the equation for y and solve for x.
3. **"Explain how to change an equation written in standard form to slope-intercept form."** Sample: Solve the equation for y.

Lesson Practice

a.

x	y
2	2
4	1
6	0

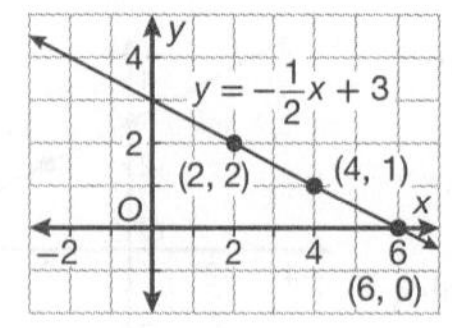

b.

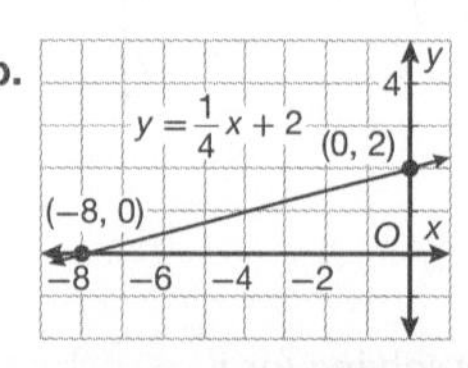

a. Graph the equation $y = -\frac{1}{2}x + 3$ by constructing a table of values. *(Ex 1)* (Hint: Choose x-values that are multiples of 2.)

b. Graph $-x + 4y = 8$ using the intercepts. *(Ex 2)*

Calculate the slope of the lines that contain the following pairs of points. Tell whether the line rises, falls, is horizontal, or is vertical. *(Ex 3)*

c. $(-3, 5)$, $(5, -6)$ $\quad -\frac{11}{8}$; falls

d. $(0, 4)$, $(-2, 0)$ $\quad$ 2; rises

e. $(-4, 3)$, $(8, 3)$ $\quad$ 0; horizontal

f. Identify the slope and y-intercept of the line $y = \frac{1}{3}x + 2$. Graph the line. *(Ex 4)*

g. **Geography** A section of the Uncanoonuc Mountains, called the South Mountain USC Trail, is located in New Hampshire. The trail has a vertical change of about 24 feet vertically for every 50 feet it moves along horizontally. What is the slope of the trail? *(Ex 5)* $\frac{12}{25}$

Practice Distributed and Integrated

f. $m = \frac{1}{3}$; (0, 2);

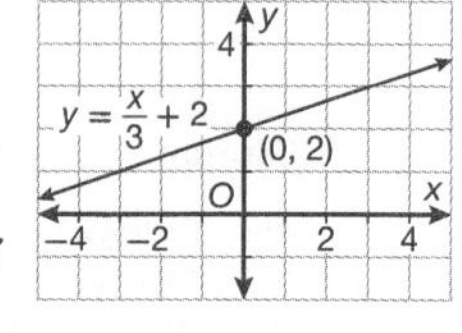

Determine the constant k, and solve the problem.

***1.** *(12)* **Multi-Step** The number of elk varied inversely as the number of deer and directly as the number of antelope. When there were 75 elk, there were 85 deer and 15 antelope. How many deer were there when there were 20 elk and 30 antelope? Round the answer down to the nearest whole number. $k = 425$; 637 deer

***2.** *(12)* **Formulate** The number of daisies varied inversely as the number of sunflowers and directly as the number of roses. When there were 65 daisies, there were 15 roses and 3 sunflowers. How many sunflowers were there when there were 5 daisies and 100 roses? $k = 13$; 260 sunflowers

3.

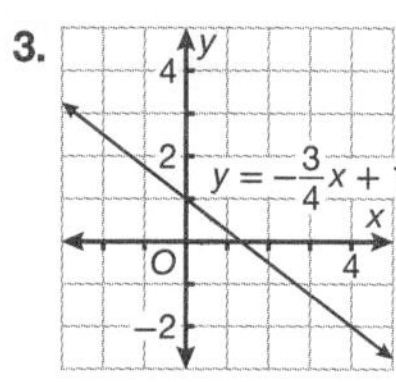

***3.** *(13)* Graph the equation $y = -\frac{3}{4}x + 1$ by constructing a table of values.

***4.** *(13)* Graph $-2x - y = 3$ using the intercepts. See Additional Answers.

***5.** *(8)* **Error Analysis** Two farmers solved the following problem:

Strawberries varied jointly as plums and tomatoes. If 500 strawberries went with 4 plums and 25 tomatoes, how many plums would go with 40 strawberries and 2 tomatoes?

Farmer A
$500 = k(4)(25)$
$k = 5$
$40 = 5(p)(2)$
$p = 4$ plums

Farmer B
$500 = k\frac{(25)}{(4)}$
$k = 80$
$40 = 80\frac{(25)}{(p)}$
$p = 50$ plums

Which farmer solved the problem using the correct steps? Explain your reasoning. Farmer A; Farmer B solved the problem as if it involved both direct and inverse variation.

INCLUSION

Visually impaired students may have difficulty plotting points on a coordinate grid. If possible show the examples using a projection method which enlarges the coordinate plane. Supply students with enlarged copies of the coordinate plane to use with the lesson.

Calculate the slope of the lines that contain the following pairs of points. Tell whether the line rises, falls, is horizontal, or is vertical.

*6. (13) $(-2, 0), (7, -5)$ $-\frac{5}{9}$; falls

7. (13) $(0, 4), (-2, 0)$ 2; rises

*8. (13) Identify the slope and y-intercept of the line $y = -\frac{5}{4}x + 2$. $m = -\frac{5}{4}$; (0, 2)

Analyze **Determine whether each expression is a polynomial. If the expression is a polynomial, rewrite it in standard form. If the expression is not a polynomial, explain why.**

*9. (11) $25x^3 + x^{-7} + 2xy$ not a polynomial because of the negative exponent

10. (11) $0.25x^4 + 5x^{\frac{4}{2}}$ polynomial; $0.25x^4 + 5x^2$

11. (7) **Geography** The table shows the relationship of the annual estimated population for three cities in the year 2005. The population in Modesto, California, is represented by the variable x.

2005 City Population

City	Population
Dallas	$5.879x$
St. Louis	$1.704x$
Modesto	x
Total of 3 cities	1,775,721

a. Formulate Write a linear equation to approximate the population in Modesto in 2005. $x + 1.704x + 5.879x = 1{,}775{,}721$

b. Estimate Find the approximate population of Modesto in 2005. Round to the nearest thousand. 207,000

Evaluate.

12. (1) $-2 - 3(-2 - 2) - 5(-5 + 7)$ 0

13. (1) $-[-2(-5 + 2) - (-2 - 3)]$ −11

14. (2) $a^2 - y^3(a - y^2)y^2$ if $a = -2$ and $y = 3$ 2677

15. (7) **Geometry** Find x and y. $x = 45, y = 90$

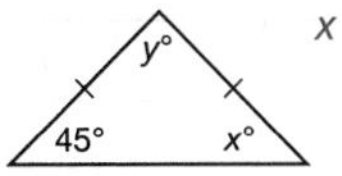

17.

16. (10) **Justify** Explain why the inequality has no solution. $3x - 5 \geq 3(x + 7)$ It produces a false statement, $-5 \geq 21$.

17. (10) Solve the inequality, and graph its solution. $7x - 5 < 7(x + 5) + 2$ $-5 < 37$

18. (10) **Civil Engineering** One cubic foot of pennies contains approximately 4.9×10^4 pennies. If approximately 1.8×10^{12} pennies would fit in the Empire State Building in New York City, what is the building's approximate volume in cubic feet? Write your answer in scientific notation. Round to the nearest tenth.
approximately 3.7×10^7 cubic feet

Solve for p.

19. (7) $(7p - 6) + 3p - (-2 - p) = 73$
$p = 7$

20. (7) $\frac{7(p + 3)}{2} = 21$ $p = 3$

21. (7) $4p + (p - 4)(2) = 8p - 7$ $p = -\frac{1}{2}$

CHALLENGE

Have students measure the classroom and use the information in Problem 18 to determine the number of pennies that would fit in the classroom.

3 Practice

Math Conversations

Discussions to strengthen understanding.

Problem 11
Extend the Problem

Find the populations of Dallas and St. Louis in 2005. Explain how you found your answers.
Dallas: 1,216,953 St. Louis: 352,728
Sample: To find the population for Dallas, I multiplied 5.879 times the population of Modesto. To find the population for St. Louis, I multiplied 1.704 times the population of Modesto.

Problem 15

"What type of triangle is shown in the problem?" isosceles

"What is true about the measures of the base angles of an isosceles triangle?" They are equal.

Problem 22

Error Alert

Students may think two matrices need to have the same dimensions to be multiplied. Remind students that the product of two matrices, $A \times B$ is possible if the number of columns in A is equal to the number of rows in B.

Problem 24

Extend the Problem

Find the total number of oranges and grapefruit produced in 2002. 14.636 million tons

Problem 29

Remind students that they can use the vertical line test to determine if each set of ordered pairs is a function.

Use the matrices to find the products. Check the answer on a graphing calculator.

$$A = [-1 \quad 2],\ B = \begin{bmatrix} 4 & 0 & 2 \\ -3 & 5 & 1 \end{bmatrix},\ C = \begin{bmatrix} 7 & 1 \\ -2 & 0 \\ 0 & -3 \end{bmatrix}$$

22. (9) Find AB. $AB = [-10 \quad 10 \quad 0]$

23. (9) Find ABC. $ABC = [-90 \quad -10]$

24. (11) **Citrus Production** The production of oranges and grapefruit (in millions of tons) in the U.S. for the years 2000 through 2006 is modeled by the polynomial functions below. The variable x represents the number of years since 2000.

Oranges $f(x) = -0.044x^3 + 0.258x^2 - 0.657x + 12.883$

Grapefruit $g(x) = 0.004x^3 - 0.065x^2 - 0.040x + 2.695$

What polynomial function is a model for the combined production of oranges and grapefruit in the United States for the years 2000–2006? $f(x) + g(x) = -0.040x^3 + 0.193x^2 - 0.697x + 15.578$

Write each fraction or decimal as a percent.

25. (6) 0.005 0.5%

26. (6) $\frac{1}{6}$ $16.\overline{6}\%$

27. (6) $\frac{5}{16}$. 31.25%

***28.** (12) **Meteorology** According to the Saffir-Simpson scale, hurricanes fall into five categories based on wind speed. The table below shows the relationship between category, wind speed, and storm surge (the height of waves). Analyze the data to determine the relationship between wind speed and storm surge. Is it a direct, joint, or inverse variation?

Category	Minimum Wind Speed (mph)	Minimum Storm Surge (ft)
1	74	4
2	96	6
3	111	9
4	131	13
5	155	19

28. As the wind speed increases, so does the storm surge. This could be a direct variation. But the ratio of wind speed and storm surge is not a constant, so the relationship is not a direct variation.

29. (4) **Multiple Choice** Which of the following sets of ordered pairs are functions? C

A (−7, 6), (−7, 3), (4, 3) **B** (−2, 5), (5, −2), (−2, 7)

C (1, −1), (−1, 1), (2, 1) **D** (0, 1), (0, 2), (0, 3)

***30.** (13) **Geography** A section of the Uncanoonuc Mountains, called the West Side Trail, is located in New Hampshire. The trail has a vertical change of about 268 feet vertically for every 1000 feet it changes horizontally. What is the slope of the trail? $\frac{67}{250}$

LOOKING FORWARD

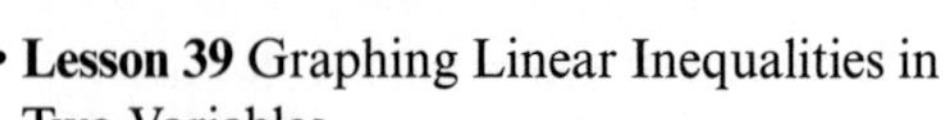

Solving and graphing linear equations prepares students for:

- **Lesson 15** Solving Systems of Equations by Graphing
- **Lesson 26** Writing the Equation of a Line
- **Lesson 29** Solving Systems of Three Equations in Three Variables
- **Lesson 34** Graphing Linear Equations II
- **Lesson 36** Using Parallel and Perpendicular Lines
- **Lesson 39** Graphing Linear Inequalities in Two Variables
- **Lesson 43** Solving Systems of Linear Inequalities
- **Lesson 45** Finding the Line of Best Fit

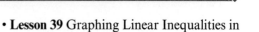

LESSON 14

Finding Determinants

Warm Up

1. (5) **Vocabulary** A(n) ________ (*element, matrix*) is a rectangular array of numbers. matrix

2. (7) Solve $4x + 6 = 22$. $x = 4$

3. (9) Simplify $\begin{bmatrix} 3 & 2 \\ -1 & 7 \end{bmatrix} \times \begin{bmatrix} 4 & -3 \\ 6 & 8 \end{bmatrix}$. $\begin{bmatrix} 24 & 7 \\ 38 & 59 \end{bmatrix}$

New Concepts

Every square matrix is associated with one real number called the **determinant** of the matrix. **If a matrix is not a square matrix, it does not have a determinant.** Enclosing the matrix within vertical lines designates the determinant of a matrix.

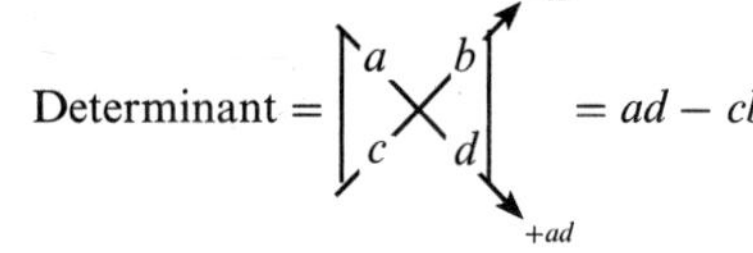

$\begin{bmatrix} 4 & 3 \\ 2 & 5 \end{bmatrix}$ matrix $\quad \begin{vmatrix} 4 & 3 \\ 2 & 5 \end{vmatrix}$ determinant

The determinant of a 2×2 square matrix is found by subtracting the product of the entries in one diagonal from the product of the entries in the other diagonal. The order in which you subtract is important and is shown by this diagram.

Determinant = $\begin{vmatrix} a & b \\ c & d \end{vmatrix} = ad - cb$

This memory device can be used to help remember which product is positive and which is negative. The minus sign points to the cold state of Maine and the plus sign points to the warm state of Florida.

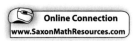

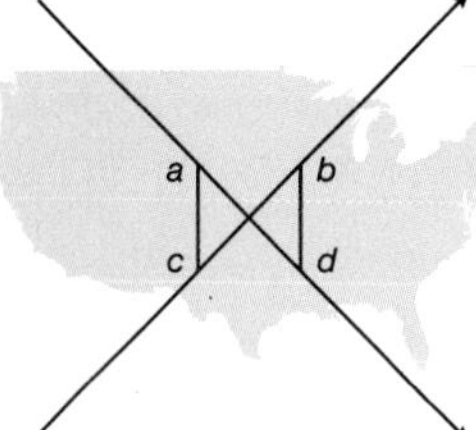

> **Caution**
>
> Subtracting the products in the incorrect order will give you the opposite of the value of the determinant.

Example 1 Finding the Determinant of a 2 × 2 Matrix

(a.) Evaluate $\begin{vmatrix} -4 & -3 \\ 2 & 7 \end{vmatrix}$.

SOLUTION Subtract *cb* from *ad*.

$$\begin{vmatrix} -4 & -3 \\ 2 & 7 \end{vmatrix} = (-4)(7) - (2)(-3) = -28 - (-6) = -22$$

(b.) Evaluate $\begin{vmatrix} -7 & 5 \\ 3 & -4 \end{vmatrix}$.

SOLUTION

$$\begin{vmatrix} -7 & 5 \\ 3 & -4 \end{vmatrix} = (-7)(-4) - (3)(5) = 28 - 15 = 13$$

Online Connection www.SaxonMathResources.com

LESSON 14

1 Warm Up

Ask students to determine the dimensions of the resulting matrix in Problem 3 before multiplying. 2×2

2 New Concepts

In this lesson, students learn how to find the determinants of 2×2 and 3×3 matrices.

Explain that only square matrices have determinants. Review the definition of a square matrix if necessary. A square matrix contains the same number of rows and columns. Discuss the definition of a **determinant** and stress that it is a real number, not a matrix. Make sure students understand the difference between the symbols [ ] and | |.

Example 1

This example shows students how to find the determinant of a 2×2 matrix. Remind students that the order in which they subtract is important.

Additional Example 1

Evaluate $\begin{vmatrix} 0 & 12 \\ -4 & -3 \end{vmatrix}$. 48

MATH BACKGROUND

The determinant function is defined only for square matrices and is a real value.

The determinant has many useful applications. It can be used to determine if a system of equations has a solution.

The determinant can also be used in transformational geometry as a 2×2 matrix which gives the ratio of the area of the new, transformed shape to the original shape. The sign of the determinant gives more information about the transformation. If the sign is positive, the image is direct, or the same way around. If the sign is negative, then the image is a mirror image.

LESSON RESOURCES

Student Edition Practice Workbook 14
Reteaching Master 14
Adaptations Master 14
Challenge and Enrichment Master C14
Technology Lab Master 14

Example 2

In this example, students solve a determinant equation in one variable.

Additional Example 2

Find x. $\begin{vmatrix} 3 & 2 \\ x-1 & 5 \end{vmatrix} = 19$

$x = -1$

Example 3a

This example shows students how to find the determinant of a 3×3 matrix using expansion by minors. Tell students that they may choose any row when finding minors. If the matrix has a row which contains a 0, choose that row for expansion.

Error Alert Stress that the operation $5\begin{vmatrix} 2 & -7 \\ -6 & 8 \end{vmatrix}$ means 5 times the determinant. It is not scalar multiplication since $\begin{vmatrix} 2 & -7 \\ -6 & 8 \end{vmatrix}$ is a determinant and not the matrix $\begin{bmatrix} 2 & -7 \\ -6 & 8 \end{bmatrix}$.

Extend the Example

Have students use row 2 or row 3 of the matrix to understand that any row chosen will produce the same determinant.

Row 2:
$-(-4)(6) + 2(37) - (-7)(-30)$
$= -112$

Row 3:
$3(-2) + 6(-31) + 8(10)$
$= -112$

Additional Example 3a

Find the determinant $\begin{vmatrix} -2 & 1 & 4 \\ 0 & 1 & -5 \\ 3 & -1 & 10 \end{vmatrix}$ using expansion by minors. -37

Example 2 **Solving Determinant Equations**

Find x. $\begin{vmatrix} x+4 & 3 \\ 2 & 4 \end{vmatrix} = 18$

SOLUTION Begin this type of problem the same as you would if you were finding the value of a determinant. Then solve for the missing value.

$(4)(x+4) - (2)(3) = 18$	Write the determinant as an equation.
$4x + 16 - 6 = 18$	Multiply.
$4x = 8$	Simplify.
$x = 2$	Divide.

There are two methods for finding the determinant of a 3×3 matrix with pencil and paper. The first method is known as expansion by minors. The second method is shown in Example 3 part b.

Expansion by Minors

If you pick an element of a matrix and cover its row and column, the determinant of the square matrix that remains is that element's **minor.**

$$\begin{bmatrix} \textcircled{a_1} & b_1 & c_1 \\ a_2 & b_2 & c_2 \\ a_3 & b_3 & c_3 \end{bmatrix} \quad \begin{bmatrix} a_1 & \textcircled{b_1} & c_1 \\ a_2 & b_2 & c_2 \\ a_3 & b_3 & c_3 \end{bmatrix} \quad \begin{bmatrix} a_1 & b_1 & \textcircled{c_1} \\ a_2 & b_2 & c_2 \\ a_3 & b_3 & c_3 \end{bmatrix}$$

To find the determinant, multiply each element in one row or column by its minor. Then subtract the middle product and add the final product.

$$\begin{vmatrix} a_1 & b_1 & c_1 \\ a_2 & b_2 & c_2 \\ a_3 & b_3 & c_3 \end{vmatrix} = a_1\begin{vmatrix} b_2 & c_2 \\ b_3 & c_3 \end{vmatrix} - b_1\begin{vmatrix} a_2 & c_2 \\ a_3 & c_3 \end{vmatrix} + c_1\begin{vmatrix} a_2 & b_2 \\ a_3 & b_3 \end{vmatrix}$$

Example 3 **Finding the Determinant of a 3 × 3 Matrix**

a. Find the determinant $\begin{vmatrix} 5 & 0 & 1 \\ -4 & 2 & -7 \\ 3 & -6 & 8 \end{vmatrix}$ using expansion by minors.

Hint

If you choose to expand a row or column that has a zero, it makes your calculations easier.

SOLUTION Find the minors for each element in one row or column.

$$\begin{vmatrix} \textcircled{5} & 0 & 1 \\ -4 & 2 & -7 \\ 3 & -6 & 8 \end{vmatrix} \quad \begin{vmatrix} 5 & \textcircled{0} & 1 \\ -4 & 2 & -7 \\ 3 & -6 & 8 \end{vmatrix} \quad \begin{vmatrix} 5 & 0 & \textcircled{1} \\ -4 & 2 & -7 \\ 3 & -6 & 8 \end{vmatrix}$$

Multiply each minor by its element and combine using the correct signs.

$$5\begin{vmatrix} 2 & -7 \\ -6 & 8 \end{vmatrix} - 0\begin{vmatrix} -4 & -7 \\ 3 & 8 \end{vmatrix} + 1\begin{vmatrix} -4 & 2 \\ 3 & -6 \end{vmatrix}$$

Evaluate the minors and simplify.

$$5[(2)(8) - (-6)(-7)] - 0[(-4)(8) - (3)(-7)] + 1[(-4)(-6) - (3)(2)]$$
$$= 5[16 - 42] - 0 + 1[24 - 6] = 5(-26) + 18 = -112$$

ENGLISH LEARNERS

The word **minor** has many meanings in the English language. Say:

"The word minor has many different definitions."

Give students some of the definitions for the word minor:

1. inferior in importance, size, or degree
2. not having reached the age of majority
3. a type of scale in music
4. not serious as in a minor illness
5. a secondary course of academic study

Give examples using some of the definitions.

"Jimmy is only 15, so he is still a minor."

"Monica has a cold. It is only a minor illness."

In this lesson, a minor is a determinant or matrix obtained from a given determinant or matrix by eliminating the row and column in which the given element lies.

b. Find the determinant $\begin{vmatrix} 3 & -2 & 1 \\ -1 & 4 & 10 \\ 2 & -3 & 5 \end{vmatrix}$.

SOLUTION To begin the other method, copy the elements of the determinant and then repeat the first two columns to the right of the third column.

$$\begin{matrix} 3 & -2 & 1 & 3 & -2 \\ -1 & 4 & 10 & -1 & 4 \\ 2 & -3 & 5 & 2 & -3 \end{matrix}$$

Multiply on the diagonals as shown and add the products.

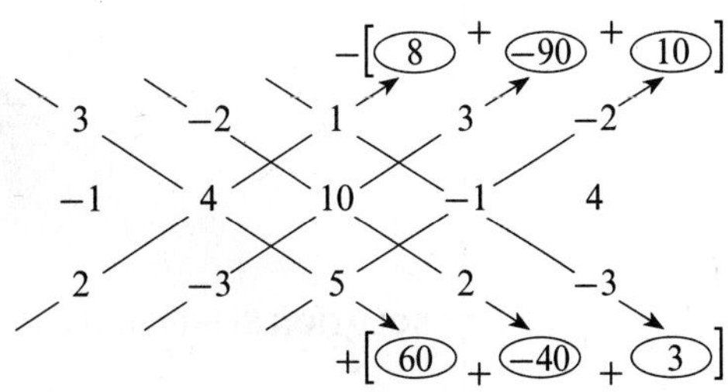

Subtract the sum of the upper products from the sum of the lower products.

$$\begin{vmatrix} 3 & -2 & 1 \\ -1 & 4 & 10 \\ 2 & -3 & 5 \end{vmatrix} = (60 - 40 + 3) - (8 - 90 + 10) = 95$$

Example 4 Using a Calculator to Find the Determinant

Find the determinant $\begin{vmatrix} 7 & 3 & -5 \\ -2 & 1 & 8 \\ 4 & -6 & 0 \end{vmatrix}$ using a calculator.

SOLUTION Store the data in a matrix.

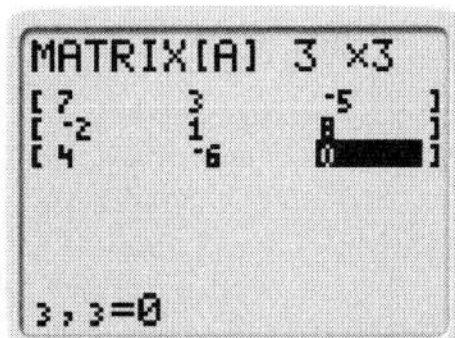

QUIT  ; MATRX x^{-1}; Choose 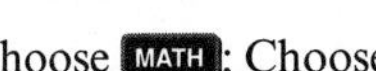; Choose 1:det(; MATRX x^{-1}; Choose the matrix; ; ENTER.

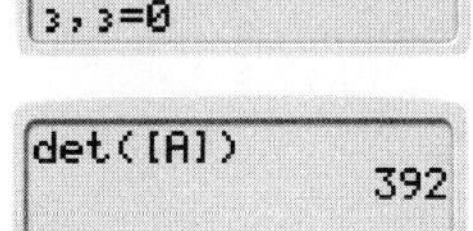

Verify Use expansion by minors to check the calculator answer.

$$7\begin{vmatrix} 1 & 8 \\ -6 & 0 \end{vmatrix} - 3\begin{vmatrix} -2 & 8 \\ 4 & 0 \end{vmatrix} + (-5)\begin{vmatrix} -2 & 1 \\ 4 & -6 \end{vmatrix} =$$

$$7[(1)(0) - (-6)(8)] - 3[(-2)(0) - (4)(8)] + (-5)[(-2)(-6) + (1)(4)] =$$
$$7[0 - (-48)] - 3[0 - 32] + (-5)[12 - 4] = 7(48) - 3(-32) + (-5)(8) = 392$$

Graphing Calculator

For help with storing data in a matrix, refer to page 27.

Example 3b

In this example, students learn how find the determinant of a 3×3 matrix by repeating the first two columns of the matrix and working with the diagonals.

Error Alert Encourage students to draw the diagonals to help them with their computations.

Additional Example 3b

Find the determinant of each matrix.

a. $\begin{vmatrix} 3 & -1 & 2 \\ 2 & 7 & 4 \\ -2 & -1 & 0 \end{vmatrix}$ 44

b. $\begin{vmatrix} 10 & 5 & -2 \\ 3 & 3 & -1 \\ 2 & -2 & 1 \end{vmatrix}$ 9

Example 4

Students are shown how to use a graphing calculator to find the determinant of a matrix. Students may need additional help storing data into a matrix.

Extend the Example

Have students use a calculator to check the answers of Example 1 and Example 3.

Additional Example 4

Find the determinant of $\begin{vmatrix} 8 & 0 & -12 \\ 5 & -7 & -8 \\ 2 & 9 & 4 \end{vmatrix}$ using a calculator.
−356

INCLUSION

When finding the determinant of a 2×2 matrix, have students draw arrows and label them as shown below.

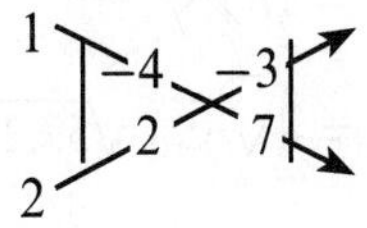

$$\begin{matrix} -4 & -3 \\ 2 & 7 \end{matrix}$$ (upper arrow labeled 1, lower arrow labeled 2)

Example 5

In this example, students are given the vertices of a triangle $[(x_1, y_1), (x_2, y_2), \text{and } (x_3, y_3)]$ and use the formula $Area = \frac{1}{2}\begin{vmatrix} x_1 & x_2 & x_3 \\ y_1 & y_2 & y_3 \\ 1 & 1 & 1 \end{vmatrix}$ to find the area of the triangle.

Error Alert Students may write the area as a negative number. Remind students to find the absolute value of the area.

Additional Example 5

Find the area of the triangle below.

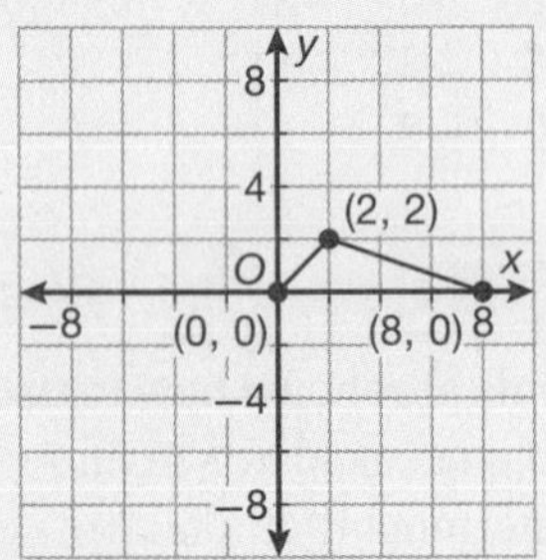

8 sq units

Math Reasoning

Connect Why do you take the absolute value to find the area?

Area is always a positive number.

Example 5 **Application: Geometry**

A triangle with vertices (x_1, y_1), (x_2, y_2), and (x_3, y_3) has an area equal to the absolute value of

$$\frac{1}{2}\begin{vmatrix} x_1 & x_2 & x_3 \\ y_1 & y_2 & y_3 \\ 1 & 1 & 1 \end{vmatrix}.$$

Find the area of the triangle below.

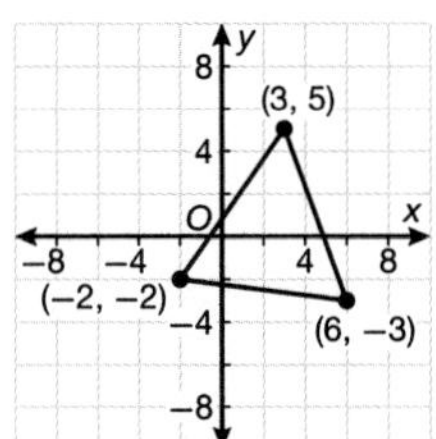

SOLUTION Substitute the coordinates of the vertices into the given matrix.

$$\frac{1}{2}\begin{vmatrix} 3 & 6 & -2 \\ 5 & -3 & -2 \\ 1 & 1 & 1 \end{vmatrix}$$

Expand by minors.

$$\begin{vmatrix} 3 & 6 & -2 \\ 5 & -3 & -2 \\ \textcircled{1} & 1 & 1 \end{vmatrix} \quad \begin{vmatrix} 3 & 6 & -2 \\ 5 & -3 & -2 \\ 1 & \textcircled{1} & 1 \end{vmatrix} \quad \begin{vmatrix} 3 & 6 & -2 \\ 5 & -3 & -2 \\ 1 & 1 & \textcircled{1} \end{vmatrix}$$

$$\frac{1}{2}\begin{vmatrix} 3 & 6 & -2 \\ 5 & -3 & -2 \\ 1 & 1 & 1 \end{vmatrix} = \frac{1}{2}\left[1\begin{vmatrix} 6 & -2 \\ -3 & -2 \end{vmatrix} - 1\begin{vmatrix} 3 & -2 \\ 5 & -2 \end{vmatrix} + 1\begin{vmatrix} 3 & 6 \\ 5 & -3 \end{vmatrix}\right]$$

Simplify.

$$\frac{1}{2}[1[(6)(-2) - (-3)(-2)] - 1[(3)(-2) - (5)(-2)] + 1[(3)(-3) - (5)(6)]] =$$

$$\frac{1}{2}[(-12 - 6) - (-6 - (-10)) + (-9 - 30)] = \frac{1}{2}[-18 - 4 + (-39)] = -\frac{61}{2}$$

The absolute value of $-\frac{61}{2}$ is $\frac{61}{2}$ or $30\frac{1}{2}$.

The area of the triangle is $30\frac{1}{2}$ square units.

ALTERNATE METHOD

For Example 5, find the length of the base and the midpoint of the base.

$$base = \sqrt{(-3 - (-2))^2 + (6 - (-2))^2} = \sqrt{65}$$

$$M = \left(\frac{6 + (-2)}{2}, \frac{-3 + (-2)}{2}\right) = (2, -2.5)$$

Find the distance from the top vertex, (3, 5) to the midpoint of the base to find the height of the triangle.

$$height = \sqrt{(5 -(-2.5))^2 + (3 - 2)^2} = \sqrt{57.25}$$

Use the formula for area of a triangle:

$$A = \frac{1}{2}bh$$

$$A = \frac{1}{2}\sqrt{65} \cdot \sqrt{57.25} \approx 30.5$$

Lesson Practice

a. Evaluate $\begin{vmatrix} 1 & -6 \\ 0 & 8 \end{vmatrix}$. 8
(Ex 1)

b. Find x. $\begin{vmatrix} x-7 & 8 \\ -1 & -5 \end{vmatrix} = 23$ $x = 4$
(Ex 2)

c. Find the determinant $\begin{vmatrix} 5 & -9 & -5 \\ -5 & -3 & 8 \\ 2 & -8 & -1 \end{vmatrix}$ using expansion by minors. 6
(Ex 3)

d. Find the determinant $\begin{vmatrix} -4 & 2 & 7 \\ 9 & 3 & -4 \\ 7 & -1 & -2 \end{vmatrix}$. −190
(Ex 3)

e. Find the determinant $\begin{vmatrix} -8 & -9 & -4 \\ -7 & 4 & 9 \\ 4 & 1 & 7 \end{vmatrix}$ using a calculator. −825
(Ex 4)

f. A triangle with vertices (x_1, y_1), (x_2, y_2), and (x_3, y_3) has an area equal to the absolute value of
(Ex 5)

$$\frac{1}{2}\begin{vmatrix} x_1 & x_2 & x_3 \\ y_1 & y_2 & y_3 \\ 1 & 1 & 1 \end{vmatrix}.$$

Find the area of the triangle.

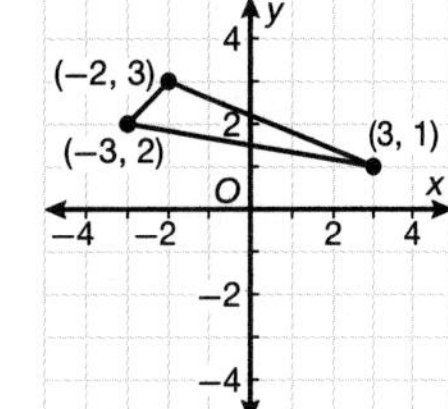

f. $\frac{1}{2}\begin{vmatrix} -2 & 3 & -3 \\ 3 & 1 & 2 \\ 1 & 1 & 1 \end{vmatrix} = 3.5$

Practice Distributed and Integrated

***1. Multi-Step** The regular price of a cell phone was \$89.99. The price was reduced by 25%.
(6)

a. Find the amount saved. Then find the new price of the cell phone. Round to the nearest hundredth. \$22.50; \$67.49

b. If the new price is later reduced by \$15, find the percent change from the original price to the lowest price at which the cell phone is sold. Round to the nearest percent. 42%

***2. Error Analysis** Two students analyzed the data table shown at right. One student determined that the relationship between the variables is an inverse variation, while the other determined that it is a direct variation. Which student is correct? What error did the other student make?
(12)

Beads

Quantity	Price
1000	\$90
900	\$100
750	\$120
600	\$150
500	\$180

Student A

Quantity	Price	$Q \times P$
1000	\$90	90,000
900	\$100	90,000
750	\$120	90,000
600	\$150	90,000
500	\$180	90,000

Student B

Quantity	Price	$Q \div P$
1000	\$90	90,000
900	\$100	90,000
750	\$120	90,000
600	\$150	90,000
500	\$180	90,000

2. Student A; Student B correctly multiplied the values but incorrectly labeled the results as a quotient, and concluded that the relationship was a direct variation.

CHALLENGE

A quadrilateral has coordinates (3, 3), (4, 0), (0, −1) and (−3, 1). Use what you know about finding the area of triangles to find the area of the quadrilateral. 15.5 sq units

Lesson Practice

Problems c–e

Have students check their answers using a graphing calculator.

Problem d

Scaffolding Suggest that students draw the diagonals as they find each product.

Problem f

Scaffolding Have students label the ordered pairs on the graph with (x_1, y_1), (x_2, y_2), and (x_3, y_3).

Check for Understanding

The questions below help assess the concepts taught in this lesson.

1. **"Explain how to find the determinant of a 3 × 3 matrix using expansion by minor."** Sample: Choose a row of the matrix. For each element in the row, multiply the element by its minor. Then subtract the middle product and add the final product.

2. **"Explain why you use the absolute value of $\frac{1}{2}\begin{vmatrix} x^1 & x^2 & x^3 \\ y^1 & y^2 & y^3 \\ 1 & 1 & 1 \end{vmatrix}$ when using the formula to find the area of a triangle."** Sample: Area cannot be a negative number.

3 Practice

Math Conversations

Discussions to strengthen understanding.

Problem 2

Extend the Problem

If the relationship between the variables remains the same, what would x equal if the value of y is 1500? 60 250? 360

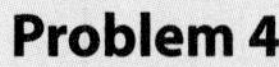

Problem 4

Error Alert

Students may assume the equation is an inverse variation because the problem contains a fraction. Have students choose values for x and y to understand that the equation is a direct variation.

Problem 6

"How can you avoid working with fractions when you are choosing values for x?" choose multiples of 3

Problem 7

"What is an intercept?" one of the points where the graph crosses an axis

"How do you find the x-intercept?" Set $y = 0$ and solve for x.

"How do you find the y-intercept?" Set $x = 0$ and solve for y.

Problems 8–10

Students may need to be given the slope formula:

$$m = \frac{y_2 - y_1}{x_2 - x_1}$$

Problem 18

Extend the Problem

If she earns $0.40 per delivery, how many papers will she have to deliver? 1250

Identify which equations are direct variations and which are inverse variations.

3. (8, 12) $y = 3x$ direct

4. (8, 12) $y = \frac{1}{2}x$ direct

5. (8, 12) $y = \frac{20}{x}$ inverse

Model **Graph the equation by using the stated method.**

6. (13) Graph the equation $y = -\frac{2}{3}x + 4$ using a table of values.

***7.** (13) Graph the equation $y = \frac{5}{4}x + 1$ using its intercepts.

6.

x	y
0	4
3	2
6	0

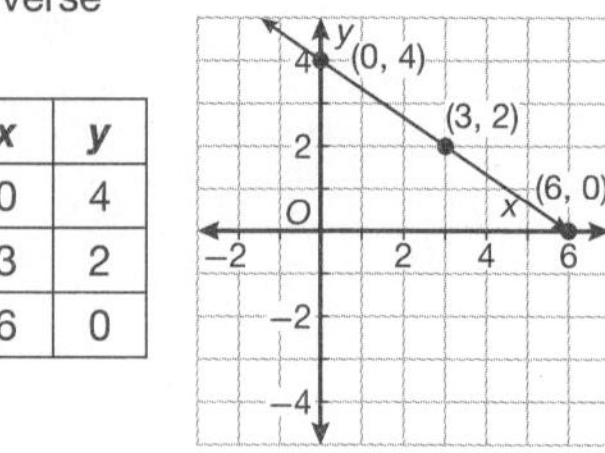

7.

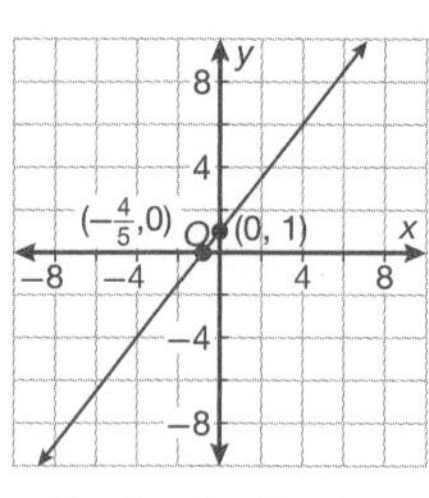

Calculate the slope of the lines that contain the following pairs of points. Tell whether the line rises, falls, is horizontal, or is vertical.

8. (13) $(-8, 2), (3, -1)$ $-\frac{3}{11}$; falls

9. (13) $(6, 4), (-5, -2)$ $\frac{6}{11}$; rises

10. (13) $(6, 2), (-5, 2)$ horizontal

***11.** (14) Evaluate $\begin{vmatrix} -1 & 2 \\ 3 & 5 \end{vmatrix}$. -11

***12.** (14) Find x. $\begin{vmatrix} 3 & 5 \\ -2x + 1 & -7 \end{vmatrix} = 24$ $x = 5$

***13.** (14) **Verify** Evaluate $\begin{vmatrix} 7 & -1 & 2 \\ -3 & 0 & -2 \\ 4 & 3 & 5 \end{vmatrix}$. Show the steps of the method specified.

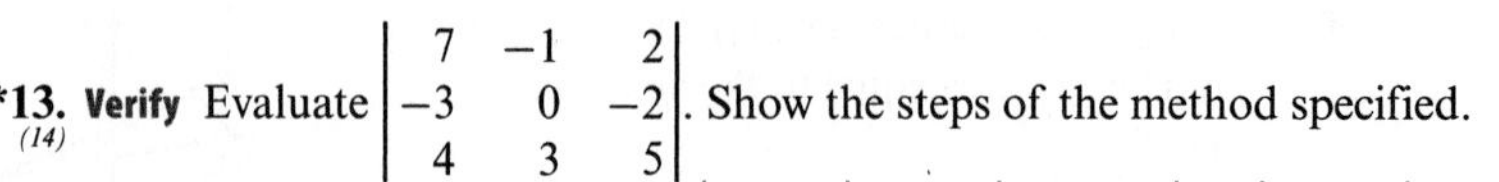

a. Use expansion by minors. $7\begin{vmatrix} 0 & -2 \\ 3 & 5 \end{vmatrix} - (-1)\begin{vmatrix} -3 & -2 \\ 4 & 5 \end{vmatrix} + 2\begin{vmatrix} -3 & 0 \\ 4 & 3 \end{vmatrix} = 17$

b. Set up diagonals. Find the difference of products.

13b.
$$\begin{matrix} 7 & -1 & 2 & 7 & -1 \\ -3 & 0 & -2 & -3 & 0 \\ 4 & 3 & 5 & 4 & 3 \end{matrix} =$$
$(0 + 8 - 18) - (0 - 42 + 15) =$

***14.** (14) **Graphing Calculator** Use a graphing calculator to find $\begin{vmatrix} 7 & 3 & 8 \\ 0 & -5 & 6 \\ -1 & 2 & -4 \end{vmatrix}$. -2

***15.** (14) **Geometry** Find the area of the triangle with coordinates $(-2, 5)$, $(7, 3)$, $(-4, -3)$. 38

16. (5) **Meteorology** The average temperatures were calculated, in degrees Fahrenheit, for the city of Hilo, Hawaii, and for the city of Lihue, Hawaii, from the year 1971 to 2000.

City	Jan	Feb	Mar	Apr	May	Jun
Hilo	71.4	71.5	72.0	72.5	73.7	75.1
Lihue	71.7	71.1	72.7	73.9	75.4	77.7

a. **Model** Record this information in a matrix and name it matrix A. $\begin{bmatrix} 71.4 & 71.5 & 72.0 & 72.5 & 73.7 & 75.1 \\ 71.7 & 71.1 & 72.7 & 73.9 & 75.4 & 77.7 \end{bmatrix}$

b. Let $B = \begin{bmatrix} -32 & -32 & -32 & -32 & -32 & -32 \\ -32 & -32 & -32 & -32 & -32 & -32 \end{bmatrix}$. Convert the temperatures from Fahrenheit to Celsius by applying the operations on matrix A. Round each element to the nearest tenth.

$$C = \frac{5}{9}([A] + [B])$$
$\begin{bmatrix} 21.9 & 21.9 & 22.2 & 22.5 & 23.2 & 23.9 \\ 22.1 & 21.7 & 22.6 & 23.3 & 24.1 & 25.4 \end{bmatrix}$

17. (8) **Measurement** The number of feet varies directly with the number of yards. If a rope measures 18 feet, it measures 6 yards. Josh is asked to write a proportion to find the number of yards in a rope that measures 33 feet. Josh wrote the proportion $\frac{18}{6} = \frac{x}{33}$. Identify Josh's error and solve the problem correctly.

17. The proportion is set up incorrectly because each ratio should contain the same units in the same position. The correct proportion is $\frac{6}{18} = \frac{x}{33}$ and the correct answer is 11 yards.

18. (10) **Formulate** A friend is trying to earn at least $500 this month by delivering newspapers. If she earns $0.25 per delivery, how many papers will she have to deliver? Write an inequality and solve it. $0.25x \geq 500$; $x \geq 2000$; 2000 newspapers

Solve the inequalities.

19. (10) $-1.9 < 2(x - 0.25) \leq 2.5$ $-0.7 < x \leq 1.5$

*20. (10) $-2 < \frac{2(x-7)}{3} \leq 5$ $4 < x \leq \frac{29}{2}$

(Basketball) In basketball, points are determined by throwing the ball into the basket, also called making a shot. Use the tables to answer the problems.

21. $A = \begin{bmatrix} 2 & 1 & 1 \\ 1 & 1 & 1 \\ 2 & 3 & 0 \end{bmatrix}$; $B = \begin{bmatrix} 3 \\ 2 \\ 1 \end{bmatrix}$

Player	Behind the 3-Point Line	Inside the 3-Point Line	Foul
Lan	2	1	1
Stacey	1	1	1
Robert	2	3	0

Type of Shot	Points
Behind the 3-Point Line	3
Inside the 3-Point Line	2
Foul	1

21. (5) Record Lan's, Stacey's, and Robert's points into a matrix. Name it matrix A. Record the point system into a matrix and name it matrix B.

*22. (9) Find the total points for each player by finding the product $A \cdot B$.

22. $\begin{bmatrix} 2 & 1 & 1 \\ 1 & 1 & 1 \\ 2 & 3 & 0 \end{bmatrix} \cdot \begin{bmatrix} 3 \\ 2 \\ 1 \end{bmatrix} = \begin{bmatrix} 9 \\ 6 \\ 12 \end{bmatrix}$; Lan scored 9 points, Stacey scored 6 points, and Robert scored 12 points.

Determine the kind of variation, if any, for each equation.

23. (8, 12) $y = mx + b$, for $m \neq 0, b \neq 0$ none

24. (8, 12) $y = mx + b$, for $m \neq 0$ and $b = 0$.   direct

Identify the subsets of real numbers of which each number is a member.

25. (1) 0.33   rational; real

26. (1) 0   whole, integer, rational, real

27. (1) $\sqrt{5}$ irrational, real

28. (12) (Meteorology) According to the Saffir-Simpson scale, hurricanes fall into five categories based on wind speed. The table at right shows the relationship between category, wind speed, and storm surge (the height of waves). Analyze the data to determine the relationship between wind speed and storm surge. Is it a direct, joint, or inverse variation?

Category	Maximum Wind Speed (mph)	Maximum Storm Surge (ft)
1	95	5
2	100	8
3	130	12
4	155	18
5	155+	19+

28. As the wind speed increases, so does the storm surge. This could be a direct variation. But the ratio of wind speed and storm surge is not a constant, so the relationship is not a direct variation.

29. (11) **Multiple Choice** Which polynomial is in standard form?   A

A $\frac{1}{2}x^3 - x$

B $\frac{1}{3} - \frac{1}{3}x^3$

C $4x^2 + 3x^3 + 2x^4$

D $x^4 + x^5$

30. (11) (Simple Interest) Al's grandfather deposited the amounts shown in Bank A as gifts on Al's birthday during the years 2002 through 2005. His aunt deposited the amounts shown in Bank B. The value of the accounts on 7/2/06 is represented by these polynomials, where $x = 1 + r$, and r is the interest rate for both accounts:

Bank A $500x^4 + 1000x^3 + 600x^2 + 500x$

Bank B $1000x^4 + 200x^3 + 200x^2 + 200x$

Date	Bank A	Bank B
7/2/02	$500	$1000
7/2/03	$1000	$200
7/2/04	$600	$200
7/2/05	$500	$200

a. Write the polynomial that represents the total value of both accounts on 7/2/06.
$1500x^4 + 1200x^3 + 800x^2 + 700x$

b. What is the total value of both accounts on 7/2/06 if the interest rate is 5%? $4829.41

Problem 19

Remind students that they can eliminate the decimal numbers by multiplying each term of this problem by 100.

LOOKING FORWARD

Working with determinants prepares students for:

- **Lesson 16** Using Cramer's Rule
- **Lesson 32** Solving Linear Systems with Matrix Inverses
- **Lesson 99** Using Vectors
- **Lesson 104** Finding Transformations

LESSON 15

1 Warm Up

For problem 3, remind students the ordered pair is (x, y).

2 New Concepts

In this lesson, students learn to solve a system of equations by graphing.

Discuss the definition of **consistent system, inconsistent system, dependent system,** and **independent system.** Explain that the solution to a system of equations occurs at the point at which the lines intersect.

Example 1

Remind students that the solution to a system is an ordered pair which makes the equations true.

Additional Example 1

a. Solve this system by graphing.
$y - 2x + 4 = 0$
$y + x = -1$ (1, −2)

b. Make a table of values for each equation to solve the system in part **a**.
See Additional Answers.

LESSON 15

Solving Systems of Equations by Graphing

Warm Up

1. (13) **Vocabulary** The ________ of a line is the change in the y-coordinates divided by the change in the x-coordinates. slope

2. (13) Give the slope and the y-intercept of the line with equation $y = -3x + 5$. −3; 5

3. (2) Determine if the point (2, 1) satisfies $y = 3x - 5$ and $y = x + 3$. no

New Concepts

A **system of equations** is a collection of two or more equations containing two or more of the same variables. A **linear system** contains two linear equations in two like unknowns. Linear systems can be solved by graphing. Both of the equations are graphed on the same coordinate grid. The coordinates of the point where the lines **intersect,** or cross, give the solution.

Example 1 Solving Systems Using Tables and Graphs

a. Solve this system by graphing.

$$3y - x = 9$$
$$y + x = -1$$

SOLUTION Solve each equation for y to get the slope-intercept form. Then graph the equations.

$$y = \frac{1}{3}x + 3$$
$$y = -x - 1$$

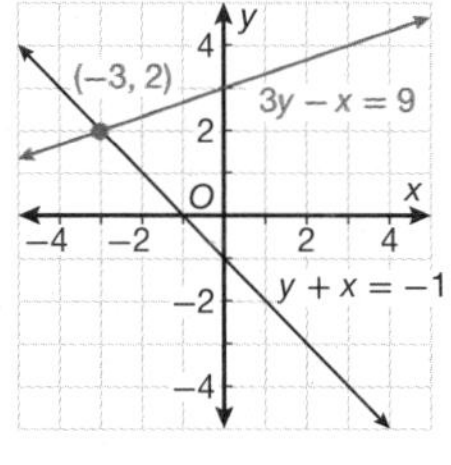

The solution of the system is $(-3, 2)$.

b. Make a table of values for each equation to solve the system in part **a**.

SOLUTION $3y - x = 9$

x	y
−6	1
−3	2
0	3
3	4

$y = -x - 1$

x	y
−6	5
−3	2
0	−1
3	−4

Hint

When choosing values of x to graph an equation, include negative values and zero.

When $x = -3$ the y values are the same for both equations. The solution to the system is $(-3, 2)$.

Online Connection www.SaxonMathResources.com

LESSON RESOURCES

Student Edition Practice Workbook 15
Reteaching Master 15
Adaptations Master 15
Challenge and Enrichment Master C15
Technology Lab Masters 15A, 15B, 15C

MATH BACKGROUND

A system of linear equations is solved when one ordered pair makes both equations true. Graphically, this is seen by the intersection of two lines. In this lesson students will see systems that have one solution, systems with no solutions, and systems with infinite solutions. In later lessons, students will learn to solve these same systems algebraically.

Graphing a system of equations by hand can often lead to imprecise graphs and thus, inexact solutions, but it is important to point out that the graph is a visual representation of the solution. Students are able to clearly see for example, that parallel lines will never intersect and therefore will have no solution. Have students practice finding the intersection on a graphing calculator to acquire a more precise solution.

Not all solutions to a linear system will intersect at integer values of x and y. A graphing calculator enables more exact solutions to be found.

Math Reasoning

Verify Use an algebraic method to verify that the solution (1.6, −0.6) is correct.

Substitute 1.6 for x and −0.6 for y into both equations, then simplify. Both sides of the equation should be equal for $y = \frac{3}{2}x - 3$ and $y = -x + 1$.

Example 2 Using a Graphing Calculator to Solve Systems

Solve this system by graphing.

$$3x - 2y = 6$$
$$y + x = 1$$

SOLUTION Solve each equation for y to get the slope-intercept form. Then graph the equations and find the point of intersection using a graphing calculator.

$$y = \frac{3}{2}x - 3$$
$$y = -x + 1$$

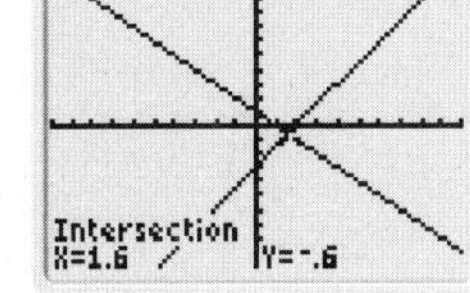

The lines intersect at (1.6, −0.6), so (1.6, −0.6) is the solution of the system.

Solutions of systems are ordered pairs. There are three possibilities for the number of solutions to a linear system: one ordered pair, an infinite number of ordered pairs, or no ordered pairs.

A linear system that has at least one solution is called a **consistent system.**

A system with no solution is called an **inconsistent system.**

A linear system is a **dependent system** when one of the equations in the system contains all solutions common to the other equation in the system.

Otherwise the system is an **independent system.**

Classifying Systems of Equations

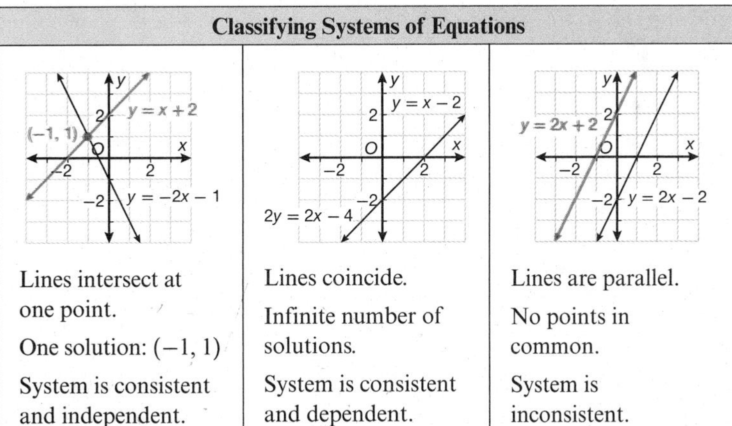

Lines intersect at one point. One solution: (−1, 1) System is consistent and independent.	Lines coincide. Infinite number of solutions. System is consistent and dependent.	Lines are parallel. No points in common. System is inconsistent.

Example 2

Point out that graphing calculators will only accept equations in the "$y =$" form.

Error Alert Most mistakes made when graphing to solve systems occur when the equation is not correctly solved for y. Remind students to check their work before entering the equations.

Additional Example 2

Solve this system by graphing.

$-5x = -y + 2$
$3x + y = -1$

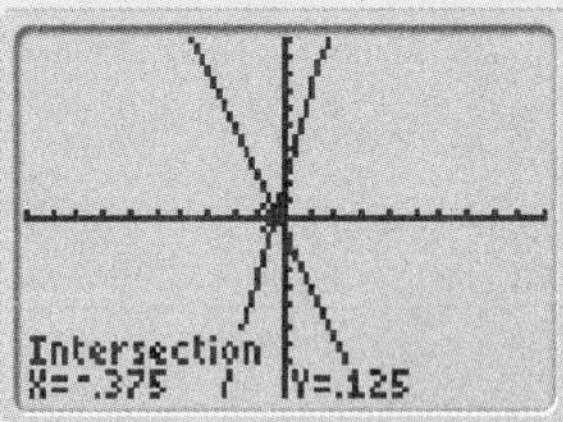

The lines intersect at the point (−0.375, 0.125) so the solution is (−0.375, 0.125).

Error Alert

Students may glance at the graph on their calculator screens and "guess" the point of intersection. Make sure students know the right procedure to find the exact point of intersection.

TEACHER TIP

When classifying systems of equations, tell students that both consistency and dependence describe the solution to the system. Consistency refers to the system having at least one solution while dependency refers to one equation containing all the solutions common to the other equation.

ENGLISH LEARNERS

Explain the meaning of the word **consistent.** Say:

"The word consistent means something that is in agreement, orderly, or logical."

Discuss the meaning in context with things in everyday life. A student can be consistent if he or she attends school every day and is well prepared. Paint can be consistent if it does not contain any variation of color.

Cooking directions often require mixing until a certain consistency is obtained.

Use consistent and inconsistent with each example problem throughout this lesson. If the system is made up of parallel lines, state that there is no solution AND the system is inconsistent. Let students hear both phrases at the same time so they can understand the connection.

Example 3

Remind students that solutions must be given for consistent systems.

Extend the Example

Have students give an example of a system of equations that is consistent and independent.
Sample: $y = x$ and $y = 2x - 5$

Have students give an example of a system of equations that is inconsistent.
Sample: $y = -3x + 4$ and $y = -3x + 2$

Additional Example 3

Determine if the following linear systems are consistent and independent, consistent and dependent, or inconsistent. If the system is consistent, give the solution.

a. $3x + 2y = 4$
$6x + 4y = 8$ Consistent and dependent. Infinite set of ordered pairs.

b. $x = 3$
$x + y = 6$ Consistent and independent. (3, 3)

c. $y = 2x + 1$
$y = 2x - 3$ Inconsistent

Example 4

Tell students to check their solution algebraically after finding the intersection point to be sure the equations were entered correctly.

Additional Example 4

A cell phone company charges \$0.60 for each text message for customers not enrolled in a plan. Customers in the plan pay \$10 each month and \$0.10 for each text message. After how many text messages will the total cost be the same for members and nonmembers? The cost for members and nonmembers is \$12.00 when 20 text messages have been sent.

Example 3 Classifying Linear Systems

Determine if the following linear systems are consistent and independent, consistent and dependent, or inconsistent. If the system is consistent, give the solution.

a.

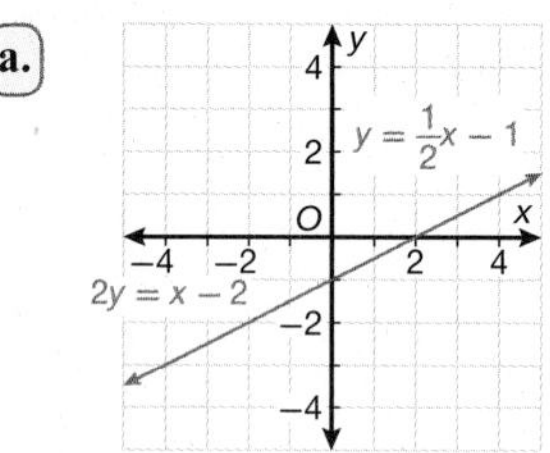

SOLUTION consistent and dependent; infinite set of ordered pairs

b.

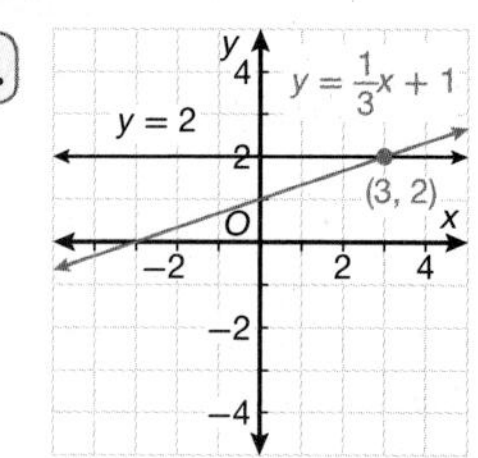

SOLUTION consistent and independent; (3, 2)

c.

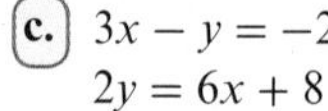

$3x - y = -2$
$2y = 6x + 8$

SOLUTION Inconsistent

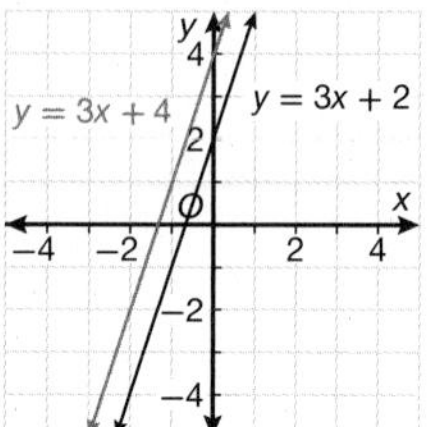

> **Math Reasoning**
>
> **Generalize** How can it be determined that a system is inconsistent without graphing?
>
> Put the equations into slope-intercept form. Determine the slope of each line. If the slopes are the same and the intercepts are different, the lines are parallel and never intersect. Since there are no points in common, the system is inconsistent.

Example 4 Application: Consumer Math

Music Masters sells MP3s for \$0.95 each to nonmembers. Members pay \$5 per year and \$0.90 for each MP3 purchase. After how many MP3 purchases will the total cost be the same for members and nonmembers?

SOLUTION Write two equations in two variables to represent the cost of each type of membership. Solve using a graphing calculator and check by substituting the solution into the equations.

Let x represent the number of MP3s purchased.
Let y represent the cost of the purchase.

Members: $y = 5 + 0.9x$

Nonmembers: $y = 0.95x$

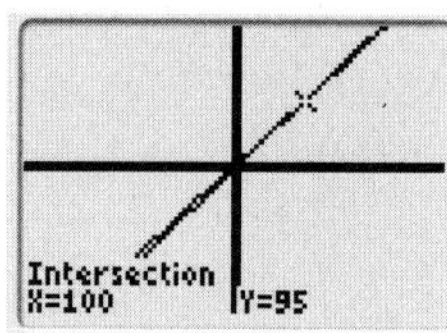

When $x = 100$, the y values are the same for both equations. The cost for members and nonmembers is \$95 when 100 MP3s have been purchased.

> **Graphing Calculator Tip**
>
> 
>
> The graphs of the lines $y = 0.95x$ and $y = 5 + 0.9x$ appear to be parallel in a standard window. Use the Zoom Out feature to see that the lines do intersect.

INCLUSION

Suggest students use the diagram to help them classify systems of equations.

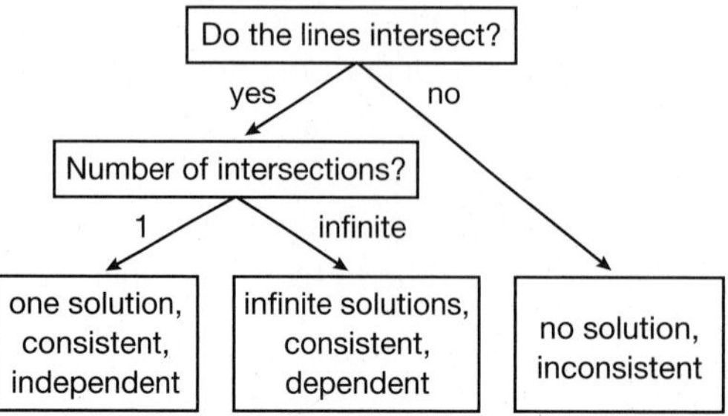

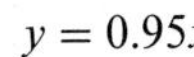

Check

$y = 0.95x$	$y = 5 + 0.9x$
$95 = 0.95(100)$	$95 = 5 + 0.9(100)$
$95 = 95$	$95 = 5 + 90$
	$95 = 95$

a. (−1, −8)

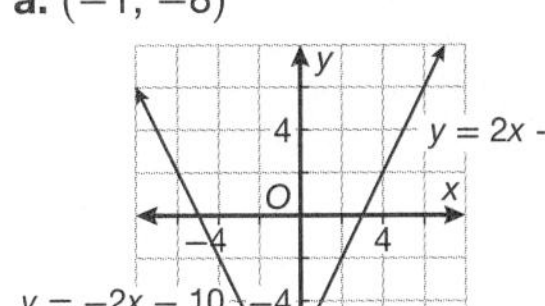

Lesson Practice

a. Solve this system by graphing.
(Ex 1)

$$2x - y = 6$$
$$y + 2x = -10$$

b. Make a table of values for each equation to solve the system in part **a.**
(Ex 1)

$2x - y = 6$

x	y
−2	−10
−1	−8
0	−6
1	−4

$y + 2x = -10$

x	y
−2	−6
−1	−8
0	−10
1	−12

c. (−6, −11)

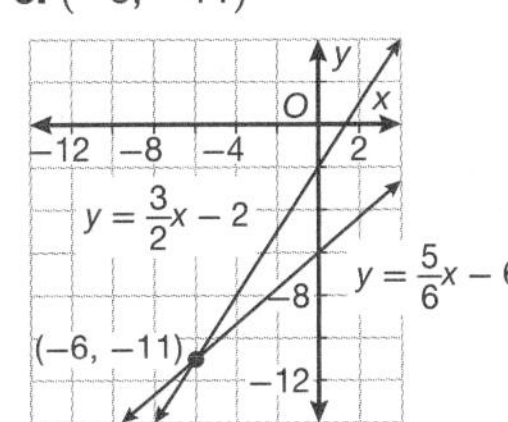

c. Solve this system by graphing.
(Ex 2)

$$5x - 6y = 36$$
$$2y - 3x = -4$$

d. Determine if the linear system at the right is consistent and independent, consistent and dependent, or inconsistent. If the system is consistent, give the solution. consistent and independent; (−3, 3)
(Ex 3)

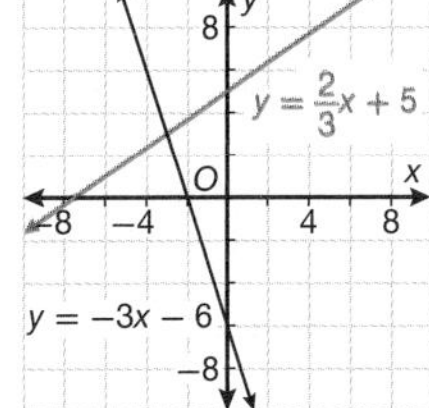

e. Determine if the linear system at the right is consistent and independent, consistent and dependent, or inconsistent. If the system is consistent, give the solution. inconsistent
(Ex 3)

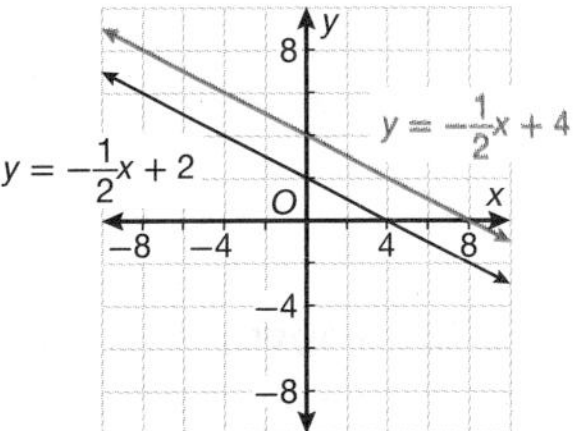

f. Determine if the linear system at the right is consistent and independent, consistent and dependent, or inconsistent. If the system is consistent, give the solution. consistent and dependent; infinite set of ordered pairs
(Ex 3)

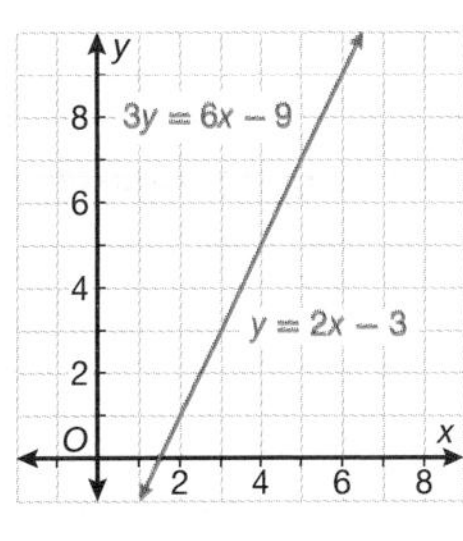

Lesson Practice

Problem b

Scaffolding Tell students to solve each equation for y before substituting values for x. Remind students to choose the same values for x for each equation. When the same ordered pair makes both equations true, that ordered pair is the solution to the system.

Problem d

Point out that the scale is by 2. Tell students to check the scale before finding the ordered pair.

Problem f

Remind students that although the graph appears to be of one line, it is actually a system of equations in which the lines coincide.

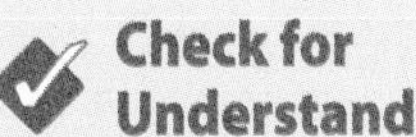

Check for Understanding

The question below helps assess the concepts taught in this lesson.

"Using the terms for classifying systems of equations, what type of system is not possible? Explain." It is not possible to have a system that is inconsistent and dependent, because a dependent system has solutions and an inconsistent system does not.

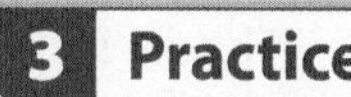

3 Practice

Math Conversations

Discussion to strengthen understanding

Problem 9

Remind students that a determinant can only be found for an $n \times n$ matrix.

Problem 11

Guide the students by asking them the following questions.

"What is the formula for slope?" $m = \frac{y_2 - y_1}{x_2 - x_1}$

"What values can be used for x_1, x_2, y_1, y_2?" $x_1 = 3$, $x_2 = -6$, $y_1 = 8$, $y_2 = y$

"What is the value of m?" $\frac{4}{9}$

"Write the equation using the known values." $\frac{4}{9} = \frac{y-8}{-6-3}$

"What is the value of y?" $y = 4$

Problem 13

Extend the problem

"What is the actual percent decrease?" Round to the nearest whole percent. 33.3%

"If the price of a product costing \$9 was reduced by 50%, what would the new price be?" \$4.50

---

g. (Ex 4) Superfit Gym charges nonmembers \$20 for each fitness class. Members pay \$75 per year and \$5 for each fitness class. After how many fitness classes will the total cost be the same for members and nonmembers?
$y = 20x$ and $y = 5x + 75$; 5 fitness classes

Practice Distributed and Integrated

Given $h(x) = 6x + 3$ and $p(x) = 2x^2 - x$, find each of the following.

*1. (4) $p(-5)$ 55

2. (4) $h\left(\frac{1}{2}\right)$ 6

Identify whether the equation is a direct, inverse, or joint variation.

3. (12) $\frac{1}{3}y = x$ direct

*4. (12) $y = \frac{1}{2}xz$ joint

5. (12) $xy = 10$ inverse

Geometry For each equation identify the kind of variation it represents.

6. (12) Circumference $= 2\pi \times$ Radius direct

7. (12) Area of a circle $= \pi(\text{Radius})^2$ direct

*8. (6) **Multi-Step** A jacket is on sale for 75% off the original price of \$39.99. Find the amount of the price reduction. Then find the new price, which includes a sales tax of 5%. \$29.99; \$10.50

9. (14) **Multiple Choice** Evaluate $\begin{vmatrix} -1 & 3 \\ 2 & 3 \\ 7 & -4 \end{vmatrix}$. D

A 0 B -9

C -29 D This matrix does not have a determinant.

10. (13) Given the equation $8x - 2y = -10$,

a. identify the slope and the y-intercept. $m = 4$; $b = 5$

b. graph the line. See Additional Answers.

16. No points in common. The system is inconsistent.

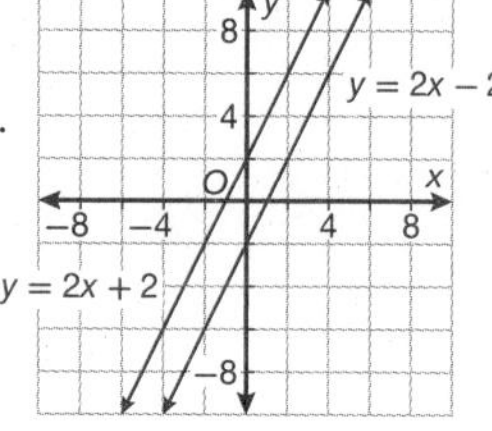

Use the slope formula to find the missing coordinate.

*11. (13) The slope of a line is $\frac{4}{9}$. The points (3, 8) and $(-6, y)$ lie on the line. Find y. $y = 4$

12. (13) The slope of a line is $-\frac{7}{3}$. The points $(4, -4)$ and $(x, 3)$ lie on the line. Find x. $x = 1$

*13. (6) **Error Analysis** The price of a product decreased from \$9 to \$6. A student incorrectly computed the percent of decrease to be 50%. What was the student's error?

13. The student found the decrease in price correctly, but found the percent change by dividing the amount of change by the new price instead of the original price.

14. (14) Evaluate $\begin{vmatrix} -5 & 2 \\ 1 & -3 \end{vmatrix}$. 13

15. (14) Find x. $\begin{vmatrix} 2x & 3 \\ -x-4 & -1 \end{vmatrix} = 10$ $x = -2$

*16. (15) **Graphing Calculator** Graph to solve the system. Then classify the system.
$2x - y = -2$
$2y = 4x - 4$.

104 Saxon Algebra 2

*17. (11) **Woodworking** A lathe operator has a piece of wood in the shape of a square prism with dimensions $2x$, $2x$, and h. He wants to make the largest possible cylinder by turning the wood on the lathe and cutting it down. The cylinder will have radius x and height h. Write a polynomial that represents the volume of wood he will cut off to make the cylinder. (The formula for the volume of a cylinder is $V = \pi r^2 h$.) $4x^2h - \pi x^2 h$ or $(4 - \pi)x^2 h$

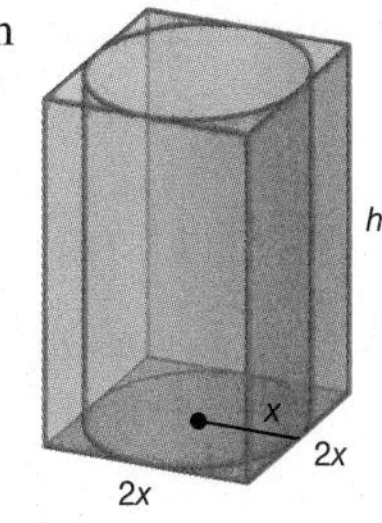

18. (12) **Physics** According to Ohm's Law, a direct current flowing in a wire is inversely proportional to the resistance of the wire. If the current in a wire is 0.01 amperes (A) and the resistance is 1200 ohms (Ω), what resistance will result in a current of 0.1 A? 120 Ω

19. (7) **Travel** Aaron is traveling 955 miles from Phoenix, Arizona, to Jackson, Wyoming. He leaves Phoenix, driving 410 miles before stopping for gas in Cortez, Colorado. He makes one last stop in Rock Springs, Wyoming, before traveling the final 180 miles to his destination. Write and solve an equation to find the number of miles Aaron drove between Cortez and Rock Springs. $410 + d + 180 = 955$; $d = 365$ miles

*20. (4) **Formulate** Write a function that represents the data set $(-4, 16)$, $(1, 1)$, $(3, 9)$, $(4, 16)$, $(7, 49)$. $f(x) = x^2$

21. (10) **Business** A snow cone vendor wants to make at least \$2,500 the first month. If he charges \$1.25 per snow cone, how many snow cones will he have to sell? Write and solve an inequality to find how many snow cones he will have to sell.
$1.25x \geq 2500$; $x \geq 2000$; 2000 snow cones

22. (10) **Verify** Solve $-2(7x + 1) \leq -8x - 9$. Check the answer by substituting an integer that makes the inequality true. $x \geq \frac{7}{6}$

23. (9) **Scoring** Andrew, Max, and Gracie are all taking a test where each type of question is given a certain point value. Use matrix multiplication to find out who scored the greatest number of points on the test.

Questions answered correctly

	Type 1	Type 2	Type 3
Andrew	7	5	4
Max	6	7	3
Gracie	7	4	5

Point Value	
Type 1	3
Type 2	5
Type 3	10

23. $\begin{bmatrix} 7 & 5 & 4 \\ 6 & 7 & 3 \\ 7 & 4 & 5 \end{bmatrix}\begin{bmatrix} 3 \\ 5 \\ 10 \end{bmatrix} = \begin{bmatrix} 86 \\ 83 \\ 91 \end{bmatrix}$; Gracie scored the greatest number of points.

Use the matrices to find the products, if possible.

$$A = \begin{bmatrix} -1 \\ 5 \\ 3 \end{bmatrix} \qquad B = \begin{bmatrix} -2 & 0 & 2 \end{bmatrix}$$

24. (9) AB

25. (9) BA [8]

24. $\begin{bmatrix} 2 & 0 & -2 \\ -10 & 0 & 10 \\ -6 & 0 & 6 \end{bmatrix}$

CHALLENGE

Graph the following equations on a calculator. State the solution(s). Explain why this is NOT a linear system of equations.

$y = x^2 - 4 \qquad y = \frac{1}{2}x + 1$

$(-2, 0)$ and $(2.5, 2.25)$; A linear system of equations consists of lines and will have exactly 1, none, or infinite solutions. Because $y = x^2 - 4$ is not linear and this system has 2 solutions, this is not a linear system.

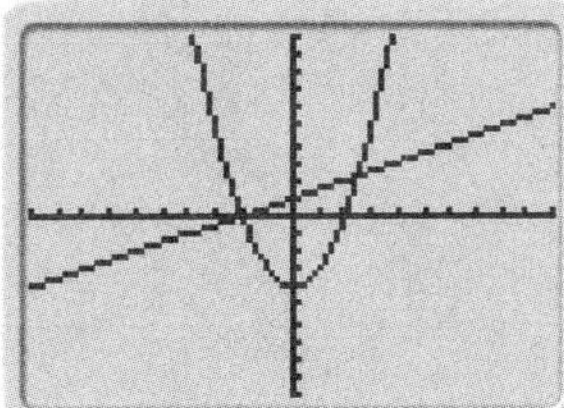

Problem 17

Guide the students by asking them the following questions.

"How can you find the volume of the wood that will be removed?" I can find the volume of the square prism and then subtract the volume of the cylinder. The wood that will be removed is the difference between the two.

"What is the volume of the square prism?" $(2x)(2x)(h) = 4x^2h$

"What is the volume of the cylinder? Explain." $V = \pi r^2 h$. The cylinder will have radius x so I substitute $r = x$ in the equation. The volume of the cylinder is $V = \pi x^2 h$.

Problem 20

Tell students to think about how the x-value of each ordered pair relates to the corresponding y-value. Alternatively, have students graph the ordered pairs to sketch the function.

Problem 22

Error Alert When solving inequalities, students might forget to flip the inequality symbol when dividing by a negative. Have students substitute 0 or another integer (as suggested in the problem) to verify the answer is correct.

Problem 26

When solving multiple choice problems, remind students to first try any answer choice that can be checked quickly. With choice **C**, students see that (0, 0) cannot be true. So **C** is eliminated.

26. (15) **Multiple Choice** Which is a solution to the system below? **B**

$$-x + 2y = 6$$
$$-3x + 4y = 4$$

A (7, 5) **B** (8, 7) **C** (0, 0) **D** (−16, −11)

***27.** (15) **Graphing Calculator** Use a graphing calculator to determine the solution of the system.

$$-2x - y = 2$$
$$3x + 2y = 1$$

***28.** (15) **Write** The solution of a system is a single point. Classify the system and describe the graph.

29. (8) **Meaurement** In a certain recipe, the amount of sugar is directly proportional to the amount of flour. If 3 cups of sugar are used with 8 cups of flour, how many cups of sugar are used with 12 cups of flour? 4.5 cups

30. (3) **Population** The U.S. population is approximately 2.99×10^8. In one year, the United States produced 4.78×10^{11} pounds of garbage. Approximately how much garbage did the average American produce that year? 1.60×10^3 pounds

28. The graph consists of two lines intersecting at exactly one point. Since there is exactly one solution, the point of intersection, the system is consistent and independent.

27.

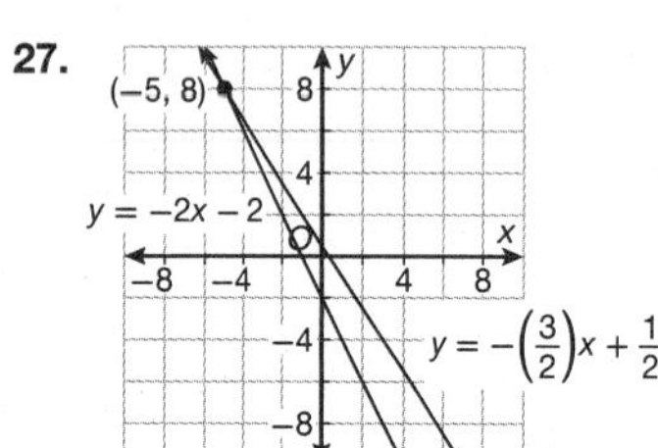

LOOKING FORWARD

Solving Systems of Equations by Graphing prepares students for

- **Lesson 21** Solving Systems of Equations Using the Substitution Method
- **Lesson 24** Solving Systems of Equations Using the Elimination Method
- **Lesson 29** Solving Systems of Three Equations in Three Variables
- **Lesson 43** Solving Systems of Linear Inequalities

LESSON 16

Using Cramer's Rule

Warm Up

1. **Vocabulary** A ________ ***(denominator, determinant)*** is a real number associated with a square matrix. (14) determinant

2. Find the determinant of $\begin{vmatrix} 4 & -3 \\ 5 & 2 \end{vmatrix}$. (14) 23

3. Solve the system. $\begin{aligned} 2x + y &= 2 \\ 4x - y &= 10 \end{aligned}$ (15) (2, −2)

New Concepts

Cramer's rule is a method for solving systems of linear equations using determinants. Elimination can be used to solve a general system of linear equations for x and y, as shown here.

$$\begin{aligned} ax + by = e \;\rightarrow\; (d) \;\rightarrow\;& \quad dax + dby = de \\ cx + dy = f \;\rightarrow\; (-b) \;\rightarrow\;& \quad -bcx - bdy = -bf \\ & \quad (ad - bc)x = de - bf \;\rightarrow\; x = \frac{de - bf}{ad - bc} \end{aligned}$$

$$\begin{aligned} ax + by = e \;\rightarrow\; (-c) \;\rightarrow\;& \quad -cax - cby = -ce \\ cx + dy = f \;\rightarrow\; (a) \;\rightarrow\;& \quad acx + ady = af \\ & \quad (ad - bc)y = af - ce \;\rightarrow\; y = \frac{af - ce}{ad - bc} \end{aligned}$$

Observe that the denominators of x and y are the same and that their numerators are different. The same results are found by simplifying the following expressions.

$$x = \frac{\begin{vmatrix} e & b \\ f & d \end{vmatrix}}{\begin{vmatrix} a & b \\ c & d \end{vmatrix}} = \frac{ed - fb}{ad - cb} \qquad y = \frac{\begin{vmatrix} a & e \\ c & f \end{vmatrix}}{\begin{vmatrix} a & b \\ c & d \end{vmatrix}} = \frac{af - ce}{ad - cb}$$

Math Language

When a constant is multiplied by a variable, it is called a **coefficient.**

Note that the elements of the determinants in the denominators are the coefficients of x and y in the given equations. For this reason, this matrix is called the **coefficient matrix.** The matrices in the numerators are different. In the matrices in the numerators, the constants replace the coefficients of x when we solve for x, and the constants replace the coefficients of y when we solve for y.

Cramer's Rule

The solution of the linear system $\begin{aligned} ax + by &= e \\ cx + dy &= f \end{aligned}$ is

$x = \dfrac{\begin{vmatrix} e & b \\ f & d \end{vmatrix}}{D}$ and $y = \dfrac{\begin{vmatrix} a & e \\ c & f \end{vmatrix}}{D}$, where D is the determinant of the coefficient matrix.

Online Connection
www.SaxonMathResources.com

MATH BACKGROUND

Cramer's rule can also be applied to a system of three equations in three variables.

The system below can be written as four separate matrices as shown:

$$\begin{aligned} a_1x + b_1y + c_1z &= d_1 \\ a_2x + b_2y + c_2z &= d_2 \\ a_3x + b_3y + c_3z &= d_3 \end{aligned}$$

$$D = \begin{bmatrix} a_1 & b_1 & c_1 \\ a_2 & b_2 & c_2 \\ a_3 & b_3 & c_3 \end{bmatrix}, D_x = \begin{bmatrix} d_1 & b_1 & c_1 \\ d_2 & b_2 & c_2 \\ d_3 & b_3 & c_3 \end{bmatrix}$$

$$D_y = \begin{bmatrix} a_1 & d_1 & c_1 \\ a_2 & d_2 & c_2 \\ a_3 & d_3 & c_3 \end{bmatrix}, D_z = \begin{bmatrix} a_1 & b_1 & d_1 \\ a_2 & b_2 & d_2 \\ a_3 & b_3 & d_3 \end{bmatrix}$$

To solve for each variable:

$$x = \frac{\det D_x}{\det D}, y = \frac{\det D_y}{\det D}, z = \frac{\det D_z}{\det D}$$

1 Warm Up

Problem 2

Remind students the determinant of a matrix is defined by

$$\begin{vmatrix} a & b \\ c & d \end{vmatrix} = ad - cb.$$

2 New Concepts

In this lesson, students learn to solve systems of equations using Cramer's rule.

Discuss Cramer's rule with students. Point out that the denominators are equal to the determinant of the coefficient matrix:

$$D = \begin{vmatrix} a & b \\ c & d \end{vmatrix}$$

LESSON RESOURCES

Student Edition Practice Workbook 16
Reteaching Master 16
Adaptations Master 16
Challenge and Enrichment Master C16

Example 1

Tell students they are going to use determinants and Cramer's rule to solve systems of linear equations.

Additional Example 1

Use Cramer's rule to solve

$$\begin{aligned} x + y &= 1 \\ x + 2y &= 4 \end{aligned}.$$

(−2, 3)

Extend the Example

Have students graph the system of equations without a calculator. Ask students which method they prefer, graphing or using Cramer's rule, and why.

Error Alert Students may have difficulty writing the matrices in the numerators. Have them identify the constants.

Example 2

Explain to students that the determinant of the coefficient matrix provides a way to tell if the system has an infinite number of solutions or no solutions.

Additional Example 2a

a. Use Cramer's rule to solve

$$\begin{aligned} 2x + 4y &= 12 \\ x + 2y &= -2 \end{aligned}.$$

no solution

Example 1 Using Cramer's Rule to Solve Systems of Equations

Use Cramer's rule to solve $\begin{aligned} 3x + 2y &= -1 \\ 4x - 3y &= 10 \end{aligned}$.

SOLUTION The denominator of both x and y is the determinant of the coefficient matrix.

$$x = \frac{\begin{vmatrix} & \\ & \end{vmatrix}}{\begin{vmatrix} 3 & 2 \\ 4 & -3 \end{vmatrix}} \qquad y = \frac{\begin{vmatrix} & \\ & \end{vmatrix}}{\begin{vmatrix} 3 & 2 \\ 4 & -3 \end{vmatrix}}$$

The numerator determinants are the same, except that the constants −1 and 10 replace the coefficients of x when we solve for x and replace the coefficients of y when we solve for y.

$$x = \frac{\begin{vmatrix} -1 & 2 \\ 10 & -3 \end{vmatrix}}{\begin{vmatrix} 3 & 2 \\ 4 & -3 \end{vmatrix}} = \frac{3 - 20}{-9 - 8} = 1 \qquad y = \frac{\begin{vmatrix} 3 & -1 \\ 4 & 10 \end{vmatrix}}{\begin{vmatrix} 3 & 2 \\ 4 & -3 \end{vmatrix}} = \frac{30 + 4}{-9 - 8} = -2$$

Caution

The order of the elements in the coefficient matrix is always the same.

Sometimes when using Cramer's rule, the determinant of the coefficient matrix is equal to zero. This makes the denominator of the solutions equal to zero, which makes the expression undefined.

Classifying Systems by Their Solutions		
If $D \neq 0$, the system has exactly **one unique solution.** A system that has any number of solutions is considered consistent.	If $D = 0$ but neither of the numerators is zero, the system has **no solution** and is considered inconsistent.	If $D = 0$ and at least one of the numerators is zero, the system has an **infinite number of solutions,** which means it is dependent and consistent.

Example 2 Interpreting a Denominator of Zero

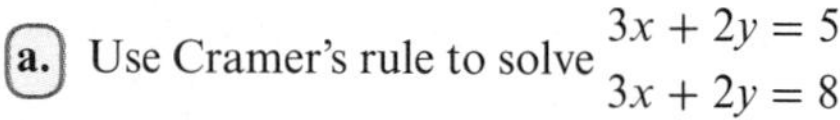

a. Use Cramer's rule to solve $\begin{aligned} 3x + 2y &= 5 \\ 3x + 2y &= 8 \end{aligned}$.

SOLUTION Set up and simplify the equations for x and y using the coefficient matrix and the constants.

$$x = \frac{\begin{vmatrix} 5 & 2 \\ 8 & 2 \end{vmatrix}}{\begin{vmatrix} 3 & 2 \\ 3 & 2 \end{vmatrix}} = \frac{10 - 16}{6 - 6} = \frac{-6}{0} \qquad y = \frac{\begin{vmatrix} 3 & 5 \\ 3 & 8 \end{vmatrix}}{\begin{vmatrix} 3 & 2 \\ 3 & 2 \end{vmatrix}} = \frac{24 - 15}{6 - 6} = \frac{9}{0}$$

Division by zero is undefined, so using Cramer's rule did not provide a solution. Neither of the numerators is zero, so there is no solution. This is because the graphs of the equations are parallel lines and parallel lines never intersect.

ENGLISH LEARNERS

For examples 1 and 2, explain the meaning of the word **coefficient.** Say:

"The word coefficient is a number that is multiplied by a variable or group of variables."

Write the following system of equations on the board and have students identify the coefficients in the system.

$$\begin{aligned} 2x - y &= -5 \\ -3x + 2y &= 10 \end{aligned}$$

Point to each of the coefficients and say:

"The number 2 is the coefficient of x in the first equation. The coefficient of y is −1. For the second equation, the coefficients are −3 for x and 2 for y."

Have the students arrange the coefficients in a coefficient matrix.

$$\begin{bmatrix} 2 & -1 \\ -3 & 2 \end{bmatrix}$$

Math Reasoning

Generalize Multiplying $3x + 2y = 5$ by 2 results in $6x + 4y = 10$, which is the same line. Give one more equation of this line.

Sample: $9x + 6y = 15$

b. Use Cramer's rule to solve the system. $\begin{aligned} 3x + 2y &= 5 \\ 6x + 4y &= 10 \end{aligned}$

SOLUTION Set up and simplify the equations for x and y.

$$x = \frac{\begin{vmatrix} 5 & 2 \\ 10 & 4 \end{vmatrix}}{\begin{vmatrix} 3 & 2 \\ 6 & 4 \end{vmatrix}} = \frac{20 - 20}{12 - 12} = \frac{0}{0} \qquad y = \frac{\begin{vmatrix} 3 & 5 \\ 6 & 10 \end{vmatrix}}{\begin{vmatrix} 3 & 2 \\ 6 & 4 \end{vmatrix}} = \frac{30 - 30}{12 - 12} = \frac{0}{0}$$

In addition to the denominators being zero, both of the numerators are equal to zero, so there is an infinite number of solutions to this system. This is because the graphs of the equations are the same line.

Example 3 Application: Science

The molecular weight of H_2O is 18 atomic mass units, which means that 2 hydrogen (H) atoms and 1 oxygen (O) atom have a combined weight of 18 amu. Write a system of equations that describes the data in the table and use Cramer's rule to find the atomic weights of hydrogen and carbon (C).

Name	Formula	Molecular weight
Benzene	C_6H_6	78
Naphthalene	$C_{10}H_8$	128

Reading Math

The subscript number after each letter in a formula stands for the number of atoms of each element in that compound.

SOLUTION Using C and H as the variables, the system that represents the data is

$$\begin{aligned} 6C + 6H &= 78 \\ 10C + 8H &= 128 \end{aligned}$$

Solving this system with Cramer's rule will result in the weights of each element.

Remember that the coefficient matrix will be in the denominator for each variable. Use the constants in the numerator.

$$C = \frac{\begin{vmatrix} 78 & 6 \\ 128 & 8 \end{vmatrix}}{\begin{vmatrix} 6 & 6 \\ 10 & 8 \end{vmatrix}} = \frac{624 - 768}{48 - 60} = \frac{-144}{-12} = 12$$

$$H = \frac{\begin{vmatrix} 6 & 78 \\ 10 & 128 \end{vmatrix}}{\begin{vmatrix} 6 & 6 \\ 10 & 8 \end{vmatrix}} = \frac{768 - 780}{48 - 60} = \frac{-12}{-12} = 1$$

Check The atomic weight of carbon is 12 amu and that of hydrogen is 1 amu. Substitute the values back into each equation to make sure they are correct.

$$6(12) + 6(1) = 72 + 6 = 78$$
$$10(12) + 8(1) = 120 + 8 = 128$$

Additional Example 2b

b. Use Cramer's rule to solve

$$\begin{aligned} 2x + y &= 6 \\ 6x + 3y &= 18 \end{aligned}$$

infinite number of solutions

Extend the Example

Have students check their answers in parts **a** and **b** by finding and comparing the slopes and y-intercepts of the equations.

Example 3

Tell students Cramer's rule can be used in science to find the atomic weights of atoms.

Additional Example 3

Write a system of equations that describes the data in the table and use Cramer's rule to find the atomic weights of potassium and oxygen.

Name	Formula	Molecular Weight
Potassium dioxide	KO_2	71
Potassium oxide	K_2O	94

Potassium: 39 amu; Oxygen: 16 amu

TEACHER TIP

Encourage students to first write the determinant of the coefficient matrix for C and H.

INCLUSION

Have students use the periodic table to check their work. The sum of the weights of the atoms should equal the molecular weight.

Example:

$$\begin{aligned} H_2O &= 2(H) + O \\ &= 2(1) + 16 \\ &= 2 + 16 \\ &= 18 \end{aligned}$$

Lesson Practice

Problem a

Scaffolding When solving for a variable, encourage students to first write the coefficient matrix for the denominators, then use the constants in the numerator to replace the coefficients of x and y, respectively.

Problem b

Error Alert Some students may forget that a fraction with a denominator of zero does not equal zero. Remind them that they cannot divide "nothing" into "something."

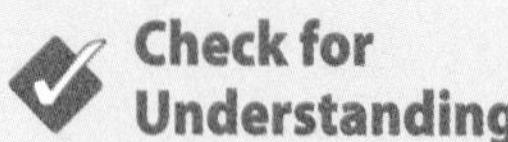

Check for Understanding

The question below helps assess the concepts taught in this lesson.

"How do you use Cramer's rule to solve a system of linear equations?" Sample: Write matrices in the numerators and use the constants when solving for x and y. Use the coefficient matrix in the denominator, then solve.

3 Practice

Math Conversations

Discussion to strengthen understandings

Problem 1

Have students define a function before answering the question.

Problem 4

Extend the Problem

Have students solve the system using Cramer's rule.

Lesson Practice

a. (Ex 1) Use Cramer's rule to solve the system. $\begin{aligned} 2x + 2y &= 3 \\ 3x + 8y &= 7 \end{aligned}$ $\left(1, \frac{1}{2}\right)$

b. (Ex 2) Use Cramer's rule to solve the system. $\begin{aligned} 2y - x &= 6 \\ 2y - x &= -2 \end{aligned}$ no solution

c. (Ex 2) Use Cramer's rule to solve the system. $\begin{aligned} x + 2y &= -4 \\ 3x + 6y &= -12 \end{aligned}$ infinite number of solutions

d. (Ex 3) The molecular weight of H_2O is 18 atomic mass units, which means that 2 hydrogen (H) atoms and 1 oxygen (O) atom have a combined weight of 18 amu. Write a system of equations that describes the data in the table and use Cramer's rule to find the atomic weights of nitrogen (N) and oxygen (O). $2x + 4y = 92$ and $2x + y = 44$; N: 14; O: 16

Name	Formula	Molecular weight
Nitrogen oxide	N_2O_4	92
Nitrous oxide	N_2O	44

Practice Distributed and Integrated

1. (4) **Multi-Step** One T-shirt costs $15.50. This can be expressed as the ordered pair (1, 15.5). The store is having a buy-one-get-one-free sale on T-shirts. Find the total cost if 2, 3, 4, 5, and 6 T-shirts are purchased. Express the answers as ordered pairs in set notation. Identify the domain and range. Determine if the set of ordered pairs represents a function. Explain.

1. {(2, 15.5), (3, 31), (4, 31), (5, 46.5), (6, 46.5)}; Domain: 2, 3, 4, 5, 6; Range: 15.5, 31, 46.5; The set of ordered pairs represents a function since for every value of x there is exactly one y value.

***2.** (15) **Error Analysis** After examining the two function tables below, a student concluded that the two equations were inconsistent.

$y = -\frac{7}{3}x + 3$

x	−2	−1	0	1
y	$-\frac{5}{2}$	−1	2	5

$y = \frac{1}{3}x - 1$

x	−2	−1	0	1
y	$-\frac{5}{3}$	$-\frac{4}{3}$	−1	$-\frac{2}{3}$

a. Describe the student's error.

b. How can this error be avoided?

c. Solve the system. $\left(\frac{3}{2}, -\frac{1}{2}\right)$

2a. The student assumed incorrectly that because there were no matching values in the table, the system did not have a solution.

b. This problem can be avoided by graphing the system and determining if the lines intersect.

3. (4) **Model** One day the value of one U.S. dollar was equivalent to 0.77 euro. On the same day, one U.S. dollar was equivalent to 1.24 Canadian dollars. Write a function to represent the value of Canadian dollars in euros. $f(c) = \frac{0.77c}{1.24}$

***4.** (5) **Graphing Calculator** Solve the system: $\begin{aligned} x - 2y &= 6 \\ -6x + 3y &= 1 \end{aligned}$. Round to the nearest tenth. (−2.2, −4.1)

ENGLISH LEARNERS

The **euro** is the currency of the Eurozone, which consists of the European countries of Austria, Belgium, Cyprus, Finland, France, Germany, Greece, Ireland, Italy, Luxembourg, Malta, the Netherlands, Portugal, Slovenia, and Spain.

The euro comes in coins and banknotes. Encourage students to look for pictures of the euro coins and banknotes online.

5. The number of students attending a certain sports event decreased from 2080 to
(6) 1575 from one school year to the next.

a. Estimate Estimate the percent of change. about a 25% decrease

b. Find the actual percent of change. Round to the nearest percent. 24%

Which of the following depict functions? Identify the domain and the range.

6. (4)

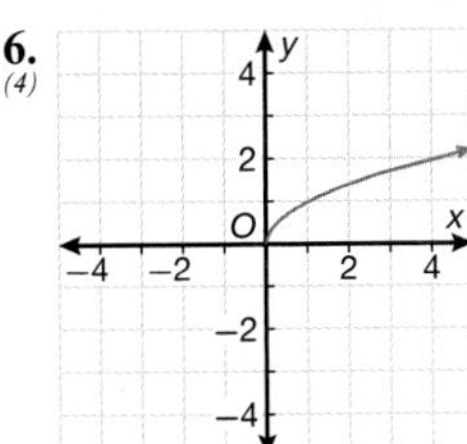

function; D: $x \geq 0$; R = all real numbers

7. (4)

x	y
−2	−1
−2	3
−2	7

not a function; D = {−2}; R = {−1, 3, 7}

8. Measurement This figure consists of a cylinder with a hemisphere on top. Write a
(11) polynomial in x that represents the total surface area of the figure. For reference, formulas for surface area are given below.

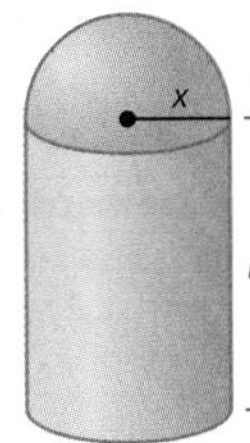

Cylinder: $SA = 2\pi r^2 + 2\pi rh$

Sphere: $SA = 4\pi r^2$

(Hint: The figure has only one circular base.) $3\pi x^2 + 2\pi xh$

Given matrices A, B, and C, multiply, if possible.

$$A = \begin{bmatrix} 1 & 1 \\ 2 & 3 \end{bmatrix} \quad B = \begin{bmatrix} 3 & 2 \\ -1 & 1 \end{bmatrix} \quad C = \begin{bmatrix} 0 & 2 & 0 \\ 3 & 1 & 4 \end{bmatrix}$$

9. CA not possible (9)

10. AB $\begin{bmatrix} 2 & 3 \\ 3 & 7 \end{bmatrix}$ (9)

11. BC $\begin{bmatrix} 6 & 8 & 8 \\ 3 & -1 & 4 \end{bmatrix}$ (9)

Solve.

12. (7) $\frac{4}{7} + \frac{x + 2}{3} = \frac{5}{3}$ $x = \frac{9}{7}$ or $1\frac{2}{7}$

13. (7) $\frac{5}{3} - \frac{x - 4}{2} = \frac{1}{2}$ $\frac{19}{3}$ or $6\frac{1}{3}$

14. (7) $x - 7 + \frac{x}{4} = -\frac{1}{3}$ $\frac{16}{3}$ or $5\frac{1}{3}$

***15.** (15) **Demography** The population of Sacramento, California, in 2005 was 451,743 and increased by 2038 people by 2006. The population of Miami, Florida, in 2005 was 386,619 and increased by 17,429 people by 2006. If the population of these cities continued to grow at these rates, then the following equations would represent the population of the cities, where x is the number of years after 2005 and y is the population.

$y = 2038x + 451{,}743$ Sacramento's Population

$y = 17{,}429x + 386{,}619$ Miami's Population.

a. In what year would the populations of Sacramento and Miami be equal? 2009

b. About how many people are in each city when the populations are equal? 460,000

Problems 9–11

Remind students that to multiply two matrices the number of columns in the first matrix must equal the number of rows in the second matrix.

Example: $C_{2\times3} \times A_{2\times2}$ is not possible because $2 \neq 3$.

Problems 12–14

Ask: **"What are the steps to use to solve for x?"** Sample: Multiply the equation by the least common multiple to eliminate the fractions. Then add or subtract terms to have variables on one side of the equation. Simplify both sides of the equation. Solve for x.

Problem 18

Have students rewrite the compound inequality as two inequalities, $-10 > n$ or $n < -10$ and $n > -1$. Then suggest students graph both inequalities on the same number line.

Problem 22

Remind students that they can check the solution by substituting the values for x and y into the equations.

Problem 25

Error Alert

Students may not remember that the denominator for both x and y is the coefficient matrix. Have students work backward. Given the system of equations, have them write the coefficient matrix.

16. Find x. $\begin{vmatrix} x & 2 & 1 \\ -1 & 1 & 0 \\ 0 & 0 & 1 \end{vmatrix} = 5$ $x = 3$
(14)

17. **Aquarium Design** The aquariums shown each require the same-sized shelf, but they hold different amounts of water. Write a polynomial that represents how much more water the cube-shaped aquarium holds than the cylindrical aquarium. (Hint: The formula for the volume of a cylinder is $V = \pi r^2 h$.) $x^3 - \frac{\pi}{4}x^3$ or $\left(1 - \frac{\pi}{4}\right)x^3$
(11)

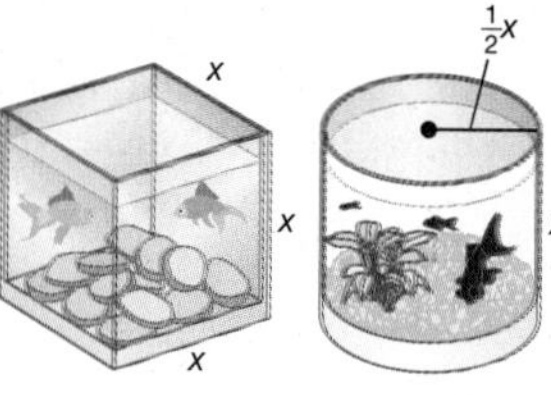

18. **Explain** Why is there no solution for the compound inequality $-10 > n > -1$? A number cannot be greater than -1 and less than -10.
(10)

Solve the inequalities.

19. $3x + 1 > -2$ or $6 < 2x - 4$ $x > -1$
(10)

20. $\frac{1}{3}x + 5 \leq 6$ or $-8 \leq \frac{1}{2}x - 7$ $-2 \leq x \leq 3$
(10)

*21. **Construction** A contractor is replacing the tile in two bathrooms. For one bathroom, she purchased 416 large tiles and 256 small tiles at a cost of \$233.60. For the other bathroom, she purchased 400 large tiles and 512 small tiles at a cost of \$251.20. How much does each size tile cost? large tile: \$0.50; small tile: \$0.10
(16)

Use Cramer's rule to solve each system.

*22. (16) $\begin{aligned} -3x + 4y &= 8 \\ x + 4y &= 4 \end{aligned}$ $(-1, 1.25)$

*23. (16) $\begin{aligned} -3x + 5y &= 8 \\ -3x + 5y &= 4 \end{aligned}$ no solution

*24. (16) $\begin{aligned} 2x + 4y &= 10 \\ -5x - 10y &= -25 \end{aligned}$ Infinitely many solutions

*25. **Multiple Choice** Match the solution with the system of equations. C
(16)

$$x = \frac{\begin{vmatrix} 8 & 2 \\ 1 & -1 \end{vmatrix}}{\begin{vmatrix} 5 & 2 \\ 3 & -1 \end{vmatrix}} \qquad y = \frac{\begin{vmatrix} 5 & 8 \\ 3 & 1 \end{vmatrix}}{\begin{vmatrix} 5 & 2 \\ 3 & -1 \end{vmatrix}}$$

A $\begin{aligned} 8x + 2y &= 5 \\ x - y &= 3 \end{aligned}$

B $\begin{aligned} 5x + 8y &= 2 \\ 3x + y &= -1 \end{aligned}$

C $\begin{aligned} 5x + 2y &= 8 \\ 3x - y &= 1 \end{aligned}$

D $\begin{aligned} 8x + y &= 5 \\ 2x - y &= 2 \end{aligned}$

*26. **Write** When using Cramer's rule to solve systems of equations, what types of systems could exist if the determinant of the coefficient matrix equals zero? Describe the graphs of the lines. The system could be inconsistent and the lines parallel, or the system could be dependent and consistent and the lines coincide.
(16)

CHALLENGE

Use Cramer's rule to solve

$$x + \frac{y}{2} = 2$$
$$\frac{x}{2} - \frac{3y}{4} = -4$$

$\left(-\frac{1}{2}, 5\right)$

***27.** (14) **Geometry** A quadrilateral with vertices (x_1, y_1), (x_2, y_2), (x_3, y_3), and (x_4, y_4) has an area equal to the absolute value of

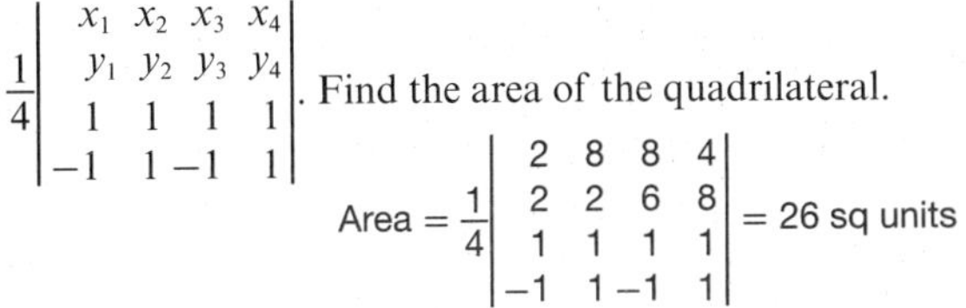

$$\frac{1}{4}\begin{vmatrix} x_1 & x_2 & x_3 & x_4 \\ y_1 & y_2 & y_3 & y_4 \\ 1 & 1 & 1 & 1 \\ -1 & 1 & -1 & 1 \end{vmatrix}$$

. Find the area of the quadrilateral.

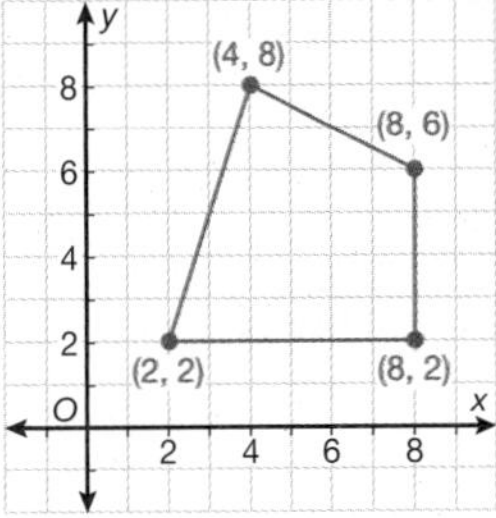

$$\text{Area} = \frac{1}{4}\begin{vmatrix} 2 & 8 & 8 & 4 \\ 2 & 2 & 6 & 8 \\ 1 & 1 & 1 & 1 \\ -1 & 1 & -1 & 1 \end{vmatrix} = 26 \text{ sq units}$$

28. (13) Find the x- and y-intercepts of the line with equation $3x - \frac{1}{2}y = 6$.
(0, −12); (2, 0)

29. (5) **Meteorology** The average temperatures were calculated, in degrees Fahrenheit, for the city of Kodiak, Alaska, and for the city of Valdez, Alaska, from the year 1971 to 2000.

City	Jan	Feb	Mar	Apr	May	Jun
Kodiak	29.7	29.9	32.6	37.3	43.5	49.2
Valdez	21.9	24.8	29.8	37.7	45.8	52.2

a. Model Record this information in a matrix and name it Matrix A.

b. Let $B = \begin{bmatrix} -32 & -32 & -32 & -32 & -32 & -32 \\ -32 & -32 & -32 & -32 & -32 & -32 \end{bmatrix}$. Convert the temperatures from Fahrenheit to Celsius by applying the operations on Matrix A. Round each element to the nearest tenth.

29a. $\begin{bmatrix} 29.7 & 29.9 & 32.6 & 37.3 & 43.5 & 49.2 \\ 21.9 & 24.8 & 29.8 & 37.7 & 45.8 & 52.2 \end{bmatrix}$

$C = \frac{5}{9}([A] + [B])$ **29b.** $\begin{bmatrix} -1.3 & -1.2 & 0.3 & 2.9 & 6.4 & 9.6 \\ -5.6 & -4 & -1.2 & 3.2 & 7.7 & 11.2 \end{bmatrix}$

30. (13) **Geography** Christine is hiking a trail to the summit of a mountain. The mountain has a vertical change of 15 feet upward for every 25 feet of horizontal distance.

a. What is the slope of the mountain? $m = \frac{3}{5}$

b. If the trail has changed vertically by 450 feet, how much has it changed horizontally?
$x = 750$ feet

Problem 28

Encourage students to write the equation in slope-intercept from before finding the x- and y-intercepts.

Problem 29

Ask: "How is $C = \frac{5}{9}([A] + [B])$ like the formula $C = \frac{5}{9}(F - 32)$?" Sample: The elements in Matrix A are the Fahrenheit temperatures, and Matrix B is −32 in the equation. The computation is the same.

Problem 30

Remind students that the slope is the $\frac{\text{rise}}{\text{run}}$ or $\frac{\Delta y}{\Delta x}$.

LOOKING FORWARD

Solving systems of equations by Cramer's rule prepares students for

- **Lesson 29** Systems of Three Equations and Three Variables
- **Investigation 3** Graphing Three Linear Equations in Three Variables

LAB

4

Materials

- graphing calculator

Discuss

In this lab, students will examine line tools such as line thickness, path symbol, dot and inequalities. They will alter window values and use the zoom menu to change the graph display.

Define inequality symbols, path symbol, dot tool, zoom in and zoom out.

TEACHER TIP

It is impossible to adequately represent inequalities containing $<$ or $>$ or a calculator. Dotted lines cannot be represented when shading is used.

Adjusting the Viewing Window

Recall the absolute value function is found using MATH : NUM: 1 :abs(.

Problem 2

Add 1.5 to Xmin and Xmax. Add 1 to Ymin and Ymax. Do not change the x or y scale.

LAB

4

Changing the Line and Window of a Graph

Graphing Calculator Lab (Use with Lessons 17 and 39)

Graphing Calculator Tip

For help with graphing equations, see the graphing calculator keystrokes on page 19.

Adjusting the Viewing Window

The viewing window of the graphing calculator can be adjusted to best display a graph.

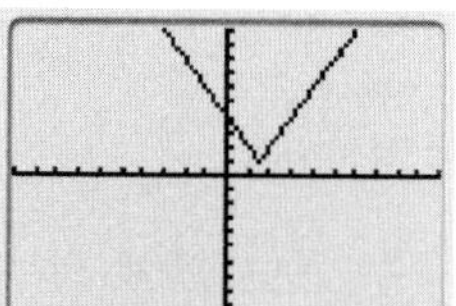

1. Graph the function $y = |2x - 3| + 1$.

2. Center the window on the vertex.

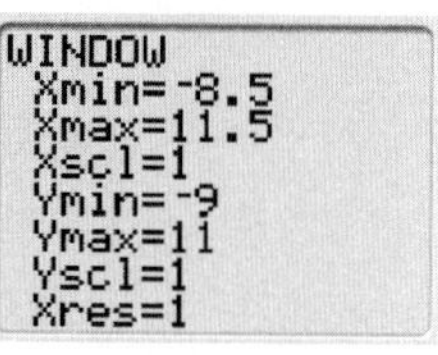

The vertex of this function is located at (1.5, 1). To center the graph on this vertex, the x- and y-values need to be translated: $(x, y) \rightarrow (x + 1.5, y + 1)$. Press WINDOW, use the arrow keys ◄ ▲ ▼ ► to highlight Xmin, enter the value -8.5, and press ENTER. Repeat for Xmax, Ymin, and Ymax. Press GRAPH to display the graph centered on the vertex.

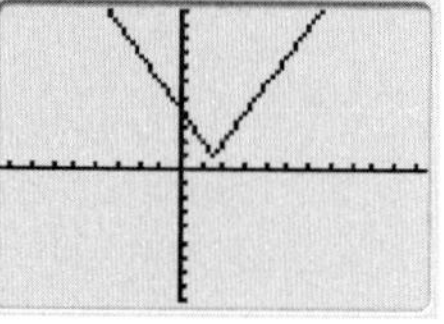

3. Use the zoom features to better see the graph.

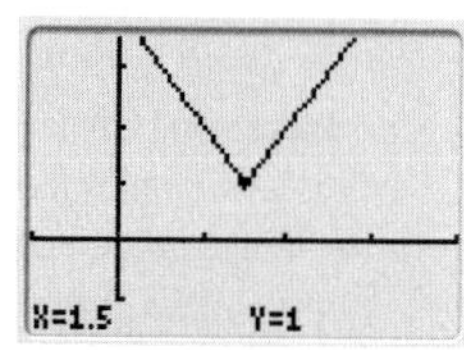

To zoom in on a certain area of a graph, press ZOOM and press 2 to select **2: Zoom In**. The graph will then be displayed with a cursor. Use the arrow keys ◄ ▲ ▼ ► to move the cursor to the area you would like to zoom in on, and then press ENTER. Follow the same method but select **3: Zoom Out** to zoom the graph out.

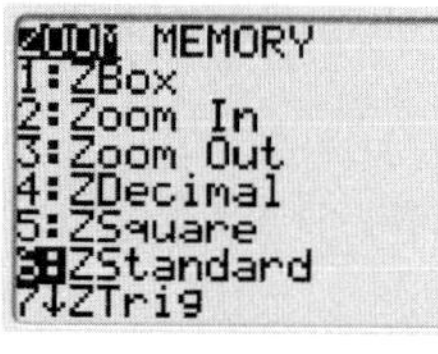

To return a graph to the standard settings where $-10 \leq x \leq 10$ and $-10 \leq y \leq 10$, press ZOOM, use the arrow keys ◄ ▲ ▼ ► to select **6: ZStandard** and press ENTER.

Using Different Drawing Tools

A graphing calculator can be used to change the style of a line.

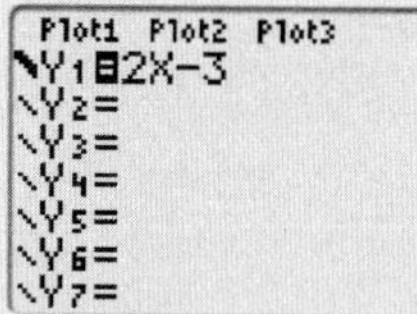

1. Graph the equation $y = 2x - 3$.

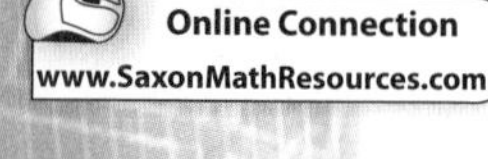

2. Change the graph to thick-line style.

Press Y= and ◀ ◀ to highlight the line symbol to the left of the equation $y = 2x - 3$.

Press ENTER to change to the thick-line symbol. Press GRAPH to see the thick-line graph displayed.

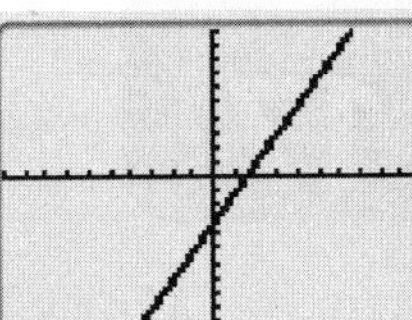

3. Change the graph to a less-than-line style.

Press Y= and highlight the line symbol again.

Press ENTER twice this time until you see the less-than-line symbol. Press GRAPH to see the less-than-line graph of $y \leq 2x - 3$ displayed. (The same method can be used to graph $y \geq 2x - 3$ by selecting the greater-than-line tool.)

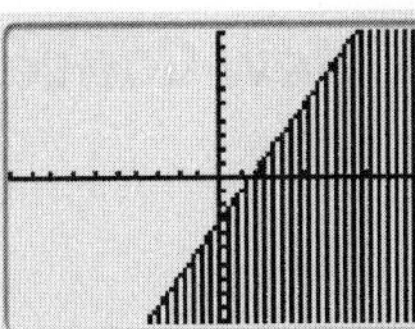

4. Investigate the other drawing tools.

After the less-than-line symbol is the path symbol. This tool traces the graph and draws the path. This is especially helpful in drawing parametric equations.

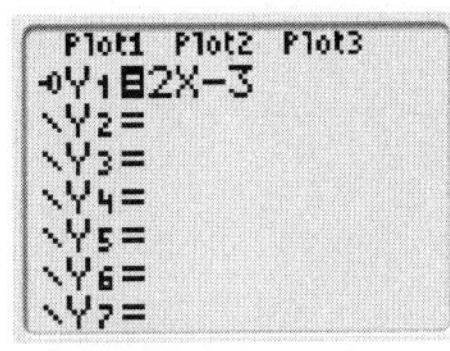

After the path symbol is the animate symbol. This tool traces the graph without drawing the path. This tool is primarily used in physics applications.

The last tool is the dot tool, which will represent each plotted point as a dot. This tool is helpful when drawing step functions or other noncontinuous functions.

Graphing Calculator Practice

a. Use the graphing calculator to graph $y \geq 5 - x$. See Additional Answers.

b. Use the graphing calculator to graph $y = x^2 - 4x + 9$ and center the graph on (2, 5). See Additional Answers.

c. Use the graphing calculator to graph $y = |6x + 3| - 5$ and zoom in on the vertex. See Additional Answers.

Problem 3

Have students examine the window after each Zoom In and Zoom Out command. This will help students understand the concept of zooming.

Extend the Problem

Investigate ZSquare, or zoom square. The calculator screen is a rectangle and not a true square. The zoom square function creates a square window. It does not distort the graph as rectangular windows do.

Using Different Drawing Tools

The drawing tool that is selected will stay in memory until the graph is deselected or deleted. To deselect a graph move the cursor on top of the = symbol and press enter.

The animate symbol can also be used to animate projectiles when graphing parametric equations.

Practice Problem 2

Find the minimum of the parabola by using the techniques in Lab #3. Then if (2, 5) is the vertex, remember to add 2 to Xmin and Xmax. Add 5 to Ymin and Ymax. Do not change the x or y scale.

Lab 4 115

1 Warm Up

Use the Warm Up to review the steps in solving inequalities.

2 New Concepts

In this lesson, students learn to solve absolute value equations and absolute value inequalities.

Introduce the concept of **absolute value** by discussing distances on a number line. Explain to students that they will extend this concept to include variables and, later in the lesson, to include functions.

LESSON 17

Solving Equations and Inequalities with Absolute Value

Warm Up

1. **Vocabulary** A __________ ***(conjunction, disjunction)*** is a compound inequality containing the word *and.* (10) conjunction

2. Solve $x \geq -1$ and $x \leq 4$. (10) $-1 \leq x \leq 4$

3. Solve $x \geq -1$ or $x \leq 4$. (10) all real numbers

New Concepts

The **absolute value** of a number is the distance along the x-axis from the origin to the graph of the number. It is important to note that the absolute value of every number except zero is greater than zero.

$$\text{If } x > 0, |x| = x.$$
$$|7| = 7$$

$|7| = 7$

−7 −6 −5 −4 −3 −2 −1 0 1 2 3 4 5 6 7

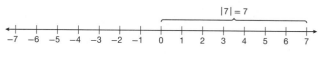

$$\text{If } x = 0, |x| = x.$$
$$|0| = 0$$

$|0| = 0$

−3 −2 −1 0 1 2 3

$$\text{If } x < 0, |x| = -x.$$
$$|-7| = -(-7) = 7$$

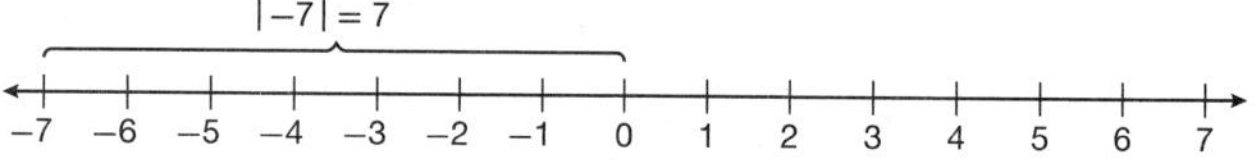

Reading Math

The equation $|x - a| = k$ can be read as "the distance from x to a is k units."

To solve absolute value equations, use inverse operations to isolate the absolute value expression on one side of the equation. Then consider the two cases below.

If $|x - a| = k$

$$x - a = -k \quad \text{or} \quad x - a = k$$
$$\text{then } x = a - k \quad \text{or} \quad x = a + k$$

The two equations above are derived, or obtained, from the original absolute value equation. Derived equations may result in **extraneous solutions.** These solutions do not satisfy the original absolute value equation. Therefore, you need to check all possible solutions.

LESSON RESOURCES

- Student Edition Practice Workbook 17
- Reteaching Master 17
- Adaptations Master 17
- Challenge and Enrichment Master C17

MATH BACKGROUND

Graphing is an important visual tool for helping students understand absolute value equations and inequalities. The solutions to absolute value inequalities can easily be checked by graphing the solution set on a number line and then choosing test points both within and outside the solution set. A test point within the solution set should provide a true statement when inserted in the original inequality. A test point outside the solution set should result in an incorrect statement.

For example, suppose the solution set of an inequality is $x \geq 5$ and $x \leq -3$. Choose a test point in each of the three regions: $x = 9$, $x = 0$, and $x = -5$. When the test points are inserted in the original absolute value inequality, the points $x = 9$ and $x = -5$ should give true statements. The point $x = 0$, because it is not within the solution set, should give a false statement. If not, there is an error in the solution of the problem.

Example 1 Solving Absolute Value Equations

a. Solve $|x-6| = 4$. Graph the solution.

SOLUTION

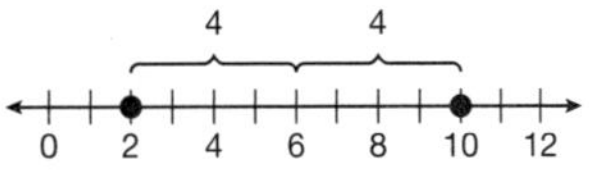

$x - 6 = -4$ or $x - 6 = 4$

$x = -4 + 6$ $\quad$ $x = 4 + 6$

$x = 2$ $\quad$ $x = 10$

Check $|2-6| = |-4| = 4$ $\quad$ $|10-6| = |4| = 4$

The solutions are 2 and 10.

b. Solve $|2x+4| - 5 = 1$.

SOLUTION

$$|2x+4| - 5 = 1$$
$$|2x+4| = 6$$

$2x + 4 = 6$ or $2x + 4 = -6$

$2x = 2$ $\quad$ $2x = -10$

$x = 1$ $\quad$ $x = -5$

Check $|2(1)+4| - 5 \stackrel{?}{=} 1$ $\quad$ $|2(-5)+4| - 5 \stackrel{?}{=} 1$

$|2+4| \stackrel{?}{=} 6$ $\quad$ $|-10+4| \stackrel{?}{=} 6$

$6 = 6$ ✓ $\quad$ $|-6| \stackrel{?}{=} 6$

$6 = 6$ ✓

The solutions are 1 and -5.

Hint

An extraneous solution may occur anytime there is a variable outside the absolute value symbol.

c. Solve $|3x+5| = -10$.

SOLUTION No solution. The absolute value of a number is never negative, as it represents distance.

d. Solve $|3x+18| = 6x$. Check for extraneous solutions.

SOLUTION $3x + 18 = 6x$ or $3x + 18 = -6x$

$18 = 3x$ $\quad$ $18 = -9x$

$6 = x$ $\quad$ $-2 = x$

Check Evaluate $|3x+18| = 6x$ for $x = 6$ and $x = -2$.

$|3(6)+18| \stackrel{?}{=} 6(6)$ $\quad$ $|3(-2)+18| \stackrel{?}{=} 6(-2)$

$|18+18| \stackrel{?}{=} 36$ $\quad$ $|-6+18| \stackrel{?}{=} -12$

$|36| \stackrel{?}{=} 36$ $\quad$ $|12| \stackrel{?}{=} -12$

$36 = 36$ ✓ $\quad$ $12 \neq -12$

The solution is 6. -2 is an extraneous solution.

Example 1

This example demonstrates the method of solving an absolute value equation in which the variable appears only within the absolute value symbol.

Error Alert Students may mistakenly check for extraneous solutions by substituting the possible solutions into the derived equations rather than the original absolute value equation. This error will make all *possible* solutions seem to be *acceptable* solutions. If students substitute the possible solution $x = -3$ into the derived equation $3x + 18 = -6x$ for example 1d, the solution seems to be correct. Instead, they must check by substituting $x = -3$ into the original absolute value equation, $|3x + 18| = 6x$, to find that the solution is extraneous.

Additional Example 1

a. Solve $|x - 4| = 7$. Graph the solution. -3 and 11

b. Solve $|3x + 1| - 4 = 6$. 3 and $-\frac{11}{3}$

c. Solve $|9x + 7| = -2$. no solution

d. Solve $|4x + 12| = 8x$. Check for extraneous solutions. 3

INCLUSION

Relate the mathematical conjunctions that students study in this lesson to the grammar conjunctions that they have studied in language classes. Students have learned that conjunctions such as *and, but, or,* and *because* are used to link words, phrases, and clauses. For example:

> A car *and* a truck drove along the road.
> Jan walked slowly *because* she was tired.

Draw students' attention to the root word *junction,* which means "a place where things meet." The prefix *con-* means "together," and the prefix *dis-* means "apart."

Sketch two number lines on the board, and graph the inequalities $|x| < 4$ and $|x| > 4$.

Lead students in discussing how the prefixes and root word of *conjunction* and *disjunction* relate to the graphs you have drawn.

Example 2

The examples show how to solve absolute value inequalities with conjunctions. In part b., students need to first isolate the absolute value term, before solving the inequality.

Additional Example 2

a. Solve $|x - 9| \leq 3$. Graph the solution. $6 \leq x \leq 12$

4 6 8 10 12 14

b. Solve $-3|4x| + 5 \leq 8$.
no solution

TEACHER TIP

Use the line graphs on this page to explain the difference meanings and the difference in plotting inequalities that use the symbols < and > and those that use the symbols ≤ and ≥.

Absolute value inequalities can be solved by rewriting and solving them as compound inequalities. Absolute value inequalities are either conjunctions or disjunctions.

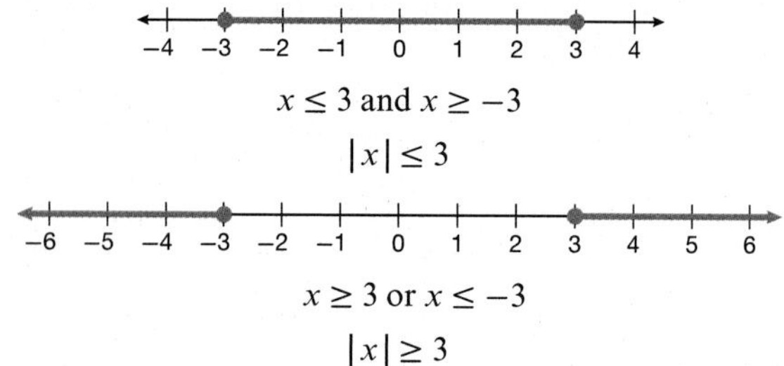

$x \leq 3$ and $x \geq -3$

$|x| \leq 3$

$x \geq 3$ or $x \leq -3$

$|x| \geq 3$

Conjunctions can be replaced with absolute value statements of less than. Disjunctions can be replaced with absolute value statements of greater than.

If a is a positive number, then

$|x| < a$ is the same as the conjunction $x < a$ and $x > -a$ or $-a < x < a$

$|x| > a$ is the same as the disjunction $x > a$ or $x < -a$

Note that statements like $|x| < -4$ and $|x| > -4$ are special cases. The first inequality has no solution, while the second is all real numbers.

Reading Math

"And" means to include in the solution all numbers common to both inequalities.

Example 2 Solving Absolute Value Inequalities with Conjunctions

a. Solve $|x - 5| \leq 2$. Graph the solution.

SOLUTION Rewrite the inequality as a conjunction, then solve for x.

$$x - 5 \leq 2 \quad \text{and} \quad x - 5 \geq -2$$
$$x \leq 7 \quad \text{and} \quad x \geq 3$$

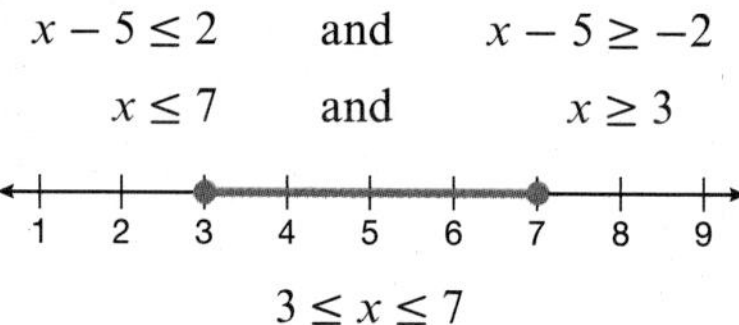

$3 \leq x \leq 7$

b. Solve $-2|3x| + 4 \geq 6$.

SOLUTION Always isolate the absolute value term before rewriting the inequality as a conjunction or disjunction.

$$-2|3x| + 4 \geq 6 \quad \longrightarrow \quad -2|3x| \geq 2 \quad \longrightarrow \quad |3x| \leq -1$$

Since the absolute value of a number is always greater than or equal to zero, there is no solution.

ALTERNATE METHOD FOR EXAMPLE 2

Students may prefer to solve the absolute value inequalities using a more visual method by first graphing each part of the conjunction with one graph above the other, and then observing where the graphs overlap to create the solution graph, as shown here.

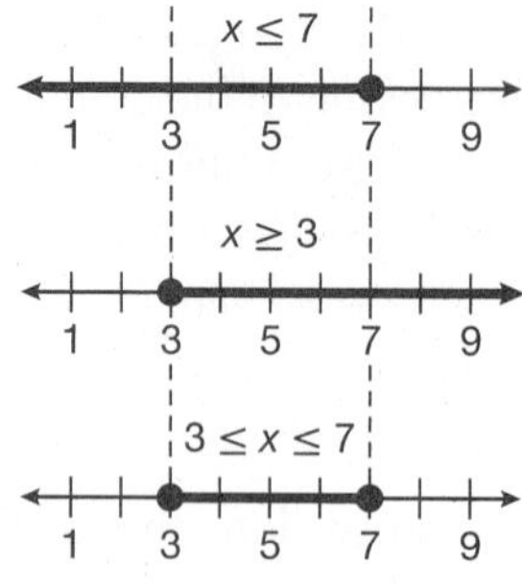

Example 3 Solving Absolute Value Inequalities with Disjunctions

a. Solve $|2x - 5| > 9$. Graph the solution.

SOLUTION Rewrite the inequality as a disjunction and then solve for x.

$$2x - 5 > 9 \quad \text{or} \quad 2x - 5 < -9$$
$$2x > 14 \qquad\qquad 2x < -4$$
$$x > 7 \quad \text{or} \quad x < -2$$

−3 −2 −1 0 1 2 3 4 5 6 7 8

$x < -2$ or $x > 7$

b. Solve $-|4x - 2| < 1$.

SOLUTION Isolate the absolute value term.

$$-|4x - 2| < 1 \quad \rightarrow \quad |4x - 2| > -1$$

Since the absolute value of a number is always greater than or equal to zero, the inequality will be true for any number substituted for x.

The solution is all real numbers.

Reading Math

"Or" means to include in the solution all numbers described by both inequalities.

The graphs in the previous examples are one-dimensional because the only variable is x. An **absolute value function** is a function that contains an absolute value expression. The graph of the equation $y = |x|$, or $f(x) = |x|$, will be two-dimensional because there are two variables, x and y.

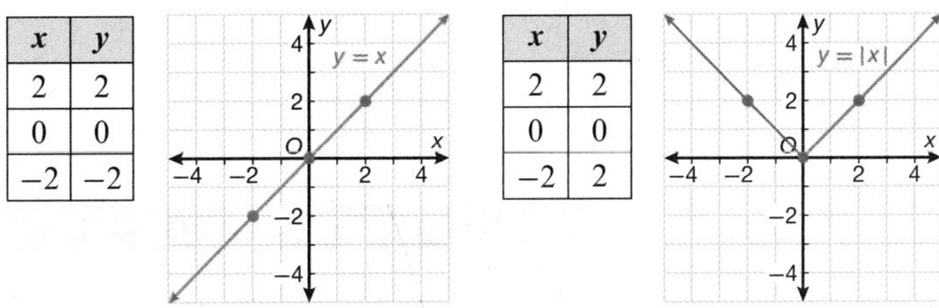

x	y
2	2
0	0
−2	−2

x	y
2	2
0	0
−2	2

The graph on the left is the graph of $y = x$. The graph on the right is the graph of $f(x) = |x|$, the parent function of absolute value functions. It does not go below the x-axis because y equals the absolute value of x and the absolute value of a number is never negative.

A **parent function** is the simplest function of a particular type. New functions can be graphed by **transformations,** or changes, to the graph of the parent function. These changes may involve a change in the size, shape, orientation, or position of the parent function.

Math Reasoning

Generalize Give the parent function for a linear function. $y = x$

ALTERNATE METHOD FOR EXAMPLE 3

Have students explore absolute value functions by plotting a function on a graphing calculator and varying the values of the constants a, h, and k that they use in the equation. Encourage students to experiment with varying one of the constants at a time to determine how an increase or a decrease in its value affects the function's appearance.

Example 3

Students learn to solve absolute value inequalities with disjunctions in this example.

Additional Example 3

a. Solve $|3x - 6| > 3$. Graph the solution. $x < 1$ or $x > 3$

−2 0 2 4 6

b. Solve $-|5x - 4| < 6$.
all real numbers

Error Alert Students may mistakenly believe that the answer to Example 3b is "no solution" by using the following reasoning: Multiply both sides by −1 to get $|4x - 2| < -1$. Because an absolute value must be positive, the problem has no solution. Remind students that when they multiply an inequality by a negative number, the inequality changes direction. In this case, the "less than" sign becomes "greater than," and the solution is all real numbers.

TEACHER TIP

When students choose the x and y values that they will use to plot the graph of an absolute value function, encourage them to choose points that they believe will provide a clear idea of the function's shape. For example, to plot the function $f = |x|$, choosing a positive number, a negative number, and zero show that the function has the shape of a "V." If students plot the points and the shape of the function is not obvious, or they cannot discern the vertex, suggest that they choose more points to plot.

Lesson 17 119

Example 4

The example demonstrates how to solve a real life problem using an absolute value inequality.

Additional Example 4

Brian wants to plant a garden that is within 3.5 meters of being 15 meters wide. Write an absolute value equation to determine the least and greatest width of the garden. Solve the equation and graph the solution.
$11.5 \leq w \leq 18.5$

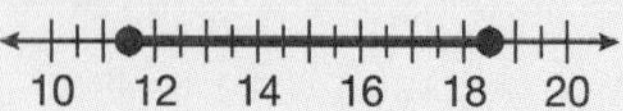

Lesson Practice

Problem b

Error Alert Remind students to first isolate the absolute value before performing any other steps.

Problem d

Scaffolding Remind students that extraneous solutions may occur for a variable outside the absolute value symbol. In this case, both solutions are correct.

Check for Understanding

The questions below help assess the concepts taught in this lesson.

1. **What are examples of real life problems that have absolute values?** Sample: distances or ranges in values
2. **Why do some absolute value problems have no *correct* solution?** Absolute values must be positive.

Hint

Since $f(x) = |x + 4| = |x - (-4)|$, the h value is negative, not positive.

Exploration Transforming $f(x) = |x|$

Use a table of values to graph each of the following equations.

a. $f(x) = -|x|$ **b.** $f(x) = \frac{1}{2}|x|$ **c.** $f(x) = |x - 4|$

d. $f(x) = |x + 4|$ **e.** $f(x) = |x| - 4$ **f.** $f(x) = |x| + 4$

a.–h. See Additional Answers.

The graph of the absolute value function $y = a|x - h| + k$ can be used to model the transformations of the graph of the parent function $f(x) = |x|$.

g. Use the graphs of the functions to describe the effect of h and k on the graph of the parent function.

h. How is the shape and orientation of the graph determined?

i. Can the equation $y = a|x - h| + k$ be used to determine the **vertex**, or turning point, of the graph? Yes. The vertex is at the point (h, k).

Hint

The number inside the absolute value symbol will be the "starting point"; the number outside the absolute value symbol will be the variance.

Example 4 Application: Chemistry

For hydrogen to be a liquid, it must be within 2° of −257°C. Write an absolute value equation to determine the least and greatest temperatures at which hydrogen will remain a liquid. Solve the equation and graph the solution.

SOLUTION Let t = temperature.

$$|t - (-257)| = 2$$
$$|t + 257| = 2$$
$$t + 257 = 2 \quad \text{and} \quad t + 257 = -2$$
$$t = -255 \qquad t = -259$$

The least temperature is −259°C and the greatest temperature is −255°C.

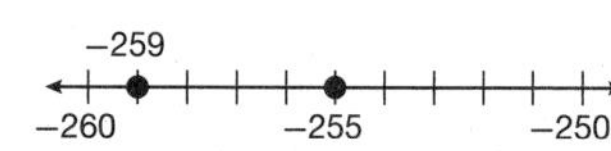

Lesson Practice

a. (Ex 1) Solve $|x + 3| = 7$. Graph the solution. See Additional Answers.

b. (Ex 1) Solve $|3x - 3| + 5 = 8$. $x = 0$ or $x = 2$

c. (Ex 1) Solve $|7x - 2| = -8$. no solution

d. (Ex 1) Solve $|4x - 1| = 2x$. Check for extraneous solutions. $x = \frac{1}{2}$ or $\frac{1}{6}$

e. (Ex 2) Solve $|x + 2| < 8$. Graph the solution. See Additional Answers.

f. (Ex 2) Solve $3|5x| - 6 \leq 6$. $x \leq \frac{4}{5}$ and $x \geq -\frac{4}{5}$

g. (Ex 3) Solve $|-2x + 9| \geq 7$. Graph the solution. See Additional Answers.

h. (Ex 3) Solve $-|2x + 3| \leq 5$. all real numbers

i. (Ex 4) For nitrogen to be a liquid, it must be within 13° of −333°F. Write an absolute value equation to determine the least and greatest temperatures at which nitrogen will remain a liquid. Solve the equation and graph the solution. $|t + 333| = 13$; min: −346; max: −320

−350 −345 −340 −335 −330 −325 −320 −315

ENGLISH LEARNERS

The term **extraneous** may be unfamiliar to students. Say:

"The word extraneous means not belonging."

Draw students' attention to the root word *extra.* Write the word extraneous on the board and underline *extra.* Lead students in discussing what this root word may imply about the meaning of *extraneous.* Say:

"If you have extra pencils, you have more than what you need."

Have students give examples of things that can be considered extraneous.

Practice Distributed and Integrated

***1.** (17) **Construction Engineering** A company's safety regulations require the wire rope used to suspend a 100-ton load to have a thickness that is within $\frac{3}{8}$ inch of $1\frac{3}{4}$ inches. Write and solve an absolute value equation to find the minimum safe thickness of rope. $|t - 1\frac{3}{4}| = \frac{3}{8}$; $1\frac{3}{8}$ inches

2. (13) **Explain** Two points, (3, −7) and (3, 5), lie on a line. Using the slope formula, explain why the slope does not exist. What kind of line do these points lie on?

***3.** (17) **Generalize** Will the inequality $3|x - 7| > -12$ have a solution?

Use Cramer's rule to solve each system.

***4.** (16) $4x - 2y = 6$, $10x - 5y = 15$ infinitely many solutions

5. (16) $-5x + 2y = 7$, $10x - 4y = 3$ no solution

6. (16) $-3x + 2y = 4$, $x + 2y = 10$ (1.5, 4.25)

***7.** (15) **Multiple Choice** Which is *not* a solution to the system below? **B**

$$2x - 5y = -3$$
$$-10x + 25y = 15$$

A (1, 1) B (0, 0)

C (6, 3) D All of these are solutions.

Find the product.

8. (9) $\begin{bmatrix} 1 & 0 & -2 \\ 0 & 3 & -1 \\ 2 & 0 & 4 \end{bmatrix} \cdot \begin{bmatrix} 4 & -3 \\ 1 & 2 \\ 0 & -1 \end{bmatrix}$ $\begin{bmatrix} 4 & -1 \\ 3 & 7 \\ 8 & -10 \end{bmatrix}$

9. (9) $\begin{bmatrix} 2 & -3 & 1 & -2 \end{bmatrix} \cdot \begin{bmatrix} 0 & 1 \\ -3 & 2 \\ 1 & 0 \\ 4 & 6 \end{bmatrix}$ $[2 \ -16]$

10. (8) **Temperature** Juanita is conducting an experiment where the temperature of a liquid varies directly with time. Her observations are recorded in the table below.

Temperature	80 degrees	120 degrees	? degrees
Time	120 seconds	180 seconds	240 seconds

a. Using the values in the table, identify the constant of variation. $k = \frac{2}{3}$

b. Find the missing temperature in the table. 160 degrees

c. Determine an accurate prediction for the temperature of the liquid after 360 seconds. 240 degrees

11. (13) **Multiple Choice** Identify the slope of the line with the equation $2x + 9y = 18$. **D**

A 2 B $\frac{2}{9}$ C $-\frac{9}{2}$ D $-\frac{2}{9}$

2. When the coordinates are substituted into the formula, the denominator results in a zero; Vertical line.

3. Yes. After isolating the absolute value expression, it is greater than a negative number. Since absolute value is always positive, x can be replaced with any number and the inequality will be true.

3 Practice

Math Conversations

Discussions to strengthen understanding.

Problem 10

Error Alert

Students may become confused between a constant of variation and its inverse. Consider the two possibilities for this problem:

(Time) = k(Temperature) → $k = \frac{3}{2}$

(Temperature) = k(Time) → $k = \frac{2}{3}$

Either form is acceptable, provided the student maintains consistency in applying the constant of variation. If the student chooses the first constant of variation, but reverses the placement of time and temperature, the incorrect solution to part b would be 360 degrees, an unreasonable answer. Draw students' attention to this possible error and encourage them to check for reasonableness when applying the constant of variation.

Problem 11

Extend the Problem

"What is the equation written in the form $y = mx + b$?"
$y = -\frac{2}{9}x + 2$

"What is the point at which the line crosses the y-axis?" (0, 2)

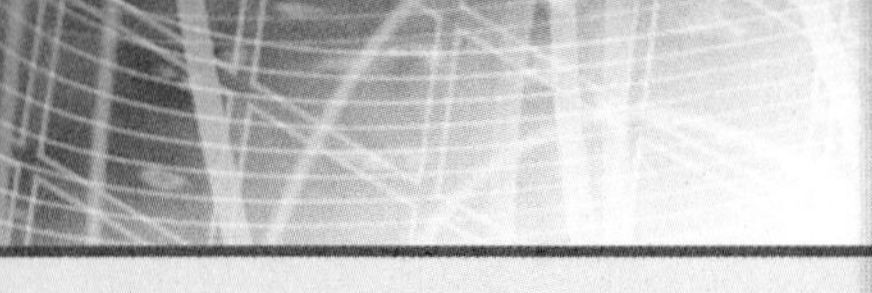

Problem 12

Guide the students by asking them the following questions.

"What should you do to determine the constant of variation for each pitcher?" For each pitcher, insert one row of the ball's speed and the corresponding force into the equation $F = kv^2$, and solve for k.

"A student says the force of the wind resistance varies directly with the ball's speed for each pitcher. Do you agree? Explain." No; the force varies directly with the *square* of the ball's speed.

Problem 16

Ask students, **"What two steps could you take before solving the system of inequalities to change the fractions in the first inequality to integers?"** First, change the mixed fraction $1\frac{2}{3}$ to the improper fraction $\frac{5}{3}$. Then, multiply both sides of the inequality by 3 so that there are only integers in the equality.

Problem 19

Ask students, **"How can you tell just by the form of the absolute value equation that it might have an extraneous solution?"** The equation has a variable outside the absolute value symbol.

12. (8) **Baseball** When a baseball pitcher throws a baseball, the ball is slowed down by wind resistance. The relationship between the force (F) of wind resistance and velocity (v) of the baseball is a direct variation of the form $F = kv^2$. The data tables below represent sample pitches from two ball games.

Pitcher A

Ball Speed (mph)	Force
90	1620
91	1656
92	1693
93	1730
94	1767
95	1805

Pitcher B

Ball Speed (mph)	Force
90	2025
91	2070
92	2116
93	2162
94	2209
95	2256

a. Find the constant of variation for each pitcher. Pitcher A: 0.2; Pitcher B: 0.25

b. Based on your results, which pitcher was throwing the ball faster? Pitcher B

c. What could account for the difference in the force of wind resistance? Sample: The weather can be a factor in wind resistance.

13. (16) **Multi-Step** Use Cramer's Rule to solve the system. Check your solution by graphing. $\left(2, \frac{4}{3}\right)$ See Additional Answers.

$$-2x + 3y = 0$$
$$x + 3y = 6$$

14. (11) **Error Analysis** A student says that the polynomial $ab^4 + a^2b^2 - 3$ is of higher degree than the polynomial $a^2b^3 + ab + 2$. What is the error? Explain.

14. The polynomials have the same degree, 5. The monomial with greatest degree in the first polynomial is ab^4, which has degree 5, and the monomial with greatest degree in the second polynomial is a^2b^3, which also has degree 5.

Solve the equation or inequality.

15. (7) $\frac{y-2}{4} = 7y - 2 - 6(y + 1)$ $y = 10$

16. (10) $2 + \frac{1}{3}x \le 1\frac{2}{3}$ and $-2x - 5 \le 7$ $-6 \le x \le -1$

17. (10) $-\frac{1}{3} - \frac{2x}{3} > \frac{1}{3}$ and $-7x - \frac{1}{2} < 6\frac{1}{2}$ no solution

***18.** (17) $|-2x + 7| - 3 = 10.$ $x = -3$ or $x = 10$

***19.** (17) **Verify** Solve $|8x - 3| = 16x$. Check for extraneous solutions by substituting the solution into the equation. $x = \frac{1}{8}$; The result for substituting $-\frac{3}{8}$ is $|-6| = -6$, which is false.

***20.** (17) Solve $|3x + 2| \le 14$. Graph the solution. $-\frac{16}{3} \le x \le 4$;

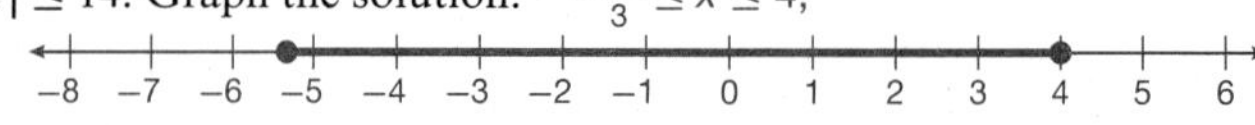

21. (15) **Geometry**

a. Graph the system below. Describe the shape that the lines form.

$$3x - 2y = 2$$
$$-3x - 2y = -34$$
$$x - 2y = 6$$

See Additional Answers.

b. Find the vertices of the shape. (6, 8), (10, 2), (–2, –4)

22. (14) A triangle has vertices (1, 2), (1, –4), and (4, –4). Find the area of the triangle by writing and solving a determinant. $\frac{1}{2}\begin{vmatrix} 1 & 1 & 4 \\ 2 & -4 & -4 \\ 1 & 1 & 1 \end{vmatrix} = 9$ square units

CHALLENGE

Have students extend what they have learned about graphing absolute value functions to graph several absolute value inequalities. Provide the example of graphing $f(x) \ge |x|$.

Explain that first students should graph the equation $f(x) = |x|$. Next, they should test a point above and a point below the graph of the equation to see which makes a true inequality. The region that contains the correct test point correctly solves the inequality. Students can indicate this region by shading.

Have students graph $f(x) \le |x - 3|$ and $f(x) > 2|x|$.

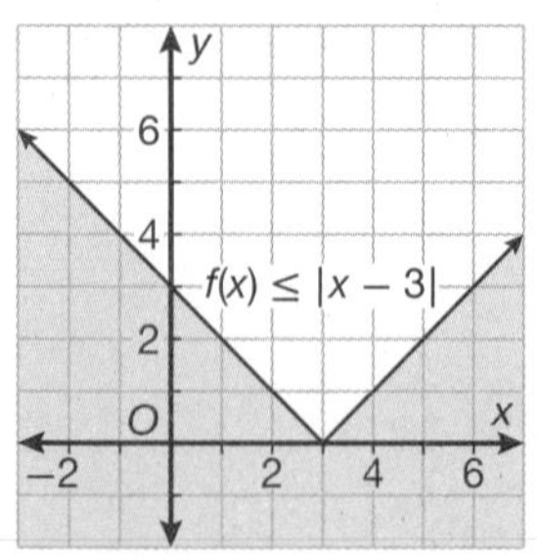

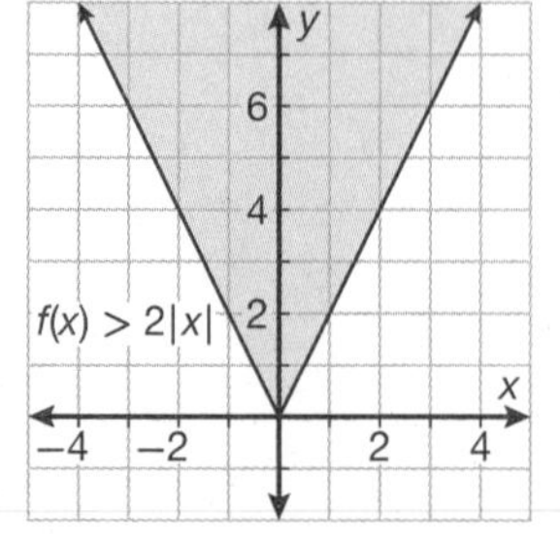

Use a table to graph the equation. (Hint: Choose x-values that are multiples of the slope's denominator.)

23. (13) $y = -\frac{5}{3}x - 2$ See Additional Answers.

24. (13) $y = -\frac{1}{2}x + 5$ See Additional Answers.

***25.** (14) **Graphing Calculator** Use a graphing calculator to evaluate

$$2\begin{vmatrix} -2 & 1 & 4 \\ -5 & 7 & 0 \\ 8 & -3 & 1 \end{vmatrix} - 3\begin{vmatrix} 0 & 1 & 4 \\ 1 & 7 & 0 \\ -6 & -3 & 1 \end{vmatrix} - 1\begin{vmatrix} 0 & -2 & 4 \\ 1 & -5 & 0 \\ -6 & 8 & 1 \end{vmatrix} - 5\begin{vmatrix} 0 & -2 & 1 \\ 1 & -5 & 7 \\ -6 & 8 & -3 \end{vmatrix}.$$ -1005

26. (3) **Solar System** The average distance between the earth and sun is approximately 1.495×10^{11} m. Earth's orbit around the sun is nearly circular. For estimation purposes, assume that Earth's orbit is circular.

a. Estimate the distance in kilometers that the earth travels around the sun in one year. Write your answer in scientific notation. Round to the nearest hundredth. $2 \times \pi \times (1.495 \times 10^{11})$ m $= 9.39 \times 10^{11}$ m $= 9.39 \times 10^{8}$ km

b. Estimate the average speed at which the earth travels around the sun in km/s. Use 365.25 days per year.

26. b.
365.25 days $\times \frac{24 \text{ hr}}{\text{day}} \times \frac{60 \text{ min}}{\text{hr}} \times \frac{60\text{s}}{\text{min}} =$ 3.156×10^7 s.
So, $\frac{9.39 \times 10^8 \text{ km}}{3.156 \times 10^7 \text{ s}} =$ 29.75 km/s.

***27.** (13) Find the slope of the line between $(-2, -7)$ and $(2, 1)$. Determine if the line rises, falls, or is horizontal or vertical. $m = 2$; rises

***28.** (8) **Landscaping** When mixing concentrated fertilizer for a garden, the amount of fertilizer varies directly with the amount of water. If 2 cups of fertilizer are used in 16 gallons of water, how much fertilizer is used in 48 gallons of water? 6 cups

Determine the kind of variation, if any, for each equation.

29. (12) $y = ax^2 + bx + c$, for $a, b, c \neq 0$ no variation

30. (12) $y = ax^2 + bx + c$, for any values of a, b, and c. direct when b and $c = 0$ or when a and $c = 0$

LOOKING FORWARD

Solving equations and inequalities with absolute value prepares students for

- **Lesson 22** Analyzing Discrete and Continuous Functions
- **Lesson 69** Simplifying Complex Expressions

Problem 28
Extend the Problem

"What is the direct variation equation for the problem?" $F = \frac{1}{8}w$

"How much water would be needed if 8 cups of fertilizer were used?" 64 cups

LESSON
18

1 Warm Up

Use problems 2 and 3 in the Warm Up to review canceling techniques to be used in this lesson.

2 New Concepts

In this lesson, students learn to convert units of measure using dimensional analysis.

Example 1

Students will find the correct conversion factor.

Additional Example 1

a. Change 5 pounds to ounces. 80 ounces

b. Change 900 feet to yards. 300 yards

Example 2

Remind students that square units are only cancelled by the same square units.

Additional Example 2

a. Convert 17 yd^2 to in^2. 22,032 in^2

b. Convert 2500 seconds to hours. $\frac{25}{36}$ hr

LESSON
18 Calculating with Units of Measure

Warm Up

1. Vocabulary 1 foot and 12 inches are equivalent. (*equivalent, proportional*)

2. (3) Simplify $\frac{x^4 \cdot x^2}{x^3}$. x^3

3. (SB) Simplify $\frac{6}{7} \times \frac{5}{6} \times \frac{3}{5} \times \frac{2}{3}$. $\frac{2}{7}$

New Concepts

You can use unit **conversion factors** to change one unit of measure to another. Dimensional analysis involves choosing the appropriate conversion factor to produce the appropriate unit.

Reading Math

The slash (/) is used to symbolize the canceling of factors or, as in this lesson, units.

Example 1 Choosing the Appropriate Conversion Factor

a. Change 600 inches to feet.

SOLUTION Put 600 in. over 1.

$$\frac{600\text{ in.}}{1}$$

There are 12 inches in a foot, so the conversion factor is either $\frac{1\text{ ft}}{12\text{ in.}}$ or $\frac{12\text{ in.}}{1\text{ ft}}$. If you choose $\frac{1\text{ ft}}{12\text{ in.}}$ as the conversion factor, the inches will cancel.

$$\frac{600\,\cancel{\text{in.}}}{1} \times \frac{1\text{ ft}}{12\,\cancel{\text{in.}}} = 50\text{ ft}$$

b. Change 8 hours to minutes.

SOLUTION Put 8 hours over 1.

$$\frac{8\text{ hr}}{1}$$

There are 60 minutes in an hour, so the conversion factor is either $\frac{1\text{ hr}}{60\text{ min}}$ or $\frac{60\text{ min}}{1\text{ hr}}$. You want the hours to cancel, so choose $\frac{60\text{ min}}{1\text{ hr}}$.

$$\frac{8\,\cancel{\text{hr}}}{1} \times \frac{60\text{ min}}{1\,\cancel{\text{hr}}} = 480\text{ min}$$

Sometimes you may need to use more than one conversion factor.

Example 2 Using Multiple Conversion Factors

a. Convert 42 yd^2 to in^2.

SOLUTION Put 42 yd^2 over 1.

$$\frac{42\text{ yd}^2}{1}$$

There are 3 feet in a yard and 12 inches in a foot, so

$$\frac{42\,\cancel{\text{yd}^2}}{1} \times \frac{3\,\cancel{\text{ft}}}{1\,\cancel{\text{yd}}} \times \frac{3\,\cancel{\text{ft}}}{1\,\cancel{\text{yd}}} \times \frac{12\text{ in.}}{1\,\cancel{\text{ft}}} \times \frac{12\text{ in.}}{1\,\cancel{\text{ft}}} = 54{,}432\text{ in}^2$$

b. Convert 3000 seconds to hours.

SOLUTION Put 3000 s over 1.

$$\frac{3000\text{ s}}{1}$$

There are 60 seconds in a minute and 60 minutes in an hour, so

$$\frac{3000\,\cancel{\text{s}}}{1} \times \frac{1\,\cancel{\text{min}}}{60\,\cancel{\text{s}}} \times \frac{1\text{ hr}}{60\,\cancel{\text{min}}} = \frac{5}{6}\text{ hr}$$

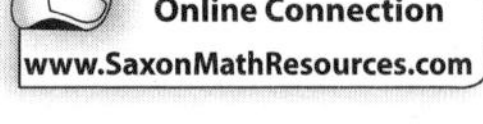

MATH BACKGROUND

Dimensional Analysis is also called the Unit-Factor Method or the Factor-Label Method. It depends on the understanding that any value can be multiplied by 1 and maintains its value.

$\frac{1\text{ ft}}{12\text{ in.}} = 1$, so this factor can be used to change inches to feet when it is multiplied by any number of inches. The measurement that is multiplied by the factor does not change because the factor is equal to 1.

Dimensional Analysis can be used to change between measures in the same system, such as inches to feet, or between different systems, such as feet to meters.

LESSON RESOURCES

Student Edition Practice Workbook 18
Reteaching Master 18
Adaptations Master 18
Challenge and Enrichment Master C18

Example 3 Converting Rates

Convert 50 feet per second to miles per hour.

SOLUTION Write 50 feet per second as a fraction. $\frac{50 \text{ ft}}{1 \text{ s}}$

Convert feet to miles and seconds to hours. There are 5280 feet in a mile, so the conversion factor is $\frac{1 \text{ mi}}{5280 \text{ ft}}$. There are 60 seconds in a minute and 60 minutes in an hour, so the other conversion factor is $\frac{3600 \text{ s}}{1 \text{ hr}}$.

$$\frac{50 \cancel{\text{ft}}}{1 \cancel{\text{s}}} \times \frac{1 \text{ mi}}{5280 \cancel{\text{ft}}} \times \frac{3600 \cancel{\text{s}}}{1 \text{ hr}} = \frac{(50)(3600)}{5280} \frac{\text{mi}}{\text{hr}}$$

Using a calculator, this simplifies to about 34 mph.

Math Language

Per means "for each" and implies division.

The **accuracy** of a measurement refers to how closely it corresponds to the actual value being measured. The **precision** of a measurement refers to the number of **significant digits** it contains. The following table illustrates how to find the number of significant digits in a measured value.

Significant Digits

Rule	Example	Number of Significant Digits
Nonzero digits are significant.	325.6	4
Zeros between significant digits are significant.	5003.09	6
Leading zeros are not significant.	0.00047	2
Zeros after the last nonzero digit that are also to the right of a decimal point are significant.	0.0001800	4

The following rules are used to determine the number of significant digits that should be in the answer to a calculation with measurements:

Rules for Significant Digits in Measurements
When adding or subtracting, the answer should have the same number of decimal places as the measurement with the fewest decimal places. When multiplying or dividing, the answer should have the same number of significant digits as the measurement with the fewest significant digits.

Example 4 Using Significant Digits

Simplify each expression.

a. 5.38 mi + 6.495 mi + 0.5 mi

SOLUTION Add the three distances.

5.38 mi + 6.495 mi + 0.5 mi = 12.375 mi

Since 0.5 mi has only one decimal place, the answer must be rounded to one decimal place, resulting in 12.4 mi.

b. 2.09 ft × 0.050 ft × 303 ft

SOLUTION Multiply the three lengths.

2.09 ft × 0.050 ft × 303 ft = 31.6635 ft^3

Since 0.050 ft has only two significant digits, the answer can only have two significant digits, resulting in 32 ft^3.

INCLUSION

Allow students to create a list of common conversions. Students can then refer to the list to find those factors that have both the unit of measure that they have as well as the unit they wish to convert to.

Example 3

These values are called rates because they are in the form *per unit*.

Additional Example 3

Convert 45 miles per hour to feet per second. 66 feet per second

Extend the Example

Have students check their answers by comparing the distance that can be covered in 5 minutes at 50 feet per second and 34 miles per hour.

TEACHER TIP

Students should understand that when adding or subtracting measurements with whole numbers the answer would only be as accurate as the smallest place value of any measurement. For example, 45 m + 1020 m = 1070 m.

Example 4

Students will practice using significant digits in addition and multiplication problems.

Additional Example 4

Simply each expression

a. 6.37 in. + 4.257 in. + 0.8 in. 11.4 in.

b. 3.04 ft × 4.275 ft × 3.1 ft 40 ft

Extend the Example

Challenge students to come up with new numbers for example 4b that would give an answer with 3, 4, and 5 significant digits.

Example 5

Remind the students not to round to significant digits until all calculations are done.

Additional Example 5

The speed of sound on Earth at 0 altitude is 761 miles per hour. What is this speed in feet per second? 1116.1333 feet per second

Lesson Practice

Problem d

Scaffolding Before converting, have students write the first term in the conversion and the answer desired with space to fill in with the correct conversion factors.

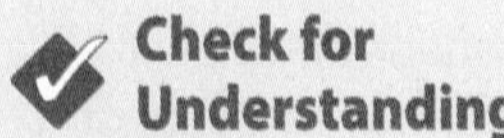

Check for Understanding

The questions help assess the concepts taught in this lesson.

1. **Explain how to choose a conversion factor.** Sample: The conversion factor should have the unit that the problem contains in the denominator and the unit to convert to in the numerator.
2. **Explain why measurement conversions require the use of significant digits.** Sample: When you calculate with measurements, precision is important. Using significant digits rounds the answer to the least precise number of digits that was used in the calculation.

3 Practice

Math Conversations

Discussion to strengthen understanding.

Problem 1

When using Cramer's rule, determinants must be used to solve the system of linear equations.

Problem 4

Remind students to first isolate the absolute value.

Example 5 **Application: Sports**

Natcar is an annual robotic car race. In 2007, the winning car completed the course with an average speed of 7.57 feet per second. What is this speed in miles per hour?

SOLUTION Write the given speed as a fraction.

$$\frac{7.57 \text{ ft}}{1 \text{ s}}$$

One of the conversion factors needs to have *ft* in its denominator and the other needs *s* in its numerator.

$$\frac{7.57 \cancel{\text{ft}}}{1 \cancel{\text{s}}} \times \frac{1 \text{ mi}}{5280 \cancel{\text{ft}}} \times \frac{3600 \cancel{\text{s}}}{1 \text{ hr}} = \frac{(7.57)(3600)}{5280} \frac{\text{mi}}{\text{hr}}$$

This answer simplifies to about 5.16 mph.

Math Reasoning

Predict If the builder of a car wanted it to reach 10 mph, about how fast would it need to go in feet per second?

This is about twice as fast as the car in the example, so about 15 feet per second.

Lesson Practice

a. Change 720 inches to feet. 60 ft (Ex 1)

b. Change 6 hours to minutes. 360 minutes (Ex 1)

c. Convert 52 yd^2 to in^2. 67,392 in^2 (Ex 2)

d. Convert 2700 seconds to hours. $\frac{3}{4}$ hr (Ex 2)

e. Convert 80 feet per second to miles per hour. $\frac{(80)(3600)}{5280} \frac{\text{mi}}{\text{hr}}$ or about 55 mph (Ex 3)

f. Simplify the expression 6.21 mi + 3.672 mi + 0.8 mi. 10.7 mi (Ex 4)

g. Simplify the expression 8.08 ft × 0.020 ft × 407 ft. 66 ft^3 (Ex 4)

h. RaceUSA is an annual boxcar race. In 2007, the winning car completed the course with an average speed of 24 feet per second. What is this speed in miles per hour? $\frac{(24)(3600)}{5280} \frac{\text{mi}}{\text{hr}}$ or about 16 mph (Ex 5)

Practice Distributed and Integrated

Use Cramer's rule to solve each system.

*1. (16) $x = y + 1$, $3x + 2y = 8$ (2, 1)

2. (16) $3x - y = 22$, $2x + 3y = -11$ (5, −7)

3. (16) $x + y = 20$, $5x + 10y = 200$ (0, 20)

Solve.

*4. (17) $-5|2x - 7| - 4 = -34$ $x = 6.5$ or $x = 0.5$

5. (17) $\left|\frac{1}{2}x + 1\right| \leq -\frac{1}{2}$ no solution

6. (17) $|8 - 3x| > 9$ $x < -\frac{1}{3}$ or $x > 5\frac{2}{3}$

ALTERNATIVE METHOD

When adding or subtracting significant digits, it may be easier to line up the digits added vertically so the least precise value can be clearly seen.

Add 4.65 in. + 3.1 in. + 9.875 in. and round to the correct number of significant figures.

After lining up the numbers students can clearly see how much we need to round in order to obtain the correct number of significant digits.

4.65 in. (2 decimal places)
3.1 in. (1 decimal place)
+ 9.875 in. (3 decimal places)
17.625 in.
17.6 in. rounded to 1 decimal place

Identify whether the equation is a direct, inverse, or joint variation. Find the constant of variation.

7. $\frac{y}{x} = \sqrt{2}$ direct; $\sqrt{2}$ (12)

8. $y = \frac{15}{x}$ inverse; 15 (12)

*9. (Chemical Mixture) A chemist has one solution that is 10% iodine and another that is 50% iodine. How many milliliters of each should the chemist use to make 100 mL of a mixture that is 20% iodine? 75 mL of the 10% solution and 25 mL of the 50% solution (15)

a. **Formulate** Set up a system of equations that models the problem. $p + d = 100$, $0.5p + 0.1d = 0.2(100)$

b. **Graphing Calculator** Use a graphing calculator to solve the system.

10. **Multiple Choice** In the data set at right, what is the relationship between x and y? C (12)

A joint variation B direct variation

C inverse variation D none of the above

x	1	2	3	4
y	4	2	$1\frac{1}{3}$	1

11. (Sports) Suppose you and a friend are practicing basketball. To make practice more interesting, you invent a game. Every time you make a basket, you will gain 2 points. Every time your friend makes a basket, you will lose 1 point. Likewise, every time your friend makes a basket, he will gain 2 points, and every time you make a basket, he will lose 1 point. Both of you start with 0 points. At the end of the game, you have 16 points and your friend has 10. (15)

a. **Formulate** Write a system of equations to represent this situation.

b. How many baskets did each of you make? You made 14 baskets and your friend made 12.

11a. $2x - y = 16$, $2y - x = 10$; x = the number of baskets you make; y = the number of baskets your friend makes

12. **Geometry** As the diameter (d) of a circle increases in size, the circumference (C) increases. Likewise, as the diameter decreases in size, so does the circumference. The constant of variation between C and d is π. Describe the kind of variation between circumference and diameter. Write the equation. direct variation; The equation is $C = \pi d$. (12)

13. **Error Analysis** Explain the error in the work below. Then find the correct determinant. (14)

$$\begin{vmatrix} -2 & 6 \\ 3 & -1 \end{vmatrix} = (6)(3) - (-2)(-1) = 18 - 2 = 16$$

13. The products were subtracted in the wrong order; −16

Convert the units and unit rates.

*14. Change 0.075 hours to seconds. 270 sec (18)

*15. Convert 1224 in^2 to yd^2. $\frac{17}{18}$ yd^2 (18)

*16. Convert 0.26 miles per hour to feet per minute. $22.88 \frac{ft}{min}$ (18)

*17. (Space Travel) The Endeavor, a space shuttle, has speeds of about 27,404 feet per second. Convert the speed into kilometers per hour and miles per hour. 30,070 km/h ≈ 18,685 mph (18)

18. **Verify** Show that $|2x + 3| = 16x$ has two solutions, one of which is extraneous. (17)

*19. **Analyze** Write the four resulting inequalities that are used to solve $|-3x + 5| \geq |x|$. (17) $-3x + 5 \geq x$, $-3x + 5 \leq -x$, $3x - 5 \geq x$, $3x - 5 \leq -x$

18. $x = \frac{3}{14}$ is a solution of the equation because $\left|2\left(\frac{3}{14}\right) + 3\right| = 16\left(\frac{3}{14}\right)$. $-\frac{1}{6}$ is an extraneous solution because $16\left(-\frac{1}{6}\right) = -\frac{8}{3}$ and absolute value can never equal a negative number.

Problem 9

Use a weighted average to obtain the different amounts of each solution the chemist should use.

Problem 14
Extend the Problem

Explain whether it would be easier to change the measure to minutes using 0.075 hours or 270 seconds.

Error Alert Sometimes students have difficulty arranging the units correctly so that they will cancel in the dimensional analysis problem. Remind them to write conversion factors so that they are in the inverse position of the unit of measure they are to cancel.

Problem 17

Students may want to try to convert from feet to kilometers. If they don't have the conversion for this they can first convert to another set of units with a simple English to Metric conversion (1 in. = 2.54 cm).

TEACHER TIP

Emphasize that significant digits are needed to correctly show the accuracy of a measurement. The calculation cannot make the answer more accurate than the given values to begin with. All answers in word problems should be rounded to the correct number of significant figures.

ENGLISH LEARNERS

For this lesson, explain the meaning of the word **unit.** Say:

"The word *unit* is a way to describe the amount of a measurement."

Explain that there are different units for very small amounts as well as very large amounts, such as an inch or a mile. Connect the practicality of units by showing that it is easier to say 5 miles rather than 316,800 inches and is also easier to use in mathematical calculations.

Have students give examples of when large units of measure would be appropriate, and when small units of measure would be appropriate.

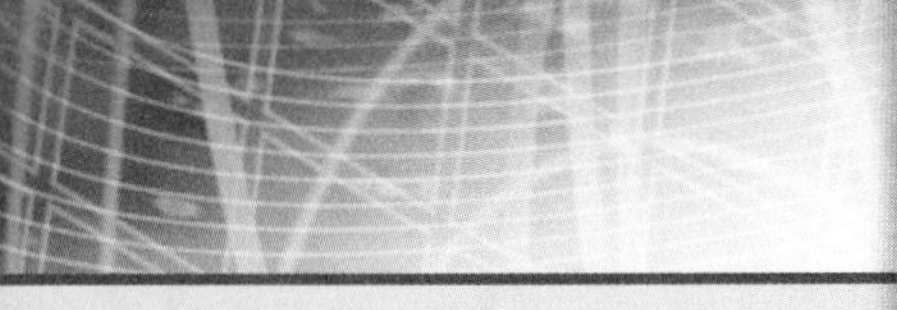

Problem 21

Students who have difficulty writing the answer to the problem can graph an equation using the intercepts, and write each step they take.

20. (17) **Chemical Elements** For oxygen to be a liquid, it must be within 35.845° of −332.925°F.

a. Write an absolute value equation to determine the least and greatest temperatures at which oxygen will remain a liquid. $|t + 332.925| < 35.845$

b. Solve the equation. $-368.77 < t < -297.08$

21. (13) **Explain** Give a written explanation on how to graph an equation using intercepts.

21. First, find the x-intercept by letting $y = 0$ and solving for x. Next, find the y-intercept by letting $x = 0$ and solving for y. Then plot and connect the intercepts and extend a line through the points with arrowheads on the ends of the line.

22. (11) **Analyze** Give an example of two trinomials whose sum has 6 terms. Sample: Let $P_1 = x^6 + x^5 + x^4$ and $P_2 = x^3 + x^2 + x$. Then $P_1 + P_2 = x^6 + x^5 + x^4 + x^3 + x^2 + x$.

Solve for x.

***23.** (7, 14) $\begin{vmatrix} \frac{x}{2} & 4 \\ 3 & -10 \end{vmatrix} = -(-x + 7)$ $x = -\frac{5}{6}$

24. (7, 14) $\begin{vmatrix} -3 & 2 \\ 4x - 1 & 2x - \frac{1}{3} \end{vmatrix} = -16x + 7$ $x = 2$

Multi-Step Given the slope and a point on the line, graph the line. Determine the y-intercept of the line.

25. (13) $m = \frac{5}{3}$ $(-3, 1)$

26. (13) $m = -\frac{4}{5}$ $(5, -5)$

***27.** (3, 18) **Solar System** The earth revolves about the sun at about 29.8 kilometers per second. Convert the rate into meters per hour. Write the answer in scientific notation rounded to the thousandths. $1.073 \times 10^8 \frac{\text{m}}{\text{hr}}$

$A = \begin{bmatrix} 6 & -3 \\ 1 & 4 \end{bmatrix}$ **and** $B = \begin{bmatrix} 0 & 4 \\ -2 & 6 \end{bmatrix}$. **Find each product.**

28. (9) Find AB. $\begin{bmatrix} 6 & 6 \\ -8 & 28 \end{bmatrix}$

29. (9) Find BA. $\begin{bmatrix} 4 & 16 \\ -6 & 30 \end{bmatrix}$

30. (9) Find A^2. $\begin{bmatrix} 33 & -30 \\ 10 & 13 \end{bmatrix}$

25. (0, 6)

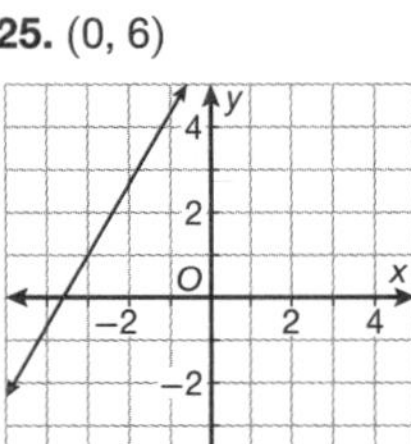

26. (0, −1)

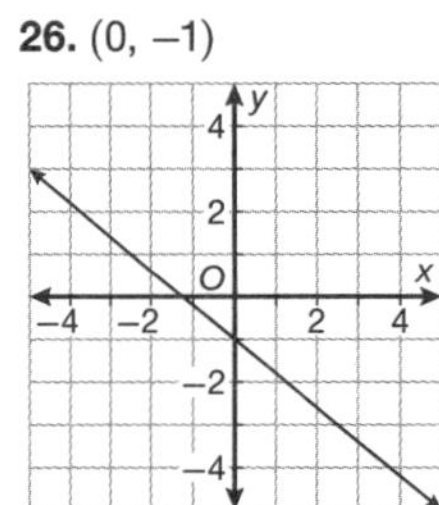

CHALLENGE

Explain why 1000 has only one significant digit but 1000.0 has five. In 1000 there is only one digit that is nonzero, so it has one significant digit. In 1000.0 the zero to the right of the decimal point is significant, so all the zeros between it and 1 are also significant.

LOOKING FORWARD

Using conversions of units prepares students for

- **Lesson 33** Applying Counting Principles
- **Lesson 113** Using Geometric Series

LESSON 19

Multiplying Polynomials

Warm Up

1. **Vocabulary** The 5 in the term $5x$ is called the _________. coefficient
(11)
2. Simplify using the Distributive Property: $5(3 + 4)$. $5(3) + 5(4) = 15 + 20 = 35$
(1)
3. Combine like terms: $3x^2 + 5x - 8x^2 - x$. $-5x^2 + 4x$
(2)
4. Simplify $2a^3 \cdot 3a^3$. $6a^6$
(3)

New Concepts

To multiply two polynomials, each term of the first polynomial is multiplied by each term of the other polynomial. After each of these products is found, the like terms are combined. To multiply two binomials a method called FOIL is often used. The letters in FOIL stand for where the terms are found in the binomials.

The FOIL Method
Multiply $(x + 3)(x - 5)$.
The **F**irst terms are x and x. Their product is x^2.
The **O**utside terms are x and -5. Their product is $-5x$.
The **I**nside terms are 3 and x. Their product is $3x$.
The **L**ast terms are 3 and -5. Their product is -15.
Combine the like terms in $x^2 - 5x + 3x - 15$.
$(x + 3)(x - 5) = x^2 - 2x - 15$

Example 1 Multiplying Using the FOIL Method

Multiply using the FOIL method.

Math Reasoning

Write Explain in writing why $(-5 + a)(8 + a)$ would produce the same result as $(a + 8)(a - 5)$.

Both addition and multiplication are commutative. So, $-5 + a = a - 5$, $8 + a = a + 8$, and $(-5 + a)(8 + a) = (a + 8)(a - 5)$.

Online Connection www.SaxonMathResources.com

a. $(a + 8)(a - 5)$

SOLUTION

F: $a \cdot a = a^2$ **O:** $a \cdot (-5) = -5a$ **I:** $8 \cdot a = 8a$ **L:** $8 \cdot (-5) = -40$

$= a^2 - 5a + 8a - 40$ Multiply.

$= a^2 + 3a - 40$ Combine like terms.

b. $(2x - 3)(3x + 2)$

SOLUTION

F: $2x \cdot 3x = 6x^2$ **O:** $2x \cdot 2 = 4x$ **I:** $-3 \cdot 3x = -9x$ **L:** $-3 \cdot 2 = -6$

$= 6x^2 + 4x - 9x - 6$ Multiply.

$= 6x^2 - 5x - 6$ Combine like terms.

LESSON 19

1 Warm Up

Remind students to add or subtract the coefficients of the same terms when combining like terms.

2 New Concepts

In this lesson, students learn to multiply polynomials.

Discuss the definition of term, polynomial, trinomial, and binomial.

Example 1

Make sure students understand how to use the FOIL method.

Additional Example 1

Multiply using the FOIL method.

a. $(x + 6)(x - 4)$ $x^2 + 2x - 24$

b. $(3x - 4)(4x + 5)$ $12x^2 - x - 20$

MATH BACKGROUND

Methods for multiplying polynomials depend on the Distributive Property of Multiplication over Addition. The fact that

$$(a + b)(c + d) = ac + ad + bc + bd$$

depends on the fact that

$$a(c + d) + b(c + d) = (a + b)(c + d)$$

or, in even more fundamental terms,

$$ax + bx = (a + b)x.$$

When introducing the FOIL method, some students may benefit from starting with a few examples using only constants.

LESSON RESOURCES

Student Edition Practice Workbook 19
Reteaching Master 19
Adaptations Master 19
Challenge and Enrichment Masters C19, E19

Example 2

Walk through one term of the binomial at a time. Check for understanding at each step.

Additional Example 2

Multiply

$(p + 2)(-2p^2 + p - 2)$.
$-2p^3 - 3p^2 - 4$

Example 3

Point out that multiplying the first pair of binomials results in a trinomial. Then student should apply the method for multiplying a binomial by a trinomial.

It may not immediately be clear to students how the Associative Property of Multiplication relates to polynomial expressions. Compare

a. $(5 \times 3) \times 2 = 5 \times (3 \times 2)$

b. $[(r + 3) \times (r - 2)] \times (r + 5)$
$= (r + 3) \times [(r - 2) \times (r + 5)]$

Show how each polynomial term in B parallels each constant in A.

Additional Example 3

Multiply $(a + 4)(a - 3)(a + 6)$ in two different ways using the Associative Property of Multiplication.
$a^3 + 7a^2 - 6a - 72$

Example 2 Multiplying a Binomial by a Trinomial

Multiply $(a + 5)(3a^2 - 2a + 7)$.

SOLUTION Multiply each term of the binomial by each term of the trinomial.

$(a + 5)(3a^2 - 2a + 7)$

$= a(3a^2) + a(-2a) + a(7) + 5(3a^2) + 5(-2a) + 5(7)$

$= 3a^3 - 2a^2 + 7a + 15a^2 - 10a + 35$ Multiply.

$= 3a^3 + 13a^2 - 3a + 35$ Combine like terms.

More than two polynomials can be multiplied together. The Associative Property of Multiplication holds for polynomials. Multiply two of the polynomials and then multiply that product by the remaining polynomial.

Math Reasoning

Verify Does multiplying $(r + 3)(r + 5)$ and then multiplying that result by $(r - 2)$ lead to the same result as the two methods shown in Example 3?

yes

Example 3 Multiplying Three Binomials

Multiply $(r + 3)(r - 2)(r + 5)$ in two different ways using the Associative Property of Multiplication.

SOLUTION

Multiply $(r + 3)(r - 2)$.

$(r + 3)(r - 2)$

$= r(r) + r(-2) + 3(r) + 3(-2)$ Use FOIL.

$= r^2 - 2r + 3r - 6$ Multiply.

$= r^2 + r - 6$ Combine like terms.

$(r + 5)(r^2 + r - 6)$ Multiply by $(r + 5)$.

$= r(r^2) + r(r) + r(-6) + 5(r^2) + 5(r) + 5(-6)$ Distribute.

$= r^3 + r^2 - 6r + 5r^2 + 5r - 30$ Multiply.

$= r^3 + 6r^2 - r - 30$ Combine like terms.

SOLUTION

Multiply $(r - 2)(r + 5)$.

$(r - 2)(r + 5)$

$= r(r) + r(5) + (-2)r + (-2)5$ Use FOIL.

$= r^2 + 5r - 2r - 10$ Multiply.

$= r^2 + 3r - 10$ Combine like terms.

$(r + 3)(r^2 + 3r - 10)$ Multiply by $(r + 3)$.

$= r(r^2) + r(3r) + r(-10) + 3(r^2) + 3(3r) + 3(-10)$ Multiply.

$= r^3 + 3r^2 - 10r + 3r^2 + 9r - 30$ Multiply.

$= r^3 + 6r^2 - r - 30$ Combine like terms.

ALTERNATE METHOD FOR EXAMPLE 2

Multiplying a binomial by a trinomial can be done using the vertical method. Tell students to put the expression with the most terms on top.

$$\begin{array}{r} 3a^2 - 2a + 7 \\ \times \qquad a + 5 \\ \hline \end{array}$$

Multiply each term of the top expression by 5.

$$15a^2 - 10a + 35$$

Then multiply each term by a.

$$3a^3 - 2a^2 + 7a$$

Combine the two expressions.

$$3a^3 + 13a^2 - 3a + 35$$

Some binomial products appear so frequently that memorizing the patterns they form results in convenience and efficiency while solving problems.

Caution

$(a+b)^2 \neq a^2 + b^2$

$(a-b)^2 \neq a^2 - b^2$

Special Product Patterns	
Sum and difference	$(a+b)(a-b) = a^2 - b^2$
Square of a sum	$(a+b)^2 = (a+b)(a+b) = a^2 + 2ab + b^2$
Square of a difference	$(a-b)^2 = (a-b)(a-b) = a^2 - 2ab + b^2$

Example 4 Multiplying Using Special Product Patterns

Multiply.

a. $(2y-5)^2$

SOLUTION

$(2y-5)^2$

$= (2y-5)(2y-5)$

$= (2y)^2 - 2(2y)(5) + (5)^2$

$= 4y^2 - 20y + 25$

b. $(5x+2y)(5x-2y)$

SOLUTION

$(5x+2y)(5x-2y)$

$= (5x)^2 - (2y)^2$

$= 25x^2 - 4y^2$

c. $(3q+2r)^2$

SOLUTION

$(3q+2r)^2$

$= (3q+2r)(3q+2r)$

$= (3q)^2 + 2(3q)(2r) + (2r)^2$

$= 9q^2 + 12qr + 4r^2$

Many problems involving unknown quantities in geometric figures and designs can be solved using polynomials to represent dimensions.

Example 5 Application: Geography

The National Mall in Washington, D.C., forms a rectangle and includes many important sites. The length of the mall from the steps of the U.S. Capitol to the Lincoln Memorial can be expressed as $(x - 0.1)$ miles. The width of the mall is measured across the Washington Monument and can be expressed as $(x - 0.9)$ miles. Write a polynomial to express the area of the National Mall.

SOLUTION

The area of a rectangle is equal to the length times the width.

Area of the mall $= (x-0.1)(x-0.9)$

$= x(x) + x(-0.9) + (-0.1)x + (-0.1)(-0.9)$ Use FOIL.

$= x^2 - 0.9x - 0.1x + 0.09$ Multiply.

$= x^2 - x + 0.09$ Combine like terms.

The area of the National Mall is $x^2 - x + 0.09$ square miles.

INCLUSION

For parts **a**, **b**, **c** in Example 4, have students use the FOIL method to verify the answers.

Example 4

Make sure to name the patterns as you demonstrate them: (a) square of a difference, (b) sum and difference, (c) square of a sum. Show how each term in the examples parallels the *a*'s and *b*'s of the patterns.

Additional Example 4

Multiply.

a. $(3y-4)^2$ $9y^2 - 24y + 16$

b. $(6x+4y)(6x-4y)$
$36x^2 - 16y^2$

c. $(5q+3r)^2$
$25q^2 + 30qr + 9r^2$

Error Alert Students sometimes over generalize the sum and difference pattern to factors like the following:

$$(2x+2)(x-2).$$

Point out why the middle term "disappears" when the only difference between the factors is the sign. Since the sum of a term and its opposite is zero, the sum of the product of the outer terms and the inner terms is zero.

Example 5

Additional Example 5

A triangular garden has a base given by the expression $(x+3)$ ft and a height given by the expression $(2x+8)$ ft. Write a polynomial expression for the area of the triangular garden.
$x^2 + 7x + 12$

Error Alert Students may have difficulty using the FOIL method with decimals. Remind students that when multiplying a tenth by a tenth the decimal point moves two places to the left.

Extend the Example

To find the area of the National Mall have students check the answer by using the Distributive Property.

Lesson Practice

Problem d

Scaffolding If students do not immediately see what the two ways are, ask them to state the Associative Property of Equality. Then ask them to identify the three factors being multiplied. If more help is needed, try writing $a \cdot b \cdot c$ above and aligned with $(r + 3)(r - 6)(r + 2)$.

Check for Understanding

The questions below help assess the concepts taught in this lesson.

Explain how to use FOIL when multiplying $(2x + 3)(x - 4)$.
Multiply the first terms: $2x \cdot x = 2x^2$; the outer terms: $2x \cdot -4 = -8x$; the inside terms: $3 \cdot x = 3x$; the last terms: $3 \cdot -4 = -12$. Combine like terms: $2x^2 - 5x - 12$.

3 Practice

Math Conversations

Discussions to strengthen understanding.

Problem 9

If students have difficulty, walk through one conversion at a time: feet per hour first and then miles per hour:

$$x\frac{\text{ft}}{\text{sec}} = (3600x)\frac{\text{ft}}{\text{hr}}$$
$$= \left(\frac{3600x}{5280}\right)\frac{\text{mi}}{\text{hr}}$$

Make it concrete with actual values: 88 feet per second:

$$88\frac{\text{ft}}{\text{sec}} = 3600 \times 88\frac{\text{ft}}{\text{hr}}$$
$$= \frac{3600 \times 88}{5280}\frac{\text{mi}}{\text{hr}}$$
$$= \frac{316800}{5280}\frac{\text{mi}}{\text{hr}} = 60\frac{\text{mi}}{\text{hr}}$$

Lesson Practice

a. (Ex 1) Multiply using the FOIL method. $(a + 7)(a - 4)$ $a^2 + 3a - 28$

b. (Ex 1) Multiply using the FOIL method. $(4x + 5)(3x - 2)$ $12x^2 + 7x - 10$

c. (Ex 2) Multiply $(a + 9)(2a^2 - 6a + 5)$. $2a^3 + 12a^2 - 49a + 45$

d. (Ex 3) Multiply $(r + 3)(r - 6)(r + 2)$ in two different ways using the Associative Property of Equality.

d.
$(r + 3)(r - 6)$
$r^2 - 3r - 18$
$(r + 2)(r^2 - 3r - 18)$
$r^3 - r^2 - 24r - 36$
or
$(r - 6)(r + 2)$
$r^2 - 4r - 12$
$(r + 3)(r^2 - 4r - 12)$
$r^3 - r^2 - 24r - 36$

e. (Ex 4) Multiply $(4y + 3)^2$. $16y^2 + 24y + 9$

f. (Ex 4) Multiply $(7a + 3b)(7a - 3b)$. $49a^2 - 9b^2$

g. (Ex 4) Multiply $(5q + 4r)^2$. $25q^2 + 40qr + 16r^2$

h. (Ex 5) The food court at the Galleria Mall forms a rectangle with eateries on all sides. The length of the food court can be expressed as $(x - 15)$ yards. The width of the food court can be expressed as $(x - 12)$ yards. Write a polynomial to express the area of the food court at the Galleria Mall.
The area of the Galleria Mall is $x^2 - 27x + 180$ square yards.

Practice Distributed and Integrated

Simplify each expression.

1. (18) 2.25 yd + 7.6 yd + 0.58 yd   10.4 yd

2. (18) 2.08 ft × 0.033 ft × 15.5 ft   1.1 ft³

3. (8, 12) **Geometry** Which type of variation is represented by the equation Area = length × width, if the Area = 25 ft²? Find the constant of variation.   inverse; 25

4. (8, 12) **Analyze** Which type of variation is represented by the equation $d = r \times t$ if d is held constant? r is held constant? t is held constant?   inverse; direct; direct

5. (18) Kellie's last three walks were 2.25 mi, 3.2 mi, and 2.31 mi. What is the sum of the distances Kellie walked?   7.8 mi.

6. (17) **Multiple Choice** Solve $|2x + 1| < 4$.   A

A $-\frac{5}{2} < x < \frac{3}{2}$ **B** $\frac{3}{2} < x < -\frac{5}{2}$

C $x < -\frac{5}{2}$ or $x > \frac{3}{2}$ **D** $x < \frac{3}{2}$

***7.** (11, 19) **Packaging Technology** An engineer has a box in the shape of a cube. She wants to know how the volume is affected if she adds 1 unit to each base edge and subtracts 2 units from the height. Does the volume increase, decrease, or remain the same? Explain your answer.

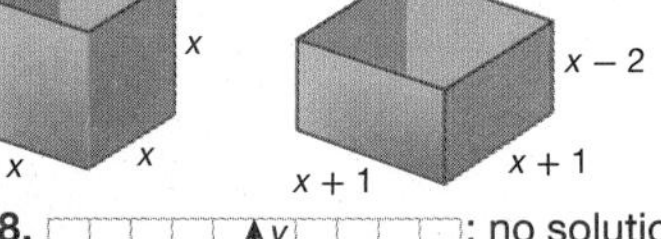

8. (13) Graph to determine the solution of $\begin{cases} x + 2y = 2 \\ y = -\frac{1}{2}x - 3 \end{cases}$.

9. (18) **Explain** How can feet per second be converted to miles per hour?

7. The volume decreases by $3x + 2$ cubic units. The volume of the cube is $x \cdot x \cdot x = x^3$. The volume of the other box is $(x + 1)(x + 1)(x - 2) = x^3 - 3x - 2$. The difference in volumes is $x^3 - (x^3 - 3x - 2) = 3x + 2$.

8.
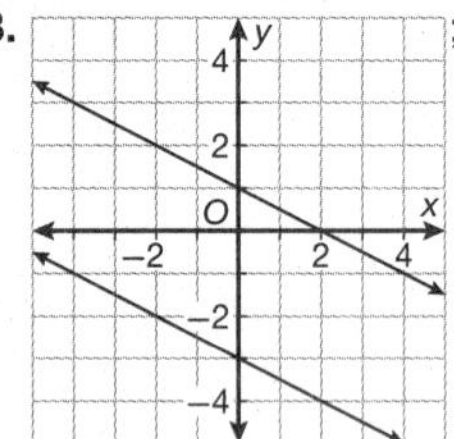

; no solution

9. Convert feet per second to feet per hour, then feet per hour to miles per hour; or convert feet per second to miles per second, then miles per second to miles per hour. $\frac{x \text{ feet}}{\text{second}} \cdot \frac{3600 \text{ seconds}}{1 \text{ hour}} \cdot \frac{1 \text{ mile}}{5280 \text{ feet}} = \frac{y \text{ miles}}{\text{hour}}$

ENGLISH LEARNERS

For this lesson, explain that **foil** is a word with several meanings in English. One is a thin sheet of metal used in the kitchen; aluminum foil.

The verb foil means to keep someone from getting what he or she wants. Using the FOIL method will *foil* these math problems that are trying not to be solved.

Giving meaning to the mnemonic will help English learners remember the method.

Otherwise, when the mnemonic appears to be a random combination of letters, the mnemonic is just another rote fact to memorize rather than a help.

*10. **Chemical Mixture** Ocean water is about 3.5% salt. A chemist has a solution that (15) is 25% salt and 75% water. If the chemist needs to make 1600 mL of a solution that is 15% salt, about how much ocean water should the chemist use? Round the answer to the nearest whole number.

a. Set up a system of equations that models the problem. $c + s = 1600$; $0.035c + 0.25s = 0.15(1600)$

b. **Graphing Calculator** Use a graphing calculator to solve the system. 774 mL

11. **Data Analysis** Each of the data sets shown is either a direct or an inverse variation. (12) For each data set, find the constant of variation.

a. 1.5

x	y
1	1.5
2	3
3	4.5
4	6
5	7.5

b. 4

x	y
1	4
2	2
3	$\frac{4}{3}$
4	1
5	$\frac{4}{5}$

c. $\frac{2}{3}$

x	y
2	$\frac{4}{3}$
3	2
4	$\frac{8}{3}$
5	$\frac{10}{3}$

*12. **Generalize** In the diagram, there is a volume (V) of air in a cylinder with a movable (12) pressure device that applies pressure (P) on the column of air. When downward pressure is applied, the volume of air decreases. When pressure is released by moving the pressure device up, the volume of air increases. What would need to be true for the relationship between P and V to be an inverse variation? What would be the equation to model this situation? The product of P and V for different values of each would need to equal a constant, k; The equation would be $PV = k$.

Multiply.

*13. $(8x + 6)(7x - 9)$ $56x^2 - 30x - 54$ (19)

*14. $(y - 3)(y^2 + 2y - 5)$ $y^3 - y^2 - 11y + 15$ (19)

15. **Error Analysis** Two students converted 200 feet per second to miles per hour. Which (18) student is correct? Explain the error in the other student's work. Student B is correct; Student A used the wrong conversion factor for the number of seconds in one hour.

Student A

$$\frac{200 \text{ ft}}{1 \text{ s}} \times \frac{1 \text{ mi}}{5280 \text{ ft}} \times \frac{360 \text{ s}}{1 \text{ hr}} = \frac{(200)(360)}{5280} \frac{\text{mi}}{\text{hr}}$$

Using a calculator, this simplifies to about 13.6 miles per hour.

Student B

$$\frac{200 \text{ ft}}{1 \text{ s}} \times \frac{1 \text{ mi}}{5280 \text{ ft}} \times \frac{3600 \text{ s}}{1 \text{ hr}} = \frac{(200)(3600)}{5280} \frac{\text{mi}}{\text{hr}}$$

Using a calculator, this simplifies to about 136 miles per hour.

ALTERNATIVE METHOD FOR PROBLEM 13

Multiplication of binomials can be done using the Distributive Property.

$$(8x + 6)(7x - 9) = 8x \cdot 7x + 8x \cdot -9 + 6 \cdot 7x + 6 \cdot -9$$
$$= 56x^2 - 72x + 42x - 54$$
$$= 56x^2 - 30x - 54$$

Problem 14

Guide students by asking them the following questions.

"What expression do you get when you multiply y by $y^2 + 2y - 5$?" $y^3 + 2y^2 - 5y$

"What expression do you get when you multiply -3 by $y^2 + 2y - 5$?" $-3y^2 - 6y + 15$

"When you combine the two expressions what do you get?" $y^3 - y^2 - 11y + 15$

Problem 15

Have students look only at the left side of the equation for Student A and Student B. Encourage students to check each ratio. Students should see that the first two ratios are the same and that it is the third ratio for Student A that is incorrect.

Problem 17

Guide students by asking them the following questions.

"How do you find how many minutes are in 72 hours?" Multiply 72 by 60.

"How many minutes is that?" 4320 minutes

"How do you find how many seconds are in 4,320 minutes?" Multiply 4320 by 60.

"How many seconds is that?" 259,200 seconds

"How many seconds are in 72 hours?" 259,200 seconds

Problem 23

If students have difficulty writing the absolute value expression, have them work backward. Have them plot the points, find the distance, then write the expression.

Problems 24 and 25

Point out to students that both problems use the special product patterns: Problem 24 is the square of a sum and Problem 25 is a sum and difference.

Convert each of the following measurements.

16. (18) 8 yd^2 to in^2 10,368 in^2

17. (18) 72 hours to seconds 259,200 s

18. (15) **Multiple Representations** The ordered pairs $(-1, -\frac{5}{2})$, $(0, -1)$, $(2, 2)$, and $(4, 5)$ are values in one function of a system that is consistent and dependent. Complete the table to represent ordered pairs of the other function in the same system.

x	0	2	4	6
y	–1	2	5	8

19. (18) **Multi-Step** While bicycling one weekend, Jess recorded the total distance and time he traveled each time that he stopped. The table shows his records.

Time (hours)	Distance Traveled (miles)
0.5	6
1	12
1.5	18
3	36

a. What was Jess's average speed, in miles per hour, for the total trip? 12 miles per hour

b. Convert Jess's speed in miles per hour to feet per second. 17.6 feet per second

c. How long, in seconds, would it take Jess to travel 500 feet? About 28.4 seconds.

Simplify.

20. (3) $\frac{5x^2y}{7y^5} \cdot \frac{28z}{115x^{-2}y^{-3}}$ $\frac{4x^4z}{23y}$

21. (3) $\frac{3x^2yz^{-4}}{18xy^{-2}} \div \frac{9y^4}{54x^6z^8}$ $\frac{x^7z^4}{y}$

***22.** (17) **Chemical Elements** For helium to be a liquid, it must be within 3.0935° of –454.9065°F.

a. Formulate Write an absolute value equation to determine the least and greatest temperatures at which helium will remain a liquid. $|t + 454.9065| = 3.0935$

b. Solve the equation. $t = -458$ or $t = -451.813$

***23.** (17) **Analyze** Write the distance from each point to the origin as an absolute value expression. Then simplify the expression.

a. (5, 0) $|5| = 5$
b. (–7, 0) $|-7| = 7$
c. (0, 9) $|9| = 9$
d. (0, –8) $|-8| = 8$

Simplify the expressions.

***24.** (19) $(-3y + 7)^2$ $9y^2 - 42y + 49$

***25.** (19) $(4a + 6b)(4a - 6b)$ $16a^2 - 36b^2$

134 *Saxon Algebra 2*

26. **Generalize** Consider the following polynomials: $P_1 = 2x^5 + x^3$, $P_2 = -2x^5 - x^3 + x$,
(11) $P_3 = x^2$, and $P_4 = x^5$. Find the number of terms in each of these sums: $P_1 + P_2$, $P_1 + P_3$, and $P_1 + P_4$. Use the results to make a generalization about the number of terms in the sum of two polynomials compared to the number of terms in the polynomials that make up that sum.

27. **Solar System** The mass of the moon is 7.3477×10^{22} kg. If the mass of Earth is
(3) 5.9736×10^{24} kg, how many times larger is Earth than the moon? 81.30 times larger

*28. **Exterior Design** The diagram at the right shows the area in
(19) Lucy's backyard that she is preparing for planting.

a. Write an expression for the area of the garden. $(x + 2)(3x^2 - 5x + 8)$

b. Simplify the expression using multiplication. $3x^3 + x^2 - 2x + 16$

c. Find the area of the garden if $x = 3$ feet. 100 ft^2

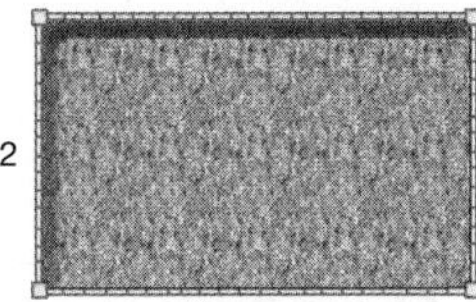

Calculate the slope of the lines that contain the following pairs of points. Tell whether the line rises, falls, is horizontal, or is vertical.

29. $\left(-\frac{1}{2}, \frac{1}{2}\right)$ and $\left(-\frac{1}{2}, \frac{3}{4}\right)$ undefined; vertical
(13)

30. $\left(-1, \frac{1}{2}\right)$ and $\left(3, \frac{1}{2}\right)$ 0; horizontal
(13)

26. $P_1 + P_2$ has 1 term, $P_1 + P_3$ has 3 terms, and $P_1 + P_4$ has 2 terms. The sum of two polynomials can have more terms than either polynomial, fewer terms than either polynomial, or the same number of terms as either polynomial.

Problem 27

Encourage students to write the division problem in vertical format:

$$\frac{5.9736}{7.3477} \times \frac{10^{24}}{10^{22}} = 0.8129 \times 10^2$$
$$= 81.29$$

or about 81.3.

Problem 28

Extend the Problem

Have students write an expression for the perimeter of the garden.

$$2(x + 2) + 2(3x^2 - 5x + 8)$$

Then have them find the perimeter of the garden if $x = 3$ feet.

$$P = 2(x + 2) + 2(3x^2 - 5x + 8)$$
$$= 2(3 + 2) + 2(3 \cdot 9 - 5 \cdot 3 + 8)$$
$$= 2(5) + 2(27 - 15 + 8)$$
$$= 10 + 2(20)$$
$$= 10 + 40$$
$$= 50 \text{ ft}$$

Problems 29 and 30

Error Alert

Students may calculate the slope as $\frac{\Delta x}{\Delta y}$. Remind students that slope is $\frac{\text{rise}}{\text{run}}$, which is the same as $\frac{\Delta y}{\Delta x}$.

CHALLENGE

Advanced students may be able to write the resulting polynomials for the products in problems 24 and 25 by inspection, without doing the calculations. Challenge them to evaluate without writing out the intermediate multiplications.

LOOKING FORWARD

Multiplying polynomials prepares students for

- **Lesson 23** Factoring Polynomials
- **Lesson 31** Multiplying and Dividing Rational Expressions

LESSON 20

1 Warm Up

Problem 2

Use the Warm Up to review the method of evaluating functions.

2 New Concepts

In this lesson, students learn different ways to add, subtract, multiply, and divide functions. Remind students that *numerically* refers to operations performed with numbers and *algebraically* refers to operations performed with variables and numbers.

Example 1

The examples help students contrast the numerical and algebraic methods of finding the sum and difference of two functions.

Additional Example 1

Given $h(x) = x + 3$; $D = \{\text{Reals}\}$, $g(x) = x - 4$; $D = \{\text{Integers}\}$

a. Find $(h + g)(3)$ numerically.
$(h + g)(3) = 5$

b. Find the algebraic sum.

$(h + g)(x)$.
$(h + g)(x) = 2x - 1$ {Integers}

LESSON 20

Performing Operations with Functions

Warm Up

1. **Vocabulary** A ________ is a mapping between two sets that associates with each element in the domain a unique element in the range. (7) function

2. Evaluate $f(x) = 3x + 5$, for $x = -2$. (4) -1

3. True/False: The points (0, 4), (1, 7), and (1, –2) represent a function. (4) False

New Concepts

You can add, subtract, multiply, and divide functions in several ways.

Notation for Operations with Functions

Operation	Notation
Addition	$(f + g)(x) = f(x) + g(x)$
Subtraction	$(f - g)(x) = f(x) - g(x)$
Multiplication	$(fg)x = f(x) \cdot g(x)$
Division	$(f/g)(x) = \frac{f(x)}{g(x)}$, when $g(x) \neq 0$

The domain of the sum of two functions is all the numbers that are common to both of the original domains.

Example 1 Finding the Sum and Difference of Functions Numerically and Algebraically

Given $g(x) = x + 4$; $D = \{\text{Integers}\}$, $h(x) = x - 2$; $D = \{\text{Reals}\}$

a. Find $(h + g)(2)$ numerically.

SOLUTION Note that $D = \{\text{Integers}\}$ is common to both functions. Find $h(2)$ and $g(2)$. Then add.

$$h(2) = 2 - 2 \qquad g(2) = (2) + 4$$
$$h(2) = 0 \qquad g(2) = 6$$
$$(h + g)(2) = (0) + (6) = 6$$

The numerical sum of $(h + g)(2) = 6$.

b. Find the algebraic sum $(h + g)(x)$.

$$h(x) = x - 2$$
$$\underline{g(x) = x + 4}$$
$$h(x) + g(x) = 2x + 2$$

The algebraic sum of $(h + g)(x) = 2x + 2$.

Math Reasoning

Verify Check that $(h + g)(2) = 6$ using the algebraic sum. Show your work.

$(h + g)(2)$
$= 2(2) + 2 = 6$

LESSON RESOURCES

Student Edition Practice Workbook 20
Reteaching Master 20
Adaptations Master 20
Challenge and Enrichment Master C20

MATH BACKGROUND

The concept of functions can be challenging for students. It is helpful to present functions in different ways. First, functions are something you *do* (i.e., mapping from a domain to a range). Functions are also visual, as the geometrical method of finding the sum and difference of functions shows. Finally, functions can be presented as equations. This method is used in performing operations with functions algebraically. It is important to note, however, that not all functions can be written as simple equations. Students may notice that the addition of functions is both commutative and associative, but functions are not distributive. For example, $(f + g)(x) = (g + f)(x)$ and $[(f + g) + h](x) = [f + (g + h)](x)$. However, suppose $f(x) = x^2$. Then $f(4a) \neq 4f(a)$, because $f(4a) = (4a)^2 = 16a^2$, but $4f(a) = 4a^2$.

c. Find $(g - h)(-2)$ numerically.

SOLUTION Find $g(-2)$ and $h(-2)$.

$$g(-2) = (-2) + 4 \qquad h(-2) = (-2) - 2$$
$$g(-2) = 2 \qquad h(-2) = -4$$
$$(g - h)(-2) = (2) - (-4) = 6$$

The numerical difference of $(g - h)(-2) = 6$.

d. Find the algebraic difference $(g - h)(x)$.

$$g(x) - h(x) = (x + 4) - (x - 2) = x + 4 - x + 2 = 6$$

The algebraic difference of $(g - h)(x) = 6$.

You can also find the sum and difference of functions using a coordinate plane.

Example 2 Finding the Sum and Difference of Functions Geometrically

Given $f(x) = 3$; $D = \{\text{Reals}\}$, $g(x) = 2x$; $D = \{\text{Reals}\}$

a. Find $(f + g)(x)$ geometrically.

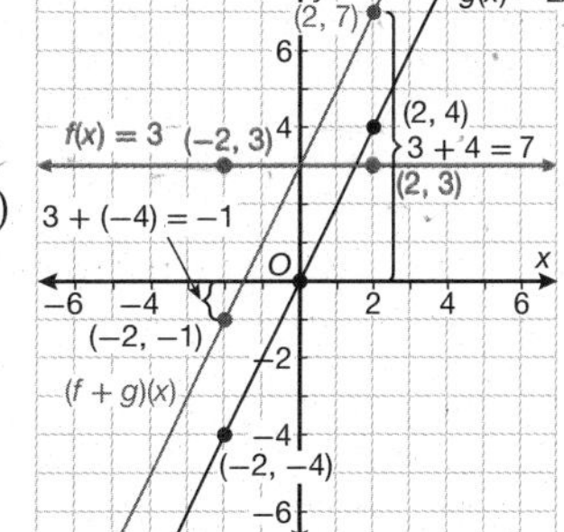
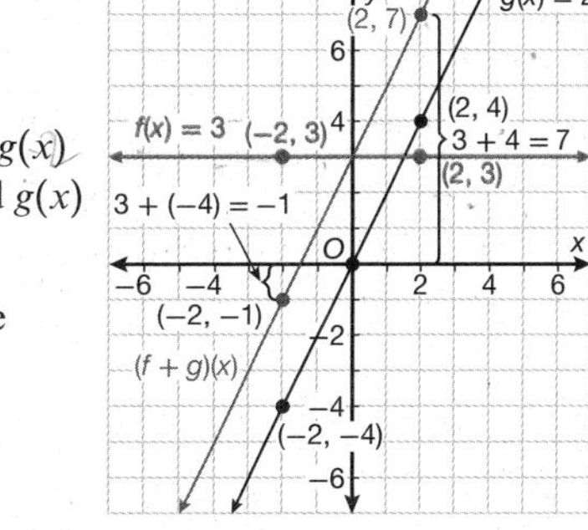

SOLUTION

Step 1: Write $(f + g)(x)$ as $f(x) + g(x)$ and replace both notations $f(x)$ and $g(x)$ with y.

Step 2: Graph the equations on the coordinate plane.

Step 3: Given D for both f and g is $\{\text{Reals}\}$, let $x = 2$ and $x = -2$.

Step 4: Find the vertical distance from the x-axis to the y-coordinates $f(2)$ and $g(2)$. Find $(2, 0)$ on the x-axis and count the units vertically up or down to the y-coordinate of each function, f and g. Add the vertical distances from the x-axis to $f(2)$ and $g(2)$: $3 + 4 = 7$. Plot the point $(2, 7)$.

Step 5: Find the y-coordinate of each function at $x = -2$. Add the vertical distances from the x-axis to $f(-2)$ and $g(-2)$: $3 + (-4) = -1$. Plot the point $(-2, -1)$. Draw a line through $(2, 7)$ and $(-2, -1)$.

Math Reasoning

Verify How can the algebraic sum $(f + g)(x)$ be used to verify that the line graphed as the sum of f and g is correct?

The slope and y-intercept of the graphed line $(f + g)(x)$ should be the same as $(f + g)(x) = 2x + 3$.

Online Connection
www.SaxonMathResources.com

Error Alert When finding the difference of the functions numerically, students may believe that the negative sign can be brought outside the function $h(-2)$. To avoid this error, have them calculate $-h(2)$ and $h(-2)$ for the function $h(x) = x - 2$.
$-h(2) = 0$; $h(-2) = -4$

Additional Example 1

Given $h(x) = x - 7$; $D = \{\text{Reals}\}$, $g(x) = x + 8$; $D = \{\text{Integers}\}$

c. Find $(g - h)(-4)$ numerically.
$(g - h)(-4) = 15$

d. Find the algebraic difference. $(g - h)(x)$. $(g - h)(x) = 15$

Example 2

The examples demonstrate the method of finding the sum and difference of functions by graphing the functions on a coordinate grid.

Additional Example 2a

Given $f(x) = -2$; $D = \{\text{Reals}\}$, $g(x) = 3x$; $D = \{\text{Reals}\}$

a. Find $(f + g)(x)$ geometrically.

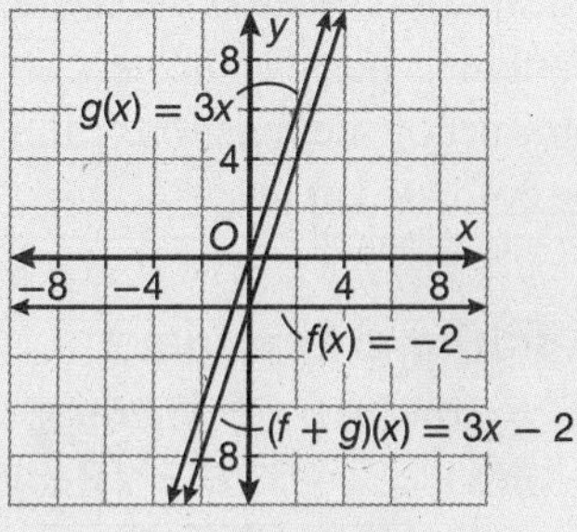

ENGLISH LEARNERS

Write the words **numerically, algebraically,** and **geometrically** on the board. Say the words aloud so that students can hear the suffix *–ally* that the words have in common.

Discuss with students the root words of numerically, algebraically, and geometrically. Students should understand that each term has the suffix *–ally* appended to a different root word.

Explain that the suffix *–ally* means "in the manner of." Lead students in applying this meaning to the definitions of the words *numerically, algebraically,* and *geometrically*.

Have students connect the root words *numeric, algebraic,* and *geometric* to other uses. For example, a numeric expression contains only numbers, but an algebraic expression contains variables as well. A cube is an example of a geometric solid.

Lesson 20 137

Additional Example 2b

b. Find $(f-g)(x)$ geometrically.

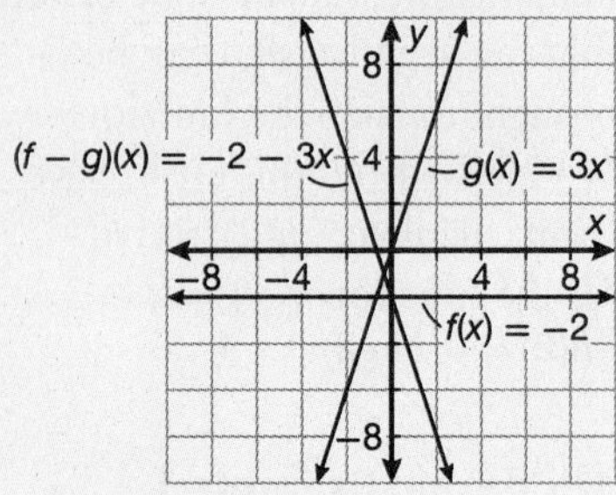

Example 3

The examples contrast the methods of multiplying functions numerically and algebraically. Students will discover that limiting the domain of one function also limits the domain when that function is multiplied by another function.

TEACHER TIP

It is important for students to compare and contrast Examples 3a and 3b. Although the problems are similar, Example 3a has a solution because the common domain is negative integers and the question asks for the product of the functions to be evaluated at -4. Example 3b has no solution because the common domain is positive integers, so the product of the functions cannot be evaluated at -4.

Additional Example 3

a. Find $(hg)(-3)$ where $h(x) = x + 1$; $D = \{\text{Reals}\}$, and $g(x) = x - 1$; $D = \{\text{Negative integers}\}$. $(hg)(-3) = 8$

b. Find $(fg)(-2)$ where $f(x) = x + 4$; $D = \{\text{Reals}\}$, and $g(x) = x - 2$; $D = \{\text{Positive integers}\}$. The problem has no answer.

b. Find $(f-g)(x)$ geometrically.

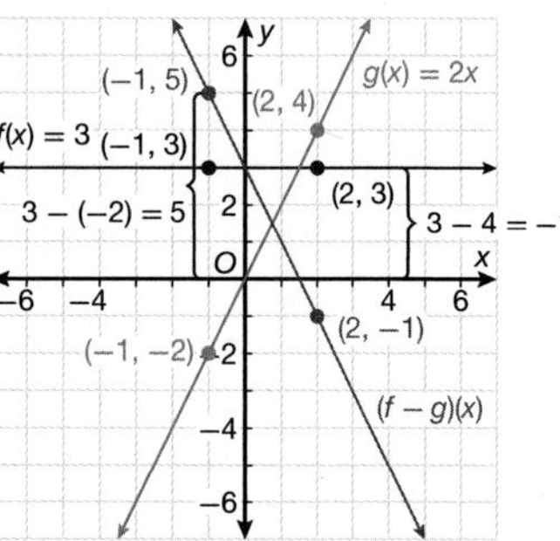

SOLUTION

Step 1: Write $(f-g)(x)$ as $f(x) - g(x)$ and replace both notations $f(x)$ and $g(x)$ with y.

Step 2: Graph the equations.

Step 3: Given D for both f and g is $\{\text{Reals}\}$, let $x = 2$ and $x = -1$.

Step 4: Find the vertical distance from the x-axis to the y-coordinates $f(2)$ and $g(2)$. Find $(2, 0)$ on the x-axis and count the units vertically up or down to the y-coordinate of each function, f and g. Subtract the vertical distances from the x-axis to $f(2)$ and $g(2)$: $3 - 4 = -1$. Plot the point $(2, -1)$.

Step 5: Repeat the process in **Step 4** for $x = -1$. Plot the point $(-1, 5)$. Draw a line through $(2, -1)$ and $(-1, 5)$.

Example 3 Multiplying Functions Numerically and Algebraically

a. Find $(hg)(-4)$ where $h(x) = x + 3$; $D = \{\text{Reals}\}$, and $g(x) = x - 6$; $D = \{\text{Negative integers}\}$.

SOLUTION

Method 1: Note that the common domain is the negative integers. Find $h(-4)$ and $g(-4)$, then multiply these answers.

$$h(-4) = -4 + 3 \qquad g(-4) = (-4) - 6$$
$$h(-4) = -1 \qquad g(-4) = -10$$
$$(hg)(-4) = (-1)(-10) = 10$$

Method 2: Find $hg(x)$ algebraically. Then find $hg(-4)$.

$$(hg)(x) = (x + 3)(x - 6)$$
$$(hg)(x) = x^2 - 3x - 18$$
$$(hg)(-4) = (-4)^2 - 3(-4) - 18$$
$$(hg)(-4) = 16 + 12 - 18$$
$$(hg)(-4) = 10$$

b. Find $(fg)(-4)$ where $f(x) = x + 3$; $D = \{\text{Reals}\}$, and $g(x) = x - 5$; $D = \{\text{Positive integers}\}$.

SOLUTION

The common domain is the positive integers. Since -4 is a negative integer, $(fg)(-4)$ cannot be found. The problem has no answer.

ALTERNATE METHOD FOR EXAMPLE 3

An alternative way to explain why a domain could prevent a problem from having an answer is to plot the functions in Example 3b on the board. When the function $g(x) = x - 5$ is plotted, all negative x values (i.e., the entire left half of the coordinate grid) should be shaded out because the domain is limited to positive integers. Students can see that, although $(fg)(x)$ has solutions, it has no solution at $x = -4$.

Math Reasoning

Generalize Find $(f/g)(0)$ for $f(x) = 2x + 1$ and $g(x) = x$. Explain your answer.

No solution.
$\frac{f(x)}{g(x)} = \frac{2x+1}{x} = \frac{1}{0}$
Division by zero is undefined.

Example 4 Dividing Functions Algebraically and Numerically

Find $(f/g)(6)$ if $f(x) = x + 2$; $D = \{\text{Integers}\}$, and $g(x) = x + 3$; $D = \{\text{Positive whole numbers}\}$.

SOLUTION Note that $D = \{\text{Positive whole numbers}\}$ is the common domain.

Method 1: Find $f(6)$ and $g(6)$ and then divide these answers.

$$f(6) = 6 + 2 \qquad g(6) = 6 + 3$$
$$f(6) = 8 \qquad g(6) = 9$$
$$(f/g)(6) = \frac{8}{9}$$

Method 2: Find $(f/g)(x)$ algebraically. Then find $(f/g)(6)$.

$$(f/g)(x) = \frac{f(x)}{g(x)} = \frac{x+2}{x+3}$$

The algebraic solution for $(f/g)(x)$ is $\frac{x+2}{x+3}$. Now find $(f/g)(6)$.

$$\frac{6+2}{6+3} = \frac{8}{9}$$

Example 5 Application: Business

Betsy makes memory wire bracelets to earn extra cash. The cost of making a bracelet is given by the function $f(x) = \$2 + \$5.75x$. Her income from the sale of bracelets is given by the function $g(x) = \$10x$. The number of bracelets is represented by x. Find the function representing her profit, $p(x)$. Then find the profit resulting from the sale of 5 bracelets.

SOLUTION Her profit is represented by the function $p(x) = g(x) - f(x)$ since the income from each bracelet, $g(x)$, minus the cost of making each bracelet, $f(x)$, gives the profit, $p(x)$, for each bracelet, x.

$$p(x) = g(x) - f(x) = 10(x) - (2 + 5.75(x))$$
$$10x - 2 - 5.75(x) = 4.25x - 2$$

So $p(x) = 4.25x - 2$. The profit resulting from the sale of 5 bracelets is found by evaluating $p(5)$.

$$p(5) = 4.25(5) - 2 = 21.25 - 2 = 19.25$$

Betsy's profit on 5 bracelets is $19.25.

Lesson Practice

a. Given $f(x) = 3x - 5$; $D = \{\text{Reals}\}$, $g(x) = x - 3$; $D = \{\text{Integers}\}$ find $(f + g)(6)$ numerically. *(Ex 1)*

b. Given $f(x) = 3x - 5$; $D = \{\text{Reals}\}$, $g(x) = x - 3$; $D = \{\text{Integers}\}$ find the algebraic sum $(f + g)(x)$. *(Ex 1)*

c. Given $f(x) = 7x - 8$; $D = \{\text{Reals}\}$, $g(x) = x + 5$; $D = \{\text{Integers}\}$ find $(f - g)(3)$ numerically. *(Ex 1)*

a. $f(6) = 3(6) - 5 = 18 - 5 = 13$; $g(6) = (6) - 3 = 6 - 3 = 3$; $13 + 3 = 16$

b. $f(x) = 3x - 5$
$g(x) = x - 3$
$(f + g)(x) = 4x - 8$

c. $f(3) = 7(3) - 8 = 13$; $g(3) = 3 + 5 = 8$; $(f - g)(3) = 13 - 8 = 5$

INCLUSION

Draw a coordinate grid on the board. Then have students demonstrate how the domain restrictions– *reals, integers, whole numbers, positive integers,* and *negative integers*– affect functions added or subtracted geometrically on the coordinate grid.

Example 4

This example demonstrates the methods of dividing functions numerically and algebraically.

Additional Example 4

Find $(f/g)(4)$ if $f(x) = x + 3$; $D = \{\text{Integers}\}$, and $g(x) = x + 5$; $D = \{\text{Positive whole numbers}\}$. $(f/g)(4) = \frac{7}{9}$

Example 5

This example provides a real life example of performing operations with functions.

Additional Example 5

A baker's cost of making a cake is $f(x) = \$3 + \$4.25x$. His income from the sale of a cake is given by $g(x) = \$12x$, where x is the number of cakes. Find the function representing the profit, $p(x)$. Then find the profit for selling 4 cakes. $p(x) = 7.75x - 3$; $p(4) = 28$; The profit for 4 cakes is $28.

Lesson Practice

Problem d

Error Alert Students may forget to apply the subtraction sign to the entire expression $x + 5$. Suggest that students use parentheses around the $f(x)$ and $g(x)$ functions. Remind them that the subtraction sign applies to each term within the parentheses.

Problem h

Scaffolding Encourage students to begin each problem by writing out the common domain.

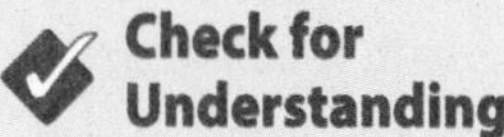

Check for Understanding

The questions below help assess the concepts taught in this lesson.

1. **"What is a benefit of using $f(x)$ notation rather than simply x and y when performing operations with functions?"** Sample: The $f(x)$ notation stresses the dependence of the functions on the domain.

2. **"When adding or subtracting functions, which method do you prefer to use? Why?"** Sample: The geometric method is a more visual method of adding and subtracting fractions.

3 Practice

Math Conversations

Discussions to strengthen understanding.

Problem 1

Error Alert
Students may believe that digits to the right of the decimals should be added in the same way that those to the left are added. In this case, they might add $65+1+843=909$. Remind students that these are decimal values, not whole numbers.

d. $f(x) = 7x - 8$; $g(x) = x + 5$; $(f - g)(x) = 6x - 13$

d. (Ex 1) Given $f(x) = 7x - 8$; $D = \{\text{Reals}\}$, $g(x) = x + 5$; $D = \{\text{Integers}\}$ find the algebraic difference $(f - g)(x)$.

e. (Ex 2) Given $f(x) = 8$; $D = \{\text{Reals}\}$, $g(x) = 3x$; $D = \{\text{Reals}\}$ find $(f + g)(x)$ geometrically. See Additional Answers.

f. (Ex 2) Given $f(x) = 8$; $D = \{\text{Reals}\}$, $g(x) = 3x$; $D = \{\text{Reals}\}$ find $(f - g)(x)$ geometrically. See Additional Answers.

g. (Ex 3) Find $(hg)(-4)$ where $h(x) = x + 6$; $D = \{\text{Reals}\}$, and $g(x) = x - 5$; $D = \{\text{Negative integers}\}$. -18

h. The common domain is positive integers only; therefore $(fg)(-4)$ cannot be found.

h. (Ex 3) Find $(fg)(-4)$ where $f(x) = x + 9$; $D = \{\text{Reals}\}$, and $g(x) = x - 4$; $D = \{\text{Positive integers}\}$.

i. (Ex 4) Find $(f/g)(7)$ where $f(x) = x + 3$; $D = \{\text{Integers}\}$, and $g(x) = x + 5$; $D = \{\text{Whole numbers}\}$. $\frac{10}{12} = \frac{5}{6}$

j. $p(x) = 5.75x - 3$; $p(6) = \$31.50$; Patty's profit on 6 pastries is $31.50.

j. (Ex 5) Patty sells pastries to bakeries to earn extra cash. The cost of making one pastry is given by the function $f(x) = \$3 + \$6.25x$. Her income from the sale of pastries is given by the function $g(x) = \$12x$. The number of pastries is represented by x. Find the function representing Patty's profit $p(x)$. Then find her profit from the sale of 6 pastries.

Practice Distributed and Integrated

1. (18) **Write** Explain how to simplify this problem: 12.65 in. + 30.1 in. + 15.843 in. First add the numbers together, which is 58.593. Then you have to round to one decimal place because of significant digits, which is 58.6 in.

2. (16) **Multi-Step** The solution to the system of equations $\begin{aligned} x + y &= 5 \\ px + qy &= -4 \end{aligned}$ is (3, 2).
   a. Use Cramer's rule to set up equations for x and y. See Additional Answers.
   b. Set $x = 3$ and $y = 2$. Simplify to write an equation with variables p and q. $3p + 2q = -4$
   c. Graph the line from part **b.** See Additional Answers.
   d. Choose a point (p, q) along the line in part **c.** Substitute those values for p and q into the original system to write a system of equations with variables x and y. See Additional Answers.
   e. Graph your system from part **d** to check your answer. How can you tell if your answer is correct? See Additional Answers.

Solve the equations.

3. (7) $3(5r - 10) = 8(2r - 4) + 5r$ $r = \frac{1}{3}$

4. (7) $\frac{3}{4}\left(\frac{1}{2}x - 4\right) = (x - 7)$ $x = \frac{32}{5}$

*5. (16) **Graphing Calculator** Solve the system using Cramer's Rule. Verify the solution by using a graphing calculator. (12, 10)
$$\begin{cases} 2x + 3y = 54 \\ -x + 6y = 48 \end{cases}$$

6. (19) **Geometry** Write an expression for the area of the triangle and simplify. $\frac{1}{2}(2x + 4)(x + 6)\text{ in}^2 = x^2 + 8x + 12\text{ in}^2$

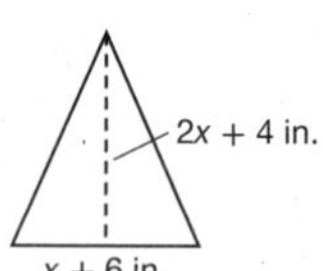

ALTERNATE METHOD FOR PROBLEM 4

If students have difficulty multiplying fractions, they may find this problem easier to solve by eliminating the fractions.

First, multiply by 4.

$$3\left(\frac{1}{2}x - 4\right) = 4(x - 7)$$
$$\frac{3}{2}x - 12 = 4x - 28$$

Next, multiply by 2.

$$3x - 24 = 8x - 56$$
$$32 = 5x$$
$$\frac{32}{5} = x$$

*7. **Transportation** The rate of one knot equals one nautical mile per hour. One nautical mile is 1852 meters. What is the speed in meters per second of a ship traveling at 20 knots? 10.3 m/s
(18)

*8. **Bird Flight** The peregrine falcon is perhaps the fastest animal on earth. In a stoop, or dive, the peregrine has been clocked at speeds of over 180 miles per hour. Convert this to feet per seconds. 264 feet per second
(18)

9. A scientist has one solution that is 10% iodine and another that is 40% iodine. How much of each should the scientist use to produce 100 mL of a mixture that is 25% iodine? 50 mL of 10% solution and 50 mL of 40% solution
(15)

Multiply the polynomials.

10. $(x + 7)(x - 9)$ $x^2 - 2x - 63$
(19)

11. $(x + 3)^2(x - 2)$ $x^3 + 4x^2 - 3x - 18$
(19)

12. **Write** Explain how to multiply $(2x + 8)(3x - 6)$ using the FOIL method.
(19)

13. **Justify** Is the equation $xyz = 0$ a joint variation? Why or why not?
(12)

12. Multiply the first terms in each binomial together $(2x)(3x)$, then multiply the outer two terms $(2x)(-6)$, then multiply the inner two terms $(8)(3x)$, and then the last two terms $(8)(-6)$. Combine any like terms together to simplify to $6x^2 + 12x - 48$.

13. No, this is not a joint variation. If $xyz = 0$, then x, y, or z is equal to zero. But the term $\frac{0}{0}$ is not defined. Therefore, $xyz = 0$ is not a joint variation.

*14. **Graphing Calculator** The population of Tulsa, Oklahoma, in 2005 was 381,479 and increased by 1393 people by 2006. The population of Tampa, Florida, in 2005 was 325,800 and increased by 7088 people by 2006. If the population of these cities continued to grow at these rates, then the following equations would represent the population of the cities, where x is the number of years after 2005 and y is the population.
(16)

$y = 1393x + 381{,}479$ Tulsa's Population

$y = 7088x + 325{,}800$ Tampa's Population

a. In what year would the populations of Tulsa and Tampa be equal? 2014

b. About how many people would be in each city when the populations are equal? 395,098

*15. **Architecture** A concrete support for a highway bridge consists of (from the bottom up) a rectangular prism, a trapezoidal prism, and another rectangular prism, with the dimensions shown. Write a polynomial in standard form to represent the total volume. (Hint: The formula for the area of a trapezoid is $A = \frac{1}{2}(b_1 + b_2)h$.) $3x^3 + 18x^2 + 6x$
(11)

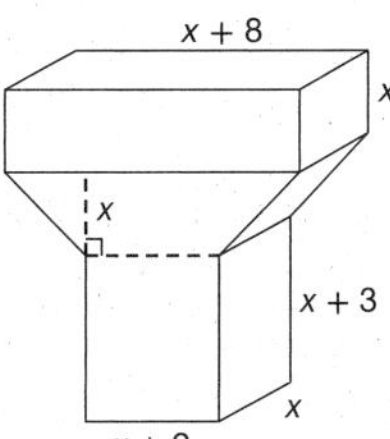

Find the percent of change in each situation. Round to the nearest tenth.

16. The population changes from 135,000 people to 150,000 people. $11.\overline{1}$% increase
(6)

17. A price changes from \$2.49 for a cup of tea to \$2.59. 4.0% increase
(6)

18. The energy usage changes from 25,500 trillion Btu to 22,500 trillion Btu. 11.8% decrease
(6)

Determine the kind of variation, if any, for each equation.

19. $y = \frac{1}{x}$, for $x \neq 0$ inverse
(12)

20. $z = \frac{1}{xy + a}$, for $x, y \neq 0$ and any value of a joint when $a = 0$
(12)

CHALLENGE

Given $f(x) = x + 2$; $D = \{\text{Reals}\}$, $g(x) = x - 3$; $D = \{\text{Integers}\}$, and $h(x) = x - 4$; $D = \{\text{Negative integers}\}$

Find the following both numerically and algebraically:

a. $(fgh)(-3)$
$(fgh)(x) = x^3 - 5x^2 - 2x + 24; (fgh)(-3) = -42$

b. $(fgh)(7)$ no solution

c. $\left(\frac{f + g}{h}\right)(-4)$
$\left(\frac{f+g}{h}\right)(x) = \frac{2x - 1}{x - 4}; \left(\frac{f+g}{h}\right)(-4) = \frac{9}{8}$

d. $\left(\frac{fg}{h}\right)(-2)$
$\left(\frac{fg}{h}\right)(x) = \frac{x^2 - x - 6}{x - 4}; \left(\frac{fg}{h}\right)(-2) = 0$

Problem 16

Extend the Problem

Ask students, **"Suppose, instead, that the population had increased 25%. What would the new population be?"** 168,750 people

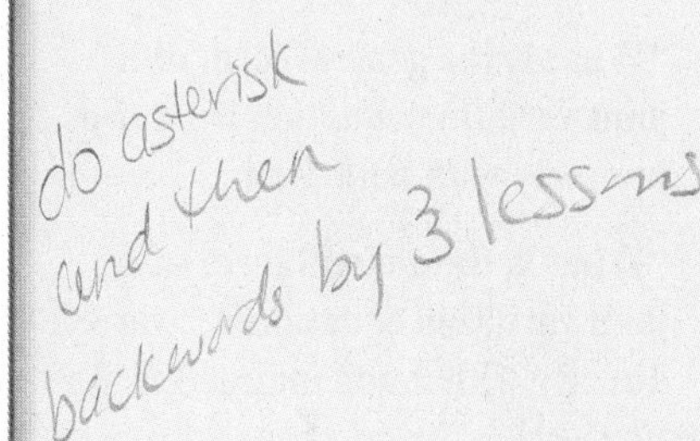

21. Write the determinant as an equation, and then solve the equation. $-x + 4x - 12x = -4x + 10$; $x = -2$
(14)

$$\begin{bmatrix} -x & 2 & -2 \\ 0 & -3 & 1 \\ 2x & 8 & -3 \end{bmatrix} = -4x + 10$$

22. Student A is correct; Student B forgot to distribute the negative through both terms in the second set of parentheses.

***22. Error Analysis** Two students were evaluating $(f - g)(3)$, given $f(x) = 5x - 2$ and $g(x) = 9x + 20$. Who is correct? Explain the error.
(20)

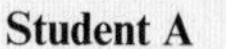

Student A	Student B
$(f-g)(3) = 5(3) - 2 - (9(3) + 20)$	$(f-g)(3) = 5(3) - 2 - (9(3) + 20)$
$= 15 - 2 - 27 - 20$	$= 15 - 2 - 27 + 20$
$= -34$	$= 6$

23. Geometry Write a polynomial in standard form that represents the shaded area formed by the two rectangles. $2x^2 - 3x + 15$
(11, 19)

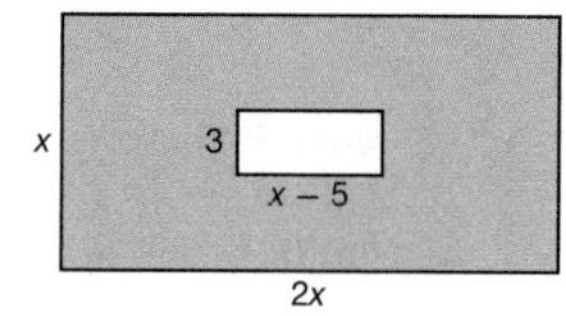

24. Spending and Saving The amount of money Hannah has saved is given by the function $f(x) = 20x + 100$. Jess, Hannah's sister, has started spending her money and this is given by the function $g(x) = -10x + 400$. The number of weeks the girls are spending and saving is represented by x.
(20)

a. **Formulate** Find the function representing the amount of money that the girls have combined, $h(x)$. $h(x) = (f + g)(x) = 20x + 100 + (-10x) + 400 = 10x + 500$

b. Find the amount of money that the girls would have together in 3 weeks. $h(3) = 10(3) + 500 = \$530$

c. Who will have more money in 15 weeks?

24c. Hannah will have more money. In 15 weeks she will have $400, and Jess will have $250; $f(15) = 20(15) + 100 = 400$; $g(15) = -10(15) + 400 = 250$

***25.** Given $f(x) = 6x + 13$ and $g(x) = 7x - 15$, find $(f + g)(x)$. $(f + g)(x) = 13x - 2$
(20)

***26.** Explain how to find $(f \cdot g)(x)$, given $f(x) = 5x - 9$ and $g(x) = 9x + 8$. Multiply the two binomials using FOIL. $(f \cdot g)(x) = (5x - 9)(9x + 8) = 45x^2 - 41x - 72$
(20)

***27. Multiple Choice** Given $f(x) = -2x + 11$ and $g(x) = 6x - 1$, find $(f + g)(8)$. **A**
(20)

A 42 **B** 52 **C** 74 **D** 76

28. Solve $|-3x - 4| \geq 2$, then graph the solution. Is $x = 4$ a solution to the inequality? See Additional Answers.
(17)

29. Multiple Representations Write the absolute value function shown in the graph. $f(x) = |x - 4| + 2$
(17)

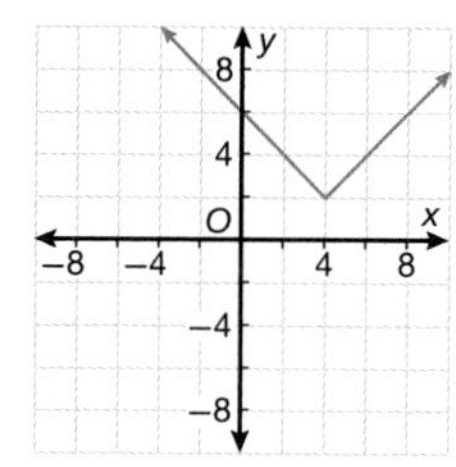

***30. Chemical Elements** For neon to be a liquid, it must be within 1.2715° of –247.1755°C.
(17)

a. **Formulate** Write an absolute value inequality to determine the least and greatest temperatures at which neon will remain a liquid. $|t + 247.1755| = 1.2715$

b. Solve the equation. $t = -248.447$ or $t = -245.904$

Problem 20

Guide the students by asking them the following questions.

"What are the three types of variations?" direct, inverse, and joint

"What are the general forms of equations that have direct and inverse variation?" Direct variation has the form $y = kx$. Inverse variation has the form $y = \frac{k}{x}$.

"What is the general form of a joint variation equation if z varies directly with both x and y? $z = kxy$

"What is the general form of a joint variation equation if z varies inversely with both x and y? $z = \frac{k}{xy}$

"What is the general form of a joint variation equation if z varies directly with x and indirectly with y? $z = \frac{kx}{y}$

Problem 24

Ask students, **"What are two methods you could use to solve part b?"** You could first find $f(3)$ and $g(3)$, and then find the sum, $h(3) = f(3) + g(3)$. You could also use the algebraic sum from part a, $h(3) = 10(3) + 500 = \$530$.

"Which of these methods do you feel would be most useful if you want to find the amount of money the girls would have together at different times in the future?" Sample: Finding the algebraic sum would be most useful because you could use it for different numbers of weeks.

Problem 25

Point out to students that if the domains of the functions are not specified, they can assume both domains are {Reals}.

LOOKING FORWARD

Performing operations with functions prepares students for

- **Lesson 24** Solving Systems of Equations Using the Elimination Method
- **Lesson 31** Multiplying and Dividing Rational Expressions
- **Lesson 37** Adding and Subtracting Rational Expressions

INVESTIGATION 2

Solving Parametric Equations

House Painting A house painter charges \$30 per hour. On average, she paints 200 square feet of a wall per hour.

In t hours, the painter paints x square feet and earns y dollars. The following equations describe the area painted and amount earned in terms of t.

$$x = 200t$$
$$y = 30t$$

1. Suppose the painter works for 7 hours.

a. How many square feet does she paint? 1400

b. How much does she earn? \$210

2. Complete the table.

t (hours)	0	1	2	3	4	5
x (square feet)	0	200	400	600	800	1000
y (dollars)	0	30	60	90	120	150

3. Model Use the table to write six (x, y) coordinate pairs. (Do not use the t-values.) Graph and connect the points. See Additional Answers.

4. Write Describe the graph. What is the real-world meaning of the point (200, 30)? Painting 200 ft² earns \$30.

Hint

Time is often the parameter when a real-world situation is modeled by parametric equations.

When two variables are expressed in terms of a third variable, the equations used are called **parametric equations.** In the activity above, the parametric equations are $x = 200t$ and $y = 30t$. The variable in both equations, t, is the **parameter.**

5. Graphing Calculator A graphing calculator can graph parametric equations.

NORMAL SCI ENG
FLOAT 0 1 2 3 4 5 6 7 8 9
RADIAN DEGREE
FUNC PAR POL SEQ
CONNECTED DOT
SEQUENTIAL SIMUL
REAL a+bi re^θi
FULL HORIZ G-T
SET CLOCK 01/01/01 01:05

a. To put the calculator in parametric mode, press MODE. Use the arrow keys to highlight "PAR," and then press ENTER.

b. Press the Y= button to enter the parametric equations. In $X1_T$, enter 200, and then press the X,T,θ,n key to insert the variable t. In $Y1_T$, enter 30, and then press X,T,θ,n.

c. Press the WINDOW key. Enter 0 for Tmin, 10 for Tmax, and 1 for Tstep. Enter 0 for Xmin, 2000 for Xmax, and 500 for Xscl. Enter 0 for Ymin, 300 for Ymax , and 100 for Yscl.

d. Press GRAPH to graph the equation. Compare the graph to the one from question 3 above. The graphs are the same.

Online Connection
www.SaxonMathResources.com

A projectile is an object that falls to earth due to the force of gravity. Parametric equations can describe the path of a projectile.

INVESTIGATION 2

Materials

- graphing calculator

Alternate Materials

- graph paper
- calculator

Discuss

In this investigation, students define and graph parametric equations. Define **parametric equations** and **parameter.**

Error Alert

Students may be confused by the parameter. Use the table of values to stress that it is the quantity that is changing. Indicate that parametric equations are another way of representing functions that students may have worked with in the rectangular system.

MATH BACKGROUND

A set of parametric equations consists of a pair of algebraic equations which will be satisfied by the coordinates of every point on a particular relation. Parametric equations are expressed as linear functions of t. The two parametric equations must be used together. Parametric equations can be derived from, and converted back to, their equivalent rectangular equation forms.

In many cases, the parametric form is used to clearly examine motion with respect to time such as the path of a projectile.

INVESTIGATION RESOURCES

Reteaching Master Investigation 2

Problem 6

The term $-16t^2$ involves the force of gravity and is part of the projectile motion model. It will be used in any projectile motion problem in this investigation.

Discuss

Indicate the relationship between the table of values and the WINDOW settings. Students may have difficulty determining the window values when working independently.

Error Alert

A common mistake is to enter only one of the parametric equations. Students will see only the axes unless both the equations are entered.

Problem 8

In addition to tracing, use the calculator table to examine the values of t, x, and y side-by-side to answer part **d.** Why does the table have no realistic values after $t = 0$? The value of y becomes negative at $t = 7$. This would mean that the ball was underground, which is not the case.

TEACHER TIP

After Question 8, have students write and share application ideas that can be represented by parametric equations.

(Golf) A golfer hits his first shot on a hole. When the golf ball leaves the club, it is traveling 120 feet per second horizontally and 96 feet per second vertically.

The parametric equations that describe the golf ball's motion are

$$x = 120t$$
$$y = -16t^2 + 96t$$

where x is the horizontal distance the golf ball has traveled and y is the height of the ball.

Math Reasoning

Formulate Using the parametric equations describing the path of the golf ball, how can an equation be written for y in terms of x?

Isolate t in the equation $x = 120t$, and then substitute the expression $t = \frac{x}{120}$ for t in the equation $y = -16t^2 + 96t$. Simplify. The result is $y = -0.001x^2 + 0.8x$

Notice where the initial speeds appear in the equations. The initial horizontal speed, 120 ft/s, is the coefficient of t in the equation for x. The initial vertical speed, 96 ft/s, is the coefficient of t in the equation for y.

6. Complete the table.

t (seconds)	0	1	2	3	4	5	6
x (feet)	0	120	240	360	480	600	720
y (feet)	0	80	128	144	128	80	0

7. Write Use the table to write (x, y) coordinate pairs. Graph and connect the points. Describe the graph. The graph is a parabola that opens downward. See Additional Answers.

8. Graphing Calculator Use a graphing calculator to graph the parametric equations.

a. Press the Y= button. Enter the parametric equations, using the x^2 button to enter the exponent.

b. Press the WINDOW key. Enter 0 for Tmin, 6 for Tmax, and 0.5 for Tstep. Enter 0 for Xmin, 900 for Xmax, and 100 for Xscl. Enter –50 for Ymin, 200 for Ymax, and 25 for Yscl. Then press GRAPH to see the graph.

c. Press the TRACE key. Notice the blinking cursor at the origin, and the x-, y-, and t-values for that point at the bottom of the screen.

d. Use the right and left arrows to move along the graph. Watch the values of the variables change. When does the golf ball reach its highest point, and what is its height at that time? How long does it take the golf ball to hit the ground, and how many feet does it travel horizontally?

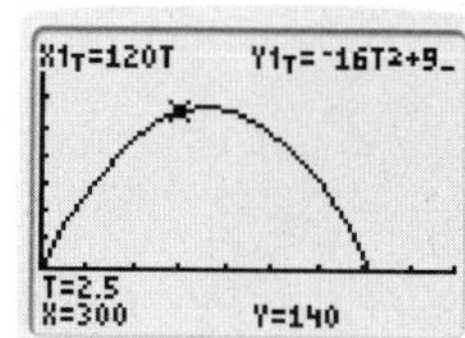

Math Reasoning

Generalize Gravity on the moon is about one-sixth as strong as it is on the earth. Would a golf ball hit in the same way on the moon go higher, farther, or both, than the one in this Activity did on the earth?

both

8d. The golf ball reaches its highest point, 144 feet high, in 3 seconds. It takes the golf ball 6 seconds to reach the ground, and it travels 720 feet.

g. $x = 60t$
$y = -16t^2 + 128t$

h.

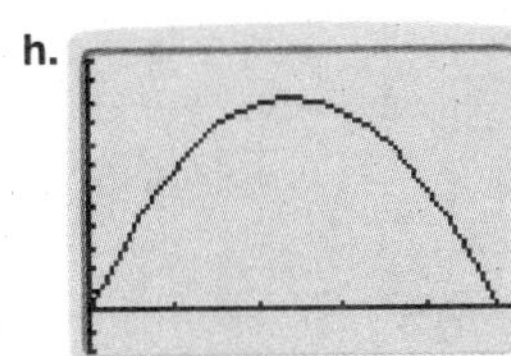

i. The x-coordinate gives the horizontal distance the ball has traveled at a given time; the y-coordinate gives the height of the ball at that time.

j. The golf ball reaches its highest point, 256 feet high, in 4 seconds. It takes the golf ball 8 seconds to reach the ground, and it travels 480 feet.

k. The second shot had a greater vertical velocity than the first, so it went higher. The first shot had a greater horizontal velocity than the second did, so it traveled a greater horizontal distance.

e.

f. The bus can travel 480 miles on one tank of fuel. It can be driven 12 hours before refueling.

Suppose t represents a Great Dane puppy's age in months, x is its shoulder height in inches, and y is its weight in pounds. Then these parametric equations approximate the typical growth of a puppy from age 2 months to age 12 months.

$$x = 1.8t + 11.4$$
$$y = 10t$$

a. Complete the table.

t (months)	2	4	6	9	12
x (inches)	15	18.6	22.2	27.6	33
y (pounds)	20	40	60	90	120

b. Graph the (x, y) coordinate pairs. Describe the graph. See Additional Answers.

c. **Predict** According to the graph, how heavy will a 24-inch-tall puppy be?
70 pounds

A bus traveling at 40 miles per hour uses 5 gallons of fuel per hour. The fuel tank has a capacity of 60 gallons.

d. Let t be the time in hours, x be the distance traveled, and y be the number of gallons remaining in the fuel tank. Write parametric equations for x and y in terms of t. $x = 40t$; $y = 60 - 5t$

e. Make a table of values and graph the (x, y) coordinate pairs. Describe the graph. The graph is a straight line with a negative slope.

f. Use the graph to determine how far the bus can travel on one tank of fuel. How many hours can the bus be driven before it needs refueling?

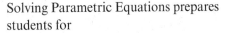

Graphing Calculator Suppose the golfer in the activity on page 144 hits a second shot. This time, the horizontal speed of the ball is only 60 feet per second, but the vertical speed is 128 feet per second.

g. Write a pair of parametric equations for the horizontal distance traveled by the golf ball (x) and the height of the golf ball (y).

h. Graph the equations on a graphing calculator. Adjust Tmax, Xmax, and/or Ymax to see the complete flight of the ball.

i. Use TRACE to move along the graph. What do the coordinates of each point mean?

j. For this shot, when does the golf ball reach its highest point, and what is its height at that time? How long does it take the golf ball to hit the ground, and how many feet does it travel?

k. **Write** Compare the maximum heights and the distances traveled for the two shots. Explain why the differences make sense.

Investigation Practice

Math Conversations

Discussion to strengthen understanding.

Problem a

Scaffolding Have students follow the steps to complete the problem.

1. Substitute the value of t and solve for x and y.
2. Use the table and graphing calculator instructions in problems 5 and 8 to graph the set of parametric equations.
3. Trace or use the table to make the prediction. Does your prediction make sense?
Yes, 70 pounds is between 22.2 and 27.6 inches in the table.

Problem d

The problem describes a line or linear system. Use the equations in the House Painting problem as a model. Use the form:

$$x = at + b$$
$$y = ct + d$$

Extend the Problem

Write an equation in rectangular form by eliminating the parameter t. Graph this line in function mode. Is it equivalent to your parametric model?
$x = 40t$, $y = 60 - 5t$
$y = -\frac{x}{8} + 60$; yes

Problem g

Adjust the model from the golf problem. Do not forget the term $-16t^2$.

ENGLISH LEARNERS

For this lesson, explain the meaning of the word **parameter.** Say:

"Parameter is a quantity that changes."

Discuss examples such as throwing a football or hitting a baseball.

Before the baseball is released, time = 0 and the position of the baseball is (0, 0). As the ball is released, its position (x, y) changes as time changes.

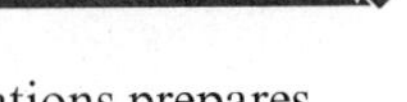

LOOKING FORWARD

Solving Parametric Equations prepares students for

- **Lesson 12** Solving Systems of Equations Using the Substitution Method

Lesson Planner

Lesson	New Concepts
21	Solving Systems of Equations Using the Substitution Method
LAB 5	*Graphing Calculator Lab:* Storing and Plotting a List of Data
22	Analyzing Continuous, Discontinuous, and Discrete Functions
23	Factoring Polynomials
24	Solving Systems of Equations Using the Elimination Method
LAB 6	*Graphing Calculator Lab:* Calculating 1- and 2-Variable Statistical Data
25	Finding Measures of Central Tendency and Dispersion
	Cumulative Test 4, Performance Task 4
26	Writing the Equation of a Line
27	Connecting the Parabola with the Quadratic Function
28	Simplifying Rational Expressions
29	Solving Systems of Equations in Three Variables
30	Applying Transformations to the Parabola and Determining the Minimum or Maximum
	Cumulative Test 5, Performance Task 5
INV 3	Graphing Three Linear Equations in Three Variables

Resources for Teaching

- Student Edition
- Teacher's Edition
- Student Edition eBook
- Teacher's Edition eBook
- Resources and Planner CD
- Solutions Manual
- Instructional Masters
- Technology Lab Masters
- Warm Up and Teaching Transparencies
- Instructional Presentations CD
- Online activities, tools, and homework help **www.SaxonMathResources.com**

Resources for Practice and Assessment

- Student Edition Practice Workbook
- Course Assessments
- Standardized Test Practice
- College Entrance Exam Practice
- Test and Practice Generator CD using ExamView™

Resources for Differentiated Instruction

- Reteaching Masters
- Challenge and Enrichment Masters
- Prerequisite Skills Intervention
- Adaptations for Saxon Algebra 2
- Multilingual Glossary
- English Learners Handbook
- TI Resources

Pacing Guide

Resources and Planner CD for lesson planning support

45-Minute Class

Day 1	Day 2	Day 3	Day 4	Day 5	Day 6
Lesson 21	Lesson 22	Lesson 23	Lab 5 Lesson 24	Lab 6 Lesson 25	Cumulative Test 4
Day 7	**Day 8**	**Day 9**	**Day 10**	**Day 11**	**Day 12**
Lesson 26	Lesson 27	Lesson 28	Lesson 29	Lesson 30	Cumulative Test 5
Day 13					
Investigation 3					

Block: 90-Minute Class

Day 1	Day 2	Day 3	Day 4	Day 5	Day 6
Investigation 2 Lesson 21	Lab 5 Lesson 22 Lesson 23	Lesson 24 Lab 6 Lesson 25	Cumulative Test 4 Lesson 26	Lesson 27 Lesson 28	Lesson 29 Lesson 30
Day 7					
Cumulative Test 5 Investigation 3					

** For suggestions on how to implement Saxon Math in a block schedule, see the Pacing section at the beginning of the Teacher's Edition.*

Differentiated Instruction

Below Level		Advanced Learners	
Warm Up	SE pp. 146, 155, 163, 170, 180, 187, 194, 201, 207, 215	Challenge	TE pp. 152, 161, 168, 175, 185, 190, 192, 197, 204, 211, 213, 217
Skills Bank	SE pp. 862–885	Extend the Example	TE pp. 147, 158, 164, 171, 183, 188, 189, 194, 196, 210, 216
Reteaching Masters	Lessons 21–30, Investigation 3	Extend the Exploration	TE p. 195
Warm Up Transparencies	Lessons 21–30	Extend the Problem	TE pp. 152, 162, 168, 176, 185, 186, 191, 193, 198, 199, 200, 204, 206, 214, 219, 220
Prerequisite Skills Intervention	1–4, 10, 63, 67–72, 84	Challenge and Enrichment Masters	Challenge C21–C30 Enrichment E25, E28
English Learners		**Special Needs**	
EL Tips	TE pp. 147, 156, 164, 171, 181, 188, 195, 202, 208, 216, 223	Inclusion Tips	TE pp. 148, 150, 157, 165, 173, 183, 191, 198, 205, 210, 212, 219
Multilingual Glossary	Booklet and Online	Adaptations for Saxon Algebra 2	Lessons 21–30; Cumulative Test 4, 5
English Learners Handbook			
For All Learners			
Exploration	SE p. 195	Alternate Method	TE pp. 149, 151, 158, 160, 167, 172, 174, 189, 203, 209
Caution	SE pp. 180, 182, 194, 202, 210, 211, 218	Online Tools	
Hints	SE pp. 146, 147, 155, 157, 163, 164, 165, 171, 187, 197, 203, 207, 209, 222, 223, 224, 225		
Error Alert	TE pp. 148, 150, 151, 153, 154, 158, 159, 160, 166, 168, 171, 174, 183, 185, 186, 190, 197, 202, 208, 216, 222, 225		

SE = Student Edition; TE = Teacher's Edition

Math Vocabulary

Lesson	New Vocabulary		Maintained	EL Tip in TE
21	substitution method		solution	coincide
22	continuous function discontinuous function	point of discontinuity		discontinuous discontinuity
23	difference of two squares factor greatest common monomial factor	perfect square trinomial prime polynomial	factors	factor polynomial
24	elimination method		consistent dependent	elimination
25	box-and-whisker plot mean measure of central tendency measure of dispersion median	mode outlier range of a data set standard deviation statistics	discrete	deviation
26	point-slope form standard form of a linear equation		vertical	form
27	axis of symmetry first quartile parabola quadratic equation quadratic function reflection	standard form of a quadratic function third quartile vertex of a parabola zeros of a function	linear	roots vertex
28	rational expression		polynomial	rational
29	ordered triple		inconsistent	plane
30	compressed maximum value of a function minimum value of a function	shift stretched vertex form of a quadratic function	parabola reflection transformation vertex	translation
INV 3	three-dimensional coordinate system z-axis		ordered triples	revenue

SECTION OVERVIEW 3

Math Highlights

Enduring Understandings – The "Big Picture"

After completing Section 3, students will understand:

- How to solve systems of equations using the substitution method and the elimination method.
- How to apply transformations to parabolas and determine the minimum and maximum.
- How to find measures of central tendency and variance.
- How to solve and graph systems of three equations and three variables.

Essential Questions

- How do I simplify rational expressions?
- How can I factor polynomials?
- How do I write the equation of a line?

Math Content Strands

Exponential and Logarithmic Functions

• Lesson 23	Factoring Polynomials

Linear Functions

• Lesson 22	Analyzing Continuous, Discontinuous, and Discrete Functions
• Lesson 26	Writing the Equation of a Line

Linear Systems

• Lesson 21	Solving Systems of Equations Using the Substitution Method
• Lesson 24	Solving Systems of Equations Using the Elimination Method
• Lesson 29	Solving Systems of Equations in Three Variables
• Investigation 3	Graphing Three Linear Equations in Three Variables

Probability and Statistics

• Lab 5	Storing and Plotting a List of Data
• Lab 6	Calculating 1- and 2-Variable Statistical Data
• Lesson 25	Finding Measures of Central Tendency and Dispersion

Quadratic Functions

• Lesson 27	Connecting the Parabola with the Quadratic Function
• Lesson 30	Applying Transformations to the Parabola and Determining the Minimum or Maximum

Rational and Radical Functions

• Lesson 28	Simplifying Rational Expressions

Connections in Practice Problems

	Lessons
Data Analysis	23, 25, 26, 28
Coordinate Geometry	24, 29, 30
Geometry	21, 22, 23, 24, 25, 26, 27, 28, 29, 30, Inv. 3
Measurement	21
Statistics	27

Math Processes

Reasoning and Communication

	Lessons
• Analyze	21, 23, 24, 25, 26, 28, 29, 30, Inv. 3
• Error analysis	21, 22, 23, 24, 25, 26, 27, 28, 29, 30
• Estimate	21, 24, 30
• Formulate	21, 25
• Generalize	Inv. 3
• Justify	21, 22, 23, 24, 26, 27, 29, 30
• Math reasoning	21, 24, 27, 28, 29, 30
• Model	24, 30, Inv. 3
• Multiple choice	21, 22, 23, 24, 25, 26, 27, 28, 29, 30
• Multi-step	21, 22, 23, 24, 25, 26, 27, 28, 29, 30, Inv. 3
• Predict	21
• Verify	21, 23, 26, 27, 28, 29
• Write	22, 23, 25, 26, 27, 28, 29
• Graphing Calculator	21, 22, 23, 24, 25, 26, 27, 28, 29, 30, Inv. 3

Connections

In Examples: Consumer math, Demography, Engineering, the Golden Ratio in Art, Investing, Sports, Vacationing

In Practice problems: Artwork, Aviation, Basketball, Business school, Carnival, Coffee, Computer graphics, Drumming, Engines, Envelopes, Exercise, Fitness, Fuel economy, Grizzly bears, Imports, Mailing weights, Medicine, Mountains, Nutrition, Packaging technology, Planets, Population, Pyramids, Quilting, Rocket, Rugby, Running, Sightseeing, Skateboarding, Soccer, Sports, Tall structures, Track and field, Travel

Content Trace

Lesson	Warm Up: Prerequisite Skills	New Concepts	Where Practiced	Where Assessed	Looking Forward
21	Lessons 2, 13, 15	Solving Systems of Equations Using the Substitution Method	Lessons 21, 22, 23, 24, 25, 26, 27, 28, 29, 30, 31, 33, 34, 35, 39, 40, 72, 105	Cumulative Tests 5, 7, 9, 11, 17, 23	Lessons 24, 29
22	Lesson 4	Analyzing Continuous, Discontinuous, and Discrete Functions	Lessons 22, 23, 24, 25, 26, 28, 29, 30, 35, 37, 39	Cumulative Tests 5, 7, 9, 14	Lessons 27, 109
23	Skills Bank	Factoring Polynomials	Lessons 23, 24, 25, 26, 27, 28, 29, 30, 31, 32, 33, 34, 35, 38, 39, 40, 43, 44, 46, 47, 49, 57, 59, 101, 115	Cumulative Tests 5, 6, 8, 11, 16	Lessons 65, 66, 76, 89
24	Lessons 15, 21	Solving Systems of Equations Using the Elimination Method	Lessons 24, 25, 26, 27, 28, 29, 30, 31, 32, 33, 34, 35–37, 38, 40, 42, 48, 49, 52, 57	Cumulative Tests 5, 6, 8, 10, 15	Lessons 29, 43, 54
25	Skills Bank, Lesson 22	Finding Measures of Central Tendency and Dispersion	Lessons 25, 26, 28, 30, 32, 34, 40, 52, 54, 113	Cumulative Tests 5, 10, 14, 22	Lessons 73, 80, 118
26	Lesson 13	Writing the Equation of a Line	Lessons 26, 27, 28, 29, 30, 33, 36, 40, 41, 42, 50	Cumulative Tests 6, 7, 8, 12, 17	Lessons 34, 36, 39
27	Lessons 7, 13, 17, 19	Connecting the Parabola with the Quadratic Function	Lessons 27, 28, 30, 32, 36, 38, 39, 43, 44, 45, 46, 47, 48, 57	Cumulative Tests 6, 7, 11, 13	Lessons 30, 35, 39
28	Lessons 11, 19, 23	Simplifying Rational Expressions	Lessons 28, 29, 30, 31, 32, 39, 42, 43, 104, 113	Cumulative Tests 6, 7, 9, 12, 19	Lessons 31, 37, 40, 44
29	Lessons 2, 21, 24	Solving Systems of Equations in Three Variables	Lessons 29, 30, 32, 36, 38, 39, 43, 44, 47, 50, 52	Cumulative Tests 6, 7, 8, 10, 13, 16	Lessons 43, 54
30	Lesson 27	Applying Transformations to the Parabola and Determining the Minimum or Maximum	Lessons 30, 31, 32, 34, 36, 38, 39, 42, 43, 44, 50, 54, 113	Cumulative Tests 6, 7	Lessons 35, 58, 78, 83
INV 3	N/A	Graphing Three Linear Equations in Three Variables	Lessons 31, 33, 61	Cumulative Test 8	Lessons 32, 43

Ongoing Assessment

	Type	Feature	Intervention *
BEFORE instruction	Assess Prior Knowledge	• Diagnostic Test	• Prerequisite Skills Intervention
BEFORE the lesson	Formative	• Warm Up	• Skills Bank • Reteaching Masters
DURING the lesson	Formative	• Lesson Practice • Math Conversations with the Practice problems	• Additional Examples in TE • Test and Practice Generator (for additional practice sheets)
AFTER the lesson	Formative	• Check for Understanding (closure)	• Scaffolding Questions in TE
AFTER 5 lessons	Summative	After Lesson 25 • Cumulative Test 4 • Performance Task 4 After Lesson 30 • Cumulative Test 5 • Performance Task 5	• Reteaching Masters • Test and Practice Generator (for additional tests and practice)
AFTER 20 lessons	Summative	• Benchmark Tests	• Reteaching Masters • Test and Practice Generator (for additional tests and practice)

* for students not showing progress during the formative stages or scoring below 80% on the summative assessments

Evidence of Learning – What Students Should Know

Because the Saxon philosophy is to provide students with sufficient time to learn and practice each concept, a lesson's topic will not be tested until at least five lessons after the topic is introduced.

On the Cumulative Tests that are given during this section of ten lessons, students should be able to demonstrate the following competencies:

- Solve equations and inequalities with absolute value.
- Use Cramer's Rule.
- Solve systems of equations using the substitution method and the elimination method.
- Factor polynomials.
- Analyze discrete and continuous functions.

Test and Practice Generator CD using ExamView™

The Test and Practice Generator is an easy-to-use benchmark and assessment tool that creates unlimited practice and tests in multiple formats and allows you to customize questions or create new ones. A variety of reports are available to track student progress toward mastery of the standards throughout the year.

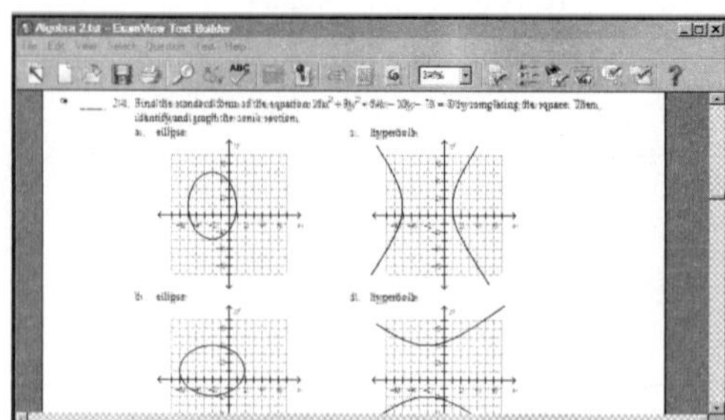

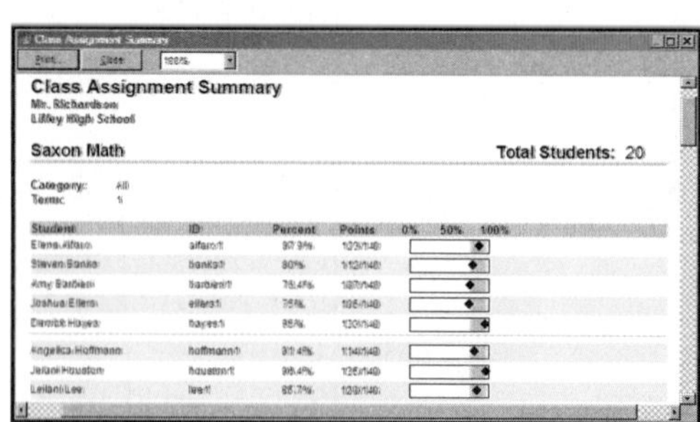

Assessment Resources

Resources for Diagnosing and Assessing

- **Student Edition**
  - Warm Up
  - Lesson Practice
- **Teacher's Edition**
  - Math Conversations with the Practice problems
  - Check for Understanding (closure)
- **Course Assessments**
  - Cumulative Tests
  - Performance Tasks
  - Benchmark Tests
  - Diagnostic Test

Resources for Test Prep

- **Student Edition Practice**
  - Multiple-choice problems
  - Multiple-step and writing problems
  - Daily cumulative practice
- **Standardized Test Practice**
- **College Entrance Exam Practice**
- **Test and Practice Generator CD using ExamView™**

Resources for Intervention

- **Student Edition**
  - Skills Bank
- **Teacher's Edition**
  - Additional Examples
  - Scaffolding questions
- **Prerequisite Skills Intervention**
  - Skill worksheets
- **Reteaching Masters**
  - Lesson instruction and practice sheets
- **Test and Practice Generator CD using ExamView™**
  - Lesson practice problems
  - Additional tests

Cumulative Tests

The assessments in Saxon Math are frequent and consistently placed after every five lessons to offer a regular method of ongoing testing. These cumulative assessments check mastery of concepts from previous lessons.

Performance Tasks

The Performance Tasks can be used in conjunction with the Cumulative Tests and are scored using a rubric.

After Lesson 25

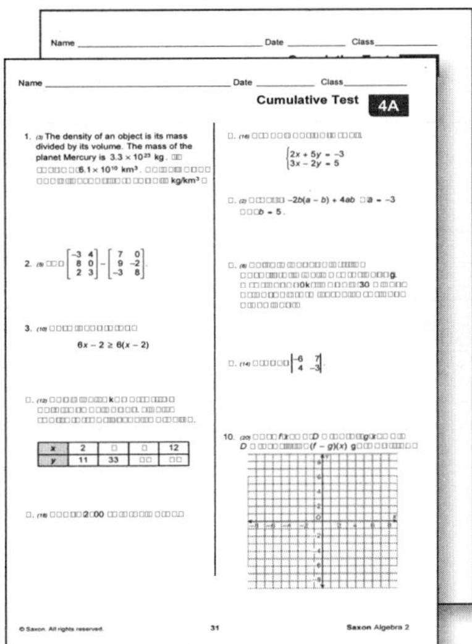

Name ______ Date ______ Class ______

Cumulative Test 4A

1. (3) The density of an object is its mass divided by its volume. The mass of the planet Mercury is 3.3×10^{23} kg. … 6.1×10^{10} km³ … kg/km³

2. (5) … $\begin{bmatrix} -3 & 4 \\ 8 & 0 \\ 2 & 3 \end{bmatrix} - \begin{bmatrix} 7 & 0 \\ 9 & -2 \\ -3 & 8 \end{bmatrix}$.

3. (10) … $6x - 2 \geq 6(x - 2)$

(12) …

x	2			12
y	11	33		

(16) … 2000 …

(16) … $\begin{cases} 2x + 5y = -3 \\ 3x - 2y = 5 \end{cases}$

(2) … $-2b(a - b) + 4ab$ … $a = -3$ … $b = 5$.

(8) … 30 …

(14) … $\begin{vmatrix} -6 & 7 \\ 4 & -3 \end{vmatrix}$.

10. (20) … $f(x)$ … D … $g(x)$ … D … $(f - g)(x)$ …

© Saxon. All rights reserved. 31 Saxon Algebra 2

After Lesson 30

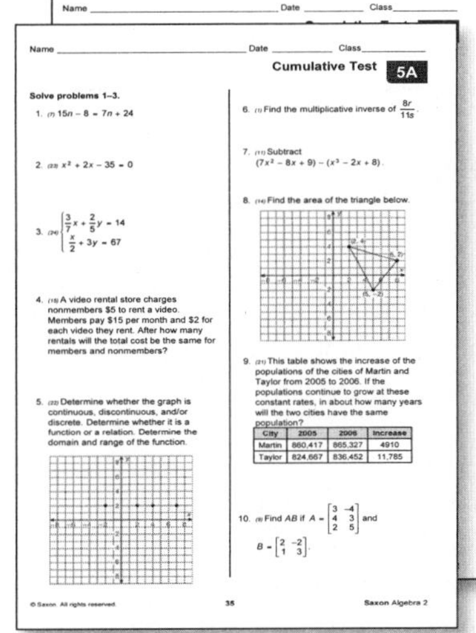

Name ______ Date ______ Class ______

Cumulative Test 5A

Solve problems 1–3.

1. (7) $15n - 8 = 7n + 24$

2. (23) $x^2 + 2x - 35 = 0$

3. (24) $\begin{cases} \frac{3}{7}x + \frac{2}{5}y = 14 \\ \frac{x}{2} + 3y = 67 \end{cases}$

4. (15) A video rental store charges nonmembers $5 to rent a video. Members pay $15 per month and $2 for each video they rent. After how many rentals will the total cost be the same for members and nonmembers?

5. (22) Determine whether the graph is continuous, discontinuous, and/or discrete. Determine whether it is a function or a relation. Determine the domain and range of the function.

6. (1) Find the multiplicative inverse of $\frac{8r}{11s}$.

7. (11) Subtract $(7x^2 - 8x + 9) - (x^2 - 2x + 8)$.

8. (14) Find the area of the triangle below.

9. (21) This table shows the increase of the populations of the cities of Martin and Taylor from 2005 to 2006. If the populations continue to grow at these constant rates, in about how many years will the two cities have the same population?

City	2005	2006	Increase
Martin	860,417	865,327	4910
Taylor	824,667	836,452	11,785

10. (9) Find AB if $A = \begin{bmatrix} 3 & -4 \\ 4 & 3 \\ 2 & 5 \end{bmatrix}$ and $B = \begin{bmatrix} 2 & -2 \\ 1 & 3 \end{bmatrix}$.

© Saxon. All rights reserved. 35 Saxon Algebra 2

For use with Performance Tasks

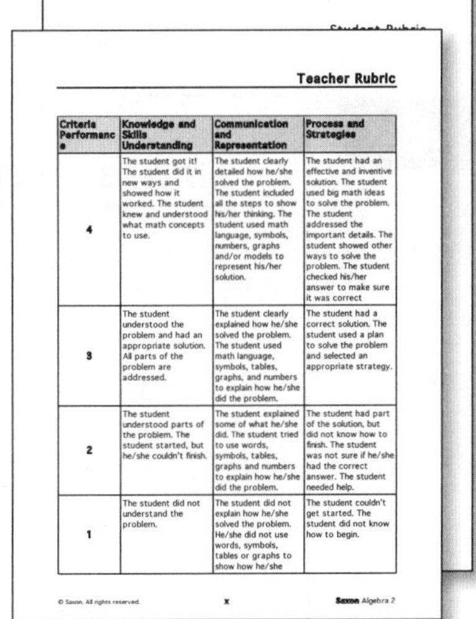

Teacher Rubric

Criteria Performance	Knowledge and Skills Understanding	Communication and Representation	Process and Strategies
4	The student got it! The student did it in new ways and showed how it worked. The student knew and understood what math concepts to use.	The student clearly detailed how he/she solved the problem. The student included all the steps to show his/her thinking. The student used math language, symbols, numbers, graphs and/or models to represent his/her solution.	The student had an effective and inventive solution. The student used big math ideas to solve the problem. The student addressed the important details. The student showed other ways to solve the problem. The student checked his/her answer to make sure it was correct
3	The student understood the problem and had an appropriate solution. All parts of the problem are addressed.	The student clearly explained how he/she solved the problem. The student used math language, symbols, tables, graphs, and numbers to explain how he/she did the problem.	The student had a correct solution. The student used a plan to solve the problem and selected an appropriate strategy.
2	The student understood parts of the problem. The student started, but he/she couldn't finish.	The student explained some of what he/she did. The student tried to use words, symbols, tables, graphs and numbers to explain how he/she did the problem.	The student had part of the solution, but did not know how to finish. The student was not sure if he/she had the correct answer. The student needed help.
1	The student did not understand the problem.	The student did not explain how he/she solved the problem. He/she did not use words, symbols, tables or graphs to show how he/she	The student couldn't get started. The student did not know how to begin.

© Saxon. All rights reserved. x Saxon Algebra 2

1 Warm Up

Problem 2

Remind students when solving for y, to put the equation in slope-intercept form.

2 New Concepts

In this lesson, students learn to solve a system of equations using the substitution method.

Discuss what is meant by the **substitution method.** Tell students this is only one of the procedures they can follow to solve systems of equations and it involves substitution of known values to solve for the unknown variables.

Example 1

When solving for one of the variables, suggest that students choose the equation where the variable is the easiest to isolate.

Additional Example 1

Solve the system of equations by substitution.

$4y - x = 12$
$y - 4x = 18$
(−4, 2)

LESSON 21 Solving Systems of Equations Using the Substitution Method

Warm Up

1. **Vocabulary** A ________ of a system is an ordered pair or a set of ordered pairs that satisfy all the equations in the system. (15) **C**
A check   B evaluation   C solution

2. Solve for y: $-6x + 3y = -9$. (13) $y = 2x - 3$

3. Distribute $7xy(5x - 3 + 4y)$. (2) $35x^2y - 21xy + 28xy^2$

New Concepts

One way a system of equations can be solved is through graphing. Sometimes a solution to a system may be difficult to determine on a graph, especially if the solution is an intersection point with values that are fractions or decimals.

However, there is an algebraic way to find the exact solution of a system of equations. The **substitution** method is a method used to solve systems of equations by solving an equation for one variable and substituting the resulting expression into the other equation.

Example 1 Solving a System of Equations by Substitution

Solve the system of equations by substitution. $\begin{aligned} 2y - x &= -6 \\ y - 2x &= 1 \end{aligned}$

SOLUTION

Step 1: Choose an equation and solve for one of the variables.

$$y - 2x = 1$$
$$y = \boxed{2x + 1}$$ ← This expression will be used in the next step.

Step 2: Substitute the expression for y into the other equation. Solve for x.

$$2\boxed{y} - x = -6$$
$$2(2x + 1) - x = -6$$ Substitute for y.
$$x = -\frac{8}{3}$$ Solve for x.

Step 3: Substitute the value of x into either equation to solve for y.

$$2y - \boxed{x} = -6$$
$$2y - \left(-\frac{8}{3}\right) = -6$$
$$y = -\frac{13}{3}$$

The solution is $\left(-\frac{8}{3}, -\frac{13}{3}\right)$.

Hint

Check the answer by substituting the x-value and the y-value into both equations. The answer is correct if the values make both equations true.

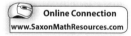

Online Connection www.SaxonMathResources.com

LESSON RESOURCES

Student Edition Practice Workbook 21
Reteaching Master 21
Adaptations Master 21
Challenge and Enrichment Masters C21

MATH BACKGROUND

To solve a system of equations, there must be as many equations as variables. If there are two equations, then there must be two variables; three equations, three variables.

Solving systems of equations by substitution lends itself to the use of the slope-intercept form, $y = mx + b$, and the Distributive Property, $a(b + c) = ab + bc$, when solving for one of the variables.

Evaluating expressions using substitution is also used in solving systems of equations when substituting the values for x and y back into the original equations in order to check the answer.

If a system of equations forms intersecting lines, then the equations have one common solution. When solving independent systems algebraically, the result is a coordinate. Recall the three types of possible systems.

Classifying Systems			
Type of Lines	**Graph of Lines**	**Type of Solution**	**Type of System**
Intersecting Lines	The lines have one point in common.	Consistent	Independent
Coinciding Lines	The lines overlap and share all points in common.	Consistent	Dependent
Parallel Lines	The lines have no points in common.	Inconsistent	No solution

If a system of equations forms coinciding lines, then the equations are describing the same line. Thus, all of the points on the line are solutions to the system. When solving dependent systems algebraically, the result is a true numerical statement (one without variables) such as $0 = 0$ or $5 = 5$.

Example 2 Recognizing a System of Coinciding Lines

Solve the system of equations by substitution.

$$y = x - 2$$
$$2y = 2x - 4$$

SOLUTION

Step 1: Choose an equation and solve for one of the variables. Use the first equation, since it has been solved for y.

$$y = \boxed{x - 2}$$

Hint

If the two equations in the system are rewritten into the slope-intercept form, then it is easier to identify coinciding lines.

Step 2: Substitute the expression for y into the other equation. Solve for x.

$$2\boxed{y} = 2x - 4$$
$$2(x - 2) = 2x - 4 \quad \text{Substitute for } y.$$
$$2x - 4 = 2x - 4$$
$$0 = 0 \quad \text{True.}$$

The substitution produced an equation that is always true. Therefore, these two equations form coinciding lines. Since all of the coordinates on the line are solutions, write the solution as $\{(x, y) \mid y = x - 2\}$.

If a system of equations forms parallel lines, then the lines have no points in common. When attempting to solve systems with no solution, the result is a false numerical statement such as $0 = 6$ or $-4 = 4$.

Example 2

Extend the Example

Have students multiply the first equation by 2 to yield the equation $2y = 2x - 4$. Point out to students that the first equation is now identical to the second equation. Then have students multiply the second equation by $\frac{1}{2}$ to yield $y = x - 2$. Again, point out to students that the two equations are now identical. Have students explain how this method can be used to identify dependent systems. The method shows that the two equations are identical, therefore the two equations represent the same line. So, the lines coincide and the system is dependent.

Additional Example 2

Solve the system of equations by substitution.

$3y = -3x - 9$

$y = -x - 3$

$\{(x, y) | y = -x - 3\}$

ENGLISH LEARNERS

To help students understand the meaning of **coincide,** define the word as a verb—to occupy the same space or to occupy equivalent positions.

Coincide also means in accord or agreement. Synonyms that may help students are concur or agree.

Coincide as a verb can also mean to happen at or near the same point of time. For example: The day off from school coincides with Sam's birthday.

Have students think of situations when they may have used the word coincide as a verb meaning either to agree or to happen at the same time.

Example 3

Have students write the second equation in slope-intercept form ($y = 2x - 2$). Point out to students that both equations have the same slope with different y-intercepts and are therefore parallel.

Additional Example 3

Solve the system of equations by substitution.

$$-3x + y = -2$$
$$y = 3x - 3$$

no solution

Example 4

Error Alert Students may forget to multiply each term on both sides of the equation by 2. Remind students that an equation is like a balance scale—what is done to one side must be done to the other.

Additional Example 4

Solve the system of equations by substitution.

$$4x + 3y = 5$$
$$3x - 2y = 8$$

(2, −1)

Example 3 Recognizing a System of Parallel Lines

Solve the system of equations by substitution. $y = 2x + 2$, $-2x + y = -2$

SOLUTION

Step 1: Choose an equation and solve for one of the variables. Use the first equation. Since y has been solved for, move to the next step.

$$y = \boxed{2x + 2}$$

Step 2: Substitute the expression for y into the other equation. Solve for x.

$$-2x + \boxed{y} = -2$$
$$-2x + (2x + 2) = -2 \quad \text{Substitute for } y.$$
$$+2 = -2 \quad \text{False.}$$

The substitution produced an equation that is always false. Therefore, these two equations form parallel lines. Since parallel lines do not intersect, this system has no solution.

Example 4 Substituting with Fractions

Solve the system of equations by substitution. $3x + 2y = -3$, $4x - 3y = 13$

Math Reasoning

Analyze How can the expression $\frac{-3x-3}{2}$ be written so the denominator is eliminated?

Divide each term in the numerator by 2 and write it using a decimal.

SOLUTION Choose an equation and solve for one of the variables.

$$3x + 2y = -3$$
$$2y = -3x - 3$$
$$y = \frac{-3x - 3}{2}$$
$$4x - 3\boxed{y} = 13$$
$$4x - 3\left(\frac{-3x - 3}{2}\right) = 13 \quad \text{Substitute the expression for } y \text{ into the other equation.}$$
$$4x(2) - 3\left(\frac{-3x - 3}{2}\right)(2) = 13(2) \quad \text{Eliminate the denominator by multiplying every term on both sides by 2.}$$
$$8x - 3(-3x - 3) = 26 \quad \text{Simplify.}$$
$$x = 1 \quad \text{Solve for } x.$$
$$3x + 2y = -3 \quad \text{Choose an equation for substituting the value of } x.$$
$$3(1) + 2y = -3 \quad \text{Substitute the value for } x \text{ into the equation.}$$
$$y = -3 \quad \text{Solve for } y.$$

The solution is (1, −3).

INCLUSION

Solving for x may present a challenge to students. Suggest that students highlight or put a box around x to help them focus on the variable x that is being isolated. It may also be helpful in determining the inverse operations needed to solve for x.

Example 5 Application: Demography

Predict This table shows the increase of the population of Maine and of Hawaii from 2004 to 2005. If the populations continue to grow at these constant rates, in what year will these two states have the same population?

State	2004	2005	Increase
Maine	1,317,253	1,321,505	4252
Hawaii	1,262,840	1,275,194	12,354

SOLUTION

1. **Understand** The population of the states and the rate at which the population is increasing are given. Find the year that Maine and Hawaii will have the same population.

2. **Plan** Set up a system of equations and find the point of intersection. Use the substitution method to ensure a better estimate.

3. **Solve** Formulate and solve the system of equations. Let $x = 0$ represent the year 2004.

$$y = 4252x + 1{,}317{,}253$$
$$y = 12{,}354x + 1{,}262{,}840$$

Step 1: Choose an equation and solve for one of the variables.

$$y = \boxed{4252x + 1{,}317{,}253}$$

Step 2: Substitute.

$$\boxed{4252x + 1{,}317{,}253} = 12{,}354x + 1{,}262{,}840$$
$$54{,}413 = 8102x$$
$$x \approx 6.716 \text{ years later}$$

The projected year is sometime during the year of 2010.

4. **Check** Verify your solution by substituting your value for x into each equation.

$$y = 4252\,(6.716) + 1{,}317{,}253 \longrightarrow y \approx 1{,}345{,}809$$
$$y = 12{,}354\,(6.716) + 1{,}262{,}840 \longrightarrow y \approx 1{,}345{,}809$$

About 6.716 years after 2004, Maine and Hawaii should have the same population.

Graphing Calculator 

Use the intersection feature described in Lab 3 on p. 85 to verify the solution to this system of equations.

Lesson Practice

a. Solve the system of equations by substitution. $y + 3x = -4$, $3y - 2x = -2$ (Ex 1)
$\left(-\frac{10}{11}, -\frac{14}{11}\right)$

b. Solve the system of equations by substitution. $3y = 12 - 6x$, $y = -2x + 4$ (Ex 2)
$\{(x, y) \mid y = -2x + 4\}$

Example 5

Remind students that when checking their answer, they should substitute the values for x and y into both original equations. For the solution to be correct, both equations must be true.

Lesson Practice

Problem b

Scaffolding Point out that the second equation is already in slope-intercept form, so they should use that equation for the substitution.

ALTERNATE METHOD FOR PROBLEM a

Encourage students to use Cramer's Rule to find the solution. First, have students rewrite the equations and then find the determinant of the coefficient matrix.

$$D = \begin{vmatrix} 3 & 1 \\ -2 & 3 \end{vmatrix} = 9 - (-2) = 11$$

Then have students solve for x and y.

$$x = \frac{\begin{vmatrix} -4 & 1 \\ -2 & 3 \end{vmatrix}}{11} = \frac{-12 - (-2)}{11} = -\frac{10}{11}$$

$$y = \frac{\begin{vmatrix} 3 & -4 \\ -2 & -2 \end{vmatrix}}{11} = \frac{-6 - 8}{11} = -\frac{14}{11}$$

Problem c

Error Alert Students may make a calculating error. Show students the steps so that they can see the second equation has the same slope as the first equation.

Check for Understanding

The questions below help assess the concepts taught in this lesson.

1. **"Explain how to solve the following system of equations using the substitution method."**

   $3y - x = 5$

   $y - x = 1$

   Put the second equation into slope-intercept form: $y = x + 1$. Substitute $x + 1$ into the first equation and solve for x. Then solve for y by substitution.

2. **"How do you recognize a system of coinciding lines?"** A true numerical statement written without variables, such as $0 = 0$, is obtained.

3 Practice

Math Conversations

Discussions to strengthen understanding.

Problem 1

Guide the students by asking them the following questions.

"Which equation should you use to solve for y?" $3x + y = 10$

"What is $3x + y = 10$ in slope-intercept form?" $y = -3x + 10$

"After the substitution, what simplified equation do you get?" $13x = 39$

Problem 7

"What is absolute value?" the distance from 0 on a number line

"What disjunction do you write for the equation given?" $x + 3 = 16$ or $x + 3 = -16$

---

c. (Ex 3) Solve the system of equations by substitution. $\begin{aligned} y &= 6x - 5 \\ 2y - 10 &= 12x \end{aligned}$ no solution

d. (Ex 4) Solve the system of equations by substitution. $\begin{aligned} 3y - 7x &= 5 \\ 4x - 9y &= 2 \end{aligned}$ $\left(-1, -\frac{2}{3}\right)$

e. (Ex 5) The table shows the increase in the number of rushing yards for two football players from 2005 to 2006. If each player's yardage continues to grow at these constant rates, in what year will these two players have the same total rushing yards? The two players will have the same total rushing yards sometime during 2010.

Player	2005	2006	Increase
Corey	733	812	79
Marion	538	654	116

Practice Distributed and Integrated

Use substitution to solve each system of linear equations.

*1. (21) $\begin{aligned} 3x + y &= 10 \\ -2x - 5y &= -11 \end{aligned}$ $x = 3, y = 1$

*2. (21) $\begin{aligned} -x + 3y &= 10 \\ 3x + 4y &= -4 \end{aligned}$ $x = -4, y = 2$

3. (17) Graph $|-2x - 1| \geq 3$. −2 −1 0 1 2

*4. (20) Find $(f + g)(3)$ if $f(x) = -2x + 4$ and $g(x) = -(x^2)$. -11

5. (9) Find the product. $\begin{bmatrix} 2 & -1 \\ 3 & 1 \\ 1 & 5 \end{bmatrix} \times \begin{bmatrix} 2 & 0 & -1 \\ 1 & 5 & 3 \end{bmatrix}$ $\begin{bmatrix} 3 & -5 & -5 \\ 7 & 5 & 0 \\ 7 & 25 & 14 \end{bmatrix}$

*6. (21) **Verify** Use the system of equations: $\begin{aligned} 2y - 4x &= 6 \\ y + 5x &= -10 \end{aligned}$.

a. Solve the system of equations by solving the first equation for y, then substituting. $\left(-\frac{13}{7}, -\frac{5}{7}\right)$

b. Verify your answer by solving the second equation for y, then substituting. Show your work.

6b. $y = -5x - 10$, so substitute into $2\boxed{y} - 4x = 6$. $2(-5x - 10) - 4x = 6$ gives $x = -\frac{26}{14} = -\frac{13}{7}$. Solve for y: $y = 2\left(-\frac{13}{7}\right) + 3$ gives $y = \frac{-5}{7}$. The solution is $\left(-\frac{13}{7}, -\frac{5}{7}\right)$.

Solve each equation.

7. (17) $|x + 3| = 16$ $x = 13, x = -19$

8. (17) $|2x + 3| = 2 - x$ $x = -\frac{1}{3}, x = -5$

9. (17) $2|x + 6| = 8x$ $x = 2, x = -\frac{6}{5}$

*10. (20) **Error Analysis** Two students evaluated $(f - g)(2)$, given $f(x) = 5x - 2$ and $g(x) = 8x + 10$. Who is correct? Explain the error.

Student A	Student B
$(f - g)(2) = 5(2) - 2 - (8(2) + 10)$ $= 10 - 2 - 16 - 10$ $= -18$	$(f - g)(2) = 5(2) - 2 - (8(2) + 10)$ $= 10 - 2 - 16 + 10$ $= 2$

10. Student A is correct; Student B forgot to distribute the negative through both terms in the second set of parentheses.

150 Saxon Algebra 2

*11. **Geometry** Write an expression for the area of the triangle. (19) $\frac{1}{2}(x + 3)(4x + 2)$ in^2 or $2x^2 + 7x + 3$ in^2

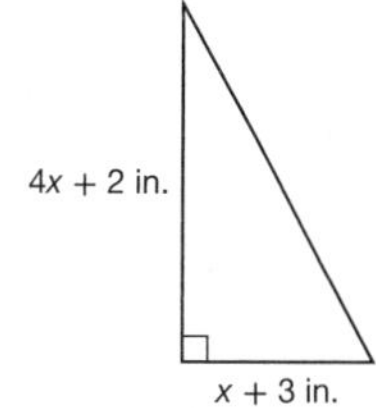

12. Evaluate the determinant: $\begin{vmatrix} -2 & 6 \\ 1 & 5 \end{vmatrix}$ −16 (14)

*13. **Multiple Choice** Phyllis collects silver dollars and half-dollars. She has 5 times as many half-dollars as silver dollar coins. She has 192 coins. Which solution gives the number of silver dollars Phyllis has? **C** (16)

A $\dfrac{\begin{vmatrix} 192 & 1 \\ 0 & -5 \end{vmatrix}}{6}$ B $\dfrac{\begin{vmatrix} 1 & 192 \\ -5 & 0 \end{vmatrix}}{-6}$ C $\dfrac{\begin{vmatrix} 1 & 192 \\ -1 & 0 \end{vmatrix}}{6}$ D $\dfrac{\begin{vmatrix} 192 & 1 \\ 0 & 1 \end{vmatrix}}{-6}$

14. **Multiple Choice** Tickets to the community theatre cost $20. It is also possible to purchase a season pass for $170. Use an inequality to determine how many productions you can attend at the $20 price before spending more than it costs for the season pass. **B** (10)

A 7 B 8 C 9 D 10

15. Given $f(x) = 4x - 1$ and $g(x) = 2x - 1$, find the sum $(f + g)(x)$. $6x - 2$ (20)

16. **Estimate** Estimate the new amount when 14.082 is increased by 9.68%. Explain your reasoning. Sample: About 15.5; Find 10% of 14, which is 1.4 and add 1.4 to 14.1. (6)

*17. **Formulate** Bill leaves his house for Makayla's house riding his bicycle at 8 miles per hour. At the same time, Makayla leaves her house heading toward Bill's house walking at 3 miles per hour. Write a system of equations that could be used to determine how long it takes for them to be the same distance d from Makayla's house in h hours. They live 8.25 miles apart. $d = 3h$; $d = 8.25 - 8h$ (21)

18. **Computer Graphics** A computer programmer wants a shape to move and expand on the screen. The programmer decides to multiply the coordinates of each vertex of the shape by the matrix $\begin{bmatrix} 4 & 6 \\ 2 & 3 \end{bmatrix}$. The area of the shape is multiplied by a factor that equals the determinant of this matrix. By what factor is the area multiplied? Explain. 0; This transformation squashes the shape to a line segment, which has area 0. (14)

19. Write the polynomial $3x + 6x^5 - 3x^2 + 43 - 5x^3$ in standard form. (11)

20. **Measurement** This figure consists of a cylinder with a hemisphere on top. Write a polynomial in terms of x that represents the total volume of the figure. Formulas for volume are given below. (11)

Cylinder: $V = \pi r^2 h$

Sphere: $V = \frac{4}{3}\pi r^3$

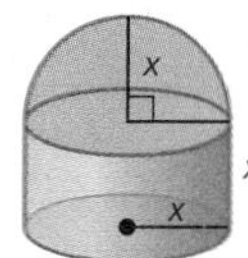

(Hint: The figure has only one circular base.) $\frac{5}{3}\pi x^3$

Problem 12

Remind students that the determinant of a 2 × 2 matrix is defined as

$$D = \begin{vmatrix} a & b \\ c & d \end{vmatrix} = ad - cb$$

Problem 15

Tell students that the operation $(f + g)(x)$ is the same as $f(x) + g(x)$.

Problem 20

Error Alert

Although a hint is given, students still may not take half the volume of the sphere. Before students start the problem, have them identify each figure so that they realize they are not given a whole sphere.

ALTERNATE METHOD FOR PROBLEM 14

Students can solve this problem using a pattern and making a chart like the one below.

7 × $20 = $140

8 × $20 = $160

9 × $20 = $180

Nine productions are too many. The amount, $180, is more than it costs for the season pass. So, the correct answer is 8, or B.

Problem 24

TEACHER TIP

Encourage students to first simplify each term.

$$\frac{a^{-3}x}{y^{-3}} = \frac{xy^3}{a^3}$$

$$\frac{xxx^{-2}}{y^{-2}yy} = \frac{x^2y^2}{x^2y^2} = 1$$

Problem 25

Remind students $y = kx$ represents a direct variation. Have them first solve for the constant k.

$$k = \frac{y}{x} = \frac{57}{150} = 0.38$$

Then solve for y.

$$y = 0.38(25) = 9.5$$

Problem 26

Since the problem asks to find the average speed in miles per hour, remind students to put 10 minutes in terms of hours.

Problem 29

Extend the Problem

Verify your answer by multiplying the binomials first, then substitute.

$(x + 12)(x - 32)$

$x^2 - 20x - 384$

$(82)^2 - 20(82) - 384$

$6724 - 1640 - 384$

4700

21. **Justify** Is the equation $abc = 0$ a joint variation? Why or why not?
(12)

21. No, this is not a joint variation. If $abc = 0$, then either a, b, or c is equal to zero. But the term $\frac{0}{0}$ is not defined. Therefore, $abc = 0$ is not a joint variation.

22. **Basketball** The table shows the types of shots made in a game by the three top scoring L.A. Lakers and the point value of each type of shot. Use matrix multiplication to find out which player scored the most points in the game.
(9)

Shots Made

Player	3 Point	2 Point	1 Point
K. Bryant	1	5	6
M. Evans	2	5	5
L. Walton	1	7	1

22. $\begin{bmatrix} 1 & 5 & 6 \\ 2 & 5 & 5 \\ 1 & 7 & 1 \end{bmatrix} \begin{bmatrix} 3 \\ 2 \\ 1 \end{bmatrix} = \begin{bmatrix} 19 \\ 21 \\ 18 \end{bmatrix}$; M. Evans scored the most points in the game.

23. **Pyramids** The Great Pyramid of Giza has a height of 138 m and a horizontal distance from the side to the center of about 115 m. What is the slope of the pyramid to the nearest tenth? $m = 1.2$
(13)

24. Simplify the product: $\frac{a^{-3}x}{y^{-3}}\left(\frac{xxx^{-2}}{y^{-2}yy} - 3\right)$ $-2a^{-3}xy^3$
(19)

25. **Planets** The weight of an object on Mercury varies directly with the weight of that object on Earth. An object that weighs 150 lb on Earth weighs 57 lb on Mercury. Find the weight of an object on Mercury that weighs 25 lb on Earth. 9.5 pounds
(8)

26. Margaret wants to determine her average speed on her way to work. She knows she drives for about 10 minutes through her neighborhood, then $\frac{1}{2}$ hour on the highway, and finally 10 minutes to her office. Her odometer tells her the total distance from her home to her work is 40 miles. Write and solve an equation to find her average speed in miles per hour.
(7)

26. $\frac{1}{6}x + \frac{1}{2}x + \frac{1}{6}x = 40$
$\frac{5}{6}x = 40$
$x = 48$ mph

27. Your dinner total at your favorite restaurant is \$24. Use the distributive property to mentally calculate a 15% tip. \$3.60
(1)

*28. **Graphing Calculator** Find the product. Check using the graphing calculator.
(9)

$$\begin{bmatrix} 1 & 0 \\ 0 & 1 \\ 1 & 0 \end{bmatrix} \times \begin{bmatrix} -2 & 3 & -4 \\ 0 & -1 & 1 \end{bmatrix} \quad \begin{bmatrix} -2 & 3 & -4 \\ 0 & -1 & 1 \\ -2 & 3 & -4 \end{bmatrix}$$

*29. **Multi-Step** The length of a regulation basketball court is represented by the expression $(x + 12)$ feet. The width of a regulation basketball court is represented by the expression $(x - 32)$ feet.
(19)

a. Write an expression that represents the area of a regulation NBA basketball court. $(x + 12)(x - 32)$ ft^2

b. Evaluate the area of the court if $x = 82$. 4700 ft^2

30. Solve and graph the inequality: $-2(x + 3) \leq 4$. $x \geq -5$
(10)

−8 −6 −4 −2 0 2

CHALLENGE

Jason has nickels and dimes in his pocket. There are 32 coins in total. The value of the coins is \$2.45. How many nickels and dimes does Jason have in his pocket? Write a system of equations and solve using the substitution method.
Nickels: 15; Dimes: 17

LOOKING FORWARD

Solving systems of equations by the substitution method prepares students for

- **Lesson 24** Solving Systems of Equations Using the Elimination Method
- **Lesson 29** Solving Systems of Equations in Three Variables

LAB 5

Storing and Plotting a List of Data

Graphing Calculator Lab *(Use with Lesson 22)*

A graphing calculator can be used to store and plot data. Use the graphing calculator to analyze the following two sets of data.

Data Set 1	Data Set 2
–5	7
–4	5
–4	6
–1	3
2	1
2	–1
3	–2
5	–2
7	–5

Storing a List of Data

1. Enter the Data Set 1 into the calculator.
   a. Press STAT to open the statistics menu. **[1: Edit…]** will already be highlighted. Press ENTER.
   b. If there is data already displayed in the lists, then clear the list. To clear L1 use the arrow keys to highlight the L1 column heading and press CLEAR ENTER. Repeat the step to clear L2 if necessary.
   c. Once the columns are empty, use the arrow keys to move to the first entry in the L1 column. Press (–) 5 ENTER to enter the first data point. Continue inputting the data set, pressing ENTER after each number.

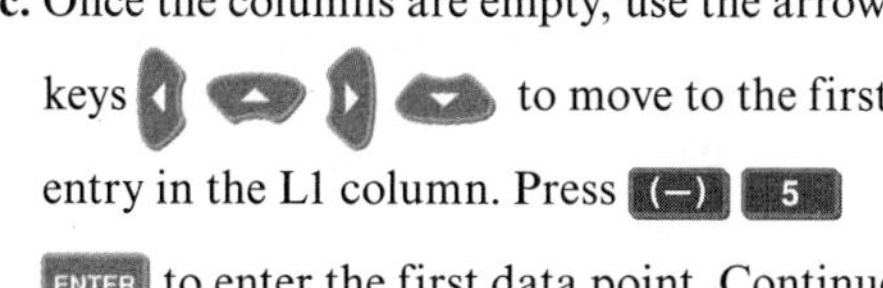

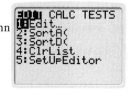

2. Enter the Data Set 2 into the calculator.
   a. Once L1 is inputted, press to move to the L2 column and press 7 ENTER to enter the first data point. Continue inputting data set 2, pressing ENTER after each number.
   b. The data sets are now inputted as L1 and L2 and can be analyzed and plotted.

Plotting Data

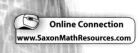

Before plotting the data sets, make sure that the graph is clear. Press Y= and use the arrow keys to select any equations in the Y= equation editor. Press CLEAR ENTER to delete them.

LAB 5

Materials

• graphing calculator

Discuss

In this lab, students will store and plot a set of data using the statistics menu.

Define **scatter plot.**

TEACHER TIP

ClrList can be used to quickly clear the columns of data. For example, ClrList L1, L2 will clear the data in lists 1 and 2.

Storing a List of Data

Instruct students to reset the viewing window if all the data points are not displayed. For this example, Xmin = –6, Xmax = 8, Xscl = 1, Ymin = –6, Ymax = 8, and Yscl = 1.

Error Alert

If students input data incorrectly, the data values can be easily changed by scrolling through the data list and typing over the incorrect values. Use the notation at the bottom of the screen to help. L2(9) = –5 indicates that –5 is the ninth value in List 2.

Plotting Data

Investigate changes in the Xlist and Ylist. What happens if L1 and L2 values are switched?
L2 values are plotted along the *x*-axis and L1 values are plotted along the *y*-axis.

Describe the scatter plot if L1 is used for the Xlist and Ylist.
The scatter plot is a line.

Error Alert

When finishing with the statistics menu, students should turn the Plots off. Leaving Plots on may interfere with graphing functions.

Practice Problem 2

TEACHER TIP

Use Data Set 1 for List 1 and *y*-values and Data Set 2 for List 2 and *x*-values. Remember to reset the viewing window. For this example, Xmin = −9, Xmax = 7, Xscl = 1, Ymin = 3, Ymax = 6, and Yscl = 1.

1. Turn on the plot feature.
   a. Press 2nd MODE to return to the home screen. Press 2nd Y= to open the [STAT PLOT] menu. Press ENTER to open the first Stat plot.
   b. Press ENTER to turn Plot1 on. This will display the plot on the graph.

2. Customize the graph as a scatter plot.
   a. Press ▼ to move to **[Type:]**. The first graph should be highlighted. This will display the data as a scatter plot. (If not, use the arrow keys ◀ ▲ ▶ ▼ to highlight the scatter plot and press ENTER.)
   b. Press ▼ to move to **[Xlist:]**. L1 should be displayed, meaning it will use the data entered from data set 1 for the *x*-values. (If L1 is not displayed, press 2nd 2 ENTER.)
   c. Press ▼ to move to **[Ylist:]**. L2 should be displayed, meaning it will use the data entered from data set 2 for the *y*-values. (If L2 is not displayed, press 2nd 2 ENTER.)
   d. Press ▼ to move to **[Mark:]**. Make sure the first symbol, the square, is highlighted. This means that the data points in the scatter plot will be displayed as squares.

3. Plot the data on the graph.
   a. Press GRAPH. The scatter plot of data sets 1 and 2 is now displayed.

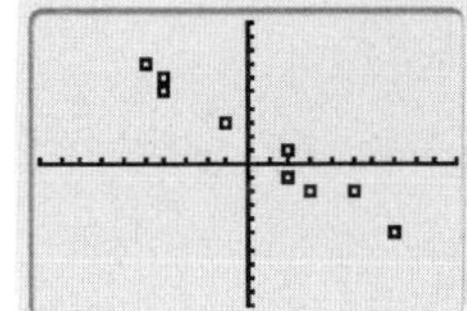

Graphing Calculator Practice

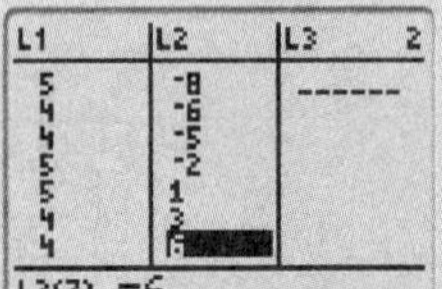

1. Use the graphing calculator to enter the following data sets as L1 and L2.

2. Use the graphing calculator to make a scatter plot, with L2 as *x*-values and L1 as *y*-values.

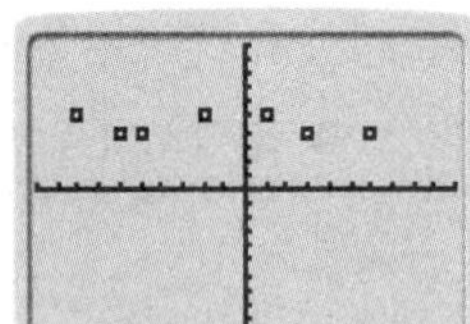

Data Set 1	Data Set 2
5	−8
4	−6
4	−5
5	−2
5	1
4	3
4	6

154 *Saxon* *Algebra 2*

LESSON 22

Analyzing Continuous, Discontinuous, and Discrete Functions

Warm Up

1. **Vocabulary** The vertical line test states that a relation is a function if any vertical line intersects the graph of the relation no more than ________. once
(4)

2. Identify the domain and range of $\{(5, 2), (7, 0), (-1, 9)\}$.
(4) Domain: 5, 7, −1; Range: 2, 0, 9

3. Identify the range of $f(x) = 2x + 7$ given the domain of $\{0, 3, 4\}$.
(4) Range: 7, 13, 15

New Concepts

A relation pairs input values x from the domain with output values y from the range. A function is a specific type of relation where every value in the domain must be matched to only one value in the range.

> **Hint**
> A graph of a continuous function can be drawn without lifting the pencil.

A **continuous function** is a function with a graph that has no gaps, jumps, or asymptotes. Any function that has gaps, jumps or asymptotes is considered a **discontinuous function.** A **discrete function** is a type of function made up of separate, disconnected points.

Continuous Functions

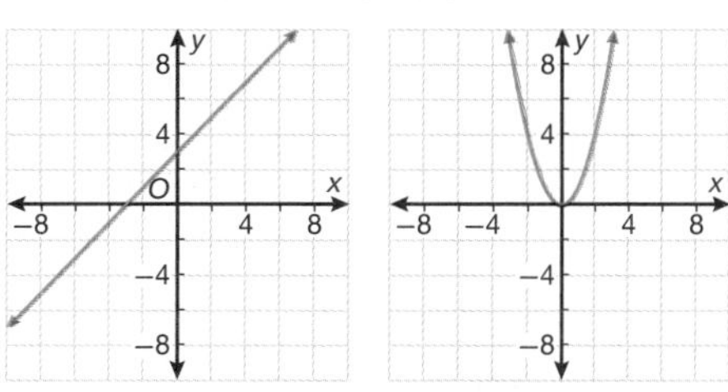

Discontinuous Functions

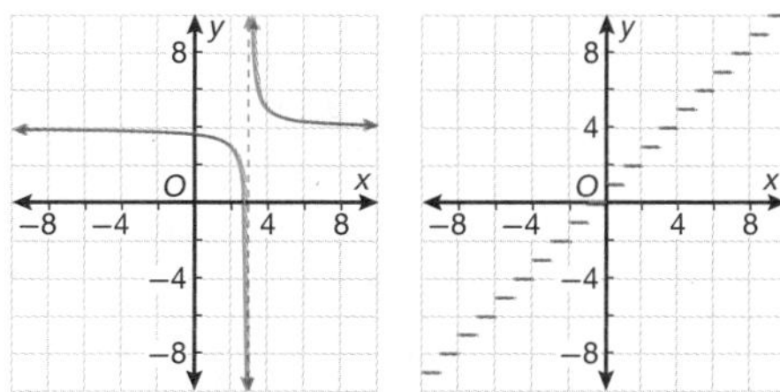

Discrete Functions

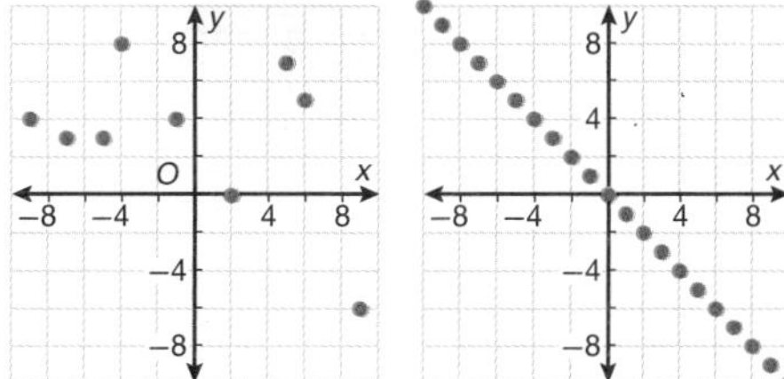

Online Connection
www.SaxonMathResources.com

LESSON 22

1 Warm Up

Problem 2

Review the definitions of *domain* and *range* with students.

2 New Concepts

In this lesson, students identify domain and range and learn to identify types of functions.

Discuss the definition of continuous function, discontinuous function, and discrete function. Explain that these types of functions also have a domain and range.

MATH BACKGROUND

In Lesson 4, students learned how to identify functions, domain, and range.

The knowledge of functions is extended in various steps, to further understanding of the characteristics of functions. Although students will analyze graphs such as $xy = 4$, $y = x^2$, $y = |x| + 2$, they will not be formally introduced to these functions at this time.

LESSON RESOURCES

Student Edition Practice Workbook 22
Reteaching Master 22
Adaptations Master 22
Challenge and Enrichment Master C22

Example 1

Remind students that in Lesson 4 they learned how to identify domain and range.

Additional Example 1

Graph the function and state the domain and range of:

a. the discrete function

$f = \{(-7, 1), (-4, 3), (-1, 5), (4, 7)\}$.

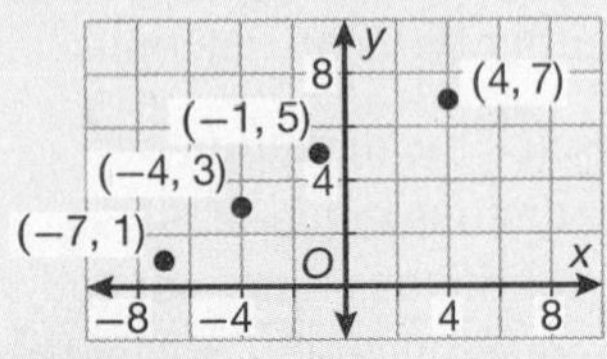

Domain: {−7, −4, −1, 4}; range: {1, 3, 5, 7}

b. the continuous function

$g(x) = -2x + 4$

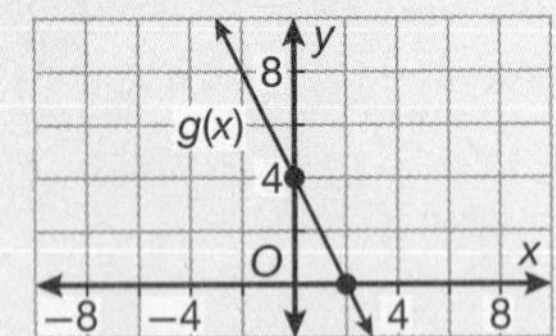

Domain and range: all real numbers

Example 2

Students will determine if and where discontinuity occurs within a graph of a function.

Additional Example 2

a.

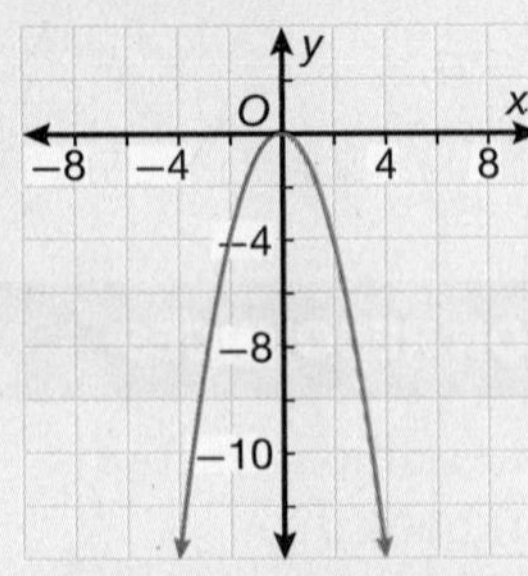

Continuous function

b.

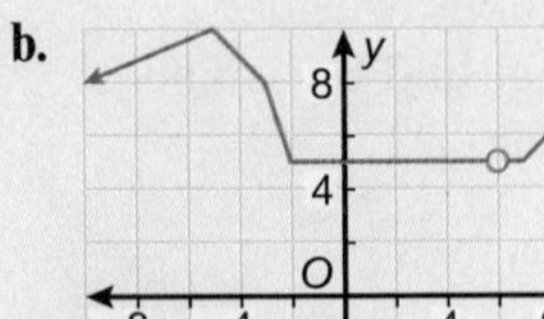

Discontinuous function; point of discontinuity at about (6, 5)

Example 1 Graphing Discrete and Continuous Functions

Graph the function and state the domain and range of:

a. the discrete function

$f = \{(2, 3), (4, 5), (6, 7), (-1, 0)\}$.

SOLUTION

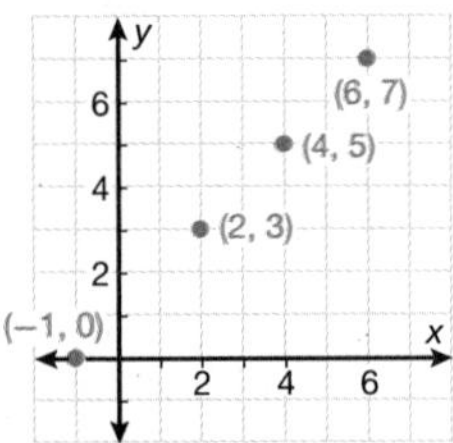

Domain: {2, 4, 6, −1}
Range: {3, 5, 7, 0}

b. the continuous function

$g(x) = x + 2$.

SOLUTION

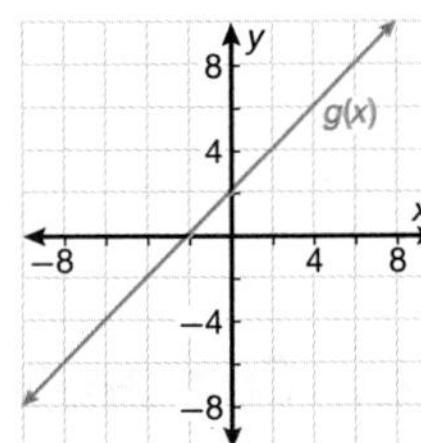

Domain and Range: all real numbers

Discontinuous functions have specific places where they are not continuous.

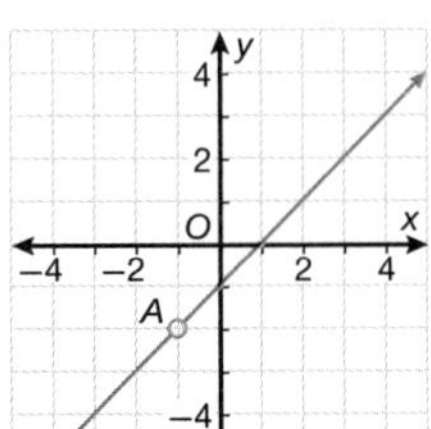

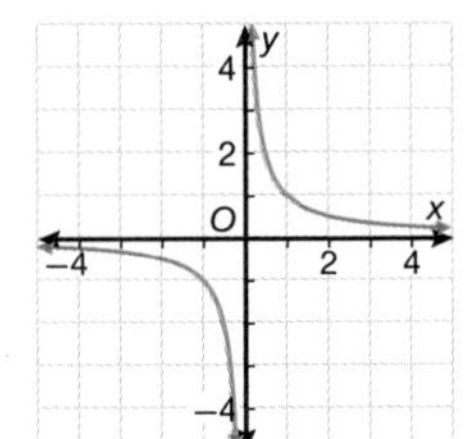

The point A above is called a **point of discontinuity** because it is the point at which the graph of the relation or function is not connected. The second graph above is discontinuous at the line $x = 0$. Therefore, the second graph is discontinuous but has no point of discontinuity.

Example 2 Identifying Types of Functions

Determine if each graph is continuous, discontinuous, or discrete. If the function is discontinuous, then name the x-value(s) where the discontinuity occurs.

a.

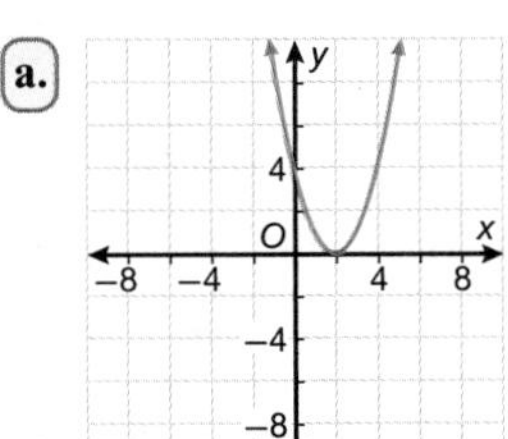

SOLUTION Continuous function

b.

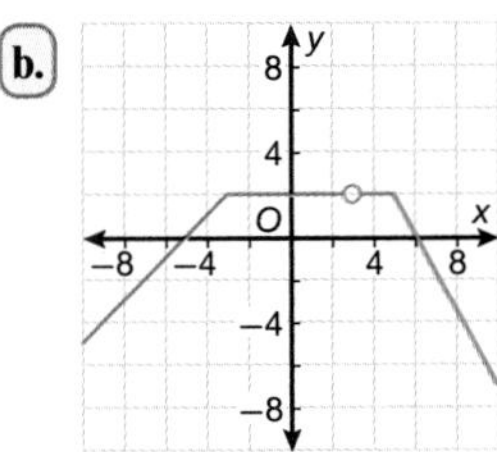

SOLUTION Discontinuous function; point of discontinuity at about (3, 2).

ENGLISH LEARNERS

To help students understand the meaning of **discontinuity** and **discontinuous,** define the prefix dis- and show how it is used with other words.

"The basic meaning of the prefix dis- is 'not' or 'not any.'"

Other words: disbelieve: not to believe; discomfort: not having comfort; disrespect: not having respect; disappear: not to appear.

discontinuity and discontinuous: not continuous

156 *Saxon* *Algebra 2*

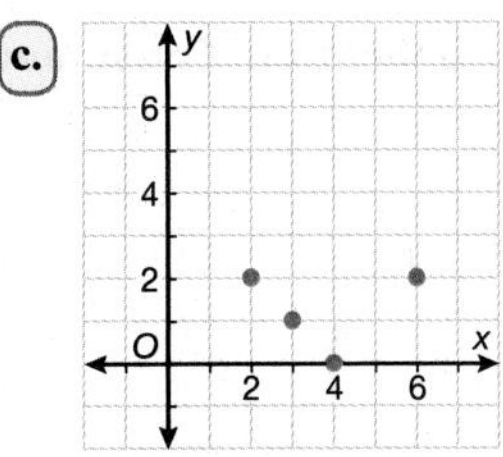

SOLUTION Discrete function

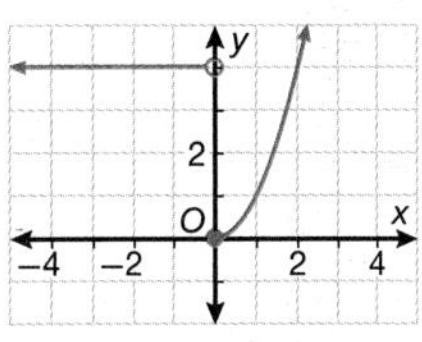

The vertical line test can be used on continuous, discontinuous, and discrete relations to determine if the relations are functions. The discontinuous relation shown at right is a function because it passes the vertical line test even at the point of discontinuity. Recall that to pass the vertical line test, any vertical line can only intersect the graph at one point. The domain of this function is all real numbers and the range is $y \geq 0$.

Example 3 Identifying Functions and Domain and Range

Determine if each graph is continuous, discontinuous, or discrete. Determine if it is a function or a relation. Determine the domain and range of each.

> **Hint**
>
> To find the domain, imagine the graph pressed to the *x*-axis. How much of the *x*-axis is covered?

a. 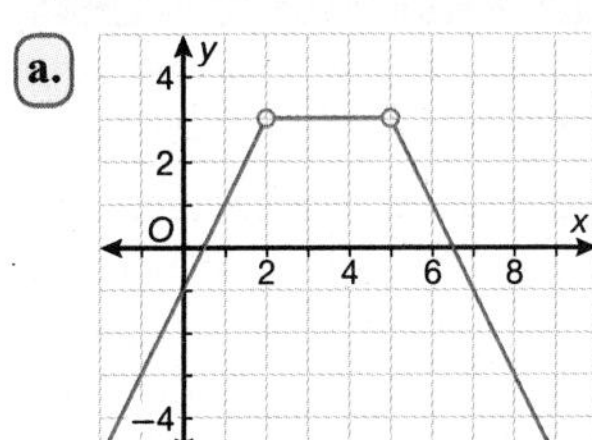

SOLUTION Discontinuous function; Domain: All real numbers except $x = 2, 5$; Range: $y \leq 3$

b. 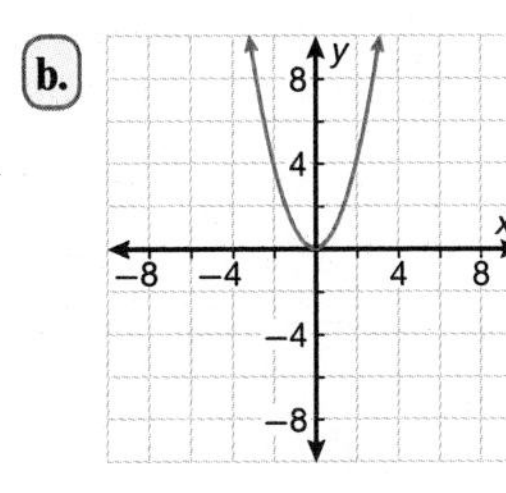

SOLUTION Continuous function; Domain: All real numbers; Range: $y \geq 0$

c. 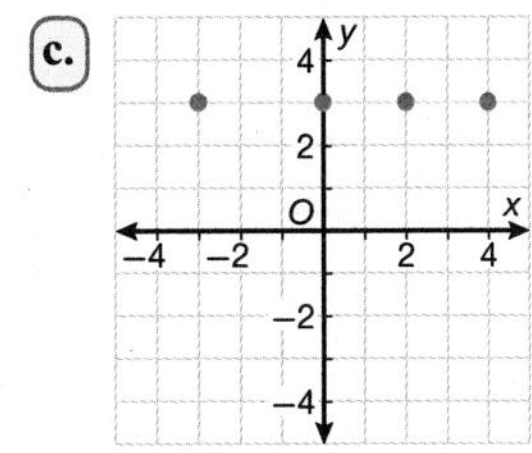

SOLUTION Discrete function; Domain: $x = -3, 0, 2, 4$; Range: $y = 3$

INCLUSION

For Example 3b, have students list ordered pairs for the points on the graph. Then have them describe the domain and range.

c. 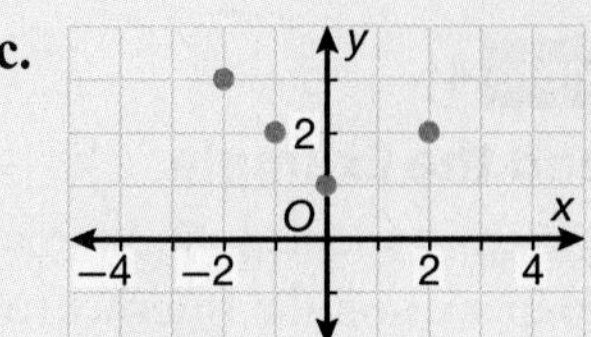

Discrete function

Example 3

Review the definitions of continuous function, discontinuous function, and discrete function.

Additional Example 3

Determine if each graph is continuous, discontinuous, or discrete. Determine if it is a function or a relation. Determine the domain and range of each.

a. 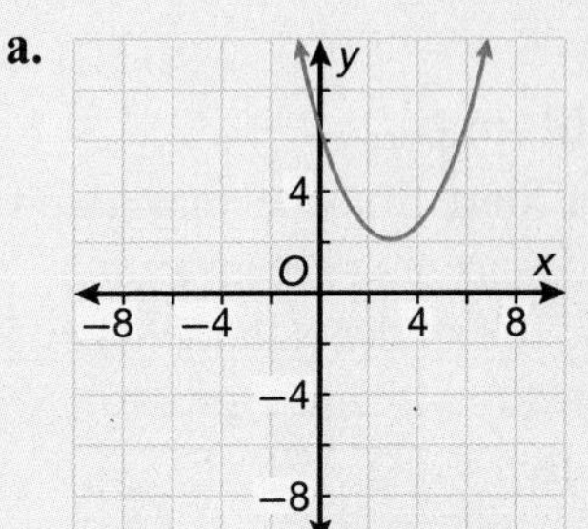

Continuous function; domain: all real numbers; range: $y \geq 2$

b. 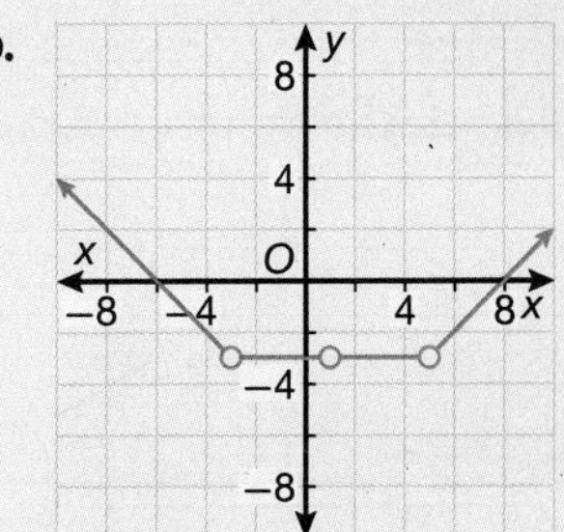

Discontinuous function; domain: all real numbers except $x = -3, 1, 5$; range: $y \geq -3$

c. 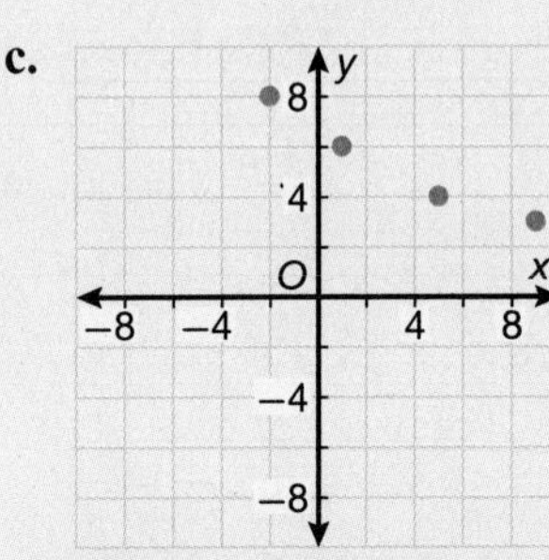

Discrete function; domain: $x = -2, 1, 5, 9$; range: $y = 8, 6, 4, 3$

Example 4

Extend the Example

Encourage students to look in a newspaper or on the Internet to find a function that shows sales of an item for a period of time. Have them show that the graph is a function by using the vertical line test and analyzing the domain and range. Challenge students to list the domain and range of the graph. See student work.

Lesson Practice

Problem a

Scaffolding Students may find it easier to first state the domain and range, and then graph the discrete function.

Problem b

Error Alert Students may graph $x = 5$ since they see an x in $h(x)$. Tell students that $h(x) = 5$ is function notation for the equation $y = 5$.

Math Reasoning

Verify Use a graphing calculator to store and plot the points. Then compare the display to the graph in the solution.

Example 4 Application: Consumer Math

A company records its sales of new cars for a six day period. The results are listed in the table below. Graph the points. Identify the domain and range. Show that the graph is a function by using the vertical line test and analyzing the domain and range.

Day	Number of Cars Sold
1	10
2	4
3	18
4	7
5	20
6	5

SOLUTION Domain: 1, 2, 3, 4, 5, 6; Range: 10, 4, 18, 7, 20, 5; A vertical line may be placed on the graph to show that the relation passes the vertical line test and therefore is a function. Examining the domain and range indicates that for every x there is exactly one y.

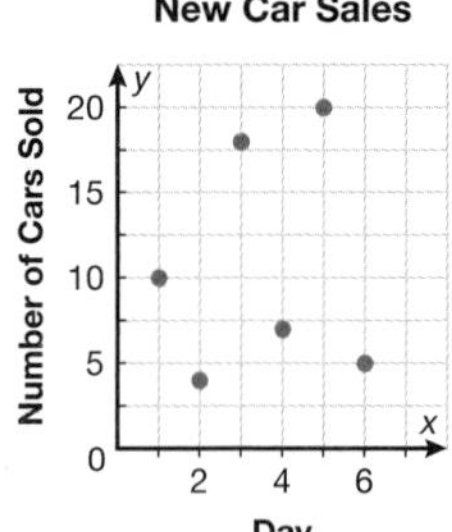

a.
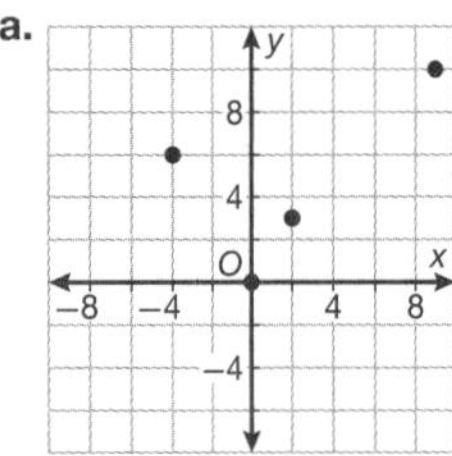

b.
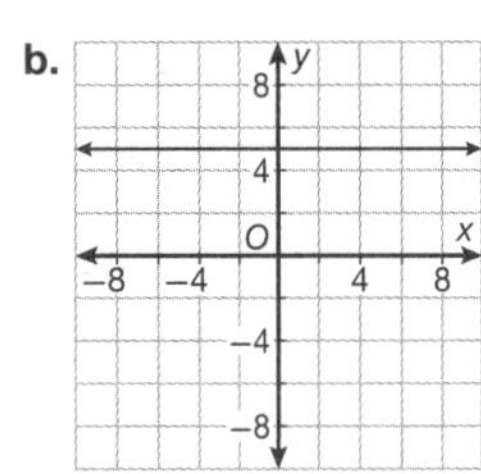

Lesson Practice

a. *(Ex 1)* Graph and state the domain and range of the discrete function $G = \{(0, 0), (2, 3), (-4, 6), (9, 10)\}$. Domain: 0, 2, −4, 9; Range: 0, 3, 6, 10

b. *(Ex 1)* Graph and state the domain and range of the continuous function $h(x) = 5$. Domain: all real numbers; Range: $y = 5$

c. *(Ex 2)* Determine if the graph is continuous, discontinuous, or discrete. If the function is discontinuous, name the x-value(s) where the discontinuity occurs. Discontinuous function, point of discontinuity at $x = 4$

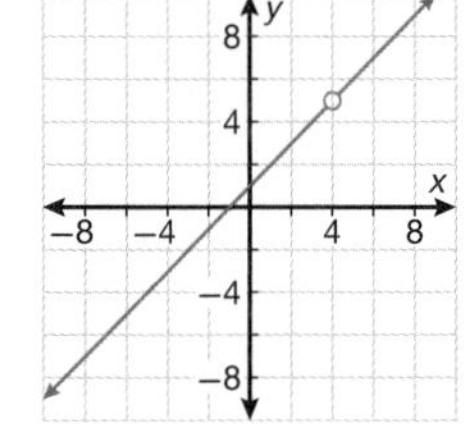

d. *(Ex 2)* Determine if the graph is continuous, discontinuous, or discrete. If the function is discontinuous, name the x-value(s) where the discontinuity occurs. Continuous function

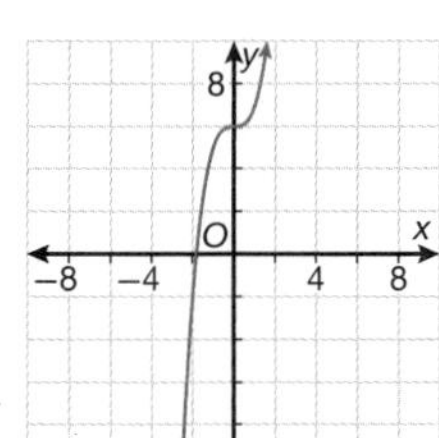

ALTERNATE METHOD FOR EXAMPLE 4

Instead of looking at the graph, have students write ordered pairs for the data in the table. Then write the domain and range. By looking at the ordered pairs, students can see that for every x there is exactly one y.

e. (Ex 2) Determine if the graph is continuous, discontinuous, or discrete. If the function is discontinuous, then name the x-value(s) where the discontinuity occurs. Discrete function

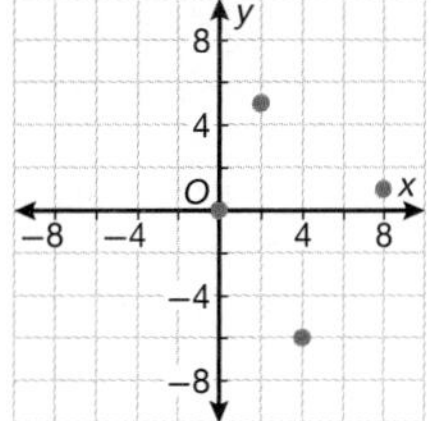

f. (Ex 3) Determine if the graph is continuous, discontinuous, or discrete. Determine if it is a function or a relation. Determine the domain and range. Continuous relation; Domain: $x \geq 0$; Range: all real numbers

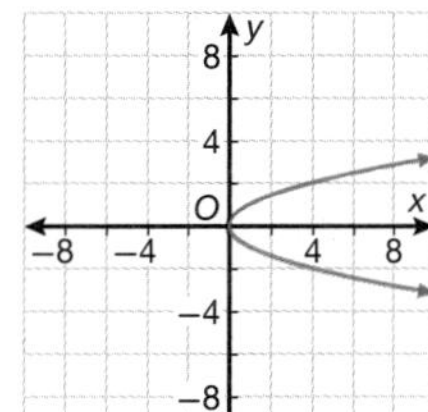

g. (Ex 3) Determine if the graph is continuous, discontinuous, or discrete. Determine if it is a function or a relation. Determine the domain and range. Discontinuous function; Domain: $0 \leq x < 4$; Range: $y = 0, 2$

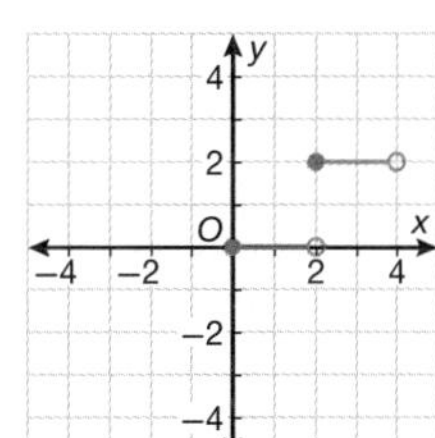

h. (Ex 3) Determine if the graph is continuous, discontinuous, or discrete. Determine if it is a function or a relation. Determine the domain and range. Discrete function; Domain: $x = 0, 1, -2, 6$; Range: $y = 0, 3, 5, 7$

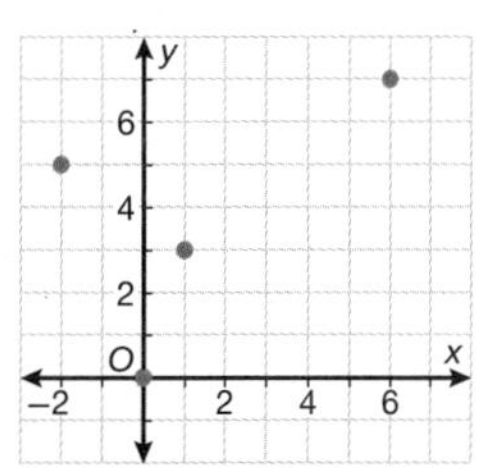

i. Domain: 1, 2, 3, 4, 5; Range: 2, 0, 3, 1; A vertical line test will verify that the relation is a function. Examining the domain and range indicates that for every x there is exactly one y.

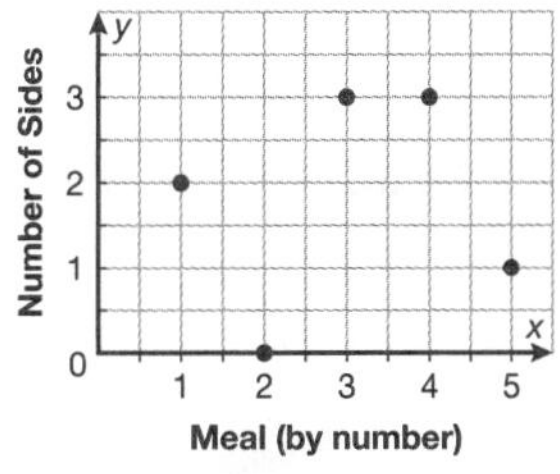

i. (Ex 4) A restaurant's carryout menu list meals by numbers. Beside each meal is the total number of side orders that can be added to a particular meal. The results are listed in the table below. Graph the points. Identify the domain and range. Show that the graph is a function by using the vertical line test and analyzing the domain and range.

Meal	Number of Sides
1	2
2	0
3	3
4	3
5	1

Problem f

Error Alert Students may look at the graph quickly and say it is a function. Remind students to use the vertical line test to determine if the graph is a function or a relation. For the domain, remind students to look at the x-axis and determine which values of x are included in the graph.

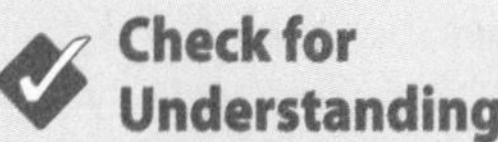

Check for Understanding

The questions below help assess the concepts taught in this lesson.

"How can you tell if a graph of a function is continuous or discontinuous?" A function such as $y = x + 3$ is continuous because you can trace the graph without lifting your pencil. A graph of a discontinuous function has gaps, jumps, or asymptotes.

"How do you identify the point of discontinuity?" Look at the graph and find the point where the graph of a relation or function is not connected.

3 Practice

Math Conversations

Discussions to strengthen understanding

Problem 3

Guide students by asking them the following questions:

"$f(x) = 3x$ is the same as graphing what equation?" $y = 3x$

"What does the graph $y = 3x$ look like?" It is a line going through the origin with a positive slope.

"Is the graph continuous or discrete?" continuous

"Look at the x-axis. What is the domain or x-values?" all real numbers

"Look at the y-axis. What is the range or y-values?" all real numbers

Problem 10

Error Alert

Students may divide 119,727 by 20,320 because 119,727 is the greater number. Remind students that slope $= \frac{\text{rise}}{\text{run}}$. Tell students that in this problem the elevation is the *rise,* and the horizontal run is the *run.*

Problems 11 and 12

TEACHER TIP

Review the rules of exponents. Use examples to show multiplication of powers with the same base $(10^2 \cdot 10^3 = 10^5)$, division of powers with the same base $\left(\frac{10^5}{10^3} = 10^2\right)$, and multiplication of a power raised to a power $((10^5)^2 = 10^{10})$.

Practice Distributed and Integrated

1. (Population) According to the 2000 census the three largest states by population in the U.S. are California, Texas, and New York. The total population of the three states is 73,699,925. The population of California is 13,019,828 more than the population of Texas and the population of New York is 1,875,363 less than the population of Texas. Find the population of Texas. 20,851,820
(7)

Graph and state the domain and range of each function. State whether the function is discrete or continuous.

*2. $\{(1, -2), (3, 0), (-6, 5), (6, 3)\}$ (22)

*3. $f(x) = 3x$ (22)

2. Discrete; Domain: 1, 3, −6, 6; Range: −2, 0, 5, 3

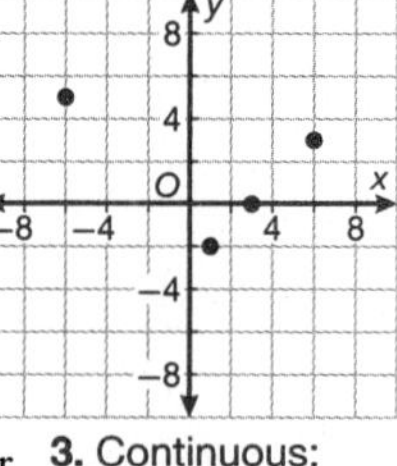

*4. Find $(f)(g)(-2)$ if $f(x) = 3x + 1$ and $g(x) = x + 6$. −20
(20)

5. Use Cramer's Rule to solve the system of equations. $\begin{aligned} 3x + 7y &= -18 \\ -4x + 11y &= -37 \end{aligned}$ $x = 1, y = -3$
(16)

6. (Rocket) A physics class is about to test their first rocket out on the football field. The teacher fires the rocket at a 75° angle. At ignition, the rocket travels 38 feet per second horizontally and 110 feet per second vertically.
(Inv 2)
In t seconds, the rocket will travel x and y feet. The parametric equations that the rocket will travel are

$$x = 38t$$
$$y = -16t^2 + 110t$$

a. How many seconds does it take the rocket to hit the ground? Round your answer to the nearest thousandth of a second. 6.875 seconds

b. How far does the rocket travel? 261.25 feet

c. Approximately how far has the rocket traveled when it has reached its highest point in flight? Round your answer to the nearest foot. Approximately 131 feet

3. Continuous; Domain: all real numbers; Range: all real numbers

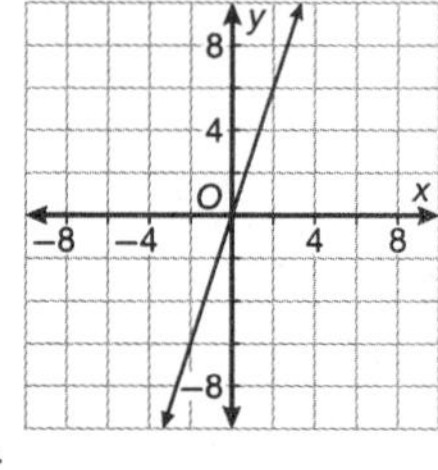

State the degree of each polynomial.

7. $x^4 + 2x - x^7$ 7
(11)

8. $5x^2 + 2x^5 - 3$ 5
(11)

*9. The Temple of Kukulcan, located in the ancient Mayan city of Chichen Itza, was built on a square base. If the expression $(4x + 12)$ represents one side of the base, write an expression that represents the area of the base.
(19)
$(4x + 12)^2 = (4x + 12)(4x + 12) = 16x^2 + 96x + 144$

10. (Mountains) Mt. McKinley in Alaska is the highest mountain in North America with an elevation of 20,320 ft. From its center the mountain runs horizontally approximately 119,727 ft. Find the approximate slope of Mt. McKinley. Round your answer to the thousandths place. 0.170
(13)

Simplify the expressions. Use negative exponents when necessary.

11. $\frac{(4x)^{-2}y^0(y^{-2})^2y}{32^{-1}x^2(yx^0)^{-3}}$ $2x^{-4}$
(3)

12. $\frac{9x^{-4}(y^3x^2)^{-2}}{2^{-3}x^2y^3x(x^{-4}y^2)}$ $72x^{-7}y^{-11}$
(3)

ALTERNATE METHOD FOR PROBLEM 5

Challenge students to use the substitution method.

Solve for y in the first equation.

$$y = \frac{-3x - 18}{7}$$

Substitute y into the second equation and solve for x.

$$-4x + \frac{11(-3x - 18)}{7} = -37$$

$$-28x - 33x - 198 = -259$$
$$-61x = -61$$
$$x = 1$$

Then solve for y.

$$3x + 7y = -18$$
$$3(1) + 7y = -18$$
$$7y = -21$$
$$y = -3$$

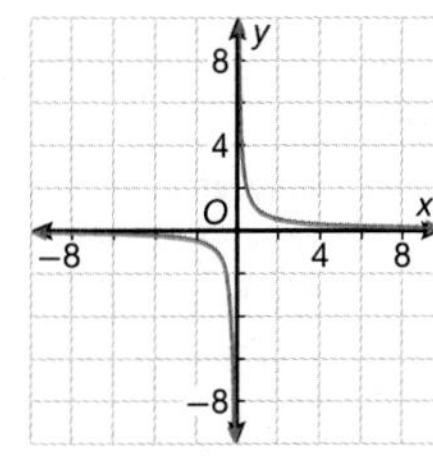

*13. James examines the graph at right and states that the domain of the function is all real numbers. Identify the error in his decision. (22) The graph is discontinuous at the line $x = 0$. The domain is all real numbers except $x = 0$.

14. **Error Analysis** Two students solve the inequality $32 + \frac{|x - 7|}{13} < 7$ and their answers are below. (17)

Which student is correct? Explain how you know.

Ben: No solution.

Ralph: $x = 332$ or $x = 318$.

14. Ben is correct. $\frac{|x-7|}{13} < -25$ results in $|x - 7| < -325$. Since the absolute value of a number is always greater than or equal to zero, there is no solution.

Calculate the percent of change.

15. from 5 to 8.2 (6) 64%

16. from 5 to 9.4 (6) 88%

17. **Rugby** Jonny Wilkinson, the fly half of the England rugby team, is at the 41 meter line on the rugby pitch. He runs up to kick the ball for a field goal. The ball moves at a horizontal speed of 11 meters per second and a vertical speed of 23 meters per second. (Inv 2)

In t seconds, the rugby ball will travel x and y meters. The parametric equations that the ball will travel are

$$x = 11t$$
$$y = -4.9t^2 + 23t$$

a. How many seconds does it take for the ball to get to the field goal post? Round to the nearest hundredth of a second. 3.73 seconds

b. The field goal posts are 1.2 meters tall. Assume Jonny kicks the ball directly center of the field goal. Will the ball travel through the goal posts? Explain why or why not. Yes, because at 3.73 seconds the ball is still 17.62 meters above the ground, enabling the ball to be high enough to go through the field goal posts.

*18. **Multi-Step** Kate and Riley are reading the same book. Kate reads $\frac{1}{3}$ page per minute, and Riley reads $\frac{3}{4}$ page per minute. Kate has already read 70 pages, while Riley has read 30 pages. If they both resume reading together, eventually Riley will catch up to Kate. (21)

a. On what page will that occur?

b. How many minutes have they read when Riley catches up? To solve for m, substitute $p = 102$ into $m = 3p - 210$. $m = 96$ minutes or 1 hr 36 min.

18a. For Kate: $p = \frac{1}{3}m + 70$. For Riley: $p = \frac{3}{4}m + 30$. To solve for the page, solve Kate's equation for m and substitute m into Riley's equation. $m = 3p - 210$. So, $p = \frac{3}{4}(3p - 210) + 30 = \frac{9}{4}p - \frac{630}{4}$. Solving for p gives $p = 102$. So, Riley will catch up to Kate at page 102.

19. **Engines** Two-stroke engines require a pre-mix of gas and oil. The amount of gas used varies directly with the amount of oil used. In most two-stroke engines 3 gal of gas requires 19.2 oz of oil. (8)

a. Write the proportion that can be used to find how many ounces of oil to use with 5 gal of gas. $\frac{3}{5} = \frac{19.2}{x}$

b. Solve the proportion in part **a.** $x = 32$ oz

c. Check the answer from part **b.** with the proportion from part **a.** $\frac{3}{5} = \frac{19.2}{32} \Rightarrow 3(32) = 5(19.2) \Rightarrow 96 = 96$

CHALLENGE

Graph the function. Determine if the graph is continuous, discontinuous, and/or discrete. Determine the domain and range.

$f(x) = 2|x|$

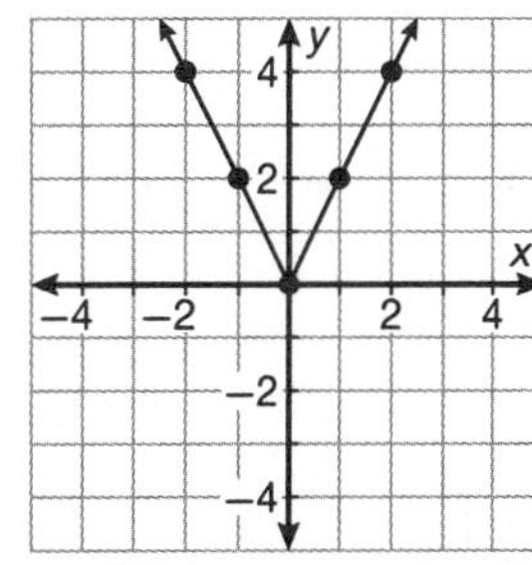

Continuous function; domain: all real numbers; range: $y \geq 0$

Problems 15 and 16

Tell students that to find the percent of change, they need to first find the difference of the two amounts. The difference is the numerator. The denominator is the original amount.

Problem 19

Students may have difficulty setting up the proportion. Have them write ordered pairs for the data given.

(19.2, 3), (x, 5)

Then substitute the value into the direct variation proportion.

$\frac{y_1}{x_1} = \frac{y_2}{x_2} \rightarrow \frac{3}{19.2} = \frac{5}{x}$.

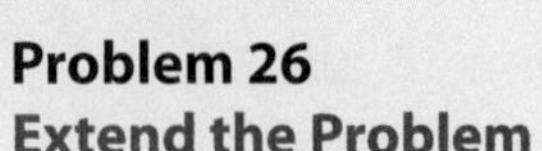

Problem 26
Extend the Problem

After students write their compound inequalities, encourage them to graph the two inequalities on a number line.

Problem 29

Tell students there is more than one way to simplify the expression.

Problem 30

Remind students that slope is defined as

$m = \frac{\text{change in } y}{\text{change in } x} = \frac{y_2 - y_1}{x_2 - x_1}$.

Have students look at the sign to tell if the line is rising (positive sign) or falling (negative sign).

Student sketches can be very simple. Encourage students to roughly sketch and connect the two points.

20. (8) Convert 420 inches to feet. 35 feet

21. (14) **Geometry** If one corner of a parallelepiped is at the origin, then all the vertices of the shape can be determined by knowing that the three other vertices with edges to the origin are at (1, 3, 4), (−3, 2, 1), and (4, −2, 3). The volume of the parallelepiped is the determinant of the matrix with these coordinates as rows. Find the volume of the parallelepiped. 39 cubic units

22. (9) **Multiple Choice** The following matrix is the product of which two matrices? [19] C

A $\begin{bmatrix}6 & -1\end{bmatrix}\begin{bmatrix}3\\1\end{bmatrix}$ **B** $\begin{bmatrix}3\\1\end{bmatrix}\begin{bmatrix}6 & -1\end{bmatrix}$ **C** $\begin{bmatrix}1 & 0 & 3\end{bmatrix}\begin{bmatrix}4\\-2\\5\end{bmatrix}$ **D** $\begin{bmatrix}4\\-2\\5\end{bmatrix}\begin{bmatrix}1 & 0 & 3\end{bmatrix}$

23. (12) **Justify** Is the equation $xy = 0$ an inverse variation? Why or why not?

Use substitution to solve the system of equations.

***24.** (21) $\begin{aligned}-x + y &= -2\\ x + y &= 8\end{aligned}$ (5, 3)

***25.** (21) $\begin{aligned}3x + y &= 4\\ -3x + y &= 8\end{aligned}$ $\left(-\frac{2}{3}, 6\right)$

26. (10) **Write** Write a compound inequality using *and* and a compound inequality using *or*. Explain the difference when you connect two inequalities with *and* and when you connect two inequalities with *or*.

27. (8) Find the constant of variation if x varies directly with y and $x = 28$ when $y = 7$. 4

***28.** (6) **Graphing Calculator** The US minimum wage increased from \$0.75 in 1950 to \$5.15 in 2000. Use your calculator to find the percent increase to the nearest percent. 587%

29. (1) **Justify** Simplify: 3 • 4 • 7. Justify your answer by identifying which property you used for each step. Sample: 3(4 • 7), Associative Property of Multiplication; 3(28), Multiply; 84, Multiply.

30. (13) **Multi-Step** Use Point 1 (−8, −3) and Point 2 (1, −8).

a. Find the slope of the line that goes through Point 1 and Point 2. $m = -\frac{5}{9}$

b. Based on the slope, is the line rising or falling? falling

c. Sketch a graph of the line that goes through Point 1 and Point 2. see graph

d. Based on the graph, is the line rising or falling? falling

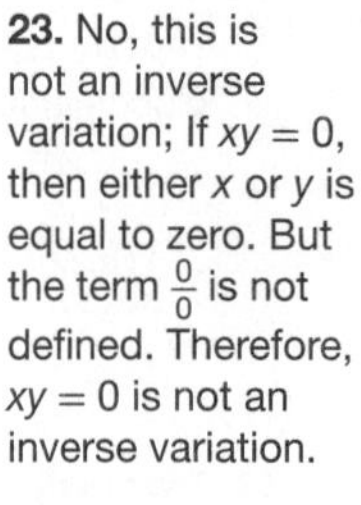

23. No, this is not an inverse variation; If $xy = 0$, then either x or y is equal to zero. But the term $\frac{0}{0}$ is not defined. Therefore, $xy = 0$ is not an inverse variation.

26. Sample: *and* inequality: $3 < x < 8$; *or* inequality: $2 < x$ or $x < -3$. Compound inequalities with *and* represent the intersection of the solutions. Compound inequalities with *or* represent the union of the solutions.

30.

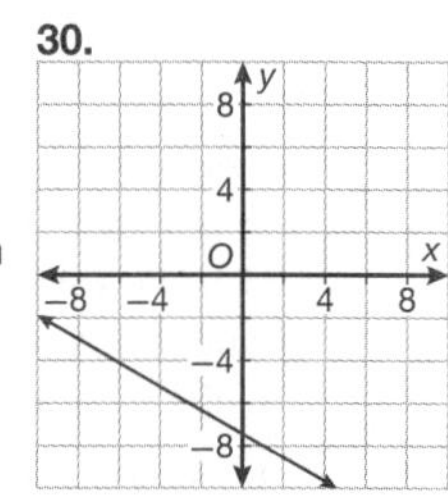

LOOKING FORWARD

Analyzing discrete and continuous functions prepares students for

- **Lesson 27** Connecting the Parabola with the Quadratic Function
- **Lesson 109** Making Graphs and Using Equations of Hyperbolas

LESSON 23 Factoring Polynomials

Warm Up

1. **Vocabulary** Numbers or expressions that are multiplied to form a product are called factors.
(SB)

2. Write all the positive integer factor pairs for the product 15. (1)(15), (3)(5)
(SB)

3. Write all the integer factor pairs for the product −35.
(SB)

3. (1)(−35), (−1)(35), (5)(−7), (−5)(7)

4. Write all the integer factor pairs for the product 16. Use both positive and negative factors. (1)(16), (−1)(−16), (2)(8), (−2)(−8), (4)(4), (−4)(−4)
(SB)

New Concepts

To completely **factor** a number means to express it as a product of prime factors. For example, $18 = 2 \cdot 3 \cdot 3$, or $2 \cdot 3^2$. Similarly, to completely factor a polynomial of two or more terms means to express it as a product of prime polynomial factors. A **prime polynomial** is a polynomial that cannot be factored. Use what you know about multiplying polynomials to factor them. As the first step in factoring any polynomial, factor out the **greatest common monomial factor** if it is other than 1.

Math Language

Unless otherwise specified, *factor a polynomial* means *completely factor the polynomial.*

Example 1 Factoring Out the Greatest Common Monomial Factor

Factor each polynomial.

a. $3x^2 + 6x - 3$

SOLUTION

$3x^2 + 6x - 3 = 3 \cdot x \cdot x + 2 \cdot 3 \cdot x - 3 \cdot 1$ 3 is the GCF.

$= 3(x^2 + 2x - 1)$

$x^2 + 2x - 1$ cannot be factored, so the factoring is complete. Check by using the distributive property to multiply.

Check $3(x^2 + 2x - 1) = 3x^2 + 6x - 3$

b. $-4x^3 - 10x$

SOLUTION When the leading coefficient is negative, include the negative in the monomial that you factor out. This will yield a positive leading coefficient in the polynomial inside the parentheses.

$-4x^3 - 10x = -2 \cdot 2 \cdot x \cdot x \cdot x - 2 \cdot 5 \cdot x$ 2x is the GCF.

$= -2x(2x^2 + 5)$ Factor out $-2x$. Then $2x^2 + 5$ has a positive leading coefficient.

MATH BACKGROUND

A factor of a polynomial divides evenly into the polynomial. Factoring is the opposite process of multiplying polynomials.

The difference between factoring numbers and factoring polynomials is that not only do we look for the greatest common numerical factor, but we also look for the greatest common monomial factor as well.

While some equations can be solved by factoring, there are equations that must be solved using the quadratic formula or other methods.

LESSON 23

1 Warm Up

Use problems 2 and 3 in the Warm Up to review factoring techniques to be used in this lesson.

2 New Concepts

Discuss the definitions of a prime number and the greatest common monomial factor. In order to factor, there must be a common number or variable in all terms in the polynomial.

Example 1

Students will factor out the greatest common monomial factor from the polynomial to answer the questions.

Additional Example 1

Factor each polynomial.

a. $6x^2 + 18x + 24$ $6(x^2 + 3x + 4)$

b. $-9x^3 - 12x$ $-3x(3x^2 + 4)$

TEACHER TIP

Encourage students to check all factoring results by multiplying.

LESSON RESOURCES

Student Edition Practice Workbook 23
Reteaching Masters 23
Adaptations Masters 23
Challenge and Enrichment Masters C23

The following table shows some useful factoring strategies to try after factoring out the greatest common monomial factor (if it is other than 1).

Factoring Polynomials where b, c, u and v are nonzero integers.		
Type of Polynomial	**Factoring Pattern**	**Examples**
Basic Quadratic Trinomial	$x^2 + bx + c = (x + u)(x + v)$ $u + v = b$ and $uv = c$	$x^2 + 9x + 20 = (x + 4)(x + 5)$ $4 + 5 = 9$ and $4 \cdot 5 = 20$
Perfect Square Trinomial	$a^2 + 2ab + b^2 = (a + b)^2$ $a^2 - 2ab + b^2 = (a - b)^2$	$x^2 + 8x + 16 = (x + 4)^2$ $x^2 - 6x + 9 = (x - 3)^2$
Difference of Two Squares	$a^2 - b^2 = (a + b)(a - b)$	$x^2 - 9 = (x + 3)(x - 3)$

Example 2 Students will practice factoring perfect square trinomials.

Additional Example

a. Factor $x^2 + 14x + 49$.
$(x + 7)(x + 7) = (x + 7)^2$

b. Factor $9x^2 + 30xy + 25y^2$
$(3x + 5y)^2$

Example 2 Factoring a Perfect Square Trinomial

a. Factor $x^2 - 10x + 25$.

Hint

In the quadratic trinomial $x^2 - 10x + 25$, x^2 is the quadratic term, $-10x$ is the linear term, and 25 is the constant term.

SOLUTION

In a perfect square trinomial, the square of half the coefficient of the linear term is the constant term. So, $x^2 - 10x + 25$ is a perfect square trinomial because half of -10 is -5, and the square of -5 is 25. Use the factoring pattern $a^2 - 2ab + b^2 = (a - b)^2$.

$$a^2 - 2ab + b^2 = (a - b)^2$$
$$x^2 - 10x + 25 = (x - 5)^2$$
$$x^2 - 10x + 25 = (x - 5)^2$$

Check $(x - 5)^2 = (x - 5)(x - 5)$
$= x^2 - 5x - 5x + 25$
$= x^2 - 10x + 25$ ✓

b. Factor $4m^2 + 12mn + 9n^2$.

SOLUTION

Use the factoring pattern $a^2 + 2ab + b^2 = (a + b)^2$

$$a^2 + 2ab + b^2 = (a + b)^2$$
$$4m^2 + 12mn + 9n^2 = (2m + 3n)^2$$

Check $(2m + 3n)^2 = (2m + 3n)(2m + 3n)$
$= 4m^2 + 6mn + 6mn + 9n^2$
$= 4m^2 + 12mn + 9n^2$

ENGLISH LEARNERS

To help students during the examples, explain the meaning of the words **polynomial** and **factor.**

Poly means many. This indicates that the polynomial is the addition of many monomials.

A factor is a common number or variable that is in every term of the equation. It is equivalent to the technique of reducing fractions, but variables will also be factored in addition to numbers.

Example 3 Factoring a Difference of Two Squares

Factor $x^2 - 49$.

SOLUTION $x^2 - 49 = x^2 - 7^2$, so it is a difference of two squares.

$$x^2 - 49 = (x + 7)(x - 7)$$

Check $(x + 7)(x - 7) = x^2 - 7x + 7x - 49$

$= x^2 - 49$ ✓

The Zero Product Property says that if a product is zero, then at least one of its factors is zero. You can use this property to solve some polynomial equations.

Hint

The Zero Product Property applies to any number of factors. If $abc = 0$, then $a = 0$ or $b = 0$ or $c = 0$.

Zero Product Property
Let a and b be real numbers. If $ab = 0$, then $a = 0$ or $b = 0$.

Example 4 Solving a Basic Quadratic Trinomial Equation

Solve $x^2 + 3x - 10 = 0$.

SOLUTION First factor the quadratic polynomial $x^2 + 3x - 10$. Find two numbers whose product is -10 and whose sum is 3. The factor pairs for -10 are $(1)(-10)$, $(-1)(10)$, $(2)(-5)$, and $(-2)(5)$. The factor pair whose sum is 3 is $(-2)(5)$. So, the factored expression for $x^2 + 3x - 10$ is $(x - 2)(x + 5)$. Now use the Zero Product Property to solve the equation.

$x^2 + 3x - 10 = 0$ Original equation

$(x - 2)(x + 5) = 0$ Factor.

$(x - 2) = 0$ or $(x + 5) = 0$ Zero Product Property

$x = 2$ or $x = -5$ Solve each equation.

Check To check a solution, substitute it for the variable in the original equation. If it makes the equation true, it is a correct solution.

$x^2 + 3x - 10 = 0$	$x^2 + 3x - 10 = 0$
$2^2 + 3(2) - 10 \stackrel{?}{=} 0$	$(-5)^2 + 3(-5) - 10 \stackrel{?}{=} 0$
$4 + 6 - 10 \stackrel{?}{=} 0$	$25 - 15 - 10 \stackrel{?}{=} 0$
$0 = 0$ ✓	$0 = 0$ ✓

The solutions are 2 and -5 because they both make the original equation true.

Example 3

Students will use the difference of two squares method to factor the expression.

Additional Example 3

Factor $x^2 - 9$.
$(x + 3)(x - 3)$

Example 4

Students will learn to factor a quadratic polynomial by solving for the correct factored pair.

Additional Example 4

Solve $x^2 + 2x - 24 = 0$.
$(x - 4)(x + 6) = 0$
$x = 4$ or $x = -6$

Extend the Example

Have students check their work by taking the answers found and substituting them back into the equation. The value of the left side should be equal to zero.

TEACHER TIP

When factoring a quadratic trinomial equation, look at the sign of the constant term. If it is negative, the binomial factors will have opposite signs. If it is positive, the factors will have the same signs (the sign of the linear term).

INCLUSION

In order to help students learn to recognize how the polynomials factor, allow them to practice by working backwards.

Have the students start with two factors and multiply them together in order to solve for the polynomial. This will help students begin to recognize different types of polynomials.

Allow students to multiply other difference of two squares expressions.
Sample: $(x + 9)(x - 9)$

Example 5

Students will apply factoring to solve a problem involving the golden ratio in art.

Additional Example 5

An artist wants to make a rectangular tapestry with an area of 250 square feet whose length and width are in the ratio 1.6 to 1. What length and width should she use? 12.5 feet and 20 feet

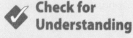

Lesson Practice

Problem b

Error Alert Students may forget to factor out the negative in the second term. When the negative is factored, the second term, originally positive, becomes negative.

Problem c

Scaffolding Find the greatest common factor of all three terms. Check to see if all three terms have common variables to be factored. Factor the greatest common factor and the common variable expression out of the polynomial.

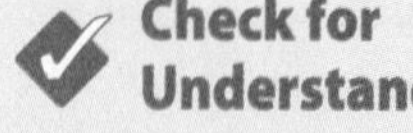

The questions below help assess the concepts taught in this lesson.

1. **How do you factor a perfect square trinomial?** Sample: Find a value that is half the coefficient of the linear term and the square root of the constant term.
2. **How can you verify that the solution(s) to an equation are correct?** Sample: Substitute each solution back into the original equation.

Math Reasoning

Write The golden ratio is the number $\frac{1+\sqrt{5}}{2}$. Explain why it is irrational. Then approximate its value to the nearest thousandth.

Since the number $\sqrt{5}$ is irrational, the golden ratio is also irrational; 1.618

Example 5 Application: The Golden Ratio in Art

The Golden Ratio is approximately 1.6 to 1. It has been used by artists for centuries to create visually pleasing art works. An artist wants to make a rectangular tapestry with an area of 90 square feet whose length and width are in the ratio 1.6 to 1. What length and width should she use?

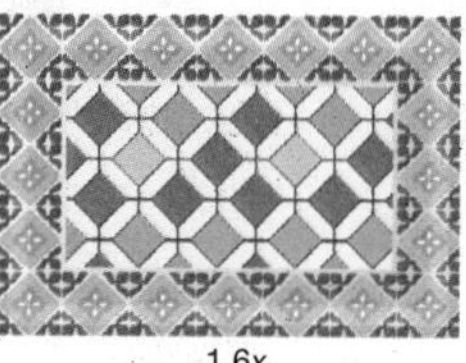

SOLUTION

Understand The dimensions of the rectangle can be represented by x and $1.6x$.

Plan Write and solve an equation for the area of the rectangle.

Solve

$(1.6x)(x) = 90$	Length times width equals area.
$1.6x^2 = 90$	Multiply both sides by 10 to eliminate decimals.
$16x^2 = 900$	
$16x^2 - 900 = 0$	Subtract 900 from both sides.
$(4x - 30)(4x + 30) = 0$	Factor the difference of two squares.
$4x - 30 = 0$ or $4x + 30 = 0$	Apply the Zero Product Property.
$x = 7.5$ or $x = -7.5$	Solve each equation. Use the positive solution 7.5.

$x = 7.5$ and $1.6x = (1.6)(7.5) = 12$.

The artist should use the dimensions 7.5 feet and 12 feet.

Check The ratio is correct: $\frac{12}{7.5} = 1.6$. The area is correct: $(12)(7.5) = 90$. ✓

Lesson Practice

a. Factor $12x^2 + 4x + 8$. $4(3x^2 + x + 2)$ *(Ex 1)*

b. Factor $-20x^3 + 5x^2$. $-5x^2(4x - 1)$ *(Ex 1)*

c. Factor $x^2 + 12x + 36$. $(x + 6)^2$ *(Ex 2)*

d. Factor $9x^2 + 30xy + 25y^2$. $(3x + 5y)^2$ *(Ex 2)*

e. Factor $x^2 - 1$. $(x + 1)(x - 1)$ *(Ex 3)*

f. Solve $x^2 - 10x + 21 = 0$. $x = 3, x = 7$ *(Ex 4)*

g. A rectangular wooden deck is 50 feet long and 40 feet wide. The owner wants to increase both dimensions by the same amount, resulting in a 50% increase in area. Write and solve an equation to find out how much he should increase each dimension. $(x + 50)(x + 40) = 3000$; 10 feet *(Ex 5)*

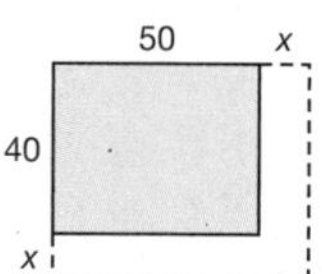

166 *Saxon* Algebra 2

Practice Distributed and Integrated

Evaluate each expression.

1. (2) $-a(a-b)$ if $a = -\frac{1}{2}$ and $b = \frac{1}{3}$ $-\frac{5}{12}$ **2.** (2) $-xy(-x^2 - y)$ if $x = -\frac{1}{2}$ and $y = \frac{1}{4}$ $-\frac{1}{16}$

3. (4) Determine whether $f(x) = 3x + x^2$ is a function. Function

4. (18) Convert 120 inches per second to feet per minute. 600 ft/min.

5. (19) Find the product: $\frac{-3^{-2}x}{y}\left(\frac{9y^0x}{-x} - \frac{3x}{y}\right)$. $\frac{x}{y} + \frac{x^2}{3y^2}$

Solve each equation for x.

6. (7) $0.003x + 0.02x - 0.03 = 0.177$ 9 **7.** (7) $2\frac{1}{3}x + 1\frac{3}{5} = 7\frac{2}{5}$ $\frac{87}{35}$ **8.** (7) $\frac{1}{2}x + 4 = 6\frac{1}{5}$ $\frac{22}{5}$

***9.** (22) Graph and state the domain and range of the discrete function: $\{(-2, -2), (4, 1), (-1, 6), (0, 2)\}$. Domain: −2, 4, −1, 0; Range: −2, 1, 6, 2

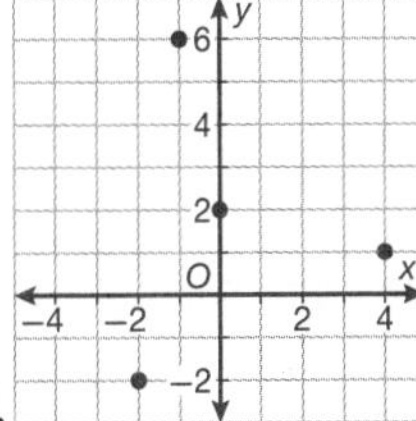

Factor each polynomial.

***10.** (23) $-3x^3 + 6x^2 + 3x$ $-3x(x^2 - 2x - 1)$ ***11.** (23) $-2x^2 + 5x + 3$ $-(2x + 1)(x - 3)$ ***12.** (23) $x^2 - 5x + 6$ $(x - 3)(x - 2)$

***13.** (23) **Analyze** Is $x^2 - 25$ a Basic Quadratic Polynomial, a Perfect Square Trinomial, or a Difference of Two Squares? Explain how you can tell by looking at the polynomial. It is a Difference of Two Squares. The polynomial has two terms, each of which is a square.

14. (20) **Geometry** In the diagram of a rectangle, $f(x) = 2x + 5$ and $g(x) = 5x + 4$. Find the perimeter of the rectangle in terms of x. $14x + 18$

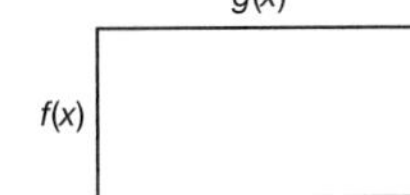

15. (7) **Verify** Is $x = -1$ the solution to the equation $5(4x - 1) = -7(9 + 4x) + 8 - 2x$? yes

16. (13) **Write** Give a written explanation on how to graph a linear equation using intercepts.

16. First, we must find the x-intercept by letting $y = 0$ and solving for x. Next, we find the y-intercept by letting $x = 0$ and solving for y. We then plot and connect the intercepts and extend a line through the points with arrowheads on the ends of the line.

17. (17) **Multi-Step** At a sugar plantation processing plant, a machine fills a bag with 5 pounds of white sugar. For quality control, another machine weighs each bag in ounces and rejects bags that differ from 5 pounds by more than y ounces.

a. Write an absolute-value function to show the minimum and maximum weight of sugar that could be in each bag. $80 - y \le w \le 80 + y$, so $|w - 80| \le y$

b. Graph the solution of the function.

80 − y 80 + y
50 60 70 80 90

18. (16) **Verify** **a.** Use Cramer's Rule to solve the system. $x + 2y = 0$, $x + 3y = 6$ (−12, 6)

b. Check your solution by graphing.

ALTERNATE METHOD FOR PROBLEM 15

This problem is solved by simply substituting $x = -1$ into the equation and verifying that both sides of the equation are equal. This problem could also be solved by solving for x using algebra.

$$5(4x - 1) = -7(9 + 4x) + 8 - 2x$$
$$20x - 5 = -63 - 28x + 8 - 2x$$
$$50x + 50 = 0$$
$$50x = -50$$
$$x = -1$$

3 Practice

Math Conversations

Discussions to strengthen understanding.

Problem 14

The perimeter of a rectangle is $P = 2 \cdot l + 2 \cdot w$

Problem 16

Extend the Problem

"What is the equation of a line?"
$y = mx + b$ or $(y_2 - y_1) = m(x_2 - x_1)$

Problem 19

Error Alert

Students may multiply the matrix incorrectly. To find the product of the matrix, multiply the first row of the first matrix by the first column of the second matrix.

Problem 20

The degree of a polynomial is equal to the degree of the monomial with the highest degree.

Problem 24

Extend the Problem

Find the weight of an object on the Sun that weighs 3 pounds on Earth. (Hint: Convert pounds to ounces first.)

$3 \text{ lbs} = \frac{16 \text{ oz}}{1 \text{ lbs}} = 48 \text{ oz}$

$\frac{48 \text{ oz}}{x} = \frac{12 \text{ oz}}{336 \text{ oz}}$

$x = \frac{336 \text{ oz} \times 48 \text{ oz}}{12 \text{ oz}}$

$x = 1344 \text{ oz}$

*19. (9) **Graphing Calculator** Find the product. Check using the graphing calculator.

$$\begin{bmatrix} 1 & 0 \\ 0 & 1 \\ 1 & 0 \end{bmatrix} \times \begin{bmatrix} -1 & 4 & -8 \\ 0 & -3 & 1 \end{bmatrix} \quad \begin{bmatrix} -1 & 4 & -8 \\ 0 & -3 & 1 \\ -1 & 4 & -8 \end{bmatrix}$$

20. (11) **Multiple Choice** What is the degree of the polynomial $3x + 2x + 1$? **B**

A 0 **B** 1 **C** 2 **D** 3

*21. (21) For the system of equations below, find values of b and c so that the system is characterized as follows. $\begin{matrix} x - 3y = 12 \\ 3x + by = c \end{matrix}$

a. consistent and dependent $b = -9, c = 36;$

b. inconsistent $b = -9, c \neq 36;$

c. consistent and independent $b \neq -9$

22. (10) **Error Analysis** Describe and correct the error.

$4x - 3 > x - 2$

$4x > x - 5$

$x > -5$

When isolating the variable, 3 was subtracted from 2 instead of added. The variable terms were not combined correctly either. $4x - 3 > x - 2$; $4x > x + 1$; $3x > 1$; $x > \frac{1}{3}$

23. (9) **Justify** Show and explain each step in finding the product AB.

$$A = \begin{bmatrix} 5 & 2 & 14 \\ 9 & 11 & 18 \\ 3 & 7 & 6 \end{bmatrix} B = \begin{bmatrix} 15 & 6 \\ 7 & 13 \\ 10 & 16 \end{bmatrix}$$

See Additional Answers.

24. (8) **Planets** The weight of an object on the Sun varies directly with the weight of that object on Earth. An object that weighs 12 oz on Earth weighs 336 oz on the Sun. Find the weight of an object on the Sun that weighs 7 oz on Earth. 196 ounces

*25. (22) **Data Analysis** Death Valley has the lowest elevation in North America. Below is a table of the temperature over the course of one day in the desert.

Time	1 a.m.	6 a.m.	10 a.m.	2 p.m.	4 p.m.	8 p.m.	11 p.m.
Temperature	83°	75°	90°	101°	105°	99°	90°

a. Graph the time and temperature data. Connect the points with line segments. See Additional Answers.

b. Explain why the temperature data creates a continuous relation.

c. Determine if the graph is a function. Explain.

25b. Given a specific time of day, temperature can always be measured and temperature does not immediately switch, which creates a connected graph.

c. Yes. For every time given, there is exactly one temperature. The graph also passes the vertical line test.

26. (15) **Nutrition** Nutritionists recommend a daily diet consisting of at least 85 g of carbohydrate and at least 50 g of protein. A cup of fried rice contains 48.7 g of carbohydrate and 9.1 g of protein. A cup of sweet and sour prawn contains 28.6 g of carbohydrate and 16.5 g of protein. How many cups of each dish will give the minimum daily allowance of carbohydrate and protein? Let r represent the number of cups of fried rice and p the number of cups of prawn.

26. The system $\begin{cases} 48.7r + 28.6p = 85 \\ 9.1r + 16.5p = 50 \end{cases}$ has solution $r = -0.05$ and $p = 3.0582$. In effect, this means 0 cups of fried rice and 3 cups of prawn.

CHALLENGE

Solve $x^2 + x - \frac{3}{4} = 0.$

$x = \frac{1}{2}$

$x = -\frac{3}{2}$

*27. (Envelopes) The United States Postal Service will mail an envelope that is no greater (23) than $2x + 1.5$ inches long and no greater than $x + 1$ inches high. The total area of an envelope with the maximum dimensions is approximately 69 in^2. Calculate the approximate maximum dimensions of an envelope that can be mailed through the USPS.

28. (Population) The table below lists the population estimates in millions for (13) Hawaii from 2000 to 2002.

Year	2000	2001	2002
Population	1.21	1.22	1.23

a. Write the data above as ordered pairs where x is the number of years after 2000 and y is the population in millions. (0, 1.21), (1, 1.22), and (2, 1.23)

b. Use slope and y-intercept to find the equation of the line representing this data. $y = 0.01x + 1.21$

Factor each expression.

*29. (23) $4x^2 - 25$ $(2x + 5)(2x - 5)$

*30. (23) $x^2 + 3x - 18$ $(x + 6)(x - 3)$

27. $(2x + 1.5)(x + 1) = 69$; $2x^2 + 3.5x + 1.5 = 69$, so $2x^2 + 3.5x - 67.5 = 0$; $(2x + 13.5)(x - 5) = 0$. So, $x = -6.75$ or $x = 5$. If $x = -6.75$, $2x + 1.5$ is negative. So, $x = 5$ is the solution. The maximum length is 11.5 inches and the maximum height is 6 inches.

Problem 27

Using the area equation, set the length times the width equal to the maximum area. Solve for x, which will give the maximum length and width. (First, set the entire equation equal to zero.)

LOOKING FORWARD

Using factoring prepares students for

- **Lesson 35** Solving Quadratic Equations I
- **Lesson 38** Dividing Polynomials Using Long Division
- **Lesson 61** Understanding Advanced Factoring
- **Lesson 66** Solving Polynomial Equations
- **Lesson 76** Finding Polynomial Roots I

LESSON
24

1 Warm Up

Use the Warm Up to review solving systems of equations by graphing and substitution.

2 New Concepts

In this lesson, students learn a third way to solve a system of equations—the elimination method.

Discuss the meaning of a *solution* to a system of equations. Students should realize that finding a solution is equivalent to finding the points, if any, at which the equations intersect.

Discuss the definition of the **elimination method.** Ask students what they are attempting to eliminate when they use this method.

Be sure they understand that the choice of which variable to retain is unimportant. They should choose the simplest method of eliminating the other variable(s).

LESSON
24 Solving Systems of Equations Using the Elimination Method

Warm Up

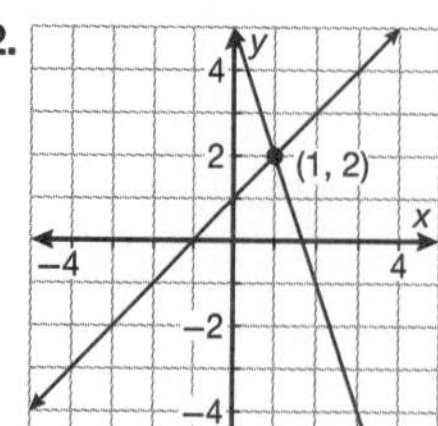

1. **Vocabulary** A system of equations with an infinite number of solutions is a(n) ________ (***consistent, inconsistent***) and a(n) ________ (***independent, dependent***) system. consistent, dependent
(15)

2. Solve $\begin{aligned} y &= x + 1 \\ y + 3x &= 5 \end{aligned}$ by graphing. (1, 2)
(15)

3. Solve $\begin{aligned} y &= x + 9 \\ 2x - y &= -13 \end{aligned}$ by substitution. (–4, 5)
(21)

New Concepts

Recall that a linear system with no solutions is an inconsistent system while a system with *at least* one solution is a consistent system. If there is exactly one solution to a system, it is independent. If there are infinitely many solutions, the system is dependent.

The solution of a system is the intersection of the graphs of the equations of the system, making it possible to describe a system just by looking at its graph.

Inconsistent System	Consistent System	
	Independent System	Dependent System
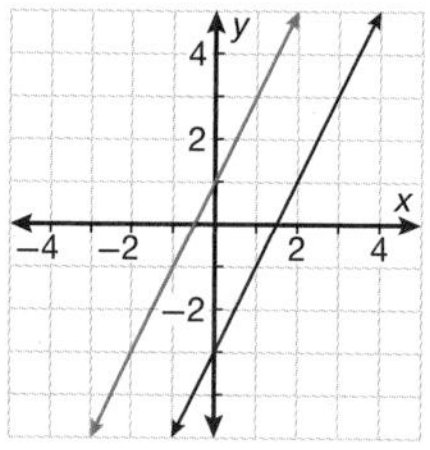	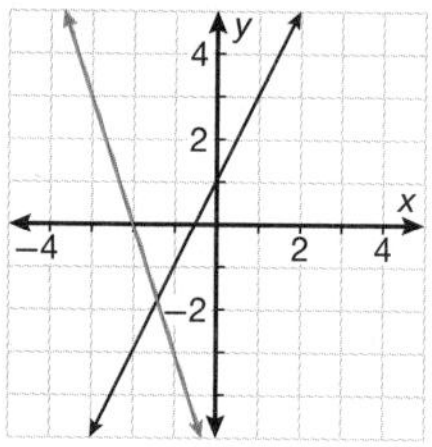	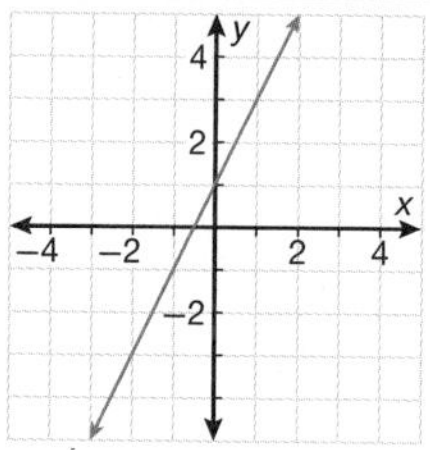

Therefore, one method of solving a linear system is by graphing and finding the intersection point or points if they exist. Another method previously discussed is the substitution method, which involves substituting an equivalent expression for x or y in one equation to get an equation in one variable. When that equation is solved, the value of that variable is then substituted into either original equation and the second variable is solved for.

Math Language

The **elimination method** is sometimes referred to as the **addition method.**

The last method for solving a linear system is the **elimination method.** When the elimination method is used, the two equations are added. The sum of one of the variables is 0, leaving an equation in one variable, which is solved. This value is then substituted into either original equation to solve for the second variable.

Sometimes extra steps are needed to be sure that the sum of one of the variables is 0. This could mean multiplying one or both equations by a constant.

LESSON RESOURCES

Student Edition Practice Workbook 24
Reteaching Master 24
Adaptations Master 24
Challenge and Enrichment Master 24
Graphing Calculator Lab Master 24

MATH BACKGROUND

In order to solve a single equation, the equation must have only one unknown. For example, the equation $y - 3 = 8$ can be solved, but the equation $x + 6 = y - 3$ cannot. A system of equations can be solved (or determined to have no solution) provided that the number of unknowns equals or is less than the number of equations. Using elimination to solve a system of equations is simply a method of reducing the problem to solving a single equation with a single unknown.

Elimination is a powerful method because it can easily be extended to solve larger systems involving more than two linear equations. Elimination can also be used for systems that involve equations which are non-linear.

Example 1 Solving Systems Using the Elimination Method

a. Solve $\begin{array}{l} 15 = 3x - 2y \\ x = -11 - 2y \end{array}$ and classify the system.

SOLUTION Begin by writing each equation in standard form.

$$\begin{array}{l} 15 = 3x - 2y \\ x = -11 - 2y \end{array} \rightarrow \begin{array}{l} 3x - 2y = 15 \\ x + 2y = -11 \end{array}$$

Add vertically. The y-terms will be eliminated. Solve for x and substitute the value for x into either original equation to find y.

$$\begin{array}{r} 3x - 2y = 15 \\ + x + 2y = -11 \\ \hline 4x \quad = 4 \\ x = 1 \end{array} \longrightarrow \begin{array}{r} 15 = 3x - 2y \\ 15 = 3(1) - 2y \\ 15 = 3 - 2y \\ 12 = -2y \\ -6 = y \end{array}$$

The solution is $(1, -6)$. The system is consistent and independent.

Check Substitute 1 for x and -6 for y into both original equations.

$$\begin{array}{ll} 15 = 3x - 2y & x = -11 - 2y \\ 15 \stackrel{?}{=} 3(1) - 2(-6) & 1 \stackrel{?}{=} -11 - 2(-6) \\ 15 = 15 \ \checkmark & 1 = 1 \ \checkmark \end{array}$$

b. Solve $\begin{array}{l} 2x + 5y = -34 \\ -3x + 2y = -44 \end{array}$ and classify the system.

SOLUTION The equations are already in standard form. Multiply the first equation by 3 and the second equation by 2.

$$\begin{array}{l} 2x + 5y = -34 \\ -3x + 2y = -44 \end{array} \rightarrow \begin{array}{l} 3(2x + 5y) = 3(-34) \\ 2(-3x + 2y) = 2(-44) \end{array} \rightarrow \begin{array}{l} 6x + 15y = -102 \\ -6x + 4y = -88 \end{array}$$

Add the equations. Solve for x and y.

$$\begin{array}{r} 6x + 15y = -102 \\ + -6x + 4y = -88 \\ \hline 19y = -190 \\ y = -10 \end{array} \longrightarrow \begin{array}{r} 2x + 5y = -34 \\ 2x + 5(-10) = -34 \\ 2x - 50 = -34 \\ 2x = 16 \\ x = 8 \end{array}$$

The solution is $(8, -10)$. The system is consistent and independent.

Check Substitute 8 for x and -10 for y into both original equations.

$$\begin{array}{ll} 2x + 5y = -34 & -3x + 2y = -44 \\ 2(8) + 5(-10) \stackrel{?}{=} -34 & -3(8) + 2(-10) \stackrel{?}{=} -44 \\ -34 = -34 \ \checkmark & -44 = -44 \ \checkmark \end{array}$$

Math Reasoning

Justify Why is the value of x substituted into one of the original equations and not one of the equations written in standard form?

An error could have been made while writing the equations in standard form.

Hint

To eliminate like terms, multiply each equation by a constant to make the terms opposites.

Example 1

The examples demonstrate the elimination method of solving systems when the equations are consistent and independent. In Example 1a, a variable can be eliminated simply by adding the equations without any modification. In Example 1b, in order to eliminate a variable, the equations must be multiplied by integers before adding them.

TEACHER TIP

Demonstrate for students how to change an equation to standard form, $ax + by = c$. Students will learn more about this procedure in Lesson 26.

Extend the Example

Ask students to solve Example 1b again by eliminating y instead of x. In this case, they should multiply the first equation by 2 and the second equation by -5 before adding the equations.

Additional Example 1

a. Solve $\begin{array}{l} 2x = 2 - 4y \\ 4y = x - 7 \end{array}$ and classify the system. $(3, -1)$, consistent and independent

b. Solve $\begin{array}{l} -7 = 9x + 8y \\ -5 + x = 2y \end{array}$ and classify the system. $(1, -2)$, consistent and independent

Error Alert Students may believe that once they have found one variable for a system, they have found the solution. Be sure they understand that a solution consists of an ordered pair, (x, y). Remind them that when they solve systems by the graphical method, the solution is one or more points. A point is described by an ordered pair, not just an x- or a y-value alone.

ENGLISH LEARNERS

Ask students to listen carefully as you say the word **elimination.** Have them identify the root word (eliminate) and the suffix (-tion).

Write these equations on the board:

$$\begin{array}{r} 6x + 15y = -102 \\ + \quad -6x + 4y = -88 \\ \hline 19y = -190 \\ y = -10 \end{array}$$

Ask students to identify the variable that was eliminated. *x*

Have students use either the word eliminate or the word elimination in a non-mathematical way. For example, one possible sentence is, "You can eliminate your hunger by eating a snack."

Ask students to develop a simple model that demonstrates the definition of the word elimination. For example, students may place several pencils in a line and then eliminate one from the line.

Example 2

Students will discover in these examples that clearing fractions can make solving systems of equations with fractional coefficients much easier.

TEACHER TIP

Stress the importance of checking the solution ordered pair in *both* of the original equations. If one or both of the equations does not check correctly, students should review their answer to find the mistake.

Additional Example 2

a. Solve. $\begin{array}{l}\frac{2}{3}x = 4y \\ 9 = 2x - 3y\end{array}$ (6, 1)

b. Solve. $\begin{array}{l}\frac{3}{4}x + \frac{y}{3} = 10 \\ \frac{x}{2} + 5y = 64\end{array}$ (8, 12)

Math Reasoning

Analyze How is multiplying one equation by −1 and then adding the equations the same as subtracting one equation from the other?

Every term in the second equation becomes its opposite.

Example 2 Solving Systems with Fractional Coefficients

a. Solve $\begin{array}{l}\frac{3}{4}x = 3y \\ 15 + 7y = 3x\end{array}$.

SOLUTION Begin by writing each equation in standard form.

$$\begin{array}{l}\frac{3}{4}x = 3y \\ 15 + 7y = 3x\end{array} \rightarrow \begin{array}{l}\frac{3}{4}x - 3y = 0 \\ 3x - 7y = 15\end{array}$$

Clear the fraction in the first equation by multiplying the equation by 4. Then multiply one of the equations by −1 to make the x-terms opposites.

$$\begin{array}{l}4\left(\frac{3}{4}x - 3y\right) = 4(0) \\ 3x - 7y = 15\end{array} \rightarrow \begin{array}{l}3x - 12y = 0 \\ 3x - 7y = 15\end{array} \rightarrow \begin{array}{l}3x - 12y = 0 \\ -3x + 7y = -15\end{array}$$

Solve for x and y.

$$\begin{array}{r}3x - 12y = 0 \\ + -3x + 7y = -15 \\ \hline -5y = -15 \\ y = 3\end{array} \rightarrow \begin{array}{r}15 + 7y = 3x \\ 15 + 7(3) = 3x \\ 15 + 21 = 3x \\ 36 = 3x \\ 12 = x\end{array}$$

The solution is (12, 3).

b. Solve $\begin{array}{l}\frac{5}{6}x + \frac{7}{8}y = 25 \\ \frac{x}{3} + 2y = 76\end{array}$.

SOLUTION Clear the fractions in the first equation by multiplying it by the least common denominator 24. Multiply the second equation by 3.

After the fractions are cleared, multiply the second equation by −20 + 0 eliminate the x-terms.

$$\begin{array}{l}24\left(\frac{5}{6}x + \frac{7}{8}y\right) = 24(25) \\ 3\left(\frac{x}{3} + 2y\right) = 3(76)\end{array} \rightarrow \begin{array}{l}20x + 21y = 600 \\ x + 6y = 228\end{array} \rightarrow \begin{array}{l}20x + 21y = 600 \\ -20x - 120y = -4560\end{array}$$

Solve for x and y.

$$\begin{array}{r}20x + 21y = 600 \\ + -20x - 120y = -4560 \\ \hline -99y = -3960 \\ y = 40\end{array} \rightarrow \begin{array}{r}\frac{x}{3} + 2y = 76 \\ \frac{x}{3} + 2(40) = 76 \\ \frac{x}{3} = -4 \\ x = -12\end{array}$$

The solution is (−12, 40).

ALTERNATE METHOD FOR EXAMPLE 2

Suggest the following simple method for finding the least common multiple in Example 2b. First, choose the greater of the two denominators of the fractions in the equation, in this case 8. Then, begin listing the multiplies of that number: 8, 16, 24, ... Stop when you get to a number that is also a multiple of the other denominator, in this case 24. This is the least common multiple you should use for multiplying the equation.

Example 3 Solving Systems with Infinitely Many and No Solutions

a. Solve $\begin{aligned} 2x - y &= 3 \\ -6x + 3y &= -9 \end{aligned}$ and classify the system.

SOLUTION Multiply the first equation by 3 to make opposite x-terms.

$$\begin{aligned} 3(2x - y) &= 3(3) \\ -6x + 3y &= -9 \end{aligned} \rightarrow \begin{aligned} 6x - 3y &= 9 \\ -6x + 3y &= -9 \end{aligned}$$

Solve for x and y.

$$\begin{aligned} 6x - 3y &= 9 \\ + -6x + 3y &= -9 \\ \hline 0 &= 0 \end{aligned}$$

$0 = 0$ is a true statement.

There are infinitely many solutions. The system is consistent and dependent. The lines coincide.

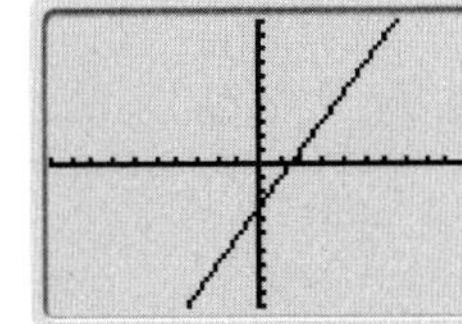

Math Language

Two lines that **coincide** share the same points.

b. Solve $\begin{aligned} 3x - 4y &= -24 \\ 6x - 8y &= 16 \end{aligned}$ and classify the system.

SOLUTION Multiply the first equation by -2 to make opposite x-terms.

$$\begin{aligned} -2(3x - 4y) &= -2(-24) \\ 6x - 8y &= 16 \end{aligned} \rightarrow \begin{aligned} -6x + 8y &= 48 \\ 6x - 8y &= 16 \end{aligned}$$

Solve for x and y.

$$\begin{aligned} -6x + 8y &= 48 \\ + 6x - 8y &= 16 \\ \hline 0 &= 64 \end{aligned}$$

$0 = 64$ is a false statement.

There are no solutions. The system is inconsistent. The lines are parallel.

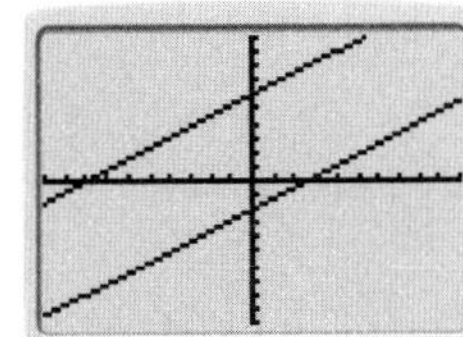

Example 3

Students will learn how to interpret the results when they solve a system of equations and obtain a true statement, such as $0 = 0$, or a false statement, such as $0 = 64$.

Additional Example 3

a. Solve $\begin{aligned} -3x + 2y &= 5 \\ 9x &= 6y - 15 \end{aligned}$ and classify the system. infinitely many solutions, consistent and dependent

b. Solve $\begin{aligned} 4x &= 7 + 3y \\ 12x - 9y &= 15 \end{aligned}$ and classify the system. no solutions, inconsistent

INCLUSION

Have students give a verbal, step-by-step description of one or more of the examples in this lesson. Encourage them to explain the reasons for each step rather than simply reading from the text. The verbal explanations that students give are a good opportunity to uncover any misconceptions they may have about the procedures.

Example 4

This example demonstrates the use of elimination to solve systems of equations involving real life situations.

Additional Example 4

Tamara and her sister bought school supplies. Tamara bought 5 spiral notebooks and 6 book covers for \$10.75. Her sister bought 4 spiral notebooks and 5 book covers for \$8.75. Find the cost for each spiral notebook and each book cover. spiral notebook: \$1.25, book cover: \$0.75

Lesson Practice

Problem a

Error Alert Caution students to be careful about signs before the coefficients and constants in the equations, especially when changing the equations to standard form. Suggest that students look for this error if the solution to the problem does not check correctly.

Problem d

Scaffolding Remind students to multiply both sides of an equation by the lowest common multiple *before* eliminating a variable.

Check for Understanding

The questions below help assess the concepts taught in this lesson.

"What is a way to eliminate the fractions in an equation without finding the lowest common multiple?" Sample: Multiply by each denominator in the equation separately, or alternatively, multiply by the product of all denominators.

"How do you decide which variable to eliminate when solving a system of equations?" Sample: A variable that has a coefficient of 1 or a coefficient that is a multiple of the corresponding coefficient in the other equation may be easiest to eliminate.

Example 4 **Application: Vacationing**

In 2007, the costs to take the elevator to the top of the Eiffel Tower were such that a group of 6 adults and 4 children paid 94.20 euros and a group of 5 adults and 14 children paid 145.70 euros. Find the cost for each adult and each child.

Math Reasoning

Estimation How can estimation be used to check the answer for reasonableness?

Use $a \approx 12$ and $c \approx 6$, then $6a + 4c = 72 + 24 = 96$, which is close to 94.2.

SOLUTION Write a system where a represents the cost for an adult and c the cost for a child. Multiply so that one of the variables will be eliminated.

$$\begin{aligned}6a + 4c &= 94.20\\ 5a + 14c &= 145.70\end{aligned} \longrightarrow \begin{aligned}-5(6a + 4c) &= -5(94.20)\\ 6(5a + 14c) &= 6(145.70)\end{aligned} \longrightarrow \begin{aligned}-30a - 20c &= -471\\ 30a + 84c &= 874.2\end{aligned}$$

Solve for x and y.

$$\begin{aligned}-30a - 20c &= -471\\ +\ 30a + 84c &= 874.2\\ \hline 64c &= 403.2\\ c &= 6.3\end{aligned} \longrightarrow \begin{aligned}6a + 4c &= 94.2\\ 6a + 4(6.3) &= 94.2\\ 6a + 25.2 &= 94.2\\ 6a &= 69\\ a &= 11.5\end{aligned}$$

The cost for one adult is 11.50 euros and the cost for one child is 6.30 euros.

Lesson Practice

Solve and classify each system.

a. (Ex 1) $-2y = -6x + 62$, $-x = -22 - 2y$ — a. (8, −7), consistent and independent

b. (Ex 1) $-x - y = -3$, $3x = 2y - 11$ — (−1, 4), consistent and independent

Solve.

c. (Ex 2) $5x + 7y = -36$, $\frac{2}{3}x - 8y = 22$ — (−3, −3)

d. (Ex 2) $\frac{1}{2}x - y = 15$, $\frac{1}{4}x + \frac{1}{3}y = 0$ — (12, −9)

Solve and classify each system.

e. (Ex 3) $-7 = y + 3x$, $15x = 50 - 5y$ — no solutions, inconsistent

f. (Ex 3) $4x = 10 + 2y$, $5 = 2x - y$ — infinitely many solutions, consistent and dependent

g. (Ex 4) In 2007, the costs of tickets to the top of the Gateway Arch in St. Louis, Missouri, were such that a group of 10 adults and 3 children paid \$109 and a group of 5 adults and 3 children paid \$59. Find the cost for each adult and each child. adult: \$10, child: \$3

ALTERNATE METHOD FOR PROBLEM e

Instead of eliminating a variable in this system by multiplying the top equation by −5, students can equivalently divide the bottom equation by −5 before adding the equations.

Practice Distributed and Integrated

Solve for x.

1. (14) $\begin{vmatrix} -2 & 1 \\ 1 & x \end{vmatrix} = 16$ $x = -\frac{17}{2}$ **2.** (14) $\begin{vmatrix} -3+x & x \\ 1 & 6 \end{vmatrix} = 5$ $x = \frac{23}{5}$ **3.** (14) $\begin{vmatrix} 4 & -5 \\ 2 & x \end{vmatrix} = 8$ $x = -\frac{1}{2}$

4. (18) Convert 120 inches per second to feet per minute. 600 ft/min.

5. (13) Calculate the slope of the line that passes through the points (2, 1) and (0, 5). −2

Find each product.

6. (9) $\begin{bmatrix} -5 & 2 \\ 0 & 1 \end{bmatrix} \times \begin{bmatrix} 3 & 4 \\ 1 & 8 \end{bmatrix}$ **7.** (9) $[-1 \ 5] \times \begin{bmatrix} 6 \\ 8 \end{bmatrix}$ [34] **8.** (9) $[-3 \ 4] \times \begin{bmatrix} 1 \\ 7 \end{bmatrix}$ [25]

6. $\begin{bmatrix} -13 & -4 \\ 1 & 8 \end{bmatrix}$

***9.** (23) Factor the polynomial: $x^4 - 16$. $(x+2)(x-2)(x^2+4)$

Solve each system of equations using elimination.

***10.** (24) $\begin{aligned} 2x - 5y &= 5 \\ -5x + y &= -1 \end{aligned}$ $x = 0, y = -1$ ***11.** (24) $\begin{aligned} -4x + 7y &= -47 \\ 3x - 5y &= 34 \end{aligned}$ $x = 3, y = -5$

***12.** (24) $\begin{aligned} 5x + y &= 14 \\ -3x - 4y &= -5 \end{aligned}$ $x = 3, y = -1$ ***13.** (24) $\begin{aligned} 2x - 5y &= -3 \\ -10x + 25y &= 15 \end{aligned}$ infinitely many solutions

***14.** (23) **Geometry** Find the possible value(s) of x if Volume = 104. $2(x+8)(x-1) = 104$. Dividing the 2 from both sides and multiplying out gives $x^2 + 7x - 8 = 52$. Then $x^2 + 7x - 60 = 0$ so $(x + 12)(x - 5) = 0$. x can't be negative, so $x = 5$.

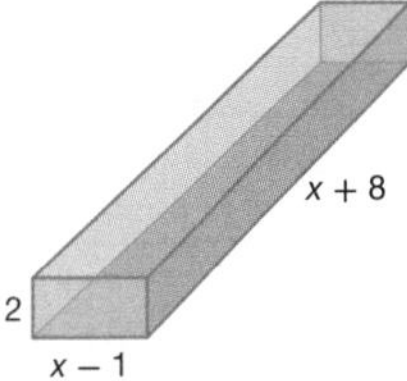

15. (21) Solve $\begin{aligned} 2x + y &= -4 \\ x + y &= 7 \end{aligned}$ by substitution. (−11, 18)

16. (19) **Model** Model FOIL for the multiplication of any two binomials in the form $(a + b)(c + d)$.

16.
First terms $a \cdot c = ac$
Outer terms $a \cdot d = ad$
Inner terms $b \cdot c = bc$
Last terms $b \cdot d = bd$
Add the terms:
$ac + ad + bc + bd$
Combine any like terms at the end.

17. (9) **Multi-Step** Use $A = \begin{bmatrix} 5 & 3 \\ 6 & 5 \end{bmatrix}$ $B = \begin{bmatrix} 7 & 4 \\ 8 & 7 \end{bmatrix}$.

a. Find AB. $\begin{bmatrix} 59 & 41 \\ 82 & 59 \end{bmatrix}$ **b.** Find BA. $\begin{bmatrix} 59 & 41 \\ 82 & 59 \end{bmatrix}$

c. Is $AB = BA$? Yes; $\begin{bmatrix} 59 & 41 \\ 82 & 59 \end{bmatrix} = \begin{bmatrix} 59 & 41 \\ 82 & 59 \end{bmatrix}$

***18.** (24) **Sightseeing** The cost of tickets to the observatory on the 86th floor of the Empire State Building in 2007 were such that 5 adult tickets and 4 senior citizen tickets cost \$154 and 3 adult tickets and 8 senior citizen tickets cost \$182. Find the cost of each type of ticket. Adult: \$18, Senior citizen: \$16

CHALLENGE

Solve $\begin{aligned} 2y &= 1 - 3x \\ 2x - 8 &= -5y \\ 10 - 2y &= -6x \end{aligned}$. (−1, 2)

Solve $\begin{aligned} 3x &= 2y + 7 \\ 14 + 4y &= 6x \\ 9x + 5 &= 6y \end{aligned}$. no solution

3 Practice

Math Conversations

Discussions to strengthen understanding

Problem 9

Error Alert

A common error is factoring $x^2 + a^2$ to $(x + a)(x + a)$. Advise students that the product of $(x + a)(x + a)$ has a middle term, $2ax$.

Problem 19

Students may have a tendency to forget the effect of coefficients and to consider only positive integers for the variables when solving this problem. Encourage them to think about other possibilities by asking the following questions.

"Suppose P_1 and P_2 are ax^3 and bx^2 respectively. Would P_1 be greater than P_2 if $a = \frac{1}{2}$, $b = \frac{1}{4}$, and $x = 3$?" yes

"Would P_1 be greater than P_2 if $a = 2$, $b = 2$, and $x = \frac{1}{2}$?" no

Problem 20

Extend the Problem

"Find $(gf)(x)$. Do the functions obey the Commutative Property of Multiplication?" $3x^2 - 18x + 27$; yes

Problem 26

Guide the students by asking them the following questions.

"What is meant by the terms *conjunction* and *disjunction?*" A conjunction has the form $|x| < a$ or $|x| \leq a$. A disjunction has the form $|x| > a$ or $|x| \geq a$.

"How can you determine whether this is a conjunction or a disjunction? The most the bear can eat is the maximum, and the least it can eat is the minimum. This fits the definition of a conjunction.

19. (11) **Justify** If polynomial P_1 has a greater degree than polynomial P_2, does P_1 have a greater value than P_2? Explain your answer and justify it by giving examples. See Additional Answers.

20. (20) If $f(x) = 3x - 9$ and $g(x) = x - 3$, find $(fg)(x)$. $3x^2 - 18x + 27$

21. (14) **Coordinate Geometry** A quadrilateral with vertices (x_1, y_1), (x_2, y_2), (x_3, y_3), and (x_4, y_4) has an area equal to the absolute value of $\frac{1}{4}\begin{vmatrix} x_1 & x_2 & x_3 & x_4 \\ y_1 & y_2 & y_3 & y_4 \\ 1 & 1 & 1 & 1 \\ -1 & 1 & -1 & 1 \end{vmatrix}$.

Find the area of the quadrilateral. Area $= \frac{1}{4}\begin{vmatrix} 1 & 7 & 7 & 3 \\ 2 & 2 & 6 & 8 \\ 1 & 1 & 1 & 1 \\ -1 & 1 & -1 & 1 \end{vmatrix} = 26$ sq. units

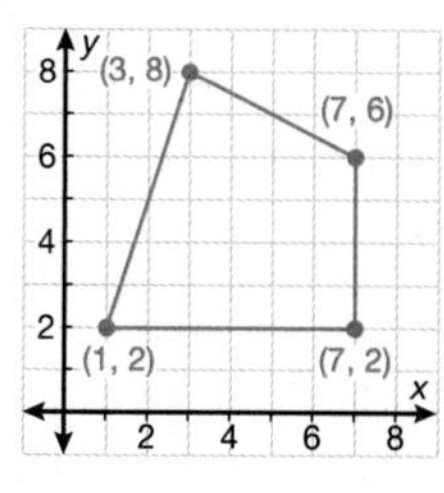

***22.** (13) **Graphing Calculator** The table shows the total number of birdhouses Sal made, y, after x amount of days.

Number of Days	2	3	7
Birdhouses	$5\frac{1}{3}$	8	$18\frac{2}{3}$

a. Plot the data on your graphing calculator. a. and b. See graph.

b. Find the line that best fits the data using linear regression and graph the line on your graphing calculator.

c. Use the line to predict the number of birdhouses Sal can make in 10 days. approximately $26\frac{2}{3}$ birdhouses

***23.** (24) **Error Analysis** Find and correct the error a student made below. The student did not multiply the right side of the second equation by −1. The correct solution is (2, 1).

$$\begin{aligned} 4x + y &= 9 \\ 4x - 3y &= 5 \end{aligned} \quad \longrightarrow \quad \begin{aligned} 4x + y &= 9 \\ -4x + 3y &= 5 \end{aligned}$$

$$\begin{aligned} 4x + y &= 9 \\ + -4x + 3y &= 5 \\ \hline 4y &= 14 \\ y &= 3.5 \end{aligned} \quad \longrightarrow \quad \begin{aligned} 4x + y &= 9 \\ 4x + 3.5 &= 9 \\ 4x &= 5.5 \\ x &= 1.375 \end{aligned}$$

The solution is (1.375, 3.5).

24. (10) **Multi-Step** At the local bowling alley there is a tournament underway. One of the bowlers has played two games and has a total score of 530. To win the tournament, a total score of 750 for three games is needed. Use the information given to write an inequality describing the possible number of points the bowler can score and win the tournament. What is the minimum score possible in order to win the tournament? $530 + x \geq 750$; $x \geq 220$; Minimum score: 220

25. (18) **Estimate** A cheetah runs at a speed of 70 miles per hour. Estimate a cheetah's speed in feet per second. 102.67 feet per second or about 103 feet per second.

26. (17) **Grizzly Bears** The table below shows amounts of three foods that a 200-lb grizzly bear can eat in a day. Which term, *disjunction* or *conjunction*, would represent the amount of these foods required for a 200-lb grizzly bear? Explain.

Type	Deer	Salmon	Vegetation
Amount (lb)	24	30	67

26. Conjunction – the amount must be greater than/equal to the minimum AND less than/equal to the maximum.

27. (8) **Multiple Choice** The amount of water added to a dry concrete mix varies directly with the amount of dry concrete. If 80 lb of dry concrete requires 6 pt of water, how much water is needed for 200 lb of dry concrete? Circle the letter that best represents the amount of water needed. **A**

A 15 pt **B** 10 pt **C** 8 pt **D** 6.5 pt

State whether the function is discrete or continuous.

***28.** (22) (1, 5), (0, 9), (2, 7), (−5, 4) discrete

***29.** (22) (2, 5), (4, 8), (6, 9), (−9, −6) discrete

30. (22) **Sports** A baseball when hit travels in a parabolic path. If time is represented by the x-values and the height of the ball is represented by the y-values, the graph at right can be drawn. Does this example represent a continuous, discontinuous, and/or discrete function? Justify your answer. This is a continuous function; The graph can be drawn without lifting the pencil from the paper.

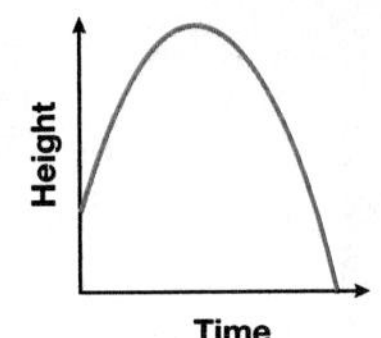

Problem 27

Encourage students to think about the first sentence in the problem and then write an equation representing the direct variation between the water, w, and the dry concrete mix, m: $w = km$.

LOOKING FORWARD

Solving systems by elimination prepares students for

- **Lesson 29** Solving Systems of Equations in Three Variables
- **Lesson 43** Solving Systems of Linear Inequalities
- **Lesson 54** Using Linear Programming

Materials

- graphing calculator

Discuss

In this lab, students will calculate one- and two-variable statistical data. One-variable data will be displayed using a box-and-whisker plot.

Define mean, median, standard deviation, quartile, and box-and-whisker plot.

TEACHER TIP

Discuss the meaning of each of the statistical variables as they are displayed.

Calculating Statistics for 1-Variable Data

One-variable data lists the following information for all data values in the chosen list: mean, sum, sum of x^2, sample standard deviation, population standard deviation, number of data points, minimum, first quartile, median, third quartile, maximum.

Calculating 1- and 2-Variable Statistical Data

Graphing Calculator Lab ***(Use with Lesson 25, Inv. 7, 73, 80, and Inv. 8)***

Graphing Calculator Tip

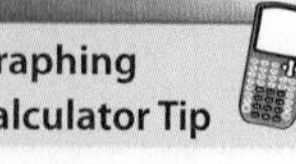

For help with entering data into lists, see graphing calculator lab 5 on pg. 153.

A graphing calculator can be used to analyze data sets of 1 and 2 variables.

Data Set 1	Data Set 2
–5	–10
–3	–6
–2	–4
–1	–2
0	0
2	4
3	6
4	8

Calculating Statistics for 1-Variable Data

1. Use the graphing calculator to enter the data sets into L1 and L2.

2. Calculate 1-variable statistical data.

From the home screen, press STAT, and then press ▶ to open the **[CALC]** menu. Press ENTER to select **[1: 1-Var Stats]**. Input L1 by pressing 2nd 1. Then press ENTER and the calculator will analyze the data values in L1. Press ▼ to scroll through the information.

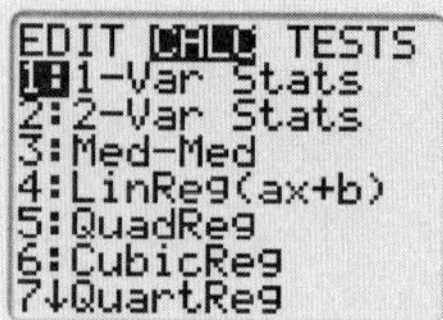

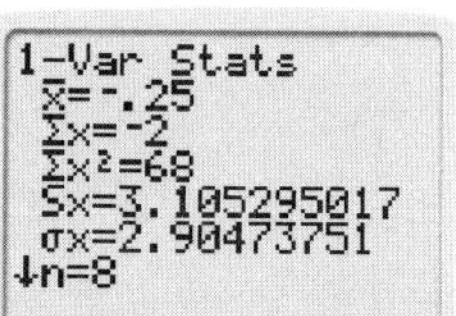

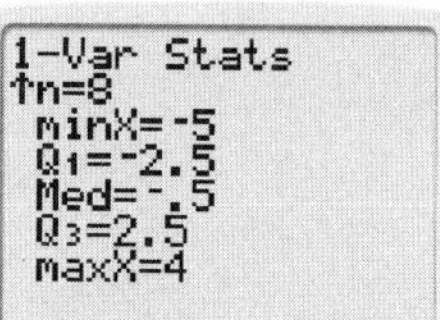

Calculating Statistics for 2-Variable Data

Use the above sets of data already entered into L1 and L2.

a. From the home screen, press STAT, and then press ▶ to open the **[CALC]** menu. Press ▼ to scroll to **[2: 2-Var Stats]**. Then press ENTER. Input L1 and L2 by pressing 2nd 1 , 2nd 2. Then press ENTER and the calculator will analyze the data values in L1 and L2.

b. The data listed for L1 is referred to as x. The data for L2 is referred to as y. There is one new statistic: **Σxy** is the sum of the products of the paired data values.

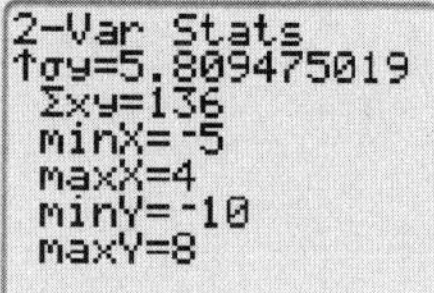

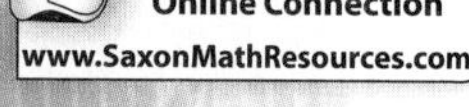

Online Connection
www.SaxonMathResources.com

Display 1-Variable Statistical Data Through a Box-and-Whisker Plot

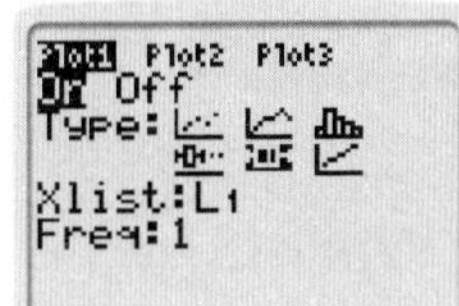

1. Customizing a box-and-whisker plot.
   a. Press 2nd Y= to open the [STAT PLOT] menu. Press ENTER to open the first Stat plot.
   b. Press ENTER to turn Plot1 on. This will display the plot on the graph.
   c. Press ▼ to move to [Type:]. Press ▶ until the box-plot symbol is highlighted and press ENTER.
   d. Press ▼ to move to [Xlist:]. L1 should be displayed, meaning it will use the data values from data set 1. (If L1 is not displayed, press 2nd 1 ENTER.)
   e. Press ▼ to move to [Freq:]. Press 1 ENTER.

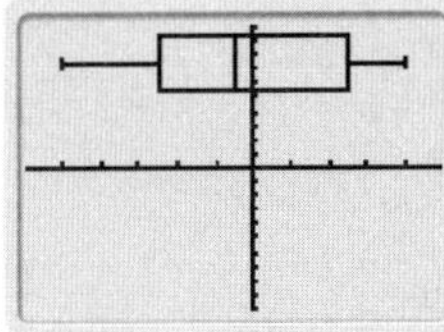

2. Graphing a box-and-whisker plot.
   Press ZOOM and use the arrow key ▼ to select [9: ZoomStat] and press ENTER. The box-and-whisker plot of L1 will now be displayed.

Graphing Calculator Practice

Use the graphing calculator to analyze the following data sets.

Data Set 1	Data Set 2
–12	5
–4	6
13	16
21	21
30	23

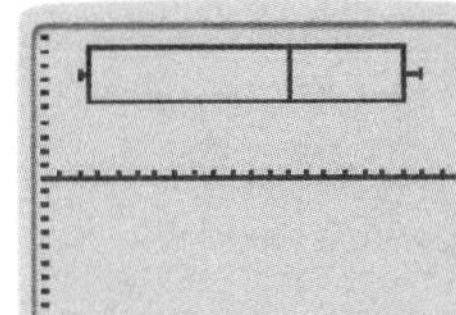

a. Graph a box-and-whisker plot for data set 2.

b. Calculate the value of Σxy for data sets 1 and 2. 1255

TEACHER TIP

Frequency refers to the number of times the data elements occur in the list.

Display 1-Variable Statistical Data Through a Box-and-Whisker Plot

Trace the box-and-whisker plot from left to right. What information is displayed?
Minimum = −5, first quartile = −2.5, median = −0.5, third quartile = 2.5, maximum = 4

TEACHER TIP

The modified box-and-whisker plot calculator option plots outliers in addition to the box-and-whisker plot.

Practice Problem 1

TEACHER TIP

The Xlist must be L2 for data set 2 to be displayed.

Practice Problem 2

TEACHER TIP

Since two data sets are used, use 2-variable statistics calculations.

LESSON 25

1 Warm Up

In problems 2 and 3 remind students of decimal placement.

2 New Concepts

In this lesson, students learn to find measures of central tendency and dispersion.

Discuss the definitions of **statistics, measure of central tendency, mean, median,** and **mode.** Explain that statistics is used to analyze and find trends in sets of data.

Example 1

This example shows students how to find three measures of central tendency: mean, median, and mode. Remind students to review the definitions of the terms to ensure they calculate the correct value.

Additional Example 1

Calculate the mean, median, and mode for the following set of data:

16, 13, 12, 15, 18, 14, 14

mean: ≈14.6; median: 14; mode: 14

LESSON 25

Finding Measures of Central Tendency and Dispersion

Warm Up

1. **Vocabulary** A set of separate numbers is referred to as discrete (*discrete, continuous*) data. (22)

2. Subtract 25.5 − 37.75. −12.25 (SB)

3. Simplify $(-0.25)^2$. 0.0625 (SB)

New Concepts

Statistics is the branch of mathematics that involves the collection, analysis, and comparison of sets of numerical data.

A **measure of central tendency** is used to represent the middle of a set of data.

Measures of Central Tendency
The **mean,** or average, of n numbers is the sum of the numbers divided by n. The mean is denoted by $\overline{x}$, read "x-bar." For the data set $x_1, x_2, \ldots, x_n$, the mean is $\overline{x} = \frac{x_1 + x_2 + \ldots + x_n}{n}$.
The **median** of n numbers is the middle number when the numbers are written in order. If n is even, the median is the mean of the two middle numbers.
The **mode** of n numbers is the number that appears most frequently in the list. There may be one mode, no mode, or more than one mode.

Caution

The data must be in either ascending or descending order to properly determine the median.

Example 1 Finding Measures of Central Tendency

Luann earned the following grades on her algebra quizzes:

18, 15, 20, 16, 17, 19, 19

Calculate the mean, median, and mode for Luann's quiz grades.

SOLUTION

Mean: $\overline{x} = \frac{18 + 15 + 20 + 16 + 17 + 19 + 19}{7} = \frac{124}{7} \approx 17.7$

Median: Arrange the data in order. 15, 16, 17, 18, 19, 19, 20

The median is the middle number, 18.

Mode: The mode is the number that appears most often, 19.

A **measure of dispersion** is a statistic that indicates how spread out, or dispersed, data values are. Three common measures of dispersion are the range, variance, and standard deviation.

LESSON RESOURCES

Student Edition Practice Workbook 25
Reteaching Master 25
Adaptations Master 25
Challenge and Enrichment Masters C25, E25

MATH BACKGROUND

The box-and-whisker plot is a very useful tool when large data sets are involved or when two data sets are being compared. The plots show the spread, overall range, and median of the data sets at a glance. The reader can also quickly determine outliers that might skew the central tendencies.

The box part of the box-and-whisker plot is obvious. But the whiskers in the plot are not as obvious. The whiskers in the box-and-whisker plot are the two lines outside the box that connect the box to the minimum value in the data set and the maximum value in the data set.

Measures of Dispersion
The **range of a data set** is the difference between the largest and smallest data values. The **variance** of a data set is the average of the squared differences from the mean. The **standard deviation** measures, on average, how far away from the mean the data values are. The standard deviation σ, which is the Greek letter sigma, is the square root of the variance and is calculated using the following formula for a data set with n terms, $x_1, x_2, \ldots, x_n$: $\sigma = \sqrt{\frac{(x_1 - \overline{x})^2 + (x_2 - \overline{x})^2 + \ldots + (x_n - \overline{x})^2}{n}}$

Graphing Calculator Tip

$\sqrt{\ }$ means "square root." Press the $\sqrt{\ }$ key first, then enter the data.

Example 2 Finding Measures of Dispersion

Find the range and standard deviation for the following sets of data.

a. 5, 7, 12, 14, 17

SOLUTION

The range is the difference between the largest and smallest data values.

The range is 17 − 5 = 12.

To find the standard deviation, first calculate the mean.

$$\overline{x} = \frac{5 + 7 + 12 + 14 + 17}{5} = \frac{55}{5} = 11$$

$$\sigma = \sqrt{\frac{(5 - 11)^2 + (7 - 11)^2 + (12 - 11)^2 + (14 - 11)^2 + (17 - 11)^2}{5}}$$

$$= \sqrt{\frac{98}{5}} \approx 4.4$$

b. 10, 12, 7, 11, 20, 7, 6, 8, 9

SOLUTION

The range is 20 − 6 = 14.

To find the standard deviation, first calculate the mean.

$$\overline{x} = \frac{10 + 12 + 7 + 11 + 20 + 7 + 6 + 8 + 9}{9} = \frac{90}{9} = 10$$

$$\sigma = \sqrt{\frac{(10 - 10)^2 + (12 - 10)^2 + \ldots + (8 - 10)^2 + (9 - 10)^2}{9}}$$

$$\sigma = \sqrt{\frac{0^2 + 2^2 + \ldots + (-2)^2 + (-1)^2}{9}} = \sqrt{\frac{144}{9}} = \sqrt{16} = 4$$

The standard deviation is 4.

An **outlier** is an item in a data set that is much larger or much smaller than the other items in the set. The presence of an outlier in a set of data can have a misleading effect on the measures of central tendency and dispersion.

Example 2

Remind students that they must perform the operations in parentheses first. Second, they must square the difference for each term. Third, they must add all of the products together. Fourth, they must divide the sum by the divisor. Finally, they must take the square root.

Additional Example 2

Find the range and standard deviation for the following sets of data.

a. 3, 4, 5, 7, 9
range: 6; standard deviation: ≈2.2

b. 12, 13, 15, 16, 17
range: 5; standard deviation: ≈1.9

ENGLISH LEARNERS

For this lesson, explain the meaning of the word **deviation.** Say:

"Deviation means something that is not considered normal."

For example, the behavior of someone that is acting very rudely toward another person is considered a deviation from normal or standard behavior. In math, a standard deviation is a measure of how far data points are from a standard—the mean.

A low standard deviation means that the data points are very close in value to the mean. A high standard deviation means the data points are scattered farther away in value from the mean.

Data set with a low standard deviation:

11, 12, 12, 13, 13

Data set with a high standard deviation:

11, 15, 25, 36, 45

Example 3

Have student volunteers explain in their own words what an outlier is and why it gives a misleading effect on central tendency and dispersion.

Additional Example 3

Identify the outlier in the data set. Then find the mean, median, mode, range, and standard deviation of the data set when the outlier is included and when it is not.

3, 3, 6, 6, 6, 7, 8, 9, 35

outlier: 35; range with outlier: 32; range without outlier: 6; mode with and without outlier: 6; median with outlier: 6; median without outlier: 6; mean with outlier: 9.2; mean without outlier: 6; standard deviation with outlier: 9.3; standard deviation without outlier: 2

Caution

Be sure to reduce the number of data items by the number of outliers before calculating mean and standard deviation.

Math Reasoning

Verify Use a graphing calculator to check the solution in Example 3.

Example 3 Examining the Effect of an Outlier

Identify the outlier in the data set. Then find the mean, median, mode, range, and standard deviation of the data set when the outlier is included and when it is not.

2, 2, 3, 3, 4, 4, 4, 6, 68

SOLUTION

The outlier is 68.

The range with the outlier is $68 - 2 = 66$.

The range without the outlier is $6 - 2 = 4$.

The mode with and without the outlier is 4.

The median with the outlier is 4.

The median without the outlier is 3.5, which is the mean of the numbers 3 and 4.

The mean with the outlier is:

$$\overline{x} = \frac{2 + 2 + \ldots + 68}{9} = \frac{96}{9} \approx 10.7$$

The mean without the outlier is:

$$\overline{x} = \frac{2 + 2 + \ldots + 6}{9} = \frac{28}{8} = 3.5$$

The standard deviation with the outlier is:

$$\sigma = \sqrt{\frac{(2 - 10.7)^2 + \ldots + (68 - 10.7)^2}{9}} = \sqrt{\frac{3710.01}{9}} \approx \sqrt{412.2} \approx 20.3$$

The standard deviation without the outlier is:

$$\sigma = \sqrt{\frac{(2 - 3.5)^2 + \ldots + (6 - 3.5)^2}{8}} = \sqrt{\frac{12}{8}} = \sqrt{1.5} \approx 1.2$$

One convenient way to organize data is with a **box-and-whisker plot.**

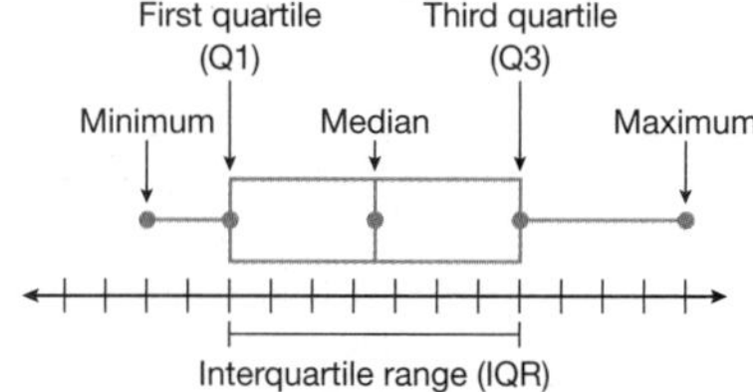

The **first quartile** is the median of the lower half of the data set. The **third quartile** is the median of the upper half of the data set.

Example 4 Organizing Data with a Box-and-Whisker Plot

Draw a box-and-whisker plot to display the following data:

31, 29, 28, 20, 35, 22, 32, 22, 32.

SOLUTION

Write the data in ascending order: 20, 22, 22, 28, 29, 31, 32, 32, 35.

The median of the data is 29.

The lower quartile 22 is the median of the lower half of the data.

The upper quartile 32 is the median of the upper half of the data.

The minimum is 20. The maximum is 35.

Draw the box-and-whisker plot.

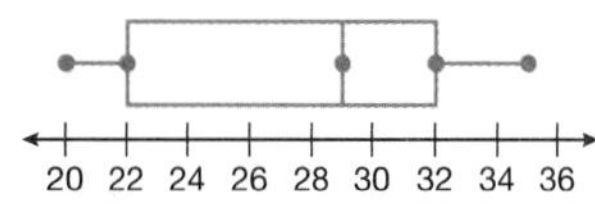

Reading Math

σ is the lower case Greek letter sigma and represents standard deviation. $\bar{x}$ is read "x bar" and represents the mean.

Example 5 Application: Sports

The National League leaders in home runs for the 2003 through 2006 seasons are found in the table below. What was the mean number of home runs hit by the league leader for those seasons and what was the standard deviation for that statistic?

Season	Leader	Home Runs
2003	Jim Thome	51
2004	Adrian Beltre	48
2005	Andruw Jones	47
2006	Ryan Howard	49

SOLUTION

The mean is $\bar{x} = \frac{51 + 48 + 47 + 49}{4} = \frac{195}{4} = 48.75$.

The standard deviation is

$$\sigma = \sqrt{\frac{(51 - 48.75)^2 + \ldots + (49 - 48.75)^2}{4}} = \sqrt{\frac{8.75}{4}} = \sqrt{2.1875} \approx 1.5.$$

Lesson Practice

a. (Ex 1) Jacob paid the following dollar amounts for lunch in one week: 4.5, 6.5, 7, 5, 7, 5, 7. Calculate the mean, median, and mode for Jacob's lunch costs. Mean: 6; Median: 6.5; Mode: 7

b. (Ex 2) Find the range and standard deviation for the following set of data: 11, 8, 2, 7, 12. Range: 10; Standard deviation: 3.5

c. (Ex 2) Find the range and standard deviation for the following set of data: 14, 9, 19, 16, 8, 17, 25, 21, 15. Range: 17; Standard deviation: 5.1

d. (Ex 3) Identify the outlier in the data set {6, 4, 7, 47, 5, 5, 6, 5}. Then find the mean, median, mode, range, and standard deviation of the data set when the outlier is included and when it is not.

d. The outlier is 47. The range with the outlier is 43. The range without the outlier is 3. The mode with and without the outlier is 5. The median with the outlier is 5.5. The median without the outlier is 5. The mean with the outlier is 10.6. The mean without the outlier is 5.4. The standard deviation with the outlier is 13.8. The standard deviation without the outlier is 0.9.

INCLUSION

This lesson contains several new vocabulary terms. Suggest that students use index cards to review the definitions for each new term. Have students write the new term on one side of the index card and the definition on the other side. Students should also include on the definition side of the card an example of how to calculate the value and any formulas needed.

Example 4

Error Alert Make sure students use the median to create their box-and-whisker plots instead of mean or mode.

Additional Example 4

Draw a box-and-whisker plot to display the following data:

32, 44, 42, 34, 40, 34, 33, 30, 46

median: 34; lower quartile: 32.5; upper quartile: 43; minimum: 30; maximum: 46

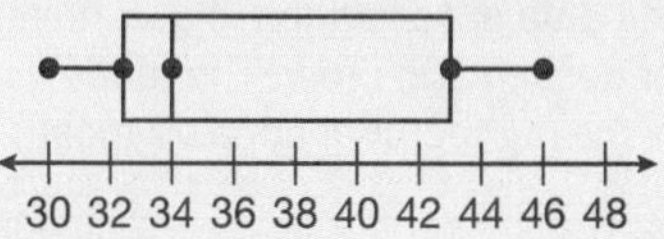

Example 5

Extend the Example

Have students create a box-and-whisker plot for the home run data in the example.

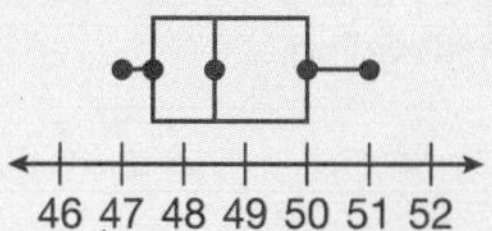

Additional Example 5

The highest averages of the students in Mr. Rogers's Algebra II class are shown in the table below. What is the mean of the scores and the standard deviation?

Student	Average
Alfonso	93
Bobbi Jo	91
Raul	98
Matsuko	90

mean: 93; standard deviation: ≈3.1

Lesson Practice

Problem a

Error Alert Remind students to check the definitions of the terms before they make their calculations to ensure they are calculating the correct value.

e.

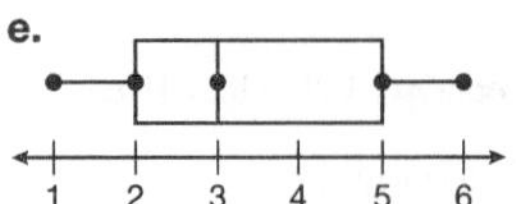

e. (Ex 4) Draw a box-and-whisker plot to display the following data: 3, 5, 1, 2, 4, 2, 6.

f. (Ex 5) Annual snowfall amounts in inches for Buffalo, New York, for 2000–2007 are listed in the table.

What was the mean amount of snowfall in Buffalo during those years and what was the standard deviation? The mean is about 111.4. The standard deviation is about 25.1.

Season	Amount (inches)
2000–01	158.7
2001–02	132.4
2002–03	111.3
2003–04	100.9
2004–05	109.1
2005–06	78.2
2006–07	88.9

Practice Distributed and Integrated

Simplify each expression using the properties of real numbers.

1. (1) $-5[(2-1-3)-(5-8)-6]$ 25

2. (1) $2(2-6)-(-1-1)-3$ −9

3. (3) Simplify: $-3x^6(x^{-1}y^{-8})^{-3}$ $-3x^9y^{24}$

4. (10) Solve for x and graph the solution. $3x+1>x+13$ $x>6$

−8 −6 −4 −2 0 2 4 6 8

5. (9) Find the product $\begin{bmatrix}-2 & 10\\ 3 & 2\end{bmatrix}\times\begin{bmatrix}-1 & 0\\ 0 & 1\end{bmatrix}$. $\begin{bmatrix}2 & 10\\ -2 & 3\end{bmatrix}$

6. (19) Simplify the product: $3x^2(2x^2-3x)$. $6x^4-9x^3$

***7.** (23) Factor the polynomial: $2x^2+9x-5$. $(x+5)(2x-1)$

Solve each system of linear equations using substitution.

8. (21) $4x+y=-11$, $-x+y=9$ $x=-4, y=5$

9. (21) $x+y=4$, $x-y=6$ $x=5, y=-1$

Find the mean and median for each data set.

***10.** (25) {2, 2, 3, 10, 11, 13, 15} mean: 8; median: 10

***11.** (25) {1, 2, 3, 3} mean: 2.25; median: 2.5

***12.** (25) {1, 1, 13, 15, 14} mean: 8.8; median: 13

***13.** (23) **Geometry** The area of a new window is $x^2-24x+144$ in^2. What are the dimensions of the new window? $l=x-12$ in., $w=x-12$ in.

14. (20) **Multiple Choice** Given $f(x)=-3x+11$ and $g(x)=4x-10$, find $(f+g)(12)$. B

A −9 **B** 13 **C** 85 **D** 105

Problem e

Scaffolding Suggest that students make their box-and-whisker plot on graph paper.

Check for Understanding

The questions below help assess the concepts taught in this lesson.

"What is the difference among the terms mean, median, and mode?" Sample: The mean is the average of the numbers. The median is the number in the middle, when the data are arranged in ascending or descending order. The mode is the number that appears most frequently.

"What is an outlier and how does it affect the measures of central tendency and dispersion?" Sample: An outlier is a number that is much smaller or larger than the other numbers in the data set. An outlier will make some measures of central tendency and dispersion inaccurate and misleading.

3 Practice

Math Conversations

Discussion to strengthen understandings

Problem 1

Guide students by asking them the following question.

"What is the order of operations?" Parentheses, Exponents, Multiplication and Division from left to right, Addition and Subtraction from left to right

Solve each system using elimination.

*15. (24) $\begin{cases} 5x + y = 19 \\ -2x - y = -7 \end{cases}$ (4, −1)

*16. (24) $\begin{cases} -x + 3y = 12 \\ 6x - y = -21 \end{cases}$ (−3, 3)

*17. (24) $\begin{cases} 2x + y = 8 \\ x - y = 10 \end{cases}$ (6, −4)

18. (11) **Write** Describe how the graph of polynomial function $P_1 + P_2$ compares to the graph of polynomial function P_1 if P_2 does not equal 0, but has degree 0. Explain.

18. The graph of $P_1 + P_2$ is a vertical translation (shift) of the graph of P_1. Possible explanation: If P_2 does not equal 0, but has degree 0, then it is a nonzero constant function. So, $P_1 + P_2$ is the function obtained by adding the nonzero constant P_2 to P_1.

19. (18) **Drumming** Mike "Da Man" Mangini holds the title as the world's fastest drummer. At the 2005 Summer NAMM Session, Mike drummed out 1,247 singles in 60 seconds.

a. How many singles could Mike drum in one hour? 74,820 singles

b. Not only does Mike have fast hands, he has fast feet, pounding down a toe-stomping 13,222 singles with his feet in 15 minutes. How many singles could Mike drum with his feet in one hour? 52,888 singles

c. How much faster does Mike drum with his hands than with his feet? 21,932 more singles per hour

20. (23) **Quilting** Kylie is making a rectangular quilt out of 4 inch squares. So far, her quilt is 36 inches by 56 inches. She wants to add a border around her quilt that is the same number of squares on each side. A standard twin comforter covers approximately 4800 square inches.

a. How many squares should she add to each side if she wants her quilt to cover the same area? 3

b. Verify that her quilt will cover the same area. Adding a border of 3, is the same as adding 24 inches to each side. Therefore (36 + 24)(56 + 24) = 4800 sq. inches.

21. (9) **Data Analysis** Alea, Cory, and Troy had lunch together. Alea bought 1 drink, 2 sandwiches, and 2 snacks. Cory bought 2 drinks, 2 sandwiches, and 1 snack. Troy bought 2 drinks, 1 sandwich, and 3 snacks. The cost of a drink is \$1.50, a sandwich is \$4.00, and a snack is \$1.00.

a. Organize the information into the tables below.

Lunch

Person	Drink	Sandwich	Snack
Alea	1	2	2
Cory	2	2	1
Troy	2	1	3

Cost	
Drink	\$1.50
Sandwich	\$4.00
Snack	\$1.00

b. Create two matrices to represent the tables in part a.

c. Who spent the most money? Cory

21b. Lunch = $\begin{bmatrix} 1 & 2 & 2 \\ 2 & 2 & 1 \\ 2 & 1 & 3 \end{bmatrix}$ Cost = $\begin{bmatrix} 1.50 \\ 4.00 \\ 1.00 \end{bmatrix}$

*22. (14) **Graphing Calculator** a. Write the determinant as an equation. $2x^2 - 32 = 0$

$$\begin{vmatrix} -x & 2 & -2 \\ 0 & -3 & 1 \\ 8 & 2x & 0 \end{vmatrix} = 0$$

b. Solve for x. $x = 4$ or $x = -4$

c. Check your answer by substituting for x and finding the determinant with a graphing calculator.

22c. $\begin{vmatrix} -4 & 2 & 2 \\ 0 & -3 & -1 \\ 8 & 8 & 0 \end{vmatrix} = 0$; $\begin{vmatrix} 4 & 2 & -2 \\ 0 & -3 & 1 \\ 8 & -8 & 0 \end{vmatrix} = 0$

CHALLENGE

Haley and her grandfather decide to make a rectangular patio. If one side of the patio is $(3x - 7)$ and the other side is $(2x - 5)$ what is the expression that represents the area of the new patio?

$(3x - 7)(2x - 5) = 6x^2 - 29x + 35$

Problem 19

Error Alert

A common error for students is the failure to make the correct unit conversions. Remind students that there are 60 seconds in one minute and 60 minutes in one hour.

Problem 21

Extend the Problem

What are the mean and median for the lunch totals? mean: \$11.17; median: \$11.50

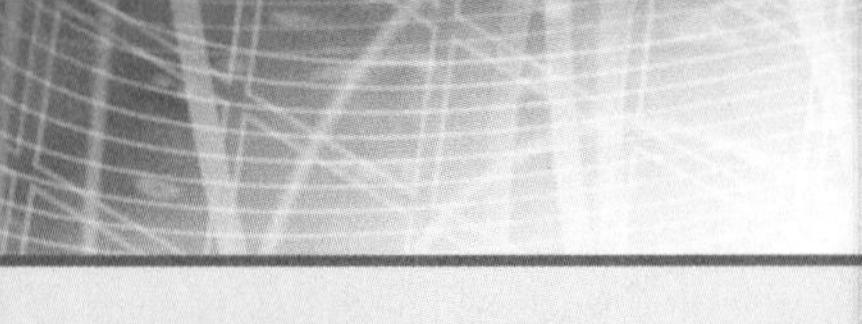

Problem 23

Error Alert

Remind students that the per minute charge does not occur until over 250 minutes are used. The variable in their equation must be for the minutes over 250 minutes, not the total minutes used in the month.

Problem 25

Guide students by asking them the following questions.

"What is the formula for the area of a square?" Area = (length of side)^2

"What is the length of one side in this problem?" $(2x - 5)$

"What is the formula for the area of this square?" Area = $(2x - 5)^2$

Problem 30

Guide students by asking them the following question.

"What is the definition of a direct variation relationship?" A relationship between two variables whose ratio is constant.

Extend the Problem

"Suppose that you made 64 ounces of pasta. How many servings did you make?" 32

23. (7) **Multi-Step** A cell phone plan costs \$29.95 a month and \$0.40 per minute used over 250 minutes. There is a one time only activation fee of \$25.00. The first month's bill is \$114.95.

a. Write an equation to solve for the minutes over 250 used. $29.95 + 0.40m + 25 = 114.95$

b. Solve the equation from part **a**. $m = 150$ minutes

c. Show the work to check the answer to part **b**.

23c. $29.95 + 0.40(150) + 25 = 29.95 + 60 + 25 = 114.95$

d. How many total minutes were used? 400 minutes

***24.** (24) **Formulate** Create a linear system that requires that both equations be multiplied by a constant before they are added together. Tell which constants should be used and why.

24. Possible answer: $\begin{cases} 5x + 2y = 7 \\ 3x - 9y = -6, \end{cases}$ multiply the first equation by 3 and the second by −5 so that the coefficients of the x-terms are 15 and −15. 15 is the LCM of 5 and 3.

25. (19) **Write** The length of one side of a square patio is represented by the expression $(2x - 5)$. Write an expression that represents the area of the patio.
$(2x - 5)^2 = 4x^2 - 20x + 25$

26. (17) **Exercise** For a 30-year-old to work out within her cardio range, her heart rate should be within 24 beats per minute of 147 bpm.

a. Write an absolute-value equation to determine the lowest and highest heart rate at which she will be in her cardio range. $|x - 147| = 24$

b. Solve the equation. $x = 123$ or 171

27. (13) **Error Analysis** Ani is asked find the slope of the line through the points (11, 6) and (7, 4), and then to tell whether the line rises or falls. Her solution is shown below. Identify whether there is an error in her solution. If so, give the correct solution.

Ani's solution:

$\frac{4 - 6}{7 - 11} = \frac{-2}{-4} = \frac{1}{2}$, so $m = \frac{1}{2}$. Because the slope is a fraction, the line falls.

27. The line does not fall. The slope is correct, but the line rises because the slope is positive.

28. (22) Determine if each graph is continuous, discontinuous, and/or discrete. Determine if each graph is a function or a relation. Determine the domain and range of each.

a.

b.

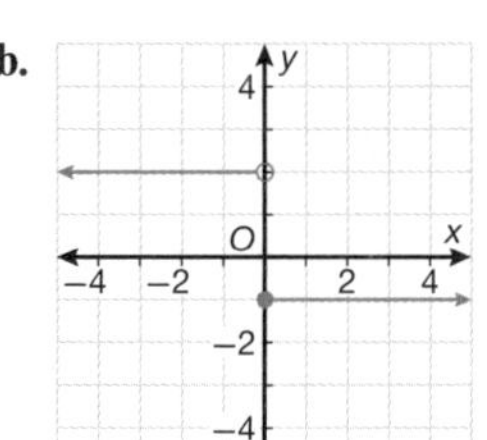

28a. Continuous function; Domain: all real numbers; Range: $y \geq 0$
b. Discontinuous function; Domain: all real numbers; Range: −1, 2

***29.** (25) **Skateboarding** The table below shows the number of Americans who participated in skateboarding more than once during 1997–2000. Find the mean and standard deviation of the data. Mean: 8.7; Standard deviation: ≈ 1.71.

Year	1997	1998	1999	2000
Participants (in millions)	8.2	7.2	7.8	11.6

30. (8) **Analyze** The table shows the amount of pasta required for each number of servings. Is this a direct variation relationship? If so, what is the constant of variation? If not, explain why. Yes; the constant of variation is 2.

Servings	Pasta
4	8 oz
13	26 oz
17	34 oz
29	58 oz

LOOKING FORWARD

Finding measures of central tendency and dispersion prepares students for

- **Lesson 73** Using Sampling
- **Lesson 80** Finding the Normal Distribution
- **Lesson 118** Recognizing Misleading Data

LESSON 26

Writing the Equation of a Line

Warm Up

1. **Vocabulary** A _______ line has an undefined slope. vertical
(13)

2. Calculate the slope of the line that contains the points $(-2, 3)$ and $(4, -1)$.
(13) 2. $-\frac{2}{3}$

3. Identify the slope and y-intercept of the line $y = 2x - 5$.
(13) slope = 2; y-int. = -5

4. **Multiple-Choice** Which line has a slope of 0? A
(13)
 - **A** A line that contains $(-2, -2)$ and $(7, -2)$
 - **B** A line that contains $(4, -2)$ and $(-1, 2)$
 - **C** A line that contains $(5, -7)$ and $(3, -2)$
 - **D** A line that contains $(0, 0)$ and $(5, 5)$

5. Find the slope of the line described by $2x + 3y = 12$. $-\frac{2}{3}$
(13)

New Concepts

Linear equations are often written in slope-intercept form because that is the easiest way to sketch a graph.

Hint

The slope-intercept form of a line is $y = mx + b$, where m = slope and b = y-intercept.

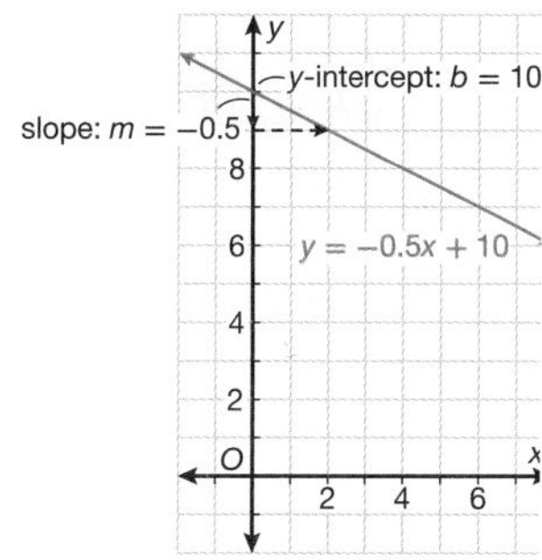

However, an equation is often written in another form. For example, suppose you have $30 dollars to spend on pens and notebooks. Notebooks are $3 each and pens are $1.50 per package. The following equation models all the possible combinations of pen and notebook purchases.

Let x = the number of packages of pens

Let y = the number of notebooks

$$1.5x + 3y = 30$$

This equation is written in standard form. Solving for y in the equation gives the slope-intercept form.

$$y = -0.5x + 10$$

The **standard form of a linear equation** is written below. For an equation in standard form, A, B, and C are real numbers and A and B are not both zero.

$$Ax + By = C$$

Online Connection
www.SaxonMathResources.com

LESSON 26

1 Warm Up

Remind students that the slope of a line is $\frac{\text{rise}}{\text{run}}$.

2 New Concepts

In this lesson, students learn to write the equation of a line in different forms.

Explain that the graph of a line is the same whether its equation is written in standard form, slope-intercept form, or point-slope form. The form of the equation of the line can depend on what is known about the line. For example, if the slope and y-intercept are known, it is natural to use slope-intercept form. If the slope and a point other than the y-intercept are known, or if two points on the line are known, point-slope form would be used. If you know the equation of the line in one form, you can always write the equation in any of the other forms.

MATH BACKGROUND

Students have already used equations to graph lines and are familiar with finding the slope of a line.

It is important that students can efficiently solve equations for a given variable. Students need this skill to translate among the different forms of linear equations.

LESSON RESOURCES

Student Edition Practice Workbook 26
Reteaching Masters 26
Adaptations Masters 26
Challenge and Enrichment Master C26

Example 1

Work through the steps of writing the equation in standard form if necessary.

Extend the Example

Use the equation written in standard form to show that 20°C is equivalent to 68°F.
$5(68) - 9(20) = 160$; $160 = 160$

Additional Example 1

Write the equation in standard form.

$y = -\frac{1}{2}x + 7x + 2y = 14$

Example 2

Remind students that you must know both the slope and the y-intercept of a line to use the slope-intercept form.

Additional Example 2

A line has slope -10 and crosses the y-axis at the point $(0, -5)$. What is the equation of the line written in slope-intercept form?
$y = -10x - 5$

Example 3

Tell students point-slope form can be used when you know the slope of the line and a point other than the y-intercept.

Extend the Example

Have students find the y-intercept of the line. 32

Additional Example 3

A line has slope $-\frac{2}{3}$ and passes through the point $(-2, 5)$. What is the equation of this line written in slope-intercept form?
$y = -\frac{2}{3}x + \frac{11}{3}$

Example 1 Writing an Equation in Standard Form

The equation for converting Fahrenheit temperatures (F) to Celsius (C) is written in this form:

$$F = \frac{9}{5}C + 32$$

Write the equation in standard form.

SOLUTION

Step 1: Move all terms with variables to the same side of the equation.

$$F - \frac{9}{5}C = 32$$

Step 2: Multiply by a factor that results in integer coefficients for F and C and an integer on the right side of the equation. Multiply both sides by 5.

$$5F - 9C = 160$$

> **Math Reasoning**
>
> **Verify** The Fahrenheit-Celsius formula is based on the fact that water boils at 212°F and 100°C, and water freezes at 32°F and 0°C. Use these coordinates to verify the accuracy of the formula.
>
> $212 = \frac{9}{5}(100) + 32$
> $212 \stackrel{?}{=} 180 + 32$
> $212 = 212$ ✓
> $32 = \frac{9}{5}(0) + 32$
> $32 \stackrel{?}{=} 0 + 32$
> $32 = 32$ ✓

If you know the slope m and the y-intercept b of a line, then you can write the equation of the line. The slope-intercept form of a linear equation is written as:

$$y = mx + b.$$

Example 2 Writing an Equation in Slope-Intercept Form

A line has slope 3 and crosses the y-axis at the point $(0, 7)$. What is the equation of this line written in slope-intercept form?

SOLUTION

Recall the slope-intercept form of a linear equation: $y = mx + b$. For this equation $m = 3$ and $b = 7$. Substitute the known values in the equation.

$$y = 3x + 7$$

If you know the slope m and an ordered pair (x_1, y_1) of any point on the line, then you can use the **point-slope form** to write the equation of the line.

$$y - y_1 = m(x - x_1)$$

Example 3 Using the Point-Slope Formula

A line has slope -2 and passes through the point $(10, 12)$. What is the equation of this line written in slope-intercept form?

SOLUTION

Substitute the known values into the point-slope form of the linear equation, then solve the equation for y to write in slope-intercept form.

$$y - 12 = -2(x - 10)$$
$$y = -2x + 20 + 12$$
$$y = -2x + 32$$

ENGLISH LEARNERS

To help students better understand the forms for the equation of a line, discuss the meaning of the word **form**.

The word form has many different meanings in the English language. Some meanings include:

"the shape and structure of something as distinguished from its material"

"a printed or typed document with blank spaces for insertion of requested information"

The meaning of the word for this lesson is:

"a mathematical expression of a particular type"

Stress that no matter what form is used to write the equation, the graph of the equation is the same line.

Math Reasoning

Justify Explain how the slope formula and the point-slope formula are related.

The slope formula is the point-slope formula solved for m.

If you know the coordinates of two points on a line, you can use these to find the slope, m. To find the slope, solve the point-slope form of the equation to find a formula for m:

$$m = \frac{y - y_1}{x - x_1}$$

Once you have calculated m, you can substitute the value of m and one of the points in the point-slope form, then solve for y to write the equation in slope-intercept form.

Example 4 Writing the Equation of a Line Given Two Points

The chart below shows the number of units sold for a new product and the amount left to reach before the product breaks even and then becomes profitable. The points are graphed and shown to be part of the same line. Write the equation of this line in slope-intercept form.

Units Sold	Amount Before Break Even
1,000	−5,000
2,000	−2,500
3,000	0

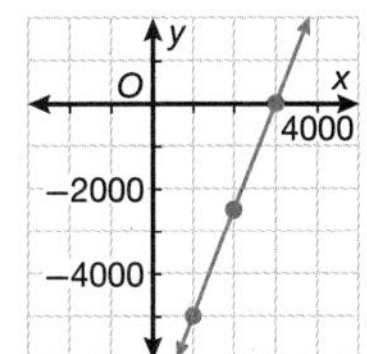

SOLUTION

Step 1: Use the formula for slope with any two points to find the value of m.

Let $(x, y) = (1000, -5000)$ and $(x_1, y_1) = (2000, -2500)$.

$$m = \frac{y - y_1}{x - x_1}$$

$$m = \frac{-5000 + 2500}{1000 - 2000}$$

$$= \frac{-2500}{-1000}$$

$$= 2.5$$

Step 2: Use the point-slope form with one of the points given, then solve for y to find the equation in slope-intercept form.

$$y - (-5000) = 2.5(x - 1000)$$

$$y - (-5000) = 2.5(x - 1000)$$

$$y + 5000 = 2.5x - 2500$$

$$y = 2.5x - 7500$$

ALTERNATE METHOD FOR EXAMPLE 4

Students can use the point (3000, 0) when finding the slope and writing the equation of the line. This eliminates some steps in calculation.

$$m = \frac{-5000 - 0}{1000 - 3000} = \frac{-5000}{-2000} = 2.5$$

$$y - 0 = 2.5(x - 3000)$$

$$y = 2.5x - 7500$$

Example 4

In this example the slope of the line is not known. Review the slope formula with students.

$$m = \frac{y - y_1}{x - x_1}$$

Extend the Example

Have students find the slope of the line using the points (2000, −2500) and (3000, 0) to see that the slope is the same as found in the example.

Additional Example 4

The chart shows the amount of money earned for hours worked. The relationship is linear. Write the equation of the line in slope-intercept form.

Hours	Amount Earned (dollars)
20	175
28	245
36	315

$y = 8.75x$

Example 5

This example uses the skills learned in Example 4 to model a real-world situation.

Additional Example 5

A cellular phone company charges a one-time setup fee and a monthly charge. The table shows data for the total cost based on the number of months. Use the data to write the equation of the line in slope-intercept form.

Months	Total Cost (dollars)
2	115
5	235
10	435

$y = 40x + 35$

Lesson Practice

Problem c

Error Alert Watch for students who think -24 is the y-intercept and write the equation as $y = 1.5x - 24$. Ask **"What is the point $(-24, 0)$?"** Samples: The point where the line crosses the x-axis. -24 is the x-intercept.

Check for Understanding

The questions below help assess the concepts taught in this lesson.

1. **"The equation of a line is written in slope-intercept form. Explain how to change the equation of the line to standard form."** Sample: Collect all terms containing variables on one side of the equation.

2. **"Explain how to find the y-intercept of the line $-10x + 5y = 30$."** Sample: Solve the equation for y to put the equation in slope-intercept form, $y = mx + b$. The value of b is the y-intercept.

Math Reasoning

Analyze The equation that can be used to predict the height of a child has an infinite domain and range. How does this affect the accuracy of the equation?

Since people stop growing in height after a certain age, the equation will no longer apply after a certain age.

Example 5 Mathematical Modeling with Linear Equations

The Centers for Disease Control has developed growth charts that pediatricians use to see if a child's height is within a certain average. The chart shows data for a boy's height in the 50th percentile. The three points lie on a line. Use the data to write the equation of the line in slope-intercept form.

Age (years)	Height (inches)
2	35
3	37.5
5	42.5

SOLUTION

Step 1: Use the formula for slope with any two points to find m.

Let $(x, y) = (3, 37.5)$ and $(x_1, y_1) = (5, 42.5)$.

$$m = \frac{y - y_1}{x - x_1}$$
$$= \frac{37.5 - 42.5}{3 - 5}$$
$$= \frac{-5}{-2}$$
$$= 2.5$$

Step 2: Use the point-slope form with one of the points given, then solve for y to find the equation in slope-intercept form.

$$y - 35 = 2.5(x - 2)$$
$$y = 2.5x - 5 + 35$$
$$y = 2.5x + 30$$

Lesson Practice

a. (Ex 1) The equation for converting Celsius (C) temperatures to Fahrenheit (F) is usually written in the form $C = \frac{5}{9}(F - 32)$. Write the equation in standard form. $5F - 9C = 160$

b. (Ex 2) A line with a slope of -2 crosses the y-axis at the point $(0, 15)$. What is the equation of this line written in slope-intercept form? $y = -2x + 15$

c. (Ex 3) A line with a slope of 1.5 passes through the point $(-24, 0)$. What is the equation of this line in slope-intercept form? $y = 1.5x + 36$

d. (Ex 4) A line passes through points $(10, 0)$ and $(16, 12)$. What is the equation of the line written in slope-intercept form? $y = 2x - 20$

e. (Ex 5) A coastal city is tracking the movements of a hurricane that is expected to make landfall in the region. The table shows the distance from landfall for successive days. These points are on the same line when graphed. Write the equation of this line in slope-intercept form.
$y = -125x + 625$

Day	Distance from landfall (miles)
1	500
2	375
3	250

CHALLENGE

Find the slope of the line $15x - 8y = 3$.
$m = 1.875$

Practice Distributed and Integrated

Classify each polynomial by degree and number of terms.

1. (11) $3x^4$ quartic; monomial

2. (11) $-x^3 + 5x$ cubic; binomial

3. (11) $2x^2 - 5x + 1$ quadratic, trinomial

4. (5) Find the sum: $\begin{bmatrix} 0 & 1 \\ 1 & 0 \end{bmatrix} + 6\begin{bmatrix} 2 & -2 \\ -3 & 1 \end{bmatrix}$ $\begin{bmatrix} 12 & -11 \\ -17 & 6 \end{bmatrix}$

5. (18) Convert 450 feet to yards. 150 yards

Factor each polynomial.

***6.** (23) $-15x^2 + 5x$ $-5x(3x - 1)$

***7.** (23) $4x^2 - 9$ $(2x + 3)(2x - 3)$

***8.** (23) $6x^2 + 19x - 7$ $(3x - 1)(2x + 7)$

***9.** (25) Find the mode of the data set: {100, 120, 128, 128, 129, 130, 130}. 128, 130

Find the equation of the line that passes through the two points given.

***10.** (26) (0, 3) and (4, −4) $y = -\frac{7}{4}x + 3$

***11.** (26) (1, 5) and (4, 2) $y = -x + 6$

***12.** (26) (−3, 2), (5, 0) $y = -\frac{1}{4}x + \frac{5}{4}$

13. (1) **Analyze** Identify which property of real numbers is being demonstrated. Explain why this property might be helpful in solving this problem without a calculator.

$$(4 \cdot 6) \cdot 5 = 4 \cdot (6 \cdot 5) = 4 \cdot 30 = 120$$

13. Associative Property of Multiplication; $(6 \cdot 5)$ is a multiple of 10, so it is easier to multiply $4 \cdot 30$ than $24 \cdot 5$.

14. (22) **Multi-Step** **a.** Graph $y = x^2 + 2$.

14a.

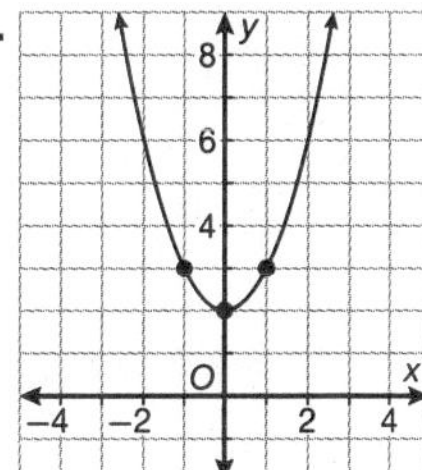

b. Is this relation a function? yes

c. Determine if the graph is continuous, discontinuous, and/or discrete. continuous function

15. (7) **Multiple Choice** Choose the letter that best represents the solution to the equation: $\frac{2}{5}c + 3 = -5c + \frac{3}{4}$. D

A $-2\frac{2}{5}$ **B** $\frac{12}{13}$ **C** $\frac{1}{11}$ **D** $-\frac{5}{12}$

16. (10) **Geometry** Write a compound inequality using the fact that the sum of the lengths of any two sides of a triangle is greater than the length of the third side (Triangle Inequality) using the diagram. (*Hint*: Remember that length cannot be negative.) $2 < x < 10$

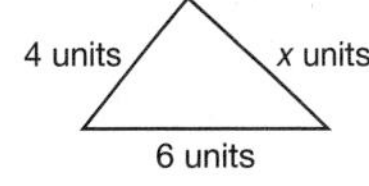

***17.** (23) **Multi-Step** A homeowner painted her bathroom. She has a mirror that is 30 inches high and 20 inches wide. She decides to decrease both mirror dimensions by the same amount, and she will now have to paint the newly exposed wall. She only has enough paint to cover 225 square inches.

a. Calculate the new area of the mirror. $(30)(20) - 225 = 375$ square inches;

b. Write and solve an equation to find out how much she should decrease each dimension. $(30 - x)(20 - x) = 375$, so $x^2 - 50x + 225 = 0$ gives $(x - 5)(x - 45) = 0$. She should decrease each dimension by 5 inches.

3 Practice

Math Conversations

Discussions to strengthen understanding.

Problem 13

Extend the Problem

"How can you use the property to solve (12 × 15) × 2 without using a calculator?" Sample: Multiply 15 × 2, then multiply that product by 12. 15 × 2 = 30; 12 × 30 = 360.

INCLUSION

Students may have difficulty distinguishing among the different forms for the equation of a line. Have students underline key words in the problem statement to help them decide which form to use based on the information given.

Problem 23

Error Alert

Students may attempt to solve the problem using a single linear equation. Explain that this is a mixture problem and is solved using a system of linear equations.

"What are the two unknowns in the problem?" the number of pounds of Sumatra beans in the blend and the number of pounds of Kona Hawaiian beans in the blend

"What does each equation in the system represent?" One equation represents the total number of beans in the blend and the other represents the cost.

18. (Inv 2) **Soccer** Mia Hamm is running with the ball and is about to make a chip shot aiming to kick the ball above the goalie's head. Mia is 31 feet from the goal and kicks the ball at a horizontal speed of 14 feet per second and a vertical speed of 37 feet per second.

In t seconds, the soccer ball will travel x and y feet. The parametric equations that the ball will travel are

$$x = 14t$$
$$y = -16t^2 + 37t$$

a. How many seconds does it take the ball to travel to the goal? Round your answer to the nearest hundredth of a second. 2.21 seconds

b. The goalie is 5.5 feet tall and the goal is 8 feet tall. If the ball lands below the goalie's head, it is assumed that the goal has been blocked. Will Mia make the goal? Explain why or why not.

18b. No. The ball will reach the goal, but only at a height of 3.6 feet, meaning that the goal has been blocked.

19a.

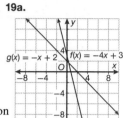

19. (20) **Multi-Step** Given $f(x) = -4x + 3$ and $g(x) = -x + 2$.

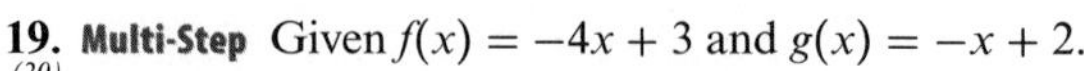

a. Graph $f(x)$ and $g(x)$ on the same grid.

b. Graph the difference $(f - g)(x)$.

c. Use algebra to verify the difference $(f - g)(x)$.
$(f - g)(x) = -4x + 3 - (-x + 2) = -4x + 3 + x - 2 = -3x + 1$

20. (13) **Error Analysis** The work below uses the slope-intercept form of a linear equation to graph the equation $3x - 2y = 9$. Inspect the work. Is it correct? If not, explain the error and find the correct solution. If it is correct, explain in words each step of the work.

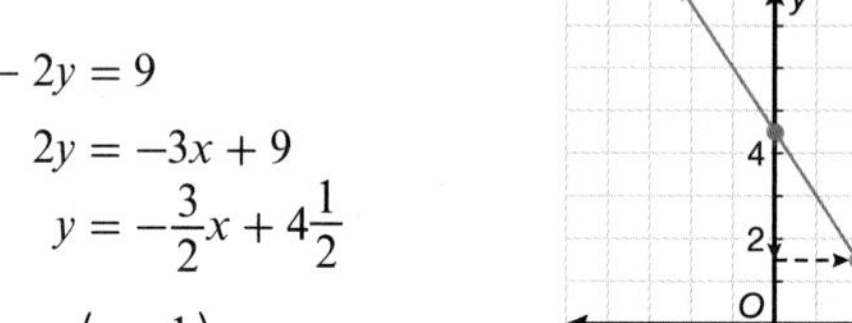

$$3x - 2y = 9$$
$$2y = -3x + 9$$
$$y = -\frac{3}{2}x + 4\frac{1}{2}$$

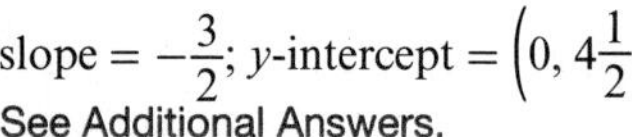

slope $= -\frac{3}{2}$; y-intercept $= \left(0, 4\frac{1}{2}\right)$

See Additional Answers.

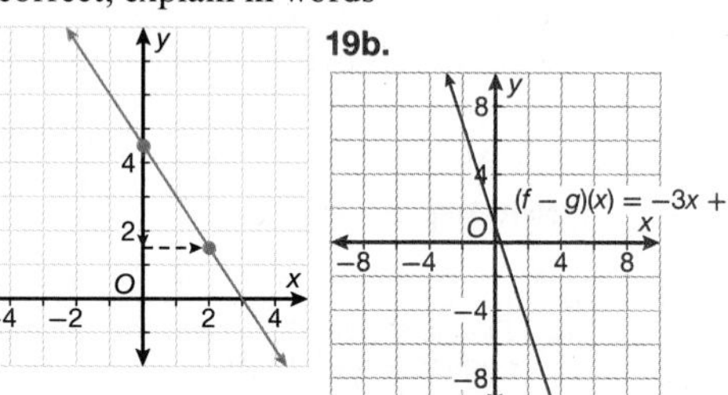

21. (17) **Fitness** An adult is considered to be in a healthy weight range if his or her BMI is within 3.2 of 21.7.

a. Write an absolute value inequality to determine the minimum and maximum BMI range that is considered healthy. $|x - 21.7| < 3.2$

b. Solve the inequality. $18.5 < x < 24.9$

22. (18) **Running** The record for the fastest mile ever run by a human belongs to Hicham El Guerrouj of Morocco. He ran one mile in 3.719 minutes. Determine El Guerrouj's speed in miles per hour. about 16.133 mph

23. (21) **Coffee** A coffee blend contains Sumatra beans, which cost \$12/lb, and Kona Hawaiian beans, which cost \$45/lb. If the blend costs \$30/lb, about how much of each type of coffee is in 50 lb of the blend?

23. Let s represent the total weight of Sumatra beans and k represent the total weight of Kona beans in the blend. For the first equation, $12s + 45k = 30(s + k)$, so $s = \frac{5}{6}k$.
$s = \frac{5}{6}k$
$s + k = 50$
Substituting the first equation for s into second equation, $\frac{5}{6}k + k = 50$. So, $k = 27.3$ lb. Then, $s = 22.7$ lb.

***24.** (24) **Write** Explain how using the elimination methods to solve systems with infinitely many solutions is similar to and different from using the elimination method to solve systems with no solutions. See Additional Answers.

CHALLENGE

Find the slope of the line $\frac{1}{10}(y - 3) = x + 5$
$m = 10$

25. Verify Find the determinant using expansion by minors. Verify the solution using a graphing calculator. 11
(14)

$$\begin{vmatrix} -1 & 2 & -2 \\ 2 & 4 & 1 \\ -1 & 1 & -3 \end{vmatrix}$$

***26. Justify** Is the equation $2\pi x + 3y = 20$ in standard form? Explain your reasoning.
(26)

26. Yes, this equation is in standard form. The number π is a real number and part of the coefficient of x. For this equation, $a = 2\pi$.

27. Data Analysis Amara, Kate, and Ava are all taking a test where each type of question is given a certain point value. Use matrix multiplication to find out who scored the greatest number of points on the test.
(9)

Questions Answered Correctly

	Type 1	Type 2	Type 3
Amara	2	3	7
Kate	5	5	4
Ava	9	6	3

Point Value

Type 1	4
Type 2	6
Type 3	8

27. $\begin{bmatrix} 2 & 3 & 7 \\ 5 & 5 & 4 \\ 9 & 6 & 3 \end{bmatrix}\begin{bmatrix} 4 \\ 6 \\ 8 \end{bmatrix} = \begin{bmatrix} 82 \\ 82 \\ 96 \end{bmatrix}$

Ava scored the greatest number of points.

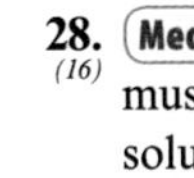

28. Medicine A 7% saline (salt) solution can help people with cystic fibrosis, but it must be mixed by hand from commercially available solutions of 0.9% and 10% solutions. About how much of each commercial solution is needed to make 6 mL of the 7% solution?
(16)

a. Set up equations relating the number of mL of each solution to the saline concentrations. Let a represent the number of mL of the 0.9% solution and b the number of mL of the other solution.

b. Use Cramer's Rule to solve the system of equations.

28b. $b = \dfrac{\begin{vmatrix} 1 & 6 \\ 0.009 & 0.42 \end{vmatrix}}{\begin{vmatrix} 1 & 1 \\ 0.009 & 0.1 \end{vmatrix}} = \dfrac{0.375}{0.091} \approx$ 4 mL of 10% solution

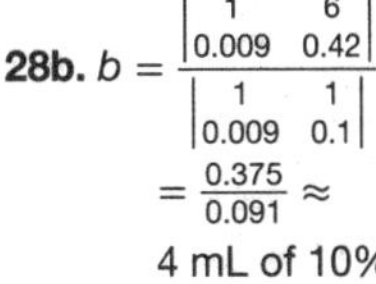

***29. Graphing Calculator** When you step on the brakes to stop a car, the car still continues forward. The distance traveled is called the "stopping distance." The faster a car is moving, the longer the stopping distance. The table shows the stopping distance at three different speeds for a passenger car traveling on dry pavement. Use the linear regression capabilities of your graphing calculator to write an equation in slope-intercept form for the stopping distance. $y = 3.55x - 79.4$
(26)

Initial Traveling Speed (mile/hour)	Stopping Distance (feet)
35	46.430
49	91.097
62	142.364

28a. $a + b = 6$
$0.009a + 0.1b = 0.07(6) = 0.42$

$a = \dfrac{\begin{vmatrix} 6 & 1 \\ 0.42 & 0.1 \end{vmatrix}}{\begin{vmatrix} 1 & 1 \\ 0.009 & 0.1 \end{vmatrix}} = \dfrac{0.18}{0.091} \approx 2$ mL of 0.9% solution

30. Write Explain how to multiply $(x + 2)(2x - 1)$ using the FOIL method. You multiply the first terms in each binomial $(x)(2x)$, then multiply the outer terms $(x)(-1)$, then multiply the inner terms $(2)(2x)$, and then the last terms $(2)(-1)$. Combine like terms together to simplify; $2x^2 + 3x - 2$.
(19)

Problem 28

Error Alert

Students may accidentally write the system interchanging the variables in the equations. Tell students to define each of the variables, and double check the information given about each of the variables before writing the equations.

Problem 29

Extend the Problem

Have students graph the linear equation on their graphing calculators. Discuss with students why it is necessary to write an equation in slope-intercept form to graph it using the graphing calculator.

LOOKING FORWARD

Writing the equation of a line prepares students for:

- **Lesson 34** Graphing Linear Equations II
- **Lesson 36** Using Parallel and Perpendicular Lines
- **Lesson 39** Graphing Linear Inequalities in Two Variables

LESSON 27

1 Warm Up

Remind students for Problem 4 that the square of a binomial written in the form $(a + b)^2$ is $a^2 + 2ab + b^2$.

2 New Concepts

In this lesson, students learn the standard form of a quadratic function and construct and examine the graph of a quadratic function.

Example 1b

Remind students of the order of operations and discuss why $(x - 4)^2$ was performed before the 2 was distributed.

Additional Example 1

a. Write $2y + 2 = 5x^2 + 7x$ in standard form.
$y = \frac{5}{2}x^2 + \frac{7}{2}x - 1$

b. Write $f(x) = -3(x + 4)^2 + 5$ in standard form.
$f(x) = -3x^2 - 24x - 43$

LESSON 27

Connecting the Parabola with the Quadratic Function

Warm Up

1. **Vocabulary** An equation of the form $3x - 6 = 9$ is a <u>linear</u> equation. (7)
2. Find the x- and y-intercepts of $6x - 4y = -12$. $x = -2, y = 3$ (13)
3. Identify the domain and range of the equation $y = |x|$. D: all real numbers, R: $y \geq 0$ (17)
4. Multiply: $(x + 8)(x + 8)$. $x^2 + 16x + 64$ (19)

New Concepts

A **quadratic equation** is one that can be written in the form $ax^2 + bx + c = 0$, where $a \neq 0$. Examples of quadratic equations include $x^2 = 25$, $3x^2 - 8 = 1$, and $-2x^2 - 8x = 0$.

A **quadratic function** is a function that can be written in the form $f(x) = ax^2 + bx + c$, which is called **standard form of a quadratic function,** where $a \neq 0$ and a, b, and c are real numbers. Because $f(x) = y$, a quadratic function can also be written as $y = ax^2 + bx + c$.

Caution

Remember to follow the order of operations when simplifying $f(x) = 2(x - 4)^2 + 9$. Square $(x - 4)$ before distributing the 2.

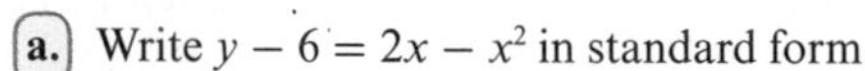

Example 1 Converting to Standard Form

a. Write $y - 6 = 2x - x^2$ in standard form.

SOLUTION

Isolate y and list the terms in decreasing order.

$$y - 6 = 2x - x^2$$
$$y = 2x - x^2 + 6$$
$$y = -x^2 + 2x + 6$$

b. Convert $f(x) = 2(x - 4)^2 + 9$ into standard form.

SOLUTION

Expand and simplify.

$$f(x) = 2(x - 4)^2 + 9$$
$$= 2(x^2 - 8x + 16) + 9$$
$$= 2x^2 - 16x + 32 + 9$$
$$= 2x^2 - 16x + 41$$

Online Connection
www.SaxonMathResources.com

The parent function of a quadratic function is $f(x) = x^2$. So, in standard form, $a = 1$, $b = 0$, and $c = 0$.

LESSON RESOURCES

Student Edition Practice Workbook 27
Reteaching Masters 27
Adaptations Masters 27
Challenge and Enrichment Masters C27

MATH BACKGROUND

Students are familiar with linear equations and the different forms of linear equations including standard form, $Ax + By + C = 0$. The standard form of a quadratic equation $ax^2 + bx + c = 0$ is similar to other polynomial equations of degree greater than or equal to 1 written in standard form. For example, the standard form of a cubic equation is $ax^3 + bx^2 + cx + d = 0$.

Each of these equations can be converted to a function in standard form by replacing 0 with $f(x)$. Generally, the standard form is helpful in identifying types of equations, since the variable with the highest degree is written first in standard form.

The graph of the parent function, $f(x) = x^2$, is shown below.

x	−3	−2	−1	0	1	2	3
y	9	4	1	0	1	4	9

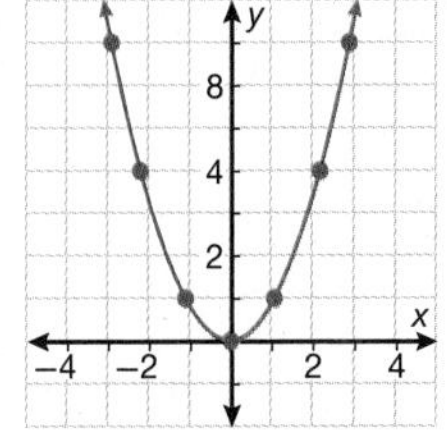

This curve is called a **parabola.** The graph of every quadratic function is a parabola. All parabolas have the same symmetric U shape. For the graph of $f(x) = x^2$, the point (0, 0) is the **vertex of the parabola.** The vertex indicates where the curve changes direction. It is the lowest (or highest) point on a parabola.

The **zeros** of a quadratic function are the values of x for which the function equals 0. Therefore on the graph of a quadratic function, the zeros are the x-intercepts, or where the graph intersects the x-axis. The y-intercept is the point where the graph intersects the y-axis and can be calculated by substituting x with 0.

Math Reasoning

Analyze In standard form, the value of c is always the y-intercept. Why?

When 0 is substituted for x into the equation, the value of the expression is c.

Exploration Finding the Zeros and Vertex of a Parabola

Find the zeros and vertex of $y = -x^2 + 3x - 2$.

1. Graph $y = -x^2 + 3x - 2$.
2. Press 2nd TRACE to access the **CALC** menu and select **2: zero.** Choose a point to the left and to the right of one of the x-intercepts and press enter; the coordinates of the first root (x-intercept) will be displayed. Repeat for the other x-intercept. What are the x-intercepts? 1 and 2

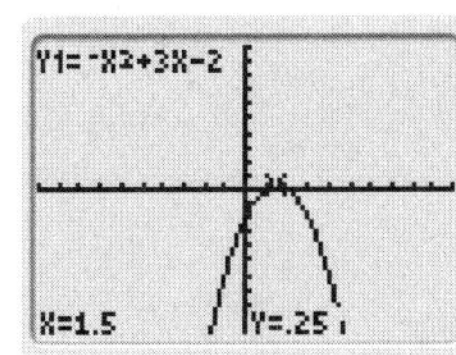

3. To find the y-intercept, press TRACE and enter 0, after **X=.** What is the y-intercept? −2
4. Since the vertex is halfway between the x-intercepts, the x-coordinate of the vertex is $\frac{1+2}{2}$, or 1.5. With TRACE still chosen, enter 1.5 for x.

What is the y-value? Where is the vertex located? 0.25; (1.5, 0.25)

The **TABLE** menu, which can be accessed from 2nd GRAPH, can also be helpful when analyzing the graph of a quadratic function. The x-intercepts can be found by locating zeros in the second column.

X	Y1
-3	-20
-2	-12
-1	-6
0	-2
1	0
2	0
3	-2

X=1

Exploration

Extend the Exploration

Graph the function $y = x^2 - 4x + 3$. Find the zeros and vertex of the function.

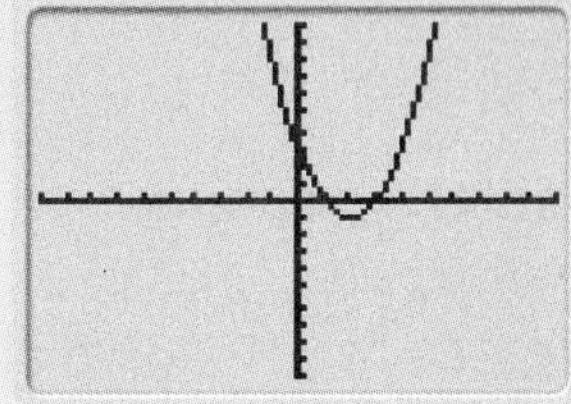

The zeros are 1 and 3. The vertex is (2, −1).

ENGLISH LEARNERS

There are many new vocabulary words in this lesson including vertex, parabola, and quadratic.

Discuss and reinforce the meanings of each vocabulary word.

The **vertex** of a parabola is its lowest or highest point. Have student name other figures with vertices, such as triangles and quadrilaterals, and discuss how their vertices are similar to and different from the vertex of a parabola.

Lesson 27 195

Example 2

Since parabolas are symmetric, suggest that students choose number pairs that are reflections of each other over the axis of symmetry when making a table of values.

Extend the Example

Have students graph $f(x) = 2x^2 - x - 6$. Discuss how the graph of this function differs from the graph of the function $f(x) = x^2 - x - 6$.

The graph of $f(x) = 2x^2 - x - 6$ is narrower.

Additional Example 2

a. Graph $f(x) = x^2 + 6x + 9$.

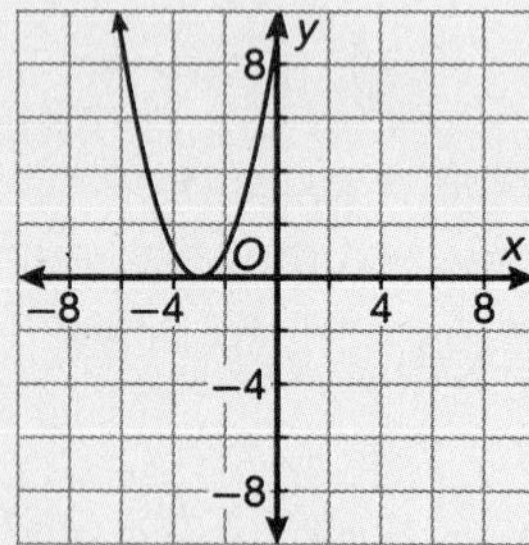

b. Identify the x- and y-intercepts of $f(x) = x^2 + 6x + 9$.
x-intercept: $(-3, 0)$
y-intercept: $(0, 9)$

c. Identify the domain and range of $f(x) = x^2 + 6x + 9$.
The domain is all real numbers.
The range is all real numbers greater than or equal to 0.

When working with quadratic equations in standard form, the x-coordinate of the vertex of the parabola can be found using $x = -\frac{b}{2a}$. The y-coordinate can then be found using substitution. The vertex is on the axis of symmetry of the parabola.

The **axis of symmetry** is a line that divides a figure into two congruent mirror images. Therefore, the **reflection** of each point on the left side of a parabola is located on the right side of the parabola. The equation of the axis of symmetry is $x = -\frac{b}{2a}$.

Example 2 Graphing Quadratic Functions

a. Graph $f(x) = x^2 - x - 6$.

SOLUTION Use $x = -\frac{b}{2a}$ to find the x-coordinate of the vertex, then substitute to find the y-coordinate.

$$x = -\frac{b}{2a} = -\frac{(-1)}{2(1)} = \frac{1}{2}$$

$$y = x^2 - x - 6 = \left(\frac{1}{2}\right)^2 - \left(\frac{1}{2}\right) - 6 = -6\frac{1}{4}$$

Vertex: $\left(\frac{1}{2}, -6\frac{1}{4}\right)$; Axis of symmetry: $x = \frac{1}{2}$.

Plot the axis of symmetry and the vertex.

Next, make a table of ordered pairs. Plot the points and connect with a smooth line.

x	$x^2 - x - 6$	y
−3	$(-3)^2 - (-3) - 6$	6
−2	$(-2)^2 - (-2) - 6$	0
−1	$(-1)^2 - (-1) - 6$	−4
0	$(0)^2 - (0) - 6$	−6
1	$(1)^2 - (1) - 6$	−6
2	$(2)^2 - (2) - 6$	−4
3	$(3)^2 - (3) - 6$	0

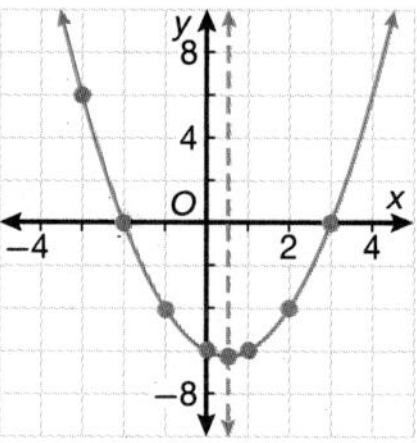

b. Identify the x- and y-intercepts of $f(x) = x^2 - x - 6$ on its graph. Then use a calculator to determine the exact values.

SOLUTION The x-intercepts are the x-coordinates of the points where the graph intersects the x-axis at $(-2, 0)$ and $(3, 0)$. The y-intercept is the y-coordinate of the point where the graph intersects the y-axis at $(0, -6)$.

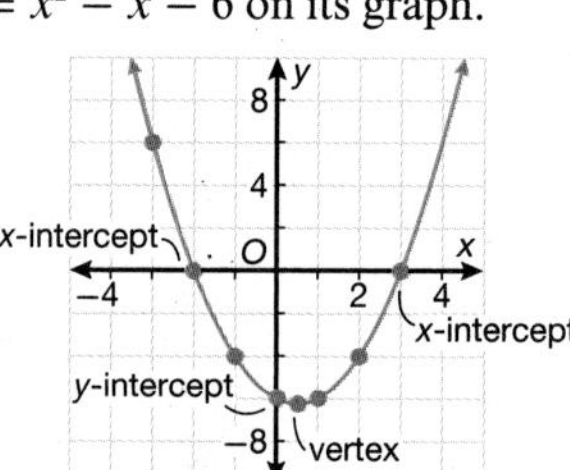

196 Saxon Algebra 2

ALTERNATE METHOD FOR EXAMPLE 2

Since the graph of a parabola is symmetric and the vertex is the turning point of the parabola, the vertex occurs on the axis of symmetry midway between the x-intercepts. So, rather than use $x = -\frac{b}{2a}$ to find the x-coordinate of the vertex, the average of the x-intercepts will give the same result. In both cases, the x-value will be substituted into the quadratic function to find the y-coordinate of the vertex.

c. Identify the domain and range of $f(x) = x^2 - x - 6$.

SOLUTION The domain consists of the x-values. Any real number can be squared, so the domain is the set of all real numbers. The range consists of all the possible outputs. The parabola has a vertex at $(0.5, -6.25)$. There are no outputs below the vertex. Therefore, the least possible value for $f(x)$ is -6.25. The range is all real numbers greater than or equal to -6.25.

The height of an object that is dropped can be modeled by the quadratic function $h(t) = -16t^2 + b$, where t is the time in seconds, and b is the original height the object is dropped from. To find the time it takes to reach the ground, find the t-intercept where $h(t) = 0$.

Hint

Even if the graph of a quadratic function has two zeros, one of them may not make sense in a real-world application and can therefore be ignored.

Example 3 Application: Engineering

A bridge built over a stream can be modeled on the coordinate plane by the function $f(x) = -\frac{1}{4}x^2 + 16$, where the x-axis represents ground level and the units on the graph represent feet. Find the horizontal distance the bridge spans.

SOLUTION

Understand The question asks for the distance between where the bridge touches the ground on either side of the stream.

Plan Find the x-intercepts and use their values to find the distance.

Solve Use a graphing calculator. The intercepts are -8 and 8.

Because the axis of symmetry is the y-axis, add the absolute values of the x-intercepts: $8 + 8 = 16$. The bridge spans a distance of 16 feet.

Check The **TABLE** feature confirms that $y = 0$ when $x = -8$ and 8.

Lesson Practice

a. *(Ex 1)* Write $11 - x^2 = y + 7x$ in standard form. $y = -x^2 - 7x + 11$

b. *(Ex 1)* Convert $f(x) = -(x + 1)^2 - 5$ into standard form. $f(x) = -x^2 - 2x - 6$

c. *(Ex 2)* Graph $f(x) = x^2 - 5x + 4$.

d. *(Ex 2)* Estimate the x- and y-intercepts and the coordinates of the vertex of $f(x) = x^2 + 11x + 28$ from its graph. Then use a calculator to determine the exact values.

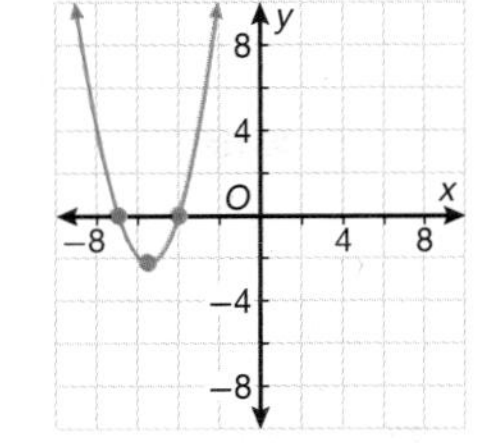

e. *(Ex 2)* Identify the domain and range of $f(x) = -x^2 - 4.5$.

f. *(Ex 3)* A coin is thrown off the roof of a building that is 35 feet above the sidewalk. The height of the coin, in feet, at any second, x, during the fall can be found using the function $f(x) = -16x^2 + 35$. How long does it take for the coin to hit the sidewalk? Round your answer to the nearest hundredth of a second. About 1.48 seconds

c.

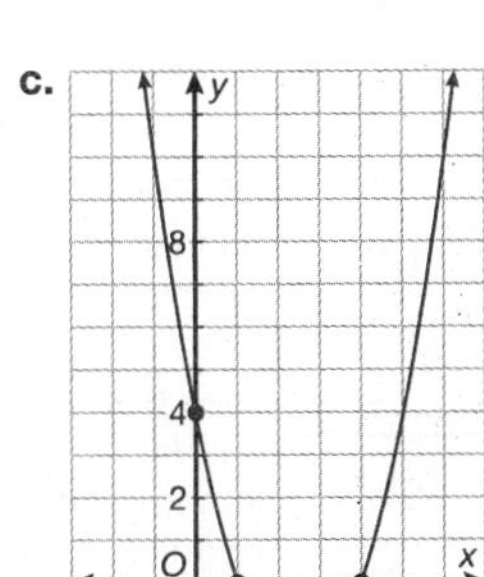

d. $x = -7$, $x = -4$, $y = 28$, $(-5.5, -2.25)$

e. D: all real numbers; R: all real numbers less than or equal to -4.5

Example 3

Make sure students understand why the function is quadratic. Discuss the characteristics of the equation that make it a quadratic function.

Additional Example 3

An arch is modeled on the coordinate plane by the function $f(x) = -\frac{1}{5}x^2 + 20$, where the x-axis represents ground level and the units on the graph represent feet. Find the horizontal distance the arch spans. 20 feet

Lesson Practice

Problem b

Error Alert Students may distribute the -1 before squaring $(x + 1)$. Ask, **"Which operation is performed first according to the order of operations?"** squaring the binomial in parentheses

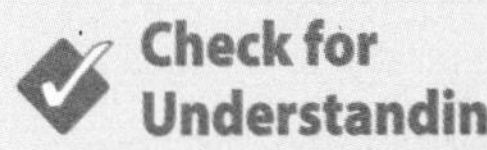

Check for Understanding

The questions below help assess the concepts taught in this lesson.

1. **"How is the axis of symmetry helpful when graphing a parabola?"** Sample: It is helpful because after two or three points are plotted to the right (or left) side of the axis of symmetry, those points can be reflected over the axis of symmetry. Then a smooth curve can be drawn through the plotted points.
2. **"How do you write a quadratic equation in standard form?"** Sample: Isolate y on one side of the equation and list the terms in decreasing order of degree.

CHALLENGE

A ball is dropped from a height of 60 feet. How long does it take the ball to reach the ground?
about 1.9 seconds

3 Practice

Math Conversations

Discussions to strengthen understanding

Problem 6

"What is the first step in factoring the polynomial?" Factor out the common monomial factor 2. **"What is the next step?"** Factor the trinomial into two binomials.

Problem 9

Extend the Problem

Have students identify the slope of the line. $m = 2$

Practice Distributed and Integrated

Convert each function to standard form.

*1. (27) $f(x) = (2x + 3)^2$ $f(x) = 4x^2 + 12x + 9$

*2. (27) $f(x) = 2(x + 5) + x^2$ $f(x) = x^2 + 2x + 10$

*3. (27) $f(x) = (x - 5)^2$ $f(x) = x^2 - 10x + 25$

Graph each function.

*4. (27) $f(x) = (-x + 1)^2$

*5. (27) $f(x) = x^2 - 3$

4.

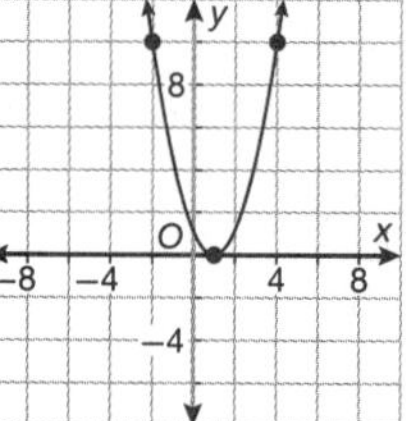

5.

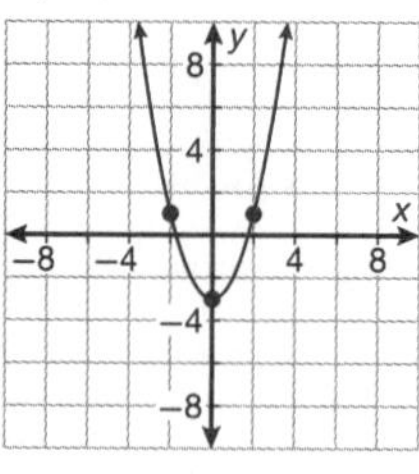

Factor each polynomial.

6. (23) $2x^2 - 4x - 30$ $2(x + 3)(x - 5)$

7. (23) $-4x^3 + 20x^2 + 12x$ $-4x(x^2 - 5x - 3)$

8. (18) Convert 3 liters per minute to milliliters per second. 50 mL/sec

9. (13) Identify the y-intercept given the linear equation $y - 4 = 2(x - 2)$. (0, 0)

Find the constant of variation for the given values of x and y given that x varies inversely with y.

10. (12) $x = 3, y = 12$ 36

11. (12) $x = 10, y = 5$ 50

12. (12) $x = 4, y = 9$ 36

*13. (24) **Multi-Step** Shirley has 47 coins in a jar. The jar contains only dimes and nickels and the value of the coins is \$3.20.

a. Using d for dimes and n for nickels, write an equation representing the number of coins. $d + n = 47$

b. Write an equation to show that the value of the dimes plus the value of the nickels is \$3.20 in all. $0.10d + 0.05n = 3.20$

c. Write and solve a linear system to find the number of dimes and number of nickels in Shirley's jar. $d + n = 47$, $0.10d + 0.05n = 3.20$ 17 dimes and 30 nickels

14. (7) Solve the equation for r: $3(5r - 10) = 8(2r - 4) + 5r$. B

A $r = \frac{1}{4}$ B $r = \frac{1}{3}$ C $r = 2$ D $r = 3$

*15. (27) **Justify** Tell why the range of a quadratic function will never be the set of all real numbers.

16. (21) **Write** Without solving the system, can you tell how many solutions this system of equations has? Explain.

$$y + 1 = 3x$$
$$2y - 6x = -2$$

17. (12) **Geometry** Identify the kind of variation each equation represents.

a. Volume of a rectangular prism = length × width × height joint

b. Volume of a cube = $(\text{length})^3$ direct

15. Sample: The range values will always be ≥ the minimum or ≤ the maximum value of the function, which will be a subset of the real numbers.

16. The system has an infinite number of solutions because the lines overlap and share all points in common. Each coefficient in the second equation is simply twice the coefficient in the first equation. So, solving for y in each equation gives the same result, $y = 3x - 1$.

INCLUSION

Help students write an algorithm of the steps for finding the zeros of the function and vertex of a parabola using a graphing calculator.

18. Multiple Choice Choose the letter that best represents the graph of $y = -4x + 2$. C
(13)

A
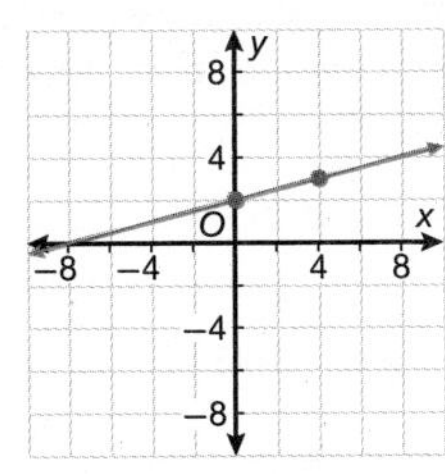

B
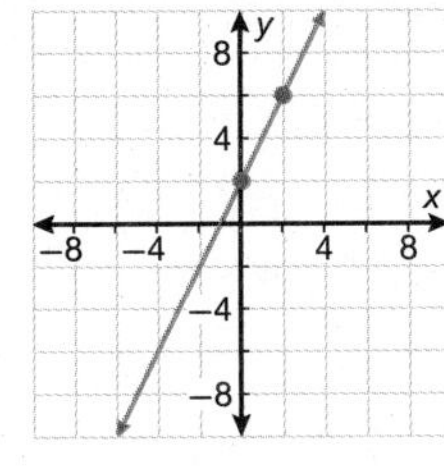

C
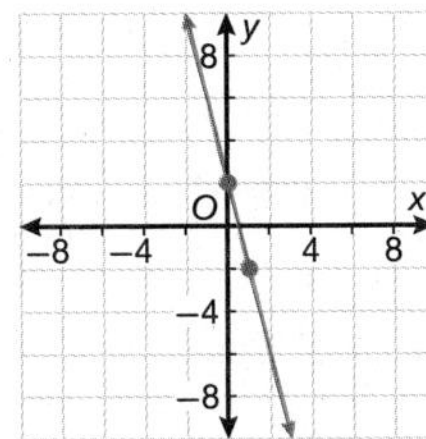

D
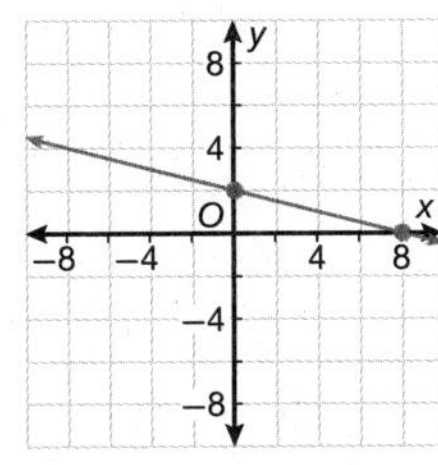

***19. Multi-Step** A rectangular wooden deck is 40 feet long and 30 feet wide. The owner wants to increase the width and length to double the area of the deck. He also wants the increase in length to be twice as much as the increase in width.
(23)

a. Calculate the new area of the deck. $2(40)(30) = 2400$ square feet

b. Write and solve an equation to find out how much the owner should increase each dimension. $(40 + 2x)(30 + x) = 2400$; length: 20 feet, width: 10 feet

***20. Error Analysis** Two students were asked which of these lines coincide. Their answers are below. Which student is correct? What is the relationship between the lines of the incorrect answer? Randy is correct. Equations 1 and 3 are parallel.
(21)

Equation 1: $y + 3x = 7$ Equation 2: $y = -3x + 5$ Equation 3: $10 - 2y = 6x$

Becky: Equations 1 and 3 coincide.

Randy: Equations 2 and 3 coincide.

21. Justify Justify the claim that the determinant of the product of matrices $\begin{bmatrix} 3.1 & -2.2 \\ 0.6 & 4.5 \end{bmatrix}$ and $\begin{bmatrix} -1.9 & 4.8 \\ -2.2 & 3.0 \end{bmatrix}$ equals the product of the determinants of these matrices.
(14)

22. Fuel Economy A dragster can consume 6 gallons of gasoline in $\frac{1}{4}$ mile. What is the fuel economy in miles per gallon? How far would a car with a 20-gallon tank get before needing a refill? $\frac{0.25 \text{ miles}}{6 \text{ gallons}} \approx 0.042$ miles per gallon.; $\frac{0.042 \text{ miles}}{1 \text{ gallon}} \times 20$ gallons $= 0.84$ miles.
(18)

23. Imports The total imports of goods and services, in millions of dollars, for the U.S. in 2004, 2005, and 2006 was 5,971,007. The imports in 2005 were 228,100 more than in 2004 and 206,784 less than in 2006. What were the imports in millions of dollars in 2005? 1,997,441
(7)

21. $\left|\begin{bmatrix} 3.1 & -2.2 \\ 0.6 & 4.5 \end{bmatrix}\begin{bmatrix} -1.9 & 4.8 \\ -2.2 & 3.0 \end{bmatrix}\right| = \begin{vmatrix} -1.05 & 8.28 \\ -11.04 & 16.38 \end{vmatrix} = 74.2122$

$\begin{vmatrix} 3.1 & -2.2 \\ 0.6 & 4.5 \end{vmatrix} \times \begin{vmatrix} -1.9 & 4.8 \\ -2.2 & 3.0 \end{vmatrix} = 15.27 \times 4.86 = 74.2122$

Problem 18
Extend the Problem

Have students find the equation of the line in choice D.
$y = -\frac{1}{4}x + 2$

Problem 20

"What is another name for a system whose lines coincide?"
a dependent system

Lesson 27 199

Problem 27

Extend the Problem

Ask students if the data includes an outlier. no

24. (19) While buying a bird feeder, Karl discovers one in the shape of a rectangular prism. Karl is trying to determine the volume of bird food that the feeder will hold. He knows that the dimensions are as follows:

Length: x inches   Width: $(x - 3.75)$ inches   Height: $(x - 0.25)$ inches

Write an expression for the volume of the bird feeder that Karl can use in his calculations. $(x)(x - 3.75)(x - 0.25) = (x^2 - 3.75x)(x - 0.25) = x^3 - 4x^2 + 0.9375x$

25. (11) **Error Analysis** A student says that the polynomial $ab^4 + a^2b^2 - 3$ is of higher degree than the polynomial $a^2b^3 + ab + 2$. Is this correct? Explain.

25. The polynomials have the same degree, 5 The monomial with greatest degree in the first polynomial is ab^4, which has degree 5, and the monomial with greatest degree in the second polynomial is a^2b^3, which also has degree 5.

26. (20) **Statistics** The proceeds for three major fundraisers are represented by $f(x) = 35x - 100$, $g(x) = 52x - 60$, and $h(x) = 100x - 250$. Write a function $m(x)$ that would represent the mean of the proceeds in terms of x.

***27.** (25) The table shows the average salaries of various engineering jobs in 2006. Find the range and median of this data. Range: from \$43,679 to \$61,156 = \$17,477; Median: \$50,236

Job	Aerospace	Agricultural	Civil	Computer	Environmental	Mechanical	Petroleum
Average Salary	\$50,993	\$46,172	\$43,679	\$52,464	\$47,384	\$50,236	\$61,156

28. (17) **Verify** Show that $|1 - 3x| = 5x$ has two solutions, one of which is extraneous.

***29.** (26) **Medicine** The Centers for Disease Control has developed growth charts that pediatricians use to see if a child's height is within a certain average. The chart shows data for a girl's height in the 50th percentile. The three points are on a line. Use the data to write the equation of the line in slope-intercept form. $y = 3x + 28$

Age (years)	Height (inches)
3	37
4	40
5	43

***30.** (9) **Graphing Calculator** $A = \begin{bmatrix} -5 & 3 \\ 1 & 2 \end{bmatrix}$ $B = \begin{bmatrix} -6 & 0 \\ 0 & -6 \end{bmatrix}$ Use a graphing calculator to find AB and BA. Is $AB = BA$?

$AB = \begin{bmatrix} 30 & -18 \\ -6 & -12 \end{bmatrix}$ $BA = \begin{bmatrix} 30 & -18 \\ -6 & -12 \end{bmatrix}$; Yes

26. $m(x) = \frac{(f(x) + g(x) + h(x))}{3} = \frac{(35x - 100) + (52x - 60) + (100x - 250)}{3} = \frac{187x - 410}{3}$

28. $x = \frac{1}{8}$ is a solution of the equation because $\left|1 - 3\left(\frac{1}{8}\right)\right| = 5\left(\frac{1}{8}\right)$. $x = -\frac{1}{2}$ is an extraneous solution because $5\left(-\frac{1}{2}\right) = -\frac{5}{2}$ and absolute value can never equal a negative number.

LOOKING FORWARD 

Connecting the parabola with the quadratic function prepares students for:

- **Lesson 30** Applying Transformations to the Parabola and Determining the Minimum or Maximum
- **Lesson 35** Solving Quadratic Equations I
- **Lesson 39** Graphing Linear Inequalities in Two Variables

Simplifying Rational Expressions

Warm Up

1. **Vocabulary** A polynomial is a monomial or the sum or difference of monomials. (11)

2. Multiply $-4x^2(6x^2y^3 + 2xy^2 - 1)$. $-24x^4y^3 - 8x^3y^2 + 4x^2$ (19)

3. Factor $-12x^6 + 15x^5y$. $-3x^5(4x - 5y)$ (23)

4. Which is a difference of squares? D (23)
   A $(16x^2 + y^2)$ B $(8 - 4y^2)$ C $(9 - 50y^6)$ D $(x^{10} - 100)$

New Concepts

A **rational expression** is the quotient of two polynomials, such as $\frac{2x^2+4x-4}{x+3}$, with a denominator of a degree that is greater than or equal to one. As with any fraction, the denominator cannot equal zero. Therefore, $\frac{2x^2+4x-4}{x+3}$ is not defined when $x = -3$ because $-3 + 3 = 0$.

In any function, an excluded value is a domain value that makes the function undefined. For the function above, -3 is an excluded value. Not all rational expressions have excluded values and some have more than one excluded value.

No excluded values	More than one excluded value
$\frac{-3x-6}{4}$, $\frac{4x^2+16}{x^2+1}$	$\frac{5}{x^2+3x+2}$, excluded values: -1 and -2

Math Reasoning

Analyze Why will the expression $x^2 + 1$ never be equal to 0 for any value of x?

The square of any number is either 0 or a positive number, so when 1 is added, the denominator is a positive number.

A rational expression is simplified when there are no common factors, other than 1, in the numerator and denominator.

Simplified	Not simplified
$\frac{x^3}{2}$, $\frac{x+3}{x+4}$	$\frac{x^6y^2}{x^4}$, common factor: x^4 $\frac{(x+3)(x-7)}{(x-7)}$, common factor: $(x-7)$

Rational expressions with monomial numerators and denominators are best simplified by using the Quotient of Powers Property, which states that to divide two powers with the same base, subtract the exponents.

Quotient of Powers Property
For $a \neq 0$, and integers m and n, $\frac{a^m}{a^n} = a^{m-n}$.

Online Connection
www.SaxonMathResources.com

LESSON 28

1 Warm Up

Remind students to use the Power of a Power Property to write x^{10} as $(x^5)^2$.

2 New Concepts

In this lesson, students learn how to simplify rational expressions.

Discuss the definitions of rational expression and excluded value. Discuss the difference between a rational expression that is simplified and one that is not. A rational expression is simplified when the numerator and denominator have no common factors other than 1.

Students will use the Quotient of Powers Property to simplify monomial numerators and denominators.

MATH BACKGROUND

Students are familiar with simplifying fractions whose numerators and denominators are integers. A fraction is simplified when its numerator and denominator have no common factor other than 1. The same is true for a rational expression. The difference is that the numerator and denominator of a rational expression are polynomials instead of integers.

Division by zero is undefined, so the denominator of a fraction cannot equal zero. This is also true for the denominator of a rational expression.

LESSON RESOURCES

Student Edition Practice Workbook 28
Reteaching Masters 28
Adaptations Masters 28
Challenge and Enrichment Masters C28, E28

Example 1

Students use the Quotient of Powers Property to simplify rational expressions whose numerators and denominators are monomials.

Error Alert Watch for students who answer x^3 for Example 1b. Discuss the meaning of a negative exponent. Use the examples below to reinforce the difference between a positive and a negative exponent.

$2^3 = 8$

$2^{-3} = \frac{1}{2^3} = \frac{1}{8}$

Additional Example 1

Identify any excluded values. Then simplify the expression.

a. $\frac{4y^5}{8y^2}$ Excluded value is 0. $\frac{y^3}{2}$

b. $\frac{z}{z^5}$ Excluded value is 0. $\frac{1}{z^4}$

Example 2

Error Alert Remind students that they must find the excluded value(s) before beginning to simplify the expression. Use Example 2a to help students understand they cannot find the excluded value after the expression has been simplified.

Additional Example 2

Identify any excluded values. Then simplify the expression.

$\frac{2(x^2 - 4)}{x + 2}$ Excluded value is –2.

$2(x - 2)$

Example 1 Simplifying by Using the Quotient of Powers Property

Identify any excluded values. Then simplify the expression.

a. $\frac{2m^3}{m^2}$

SOLUTION The excluded value is 0 because $0^2 = 0$.

$$\frac{2m^3}{m^2} = 2m^{3-2} = 2m$$

b. $\frac{x^4}{x^7}$

SOLUTION The excluded value is 0 because $0^7 = 0$.

$$\frac{x^4}{x^7} = x^{4-7} = x^{-3} = \frac{1}{x^3}$$

All rational expressions can be simplified by dividing out the common factors that appear in both the numerator and denominator.

Caution

Be sure to determine any excluded values before simplifying the expression.

Example 2 Simplifying by Dividing Out Common Factors

Identify any excluded values. Then simplify the expression.

a. $\frac{4x + 8}{8x + 16}$

SOLUTION To find what value of x makes the denominator 0, set the denominator equal to 0 and solve for x.

$8x + 16 = 0$

$8x = -16$

$x = -2$ The excluded value is –2.

Factor out the GCF from the numerator and denominator.

$$\frac{4x + 8}{8x + 16} = \frac{4(x + 2)}{8(x + 2)}$$

$$= \frac{{}^{1}\cancel{4}\cancel{(x+2)}}{{}_{2}\cancel{8}\cancel{(x+2)}} = \frac{1}{2}$$ Divide out 4 and $(x + 2)$.

b. $\frac{3b^2 - 27}{b + 3}$

SOLUTION The excluded value is –3.

$$\frac{3b^2 - 27}{b + 3} = \frac{3(b^2 - 9)}{b + 3}$$ Factor out the GCF of 3 in the numerator.

$$= \frac{3(b + 3)(b - 3)}{b + 3}$$ Factor the difference of squares.

$$= \frac{3\cancel{(b + 3)}(b - 3)}{\cancel{b + 3}}$$ Divide out the common factor, $b + 3$.

$$= 3(b - 3)$$

Math Language

Opposite binomials are binomials of the form $a - b$ and $b - a$.

When –1 is factored out of $b - a$, the result is $-1(-b + a)$, which can be written as $-1(a - b)$. This result allows opposite binomials to be factored out of a rational expression.

ENGLISH LEARNERS

In the English language **rational** is an adjective meaning "having reason or understanding." When we describe someone's thinking as rational, we mean his or her thinking is sound and sane.

A second meaning of "rational" refers to numbers and expressions in mathematics. A rational number is a number that can be expressed as the quotient of two integers. A rational expression is the quotient of two polynomials.

Example 3 Simplifying by Factoring Out –1

Identify any excluded values for $\frac{6x-12}{6-3x}$. Then simplify the expression.

SOLUTION Solve $6 - 3x = 0$ to find the excluded value.

$$6 - 3x = 0$$
$$-3x = -6$$
$$x = 2$$

The excluded value is 2.

Factor the numerator and denominator to simplify.

$$\frac{6x-12}{6-3x} = \frac{6(x-2)}{3(2-x)}$$

The factors $(x - 2)$ and $(2 - x)$ are opposite binomials.

$$= \frac{6(x-2)}{3(-1)(x-2)}$$

Factor –1 out of the binomial in the denominator.

$$= \frac{\overset{2}{\cancel{6}}\cancel{(x-2)}}{\underset{1}{\cancel{3}}(-1)\cancel{(x-2)}} = \frac{2}{-1} = -2$$

Example 4 Simplifying Rational Expressions with Trinomials

Identify any excluded values for $\frac{-2x^2-4x+30}{3x^2+21x+30}$. Then simplify the expression.

SOLUTION To find the excluded values, set the denominator equal to 0.

$$0 = 3x^2 + 21x + 30$$
$$0 = 3(x^2 + 7x + 10)$$
$$0 = 3(x + 2)(x + 5) \longrightarrow x + 2 = 0 \quad \text{or} \quad x + 5 = 0$$
$$x = -2 \quad \text{or} \quad x = -5$$

The excluded values are –2 and –5.

Now, factor and divide out common factors.

$$\frac{-2x^2-4x+30}{3x^2+21x+30} = \frac{-2(x^2+2x-15)}{3(x+2)(x+5)} = \frac{-2\cancel{(x+5)}(x-3)}{3(x+2)\cancel{(x+5)}} = \frac{-2(x-3)}{3(x+2)}$$

Example 5 Application: Sports

A basketball is a sphere. Write a simplified rational expression for the volume to surface area ratio of a basketball. Then find the volume to surface area ratio for a basketball whose diameter is 9 inches.

Hint

The radius is one-half of the diameter.

SOLUTION

For a sphere, $V = \frac{4}{3}\pi r^3$ and $SA = 4\pi r^2$. The ratio is $\frac{\frac{4}{3}\pi r^3}{4\pi r^2} = \frac{\frac{4}{3}r}{4} = \frac{1}{3}r$.

Substitute $\frac{9}{2}$ for r: $\frac{1}{3}\left(\frac{9}{2}\right) = \frac{3}{2}$.

The volume to surface area ratio of a basketball with a 9-inch diameter is $\frac{3}{2}$.

ALTERNATE METHOD FOR EXAMPLE 3

–1 can be factored out of the numerator instead of the denominator.

$$\frac{6x-12}{6-3x} = \frac{6(x-2)}{3(2-x)}$$
$$= \frac{6(-1)(2-x)}{3(2-x)}$$
$$= 2(-1)$$
$$= -2$$

Example 3

Remind students to first look for a common monomial to factor out of the numerator and denominator.

Additional Example 3

Identify any excluded values for the expression $\frac{10(4-3x)}{15(3x-4)}$. Then simplify the expression. Excluded value is $\frac{4}{3}$. $-\frac{2}{3}$

Example 4

This example shows students how to simplify rational expressions with trinomials in the numerator and denominator. The denominator must be factored to find the excluded values.

Additional Example 4

Identify any excluded values for $\frac{4x^2-10x+6}{-2x^2-x+3}$. Then simplify the expression. Excluded values are 1 and $-\frac{3}{2}$. $\frac{-2(2x-3)}{(2x+3)}$

Example 5

Point out to students that the volume to surface area ratio of *every* sphere is $\frac{1}{3}r$.

Additional Example 5

A cardboard box is shaped like a cube. Write a simplified rational expression for the surface area to volume ratio of the box. Then find the surface area to volume ratio for a cube whose side length is 12 feet. $\frac{6}{s}$; $\frac{1}{2}$

Lesson Practice

Problem g

Scaffolding Write the surface area to volume ratio for a sphere. Then simplify. Divide 2160 by 2 to find the radius of the moon. Substitute the length of the radius into the ratio for r.

Check for Understanding

The questions below help assess the concepts taught in this lesson.

1. **"Explain how to find the excluded value of a rational expression."** Sample: Find the domain value for which the expression is undefined. Some rational expressions do not have excluded values and some have more than one excluded value.
2. **"Explain how to simplify a rational expression whose numerator and denominator are opposite binomials."** Sample: Factor –1 out of one of the opposite binomials.

3 Practice

Math Conversations

Discussions to strengthen understanding

Problems 6 and 7

"What is the solution to a system of linear equations?" The point where the lines intersect.

"Can a system of two linear equations have exactly two solutions?" Sample: No, a system of two linear equations has one solution, no solution, or an infinite number of solutions.

Extend the Problem

Have students identify the systems as consistent or inconsistent and dependent or independent. Both problems are consistent and independent.

Lesson Practice

Identify any excluded values. Then simplify the expression.

a. (Ex 1) $\frac{3p^8}{9p^3}$ $0, \frac{p^5}{3}$

b. (Ex 1) $\frac{a}{6a^4}$ $0, \frac{1}{6a^3}$

c. (Ex 2) $\frac{x^2 + 7x}{6x + 42}$ $-7, \frac{x}{6}$

d. (Ex 2) $\frac{-2x^2 + 2}{10x - 10}$ $1, \frac{-(x+1)}{5}$

e. (Ex 3) $\frac{a^2 - 81}{81 - 9a}$ $9, -\frac{a+9}{9}$

f. (Ex 4) $\frac{2x^2 - 4x - 6}{2x^3 - 2x}$ $-1, 0, 1, \frac{x-3}{x(x-1)}$

g. (Ex 3) The moon is a sphere. Write a simplified rational expression for the surface area to volume ratio of the moon. Then find the surface area to volume ratio for the moon given that its diameter is 2160 miles. $\frac{3}{r}, \frac{1}{360}$

Practice Distributed and Integrated

*1. (27) Convert $f(x) = (-x + 1)^2$ to standard form. $x^2 - 2x + 1$

Identify any excluded values, then simplify each expression.

*2. (28) $\frac{-2q^3}{16q}$ $q \neq 0, \frac{-q^2}{8}$

*3. (28) $\frac{s + 1}{15(s + 1)^2}$ $s \neq -1, \frac{1}{15s + 15}$

*4. (28) $\frac{x^2}{x}$ $x \neq 0, x$

*5. (28) $\frac{4x^5}{12x}$ $x \neq 0, \frac{x^4}{3}$

Use Cramer's Rule to solve the following systems of equations.

6. (16) $x + y = 5$, $x - y = 5$ $x = 5, y = 0$

7. (16) $-5x + y = 7$, $x - 3y = 7$ $x = -2, y = -3$

Simplify each of the following expressions.

8. (3) $x^3y^{-3}x^{-5}y^8y^7$ $\frac{y^2}{x^2}$

9. (3) $\frac{xx^{-2}y^5x^{-1}y^{-1}}{x^8y^{-3}y^2x^{-4}}$ $\frac{y^5}{x^6}$

10. (3) $\frac{2x^6y^{-4}}{24xy^{-1}}$ $\frac{x^5}{12y^3}$

Change each of the following to percents.

11. (6) $\frac{3}{5}$ 60%

12. (6) 0.8 80%

13. (6) 0.025 2.5%

14. (10) **(Carnival)** The entry cost at the local fair is \$9.00. Each ride costs \$1.50. If Matthew has \$45, how many rides could he go on? Write an inequality to help you answer the problem. $9 + 1.50x \leq 45$; $1.50x \leq 36$; $x \leq 24$; 24 rides

15. (18) **Write** Write a situation explaining the problem: $\frac{20 \text{ hr}}{1} \times \frac{60 \text{ min}}{1 \text{ hr}} \times \frac{60 \text{ s}}{1 \text{ min}} = 72{,}000 \text{ s}$ converting 20 hours into 72,000 seconds

*16. (28) **Analyze** Compare and contrast the Quotient of Powers Property to the Product of Powers Property. Both properties require that the bases be the same before the exponents can be added or subtracted. In the Product of Powers Property, the exponents are added; in the Quotient of Powers Property, they are subtracted.

204 *Saxon* Algebra 2

CHALLENGE

Identify any excluded values for $\frac{x^3 + 3x^2 + 3x + 1}{-x^2 + 6x + 7}$. Then simplify the expression. Excluded values: –1 and 7; $\frac{(x+1)^2}{7 - x}$

17. (17) **Multiple Choice** Solve $-3|4x| - 2 \geq 22$. D

A $-2 \leq x \leq 2$ B $x \leq -2$ or $x \geq 2$

C All real numbers D No solution

***18.** (26) (**Aviation**) The Federal Aviation Administration tracks airline delays for airports around the country. During the first half of 2007, the flights delayed at Dallas-Fort Worth Airport averaged 4,500 per month. Use this information to write an equation in slope-intercept form that could be used to predict the total number of delays throughout the year. Let x equal the month of the year and y equal the cumulative delays. $y = 4500x$

***19.** (25) **Data Analysis** A chemist weighs samples obtained from a production run. The weights of the samples are 13 g, 14 g, 65 g, 11 g, 15 g, 14 g, 14 g, 12 g, 13 g, 15 g, 14 g, and 12 g.

a. Find the mean of the data. $\bar{x} \approx 17.7$

b. Find the standard deviation. $\sigma \approx 14.3$

c. Identify any outliers. 65

d. Describe how any outlier affects the mean and the standard deviation of this data set. The outlier increases the mean from ≈ 13.4 to ≈ 17.7 and increases the standard deviation from ≈ 1.2 to ≈ 14.3.

20. (11) (**Packaging Technology**) An engineer has a box in the shape of a cube. He wants to know how the volume is affected if he adds 2 units to each base edge and subtracts 3 units from the height. How does the change in dimension affect the volume? Explain your answer.

20. The volume changes by $-x^2 + 8x + 12$ cubic units. The volume of the cube is x^3. The volume of the other box is $(x + 2)(x + 2)(x - 3) = x^3 + x^2 - 8x - 12$. The difference in volume is $x^3 - (x^3 + x^2 - 8x - 12) = -x^2 + 8x + 12$.

21. (13) **Multi-Step** Use $-7x + 14y = -84$.

a. Find the x-intercept. x-intercept = (12, 0)

b. Find the y-intercept. y-intercept = (0, −6)

22. (24) **Geometry** Two angles are complementary and the difference between the larger angle and twice the smaller angle is 30°. Write a system to represent the scenario and solve the system to find the measures of the angles.

$x + y = 90$
$x - 2y = 30$; The angles measure 20° and 70°.

23. (16) **Error Analysis** Two students solved the system of equations $\begin{matrix} 7 - 5y - 4x = 0 \\ 16 - 2y - 5x = 0 \end{matrix}$. Find the error or errors in these students' work and solve the system correctly.

Student A $\begin{matrix} 4x + 5y = 7 \\ 5x + 2y = 16 \end{matrix}$ $x = \dfrac{\begin{vmatrix} 7 & 5 \\ 16 & 2 \end{vmatrix}}{\begin{vmatrix} 4 & 5 \\ 5 & 2 \end{vmatrix}} = \dfrac{-66}{-17} \approx 3.88$ and $y = \dfrac{\begin{vmatrix} 5 & 7 \\ 2 & 16 \end{vmatrix}}{\begin{vmatrix} 4 & 5 \\ 5 & 2 \end{vmatrix}}$

$= \dfrac{66}{-17} \approx -3.88$

Student B $\begin{matrix} -5y - 4x = -7 \\ -2y - 5x = -16 \end{matrix}$ $y = \dfrac{\begin{vmatrix} -7 & -4 \\ -16 & -5 \end{vmatrix}}{\begin{vmatrix} -5 & -4 \\ -2 & -5 \end{vmatrix}} = \dfrac{-29}{17} \approx -1.71$ and $x = \dfrac{\begin{vmatrix} -5 & -7 \\ -2 & -16 \end{vmatrix}}{\begin{vmatrix} -5 & -4 \\ -2 & -5 \end{vmatrix}}$

$= \dfrac{66}{17} \approx 3.88$

23. Student A interchanged columns of the matrix in the numerator instead of replacing the first column with the coefficients of x. Correct solutions may take different approaches, but will produce the same answers as Student B.

Problem 17

"Is the absolute value of $4x$ a positive number or a negative number?" Positive

"If you multiply a positive number by a negative number and subtract a positive number, will the value of the expression be positive or negative?" Negative

"Will the value of the left side of the inequality be positive or negative?" Negative

"Can a negative number ever be greater than or equal to 22?" No

Problem 19

"What is an outlier?" a value in a data set that is much greater or less than the other values

Problem 22

Error Alert

Watch for students who confuse complementary and supplementary angles.

Ask, **"What are complementary angles?"** two angles whose measures sum to 90°

INCLUSION

Have students cross out each factor as they divide out the common factors. It may help students to rewrite the expression each time a common factor is divided out.

Problem 25

"What is another way to find the equation of the line?" Sample: Use the slope formula to find the slope of the line. Then use point-slope form to write the equation of the line. Solve for y to write the equation in slope-intercept form.

Problem 27

Extend the Problem

"What type of function is shown?" a piecewise function

"What error did Courtney make in determining the relation failed the vertical line test?" She thought the domain of the linear part of the function included 0.

Problem 28

"What are the roots of a quadratic function?" the points where the graph of the function crosses the x-axis

Extend the Problem

"What is the graph of this function?" a parabola

"Does the parabola open up or down?" up

"How do you know the parabola opens up?" The coefficient of the x^2 term is positive.

*24. (20) **Graphing Calculator** Given $f(x) = 2x - 2$ and $g(x) = x^2$, find $(f + g)(x)$. Graph $(f + g)(x)$ using a graphing calculator. Explain what the graph shows. See Additional Answers.

25. (15) **Multi-Step** Set up and solve a system to find an equation of the line through points (2, 5) and (4, −3). Put the equation in the form $y = mx + b$.

a. Substitute the point (2, 5) for (x, y) in the form $y = mx + b$ to get a linear equation in unknowns m and b. $5 = 2m + b$

b. Substitute the point (4, −3) into the form $y = mx + b$ to get another linear equation in m and b. $-3 = 4m + b$.

c. Solve the system for m and b. $m = -4$, $b = 13$

d. What is the equation of the line? $y = -4x + 13$

26. (21) **Business School** This table shows the change in rank of two undergraduate business schools from 2006 to 2007. If the rankings continue to change at these constant rates, in what year will University of Florida and University of Wisconsin have the same rank? 2010

School	2006	2007	Change
University of Florida	47	43	−4
University of Wisconsin	27	28	+1

27. (22) **Error Analysis** Courtney determines that the relation shown at right fails the vertical line test. Write a response to correct her decision. The graph passes the vertical line test because any vertical line intersects the graph no more than once. The point of discontinuity does not change this fact.

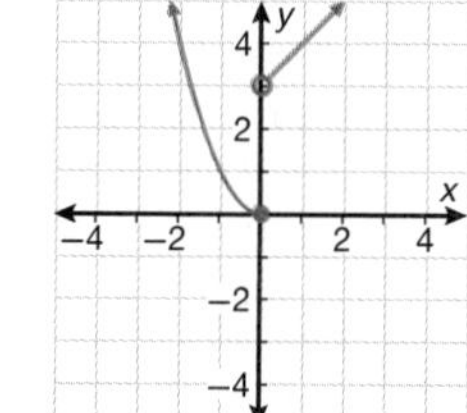

28. $f(-9) = (-9)^2 + 7(-9) - 18 = 81 - 63 - 18 = 0$, $f(2) = (2)^2 + 7(2) - 18 = 4 + 14 - 18 = 0$

*28. (27) **Verify** Verify that the roots of $f(x) = x^2 + 7x - 18$ are −9 and 2 by substituting −9 and 2 into the function.

*29. (25) **Analyze** Cassie's job is to analyze a set of 100 scores that range from 0 to 10 from a recent survey. The set of values includes exactly 6 scores that are zero. She decides not to include the 6 zero scores in the analysis, based on the false assumption that zero is not really a number since it has no value.

a. Is it possible to determine whether the mean will be greater than, less than, or equal to the value using all 100 scores? Greater than; The sum is the same for both, and she will divide by 94 rather than 100.

b. Is it possible to determine whether the standard deviation will be greater than, less than, or equal to the value using all 100 scores? Explain your answers. Less than; The set of 94 values ranges from 1 to 10 and so is not as spread out as the set of 100 values.

30. (23) **Artwork** Jacob would like to buy a frame for some artwork he painted. His painting is 20 feet by 16 feet. He wants an equal-sized border around the outside of the painting, and he wants to increase the amount of area that the painting covers by 50%.

a. Write an expression to solve for the width of the border around the painting.

b. Calculate what size frame he should buy. Using the equation from part (a) gives $4(x^2 + 18x - 40) = 4(x + 20)(x - 2) = 0$. The increase is $x = 2$, so each dimension should increase by $2x$ or 4 feet. Therefore, the frame should be 24 feet by 20 feet.

30a. Let x represent the width of the additional border around the painting. Each dimension will increase by $2x$ (an x increase on each side). $(20 + 2x)(16 + 2x) = 1.5(16)(20)$ square feet, so $4x^2 + 72x + 320 = 480$ or $4x^2 + 72x - 160 = 0$

LOOKING FORWARD

Simplifying rational expressions prepares students for:

- **Lesson 31** Multiplying and Dividing Rational Expressions
- **Lesson 37** Adding and Subtracting Rational Expressions
- **Lesson 40** Simplifying Radical Expressions
- **Lesson 44** Rationalizing Denominators

LESSON 29

Solving Systems of Equations in Three Variables

Warm Up

1. **Vocabulary** A system of simultaneous equations that have no common solution is called inconsistent. (21)

2. Evaluate the expression $-2x - 5y$ when $x = -5$ and $y = -3$. 25 (2)

3. Solve the system of equations using the elimination method: $x + y = 5$, $x - y = 1$ (3, 2) (24)

New Concepts

Systems of equations are not limited to two equations and two variables. A linear equation in three variables is of the form $Ax + By + Cz = D$. Systems of equations in three variables require three equations to solve. The solution to a system of three equations in three variables is an **ordered triple** and is noted (x, y, z). Similar to systems of two equations, systems of three equations can be solved using elimination.

Hint

The order in which the equations are eliminated is not important. It is important that all three equations are used.

To solve a system of three equations in three variables

Step 1: Use two of the three equations to eliminate one of the variables.
Step 2: Use the remaining equation and one of the equations used in Step 1 to eliminate the same variable as in Step 1. From Steps 1 and 2, there is now a system of two equations in two variables.
Step 3: Solve the system of equations resulting from Steps 1 and 2.
Step 4: Substitute the values for the two variables found in Step 3 into one of the original equations to solve for the third variable.
Step 5: Check the solution by substituting the values for the three variables into each of the three original equations.

A solution to a system in three variables means that there is an ordered triple that satisfies all three equations. A solution is either a single point or a line. If the three planes do not share a common point, then there is no solution.

There are three possible results when solving systems of three equations: one solution, infinitely many solutions, and no solution.

Number of Solutions	Type of Solution	Graphic Representation
one	consistent/ independent	planes intersect at exactly one point
infinitely many	consistent/dependent	same plane or planes intersect in a line
none	inconsistent	parallel planes or planes that each intersect at exactly one of the other planes

LESSON 29

1 Warm Up

To avoid errors in sign, suggest to students that they not use mental math to solve Problem 2.

2 New Concepts

In this lesson, students learn how to solve systems of three equations and three variables.

Discuss the definition of **ordered triple.** Draw a right-hand Cartesian coordinate system and plot the ordered triple (1, 3, 2) as shown below.

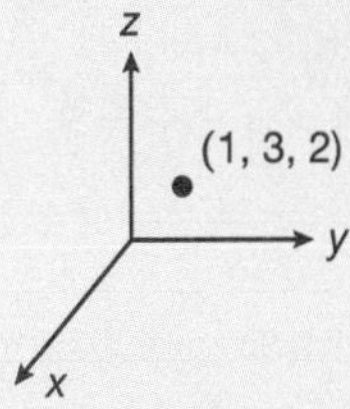

Discuss the possible solutions to a system of three equations and three unknowns:

1. The planes can intersect in a single point.
2. All three planes can be parallel.
3. Each plane in the system intersects exactly one of the other planes in the system.
4. The planes intersect in a line.
5. All three equations represent the same plane.

MATH BACKGROUND

Students have solved systems of two equations and two variables and know that these systems can have one solution, infinitely many solutions, or no solution. The same is true for systems of three equations and three variables.

Each equation in a system of two equations and two unknowns is a line. Each equation in a system of three equations and three unknowns is a plane.

Students solved systems of linear equations using graphing, the substitution method, and the elimination method. All the systems in this lesson are solved using the elimination method.

LESSON RESOURCES

Student Edition Practice Workbook 29
Reteaching Masters 29
Adaptations Masters 29
Challenge and Enrichment Masters C29

Example 1

In this example, students learn the steps for solving a system of three equations that has one solution.

Remind students that they can use any of the original equations in step 4.

Error Alert Watch for students who eliminate a different variable in step 2. Stress that the same variable must be eliminated in steps 1 and 2.

Additional Example 1

Solve the system of equations.

$$3x + 2y - z = -15$$
$$5x + 3y + 2z = 0$$
$$3x + y + 3z = 11$$

$(-4, 2, 7)$

Example 1 **System of Three Equations with One Solution**

Solve the system of equations.

$$\begin{aligned} x + y + z &= 4 \\ 9x + 3y + z &= 0 \\ 4x + 2y + z &= 1 \end{aligned}$$

SOLUTION

Step 1: Eliminate one variable using the first and second equations.

$$\begin{array}{ll} -1(x + y + z) = -1(4) & -x - y - z = -4 \\ \underline{+9x + 3y + z = 0} & \underline{+9x + 3y + z = \;\; 0} \\ & 8x + 2y \quad = -4 \end{array}$$

Step 2: Eliminate the same variable using the second and third equations.

$$\begin{array}{ll} -1(9x + 3y + z) = -1(0) & -9x - 3y - z = 0 \\ \underline{+4x + 2y + z = 1} & \underline{+4x + 2y + z = 1} \\ & -5x - y \quad = 1 \end{array}$$

Step 3: Solve the system of equations resulting from Steps 1 and 2.

$$\begin{array}{lll} 8x + 2y = -4 & 8x + 2y = -4 & 8x + 2y = -4 \\ 2(-5x - y) = 2(1) & \underline{+ -10x - 2y = \;\; 2} & 8(1) + 2y = -4 \\ & -2x \quad = -2 & 8 + 2y - 8 = -4 - 8 \\ & \frac{\cancel{-2}x}{\cancel{-2}} = \frac{-2}{-2} & 2y = -12 \\ & x = 1 & \frac{\cancel{2}y}{\cancel{2}} = \frac{-12}{2} \\ & & y = -6 \end{array}$$

Step 4: Substitute the values of the two variables found in Step 3 into one of the original equations to solve for the third variable.

$$\begin{aligned} x + y + z &= 4 \\ (1) + (-6) + z &= 4 \\ -5 + z &= 4 \\ -5 + z + 5 &= 4 + 5 \\ z &= 9 \end{aligned}$$

Since $x = 1$, $y = -6$, and $z = 9$, the ordered triple is $(1, -6, 9)$.

Step 5: Check the ordered triple in each of the original equations.

$$\begin{array}{lll} x + y + z = 4 & 9x + 3y + z = 0 & 4x + 2y + z = 1 \\ (1) + (-6) + (9) \stackrel{?}{=} 4 & 9(1) + 3(-6) + (9) \stackrel{?}{=} 0 & 4(1) + 2(-6) + (9) \stackrel{?}{=} 1 \\ 4 = 4 \checkmark & 0 = 0 \checkmark & 1 = 1 \checkmark \end{array}$$

All three statements are true. Therefore, the single solution to the system of three equations is $(1, -6, 9)$.

Math Reasoning

Write How would you determine if a given ordered triple is a solution to a system of three equations in three variables?

Substitute the values of the ordered triple into the three equations. If the resulting statements are true, then the ordered triple is a solution to the system of equations.

ENGLISH LEARNERS

Discuss the mathematical meaning of plane.

A **plane** is a two-dimensional figure that has length and width. Though planes are drawn as if they have dimensions that can be measured, they do not. Planes extend infinitely in all directions just as lines extend infinitely in both directions.

Example 2 System of Three Equations with Infinitely Many Solutions

Solve the system of equations.
$$2x + 3y + 4z = 12$$
$$-6x - 12y - 8z = -56$$
$$4x + 6y + 8z = 24$$

SOLUTION

Step 1: Eliminate one variable using the first and second equations.

$$\begin{array}{rl} 2(2x + 3y + 4z) = 2(12) & \quad 4x + 6y + 8z = 24 \\ \underline{-6x - 12y - 8z = -56} & \quad \underline{-6x - 12y - 8z = -56} \\ & \quad -2x - 6y \qquad = -32 \end{array}$$

Step 2: Eliminate the same variable using the second and third equations.

$$\begin{array}{r} -6x - 12y - 8z = -56 \\ \underline{+4x + 6y + 8z = 24} \\ -2x - 6y \qquad = -32 \end{array}$$

Step 3: Solve the system of equations resulting from Steps 1 and 2.

$$-2x - 6y = -32$$
$$-2x - 6y = -32$$

Use elimination to solve for the solution to the system of two equations.

$$\begin{array}{rl} -1(-2x - 6y) = -1(32) & \quad 2x + 6y = 32 \\ \underline{+ -2x - 6y = -32} & \quad \underline{+ -2x - 6y = -32} \\ & \quad 0 = 0 \end{array}$$

The result is an identity statement. Therefore, there are infinitely many solutions to the system of equations. Those solutions form a line and the equation of the line is $-2x - 6y = 32$.

Hint

It does not matter which variable you eliminate in step 1 as long as you eliminate the same variable in step 2.

Example 3 System of Three Equations with No Solutions

Solve the system of equations.
$$x + 2y - 3z = 4$$
$$2x + 4y - 6z = 3$$
$$-x + 5y + 3z = 1$$

SOLUTION

Step 1: Eliminate one variable using the first and second equations.

$$\begin{array}{rl} -2(x + 2y - 3z) = -2(4) & \quad -2x - 4y + 6z = -8 \\ \underline{+2x + 4y - 6z = 3} & \quad \underline{+2x + 4y - 6z = 3} \\ & \quad 0 = -5 \end{array}$$

The result is a false statement. Therefore, there is no solution to the system of equations. Notice that the coefficients of the first and second equations are multiples of each other, but their constants are not. Therefore, these equations form parallel planes and do not share a common point.

Example 2

In this example, students are shown a system of equations with infinitely many solutions. Tell students that in this example, two of the planes coincide. The third plane intersects the coinciding planes in a line.

Additional Example 2

Solve the system of equations.

$2x + 4y - z = 8$

$x + 5y + z = 0$

$6x + 12y - 3z = 24$

infinitely many solutions

Example 3

In this example, students are shown a system of equations with no solution. The planes $x + 2y - 3z = 4$ and $2x + 4y - 6z = 3$ are parallel planes.

Additional Example 3

Solve the system of equations.

$3x - 5y + 2z = 10$

$x + y - 4z = 9$

$2x + 2y - 8z = 1$

No solution

ALTERNATE METHOD FOR EXAMPLE 3

The coefficients of the variables of the second equation are multiples of the coefficients of the variables of the first equation. However, the constants on the right side are not multiples. Therefore, the system has no solution.

Example 4

This example shows students additional examples of inconsistent and consistent dependent systems. Write the systems on the board and show students the equations that are multiples of each other.

Additional Example 4

a. Solve the system of equations.

$$12x + 18y + 20z = 30$$
$$-6x - 9y - 10z = 4$$
$$24x + 36y + 40z = 15$$

no solution

Extend the Example

Have students discuss the equations in Additional Example 4a. This system is formed by three planes, two of which are parallel planes.

b. Solve the system of equations.

$$x - y - 2z = 3$$
$$-2x + 2y + 4z = -6$$
$$5x - 5y - 10z = 15$$

infinitely many solutions

Extend the Example

Have students discuss the equations in Additional Example 4b. This system is formed by three planes that intersect in a line.

A system that has at least one solution is **consistent**, so systems with one solution or infinitely many solutions are consistent.

A system of simultaneous equations that have no common solution is **inconsistent**.

Example 4 Types of Systems of Three Equations

(a.) Solve the system of linear equations. Determine whether the system is consistent or inconsistent.

$$-x - 5y + 3z = 7$$
$$5x + y + 3z = 9$$
$$2x + 10y - 6z = -4$$

SOLUTION Notice that the coefficients of x for the first and third equations are multiples. The coefficients of y for these same two equations are also multiples, as are the coefficients of z. The constants for these two equations are *not* multiples.

$$\begin{array}{lcl} -x - 5y + 3z = 7 & & -x - 5y + 3z = 7 \\ 5x + y + 3z = 9 & \longrightarrow & 5x + y + 3z = 9 \\ 2x + 10y - 6z = -4 & & -2(-x - 5y + 3z) = -4 \end{array}$$

Combine the first and third equations to solve.

$$\begin{array}{lcr} 2(-x - 5y + 3z) = 2(7) & & -2x - 10y + 6z = 14 \\ \underline{2x + 10y - 6z = -4} & \longrightarrow & \underline{2x + 10y - 6z = -4} \\ & & 0 = 10 \end{array}$$

Math Reasoning

Analyze Why must linear systems be independent, dependent, or inconsistent?

Because graphs intersect, coincide or are parallel.

Because the coefficients of the variables are multiples for each of the variables and the constants are not multiples, there is no solution. This means the system is inconsistent.

(b.) Solve the system of linear equations. Determine whether the system is consistent or inconsistent.

$$5x - 9y - 6z = 11$$
$$-5x + 9y + 6z = -11$$
$$2x - 4y - 3z = 6$$

SOLUTION Notice that the first and second equations are multiples of each other, which means they are parallel planes.

Combine the second and third equations to solve.

$$\begin{array}{lcr} 2(2x - 4y - 3z) = 2(6) & & -5x + 9y + 6z = -11 \\ \underline{(4x - 8y - 6z = 12)} & \longrightarrow & \underline{4x - 8y - 6z = 12} \\ & & -x + y = 1 \end{array}$$

There are an infinite number of solutions that form a line. The equation of the line is $-x + y = 1$.

Caution

You cannot assume that equations that do not fit the criteria in Example 4 parts a and b have one solution. You may have to solve the system of equations to find the number of solutions.

INCLUSION

Discuss with students examples of consistent and inconsistent. For example, for students who are always on time for school, the behavior is considered consistent. If a student is sometimes on time and sometimes late, then the behavior is inconsistent.

Example 5 Application: Investing

A person invests \$12,000 for one year; some is invested at 5%, some at 10%, and the remainder at 13% interest. The combined interest earned at the end of the year from these investments was \$920. The amount invested at 10% is \$4,000 less than the amount invested at 5% and 13% combined. Find the amount of money invested at each rate.

SOLUTION

Money is invested in three accounts and each account earns a different rate of interest: 5%, 10%, and 13%.

Define the variables: Let x = amount invested in 5% account, y = amount invested in 10% account, and z = amount invested in 13% account.

The total amount invested is \$12,000. So,

$$x + y + z = 12000$$

At the end of the year, the total amount of interest earned from all three accounts was \$920. The interest earned on an account for one year can be found by multiplying the interest rate by the amount invested.

$$0.05x + 0.10y + 0.13z = 920$$

The amount invested in the 10% account is \$4,000 **less** than the total amount in the 5% and 13% accounts.

$$y = (x + z) - 4000 \text{ or } -x + y - z = -4000$$

Now we have a system of three linear equations with three variables.

Write the system of equations, then solve.

$$\begin{aligned} x + y + z &= 12,000 \\ 0.05x + 0.1y + 0.13z &= 920 \\ -x + y - z &= -4,000 \end{aligned}$$

$$\begin{array}{r} x + y + z = 12000 \\ \underline{-x + y - z = -4000} \\ 2y \quad = 8000 \\ y = 4000 \end{array}$$

Substitute the y-value of 4000 in the second and third equations.

$$\begin{aligned} -x + 4000 - z &= -4000 \\ -x - z &= -8000 \end{aligned} \qquad \begin{aligned} 0.05x + 400 + 0.13z &= 920 \\ 0.05x + 0.13z &= 520 \end{aligned}$$

Combine the two simplified equations to eliminate a variable.

$$\begin{aligned} -x - z &= -8000 \\ 20(0.05x + 0.13z) &= 20(520) \end{aligned}$$

$$\begin{array}{r} -x - z = -8000 \\ \underline{x + 2.6z = 10400} \\ 1.6z = 2400 \\ z = 1500 \end{array}$$

Substitute the z-value of 1500 to find x.

$$\begin{aligned} -x - 1500 &= -8000 \\ x &= 6500 \end{aligned}$$

The amount placed in each account is: \$6,500 in the 5% account, \$4,000 in the 10% account, and \$1,500 in the 13% account.

Caution

Always organize your thoughts and write a plan before attempting to write a system of equations.

Example 5

Work through each of the steps used in solving the problem. It is crucial that the variables be defined properly and the equations set up correctly.

Additional Example 5

A person invests \$10,000 for one year; some is invested at 3%, some at 4%, and the remainder at 6% interest. The combined interest earned at the end of the year from these investments is \$475. The amount invested at 6% is the sum of the amounts invested at 3% and 4%. Find the amount of money invested at each rate. (2500, 2500, 5000)

CHALLENGE

Solve the system of equations using substitution. Solve the first equation for z and substitute that value into the second and third equations for z.

$x + y + z = 18$

$2x - 4y + z = 12$

$3x + 2y - z = 4$

(4, 2, 12)

Lesson Practice

Problem a

Error Alert Remind students to check the solution in *every* equation in the system.

Problems a–e

Scaffolding Have students look for equations that are multiples of each other before beginning to solve the system.

Check for Understanding

The questions below help assess the concepts taught in this lesson.

1. **"Explain what it means for a system of three equations and three variables to have exactly one solution."** Sample: The planes intersect in a single point in three space.
2. **"What are the three possible results when solving a system of equations?"** Sample: The system can have exactly one solution, infinitely many solutions, or no solutions.

3 Practice

Math Conversations

Discussion to strengthen understanding

Problems 3 and 4

"What type of binomials are problems 3 and 4?" the difference of two squares

Lesson Practice

Solve the systems of equations.

a. (Ex 1) $6x - 3y + 3z = 3$, $3x + 3y - z = 5$, $5x + 2y - 2z = 4$ $\left(\frac{2}{3}, \frac{4}{3}, 1\right)$

b. (Ex 2) $-3x - y - 4z = 15$, $9x + 3y + 12z = -45$, $-6x + 2y - 8z = -30$

b. infinitely many solutions

c. (Ex 3) Solve the system of equations. $4x - 2y + z = 2$, $2x + 4y - 3z = 0$, $-12x + 6y - 3z = 6$ no solution

How many solutions does the system of equations have and what type of system is it?

d. (Ex 4) $4x + 9y - 22z = 10$, $3x - y + 2z = -3$, $-15x + 5y - 10z = -15$

e. (Ex 4) $5x - 3y + z = 13$, $-28x + 24y - 4z = 20$, $-7x + 6y - z = 5$

d. no solution, inconsistent
e. infinitely many solutions, consistent

f. (Ex 5) A person invests \$5,400 for one year; some is invested at 12%, some at 15%, and the remainder at 18%. The combined interest earned at the end of the year from these investments was \$822. The amount invested at 12% is \$2,600 less then the amount invested at 15% and 18% combined. Find the amount of money invested at each rate. 12%: \$1400; 15%: \$2200; 18%: \$1800

Practice Distributed and Integrated

Solve each system of equations.

*1. (29) $x - 5y + 2z = 2$, $2x - y + z = 1$, $7x - 3y + z = 8$ (1, –1, –2)

*2. (29) $-4x + 2y - z = 2$, $4x + 8y - 6z = 0$, $4x - 2y + z = 2$ no solution

Factor the polynomials.

3. (23) $144x^2 - 1$ $(12x + 1)(12x - 1)$

4. (23) $9x^2 - 25$ $(3x + 5)(3x - 5)$

Given the functions $f(x) = 2x + 1$ and $g(x) = x^2$,

5. (20) find $(f - g)(4)$. –7

6. (20) find $(f + g)(-3)$. 4

Given the functions $f(x) = -x - 7$ and $g(x) = -(x^2 + 3)$,

7. (20) find $(g + f)(0)$. –10

8. (20) find $(g - f)(-1)$. 2

Solve each equation.

9. (17) $|x + 3| = 4$ $x = 1, x = -7$

10. (17) $|2x + 6| + 2 = 1$ no solution

11. (17) $|1 - 3x| + 5 = 6$ $x = 0, x = \frac{2}{3}$

212 Saxon Algebra 2

INCLUSION

Have students label the equations in a system as 1, 2, and 3 and write the number beside the equation each time they work with it.

12. **Write** Explain FOIL for the multiplication of any two binomials in the form $(a + b)(a + b)$.
(19)

12. First terms $a \cdot a = a^2$
Outer terms $a \cdot b = ab$
Inner terms $b \cdot a = ab$
Last terms $b \cdot b = b^2$
Add the terms: $a^2 + ab + ab + b^2$
The outer and inner terms in this case will always be the same, leaving you with the product $a^2 + 2ab + b^2$.

Convert the following to feet per minute.

13. 18 in./hour 0.025 ft/min
(18)

14. 144 in./min 12 ft/min
(18)

*15. **Verify** Is the ordered triple $(-1, 2, -3)$ a solution of the system?
(29)

$$-x + y - z = 6$$
$$-x - 2y + 2z = -9$$
$$3x - y + 2z = -11$$

yes

16. Given the equation $6x + 3y = -9$, identify the slope and y-intercept.
(13)
$m = -2$; $b = -3$

17. **Error Analysis** A student solved the inequality $-4x - 2 \geq 14$ and got the solution $x \geq -4$. Explain and correct the error.
(10)

17. Possible answer: The student forgot to change the inequality sign when dividing by -4. $x \leq -4$

*18. **Graphing Calculator** Calculate the determinant of $\begin{bmatrix} 4 & -2 & 1 \\ 3 & 0 & 2 \\ 2 & -1 & 1 \end{bmatrix}$ using a graphing calculator. 3
(14)

*19. **Multiple Choice** Using the data in the table, what is the equation in standard form of the line that passes through the three points? C
(26)

A $y = -12.50x + 7.5$
B $y = 12.50x + 7.5$
C $125x + 10y = 75$
D $-125x + 10y = 75$

x	y
1	−5
2	−17.5
3	−30

*20. **Coordinate Geometry** A rectangle is drawn on a coordinate grid with one side along the x-axis and one vertex at $(4 + v, 0)$. The area of the rectangle is $v^2 - 7v + 10$. Determine an expression for an adjacent vertex. Explain your answer.
(23)
See Additional Answers.

21. If x varies directly with y and the constant of variation is 3, what is the value of x when $y = 12$? 36
(8)

22. **Justify** A man records his height every 5 years. Examine the table below. Does this table represent a continuous, discontinuous, and/or discrete function? Justify your answer.
(22)

Age	5	10	15	20
Height	36 in.	48 in.	60 in.	72 in.

Continuous function; This is a linear function with no holes or points of discontinuity.

23. **Multi-Step** An online nut store sells nuts and raisins by the pound. Cora bought 4 pounds of nuts and 2 pounds of raisins for \$37.20. Mark bought 2 pounds of nuts and 4 pounds of raisins for \$26.40.
(21)

a. Write a system of equations that represents the price of the nuts, n, and the price of the raisins, r. See Additional Answers.

b. How much should a pound of nuts and a pound of raisins cost together? Explain. See Additional Answers.

22.
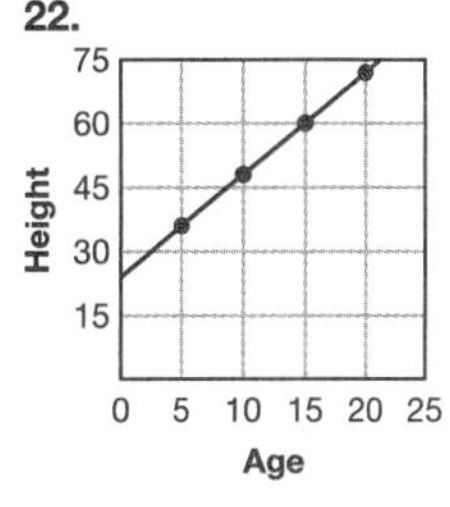

Problem 16

"In what form is the equation of the line written?" standard form

"What form should the equation be written in to identify the slope and y-intercept of the line?" slope-intercept form

"How do you change an equation written in standard form into slope-intercept form?" Solve the equation for y.

Problem 19

Error Alert

Watch for students who leave the equation in slope-intercept form and answer A.

CHALLENGE

Solve the system of equations using substitution. Solve the first equation for y and substitute that value into the second and third equations for y.

$$x + 3y + 7z = 68$$
$$-3x + y - z = -14$$
$$5x + 2y + z = 13$$

(1, −1, 10)

Problem 25

Extend the Problem

Have students find $f(8) + g(8)$ to check their answer.

$f(8) = -16 + 11 = -5$
$g(8) = 48 - 1 = 47$
$f(8) + g(8) = -5 + 47 = 42$

Problem 28

"How will you solve the problem?" Sample: Using a system of three equations and three unknowns.

"What are the three unknowns in the system?" Sample: x is the population of New York, y is the population of Florida, and z is the population of Illinois.

*24. **Write** Describe the steps used when solving a linear system by the elimination method. See Additional Answers. (24)

25. **Multiple Choice** Given $f(x) = -2x + 11$ and $g(x) = 6x - 1$, find $(f + g)(8)$. A (20)
A 42 B 52 C 74 D 76

26. The Olympic record time for swimming the 100-meter freestyle is held by P. van den Hoogenband, who swam it in 47.84 seconds on September 19, 2000. What is his time in feet per second? ≈ 6.858 feet per second (18)

27. **Error Analysis** Explain the error in the statement and provide numerical support: The transformation that occurs from $f(x) = |x|$ to $f(x) = |x - 3|$ results in a graph that shifts to the left 3 units. (17)

27. The transformation moves the graph to the right 3 units. The original function equals 1 at $x = -1$ and $x = 1$. The new function equals 1 at $x = 2$ and $x = 4$.

*28. **Population** The table shows the population in millions for the two most populated states. If the populations of the next three most populated states, New York, Florida, and Illinois, are added, the total population is 102.2 million. The difference between the populations of New York and Florida is 3 million. The difference between the populations of Florida and Illinois is 3.6 million. Find the populations of New York, Florida, and Illinois. (29)

State	Population in Millions
California	33.9
Texas	20.9
New York	19
Florida	16
Illinois	12.4

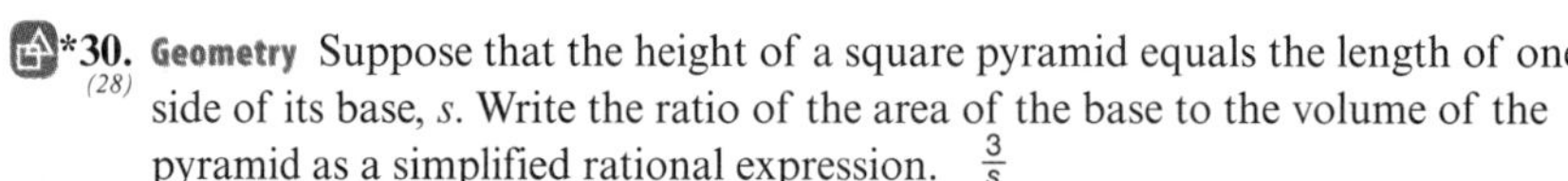

29. Use Cramer's Rule to solve the system $\begin{matrix} x + y = 2 \\ 2x - y = 7 \end{matrix}$. $x = 3; y = -1$ (16)

*30. **Geometry** Suppose that the height of a square pyramid equals the length of one side of its base, s. Write the ratio of the area of the base to the volume of the pyramid as a simplified rational expression. $\frac{3}{s}$ (28)

LOOKING FORWARD

Solving systems of three equations and three variables prepares students for:

- **Lesson 43** Solving Systems of Linear Inequalities
- **Lesson 54** Using Linear Programming

LESSON 30

Applying Transformations to the Parabola and Determining the Minimum or Maximum

Warm Up

1. **Vocabulary** The graph of a quadratic function is a U-shaped curve called a parabola. (27)

2. The parent quadratic function is ________. $f(x) = x^2$ (27)

3. Write $y = 2(x - 3)^2 + 5$ in standard form. $y = 2x^2 - 12x + 23$ (27)

4. Where is the vertex of the graph of $y = x^2$ located? (0, 0) (27)

New Concepts

A transformation is a change in the location or shape of a graph. One type of transformation is a **shift,** or slide.

Math Language

A shift can also be called a **translation.**

Example 1 Examining Shifts in Parabolas

Graph $y = (x - 3)^2$ and $y = x^2 + 4$. For each, determine the vertex and the equation of the axis of symmetry, and explain how the graph shifted relative to the parent function $y = x^2$.

SOLUTION To help answer the question, the parent function is also graphed. Use $x = -\frac{b}{2a}$ to find the x-coordinate of the vertex and the axis of symmetry. Then make a table of values to find other points on the parabola.

x	0	1	2	3	4	5	6
y	9	4	1	0	1	4	9

x	−2	−1	0	1	2
y	8	5	4	5	8

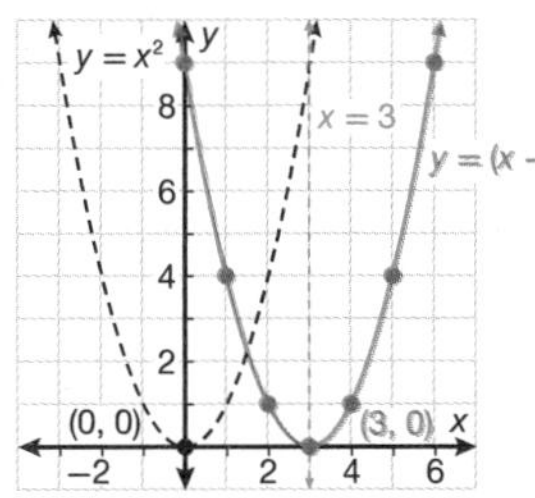

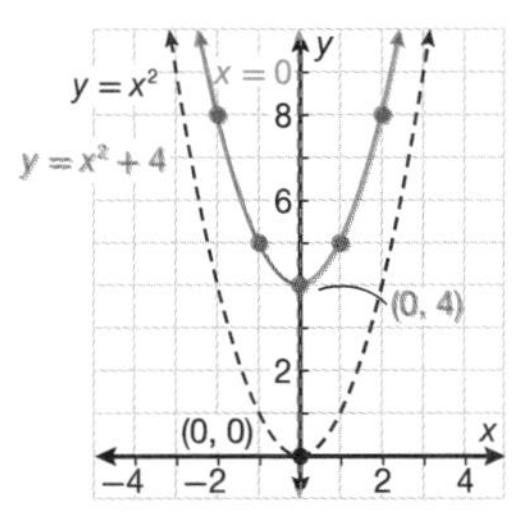

The vertex of $y = (x - 3)^2$ is (3, 0) and the axis of symmetry is $x = 3$. Relative to the parent function, the graph shifted 3 units to the right. The vertex of $y = x^2 + 4$ is (0, 4) and the axis of symmetry is $x = 0$. Relative to the parent function, the graph shifted 4 units up.

The **vertex form of a quadratic function** is $f(x) = a(x - h)^2 + k$ where $a \neq 0$, and (h, k) represents the vertex of the parabola. The functions in Example 1, written in vertex form, show the values of a, h, and k: $y = 1(x - 3)^2 + 0$ and $y = 1(x - 0)^2 + 4$. Notice that, compared to the parent function, h indicates a horizontal shift and k indicates a vertical shift of the vertex of the parabola from the origin.

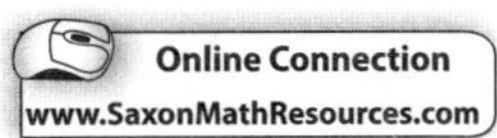

LESSON 30

1 Warm Up

Remind students to follow the order of operations in Problem 3.

2 New Concepts

In this lesson transformations are used to explain and explore shifts in parabolas.

Example 1

Ask students to identify the vertex and the axis of symmetry of the parent function $y = x^2$.

Additional Example 1

Graph $y = (x + 7)^2$. Determine the vertex and the equation of the axis of symmetry and explain how the graph shifted relative to the parent function $y = x^2$.

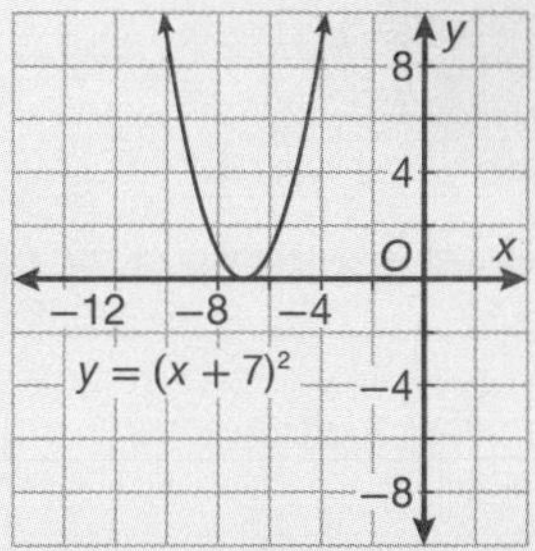

Vertex: (0, −7); Axis of symmetry: $x = -7$; The graph shifted 7 units to the left.

MATH BACKGROUND

In Lesson 27, students learned that the graph of a quadratic function is a parabola.

The parent function $y = x^2$ can be written in vertex form as $y = 1(x - 0)^2 + 0$. From this form students can determine that it opens upward, its vertex is (0, 0), and its axis of symmetry is the y-axis.

It is important that students understand how changing the signs and values of a, h, and k changes the graph of the function.

LESSON RESOURCES

Student Edition Practice Workbook 30
Reteaching Masters 30
Adaptations Masters 30
Challenge and Enrichment Masters C30

Example 2

This example uses a quadratic function in vertex form and the axis of symmetry to graph a parabola.

Error Alert Watch for students who identify the vertex as $(-3, 1)$ instead of $(3, 1)$.

Extend the Example

Have students name the reflection of the points $(0, 10)$, $(1, 5)$, and $(2, 2)$.

$(6, 10)$, $(5, 5)$, and $(4, 2)$

Additional Example 2

Graph $f(x) = (x + 2)^2 - 1$.

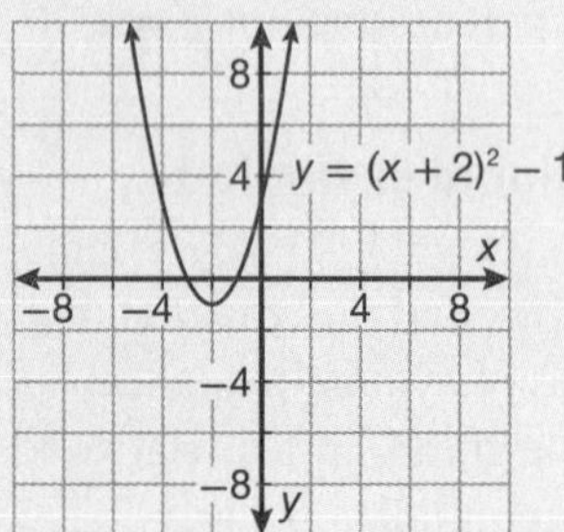

Justify

What are the advantages of using the vertex form versus the standard form of an equation?

The coordinates of the vertex can be read directly from an equation in vertex form.

The vertex form of a quadratic equation, the axis of symmetry and the reflective properties of a parabola can be used to sketch the graph of the parabola. Recall that the reflection of each point on the left side of a parabola is located on the right side of the parabola.

Example 2 Using the Vertex Form and Symmetry to Graph a Quadratic Function

Graph $f(x) = (x - 3)^2 + 1$.

SOLUTION

Step 1: Identify the vertex (h, k) and plot it.

$$f(x) = (x - \boxed{3})^2 + \boxed{1}$$

The vertex is $(3, 1)$.

Step 2: Sketch the axis of symmetry. The axis of symmetry always passes through the vertex, so the equation of the line is $x = 3$.

Step 3: Plot a few points on one side of the axis of symmetry.

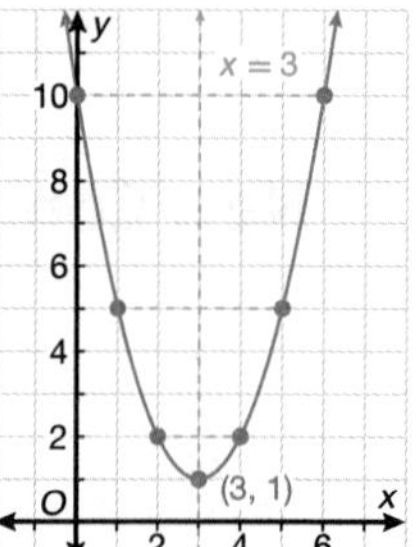

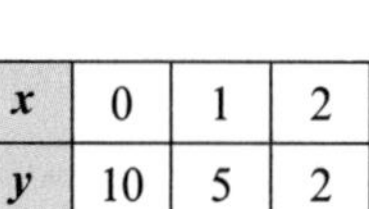

x	0	1	2
y	10	5	2

Find the reflection of each of those points across the axis of symmetry, then join the points with a smooth curve.

The sign of a in $f(x) = a(x - h)^2 + k$ tells whether the parabola opens upward or downward. When a is positive, the parabola opens upward, its vertex is a low point, and its y-coordinate is the **minimum value of the function.** When a is negative, it opens downward, its vertex is a high point, and its y-coordinate is the **maximum value of the function.**

Minimum and Maximum Values	
Opens Upward	**Opens Downward**
$f(x) = x^2$	$f(x) = -x^2$
The domain is all real numbers. The range is all values greater than or equal to the minimum.	The domain is all real numbers. The range is all values less than or equal to the maximum.

ENGLISH LEARNERS

A **translation** can also be called a shift or a slide. A translation is a type of transformation. When the values of a, h, or k are changed in the equation of a parabola, the parabola is transformed.

Reinforce how the graph of a parabola is transformed when each value is changed.

1. If the sign of a changes, the parabola is reflected across the line $y = k$.
2. If the vertex (h, k) changes, the parabola is translated left or right, and up or down.
3. Changing the absolute value of a makes the parabola widen or narrow.

The absolute value of a tells whether the parabola is vertically **compressed** or vertically **stretched**. When $0 < |a| < 1$, the parabola is vertically compressed, so it is wider than the parent function. When $|a| > 1$, the parabola is vertically stretched, so it is narrower than the parent function.

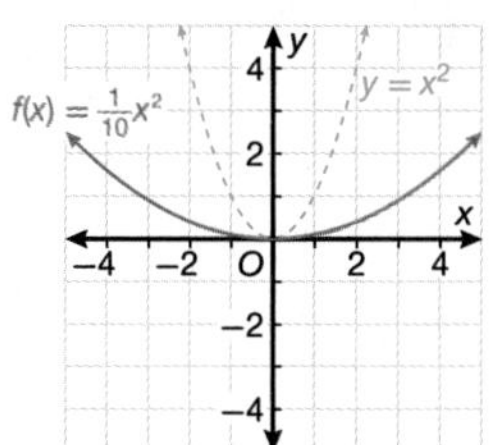

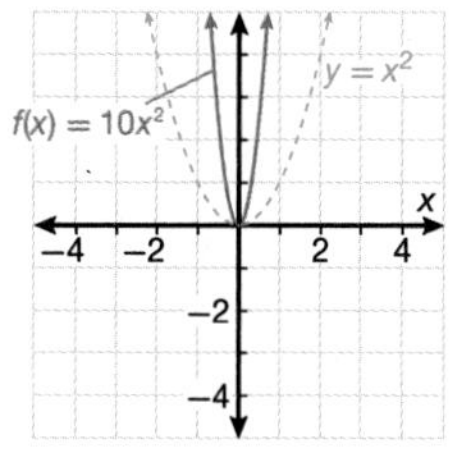

Example 3 Using the Value of a to Identify Graphs of Quadratic Functions

Match each function with its graph.

$$y = 3x^2, \quad y = -3x^2, \quad y = \frac{1}{3}x^2, \quad y = -\frac{1}{3}x^2$$

Graph A

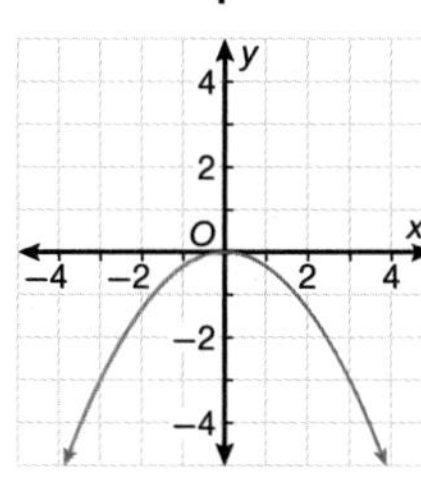

Graph B

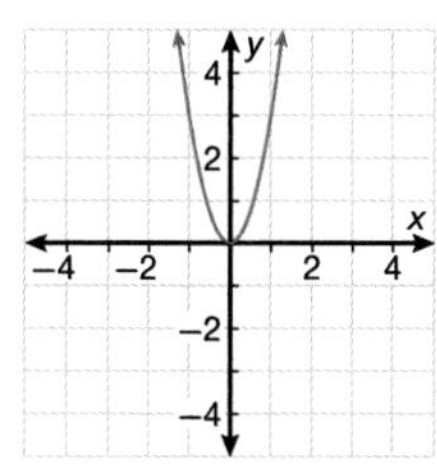

Graph C

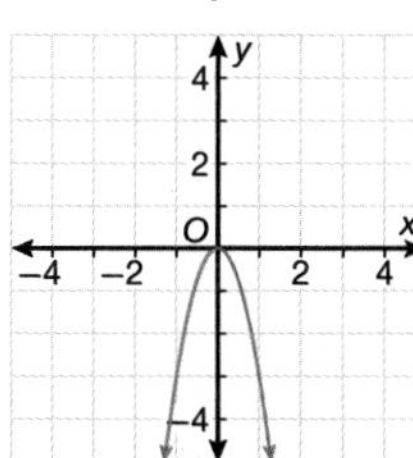

Graph D

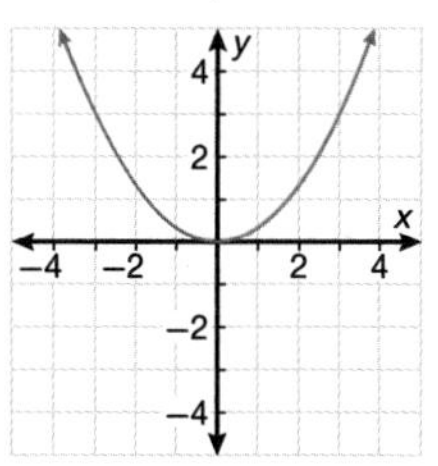

SOLUTION Graphs B and D both open upward, so the value of a in each is positive. Since Graph B is narrower, the absolute value of a is greater than that in Graph D, so Graph B shows $y = 3x^2$ and Graph D shows $y = \frac{1}{3}x^2$. Graphs A and C both open downward, so the value of a in each is negative. Since Graph C is narrower, the absolute value of a must be greater than in Graph A. Therefore, Graph A shows $y = -\frac{1}{3}x^2$ and Graph C shows $y = -3x^2$.

Math Reasoning

Analyze Which graphs are reflections of each other over the x-axis?

Graphs A and D are reflections over the x-axis. Graphs B and C are reflections over the x-axis.

Example 3

Remind students to consider both the sign of a and its absolute value. Use the sign to determine whether the parabola opens upward or downward, and the absolute value to determine how much the graph is vertically compressed or stretched.

Additional Example 3

Match each function with its graph.

$y = 5x^2$ $\quad$ $y = \frac{1}{5}x^2$

$y = -5x^2$ $\quad$ $y = -\frac{1}{5}x^2$

a.

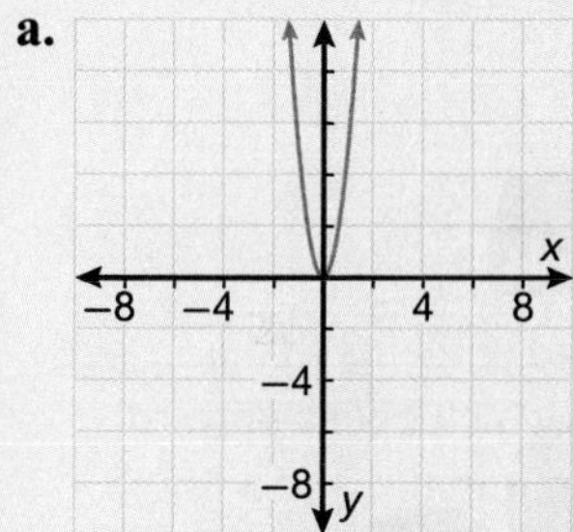

b.

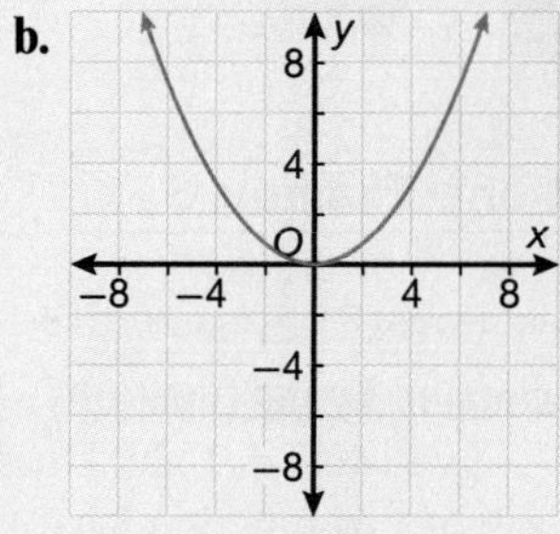

c.

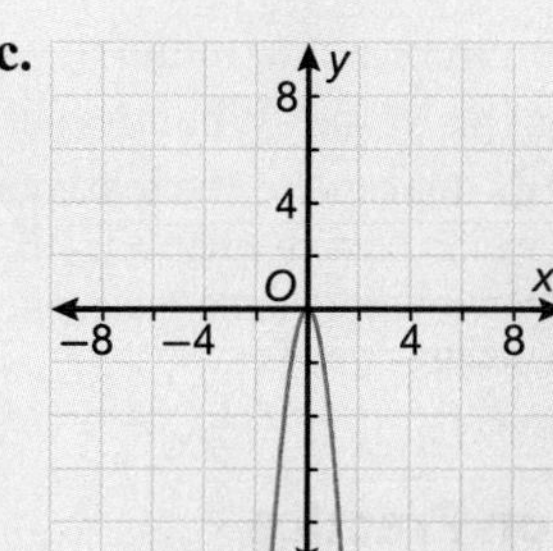

d.

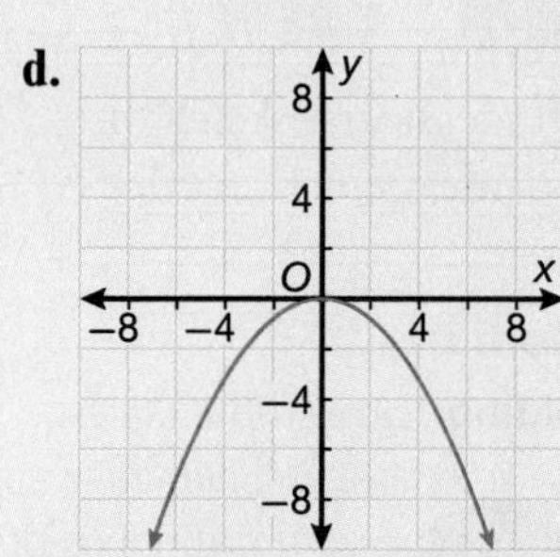

a. $y = 5x^2$ b. $y = 0.20x^2$
c. $y = -5x^2$ d. $y = -0.20x^2$

CHALLENGE

Write $y = 2x^2 + 16x + 32$ in vertex form and describe its graph.

$y = 2(x + 4)^2$; The vertex is $(-4, 0)$. The axis of symmetry is $x = -4$. The parabola opens upward and is narrower than the parent function.

Lesson 30 217

Example 4

In this example, students are shown how to find the equation of a parabola in vertex form using its graph.

Additional Example 4

Find the equation of the parabola shown.

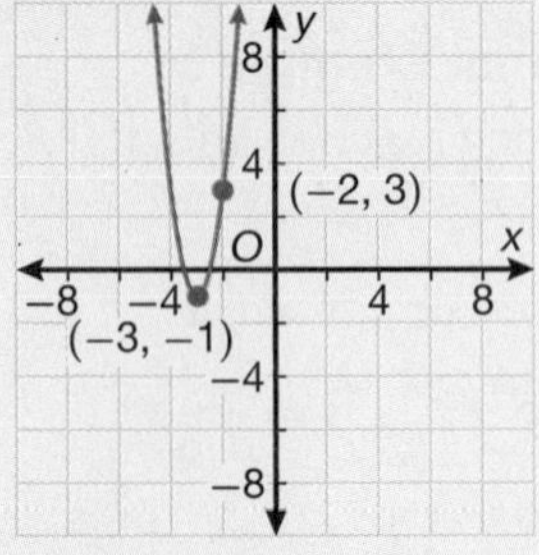

$y = 4(x + 3)^2 - 1$

Example 5

Remind students that a graph which opens upward has a minimum and a graph which opens downward has a maximum.

Additional Example 5

A company's profit over the past x weeks can be approximated by the function $f(x) = -(x - 46)^2 + 1520$. Does the graph of this function have a minimum or a maximum? What is this value? What does it represent? maximum; The maximum is 1520 which occurs when $x = 46$. The maximum represents the profit over 46 weeks.

Lesson Practice

Problem a

Have students first sketch the graph of the parent function $y = x^2$.

Problem b

Scaffolding Have students first identify a, h, and k. Then have them name the vertex and axis of symmetry. Tell them to use this information to help sketch the graph.

Given the coordinates of the vertex of a parabola and another point on the parabola, the equation of the parabola can be determined using the vertex form.

Example 4 Finding the Equation of a Parabola

Find the equation of the parabola shown.

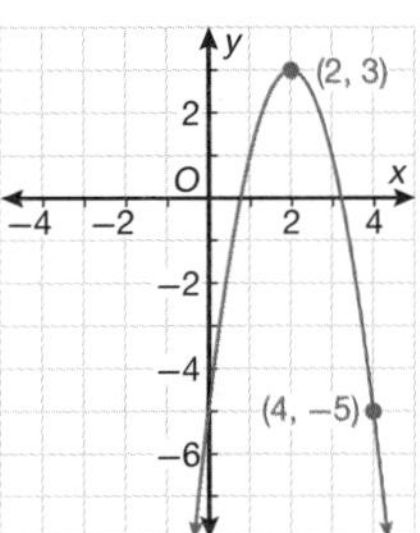

SOLUTION Substitute the coordinates of the vertex for h and k into the vertex form of a quadratic function.

$$y = a(x - 2)^2 + 3$$

Substitute the coordinates of the other point labeled for x and y, then solve for a.

$-5 = a(4 - 2)^2 + 3$

$-5 = 4a + 3$

$-8 = 4a$

$-2 = a$

→ Substitute the value of a into the equation: $y = -2(x - 2)^2 + 3$.

Caution

It is easy to assume that there is a minimum when the value of a is negative. Think about the shape of the graph before answering.

Example 5 Application: Investing

The value of a stock, in dollars, over the past x weeks can be approximated by the function $f(x) = -0.185(x - 34)^2 + 220$. Does the graph of this function have a minimum or maximum? What is this value? What does it represent?

SOLUTION The value of a is negative, so the graph opens downward and has a maximum. The maximum is \$220, which occurs when $x = 34$. So, the maximum represents the value of the stock over 34 weeks.

Lesson Practice

a. Graph $y = (x + 5)^2$ and $y = x^2 - 2$. For each, determine the vertex and axis of symmetry, and explain how the graph is shifted relative to the parent function $y = x^2$. *(Ex 1)*

a. The vertex of $y = (x + 5)^2$ is $(-5, 0)$ and the axis of symmetry is $x = -5$; relative to the parent function, it is shifted 5 units left. The vertex of $y = x^2 - 2$ is $(0, -2)$ and the axis of symmetry is $x = 0$; relative to the parent function, it is shifted 2 units down.

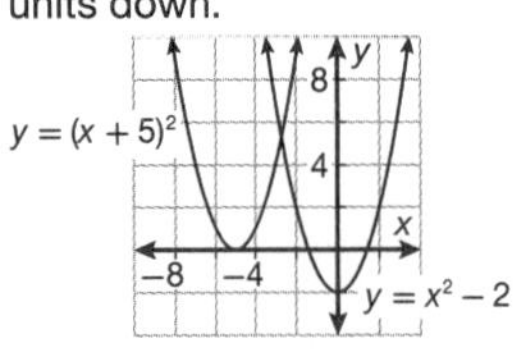

b. Graph $f(x) = (x + 4)^2 + 3$. *(Ex 2)*

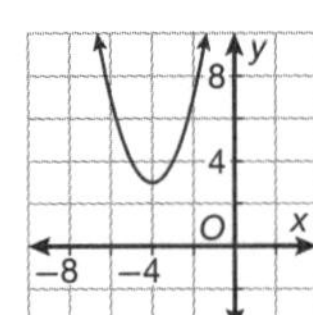

c. Graph A: $y = 4x^2$, Graph B: $y = -0.25x^2$, Graph C: $y = 0.25x^2$, Graph D: $y = -4x^2$

c. (Ex 3) Match each function with its graph.

$y = 0.25x^2, \quad y = 4x^2, \quad y = -0.25x^2, \quad y = -4x^2$

Graph A

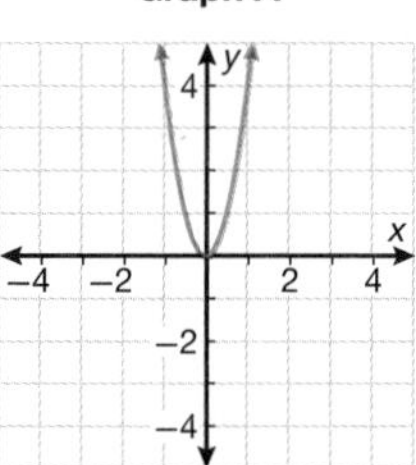

Graph B

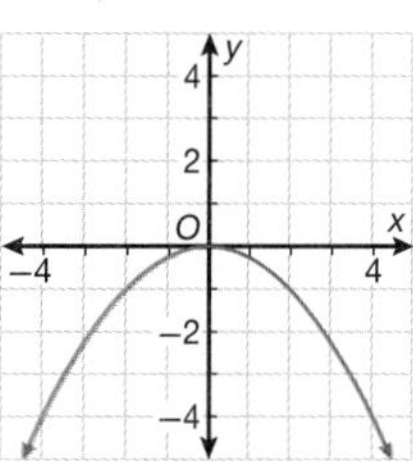

Graph C

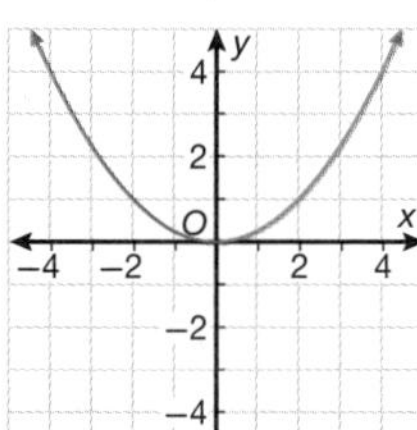

Graph D

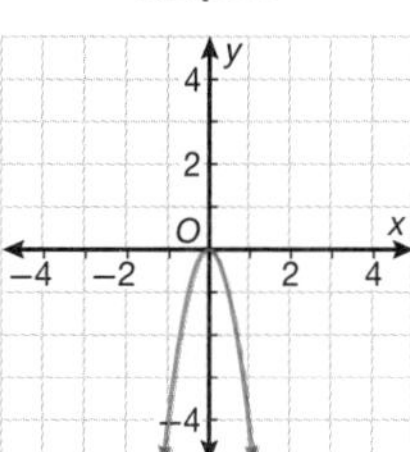

d. (Ex 4) Find the equation of the parabola shown.
$y = \frac{1}{5}(x + 1)^2 - 8$

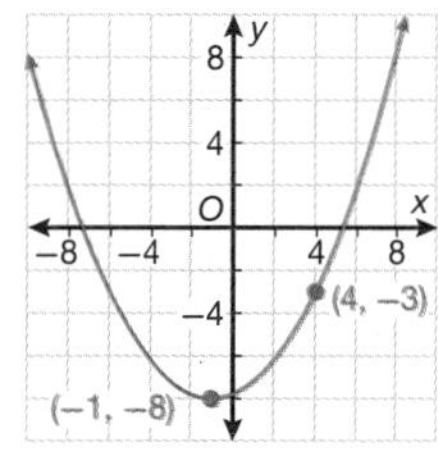

e. The value of a is positive, so the graph opens upward and the function has a minimum. The minimum occurs at the vertex (18, 39.50), so the minimum is $39.50. It represents the value of the stock at week 18.

e. (Ex 5) The value of stock, in dollars, over the past x weeks can be approximated by the function $f(x) = 0.445(x - 18)^2 + 39.50$. Does the graph of this function have a minimum or maximum? What is this value? What does it represent?

Practice Distributed and Integrated

Determine the vertex and axis of symmetry of each function.

***1.** (30) $y = x^2 + 3$ vertex: (0, 3); $x = 0$

***2.** (30) $y = 2(x - 1)^2 + 3$ vertex: (1, 3); $x = 1$

***3.** (30) $y = -(x + 2)^2$ vertex: (−2, 0); $x = -2$

***4.** (30) $y = 3x^2 + 5$ vertex: (0, 5); $x = 0$

***5.** (29) Solve the system of equations:
$$\begin{aligned} x + 3y - z &= 10 \\ 2x + 5y + z &= 9 \\ -3x + y - 3z &= 8 \end{aligned}$$
$x = 1, y = 2, z = -3$

6. (27) Determine the domain and range of the function $f(x) = 2x^2$. Domain: all real numbers; Range: All real numbers greater than or equal to 0.

Check for Understanding

The questions below help assess the concepts taught in this lesson.

1. **"Explain how to use a quadratic equation in vertex form to help you sketch its graph."** Sample: You can use the equation to determine whether the parabola has a maximum or a minimum, determine that value and use it to find the vertex and axis of symmetry.

2. **"Explain the difference between the graphs of the function $y = -2x^2$ and $y = -2(x - 4)^2 + 1$."** Sample: The graph of $y = -2x^2$ has its vertex at (0, 0) and its axis of symmetry is the y-axis. The graph of $y = -2(x^2 - 4)^2 + 1$ has its vertex at (4, 1) and the equation of its axis of symmetry is $x = 4$.

3 Practice

Math Conversations

Discussion to strengthen understanding

Problem 6
Extend the Problem

"What is the graph of the function $f(x) = 2x^2$?" a parabola

"Does the parabola have a maximum or a minimum?" a minimum

"How can you determine the range of the function with respect to its minimum value?" The range is all real numbers greater than or equal to the y-coordinate of its minimum.

INCLUSION

Have students circle h and k in each of the equations written in vertex form to help identify the vertex.

Lesson 30 219

Problem 12
Extend the Problem
What is the y-intercept of each function? 381 and 442

Find each product.

7. (19) $2x^2(2x - 4)$ $4x^3 - 8x^2$

8. (19) $\frac{4x^2}{3x^3}(x^3 + 9)$ $x \neq 0, \frac{4}{3}x^2 + \frac{12}{x}$

Determine whether each of the following are functions.

9. (4) $y^2 = x + 5$ Not a function

10. (4) $y + 3x^3 = 2x + 1$ Function

11. (4) $y^2 - x^2 = 3$ Not a function

*12. (30) **Tall Structures** The height of an object, in meters, dropped from the roof of the Empire State Building after x seconds can be approximated by the function $y = -5x^2 + 381$, whereas the height of an object dropped from the Sears Tower can be approximated by $y = -5x^2 + 442$. Without graphing, tell how the graphs of each function compare to the parent quadratic function and to each other. See Additional Answers.

*13. (29) **Estimate** Use

$$-5x - z = -4 - 9y$$
$$15x - 12 + 4z = 6y$$
$$20x - 36y = -4z + 16$$

a. Rewrite the equations by lining up the variables.

b. Estimate the number of solutions. Explain your answer.

c. Solve the system of equations to verify your estimate. Infinitely many solutions

13a. $-5x + 9y - z = -4$
$15x - 6y + 4z = 12$
$20x - 36y + 4z = 16$

13b. Infinitely many solutions; The first and third equations are multiples of each other.

*14. (28) **Travel** The London Eye is a large Ferris wheel in England. Write the circumference to area ratio of the Eye as a simplified rational expression. Then find the ratio given that the diameter of the Eye is 135 meters. $\frac{2}{r} = \frac{4}{135} \approx 0.03$

*15. (15) **Graphing Calculator** Solve the system of equations using a graphing calculator. (1, 1)

$$5y = 7 - 2x$$
$$6x + 3y = 9$$

16. (14) **Multi-Step** a. Calculate the determinant of $\begin{bmatrix} 0 & -2 & 3 \\ 1 & 4 & 2 \\ -3 & -1 & 1 \end{bmatrix}$. 47

b. Write the result of interchanging the first two rows of the matrix above.

c. Compare the determinants of the matrices in parts a and b. Explain what you see. They are equal because the calculations are the same.

16b. $\begin{bmatrix} 1 & 4 & 2 \\ 0 & -2 & 3 \\ -3 & -1 & 1 \end{bmatrix}$

17. (25) **Model** Each week, Damien records his car's miles per gallon. Over a period of 10 weeks, he records: 18, 17, 19, 18, 18, 25, 29, 30, 26, 19. Make a box-and-whisker plot of his data.

18. (24) **Justify** Which property of equality allows one equation to be added to another equation? Explain. See Additional Answers.

19. (23) **Error Analysis** Explain the error in the student's work below.

$$3x^2 - x - 4 = 0$$
$$2x = 4$$
$$x = 2$$

19. The student added unlike terms resulting in a linear equation. The student should have factored to solve.

17.
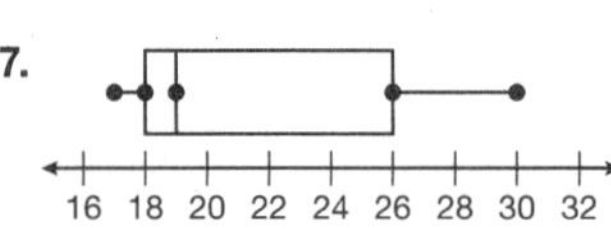

220 Saxon Algebra 2

20. **Analyze** Describe how a graph of 2 linear equations looks when the system has:
(21)
a. exactly one solution. The lines intersect at a single point.
b. an infinite number of solutions. The lines coincide, sharing all points.
c. no solution. The lines are parallel.

21. **Multiple Choice** Solve $|2x + 1| < 4$. A
(17)
A $-\frac{5}{2} < x < \frac{3}{2}$ **B** $\frac{3}{2} < x < -\frac{5}{2}$
C $x < -\frac{5}{2}$ or $x > \frac{3}{2}$ **D** $x < \frac{3}{2}$

22. **Mailing Weights** A customer visits the post office to weigh a package. The cost of mailing a package depends on its weight. Examine the table. Does this table represent a continuous, discontinuous, and/or discrete function? Justify your answer. This is a discontinuous function; The points of discontinuity are at $x = 5, 10, 15$.
(22)

Weight	Cost
$0 \le x < 5$	\$2.00
$5 \le x < 10$	\$4.00
$10 \le x < 15$	\$6.00

23. **Basketball** The length of a regulation high school basketball court is represented by the expression $(x + 24)$ feet. The width of a regulation high school basketball court is represented by the expression $(x - 10)$ feet.
(19)
a. Write an expression that represents the area of a regulation high school basketball court. $(x + 24)(x - 10) = x^2 + 14x - 240$ ft^2
b. Evaluate the area of the court if $x = 60$. $(60)^2 + 14(60) - 240 = 4200$ ft^2

24. **Track and Field** Katie ran two miles to get ready for Thursday's meet. How many feet did Katie run? 10,560 ft.
(18)

25. **Coordinate Geometry** A triangle on a coordinate grid has vertices at (3, 0), (−5, 0), and (0, −6). Write the distance from each vertex to the origin as an absolute value expression. Then simplify the expression. $|3| = 3, |-5| = 5, |-6| = 6$
(17)

26. **Multi-Step** Given the polynomial functions $f(x) = x^3 - x$, $g(x) = x^2 + 1$, and $h(x) = x^2 - 1$:
(11)
a. Write the polynomial function $g(x) + h(x)$. $g(x) + h(x) = 2x^2$
b. Write the composite function $f(g(x) + h(x))$ in standard form. $f(g(x) + h(x)) = 8x^6 - 2x^2$

27. **Multiple Choice** Solve $-|2x + 9| \le -3$. B
(17)
A $-6 \le x \le -3$ **B** $x \le -6$ or $x \ge -3$
C All real numbers **D** No solution

***28.** **Error Analysis** Two students are asked to find the axis of symmetry for the parabola of the function $f(x) = -(x + 4)^2 + 1$. Student A said the line was $x = 4$ and Student B said the line was $x = -4$. Which student is incorrect? Explain the error.
(30)

29. **Justify** Identify the domain and range of $f(x) = 2x^2 - 7$. Explain how you know.
(27)

30. **Geometry** The Mendez family is going to start a vegetable garden by their house and is going to enclose it within a fence on three sides. If the total amount of fencing they purchase is 300 feet, write an equation in standard form for finding all possible lengths and widths for the garden. $2W + L = 300$.
(26)

28. Student A is incorrect. The function can be written as $y = -(x - (-4))^2 + 1$, which shows more clearly that $h = -4$. Since the axis of symmetry passes through the vertex $(-4, 1)$, the axis of symmetry is $x = -4$.

29. D: all real numbers, R: all real numbers greater than or equal to −7; Any number can be substituted in for x, but because any real number squared is greater than or equal to 0, −7 is the lowest possible output for the function.

Problem 21

Error Alert

Watch for students who ignore the absolute value symbol and choose answer D.

Problem 23

"What shape is a basketball court?" rectangular

"What is the formula for the area of a rectangle?" $A = lw$

LOOKING FORWARD

Applying transformations to the parabola prepares students for:

- **Lesson 35** Solving Quadratic Equations I
- **Lesson 58** Completing the Square
- **Lesson 78** Solving Quadratic Equations II
- **Lesson 83** Writing Quadratic Equations from Roots

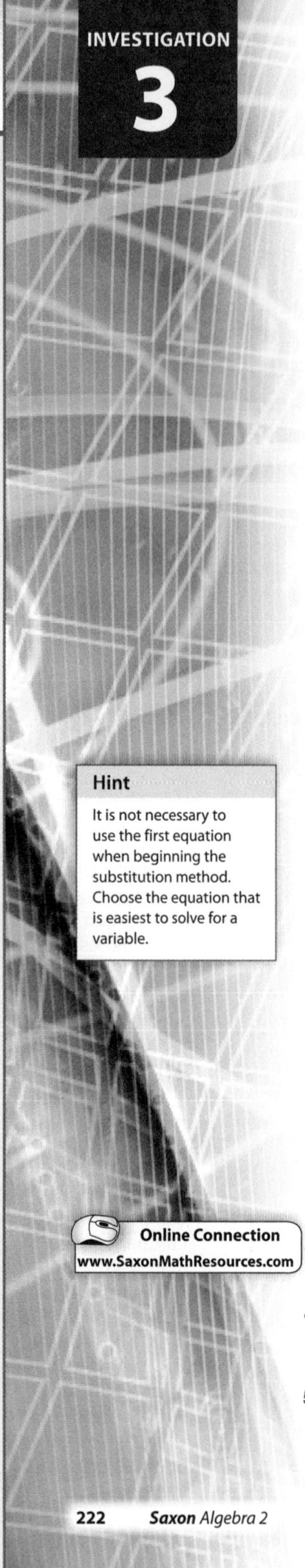

INVESTIGATION 3

Materials

- Graph paper
- Straightedge

Discuss

Review the substitution method. Focus on how the elimination method and substitution method produce equations in one variable in both a system of two equations or a system of three equations. Discuss the different types of solutions to a system of two equations and three equations. Explain to students that graphing equations in three variables requires a three-dimensional coordinate system.

INVESTIGATION 3

Applying the Substitution Method to a System in Three Variables

The same method of substitution, which has been used to find a solution to a system of equation in two variables, can be applied to a system of equations in three variables. Use the following steps to scrutinize the method. Then apply the method to a system of equations in three variables.

The system consisting of the equations $2x - y = -10$ and $-x + y = 4$ is graphed at the right. Solve the system, using the substitution method, by following the steps.

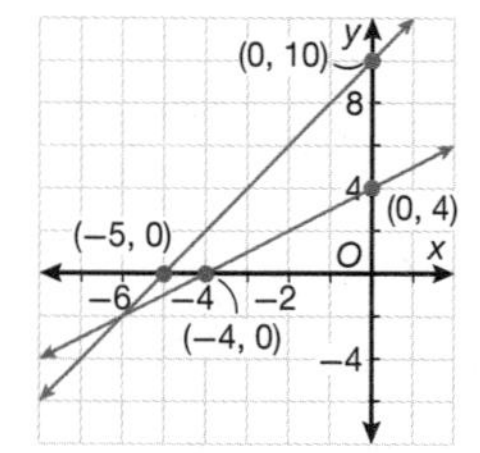

1. The first step, when solving a system using the substitution method, is choosing an equation and solving it for a variable. Solve for y in the second equation. $y = x + 4$

2. Explain how the resulting expression is used in the second step of the substitution method. Record the equation found after completing this step. The resulting expression is substituted into the other equation; $2x - (x + 4) = -10$

3. **Generalize** Notice that the equation is written in one variable. Explain how forming a one-variable equation contributes to finding a solution to the system. Sample: Forming a one-variable equation produces a solvable equation

4. **Verify** Find the values of x and y. Explain how the values are determined.

5. **Explain** How is the solution of the system checked?

Hint

It is not necessary to use the first equation when beginning the substitution method. Choose the equation that is easiest to solve for a variable.

In order to solve a two-variable system, it is necessary to have at least two equations. In the same way, to solve a three-variable system there must be at least three equations.

Use the substitution method to solve the system:

$$x - 3y + 2z = 11$$
$$-x + 4y + 3z = 5$$
$$2x - 2y - 4z = 2$$

6. Apply the first step of the substitution method, found in Step 1, by solving the first equation for x. $x = 3y - 2z + 11$

Online Connection
www.SaxonMathResources.com

4. Solve for x in the equation from step 2, which is $x = -6$. Then substitute the value for x into one of the original the equations, which is $6 + y = 4$. Then solve this equation for y, which is $y = -2$.

5. Sample: Substitute x and y into each equation. If both values satisfy both equations, then this verifies the answer.

MATH BACKGROUND

An equation of the form $ax + by + cz = d$, where a, b, c, and d are constants, with a, b, and c nonzero, is a linear equation in three variables. When the ordered triple (x, y, z) satisfies the equation $ax + by + cz = d$, it is said to be a solution of the equation. The graph of a linear equation in three variables is a plane.

7. Substituting is the next step. The equation produced by substituting the resulting expression from Step 1 into the second equation is $-(3y - 2z + 11) + 4y + 3z = 5$. Write this equation in simplified form and draw a box around it. $y + 5z = 16$

8. Substitute the same expression from Step 1 into the third equation. Write the equation formed, simplify it, and draw a box around it. $4y - 8z = -20$

For an equation to be solvable, the equation must be written in one variable. Therefore, the process of substitution must be repeated until this situation arises.

9. How many variables are there in the equations that were boxed? What are the variables? two; y and z

10. Apply the substitution method for solving a system of equations in two variables to solve the smaller system of equations formed by the two boxed-equations. What are the values of y and z? $y = 1$; $z = 3$

11. **Generalize** Find the value of x. How is the third variable of a system of equations in three variables determined? $x = 8$; By substituting the other two variables into one of the original equations

The solution to this system is a point with three coordinates. Points with three coordinates are graphed on a three-dimensional coordinate system. A **three-dimensional coordinate system** is a space that is divided into eight regions by an x-axis, a y-axis, and a z-axis.

The **z-axis** is the third axis in a three-dimensional coordinate plane and is typically drawn as a vertical line. The y-axis is drawn as a horizontal line and the x-axis is drawn as if it is going into the page, as shown in the graph. Coordinates in a three-dimensional plane are called ordered triples and are written in the form (x, y, z). The arrows in the graph show how to plot the point (2, 4, 6).

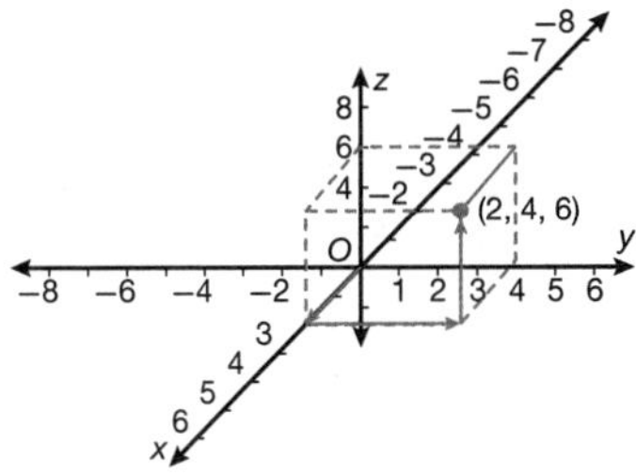

An ordered triple is one type of solution to a system of equations in three variables. The graph of an equation in three variables is a plane and is written as $Ax + By + Cz = D$, where A, B, and C are nonzero real numbers. If a system of equations in three variables has a single ordered triple as a solution, then

- the coordinates of that point satisfies all three equations and
- the point is the intersection of the three planes.

Problem 10

Error Alert

Students who do not show all of their steps may have distribution errors, addition errors, or simplification errors. To avoid errors, have students show all of their work and have them box their answers in Problem 7 and Problem 8.

Problem 11

Extend the Problem

What is the result produced by applying the substitution method to a system of three equations which has infinitely many solutions? How is the solution written? It produces a true numerical statement; the solution is written as a line.

TEACHER TIP

Discuss the other types of solutions of systems of three equations, a line, a plane, or no solution, by connecting the algebraic and graphic interpretations.

INCLUSION

Students often perform the steps of the substitution method correctly, but make computational errors that may produce incorrect answers. Suggest that these student use graph paper to write each step out in an organized way.

Problem 12

There are more points that can be used to define a plane besides the intercept points. Point out to students that they can use non-intercept points, although intercept points are the easiest to calculate and plot.

Problem 13

Error Alert

When drawing a three dimensional coordinate system it can be helpful to impose a rectangular prism to show where a coordinate is plotted.

Problem 14

TEACHER TIP

Remind students that three non-collinear points define a plane.

In a system of equations in three variables, the intersection of all three planes is the solution to the system.

One Solution	Infinitely Many Solutions
The planes intersect at a single point.	The planes intersect in a line.

To graph the equation $2x + 3y + 6z = 12$, use the intercept method that is used to graph a linear equation.

12. **Explain** If setting $y = 0$ and solving for x is the process for determining the x-intercept of a linear equation, then what is the process for determining the x-intercept for the equation $2x + 3y + 6z = 12$?
Set $y = 0$, set $z = 0$, and then solve for x.

13. (6, 0, 0,), (0, 4, 0), (0, 0, 2)

13. **Formulate** What are the x-, y-, and z-intercepts for the equation $2x + 3y + 6z = 12$? Write the answer in ordered triples.

Caution

The plane formed by the shaded triangle is not limited to the triangle. However, the shaded triangle is contained in the plane.

14. **Model** Copy and complete the drawing by plotting the other intercept. Then draw the two other lines through the other points to form a triangle. Shade the triangle to give the illusion of a plane.

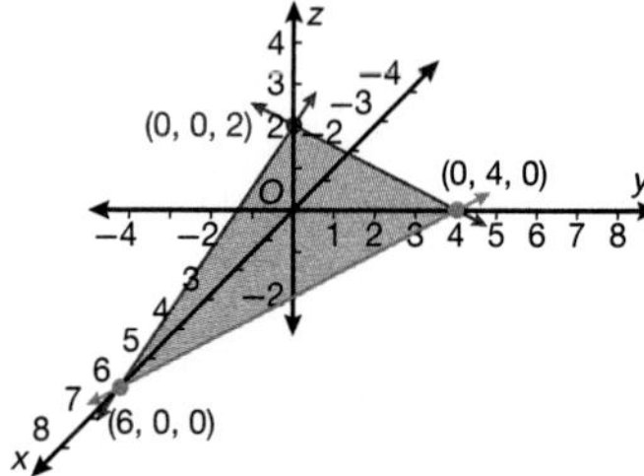

A system of equations in three variables may not have a solution. This occurs when there is no point that lies in all three planes. These systems may have equations that form three planes in the following ways:

No Solution

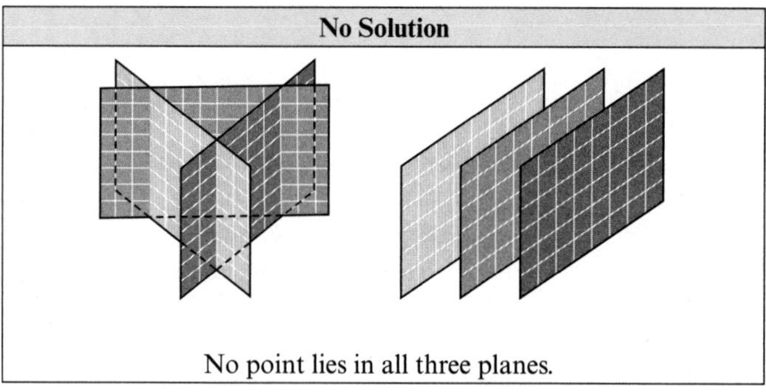

No point lies in all three planes.

ENGLISH LEARNERS

For Problem 14, explain the meaning of the word **illusion.** Say,

"Illusion means to make something appear to be what it is not."

Explain to students that shading is often used to make a two-dimensional figure appear to be three-dimensional.

Have students give example of other illusions with which they are familiar.
Sample: optical illusions, magician's illusions

Investigation Practice

a. **Multi-Step** Solve the system using the substitution method. If the solution is a single point, then graph the coordinate using arrows on a three-dimensional coordinate system.

$$x + 4y - 5z = 7$$
$$3x + 2y + 3z = 7$$
$$2x + y + 5z = 8 \quad (2, -1, 1)$$

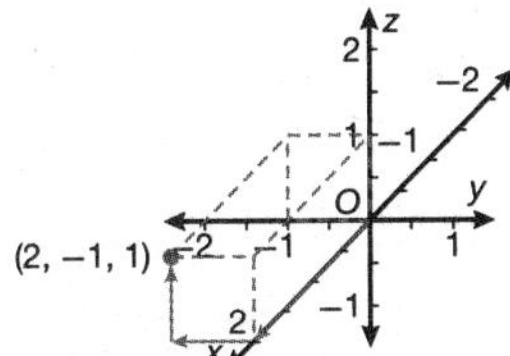

b. **Multi-Step** Find the intercepts of the equation $2x - y + 3z = 6$. Graph the intercepts of the equation on a graph and shade the plane that is formed by the intercepts. (0, 0, 2), (0, −6, 0), (3, 0, 0)

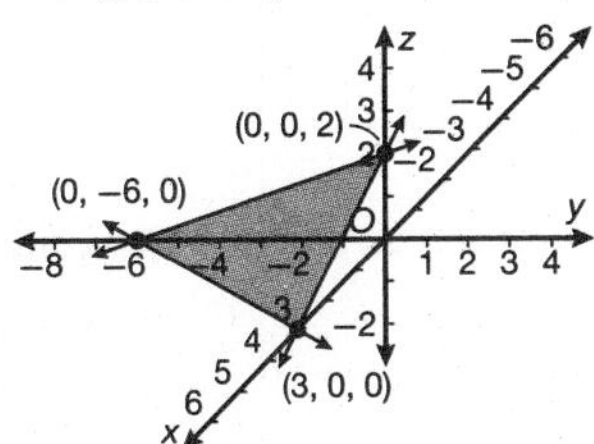

Investigation Practice

Math Conversations

Discussion to strengthen understanding.

Problem a

Error Alert

If students get an incorrect answer, then have them check their work by using another method or substituting the coordinates into each original equation.

LOOKING FORWARD

Applying the substitution method with a system of three equation prepares students for

- **Lesson 32** Solving Linear Systems with Matrix Inverses
- **Lesson 43** Solving Systems of Linear Inequalities

Lesson Planner

Lesson	New Concepts
31	Multiplying and Dividing Rational Expressions
32	Solving Linear Systems with Matrix Inverses
33	Applying Counting Principles
34	Graphing Linear Equations II
35	Solving Quadratic Equations I
	Cumulative Test 6, Performance Task 6
36	Using Parallel and Perpendicular Lines
37	Adding and Subtracting Rational Expressions
38	Dividing Polynomials Using Long Division
39	Graphing Linear Inequalities in Two Variables
40	Simplifying Radical Expressions
	Cumulative Test 7, Performance Task 7
INV 4	Investigation: Understanding Cryptography

Resources for Teaching

- Student Edition
- Teacher's Edition
- Student Edition eBook
- Teacher's Edition eBook
- Resources and Planner CD
- Solutions Manual
- Instructional Masters
- Technology Lab Masters
- Warm Up and Teaching Transparencies
- Instructional Presentations CD
- Online activities, tools, and homework help **www.SaxonMathResources.com**

Resources for Practice and Assessment

- Student Edition Practice Workbook
- Course Assessments
- Standardized Test Practice
- College Entrance Exam Practice
- Test and Practice Generator CD using ExamView™

Resources for Differentiated Instruction

- Reteaching Masters
- Challenge and Enrichment Masters
- Prerequisite Skills Intervention
- Adaptations for Saxon Algebra 2
- Multilingual Glossary
- English Learners Handbook
- TI Resources

Pacing Guide

Resources and Planner CD for lesson planning support

45-Minute Class

Day 1	Day 2	Day 3	Day 4	Day 5	Day 6
Lesson 31	Lesson 32	Lesson 33	Lesson 34	Lesson 35	Cumulative Test 6
Day 7	**Day 8**	**Day 9**	**Day 10**	**Day 11**	**Day 12**
Lesson 36	Lesson 37	Lesson 38	Lesson 39	Lesson 40	Cumulative Test 7
Day 7					
Investigation 4					

Block: 90-Minute Class

Day 1	Day 2	Day 3	Day 4	Day 5	Day 6
Lesson 31 Lesson 32	Lesson 33 Lesson 34	Lesson 35 Cumulative Test 6	Lesson 36 Lesson 37	Lesson 38 Lesson 39	Lesson 40 Cumulative Test 7
Day 7					
Investigation 4 Lesson 41					

** For suggestions on how to implement Saxon Math in a block schedule, see the Pacing section at the beginning of the Teacher's Edition.*

Differentiated Instruction

Below Level		Advanced Learners	
Warm Up	SE pp. 226, 233, 240, 246, 253, 259, 266, 273, 279, 286	Challenge	TE pp. 231, 238, 243, 251, 257, 264, 271, 278, 284, 290, 292
Skills Bank	SE pp. 862–885	Extend the Example	TE pp. 226, 228, 235, 242, 260, 267, 274, 281, 286, 287, 288, Inv. 4
Reteaching Masters	Lessons 31–40, Investigation 4	Extend the Problem	TE pp. 230, 231, 238, 239, 244, 251 258, 265, 271, 283, 285, 292, 293, 294
Warm Up Transparencies	Lessons 31–40	Challenge and Enrichment	Challenge: C31–C40 Enrichment E35, E40
Prerequisite Skills Intervention	Lessons 1, 2, 6, 61, 72, 74, 74, 76, 90		

English Learners		Special Needs	
EL Tips	TE pp. 228, 234, 241, 248, 255, 261, 267, 274, 280, 288, 294	Inclusion Tips	TE pp. 227, 229, 230, 235, 242, 249, 250, 254, 260, 262, 268, 269, 275, 282, 291
Multilingual Glossary	Booklet and Online	Adaptations for Saxon Algebra 2	Lessons 31–40; Cumulative Tests 6, 7
English Learners Handbook			

For All Learners			
Exploration	SE p. 233	Alternate Method	TE pp. 236, 237, 245, 247, 256, 263, 270, 281, 287, 289
Caution	SE pp. 227, 228, 235, 279, 287	Online Tools	
Hints	SE pp. 226, 228, 233, 236, 246, 247, 253, 255, 259, 274, 281, 288, 289, 293		
Error Alert	TE pp. 227, 228, 230, 234, 236, 241, 243, 247, 254, 256, 257, 262, 263, 265, 269, 276, 282, 284, 287, 288, 289, 290, 291, 294		

SE = Student Edition; TE = Teacher's Edition

Math Vocabulary

Lesson	New Vocabulary		Maintained	EL Tip in TE
31	reciprocal		undefined	reciprocal
32	matrix of coefficients matrix of constants matrix of variables	multiplicative inverse of a square matrix singular matrix	matrix	matrices matrix
33	addition counting principle dependent events event experiment fundamental counting principle independent events	mutually exclusive outcomes sample space tree diagram trial	median	exclusive mutual
34	horizontal line linear function		slope	transform transformations
35	double root roots of an equation		quadratic	double
36			point-slope	parallel perpendicular
37			rational	Least Common Multiple
38			inequality	dividend divisor quotient remainder
39	boundary line half-plane linear inequality in two variables		slope-intercept undefined	< and > symbols
40	index like radicals principal root radical	radical symbol radicand rationalizing the denominator	square root	approximate evaluate simplify
INV 4				decrypt encrypt

SECTION OVERVIEW 4

Math Highlights

Enduring Understandings – The "Big Picture"

After completing Section 4, students will understand:

- How to add, subtract, multiply, and divide rational expressions.
- How to solve and graph linear equations in one or two variables.
- How to use matrix inverses to solve linear systems.

Essential Questions

- How is cryptography used in computers and the Internet?
- How are counting principles used in probability and statistics?
- What is the Zero Product Property?

Math Content Strands

Linear Functions

• Lesson 34	Graphing Linear Equations II
• Lesson 36	Using Parallel and Perpendicular Lines
• Lesson 39	Graphing Linear Inequalities in Two Variables

Matrices

• Lesson 32	Solving Linear Systems with Matrix Inverses Exploration: Exploring Matrix Inverses

Polynomials and Polynomial Functions

• Lesson 38	Dividing Polynomials Using Long Division

Probability and Statistics

• Lesson 33	Applying Counting Principles

Quadratic Functions

• Lesson 35	Solving Quadratic Equations I

Rational and Radical Functions

• Lesson 31	Multiplying and Dividing Rational Expressions
• Lesson 37	Adding and Subtracting Rational Expressions
• Lesson 40	Simplifying Radical Expressions

Sequences Series, and Logic

• Investigation 4	Understanding Cryptography

Connections in Practice Problems

	Lessons
Coordinate Geometry	31, 35, 40
Data Analysis	36
Geometry	31, 32, 33, 34, 35, 36, 37, 38, 39, 40
Measurement	33
Probability	32, 34, 35, 37, 38,
Statistics	39

Math Processes

Reasoning and Communication

	Lessons
• Analyze	31, 32, 33, 34, 35, 36, 37, 38, 39, 40, Inv. 4
• Error analysis	31, 32, 33, 34, 35, 36, 37, 38, 39, 40
• Estimate	34
• Formulate	35, 36
• Generalize	31, 35, Inv. 4
• Justify	33, 35, 36, 37, 38
• Model	39
• Multiple choice	31, 32, 33, 34, 35, 36, 37, 38, 39, 40
• Multi-step	31, 32, 33, 34, 36, 37, 38, 39, 40, Inv. 4
• Predict	40
• Verify	31, 32, 34, 36, 37, 39, 40
• Write	31, 32, 33, 34, 35, 36, 37, 38, 40
• Graphing Calculator	31, 32, 33, 34, 35, 36, 37, 38, 39, 40, Inv. 4

Connections

In Examples: Analyzing nutrition and cost, Determining a dimension, Food preparation, Physics, Right triangles, Sports, Travel time, Vertical motion, Wheelchair accessibility

In Practice problems: Airplanes, Average velocity, Aviation, Baseball equipment, Basketball, Berries, Biology, Business, Cab fares, Chemistry, Construction, Currency exchange, Economics, Engineering, Exercise, Flags, Geography, Hourly pay, Investing, Item costs, Medicine, Money, Motion, Mountains, Nutrition, Olympic swimming pool size, Population, Recreational planning, River current, Roofing, Shipping boxes, Small business, Sports, Ticket prices, U.S. Postal Service, Women's basketball, Woodworking, Work

Content Trace

Lesson	Warm Up: Prerequisite Skills	New Concepts	Where Practiced	Where Assessed	Looking Forward
31	Lessons Skills Bank 2, 28	Multiplying and Dividing Rational Expressions	Lessons 31, 32, 33, 34, 35, 36, 37, 40, 42, 43, 45, 47, 49, 50, 52, 54, 57, 64, 1204, 107, 112, 113, 116	Cumulative Tests 7, 9, 10, 11, 14, 17, 21	Lessons 37, 40, 44, 48
32	Lessons 5, 9	Solving Linear Systems with Matrix Inverses	Lessons 32, 33, 34, 35, 36, 37, 38, 39, 40, 41, 42, 43, 45, 46, 57, 72, 79, 99, 101, 102, 105, 110, 112, 114, 115	Cumulative Tests 7, 12, 14, 18, 19	Lessons 56, 99, 112
33	Lesson 25	Applying Counting Principles	Lessons 33, 34, 36, 37, 38, 39, 40, 41, 42, 44, 45, 46, 53, 55, 101, 103, 106, 108, 109, 111, 115, 116, 118	Cumulative Tests 7, 8, 10, 13, 15, 16	Lessons 55, 60
34	Lessons 7, 13	Graphing Linear Equations II	Lessons 34, 35, 36, 37, 38, 39, 40, 41, 42, 44, 45, 50, 57, 104	Cumulative Tests 7, 9, 12, 17	Lessons 36, 39, 43, 50
35	Lessons 23, 27	Solving Quadratic Equations I	Lessons 35, 36, 37, 38, 39, 40, 41, 42, 44, 45, 46, 47, 53, 63, 64, 107, 108, 110, 111, 112	Cumulative Tests 7, 8, 10, 11, 23	Lessons 58, 65, 66, 78
36	Lesson 13	Using Parallel and Perpendicular Lines	Lessons 36, 37, 38, 39, 40, 41, 42, 43, 44, 45, 46, 47, 48, 49, 51, 52, 53, 59, 60, 65, 66, 100, 109, 117	Cumulative Tests 8, 10, 14, 18	Lessons 41, 45
37	Lessons 1, 23	Adding and Subtracting Rational Expressions	Lessons 37, 38, 39, 40, 41, 42, 45, 46, 47, 48, 51, 52, 53, 55, 62, 66, 99, 110, 112, 113	Cumulative Tests 8, 9, 10, 12, 16, 20	Lessons 40, 44, 58, 61, 65
38	Lessons 4, 10, 39	Dividing Polynomials Using Long Division	Lessons 38, 39, 40, 41, 42, 43, 44, 45, 46, 47, 52, 55, 59, 60, 65, 71, 100, 107, 115	Cumulative Tests 8, 9, 12, 15	Lessons 51, 66, 95
39	Lesson 13	Graphing Linear Inequalities in Two Variables	Lessons 39, 40, 41, 42, 43, 44, 45, 46, 47, 48, 49, 51, 53, 56, 57, 59, 64, 65, 101, 105, 116, 118	Cumulative Tests 8, 10, 17	Lessons 43, 89, 93, 102
40	Lessons 2, 3, 19, 25	Simplifying Radical Expressions	Lessons 40, 41, 42, 43, 44, 45, 46, 47, 48, 49, 50, 52, 53, 55, 57, 58, 59, 63, 65, 72, 100, 103, 112, 114, 116, 119	Cumulative Tests 8, 9, 10, 11, 13, 14, 16, 19	Lessons 44, 48, 59, 70, 75
INV 4	N/A	Investigation: Understanding Cryptography	Lesson 77	Cumulative Test 9	Lesson 54

SECTION OVERVIEW 4

Ongoing Assessment

	Type	Feature	Intervention *
BEFORE instruction	Assess Prior Knowledge	• Diagnostic Test	• Prerequisite Skills Intervention
BEFORE the lesson	Formative	• Warm Up	• Skills Bank • Reteaching Masters
DURING the lesson	Formative	• Lesson Practice • Math Conversations with the Practice problems	• Additional Examples in TE • Test and Practice Generator (for additional practice sheets)
AFTER the lesson	Formative	• Check for Understanding (closure)	• Scaffolding Questions in TE
AFTER 5 lessons	Summative	After Lesson 35 • Cumulative Test 6 • Performance Task 6 After Lesson 40 • Cumulative Test 7 • Performance Task 7	• Reteaching Masters • Test and Practice Generator (for additional tests and practice)
AFTER 20 lessons	Summative	• Benchmark Tests	• Reteaching Masters • Test and Practice Generator (for additional tests and practice)

* for students not showing progress during the formative stages or scoring below 80% on the summative assessments

Evidence of Learning – What Students Should Know

Because the Saxon philosophy is to provide students with sufficient time to learn and practice each concept, a lesson's topic will not be tested until at least five lessons after the topic is introduced.

On the Cumulative Tests that are given during this section of ten lessons, students should be able to demonstrate the following competencies:

- Simplify rational expressions.
- Solve systems of three equations and three variables.
- Find measures of central tendency and dispersion.
- Write the equation of a line.
- Solve linear systems with matrix inverses.
- Multiply and divide rational expressions.
- Apply counting principles to probability and statistics.

Test and Practice Generator CD using ExamView™

The Test and Practice Generator is an easy-to-use benchmark and assessment tool that creates unlimited practice and tests in multiple formats and allows you to customize questions or create new ones. A variety of reports are available to track student progress toward mastery of the standards throughout the year.

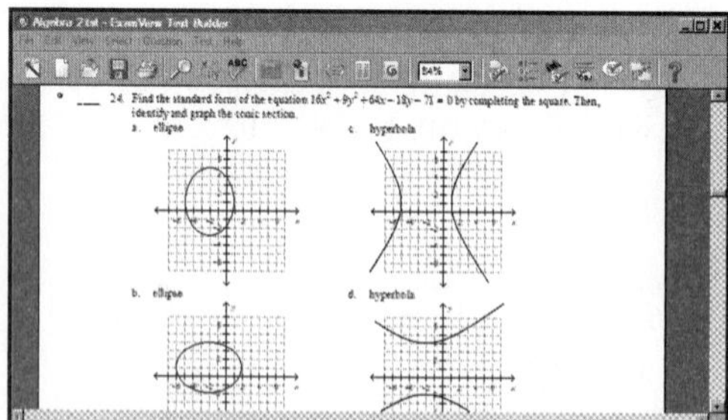

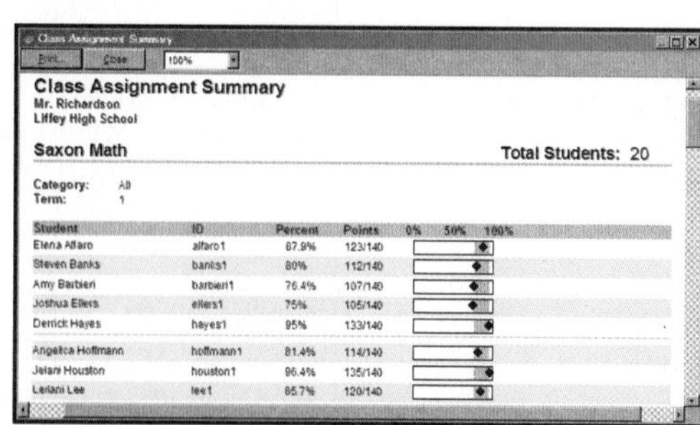

Assessment Resources

Resources for Diagnosing and Assessing

- **Student Edition**
  - Warm Up
  - Lesson Practice
- **Teacher's Edition**
  - Math Conversations with the Practice problems
  - Check for Understanding (closure)
- **Course Assessments**
  - Diagnostic Test
  - Cumulative Tests
  - Performance Tasks
  - Benchmark Tests

Resources for Test Prep

- **Student Edition**
  - Multiple-choice practice problems
  - Multiple-step and writing problems
  - Daily cumulative practice
- **Standardized Test Practice**
- **College Entrance Exam Practice**
- **Test and Practice Generator CD using ExamView™**

Resources for Intervention

- **Student Edition**
  - Skills Bank
- **Teacher's Edition**
  - Additional Examples
  - Scaffolding questions
- **Prerequisite Skills Intervention**
  - Worksheets
- **Reteaching Masters**
  - Lesson instruction and practice sheets
- **Test and Practice Generator CD using ExamView™**
  - Lesson practice problems
  - Additional tests

SECTION OVERVIEW 4

Cumulative Tests

The assessments in Saxon Math are frequent and consistently placed after every five lessons to offer a regular method of ongoing testing. These cumulative assessments check mastery of concepts from previous lessons.

Performance Tasks

The Performance Tasks can be used in conjunction with the Cumulative Tests and are scored using a rubric.

After Lesson 35

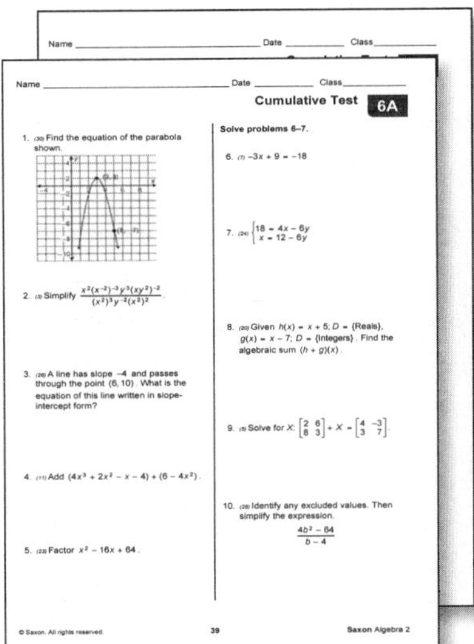

Name ________ Date ________ Class ________

Cumulative Test 6A

1. (30) Find the equation of the parabola shown.

2. (3) Simplify $\frac{x^2(x^{-2})^{-3}y^3(xy^2)^{-2}}{(x^2)^3y^{-2}(x^2)^2}$.

3. (26) A line has slope -4 and passes through the point $(6, 10)$. What is the equation of this line written in slope-intercept form?

4. (11) Add $(4x^3 + 2x^2 - x - 4) + (6 - 4x^2)$.

5. (23) Factor $x^2 - 16x + 64$.

Solve problems 6–7.

6. (7) $-3x + 9 = -18$

7. (24) $\begin{cases} 18 = 4x - 6y \\ x = 12 - 6y \end{cases}$

8. (20) Given $h(x) = x + 5$; $D = \{\text{Reals}\}$, $g(x) = x - 7$; $D = \{\text{Integers}\}$. Find the algebraic sum $(h + g)(x)$.

9. (5) Solve for X: $\begin{bmatrix} 2 & 6 \\ 8 & 3 \end{bmatrix} + X = \begin{bmatrix} 4 & -3 \\ 3 & 7 \end{bmatrix}$.

10. (28) Identify any excluded values. Then simplify the expression.
$$\frac{4b^2 - 64}{b - 4}$$

© Saxon. All rights reserved. 39 Saxon Algebra 2

After Lesson 40

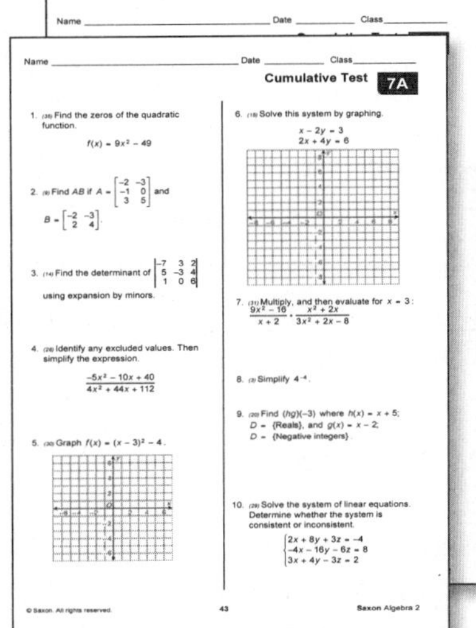

Name ________ Date ________ Class ________

Cumulative Test 7A

1. (35) Find the zeros of the quadratic function.
$$f(x) = 9x^2 - 49$$

2. (8) Find AB if $A = \begin{bmatrix} -2 & -3 \\ -1 & 0 \\ 3 & 5 \end{bmatrix}$ and $B = \begin{bmatrix} -2 & -3 \\ 2 & 4 \end{bmatrix}$.

3. (14) Find the determinant of $\begin{vmatrix} -7 & 3 & 2 \\ 5 & -3 & 4 \\ 1 & 0 & 6 \end{vmatrix}$ using expansion by minors.

4. (28) Identify any excluded values. Then simplify the expression.
$$\frac{-5x^2 - 10x + 40}{4x^2 + 44x + 112}$$

5. (30) Graph $f(x) = (x - 3)^2 - 4$.

6. (18) Solve this system by graphing.
$$x - 2y = 3$$
$$2x + 4y = 6$$

7. (31) Multiply, and then evaluate for $x = 3$: $\frac{9x^2 - 16}{x + 2} \cdot \frac{x^2 + 2x}{3x^2 + 2x - 8}$

8. (3) Simplify 4^{-4}.

9. (20) Find $(hg)(-3)$ where $h(x) = x + 5$; $D = \{\text{Reals}\}$, and $g(x) = x - 2$; $D = \{\text{Negative integers}\}$.

10. (29) Solve the system of linear equations. Determine whether the system is consistent or inconsistent.
$$\begin{cases} 2x + 8y + 3z = -4 \\ -4x - 16y - 6z = 8 \\ 3x + 4y - 3z = 2 \end{cases}$$

© Saxon. All rights reserved. 43 Saxon Algebra 2

For use with Performance Tasks

Teacher Rubric

Criteria Performance	Knowledge and Skills Understanding	Communication and Representation	Process and Strategies
4	The student got it! The student did it in new ways and showed how it worked. The student knew and understood what math concepts to use.	The student clearly detailed how he/she solved the problem. The student included all the steps to show his/her thinking. The student used math language, symbols, numbers, graphs and/or models to represent his/her solution.	The student had an effective and inventive solution. The student used big math ideas to solve the problem. The student addressed the important details. The student showed other ways to solve the problem. The student checked his/her answer to make sure it was correct
3	The student understood the problem and had an appropriate solution. All parts of the problem are addressed.	The student clearly explained how he/she solved the problem. The student used math language, symbols, tables, graphs, and numbers to explain how he/she did the problem.	The student had a correct solution. The student used a plan to solve the problem and selected an appropriate strategy.
2	The student understood parts of the problem. The student started, but he/she couldn't finish.	The student explained some of what he/she did. The student tried to use words, symbols, tables, graphs and numbers to explain how he/she did the problem.	The student had part of the solution, but did not know how to finish. The student was not sure if he/she had the correct answer. The student needed help.
1	The student did not understand the problem.	The student did not explain how he/she solved the problem. He/she did not use words, symbols, tables or graphs to show how he/she	The student couldn't get started. The student did not know how to begin.

© Saxon. All rights reserved. x Saxon Algebra 2

LESSON 31

1 Warm Up

Caution students to be careful about the signs of cubed numbers in problem 4.

2 New Concepts

In this lesson, students will extend the skills they have learned for multiplying and dividing rational *numbers* to multiplying and dividing rational *expressions.*

Discuss the definition of **reciprocal.** Remind students that the reciprocal of $\frac{a}{b}$ is $\frac{b}{a}$.

Example 1

This example demonstrates methods of multiplying and evaluating rational expressions.

Extend the Example

Ask students to describe how to simplify the expression in Example 1a before multiplying the integers. Change $\frac{12}{3}$ to 4.

Additional Example 1

a. Multiply, then evaluate for $a = 3, b = 4$: $\frac{6a^3b^3}{7b^5} \cdot \frac{21ab^4}{4a^5}$.

$\frac{9b^2}{2a}$; 24

LESSON 31

Multiplying and Dividing Rational Expressions

Warm Up

1. **Vocabulary** A rational expression is ________ if its denominator equals zero. undefined
(28)

2. Multiply. $\frac{3}{10} \cdot \frac{5}{9}$ $\frac{1}{6}$
(SB)

3. Divide. $\frac{2}{5} \div \frac{1}{20}$ 8
(SB)

4. Evaluate $4xy^3$ for $x = 3, y = -2$. −96
(2)

New Concepts

To multiply rational expressions, multiply the numerators and multiply the denominators. To simplify a rational expression, factor and then divide out all common factors. To evaluate an algebraic expression for given values of the variables, substitute the given values, and then simplify the numerical expression.

Recall that a rational expression is undefined if its denominator equals zero. In this lesson, assume that all rational expressions are defined unless otherwise specified.

Example 1 Multiplying Rational Expressions

a. Multiply, and then evaluate for $a = 4, b = 5$: $\frac{5ab^2}{6b^2} \cdot \frac{12a^2b^2}{3ab^3}$.

SOLUTION Multiply:

$\frac{5ab^2}{6b^2} \cdot \frac{12a^2b^2}{3ab^3} = \frac{60a^3b^4}{18ab^5}$ — Multiply numerators and denominators.

$= \frac{\cancel{6} \cdot 10 \cdot \cancel{a} \cdot a^2 \cdot \cancel{b^4}}{3 \cdot \cancel{6} \cdot \cancel{a} \cdot b \cdot \cancel{b^4}}$ — Factor. Then divide out common factors.

$= \frac{10a^2}{3b}$ — Write the algebraic expression in simplified form.

Evaluate the expression for $a = 4, b = 5$:

$\frac{10a^2}{3b} = \frac{10 \cdot 4^2}{3 \cdot 5}$ — Substitute 4 for *a* and 5 for *b*.

$= \frac{2 \cdot \cancel{5} \cdot 4^2}{3 \cdot \cancel{5}}$ — Factor as needed to divide out all common factors.

$= \frac{32}{3}$ — Write the numerical expression in simplified form.

The product is the expression $\frac{10a^2}{3b}$. Its value is $\frac{32}{3}$ for the given values of *a* and *b*.

Hint

Another way to simplify $\frac{10 \cdot 4^2}{3 \cdot 5}$ is to multiply, divide, and then simplify.

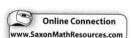

LESSON RESOURCES

Student Edition Practice Workbook 31
Reteaching Master 31
Adaptations Master 31
Challenge and Enrichment Master C31

MATH BACKGROUND

A *rational expression* is defined as a ratio of polynomials. Rational expressions can be multiplied, divided, simplified, and evaluated.

A rational expression is simplified when it has no factor common to both numerator and denominator. Factoring concepts learned from previous lessons will be used to help simplify the rational expressions.

Multiplying and dividing rational expressions follow the same rules as multiplying and dividing fractions. These rules will be applied again as students learn to simplify complex fractions in later lessons.

b. Multiply, and then identify all values of x that make the expression undefined: $\frac{15x - 3x^2}{x^2 - 9} \cdot \frac{x^2 - 8x + 15}{x^2 - 10x + 25}$.

SOLUTION

Caution

To identify values that make an expression undefined, use the given expression, not the simplified result.

$$\frac{15x - 3x^2}{x^2 - 9} \cdot \frac{x^2 - 8x + 15}{x^2 - 10x + 25}$$

$$= \frac{3x(5 - x)}{(x - 3)(x + 3)} \cdot \frac{(x - 3)(x - 5)}{(x - 5)(x - 5)}$$ Factor.

$$= \frac{3x(-1)\cancel{(x - 5)}\cancel{(x - 3)}\cancel{(x - 5)}}{\cancel{(x - 3)}(x + 3)\cancel{(x - 5)}\cancel{(x - 5)}}$$ Rewrite $(5 - x)$ as $(-1)(x - 5)$ so that the common factor $(x - 5)$ appears. Then multiply. Then divide out common factors.

$$= \frac{-3x}{(x + 3)}$$

Identify values of x that make the *given* expression undefined:

The given expression is $\frac{15x - 3x^2}{x^2 - 9} \cdot \frac{x^2 - 8x + 15}{x^2 - 10x + 25}$, which is equivalent to $\frac{3x(5 - x)}{(x - 3)(x + 3)} \cdot \frac{(x - 3)(x - 5)}{(x - 5)(x - 5)}$. The factors in the denominator are $(x - 3)$, $(x + 3)$, and $(x - 5)$. These factors are zero when x is 3, -3, and 5, respectively. So, the values of x that make the given expression undefined are 3, -3, and 5.

c. Multiply $\frac{5x + 10}{3x^2 + 2x - 1} \cdot \frac{9x^2 - 1}{x + 2} \cdot \frac{x + 1}{15x + 5}$.

SOLUTION

$$\frac{5x + 10}{3x^2 + 2x - 1} \cdot \frac{9x^2 - 1}{x + 2} \cdot \frac{x + 1}{15x + 5}$$

$$= \frac{\cancel{5(x + 2)}}{\cancel{(3x - 1)(x + 1)}} \cdot \frac{\cancel{(3x + 1)(3x - 1)}}{\cancel{x + 2}} \cdot \frac{\cancel{x + 1}}{\cancel{5(3x + 1)}}$$ Factor. Divide by the common factors and then multiply.

$$= 1$$

d. Multiply: $\frac{x + 4}{x^2 - 4x} \cdot (2x^2 - 9x + 4)$

SOLUTION

$$\frac{x + 4}{x^2 - 4x} \cdot \frac{2x^2 - 9x + 4}{1}$$ Rewrite the polynomial as a rational expression with a denominator of 1. Then factor, multiply, and divide out common factors.

$$= \frac{x + 4}{x\cancel{(x - 4)}} \cdot \frac{(2x - 1)\cancel{(x - 4)}}{1}$$

$$= \frac{(x + 4)(2x - 1)}{x}$$

b. Multiply, and then identify all values of x that make the expression undefined: $\frac{15x - 5x^2}{x^2 - 4} \cdot \frac{x^2 - 5x + 6}{x^2 - 6x + 9}$.

$\frac{-5x}{(x + 2)}$; $x \neq -2, 2, 3$

c. Multiply: $\frac{3x + 9}{5x^2 + 9x - 2} \cdot \frac{25x^2 - 1}{x + 3} \cdot \frac{x + 2}{15x + 3}$. 1

d. Multiply: $\frac{x + 3}{x^2 + 3x} \cdot (5x^2 + 14x - 3)$

$\frac{(x + 3)(5x - 1)}{x}$

Error Alert Students may not recognize an expression of the form $\frac{a - x}{x - a}$ as factorable. After explaining the error to students, write several examples of this type of expression on the board. Have students factor out -1 from the numerator of each to see that it becomes $\frac{(-1)(x - a)}{(x - a)} = -1$.

TEACHER TIP

Students may not be able to recognize when they have finished a problem. They may believe that a problem having parentheses should be simplified further. Point out that the problem is simplified if it is completely factored and all common factors are eliminated.

INCLUSION

Some students may become confused with all of the factors that appear in some of the expressions. Have them write each polynomial in the problem on index cards laid out on a desk to mimic the layout of the problem. Then, have them look for any polynomials that can be factored, and replace them with the factors, also written on cards. Students can then try to match and remove identical cards (factors) in the numerator and denominator to simplify the expression.

Example 2

In this example, students will learn to divide various types of rational expressions by changing the division problem to multiplication by a reciprocal.

Error Alert When dividing rational expressions, students sometimes invert the first expression rather than the expression after the division sign. Remind students that division is not commutative, and the order in which they apply the reciprocal method is important.

Extend the Example

Evaluate the expression in Example 2a for $x = 0.5$, $y = 0.25$. 0.375

Additional Example 2

a. Divide, and then evaluate for $x = -4$, $y = 2$: $\frac{8x^4}{7xy} \div \frac{2x^2}{7xy^3}$. $4x^2y^2$; 256

b. Divide, and then identify all values of x that make the expression undefined: $\frac{x+2}{x-5} \div \frac{x^2-7x}{x^2-5x}$. $\frac{x+2}{x-7}$; $x \neq 0, 5, 7$

Dividing by a Rational Expression

The **reciprocal** of a real number $\frac{c}{d}$ is $\frac{d}{c}$, provided that $c \neq 0$ and $d \neq 0$.

To divide by a rational expression, multiply by its reciprocal: $\frac{a}{b} \div \frac{c}{d} = \frac{a}{b} \cdot \frac{d}{c}$, where b, c, and d are all nonzero.

Hint

One quick way to check simplification is to substitute values for the variables in the original expression and evaluate. They should be the same.

Example 2 Dividing Rational Expressions

a. Divide, and then evaluate for $x = -2$, $y = 3$: $\frac{12x^3}{5y} \div \frac{4x^5}{5x^3y^2}$.

SOLUTION

$$\frac{12x^3}{5y} \div \frac{4x^5}{5x^3y^2} = \frac{12x^3}{5y} \cdot \frac{5x^3y^2}{4x^5}$$ Multiply by the reciprocal.

$$= \frac{60x^6y^2}{20x^5y}$$ Multiply numerators and denominators.

$$= \frac{3 \cdot \cancel{20} \cdot x \cdot \cancel{x^5} \cdot \cancel{y} \cdot y}{\cancel{20} \cdot \cancel{x^5} \cdot \cancel{y}}$$ Factor. Then divide out common factors.

$$= \frac{3xy}{1}$$ Write the algebraic expression in simplified form.

$$= 3xy$$

Evaluate for $x = -2$, $y = 3$:

$3xy = 3(-2)(3)$ Substitute −2 for x and 3 for y, and then simplify.

$= -18$

The quotient is the expression $3xy$. Its value is −18 for the given values of x and y.

Caution

Do not divide out terms of polynomials.

$\frac{x+1}{x-3} \neq \frac{1}{-3}$

(unless $x = 0$).

b. Divide, and then identify all values of x that make the expression undefined: $\frac{x+1}{x-2} \div \frac{x^2-3x}{x^2-2x}$.

SOLUTION Divide:

$$\frac{x+1}{x-2} \div \frac{x^2-3x}{x^2-2x} = \frac{x+1}{x-2} \cdot \frac{x^2-2x}{x^2-3x}$$ Multiply by the reciprocal.

$$= \frac{x+1}{x-2} \cdot \frac{x(x-2)}{x(x-3)}$$ Factor.

$$= \frac{(x+1)\cancel{x}\cancel{(x-2)}}{\cancel{(x-2)}\cancel{x}(x-3)}$$ Divide out common factors.

$$= \frac{x+1}{x-3}$$

Identify values of x that make the *given* expression undefined:

The given expression in factored form is $\frac{x+1}{x-2} \div \frac{x(x-3)}{x(x-2)}$. In a division expression of the form $\frac{a}{b} \div \frac{c}{d}$, b, c, and d must all be nonzero. So, in this case, $x - 2$, $x(x-3)$, and $x(x-2)$ must all be nonzero. Therefore, the factors $(x-2)$, x, and $(x-3)$ must all be nonzero. So the values of x that make the given division expression undefined are 2, 0, and 3.

ENGLISH LEARNERS

Draw students' attention to the word **reciprocal** at the top of this page. Say the word aloud, and have students copy your pronunciation of the word.

Explain that the word reciprocal is sometimes called the multiplicative inverse. Discuss with students how to find the reciprocal of a number by doing the following:

Write various numbers on the board, and have students find their reciprocals. Each time, as you write the number, say: **"What is the reciprocal of _____?"** Students should respond by saying, "The reciprocal of _____ is _____."

Connect this discussion to the rational expressions on this page. Have students demonstrate how to find reciprocals for some of the expressions shown. In each case, encourage students to correctly use the word reciprocal.

Example 3 Simplifying a Rational Expression Containing Multiplication and Division

Simplify: $\frac{45}{x^2 + 2x - 15} \cdot \frac{2x^2 + 10x}{5x^2y} \div \frac{1}{x - 3}$

SOLUTION

$$\frac{45}{x^2 + 2x - 15} \cdot \frac{2x^2 + 10x}{5x^2y} \div \frac{1}{x - 3}$$

$$= \frac{45}{x^2 + 2x - 15} \cdot \frac{2x^2 + 10x}{5x^2y} \cdot \frac{x - 3}{1}$$ Multiply by the reciprocal.

$$= \frac{\cancel{5} \cdot 9}{\cancel{(x+5)}\cancel{(x-3)}} \cdot \frac{2 \cdot \cancel{x} \cdot \cancel{(x+5)}}{\cancel{5} \cdot \cancel{x} \cdot x \cdot y} \cdot \frac{\cancel{(x-3)}}{1}$$ Factor and divide out common factors.

$$= \frac{18}{xy}$$

Example 4 Application: Determining a Dimension

An engineer is designing two storage tanks. One tank is to be a sphere and the other a cylinder. He wants the tanks to have the same volume and the same radius. What must be the height of the cylinder, in terms of the radius?

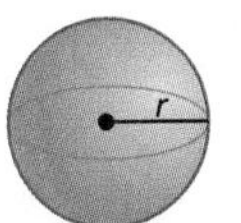

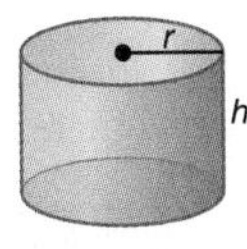

SOLUTION

$$V_{sphere} = V_{cylinder}$$

$$\frac{4\pi}{3}r^3 = \pi r^2 h$$

$$\frac{1}{\pi r^2} \cdot \frac{4\pi}{3}r^3 = \frac{1}{\pi r^2} \cdot \pi r^2 h$$ Multiply both sides by the reciprocal of πr^2.

$$\frac{1}{\pi r^2} \cdot \frac{4\pi}{3}r^3 = h$$

$$\frac{1}{\cancel{\pi} \cdot \cancel{r^2}} \cdot \frac{4 \cdot \cancel{\pi} \cdot r \cdot \cancel{r^2}}{3} = h$$ Factor and divide out common factors.

$$\frac{4r}{3} = h$$

Check Substitute $\frac{4r}{3}$ for h in the expression for the volume of a cylinder. The result is the expression for the volume of a sphere, so the answer is correct:

$$V_{cylinder} = \pi r^2 h = \pi r^2 \cdot \frac{4r}{3} = \frac{4\pi r^3}{3} = V_{sphere}$$

Math Reasoning

Analyze Suppose the engineer wanted the tanks to have the same surface area. What must be the height of the cylinder in terms of the radius? $h = r$

INCLUSION

You may choose to encourage students to factor and divide out in two separate steps. So Example 3 could be written as:

$\frac{5 \cdot 9}{(x + 5)(x - 3)} \cdot \frac{2 \cdot x \cdot (x + 5)}{5 \cdot x \cdot x \cdot y} \cdot \frac{(x - 3)}{1}$ and then rewritten with common factors crossed out.

$\frac{\cancel{5} \cdot 9}{\cancel{(x+5)}\cancel{(x-3)}} \cdot \frac{2 \cdot \cancel{x} \cdot \cancel{(x+5)}}{\cancel{5} \cdot \cancel{x} \cdot x \cdot y} \cdot \frac{\cancel{(x-3)}}{1}$. This way students can easily check their work if an error is made.

Example 3

This example demonstrates a method of simplifying a rational expression that contains both multiplication and division.

Additional Example 3

Simplify:

$\frac{21}{x^2 + x - 6} \cdot \frac{2x^2 + 6x}{3x^3y} \div \frac{1}{x - 2} \cdot \frac{14}{x^2y}$

Example 4

Students will apply the methods they have learned for multiplying and dividing rational expressions to a real life situation.

Additional Example 4

A packing company designs two storage boxes. The volume of one box is given by $V_1 = 20h^3$. The volume of the other box is given by $V_2 = 14h^2w$, where h is the height and w is the width of the box. The boxes need to have the same volume and height. What must be the width of the second box in terms of its height? $\frac{10h}{7}$

Lesson Practice

Problem b

Error Alert Students may forget to factor x out of expressions having x in both terms, such as $5x^2 - 20x$. Tell students to avoid factoring errors by multiplying mentally to be sure the result is the original term.

Problem e

Scaffolding Have students simplify terms before dividing. For example, $\frac{9x^8y^2}{14xy^6}$ is simplified to $\frac{9x^7}{14y^4}$.

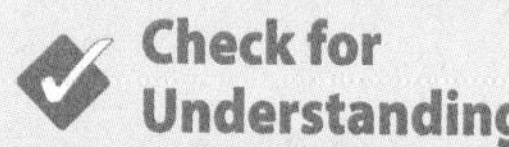

Check for Understanding

The questions below help assess the concepts taught in this lesson.

1. **"Why is it better to multiply or divide expressions before evaluating them?"** Multiplying or dividing first simplifies the expression and reduces chance of error.
2. **"Why can't you identify values that make an expression undefined after simplifying?"** Some terms for which x is undefined have been factored out.

3 Practice

Math Conversations

Discussion to strengthen understanding

Problem 4

Extend the Problem

"Using the same ratio of fertilizer to water, how many gallons of water are needed if you are going to add 18 cups of fertilizer?" 144 gal

Lesson Practice

a. (Ex 1) Multiply, and then evaluate for $x = 5$: $\frac{4x^2 - 9}{x + 1} \cdot \frac{x^2 + x}{4x^2 + 12x + 9}$. $\frac{x(2x - 3)}{2x + 3}$; $\frac{35}{13}$

b. (Ex 1) Multiply, and then identify all values of x that make the expression undefined: $\frac{x^2 + 5x - 14}{x^2 + x - 6} \cdot \frac{x^2 - x - 12}{5x^2 - 20x}$. $\frac{x + 7}{5x}$; $-3, 0, 2, 4$

c. (Ex 1) Multiply: $\frac{x^2 - 4}{7x^2 + 14x - 56} \cdot \frac{7x - 21}{x + 4} \cdot \frac{x + 4}{x^2 - x - 6}$. $\frac{1}{x + 4}$

d. (Ex 1) Multiply: $\frac{3x - 9}{6x^2 + 12x} \cdot (x^2 - 4x - 12)$. $\frac{(x - 3)(x - 6)}{2x}$

e. (Ex 2) Divide, and then evaluate for $x = -1$, $y = -6$: $\frac{3x^2y^5}{7xy^8} \div \frac{9x^8y^2}{14xy^6}$ $\frac{2y}{3x^6}$; -4

f. (Ex 2) Divide, and then identify all values of x that make the expression undefined: $\frac{1}{x^2 + 2x} \div \frac{2x - 1}{x^3 + 7x^2 + 10x}$ $\frac{x + 5}{2x - 1}$; $0, -2, -5, \frac{1}{2}$

g. (Ex 3) Simplify: $\frac{16 - x^2}{4xy} \cdot \frac{x^2y}{x - 4} \div \frac{x + 4}{4}$ $-x$

h. (Ex 4) A cube and a cylinder are to have the same volume. The diameter x of the cylinder is equal to the length of the edge of the cube. What must be the height of the cylinder, in terms of x? $h = \frac{4x}{\pi}$

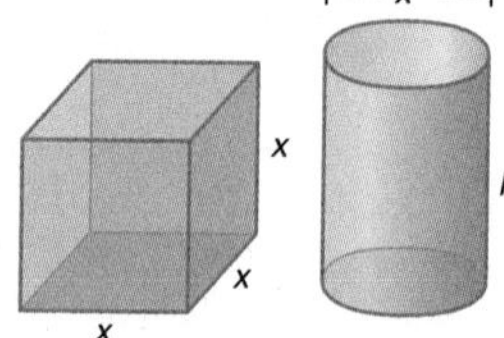

Practice Distributed and Integrated

1. (9) **Generalize** Given the dimensions of four matrices, A: 2×4, B: 2×2, C: 4×2, D: 4×4, determine all of the possible multiplication pairs and the dimensions of each product matrix. BA: 2×4, CB: 4×2, DC: 4×2, AC: 2×2, CA: 4×4, AD: 2×4

***2.** (31) If $f(x) = \frac{x^2 - 100}{x^2 + 20x + 100}$ and $g(x) = \frac{10x + 100}{3x - 30}$, what is $f(x) \cdot g(x)$ in simplest form? $\frac{10}{3}$

***3.** (28) **Engineering** The Channel Tunnel is a tunnel that runs under the English Channel. It is cylindrical in shape. Write the volume to lateral area ratio as a simplified rational expression. Then find the ratio given that the tunnel has an inner diameter of 7.6 meters. (Hint: The lateral area of a cylinder is the same as the surface area minus the area of the bases.) $\frac{r}{2} = 1.9$

4. (8) When mixing concentrated fertilizer for a garden, the amount of fertilizer varies directly with the amount of water. If 2 cups of fertilizer are used in 16 gallons of water, how much fertilizer is used in 48 gallons of water? 6 cups

5. (10) **Geometry** Write a compound inequality using the fact that the sum of the lengths of any two sides of a triangle is greater than the length of the third side (Triangle Inequality) using the diagram. (Hint: Remember that length cannot be negative.) $4 + x > 6$ and $4 + 6 > x$ and $6 + x > 4$; $2 < x < 10$

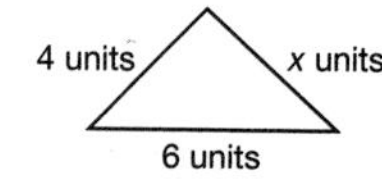

230 Saxon Algebra 2

INCLUSION

Visual learners may benefit from circling, rather than marking out, common factors. In this way, they can clearly identify the remaining terms.

Use the description to write the vertex form of a quadratic equation.

***6.** The parent function is shifted 4 units right and 6 units down. $y = (x - 4)^2 - 6$
(30)

***7.** The parent function is reflected across the x-axis, and then shifted 3 units up.
(30) $y = -x^2 + 3$

8. (**Woodworking**) A lathe operator has a piece of wood in the shape of a square prism with dimensions $2x$, $2x$, and h. He wants to make the largest possible cylinder by turning the wood on the lathe and cutting it down. The cylinder will have radius x and length h. Write a polynomial that represents the volume of wood he will cut off to make the cylinder. $4x^2h - \pi x^2h$ or $(4 - \pi)x^2h$
(11)

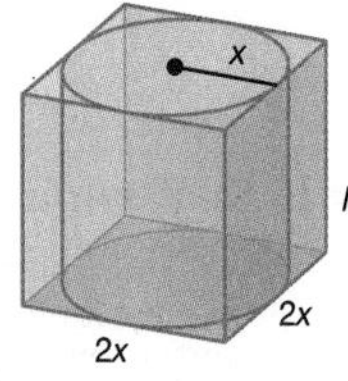

Multiply.

***9.** $\frac{3a^3b^2}{5a^5} \cdot \frac{10a^3b}{7a^4b^2}$ $\frac{6b}{7a^3}$
(31)

***10.** $\frac{2xy}{3y^{11}} \cdot \frac{6x^2y}{3xy}$ $\frac{4x^2}{3y^{10}}$
(31)

11. **Verify** Use FOIL to verify that $a = c + d$ and $b = cd$ in the formula:
(23)

$x^2 + ax + b = (x + c)(x + d)$. $(x + c)(x + d) = x(x) + x(d) + c(x) + c(d)$
$= x^2 + dx + cx + cd = x^2 + (d + c)x + cd$

12. (**Mountains**) Mt. Elbert in Colorado has an elevation of 14,433 ft and from the center, it runs horizontally approximately 22,105 ft. Find the approximate slope of Mt. Elbert, round your answer to the thousandths place. 0.653
(13)

13. **Multiple Choice** Which polynomial is in standard form? A
(11)

A $\frac{1}{2}x^3 - x$ **B** $\frac{1}{3} - \frac{1}{3}x^3$ **C** $4x^2 + 3x^3 + 2x^4$ **D** $x^4 + x^5$

14. Convert 87 ft^2 to square inches. 12,528 in^2
(18)

15. **Analyze** Find the largest two consecutive even integers with a total sum less than or equal to 130. $n + n + 2 \le 130$; $2n + 2 \le 130$; $2n \le 128$; $n \le 64$; 64 and 66
(10)

16. **Error Analysis** Explain the error in the student's work. Then find the correct determinant.
(14)

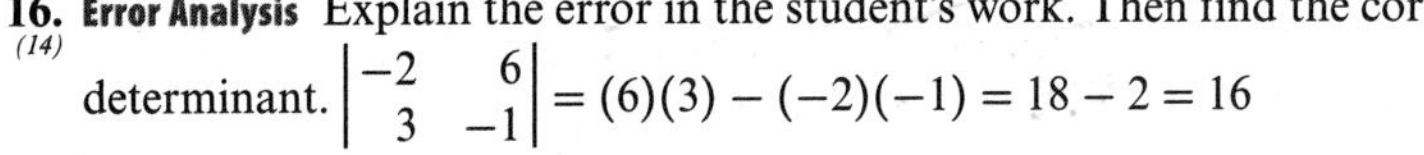
$\begin{vmatrix} -2 & 6 \\ 3 & -1 \end{vmatrix} = (6)(3) - (-2)(-1) = 18 - 2 = 16$

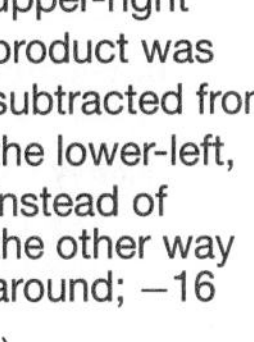
16. The upper-right product was subtracted from the lower-left, instead of the other way around; -16

***17.** **Graphing Calculator** Solve the system of equations using a graphing calculator. $\left(\frac{1}{2}, -1\right)$
(15)

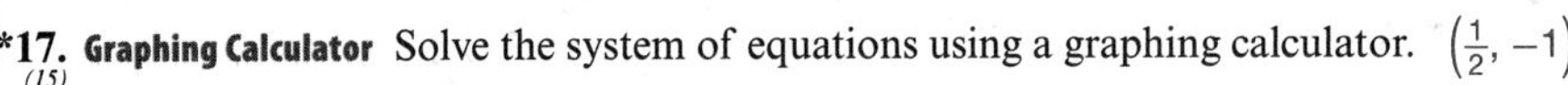

$$2x - 3y = 4$$
$$4x + y = 1$$

18. **Multi-Step** $|ax + b| \le c$, where $a > 0$ and $c > 0$.
(17)

a. Solve the inequality for x in terms of a, b, and c. $\frac{-(c + b)}{a} \le x \le \frac{c - b}{a}$

b. Apply this general solution to solve $|2x + 3| \le 5$. $-4 \le x \le 1$

Problem 6

Error Alert

Students might think that because shifting to the right is in the positive direction, the amount of the shift should be *added* to the parent function. Remind students of the general form of the quadratic function, $y = a(x - h)^2 + k$.

Problem 12

Guide the students by asking them the following question.

"What is the general method for finding slope?" slope $= \frac{rise}{run}$

"Which number represents rise?" 14,433

"Which number represents run?" 22,105

Problem 15

Extend the Problem

Ask students, **"How would the problem change if it had asked for two consecutive *odd* integers?"** Steps for solving the problem would have been the same, but the answer would have been 63 and 65.

CHALLENGE

Simplify:

$$\frac{5x^4 + 10x^3 + 2x + 4}{y(x + 1)} \cdot \frac{x - 2}{x - 7} \cdot \frac{x + 1}{x^2 - 4x + 4} \div \frac{x + 2}{y^2(x - 7)}.$$

Then, evaluate the expression for $x = 3$, $y = 1$. $\frac{y(5x^3 + 2)}{x - 2}$; 137

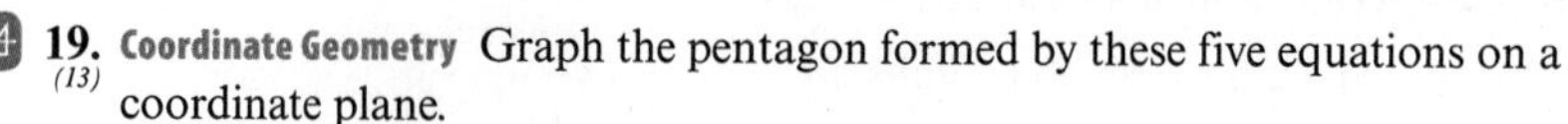

Problem 19

"Looking just at the equations, describe how the lines for the fourth and fifth equations are alike and how they are different." The lines intersect the y-axis at the same point, but they have different slopes.

19. **Coordinate Geometry** Graph the pentagon formed by these five equations on a coordinate plane.
(13)

$$x = 3 \qquad x = -3 \qquad y = -4 \qquad y = \frac{2}{3}x + 3 \qquad y = -\frac{2}{3}x + 3$$

a. Is the pentagon regular? no

b. What are the coordinates of the vertices of the pentagon? (0, 3), (3, 1), (3, −4), (−3, −4), and (−3, 1)

*20. **Error Analysis** A student said the graph of the function $y = (x - 6)^2$ is a shift of the parent function 6 units to the left because h is negative. Explain and correct the error in the student's thinking. The value of h is positive; the minus sign is included in the vertex form of the equation: $y = a(x - h)^2 + k$. So, the graph is a shift 6 units to the right.
(30)

21. **Multiple Choice** Multiply $(x + 11)(x - 8)$. B
(19)

A $x^2 - 19x + 88$ **B** $x^2 + 3x - 88$ **C** $x^2 - 3x - 88$ **D** $x^2 + 19x - 88$

Identify the following equations as direct or inverse variations.

22. $y = 3x$ direct
(12)

23. $y = \frac{20}{x}$ inverse
(12)

24. **Analyze** Describe how a graph of 2 linear equations looks when the system has:
(21)

a. exactly one solution. The lines intersect at a single point.

b. an infinite number of solutions. The lines coincide, sharing all points.

c. no solution. The lines are parallel.

*25. **Write** Describe how to find the following product in simplest form: $\frac{a^2 - 49}{a - 7} \cdot \frac{a}{2a^2 + 14a}$.
(31)

25. Possible answer: Factor $a^2 - 49$, getting $(a + 7)(a - 7)$. Factor $2a^2 + 14a$, getting $2a(a + 7)$. Divide out the common factors a, $(a + 7)$, and $(a - 7)$. The product in simplest form is $\frac{1}{2}$.

*26. **Multi-Step a.** Simplify $\frac{4x^2 - 13x + 3}{9 - 6x + x^2}$. $\frac{4x - 1}{x - 3}$
(28)

b. Evaluate the simplified expression for $x = 9$. $5\frac{5}{6}$

27. **Money** A parking meter contains 157 coins worth $26.95. If the meter only accepts quarters and dimes, how many of each type of coin are in the meter?
(24)
75 quarters and 82 dimes

Given $f(x) = 5x - 9$ and $g(x) = 9x + 8$.

28. Find $(f \cdot g)(3)$. 210
(20)

29. Find $\left(\frac{f}{g}\right)(2)$. $\frac{1}{26}$
(20)

30. Find the intercepts of the equation $10x + 3y - 8z = 12$. x: (1.2, 0, 0), y: (0, 4, 0), z: (0, 0, −1.5)
(Inv 3)

LOOKING FORWARD

Multiplying and dividing rational expressions prepares students for

- **Lesson 37** Adding and Subtracting Rational Expressions
- **Lesson 40** Simplifying Radical Expressions
- **Lesson 44** Rationalizing Denominators
- **Lesson 48** Understanding Complex Fractions

LESSON
32

Solving Linear Systems with Matrix Inverses

Warm Up

1. **Vocabulary** A ________ is a rectangular array of elements. matrix
(5)

2. Multiply the matrix by the scalar. $-2[1\ \ 3\ \ -4]$ $[-2\ \ -6\ \ 8]$
(9)

3. Multiply the matrices. $\begin{bmatrix} 1 & 2 \\ 2 & 3 \end{bmatrix} \cdot \begin{bmatrix} 0 & 4 \\ 1 & 5 \end{bmatrix}$ $\begin{bmatrix} 2 & 14 \\ 3 & 23 \end{bmatrix}$
(9)

New Concepts

Exploration Exploring Matrix Inverses

1. Find products AB and BA for $A = \begin{bmatrix} -2 & 0 \\ 5 & 1 \end{bmatrix}$ and $B = \begin{bmatrix} -0.5 & 0 \\ 2.5 & 1 \end{bmatrix}$. $\begin{bmatrix} 1 & 0 \\ 0 & 1 \end{bmatrix}$

2. Find products PQ and QP for $P = \begin{bmatrix} 8 & 5 \\ 6 & 4 \end{bmatrix}$ and $Q = \begin{bmatrix} 2 & -2.5 \\ -3 & 4 \end{bmatrix}$. $\begin{bmatrix} 1 & 0 \\ 0 & 1 \end{bmatrix}$

3. Find products ST and TS for $S = \begin{bmatrix} 3 & 1 \\ 11 & 4 \end{bmatrix}$ and $T = \begin{bmatrix} 4 & -1 \\ -11 & 3 \end{bmatrix}$. $\begin{bmatrix} 1 & 0 \\ 0 & 1 \end{bmatrix}$

4. What do you notice about the products of the matrices in Problems 1–3? The products are all $\begin{bmatrix} 1 & 0 \\ 0 & 1 \end{bmatrix}$.

5. Explain what is special about the matrix you found to be the product in Problems 1–3. It is the multiplicative identity matrix.

Hint

Recall that an identity matrix has ones on the diagonal and zeros everywhere else.

If A is any $n \times n$ matrix and I is the $n \times n$ identity matrix, then $AI = IA = A$. The **multiplicative inverse of a square matrix,** if it exists, is a matrix such that the product of it and another matrix forms an identity matrix. The inverse of matrix A is notated A^{-1}. So, two matrices A and B are inverses of each other if $A \cdot B = B \cdot A = I$. Likewise, $A \cdot A^{-1} = A^{-1} \cdot A = I$.

Hint

Matrix multiplication is not commutative. Check the product in both orders to verify that the matrices are inverses.

Example 1 Verifying Inverses

Determine whether the matrices are inverses.

a. $P = \begin{bmatrix} 2 & 6 \\ 1 & 4 \end{bmatrix}$ and $Q = \begin{bmatrix} 2 & -3 \\ -0.5 & 1 \end{bmatrix}$

SOLUTION

Determine whether $P \cdot Q = I$ and $Q \cdot P = I$.

$$P \cdot Q = \begin{bmatrix} 2 & 6 \\ 1 & 4 \end{bmatrix} \cdot \begin{bmatrix} 2 & -3 \\ -0.5 & 1 \end{bmatrix} = \begin{bmatrix} 4-3 & -6+6 \\ 2-2 & -3+4 \end{bmatrix} = \begin{bmatrix} 1 & 0 \\ 0 & 1 \end{bmatrix} = I$$

$$Q \cdot P = \begin{bmatrix} 2 & -3 \\ -0.5 & 1 \end{bmatrix} \cdot \begin{bmatrix} 2 & 6 \\ 1 & 4 \end{bmatrix} = \begin{bmatrix} 4-3 & 12-12 \\ -1+1 & -3+4 \end{bmatrix} = \begin{bmatrix} 1 & 0 \\ 0 & 1 \end{bmatrix} = I$$

$P \cdot Q = I$ and $Q \cdot P = I$, so P and Q are inverses.

Online Connection
www.SaxonMathResources.com

MATH BACKGROUND

A linear system is a set of linear equations. In past lessons students have learned to solve a linear system of two equations in two unknowns using graphing, substitution, or elimination.

Another method for solving a linear systems includes the use of matrices. It is possible to write a system of equations in matrix form and then use the inverse of a matrix to find the solution. This method is especially helpful for solving equations with three or more variables.

LESSON
32

1 Warm Up

Use Warm Up problem 3 to review the order in which elements are multiplied and added during matrix multiplication.

2 New Concepts

In this lesson, students learn how to find the inverse of a matrix. They then use the inverse matrix to solve a matrix equation and to solve a linear system.

Discuss the definition of the **multiplicative inverse of a square matrix.** Remind students that the product of a real number and its multiplicative inverse is 1: $a \cdot \frac{1}{a} = 1$. Similarly, the product of a matrix and its inverse is the identity matrix.

Example 1

Students multiply to determine if matrices are inverses.

Additional Example 1

Determine whether the matrices are inverses.

a. $P = \begin{bmatrix} 3 & 1 \\ 2 & 1 \end{bmatrix}$ and $Q = \begin{bmatrix} 1 & -1 \\ -2 & 3 \end{bmatrix}$ yes

LESSON RESOURCES

Student Edition Practice Workbook 32
Reteaching Master 32
Adaptations Master 32
Challenge and Enrichment Master C32

Additional Example 1

Determine whether the matrices are inverses.

$R = \begin{bmatrix} 4 & 2 \\ 1 & 6 \end{bmatrix}$ and $S = \begin{bmatrix} -3 & 4 \\ 2 & 2 \end{bmatrix}$

no

Error Alert Students may assume that the determinant $|A|$ must be positive because it uses the same notation as the absolute value symbol, | |. Caution students that the determinant may be positive or negative, and the similarity in symbols should not influence the result.

Example 2

Students use the determinant of a matrix to find its inverse.

Additional Example 2

Find the inverse of each matrix, if it exists.

a. $T = \begin{bmatrix} 4 & -1 \\ -2 & 3 \end{bmatrix}$ $T^{-1} = \begin{bmatrix} 0.3 & 0.1 \\ 0.2 & 0.4 \end{bmatrix}$

b. $Y = \begin{bmatrix} 4 & 12 \\ 3 & 9 \end{bmatrix}$ No inverse exists.

c. $A = \begin{bmatrix} 2 & 0 & 1 \\ 1 & 0 & 1 \\ 2 & 1 & 0 \end{bmatrix}$

$A^{-1} = \begin{bmatrix} 1 & -1 & 0 \\ -2 & 2 & 1 \\ 1 & 2 & 0 \end{bmatrix}$

b. $R = \begin{bmatrix} 3 & 2 \\ 5 & 1 \end{bmatrix}$ and $S = \begin{bmatrix} 4 & 1 \\ -2 & 3 \end{bmatrix}$

SOLUTION Determine whether $R \cdot S = I$ and $S \cdot R = I$.

$$R \cdot S = \begin{bmatrix} 3 & 2 \\ 5 & 1 \end{bmatrix} \cdot \begin{bmatrix} 4 & 1 \\ -2 & 3 \end{bmatrix} = \begin{bmatrix} 12-4 & 3+6 \\ 20-2 & 5+3 \end{bmatrix} = \begin{bmatrix} 8 & 9 \\ 18 & 8 \end{bmatrix} \neq I$$

$R \cdot S \neq I$, so R and S are not inverses.

Reading Math

If A is the matrix $\begin{bmatrix} a & b \\ c & d \end{bmatrix}$, then these all represent the determinant of A:

- det A
- $\det\begin{bmatrix} a & b \\ c & d \end{bmatrix}$
- $|A|$
- $\begin{vmatrix} a & b \\ c & d \end{vmatrix}$

Recall, that to find the determinant of a 2 × 2 matrix, use the following method.

$$\det \begin{bmatrix} a & b \\ c & d \end{bmatrix} = \begin{bmatrix} a & b \\ c & d \end{bmatrix} = ad - cb$$

An $n \times n$ matrix A has an inverse if and only if $\det A \neq 0$. The inverse of matrix A is denoted A^{-1}. If A does not have an inverse, then A is called a **singular matrix**.

Inverse of a 2 × 2 Matrix
If $A = \begin{bmatrix} a & b \\ c & d \end{bmatrix}$ and $ad - cb \neq 0$, then the inverse of A is: $A^{-1} = \frac{1}{\lvert A \rvert}\begin{bmatrix} d & -b \\ -c & a \end{bmatrix} = \frac{1}{ad-cb}\begin{bmatrix} d & -b \\ -c & a \end{bmatrix}$.

Example 2 **Finding Inverses**

Find the inverse of each matrix, if it exists.

a. $T = \begin{bmatrix} 3 & 4 \\ -1 & 2 \end{bmatrix}$

SOLUTION First find the determinant:
$|T| = (3)(2) - (-1)(4) = 6 + 4 = 10.$

$$T^{-1} = \frac{1}{10}\begin{bmatrix} 2 & -4 \\ 1 & 3 \end{bmatrix} = \begin{bmatrix} 0.2 & -0.4 \\ 0.1 & 0.3 \end{bmatrix}$$

b. $Y = \begin{bmatrix} 2 & 4 \\ 5 & 10 \end{bmatrix}$

SOLUTION Find the determinant: $|Y| = (2)(10) - (5)(4) = 20 - 20 = 0.$
The inverse of Y does not exist because $|Y| = 0$.

c. $A = \begin{bmatrix} -2 & 1 & -1 \\ 2 & 0 & 4 \\ 0 & 2 & 5 \end{bmatrix}$

SOLUTION Use a graphing calculator to find the inverse matrix. Then use the calculator to verify that $AA^{-1} = I$ and $A^{-1}A = I$.

Graphing Calculator Tip

For help in inputting matrices and finding inverses with the graphing calculator, see the lab on page 27.

```
[A]-1
 [[-4 -3.5 2 ]
  [-5 -5   3 ]
  [2   2  -1]]
```

```
[A]*[A]-1
 [[1 0 0]
  [0 1 0]
  [0 0 1]]
```

```
[A]-1*[A]
 [[1 0 0]
  [0 1 0]
  [0 0 1]]
```


ENGLISH LEARNERS

Draw students' attention to places in the lesson where the words **matrix** and **matrices** are written. Write both words on the board, and help students correctly pronounce and define the words.

Explain to students that forming the plural of a word ending in *-x* by changing the *-x* to *-ces* is not as common as simply adding *-es* to a word ending in *-x*. Students should be alert to both possibilities.

Have students use the word matrix in a sentence. Then, have them use the word matrices in a sentence.

Write the following words on the board:

tax taxes
index indices indexes
prefix prefixes

Be sure students are able to connect the discussion of plural forms to other words ending in *x*, such as those listed above.

A **matrix equation** represents a system of equations in matrix form where the variable is a matrix.

Using an Inverse to Solve a Matrix Equation

If matrix A has an inverse and the matrix equation $AX = B$ has a solution, then the solution is $X = A^{-1}B$.	$AX = B$	
	$A^{-1}AX = A^{-1}B$	Multiply both sides by A^{-1}.
	$IX = A^{-1}B$	$A^{-1}A = I$ by definition of inverse.
	$X = A^{-1}B$	$IX = X$ by definition of identity.

Caution

To solve $AX = B$, you must multiply both sides of the equation by A^{-1} from the left.

$(A^{-1})AX = (A^{-1})B$

Example 3 Solving a Matrix Equation

Solve for matrix X. $\underbrace{\begin{bmatrix} 12 & 7 \\ 5 & 3 \end{bmatrix}}_{A} X = \underbrace{\begin{bmatrix} 2 & -1 \\ 3 & 2 \end{bmatrix}}_{B}$

SOLUTION

$$X = A^{-1}B = \begin{bmatrix} 3 & -7 \\ -5 & 12 \end{bmatrix}\begin{bmatrix} 2 & -1 \\ 3 & 2 \end{bmatrix} = \begin{bmatrix} -15 & -17 \\ 26 & 29 \end{bmatrix}$$

Check $AX = \begin{bmatrix} 12 & 7 \\ 5 & 3 \end{bmatrix}\begin{bmatrix} -15 & -17 \\ 26 & 29 \end{bmatrix} = \begin{bmatrix} -180 + 182 & -204 + 203 \\ -75 + 78 & -85 + 87 \end{bmatrix}$

$= \begin{bmatrix} 2 & -1 \\ 3 & 2 \end{bmatrix} = B$

When the matrix equation $AX = B$ is used to represent a system of equations, A is called the **matrix of coefficients,** X is called the **matrix of variables,** and B is called the **matrix of constants.**

Example 4 Using an Inverse Matrix to Solve a Linear System

Solve the system.

$$3x + 2y + z = 1$$
$$x - y - 3z = 12$$
$$-x + y + 4z = -15$$

SOLUTION

Write the system as a matrix equation. $\underbrace{\begin{bmatrix} 3 & 2 & 1 \\ 1 & -1 & -3 \\ -1 & 1 & 4 \end{bmatrix}}_{A}\underbrace{\begin{bmatrix} x \\ y \\ z \end{bmatrix}}_{X} = \underbrace{\begin{bmatrix} 1 \\ 12 \\ -15 \end{bmatrix}}_{B}$

Solve the equation. $X = A^{-1}B = \begin{bmatrix} 0.2 & 1.4 & 1 \\ 0.2 & -2.6 & -2 \\ 0 & 1 & 1 \end{bmatrix}\begin{bmatrix} 1 \\ 12 \\ -15 \end{bmatrix} = \begin{bmatrix} 2 \\ -1 \\ -3 \end{bmatrix}$

The solution to the system is $x = 2$, $y = -1$, $z = -3$.

INCLUSION

Have students work in pairs to solve the matrix equation in Example 3 verbally. Instruct students to take turns explaining to their partners the steps needed to find the determinant, $|A|$, the inverse matrix, A^{-1}, and the solution matrix, X.

TEACHER TIP

Emphasize to students the importance of the discussion in the key concept box at the top of the page. Students have previously learned to solve real number multiplication equations simply by dividing:

$$ax = b$$
$$x = \frac{b}{a}$$

Here, students learn that for matrices, they must multiply, and the direction from which they multiply a matrix is important, as matrix multiplication is not commutative.

Example 3

In this example, students use an inverse matrix to solve a matrix equation.

Extend the Example

Have students multiply the equation from the right to prove to themselves the importance of the direction of multiplication when working with matrices.

$BA^{-1} = \begin{bmatrix} 11 & -26 \\ -1 & 3 \end{bmatrix} \neq A^{-1}B$

Additional Example 3

Solve for matrix X.

$\begin{bmatrix} 5 & 4 \\ 6 & 5 \end{bmatrix} X = \begin{bmatrix} 3 & 4 \\ 0 & 2 \end{bmatrix}$.

$X = \begin{bmatrix} 15 & 12 \\ -18 & -14 \end{bmatrix}$

Example 4

Students use an inverse matrix to solve a linear system. Encourage students to use a graphing calculator to find the inverse matrix A^{-1}, and then multiply by B to find the solution matrix X.

Additional Example 4

Solve the system.

$$4x + y + 3z = 2$$
$$2x - y + 2z = 8$$
$$-2x - y - z = -6$$

$x = 20$, $y = -12$, $z = -22$

Example 5

This example demonstrates the use of matrix multiplication when solving a real world system of equations.

Additional Example 5

Karen sells her drawings at craft shows. At one show she sells 2 small, 2 medium, and 2 large drawings for a total of \$63.50. At another show she sells 1 small, 2 medium, and 4 large drawings for \$95.25. At a third show she sells 0 small, 2 medium, and 4 large drawings for \$91.00. What was the price of each size drawing? small \$4.25; medium \$9.50; large \$18.00

Lesson Practice

Problem a

Error Alert Even if students understand how to solve matrix problems, working with negative signs and decimals may lead to errors. Remind students to find both QW and WQ in order to check their work. Also, encourage them to use a graphing calculator when possible as a check.

Hint

Remember
1 kilogram = 1000 grams

Example 5 Application: Analyzing Nutrition and Cost

A 460-gram package of trail mix costs \$4.42 and contains 59 grams of protein. The mix contains peanuts (\$12 per kilogram, 25% protein), raisins (\$5.50 per kilogram, 3% protein), and almonds (\$14 per kilogram, 13% protein). How much of each ingredient is in the trail mix?

SOLUTION Write a system.

$p + r + a = 460$ masses of ingredients, using grams

$0.25p + 0.03r + 0.13a = 59$ masses of protein in the ingredients

$0.012p + 0.0055r + 0.014a = 4.42$ costs of ingredients, using grams

Write the matrix equation. $$\underbrace{\begin{bmatrix} 1 & 1 & 1 \\ 0.25 & 0.03 & 0.13 \\ 0.012 & 0.0055 & 0.014 \end{bmatrix}}_{A} \underbrace{\begin{bmatrix} p \\ r \\ a \end{bmatrix}}_{X} = \underbrace{\begin{bmatrix} 460 \\ 59 \\ 4.42 \end{bmatrix}}_{B}$$

Solve the equation. $$X = A^{-1}B = \begin{bmatrix} 160 \\ 200 \\ 100 \end{bmatrix}$$

The solution to the system is $p = 160$, $r = 200$, $a = 100$. The trail mix contains 160 grams of peanuts, 200 grams of raisins, and 100 grams of almonds.

Check The total mass of ingredients is $160 + 200 + 100 = 460$ grams.
The total mass of protein is $(0.25)(160) + (0.03)(200) + (0.13)(100) = 59$ grams.

The total cost is $(0.012)(160) + (0.0055)(200) + (0.014)(100) = \$4.42$.

Lesson Practice

a. (Ex 1) Determine whether $Q = \begin{bmatrix} -1 & 2 \\ 1.5 & -2.5 \end{bmatrix}$ and $W = \begin{bmatrix} 5 & 4 \\ 3 & 2 \end{bmatrix}$ are inverses. yes

b. (Ex 1) Determine whether $A = \begin{bmatrix} 2 & -1 \\ -4 & 3 \end{bmatrix}$ and $B = \begin{bmatrix} \frac{1}{2} & -1 \\ -\frac{1}{4} & \frac{1}{3} \end{bmatrix}$ are inverses. no

c. (Ex 2) Find the inverse of $A = \begin{bmatrix} 5 & -2 \\ -3 & 1 \end{bmatrix}$, if it exists. $A^{-1} = \begin{bmatrix} -1 & -2 \\ -3 & -5 \end{bmatrix}$

d. (Ex 2) Find the inverse of $B = \begin{bmatrix} 2 & 0 \\ 0 & 2 \end{bmatrix}$, if it exists. $B^{-1} = \begin{bmatrix} 0.5 & 0 \\ 0 & 0.5 \end{bmatrix}$

e. (Ex 2) Use a calculator to find and verify the inverse of $A = \begin{bmatrix} 2 & 1 & -2 \\ 5 & 3 & 0 \\ 4 & 3 & 8 \end{bmatrix}$.

e.

```
[A]-1
    [[12  -7 3 ]
     [-20 12 -5]
     [1.5 -1 .5]]
```

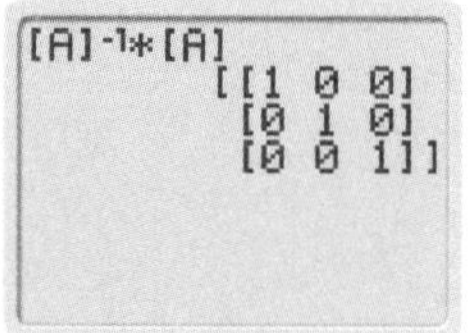


```
[A]-1*[A]
    [[1 0 0]
     [0 1 0]
     [0 0 1]]
```

f. (Ex 3) Solve for matrix X. $\underbrace{\begin{bmatrix} 3 & 7 \\ 1 & 4 \end{bmatrix}}_{A} X = \underbrace{\begin{bmatrix} -1 & -8 \\ -3 & -24 \end{bmatrix}}_{B}$ $X = \begin{bmatrix} 3.4 & 27.2 \\ -1.6 & -12.8 \end{bmatrix}$

ALTERNATE METHOD FOR EXAMPLE 5

If students have difficulty organizing the information given in Example 5 into a system of equations, have them write the details on a white board in a table format. The rows of the table can then be rewritten as equations.

g. Solve the system. $-5x - y + z = -16$ $x = 2, y = 0, z = -6$
(Ex 4)
$$3x + 2y - z = 12$$
$$x + y + 2z = -10$$

h. A 350-gram entrée contains black beans (3% fat and 23% protein), chicken breast (20% fat and 80% protein), and rice (2% fat and 8% protein). The entrée has 24.7 grams of fat and 115.3 grams of protein. How much of each ingredient is in the entrée? 150 grams of beans, 90 grams of chicken, 110 grams of rice
(Ex 5)

Practice Distributed and Integrated

***1.** **Verify** Is the ordered triple (5, −3, −1) a solution of the following system? no
(29)
$2x + y + 2z = 5$
$x - 4y + 3z = 14$
$-x + 4y - 3z = -6$

2. **Multi-Step** A data set consists of the following numbers: −4, −7, 12, −2, 8, 3, −1, 2, 4, −52
(25)
a. Find the mean of the data. −3.7 **b.** Find the standard deviation. ≈ 17.0

c. Identify any outliers. −52

d. Describe how any outlier affects the mean and the standard deviation of this data set. The outlier decreases the mean from ≈ 1.7 to −3.7, and increases the standard deviation from ≈ 5.6 to ≈ 17.0.

3. Solve the inequality: $3t + 4 < 2(t + 3) + t$. Show your work. all real numbers
(10)
$3t + 4 < 2(t + 3) + t$; $3t + 4 < 3t + 6$; $4 < 6$

***4.** **Multiple Choice** Which shows all the values of x that make the division expression $\frac{x^2 - 1}{x} \div \frac{3 - x}{2x + 2}$ undefined? A
(31)
A 0, 3, −1 **B** 0, −3, 1 **C** 2, 3, −1 **D** 2, −3, 1

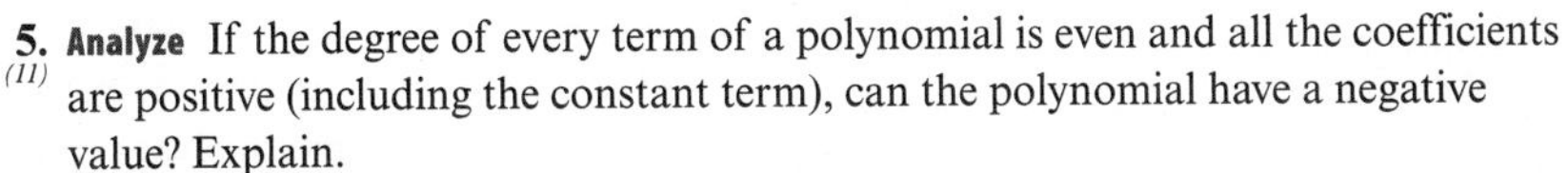

5. **Analyze** If the degree of every term of a polynomial is even and all the coefficients are positive (including the constant term), can the polynomial have a negative value? Explain.
(11)

5. No; Possible explanation: Any even power of x is nonnegative, and any positive coefficient times any nonnegative value is nonnegative. So, the value of the polynomial is the sum of nonnegative values, and that sum is therefore nonnegative.

***6.** Write the matrix equation for the system and solve. $\begin{bmatrix} 3 & -1 \\ -2 & 1 \end{bmatrix}\begin{bmatrix} x \\ y \end{bmatrix} = \begin{bmatrix} 5 \\ -4 \end{bmatrix}$ (1, −2)
(32)
$3x - y = 5$ and $y = 2x - 4$

7. **Multiple Choice** Choose the letter that best represents the equation of the graph: C
(13)

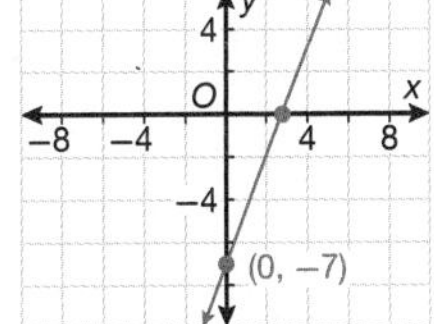

A $y = \frac{2}{5}x - 7$ **B** $y = -\frac{5}{2}x - 7$

C $y = \frac{5}{2}x - 7$ **D** $y = -\frac{2}{5}x - 7$

8. **Verify** Verify that (1.3, −2.7) is a solution of $\begin{matrix} 5.3x - 0.8y = 9.05 \\ -3.0x + 1.4y = -7.68 \end{matrix}$.
(15)

$5.3(1.3) - (0.8)(-2.7) = 9.05$; $-3.0(1.3) + 1.4(-2.7) = -7.68$

ALTERNATE METHOD FOR PROBLEM G

After students solve Problem g using matrices, have them solve the problem by other methods, such as elimination. Then have them check that the solution matches the answer they found using matrices.

Problem g

Scaffolding Review with students the steps for solving a system of equations using matrices. First, write the system as a matrix equation. Next, find the determinant of A in order to find the inverse matrix A^{-1}. Finally, multiply from the left: $X = A^{-1}B$.

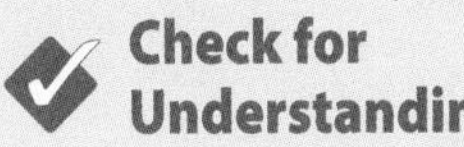

Check for Understanding

The questions below help assess the concepts taught in this lesson.

1. **"How is an inverse matrix similar to a multiplicative inverse?"** The product of a real number and its inverse is 1, just as the product of a matrix and its inverse is the identity matrix.

2. **"Why are matrices useful for solving systems of equations?"** Possible answer: You can use a graphing calculator to find the inverse of the matrix, and find the solution matrix by simply multiplying two matrices. This is sometimes easier than trying to manipulate equations.

3 Practice

Math Conversations

Discussions to strengthen understanding

Problem 4

Error Alert

Students may not realize they should include, in addition to $x = 0$, the x values for which $2x + 2$ and $3 - x$ are zero. Remind them that any time a variable appears in the denominator, that term is undefined for zero.

Problem 9

Error Alert

Students may divide out variables in the numerator and denominator of the different terms before inverting the second term. Remind them that dividing out should be done after the problem has been rewritten using multiplication.

Problem 14

Extend the Problem

Ask students the following questions.

"What type of graph does this function have?" parabola

"What is the parabola's vertex?" $(h, k) = \left(\frac{1}{2}, -5\right)$

"What is the parabola's axis of symmetry?" $x = h = \frac{1}{2}$

"What is the direction of its opening?" downward

"How would the graph change if −2 were replaced by −4?" The parabola would be narrower.

***9.** (31) Divide. $\frac{36x^5y^{10}}{7y^4} \div \frac{12y^4}{21x^2}$ $9x^7y^2$

10. (27) **Recreational Planning** A playground that is to be rectangular in shape has an area modeled by the function $f(x) = -x^2 + 12x$ where x represent the length of one side of the playground in meters.

a. What value of x gives the playground the greatest possible area? 6 meters

b. What is the greatest possible area? 36 square meters

***11.** (30) **Graphing Calculator** An object dropped from a height 40 feet above the ground after x seconds is represented by $y = -16x^2 + 40$. When the object is dropped from 10 feet above the ground, the function becomes $y = -16x^2 + 10$.

a. Graph the functions on a graphing calculator and describe the transformation that changes the graph of the first function to the second.

b. For which quadrant or quadrants does the graph make sense? Why?

Write matrix equations for the systems of equations

***12.** (32)
$$2x + 4y + z = 16$$
$$x - 5y + z = -5$$
$$x + y + z = 7$$

***13.** (32)
$$3x + 4z = 13$$
$$15y - 2z = 20$$
$$6z = 6$$
$\begin{bmatrix} 3 & 0 & 4 \\ 0 & 15 & -2 \\ 0 & 0 & 6 \end{bmatrix}\begin{bmatrix} x \\ y \\ z \end{bmatrix} = \begin{bmatrix} 13 \\ 20 \\ 6 \end{bmatrix}$

14. (27) Written in vertex form, what are the values of a, h, and k in $f(x) = -2\left(x - \frac{1}{2}\right)^2 - 5$? $a = -2, h = \frac{1}{2}, k = -5$

15. (11) **Write** Describe how to rewrite the polynomial $x + 4x + 12 - 5x^2 - x$ as an equivalent polynomial in standard form.

***16.** (32) **Nutrition** A sandwich consists of Swiss cheese, ham, and rye bread. The sandwich contains 37.4 grams of carbohydrates, 46 grams of fat, and 36.6 grams of protein. How much of each ingredient is in the sandwich?

	Swiss Cheese	Ham	Rye Bread
Carbohydrates	6%	9%	77%
Fat	64%	48%	11%
Protein	30%	43%	12%

17. (28) **Error Analysis** Explain and correct the error a student made below.

$$\frac{10 - 2r}{r^2 - 10r + 25} = \frac{2(5 - r)}{(r - 5)(r - 5)} = \frac{2(\cancel{r - 5})}{(\cancel{r - 5})(r - 5)} = \frac{2}{r - 5}$$

18. (12) **Geometry** For each equation identify the kind of variation it represents.

a. Area of a circle = $\pi(\text{radius})^2$ direct

b. Area of a rectangle = length × width joint

***19.** (31) **Multi-Step** A container manufacturer is considering doubling the height of a cylindrical container. a–c. See Additional Answers.

a. Find the ratio of surface area to volume for the small container.

b. Find the ratio of surface area to volume for the large container.

c. A smaller ratio of surface area to volume results in a more economical container. Which container is more economical? Explain.

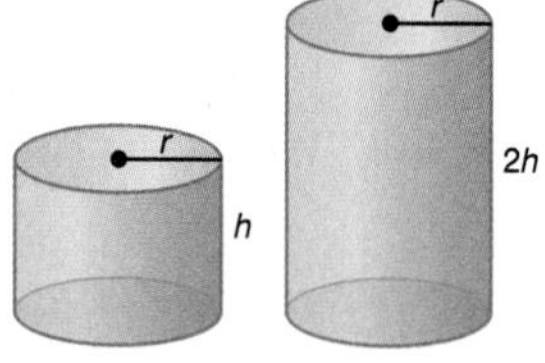

11a.

A vertical shift of 30 units down transforms the first graph to the second.

12. $\begin{bmatrix} 2 & 4 & 1 \\ 1 & -5 & 1 \\ 1 & 1 & 1 \end{bmatrix}\begin{bmatrix} x \\ y \\ z \end{bmatrix} = \begin{bmatrix} 16 \\ -5 \\ 7 \end{bmatrix}$

11b. Quadrant I; time is positive and the lowest height is ground level. (Quadrant IV could make sense if scenario involved negative elevations.)

15. Possible answer: Combine the like terms x, $4x$, and $-x$ to get $4x$, and then write the terms in descending order by degree to get $-5x^2 + 4x + 12$.

16. 20 grams of Swiss cheese, 60 grams of ham, 40 grams of rye bread

17. The student changed $5 - r$ to $r - 5$ without first factoring out −1. The numerator should be $-2(r - 5)$, making the simplified expression $-\frac{2}{r - 5}$.

CHALLENGE

Students have learned in this lesson that multiplication of matrices is not commutative. Have them determine whether the Associative Property of Addition and the Associative Property of Multiplication hold for the following matrices:

$$A = \begin{bmatrix} 1 & 2 \\ -1 & 0 \end{bmatrix}, B = \begin{bmatrix} 0 & 1 \\ 3 & -1 \end{bmatrix}, C = \begin{bmatrix} 1 & 1 \\ 2 & -1 \end{bmatrix}.$$

The Associative Property of Addition: yes; $(A + B) + C = A + (B + C) = \begin{bmatrix} 2 & 4 \\ 4 & -2 \end{bmatrix}$.

The Associative Property of Multiplication: yes: $(AB)C = A(BC) = \begin{bmatrix} 4 & 7 \\ -2 & 1 \end{bmatrix}$.

20. (17) **Exercise** For a 20-year old to workout within his cardio range, his heart rate should be within 25 beats per minute of 155 bpm.

  a. Write an absolute value inequality to determine the lowest and highest heart rate at which he will be in his cardio range. $|x - 155| < 25$

  b. Solve the inequality. $130 < x < 180$

21. (3) Simplify $\dfrac{x^2x^0x^{-1}(x^{-2})^2yx^{-3}}{(x^2y)^{-3}xyx^{-2}x^2}$. $\frac{y^3}{x}$

22. (19) **Basketball** The length of a regulation high school basketball court is represented by the expression $(x + 24)$ feet. The width of a regulation high school basketball court is represented by the expression $(x - 10)$ feet.

  a. Write an expression that represents the area of a regulation high school basketball court. $(x + 24)(x - 10) = x^2 + 14x - 240 \text{ ft}^2$

  b. Evaluate the area of the court if $x = 60$. $(60)^2 + 14(60) - 240 = 4200 \text{ ft}^2$

***23.** (32) **Analyze** Suppose matrix A has an inverse and the matrix equation $AX = B$ has a solution. Explain why $X = A^{-1}B$ is the solution, but $X = BA^{-1}$ is not the solution.

24. (20) Given $f(x) = -7x + 4$ and $g(x) = 9x + 2$, represent $(f + g)(x)$ geometrically.

25. (28) **Probability** A mathematician has a number of red, white, and blue marbles. The number of red marbles is the same as the number of blue marbles and the number of white marbles is the square of the number of red marbles. If the mathematician puts all the marbles in a bag and randomly chooses one marble, what simplified rational expression represents the probability of pulling out one red marble? $\frac{1}{2 + x}$

23. Possible answer: To solve $AX = B$, both sides must be multiplied by A^{-1}. To get $X = BA^{-1}$, A^{-1} would have to be written as a matrix factor on the right of both sides of $AX = B$, and the result would be $AX A^{-1} = BA^{-1}$. But the left side of this equation does not equal X.

24.

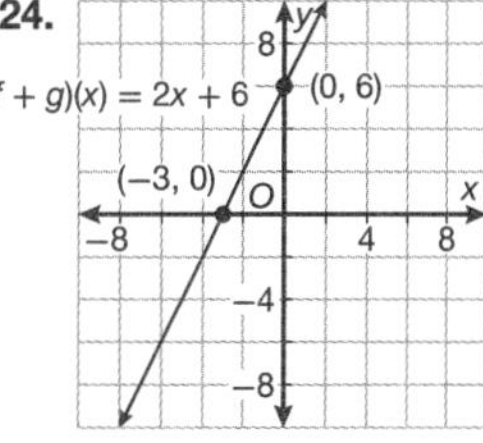

Solve.

26. (24) $\frac{3}{8}x - \frac{1}{3}y = -9$
$2x + 4y = 4$ $\quad x = -16, y = 9$

27. (7) $\dfrac{-3 - x}{2} - \dfrac{x}{2} = 7$ $\quad -\frac{17}{2}$

***28.** (29) Use
$9x = y - 3z - 21$
$4y - 6z = 8x + 10$
$56x - 28y = 2 - 42z$

  a. Write the equations in standard form.

  b. Predict the number of solutions. Explain your answer.

  c. Solve the system of equations to verify your prediction. No solution

28a. $9x - y + 3z = -21$
$-8x + 4y - 6z = 10$
$56x - 28y + 42z = 2$

28b. No solution; The second and third equations have coefficients that are multiples of each other but the constants are not multiples.

29. (23) Solve $x^2 - 5x - 36 = 0$ $\quad x = 9$ or $x = -4$

30. (14) **Error Analysis** Explain the error in the work below. Then find the correct determinant.

$$\begin{vmatrix} 1 & 2 & -2 \\ -1 & 4 & 3 \\ 0 & 1 & 2 \end{vmatrix} = 1\begin{vmatrix} 4 & 3 \\ 1 & 2 \end{vmatrix} - 1\begin{vmatrix} 2 & -2 \\ 1 & 2 \end{vmatrix} + 0\begin{vmatrix} 2 & -2 \\ 4 & 3 \end{vmatrix} = 5 - 6 + 0 = -1$$

The middle term should be subtracted; the determinant is $5 - (-6) + 0 = 11$.

Problem 21

Ask students, **"What is the meaning of a negative exponent?"** A negative exponent means you take the reciprocal of the base and raise it to the absolute value of the negative exponent.

"What should your first step be if you have $(x^2y)^{-3}$ in the denominator?" Write it as $(x^2y)^3$ in the numerator.

"How do you apply the 3 exponent in $(x^2y)^3$?" Apply the cube to each variable in the parentheses, so that the expression becomes x^6y^3.

Problem 23

Extend the Problem

Have students provide sample matrices for A and B and prove that $A^{-1}B \neq BA^{-1}$.

LOOKING FORWARD

Solving linear systems with matrix inverses prepares students for

- **Lesson 56** Finding Angles of Rotation
- **Lesson 99** Using Vectors
- **Lesson 112** Using Sum and Difference Identities

LESSON 33

1 Warm Up

To find the median remind students to place the numbers in order from least to greatest. The median is the middle number. If two data values are in the middle, the mean of those numbers is the median.

2 New Concepts

In this lesson, students learn to apply different types of counting principles. These principles give the number of possible outcomes in a situation.

Example 1

This example shows students to use a tree diagram to find the number of possible outcomes.

Additional Example 1

A restaurant offers a single dip of ice cream and a single topping for dessert. The ice cream choices are chocolate, vanilla, and toffee. The topping choices are chocolate, caramel, and strawberry. How many different desserts can be ordered? 9

LESSON 33 Applying Counting Principles

Warm Up

1. (25) **Vocabulary** The middle number in an ordered list of numbers is called the median.

2. (25) Find the mean of this data set: 12, 20, 20, 30. 20.5

3. (25) Find the median of this data set: 10, 20, 40, 30, 32, 38. 31

New Concepts

In counting theory, an **experiment** is any process that results in one or more **outcomes.** If a process is repeated one or more times, each time it is performed is sometimes called a **trial,** and the experiment consists of all the trials.

Math Language

A **tree diagram** is a branching diagram that shows all possible combinations or outcomes of an experiment.

Example 1 Using a Tree Diagram

A cafeteria offers turkey, ham, and chicken salad sandwiches. The bread choices are rye and wheat. How many different sandwiches can be ordered?

SOLUTION

Ordering a sandwich can be considered a trial of an experiment. Each different sandwich is an outcome. Make a tree diagram to show all possible outcomes.

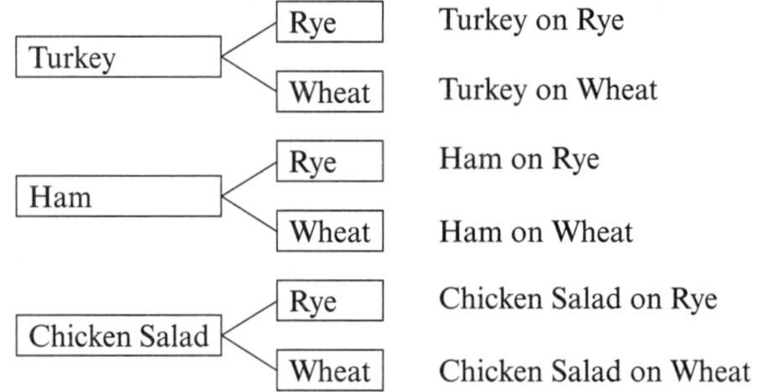

There are 6 different sandwiches that can be ordered.

The **sample space** for an experiment is the set of all possible outcomes. A tree diagram was used in Example 1 to show a sample space. An **event** is any subset of a sample space, so an event is any outcome or set of outcomes. If you need only to count outcomes rather than actually show them, one method you can sometimes use is to apply the **Addition Counting Principle.**

Addition Counting Principle
Suppose a trial can result in any of n_1 outcomes from one category, any of n_2 outcomes from another category, and so on. If there are k different categories of outcomes, then the total number of outcomes that can result is $n_1 + n_2 + \ldots + n_k$.

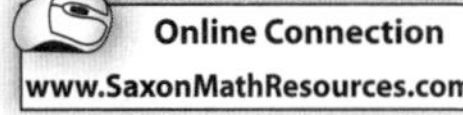

LESSON RESOURCES

Student Edition Practice Workbook 33
Reteaching Master 33
Adaptations Master 33
Challenge and Enrichment Master C33

MATH BACKGROUND

Possible outcomes can be easily listed and counted when dealing with a limited amount of choices. For example, the letters ABC can be arranged in six different ways: ABC, ACB, BAC, BCA, CBA, and CAB. Difficulties arise when dealing with numerous choices. Calculations become more complex if items can be repeated, if the order of the arrangement matters, or if certain events can happen at the same time.

The Addition Counting Principle and the Fundamental Counting Principle are used to calculate the number of outcomes. By determining sample space, they both set the stage for future work in probability.

Two events in a sample space are **mutually exclusive** if they have no outcomes in common. To find the number of outcomes in an event that consists of mutually exclusive events, use the Addition Counting Principle.

Example 2 Using the Addition Counting Principle

Find the number of outcomes in each event.

a. Draw an ace or a face card by drawing a card at random from a standard deck.

SOLUTION

The events *draw an ace* and *draw a face card* are mutually exclusive. There are 4 aces. There are 12 face cards: 4 jacks, 4 queens, and 4 kings.

$4 + 12 = 16$

There are 16 outcomes in the event *draw an ace or a face card.*

b. Choose a prime number or a multiple of 6 or a multiple of 10 by choosing a number at random from the whole numbers 1 through 20.

SOLUTION

The three events *choose a prime number, choose a multiple of 6,* and *choose a multiple of 10* are mutually exclusive. There are 8 prime numbers: 2, 3, 5, 7, 11, 13, 17, and 19. There are 3 multiples of 6: 6, 12, and 18. There are 2 multiples of 10: 10 and 20.

$8 + 3 + 2 = 13$

There are 13 outcomes in the event *choose a prime number or a multiple of 6 or a multiple of 10.*

Math Language

An event that is the union or intersection of two events is a **compound event.** The event *draw an ace or a face card* is a compound event.

The **Fundamental Counting Principle** uses multiplication instead of addition.

Fundamental Counting Principle
Suppose k items are to be chosen. If there are n_1 ways to choose the first item, n_2 ways to choose the second item, and so on, then there are $n_1 \cdot n_2 \cdot \ldots \cdot n_k$ ways to choose all k items.

Example 3 Using the Fundamental Counting Principle

A student is choosing a three-letter password to use for email.

a. How many passwords are possible if letters may be repeated?

SOLUTION

Because letters may be repeated, there are 26 choices for each letter.

$26 \cdot 26 \cdot 26 = 17{,}576$

There are 17,576 possible passwords.

Example 2

This example gives students practice using the Addition Counting Principle.

Additional Example 2

Find the number of outcomes in each event.

a. In a local restaurant, you have a choice of three beef dishes, four chicken dishes, or two vegetarian dishes. 9

b. Choose a prime number or a multiple of 4 or a multiple of 9 by choosing a random number from the whole numbers 1 through 20. 15

Example 3

Students practice using the Fundamental Counting Principle to calculate the possible number of passwords.

Error Alert Although there are 26 letters, the different uppercase and lowercase letters brings the total to 52. Point out that email addresses are usually not case sensitive and so the number of possible letters is 26.

Additional Example 3

A student is choosing a four-letter password for email.

a. How many passwords are possible if letters may be repeated? 456,976

ENGLISH LEARNERS

Explain the meaning of the words **mutual** and **exclusive.** Say:

"The word mutual means common or at the same time. The word exclusive means things that are not shared. In math, the phrase mutually exclusive means things that cannot happen at the same time."

Write the following on the board.

1. The animal is a cat. The animal is a dog.
2. The number is odd. The number is even.
3. The number is prime. The number is a multiple of 5. Say:

"These events are mutually exclusive because they cannot happen at the same time."

Have students think of other events and then state whether they are mutually exclusive or not.

b. How many passwords are possible if letters may not be repeated? 358,800

Example 4

Be sure to discuss the meaning of independent and dependent events.

Additional Example 4

A collection of coins contains a penny, a dime, a nickel, a quarter, and a dollar. Determine whether the events in each case are independent or dependent.

a. Choose a penny then choose a nickel, if the penny is not replaced before the nickel is chosen. dependent

b. Choose a penny then a nickel if the penny is replaced before the nickel is chosen. independent

Example 5

In this example, students use the Fundamental Counting Principle in a real life application.

Additional Example 5

There are 8 students working on the school newspaper. The 8 students will be lined up in a row for a picture. How many different ways can the students be arranged? 40,320

Extend the Example

If one more student was included in the picture, how many MORE ways can the students be arranged? 322,560

TEACHER TIP

Point out to students that in independent events the number of possible outcomes remains the same, but in dependent events the number of possible outcomes changes with each event.

(b.) How many passwords are possible if letters may not be repeated?

SOLUTION

Because letters may not be repeated, there are 26 choices for the first letter, 25 choices for the second letter, and 24 choices for the third letter.

$26 \cdot 25 \cdot 24 = 15{,}600$

There are 15,600 possible passwords.

Two events are **independent** if the probability of one event is not affected by whether or not the other event occurs. Two events are **dependent** if the probability of one event is affected by whether or not the other event occurs.

Example 4 Comparing Independent and Dependent Events

The letters A through E are written on 5 index cards. A card is chosen at random and then another card is chosen at random. Determine whether the events in each case are independent or dependent.

(a.) Choose A and then choose B, if the first card is replaced before the second card is chosen.

SOLUTION

The events are independent because there is a 1 in 5 probability of choosing B second, regardless of what is chosen first.

(b.) Choose A and then choose B, if the first card is not replaced before the second card is chosen.

SOLUTION

The events are dependent. If A is chosen first, there is a 1 in 4 probability of choosing B second. But if A is not chosen first, then it is possible that B is chosen first, in which case there is a zero probability of choosing B second.

Math Reasoning

Analyze How is finding the probability of independent events different than finding the probability of dependent events?

Sample:The number of outcomes for independent events stays consistent, but for dependent events it changes with each event.

Example 5 Application: Sports

There are 6 positions in volleyball: left front, center front, right front, left back, center back, and right back. How many ways can 6 players be placed in the 6 positions?

Net		
LF	CF	RF
LB	CB	RB

SOLUTION

Use the Fundamental Counting Principle.

$6 \cdot 5 \cdot 4 \cdot 3 \cdot 2 \cdot 1 = 720$

There are 720 ways to place 6 players in the 6 positions.

Check The method makes sense because any of the 6 players can be LF. Then any of the 5 remaining players can be CF, and so on: any of 4 can be RF, any of 3 can be LB, either of 2 can be CB, and the last player would be RB.

INCLUSION

Students who are not visual learners may benefit from checking their tree diagrams by using the Fundamental Counting Principle. For example, when students are creating tree diagrams, encourage them to use the Fundamental Counting Principle to check the number of possible outcomes.

For example, problem a in lesson practice states that students are choosing 1 T-shirt and 1 pair of pants from 4 T-shirts and 2 pairs of pants. The Fundamental Counting Principle shows that the number of possible outcomes is $4 \times 2 = 8$.

a. 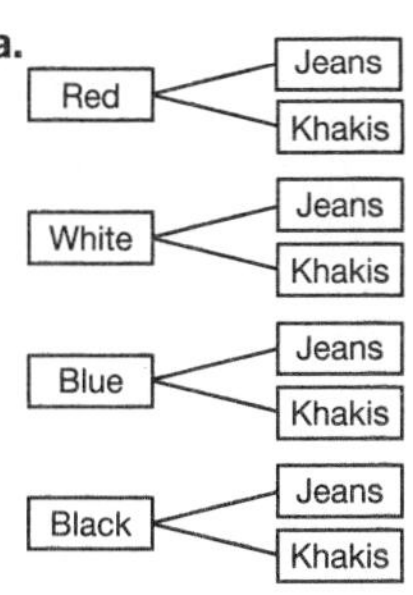

c. 9 outcomes: 25, 36, 24, 32, 40, 23, 29, 31, 37.

Lesson Practice

a. *(Ex 1)* A student has four choices for a T-shirt: red, white, blue, and black. He has 2 choices for pants: jeans or khakis. How many different outfits can he make, using one T-shirt and one pair of pants? Make a tree diagram to show all possible outcomes. 8

b. *(Ex 2)* A card is drawn at random from a standard 52-card deck. How many outcomes are in the event *draw a heart or a club*? 26

c. *(Ex 2)* A number is chosen at random from the whole numbers 21 through 40. How many outcomes are in the event *choose a perfect square or a multiple of 8 or a prime number*? List all the outcomes.

d. *(Ex 3)* A student is choosing a four-digit password to use for her bank account. How many passwords are possible if digits may be repeated? 10,000

e. *(Ex 3)* A student is choosing a four-digit password to use for her bank account. How many passwords are possible if digits may not be repeated? 5,040

There are five tiles in a bag, labeled W, O, R, D, and S. A tile is chosen at random and then another tile is chosen at random. Determine whether the following events are independent or dependent. *(Ex 4)*

f. Choose W and then choose S, if the first tile is replaced before the second tile is chosen. independent

g. Choose W and then choose S, if the first tile is not replaced before the second tile is chosen. dependent

h. *(Ex 5)* There are 9 players in a starting baseball lineup. How many ways can batting positions 1, 2, and 3 be filled, choosing from 9 players? 504

Practice Distributed and Integrated

 ***1.** *(30)* **Geometry** The function representing the area of a rectangle whose length is 12 units longer than its width is $f(x) = (x + 6)^2 - 36$ where x is the width of the rectangle. Graph this function. For which quadrant or quadrants does the graph make sense? Why? Because width, length and area can only be positive, the graph only makes sense for values in Quadrant I.

1. (graph: y-axis labeled 20, 40; x-axis labeled −40, −20, 20, 40; O)

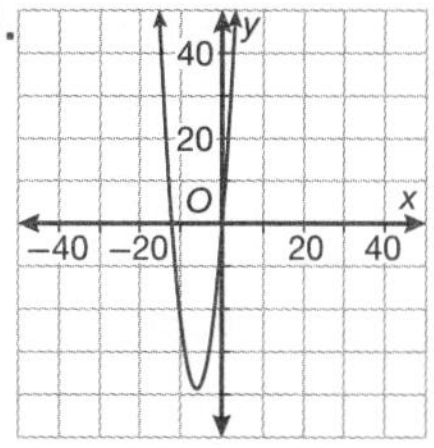

2. *(10)* Solve and graph the compound inequality $4 < 2(x - 2) \leq 16$.
$4 < x \leq 10$; 

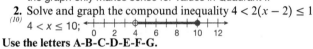

Use the letters A-B-C-D-E-F-G.

***3.** *(33)* How many seven-letter passwords are possible if letters can be repeated? 823,543

***4.** *(33)* How many seven-letter passwords are possible if letters cannot be repeated? 5,040

5. *(26)* Find the equation of the line through (−3, −5) and (4, −5). $y = -5$

6. *(Inv 2)* **Airplanes** As an airplane ascends after takeoff, its altitude increases at a rate of 45 ft/s while its distance on the ground from the airport increases at 210 ft/s. Write parametric equations to model the location of the plane. $x = 210t$ and $y = 45t$

 **CHALLENGE**

An on-line site is setting rules for customer created passwords. The password must consist of letters (not case sensitive) and digits (from 0 – 9). The password is 6 characters long.

How many passwords can be created if the digits and letters can be repeated and can be in any order? $36^6 = 2{,}176{,}782{,}336$

Repeat the above scenario, but now digits and letters CANNOT be repeated. $(36)(35)(34)(33)(32)(31) = 1{,}402{,}410{,}240$

How many passwords can be created if the digits must be in the first two places and letters in the remaining places? The digits and letters can be repeated. $(10^2)(26^4) = 45{,}697{,}600$

Repeat the above scenario, but now the digits and letters CANNOT be repeated. $(10)(9)(26)(25)(24)(23) = 32{,}292{,}000$

Which situation results in the most possible passwords? Digits and letters in any order and they can be repeated.

Lesson Practice

Problem h

Error Alert Students often believe the number of outcomes is found by 3 • 2 • 1 because there are 3 places. Remind students that there are 9 possible players for the first position, then 8 left for the second position, then 7 left for the third position.

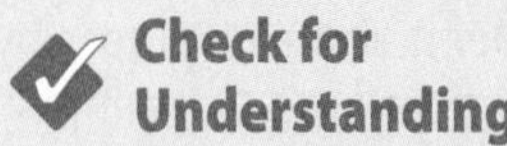

The questions below help assess the concepts taught in this lesson.

"What is the difference between independent events and dependent events?" Events are independent if one does not affect the probability of the other. Events are dependent if one event does affect the probability of the other.

"What is an example of independent events?" flipping two coins

"What is an example of dependent events?" selecting two marbles from a bag without replacement

3 Practice

Math Conversations

Discussion to strengthen understanding

Problem 1

Guide students by asking them the following questions.

"Can the length or width of a rectangle be a negative number? Explain." No, the length and width must be positive numbers in real life situations.

"In which quadrant must the solution to this function lie?" The solution must be in Quadrant I.

Problem 9

Remind students to collect like terms when they add the functions.

Extend the Problem

What is the sum of the functions in part a and b?
$4x^5 - 24x^3 + 2\frac{1}{2}x^2 + 4x - 3$

Problem 18

Have students compare slopes by putting both equations in slope-intercept form. Then tell them to compare y-intercepts.

*7. Write the matrix equation that represents the system of equations.
(32)

$$\begin{aligned} p + q + r &= 6 \\ 0.4p + 0.5q + 2r &= 5.7 \\ 2.2p + 3.4q + r &= 12 \end{aligned} \qquad \begin{bmatrix} 1 & 1 & 1 \\ 0.4 & 0.5 & 2 \\ 2.2 & 3.4 & 1 \end{bmatrix}\begin{bmatrix} p \\ q \\ r \end{bmatrix} = \begin{bmatrix} 6 \\ 5.7 \\ 12 \end{bmatrix}$$

8. **Error Analysis** Two students evaluated $(f - g)(7)$, given $f(x) = 5x + 8$ and $g(x) = 9x + 2$. Who is correct? Explain the error.
(20)

Student A	Student B
$(f - g)(7)$ $= 5(7) + 8 - (9(7) + 2)$ $= 35 + 8 - 63 - 2$ $= -22$	$(f - g)(7)$ $= 5(7) + 8 - (9(7) + 2)$ $= 35 + 8 - 63 + 2$ $= -2$

8. Student A is correct; Student B forgot to distribute the negative through both terms in the second set of parentheses.

9. Given the polynomial functions $f(x) = \frac{1}{2}x^2 - 3$, $g(x) = 2x^2$, and $h(x) = 4x$,
(11, 19)
 a. write the sum $(f + g + h)(x)$ in standard form. $2\frac{1}{2}x^2 + 4x - 3$
 b. write the product $(f \cdot g \cdot h)(x)$ in standard form. $4x^5 - 24x^3$

*10. **Justify** Is multiplication of rational expressions commutative? Is division of rational expressions commutative? Justify your answers. See Additional Answers.
(31)

11. **Multiply** Assume all expressions are defined. $\frac{2x^4y^5}{3x^2} \cdot \frac{15x^2}{8x^3y^2}$ $\frac{5xy^3}{4}$
(31)

*12. Using the numbers 2-4-6 and the letters P-A-R-K, how many one-digit, two-letter passwords can be made, if repeats are allowed and the password starts with a digit? 48
(33)

13. **Multi-Step** $\begin{vmatrix} x & 2 \\ -6 & 4 \end{vmatrix} = 8$
(14)
 a. Write the determinant as an equation. $4x + 12 = 8$
 b. Solve for x. -1
 c. Check your answer by substituting for x and finding the determinant with a calculator. $\begin{vmatrix} -1 & 2 \\ -6 & 4 \end{vmatrix} = 8$

*14. Find the inverse of $M = \begin{bmatrix} 4 & 8 \\ 2 & 6 \end{bmatrix}$, if it exists. $M = \begin{bmatrix} 0.75 & -1 \\ -0.25 & 0.5 \end{bmatrix}$
(32)

17a.
$c + a = 45$
$10.95c + 14.95a = 516.75$

Write each equation in standard form.

15. $y = 1.5x + 3$ $1.5x - y = -3$
(26)

16. $y = -0.05x + 20$ $0.05x + y = 20$
(26)

17. **Ticket Prices** A zoo charges $10.95 for each child's admission and $14.95 for each adult admission. If a busload of 45 people attend, and together they pay $516.75, how many adults and how many children are admitted?
(16)
 a. Set up equations relating the number of children and adults to the total admissions. Let c represent the number of children and a the number of adults.
 b. Use Cramer's Rule to solve the system of equations. $c = 39$ children; $a = 6$ adults

18. **Write** Without solving the system, can you tell how many solutions this system of equations has? Explain. $\begin{aligned} y + x &= 2 \\ y + 1 &= -x \end{aligned}$ The system has no solutions because the lines are parallel and have no points in common. Solving for y in each equation gives the same slope and two different y-intercepts.
(21)

19. Simplify: $\frac{(xm^{-2})^0x^0m^0}{xx^2m^0(2x)^{-2}}$ $4x^{-1}$
(19)

*20. **Write** Describe how to determine the number of different arrangements of the letters M, A, T, and H.
(33)

20. Possible answer: There are 4 choices for the first letter in an arrangement, 3 choices for the second letter, 2 choices for the third letter, and 1 choice for the fourth letter. So the number of arrangements is $4 \cdot 3 \cdot 2 \cdot 1 = 24$.

21. **Multiple Choice** Factor the expression $-12x^4 + 6x^2 + 18x$. A
(23)
A $-6x(2x^3 - x - 3)$ B $-6(2x^4 - x^2 - 3)$
C $-6x(2x^3 + x + 3)$ D $-6(2x^4 + x^2 + 3)$

*22. **Graphing Calculator** Use a graphing calculator to determine the y-intercept of the quadratic function $y = x^2 + x - 2$. y-intercept: -2
(27)

*23. **Sports** There were 12 players on the United States team that competed in the 2006 Women's Basketball (under 19) World Championship tournament. How many ways can 5 starters be chosen from 12 players? 95,040
(33)

24. **Motion** A speed boat leaves a nearby shore of a lake and moves at 25 knots toward the opposite shore, 2 nautical miles away. At the same time, a pleasure boat leaves the opposite shore and moves at 10 knots toward the speed boat. When will the boats meet?
(16)
a. Set up a system of equations representing the position of each boat relative to the nearby shore. $x = 25t$, $x = 2 - 10t$
b. Use Cramer's Rule to solve the system. $t = \frac{2}{35}$ hour

*25. **Measurement** Write a rational expression in simplest form for the ratio of area to perimeter for the right triangle. $\frac{x}{2}$
(31)

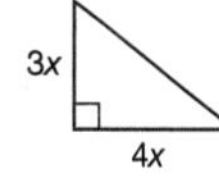

*26. Find the intercepts of the equation $40 + 8y - 2z = -5x$.
(Inv 3) x: $(-8, 0, 0)$, y: $(0, -5, 0)$, z: $(0, 0, 20)$

27. **Analyze** The first quartile of some test scores is 55 and the third quartile is 74.
(25)
a. Is it possible for the median of the test scores to be 77? Explain why or why not.
b. The maximum score is 93 and the range of the test scores is 55. What is the minimum test score? $93 - 55 = 38$
c. What is the range of test scores that will place a student in the middle 50% of the class? scores between 55 and 74

27a. No. Possible answer: The value of the median is between the first and third quartiles

28. **Multi-Step** a. Write an equation in two variables to represent that the sum of two numbers is 73. $x + y = 73$
(24)
b. Write an equation with the same variables to represent that twice the second number minus the first number is 2. $2y - x = 2$
c. Write and solve a linear system to find the two numbers. $x + y = 73$, $2y - x = 2$; $x = 48$, $y = 25$

29. Convert 61 yd^2 to square inches 79,056 in^2
(18)

*30. What is the inverse of the matrix $\begin{bmatrix} 2 & 2 \\ 4 & 5 \end{bmatrix}$? $\begin{bmatrix} 2.5 & -1 \\ -2 & 1 \end{bmatrix}$
(32)

Problem 24

Guide students by asking them the following questions.

"If x is the distance from the nearby shore, what is the equation for the speed boat?" $x = 25t$

"What is the equation for the pleasure boat? Remember the boats are traveling in opposite directions." $x = 2 - 10t$

"What is true about x when the boats meet? Explain." The variable x represents the distance of the boat from the nearby shore. When the boats meet, their distance from the nearby shore is the same. So x must be equal to the same amount when the boats meet.

"Explain how to use Cramer's Rule to solve the system." Cramer's Rule can be used because the determinant is not 0. The determinant of $\begin{bmatrix} 1 & -25 \\ 1 & 10 \end{bmatrix}$ is 35.

So $t = \frac{\begin{vmatrix} 1 & 0 \\ 1 & 2 \end{vmatrix}}{35} = \frac{2}{35}$ of an hour.

Problem 25

Guide students by asking them the following questions.

"What is the length of the hypotenuse of the triangle? Explain." Because the legs are $3x$ and $4x$, this is a 3–4–5 triangle. The hypotenuse is $5x$.

"What is the area of the triangle?" $\frac{1}{2}(4x)(3x) = 6x^2$

"What is the perimeter of the triangle?" $3x + 4x + 5x = 12x$

"What is the simplest form of the ratio of area to perimeter? $\frac{x}{2}$

ALTERNATE METHOD FOR PROBLEM 22

The y-intercept can be found by inspection of the equation. The graph will cross the y-axis when $x = 0$. So $y = 0^2 + 0 - 2 = -2$. The y-intercept is -2.

LOOKING FORWARD

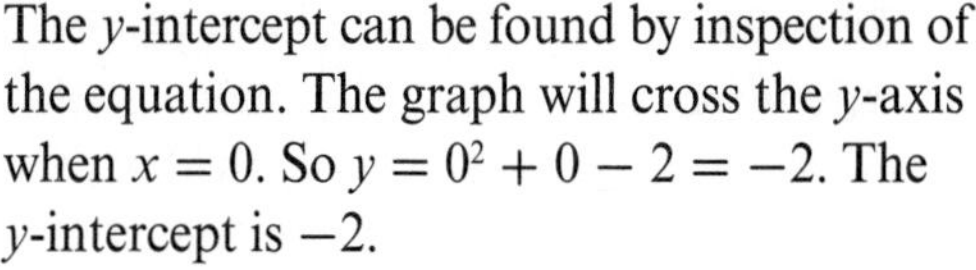

Applying counting principles prepares students for

- **Lesson 55** Finding Probability
- **Lesson 60** Distinguishing Between Mutually Exclusive and Independent Events

LESSON 34

1 Warm Up

In problem 3, students must substitute 2 for y.

2 New Concepts

In this lesson, students learn to graph linear equations and transformations of $f(x) = x$.

Example 1

Students identify the graph of a linear function.

Additional Example 1

Determine whether each graph represents a linear function.

a.

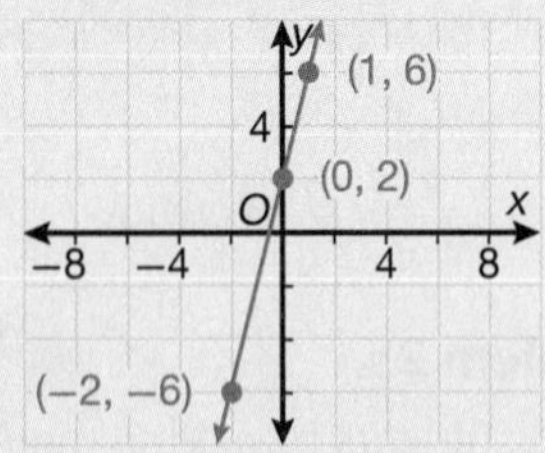

Yes, this is a linear function.

b.

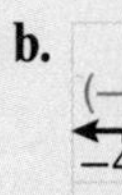

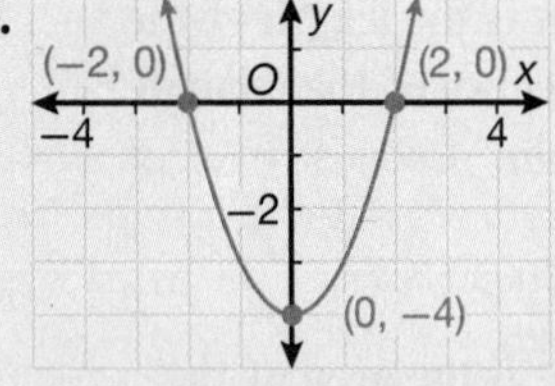

This is a function, but not a linear function.

LESSON 34

Graphing Linear Equations II

Warm Up

1. (13) **Vocabulary** The expression $\frac{\text{rise}}{\text{run}}$ is the ____slope____ of a line.

2. (13) What is the y-intercept of the line whose equation is $y = 2x + 5$? 5

3. (7) One point on the line with equation $-x + 3y = 4$ is (___, 2). 2

New Concepts

A relation is a set of ordered pairs, usually denoted (x, y). A function is a relation in which there is exactly one value of y for every value of x. To determine whether a graph is the graph of a function, you can use the vertical line test.

A function with a constant rate of change is called a **linear function,** and its graph is a line. Every non-vertical line represents a linear function.

Example 1 Identifying Graphs of Linear Functions

Determine whether each graph represents a linear function.

a. Rate of change from $(-3, 0)$ to $(0, 2)$:

$$\frac{2-0}{0-(-3)} = \frac{2}{3}$$

Rate of change from $(0, 2)$ to $(5, 4)$:

$$\frac{4-2}{5-0} = \frac{2}{5}$$

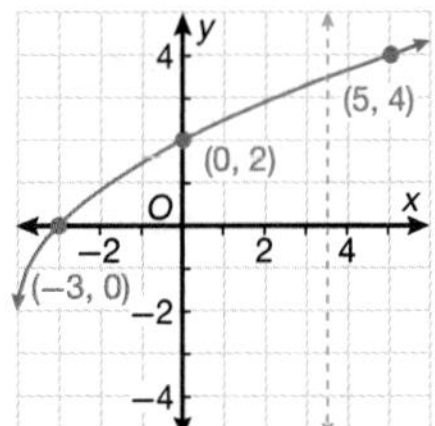

SOLUTION No vertical line intersects the graph in more than one point, so it represents a function. However, it is not a linear function because it does not have a constant rate of change.

Hint

To be sure that a graph represents a linear function, you either need to know that it is a line, or you need to know its equation.

b. Rate of change from $(-4, 0)$ to $(0, 2)$:

$$\frac{2-0}{0-(-4)} = \frac{2}{4} = \frac{1}{2}$$

Rate of change from $(0, 2)$ to $(2, 3)$:

$$\frac{3-2}{2-0} = \frac{1}{2}$$

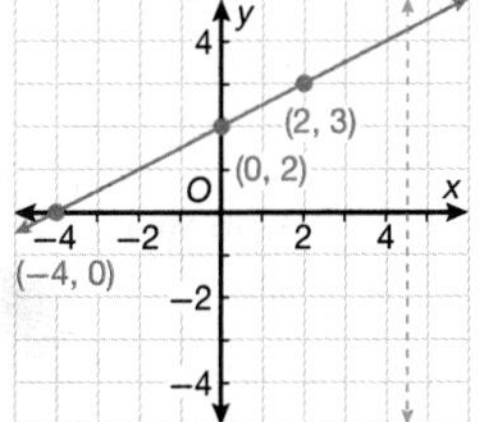

SOLUTION No vertical line intersects the graph in more than one point, so it represents a function. And, it is a linear function because it has a constant rate of change.

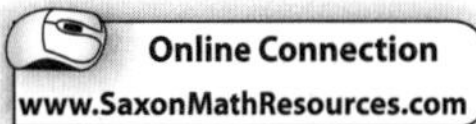

A linear function can be represented by a linear equation. There are three forms of a linear equation that are commonly used.

LESSON RESOURCES

Student Edition Practice Workbook 34
Reteaching Master 34
Adaptations Master 34
Challenge and Enrichment Master C34

MATH BACKGROUND

Students have learned to graph lines using different information. Students can graph a line given:

- two points
- a slope and a y-intercept
- a slope and any point on the line

Graphs of other functions can be graphed in similar ways. But because the functions may not be linear, more information is needed.

The idea of graphing by transforming a parent function is useful for many of these graphs. With the methods learned in this lesson, students can compare almost any function to the parent function and sketch the new graph.

Forms of a Linear Equation		
Standard Form	$Ax + By = C$	A and B are not both zero.
Slope-Intercept Form	$y = mx + b$	m is the slope and b is the y-intercept.
Point-Slope Form	$y - y_1 = m(x - x_1)$	m is the slope and (x_1, y_1) is a point on the line.

Hint

It is easy to compute with zeros, so it is often helpful to include one or both intercepts when making a table of values.

Example 2 Graphing Linear Equations, Given Standard Form

Graph each linear equation.

a. $3x + 2y = 12$

SOLUTION Make a table of ordered pairs, plot the ordered pairs, and draw a line through them.

x	0	4	2
y	6	0	3

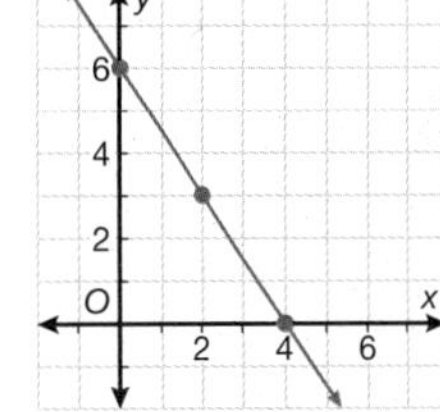

b. $-2x + 5y = -20$

SOLUTION Solve the equation for y to get slope-intercept form.

$$-2x + 5y = -20$$
$$5y = 2x - 20$$
$$y = \frac{2}{5}x - 4$$

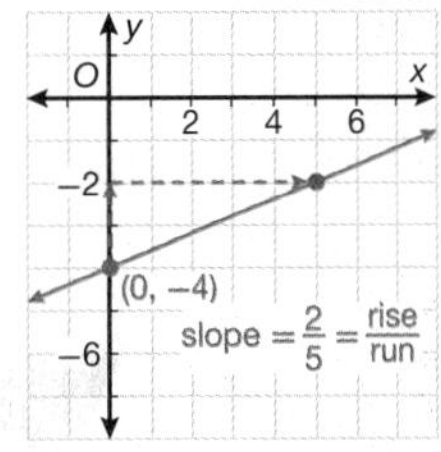

The y-intercept is -4, so the line crosses the y-axis at $(0, -4)$. Plot $(0, -4)$. Then use the slope: from $(0, -4)$, count 2 up and 5 right to plot another point on the line. Draw the line through the points.

Hint

There are different ways to count using slope. For example, $-\frac{1}{2} = \frac{2}{-4} = \frac{\text{rise}}{\text{run}}$, so in Example 3, you can count 2 up and 4 left to plot another point on the line.

Example 3 Graphing a Linear Equation, Given Point-Slope Form

Graph $y - 3 = -\frac{1}{2}(x + 2)$.

SOLUTION $y - 3 = -\frac{1}{2}(x + 2)$ is in the point-slope form $y - y_1 = m(x - x_1)$. The slope is $m = -\frac{1}{2}$ and a point on the line is $(x_1, y_1) = (-2, 3)$. Plot $(-2, 3)$ and then count 1 down and 2 right to plot another point on the line. Draw the line through the points.

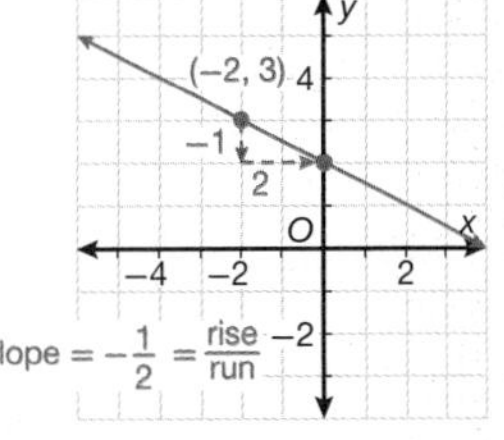

The most basic linear function is $y = x$. It is called the *parent function* of all linear functions. All other linear functions are *transformations* of $y = x$. Reflections, shifts, stretches, and compressions are types of transformations.

Example 2

Students learn to graph a linear equation in the standard form.

TEACHER TIP

Remind students that although equations can be graphed using a graphing calculator, they must still be solved for y. Encourage students to graph standard form equations using intercepts for a quick graph.

Additional Example 2

Graph each linear equation.

a. $x + 3y = 12$

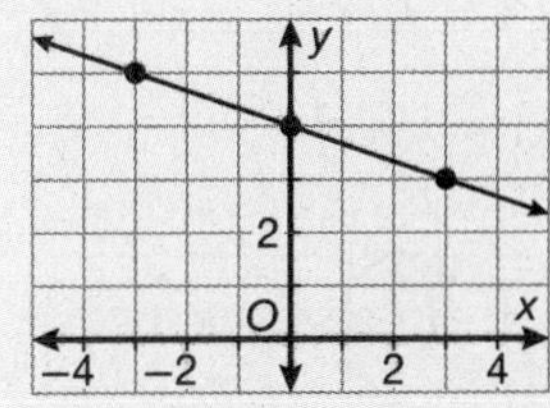

b. $-3x + 4y = -4$

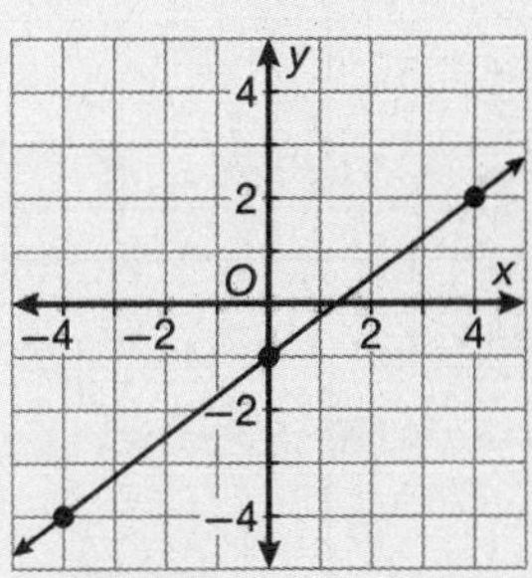

Example 3

Students learn to graph a linear equation in point-slope form.

Additional Example 3

Graph $y + 2 = \frac{2}{3}(x - 1)$.

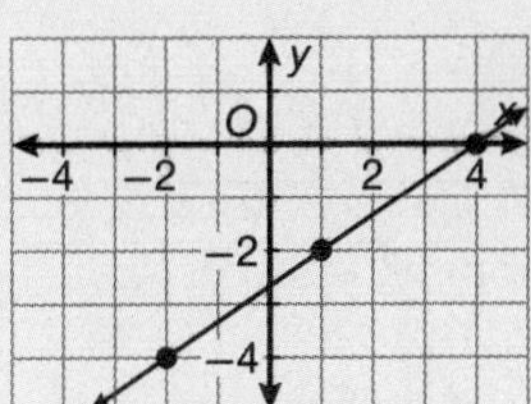

ALTERNATE METHOD FOR EXAMPLE 2

In part b, students can graph using x- and y-intercepts rather than converting to the slope-intercept form.

To find the x-intercept, let $y = 0$:

$$-2x + 5(0) = -20$$
$$-2x = -20$$
$$x = 10$$

To find the y-intercept, let $x = 0$:

$$-2(0) + 5y = -20$$
$$5y = -20$$
$$y = -4$$

Plot points $(10, 0)$ and $(0, -4)$ and graph the line.

Example 4

In this example, students explore transformations of the parent function $f(x) = x$.

Additional Example 4

Graph each transformation of $f(x) = x$.

a. $g(x) = 4x$

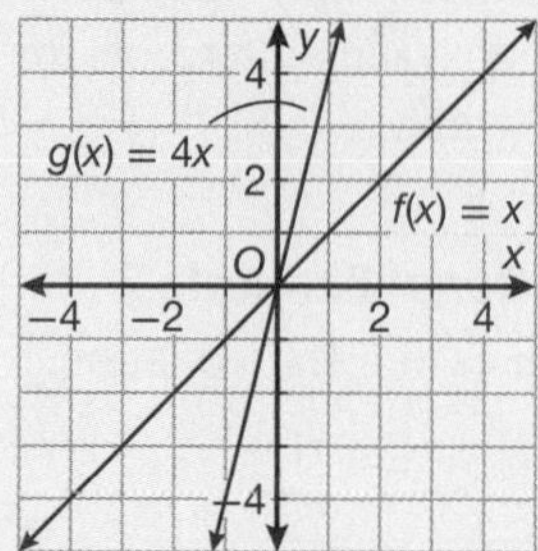

b. $g(x) = x + 2$

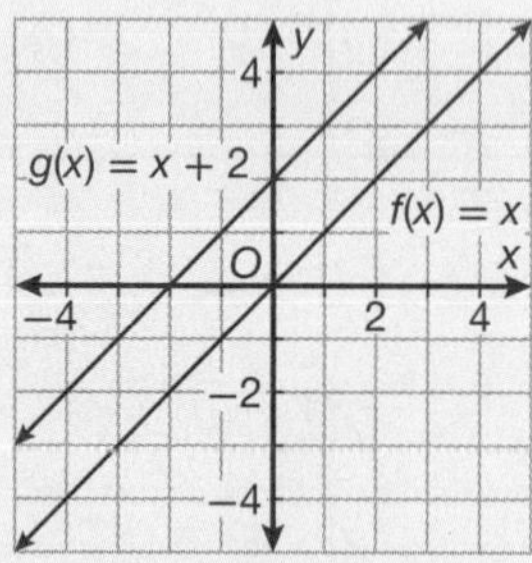

c. $g(x) = -2x$

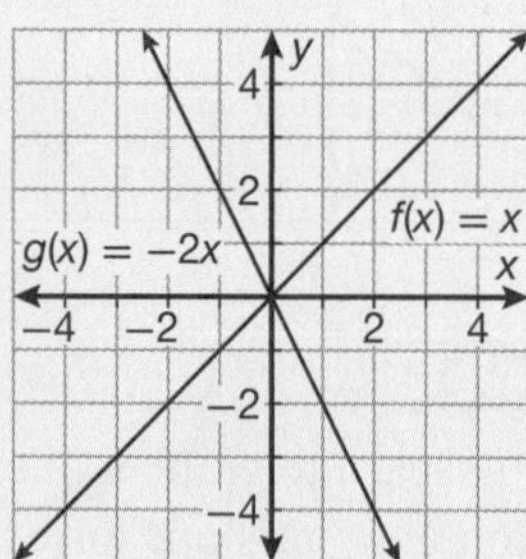

d. $g(x) = 2x + 1$

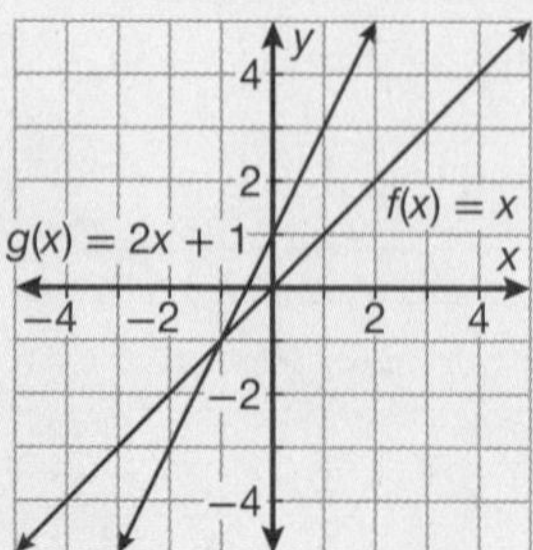

Transformations of $f(x) = x$
$-f(x)$ is a reflection over the x-axis.
$f(x) + c$ is a vertical shift c units up if c is positive.
$f(x) + c$ is a vertical shift c units down if c is negative.
$c \cdot f(x)$ is a vertical stretch by a factor of c if $c > 1$.
$c \cdot f(x)$ is a vertical compression by a factor of c if $0 < c < 1$.

Example 4 Graphing Transformations of f(x) = x

Graph each transformation of $f(x) = x$.

a. $g(x) = -x$

SOLUTION $g(x) = -x = -f(x)$, which is the reflection of $f(x)$ over the x-axis.

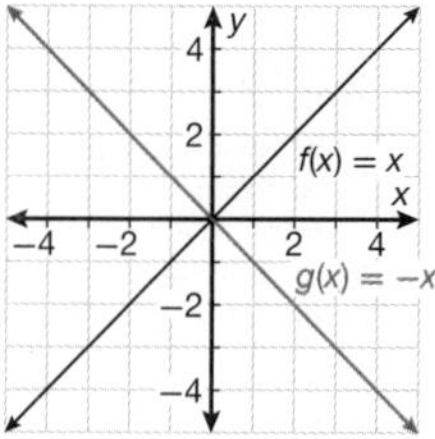

b. $g(x) = x - 3$

SOLUTION $g(x) = x - 3 = f(x) - 3$, which is a vertical shift of $f(x)$ down 3 units.

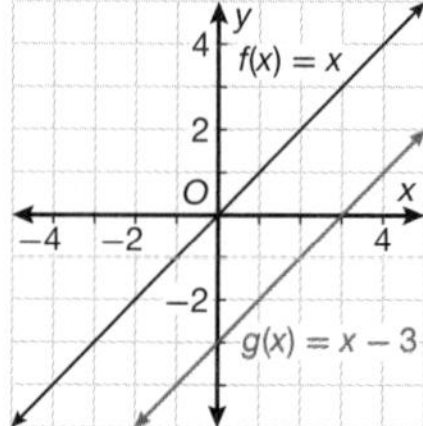

c. $g(x) = 2x$

SOLUTION $g(x) = 2x = 2 \cdot f(x)$, which is a vertical stretch of $f(x)$ by a factor of 2.

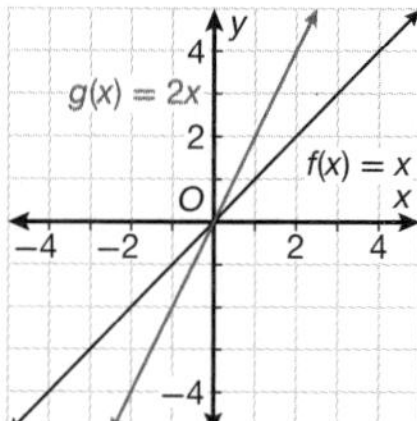

Graphing Calculator Tip

To enter $g(x) = -\frac{1}{3}x + 2$, use these key strokes: Y=, then (−) 1 ÷ 3 X,T,θ,n + 2, then GRAPH. Adjust the viewing window as needed.

d. $g(x) = -\frac{1}{3}x + 2$

SOLUTION $g(x) = -\frac{1}{3}x + 2 = -\frac{1}{3}f(x) + 2$, which consists of three transformations of $f(x)$:

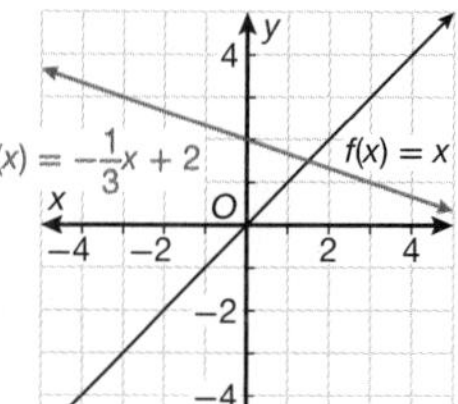

- a vertical compression by a factor of $\frac{1}{3}$
- a reflection over the x-axis
- a vertical shift 2 units up

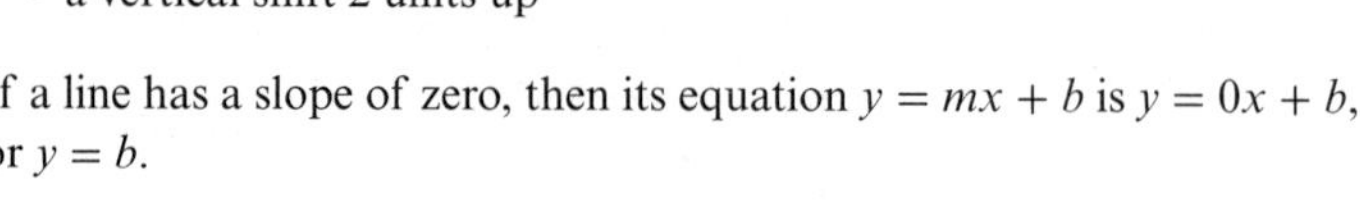

If a line has a slope of zero, then its equation $y = mx + b$ is $y = 0x + b$, or $y = b$.

ENGLISH LEARNERS

Some students might have trouble with the term **transformations.** Tell students that **transform** means "to change shape or form." In mathematics, transformations are changes in the parent function, $f(x) = x$.

This lesson describes five types of transformations: reflection, vertical shift down, vertical shift up, vertical stretch, and vertical compression.

For example, $g(x) = -x$ is a reflection over the x-axis. The function $g(x) = x - 3$ is a vertical shift down. The function $g(x) = x + 3$ is a vertical shift up. The function $g(x) = 2x$ is a vertical stretch. The function $g(x) = \frac{1}{3}x$ is a vertical compression.

Model for students how to identify each type of transformation using additional example 4.

Horizontal and Vertical Lines
Let b be any constant.
$y = b$ is a linear function whose graph is a **horizontal line** with a slope of zero.
$x = b$ is not a function; its graph is a vertical line with an undefined slope.

Example 5 Graphing Horizontal and Vertical Lines

Math Language

An **undefined slope** is also called **no slope.** Remember that slope is a number. A zero in a denominator indicates no slope because there is no number that has zero in the denominator.

a. Graph $y = 3$.

SOLUTION Make a table of ordered pairs. Use 3 for y and any number for x.

x	−4	0	2
y	3	3	3

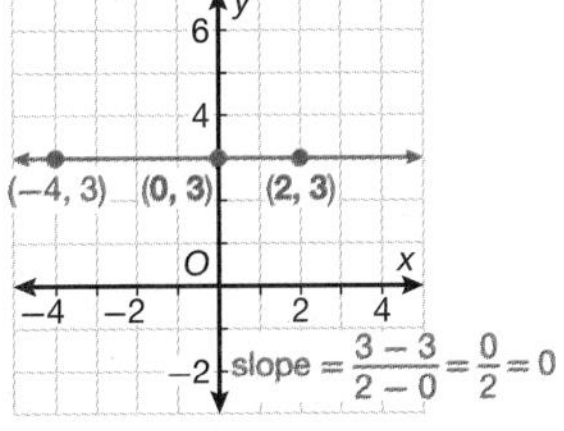

b. Graph $x = -2$.

SOLUTION Make a table of ordered pairs. Use −2 for x and any number for y.

x	−2	−2	−2
y	3	1	0

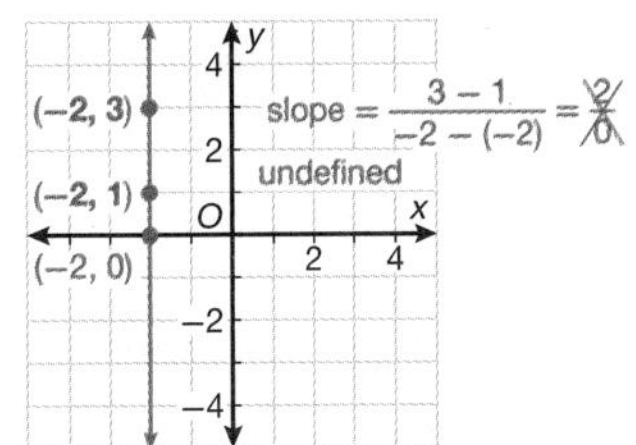

Example 6 Application: Wheelchair Accessibility

The Americans with Disabilities Act specifies that the maximum slope for a wheelchair ramp should be 1:12. A builder needs to install a wheelchair ramp from point P to the entrance door shown in the diagram. Graph a line that can be used to represent the ramp. Write an equation of the line in slope-intercept form.

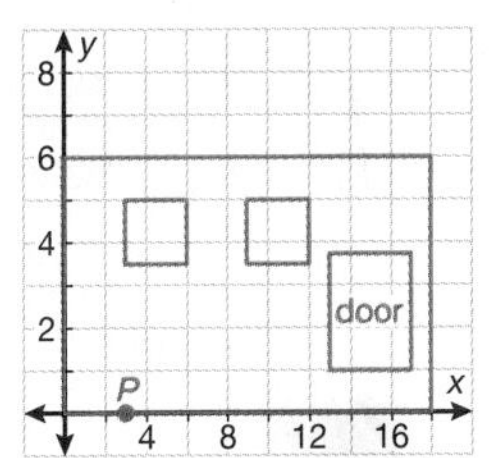

SOLUTION Draw a line through point P with a rise of 1 and a run of 12. Use the given point and given slope to write an equation of the line in point-slope form. Then solve for y to obtain slope-intercept form.

$$y - y_1 = m(x - x_1)$$

$$y - 0 = \frac{1}{12}(x - 3)$$

$$y = \frac{1}{12}(x - 3)$$

$$y = \frac{1}{12}x - \frac{1}{4}$$

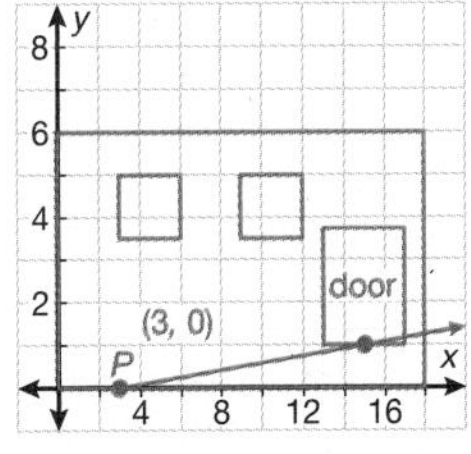

Check The graph is correct because the rise is 1, the run is 12, and it passes through $P(3, 0)$. The equation $y = \frac{1}{12}x - \frac{1}{4}$ is correct because its slope is $\frac{1}{12}$ and the ordered pair (3, 0) is a solution.

Example 5

Students graph horizontal and vertical lines.

Additional Example 5

a. Graph $y = 5$.

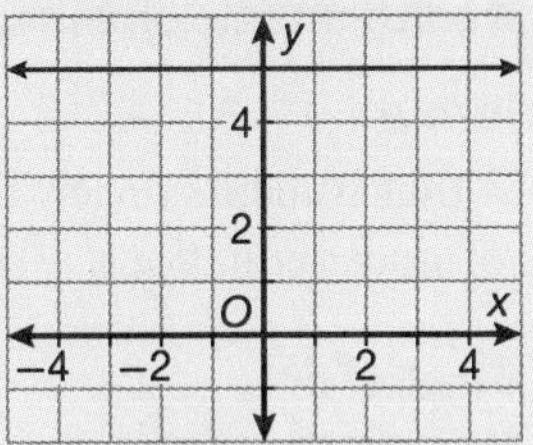

b. Graph $x = 2$.

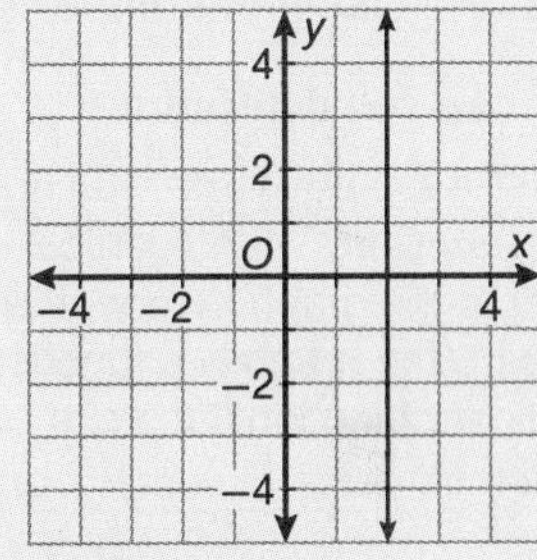

Example 6

Students define and graph a linear equation representing a real-life situation.

Additional Example 6

The roof of a barn has pitch of 1:8.

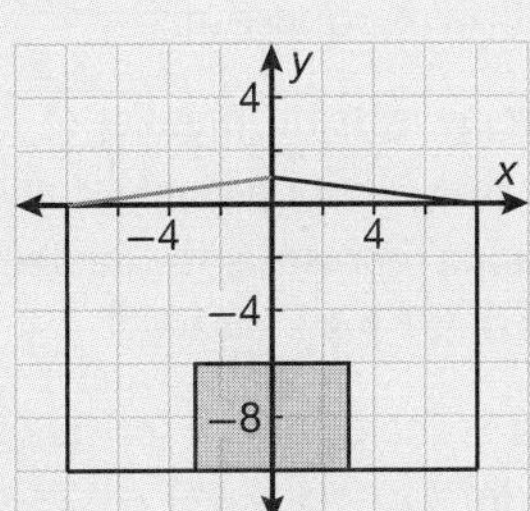

Graph a line that can be used to represent the left side of the roof. Write an equation of the line in slope-intercept form.

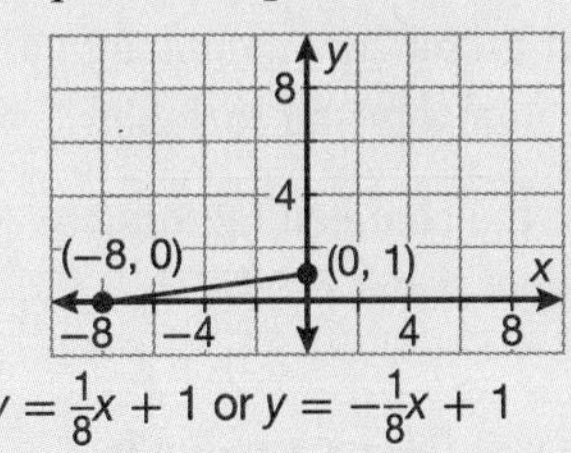

$y = \frac{1}{8}x + 1$ or $y = -\frac{1}{8}x + 1$

INCLUSION

Have students write each form of a linear equation so they can refer to it when needed.

Slope intercept form: $y = mx + b$

Point-Slope form: $y - y_1 = m(x - x_1)$

Standard Form: $Ax + By = C$

Lesson Practice

Problems a and b

Scaffolding Have students first use the vertical line test to check if the graph is a function. If it is a function, have students check if it has a constant rate of change.

Problem e

Suggest that students review the forms of linear equations.

Check for Understanding

The question below helps assess the concepts taught in this lesson.

"How can you determine whether a graph represents a linear function?" If no vertical line intersects the graph in more than one point, the graph is a function. It is a linear function if it has a constant slope.

3 Practice

Math Conversations

Discussion to strengthen understandings

Problem 1

Guide students by asking them the following questions.

"If x represents the number of quarts that Nikita picked, what expression represents the number of quarts that Chuck picked?" $x + 11$

"What is the equation for this scenario?" $x + (x + 11) = 173$

Problem 2

Guide students by asking them the following questions.

"What factors are common to all of the numbers and variables?" ab

"Once the common factors are pulled out, what is left?" $ab(-2 + x + x^2)$

"How can this expression be simplified to make factoring easier?" Rearrange the expression to $x^2 + x - 2$ and then factor.

c.

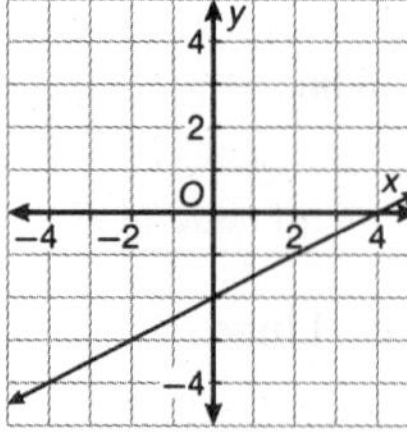

d.

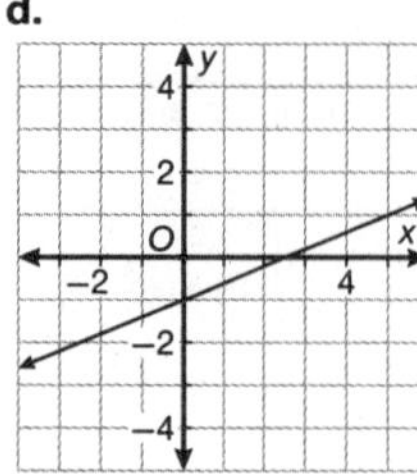

e.

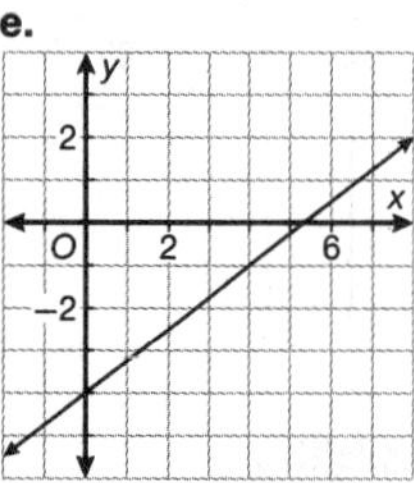

Lesson Practice

Determine whether the graph represents a linear function. (Ex 1)

a. 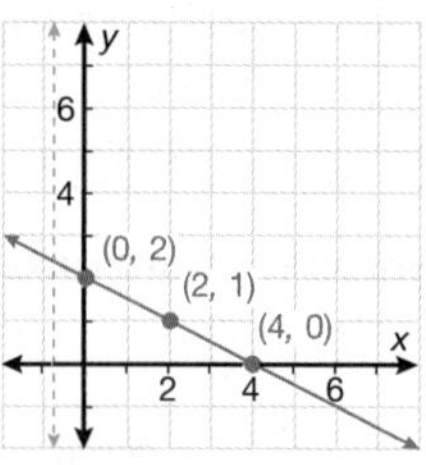

yes

b. 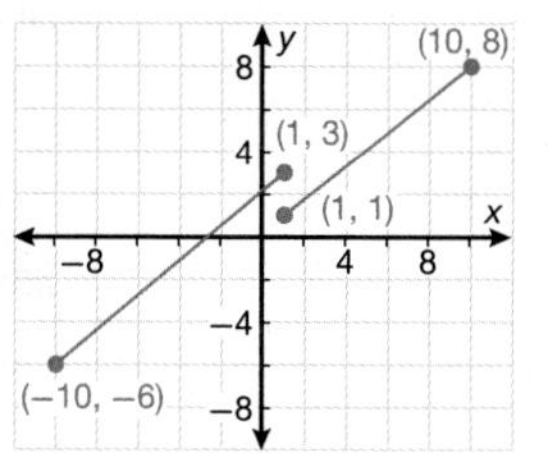

no

c. Graph $2x - 4y = 8$ using a table. (Ex 2)

d. Graph $2x - 5y = 5$ by solving for y to obtain slope-intercept form. (Ex 2)

e. Graph $y + 1 = \frac{3}{4}(x - 4)$. (Ex 3)

Graph by transforming the parent function $f(x) = x$. (Ex 4) See Additional Answers.

f. $g(x) = -6x$ **g.** $g(x) = x + 5$

h. $g(x) = 4x - 7$ **i.** $g(x) = -3x + 1$

Graph. (Ex 5)

j. $x = 4$ See Additional Answers. **k.** $y = -5$ See Additional Answers.

l. (Ex 6) The diagram shows two walls and a door of a shed. $\overline{PQ}$ represents a wall. Graph a line through point P to represent a roof with a slope of $\frac{3}{5}$. Write an equation of the line in slope-intercept form. See Additional Answers.

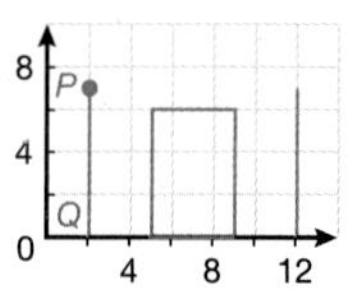

Practice Distributed and Integrated

1. (7) **Berries** Chuck and Nikita picked 173 quarts of berries. How many did each pick if Chuck picked 11 more quarts than Nikita? Chuck = 92 quarts, Nikita = 81 quarts

2. (23) Factor: $-2ab + abx + abx^2$. $ab(x + 2)(x - 1)$

Evaluate.

3. (2) $x^2 - y^2(x - y)$ if $x = \frac{1}{2}$ and $y = \frac{1}{3}$. $\frac{25}{108}$

4. (2) $ax - a(a - x)$ if $a = -\frac{1}{2}$ and $x = \frac{1}{4}$. $-\frac{1}{2}$

5. (21) Use substitution to solve: $\begin{matrix} x + 2y = 5 \\ 3x - y = 7 \end{matrix}$. $\left(\frac{19}{7}, \frac{8}{7}\right)$

6. (19) Expand: $\frac{4x^{-2}y^{-2}}{z^2}\left(\frac{3x^2y^2z^2}{4} + \frac{2x^0y^{-2}}{z^2y^2}\right)$. $3 + 8x^{-2}y^{-6}z^{-4}$

Simplify.

7. (3) $\frac{(0.0003 \times 10^8)(6000)}{(0.006 \times 10^{15})(2000 \times 10^5)}$ 1.5×10^{-13}

8. (3) $\frac{3m}{x} - \frac{2x^{-1}}{m^0m^{-1}} + \frac{5x^2m^2}{x^3m}$ $6mx^{-1}$

INCLUSION

The number of graphs that must be constructed in problems **f–i** might overwhelm some students. Prepare in advance copies of a graph template that has the parent function already graphed. Allow students to use these templates to graph the transformations.

9. Write the equation $y = \frac{2}{3}x + \frac{4}{5}$ in standard form. $\frac{2}{3}x - y = -\frac{4}{5}$
(26)

10. Solve for C: $[2 \quad -29 \quad 5] + C = [31 \quad -18 \quad 14]$. $[29 \quad 11 \quad 9]$
(5)

***11.** **Multiple Choice** Which statement is true about the graph of $y = 3x + 2$? **B**
(34)

A The rate of change between any two points on the graph is 2.

B The rate of change between any two points on the graph is 3.

C The rate of change decreases along the graph from left to right.

D The rate of change increases along the graph from left to right.

***12.** **Analyze** Given the functions $f(x) = \frac{3x-2}{x+2}$, $g(x) = \frac{10x^2+20x}{3x^2-2x}$, and $h(x) = 10$, compare the function product $f(x) \cdot g(x)$ and the constant function $h(x) = 10$. Describe how they are related.
(31)

12. Possible answer: They are identical except that $f(x) \cdot g(x)$ is undefined at the values $x = 0$, $x = -2$, and $x = \frac{2}{3}$.

13. **Population** The table lists the population estimates, in hundreds of thousands, for Vermont from 2000 to 2002.
(13)

Year	2000	2001	2002
Population	6.1	6.13	6.16

a. Write the data above as ordered pairs where x is the number of years after 2000 and y is the population in hundreds of thousands.

13a. (0, 6.1), (1, 6.13), and (2, 6.16)

b. **Estimate** Use slope and y-intercept to find the equation of the line representing this data. $y = 0.03x + 6.1$

14. a. Multiply the first equation in $\begin{matrix} 0.2x + 0.5y = -1 \\ x - y = 16 \end{matrix}$ by 10. How does this make solving the system easier?
(24)

14a. $\begin{matrix} 2x + 5y = -10 \\ x - y = 16 \end{matrix}$, all the coefficients are now whole numbers.

b. Solve the system. (10, −6)

***15.** **Graphing Calculator** Use a graphing calculator to graph $y = (x + 2)^2$ and $y = x^2$ on the same coordinate axes. How do the graphs compare? The vertex of the graph of $y = (x + 2)^2$ is 2 units further to the left.
(30)

16. **River Current** A motor boat makes a 175-kilometer trip down the Mississippi River to New Orleans in 3.3 hours. But it takes an hour longer for the boat to return upstream to its starting point. How fast is the river's current? about 6.17 km/h
(15)

***17.** **Probability** A circle has a radius of 4 and center (0, 0). Suppose a point is chosen at random inside the circle. What is the probability that the chosen point is in quadrant I and below the line $y = x$? $\frac{1}{8}$
(34)

18. **Geometry** You are given the equation of a line on a coordinate grid. You are then given three other equations of lines that combine with the first to form a rectangle. How many of the three lines have an inconsistent solution with the original line? How many of the three lines have a consistent solution with the original line?
(21)
1; 2

19. **Multi-Step** Find the inverse of matrix A. Then prove your answer is correct. Do not use a calculator. $A = \begin{bmatrix} 3 & 8 \\ 2 & 4 \end{bmatrix}$
(32)

19. $A^{-1} = \begin{bmatrix} -1 & 2 \\ \frac{1}{2} & -\frac{3}{4} \end{bmatrix}$; $AA^{-1} = \begin{bmatrix} 3 & 8 \\ 2 & 4 \end{bmatrix}\begin{bmatrix} -1 & 2 \\ \frac{1}{2} & -\frac{3}{4} \end{bmatrix} = \begin{bmatrix} -3+4 & 6-6 \\ -2+2 & 4-3 \end{bmatrix} = \begin{bmatrix} 1 & 0 \\ 0 & 1 \end{bmatrix} = I$,

$A^{-1}A = \begin{bmatrix} -1 & 2 \\ \frac{1}{2} & -\frac{3}{4} \end{bmatrix}\begin{bmatrix} 3 & 8 \\ 2 & 4 \end{bmatrix} = \begin{bmatrix} -3+4 & -8+8 \\ \frac{3}{2}-\frac{3}{2} & 4-3 \end{bmatrix} = \begin{bmatrix} 1 & 0 \\ 0 & 1 \end{bmatrix} = I$

Problem 9

Extend the Problem

At what points does the line intersect the x- and y-axis? $(-\frac{6}{5}, 0)$ and $(0, \frac{4}{5})$

Problem 16

"When the boat is going downstream, what is the actual speed of the boat relative to the shore?" the speed of the boat plus the speed of the current

"If x equals the speed of the boat and y equals the speed of the current, what is the equation of the boat going downstream?" 175 km = $(x + y)$3.3 h

"What is the equation for the boat going upstream?" 175 km = $(x - y)$4.3 h

"How will you arrive at the answer?" This is a system of linear equations. I can solve by substitution, elimination, or by using Cramer's Rule.

CHALLENGE

Write 3 linear equations such that, when graphed, the lines form a right triangle. Graph the lines to show the triangle.

Sample answer:

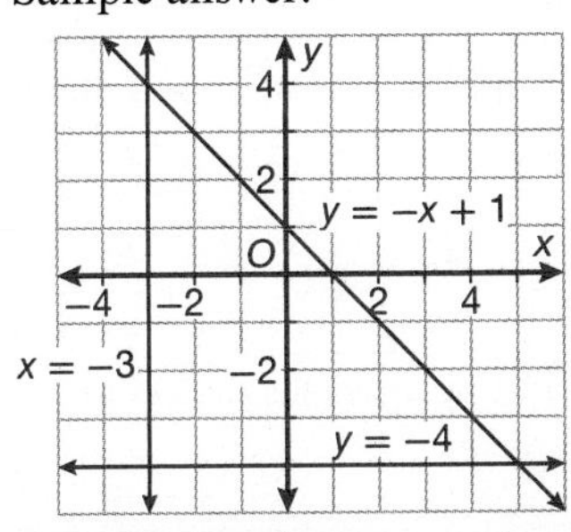

$x = -3$, $y = -4$, $y = -x + 1$

Problem 20

Error Alert

Some students might lose track of the negative signs when they are multiplying. Remind students to use care when multiplying these expressions.

Problem 26

Remind students that in the Fundamental Counting Principle the items are multiplied instead of added.

Problem 29

Guide students by asking them the following questions.

"How many variables are in this system of equations?" 2

"What do the variables represent?" They are an ordered pair (x, y).

"Which variable has a value of 2?" x

What is the value of y? $y = 1$

"What is the solution to this linear system of equations?" (2, 1)

20. (19) **Multiple Choice** Multiply $(x + 7)(x - 9)$ C

A $x^2 - 16x + 63$ **B** $x^2 - 2x + 63$ **C** $x^2 - 2x - 63$ **D** $x^2 + 2x - 63$

21. (7) **Verify** Is $x = 4$ the solution to the equation $6x - 4 = 20$?
Yes; $6(4) - 4 = 24 - 4 = 20$

22. (25) **Shipping Boxes** The table shows the measurements in inches of the side lengths of various shipping boxes available from the United States Postal Service.

Box	Measurement 1	Measurement 2	Measurement 3
1	11.875	3.375	13.625
2	11	8.5	5.5
3	7.5	5.125	14.375

Which measurement has the greatest range of side lengths? What is that range?

***23.** (34) **Roofing** The minimum slope (pitch) that is normally recommended for an asphalt shingle roof is $\frac{1}{3}$. Rectangle $ABCD$ represents the front wall of a building. Graph a line through point A to represent a roof with a slope of $\frac{1}{3}$. Write an equation of the line in slope-intercept form.

24. (33) **Passwords** A voicemail system password is 1 letter followed by a 3-digit number less than 600. How many different voicemail passwords are possible? 15,600

25. (15) **Analyze** Explain the difficulty you encounter when trying to use Cramer's Rule to solve the system $\begin{aligned} 4x - 12y &= -4 \\ -6x + 18y &= 6 \end{aligned}$ All related matrices have determinant 0, so the solutions are 0/0, indicating infinitely many possibilities. The two equations are equivalent, so there are infinitely many solutions.

26. (33) **Error Analysis** A student is choosing a four-letter password. She wants to know how many passwords are possible if letters may not be repeated. To find out, she adds: $26 + 25 + 24 + 23 = 98$. What is the error? Find the correct answer.

27. (23) **Analyze** Is $x^2 + 7x + 12$ a basic quadratic polynomial, a perfect square trinomial, or a difference of two squares? Explain how you can tell by looking at the polynomial.

***28.** (34) **Write** Describe how to obtain the graph of $y = \frac{3}{4}x - 3$ by transforming the graph of $y = x$. Possible answer: Compress (shrink) the graph of $y = x$ vertically by a factor of $\frac{3}{4}$ and then shift (translate) the resulting graph 3 units down.

29. (15) **Error Analysis** A student solved the linear system $\begin{aligned} x + y &= 3 \\ x - y &= 1 \end{aligned}$ and got 2 as the answer. Explain and correct the student's error.

30. (23) Use $x^2 + 16x + 64$. Rewrite the expression in the form of a perfect square trinomial. $(x)^2 + 2(x)(8) + (8)^2$

22. Measurement 3; 8.875 inches

23. $y = \frac{1}{3}x + \frac{16}{3}$

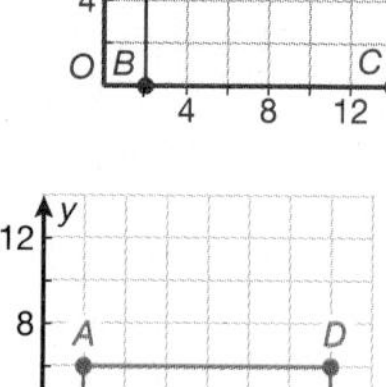

26. The student used the Addition Counting Principle instead of the Fundamental Counting Principle. The correct answer is $26 \cdot 25 \cdot 24 \cdot 23 = 358{,}800$.

27. It is a basic quadratic polynomial. 7 is the sum of 3 and 4, and 12 is the product of 3 and 4. So, the factors are in the form $(x + u)(x + v)$ where $u + v = 7$ and $uv = 12$.

29. A solution to a linear system of two equations is an ordered pair, not a single number. The pair (2, 1) is the solution to this system.

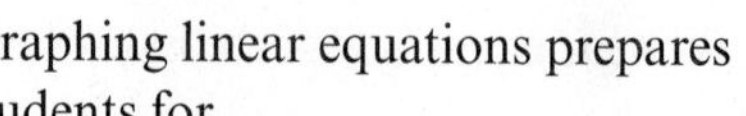

Graphing linear equations prepares students for

- **Lesson 36** Using Parallel and Perpendicular Lines
- **Lesson 39** Graphing Linear Inequalities in Two Variables
- **Lesson 43** Solving Systems of Linear Inequalities
- **Lesson 50** Finding Inverses of Relations and Functions

LESSON 35

Solving Quadratic Equations I

Warm Up

1. (27) **Vocabulary** A parabola is a graph of a quadratic function.
2. (23) Factor $8x^2 + 4x$ completely. $4x(2x + 1)$
3. (23) Factor $16x^2 - 20x - 6$ completely. $2(4x + 1)(2x - 3)$

New Concepts

Every quadratic function can be written in the standard form $f(x) = ax^2 + bx + c$, where $a \neq 0$. The zeros of a function $f(x)$ are the x-values that make $f(x) = 0$. To find the zeros of a quadratic function, solve the related equation $ax^2 + bx + c = 0$. Many quadratic equations can be solved by factoring and applying the Zero Product Property, which says that if a product is zero, then at least one of its factors is zero.

Hint

The Zero Product Property applies to any number of factors. For example, if $abc = 0$, then $a = 0$ or $b = 0$ or $c = 0$.

Zero Product Property
Let a and b be real numbers. If $ab = 0$, then $a = 0$ or $b = 0$.

Example 1 **Finding the Zeros of Quadratic Functions**

Find the zeros of each quadratic function.

Hint

The function $f(x) = 4x^2 - 25$ is in standard form $f(x) = ax^2 + bx + c$ with $b = 0$.

a. $f(x) = 4x^2 - 25$

SOLUTION

$4x^2 - 25 = 0$ Write the related quadratic equation.

$(2x + 5)(2x - 5) = 0$ Factor.

$2x + 5 = 0$ or $2x - 5 = 0$ Zero Product Property

$2x = -5$ $\quad 2x = 5$ Solve each equation.

$x = -\frac{5}{2}$ $\quad x = \frac{5}{2}$

The zeros are $-\frac{5}{2}$ and $\frac{5}{2}$.

b. $f(x) = 2x^2 + x$

SOLUTION

$2x^2 + x = 0$ Write the related quadratic equation.

$x(2x + 1) = 0$ Factor.

$x = 0$ or $2x + 1 = 0$ Zero Product Property

$2x = -1$

$x = -\frac{1}{2}$

The zeros are 0 and $-\frac{1}{2}$.

Online Connection www.SaxonMathResources.com

The **roots of an equation** are the solutions to the equation.

MATH BACKGROUND

Solving quadratic functions is a prelude to using factoring to solve polynomial equations and to identify all real roots of polynomial equations. Students develop skills necessary to solve a quadratic function that is a difference of squares, a cubic function (third-degree) with a monomial factor and a difference of squares, and a quartic function (fourth-degree) with a difference of squares.

The quadratic function's graph is the parabola. The graph of a cubic function is S shaped. The graph of the quartic function is W shaped.

LESSON 35

1 Warm Up

Remind students to look for the greatest common factor when factoring.

2 New Concepts

In this lesson, students learn to solve quadratic equations by finding roots, zeros, and x-intercepts.

Example 1

Review with students how to factor an expression that is a difference of two squares.

Additional Example 1

Find the zeros of each quadratic function.

a. $f(x) = 9x^2 - 64$
The zeros are $\frac{8}{3}$ and $-\frac{8}{3}$.

b. $f(x) = x^2 - 5x$
The zeros are 0 and 5.

LESSON RESOURCES

Student Edition Practice Workbook 35
Reteaching Master 35
Adaptations Master 35
Challenge and Enrichment Masters C35, E35

Example 2

Students will factor to find the roots of a quadratic equation.

Error Alert Most errors are made when students mentally use the Zero Product Property when the equation is in factored form. For example, students might believe the roots of $(x + 2)(x - 3) = 0$ are $+2$ and -3. Encourage students to either write each factor using the Zero Product Property or check their solutions in the original equation to see that the roots are -2 and 3.

Additional Example 2

Find the roots of the quadratic function.

$x^2 = -3x + 28$ The roots are -7 and 4.

Example 3

Students will describe the relationship between the roots, the zeros and the x-intercepts of a quadratic equation.

Additional Example 3

Find the roots of each equation. Graph the related function and describe the relationship between the roots, the zeros, and the x-intercepts.

a. $x^2 - 10x + 25 = 0$

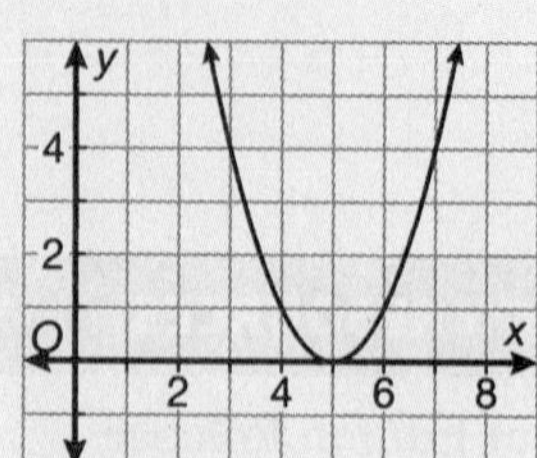

5 is the double root of the equation, the only zero of the related function $f(x) = x^2 - 10x + 25$, and the only x-intercept of the graph.

Math Language

Functions have zeros or x-intercepts.

Equations have solutions or roots.

Example 2 Solving Quadratic Equations

Find the roots of the quadratic equation.

$x^2 = -2x + 15$

SOLUTION

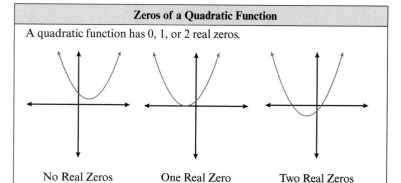

$x^2 = -2x + 15$	Write the given equation.
$x^2 + 2x - 15 = 0$	Add $2x - 15$ to both sides to get zero on one side.
$(x + 5)(x - 3) = 0$	Factor.
$x + 5 = 0$ or $x - 3 = 0$	Zero Product Property
$x = -5$ $\quad$ $x = 3$	Solve each equation.

The roots are -5 and 3.

The graph of a quadratic function shows how many zeros the function has.

Zeros of a Quadratic Function

A quadratic function has 0, 1, or 2 real zeros.

No Real Zeros $\quad$ One Real Zero $\quad$ Two Real Zeros

When a quadratic function has exactly one real zero, that zero is a **double root** of the related equation.

Math Reasoning

Generalize When a quadratic function has exactly one real zero, at how many points does the graph intersect the x-axis?

one

Example 3 Comparing Roots, Zeros, and x-Intercepts

Find the roots of each equation. Graph the related function and describe the relationship between the roots, the zeros, and the x-intercepts.

a. $x^2 - 6x + 9 = 0$

SOLUTION

$x^2 - 6x + 9 = 0$

$(x - 3)(x - 3) = 0$

$x = 3$

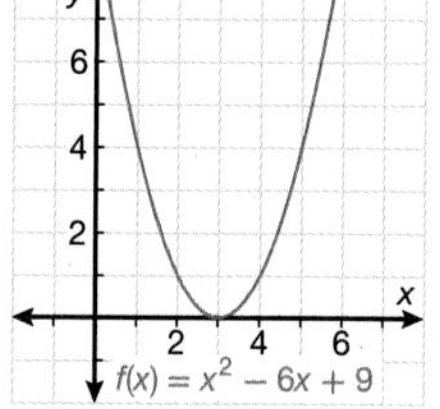

3 is the double root of the equation, the only zero of the related function $f(x) = x^2 - 6x + 9$, and the only x-intercept of the graph.

INCLUSION

Students may benefit from using the Zero Product Property on each factor individually. If needed in Example 2, encourage students to write:

$$\begin{array}{r} x + 5 = 0 \\ -5 \ -5 \\ \hline x = -5 \end{array} \quad \text{and} \quad \begin{array}{r} x - 3 = 0 \\ +3 \ +3 \\ \hline x = 3 \end{array}$$

Graphing Calculator Tip

Verify your graph with a graphing calculator. To enter $f(x) = 3x^2 + 6x$, use these key strokes:

Adjust the viewing window as needed.

b. $3x^2 + 6x = 0$

SOLUTION

$3x^2 + 6x = 0$

$3x(x + 2) = 0$

$3x = 0 \quad \text{or} \quad x + 2 = 0$

$x = 0 \quad \text{or} \quad x = -2$

0 and −2 are the roots of the equation, the zeros of the related function $f(x) = 3x^2 + 6x$, and the x-intercepts of the graph.

Example 4 Writing a Quadratic Function, Given its Zeros

Write a quadratic function that has zeros $-\frac{5}{3}$ and 1.

SOLUTION Reverse the process of solving a quadratic equation.

$\left(x + \frac{5}{3}\right)(x - 1) = 0$	Write the related equation in factored form.
$3\left(x + \frac{5}{3}\right)(x - 1) = 3(0)$	Multiply both sides by 3 to eliminate the fraction.
$(3x + 5)(x - 1) = 0$	Distribute the 3.
$3x^2 + 2x - 5 = 0$	Multiply the binomials.

The quadratic function $f(x) = 3x^2 + 2x - 5$ has zeros $-\frac{5}{3}$ and 1.

Hint

Velocity is a vector quantity, which means it has both magnitude and direction. If an object is thrown straight down at a speed of 20 feet per second, its initial velocity is −20 feet per second.

Example 5 Application: Vertical Motion

The height of a free-falling object is given by the function $h(t) = -16t^2 + v_0t + h_0$, where h_0 is the initial height in feet, v_0 is the initial velocity in feet per second, and $h(t)$ is the height in feet at time t seconds. How long does it take for an object to hit the ground after it is thrown straight down at a speed of 20 feet per second from a height of 84 feet?

SOLUTION

$h(t) = -16t^2 + v_0t + h_0$

$0 = -16t^2 - 20t + 84$	Substitute given values for v_0 and h_0.
$0 = -4(4t^2 + 5t - 21)$	Factor out −4.
$0 = -4(4t - 7)(t + 3)$	Factor the trinomial.
$4t - 7 = 0 \quad \text{or} \quad t + 3 = 0$	Use the Zero Product Property.
$t = 1.75 \quad \text{or} \quad t = -3$	Ignore $t = -3$. Time cannot be negative.

It takes the object 1.75 seconds to hit the ground.

ENGLISH LEARNERS

To help students understand the meaning of double root, define the word **double**: something that is composed of two like parts or members.

Double as an adjective comes from Anglo-French duble, from Latin duplus. Double can be used not only as an adjective, but also as a noun and a verb.

Double also means twice as great, twice as many, twice as much. Other words with double: double-decker: something with two decks; doubleheader: two games played consecutively.

A double root is a zero that appears twice after factoring and applying the Zero Product Property.

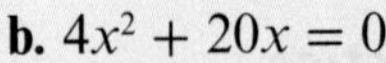

b. $4x^2 + 20x = 0$

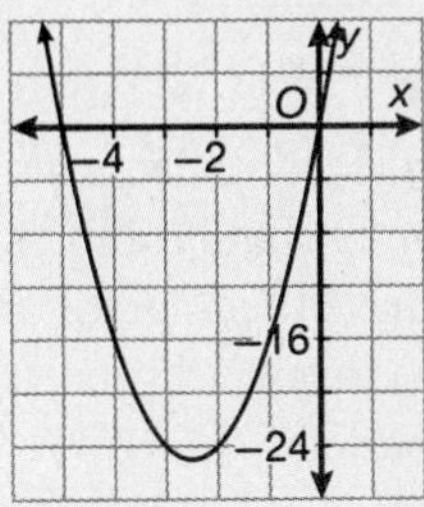

0 and −5 are the roots of the equation, the zeros of the related function $f(x) = 4x^2 + 20x$, and the x-intercepts of the graph.

Example 4

Remind students that fractions can be eliminated by multiplying both sides of the equation by the least common denominator.

Additional Example 4

Write a quadratic function that has zeros $-\frac{3}{2}$ and 4.

$f(x) = 2x^2 - 5x - 12$

Example 5

Remind students to first substitute the given values into the function, then factor and solve for t.

Additional Example 5

The height of a free-falling object (neglecting air resistance) is given by the function $h(t) = -16t^2 + v_0t + h_0$, where h_0 is the initial height in feet, v_0 is the initial velocity in feet per second, and $h(t)$ is the height in feet at time t seconds. How long does it take for an object to hit the ground after it is thrown straight down at a speed of 12 feet per second from a height of 108 feet? 2.25 seconds

Lesson Practice

Problem c

Scaffolding Have students write the equation in standard form first. Then have them factor and use the Zero Product Property to find the roots.

Problem f

Error Alert Students may write incorrect signs when putting the related equation in factored form. Write a simple binomial product, such as $(x + 3)(x - 1) = 0$, and have students find the roots.

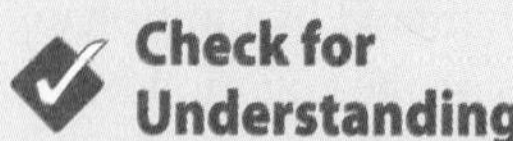

Check for Understanding

The questions below help assess the concepts taught in this lesson.

"How are the roots of $22x = 8x^2 + 12$ found?" Add $-22x$ to both sides. Factor the equation. Use the Zero Product Property and solve each equation. The roots are $\frac{3}{4}$ and 2.

"What are the zeros of a function?" The zeros are the x-values to make $f(x) = 0$.

3 Practice

Math Conversations

Discussion to strengthen understanding

Problem 5

Guide students by asking them the following questions.

"What do you need to find?" the slope

"How do you find the slope?"
$\frac{y_2 - y_1}{x_2 - x_1} = \frac{-2-4}{3-(-3)} = \frac{-6}{6} = -1$

"What is the point-slope form?"
$y - y_1 = m(x - x_1)$

"What equation do you have after substituting the values for y_1, m, and x_1?" $y - 4 = -1(x + 3)$

"What is the equation in slope-intercept form?" $y = -x + 1$

d. -4 is the double root of the equation, the only zero of the related function $f(x) = x^2 + 8x + 16$, and the only x-intercept of the graph.

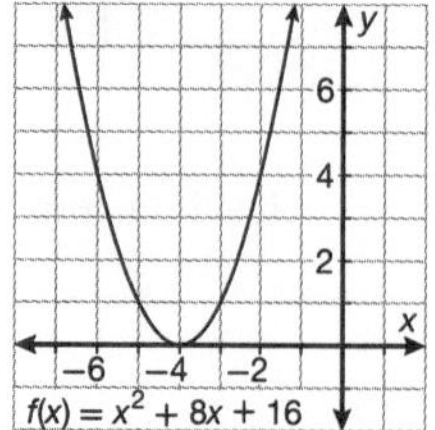

Lesson Practice

Find the zeros of each quadratic function. (Ex 1)

a. $f(x) = 25x^2 - 1$. $-\frac{1}{5}$ and $\frac{1}{5}$

b. $f(x) = x^2 - 7x$. 0 and 7

c. Find the roots of $3x^2 - x = 2$. $-\frac{2}{3}$ and 1

Find the roots of each equation. Graph the related function and describe the relationship between the roots, the zeros, and the x-intercepts. (Ex 3)

d. $x^2 + 8x + 16 = 0$

e. $f(x) = x^2 + 2x - 8$ See Additional Answers.

f. (Ex 4) Write a quadratic function that has zeros -5 and $\frac{3}{4}$. Sample: $f(x) = 4x^2 + 17x - 15$

g. (Ex 5) The height of a free-falling object is given by the function $h(t) = -16t^2 + v_0t + h_0$, where h_0 is the initial height in feet, v_0 is the initial velocity in feet per second, and $h(t)$ is the height in feet at time t seconds. How long does it take for an object to hit the ground after it is thrown straight *up* at a speed of 8 feet per second from a height of 80 feet? 2.5 seconds

Practice Distributed and Integrated

Simplify.

1. (3) $\frac{(b^2c^{-2})^{-3}c^{-3}}{(b^2c^0b^{-2})^4}$ $\frac{c^3}{b^6}$

2. (3) $\frac{(2x^2ya)^{-3}ya^3}{x^2y(ay)^{-2}y}$ $\frac{a^2}{8x^8y^2}$

Solve.

3. (7) $3(-2x - 3) - 2^2 = -(-3x - 5) - 2$ $-\frac{16}{9}$

4. (23) $x^2 + 26x - 56 = 0$ $x = -28$ or $x = 2$

5. (26) Find the equation of the line that passes through $(-3, 4)$ and $(3, -2)$. $y = -x + 1$

Use elimination to solve.

6. (24) $4x - 3y = -1$; $2x + 5y = 19$ (2, 3)

7. (24) $5x + \frac{1}{2}y = -4$; $-x + y = 3$ (−1, 2)

8. (5) Solve for a and b: $\begin{bmatrix} a \\ 64 \end{bmatrix} = \begin{bmatrix} 102 \\ a - b \end{bmatrix}$. $a = 102, b = 38$

9. (20) Find $(f \cdot g)(x)$, given $f(x) = 4x - 3$ and $g(x) = 8x + 9$. $f(x) \cdot g(x) = (4x - 3)(8x + 9) = 32x^2 + 12x - 27$

10. (22) **Formulate** Describe a plan for determining if a function is continuous. See student work. A continuous function can be drawn without lifting the pencil from the paper.

*__11.__ (35) **Multiple Choice** What are the zeros of the function $f(x) = x^2 - 5x + 6$? C

A 0 and 6 B 0 and −6 C 2 and 3 D 2 and −3

12. (32) **Probability** Suppose you roll a pair of number cubes twice. What is the probability of rolling a sum greater than 10 on both rolls? $\frac{1}{144}$

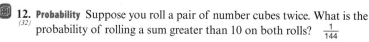

ALTERNATE METHOD FOR PROBLEM B

Instead of factoring, encourage students to make a table of values to find the zeros.

x	$f(x)$
0	0
1	−6
2	−10
3	−12
4	−12
5	−10
6	−6
7	0

*13. **Error Analysis** A student described this line as having no slope, or zero slope. (34) What is wrong with this description? The line has no slope, or an undefined slope. It does not have a zero slope. A horizontal line has a zero slope.

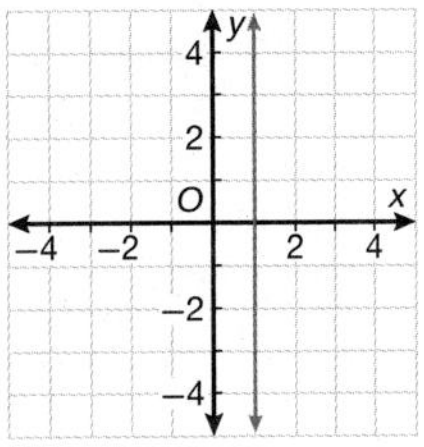

14. If a polynomial of degree 3 is added to a polynomial of degree 4, what are all (11) possible values for the degree of the result? only 4

15. **Analyze** The product $\frac{x^2-4}{x^2-3x-4} \cdot \frac{x-4}{x+2}$ in simplest form is $\frac{x-2}{x+1}$, as shown: (31)

$\frac{x^2-4}{x^2-3x-4} \cdot \frac{x-4}{x+2} = \frac{\cancel{(x+2)}(x-2)}{(x+1)\cancel{(x-4)}} \cdot \frac{\cancel{(x-4)}}{\cancel{(x+2)}} = \frac{x-2}{x+1}$. When 4 is substituted for x in $\frac{x-2}{x+1}$, the value is $\frac{2}{5}$. Explain why the value of $\frac{x^2-4}{x^2-3x-4} \cdot \frac{x-4}{x+2}$ is not $\frac{2}{5}$ when $x = 4$. The given multiplication expression is undefined when $x = 4$.

16. **Write** A square is drawn on a coordinate grid with one side along the x-axis and (23) one vertex at $(a - 1, 0)$. The area of the square is $a^2 - 8a + 16$. Determine an expression for an adjacent vertex. Explain. See Additional Answers.

*17. **Justify** Explain why this paragraph describes a method of graphing the equation: (34) $y + 1 = \frac{1}{4}(x - 2)$: Plot the ordered pair $(2, -1)$. Then from that point, count 1 unit up and 4 units to the right to plot another point. Then draw a line through the two plotted points.

18.

18. Solve and graph the compound inequality: $4 < 2(x - 2) \leq 16$. $4 < x \leq 10$; (10)

19. **Average Velocity** If an object is thrown straight down with initial velocity 8 feet (31) per second, the number of feet it travels in t seconds is given by the expression $16t^2 + 8t$ (neglecting air resistance). **19a.** $\frac{16t^2 + 8t}{t} = 16t + 8$

a. Write a rational expression for the average velocity of the object before it hits the ground over the time interval from 0 seconds to t seconds. Then simplify the expression. (Average velocity equals distance traveled divided by elapsed time.)

b. Evaluate the expression to find the average velocity of the object over the time interval from 0 seconds to 2.5 seconds. 48 feet per second

17. Possible answer: The equation $y + 1 = \frac{1}{4}(x - 2)$ is a linear equation in the point-slope form $y - y_1 = m(x - x_1)$. So its graph is a line, $(x_1, y_1) = (2, -1)$ is a point on the line, and $m = \frac{1}{4}$ is the slope of the line.

20. **Chemistry** How many liters of a 15% acid solution should be mixed with a 35% (24) acid solution to make 7 liters of a 20% acid solution? 5.25 liters of the 15% solution and 1.75 liters of the 35% solution

*21. **Write** State all possible numbers of real zeros a quadratic function can have. (35) Explain what information the number of real zeros provides about the point(s) of intersection of the graph and the x-axis. 0, 1, or 2 real zeros; The number of real zeros is the number of points in which the graph intersects the x-axis.

22. Is the equation $y = \sqrt{2}x$ a direct or inverse variation? direct (12)

*23. **Geometry** The area of the right triangle is 24 square units. Find the (35) value of x. 6

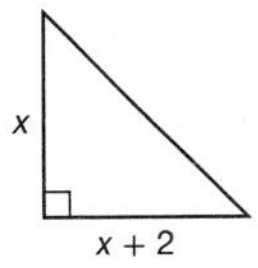

*24. **Currency Exchange** During 2006, the average exchange rate for euros and (34) U.S. dollars was \$1.2563 per euro. This relationship is given by the function $y = 1.2563x$, where y represents dollars and x represents euros. Describe how to transform the graph of the parent function $y = x$ to obtain the graph of $y = 1.2563x$. Possible description: Stretch (dilate) the graph of $y = x$ vertically by a factor of 1.2563

Problem 15

Remind students to substitute $x = 4$ into the original product. When students do the substitution, they get 0 in the denominator, making the product undefined at $x = 4$.

Problem 23

Point out that students are finding the solution to a quadratic function. Remind them to use the Zero Product Property and factoring to solve for x.

CHALLENGE

Danielle framed a photo. The photo, with matting and frame, is 10 inches by 5 inches. She wants to add more matting by increasing the length and the width by the same amount. The new area of the framed photo would increase by 54 square inches. Find the new dimensions. Explain how you got your answer. The area of the enlarged frame photo is $(x + 10)(x + 5) = 50 + 54$.

Simplifying I have: $x^2 + 15x - 54 = 0$. This factors to $(x - 3)(x + 18) = 0$. I use the zero product property to find that $x = 3$ and $x = -18$. I use the positive solution to find the new length and width. The new dimensions are 13 inches by 8 inches.

TEACHER TIP

For Problem 25, remind students that real numbers are all rational and irrational numbers. Therefore if choice D, irrational numbers cannot be listed, then choice A can be eliminated also.

Problem 27

Encourage students to put all equations into slope-intercept form. Then have them look for the two equations that have the same slope and different y-intercepts.

Problem 28

Remind students to use the positive value for x, or $x = 3$.

Problem 29

Extend the Problem

Have students find the area of the rectangle in feet. $\frac{5}{9}$ square feet

25. (22) **Multiple Choice** An example of a set of numbers that can be listed is: **B**

A real numbers
B integers
C rational numbers
D irrational numbers

***26.** (26) **Graphing Calculator** When you're traveling in a car that comes to an abrupt halt, the car continues forward even though the brakes have been pressed. The distance traveled is called the "stopping distance." The table below shows the stopping distance at three different speeds for a car traveling on wet pavement. Use your graphing calculator and the linear regression capabilities to write an equation in slope-intercept form for the stopping distance. $y = 5.51x - 144.94$

Initial Traveling Speed (mile/hour)	Stopping Distance (feet)
35	53.389
49	114.159
62	202.678

27. (21) **Coordinate Geometry** Which set of equations could be represented by this graph? **D**

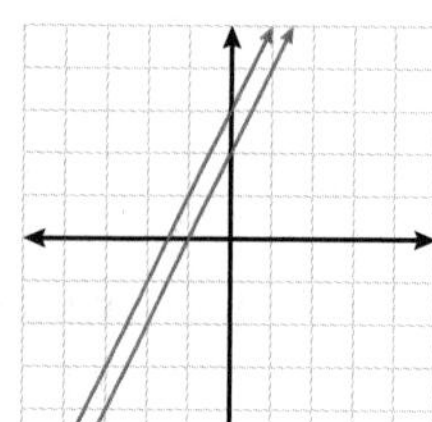

A $y = 2x + 4$, $2y - 2x = 8$

B $y = 2x + 4$, $12 - 3y = -6x$

C $2y = 4x - 12$, $y = 2x + 6$

D $-4x = 8 - 2y$, $y = 2x + 6$

28. (32) **Nutrition** A spaghetti entrée consists of spaghetti, ground beef, and tomato sauce. The entrée contains 118.68 grams of carbohydrates, 40.12 grams of fat, and 41.2 grams of protein. How much of each ingredient is in the entrée? To find the answer, write a system of equations and use an inverse matrix to solve it. Use the table below. 110 grams of spaghetti, 56 grams of ground beef, 34 grams of tomato sauce

	Spaghetti	Ground Beef	Tomato Sauce
Carbohydrates	81%	0%	87%
Fat	5%	60%	3%
Protein	14%	40%	10%

***29.** (35) **Flags** There is no required size for a United States flag, but the ratio of width to length that is recommended in most cases is 1 : 1.9. Write and solve a quadratic equation to find the length and width of a United States flag that has an area of 17.1 square feet.

29. $x(1.9x) = 17.1$
$1.9x^2 = 17.1$
$\frac{1.9x^2}{1.9} = \frac{17.1}{1.9}$
$x^2 = 9$
$x = -3$ or $x = 3$
Choose the positive solution. $x = 3$ and $1.9x = 5.7$. The dimensions are 3 feet and 5.7 feet.

30. (18) What is the perimeter of this rectangle in feet? 3 ft.

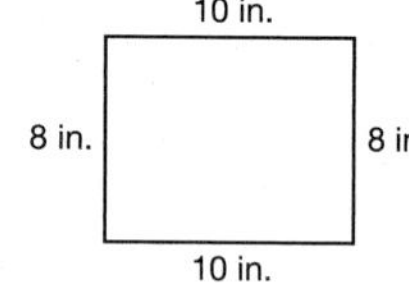

LOOKING FORWARD

Solving quadratic equations prepares students for

- **Lesson 58** Completing the Square
- **Lesson 65** Using the Quadratic Formula
- **Lesson 66** Solving Polynomial Equations
- **Lesson 78** Solving Quadratic Equations II

LESSON 36

Using Parallel and Perpendicular Lines

Warm Up

1. **Vocabulary** If you know the slope of a line and the coordinates of a point on the line, you can use the point-slope formula to write the equation of the line. (13)

2. Find the slope of the line that crosses (1, 4) and (5, 9). 1.25 (13)

3. Write the equation $3x - 7y = 28$ in slope-intercept form. $y = \frac{3}{7}x - 4$ (13)

New Concepts

From geometry you know that parallel lines do not intersect and that perpendicular lines meet at right angles. When parallel and perpendicular lines are graphed on an coordinate plane, the equations of these lines have special properties.

Parallel lines have identical slopes and different y-intercepts. Perpendicular lines have slopes that are reciprocals of each other and have opposite signs. The product of the slopes of two perpendicular lines is -1.

Hint

For parallel lines: $m_1 = m_2$.
For perpendicular lines: $m_1m_2 = -1$

Example 1 Graphs of Parallel and Perpendicular Lines

a. Show that L_1 and L_2 are parallel.

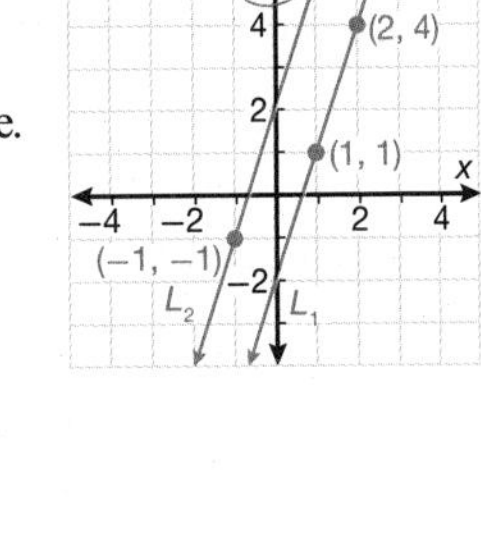

SOLUTION

Use the slope formula to find the slope of each line.

L_1	L_2
$m_1 = \frac{y_2 - y_1}{x_2 - x_1}$	$m_2 = \frac{y_2 - y_1}{x_2 - x_1}$
$m_1 = \frac{4 - 1}{2 - 1}$	$m_2 = \frac{5 - (-1)}{1 - (-1)}$
$m_1 = 3$	$m_2 = 3$

Since the slopes are identical and the lines do not have the same y-intercepts, the lines are parallel.

b. Show that L_1 and L_2 are perpendicular.

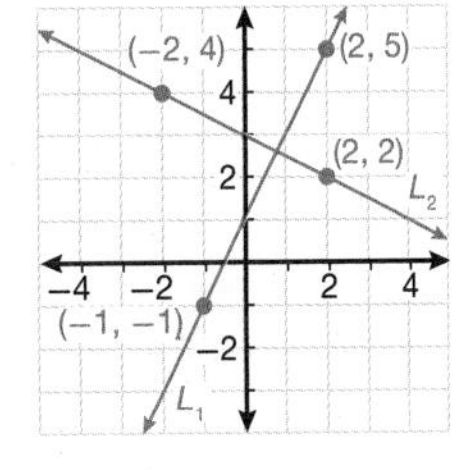

SOLUTION

Use the slope formula to find the slope of each line.

L_1	L_2
$m_1 = \frac{y_2 - y_1}{x_2 - x_1}$	$m_2 = \frac{y_2 - y_1}{x_2 - x_1}$
$m_1 = \frac{5 - (-1)}{2 - (-1)}$	$m_2 = \frac{4 - 2}{2 - 2}$
$m_1 = 2$	$m_2 = -0.5$

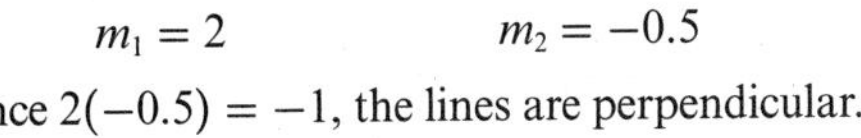

Since $2(-0.5) = -1$, the lines are perpendicular.

Math Reasoning

Generalize For a linear equation in standard form, $Ax + By = C$, what is the slope-intercept form in terms of the coefficients A, B, and C?

$y = \frac{A}{B}x + \frac{C}{B}$

LESSON 36

1 Warm Up

Remind students they can use the slope formula for problem 2.

2 New Concepts

In this lesson, students write equations for parallel and perpendicular lines.

Example 1

Remind students that the slope formula is $m = \frac{y_2 - y_1}{x_2 - x_1}$.

Additional Example 1

a. Show that L_1 and L_2 are parallel.

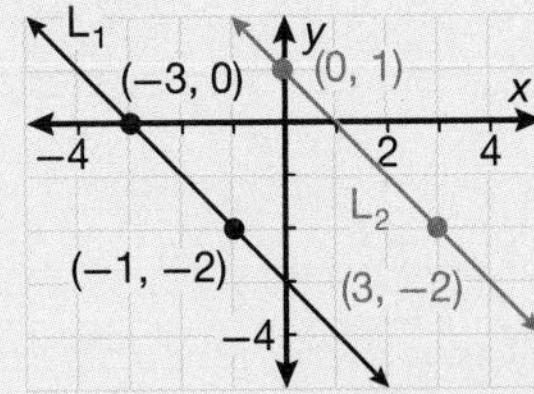

Slope of $L_1 = -1$; Slope $L_2 = -1$

b. Show that L_1 and L_2 are perpendicular.

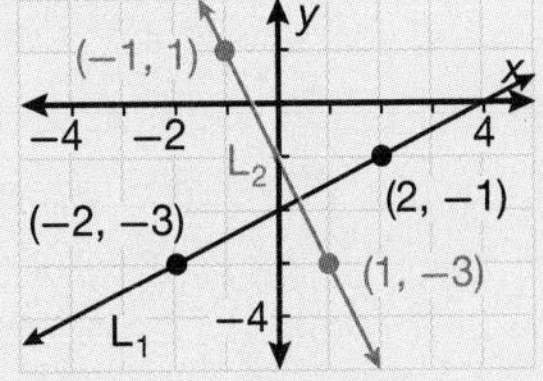

Slope of $L_1 = \frac{1}{2}$ Slope of $L_2 = -2$
$\frac{1}{2}(-2) = -1$

LESSON RESOURCES

Student Edition Practice Workbook 36
Reteaching Master 36
Adaptations Master 36
Challenge and Enrichment Master C36

MATH BACKGROUND

In previous lessons, students have used parallel and perpendicular lines to describe geometrical shapes and help them determine the number of solutions to a system of equations. Students have also learned to use slopes and points to write equations of a line.

This lesson combines these concepts by having students write equations for parallel and perpendicular lines.

Finding the slopes of parallel and perpendicular lines and determining if the lines are parallel or perpendicular lends itself to geometry proofs, such as proving that a quadrilateral is a rectangle and whether a triangle has a right angle.

Example 2

Extend the Example

Have students graph $y = 3x + 4$ and $y = 3x - 3$ so that they can verify that the lines are parallel.

Additional Example 2

a. Find the equation of the line parallel to $y = -2x + 3$ that crosses $(-4, 2)$. $y = -2x - 6$

b. Find the equation of the line that passes through the point $(4, -1)$ and is perpendicular to the line $y = 2x + 3$.
$y = -\frac{1}{2}x + 1$

Example 2 **Writing Equations of Parallel and Perpendicular Lines**

a. Find the equation of the line parallel to $y = 3x + 4$ that crosses $(2, 3)$.

SOLUTION

Step 1:

The equation of the line parallel to $y = 3x + 4$ has the same slope: $m = 3$

Step 2:

Use the point-slope formula to find the equation of the line.

$$m = \frac{y - y_1}{x - x_1}$$

$$3 = \frac{y - 3}{x - 2}$$ Substitute the coordinate point (2, 3) for (x_1, y_1) and 3 for the slope m.

$$3(x - 2) = y - 3$$

$$y = 3x - 6 + 3$$ Solve for y by multiplying each side by $(x - 2)$, then adding 3 to both sides.

$$y = 3x - 3$$

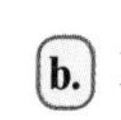

b. Find the equation of the line that passes through the point $(-1, 3)$ and is perpendicular to the line $y = -0.5x - 1$.

SOLUTION

Step 1:

Find the slope that is the opposite reciprocal of -0.5.

$$m = -\left(-\frac{1}{0.5}\right) = 2$$

Step 2:

Use the point-slope formula to find the equation of the line.

$$m = \frac{y - y_1}{x - x_1}$$

$$2 = \frac{y - 3}{x - (-1)}$$ Substitute the coordinate point $(-1, 3)$ for (x_1, y_1) and 2 for the slope m.

$$2(x - (-1)) = y - 3$$

$$y = 2x + 2 + 3$$ Solve for y by multiplying each side by $(x - (-1))$, then adding 3 to both sides.

$$y = 2x + 5$$

INCLUSION

Visual learners may benefit from using colored pencils when finding the slope from two points. For example, have students circle or underline x_1 and y_1 with a blue pencil. Then have students circle or underline x_2 and y_2 with a red pencil. When students write the points using the formula, they will see red minus blue in the numerator and red minus blue in the denominator.

Example 3 Determining if Two Lines Are Perpendicular or Parallel

a. Given two equations, determine if they are perpendicular or parallel.

$$5x + 3y = 27 \qquad 15x + 9y = -72$$

SOLUTION

Write each equation in slope-intercept form.

$$5x + 3y = 27 \qquad 15x + 9y = -72$$
$$3y = -5x + 27 \qquad 9y = -15x - 72$$
$$y = -\frac{5}{3}x + 9 \qquad y = -\frac{5}{3}x - 9$$

Because the slopes are equal, the lines are parallel.

b. The points A, B, and C are collinear. The points D, E, and F are also collinear. Compare the equations of the lines through those sets of points.

	A	B	C	D	E	F
x	1	3	4	2	4	6
y	0.5	5.5	8	0.7	−0.1	−0.9

Math Reasoning

Formulate Use the point-slope formula to find the equations of the two lines in Example 3. Use the coordinates for C and F.

The equation for points A, B, C: $y = \frac{5}{2}x - 2$. The equation for points D, E, F: $y = -.4x + 1.5$.

SOLUTION

Step 1:

Use the slope formula with points A and B and D and E.

$$m_1 = \frac{0.5 - 5.5}{1 - 3} \qquad m_2 = \frac{0.7 - (-0.1)}{2 - 4}$$
$$m_1 = \frac{-5}{-2} \qquad m_2 = \frac{0.8}{-2}$$
$$m_1 = \frac{5}{2} \qquad m_2 = -0.4$$

Step 2:

To test if the lines are perpendicular, multiply the two slopes.

$$m_1m_2 = \left(\frac{5}{2}\right)(-0.4)$$
$$= -\frac{2}{2}$$
$$= -1$$

Because the product of the slopes is −1, the lines are perpendicular.

Example 3

Remind students that the slopes of parallel lines are equal and that the slopes of perpendicular lines are negative reciprocals.

Additional Example 3

a. Given two equations, determine if they are perpendicular or parallel.

$8x + 16y = 16 \quad 6x - 3y = 12$

perpendicular

b. The points A, B, and C are collinear. The points D, E, and F are also collinear. Compare the equations of the lines through those set of points.

	A	B	C	D	E	F
x	1	3	4	2	3	4
y	2.5	3.5	4	−3	−2.5	−2

Because the slopes are equal, the lines must be parallel.

ENGLISH LEARNERS

To help students understand the meaning of **parallel** and **perpendicular,** define parallel (lines) as lying in the same plane but never meeting, and perpendicular (lines) as meeting at right angles.

Parallel also means having the same direction, course, or tendency, such as parallel forces.

Cities have parallel and perpendicular streets. Enlarge a local map and have students name parallel and perpendicular streets.

Say:

"Street ______ is parallel to street ______. And street ______ is perpendicular to street ______."

Have students name streets and describe them using the words parallel and perpendicular.

Example 4

Students use reasoning to find equations for horizontal and vertical lines.

Error Alert Students often forget that the graph of $y = 2$ is a horizontal line. Point out that 2 is a constant and that for every value of x, $y = 2$.

Additional Example 4

a. Find the equation of the line perpendicular to the graph of $y = -4$ that passes through the point $(-5, -2)$. $x = -5$

b. Find the equation of the line perpendicular to the graph of $x = -3$ that passes through the point $(2, 3)$. $y = 3$

Example 5

Remind students that a right triangle has a right angle.

Additional Example 5

Use what you have learned about the properties of perpendicular lines to prove that ΔABC is a right triangle.

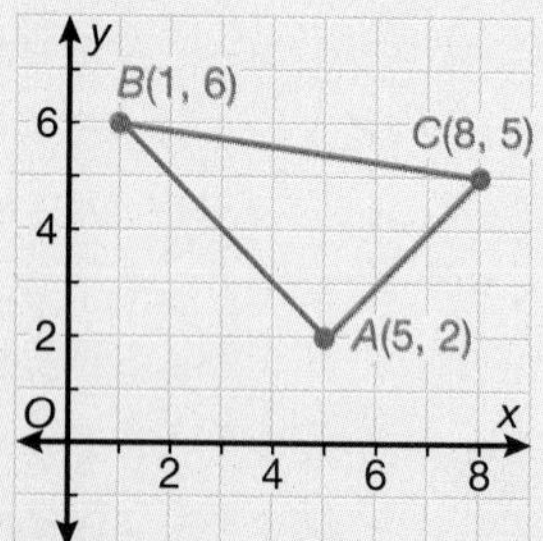

Find the slopes of $\overline{AB}$ and $\overline{AC}$.

$m = \frac{2-6}{5-1}$ $\quad$ $m = \frac{2-5}{5-8}$

$m = \frac{-4}{4}$ $\quad$ $m = \frac{-3}{-3}$

$m = -1$ $\quad$ $m = 1$

Because the product of the slopes is -1, $\angle ABC$ is a right angle. Therefore, ΔABC is a right triangle.

Reading Math

$L_1 \parallel L_2$ is read "L_1 is parallel to L_2."

$L_1 \perp L_2$ is read "L_1 is perpendicular to L_2."

Example 4 Finding the Equations of Horizontal and Vertical Lines

a. Find the equation of the line perpendicular to the graph of $y = 2$ that passes through the point $(4, -1)$.

SOLUTION

The graph of $y = 2$ is a horizontal line. The equation of a line perpendicular to $y = 2$ is a vertical line of the form $x = c$ for some constant c.

Use the x-coordinate of the point $(4, -1)$ to find the equation.

The equation $x = 4$ is perpendicular to the graph of $y = 2$ and passes through the point $(4, -1)$.

b. Find the equation of the line perpendicular to the graph of $x = 15$ that passes through the point $(7, -1)$.

SOLUTION

The graph of $x = 15$ is a vertical line. The equation of a line perpendicular to $x = 15$ is a horizontal line of the form $y = c$ for some constant c.

Use the y-coordinate of the point $(7, -1)$ to find the equation.

The equation $y = -1$ is perpendicular to the graph of $x = 15$ and passes through the point $(7, -1)$.

Example 5 Application: Right Triangles

Geometry Use what you have learned about the properties of perpendicular lines to prove that ΔABC is a right triangle.

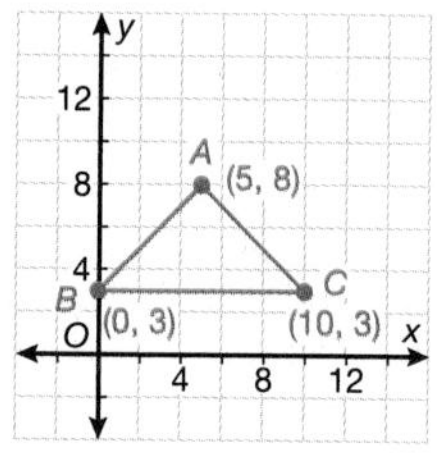

SOLUTION

If ΔABC is a right triangle, then $\angle BAC$ is a right angle and $\overline{AB} \perp \overline{AC}$. Use the slope formula with points A and B and with A and C to see if $\overline{AB}$ and $\overline{AC}$ are perpendicular.

$$m\overline{AB} = \frac{8-3}{5-0} \qquad m\overline{AC} = \frac{8-3}{5-10}$$

$$m\overline{AB} = \frac{5}{5} \qquad m\overline{AC} = \frac{5}{-5}$$

$$m\overline{AB} = 1 \qquad m\overline{AC} = -1$$

Since the product of the slopes is -1, then $\angle BAC$ is a right angle. ΔABC is a right triangle.

INCLUSION

For example 4, students may benefit from graphing the problem in order to check their answer. Guide students to graph $y = 2$ on grid paper using a colored pencil. Then have them graph the point $(4, -1)$ and the equation $x = 4$ using a different-colored pencil.

Have students repeat this exercise for part b.

Lesson Practice

a. The lines are parallel.

a. (Ex 1) The points (1, −4) and (2, −1) are collinear. The points (3, 19) and (5, 25) are also collinear. What can you say about the lines that cross these points?

b. (Ex 1) The points (1, 16.88) and (3, 16.63) are collinear. The points (2, 24) and (4, 40) are also collinear. What can you say about the lines that cross these points? The lines are perpendicular.

c. (Ex 2) Write the equation of the line that is parallel to the graph of $y = -13x + 10$ and crosses the point (0, 15). $y = -13x+15$

d. (Ex 2) Write the equation of the line that is perpendicular to the graph of $y = 25x + 99$ and crosses the point (1, 37). $y = -.04x + 37.04$

e. (Ex 3) What is the relationship between the graphs of $y = -27x + 15$ and $y = -27x + 5$. The lines are parallel.

f. (Ex 3) What is the relationship between the graphs of $y = -0.125x + 10$ and $y = 8x + 1$. The lines are perpendicular.

g. (Ex 4) Find the equation of the line perpendicular to the graph of $y = 5$ that passes through the point (21, 1). $x = 21$.

h. (Ex 4) Find the equation of the line perpendicular to the graph of $x = 7$ that passes through the point (−3, 5). $y = 5$

i. (Ex 5) The graph of $y = \frac{4}{3}x + \frac{22}{3}$ is tangent to the circle at (−1, 6). The center of the circle is at (3, 3). Use what you know about perpendicular lines to show that the tangent is perpendicular to the diameter at that point. The slope of the line that crosses (−1, 6) and (3, 3) is $-\frac{3}{4}$

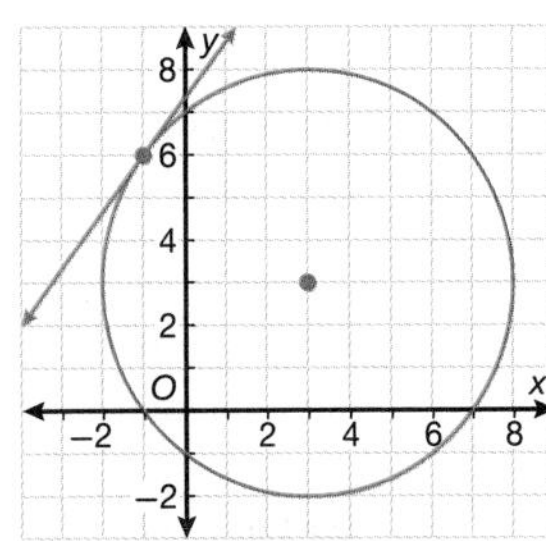

Practice Distributed and Integrated

Use the slope formula to find the slope of each line.

***1.** (26) (−3, 7)(1, 0) $-\frac{7}{4}$

***2.** (26) (2, −5)(0, −6) $\frac{1}{2}$

Determine the kind of variation, if any, for each equation.

3. (12) $y = mx + b$, for $m, b \neq 0$ No variation

4. (12) $y = mx + b$, for $m \neq 0$ and any value of b Direct when $b = 0$

Simplify. Write answers with all exponential expressions in the numerator.

5. (3) $\frac{xx^2(x^0y^{-1})^2}{x^2x^{-5}(y^2)^5}$ x^6y^{-12}

6. (3) $\frac{m^2p^0(m^{-2}p)^2}{m^{-2}p^{-1}(m^{-3}p^2)^3}$ m^9p^{-3}

Solve.

7. (27) $x^2 + 2 = 4x + 7$ $x = -1, x = 5$

8. (24) $12x - 5y = 24$; $20y - 4x = 3$ $x = 2.25, y = 0.6$

ALTERNATE METHOD FOR PROBLEM 8

Have students use Cramer's rule to solve for x and y. Encourage students to rewrite the system before applying the rule.

$$12x - 5y = 24$$
$$-4x + 20y = 3$$

$$x = \frac{\begin{vmatrix} 24 & -5 \\ 3 & 20 \end{vmatrix}}{\begin{vmatrix} 12 & -5 \\ -4 & 20 \end{vmatrix}} = \frac{495}{220} = 2.25$$

$$y = \frac{\begin{vmatrix} 12 & 24 \\ -4 & 3 \end{vmatrix}}{\begin{vmatrix} 12 & -5 \\ -4 & 20 \end{vmatrix}} = \frac{132}{220} = 0.6$$

Lesson Practice

Problem f

Error Alert Students may not recognize the relationship of the graphs because of the decimal slope. Encourage them to write the decimal in fraction form in lowest terms.

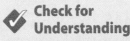

Check for Understanding

The questions below help assess the concepts taught in this lesson.

"How is an equation of a line that is parallel to $y = -2x + 6$ and crosses the point (−2, −3) found?" Use the point-slope equation. Substitute −2 for m, and (−2, −3) for (x_1, y_1). Simplify. Then write the equation in slope-intercept form.

"How do you know when two lines are parallel or perpendicular?" Look at the values of the slopes. If the slopes are equal, the lines are parallel. If the product of the slopes is −1, the lines are perpendicular.

3 Practice

Math Conversations

Discussions to strengthen understanding

Problem 1

Guide students by asking them the following questions.

"What is the slope formula?" $m = \frac{y_2 - y_1}{x_2 - x_1}$

"What is the slope?" $-\frac{7}{4}$

Problem 13

Remind students that the determinant for a 2×2 matrix is defined as

$$D = \begin{vmatrix} a & b \\ c & d \end{vmatrix} = ad - bc.$$

Encourage students to write the initial equation, $-x = -4x - 15$, and then solve for x.

Problem 15

After students write a quadratic equation, remind them to solve the equation by factoring and applying the Zero Product Property.

Problem 18

Tell students the rate of change is the slope of the line. Encourage them to use the slope formula to find the rate of change.

9. (26) Write the equation in standard form: $y = \frac{1}{11}x + \frac{1}{7}$. $\frac{1}{11}x - y = -\frac{1}{7}$

10. (28) **Analyze** Explain how to create a rational expression with four excluded values. Then give an example.

10. Possible answer: Write the denominator as a product of four algebraic expressions so that when each expression is set equal to zero, the solution is different. The excluded values for $\frac{1}{x(x-1)(x+1)(x-2)}$ are 0, 1, −1, and 2.

11. (23) **Error Analysis** Carmen factored the polynomial $x^2 + 5x - 6$ into $(x - 5)(x - 1)$. Describe her error. Instead of correctly using $x^2 + bx + c = (x + u)(x + v)$ with $u + v = b$ and $uv = c$, Carmen wrote $u + v = c$, and $uv = b$.

12. (22) **Verify** Show that the graph $y = 3x - 6$ is a continuous function. The graph of the linear function is a connected graph.

12.

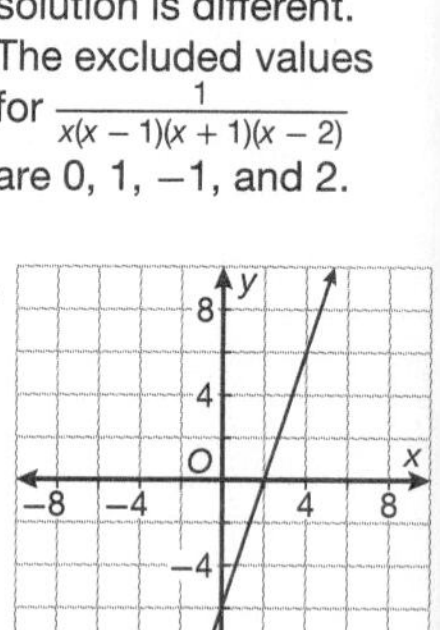

***13.** (14) **Graphing Calculator** Calculate the value of x in the matrix below. Substitute the value of x and use a graphing calculator to verify your answer. $\begin{vmatrix} -4 & 3 \\ 5 & x \end{vmatrix} = -x$ $x = -5$

14. (31) Multiply. Assume that all expressions are defined. $\frac{x}{15} \cdot \frac{x^7}{2x} \cdot \frac{20}{x^4}$ $\frac{2x^3}{3}$

***15.** (35) **Olympic Swimming Pool Size** An Olympic swimming pool has an area of 1250 square meters, and its length is 25 meters more than its width. Write and solve a quadratic equation to find the length and width of an Olympic swimming pool.

16. (32) **Geometry** In the triangle, x is 5 greater than y, and y is 21 less than 3 times z, and the perimeter is 180. What is the value of each variable? To find the answer, write a system of equations and use an inverse matrix to solve it. $x = 77, y = 72, z = 31$

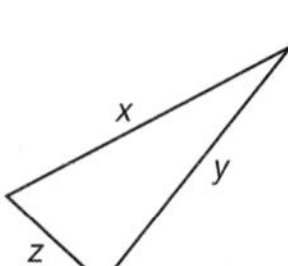

17. (29) **Data Analysis** The table represents the number of ice creams sold at an ice cream shop for the months of January (01), May (05), and October (10).

Month	Sales
01	124
05	4,476
10	3,796

Let x be the month and y be the sales. Use the data in the table to create a system of three equations to find a quadratic equation of the form $y = ax^2 + bx + c$ that models the data. $y = -136x^2 + 1{,}904x - 1644$

***18.** (34) **Cab Fares** The normal fares for taxicab rides in New York City in the year 2006 satisfied a linear function. The table shows the fares for rides of several different distances. Rate of change = 2; Possible description: The fare increases \$2.00 per mile, or \$0.40 for every 0.2 mile.

Number of Miles (x)	0.2	0.4	1	5
Fare in Dollars (y)	2.90	3.30	4.50	12.50

Graph the function, state the rate of change, and describe what it means.

18.

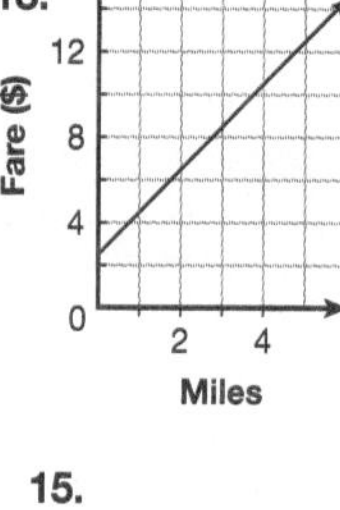

19. (Inv 2) A helicopter takes off with a horizontal speed of 5 ft/s and a vertical speed of 20 ft/s. Write parametric equations to show the motion of the helicopter. $x = 5t$ and $y = 20t$

15.
$x(x + 25) = 1250$
$x^2 + 25x = 1250$
$x^2 + 25x - 1250 = 0$
$(x + 50)(x - 25) = 0$
$x = -50$ or $x = 25$
Choose the positive solution. $x = 25$ and $x + 25 = 50$. The dimensions are 25 meters and 50 meters.

CHALLENGE

Use what you have learned about the properties of parallel lines to show that quadrilateral $ABCD$ is a parallelogram, but not a rectangle.

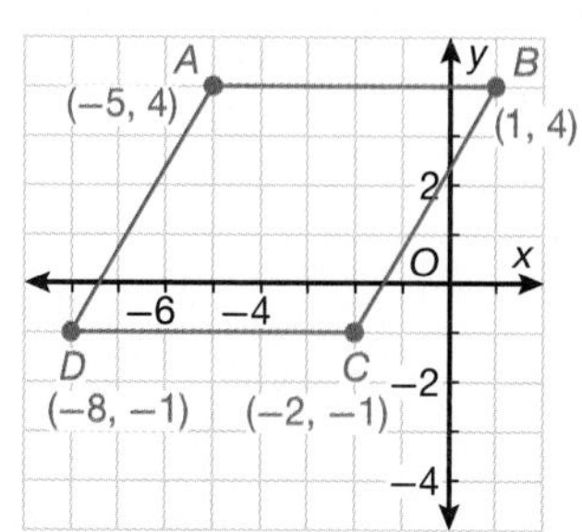

The slopes of $\overline{AB}$ and $\overline{CD}$ are 0, so $\overline{AB}$ is parallel to $\overline{CD}$. The slopes of $\overline{BC}$ and $\overline{AD}$ are $\frac{5}{3}$, so $\overline{BC}$ and $\overline{AD}$ are parallel. So quadrilateral $ABCD$ is a parallelogram. Because the product of the slopes is not −1, the quadrilateral is not a rectangle.

*20. **Error Analysis** Two students are finding the equation of the line parallel to
(36) $y = 5x - 3$ that crosses (1, 4) but get different results. Which student made the mistake? Explain. Student B incorrectly transposed the coordinates.

Student A	Student B
$5 = \frac{y-4}{x-1}$	$5 = \frac{y-1}{x-4}$
$5x - 5 = y - 4$	$5x - 20 = y - 1$
$y = 5x - 1$	$y = 5x - 19$

21. **Multiple Choice** Which data set gives a median of 8 and a mode of 4? **B**
(25)
A {4, 5, 6, 8, 8, 9, 12} B {4, 4, 8, 9, 10}
C {2, 3, 4, 8, 8, 9} D {2, 3, 4, 4, 8, 8}

*22. **Write** Is the triangle defined by vertices (−4, 6), (4, 4), and (1, −8) a right triangle?
(36) How do you know? Yes. The line containing (−4, 6) and (4, 4) is perpendicular to the line containing (4, 4) and (1, −8).

23. **Small Business** The profits, for x weeks, in one year for a small business can be
(30) modeled by the function $y = 0.45(x - 22)^2 - 840.50$. Does the graph of the function have a maximum or a minimum? What is that value? During what week did it occur? The minimum is \$840.50; week 22

*24. Find the roots of $x^2 + 7x + 6 = 0$. $x = -1$ and $x = -6$
(35)

25. **Justify** In $f(x) = ax^2 + bx + c$, why is a the only constant that is not allowed
(27) to be zero? If a were zero, then there would be no term raised to the second power because zero times any number is zero. The function would be linear.

*26. **Multiple Choice** There are 8 runners in a race. How many ways can runners finish in
(33) first, second, and third place? **C**
A 21 B 24 C 336 D 512

27. **Multi-Step** The matrix $\begin{bmatrix} a & c \\ b & d \end{bmatrix}$ represents a parallelogram, with vertices at (0, 0),
(14) (a, b), (c, d), and $(a + c, b + d)$.
a. Graph this parallelogram in the first quadrant, putting (a, b) clockwise from (c, d).
b. To find the area of this parallelogram, draw a rectangle around it and subtract off the areas of triangles and rectangles. Area of parallelogram is $(a + c)(b + d) - ab - cd - 2bc$.
c. Show that the area of the parallelogram equals the determinant of the matrix. Area of parallelogram simplifies to the determinant $ad - bc$.

*28. **Women's Basketball** There are 12 teams in the Atlantic Coast Conference of college
(33) women's basketball. How many ways can teams finish in first, second, and third place? 1320

29. **Write** Describe how symmetry can be used to graph $y = (x - 2)^2 + 2$.
(30)

30. **Multiple Choice** What is the value of $\frac{x^2 + x}{x^2 - 9} \cdot \frac{3x - x^2}{3x + 3}$ if $x = 6$? **A**
(31)
A $-\frac{4}{3}$ B $-\frac{4}{9}$ C $\frac{4}{9}$ D $\frac{4}{3}$

29. Plot the vertex (2, 2), find the value of y for several values of x that are either all less than 2 or greater than 2, and plot those ordered pairs. Sketch the axis of symmetry, $x = 2$, and plot the points that are mirror images of the points already found.

27a.
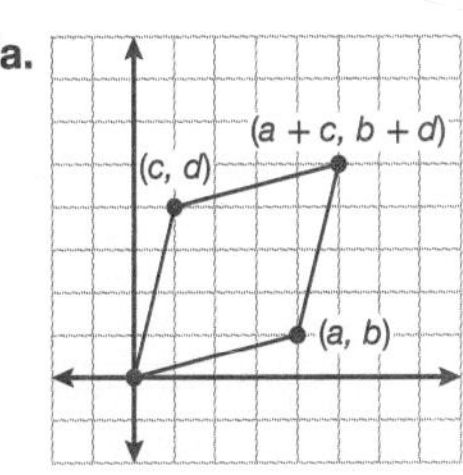

TEACHER TIP

In problem 21, remind students the mode is the number occurring the most. Choices A and C can be eliminated.

Problem 22

Encourage students to plot the points on a grid, then use the properties of perpendicular lines to show whether the triangle has a right angle.

Problem 26

Error Alert

Students may multiply 8 by 3 to get 24. Review the Fundamental Counting Principle. Discuss how to solve the problem by multiplying the number of possibilities for each option.

$8 \cdot 7 \cdot 6 = 336$

Problem 30

Extend the Problem

Have students find the simplified form of the expression.

$-\frac{x^2}{3(x + 3)}$

LOOKING FORWARD

Using parallel and perpendicular lines prepares students for

- **Lesson 41** Using the Pythagorean Theorem and the Distance Formula
- **Lesson 45** Finding the Line of Best Fit

LESSON 37

1 Warm Up

Remind students to find a common denominator when adding fractions in problem 2.

2 New Concepts

In this lesson, students learn to add and subtract rational expressions with like and unlike denominators.

Example 1

Students will add and subtract expressions with like denominators.

Additional Example 1

a. Simplify the following expression.

$$\frac{7}{9x} + \frac{10}{9x} \quad \frac{17}{9x}$$

b. Simplify the following expression.

$$\frac{8x}{x^2 + x - 12} - \frac{11}{x^2 + x - 12}$$

$$\frac{8x - 11}{x^2 + x - 12}$$

LESSON RESOURCES

Student Edition Practice Workbook 37
Reteaching Master 37
Adaptations Master 37
Challenge and Enrichment Master C37

LESSON 37

Adding and Subtracting Rational Expressions

Warm Up

1. **Vocabulary** In the expression $\frac{a}{b}$, if a and b are integers and $b \neq 0$, then $\frac{a}{b}$ is a ________ number. rational
(1)

2. Add the fractions. $\frac{2}{7} + \frac{4}{5}$ $\frac{38}{35}$ or $1\frac{3}{35}$
(1)

3. Factor the expression. $12x^2 - 28x + 15$ $(6x - 5)(2x - 3)$
(23)

New Concepts

Both rational numbers and rational expressions are expressed as ratios.

Rational Number	Rational Expression
$\frac{a}{b}$, for integers a and b, $b \neq 0$	$\frac{f(x)}{g(x)}$, for polynomials $f(x)$ and $g(x)$, $g(x) \neq 0$, $g(x)$ of degree ≥ 1

Recall that a rational expression is undefined for values of the variable that cause the denominator to equal zero. In this lesson assume that all rational expressions are defined unless otherwise indicated.

Math Reasoning

Write If $f(x)$ is a polynomial of degree 1, and not equal to zero, explain why $\frac{1}{f(x)}$ is a rational expression.

Its denominator contains a variable.

Example 1 Combining Expressions with Like Denominators

a. Simplify the following expression.

$$\frac{1}{2x} + \frac{3}{2x}$$

SOLUTION

When two rational expressions have the same denominator, add the numerators.

$$\frac{1}{2x} + \frac{3}{2x} = \frac{4}{2x} = \frac{2}{x}$$

b. Simplify the following expression.

$$\frac{x}{x^2 - 2x + 1} - \frac{1}{x^2 - 2x + 1}$$

SOLUTION

When two rational expressions have the same denominator, subtract the numerators.

$$\frac{x}{x^2 - 2x + 1} - \frac{1}{x^2 - 2x + 1} = \frac{x - 1}{x^2 - 2x + 1}$$

Note that the denominator can be factored. $\frac{x-1}{x^2 - 2x + 1} = \frac{x-1}{(x-1)^2}$

Both the numerator and the denominator have an $(x - 1)$ term in common, which can be further simplified. $\frac{x-1}{(x-1)^2} = \frac{1}{x-1}$

266 *Saxon* *Algebra 2*

MATH BACKGROUND

Students have learned in previous lessons to add and subtract fractions by finding common denominators. The same rules apply when adding and subtracting rational expressions. Students will now be able to substitute rational expressions into formulas and simplify. For example, if the length and width of a rectangle are $\frac{3}{x^2}$ and $\frac{1}{x}$, students will use the rules in this lesson to simplify the perimeter to $\frac{6 + 2x}{x^2}$.

c. Simplify the following expression.

$$\frac{2x}{x^2-4x+3}-\frac{x+2}{x^2-4x+3}+\frac{-1}{x^2-4x+3}$$

SOLUTION

When two or more rational expressions have the same denominator, add or subtract the numerators. With binomial expressions in the numerator, distribute the sign to both terms.

$$\frac{2x}{x^2-4x+3}-\frac{x+2}{x^2-4x+3}+\frac{-1}{x^2-4x+3}=\frac{2x-x-2-1}{x^2-4x+3}$$
$$=\frac{x-3}{x^2-4x+3}$$

Note that the denominator can be factored. $\frac{x-3}{x^2-4x+3}=\frac{x-3}{(x-1)(x-3)}$

Both the numerator and the denominator have an $(x-3)$ term in common, which can be further simplified. $\frac{x-3}{(x-1)(x-3)}=\frac{1}{x-1}$

Example 2 Finding the LCD of Two Rational Expressions

a. Find the least common denominator of the two rational expressions.

$\frac{1}{2x}$ $\frac{1}{7x}$

> **Math Language**
>
> The **least common denominator** is the least common multiple of the denominators of the fractions.

SOLUTION

Finding the LCD of the two rational expressions, in this case, means finding the LCM of $2x$ and $7x$.

$2x$ $4x$ $6x$ $8x$ $10x$ $12x$ $14x$

$7x$ $14x$

The LCD is $14x$, resulting in the rational expressions $\frac{7}{14x}$ and $\frac{2}{14x}$.

b. Find the least common denominator of the two rational expressions.

$\frac{1}{x^2-4}$ $\frac{1}{x^2+5x+6}$

SOLUTION

With more complicated rational expressions, follow these steps.

Step 1: Write each term in factored form.

$\frac{1}{(x-2)(x+2)}$ $\frac{1}{(x+2)(x+3)}$

Step 2: Multiply by the *least* number of factors they do not have in common:

$\frac{(x+3)}{(x-2)(x+2)(x+3)}$ $\frac{(x-2)}{(x-2)(x+2)(x+3)}$

Additional Example 1

c. Simplify the following expression.

$$\frac{15x^2+3x}{x^2+3x-18}-\frac{x+4}{x^2+3x-18}+\frac{10}{x^2+3x-18}\ \frac{15x^2+2x+6}{x^2+3x-18}$$

Example 2

Students learn to find the LCD of two rational expressions.

Additional Example 2

a. Find the least common denominator of the two rational expressions.

$\frac{1}{8x}$ $\frac{1}{11x}$

The LCD is $88x$, resulting in the rational expressions $\frac{11}{88x}$ and $\frac{8}{88x}$.

b. Find the least common denominator of the two rational expressions.

$\frac{1}{x^2-2x-35}$ $\frac{1}{x^2+4x-5}$

The LCM is $(x+5)(x-7)(x-1)$, resulting in the rational expressions $\frac{(x-1)}{(x+5)(x-7)(x-1)}$ and $\frac{(x-7)}{(x+5)(x-7)(x-1)}$

Extend the Example

Have students determine if the LCD in part a would change if students found the LCD for $\frac{1}{2x}, \frac{1}{7x}$, and $\frac{1}{14}$. The LCD would not change because 14 is already a factor in the current LCD of $14x$.

ENGLISH LEARNERS

To help students understand the meaning of **Least Common Multiple,** discuss the meaning of each word separately.

Least means the lowest value. Common means ordinary. In math, common means something shared. So $3x$ and $5x$ have a common factor of x. Multiple means something that consists of more than one part. In math, a multiple is a number that is a product of two numbers.

Discuss the meaning of multiple first by having students list multiples of 5. Say:

"Some multiples of 5 are 5, 10, 15, 20, 25, 30, and 35."

Next have students state the multiples of 10. Students should say: **"The multiples of 10 are 10, 20, 30, 40, 50, 60 and 70."**

Say: **"The common multiples are 10, 20, and 30. The Least Common Multiple is 10."**

Example 3

Remind students that division by 0 is undefined.

Additional Example 3

Find any values of x for which the following expression is undefined.

$\frac{1}{3x^2 + 6x - 24}$ 2 and −4

Example 4

Remind students that the least common multiple is used to find the least common denominator.

Additional Example 4

a. Add the two rational expressions.

$\frac{3}{4x^5} + \frac{7}{12x^3}$ $\frac{9 + 7x^2}{12x^5}$

b. Subtract the two rational expressions.

$\frac{1}{x^2 - x - 6} - \frac{1}{x^2 + 6x + 8}$

$\frac{7}{(x + 2)(x - 3)(x + 4)}$

Math Reasoning

Analyze Suppose that $\frac{1}{ax^2 + bx + c}$ has no restrictions on x. What can you can conclude about this expression?

The quadratic has no real roots.

Example 3 Undefined Values of a Rational Expression

Find any values of x for which the following expression is undefined:

$$\frac{1}{2x^2 + 4x - 6}$$

SOLUTION

A rational expression $\frac{f(x)}{g(x)}$ is undefined when $g(x) = 0$. Follow these steps to find these undefined values:

Step 1: Write each term in factored form.

$$\frac{1}{(2x - 2)(x + 3)}$$

Step 2: Determine the values where each factor is zero.

$2x - 2 = 0 \qquad x + 3 = 0$

$x = 1 \qquad x = -3$

So, the rational expression is undefined for $x = 1$ and $x = 3$.

Example 4 Combining Expressions with Unlike Denominators

a. Add the two rational expressions.

$$\frac{1}{3x^3} + \frac{1}{6x^2}$$

SOLUTION

Find the least common denominator by finding the LCM.

$$\frac{1 \cdot 2}{3x^3 \cdot 2} + \frac{1 \cdot x}{6x^2 \cdot x}$$

$$= \frac{2 + x}{6x^3}$$

b. Subtract the two rational expressions.

$$\frac{1}{x^2 - 1} - \frac{1}{x^2 + 3x + 2}$$

SOLUTION

Factor each denominator to find the LCM.

$$\frac{1}{(x - 1)(x + 1)} - \frac{1}{(x + 1)(x + 2)}$$

$$= \frac{(x + 2)}{(x - 1)(x + 1)(x + 2)} - \frac{(x - 1)}{(x + 1)(x + 2)(x - 1)}$$

$$= \frac{3}{(x - 1)(x + 1)(x + 2)}$$

INCLUSION

In order to help students learn to write equivalent fractions, you can show them the "cover up" method.

Be sure that students have completely factored each denominator. Then, have the students find the least common denominator of the expression. Next, have them look at the denominator of the first fraction to be added or subtracted and cover up the parts of the fraction that are used in the least common denominator with their hand.

It should then be clear which parts of the denominator must be multiplied into the numerator.

Example 5 Application: Travel Time

On a roundtrip by car, it took 2 hours longer on the return trip than it did on the first leg of the trip. How much faster did the car go on the first part of the trip?

SOLUTION

Use the equation for speed:

$$\text{Speed} = \frac{\text{distance}}{\text{time}}$$

First part of the trip	Return trip
$s_1 = \frac{d}{t}$	$s_2 = \frac{d}{t+2}$

$$s_1 - s_2 = \frac{d}{t} - \frac{d}{t+2}$$

$$= \frac{d(t+2)}{t(t+2)} - \frac{dt}{t(t+2)} = \frac{2d}{t(t+2)}$$

Math Language

The **equation for speed** is a variation of the equation for distance: $d = rt$, where r is the rate, t is the time, and d is the distance. Solving the equation for rate gives $r = d \div t$.

Lesson Practice

a. (Ex 1) Simplify the expression. $\frac{7}{5x^3} + \frac{3}{5x^3}$ $\frac{2}{x^3}$

b. (Ex 1) Simplify the expression. $\frac{x}{x^2-1} - \frac{1}{x^2-1}$ $\frac{1}{x+1}$

c. (Ex 1) Simplify. $\frac{4x}{3x^2+19x-14} + \frac{1}{3x^2+19x-14} - \frac{x+3}{3x^2+19x-14}$ $\frac{1}{x+7}$

d. (Ex 2) Find the LCD: $\frac{1}{6x^3}$ $\frac{1}{7x^2}$ $42x^3$

e. (Ex 2) Find the LCD: $\frac{1}{7x^2+32x-15}$ $\frac{1}{2x^2+3x-35}$ $(7x-3)(x+5)(2x-7)$

f. (Ex 3) For what values of x is the denominator zero? $\frac{1}{7x^2-66x+27}$ $x = 9, x = \frac{3}{7}$

g. (Ex 4) Add the two rational expressions. $\frac{1}{5x^4} + \frac{1}{7x^5}$ $\frac{7x+5}{35x^5}$

h. (Ex 4) Subtract the two rational expressions. $\frac{13-3x}{(2x-3)(4x-5)(x+8)}$

$$\frac{1}{8x^2-22x+15} - \frac{1}{2x^2+13x-24}$$

i. (Ex 5) On a canoe trip, it took 45 minutes longer going upstream than it did downstream. How much slower was the upstream part of the trip, in miles per hour? $\frac{3d}{t(4t+3)}$

INCLUSION

In order to help students understand why they must multiply the numerator with missing quantities from the least common denominator, allow them to split up the problem in order to see that they are in reality multiplying the fraction by a form of 1 and any number multiplied by 1 does not change in value.

For example: Add the rational expression:

$$\frac{1}{x} + \frac{1}{x+1}$$

$$\frac{(x+1)}{(x+1)} = 1 \text{ and } \frac{(x)}{(x)} = 1$$

$$= \frac{1}{x} \cdot \frac{(x+1)}{(x+1)} + \frac{1}{x+1} \cdot \frac{(x)}{(x)}$$

$$= \frac{x+1}{x(x+1)} + \frac{x}{x(x+1)} = \frac{2x+1}{x(x+1)}$$

Example 5

Students will apply their knowledge of adding and subtracting rational expressions to create equations to solve problems for any values.

Additional Example 5

A car made two trips. During the second trip the car traveled twice as fast and covered 40 more miles. What was the total time for both trips?

$t_1 + t_2 = \frac{3d+40}{2r}$

Lesson Practice

Problem a

Remind students to simplify after adding the rational expressions.

Problem c

Error Alert Students may add in the numerator incorrectly if they forget to distribute the negative to both terms in the expression.

$$-\frac{x+3}{3x^2+19x-14} = \frac{-x-3}{3x^2+19x-14}$$

Check for Understanding

The questions below help assess the concepts taught in this lesson.

"How is the LCM of two rational expressions with a polynomial in the denominator found?" Sample: Begin by writing each term in factored form. Next, multiply each term by the least number of factors that they do not have in common.

"For what values is a rational expression undefined?" Sample: A rational expression will be undefined if the denominator is equal to zero. To solve for the values that cause this, write each term in factored form. Then set each factor equal to zero and solve for x.

3 Practice

Math Conversations

Discussion to strengthen understanding

Problem 9

When simplifying rational expressions, be sure to solve the expression in steps. First, add the expressions in each denominator. Next, divide the expressions to get a single numerator and denominator. Finally, subtract the reduced expression.

Problem 13

Guide the students by asking them the following questions.

"What is the formula for speed?" $d = rt$

"The question asks how much faster the return trip is. What element of the speed formula should be subtracted?" speed: $(s_2 - s_1)$

Practice Distributed and Integrated

1. (24) Use elimination to solve the system $\begin{matrix} 5x + 2y = 70 \\ 3x - 2y = 10 \end{matrix}$. (10, 10)

2. (26) Find the equation of the line that has a slope of $-\frac{3}{8}$ and passes through (4, 4). $y = -\frac{3}{8}x + \frac{11}{2}$

***3.** (37) Simplify: $\frac{k^2}{2p} + c - \frac{4}{p^2c}$. $\frac{k^2pc + 2p^2c^2 - 8}{2p^2c}$

***4.** (36) Find the equation of the line that passes through the point (3, 5) and is parallel to the line $y = \frac{1}{6}x - 2$. $y = \frac{1}{6}x + \frac{9}{2}$

5. (20) Expand: $\frac{x^2y^{-2}}{z^2}\left(\frac{z^2}{y^2(2x^{-2})^{-1}} - \frac{4x^2y^0}{z^{-2}}\right)$. $2y^{-4} - 4x^4y^{-2}$

6. (9) Multiply: $\begin{bmatrix} 4 & -1 \\ 3 & 7 \end{bmatrix} \cdot \begin{bmatrix} 2 & 4 & 3 \\ 1 & 0 & 8 \end{bmatrix}$. $\begin{bmatrix} 7 & 16 & 4 \\ 13 & 12 & 65 \end{bmatrix}$

Factor completely.

7. (23) $x^2 + x - 6$ $(x + 3)(x - 2)$

8. (23) $x^3 - 9x$ $x(x + 3)(x - 3)$

***9.** (37) Find the difference. $\frac{1}{1 + \frac{1}{x+1}} - \frac{1}{1 + \frac{1}{x-1}}$. $\frac{2}{x(x+2)}$

10. (13) Given $f(x) = 2x - 7$ and $g(x) = -5x + 8$, graph $f(x)$ and $g(x)$ on the same grid.

10. 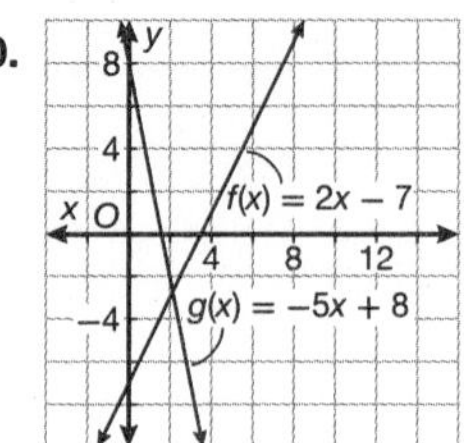

11. (17) **Write** Determine the four resulting inequalities that are used to solve $|x| > |2 + 7x|$.
$x > 2 + 7x$; $x > -2 - 7x$; $x < 2 + 7x$; $x < -2 - 7x$

12. (27) **Multi-Step** **a.** Tell how to determine the values of a, b, and c for any quadratic function written in standard form. a is the coefficient of the squared term, b is the coefficient of the linear term, and c is the constant.

b. Write a quadratic equation in standard form where $a = -1$, $b = -2$, and $c = 3$.
$f(x) = -x^2 - 2x + 3$

***13.** (37) **Aviation** Because of the jet stream, on a roundtrip flight from Washington, D.C. to California, the first part of the trip will take half an hour longer than the return trip. How much faster is the plane flying on the return trip? $\frac{d}{t(2t+1)}$

14. (31) **Error Analysis** A student multiplied rational expressions as follows:

$$\frac{x^2 - 1}{x^2 + 2x + 1} \cdot \frac{x + 1}{x - 3} = \frac{-1}{2x + 1} \cdot \frac{1}{-3} = \frac{1}{3(2x + 1)}.$$

What is the error? Find the correct product. The error is dividing out terms of polynomials. The correct product is $\frac{x-1}{x-3}$

15. (15) **Multiple Choice** Which is the solution to the linear system $\begin{matrix} y = x \\ y = 3x - 2 \end{matrix}$? C

A (3, 3) **B** (2, 4) **C** (1, 1) **D** There is no solution.

ALTERNATE METHOD FOR PROBLEM 7

$x^2 + x - 6$

$= (x\_\_\_) \cdot (x\_\_\_)$ — We know x multiplied by x will result in x^2.

$= (x + \_\_\_) \cdot (x - \_\_\_)$ — By looking at the second and third sign, you know the expression will have a positive and negative sign.

$= (x + 3) \cdot (x - 2)$

3 and 2 are the last factors in the binomials because 3 times 2 equals 6 and 3 minus 2 equals 1. The 3 belongs with the positive factor and the 2 belongs with the negative factor, so that the middle term is positive.

16. Error Analysis (24) Find and correct the error a student made below.

$$\begin{aligned}2x + 2y &= 6\\ -2x + y &= -12\end{aligned} \longrightarrow \begin{aligned}2x + 2y &= 6\\ + -2x + y &= -12\\ \hline 2y &= -6\\ y &= -3\end{aligned} \longrightarrow \begin{aligned}-2x + y &= -12\\ -2x - 3 &= -12\\ -2x &= -9\\ x &= 4.5\end{aligned}$$

The solution is (4.5, –3).

16. The student made an error in adding the y-terms: $2y + y = 3y$. The correct solution is (5, –2).

***17. Economics** (36) The exchange rate from dollars to different currencies is shown in the table. A company charges a fee of \$3 for amounts up to \$50 and \$5 for amounts above \$50. Write the equations for exchanging Euros to dollars. What do the graphs of the equations have in common?

Currency	US \$
1 euro =	1.377
1 Canadian dollar =	0.9472
1 British pound =	2.0284

$y = 1.377x + 3$ and $y = 1.377x + 5$; the lines are parallel

18. Probability (35) The right triangle is inscribed in the circle. The area of the triangle is 120 square units. Suppose a point is chosen at random inside the circle. What is the probability that the chosen point is inside the triangle? $\frac{120}{169\pi}$

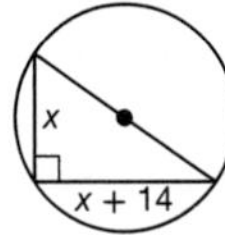

19. Multi-Step (34) **a.** Graph the equations $y = \frac{1}{2}x - 2$ and $y = \frac{1}{2}x + 3$.

b. What is the slope of each line? $\frac{1}{2}$

c. State a property of lines and their slopes that is illustrated by the graphs. Non-vertical lines are parallel if and only if they have the same slope and different y-intercepts.

19a.

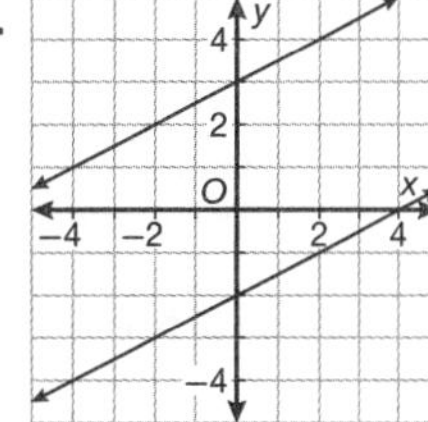

***20. Write** (37) What must be true if the LCM of rational expressions $\frac{f(x)}{g(x)}$ and $\frac{h(x)}{i(x)}$ is $g(x)i(x)$? Both $g(x)$ and $i(x)$ have no common factors.

***21. Graphing Calculator** (14) Use a graphing calculator to solve.

$$\det\begin{bmatrix}2 & -3 & 5\\ 2 & 0 & -1\\ 2 & 3 & 1\end{bmatrix}$$ 48

22. Analyze (33) A card is chosen from a standard 52-card deck. Consider these four events: *Choose a red card. Choose a face card. Choose the jack of spades. Choose a black jack.* How many pairs of mutually exclusive events can be made from the events? List all the pairs. 2 pairs: Choose a red card; choose the jack of spades. Choose a red card; choose a black jack

23. Basketball (19) The length of a regulation high school basketball court is represented by the expression $(x + 24)$ feet. The width of a regulation high school basketball court is represented by the expression $(x - 10)$ feet.

a. Write an expression that represents the area of a regulation high school basketball court. $(x + 24)(x - 10) = x^2 + 14x - 240$ ft²

b. Evaluate the area of the court if $x = 60$. $(60)^2 + 14(60) - 240 = 4200$ ft²

***24. Justify** (36) Suppose that $y_1 = m_1x + b_1$ and $y_2 = m_2x + b_2$ are each perpendicular to $y_3 = m_3x + b_3$. Justify the statement $y_1 \parallel y_2$. Since $m_1 = -\frac{1}{m_3}$ and $m_2 = -\frac{1}{m_3}$, then $m_1 = m_2$. Therefore, y_1 and y_2 are parallel.

Problem 23

Extend the Problem

Have students write the perimeter of the basketball court in terms of x. $4x + 28$

Problem 24

Guide the students by asking them the following questions.

"What can be said about the slopes of parallel lines?"
Parallel lines have equal slopes.

"What can be said about the slopes of perpendicular lines?"
A line is perpendicular to another line if their product is –1.

"What can be said about the slopes of lines y_1 and y_2"
If y_1 and y_2 are both perpendicular to y_3, then they would have the same slope and be parallel to each other.

CHALLENGE

Simplify the expression.

$$\frac{x^2}{2x(x^2+1)} + \frac{11}{x^2} - \frac{4x^3}{\frac{7}{x^2}}$$

$$\frac{-8x^9 - 8x^7 + 7x^3 + 154x^2 + 154}{14x^4 + 14x^2}$$

Problem 28

Remember that dividing is equivalent to multiplying by the reciprocal of the expression. To solve, simply find the reciprocal $g(x)$ and then multiply the expressions. Before simplifying the expression, first check to see if any factors can be divided out.

Problem 30

Create an equation for each purchase. Set small tiles equal to variable x and large tiles to variable y. With the two equations, solve for the two variables.

25. (21) **Verify** Solve the system of equations by solving the first equation for y then substituting. Verify your answer by solving the second equation for y, then substituting.

$2y - 3x = -10$

$4x = 7 - y$ $\left(\frac{24}{11}, -\frac{19}{11}\right)$

26. (32) **Item Costs** An office worker ordered breakfast items for coworkers as shown below. Monday: 6 muffins, 6 bagels, and 6 fruit cups; total bill \$24.00
Tuesday: 4 muffins, 12 bagels, and 4 fruit cups; total bill \$22.80
Wednesday: 8 muffins, 12 bagels, and 10 fruit cups; total bill \$39.30

\$1.20 per muffin
\$0.85 per bagel
\$1.95 per fruit cup

What was the cost of each item? To find the answer, write a system of equations and use an inverse matrix to solve it.

27. (22) **Geometry** Examine the polygons given below. Each polygon has been divided up into triangles. Complete the table. Graph the function. State the domain and range. Determine if the graph is continuous, discontinuous, and/or discrete.

Number of sides of the polygon	Number of triangles
3	1
4	2
5	3
6	4
7	5
8	6

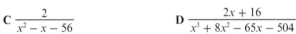

Domain: 3, 4, 5, 6, 7, 8; Range: 1, 2, 3, 4, 5, 6; Discrete, Discontinuous

28. (31) **Multi-Step** Given the rational functions $f(x) = \frac{2x-1}{x+5}$ and $g(x) = \frac{14x-7}{14x^2+70x}$:

a. Find the function quotient $f(x) \div g(x)$ in simplest form. $2x$

b. Find the value of $f(x) \div g(x)$ if $x = 10$. 20

27.

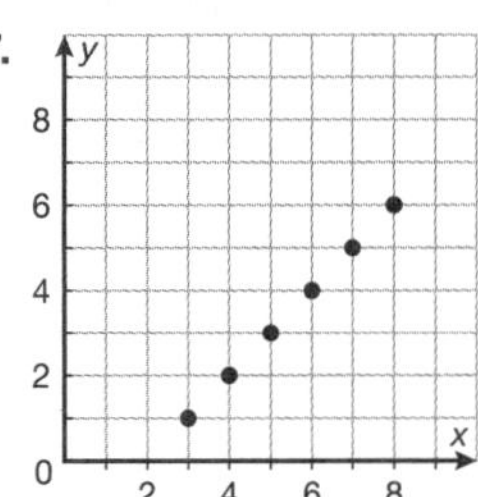

***29.** (37) What is the sum of $\frac{1}{x^2+x-72}$ and $\frac{1}{x^2-x-56}$? D

A $\frac{2}{x^2+16x+63}$

B $\frac{2}{x^2+x-72}$

C $\frac{2}{x^2-x-56}$

D $\frac{2x+16}{x^3+8x^2-65x-504}$

30. (16) **Construction** A contractor is replacing the tile in two bathrooms. For one bathroom, she purchased 416 large tiles and 256 small tiles at a cost of \$233.60. For the other bathroom, she purchased 400 large tiles and 512 small tiles at a cost of \$251.20. How much does each size tile cost? large tile: \$0.50; small tile: \$0.10

LOOKING FORWARD

Using addition and subtraction of rational expressions prepares students for

- **Lesson 40** Simplifying Radical Expressions
- **Lesson 44** Rationalizing Denominators
- **Lesson 58** Completing the Square
- **Lesson 61** Understanding Advanced Factoring
- **Lesson 65** Using the Quadratic Formula

LESSON 38

Dividing Polynomials Using Long Division

Warm Up

1. **Vocabulary** An expression that contains the symbols < or > is called a(n) inequality. (10)

2. Multiply: $(x + 3)(x + 7)$. $x^2 + 10x + 21$ (39)

3. Determine $f(-5)$ if $f(x) = 2x^2 - 3x$. 65 (4)

New Concepts

Polynomial long division is a similar process to integer long division: The quotient can have a remainder of zero or not.

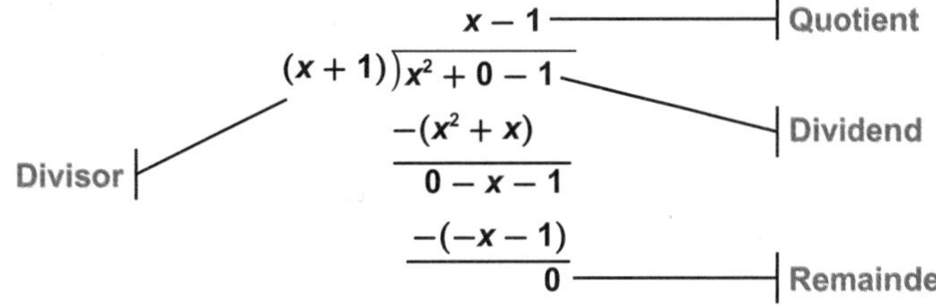

Math Reasoning

Analyze Suppose m and n are two different integers. If m is a prime number and $n > 1$, how do you know that $\frac{m}{n}$ has a nonzero remainder?

All prime numbers are only divisible by themselves and 1.

Example 1 Dividing a Polynomial by a Monomial

Divide: $(12x^3 - 6x^2 + 6x + 4)$ by $3x$.

SOLUTION

Use polynomial long division.

$$\begin{array}{r} 4x^2 - 2x + 2 \\ 3x\overline{)12x^3 - 6x^2 + 6x + 4} \\ -(12x^3) \qquad\qquad\qquad \\ \hline 0 - 6x^2 + 6x + 4 \\ -(-6x^2) \qquad\qquad \\ \hline 0 + 6x + 4 \\ -(6x) \quad \\ \hline 0 + 4 \end{array}$$

The quotient and remainder can be written as:

$$(4x^2 - 2x + 2) + \frac{4}{3x}$$

Check

$$\left(4x^2 - 2x + 2 + \frac{4}{3x}\right)(3x) = (12x^3 - 6x^2 + 6x) + (4)$$

$$= 12x^3 - 6x^2 + 6x + 4 \checkmark$$

Online Connection www.SaxonMathResources.com

MATH BACKGROUND

In algebra, polynomial long division is used for dividing a polynomial by another polynomial of the same or lower degree, a generalized version of the familiar arithmetic technique called long division. It can be done easily by hand, because it separates an otherwise complex division problem into smaller ones.

This method is comparable to long division of integers. The result can also have a remainder and it is written as the value of the remainder divided by the divisor.

LESSON 38

1 Warm Up

Use problems 2 and 3 in the Warm Up to review techniques for working with polynomials and solving functions for specific variables.

2 New Concepts

In this lesson, students learn to divide polynomials using long division.

Discuss the definitions of a polynomial, monomial, and long division of integers. Dividing polynomials follow the same rules as long division with integers.

Example 1

Students will use long division to divide polynomials by monomials.

Additional Example 1

Divide:

$(32x^4 - 104x^3 + 56x^2 + 8x + 4)$ by $8x$. $(4x^3 - 13x^2 + 7x + 1) + \frac{1}{2x}$

LESSON RESOURCES

Student Edition Practice Workbook 38
Reteaching Master 38
Adaptations Master 38
Challenge and Enrichment Master C38

Example 2

Students will divide a polynomial with a linear polynomial using long division.

Additional Example 2

Divide:

$(3x^4 + 11x^3 - 55x^2 + 113x + 79)$ by $x + 7$. $(3x^3 - 10x^2 + 15x + 8) + \frac{23}{x+7}$

Example 3

Students will divide a polynomial by a lower-degree polynomial using long division.

Extend the Example

Have the students check their work by taking the quotient, multiplying it by the divisor and adding the remainder. The answer should be the dividend.

$(x^2 + 11)(4x^2 - x - 44)$
$= 4x^4 - x^3 - 44x^2 + 44x^2 - 11x - 484$
$= 4x^4 - x^3 - 11x - 484$

Additional Example 3

Divide:

$(4x^4 + 8x^3 - 55x^2 + 24x)$ by $x^2 + 3$. $(4x^2 + 8x - 67) + \frac{201}{x^2+3}$

TEACHER TIP

Remind students that each variable must be represented in the dividend in descending order. So if the polynomial begins with x^4, the dividend must be written with x^3, x^2, and x.

Hint

Distribute the −1 to each of the numbers when subtracting the product of the quotient and the divisor.

Example 2 Dividing a Polynomial by a Linear Polynomial

Divide: $(x^4 + 2x^3 - 13x^2 - 38x - 24)$ by $(x + 4)$.

SOLUTION

$$
\begin{array}{r}
x^3 - 2x^2 - 5x - 18 \\
(x+4)\overline{\big)\,x^4 + 2x^3 - 13x^2 - 38x - 24} \\
-(x^4 + 4x^3) \qquad\qquad\qquad\qquad \\
\hline
0 - 2x^3 - 13x^2 - 38x - 24 \\
-(-2x^3 - 8x^2) \qquad\qquad\quad \\
\hline
0 - 5x^2 - 38x - 24 \\
-(-5x^2 - 20x) \qquad \\
\hline
0 - 18x - 24 \\
-(-18x - 72) \\
\hline
0 + 48
\end{array}
$$

The quotient and remainder are

$(x^3 - 2x^2 - 5x - 18) + \dfrac{48}{x+4}$

Check

$$\left(x^3 - 2x^2 - 5x - 18 + \frac{48}{x+4}\right)(x+4) = (x^4 + 2x^3 - 13x^2 - 38x - 72) + 48$$
$$= x^4 + 2x^3 - 13x^2 - 38x - 24 \ \checkmark$$

Example 3 Dividing a Polynomial by a Lower-Degree Polynomial

Divide: $(4x^4 - x^3 - 11x - 484)$ by $(x^2 + 11)$.

SOLUTION

Even though there is no quadratic term in the dividend, include a place for it.

$$
\begin{array}{r}
4x^2 - x - 44 \\
(x^2+11)\overline{\big)\,4x^4 - x^3 + 0x^2 - 11x - 484} \\
-(4x^4 \qquad + 44x^2) \qquad\qquad\quad \\
\hline
0 - x^3 - 44x^2 - 11x - 484 \\
-(-x^3 \qquad\quad - 11x) \qquad\quad \\
\hline
0 - 44x^2 + 0 - 484 \\
-(-44x^2 \qquad - 484) \\
\hline
0
\end{array}
$$

The quotient is $(4x^2 - x - 44)$. There is no remainder.

ENGLISH LEARNERS

To help students distinguish among **divisor, quotient, dividend,** and **remainder,** discuss the meanings of these four words.

Divisor comes from divide with an ending of "or." Words ending in "or" indicate the word is doing something. Other words ending in "or" include counselor and advisor. So divisor is the number that divides into another number.

Quotient is a mathematical term that means the result of division. So the quotient is the answer.

Dividend can be a payment made or cash shared. In math, dividend is the number being divided into.

Remainder refers to something that is left over. In long division, remainder is that number or expression that is left after division.

274 *Saxon Algebra 2*

Example 4 Testing if One Polynomial Is a Factor of Another

a. Is $(x + 2)$ a factor of $2x^3 - x^2 - 7x + 6$?

SOLUTION

Use polynomial long division.

$$
\begin{array}{r}
2x^2 - 5x + 3 \\
(x + 2)\overline{)2x^3 - x^2 - 7x + 6} \\
-(2x^3 + 4x^2) \\
\hline
0 - 5x^2 - 7x + 6 \\
-(-5x^2 - 10x) \\
\hline
0 + 3x + 6 \\
-(3x + 6) \\
\hline
0
\end{array}
$$

Because the remainder is zero, $(x + 2)$ is a factor.

b. Is $(x + 3)$ a factor of $6x^3 - 6x^2 - 6x + 6$?

SOLUTION

Use polynomial long division.

$$
\begin{array}{r}
6x^2 - 24x + 66 \\
(x + 3)\overline{)6x^3 - 6x^2 - 6x + 6} \\
-(6x^3 + 18x^2) \\
\hline
0 - 24x^2 - 6x + 6 \\
-(-24x^2 - 72x) \\
\hline
66x + 6 \\
(66x + 198) \\
\hline
204
\end{array}
$$

Because the remainder is not zero, $(x + 3)$ is not a factor.

Example 5 Application

What is the ratio of the volume to the surface area for the rectangular prism?

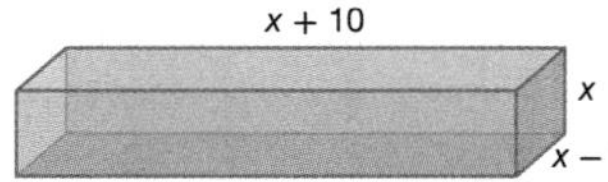

SOLUTION

$$\frac{\text{volume}}{\text{surface area}} = \frac{x(x + 10)(x - 1)}{2x(x + 10) + 2(x - 1)(x + 10) + 2x(x - 1)}$$

$$= \frac{x(x + 10)(x - 1)}{6x^2 + 36x - 20}$$

Since the numerator and denominator do not share any factors, the ratio has a nonzero remainder.

Math Reasoning

Verify Show that the ratio of the volume to the surface area has no common factors.

The factored form of the ratio is $\frac{x(x + 10)(x - 1)}{2(x^2 + 18x - 10)}$, which has no common factors.

Example 4

Students will use long division to determine if a polynomial is a factor of another polynomial.

Additional Example 4

a. Is $(x + 5)$ a factor of $(8x^3 + 37x^2 - 11x + 20)$?
Yes, because the remainder is zero.

b. Is $(x + 6)$ a factor of $(4x^3 + 35x^2 + 73x + 150)$?
No, because the remainder is not zero.

Example 5

Students will apply long division of polynomials to find the ratio between volume and surface area of a rectangular prism.

Additional Example 5

What is the ratio of the volume to surface area of a rectangular prism if the length is $(x + 20)$, the width is $(x - 5)$ and the height is x? $\frac{\text{volume}}{\text{surface area}} = \frac{x(x + 20)(x - 5)}{2x(x + 20) + 2x(x - 5) + 2(x + 20)(x - 5)} = \frac{x(x + 20)(x - 5)}{6x^2 + 60x - 200}$
Since there are no common factors, there is also a nonzero remainder.

INCLUSION

In order to help students learn to recognize how polynomials divide, allow them to create a template that will guide them through the division. Create in the dividend a polynomial that can be filled in with constants in front of the variables such as:

$$(\_x^4 - \_x^3 + \_x^2 + \_x + \_)$$

This will allow them to remember to put in a 0 for any constant that is not in the polynomial and will help guide them through the division.

Lesson Practice

Problem a

Error Alert Students may not remember to add the remainder at the end of the long division. Remind the students that any leftover terms are written as $\frac{\text{remainder}}{\text{divisor}}$.

Problems d and e

Scaffolding Before dividing, be sure to set up the long division with correct dividend and divisor. Be sure to keep signs correct and to subtract straight down in the long division columns. Any leftover values will be the remainder. If the division has a remainder, then the quotient will not be a factor of the dividend.

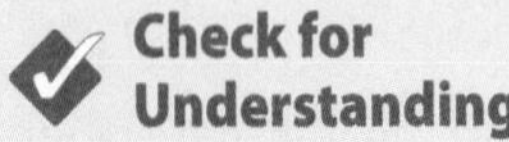

Check for Understanding

The questions below help assess the concepts taught in this lesson.

1. **"What are some of the similarities between polynomial long division and integer long division?"** Sample: Polynomial long division is similar to integer long division and the quotient may or may not have a remainder.
2. **"How is the remainder in polynomial long division written?"** Sample: The remainder is written as the remainder value divided by the divisor.

3 Practice

Math Conversations

Discussion to strengthen understanding

Problems 5 and 6

Remind students that mutually exclusive means the events cannon happen at the same time.

Lesson Practice

a. (Ex 1) Divide $12x^3 - 9x^2 - 237x + 40$ by $3x$. $4x^2 - 3x - 79 + \frac{40}{3x}$

b. (Ex 2) Divide $6x^4 - 23x^3 - 34x^2 + 207x - 180$ by $x - 3$. $6x^3 - 5x^2 - 49x + 60$

c. (Ex 3) Divide $2x^4 + 7x^3 - 241x^2 - 192x + 3024$ by $x^2 - 5x - 36$. $2x^2 + 17x - 84$

d. (Ex 4) Is $x - 6$ a factor of $2x^3 + x^2 - 177x + 594$? Yes

e. (Ex 4) Is $x + 27$ a factor of $7x^3 + 178x^2 - 107x - 78$? No

f. (Ex 5) What is the ratio of the volume to surface area in the figure below? Does this expression have a nonzero remainder? $\frac{15x^2 + 75x}{62x + 160}$; it has a nonzero remainder.

Practice Distributed and Integrated

Use the descriptions below to write the vertex form of a quadratic equation.

1. (30) The parent function is shifted 10 units left. $y = (x + 10)^2$

2. (30) The parent function is shifted 1 unit right and 3 units down. $y = (x - 1)^2 - 3$

***3.** (38) Divide $x^3 - 10x^2 - 69x + 30$ by $(x + 5)$. $x^2 - 15x + 6$

4. (32) Given $A = \begin{bmatrix} 4 & -2 \\ 8 & 4 \end{bmatrix}$ and $B = \begin{bmatrix} -2 & 0 \\ 0 & -2 \end{bmatrix}$, solve $AX = B$. $X = \begin{bmatrix} -.25 & -.125 \\ .5 & -.25 \end{bmatrix}$

A number cube is rolled. Determine if the following events are mutually exclusive.

5. (33) *Roll an odd number* or *roll a 6* Yes

6. (33) *Roll an even number* or *roll a number less than 3* No

***7.** (37) Find the difference. $\frac{1}{x+3} - \frac{1}{x+2} - \frac{1}{x+1}$ $\frac{-x^2 - 6x - 7}{x^3 + 6x^2 + 11x + 6}$

8. (16) Use Cramer's Rule to solve $\begin{matrix} 3x - 12y = -15 \\ x + 2y = 7 \end{matrix}$. $x = 3, y = 2$

Find the determinants of the following matrices.

9. (14) What is $|A|$ if $A = \begin{bmatrix} 2 & -12 \\ 7 & 13 \end{bmatrix}$? 110

10. (14) What is $|B|$ if $B = \begin{bmatrix} -1 & -24 \\ 0.25 & 0.5 \end{bmatrix}$? 5.5

***11.** (13) What are the slope and y-intercept of $3x + 10y = -1$? Slope: -0.3; y-intercept: -0.1

12. (12) **Geometry** As the diameter (d) of circle increases in size, the circumference (C) increases. Likewise, as the diameter decreases in size, so does the circumference. The constant of variation between C and d is π. Describe the kind of variation between the circumference and diameter in a circle. Write the equation. Direct variation; The equation is $C = \pi d$.

276 **Saxon** *Algebra 2*

*13. **Write** State all the possible numbers of y-intercepts a quadratic function graph can have. Explain. See Additional Answers.
(35)

*14. **Justify** Consider the polynomial $x^2 + ax + bx + ab$. What is the remainder when this polynomial is divided by $x + a$? How do you know? The remainder is zero because the polynomial is equivalent to $(x + a)(x + b)$.
(38)

15. **(Hourly Pay)** An employee makes three different rates of pay based on the type of work. The rates of pay are \$16 per hour, \$24 per hour, and \$32 per hour. The combined number of hours worked at the rate of \$16 per hour and \$24 per hour was 10 times the hours worked at the rate of \$32 per hour. If in one week the employee earned \$808 for working 44 hours, how many hours were worked at each rate of pay? \$16: 35; \$24: 5; \$32: 4
(29)

*16. **Error Analysis** Two students are dividing $-14x^3 + 46x^2 + 44x - 16$ by $x - 2$ but get different results. Which student made the mistake? Student B incorrectly subtracts $36x$ instead of adding.
(38)

Student A	Student B
$\begin{array}{r} -14x^2 + 18x + 80 \\ (x-2)\overline{)-14x^3 + 46x^2 + 44x - 16} \\ -(-14x^3 + 28x^2) \\ \hline 0 + 18x^2 + 44x - 16 \\ -(18x^2 - 36x) \\ \hline 0 + 80x - 16 \\ -(80x - 160) \\ \hline 144 \end{array}$	$\begin{array}{r} -14x^2 + 18x - 8 \\ (x-2)\overline{)-14x^3 + 46x^2 + 44x - 16} \\ -(-14x^3 + 28x^2) \\ \hline 0 + 18x^2 + 44x - 16 \\ -(18x^2 - 36x) \\ \hline 0 + 8x - 16 \\ -(8x - 16) \\ \hline 0 \end{array}$

*17. **Graphing Calculator** Use a graphing calculator to determine the minimum of the quadratic equation $f(x) = x^2 - 4x - 2$. (2, −6)
(27)

*18. **Multiple Choice** Which is the equation of the line perpendicular to $y = 4x + 10$ that passes through (1, 1)? **B**
(36)

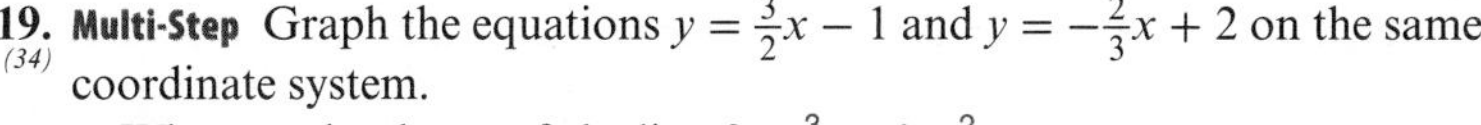

A $y = 4x + \frac{5}{4}$ **B** $y = -\frac{1}{4}x + \frac{5}{4}$ **C** $y = -4x + \frac{5}{4}$ **D** $y = \frac{1}{4}x + \frac{5}{4}$

19. **Multi-Step** Graph the equations $y = \frac{3}{2}x - 1$ and $y = -\frac{2}{3}x + 2$ on the same coordinate system.
(34)

19. (graph) $y = -\frac{2}{3}x + 2$; $y = \frac{3}{2}x - 1$; axes x, y, O, 4, −4, −2, 2, −4

a. What are the slopes of the lines? $\frac{3}{2}$ and $-\frac{2}{3}$

b. What is the product of the slopes? −1

c. State a property of lines and their slopes that is illustrated by the graphs. Two non-vertical lines are perpendicular if and only if the product of their slopes is −1.

20. **(Geography)** Crater Lake in southern Oregon lies inside a volcanic basin and is nearly circular in shape. Write the area to circumference ratio of the lake as a simplified rational expression. Then find the ratio given that the radius of the lake is about 3 miles. $\frac{r}{2} = \frac{3}{2} = 1.5$
(28)

21. **Error Analysis** A card is drawn at random from a standard 52-card deck. How many outcomes are in the event *draw an ace or a spade*? A student solved this problem by reasoning as follows: There are 4 aces and 13 spades, so there are $4 + 13 = 17$ outcomes in the event. What is the error? Find the correct answer.
(33)

21. The student incorrectly reasoned that the events draw an ace and draw a spade are mutually exclusive. The events are not mutually exclusive because the ace of spades is both an ace and a spade. The sum 4 + 13 includes the ace of spades twice. To get the correct answer, subtract 1 from that sum. The correct answer is 16.

Problem 16

When performing polynomial long division, remind students to use algebraic addition. Students should multiply the polynomial by −1, and then add.

Problem 18

Guide the students by asking them the following questions.

"What is true about the slopes of perpendicular lines?" The slopes are negative inverses of each other.

"How can you find the y-intercept for this equation?" Find the negative reciprocal of the slope in the problem. Then substitute $x = 1$ and $y = 1$ into the equation $y = mx + b$ and solve for b.

TEACHING TIP

When solving multiple choice problems, tell students to eliminate answers if possible. For example, in problem 18, the slope of the perpendicular line must be $-\frac{1}{4}$. The answer must be B.

Problem 21

Remember that there are four possible aces and thirteen spades, but ones of those spades is an ace.

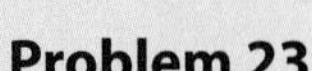

Problem 23

Create an equation using the percentages and three variables. This will set up three equations with three unknowns that can then be found by solving.

Problem 25

By using the zero product property, each factored polynomial can be set equal to zero to solve for each x individually.

Problem 26

Students may try to solve this problem numerically, but it should be set as the difference between two sets of equations. Remember that $d = rt$.

Problem 28

Guide the students by asking them the following question.

"What is the definition of a factor?" A factor is a number or expression that divides into another number or expression with no remainder.

Problem 29

Remind students to write two ordered pairs using age and height for x and y. Next tell students to find the slope and substitute into $y = mx + b$ to find the y-intercept.

22. (24) **Multi-Step a.** Rewrite the system $\begin{matrix} y = 5 - 7x \\ 10 = 14x + 2y \end{matrix}$ so that both equations are in standard form.

b. By inspection, what do you think the solution is? Why?

c. Solve and classify the system. infinitely many solutions, consistent and dependent

22a. $\begin{matrix} 7x + y = 5 \\ 14x + 2y = 10 \end{matrix}$

22b. Possible answer: infinitely many solutions, all the like terms would become opposites if the first equation was multiplied by −2

23. (32) **Analyze** Students at a high school were asked if they visited a museum, public library, or historical site during the last month. The table shows data about the results of the survey. How many students in each grade were surveyed? To find the answer, write a system of equations and use an inverse matrix to solve it.

	Ninth Graders	Tenth Graders	Eleventh Graders	Total
Museum	20%	30%	25%	143
Public Library	40%	50%	45%	258
Historical Site	20%	20%	35%	142

23. 205 ninth graders, 190 tenth graders, 180 eleventh graders

24. (30) **Generalize** Describe shifts, stretches, and compressions of parabolas and discuss how those changes appear in the equations of parabolas.

25. (23) **Write** Explain in words how the Zero Product Property is useful in solving polynomial equations.

***26.** (37) **Aviation** Because of a strong head wind the return trip on an airplane takes 1.5 hours longer than the first part of the trip. How much slower did the airplane travel on the return trip? $\frac{1.5d}{t^2 + 1.5t}$

27. (27) **Justify** Graph $f(x) = -x^2 + 3$. Tell why the range of the function is the set of real numbers less than or equal to 3. The point (0, 3) is the highest point on the parabola; the y-values do not extend above 3.

27.

***28.** (38) **Multiple Choice** Which of the following is a factor of $3x^3 + 8x^2 - 31x + 20$? C

A $(x + 2)$ **B** $(3x + 4)$ **C** $(x - 1)$ **D** $(x + 6)$

29. (26) **Medicine** The Centers for Disease Control has developed growth charts that pediatricians use to see if a child's height is within a certain average. The chart below shows data for a boy's height in the 75th percentile. The three points are on a line. Use the data to write the equation of the line in slope-intercept form.
$y = 3x + 29.5$

Age (years)	Height (inches)
3	38.5
4	41.5
5	44.5

25. When a polynomial is factored and is equal to zero, since the product of the terms equals zero, at least one of its terms equals zero. Setting each term containing a variable equal to zero enables you to solve for a possible value of the variable.

***30.** (37) **Probability** Two six-sided number cubes have labels $\frac{1}{x}$, $\frac{1}{2x}$, $\frac{1}{3x}$, $\frac{1}{4x}$, $\frac{1}{5x}$, and $\frac{1}{6x}$. If both number cubes are rolled, what is the probability that the sum of the expressions is $\frac{1}{x}$? $\frac{1}{36}$

24. A change in the value of h shifts the parent function to the right when h is positive and to the left when h is negative. A change in the value of k shifts the parent function up when k is positive and down when k is negative. When the absolute value of a is greater than 1, the graph is stretched away from the x-axis, appearing narrower than the parent function. When the absolute value of a is between 0 and 1, the graph is compressed towards the x-axis, appearing wider than the parent function.

CHALLENGE

Divide:

$(x^7 + 3x^6 + 7x^5 + 9x^4 + 14x^3 + 17x^2 + 41x + 44)$ by $(x^2 + 3x + 4)$. Is there a remainder?
$(x^5 + 3x^3 + 2x + 11)$ There is no remainder.

LOOKING FORWARD

Using division of polynomial expressions prepares students for

- **Lesson 51** Using Synthetic Division
- **Lesson 66** Solving Polynomial Equations
- **Lesson 95** Factoring Higher-Order Polynomials

LESSON 39

Graphing Linear Inequalities in Two Variables

Warm Up

1. slope-intercept

1. **Vocabulary** The equation $y = \frac{1}{4}x - 2$ is written in ________ form. (13)
2. Find the slope of the line that passes through (9, 3) and (−7, 5). $-\frac{1}{8}$ (13)
3. The slope of a vertical line is ________. undefined (13)
4. True or False: The y-intercept of $2x - y = -4$ is 4. true (13)

New Concepts

When two expressions have the same value, they can be joined by an equal sign. If two expressions do not have the same value, they can be joined by one of the inequality signs shown below.

Less than	Greater than	Less than or equal to	Greater than or equal to
$<$	$>$	$\leq$	$\geq$

A **linear inequality in two variables** relates two variables, often x and y, with an inequality sign. A solution (x, y) makes the inequality true when the values of x and y are substituted into the inequality.

Example 1 Determining if an Ordered Pair is a Solution of a Linear Inequality

Determine if each point is a solution of the inequality.

a. $y > -3x + 5$, (2, 9)

SOLUTION

$9 \overset{?}{>} -3(2) + 5$

$9 > -1$ True; (2, 9) is a solution.

b. $3y - x < -18$, (−3, −7)

SOLUTION

$3(-7) - (-3) \overset{?}{<} -18$

$-18 < -18$ False; (−3, −7) is not a solution.

c. $-2y \leq 1 - x$, (−3, 4)

SOLUTION

$-2(4) \overset{?}{\leq} 1 - (-3)$

$-8 \leq 4$ True; (−3, 4) is a solution.

Caution

A number can not be less than (or greater than) itself. In Example 2b, the point would be a solution if the inequality symbol were $\leq$ rather than $<$.

Online Connection www.SaxonMathResources.com

LESSON 39

1 Warm Up

For problem 4, remind students that the y-intercept occurs when $x = 0$.

2 New Concepts

In this lesson, students learn to solve two-variable, linear inequalities graphically.

Discuss the meaning of **boundary line** and **half-plane.** Explain that inequalities have an infinite number of solutions.

Example 1

Remind students that a solution to an inequality makes the inequality true.

Additional Example 1

Determine if each point is a solution of the inequality.

a. $y > 7 + 2x$, (0, 0) False

b. $-5y \leq 4x + 3$, (−1, 2) True

c. $2x - 3y \geq 7$, (−3, −1) False

MATH BACKGROUND

Students have had previous experience with graphing lines and testing solutions by substituting ordered pairs into an equation. In this lesson, this concept is expanded so that students are graphing and testing solutions for inequalities.

The benefits of using inequalities extend from algebra to geometry to real-life applications. Students may need to find the length of a side that can be "no more than $x + 3$." Students may need to find the number of purchases that can be made if they can spend "no less than y." Using the knowledge from graphing linear equalities, students can expand the concepts to linear inequalities.

LESSON RESOURCES

Student Edition Practice Workbook 39
Reteaching Master 39
Adaptations Master 39
Challenge and Enrichment Master C39

Example 2

Remind students that 0 can be a good choice when making a table of values.

Additional Example 2

Graph $-2y + 6 \geq 3x$ by making a table of values.

Step 1:

x	0	2	4	6
y	3	0	−3	−6

Steps 2 and 3:

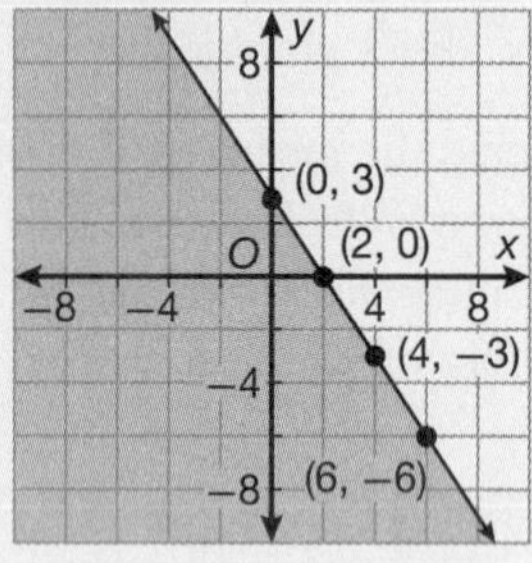

TEACHER TIP

Explain to students that the first step in graphing an inequality is to graph the boundary line. To graph the boundary line, rewrite the inequality with an equal sign. Then graph that line.

When graphing lines, students may have a 'favorite' way. Encourage them to use a variety of methods—making a table of values, finding the slope and y-intercept, finding a point and using the slope. If they use two methods on a single problem, they are providing an instant check.

Exploration Finding Solutions of Linear Inequalities on the Coordinate Plane

Graph $y = \frac{4}{3}x - 2$. Then graph each of the following points and tell if the point is *above the line, on the line,* or *below the line.*

$(6, 2), (-3, -6), (1, 4), (-5, -5), (0, -2), (4, -1)$ below, on, above, above, on, below

Which of the points satisfies $y < \frac{4}{3}x - 2$? How are these solutions related to the graph? (6, 2) and (4, −1), they are below the line

Which satisfy $y \geq \frac{4}{3}x - 2$? How are these solutions related to the graph? (−3, −6), (1, 4), (−5, −5), and (0, −2), they are above or on the line

Reading Math

A dashed line indicates that the points on the line are not solutions of the inequality. A solid line indicates that they are solutions.

The graph of a linear inequality in two variables is the set of all points that satisfy the inequality. To graph a linear inequality, first graph the related linear equation (just suppose the inequality sign is an equal sign). Make the line dashed when the symbol is $<$ or $>$ and solid when the symbol is $\leq$ or $\geq$. This line is the **boundary line.** It separates the plane into two **half-planes.** Shade the half-plane that includes the solutions of the inequality.

To determine which half-plane contains the solutions of the inequality, use a test point. If the test point satisfies the inequality, then all the points in the half-plane that contains the test point will also satisfy the inequality. The test point should not be a point on the boundary line. The point (0, 0) makes a good test point when it is not on the boundary.

Example 2 Using a Table of Values to Graph a Linear Inequality in Two Variables

Graph $3y + x \geq -9$ by making a table of values.

SOLUTION

Step 1: Find ordered pairs that satisfy the equation $3y + x = -9$. Use the x- and y-intercepts as well as other points.

x	0	−9	−6	−3	3
y	−3	0	−1	−2	−4

Step 2: Connect the points with a solid line.

Step 3: Use the test point (0, 0) to determine which half-plane to shade.

$$3y + x \geq -9$$

$$3(0) + 0 \overset{?}{\geq} -9$$

$$0 \geq -9 \quad \text{True}$$

The point (0, 0) is a solution. Shade the half-plane that contains (0, 0).

When the inequality is written in slope-intercept form, you can choose which half-plane to shade by looking at the direction of the inequality sign. Shade above the line for $>$ and $\geq$, and below the line for $<$ and $\leq$.

ENGLISH LEARNERS

To help students understand and remember the **< and > symbols,** first write the symbols and the appropriate words on the board. Be sure to say them as you point to them.

Then use this explanation. When reading from left to right, a reader encounters the small (or lesser) side of $<$ first. Consequently, $<$ is a 'less than' sign. When reading from left to right, a reader encounters the large (or greater) side of $>$ first. Consequently, $>$ is a 'greater than' sign.

Write (and say) a few simple relationships so students see the symbols used correctly.

$3 < 5$ and $5 > 3$; $-6 < 2$ and $2 > -6$

$-12 < -5$ and $-5 > -12$

Use words to show the symbols also. The 9th grade class has a greater number of students than the 12th grade class.

Number of 9th graders > Number of 12th graders.

Example 3 Using Slope-Intercept Form to Graph a Linear Inequality in Two Variables

a. Graph $5y + x < 20$ using slope-intercept form.

SOLUTION

Step 1: Write the inequality in slope-intercept form.

$$5y + x < 20$$
$$5y < -x + 20$$
$$y < -\frac{1}{5}x + 4$$

Step 2: Graph $y = -\frac{1}{5}x + 4$ by plotting (0, 4) and a second point by moving 1 unit down and 5 units right. Connect the points with a dashed line to indicate that the points on the line are not solutions.

Step 3: Shade below the line because the inequality symbol is <.

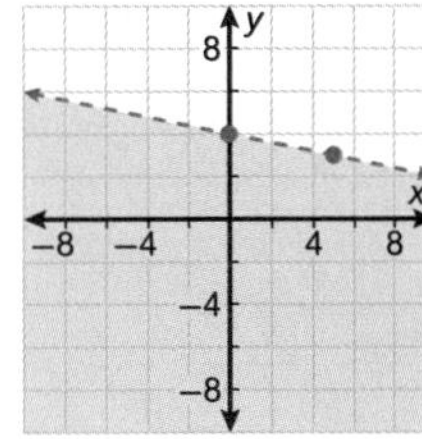

The test point (0, 0) verifies this.

$$5y + x < 20$$
$$5(0) + 0 \stackrel{?}{<} 20$$
$$0 < 20 \quad \text{True}$$

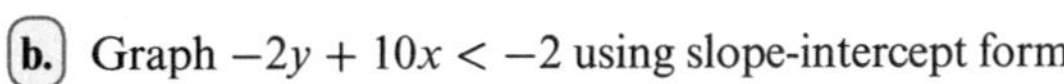

b. Graph $-2y + 10x < -2$ using slope-intercept form.

SOLUTION

Step 1: Write the inequality in slope-intercept form. Don't forget to switch the direction of the inequality sign when multiplying or dividing by a negative number.

$$-2y + 10x < -2$$
$$-2y < -10x - 2$$
$$y > 5x + 1$$

Step 2: Plot (0, 1) and find a second point by moving 5 units up and 1 unit right. Connect the points with a dashed line.

Step 3: Shade above the line because the inequality symbol is > in slope-intercept form.

The test point (0, 0) verifies this.

$$-2y + 10x < -2$$
$$-2(0) + 10(0) \stackrel{?}{<} -2$$
$$0 < -2 \quad \text{False}$$

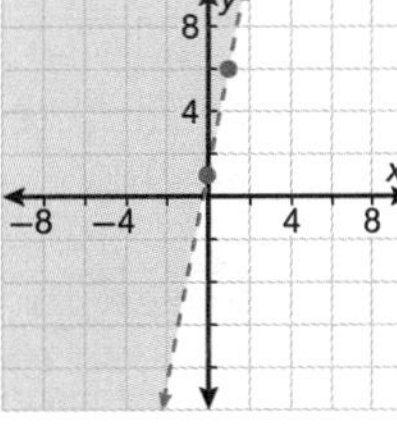

Hint

Look at the y-axis to help decide which half-plane is above the line.

ALTERNATE METHOD FOR EXAMPLE 3

Suggest that students graph the lines by making a table of values. Use at least three points to be sure that there are no calculation errors. Using $x = 0$ and $y = 0$ gives two of the easiest-to-graph points.

Or, have students check their work by using a graphing calculator. (See Example 4.)

Example 3

Review the slope-intercept form of a linear equation. Remind students that the inequality sign changes direction when multiplying or dividing by a negative number.

Additional Example 3

a. Graph $2x - 3y \geq 7$ using slope-intercept form.

Step 1: $y \leq \frac{2}{3}x - \frac{7}{3}$

Steps 2 and 3:

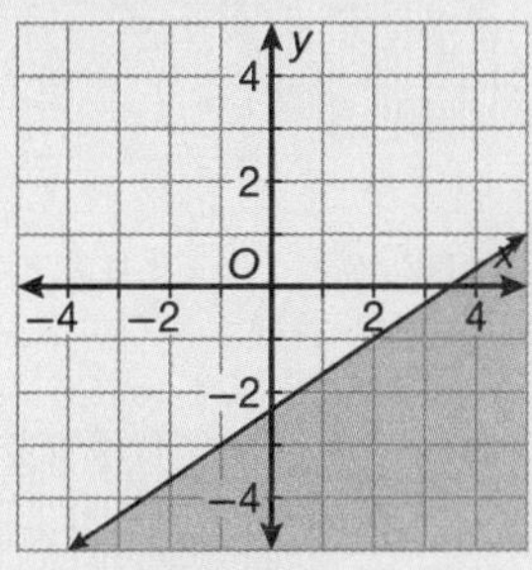

b. Graph $3x + 6y \leq 0$ using slope-intercept form.

Step 1: $y \leq -\frac{1}{2}x$

Steps 2 and 3:

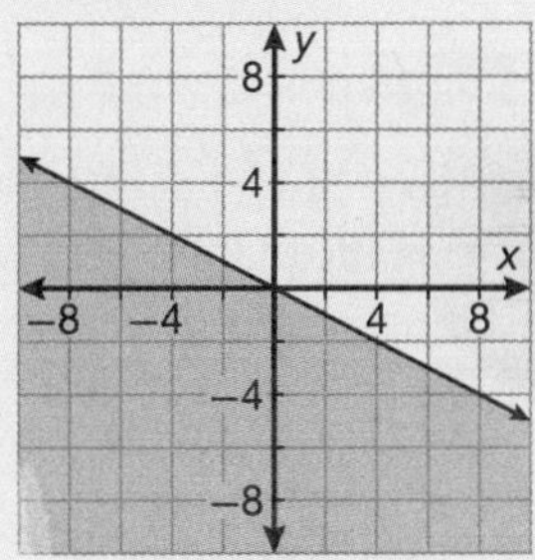

Extend the Example

Challenge students to graph $y \geq x^2$.

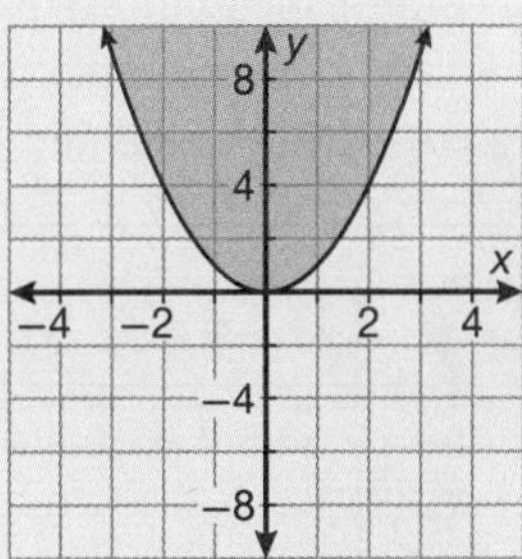

Example 4

Remind students that most graphing calculators require the equation to be in slope-intercept form before graphing.

Additional Example 4

a. Graph $4x - 2y \le 10$ on a graphing calculator.

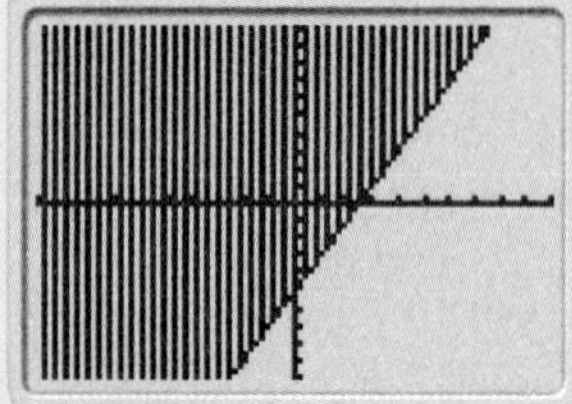

b. Graph $y > -x$ on a graphing calculator.

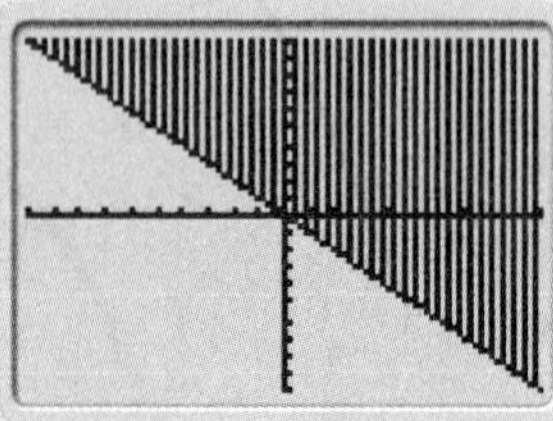

Example 5

Error Alert Students often write the wrong inequality signs when translating word problems to equations.

Additional Example 5

Tran is buying hamburger patties and veggie patties for a cookout. Hamburger patties cost 75¢ each. Veggie patties cost 60¢ each. Tran cannot spend more than \$30. Graph the inequality that represents the possible numbers of each type of patty.

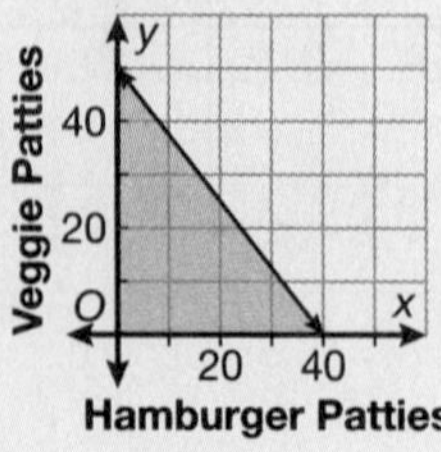

Example 4 **Using Technology to Graph a Linear Inequality in Two Variables**

a. Graph $y \le 4$ on a graphing calculator.

SOLUTION In the **[Y=]** editor, after y, enter 4. To indicate shading below the line, use the arrow key to highlight the symbol to the left of Y_1. Press enter until the symbol shows the lower left portion of the square shaded, then graph.

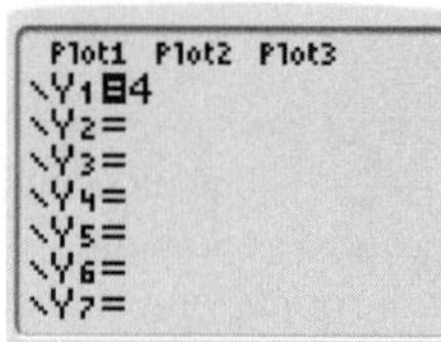

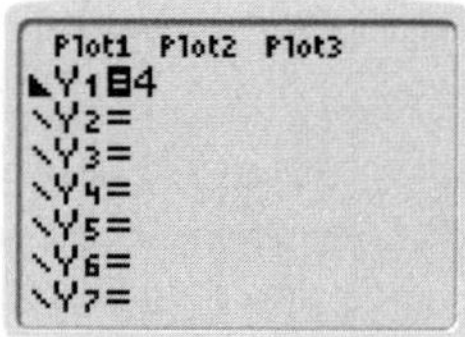

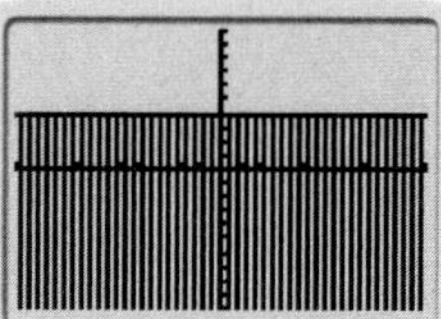

b. Graph $3x - y \le 2$ on a graphing calculator.

SOLUTION First write the inequality in slope-intercept form.

$$3x - y \le 2$$
$$-y \le -3x + 2$$
$$y \ge 3x - 2$$

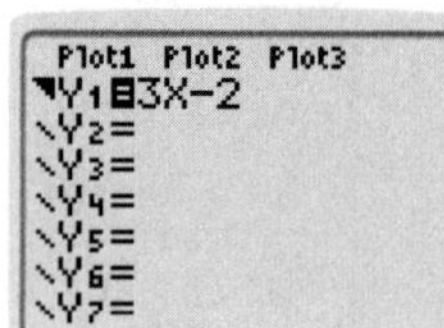

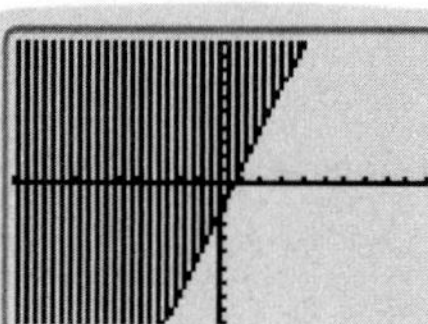

Example 5 **Application: Food Preparation**

Nellie is making a peanut butter and jelly snack for a school function. Each tablespoon of jelly has 15 grams of carbohydrates and each tablespoon of peanut butter has 3 grams of carbohydrates. She wants the snack to have no more than 90 grams of carbohydrates. Graph the inequality that represents the possible amounts of each ingredient.

SOLUTION Let x represent the tablespoons of jelly and y the tablespoons of peanut butter. The phrase *no more than* indicates *less than or equal to*. Then the inequality is $15x + 3y \le 90$.

Write $15x + 3y \le 90$ in slope-intercept form.

$$15x + 3y \le 90$$
$$3y \le -15x + 90$$
$$y \le -5x + 30$$

Graph $y = -5x + 30$ with a solid line. Shade below the line.

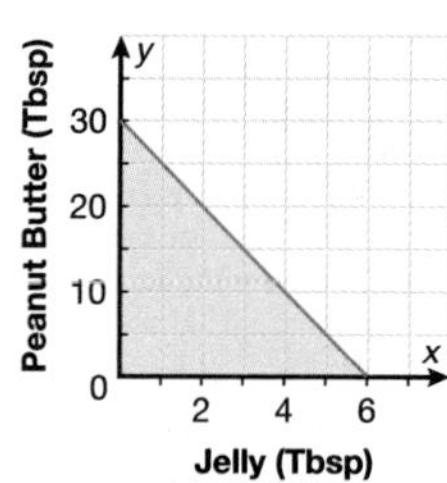

The inequality could also be graphed by plotting the points that contain the intercepts (0, 30) and (6, 0). The test point (0, 0) makes the original inequality true and should be in the solution set.

Math Reasoning

Analyze Do all the solutions make sense in context of the application? Explain.

No, only solutions in Quadrant I make sense because the number of tablespoons cannot be negative.

INCLUSION

Have students rephrase parts of word problems to help them understand the language of inequalities better. For example, students are likely to say, "I only have six dollars." That means that students can buy 'no more than' six dollars worth of goods.

Lesson Practice

d.

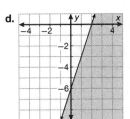

Determine if each point is a solution of the inequality.

a. $y \geq 7 - 4x, (-2, 1)$ no
(Ex 1)

b. $-2y + x < 0, (0, 0)$ no
(Ex 1)

c. $4y - 6x > 15, (4, 13)$ yes
(Ex 1)

d. Graph $2y - 6x \leq -12$ by making a table of values.
(Ex 2)

e. Graph $4y + 4 > x$ using slope-intercept form.
(Ex 3)

e.
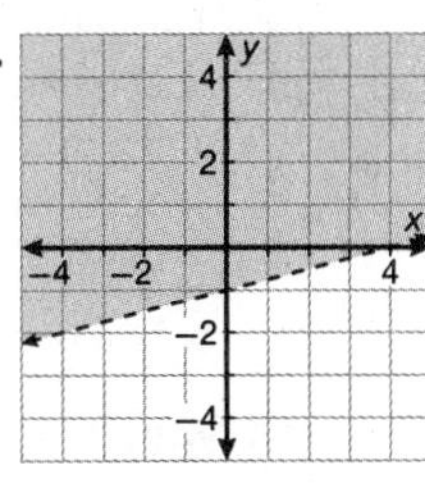

f. Graph $4 - 2y > -x$ using slope-intercept form.
(Ex 3) See Additional Answers.

g.

g. Graph $y \geq 0$ on a graphing calculator.
(Ex 4)

h. Graph $3y + 9 \geq 3x$ on a graphing calculator.
(Ex 4) See Additional Answers.

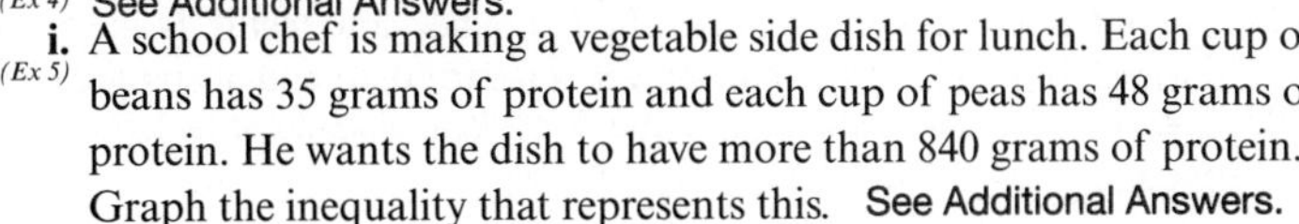

i. A school chef is making a vegetable side dish for lunch. Each cup of beans has 35 grams of protein and each cup of peas has 48 grams of protein. He wants the dish to have more than 840 grams of protein. Graph the inequality that represents this. See Additional Answers.
(Ex 5)

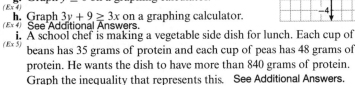

Practice Distributed and Integrated

Determine if the given points are solutions of the inequalities.

***1.** $y < 6x - 2, (3, 18)$ no
(39)

***2.** $y + 2x \geq -4, (-1, -2)$ yes
(39)

3. Add: $m + \frac{x}{c} + \frac{c}{x^2b}$ $\frac{mbcx^2 + bx^3 + c^2}{bcx^2}$
(20)

4. Solve. $\begin{aligned} -8x - 22 + 2y &= 2z \\ -6x + 2y &= 16 + z \\ 6 + 3y + z &= -x \end{aligned}$ (−3, −1, 0)
(29)

Solve by substitution:

5. $\begin{aligned} x &= y + 1 \\ 3x + 2y &= 8 \end{aligned}$ (2, 1)
(21)

6. $\begin{aligned} 3x - y &= 22 \\ 2x + 3y &= -11 \end{aligned}$ (5, −7)
(21)

7. $\begin{aligned} -7x + y &= 8 \\ 5x - y &= -6 \end{aligned}$ (−1, 1)
(21)

8. Divide $6x^3 + 23x^2 - 20x - 9$ by $3x + 1$. $2x^2 + 7x - 9$
(38)

9. Find the excluded values of $\frac{x^2 - 25}{3x^2 + 15x}$. 0, −5
(28)

10. Factor the polynomial $2x^4 + 4x^3 - 4x$. $2x(x^3 + 2x^2 - 2)$
(23)

11. Verify Show why the x's cannot be divided out in $\frac{x + 2}{x + 5}$.
(28)

***12. Multiple Choice** The graph of which inequality is shown? A
(39)

A $-3y - 4x \geq 24$ B $-3y - 4x \leq 24$

C $-3y - 4x > 24$ D $-3y - 4x < 24$

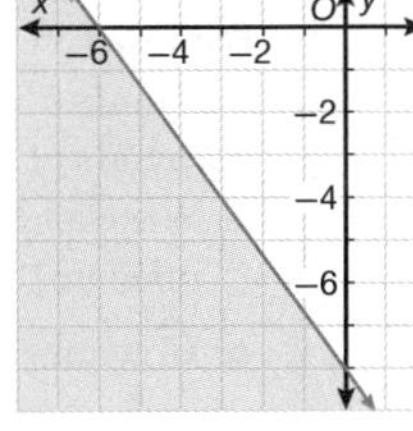

11. Possible answer: substitute 3 for x to see what happens: $\frac{\cancel{3} + 2}{\cancel{3} + 5} = \frac{2}{5}$ and $\frac{3 + 2}{3 + 5} = \frac{5}{8}$, and $\frac{2}{5} \neq \frac{5}{8}$.

Lesson Practice

Problem h

Scaffolding Tell students to write the inequality in slope-intercept form. Remind students to check a point to determine if their graph is correct.

Check for Understanding

The questions below help students see how this lesson builds on prior knowledge.

1. **"How is graphing a linear inequality similar to graphing a linear equation?"** You can graph a boundary line or a linear equation by making a table of values, or writing it in slope-intercept form.

2. **"What is the difference between graphing a linear inequality and graphing a linear equation?"** In graphing linear inequalities, you graph the line and then shade the appropriate area. Also, the line may be dashed or solid, depending on the sign.

3 Practice

Math Conversations

Discussions to strengthen understanding

Problem 9

Extend the Problem

"Write the simplified form of the expression." $\frac{x - 5}{3x}$

Problem 11

If students are struggling to start the problem, suggest that they substitute a number in for x, and verify it that way.

Problem 13

Error Alert

Students are likely to have difficulty setting up the initial equations. Have them list the possibilities (like the sneakers, don't like the sneakers, no opinion). Then have them write down the relationships that are given. Remind students that all categories must total 100%.

Problem 19

Students may need to sketch the graphs to help them visualize this problem.

*13. (37) **Statistics** The fraction of students who are interested in a new brand of sneakers is twice the fraction of those who are not. The fraction of students who are not interested is $\frac{1}{x}$. Those who expressed no opinion in the sneakers were 10% of the students who were interested. What percent of students were interested? 62.5%

14. (16) **Baseball Equipment** Last month, a baseball coach bought 4 bats and 9 balls for $355. This month, the coach bought 2 bats and a dozen balls for $290. The prices did not change from last month to this month. How much did each bat and ball cost?

a. Set up equations relating the monetary values of the bats and balls last month and this month. Let T represent the cost (in dollars) per bat, and B represent the cost per ball.

14a. $4T + 9B = 355$; $2T + 12B = 290$

b. Use Cramer's Rule to solve the system of equations. $T = \$55$ per bat; $B = \$15$

*15. (39) **Verify** Using the graph, choose a point in the shaded region and test it. Choose a point in the unshaded region and test it. Is the graph correct? Explain. Possible answer: shaded (0, 0) and unshaded (−4, 0), since $0 < 2$ is a true statement, and $4 < 2$ is a false statement, the graph is correct.

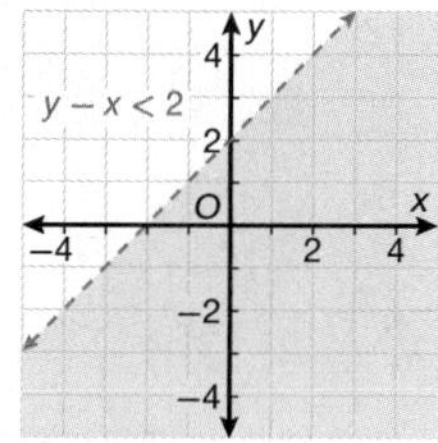

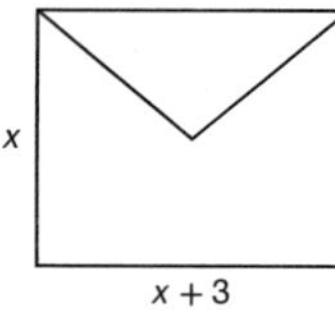
*16. (22) **Graphing Calculator** Graph $y = 4$ on your graphing calculator. Determine if this relation is a function. Determine if the graph is continuous, discontinuous, and/or discrete. continuous function

*17. (35) **U.S. Postal Service** The United States Postal Service uses size, shape, and weight to determine pricing for first class mail. One category of first class mail is large envelope. The maximum length of a large envelope is 3 inches greater than its maximum width, and its maximum area is 180 square inches. Write and solve a quadratic equation to find the maximum length and maximum width of a large envelope. See Additional Answers.

x / $x + 3$

18. (23) **Multi-Step** Use $x^2 + 8x - 48$.

a. Find the factors of −48.

18a. (1)(−48), (−1)(48), (2)(−24), (−2)(24), (3)(−16), (−3)(16), (4)(−12), (−4)(12), (6)(−8), (−6)(8)

b. Which of the factors have a sum of 8? −4 and 12

c. What is the factored form of the polynomial? $(x - 4)(x + 12)$

19. (34) **Multiple Choice** If the graph of $y = x$ is reflected over the x-axis, and then the resulting graph is translated 4 units up, which equation is represented by the final graph? **D**

A $y = -\frac{1}{4}x$ **B** $y = -4x$ **C** $y = x - 4$ **D** $y = -x + 4$

20. (21) **Multi-Step** A store sells granola and dried fruit by the pound. Dillon bought 4 pounds of granola and 2 pounds of dried fruit for $22. Carmen bought 2 pounds of granola and 4 pounds of dried fruit for $26.

a. Write a system of equations that represents the price of the granola, g, and the price of the dried fruit, f.

20a. $4g + 2f = 22$; $2g + 4f = 26$

b. How much should one pound of granola and one pound of dried fruit cost individually and together? $g = \$3$, $f = \$5$, $g + f = \$8$

CHALLENGE

Graph $y < x$ and $y > 5$ on the same axes. Use both the graph and the equations to determine if (7, 6) is a solution to both equations. Yes; $6 < 7$, $6 > 5$

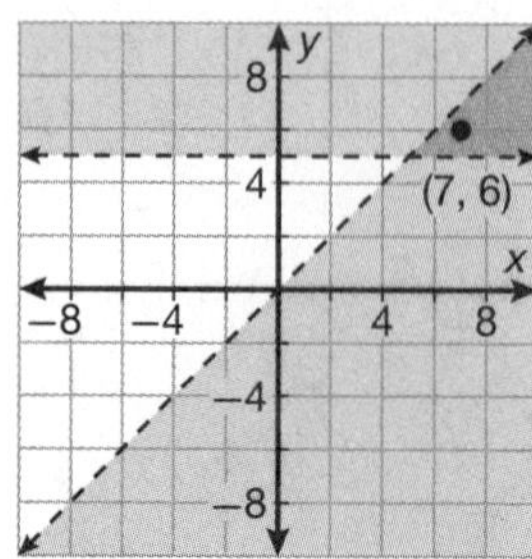

***21. Model** The figure at the right is a Venn diagram. It shows that jacks and clubs are not mutually exclusive events when choosing a card from a standard 52-card deck. Draw a Venn diagram to show that kings and hearts are not mutually exclusive events when choosing a card from a standard 52-card deck. See Additional Answers.
(33)

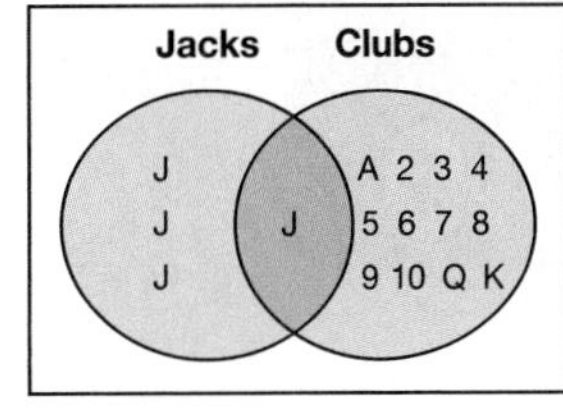

22. Analyze What system of equations is represented by the matrix equation shown below? Solve the system mentally.
(32)

$$\begin{bmatrix} 2 & 0 & 0 \\ 0 & 3 & 0 \\ 0 & 0 & 5 \end{bmatrix} \begin{bmatrix} x \\ y \\ z \end{bmatrix} = \begin{bmatrix} 10 \\ 12 \\ 50 \end{bmatrix}$$

$2x = 10$
$3y = 12$; The solution is $x = 5, y = 4, z = 10$.
$5z = 50$

23. Error Analysis A student divided rational expressions as follows: $\frac{20x^2}{y} \div \frac{y}{x^3} =$ $\frac{20x^2}{y} \div \frac{y}{x \cdot x^2} = \frac{20}{x}$. What error did the student make? Find the correct quotient.
(28)

23. The student did not multiply by the reciprocal. The correct quotient is $\frac{20x^5}{y^2}$.

***24. Model** Show that the ratio of an odd number to an even number, when each is expressed as a polynomial, has a nonzero remainder. $\frac{2n+1}{2n} = 1 + \frac{1}{2n}$, where $n \neq 0$
(38)

25. Verify Suppose a rocket is fired straight into the air such that the graph of the function representing the height of the rocket after x seconds has its vertex at (3.75, 225) and passes through the point (5, 200). Verify that the value of a in the equation written in vertex form is -16. See Additional Answers.
(30)

***26. Geometry** What is the ratio of the volume to the surface area for the rectangular prism shown? Does the ratio have a remainder? $\frac{x^3 + 16x^2 + 15x}{6x^2 + 64x + 30}$; yes, the ratio does have a remainder.
(38)

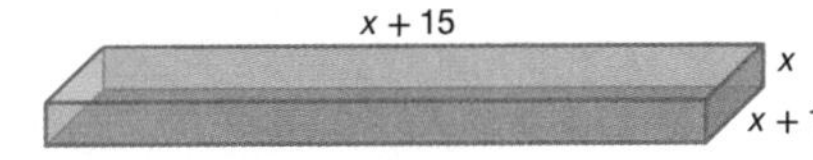

27. Investing A person invests \$50,000 for one year; some is invested at 7%, some at 8%, and the remainder at 12%. The combined interest earned at the end of the year from these investments was \$4,770. The amount invested at 8% is \$4,000 more than the amount invested at 7% and 12% combined. Find the amount of money invested at each rate. 7%: \$3,000; 8%: \$27,000; 12%: \$20,000
(29)

***28. Money** Nelson is building a tower of coins with half-dollars and dimes. He wants the tower to be less than 15 centimeters high. Each half dollar is 2.15 mm thick and each dime is 1.35 mm thick. Write an inequality that represents how many of each coin are needed. Then show how to use the inequality to see if using 30 half-dollars and 70 dimes is a possibility.
(39)

28. $2.15x + 1.35y < 150$ where x is the number of half-dollars and y is the number of dimes. 30 half-dollars and 70 dimes is not a possibility because the inequality becomes $159 < 150$ which is a false statement.

29. Business Mr. Jing makes and sells carved animals. His monthly profit function can be modeled by $f(x) = -0.15x^2 + 7x$ where x represents the number of carved animals he sells each month.
(27)

a. For how many animals does he make the maximum profit? How much profit is it? 23 animals, \$81.65

b. At what point would Mr. Jing begin to lose money? when he sells 47 animals

***30.** Write the equation of the line in slope intercept form that is parallel to $y = 5x - 3$ and goes through (1, 4). $y = 5x - 1$
(36)

Problem 24

Help students determine that they should represent an even number as $2x$. Two times any number will always give an even number.

Problem 25
Extend the Problem

Have students find the time t when the rocket will first hit the ground. 7.5 seconds

LOOKING FORWARD

Graphing linear inequalities in two variables prepares students for

- **Lesson 43** Solving Systems of Linear Inequalities
- **Lesson 89** Solving Quadratic Inequalities
- **Lesson 93** Solving Exponential Equations and Inequalities
- **Lesson 102** Solving Logarithmic Equations and Inequalities

LESSON 40

1 Warm Up

In problem 3, remind students that like terms must have the same variables with exactly the same exponents. Like terms are combined by adding coefficients.

2 New Concepts

In this lesson, students learn to simplify radical expressions by using the product rule or by rationalizing the denominator.

Example 1

Students find roots of numbers that are perfect nth powers.

Additional Example 1

Simplify each expression. Assume any variables are positive.

a. $\sqrt[3]{-0.008}$ -0.2

b. $\sqrt[3]{-\frac{27}{64}}$ $-\frac{3}{4}$

c. $\sqrt[4]{625}$ 5

LESSON 40

Simplifying Radical Expressions

Warm Up

1. (25) **Vocabulary** $\sqrt{16} = 4$. 4 is the ________ of 16. square root
2. (19) Multiply $(2x - 5)(2x + 5)$. $4x^2 - 25$
3. (2) Combine like terms: $3x^2 + 5x^3 - 8x^3 + x^2 - 5x^2$ $-3x^3 - x^2$
4. (3) Simplify $7^3 \cdot 7^2$ 16,807
5. (3) Simplify $(3^2)^3$ 729

New Concepts

Because $4^2 = 16$, 4 is a **square root** of 16. However, $(-4)^2 = 16$, so -4 is also a square root of 16. To indicate that the positive, or **principal,** square root is desired, the **radical symbol** is used. Therefore, $\sqrt{16}$ equals 4 and only 4. The expression under a radical sign is the **radicand.** $\sqrt{16}$ is a **radical,** or radical expression, and 16 is the radicand.

Math Reasoning

Analyze Why is -2 not a cube root of 8?

Because $(-2)^3 = -8$

There are roots other than square roots. For example, because $2^3 = 8$, 2 is a cube root of 8. Because $3^4 = 81$ and $(-3)^4 = 81$, -3 and 3 are fourth roots of 81.

n Roots
Given that a and b are real numbers and n is an integer greater than 1, if $a^n = b$, then a is an nth root of b.
Given that a and b are not negative and n is an even integer greater than 1, or given that a and b are real numbers and n is an odd integer greater than 1, if $a^n = b$, then $\sqrt[n]{b} = a$.

For $\sqrt[n]{b}$, n is the **index.** When n is not shown, it is assumed to be 2.

Example 1 Simplifying Radicals

Simplify each expression.

a. $\sqrt[5]{-32}$

SOLUTION $\sqrt[5]{-32} = -2$ because $(-2)^5 = -32$.

b. $\sqrt[3]{27}$

SOLUTION $\sqrt[3]{27} = 3$ because $3^3 = 27$.

c. $\sqrt[4]{16}$

SOLUTION $\sqrt[4]{16} = 2$ because $2^4 = 16$. Although -2 is a fourth root of 16, the radical sign indicates that only the positive root is to be given.

LESSON RESOURCES

Student Edition Practice Workbook 40
Reteaching Master 40
Adaptations Master 40
Challenge Enrichment Master C40, E40

MATH BACKGROUND

For every positive integer n, any solution of the equation $x^n = b$ is called an nth root of b and is indicated by the expression $\sqrt[n]{b}$. Roots are classified based on whether n is odd or even, and whether $b < 0$, $b = 0$, or $b > 0$. The situation is simple when $b = 0$, since $\sqrt[n]{b} = 0$ for all values of n. And, when n is odd, there is only one root. It is positive if $b > 0$ and negative if $b < 0$.

When n is even, defining the expression $\sqrt[n]{b}$ is a little more complicated. First of all, b must be positive for the expression to be a real number. For example, $\sqrt[6]{-64}$ is not defined in the set of real numbers, although in the set of complex numbers it has the value $2i$. Thus, for any real number b, $\sqrt[n]{b^n} = |b|$ when n is even. Notice that if $b \geq 0$, then $\sqrt{b^2} = b$. If $b < 0$, then $\sqrt{b^2} = -b$.

The Product Rule for Radicals
Given that a and b are real numbers and n is an integer greater than 1, $\sqrt[n]{ab} = \sqrt[n]{a} \cdot \sqrt[n]{b}$ and $\sqrt[n]{a} \cdot \sqrt[n]{b} = \sqrt[n]{ab}$

The product rule states that $\sqrt{10}$ can be written as $\sqrt{2} \cdot \sqrt{5}$. This rule is helpful when one of the radicals in the product can be simplified. For instance, $\sqrt{20} = \sqrt{4} \cdot \sqrt{5}$. Now, $\sqrt{4}$ can be simplified: $\sqrt{20} = 2\sqrt{5}$.

Types of Real Roots
If n is even, $\sqrt[a]{x^n} = x^{\frac{n}{a}}$.
If n is odd, $\sqrt[a]{x^n} = x^{\frac{n-1}{a}} \cdot \sqrt{x}$

Example 2 **Using the Product Rule for Radicands**

Simplify each expression.

a. $\sqrt{8} \cdot \sqrt{5}$

SOLUTION Either multiply and then simplify, or simplify and then multiply.

Option 1: $\sqrt{8} \cdot \sqrt{5} = \sqrt{40} = \sqrt{4} \cdot \sqrt{10} = 2\sqrt{10}$

Option 2: $\sqrt{8} \cdot \sqrt{5} = \sqrt{4} \cdot \sqrt{2} \cdot \sqrt{5} = 2\sqrt{2} \cdot \sqrt{5} = 2\sqrt{10}$

Caution

Simplifying before multiplying does not always mean that the product will not need to be simplified further.

b. $\sqrt[3]{54}$

SOLUTION

$\sqrt[3]{54} = \sqrt[3]{27} \cdot \sqrt[3]{2}$ Find a factor of 54 that has a cube root.

$= 3\sqrt[3]{2}$ The cube root of 27 is 3.

c. $\sqrt{567}$

SOLUTION

$$\begin{aligned}\sqrt{567} &= \sqrt{9 \cdot 63} \\ &= 3\sqrt{9 \cdot 7} \\ &= 3 \cdot 3\sqrt{7} \\ &= 9\sqrt{7}\end{aligned}$$

When radical expressions have the same radicand and index, they are **like radicals** and can be combined. This is analogous to combining like terms.

Combine like terms: $2x + 3x = 5x$

Combine like radicals: $2\sqrt{x} + 3\sqrt{x} = 5\sqrt{x}$

TEACHER TIP

If students are simplifying square roots, they should look for perfect square factors of the radicand. In most problems students encounter, the numerical factors will be 4, 9, or 25. If students are simplifying cube roots, they should look for perfect cube factors. The most frequently-encountered numerical factors will be 8, 27, and 64.

Example 2

Students use the product rule to simplify radical expressions.

Additional Example 2

Simplify each expression.

a. $\sqrt{3} \cdot \sqrt{6}$ $3\sqrt{2}$

b. $\sqrt[3]{750}$ $5\sqrt[3]{6}$

c. $\sqrt{176}$ $4\sqrt{11}$

Error Alert Students may write an expression such as $\sqrt{80}$ as $2\sqrt{20}$, failing to notice that there remains a factor of 4 in the radicand 20. Remind students to check answers for any more perfect square factors.

Extend the Example

Simplify by factoring.

a. $\sqrt{2x^2 + 12x + 18}$ $(x + 3)\sqrt{2}$

b. $\sqrt[3]{(a + b)^4}$ $(a + b)\sqrt[3]{a + b}$

ALTERNATE METHOD FOR EXAMPLE 2

Put a two-column chart on the board, labeling the columns *Number* and *Perfect Square.* Write 2, 3, and 5 in the first column and have students complete the second column. $2^2 = 4$, $3^2 = 9$, $5^2 = 25$ Explain that to simplify a square root, students should look for perfect square factors. So, the square root of any multiple of 4 can be simplified. Illustrate with $\sqrt{8}$, $\sqrt{20}$, and $\sqrt{40}$. $2\sqrt{2}$, $2\sqrt{5}$, $2\sqrt{10}$

Add the expressions x, x^2, x^3, and x^4 to the chart and have students write their squares. $(x)^2 = x^2$, $(x^2)^2 = x^4$, $(x^3)^2 = x^6$, $(x^4)^2 = x^8$

Point out that any variable with an even exponent is a perfect square. Illustrate this with an example such as $\sqrt{x^6} = \sqrt{x^3 \cdot x^3} = x^3$, where x is a non-negative real number. Model for students how to simplify variables with odd exponents using an example such as $\sqrt{x^7} = \sqrt{x^6 \cdot x} = x^3\sqrt{x}$.

Example 3

Students simplify radical expression by adding like radicals.

Additional Example 3

Simplify each expression. First simplify each term to identify any like radicals.

a. $8\sqrt{80} - 12\sqrt{45}$ $-4\sqrt{5}$

b. $5\sqrt[3]{32} - 2\sqrt[3]{108}$ $4\sqrt[3]{4}$

c. $8\sqrt{32} + 2\sqrt[4]{4} + \sqrt{2}$
$35\sqrt{3}$

Extend the Example

Show that there are real numbers for which this statement is false.

$\sqrt[3]{x} - \sqrt[3]{y} = \sqrt[3]{x - y}$ Sample: $x = 8, y = 1$

TEACHER TIP

Remind students to make the tops of the radical signs long enough to include the entire radicand. Point out that there is a difference between $\sqrt{8a}$ and $\sqrt{8}a$.

Example 3 **Combining Radical Expressions**

Simplify each expression.

a. $12\sqrt[3]{8} - \sqrt[3]{8} + 5\sqrt{8} + 9\sqrt{8}$

SOLUTION

$12\sqrt[3]{8} - \sqrt[3]{8} + 5\sqrt{8} + 9\sqrt{8}$

$= 11\sqrt[3]{8} + 14\sqrt{8}$ Combine like radicals.

$= 11 \cdot 2 + 14\sqrt{4} \cdot \sqrt{2}$ $\sqrt[3]{8} = 2$ and $\sqrt{8} = \sqrt{4}\sqrt{2}$.

$= 22 + 28\sqrt{2}$

b. $\sqrt{242} + \sqrt{72} - \sqrt{48}$

SOLUTION Simplify each term to identify any like terms.

$\sqrt{242} + \sqrt{72} - \sqrt{48}$

$= \sqrt{121} \cdot \sqrt{2} + \sqrt{36} \cdot \sqrt{2} - \sqrt{16} \cdot \sqrt{3}$ Use the Product Rule.

$= 11\sqrt{2} + 6\sqrt{2} - 4\sqrt{3}$ Simplify.

$= 17\sqrt{2} - 4\sqrt{3}$ Combine like terms.

c. $\sqrt[4]{32} + \sqrt[4]{2} + \sqrt[4]{162}$

SOLUTION

$\sqrt[4]{32} + \sqrt[4]{2} + \sqrt[4]{162}$

$= \sqrt[4]{16} \cdot \sqrt[4]{2} + \sqrt[4]{2} + \sqrt[4]{81} \cdot \sqrt[4]{2}$ Use the Product Rule.

$= 2\sqrt[4]{2} + \sqrt[4]{2} + 3\sqrt[4]{2}$ Take the fourth roots of 16 and 81.

$= 6\sqrt[4]{2}$ Combine like terms.

Hint

Make a list of square, cube, and fourth roots to look at while simplifying radicals.

All the concepts in this lesson can be extended to variables. Keep in mind, however, that for a positive root to be taken, a variable must represent a positive number. For example, the product rule can be used to expand a variable representing positive values as shown below:

$$\sqrt{x^6} = \sqrt{x^2} \cdot \sqrt{x^2} \cdot \sqrt{x^2} = x \cdot x \cdot x = x^3$$

Example 4 **Simplifying Radicals with Variables**

Simplify each expression. All variables represent non-negative real numbers.

a. $\sqrt{x^4}$

SOLUTION $\sqrt{x^4} = x^2$ because $(x^2)^2 = x^4$.

b. $\sqrt{18h^{17}}$

SOLUTION

$\sqrt{18h^{17}} = \sqrt{9} \cdot \sqrt{2} \cdot h^{\frac{17-1}{2}} \cdot \sqrt{h}$

$= 3 \cdot \sqrt{2} \cdot h^8 \cdot \sqrt{h}$

$= 3h^8\sqrt{2h}$

Hint

With conjugates, the middle two terms of the product will always be opposites.

ENGLISH LEARNERS

Contrast the instructions **simplify, evaluate,** and **approximate** as they are used with radical expressions.

To simplify is to factor out perfect powers from the number under the square root sign. Or, simplifying means to remove radicals from the denominator.

Example: $\sqrt{40} = \sqrt{4 \cdot 10} = 2\sqrt{10}$

To evaluate is to substitute a given number for a variable. Example: For $x = 8$, $\sqrt{5x} = \sqrt{40}$.

To approximate is to use a calculator to find a decimal value for a radical expression. Example: $6\sqrt{5} \approx 13.4164$

You may need to remind students that an irrational number such as $\sqrt{5}$ equals a decimal in which the digits go on forever and never form a repeating pattern.

c. $\sqrt[4]{48x} + \sqrt[4]{3x} + \sqrt[4]{243x}$

SOLUTION Simplify each term to identify any like terms.

$\sqrt[4]{48x} + \sqrt[4]{3x} + \sqrt[4]{243x}$

$= \sqrt[4]{16} \cdot \sqrt[4]{3x} + \sqrt[4]{3x} + \sqrt[4]{81} \cdot \sqrt[4]{3x}$ — Use the Product Rule.

$= 2\sqrt[4]{3x} + \sqrt[4]{3x} + 3\sqrt[4]{3x}$ — Take the fourth roots of 16 and 81.

$= 6\sqrt[4]{3x}$ — Combine like terms.

d. $\sqrt[4]{16x^2} + \sqrt{4x} + \sqrt[3]{27}$

SOLUTION

$\sqrt[4]{16x^2} + \sqrt{4x} + \sqrt[3]{27}$

$= \sqrt[4]{16} \cdot \sqrt[4]{x^2} + \sqrt{4} \cdot \sqrt{x} + 3$ — Use the Product Rule.

$= 2\sqrt[4]{x^2} + 2\sqrt{x} + 3$ — Take the indicated roots of 16 and 4.

$= 2x^{\frac{2}{4}} + 2\sqrt{x} + 3$ — Take the 4th root of x^2.

$= 2\sqrt{x} + 2\sqrt{x} + 3$ — Simplify

$= 4\sqrt{x} + 3$ — Combine like terms.

Example 5 Application: Physics

The pendulum in the Pantheon in Paris makes one complete swing in $\sqrt{\frac{110\pi^2}{4}}$ seconds. Simplify this expression.

The length of a pendulum is given by the equation $l = \frac{8s^2}{\pi^2}$, where l is the length in feet and s is the time in seconds the pendulum takes to make a complete swing. Using your simplified expression from the first part of the problem, write an expression to find the length of the pendulum and simplify it to find the length of the pendulum.

SOLUTION Simplify the expression using the product rule for radicals.

$\sqrt{\frac{110\pi^2}{4}} = \sqrt{\pi^2} \cdot \sqrt{\frac{1}{4}} \cdot \sqrt{110}$ — Use the Product Rule.

$\pi \cdot \frac{1}{2} \cdot \sqrt{110}$ — Take the indicated roots.

$\frac{\pi\sqrt{110}}{2}$ — Simplify.

Now, plug this expression into the formula given for the length of a pendulum.

$l = \frac{8s^2}{\pi^2}$

$$l = \frac{8\left(\frac{\pi\sqrt{110}}{2}\right)^2}{\pi^2} = \frac{8\left(\frac{\pi^2 110}{4}\right)}{\pi^2} = \frac{2\pi^2 110}{\pi^2} = 2 \cdot 110 = 220$$

So the pendulum is 220 feet long.

Example 4

Additional Example 4

Simplify each expression. All variables represent non-negative real number.

a. $\sqrt[3]{-y^6}$ $(-y)^2$

b. $\sqrt{50m^9}$ $5m^4\sqrt{2m}$

c. $\sqrt[3]{625a^5} + a\sqrt[3]{-40a^2}$ $3a\sqrt[3]{5a^2}$

d. $\sqrt[4]{y2^{16}} + 8\sqrt{y^8}$ $9y^4$

Example 5

Students use a radical expression to solve an application problem.

Additional Example 5

This formula gives the volume of a sphere in terms of the diameter.

$V = \frac{1}{6}\pi d^3$

a. Solve for the diameter in simplest form.
$d = \sqrt[3]{\frac{6V}{\pi}}$

b. How large a sphere is needed to hold one thousand cubic meters of water? Give the diameter to three decimal places. 12.407 m

Lesson Practice

Problem i

Error Alert When students substitute the expression for the time in seconds into the equation, they will have to square the entire expression. Students might not square some parts of the expression. Remind them to square each separate term; in this case, both $\sqrt{2\pi^4}$ and $\sqrt[4]{2}$.

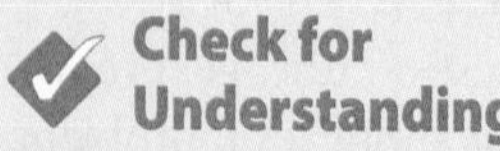

Check for Understanding

The questions below help assess the concepts taught in this lesson.

"When does a radical expression contain 'like radicals'?" Sample: When two or more of the radicals have the same radicand and root. The coefficients of the radicals may vary.

"When is a square root in simplest form?" Sample: The radicand has no perfect square factors.

3 Practice

Math Conversations

Discussions to strengthen understanding.

Problem 11

Error Alert

Check that students understand the resulting expression must be equivalent.

Multiplying by $\frac{1}{\sqrt[4]{3^3}}$ will rationalize the denominator, but the result won't be equivalent to the original expression. Emphasize students must multiply by a fraction equal to 1; in this case, $\frac{\sqrt[4]{3^3}}{\sqrt[4]{3^3}}$.

Lesson Practice

Simplify each expression. Assume all variables represent non-negative real numbers.

a. $\sqrt[3]{-125}$ -5 (Ex 1)

b. $-\sqrt{9}$ -3 (Ex 1)

c. $\sqrt[5]{-1}$ -1 (Ex 1)

d. $\sqrt{45} \cdot \sqrt{2}$ $3\sqrt{10}$ (Ex 2) **e.** $\sqrt[5]{64}$ $2\sqrt[5]{2}$ (Ex 2) **f.** $\sqrt{50} - \sqrt{32}$ $\sqrt{2}$ (Ex 3)

g. $\sqrt{98w^{10}}$ $7w^5\sqrt{2}$ (Ex 4) **h.** $-\sqrt[4]{y} + 2\sqrt{y} - 7\sqrt[4]{y} - \sqrt{y}$ (Ex 4)

h. $-8\sqrt[4]{y} + \sqrt{y}$

i. (Ex 5) Refer to the formula given in example 5. If a pendulum makes one complete swing in $\sqrt{2\pi^4} \cdot \sqrt[4]{2}$ seconds, write a simplified expression for the length of the pendulum. $16\pi^2\sqrt{2}$

Practice Distributed and Integrated

***1.** (39) Make a table of values to satisfy the inequality $2x - 4y \geq 12$.

1. Sample answer:

x	y
–1	–4
0	–3
1	–6

Write the equation in standard form for the line that crosses the two points.

2. (26) (4, 5.5), (–1, 2.5) $6x - 10y = -31$

3. (26) (3, 5), (6, 4) $x + 3y = 18$

Multiply then simplify.

***4.** (40) $\sqrt{30} \cdot \sqrt{6}$ $6\sqrt{5}$

***5.** (40) $\sqrt{180} \cdot \sqrt{10}$ $30\sqrt{2}$

Factor:

6. (23) $5x^2y^2 - 2xy + 10xy^2$ $xy(5xy - 2 + 10y)$

7. (23) $x^2y^3m^5 + 12x^3ym^4 - 3x^2y^2m^2$ $x^2ym^2(y^2m^3 + 12xm^2 - 3y)$

8. (20) Given the rational functions $f(x) = \frac{1}{x}$ and $g(x) = \frac{x^2}{x+4}$, find the value of $f(x) \cdot g(x)$ if $x = -2$. -1

Solve:

9. (35) $-x + x^2 = 12$ $4, -3$

10. (35) $-48x = -2x^2 - x^3$ $0, -8, 6$

***11.** (40) **Multi-Step a.** Expand the expression $\sqrt{x^8}$ as much as possible. Do not simplify.

b. Explain how can you rewrite your answer from part **a** so the expression can be easily simplified.

c. Simplify the expression as much as possible. The variable represents non-negative real numbers. x^4

11a. $\sqrt{x \cdot x \cdot x \cdot x \cdot x \cdot x \cdot x \cdot x}$

11b. Rewrite each pair of x's as x^2 so the square root can be taken easily: $\sqrt{x^2 \cdot x^2 \cdot x^2 \cdot x^2}$

12. (28) **Error Analysis** Explain and correct the error a student made below.

$$\frac{x^2}{x^5} = x^{5-2} = x^3$$

The student subtracted the exponents in the wrong order. The exponent of the denominator should be subtracted from the exponent in the numerator. $x^{2-5} = x^{-3} = \frac{1}{x^3}$.

CHALLENGE

A modern sculpture in a park will include a huge cube and sphere. They have the same surface area, 60 m^2. Use this information to find exact values for the following. Hint: For the sphere, $S = 4\pi r^2$ and $V = \frac{4}{3}\pi r^3$.

a. edge of the cube $\sqrt{10}$ m

b. volume of the cube $10\sqrt{10}$ m³

c. radius of the sphere $\frac{\sqrt{15\pi}}{\pi}$ m

d. volume of the sphere $\frac{20\sqrt{15\pi}}{\pi}$ m³

e. ratio of volume of cube to volume of sphere $\frac{\sqrt{6\pi}}{6}$

13. **Multiple Choice** If $A = \begin{bmatrix} 2 & 3 \\ 3 & 4 \end{bmatrix}$ and $B = \begin{bmatrix} -1 & 2 \\ 5 & 0 \end{bmatrix}$, what is the solution to the matrix equation $AX = B$? **A**
(32)

A $X = \begin{bmatrix} 19 & -8 \\ -13 & 6 \end{bmatrix}$ **B** $X = \begin{bmatrix} 11 & -8 \\ -13 & 6 \end{bmatrix}$

C $X = \begin{bmatrix} 19 & 8 \\ -13 & 6 \end{bmatrix}$ **D** $X = \begin{bmatrix} 19 & -8 \\ 13 & 6 \end{bmatrix}$

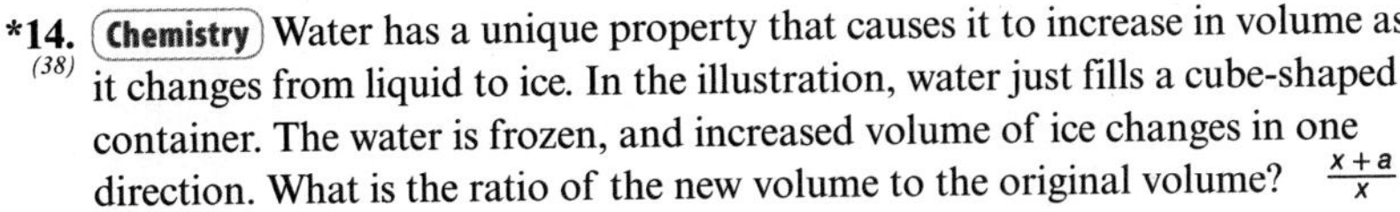

***14.** **(Chemistry)** Water has a unique property that causes it to increase in volume as it changes from liquid to ice. In the illustration, water just fills a cube-shaped container. The water is frozen, and increased volume of ice changes in one direction. What is the ratio of the new volume to the original volume? $\frac{x+a}{x}$
(38)

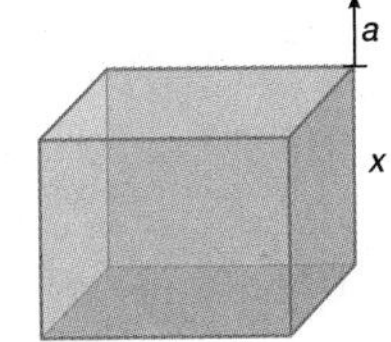

15. **Multiple Choice** Subtract. $\frac{2}{x^2 - 4x - 45} - \frac{1}{x^2 + 9x + 20}$ **B**
(37)

A $\frac{x+17}{x^2 - 61x - 180}$ **B** $\frac{x+17}{x^3 - 61x - 180}$ **C** $\frac{1}{x^3 - 61x - 180}$ **D** $\frac{1}{x^2 - 61x - 180}$

16. **Error Analysis** A chemist weighs samples obtained from a production run. The weights of the samples are 12 g, 14 g, 65 g, 11 g, 15 g, 12 g, 13 g, 15 g, 14 g, and 11 g. She eliminated the outlier and calculated the mean of the data. What is her error?
(25)

The denominator should be 9 instead of 10, since the outlier was eliminated.

$$\overline{x} = \frac{12 + 14 + 11 + 15 + 12 + 13 + 15 + 14 + 11}{10} = \frac{117}{10} = 11.7$$

17. **Geometry** For the circle shown, the line $y_1 = \frac{4}{3}x + \frac{1}{3}$ passes through the center of the circle at (2, 3). How do you know that the equation of the tangent at (−2, 6) is parallel to y_1? Since the slope from the center to (−2, 6) is $-\frac{3}{4}$, the line perpendicular to y_1 crosses (−2, 6). Since a tangent is perpendicular to the circle, then the line crossing (−2, 6) is parallel to y_1
(36)

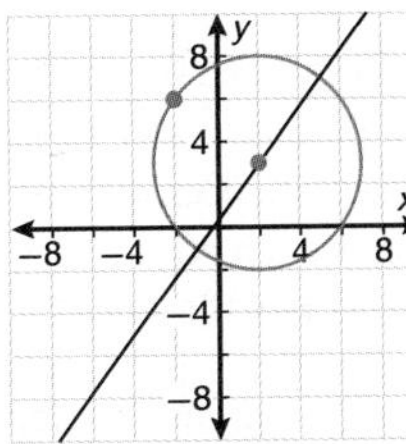

18. **Predict** Use your knowledge of the factoring formulas to find the product of $(5x^6 + 3)$ and $(5x^6 - 3)$ without multiplying the polynomials. Explain your prediction. $25x^{12} - 9$; Since the two factors fit the factored form of the difference of 2 squares, use the formula in reverse.
(23)

19. **Analyze** Does the table of values represent a linear function? Explain your answer without graphing.
(34)

x	−4	0	2	8
y	11	5	2	−7

20. **(Sports)** There are 4 teams in the National Football Conference East division. How many ways can the teams finish in first, second, third, and fourth place? 24
(33)

21. **Write** Describe how to graph $y - 1 \leq 5x$ on a graphing calculator.
(39)

21. First write the inequality in slope-intercept form: $y \leq 5x + 1$. Type $5x + 1$ next to Y. Move to the left of Y and press enter until the symbol shows the lower half of a square shaded. Then press the Graph key. Adjust the viewing window if needed.

19. Yes. Possible explanation: The rate of change is constant. The rates of change are listed below.
from (−4, 11) to (0, 5): $\frac{5-11}{0+4} = \frac{-6}{4} = -\frac{3}{2}$;
from (0, 5) to (2, 2): $\frac{2-5}{2-0} = \frac{-3}{2} = -\frac{3}{2}$;
from (2, 2) to (8, −7): $\frac{-7-2}{8-2} = \frac{-9}{6} = -\frac{3}{2}$

Problem 13

You may need to review multiplication of 2 × 2 matrices. If $A = \begin{bmatrix} a_1 & b_1 \\ a_2 & b_2 \end{bmatrix}$ and $B = \begin{bmatrix} c_1 & d_1 \\ c_2 & d_2 \end{bmatrix}$, then the product $A \times B = \begin{bmatrix} a_1c_1 + b_1c_2 & a_1d_1 + b_1d_2 \\ a_2c_1 + b_2c_2 & a_2d_1 + b_2d_2 \end{bmatrix}$.

Problem 17

Suggest that students start by finding the slope of the line through the points (−2, 6) and (2, 3). $m = \frac{6-3}{-2-2} = -\frac{3}{4}$

This shows the radius that connects (−2, 6) and (2, 3) is perpendicular to line y_1 because their slopes are negative reciprocals. So, both y_1 and the tangent line through (−2, 6) and (2, 3) are perpendicular to the radius that connects (−2, 6) and (2, 3).

Problem 18

Error Alert

The formula students need is $(a + b)(a - b) = (a^2 - b^2)$. Remind students to square both the coefficient and the variable term when squaring $5x^6$.

INCLUSION

Some students may not understand why they cannot just use a calculator to simplify a radical expression. Write on the board $\sqrt{4} \times \sqrt{2}$. Ask students to write some different names for this expression. Possibilities include $\sqrt{8}$, $2\sqrt{2}$, $\sqrt{4 \cdot 2}$, and $\sqrt{2^3}$.

Then have students use a calculator to find an approximation for $\sqrt{8}$ that includes as many decimal places as possible; for example, 2.8284271247. Point out that the digits are not making a repeating pattern. Emphasize that this is not an exact value for $\sqrt{8}$, it is only an approximation. In some practical applications, the difference between exact and approximate can be quite important.

Problem 22

Extend the Problem

Compare the area of the circle to that of an equilateral triangle with side s. The area formula is $A = \frac{s^2}{4}\sqrt{3}$. area of triangle is $\frac{x^2\sqrt{3}}{36}$; ratio of circle area to triangle area is $\frac{3\sqrt{3}}{\pi}$; circle area is 165% of triangle area

Problem 29

You may want to point out that $\sqrt[n]{b}$ is negative for any odd value of n when $b = -1$. To demonstrate this, point out that $(-1)^3 = -1$, $(-1)^5 = -1$, $(-1)^7 = -1$, and so on.

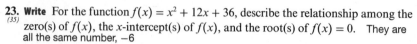

22. (31) **Multi-Step** Consider this question: Which is the larger area that a piece of rope of length x will enclose, a circle or a square?

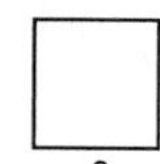

a. Write a simplified expression for the area of the circle in terms of x. $\frac{x^2}{4\pi}$

b. Write a simplified expression for the area of the square in terms of x. $\frac{x^2}{16}$

c. Which area is larger? Find the ratio of the areas.

d. Express the larger area as a percent of the smaller area. Round to the nearest percent. The circle area is 127% of the square area.

22c. The circle area is larger. The ratio of the circle area to the square area is $\frac{16}{4\pi}$.

23. (35) **Write** For the function $f(x) = x^2 + 12x + 36$, describe the relationship among the zero(s) of $f(x)$, the x-intercept(s) of $f(x)$, and the root(s) of $f(x) = 0$. They are all the same number, -6

***24.** (27) **Graphing Calculator** Determine the vertex of the function $f(x) = x^2 - 6x + 1$ using a graphing calculator. $(3, -8)$

***25.** (40) **Biology** The metabolism rate of an 18 pound animal is approximately $73\sqrt[4]{625}$ Calories per day. Simplify the metabolism rate. About 365 Calories per day

26. (24) **Work** In one month, Angela worked a total of 20 hours, some of it spent babysitting and the rest spent washing cars. She earned a total of \$96.25. If she gets paid \$5.50 per hour for babysitting and \$2.75 per hour for washing cars, how many hours of each type of work did she do? 15 hrs babysitting, 5 hrs washing cars

27. (39) **Sports** In American football, a touchdown with a conversion is worth 7 points and a field goal is worth 3 points. Suppose the only scoring in a game was due to touchdowns with conversions and field goals. Write the inequality that represents how many of each could have occurred if the total number of points earned in the game was less than or equal to 105. Give a solution that would be on the boundary line if the inequality were graphed. $7x + 3y \leq 105$, Possible answer: 12 touchdowns with conversions and 7 field goals

28. (21) **Coordinate Geometry** You are given equations of three lines on a coordinate grid that intersect to form a triangle. Explain in words how you could find the vertices of the triangle.

28. Solve a system of two of the equations using substitution to calculate the x and y coordinates of one vertex. Repeat with a different pair of equations from the set. Repeat with the last pair of equations. Those will be the three vertices of the triangle.

***29.** (40) **Verify** Supply two examples to show that b and the value of $\sqrt[n]{b}$ can be negative when n is odd. $\sqrt[3]{-125} = -5$ and $\sqrt[7]{-1} = -1$

***30.** (26) **Aviation** The Federal Aviation Administration tracks airline delays for airports around the country. From the beginning of the year to the end of March, there were 6,000 delays at Atlanta-Hartsfield Airport. By the end of May, there were 10,000 cumulative delays. Use this information to write an equation in slope-intercept form that could be used to predict the total delays throughout the year. Let x equal the month of the year as a number and y equal the cumulative delays. $y = 2000x$

CHALLENGE

Factor each of the following completely over the set of polynomials with real coefficients.

a. $g^2 - 27$ $(g + 3\sqrt{3})(g - 3\sqrt{3})$

b. $x^2 + 10\sqrt{2}x + 50$ $(x + 5\sqrt{2})^2$

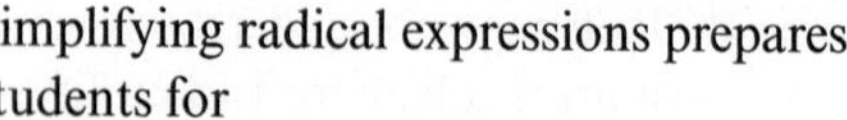

Simplifying radical expressions prepares students for

- **Lesson 44** Rationalizing Denominators
- **Lesson 48** Understanding Complex Fractions
- **Lesson 59** Using Fractional Exponents
- **Lesson 70** Solving Radical Equations
- **Lesson 75** Graphing Radical Functions

INVESTIGATION 4

Understanding Cryptography

Computer Internet security is a top priority for governments and private companies. For information to be secure, it needs to be encrypted when sent out over the Web and decrypted when received. This way only the sender and receiver know the contents of the message. In the area of cryptography, different methods of keeping messages secure have been developed.

One of the simplest ways of encrypting a message is to use a substitution cipher. A number replaces each letter of the alphabet, so that all messages consist of a string of numbers. Without the cipher, it is difficult to decipher the message.

Use a spreadsheet to create a substitution cipher.

1. Use the cipher in the table below and transfer it to a spreadsheet. Input the letters A–Z in cells A1 to A26, and input the numeric cipher in B1 to B26. See student work.

A	B	C	D	E	F	G	H	I	J	K	L	M	N	O	P	Q	R	S	T	U	V	W	X	Y	Z
1	3	5	7	9	11	13	15	17	19	21	23	25	2	4	6	8	10	12	14	16	18	20	22	24	26

The cipher is the key to encrypting and decrypting messages. A spreadsheet automates the process of using such a cipher.

Math Reasoning

Generalize Suppose you wanted the cipher to include word spaces and special characters. How would you change the cipher?

Assign a number to each of those symbols.

2. Input the letters of the words SECRET MESSAGE in cells D1 through D13. The space between the words is not encrypted. See student work.
3. The VLOOKUP formula searches for a value in the leftmost column of the table (A) and then returns a value in the same row from a column you specify (B). Input this formula into cell E1: **=VLOOKUP(D1,$A$1:$B$26,2).** Then copy and paste the formula into cells E2 to E13. See student work.

	A	B	C	D	E
1	A	1		S	=VLOOKUP(D1,$A$1:$B$26,2)
2	B	3		E	
3	C	5		C	
4	D	7		R	
5	E	9		E	
6	F	11		T	
7	G	13		M	
8	H	15		E	
9	I	17		S	
10	J	19		S	
11	K	21		A	
12	L	23		G	
13	M	25		E	
14	N	2			
15	O	4			
16	P	6			
17	Q	8			
18	R	10			
19	S	12			
20	T	14			
21	U	16			
22	V	18			
23	W	20			
24	X	22			
25	Y	24			
26	Z	26			

INVESTIGATION 4

Materials

Pencil, Paper, Computer spreadsheet, Graphing Calculator

Discuss

Students investigate cryptography by creating ciphers, encrypting and decrypting code. Spreadsheets and graphing calculators help to streamline the process. Encoding matrices are used to create a more secure coding method.

Discuss the definitions of cryptography, encrypt, decrypt, and cipher

TEACHER TIP

A cipher is an invention of the cryptographer. This cipher is just one example of an infinite number of ciphers that can be created.

VLOOKUP is a function of the spreadsheet that will match each letter with the assigned value of the cipher.

Problems 1–3

Extend the Problem

Create a substitution cipher that assigns each letter, number and symbol on the keyboard to a value. Use a spreadsheet to create this cipher.

MATH BACKGROUND

The word cryptography is derived from the Greek and means "hidden", and "to write or to speak". The study of cryptography refers to coding or the analysis of codes. Before the 20th century, cryptography dealt with communication secrecy used by military and political leaders and spies. Early Christians used this science to escape persecution for their religious writing. Since the early 20th century, the invention of mechanical encryption devices improved upon the crude ciphers and devices used in ancient Greece. The development of computers has lead to the creation of complex ciphers and has changed the face of cryptography. It is now a branch of mathematics, computer science, and engineering.

4. Write the encrypted message as a string of numbers. 12 9 5 10 9 14 25 9 12 12 1 13 9

5. Use the spreadsheet to encrypt the following messages. List the message as a string of numbers. If necessary, copy and paste the spreadsheet formula to more cells.

   a. QUADRATIC 8 16 1 7 10 1 14 17 5

   b. ALGEBRA 1 23 13 9 3 10 1

The spreadsheet you created can be used to encrypt messages. A variation of this spreadsheet can be used to decrypt messages. Suppose your teacher has sent you the following message using the same encryption cipher.

8 16 17 26 14 15 17 12 11 10 17 7 1 24

You need to create a decryption spreadsheet.

6. **Multi-Step** Create a new spreadsheet. Check students' work for parts a–c.

   a. Input the numeric cipher *in ascending order* to cells A1 to A26, and input the alphabet to B1 to B26. The letters will no longer be in alphabetical order.

   b. Input the encrypted message above to cells D1 to D14.

   c. Input this formula into cell E1: **=VLOOKUP(D1,$A$1:$B$26,2).** Then copy and paste the formula into cells E2 to E14.

	A	B	C	D	E
1	1	A		8	=VLOOKUP(D1,$A$1:$B$26,2)
2	2	N		16	
3	3	B		17	
4	4	O		26	
5	5	C		14	
6	6	P		15	
7	7	D		17	
8	8	Q		12	
9	9	E		11	
10	10	R		10	
11	11	F		17	
12	12	S		7	
13	13	G		1	
14	14	T		24	
15	15	H			
16	16	U			
17	17	I			
18	18	V			
19	19	J			
20	20	W			
21	21	K			
22	22	X			
23	23	L			
24	24	Y			
25	25	M			
26	26	Z			

   d. What is your teacher's message? QUIZ THIS FRIDAY

An additional level of security can be added to the substitution cipher. This involves using matrix multiplication.

7. Encrypt the following message using the cipher you previously produced. TOP SECRET MESSAGE 14 4 6 12 9 5 10 9 14 25 9 12 12 1 13 9

Problem 5

Pasting each example in separate cells would allow students and the teacher to monitor progress easily.

How could you check your answers by examining the numbers?

The assignment of numbers to letters should be consistent. Also, in the Mississippi River example, repeated letters should result in repeated numbers.

TEACHER TIP

Notice that the command used in example 6 E1:=**VLOOKUP** (D1,$A$1:$B$26, 2) is the same as in the encryption example 3. The function **VLOOKUP** treats numbers and letters the same. In each example, it accesses the cells where the cipher is located.

Problem 7

The same process is used in question 7 that was used in questions 6 and 3.

Extend the Problem

Code a message to a classmate and have him/her use the spreadsheet to decrypt the message.

Have each student create their own cipher for the letters $A - Z$. They then will encrypt a message and challenge the class to break their code.

TEACHER TIP

Stress the importance of a secure code. Students should realize the importance of protecting their personal information.

ENGLISH LEARNERS

Define **encrypt** and **decrypt**. Say:

"To encrypt means to change text into code. To decrypt means to decode or change code into text."

Indicate that the science of cryptography has been used since the beginning of time to communicate secretly with other people. Discuss uses of cryptography such as communication during wartime, protecting the government, the World Bank, and all financial institutions.

8. Write the string of numbers in two 3 × 3 cipher matrices. The first number goes in the first row first column, the second number goes in the second row first column. The first matrix is started. Complete the two matrices.

$$\begin{bmatrix} 14 & 12 & \_ \\ 4 & \_ & \_ \\ 6 & \_ & \_ \end{bmatrix}\begin{bmatrix} 25 & \_ & \_ \\ 9 & \_ & \_ \\ \_ & \_ & \_ \end{bmatrix} \quad \begin{bmatrix} 14 & 12 & 10 \\ 4 & 9 & 9 \\ 6 & 5 & 14 \end{bmatrix}\begin{bmatrix} 25 & 12 & 9 \\ 9 & 1 & 0 \\ 12 & 13 & 0 \end{bmatrix}$$

9. **Graphing Calculator** Multiply the cipher matrices by the encoding matrix shown below.

$$\begin{bmatrix} 1 & -1 & 2 \\ 0 & 0 & -5 \\ 2 & -3 & 2 \end{bmatrix} \quad \begin{bmatrix} 34 & -44 & -12 \\ 22 & -31 & -19 \\ 34 & -48 & 15 \end{bmatrix}\begin{bmatrix} 43 & -52 & 8 \\ 9 & -9 & 13 \\ 12 & -12 & -41 \end{bmatrix}$$

10. 34 22 34 −44 −31 −48 −12 −19 15 43 9 12 −52 −9 −12 8 13 −41

10. Write the newly encrypted message as a string of numbers.

11. **Analyze** Why is this encryption method more secure than a substitution cipher? The matrix product creates a message that cannot be hacked one letter at a time.

Decrypting a message using the cipher-matrix system requires that you know both the encrypted and the encoding matrices. Suppose your teacher has a message encoded in the encrypted matrices:

$$\begin{bmatrix} 38 & -50 & -8 \\ 39 & -51 & -71 \\ 19 & -20 & -9 \end{bmatrix}\begin{bmatrix} 23 & -28 & -24 \\ 41 & -57 & -10 \\ 37 & -47 & 9 \end{bmatrix}\begin{bmatrix} 9 & -9 & 18 \\ 0 & 0 & 0 \\ 0 & 0 & 0 \end{bmatrix}$$

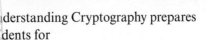

12. **Graphing Calculator** Follow these steps to decrypt the message.

a. Store the encoding matrix in your calculator as matrix [A].

b. Store the encrypted matrices as separate matrices in the calculator.

c. Multiply each encrypted matrix by the inverse of the encoding matrix.

d. Write the partially decrypted message as a string of numbers.

e. Use the decryption spreadsheet to decipher the message. What is the message? THIS MESSAGE IS SECURE

12d. 14 15 17 12 25 9 12 12 1 13 9 17 12 12 9 5 16 10 9

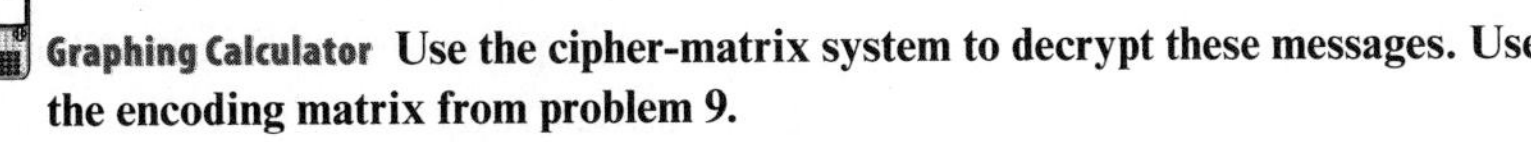

Investigation Practice

Graphing Calculator **Use the cipher-matrix system to decrypt these messages. Use the encoding matrix from problem 9.**

a. $\begin{bmatrix} 16 & -17 & -30 \\ 25 & -30 & -45 \\ 25 & -29 & -18 \end{bmatrix}\begin{bmatrix} 31 & -43 & -87 \\ 11 & -12 & -25 \\ 33 & -46 & -20 \end{bmatrix}\begin{bmatrix} 9 & -9 & 18 \\ 0 & 0 & 0 \\ 0 & 0 & 0 \end{bmatrix}$ THIS IS A CODED MESSAGE

b. $\begin{bmatrix} 38 & -50 & 22 \\ 55 & -75 & 65 \\ 17 & -21 & -34 \end{bmatrix}\begin{bmatrix} 38 & -52 & -12 \\ 27 & -37 & -91 \\ 51 & -68 & 63 \end{bmatrix}\begin{bmatrix} 22 & -22 & 44 \\ 0 & 0 & 0 \\ 0 & 0 & 0 \end{bmatrix}$ THE PASSWORD IS MATRIX

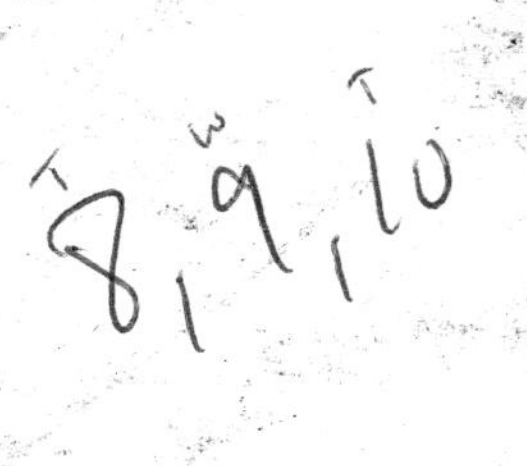

LOOKING FORWARD

Understanding Cryptography prepares students for

- **Lesson 54** Using Linear Programming

Problem 8

Tell students to use 0 as a placeholder in a matrix.

Problem 9

This is an example of an encoding matrix which is created by the cryptographer.

Problem 12

b. Write the matrices on paper before entering the values into the calculator.

c. Multiply the cipher matrix by the encoding matrix to encrypt a message and multiply the encrypted matrix by the inverse of the encoding matrix to decrypt a message.

d. Start with the value in row 1 and column 1. Continue moving down the column, row by row.

e. Follow the process in example 6.

Investigation Practice

Math Conversations

Discussion to strengthen understanding

Problem a

To use the command E1: = VLOOKUP(D1,$A$1:$B$26, 2) cells A, B, D, and E must be used.

Problem b

Multiply your matrices by the given encoding matrix.

Lesson Planner

Lesson	New Concepts
41	Using the Pythagorean Theorem and the Distance Formula
LAB 7	*Graphing Calculator Lab:* Calculating Permutations and Combinations
42	Finding Permutations and Combinations
43	Solving Systems of Linear Inequalities
44	Rationalizing Denominators
LAB 8	*Graphing Calculator Lab:* Applying Linear and Median Regression
45	Finding the Line of Best Fit
	Cumulative Test 8, Performance Task 8
46	Finding Trigonometric Functions and their Reciprocals
47	Graphing Exponential Functions
48	Understanding Complex Fractions
49	Using the Binomial Theorem
50	Finding Inverses of Relations and Functions
	Cumulative Test 9, Performance Task 9
INV 5	Investigation: Finding the Binomial Distribution

Resources for Teaching

- Student Edition
- Teacher's Edition
- Student Edition eBook
- Teacher's Edition eBook
- Resources and Planner CD
- Solutions Manual
- Instructional Masters
- Technology Lab Masters
- Warm Up and Teaching Transparencies
- Instructional Presentations CD
- Online activities, tools, and homework help **www.SaxonMathResources.com**

Resources for Practice and Assessment

- Student Edition Practice Workbook
- Course Assessments
- Standardized Test Practice
- College Entrance Exam Practice
- Test and Practice Generator CD using ExamView™

Resources for Differentiated Instruction

- Reteaching Masters
- Challenge and Enrichment Masters
- Prerequisite Skills Intervention
- Adaptations for Saxon Algebra 2
- Multilingual Glossary
- English Learners Handbook
- TI Resources

Pacing Guide

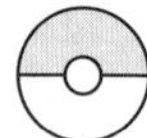
Resources and Planner CD for lesson planning support

45-Minute Class

Day 1	Day 2	Day 3	Day 4	Day 5	Day 6
Lesson 41	Lesson 42	Lesson 43	Lesson 44	Lesson 45	Cumulative Test 8
Day 7	**Day 8**	**Day 9**	**Day 10**	**Day 11**	**Day 12**
Lesson 46	Lesson 47	Lesson 48	Lesson 49	Lesson 50	Cumulative Test 9
Day 13					
Investigation 5					

Block: 90-Minute Class

Day 1	Day 2	Day 3	Day 4	Day 5	Day 6
Investigation 4 Lesson 41	Lab 7 Lesson 42 Lesson 43	Lesson 44 Lab 8 Lesson 45	Cumulative Test 8 Lesson 46	Lesson 47 Lesson 48	Lesson 49 Lesson 50
Day 7					
Cumulative Test 9 Investigation 5					

** For suggestions on how to implement Saxon Math in a block schedule, see the Pacing section at the beginning of the Teacher's Edition.*

Differentiated Instruction

Below Level		Advanced Learners	
Warm Up	SE pp. 296, 304, 312, 318, 325, 331, 337, 343, 348, 355	Challenge	TE pp. 300, 302, 307, 309, 311, 315, 321, 330, 335, 341, 345, 351, 360
Skills Bank	SE pp. 862–885	Extend the Example	TE pp. 297, 304, 305, 308, 313, 319, 333, 338, 343, 351
Reteaching Masters	Lessons 41–50, Investigation 5	Extend the Problem	TE pp. 301, 310, 317, 321, 329, 341, 346, 347, 354
Warm Up Transparencies	Lessons 41–50	Challenge and Enrichment	Challenge: C41–C50 Enrichment: E41, E45
Prerequisite Skills Intervention	Lessons 6, 31, 90		
English Learners		**Special Needs**	
EL Tips	TE pp. 301, 310, 313, 319, 329, 332, 340, 344, 350, 356, 362	Inclusion Tips	TE pp. 297, 306, 314, 328, 334, 338, 346, 349, 353, 357
Multilingual Glossary	Booklet and Online	Adaptations for Saxon Algebra 2	Lessons 41–50; Cumulative Tests 8, 9
English Learners Handbook			
For All Learners			
Exploration	SE pp. 296, 308, 327, 355	Alternate Method	TE pp. 298, 299, 305, 308, 316, 320, 333, 339, 352, 358, 359
Caution	SE pp. 339, 344, 349	Online Tools	
Hints	SE pp. 298, 304, 305, 312, 313, 318, 319, 327, 343, 349, 356, 357, 408		
Error Alert	TE pp. 297, 298, 300, 303, 307, 309, 310, 311, 314, 317, 319, 320, 321, 323, 324, 327, 328, 329, 330, 332, 339, 340, 344, 349, 350, 358, 360		

SE = Student Edition; TE = Teacher's Edition

Math Vocabulary

Lesson	New Vocabulary		Maintained	EL Tip in TE
41	distance formula hypotenuse legs of a right triangle	right triangle	radical	distance formula
42	combination factorial	permutations	event	arrangement combination
43	system of linear inequalities		solution	boundary
44	conjugates		radicand	binomial bi- monomial mono- -nomial
45	correlation correlation coefficient	line of best fit regression	*y*-intercept	correlation
46	cosecant cosine cotangent	secant sine tangent trigonometric function trigonometric ratio trigonometry	hypotenuse reciprocals	adjacent opposite
47	asymptote exponential function horizontal asymptote		base	-ly (suffix)
48	complex fraction		reciprocal	simplify
49	binomial experiment binomial probability	Binomial Theorem	combination	evaluate solve expand
50	inverse function inverse relation		range	inverse
INV 5			binomial experiment	binomial distribution

SECTION OVERVIEW 5

Math Highlights

Enduring Understandings – The "Big Picture"

After completing Section 5, students will understand:

- How to find permutations and combinations.
- How to find trigonometric functions and their reciprocals.
- How to find the line of best fit.
- How to identify and use the Pythagorean Theorem and the distance formula.

Essential Questions

- How are exponential functions graphed?
- What is the difference between an inverse and a reciprocal?
- How are systems of linear inequalities solved?
- What is the binomial theorem and how is it used?

Math Content Strands

Exponential and Logarithmic Functions

• Lesson 47	Graphing Exponential Functions

Linear Functions

• Lab 8	Graphing Calculator Lab: Applying Linear and Median Regression
• Lesson 45	Finding the Line of Best Fit
• Lesson 50	Finding Inverses of Relations and Functions

Linear Systems

• Lesson 43	Solving Systems of Linear Inequalities

Probability and Statistics

• Lab 7	Graphing Calculator Lab: Calculating Permutations and Combinations
• Lesson 42	Finding Permutations and Combinations
• Lesson 49	Using the Binomial Theorem
• Investigation 5	Finding the Binomial Distribution

Rational and Radical Functions

• Lesson 44	Rationalizing Denominators
• Lesson 48	Understanding Complex Fractions

Trigonometry

• Lesson 41	Using the Pythagorean Theorem and the Distance Formula
• Lesson 46	Finding Trigonometric Functions and their Reciprocals

Connections in Practice Problems

	Lessons
Coordinate Geometry	41, 46
Data Analysis	43, 48, 49
Geometry	41, 42, 43, 44, 45, 46, 47, 48, 49, 50
Measurement	44, 45
Probability	42, 47, 50

Math Processes

Reasoning and Communication

	Lessons
• Analyze	42, 43, 44, 45, 46, 47, 49, 50, Inv. 5
• Error analysis	41, 42, 43, 44, 45, 46, 47, 48, 49, 50
• Estimate	49
• Formulate	46, 47, 48
• Generalize	43, 44, 45, 47, 50
• Justify	41, 43, 44, 46, 48, 50
• Math reasoning	41, 45, 46, 49
• Model	41, 42, 50
• Multiple choice	41, 42, 43, 44, 45, 46, 47, 48, 49, 50
• Multi-step	41, 42, 43, 44, 45, 46, 47, 48, 49, 50, Inv. 5
• Predict	Inv. 5
• Verify	42, 44, 45, 46, 47, 48, 49, 50, Inv. 5
• Write	41, 42, 43, 44, 45, 46, 47, 48, 49, 50
• Graphing Calculator	41, 42, 43, 44, 45, 46, 47, 48, 49, 50

Connections

In Examples: Athletic tickets; Cartography; Compound interest; Distance, Time, and gravity; Navigation; Spinner probabilities; Solar heating; Tickets to an entertainment event

In Practice problems: Airplane altitude, Architecture, Baseball, Basketball, Births, Business school, Cartography, Chess tournament, Compound interest, Density, Depreciation, Dog show, Economics, Engine size, Geography, Gravity, Grizzly bears, Health, Hiking, Lottery, Money, Nutrition and cost, Physics, Rainfall, Running, Savings, Sightseeing, Small business, Sports, Student government, Swimming, Temperature, Tennis, Test preparation, Ticket prices, Ticket sales, Tourism, Utilities, Velocity, Window display

Content Trace

Lesson	Warm Up: Prerequisite Skills	New Concepts	Where Practiced	Where Assessed	Looking Forward
41	Lessons 19, 35, 40	Using the Pythagorean Theorem and the Distance Formula	Lessons 41, 42, 43, 44, 45, 46, 47, 48, 49, 50, 51, 53, 55, 57, 60, 64, 72, 86, 99, 102	Cumulative Tests 9, 10, 12, 15	Lessons 46, 52, 56
42	Lesson 33	Finding Permutations and Combinations	Lessons 42, 43, 44, 45, 46, 47, 48, 49, 50, 51, 52, 53, 55, 56, 57, 59, 106, 110, 118, 119	Cumulative Tests 9, 11, 14, 18	Lessons 49, 55, 60, 68
43	Lesson 39	Solving Systems of Linear Inequalities	Lessons 43, 44, 45, 46, 47, 49, 50, 51, 52, 53, 55, 57, 60	Cumulative Tests 9, 10, 15	Lessons 89, 93, 94
44	Lesson 40	Rationalizing Denominators	Lessons 44, 45, 47, 48, 49, 51, 53, 54, 55, 58, 59, 60, 63, 64, 65, 68, 78, 107	Cumulative Tests 9, 10, 11, 14, 18, 23	Lessons 48, 70, 75, 84, 88
45	Lessons 2, 13, 26	Finding the Line of Best Fit	Lessons 45, 46, 47, 49, 50, 51, 52, 54, 55, 56, 58, 59, 60, 61, 63, 64, 117, 119	Cumulative Tests 9, 12	Lessons 116, 117, 118, 119
46	Lessons 7, 31, 41	Finding Trigonometric Functions and their Reciprocals	Lessons 46, 47, 49, 50, 51, 52, 53, 54, 55, 56, 58, 59, 60, 61, 63, 65, 68, 110	Cumulative Tests 10, 12, 16, 23	Lessons 52, 63, 67
47	Lessons 3, 27	Graphing Exponential Functions	Lessons 47, 48, 49, 53, 55, 56, 61, 107, 115, 117	Cumulative Tests 10, 17	Lessons 57, 72
48	Lessons 31, 37	Understanding Complex Fractions	Lessons 48, 49, 51, 53, 54, 56, 63, 67, 98, 106, 109, 113	Cumulative Tests 10, 12, 13, 18	Lessons 53, 59
49	Lesson 42	Using the Binomial Theorem	Lessons 49, 50, 51, 52, 53, 55, 56, 59, 61, 62, 65, 66, 68, 106, 107, 108, 113, 114	Cumulative Tests 10, 13, 18, 21	Lessons 53, 55, 66
50	Lessons 4, 7, 30	Finding Inverses of Relations and Functions	Lessons 50, 52, 53, 55, 58, 59, 61, 62, 63, 64, 66, 70, 71, 76, 80, 81, 111, 116	Cumulative Tests 10, 11, 15	Lessons 53, 67, 75
INV 5	N/A	Investigation: Finding the Binomial Distribution	Lessons 54, 63, 66, 68, 79	Cumulative Test 11	Lesson 83

Ongoing Assessment

	Type	Feature	Intervention *
BEFORE instruction	Assess Prior Knowledge	• Diagnostic Test	• Prerequisite Skills Intervention
BEFORE the lesson	Formative	• Warm Up	• Skills Bank • Reteaching Masters
DURING the lesson	Formative	• Lesson Practice • Math Conversations with the Practice problems	• Additional Examples in TE • Test and Practice Generator (for additional practice sheets)
AFTER the lesson	Formative	• Check for Understanding (closure)	• Scaffolding Questions in TE
AFTER 5 lessons	Summative	After Lesson 45 • Cumulative Test 8 • Performance Task 8 After Lesson 50 • Cumulative Test 9 • Performance Task 9	• Reteaching Masters • Test and Practice Generator (for additional tests and practice)
AFTER 20 lessons	Summative	• Benchmark Tests	• Reteaching Masters • Test and Practice Generator (for additional tests and practice)

* for students not showing progress during the formative stages or scoring below 80% on the summative assessments

Evidence of Learning – What Students Should Know

Because the Saxon philosophy is to provide students with sufficient time to learn and practice each concept, a lesson's topic will not be tested until at least five lessons after the topic is introduced.

On the Cumulative Tests that are given during this section of ten lessons, students should be able to demonstrate the following competencies:

- Graph and solve linear equations; solve quadratic equations.
- Estimate a line of best fit.
- Find the length of a side of a right triangle, given the lengths of the other two sides.
- Identify solutions to, and graph, a system of linear inequalities.
- Classify lines using slope.
- Write the equation of a line given two points.

Test and Practice Generator CD using ExamView™

The Test and Practice Generator is an easy-to-use benchmark and assessment tool that creates unlimited practice and tests in multiple formats and allows you to customize questions or create new ones. A variety of reports are available to track student progress toward mastery of the standards throughout the year.

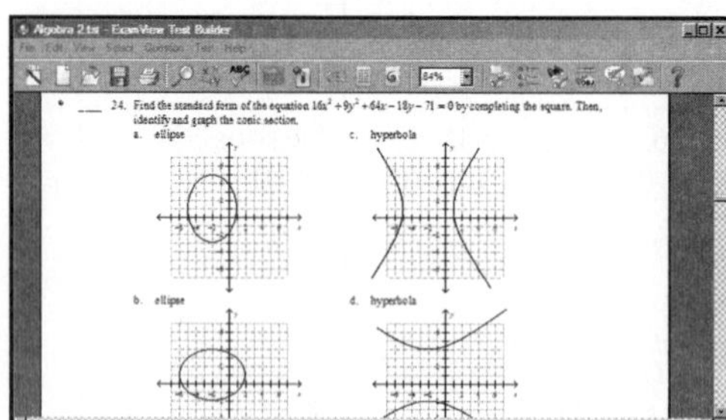

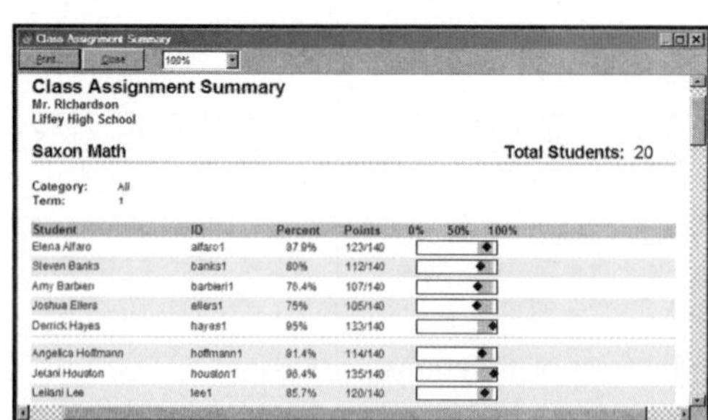

Assessment Resources

Resources for Diagnosing and Assessing

- **Student Edition**
  - Warm Up
  - Lesson Practice
- **Teacher's Edition**
  - Math Conversations with the Practice problems
  - Check for Understanding (closure)
- **Course Assessments**
  - Diagnostic Test
  - Cumulative Tests
  - Performance Tasks
  - Benchmark Tests

Resources for Intervention

- **Student Edition**
  - Skills Bank
- **Teacher's Edition**
  - Additional Examples
  - Scaffolding questions
- **Prerequisite Skills Intervention**
  - Worksheets
- **Reteaching Masters**
  - Lesson instruction and practice sheets
- **Test and Practice Generator CD using ExamView™**
  - Lesson practice problems
  - Additional tests

Resources for Test Prep

- **Student Edition**
  - Multiple-choice practice problems
  - Multiple-step and writing problems
  - Daily cumulative practice
- **Standardized Test Practice**
- **College Entrance Exam Practice**
- **Test and Practice Generator CD using ExamView™**

Cumulative Tests

The assessments in Saxon Math are frequent and consistently placed after every five lessons to offer a regular method of ongoing testing. These cumulative assessments check mastery of concepts from previous lessons.

Performance Tasks

The Performance Tasks can be used in conjunction with the Cumulative Tests and are scored using a rubric.

After Lesson 45

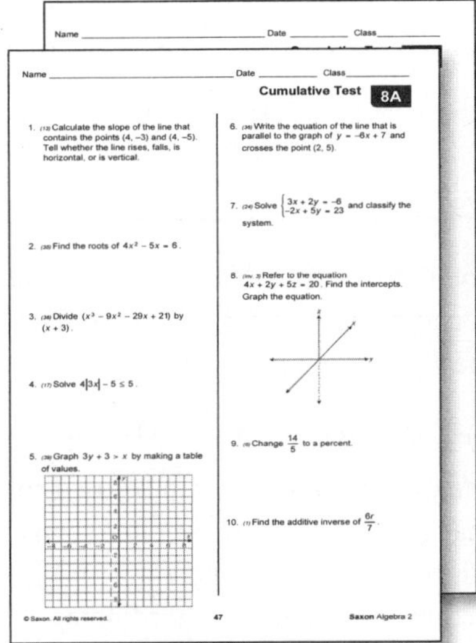

Name ______ Date ______ Class ______

Cumulative Test 8A

1. Calculate the slope of the line that contains the points (4, –3) and (4, –5). Tell whether the line rises, falls, is horizontal, or is vertical.
2. Find the roots of $4x^2 - 5x = 6$.
3. Divide $(x^3 - 9x^2 - 29x + 21)$ by $(x + 3)$.
4. Solve $4|3x| - 5 \le 5$.
5. Graph $3y + 3 > x$ by making a table of values.
6. Write the equation of the line that is parallel to the graph of $y = -6x + 7$ and crosses the point (2, 5).
7. Solve $\begin{cases} 3x + 2y = -6 \\ -2x + 5y = 23 \end{cases}$ and classify the system.
8. Refer to the equation $4x + 2y + 5z = 20$. Find the intercepts. Graph the equation.
9. Change $\frac{14}{5}$ to a percent.
10. Find the additive inverse of $\frac{6r}{7}$.

© Saxon. All rights reserved. 47 Saxon Algebra 2

After Lesson 50

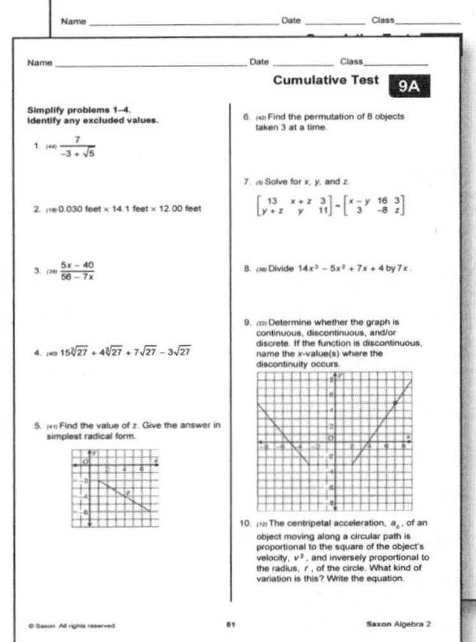

Name ______ Date ______ Class ______

Cumulative Test 9A

Simplify problems 1–4. Identify any excluded values.

1. $\frac{7}{-3 + \sqrt{5}}$
2. 0.030 feet × 14.1 feet × 12.00 feet
3. $\frac{5x - 40}{56 - 7x}$
4. $15\sqrt[3]{27} + 4\sqrt[3]{27} + 7\sqrt{27} - 3\sqrt{27}$
5. Find the value of z. Give the answer in simplest radical form.
6. Find the permutation of 8 objects taken 3 at a time.
7. Solve for x, y, and z. $\begin{bmatrix} 13 & x + z & 3 \\ y + z & y & 11 \end{bmatrix} = \begin{bmatrix} x - y & 16 & 3 \\ 3 & -8 & z \end{bmatrix}$
8. Divide $14x^3 - 5x^2 + 7x + 4$ by $7x$.
9. Determine whether the graph is continuous, discontinuous, and/or discrete. If the function is discontinuous, name the x-value(s) where the discontinuity occurs.
10. The centripetal acceleration, a_c, of an object moving along a circular path is proportional to the square of the object's velocity, v^2, and inversely proportional to the radius, r, of the circle. What kind of variation is this? Write the equation.

© Saxon. All rights reserved. 51 Saxon Algebra 2

For use with Performance Tasks

Teacher Rubric

Criteria Performance	Knowledge and Skills Understanding	Communication and Representation	Process and Strategies
4	The student got it! The student did it in new ways and showed how it worked. The student knew and understood what math concepts to use.	The student clearly detailed how he/she solved the problem. The student included all the steps to show his/her thinking. The student used math language, symbols, numbers, graphs and/or models to represent his/her solution.	The student had an effective and inventive solution. The student used big math ideas to solve the problem. The student addressed the important details. The student showed other ways to solve the problem. The student checked his/her answer to make sure it was correct
3	The student understood the problem and had an appropriate solution. All parts of the problem are addressed.	The student clearly explained how he/she solved the problem. The student used math language, symbols, tables, graphs, and numbers to explain how he/she did the problem.	The student had a correct solution. The student used a plan to solve the problem and selected an appropriate strategy.
2	The student understood parts of the problem. The student started, but he/she couldn't finish.	The student explained some of what he/she did. The student tried to use words, symbols, tables, graphs and numbers to explain how he/she did the problem.	The student had part of the solution, but did not know how to finish. The student was not sure if he/she had the correct answer. The student needed help.
1	The student did not understand the problem.	The student did not explain how he/she solved the problem. He/she did not use words, symbols, tables or graphs to show how he/she	The student couldn't get started. The student did not know how to begin.

© Saxon. All rights reserved. x Saxon Algebra 2

LESSON 41

1 Warm Up

In problem 2, have students also find a two-place decimal approximation for $\sqrt{300}$. 17.32

2 New Concepts

In this lesson, students use the Pythagorean Theorem to develop the distance formula.

Exploration

Students carry out a dissection proof of the Pythagorean Theorem.

Additional Example

This alternate dissection proof works for any right triangle.

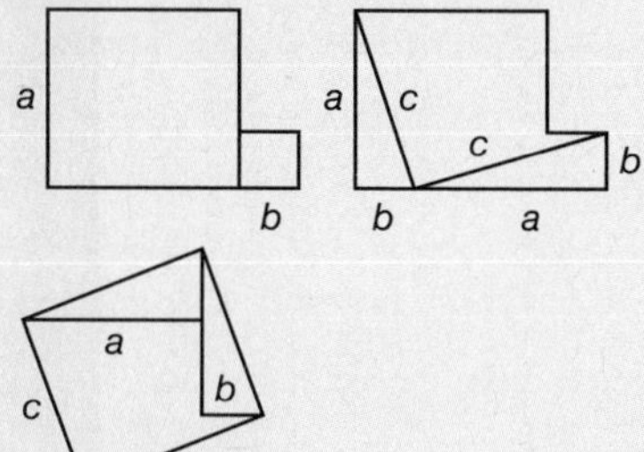

Steps 1–2: Start with two squares. Draw hypotenuse c twice.

Step 3: Rearrange the three pieces to make a square with side c.

The sum of the areas of the two smaller squares ($a^2 + b^2$) equals the area of the larger square (c^2) formed, illustrating the Pythagorean Theorem $a^2 + b^2 = c^2$.

LESSON RESOURCES

Student Edition Practice Workbook 41
Reteaching Master 41
Adaptations Masters 41
Challenge and Enrichment Masters C41, E41

LESSON 41 Using the Pythagorean Theorem and the Distance Formula

Warm Up

1. (40) **Vocabulary** $\sqrt{75}$ is a ________ expression. (*rational*|*radical*). radical
2. (40) Simplify $\sqrt{300}$. $10\sqrt{3}$
3. (19) Expand $(x - 5)^2$. $x^2 - 10x + 25$
4. (35) Solve $x^2 + 7x = -10$ by factoring. $-5, -2$

New Concepts

A **right triangle** is a triangle with one right angle. The sides that form the right angle are the **legs** of a right triangle and the side opposite the right angle is the **hypotenuse**.

Exploration Visualizing the Pythagorean Theorem

Materials needed: grid paper, scissors

Step 1:
On grid paper, draw a right triangle so that the base is 3 squares long and the height is 4 squares high.

Step 2:
Elsewhere on the paper, draw a 3 by 3 square, a 4 by 4 square, and a 5 by 5 square. Cut out these three squares.

Step 3:
Place the squares so that one side of each square aligns with one of the sides of the triangle.

Step 4:
Move the 4 by 4 square onto the 5 by 5 square. Cut the 3 by 3 square into pieces to completely fill in the rest of the 5 by 5 square. The two smaller squares should completely cover the larger square. That is, the sum of the areas of the smaller squares equals the area of the larger square.

Because the area of a square is found by squaring the length of one side of the square, the result of the exploration suggests the Pythagorean Theorem. The converse of the Pythagorean Theorem is also true.

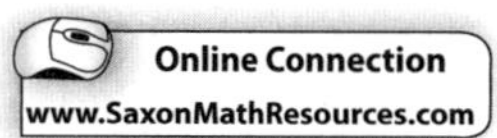

The Pythagorean Theorem
If a triangle is a right triangle, the sum of the squares of the lengths of the legs equals the square of the length of the hypotenuse. For legs a and b, and hypotenuse c, $a^2 + b^2 = c^2$.

MATH BACKGROUND

Although directed distance occurs in advanced mathematics, in most elementary applications both distance and length are positive. So, the distance between the graphs of a and b on a number line is the absolute value of their difference: $|a - b|$ or $|b - a|$. In the same way, the distance between points on the same horizontal line is $|x_2 - x_1|$ or $|x_1 - x_2|$; on the same vertical line, $|y_2 - y_1|$ or $|y_1 - y_2|$.

Using the Pythagorean Theorem, a distance formula can be derived for any two points in the plane $P_1\ (x_1, y_1)$ and $P_2\ (x_2, y_2)$.

$$d(P_1, P_2) = \sqrt{(x_2 - x_1)^2 + (y_2 - y_1)^2}$$

Then, the distance formula can be used to prove that the midpoint M of a line segment with endpoints $P_1(x_1, y_1)$ and $P_2(x_2, y_2)$ is computed by averaging the coordinates.

$$M\left(\frac{x_1 + x_2}{2}, \frac{y_1 + y_2}{2}\right)$$

The Converse of the Pythagorean Theorem
If the sum of the squares of the lengths of the two shorter sides of a triangle equals the square of the length of the longest side, then the triangle is a right triangle.

Use the Converse of the Pythagorean Theorem when checking if three sides of a triangle are the sides of a *right* triangle.

Example 1 Determining if a Triangle is a Right Triangle

a. The sides of a triangle measure 15 cm, 36 cm, and 39 cm. Is the triangle a right triangle?

SOLUTION Substitute 15 and 36 for a and b, and 39 for c, in $a^2 + b^2 = c^2$.

$$a^2 + b^2 = c^2$$
$$15^2 + 36^2 \stackrel{?}{=} 39^2$$
$$225 + 1296 \stackrel{?}{=} 1521$$
$$1521 = 1521 \checkmark$$

The triangle is a right triangle.

Math Reasoning

Justify Why could 36 be substituted for a and 15 be substituted for b instead?

The sum of their squares is the same due to the Commutative Property of Addition.

b. The sides of a triangle measure 21 in., 70 in., and 75 in. Is the triangle a right triangle?

SOLUTION Substitute 21 and 70 for a and b, and 75 for c, in $a^2 + b^2 = c^2$.

$$a^2 + b^2 = c^2$$
$$21^2 + 70^2 \stackrel{?}{=} 75^2$$
$$441 + 4900 \stackrel{?}{=} 5625$$
$$5341 \neq 5625$$

The triangle is not a right triangle.

Use the Pythagorean Theorem when determining the length of any side of a right triangle, given the lengths of the other two sides.

Example 2 Finding the Length of a Missing Side of a Right Triangle

a. Find the value of x.

x in. 30 in. 24 in.

SOLUTION

$a^2 + b^2 = c^2$	
$x^2 + 24^2 = 30^2$	Substitute x and 24 for the legs, a and b and 30 for c.
$x^2 + 576 = 900$	Square 24 and 30.
$x^2 = 324$	Subtract 576 from each side.
$x = 18$	Take the square root of both sides.

INCLUSION

Materials: drinking straws, scissors, ruler

Review the triangle inequality: For any triangle, the measure of a given side must be less than the sum of the other two sides, but greater than the difference between those sides. So, for example, the lengths 2, 3, and 7 cannot be used to make a triangle. Have students use the straws to find triples that will, and won't, make triangles.

Then introduce the 3-4-5 right triangle. These dimensions, or multiples of them, are probably the ones most often used in textbook problems. Have students make a few right triangles using triples such as (3, 4, 5), (6, 8, 10), (5, 12, 13).

Finally, have students fold a square in half along the diagonal. Allow time for them to convince themselves that the diagonal is not an integer. Explain that a formula must be used for this right triangle; in fact, for most right triangles. There are just a few triangles—like the 3-4-5—that "come out even."

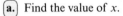

Example 1

Students decide if a triangle is a right triangle by finding out if the side lengths satisfy the Pythagorean Theorem.

Error Alert Check that students square each leg length and then add, rather than adding the lengths and squaring their sum.

Additional Example 1

a. The sides of a triangle measure 9 ft, 40 ft, and 41 ft. Is the triangle a right triangle? Yes

b. The sides of a triangle measure 20 cm, 21 cm, and 25 cm. Is the triangle a right triangle? No

Extend the Example

In a right triangle with hypotenuse c, if $c^2 > a^2 + b^2$, then the triangle is obtuse. If $c^2 < a^2 + b^2$, then the triangle is acute. Have students determine if the triangles with the given sides are acute or obtuse.

a. 12 m, 15 m, 17 m acute

b. 21 yd, 36 yd, 45 yd obtuse

Example 2

Students use the Pythagorean Theorem to find an unknown length in a right triangle.

Additional Example 2

a. Find the value of x. 77

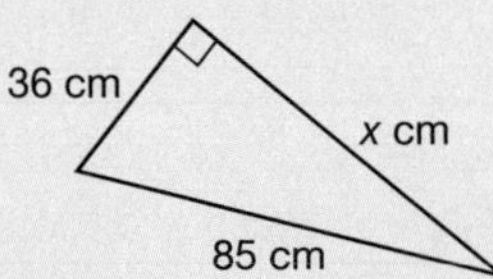

Error Alert Remind students that the hypotenuse is always across from the right angle, and it is always the longest side. This length must be substituted for c in the Pythagorean Theorem, and not for a or b.

Additional Example 2, cont.

b. Find the value of y. 13

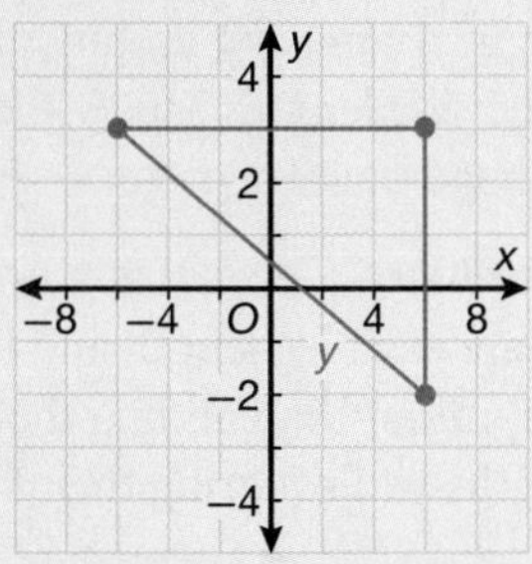

c. Find the value of z. Give the answer in simplest radical form and to the nearest tenth. $3\sqrt{13}$; about 10.8 units

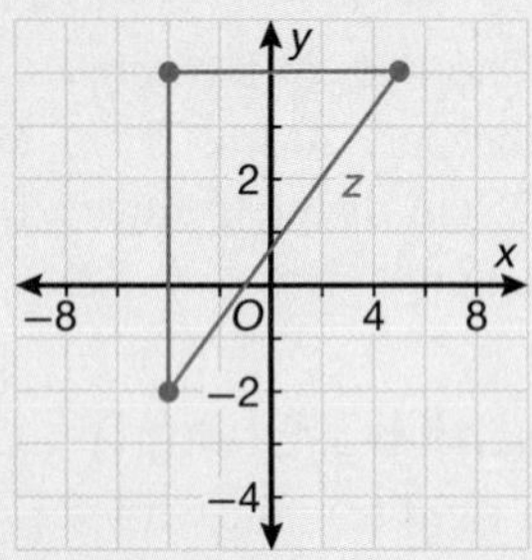

Error Alert Students who are making errors when substituting coordinates into the distance formula can be asked to plot the given points, connect them to make a line segment, and then draw the right triangle with that line segment as the hypotenuse.

Hint

Use the fact that the hypotenuse is the longest side of a right triangle to check if your answer is reasonable.

b. Find the value of y.

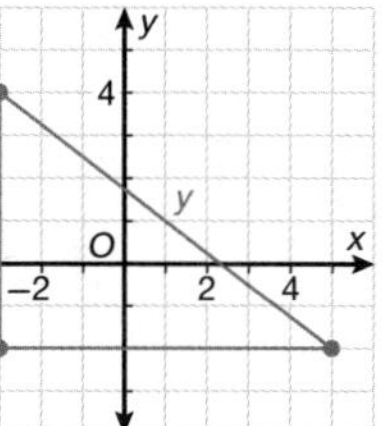

SOLUTION Count the number of units to find the lengths of the legs.

The vertical segment is 6 units long. The horizontal segment is 8 units long.

$$a^2 + b^2 = c^2$$
$$6^2 + 8^2 = y^2$$
$$36 + 64 = y^2$$
$$100 = y^2$$
$$10 = y$$

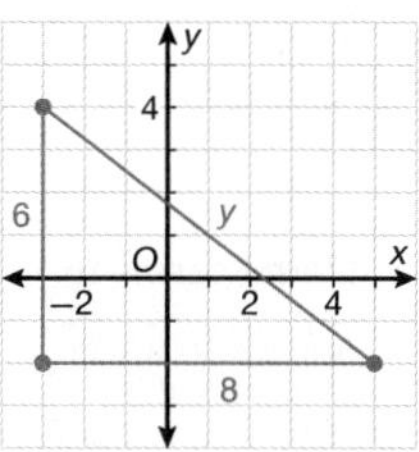

c. Find the value of z. Give the answer in simplest radical form and to the nearest tenth.

SOLUTION The vertical segment is 4 units long. The horizontal segment is 8 units long.

$$a^2 + b^2 = c^2$$
$$4^2 + 8^2 = z^2$$
$$16 + 64 = z^2$$
$$80 = z^2$$
$$\sqrt{80} = z$$
$$\sqrt{80} = \sqrt{16} \cdot \sqrt{5} = 4\sqrt{5}$$

The value of z is exactly $4\sqrt{5}$ units, or about 8.9 units, long.

The distance between any two points can be found by using the Pythagorean Theorem. As Examples 2b and 2c show, the horizontal distance is the difference between the x-coordinates and the vertical distance is the difference between the y-coordinates. Because the length of the hypotenuse is the square root of the sum of the squares of the leg lengths, the distance between any two points can be represented by the **distance formula** shown below.

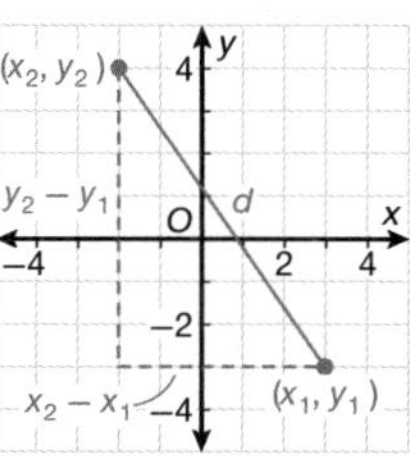

Distance Formula
The distance d between any two points with coordinates (x_1, y_1) and (x_2, y_2) is $d = \sqrt{(x_2 - x_1)^2 + (y_2 - y_1)^2}$.

ALTERNATE METHOD FOR EXAMPLE 2

Materials: cm grid paper, cm ruler

Present this problem: Find the lengths of the sides of a triangle with vertices at $(-3, 4)$, $(-3, -2)$, and $(5, -2)$.

Have students plot the vertices and connect them to make the triangle. Say: **"Use the centimeter ruler to measure the three sides."** 6 cm, 8 cm, 10 cm

Ask: **"Could you find these lengths without actually drawing the triangle and measuring the sides? How?"** Discuss students' ideas. Emphasize finding vertical and horizontal lengths by using the absolute value of the difference of the coordinates.

Explain that this triangle is not typical in that most right triangles have hypotenuses that are not rational numbers. So, measuring isn't a very accurate or particularly useful way of finding lengths of hypotenuses.

Example 3 Finding the Distance between Two Points

Find the distance between each pair of points. Give the answer in simplest radical form and to the nearest tenth.

a. $A(-4, 11)$, $B(1, -1)$

SOLUTION Label $(-4, 11)$ as (x_1, y_1) and $(1, -1)$ as (x_2, y_2).

$$d = \sqrt{(x_2 - x_1)^2 + (y_2 - y_1)^2} = \sqrt{(1 - (-4))^2 + (-1 - 11)^2}$$
$$= \sqrt{(5)^2 + (-12)^2} = \sqrt{25 + 144}$$
$$= \sqrt{169} = 13$$

b. $A(-6, 5)$, $B(-2, -7)$

SOLUTION Label $(-6, 5)$ as (x_1, y_1) and $(-2, -7)$ as (x_2, y_2).

$$d = \sqrt{(x_2 - x_1)^2 + (y_2 - y_1)^2}$$
$$= \sqrt{(-2 - (-6))^2 + (-7 - 5)^2}$$
$$= \sqrt{(4)^2 + (-12)^2} = \sqrt{16 + 144} = \sqrt{160} = \sqrt{16}\sqrt{10} = 4\sqrt{10} \approx 12.6$$

Math Reasoning

Justify Can $(1, -1)$ be labeled as (x_1, y_1) and $(-4, 11)$ as (x_2, y_2)? Explain.

Yes, subtraction is not commutative, but the differences are squared.

Example 4 Finding a Missing Coordinate

Find the value of k so that the distance between $(2, k)$ and $(-2, 8)$ is 4.

SOLUTION

Substitute values into $d = \sqrt{(x_2 - x_1)^2 + (y_2 - y_1)^2}$ and simplify.

$$4 = \sqrt{(-2 - 2)^2 + (8 - k)^2}$$
$$= \sqrt{(-4)^2 + 8^2 - 16k + k^2} = \sqrt{16 + 64 - 16k + k^2} = \sqrt{80 - 16k + k^2}$$

Solve $4 = \sqrt{80 - 16k + k^2}$ by factoring.

$16 = 80 - 16k + k^2$	Square both sides of the equation.
$0 = k^2 - 16k + 64$	Make one side 0. Rearrange terms.
$0 = (k - 8)(k - 8)$	Factor the trinomial.

Solve $k - 8 = 0$ to find that $k = 8$.

Example 5 Application: Cartography

A cartographer constructs a map of New Mexico over a grid system such that Silver City is at (63, 142) and Las Cruces is at (192, 98). Find the distance between the cities to the nearest kilometer if each unit represents one kilometer.

SOLUTION

$$d = \sqrt{(x_2 - x_1)^2 + (y_2 - y_1)^2}$$
$$= \sqrt{(192 - 63)^2 + (98 - 142)^2}$$
$$= \sqrt{(129)^2 + (-44)^2} = \sqrt{16{,}641 + 1936} \approx 136$$

The distance between Silver City and Las Cruces is about 136 kilometers.

Example 3

Students use the distance formula to find the distance between two points from the coordinates of their ordered pairs.

Additional Example 3

Find the distance between each pair of points. Give the answer in simplest radical form and to the nearest tenth.

a. $A(-2, 8)$, $B(6, -7)$ 17

b. $A(6, -1)$, $B(-4, 5)$ $2\sqrt{34}$; 11.7

Example 4

Students use the distance formula to find a missing coordinate in one of two ordered pairs when given the distance between the points.

Additional Example 4

Find the value of k so that the distance between $(12, k)$ and $(-8, -11)$ is 29. $k = 10$ or $k = -32$

Example 5

Students use the distance formula to solve an application problem.

Additional Example 5

In a city based on a square grid system, what is the straight line distance from Tenth Avenue and 112th Street to Third Avenue and 58th Street? Write the equation you used. Round to the nearest block.
$d = \sqrt{(10 - 3)^2 + (112 - 58)^2}$; 54 blocks

ALTERNATE METHOD FOR EXAMPLE 3

Some students may be confused by the subscripted variables in the distance formula. If so, start with two points (a, b) and (c, d). Develop the formula using these variables and the diagram shown at the right. The variable x is the distance between the two points.

$$x = \sqrt{(b - d)^2 + (c - a)^2}$$

or $x = \sqrt{(a - c)^2 + (b - d)^2}$

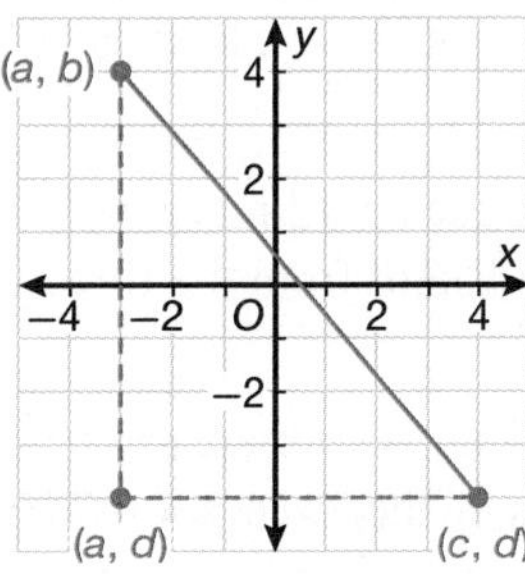

TEACHER TIP

Primitive Pythagorean triples are sets of numbers that (1) satisfy the Pythagorean Theorem and (2) have no common factors other than 1. Here are some examples.

(3, 4, 5)	(5, 12, 13)
(7, 24, 25)	(8, 15, 17)
(20, 21, 29)	(9, 40, 41)

Lesson Practice

a. The sides of a triangle measure 14 m, 20 m, and 25 m. Is the triangle a right triangle? no
(Ex 1)

b. The sides of a triangle measure 12 mm, 16 mm, and 20 mm. Is the triangle a right triangle? yes
(Ex 1)

c. Find the value of x. 12
(Ex 2)

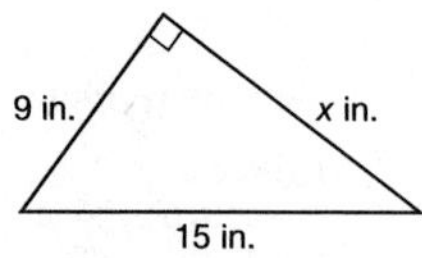

d. Find the value of y. 17
(Ex 2)

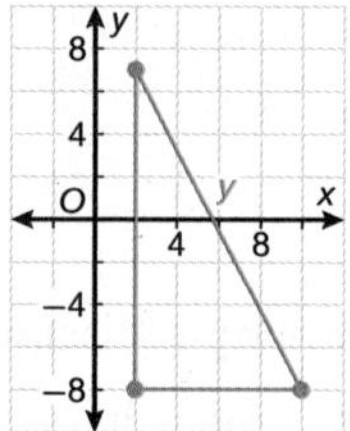

e. Find the value of z. Give the answer in simplest radical form and to the nearest tenth. $2\sqrt{5} \approx 4.5$
(Ex 2)

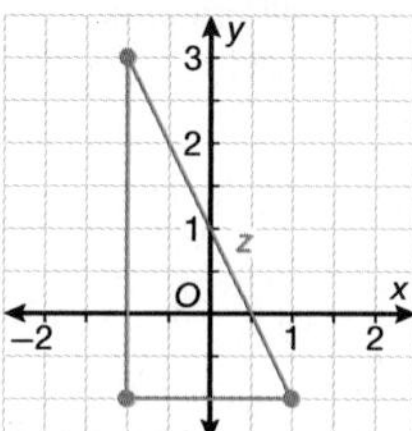

Find the distance between each pair of points. Give the answer in simplest radical form and to the nearest tenth.
(Ex 3)

f. $A(6, 9)$, $B(-18, -1)$ 26

g. $A(5, -5)$, $B(9, -11)$ $2\sqrt{13} \approx 7.2$

h. Find two possible values of k so that the distance between $(1, k)$ and $(6, -3)$ is 13. 9 and −15
(Ex 4)

i. A cartographer constructs a map of New Mexico over a grid system such that Silver City is at (200, 205) and Los Alamos is at (225, 287). Find the distance between the cities to the nearest kilometer if each unit represents one kilometer. About 86 km
(Ex 5)

Practice Distributed and Integrated

Find the distance between the points.

***1.** $(-3, 8)$ and $(3, 0)$ 10
(41)

***2.** $(-1, -1)$ and $(13, 6)$ ≈ 15.65
(41)

3. Write the equation of the line that is perpendicular to $y = \frac{1}{3}x - 1$ and passes through the point $(2, -3)$. $y = -3x + 3$
(26)

Simplify.

***4.** $3\sqrt{3} \cdot 4\sqrt{12} - 5\sqrt{300}$ $72 - 50\sqrt{3}$
(40)

***5.** $4\sqrt{3}(2\sqrt{3} - \sqrt{6})$ $24 - 12\sqrt{2}$
(40)

Add.

6. $2 + \frac{1}{x}$ $\frac{2x + 1}{x}$
(37)

7. $\frac{5x^2}{y} + p^2 - \frac{3x}{py}$ $\frac{5x^2p + p^3y - 3x}{py}$
(37)

Lesson Practice

Problem c

Scaffolding Students can start by identifying the hypotenuse and the legs. hypotenuse: 15 in.; legs: 9 in. and x in.

Ask: **"How do these relate to the variables *a*, *b*, and *c* in the Pythagorean Theorem?"** Sample: $a = 9$, $b = x$, $c = 15$

Problem g

Error Alert Remind students that "simplest radical form" means that the number under the square root sign must have no perfect square factors.

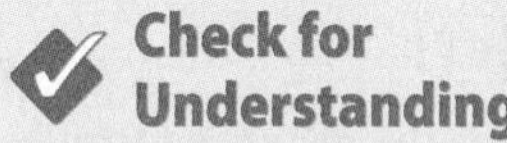

Check for Understanding

The questions below help assess the concepts taught in this lesson.

1. **"How can you determine if three given side lengths form a right triangle?"** The lengths must make the Pythagorean Theorem true.
2. **"How does finding the length of a slanted line segment on a coordinate plane differ from finding the length of a horizontal or vertical line segment?"** slanted: use the distance formula; vertical: use the absolute value of the difference of the y-coordinates; horizontal: use the absolute value of the difference of the x-coordinates

3 Practice

Math Conversations

Discussions to strengthen understanding

Problem 3

Remind students that the slopes of perpendicular lines are negative reciprocals. So, students can use the point-slope equation of a line with −3 as the slope and (2, −3) as the point. The point-slope equation is $y - y_1 = m(x - x_1)$.

CHALLENGE

Three points have coordinates (2, 9), (8, 3), and (6, −3).

a. Find the coordinates of the point equidistant from the three given points. (1, 2)

b. How far is your answer to Part A from each of the given points? Give the answer in simplest radical form and to the nearest tenth. $5\sqrt{2}$; 7.1

8. Find the equation of the line that passes through the point (2, 2) and is parallel
(36) to $y = -\frac{3}{7}x + 4$. $y = -\frac{3}{7}x + \frac{20}{7}$

Expand.

9. (20) $xy^{-2}\left(\frac{x^0y^2}{x} - \frac{3x^0y^2}{x^2}\right)$ $1 - 3x^{-1}$

10. (20) $\frac{xy^{-2}}{p^2}\left(\frac{p^2y^2}{x} + \frac{5x^2y^3}{p^{-2}}\right)$ $1 + 5x^3y$

11. (28) **Geography** The state of Wyoming is roughly square in shape. Write the area to perimeter ratio of the state as a simplified rational expression. Then find the ratio given that the length of each side of the state is roughly 300 miles long. $\frac{s}{4} = 75$

***12.** (41) **Multi-Step** If the origin represents a pier, and one boat travels 4 units due east and 6 units due north, while a second boat travels 4 units due west and 6 units due south, how far apart are the boats in units? Write the answer as both a simplified radical expression and as a decimal rounded to the nearest tenth. Then approximate the distance given that each unit represents 2.5 miles. $4\sqrt{13}$, or about 14.4 units; about 36 miles

13. (30) **Multi-Step a.** Identify the vertex and axis of symmetry of $y = (x + 3)^2 - 5$. $(-3, -5)$; $x = -3$

b. Find the values of y when $x = -6, -5$, and -4. 4, −1, −4

c. Use symmetry to find the values of y when $x = -2, -1$, and 0. −4, −1, 4

***14.** (40) **Geometry** The radius of a right circular cylinder can be represented by $\frac{\sqrt{V}}{\sqrt{\pi h}}$, where V is the volume of the cylinder and h is the height. Simplify the expression by multiplying by $\frac{\sqrt{\pi h}}{\sqrt{\pi h}}$. $\frac{\sqrt{V\pi h}}{\pi h}$

15. (33) **Multiple Choice** How many three-digit passwords are possible if digits may be repeated? **D**

A 27 **B** 30 **C** 720 **D** 1000

16. (38) **Write** Suppose that $f(x)$ is a polynomial of degree m, and $g(x)$ is a polynomial of degree $n < m$. What can you conclude about $\frac{f(x)}{g(x)}$ if it has a zero remainder?

17. (34) **Error Analysis** A student solved the equation $x^2 - 16 = 0$ as shown below. $x^2 - 16 = 0 \rightarrow (x - 4)^2 = 0 \rightarrow x = 4$. What is the error? Solve the equation correctly.

***18.** (41) **Multiple Choice** The legs of a right triangle are 18 mm and 80 mm. What is the length of the hypotenuse? **B**

A 80 mm **B** 82 mm **C** 89 mm **D** 98 mm

19. (34) **Model** Graph the line represented by the table of values.

x	−2	0	2	4
y	−5	−2	1	4

***20.** (39) **Justify** Why does (0, 0) usually make for a good test point for determining which half-plane to shade? When can it not be used?

21. (35) **Graphing Calculator** Use a graphing calculator to estimate the root(s) of the equation $x^2 - 78 = 0$ to the nearest integer(s). −9 and 9

16. $\frac{f(x)}{g(x)}$ is a polynomial of degree $m - n$.

17. The student factored incorrectly.
$x^2 - 16 = 0$
$(x + 4)(x - 4) = 0$
$x + 4 = 0$ or $x - 4 = 0$
$x = -4$ or $x = 4$

19.

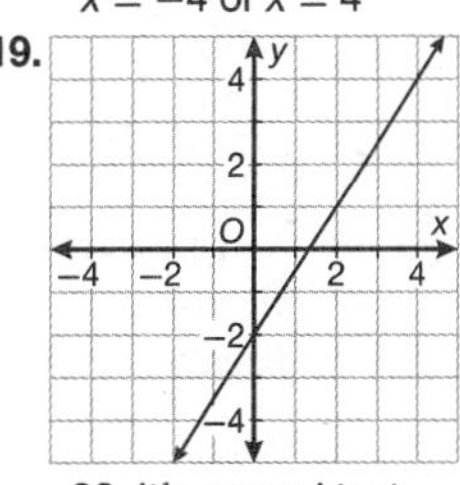

20. It's a good test point because it makes the math quicker and easier and less prone to errors; it cannot be used when it is on the boundary line.

Problem 12

Guide the students by asking them the following questions.

"How can you label the *x*- and *y*-axes to show the compass directions north, south, east, and west?" Put north on the top, south on the bottom, east on the right, west on the left.

"What two ordered pairs represent the distance between the boats?" (4, 6) and (−4, −6)

"How can you find the distance between the boats?" Use the distance formula with the two points (4, 6) and (−4, −6).

Problem 13

Extend the Problem

Find the x-intercepts in simplified radical form and approximated to the nearest hundredth. $-3 + \sqrt{5}, -3 - \sqrt{5}$, −0.76, −5.24

Problem 14

Extend the Problem

The volume of a right circular cone is one-third that of the right circular cylinder with the same height and base. Find a simplified radical expression for the radius of the cone. $\frac{\sqrt{3V\pi h}}{\pi h}$

ENGLISH LEARNERS

Explain that there are a number of different equations in mathematics that are known as the **distance formula**. Thus, each is more precisely called a distance formula, there being no such thing as "the" distance formula.

Write $d = st$ on the board and have a volunteer explain what it means and what it's used for. Sample: Distance equals speed multiplied by time; used to compute distance covered by a moving object

Ask: **"What is the purpose of the distance formula taught in this lesson?"** Sample: find distance between two points on a coordinate plane from the coordinates of their points

Students who have studied geometry may also have encountered this formula for the shortest distance from a given point $P_1(x_1, y_1)$ to a line with the equation $Ax + By + C = 0$.

$$d = \frac{|Ax_1 + By_1 + C|}{\sqrt{A^2 + B^2}}$$

22. (32) **Nutrition and Cost** A one-kilogram container of mixed nuts costs \$17.70 and contains 86 grams of protein. The mix contains almonds (\$15 per kilogram, 13% protein), cashews (\$18 per kilogram, 9% protein), and pecans (\$19 per kilogram, 5% protein). How much of each type of nut is in the mix? To find the answer, write a system of equations and use an inverse matrix to solve it. 0.2 kg of almonds, 0.5 kg of cashews, 0.3 kg of pecans

23. (29) **Ticket Sales** At a college basketball game 350 tickets were sold. Tickets cost \$5 for children and senior citizens, \$7 for students, and \$10 for all others. The total income from ticket sales was \$2,665. The combined number of \$7 and \$10 tickets sold was 6 times more than the number of \$5 tickets sold. How many tickets of each type were sold? \$5: 50; \$7: 195; \$10: 105

*24. (40) **Justify** Explain why the expression $\frac{3}{\sqrt{5}}$ is allowed to be written as $\frac{3}{\sqrt{5}} \cdot \frac{\sqrt{5}}{\sqrt{5}}$.

24. Any number divided by itself is 1, so the expression is being multiplied by 1. By the Identity Property of Multiplication,

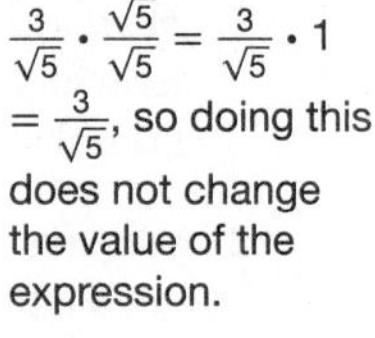

$\frac{3}{\sqrt{5}} \cdot \frac{\sqrt{5}}{\sqrt{5}} = \frac{3}{\sqrt{5}} \cdot 1 = \frac{3}{\sqrt{5}}$, so doing this does not change the value of the expression.

25. (37) **Physics** A satellite has an orbital acceleration of $\frac{v^2}{r}$, where v is the speed of the satellite and r is the distance from the satellite to the Earth's center. Find the difference in acceleration between satellite 1 and satellite 2. $\frac{v^2}{4r}$

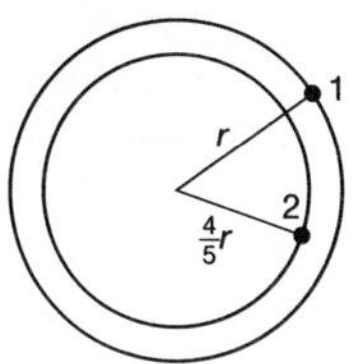

26. (25) **Rainfall** Annual rainfall amounts in inches for Austin, Texas for 2006 are listed in the table below. What was the mean amount of rainfall in Austin during that year and what was the standard deviation? The mean is $\bar{x} \approx 2.89$, and the standard deviation is: $\sigma \approx 2.06$

Month	J	F	M	A	M	J	J	A	S	O	N	D
Amount (in.)	1.80	0.89	7.54	2.89	5.28	3.18	0.48	0.22	3.00	3.93	1.29	4.20

*27. (41) **Error Analysis** Find and correct the error a student made in finding the distance between the point (7, 2) and the point (8, −5).

$$d = \sqrt{(8-7)^2 - (-5-2)^2}$$
$$= \sqrt{1^2 - (-7)^2}$$
$$= \sqrt{1-49}$$
$$= \sqrt{-48}$$

The student wrote the formula incorrectly. There should be a plus sign between the two quantities that are squared. The correct distance is $\sqrt{1+49} = \sqrt{50} = 5\sqrt{2}$

29.

s	t	$\neg t$	$s \wedge \neg t$
T	T	F	F
T	F	T	T
F	T	F	F
F	F	T	f

28. (26) **Justify** Is the equation $2\pi x + 3y = 20$ in standard form? Explain your reasoning. Yes, this equation is in standard form. The number π is a real number and part of the coefficient of x.

29. (Inv 1) Create a truth table for $s \wedge \neg t$.

30. (22) **Coordinate Geometry** Use the set of ordered pairs {(2, 3), (2, 1), (2, 0), (2, 4)}. Is the graph of this relation continuous, discontinuous, or discrete? Graph of a discrete, vertical set of points.

Problem 22

If students need a hint, tell them the system will have three equations and give them the equation for price:
$\$15a + \$18c + \$19p = \$17.70$

The other two equations show the total mass and amount of protein:
$a + c + p = 1$ kg
$0.13a + 0.09c + 0.05p = 0.086$ kg

Problem 23

Point out there are three categories of ticket prices, not four. Students might use the variables a, b, and c with a = number of child/senior tickets, b = number of student tickets, c = number of other tickets. If students need help getting started, give them one of the three equations in the system:
$a + b + c = 350$
$5a + 7b + 10c = 2665$
$b + c = 6a$

Problem 25

If students have difficulty, have them solve a simpler problem by using $0.8r$ as the radius for satellite 2. They will get $14.75\frac{v^2}{r}$, which is equivalent to $\frac{59v^2}{4r}$.

Problem 28

Remind students that the standard form is $Ax + By = C$. The constants A, B, and C can be any real numbers. You may need to point out that π is a constant, not a variable.

CHALLENGE

A circle is centered at the origin with radius 25. Find all the ordered pairs on this circle that have integral coordinates. (0, ±25), (±25, 0), (±7, ±24), (±24, ±7), (±15, ±20), (±20, ±15)

LOOKING FORWARD

Applying the distance formula and the Pythagorean Theorem prepares students for

- **Lesson 46** Finding Trigonometric Functions and their Reciprocals
- **Lesson 52** Using Two Special Right Triangles
- **Lesson 56** Finding Angles of Rotation

LAB 7

Calculating Permutations and Combinations

Graphing Calculator Lab (*Use with Lesson 42*)

A graphing calculator can be used to calculate permutations and combinations. Use the graphing calculator to calculate ${}_{18}P_5$ and ${}_{14}C_3$.

Reading Math

${}_nP_r$ is read "the permutation of *n* things taken *r* at a time."

${}_nC_r$ is read "the combination of *n* things taken *r* at a time."

To Calculate a Permutation: ${}_{18}P_5$

1. Press 1 8 to enter n, the total number of objects to choose from. The subscript n is always located on the left hand side of the general form ${}_nP_r$.

MATH NUM CPX PRB
1:rand
2:nPr
3:nCr
4:!
5:randInt(
6:randNorm(
7:randBin(

2. Press MATH and then the arrow key ◀, to open the **[PRB]** menu. Use the down arrow ▼ to highlight [2:${}_nP_r$], and press ENTER.

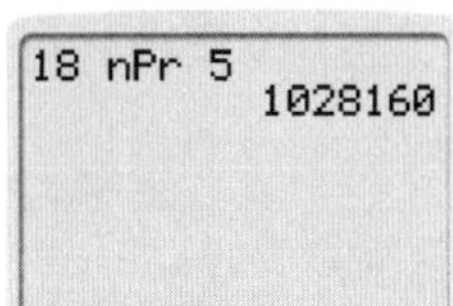

3. Press 5 to enter r, the number of objects chosen. The subscript r is always located on the right hand side of the general form ${}_nP_r$.
4. Press ENTER and the value of ${}_{18}P_5$ is displayed.

To Calculate a Combination: ${}_{14}C_3$

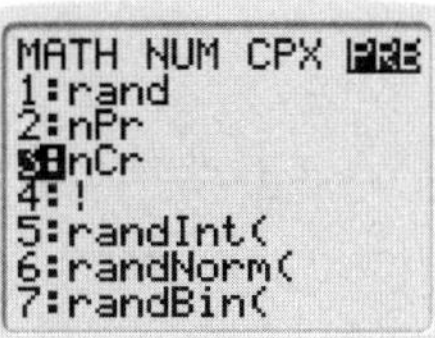

1. Press 1 4 to enter n, the total number of objects to choose from. The subscript n is always located on the left hand side of the general form ${}_nC_r$.
2. Press MATH, and then the arrow key ◀, to open the **[PRB]** menu. Press the down arrow ▼ twice to highlight [3:${}_nC_r$], and press ENTER.

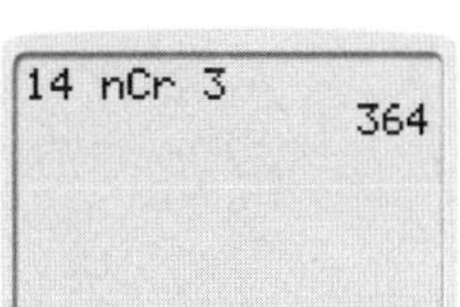

3. Press 3 to enter r, the number of objects chosen. The subscript r is always located on the right hand side of the general form ${}_nC_r$.
4. Press ENTER and the value of ${}_{14}C_3$ is displayed.

Lab Practice

a. Use the graphing calculator to calculate ${}_{12}P_7$. 3,991,680

b. Use the graphing calculator to calculate ${}_{22}P_3$. 9240

c. Use the graphing calculator to calculate ${}_{12}C_7$. 792

d. Use the graphing calculator to calculate ${}_{22}C_3$. 1540

LAB 7

Materials

- graphing calculator

Discuss

In this lab, students use the graphing calculator to determine the value of permutations and combinations.

Tell students that **PRB** stands for probability.

Practice Problems

Error Alert Remember to type the value of *n* on the home screen before choosing the permutation or combination function from the math menu. The message ERR: SYNTAX will be displayed if the function is chosen first.

Additional Practice Problems

1. Give an example to show why ${}_3P_2 = {}_3P_3$.
   Consider the objects *a*, *b*, *c*.
   ${}_3P_2 = 6$ {*ab*, *ac*, *bc*, *ba*, *ca*, *cb*}
   ${}_3P_3 = 6$ {*abc*, *acb*, *bac*, *bca*, *cba*, *cab*}
2. Compute the values of ${}_4C_0$, ${}_4C_1$, ${}_4C_2$, ${}_4C_3$, ${}_4C_4$. Notice the symmetry in the values. What is the relationship between these values and Pascal's triangle?
   The values are 1, 4, 6, 4, and 1. They represent the fourth row of Pascal's triangle if the top row is labeled Row 0.

LESSON 42

1 Warm Up

For problem 5, review the Fundamental Counting Principle: All possible outcomes in a given situation can be found by multiplying the ways each event can happen.

2 New Concepts

In this lesson, students learn to distinguish between permutations and combinations, including permutations with repeated elements. Formulas that involve factorials are used to compute numerical answers.

Example 1

Students evaluate expressions with factorials.

Additional Example 1

Evaluate.

a. $(7 - 1)!$ 720

b. $\frac{8!}{2!\,2!\,3!}$ 1,680

Extend the Example

Evaluate these expressions.

a. $\frac{5!}{2!(5-2)!} + \frac{9!}{3!(9-3)!}$ 94

b. $\frac{5!}{2!(5-2)!} \times \frac{9!}{3!(9-3)!}$ 840

LESSON RESOURCES

Student Edition Practice Workbook 42
Reteaching Masters 42
Adaptations Masters 42
Challenge and Enrichment Master C42

LESSON 42 Finding Permutations and Combinations

Warm Up

1. **Vocabulary** An ________ is an outcome of a probability experiment. event
(33)
2. What is the sample space for tossing a six-sided number cube? {1, 2, 3, 4, 5, 6}
(33)
3. Find the sample space of tossing a two-sided coin two times. {HH, TT, HT, TH}
(33)
4. Determine if the events are dependent or independent: flipping a coin and then tossing a number cube. independent
(33)
5. Use the Fundamental Counting Principle to find how many different outfits consisting of one shirt, one pair of pants, and one pair of shoes can be made from 3 shirts, 2 pairs of pants, and 4 pairs of shoes.
(33)
$3 \times 2 \times 4 = 24$ outfits

New Concepts

A **factorial** of a positive integer is the product of all positive integers up to and including that integer. Note that 0 factorial (0!) is defined to be 1.

Hint

$4! = 4(4-1)(4-2)(4-3)$
$4! = 4 \times 3 \times 2 \times 1 = 24$

***n* Factorial**
The factorial of n is denoted as $n!$ $n! = n(n-1)(n-2)(n-3) \ldots 1$ Zero factorial is defined to be 1. $0! = 1$.

Example 1 **Evaluating Expressions Containing Factorials**

Evaluate the following expressions that contain factorials:

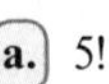

a. 5!

SOLUTION

$5! = 5 \times 4 \times 3 \times 2 \times 1 = 120$

A factorial of a positive integer is the multiplication of all positive integers up to and including the integer.

b. $\frac{10!}{2!(10-2)!}$

SOLUTION

$\frac{10!}{2!(10-2)!} = \frac{10!}{2!8!}$

$= \frac{10 \times 9 \times \cancel{8!}}{2 \times \cancel{8!}}$

$= \frac{90}{2} = 45$

To help simplify expressions with factorials, expand the numerator just enough to cancel duplicate factors in the denominator.

Online Connection
www.SaxonMathResources.com

MATH BACKGROUND

Many applications in set theory involve the selection and arrangement of a certain subset of a set. If the order of the elements in the subset matters, then the Fundamental Counting principle can be used to derive the permutations formula for the number of permutations of a set of n objects taken r at a time, $P(n, r)$. Notice that 0! must be defined as 1 so that $P(n, n)$ will equal the familiar $n!$

When some elements in the set n are identical or have similar properties, then the permutations formula is the one given with Example 2c. If the arrangement or order of the set elements is of no importance, then a combinations formula $C(n, r)$ may be used.

In abstract algebra, a permutation is defined as a bijection from a finite set onto itself. (A bijective function is both one-to-one and onto.) This leads to the development of the concept of permutation groups.

Graphing Calculator Tip

For directions on calculating permutations and combinations, see Graphing Calculator Lab #7.

A **permutation** is a selection of items where order is important.

Permutations
The permutation of n objects taken r at a time is: $$P(n, r) = \frac{n!}{(n-r)!}$$

The permutation of 6 objects taken 3 at a time is:

$$P(6, 3) = \frac{6!}{(6-3)!} = \frac{6!}{3!} = 120$$

A permutation of n objects arranged into one group of size n, without repetition of objects, can be found by using the formula: $P(n, n) = n!$

For example, the permutations of three letters (**A, B, C**) arranged into groups of three can be calculated as $P(3, 3) = 3! = 3 \times 2 \times 1 = 6$. We can check our calculation by showing all possible arrangements of the three letters, without repetition. The 6 arrangements are **ABC, ACB, BAC, BCA, CAB,** and **CBA.**

When letters are repeated, permutations are not distinguishable from each other. For example, for the letters (**B, B, O**) there are only three distinguishable permutations of the letters: **BOB, BBO,** and **OBB.**

The number of distinguishable permutations of n objects where one object is repeated q_1 times, another object is repeated q_2 times, and so on is: $\frac{n!}{q_1! \cdot q_2! \cdot \ldots q_k!}$. The number of permutations of the letters **BOB** is $\frac{3!}{2!1!} = \frac{6}{2} = 3$.

Example 2 Finding Permutations

a. Find the permutation of 8 objects.

SOLUTION

$8! = 8 \times 7 \times 6 \times 5 \times 4 \times 3 \times 2 \times 1$ The permutation of n objects is $n!$

There are 40,320 possible permutations of 8 objects.

b. Find the permutation of 6 objects taken 2 at a time.

SOLUTION

Use the formula for the permutation of n objects taken r at a time.

$$P(n, r) = \frac{n!}{(n-r)!} \longrightarrow P(6, 2) = \frac{6!}{(6-2)!}$$

$$= \frac{6!}{4!}$$

$$= \frac{6 \times 5 \times \cancel{4!}}{\cancel{4!}}$$

$$= 30$$

There are 30 possible permutations of 6 objects taken 2 at a time.

Hint

You can check your answer by finding the sample space using the digits 1 through 6 to represent the objects.

TEACHER TIP

A number of different notations are used for permutations:

$P(n, r)$, ${}_nP_r$, $P_{n,r}$, P^n_r, ${}^nP_r$

Using $P(n, r)$ helps to emphasize that the formula defines a function of the two variables n and r.

Example 2

Students compute permutations, with and without repeated elements.

Additional Example 2

a. Find the permutation of 9 objects. 362,880

b. Find the permutation of 12 objects taken 3 at a time. 1,320

Extend the Example

A photograph is taken of a 7-person committee. In how many ways can the people be lined up if the chairperson is in the center of the group? 6! = 720

ALTERNATE METHOD FOR EXAMPLE 2

Use the word game anagrams as a way of introducing permutations of things not all different. Explain that the letters of ASTRONOMER can be rearranged to form the phrase MOON STARER. Have students share their experiences solving anagrams. Then present this problem: The anagram puzzle is to rearrange UPON COAST to find the name of a sea creature. How many different possible arrangements are there of the letters in the phrase UPON COAST?

Point out that there are 9 letters in all, but two of them are repeated. Ask: **"How many permutations are there of 9 letters?"** 9! **"What happens to that number if two of the letters are the same?"** It is divided in half.

Have students evaluate $\frac{9!}{2!}$ to find the number of permutations and then solve the anagram. 181,440; AN OCTOPUS

Additional Example 2, cont.

c. At a video store, how many ways can 4 copies of an animal video, 5 copies of an exercise video, and 3 copies of a western be arranged on a shelf? $\frac{12!}{4!\,5!\,3!} = 27{,}720$

TEACHER TIP

When reuse is permitted, the number of permutations of n different elements taken r at a time is n^r. For example, there are 6,561 possible 4-digit numbers that can be made from the digits 1–9 if the digits can be used more than once.

Example 3

Students solve combinations problems, including examples in which they must multiply or add numbers of outcomes.

Additional Example 3

a. Find the combination of 10 objects taken 3 at a time. 120

---

c. Find the number of distinguishable permutations of the letters in the word **CONNECTION.**

SOLUTION

CONNECTION has 10 letters with **C** repeated 2 times, **O** repeated 2 times, and **N** repeated 3 times. Let n = number of letters in the word **CONNECTION,** q_1 = number of **C**s, q_2 = number of **O**s, and q_3 = number of **N**s.

The number of distinguishable permutations can be found using: $\frac{n!}{q_1!q_2!q_3!}$

$$\frac{10!}{2!2!3!} = \frac{3{,}628{,}800}{2 \times 2 \times 6}$$
$$= 151{,}200$$

There are 151,200 distinguishable permutations of the letters in the word **CONNECTION.**

A **combination** is a selection of items where order does not matter.

Combinations
The combination of n objects taken r at a time is: $C(n, r) = \frac{n!}{r!(n-r)!}$

The combination of 5 objects taken 2 at a time is:

$$C(5, 2) = \frac{5!}{2!(5-2)!} = \frac{5!}{2!3!} = \frac{5 \times \overset{2}{\cancel{4}} \times \cancel{3} \times \cancel{2} \times \cancel{1}}{\cancel{2} \times \cancel{1} \times \cancel{3} \times \cancel{2} \times \cancel{1}} = 5 \times 2 = 10$$

To decide if a permutation or combination is needed, ask yourself if order is important.

The arrangement of digits for an alarm system code requires a specific order; the code 352 is different from the code 235, so a permutation is used to determine the number of possible codes.

The arrangement of names of people in a study group does not require a specific order, so a combination is used to calculate the number of possible arrangements.

Example 3 Finding Combinations

a. Find the combination of 7 objects taken 4 at a time.

SOLUTION

Use the formula for the combination of n objects taken r at a time. So,

$$C(n, r) = \frac{n!}{r!(n-r)!} \longrightarrow C(7, 4) = \frac{7!}{4!(7-4)!}$$
$$= \frac{7!}{4!3!}$$
$$= 35$$

There are 35 combinations of 7 objects taken 4 at a time.

INCLUSION

Some students may have difficulty using the formula for permutations of a set that contains repeated elements. Illustrate the use of the formula using easier examples. Ask: **"How many 5-digit numbers can be made from the digits 1, 2, 3, 4, 5?"** 120 **"What happens if I change the digits to 1, 1, 2, 3, 4?"** The number is cut in half and is only 60. **"if the digits are 1, 1, 1, 2, 3?"** The number is one-sixth as great and is only 20.

Show that the problem can be solved for the digits 1, 1, 1, 2, 3 by dividing 5! by 3! Point out that the number of possibilities decreases when there are repeated digits.

Then present problems in which more than one digit is repeated; for example: How many possible 5-digit numbers can be made using the digits 1, 1, 1, 2, 2

$$\frac{5!}{3!\,2!} = \frac{5 \times 4 \times 3 \times 2 \times 1}{(3 \times 2 \times 1) \times (2 \times 1)} = 10$$

Math Language

Multiple **independent events:**

If Event A and Event B can both occur, then multiply their outcomes.

If Event A or Event B can occur, then add their outcomes.

(b.) How many different pizza varieties can be created if there are two choices of crust, thick or thin, and two out of three possible toppings are selected?

SOLUTION

The combination of the 2 types of crusts is $C(2, 1)$. The combination of 2 out of 3 toppings is $C(3, 2)$. So, the number of pizza varieties that can be created is:

$$C(2, 1) \times C(3, 2) = \frac{2!}{1!(2-1)!} \times \frac{3!}{2!(3-2)!}$$
$$= \frac{2}{1} \times \frac{3 \times \cancel{2}}{\cancel{2} \times 1}$$
$$= 6$$

(c.) To travel from New York to Boston you could take one of three trains or one of four buses. How many different options for traveling between the two cities do you have?

Hint

When each combination represents a separate outcome, add the combinations.

SOLUTION

The combination of trains is $C(3, 1)$. The combination of buses is $C(4, 1)$. So the number of travel options is $C(3, 1) + C(4, 1)$

$$C(3, 1) + C(4, 1) = \frac{3!}{1!(3-1)!} + \frac{4!}{1!(4-1)!} = \frac{3}{1} + \frac{4}{1} = 7$$

Example 4 Distinguishing Between Permutations and Combinations

(a.) Explain whether the following is a combination or a permutation and find the solution. How many two-letter arrangements can be formed from the letters **CAT**?

SOLUTION

Order makes a difference in this problem because **CA** and **AC** are not the same arrangement. The solution is found using permutations: $P(3, 2) = \frac{3!}{(3-2)!} = 6$. There are 6 possible arrangements {CA, AC, CT, TC, AT, TA}.

(b.) Explain whether the following is a combination or a permutation and find the solution. How many two-man crews can be selected from the set of three males: {Charlie, Anton, Tom}?

SOLUTION

For this problem, order does *not* make a difference. The two-man crew of Charlie/Anton is the same as the two-man crew Anton/Charlie. The solution is found using combinations: $C(3, 2) = \frac{3!}{2!(3-2)!} = 3$. There are only 3 different two-man crews {Charlie/Anton, Charlie/Tom, Anton/Tom}.

CHALLENGE

This step-by-step example shows students a problem in which *both* combinations and permutations are used to find the solution.

Suppose a toy store has 7 different teddy bears and 4 different baby dolls. In how many ways can 3 teddy bears and 2 dolls be arranged on a display shelf?

Step 1: Find the number of combinations for the teddy bears. $C(7, 3) = 35$

Step 2: Find the combinations for the baby dolls. $C(4, 2) = 6$

Step 3: Multiply to find the number of combinations of the 5 toys. $35 \cdot 6 = 210$

Step 4: Find the number of permutations of 5 toys taken 5 at a time. $P(5, 5) = 120$

Step 5: There are 120 permutations for each combination. Multiply. $120 \cdot 210 = 25{,}200$

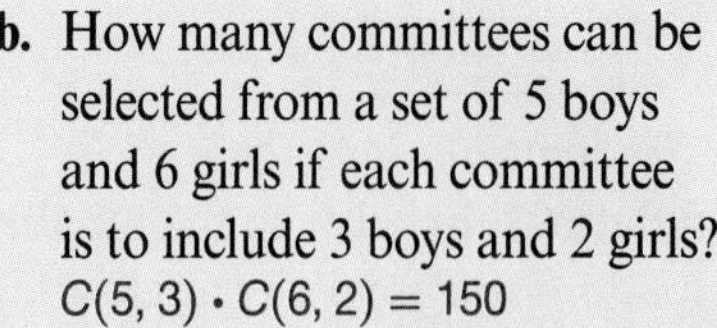

b. How many committees can be selected from a set of 5 boys and 6 girls if each committee is to include 3 boys and 2 girls?
$C(5, 3) \cdot C(6, 2) = 150$

c. On a final examination, students can choose to answer 7 out of 10 multiple-choice questions or 3 out of 5 essay questions. How many different choices do students have for completing this exam?
$\frac{10!}{7!(10-7)!} + \frac{5!}{3!(5-3)!} = 130$

Example 4

Students analyze problems to decide if they describe combinations or permutations; that is, they determine if the order of the elements makes a difference in the arrangement.

Error Alert In Part a, some students may assume, incorrectly, that a letter may be used twice. Explain that they are to assume reuse is *not* allowed unless it is specifically mentioned as an option in the statement of the problem.

Additional Example 4

Explain whether each situation is a combination or a permutation and find the solution.

a. How many 4-letter passwords can be made from the first 10 letters of the alphabet if no letter is used more than once in the same password?
permutation; $P(10, 4) = 5{,}040$

b. How many sets of officers of 3 people can be selected from a club that has 22 members?
combination; $C(22, 3) = 1{,}540$

TEACHER TIP

The combinations formula appears again when students study the binomial expansion of $(a + b)^n$. The coefficient of the rth term is $C(n, r - 1)$.

Exploration

Students discover the relationship between the number pattern in Pascal's Triangle and the formula for the combination of n things taken r at a time.

Additional Example

Use Pascal's Triangle to explain why $C(10, 3)$ and $C(10, 7)$ are equal. Sample: They are placed symmetrically in the tenth row of the triangle and are therefore equal in value. Both equal 120.

Extend the Example

Use the pattern in Pascal's Triangle to simplify the expression $C(n, r - 1) + C(n, r)$. Explain the meaning of this relationship in words. $C(n + 1, r)$; Each number in Pascal's Triangle equals the sum of the two numbers above it.

Example 5

Students multiply combinations to solve an applications problem.

Additional Example 5

At a family reunion there are 8 children, 20 adults, and 5 seniors. When the drawings are held for door prizes, there will be 5 prizes for children, 2 for adults, and 2 for seniors. How many possible sets of winners are there? $C(8, 5) \cdot C(20, 2) \cdot C(5, 2) = 106{,}400$

Extend the Example

From a group of 7 people, find the number of different ways to select at most 4 people. Hint: You can choose 0, 1, 2, 3, or 4 people. 99

Hint

Notice that Entry 0 in each row is 1.

Exploration Pascal's Triangle and Combinations

By labeling the top row as Row 0 and the first entry in each row as Entry 0, Pascal's Triangle shows a direct relationship to combinations. For example, to count the number of ways to choose 1 object from 3 objects, look at Entry 1 in Row 3. This entry is 3. $C(3, 1) = 3$

1	Row 0
1 1	Row 1
1 2 1	Row 2
1 3 3 1	Row 3
1 4 6 4 1	Row 4
1 5 10 10 5 1	Row 5

Explore the different combinations represented in Pascal's Triangle by identifying all of the combinations in the first 5 rows. Justify your results by solving for each combination identified.

SOLUTION

Combinations:

$C(0, 0) = 1$; $C(1, 0) = 1$; $C(1, 1) = 1$; $C(2, 0) = 1$; $C(2, 1) = 2$; $C(2, 2) = 1$; $C(3, 0) = 1$; $C(3, 1) = 3$; $C(3, 2) = 3$; $C(3, 3) = 1$; $C(4, 0) = 1$; $C(4, 1) = 4$; $C(4, 2) = 6$; $C(4, 3) = 4$; $C(4, 4) = 1$; $C(5, 0) = 1$; $C(5, 1) = 5$; $C(5, 2) = 10$; $C(5, 3) = 10$; $C(5, 4) = 5$; $C(5, 5) = 1$.

Example 5 Application: Athletic Tickets

A school has scheduled 5 football games, 6 basketball games, 3 volleyball games, and 4 soccer games. You have a ticket that allows you to attend 5 games. In how many ways can you attend 2 football games, 2 basketball games, and either a volleyball or soccer game?

SOLUTION

1. Understand Since the order of arrangements does not matter, this is a combination problem.

2. Plan To find the number of ways to use your tickets, make a table to help solve the problem.

Five-Game Ticket

Attend 2 games	Attend 2 games	Attend 1 game
Football: 5	Basketball: 6	Volleyball or soccer: 7

Use combinations to solve. Multiply the combination for each event to find the possible ways to use your tickets.

3. Solve C(5 football, pick 2) × C(6 basketball, pick 2) × (7 volleyball or soccer, pick 1)

$$= C(5, 2) \times C(6, 2) \times C(7, 1) = \frac{5!}{2!3!} \times \frac{6!}{2!4!} \times \frac{7!}{1!6!} = 1{,}050$$

Check Use your calculator to check your calculations for each combination, and then multiply the results. ${}_5C_2 = 10$; ${}_6C_2 = 15$; ${}_7C_1 = 7$; $10 \times 15 \times 7 = 1{,}050$

ALTERNATE METHOD FOR EXPLORATION

Explain the notation $\binom{n}{r}$ as another way to write the combination of n things taken r at a time. Then put the pattern at the right on the board. Have students evaluate the combinations and they will get Pascal's Triangle. Ask students to add one more row to the pattern in the triangle.

$$\binom{0}{0}$$
$$\binom{1}{0} \quad \binom{1}{1}$$
$$\binom{2}{0} \quad \binom{2}{1} \quad \binom{2}{2}$$
$$\binom{3}{0} \quad \binom{3}{1} \quad \binom{3}{2} \quad \binom{3}{3}$$
$$\binom{4}{0} \quad \binom{4}{1} \quad \binom{4}{2} \quad \binom{4}{3} \quad \binom{4}{4}$$

Lesson Practice

a. Evaluate 6! 720 (Ex 1)

b. Evaluate $\frac{6!}{4!(6-4)!}$ 15 (Ex 1)

c. Find the number of permutation of 7 objects. c. $7! = 7 \times 6 \times 5 \times 4 \times 3 \times 2 \times 1 = 5040$ (Ex 2a)

d. Find the permutation of 12 objects taken 3 at a time. (Ex 2b)

d. $\frac{12!}{(12-3)!} = \frac{12 \times 11 \times 10 \times 9!}{9!} = 1{,}320$

e. **OHIO** has 4 letters with **O** repeated twice. Find the number of distinguishable permutations of letters in **OHIO**. $\frac{4!}{2!} = \frac{24}{2} = 12$ (Ex 2c)

f. Find the combination of 10 objects taken 7 at a time. $C(10, 7) = 120$ (Ex 3a)

g. Find the number of salad varieties using one of four salad dressings and two of four additional vegetables. $C(4, 1) \times C(4, 2) = 4 \times 6 = 24$ (Ex 3b)

h. How many different 4-card hands are possible if you draw 4 cards from a standard deck of 52 cards? Is this a permutation or combination problem? $C(52, 4) = 270{,}725$ This is a combination problem. (Ex 4)

i. How many different ways can 4 cards be picked from a standard deck of 52 cards and be played in a game? Is this a permutation or a combination problem? $P(52, 4) = 6{,}497{,}400$; permutation (Ex 4)

j. In how many ways can 3 blue, 2 red, and 5 green markers be distributed to 10 students? $P = \frac{10!}{3!2!5!} = 2{,}520$ (Ex 5)

Practice Distributed and Integrated

Use multipliers to convert.

1. 32 mi³ to cubic inches (18) $32(5280)(5280)(5280)(12)(12)(12) \approx 8.14 \times 10^{15}$ in.³

2. 10 square miles to square feet (18) $(10)(5280)(5280) = 278{,}784{,}000$ ft²

Use the point-slope formula to write the equation of the line with slope m that passes through the given point.

3. $m = -1$, (4, 5.5) (26) $y = -x + 9.5$

4. $m = 1.8$, (−10, 0) (26) $y = 1.8x + 18$

Find the distance between the following points.

*5. (−2, 2) and (4, 6). (41) $2\sqrt{13}$

*6. (−3, 2) and (5, 2) (41) 8

Evaluate.

*7. $P(5, 3)$ (42) 60

*8. $C(8, 4)$ (42) 70

*9. 11! (42) 39,916,800

Find the sum.

10. $\frac{1}{x+1} + \frac{1}{x+2} + \frac{1}{x+3}$ (37)

10. $\frac{3x^2 + 12x + 11}{x^3 + 6x^2 + 11x + 6}$

11. $\frac{1}{1 + \frac{1}{x+1}} + \frac{1}{1 + \frac{1}{x-1}}$ (37) $\frac{2x^2 + 2x - 2}{x(x+2)}$

12. **Verify** Show that $\begin{matrix} 2x + 3y = 13 \\ 4x - 9y = -79 \end{matrix}$ can be solved by eliminating either the x-terms or the y-terms. (24) See Additional Answers.

CHALLENGE

When a set of objects is arranged around a circle rather than in a linear row, the number of permutation is less. For a set of n elements, it is $(n - 1)!$

a. Find the number of ways 8 people can sit at a round table. 5,040

b. How many arrangements of 6 keys are there on a ring? Hint: The clockwise and counterclockwise arrangements are the same. 60

Lesson Practice

Problem e

Error Alert Since there are only 12 possible permutations, students who have difficulty can solve the problem by making an organized list.

Problem g

Scaffolding Have students start by finding the number of combinations of vegetables. That equals 4 things taken 2 at a time, or $C(4, 2) = 6$. Each of these can be paired with one of four salad dressings, so the answer is $6 \cdot 4$.

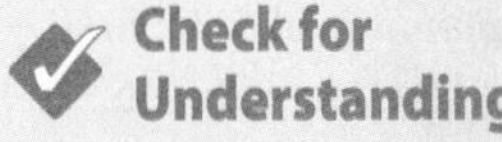

Check for Understanding

The questions below help assess the concepts taught in this lesson.

1. **"How can you find $(n + 1)!$ if you know $n!$?"** Multiply $n!$ times $(n + 1)$.

2. **"Compare the formulas for permutations and combinations, $P(n, r)$ and $C(n, r)$. How are they different?"** Sample: In the combinations formula, the denominator is multiplied by $r!$. Or, $C(n, r) = \frac{P(n, r)}{r!}$

3 Practice

Math Conversations

Discussions to strengthen understanding

Problems 5–6

If students do not remember the distance formula, have them graph the points and connect them to make the hypotenuse of a right triangle. Then the Pythagorean Theorem can be used to find the length of the hypotenuse.

Problem 18

Error Alert

If students choose the wrong answer, remind them that an x-intercept must make $x^2 + 2x + 1$ equal 0 when it is substituted for x.

Problem 19

Guide the students by asking them the following questions.

"Your first step is to classify the triples into two groups. What will those groups be?" Those that satisfy the Pythagorean Theorem and those that don't.

"The denominator of your first probability fraction will be 6. Why?" There are 6 pieces of paper.

"What will be the denominator of the second probability fraction?" 5

"Why?" After the first drawing, there will be only 5 pieces of paper left.

Problem 20

You may need to tell students that the inequality in the problem has two variables. Have them graph an example such as $y \geq x - 2$ to help them interpret the problem.

Problem 21

"How do the denominators in the answer choices give you a hint about solving this problem?" Sample: It is likely that the binomial $(x - 4)$ is a factor of the denominator.

Problem 22

Extend the Problem

A city is 26 km from Hamilton and its coordinates are $(k, 14)$. Find the value of k. 156 or 108

*13. **Dog Show** In a dog show, how many ways can 3 beagles, 2 poodles, and 5 greyhounds line up if the dogs of the same breed are considered identical? 2520
(42)

14. **Error Analysis** Given the matrix $A = \begin{bmatrix} 1 & 2 \\ 1 & -3 \end{bmatrix}$, a student found the inverse matrix as follows:
(32)

$$A^{-1} = \frac{1}{-5}\begin{bmatrix} -1 & 1 \\ 2 & 3 \end{bmatrix} = \begin{bmatrix} 0.2 & -0.2 \\ -0.4 & -0.6 \end{bmatrix}.$$

What is the error? Find the correct inverse matrix.

14. The student used $\frac{1}{ad - cb}\begin{bmatrix} -a & c \\ b & -d \end{bmatrix}$ instead of $\frac{1}{ad - cb}\begin{bmatrix} d & -b \\ -c & a \end{bmatrix}$. The correct inverse matrix is $A^{-1} = \frac{1}{-5}\begin{bmatrix} -3 & -1 \\ -2 & 1 \end{bmatrix} = \begin{bmatrix} 0.6 & 0.2 \\ 0.4 & -0.2 \end{bmatrix}$

15. **Multi-Step** The graph of a polynomial function is continuous. That is, there are no breaks in the graph. The x-intercepts of a function are the x-coordinates of the points at which the graph of the function crosses the x-axis.
(11)

a. Complete the table of values for the polynomial function $f(x) = x^3 - 4x - 2$.

x	−2	−1	0	1	2	3
$f(x)$	−2	1	−2	−5	−2	13

b. The function $f(x) = x^3 - 4x - 2$ has three x-intercepts. Between what pair of consecutive integer values of x does each x-intercept lie?
−2 and −1, −1 and 0, 2 and 3

*16. **Write** Describe the difference between a permutation and a combination if you select two-letter sets from the three-letter set {A, B, C}.
(42)

16. Possible answer: For permutations order matters; there are 6 two-letter permutations: AB, AC, BA, BC, CA, and CB. For combinations order doesn't matter; there are 3 two-letter combinations: AB, AC, and BC.

*17. **Graphing Calculator** Use a graphing calculator to graph $f(x) = -x^2 - 8x - 11$. Explain how the graph differs from the parent function $y = x^2$.
(30)

17. The graph of $-x^2 - 8x - 11$ opens downward and is shifted 4 units to the left and 5 units up relative to the parent function.

18. **Multiple Choice** What are the x-intercept(s) of the function $f(x) = x^2 + 2x + 1$? A
(35)

A −1 only **B** 1 only **C** −1 and 1 **D** −1 and −2

*19. **Probability** A teacher writes the numbers shown below on 6 sheets of paper and a student randomly chooses two papers from the hat, without replacement. What is the probability that the two papers chosen show measures that could be the sides of a right triangle? $\frac{2}{5} = 40\%$
(41)

30, 72, 78	24, 45, 51	12, 18, 20	25, 60, 65	9, 40, 41	14, 50, 54

20. **Analyze** Suppose you test a point that is on the boundary line of the graph of an inequality. What information does the result give about making the graph? What information does it not give about making the graph? It indicates if the boundary line should be dashed or solid. It does not indicate which half-plane to shade.
(39)

21. **Multiple Choice** Which of the following shows $\frac{3x^2 + 6x + 3}{x^2 - 3x - 4}$ completely simplified? C
(28)

A $-\frac{1}{4}$ **B** $\frac{1}{x - 4}$ **C** $\frac{3(x + 1)}{x - 4}$ **D** $\frac{(x + 1)^2}{x - 4}$

*22. **Cartography** A cartographer constructs a map of Montana over a grid system such that Hamilton is at (132, 4) and Missoula is at (146, 72). Find the distance between the cities to the nearest kilometer if each unit represents one kilometer.
(41)
about 69 kilometers

ENGLISH LEARNERS

Point out that **combination** is often used in everyday language in situations that are permutations problems. For example, someone might talk about the number of "combinations" of words than can be made from a set of letters. Since the order of the letters makes a difference, these are permutations, not combinations.

The word **arrangement** can be used for both permutations and combinations. Have students use the three terms in sentences to show they understand the distinctions among them.

23. Multi-Step (31) If an object is thrown straight down with an initial velocity of 32 feet per second, the number of feet it travels in t seconds is given by the expression $16t^2 + 32t$ (neglecting air resistance).

a. Write a rational expression for the average velocity of the object before it hits the ground over the time interval from 0 seconds to t seconds. Then simplify the expression. (Average velocity equals distance traveled divided by elapsed time.) **a.** $\frac{16t^2 + 32t}{t} = 16t + 32$

b. Evaluate the expression to find the average velocity of the object over the time interval from 0 seconds to 2 seconds. 64 feet per second

24. Error Analysis (38) Two students are dividing $2x^5 - 7x^4 - 4x^3 + 27x^2 - 18x$ by $x + 1$ but get different results. Which student made the mistake? Student A incorrectly added the squared term.

Student A	Student B
$2x^4 - 9x^3 + 5x^2 + 32x$	$2x^4 - 9x^3 + 5x^2 + 22x$
$(x + 1)\overline{)2x^5 - 7x^4 - 4x^3 + 27x^2 - 18x}$	$(x + 1)\overline{)2x^5 - 7x^4 - 4x^3 + 27x^2 - 18x}$
$-(2x^5 + 2x^4)$	$-(2x^5 + 2x^4)$
$0 - 9x^4 - 4x^3$	$0 - 9x^4 - 4x^3$
$-(-9x^4 - 9x^3)$	$-(-9x^4 - 9x^3)$
$0 + 5x^3 + 27x^2$	$0 + 5x^3 + 27x^2$
$-(5x^3 + 5x^2)$	$-(5x^3 + 5x^2)$
$0 + 32x^2 - 18x$	$0 + 22x^2 - 18x$
$-(32x^2 + 32x)$	$-(22x^2 + 22x)$
$0 - 50x$	$0 - 40x$

25. Model (33) A lunch special includes soup (tomato or chicken noodle), a sandwich (tuna, roast beef, or ham), and a beverage (juice or milk). Draw a tree diagram to show all the different possible lunches. How many different lunches are possible? See Additional Answers. 12;

26. Multi-Step (29) Use $y = -5x + 2z - 18$, $-6x = 2y - 3z + 23$, $z = -10 - 4x + y$

a. Write the equations with the variables aligned. **a.** $5x + y - 2z = -18$, $-6x - 2y + 3z = 23$, $4x - y + z = -10$

b. Estimate the number of solutions. Explain your answer. **b.** One solution; No two equations are multiples of each other in any way.

c. Solve the system of equations to verify your estimate. $(-3, -1, 1)$

27. (Physics) (36) To convert from Fahrenheit to Celsius, use the formula $F = \frac{9}{5}C + 32$. Find the formula to convert Celsius to Fahrenheit and determine if the graphs of the equations are parallel, perpendicular, or neither. $C = \frac{5}{9}(F - 32)$. The lines are neither parallel nor perpendicular.

***28. Multi-Step** (40) **a.** Identify the like radicals in the expression $4\sqrt[3]{5k} - 4\sqrt{5} + \sqrt[3]{4k} + \sqrt{5}$ $-4\sqrt{5}$ and $\sqrt{5}$

b. Simplify the expression by combining the like radicals. $4\sqrt[3]{5k} - 3\sqrt{5} + \sqrt[3]{4k}$

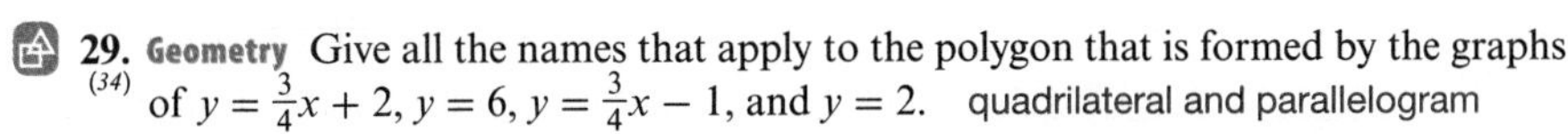

29. Geometry (34) Give all the names that apply to the polygon that is formed by the graphs of $y = \frac{3}{4}x + 2$, $y = 6$, $y = \frac{3}{4}x - 1$, and $y = 2$. quadrilateral and parallelogram

30. Model (27) Make sketches of parabolas to show that there can be zero, one, or two x-intercepts in the graph of a quadratic function. See Additional Answers.

CHALLENGE

Whenever r elements are selected from a set of n elements, there are $n - r$ elements left behind. What does this tell you about $C(n, r)$ and $C(n, n - r)$? They are equal.

LOOKING FORWARD

Counting with permutations and combinations prepares students for

- **Lesson 49** Using the Binomial Theorem
- **Lesson 55** Finding Probability
- **Lesson 60** Distinguishing Between Mutually Exclusive and Independent Events
- **Lesson 68** Finding Conditional Probability

Problem 28

Error Alert

Remind students that "like radicals" must have (1) the same index and (2) exactly the same number or expression under the radical sign. Ask:

"Two of the radicals have 3 as the index. What is the index of the other two radicals? How do you know?" 2; square roots have an index of 2

Problem 29

Guide the students by asking them the following questions.

"Describe the two lines with the equations $y = 6$ and $y = 2$." They are parallel horizontal lines that cross the y-axis at 6 and 2.

"How do you know the other two lines are also parallel?" They have the same slope.

"How do you know the figure cannot be a rectangle or a square?" Sample: Since two of the lines are horizontal, the other two would have to be vertical with equations of the form $x = a$.

LESSON
43

1 Warm Up

For problems 2 and 3, remind students to substitute the values of x and y in the ordered pair into the inequality.

2 New Concepts

In this lesson, students learn to solve systems of inequalities.

Example 1

Point out for $>$ and $<$ the boundary line is dashed and for $\leq$ and $\geq$ the boundary line is solid.

Additional Example 1

a. Determine whether $(-2, -1)$ and $(3, 1)$ are solutions of the system of linear inequalities.

$y > -2$

$2x + y \geq -2$

$(-2, -1)$ is not a solution.
$(3, 1)$ is a solution.

b. Graph the system.

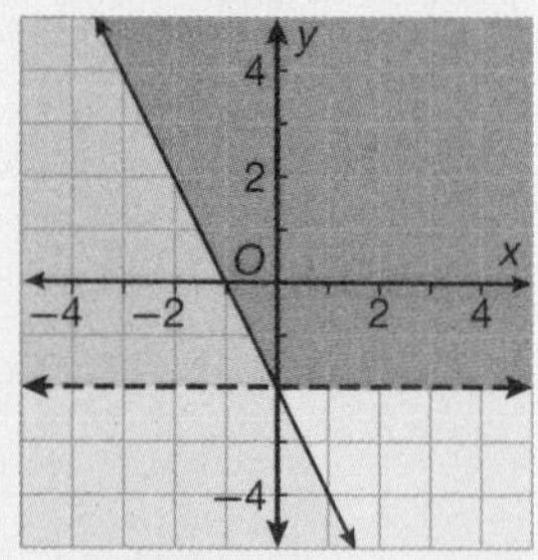

LESSON RESOURCES

Student Edition Practice Workbook 43
Reteaching Master 43
Adaptations Master 43
Challenge and Enrichment Master C43

LESSON 43

Solving Systems of Linear Inequalities

Warm Up

1. **Vocabulary** An ordered pair that makes a linear inequality true is a ______ of that inequality. solution
(39)

2. Is $(3, 5)$ a solution of $2x + y > 10$? yes
(39)

3. Is $(-1, 4)$ a solution of $-3x + 2y \leq 11$? yes
(39)

New Concepts

A **system of linear inequalities** is formed by two or more linear inequalities. An ordered pair is a solution of a system if it is a solution of every inequality in the system.

Math Language

To graph an inequality or system means to graph its **solution set.** The solution set is the set of all solutions.

To graph a linear inequality, first graph its boundary line. Then shade the entire half-plane that contains its solutions. To decide which half-plane to shade, pick a point in either half-plane. If the point is a solution, then shade that half-plane; if the point is not a solution, then shade the other half-plane. The graph of the system is the intersection of the graphs of the inequalities in the system.

Example 1 Identifying Solutions and Graphing a System

a. Determine whether $(2, 1)$ and $(2, 2)$ are solutions of the system of linear inequalities.

$y < 3$

$x + 2y \leq 4$

SOLUTION Substitute the ordered pairs for x and y.

Substitute $(2, 1)$.

$y < 3 \rightarrow 1 < 3$ true

$x + 2y \leq 4 \rightarrow 2 + 2(1) \leq 4$ true

$(2, 1)$ is a solution.

Substitute $(2, 2)$.

$y < 3 \rightarrow 2 < 3$ true

$x + 2y \leq 4 \rightarrow 2 + 2(2) \leq 4$ false

$(2, 2)$ is not a solution.

b. Graph the system.

SOLUTION

Graph the dashed boundary line $y = 3$. The solution set for $y < 3$ consists of all points below the line.

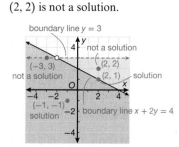

Graph the solid boundary line $x + 2y = 4$. The solution set for $x + 2y \leq 4$ consists of all points on the line and all points below the line. The solution set for the system consists of all points that are solutions of both inequalities. It is represented by the dark shaded region and the thick portion of the solid boundary line, not including $(-2, 3)$.

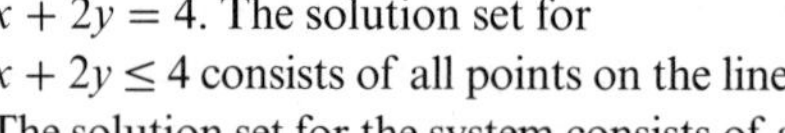

Hint

For $<$ and $>$, the boundary line is dashed, indicating that points on the line are not solutions. For $\leq$ and $\geq$, the boundary line is solid, indicating that points on the line are solutions.

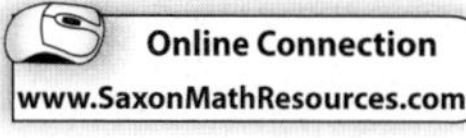
Online Connection
www.SaxonMathResources.com

MATH BACKGROUND

Graphing linear inequalities can also be applied to linear programming. Linear programming is used to find optimal values, such as maximum profits or productivity.

In linear programming, the system of inequalities is called *constraints*. The solution of the system is called a *feasible region*. Any point in this region satisfies the system, or constraints.

The quantity to be maximized or minimized is represented by a function. This function is called the *objective function*.

In linear programming, the maximum and minimum values occur at one of the vertices of the feasible region.

Example 2 Graphing Systems with Parallel Boundary Lines

a. Graph the system of linear inequalities. Describe the solution set.

$3x - 4y > 8$

$y \geq \frac{3}{4}x + 1$

SOLUTION

Solve $3x - 4y > 8$ for y.

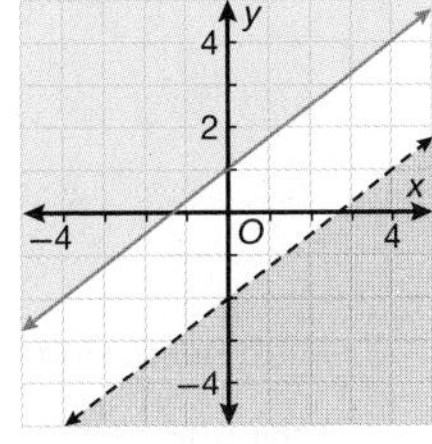

$3x - 4y > 8$

$-4y > -3x + 8$

$\frac{-4y}{-4} < \frac{-3x + 8}{-4}$

$y < \frac{3}{4}x - 2$

The graph of $3x - 4y > 8$ consists of all points below the boundary line. The graph of $y \geq \frac{3}{4}x + 1$ consists of all points on the boundary line and all points above the line. The boundary lines are parallel, so the graphs do not intersect. The solution set of the system is the empty set.

> **Hint**
>
> Remember to reverse the inequality symbol when you multiply or divide both sides of an inequality by a negative number.

b. Graph the system on a graphing calculator. Describe the solution set.

$y \geq -x + 1$

$x + y \leq 5$

SOLUTION

The equations of the boundary lines must be entered in the form $y = mx + b$, so solve $x + y \leq 5$ for y. Enter $y = -x + 1$ and $y = -x + 5$.

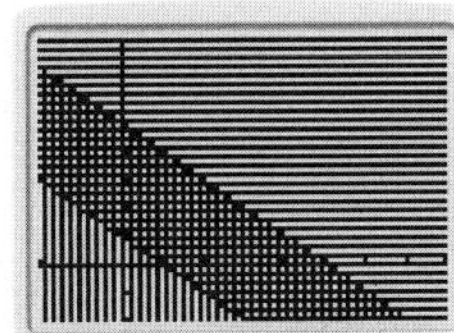

Then use the SHADE feature to shade the appropriate half-plane for each inequality. The boundary lines are parallel. The solution set consists of all points on both boundary lines and all points between the boundary lines.

> **Graphing Calculator Tip**
>
> To shade in the Y= editor, move the cursor to the graph style icon in the first column, just left of Y_1. Then press ENTER repeatedly until you get the appropriate icon.

Example 3 Graphing a System of Three Linear Inequalities

Graph the system of linear inequalities. Describe the solution set.

$x \geq -4$

$5x - 2y \leq 0$

$x - 3y \geq 6$

SOLUTION

The solution set of the system consists of all points on the triangle formed by the three boundary lines and all points inside the triangle.

ENGLISH LEARNERS

For this lesson, explain the meaning of the word **boundary**, say: "The word boundary is a noun that means something that indicates a limit or bounds."

Discuss examples of other types of boundaries, such as a territory in or near boundary, boundaries in a game, boundaries of space and time, and so on.

Have students identify the boundary lines in Examples 2 and 3 and explain why these lines are called "boundary lines."

Connect the meaning of boundary as a limit using the graphs in Examples 2 and 3. Tell students that the boundary line is a way of limiting the values of x and y for that system.

Example 2

Extend the Example

For part b, have students graph the system of equations without using the calculator. Remind them to use the slope-intercept form.

Additional Example 2

a. Graph the system of linear inequalities. Describe the solution set.

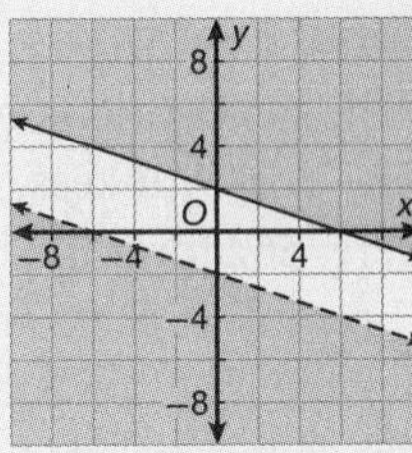

$x + 3y < -6$

$y \geq -\frac{1}{3}x + 2$

The solution set of the system is the empty set.

b. Graph the system on a graphing calculator. Describe the solution set.

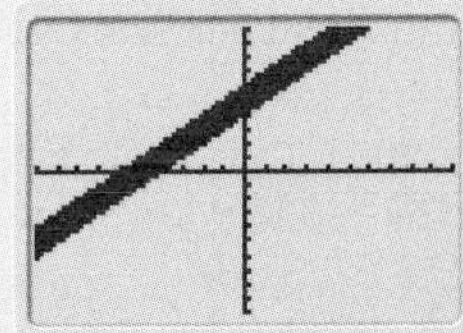

$y \geq x + 2$

$x - y \geq -3$

The solution set consists of all points on both boundary lines and all points between the boundary lines.

Example 3

Encourage students to use different patterns for the shaded regions.

Additional Example 3

Graph the system of linear inequalities. Describe the solution set.

$x - y \geq 3$

$x + y \leq -2$

$x \leq 2$

The solution set of the system consists of all points on the corner formed by the three boundary lines and all points inside the corner.

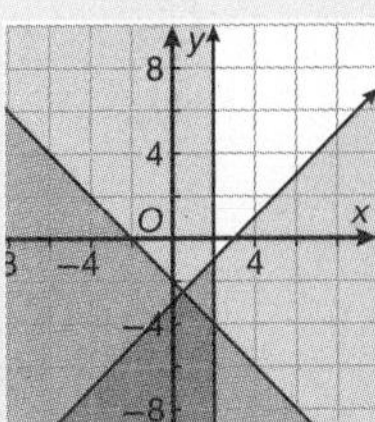

Example 4

Error Alert Students often reverse the inequality symbol when writing a system of linear inequalities. Point out the word *maximum*. Define maximum as the upper limit without going over. Then have students identify which inequality symbol represents *maximum*.

Additional Example 4

Two of the ticket prices for a 2007 New York Yankees baseball game were: \$62 for a Box seat and \$15 for a Bleachers seat. Suppose you are a softball coach. You want to buy tickets for the team. You decide to buy up to 20 tickets and to spend up to \$600. Let x represent a number of Box seats and y represent a number of Bleacher seats. Write and graph a system of linear inequalities to represent all the possible combinations of Box seats and Bleacher seats you can buy.

$x + y \leq 20$

$62x + 15y \leq 600$

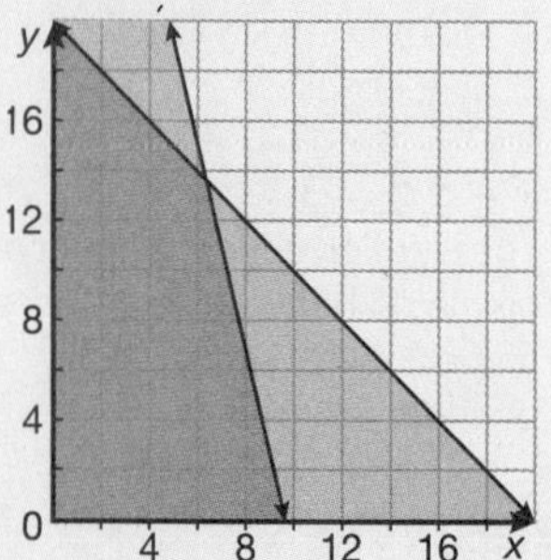

Lesson Practice

Problem c

Scaffolding Before graphing the inequalities, have students change $x + y < 3$ into slope-intercept form. Be sure students recognize that the two graphs are parallel.

Example 4 **Application: Tickets to an Entertainment Event**

Ticket prices for a major league baseball game are \$63 for a main box seat and \$20 for a tier reserved seat. Suppose you are a CEO of a company, and you want to buy tickets for some of your employees. You decide to buy up to 30 tickets and to spend up to \$1000. Write and graph a system of linear inequalities to represent all the possible combinations of main box seats and tier reserved seats you can buy.

SOLUTION Write the system. Let x equal the number of main box seats and y equal the number of tier reserve seats.

$x + y \leq 30$ The maximum sum of tickets is 30.

$63x + 20y \leq 1000$ The maximum amount to spend is \$1000.

Graph the system.

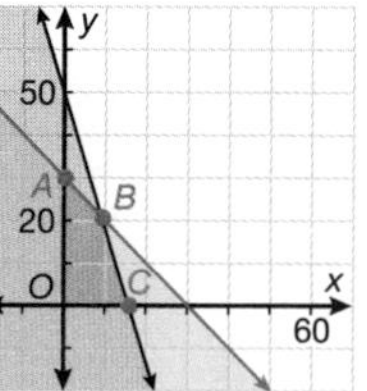

The solution set of the system consists of all points in the region where the shading overlaps and all points on the boundary of that region. However, only points with nonnegative integer coordinates make sense for this application because x and y represent numbers of tickets. Therefore, all the possible combinations of main box seats and tier reserved seats you can buy are represented by all points (x, y) on and inside polygon $OABC$, where x and y are integers.

Math Reasoning

Write Is the number of points on and inside polygon *OABC* finite or infinite? Is the number of possible combinations of tickets finite or infinite? Explain.

The number of points is infinite but the number of ticket combinations is finite since you can't buy a fraction of a ticket.

Lesson Practice

a. (Ex 1) Determine whether $(-5, 0)$, $(-6, 0)$, and $(1, -2)$ are solutions of the system of linear inequalities. $(-5, 0)$ yes; $(-6, 0)$ no; $(1, -2)$ yes

$$x \geq -5$$
$$2x + 3y < -3$$

b. (Ex 1) Graph the system of linear inequalities.

$$x \geq -5$$
$$2x + 3y < -3$$

c. (Ex 2) Graph the system of linear inequalities. Describe the solution set. The boundary lines are parallel. The solution set consists of all points between the boundary lines.

$$y > -x - 2$$
$$x + y < 3$$

d. (Ex 2) Graph the system of linear inequalities on a graphing calculator. Describe the solution set. The boundary lines are parallel, so the graphs do not intersect. The solution set of the system is the empty set.

$$y \geq -\frac{3}{4}x + 4$$
$$3x + 4y \leq 4$$

e. (Ex 3) Graph the system of linear inequalities. Describe the solution set.

$$y < 4$$
$$2x + y \geq 4$$
$$x - 2y \leq -2$$ See Additional Answers.

INCLUSION

Encourage students to use different color pens or pencils when graphing each inequality. Tell students to graph an inequality and shade the region with one color pen, and to do the same for the other inequality using a different color pen.

f.

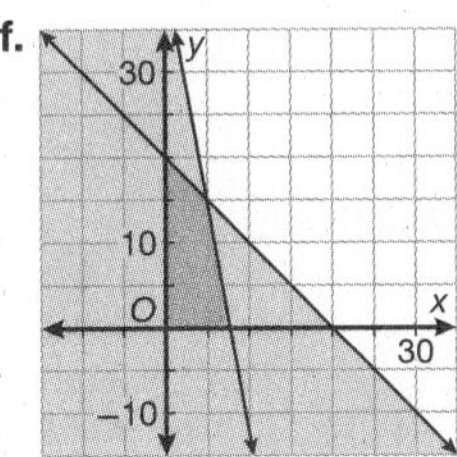

f. (Ex 4) Two of the ticket prices for a major league baseball game are \$65 for a tier box MVP seat and \$12 for a bleachers seat. Suppose you want to buy tickets for some of your friends. You decide to buy up to 20 tickets and to spend up to \$500. Let x represent a number of tier box MVP seats and y represent a number of bleachers seats. Write and graph a system of linear inequalities to represent all the possible combinations of tier box MVP seats and bleachers seats you can buy.

Practice Distributed and Integrated

Factor.

1. (23) $63x^3 + 108x^2 + 81x$ $9x(7x^2 + 12x + 9)$ **2.** (23) $x^{10} - 400$ $(x^5 - 20)(x^5 + 20)$

Determine if there are any excluded values. If so, list them.

3. (28) $\frac{10}{5x^2 - 20x - 60}$ 6, −2 **4.** (28) $\frac{4 - x}{3}$ There are no excluded values

***5.** (43) **Justify** Explain why all solutions of the system below lie in quadrant III.

$$y > \frac{1}{2}x$$
$$y < -2$$

5. Possible answer: There are solutions in quadrant III, such as (−8, −3). Every solution of $y > \frac{1}{2}x$ lies in quadrant I, II, or III. Every solution of $y < -2$ lies in quadrant III or IV. Therefore, every solution of the system lies in quadrant III.

6. (30) (**Small Business**) The profits, in dollars, for x weeks in one year for a small business can be modeled by the function $y = -0.55(x - 12)^2 + 630$. Does the graph of the function have a maximum or a minimum? What is that value and during what week did it occur? The maximum is \$630; week 12

7. (16) **Analyze** Explain the difficulty you encounter when trying to use Cramer's Rule to solve the system $\begin{array}{l} 4x - 12y = -4 \\ -6x + 18y = -6 \end{array}$

7. The coefficient matrix has determinant 0. The numerator matrices, however, are non-zero, indicating that there are no solutions. Indeed, the two equations are inconsistent.

***8.** (43) (**Ticket Prices**) Two of the ticket prices for a baseball game are \$45 for a right field box seat and \$90 for a pavilion box seat. Suppose it is the year 2007 and you are a business owner. You decide to buy tickets to give away as prizes to customers. You decide to buy up to 15 tickets and to spend up to \$900. Let x represent a number of right field box seats and y represent a number of pavilion box seats.

a. Write and graph a system of linear inequalities that represents the situation.

b. Describe the points in the graph of the system that represent all the possible combinations of right field box seats and pavilion box seats you can buy.

c. Determine the point of intersection of the boundary lines in the graph and explain its meaning. (10, 5); Possible explanation: It represents 10 right field box seats and 5 pavilion box seats at a total cost of \$900, the maximum that can be spent.

8a. $x + y \leq 15$
$45x + 90y \leq 900$
See Additional Answers.

8b. The points in the graph of the system that represent all the possible combinations of Right Field Box seats and Pavilion Box seats you can buy are all points with both coordinates nonnegative integers.

9. (20) (**Tennis**) The length of a regulation tennis court is given by the function $f(x) = x + 42$ feet. The width of a regulation tennis court is given by the function $g(x) = x$ feet. Write a function $h(x)$ that represents how many feet longer the court is than it is wide. $h(x) = f(x) - g(x) = x + 42 - (x) = 42$. The tennis court is 42 feet longer than it is wide.

CHALLENGE

Bridget works 50 hours or less a week. She earns \$40 per hour tutoring math and \$25 per hour tutoring french. Bridget needs to earn at least \$600 per week.

Write a system of linear inequalities. Graph the system. What is the best way for Bridget to spend her time? Explain.

$x + y \leq 50$
$40x + 25y \geq 600$

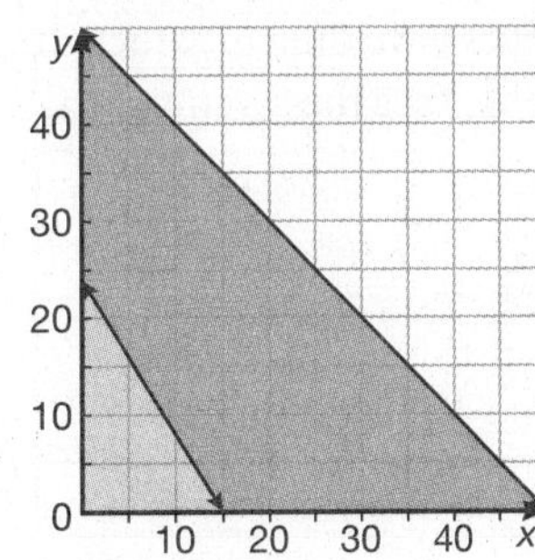

Accept reasonable explanations.

Check for Understanding

The questions below help assess the concepts taught in this lesson.

"How do you graph a linear inequality?" Graph its boundary line. Pick a point in either half-plane. If the point is a solution, shade that half-plane. If it isn't, shade the other half-plane.

"Explain how to decide if a boundary line is dashed or solid."

The boundary line is solid for ≤ or ≥. The boundary line is dashed for <or >.

"Describe the graph and solution set for the system $2x - y \geq 3$ and $y > 2x + 4$." The boundary lines are parallel The solutions do not intersect. The solution set is the empty set.

3 Practice

Math Conversations

Discussions to strengthen understanding

Problem 5

"The solution to $y > \frac{1}{2}x$ lies in what quadrants?" Quadrants I, II, III

"The solution to $y < -2$ lies in what quadrants?" Quadrants III and IV

"In what quadrant lies the intersection of the two graphs?" Quadrant III

"Why do all solutions lie in quadrant III?" Quadrant III is where the graphs intersect.

Problem 7

Remind students to use the coefficient matrix for the denominators for x and y. Review classification of systems by their solution. If $D = 0$ but neither numerator is 0, then the system is inconsistent. If $D = 0$ and at least one of the numerators is 0, then the system is dependent and consistent.

Problem 12

Point out that the two boundary lines are parallel. The shaded regions are different. If students have difficulty seeing that A is the correct answer choice, then have them do a rough sketch of each system.

Problem 13

TEACHER TIP

Have students use the FOIL method to multiply $(a + b)$ $(a - b)$. Elicit the response that after multiplying the binomial the middle terms, ab and $-ab$, cancel. The binomial $a^2 - b^2$ is left.

Problem 20

Students may focus too much on the distance formula and not on the steps presented. Have students find the distance between the two points. Then compare their work to the work given.

*10. **Graphing Calculator** Use a graphing calculator to solve. (32)
$$\begin{aligned} 9z - 7 &= 10x + 7y \\ -x - 3 &= -8y + 11z \\ z &= -2 - x + y \end{aligned}$$
$(-1, 3, 2)$

11. **Generalize** Suppose that $y_1 = m_1x + b_1$ is perpendicular to $y_2 = m_2x + b_2$. What must be true for b_1 to equal b_2? (36) The lines must intersect at the y-axis.

*12. **Multiple Choice** Which system has no solution? (43) **A**

A $y \le 2x + 2$, $y \ge 2x + 3$ B $y \le 2x + 2$, $y \le 2x + 3$ C $y \ge 2x + 2$, $y \le 2x + 3$ D $y \ge 2x + 2$, $y \ge 2x + 3$

13. **Write** In the difference of 2 squares, explain why the product of the two binomials $(a + b)$ and $(a - b)$ is $a^2 - b^2$. (23)

13. Possible response: Since the binomials have the same terms with different signs when they are multiplied the second and third terms end up the same terms with different signs so that they cancel out.

Determine whether the given points are solutions of the systems of linear inequalities.

*14. (43) $y + x \le 6$, $2x - 3y > 12$ $(6, 0)$ no

*15. (43) $10x + 5y \ge 16$, $4x - 6y < 22$ $(1, 3)$ yes

16. **Multiple Choice** What are the excluded value(s) for $\frac{x+4}{2x^2 - x - 21}$? (28) **C**

A -4 B -3 C -3 and 3.5 D -4, -3, and 3.5

17. a. Show the steps to multiply $\sqrt{12} \cdot \sqrt{24}$ by simplifying each radical first. (40)
$\sqrt{4}\sqrt{3} \cdot \sqrt{4}\sqrt{6} = 2\sqrt{3} \cdot 2\sqrt{6} = 4\sqrt{18} = 4\sqrt{9}\sqrt{2} = 12\sqrt{2}$

b. Show the steps to multiply $\sqrt{12} \cdot \sqrt{24}$ by multiplying the radicands first.
$\sqrt{288} = \sqrt{144}\sqrt{2} = 12\sqrt{2}$

18. **Justify** Suppose that the graph of $y = ax^2 + bx + c$, for real numbers a, b, and c, does not cross the x-axis. Is there a linear polynomial $x + d$, for real number d, such that $\frac{ax^2 + bx + c}{x + d}$ has a zero remainder? Explain. (38) No, because the quadratic has no real roots and therefore there are no linear polynomials that result in a zero remainder.

19. **Data Analysis** Students at a high school were asked how they traveled to and from school. The table shows data about the results of the survey. How many students in each grade were surveyed? To find the answer, write a system of equations and use an inverse matrix to solve it. (32)

19. 160 tenth graders, 170 eleventh graders, 200 twelfth graders

	Tenth Graders	Eleventh Graders	Twelfth Graders	Total
Walk	30%	20%	16%	114
School Bus	50%	50%	40%	245
Other	20%	30%	44%	171

*20. **Error Analysis** Find and correct the error a student made in finding the distance between the point at $(-1, 3)$ and the point at $(0, 2)$. (41)
$$\begin{aligned} d &= \sqrt{(0 - (-1))^2 + (2 - 3)^2} \\ &= \sqrt{1^2 + (-1)^2} \\ &= \sqrt{4} \\ &= 2 \end{aligned}$$

20. The student incorrectly added the sum of the squares in the radicand. $\sqrt{1^2 + \sqrt{1^2}} = \sqrt{2}$.

ALTERNATE METHOD FOR PROBLEM 16

If students have difficulty factoring, have them substitute the given values.

$x = -4$

$$\frac{-4 + 4}{32 + 4 - 21} = \frac{0}{15} = 0$$

Students can rule out choices A and D.

$x = -3$

$$\frac{-3 + 4}{18 + 3 - 21} = \frac{1}{0}$$

$x = 3.5$

$$\frac{3.5 + 4}{24.5 - 3.5 - 21} = \frac{7.5}{0}$$

Choice C is the correct answer.

21. (Business School) This table shows the change in rank according to Business Week of two undergraduate business schools from 2006 to 2007. If the rankings continue to change at these constant rates, at what rank will College A and College B be equal?
(21)

School	2006	2007	Change
College A	47	43	–4
College B	27	28	+1

21. Let y be rank and x be time in years.
$\begin{cases} y = -4x + 43 \\ y = x + 28 \end{cases}$
$y = 31$

State the expanded form.

***22.** 8! $8 \cdot 7 \cdot 6 \cdot 5 \cdot 4 \cdot 3 \cdot 2 \cdot 1$
(42)

***23.** $\frac{10!}{3!}$ $10 \cdot 9 \cdot 8 \cdot 7 \cdot 6 \cdot 5 \cdot 4$
(42)

24. **Geometry** Suppose 5 inch by 5 inch squares and 5 inch by 10 inch rectangles are placed end to end to make a long strip that is 5 inches high. Write and graph the inequality that shows how many of each shape can be used if the area of the strip must remain less than 1500 square inches. $25x + 50y < 1500$ See Additional Answers.
(39)

25. **Multi-Step** A container manufacturer is comparing a cubic container and a cylindrical container with the dimensions shown.
(31)

a. Write a rational expression in simplest form for the ratio of surface area to volume for the cubic container. $\frac{6}{x}$

b. Write a rational expression in simplest form the ratio of surface area to volume for the cylindrical container. $\frac{6}{x}$

c. Explain the meaning of the results in parts *a* and *b*. Possible answer: For every value of x, the two containers have the same ratio of surface area to volume.

26. **Error Analysis** A student was asked to convert a function written in vertex form to its standard form. The student's work is shown below. Find and correct the error the student made. The student did not fully distribute the –2. The correct answer is $f(x) = -2x^2 + 16x - 33$.
(27)

$$\begin{aligned} f(x) &= -2(x-4)^2 - 1 \\ &= -2(x^2 - 8x + 16) - 1 \\ &= -2x^2 - 8x + 16 - 1 \\ &= -2x^2 - 8x + 15 \end{aligned}$$

29. Order is important: seniors: $P(9,3) = 504$; juniors: $P(6,3) = 120$; Because the multiple events must both occur, the total possible out comes is the product; $504 \times 120 = 60{,}480$

Divide and identify the roots.

27. $15x^3 - 17x^2 - 66x + 56$ by $x + 2$ $15x^2 - 47x + 28$; the roots are $-2, \frac{4}{5}, \frac{7}{3}$
(38)

28. $-8x^3 + 50x^2 - 93x + 45$ by $x - 3$ $26x - 8x^2 - 15$; the roots are $3, \frac{3}{4}, \frac{5}{2}$
(38)

***29.** (Student Government) There are nine seniors and six juniors running for the class officer positions (President, Secretary, and Treasurer). Each class must elect 3 officers. How many possible outcomes are there for this election? Explain.
(42)

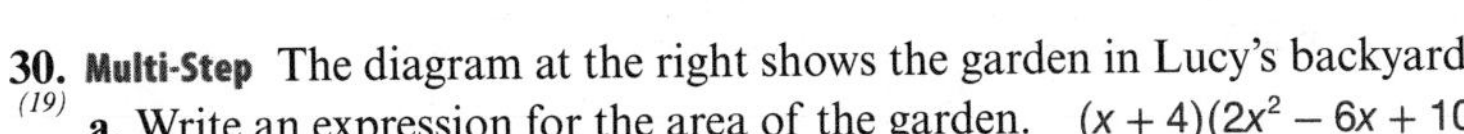

30. **Multi-Step** The diagram at the right shows the garden in Lucy's backyard.
(19)

a. Write an expression for the area of the garden. $(x + 4)(2x^2 - 6x + 10)$

b. Simplify the expression using multiplication. $2x^3 + 2x^2 - 14x + 40$

c. Find the area of the garden if $x = 4$ feet. 144 ft²

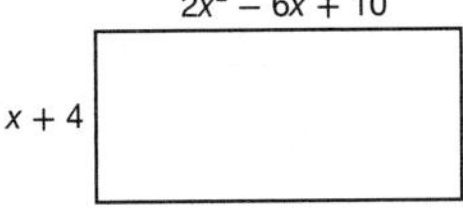

Problem 21

Students may have difficulty writing the system of equations. As an alternative, have them extend the table and continue the pattern.

2007	2008	2009	2010
43	39	35	31
28	29	30	31

Problem 23

Remind students that factorials in expanded notation is $n! = n(n-1)(n-2) \cdot \ldots \cdot 3 \cdot 2 \cdot 1$. Have students expand the numerator and denominator. Then simplify.

Problem 24

Error Alert

Students may write the incorrect inequality sign. Encourage students to reread the problem and to translate "remain less than" in terms of an inequality sign.

Problem 29

Remind students $_nP_r = \frac{n!}{(n-r)!}$. In this problem,

$_9P_3 = \frac{9!}{6!} = 9 \cdot 8 \cdot 7 = 504$ and

$_6P_3 = \frac{6!}{3!} = 6 \cdot 5 \cdot 4 = 120$.

Problem 30

Extend the Problem

Encourage students to write an expression for the perimeter of the garden, simplify the expression, and then find the perimeter of the garden if $x = 4$ feet.

$$\begin{aligned} P &= 2l + 2w \\ &= 2(2x^2 - 6x + 10) + 2(x + 4) \\ &= 4x^2 - 10x + 28 \\ &= 4(4^2) - 10(4) + 28 \\ &= 52 \text{ feet} \end{aligned}$$

LOOKING FORWARD

Solving systems of equations prepares students for

- **Lesson 89** Solving Quadratic Inequalities
- **Lesson 93** Solving Exponential Equations and Inequalities
- **Lesson 94** Solving Rational Inequalities

LESSON 44

1 Warm Up

Use the Warm Up to review multiplication of radicals.

2 New Concepts

In this lesson, students learn techniques for rationalizing expressions that have radicals in the denominator, either as monomials or as binomials.

Example 1

Students rationalize a denominator that is a monomial.

Additional Example 1

a. Simplify $\frac{4}{3\sqrt{7}}$. $\frac{4\sqrt{7}}{21}$

b. Simplify $\frac{1}{\sqrt{12}}$. $\frac{\sqrt{3}}{6}$

TEACHER TIP

Point out that some expressions may need to be further simplified *after* the rationalization. For example, $\frac{6\sqrt{3}}{20}$ would need to be further simplified to $\frac{3\sqrt{3}}{10}$.

LESSON 44 Rationalizing Denominators

Warm Up

1. **Vocabulary** In the radical expression $3\sqrt{2}$, 2 is called the radicand. (40)
2. Multiply and write the product in simplest form: $\frac{-2x+10}{x^2-25} \cdot \frac{x+5}{6}$ $-\frac{1}{3}$ (40)
3. Simplify: $2\sqrt{3} \cdot 4\sqrt{2}$ $8\sqrt{6}$ (40)
4. Simplify: $4\sqrt{5} \cdot \sqrt{5}$ 20 (40)

New Concepts

The expressions $\frac{3}{2\sqrt{5}}$ and $\frac{4+\sqrt{3}}{2-3\sqrt{3}}$ have irrational denominators because $\sqrt{5}$ and $\sqrt{3}$ are irrational. To rationalize the denominator of an expression, write an equivalent expression so that there are no radicals in any denominator and no denominators in any radical. An expression containing square root radicals is in simplest form when no radicand has a perfect square root factor and there are no irrational radical expressions in any denominator.

Hint

$\frac{3\sqrt{5}}{2\sqrt{25}}$ has a rational denominator, but is not in simplest form because the radicand 25 is a perfect square.

Example 1 Monomials in Numerator and Denominator

a. Simplify $\frac{3}{2\sqrt{5}}$.

SOLUTION

$$\frac{3}{2\sqrt{5}} = \frac{3}{2\sqrt{5}} \cdot \frac{\sqrt{5}}{\sqrt{5}}$$

Multiply the numerator and denominator by $\sqrt{5}$ to eliminate radical from the denominator.

$$= \frac{3\sqrt{5}}{2\sqrt{5}\sqrt{5}}$$

$$= \frac{3\sqrt{5}}{2 \cdot 5}$$

$\sqrt{5} \cdot \sqrt{5} = \sqrt{25} = 5$

$$= \frac{3\sqrt{5}}{10}$$

b. Simplify $\sqrt{\frac{1}{8}}$.

SOLUTION

$$\sqrt{\frac{1}{8}} = \sqrt{\frac{1}{8} \cdot \frac{2}{2}}$$

The radicand is a fraction. Multiply the numerator and denominator of the radicand by 2 to get a perfect square in the denominator.

$$= \sqrt{\frac{2}{16}}$$

$$= \frac{\sqrt{2}}{\sqrt{16}}$$

$\sqrt{\frac{a}{b}} = \frac{\sqrt{a}}{\sqrt{b}}$

$$= \frac{\sqrt{2}}{4}$$

Hint

Here is another method:

$$\sqrt{\frac{1}{8} \cdot \frac{8}{8}} = \sqrt{\frac{8}{64}} = \frac{\sqrt{8}}{8} = \frac{\sqrt{4}\sqrt{2}}{8} = \frac{2\sqrt{2}}{8} = \frac{\sqrt{2}}{4}$$

LESSON RESOURCES

Student Edition Practice Workbook 44
Reteaching Master 44
Adaptations Master 44
Challenge and Enrichment Master C44

MATH BACKGROUND

Rationalizing a denominator is useful because it can make mentally estimating expressions easier. This was especially true before calculators and computers were widely available. Consider the expressions in Example 1a. Students often memorized approximate values for radicals, such as $\sqrt{5} \approx 2.2$. The expression $\frac{3}{2\sqrt{5}}$ would have to be mentally estimated as $3 \div 2 \div 2.2$.

The rationalized form $\frac{3\sqrt{5}}{10}$ could easily be estimated mentally as $3 \times 2.2 = 6.6$, and $6.6 \div 10 = 0.66$. By rationalizing the expression first, you avoid having to mentally divide by a decimal.

To rationalize some binomial denominators, you need to multiply by a conjugate.

Radical Conjugates

If a, b, c, and d are rational numbers, then $a\sqrt{b} + c\sqrt{d}$ and $a\sqrt{b} - c\sqrt{d}$ are **conjugates** of each other, and their product is a rational number.

If denominator has the form	Multiply numerator and denominator by
$a\sqrt{b} + c\sqrt{d}$	$a\sqrt{b} - c\sqrt{d}$
$a\sqrt{b} - c\sqrt{d}$	$a\sqrt{b} + c\sqrt{d}$

Example 2 Monomial in Numerator, Binomial in Denominator

a. Simplify $\frac{2}{-4+\sqrt{3}}$.

SOLUTION

$\frac{2}{-4+\sqrt{3}} = \frac{2}{-4+\sqrt{3}} \cdot \frac{-4-\sqrt{3}}{-4-\sqrt{3}}$ — $-4-\sqrt{3}$ is the conjugate of $-4+\sqrt{3}$.

$= \frac{2(-4-\sqrt{3})}{(-4+\sqrt{3})(-4-\sqrt{3})}$ — Multiply.

$= \frac{-8-2\sqrt{3}}{(-4)^2-(\sqrt{3})^2}$ — Use $(a+b)(a-b) = a^2 - b^2$ in the denominator.

$= \frac{-8-2\sqrt{3}}{16-3}$ — Simplify the powers.

$= \frac{-8-2\sqrt{3}}{13}$ — Simplify the denominator.

Hint

$-\frac{8}{13} - \frac{2\sqrt{3}}{13}$ is an alternate simplified form for Example 2a.

b. Simplify $\frac{3}{\sqrt{5}+\sqrt{2}}$.

SOLUTION

$\frac{3}{\sqrt{5}+\sqrt{2}} = \frac{3}{\sqrt{5}+\sqrt{2}} \cdot \frac{\sqrt{5}-\sqrt{2}}{\sqrt{5}-\sqrt{2}}$ — $\sqrt{5}-\sqrt{2}$ is the conjugate of $\sqrt{5}+\sqrt{2}$.

$= \frac{3(\sqrt{5}-\sqrt{2})}{(\sqrt{5}+\sqrt{2})(\sqrt{5}-\sqrt{2})}$ — Multiply.

$= \frac{3(\sqrt{5}-\sqrt{2})}{(\sqrt{5})^2-(\sqrt{2})^2}$ — Use $(a+b)(a-b) = a^2 - b^2$ in the denominator.

$= \frac{3(\sqrt{5}-\sqrt{2})}{5-2}$ — Simplify the powers.

$= \frac{3(\sqrt{5}-\sqrt{2})}{3}$ — Simplify the denominator.

$= \sqrt{5}-\sqrt{2}$ — Simplify.

Example 2

Students rationalize expressions in which a radical is part of a binominal in the denominator.

Error Alert A common mistake is to use the incorrect sign when multiplying by the conjugate. In example 2a, students may mistakenly multiply by $\frac{-4+\sqrt{3}}{-4+\sqrt{3}}$ and incorrectly write down the squared terms in the denominator. Write both $(a+b)(a+b)$ and $(a+b)(a-b)$ on the board. Have students multiply both to see that the difference in two squares is $(a+b)(a-b) = a^2 - b^2$. Point out that the middle term, which would contain a radical, is eliminated.

Extend the Example

Suppose the radical in example 2a was in the first term of the denominator instead of the second: $\frac{2}{\sqrt{3}-4}$. Have students identify the conjugate for the denominator. $\sqrt{3}+4$ Ask them to solve the problem in this form and verify that the answer is the same, even though the conjugate is in a different form.

Additional Example 2

a. Simplify $\frac{3}{-3+\sqrt{5}}$. $\frac{-9-3\sqrt{5}}{4}$

b. Simplify $\frac{5}{\sqrt{7}+\sqrt{2}}$. $\sqrt{7}-\sqrt{2}$

ENGLISH LEARNERS

Write the terms **monomial** and **binomial** on the board. Have students say them aloud and define both words.

Discuss the meanings of the prefixes and suffixes of the words. Explain that **mono-** means "one," **bi-** means "two," and **-nomial** means "term" or "part." Relate these meanings to the definitions of the words.

Have students name other words that use the prefixes mono- and bi-, and discuss the meanings of those words. Examples include monolingual, bilingual, monotone, and bicycle.

Help students connect the definitions of mono- and bi- to the discussion in this lesson. Have them find examples in the lesson of monomials and binomials.

Example 3

Students simplify an expression that has radical binomials in both the numerator and denominator.

Additional Example 3

Simplify $\frac{5+\sqrt{5}}{4-3\sqrt{5}}$. $\frac{35+19\sqrt{5}}{-29}$

Lesson Practice

Problem b

Scaffolding Remind students to apply the rule for radicals with fractions before solving the problem: $\sqrt{\frac{a}{b}} = \frac{\sqrt{a}}{\sqrt{b}}$.

Problem d

Error Alert Students may reverse the signs of both radicals in the denominator. Point out that only the second sign is reversed in $(a+b)(a-b) = a^2 - b^2$.

Check for Understanding

The questions below help assess the concepts taught in this lesson.

1. **"Do you always end up with a radical in the numerator when you rationalize the denominator? Explain."** No; the numerator might have a perfect square root, which can be simplified to an integer.
2. **"Why is rationalizing the denominator a form of simplifying?"** Sample: Eliminating radicals in the denominator makes the expression easier to estimate.

Example 3 Binomials in Numerator and Denominator

Simplify $\frac{4+\sqrt{3}}{2-3\sqrt{3}}$.

SOLUTION

$\frac{4+\sqrt{3}}{2-3\sqrt{3}}$

$= \frac{4+\sqrt{3}}{2-3\sqrt{3}} \cdot \frac{2+3\sqrt{3}}{2+3\sqrt{3}}$ — $2+3\sqrt{3}$ is the conjugate of $2-3\sqrt{3}$.

$= \frac{(4+\sqrt{3})(2+3\sqrt{3})}{(2-3\sqrt{3})(2+3\sqrt{3})}$ — Multiply.

$= \frac{8+12\sqrt{3}+2\sqrt{3}+3\sqrt{3}\sqrt{3}}{(2)^2-(3\sqrt{3})^2}$ — Use FOIL method in the numerator. Use $(a+b)(a-b) = a^2 - b^2$ in the denominator.

$= \frac{8+14\sqrt{3}+9}{4-27}$ — Simplify.

$= \frac{17+14\sqrt{3}}{-23}$

Lesson Practice

Simplify.

a. (Ex 1) $\frac{2}{5\sqrt{7}}$ $\frac{2\sqrt{7}}{35}$

b. (Ex 1) $\sqrt{\frac{3}{20}}$ $\frac{\sqrt{15}}{10}$

c. (Ex 2) $\frac{2}{2-\sqrt{7}}$ $\frac{4+2\sqrt{7}}{-3}$ or $\frac{-4-2\sqrt{7}}{3}$

d. (Ex 2) $\frac{1}{4\sqrt{6}+\sqrt{3}}$ $\frac{4\sqrt{6}-\sqrt{3}}{93}$

e. (Ex 3) $\frac{3+\sqrt{5}}{1-\sqrt{5}}$ $-2-\sqrt{5}$

Practice Distributed and Integrated

Simplify:

***1.** (44) $\frac{5}{3\sqrt{3}}$ $\frac{5\sqrt{3}}{9}$

***2.** (44) $\frac{4}{2+\sqrt{7}}$ $-\frac{8-4\sqrt{7}}{3}$

***3.** (44) $\sqrt{\frac{9}{10}}$ $\frac{3\sqrt{10}}{10}$

***4.** (41) **Hiking** If the origin represents a campsite, and one hiker hikes 3 units due east and 4 units due south, while a second hiker hikes 5 units due west and 7 units due south, how much further from the campsite is the second hiker hike than the first? Write the answer as a decimal to the nearest tenth of a mile, given that each unit represents 1.5 miles. 5.4 miles

5. (24) Solve $\begin{matrix} 4x = 12 - 5y \\ 24 = 8x + 10y \end{matrix}$. infinitely many solutions

ALTERNATE METHOD FOR EXAMPLE 3

Some students may find applying the Distributive Property easier. For the numerator in this problem, they could use the following steps:

$(4+\sqrt{3})(2+3\sqrt{3})$

$4(2+3\sqrt{3}) + \sqrt{3}(2+3\sqrt{3})$

$8+12\sqrt{3}+2\sqrt{3}+3\sqrt{3}\sqrt{3}$

$17+14\sqrt{3}$

320 *Saxon* Algebra 2

*6. **Error Analysis** The graph at the right is a student's incorrect graph of the system below. What is the error? Graph the system correctly.
(43)
See Additional Answers.

$y \geq \frac{1}{2}x + 2$

$2x - y \leq 2$

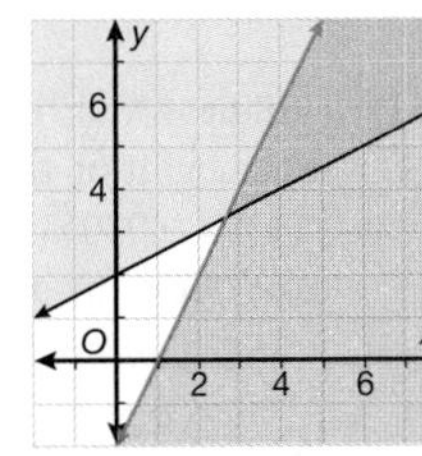

*7. Describe a substitution cipher. Each letter of the alphabet is replaced with a number.
(Inv 4)

*8. **Justify** Are there more arrangements of 10 items taken 4 at a time with order not important, or 10 items taken 6 at a time with order not important?
(43)
See Additional Answers.

*9. **Physics** The time in seconds it takes for an object to fall from a certain height can be given by $\frac{\sqrt{h}}{\sqrt{16}}$ where h is the initial height of the object in feet.
(40)

Find how long it takes for a rock to fall from the top of the Hoover Dam which has a height of 726 feet. About 6.7 seconds

*10. **Multiple Choice** The graph of which inequality is shown? B
(39)

A $x \leq -2$ **B** $x < -2$

C $y \leq -2$ **D** $y < -2$

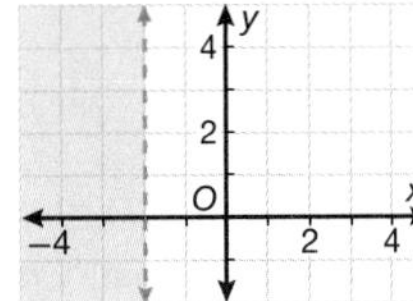

*11. **Generalize** Suppose the polynomial $ax^2 + bx + c$ has no real roots. Is there a linear factor $x + d$ such that the remainder is zero? Explain. No. The quadratic has no factors of the form $x + d$; therefore, dividing by $x + d$ will result in a nonzero remainder.
(38)

12. **Geometry** Are the events mutually exclusive? Explain your answer.
(33)

a. Draw an obtuse triangle and draw an isosceles triangle.

b. Draw an acute triangle and draw a right triangle. Yes. A triangle cannot be both acute and right.

12a. No. A triangle can be both obtuse and isosceles;

13. **Analyze** Suppose that $y_1 \parallel y_2$, $y_2 \perp y_3$, and $y_3 \perp y_4$. What must be true for y_1 and y_4 to share the same y-intercept? $y_1 = y_4$
(36)

14. Factor $x^3y^2z^3 + x^2yz^2 - 3x^3yz$. $x^2yz(xyz^2 + z - 3x)$
(23)

15. Given $f(x) = \frac{x}{x+1}$ and $g(x) = \frac{3}{2x}$, find $g(f(x))$ in simplest form. $\frac{3(x+1)}{2x}$
(34)

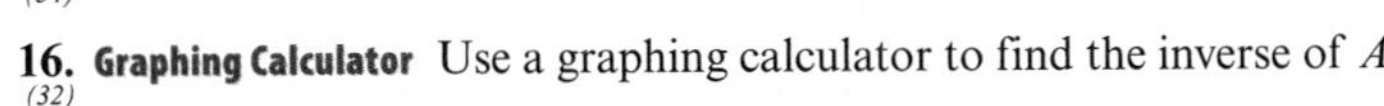

16. **Graphing Calculator** Use a graphing calculator to find the inverse of $A = \begin{bmatrix} 6 & -2 \\ 4 & 12 \end{bmatrix}$. $A' = \begin{bmatrix} 0.15 & 0.025 \\ -0.05 & 0.075 \end{bmatrix}$
(32)

17. How does the graph of $y = 5x^2$ differ from the graph of $y = x^2$?
(30)
The graph of $y = 5x^2$ is narrower.

18. **Multi-Step** Use
(29)

$$2x + 3y = 2z$$
$$4x = -5y + 4z.$$
$$3x + 5z = 2y$$

a. Write the equations with the variables aligned.

b. Estimate the number of solutions. Explain your answer.

c. Solve the system of equations to verify your estimate. (0, 0, 0)

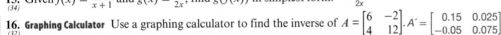

18a.
$$2x + 3y - 2z = 0$$
$$4x + 5y - 4z = 0$$
$$3x - 2y + 5z = 0$$

18b. One solution; No two equations are multiples of each other in any way.

CHALLENGE

Give students the following example:

$$\frac{1}{\sqrt[3]{ab}} = \frac{1}{\sqrt[3]{ab}} \cdot \frac{\sqrt[3]{a^2b^2}}{\sqrt[3]{a^2b^2}} = \frac{\sqrt[3]{a^2b^2}}{\sqrt[3]{a^3b^3}} = \frac{\sqrt[3]{a^2b^2}}{ab}$$

Then have them simplify these expressions:

$\frac{1}{\sqrt[3]{4}}$ $\frac{\sqrt[3]{2}}{2}$ $\frac{18}{\sqrt[3]{3}}$ $6\sqrt[3]{3^2}$

3 Practice

Math Conversations

Discussions to strengthen understanding

Problem 9

Error Alert

Students may believe that the radical sign in $\sqrt{h}$ must be eliminated in order to rationalize the expression. Remind students that a simplified expression can have a radical sign in the numerator, but not in the denominator.

Problem 12

Guide students by asking the following questions:

"What is an obtuse triangle?" a triangle with an angle greater than 90°

"What is an isosceles triangle?" a triangle with two congruent sides

"What is an acute triangle?" a triangle with all angles less than 90°

"What is a right triangle?" a triangle with one 90° angle

Problem 15

Extend the Problem

Ask students if $g(f(x))$ is the same as $f(g(x))$. Have them prove their answer. no; $f(g(x)) = \frac{3}{3+2x}$.

Problem 17

Extend the Problem

After students have found the correct answer for the problem, ask the following questions:

"How could you rewrite the equation $y = 5x^2$ in order to move the vertex five units higher?"
$y = 5x^2 + 5$

"How could you rewrite the equation $y = 5x^2$ in order to move the vertex five units lower?"
$y = 5x^2 - 5$

Problem 27

Ask students if the boundary should be included in the solution, and why. No; the inequality is greater than 6. It does not include the possibility of equaling 6, which would be on the boundary.

Problem 30

Ask students how they would write the dividend when using long division to solve this problem. The dividend should be written as $3x^3 + 0x^2 + 0x - 3$ in order to save places for the degrees of x that are not present in the dividend.

19. (27) **Utilities** A utility cable is hung between two poles that are 150 feet apart. The height of the cable between the two poles can be modeled by $f(x) = 0.0005x^2 + 35$ where x is the distance from the halfway point to either pole. How far up each pole is the cable attached? Round to the nearest tenth of a foot. About 37.8 feet

20. (27) Written in standard form, what are the values of a, b, and c in $f(x) = 3x^2$? $a = 3, b = 0, c = 0$

21. (35) **Write** Consider a quadratic function $f(x) = ax^2 + bx + c$ with $a < 0$ and whose vertex is in Quadrant III. How many real zeros does the function have? Explain.

21. No real zeros; Possible explanation: Because $a < 0$, the graph opens down. Because the graph opens down and the vertex is in Quadrant III, the graph does not intersect the x-axis.

22. (26) **Error Analysis** Two students used the point-slope form to write the equation of a line with slope 3 that passes through the point (5, 2). One student wrote the equation as $y = 3x - 13$, while the other wrote the equation as $y = 3x - 1$. Which student is correct? What error did the other student make?

Student A	Student B
$y - 5 = 3(x - 2)$	$y - 2 = 3(x - 5)$
$y = 3x - 6 + 5$	$y = 3x - 15 + 2$
$y = 3x - 1$	$y = 3x - 13$

22. Student B. Student A incorrectly exchanges the x and y coordinates in the point-slope form.

23. (23) **Measurement** Convert $36x^2 + 72x + 96$ inches to feet. $3x^2 + 6x + 8$ ft

24. (23) Factor $16m^2p^3y - 8y^4mp^3 + 4m^2p^2y^2$ $4mp^2y(4mp - 2py^3 + my)$

25. (23) The United States Postal Service will mail a letter that is no greater than $2x + 1.5$ inches long and no more than $x + 1$ inches high. The total area of an envelope with the maximum dimensions is approximately 69 in². Calculate the approximate maximum dimensions of an envelope that can be mailed through the USPS. The maximum length is 11.5 inches and the maximum height is 6 inches.

26. (38) Divide $x^4 - 2$ by $x + 1$ and check.

27. (43) **Write** Assume you have graphed the boundary line for $x + 2y > 6$. Describe two ways to determine which half-plane to shade. See Additional Answers.

28. (41) **Multi-Step** If the origin represents a parking lot, and one mountain biker is located at $(6, k)$ and another is located at $(-2, -7)$:

a. Find two possible values of k if the bikers are 10 units apart. -1 or -13

b. Determine the first biker's coordinates given that his distance from the parking lot is about 6.1 units. $(6, -1)$

29. (42) **Error Analysis** At an ice cream store, there are five different flavors of frozen yogurt. A customer orders three scoops. One customer says that there could be 60 different variations, and another customer says there could be only 10. Who is correct? Explain your reasoning. See Additional Answers.

30. (38) Divide $3x^3 - 3$ by $-x - 2$ and check.
$-3x^2 + 6x - 12 - \frac{27}{-x-2}$; $\left(-3x^2 + 6x - 12 - \frac{27}{-x-2}\right)(-x - 2) = 3x^3 + \frac{27(x+2)}{-x-2} + 24 = 3x^3 - 3$

26. $x^3 - x^2 + x - 1 - \frac{1}{x+1}$; $\left(x^3 - x^2 + x - 1 - \frac{1}{x+1}\right)(x + 1) = x^4 - 1 - \frac{x+1}{x+1} = x^4 - 2$

LOOKING FORWARD 

Rationalizing denominators prepares students for

- **Lesson 48** Understanding Complex Fractions
- **Lesson 70** Solving Radical Equations
- **Lesson 75** Graphing Radical Functions
- **Lesson 84** Solving Rational Equations
- **Lesson 88** Solving Abstract Equations

LAB 8

Applying Linear and Median Regression

Graphing Calculator Lab (*Use with Lesson 45*)

The graphing calculator can be used to calculate and plot a line of best fit using linear and median regression. Use the following data:

x	−8	−6	−5	−4	−2	−1	1	3	4	5	6	8
y	13	13	12	11	9	9	7	6	4	4	2	2

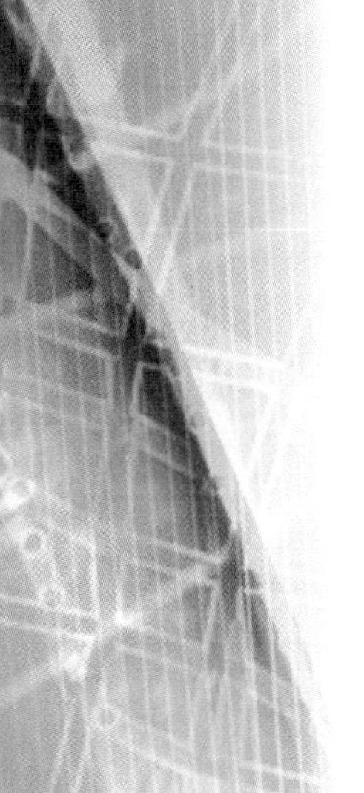

Graphing Calculator Tip

For directions on how to store and plot data using lists, see Graphing Calculator Lab 5.

Calculating and Plotting Linear Regression Lines

1. Store and plot the data points from the table above.
   a. Store the x-values in L1 and the y-values in L2.
   b. Plot the data points on a coordinate graph.
   c. Change the viewing window to $Y_{min} = 0$ and $Y_{max} = 15$ to display all the points. (For help in changing the window of a graph, see Graphing Calculator Lab 4.)

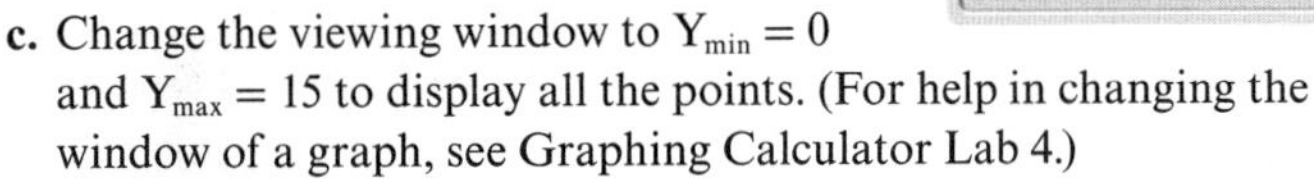

2. Once the data is stored into the lists, the linear regression line can be calculated.
   a. Press STAT ▶ to open the **[CALC]** menu.
   b. Press ▼ to select **[4: LinReg(ax + b)]** and press ENTER.
   c. Press 2nd 1 to enter L1 as the x-values. Then, press , 2nd 2 to enter L2 as the y-values.
   d. Press ENTER, and the values for a and b will be displayed. These values, substituted in the equation $y = ax + b$, form the Linear Regression line.

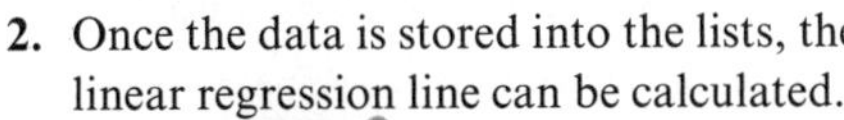

EDIT CALC TESTS
1:1-Var Stats
2:2-Var Stats
3:Med-Med
4:LinReg(ax+b)
5:QuadReg
6:CubicReg
7↓QuartReg

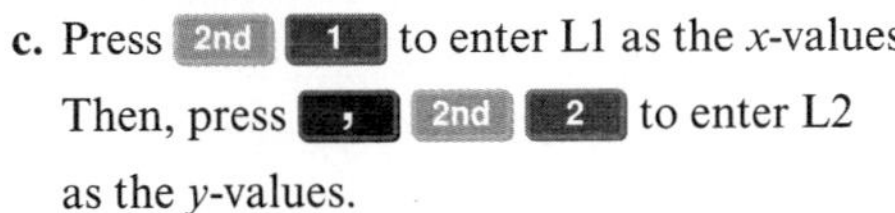

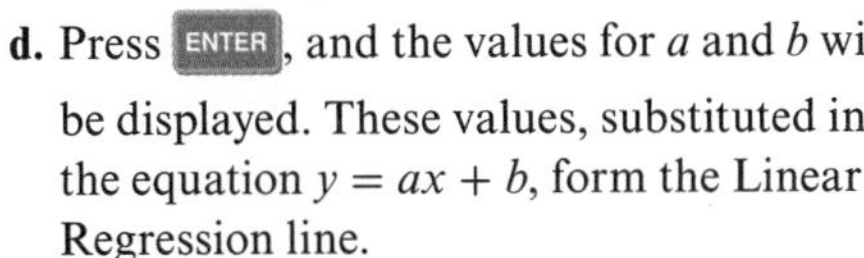

LinReg
y=ax+b
a=-.7802413696
b=7.731686781

3. The Linear Regression line can now be graphed and compared to the plotted data points.
   a. Press Y=, to open the **[Y=]** editor.
   b. Press VARS to open the Variables menu.
   c. Press the ▼ key to highlight **[5: Statistics...]** and press ENTER. Press the ▶ key twice to open the **[EQ]** menu. Select **[1: RegEQ]** and press ENTER. The equation for the Linear Regression line is stored in the RegEQ (regression equation) tool and will now be displayed next to Y_1=.

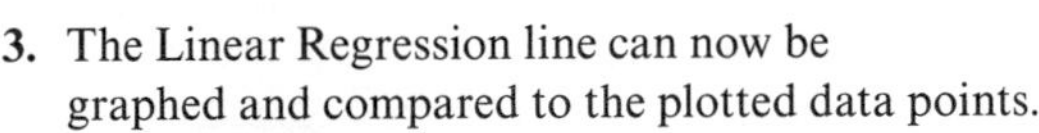

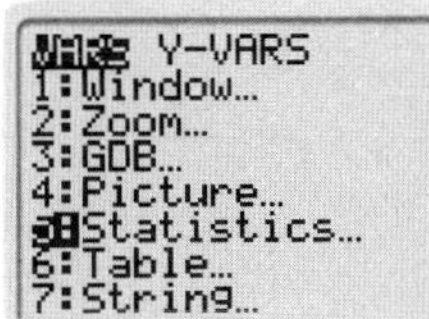

Online Connection
www.SaxonMathResources.com

LAB 8

Materials
- graphing calculator

Discuss

In this lab, students use the graphing calculator to determine and graph the Linear Regression line and the Median Regression line.

Define **Linear Regression line** and the **Median Regression line.**

Problem 1c

Use the suggested window changes. The other window values represent the standard viewing window.

TEACHER TIP

The **LinReg ($ax + b$)** calculator function calculates the line of best fit using the least-squares method. The slope is a and the y-intercept is b. There is another **8: LinReg ($a + bx$)** function in the **CALC** menu. In the form $y = a + bx$, the slope is b and a is the y-intercept.

Problem 2

Error Alert

If students make a typing mistake, tell them to repeat steps a through c.

Problem 3

To display the regression line without the data points, turn the plot off. To do this in the **Y =** editor, use the up arrow key to move to the highlighted **Plot**. Press enter.

Problem 4

The **Med-Med** calculator function calculates the line of best fit using the median-median line or resistant line in the form $y = ax + b$. The slope is a and the y-intercept is b.

Practice Problems a and b

Suggest that when students write the regression equations on paper, they round coefficients and constant terms to the nearest hundredth place.

Practice Problem c

To graph both regression lines, have students refer to Step 3 and Step 4 of the example problems.

Error Alert It is convenient to use L1 for x values and L2 for y values. In the **Stat Plot** window, the L1 must be assigned to Xlist and L2 must be assigned to Ylist.

d. Press GRAPH and the Linear Regression line will be graphed next to the plotted points.

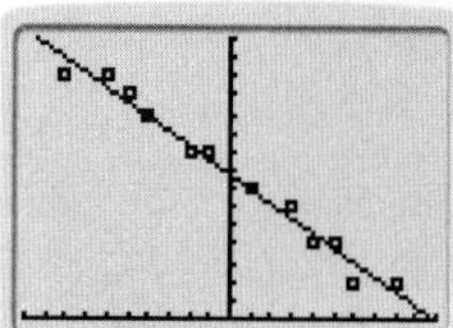

4. The RegEQ tool can also be used to graph the Median Fit line.

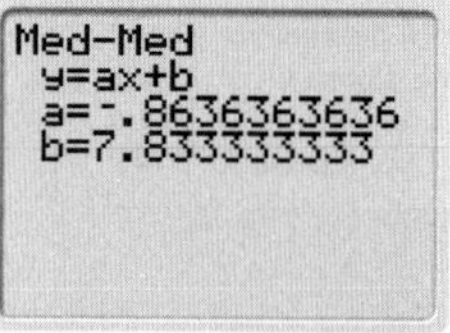

a. Press 2nd MODE to return to the home screen. Press STAT ▶ to open the **[CALC]** menu again, but use the ▼ key to highlight **[3: Med-Med]** and press ENTER.

b. Press 2nd 1 , 2nd 2 to enter L1 and L2 as the x- and y-values.

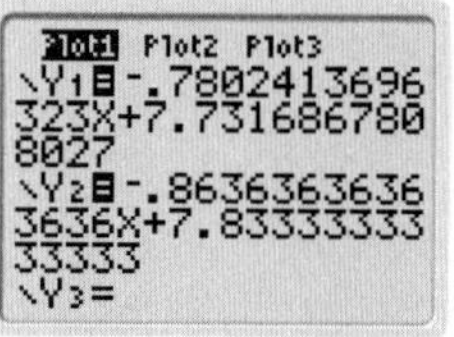

c. Press ENTER and the values of a and b for the Median Fit line will be displayed. This equation will now be saved in the RegEQ tool.

d. Press Y= to open the **[Y=]** editor and move the cursor to Y_2=. Repeat Step 3, to insert the equation stored in the RegEQ tool.

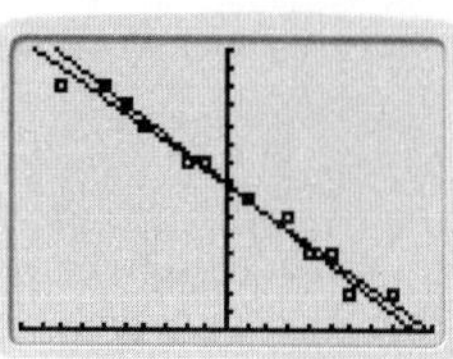

e. Press GRAPH and now the Median Regression line is graphed along with the Linear Regression line, and can be compared.

Lab Practice

Use the following data:

x	23	19	11	8	6	2	0	–1	–7	–9	–19	–22
y	0	2	5	7	6	9	11	13	12	18	19	21

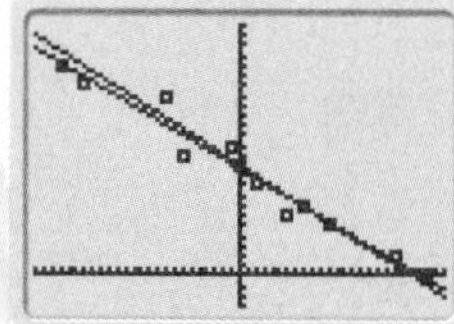

a. Find the equation of the Linear Regression line. $y = -0.48x + 10.69$

b. Find the equation of the Median Regression line. $y = -0.52x + 11.01$

c. Graph the data and both regression lines on the graphing calculator.

LESSON 45 Finding the Line of Best Fit

Warm Up

1. **Vocabulary** The y-coordinate of the point where a graph crosses the y-axis is the ________. *y-intercept* (13)

2. Identify the slope and y-intercept in $2x - 4y = 8$. Slope: $\frac{1}{2}$, y-int: -2 (13)

3. Evaluate $15.5x + 70$ when $x = 90$. 1465 (2)

4. Write the equation of the line graphed at right. $y = -4x - 3$ (26)

5. Tell whether the slope of line graphed at the right is positive, negative, zero, or undefined. negative (13)

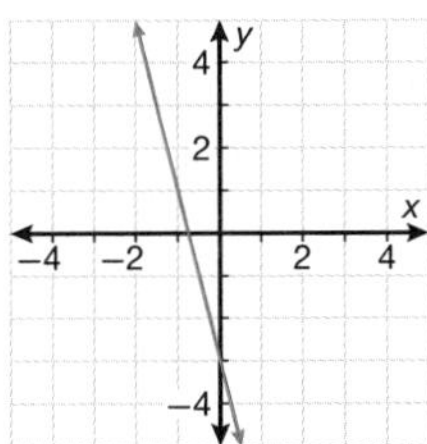

New Concepts

Regression is the process of identifying a relationship between variables. A measure of the strength and direction of the relationship between two variables or data sets is called **correlation.**

When the points tend to gather about a line, there is a linear relationship, or linear correlation. A scatter plot of the points will indicate whether there is a positive correlation or a negative correlation. When the points are widely scattered, there will be little to no correlation.

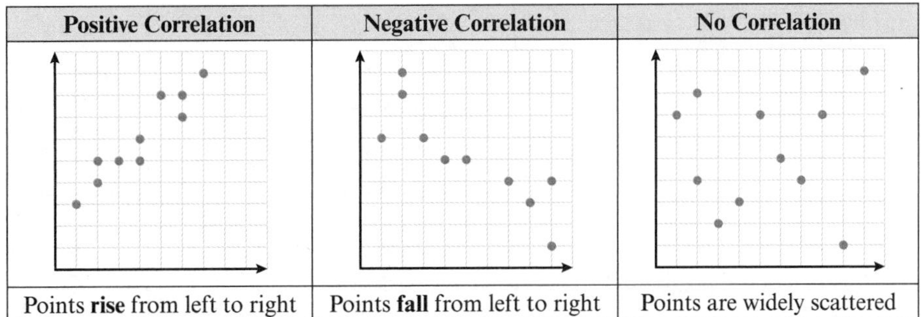

Positive Correlation
Negative Correlation
No Correlation
Points **rise** from left to right
Points **fall** from left to right
Points are widely scattered

A line that best fits the points in a scatter plot is a **line of best fit.** It is also called a regression line. A line of best fit will have about the same number of points above and below it. Also, it may or may not go through one or more of the points on the graph.

MATH BACKGROUND

To help students understand the meaning of *regression,* explain to students that regression is a method of analyzing data points to determine the relationship among the data. If there is a relationship, an equation can be used to predict additional data points. The accuracy of the predicted values depends on how closely related the data points actually are and how accurate the best-fit line is.

While this lesson discusses linear regression, data points can also be evaluated that are modeled by quadratic, cubic, power, logarithmic, and exponential functions.

LESSON 45

1 Warm Up

Use the Warm Up to review the prerequisite skills for this lesson. Remind students that when an equation is written in the slope-intercept form ($y = mx + b$) that m is the slope and b is the y-intercept.

2 New Concepts

In this lesson students learn to find the line of best fit given a set of data and to estimate and to calculate the correlation coefficient, r.

Discuss the definitions of **regression, correlation, line of best fit,** and **correlation coefficient.**

LESSON RESOURCES

Student Edition Practice Workbook 45
Reteaching Master 45
Adaptations Master 45
Challenge and Enrichment Masters C45, E45

Example 1

This example demonstrates how to create a scatter plot and describe the correlation. The example shows how to sketch a line of best fit, write the equation of the line, and describe the slope in terms of the given data.

Additional Example 1

Using the data in the table at the bottom of the page, sketch a line of best fit, write the equation of the line, and describe the slope in terms of the given data.

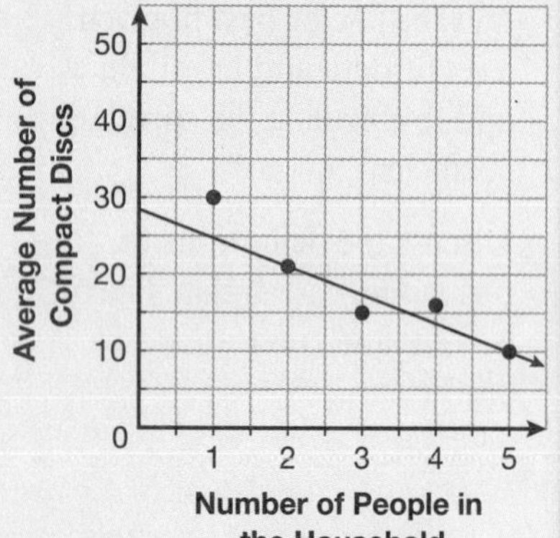

Equation of the line is using points (2, 22) and (5, 10): $y = -4x + 30$. The slope indicates that the number of compact discs decreases by 4 for every increase of 1 person in the household.

Example 1 **Describing Correlation and Estimating a Line of Best Fit**

Create a scatter plot of the data and describe the correlation. Sketch a line of best fit, write the equation of the line, and describe the slope in terms of the data.

Number of People in Household	1	2	3	4	5	6
Average Pieces of Mail per Day	4	6	6	9	8	6

SOLUTION Plot the points (people, mail). The points tend to rise from left to right. There is a positive correlation. Sketch a line of best fit and use two points on the line to write the equation.

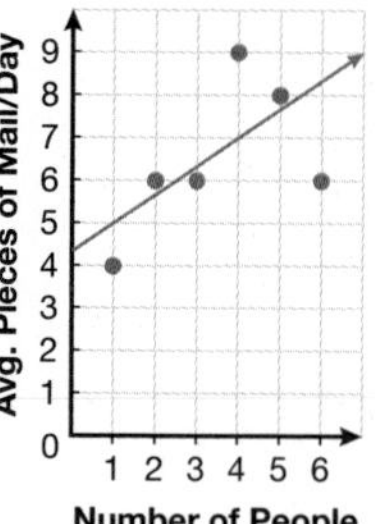

$$(1, 5), (4, 7): m = \frac{7-5}{4-1} = \frac{2}{3}$$

$$y - y_1 = m(x - x_1)$$

$$y - 5 = \frac{2}{3}(x - 1)$$

$$y = \frac{2}{3}x + 4\frac{1}{3}$$

The slope indicates that the number of pieces of mail increases by 2 for every increase of 3 people in the household.

Math Reasoning

Generalize Describe a data set whose *r*-value is –0.8.

From left to right the points fall and they are fairly close to forming a line.

The strength and direction of a linear correlation is measured by the **correlation coefficient**, *r*. The values of *r* can range from –1 to 1, where negative values indicate a negative correlation and positive values indicate a positive correlation. The further *r* is from 0, in either direction, the closer the points are to a straight line. When there is no linear correlation, *r* equals zero.

$r \approx -0.93$

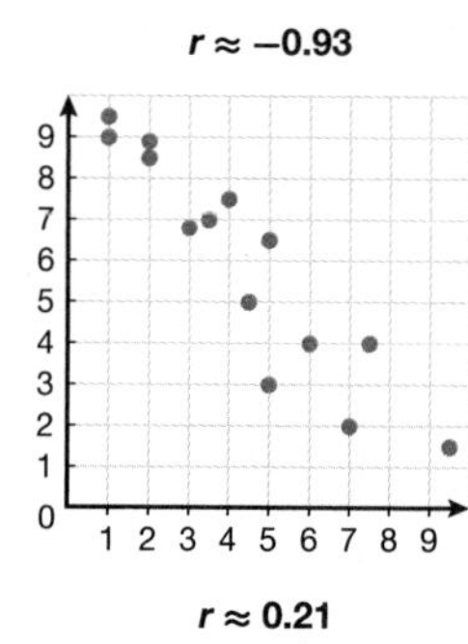

$r \approx -0.67$

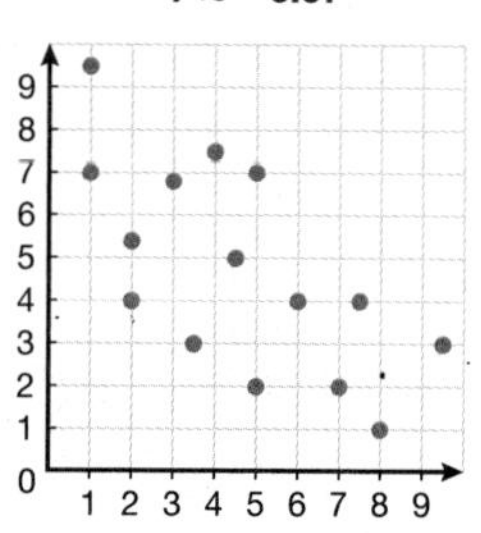

$r \approx 0.21$

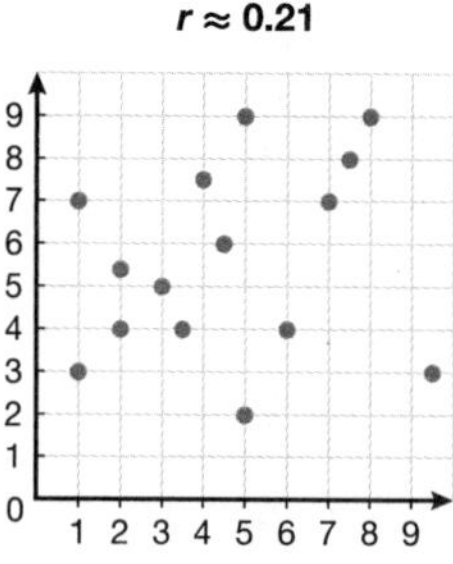

$r \approx 0.81$

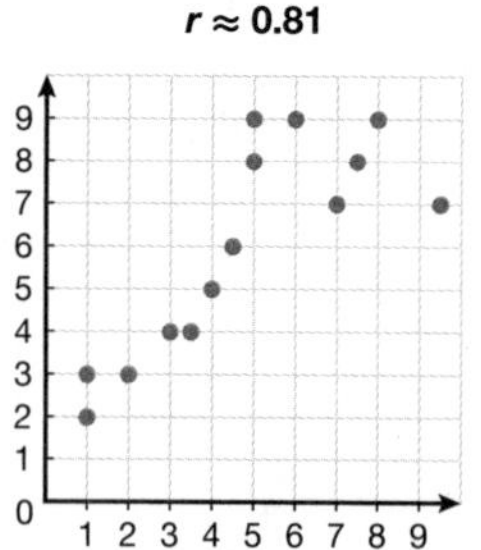

Additional Example 1 Data Table

Number of People in Household	1	2	3	4	5
Average Number of Music Compact Discs	30	22	15	16	10

Example 2 Estimating the Value of r

> **Hint**
>
> Predicting within a given range of data is more accurate than predicting outside the range of data.

Create a scatter plot of the data and estimate the correlation coefficient. Then predict the number of people who took the stairs to the fourth floor.

Building Floor Number	1	2	3	5	6	7	8
Number of People who Took Stairs	22	18	14	9	8	0	3

SOLUTION Plot the points (floor, people).

The points fall, so the r-value is negative. They are very close to forming a line, so the value is near -1, but not -1 because the points do not form a line exactly. A good estimate of the r-value would be -0.97.

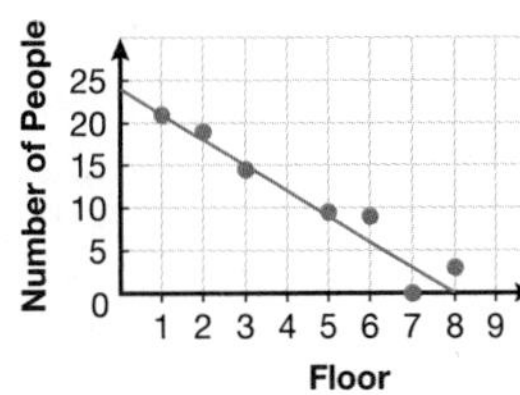

Sketching a line of best fit shows that a good prediction for the number of people who take the stairs to the fourth floor is 12.

Exploration Collecting and Analyzing Data

Materials needed: tennis ball, stop watch

Step 1:

Have one student bounce a tennis ball and one student time how long it takes for the ball to stop bouncing. Meanwhile, the other students should be counting the number of times the ball bounces during that time. It will help for students to agree on the number of bounces if the timer yells "stop" when he or she stops the stop watch.

Step 2:

Record the number of seconds the ball bounced as well as the number of bounces in a table similar to the one below.

Time (sec)										
Number of Bounces										

Step 3:

Repeat the activity nine more times for a total of 10 data points.

Step 4:

Have each student plot the points, sketch a line of best fit, determine the equation of the line, and estimate the correlation coefficient. Have students share and discuss their results.

A graphing calculator can be used to determine the correlation coefficient and line of best fit for a set of data.

Example 2

This example shows students how to create a scatter plot and then predict the correlation coefficient.

Additional Example 2

Create a scatter plot of the data and estimate the correlation coefficient. Then predict the number of apartments on the third floor.

Building Floor Number	1	2	4	5	6
Number of Apartments	22	19	15	13	11

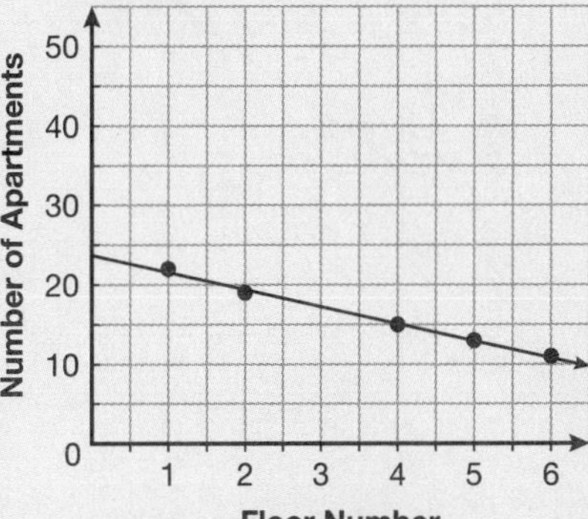

The correlation coefficient is about -1. The number of apartments on the third floor is 17.

Exploration

Error Alert To ensure that students get consistent results, make sure students bounce the ball in the same manner for each trial. Students might want to just drop the ball from the same height each time instead of bouncing the ball.

Example 3

This example demonstrates how to make a scatter plot by hand and then use a graphing calculator to find the correlation coefficient using sample data.

Additional Example 3

The number of dogs registered for 5 years is listed in the data table at the bottom of the page.

Make a scatter plot. Use a calculator to find the correlation coefficient. Predict the number of registered dogs in 2008.

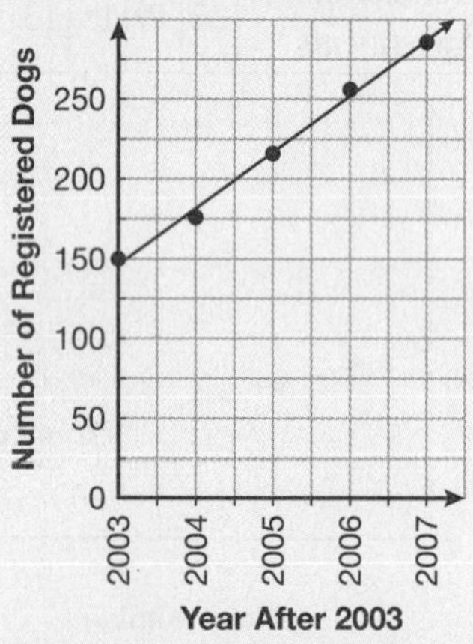

The correlation coefficient is about 0.997. The number of registered dogs in 2008 is about 322.

Lesson Practice

Problem a

Error Alert Make sure students choose two points that fall near the best fit line to get the best equation for the line.

Check for Understanding

The questions below help assess the concepts taught in this lesson.

"What is the process for identifying a relationship between variables?" regression

"What term is used to describe the strength of the relationship between variables?" correlation

"When points tend to gather about a line, what type of relationship do the points have?" linear relationship or linear correlation

Example 3 Using a Graphing Calculator

Enrollment at a high school for the years 2000 through 2007 are shown. Make a scatter plot of the data. Then use a graphing calculator to find the correlation coefficient. Predict the enrollment for 2008.

Year	2000	2001	2002	2003	2004	2005	2006	2007
Number of Students	149	175	198	240	262	332	418	451

Graphing Calculator Tip

For help using your calculator for regression, see the Lab on page 323. For the correlation coefficient, turn on the diagnostics feature. Press 2nd 0 to open the **CATALOG** menu. Scroll down to **DiagnosticsOn** and press ENTER twice.

SOLUTION

To avoid a large gap on the x-axis, write the years as the number of years after 2000.

Enter the data into a graphing calculator. Choose **LinReg($ax + b$)** from the CALC menu. Then type the list names.

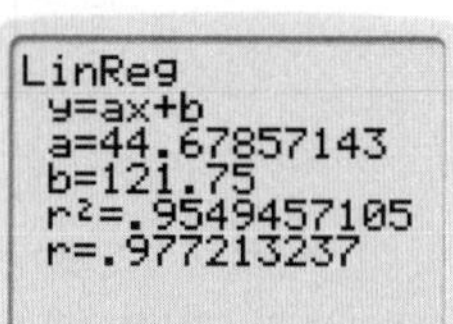

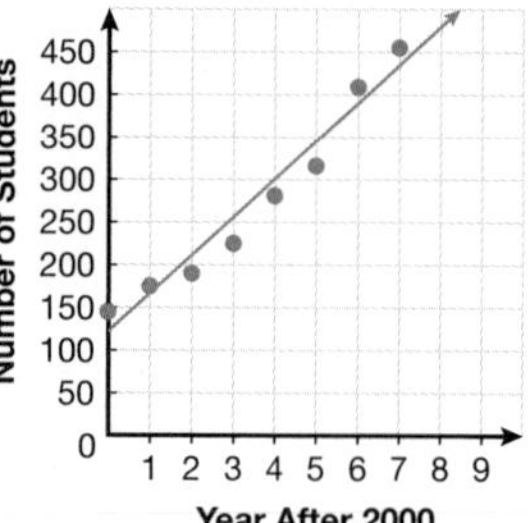

The r-value is about 0.98. The line of best fit is also shown. It is $y \approx 44.7x + 121.75$. Sketch this on the graph to predict that enrollment in 2008 is 479 students.

Lesson Practice

a. *(Ex 1)* Create a scatter plot of the data and describe the correlation. Sketch a line of best fit, write the equation of the line, and describe the slope in terms of the data.

Minutes Studied for Quiz	5	9	20	15	12	18
Number of Incorrect Answers	4	1	0	1	3	1

a. Negative correlation, Possible answer: $y = -\frac{1}{4}x + 5$, For every increase of four minutes in studying, there is a decrease of one incorrect answer.

b. *(Ex 2)* Create a scatter plot of the data and estimate the correlation coefficient. Then predict the amount of the heating bill when the average temperature is 40°F. $r \approx -0.8$, Sample: $78

Average Temperature, °F	15	22	24	30	49	56	59
Monthly Heating Bill, $	130	98	75	81	82	65	51

c. *(Ex 3)* Enrollments at a fitness center for the years 2000 through 2007 are shown. Make a scatter plot of the data. Then use a graphing calculator to find the correlation coefficient. Predict the enrollment for 2008.
$r \approx 0.76$, Sample: 590 members

Year	2000	2001	2002	2003	2004	2005	2006	2007
Number of Members	310	295	412	488	322	592	514	522

Additional Example 3 Data Table

Year	Number of Dogs
2003	150
2004	176
2005	216
2006	256
2007	286

INCLUSION

Using a graphing calculator to find the correlation coefficient can be confusing to some students. Prepare step-by-step instructions that lead students through the process. The owner's manual for specific calculators contains instructions that can be used in preparing the instruction sheet. Allow students to use the instructions as needed until they memorize the process.

Practice Distributed and Integrated

*1. **Multi-Step** (45)

x	1	5	2	7	4	8	4	7
y	−75	−20	−32	−31	−44	−16	−64	−39

a. Make a scatter plot of the data set. See Additional Answers.
b. Sketch a line of best fit. See Additional Answers.
c. Give the equation of the line. $y = \frac{20}{3}x - 73\frac{1}{3}$

*2. **Graphing Calculator** (45) Use a graphing calculator to find the value of r for the data set below. Tell what this value means. $r \approx -0.71$, there is a moderate negative correlation between the weight and price of a bicycle.

Weight of Bicycle (lb)	21.1	20.4	38.4	41.3	29.9	29.5	14.2	15.6	26.9
Price of Bicycle ($)	650	710	490	330	650	535	4500	5610	2200

*3. **Measurement** (43) Find the area of the graph of the system of linear inequalities.

$y \le 10$ and $y \ge \frac{3}{4}x + 2$ and $y \ge -\frac{5}{2}x + 15$ $21\frac{2}{3}$ square units

4. **Window Display** (42) A video store wants to display 4 identical DVD movies, 3 identical CDs, and 2 identical hand-held devices. How many distinguishable displays are possible? displays: $\frac{9!}{4!3!2!} = 1{,}260$

5. **Verify** (41) Show that 16 cm, 40 cm, and 43 cm *cannot* be the lengths of the sides of a right triangle. $16^2 + 40^2 = 256 + 1600 = 1856$ and $43^2 = 1849$

Simplify.

6. (40) $2\sqrt{27} - 3\sqrt{75}$ $-9\sqrt{3}$

7. (40) $3\sqrt{2}\left(2\sqrt{2} - \sqrt{6}\right) \cdot 4\sqrt{3} + 2$ $48\sqrt{3} - 70$

8. (44) $\frac{3}{5\sqrt{12}}$ $\frac{\sqrt{3}}{10}$

9. (44) $\frac{14}{3\sqrt{75}}$ $\frac{14\sqrt{3}}{45}$

10. (44) $\frac{2}{3\sqrt{6}}$ $\frac{\sqrt{6}}{9}$

11. **Multiple Choice** (40) Simplify $\sqrt[3]{250}$. D

A 10 B $\sqrt[3]{10}$ C $2\sqrt[3]{5}$ D $5\sqrt[3]{2}$

12. **Sightseeing** (39) In 2007, tickets to the Space Needle's Observation Deck in Seattle Washington cost $16 per adult and $8 per child. A group of tourists has up to $200 to spend on tickets. Write and graph an inequality that shows how many of each ticket they could buy. Use the graph to explain whether they could buy 6 adult tickets and 15 children's tickets. See Additional Answers.

13. **Error Analysis** (45) A student claimed that the correlation coefficient for a set of data was 1.25. Why is the student incorrect? The value of the correlation coefficient cannot exceed 1.

14. **Physics** (38) One of the properties of metals is that they expand in size when heated. The coefficient of thermal expansion is an indication of how a particular metal increases in size. A metal cube is heated. The cube has side lengths, x. After heating, the linear dimensions of the cube increase by a value of a. What is the ratio of the new volume to the original volume? $\frac{x^3 + 3ax^2 + 3a^2x + a^3}{x^3}$

ENGLISH LEARNERS

Some students might have trouble with the term **correlation.** Tell students that correlation means "a relationship existing among things." In mathematics, you investigate relationships among variables or data points.

In this lesson, you investigate the relationship among data points that are linear in nature and determine a line that best fits (or models) the data points.

The correlation coefficient, r, is a number that shows how linear a data set actually is. If r equals 0, there is no linear correlation or relationship. The closer the coefficient is to 1 and −1, the more linear the data set is.

As another sample data set, create a table of shoe size and height (in inches) of several students in your class. Model how to create a scatter plot. Have a student volunteer estimate the correlation coefficient and explain how he or she determined the number. Then find the actual coefficient using a graphing calculator.

3 Practice

Math Conversations

Discussion to strengthen understanding

Problem 1

Guide the students by asking them the following question.

"When making the scatter plot for this data set, what increments would you use for the x- and y-axis?" x-axis increments of 1; y-axis increments of 10

Problem 2

Error Alert

Make sure students have their graphing calculators set on diagnostics display mode. When the diagnostics mode is on, the correlation coefficient will display automatically. For some calculators, the DiagnosticOn and DiagnosticOff instruction is in the Catalog.

Problem 5

Guide the students by asking them the following questions.

"What is the mathematical relationship among the three sides of a right triangle?" If the sides form a right triangle then according to the Pythagorean Theorem, $a^2 + b^2 = c^2$, where c is the longest side.

"Does $a^2 + b^2 = c^2$ given the lengths of the triangle sides?" no

Problem 12

Guide the students by asking them the following question.

"If x equals the number of adult tickets and y equals the number of child tickets, what equation expresses the relationship between these two terms?" $16x + 8y \le 200$

Extend the Problem

Have students determine the slope and y-intercept of this equation. slope = −2; y-intercept = 25

Problem 20

Guide the students by asking them the following questions.

"If two equations are parallel, what has to be true about the slopes of the lines?" The slopes of the lines have to be equal.

"If the line parallel to the given line crosses the origin, what is its y-intercept?" zero

Problem 29

Error Alert

Remind students to collect like terms in the numerator.

15. **Generalize** When do roots of negative numbers exist and when are they undefined? (40)
15. Roots of negative numbers exist when the index of the radical is an odd number. They are undefined when the index is an even number.

16. **Geography** On a map, a square is drawn around Washington DC. Write the perimeter to area ratio of the square as a simplified rational expression. Then find the ratio given that the length of each side of the square is 10 miles long. (28) $\frac{4}{s} = \frac{2}{5}$

17. **Write** Can a rational number be a rational expression? Can a rational expression be a rational number? Explain. (37) If rational number $\frac{a}{b}$ is equal to rational expression $\frac{f(x)}{g(x)}$, both $f(x) = a$ and $g(x) = b$.

Expand.

18. $(x - 1)^3$ (19) $x^3 - 3x^2 + 3x - 1$

19. $(x + 5)^3$ (19) $x^3 + 15x^2 + 75x + 125$

20. Which is the equation of the line parallel to $y = -5x + 7$ that crosses the origin? (36) A

A $y = -5x$ **B** $y = -\frac{1}{5}x + 7$ **C** $y = 5x$ **D** $y = \frac{1}{5}x + 7$

21. **Error Analysis** A student solved the equation $4x^2 - 20x + 25 = 0$ as shown below. (35)

$$4x^2 - 20x + 25 = 0$$
$$(2x + 5)(2x - 5) = 0$$
$$2x + 5 = 0 \quad \text{or} \quad 2x - 5 = 0$$
$$2x = -5 \quad \text{or} \quad 2x = 5$$
$$x = -\frac{5}{2} \quad \text{or} \quad x = \frac{5}{2}$$

What is the error? Solve the equation correctly.

The student factored incorrectly.
$$4x^2 - 20x + 25 = 0$$
$$(2x - 5)^2 = 0$$
$$2x - 5 = 0$$
$$2x = 5$$
$$x = \frac{5}{2}$$

22. **Temperature** The function $C = \frac{5}{9}(F - 32)$ describes the relationship between Celsius temperature and Fahrenheit temperature. Write the function in point-slope form. Graph the function, state the rate of change, and describe what it means. (34) See Additional Answers.

23. **Analyze** These characters are written on 10 index cards, a different character on each card: A, B, C, D, E, 1, 2, 3, 4, and 5. A letter card is chosen and then a number card is chosen. How many outcomes are in the event *choose a vowel and then choose an odd number*? List all those outcomes. (33) 6 outcomes: A1, A3, A5, E1, E3, E5

24. **Geometry** An isosceles right triangle is inscribed in a circle as shown. Its hypotenuse is the diameter of the circle. Write the ratio of the area of the circle to the area of the right triangle in simplest form. (31) π

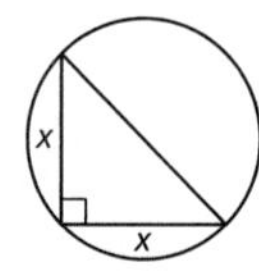

25. **Write** Describe how to determine whether two matrices are inverses. (32)

25. Sample: Multiply the matrices in both orders. If the product is the identity matrix both times, then the matrices are inverses.

Solve.

26. $-x + x^2 = 12$ (35) 4, −3

27. $-48x = -2x^2 - x^3$ (35) 0, −8, 6

28. Write a quadratic function in vertex form where $a = -1$, $h = -2$, and $k = 3$. (27) $f(x) = -(x + 2)^2 + 3$

Add.

29. $\frac{4x}{x + 4} + \frac{6}{x + 2}$ (37) $\frac{4x^2 + 14x + 24}{(x + 4)(x + 2)}$

30. $\frac{3m}{m^2 + 3m + 2} - \frac{5m}{m + 1}$ (37) $\frac{-5m^2 - 7m}{(m + 2)(m + 1)}$

CHALLENGE

Have students rewrite the function in problem 22 to solve for Fahrenheit temperature instead of Celsius temperature.

$F = \frac{9}{5}C + 32$

LOOKING FORWARD

Finding the line of best fit prepares students for

- **Lesson 116** Finding Best Fit Models
- **Lesson 117** Solving Systems of Nonlinear Equations
- **Lesson 118** Recognizing Misleading Data
- **Lesson 119** Solving Trigonometric Equations

LESSON 46

Finding Trigonometric Functions and their Reciprocals

Warm Up

1. **Vocabulary** The longest side of a right triangle is the hypotenuse. (41)

2. Solve $4.2 = \frac{x}{35}$. 147 (7)

3. Solve $0.06x = 42$. 700 (7)

4. What is the reciprocal of $\frac{3}{4}$? $\frac{4}{3}$ (31)

5. Can the sides of a right triangle measure 20 inches, 25 inches, and 30 inches? no (41)

New Concepts

This lesson introduces **trigonometry,** which is the study of right triangles. A **trigonometric ratio** is a ratio of the lengths of any two sides of a right triangle. A function whose rule is a trigonometric ratio is a **trigonometric function.** Three common trigonometric functions are sine, cosine, and tangent, abbreviated sin, cos, and tan, respectively.

Trigonometric Functions		
The **sine** of angle A is the ratio of the length of the **opposite** side to the length of the **hypotenuse.**	$\sin A = \frac{\text{opp}}{\text{hyp}} = \frac{BC}{AB}$	B; side opposite ∠A; hypotenuse; C; A; side adjacent ∠A
The **cosine** of angle A is the ratio of the length of the **adjacent** side to the length of the **hypotenuse.**	$\cos A = \frac{\text{adj}}{\text{hyp}} = \frac{AC}{AB}$	
The **tangent** of angle A is the ratio of the length of the **opposite** side to the length of the **adjacent** side.	$\tan A = \frac{\text{opp}}{\text{adj}} = \frac{BC}{AC}$	

Math Language

The side **adjacent** to an angle is one of the sides that forms the angle but is not the hypotenuse.

To determine the sine, cosine, and tangent functions for $\angle B$ in the diagram above, be sure to use AC for the length of the opposite side and BC for the length of the adjacent side.

The trigonometric functions are only related to the acute angles of a right triangle. It does not make sense to find the sine, cosine, or tangent of $\angle C$.

LESSON 46

1 Warm Up

For Problem 4, remind students of the definition of reciprocal. Two numbers are **reciprocals** if their product is 1. To find the reciprocal of a number, write it in fraction form, then interchange numerator and denominator.

2 New Concepts

This lesson introduces students to **trigonometry,** the study of right triangles. In order to understand the three fundamental trigonometric ratios (**sine, cosine,** and **tangent**), it is essential that students differentiate among the **hypotenuse,** the adjacent side and the opposite side. In the diagram, point out that side CA is adjacent to $\angle A$, but opposite $\angle B$. The assignments *opposite* and *adjacent* depend on the angle being studied. However, the hypotenuse is always the side opposite the right angle.

MATH BACKGROUND

From studying the Pythagorean Theorem, students are already aware that right triangles behave in ways that other triangles do not. The entire branch of mathematics called trigonometry studies these behaviors.

Every right triangle is made up of six parts: three sides and three angles. The longest side of the triangle, opposite the right angle, is called the hypotenuse. The other sides are called legs. Of the three angles in a right triangle, one is a right angle and the others are acute and complementary. Although not necessary, the right angle is usually named C and the hypotenuse c in ΔABC.

Often, the measures of only a few of a right triangle's six parts are known. Trigonometry allows us to find the unknown measures. If at least one of the acute angles and one of the side lengths is known, the entire triangle can be "solved."

LESSON RESOURCES

Student Edition Practice Workbook 46
Reteaching Master 46
Adaptations Master 46
Challenge and Enrichment Master C46

Example 1

Point out that the trigonometric ratios are being found for angle A. Be sure students see that side BC lies opposite angle A.

Additional Example 1

Find the values of the sine, cosine, and tangent of $\angle B$.

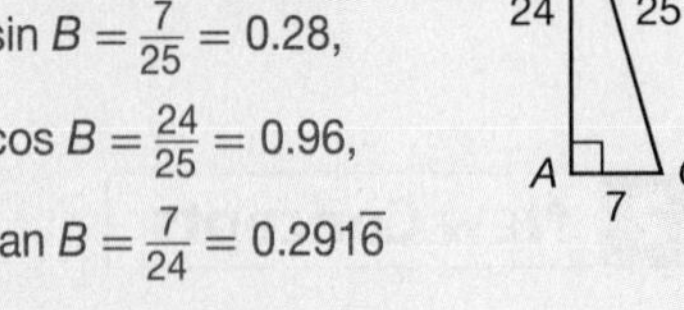

$\sin B = \frac{7}{25} = 0.28,$

$\cos B = \frac{24}{25} = 0.96,$

$\tan B = \frac{7}{24} = 0.291\overline{6}$

TEACHER TIP

Give students the mnemonic acronym SOH-CAH-TOA to help them remember the ratios. For example, SOH tells them that "Sine equals Opposite over Hypotenuse." Suggest that when working with a triangle, they label the sides with "O" or "H."

Example 2

Error Alert Students might confuse cosine and cosecant. Take a moment to review the abbreviations for all six functions.

Additional Example 2

Find the value of the cosecant, secant, and cotangent of $\angle B$.

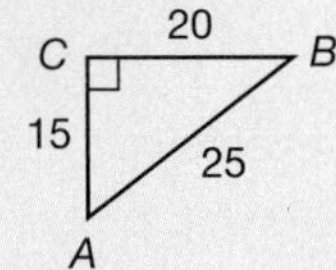

$\csc B = \frac{25}{15} = 1.\overline{6},$

$\sec B = \frac{25}{20} = 1.25,$

$\cot B = \frac{20}{15} = 1.\overline{3}$

Example 1 Finding the Values of Sine, Cosine, and Tangent

Find the values of the sine, cosine, and tangent of $\angle A$.

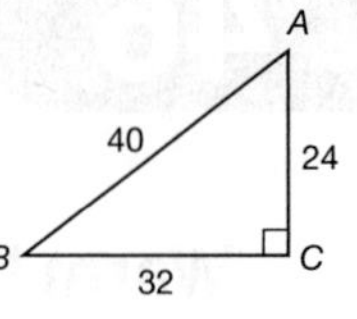

SOLUTION Identify the hypotenuse: $\overline{AB}$.

Identify the side opposite $\angle A$: $\overline{BC}$.

Identify the side adjacent $\angle A$: $\overline{AC}$.

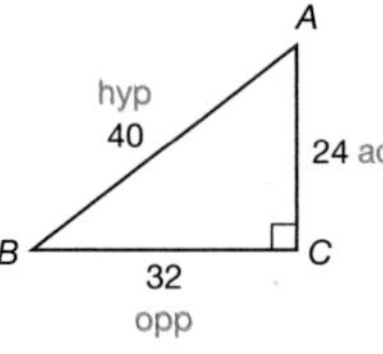

$$\sin A = \frac{\text{opp}}{\text{hyp}} = \frac{32}{40} = \frac{4}{5} = 0.8$$

$$\cos A = \frac{\text{adj}}{\text{hyp}} = \frac{24}{40} = \frac{3}{5} = 0.6$$

$$\tan A = \frac{\text{opp}}{\text{adj}} = \frac{32}{24} = \frac{4}{3} = 1.\overline{3}$$

Three other trigonometric functions are **cosecant, secant,** and **cotangent,** abbreviated csc, sec, and cot, respectively. They are the reciprocals of the sine, cosine, and tangent functions, respectively.

Math Reasoning

Verify Show how $\frac{1}{\sin A} = \frac{\text{hyp}}{\text{opp}}$.

$\left[\frac{1}{\sin A} = \frac{1}{\frac{\text{opp}}{\text{hyp}}} = 1 \div \frac{\text{opp}}{\text{hyp}} = 1 \times \frac{\text{hyp}}{\text{opp}} = \frac{\text{hyp}}{\text{opp}}\right]$

Reciprocal Trigonometric Functions		
The **cosecant** of angle A is the reciprocal of the **sine** function.	$\csc A = \frac{1}{\sin A} = \frac{\text{hyp}}{\text{opp}} = \frac{AB}{BC}$	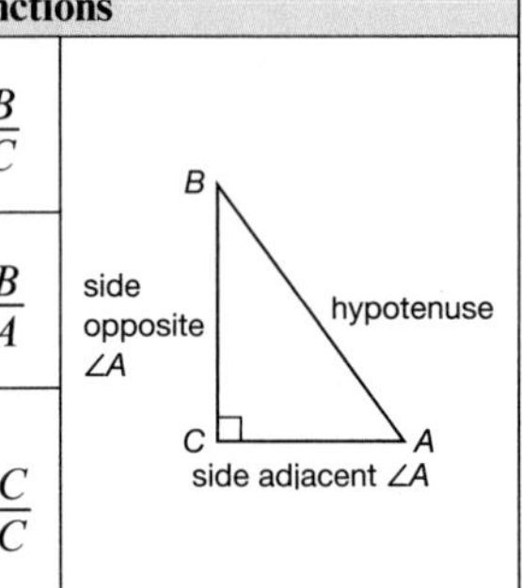
The **secant** of angle A is the reciprocal of the **cosine** function.	$\sec A = \frac{1}{\cos A} = \frac{\text{hyp}}{\text{adj}} = \frac{AB}{CA}$	
The **cotangent** of angle A is the reciprocal of the **tangent** function.	$\cot A = \frac{1}{\tan A} = \frac{\text{adj}}{\text{opp}} = \frac{AC}{BC}$	

Example 2 Finding the Values of Cosecant, Secant, and Cotangent

Find the values of the cosecant, secant, and cotangent of $\angle B$.

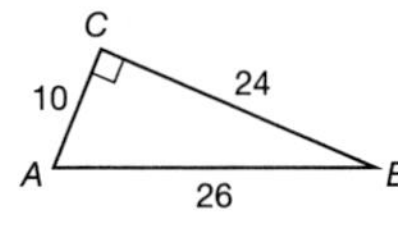

SOLUTION Identify the hypotenuse: $\overline{AB}$.

Identify the side opposite $\angle B$: $\overline{AC}$.

Identify the side adjacent $\angle B$: $\overline{BC}$.

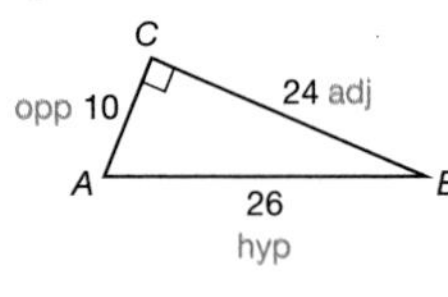

$$\csc B = \frac{\text{hyp}}{\text{opp}} = \frac{26}{10} = \frac{13}{5} = 2.6$$

$$\sec B = \frac{\text{hyp}}{\text{adj}} = \frac{26}{24} = \frac{13}{12} = 1.08\overline{3}$$

$$\cot B = \frac{\text{adj}}{\text{opp}} = \frac{24}{10} = \frac{12}{5} = 2.4$$

The trigonometric ratios are related to the angle measures, rather than to the lengths of the sides. For instance, the ratios for a right triangle whose sides measure 3, 4, and 5 will be the same as for those whose sides measure twice as much, 6, 8, and 10, or three times as much, 9, 12, and 15. This is because the angle measures of similar triangles are the same.

ENGLISH LEARNERS

To help students understand the meanings of opposite and adjacent, tell them that **opposite** means across from and **adjacent** means next to.

Discuss the word opposite. When used to give directional information, opposite can mean on the other side. Adjacent means near or close. So, in a triangle, the opposite leg is the one farthest from the angle; the adjacent leg is the one nearest the angle.

Show students several examples of right triangles and ask them to identify the legs that lie opposite and adjacent to a named acute angle.

Connect the terms opposite and adjacent to their other uses in mathematics. The opposite of a number lies across 0 from the number; an adjacent angle is an angle that lies next to a given angle, sharing a side.

332 *Saxon Algebra 2*

The values of the trigonometric ratios for given angles are listed in trigonometric tables, and are also stored in scientific and graphing calculators.

Graphing Calculator Tips

To put the calculator in degree mode, press MODE and use the arrow keys to switch from Radian to Degree.

Example 3 Finding the Side of a Triangle

Find the value of x. Round to the nearest tenth.

42°
32
x

SOLUTION

Identify the known and unknown lengths as the hypotenuse and the opposite side to the given angle.

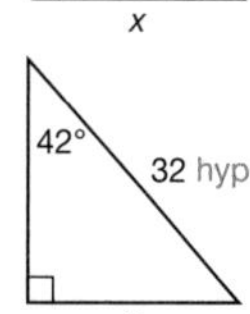

Use a trigonometric function that uses the hypotenuse and opposite side and substitute the given information.

$\sin 42° = \frac{\text{opp}}{\text{hyp}}$

$\sin 42° = \frac{x}{32}$ Solve for x.

$x = 32(\sin 42°)$ Use a calculator to find x.

$x \approx 21.4$

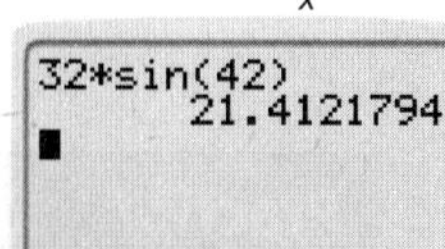

Example 4 Application: Navigation

The top of the Yaquina Bay Lighthouse on the coast of Oregon is 162 feet above sea level. The angle of elevation from a boat to the top of the lighthouse is 35°. Find the distance from the boat to the base of the lighthouse to the nearest foot.

SOLUTION Draw a diagram with the relevant information.

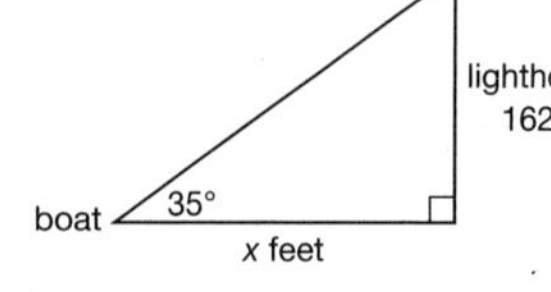

$\tan 35° = \frac{\text{opp}}{\text{adj}}$

$\tan 35° = \frac{162}{x}$ Solve for x.

$x = \frac{162}{\tan 35°}$ Use a calculator to find x.

$x \approx 231$

The boat is about 231 feet away from the base of the lighthouse.

Lesson Practice

a. Find the values of the sine, cosine, and tangent of $\angle A$.
(Ex 1)

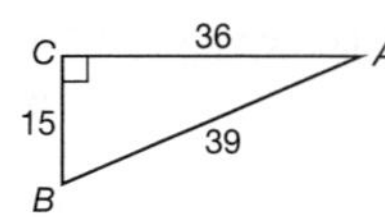

$\sin A = \frac{5}{13} \approx 0.3846$

$\cos A = \frac{12}{13} \approx 0.9231$

$\tan A = \frac{5}{12} \approx 0.4167$

ALTERNATE METHOD FOR EXAMPLE 3

Some students develop a preference for using sine or cosine. Show them that they can use the Triangle Sum Property, then use cosine to solve for x.

Use the Triangle Sum Property to find the measure of the third angle:

$90° + 42° + a = 180°$

$a = 48°$

Side x lies adjacent to a 48° angle, so

$\cos 48° = \frac{x}{32}$

$32(\cos 48°) = x$

$21.4 \approx x$

Example 3

Point out that there is only one possible value for x. All triangles with 90°, 42° and 48° angles are similar. Of those similar triangles, all those in which the hypotenuse is 32 are congruent.

Extend the Example

Challenge students to find the length of the third side using the cosine ratio. Then have them verify their answer using the Pythagorean Theorem.
about 23.8

TEACHER TIP

Study the calculator screenshot with students and be sure they can reproduce the results on their own calculators. Tell them that it is not necessary to press the multiplication (×) key or to input the final parentheses in this case. They can enter

   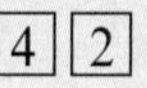 .

Example 4

Remind students that the angle of elevation is the angle formed by the line of sight and the horizontal. Be sure students can distinguish between the line-of-sight distance and the horizontal distance.

Additional Example 4

A radio signal is sent by the boat to a receiver at the top of the lighthouse. What is the distance traveled by the signal?
about 282 ft

Lesson Practice

Problem c

Scaffolding Have students assign terms *opposite*, *adjacent*, and *hypotenuse* to the labeled sides. Then, have them determine which trigonometric ratio uses those sides. Finally, have them write and solve an equation.

Check for Understanding

The questions below help assess the concepts taught in this lesson.

"Explain how to find the sine of an angle." To find the sine of an angle, write a ratio in fraction form. The numerator in the ratio is the length of the side that is opposite the angle. The denominator in the ratio is the length of the triangle's hypotenuse.

"How can you find x, y, and z in the triangle?"

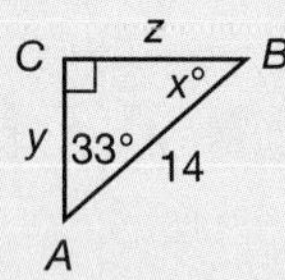

You can use the fact that the three angles in a triangle add up to 180° to find x. Then, you can use the sine and cosine ratios to find y and z.

3 Practice

Math Conversations

Discussions to strengthen understanding

Problems 6 and 7

Have students label the sides of the triangle with respect to angle x as *adjacent*, *opposite*, and *hypotenuse*.

b. (Ex 2) Find the values of the cosecant, secant, and cotangent of $\angle A$. $\csc A = \frac{5}{3} = 1.\overline{6}$

$\sec A = \frac{5}{4} = 1.25$

$\cot A = \frac{4}{3} = 1.\overline{3}$

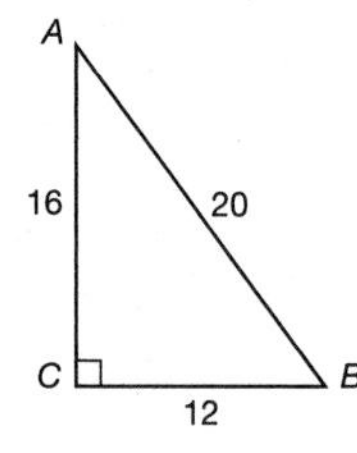

c. (Ex 3) Find the value of x. Round to the nearest tenth. 64.2

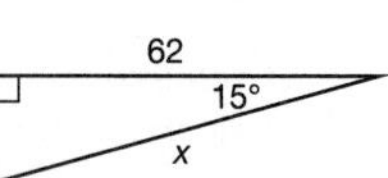

d. (Ex 4) A surveyor is located 380.7 feet from the base of the Chrysler Building in New York, NY. The angle of elevation from the surveyor to the top of the building is 70°. Find the height of the Chrysler Building to the nearest foot. 1046 feet

Practice Distributed and Integrated

For each equation and point, find the equation of the lines that are parallel and perpendicular to the line, and that pass through the point.

1. (36) $y = 3x - 6$; $(3, 4)$ parallel: $y = 3x - 5$ perpendicular: $y = -\frac{1}{3}x + 5$

2. (36) $y = -2x + 8$; $(-7, 0)$

2. parallel: $y = -2x - 14$ perpendicular: $y = \frac{1}{2}x + \frac{7}{2}$

Convert:

3. (20) 1800 seconds to hours. 0.5 hr

4. (20) 16 yd^2 to in^2. 20,736 in^2

5. (30) Write the vertex form of a quadratic equation if the parent function is shifted 5 units right. $y = (x - 5)^2$

Use the right triangle to find the value of the following trigonometric functions:

***6.** (46) $\tan(x)$ $\frac{56}{33}$

***7.** (46) $\csc(x)$ $\frac{65}{56}$

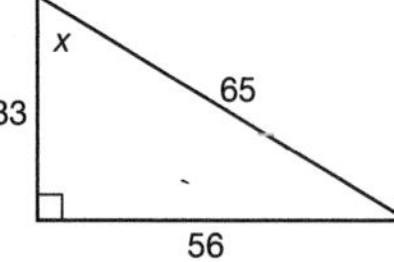

Factor the expressions:

8. (23) $-12x^4 - 18x^2 - 6$ $-6(2x^4 + 3x^2 + 1)$

9. (23) $x^2 - 28x + 196$ $(x - 14)^2$

Write the equation of the line with slope m that passes through the point, in slope-intercept form.

10. (26) $m = -8, (-2, 9)$ $y = -8x - 7$

11. (26) $m = \frac{4}{9}, (6, 3)$ $y = \frac{4}{9}x + \frac{1}{3}$

***12.** (46) **Multiple Choice** What is the value of the cosecant of $\angle M$? C

A 0.6 B 0.8

C 1.25 D $1.\overline{7}$

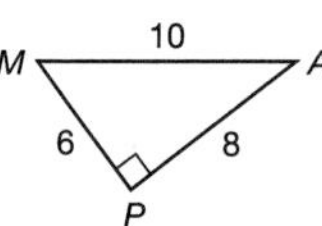

***13.** (16) **Coordinate Geometry** Use Cramer's Rule to find the intersection of the lines with equations $9x + 3y = 21$ and $2x - 2y = 2$. The intersection is at (2, 1).

INCLUSION

Help students identify the opposite and adjacent sides by having them trace the two sides of the angle in question with a highlighter. One of the sides will be the adjacent side; the other will be the hypotenuse. (The adjacent side helps form the right angle. The hypotenuse is the longest side.) The opposite side is the remaining leg — the one not highlighted.

For $\angle B$:

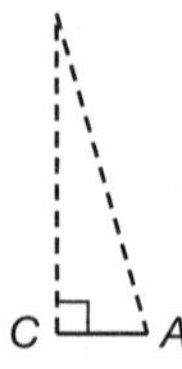

14. (35) **Gravity** The height of a free-falling object (neglecting air resistance) is given by the function $h(t) = -16t^2 + v_0t + h_0$, where h_0 is the initial height in feet, v_0 is the initial velocity in feet per second, and $h(t)$ is the height in feet at t seconds. An object is dropped from a height of 56 feet. How long does it take for the object to reach a height of 20 feet? (Hint: The initial velocity of a dropped object is zero.)
1.5 seconds

15. (43) **Analyze** What ordered pair of integers in the solution set of the system below has the least sum? Explain your answer.

$$y < \frac{3}{4}x - 3$$
$$y > \frac{1}{3}x + 4$$

(17, 10); Possible explanation: The boundary lines intersect in the point (16.8, 9.6). All solutions of the system are above and to the right of (16.8, 9.6), so every solution has an x-coordinate greater than 16.8 and a y-coordinate greater than 9.6. So the solution with the least coordinates, and therefore the least sum, is (17, 10).

***16.** (45) **Multi-Step** The graph compares students' quiz and test grades.

a. Write an equation for the line of best fit. Possible answer: $y = \frac{5}{6}x + 15$

b. Describe the slope in terms of the data.
Possible answer: Every increase of 6 points on the quiz grade is an increase of 5 points on the test grade.

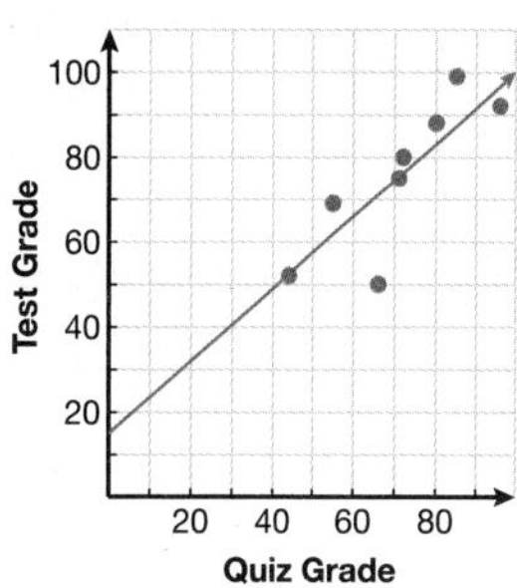

17. (39) **Error Analysis** Find and correct the error made below where a student was determining if (4, −8) was a solution to $2y + 3 \leq -4x$. The student replaced x with the y-value and vice versa.

$2(4) + 3 \overset{?}{\leq} -4(-8)$

$8 + 3 \overset{?}{\leq} 32$

$11 \leq 32$ True, (4, −8) is a solution.

$2(-8) + 3 \leq -4(4)$

$-16 + 3 \leq -16$

$-13 \leq -16$ False, (4, − 8) is not a solution.

18. (23) **Multiple Choice** Circle the letter that represents the complete factorization of $x^2 - 9x - 36$. C

A $(x + 6)(x - 6)$ **B** $(x + 4)(x - 9)$

C $(x + 3)(x - 12)$ **D** $(x + 2)(x - 18)$

19. (40) **Density** The side length of a metal cube, in centimeters, is given by $\frac{\sqrt[3]{m}}{\sqrt[3]{p}}$, where m is its mass in grams and p is its density.

a. Write the expression in simplified form. $\frac{\sqrt[3]{mp^2}}{p}$

b. Approximate the side length of a 1000 gram cube of nickel given that the density of nickel is 88 g/cm³. About 2.2 cm.

***20.** (45) **Justify** Why does a table showing number of feet and the corresponding number of inches have a correlation of 1? The number of inches is always 12 times the number of feet, so all the points lie on the straight line $y = 12x$. A perfectly straight line has correlation of 1.

21. (33) **Baseball** There are 5 teams in the American League East division of professional baseball. How many ways can teams finish in first and second place? 20

CHALLENGE

Have students solve the following problem:

When a hiker looks at a mountain peak from his tent, the angle of elevation is 38°. When he hikes 1500 meters closer to the mountain, the angle of elevation is 60°. What is the height of the mountain?
about 2135 meters

Problem 14

If students have trouble writing the equation to be solved, say, "We need to find the value of t for which $h(t)$ is 20. Substitute 20 for $h(t)$. Substitute 0 for v_0 and 56 for h_0."

Problem 16

Guide students with the following prompts:

"What is the y-intercept of the line?" about 15

"Estimate the coordinates of two points on the line." about (30, 40) and (90, 90)

"What is the slope through those two points?" $\frac{5}{6}$

"What is the equation of a line with y-intercept 15 and slope $\frac{5}{6}$?"
$y = \frac{5}{6}x + 15$

Problem 21

Error Alert

Students might not realize that the order matters in this case. For example, Red Sox and Yankees finishing first and second, respectively, is different from Yankees and Red Sox finishing first and second, respectively. Students should use ${}_5P_2$ instead of ${}_5C_2$.

Problem 28

Encourage students to make a sketch for the problem. The bottom of the staircase is the origin, so the bottom of the handrail is at (0, 3).

Problem 30

Guide students by asking the following questions:

"What is the area of the square?" x^2

"What are the height and base of the triangle?" $h = x$; $b = x - a$

"The shaded region is the triangle. What is the area of the shaded region?" $0.5x(x - a)$

"What is the area of the unshaded region?" $x^2 - 0.5x(x - a)$

"What is the unsimplified ratio of the shaded area to the unshaded area?" $\frac{0.5x(x - a)}{x^2 - 0.5x(x - a)}$

22. **(Physics)** Through the process of annealing, metals are made more flexible, allowing a piece of metal to be flattened without breaking. Suppose a rectangular piece of metal with square ends of dimension $x - 10$ goes through the annealing process and is flattened into a thin sheet. What is the ratio of the new surface area to the original? Does the quotient have a zero remainder? Explain. $\frac{3x^2 + 40x - 500}{3x^2 - 40x + 100}$; the quotient does not have a zero remainder because there are no common factors for the numerator and denominator.
(38)

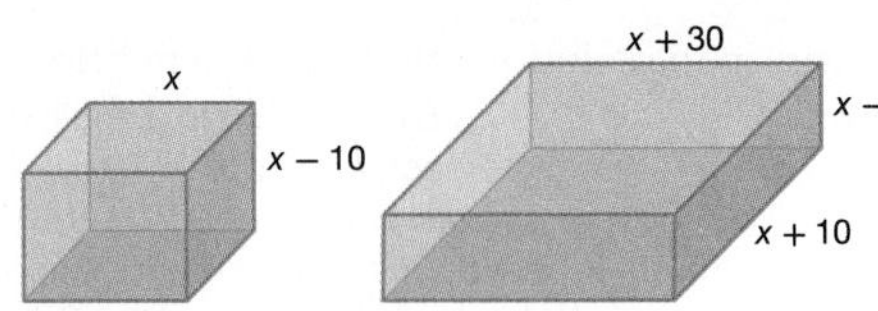

23. **(Cartography)** A cartographer constructs a map of North Dakota over a grid system such that Bismarck is at (225, 87) and Minot is at (192, 232). Find the distance between the cities to the nearest kilometer if each unit represents one kilometer. About 149 kilometers
(41)

*24. **Graphing Calculator** If $A = \begin{bmatrix} 2 & 4 \\ 6 & 8 \end{bmatrix}$ and $B = \begin{bmatrix} 10 & 12 \\ 14 & 16 \end{bmatrix}$, use a graphing calculator to find $AX = B$. $X = \begin{bmatrix} -3 & -4 \\ 4 & 5 \end{bmatrix}$
(32)

*25. **Write** How are the sine and cosine functions alike? How are they different?
(46)

26. **Error Analysis** A student was asked to convert a function written in vertex form to its standard form. The student's work is shown below. Find and correct the error the student made. The student did not include the middle term when squaring the binomial. The correct answer is $f(x) = -x^2 - 6x + 5$.
(27)

$$f(x) = -(x + 3)^2 + 14$$
$$= -(x^2 + 9) + 14$$
$$= -x^2 - 9 + 14$$
$$= -x^2 + 5$$

25. Possible answer: They are alike in that both use the length of the hypotenuse in the denominator of the ratio. The sine function has the opposite side in the numerator and the cosine function has the adjacent side in the numerator.

27. **(Chess Tournament)** Ten people enter a chess tournament. How many ways can matches be determined for the first round? $C(10, 2) = 45$
(42)

28. **Formulate** A staircase needs to be built that crosses a horizontal distance of 10 feet and a vertical distance of 15 feet. Write an equation of a line that could model the handrail that is 3 feet above the stairs. $y = 1.5x + 3$
(36)

*29. **(Sports)** A baseball diamond is shaped like a square that is 90 feet on each side. A line drawn from second base to home plate forms a right triangle with acute angles measuring 45°.
(46)

a. Show how to use a trigonometric function to find the distance from second base to home base to the nearest tenth of a foot. $\begin{bmatrix} \sin 45 = \frac{90}{x} \\ 127.3 \approx x \end{bmatrix}$

b. Check your answer to part a by using the Pythagorean Theorem. $x = \sqrt{90^2 + 90^2} \approx 127.3$

30. **Geometry** What is the ratio of the area of the shaded region to that of the unshaded region in the square to the right? $\frac{x - a}{x + a}$
(37)

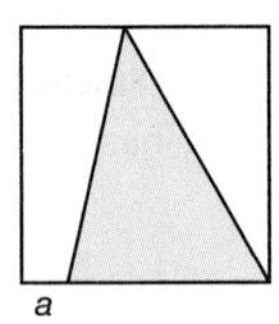

336 *Saxon Algebra 2*

LOOKING FORWARD

Identifying trigonometric ratios and using them to solve triangles prepares students for:

- **Lesson 52** Using Two Special Right Triangles
- **Lesson 63** Understanding the Unit Circle and Radian Measures
- **Lesson 67** Finding Inverse Trigonometric Functions

LESSON 47 Graphing Exponential Functions

Warm Up

1. **Vocabulary** In the expression 2^3, the exponent is 3 and the ___base___ is 2.
(3)
2. What is the value of $\left(\frac{2}{5}\right)^3$? $\frac{8}{125}$
(3)
3. What is the minimum value of the function $y = x^2 - 5$? −5
(27)

New Concepts

A function of the form $y = ab^x$ is an **exponential function** if x is a real number, $a \neq 0$, $b > 0$, and $b \neq 1$. The parent function of all exponential functions with base b is $y = b^x$.

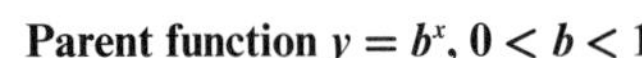

Parent function $y = b^x$, $b > 1$ **Parent function $y = b^x$, $0 < b < 1$**

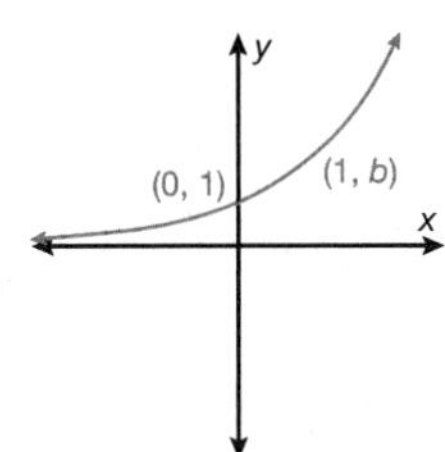

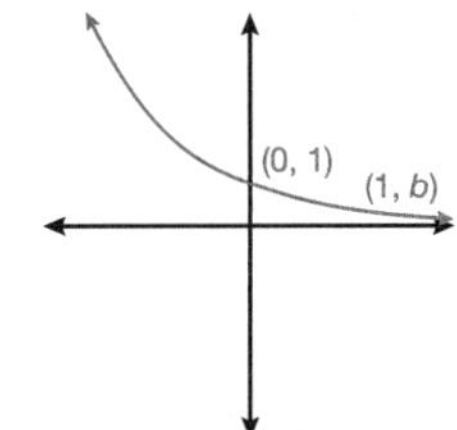

For each graph above, the line $y = 0$, or the x-axis, is an asymptote. An **asymptote** is a line that a graph approaches as the value of a variable becomes extremely large or small. The line $y = k$ is a **horizontal asymptote** of a graph if y approaches k as x increases or decreases without bound. The base of an exponential function must be positive, but the exponent can be negative. To graph exponential functions, use the property

$b^{-m} = \left(\frac{1}{b}\right)^m$. For example, $2^{-3} = \left(\frac{1}{2}\right)^3 = \frac{1}{8}$ and $\left(\frac{3}{2}\right)^{-2} = \left(\frac{2}{3}\right)^2 = \frac{4}{9}$.

Example 1 Graphing $y = b^x$

Graph $y = 2^x$. Identify the domain, the asymptote, and the range.

SOLUTION Make a table, plot the ordered pairs, and draw a smooth curve through them.

x	−3	−2	−1	0	1	2	3
$y = 2^x$	$\frac{1}{8}$	$\frac{1}{4}$	$\frac{1}{2}$	1	2	4	8

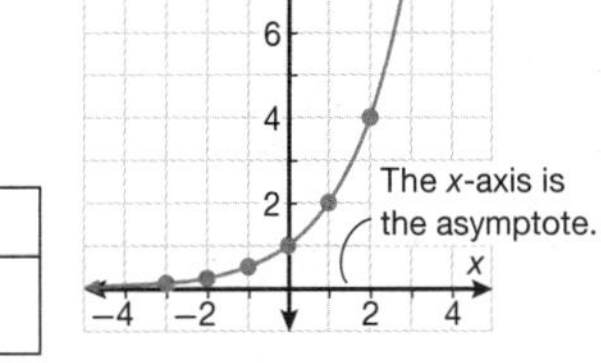

The domain is the set of all real numbers; the graph extends without end to the left and to the right. The asymptote is the line $y = 0$; as x decreases without bound, y approaches 0. The range is the set of all positive real numbers; the graph gets closer and closer to the x-axis from above, and it extends up without end.

Math Reasoning

Verify The domain of $y = 2^x$ includes numbers such as $x = \frac{1}{2}$ and $x = \sqrt{5}$.

Verify these approximate function values on the graph:

$2^{\frac{1}{2}} = \sqrt{2} \approx 1.4$

$2^{\sqrt{5}} \approx 4.7$

See student work.

LESSON 47

1 Warm Up

For Problem 2, review the rules of exponents:

$\left(\frac{a}{b}\right)^n = \frac{a^n}{b^n}$; $(ab)^n = a^n b^n$; $a^m a^n = a^{m+n}$

$a^0 = 1$; $a^1 = a$

2 New Concepts

Carefully review the restrictions on **exponential functions,** pointing out that $y = 3x^2$ is not an exponential function because the base (x) is not a constant greater than 0.

Example 1

This function takes the form $y = b^x$, where b is 2. So, the graph contains (0, 1) and (1, 2).

Additional Example 1

Graph $y = 3^x$. Identify the domain, the asymptote, and the range.

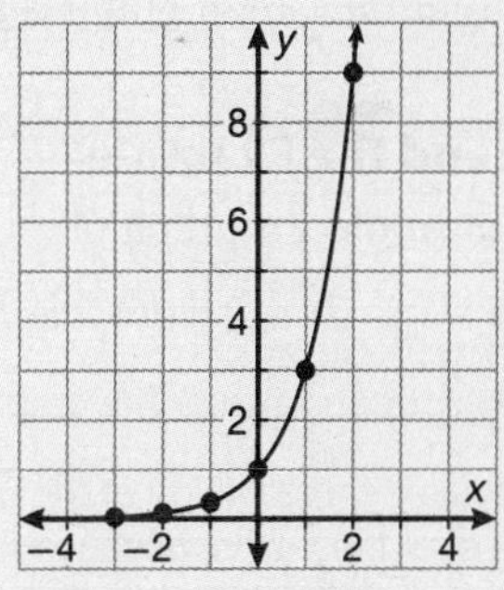

Domain: R Range: $y > 0$
Asymptote: x-axis ($y = 0$)

MATH BACKGROUND

The concept of asymptotes is new to students. With previous functions (with the exception of horizontal lines), as x increased or decreased, the value of y increased or decreased without bound. For example, in $y = x^2$, as the value of x increases, the value of y increases without limit.

With exponential functions, there is always an asymptote. An asymptote is a line to which the graph of a function continues to get closer. Point out that while the exponential graph *approaches* the asymptote, it never *touches* the asymptote. In the graph of $y = 2^x$, as x gets smaller, the value of y gets *asymptotically close* to 0, but never reaches 0. There is no value of x for which $2^x = 0$.

LESSON RESOURCES

Student Edition Practice Workbook 47
Reteaching Master 47
Adaptations Master 47
Challenge and Enrichment Master C47

Example 2

The graph of $y = \left(\frac{1}{b}\right)^x$ is a reflection of $y = b^x$ over the y-axis because $\left(\frac{1}{b}\right)^x = (b)^{-x}$. So, one graph contains (x, y), while the other contains $(-x, y)$. For each point (x, y) on $y = b^x$, the point $(-x, y)$ lies on $y = \left(\frac{1}{b}\right)^x$.

Additional Example 2

Graph $y = 4^x$ and $y = \left(\frac{1}{4}\right)^x$.

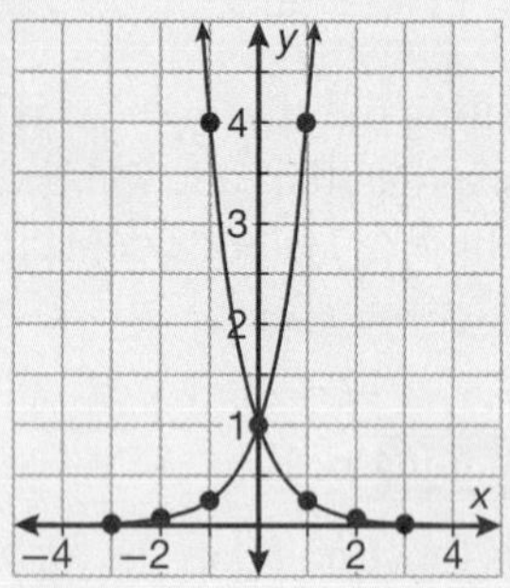

Example 3

Before looking at the graphs, have students use the transformation rules to predict how the three graphs are related. Point out that the parent graph is y_1.

Extend the Example

What would the graph of $y_4 = -\left[\frac{1}{4} \cdot 3^x - 2\right]$ look like? How do you know? The graph of y_4 would be a reflection of the graph of y_3 over the x-axis, because for each value of x, the value of y in y_4 is the opposite of its value in y_3. So, for example, if $\left(2, \frac{1}{4}\right)$ lies on y_3, then $\left(2, -\frac{1}{4}\right)$ lies on y_4. Each point is reflected over the x-axis, so the entire graph is reflected over the x-axis.

Example 2 **Graphing $y = b^x$ and $y = \left(\frac{1}{b}\right)^x$**

Graph $y = \left(\frac{3}{2}\right)^x$ and $y = \left(\frac{2}{3}\right)^x$.

SOLUTION

Make a table of values and graph each function.

x	−3	−2	−1	0	1	2	3
$y = \left(\frac{3}{2}\right)^x$	$\frac{8}{27}$	$\frac{4}{9}$	$\frac{2}{3}$	1	$\frac{3}{2}$	$\frac{9}{4}$	$\frac{27}{8}$
$y = \left(\frac{2}{3}\right)^x$	$\frac{27}{8}$	$\frac{9}{4}$	$\frac{3}{2}$	1	$\frac{2}{3}$	$\frac{4}{9}$	$\frac{8}{27}$

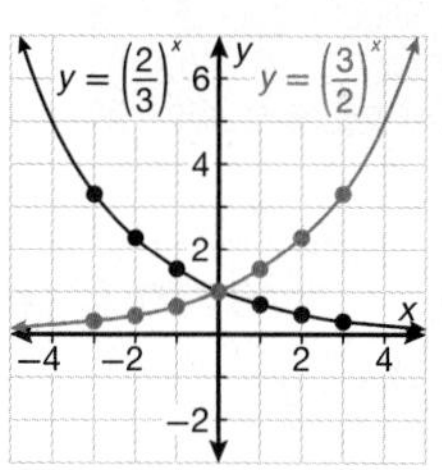

Transformations of the Parent Function $y = b^x$	
$y = ab^x$	vertical stretch if $\lvert a \rvert > 1$
	vertical compression if $0 < \lvert a \rvert < 1$
	reflection over x-axis if $a < 0$
$y = b^{x-h} + k$	shift horizontally h units, vertically k units

Example 3 **Graphing Transformations of $y = b^x$**

Graph the functions $y_1 = 3^x$, $y_2 = \frac{1}{4} \cdot 3^x$, and $y_3 = \frac{1}{4} \cdot 3^x - 2$. Describe the graphs, including domains and ranges.

SOLUTION

Make a table of values and graph each function.

x	−2	−1	0	1	2
$y_1 = 3^x$	$\frac{1}{9}$	$\frac{1}{3}$	1	3	9
$y_2 = \frac{1}{4} \cdot 3^x$	$\frac{1}{36}$	$\frac{1}{12}$	$\frac{1}{4}$	$\frac{3}{4}$	$\frac{9}{4}$
$y_3 = \frac{1}{4} \cdot 3^x - 2$	$-\frac{71}{36}$	$-\frac{23}{12}$	$-\frac{7}{4}$	$-\frac{5}{4}$	$\frac{1}{4}$

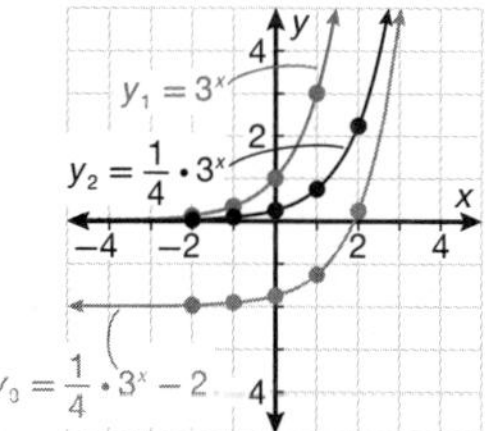

Math Reasoning

Analyze What is the horizontal asymptote for the graph of y_3?

$y = -2$

y_1 is the parent function of all exponential functions with base 3. The domain of all the functions is the set of all real numbers. The range of y_1 and y_2 is the set of all positive real numbers. The range of y_3 is the set of all real numbers greater than −2.

The graph of y_2 is a vertical compression of the graph of y_1 by a factor of $\frac{1}{4}$.

The graph of y_3 is a vertical shift 2 units down of the graph of y_2.

A function of the form $y = -b^x$ has the form $y = ab^x$, with $a = -1$. The graph of $y = -b^x$ is a reflection over the x-axis of the graph of $y = b^x$.

INCLUSION

In the graph in Example 3, students might have difficulty seeing the transformations that relate one graph to another.

Have them recreate the graphs on graph paper, using a different color to plot the points for each graph. Then, show them how the graph of y_2 is a compression of y_1, since each corresponding x-value yields a smaller y-value in y_2 than in y_1.

Next, have students count down two units from each point in y_2 to see that y_3 is a translation of y_2 two units down.

Example 4 Graphing Transformations of $y = b^x$ with a Calculator

Caution

$y = (-1.4)^x$ has a negative base and is not an exponential function.

$-(1.4)^x = -1 \cdot (1.4)^x$

$-(1.4)^x \neq (-1.4)^x$

Use a graphing calculator to graph the functions $y_1 = (1.4)^x$, $y_2 = -(1.4)^x$, and $y_3 = -2\,(1.4)^x$. Describe the graphs.

SOLUTION

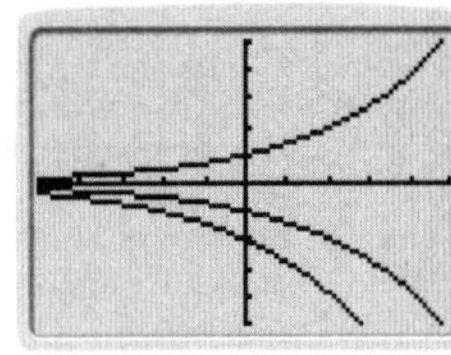

y_1 is the parent function of all exponential functions with base 1.4.

The graph of y_2 is a reflection of the graph of y_1 over the x-axis.

The graph of y_3 is a vertical stretch of the graph of y_2 by a factor of 2.

Example 5 Application: Compound Interest

The amount A in an account that earns interest is given by the exponential function $A = P\left(1 + \frac{r}{n}\right)^{nt}$, where P is the initial deposit, r is the annual interest rate, n is the number of times per year the interest is compounded, and t is the number of years. Suppose \$20,000 is deposited in a college savings account when a person is born. How much will be in the account on that person's 18th birthday if the account earns 9% compounded quarterly? If it is compounded daily?

SOLUTION

Math Reasoning

Write Is the function $A = P\left(1 + \frac{r}{n}\right)^{nt}$ in the form $y = ab^x$? Explain.

Yes; Sample: $A = P\left(1 + \frac{r}{n}\right)^{nt}$ is in the form $y = ab^x$ with $a = P$, $b = 1 + \frac{r}{n}$, and $x = nt$.

Understand Quarterly means 4 times per year. Daily means 365 times per year.

Plan Evaluate the function, letting $n = 4$ and $n = 365$.

Solve

Compounded Quarterly:	Compounded Daily:
$A = P\left(1 + \frac{r}{n}\right)^{nt}$	$A = P\left(1 + \frac{r}{n}\right)^{nt}$
$A = 20{,}000\left(1 + \frac{0.09}{4}\right)^{4 \cdot 18}$	$A = 20{,}000\left(1 + \frac{0.09}{365}\right)^{365 \cdot 18}$
$A = 20{,}000(1 + 0.0225)^{72}$	$A = 20{,}000\left(1 + \frac{0.09}{365}\right)^{6570}$
$A = 99{,}263.32$	$A = 101{,}041.63$

There will be \$99,263.32 in the account if compounded quarterly and \$101,041.63 if compounded daily.

Check The amounts from quarterly compounding and daily compounding are reasonable because the quarterly compounding should be less than the amount from the daily compounding.

ALTERNATE METHOD FOR EXAMPLE 5

Show students how to enter interest calculations into a graphing calculator, reminding them to use parentheses when necessary. Show them how to use the ENTRY key (by pressing 2nd ENTER) to copy a previous calculation. Then, have them use the arrow keys to move through the expression, changing each instance of n from 4 to 365. Remind them to use the INS key to make room for additional digits.

```
20000*(1+0.09/4)
^(4*18)
        99263.31998
20000*(1+0.09/36
5)^(365*18)
        101041.627
```

Example 4

Error Alert Be sure students use parentheses when entering functions into a calculator. Remind them that -1.4^x is not the same as $(-1.4)^x$.

Additional Example 4

Use a graphing calculator to graph the functions $y_1 = (2.9)^x$, $y_2 = -(2.9)^x$, and $y_3 = -0.5(2.9)^x$. Describe the graphs.

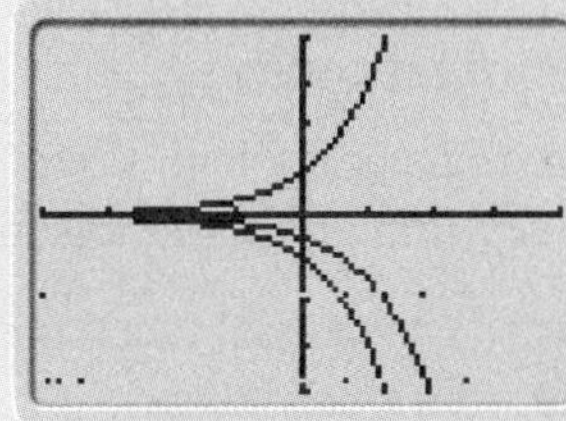

y_1 is the parent function. The graph of y_2 is a reflection of y_1 over the x-axis. The graph of y_3 is a compression of y_2 by a factor of 0.5.

Example 5

Be sure students understand that compound interest is interest paid on principal *and* previously-earned interest. Contrast with simple interest, which is interest paid only on principal.

Additional Example 5

\$4000 is deposited in an account. How much will be in the account after 7 years if interest is compounded monthly at a rate of 2.75%? *\$4,848.04*

TEACHER TIP

In interest calculations, encourage students to identify P, r, n, and t on paper before entering them into the interest formula. Have them copy the formula, then write it again, substituting the value of each variable. Remind them to use the correct order of operations and perform only one step at a time.

Lesson Practice

Problem a

Scaffolding Have students make a table of values using x-values that are the integers from -4 to 4.

Problem e

Error Alert Students might use 6 for r. Remind them that r is the interest expressed as a decimal. Since $6\% = 0.06$, they should use 0.06 for r.

Check for Understanding

The questions below help assess the concepts taught in this lesson.

"How is an exponential function different from a polynomial function?" An exponential function shows a constant greater than 0 raised to a variable. A polynomial function shows the sum of variables raised to powers greater than or equal to 0.

"If you have graphed $y = 4^x$, how can you find the graph of $y = 4^x - 3$? of $y = 0.25(4^x)$?" The graph of $y = 4^x - 3$ is a translation of $y = 4^x$ three units downward. Take each point on $y = 4^x$ and move it down three units. The graph of $y = 0.25(4^x)$ is a compression of $y = 4^x$ by a factor of 0.25. Take each point on $y = 4^x$ and multiply its y-coordinate by 0.25.

Lesson Practice

a.

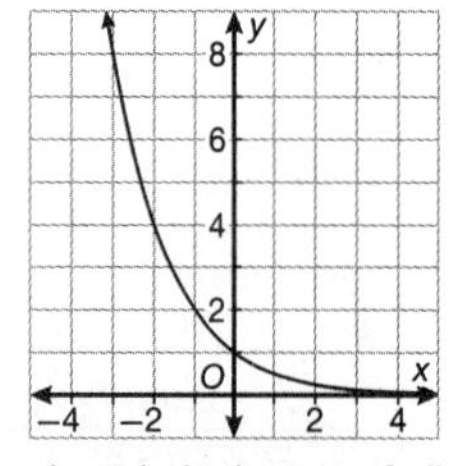

The domain is the set of all real numbers. The asymptote is the line $y = 0$ (the x-axis). The range is the set of all positive real numbers.

a. *(Ex 1)* Graph $y = \left(\frac{1}{2}\right)^x$. Identify the domain, the asymptote, and the range.

b. *(Ex 2)* Graph $y = \left(\frac{3}{4}\right)^x$ and $y = \left(\frac{4}{3}\right)^x$. Describe the graphs. See Additional Answers.

c. *(Ex 3)* Graph the functions $y_1 = 2^x$, $y_2 = \frac{1}{2} \cdot 2^x$ and $y_3 = \frac{1}{2} \cdot 2^x + 3$. Describe the graphs, including domains and ranges. See Additional Answers.

d. *(Ex 4)* Use a graphing calculator to graph the functions $y_1 = (1.6)^x$, $y_2 = -(1.6)^x$, and $y_3 = -\frac{1}{2}(1.6)^x$. Describe the graphs. See Additional Answers.

e. *(Ex 5)* Suppose \$1,000 is deposited in a savings account. How much will be in the account in 2 years if the account earns 6% compounded quarterly? If it is compounded monthly? See Additional Answers.

Practice Distributed and Integrated

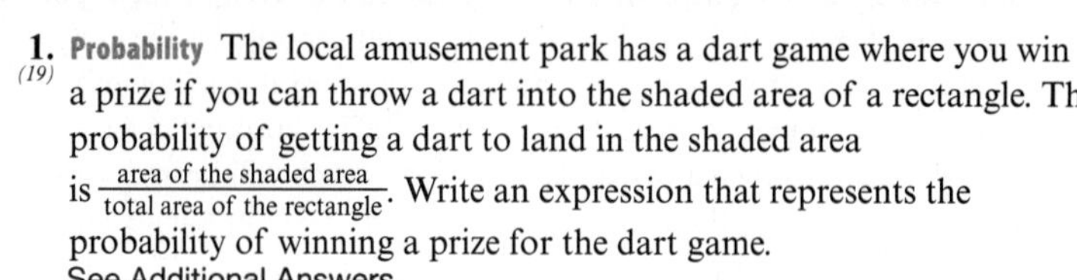

1. *(19)* **Probability** The local amusement park has a dart game where you win a prize if you can throw a dart into the shaded area of a rectangle. The probability of getting a dart to land in the shaded area is $\frac{\text{area of the shaded area}}{\text{total area of the rectangle}}$. Write an expression that represents the probability of winning a prize for the dart game. See Additional Answers.

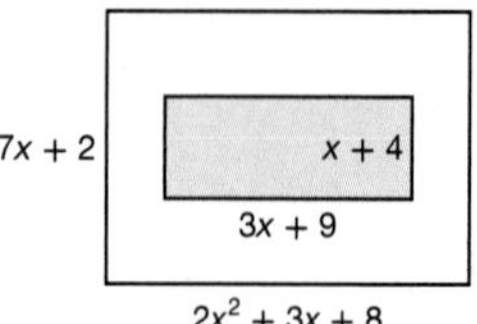

2. *(38)* **Multiple Choice** Which of the following is the remainder when dividing $3x^3 - 16x^2 + 12x + 16$ by $(x + 1)$? **B**

A -16 B -15 C 0 D 15

3. *(27)* **Generalize** If the x-intercepts of a quadratic function are x_1 and x_2, give a general equation for the x-coordinate of the vertex. $x = \frac{x_1 + x_2}{2}$

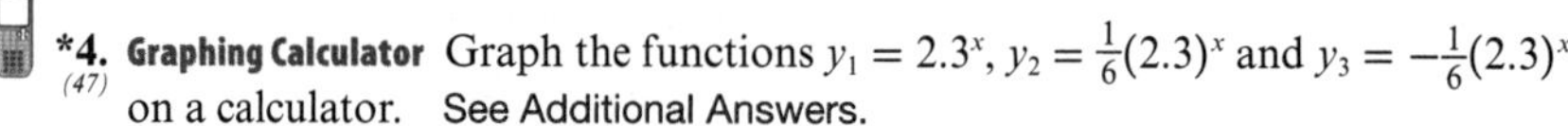

***4.** *(47)* **Graphing Calculator** Graph the functions $y_1 = 2.3^x$, $y_2 = \frac{1}{6}(2.3)^x$ and $y_3 = -\frac{1}{6}(2.3)^x$ on a calculator. See Additional Answers.

8b. Possible description: All meaningful solutions are the ordered pairs of the solution set on and inside the triangle whose left side is the segment from (0, 20) to (0, 16).

Add:

5. *(37)* $\frac{5x^2}{pm} - 4 + \frac{c}{p^2m}$ $\frac{5x^2p - 4p^2m + c}{p^2m}$

6. *(37)* $3xy^2m + \frac{4}{x}$ $\frac{3x^2y^2m + 4}{x}$

7. *(18)* **Running** The expression representing a runner's speed is $120x^2 - 60x - 240$ feet per minute. Find the expression for the runner's speed in feet per second. $2x^2 - x - 4$ ft/s

***8.** *(43)* **Multi-Step** A college student earns \$10 per hour working in the library and \$15 per hour on a landscaping crew. He decides to work not more than 20 hours in a week, and his goal is to earn at least \$240 in a week. Let x represent a number of hours working in the library and y represent a number of hours working on the landscaping crew. **a–b.** See Additional Answers.

a. Write and graph a system of linear inequalities that represents the situation.

b. Describe the portion of the solution set that contains meaningful solutions for this situation.

c. Determine the vertices of the polygon you described in part b. Describe what each vertex represents. See Additional Answers.

ENGLISH LANGUAGE LEARNERS

In compound interest problems, students need to translate words such as monthly, daily, and quarterly into numbers. Tell them that the suffix –ly adds the meaning happening once every to a measure of time.

Daily means happening once every day, monthly means happening once every month, etc.

Ask students to identify some things that happen hourly, daily, weekly, and monthly.

For example, the Chess Club meets weekly; the soccer team practices daily; grades are given out monthly.

Have students make a list of the number of times per year interest is compounding under the various compounding schedules. For example, monthly compounding is done 12 times per year.

***9.** (39) **Formulate** Write a list of rules describing which half-plane to shade and what type of line to use (dashed or solid) based on the inequality symbol in an inequality.

10. (35) **Gravity** The height of a free-falling object (neglecting air resistance) is given by the function $h(t) = -16t^2 + v_0t + h_0$, where h_0 is the initial height in feet, v_0 is the initial velocity in feet per second, and $h(t)$ is the height in feet at time t seconds. How long does it take for an object to hit the ground after it is thrown straight up at a speed of 36 feet per second from a height of 52 feet? 3.25 seconds

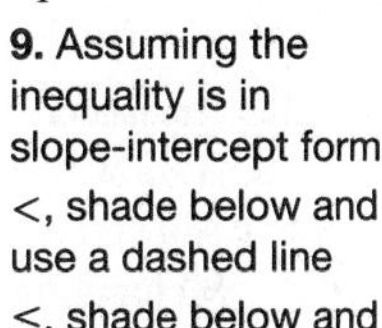

9. Assuming the inequality is in slope-intercept form:
<, shade below and use a dashed line
≤, shade below and use a solid line
>, shade above and use a dashed line
≥, shade above and use a solid line

11. (15) Graph the system below. Describe the shape that the lines form.

$0.9x - 1.5y = 0.21$
$-1.2x + 2.0y = -0.28$ All three lines coincide.
$0.6x - y = 0.14$

***12.** (47) **Savings** London deposited \$3000 into a savings account when she got her first job after graduating from college. How much will be in her account when she finishes graduate school in 2 years if the account earns 8.3% compounded daily? \$3541.65

11.

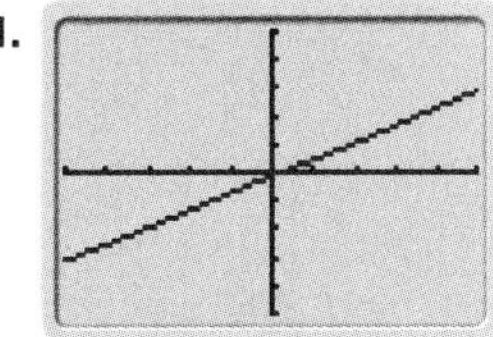

Determine whether the ordered triples are solutions of the systems.

13. (29) Is (2, −5, 3) a solution of the system $\begin{aligned} 4x + 3y + 5z &= 8 \\ -6x + 3y + 7z &= -6 \\ 8x + y - 2z &= 5 \end{aligned}$? yes

14. (29) Is (0, 1, 2) a solution of the system $\begin{aligned} 10x + 9y + 6z &= 21 \\ -x + 4y - 7z &= -10 \\ -9x + 5y + 2z &= 9 \end{aligned}$? yes

***15.** (44) **Write** Explain why multiplying a radical denominator by its radical conjugate eliminates the radical from the denominator. See Additional Answers.

16. (16) **Analyze** Explain the difficulty you encounter when trying to use Cramer's Rule to solve the system $\begin{aligned} 4x - 12y &= -4 \\ -6x + 18y &= -6 \end{aligned}$

16. The coefficient matrix has determinant 0. The numerator matrices, however, are non-zero, indicating that there are no solutions. Indeed, the two equations are inconsistent.

17. (41) **Verify** Show that 30 cm, 72 cm, and 78 cm can be the lengths of the sides of a right triangle. $30^2 + 72^2 = 900 + 5184 = 6084$ and $78^2 = 6084$

***18.** (45) **Depreciation** The table shows the trade-in value for seven cars in good condition with typical mileage and standard equipment. Make a scatter plot of the data, using the number of years before and after 2000 on the x-axis. Sketch a line of best fit.

	A	B	C	D	E	F	G
Year	1987	1992	1996	1999	2002	2005	2007
Value (\$)	450	650	1950	2050	3435	4265	8610

See Additional Answers.

3 Practice

Math Conversations

Discussions to strengthen understanding

Problem 12

Guide students by asking them the following questions.

"What is P?" The initial investment, \$3000

"What is r?" The interest rate, 8.3% or 0.083

"What is n?" The number of times interest is compounded per year, 365

"What is t?" The number of years, 2

Problem 15

Remind students that the conjugate of the radical expression $a + \sqrt{b}$ is $a - \sqrt{b}$.

Problem 18

Extend the Problem

Write an equation for the line of best fit. Name the y-intercept and two points on your line.
Sample: Using $b = 3640$ and the points (1,3979) and (2,4318), the equation of the line is $y = 339x + 3640$.

CHALLENGE

\$1000 is invested in an account that earns 6.5% interest. Find the amount in the account after 3 years if interest is compounded

a. yearly \$1207.95

b. quarterly \$1213.41

c. monthly \$1214.67

d. daily \$1215.29

e. hourly \$1215.31

Have students use their answers to predict the amount in the account if interest is compounded every minute. Ask them to justify their predictions. Sample: The amount will still be about \$1215.31. As n increased from 1 to 4 to 12 to 365 to 8,760, the amount of increase in the amount of money got much smaller. So, compounding every minute will not make much difference over compounding hourly.

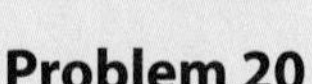

19. *(40)* **Error Analysis** A student submitted the work below and reported that $\sqrt{8} \cdot \sqrt{6}$ simplifies to $2\sqrt{12}$. Explain her error.

$\sqrt{8} \cdot \sqrt{6} = \sqrt{4} \cdot \sqrt{2} \cdot \sqrt{6} = 2\sqrt{2}\sqrt{6} = 2\sqrt{12}$

The student did not completely simplify the expression because the square root of 12 can be simplified. $2\sqrt{12} = 2\sqrt{4}\sqrt{3} = 4\sqrt{3}$

20. *(31)* **Geometry** Write a rational expression in simplest form for the ratio of the triangle's perimeter to its area. $\frac{2}{3x}$

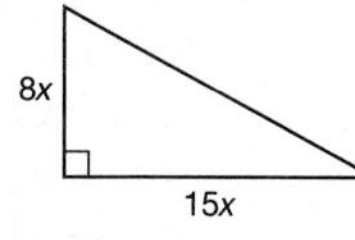

21. *(36)* **Economics** The exchange rate from dollars to different currencies is shown. A company charges a fee of \$2.50 for amounts up to \$50 and \$7.50 for amounts above \$50. Write the equations for exchanging British pounds to dollars. What do the graphs of the equations have in common? $y = 2.0284x - 2.5$ and $y = 2.0284x - 7.5$; same slope

Currency	US \$
1 Euro =	1.377
1 Canadian dollar =	0.9472
1 British pound =	2.0284

22. *(13)* **Error Analysis** A student incorrectly graphed the equation $x = -2$ as shown. What equation does the graph represent? Explain how you know.
$y = -2$; Possible explanation: The y-coordinate of every point on the line is -2.

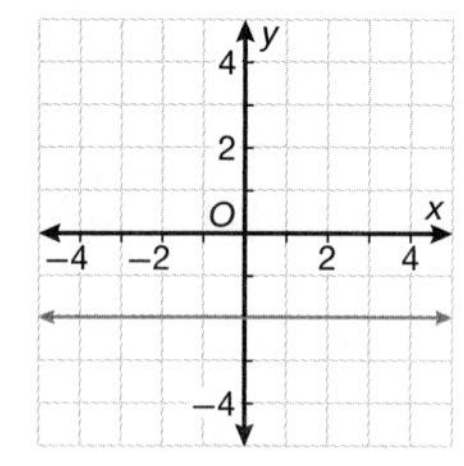

23. *(28)* **Multi-Step** Consider the expression $\frac{3x - 6}{2}$.

a. Is the expression simplified? Tell why or why not.

b. Are there any excluded values? Explain. No, the denominator will never be 0.

23a. Yes, the GCF in the numerator is 3, which does not cancel out with the 2 in the denominator.

***24.** *(46)* **Tourism** The angle of elevation from a tourist on the beach in Cape May, New Jersey to the top of the lighthouse is 38°. The lighthouse has a height of 158 feet. To the nearest foot, how far away is the tourist from the base of the lighthouse? 202 feet

25. *(15)* Graph the system below. Describe the shape that the lines form. See Additional Answers.

$$4x - 2y = 2$$
$$-6x - 3y = 3$$
$$x - 2y = 6$$

26. *(42)* **Multiple Choice** How many different committees of three people can be formed from a group of 15? **A**

A 455 **B** 910 **C** 1365 **D** 2370

Write the distance from each point to the origin as an absolute value expression. Then simplify the expression.

27. *(17)* (5, 0) $|5| = 5$ **28.** *(17)* (−7, 0) $|-7| = 7$ **29.** *(17)* (0, 9) $|9| = 9$

***30.** *(44)* Which of the following shows the simplified radical expression for $\frac{4\sqrt{7} - 2}{5\sqrt{7} + 3}$? **A**

A $\frac{73 - 11\sqrt{7}}{83}$ **B** $\frac{54}{83}$ **C** $\frac{134 + 22\sqrt{7}}{184}$ **D** $\frac{108}{146 + 19\sqrt{7}}$

Problem 20

"What Pythagorean triple can be used to find the hypotenuse in a right triangle with leg lengths in the ratio 8:15? 8, 15, 17

Problem 22

"What is the y-coordinate of each point on the line? -2

"What equation describes each point on the line? $y = -2$

Problem 24

Guide students by asking them the following questions.

"Relative to the 38° angle, which side is known?" The opposite side

"Relative to the 38° angle, which side needs to be found?" The adjacent side

"Which trigonometric ratio uses the lengths of the opposite and adjacent sides?" The tangent ratio

Problem 25

Suggest that students use intercepts to help them graph each equation. For example, they can use inspection to find that (0.5, 0) and (0, −1) lie on $4x - 2y = 2$.

Problem 30

Error Alert

Students sometimes have trouble squaring a radical product because they fail to square each of its parts. For example, they might write $(5\sqrt{7})^2$ as $5 \cdot 7$. Remind students to use the properties of exponents to write $(5\sqrt{7})^2$ as $5^2 \cdot (\sqrt{7})^2$, or $25 \cdot 7$.

LOOKING FORWARD

The study of exponential functions prepares students for the following lessons:

- **Lesson 57** Finding Exponential Growth and Decay
- **Lesson 72** Using the Properties of Logarithms

LESSON 48

Understanding Complex Fractions

Warm Up

1. **Vocabulary** $\frac{2}{x}$ is the reciprocal of $\frac{x}{2}$. (31)

2. Divide and write the quotient in simplest form: $\frac{3}{10} \div \frac{6}{5}$. $\frac{1}{4}$ (31)

3. What is the Least Common Denominator of $\frac{1}{4x}$, $\frac{5}{6x}$, and $\frac{x}{x+5}$? $12x(x+5)$ (37)

New Concepts

A **complex fraction** is a fraction that contains one or more fractions in its numerator or denominator.

Some examples of complex fractions are shown below.

$$\frac{(x-2)}{\frac{5}{x}} \qquad \frac{2+\frac{1}{3}}{2x+5} \qquad \frac{x+\frac{2}{x}}{x-\frac{1}{3x}}$$

Simplifying Complex Fractions	
Method 1:	Simplify as needed to write the numerator and the denominator each as a single term. Then divide.
Method 2:	Multiply the numerator and the denominator by the Least Common Denominator (LCD) of all the fractions in the complex fraction. Then simplify.

Example 1 Simplifying a Numerical Complex Fraction (Method 1)

Simplify $\dfrac{\frac{1}{6}+\frac{3}{4}}{2+\frac{1}{5}}$.

SOLUTION

$\dfrac{\frac{1}{6}+\frac{3}{4}}{2+\frac{1}{5}} = \dfrac{\frac{2}{12}+\frac{9}{12}}{\frac{10}{5}+\frac{1}{5}}$ Add the terms in the numerator. Add the terms in the denominator.

$= \dfrac{\frac{11}{12}}{\frac{11}{5}}$ Simplify.

$= \frac{11}{12} \cdot \frac{5}{11}$ To divide by a fraction, multiply by its reciprocal.

$= \frac{5}{12}$

Hint

You need to use an LCD in Method 1, but not necessarily the LCD of *all* fractions in the complex fraction. The LCD of $\frac{1}{6}$ and $\frac{3}{4}$ is 12.

Online Connection
www.SaxonMathResources.com

MATH BACKGROUND

Fractions are usually classified as simple, compound, or complex. Simple fractions consist of a fraction with a whole number numerator and denominator. Compound fractions are also known as mixed numbers. These consist of a whole number and a simple fraction. A complex fraction consists of a fraction in which the numerator, the denominator, or both, contain a fraction.

Simplifying complex fractions is necessary to make calculations easier or make numbers easier to compare. Several methods can be used when simplifying. It is left to the student to choose the method most appropriate for a given situation.

LESSON 48

1 Warm Up

Remind students that a reciprocal is sometimes called the multiplicative inverse.

2 New Concepts

In this lesson, students simplify complex fractions.

Discuss the definition of **complex fraction.** Explain that complex fractions are simplified when the numerator and denominator are each written as a single term.

Example 1

Remind students that a fraction bar represents division.

Additional Example 1

Simplify $\dfrac{\frac{3}{5}+\frac{1}{10}}{4+\frac{3}{8}}$. $\frac{4}{25}$

Extend the Example

"Explain why converting the fractions to decimals may or may not be a good method for solving this problem." Although $\frac{3}{4}$ and $\frac{1}{5}$ can be changed to 0.75 and 0.2 respectively, the fraction $\frac{1}{6}$ is a repeating decimal. This means our answer may not be an exact value.

LESSON RESOURCES

Student Edition Practice Workbook 48
Reteaching Master 48
Adaptations Master 48
Challenge and Enrichment Master C48

Example 2

This example uses the LCD of both the numerator and the denominator to multiply and eliminate the fractions.

Error Alert Students might believe that the LCD of x and $x - 5$ is simply $x - 5$. Remind students that the x's do not divide out in $\frac{x-5}{x}$.

Additional Example 2

Simplify.

a. $\dfrac{\frac{3}{a}+\frac{1}{b}}{4-\frac{2}{a^2}}$ $\frac{3ab+a^2}{4a^2b-2b} = \frac{a(3b+a)}{2b(2a^2-1)}$

b. $\dfrac{\frac{1}{x+2}+\frac{5}{x^2}}{\frac{3x}{x+2}}$ $\frac{x^2+5x+10}{3x^3}$

TEACHER TIP

Tell students that after multiplying the numerator and denominator by the LCD, neither the numerator nor the denominator will contain fractions. If fractions still remain, tell students they may have chosen an incorrect LCD.

Example 3

Formulas involving fractions can be simplified to make substitution of values easier.

Additional Example 3

Express the volume formula from Example 3 in simplest form in terms of h and R if the radius r of the smaller base is one-third the radius R of the larger base.

$\frac{13\pi hR^2}{27}$

Example 2 Simplifying Algebraic Complex Fractions (Method 2)

Caution

Do not divide out factors of individual terms to attempt to simplify in a rational expression.

$\frac{3ab+2b}{5ab-a} \neq \frac{3+2b}{5-a}$.

a. Simplify $\dfrac{3+\frac{2}{a}}{5-\frac{1}{b}}$.

SOLUTION

$$\frac{3+\frac{2}{a}}{5-\frac{1}{b}} = \frac{\left(3+\frac{2}{a}\right)\cdot ab}{\left(5-\frac{1}{b}\right)\cdot ab}$$

The LCD of $\frac{2}{a}$ and $\frac{1}{b}$ is ab. Multiply the numerator and denominator by ab.

$$= \frac{3ab+2b}{5ab-a}$$

Distribute ab to simplify.

b. Simplify $\dfrac{\frac{3}{x}+\frac{1}{x-5}}{\frac{4x}{x-5}}$.

SOLUTION

$$\frac{\frac{3}{x}+\frac{1}{x-5}}{\frac{4x}{x-5}} = \frac{\left(\frac{3}{x}+\frac{1}{x-5}\right)\cdot x(x-5)}{\left(\frac{4x}{x-5}\right)\cdot x(x-5)}$$

The LCD of $\frac{3}{x}$, $\frac{1}{x-5}$, and $\frac{4x}{x-5}$ is $x(x-5)$. Multiply the numerator and denominator by $x(x-5)$.

$$= \frac{3(x-5)+x}{4x\cdot x}$$

Simplify.

$$= \frac{4x-15}{4x^2}$$

Example 3 Application: Solar Heating

Math Language

A **frustum** of a cone is formed by a plane cutting through a cone, perpendicular to its vertical axis. It has two parallel circular bases of different sizes.

A solar collector in the shape of a frustum of a cone heats collected water by reflecting the sun's rays from its lateral surface toward its vertical axis. Express the volume formula in simplest form in terms of h and R if the radius r of the smaller base is half the radius R of the larger base.

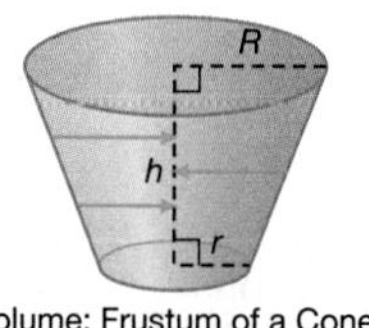

Volume: Frustum of a Cone

$V = \frac{\pi h(r^2+rR+R^2)}{3}$

SOLUTION

Substitute $\frac{R}{2}$ for r, and then simplify.

$$V = \frac{\pi h(r^2+rR+R^2)}{3} = \frac{\pi h\left(\left(\frac{R}{2}\right)^2+\left(\frac{R}{2}\right)R+R^2\right)}{3} = \frac{\pi h\left(\frac{R^2}{4}+\frac{R^2}{2}+R^2\right)}{3}$$

$$= \frac{\pi h\left(\frac{R^2}{4}+\frac{R^2}{2}+R^2\right)\cdot 4}{3\cdot 4} = \frac{\pi h(R^2+2R^2+4R^2)}{12} = \frac{7\pi hR^2}{12}$$

Check The expression is in simplest form in terms of h and R.

ENGLISH LEARNERS

The word simplify is used several times in Example 2. Explain the meaning of the word **simplify**. Say:

"The word simplify means to make something easier. In math, the word simplify means to perform an operation that will make the expression simpler."

Sometimes the operation is reducing a fraction. Write the following on the board:

Simplify $\frac{1}{2}+\frac{1}{4}$. Say, **"Simplify by changing $\frac{1}{2}$ to $\frac{2}{4}$ and adding the fractions."** The answer is $\frac{3}{4}$.

Sometimes the simplifying operation is using the Distributive Property. Write the following on the board: Simplify $2x(x+5)$. Say, **"Simplify by distributing the $2x$."** The answer is $2x^2+10x$.

Lesson Practice

a. (Ex 1) Simplify $\dfrac{\frac{1}{10}-1}{\frac{5}{8}+\frac{3}{20}}$. $-\frac{36}{31}$

b. (Ex 2) Simplify $\dfrac{\frac{5}{x}-1}{\frac{3}{y}+1}$. $\frac{5y-xy}{3x+xy}$

c. (Ex 2) Simplify $\dfrac{\frac{a}{b}-\frac{c}{d}}{\frac{a}{b}+\frac{c}{d}}$. $\frac{ad-bc}{ad+bc}$

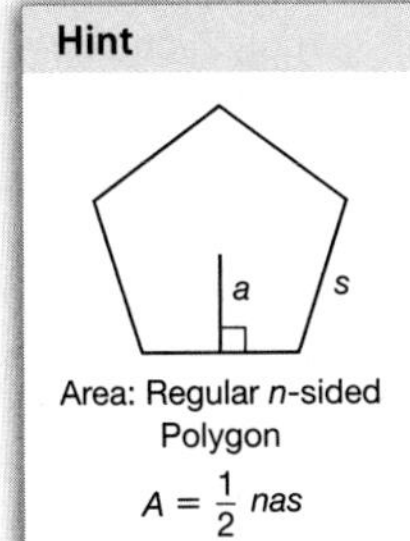

d. (Ex 3) The Pentagon building in Washington D.C. has the approximate shape of a regular pentagon. In a regular pentagon, the apothem a and the side length s are related by $a=\frac{\frac{s}{2}}{0.727}$ (where 0.727 is correct to the nearest thousandth). Express the formula for the area of a regular pentagon in simplest form in terms of s. $A=\frac{5s^2}{2.908}$ or $A=1.719s^2$

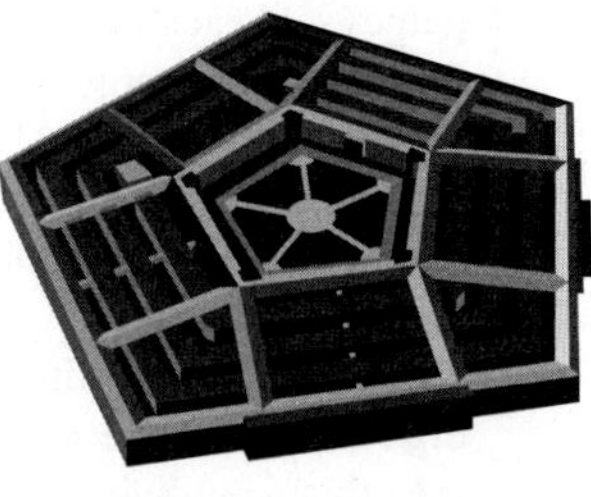

Practice Distributed and Integrated

Simplify:

***1.** (48) $\dfrac{\frac{x}{m+p}}{\frac{y}{m+p}}$ $\frac{x}{y}$

***2.** (48) $\dfrac{x+\frac{4xy}{x}}{\frac{1}{x}-y}$ $\frac{x^2+4xy}{1-xy}$

***3.** (48) $\dfrac{\frac{m}{p}+\frac{3}{xp}}{\frac{y}{p}}$ $\frac{mx+3}{xy}$

4. (20) **Basketball** The length of a regulation NCAA basketball court is given by the function $f(x)=x+24$ feet. The width of a regulation NCAA basketball court is given by the function $g(x)=2x-90$ feet. Write a function $h(x)$ that represents how many feet longer the court is than it is wide. $h(x)=-x+114$ feet

5. (Inv 2) **Airplane Altitude** A plane's altitude increases at a rate of 40 ft/s as it ascends after takeoff. Its ground distance from the airport is increasing at a rate of 240 ft/s. What is the location of the plane 20 seconds after takeoff? altitude of 800; ground distance of 4800 ft from the airport

6. (36) **Justify** Is the triangle defined by vertices (−3, 6), (4, 4), and (1, −8) a right triangle? Explain your answer. No because none of the pairs of lines that cross pairs of vertices is perpendicular.

7. (44) **Geometry** The area of a rectangular garden is 30 ft^2. The width of the garden is $(\sqrt{3}+1)$ ft. Find a simplified expression for the length of the garden. $(15\sqrt{3}-15)$ ft or $15(\sqrt{3}-1)$ ft

Lesson Practice

Problem a

Scaffolding Tell students to first decide whether it is easier to find the LCD for the whole fraction or the LCD of the numerator and denominator separately. Then multiply by the LCD.

Check for Understanding

The questions below help assess the concepts taught in this lesson.

1. **"What happens when the numerator and denominator of a complex fraction are multiplied by the LCD?"** When numerator and denominator are multiplied by the LCD, all fractions are divided out. So the numerator and denominator will no longer contain expressions with fractions.

2. **"How can you check that you simplified a complex fraction correctly?"** If the complex fraction contains numbers only, I can change the fractions to decimals and solve. If the complex fraction contains variables, I can substitute a number to see if the answer remains the same in the simplified form.

CHALLENGE

Simplify.

$$\dfrac{\dfrac{\frac{1}{x+3}+\frac{4}{x}}{\frac{2}{x+3}-\frac{1}{x}}}{\frac{1}{x-3}+\frac{3}{x}}$$ $\frac{x^2+4x-12}{4x-9}$

3 Practice

Math Conversations

Discussions to strengthen understanding

Problem 13

Extend the Problem

"What is the population standard deviation for this data with the outlier?" $\sigma = 14.38$

"What is the population standard deviation without the outlier?" $\sigma = 1.4$

Use the description to write the vertex form of a quadratic equation.

8. (30) The parent function is shifted 5 units right. $y = (x - 5)^2$

9. (30) The parent function is shifted 2 units to the left and 7 units up. $y = (x + 2)^2 + 7$

10. (40) **Write** Explain why absolute value symbols are used in the following sentence. For any real number x, $\sqrt{x^2} = |x|$.

10. If the absolute value signs were missing, then for $x = -2$, $\sqrt{(-2)^2} = \sqrt{4} = -2$, but that is not true because the radical symbol indicates that only the positive root, 2, can be given.

11. (22) **Data Analysis** A store records the number of video games sold each month. Examine the table. Does this table represent a continuous, discontinuous, and/or discrete function? Justify your answer. Discrete, discontinuous function; The graph consists of four points.

Month	Games Sold
1	10
2	8
3	9
4	20

***12.** (42) **Verify** If you have 5 digits that can be arranged in any order, then specify that one digit must be in the second position; verify that the number of arrangements of the other four digits must be 4!

13. (25) **Error Analysis** A chemist weighs samples obtained from a production run. The weights of the samples are 12 g, 14 g, 65 g, 11 g, 15 g, 14 g, 14 g, 12 g, 13 g, 15 g, 14 g, and 11 g. He eliminated the outlier and drew a box-and-whisker plot to represent the data. What is his error? See Additional Answers.

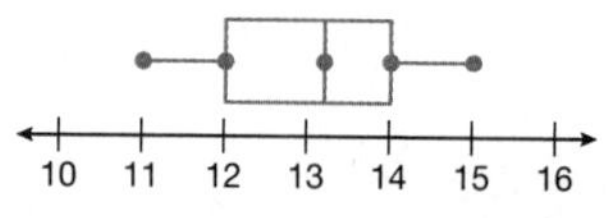

12. Once a position is specified, there are only four digits left that can be arranged in any order: $4! = 4 \times 3 \times 2 \times 1 = 24$ arrangements

***14.** (48) Simplify $\dfrac{\dfrac{5}{2x} - \dfrac{2}{x+5}}{\dfrac{1}{2(x+5)} + \dfrac{1}{x}}$. $\dfrac{x + 25}{3x + 10}$

15. (27) **Formulate a.** Use a table to graph $f(x) = (x - 2)^2 + 6$. See Additional Answers.

b. Compare the graph to its function. Formulate a conjecture about how you can find the vertex of a parabola based on its related function given in vertex form. The vertex is (h, k) for a function in the form $y = (x - h)^2 + k$.

Simplify:

16. (40) $5\sqrt{18} - 10\sqrt{50} + 3\sqrt{72}$ $-17\sqrt{2}$

17. (40) $3\sqrt{18}(4\sqrt{2} - 2\sqrt{3})$ $72 - 18\sqrt{6}$

18. (44) $2\sqrt{\frac{2}{9}} - 3\sqrt{\frac{9}{2}}$ $\frac{-23\sqrt{2}}{6}$

19. (44) $-3\sqrt{\frac{2}{3}} + 2\sqrt{\frac{3}{2}}$ 0

20. (40) $3\sqrt{24}(2\sqrt{6} - 3\sqrt{12})$ $72 - 108\sqrt{2}$

21. (30) **Multi-Step a.** Graph the function $y = (x - 5)^2 + 1$.

b. On the same graph, sketch the reflection of the parabola across the x-axis.

c. Give the equation of the function represented by the reflected parabola.

21. Function for reflected parabola: $y = -1(x - 5)^2 - 1$

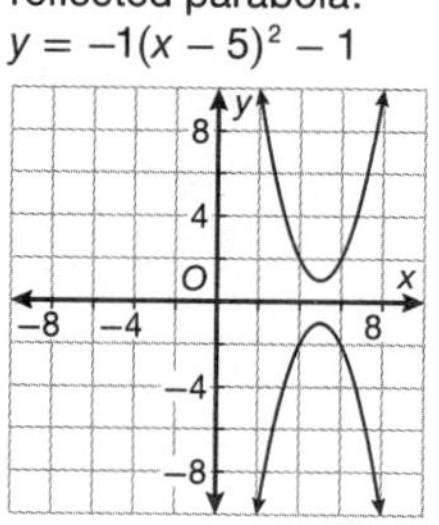

INCLUSION

When students are simplifying square roots as in problems 18 and 19, have them write the numerator and denominator separately under the square root so they remember to take the square root of both.

For example, problem 18 would be rewritten as $2\frac{\sqrt{2}}{\sqrt{9}} - 3\frac{\sqrt{9}}{\sqrt{2}}$. Taking square roots we see $2\frac{\sqrt{2}}{3} - 3\frac{3}{\sqrt{2}}$. Then have students rationalize the second term and simplify.

22. **Multiple Choice** To solve by elimination, which linear system will require that both equations first be multiplied by a constant before the equations are added? D
(24)

A $4x - 4y = 0$
$-4x + 6y = 2$

B $4x - 4y = 0$
$4x + 5y = 9$

C $4x - 4y = 0$
$-\frac{1}{4}x + \frac{5}{4}y = 1$

D $4x - 4y = 0$
$3x + 5y = 8$

23. **Error Analysis** Two students are adding the rational expressions $\frac{1}{x+3}$ and $\frac{1}{x-3}$ but get different results. Which student made the mistake? Student A incorrectly multiplies the second term's numerator by $(x - 3)$.
(37)

Student A	Student B
$\frac{1}{x+3} + \frac{1}{x-3} = \frac{x-3}{(x+3)(x-3)} + \frac{x-3}{(x-3)(x+3)} = \frac{2x-6}{x^2-9}$	$\frac{1}{x+3} + \frac{1}{x-3} = \frac{x-3}{(x+3)(x-3)} + \frac{x+3}{(x-3)(x+3)} = \frac{2x}{x^2-9}$

***24.** **Write** Describe the transformations you need to make to the graph of $y = \left(\frac{1}{5}\right)^x + 3$ to get the graph of $y = 5^x + 1$. Reflect about the y-axis and translate 2 units down.
(47)

***25.** **Graphing Calculator** Solve the system of equations using a graphing calculator.
(15)

$$5x + y = 15$$
$$2y = 5 + 10x$$

(1.25, 8.75)

***26.** **Verify** Simplify the expression on the left side of the equation; verify that it is equal to the right side.
(48)

$$\frac{\frac{4}{x+2} - \frac{2}{x+3}}{\frac{2}{x+3}} = \frac{x+4}{x+2}$$

See student work.

27. **Money** Dejah is collecting pennies and nickels for a charity event. She's going to continue until her collection of coins weighs at least 2 kilograms. Every penny weighs 2.5 grams and every nickel weighs 5 grams. Write and graph an inequality that represents how many of each coin are needed. See Additional Answers.
(39)

28. **Swimming** In order to qualify for the 2008 Olympic Swim Team, a male swimmer must swim the 100-meter freestyle in under 51.59 seconds.
(18)

a. What is this time in feet per second? (Hint:1 meter = 3.2808399 feet) about 6.36 feet per second

b. If a male swimmer swims the 100-meter freestyle in 48.62 seconds, what is his time in feet per second? about 6.75 feet per second

***29.** **Compound Interest** Ann deposits \$2,800 in a savings account. How much will be in her account in 3 years if the account earns 4% compounded annually? If it is compounded semi-annually? \$3149.62; \$3153.25
(47)

30. **Write** When using the Pythagorean Theorem to find a missing side of a right triangle, how is finding the length of a leg different from finding the length of the hypotenuse? Sample: Finding the length of a leg requires using the Subtraction Property of Equality to isolate the squared term, while finding the length of a hypotenuse does not.
(41)

LOOKING FORWARD

Understanding complex fractions prepares students for

- **Lesson 53** Performing Compositions of Functions
- **Lesson 59** Using Fractional Exponents

Problem 22

Extend the Problem

"Explain what the slopes of the lines in the linear system described in D tell you about the number of solutions." The slope of $4x - 4y = 0$ is 1. The slope of $3x + 5y = 8$ is $-\frac{3}{5}$. Because the slopes are different, it means the lines are not parallel and these are not the same lines. Therefore, the lines intersect once so the system has 1 solution.

"What is the solution for the linear system described in D?" $x = 1, y = 1$

Problem 25

Extend the Problem

"If you had to solve this system without a graphing calculator, would you use graphing, substitution or elimination? Explain your reasoning." Sample: I would use substitution because $5x + y = 15$ could be rewritten as $y = 15 - 5x$ and then substituted in to the second equation.

Problem 29

Guide the students by asking them the following questions.

"What is the formula for finding compound interest?"
$A = P\left(1 + \frac{r}{n}\right)^{nt}$

"What are the values for P, r, n, and t if the interest is compounded annually?" $P = 2800$, $r = 0.04$, $n = 1$, $t = 3$

"What is meant by semi-annually?" Semi-annually means twice a year.

"What are the values for P, r, n, and t if the interest is compounded semi-annually?" $P = 2800$, $r = 0.04$, $n = 2$, $t = 3$

LESSON 49

1 Warm Up

Remind students to expand problem 2 by multiplying $(x + 2)(x + 2)$.

2 New Concepts

In this lesson, students learn to expand binomials and calculate probabilities using the binomial theorem.

Discuss the definition of **binomial experiment** before Example 4. Explain that a binomial experiment has exactly two possible outcomes for each trial.

Example 1

Remind students a number or variable raised to the zero power is equal to 1.

Additional Example 1

Expand $(a + b)^3$.

$a^3 + 3a^2b + 3ab^2 + b^3$

LESSON RESOURCES

Student Edition Practice Workbook 49
Reteaching Master 49
Adaptations Master 49
Challenge and Enrichment Master C49

LESSON 49 Using the Binomial Theorem

Warm Up

1. **Vocabulary** A combination is a selection of items where order doesn't matter. (42)
2. Expand $(x + 2)^2$ $x^2 + 4x + 4$ (42)
3. Evaluate 5! 120 (42)
4. Evaluate ${}_6C_2$ 15 (42)
5. Evaluate $\frac{2!}{6!}$ $\frac{1}{360}$ (42)

New Concepts

Expand a few powers of the binomial $(a + b)$.

Math Reasoning

Generalize What pattern do you observe in the exponents for each term?

The exponent of *a* decreases and the exponent of *b* increases.

$$(a + b)^0 = 1a^0b^0$$
$$(a + b)^1 = 1a^1b^0 + 1a^0b^1$$
$$(a + b)^2 = 1a^2b^0 + 2a^1b^1 + 1a^0b^2$$
$$(a + b)^3 = 1a^3b^0 + 3a^2b^1 + 3a^1b^2 + 1a^0b^3$$

The coefficients form a pattern known as Pascal's Triangle.

$(a + b)^0$	1
$(a + b)^1$	1 1
$(a + b)^2$	1 2 1
$(a + b)^3$	1 3 3 1
$(a + b)^4$	1 4 6 4 1

Example 1 Expanding a Binomial Using Pascal's Triangle

Expand $(a + b)^4$.

SOLUTION

Use the fourth row of Pascal's Triangle to write the coefficients.

$$(a + b)^4 = 1a^4b^0 + 4a^3b^1 + 6a^2b^2 + 4a^1b^3 + 1a^0b^4$$
$$= a^4 + 4a^3b + 6a^2b^2 + 4ab^3 + b^4$$

Another way to show the coefficients is by writing them as combinations.

Hint

The top row of Pascal's Triangle is called the zero row.

$(a + b)^0$	${}_0C_0$
$(a + b)^1$	${}_1C_0$ ${}_1C_1$
$(a + b)^2$	${}_2C_0$ ${}_2C_1$ ${}_2C_2$
$(a + b)^3$	${}_3C_0$ ${}_3C_1$ ${}_3C_2$ ${}_3C_3$
$(a + b)^4$	${}_4C_0$ ${}_4C_1$ ${}_4C_2$ ${}_4C_3$ ${}_4C_4$

Online Connection
www.SaxonMathResources.com

The pattern can be summarized in the **Binomial Theorem.**

MATH BACKGROUND

The binomial theorem is used in algebra and in statistics. In algebra, the binomial theorem is used to quickly expand an expression to a power. Using this expansion method, expressions such as $(x + 2)^7$ can be simplified without having to distribute.

Pascal's Triangle is used to explore the coefficients for the binomial expansion as we see that each term can be written as a combination. This leads to the use of the binominal theorem in finding probabilities in a binomial experiment.

Math Language

The Greek capital letter *sigma*, Σ, is used to notate the sum of a series.

Binomial Theorem

If n is a nonnegative integer, then

$$(a+b)^n = ({}_nC_0)a^nb^0 + ({}_nC_1)a^{n-1}b^1 + ({}_nC_2)a^{n-2}b^2 + \ldots + ({}_nC_{n-1})a^1b^{n-1} + ({}_nC_n)a^0b^n$$

$$= \sum_{r=0}^{n}({}_nC_r)a^{n-r}b^r \text{ where } {}_nC_r = \frac{n!}{r!(n-r)!}$$

Example 2 Expanding a Binomial Using the Binomial Theorem

Use the Binomial Theorem to expand each power.

a. $(x+y)^5$

SOLUTION

Use the binomial theorem to expand $(a+b)^n$, where $a = x$, $b = y$, and $n = 5$.

$$(x+y)^5 = ({}_5C_0)x^5y^0 + ({}_5C_1)x^4y^1 + ({}_5C_2)x^3y^2 + ({}_5C_3)x^2y^3 + ({}_5C_4)x^1y^4 + ({}_5C_5)x^0y^5$$

Evaluate the coefficients and simplify.

$$(x+y)^5 = x^5 + 5x^4y + 10x^3y^2 + 10x^2y^3 + 5xy^4 + y^5$$

Hint

$5! = 5 \cdot 4 \cdot 3 \cdot 2 \cdot 1$

${}_5C_2 = \frac{5!}{2!3!} = \frac{5 \cdot 4 \cdot 3!}{2!3!} = \frac{5 \cdot 4}{2!}$

b. $(2r-s)^3$

SOLUTION

Use the binomial theorem to expand $(a+b)^3$. Substitute $2r$ for a and $-s$ for b.

$$(a+b)^3 = ({}_3C_0)a^3b^0 + ({}_3C_1)a^2b^1 + ({}_3C_2)a^1b^2 + ({}_3C_3)a^0b^3$$
$$= (2r)^3 + 3(2r)^2(-s) + 3(2r)(-s)^2 + (-s)^3$$
$$= (2)^3r^3 + 3(2)^2r^2(-s) + 3(2r)(-s)^2 + (-s)^3$$
$$= 8r^3 - 12r^2s + 6rs^2 - s^3$$

Caution

$(2r)^3 \neq 2r^3$

$(2r)^3 = 2^3r^3$

Example 3 Finding the *n*th Term of a Binomial

Find the fifth term of the expansion of $(p+q)^{10}$.

SOLUTION

First, use the Binomial Theorem to write the expansion in summation notation.

$$(p+q)^{10} = \sum_{r=0}^{10}({}_{10}C_r)p^{10-r}q^r$$

In the fifth term, $r = 4$.

$$({}_{10}C_r)p^{10-r}q^r = ({}_{10}C_4)p^{10-4}q^4$$
$$= \frac{10!}{(10-4)!4!}p^{10-4}q^4$$
$$= \frac{10 \cdot 9 \cdot 8 \cdot 7}{4 \cdot 3 \cdot 2 \cdot 1}p^6q^4$$
$$= 210p^6q^4$$

INCLUSION

When students are required to substitute in terms for a and b when expanding binomials, encourage them to write the complete expansion using a and b but leave space between the terms. Then when the substitution is made in the next step, students can write the substituted value directly below the expansion.

For example, expanding $(3x+2y)^3$ can be written as: $1a^3b^0 + 3a^2b^1 + 3a^1b^2 + 1a^0b^3$. Now simplify and substitute $a = 3x$ and $b = 2y$.

$$a^3 \quad + 3a^2b \quad + 3ab^2 \quad + b^3$$

$$(3x)^3 + 3(3x)^2(2y) + 3(3x)(2y)^2 + (2y)^3$$

Example 2

Part b shows how to expand an expression involving subtraction by rewriting the second term with a negative.

Error Alert When substituting $-s$ for b in part b, remind students to include the negative when raised to a power.

Additional Example 2

Use the Binomial Theorem to expand each power.

a. $(a+b)^6$ $a^6 + 6a^5b + 15a^4b^2 + 20a^3b^3 + 15a^2b^4 + 6ab^5 + b^6$

b. $(3x-2)^4$ $81x^4 - 216x^3 + 216x^2 - 96x + 16$

Example 3

This example shows how to find a particular term without having to write out the entire expansion.

Error Alert Students may be confused by the fact that $r = 4$ for the fifth term. Have students write out the combinations for the 10th row to see that the first five terms are: ${}_{10}C_0$, ${}_{10}C_1$, ${}_{10}C_2$, ${}_{10}C_3$, ${}_{10}C_4$. The fifth term is ${}_{10}C_4$, thus $r = 4$.

Additional Example 3

Find the eighth term of the same expansion. $120p^3q^7$

Calculator Use

You may also find ${}_{10}C_4$ using your calculator. Most calculators require you to enter 10, then the combination function, then enter 4.

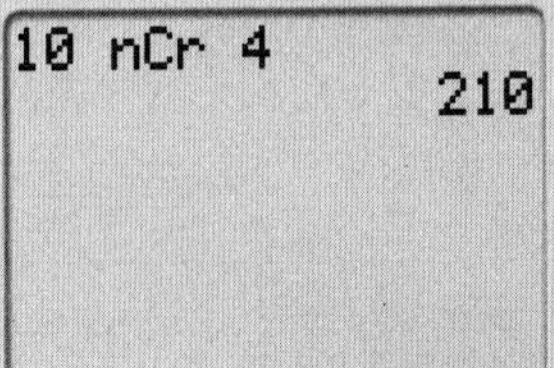

TEACHER TIP

Point out that several things must be true for a binomial experiment. A binomial experiment must have: exactly two outcomes, a fixed number of trials, each probability must remain the same throughout the experiment, and the outcomes must be independent.

Error Alert Students might think an event such as rolling a number cube is not a binomial experiment because there are more than two outcomes. Explain that the two outcomes in a binomial experiment can be thought of as a "success" and a "failure." So we can think of an event occurring and then the event NOT occurring. For example, when rolling a number cube, the probability of rolling a 3 is $\frac{1}{6}$. The probability of NOT rolling a 3 is $\frac{5}{6}$.

Example 4

Remind students that the probability of an event is written using $P(\text{Event})$.

Additional Example 4

Suppose you toss a coin 5 times. Use the Binomial Theorem to find each probability.

a. $P(\text{exactly 3 tails})$ $\frac{5}{16}$

b. $P(\text{at least 3 tails})$ $\frac{1}{2}$

The Binomial Theorem can also be used to find probabilities for a **binomial experiment.** A binomial experiment has exactly two possible outcomes for each trial, where one outcome is a success (p) and one outcome is a failure (q). The probability of success is the same for each trial. Because there are only two outcomes, $p + q = 1$ or $q = 1 - p$.

These are some examples of binomial experiments.

Experiment	Success	Failure	P(success)	P(failure)
100 flips of a coin	Heads	Tails	$p = 0.5$	$p = 0.5$
20 rolls of a number cube	Roll a 2	Roll 1, or 3–6	$p = \frac{1}{6}$	$p = \frac{5}{6}$

Binomial Probability

If p is the probability of success and q is the probability of failure in one trial of a binomial experiment, then the **binomial probability** of exactly n successes in m trials is given by

$${}_mC_n p^n q^{m-n}$$

Example 4 Finding a Binomial Probability

Suppose you toss a coin 4 times. Use the Binomial Theorem to find each probability.

a. $P(\text{exactly 2 tails})$

SOLUTION There are ${}_4C_2$ ways of getting 2 tails.

$$P(\text{exactly 2 tails}) = ({}_4C_2)p^2q^2$$
$$= ({}_4C_2)\left(\frac{1}{2}\right)^2\left(\frac{1}{2}\right)^2$$
$$= \frac{6}{16} = \frac{3}{8}$$

The probability of getting exactly 2 tails in 4 tosses is $\frac{3}{8}$.

b. $P(\text{at least 2 tails})$

SOLUTION Instead of adding the probabilities of getting exactly 2, 3, and 4 tails, it may be easier to subtract the probabilities of getting exactly 0 or 1 tail from 1.

$$P(\text{at least 2 tails}) = 1 - P(0 \text{ tails}) - P(1 \text{ tail})$$
$$= 1 - ({}_4C_0)p^0q^4 - ({}_4C_1)p^1q^3$$
$$= 1 - \left(\frac{1}{2}\right)^4 - 4\left(\frac{1}{2}\right)\left(\frac{1}{2}\right)^3$$
$$= \frac{11}{16}$$

The probability of getting at least 2 tails in 4 tosses is $\frac{11}{16}$.

ENGLISH LEARNERS

Problems often have directions such as **evaluate, expand** or **solve.** This lesson directs students to expand. Discuss the meanings of these words.

Evaluate means to assess the value of something. In math, evaluate means to replace a variable with numbers or other variables and simplify.

Solve means to find the solution of something. In math, this indicates to find the answer to a problem.

Expand means to make something bigger. Expanding binomials means to multiply the polynomials together the indicated number of times. This results in an expression with more terms.

Graphing Calculator Tip

For help calculating combinations see the lab on page 303.

Example 5 Using a Calculator to Find Binomial Probability

Use a calculator to find the probability of getting exactly 50 heads if you toss a coin 100 times.

SOLUTION

There are ${}_{100}C_{50}$ ways of getting exactly 50 heads.

$$P(\text{50 heads}) = ({}_{100}C_{50})h^{50}t^{50}$$
$$= ({}_{100}C_{50})\left(\frac{1}{2}\right)^{50}\left(\frac{1}{2}\right)^{50}$$
$$\approx 0.08$$

Example 6 Application: Spinner Probabilities

Suppose you spin the following spinner 3 times. What is the probability that you will spin white exactly 2 times?

SOLUTION

Understand The probability of spinning white is $\frac{2}{3}$ and the probability of spinning black is $\frac{1}{3}$.

Plan Find the probability of spinning white 2 times.

Solve $P(\text{spinning white 2 times}) = ({}_3C_2)p^2q^1$

$$= ({}_3C_2)\left(\frac{2}{3}\right)^2\left(\frac{1}{3}\right)^1$$
$$= 3\left(\frac{4}{27}\right)$$
$$= \frac{12}{27} = \frac{4}{9}$$

The probability of spinning white exactly 2 times is $\frac{4}{9}$.

Lesson Practice

a. (Ex 1) Use Pascal's Triangle to expand $(2x + 4)^3$. $8x^3 + 48x^2 + 96x + 64$

Use the Binomial Theorem to expand each expression. (Ex 2)

b. $(f + 2)^5$ $f^5 + 10f^4 + 40f^3 + 80f^2 + 80f + 32$

c. $(1 - 7x)^3$ $1 - 21x + 147x^2 - 343x^3$

d. (Ex 3) Find the fourth term of the expansion of $(x + 3)^{10}$. $3240x^7$

e. (Ex 4) Find the probability of getting exactly 5 tails if a coin is tossed 6 times. $\frac{3}{32}$

f. (Ex 4) Find the probability of getting at least 1 tail if a coin is tossed 6 times. $\frac{63}{64}$

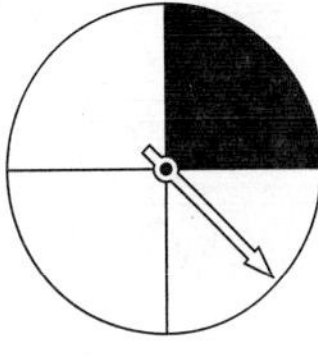

g. (Ex 6) Suppose you spin the following spinner 4 times. What is the probability that you will spin white exactly 1 time? $\frac{3}{64}$

Example 5

Remind students to use parentheses when inputting terms in the calculator.

Additional Example 5

Use a calculator to find the probability of getting exactly 70 heads if you toss a coin 150 times. 0.047

Extend the Additional Example

"What is the probability of getting between 48 and 52 heads, inclusive?" approximately 0.38

Example 6

Additional Example 6

Suppose you spin the spinner 4 times. What is the probability you will spin white exactly 3 times? $\frac{32}{81}$

Lesson Practice

Problem a

Scaffolding Have students first write the expansion of $(a + b)^3$. Then tell students to substitute $a = 2x$ and $b = 4$ to find the expansion $(2x + 4)^3$.

Check for Understanding

The questions below help assess the concepts taught in this lesson.

1. **"How can you find the 8th row of Pascal's triangle without knowing the first seven rows?"** I can use combinations. The 8th row will be ${}_8C_0$, ${}_8C_1$, ${}_8C_2$, ${}_8C_3$, ${}_8C_4$, ${}_8C_5$, ${}_8C_6$, ${}_8C_7$, and ${}_8C_8$.
2. **"What do p and q represent?"** p is the probability the event occurs. q is the probability the event does not occur.

CHALLENGE

A binomial probability distribution is the set of probabilities associated with the outcomes in a binomial experiment. The sum of the probabilities will equal 1.

Suppose the probability of winning a raffle is 0.6. Find the binomial probability distribution for 4 trials by completing the table. Then verify that the sum of the probabilities is 1.

Wins		
4	${}_4C_4(0.6)^4(0.4)^0$	0.1296
3	${}_4C_3(0.6)^3(0.4)^1$	0.3456
2	${}_4C_2(0.6)^2(0.4)^2$	0.3456
1	${}_4C_1(0.6)^1(0.4)^3$	0.1536
0	${}_4C_0(0.6)^0(0.4)^4$	0.0256

0.1296 + 0.3456 + 0.3456 + 0.1536 + 0.0256 = 1

3 Practice

Math Conversations

Discussions to strengthen understanding

Problem 1

Remind students to factor the numerator in order to simplify.

Problem 12

Remind students that a binomial experiment has exactly 2 outcomes. If the probability of getting a hit is 0.32, then the probability of NOT getting a hit is $1 - 0.32 = 0.68$.

Problem 14

Guide the students by asking them the following questions.

"What are the meanings of continuous, discontinuous and discrete functions?" A continuous function is a function with no gaps. A discontinuous function has gaps, jumps, or asymptotes. A discrete function is a type of discontinuous function that is made up of separate disconnected points.

"Is the function continuous or discontinuous? Explain." It is discontinuous because the cost jumps from \$2.00 up to \$4.00 and so on.

"Is the function discrete? Explain." No, it is not discrete because although it jumps, its cost stays level for a while before taking another jump. These are not discrete points.

Practice Distributed and Integrated

Simplify.

1. (23) $\dfrac{4xy + 4x^2y^2}{4xy}$ $1 + xy$

2. (23) $p^5x^3 + p^4x^2 - p^3x$ $p^3x(p^2x^2 + px - 1)$

***3.** (48) $\dfrac{ax^2 - \frac{4}{a}}{\frac{x^2}{a} + 6}$ $\dfrac{a^2x^2 - 4}{x^2 + 6a}$

***4.** (48) $\dfrac{\frac{m^2p}{x} - 6}{m^2p - \frac{4}{x}}$ $\dfrac{m^2p - 6x}{m^2px - 4}$

5. (40) $6\sqrt{18} + 5\sqrt{8} - 3\sqrt{50}$ $13\sqrt{2}$

6. (40) $2\sqrt{5}(3\sqrt{15} - 2\sqrt{5})$ $30\sqrt{3} - 20$

7. (24) Solve by using either substitution or elimination. $3x - 2y = 10$, $y = -\dfrac{1}{2}$ $(3, -\frac{1}{2})$

Expand.

***8.** (49) $(b - 2)^4$ $b^4 - 8b^3 + 24b^2 - 32b + 16$

***9.** (49) $(2x + y)^6$ $64x^6 + 192x^5y + 240x^4y^2 + 160x^3y^3 + 60x^2y^4 + 12xy^5 + y^6$

10. (36) Find the equation of the line that passes through (2, 4) and is perpendicular to the line that passes through the points (2, 4) and (−3, −2). $y = -\frac{5}{6}x + \frac{17}{3}$

11. (31) **Analyze** Given the functions $f(x) = \frac{2x - 2}{x}$ and $g(x) = \frac{x^2 + 3x}{x - 1}$, describe the graph of the product function $f(x) \cdot g(x)$. Include points of discontinuity in the description. (Note: If a function is undefined at some value of x, then there is a point of discontinuity in the function graph at that value of x.) See Additional Answers.

***12.** (49) **(Baseball)** A baseball player has a batting average of 0.32 (32 hits in 100 times at bat). Find each probability for the next 4 times at bat.

a. P(exactly 2 hits) about 0.28 **b.** P(at least 1 hit) about 0.79

13. (45) **Multi-Step**

x	0	1	3	3	4	5	5	6	7	7	7
y	8	11	5	8	6	3	7	5	7	3	1

a. Make a scatter plot of the data See Additional Answers.

b. Sketch the line of best fit and write its equation. $y = -\frac{3}{4}x + 9$

c. Estimate the value of r. $r \approx -0.7$

14. (22) **Data Analysis** A customer visits the post office to weigh a package. The cost of mailing a package depends on its weight. Examine the table below. Does this table represent a continuous, discontinuous, or discrete function? Justify your answer. This is a discontinuous function; The points of discontinuity are at $x = 5, 10, 15, 20, 25$.

Weight	Cost
$0 \le x < 5$	\$2.00
$5 \le x < 10$	\$4.00
$10 \le x < 15$	\$6.00
$15 \le x < 20$	\$8.00
$20 \le x < 25$	\$10.00

ALTERNATE METHOD FOR PROBLEM 1

Tell students that when there is a polynomial in the numerator and one term in the denominator, the expression can be written as the sum of two fractions.

So $\dfrac{4xy + 4x^2y^2}{4xy}$ becomes $\dfrac{4xy}{4xy} + \dfrac{4x^2y^2}{4xy}$. By dividing common factors, we see $\dfrac{4xy}{4xy} + \dfrac{4x^2y^2}{4xy} = 1 + xy$

15. **Ticket Prices** Two of the ticket prices for a 2007 baseball game were: \$27 for an outfield grandstand seat and \$45 for a right field box seat. Suppose you are an automobile dealer. You decide to buy tickets to give away during a sale. You decide to buy up to 24 tickets and to spend up to \$720. Let x represent a number of outfield grandstand seats and y represent a number of right field box seats. See Additional Answers.
(43)

a. Write and graph a system of linear inequalities that represents the situation.

b. Describe the points in the graph of the system that represent all the possible combinations of outfield grandstand seats and right field box seats you can buy.

c. Determine the point of intersection of the boundary lines in the graph and explain its meaning.

16. **Multiple Choice** Which could be the sides of a right triangle? A
(41)
A 21, 72, and 75 B 30, 35, and 45 C 35, 58, and 48 D 41, 82, and 90

17. **Health** An adult is considered to be in a healthy weight range if his or her BMI (Body Mass Index) is within 3.2 of 21.7. Write an absolute value equation to determine the minimum and maximum BMI that is considered healthy. And then solve the equation $|x - 21.7| = 3.2$; $x = 18.5$, $x = 24.9$
(17)

*18. **Write** Describe how to expand the binomial $(y + z)^5$ using Pascal's Triangle.
(49)

18. Possible answer: Use the 5th row of Pascal's Triangle to get the coefficients 1, 5, 10, 10, 5, and 1. The exponent of y decreases by 1 for each term and the exponent of z increases by 1 for each term.

19. **Geometry** The table below shows the measurements in inches of various shipping boxes available from the United States Postal Service.
(25)

Box	Measurement 1	Measurement 2	Measurement 3
1	11.875	3.375	13.625
2	11	8.5	5.5
3	7.5	5.125	14.375

a. What is the range of volumes?

b. If you had to choose from these boxes to ship something, how could the range of volumes be useful?

20. **Lottery** A lottery game contains 24 numbers. In order to win, four numbers must be chosen that match the winning numbers. If the winning numbers are selected one at a time and not replaced, how many possible ways are there for the winning numbers to be determined? $P(24, 4) = 255{,}024$
(42)

21. **Estimate** The graphs of the parent quadratic function and a second function are shown. Use the graph to estimate the value of a for the equation of the second function. Possible answer: −3 (Answer must be less than −1)
(30)

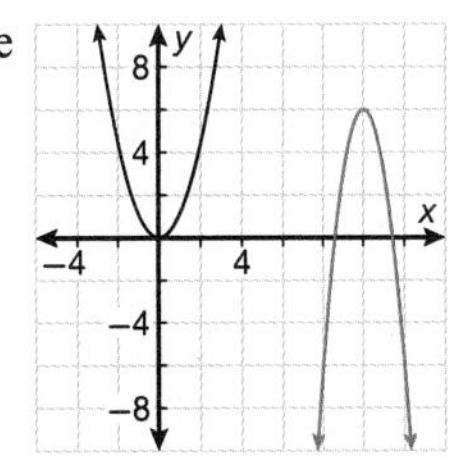

19a. The volumes are approximately 546, 514 and 553 cubic inches. The range is 39 cubic inches.

b. Possible answer: The largest and smallest volumes are used to find the range. None of these boxes could be used to ship something with a volume of greater than 553 cubic inches.

Problem 17

Error Alert

Students might be confused about when to use only the endpoints of a given range of values. Tell students to look for a specific word or phrase which would indicate what is required. Because this problem asks for the minimum and maximum BMI, this means the endpoints only are included.

INCLUSION

Linguistic, or verbal, learners may benefit from writing out each possibility when finding probabilities for a binomial probability. Problem 12b asks for the probability of at least 1 hit if the batter is at bat 4 times. Have students write:

$P(\text{at least 1 hit}) = P(\text{exactly 1 hit}) + P(\text{exactly 2 hits}) + P(\text{exactly 3 hits}) + P(\text{exactly 4 hits})$. Point out that the missing probability is $P(\text{exactly 0 hits})$. So in this case to find $P(\text{at least 1 hit})$, students can find $1 - P(\text{exactly 0 hits})$.

Problem 24

Guide the students by asking them the following questions.

"Draw a sketch of the towers and sky bridge. Label each part."

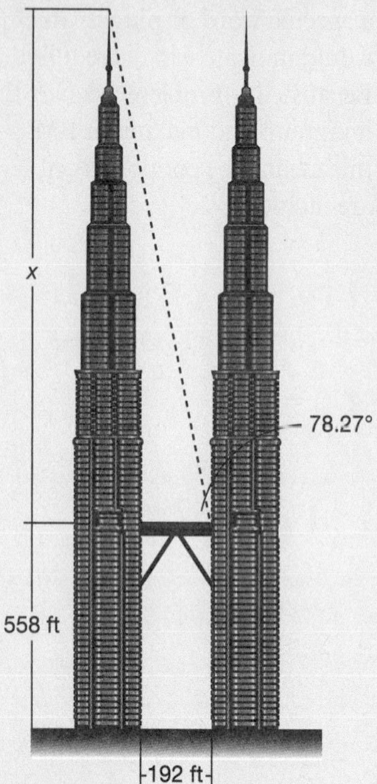

"Will you use sine, cosine, or tangent to find the missing length? Explain." Because the length of the bridge represents the side adjacent to the angle, and I need to find the opposite side x, I will use tan.

"Explain how to find the value of x in the diagram." $\tan 78.27° = \frac{x}{192}$ so $x \approx 924.69$ ft.

"What is the height of the tower?" I add 924.69 feet to 558 ft and get about 1483 feet.

Problem 27

Because y is raised to a different power in each answer choice, it is only necessary to find the power of y in the 5th term to determine the answer. Because y is first in the expression $(y - 3)^8$, it will be descending y^8, y^7, y^6, y^5, y^4, etc. The 5th term will include y^4.

Extend the Problem

"What is the 3rd term of $(y - 3)^8$?" $252y^6$

22. (44) **Error Analysis** A student worked out the problem below using radical conjugates. Is the procedure correct? If not, identify and correct the error.
Simplify: $\frac{2\sqrt{2} + 6}{3\sqrt{2} + \sqrt{5}}$. See Additional Answers.

Student work: $\frac{2\sqrt{2} + 6}{3\sqrt{2} + \sqrt{5}} \cdot \frac{2\sqrt{2} - 6}{3\sqrt{2} - \sqrt{5}} = \frac{8 - 36}{18 - 5} = -\frac{28}{13}$

23. (36) **Multi-Step** The speed of an object at time t is based on its initial speed (v_o) and its acceleration (a): $v = v_o + at$.

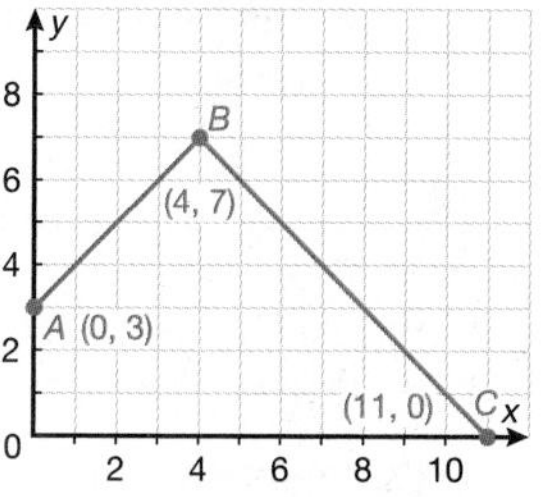

a. Find the equations of the lines from A to B and B to C and describe the motion of the object.

b. What is the relationship between the equations of motion? The two lines are perpendicular.

23a. The object starts with an initial speed of 3 and acceleration of 1 $(y = x + 3)$. After 4 seconds it decelerates, until it stops after 11 seconds $(y = -x + 11)$.

24. (46) **Architecture** The Petronas Towers in Malaysia are two twin towers joined by a sky bridge that is 192 feet long and 558 feet above the ground. The angle of elevation from either end of the sky bridge to the top of the opposite tower is about 78.27°. Find the height of the towers to the nearest foot. 1483 feet

25. (28) **Verify** Prove that $2x - 7 = -(7 - 2x)$. Supply a reason for every step. See Additional Answers.

***26.** (40) **Graphing Calculator** Graph $y = \sqrt[3]{x}$ and $y = \sqrt[4]{x}$ on a graphing calculator. (Use the equivalent equations of $y = x^{\frac{1}{3}}$ and $y = x^{\frac{1}{4}}$.) How do the graphs confirm the differences in rules for $\sqrt[n]{b}$ as far as n being odd or even?

26. The graph for the cube root exists for all values of x, the graph for the fourth root exists for only nonnegative values of x.

***27.** (49) **Multiple Choice** What is the fifth term of the expansion of $(y - 3)^8$? **B**
A $-13{,}608y^3$ **B** $5670y^4$ **C** $1890y^5$ **D** $1458y^6$

***28.** (48) **Multi-Step** Use the formula $r = \frac{d}{t}$ relating rate, distance, and time. A car traveled a distance of $3x + 60$ miles in 2 hours. A second car traveled $2x + 40$ miles in 3 hours.

a. Write a rational expression to represent the ratio of the rate of the first car to the rate of the second car.

28a. $\frac{\frac{3x + 60}{2}}{\frac{2x + 40}{3}}$

b. Simplify the rational expression. What does this expression tell you about the rates of the two cars? $\frac{9}{4}$; The first car traveled $\frac{9}{4}$ or 2.25 times as fast as the second.

29. (39) **Error Analysis** Explain the error(s) the student made when graphing $-4 > y$.

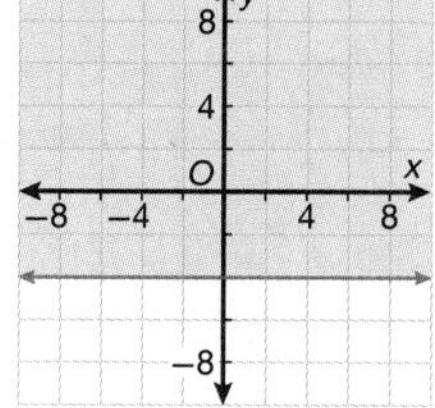

***30.** (47) **Multiple Choice** Which of the following equations does **not** represent an exponential function? **B**
A $y = -3^x$ **B** $y = x^3$ **C** $y = \left(\frac{1}{3}\right)^x$ **D** $y = 3^{-x}$

29. The student should have used a dashed line because points on the boundary are not included. Also, the student should have shaded below the line because if −4 is greater than y, then y is less than −4.

LOOKING FORWARD

Using the binomial theorem prepares students for

- **Lesson 53** Performing Compositions of Functions
- **Lesson 55** Finding Probability
- **Lesson 66** Solving Polynomial Equations

LESSON
50 Finding Inverses of Relations and Functions

Warm Up

1. **Vocabulary** If (x, y) is an ordered pair in a relation, then x is an element of the domain and y is an element of the ___range___. (4)

2. Solve $2y - 8 = 4x$ for y. $y = 2x + 4$ (7)

3. What is the reflection image of (2, 6) over the y-axis? (−2, 6) (30)

New Concepts

A relation is a set of ordered pairs. If r represents a relation, then the **inverse relation** is the set of ordered pairs obtained by reversing the coordinates in each ordered pair of r. So if (a, b) is in relation r, then (b, a) is in the inverse relation. The inverse of a relation may or may not be a function. If a relation and its inverse are both functions, they are **inverse functions**.

> **Math Language**
>
> A **function** is a relation in which each element in the domain is paired with exactly one element in the range.

Example 1 Describing a Relation and its Inverse

Find the inverse of relation r. Determine whether each relation is a function. Describe the graphs.

Relation r

Domain	x	1	1	3
Range	y	2	4	5

SOLUTION Reverse the coordinates in each ordered pair.

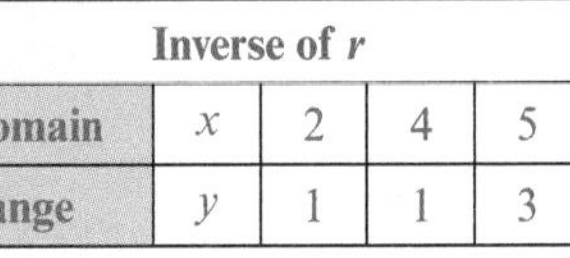

Inverse of r

Domain	x	2	4	5
Range	y	1	1	3

Relation r is not a function because the domain element 1 is paired with two different range elements: 2 and 4. The inverse of r is a function because each element in the domain is paired with exactly one element in the range.

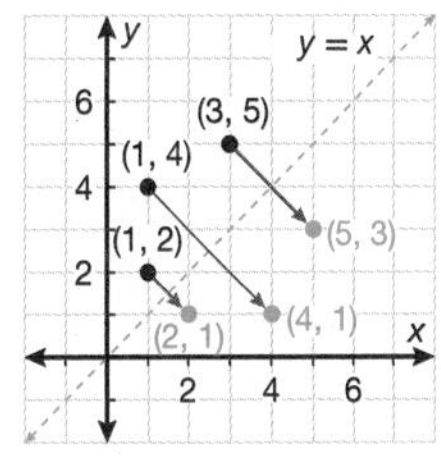

Each point in the graph of the inverse of r is the reflection image of the corresponding point in relation r. The line of reflection is $y = x$.

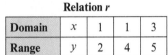

The line $y = x$ is important in the graph of any pair of inverse relations.

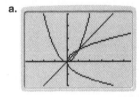

Exploration Graphing a Function and its Inverse

a. Use a graphing calculator to graph the following functions. Use a window of [−2, 4] for both x and y.

$Y1{:}\ f(x) = x^2$ $\quad Y2{:}\ g(x) = \sqrt{x}$ $\quad Y3{:}\ h(x) = -\sqrt{x}$ $\quad Y4{:}\ I(x) = x$

b. Describe the inverse of f. the functions g and h combined

c. Is the inverse of f a function? Explain. No; It does not pass the vertical line test.

d. Describe the role of the identity function I. Its graph is the line of reflection.

> **Graphing Calculator Tip**
>
> To get undistorted graphs on a calculator, use ZOOM 5:ZSquare after setting the [−2, 4] window.

Online Connection
www.SaxonMathResources.com

LESSON 50

1 Warm Up

Use problems 2 and 3 in the Warm Up to review solving for variables in an equation and observing a reflection on a graph.

2 New Concepts

In this lesson, students learn to solve for inverse functions, mainly for equations of lines.

Discuss the definitions of an ordered pair and an **inverse function**. In order to solve for an inverse function, switch the x and y variables and solve for y.

Example 1

Students will find the inverse relationship using a given domain and range table.

Additional Example 1

Find the inverse of relation r.

Relation r

Domain	x	3	2	7
Range	y	8	4	11

Inverse of r

Domain	x	8	4	11
Range	y	3	2	7

MATH BACKGROUND

There is symmetry between a function and its inverse. Specifically, if the inverse of f is f^{-1}, then the inverse of f^{-1} is the original function f. This can be expressed by the following formula: $(f^{-1})^{-1} = f$

Graphically, the inverse function is defined as the graph of f in which the roles of x and y have been reversed. This can also be described as the reflection of f over the graph of $y = x$.

ADDITIONAL RESOURCES

Student Edition Practice Workbook 50
Reteaching Master 50
Adaptations Master 50
Challenge and Enrichment Master C50

Example 2

Students will find the algebraic inverse of a linear function.

Additional Example 2

Find an equation for the inverse of $y = 8x + 14$.

$$y = 8x + 14$$
$$x = 8y + 14$$
$$x - 14 = 8y$$
$$\frac{1}{8}x - \frac{7}{4} = y$$

Example 3

Students will find an inverse that is a radical expression. They will then determine whether each relation is a function using a graphing calculator.

Additional Example 3

Find an equation for the inverse of $y = \frac{2}{7}x^3 + 8$. Use a graphing calculator and the vertical and horizontal line tests to determine whether each relation is a function.

$$y = \frac{2}{7}x^3 + 8$$
$$x = \frac{2}{7}y^3 + 8$$
$$x - 8 = \frac{2}{7}y^3$$
$$\frac{7}{2}(x - 8) = y^3$$
$$\frac{7}{2}x - 28 = y^3$$
$$\sqrt[3]{\frac{7}{2}x - 28} = y$$

The inverse of $y = \frac{2}{7}x^3 + 8$ is $y = \sqrt[3]{\frac{7}{2}x - 28}$. This is a function because no vertical line intersects its graph at more than one point. The inverse is also a function because no horizontal line intersects the graph of the original function in more than one point.

If a relation is given by an equation, interchange the variables to find the equation for the inverse.

Math Reasoning

Generalize In what form are both equations $y = 2x + 6$ and $y = \frac{1}{2}x - 3$? Is the inverse of *any* equation of the form $y = mx + b$ where $m \neq 0$, a function?

slope-intercept; yes

Example 2 Finding the Inverse of a Linear Function

Find an equation for the inverse of $y = 2x + 6$.

SOLUTION

$y = 2x + 6$	Original equation.
$x = 2y + 6$	Interchange the variables.
$x - 6 = 2y$	Solve for y.
$\frac{1}{2}x - 3 = y$	

The inverse of $y = 2x + 6$ is $y = \frac{1}{2}x - 3$.

The vertical line test to determine whether a relation is a function leads to a horizontal line test to determine whether the inverse of a relation is a function.

Horizontal and Vertical Line Tests
Vertical Line Test A relation is a function if and only if no vertical line intersects the relation's graph in more than one point.
Horizontal Line Test A relation's inverse is a function if and only if no horizontal line intersects the relation's graph in more than one point.

Example 3 Finding an Inverse that is a Radical Expression

Find an equation for the inverse of $y = \frac{1}{4}x^3 - 2$. Use a graphing calculator and the vertical and horizontal line tests to determine whether each relation is a function.

SOLUTION

$y = \frac{1}{4}x^3 - 2$	Original equation
$x = \frac{1}{4}y^3 - 2$	Interchange the variables.
$x + 2 = \frac{1}{4}y^3$	Add 2 to each side.
$4x + 8 = y^3$	Multiply each side by 4.
$\sqrt[3]{4x + 8} = y$	Write the cube root of each side to solve for y.

Hint

The graph of $y = \frac{1}{4}x^3 - 2$ appears to be almost horizontal near the point $(0, -2)$. Use coordinates of some nearby points to verify that it is not really horizontal.

The inverse of $y = \frac{1}{4}x^3 - 2$ is $y = \sqrt[3]{4x + 8}$. $y = \frac{1}{4}x^3 - 2$ is a function because no vertical line intersects its graph in more than one point. The inverse, $y = \sqrt[3]{4x + 8}$, is also a function because no horizontal line intersects the graph of $y = \frac{1}{4}x^3 - 2$ in more than one point.

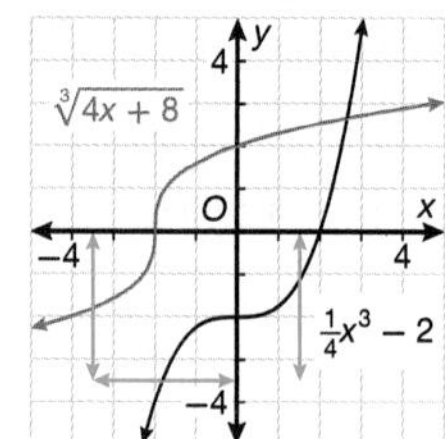

ENGLISH LEARNERS

Define an **inverse** and show that it is the opposite of something else. For example, if an object is inverted it has been turned upside down.

Discuss the technique for solving for an inverse function by showing that the only change in the equation is the roles of x and y. Once these are switched, then y can be solved for.

Use simple lines on a graph and their inverses to show how a line and its inverse are related. Apply this relationship to simple graphs first, and then move to functions that are more complicated.

Connect the association between a function and its inverse graphs and how they can be visually used to apply the vertical and horizontal line tests.

356 Saxon Algebra 2

The inverse relations in Example 3 are inverse functions, and the domain and range of both functions is the set of all real numbers. In some cases, an inverse is not a function, but a domain can be restricted to make it a function. The inverse of a function f is denoted f^{-1}.

Hint

An alternate approach using a different domain for $f(x)$ yields these inverse functions: $f(x) = x^2 + 2, x \leq 0$ and $f^{-1}(x) = -\sqrt{x - 2}$.

Example 4 Restricting a Domain to Form Inverse Functions

Restrict the domain of $y = x^2 + 2$ so that its inverse is a function. Identify the domain and range of each function.

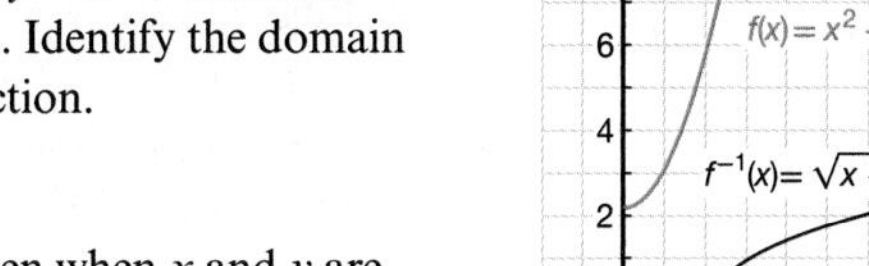

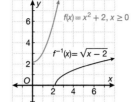

SOLUTION

Require that $x \geq 0$. Then when x and y are interchanged, $y \geq 0$, and the inverse consists only of $y = \sqrt{x - 2}$.

So if $f(x) = x^2 + 2$ with domain $x \geq 0$ and range $y \geq 2$, then its inverse function is $f^{-1}(x) = \sqrt{x - 2}$ with domain $x \geq 2$ and range $y \geq 0$.

Formulas used in applications have variables that represent specific quantities, such as d for distance and t for time. When finding the inverse of a formula, it is better to *not* interchange variables. For example, if d and t were interchanged, then d would represent time and t would represent distance; this would be confusing.

Example 5 Application: Distance, Time, and Gravity

The Sears Tower in Chicago is 1451 feet tall. The distance traveled by a free-falling object is given by $d = 16t^2$, where d is distance in feet and t is time in seconds. How long would it take an object to reach the ground if dropped from the top of the Sears Tower?

SOLUTION

Write t as a function of d. That will be the inverse function. Substitute 1451 for d and evaluate t.

$d = 16t^2, t \geq 0$ The domain is restricted naturally. Time cannot be negative.

$\frac{d}{16} = t^2$ Do not interchange variables. Solve for t.

$\sqrt{\frac{d}{16}} = t$ The inverse function is $t = \sqrt{\frac{d}{16}}$.

$\sqrt{\frac{1451}{16}} = t$ Substitute 1451 for d.

$9.5 \approx t$ Use a calculator to approximate.

It will take about 9.5 seconds for the object to reach the ground.

Check Substitute 9.5 for t in the original formula.

$d = 16t^2 = 16(9.5)^2 = 1444$, which is close to 1451. The answer is reasonable.

Example 4

Students will solve for the inverse of a given function and determine the domain and range of each.

Additional Example 4

Restrict the domain of $y = 3x^2 - 9$ so that its inverse is a function. Identify the domain and range of each function. Require that $x \geq 0$. When x and y are interchanged, $y \geq 0$, and the inverse will consist only of $y = \sqrt{\frac{x}{3}} + 3$.

Function	Domain	Range
$f(x) = 3x^2 - 9, x \geq 0$	$x \geq 0$	$y \geq -9$
$f^{-1}(x) = \sqrt{\frac{x}{3}} + 3$	$x \geq -9$	$y \geq 0$

Example 5

Students will apply their knowledge of inverses to solve a real world example.

Additional Example 5

The distance traveled by a boat over a period of time was recorded as $d = 8t^3 + 7$ where d is distance in miles and t is time in hours. How long did the boat travel if $d = 519$? 4 hours

TEACHER TIP

Emphasize that inverse functions can be used in many situations to solve for other variables in a problem. It is very useful when an equation is given as a function of another variable.

INCLUSION

Students may have trouble visualizing the graph of an inverse. Have the students start by graphing a simple line and its inverse such as $y = 2x$ and $y = \frac{x}{2}$. Then have the students fold their paper diagonally to show that the inverses are mirror images of each other. This will allow them to see the relationship between a line and its inverse.

If students are struggling to find the domain and range of a function, first have them graph the functions. The domains and ranges should be easily viewed by seeing where the minimums and maximums are.

The horizontal and vertical line tests can also be easily explained by showing the tests graphically.

Lesson Practice

Problem b

Error Alert Students may end up with an answer that has an incorrect sign in the equation. To avoid this, be sure to remind students to use inverse operations when solving for y.

Problem c

Scaffolding Before solving, graph the original function $y = -\frac{1}{2}x^3 + 1$. Next, solve for its inverse and graph that function as well. Determine whether each relation is a function using the vertical and horizontal line tests.

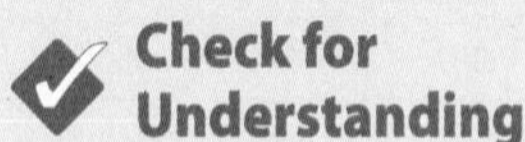

Check for Understanding

The questions below help assess the concepts taught in this lesson.

What are the steps to solving for an inverse of a linear function? Sample: Begin by interchanging the variables of the equation and then solve for y.

What tests must be used to determine whether the inverse of a relation is a function? Sample: Start with the vertical line test to determine if the relation is a function. If the relation is a function, perform the horizontal line test to verify the inverse of the relation is a function.

a. Inverse of r

Domain	x	2	2	1
Range	y	0	3	-3

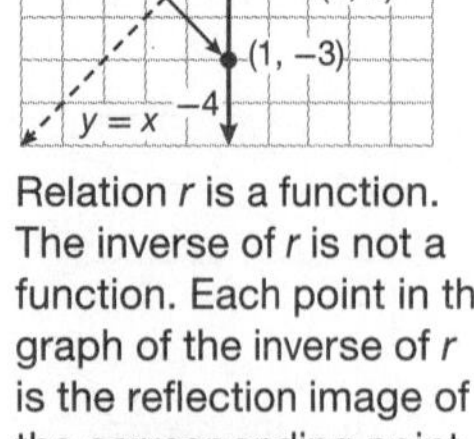

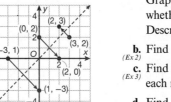

Relation r is a function. The inverse of r is not a function. Each point in the graph of the inverse of r is the reflection image of the corresponding point in relation r. The line of reflection is $y = x$.

c. The inverse is $y = \sqrt[3]{-2x + 2}$. Both relations are functions.

Lesson Practice

Relation r

Domain	x	0	3	-3
Range	y	2	2	1

a. (Ex 1) Find the inverse of relation r. Graph both relations. Determine whether each relation is a function. Describe the graphs.

b. (Ex 2) Find an equation for the inverse of $y = -\frac{1}{3}x - 1$. $y = -3x - 3$

c. (Ex 3) Find an equation for the inverse of $y = -\frac{1}{2}x^3 + 1$. Determine whether each relation is a function. (Hint: Use a graphing calculator if necessary.)

d. (Ex 4) Find an equation for the inverse of the function $y = \frac{1}{2}x^2 - 4$. Identify the domain and range of each relation. See Additional Answers.

e. (Ex 4) Restrict the domain of $y = \frac{1}{2}x^2 - 4$ if needed so that its inverse is a function. Identify the domain and range of the inverse functions. See Additional Answers.

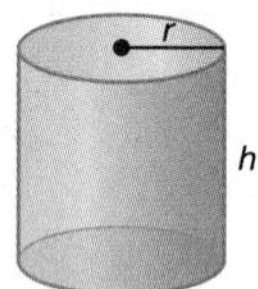

f. (Ex 5) The volume of a cylinder is given by $V = \pi r^2 h$. A manufacturer wants a cylindrical container to have a volume of one cubic foot, and the height to be twice the radius. Write an inverse function that gives r as a function of V, and find the required radius to the nearest tenth of an inch. $r = \sqrt[3]{\frac{V}{2\pi}}$; $r \approx 6.5$ inches

Practice Distributed and Integrated

Multiply:

1. (19) $(3x^3 - 2x)(2x^2 - x - 4)$
$6x^5 - 3x^4 - 16x^3 + 2x^2 + 8x$

2. (19) $(4x + 2)(x^3 - 2x + 4)$
$4x^4 + 2x^3 - 8x^2 + 12x + 8$

Write the equation in standard form for the line that crosses the two points.

3. (26) $(-3, 0), (-5, 1)$ $x + 2y = -3$

4. (26) $(-7, 9), (-10, 11)$ $2x + 3y = 13$

Expand:

***5.** (49) $(2 - m)^7$
$-m^7 + 14m^6 - 84m^5 + 280m^4 - 560m^3 + 672m^2 - 448m + 128$

***6.** (49) $(3g + 2h)^3$ $27g^3 + 54g^2h + 36gh^2 + 8h^3$

Find the inverse of each function.

***7.** (50) $y = 3x^2 - 1$
$y = \pm\frac{\sqrt{3x + 3}}{3}$

***8.** (50) $y = \sqrt{x}$ $y = x^2$

***9.** (50) $y = \frac{1}{2}x + 6$ $y = 2x - 12$

***10.** (45) **Graphing Calculator** The table shows the category and amount of damage to the United States from seven hurricanes that hit the US after the year 2000. Use a graphing calculator to find the value of r for the data set. Tell what this value means. $r \approx 0.82$, there is a strong positive correlation between the category of a hurricane and the amount of damage that results.

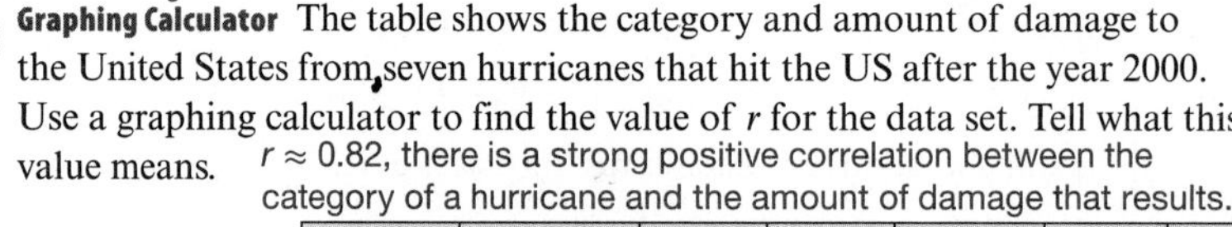

	Wilma	Charley	Ivan	Rita	Isabel	Lili	Francis
Category	3	4	3	3	2	1	2
Damage to US ($, billions)	20.6	15	14.2	11.3	3.37	0.86	8.9

ALTERNATE METHOD FOR PROBLEM 5

If students forget the Binomial Theorem, show them that $(2 - m)^7$ is a series of multiplications that can be solved for step by step.

$$(2 - m)^2 = 4 - 2m + m^2$$

$$\begin{aligned}(2 - m)^3 &= (2 - m)^2(2 - m)^1 \\ &= (4 - 2m + m^2)(2 - m)^1 \\ &= -m^3 + 4m^2 - 8m + 8\end{aligned}$$

$$\begin{aligned}(2 - m)^4 &= (2 - m)^2(2 - m)^2 \\ &= (4 - 2m + m^2)(4 - 2m + m^2) \\ &= m^4 - 4m^3 + 12m^2 - 16m + 16\end{aligned}$$

$$\begin{aligned}(2 - m)^7 &= (2 - m)^3(2 - m)^4 \\ &= (-m^3 + 4m^2 - 8m + 8)(m^4 - 4m^3 + 12m^2 - 16m + 16)\end{aligned}$$

$$(2 - m)^7 = -m^7 + 14m^6 - 84m^5 + 280m^4 - 560m^3 + 672m^2 - 448m + 128$$

11. (31) **Velocity** The velocity of a certain automobile during the first 40 seconds starting from rest is approximated by the rational function $f(t) = \frac{90t}{t+6}$, where t is the number of elapsed seconds and $f(t)$ is velocity in feet per second.

Write a division expression for the average acceleration of the automobile over the time interval from 0 seconds to t seconds. Then simplify the expression. (Average acceleration equals change in velocity divided by elapsed time.) $\frac{90t}{t+6} \div t$; $\frac{90}{t+6}$

***12.** (49) **Probability** You have a fifty-fifty chance of correctly guessing each answer on a test. Suppose you guess at 10 true/false questions. Find the probability that you will get exactly 4 questions correct. $\frac{105}{512}$

13. (17) **Multiple Choice** Solve $|2x + 1| < 4$. A

A $-\frac{5}{2} < x < \frac{3}{2}$ B $\frac{3}{2} < x < -\frac{5}{2}$

C $x < -\frac{5}{2}$ or $x > \frac{3}{2}$ D $x < \frac{3}{2}$

14. (42) **Error Analysis** In selecting five items out of ten, a student says there would be ten times more permutations than combinations. Is the student correct? If not provide the correct answer. The student is incorrect. There are 120 times more permutations than combinations. $P(10, 5) = 30{,}240$; $C(10, 5) = 252$

15. (25) **Model** The table below shows the measurements in inches of various shipping boxes available from the United States Postal Service. Draw a box-and-whisker plot to represent the approximate areas of all sides of the boxes. Consider that a box has 6 faces. See Additional Answers

Box	Measurement 1	Measurement 2	Measurement 3
1	11.875	3.375	13.625
2	11	8.5	5.5
3	7.5	5.125	14.375

17b. $|f - 45.5| \leq 21.5$ gives $f - 45.5 \leq 21.5$ and $f - 45.5 \geq -21.5$. Therefore, $f \leq 67$ and $f \geq 24$, which is the same result as part a

16. (30) **Multi-Step** The graph of a quadratic function has a vertex (2, −3) and passes through the point (5, −12). Give the equation of the function. Tell if the function has a maximum or minimum. $y = -(x - 2)^2 - 3$; maximum

17. (17) **Grizzly Bears** The table shows amounts of three foods that a 200-lb grizzly bear can eat in a day.

Type	Amount (lbs)
Deer	24
Salmon	30
Vegetation	67

a. Write an inequality to show the amounts of these foods that a 200-lb grizzly bear can eat in a day. $24 \leq f \leq 67$

b. Verify that your answer is equivalent to the absolute value inequality $|f - 45.5| \leq 21.5$.

18. (40) **Multiple Choice** Which number has two fourth roots? C

A −27 B 4 C 16 D 125

19. (27) **Geometry** **a.** Write a quadratic equation in standard form to represent the area of the shaded region. $y = -x^2 + 35$

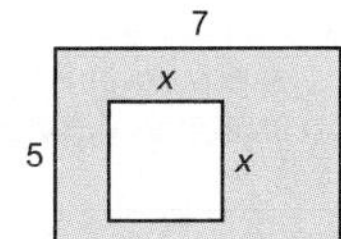

b. Identify the values of a, b, and c in the equation in part a. $a = -1, b = 0, c = 35$

3 Practice

Math Conversations

Discussions to strengthen understanding

Problem 6

When expanding, start with the FOIL method. First expand $(3g + 2h)(3g + 2h)$, then multiply the resulting answer by $(3g + 2h)$ to expand for a cubic exponent.

Problem 11

Find the acceleration at 10 and 20 seconds. Show work.

$a_{10} = \frac{90}{10 + 6} = 5.625$

$a_{20} = \frac{90}{20 + 6} \approx 3.46$

Problem 24

For this problem, draw a graph with Indianapolis at the origin (0, 0) and Raleigh at (6, −3). Use the distance formula $\left(d = \sqrt{(x_2 - x_1)^2 + (y_2 - y_1)^2}\right)$ to find the distance between the two points. Remember that one unit equals 120 km, so to find the total distance multiply the distance found by 120 to find the exact kilometers. Round if necessary.

Problem 25

Error Alert

Students may square $g(x)$ incorrectly by only writing $\frac{1}{x^2 + 4}$. Show them that squaring fractions is the same as multiplying the numerator by itself and the denominator by itself.

$$\left(\frac{1}{x+2}\right)^2 = \frac{1}{x+2} \cdot \frac{1}{x+2}$$
$$= \frac{1}{(x+2)(x+2)}$$
$$= \frac{1}{(x^2 + 4x + 4)}$$

Problem 30

When you "factor out the GCF" in a polynomial, you are dividing out a part of each term that is common in all three terms. By dividing out the greatest common factor, a polynomial is more likely to be reduced further with cancellation or other algebraic techniques.

20. (19) **Error Analysis** Two students completed the problem $(x - 8)(x + 8)$. Who is correct? Explain your answer. Student B is correct. Student A forgot to make the 8 negative in the inner multiplication

Student A	Student B
$= x^2 + 8x + 8x - 64$ $= x^2 + 16x - 64$	$= x^2 + 8x - 8x - 64$ $= x^2 - 64$

21. (43) **Justify** Explain why the system $\begin{matrix} y > 3x + 1 \\ y < 3x - 1 \end{matrix}$ has no solution. See Additional Answers.

22. (20) **(Births)** From 1990 to 1999, the number of births $b(x)$ in the U.S. can be modeled by the function $b(x) = -27x + 4103$, and the number of deaths $d(x)$ can be modeled by the function $d(x) = 23x + 2164$. Write a function for the net increase in population, $p(x) = b(x) - d(x)$ from 1990 to 1999. $p(x) = b(x) - d(x) = -27x + 4103 - (23x + 2164) = -50x + 1939$

23. (28) **Justify** Explain why $4x^2 + 3x$ is a rational expression.

23. It can be written as a fraction with a denominator of 1 and 1 is a constant monomial, so the fraction is a quotient of two polynomials.

24. (41) **(Cartography)** A student constructs a map of the eastern United States over a grid system such that Indianapolis, IN is the origin and Raleigh, NC is at (6, −3). Find the distance between the cities to the nearest kilometer if each unit represents 120 kilometers. About 805 kilometers

25. (31) If $g(x) = \frac{1}{x+2}$, what is $g(x)^2$ in simplest form? $\frac{1}{(x+2)^2}$

26. (46) **Analyze** Why are the sine and cosine values of an acute angle in a right triangle always less than 1? See Additional Answers.

27. (34) **(Engine Size)** In past years, engine size for American automobiles was usually measured in cubic inches. Today, most engine sizes are measured in liters. The table shows three typical engine sizes for modern automobiles in both liters and cubic inches.

Liters (x)	2.3	2.5	3.0
Cubic Inches (y)	140.3	152.5	183

Graph the linear function that relates liters and cubic inches, state the rate of change, and describe what it means. Rate of change = 61; Possible description: There are 61 cubic inches in every liter.

27.

Cubic Inches: 40, 80, 120, 160

Liters: 1, 2, 3

28. (29) Use
$9x = y - 3z - 21$
$4y - 6z = 8x + 10$
$56x - 28y = 2 - 42z$.

$9x - y + 3z = -21$
$-8x + 4y - 6z = 10$
$56x - 28y + 42z = 2$

a. Rewrite the equations lining up the variables.

b. Estimate the number of solutions. Explain your answer. See Additional Answers.

c. Solve the system of equations to verify your estimate. No solution

29. (41) **Analyze** In the Pythagorean Theorem, why are a, b, and c all greater than 0?

29. The variables represent the lengths of the sides and the sides of a triangle must have a length greater than 0.

30. (11) **Write** Explain in words what you are doing when you "factor out the GCF" to factor a polynomial. The GCF is the greatest common factor, which means that each term in the polynomial can be divided by the GCF with no remainder. So, factoring out the GCF means to divide each polynomial term by the GCF.

CHALLENGE

Find an equation for the inverse of the function $y^3 = \left(\frac{x}{4}\right)^2 + 8$.

$$y^3 = \frac{x^2}{16} + 8$$
$$x^3 = \frac{y^2}{16} + 8$$
$$x^3 - 8 = \frac{y^2}{16}$$
$$16(x^3 - 8) = y^2$$
$$\pm\sqrt{16(x^3 - 8)} = y$$
$$y = \pm\sqrt{16(x^3 - 8)}$$

LOOKING FORWARD

Finding inverses of relations and functions prepares students for

- **Lesson 53** Performing Compositions of Functions
- **Lesson 67** Finding Inverse Trigonometric Functions
- **Lesson 75** Graphing Radical Functions

INVESTIGATION 5

Finding the Binomial Distribution

Suppose you are flipping a coin two times. However simple the task, this coin-flipping activity is an example of a binomial experiment. There are four conditions that need to be met for a probability experiment to qualify as a binomial experiment. The four conditions are listed below and next to each item is an explanation of how the coin-flipping experiment complies.

Binomial Experiment	Does the Test Scenario Comply?
There are *n* trials in the experiment	Yes. There are 2 trials.
Only two possible outcomes per trial	Yes. The coin lands either heads or tails.
Each trial is independent	Yes. The result of one trial does not influence the result of any other.
The probability of success is the same from trial to trial	Yes. Each toss has a 1 in 2 (or 50%) chance of heads (or tails).

1. Suppose you were flipping a coin 100 times. Is this also an example of a binomial experiment? Why? Yes, because the four conditions are still met.
2. Suppose you were flipping two coins twice. Is this an example of a binomial experiment? Why? No, because condition 2 is not met (there are four possible outcomes).
3. Suppose you were rolling a six-sided number cube twice. Is this an example of a binomial experiment? Why? No, because condition 2 is not met (there are six possible outcomes each time).

Math Reasoning

Verify Two six-sided number cubes are rolled, and the values are added. Show that there are 36 possible outcomes, but not all outcomes are unique.

Some events that are usually not binomial experiments can be structured in such a way that they are. Consider two six-sided number cubes. There are 36 possible outcomes when you roll the number cubes, so this is not a binomial experiment.

4. Now suppose that you want to keep track of how often the sum of the number cubes is greater than 3 after rolling the two cubes 15 times. Determine if this is a binomial experiment by completing the table. Yes, it is a binomial experiment.

Binomial Experiment	Does the Test Scenario Comply?
There are *n* trials in the experiment	Yes. There are 15 trials.
Only two possible outcomes per trial	Yes. The sum of the faces on the number cubes is greater than 3 or not.
Each trial is independent	Yes. The result of one trial does not influence the result of any other.
The probability of success is the same from trial to trial	Yes. $P(3 \text{ or less}) = \frac{2}{11}$ and $P(>3) = \frac{9}{11}$

There are 11 possible sums from 36 unique combinations.

INVESTIGATION 5

Materials

Pencil, paper, computer spreadsheet

Discuss

Students will create a binomial experiment and calculate the binomial distribution of the experiment using a spreadsheet.

TEACHER TIP

Explain that a "success" does not necessarily refer to a "good" outcome. Either of the two possible outcomes can be called the success.

Problem 4

To help students determine the probabilities for the sum of the results of rolling two number cubes, help them write an organized list of outcomes. Get them started by listing the outcomes when the first roll results in a one.

1, 1   1, 2   1, 3   1, 4   1, 5   1, 6

MATH BACKGROUND

A binomial distribution describes the behavior of a variable X if:

a. The number of outcomes is fixed.

b. Each outcome is independent.

c. Each outcome represents a success or a failure.

d. The probability of success, *p,* is the same for each outcome

If these conditions are met, then X has a binomial distribution. The sample distribution of X is only accurately represented by the binomial distribution when the population size is at least ten times larger than the sample size. To find the probability of a binomial distribution use a calculator formula, a binary table, or a computer program such as a spreadsheet.

INVESTIGATION RESOURCES

Reteaching Master Investigation 5

5. Consider a probability experiment where you keep track of how many results are even and how many are odd that involves rolling a six-sided number cube five times.
   a. **Verify** Show that this is a binomial experiment. Check students' work.
   b. **Predict** If you perform the experiment, how many even number outcomes will there be? Check students' work.
6. Perform the binomial experiment from question 5.
   a. Create a frequency diagram of your results. Check students' work.
   b. Create a bar graph. Check students' work.
   c. Compare your results to the prediction you previously made. Answers will vary.

You can use a spreadsheet to simulate a probability experiment. In fact, using a spreadsheet, you can simulate the binomial experiment similar to the one from question 5. In this case you will simulate rolling a number cube 25 times to see how many times the results are an even number and how many times the results are an odd number.

Math Reasoning

Analyze The MOD function can be used to find the remainder when one number is divided by another. Why is Mod(#, 2) a test for even or odd?

If there is no remainder, the number is even. If the remainder is 1, the number is odd.

7. **Multi-Step** Use a spreadsheet for the following activity. Check students' work.
   a. Input the following formula to cell A1: **=RANDBETWEEN(1, 6).** This formula generates a random integer from 1 to 6, each number representing one of the faces of the number cube.
   b. Copy and paste this formula from cell A2 to A5.
   c. Press the F9 key, and you'll see that the numbers change randomly. The goal is to keep track of when the results are even and when they are odd.
   d. Input the following formula to cell B1: **=IF(MOD(A1, 2)=0, "Even", "Odd").** This tests if the outcome is an even or odd number.
   e. Copy and paste the formula to cells B2 to B5.
   f. Input the following formula to cell B7: **=COUNTIF(B1:B5, "Even").** Input the following formula to cell B8: **=COUNTIF(B1:B6, "Odd").** These formulas will count the number of even and odd numbers for each trial.
   g. Run 25 trials (by repeatedly using the F9 key). Keep track of the number of even and odd results.
   h. Create a bar graph of your results.
   i. How do your results compare to your prediction in question 5?
8. Run an additional 75 trials to have a total of 100 trials.
   a. Create a bar graph of your results.
   b. How do your results compare to your previous predictions?

Test Prep Does it help to guess if you don't know the answer to a question? What are your chances of getting a good score on a test if all you do is guess?

Suppose you are taking a 20-item, multiple-choice test. There are five possible answer choices, A through E, for each item. Your plan is to guess the answer to each of the 20 questions. What is the probability that you will get 0, 1, ... up to 20 questions correct?

TEACHER TIP

The spreadsheet allows multiple trials of the experiment to be completed quickly.

Problem 7

If the student receives an error alert, have them check for any syntax problems. They may have forgotten a parenthesis or a quotation mark.

If there are no syntax errors, they may need to go to the Tools menu, click on Add-Ins, and install Analysis ToolPak.

ENGLISH LEARNERS

Define **binomial distribution.** Say:

"A binomial distribution is a list of all probabilities of a binomial experiment. A histogram is a picture that organizes this list in a clear form. If a binomial experiment uses many trials, the binomial distribution histogram will be similar to the binomial experiment histogram." Put an example of a distribution list and its correlating histogram on the board to illustrate.

9. **Verify** A binomial experiment needs to satisfy the four conditions stated below. Complete the table to verify that guessing on the 20-item test is a binomial experiment.

Binomial Experiment	Does the Test Scenario Comply?
a. There are n trials in the experiment	Yes. There are 20 questions in the test.
b. Only two possible outcomes per trial	Yes. The guess is either correct or incorrect.
c. Each trial is independent	Yes. The result of one guess does not influence the result of any other guesses.
d. The probability of success is the same from trial to trial	Yes. Each guess has a 1 in 5 (or 20%) chance of success.

10. **Predict** If you randomly guess on 20 questions, how many are you likely to get right? Answers will vary.

11. **Multi-Step** Use a spreadsheet for the following activity. Check students' work.
   a. Input the following formula to cell A1: **=RANDBETWEEN(1, 5).** Copy and paste this formula to cells A2 to A20. These 20 numbers represent the correct answers to the items in the test.
   b. Repeat part **a** for cells B1 to B20. These 20 numbers represent the 20 random guesses.
   c. Input the following formula to cell C1: **=IF(A1-B1=0, "Correct", "N").** This tests if the guess for a particular row is correct or not. (A guess is correct when both numbers in a row are equal.)
   d. Run 30 trials (by using the F9 key) and record the cumulative number of correct guesses in a table with one column to record trial numbers and one column to record number of correct answers.
   e. Which number of correct guesses has the highest probability?
   f. How does your answer to part e compare to your original prediction? Answers will vary.

e. Answers will vary.

Investigation Practice

Determine if each of the probability experiments is a binomial experiment or not. If not, explain why.

a. Rolling two six-sided number cubes 500 times to see the probability of rolling a 12 a total of 100 times. binomial

b. Taking a 20-question multiple choice test and guessing on half the items. Not binomial; conditions different for half the questions

c. Conduct a binomial experiment that involves simulating rolling two six-sided number cubes 50 times to determine the frequency of getting a 12. Create a bar graph of your results. Check students' work.

LOOKING FORWARD

Calculating the binomial distribution prepares students for

- **Lesson 83** Writing Quadratic Equations from Roots

Problem 11

Reinforce the purpose of each step.

a. This step creates possible answers for the multiple choice test.

b. This step creates a list of answer guesses and a test key.

c. A correct guess will occur when the answer in column A matches the corresponding answer in column B.

Investigation Practice

Math Conversations

Discussions to strengthen understanding

Problem a

"How many trials are there in the experiment?" 500

"How many possible outcomes are there and what are they?" There are two possible outcomes. You either roll a 12 a total of 100 times, or you don't.

"Is each trial independent?" Yes, the result of one trial does not effect the result of any other trial.

"Does the probability of success change from one trial to the next?" No, the probability is $\frac{1}{11}$ from one trial to the next.

Lesson Planner

Lesson	New Concepts
51	Using Synthetic Division
LAB 9	*Graphing Calculator Lab:* Using the Trigonometry Keys and Adjusting to a Trigonometric Window
52	Using Two Special Right Triangles
53	Performing Compositions of Functions
54	Using Linear Programming
55	Finding Probability
	Cumulative Test 10, Performance Task 10
56	Finding Angles of Rotation
57	Finding Exponential Growth and Decay
58	Completing the Square
59	Using Fractional Exponents
60	Distinguishing Between Mutually Exclusive and Independent Events
	Cumulative Test 11, Performance Task 11
INV 6	Investigation: Deriving the Quadratic Formula

Resources for Teaching

- Student Edition
- Teacher's Edition
- Student Edition eBook
- Teacher's Edition eBook
- Resources and Planner CD
- Solutions Manual
- Instructional Masters
- Technology Lab Masters
- Warm Up and Teaching Transparencies
- Instructional Presentations CD
- Online activities, tools, and homework help **www.SaxonMathResources.com**

Resources for Practice and Assessment

- Student Edition Practice Workbook
- Course Assessments
- Standardized Test Practice
- College Entrance Exam Practice
- Test and Practice Generator CD using ExamView™

Resources for Differentiated Instruction

- Reteaching Masters
- Challenge and Enrichment Masters
- Prerequisite Skills Intervention
- Adaptations for Saxon Algebra 2
- Multilingual Glossary
- English Learners Handbook
- TI Resources

Pacing Guide

Resources and Planner CD for lesson planning support

45-Minute Class

Day 1	Day 2	Day 3	Day 4	Day 5	Day 6
Lesson 51	Lab 9 Lesson 52	Lesson 53	Lesson 54	Lesson 55	Cumulative Test 10
Day 7	**Day 8**	**Day 9**	**Day 10**	**Day 11**	**Day 12**
Lesson 56	Lesson 57	Lesson 58	Lesson 59	Lesson 60	Cumulative Test 11
Day 13					
Investigation 6					

Block: 90-Minute Class

Day 1	Day 2	Day 3	Day 4	Day 5	Day 6
Lesson 51 Lesson 52 Lab 9	Lesson 53 Lesson 54	Lesson 55 Cumulative Test 10	Lesson 56 Lesson 57	Lesson 58 Lesson 59	Lesson 60 Cumulative Test 11
Day 7					
Investigation 6 Lesson 61					

* *For suggestions on how to implement Saxon Math in a block schedule, see the Pacing section at the beginning of the Teacher's Edition.*

Differentiated Instruction

Below Level		Advanced Learners	
Warm Up	SE pp. 364, 372, 378, 384, 391, 399, 406, 413, 420, 427	Challenge	TE pp. 369, 376, 383, 390, 396, 405, 410, 419, 424, 426, 430, 432
Skills Bank	SE pp. 862–885	Extend the Example	TE pp. 365, 370, 380, 385, 398, 400, 414, 415, 416, 421, 422, 423, 428, 429
Reteaching Masters	Lessons 51–60, Investigation 6	Extend the Problem	TE pp. 369, 375, 382, 398, 404, 410, 411, 418, 419, 430, 431, 432
Warm Up Transparencies	Lessons 51–60	Challenge and Enrichment Masters	Challenge: C51–C60 Enrichment: E53, E57
Prerequisite Skills Intervention	Skills 7, 8, 23, 24, 25, 32. 82		
English Learners		**Special Needs**	
EL Tips	TE pp. 366, 375, 380, 386, 395, 400, 411, 415, 425, 431, 434	Inclusion Tips	TE pp. 365, 373, 381, 385, 387, 393, 398, 401, 407, 409, 414, 417, 422, 429
Multilingual Glossary	Booklet and Online	Adaptations for Saxon Algebra 2	Lessons 51–60; Cumulative Tests 10, 11
English Learners Handbook			
For All Learners			
Exploration	SE p. 414	Alternate Method	TE pp. 368, 388, 389, 400, 402, 408, 416, 421, 423, 428
Caution	SE pp. 364, 399, 413, 421	Online Tools	
Hints	SE pp. 364, 365, 384, 400, 401, 421, 422		
Error Alert	TE pp. 366, 369, 373, 374, 380, 381, 386, 387, 395, 396, 397, 402, 405, 407, 409, 410, 411, 414, 415, 417, 418, 420, 422, 424, 425, 426, 429, 431, 432, 433, 435		

SE = Student Edition; TE = Teacher's Edition

Math Vocabulary

Lesson	New Vocabulary		Maintained	EL Tip in TE	
51	synthetic division synthetic substitution		divisor	predict	
52	special right triangles		tangent	annealing	
53	composite function composition of function		function	composition	
54	constraint feasible region	linear programming objective function	inequality	vertices	
55	conditional probability equally likely outcomes experimental probability favarable outcome geometric probability likelihood	probability experiment probability random event random theoretical probability	sample space	probability	
56	angle of rotation coterminal angles initial side reference angle	rotation standard position terminal side	Pythagorean Theorem	coterminal angles	
57	decreasing function exponential decay exponential growth	growth factor half-life increasing function natural logarithm	exponential formula	exponential decay exponential growth	
58	completing the square		quadratic	factors	
59	*n*th roots rational exponents		exponent	base exponent index *n*th root radical sign	radicand rational number
60	compound event disjoint events	inclusive events	mutually exclusive permutation	independent events mutually exclusive events	
INV 6	quadratic formula			perfect-square trinomial	

SECTION OVERVIEW 6

Math Highlights

Enduring Understandings – The "Big Picture"

After completing Section 6, students will understand:

- How to divide polynomials.
- How to perform compositions of functions.
- How to determine probabilities for different situations.
- How to recognize and solve exponential growth and decay problems.
- How to solve quadratic equations by completing the square.

Essential Questions

- When can synthetic division be used to divide polynomials?
- When is a function composition commutative?
- What is the difference between an independent event and a mutually exclusive event?
- What are the steps for completing the square in a quadratic equation?

Math Content Strands

Exponential and Logarithmic Functions

• Lesson 57	Finding Exponential Growth and Decay

Linear Functions

• Lesson 53	Performing Compositions of Functions

Linear Systems

• Lesson 54	Using Linear Programming

Polynomials and Polynomial Functions

• Lesson 51	Using Synthetic Division

Probability and Statistics

• Lesson 55	Finding Probability
• Lesson 60	Distinguishing Between Mutually Exclusive and Independent Events

Quadratic Functions

• Lesson 58	Completing the Square
• Investigation 6	Investigation: Deriving the Quadratic Formula

Rational and Radical Functions

• Lesson 59	Using Fractional Exponents

Trigonometry

• Lesson 52	Using Two Special Right Triangles
• Lab 9	Graphing Calculator: Using the Trigonometry Keys and Adjusting to a Trigonometric Window
• Lesson 56	Finding Angles of Rotation

Connections in Practice Problems

	Lessons
Coordinate Geometry	54, 55, 57, 58, 59, 60
Data Analysis	52
Geometry	51, 52, 53, 54, 55, 56, 57, 58, 59, 60
Probability	51, 53, 56
Statistics	60

Math Processes

Reasoning and Communication

	Lessons
• Analyze	51, 52, 53, 54, 55, 56, 57, 59, Inv. 6
• Connect	56
• Error analysis	51, 52, 53, 54, 55, 56, 57, 58, 59, 60
• Estimate	51, 52, 58, 60
• Explain	55, 60
• Formulate	57, 58, Inv. 6
• Generalize	51, 53, 54, 58, 60, Inv. 6
• Justify	54, 56, 58, 59, 60
• Math reasoning	53, 54, 55
• Model	52, 57, Inv. 6
• Multiple choice	51, 52, 53, 54, 55, 56, 57, 58, 59, 60
• Multi-step	51, 52, 53, 54, 55, 56, 57, 58, 59, 60, Inv. 6
• Predict	52, 55
• Verify	51, 52, 54, 56, 59, 60
• Write	51, 52, 53, 54, 55, 56, 57, 58, 59, 60
• Graphing calculator	51, 52, 53, 54, 55, 56, 57, 58, 59, 60

Connections

In Examples: Air traffic control, Business, Cubic house, Distance, Giant panda population, Meteorology, Predicting population, Projectile motion, Sales and discounts, Veterinary medicine

In Practice problems: Acceleration, Agriculture, Aquarium design, Architecture, Aviation, Birth trends, Carpentry, Cartography, Catering, CD investment, Chemistry, Compound interest, Computer graphics, Cost of lobster, Deck building, Decorative tiles, Doppler effect, Electricity, Electronics, Employment, Exercise, Food preparation, Geography, Gravity, History, Investments, Irrigation, Life insurance, Marine biology, Medicine, Monuments, Mountain bikers, Music, Pass codes, Pendulums, Pet shelter, Physics, Playing cards, Population, Projectile motion, Rainfall, Saving money, Sea level, Skateboarding, Speed, Temperature, Ticket prices

Content Trace

Lesson	Warm Up: Prerequisite Skills	New Concepts	Where Practiced	Where Assessed	Looking Forward
51	Skills Bank, Lessons 2, 11, 19, 38	Using Synthetic Division	Lessons 51, 52, 53, 54, 55, 58, 59, 60, 62, 64, 67, 71, 78, 102, 108, 110, 118	Cumulative Tests 11, 12, 16, 18	Lessons 61, 66
52	Skills Bank, Lessons 41, 46	Using Two Special Right Triangles	Lessons 52, 53, 54, 55, 58, 59, 60, 61, 62, 64, 65, 66, 70, 71, 72, 73, 74, 75, 76, 77, 78, 79, 80, 81, 82, 85, 87, 96	Cumulative Tests 11, 13, 20	Lessons 63, 67, 71, 77, 112, 115
53	Lessons 4, 23	Performing Compositions of Functions	Lessons 53, 54, 55, 56, 57, 58, 59, 60, 61, 63, 64, 65, 66, 70, 71, 73, 79, 81, 83, 87, 110	Cumulative Tests 11, 12, 17, 22	Lessons 76, 117
54	Lessons 4, 10, 39	Using Linear Programming	Lessons 54, 55, 56, 57, 58, 60, 61, 62, 63, 67, 68, 70, 71, 72, 78	Cumulative Tests 11, 14	Lessons 75, 88, 109
55	Skills Bank, Lessons 33, 42	Finding Probability	Lessons 55, 56, 57, 58, 59, 60, 61, 62, 63, 64, 65, 66, 67, 68, 69, 70, 73, 75, 76, 79, 85, 90, 91, 115	Cumulative Tests 11, 13, 16	Lessons 60, 68
56	Lessons 2, 3, 41	Finding Angles of Rotation	Lessons 56, 57, 59, 61, 62, 63, 64, 65, 66, 67, 68, 69, 74, 77, 78, 80, 84, 86, 91, 100	Cumulative Tests 12, 15, 20	Lessons 67, 71, 77, 96, 119
57	Lessons 3, 47, 50	Finding Exponential Growth and Decay	Lessons 57, 58, 59, 60, 61, 62, 63, 64, 65, 66, 67, 69, 71, 72, 73, 74, 75, 76, 78, 79, 80, 82, 89, 92, 95	Cumulative Tests 12, 13, 18	Lessons 64, 72, 81, 87
58	Lessons 3, 23, 27	Completing the Square	Lessons 58, 59, 60, 61, 62, 63, 64, 65, 66, 67, 68, 69, 70, 71, 73, 76, 77, 84, 86	Cumulative Tests 12, 14, 15, 21	Lessons 62, 65, 74, 78
59	Lessons 3, 40	Using Fractional Exponents	Lessons 59, 60, 61, 62, 63, 64, 65, 66, 67, 68, 69, 70, 71, 73, 77, 78, 79, 80, 83, 87, 90	Cumulative Tests 12, 13, 16, 23	Lessons 70, 75, 84, 94, 100
60	Lessons 33, 47	Distinguishing Between Mutually Exclusive and Independent Events	Lessons 60, 61, 62, 63, 64, 66, 67, 68, 69, 70, 74, 76, 77, 78, 79, 80, 81, 82, 83, 84, 86, 87	Cumulative Tests 12, 16	Lessons 68, 73, 80
INV 6	N/A	Investigation: Deriving the Quadratic Formula	Lessons 72, 91, 97	Cumulative Test 13	Lessons 65, 74, 78

SECTION OVERVIEW 6

Ongoing Assessment

	Type	Feature	Intervention *
BEFORE instruction	Assess Prior Knowledge	• Diagnostic Test	• Prerequisite Skills Intervention
BEFORE the lesson	Formative	• Warm Up	• Skills Bank • Reteaching Masters
DURING the lesson	Formative	• Lesson Practice • Math Conversations with the Practice problems	• Additional Examples in TE • Test and Practice Generator (for additional practice sheets)
AFTER the lesson	Formative	• Check for Understanding (closure)	• Scaffolding Questions in TE
AFTER 5 lessons	Summative	After Lesson 55 • Cumulative Test 10 • Performance Task 10 After Lesson 60 • Cumulative Test 11 • Performance Task 11	• Reteaching Masters • Test and Practice Generator (for additional tests and practice)
AFTER 20 lessons	Summative	• Benchmark Tests	• Reteaching Masters • Test and Practice Generator (for additional tests and practice)

* for students not showing progress during the formative stages or scoring below 80% on the summative assessments

Evidence of Learning – What Students Should Know

Because the Saxon philosophy is to provide students with sufficient time to learn and practice each concept, a lesson's topic will not be tested until at least five lessons after the topic is introduced.

On the Cumulative Tests that are given during this section of ten lessons, students should be able to demonstrate the following competencies:

- Find permutations and combinations.
- Perform operations with rational expressions.
- Solve quadratic equations.
- Solve systems of linear inequalities by graphing and linear programming.
- Find the inverse of relations and functions.
- Perform compositions of functions.
- Use the trigonometric ratios to find side lengths of right triangles.
- Simplify fractions by rationalizing denominators.

Test and Practice Generator CD using ExamView™

The Test and Practice Generator is an easy-to-use benchmark and assessment tool that creates unlimited practice and tests in multiple formats and allows you to customize questions or create new ones. A variety of reports are available to track student progress toward mastery of the standards throughout the year.

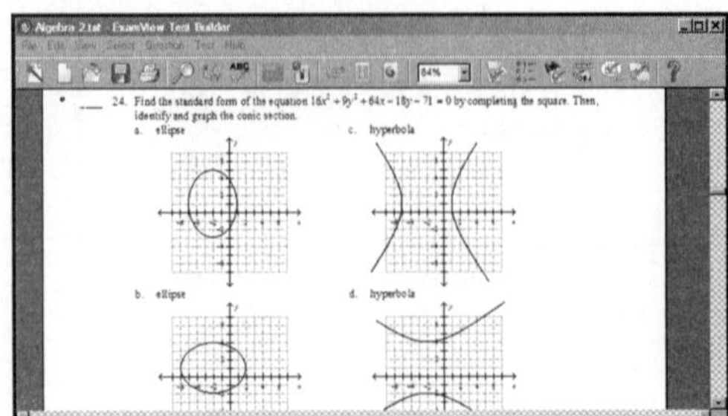

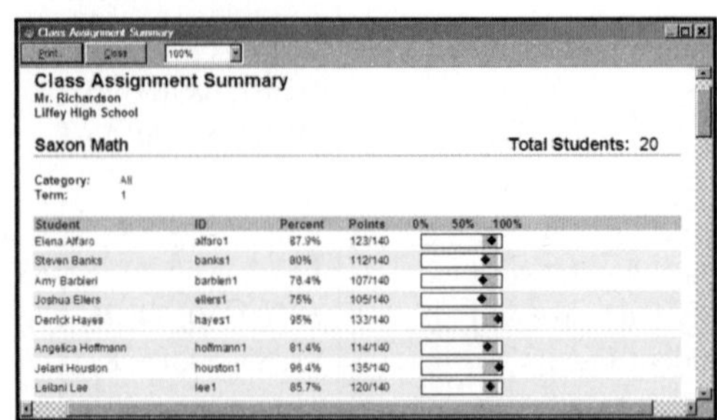

Assessment Resources

Resources for Diagnosing and Assessing

- **Student Edition**
  - Warm Up
  - Lesson Practice
- **Teacher's Edition**
  - Math Conversations with the Practice problems
  - Check for Understanding (closure)
- **Course Assessments**
  - Diagnostic Test
  - Cumulative Tests
  - Performance Tasks
  - Benchmark Tests

Resources for Test Prep

- **Student Edition**
  - Multiple-choice practice problems
  - Multiple-step and writing problems
  - Daily cumulative practice
- **Standardized Test Practice**
- **College Entrance Exam Practice**
- **Test and Practice Generator CD using ExamView™**

Resources for Intervention

- **Student Edition**
  - Skills Bank
- **Teacher's Edition**
  - Additional Examples
  - Scaffolding questions
- **Prerequisite Skills Intervention**
  - Worksheets
- **Reteaching Masters**
  - Lesson instruction and practice sheets
- **Test and Practice Generator CD using ExamView™**
  - Lesson practice problems
  - Additional tests

Cumulative Tests

The assessments in Saxon Math are frequent and consistently placed after every five lessons to offer a regular method of ongoing testing. These cumulative assessments check mastery of concepts from previous lessons.

Performance Tasks

The Performance Tasks can be used in conjunction with the Cumulative Tests and are scored using a rubric.

After Lesson 55

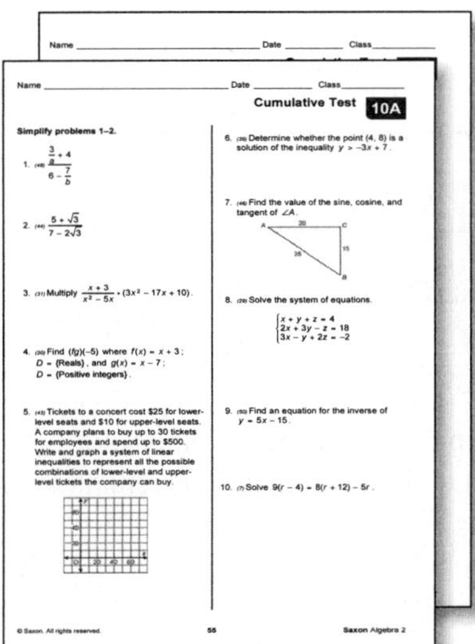

Name ________________ Date ________ Class ________

Cumulative Test 10A

Simplify problems 1–2.

1. (48) $\dfrac{\frac{3}{a} + 4}{6 - \frac{7}{b}}$
2. (44) $\dfrac{5 + \sqrt{3}}{7 - 2\sqrt{3}}$
3. (31) Multiply $\dfrac{x + 3}{x^2 - 5x} \cdot (3x^2 - 17x + 10)$.
4. (20) Find $(fg)(-5)$ where $f(x) = x + 3$; $D = \{\text{Reals}\}$, and $g(x) = x - 7$; $D = \{\text{Positive integers}\}$.
5. (43) Tickets to a concert cost $25 for lower-level seats and $10 for upper-level seats. A company plans to buy up to 30 tickets for employees and spend up to $500. Write and graph a system of linear inequalities to represent all the possible combinations of lower-level and upper-level tickets the company can buy.
6. (39) Determine whether the point (4, 8) is a solution of the inequality $y > -3x + 7$.
7. (46) Find the value of the sine, cosine, and tangent of $\angle A$.
8. (29) Solve the system of equations.
   $\begin{cases} x + y + z = 4 \\ 2x + 3y - z = 18 \\ 3x - y + 2z = -2 \end{cases}$
9. (50) Find an equation for the inverse of $y = 5x - 15$.
10. (7) Solve $9(r - 4) = 8(r + 12) - 5r$.

© Saxon. All rights reserved. 55 Saxon Algebra 2

After Lesson 60

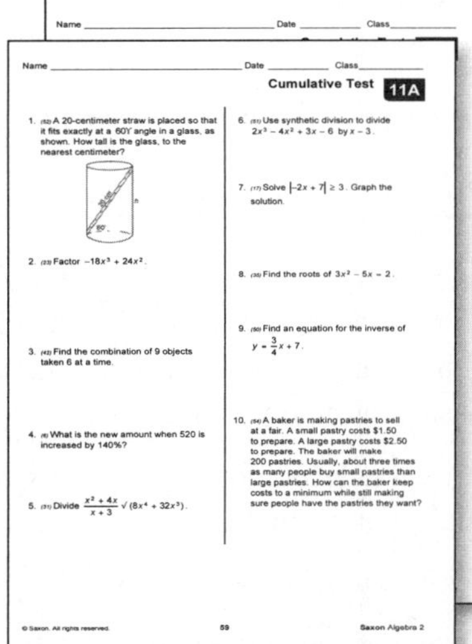

Name ________________ Date ________ Class ________

Cumulative Test 11A

1. (52) A 20-centimeter straw is placed so that it fits exactly at a 60Y angle in a glass, as shown. How tall is the glass, to the nearest centimeter?
2. (23) Factor $-18x^3 + 24x^2$.
3. (42) Find the combination of 9 objects taken 6 at a time.
4. (6) What is the new amount when 520 is increased by 140%?
5. (31) Divide $\dfrac{x^2 + 4x}{x + 3} \div (8x^4 + 32x^3)$.
6. (51) Use synthetic division to divide $2x^3 - 4x^2 + 3x - 6$ by $x - 3$.
7. (17) Solve $|-2x + 7| \geq 3$. Graph the solution.
8. (35) Find the roots of $3x^2 - 5x - 2$.
9. (50) Find an equation for the inverse of $y = \frac{3}{4}x + 7$.
10. (54) A baker is making pastries to sell at a fair. A small pastry costs $1.50 to prepare. A large pastry costs $2.50 to prepare. The baker will make 200 pastries. Usually, about three times as many people buy small pastries than large pastries. How can the baker keep costs to a minimum while still making sure people have the pastries they want?

© Saxon. All rights reserved. 59 Saxon Algebra 2

For use with Performance Tasks

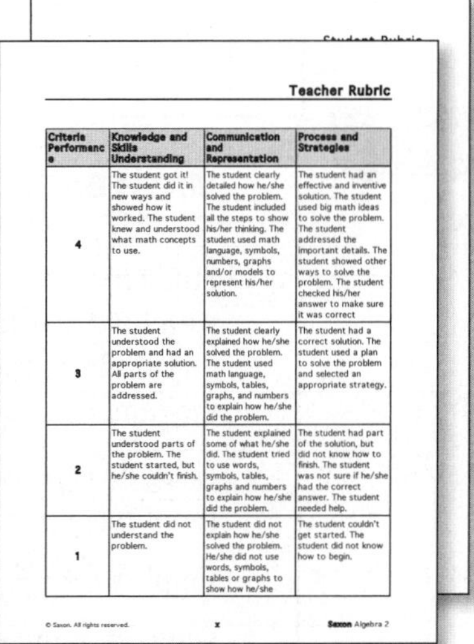

Teacher Rubric

Criteria Performance	Knowledge and Skills Understanding	Communication and Representation	Process and Strategies
4	The student got it! The student did it in new ways and showed how it worked. The student knew and understood what math concepts to use.	The student clearly detailed how he/she solved the problem. The student included all the steps to show his/her thinking. The student used math language, symbols, numbers, graphs and/or models to represent his/her solution.	The student had an effective and inventive solution. The student used big math ideas to solve the problem. The student addressed the important details. The student showed other ways to solve the problem. The student checked his/her answer to make sure it was correct
3	The student understood the problem and had an appropriate solution. All parts of the problem are addressed.	The student clearly explained how he/she solved the problem. The student used math language, symbols, tables, graphs, and numbers to explain how he/she did the problem.	The student had a correct solution. The student used a plan to solve the problem and selected an appropriate strategy.
2	The student understood parts of the problem. The student started, but he/she couldn't finish.	The student explained some of what he/she did. The student tried to use words, symbols, tables, graphs and numbers to explain how he/she did the problem.	The student had part of the solution, but did not know how to finish. The student was not sure if he/she had the correct answer. The student needed help.
1	The student did not understand the problem.	The student did not explain how he/she solved the problem. He/she did not use words, symbols, tables or graphs to show how he/she	The student couldn't get started. The student did not know how to begin.

© Saxon. All rights reserved. x Saxon Algebra 2

LESSON 51

1 Warm Up

Remind students to use the Distributive Property when multiplying in problem 2.

2 New Concepts

In this lesson, students use synthetic division to divide and evaluate polynomials.

Discuss the process of long division and synthetic division. Explain how to write the remainder over the divisor.

Example 1

Review long division with numbers. Focus on the process and steps. Then guide students through example 1.

Additional Example 1

Divide $4x^4 + 4x^3 - 12x^2 + 11x + 26$ by $x^2 + 3x - 1$.

$4x^2 - 8x + 16 + \frac{-45x + 42}{x^2 + 3x - 1}$

LESSON 51

Using Synthetic Division

Warm Up

1. (38) **Vocabulary** If $x^2 - 9$ is divided by $x - 3$, then $x^2 - 9$ is the dividend and $x - 3$ is the ___divisor___.
2. (19) Multiply. $(2x + 1)(x^2 + 2x - 3)$ $2x^3 + 5x^2 - 4x - 3$
3. (11) Find $f(2)$ for $f(x) = x^4 + x^3 - 3x - 1$. 17
4. (2) Divide $\frac{6x + 15y}{3}$ $2x + 5y$
5. (SB) $12.18 \div 2.1$ 5.8

New Concepts

To divide a polynomial by another polynomial, you can use long division. The process is similar to long division with numbers.

Caution

Be sure to write the dividend and the divisor with the terms in descending order of degree. Use placeholders for any missing terms.

Hint

To determine the first term in the quotient, divide the first term in the dividend by the first term in the divisor.

$\frac{5x^4}{x^2} = 5x^2$ ← 1st term

Caution

Remember to distribute the negative sign when subtracting the product from the dividend.

Online Connection
www.SaxonMathResources.com

Example 1 Using Long Division to Divide Polynomials

Divide $5x^4 - 10x^2 + 3x - 1$ by $x^2 + 2x - 3$.

SOLUTION Determine the first term in the quotient, and then multiply it by the divisor. Next subtract the product from the dividend. Then bring down the next term in the dividend.

$$x^2 + 2x - 3 \overline{)\ \boxed{5x^4} + 0x^3 - 10x^2 + 3x - 1}$$

Quotient: $5x^2$; Divisor: $x^2 + 2x - 3$; Dividend: $5x^4 + 0x^3 - 10x^2 + 3x - 1$

$$-(5x^4 + 10x^3 - 15x^2)$$

$$\boxed{-10x^3} + 5x^2 + 3x$$

Determine the second term in the quotient. Continue the process above until all of the terms in the dividend have been exhausted.

$$5x^2 - 10x + 25$$

$$x^2 + 2x - 3 \overline{)\ 5x^4 + 0x^3 - 10x^2 + 3x - 1}$$

$$-5x^4 - 10x^3 + 15x^2$$

$$\boxed{-10x^3} + 5x^2 + 3x$$

$$-(-10x^3 - 20x^2 + 30x)$$

$$\boxed{25x^2} - 27x - 1$$

$$-(25x^2 + 50x - 75)$$

$$-77x + 74$$

The quotient is $5x^2 - 10x + 25$ and the remainder is $-77x + 74$.

LESSON RESOURCES

Student Edition Practice Workbook 51
Reteaching Master 51
Adaptations Master 51
Challenge and Enrichment Master C51

MATH BACKGROUND

Students have a great deal of experience with long division of numbers. The process that students learned in elementary school is the same for long division with polynomials.

Long division can be used as a tool for simplifying polynomials. For example, to simplify $\frac{x^2 + 9x + 18}{x + 3}$, you could factor the numerator and eliminate the common factor, $x + 3$. The result is $x + 6$.

Or you could use long division instead, dividing $x^2 + 9x + 18$ by $x + 3$. The result is the same, $x + 6$.

As in long division with numbers, long division with polynomials has remainders; the remainder of polynomial division is in fraction form.

364 *Saxon* Algebra 2

When the divisor is a linear binomial of the form $x - k$, you can use synthetic division. **Synthetic division** is an abbreviated form of long division in which only coefficients are written.

Synthetic Division
To divide polynomial $f(x)$ by $x - k$, begin by writing k and the coefficients of $f(x)$ on the first line.

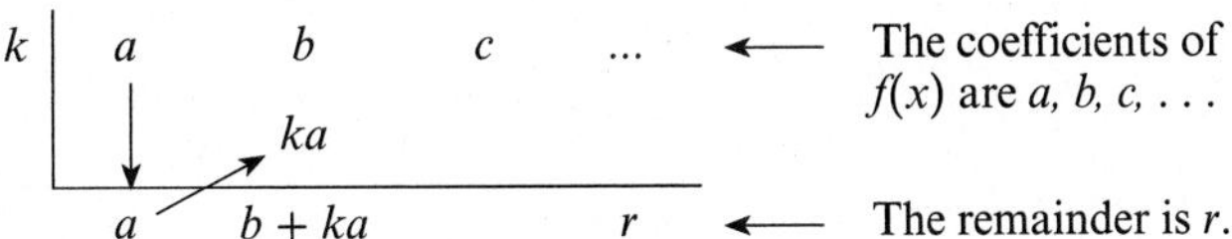

Bring down a; this is the first coefficient of the quotient.

Multiply a by k. Write the result, ka, under b.

Add b and ka. The result, $b + ka$, is the second quotient coefficient.

Continue the pattern. Multiply each new quotient coefficient by k and add the result to the next coefficient of $f(x)$. The result of the last addition is the remainder r.

Example 2 Using Synthetic Division to Divide by a Linear Binomial

Divide $3x^3 - x^2 - 10x + 11$ by $x + 2$.

SOLUTION $x + 2 = x - (-2)$, so $k = -2$.

$$\begin{array}{r|rrrr} -2 & 3 & -1 & -10 & 11 \\ & & -6 & 14 & -8 \\ \hline & 3 & -7 & 4 & 3 \end{array}$$

Dividend coefficients

Remainder

Quotient coefficients

The quotient is $3x^2 - 7x + 4$ and the remainder is 3.

$$\frac{3x^3 - x^2 - 10x + 11}{x + 2} = 3x^2 - 7x + 4 + \frac{3}{x + 2}$$

Hint

Remember to write the remainder over the divisor. The remainder of 3 is written as $\frac{3}{x+2}$.

If both sides of the equation above are multiplied by $x + 2$, the result can be written $3x^3 - x^2 - 10x + 11 = (x + 2)(3x^2 - 7x + 4) + 3$.

If $f(x) = 3x^3 - x^2 - 10x + 11$, then $f(-2)$ can be evaluated as follows:

$$f(x) = (x + 2)(3x^2 - 7x + 4) + 3$$
$$f(-2) = (-2 + 2)(3(-2)^2 - 7(-2) + 4) + 3$$
$$= 0 + 3 = 3$$

Notice that $k = -2$, the remainder r is 3, and $f(k) = f(-2) = 3 = r$.

This demonstrates the Remainder Theorem.

Remainder Theorem
If a polynomial $f(x)$ is divided by $x - k$, the remainder is $r = f(k)$.

Example 2

In this example, students learn a simplified method for dividing polynomials.

Extend the Example

Have students use long division to divide. Encourage them to name the method they like best and describe why.

Additional Example 2

Divide $2x^3 - x^2 - 5x + 2$ by $x - 1$. $2x^2 + x - 4 + \frac{-2}{x - 1}$

INCLUSION

Have students who have impaired vision place an index card to the left of each dividend coefficient. Have them use the card to guide their vertical columns for the results.

Example 3

Have students verify the solution by using substitution to evaluate $f(5)$.

Additional Example 3

Find $f(3)$ for $f(x) = -3x^4 + 4x^3 + 2x^2 + 3x - 3$. $f(3) = -111$

Example 4

Error Alert Students often make arithmetic errors when using synthetic division. Have them use a calculator to check their work.

Additional Example 4

The yearly enrollment at a college for its first four years can be modeled by the function $f(x) = 3x^3 + 4x^2 - 18x + 400$, where x is the year and $f(x)$ is the enrollment. Use $f(x)$ to predict the enrollment for the fifth year. The enrollment for the fifth year will be 785.

By the Remainder Theorem, you can divide $f(x)$ by $x - k$ to find $f(k)$. If synthetic division is used to divide, the process is called **synthetic substitution.**

Hint

To verify the solution in Example 3, evaluate $f(5)$ directly by substituting 5 for x in the polynomial.

Example 3 Using Synthetic Substitution to Evaluate a Polynomial

Find $f(5)$ for $f(x) = -2x^4 + 6x^3 + 15x - 1$.

SOLUTION

Divide $f(x)$ by $x - 5$ to find $f(5)$.

$$\begin{array}{r|rrrrr} 5 & -2 & 6 & 0 & 15 & -1 \\ & & -10 & -20 & -100 & -425 \\ \hline & -2 & -4 & -20 & -85 & -426 \end{array}$$

The remainder is -426, so $f(5) = -426$.

Example 4 Application: Predicting Population

Based on the U.S. census results for the years 1950 through 2000, the population of Nevada can be modeled by the function $P(x) = 12x^3 - 16x^2 + 150x + 154$, where x is the number of decades since 1950 and $P(x)$ is the population in thousands. Use $P(x)$ to predict the population of Nevada in the year 2010.

SOLUTION

Understand Make a table to help understand the problem.

Year	1950	1960	1970	1980	1990	2000	2010
Number of decades since 1950	0	1	2	3	4	5	6

Math Reasoning

Predict Use $P(x)$ to predict population in the year 2050. Do you think $P(x)$ is a good model for predictions that far in the future?

12,054,000
Sample: $P(x)$ is not a good model that far in the future. It is unlikely that the population of Nevada will be 12 billion in 2050.

Plan Use synthetic substitution to evaluate $P(6)$.

Solve

$$\begin{array}{r|rrrr} 6 & 12 & -16 & 150 & 154 \\ & & 72 & 336 & 2916 \\ \hline & 12 & 56 & 486 & 3070 \end{array}$$

Using $P(x)$ to predict, the population of Nevada in the year 2010 will be about 3070 thousand, or 3,070,000.

Check Evaluate $P(6)$ directly.

$P(6) = 12(6)^3 - 16(6)^2 + 150(6) + 154$

$= 3070$, so the answer is verified.

ENGLISH LEARNERS

To help students understand the meaning of **predict,** define predict as a verb: to know or to tell what will happen on the basis of observation or experience.

Discuss synonyms for predict, such as foretell, foreshadow, forecast, and anticipate. Students may be familiar with the word foreshadow and have used it when discussing literature.

Have students identify the basis of the prediction in example 4 as well as what they are trying to predict.

Connect the meaning of predict by pointing out that the function $P(x)$ is used to predict the population of Nevada. Encourage students to predict the 2050 population of Nevada.

366 Saxon Algebra 2

Lesson Practice

a. $2x^2 + 3x - 5 + \frac{-22x + 22}{x^2 - x + 4}$

b. $-2x^2 - 5x - 10 + \frac{-31}{x - 3}$

a. Use long division to divide $2x^4 + x^3 - 5x + 2$ by $x^2 - x + 4$. (Ex 1)

b. Use synthetic division to divide $-2x^3 + x^2 + 5x - 1$ by $x - 3$. (Ex 2)

c. Use synthetic substitution to find $f(-2)$ for $f(x) = x^5 - 2x^3 - x^2 + 10$. (Ex 3) −10

d. The yearly enrollment at a high school for its first six years can be modeled by the function $f(x) = -x^3 + 12x^2 - 8x + 800$, where x is the year and $f(x)$ is the enrollment. Use $f(x)$ to predict the enrollment for the seventh year. (Ex 4) 989

Practice Distributed and Integrated

Use synthetic division to divide.

*1. $2x^4 - x$ by $(x - 2)$ (51) $2x^3 + 4x^2 + 8x + 15 + \frac{30}{x - 2}$

*2. $2 + 4x - 2x^2 + 4x^3$ by $(-3 + x)$ (51) $4x^2 + 10x + 34 + \frac{104}{x - 3}$

Find the distance between the given points.

3. $(-3, 5)$ and $(-1, 2)$ (41) $\sqrt{13}$

4. $(2, 4)$ and $(6, -2)$ (41) $2\sqrt{13}$

5. $(-3, 5)$ and $(4, -2)$ (41) $7\sqrt{2}$

*6. (14) **(Computer Graphics)** A computer programmer wants a shape to rotate and expand on the screen. The programmer multiplies the coordinates of each vertex by the matrix $\begin{bmatrix} 1.5 & 0.71 \\ -0.71 & 1.5 \end{bmatrix}$. The area of the shape expands by an amount that equals the determinant of this matrix. By what amount does that area expand? 2.7541

Add.

7. (37) $\frac{m^2}{x^2a} + \frac{5}{ax} - \frac{m}{a}$ $\quad \frac{m^2 + 5x - mx^2}{ax^2}$

8. (37) $\frac{a}{x^2} - a - \frac{3x}{2a^4}$ $\quad \frac{2a^5 - 2a^5x^2 - 3x^3}{2a^4x^2}$

9. (25) **Multiple Choice** Which data set is represented by the box-and-whisker plot shown? C

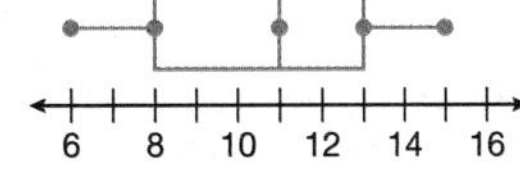

A {15, 8, 10, 13, 11, 12, 6, 13, 7, 15}

B {6, 9, 10, 12, 7, 8, 12, 15, 12, 14}

C {8, 10, 12, 6, 15, 12, 6, 13, 14, 8}

D {6, 11, 12, 7, 12, 8, 14, 15, 9, 12}

Simplify.

10. (44) $\frac{3}{4\sqrt{15}}$ $\quad \frac{\sqrt{15}}{20}$

11. (44) $\frac{5\sqrt{3} - \sqrt{2}}{4\sqrt{3} + 3\sqrt{2}}$ $\quad \frac{66 - 19\sqrt{6}}{30}$

12. (44) $\frac{5}{2\sqrt{7} - \sqrt{5}}$ $\quad \frac{10\sqrt{7} + 5\sqrt{5}}{23}$

Use synthetic substitution to evaluate the polynomials.

*13. (51) Find $f(3)$ for $f(x) = 3x^3 - 7x + 15$ 75

*14. (51) Find $f(6)$ for $f(x) = -3x^5 - 12x^4 + 30x^3 - 16x^2 - x$ −32,982

Lesson Practice

Problem b

Scaffolding Before students do the division, have them name the value for k and the dividend coefficients.

Check for Understanding

The question below helps assess the concepts taught in this lesson.

"Explain how to divide $2x^3 - x^2 - 4x + 1$ by $x + 1$ using synthetic division." $k = -1$. The dividend coefficients are 2, −1, 4, 1. Bring down 2. Multiply. Place −2 under −1 and add. Continue pattern.

3 Practice

Math Conversations

Discussions to strengthen understanding

Problem 2

Guide students by asking the following questions.

"Reverse $-3 + x$. What is the result?" $x - 3$

"$x - 3 = x - k$. What is the value of k? What are the dividend coefficients?" 3; 4, −2, 4, 2

"What do you do first?" Bring down the first dividend coefficient, 4.

"What is the next step?" Multiply 3 by 4 to get 12. Place 12 under the second dividend coefficient, −2.

"Add. What is the result?" 10

"What are the quotient coefficients? What is the remainder?" 4, 10, 34; 104

Problem 20

Encourage students to draw a picture of the problem, using grid paper. Have them convert units to miles. Review the Pythagorean Theorem if necessary.

*15. (48) **Electronics** If two resistors in an electrical circuit have resistances R_1 and R_2 (both in ohms), then the total resistance R_t (in ohms) is given by $R_t = \frac{1}{\frac{1}{R_1} + \frac{1}{R_2}}$.

a. Simplify the complex fraction. $R_t = \frac{R_1R_2}{R_1 + R_2}$

b. If there are two resistors in an electrical circuit with resistances 3 ohms and 6 ohms, what is the total resistance of the circuit? 2 ohms

16. (39) **Verify** Determine if the graph is correct by choosing points in the shaded and unshaded regions and testing them. shaded (3, 0); unshaded (−3, 0); The shading is correct but the line should be dotted because $y - x \neq 2$.

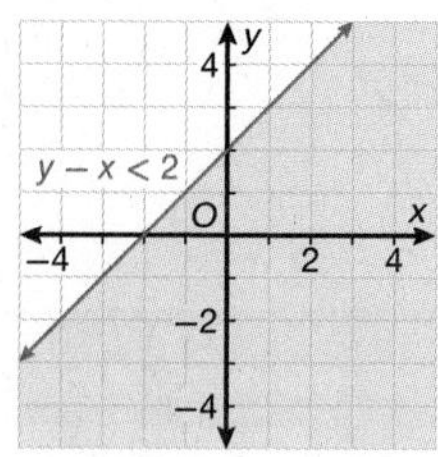

17. (37) **Generalize** Suppose that $f(x)$ is a polynomial of degree m and $g(x)$ is a polynomial of degree n. What must be true for rational expression $\frac{f(x)}{g(x)}$ to be of degree $m - 2$ in the numerator and $n - 2$ in the denominator? Both $f(x)$ and $g(x)$ must have a common factor of degree 2.

18. (11) **Error Analysis** Explain the error in the student's work.

$(3x^4 - 2x^3 + 1) - (x^4 - x^3 + 5)$

$= 3x^4 - 2x^3 + 1 - x^4 - x^3 + 5$

$= 2x^4 - 3x^3 + 6$

The student subtracted only the first term of $x^4 - x^3 + 5$; she added the other terms.

*19. (45) **Graphing Calculator** The table shows the elevation of where each record cold temperature reading took place. Use a graphing calculator to find the value of r and the equation for the line of best fit. Use it to predict the record cold temperature for an elevation of 5000 feet. $r \approx -0.79$, $y \approx -0.00434x - 21.6$, −43.3°F

	Arizona	Idaho	Wyoming	Rhode Island	Alabama	Tennessee	Virginia	Mississippi
Elev. (ft)	8180	6285	6650	425	760	2471	3870	420
Temp. (°F)	−40	−60	−66	−25	−27	−32	−30	−19

20. (41) **Mountain Bikers** If the origin represents a parking lot, and one mountain biker bikes 2 units due north and 9 units due west, while a second mountain biker bikes 8 units due north and 5 units due east, how much farther from the parking lot is the second mountain biker than the first? Write the answer as a decimal to the nearest tenth of a mile, given that each unit represents 3 miles. 0.6 miles

21. (27) **Estimate** Estimate the values of the x- and y-intercepts. $x \approx -4.5$ and 6.5, $y \approx -4.9$

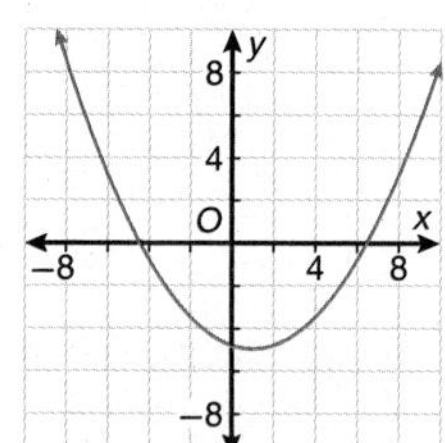

ALTERNATE METHOD FOR EXAMPLE 15

In part b, some students may use the given equation rather than the simplified version from part a.

Substitute the values for R_1 and R_2 into the original equation to find R_t.

$$R_t = \frac{1}{\frac{1}{3} + \frac{1}{6}}$$

$$R_t = \frac{1}{\frac{2}{6} + \frac{1}{6}}$$

$$R_t = \frac{1}{\frac{1}{2}} = 2 \text{ ohms}$$

22. **Multiple Choice** What is the value of the cotangent of $\angle A$ if the tangent of
(46) $\angle A$ is 0.75? D

A 0.6 B 0.75 C 1.25 D $1.\overline{3}$

23. **Multi-Step** Al's grandfather deposited the
(11) amounts shown in Bank A as gifts on Al's birthday during the years 2002 through 2005. His aunt deposited the amounts shown in Bank B. The value of the accounts on 7/2/06 is represented by these polynomials, where $x = 1 + r$, and r is the interest rate for both accounts:

	Bank A	Bank B
7/2/02	\$500	\$1000
7/2/03	\$1000	\$200
7/2/04	\$600	\$200
7/2/05	\$500	\$200

Bank A $500x^4 + 1000x^3 + 600x^2 + 500x$

Bank B $1000x^4 + 200x^3 + 200x^2 + 200x$

a. Write the polynomial that represents the total value of both accounts on 7/2/06. $1500x^4 + 1200x^3 + 800x^2 + 700x$

b. What is the total value of both accounts on 7/2/06 if the interest rate is 5%? \$4829.41

24. **Verify** Show that the equation of the line parallel to $y = mx + b$ through (x_1, y_1) is
(36) $y = mx + (y_1 - mx_1)$. $m = \frac{y - y_1}{x - x_1}$; $m(x - x_1) = y - y_1$; $y = mx + y_1 - mx_1$

25. **Write** Explain how to graph $y = \frac{3}{4}x + 9$ using a table. Be sure to show each step.
(13) See Additional Answers.

26. **Probability** Two cards are drawn at random from a deck of 52 cards, without
(42) replacement. What is the probability that both cards drawn are aces? $\frac{1}{221}$

27. **Error Analysis** The factored form of $x^2 + 5x + 6$ is given as $(x - 1)(x + 6)$. Find
(23) and explain the error and give the correct factorization. Although $6 + (-1) = 5$, $6 \times (-1) \neq 6$. $(x + 2)(x + 3)$

*28. **Geometry** The sides of a cube have length s. If each dimension of the cube is
(49) increased by 0.5, write a binomial expression for the volume of the cube. Expand the binomial. $(s + 0.5)^3$; $s^3 + 1.5s^2 + 0.75s + 0.125$

29. **Employment** A student earns \$8 per hour working for the recreation department
(43) and \$12 per hour at a candy store. She is not allowed to work more than 16 hours in a week, and her goal is to earn at least \$150 in a week. Let x represent a number of hours working for the recreation department and y represent a number of hours working at the candy store.

a. Write and graph a system of linear inequalities that represents the situation. See Additional Answers.

b. Describe the portion of the solution set that contains meaningful solutions for this situation. See Additional Answers.

c. Determine the vertices of the polygon you described in part **b.** Describe what each vertex represents. See Additional Answers.

*30. **Generalize** Write the expansion of $(a + b)^5$. Make a generalization about terms that
(49) have the same coefficient in a binomial expansion of the form $(a + b)^n$.
See Additional Answers.

Problem 23

Error Alert

Students might forget to change 5% to a decimal. Present a simple interest problem to remind students that they need to change the percent to a decimal.

Problem 25

Extend the Problem

Have students explain how to graph $y = \frac{3}{4}x + 9$ using the x- and y-intercepts. They should show each step.

Substitute 0 for x to find y.

$y = \frac{3}{4} \cdot 0 + 9 = 9$

Substitute 0 for y to find x.

$0 = \frac{3}{4}x + 9$

$-9 = \frac{3}{4}x$

$-12 = x$

The graph of $y = \frac{3}{4}x + 9$ passes through points (0, 9) and (−12, 0).

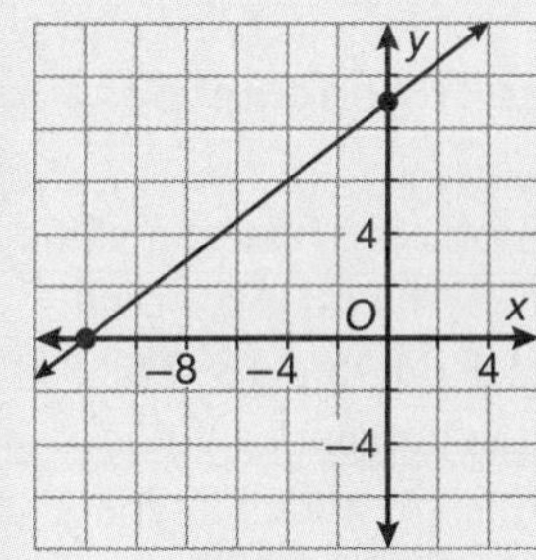

CHALLENGE

Use long division to divide $x^2 - \frac{1}{6}x - \frac{1}{3}$ by $x + \frac{1}{2}$. Check your answer, using synthetic division. $x - \frac{2}{3}$

LOOKING FORWARD

Using long division and synthetic division prepares students for

- **Lesson 61** Understanding Advanced Factoring
- **Lesson 66** Solving Polynomial Equations

LAB 9

Materials

graphing calculator

Discuss

In this lab, students will calculate trigonometric function values in degrees and radians.

TEACHER TIP

Discuss the meaning of each angle measurement. A degree is part of the sexagesimal system in which a regular hexagon is inscribed in a circle and divided into six equilateral triangles. Each central angle measures 60°. A radian is a unit of measurement calculated by dividing the arc length of a central angle by the radius of the circle. $2\pi = 360°$ or $1° \approx .01745$

Using the Trigonometric Keys

If a trigonometric function value is undefined, the calculator will display ERR:DOMAIN. For example the tangent of 90° is undefined, so if students type TAN 9 0) in degree mode, they will receive the error message.

LAB 9

Using the Trigonometry Keys and Adjusting to a Trigonometric Window

Graphing Calculator Lab (*Use with Lessons 52, 67, 82, 86, 90, and 103*)

A graphing calculator can be used to calculate and graph trigonometric functions in both degrees and radians.

Using the Trigonometric Keys

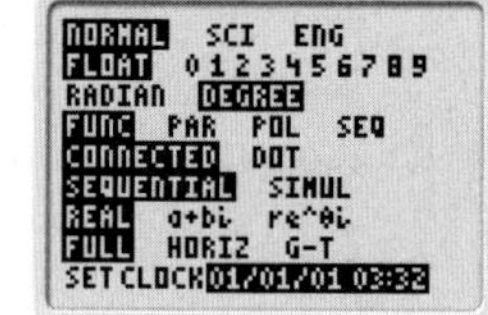

1. Press MODE, and press the down arrow key twice ▼ ▼, and then press the right arrow key ▶ to highlight **[DEGREE]** and press ENTER. The calculator will now be in degree mode. Any trigonometric functions calculated will interpret input in terms of degrees.

2. Press SIN 4 5) ENTER, to calculate sin(45°). Because the calculator is in degree mode, it will automatically assume that the input 45 is the same as 45°.

3. Press MODE ▼ ▼ ENTER, to change the mode back to **[RADIAN]** mode.

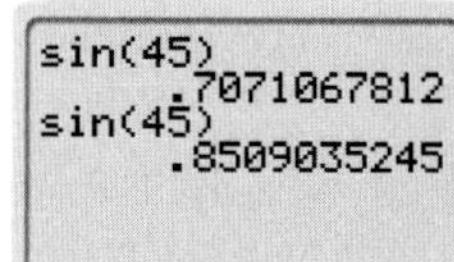

4. While the calculator is in radian mode, it will assume the input of a trigonometric function is in radians. Press SIN 4 5) again. This time the calculator will assume the input 45 is the same as 45 radians. Press ENTER. The value of sin(45) will display as two different values, because the first is calculated for 45° and the second is calculated for 45 radians.

5. The inverse trigonometric functions are also affected by the mode. The output of an inverse trigonometric function is always the measure of an angle. Therefore, when the calculator is in radian mode, the output (measure of the angle) will be in radians. Similarly, the output will be in degrees when the calculator is in degree mode.

Adjusting to a Trigonometric Window

1. Make sure the calculator is in radian and function mode, by pressing MODE and verifying that **[RADIAN]** and **[FUNC]** are highlighted.

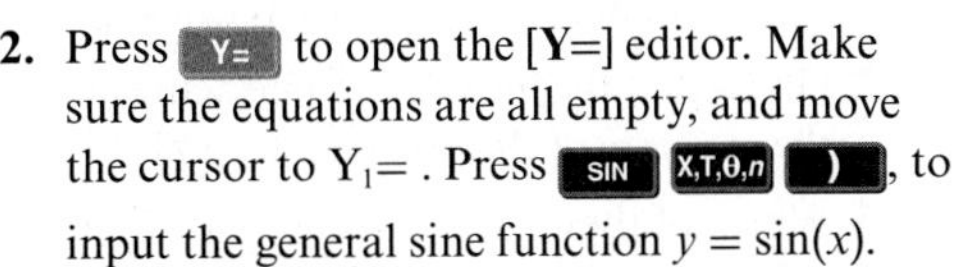

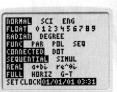

2. Press Y= to open the [Y=] editor. Make sure the equations are all empty, and move the cursor to $Y_1=$. Press SIN X,T,θ,n) , to input the general sine function $y = \sin(x)$.

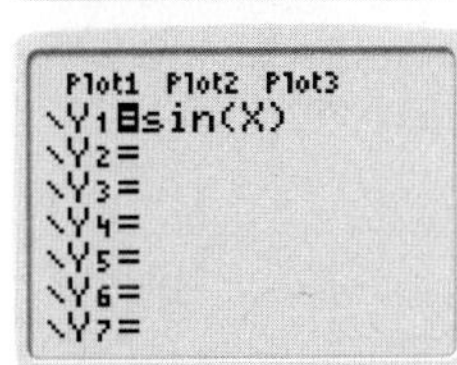

Graphing Calculator Tip

For help in adjusting the viewing window, see graphing calculator lab 4.

3. Press WINDOW to open the viewing window variables. To graph the sine function in radian mode, the window variables need to be changed accordingly.

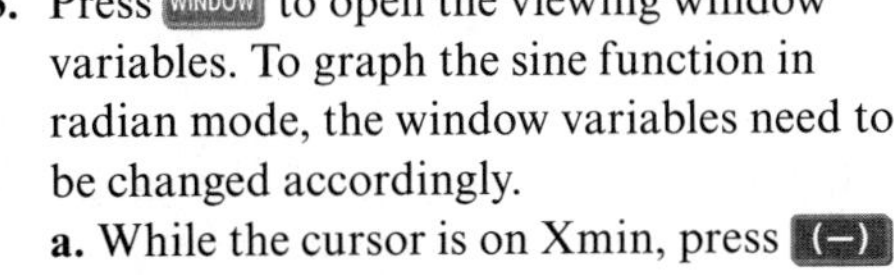

   a. While the cursor is on Xmin, press (–) 2 2nd ^ to change the minimum x-value to -2π.

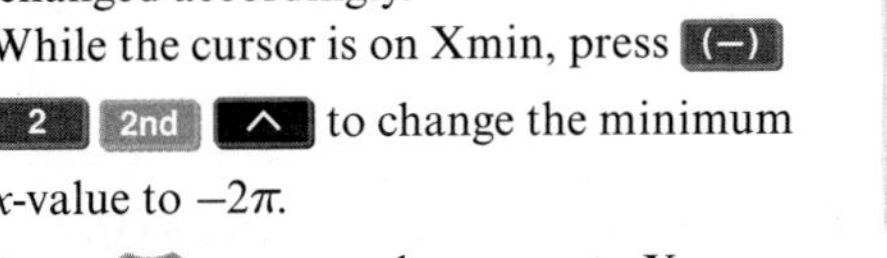

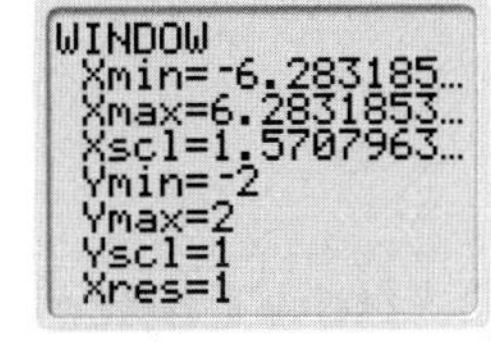

   b. Press ▼ to move the cursor to Xmax. Press 2 2nd ^ to change the maximum x-value to 2π.
   c. Press ▼ to move the cursor to Xscl. Press 2nd ^ ÷ 2 to change the x-scale to $\frac{\pi}{2}$.
   d. Press ▼ to move the cursor to Ymin and press (–) 2.

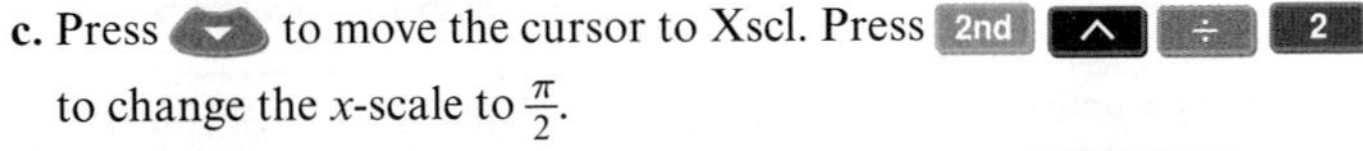

   e. Press ▼ to move the cursor to Ymax and press 2.
   f. Press ▼ to move the cursor to Yscl and press 1.
   g. Press ▼ to move the cursor to Xres and press 1.

4. Press GRAPH. Two periods of the sine function are displayed in radian mode.

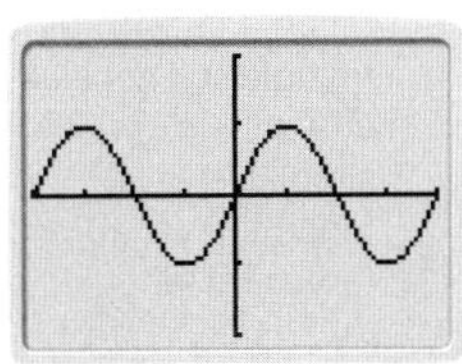

Lab Practice

a. Calculate $\cos(\pi)$ in radian mode. –1

b. Calculate $\cos(\pi)$ in degree mode. 0.998

c. Calculate $\cos(0)$ in degree and radian mode. Both are 1.

d. Graph $y = \cos(x)$, with the same viewing window as above.

Problem 1

Radian mode must always be used to graph trigonometric functions to obtain an accurate graph.

Problem 3

To graph one period of the sine function, change the minimum x-value to 0.

The values for the domain consist of radian values. The range values are real numbers and depend upon the function that is being graphed.

TEACHER TIP

Option 7 in the zoom window or ZTrig will create an acceptable window for a trigonometric function. However, students should be able to choose and type window values according to the function they are graphing.

Extend the Example

Graph $y = \tan(x)$ using the same viewing window.

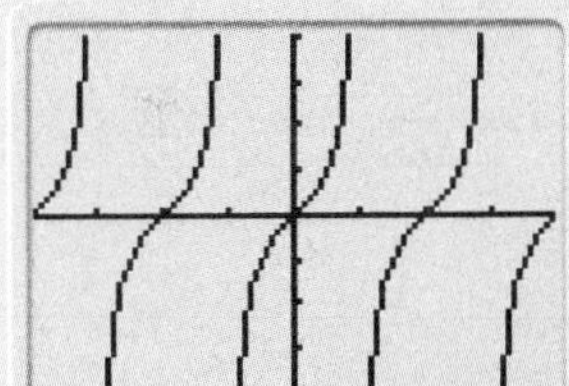

LESSON 52

1 Warm Up

Use the Warm Up to review right triangles.

2 New Concepts

In this lesson, students find side lengths of 30°-60°-90° triangles and 45°-45°-90° triangles using their properties.

Review the meaning of rationalize. Students should understand that a radical expression is not in simplest form if it contains radicals in the denominator.

Example 1

Students find the unknown side lengths of 45°-45°-90° triangles.

Additional Example 1

Find the length of x using the properties of a 45°-45°-90° triangle.

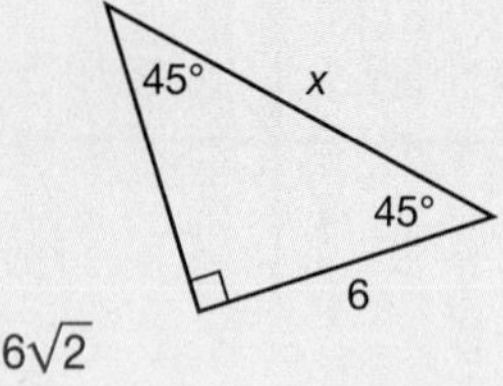

$6\sqrt{2}$

LESSON RESOURCES

Student Edition Practice Workbook 52
Reteaching Master 52
Adaptations Master 52
Challenge and Enrichment Master C52

LESSON 52 Using Two Special Right Triangles

Warm Up

1. **Vocabulary** In a right triangle, the ratio of the length of the opposite leg to the length of the adjacent leg is called the ___tangent___ of the angle. (46)

2. Given that the measure of one acute angle of a right triangle is 24°, what is the measure of the other acute angle? 66° (SB)

3. Which of these triangles is a right triangle? A (SB)

A 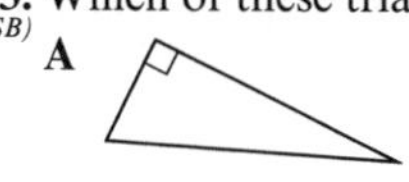 B 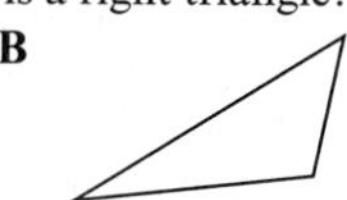 C 

4. Find the unknown length for a right triangle with one leg that is 12 cm and a hypotenuse that is 13 cm. 5 cm (41)

New Concepts

Some right triangles are used so frequently that it is helpful to remember some of their particular properties. These triangles, called **special right triangles,** are the 30°-60°-90° triangle and the 45°-45°-90° triangle. The name of each triangle gives the measures of its angles.

Math Reasoning

Verify Use the Pythagorean Theorem to show that the length of the hypotenuse of a 45°-45°-90° triangle is the length of one of the legs times $\sqrt{2}$.

Since a 45°-45°-90° triangle is isosceles, $a^2 + a^2 = c^2$, which simplifies to $2a^2 = c^2$. Since the variables represent length, $a\sqrt{2} = c$.

Properties of a 45°-45°-90° Triangle: Side Lengths

In a 45°-45°-90° right triangle, both legs are congruent and the length of the hypotenuse is the length of a leg multiplied by $\sqrt{2}$.

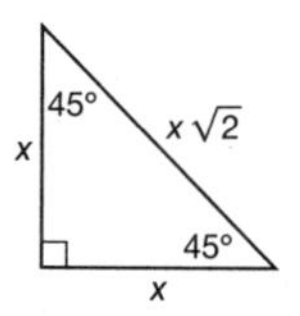

A triangle with sides 1-1-$\sqrt{2}$ is a 45°-45°-90° reference triangle. The properties of the 45°-45°-90° triangle can be used to find missing measures of a triangle if the length of one leg is known.

Example 1 Finding the Side Lengths in a 45°-45°-90° Triangle

Find the length of a when c is $5\sqrt{2}$ centimeters, using the properties of a 45°-45°-90° triangle.

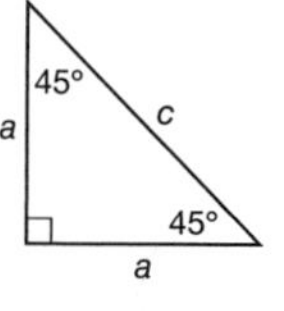

SOLUTION

Since the length of the hypotenuse of a 45°-45°-90° triangle is $\sqrt{2}$ times the length of a its leg, $a = \frac{5\sqrt{2}}{\sqrt{2}}$ or 5 centimeters.

Check The hypotenuse of the given triangle is $5\sqrt{2}$ cm. Use the reference triangle and a graphing calculator to verify the answer.

$$(\sin 45°)(5\sqrt{2}) = 3$$

Online Connection
www.SaxonMathResources.com

MATH BACKGROUND

Students have learned ways other than using trigonometric functions for determining the lengths of sides of right triangles. For example, if the legs of a right triangle have lengths a and b, and the hypotenuse has length c. According to the Pythagorean theorem, $a^2 + b^2 = c^2$.

If the vertices of the triangle are identified by ordered pairs on a coordinate grid, the distance formula can be used to find an unknown side length: $d = \sqrt{(x_2 - x_1)^2 + (y_2 - y_1)^2}$.

In this lesson, trigonometric properties of special right triangles are used to determine side lengths.

Math Reasoning

Verify Use the diagram and the Pythagorean Theorem to show that for a 30°-60°-90° triangle, the length of b is equal to a times $\sqrt{3}$.

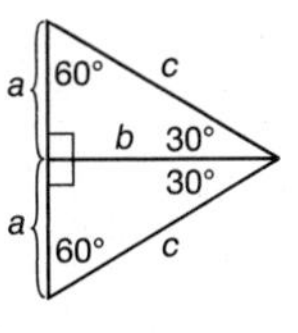

$a^2 + b^2 = c^2$
$a^2 + b^2 = (2a)^2$
$b^2 = 3a^2$
$b^2 = a\sqrt{3}$

Properties of 30°-60°-90° Triangles

In a 30°-60°-90° triangle, the length of the hypotenuse is twice the length of the shorter leg, and the length of the longer leg is the length of the shorter leg times $\sqrt{3}$.

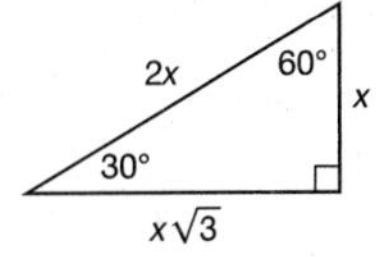

A triangle with sides 1-2-$\sqrt{3}$ is a 30°-60°-90° reference triangle. The properties of the 30°-60°-90° triangle can be used to find missing measures of a triangle if the length of one leg is known.

Example 2 Finding Side Lengths in a 30°-60°-90° Triangle

Find b when c is $\sqrt{6}$ centimeters, using the properties of a 30°-60°-90° triangle.

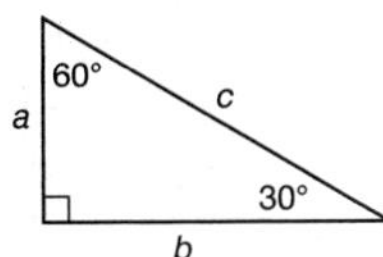

SOLUTION

Since the length of the hypotenuse of a 30°-60°-90° triangle is 2 times the length of the shorter leg, $a = \frac{\sqrt{6}}{2}$. Since the length of the longer leg is $\sqrt{3}$ times the length of the shorter leg, $b = \frac{\sqrt{6}\sqrt{3}}{2} = \frac{3\sqrt{2}}{2}$ or approximately 2.12 centimeters.

Math Reasoning

Verify Use the reference triangle and a graphing calculator to verify the answer.

Example 3 Application: Distance

A 10-foot ladder leaning against a building makes a 45° angle with the ground. How far up the building does the ladder reach?

SOLUTION

Draw a sketch.

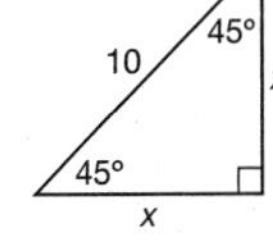

Since the length of the hypotenuse of a 45°-45°-90° is $\sqrt{2}$ times the length of a leg, then $10 = x\sqrt{2}$. Solve for x.

$$10 = x\sqrt{2}$$

$$\frac{10}{\sqrt{2}} = x$$

$$5\sqrt{2} = x$$

The ladder extends $5\sqrt{2}$, or about 7 feet up the side of the building.

INCLUSION

Have students copy the 30°-60°-90° triangle as shown. Explain to them how to use the arrows to find the length of a side. For example, the guiding arrow shows that the length of the longer leg is found by multiplying the shorter leg by the $\sqrt{3}$. To find the length of the shorter leg, use the inverse of multiplication by dividing the longer leg by the $\sqrt{3}$.

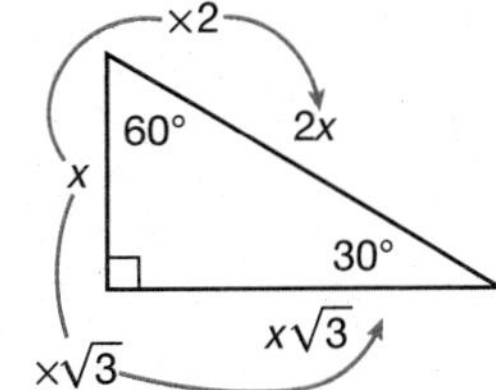

Example 2

Students find the length of an unknown side of a 30°-60°-90° triangle.

Extend the Example

Use the properties to find the values for sine of 30° and the sine of 60°. $\sin 30° = \frac{1}{2}$; $\sin 60° = \frac{\sqrt{3}}{2}$

Error Alert

Students may make the mistake of multiplying the length of the shorter leg by $\sqrt{2}$ to find the length of the longer leg. Help them remember, by explaining that the number $\sqrt{3}$ and the name 30°-60°-90° triangle both have the number 3 written in them.

Additional Example 2

Find the length of s using the properties of a 30°-60°-90° triangle.

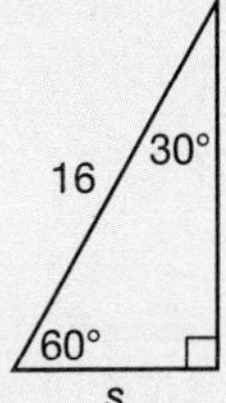

$s = 8$

Example 3

Students use the properties of special right triangles to solve a real life application.

Additional Example 3

A 25-foot ladder leaning against a building makes a 60° angle with the ground. About how far up the building does the ladder reach? Round to the nearest foot.
approximately 22 feet

Lesson Practice

Problem b

Error Alert Students may multiply by $\sqrt{2}$ instead of dividing by $\sqrt{2}$.

Problem c

Scaffolding Students must be sure to use corresponding sides of the triangles when using the scale factor to solve the problem.

Check for Understanding

The questions below help assess the concepts taught in this lesson.

1. **"Why is it useful to learn about special right triangles?"** You can solve problems faster
2. **What is the relationship between the lengths of the hypotenuse and the shorter side of any 30°-60°-90° triangle?"** hypotenuse = 2 × (short side)

3 Practice

Math Conversations

Discussions to strengthen understanding

Problem 1

Ask, **"What is true about the slopes of parallel lines?"** The slopes of parallel lines are equal.

Problem 6

Guide the students by asking them the following questions.

"What step should you take in the problem before adding or subtracting the terms?" Find a common denominator.

"How can you find a common denominator when c has no denominator?" Write it as $\frac{c}{1}$.

Lesson Practice

a. (Ex 1) Find the length of x.

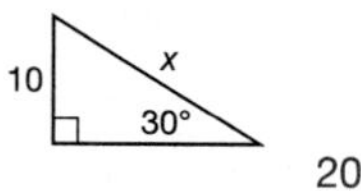

20

b. (Ex 2) Find the length of p. 5

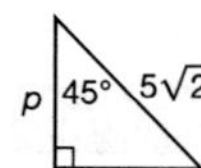

c. (Ex 3) The diagram shows a boy flying a kite. The kite forms a 45° angle as shown. Find the height of the kite from the ground. (Hint: The triangle is not touching the ground. Remember to add the distance between the triangle base and the ground to the height of the kite.) 20.4 feet

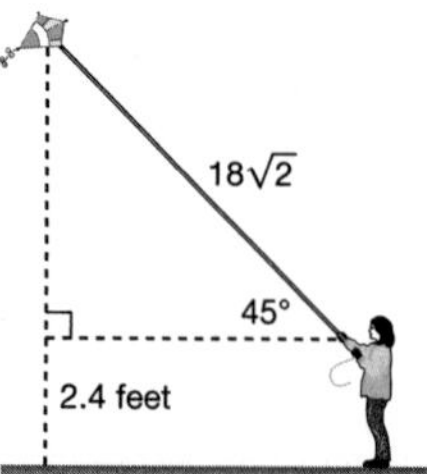

Practice Distributed and Integrated

1. (36) Find the equation of the line parallel to the line $3y - x = 3$, and passing through the point $(2, -1)$. $y = \frac{1}{3}x - \frac{5}{3}$

Use elimination to solve.

2. (24) $\begin{aligned} 8y - 3x &= 22 \\ 2y + 4x &= 34 \end{aligned}$ (6, 5)

3. (24) $\begin{aligned} 3x + y &= 11 \\ 3x - 2y &= 2 \end{aligned}$ $\left(\frac{8}{3}, 3\right)$

4. (24) $\begin{aligned} 3x + 4y &= 20 \\ -4x + 3y &= 15 \end{aligned}$ (0, 5)

Add.

5. (37) $2 + \frac{a}{2x^2}$ $\frac{4x^2 + a}{2x^2}$

6. (37) $\frac{4}{cx} + c - \frac{3}{4c^2x}$ $\frac{16c + 4c^3x - 3}{4c^2x}$

Use the properties of special right triangles to find x and y.

***7.** (52) $x = 4; y = 4\sqrt{2}$

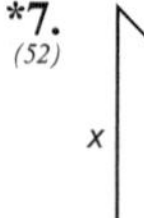

***8.** (52) $x = \sqrt{3}; y = \sqrt{6}$

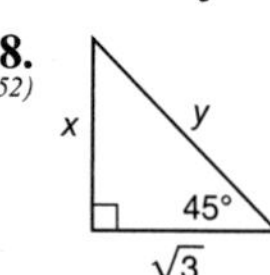

*9. Divide $(4x^4 + 21x^3 + 10x^2 + 25x) \div (x^2 + 5x)$ using polynomial long division. $4x^2 + x + 5$
(51)

10. **Aviation** The radical expression $3.56\sqrt{A}$ can be used to approximate the distance in kilometers to the horizon from an altitude of A meters. What is the approximate distance to the horizon observed by a pilot flying a Boeing 747 at an altitude of 13,225 meters? about 409 km
(40)

11. What are all the values of x for which the multiplication expression $\frac{x+5}{x+2} \cdot \frac{x}{x^3 + 2x^2 + x}$ is undefined? −2, 0, and −1
(31)

*12. **Write** Explain why all 45°-45°-90° triangles are similar.
(52)

12. The trigonometric ratios associated with the inner angles measuring 45° are the same regardless of the lengths of the sides of the triangles. Since the ratios are the same and the angles are congruent, the corresponding sides of the triangles are proportional.

13. **Physics** Through the process of annealing, metals are made more flexible, allowing a piece of metal to be flattened without breaking. Suppose a rectangular piece of metal with square ends of dimension $(x - 15)$ goes through the annealing process and is flattened into a thin sheet. What is the ratio of the new surface area to the original? $\frac{3x^2 + 20x - 1475}{3x^2 - 60x + 225}$
(38)

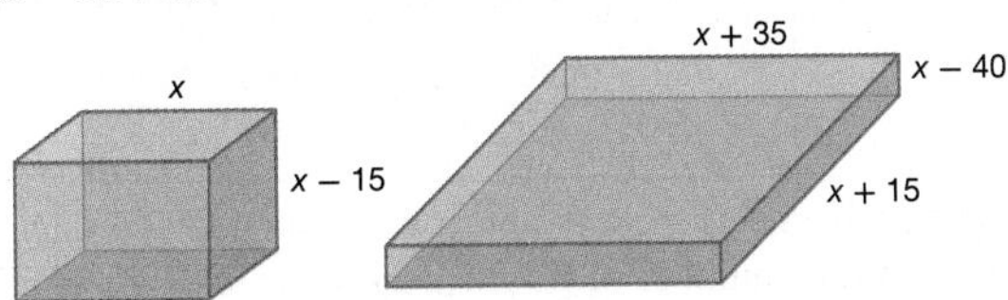

14. **Multiple Choice** A ________ function is a function with a connected graph. B
(22)
A discrete B continuous C discontinuous D relation

*15. **Multi-Step**
(51)
a. Divide the polynomial $x^5 + 4x^4 - 13x^3 - 52x^2 + 36x + 144$ by $x^2 - x - 6$ using long division. Quotient: $x^3 + 5x^2 - 2x - 24$

b. Divide the quotient of part **a** by $(x + 5)$ to find its quotient and remainder using synthetic division. Quotient: $x^2 - 2$; Remainder: −14

16. **Monuments** A painter at the top of one of the two towers at the Tower Bridge in London throws a length of rope down from his position 63 meters above the ground to another painter who secures the rope to the ground so that it makes a 68° angle with the ground. To the nearest meter, what is the length of the rope from the ground to the top of the tower? 68 meters
(46)

17. **Error Analysis** Find and explain the error in solving the system. Correct the error and solve:
(29)

$$\begin{aligned} -9x + 4y + 5z &= -16 \\ x - 4y - 6z &= 25 \\ -x + y - z &= -3 \end{aligned}$$

In step 2 the variable y should have been canceled as it was in step 1: (−1, −5, −1).

Step 1:

$$\begin{aligned} -9x + 4y + 5z &= -16 \\ + \; x - 4y - 6z &= 25 \\ \hline -8x \quad\quad - z &= 9 \end{aligned}$$

Step 2:

$$\begin{aligned} x - 4y - 6z &= 25 \\ + \; -x + y - z &= -3 \\ \hline -3y - 7z &= 22 \end{aligned}$$

*18. **Estimate** The hypotenuse of a 30°-60°-90° triangle is 20 inches. Estimate the length of the side opposite the 60° angle. Give your answer to the nearest whole inch. 17 inches
(52)

Problem 11

Error Alert

Students may factor an x in the denominator and then incorrectly cancel it with the x in the numerator before determining the undefined values. Remind them that values for which the expression is undefined must be determined before they simplify.

Problem 14

Extend the Problem

After students find the correct answer to the problem, ask, **"What is a discrete function?"** A discrete function is a function which is defined only for a set of numbers that can be listed.

ENGLISH LEARNERS

For problem 13, explain the meaning of the word **annealing.** Say:

"Annealing means to heat and then cool a material usually in order to make it tougher and less likely to break."

Discuss with students that glass and metals such as copper, steel, and brass go through the annealing process.

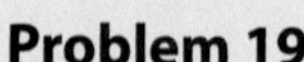

Problem 19

Guide the students by asking them the following questions.

"What is the general form for the equation of a parabola?" $y = a(x - h)^2 + k$

Extend the Example

"How does the value of $|a|$ affect the graph's width?" If $|a|$ increases, the parabola becomes narrower. If $|a|$ decreases, the parabola becomes wider.

"How does the value of a affect the direction of the graph's opening?" If a is positive, the opening is upward. If a is negative, the opening is downward.

"How does the value of h affect the graph?" A decrease in h means the vertex shifts to the left. An increase in h means the vertex shifts to the right.

"How does the value of k affect the graph?" A decrease in k means the vertex shifts down. An increase in k means the vertex shifts up.

19. (27) **Multiple Choice** What is the value of h in the vertex form of $f(x) = x^2 - 3$? **B**
A -3 B 0 C 1 D 3

20. (19) **Model** Model FOIL for the multiplication of any two binomials in the form $(a + b)(a - b)$.

21. (30) **Predict** Describe how the graph $y = 0.25(x + 6)^2$ differs from the graph of the parent function. It is wider and is shifted 6 units to the left.

22. (43) **Geometry** Find the area of the shape formed by the linear inequalities $x \geq 1, y \geq 1, y \leq 5, y \leq -2x + 9$. 8 square units

23. (15) **Data Analysis** One day Irma hikes up a mountain. The table shows times of day and her distances from the base of the mountain. She camps overnight, and then hikes down the same path the next day.

23a. first day: $d = t$; second day: $d = 8 - 1.125t$

Time of Day	8 am	10 am	12 pm	2 pm	4 pm
Distances 1st day (mi)	0	2	4	6	8
Distances 2nd day (mi)	8	5.75	3.5	1.25	0

a. Write equations that relate her distances from the bottom to the times of day. Represent the distance by d and the number of hours after 8 a.m. by t.

b. Graph those equations.

c. Is there a point on the path at which Irma arrives at the same time of day on both days? Explain. Yes, at about 3.76 hours and 3.76 miles

24. (49) **Error Analysis** A student expanded the binomial $(m - 2)^3$ as shown. Explain the error.

$$(m - 2)^3 = {}_3C_0m^32^0 + {}_3C_1m^22^1 + {}_3C_2m^12^2 + {}_3C_3m^02^3$$
$$= m^3 + 3m^2(2) + 3m(2)^2 + (2)^3$$
$$= m^3 + 6m^2 + 12m + 8$$

The student did not rewrite $(m - 2)^3$ as $(m + -2)^3$.

25. (23) **Architecture** The volume of a building is $5x^2 + 50x - 280$ yd³. If the height of the building is 5 yd, find the length and width of the building. $x + 14$ yd and $x - 4$ yd

***26.** (50) **Multi-Step** Consider the function $y = 3x + 2$.

a. Find an equation for its inverse. $y = \frac{x - 2}{3}$

b. Graph the function and its inverse on the same grid.

c. How are the slopes of the function and its inverse related?

26b.

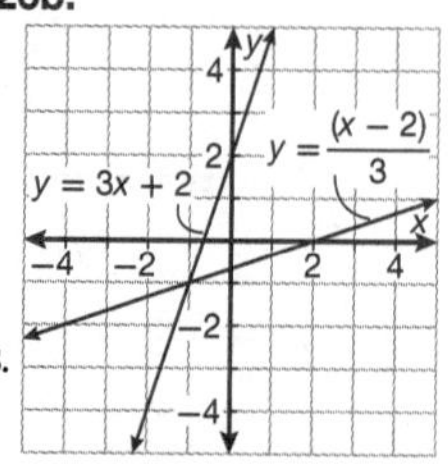

26c. The slopes are reciprocal to each other. Each line is the reflection of the other across the line $y = x$.

27. (42) **Playing Cards** A deck of cards has 4 suits of 13 cards each for a total of 52 cards.

a. How many ways can one 5-card hand be dealt? $C(52, 5) = 2{,}598{,}960$

b. How many ways can one 5-card hand be dealt that includes 2 hearts and 3 cards from the other suits? $13 \times 12 \times C(39, 3) = 1{,}425{,}684$

CHALLENGE

Suppose the triangle shown has a height h of 32 cm. Use trigonometric ratios to find the side length s. Round the answer to the nearest centimeter.

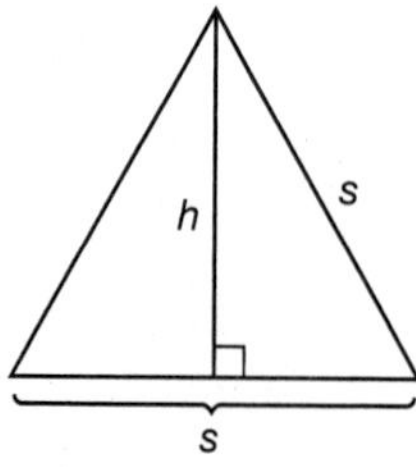

$s = 37$ cm

376 Saxon Algebra 2

28. **Model** The table shows the measurements in inches of various shipping boxes. Draw a box-and-whisker plot to represent the lengths of all edges of the boxes. Consider that a box has 12 edges.
(25)

Box	Length	Width	Height
1	11.875	3.375	13.625
2	11	8.5	5.5
3	7.5	5.125	14.375

29. **(Physics)** A satellite has an orbital acceleration of $\frac{v^2}{r}$, where v is the speed of the satellite and r is the distance from the satellite to the Earth's center. Find the difference in acceleration between satellite 1 and satellite 2. Assume that each is traveling at the same speed, v. $-\frac{v^2}{2r}$
(37)

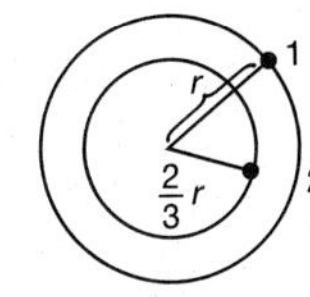

***30.** **Graphing Calculator** The table shows the average number of tropical storms per year compared to the average number of hurricanes per year. Use a graphing calculator to find the value of r and the equation for the line of best fit. Use it to predict the average number of hurricanes per year when there was an average of 9.5 tropical storms. $r \approx 0.99$, $y \approx 0.4276x + 1.49$, 5.6 hurricanes per year
(45)

Tropical Storms	8.7	10.6	10.7	11.1	11.4	12.6	14.5
Hurricanes	5.3	6.1	6	6.2	6.3	6.8	7.8

28.

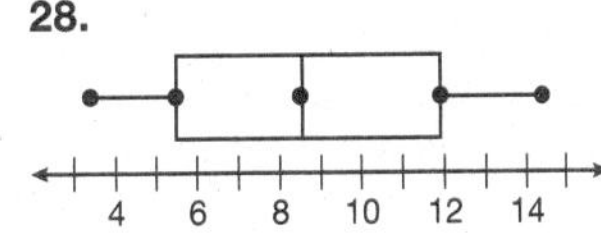

20. First terms $a \cdot a = a^2$

Outer terms $a \cdot -b = -ab$

Inner terms $b \cdot a = ab$

Last terms $b \cdot -b = -b^2$

Add the terms: $a^2 - ab + ab - b^2$

The outer and inner terms in this case will always be opposites and cancel out, leaving you with the product: $a^2 - b^2$.

23b.

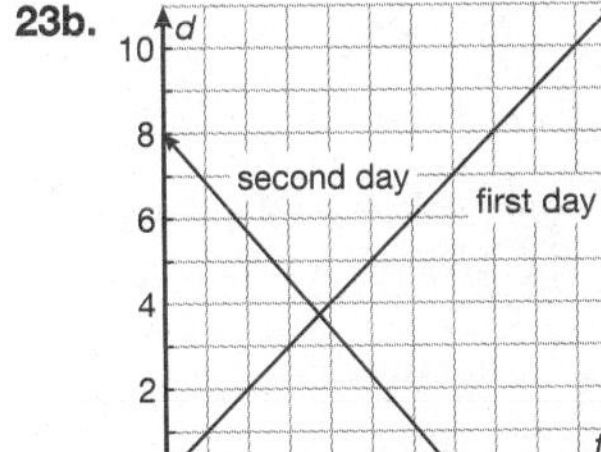

Problem 26

Guide the students by asking them the following questions.

"What is the next step for finding the inverse function, after interchanging the variables?" Solve for y.

"How can a graphing the functions verify that the functions are inverses of each other?" the graphs will be a reflection of each other over the line $y = x$

LOOKING FORWARD

Using two special right triangles prepares students for

- **Lesson 63** Understanding the Unit Circle and Radian Measures
- **Lesson 67** Finding Inverse Trigonometric Functions
- **Lesson 71** Using the Law of Sines
- **Lesson 77** Using the Law of Cosines
- **Lesson 112** Using Sum and Difference Identities
- **Lesson 115** Finding Double Angle and Half Angle Identities

LESSON

53

1 Warm Up

Remind students to distribute and then simplify in question 2.

2 New Concepts

In this lesson students learn to perform compositions of functions.

Example 1

This example demonstrates how to find a composite function and find the domain and range of the composite function.

Additional Example 1

Let $f(x) = 2x + 3$ and $g(x) = 3x$.

a. Find the composite function $f(g(x))$.
$f(3x) = 6x + 3$

b. Find the domain and range of the composite function from part **a**.
The domain and range of the composite function is all real numbers.

LESSON

53 Performing Compositions of Functions

Warm Up

1. **Vocabulary** A rule for using one number (an input) to calculate another number (an output) is called a __function__.
(4)

2. Write as a single simplified polynomial: $x(3x - 4) - 2(3x - 4)$. $3x^2 - 10x + 8$
(4)

3. Evaluate the function $f(x) = x^2 - 3x$ at $x = -1$. 4
(4)

4. Let $f(x) = x^2 - 5$. What are the domain and range of this function?
(4)

4. Domain: $(-\infty, \infty)$; Range: $(-5, \infty)$

5. Simplify $\dfrac{x^2 - x - 6}{x^2 - 4}$. $\dfrac{x - 3}{x - 2}$
(23)

New Concepts

Sometimes two processes need to be combined into one using functions.

Reading Math

The composition $f(g(x))$ is read "f of g of x."

Composition of Functions

If $f(x)$ and $g(x)$ are functions, the **composite function** $f(g(x))$ uses output values from $g(x)$ as input values for $f(x)$. That is, the range values of $g(x)$ become the domain values for $f(x)$. The composition is written $f(g(x))$ or $(f \circ g)(x)$.

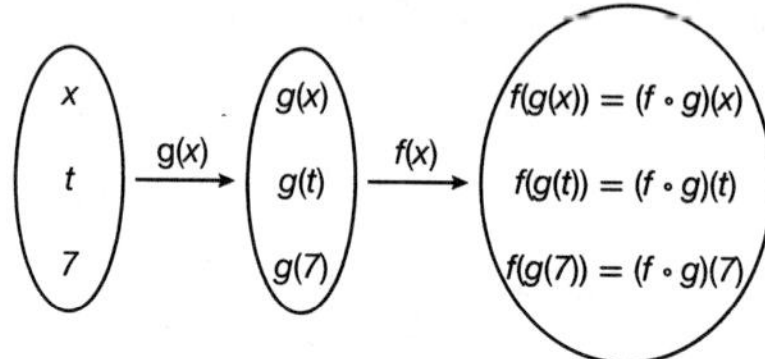

The **composition of functions** is not commutative. That is, for the functions $f(x)$ and $g(x)$, $f(g(x)) \neq g(f(x))$.

Example 1 Performing a Composition and Finding Its Domain and Range

Let $f(x) = 3x + 5$ and $g(x) = x^2$.

a. Find the composite function $f(g(x))$.

SOLUTION

$f(g(x)) = f(x^2)$ Substitute the output x^2 for $g(x)$.

$= 3x^2 + 5$ Use the output from $g(x)$ as input for $f(x)$.

b. Find the domain and range of the composite function from part **a**.

SOLUTION

The domain of $g(x)$ contains all real numbers. The range of $g(x)$ contains only the nonnegative real numbers. The range of $g(x)$ is the domain of $f(x)$. The range of the composite function $f(g(x))$ contains the real numbers greater than or equal to 5.

Online Connection
www.SaxonMathResources.com

LESSON RESOURCES

Student Edition Practice Workbook 53
Reteaching Master 53
Adaptations Master 53
Challenge and Enrichment Masters C53, E53

MATH BACKGROUND

It is important to clarify what the terms *range* and *domain* mean. The range of a function is the set of possible values for the dependent variable (output variables) of a function. The domain is the set of possible values for the independent variables (input variables) of a function. In the general equation $y = mx + b$, the domain is the possible values of x and the range is the possible values of y.

Reading Math

The composite function $f \circ g$ is read "*f* of *g*."

Example 2 Evaluating a Composition

Let $f(x) = x^2 - 4x$ and $g(x) = 2x$. Evaluate the composition $(f \circ g)(3)$ using two different methods.

SOLUTION

Method 1: Use 3 as the input for the function $g(x) = 2x$.

$g(3) = 2(3) = 6.$

Now take 6 as the input for function $f(x) = x^2 - 4x$.

$$f(6) = 6^2 - 4(6)$$
$$= 36 - 24$$
$$= 12$$

So $(f \circ g)(3) = 12$.

Method 2: Replace the function $g(x)$ as the input for the function $f(x)$, then substitute 3 for the value of x.

$f(g(x)) = f(2x)$ — Substitute $g(x)$ with $2x$.

$= (2x)^2 - 4(2x)$ — Use the output from g as the input for f.

$= 4x^2 - 8x$ — Simplify.

Now evaluate the function for $x = 3$: $(f \circ g)(3) = 4(3)^2 - 8(3) = 12$

Example 3 Determining Whether Function Composition Is Commutative

Let $f(x) = 2x - 3$ and $g(x) = 7x$.

a. Find the composition functions $(f \circ g)(x)$ and $(g \circ f)(x)$.

SOLUTION $(f \circ g)(x) = f(7x)$ — Substitute $g(x)$ with $7x$.

$= 2(7x) - 3$ — Use $7x$ as the input for f.

$= 14x - 3$ — Simplify.

On the other hand,

$(g \circ f)(x) = g(2x - 3)$ — Substitute $f(x)$ with $2x - 3$.

$= 7(2x - 3)$ — Use $2x - 3$ as the input for g.

$= 14x - 21$ — Simplify.

b. Evaluate the composition functions $(f \circ g)(x)$ and $(g \circ f)(x)$ for $x = 3$.

SOLUTION $(f \circ g)(3) = 14(3) - 3 = 39$

$(g \circ f)(3) = 14(3) - 21 = 21$

Notice that the simplified expressions for the composition functions $(f \circ g)(x)$ and $(g \circ f)(x)$ are not equal. The values of the expressions at $x = 3$ are not equal either. Therefore the order of the composition of functions matters and is not commutative.

Example 2

This example shows students how to evaluate a composition function using two different methods.

Additional Example 2

Let $f(x) = x^3 - 2x$ and $g(x) = 3x$. Evaluate the composition function $(f \circ g)(2)$ using two different methods. 204

Example 3

This example demonstrates that function composition is not commutative.

Additional Example 3

Let $f(x) = 4x - 6$ and $g(x) = 3x$.

a. Find the composition functions $(f \circ g)(x)$ and $(g \circ f)(x)$.
$(f \circ g)(x) = 4(3x) - 6 = 12x - 6$
$(g \circ f)(x) = 3(4x - 6) = 12x - 18$

b. Evaluate the composition functions $(f \circ g)(x)$ and $(g \circ f)(x)$ for $x = 2$.
$(f \circ g)(2) = 12(2) - 6 = 18$
$(g \circ f)(2) = 12(2) - 18 = 6$

TEACHER TIP

If students are given a choice on how they solve a function similar to those in Example 2, encourage them to use Method 1. Students should make fewer errors in their calculations when using that method because there are fewer terms to track.

Example 4

This example demonstrates how to determine the composition of three functions.

Additional Example 4

Let $f(x) = -x$, $g(x) = 2x + 3$, and $h(x) = x^2$. Find the composite function $f(g(h(x)))$.
$f(g(h(x))) = -2x^2 - 3$

Example 5

This example shows how composition of functions can be used to model and solve a real-life problem.

Extend the Example

Have students check their answer by simplifying the expressions before they create the composite function.

$d(t(p)) = 0.9(0.7p) = 0.63p$

Additional Example 5

A local travel agency is offering a special on selected trips to several cities in the United States. If you book within the next 30 days, you get 25% off the total price. If you pay cash for the trip at the same time that you book it, you receive a 10% discount. Find a function that describes how much a customer pays for the trip if the customer pays cash for the trip at the same time that it is booked.
Let p = original price of trip.
$t(p) = p - 0.25p$
$d(p) = p - 0.1p$
$d(t(p)) = (p - 0.25p) - 0.1(p - 0.25p) = 0.675p$

Error Alert Students must watch the signs of the numbers when they distribute to simplify the composite function.

Math Reasoning

Verify If $f(x) = 7$ and $g(x) = 3x + 39$, then show that $f(g(x)) = 7$.

Function f has output 7 for all input, so it doesn't matter what function g is.

Example 4 Determining the Composition of Three Functions

Let $f(x) = -2x$, $g(x) = 4x - 5$, and $h(x) = x^2$. Find the composite function $f(g(h(x)))$.

SOLUTION

$f(g(h(x))) = f(g(x^2))$	Substitute $h(x)$ with x^2.
$= f(4(x^2) - 5)$	Use x^2 as the input for $g(x)$.
$= f(4x^2 - 5)$	Simplify.
$= -2(4x^2 - 5)$	Use $4x^2 - 5$ as the input for $f(x)$.
$= -8x^2 + 10$	Simplify.

Example 5 Application: Sales and Discounts

A store is holding a sale. All items are being sold with a discount of 30%. Employees receive an additional 10% discount. Find a function that describes how much employees pay for an item with price p.

SOLUTION

Understand If an item's original price is \$10, the sale price is 30% off, or \$3 less, which is \$7. Employees receive a discount of 10%, which is \$0.70. So for an item with an original price of \$10, employees pay \$6.30. To find this result, we applied a 30% discount then the 10% employee discount.

Plan Notice that we use the output from the 30% sale function as the input to the 10% off employee discount function. The sale function can be written as $s(p) = p - 0.3p$, where p is the original price of an item without discounts. The employee discount function can be written as $d(p) = p - 0.1p$. Because two separate discounts are applied to the price p of the item, we need to find a composite function $d(s(p))$.

Solve

$d(s(p)) = d(p - 0.3p)$	Substitute $s(p)$ with $p - 0.3p$.
$= (p - 0.3p) - 0.1(p - 0.3p)$	Substitute $p - 0.3p$ for the item price p in the function $d(s) = p - 0.1p$.
$= p - 0.3p - 0.1p + 0.03p$	Use the Distributive Property to simplify.
$= 0.63p$	Simplify.

Employees pay 0.63 times the original price of an item.

Check Another way to solve the problem is to simplify first.

$s(p) = p - 0.3p = 0.7p$

$d(p) = p - 0.1p = 0.9p$

Then $d(s(p)) = d(0.7p) = 0.9(0.7p) = 0.63p$. This is the same function as above, so the solution checks.

ENGLISH LEARNERS

Some students might have trouble with the term **composition**. Tell students that in mathematics, a composition is two functions put together to make a single function.

Connect the meaning of composition to the idea of multiple discounts. For example, stores often give multiple discounts on merchandise or services. If you combine the individual functions for each discount into one function, you can quickly and easily determine the total price of the merchandise or service.

Discuss other meanings of the term composition, such as a composition can be an essay written in English class or an original piece of music.

Have students identify the functions in Example 5 and then model for students how to create a composition of the two functions. Have students complete Additional Example 5 at their desks. Have a student volunteer present the solution to the class.

Lesson Practice

a. Let $f(x) = 2x - 9$ and $g(x) = (x + 1)^2$. Find the composite function $f(g(x))$. $2(x + 1)^2 - 9 = 2x^2 + 4x - 7$
(Ex 1)

b. Let $f(x) = x^2 - 2$ and $g(x) = x - 4$. What are the domain and range of $(f \circ g)(x)$? $(f \circ g)(x) = (x - 4)^2 - 2$ has domain $(-\infty, \infty)$ and range $[-2, \infty)$.
(Ex 1)

c. Let $f(x) = 3x - 7$ and $g(x) = 4x + 5$. Evaluate the composition $(f \circ g)(7)$ using two different methods.
(Ex 2)

c. $g(7) = 33$, and $f(33) = 92$, so $(f \circ g)(7) = 92$. Alternatively, $(f \circ g)(x) = 3(4x + 5) - 7 = 12x + 8$, so $(f \circ g)(7) = 12(7) + 8 = 92$.

d. Let $f(x) = x + 6$ and $g(x) = x^2$. Are $(f \circ g)(x)$ and $(g \circ f)(x)$ equal?
(Ex 3)

d. No. $(f \circ g)(x) = x^2 + 6$, and $(g \circ f)(x) = (x + 6)^2 = x^2 + 12x + 36$

e. Evaluate the composite functions $f(g(x))$ and $g(f(x))$ when $x = -1$ for the functions $f(x) = 2x - 1$ and $g(x) = -x$.
(Ex 3)

e. $f(g(x)) = -2x - 1$ and $g(f(x)) = -2x + 1$; $f(g(-1)) = -2(-1) - 1 = 1$ and $g(f(-1)) = -2(-1) + 1 = 3$

f. Let $f(x) = -3x + 1$, $g(x) = 9x$, and $h(x) = -x^2$. Find the composite function $f(g(h(x)))$. $f(g(-x^2)) = f(-9x^2) = -3(-9x^2) + 1 = 27x^2 + 1$
(Ex 4)

g. A department store is advertising a sale in which all clothes are 15% off. On Saturday morning, there is an additional 20% discount. Find a function describing how much an item with price p will cost on Saturday morning. $f(p) = (p - 0.15p) - 0.2(p - 0.15p) = 0.68p$
(Ex 5)

Practice Distributed and Integrated

Solve.

1. $2\frac{1}{4}x - 3\frac{1}{2} = -\frac{1}{16}$ $\frac{55}{36}$
(7)

2. $0.002x - 0.02 = 6.6$ 3310
(7)

3. $\frac{3 - 2x}{4} + \frac{x}{3} = 5$ $\frac{-51}{2}$
(7)

Use the properties of special right triangles to find x and y.

***4.** $x = \sqrt{5}$; $y = \sqrt{10}$
(52)

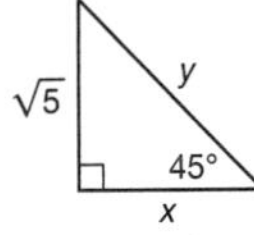

***5.** $x = 3$; $y = 3\sqrt{2}$
(39)

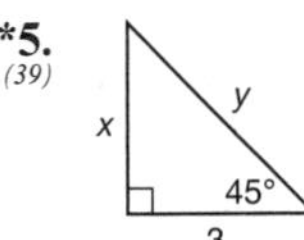

Use $3x + 10 > 4y$.

6. Find a point that is a solution. Possible answer: (1, –2)
(39)

7. Find a point that is not a solution. Possible answer: (–4, 3)
(39)

8. How many terms does the binomial expansion of $(3r + s)^{17}$ contain? 18 terms
(49)

***9.** Let $x(t) = 3$ and $y(t) = -7t + 6$. Find $x(y(t))$ and $y(x(t))$. $x(y(t)) = 3$; $y(x(t)) = y(3) = -15$
(53)

***10.** Let $p(x) = 3$ and $q(x) = -x^2 + 3x$. Find $p(q(x))$ and $q(p(x))$. $p(q(x)) = 3$; $q(p(x)) = q(3) = 0$
(53)

11. Analyze Suppose there are three tiles in a bag, labeled A, B, and C. A tile is chosen at random, then a second tile is chosen at random, and then the third tile is chosen. Each tile that is chosen is not replaced in the bag. List all the outcomes in the sample space of this experiment. How many outcomes are in the sample space? ABC, ACB, BAC, BCA, CAB, CBA; 6 outcomes
(33)

Lesson Practice

Problem f

Error Alert Suggest that students carefully keep track of the negative signs when finding the composite function.

Problem g

Scaffolding Suggest that students follow the steps used in Example 5 to find the function for this problem.

Check for Understanding

The questions below help assess the concepts taught in this lesson.

"What is a composite function?" When two functions are combined into one function, it is called a composite function.

"Are the composite functions $(f \circ g)(x)$ and $(g \circ f)(x)$ commutative?" No, they are not commutative.

"Is a composite function of more than two functions possible?" yes

3 Practice

Math Conversations

Discussions to strengthen understanding

Problem 4

Guide students by asking them the following questions.

"If this is a 45°-45°-90° triangle, what is true of the length of the legs?" The lengths of the legs have to be equal.

"Look at the triangle carefully; what is the value of x?" $\sqrt{5}$

"Can you use the Pythagorean Theorem to find the value of y?" yes

INCLUSION

When students are finding functions such as those in lesson practice g, have them simplify the terms before they combine the functions. This should minimize errors.

Problem 19

Guide students by asking them the following questions.

"Which trigonometric function can be used to find the length of $\frac{l}{2}$, where l is the length of the base?" cosine

"What is the equation to find l using the cosine of 70°?"

$\cos 70° = \frac{\frac{l}{2}}{20 \text{ inches}}$

$l = 13.68$ inches

Extend the Problem

Have students determine the value of the third angle. 40°

Problem 20

Guide students by asking them the following questions.

"What is the function when all of the known values are put into the function?"
$h(t) = -4.9t^2 + 4.9t + 29.4$

"If you factor −4.9 from the trinomial, what is the function?"
$h(t) = -4.9(t^2 - t - 6)$

"What are the possible values of t?" $t = 3$ or $t = -2$

"What is the correct answer to the problem?" $t = 3$

---

*12. **Multi-Step** (53) A bookstore gives you a 10% student discount, but you still must pay the 6% sales tax. Use composite functions to:

a. Determine how much you save if the discount is calculated first. $0.046p$

b. Determine how much you save if the tax is calculated first. $0.046p$

c. Determine which method will save you the most. It doesn't matter whether you calculate the tax or the discount first.

13. **Multi-Step** (44) A rectangle has an area of 60 square centimeters and a length of $\frac{3\sqrt{3}}{2}$ centimeters.

a. Find the width of the rectangle. $\frac{40\sqrt{3}}{3}$ cm

b. Find the perimeter of the rectangle. $\frac{89\sqrt{3}}{3}$ cm

14. (39) Find a point that is a solution of $-7x + 18 < 3y$ and a point that is not a solution. Possible answer: (3, 0) is a solution and (1, 2) is not a solution.

15. **Write** (51) Determine the polynomial divisor, dividend, and quotient represented by the synthetic division shown. Divisor: $x + 1$; Dividend: $10x^4 + 5x^3 + 4x^2 - 9$; Quotient: $10x^3 - 5x^2 + 9x - 9$

$$\begin{array}{r|rrrrr} -1 & 10 & 5 & 4 & 0 & -9 \\ & 0 & -10 & 5 & -9 & 9 \\ \hline & 10 & -5 & 9 & -9 & 0 \end{array}$$

16. **Error Analysis** (40) Find and correct the error(s) the student made.

$\frac{3}{\sqrt[3]{3}} \cdot \frac{\sqrt[3]{3}}{\sqrt[3]{3}} = \frac{3\sqrt[3]{3}}{\sqrt[3]{9}} = \frac{3\sqrt[3]{3}}{3} = \sqrt[3]{3}$

16. The student did not multiply the numerator and denominator by a radical that makes the radicand in the denominator a perfect cube. Also, the cube root of 9 is not three. The student should multiply the numerator and denominator by the cube root of 9. $\frac{3}{\sqrt[3]{3}} \cdot \frac{\sqrt[3]{9}}{\sqrt[3]{9}} = \frac{3\sqrt[3]{9}}{\sqrt[3]{27}} = \frac{3\sqrt[3]{9}}{3} = \sqrt[3]{9}$

*17. **Graphing Calculator** (47) At the start of the year, there are 23 rabbits living in a field. The growth of the rabbit population is modeled by the equation $P(x) = 1.2^x + 22$, where $P(x)$ is the number of rabbits in the field x weeks into the year. Use a graphing calculator to predict how many weeks it will take for there to be more than 100 rabbits. 24 weeks

*18. **Multiple Choice** (53) Let $h(x) = x^{-3} + x^3$ and $k(x) = x^{-1}$. What is the value of $h(k(2))$? C

A 8 **B** $\frac{1}{8}$ **C** $8\frac{1}{8}$ **D** $\frac{8}{65}$

19. **Geometry** (46) The altitude of an isosceles triangle bisects its base. Find the length of the base of an isosceles triangle whose legs measure 20 inches and whose base angles measure 70°. Round to the nearest hundredth. 13.68 inches

20. **Gravity** (35) The height of a free-falling object (neglecting air resistance) is given by the function $h(t) = -4.9t^2 + v_0 t + h_0$, where h_0 is the initial height in meters, v_0 is the initial velocity in meters per second, and $h(t)$ is the height in meters at time t seconds. How long does it take for an object to hit the ground after it is thrown straight up at a speed of 4.9 meters per second from a height of 29.4 meters? (Hint: Factor −4.9 from the trinomial.) 3 seconds

*21. **Analyze** (53) Suppose $p(u) = 2u + 5$ with domain {1, 3, 5, 7} and $r(u) = u - 3$ with domain {6, 8}. Then the domain of $p(u)$ limits the domain and range of the composite function $r(p(u))$. Can you choose new domains for functions p and r so that the domain of $r(u)$ limits the domain and range of the composite function $p(r(u))$? Sample: domain of $p(u)$ is {4, 6, 8, 10} and domain of $r(u)$ is {3, 5}.

22. (Cartography) A cartographer constructs a map of Montana over a grid system (41) such that Great Falls is at (125, 150) and Conrad is at (86, 220). Find the distance between the cities to the nearest kilometer if each unit represents one kilometer. about 80 kilometers

23. **Probability** Suppose the probability of you scoring a goal in a soccer game is $\frac{1}{3}$ for (49) every shot taken. If you take 8 shots in a game, what is the probability that you will score 2 goals? $\frac{1792}{6561}$

24. **Analyze** What must be true of a and b if the following equation is true? Explain. (37)

$$\frac{1}{x^2 + ax + bx + ab} = \frac{1}{x^2 - 1}$$

24. $\frac{1}{(x+a)(x+b)} = \frac{1}{(x+1)(x-1)}$ This means that $|a| = |b| = 1$. One of the terms is positive and the other term is negative.

25. (Irrigation) An irrigation pipeline starts from the top of a hill and has an angle of (52) elevation of 45°. If the length of the pipe line is 720 meters, what is the vertical rise of the pipe? Round your answer to the nearest meter. The vertical rise is about 509 meters.

26. **Generalize** Consider the following sequence of complex fractions. (48)

$$1, \frac{1}{1+1}, \frac{1}{1+\frac{1}{1+1}}, \frac{1}{1+\frac{1}{1+\frac{1}{1+1}}}, \frac{1}{1+\frac{1}{1+\frac{1}{1+\frac{1}{1+1}}}}, \frac{1}{1+\frac{1}{1+\frac{1}{1+\frac{1}{1+\frac{1}{1+1}}}}}, \ldots$$

Simplify the first 6 terms. Describe any patterns you see. Can you predict the next term without writing and simplifying the complex fraction?

26. $1, \frac{1}{2}, \frac{2}{3}, \frac{3}{5}, \frac{5}{8}, \frac{8}{13}$; numerators and denominators are consecutive Fibonacci numbers; $\frac{13}{21}$

27. **Multiple Choice** Evaluate $\frac{8!}{5!}$. B (42)

A 1.6 B 336 C 1680 D 6720

28. (Speed) The speed of an object at time t is based on its initial speed (36) v_o and its acceleration a: $v = v_o + at$.

a. Find the equations of the lines from A to B and B to C and describe the motion of the object.

b. What is the relationship between the equations of motion? The two lines are perpendicular.

28a. The object starts with an initial speed of 5 and acceleration of 2 ($y = 2x + 5$). After 2 seconds it decelerates, until it stops after 20 seconds ($y = -0.5x + 10$).

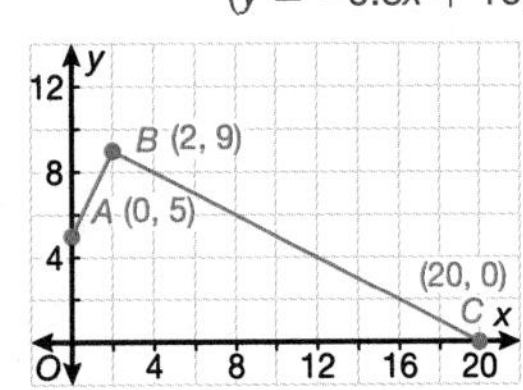

29. (Population) The population p of a city for the years from 1998 is modeled by (50) $p = 326{,}000 + 8526t$, where $t = 0$ represents the year 1998. Solve the equation for t and use it to predict the year in which the population of the city exceeds 450,000. $t = \frac{p - 326{,}000}{8526}$, $t = 15$, in the year 2013

30. (Ticket Prices) Two of the ticket prices for a football game were \$92 for a field seat (43) and \$54 for an upper view seat. You decide to buy up to 15 tickets and to spend up to \$1000. Let x represent a number of field seats and y represent a number of upper view seats.

a. Write a system of linear inequalities that represents the situation.

30a. $x + y \leq 15$
$92x + 54y \leq 1000$

b. Describe the points in the graph of the system that represent all the possible combinations of field seats and upper view seats you can buy.

30b. The points in the graph of the system that represent all the possible combinations of field seats and upper view seats you can buy are all points with both coordinates nonnegative integers.

Problem 25

Guide students by asking them the following questions.

"Make a sketch of the irrigation pipe. What is 720 meters in this triangle?" It is the hypotenuse of a right triangle.

"Which trigonometric function expresses the relationship between the hypotenuse and the length of the side opposite the angle?" the sine

"Which equation can be used to find the vertical rise of the pipe?" $\sin 45° = \frac{x}{720 \text{ meters}}$

$x = 509$ meters

CHALLENGE

A store is holding a going out of business sale. All items are being sold with a discount of 30% off on the first day. The next day there is a discount of 10% off the sale price and the following day there is an additional 10% off the sale price. Find a function that describes how much a customer pays for an item on the third day.

$d_3(d_2(d_1(p))) = 0.9[(0.9)(0.7p)] = 0.567p$

LOOKING FORWARD

Finding the compositions of functions prepares students for

- **Lesson 76** Finding Polynomial Roots I
- **Lesson 117** Solving Systems of Nonlinear Equations

LESSON 54

1 Warm Up

Use Problem 2 in the Warm Up to review graphing techniques for inequalities.

2 New Concepts

In this lesson, students learn to use linear programming in order to solve problems based on the constraints given, usually in algebraic form.

Discuss the definitions of **constraints, objective functions,** and vertices.

Example 1

Students will observe the feasible region from the constraints given and determine the minimum value for the objective function.

Additional Example 1

If in the ad campaign problem, the manager increased his budget to 15 TV ads, 25 radio ads, and reach at least 200,000 people, how would that change the constraints of the graph? The cost of the ads stays the same.
Constraints:
$0 \le x \le 15$, $0 \le y \le 25$,
$10{,}000x + 5{,}000y \ge 200{,}000$

LESSON 54

Using Linear Programming

Warm Up

1. An expression that contains the symbols < or > is called a(n) inequality.
(10)
2. Is (5, 10) a solution of $y \ge 2x - 3$. yes
(39)
3. Determine $f(-5)$ if $f(x) = 2x^2 - 3x$. 65
(4)

New Concepts

Math Language

Linear programming is useful in many fields. In business, linear programming may be used to minimize cost or optimize income.

Linear programming is a mathematical technique that allows you to make optimal decisions from a complex set of choices. In linear programming, you are looking for the maximum or minimum value of an **objective function,** subject to certain **constraints.** The constraints are given as linear equations or inequalities.

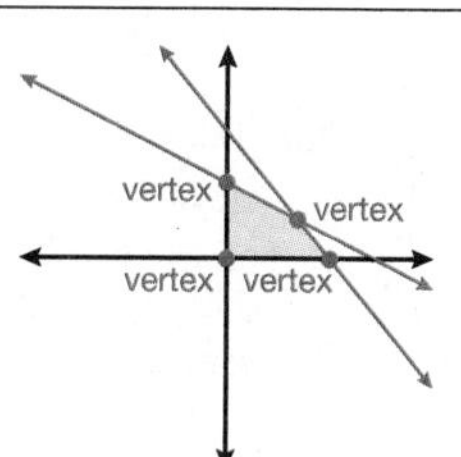

In the graph, the shaded area is known as the **feasible region** where all possible solutions are found. When evaluating a solution, a key area to focus on are the corners of the feasible region, also known as vertices.

Example 1 Graphing a Linear Programming Problem

A marketing manager is coordinating an ad campaign. TV ads are \$2000 and reach 10,000 people, and radio ads are \$500 and reach 5,000 people. The target size of the audience for this marketing campaign is at least 100,000 people. He wants to buy no more than 10 TV ads and no more than 15 radio ads. How can the marketing manager minimize his costs within these conditions?

SOLUTION

x = number of TV ads, y = number of radio ads,

Objective function: Cost $= 2000x + 500y$
Constraints: $0 \le x \le 10$, $0 \le y \le 15$, $10{,}000x + 5{,}000y \ge 100{,}000$

Hint

The minimum (or maximum) value of the objective function occurs at a vertex of the graph of the system.

Find the points within the feasible region that result in the minimum value for the objective function. Evaluate the objective function for the coordinates of the vertices:

x	y	Cost $= 2000x + 500y$
10	0	20,000
2.5	15	12,500
10	15	27,500

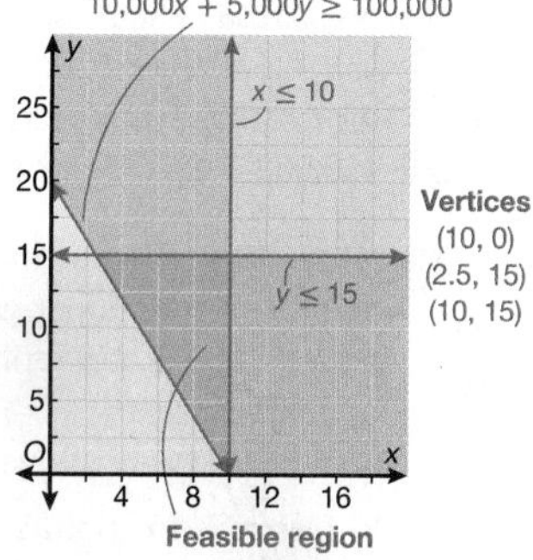

Feasible region

The solution that leads to the least amount of marketing dollars spent is $x = 2.5$ and $y = 15$. Since it makes no sense to buy half a TV ad, the real solution is 3 TV ads and 15 radio ads, for a total cost of \$13,500.

ADDITIONAL RESOURCES

Student Edition Practice Workbook 54
Reteaching Master 54
Adaptations Master 54
Challenge and Enrichment Master C54
Technology Lab Master 54

MATH BACKGROUND

Linear programming can be applied to various fields of study. It has proved useful in modeling diverse types of problems in planning, routing, scheduling, assignment, and design.

Most extensively it is used in business and economic situations, but can also be utilized for some engineering problems. Some industries that use linear programming models include transportation, energy, telecommunications, and manufacturing. Historically, ideas from linear programming have inspired many of the central concepts of optimization theory, such as duality, decomposition, and the importance of convexity and its generalizations. Likewise, linear programming is heavily used in microeconomics and business management, either to maximize the income or minimize the costs of a production scheme.

Example 2 Finding the Minimum and Maximum Values for the Objective Function

A farmer needs to decide how much corn and soybeans to grow for the next harvest. The cost of corn seed is $80 per bag, while soybeans are $50 per bag. A bag of corn requires 2 acres of farmland, while soybeans require 1 acre. The farm's acreage is 5000 acres. It takes 3 hours to plant a bag of corn and 2 hours to plant soybeans. The farmer expects to need at least 2500 hours of planting. How can the farmer manage costs for the next harvest?

SOLUTION

Let x = the number of bags of corn

Let y = the number of bags of soybeans

Objective function: Cost = $80x + 50y$

The goal is to find the minimum and maximum cost subject to these constraints:

$x \geq 0, y \geq 0$

$2x + y \leq 5000$

$3x + 2y \geq 2500$

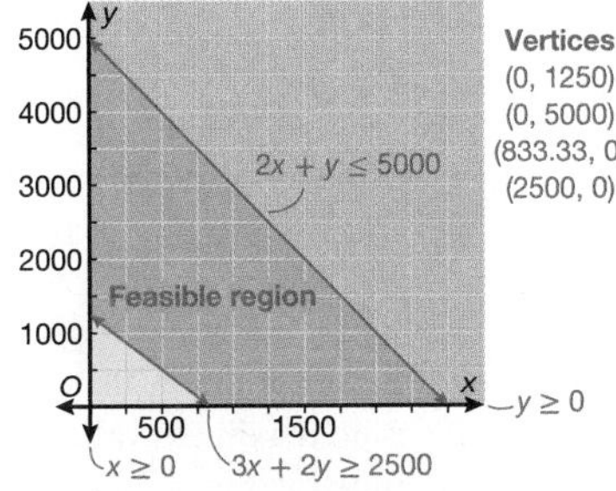

Evaluate the objective function for the coordinates of the vertices:

x	y	Cost = $80x + 50y$
0	1250	62,500
0	5000	250,000
$833\frac{1}{3}$	0	66,666.67
2500	0	200,000

The farmer has several options.

- To keep costs at an absolute minimum, purchase 1250 bags of soybeans.
- To plant all 5000 acres at the lowest cost, purchase 2500 bags of corn.

Example 2

Students will graph objective functions and determine minimum and maximum in terms of cost for the problem specified.

Additional Example 2

During the next harvest, the farmer realized that he could plant a larger bag of corn in 4 hours and a larger bag of soybeans in 6 hours. He expects to put in 3600 hours of planting. His acreage also increased to 12,000 acres. Since the size of the bags have increased, the acreage per bag has increased to 5 acres for a bag of corn and 3 acres for a bag of soybeans. Create an objective function table based on the vertices. The cost of corn and soybeans, however, remains the same.

$x \geq 0, y \geq 0$
$5x + 3y \leq 12{,}000$
$4x + 6y \geq 3600$
Vertices
(0, 4000)
(0, 600)
(2400, 0)
(900, 0)

x	y	Cost = $80x + 50y$
0	4000	200,000
0	600	30,000
2400	0	192,000
900	0	72,000

Extend the Example

Have students create a new cost function and solve for a new optimal cost based on new prices for each item.

INCLUSION

If students are having trouble understanding how to create an objective cost function based on the variables and coefficients given in the word problem, have them work backwards to derive the cost equation.

For example, first have the students calculate the cost based on buying just one of each item. Next, have the students calculated the cost for two of each item and so on. Create a table if necessary. After three or four entries in a table they should see the relationship to the variable amount of the item and the price.

Example 3

Students will graph and observe an unbounded feasible region from the constraints given in the problem.

Additional Example 3

During the next fishing season, the cost of bass and trout increase. Bass now cost 95 cents each and trout cost 45 cents each. Create a new objective function table based on the new cost function. The constraints stay the same.

x	y	Cost = $0.45x + 0.95y$
0	40,000	38,000
200,000/3	20,000/3	≈36,333
100,000	0	45,000

Error Alert Students may solve for the vertices that cross the y-axis also, not realizing that the region will end when the two lines intersect. Solving for the intersection point of the two lines is done by solving each equation for y, then setting each equation equal to each other. Solve for x and y to find the intersection vertices.

TEACHER TIP

Vertices may be difficult to solve algebraically. First have the students graph the lines with the constraints and estimate the vertices and intersection points. This will give them an idea of the vertices that they will be finding from the given constraints. This is especially helpful when solving for the intersection point of the two lines.

Example 3 An Unbounded Feasible Region

A wildlife manager needs to ensure that Lake Katherine has a sufficient number of trout and bass for the fishing season. It costs 25 cents per trout and 75 cents per bass to stock the lake. About $\frac{1}{8}$ of the trout and $\frac{1}{4}$ of the bass stocked in the lake are caught during the fishing season. It is estimated that at least 10,000 fish will be caught this season. About 1% of the trout and 5% of the bass become the prey of birds and other animals. The attrition estimate for this season is at least 1,000 fish. How can the wildlife manager keep costs to a minimum?

Math Reasoning

Justify If you name the variables differently, that is, y would represent the trout and x the bass, would the solution be different? Explain.

No. The result would be the same, although the graph would be different.

SOLUTION

Let x = the number of trout

Let y = the number of bass

Objective function: Cost = $0.25x + 0.75y$

The goal is to find the minimum and maximum cost subject to these constraints:

$$x \geq 0, y \geq 0$$

$$\frac{1}{8}x + \frac{1}{4}y \geq 10{,}000$$

$$0.01x + 0.05y \geq 1000$$

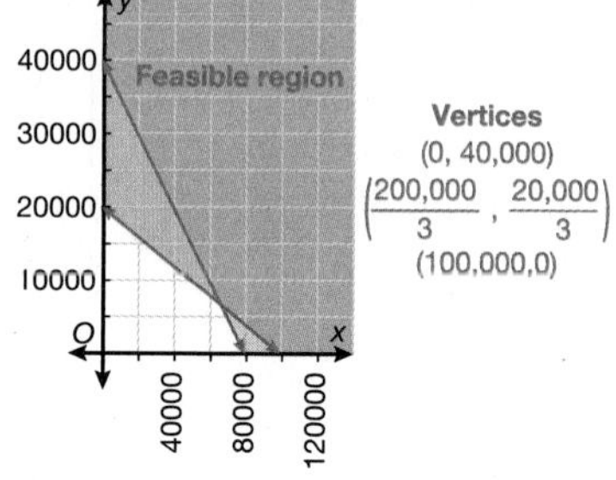

Math Reasoning

Analyze What kind of constraints would make the feasible region bounded? Provide some examples.

Sample answer: Restrict the number of trout and bass to specific amounts. For example, $0 \leq x \leq 100{,}000$ and $0 \leq y \leq 40{,}000$.

In this example, the feasible region is not enclosed. This means that there is no maximum value for the objective function. Evaluate the objective function for the coordinates of the vertices:

x	y	Cost = $0.25x + 0.75y$
0	40,000	30,000
200,000/3	20,000/3	≈21,667
100,000	0	25,000

The wildlife manager has to consider the following:

- To keeps costs low, purchase about 66,667 trout and 6,667 bass.
- Since the feasible region is unbounded, there is no maximum cost. This happens because in the fishing season it is possible that a combination of heavy fishing and a larger predator population could severely cut back on the number of fish.
- It may be necessary to stock the lake with more fish during the fishing season. Thus, the minimum obtained from the objective function may not be the true minimum for stocking the lake.

ENGLISH LEARNERS

Define **vertices** and show that the vertices are only intersections of lines based on the other constraint equations given in the problem.

Discuss constraints and how they are used to limit things in the real world. Explain how the constraint equations limit the feasible region on a graph.

Apply the objective cost functions to any type of situation in business or economics. Use a real world example to show how a company would use a cost function to evaluate profits.

Connect the constraint equations to simple line equations used together to create a feasible region. The feasible region is only created by the intersections of the constraint equations.

Example 4 Application: Business

A company makes two models of MP3 players. The M20 takes 3 hours to manufacture and the M25 takes 1 hour. The company has multiple shifts and has a 20-hour day for manufacturing the players. The M20 generates a profit of \$12, and the M25 a profit of \$7. The M20 uses 15 special chips, while the M25 uses 10. For the next manufacturing cycle, consisting of 18 days, there are 3,000 chips available. How many of each type of MP3 player should the company produce to maximize its profits? What combination of MP3 players would result in the least amount of profit?

SOLUTION

Let x = the number of M20 models

Let y = the number of M25 models

Objective function: Profit = $12x + 7y$

The goal is to find the minimum and maximum profit with these constraints:

$x \geq 0, y \geq 0$

$3x + y \leq 360$

$15x + 10y \leq 3000$

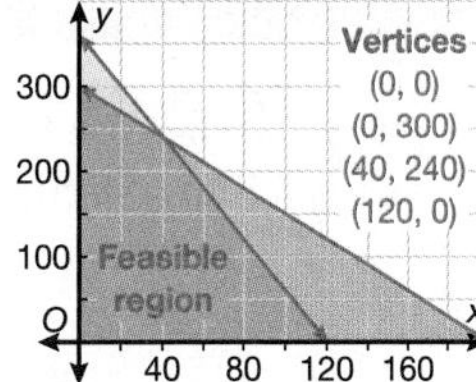

Math Reasoning

Justify How many hours will be spent manufacturing the players in 18 days? Explain.

The company spends 20 hours manufacturing the players per day. So $20 \times 18 =$ 360 hours.

Evaluate the objective function for the coordinates of the vertices:

x	y	Profit = $12x + 7y$
0	0	0
0	300	2100
40	240	2160
120	0	1440

Aside from the trivial solution of (0, 0), the solution that results in the least profit is to solely produce 120 M20s. The solution that offers the greatest profit is to produce 40 M20s and 240 M25s.

Lesson Practice

a. (Ex 1) Given the objective function $C = 25x + 30y$ and the graph and vertices shown, find the minimum and maximum values.
Minimum: 45, Maximum: 80

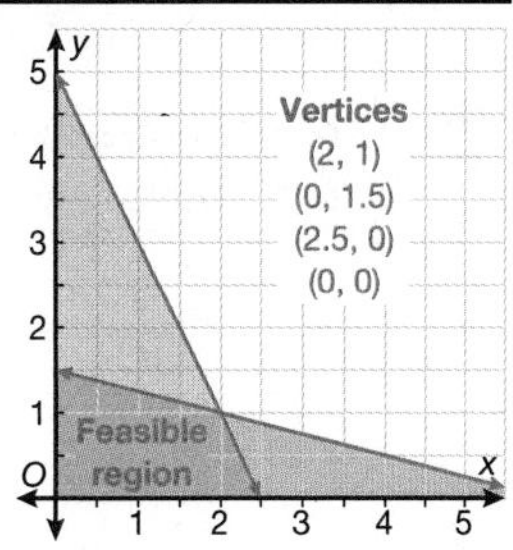

Example 4

Students use their knowledge of linear programming to apply the graphs to business applications.

Additional Example 4

Suppose in the MP3 player example, the manufacturer had to make exactly 80 M20 models. What is the range of M25 models that could be made and the range of profits that could be made?
Based on the graph, the feasible range for M25 models (y-axis) for $x = 80$ M20 models can be found by looking at the region along $x = 80$. The minimum number of M25 models that can be made is 0 and the maximum number is 120. Creating a table can show the amount of profit that can be made with either of these two amounts.

x	y	Profit = $12x + 7y$
80	0	960
80	120	1800

The number of M25 models will range from 0 to 120, and the profit margin will vary from \$960 to \$1800.

Lesson Practice

Problem a

Error Alert Students may try to solve the minimum and maximum for vertices that are outside the feasible region. When solving for the minimum and maximum be sure to choose the three vertices that intersect the x-axis, y-axis, and the intersection of the two functions.

INCLUSION

In order to help students identify applications for linear programming, have the students create a real life problem comparing two products (such as two types of digital cameras, computers, or even books with different numbers of pages.). Have the students create their own constraints from known or estimated values such as how long it would take to manufacture and profit margins.

This will allow students to understand how businesses can use linear programming to project costs and determine how many of a specific product to manufacture.

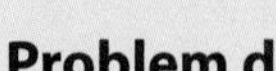

Problem d

Scaffolding In order to solve the problem, create new constraint equations based on the new total number of hours and amount of chips to be used. Solve for new vertices where functions intersect the x and y axes and each other, then calculate a maximum profit based on an objective cost table.

Check for Understanding

The questions below help assess the concepts taught in this lesson.

1. **"What is the first step in creating a graph to be used for linear programming?"** Sample: Begin by first creating constraint equations based on the information given in the problem. For two unknowns there should be two main constraint equation functions.

2. **"Vertices will be used to solve for what?"** Sample: Vertices are used to show the extremes of the objective functions of the graph.

3 Practice

Math Conversations

Discussions to strengthen understanding

Problem 1

For one constraint equation, there will be 2 vertices found. Plug each set of vertices into the objective function to find the minimum and maximum values.

b. Prepare no more than 667 chicken dishes and no more than 333 seafood dishes.

c. Since the feasible region is unbounded, there is no way to keep costs to a minimum. The organizers will have to impose a limit on spending.

d. The company should produce 720 M25 players.

b. (Ex 2) A caterer needs to prepare two different meals for a conference dinner. One is a chicken dish and the other is a seafood dish. The chicken dish costs \$2.50 to prepare and the seafood dish costs \$3.75. There will at most be 1000 people attending. Usually, twice as many people order chicken than order fish. How can the caterer keep costs to a minimum while still making sure that most people get their meal choice?

c. (Ex 3) Parade organizers are expecting at least 100,000 people to attend the annual parade. For every group of 100, the organizers would like to have a security officer available along the parade route. The cost for each officer is \$100. How can they keep costs to a minimum?

d. (Ex 4) Using the information from Example 4, suppose that for the next manufacturing cycle, consisting of 36 days, there are 9,000 chips available. How many of each type of MP3 player should the company produce to maximize its profits?

Practice Distributed and Integrated

Given the objective function P and the constraints, find the minimum and maximum values for the objective function.

*1. (54) $P = 2x + 3y$ given $x \geq 0$, $y \geq 0$, $0.4x + 0.9y \leq 25$ Minimum: 83.31; Maximum: 125

*2. (54) $P = 5x + 9y$ given $x \geq 0$, $y \geq 0$, $25x + 35y \leq 25$ Minimum: 5; Maximum: 6.4278

Simplify.

3. (48) $\dfrac{a^2x - \frac{a}{x}}{ax - \frac{4}{x}}$ $\dfrac{a^2x^2 - a}{ax^2 - 4}$

4. (48) $\dfrac{\frac{m}{m + x}}{\frac{x}{m + x}}$ $\dfrac{m}{x}$

5. (48) $\dfrac{\frac{s}{a + b} + \frac{x}{b}}{\frac{a}{s + x}}$ $\dfrac{(s + x)(bs + ax + bx)}{ab(a + b)}$

6. (22) **Multiple Choice** A point of discontinuity is a point at which the graph **B**
A increases. **B** is disconnected. **C** ends. **D** decreases.

Identify each equation as direct variation, inverse variation, or neither.

7. (12) $y = \frac{1}{2}x$ direct

8 (12) $xy = 15$ inverse

9 (12) $y = -\frac{1}{2}x + 5$ neither

10. (18) **Saving Money** Jason has 300 nickels in his money jar. How many dollars does Jason have in nickels? \$15.00

*11. (54) **Coordinate Geometry** Find the coordinates of the vertices for the feasible region. Vertices: (0, 5), (2.5, 0), (0, 0)

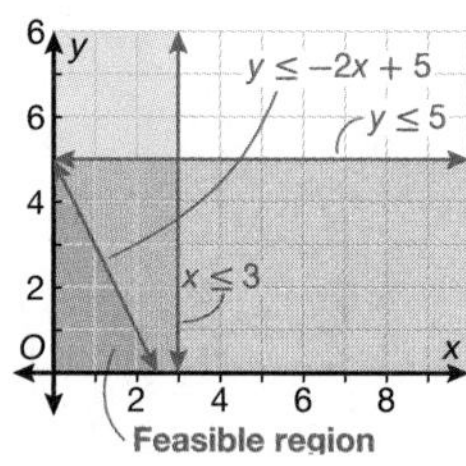

ALTERNATE METHOD FOR PROBLEM 5

Before dividing by the denominator, first add the numerators together to get one complete term. The problem can then be solved in steps. This avoids having to use distribution.

$$\frac{\frac{s}{a + b} + \frac{x}{b}}{\frac{a}{s + x}} = \frac{\frac{sb + xa + xb}{b(a + b)}}{\frac{a}{s + x}}$$

$$= \frac{sb + xa + xb}{b(a + b)} \cdot \frac{s + x}{a}$$

$$= \frac{(s + x)(bs + ax + bx)}{ab(a + b)}$$

12. (54) Give an example of a problem situation where the feasible region might include negative values. Sample: a profit and loss where loss is represented by negative values

13. (21) **Error Analysis** Two students were asked which of these lines were intersecting. Their answers are below. Which student is correct? What is the relationship between the lines that the incorrect student answered? Shelby is correct. Equations 1 and 2 are coinciding.

Equation 1: $3y + 4x = 5$; Equation 2: $8x = 10 - 6y$; Equation 3: $6y - 10 = 8x$

Dietrich: Equations 1 and 2 intersect.

Shelby: Equations 1 and 3 intersect, so equations 2 and 3 intersect as well.

14. (11) **Aquarium Design** Two aquariums each require the same amount of space on a shelf. The shapes of the aquariums are given in the picture. Write a polynomial that represents how much less water the cylindrical aquarium holds than the aquarium in the shape of a cube. (*Hint:* The formula for the volume of a cylinder is $V = \pi r^2 h$.) $x^3 - \frac{\pi}{4}x^3$ or $\left(1 - \frac{\pi}{4}\right)x^3$

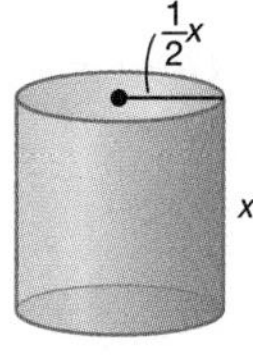

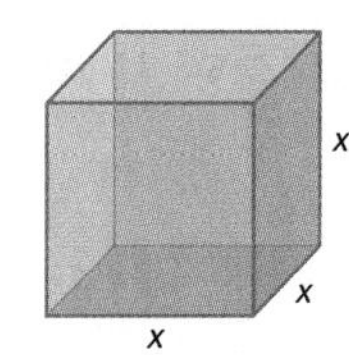

***15.** (53) **Write** Describe how to find a composite function $f(g(x))$ if the functions $f(x)$ and $g(x)$ are known. Sample: Replace each occurrence of x in the function $f(x)$ with the given function for $g(x)$, then simplify the function.

16. (52) **Analyze** A chord in a circle makes an angle of 45° with the radius. If the chord is 4 cm long, what is the radius of the circle? $2\sqrt{2}$ cm

17. (22) **Verify** Explain how to show that the graph is an example of a function. Is the function continuous, discontinuous, and/or discrete? The vertical line test can be used to determine that the graph is a function; The graph is discontinuous at $x = 0$.

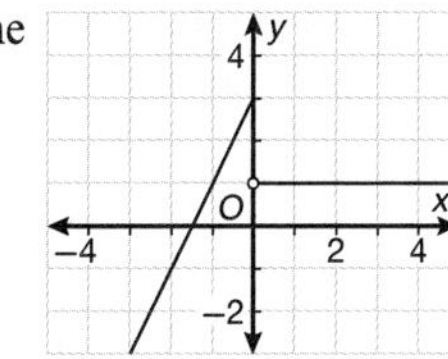

18. (25) **Rainfall** Annual rainfall amounts in inches for Austin, Texas, for 2005 are listed in the table below. If the mean amount of rainfall in Austin during that year was 1.861 inches, find x. $x = 4.302$ inches

2005	J	F	M	A	M	J	J	A	S	O	N	D
Amount (inches)	2.25	2.21	x	0.72	3.13	0.89	2.75	2.44	1.44	1.78	0.33	0.09

19. (51) **Error Analysis** Jenny and Haley each tried to divide the polynomial $2x^4 - 6x^3 + x^2 - 3x - 3$ by $x - 3$. Who is correct? Explain your reasoning.

Jenny

3	2	−6	1	−3	−3
	0	6	0	3	0
	2	0	1	0	−3

Haley

−3	2	−6	1	−3	−3
	0	−6	36	−111	342
	2	−12	37	−114	339

19. Jenny is correct. Since $(x - 3)$ is a given divisor, you must divide the polynomial by 3. Haley divided the polynomial by −3 instead of 3.

20. (30) **Justify** Max said that it is possible to write the standard form of a quadratic equation given its vertex and y-intercept. Show that Max is correct by writing the equation of a quadratic function in standard form whose vertex is (1, 9) and y-intercept is 13. See Additional Answers.

Problem 16

Use trigonometric ratios from the special right triangles to find an equivalent length for the hypotenuse of a 45°-45°-90° triangle with a base of 4 cm.

Problem 18

Guide the students by asking them the following questions.

"How would you find the total amount of rainfall?"
Multiply the average by the total number of months.

"How could you find the missing amount of rainfall?"
Take the total amount of rainfall and subtract each known amount of rainfall for the 11 months to find the amount for the missing month.

ALTERNATE METHOD FOR PROBLEM 29

Instead of factoring out the entire GCF, factor out each common item individually in order to avoid errors. Begin by arranging the equation with variables with the largest exponents listed first.

$$5x^2 + 4x^3 - x^4$$
$$= -x^4 + 4x^3 + 5x^2$$
$$= -(x^4 - 4x^3 - 5x^2)$$
$$= -x^2(x^2 - 4x - 5)$$
$$= -x^2(x + 1)(x - 5)$$

Problem 21

Remember that cotangent is the reciprocal of tangent.

Problem 25

Since $a(t)$ is only one variable with an exponent and coefficient of 1, then is $a(b(t))$ will equal $b(t)$.

21. (46) **Generalize** Tell how to find the cotangent of an angle when given the tangent of the angle. Give an example. Divide 1 by the tangent value; Sample: $\tan A = 0.6$, $\cot A = \frac{1}{0.6} = 1.6$.

22. (29) **Multiple Choice** Circle the letter that represents the number and type of solutions of the system

$$-2x - 10y - 6z = -2$$
$$x + 5y + 3z = -16 \quad \text{A}$$
$$5x + 25y + 15z = 5$$

A No solution, Inconsistent **B** One solution, Inconsistent

C One solution, Consistent **D** Infinitely many solutions, Consistent

***23.** (14) **Graphing Calculator** Use a graphing calculator to solve the following. 1422

$$\det\begin{bmatrix} 9 & 3 & 0 \\ 6 & 12 & 1 \\ -3 & -9 & 15 \end{bmatrix}$$

24. (31) **Geometry** Write a rational expression in simplest form for the ratio of the rectangular prism's surface area to its volume. $\frac{2(3x+2)}{x(x+1)}$

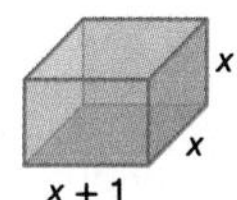

***25.** (53) Let $a(t) = t$ and $b(t) = 3.1t^2 - 2.0t + 4.3$. What is $a(b(t))$? the same as $b(t) = 3.1t^2 - 2.0t + 4.3$

***26.** (53) **Cost of Lobster** At a restaurant on the Maine coast, the supply of fresh new shell lobsters during the season (July through October) is given by the function $L(t) = -0.006t^2 + 0.733t$, where t is the number of days after July 1. If the restaurant has x lobsters for a day, it charges $C(x) = 37 - x$ dollars for each one. What function gives the restaurant's price per lobster in terms of the number of days after July 1? $C(L(t)) = 37 - (-0.006t^2 + 0.733t) = 0.006t^2 - 0.733t + 37$ dollars

27. (44) **Pendulums** The time t in seconds a pendulum takes to complete one full swing is given by the equation $t = 2\pi\sqrt{\frac{l}{9.8}}$, where l is the length of the pendulum in meters. Suppose a pendulum has a length of 5 meters. How much time will the pendulum take to complete one full swing? about 4.5 seconds

28. (45) **Multi-Step**

a. Make a scatter plot of the data set.

b. Sketch a line of best fit.

x	20	30	42	58	64	75	83	90
y	1	4	2.5	3	6	4.5	7	6.5

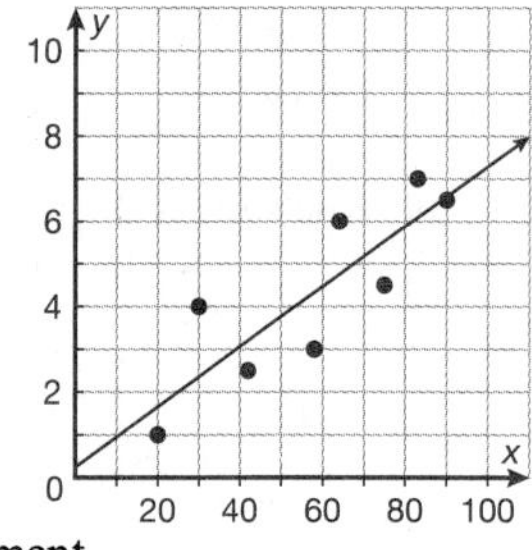

29. (23) Factor $5x^2 + 4x^3 - x^4$ completely. Always factor the GCF as the first step. $-x^2(x-5)(x+1)$

30. (Inv 5) Give an example of how to use a number cube to make a binomial experiment. Sample answer: Even numbers could be successes and odd numbers could be failures.

CHALLENGE

If a company wanted to compare a cost equation with three different products instead of only 2, estimate how that would change linear programming; would it even be linear? What types of constraints would be needed?

If there were three variables we would need to create a 3D graph in terms of x, y, and z. All constraint equations would include three variables, and the feasible region would be a 3D shape.

LOOKING FORWARD

Finding inverses of relations and functions prepares students for

- **Lesson 75** Graphing Radical Functions
- **Lesson 88** Solving Abstract Equations
- **Lesson 109** Making Graphs and Using Equations of Hyperbolas

390 *Saxon Algebra 2*

LESSON 55 Finding Probability

Warm Up

1. **Vocabulary** The total number of possible events is known as the ________. sample space
(33)

2. If there are three models of bicycles that come in four different colors, how many different bicycles are there to choose from? 12
(33)

3. **Multiple Choice** What is $\frac{3}{8}$ written as a percent?
(SB)
A 3.8% B 3.75%
C 37.5% D 375% C

4. Evaluate ${}_3P_2$. 6
(42)

5. Evaluate ${}_3C_2$. 3
(42)

New Concepts

An event is an outcome, or set of outcomes, of a sample space. The **probability** of an event is the **likelihood** of that event occurring. It is given as a number on a continuous scale from 0 to 1, where 0 means that the event is impossible and 1 means that the event will definitely occur. Probabilities can be written as fractions, decimals, or percents, so for an event that is just as likely to occur as not to occur, the probability, P, is $\frac{1}{2} = 0.5 = 50\%$.

A **probability experiment** is an occurrence whose outcome is uncertain. An event in a probability experiment can be called a **random event** because it occurs at **random,** or by chance. For example, the event of getting heads in the experiment of flipping a coin is a random event because it cannot be predicted.

Math Reasoning

Analyze What is the probability of an event that is made up of all the outcomes in the sample space? Why?

1, because the numerator and denominator in the ratio will be the same

Theoretical Probability
For equally likely outcomes, the **theoretical probability** P of an event occurring is the ratio of the number of favorable outcomes to the total number of outcomes in the sample space: $P(\text{event}) = \frac{\text{number of favorable outcomes}}{\text{total number of outcomes}}$, where a **favorable outcome** is an outcome in the event.

In theoretical probability there must be **equally likely outcomes.** That is, each outcome has the same probability of occurring. In the experiment of rolling a number cube, the likelihood of the six outcomes is the same. $P(\text{even number}) = \frac{3}{6} = \frac{1}{2}$ because there are three favorable outcomes (2, 4, 6) out of six total outcomes (1, 2, 3, 4, 5, and 6). This probability is a *theoretical probability* because it says what should happen. In theory, half of all the rolls should yield an even number, but actual experiments may yield different results.

Online Connection www.SaxonMathResources.com

Geometric probability is a theoretical probability based on geometric measurements such as length, area, or volume.

1 Warm Up

Use the Warm Up to review the prerequisite skills for this lesson.

2 New Concepts

In this lesson, students learn to find the probability that a random event will occur.

Discuss the definitions of **probability, likelihood, probability experiment, random event, random,** and **geometric probability.**

MATH BACKGROUND

Remind students that a permutation is a selection of items where order is important. The permutation is found using the formula $P(n, r) = \frac{n!}{(n-r)!}$, where n is the number of objects and r is the number of items in the selected group.

Also remind students that a combination is a selection of items where order does not matter. The combination of n objects taken r at a time is $C(n, r) = \frac{n!}{r!(n-r)!}$.

LESSON RESOURCES

Student Edition Practice Workbook 55
Reteaching Master 55
Adaptations Master 55
Challenge and Enrichment Master C55

Example 1

This example demonstrates how to calculate probability.

Additional Example 1

a. A box contains 50 raffle tickets. The tickets are numbered 1 to 50 inclusive. What is P(multiple of 10) when a ticket is drawn from the box? 0.1

b. Estimate the probability that a point chosen randomly inside the figure is in the shaded area. 50%

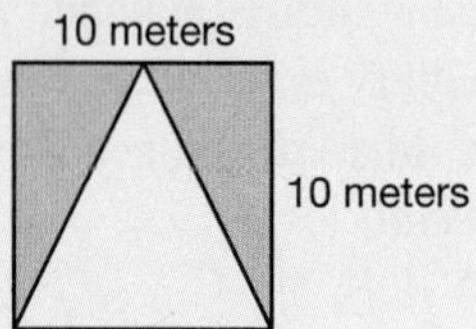

Example 2

The example shows students how to calculate probability using permutations and combinations.

Additional Example 2

a. All of the lockers in the gym are labeled with 2 digits such that each locker is labeled differently. What is the probability that a locker chosen at random has a label with the second digit being zero. 10%

b. A box contains 25 compact discs. The box contains the following types of CDs: 5 country, 5 hip hop, 5 rap, 5 jazz, and 5 classical. What is the probability that the first five CDs randomly selected from the box will be one from each group? ≈0.0588

Hint

For mutually exclusive events A and B, $P(A \text{ or } B) = P(A) + P(B)$.

Example 1 Calculating Probability

a. A calculator is programmed to generate random integers from 1 to 100 inclusive when the enter button is pressed. What is P(multiple of 20) when the enter button is pressed one time?

SOLUTION Each outcome (numbers 1 to 100) is equally likely. Use the formula $P(\text{event}) = \frac{\text{number of favorable outcomes}}{\text{total number of outcomes}}$. There are five favorable outcomes (20, 40, 60, 80, and 100) and 100 total outcomes.

$$P(\text{multiple of } 20) = \frac{5}{100} = \frac{1}{20} = 0.05$$

Notice that the event of getting a multiple of 20 is made up of the mutually exclusive events of getting 20, 40, 60, 80, and 100. The probability can also be found by adding $P(20)$, $P(40)$, $P(60)$, $P(80)$, and $P(100)$: $0.01 + 0.01 + 0.01 + 0.01 + 0.01 = 0.05$.

b. Estimate the probability that a point chosen randomly inside the figure is in the shaded region.

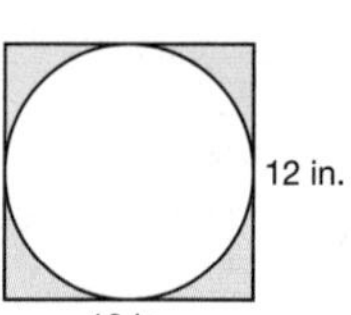

SOLUTION
$$P(\text{shaded region}) = \frac{\text{area of shaded region}}{\text{area of square}}$$
$$= \frac{\text{area of square} - \text{area of circle}}{\text{area of square}}$$
$$= \frac{s^2 - \pi r^2}{s^2} = \frac{12^2 - \pi 6^2}{12^2}$$
$$= \frac{144 - 36\pi}{144} \approx 0.2146$$

The probability that the point is in the shaded region is about 21.46%.

Example 2 Calculating Probability from Permutations and Combinations

a. All of the parking spaces in a lot are labeled with two different digits so that each parking space is labeled differently. What is the probability that a parking spot chosen at random is labeled with two even digits?

SOLUTION The total number of outcomes is a permutation because space 14 is different from space 41. The number of outcomes is ${}_{10}P_2 = 90$.

The outcomes that make up the event are numbers that begin with 0, 2, 4, 6, and 8. Each of these can be followed by an even number other than the number that makes up the first digit, so each of 0, 2, 4, 6, and 8 can be followed by four other digits. The number of favorable outcomes is therefore $5 \cdot 4 = 20$.

$$P(2 \text{ even digits}) = \frac{20}{90} = \frac{2}{9} \approx 0.22 \text{ or about } 22\%$$

b. A set of 22 books (volumes 1 through 22) are in a crate. If a student randomly chooses 5 books from the crate, what is the probability that the student picks either the first five volumes or the last five volumes?

SOLUTION The total number of outcomes is a combination because choosing volumes 1, 2, 3, 4, and 5 is the same as choosing volumes 5, 4, 3, 2, and 1. The number of outcomes is ${}_{22}C_5 = 26{,}334$.

Out of the possible 26,334 possible groupings of 5 books, there are two favorable groupings, the one with the first five volumes and the one with the last five volumes.

$$P(\text{first five or last five}) = \frac{2}{26{,}334} = \frac{1}{13{,}167} \approx 0.00008$$

When two events are independent, the occurrence of one event does not affect the probability of the other. When events are dependent, the occurrence of one event does affect the probability of the other.

Math Language

Conditional probability $P(B|A)$ is the probability of event B given that event A has occurred.

Probability of Independent and Dependent Events
For independent events A and B, $P(A \text{ and } B) = P(A) \cdot P(B)$. For dependent events A and B, $P(A \text{ and } B) = P(A) \cdot P(B\|A)$, where $P(B\|A)$ is the probability of B given that A has already occurred.

Example 3 Calculating the Probability of Independent and Dependent Events

a. A calculator is programmed to generate random integers from 1 to 100 inclusively when the enter button is pressed. If the enter button is pressed twice, what is the probability of getting a multiple of 20 and then a number greater than 90?

SOLUTION Because the occurrence of a multiple of 20 on one press does not affect the probability of getting a number greater than 90 on the next, the events are independent. Multiply the individual probabilities.

$$P(\text{multiple of } 20, > 90) = \frac{5}{100} \cdot \frac{10}{100} = \frac{1}{20} \cdot \frac{1}{10} = \frac{1}{200}$$

b. A bag contains 2 red and 6 blue marbles. What is the probability of picking a red marble, keeping it out of the bag, and then picking a blue marble?

SOLUTION Keeping the first marble out of the bag affects the probability of picking the next marble because the sample space has one less outcome. Whereas $P(\text{blue})$ would be $\frac{6}{8} = \frac{3}{4}$ if the events were independent, it is now $\frac{6}{7}$ because the events are dependent.

$$P(\text{red then blue}) = \frac{2}{8} \cdot \frac{6}{7} = \frac{12}{56} = \frac{3}{14}$$

Example 3

This example demonstrates how to calculate the probability of independent and dependent events.

Additional Example 3

a. There are balls numbered 1 to 50 inclusively in a box. You randomly pick a ball from the box and then replace it. Then, your classmate randomly picks a ball from the box. What is the probability that the first ball will have a number less than 6 and the second ball will have a number that is a multiple of 10?

$P(<6, \text{multiple of } 10) = \frac{5}{50} \cdot \frac{5}{50} = \frac{25}{2500} = \frac{1}{100}$

b. A box of candy contains 2 chocolate-covered cherries and 8 chocolate-covered caramels. What is the probability of randomly picking a cherry, keeping it out of the box, and then picking a caramel?

$P(\text{cherry then caramel}) = \frac{2}{10} \cdot \frac{8}{9} = \frac{16}{90} = \frac{8}{45}$

INCLUSION

Some students may have difficulty simplifying factorials such as $\frac{7!}{5!}$. Show them that $\frac{7 \cdot 6 \cdot 5 \cdot 4 \cdot 3 \cdot 2 \cdot 1}{5 \cdot 4 \cdot 3 \cdot 2 \cdot 1}$ is equivalent to $\frac{7 \cdot 6 \cdot 5!}{5!}$. By dividing out factorials that are equal, much of the tedium of simplifying factorials can be eliminated. Practice will reinforce that these expressions are equivalent.

Have students simplify each expression using the definition of factorial and by using cancellation.

1. $\frac{3!}{2!}$ 3
2. $\frac{4!}{2!}$ 12
3. $\frac{5!}{3!}$ 20

Example 4

This example demonstrates how to convert between probability and odds.

Additional Example 4

a. A small package contains 4 red and 3 yellow gumballs. What are the odds in favor of picking a yellow gumball? $\frac{3}{4}$

b. The odds in favor of an event are 4:1. What is the probability of the event? $P(\text{event}) = \frac{4}{5}$

Example 5

This example shows students how to create an experimental probability model.

Additional Example 5

The table at the bottom of the page shows the number of tourists that visit a small Caribbean island during each season. Construct an experimental probability model.

Like probability, the odds in favor of an event indicate the likelihood of the event occurring.

Odds of an Event
$\text{odds in favor of event} = \frac{\text{number of favorable outcomes}}{\text{number of unfavorable outcomes}}$

Odds are sometimes written as a ratio with the word *to* or with a colon.

number of favorable outcomes : number of unfavorable outcomes

Example 4 Calculating Odds

(a.) A bag contains 2 red and 6 blue marbles. What are the odds in favor of picking a red marble?

SOLUTION $\text{odds in favor of red} = \frac{\text{number of red marbles}}{\text{number of non-red marbles}} = \frac{2}{6} = \frac{1}{3}$

(b.) The odds in favor of an event are 5 : 2. What is the probability of the event?

SOLUTION The total number of outcomes is the sum of the favorable and unfavorable outcomes: $5 + 2 = 7$.

$$P(\text{event}) = \frac{\text{favorable outcomes}}{\text{all outcomes}} = \frac{5}{7}$$

A probability model shows the probability of each outcome in a sample space. The probabilities can be theoretical or experimental (based on actual data). **Experimental probability** is the ratio of the number of times an event occurs to the number of trials, or times, that an activity is performed. The sum of the probabilities in a probability model should sum to 1 (or near 1 if rounding).

Example 5 Application: Meteorology

The table shows the number of tropical storms in the Atlantic, Caribbean, and Gulf of Mexico from 1851 through 2006. Construct an experimental probability model.

Season	Jan–Apr	May–July	Aug–Oct	Nov–Dec
Number of Storms	5	198	1081	70

SOLUTION Divide the number of storms in each season by the total number of storms. The total is $5 + 198 + 1081 + 70 = 1354$. Round as needed.

Season	Jan–Apr	May–July	Aug–Oct	Nov–Dec
P(tropical storm)	0.00369	0.14623	0.79838	0.05170

Check The sum of the probabilities, $0.00369 + 0.14623 + 0.79838 + 0.05170$, is 1.

Additional Example 5 Table

Season	Jan–Apr	May–Jul	Aug–Oct	Nov–Dec
Tourists	55	2053	15,175	759

Season	Jan–Apr	May–Jul	Aug–Oct	Nov–Dec
Tourists	0.0030	0.1138	0.8411	0.0421

Lesson Practice

a. (Ex 1) A calculator is programmed to generate random integers from 1 to 10 inclusively when the enter button is pressed. What is P(perfect square) when the enter button is pressed one time? $\frac{3}{10}$

b. (Ex 1) Estimate the probability that a point chosen randomly inside the rectangle is in the shaded region. $\frac{11}{14} \approx 0.79$

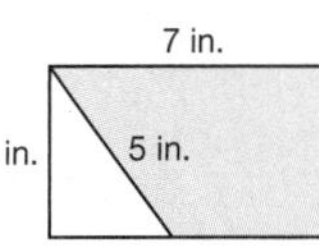

c. (Ex 2) Five of seven athletes of varying heights will be chosen for a photo. If their positions are randomly chosen, what is the probability that they are lined up from shortest to tallest from left to right? $\frac{1}{2520} \approx 0.04\%$

d. (Ex 2) A teacher has 6 papers to grade. If she randomly chooses 4 papers to grade after school, what is the probability that she chooses the papers of the four students who usually score the highest? $\frac{1}{15} \approx 6.7\%$

e. (Ex 3) A calculator is programmed to generate random numbers from 1 to 100 inclusively when the enter button is pressed. If the enter button is pressed twice, what is the probability of getting a number less than 10 and then a number greater than 50? $\frac{9}{100} \cdot \frac{50}{100} = 4.5\%$

f. (Ex 3) A bag contains 15 red and 10 blue marbles. What is the probability of picking a blue marble, keeping it out of the bag, and then picking another blue marble? $\frac{3}{20} = 15\%$

g. (Ex 4) What are the odds of rolling a six on a number cube? 1 to 5

h. (Ex 4) The probability of an event is 10%. What are the odds in favor of the event? 1 to 9

i. (Ex 5) The table shows the number of wins, losses, and overtime losses of the Buffalo Sabres in the 2006–2007 regular season. Construct an experimental probability model.

Buffalo Sabres

Wins	Losses	Overtime Losses
53	22	7

i. **Buffalo Sabres**

Wins	Losses	Overtime Losses
53	22	7
0.6463	0.2683	0.0854

Practice Distributed and Integrated

Simplify.

1. (44) $\frac{1}{-2\sqrt{24}}$ $-\frac{\sqrt{6}}{24}$

2. (44) $\frac{\sqrt{5}+3}{\sqrt{2}+\sqrt{45}}$

3. (44) $\frac{-1}{\sqrt{12}+3}$ $\frac{-2\sqrt{3}+3}{3}$

2. $\frac{\sqrt{10}-9\sqrt{5}+3\sqrt{2}-15}{-43}$

4. (40) $5\sqrt{5}(2\sqrt{5}-3\sqrt{10})$

5. (40) $3\sqrt{200}-5\sqrt{18}+7\sqrt{50}$

6. (40) $2\sqrt{3}\cdot 2\sqrt{2}(6\sqrt{6}-3\sqrt{2})$

4. $50-75\sqrt{2}$
5. $50\sqrt{2}$
6. $144-24\sqrt{3}$

7. (43) **Write** Explain why all solutions of the system $\begin{matrix} x \geq 1 \\ y > x \end{matrix}$ lie in quadrant I. See Additional Answers.

***8.** (54) Given the objective function P and the constraints, find the minimum and maximum values for the objective function. $P = 7x + 8y$ given $x \geq 0$, $y \geq 0$, $2x + 3y \leq 100$, $4x + 5y \geq 75$ Minimum: 120; Maximum: 350

ENGLISH LEARNERS

Explain the meaning of the word **probability.** Say, "Probability is the possibility or likelihood that an event will occur."

Connect the meaning of probability with familiar occurrences. For example, if you see lightning, it is highly probable that you will soon hear thunder. Conversely if you live in a desert region, it is very improbable that it will rain every day.

Discuss other familiar examples of probable and improbable events.

Have students identify the events for which they are calculating the probability in problems **a** and **b.**

Lesson Practice

Problem a

Scaffolding Remind students that the perfect squares from 1 to 10 are 1, 4, and 9. Therefore, there are three favorable outcomes.

Problem c

Error Alert Remind students to use the formula $P(n, r) = \frac{n!}{(n-r)!}$ to find the total number of outcomes. There is only one favorable outcome.

Check for Understanding

The questions below help assess the concepts taught in this lesson.

1. **"What is probability?"** the likelihood that an event will occur
2. **"What ratio do you set up to determine the probability of an event?"** $\frac{\text{number of favorable outcomes}}{\text{total number of outcomes}}$

3 Practice

Math Conversations

Discussions to strengthen understanding

Problem 1

Guide students by asking the following questions.

"Are there any perfect factors for 24?" $\sqrt{4\cdot 6}$

"If you simplify $\sqrt{4}$, what is the expression?" $\frac{1}{-2\cdot 2\cdot\sqrt{6}}$

"How do you clear $\sqrt{6}$ from the denominator?" Multiply the expression by $\frac{\sqrt{6}}{\sqrt{6}}$.

Problem 7

Have students graph the equations. The answer to the question should be apparent to students when they see the graphs.

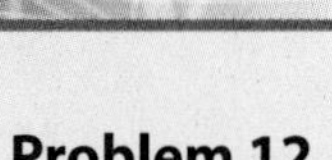

Problem 12

Error Alert

Some students might think that there are 14 kittens total in this problem. There are actually 18 kittens under consideration.

Problem 13

Remind students that the values for r can range from 1 to -1. The nearer the r value is to 1 or -1, the closer the points are to a straight line.

Problem 14

Point out that if students were standing on a street and a car or truck with a siren sounding approached and then passed them, they would experience the Doppler Effect.

9. (37) **Error Analysis** Two students are subtracting the rational expressions $\frac{2x}{2x^2 + 7x - 15}$ and $\frac{1}{x+5}$ but get different results. Which student made the mistake? Explain.

9. Student B forgets to distribute the minus sign to the two terms in the numerator.

Student A	Student B
$\frac{2x}{2x^2 + 7x - 15} - \frac{1}{x+5}$	$\frac{2x}{2x^2 + 7x - 15} - \frac{1}{x+5}$
$= \frac{2x}{(2x-3)(x+5)} - \frac{(2x-3)\bullet}{(x+5)(2x-3)}$	$= \frac{2x}{(2x-3)(x+5)} - \frac{(2x-3)}{(x+5)(2x-3)}$
$= \frac{3}{2x^2 + 7x - 15}$	$= \frac{4x-3}{2x^2 + 7x - 15}$

10. (49) **Multi-Step** Suppose one term in the expansion of $(a + b)^n$ is $1716a^7b^6$.

a. To what power was $(a + b)$ raised? 13 **b.** Which term is $1716a^7b^6$? 7th term

11. (41) **Geometry** Write the length of the diagonal of a 3 ft by 3 ft square as a simplified radical expression. $3\sqrt{2}$

***12.** (55) **Pet Shelter** In a pet shelter, there are two pairs of related kittens among 14 other kittens. What is the probability that someone randomly selecting two kittens will choose either pair of the related kittens? $\frac{2}{153} \approx 1.3\%$

13. (45) **Multiple Choice** Which value of r describes the set of points which are *farthest* from forming a line? C

A $r = -0.99$ **B** $r = -0.4$ **C** $r = 0.22$ **D** $r = 0.81$

14. (50) **Doppler Effect** When something making a sound moves in relation to a stationary listener, the frequency heard by the listener is not the same as the actual frequency of the sound at its source. In normal atmospheric conditions, if f_l is the frequency (in hertz, or cycles per second) heard by the listener, f_s is the frequency at the source, and v is the velocity of the sound source (in miles per hour), then $f_l = \frac{740f_s}{740 - v}$.

Suppose you are standing still and a police car is moving away from you with its siren blaring at 1800 hertz. You estimate its speed at about 6000 feet per minute. What frequency do you hear? about 1983 Hz

***15.** (54) **Analyze** Mobile-1 has two cell phone plans, the Star Plan and the Silver Plan. The cost for each plan is shown in the table. A small company is comparing the two plans. The company needs at least 10 cell phones, one for each sales rep, and each rep will use at least 800 minutes per month. What options does this company have? The Star Plan is $656 per month, and the Silver Plan is $625 per month. Although the Silver Plan has a higher start-up fee, over the long-term it is still the better deal.

Monthly Phone Rates

	Star Plan	Silver Plan
Start-up fee	$75	$125
Free minutes	2200	1500
Per minute rate above free minutes	7 cents	5 cents
Monthly service charge	$25 × the number of cell phones	$30 × the number of cell phones

CHALLENGE

Have students find the fully expanded expression for problem 10.

$a^{13} + 13a^{12}b + 78a^{11}b^2 + 286a^{10}b^3 + 715a^9b^4 + 1287a^8b^5 + 1716a^7b^6 + 1716a^6b^7 + 1287a^5b^8 + 715a^4b^9 + 286a^3b^{10} + 78a^2b^{11} + 13ab^{12} + b^{13}$

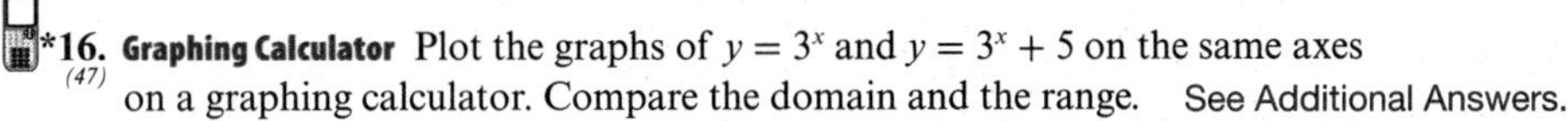

*16. **Graphing Calculator** Plot the graphs of $y = 3^x$ and $y = 3^x + 5$ on the same axes
(47) on a graphing calculator. Compare the domain and the range. See Additional Answers.

17. **Multi-Step** How many 6-letter words (including nonsense words) can be
(42) formed from the letters **A B C D E F**?

a. If the order of the six letters doesn't matter? 720

b. If the letter **B** must be in the first place? 120

c. Is the answer in part **a** different from the answer for part **b**? Explain.

17c. To find the answer for part **a** you must use 6!, but you use 5! for part **b** since there is only 1 choice for the first letter.

18. **Analyze** Suppose there are three tiles in a bag, labeled A, B, and C. A tile is
(33) chosen at random, then a second tile is chosen at random, and then a third tile is chosen at random. Each tile that is chosen is replaced in the bag. List all the outcomes in the sample space of this experiment. How many outcomes are in the sample space?

18. AAA, AAB, AAC, ABA, ABB, ABC, ACA, ACB, ACC, BAA, BAB, BAC, BBA, BBB, BBC, BCA, BCB, BCC, CAA, CAB, CAC, CBA, CBB, CBC, CCA, CCB, CCC; 27 outcomes

19. **Coordinate Geometry** The vertices of a triangle are $A(-3, 6)$, $B(2, -4)$, and
(46) $C(-3, -4)$. Find the value of the cotangent of $\angle B$. 0.5

*20. **Error Analysis** The odds in favor of an event are 3 to 5. Which student made an error
(55) in finding the probability of the event? What is the error?

Student A	Student B
$P(\text{event}) = \frac{3}{3+5}$ $= \frac{3}{8} = 37.5\%$	$P(\text{event}) = \frac{3}{5}$ $= 60\%$

Student B made the error. The denominator should be the total number of outcomes, both favorable, 3, and unfavorable, 5.

*21. **Compound Interest** You deposit p dollars into a savings account. If the account
(53) earns interest at a rate of 1% per quarter, then after one quarter your account is worth $f(p) = (1.01)p$ dollars.

a. What does the function $f(f(p))$ represent? amount the account is worth after 2 quarters

b. What's the value of $f(f(p))$? $f(1.01p) = 1.01(1.01p) = 1.0201p$

c. How much is your account worth after a year? $f(f(f(f(p)))) = (1.01)^4\,p \approx 1.04p$

22. **Architecture** Many famous works of architecture have sides whose
(23) proportions follow the Golden Ratio. To derive the Golden Ratio, look at the diagram to the right.

a. The line segment is divided into two segments, one of length a and one of longer length b. Write the ratio of the shorter segment to the longer segment. $\frac{a}{b}$

b. Now write the ratio of the longer segment to the sum of the lengths of both segments. $\frac{b}{a+b}$

c. The Golden Ratio is for values of a and b such that both ratios are equal to each other. Write this as an equation. $\frac{b}{a+b} = \frac{a}{b}$

d. Multiply both sides by the expression $b(a + b)$. $b^2 = a^2 + ab$

e. If $a = 1$ and $b = x$, find the roots of this quadratic equation using the quadratic formula. $x = \frac{1 \pm \sqrt{5}}{2}$

f. Which root can you ignore? Why? $x = \frac{1-\sqrt{5}}{2}$; because the value is negative

g. To the nearest thousandth, what is the value of the Golden Ratio? 1.618

Problem 18

Error Alert

Remind students that the tiles are placed back in the bag. Therefore, there are three possible outcomes for each draw.

***23.** (55) **Multiple Choice** The probability of an event is $\frac{x}{y}$. Which shows the odds in favor of the event? **D**

A x to y **B** y to x **C** x to $(x - y)$ **D** x to $(y - x)$

24. (50) **Temperature** The formula to convert degrees Fahrenheit to degrees Celsius is $C = \frac{5}{9}(F - 32)$.

Find the formula to convert degrees Celsius to degrees Fahrenheit by finding the inverse for this function. $F = \frac{9}{5}C + 32$

25. (52) **Explain** Explain why all 30°-60°-90° triangles are similar. See Additional Answers.

26. (40) Find the area of this isosceles triangle. Dimensions are in inches.
$2\sqrt{17}$ in²

$\sqrt{21}$ $\sqrt{21}$
4

Divide using synthetic division.

27. (51) $x^3 - 2$ by $x - 5$ $x^2 + 5x + 25 + \frac{123}{x - 5}$

28. (51) $2x^3 - 1$ by $x - 2$ $2x^2 + 4x + 8 + \frac{15}{x - 2}$

29. (26) Find the equation of the line that passes through (6, 0) and (−3, −3). $y = \frac{1}{3}x - 2$

30. (51) **Predict** The result of dividing one polynomial by another is $x^2 - 6x + 8 - \frac{2}{x - 4}$. What two polynomials might have been divided? Sample: $x^3 - 10x^2 + 32x - 34$, $x - 4$

Problem 26

"The formula for finding the area of a triangle is $A = \frac{1}{2}bh$."

"How can you find the value for h in this triangle?" Use the Pythagorean Theorem.

"What is the value for h?" $\sqrt{17}$

"What is the area of the triangle?" $\frac{1}{2}(4)(\sqrt{17}) = 2\sqrt{17}$

Problem 29

Extend the Problem

Have students state the slope of the line and the y-intercept. Have them graph the line.
The slope of the line is $\frac{1}{3}$. The equation of the line is $y = \frac{1}{3}x - 2$.

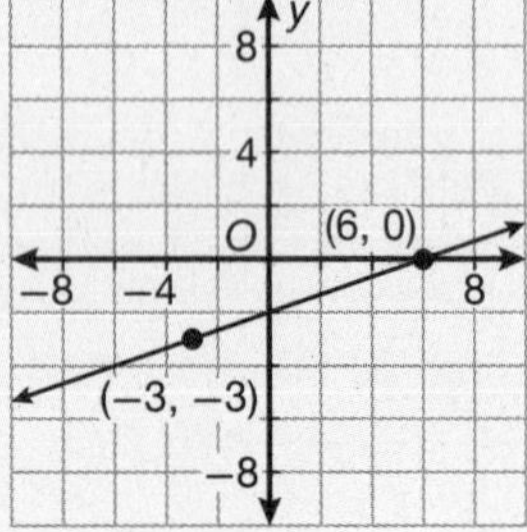

INCLUSION

Have students review material about similar triangles and 30°-60°-90° triangles before attempting to answer problem 25.

LOOKING FORWARD

Calculating probability prepares students for

- **Lesson 60** Distinguishing Between Mutually Exclusive and Independent Events
- **Lesson 68** Finding Conditional Probability

LESSON 56

Finding Angles of Rotation

Warm Up

1. (41) **Vocabulary** To find the length of the hypotenuse of a right triangle, given the lengths of the legs, use the ________. Pythagorean Theorem

2. (46) Sin A is $\frac{5}{13}$ and cos A is $\frac{12}{13}$. Find csc A and sec A. $\frac{13}{5}, \frac{13}{12}$

3. (3) Find the product of matrix A and matrix B. $\begin{bmatrix} 82 \\ 108 \end{bmatrix}$

$A = \begin{bmatrix} 2 & 7 \\ 3 & 9 \end{bmatrix}$ $\qquad B = \begin{bmatrix} 6 \\ 10 \end{bmatrix}$

New Concepts

Rotations can be important in many applications such as flying aircraft, designing views for computer games, and describing patterns in art.

Angles of Rotation

An angle is said to be in **standard position** when its vertex is at the origin and one ray is on the positive x-axis. The **terminal side** of the angle is the ray of the angle that is rotated relative to the x-axis. **The initial side** of the angle is located directly on the x-axis.

An angle formed by rotating the terminal side and keeping the initial side in place is called the **angle of rotation.** The terminal side can be rotated more than 360°.

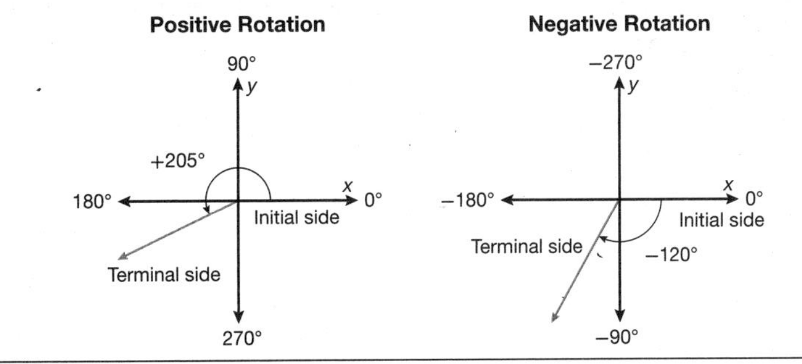

Caution

To measure positive rotation, rotate *counterclockwise* from the initial side. To measure negative rotation, rotate *clockwise* from the initial side.

Example 1 Drawing Angles of Rotation in Standard Position

Draw each of the indicated angles in standard position.

a. 45°

SOLUTION

Start at the initial side and rotate the terminal side counterclockwise to 45°.

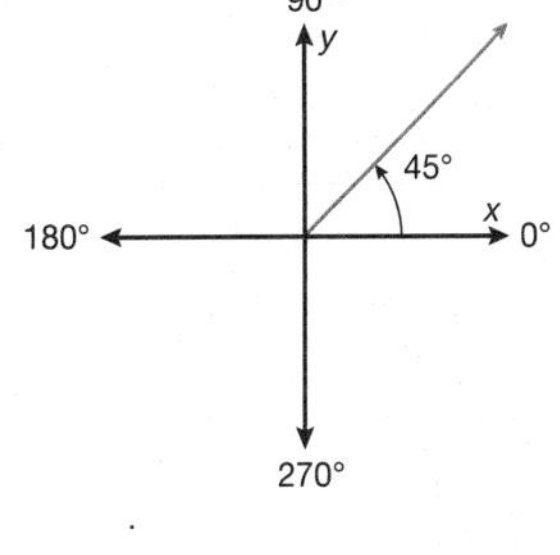

Online Connection
www.SaxonMathResources.com

LESSON 56

1 Warm Up

For problem 2, remind students of reciprocal trigonometric functions.

2 New Concepts

In this lesson, students draw angles of rotation in standard position, find the measures of coterminal angles, find reference angles, and find values of trigonometric functions.

Example 1

Remind students to rotate the terminal side of the angle counterclockwise.

Additional Example 1

Draw each of the indicated angles in standard position.

a. 60°

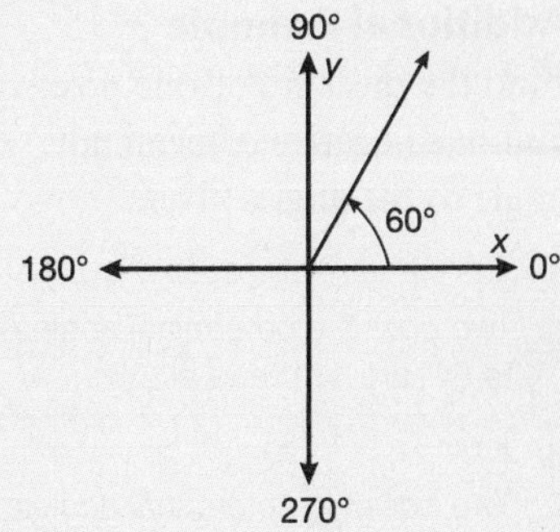

MATH BACKGROUND

In previous mathematics classes, students defined an angle as two rays formed with the same endpoint. In trigonometry, these same rays have names—initial side and terminal side.

The six trigonometric functions introduced in this lesson are used throughout the remaining trigonometry lessons. These functions are used extensively to solve sides and angles of a right triangle.

There are applications that use the trigonometric functions. Navigation is one area.

In navigation, the trigonometric functions are used to find the position of a plane or ship, or to calculate distances. Surveying is another application. Surveyors use trigonometry when measuring angles.

Understanding the trigonometric functions will help students solve problems in real-world contexts.

LESSON RESOURCES

Student Edition Practice Workbook 56
Reteaching Master 56
Adaptations Master 56
Challenge and Enrichment Master C56

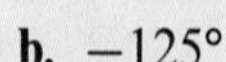

b. −125°

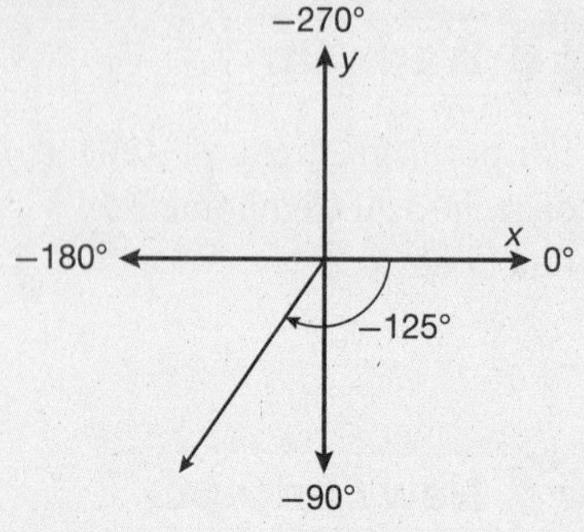

c. 380°

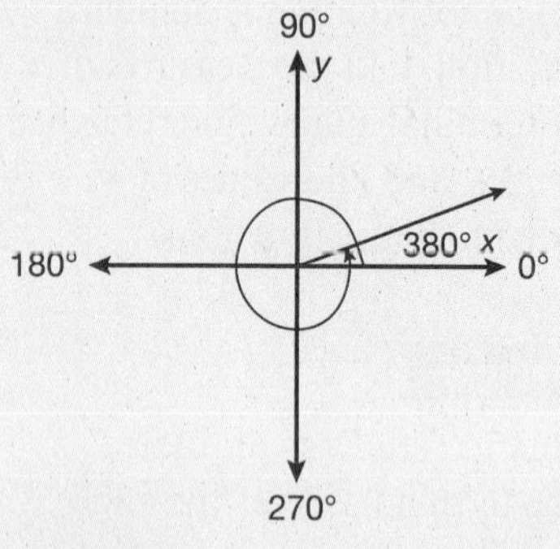

Example 2

Extend the Example

Have students draw the coterminal angles.

Additional Example 2

Find the measure of one positive and one negative coterminal angle to the angles given.

a. 54°
Two possible coterminal angles to 54° are 414° and −306°.

b. 475°
Two possible coterminal angles are 115° and −245°.

b. −225°

SOLUTION

Start at the initial side and rotate the terminal side clockwise to −225°.

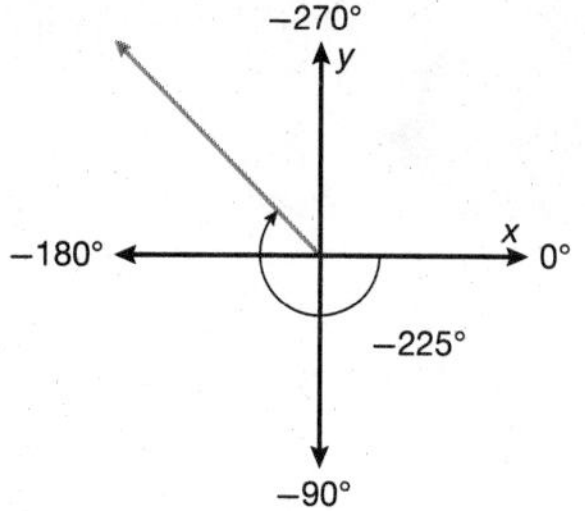

c. 440°

SOLUTION

440° can be rewritten as 360° + 80°. The terminal angle will rotate 80° counterclockwise from the initial side.

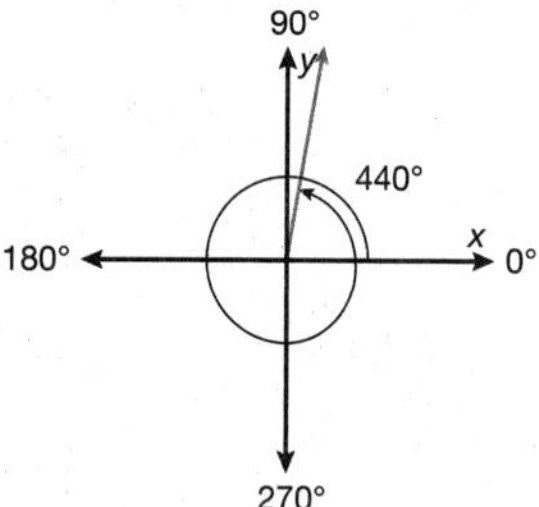

Hint

Rotating an angle 360° means the terminal side and the initial side coincide. That is, they are the same. To measure an angle larger than 360°, express it as a sum of 360° + x. If $x > 360°$, continue expressing it as 360° + … + 360° + x until $x < 360°$.

Coterminal angles are angles that share the terminal side. For example, the angles 90° and 450° are coterminal. Positive and negative angles may also be coterminal. The angle 45° is coterminal to the angle −315°. The number of coterminal angles is infinite, as any angle with measurement $x°$ can be represented as $x° + 360n$, where n is the number of times the angle rotates back to the initial side.

Example 2 Finding the Measures of Coterminal Angles

Find the measure of one positive and one negative coterminal angle to the angles given.

a. 68°

SOLUTION

To find a positive coterminal angle, add 360°. To find a negative coterminal angle, subtract 360°.

$68° + 360° = 428°$ $68° - 360° = -292°$

Two possible coterminal angles to 68° are 428° and −292°.

b. 515°

SOLUTION

To find a positive coterminal angle, subtract 360° from 515°.

$515° - 360° = 155°$

To find a negative coterminal angle, subtract 360° from 155°, which was already determined to be a coterminal angle to 515°.

$155° - 360° = -205°$

Two possible coterminal angles to 515° are 155° and −205°.

Hint

Another coterminal angle can be found by adding 360° to 515°.

515° + 360° = 875°

ENGLISH LEARNERS

To help students understand the meaning of **coterminal angles,** define the prefix co- as with, together, or jointly.

Discuss other words that have the prefix co-, such as coauthor, coworker, copilot, coexist,

Have students define coterminal angles and explain in their own words why the number of coterminal angles is infinite.

Connect the meaning of the prefix co- to the term coterminal angles: angles with the same terminal side. In Example 2, explain why there are positive and negative coterminal angles.

An angle with measurement θ in standard position forms an angle with the x axis. The acute angle formed by the terminal side of the angle of rotation and the x axis is called a **reference angle.** Reference angles always measure less than 90°.

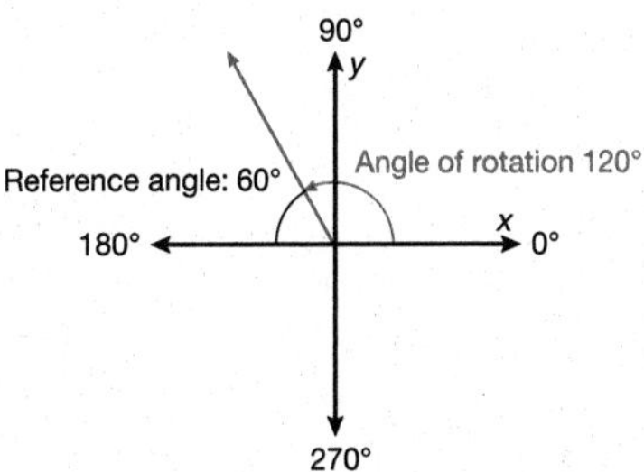

Example 3 Finding Reference Angles

Find the measure of the reference angle for each given angle.

Hint

To find reference angles for θ, $\theta < 360°$ with terminal side in:

Quadrant II - $180° - \theta$

Quadrant III - $\theta - 180°$

Quadrant IV - $360° - \theta$

a. $\theta = 155°$

SOLUTION

$180° - 155° = 25°$

The reference angle for 155° is 25°.

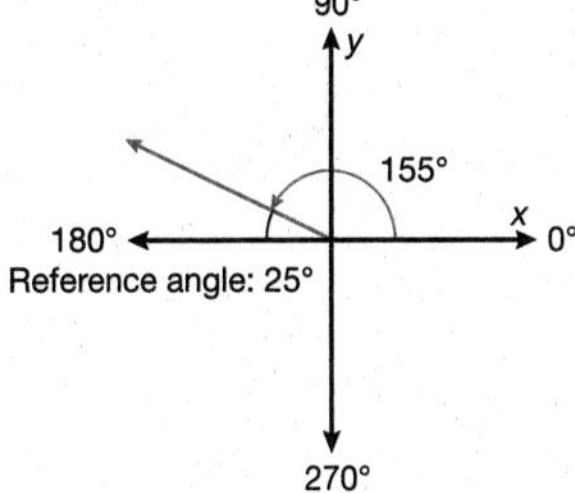

b. $\theta = 240°$

SOLUTION

$240° - 180° = 60°$

The reference angle for 240° is 60°.

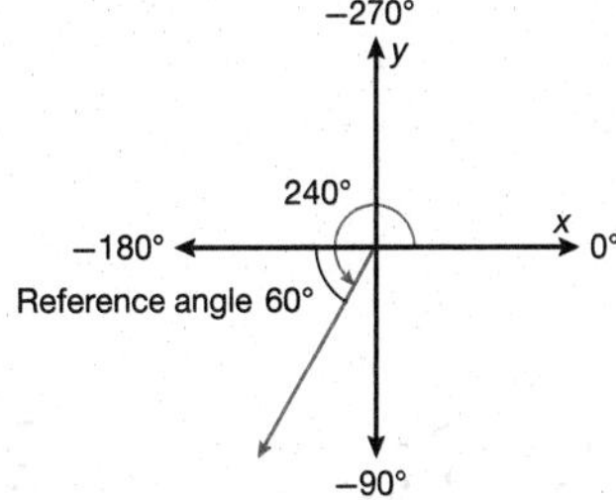

c. $\theta = -20°$

SOLUTION

Find the positive coterminal angle between 0° and 360°.

$-20° + 360° = 340°$

$360° - 340° = 20°$

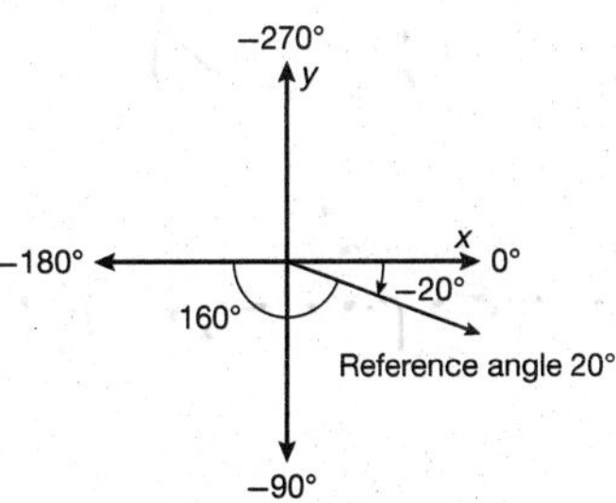

Angles in standard position and reference angles can be used to find the value of trigonometric functions for an angle with measurement θ. The distance r from a point Q with coordinates (x, y) located on the terminal side of the angle to the origin is given by $\sqrt{x^2 + y^2}$.

INCLUSION

Have students draw the given angle and show the rotation with a blue pen. In a different color pen, have students shade the reference angle.

Example 3

Review the definition of **reference angle.** Point out that reference angles always measure less than 90°.

Additional Example 3

Find the measure of the reference angle for each given angle.

a. $\theta = 115°$
The reference angle for 115° is 65°.

b. $\theta = 225°$
The reference angle for 225° is 45°.

c. $\theta = -55°$
The reference angle for −55° is 55°.

Example 4

Error Alert Students may have difficulty calculating the reciprocals for $\csc\theta$, $\sec\theta$, and $\cot\theta$. Review how to simplify fractions in a denominator.

Additional Example 4

Point Q is located on the terminal side of angle θ and has coordinates (6, 8). Find the exact value of the 6 trigonometric functions.

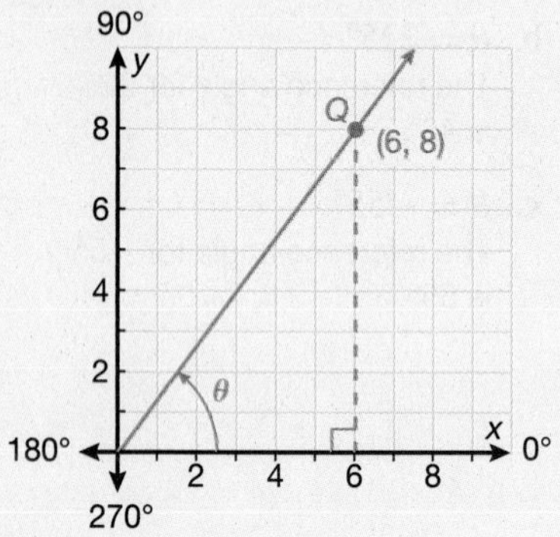

$\sin\theta = \frac{4}{5}$, $\cos\theta = \frac{3}{5}$, $\tan\theta = \frac{4}{3}$, $\csc\theta = \frac{5}{4}$, $\sec\theta = \frac{5}{3}$, $\cot\theta = \frac{3}{4}$

Example 5

To help students' understanding of polar coordinates, show the graph of (9, 35°) and (7, 305°).

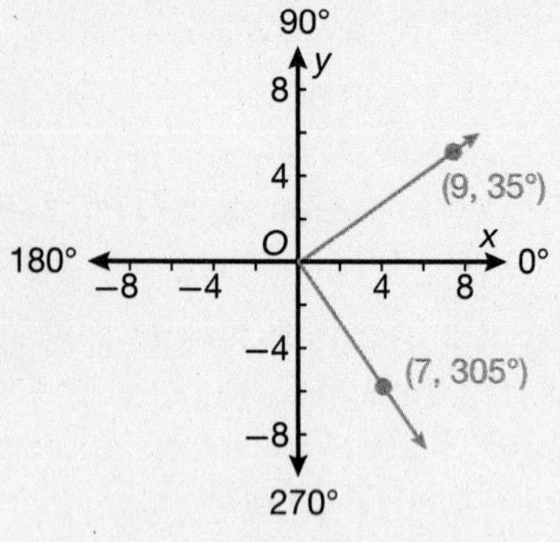

Additional Example 5

Air traffic control tells the pilot of a private plane to circle the airport. When the plane begins to circle, its polar coordinates (with respect to the airport) are (15, 60°), meaning 15 miles away and at 60°. Fifteen minutes later, the plane's polar coordinates are (12, 335°). What is the measure of the plane's angle of rotation about the airport? 275° + 360° n

---

Math Reasoning

Analyze The formula for distance is

$d = \sqrt{(x - x_1)^2 + (y - y_1)^2}$.

How does this formula relate to the formula $r = \sqrt{x^2 + y^2}$ given for the distance between Q and the origin?

The origin has coordinates (0, 0). Let Q have coordinates (x, y) and the origin be (x_1, y_1). Then the formula becomes $d = \sqrt{(x - 0)^2 + (y - 0)^2}$, which can be simplified to $d = \sqrt{x^2 + y^2}$.

Trigonometric Functions
For a point $Q(x, y)$ on the terminal side of θ in standard position and $r = \sqrt{x^2 + y^2}$,
$\sin\theta = \frac{y}{r}$ $\qquad$ $\cos\theta = \frac{x}{r}$ $\qquad$ $\tan\theta = \frac{y}{x}, x \neq 0$

Example 4 Finding Values of Trigonometric Functions

Point Q is located on the terminal side of angle θ and has coordinates $(-5, 12)$. Find the exact value of the 6 trigonometric functions for θ.

SOLUTION

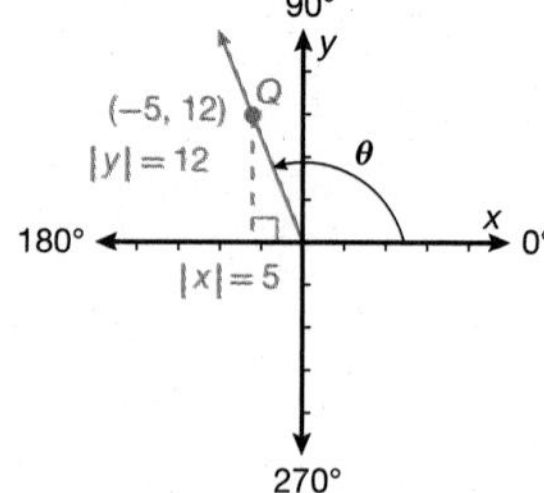

Step 1: Plot point Q and draw the angle in standard form. Then sketch a right triangle.

Step 2: Find the value of r.

$$r = \sqrt{x^2 + y^2}$$
$$= \sqrt{(-5)^2 + (12)^2}$$
$$= \sqrt{25 + 144}$$
$$= \sqrt{169}$$
$$= 13$$

Step 3: Use the values of x, y, and r to find the values of the sine, cosine, and tangent of angle θ.

$$\sin\theta = \frac{12}{13} \qquad \cos\theta = -\frac{5}{13} \qquad \tan\theta = -\frac{12}{5}$$

Step 4: Use reciprocals to find $\csc\theta$, $\sec\theta$, and $\tan\theta$.

$$\csc\theta = \frac{1}{\sin\theta} = \frac{13}{12} \qquad \sec\theta = \frac{1}{\cos\theta} = -\frac{13}{5} \qquad \cot\theta = \frac{1}{\tan\theta} = -\frac{5}{12}$$

Math Language

A vector can also be considered to be the terminal side of an angle of rotation. The coordinates (r, θ) are the polar coordinates of a point, and give the magnitude r of the vector forming an angle with measurement θ.

Example 5 Application: Air Traffic Control

Air traffic control tells the pilot of a passenger plane to circle an airport. When the plane begins to circle, its polar coordinates (with respect to the airport) are (9, 35°), meaning 9 miles away and at 35°. Ten minutes later, the plane's polar coordinates are (7, 305°). What is the measure of the plane's angle of rotation about the airport?

SOLUTION

The change in magnitude doesn't affect the angle of rotation. The information is not given of how many times the plane circled. The measure of the angle of rotation is some multiple of 360 degrees plus 305 – 35, or 270, degrees. That is, the rotation is through 270 + 360n degrees for some integer n.

ALTERNATE METHOD FOR EXAMPLE 4

Have students find the trigonometric functions in terms of the sides of the triangle, where opp = opposite side of θ, adj = adjacent side of θ, hyp = side opposite the right angle.

$$\sin\theta = \frac{\text{opp}}{\text{hyp}},\ \cos\theta = \frac{\text{adj}}{\text{hyp}},\ \tan\theta = \frac{\text{opp}}{\text{adj}},$$
$$\csc\theta = \frac{\text{hyp}}{\text{opp}},\ \sec\theta = \frac{\text{hyp}}{\text{adj}},\ \cot\theta = \frac{\text{adj}}{\text{opp}}$$

a.

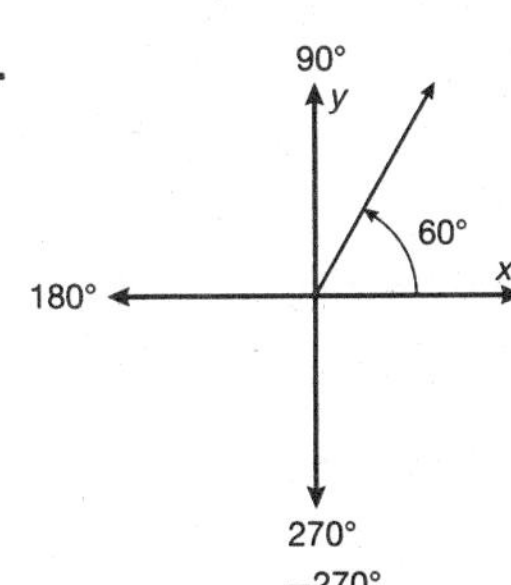

b.

-270°
y
-180°
x
0°
-120°
-90°

Lesson Practice

Draw each of the indicated angles in standard position.
(Ex 1)

a. 60° **b.** −120° **c.** 385° See Additional Answers.

Find the measure of one positive and one negative coterminal angle to the angles given.
(Ex 2)

d. 94° Sample: 454° and −266° **e.** 730° Sample: 370° and −350°

Find the measure of the reference angle for each given angle.
(Ex 3)

f. 115° 65° **g.** 200° 20° **h.** −145° 35°

i. Point P is located on the terminal side of angle θ and has coordinates (−15, −8). Find the exact values of the 6 trigonometric functions for θ. See Additional Answers.
(Ex 4)

j. A plane is located at (10, 50°). The first coordinate gives the miles from the airport and the second coordinate gives the angle. After 20 minutes, the plane's polar coordinates are (8, 355°). What is the measure of the plane's angle of rotation about the airport? 305° + 360°n
(Ex 5)

Practice Distributed and Integrated

Determine the kind of variation, if any, for each equation.

1. $y = ax^2 + bx + c$, for $a, b, c \neq 0$ no variation
(12)

2. $y = ax^2 + bx + c$, for any values of a, b, and c direct when a and $c = 0$
(12)

Point P is located on the terminal side of angle θ. Find the exact values of the 6 trigonometric functions for θ with the given coordinates for P.

***3.** $P(7, -24)$ See Additional Answers. ***4.** $P(-\sqrt{5}, 2)$ See Additional Answers.
(56) (56)

5. Identify the leading coefficient and the constant term in the polynomial $-x^3 + 5x - 2$. The leading coefficient is −1 and the constant term is −2.
(11)

6. Find the sixth term of the expansion of $(a + b)^9$. $126b^5a^4$
(49)

7. Given $f(x) = 2x - 7$ and $g(x) = -5x + 8$. Graph the sum $(f + g)(x)$.
(20)

7.

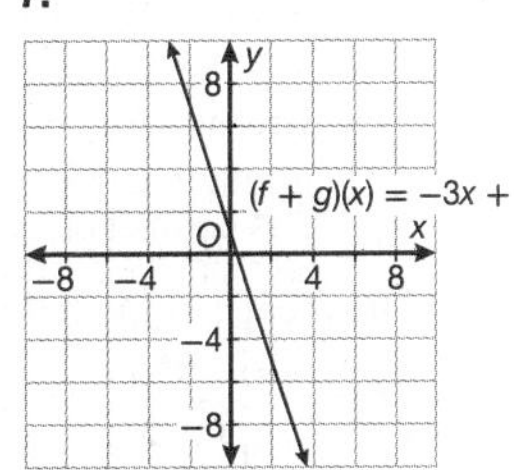

8. The odds in favor of an event are 4:12. What is the probability of the event happening? $\frac{1}{4}$
(54)

9. Justify A square room has an area of 196 square feet. What are the measurements of the room? Use a polynomial to explain. See Additional Answers.
(23)

10. Error Analysis Consider the graph shown. Donnie says the equation of this graph is $y = -5^x$. Chris disagrees; he says it is $y = (-5)^x$. Who is correct? Explain the error. Donnie is correct. The equation $y = (-5)^x$ is not usually considered an exponential function, since some values of x give complex values.
(47)

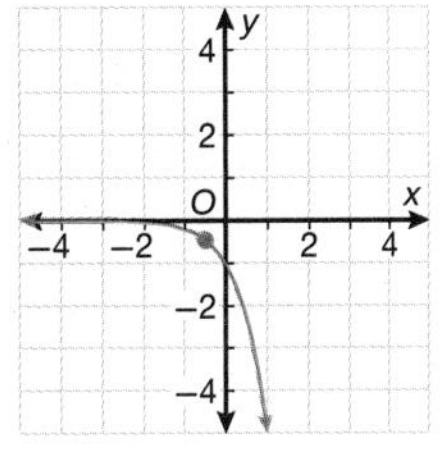

Lesson Practice

Problem h

Scaffolding Have students find the coterminal angle between 0° and 360°. Then subtract 180° from that result.

Check for Understanding

The questions below help assess the concepts taught in this lesson.

1. **"Explain how to draw a 425° angle in standard position."** Write 425° as 360° + 65°. Rotate the terminal angle 360° + 65° counterclockwise from the initial side. The angle is in Quadrant I.

2. **"How do you find the measure of the reference angle for 205°?"** Subtract 180° from 205°. The reference angle for 205° is 25°.

3 Practice

Math Conversations

Discussions to strengthen understanding

Problem 3

Guide the students by asking them the following questions.

"What quadrant is point P in?" Quadrant IV

"How do you find the value of r?" Find the square root of the sum of 49 and 576, which is 25.

"How do you find the values of the 6 trigonometric functions of angle θ?" Use the values x, y, and r in the appropriate ratios.

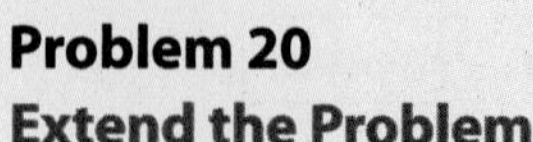

Problem 20
Extend the Problem

Have students find the reference angle. 20°

Problem 22

Have students work each denominator first. Encourage them to write fractions as improper fractions.

Problem 23

Encourage students to use single digits from 1 to 9.

Remind students the determinant of a 2 × 2 matrix is defined as

$$D = ad - cb$$

11. (18) **Exercise** Kellie's last three walks were 2.25 mi, 3.29 mi, and 2.318 mi. Use significant digits to find the sum of Kellie's walking distances. 7.86 mi

*12. (55) **Multi-Step** A brown bag contains 12 peaches and 8 nectarines.
 a. Which has the greater probability: randomly selecting 2 peaches or 2 nectarines? peaches
 b. How much greater is the probability? 20% greater

13. (27) **Multiple Choice** What is the range of the function? C
 A all real numbers between −4 and 4
 B all real numbers less than or equal to −5
 C all real numbers greater than or equal to −5
 D all real numbers

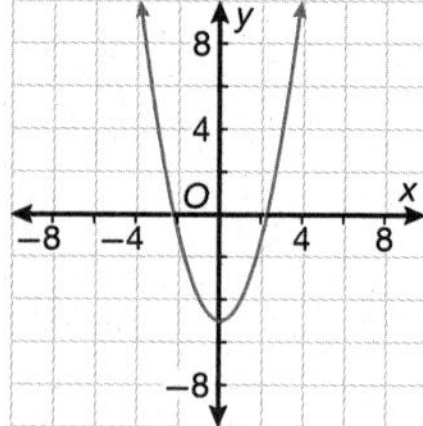

14. (49) Find the seventh term of the expansion of $(g + 2)^{12}$. $59{,}136g^6$

15. (46) **Sea Level** From an observation point 435 feet above sea level, a tourist spots a buoy at an angle of depression of 57° and another in the same line of sight at an angle of depression of 13°. To the nearest foot, how far apart are the buoys? 1602 feet

16. (15) **Investments** A couple has saved $20,000. An advisor suggests that they invest this amount in treasury bonds and in certificates of deposit (CDs). The couple can get a one-year CD that pays 5.42% (annual) interest, and a 2-year treasury bond that will yield 4.18% annually. If the couple wants to earn $1000 per year from the investment, how much should they invest in treasury bonds? about $6774

17. (39) **Food Preparation** Antonio is making a dip for a school function. Each tablespoon of olive oil has 15 grams of fat and each tablespoon of mayonnaise has 5 grams of fat. He wants the snack to have less than 75 grams of fat. Graph the inequality that represents the possible amounts of each ingredient in the dip. Choose a point in the shaded area. Tell what it means. Sample: (3, 5); The dip can have 3 tablespoons of olive oil and 5 tablespoons of mayonnaise.

17.

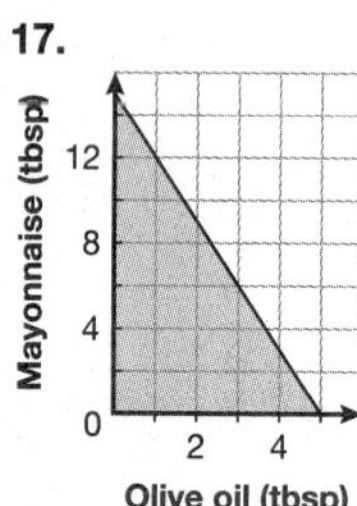

18. (45) **Error Analysis** A student said that the correlation coefficient for the data graphed is 1 because it follows a perfect pattern. Why is the student incorrect? The correlation coefficient only measures the strength and direction of linear relationships. These points do not form a straight line.

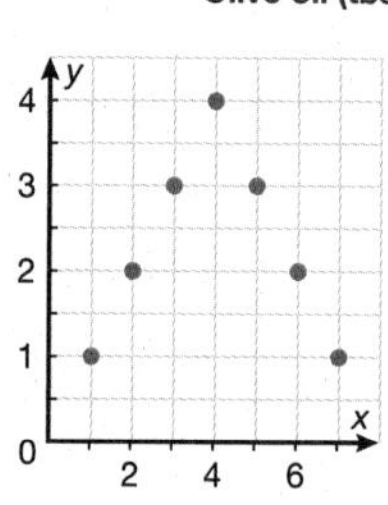

Draw each of the indicated angles in standard position. See Additional Answers.

*19. (56) 70° *20. (56) −200° *21. (56) −90°

22. (48) **Verify** Verify that the value of the complex fraction $3 + \frac{1}{7 + \frac{1}{15 + \frac{1}{16}}}$ is a good approximation of π.

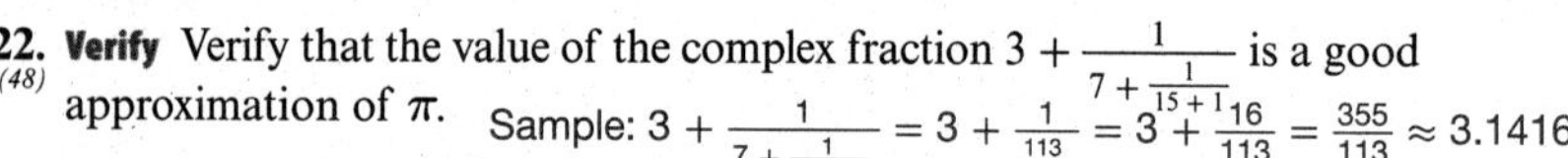

Sample: $3 + \frac{1}{7 + \frac{1}{15 + \frac{1}{16}}} = 3 + \frac{1}{\frac{113}{16}} = 3 + \frac{16}{113} = \frac{355}{113} \approx 3.1416$

23. (14) **Analyze** Create two 2 × 2 matrices that are inverses of each other. Calculate and compare their determinants. Explain your findings. The determinants are reciprocals of each other. That is, their product is 1, which is the determinant of the identity matrix, which in turn is the product of the two original matrices.

404 Saxon Algebra 2

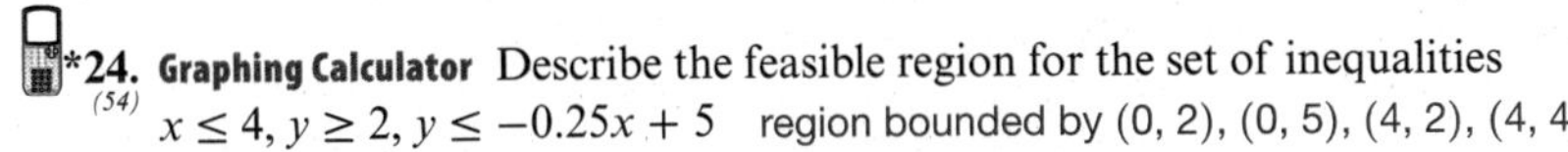

*24. **Graphing Calculator** Describe the feasible region for the set of inequalities (54)
$x \le 4$, $y \ge 2$, $y \le -0.25x + 5$ region bounded by (0, 2), (0, 5), (4, 2), (4, 4)

25. **Acceleration** A car increases its speed from 0 to 50 miles per hour. (22)
It then drives 50 miles per hour for the rest of the trip. Examine the graph shown. Does this graph represent a continuous, discontinuous, and/or discrete function? Justify your answer.   Continuous function; This function has no holes or points of discontinuity.

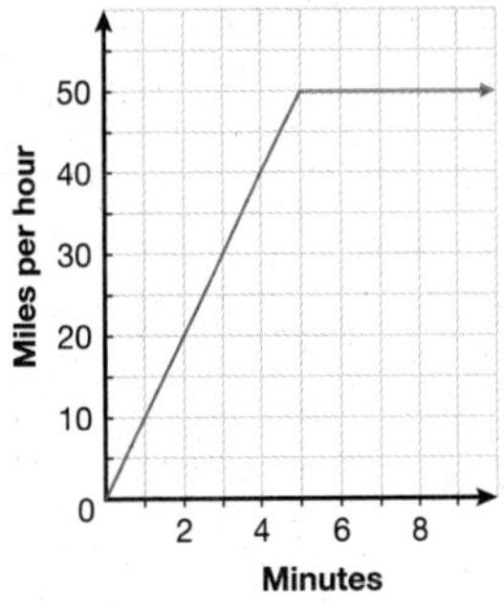

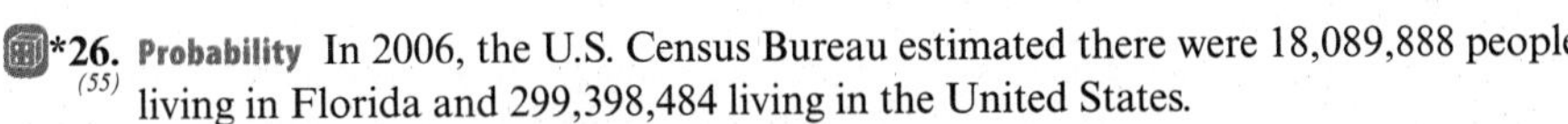

*26. **Probability** In 2006, the U.S. Census Bureau estimated there were 18,089,888 people living in Florida and 299,398,484 living in the United States. (55)

a. Estimate the probability that a person randomly selected in the United States lives in Florida.   about 6%

b. Estimate the odds in favor that a person randomly selected in the United States lives in Florida.   about 3 to 47

27. **Multi-Step** A bag of marbles contains 6 red marbles, 5 blue marbles, and 1 green marble. Two marbles are selected at random. Which is more likely: selecting 2 red marbles or 1 red and 1 blue marble? (42)

28. **Write** Describe how the graph of $y = -2.5(x - 5)^2 + 2$ differs from the graph of the parent function.   It is narrower, opens downward, and is shifted 5 units right and 2 units up. (30)

*29. A community center wants to build a rectangular playground and fence around it. The cost of fencing is \$25 per foot. The cost for painting the fence is \$14 per foot. The center cannot spend more than \$2500 on fencing. The playground cannot be any longer than 40 ft and needs to be at least 20 ft wide. What is the maximum area, in square feet, the center can get for the size of the playground?   about 241 square ft (54)

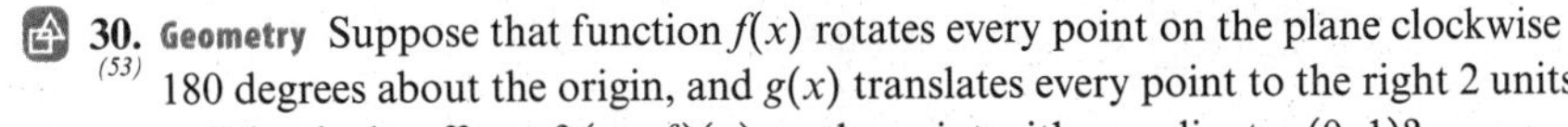

30. **Geometry** Suppose that function $f(x)$ rotates every point on the plane clockwise 180 degrees about the origin, and $g(x)$ translates every point to the right 2 units. (53)

a. What is the effect of $(g \circ f)(x)$ on the point with coordinates (0, 1)?

b. What is the effect of $(f \circ g)(x)$ on that same point? $g(x)$ takes (0, 1) to (2, 1), and $f(x)$ then takes (2, 1) to (−2, −1).

30a. $f(x)$ takes (0, 1) to (0, −1), and $g(x)$ then takes (0, −1) to (2, −1).

27. $P(\text{2 red marbles}) = \frac{\text{ways to get 2 red marbles}}{\text{total possible outcomes}} = \frac{C(6, 2)}{C(12, 2)} = \frac{15}{66} = \frac{5}{22}$

$P(\text{1 red and 1 blue}) = \frac{C(6, 1) \times C(5, 1)}{C(12, 2)} = \frac{6 \times 5}{66} = \frac{5}{11}$

It is more likely to pull 1 red and 1 blue marble

Problem 26

TEACHER TIP

Students may have difficulty solving the problem because of the large numbers presented. Reword the problem in terms of the numbers of students in the class and the entire school enrollment. Have students work the problem using those numbers. Then have them go back and work on the original problem given.

Problem 28

Error Alert

Students may switch h and k by shifting the graph 2 units to the right and 5 units up. Have them make a table of values and graph the function.

CHALLENGE

Find the five other trigonometric functions for angle θ, given $\csc \theta = \frac{5}{3}$ and the terminal side of angle θ is in Quadrant II.

$\sin \theta = \frac{3}{5}$, $\cos \theta = -\frac{4}{5}$, $\sec \theta = -\frac{5}{4}$,
$\tan \theta = -\frac{3}{4}$, $\cot \theta = -\frac{4}{3}$

LOOKING FORWARD

Angles of rotation prepares students for

- **Lesson 67** Finding Inverse Trigonometric Functions
- **Lesson 71** Using the Law of Sines
- **Lesson 77** Using the Law of Cosines
- **Lesson 96** Using Polar Coordinates
- **Lesson 119** Solving Trigonometric Equations

LESSON

57

1 Warm Up

For problem 1, write $16^{0.5}$ on the board and have students identify the exponent and the base.

2 New Concepts

In this lesson, students use exponential growth and decay functions to model application situations. They use natural logarithms to solve problems with exponential functions.

Example 1

Students apply the concept of exponential growth by computing the future value of a savings account using the expressions $P(1 + i)^n$ and Pe^{rt}, where P is the present value.

Additional Example 1

Show the expression you use to solve each problem.

A savings account earns interest at an annual rate of 6%, compounded monthly. If the present value is \$2,000, what will the future value be in 2 years? $2000\left(1 + \frac{0.06}{12}\right)^{2 \cdot 12}$, \$2,254.32

LESSON

57 Finding Exponential Growth and Decay

Warm Up

1. **Vocabulary** In an <u>exponential</u> function the independent variable is found in the exponent. (47)

2. Suppose that $f(x)$ has an inverse $g(x)$. What is $f(g(x))$? x (50)

3. Evaluate 2^{-1}. 0.5 (3)

4. True or False. A function of the form $y = ab^x$ is an exponential function if x is a real number, $a = 0$, $b > 0$, and $b \leq 1$. false (47)

New Concepts

Math Language

In the expression ab^x, b is a **growth factor** if $b > 1$. If $0 < b > 1$, then it is a decay factor.

A function is **increasing** if the output values increase as the input values increase. Its graph rises from left to right. **Exponential growth** functions are increasing functions used to model situations where a quantity always increases by the same percent for a given time period. It is modeled by the function $f(x) = ab^x$, where $a > 0$ and $b > 1$.

A function is **decreasing** if the output values decrease as the input values increase. Its graph falls from left to right. Exponential functions that are decreasing model **exponential decay.** Exponential decay is used to model situations where a quantity always decreases by the same percent in a given time period. It is modeled by the function $f(x) = ab^x$, where $a > 0$ and $0 < b < 1$.

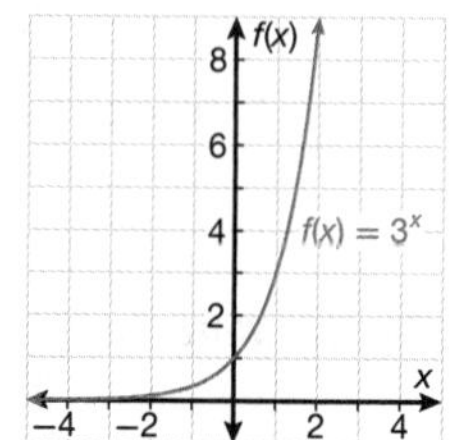

One common application of exponential growth is calculating the amount in an account that earns interest. Recall from Lesson 47 that the formula to find the amount A in an account with an initial deposit of P, interest rate r, years of interest t, and times compounded per year n is $A = P\left(1 + \frac{r}{n}\right)^{nt}$.

Reading Math

A decreasing function can also be written in the form $f(x) = ab^{-x}$, where $a > 0$, $b > 1$.

Example 1 Calculating Simple Interest

A savings account earns interest at an annual rate of 4%, compounded quarterly. If the account begins with a principal amount of \$1,000, what will its value be after 3 years?

SOLUTION

Use the formula for interest. The rate, r, is 0.04. The initial deposit is \$1000. It is compounded 4 times per year, and the time, t, is 3 year.

$$A = P\left(1 + \frac{r}{n}\right)^{nt}$$

$$A = 1000\left(1 + \frac{0.04}{4}\right)^{4(3)}$$

$$A = 1126.83$$

So the account will be worth approximately \$1126.83.

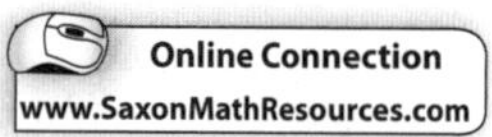

LESSON RESOURCES

Student Edition Practice Workbook 57
Reteaching Master 57
Adaptations Master 57
Challenge and Enrichment Masters C57, E57
Technology Lab Master 57

MATH BACKGROUND

The simplest exponential function has an equation of the form $y = b^x$, where b must be greater than 0 in order for the range of the function to contain only real numbers. The inverse of this function is the logarithm function with base b, specified by the equation $y = \log_b x$. Since the domain of the logarithmic function is the range of the corresponding exponential function, its domain is the set of positive numbers.

Applications in exponential growth and decay have functions of this type, often using the irrational number e as the base. The mathematical constant e is defined so that the value of the slope of the tangent line (derivative) of $f(x) = e^x$ at the point $x = 0$ is 1. Other ways of representing e are as the limit of a sequence or the sum of an infinite series. The exponential function $f(x) = e^x$ is important in calculus because it is its own derivative.

Math Language

The constant e is equal to $\left(1 + \frac{1}{n}\right)^n$ as the value of n goes to infinity.

Banks frequently compound interest continuously, meaning that n is infinite. To do this, they use the mathematical constant e, which is approximately equal to 2.718.

The formula to find the value of an account when interest is compounded continuously is $A = Pe^{rt}$.

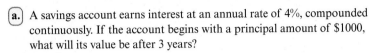

Example 2 Modeling Exponential Decay Calculating Continuous Interest

a. A savings account earns interest at an annual rate of 4%, compounded continuously. If the account begins with a principal amount of $1000, what will its value be after 3 years?

SOLUTION

Use the formula for continuously compounded interest, $A = Pe^{rt}$.

$A = Pe^{rt}$

$A = (1000)e^{(0.04)(3)}$

$A = 1127.50$

The value of the account will be approximately $1,127.50.

b. After 5 years of earning continuously compounded interest at the rate of 3.5%, a savings account is worth $3200. What was its value initially?

SOLUTION

This time, solve for P.

$A = Pe^{rt}$

$3200 = (P)e^{(0.035)(5)}$

$A = 2686.26$

The initial value of the account was $2686.26.

To solve problems using exponential growth and decay, first decide whether a situation exhibits the properties of growth or decay. Then, substitute values of x and y into the equation to solve for a and b.

Remember that x will generally represent the number of time intervals that pass in an exponential equation, and y will usually represent the total quantity of something after x periods of time.

Math Language

The **half-life** of a substance is the time it takes for one-half of the substance to decay.

Example 3 Finding Exponential Functions

The element Nobelium has a half-life of 58 minutes. Write an exponential equation to find the portion of a mass of Nobelium that is left after x minutes and find what percentage of an amount of Nobelium is left after 15 minutes.

INCLUSION

Materials: 100 pennies

Manipulative Use Have students work in pairs or small groups. Students toss the 100 pennies and remove those that land heads up. They record the number removed. They use the remaining pennies and repeat. They continue until all pennies have been removed.

Remind students that the chance that any penny will land heads up is 50%. So, about half of the pennies will be heads on each toss. But, the number of pennies decreases with each toss. So, the fraction of the original number left is $\frac{1}{2}$, then $\frac{1}{4}$, then $\frac{1}{8}$, then $\frac{1}{16}$, and so forth. Using exponents, the fraction left is $2^{-1}, 2^{-2}, 2^{-3}, 2^{-4}$, and so on. This type of pattern is called *exponential decay.*

Example 2

Students solve problems using continuously compounded interest.

Additional Example 2

a. A savings account accrues 6% interest, compounded continuously. If $2500 is deposited in the account, what will its value be after 2 years? $2,818.74

b. After 3 years of earning continuously compounded interest at the rate of 4%, a savings account is worth $2100. What was it worth initially? $1,862.53

Error Alert If students get the wrong answers for this type of problem, they might be identifying the values of P, r, and t incorrectly. Have them identify what each stands for and confirm that they have substituted numbers from the problem in correctly.

Example 3

Students write exponential functions to model word problems.

Additional Example 3

a. The half-life of Ununbium is 10 seconds. Find an exponential function to represent the percentage of Ununbium left after x seconds. $y = \left(\sqrt[10]{0.5}\right)^x$

b. The half-life of Bohrium is 1.5 hours. What percentage of a mass of Borium would be left after 35 minutes? approximately 76%

Example 4

Students find an exponential equation using a table of values.

Additional Example 4

A pendulum is released and the length of each swing of the pendulum is measured. A table of values showing the results is given below. Write an equation that relates the number of swings, x, and the distance of each swing, y. $y = (1.6)0.75^x$

Swing	Distance (ft)
0	1.6
2	0.9
4	0.51
6	0.28

Hint

The starting amount is arbitrary. Choose an amount that allows easy computation and remember to substitute half of that amount for y.

SOLUTION

The equation will be in the form $y = ab^x$. Since the question is asking for a percentage, a, which is the starting amount of material, is simply 1. We know that half of the mass decays in 58 minutes. Use this data point to find the equation.

$y = b^x$

$0.5 = b^{58}$

$b = \sqrt[58]{0.5}$

So the equation is $y = \left(\sqrt[58]{0.5}\right)^x$. Now substitute 15 for x.

$y = \left(\sqrt[58]{0.5}\right)^{15}$

$y \approx 0.84$

So approximately 84% of the Nobelium is left after 15 minutes.

Example 4 **Modeling Exponential Decay**

An experimenter measures the maximum distance a large pendulum travels from its resting point at each swing. The measurements are recorded in this table:

Swing	0	3	6	9	12	15
Distance (meters)	2.17	1.5	1.04	0.72	0.50	0.34

Using the table of values and the graph, write an exponential equation that relates the number of swings, x, and the distance of each swing, y.

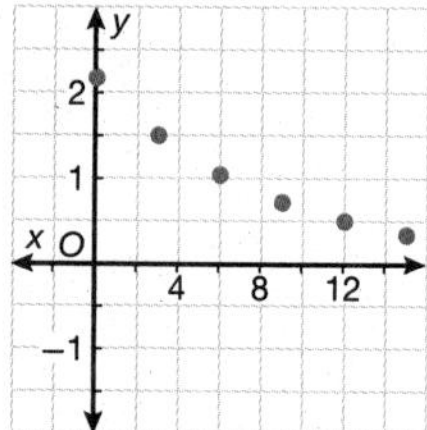

SOLUTION

The graph shows that this problem is a case of exponential decay, so the equation will be in the form $y = ab^x$, with $a > 0$ and $0 < b < 1$.

Substitute the first point from the table of values, (0, 2.17) to find the value of a.

$y = ab^x$

$2.17 = ab^0$

$2.17 = a$

So the equation is in the form $y = 2.17b^x$. Use the second point, (3, 1.5), to find b.

$y = 2.17b^x$

$1.5 = (2.17)b^3$

$b^3 = \frac{1.5}{2.17}$

$b = \sqrt[3]{\frac{1.5}{2.17}}$

$b \approx 0.88$

So the data is modeled by the equation $y = (2.17)0.88^x$.

Example 5 Application: Population Growth

The 1990 US census found that the population of the USA was approximately 248.7 million people. In 2000, the new census put the total population at 281.4 million people. Assuming the population of the USA shows exponential growth, predict what the population will be in the 2010 census.

SOLUTION

Use the two data points given in the problem to write an exponential equation. Let x = the number of years since 1990. So, $x = 0$ in 1990, and $x = 10$ in 2000. The two points are (0, 248.7) and (0, 281.4).

$$y = ab^x$$
$$248.7 = ab^0$$
$$a = 248.7$$

Now use the second point to find b.

$$y = 248.7b^x$$
$$281.4 = 248.7b^{10}$$
$$b^{10} = \frac{281.4}{248.7}$$
$$b = \sqrt[10]{\frac{281.4}{248.7}}$$
$$b \approx 1.0124$$

Now use the equation $y = (248.7)1.0124^x$ to find y when $x = 20$, which corresponds to 2010.

$$y = (248.7)1.0124^x$$
$$y = (248.7)1.0124^{20}$$
$$y \approx 318.21$$

So the population in 2010 should be approximately 318.21 million people.

Lesson Practice

a. (Ex 1) A savings account earns interest at an annual rate of 3.5%, compounded monthly. If the account begins with a principal amount of $5000, what will its value be after 4 years? $5,750.20

b. (Ex 2) A savings account earns interest at an annual rate of 3.5%, compounded continuously. If the account begins with a principal amount of $5000, what will its value be after 4 years? $5,751.37

c. (Ex 2) After 4 years, a savings account with continuously compounded interest at a rate of 4% is worth $15,320. What was the initial amount deposited into the savings account? $13,054.84

d. (Ex 3) A mass of carbon-14 atoms decays in such a way that half disappear every 5730 years. What portion of a 10 kg mass of atoms will remain after 9000 years? 3.4 kg

Example 5

Students use an exponential function to model population growth.

Additional Example 5

In 1930, the census showed that the population of the USA was 123.2 million. Find an equation modeling the exponential growth of the population between 1930 and 1990. $y = (123.2)1.0118^x$

Lesson Practice

Problems a–b

Scaffolding Have students read both problems and identify the values that are the same: the present value, the annual rate, and the time. Write on the board:

$$P(1 + i)^n \qquad Pe^{rt}$$

Discuss what the variables stand for. In the first formula, i is the annual rate divided by 12; n is 48. In the second formula, r is the annual rate; t is 4 years.

 **INCLUSION**

Have students who are visual thinkers graph the equations for the two functions $y = e^x$ and $y = \frac{1}{e^x}$. Have them identify which shows exponential growth and which shows exponential decay. Remind them that $y = e^{-x}$ is another way of writing the equation for exponential decay. Point out that e is a number, not a variable. It is similar to π, a number they know from formulas for circles.

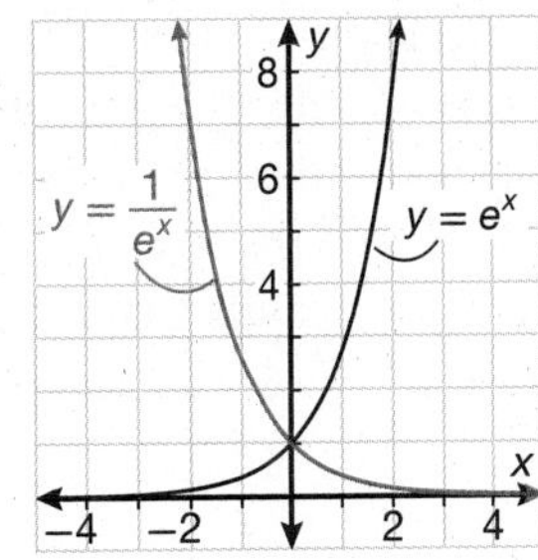

e. (Ex 4) Use the table of values to write an exponential equation and predict the value of y when $x = 15$ and $x = 45$. Round the values in your equation to four decimal places. $y = (803)0.9354^x$

x	0	10	15	45
y	803	412	294.9	39.77

f. (Ex 5) The population of Phoenix, Arizona was 983,403 in 1990. In 2000, it was 1,321,045. Predict the population of Phoenix in 2010. approximately 1,774,613

Practice Distributed and Integrated

1. (29) Is the ordered triple (4, 0, −1) a solution of the system $\begin{aligned} 2x - y + z &= 7 \\ -3x + 5y - 3z &= -9? \\ 4x - 2y + 2z &= -14 \end{aligned}$ no

Simplify.

2. (40) $4\sqrt{3} \cdot 3\sqrt{12} \cdot 2\sqrt{3}$ $144\sqrt{3}$

3. (40) $3\sqrt{75} - 4\sqrt{48}$ $-\sqrt{3}$

4. (40) $2\sqrt{5}(5\sqrt{5} - 3\sqrt{15})$ $50 - 30\sqrt{3}$

5. (31) What are all the values of x for which the division expression $\frac{x}{x-2} \div \frac{6x-2}{3x+6}$ is undefined? 2, −2, and $\frac{1}{3}$

Given the objective function P and the constraints, find the minimum and maximum values.

***6.** (54) $P = 15x + 7y$ given $x \geq 0$, $y \geq 0$, $1.5x + y \leq 35$, $0.25x + 5y \leq 15$ Minimum: 21; Maximum: 350

***7.** (54) $P = 50x + 75y$ given $x \geq 0$, $y \geq 0$, $2x + y \geq 30$, $0.75x + y \leq 20$, $0.5x + y \leq 18$ Minimum: 750; Maximum: 1450

8. (11) If a trinomial in standard form is added to a binomial in standard form and the result is written in standard form, how many terms can be in the result? 1, 2, 3, 4, or 5

9. (53) **Error Analysis** A student says: If $f(x) = \frac{5}{x}$ and $g(x) = \frac{-3}{x}$, then $f(g(x)) = \frac{5}{\frac{-3}{x}} = -\frac{5}{3}x$. Explain the reasoning.

10. (11) **Multi-Step** **a.** Complete the table of values for the polynomial function $f(x) = x^3 - 5x + 8$.

x	−3	−2	−1	0	1	2
$f(x)$	−4	10	12	8	4	6

b. Using only integer values of x, what is the smallest x-interval whose associated portion of the graph contains a relative maximum? What is the smallest x-interval whose associated portion of the graph contains a relative minimum? Justify your answers.

9. The calculation is correct, but the student doesn't mention the domains. Because $g(0)$ is undefined, the domain of the composite function does not include 0.

10b. The smallest x-interval whose associated portion of the graph contains a relative maximum is the interval from −2 to 0 because the function values increase and then decrease on that interval. The smallest x-interval whose associated portion of the graph contains a relative minimum is the interval from 0 to 2 because the function values decrease and then increase on that interval.

CHALLENGE

A mass of carbon-14 atoms has a half-life of 5730 years. Write an exponential equation to find the percentage of the mass left after x years. Then, use the equation to find the percent of the mass that is left after 430 years. $y = (\sqrt[5730]{0.5})^x$; approximately 95%

Problem e

Error Alert Instead of using an exponential equation, students may try to find patterns in the data. They must write an exponential equation for y in terms of x.

Check for Understanding

The questions below help assess the concepts taught in this lesson.

1. **"Explain why the graph of a function in the form $f(x) = b^{kx}$ has an asymptote. Assume that b is positive."** Sample: For $k > 0$, as x decreases, y approaches 0. For $k < 0$, as x increases, y approaches 0. In both cases, the x-axis is an asymptote.
2. **"An exponential function has the form $f(t) = ae^{kt}$ where t represents time. What is the initial value of this function? Why?"** The initial value is a because $ae^{kt} = a$ when $t = 0$.

3 Practice

Math Conversations

Discussions to strengthen understandings

Problem 3

Error Alert

Watch for students who try to subtract 48 from 75. Remind them they can't subtract unless the radicands are the same.

Problem 10

Extend the Problem

Graph the function $f(x) = x^3 - 5x + 8$. Then estimate the real root to the nearest tenth. $x \approx -2.8$

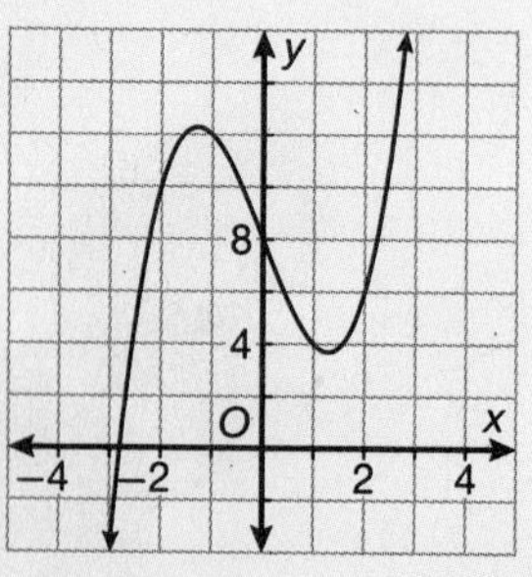

*11. **Skateboarding** In the 1999 X Games, skateboarder Tony Hawk became the first to land a 900—a rotation of 900° in the air from a half-pipe. Find an angle with measure between 0° and 360° that is coterminal with 900°. Describe the skateboarding move. 180°; two and a half complete turns
(56)

12. **Cartography** A student constructs a map of Montana over a grid system such that Lewiston is at (1, 4) and Havre is at (0.5, 10). Find the distance between the cities to the nearest kilometer if each unit represents 25 kilometers. about 150 kilometers
(41)

13. $f = \{(3, 4), (6, 8), (2, 1), (3, 6)\}$ represents a ______. D
(22)

A continuous function **B** discrete function

C continuous relation **D** discrete relation

14. **Geometry** The height of a right triangle is 6 ft and the base is 8 ft. Find the slope of the hypotenuse of the right triangle. slope = $-\frac{3}{4}$
(13)

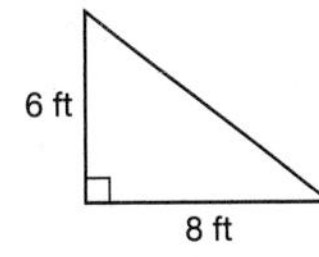

20.

Quadrant	I	II	III	IV
P(point in that quadrant)	0.25	0.25	0.25	0.25

15. **Write** Describe two ways to graph $2y - x < 6$. See Additional Answers.
(39)

16. **Error Analysis** The factored form of $9x^2 - 6x - 15$ is given as $3x(3x - 7)$. Find and explain the error and give the correct factorization.
(23)

16. Although 3 can be factored out of the expression, x cannot be factored out because there is no power of x in the constant term. $3(3x - 5)(x + 1)$

Determine whether the function shows exponential growth or decay.

*17. 1.4^x growth
(57)

*18. $10(0.4)^x$ decay
(57)

19. **Analyze** Find all the angle measures between 0° and 360° for which $\tan\theta$ is undefined. 90°, 270°
(56)

20. **Coordinate Geometry** A point is randomly chosen in one of the four quadrants of the coordinate plane. Construct a theoretical probability model to show the probabilities of the point being in each quadrant.
(55)

21. **Error Analysis** Given matrices $A = \begin{bmatrix} 2 & -3 \\ 5 & -8 \end{bmatrix}$ and $B = \begin{bmatrix} 0 & 2 \\ 1 & 4 \end{bmatrix}$, a student solved $AX = B$ as follows:
(32)

$X = BA^{-1} = \begin{bmatrix} 0 & 2 \\ 1 & 4 \end{bmatrix}\begin{bmatrix} 8 & -3 \\ 5 & -2 \end{bmatrix} = \begin{bmatrix} 10 & -4 \\ 28 & -11 \end{bmatrix}$. What is the error? Find the correct solution.

21. The student used $X = BA^{-1}$ instead of $X = A^{-1}B$. Matrix multiplication is not commutative. The correct solution is

$X = A^{-1}B$

$= \begin{bmatrix} 8 & -3 \\ 5 & -2 \end{bmatrix}\begin{bmatrix} 0 & 2 \\ 1 & 4 \end{bmatrix}$

$= \begin{bmatrix} -3 & 4 \\ -2 & 2 \end{bmatrix}$

22. **Multiple Choice** To solve $\begin{matrix} 6x - 7y = -1 \\ 3x + 2y = 5 \end{matrix}$ by elimination, what should the second equation be multiplied by in order to eliminate the x-terms? C
(24)

A −6 **B** −3 **C** −2 **D** 2

23. **Write** Identify some mathematical patterns found in Pascal's Triangle. For example, the third diagonal has the **Triangular Numbers.**
(42)

23. Sample: The fourth diagonal of Pascal's Triangle has the Tetrahedral Numbers. The sum of the numbers in each row in Pascal's Triangle is a power of 2. If the odd and even numbers in Pascal's Triangle are colored using two different colors, the Sierpinski Triangle will be shown.

24. **Model** Graph the equation $2x + 3y = 3$. See Additional Answers.
(34)

ENGLISH LEARNERS

Explain to students that two types of exponential functions represent **exponential growth** and **exponential decay.** Write the two terms on the board and underline exponent. Say, **"The equations for these functions have the independent variable x in the exponent."** Emphasize that exponential growth does not always mean growth that is surprisingly fast, even though the term is often used that way in everyday situations.

Problems 17–18

Error Alert

If students cannot decide, have them find the values of each function for $x = 0$ to 4. They can also graph $y = 1.4^x$ and $y = 10(0.4)^x$ to see the difference between the two functions. Ask them to describe what happens as the values of x get greater.

Problem 21

Check that students can find the inverse of a matrix. If they are not using a matrix calculator, then remind them that, for

$$A = \begin{bmatrix} a & b \\ c & d \end{bmatrix}$$

the inverse can be found like this:

$$A^{-1} = \frac{1}{ad - bc}\begin{bmatrix} d & -b \\ -c & a \end{bmatrix}$$

Problem 22

Guide the students by asking them the following questions.

"6x plus what equals 0?" −6x

"3x times what equals −6x?" −2

Problem 23

Suggest that students write out at least the first six rows of Pascal's Triangle.

1
1 1
1 2 1
1 3 3 1
1 4 6 4 1
1 5 10 10 5 1

Extend the Problem

How does the following combinations formula relate to Pascal's Triangle?

$${}_nC_r = \frac{n!}{r!(n - r)!}$$

Sample: The formula gives the value of the rth number in row n. The top row is row 0. So, the 5th row, 4th element equals 5.

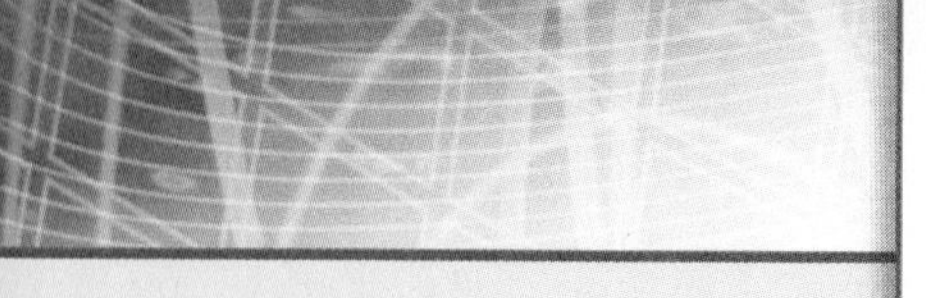

25. (40) **Electricity** Ohm's Law states that the current I, in amps, equals $\frac{\sqrt{P}}{\sqrt{R}}$ where P is power, measured in watts, and R is resistance measured in ohms. Simplify the expression. $\frac{\sqrt{PR}}{R}$

26. (14) **Analyze** If you apply expansion by minors to the 2 × 2 matrix $\begin{bmatrix} 3 & -2 \\ 4 & 1 \end{bmatrix}$, you get $3|1| - 4|-2|$. How must you define the determinant of a single number so that the result agrees with the formula for the determinant of a matrix this size? See Additional Answers.

***27.** (57) **Formulate** Write the equation of an exponential function whose graph passes through the points (0, 2) and (2, 18). Determine whether the function is increasing or decreasing. $y = 2 \cdot 3^x$; increasing

28. (43) **Catering** A caterer is ordering salmon and shrimp for an event. The salmon costs $7.50 per pound and the shrimp costs $15 per pound. She needs at least as much shrimp as salmon, and the most she can spend is $300. Let x represent the number of pounds of salmon and y represent the number of pounds of shrimp.

a. Write and graph a system of linear inequalities that represents the situation. See Additional Answers.

b. Determine the point of intersection of the boundary lines in the graph. Round to the nearest hundredth. (13.33, 13.33)

c. Assume that the salmon and shrimp can be ordered in quarter-pound increments. Determine the point closest to the point of intersection of the boundary lines that represents a possible purchase. Describe what it means.

28c. (13.25, 13.25); Possible explanation: It represents 13.25 pounds of salmon and 13.25 pounds of shrimp at a total cost of $298.13, which is $1.87 less than the maximum that can be spent.

***29.** (57) **Life Insurance** From 1950 through 1980, the total amount, I (in billions), of life insurance in the United States is shown in the table below.

Year	1950	1955	1960	1965	1970	1975	1980
Amount	234	373	586	901	1402	2314	3541

Write an exponential model that approximates this data. How much money does this model predict will be invested in life insurance by the year 2010? See Additional Answers.

***30.** (27) **Graphing Calculator** Use a graphing calculator to determine the y-intercept of the quadratic function $y - 1 = -3x^2 - 6x$. y-intercept: 1

LOOKING FORWARD

Exponential growth and decay prepares students for

- **Lesson 64** Using Logarithms
- **Lesson 72** Using the Properties of Logarithms
- **Lesson 81** Using Natural Logarithms
- **Lesson 87** Evaluating Logarithmic Expressions

412 *Saxon Algebra 2*

LESSON 58

Completing the Square

Warm Up

1. **Vocabulary** In the trinomial $ax^2 + bx + c$, c is the ________ term. constant
(11)

2. Factor the expression $x^2 + 2x + 1$. $(x + 1)^2$
(23)

3. True or False. If a number x is a perfect square, then $\sqrt{x}$ is a whole number. true
(3)

New Concepts

Recall that a perfect square trinomial can be factored into a squared binomial.

$$a^2 + 2ab + b^2 = (a + b)^2$$

$$a^2 - 2ab + b^2 = (a - b)^2$$

The Square Root Property can be used in solving quadratic equations in the form of a binomial square.

Square Root Property
If $x^2 = a$, where $a > 0$, then $x = \sqrt{a}$ or $x = -\sqrt{a}$. In general, if $x^2 = a$, then $x = \pm\sqrt{a}$ for any $a > 0$.

Caution

Do not forget that the Square Root Property yields exactly **two** solutions.

Example 1 Solving Quadratic Equations That Are Perfect Squares

a. Solve $x^2 - 10x + 25 = 9$.

SOLUTION

Step 1: Factor the perfect square trinomial.

$$x^2 - 10x + 25 = 9$$
$$x^2 - 2(5)x + 5^2 = 9$$
$$(x - 5)^2 = 9$$

Step 2: Apply the Square Root Property.

$$(x - 5)^2 = 9$$
$$x - 5 = \pm\sqrt{9}$$
$$x - 5 = \pm 3$$

Step 3: Solve for x.

$x - 5 = 3$ $\qquad$ $x - 5 = -3$

$\underline{+5 \quad +5}$ $\qquad$ $\underline{+5 \quad +5}$

$x = 8$ $\qquad$ $x = 2$

$x = 8$ or $x = 2$

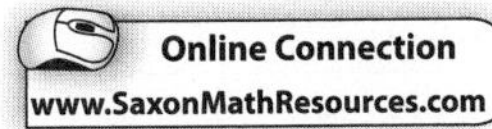
Online Connection
www.SaxonMathResources.com

LESSON 58

1 Warm Up

In problem 2, point out that $x^2 + 2x + 1$ is a perfect square. If students seem uncertain, have them square the binomial $(x + 1)$ to verify that the product is a perfect square trinomial.

2 New Concepts

In this lesson, students learn to use completing the square to solve quadratic equations of the form $ax^2 + bx + c = 0$.

Discuss solving an equation such as $x^2 = 49$ by taking the square root of both sides. Ask **"Why does the number on the right side have to be positive?"** The square root of a negative number is not a real number.

Example 1

Students solve a quadratic equation of the form $ax^2 + bx + c = d$ in which the left side of the equation is a perfect square and $d > 0$.

Additional Example 1

a. Solve: $x^2 + 6x + 9 = 64$
$x = 5$ or $x = -11$

MATH BACKGROUND

Completing the square is used to derive the quadratic formula for $ax^2 + bx + c = 0$. The first several steps produce:

$$\left(x + \frac{b}{2a}\right)^2 = \frac{b^2 - 4ac}{4a^2}$$

This equation produces real solutions only if the right side is greater than 0; that is, $ax^2 + bx + c = 0$ has real roots only if the discriminant $b^2 - 4ac$ is greater than 0.

LESSON RESOURCES

Student Edition Practice Workbook 58
Reteaching Master 58
Adaptations Master 58
Challenge and Enrichment Master C58

b. Solve: $x^2 - 14x + 49 = 10$
$x = 7 + \sqrt{10}$ or $x = 7 - \sqrt{10}$

Error Alert Check that students know how to transform $(x - p)^2 = q$ into the two equations $x - p = +\sqrt{q}$ and $x - p = -\sqrt{q}$. If students seem confused, provide practice with a few problems in which q is a perfect square.

Extend the Example

Solve:

$x^2 - \frac{2}{3}x + \frac{1}{9} = \frac{4}{9}$ $x = 1$ or $x = -\frac{1}{3}$

Exploration

Students use algebra tiles to model the process of completing the square of $x^2 + bx$. They discover that the third term must equal the square of $(b \div 2)$.

Additional Example

Make a model to show how to complete the square of $x^2 + 6x$.
$x^2 + 6x + 9$

TEACHER TIP

The models in the Exploration may be drawn on graph paper if algebra tiles are not available.

b. Solve $x^2 + 24x + 144 = 5$.

SOLUTION

Step 1: Factor the perfect square trinomial.

$$x^2 + 24x + 144 = 5$$
$$x^2 + 2(12)x + 12^2 = 5$$
$$(x + 12)^2 = 5$$

Step 2: Apply the Square Root Property.

$$(x + 12)^2 = 5$$
$$x + 12 = \pm\sqrt{5}$$

Since 5 is not a perfect square, it can be left as $\sqrt{5}$.

Step 3: Solve for x.

$$x + 12 = \pm\sqrt{5}$$
$$\underline{-12 \quad -12}$$
$$x = -12 \pm \sqrt{5}$$
$$x = -12 + \sqrt{5} \quad \text{or} \quad x = -12 - \sqrt{5}$$

Some quadratic equations cannot be solved by factoring. In these cases the method of completing the square can be used. To **complete the square,** a term can be added to a quadratic expression of the form $x^2 + bx$ to form a perfect square trinomial.

Exploration **Modeling Completing the Square**

The model represents the quadratic binomial $x^2 + 8x$.	How many more unit tiles should be added to the model to create a square?
$x^2 + 8x$	$x^2 + 8x + 16$

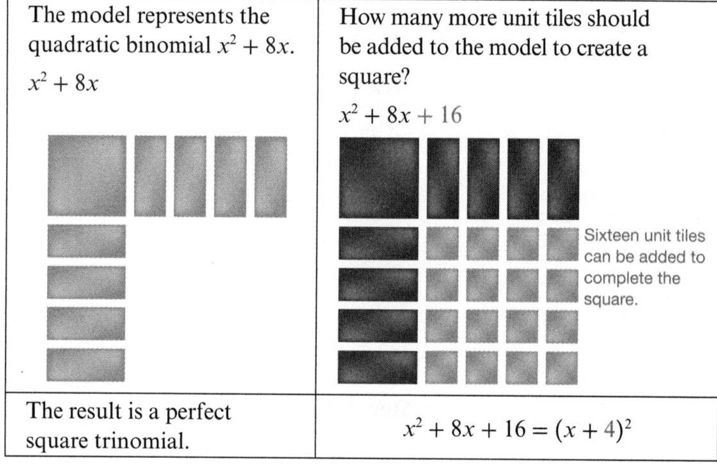
Sixteen unit tiles can be added to complete the square.

The result is a perfect square trinomial.	$x^2 + 8x + 16 = (x + 4)^2$

Draw a model of $x^2 + 10x$. Use your model to find a perfect square trinomial and its factors.

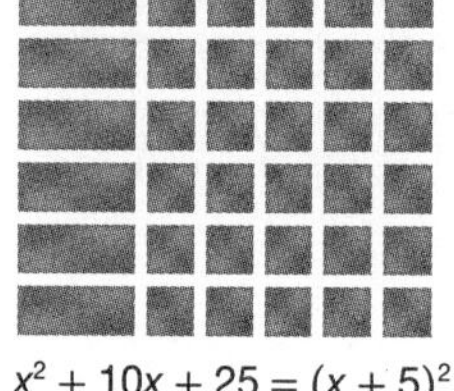

$x^2 + 10x + 25 = (x + 5)^2$

INCLUSION

To understand the idea of completing the square, students must have mastered the process of squaring binomials. Model for them the steps in squaring $(x + 10)$.

$$\begin{array}{r} x + 10 \\ \times \quad x + 10 \\ \hline 10x + 100 \\ +x^2 + 10x \quad\quad \\ \hline x^2 + 20x + 100 \end{array}$$

Ask, **"How many terms do we get in the product?"** 3 **"What is this polynomial called?"** a trinomial Point to the coefficient 20 of the x-term. **"How does this relate to the constant 10 in the original binomial?"** It is twice the constant. Point to the constant 100 in the trinomial product. **"How does this relate to the constant 10 in the original binomial?"** It is the square of the constant. Repeat with several other examples of squaring $(x + a)$. Then model some examples showing the steps in squaring $(x - a)$.

Completing the Square

Given a quadratic of the form $x^2 + bx$, add to it the square of half the coefficient of x, $\left(\frac{b}{2}\right)^2$, to create a perfect square trinomial.

$$x^2 + bx + \left(\frac{b}{2}\right)^2 = \left(x + \frac{b}{2}\right)^2$$

Example 2 Completing the Square

Complete the square and factor the resulting perfect square trinomial

$x^2 + 18x$.

SOLUTION Add the square of half the coefficient of x to the binomial. The coefficient of x is 18. Add $\left(\frac{18}{2}\right)^2 = 9^2$ to the binomial to create a perfect square trinomial.

$x^2 + 18x + 9^2 = x^2 + 18x + 81 = (x + 9)^2$

When using the method of completing the square to solve a quadratic equation, keep in mind that when you add a constant term to one side of an equation you must also add that constant to the other side of the equation.

Example 3 Solving Quadratic Equations by Completing the Square

Solve $x^2 - 14x - 8 = 0$ by completing the square.

SOLUTION

Step 1: $x^2 - 14x - 8 + 8 = 0 + 8$ Isolate the binomial $x^2 - 14x$.

$x^2 - 14x = 8$

Step 2: Add the square of half the coefficient of x to both sides of the equation.

The coefficient of x is -14; $\left(\frac{-14}{2}\right)^2 = (-7)^2 = 49$.

$x^2 - 14x + 49 = 8 + 49$

$x^2 - 14x + 49 = 57$

Step 3: $x^2 - 14x + 49 = 57$

$x^2 - 2(7)x + 7^2 = 57$ Factor the perfect square trinomial.

$(x - 7)^2 = 57$

Step 4: $x - 7 = \pm\sqrt{57}$ Apply the Square Root Property.

Step 5: $x - 7 + 7 = \pm\sqrt{57} + 7$

$x = 7 \pm \sqrt{57}$ Solve for x.

Math Reasoning

Estimate Without using a calculator, estimate the decimal approximation for the solutions to Example 3.

57 lies between $49 = 7^2$ and $64 = 8^2$; therefore, $\sqrt{57}$ lies between $\sqrt{49} = 7$ and $\sqrt{64} = 8$. So, $\sqrt{57} \approx 7.5$.

$7 + \sqrt{57} \approx 7 + 7.5 = 14.5$

$7 - \sqrt{57} \approx 7 - 7.5 = -0.5$

Example 2

Students complete the square of $x^2 + bx$ when b is even. Then, they factor the resulting trinomial.

Additional Example 2

Complete the square and factor the resulting perfect square trinomial $x^2 - 22x$.
$x^2 - 22x + 121$, $(x - 11)^2$

Extend the Example

Complete the square and factor the resulting perfect square trinomial.

a. $x^2 + 7x$ $x^2 + 7x + \frac{49}{4}$, $\left(x + \frac{7}{2}\right)^2$

b. $x^2 - 3x$ $x^2 - 3x + \frac{9}{4}$, $\left(x - \frac{3}{2}\right)^2$

Example 3

Students solve a quadratic equation of the form $x^2 + bx + c = 0$ by completing the square. Point out that students always begin by writing the equation in the form $x^2 + bx = -c$. They do this using inverse operations.

Error Alert Emphasize that the square of half the coefficient of x must be added to both sides of the equation.

Additional Example 3

Solve by completing the square: $x^2 - 10x + 19 = 0$. $5 \pm \sqrt{6}$

Extend the Example

Solve $2x^2 - 5x - 18 = 0$ by completing the square. Start by dividing each term by the coefficient of the quadratic term.
$x = -2$ or $x = \frac{9}{2}$

ENGLISH LEARNERS

Display the graph $y = x^2 - x - 6$. Write:

$x^2 - x - 6$ polynomial, trinomial
$y = x^2 - x - 6$ equation
$f(x) = x^2 - x - 6$ function

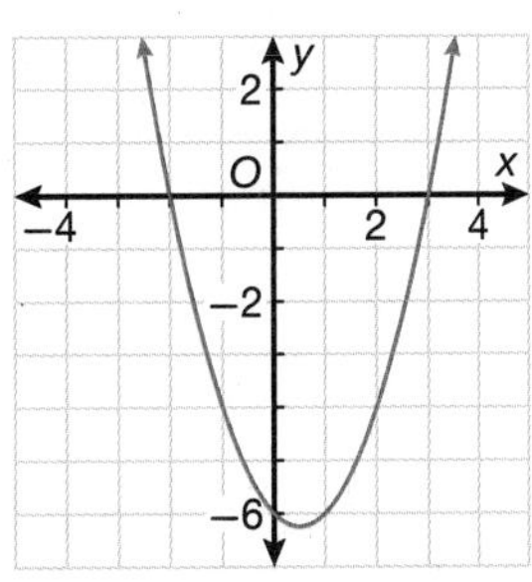

Review vocabulary by pointing out that the **factors** of the polynomial are $(x + 2)$ and $(x - 3)$. The numbers -2 and 3 are the solutions or roots of the equation, the zeros of the function, and the x-intercepts of the graph.

Example 4

Students solve a quadratic applications problem.

Extend the Example

When will the ball hit the ground? Round the answer to the nearest tenth. 4.1 seconds after the ball was hit

Additional Example 4

A diver is competing for a metal. His height in feet above the water can be modeled by the function $f(x) = -3x^2 + 6x + 24$ where x is the time in seconds after he begins the dive. Write the function in vertex form by completing the square. Then find the maximum height and the time it takes to reach that height. $f(x) = -3(x-1)^2 + 27$; It takes 1 second for the diver to reach the maximum height of 27 feet above the water.

Lesson Practice

Problem b

Scaffolding Ask students how they know the left side of the equation is a perfect square. Sample: The constant term equals 8 squared and the coefficient of the x-term equals 2 times 8.

Problem d

Error Alert If students have difficulty simplifying $\sqrt{171}$, suggest that they try 9 as a factor of 171.

Problem e

To check their answers, have students set the equation equal to zero, let h equal 4, and then divide each term by -16. They will get $t^2 - \frac{5}{4}t + \frac{1}{4} = 0$, which can be factored into $(t-1)\left(t-\frac{1}{4}\right) = 0$.

Caution

When completing the square, be sure to keep the equation equivalent to the original equation. Notice $(-16)(4)$ was added to complete the square, so $+64$ was added to keep the equation equivalent to the original equation.

Example 4 Application: Projectile Motion

During a baseball game a player hits a fly ball. The height $f(t)$, in feet, of the ball at time t, in seconds, can be described by the function $f(t) = -16t^2 + 64t + 4$. Write the equation in vertex form by completing the square. Then determine the maximum height of the ball and the time it takes to reach the maximum height.

SOLUTION

Complete the square for the trinomial expression that describes the height of the ball.

$f(t) = -16t^2 + 64t + 4$	
$= (-16t^2 + 64t) + 4$	Group the binomial $-16t^2 + 64t$
$= -16(t^2 - 4t) + 4$	Factor out -16 from $(-16t^2 + 6t)$.
$= -16(t^2 - 4t + 4) + 4 + \boxed{64}$	Complete the square.
$= -16(t-2)(t-2) + 68$	Factor. Then simplify.
$f(t) = -16(t-2)^2 + 68$	Write the function in vertex form.

To determine the maximum height of the ball use the vertex form of a function. Recall the vertex form $f(x) = a(x-h)^2 + k$ of a quadratic function. The point (h, k) is the vertex.

For the function $f(t) = -16(t - (+2)^2 + 68$, the vertex is (2, 68). Therefore, the ball reaches a maximum height of 68 feet 2 seconds after the ball was hit.

Check Use a table to graph the function. Then estimate the vertex of the parabola on the graph.

x	0	1	2	3	4
$f(x)$	4	52	68	52	4

Height of Fly Ball

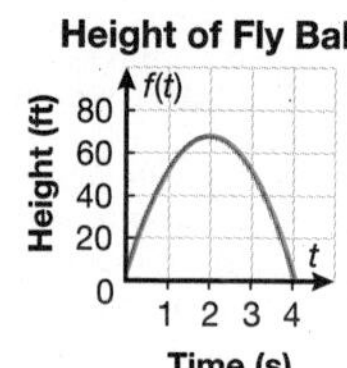

The graph verifies that the vertex occurs at (2, 68)

Lesson Practice

a. Solve $x^2 - 2x + 1 = 36$. $x = -5, 7$
(Ex 1)

b. Solve $x^2 + 16x + 64 = 6$. $x = -8 \pm \sqrt{6}$
(Ex 1)

c. Complete the square and factor the resulting perfect square trinomial
(Ex 2)

$x^2 - 20x$. $x^2 - 20x + 100 = (x-10)^2$

d. Solve $x^2 + 26x - 2 = 0$ by completing the square. $x = -13 \pm 3\sqrt{19}$
(Ex 3)

e. A pebble is thrown into the air from ground level with an initial velocity of 20 feet per second. The height of the pebble h at any given time t can be described by the equation
(Ex 4)

$$h = -16t^2 + 20t.$$

Find the time at which the height of the pebble is 4 feet. Round your answer to the hundredths place. $t = 1$ or 0.25 second

Practice Distributed and Integrated

Solve by using either substitution or elimination.

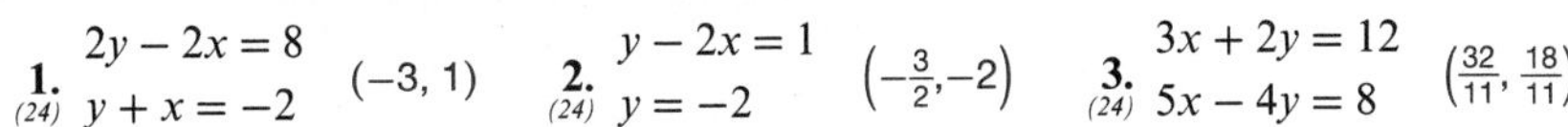

1. (24) $2y - 2x = 8$, $y + x = -2$ $(-3, 1)$

2. (24) $y - 2x = 1$, $y = -2$ $\left(-\frac{3}{2}, -2\right)$

3. (24) $3x + 2y = 12$, $5x - 4y = 8$ $\left(\frac{32}{11}, \frac{18}{11}\right)$

4. (10) Solve the inequality $-3 < d + 2$ and $d + 2 < 12$. $-5 < d < 10$

5. (10) Solve and graph the inequality $-4 \le 4x - 8 < 12$. $1 \le x < 5$

5.

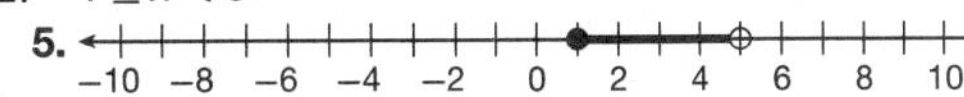

Determine the kind of variation, if any, for each equation.

6. (12) $y = \frac{1}{x}$, for $x \neq 0$ inverse

7. (12) $z = \frac{1}{xy + a}$, for $x, y \neq 0$ and any value of a joint when $a = 0$

Solve.

***8.** (58) $x^2 - 8x + 16 = 3$ $x = 4 \pm \sqrt{3}$

***9.** (58) $x^2 + 26x + 169 = 81$ $x = -4, -22$

10. (30) **(Physics)** An object dropped from a height 4 meters above the ground after x seconds is modeled by the function $y = -4.9x^2 + 4$. If measured in feet, the height is modeled by $y = -16x^2 + 1.2$. Without graphing, tell how the graphs of each function compare to each other.   The graph of $y = -4.9x^2 + 4$ is wider than the graph of $y = -16x^2 + 1.2$. It is also a vertical shift 2.8 units up.

11. (22) **Error Analysis** Sam listed the following points $\{(2, 3), (1, 6), (5, -3), (1, 2)\}$ when giving an example of a discrete function. Correct his example.

11. This is a discrete relation, not a function. Sam could change (1, 2) to $(x, 2)$ where $x \neq 1, 2, 5$. This would make his example a discrete function.

12. (51) **Multiple Choice** What is the result of dividing $x^3 - 7x + 3$ by $x - 2$?   C

A $x^2 + 2x + 3 - \frac{3}{x - 2}$ **B** $x^2 + 2x - 3$

C $x^2 + 2x - 3 - \frac{3}{x - 2}$ **D** $x^2 + 2x$

***13.** (58) **Multi-Step** Use $x^2 + 104x - 97 = 4$.

a. What is the first step before you can complete the square?   Isolate the binomial by adding 97 to both sides.

b. What constant can be added to the binomial to create a perfect square trinomial?   2704

c. What is the factored form of the perfect square trinomial? $(x + 52)^2$

d. Solve the equation for x. $x = -52 \pm \sqrt{2805}$

14. (46) **Justify** Show that it is possible to solve for x by using either the sine or cosine function.   Find the measure of the third angle by subtracting 42 from 90.

$\sin 42 = \frac{x}{32}$ $\cos 48 = \frac{x}{32}$

$21.4 \approx x$ $21.4 \approx x$

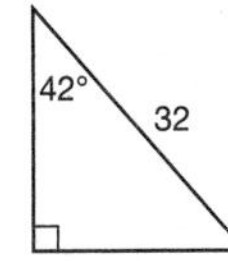

Check for Understanding

The questions below help assess the concepts taught in this lesson.

1. **"What is the result of completing the square?"** a perfect square trinomial
2. **"What must be true of the coefficient of the quadratic term before you can use completing the square?"** It must equal 1.

3 Practice

Math Conversations

Discussions to strengthen understanding

Problem 11

Guide the students by asking them the following question. **"Which two ordered pairs have the same x-value, but different y-values?"** (1, 6) and (1, 2)

Problem 14

Guide the students by asking them the following question. **"What do you know about the measure of the third angle in the triangle?"** It equals 90° − 42°.

INCLUSION

Students may need more practice recognizing perfect square trinomials. Have them find the values of b that make each expression a perfect square.

a. $x^2 + bx + 16$ 8, −8

b. $x^2 + bx + 25$ 10, −10

c. $x^2 + bx + 81$ 18, −18

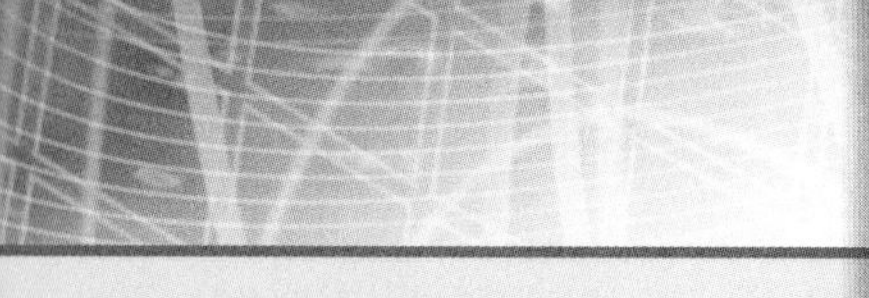

Problem 16

Error Alert

If students choose either choice B or choice D, show them that the left side of the equation equals the square of $(x - 21)^2$.

Problem 19

Extend the Problem

What is true of the scatterplot of a set of data if r equals -1 or 1? Describe the scatterplot for $r > 0$ and for $r < 0$. The scatterplot is a perfectly straight line. If $r > 0$, the data points rise from left to right. If $r < 0$, the data points fall from left to right.

Problem 22

Guide the students by asking them the following questions.

"What do you get if you fold an equilateral triangle in half along an altitude?" two right triangles

"What theorem do you use if you are missing one side in a right triangle?" Pythagorean Theorem

Problem 25

Remind students that the period is the time needed for one complete swing of the pendulum.

Extend the Problem

Find the period of a 40-cm long pendulum. 1.27 s

***15.** (57) **Formulate** Formulate an expression for the amount Stu will have in his bank account at the end of a year if he invests a principal of \$1,850 at an annual interest rate of 2.4%, compounded monthly. $1850(1.0024)^{12}$

***16.** (58) **Multiple Choice** Chose the letter that best represents the value of x in the equation $x^2 - 42x + 441 = 2$. C

A $x = -21 \pm \sqrt{2}$ **B** $x = 20, 22$

C $x = 21 \pm \sqrt{2}$ **D** $x = -20, -22$

17. (26) **Geometry** Miriam is going to create a rectangular vegetable garden along the side of her house and is going to enclose it within a fence on three sides. If the total amount of fencing she purchases is 80 feet, write an equation in standard form for finding all possible lengths and widths for the garden. $2W + L = 80$

18. (19) **Write** Explain how to multiply $(2x + 8)(3x - 6)$ using the FOIL method.

19. (45) **Formulate** Describe the correlation coefficient r using a compound inequality and absolute value symbols. $-1 \le r \le 1$ and the points get closer to forming a line as $|r|$ approaches 1.

***20.** (55) **Pass Codes** A computer generates temporary pass codes to users. Each pass code is exactly 3 letters long and it can have repeating letters. What is the probability of getting a pass code with 3 vowels (A, E, I, O, or U)? 0.71%

21. (23) **Deck Building** The area of a triangular section of a deck is $72x^2 - 98$ ft². If the base of the section of deck is $12x + 14$ ft, find the height of the section. $12x - 14$ ft

22. (52) **Agriculture** Lee and his brother own a piece of land that has the shape of an equilateral triangle with side length 200 m. They divide the land between them into two equal parts along the altitude of the triangle by putting a fence. What is the length of the fence? What area of land does each of them own? Use a graphing calculator and round your answers to the nearest hundredth. The fence is 173.21 m long. Each of the brothers own an area of 8660.5 m².

***23.** (54) **Graphing Calculator** Describe the feasible region for the set of inequalities

$x \ge 0, y \ge 0, y \le -0.75x + 8$. region bounded by (0, 0), (0, 8), (10.67, 0)

18. You multiply the first terms in each binomial $(2x)(3x)$, then multiply the outer two terms $(2x)(-6)$, then multiply the inner two terms $(8)(3x)$, and then the last two terms $(8)(-6)$. Combine any like terms to simplify.

24. (24) **Error Analysis** Find and explain the error in solving the system $\begin{aligned} x - 10y &= 10 \\ 2x - 20y &= 23 \end{aligned}$ in the step below.

$$\begin{array}{r} -2(x - 10y = 10) \\ +2x - 20y = 23 \\ \hline \end{array} \qquad \begin{array}{r} -2x + 20y = -20 \\ +2x - 20y = 23 \\ \hline 40y = 3 \end{array}$$

The variable y should have canceled: no solution.

25. (50) **Pendulums** The period T (in seconds) of a simple pendulum as a function of its length l (in meters)is given by the equation $T = 2\pi\sqrt{\frac{l}{9.8}}$. Express the length l as a function of the time t. $l = \frac{9.8T^2}{4\pi^2}$

*26. **Multi-Step** The half-life of Uranium-234 is 245,000 years.
(57)

a. Formulate an exponential function representing the amount of a grams Uranium-234 remaining after t years. $y \approx a(0.999997)^t$

b. Use the function to find how much of a 150-gram sample of Uranium-234 will be left after 182,000 years. about 90 g

27. Let $f(x) = 3x$ and $g(x) = 3x + 2$. Find the composite function $g(f(x))$. $3(3x) + 2 = 9x + 2$
(53)

28. **Justify** A student saw his friend write that $-\sqrt{81} = -9$, and he told his friend that it is wrong because a square root cannot yield a negative number. Why is the student wrong and his friend correct? It is okay because the negative sign is not part of the radicand. The square root of 81 is 9; the opposite of 9 is −9.
(40)

29. **Generalize** How might you rationalize the denominator for the expression $\frac{1}{\sqrt[3]{5}}$, when there is a *cube* root in the denominator? Multiply both numerator and denominator by $\frac{(\sqrt[3]{5})^2}{(\sqrt[3]{5})^2}$.
(44)

*30. **Projectile Motion** The world record for the World Championship Punkin Chunkin, held each year in the state of Delaware, is held by an air cannon named "2nd Amendment." The height of a pumpkin t seconds after being shot from this machine can be described by the equation $h = -16t^2 + 880t + 70.7$. After how many seconds will a pumpkin shot from this machine land on the ground? Round your answer to the tenths place. 55.1 seconds
(58)

Problem 29

Guide the students by asking them the following questions.

"What type of number is the denominator of this expression, a rational number or an irrational number?" irrational

"Why is it irrational?" The cube root of 5 cannot be expressed as the ratio of two integers.

"What does it mean to rationalize an expression?" Multiply it by a form of 1 so that the denominator is a rational number.

Problem 30

If students need a hint, ask **"What is the value of *h* when the pumpkin hits the ground? Why?"** 0; *h* stands for the height or distance above the ground.

CHALLENGE

What are the dimensions of a rectangle with a perimeter of 36 inches and an area of 36 inches squared? Solve by completing the square. Show the equation you use. Give your answer in simplest radical form and approximated to two decimal places.
$x(18 - x) = 36$, where x is the width;
$9 \pm 3\sqrt{5}$ in.; 15.71 in. and 2.29 in.

LOOKING FORWARD

Completing the square prepares students for

- **Lesson 62** Using Complex Numbers
- **Lesson 65** Using the Quadratic Formula
- **Lesson 74** Finding the Discriminant
- **Lesson 78** Solving Quadratic Equations II

LESSON
59

1 Warm Up

In problem 2, remind students of the definition of a negative exponent: For any real number a greater than 0, $a^{-n} = \frac{1}{a^n}$.

2 New Concepts

In this lesson, students extend the laws of exponents to include rational numbers.

Example 1

Students write expressions with rational exponents in radical form.

Additional Example 1

Write the rational exponents as radical expressions.

a. $(10x)^{\frac{1}{4}}$ $\sqrt[4]{10x}$

b. $p^{\frac{1}{3}}q^{\frac{5}{2}}$ $\sqrt[3]{p}\,\sqrt{q^5}$

Error Alert Some students may switch the index and the exponent of the radicand writing, for example, $x^{\frac{3}{4}}$ as $\sqrt[3]{x^4}$ rather than as $\sqrt[4]{x^3}$. Emphasize that the denominator is used as the index by reminding students that $x^{\frac{1}{3}} = \sqrt[3]{x}$.

LESSON RESOURCES

Student Edition Practice Workbook 59
Reteaching Master 59
Adaptations Master 59
Challenge and Enrichment Master C59

LESSON
59 Using Fractional Exponents

Warm Up

1. **Vocabulary** In the expression $x^{(a+b)}$ the term $(a + b)$ is the ______. (3) exponent

2. Simplify. $\frac{x^2y^4}{x^{-1}y^3}$ (3) x^3y

3. Solve $\sqrt{x} = 4$. (40) $x = 16$

New Concepts

Exponents of the form $\frac{m}{n}$, where m and n are integers and $n \neq 0$, are called **rational exponents.** Rational exponents can be written as radical expressions.

Rational Exponent Property
For m and n integers and $n \neq 0$:
$a^{\frac{1}{n}} = \sqrt[n]{a}$
$a^{\frac{m}{n}} = (\sqrt[n]{a})^m = \sqrt[n]{a^m}$

Example 1 Writing Rational Exponents as Radical Expressions

Write the rational exponents as radical expressions.

a. $3^{\frac{1}{5}}$

SOLUTION Apply the Rational Exponent Property:

$a^{\frac{1}{n}} = \sqrt[n]{a}$.

In this case, $a = 3$ and $n = 5$.

$3^{\frac{1}{5}} = \sqrt[5]{3}$

b. $9^{\frac{3}{4}}$

SOLUTION Apply the Rational Exponent Property:

$a^{\frac{m}{n}} = (\sqrt[n]{a})^m = \sqrt[n]{a^m}$.

In this case, $a = 9$, $m = 3$, and $n = 4$.

$9^{\frac{3}{4}} = \sqrt[4]{9^3}$ or $(\sqrt[4]{9})^3$

Radical expressions of the form $\sqrt[n]{a}$ are called ***n*th roots.** In this form n is the index and a is the radicand. Similar to square roots, $\sqrt[n]{a} = b$ if $b^n = a$.

Reading Math

Square roots have an index of 2 although the 2 is not written with the radical in this case.

When nth roots have an odd index, there is only one real root that maintains the sign of the radicand. For example, $\sqrt[3]{8} = 2$ and $\sqrt[3]{-8} = -2$. When nth roots have an even index and a positive radicand, there are two real roots, one positive and one negative. For example, $\sqrt[4]{16} = \pm 2$. An nth root with an even index and a negative radicand has no real roots.

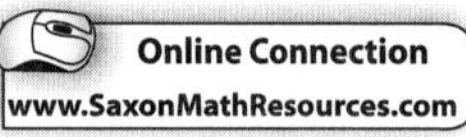

Properties of *n*th Roots
For $a > 0$ and $b > 0$,
Product Property: $\sqrt[n]{ab} = \sqrt[n]{a} \cdot \sqrt[n]{b}$
Quotient Property: $\sqrt[n]{\frac{a}{b}} = \frac{\sqrt[n]{a}}{\sqrt[n]{b}}$

MATH BACKGROUND

The radicand in radical expressions is usually assumed to be positive to avoid expressions such as $\sqrt{-5}$ which are not real numbers. Likewise, the base in the expression $a^{\frac{m}{n}}$ is assumed to be positive. To allow negative values for the base would result in some of the familiar laws of exponents not being valid.

Restricting the base to positive real numbers allows the laws developed for integral exponents to be extended in this lesson to rational exponents, and then in later lessons to all real numbers.

It is also useful to specify that the base in $a^{\frac{m}{n}}$ be nonzero. This avoids the problem of 0^0, which is defined as 1 in some branches of mathematics, and left undefined in other branches.

Example 2 Simplifying Radical Expressions

Simplify each expression. Let $x > 0$ for each problem.

a. $\sqrt[5]{243x^{10}}$

SOLUTION Factor the radicand into perfect fifths.

$\sqrt[5]{243x^{10}} = \sqrt[5]{3^5 \cdot x^5 \cdot x^5}$

Apply the Product Property.

$\sqrt[5]{3^5 \cdot x^5 \cdot x^5} = \sqrt[5]{3^5} \cdot \sqrt[5]{x^5} \cdot \sqrt[5]{x^5}$

Evaluate the radical.

$\sqrt[5]{3^5} \cdot \sqrt[5]{x^5} \cdot \sqrt[5]{x^5} = 3 \cdot x \cdot x$

Simplify.

$3 \cdot x \cdot x = 3x^2$

b. $\sqrt[5]{\dfrac{x^5}{2}}$

SOLUTION Apply the Quotient Property.

$\sqrt[5]{\dfrac{x^5}{2}} = \dfrac{\sqrt[5]{x^5}}{\sqrt[5]{2}}$

Evaluate the numerator.

$\dfrac{\sqrt[5]{x^5}}{\sqrt[5]{2}} = \dfrac{x}{\sqrt[5]{2}}$

Rationalize the denominator.

$\dfrac{x}{\sqrt[5]{2}} \cdot \dfrac{\sqrt[5]{2}}{\sqrt[5]{2}} \cdot \dfrac{\sqrt[5]{2}}{\sqrt[5]{2}} \cdot \dfrac{\sqrt[5]{2}}{\sqrt[5]{2}} \cdot \dfrac{\sqrt[5]{2}}{\sqrt[5]{2}}$

Apply the Product Property.

$\dfrac{x}{\sqrt[5]{2}} \cdot \dfrac{\sqrt[5]{2}}{\sqrt[5]{2}} \cdot \dfrac{\sqrt[5]{2}}{\sqrt[5]{2}} \cdot \dfrac{\sqrt[5]{2}}{\sqrt[5]{2}} \cdot \dfrac{\sqrt[5]{2}}{\sqrt[5]{2}} = \dfrac{x\sqrt[5]{2^4}}{\sqrt[5]{2^5}}$

Simplify.

$\dfrac{x\sqrt[5]{2^4}}{\sqrt[5]{2^5}} = \dfrac{x\sqrt[5]{16}}{2}$

Hint

When a radical is in the denominator you must always rationalize the denominator.

The properties of integer exponents covered in Lesson 3 hold true for rational exponents.

Properties of Rational Exponents
For all nonzero real numbers a and b and rational numbers m and n,
Negative Exponent Property: $a^{-n} = \dfrac{1}{a^n}$
Zero Exponent Property: $a^0 = 1$
Product of Powers Property: $a^m \cdot a^n = a^{m+n}$
Quotient of Powers Property: $\dfrac{a^m}{a^n} = a^{m-n}$
Power of a Power Property: $(a^m)^n = a^{m \cdot n}$
Power of a Product Property: $(ab)^m = a^m \cdot b^m$
Power of a Quotient Property: $\left(\dfrac{a}{b}\right)^m = \dfrac{a^m}{b^m}$

Caution

Notice the difference between the Product of Powers Property and the Power of a Power Property.

Example 2

Students simplify radical expressions by factoring out perfect nth powers or by rationalizing the denominator.

Additional Example 2

Simplify each expression.

a. $\sqrt[5]{32a^{10}b^{15}}$ $2a^2b^3$

b. $\sqrt[6]{\dfrac{x^{12}y^{30}}{128}}$ $\dfrac{x^2y^5\sqrt[6]{32}}{4}$

Extend the Example

How can you prove this formula for rationalizing the denominator of any nth root? $\dfrac{a}{\sqrt[n]{b}} = \dfrac{a\sqrt[n]{b^{n-1}}}{b}$

Numerator and denominator are multiplied by $\sqrt[n]{b^{n-1}}$.

ALTERNATE METHOD FOR EXAMPLE 2

When rationalizing the denominator for an index greater than 2, students may prefer to use rational exponents and the Product of Powers Property. Model the steps in the process like this:

$$\frac{1}{\sqrt[5]{2}} = \frac{1}{2^{\frac{1}{5}}} \cdot \frac{2^{\frac{4}{5}}}{2^{\frac{4}{5}}} = \frac{2^{\frac{4}{5}}}{2^{\frac{1}{5}+\frac{4}{5}}} = \frac{2^{\frac{4}{5}}}{2^1} = \frac{\sqrt[5]{2^4}}{2} = \frac{\sqrt[5]{16}}{2}$$

Once students understand the method, they can leave out some of the steps; for example:

$$\frac{1}{\sqrt[4]{10}} = \frac{1}{10^{\frac{1}{4}}} \cdot \frac{10^{\frac{3}{4}}}{10^{\frac{3}{4}}} = \frac{\sqrt[4]{10^3}}{10} = \frac{\sqrt[4]{1000}}{10}$$

$$\frac{1}{\sqrt[7]{3}} = \frac{1}{3^{\frac{1}{7}}} \cdot \frac{3^{\frac{6}{7}}}{3^{\frac{6}{7}}} = \frac{\sqrt[7]{3^6}}{3} = \frac{\sqrt[7]{729}}{3}$$

Example 3

Students use the Properties of Rational Exponents to simplify expressions.

Additional Example 3

Simplify each expression.

a. $125^{\frac{3}{12}} \cdot 125^{\frac{1}{12}}$ 5

b. $\frac{9^{\frac{7}{2}}}{9^{\frac{3}{2}}}$ 81

c. $(3^6)^{\frac{1}{2}}$ 27

d. $(16 \cdot 625)^{\frac{1}{4}}$ 10

Extend the Example

Simplify each expression.

a. $\left(x^{-\frac{1}{3}}y^{-\frac{2}{5}}\right)^{-15}$ x^5y^6

b. $\left(x^{-\frac{3}{5}}y^{\frac{5}{3}}\right)^{15}$ $\frac{y^{25}}{x^9}$

Error Alert Continue to emphasize that students cannot add or subtract exponents unless the base is the same.

For example, $x^{\frac{1}{3}}y^{\frac{2}{3}}$ cannot be simplified to xy.

TEACHER TIP

Although the textbook shows rational exponents written like $9^{\frac{7}{2}}$, it may be easier for students to write rational exponents using a slash fraction, for example, $9^{7/2}$. Show students both methods.

Example 4

Students use the reciprocal of the power to solve equations of the form $x^{\frac{m}{n}} = a$.

Additional Example 4

Solve each equation for the value of x.

a. $x^{\frac{1}{5}} = 5$ 3125

Example 3 **Simplifying Rational Exponents**

Simplify each expression.

a. $64^{\frac{7}{16}} \cdot 64^{\frac{1}{16}}$

SOLUTION Apply the Product of Powers Property.

$64^{\frac{7}{16}} \cdot 64^{\frac{1}{16}} = 64^{\frac{7}{16}+\frac{1}{16}} = 64^{\frac{8}{16}} = 64^{\frac{1}{2}}$

Apply the Rational Exponent Property $a^{\frac{1}{n}} = \sqrt[n]{a}$ and simplify.

$64^{\frac{1}{2}} = \sqrt{64} = 8$

b. $\frac{16^{\frac{6}{4}}}{16^{\frac{7}{4}}}$

SOLUTION Apply the Quotient of Powers Property.

$\frac{16^{\frac{6}{4}}}{16^{\frac{7}{4}}} = 16^{\frac{6}{4}-\frac{7}{4}} = 16^{-\frac{1}{4}}$

Apply the Negative Exponent Property.

$16^{-\frac{1}{4}} = \frac{1}{16^{\frac{1}{4}}}$

Apply the Rational Exponent Property $a^{\frac{1}{n}} = \sqrt[n]{a}$ and simplify.

$\frac{1}{16^{\frac{1}{4}}} = \frac{1}{\sqrt[4]{16}} = \frac{1}{2}$

c. $(12^{10})^{\frac{1}{5}}$

SOLUTION Apply the Power of a Power Property.

$(12^{10})^{\frac{1}{5}} = 12^{10 \cdot \frac{1}{5}} = 12^{\frac{10}{5}} = 12^2$

Evaluate the exponent.

$12^2 = 144$

d. $(27 \cdot 125)^{\frac{1}{3}}$

SOLUTION Apply the Power of a Product Property.

$(27 \cdot 125)^{\frac{1}{3}} = 27^{\frac{1}{3}} \cdot 125^{\frac{1}{3}}$

Evaluate the exponents and simplify.

$= 27^{\frac{1}{3}} \cdot 125^{\frac{1}{3}} = 3 \cdot 5 = 15$

Hint

Recall that the product of a fraction and its reciprocal is 1.

The Power of a Power Property can be used to help solve equations with rational exponents. To cancel a rational exponent the exponent must be multiplied by its reciprocal.

Example 4 **Solving Equations with Rational Exponents**

Solve each equation for the value of x.

a. $x^{\frac{1}{3}} = 6$

SOLUTION To cancel out the rational exponent, raise the exponential expression to the reciprocal power. The reciprocal of $\frac{1}{3}$ is 3.

$$\left(x^{\frac{1}{3}}\right)^3 = (6)^3$$
$$x^{\frac{1}{3} \cdot 3} = (6)^3$$
$$x^1 = 6^3$$
$$x = 216$$

INCLUSION

Remind students there is often more than one way to write an expression in algebra. Use examples such as $25^{\frac{1}{2}} = \sqrt{25}$ and $8^{-1} = \frac{1}{8}$. Then have students find as many different ways as possible to show $x^{\frac{2}{5}}$.

Some possibilities are:

$x^{\frac{2}{5}} = (x^{\frac{1}{5}})^2 = (x^2)^{\frac{1}{5}} = \sqrt[5]{x^2} = (\sqrt[5]{x})^2$

Have students confirm that the last two forms equal 4 when $x = 32$. They can use a scientific calculator to check the values of the other expressions. Discuss which form they think is most convenient for numerical work and why.

b. $x^{\frac{4}{5}} = 16$

SOLUTION To cancel out the rational exponent, raise the exponential expression to the reciprocal power. The reciprocal of $\frac{4}{5}$ is $\frac{5}{4}$.

$$\left(x^{\frac{4}{5}}\right)^{\frac{5}{4}} = (16)^{\frac{5}{4}}$$
$$x^{\frac{4}{5}\cdot\frac{5}{4}} = (16)^{\frac{5}{4}}$$
$$x^1 = (\sqrt[4]{16})^5$$
$$x = (2)^5 = 32$$

c. $x^{\frac{4}{3}} = 7$

SOLUTION To cancel out the rational exponent, raise the exponential expression to the reciprocal power. The reciprocal of $\frac{3}{4}$ is $\frac{4}{3}$.

$$\left(x^{\frac{4}{3}}\right)^{\frac{3}{4}} = (7)^{\frac{3}{4}} \rightarrow x^{\frac{4}{3}\cdot\frac{3}{4}} = (7)^{\frac{3}{4}} \rightarrow x^1 = \sqrt[4]{7^3} \rightarrow x = \sqrt[4]{343}$$

Example 5 Application: Cubic House

In the Netherlands, the city of Rotterdam has a complex of cubic homes designed by the Dutch architect Piet Blom. Each home has a side length of 7.5 meters. Use the equation $y = \sqrt[3]{V}$, where y is the side length and V is the volume, to find the volume of a Cube-House.

SOLUTION

Understand The side length of the cube is 7.5 meters. The equation $y = \sqrt[3]{V}$ models the side length of a cube, y, in terms of the volume of the cube, V.

Plan Substitute the side length of the Cube-House into the equation.

$7.5 = \sqrt[3]{V}$

Solve Solve the equation for the value of x.

$$7.5 = \sqrt[3]{V}$$
$$7.5 = V^{\frac{1}{3}}$$
$$(7.5)^3 = \left(V^{\frac{1}{3}}\right)^3$$
$$421.875 = V$$

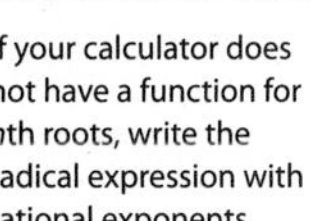

Graphing Calculator Tip

If your calculator does not have a function for *n*th roots, write the radical expression with rational exponents.

Check Substitute the value found for V back into the original equation and use a calculator to check.

$y = \sqrt[3]{421.875}$

$y = 7.5$

The volume of a Cube-House is 421.875 square meters.

Additional Example 4 (continued)

b. $x^{\frac{4}{3}} = 81$ 27

c. $x^{\frac{2}{7}} = 10$ $1000\sqrt{10}$

Extend the Example

Use a calculator with an x^y key to solve each equation. Approximate solutions to two decimal places.

a. $(x - 1)^{\frac{2}{3}} = 5$ 12.18

b. $5(2x + 3)^{\frac{1}{4}} - 8 = 0$ 1.78

Example 5

Students use rational exponents to solve an applications problem.

Extend the Example

Doubling the cube, or duplication of the cube, is one of three famous problems of antiquity that cannot be solved by a construction done with only compass and straightedge. Have students write brief reports on this ancient problem, including the solution in general form for a cube with edge x. $x_2 = x_1\sqrt[3]{2}$

Additional Example 5

Jorge can rent a cubical storage container 12 feet on each edge. He estimates he needs double this amount of storage space. What are the dimensions of a cubical storage container that has enough space for all his stuff? edge $= 12\sqrt[3]{2}$, or about 15.12 ft on each edge

ALTERNATE METHOD FOR EXAMPLE 4

Introduce raising both sides of an equation to the same power using examples such as $\sqrt{x} = 6$, which students can solve by inspection. Ask **"How can you isolate x to solve this equation?"** Square both sides. Have a volunteer show the steps:

$\sqrt{x}\cdot\sqrt{x} = 6\cdot 6$, $\sqrt{x^2} = 36$, $x = 36$

Model solving the problem using rational exponents instead of square root signs:

$x^{\frac{1}{2}} = 6$, $\left(x^{\frac{1}{2}}\right)^2 = 6^2$, $x = 36$

Repeat with a cube root problem.

$\sqrt[3]{x} = 4$, $\sqrt[3]{x}\cdot\sqrt[3]{x}\cdot\sqrt[3]{x} = 4^3$, $x = 64$

$x^{\frac{1}{3}} = 4$, $\left(x^{\frac{1}{3}}\right)^3 = 4^3$, $x = 64$

Lesson Practice

Problem d

Error Alert You may need to remind students to rationalize the denominator.

Problems e–g

Scaffolding Ask students what they plan to do with the exponents. add, subtract, multiply Then have students identify the properties of exponents that justify these steps. product of powers, quotient of powers, power of a power

Check for Understanding

The questions below help assess the concepts taught in this lesson.

"How do the numerator and denominator of a fractional exponent relate to the equivalent radical expression?" denominator is index of radical; numerator is power of radicand

"Describe two different ways to simplify a radical expression." Samples: Factor out perfect *n*th powers, rationalize the denominator, collect like radicals, convert to rational exponents and then use the laws of exponents to simplify.

3 Practice

Math Conversations

Discussions to strengthen understanding

Problem 7

Ask students to describe the steps needed to solve this problem. Sample: Solve the given equation for y to find its slope. Write the negative reciprocal of that slope. Use it and the given point in the point-slope form of an equation.

Lesson Practice

Write the rational exponent as a radical expression.
(Ex 1)

a. $7^{\frac{1}{7}}$ $\sqrt[7]{7}$

b. $4^{\frac{5}{3}}$ $\sqrt[3]{4^5}$

Simplify. Assume that all variables are positive.
(Ex 2)

c. $\sqrt[6]{64x^{18}}$ $2x^3$

d. $\sqrt[3]{\frac{x^{24}}{6}}$ $\frac{x^8\sqrt[3]{36}}{6}$

Simplify.
(Ex 3)

e. $49^{-\frac{5}{4}} \cdot 49^{\frac{3}{4}}$ $\frac{1}{7}$

f. $\frac{15^{\frac{17}{6}}}{15^{\frac{5}{6}}}$ 225

g. $\left(625^{\frac{1}{16}}\right)^4$ 5

h. $(1{,}024 \cdot 32)^{\frac{1}{5}}$ 8

Solve.
(Ex 4)

i. $x^{\frac{1}{9}} = 3$ 19,683

j. $x^{\frac{7}{6}} = 128$ 64

k. $x^{\frac{5}{2}} = 4$ $\sqrt[5]{16}$

l. The Apple Store on Fifth Ave. in New York City has a 32-foot-tall cube entrance way. Use the equation $y = \sqrt[3]{x}$, where y is the side length and x is the volume, to find the volume of the Apple Store entrance.
(Ex 5)
32,768 cubic feet

Practice Distributed and Integrated

1. Find the probability of getting exactly 0 heads if a coin is tossed 3 times. $\frac{1}{8}$
(49)

Simplify.

2. $3\sqrt{\frac{7}{5}} + 2\sqrt{\frac{5}{7}}$ $\frac{31\sqrt{35}}{35}$
(40)

3. $\frac{2}{5\sqrt{18}}$ $\frac{\sqrt{2}}{15}$
(40)

4. $\sqrt{\frac{2}{3}} + \sqrt{\frac{3}{2}}$ $\frac{5\sqrt{6}}{6}$
(40)

Complete the square and factor the resulting perfect square trinomial.

*5. $x^2 + 3x$ $x^2 + 3x + \frac{9}{4} = \left(x + \frac{3}{2}\right)^2$
(58)

*6. $x^2 - 14x$ $x^2 - 14x + 49 = (x - 7)^2$
(58)

7. Find the equation of the line that is perpendicular to $2x + y = 4$ and passes through the point $(-2, -1)$. $y = \frac{1}{2}x$
(36)

Write the rational exponent as a radical expression.

*8. $27^{\frac{1}{3}}$ $\sqrt[3]{27}$
(59)

*9. $16^{\frac{3}{4}}$ $\sqrt[4]{16^3}$
(59)

*10. $64^{\frac{1}{6}}$ $\sqrt[6]{64}$
(59)

11. **Verify** Use FOIL to verify the perfect square trinomial formulas.
(23)

a. $a^2 + 2ab + b^2 = (a + b)^2$

$(a + b)^2 = (a + b)(a + b)$
$a(a) + a(b) + b(a) + b(b)$
$a^2 + ab + ab + b^2$
$a^2 + 2ab + b^2$

b. $a^2 - 2ab + b^2 = (a - b)^2$

$(a - b)^2 = (a - b)(a - b)$
$a(a) + a(-b) + (-b)(a) + (-b)(-b)$
$a^2 - ab - ab + b^2$
$a^2 - 2ab + b^2$

CHALLENGE

A sphere is inscribed inside a cube so that the diameter of the sphere is the same as the edge of the cube.

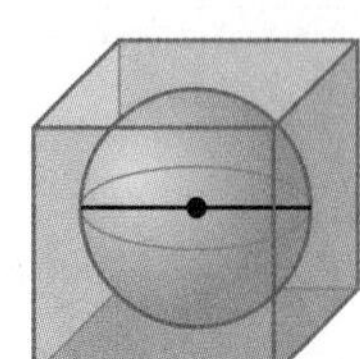

a. Show the volume formula for a cube solved for the edge (s). Show the volume formula of a sphere solved for diameter (d), using $V = \frac{4}{3}\pi r^3$ for the volume of the sphere with r equaling the radius.

$s = V^{\frac{1}{3}}, d = 2\left(\frac{3V}{4\pi}\right)^{\frac{1}{3}}$

b. If the volume of the cube is 200 m³, find the volume of the sphere to two decimal places. Write an expression to relate the two volumes.

104.72 m³, $V_s = \frac{\pi V_c}{6}$

*12. (59) **Music** Frets are small metal bars placed across the neck of a guitar so that the guitar can produce notes of a specific scale. To find the distance a fret should be placed from the bridge, multiply the length of the string by $2^{-\frac{n}{12}}$, where n is the number of notes higher than the string's root note. Where should a fret be placed to produce a G note on the A string (2 notes higher), if the length of the string is 66 cm, rounded to the nearest tenth place? 58.8 cm

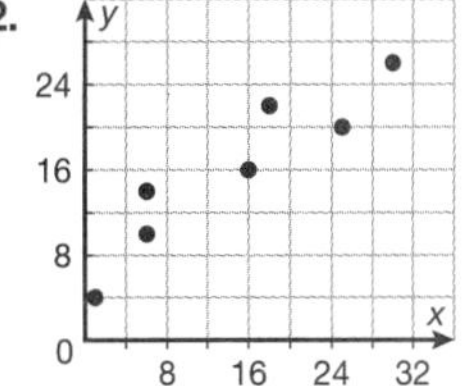

13. (39) **Multiple Choice** Which ordered pair is a solution of the system below? A

$$y \leq x$$
$$x > -4$$
$$2x - 5y > 5$$

A $(-3, -3)$ B $(-3, 3)$ C $(-5, -5)$ D $(-5, 5)$

*14. (27) **Coordinate Geometry** Graph the function $f(x) = \frac{1}{2}x^2 - 1$ by making a table. See Additional Answers.

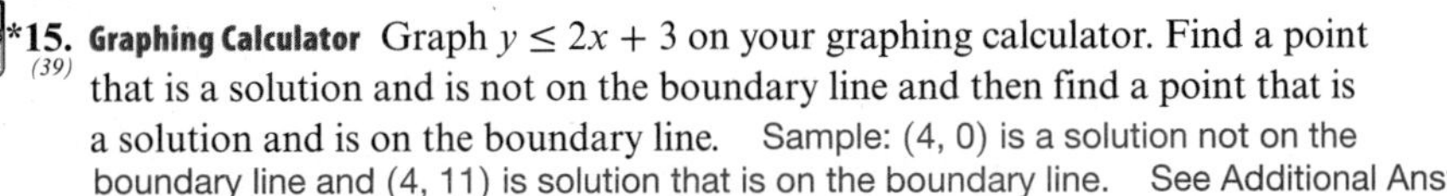

*15. (39) **Graphing Calculator** Graph $y \leq 2x + 3$ on your graphing calculator. Find a point that is a solution and is not on the boundary line and then find a point that is a solution and is on the boundary line. Sample: (4, 0) is a solution not on the boundary line and (4, 11) is solution that is on the boundary line. See Additional Answers.

*16. (59) **Verify** Explain why radical expressions with even indices and negative radicands have no real roots. Use $\sqrt[4]{-256}$ to demonstrate your explanation. See Additional Answers.

17. (38) **Analyze** Suppose that the expression $\frac{(x^2 - a^2)}{(x - d)}$, for integers a and d, has no remainder. What must be true of a and d? $|a| = |d|$

18. (42) **Decorative Tiles** A 4 in. by 8 in. picture is formed using square tiles that are 2 in. on each side. If there are 8 tiles of different colors, how many different patterns can be created? Order makes a difference, so calculate using permutations. $P(8, 8) = 8! = 40{,}320$

*19. (58) **Multi-Step** Use $x^2 - 90x - 15 = -2037$.

a. What is the first step before you can complete the square? Isolate the binomial by adding 15 to both sides.

b. What constant can be added to the binomial to create a perfect square trinomial? 2025

c. What are the factors of the perfect square binomial? $(x - 45)^2$

d. Solve the equation for x. $x = 45 \pm \sqrt{3}$

20. (51) **Carpentry** A carpenter plans to use wooden plywood to make a wardrobe. He needs a total area of $A = 20x^2 - 23x - 21$ and a minimum width of $5x + 3$. Find the length of the rectangular plywood the carpenter would use to make the wardrobe. $4x - 7$

21. (50) **Geometry** The formula for the circumference of a circle is $C = 2\pi r$. Find the inverse of the function. Use the inverse to find the radius of the circle whose circumference is 44 square inches. $r = \frac{C}{2\pi}$, about 7 inches

22. (45) **Geometry** Find the area and perimeter of each rectangle. Then sketch a scatter plot comparing the area and perimeter. Describe the correlation. There is a fairly strong positive correlation.

Dimensions	1 by 6	4 by 4	2 by 9	3 by 10	1 by 1	2 by 3	5 by 5
Area (unit²)	6	16	18	30	1	6	25
Perimeter (unit)	14	16	22	26	4	10	20

Problem 12

Sketch a drawing of a guitar, showing students where the bridge and the frets are.

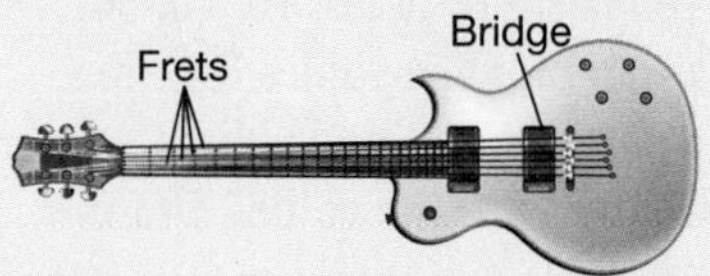

Error Alert

If students get the wrong answer, check that they noticed the negative sign in the exponent of $2^{-\frac{n}{12}}$.

Problem 13

Write the inequalities on the board and number them 1, 2, and 3. Ask **"Which answer choices does the first inequality eliminate?"** B and D **"Which answer choice does the second inequality eliminate?"** C

Problem 15

Ask students to tell you the definition of a boundary line and to give its equation for this problem. Sample: It divides the plane into two regions, one with points that are solutions, and one with points that are not solutions; $y = 2x + 3$

Problem 17

Extend the Problem

Find a value for a so that the following expression has no remainder. $a = 8$

$$\frac{x^2 - 6x + a}{x - 4}$$

ENGLISH LEARNERS

Have students copy the Rational Exponents Property: $a^{\frac{m}{n}} = (\sqrt[n]{a})^m = \sqrt[n]{a^m}$. Then write these terms on the board: **base, exponent, rational number, index, radicand, radical sign, *n*th root.** Have students use each term in a sentence to describe parts of the algebraic statement for the property.

Use a chart such as the following to help students learn how to use noun and adjective forms correctly.

Noun	Adjective
fraction	fractional
exponent	exponential
radical	radical
rational	rational

Problem 23

If students need help getting started, write the exponential equation $y = ab^x$ on the board. Tell them to use 0, 10, 20, 30, and 40 for the values for time. Using (0, 150) and substituting 0 for t gives the value 150 for a. Students can then use (10, 100) to find k.

Problem 28

Error Alert If students cannot solve the problem, remind them of how they ordered three fractions such as $\frac{2}{3}, \frac{1}{4}$, and $\frac{3}{5}$. They found a least common denominator; then wrote three equivalent fractions. You may need to show them that the LCD for this problem is $\sqrt{40}$.

***23.** (57) **(Marine Biology)** The estimated worldwide population $P(t)$ of humpback whales, in thousands, is shown in the table below for various years.

Year	1900	1910	1920	1930	1940
Number (in thousands)	150	100	66	44	29

Model the data with an exponential function, and use the model to estimate the humpback population in 1950 to the nearest hundred. $y = 150(0.96)^x$, about 19,500

24. (46) **Error Analysis** Explain and correct the error made: $\tan x = \frac{4}{3} = 1.\overline{3}$. The tangent of the angle is the ratio of the opposite side to the adjacent side, which is 3 to 4, or 0.75.

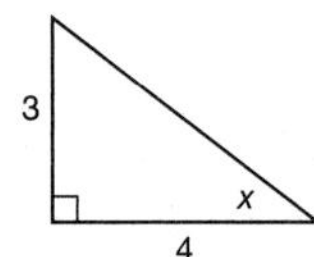

25. (55) **Multiple Choice** What is the probability that 3 out of 5 books randomly chosen from a box where all the titles are different are chosen in alphabetical order? **C**

A about 0.02% **B** about 1% **C** about 1.7% **D** about 10%

26. (52) **Justify** Explain the following statement: The triangles formed by the origin, the point (x, x), and the point $(x, 0)$, for any real x, are similar. See Additional Answers.

27. (55) **Write** What is a conditional probability? Give an example. See Additional Answers.

28. (44) Order the numbers $\frac{3}{\sqrt{5}}, \frac{3\sqrt{5}}{2\sqrt{2}}$, and $\frac{6}{\sqrt{10}}$ from least to greatest, without using a calculator. $\frac{3}{\sqrt{5}}, \frac{6}{\sqrt{10}}, \frac{3\sqrt{5}}{2\sqrt{2}}$

29. (53) **Error Analysis** A student is working with function $m(t) = t^{-3}$ and $n(t) = t^{-2}$. The student claims that the domain of $m(n(t))$ consists of all real numbers. Explain the error.

30. (56) Name two different angles that have a reference angle of 15°. Sample answer: 165°, −345°

29. The composition $m(n(t)) = t^6$. Although the domain of this function might be all real numbers, the domain of the composite is limited to the domain of the function $n(t)$, which is only positive real numbers.

CHALLENGE

Graph the equation $y = x^{\frac{n}{9}}$ for $n = 1$ to 8.

a. What happens when n is odd? when n is even? For n odd, the part of the graph left of the y-axis is below the x-axis; for n even, the part of the graph left of the y-axis is above the x-axis.

b. What happens as n gets closer to 9? The graph gets closer to the diagonal line $y = x$ when n is odd, or closer to the graph of $y = |x|$ when n is even.

LOOKING FORWARD

Fractional exponents prepares students for

- **Lesson 70** Solving Radical Equations
- **Lesson 75** Graphing Radical Functions
- **Lesson 84** Solving Rational Equations
- **Lesson 94** Solving Rational Inequalities
- **Lesson 100** Graphing Rational Functions I

LESSON **60**

Distinguishing Between Mutually Exclusive and Independent Events

Warm Up

1. **Vocabulary** The number of ways objects can be arranged when order matters is called a ________. permutation
(33)

2. Calculate ${}_8C_3$. 56
(33)

3. If a number cube is rolled, what is the probability of rolling an odd number? $\frac{1}{2}$
(47)

New Concepts

A **compound event** is an event that is made up of two or more simple events. Events that have at least one outcome in common are **inclusive events.** **Disjoint events** are events that have no outcomes in common.

> **Math Language**
>
> Inclusive events may also be described as overlapping. Disjoint events are also called mutually exclusive.

Example 1 Disjoint Events and Inclusive Events

When spinning the number wheel to the right the possible outcomes are {B1, B2, B3, B5, B6, B8, W1, W2, W3, W4, W8, W9}. Determine whether the compound events described are disjoint events or inclusive events.

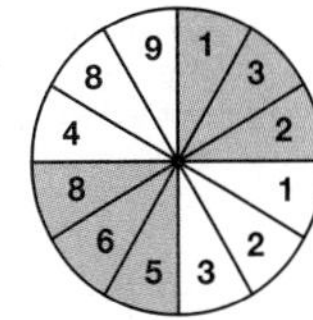

a. The spinner landing on a blue sector and the spinner landing on a 4.

SOLUTION Blue: {B1, B2, B3, B5, B6, B8}, 4: {W4} The two sets have no outcomes in common; therefore, they are disjoint events.

b. The spinner landing on a blue sector and the spinner landing on a 3.

SOLUTION Blue: {B1, B2, B3, B5, B6, B8}, 3: {B3, W3} The two sets intersect at B3; therefore, the two events are inclusive.

To calculate the probability of one or the other of two inclusive events use the formula below.

Inclusive Events
For two inclusive events A and B: $P(A \text{ or } B) = P(A) + P(B) - P(A \text{ and } B)$

Since events that are mutually exclusive, or disjoint, have no outcomes in common, $P(A \text{ and } B) = 0$.

Therefore,

$P(A \text{ or } B) = P(A) + P(B) - P(A \text{ and } B) = P(A) + P(B) - 0 = P(A) + P(B)$.

Mutually Exclusive Events
For two mutually exclusive events A and B: $P(A \text{ or } B) = P(A) + P(B)$

LESSON 60

1 Warm Up

For problem 3, remind students that a probability is a number from 0 to 1.

2 New Concepts

In this lesson, students learn to describe compound events as mutually exclusive or inclusive, and as independent or dependent.

Example 1

Students decide if two events are disjoint or inclusive.

Additional Example 1

Alice and Mary belong to both the chess club and the French club. The other chess club members are 4 boys and 3 girls. The other 5 members of the French club are all girls. Are these compound events mutually exclusive? All selections are names drawn at random.

a. event A = selecting a chess club member, event B = selecting a French club member no

b. event A = selecting a boy, event B = selecting a French club member yes

LESSON RESOURCES

Student Edition Practice Workbook 60
Reteaching Master 60
Adaptations Master 60
Challenge and Enrichment Master C60

MATH BACKGROUND

When computing compound probabilities, it is necessary to consider whether the events are independent or dependent, and whether the sample spaces for the events are overlapping or disjoint. The formula for computing the chances that two events will both happen is $P(A \text{ and } B) = P(A) \cdot P(B|A)$, where the notation $P(B|A)$ means "B under the condition that A has occurred."

When the two events are independent, $P(B|A) = P(B)$ and the formula becomes $P(A \text{ and } B) = P(A) \cdot P(B)$.

To find the chances that at least one of two events will happen, the formula is $P(A \text{ or } B) = P(A) + P(B) - P(A \text{ and } B)$. When the sample spaces are disjoint, the events are mutually exclusive. Then, $P(A \text{ and } B) = 0$ and the formula simplifies to $P(A \text{ or } B) = P(A) + P(B)$.

Example 2

Students find the probability that at least one of two events will happen. The events are either inclusive or mutually exclusive.

Additional Example 2

In a survey taken of 200 people entering a gym, 60 people plan to use the pool, 70 use the treadmill, 55 lift weights, and 40 will use both a treadmill and weights. If a gym member from this group is chosen at random, what is the probability that the member will

a. use the pool or lift weights $\frac{60}{200} + \frac{55}{200} = \frac{115}{200} = 0.575$

b. lift weights or use a treadmill $\frac{55}{200} + \frac{70}{200} - \frac{40}{200} = \frac{85}{200} = 0.425$

Extend the Example

Use the gym survey. What is the probability that a member from the survey chosen at random will not use the treadmills, the weights, or the pool? $\frac{55}{200} = 0.275$

Example 3

Students decide if two events are dependent or independent.

Additional Example 3

One student is chosen at random each week for two weeks to be class monitor. Are the following events dependent or independent? Explain.

a. The same student is chosen as monitor two weeks in a row. independent; The probability of being chosen the second week is the same as in the first week.

b. A student cannot be monitor two weeks in a row. dependent; After a name is drawn, it is not replaced. The probability of being chosen the second week is higher than the first.

Example 2 Probability of Mutually Exclusive and Inclusive Events

A jar contains 10 marbles: 5 red, 4 blue, and 1 green. The red marbles are numbered 1–5, the blue are numbered 6–9, and the green is numbered 10. A single marble is drawn from the jar.

a. Find the probability that the marble is blue or has an even number.

SOLUTION It is possible to select a blue marble with an even number. The events are inclusive and the formula $P(A \text{ or } B) = P(A) + P(B) - P(A \text{ and } B)$ can be used. Let A be the event that the marble is blue and B the event that the marble is numbered evenly.

$$P(A) = \frac{4}{10} = \frac{2}{5} \qquad P(B) = \frac{5}{10} = \frac{1}{2} \qquad P(A \text{ and } B) = \frac{2}{10} = \frac{1}{5}$$

$$P(A \text{ or } B) = P(A) + P(B) - P(A \text{ and } B) = \frac{2}{5} + \frac{1}{2} - \frac{1}{5} = \frac{7}{10} = 0.7$$

b. Find the probability that the marble is red or has a two digit number.

SOLUTION It is not possible to choose a red marble with a two digit number. The events are mutually exclusive and the formula $P(A \text{ or } B) = P(A) + P(B)$ can be used. Let A be the event that the marble is red and B the event that the marble has a two digit number.

$$P(A) = \frac{5}{10} = \frac{1}{2} \qquad P(B) = \frac{1}{10}$$

$$P(A \text{ or } B) = P(A) + P(B) = \frac{1}{2} + \frac{1}{10} = \frac{3}{5} = 0.6$$

Math Reasoning

Connect Think of an example of two events that are mutually exclusive but *not* independent.

From a jar containing red and white marbles two marbles are drawn separately without replacement. The first is red and the second is white.

Example 3 Dependent and Independent Events

A jar contains 9 white marbles and 7 green marbles. Determine whether the listed events are dependent or independent.

a. A white marble is selected and replaced. Then a green marble is selected.

SOLUTION The white marble is replaced so the first outcome has no effect on the selection of the green marble. Thus the events are independent.

b. A white marble is selected. Then without replacement another white marble is selected.

SOLUTION The first white marble is not replaced so it alters the possibilities of the next outcome. Thus the events are dependent.

The formula below can be used to calculate the probability of independent events.

Probability of Independent Events
For the probability of two independent events A and B:
$P(A \text{ and } B) = P(A) \cdot P(B)$
In general, for n independent events, $A_1, A_2, \ldots A_n$:
$P(A_1, A_2, \ldots, \text{and } A_n) = P(A_1) \cdot P(A_2) \cdot \ldots \cdot P(A_n)$

ALTERNATE METHOD FOR EXAMPLE 2

Start by pointing out that each marble must be identified by both color and number. Have students list the marbles as R1, R2, and so on. Then have students draw sample spaces for the two problems. The sample space for Part a is shown at the right. For Part b, the two circles don't overlap, so the events are mutually exclusive.

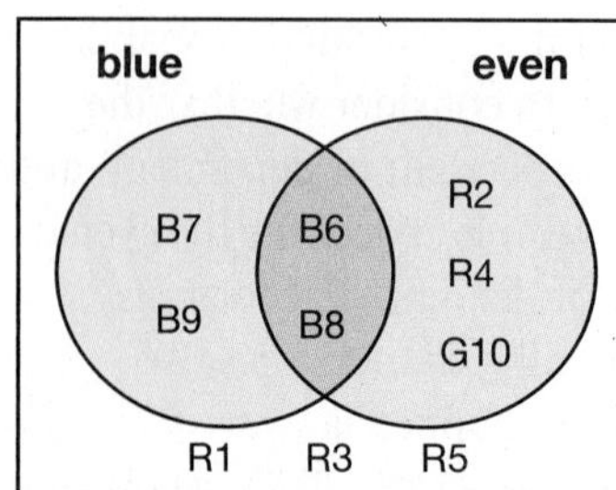

Example 4 Probability of Independent Events

Two fair coins are flipped three times. Find the probability that both coins come up one heads and one tails all three times.

SOLUTION Since each flip does not affect the next, the events are independent. The formula $P(A_1, A_2, \ldots, \text{and } A_n) = P(A_1) \cdot P(A_2) \cdot \ldots \cdot P(A_n)$ can be used.

Let A_1 be the event of one heads and one tails on the first flip, A_2 the event of one heads and one tails on the second flip, and A_3 the event of one heads and one tails on the third flip.

$$P(A_1) = \frac{1}{2} \qquad P(A_2) = \frac{1}{2} \qquad P(A_3) = \frac{1}{2}$$

$$P(A_1, A_2, \text{and } A_3) = P(A_1) \cdot P(A_2) \cdot P(A_3)$$
$$= \frac{1}{2} \cdot \frac{1}{2} \cdot \frac{1}{2} = \frac{1}{8} = 0.125$$

Math Reasoning

Verify Show the work to find the probability of one heads and one tails in one flip of two coins.

The possible outcomes of one flip of two coins are {HH, HT, TH, TT}. Two out of the four are a heads and a tails, which is half of the possibilities.

Example 5 Application: Giant Panda Population

The survival rate of giant panda cubs born in captivity is 59.4%. Find the probability that out of 4 giant panda cubs born consecutively into captivity the first two will survive and the last two will not. Round to the ten thousandths place.

SOLUTION

The survival of one panda cub does not affect the survival of the next cub, so the events are independent. The formula $P(A_1, A_2, \ldots, \text{and } A_n) = P(A_1) \cdot P(A_2) \cdot \ldots \cdot P(A_n)$ can be used.

Let A_1 be the event of one cub's survival, A_2 the event of the next cub's survival, A_3 the event of the third cub not surviving, and A_4 the event of the fourth cub not surviving.

$$P(A_1) = 0.594 \qquad P(A_2) = 0.594 \qquad P(A_3) = 0.406 \qquad P(A_4) = 0.406$$

$$P(A_1, A_2, A_3, \text{and } A_4) = P(A_1) \cdot P(A_2) \cdot P(A_3) \cdot P(A_4)$$
$$= 0.594 \cdot 0.594 \cdot 0.406 \cdot 0.406 \approx 0.05816 \approx 0.0582$$

Lesson Practice

a. (Ex 1) A number cube is rolled once. Are the events that the number rolled is odd and the number rolled is greater than 5 inclusive or mutually exclusive? mutually exclusive

b. (Ex 1) A number cube is rolled once. Are the events that the number rolled is even and the number rolled is divisible by 3 inclusive or mutually exclusive? inclusive

c. (Ex 2) A jar contains 10 green marbles and 10 orange marbles. The green marbles are numbered 1–5 and 11–15 and the orange marbles are numbered 6–10 and 16–20. Find the probability that a marble drawn from the jar is odd or green. 0.7

INCLUSION

For Example 4, review the probability of getting heads and tails when 2 coins are tossed. Have students make a tree diagram.

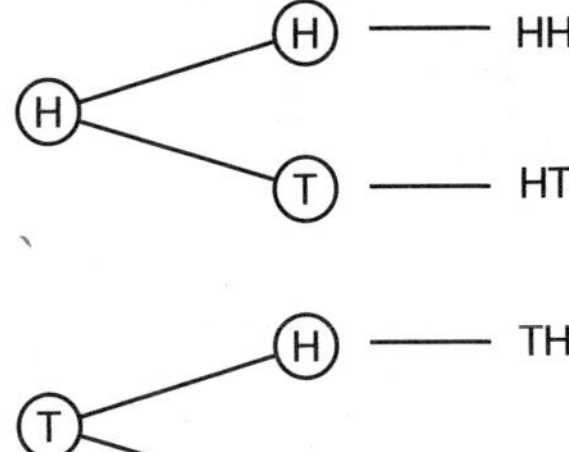

Point out there are 2 out of 4 ways to get a head and a tail. So, the chance on any one toss is $\frac{1}{2}$.

Emphasize that outcomes must be equally likely. So, the outcomes cannot be {two heads, two tails, one of each}. If students are not convinced, describe the coin toss as using a dime and a penny. Point out the outcome "heads dime, tails penny" is not the same as "heads penny, tails dime."

Example 4

Students find the probability that several events will all occur. The events are independent.

Extend the Example

When four coins are tossed, what is the probability of getting at least 2 heads? $\frac{11}{16} = 0.6875$

Additional Example 4

In a bag of marbles, 5 have stripes and 8 do not. What is the probability that a marble with stripes will be drawn three times in a row if the marble is replaced each time? $\frac{125}{2197} \approx 0.057$

Example 5

Students solve an application problem that involves the probability of independent events.

Additional Example 5

It is Wednesday. The weather report says there is a 30% chance of rain for the next 4 days. What is the probability it will rain tomorrow and Friday, but not rain on the weekend?
$0.3 \cdot 0.3 \cdot 0.7 \cdot 0.7 = 0.0441$

Lesson Practice

Problem b

Error Alert If students answer incorrectly, they may need a reminder that "divisible by 3" means the remainder is 0 when a number is divided by 3.

Problem c

Scaffolding Ask students how many outcomes there are in this experiment. 20 Then have them list the 20 outcomes in two columns, green numbers on the left and orange numbers on the right. Students will be able to see that 14 out of 20 outcomes are either odd or green.

TEACHER TIP

Drawing Venn diagrams for sample spaces can help students determine if two events can occur at the same time. If the events can happen simultaneously, they are not mutually exclusive.

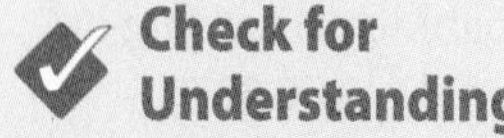

Check for Understanding

The questions below help assess the concepts taught in this lesson.

1. **"When are two events mutually exclusive?"** Sample: when their sample spaces have no outcomes in common
2. **"When are two events independent?"** Sample: when the probability of one does not depend on the occurrence of the other

3 Practice

Math Conversations

Discussions to strengthen understanding

Problem 1

Extend the Problem

Find the equation of a line that passes through (2, 2) and is parallel to the line $y = 3x - 5$.
$y = 3x - 4$

d. (Ex 2) A jar contains 10 green marbles and 10 orange marbles. The green marbles are numbered 1–5 and 11–15 and the orange marbles are numbered 6–10 and 16–20. Find the probability that a marble drawn from the jar is orange or less than 6. 0.75

e. (Ex 3) A number cube is rolled and a fair coin flipped. Are the events that a number less than 3 is rolled and heads is flipped dependent or independent? independent

f. (Ex 3) A bag contains 26 tiles lettered A–Z. Two tiles are drawn without replacement. Are the events that a vowel and a consonant are selected dependent or independent? dependent

g. (Ex 4) A jar contains 12 marbles and 7 blocks. An object is drawn from the jar then replaced. Find the probability that in 3 draws a marble, a block, then a marble is drawn. Round to the ten thousandths place. 0.1470

h. (Ex 5) **Birth Trends** The National Vital Statistics Report on births in 2004 shows that approximately 48.8% of live births are females. Find the probability that women would give birth to three daughters followed by a son. Round to the ten thousandths place. 0.0595

Practice Distributed and Integrated

1. (36) Find the equation of the line that passes through the point (2, 2) and is perpendicular to the line $y = 3x - 5$. $y = -\frac{1}{3}x + \frac{8}{3}$

2. (54) Given the objective function $P = 111x + 95y$ and the constraints $x \le 4$, $y \ge 0$, $x + 2y \le 50$, $3x + y \ge 15$, find the minimum and maximum values for the objective function. Minimum: 729; Maximum: 2629

3. (41) Find the distance between (4, −2) and (−3, −5). $\sqrt{58}$

Divide using synthetic division.

4. (51) $x^3 - 7$ by $x - 5$ $x^2 + 5x + 25 + \frac{118}{x-5}$

5. (51) $x^3 + 3x^2 + 7x + 5$ by $x + 1$ $x^2 + 2x + 5$

Divide using long division.

6. (38) $x^3 + 2$ by $x + 1$ $x^2 - x + 1 + \frac{1}{x+1}$

7. (38) $x^4 - 2$ by $x + 1$ $x^3 - x^2 + x - 1 - \frac{1}{x+1}$

***8.** (60) **Multiple Choice** A jar contains 19 black blocks and 25 gray blocks. The black blocks are numbered 1–19 and the gray blocks are numbered 20–44. Choose the answer that best represents the probability of selecting a black block or a number greater than 21. **B**

A 0.8864 **B** 0.9545 **C** 0.9773 **D** 0.9318

9. (43) **Error Analysis** A student stated that (1, 3) is a solution of the system below. What is the error?

$y \le x + 2$
$y > -x + 4$

(1, 3) is not a solution of $y > -x + 4$.

CHALLENGE

In probability problems with greater numbers, the formulas for combinations or permutations may be needed to compute numerical answers. Review the combinations formula:

$$C(n, r) = \frac{n!}{(n-r)!r!}$$

Have students show how to use combinations to solve the following problem.

The computer club has 28 girls and 32 boys. Eight names are drawn at random to choose students to go to a state conference. What is the probability that the chosen students will be half girls and half boys?

$\frac{C(28, 4) \cdot C(32, 4)}{C(60, 8)} \approx 0.288$

10. (38) **Generalize** Suppose that $ax^2 + bx + c$ is divisible by $x + d$ with no remainder, for real numbers a, b, c, and d. What can you conclude about the graph of the parabola? It intersects the x-axis at $(-d, 0)$.

11. (14) **Coordinate Geometry** Matrix multiplication can represent transforming a geometric figure. For example, suppose the three vertices of a triangle are given by the three rows of the matrix A. Then multiplying on the right by the matrix T gives a result that represents a new triangle.

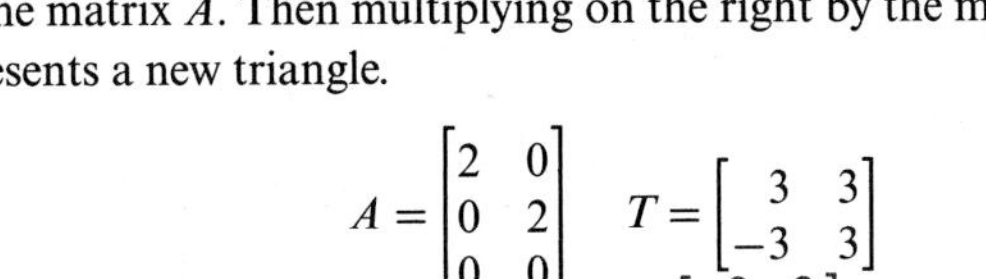

$$A = \begin{bmatrix} 2 & 0 \\ 0 & 2 \\ 0 & 0 \end{bmatrix} \quad T = \begin{bmatrix} 3 & 3 \\ -3 & 3 \end{bmatrix}$$

a. Calculate the product of these matrices.

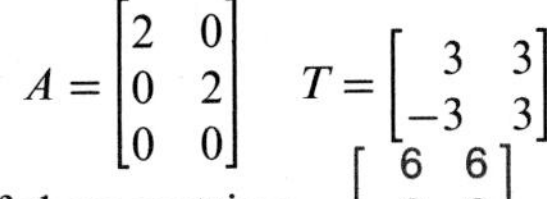

$$\begin{bmatrix} 6 & 6 \\ -6 & 6 \\ 0 & 0 \end{bmatrix}$$

b. Graph this new triangle.

b.

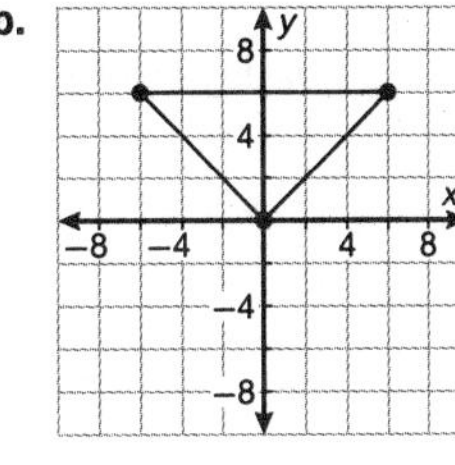

c. Calculate the areas of the original and the transformed triangles. area of original: 2 square units; area of transformed: 36 square units

d. How do these areas relate to the determinant of matrix T? The area is multiplied by 18, which is the determinant of T.

12. (52) **Estimate** The hypotenuse of a 30°-60°-90° triangle is 16 inches. Estimate the length of the side adjacent to the 30°. Give your answer to the nearest whole inch. 14 inches

***13.** (60) **Multi-Step** A number cube is rolled once and a fair coin is flipped.

a. Are the events, a number less than 5 and heads, dependent or independent? Explain why. Independent; The result of the number cube does not affect the result of the coin.

b. Find the probability of the number cube showing less than 5. Round to the hundredths place. 0.67

c. Find the probability of the coin showing heads. Round to the hundredths place. 0.5

d. Use the probabilities found in parts **b** and **c** to find the probability that a roll and flip will show a number less than 5 and heads. Round to the hundredths place. 0.34

14. (53) **Chemistry** Seventy percent of a compound is sodium chloride. If 660 grams of other chemicals are in the compound, what is the total weight of the compound? 2200 grams

15. (44) **Physics** The formula $t = \sqrt{\frac{2s}{g}}$ can be used to determine the time t, in seconds, it takes an object initially at rest to fall s meters. In this formula, g stands for the acceleration due to gravity, which on Earth is about 9.8 m/s². Use the formula to find out how long it takes a rock initially at rest to fall 110 meters. Write your answer in radical form. $\frac{\sqrt{2156}}{9.8} = \frac{2\sqrt{539}}{9.8} = \frac{\sqrt{539}}{4.9}$ about 4.7 seconds

***16.** (15) **Graphing Calculator** Use a graph to estimate the solution of $\begin{matrix} 3.1a + 2.8b = -12.2 \\ -0.9a - 1.1b = 3.85 \end{matrix}$. $(-3, -1)$

17. (51) **Explain** Can synthetic division be used to simplify $\frac{x^3 - 5x + 3}{x^2 + 2}$?

***18.** (60) **Write** Two number cubes are tossed once. Explain why the events, one cube shows 2 and the sum of the two cubes is greater than 5, are dependent.

17. No, the divisor is always a polynomial of degree 1 in synthetic division. Here the polynomial of the divisor is of degree 2, so long division or another method must solve it.

18. The events are dependent because the probability of the sum being greater than 5 changes with the knowledge that one of the cubes is showing 2.

19. (24) **Geometry** Write a rational expression in simplest form for the ratio of the rectangular prism's surface area to its volume. $\frac{4}{x}$

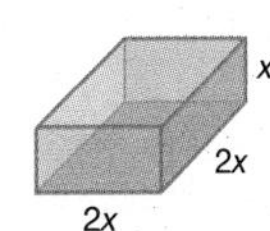

ENGLISH LEARNERS

Write these terms on the board: **mutually exclusive events, independent events.** Use an example such as the following to help students master the difference between the terms.

The numbers 1–20 are put into a hat. A number is drawn at random.

Event A = {drawing an odd number}

Event B = {drawing an even number}

These events are mutually exclusive. Their sample spaces have no outcomes in common.

$$P(A \text{ or } B) = \frac{1}{2} + \frac{1}{2} = 1$$

Event A = {drawing an odd number}
The number is replaced.
Event B = {drawing an even number}

These events are independent. The probability of event B is not affected by what happens in event A. $P(A \text{ and } B) = \frac{1}{2} \times \frac{1}{2} = \frac{1}{4}$

Problem 10
Extend the Problem

Find and graph a specific example of the generalization with $a \neq 1$. Give the x-intercepts of the graph. Sample: $2x^2 + 11x + 15$ is divisible by $(x + 3)$. The x-intercepts are -2.5 and -3.

Problem 11
Extend the Problem

a. Describe the result of multiplying the vertex matrix by matrix T. 90° counter-clockwise rotation and dilation by scale factor 3

b. Find a transformation matrix that will result in the same dilation, but in a 90° clockwise rotation.

$$\begin{bmatrix} 3 & -3 \\ 3 & 3 \end{bmatrix} \text{ or } \begin{bmatrix} 3 & 3 \\ 3 & -3 \end{bmatrix}$$

Problem 12
Error Alert

If students get 18 in., they have used 16 in. for one of the legs of the triangle instead of for the hypotenuse. Have them sketch the triangle, labeling the side opposite the 30° angle as 8 in.

Problem 16
Extend the Problem

Find the solution to 5 decimal places. $(-2.96629, -1.07303)$

Problem 19

Students should remember that volume equals the product of the dimensions, $V = lwh$. However, you may need to review the surface area formula, $SA = 2lw + 2lh + 2wh$. Suggest that students first find the ratio using the formulas, then substitute the given dimensions. They will find that

$$\frac{2lw + 2lh + 2wh}{lwh} = \frac{2}{h} + \frac{2}{w} + \frac{2}{l}.$$

Substituting x, $2x$, and $2x$ into the right side is now a relatively simple exercise.

Problem 22

Error Alert

If students choose answer B, remind them that, by definition, an inconsistent system of equations has no solutions.

Problem 24

Extend the Problem

"How would the data points in this problem compare with their mean?" The standard deviation is large, so the data points are far from the mean.

Problem 25

Error Alert

If students get 198.2 meters, their calculators are using radians rather than degrees. They can change the settings on the calculator. Or, they can multiply degrees times $\frac{\pi}{180}$ to convert to radians. The equation to solve is then $\cos\left(43\frac{\pi}{180}\right) = \frac{110}{x}$. Remind students to check that $\tan 45° = 1$. If it equals 1.61978, the calculator is set to radians.

Problem 28

If students need a hint, tell them to use $f(x) = x + 0.5x$ to show what happens in the first month.

***20.** (58) **Projectile Motion** Gravity on the planet Jupiter is almost three times stronger than on Earth. If an object is thrown into the air, with an initial velocity of 90 feet per second, from the surface of Jupiter, the height, h, of the object in feet after t seconds can be approximated by the equation $h = -42t^2 + 90t$. Find the time at which the object will return to the surface. Round your answer to the tenths place. 2.1 seconds

21. (41) **Justify** Given the lengths of three sides of a right triangle, how do you know which side is the hypotenuse? The hypotenuse is always the longest side.

22. (29) **Multiple Choice** Circle the letter that represents the number and type of solutions of the system of three equations:

$$\begin{aligned} -4x + 12y - 16z &= -28 \\ 3x - 9y + 12z &= 21 \\ -x + 3y - 4z &= -7 \end{aligned}$$

. D

A No solution, inconsistent **B** One solution, inconsistent

C One solution, consistent **D** Infinitely many solutions, consistent

23. (58) **Error Analysis** Find and explain the error in the work below. Then find the correct solution. The error is in the third line. Whenever you change one side of the equation you must change the other side in exactly the same way; $x = 17 \pm \sqrt{319}$

$$x^2 - 34x - 15 = 15 \qquad (x - 17)^2 = 30$$

$$x^2 - 34x = 30 \qquad x - 17 = \pm\sqrt{30}$$

$$x^2 - 34x + 289 = 30 \qquad x = 17 \pm \sqrt{30}$$

***24.** (59) **Statistics** Given that the variance of a data set is $425^{\frac{5}{3}}$ find the standard deviation for the data set. (Hint: standard deviation $= \sqrt{\text{variance}}$) about 155

25. (46) **History** The Red Pyramid is an Egyptian pyramid with a square base length of 220 meters. The slope is approximately 43°. Approximate the length of an edge of the pyramid to the nearest tenth. ≈ 212.7 meters

26. (57) **Medicine** If a patient ingests medicine containing a grams of a drug, the amount left in the patient's bloodstream after t hours is given by the equation $y = ab^t$. If one-fourth of the medicine is left after 3 hours, what portion is left after 4 hours? ≈ 15.7%

27. (45) **Verify** Use the table to verify that exchanging the x and y values does not change the value of r for the data set. See student work, $r \approx 0.41$

x	1	2	3	4
y	67	56	84	70

28. (53) **Investment** You invest in a business. The first month your investment gains 5%. The second month your investment loses 5%. Write a composite function to show whether the investment equals the original investment after two months.

28. first month: $f(x) = x + 0.05x = 1.05x$; second month: $g(x) = x - 0.05x = 0.95x$; composite: $g(f(x)) = 0.95(1.05)x = 0.9975x$. More has been lost than gained.

***29.** (59) **Verify** Show the steps needed to write $\sqrt{3} \cdot \sqrt[5]{3}$ as $\sqrt[10]{2{,}187}$.

$$\sqrt{3} \cdot \sqrt[5]{3} = 3^{\frac{1}{2}} \cdot 3^{\frac{1}{5}} = 3^{\frac{1}{2}+\frac{1}{5}} = 3^{\frac{7}{10}} = \sqrt[10]{3^7} = \sqrt[10]{2{,}187}$$

30. (55) **Geography** The table shows the number of states in the continental U.S. that fall into each time zone. The total exceeds 48 because some states are in two time zones. What is the probability that a randomly chosen state is not in the Pacific time zone? ≈ 0.917 or 91.7%

Time Zone	Eastern	Central	Mountain	Pacific
Number of States	22	20	13	5

CHALLENGE

The girls basketball team has a 30% chance of going to the finals. The boys team has only a 10% chance. Find each probability.

a. both teams going 3%

b. neither team going 63%

c. girls go, boys don't 27%

d. boys go, girls don't 7%

LOOKING FORWARD

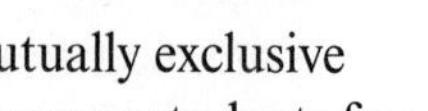

Distinguishing between mutually exclusive and independent events prepares students for

- **Lesson 68** Finding Conditional Probability
- **Lesson 73** Using Sampling
- **Lesson 80** Finding the Normal Distribution

INVESTIGATION 6

Deriving the Quadratic Formula

Model The general form of a quadratic equation is written as

$$f(x) = ax^2 + bx + c$$

The roots of the equation are found by solving the equation

$$ax^2 + bx + c = 0$$

The most common way of solving a quadratic equation is to use the **quadratic formula**

$$x = \frac{-b \pm \sqrt{b^2 - 4ac}}{2a}$$

But where does this equation come from? Is there a way of deriving this equation?

In this activity, you will use algebra tiles to model completing the square. You will need a quantity of these three models:

x^2 term	x term	Constant term (one tile represents 1, two tiles represent 2, etc.)

1. Use the tiles to model the following quadratic equation. Check students' work.

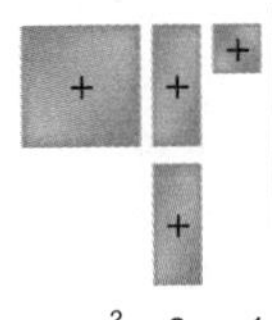

$x^2 + 2x + 1 = 0$

Math Reasoning

Analyze In the algebra tiles model, the vertical line represents the = sign. How is zero modeled?

Place no tiles to the right of the vertical line.

2. This quadratic equation is the perfect square $(x + 1)^2 = 0$. Rearrange the tiles, as shown below, to show the square. Check students' work.

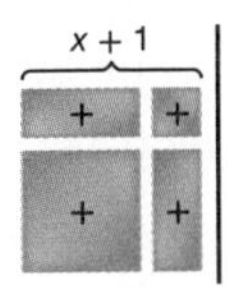

$(x + 1)^2 = 0$

3. Use tiles to show that the following quadratic equations are perfect squares.

   a. $x^2 + 4x + 4 = 0$ b. $x^2 + 6x + 9 = 0$ c. $x^2 + 8x + 16 = 0$
   See Additional Answers.

Online Connection
www.SaxonMathResources.com

INVESTIGATION 6

Materials

Pencil, paper, and algebra tiles

Discuss

Using algebra tiles, students will derive the quadratic formula. Manipulating tiles will help students determine if a quadratic equation represents a perfect square trinomial.

Define perfect-square trinomial.

TEACHER TIP

Have students place an x-tile along either side of an x^2-tile so they can see that they are proportional. Have students place a unit tile along the short edge of an x-tile to see that the width is one unit, making the area of the x-tile equal to x.

Error Alert

Students may want to place unit tiles inside the x- or x^2-tiles to find the value of x. Explain that the tiles do not work this way.

MATH BACKGROUND

The work with algebra tiles in this investigation shows that the name "perfect square" is no accident. The derivation of the quadratic formula using algebra tiles creates a perfect square which represents a perfect square trinomial. Every time the quadratic formula is used, a perfect square trinomial is created from a non perfect square trinomial. If all trinomials were perfect squares, the quadratic formula would not be needed. Students need to be aware that the quadratic formula can solve all quadratic equations, whether they are factorable or not. For some students, using the quadratic formula will be easier than factoring.

INVESTIGATION RESOURCES

Reteaching Master Investigation 6

Problem 4

Before beginning problem 4, write the equation $ax^2 + bx + c = 0$ on the board to remind students that b represents the coefficient of the x term and that c is the constant term.

Problem 6

Place the x^2-tile first. Place the x-tiles above and to the right of the x^2-tile. Finally complete the square by filling in the constant term tiles.

TEACHER TIP

In all examples, half of the x-tiles were put above the x^2-tile and half were put on the right of the x^2-tile. Therefore half of the coefficient of x or $\frac{1}{2} \cdot b = \frac{b}{2}$ equals the square root of the sum of the constant tiles or $\sqrt{c}$. The constant tiles will always create a small square whose size will depend upon the number of x-tiles.

Problems 6c and d

Scaffolding

To solve the equation $x^2 + 6x + 9 = 8$:

1. Factor into a binomial squared $(x + 3)^2 = 8$.
2. Take the square root of both sides of the equation. $x + 3 = \pm\sqrt{8}$
3. Solve by subtracting 3 from both sides of the equation. $x = -3 \pm \sqrt{8}$

4. Complete the table below with the values of c and b for each of the perfect squares.

Perfect Square	b	c
$(x + 1)^2$	2	1
$(x + 2)^2$	4	4
$(x + 3)^2$	6	9
$(x + 4)^2$	8	16

5. Write an equation that shows the relationship between c and b for perfect squares. $\left(\frac{b}{2}\right)^2 = c$

Math Reasoning

Generalize Expand the perfect square $(x + n)^2 = 0$. Since this is also a quadratic equation, what are the values of a, b, and c?

$a = 1$; $b = 2n$; $c = n^2$

Not all quadratic equations are perfect squares, but they can be turned into perfect squares.

6. **Multi-Step** Use algebra tiles.
   a. Model the equation $x^2 + 6x + 1 = 0$. See Additional Answers.
   b. What needs to be added to both sides of the equation to get a perfect square on the left side? Eight 1-tiles.
   c. Write the new equation with the perfect square on the left side. **c.** $x^2 + 6x + 9 = 8$; $(x + 3)^2 = 8$
   d. Solve the equation. $x = -3 \pm 2\sqrt{2}$

To solve the general quadratic equation, you can complete the square using the relationship between b and c you determined in problem 5.

$$ax^2 + bx + c = 0$$

7. To simplify solving the equation, divide both sides of the equation by a. Write the new form of the equation. $x^2 + \frac{b}{a}x + \frac{c}{a} = 0$
8. Subtract the constant term from each side of each equation. Write the new form of the equation. $x^2 + \frac{b}{a}x = -\frac{c}{a}$
9. Using the relationship between c and b you discovered in question 5, determine what needs to be added to the left side to complete the square. $\left(\frac{b}{2a}\right)^2$
10. Add the amount determined in problem 9 to both sides of the equation to complete the square. $x^2 + \frac{b}{a}x + \left(\frac{b}{2a}\right)^2 = -\frac{c}{a} + \left(\frac{b}{2a}\right)^2$
11. Write the left side as the square of a binomial. $\left(x + \frac{b}{2a}\right)^2 = -\frac{c}{a} + \frac{b^2}{4a^2}$
12. Simplify the right side of the equation. $\left(x + \frac{b}{2a}\right)^2 = \frac{b^2 - 4ac}{4a^2}$
13. Apply the Square Root Property. $x + \frac{b}{2a} = \pm\sqrt{\frac{b^2 - 4ac}{4a^2}}$
14. Simplify the right side of the equation. $x + \frac{b}{2a} = \frac{\pm\sqrt{b^2 - 4ac}}{2a}$
15. Solve for x: $x = \frac{-b \pm\sqrt{b^2 - 4ac}}{2a}$
16. Solve the quadratic equation $2x^2 + 6x - 3 = 0$ by substituting the values for a, b, and c.

16. $x = \frac{-6 \pm \sqrt{6^2 - 4(2)(-3)}}{2(2)} = \frac{-6 \pm \sqrt{36 + 24}}{4} = \frac{-6 \pm \sqrt{60}}{4} = \frac{-6 \pm 2\sqrt{15}}{4} = \frac{-3 \pm \sqrt{15}}{2}$

ENGLISH LEARNERS

Define perfect square trinomial. Say:

"A perfect square trinomial is a special trinomial. It can be factored into a squared binomial."

For example, $x^2 + 10x + 25$ is a perfect square trinomial because it can be factored into the squared binomial $(x + 5)^2$. This investigation will show you the relationship between the x term ($10x$) and the constant term (25) in a perfect square trinomial.

Investigation Practice

Use algebra tiles to determine which of the following quadratic equations represent perfect squares.

a. $x^2 + 10x + 25 = 0$ perfect square

b. $2x^2 + 6x + 3 = 0$ not a perfect square

c. $4x^2 + 4x + 1 = 0$ perfect square

Solve by completing the square and solve by using the quadratic formula.

d. $x^2 + 4x + 1 = 0$

e. $x^2 + 6x + 2 = 0$

d.

$$x^2 + 4x = -1$$
$$x^2 + 4x + 4 = -1 + 4$$
$$(x + 2)^2 = 3$$
$$x = -2 \pm \sqrt{3}$$

$$x = \frac{-4 \pm \sqrt{4^2 - 4(1)(1)}}{2(1)} = \frac{-4 \pm \sqrt{16 - 4}}{2} = \frac{-4 \pm \sqrt{12}}{2} = \frac{-4 \pm 2\sqrt{3}}{2} = -2 \pm \sqrt{3}$$

e.

$$x^2 + 6x = -2$$
$$x^2 + 6x + 9 = -2 + 9$$
$$(x + 3)^2 = 7$$
$$x = -3 \pm \sqrt{7}$$

$$x = \frac{-6 \pm \sqrt{6^2 - 4(1)(2)}}{2(1)} = \frac{-6 \pm \sqrt{36 - 8}}{2} = \frac{-6 \pm \sqrt{28}}{2} = \frac{-6 \pm 2\sqrt{7}}{2} = -3 \pm \sqrt{7}$$

Investigation Practice

Math Conversations

Discussions to strengthen understanding

Problems a–c

Do the tiles form a square in each problem? If a square is not formed, the quadratic equation is not a perfect square.

Remind students that $2x^2$ is represented by 2 x^2-tiles.

Problems d–e

Move the tiles to form a square. If the original tiles form a square, the equation can be factored. If the square is incomplete, add tiles to complete the square.

LOOKING FORWARD

Deriving the quadratic formula prepares students for

- **Lesson 65** Using the Quadratic Formula
- **Lesson 74** Finding the Discriminant
- **Lesson 78** Solving Quadratic Equations II

Lesson Planner

Lesson	New Concepts
61	Understanding Advanced Factoring
62	Using Complex Numbers
63	Understanding the Unit Circle and Radian Measures
Lab 10	*Graphing Calculator Lab:* Using the Log Keys
64	Using Logarithms
65	Using the Quadratic Formula
	Cumulative Test 12, Performance Task 12
66	Solving Polynomial Equations
67	Finding Inverse Trigonometric Functions
68	Finding Conditional Probability
69	Simplifying Complex Expressions
70	Solving Radical Equations
	Cumulative Test 13, Performance Task 13
INV 7	Investigation: Collecting Data

Resources for Teaching

- Student Edition
- Teacher's Edition
- Student Edition eBook
- Teacher's Edition eBook
- Resources and Planner CD
- Solutions Manual
- Instructional Masters
- Technology Lab Masters
- Warm Up and Teaching Transparencies
- Instructional Presentations CD
- Online activities, tools, and homework help **www.SaxonMathResources.com**

Resources for Practice and Assessment

- Student Edition Practice Workbook
- Course Assessments
- Standardized Test Practice
- College Entrance Exam Practice
- Test and Practice Generator CD using ExamView™

Resources for Differentiated Instruction

- Reteaching Masters
- Challenge and Enrichment Masters
- Prerequisite Skills Intervention
- Adaptations for Saxon Algebra 2
- Multilingual Glossary
- English Learners Handbook
- TI Resources

Pacing Guide

Resources and Planner CD for lesson planning support

45-Minute Class

Day 1	Day 2	Day 3	Day 4	Day 5	Day 6
Lesson 61	Lesson 62	Lesson 63	Lab 10 Lesson 64	Lesson 65	Cumulative Test 12
Day 7	**Day 8**	**Day 9**	**Day 10**	**Day 11**	**Day 12**
Lesson 66	Lesson 67	Lesson 68	Lesson 69	Lesson 70	Cumulative Test 13
Day 13					
Investigation 7					

Block: 90-Minute Class

Day 1	Day 2	Day 3	Day 4	Day 5	Day 6
Investigation 6 Lesson 61	Lesson 62 Lesson 63	Lab 10 Lesson 64 Lesson 65	Cumulative Test 12 Lesson 66	Lesson 67 Lesson 68	Lesson 69 Lesson 70
Day 7					
Cumulative Test 13 Investigation 7					

** For suggestions on how to implement Saxon Math in a block schedule, see the Pacing section at the beginning of the Teacher's Edition.*

Differentiated Instruction

Below Level		Advanced Learners	
Warm Up	SE pp. 436, 442, 447, 457, 462, 469, 476, 483, 489, 495	Challenge	TE pp. 441, 446, 452, 453, 461, 467, 474, 481, 482, 488, 492, 499, 500
Skills Bank	SE pp. 862–885	Extend the Example	TE pp. 437, 451, 470, 477, 478, 479, 484, 485, 499
Reteaching Masters	Lessons 61–70, Investigation 7	Extend the Problem	TE pp. 439, 444, 446, 454, 458, 465, 466, 474, 475, 481, 482, 488, 493, 501
Warm Up Transparencies	Lessons 61–70	Challenge and Enrichment Masters	Challenge: C61–C70 Enrichment: E65, E67
Prerequisite Skills Intervention	Lessons 6, 7, 39, 67, 81, 82		
English Learners		**Special Needs**	
EL Tips	TE pp. 437, 443, 449, 458, 463, 473, 479, 487, 491, 496, 503	Inclusion Tips	TE pp. 438, 445, 448, 451, 460, 464, 465, 467, 472, 478, 480, 485, 486, 490, 497
Multilingual Glossary	Booklet and Online	Adaptations for Saxon Algebra 2	Lessons 61–70, Cumulative Tests 12, 13
English Learners Handbook			
For All Learners			
Exploration	SE pp. 447	Alternate Method	TE pp. 439, 444, 450, 459, 470, 471, 477, 484, 498
Caution	SE pp. 478	Manipulative Use	TE pp. 484, 485
Hints	SE pp. 436, 449, 458, 459, 463, 469, 471, 477, 484, 502, 504	Online Tools	
Error Alert	TE pp. 438, 441, 443, 445, 450, 452, 455, 459, 461, 463, 465, 468, 471, 474, 475, 476, 479, 480, 481, 484, 485, 486, 491, 492, 494, 496, 501, 503, 504		

SE = Student Edition; TE = Teacher's Edition

Math Vocabulary

Lesson	New Vocabulary	Maintained	EL Tip in TE
61		linear factor root	grouping
62	complex number imaginary number imaginary part of a complex number imaginary unit real part of a complex number	quadratic equations radicand	imaginary
63	arc arc length radian unit circle	radius special triangles	radian
64	common logrithm logarithm	base exponent	logarithm
65		complex number quadratic equation quadratic formula	quadratic
66	multiplicity	roots x-intercepts	irrational rational
67	inverse cosine function inverse sine function inverse tangent function	domain unit circle	arcsine
68		probability	condition
69	absolute value of a complex number complex conjugate	complex number exponent	conjugate
70	radical equation	extraneous solutions inverse	radical radicand
INV 7		bias population sample	bias

Math Highlights

Enduring Understandings – The "Big Picture"

After completing Section 7, students will understand:

- How to simplify polynomial equations using advanced factoring.
- How to solve quadratic equations with complex solutions.
- How to evaluate trigonometric functions and their inverses.
- How to compute conditional probabilities.
- How to solve radical equations.

Essential Questions

- How can reference angles be used to evaluate trigonometric functions?
- What is the Rational Root Theorem used for?
- How can the Factor Theorem be applied to determine if a linear binomial is a factor of a polynomial?
- When is a survey considered biased?

Math Content Strands

Exponential and Logarithmic Functions

• Lab 10	Using the Log Keys
• Lesson 64	Using Logarithms

Polynomials and Polynomial Functions

• Lesson 61	Understanding Advanced Factoring
• Lesson 66	Solving Polynomial Equations

Probability and Statistics

• Lesson 68	Finding Conditional Probability
• Investigation 7	Collecting Data

Quadratic Functions

• Lesson 62	Using Complex Numbers
• Lesson 65	Using the Quadratic Formula
• Lesson 69	Simplifying Complex Expressions

Rational and Radical Functions

• Lesson 70	Solving Radical Equations

Trigonometry

• Lesson 63	Understanding the Unit Circle and Radian Measures
• Lesson 67	Finding Inverse Trigonometric Functions

Connections in Practice Problems

	Lessons
Coordinate Geometry	63, 64, 67
Geometry	61, 62, 63, 64, 65, 66, 67, 68, 69, 70
Measurement	65
Probability	61, 62, 65, 66, 68, 69, 70
Statistics	68

Math Processes

Reasoning and Communication

	Lessons
• Analyze	61, 62, 63, 64, 65, 66, 67, 68, 69, 70, Inv. 7
• Error analysis	61, 62, 63, 64, 65, 66, 67, 68, 69, 70
• Estimate	63, 68, 70
• Formulate	63, 64, 65, 66, 69
• Generalize	62, 66, 67, 68, 69, 70
• Justify	61, 64, 65
• Math reasoning	61, 62, 65, 66, 68, 69, 70
• Model	63, 67, Inv. 7
• Multiple choice	61, 62, 63, 64, 65, 66, 67, 68, 69, 70
• Multi-step	61, 62, 63, 64, 65, 66, 67, 68, 69, 70, Inv. 7
• Verify	61, 62, 65, 66, 67, 69, 70
• Write	61, 62, 63, 64, 65, 66, 67, 68, 69, 70
• Graphing Calculator	61, 62, 63, 64, 65, 66, 67, 68, 69, 70

Connections

In Examples: Acidity of rainwater, Navigation, Packaging, Physics, Planet rotation, Quality control, Three-dimensional figures, Travel

In Practice problems: Amusement parks, Buildings, Cell phones, Commuting to work, Construction, Contact lenses, Electrical engineering, Exercise, Falling objects, Finance, Housing, Jupiter, Lighthouses, Meteorology, Music, Packaging, Pass codes, Physical science, Physics, Planet rotation, Plant nutrition, Population, Projectile motion, Rainwater, School, Sports, Storage, Surveying, Temporary employees, Tennis, Tires, Transportation, Travel, Velocity of an electron, Volume, Walking shadows, Wheelchair accessibility, Windshield wipers

Content Trace

Lesson	Warm Up: Prerequisite Skills	New Concepts	Where Practiced	Where Assessed	Looking Forward
61	Lessons 11, 23, 51	Understanding Advanced Factoring	Lessons 61, 62, 63, 64, 65, 66, 67, 68, 69, 70, 71, 74, 75, 76, 77, 81, 83, 90, 111, 116	Cumulative Tests 13, 14, 17, 22	Lessons 66, 76, 85, 95
62	Lessons 1, 2, 40, 58	Using Complex Numbers	Lessons 62, 63, 64, 65, 66, 67, 68, 69, 70, 71, 72, 74, 75, 77, 78, 80, 88, 92, 97	Cumulative Tests 13, 15, 18	Lessons 65, 69, 70
63	Lessons 41, 52	Understanding the Unit Circle and Radian Measures	Lessons 63, 64, 65, 66, 67, 68, 69, 70, 71, 72, 73, 74, 75, 76, 79, 80, 85, 88, 89, 91	Cumulative Tests 13, 14, 20	Lessons 67, 71, 77, 82, 86, 90
64	Lessons 3, 47	Using Logarithms	Lessons 64, 65, 66, 68, 69, 70, 72, 73, 75, 77, 80, 84, 92, 95, 108, 115	Cumulative Tests 13, 16, 22	Lessons 72, 81, 87, 102
65	Lessons 2, 58, 62	Using the Quadratic Formula	Lessons 65, 66, 67, 68, 69, 70, 71, 72, 73, 74, 75, 76, 77, 78, 79, 80, 81, 82, 83, 84, 94	Cumulative Tests 13, 17	Lessons 78, 83, 89
66	Lessons 23, 35, 61, 65	Solving Polynomial Equations	Lessons 66, 67, 68, 69, 70, 71, 73, 74, 75, 76, 77, 78, 79, 80, 82, 83, 86, 90, 98	Cumulative Tests 14, 15	Lessons 76, 85, 101, 106
67	Lesson 63	Finding Inverse Trigonometric Functions	Lessons 67, 68, 69, 70, 72, 73, 74, 75, 76, 77, 78, 79, 80, 81, 82, 83, 84, 86, 89, 92, 93	Cumulative Tests 14, 15, 21	Lessons 71, 77, 82, 86, 90
68	Lesson 55	Finding Conditional Probability	Lessons 68, 69, 70, 71, 72, 73, 74, 75, 76, 77, 78, 79, 80, 81, 82, 83, 84, 85, 87, 89, 94, 99	Cumulative Tests 14, 20	Lessons 73, 80, 116, 118
69	Lessons 19, 40, 62	Simplifying Complex Expressions	Lessons 69, 70, 71, 72, 73, 74, 75, 76, 77, 78, 79, 80, 81, 82, 83, 84, 87, 92, 105	Cumulative Tests 14, 17, 22	Lessons 83, 85
70	Lessons 35, 40	Solving Radical Equations	Lessons 70, 71, 72, 73, 74, 75, 76, 77, 78, 79, 80, 81, 82, 83, 84, 85, 86, 87, 88, 91, 97, 99	Cumulative Tests 14, 16, 20	Lesson 75
INV 7	N/A	Investigation: Collecting Data	Lessons 71, 72, 85, 94	Cumulative Test 15	Lesson 80

Ongoing Assessment

	Type	Feature	Intervention *
BEFORE instruction	Assess Prior Knowledge	• Diagnostic Test	• Prerequisite Skills Intervention
BEFORE the lesson	Formative	• Warm Up	• Skills Bank • Reteaching Masters
DURING the lesson	Formative	• Lesson Practice • Math Conversations with the Practice problems	• Additional Examples in TE • Test and Practice Generator (for additional practice sheets)
AFTER the lesson	Formative	• Check for Understanding (closure)	• Scaffolding Questions in TE
AFTER 5 lessons	Summative	After Lesson 65 • Cumulative Test 12 • Performance Task 12 After Lesson 70 • Cumulative Test 13 • Performance Task 13	• Reteaching Masters • Test and Practice Generator (for additional tests and practice)
AFTER 20 lessons	Summative	• Benchmark Tests	• Reteaching Masters • Test and Practice Generator (for additional tests and practice)

* for students not showing progress during the formative stages or scoring below 80% on the summative assessments

Evidence of Learning – What Students Should Know

Because the Saxon philosophy is to provide students with sufficient time to learn and practice each concept, a lesson's topic will not be tested until at least five lessons after the topic is introduced.

On the Cumulative Tests that are given during this section of ten lessons, students should be able to demonstrate the following competencies:

- Apply the rules of exponents.
- Perform operations with matrices.
- Apply Cramer's Rule to solve systems of linear equations.
- Solve problems that involve percent increase or decrease.
- Identify functions and use function notation.
- Recognize and solve problems involving direct variation.
- Identify the components of polynomial expressions.

Test and Practice Generator CD using ExamView™

The Test and Practice Generator is an easy-to-use benchmark and assessment tool that creates unlimited practice and tests in multiple formats and allows you to customize questions or create new ones. A variety of reports are available to track student progress toward mastery of the standards throughout the year.

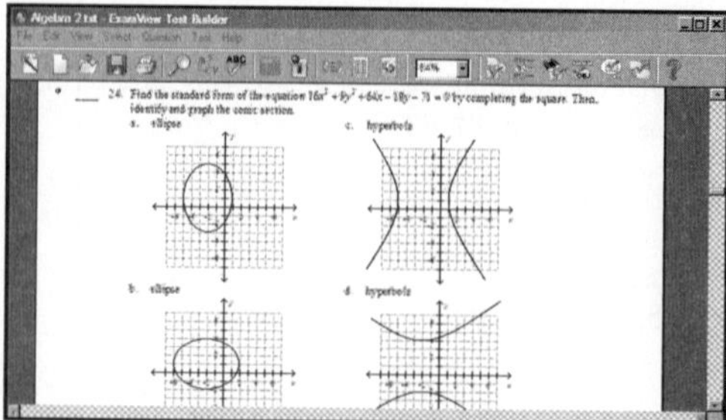

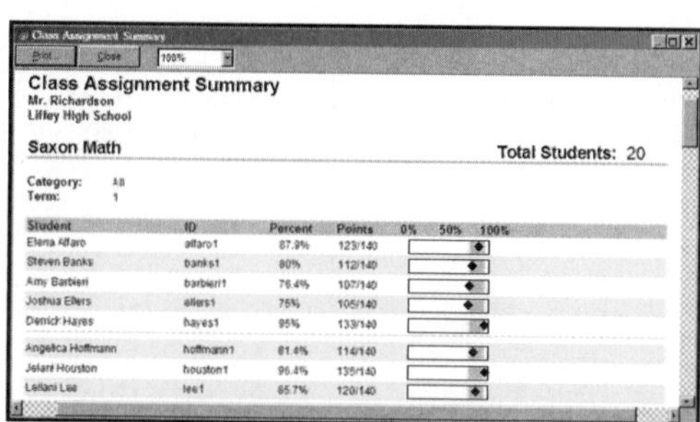

Assessment Resources

Resources for Diagnosing and Assessing

- **Student Edition**
  - Warm Up
  - Lesson Practice
- **Teacher's Edition**
  - Math Conversations with the Practice problems
  - Check for Understanding (closure)
- **Course Assessments**
  - Diagnostic Test
  - Cumulative Tests
  - Performance Tasks
  - Benchmark Tests

Resources for Intervention

- **Student Edition**
  - Skills Bank
- **Teacher's Edition**
  - Additional Examples
  - Scaffolding questions
- **Prerequisite Skills Intervention**
  - Worksheets
- **Reteaching Masters**
  - Lesson instruction and practice sheets
- **Test and Practice Generator CD using ExamView™**
  - Lesson practice problems
  - Additional tests

Resources for Test Prep

- **Student Edition**
  - Multiple-choice practice problems
  - Multiple-step and writing problems
  - Daily cumulative practice
- **Standardized Test Practice**
- **College Entrance Exam Practice**
- **Test and Practice Generator CD using ExamView™**

Cumulative Tests

The assessments in Saxon Math are frequent and consistently placed after every five lessons to offer a regular method of ongoing testing. These cumulative assessments check mastery of concepts from previous lessons.

Performance Tasks

The Performance Tasks can be used in conjunction with the Cumulative Tests and are scored using a rubric.

After Lesson 65

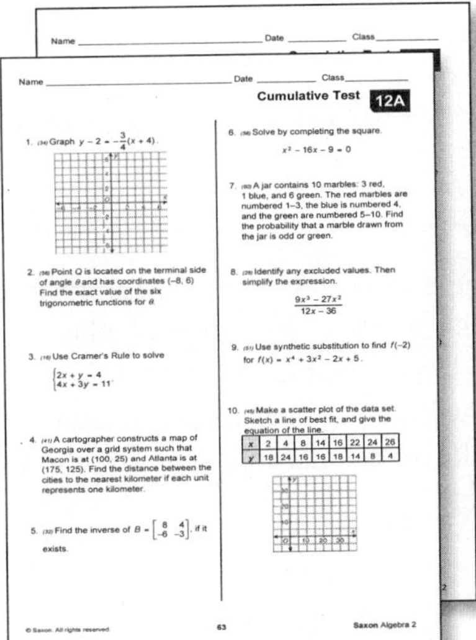
Name ______ Date ______ Class ______

Cumulative Test 12A

1. (34) Graph $y - 2 = -\frac{3}{4}(x + 4)$.
2. (36) Point Q is located on the terminal side of angle θ and has coordinates $(-8, 6)$. Find the exact value of the six trigonometric functions for θ.
3. (16) Use Cramer's Rule to solve $\begin{cases} 2x + y = 4 \\ 4x + 3y = 11 \end{cases}$
4. (41) A cartographer constructs a map of Georgia over a grid system such that Macon is at (100, 25) and Atlanta is at (175, 125). Find the distance between the cities to the nearest kilometer if each unit represents one kilometer.
5. (32) Find the inverse of $B = \begin{bmatrix} 8 & 4 \\ -6 & -3 \end{bmatrix}$, if it exists.
6. (56) Solve by completing the square. $x^2 - 16x - 9 = 0$
7. (60) A jar contains 10 marbles: 3 red, 1 blue, and 6 green. The red marbles are numbered 1–3, the blue is numbered 4, and the green are numbered 5–10. Find the probability that a marble drawn from the jar is odd or green.
8. (26) Identify any excluded values. Then simplify the expression. $\frac{9x^3 - 27x^2}{12x - 36}$
9. (51) Use synthetic substitution to find $f(-2)$ for $f(x) = x^4 + 3x^2 - 2x + 5$.
10. (45) Make a scatter plot of the data set. Sketch a line of best fit, and give the equation of the line.

x	2	4	8	14	16	22	24	26
y	18	24	16	16	18	14	8	4

© Saxon. All rights reserved. 63 Saxon Algebra 2

After Lesson 70

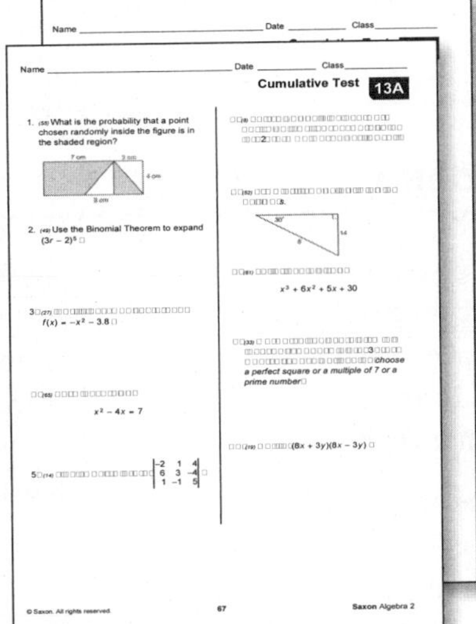
Name ______ Date ______ Class ______

Cumulative Test 13A

1. (55) What is the probability that a point chosen randomly inside the figure is in the shaded region?
2. (49) Use the Binomial Theorem to expand $(3r - 2)^5$.
3. (27) $f(x) = -x^2 - 3.8$
4. (65) $x^2 - 4x = 7$
5. (14) $\begin{vmatrix} -2 & 1 & 4 \\ 6 & 3 & -4 \\ 1 & -1 & 5 \end{vmatrix}$

$x^3 + 6x^2 + 5x + 30$

choose a perfect square or a multiple of 7 or a prime number

$(8x + 3y)(8x - 3y)$

© Saxon. All rights reserved. 67 Saxon Algebra 2

For use with Performance Tasks

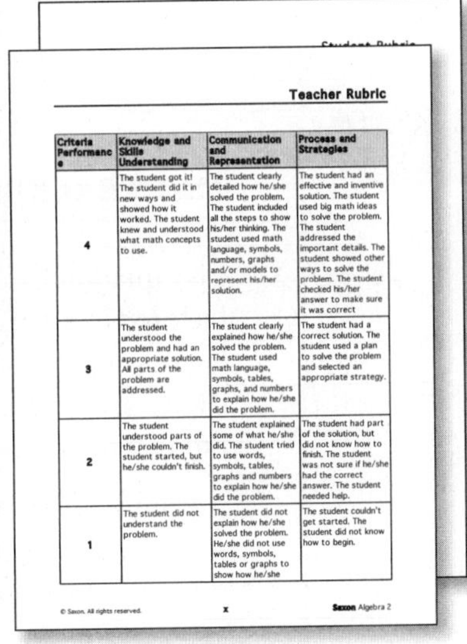
Teacher Rubric

Criteria Performance	Knowledge and Skills Understanding	Communication and Representation	Process and Strategies
4	The student got it! The student did it in new ways and showed how it worked. The student knew and understood what math concepts to use.	The student clearly detailed how he/she solved the problem. The student included all the steps to show his/her thinking. The student used math language, symbols, numbers, graphs and/or models to represent his/her solution.	The student had an effective and inventive solution. The student used big math ideas to solve the problem. The student addressed the important details. The student showed other ways to solve the problem. The student checked his/her answer to make sure it was correct
3	The student understood the problem and had an appropriate solution. All parts of the problem are addressed.	The student clearly explained how he/she solved the problem. The student used math language, symbols, tables, graphs, and numbers to explain how he/she did the problem.	The student had a correct solution. The student used a plan to solve the problem and selected an appropriate strategy.
2	The student understood parts of the problem. The student started, but he/she couldn't finish.	The student explained some of what he/she did. The student tried to use words, symbols, tables, graphs and numbers to explain how he/she did the problem.	The student had part of the solution, but did not know how to finish. The student was not sure if he/she had the correct answer. The student needed help.
1	The student did not understand the problem.	The student did not explain how he/she solved the problem. He/she did not use words, symbols, tables or graphs to show how he/she	The student couldn't get started. The student did not know how to begin.

© Saxon. All rights reserved. x Saxon Algebra 2

SECTION OVERVIEW 7

LESSON 61

1 Warm Up

Problem 2

Remind students that the GCF must be a common factor in all terms of the polynomial.

2 New Concepts

In this lesson, students use synthetic division to determine whether or not a linear binomial is a factor of a polynomial, factor the sum and difference of two cubes, and factor by grouping.

Discuss the Factor Theorem. Point out that $(x - a)$ is a factor of $P(x)$ if and only if $P(a) = 0$.

Example 1

Review the process of synthetic division. Remind students to set the divisor to $x - a$ to find a.

Additional Example 1

Determine whether the linear binomial is a factor of the polynomial.

a. $P(x) = 2x^3 - x^2 - 24x + 27$, $x - 3$ $x - 3$ is a factor.

b. $P(x) = x^3 + x^2 - 12x + 24$, $x + 2$ $x + 2$ is not a factor.

LESSON 61

Understanding Advanced Factoring

Warm Up

1. **Vocabulary** A polynomial of degree one with two terms is a ________. linear binomial (11)

2. True or False: The GCF of $-2x^4y^5 - xy^2 + 2$ is $2xy^2$. false (23)

3. Divide $4x^2 - 2x + 5$ by $x - 1$ using synthetic substitution. $4x + 2 + \frac{7}{x-1}$ (51)

New Concepts

Recall that synthetic division is used to divide a polynomial $P(x)$ by a linear binomial of the form $x - a$ and that the last number in the bottom row is the remainder and also the value of $P(a)$. If the remainder is 0, the linear binomial is a factor of the polynomial. This is known as the Factor Theorem.

Factor Theorem
For polynomial $P(x)$, $(x - a)$ is a factor of $P(x)$ if and only if $P(a) = 0$.

Hint

$x + 2 = x - (-2)$, so the value of a is -2.

For example, $x + 2$ is a factor of $x^2 + 10x + 16$ and

$$P(-2) = (-2)^2 + 10(-2) + 16$$
$$= 4 - 20 + 16$$
$$= 0.$$

Example 1 **Determining Whether a Linear Binomial is a Factor**

Determine whether the linear binomial is a factor of the polynomial.

a. $P(x) = 2x^3 - x^2 - 43x + 60$, $x - 4$

SOLUTION Use synthetic division with $a = 4$.

$$\begin{array}{r|rrrr} 4 & 2 & -1 & -43 & 60 \\ & & 8 & 28 & -60 \\ \hline & 2 & 7 & -15 & \boxed{0} \end{array}$$

Because $P(4) = 0$, $x - 4$ is a factor of $P(x) = 2x^3 - x^2 - 43x + 60$.

b. $P(x) = x^3 + x^2 - 24x + 36$, $x + 3$

SOLUTION Use synthetic division with $a = -3$.

$$\begin{array}{r|rrrr} -3 & 1 & 1 & -24 & 36 \\ & & -3 & 6 & 54 \\ \hline & 1 & -2 & -18 & \boxed{90} \end{array}$$

Because $P(-3) \neq 0$, $x + 3$ is not a factor of $P(x) = x^3 + x^2 - 24x + 36$.

When the remainder is zero, the quotient of $P(x)$ and $(x - a)$ is another factor of the polynomial. This factor may be able to be further factored by other factoring methods. For instance, in Example 1a, the quotient $2x^2 + 7x - 15$ factors into $(2x - 3)(x + 5)$. Therefore, $P(x)$ factors into $(x - 4)(2x - 3)(x + 5)$.

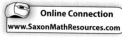

LESSON RESOURCES

Student Edition Practice Workbook 61
Reteaching Master 61
Adaptations Master 61
Challenge and Enrichment Master C61

MATH BACKGROUND

Like quadratic expressions that can be factored as a product of two binomial linear factors, a polynomial expression with a degree greater than 2 can be factored as a product of two or more factors.

Advanced factoring can be applied to solving polynomial equations, finding the roots of functions, and graphing functions.

Synthetic division, introduced in a previous lesson, is applied to determine whether or not a linear binomial is a factor. This process will also be used in later lessons to find the roots and zeros of polynomial equations.

If the remaining quotient is a cubic, it may be factorable by one of the following factoring methods.

Sum and Difference of Cubes
Sum of Two Cubes: $a^3 + b^3 = (a + b)(a^2 - ab + b^2)$
Difference of Two Cubes: $a^3 - b^3 = (a - b)(a^2 + ab + b^2)$

Example 2 Factoring the Sum and Difference of Two Cubes

Factor each expression.

a. $d^3 + 125$

SOLUTION The expression is a sum of two cubes, where $a = d$ and $b = 5$.

$d^3 + 125$
$= (d + 5)(d^2 - 5d + 25)$

b. $27x^6 + y^9$

SOLUTION The expression is a sum of two cubes, where $a = 3x^2$ and $b = y^3$.

$27x^6 + y^9 = (3x^2)^3 + (y^3)^3$
$= (3x^2 + y^3)(9x^4 - 3x^2y^3 + y^6)$

c. $3m^5 - 24m^2$

SOLUTION First factor out the GCF, $3m^2$. Then factor the difference of the two cubes, where $a = m$ and $b = 2$.

$3m^5 - 24m^2$
$= 3m^2(m^3 - 8)$
$= 3m^2(m - 2)(m^2 + 2m + 4)$

Math Reasoning

Justify Tell why $3x - 1$ is not a difference of cubes.

$3x$ is not a perfect cube.

Another method of factoring is factoring by grouping. To factor by grouping, group the terms evenly so that each group has a common factor. Factor out the GCF from each group. Then factor out the common polynomial factor.

Example 3 Factoring by Grouping

Factor each expression.

a. $x^3 + 5x^2 + 3x + 15$

SOLUTION The first two terms have a common factor as do the last two terms.

$(x^3 + 5x^2) + (3x + 15)$
$= x^2(x + 5) + 3(x + 5)$ Factor x^2 from the first group and 3 from the second.
$= (x + 5)(x^2 + 3)$ Factor out the GCF of $(x + 5)$.

Neither factor can be factored further.

Example 2

Extend the Example

Have students check answers by multiplying the polynomials.

Additional Example 2

Factor each expression.

a. $d^3 + 64$
$(d + 4)(d^2 - 4d + 16)$

b. $8x^6 + 27y^3$
$(2x^2 + 3y)(4x^4 - 6x^2y + 9y^2)$

c. $2m^5 - 250m^2$
$2m^2(m - 5)(m^2 + 5m + 25)$

Example 3

Point out that grouping the first and third terms and the second and fourth terms yields the same result.

Additional Example 3

Factor each expression.

a. $x^3 + 8x^2 + 2x + 16$
$(x + 8)(x^2 + 2)$

ENGLISH LEARNERS

To help students understand the meaning of **grouping**, define grouping as the act or process of putting things into groups.

Discuss other examples of grouping such as grouping hundreds, tens, ones; grouping objects or geometric figures into sets; and grouping children by grade level.

Have students identify the grouping that was done in Example 3.

Connect the meaning of grouping with factoring by grouping. Point out that the "things" being put into groups are the terms that have common factors.

Additional Example 3

b. $x^4 + 5x^3 - 8x - 40$
$(x + 5)(x - 2)(x^2 + 2x + 4)$

c. $x^6 + 5x^5 + 6x^4 + x^2 + 5x + 6$
$(x + 2)(x + 3)(x^4 + 1)$

Example 4

Error Alert Students may not completely factor the trinomial. Remind students to always check if the expression resulting from synthetic division can itself be factored.

Additional Example 4

The volume of a rectangular solid with a length of $x - 4$ feet has a volume of $x^3 - 25x^2 + 192x - 432$ cubic feet. Factor the expression for the volume completely. $(x - 4)(x - 12)(x - 9)$

Lesson Practice

Problem d

Error Alert Students may assign incorrect values for a and b. Remind students to divide the exponents in the first term by 3.

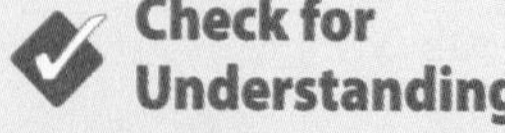

Check for Understanding

The questions below help assess the concepts taught in this lesson.

1. **"How do you factor $x^3 - 216$?"** $x^3 - 216$ is the difference of two cubes. Use $a^3 - b^3 = (a - b)(a^2 + ab + b^2)$, where $a = x$ and $b = 6$: $x^3 - 216 = (x - 6)(x^2 + 6x + 36)$.

2. **"How do you factor $xy + 6y - 4x - 24$?"** Group the first two terms and the last two terms: $(xy + 6y) + (-4x - 24)$. Factor y from the first group and -4 from the second group: $y(x + 6) + -4(x + 6)$. Factor out the GCF of $(x + 6)$: $(x + 6)(y - 4)$.

Math Reasoning

Analyze Can a polynomial with five terms be factored by using the grouping method? Explain.

No, there must be an even number of terms to obtain a common factor.

b. $x^4 + 4x^3 - x - 4$

SOLUTION Factor x^3 from the first two terms and -1 from the last two terms.

$x^4 + 4x^3 - x - 4$

$= x^3(x + 4) - 1(x + 4)$

$= (x + 4)(x^3 - 1)$ — Factor out the GCF of $(x + 4)$.

$= (x + 4)(x - 1)(x^2 + x + 1)$ — Factor the difference of cubes.

c. $x^6 + 3x^5 + 2x^4 + x^2 + 3x + 2$

SOLUTION Use two groups of three terms each.

$(x^6 + 3x^5 + 2x^4) + (x^2 + 3x + 2)$

$= x^4(x^2 + 3x + 2) + 1(x^2 + 3x + 2)$

$= (x^2 + 3x + 2)(x^4 + 1)$ — Factor out the GCF of $(x^2 + 3x + 2)$.

$= (x + 1)(x + 2)(x^4 + 1)$ — Factor the trinomial.

Example 4 Application: Three-Dimensional Figures

The volume of a rectangular solid with a length of $x - 5$ feet has a volume of $x^3 - 23x^2 + 170x - 400$ cubic feet. Factor the expression for the volume completely.

SOLUTION Since volume is the product of the length, width, and height, the expression for the length, $x - 5$, is a factor of the polynomial. Use synthetic division to find the quotient of the polynomial and $x - 5$.

$$\begin{array}{r|rrrr} 5 & 1 & -23 & 170 & -400 \\ & & 5 & -90 & 400 \\ \hline & 1 & -18 & 80 & 0 \end{array}$$

The expression for the volume factors into $(x - 5)(x^2 - 18x + 80)$. But the trinomial can still be factored: $(x - 10)(x - 8)$.

The expression for the volume factors into $(x - 5)(x - 10)(x - 8)$.

Lesson Practice

Determine whether the linear binomial is a factor of the polynomial.

a. $P(x) = 3x^3 + 19x^2 + 32x + 16$, $x + 3$ no
(Ex 1)

b. $P(x) = 4x^3 - 33x^2 + 56x - 12$, $x - 6$ yes
(Ex 1)

Factor each expression.

c. $64 - h^3$ $(4 - h)(16 + 4h + h^2)$
(Ex 2)

d. $s^6t^{12} - 125r^3$
(Ex 2) $(s^2t^4 - 5r)(s^4t^8 + 5rs^2t^4 + 25r^2)$

e. $\frac{8}{27}x^7 + x^4$
(Ex 2) $x^4\left(\frac{2}{3}x + 1\right)\left(\frac{4}{9}x^2 - \frac{2}{3}x + 1\right)$

f. $xy - 9y + 5x - 45$ $(x - 9)(y + 5)$
(Ex 3)

g. $4m^2n + 12m^2 - n - 3$
(Ex 3) $(n + 3)(2m + 1)(2m - 1)$

h. $x^5 + 12x^4 + 36x^3 + 5x^2 + 60x + 180$
(Ex 3) $(x + 6)^2(x^3 + 5)$

i. The volume of a rectangular solid with a length of $x - 15$ feet has a volume of $x^3 + 5x^2 - 600x + 4500$ cubic feet. Factor the expression for the volume completely. $(x - 15)(x + 30)(x - 10)$
(Ex 4)

INCLUSION

Have students use grid paper to help them align columns when doing synthetic division.

Practice Distributed and Integrated

Graph.

1. (13) $x = -5$ See Additional Answers.

2. (13) $2x - y = 4$ See Additional Answers.

3. (13) $7y + 7x = 21$ See Additional Answers.

4. (Inv 3) Find the intercepts of the equation $5x - 4y + 7z = 21$. x:(4.2, 0, 0), y:(0, −5.25, 0), z:(0, 0, 3)

Simplify.

5. (59) $-16^{-\frac{1}{2}}$ $-\frac{1}{4}$

6. (59) $27^{-\frac{1}{3}}$ $\frac{1}{3}$

7. (59) $9^{\frac{3}{2}}$ 27

Find an inverse for the equations.

8. (50) $y = \frac{2}{3}x - 3$ $y = \frac{3}{2}x + \frac{9}{2}$

9. (50) $y = 5x + 15$ $y = \frac{1}{5}x - 3$

10. (53) Let $K(u) = 17$ and $L(u) = -13$. Find $K(L(u))$ and $L(K(u))$. $K(L(u)) = 17$; $L(K(u)) = -13$

***11.** (54) Minimize $P = 4x + 3y$ for the constraints $x \leq 4$, $y \leq 6$, $x + y \geq 7$ (1, 6)

***12.** (57) Mary deposited \$980 at 7.0% compounded continuously. How much money will she have after 9 years? \$1840.06

13. (55) **Meteorology** The number of tornadoes in the United States in 2006 is shown in the table.

Season	Jan-Feb	Mar-Apr	May-Jun	Jul-Aug	Sep-Oct	Nov-Dec
Number of Tornadoes	59	395	258	151	160	82

What is the experimental probability that a tornado occurs in the first six months of the year? About 64.4%

***14.** (61) **Write** Tell how factoring a sum of cubes is similar to factoring a difference of cubes.

15. (45) **Probability** A student graphed a set of data points and found that the correlation coefficient was −0.73. What is the probability that the slope of the line of best fit is greater than $\frac{1}{2}$? Explain.

***16.** (60) **Geometry** The probability that a randomly selected point lies within a region can be found using the ratio of the area the point would lie in to the total area. Find the probability that a random point within the region lies within one of the smaller circles. $\frac{2}{5}$

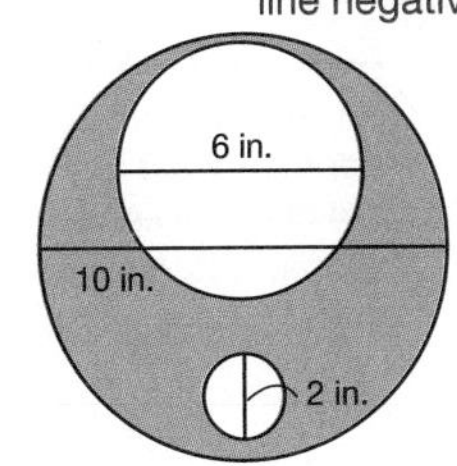

14. In both, the first factors have the cube root of each term, separated by the same sign between the terms in the original expression. Also, in both, the second factors have the square of each term in the first factor as well as the products of the two terms in the first factor, and the sign before the products is the opposite of the sign separating the terms in the original expression.

15. 0%; Sample: The points fall from left to right when the r-value is negative. So, the line of best fit also falls from left to right, making the slope of the line negative.

3 Practice

Math Conversations

Discussions to strengthen understanding

Problem 7

Guide the students by asking them the following questions.

"How can you rewrite $9^{\frac{3}{2}}$?" $\left(9^{\frac{1}{2}}\right)^3$

"What is $9^{\frac{1}{2}}$?" $9^{\frac{1}{2}} = \sqrt{9} = 3$

"What is 3^3?" 27

Problem 9

"How do you find an inverse for an equation?" Substitute y for x and x for y.

"What is the inverse equation?" $x = 5y + 15$

"What is $x = 5y + 15$ in slope-intercept form?" $y = \frac{1}{5}x - 3$

Problem 11

Remind students to evaluate the objective function at each vertex of the feasible region.

Problem 13

Extend the Problem

Have students find the experimental probability that a tornado occurs in the last six months of the year. about 36%
Then have students compare the probabilities. The experimental probability is greater for the first six months of the year than for the last six months of the year.

ALTERNATE METHOD FOR PROBLEM 2

As opposed to finding the x- and y-intercepts, have students make a table of values.

x	y
0	−4
1	−2
2	0
3	2
4	4

Have students use the table to graph $2x - y = 4$.

Problem 19

Remind students that to solve for x, x needs to be raised to the first power. Also remind students that a fraction multiplied by its reciprocal equals 1.

17. (46) **Buildings** One building is 310 feet tall and a nearby building is 374 feet tall. From the top of the taller building, you can spot the top of the shorter building at an angle of depression of 30°. How far apart are the two buildings? Round to the nearest foot. 111 feet

18. (53) **Walking Shadows** While walking the dog one night, you notice how the length of your shadow changes as you approach each lamppost. The length of the shadow seems to be $\frac{1}{5}$ of your distance to the lamppost. Your dog is dragging you along at about 3 feet per second, aiming for a lamppost. Show how to write a composite function that gives the length of your shadow in terms of time as you approach the lamppost. shadow as function of distance: $s(d) = 0.2d$; distance as function of time: $d(t) = -3t$; composite: $s(d(t)) = -0.6t$

***19.** (59) **Error Analysis** Is the work below correct? If not, find and explain the error, and give the correct solution.

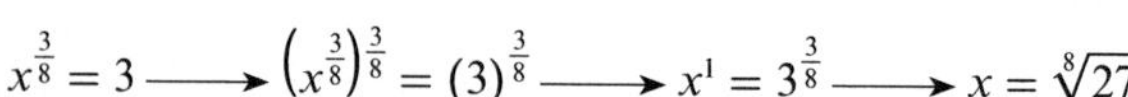

$$x^{\frac{3}{8}} = 3 \longrightarrow \left(x^{\frac{3}{8}}\right)^{\frac{3}{8}} = (3)^{\frac{3}{8}} \longrightarrow x^{1} = 3^{\frac{3}{8}} \longrightarrow x = \sqrt[8]{27}$$

19. No; The error is in the second step. To cancel a rational exponent you must raise it to the reciprocal exponent.; $\sqrt[3]{6{,}561}$

20. (49) **Analyze** Suppose you spin the spinner shown 8 times. What is the probability that you will spin black 5 times? about 0.21

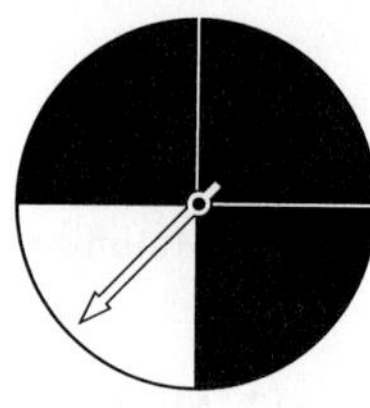

21. (58) **Verify** Use the form $x^2 + 2dx + d^2$ for a quadratic perfect square trinomial to verify the method of completing the square. Set the coefficients of x equal to each other and solve for d.

$$b = 2d \longrightarrow d = \frac{b}{2} \longrightarrow d^2 = \left(\frac{b}{2}\right)^2$$

***22.** (54) **Graphing Calculator** Describe the feasible region for the inequalities:

$$x \geq 0,\ y \geq 0,\ y \leq -0.75x + 8$$ Region bounded by: (0, 0), (0, 8), (10.67, 0)

23. (45) **Multiple Choice** Which value of r, the correlation coefficient, describes the set of points that are *closest* to forming a line? **A**

A $r = -0.75$ **B** $r = 0$ **C** $r = 0.6$ **D** $r = 0.65$

***24.** (60) **Commuting to Work** According to data collected in the 2005 American Community Survey, approximately 10.67% of workers carpool to work, 4.66% use public transportation, and 2.47% walk. Find the probability that a randomly selected worker carpools or uses public transportation. 0.1533

25. (47) **Write** A few different equations of the form $y = b^x$ are graphed to the right. Describe in your own words how the shape of the graph depends on the value of b. Sample: When $b < 1$, the curve asymptotically approaches 0 for large positive x. As you move to the left of the graph, the curve rises very quickly. When $b > 1$, the opposite is true; the curve asymptotically approaches 0 on the left, and rises quickly on the right. The closer to 1 b is, the flatter the graph.

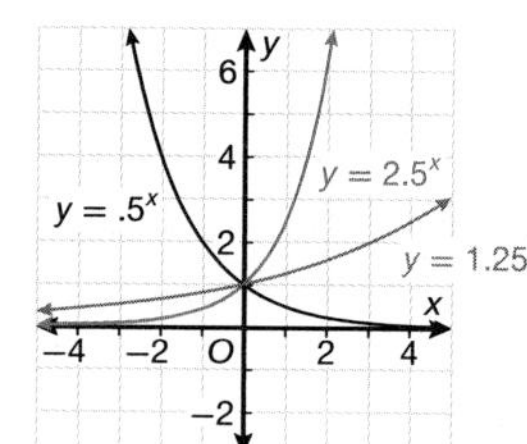

***26. Multi-Step** Use $\frac{5^{\frac{3}{5}} \cdot 5^{\frac{3}{5}}}{5^{\frac{4}{5}}}$. (59)

a. Which property of rational exponents should be applied first to simplify the expression? Explain.

26a. Product of Powers Property; Sample: By the order of operations you must evaluate powers and roots before performing multiplication and division.

b. Apply the property from part a. $\frac{5^{\frac{6}{5}}}{5^{\frac{4}{5}}}$

c. Which property of rational exponents should be applied next? Quotient of Powers Property

d. Apply the property from part c. $5^{\frac{2}{5}}$

e. If possible, finish simplifying the expression from part d. $\sqrt[5]{25}$

27. Multiple Choice In the diagram to the right, find the length of the hypotenuse of triangle LMN. **C** (52)

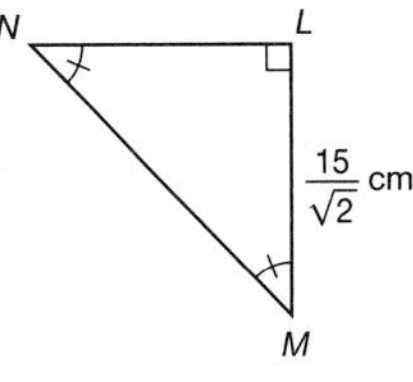

A 7.5 B $\sqrt{2}$

C 15 D $15\sqrt{3}$

***28. Multi-Step** The area of a twin size mattress is $x^2 - 275 - 11x + 25x$ square inches. (61)

a. Factor the polynomial by grouping. $(x - 11)(x + 25)$

b. Find the area given that $x = 50$. 2925 square inches

29. (Amusement Parks) The Giant Swing at Silver Dollar City in Branson, Missouri, rotates through an angle measuring 230°. Find the reference angle for this angle. 50° (56)

***30. Verify** Show that there are two different ways to group the terms in $3d + 6f + d^2 + 2df$ and that both lead to the same factorization. (61)

$(3d + 6f) + (d^2 + 2df)$ $(3d + d^2) + (6f + 2df)$

$3(d + 2f) + d(d + 2f)$ and $d(3 + d) + 2f(3 + d)$

$(d + 2f)(3 + d)$ $(d + 2f)(3 + d)$

Problem 26

Have students simplify the expression first. Then go back and identify which property they used.

Problem 27

Remind students that in a 45°-45°-90° triangle, the length of the hypotenuse is the length of a leg multiplied by $\sqrt{2}$.

Problem 28

Error Alert

Students may incorrectly factor the trinomial. Have them rewrite the polynomial as $x^2 - 11x + 25x - 275$ and then group the first two terms and the last two terms. Encourage students to proceed by factoring out x from the first group and 25 from the second.

Problem 29

Remind students that the expression to find the reference angle with the terminal side in Quadrant III is $\theta - 180°$.

Problem 30

TEACHER TIP

For the first method in problem 30, have students group the first two terms and the last two terms. Then factor. For the second way, encourage students to rewrite the expression as $3d + d^2 + 6f + 2df$. Then to repeat the process they did for the first way. Remind students the answer is the same.

CHALLENGE

Factor completely.

$6x^2 - 84x + x^2y - 14xy + 45y + 270$

$(x - 9)(x - 5)(y + 6)$

LOOKING FORWARD

Advanced factoring prepares students for

- **Lesson 66** Solving Polynomial Equations
- **Lesson 76** Finding Polynomial Roots I
- **Lesson 85** Finding Polynomial Roots II
- **Lesson 95** Factoring Higher-Order Polynomials

LESSON 62

1 Warm Up

For problem 4, remind students to look for perfect-square factors.

2 New Concepts

In this lesson, students simplify square roots of negative numbers, solve quadratic equations with imaginary numbers, and simplify expressions with complex numbers.

Discuss the definitions of real numbers, **imaginary numbers,** and **complex numbers.** Point out that the square root of a negative number is an imaginary number.

Example 1

Remind students $\sqrt{49}$ is a perfect square and $\sqrt{-1} = i$.

Additional Example 1

a. Simplify $-5\sqrt{-64}$. $-40i$

b. Simplify $\sqrt{-153}$. $3i\sqrt{17}$

LESSON 62

Using Complex Numbers

Warm Up

1. **Vocabulary** Any point on the number line is a ___real___ number. (1)
2. Simplify $(5 + 3x) - (6 - 2x)$. $-1 + 5x$ (2)
3. Solve $5x^2 - 125 = 0$. $x = \pm 5$ (58)
4. Simplify $\sqrt{150}$. $5\sqrt{6}$ (40)

New Concepts

The equation $x = \pm\sqrt{-16}$ has no real solutions because there are no real numbers that, when squared, equal -16. But the equation does have solutions when a new set of numbers, outside of the real numbers, is introduced. These numbers are the **imaginary numbers.**

Imaginary Numbers

An imaginary number is written in the form bi where b is a real number and i is the **imaginary unit.**

i is a solution of $x^2 = -1$.

Because $i^2 = -1$, $i = \sqrt{-1}$.

The square root of a negative number is an imaginary number.

$$\sqrt{-16} = \sqrt{16 \cdot -1} = \sqrt{16}\sqrt{-1} = 4i$$

Math Reasoning

Generalize For any positive real n, $\sqrt{-n} =$ ______.

$i\sqrt{n}$

Example 1 Simplifying Square Roots of Negative Numbers

a. Simplify $-2\sqrt{-49}$.

SOLUTION

$-2\sqrt{-49}$

$-2\sqrt{49 \cdot -1}$ Write -49 as the product of 49 and -1.

$-2\sqrt{49}\sqrt{-1}$ The square root of a product is the product of the square roots.

$-2 \cdot 7 \cdot i$ $\sqrt{49} = 7$ and $\sqrt{-1} = i$.

$-14i$ Multiply the real numbers.

b. Simplify $\sqrt{-117}$.

SOLUTION

$\sqrt{-117}$

$\sqrt{9 \cdot 13 \cdot -1}$ Write -117 as a product with a perfect square.

$\sqrt{9}\sqrt{13}\sqrt{-1}$ The square root of a product is the product of the square roots.

$3\sqrt{13}(i)$ $\sqrt{9} = 3$ and $\sqrt{-1} = i$.

$3i\sqrt{13}$ Commutative Property of Multiplication

Online Connection
www.SaxonMathResources.com

LESSON RESOURCES

Student Edition Practice Workbook 62
Reteaching Master 62
Adaptations Master 62
Challenge and Enrichment Master C62

MATH BACKGROUND

Besides addition and subtraction, complex numbers are also used in multiplication and division expressions. The Distributive Property can be used to multiply expressions such as $(5i + 6)(2i - 3)$. To simplify a division problem that has a complex number, $a + bi$, as its denominator, the *conjugate,* $a - bi$, is used. To simplify $\frac{3 + i}{3 + 2i}$, multiply the numerator and the denominator by the conjugate of $3 + 2i$, which is $3 - 2i$.

Knowledge of the imaginary number, bi, allows you to find solutions to any quadratic equation using the quadratic formula.

Like real numbers, the complex number, $a + bi$, also has an absolute value, $|a + bi|$.

It is defined as the distance of a complex number from the origin on the complex plane.

Example 2 Solving a Quadratic Equation with Imaginary Numbers

Solve $x^2 + 25 = 0$. Write the solutions in terms of i. Check the answers.

SOLUTION $x^2 + 25 = 0$

$x^2 = -25$ Subtract 25 from each side.

$x = \pm\sqrt{-25}$ Take the square root of each side.

$x = \pm 5i$ Simplify the square root.

The solutions are the conjugate pairs $5i$ and $-5i$.

Check

$x^2 + 25 = 0$	$x^2 + 25 = 0$
$(5i)^2 + 25 \stackrel{?}{=} 0$	$(-5i)^2 + 25 \stackrel{?}{=} 0$
$25i^2 + 25 \stackrel{?}{=} 0$	$25i^2 + 25 \stackrel{?}{=} 0$
$25(-1) + 25 \stackrel{?}{=} 0$	$25(-1) + 25 \stackrel{?}{=} 0$
$0 = 0$ ✓	$0 = 0$ ✓

Math Language

Complex solutions of quadratic equations always occur in **conjugate pairs** of the form $a + bi$ and $a - bi$.

An imaginary number bi is part of a **complex number.**

Complex Numbers
A complex number is a number that can be written in the form $a + bi$, where a and b are real numbers.
In a complex number, a is called the **real part** and bi is called the **imaginary part.** If $b = 0$, then the imaginary part is 0 and the number is a real number. If $a = 0$ and $b \neq 0$, then the real part is 0 and the number is an imaginary number.

Complex	Real	Imaginary
$2 + 3i$	$2 + 0i = 2$	$0 + 3i = 3i$

Math Reasoning

Analyze Are real numbers a subset of complex numbers or are complex numbers a subset of real numbers?

Real numbers are a subset of complex numbers.

To add or subtract complex numbers, add or subtract the real parts and then add or subtract the imaginary parts.

Add or Subtract Complex Numbers
$(a + bi) + (c + di) = (a + c) + (b + d)i$
$(a + bi) - (c + di) = (a - c) + (b - d)i$

Example 3 Simplifying Expressions with Complex Numbers

Add or subtract. Write the answer in the form $a + bi$.

a. $(7 + 4i) + (-2 - 5i)$

SOLUTION $(7 + (-2)) + (4 + (-5))i = 5 + (-1)i = 5 - i$

b. $(5 - 3i) - (5 - 11i)$

SOLUTION $(5 - 5) + (-3 - (-11))i = 0 + 8i = 8i$

ENGLISH LEARNERS

To help students understand the meaning of imaginary numbers, define **imaginary** as existing only in the imagination; not real.

Tell students a synonym for imaginary is unreal. Discuss examples of things that are imaginary or not real, such as the tooth fairy. Have students name things or events they have imagined.

Have students identify the imaginary numbers in Example 2.

Connect the meaning of imaginary with imaginary numbers by pointing out that imaginary numbers are numbers that are not real numbers. Have students make a Venn diagram to show the sets of real and imaginary numbers.

Example 2

Before starting the example, review how to solve $x^2 - 25 = 0$.

Additional Example 2

Solve $x^2 + 169 = 0$. Write the solution in terms of i. Check the answers. The solutions are $13i$ and $-13i$.

Example 3

Error Alert Students may add or subtract unlike terms. Remind them to add or subtract terms composed only of real numbers and then add or subtract the terms that contain imaginary numbers.

Additional Example 3

Add or subtract. Write the answer in the form $a + bi$.

a. $(11 + 2i) + (-6 - 7i)$ $5 - 5i$

b. $(8 - 4i) - (8 - 16i)$ $12i$

Example 4

Extend the Problem

Have students check the solutions by substituting the values for x back into the original equation.

Additional Example 4

Solve each equation. Write the solutions in the form $a + bi$.

a. $(x - 9)^2 = -25$ The solutions are $9 + 5i$ and $9 - 5i$.

b. $x^2 + 6x + 24 = 0$ The solutions are $-3 + i\sqrt{15}$ and $-3 - i\sqrt{15}$.

Lesson Practice

Problem a

Scaffolding Have students write $\sqrt{-100}$ as a product of two square roots multiplied by $\frac{1}{2}$. Then simplify each root.

Check for Understanding

The questions below help assess the concepts taught in this lesson.

1. **"Explain how to simplify $5\sqrt{-108}$."** Look for a perfect square. Write $\sqrt{-108}$ as a product of square roots: $5\sqrt{36}\sqrt{3}\sqrt{-1}$. Simplify the expression: $5 \cdot 6 \cdot \sqrt{3} \cdot i = 30i\sqrt{3}$.

2. **"How do you solve the equation $(x + 6)^2 = -45$?"** Take the square root of each side: $x + 6 = \pm\sqrt{-45}$. Simplify the square root: $x + 6 = \pm 3i\sqrt{5}$. Subtract 6 from each side: $x = -6 \pm 3i\sqrt{5}$.

Example 4 Solving Quadratic Equations

Solve each equation. Write the solutions in the form $a + bi$.

a. $(x - 3)^2 = -4$

SOLUTION $(x - 3)^2 = -4$

$x - 3 = \pm\sqrt{-4}$ Take the square root of each side.

$x - 3 = \pm 2i$ Simplify the square root.

$x - 3 = 2i$ or $x - 3 = -2i$ Solve both equations.

$x = 3 + 2i$ or $x = 3 - 2i$

The solutions are $3 + 2i$ and $3 - 2i$.

b. $x^2 + 8x + 18 = 0$

SOLUTION $x^2 + 8x = -18$ Subtract 18 from each side.

$x^2 + 8x + 16 = -18 + 16$ Complete the square.

$(x + 4)^2 = -2$ Write the left side as a perfect square.

$x + 4 = \pm\sqrt{-2}$ Take the square root of each side.

$x + 4 = \pm i\sqrt{2}$ Simplify the square root.

$x = -4 \pm i\sqrt{2}$ Subtract 4 from each side.

The solutions are $-4 + i\sqrt{2}$ and $-4 - i\sqrt{2}$.

Lesson Practice

a. (Ex 1) Simplify $\frac{1}{2}\sqrt{-100}$. $5i$

b. (Ex 1) Simplify $3\sqrt{-450}$. $45i\sqrt{2}$

c. (Ex 2) Solve $0 = 196 + x^2$. Write the solutions in terms of i. Check the answer.

c. $\pm 14i$; $196 + (\pm 14i)^2 = 196 + 196(-1) = 196 - 196 = 0$

d. (Ex 2) Solve $-6x^2 = 216$. Write the solutions in terms of i. $\pm 6i$

Add or subtract. Write the answer in the form $a + bi$. (Ex 3)

e. $(-2 + i) + (14 + 4i)$ $12 + 5i$

f. $(10 - 6i) - (-4 + 3i)$ $14 - 9i$

Solve each equation. Write the solutions in the form $a + bi$. (Ex 4)

g. $(x + 9)^2 = -9$ $-9 \pm 3i$

h. $x^2 - 2x + 2 = 0$ $1 \pm i$

Practice Distributed and Integrated

Factor.

***1.** (61) $125x^4 + 375x^3 - x - 3$ $(x + 3)(5x - 1)(25x^2 + 5x + 1)$

***2.** (61) $64x^{12} - 125y^9$ $(4x^4 - 5y^3)(16x^8 + 20x^4y^3 + 25y^6)$

ALTERNATE METHOD FOR EXAMPLE 3b

Have students use the Distributive Property, then simplify the expression by adding like terms.

$$(5 - 3i) - (5 - 11i)$$

$$5 - 3i - 5 + 11i$$

$$0 + 8i = 8i$$

Add or subtract.

3. (37) $a + \frac{a}{b}$ $\frac{ab+a}{b}$

4. (37) $\frac{ax^2}{m^2p} - c + \frac{2}{m}$ $\frac{ax^2 - cm^2p + 2mp}{m^2p}$

5. (37) $-\frac{gh^2}{x^3} + xh + \frac{g^2h^2}{gx^3}$ xh

Factor the greatest common factor.

6. (23) $35x^7y^5m - 7x^5m^2y^2 + 14y^7x^4m^2$ $7x^4y^2m(5x^3y^3 - xm + 2y^5m)$

7. (23) $6x^2ym^5 - 2x^2ym + 4xym$ $2xym(3xm^4 - x + 2)$

Simplify.

8. (59) $\frac{1}{81^{\frac{-3}{4}}}$ 27

9. (59) $(-27)^{\frac{-2}{3}}$ $\frac{1}{9}$

10. (59) $\frac{1}{-3^{-2}}$ -9

11. (49) **School** It is estimated that 15% of students walk to school. What is the probability that exactly 2 out of 5 randomly selected students will walk to school? about 0.14

12. (50) Find an equation for the inverse of $y = \frac{1}{5}x^3 + 6$. $y = \sqrt[3]{5x - 30}$

13. (55) What are the odds in favor of rolling a 3 on a number cube? 1 to 5

*14. (62) **Multiple Choice** Which is a real number? C
A $15i$ B $0 + 15i$ C $5 + 0i$ D $15 + 15i$

*15. (37) **Verify** Show that the expression $\frac{1}{1+\frac{1}{x+1}}$ is equivalent to $\frac{x+1}{x+2}$. $\frac{1}{1+\frac{1}{x+1}} = \frac{1}{\frac{x+1}{x+1}+\frac{1}{x+1}} = \frac{1}{\frac{x+2}{x+1}} = \frac{x+1}{x+2}$

*16. (62) **Electrical Engineering** A circuit has a current of $(4 - 2i)$ amps, and a second circuit has a current of $(6 - 6i)$ amps. Find the sum of the currents. $10 - 8i$ amps

17. (55) **Analyze** Explain why the odds in favor of an event with a probability of 50% are 1 to 1. 17. The probability can be written as $\frac{1}{2}$, where 1 is the number of favorable outcomes and 2 is the total number of outcomes, meaning there are $2 - 1 = 1$ unfavorable outcomes. The odds in favor of an event is the ratio of the number of favorable to unfavorable outcomes, which is 1 to 1.

18. (58) **Projectile Motion** The Leaning Tower of Pisa measures 180.4 feet. If an object is thrown into the air, with an initial velocity of 80 feet per second, from the top of the lower side, the height, h, of the object in feet after t seconds can be described by the equation $h = -16t^2 + 80t + 180.4$. Find the time at which the object will reach a height of 200 feet. Round your answer to the tenths place. 0.3 seconds and 4.7 seconds

*19. (60) A number cube is rolled once. Are the events a number greater than 3 or a multiple of 2 mutually exclusive or inclusive? Explain why. Inclusive; Both 4 and 6 are greater than 3 and multiples of 2.

*20. (61) **Transportation** The approximate volume of a moving truck, in cubic feet, can be given by $x^3 - 6x^2 + 8x + 5x^2 - 30x + 40$. Factor this expression by grouping. Then find the volume when $x = 10$. $(x + 5)(x - 2)(x - 4)$, 720 cubic feet

21. (56) **Multiple Choice** Which of the following angles is *not* coterminal with 225°? C
A 585° B −135° C 935° D −495°

22. (57) **Multi-Step** The population of an insect colony is growing at a rate of 1.5% per week.
a. Write an expression for the function $N(P)$ that gives the population one week after the population is P. $N(P) = P + 0.015P = 1.015P$
b. What composite function gives the population three weeks after the population is P? $N(N(N(P))) = 1.015^3P \approx 1.046P$

3 Practice

Math Conversations

Discussions to strengthen understanding

Problem 9

Guide the students by asking them the following questions.

"How can you rewrite the problem using a positive exponent?" $\frac{1}{(-27)^{\frac{2}{3}}}$

"How do you simplify the denominator?" Find the cube root of −27, which is −3. Then square −3, which is 9. $(\sqrt[3]{-27})^2$

Problem 16

"What do you do first to add the amps?" Add the real numbers: $4 + 6 = 10$.

"What is the next step?" Add the imaginary numbers: $-2i + -6i = -8i$.

"What is the sum of the currents?" $10 - 8i$ amps

Problem 21

Error Alert

Students may incorrectly calculate coterminal angles. Remind students that to find a coterminal angle they can add multiples of 360° to or subtract multiples of 360° from the given angle.

INCLUSION

To emphasize that the square root of a negative number is an imaginary number, encourage students to write negative radicands as follows.

$\sqrt{-72} = \sqrt{-1 \cdot 72}$

Then have them take the square root of −1 before simplifying further.

$= i\sqrt{72} = i\sqrt{2 \cdot 36} = 6i\sqrt{2}$

Problem 24

Remind students that for even-numbered roots, there is a positive and a negative root.

Problem 25

Encourage students to multiply the length by the height to get $x^2 + 6x + 8$. Then have them do long division to find the missing dimension.

Problem 27
Extend the Problem

Have students rewrite the problem and draw new diagrams to show triangles that are congruent.

Problem 29

Have students substitute $11i$ and $-11i$ for x. Have them show how $(11i)^2 = -121$ and how $(-11i)^2 = -121$. Remind students $i^2 = -1$.

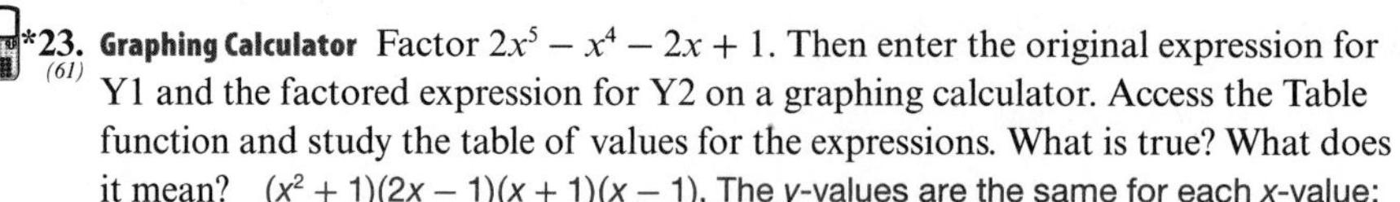

*23. (61) **Graphing Calculator** Factor $2x^5 - x^4 - 2x + 1$. Then enter the original expression for Y1 and the factored expression for Y2 on a graphing calculator. Access the Table function and study the table of values for the expressions. What is true? What does it mean? $(x^2 + 1)(2x - 1)(x + 1)(x - 1)$, The y-values are the same for each x-value; it means the graphs are the same so the factorization is correct.

24. (59) **Write** Explain why radical expressions with even indices and positive radicands have two real roots. Use $\sqrt[6]{64}$ to demonstrate your explanation.

24. Sample: The positive root of $\sqrt[6]{64}$ is 2 because $2^6 = 2 \cdot 2 \cdot 2 \cdot 2 \cdot 2 \cdot 2 = 4 \cdot 4 \cdot 4 = 64$ but $(-2)^6 = -2 \cdot -2 \cdot -2 \cdot -2 \cdot -2 \cdot -2 = 4 \cdot 4 \cdot 4 = 64$ also.

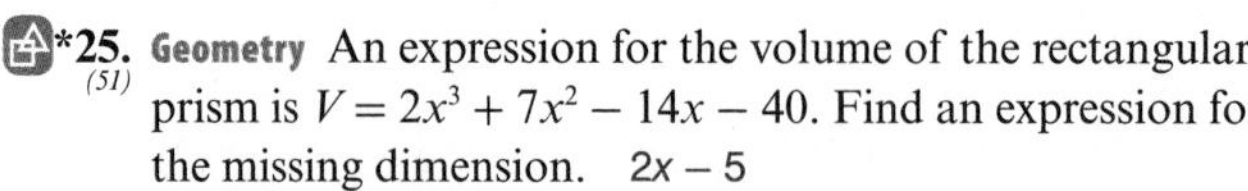

*25. (51) **Geometry** An expression for the volume of the rectangular prism is $V = 2x^3 + 7x^2 - 14x - 40$. Find an expression for the missing dimension. $2x - 5$

26. (57) **Analyze** Suppose the graph of $y = b^x + k$ passes through the points $(3, -3)$ and $(5, 0)$. Determine whether the equation models exponential growth or decay. Growth

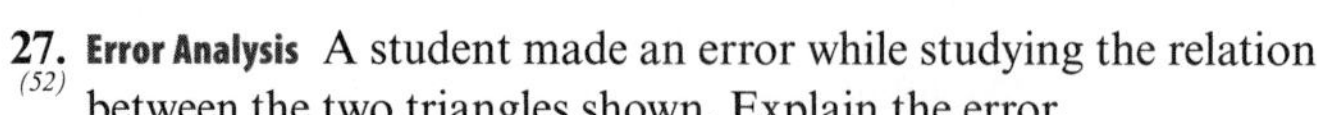

27. (52) **Error Analysis** A student made an error while studying the relation between the two triangles shown. Explain the error.

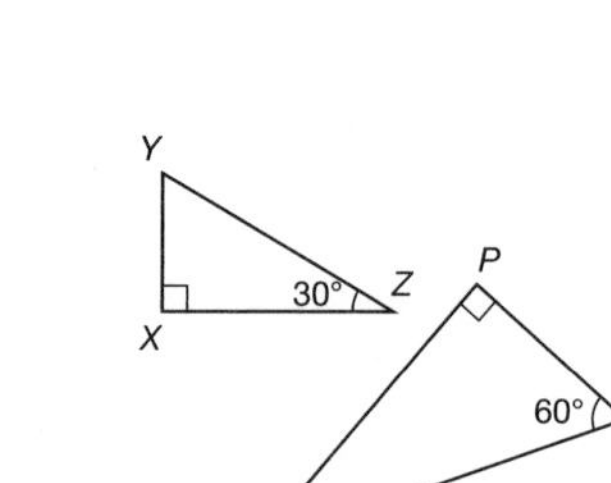

Find the missing angles.

$m\angle Y = 90° - 30° = 60°$ $m\angle R = 90° - 60° = 30°$

$m\angle X = 90°$ $m\angle Y = 60°$ $m\angle Z = 30°$

$m\angle P = 90°$ $m\angle Q = 60°$ $m\angle R = 30°$

The corresponding angles are congruent. So, the triangles are congruent.
Triangles with congruent corresponding angles are similar, not necessarily congruent.

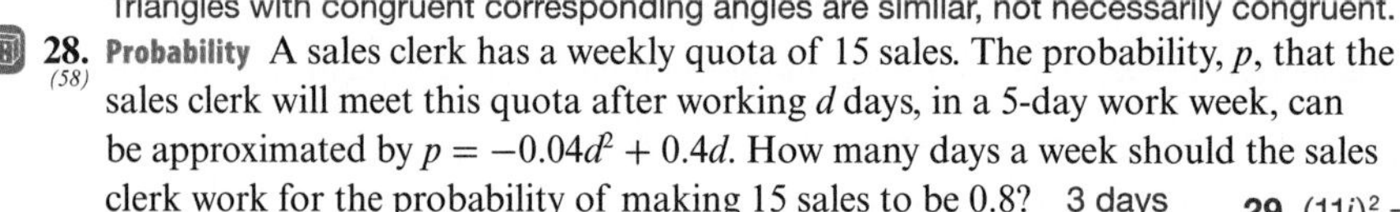

28. (58) **Probability** A sales clerk has a weekly quota of 15 sales. The probability, p, that the sales clerk will meet this quota after working d days, in a 5-day work week, can be approximated by $p = -0.04d^2 + 0.4d$. How many days a week should the sales clerk work for the probability of making 15 sales to be 0.8? 3 days

*29. (62) **Verify** Show that $11i$ and $-11i$ are solutions of $x^2 = -121$.

29. $(11i)^2 = 121i^2 = 121(-1) = -121$ and $(-11i)^2 = 121i^2 = 121(-1) = -121$

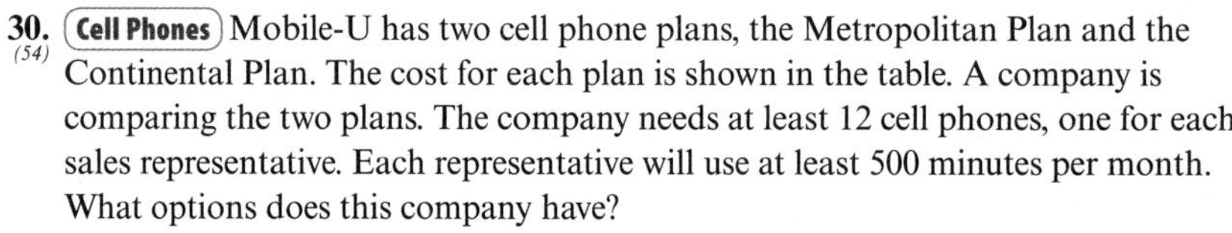

30. (54) **Cell Phones** Mobile-U has two cell phone plans, the Metropolitan Plan and the Continental Plan. The cost for each plan is shown in the table. A company is comparing the two plans. The company needs at least 12 cell phones, one for each sales representative. Each representative will use at least 500 minutes per month. What options does this company have?

	Continental Plan	Metropolitan Plan
Start-up Fee	\$50	\$100
Free minutes	2000	1200
Per minute rate above free minutes	10 cents	7 cents
Monthly charge	\$20 × # of cell phones	\$25 × # of cell phones

The Continental Plan is \$640 per month, and the Metropolitan Plan is \$636 per month. The Metropolitan Plan has a higher start-up fee, but long term offers the better deal if the company stays with the plan for at least a year.

CHALLENGE

Simplify.

$\left(\frac{5}{8} + \frac{4}{5}i\right) - \left(\frac{3}{4} - \frac{2}{3}i\right)$ $-\frac{1}{8} + \frac{22}{15}i$

LOOKING FORWARD

Understanding complex numbers prepares students for

- **Lesson 65** Using the Quadratic Formula
- **Lesson 69** Simplifying Complex Expressions
- **Lesson 70** Solving Radical Equations

LESSON **63**

Understanding the Unit Circle and Radian Measures

Warm Up

1. **Vocabulary** Half the diameter of a circle is the radius of the circle. (SB)
2. If both legs of a right triangle have length 1, then the length of the hypotenuse is $\sqrt{2}$. (41)
3. If the shortest leg of a 30°–60°–90° triangle has length 1, then the lengths of the other two sides of the triangle are $\sqrt{3}$ and 2. (52)

New Concepts

A **unit circle** is a circle with a radius of 1 unit.

Exploration Exploring the Unit Circle

Use trigonometric ratios to determine the coordinates of points on a unit circle that is centered at the origin.

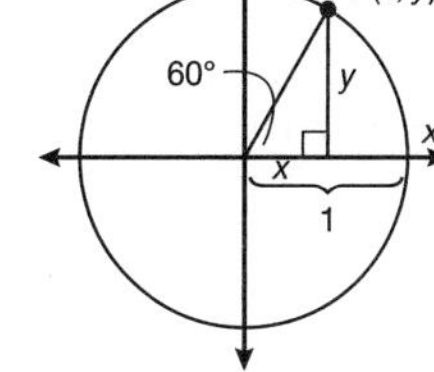

1. The figure shows a unit circle and a 60° angle in standard position. What is the length of the hypotenuse of the 30°-60°-90° triangle? How do you know? 1; It is a radius of the unit circle.
2. Use what you know about special right triangles to find the lengths of the legs of the 30°-60°-90° triangle. $x = \frac{1}{2}$; $y = \frac{\sqrt{3}}{2}$
3. What are the coordinates of point P? $\left(\frac{1}{2}, \frac{\sqrt{3}}{2}\right)$
4. What are the exact values of cos 60° and sin 60°? **4.** $\cos 60° = \frac{1}{2}$; $\sin 60° = \frac{\sqrt{3}}{2}$
5. How are the values of cos 60° and sin 60° related to the coordinates of point P? The coordinates of P are (cos 60°, sin 60°).
6. Describe how you can use a similar method to find the coordinates of point Q.
7. Explain how the values of cos 45° and sin 45° are related to the coordinates of point Q. The coordinates of point Q are (cos 45°, sin 45°).

6. Based on the 45°-45°-90° Triangle Theorem, $x = \frac{\sqrt{2}}{2}$ and $y = \frac{\sqrt{2}}{2}$. Therefore, the coordinates of point Q are $\left(\frac{\sqrt{2}}{2}, \frac{\sqrt{2}}{2}\right)$.

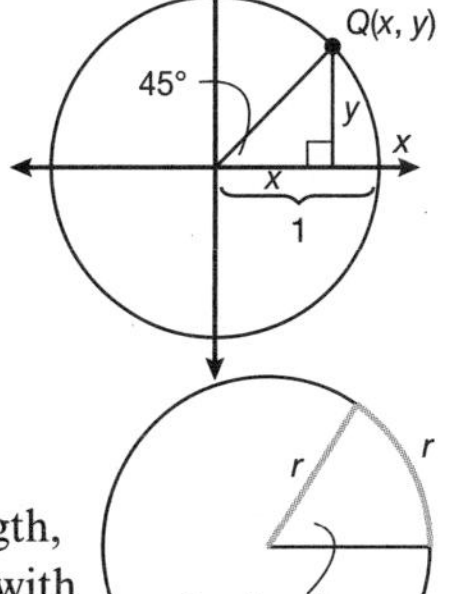

Reading Math

Remember the symbol θ is read "theta."

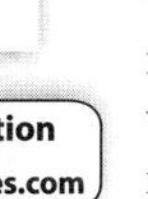
Online Connection
www.SaxonMathResources.com

Angles can be measured in degrees or in radians.

The measure of an angle in **radians** is based on arc length, the distance between two points on a circle. In a circle with radius r, the measure of a central angle θ is one radian when it intercepts an arc that has a length equal to the radius.

r
r
$\theta = 1$ radian

LESSON **63**

1 Warm Up

Use the Warm Up to review trigonometric ratios of special right triangles.

2 New Concepts

In this lesson, students learn to convert between degrees and radians. They use a unit circle to evaluate trigonometric functions.

Discuss the definition of **unit circle.** Explain that, in this lesson, a unit circle provides an alternate definition for the trigonometric ratios sine, cosine, and tangent. The unit circle is centered at (0, 0) on a coordinate grid. The values of the trigonometric functions are defined in relation to a right triangle within the unit circle.

MATH BACKGROUND

Students have previously learned to define the trigonometric functions in relation to the smaller angles of a right triangle. Angles are measured in degrees for triangles. For circles, radian measurements can be used to measure their central angles. When defining the trigonometric functions in relation to a right triangle, only the angles from 0 to $\frac{\pi}{2}$, or 0° to 90°, make sense, because the sum of the three angles of the triangle must be less than 180°.

However, when students learn about periodic functions, they will need to understand that the trigonometric ratios apply to any positive or negative angle measurement.

LESSON RESOURCES

Student Edition Practice Workbook 63
Reteaching Master 63
Adaptations Master 63
Challenge and Enrichment Master C63

Example 1

Students use conversion factors to convert between degree and radian measures.

Additional Example 1

Convert each measure from degrees to radians or from radians to degrees.

a. 60° $\frac{\pi}{3}$ radians

b. $\frac{-2\pi}{3}$ radians −120°

TEACHER TIP

The unit circle is an important topic. Allow plenty of time to discuss the circle, and help students understand the relationship between trigonometric functions on the unit circle and trigonometric functions for a right triangle.

There are 360° or 2π radians in a circle. Thus the conversion factor $\frac{2\pi}{360°}$, which is equivalent to 1, can be used to convert measures between degrees and radians.

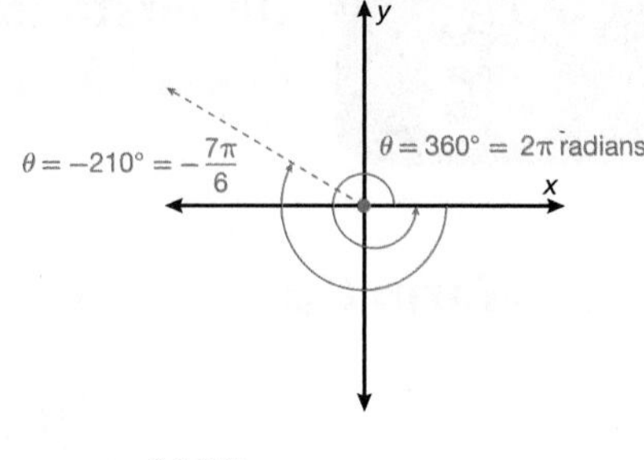

All angles are measured clockwise or counterclockwise from the positive x-axis. Measured clockwise, they are negative angles. In the figure, the −210° angle is equivalent to an angle measure of 150°.

Converting Angle Measures	
Degrees to Radians	**Radians to Degrees**
Multiply the number of degrees by $\left(\frac{\pi \text{ radians}}{180°}\right)$.	Multiply the number of radians by $\left(\frac{180°}{\pi \text{ radians}}\right)$.

Math Language

Angle measures in radians often appear without the label radians. For example, $-\frac{\pi}{6}$ radian is often written simply as $-\frac{\pi}{6}$.

Example 1 Converting Between Degrees and Radians

Convert each measure from degrees to radians or from radians to degrees.

a. −30°

SOLUTION

$-30°\left(\frac{\pi \text{ radians}}{180°}\right) = -\frac{\pi}{6}$ radians Multiply by $\left(\frac{\pi \text{ radians}}{180°}\right)$.

b. $\frac{3\pi}{4}$ radians

SOLUTION

$\left(\frac{3\pi}{4} \text{ radians}\right)\left(\frac{180°}{\pi \text{ radians}}\right) = 135°$ Multiply by $\left(\frac{180°}{\pi \text{ radians}}\right)$.

For every point $P(x, y)$ on the unit circle, the value of r is 1. Therefore, if θ is an angle in standard position whose terminal side passes through point (x, y) on the unit circle, then:

$\sin\theta = \frac{y}{r} = \frac{y}{1} = y$

$\cos\theta = \frac{x}{r} = \frac{x}{1} = x$

$\tan\theta = \frac{y}{x}$

So, the coordinates of P can be written as $(\cos\theta, \sin\theta)$.

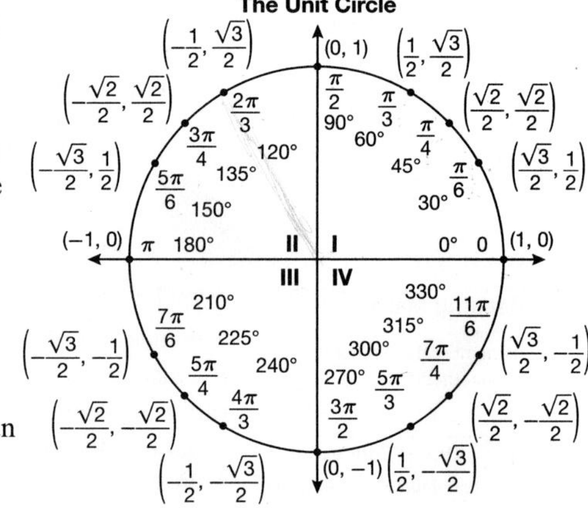

The diagram shows the equivalent degree and radian measures of special angles, and the corresponding x- and y-coordinates of points on the unit circle.

INCLUSION

A visual method of learning the values on the unit circle is to learn only the radian equivalents and coordinates in the first quadrant, and then learn how to convert to other quadrants. For example, a 30° angle in the first quadrant is equivalent to $\frac{\pi}{6}$. A 30° angle *up* from the negative x-axis in the second quadrant is 150°, and the radian equivalent is $\pi - \frac{\pi}{6} = \frac{5\pi}{6}$. The coordinates are the same, except the x-value is negative, $\left(-\frac{\sqrt{3}}{2}, \frac{1}{2}\right)$. Have students work in small groups to practice converting to each of the quadrants.

Example 2 Using the Unit Circle to Evaluate Trigonometric Functions

Use the unit circle to find each trigonometric function value. Find exact values.

a. sin 120°

SOLUTION

The terminal side of 120° passes through the point $\left(-\frac{1}{2}, \frac{\sqrt{3}}{2}\right)$ on the unit circle.

$\sin \theta = y$

$\sin 120° = \frac{\sqrt{3}}{2}$

> **Hint**
>
> The exact value of sin 120° is irrational. An approximate value is 0.866.
>
> $\sin 120° = \frac{\sqrt{3}}{2} \approx 0.866$
>
> exact approximate

b. $\tan \frac{11\pi}{6}$

SOLUTION

The terminal side of $\frac{11\pi}{6}$ passes through the point $\left(\frac{\sqrt{3}}{2}, -\frac{1}{2}\right)$ on the unit circle.

$\tan \theta = \frac{y}{x}$

$\tan \frac{11\pi}{6} = \frac{-\frac{1}{2}}{\frac{\sqrt{3}}{2}}$

$= -\frac{1}{2} \cdot \frac{2}{\sqrt{3}}$ To divide by a fraction, multiply by its reciprocal.

$= -\frac{1}{\sqrt{3}}$

$= -\frac{1}{\sqrt{3}} \cdot \frac{\sqrt{3}}{\sqrt{3}}$ Rationalize the denominator.

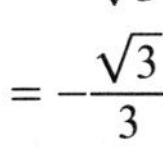

$= -\frac{\sqrt{3}}{3}$

You can use reference angles and the portion of the unit circle in Quadrant I to determine trigonometric function values.

Evaluate Trigonometric Functions using Reference Angles
To find the sine, cosine, or tangent of θ:
Step 1: Determine the measure of the reference angle of θ.
Step 2: Use the portion of the unit circle in Quadrant I to find the sine, cosine, or tangent of the reference angle.
Step 3: Use the quadrant of the terminal side of θ in standard position to determine the sign of the sine, cosine, or tangent.

Example 2

Students will use the unit circle to determine a trigonometric function value.

Additional Example 2

Use the unit circle to find each trigonometric function value. Find exact values.

a. cos 135° $\frac{-\sqrt{2}}{2}$

b. $\tan \frac{5\pi}{6}$ $-\frac{\sqrt{3}}{3}$

TEACHER TIP

Encourage students to memorize the values on the unit circle. Some students may need to make flash cards in order to quiz themselves or each other.

ENGLISH LEARNERS

Draw a circle on the board with a radian clearly marked on the circle. Have students identify what you have drawn and define the word **radian.**

Indicate the radius of the circle you have drawn. Write the word radius on the board, and help students distinguish, verbally and visually, the difference between the two words. Point out that the words and their meanings are related.

Show students circles on the board, or have them look at circles in the lesson. Ask them to identify a radius and a radian of each circle.

Have students draw a circle on the board or on paper. Next, have them use a string to measure the radius, and then demonstrate a radian. Help students use the words radius and radian correctly as they work.

The diagram shows how the signs of the trigonometric functions are determined by the quadrant that contains the terminal side of θ in standard position.

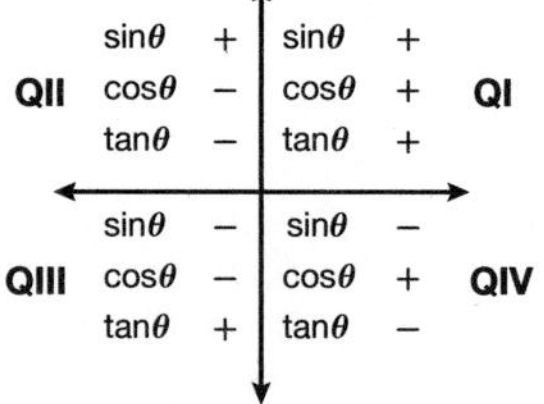

Example 3 In this example, students use reference angles to evaluate trigonometric functions.

Error Alert Students may forget to adjust the signs after finding the trigonometric functions for the reference angle. Draw a unit circle on the board, and demonstrate how the orientation of a triangle would change if it were moved from the first quadrant to any of the other quadrants. Point out when the sign of x, y, or both would change.

Additional Example 3

Find the sine, cosine, and tangent of 300°. Find exact values.

$\sin 300° = -\frac{\sqrt{3}}{2}$; $\cos 300° = \frac{1}{2}$; $\tan 300° = -\sqrt{3}$

Example 3 Using Reference Angles to Evaluate Trigonometric Functions

Find the sine, cosine, and tangent of 135°. Find exact values.

SOLUTION

Step 1: Find the measure of the reference angle.

The measure of the reference angle is 45°.

Step 2: Find the sine, cosine, and tangent of the reference angle.

$\sin 45° = \frac{\sqrt{2}}{2}$ Use $\sin \theta = y$.

$\cos 45° = \frac{\sqrt{2}}{2}$ Use $\cos \theta = x$.

$\tan 45° = 1$ Use $\tan \theta = \frac{y}{x}$.

Step 3: Determine the sign.

$\sin 135° = \frac{\sqrt{2}}{2}$ In Quadrant II, $\sin \theta$ is positive.

$\cos 135° = -\frac{\sqrt{2}}{2}$ In Quadrant II, $\cos \theta$ is negative.

$\tan 135° = -1$ In Quadrant II, $\tan \theta$ is negative.

Hint

Recall that a reference angle is an acute angle. So for $\theta < 360°$, the measure of θ is:

QII – $180° - \theta$
QIII – $\theta - 180°$
QIV – $360° - \theta$

The arc length of a circle intercepted by the central angle is related to the central angle.

Math Language

An **arc** is an unbroken part of a circle consisting of two points on the circle, called endpoints, and all the points on the circle between them.

This arc is named $\widehat{RS}$.

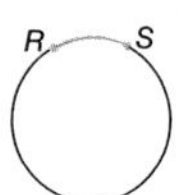

Arc Length Formula

For a circle of radius r, the **arc length** s intercepted by a central angle θ (measured in radians) is given by the following formula.

$$s = r\theta$$

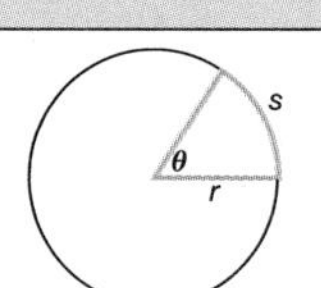

The arc length s of a circle is a portion of the circumference of a circle. This portion is the ratio between the measure of the central angle and the measure of the entire circle multiplied by the circumference of the circle. Thus, $s = \frac{\theta}{2\pi} \cdot 2\pi r$ or $s = \theta r$.

ALTERNATE METHOD FOR EXAMPLE 3

Students have previously learned the values of trigonometric functions for the special 30°-60°-90° and 45°-45°-90° right triangles. Once they have identified the reference angle, they can write the values of the trigonometric functions for the appropriate right triangle, and then adjust the signs based on the unit circle.

Example 4 Finding Arc Lengths

a. Find the length of arc s_1. Approximate to the nearest tenth.

SOLUTION

$s = r\theta$ Write the formula.

$s_1 = 5 \cdot \frac{2\pi}{3}$ Substitute s_1 for s, 5 for r, and $\frac{2\pi}{3}$ for θ.

$= \frac{10\pi}{3}$ Simplify.

≈ 10.5 cm Use a calculator to approximate.

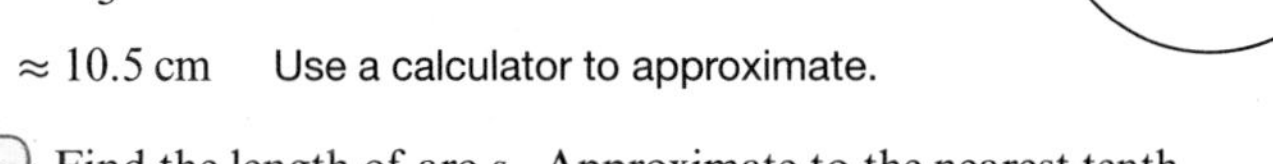

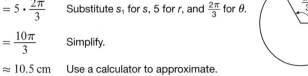

b. Find the length of arc s_2. Approximate to the nearest tenth.

SOLUTION

Step 1: Convert 225° to radians.

$$225°\left(\frac{\pi \text{ radians}}{180°}\right) = \frac{5\pi}{4} \text{ radians}$$

Step 2: Use the formula for arc length.

$s = r\theta$ Write the formula.

$s_2 = 2.5\left(\frac{5\pi}{4}\right)$ Substitue s_2 for s, 2.5 for r, and $\frac{5\pi}{4}$ for θ.

$= 3.125\pi$ Simplify.

≈ 9.8 ft Use a calculator to approximate.

Example 5 Application: Planet Rotation

Earth makes one complete rotation in 24 hours, and its radius is approximately 3955 miles. If an object is fixed on Earth's equator, how far does it travel in 1 hour due to Earth's rotation?

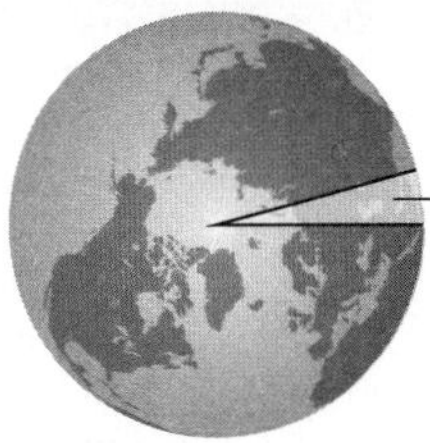

SOLUTION

The central angle that corresponds to a complete rotation is 2π radians. In 1 hour, Earth makes $\frac{1}{24}$ of a complete rotation. So, $\theta = \frac{1}{24} \cdot 2\pi = \frac{\pi}{12}$.

$s = r\theta$

$= 3955 \cdot \frac{\pi}{12}$

≈ 1035

The object travels about 1035 miles in 1 hour.

Check Find the approximate circumference of Earth: $2\pi r \approx 2\pi \cdot 3955 \approx$ 24,850 miles.

$\frac{1}{24}$ of 24,850 is slightly greater than 1000, so 1035 miles is reasonable.

Example 4

In this example, students use a circle's radius and central angle to find the length of an arc.

Extend the Example

Ask students how they could find the radius of a circle given the length of an arc and the central angle it intercepts. $r = \frac{s}{\theta}$

Additional Example 4

a. Find the length of arc s_1. Approximate to the nearest tenth.

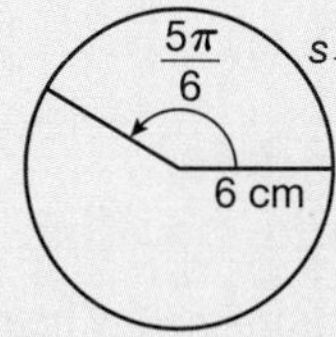

15.7 cm

b. Find the length of arc s_2. Approximate to the nearest tenth.

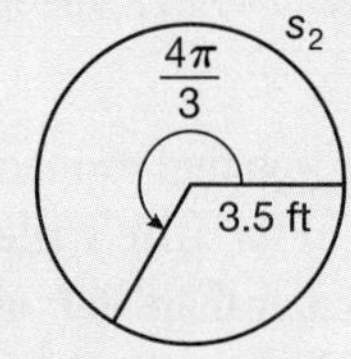

14.7 ft

Example 5

This example applies the equation $s = r\theta$ to a planet's rotation.

Additional Example 5

Mars makes one complete rotation in 25 hours, and its radius is approximately 2111 miles. How far does a point on the equator move in 1 hour due to the rotation of Mars? about 531 miles

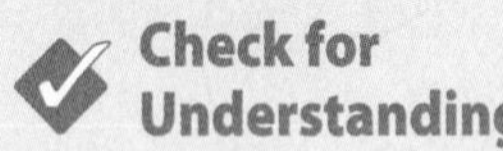

Lesson Practice

Problem a

Error Alert Remind students that they apply negative signs only when evaluating the trigonometric functions in different quadrants, not when they are converting from degree to radian measures.

Problem h

Scaffolding Ask how many minutes are shown along the circumference of a clock. 60 Help students understand that the angle is $\theta = \left(\frac{25}{60}\right)2\pi$ radians ≈ 2.6 radians.

Check for Understanding

The questions below help assess the concepts taught in this lesson.

"Is it possible to express radians without using π? Explain." Yes; π is the exact length, but an approximate length could also be given.

"How can you find trigonometric functions of negative angles or angles greater than 360° using the unit circle?" Use reference angles and consider the sign of the quadrant.

3 Practice

Math Conversations

Discussions to strengthen understanding

Problem 3

Error Alert

Students may neglect to multiply the x term in the numerator and the x^2 term in the denominator by x^2 when finding a common denominator. Remind them that every term, in both the numerator and the denominator, must be multiplied by the same factor in order to preserve the value of the expression.

Lesson Practice

a. (Ex 1) Convert 150° to radians. $\frac{5\pi}{6}$

b. (Ex 1) Convert $-\frac{4\pi}{3}$ radians to degrees. $-240°$

c. (Ex 2) Use the unit circle to find the exact value of cos 315°. $\frac{\sqrt{2}}{2}$

d. (Ex 2) Use the unit circle to find the exact value of $\tan \frac{3\pi}{4}$. -1

e. (Ex 3) Use a reference angle to find the sine, cosine, and tangent of 210°. Find exact values. $\sin 210° = -\frac{1}{2}$, $\cos 210° = -\frac{\sqrt{3}}{2}$, $\tan 210° = \frac{\sqrt{3}}{3}$

f. (Ex 4) Find the length of arc s_1. Approximate to the nearest tenth. 35.6 m

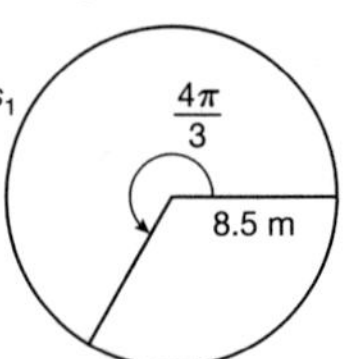

g. (Ex 4) Find the length of arc s_2. Approximate to the nearest tenth. 18.8 in.

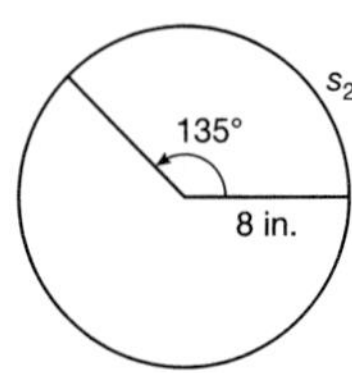

h. (Ex 5) The minute hand of a certain clock is 15 centimeters long. How far does the tip of the minute hand travel in 25 minutes, to the nearest centimeter? 39 cm

Practice Distributed and Integrated

Simplify.

1. (48) $\dfrac{\frac{1}{x}+\frac{4}{y}}{3+\frac{1}{xy}}$ $\quad \frac{y+4x}{3xy+1}$

2. (48) $\dfrac{\frac{4}{x}-3}{\frac{7}{x}+2}$ $\quad \frac{4-3x}{7+2x}$

3. (48) $\dfrac{x+\frac{1}{x^2}}{x^2-\frac{2}{x^2}}$ $\quad \frac{x^3+1}{x^4-2}$

Determine if the following probability experiments are binomial experiments. If not, explain why.

4. (Inv 5) Rolling a number cube 18 times and recording the results Not binomial; more than two outcomes

5. (Inv 5) Flipping 2 coins 20 times to test if they match half of the time Binomial

Simplify.

6. (40) $5\sqrt{45} - 2\sqrt{75} + 2\sqrt{108}$ $\quad 15\sqrt{5} + 2\sqrt{3}$

7. (40) $3\sqrt{12}\left(4\sqrt{3} - 3\sqrt{3}\right)$ $\quad 18$

Expand.

8. (19) $(x+5)^3$ $\quad x^3 + 15x^2 + 75x + 125$

9. (19) $(x+4)^3$ $\quad x^3 + 12x^2 + 48x + 64$

Solve.

10. (35) $36x^2 - 36 = 0$ 1, −1

11. (35) $24x = -11x^2 - x^3$ 0, −8, −3

12. (50) **Error Analysis** Julian is finding the inverse of the function $y = 2x^3$. Which step is incorrect?

Step One: $y = 2x^3 \longrightarrow$ Step Two: $x = 2y^3 \longrightarrow$ Step Three: $\frac{x}{2} = y^3 \longrightarrow$

Step Four: $\pm\sqrt{\frac{x}{2}} = y$

12. Step Four. He has taken the square root of the left side but the cube root of the right.

***13.** (62) Write the expression in terms of i and then add: $(15 - \sqrt{-4}) + (10 + \sqrt{-1})$.
$(15 - 2i) + (10 + i)$; $25 - i$

14. (44) **Geometry** In the triangle to the right, find x. $\frac{9\sqrt{2}}{2} \approx 6.36$ m

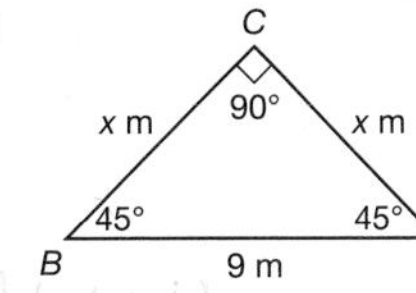

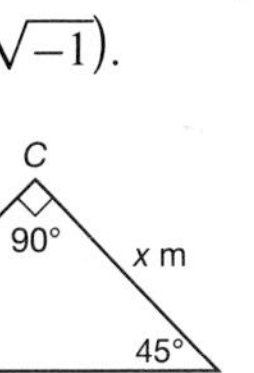

***15.** (63) **Planet Rotation** Jupiter is the largest planet. Its radius is approximately 44,365 miles. Jupiter rotates faster than Earth. It takes approximately 9.8 hours for Jupiter to make one complete rotation. If an object is fixed on Jupiter's equator, how far does it travel in 1 hour due to Jupiter's rotation? approximately 28,444 miles

16. (57) **Multiple Choice** Which of the following functions could be used to model exponential growth? D

A $y = \frac{1}{e^x}$ B $y = 2e^{-x}$ C $y = \frac{2}{e^{2x}}$ D $y = \frac{2.4}{e^{-2x}}$

17. (46) **Surveying** A surveyor stands on the roof of a building that is 180 feet above the ground and spots the top of a taller building at an angle of elevation of 34°. The two buildings are 480 feet apart. Find the height of the taller building. Round to the nearest foot. 504 feet

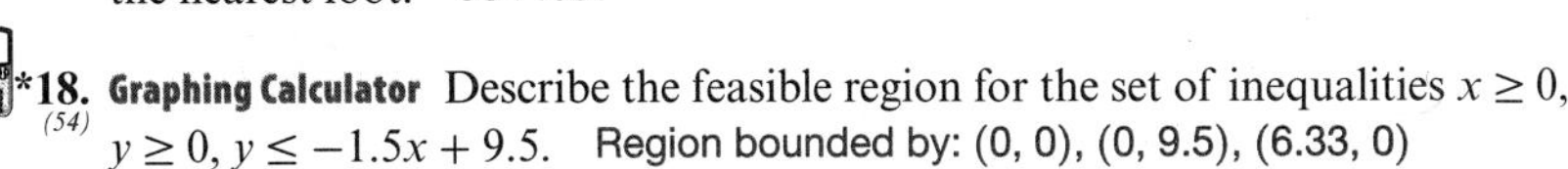

***18.** (54) **Graphing Calculator** Describe the feasible region for the set of inequalities $x \geq 0$, $y \geq 0$, $y \leq -1.5x + 9.5$. Region bounded by: (0, 0), (0, 9.5), (6.33, 0)

***19.** (60) **Formulate** A fair coin is flipped. Write the equation that can be used to solve for the probability that three flips result in heads, then four flips, and seven flips. Write a formula using exponents that can be used to find the probability that the same independent event will occur n times.

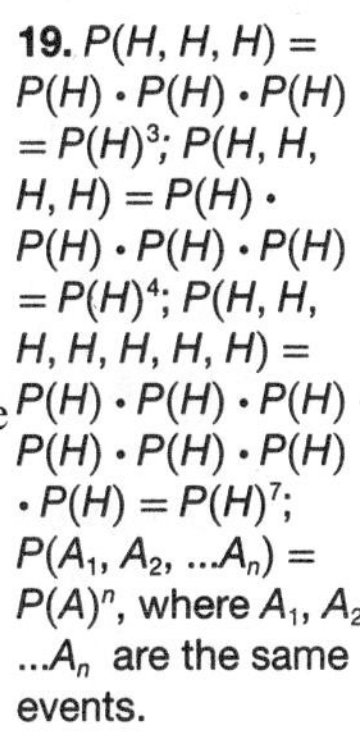

19. $P(H, H, H) = P(H) \cdot P(H) \cdot P(H) = P(H)^3$; $P(H, H, H, H) = P(H) \cdot P(H) \cdot P(H) \cdot P(H) = P(H)^4$; $P(H, H, H, H, H, H, H) = P(H) \cdot P(H) \cdot P(H) \cdot P(H) \cdot P(H) \cdot P(H) \cdot P(H) = P(H)^7$; $P(A_1, A_2, \ldots A_n) = P(A)^n$, where $A_1, A_2, \ldots A_n$ are the same events.

20. (48) **Multiple Choice** Which of the following expressions is equivalent to $\frac{\frac{1}{x} + \frac{1}{y}}{1 - \frac{1}{x}}$? C

A $\frac{1 - x}{x + y}$ B $\frac{x^2 - xy - x - y}{x^2y}$ C $\frac{x + y}{xy - y}$ D $\frac{2(1 - x)}{x + y}$

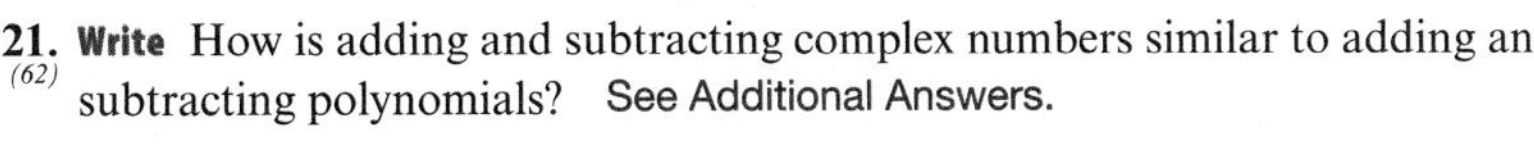

***21.** (62) **Write** How is adding and subtracting complex numbers similar to adding and subtracting polynomials? See Additional Answers.

***22.** (45) **Model** Sketch a graph of five points whose correlation coefficient is about 0.1. possible answer:

22.

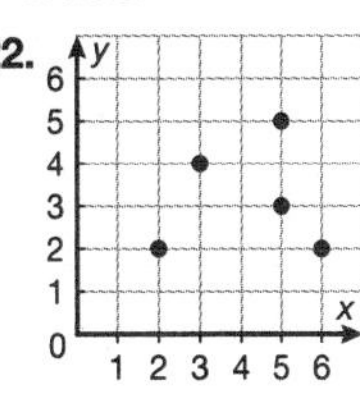

CHALLENGE

Find the sine, cosine, and tangent of the following angles. Find exact values.

a. 585° $\sin 585° = -\frac{\sqrt{2}}{2}$; $\cos 585° = -\frac{\sqrt{2}}{2}$; $\tan 585° = 1$

b. −240° $\sin(-240°) = \frac{\sqrt{3}}{2}$; $\cos(-240°) = -\frac{1}{2}$; $\tan(-240°) = -\sqrt{3}$

c. 510° $\sin 510° = \frac{1}{2}$; $\cos 510° = -\frac{\sqrt{3}}{2}$; $\tan 510° = -\frac{\sqrt{3}}{3}$

Problem 13

Writing terms in terms of i helps students visualize an easier way of adding complex numbers, rather than working with negative roots.

Problem 18

Remind students to test points in the coordinate plane to make sure they shade the correct regions for each linear graph.

Problem 21

Guide students by asking the following questions.

"What are the two parts of a complex number?" real and imaginary parts

"Can you add or subtract a real part and an imaginary part?" no

Lesson 63 453

Problem 23

Extend the Problem

"What is the interior angle of a hexagon?" 120°

"What is the reference angle for this angle?" 60°

23. (56) **Multi-Step** The formula $\theta = \frac{180°(n-2)}{n}$ gives the measure of each interior angle of an n-sided regular polygon.

a. Use the formula to find the measure of an interior angle of a regular decagon. 144°

b. Find the reference angle for this angle. 36°

24. (63) **Estimate** Use what you know about the unit circle and special angles to estimate $\cos(0.3\pi)$. Do not use a calculator. Explain your method.

24. $\cos(0.3\pi) \approx \frac{1}{2}$; 0.3π is close to $\frac{\pi}{3}$, and $\cos\frac{\pi}{3} = \frac{1}{2}$.

25. (58) **Jupiter** Gravity on the planet Jupiter is almost three times stronger than on Earth. If an object is thrown into the air, with an initial velocity of 100 feet per second, from the surface of Jupiter, the height, h, of the object in feet after t seconds can be approximated by the equation $h = -42t^2 + 100t$. Find the time at which the object will first reach 50 feet. Round your answer to the tenths place. 0.7 seconds

26. (53) **Analyze** Let $f(x) = ax + b$ and $g(x) = cx + d$. Under which conditions will the composite functions $f(g(x))$ and $g(f(x))$ be equal? $ad + b = bc + d$

27. (61) **Construction** The volume of a typical American-made brick in cubic millimeters can be represented by the polynomial $x^3 - 20x^2 - 4500x + 126{,}000$ where the length is given by $x + 70$. Fully factor the expression for the volume of a brick. $(x + 70)(x - 60)(x - 30)$

28. (59) **Coordinate Geometry** Sketch a graph of the equation $y = \sqrt[3]{x}$, where y is the side length of a cube and x is the volume of the cube. Use the graph to estimate the volume of a cube with side lengths of 2.4 in. Use the graph to estimate the side length of a cube with a volume of 6.9 in³.

***29.** (63) **Error Analysis** A student incorrectly found s, the length of the indicated arc, as shown below.

$s = r\theta$

$= 10 \cdot 60$

$= 600$ m

What is the error? Find the correct arc length.

The student used degrees instead of radians. $s = \frac{10\pi}{3}$ m ≈ 10.5 m

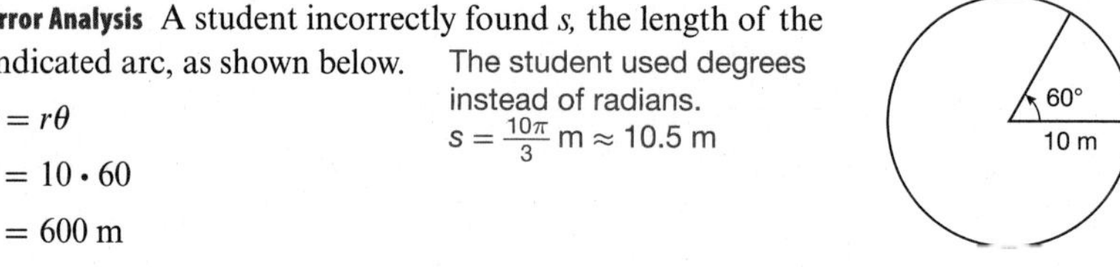

***30.** (55) **Pass codes** A computer generates temporary pass codes for users. Each pass code is exactly 3 letters long with no repeating letters. What is the probability of getting a pass code with 3 vowels (A, E, I, O, or U)? $\frac{1}{260} \approx 0.38\%$

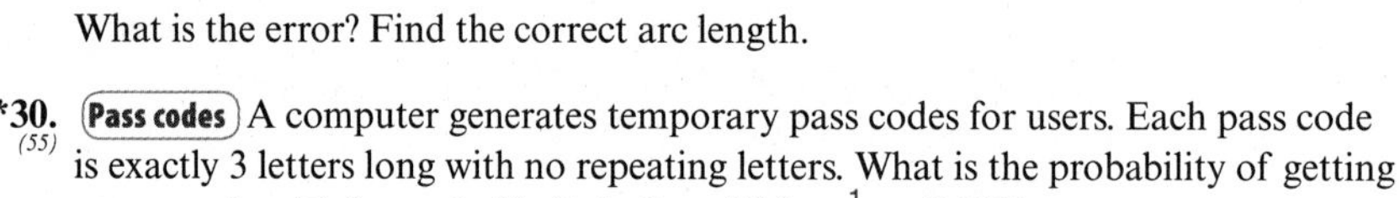

28. 13.8 in³; 1.9 in

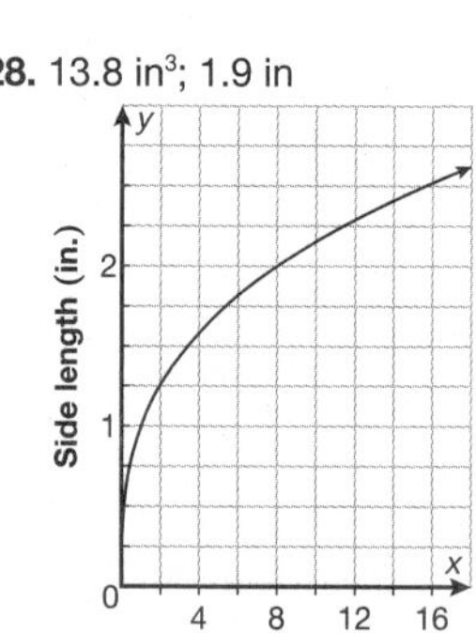

LOOKING FORWARD

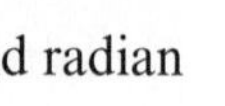

Understanding the unit circle and radian measures prepares students for

- **Lesson 67** Finding Inverse Trigonometric Functions
- **Lesson 71** Using the Law of Sines
- **Lesson 77** Using the Law of Cosines
- **Lesson 82** Graphing the Sine and Cosine Functions
- **Lesson 86** Translating Sine and Cosine Functions
- **Lesson 90** Graphing the Tangent Function

454 *Saxon Algebra 2*

LAB 10

Using the Log Keys

Graphing Calculator Lab *(Use with Lesson # 64, 72, 81, 87, 93, 102, and 110)*

Evaluating Logarithmic Expressions

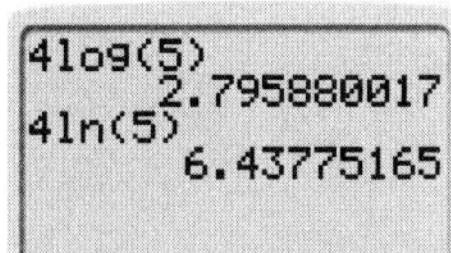

1. Calculate the common logarithmic expression 4 log (5).
   a. To enter the value **4 log (5)**, press 4 LOG 5).
   b. To calculate this value, press ENTER.
2. Calculate the natural logarithmic expression 4 ln (5).
   a. To enter the value **4 ln (5)**, press 4 LN 5).
   b. To calculate this value, press ENTER.

3. Use the Change of Base Law to calculate the logarithmic expression $\log_6(15)$.
   a. To enter the value $\log_6$ **(15)**, press
   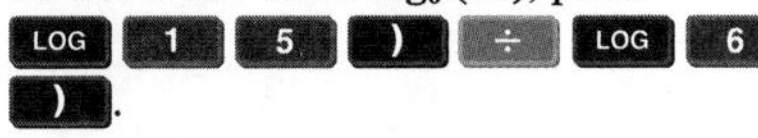

).
   b. Press ENTER to calculate this value.

Hint

Use the Change of Base Law when calculating a log that does not have a base of 10 or *e*.

Graphing Logarithmic Functions

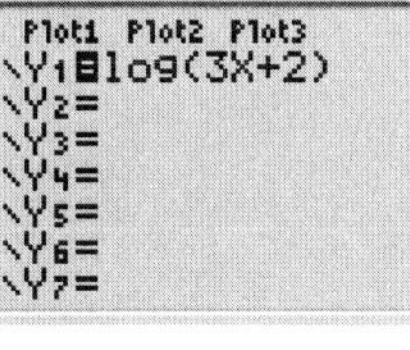

1. Graph the common logarithmic function log $(3x + 2)$.
   a. Press Y= to access the screen to enter the logarithmic function.
   b. To enter the function **log** $(3x + 2)$, press LOG 3 X,T,θ,n + 2).
   c. Press ZOOM, and then press ▼ to select the **ZStandard** window.
   d. Then press ENTER to view the graph.

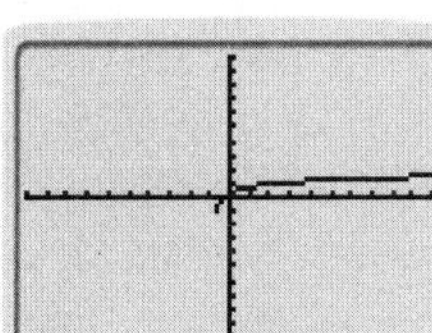

Graphing Calculator Tip

When graphing logarithmic expressions, use the standard zoom window. Adjust the window to view specific parts of the graph by zooming in or out.

Online Connection
www.SaxonMathResources.com

LAB 10

Materials

• graphing calculator

Discuss

In this lab, students will evaluate logarithmic expressions and graph logarithmic functions.

Evaluating Logarithmic Expressions

Common logarithms have base 10 and can be written as $\log_{10} x$ or $\log x$. Natural logarithms have base e and can be written as $\log_e x$ or $\ln x$.

Error Alert

If the logarithm of a negative number is entered, the calculator will display **ERR: NONREAL ANS**. The logarithm of a negative number is undefined.

TEACHER TIP

The Change of Base Law is used to evaluate logarithmic expressions without base 10 or base e: For $a > 0$, $a \neq 1$, any base b such that $b > 0$, and $b \neq 1$, $\log_a x = \frac{\log_b x}{\log_b a}$.

Graphing a Logarithmic Function

To graph a logarithmic function whose base is not 10 or e, use the Change of Base Law to enter the function into the calculator.

Problem 2

Remind students that a logarithm is an exponent. So, ln (1) means that e raised to some power is equal to 1. That power is zero, $e^0 = 1$.

Additional Problem 2

Graph $y = \log_4(9x + 1)$.

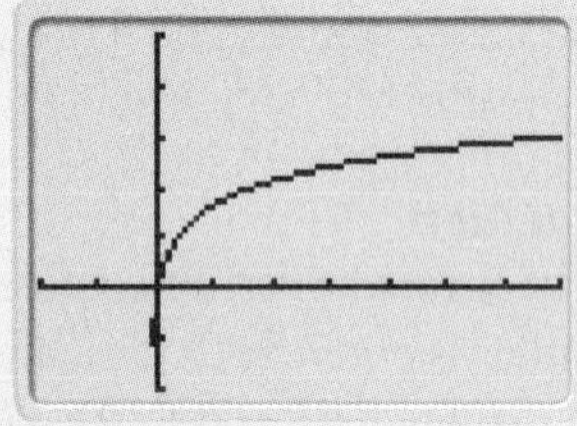

Practice Problem 5

Enter $\log_5(x + 6)$ into the calculator as $\frac{\log(x + 6)}{\log(5)}$.

2. Graph the logarithmic function $\log_6(13x)$ whose base is not natural or common.
   a. Press Y= to access the screen to enter the logarithmic function.
   b. To enter the function $\log_6(13x)$, press

   6).
   c. Press ZOOM, and then press ▼ to select the **ZStandard** window.
   d. Then press ENTER to view the graph.

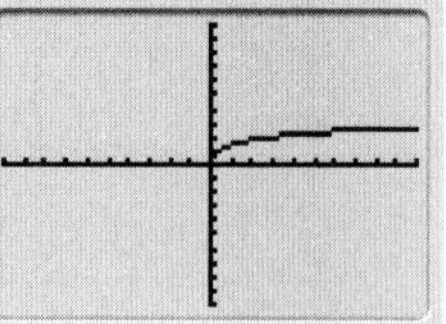

Lab Practice

1. Calculate 6 log (8). 5.42
2. Calculate 3 ln (1). 0
3. Calculate $\log_7(9)$. 1.13
4. Graph $y = \log(15x + 8)$.
5. Graph $y = \log_5(x + 6)$.

4.
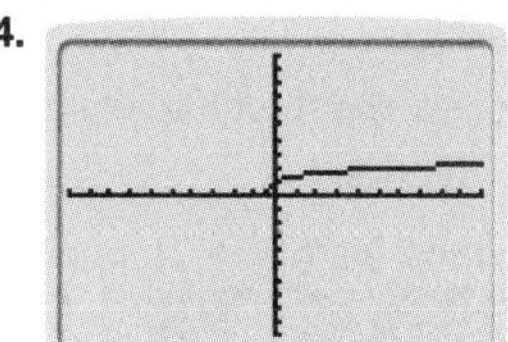

5.
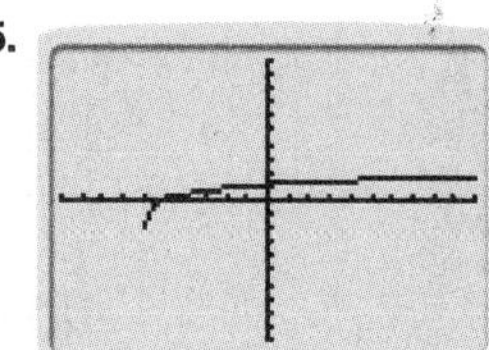

LESSON 64

Using Logarithms

Warm Up

1. **Vocabulary** In the expression 4^5, the base is 4 and the exponent is 5.
(3)
2. What is the value of 2^3? 8
(3)
3. What value of x makes the equation $10^x = 100$ true? 2
(47)

New Concepts

A **logarithm** is the exponent that is applied to a specified base to obtain a given value. Every exponential equation has a logarithmic form and vice versa.

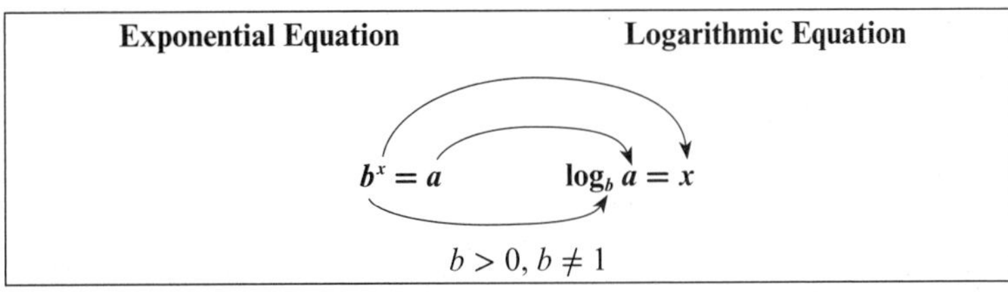

The logarithmic equation $\log_b a = x$ is read "the log base b of a equals x." Notice that x is both the exponent and the logarithm in the equations above.

Example 1 Converting from Exponential to Logarithmic Form

Write each exponential equation in logarithmic form.

a. $2^5 = 32$

SOLUTION

$2^5 = 32 \Leftrightarrow \log_2 32 = 5$ The base is the same in both the exponential equation and the logarithmic equation.

The logarithmic form is $\log_2 32 = 5$.

b. $5^1 = 5$

SOLUTION

$5^1 = 5 \Leftrightarrow \log_5 5 = 1$ The exponent is the logarithm.

The logarithmic form is $\log_5 5 = 1$.

c. $8^0 = 1$

SOLUTION

$8^0 = 1 \Leftrightarrow \log_8 1 = 0$ Any nonzero base to the zero power is 1.

The logarithmic form is $\log_8 1 = 0$.

Reading Math

Read the symbol $\Leftrightarrow$ as "if and only if." When used between two equations, it means the equations are equivalent.

Online Connection
www.SaxonMathResources.com

LESSON 64

1 Warm Up

Use Problems 2 and 3 in the Warm Up to review solving problems with exponents to prepare for problems involving logarithms.

2 New Concepts

In this lesson, students learn to use logarithms and the exponential equation.

Discuss the definitions of **logarithm, exponent,** and **base.** In order to solve logarithms, you must convert to the exponential equation.

Example 1

Students will convert an equation in exponential form into logarithmic form.

Additional Example 1

Write each exponential equation in logarithmic form.

a. $3^5 = 243$ $\log_3 243 = 5$

b. $4^{-2} = 0.0625$ $\log_4 0.0625 = -2$

c. $8^2 = 64$ $\log_8 64 = 2$

d. $6^3 = 216$ $\log_6 216 = 3$

MATH BACKGROUND

Logarithms are used in many areas of science and engineering in which quantities vary over a large range. For example, the decibel scale for the loudness of sound, the Richter scale of earthquake magnitudes, and the astronomical scale of stellar brightness are all logarithmic scales.

The natural logarithm, formerly known as the hyperbolic logarithm, is the logarithm to the base e, where e is an irrational constant approximately equal to 2.718. The natural logarithm can be defined for all positive real numbers x as the area under the curve $y = \frac{1}{t}$ from 1 to x, and can also be defined for non-zero complex numbers.

LESSON RESOURCES

Student Edition Practice Workbook 64
Reteaching Master 64
Adaptations Master 64
Challenge and Enrichment Master C64

Example 2

Students will convert an equation in logarithmic form into exponential form.

Additional Example 2

Write each exponential equation in logarithmic form.

a. $\log_7 343 = 3$ $7^3 = 343$

b. $\log_9 81 = 2$ $9^2 = 81$

c. $\log_2 1024 = 10$ $2^{10} = 1024$

Example 3

Students will apply logarithms to solve a chemistry problem involving the pH scale.

Additional Example 3

A chemist measured the pH of a liquid to test its acidity. If the hydrogen concentration is 0.000000040 moles per liter, is the liquid an acid or a base? (A base has a pH above 7 and an acid has a pH below 7.)

$\text{pH} = -\log[H^+]$
$\text{pH} = -\log(0.000000040)$
$\text{pH} \approx 7.4$
The liquid is a base.

Extend the Example

An acid was measured to have a pH of 3.8. What is the hydrogen concentration?

$\text{pH} = -\log[H^+]$
$3.8 = -\log[H^+]$
$-3.8 = \log[H^+]$
$10^{-3.8} = [H^+]$
0.00016 moles per liter $= H^+$

Reading Math

The equations in Example 1d can be written $5^{-2} = \frac{1}{25}$ and $\log_5 \frac{1}{25} = -2$.

d. $5^{-2} = 0.04$

SOLUTION

$5^{-2} = 0.04 \Leftrightarrow \log_5 0.04 = -2$ An exponent (or log) can be negative.

The logarithmic form is $\log_5 0.04 = -2$.

Example 2 Converting from Logarithmic to Exponential Form

Write each logarithmic equation in exponential form.

a. $\log_{10} 1000 = 3$

SOLUTION

$\log_{10} 1000 = 3 \Leftrightarrow 10^3 = 1000$ The base is the same in both the logarithmic equation and the exponential equation.

The exponential form is $10^3 = 1000$.

b. $\log_7 7 = 1$

SOLUTION

$\log_7 7 = 1 \Leftrightarrow 7^1 = 7$ The logarithm is the exponent.

The exponential form is $7^1 = 7$.

c. $\log_3 81 = x$

SOLUTION

$\log_3 81 = x \Leftrightarrow 3^x = 81$ The logarithm (and the exponent) can be a variable.

The exponential form is $3^x = 81$.

A logarithm with base 10 is called a **common logarithm.** If no base is written for a logarithm, the base is assumed to be 10. For example, $\log 5 = \log_{10} 5$.

Example 3 Application: Acidity of Rainwater

Because of the phenomenon of acid rain, the acidity of rainwater is important to environmental scientists. The acidity of a liquid is measured in pH, given by the function $\text{pH} = -\log[H^+]$, where $[H^+]$ represents the concentration of hydrogen ions in moles per liter. In 1999, the hydrogen ion concentration of rainwater in western Nevada was found to be approximately 0.0000032 moles per liter. What was the pH of the rainwater?

SOLUTION

$\text{pH} = -\log[H^+]$

$\text{pH} = -\log(0.0000032)$ Substitute the known value in the function.

```
-log(0.0000032)
     5.494850022
```

Use a calculator to find the value of the logarithm in base 10. Press the LOG key.

The rainwater had a pH of about 5.5.

ENGLISH LEARNERS

The term **logarithm** stands for a number that indicates a ratio, because the difference of two logarithms determines the ratio of the numbers they represent.

Explain that a logarithm is a function that is used to solve equations in which the exponent is unknown.

Graph the logs of different bases and show how the scale can vary compared to normal polynomial functions.

Connect the relationship between the logarithmic form and the exponential form. These two equations are equivalent and can be used to solve the logarithm.

Hint

The display 3.16227766E − 6 means $3.16227766 \times 10^{-6}$, which is approximately 3.2×10^{-6}, or 0.0000032.

Check

$-\log(0.0000032) \approx 5.5$ Write the result found in the Solution.

$\log(0.0000032) \approx -5.5$ Multiply both sides by −1.

$10^{-5.5} \approx 0.0000032$ Write the logarithmic equation in exponential form.

Use a calculator to verify that the value of $10^{-5.5}$ is approximately 0.0000032.

```
10^(-5.5)
      3.16227766E-6
```

Lesson Practice

Write each exponential equation in logarithmic form.
(Ex 1)

a. $3^2 = 9$ $\log_3 9 = 2$ **b.** $4^1 = 4$ $\log_4 4 = 1$

c. $9^0 = 1$ $\log_9 1 = 0$ **d.** $8^{-1} = 0.125$ $\log_8 0.125 = -1$

Write each logarithmic equation in exponential form.
(Ex 2)

e. $\log_{10} 100 = 2$ $10^2 = 100$ **f.** $\log_8 8 = 1$ $8^1 = 8$ **g.** $\log_5 125 = x$ $5^x = 125$

h. *(Ex 3)* The acidity of a liquid is measured in pH, given by the function pH = $-\log[H^+]$, where $[H^+]$ represents the concentration of hydrogen ions in moles per liter. In 1999, the hydrogen ion concentration of rainwater in northern Maine was found to be approximately 0.0000200 moles per liter. What was the pH of the rainwater, to the nearest tenth? 4.7

Practice Distributed and Integrated

Use synthetic substitution.

1. *(51)* Find $f(6)$ for $f(x) = x^4 - 4x^3 + 2x^2 + 4x - 18$. 510

2. *(51)* Find $f(-7)$ for $f(x) = x^4 + 5x^3 - 12x^2 - 4x + 8$. 134

3. *(26)* Find the equation of the line that passes through (−2, 5) and (−6, −3). $y = 2x + 9$

4. *(41)* The sides of a triangle measure 7 in., 6 in., and 8 in. Is the triangle a right triangle? No

Find the zeros of each quadratic function.

5. *(35)* $f(x) = 2x^2 + x - 15$ $\frac{5}{2}$ and −3 **6.** *(35)* $f(x) = -32x^2 - 28x$ 0 and $-\frac{7}{8}$ **7.** *(35)* $f(x) = x^2 - 9$ −3 and 3

Determine if (0, −3) is a solution of the inequalities.

8. *(39)* $5x + 2y < -4$ yes **9.** *(39)* $y - 2x > 6$ no **10.** *(39)* $16y - 2 \geq x$ no

11. *(52)* **Formulate** A parasail is attached to a boat with a rope 300 feet long. The angle of elevation from the boat to the parasail is 48 degrees. Write a formula that would help you to estimate the parasail's height above the boat. $\sin 48° = \frac{h}{300}$

ALTERNATE METHOD FOR PROBLEM 11

Draw a triangle simulating the length of the rope, the angle, and the unknown height of the parasail. Using cos θ, find the length that the parasail is away from the boat in the x-direction. Using the Pythagorean Theorem, solve for the height of the parasail.

$$\cos 48 = \frac{x}{300}$$

$$x = 300\cos(48)$$

$$x \approx 200.74 \text{ ft}$$

$$a^2 = b^2 + c^2$$

$$b^2 = c^2 - a^2$$

$$b = \sqrt{c^2 - a^2}$$

$$b \approx \sqrt{(300)^2 - (200.74)^2}$$

$$b \approx 222.94 \text{ ft}$$

Lesson Practice

Problem d

Error Alert

Students may forget to include the negative when writing the logarithmic form. Allow students to put all numbers and their signs in parentheses before they convert to logarithmic form.

Problem g

Scaffolding Begin by identifying each variable in the logarithmic expression ($a = 125$, $b = 5$, $x = x$). Write the equation in exponential form following the equation $b^x = a$.

Check for Understanding

The questions below help assess the concepts taught in this lesson.

1. **"What two equations are used to solve logarithms?"** Sample: The logarithmic equation and the exponential equation. ($b^x = a \Leftrightarrow \log_b a = x$)

2. **"What are logarithms used for?"** Sample: Logarithms are used to scale quantities over a large range. They are also used to solve equations in which the exponent is unknown.

3 Practice

Math Conversations

Discussions to strengthen understanding

Problem 3

First, find the slope using the slope formula $\left(m = \frac{(y_2 - y_1)}{(x_2 - x_1)}\right)$.

Next, using the equation of the line $y = mx + b$, use one pair of coordinates and solve for b, the y-intercept.

Problem 14
TEACHER TIP

Students will need practice identifying the relationship between the exponential form equation and the logarithmic form equation. Emphasize the relationship when showing simple logarithms. Have the students solve for the exponent in their head so they can get an idea on how the equations should relate to each other.

Problem 20

Calculate the arc length of a sector of a circle. The sector is 135°. Calculate the arc length for each length. Subtract the two lengths to find the difference.

***12.** (63) **Coordinate Geometry** Find the area of triangle OQR. Give the answer in exact form and to the nearest tenth of a square unit. $\frac{3\sqrt{3}}{2}$ square units $\approx$ 2.6 square units

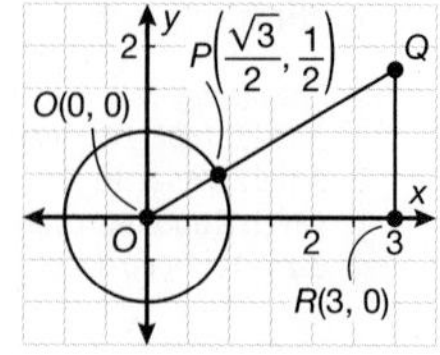

13. (50) Find an equation for the inverse of $y = 5x - 8$. Identify the domain and range of the inverse function. $y = \frac{x+8}{5}$; domain: x is any real number; range: y is any real number

***14.** (64) **Write** Explain why $\log_0 9$ and $\log_1 9$ do not exist.

14. Possible answer: $\log_0 9$ does not exist because there is no power of 0 that equals 9. $\log_1 9$ does not exist because there is no power of 1 that equals 9.

15. (53) **Population** Currently the U.S. population is growing at a rate of approximately 0.6 percent per year. According to the 2000 census, the population was about 281 million. Use composite functions to predict the U.S. population in the year 2015, and justify your prediction.

15. Function $f(p) = 1.006p$ gives the population one year after the population is p. The population of 2015 will be the composition of f with itself 15 times, evaluated at 281 million. That is, the population will be $1.006^{15}(281) \approx 307$ million.

***16.** (59) **Multi-Step** Use $\left(\frac{9}{7}\right)^{\frac{1}{4}}\left(\frac{9}{7}\right)^{\frac{1}{4}}$.

a. Which property of rational exponents should be applied first to simplify the expression? Explain.

16a. Power of a Quotient Property; By the order of operations you must evaluate exponents before multiplying.

b. Apply the property from part a. $\frac{9^{\frac14}}{7^{\frac14}} \cdot \frac{9^{\frac14}}{7^{\frac14}}$

c. Which property of rational exponents should be applied next? Product of Powers Property

d. Apply the property from part c. $\frac{9^{\frac12}}{7^{\frac12}}$

e. If possible, finish simplifying the expression from part d. $\frac{3\sqrt{7}}{7}$

***17.** (61) **Transportation** The approximate volume of a moving truck, in cubic feet, that can move four to five household rooms can be given by $x^3 - 15x^2 + 56x + 6x^2 - 90x + 336$. Factor this expression by grouping. Then find the dimensions when $x = 15$. $(x + 6)(x - 7)(x - 8)$, 21 ft by 8 ft by 7 ft

18. (57) **Geometry** The figures below show how to create Sierpinski's Triangle. Start with a solid black equilateral triangle (Iteration 0); at every iteration, join the midpoints of the sides of each black triangle to get a smaller triangle, and color the interior of that triangle white.

Iteration 0 Iteration 1 Iteration 2 Iteration 3 Iteration 4

Formulate an exponential function for the number of black triangles $N(x)$ in the xth iteration. $N(x) = 3^x$

19. (31) Find the slope of the line that passes through the points $A\left(\frac{3}{x}, \frac{1}{3}\right)$ and $B\left(\frac{1}{5}, \frac{5}{x}\right)$, where x is any non-zero real number. $-\frac{5}{3}$

***20.** (63) **Windshield Wipers** A rear windshield wiper moves through an angle of 135° on each swipe. To the nearest inch, how much greater is the length of the arc traced by the top end of the wiper blade than the length of the arc traced by the bottom end of the wiper blade? 33 inches

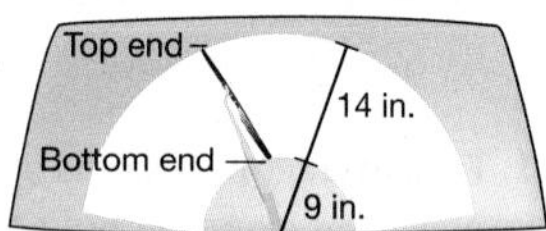

INCLUSION

For more visual students, draw the log functions on a graph for different bases. Then based on a given value, the exponent can be found. Start with a base 10 graph, and then move to other graphs so the logarithmic scale can be visually seen.

Calculators may be used to solve the logarithmic equation but be sure the students are experienced in converting the exponential equation into logarithmic form so they do not take the log of the wrong variable.

21. **Multiple Choice** Which of the following expressions is equivalent to $\frac{3}{5-\sqrt{2}}$? B
(44)

A $\frac{3-15\sqrt{2}}{21}$ B $\frac{15+3\sqrt{2}}{23}$ C $\frac{15-2\sqrt{3}}{21}$ D $\frac{21-3\sqrt{2}}{15}$

22. **Multi-Step** What number needs to be added to both sides of the equation to make $x^2 + 12x + 42 = 0$ a perfect square? Solve the equation. $-6; x = -6 \pm i\sqrt{6}$
(Inv 6)

*23. **Rainwater** The acidity of a liquid is measured in pH, given by the function $\text{pH} = -\log[\text{H}^+]$, where $[\text{H}^+]$ represents the concentration of hydrogen ions in moles per liter. In 1999, the hydrogen ion concentration of rainwater in the Chesapeake Bay region of Maryland was found to be approximately 0.0000316 moles per liter. What was the pH of the rainwater, to the nearest tenth? Show how to check your answer by writing a logarithmic equation and its equivalent exponential equation. (Hint: You will need to use the ≈ symbol instead of the = symbol.)
(64)
$4.5; -\log(0.0000316) \approx 4.5 \Rightarrow \log(0.0000316) \approx -4.5 \Rightarrow 10^{-4.5} \approx 0.0000316$

*24. **Write** Two number cubes are tossed once. Explain why the events, one cube shows a number less than 5 and the sum of the two cubes is a multiple of 2, are dependent. The events are dependent because the probability of the sum being a multiple of 2 changes with the knowledge that one of the cubes is showing less than 5.
(60)

25. **Justify** Give an example of an event that has a probability of 0. Explain why the probability is 0.
(55)

25. Possible answer: getting a 7 when rolling a number cube. The probability is 0 because there are no favorable outcomes because 7 is not in the sample space.

*26. **Graphing Calculator** Set the mode on your graphing calculator to $a + bi$ by pressing the Mode key and using the arrow keys. Then find $\sqrt{-1296} \div \sqrt{-324}$. 2
(62)

27. **Error Analysis** Rizwan tried to find the value of $\cos\theta$, where θ is an angle in standard position with the point $Q(-6, 8)$ on its terminal side. His work is shown below. What was Rizwan's error? The x-coordinate is -6, not 6. So, in the final step, $\cos\theta = \frac{-6}{10} = -0.6$.
(56)

$r = \sqrt{x^2 + y^2}$

$r = \sqrt{(-6)^2 + 8^2}$

$r = \sqrt{100}$

$r = 10$

$\cos\theta = \frac{x}{r}$

$\cos\theta = \frac{6}{10} = 0.6$

*28. **Multiple Choice** Which equation is equivalent to $\log_2 16 = x$? A
(64)

A $2^x = 16$ B $x^2 = 16$ C $16^2 = x$ D $2^{16} = x$

29. **Analyze** Compare and contrast correlation coefficient values of -0.45 and 0.45. See Additional Answers.
(45)

*30. **Falling Objects** The height, in feet, of an object that is falling or is projected into the air can be described by $h = -16t^2 + v_0t + h_0$, where h is the height in feet after t seconds, v_0 is the initial velocity of the object in feet per second, and h_0 is the initial height of the object in feet per second. A coin is tossed from the top of a 100 foot tall building, with an initial velocity of 92 feet per second. Write the equation that models the height of the coin. Find the time when the coin will reach the ground. Round your answer to the tenths place. $h = -16t^2 + 92t + 100$; $t = 6.7$ seconds
(58)

Problem 23

Use the logarithm form equation and your calculator to solve for the pH. Remember that the pH is the negative log of the hydrogen concentration.

Problem 28

Error Alert

Students may write the exponential form incorrectly due to misplacing the variables. Encourage the students to create a list with each variable written down ($a =, b =, x =$). This will help them to make fewer mistakes.

Problem 29

Guide the students by asking them the following questions.

"How would the coefficients affect the scale of the variable?"
The scale would be the same since each value is the same.

"How do the coefficients relate according to their signs?"
The coefficients have opposite signs, so one value would be positively affected and the other would be negatively affected.

Problem 30

The equation can be modeled by plugging in the values for the initial conditions given in the word problem for the initial height and velocity. To solve for the time when the coin hits the ground, set the height equal to 0 (since it is at the ground) and solve the polynomial for t.

CHALLENGE

Solve: $\frac{(\log 5 - \log 400)}{\log 225}$

$\frac{(\log 5 - \log 400)}{\log 225}$

$\approx \frac{(.699 - 2.602)}{2.352}$

$\approx -.809$

LOOKING FORWARD

Using logarithms prepares students for

- **Lesson 72** Using the Properties of Logarithms
- **Lesson 81** Using Natural Logarithms
- **Lesson 87** Evaluating Logarithmic Expressions
- **Lesson 102** Solving Logarithmic Equations and Inequalities

LESSON 65

1 Warm Up

Problem 3
Remind students that $3\sqrt{-25} = 3 \cdot 5i$, which is $15i$.

2 New Concepts

In this lesson, students learn to use the quadratic formula to solve equations.

Review deriving the quadratic formula by completing the square.

LESSON 65

Using the Quadratic Formula

Warm Up

1. (62) **Vocabulary** The square root of a negative number is an imaginary number.

2. (58) Solve by completing the square $x^2 - 26x = 13$. $x = 13 \pm\sqrt{182}$

3. (62) Simplify $3\sqrt{-25}$. $15i$

4. (2) Evaluate $b^2 - 4ac$ when $a = 2$, $b = 7$, and $c = 5$. 9

New Concepts

In general, a quadratic equation in standard form is $ax^2 + bx + c = 0$, with $a \neq 0$. The general equation can be solved for x by completing the square.

$$ax^2 + bx = -c \qquad \text{Subtract } c \text{ from each side.}$$

$$x^2 + \frac{b}{a}x = -\frac{c}{a} \qquad \text{Divide both sides by } a.$$

$$x^2 + \frac{b}{a}x + \frac{b^2}{4a^2} = -\frac{c}{a} + \frac{b^2}{4a^2} \qquad \text{Complete the square.}$$

$$\left(x + \frac{b}{2a}\right)^2 = -\frac{c}{a} + \frac{b^2}{4a^2} \qquad \text{Factor the left side.}$$

$$\left(x + \frac{b}{2a}\right)^2 = -\frac{4ac}{4a^2} + \frac{b^2}{4a^2} \qquad \text{Make common denominators on the right.}$$

$$\left(x + \frac{b}{2a}\right)^2 = \frac{b^2 - 4ac}{4a^2} \qquad \text{Combine the fractions on the right.}$$

$$x + \frac{b}{2a} = \pm\sqrt{\frac{b^2 - 4ac}{4a^2}} \qquad \text{Apply the Square Root Property.}$$

$$x = -\frac{b}{2a} \pm \sqrt{\frac{b^2 - 4ac}{4a^2}} \qquad \text{Isolate } x.$$

$$x = -\frac{b}{2a} \pm \frac{\sqrt{b^2 - 4ac}}{2a} \qquad \text{Simplify the radical.}$$

$$x = \frac{-b \pm \sqrt{b^2 - 4ac}}{2a} \qquad \text{Combine the fractions.}$$

Math Reasoning

Analyze Explain how $\frac{-c}{a} + \frac{b^2}{4a^2}$ becomes $-\frac{4ac}{4a^2} + \frac{b^2}{4a^2}$.

Multiply $\frac{-c}{a}$ by $\frac{4a}{4a}$.

The last line is the quadratic formula.

Quadratic Formula
The solutions of the quadratic equation $ax^2 + bx + c = 0$ $(a \neq 0)$ are given by $x = \dfrac{-b \pm \sqrt{b^2 - 4ac}}{2a}$.

The quadratic formula can be used to find the solutions of any quadratic equation.

LESSON RESOURCES

Student Edition Practice Workbook 65
Reteaching Master 65
Adaptations Master 65
Challenge and Enrichment Masters C65, E65

MATH BACKGROUND

Completing the square can be used to solve many quadratic equations. For example, to solve $x^2 - 6x - 3 = 0$, you can complete the square as shown below.

1. $x^2 - 6x = 3$
2. $x^2 - 6x + 9 = 3 + 9$
3. $(x-3)^2 = 12$
4. $x - 3 = \pm\sqrt{12}$
5. $x = 3 \pm \sqrt{12} = 3 \pm 2\sqrt{3}$

Step 1: Isolate the constant and divide through by the coefficient of x^2, if it is not equal to 1.

Step 2: Take half of the coefficient of x, square it, and add it to both sides.

Step 3: Factor the left side as a square of a binomial.

Step 4: Solve the equation for x.

Step 5: The quadratic equation has two possible solutions as shown.

Example 1 Solving Quadratic Equations with Real Zeros

Solve each equation.

Math Language

The **solutions** of a quadratic equation are the **zeros** of the related function.

a. $5x^2 + 34x - 7 = 0$

SOLUTION Use the quadratic formula.

$$x = \frac{-b \pm \sqrt{b^2 - 4ac}}{2a}$$

$$= \frac{-34 \pm \sqrt{34^2 - 4(5)(-7)}}{2(5)}$$ Substitute 5 for *a*, 34 for *b*, and −7 for *c*.

$$= \frac{-34 \pm \sqrt{1296}}{10}$$ Simplify the radicand and denominator.

$$= \frac{-34 \pm 36}{10} = \frac{1}{5} \text{ and } -7$$ Evaluate the square root and simplify.

The solutions are $\frac{1}{5}$ and -7.

b. $9x^2 + 6x + 1 = 0$

SOLUTION Use the quadratic formula $x = \frac{-b \pm \sqrt{b^2 - 4ac}}{2a}$.

$$x = \frac{-6 \pm \sqrt{6^2 - 4(9)(1)}}{2(9)}$$ Substitute 9 for *a*, 6 for *b*, and 1 for *c*.

$$= \frac{-6 \pm \sqrt{0}}{18}$$ Simplify.

$$= \frac{-6 \pm 0}{18} = -\frac{6}{18} = -\frac{1}{3}$$

The solution is $-\frac{1}{3}$.

Example 2 Solving Quadratic Equations with Complex Zeros

Hint

The standard form of a complex number is $a + bi$.

a. Solve the equation $3x^2 + 5x + 4 = 0$. Write the solutions as complex numbers in standard form.

SOLUTION Use the quadratic formula.

$$x = \frac{-b \pm \sqrt{b^2 - 4ac}}{2a}$$

$$= \frac{-5 \pm \sqrt{5^2 - 4(3)(4)}}{2(3)}$$ Substitute 3 for *a*, 5 for *b*, and 4 for *c*.

$$= \frac{-5 \pm \sqrt{-23}}{6}$$ Simplify the radicand and denominator.

$$= \frac{-5 \pm i\sqrt{23}}{6}$$ Write the negative root as an imaginary number.

$$= -\frac{5}{6} \pm \frac{\sqrt{23}}{6}i$$ Write the solutions in standard form.

The solutions are $-\frac{5}{6} + \frac{\sqrt{23}}{6}i$ and $-\frac{5}{6} - \frac{\sqrt{23}}{6}i$.

Example 1

These examples demonstrate how to solve quadratic equations with real zeros by using the quadratic formula.

Error Alert Remind students that negative signs are important and they must keep them with the number. Point out in Example 1 how −7 changed the sign in the radicand.

Additional Example 1

Solve each equation.

a. $x^2 - 3x = 4$

Solutions: $x = 4$ and $x = -1$

b. $3x^2 + 12x - 7 = 0$

The solutions are $x = -2 + \frac{\sqrt{57}}{3}$ and $x = -2 - \frac{\sqrt{57}}{3}$.

Example 2

These examples show students how to solve quadratic equations with complex zeros using the quadratic formula.

Additional Example 2a

Solve the equation $2x^2 + 5x + 8 = 0$. Write the solutions as complex numbers in standard form.

Solution: $x = -\frac{5}{4} \pm \frac{\sqrt{39}}{4}i$

The solutions are $x = -\frac{5}{4} + \frac{\sqrt{39}}{4}i$ and $x = -\frac{5}{4} - \frac{\sqrt{39}}{4}i$.

ENGLISH LEARNERS

For this lesson, explain the meaning of the word **quadratic.** Say:

"The term quadratic is derived from the Latin word quadratus which means "to make square." Also, a square has four sides and quad is a prefix meaning "four."

To derive the quadratic formula you must complete the square. Also, the leading term in a quadratic equation is squared. Both of these examples are references to the original Latin term.

Other words that contain the term quad are: quadruplet: four children born at one birth; quadrangle: a four-sided enclosure; quadrate: something that is square or approximately squared.

Connect the meaning of the term quadratic to its Latin origin as you explain how the quadratic formula is derived. Point out to students how you must "complete the square" to derive the quadratic formula.

Additional Example 2b

Solve the equation $x^2 - \frac{1}{3}x + \frac{1}{24} = 0$. Write the solutions as complex numbers in standard form.

Solution: $x = \frac{1}{6} \pm \frac{\sqrt{2}}{12}i$

The solutions are $x = \frac{1}{6} + \frac{\sqrt{2}}{12}i$ and $x = \frac{1}{6} - \frac{\sqrt{2}}{12}i$.

TEACHER TIP

Remind students of the meaning of the term i. The imaginary number i is the square root of -1.

$i = \sqrt{-1}$ and $i^2 = -1$

A complex number is written in the form of $a + bi$, where a and b are real numbers, $b \neq 0$, and i is the imaginary number.

Example 3

This example demonstrates how to solve quadratic equations using a graphing calculator.

Additional Example 3

Solve $x^2 - 7x + 10 = 0$ by using a graphing calculator.

The solutions are $x = 2$ and $x = 5$.

b. Solve the equation $x^2 - \frac{1}{2}x + \frac{1}{8} = 0$. Write the solutions as complex numbers in standard form.

SOLUTION To make the calculations simpler, clear the fractions before using the quadratic formula.

$8x^2 - 4x + 1 = 0$ — Multiply both sides of the equation by 8.

Use the quadratic formula: $x = \frac{-b \pm \sqrt{b^2 - 4ac}}{2a}$.

$= \frac{-(-4) \pm \sqrt{(-4)^2 - 4(8)(1)}}{2(8)}$ — Substitute 8 for a, -4 for b, and 1 for c.

$= \frac{4 \pm \sqrt{-16}}{16}$ — Simplify the radicand and denominator.

$= \frac{4 \pm 4i}{16}$ — Write the negative root as an imaginary number.

$= \frac{1 \pm i}{4}$ — Factor 4 out of the numerator and denominator.

$= \frac{1}{4} \pm \frac{1}{4}i$ — Write the solutions in standard form.

The solutions are $\frac{1}{4} + \frac{1}{4}i$ and $\frac{1}{4} - \frac{1}{4}i$.

Because the solutions of a quadratic equation are the zeros, or x-intercepts of the equation, a graphing calculator can be used to find the solutions of a quadratic equation when the solutions are real.

Example 3 Solving Quadratic Equations using a Graphing Calculator

Solve $2x^2 + x - 15 = 0$ by using a graphing calculator.

SOLUTION Graph the related function, $y = 2x^2 + x - 15$.

If needed, adjust the window so that the x-intercepts of the graph are displayed. Access the **Calc** function (2nd + Trace) and choose **zero.**

When asked for left and right bounds, choose points that are on either side of one of the x-intercepts. Repeat for the second intercept.

Math Reasoning

Verify Graph $y = 3x^2 + 5x + 4$. How does the graph confirm that there are no real solutions to $3x^2 + 5x + 4 = 0$?

The graph does not intersect the x-axis, so there are no zeros.

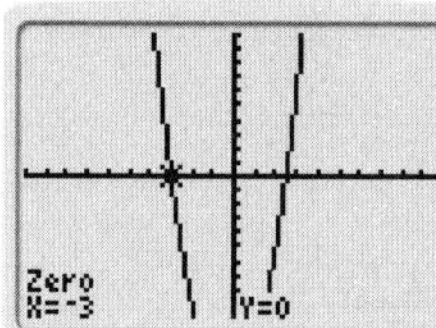

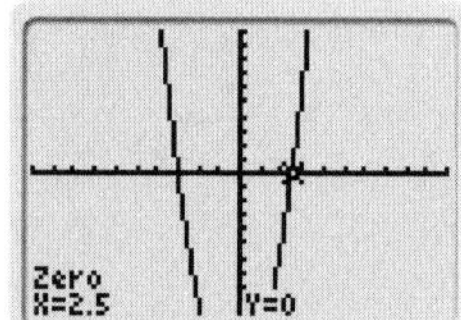

The solutions are -3 and 2.5.

INCLUSION

Students might have difficulty using the graphing calculator in Example 3 to find the solutions to the quadratic equation. Assign more advanced students to help those students that might need extra assistance. Make sure that the advanced students provide assistance only and do not work the problem for those students that need help.

Example 4 Application: Travel

Train A leaves the station at 1 p.m. and travels due north at 55 miles per hour. Train B leaves the same station at 4 p.m. and travels due east at 35 miles per hour. About how long will it take for the trains to be 500 miles apart?

SOLUTION

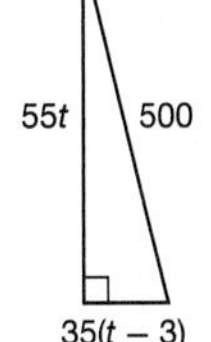

Write each distance as *rate* × *time*.
Train B is 3 hours behind Train A.
Train A: $d = rt = 55t$
Train B: $d = rt = 35(t - 3)$

$$a^2 + b^2 = c^2$$

$$(55t)^2 + (35(t-3))^2 = 500^2 \quad \text{Use the Pythagorean Theorem.}$$

$$3025t^2 + (35t - 105)^2 = 250{,}000 \quad \text{Simplify.}$$

$$3025t^2 + 1225t^2 - 7350t + 11{,}025 = 250{,}000 \quad \text{Square the binomial.}$$

$$4250t^2 - 7350t - 238{,}975 = 0 \quad \text{Combine like terms.}$$

Now use the quadratic formula.

$$t = \frac{-(-7350) \pm \sqrt{(-7350)^2 - 4(4250)(-238{,}975)}}{2(4250)}$$

$$= \frac{7350 \pm \sqrt{4{,}116{,}597{,}500}}{8500}$$

$t \approx 8.41$ and $t \approx -6.68$

Disregard the negative time. It will take about 8.41 hours for the trains to be 500 miles apart.

Check Find the distance each train traveled after 8.41 hours.

Train A: $55(8.41) = 462.55$ miles, Train B: $35(8.41 - 3) = 189.35$ miles

Use the Pythagorean Theorem: $\sqrt{462.55^2 + 189.35^2} = 499.8 \approx 500$.

Lesson Practice

Solve each equation.
(Ex 1)

a. $3x^2 - 7x + 2 = 0$ $\frac{1}{3}, 2$

b. $9x^2 + 12x + 4 = 0$ $-\frac{2}{3}$

Solve each equation. Write the solutions as complex numbers in standard form.

c. *(Ex 2)* $x^2 + 5x = -9$ $-\frac{5}{2} + \frac{\sqrt{11}}{2}i, -\frac{5}{2} - \frac{\sqrt{11}}{2}i$

d. *(Ex 2)* $-x^2 + \frac{1}{3}x - \frac{1}{9} = 0$ $\frac{1}{6} + \frac{\sqrt{3}}{6}i, \frac{1}{6} - \frac{\sqrt{3}}{6}i$

e. *(Ex 3)* Solve $8x^2 + 7x - 100 = 0$ by using a graphing calculator. $-4, 3.125$

f. *(Ex 4)* A hiker leaves a campground at 8 a.m. and heads due south at a rate of 4 miles per hour. Another hiker leaves the same campground at 9 a.m. and heads due east at a rate of 2 miles per hour. Approximately how long will it take for the hikers to be 15 miles apart? About 3.53 hours

INCLUSION

Some students might have trouble keeping track of all of the numbers in Example 4. Encourage students to write out all of their numbers when solving a complicated quadratic formula. Additional steps can be added to the solution for Example 4 to demonstrate how to keep track of all of the numbers instead of skipping some of the intermediate steps.

Example 4

In this example, students learn to use the quadratic formula to solve a real-life application.

Additional Example 4

A hiker leaves the base camp at 9 a.m. walking due north at 3 miles per hour. Two hours later, a second hiker leaves the base camp traveling due east at 5 miles per hour. Approximately how long will it take the two hikers to be 25 miles apart?
The equation is $34t^2 - 100t - 525 = 0$.
The solution is $t \approx 5.67$ hours.

Extend the Example

Have students determine about how far each hiker traveled when the hikers were 25 miles apart.
The hiker traveling at 3 miles per hour traveled 17.01 miles. The hiker traveling at 5 miles per hour traveled 18.35 miles.

Lesson Practice

Problem c

Scaffolding Remind students to put the equation in standard form before they attempt to find the solutions to the equation.

Problem d

Error Alert Some students might miss the fact that x^2 is negative. Students can multiply through by -1 before they attempt to find the solution or they must keep track of the negative sign.

Check for Understanding

The questions below help assess the concepts taught in this lesson.

"Before using the quadratic formula the equation must be written in what form?" standard form: $ax^2 + bx + c = 0$

"Is the following sentence true or false? The quadratic formula can be used to solve equations with real zeros only." false; The quadratic formula can be used to solve quadratic equations with real and complex zeros.

3 Practice

Math Conversations

Discussions to strengthen understanding

Problems 4 and 5

Remind students that the quadratic equation must be in standard form.

Problem 11

Extend the Problem

Challenge students to complete Pascal's triangle through Row 8.

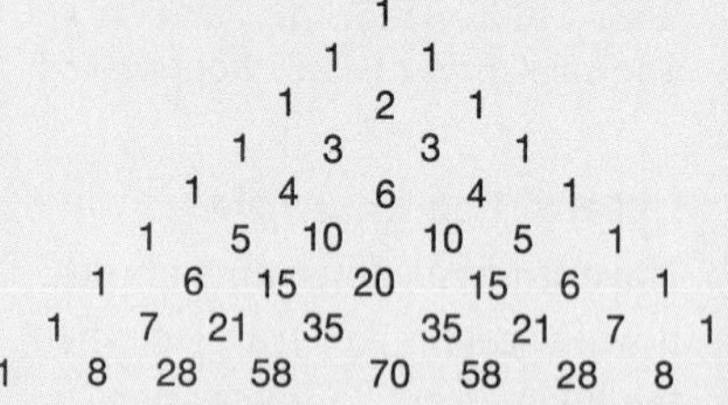

Practice Distributed and Integrated

1. (57) Secret ingredient X has a half-life of 23 hours. What portion of 360 kg will remain after 7 hours? About 291.5 kg

Use long division.

2. (38) Divide $(3x^3 + 12x^2 - 15x + 15)$ by $(3x - 9)$ $x^2 + 7x + 16 + \frac{53}{x-3}$

3. (38) Divide $(2x^3 + 14x^2 - 4x - 48)$ by $(2x + 4)$ $x^2 + 5x - 12$

Solve.

*4. (58) $x^2 = 7 + 3x$ $\frac{3}{2} \pm \frac{\sqrt{37}}{2}$

*5. (58) $x^2 = -x + 1$ $-\frac{1}{2} \pm \frac{\sqrt{5}}{2}$

Simplify.

6. (40) $2\sqrt{3}(5\sqrt{3} - 2\sqrt{6})$ $30 - 12\sqrt{2}$

7. (40) $4\sqrt{63} - 3\sqrt{28}$ $6\sqrt{7}$

8. (40) $3\sqrt{2} \cdot 2\sqrt{6} \cdot 3\sqrt{6}$ $108\sqrt{2}$

9. (55) Jordon spins a spinner with six equal-sized sections numbered 1–6. In one spin, what is the likelihood that the spinner will stop on a 1 or a 5? $\frac{1}{3}$

*10. (65) **Error Analysis** Find and correct the error a student made in solving $4x^2 - 37x + 9 = 0$.

$$x = \frac{-b \pm \sqrt{b^2 - 4ac}}{2a}$$

$$= \frac{-37 \pm \sqrt{(-37)^2 - 4(4)(9)}}{8}$$

$$= \frac{-37 \pm \sqrt{1369 - 144}}{8}$$

$$= \frac{-37 \pm \sqrt{1225}}{8} = \frac{-37 \pm 35}{8} = -\frac{1}{4} \text{ and } -9$$

The student did not take the opposite of b in the first term. The solutions are $\frac{37 \pm 35}{8} = \frac{1}{4}$ and 9 .

11. (49) List the coefficients in the 6th row of Pascal's Triangle. 1, 6, 15, 20, 15, 6, 1

12. (55) **Probability** A history test has 20 questions, 7 of which are about the Civil War. Students are asked to answer 5 of the 20 questions. What is the probability that a student randomly selecting questions will select 5 Civil War questions? $\frac{7}{5168} \approx 0.14\%$

*13. (63) **Write** Describe how to determine $\sin \frac{3\pi}{2}$ by using the unit circle.

14. (36) Find an equation of a line perpendicular to $y = \frac{1}{3}x - 4$. Possible answer: $y = -3x + 9$

15. (46) **Analyze** In what type of right triangles will the sine and cosine values of the acute angles be equal? isosceles right triangles

13. Possible answer: $\sin\theta = y$, where (x, y) is on the unit circle and the terminal side of θ passes through (x, y). The terminal side of $\frac{3\pi}{2}$ passes through $(0, -1)$. Therefore, $\sin \frac{3\pi}{2} = -1$.

Find x and y.

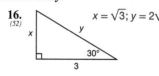

16. (52) $x = \sqrt{3}; y = 2\sqrt{3}$

x y 30° 3

17. (52) $x = 5\sqrt{3}; y = 10$

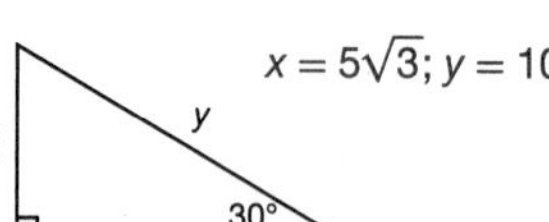

466 Saxon Algebra 2

*18. **Multi-Step** Complete parts a–d to graph a logarithmic function and use the graph to estimate a logarithm.
(64)

a. Write the equation $y = \log_2 \frac{1}{4}$ in exponential form. What value of y makes both equations true? $2^y = \frac{1}{4}$; $y = -2$

b. Writing exponential equations if needed, complete the table of values for the function $y = \log_2 x$.

x	$\frac{1}{4}$	$\frac{1}{2}$	1	2	4	8
$y = \log_2 x$	−2	−1	0	1	2	3

c. Plot the points and sketch the graph of the function. See Additional Answers.

d. Use your graph to estimate the value of $\log_2 6$. Check your estimate by evaluating the appropriate power of 2 on a calculator. $\log_2 6 \approx 2.6$; Check: $2^{2.6} \approx 6.06$

19. **Multiple Choice** Choose the letter that best represents the value of x in the equation $x^2 + 2x + 7 = 8$. **A**
(58)

A $x = -1 \pm \sqrt{2}$ B $x = -2, 0$ C $x = 2, 0$ D $x = 1 \pm \sqrt{2}$

20. **Measurement** Given that 1 strip of red ribbon = 3 inches and 1 strip of blue ribbon = 4 inches, write and graph the inequality that represents that the total number of inches must be no less than 60. $3x + 4y \geq 60$; See Additional Answers.
(39)

21. **Multi-Step** A car is sitting outside in a driveway. Consider the following statement, "If it starts raining, the car will get wet."
(Inv 1)

a. Is the converse of the statement true? Explain.

21a. No, the car could get wet by someone washing it with a hose; it doesn't have to mean it's raining.

b. Is the contrapositive true? Explain. True, if the car is outside and dry, it can't be raining.

22. **Geometry** The base of a triangle is $5\sqrt{2}$ feet, and its height is $\frac{1}{\sqrt{3}}$ feet. Find the area of the triangle. $\frac{5\sqrt{6}}{6}$ square feet
(44)

*23. **Physics** A fireworks technician wants a firework to explode 70 feet below the top of the Gateway Arch in St. Louis. The Gateway Arch has a height of 630 feet. The technician has figured the height of the firework to be modeled by $-16t^2 + 160t$, where t is the time in seconds after it is launched. The solutions of $-16t^2 + 160t = 560$ give the number of seconds it will take for the firework to reach the desired height. Solve the equation. Will the firework reach the desired height? If so, when? $5 \pm i\sqrt{10}$, The time is not a real number; the firework will never reach the desired height.
(62)

24. **Justify** Let $f(x) = 3x - 7$ and $g(x) = \frac{1}{3}x + \frac{7}{3}$.
(53)

a. Justify the claim that $f(g(x)) = x$. $f(g(x)) = 3\left(\frac{1}{3}x + \frac{7}{3}\right) - 7 = x + 7 - 7 = x$

b. Does $g(f(x)) = x$ also? Explain. Yes. $g(f(x)) = \frac{1}{3}(3x - 7) + \frac{7}{3} = x - \frac{7}{3} + \frac{7}{3} = x$

25. **Error Analysis** Find and correct the error a student made in factoring the expression below. The student tried to factor $9x^3 - 8$ as a difference of cubes and it is not because 9 is not a perfect cube. The factored expression is $(x - 7)(9x^3 - 8)$.
(61)

$$9x^4 - 63x^3 - 8x + 56$$
$$9x^3(x - 7) - 8(x - 7)$$
$$(x - 7)(9x^3 - 8)$$
$$(x - 7)(3x - 2)(6x^2 + 6x + 4)$$

Problem 23

Remind students to put the quadratic equation in standard form before they use the quadratic formula. Also, students must use care when finding the solution to this equation because the negative signs can be accidentally dropped.

INCLUSION

Some students might become frustrated when solving a multi-step problem, such as problem 18, because an error early in the problem means the entire problem is incorrect. Allow students to check individual steps of the problem with each other or with the teacher to make sure they are on track to finding the correct solution.

CHALLENGE

For problem 20, have students find the area of the triangle formed by the line and the x- and y-axes.

area = 1800 in^2

Lesson 65 467

Problem 29

Error Alert

Students should use parentheses around the $\frac{2}{3}$ exponent in order for the calculator to interpret the entry correctly.

***26.** (65) **Physical Science** The North Falls waterfalls in Silver Falls State Park in Oregon are 136 feet high. The equation $-16t^2 + 136 = 0$ gives the number of seconds it takes for a drop of water at the top of the falls to reach the pool of water below. Solve the equation by using the quadratic formula. Round to the nearest hundredth of a second. 2.92 seconds

27. (56) **Formulate** Let θ be an angle in standard position and let n be any integer. You can use the expression $\theta + n(360°)$ to indicate all the angles coterminal with θ. Write an expression for all the angles coterminal with 15°, and find 3 different ones. $15° + n(360°)$; Sample Answer: 375°, 735°, −345°

***28.** (65) **Graphing Calculator** Solve $5x^2 - 2x - 16 = 0$ by using a graphing calculator. −1.6 and 2

29. (59) **Velocity of an Electron** The velocity at which an electron orbits the nucleus of an atom is known as the Fermi-Thomas velocity and can be found using the equation $\frac{Z^{\frac{2}{3}}}{137}c$, where Z is the number of protons in the nucleus and c is the speed of light. What is the Fermi-Thomas velocity for platinum, which has 78 protons, in terms of c? Round to the nearest thousandths place. 0.133c

***30.** (64) **Analyze** Write the following equations in exponential form. What property of exponents is illustrated?

$$\log_2 1 = 0, \log_3 1 = 0, \log_{15} 1 = 0$$

$2^0 = 1$, $3^0 = 1$, $15^0 = 1$; Property: $b^0 = 1$ for all nonzero values of b.

LOOKING FORWARD 

Solving problems using the quadratic formula prepares students for

- **Lesson 78** Solving Quadratic Equations II
- **Lesson 83** Writing Quadratic Equations from Roots
- **Lesson 89** Solving Quadratic Inequalities

LESSON 66

Solving Polynomial Equations

Warm Up

1. **Vocabulary** The formula $x = \frac{-b \pm \sqrt{b^2 - 4ac}}{2a}$ is called the quadratic formula (65)
2. Factor $27cd^3 - 12cd$. $3cd(3d + 2)(3d - 2)$ (23)
3. Solve $x(x - 4) = 0$. 0 and 4 (35)
4. True or False: $x + 7$ is a factor of $x^3 + 8x^2 + x - 42$. True (61)
5. Solve $x^2 + x + 1 = 0$ by using the quadratic formula. $\frac{-1 \pm i\sqrt{3}}{2}$ (65)

New Concepts

Sometimes a polynomial equation can be solved just by factoring and using the Zero Product Property.

Hint

Recall that the **Zero Product Property** states that if $ab = 0$, then $a = 0$ or $b = 0$.

Example 1 Using Factoring to Solve Polynomial Equations

Solve each equation.

a. $2x^4 - 10x^3 - 72x^2 = 0$

SOLUTION Since one side is already equal to 0, begin by factoring the polynomial.

$2x^2(x^2 - 5x - 36) = 0$	The GCF is $2x^2$.
$2x^2(x + 4)(x - 9) = 0$	Factor the trinomial.
$2x^2 = 0$ or $x + 4 = 0$ or $x - 9 = 0$	Use the Zero Product Property.
$x = 0$ or $x = -4$ or $x = 9$	Solve each equation.

The solutions are 0, −4, and 9.

b. $4x^3 + x = 4x^2$

SOLUTION First write the equation in standard form.

$4x^3 - 4x^2 + x = 0$	Subtract $4x^2$ from each side.
$x(4x^2 - 4x + 1) = 0$	The GCF is x.
$x(2x - 1)(2x - 1) = 0$	Factor the perfect square trinomial.
$x = 0$ or $2x - 1 = 0$ or $2x - 1 = 0$	Use the Zero Product Property.
$x = 0$ or $x = \frac{1}{2}$ or $x = \frac{1}{2}$	Solve each equation.

The solutions are 0 and $\frac{1}{2}$.

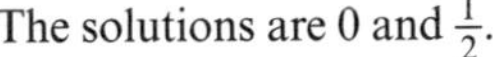

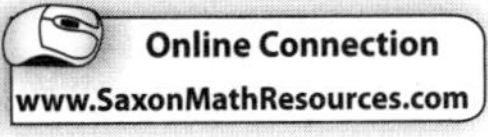

Notice in Example 1b that the solution, or root, of $\frac{1}{2}$ appears twice. This is called a double root. It has **multiplicity** 2.

MATH BACKGROUND

Students at the Algebra 2 level frequently ask: "When are we ever going to use this?" Upper-level science and engineering contain numerous real-world applications of polynomial equations including:

1. Poiseuille's equation, which relates the rate of fluid flow to the fourth power of the radius of the tube (applicable to blood flow in arteries), **2.** the power produced by a wind mill, which is proportional to the cube of the wind speed, and **3.** scientific data that has been graphed is often described by determining a best-fit polynomial equation.

Many electrical engineering problems involve not only polynomial equations, but complex variables (such as finding the current in certain alternating current circuits). In a few lessons, students will investigate complex numbers, which often result from solving polynomial equations.

LESSON 66

1 Warm Up

For problem 2, remind students to first factor out the constants and both variables.

2 New Concepts

Students solve polynomial equations by factoring, by synthetic division, by using a graphing calculator, and by combining methods.

Discuss the definition of **multiplicity**. Remind students how synthetic division works.

Explain the Rational Root Theorem and how using it with synthetic division can determine roots. Explain the Irrational Root Theorem and its relationship to the quadratic formula.

Example 1

To introduce multiplicity, ask how many roots are expected for each equation.

Additional Example 1

Solve each equation.

a. $3x^3 - 5x^2 - 2x = 0$

$-\frac{1}{3}$, 0, and 2

b. $x^3 - 12x = x^2$

−3, 0, and 4

LESSON RESOURCES

Student Edition Practice Workbook 66
Reteaching Master 66
Adaptations Master 66
Challenge and Enrichment Master C66

Example 2

Students will use factoring to determine the multiplicity of roots.

Additional Example 2

Find the roots of each equation. Give the multiplicity of each root.

a. $x^5 - 12x^4 + 36x^3 = 0$

0 is a root with multiplicity 3; 6 is a root with multiplicity 2.

b. $x^4 = 8x^2 - 6$

2 is a root with multiplicity 2; −2 is a root with multiplicity 2.

Extend the Example

Explain that students will see how multiplicity is related to the shape of the graph of the function.

Have students graph these four equations (the two examples in their books and the two additional examples above) using a graphing calculator. Challenge students to draw a relationship between the multiplicity of a root and what happens on the graph.

Students should see that the graph crosses the x-axis if the root's multiplicity is odd, and just touches the axis and reverses direction if the multiplicity is even.

Multiplicity of Roots
The multiplicity of a root r of a polynomial equation is the number of times $x - r$ is a factor of the polynomial.

Example 2 Identifying Multiplicity

Find the roots of each equation. Give the multiplicity of each root.

a. $x^5 + 8x^4 + 16x^3 = 0$

SOLUTION Factor the polynomial to use the Zero Product Property.

$x^3(x^2 + 8x + 16) = 0$ — The GCF is x^3.

$x^3(x + 4)(x + 4) = 0$ — Factor the perfect square trinomial.

$x^3 = 0$ or $x + 4 = 0$ or $x + 4 = 0$ — Use the Zero Product Property.

$x = 0$ or $x = -4$ or $x = -4$ — Solve each equation.

The roots are 0 and −4. Because $x^3 = x \cdot x \cdot x$, x is a factor 3 times, so the root of 0 has a multiplicity 3. Because $x + 4$ is a factor 2 times, the root of −4 has multiplicity 2.

b. $x^4 = 2x^2 - 1$

SOLUTION First write the equation in standard form: $x^4 - 2x^2 + 1 = 0$.

$(x^2 - 1)(x^2 - 1) = 0$ — Factor the perfect square trinomial.

$(x + 1)(x - 1)(x + 1)(x - 1) = 0$ — Factor the differences of squares.

$x + 1 = 0$ or $x - 1 = 0$ or $x + 1 = 0$ or $x - 1 = 0$

$x = -1$ or $x = 1$ or $x = -1$ or $x = 1$

The roots are −1 and 1. Because both $(x + 1)$ and $(x - 1)$ occur twice, each root has multiplicity 2.

A polynomial equation like $x^3 - 2x^2 - 11x + 12 = 0$, where the degree of the polynomial is greater than 2, can be factored by using synthetic division if one of the factors is a linear binomial and is already known. When none of the factors are already given, begin factoring the polynomial by using the Rational Root Theorem.

Math Reasoning

Analyze What can you do to use the Rational Root Theorem to find the possible rational roots of $\frac{1}{5}x^3 + 2x^2 - x + 2 = 0$?

Multiply both sides of the equation by 5.

The Rational Root Theorem
If a polynomial $P(x)$ has integer coefficients, then every rational root of $P(x) = 0$ can be written in the form $\frac{p}{q}$, where p is a factor of the constant term and q is a factor of the leading coefficient of $P(x)$.

The Irrational Root Theorem states that irrational roots come in pairs.

The Irrational Root Theorem
If a polynomial $P(x)$ has rational coefficients, and $a + b\sqrt{c}$ is a root of $P(x) = 0$, where a and b are rational and $\sqrt{c}$ is irrational, then $a - b\sqrt{c}$ is also a root of $P(x) = 0$.

ALTERNATE METHOD FOR EXAMPLE 2

If students don't immediately see that $x^2 + 8x + 16$ is a perfect square, they can use the quadratic formula. Once they solve for x, they can determine the multiplicity of the root.

Using the quadratic formula yields the following results:

$$x = \frac{-b \pm \sqrt{b^2 - 4ac}}{2a}$$

$$x = \frac{-8 + \sqrt{8^2 - 4(1)(16)}}{2(1)}$$

$$\text{or } x = \frac{-8 - \sqrt{8^2 - 4(1)(16)}}{2(1)}$$

$$x = \frac{-8 + \sqrt{64 - 64}}{2} \text{ or } x = \frac{-8 - \sqrt{64 - 64}}{2}$$

$$x = \frac{-8 + \sqrt{0}}{2} \text{ or } x = \frac{-8 - \sqrt{0}}{2}$$

$$x = \frac{-8}{2} \text{ or } x = \frac{-8}{2}$$

$$x = -4 \text{ or } x = -4$$

Example 3 Identifying All Real Roots of a Polynomial Equation

a. Identify all the real roots of $x^3 - 2x^2 - 11x + 12 = 0$.

Hint

Remember that $x - r$ is a factor if $P(r) = 0$.

SOLUTION By the Rational Root Theorem the possible rational roots are: $\frac{\pm1, \pm2, \pm3, \pm4, \pm6, \pm12}{\pm1} = \pm1, \pm2, \pm3, \pm4, \pm6, \pm12$. Use synthetic division to test roots, r, until a factor, $x - r$, is found.

$$\begin{array}{r|rrrr} 1 & 1 & -2 & -11 & 12 \\ & & 1 & -1 & -12 \\ \hline & 1 & -1 & -12 & 0 \end{array}$$

The first try works. By the Factor Theorem $P(1) = 0$, so $x - 1$ is a factor.

The quotient is also a factor, so the polynomial can be written as $(x - 1)(x^2 - x - 12)$, which factors into $(x - 1)(x - 4)(x + 3)$.

The equation can be written as $(x - 1)(x + 3)(x - 4) = 0$.

Using the Zero Product Property, the roots are 1, −3, and 4.

b. Identify all the real roots of $3x^4 - 5x^3 - 29x^2 + 3x + 4 = 0$.

SOLUTION By the Rational Root Theorem the possible rational roots are: $\frac{\pm1, \pm2, \pm4}{\pm1, \pm3} = \pm1, \pm\frac{1}{3}, \pm2, \pm\frac{2}{3}, \pm4, \pm\frac{4}{3}$. Test roots. Begin with integers.

Organize the work in a synthetic substitution table.

The remainder is 0 for $P(4)$, so $x - 4$ is a factor.

$3x^3 + 7x^2 - x - 1$ is the other factor.

Possible root	3	−5	−29	3	4
1	3	−2	−31	−28	−24
2	3	1	−27	−51	−98
4	3	7	−1	−1	0

The possible rational roots for $3x^3 + 7x^2 - x - 1 = 0$ are: $\frac{\pm1}{\pm1, \pm3} = \pm1, \pm\frac{1}{3}$.

$$\begin{array}{r|rrrr} -\frac{1}{3} & 3 & 7 & -1 & -1 \\ & & -1 & -2 & 1 \\ \hline & 3 & 6 & -3 & 0 \end{array}$$

$x + \frac{1}{3}$ is a factor. $3x^2 + 6x - 3$ is the other factor. The trinomial factors into $3(x^2 + 2x - 1)$. Solve $x^2 + 2x - 1 = 0$ by using the quadratic formula.

$$x = \frac{-2 \pm \sqrt{2^2 - 4(1)(-1)}}{2(1)} = \frac{-2 \pm \sqrt{8}}{2} = \frac{-2 \pm 2\sqrt{2}}{2} = -1 \pm \sqrt{2}$$

The polynomial equation is

$$(x - 4)\left(x + \frac{1}{3}\right)\left(x - (-1 + \sqrt{2})\right)\left(x - (-1 - \sqrt{2})\right) = 0.$$

The real roots are 4, $-\frac{1}{3}$, $-1 + \sqrt{2}$, and $-1 - \sqrt{2}$.

The x-intercepts of a polynomial function are real roots of the related equation. Therefore, a graph can be used to help find the roots of a polynomial equation.

ALTERNATE METHOD FOR EXAMPLE 3a

If students don't immediately see the factors for the quadratic expression $x^2 - x - 12$, they can use the quadratic formula to solve the related equation.

Example 3

Note that this example follows the Rational and Irrational Root Theorems. Both rational and irrational numbers are *real* numbers.

The quadratic formula can sometimes yield complex numbers (simplifying complex expressions will be covered in Lesson 69). Those situations are not addressed by these theorems.

If students understand the quadratic formula, the Irrational Root Theorem makes sense. The link should be that both have a number ± a square root. Students should be reminded that this is something they already know, but now it's been formally stated.

Error Alert Students may have difficulty because of dropped negative signs (or adding them where they don't belong) in this process. Point out that constants and coefficients have both positive and negative factors.

Also, if students identify a root, r, through synthetic division, they need to recognize that this means $x = r$, so the factor of the equation is actually $(x - r)$.

Additional Example 3

a. Identify all the real roots of $x^3 - 2x^2 - 5x + 6 = 0$. −2, 1, and 3

b. Identify all the real roots of $4x^4 - 29x^3 + 39x^2 + 32x - 10 = 0$ 5, $\frac{1}{4}$, $1 + \sqrt{3}$, $1 - \sqrt{3}$

Example 4

Remind students that the real roots of the equation are the x-intercepts.

Additional Example 4

Solve $x^3 - x^2 - 13x - 3 = 0$ by using a graphing calculator. $-3, 2 + \sqrt{5}, 2 - \sqrt{5}$

Example 5

Remind students to write out the given information. Identify the quantity that will be represented by the variable. Then write the other information in terms of that quantity.

Additional Example 5

A swimming pool is to be designed so that its length is 10 feet greater than its width and its depth is 8 feet less than its width. What must the width be if the volume must be 1056 cubic feet? 12 ft

TEACHER TIP

For additional example 5, the variable, w, will represent the width. Then the length and depth can be written in terms of w.

When using the Rational Root Theorem, students should realize that the width must be greater than 8 for the depth to be positive. So it's not necessary to do synthetic division with possible solutions (determined using the Rational Root Theorem) that are less than 8.

Example 4 Using a Calculator to Solve Polynomial Equations

Solve $x^3 + 5x^2 - 9x - 10 = 0$ by using a graphing calculator.

SOLUTION Graph the related function, $y = x^3 + 5x^2 - 9x - 10$. Use the **Calc** command to find the x-intercepts.

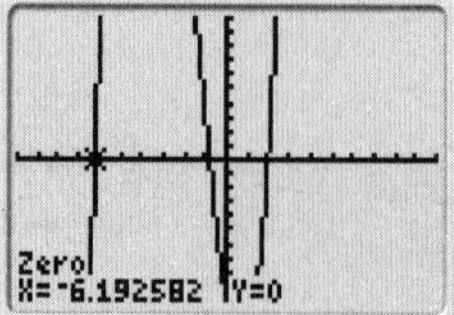

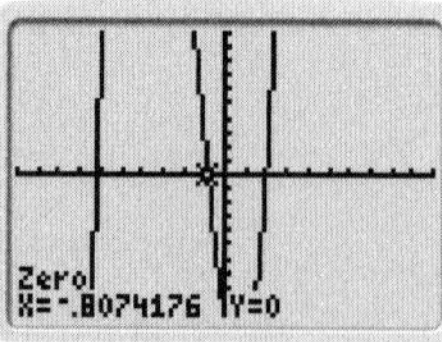

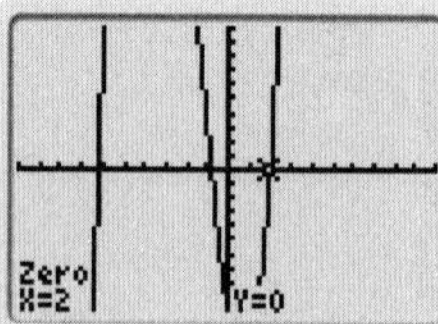

Math Reasoning

Verify Show that the Rational Root Theorem gives 2 as a possible root.

$p = -10$ and $q = 1$, so the factors of -10 are possible roots.

Since 2 is a rational root, use synthetic division with $r = 2$.

2	1	5	−9	−10
		2	14	10
	1	7	5	0

Solve $x^2 + 7x + 5 = 0$: $x = \frac{-7 \pm \sqrt{7^2 - 4(1)(5)}}{2(1)} = \frac{-7 \pm \sqrt{29}}{2}$.

The roots are 2, $\frac{-7 + \sqrt{29}}{2}$, and $\frac{-7 - \sqrt{29}}{2}$. Notice that the x-intercepts given by the graphing calculator above are estimates of the exact values of the irrational roots.

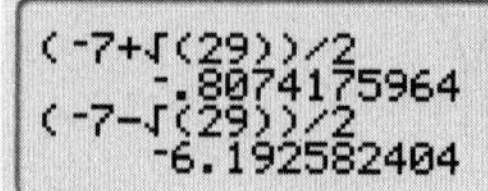

Example 5 Application: Packaging

A box is to be designed so that the height is 6 inches greater than the length and the width is 3 inches less than the length. What must the length be if the volume has to be 40 cubic inches?

SOLUTION

1. **Understand** The volume of a box, or rectangular prism, is the product of the length, width, and height: $V = lwh$.

2. **Plan** Write expressions for each dimension. If x represents the length, then $x + 6$ represents the height and $x - 3$ represents the width.

$$40 = x(x - 3)(x + 6)$$

Hint

Use the Rational Root Theorem to determine all the possible rational roots.

3. **Solve** $40 = x^3 + 3x^2 - 18x$

$$0 = x^3 + 3x^2 - 18x - 40$$

4	1	3	−18	−40
		4	28	40
	1	7	10	0

The polynomial factors into$(x - 4)(x^2 + 7x + 10)$, which factors into $(x - 4)(x + 2)(x + 5)$. The roots are 4, −2, and −5. Since the length must be positive, disregard the negative roots.

The length is 4 inches.

4. **Check** If the length is 4 inches, the height is 10 inches, and the width is 1 inch. Find the volume: $V = lwh = 4(1)(10) = 40$.

INCLUSION

Allow students to use a graphing calculator to find the first solution using their list of possible rational roots. Once they have found one solution with the graphing calculator, have them verify it using synthetic division. Then, completely solve the equation using the quadratic formula or factoring.

Lesson Practice

Solve each equation.

(Ex 1)

a. $x^4 - 3x^3 - 28x^2 = 0$ 0, 7, and −4

b. $18x^3 - 18x = 0$ 0, −1, and 1

Find the roots of each equation. Give the multiplicity of each root.

(Ex 2)

c. $2x^3 - 32x^2 + 128x = 0$

d. $x^6 + 12x^5 + 27x^4 = 0$ 0 is a root with multiplicity of 4 and −3 and −9 are roots, each with a multiplicity of 1

e. Identify all the real roots of $x^3 - 5x^2 - x + 5 = 0$. −1, 1, and 5

(Ex 3)

f. Identify all the real roots of $x^3 + 4x^2 - 5x - 14 = 0$.

(Ex 3)

g. Solve $x^3 + 2x^2 - 45x - 18 = 0$ by using a graphing calculator.

(Ex 4)

h. A box is to be designed so that the height is 3 inches greater than the length and the width is 2 inches less than the length. What must the length be if the volume has to be 18 cubic inches? 3 inches

(Ex 5)

c. 0 is a root with multiplicity of 1 and 8 is a root with multiplicity of 2

f. $2, -3 + \sqrt{2}, -3 - \sqrt{2}$

g. $6, -4 + \sqrt{13}, -4 - \sqrt{13}$

Practice Distributed and Integrated

Simplify each expression.

1. (59) $\dfrac{81^{\frac{2}{4}}}{81^{\frac{3}{4}}}$ $\frac{1}{3}$

2. (37) $\dfrac{p - 4px}{p}$ $1 - 4x$

3. (37) $\dfrac{4a}{a + 4} + \dfrac{a + 2}{2a}$ $\dfrac{9a^2 + 6a + 8}{2a(a + 4)}$

4. (37) $\dfrac{x}{x + 2} + \dfrac{3 + x}{x^2 + 4x + 4}$

5. (59) $(4^6)^{\frac{1}{3}}$ 16

6. (59) $343^{\frac{1}{3}} \cdot 343^{\frac{1}{3}}$ 49

***7.** (60) There are 7 cherries and 3 grapes in a bag. What is the probability of selecting 2 grapes at random without replacement? $\frac{1}{15}$

4. $\dfrac{x^2 + 3x + 3}{(x + 2)^2}$

8. (36) Find the equation of the line that passes through (2, −3) and is parallel to $y = -\frac{3}{8}x + 2$. $y = -\frac{3}{8}x - \frac{9}{4}$

***9.** (66) **(Packaging)** A new food product is to be sold in cylindrical cans. The designer wants the height of the can to be 6 inches greater than the radius. The manager wants the can to have a volume of about 125 in^3.

a. Write a polynomial equation in standard form that can be used to find the radius. Leave in terms of π. Hint: The formula for the volume of a cylinder is $V = \pi r^2 h$. $\pi r^3 + 6\pi r^2 - 125 = 0$

b. Find the approximate radius that should be used for the can by using a graphing calculator. Round the radius to the nearest tenth. 2.2 inches

10. (50) Find an equation for the inverse of $y = 7x^2 + 21$ for $x \geq 0$. Identify the domain and range of the inverse function. $y = \sqrt{\frac{x - 21}{7}}$; domain: $x \geq 21$; range: $y \geq 0$

11. (22) **Multiple Choice** $f(x) = x - 5$ is an example of a: A

A continuous function

B discrete function

C discontinuous function

D both B and C

ENGLISH LEARNERS

The words **rational** and **irrational** sound very similar, particularly if said quickly. A poster would be helpful for English language learners. The poster should have the titles 'Rational Numbers' and 'Irrational Numbers' and should give the definition of each, along with several examples. Students could make the posters, with several being selected to hang around the classroom.

As the Rational Root Theorem and Irrational Root Theorem are presented, refer (physically as well as verbally) to the posters.

Lesson Practice

Problem e

Scaffolding Use the Rational Root Theorem to identify possible roots of the equation. Then use synthetic division to determine an actual root. Once one root has been found, a new, lower-order polynomial equation can be written to find the next root. If possible, factor the equation or use the quadratic formula. If not, use the Rational Root Theorem and synthetic division again.

Check for Understanding

The question below helps assess the concepts taught in this lesson.

"How is the Zero Product Property used to solve polynomial equations?" Sample: The factors of the equation are set equal to zero and solved. The solutions are also solutions of the polynomial equation.

"What does the multiplicity of a root tell you?" Sample: The number of times that factor is repeated.

3 Practice

Math Conversations

Discussions to strengthen understanding

Problem 3

Guide the students by asking them the following questions.

"What is the common denominator?" $2a(a + 4)$

"What will you multiply the first fraction by?" $\frac{2a}{2a}$

"What will you multiply the second fraction by?" $\frac{a + 4}{a + 4}$

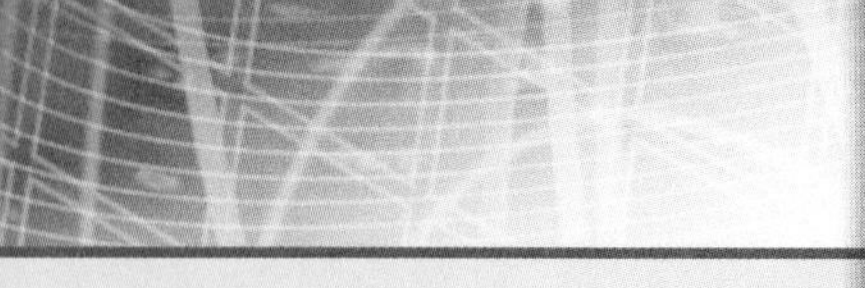

Problem 16

Error Alert Students might write the lengths of the sides as $(24 + x)$ and $(36 + x)$, instead of $(24 + 2x)$ and $(36 + 2x)$.

Problem 17

Extend the Problem

"By hand, plot the function, graphing at least 5 points."

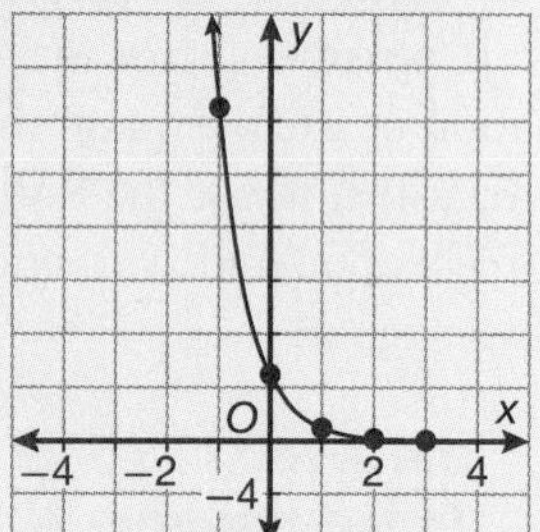

"Does your graph show that the function is decreasing (or increasing) as you stated in your answer?" Answers will vary.

12. **Write** Explain why it is necessary to add the constant term $\left(\frac{b}{2}\right)^2$ to both sides of the equation when using the method of completing the square to solve a quadratic equation. *(58)*

12. Sample: $\left(\frac{b}{2}\right)^2$ must be added to both sides of the equation to keep the equation equivalent to the original equation.

*13. **Graphing Calculator** Calculate the binomial probability, to the nearest hundredth of a percent, of 8 successes out of 50 trials, if the probability of success for each trial is 0.17. 14.95% *(Inv 5)*

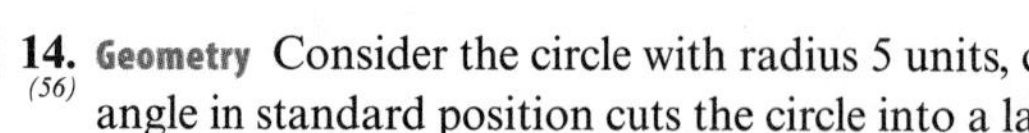

14. **Geometry** Consider the circle with radius 5 units, centered at the origin. A 270° angle in standard position cuts the circle into a larger and a smaller sector. Find the area of the larger sector. $\frac{75}{4}\pi \approx 58.9$ square units *(56)*

*15. **Error Analysis** A student converted the logarithmic equation $\log_2 64 = x$ to exponential form by writing $x^2 = 64$. What is the error? Write the correct exponential equation. Possible answer: The student wrote the logarithm as the base instead of writing the logarithm as the exponent. Correct equation: $2^x = 64$ *(64)*

*16. **Multi-Step** A 24 in. by 36 in. photo is framed and the total area of the photo and the frame is 1200 in^2. *(65)*

a. Write a quadratic expression in standard form to represent the situation. $4x^2 + 120x - 336 = 0$ or $x^2 + 30x - 84 = 0$

b. Find the width of the frame to the nearest hundredth of an inch. 2.58 inches

17. **Formulate** Write the equation of an exponential function whose graph passes through the points (0, 5) and (−2, 125). Determine whether the function is increasing or decreasing. $y = 5 \cdot \left(\frac{1}{5}\right)^x$ or $y = \left(\frac{1}{5}\right)^{x-1}$; decreasing *(57)*

*18. **Analyze** If using the quadratic formula to solve $16 = -3x^2$, what would be the values of a, b, and c? Either $a = 3, b = 0, c = 16$, or $a = -3, b = 0, c = -16$ *(65)*

*19. **Tires** The diameter of a certain tire is 24 inches. Through how many degrees does the tire rotate when the automobile travels 5 feet? Give your answer to the nearest degree. 286° *(63)*

20. **Population** In 2006, the U.S. Census Bureau estimated there were 36,457,549 people living in California and 299,398,484 living in the United States. *(55)*

a. Estimate the probability that a person randomly selected in the United States lives in California. About 12%

b. Estimate the odds in favor that a person randomly selected in the United States lives in California. About 3 to 22

21. **Probability** A student taking a test has enough time to solve 2 out of the 5 equations shown. *(62)*

$x^2 + 1 = 0, \quad x^2 + 4 = 0, \quad x^2 - 25 = 0, \quad x^2 - 16 = 0, \quad x^2 + 9 = 0$

If she chooses equations randomly, what is the probability that both equations have imaginary solutions? 30%

Use trigonometric ratios to solve for each of the variables.

22. $\cos 30° = \frac{\sqrt{3}}{2}$ and $\cos 30° = \frac{y}{12}$ *(52)* $y = 10.392$

23. $\sin 30° = \frac{1}{2}$ and $\sin 30° = \frac{x}{12}$ *(52)* $x = 6$

CHALLENGE

Determine the roots of $x^5 - 3x^4 + 3x^3 = x^2$. Use the multiplicity of each root to predict how the graph will look. Graph the function using a graphing calculator. Does it do what you predicted? If not, carefully examine the graph from $-1 \le x \le 1$. $x = 0$, multiplicity 2; $x = 1$, multiplicity 3

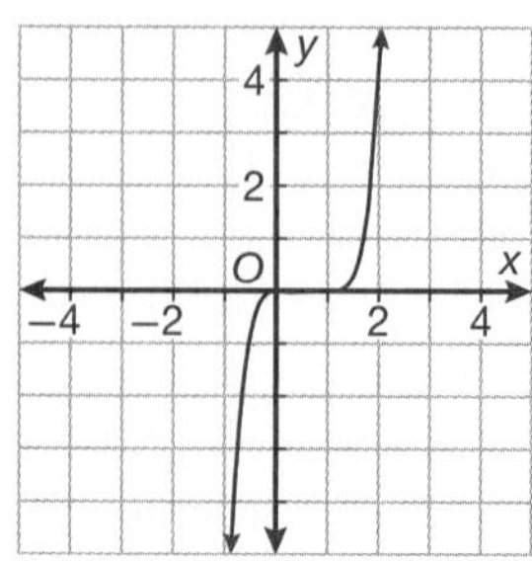

24. **Multi-Step** A student creates a chart classifying (60) his books by subject and cover.

a. Are the events math textbook or paperback textbook mutually exclusive or inclusive? Explain why. See Additional Answers.

b. Find the probability that four books, selected randomly with replacement, are math or paperback. Round to the thousandths place. 0.063

	Cover	
Subject	**Hardcover**	**Paperback**
Math	7	3
Sciences	23	14
Social Sciences	6	16
History	1	4

25. (59) **Music** Frets are small metal bars placed across the neck of a guitar so that the guitar can produce notes of a specific scale. To find the distance a fret should be placed from the bridge, multiply the length of the string by $2^{-\frac{n}{12}}$, where n is the number of notes higher than the string's root note. Where should a fret be placed on the low E string to produce a note that is 5 notes higher, if the length of the string is 64 cm, rounded to the nearest hundredths place? 47.95 cm

***26.** (61) **Generalize** Tell how to factor by grouping. See Additional Answers.

27. (49) **Probability** Find the probability of getting at least 1 tail if a coin is tossed 4 times. $\frac{15}{16}$

***28.** (66) **Multiple Choice** Which is not a possible rational root of $2x^3 + 2x^2 - 21x - 27 = 0$? C

A -3 **B** -1 **C** $\frac{2}{3}$ **D** $\frac{9}{2}$

29. (53) Let $f(x) = 8x - 6$ and $g(x) = 4x^2 + 1$. Evaluate the composition $(f \circ g)(-2)$ using two different methods. See Additional Answers.

***30.** (64) **Write** Explain why $\log_0 5$ and $\log_1 5$ do not exist. Possible answer: $\log_0 5$ does not exist because there is no power of 0 that equals 5. $\log_1 5$ does not exist because there is no power of 1 that equals 5.

Problem 25

Error Alert

Students may use a calculator to find the solution for this problem. Make sure students enter the exponent correctly by using parentheses for grouping where appropriate.

Problem 28

Extend the Problem

Have students test the possible roots -3, -1, and $\frac{9}{2}$ to determine if they are solutions to the cubic equation. -3 is a solution

LOOKING FORWARD

Solving polynomial equations prepares students for

- **Lesson 76** Finding Polynomial Roots I
- **Lesson 85** Finding Polynomial Roots II
- **Lesson 101** Making Graphs of Polynomial Functions
- **Lesson 106** Using the Fundamental Theorem of Algebra

LESSON
67

1 Warm Up

After students answer problem 1, review the definition of *radian*. Draw a circle. Start at "3 o'clock" and have students call out the radians and the angles in degrees.

2 New Concepts

In this lesson, students evaluate and define inverse trigonometric functions, then use them to solve equations and problems.

Example 1

Students find all the values of an inverse trigonometric expression.

Additional Example 1

Describe all the values of $\tan^{-1}(-\sqrt{3})$. $\frac{2\pi}{3} + 2\pi n$ and $\frac{5\pi}{3} + 2\pi n$, where n is an integer

Error Alert Emphasize the difference between $\sin x$ and $\sin^{-1} x$. In problem situations, the first is a length or distance; the second is the measure of an angle in degrees or radians.

LESSON
67 Finding Inverse Trigonometric Functions

Warm Up

1. **Vocabulary** A circle with a radius of 1 unit is called a unit circle.
(63)

2. What is $\sin 30°$? $\frac{1}{2}$
(63)

3. What is $\cos \frac{\pi}{4}$? $\frac{\sqrt{2}}{2}$
(63)

New Concepts

Evaluation of trigonometric functions for given angle measures was explained in Lesson 46. Angle measures that have given trigonometric function values can be found by using **inverse trigonometric relations.**

If a function value is:	Then one of the inverse relation values is:
$\sin \theta = a$	$\sin^{-1} a = \theta$
$\cos \theta = a$	$\cos^{-1} a = \theta$
$\tan \theta = a$	$\tan^{-1} a = \theta$

Reading Math

The symbol $\sin^{-1}$ represents the inverse sine relation, NOT a reciprocal. $\sin^{-1} a \neq \frac{1}{\sin a}$.

The inverses of the trigonometric functions are not functions themselves because there are many values of θ for a particular value of a. For example, consider $\cos^{-1}\frac{\sqrt{2}}{2}$. Angles with measures of $\frac{\pi}{4}$ and $\frac{7\pi}{4}$ radians have the cosine value $\frac{\sqrt{2}}{2}$. So do all angles that are coterminal with these angles.

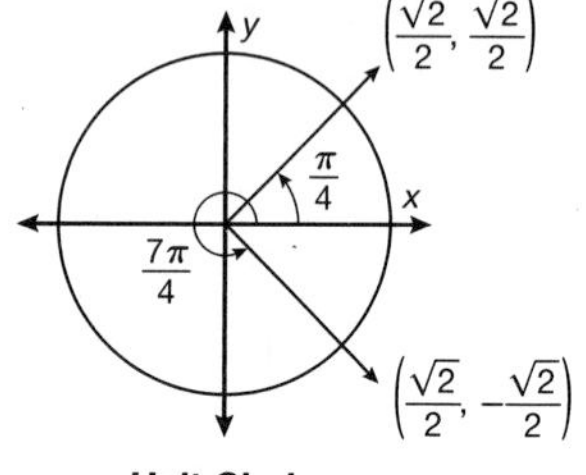

Unit Circle

Example 1 **Finding Trigonometric Inverses**

Describe all the values of $\sin^{-1}\frac{\sqrt{3}}{2}$.

Step 1: Find the values of θ between 0 and 2π radians for which $\sin \theta$ is equal to $\frac{\sqrt{3}}{2}$.

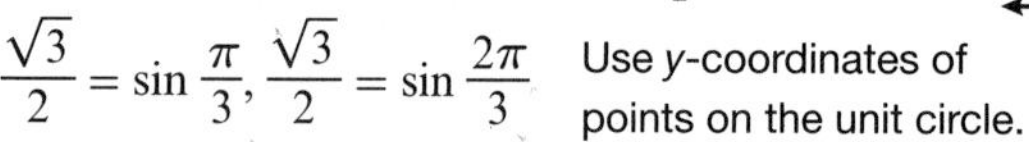

$\frac{\sqrt{3}}{2} = \sin\frac{\pi}{3}, \frac{\sqrt{3}}{2} = \sin\frac{2\pi}{3}$ Use y-coordinates of points on the unit circle.

Step 2: Describe the measures of all angles that are coterminal with $\frac{\pi}{3}$ and $\frac{2\pi}{3}$.

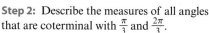

All the values of $\sin^{-1}\frac{\sqrt{3}}{2}$ are given by $\frac{\pi}{3} + (2\pi)n$ and $\frac{2\pi}{3} + (2\pi)n$, where n is an integer. Add integer multiples of 2π radians.

Hint

Substitute positive and negative integers for n in the expressions $\frac{\pi}{3} + 2\pi n$ and $\frac{2\pi}{3} + 2\pi n$. Evaluate the sine of each result.

To define inverse trigonometric functions, it is necessary to restrict the domains of the trigonometric functions. The trigonometric functions that a calculator uses have restricted domains and will give only one value in the range that you will need to generalize to find all the possible values.

Online Connection
www.SaxonMathResources.com

LESSON RESOURCES

Student Edition Practice Workbook 67
Reteaching Master 67
Adaptations Master 67
Challenge and Enrichment Masters C67, E67

MATH BACKGROUND

When a function is described by an equation in the variables x and y, the inverse of the function can be found by interchanging x and y. So, the inverse of the function described by $\{(x, y) : y = \sin x\}$ is $\{(x, y) : x = \sin y\}$. Graphing $x = \sin y$ will immediately show that this is a relation and not a function. To create an inverse sine function it is necessary to restrict the domain of the sine function to a suitable interval of π. By definition the range of the inverse sine function is $-\frac{\pi}{2} \leq x \leq \frac{\pi}{2}$. The ranges for the other inverse trigonometric functions are restricted in a similar manner.

There are a variety of common notations for the inverse trigonometric functions. For example, the inverse sine function, also called the arcsine function, can be written as $\sin^{-1}\theta$, arcsin θ, or asin θ.

$\text{Sin}\,\theta = \sin\theta$ for $\left\{\theta \mid -\frac{\pi}{2} \le \theta \le \frac{\pi}{2}\right\}$ — θ can terminate on the y-axis, the positive x-axis, or in Quadrant I or IV.

$\text{Cos}\,\theta = \cos\theta$ for $\{\theta \mid 0 \le \theta \le \pi\}$ — θ can terminate on the x-axis, the positive y-axis, or in Quadrant I or II.

$\text{Tan}\,\theta = \tan\theta$ for $\left\{\theta \mid -\frac{\pi}{2} < \theta < \frac{\pi}{2}\right\}$ — θ can terminate on the positive x-axis, or in Quadrant I or IV.

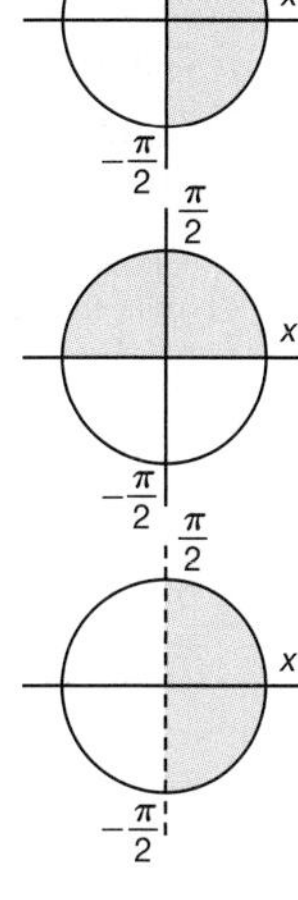

Sin θ, Cos θ, and Tan θ can be used to define the inverse trigonometric functions. For each value of a in the domain of any inverse trigonometric function, there is one and only one value of θ in the range.

Inverse Trigonometric Functions

Words	Symbol	Domain	Range
The **inverse sine function** is $\text{Sin}^{-1}a = \theta$, where $\text{Sin}\,\theta = a$.	$\text{Sin}^{-1}a$	$\{a \mid -1 \le a \le 1\}$	$\left\{\theta \mid -\frac{\pi}{2} \le \theta \le \frac{\pi}{2}\right\}$ $\{\theta \mid -90° \le \theta \le 90°\}$
The **inverse cosine function** is $\text{Cos}^{-1}a = \theta$, where $\text{Cos}\,\theta = a$.	$\text{Cos}^{-1}a$	$\{a \mid -1 \le a \le 1\}$	$\{\theta \mid 0 \le \theta \le \pi\}$ $\{\theta \mid 0° \le \theta \le 180°\}$
The **inverse tangent function** is $\text{Tan}^{-1}a = \theta$, where $\text{Tan}\,\theta = a$.	$\text{Tan}^{-1}a$	$\{a \mid -\infty < a < \infty\}$	$\left\{\theta \mid -\frac{\pi}{2} < \theta < \frac{\pi}{2}\right\}$ $\{\theta \mid -90° < \theta < 90°\}$

Reading Math

The inverse trigonometric functions are also called the arcsine, arccosine, and arctangent functions.

Example 2 Evaluating Inverse Trigonometric Functions

Find each inverse trigonometric function value that exists. Give answer in both radians and degrees.

a. $\text{Tan}^{-1}(-1)$

SOLUTION

Use the unit circle.

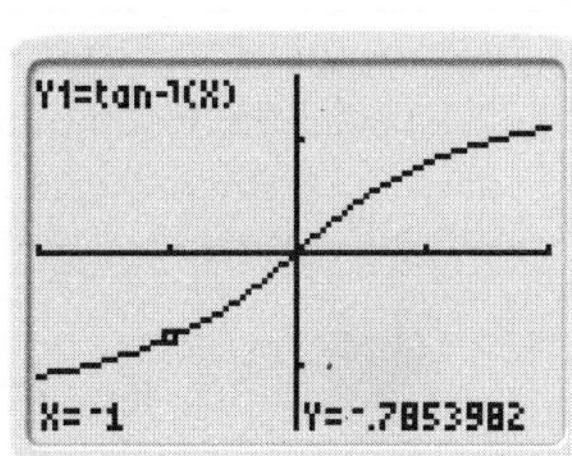

$-1 = \text{Tan}\left(-\frac{\pi}{4}\right)$ — $-\frac{\pi}{4}$ is the angle measure between $-\frac{\pi}{2}$ and $\frac{\pi}{2}$ whose tangent is -1.

$\text{Tan}^{-1}(-1) = \left(-\frac{\pi}{4}\right)$, or $\text{Tan}^{-1}(-1) = -45°$

Hint

$\text{Tan}\,\theta = \frac{y}{x}$

$\text{Tan}\left(-\frac{\pi}{4}\right) = -\frac{\frac{\sqrt{2}}{2}}{\frac{\sqrt{2}}{2}} = -1$

b. $\text{Cos}^{-1}\,2$

SOLUTION

The domain of the inverse cosine function is $\{a \mid -1 \le a \le 1\}$. Because 2 is not in this domain, $\text{Cos}^{-1}\,2$ does not exist.

TEACHER TIP

Discuss the use of the capital letter to indicate trigonometric functions with restricted domains; therefore, the inverse trigonometric function is indicated by a capital letter.

Put this diagram on the board to help students follow the discussion on restricted domains and ranges.

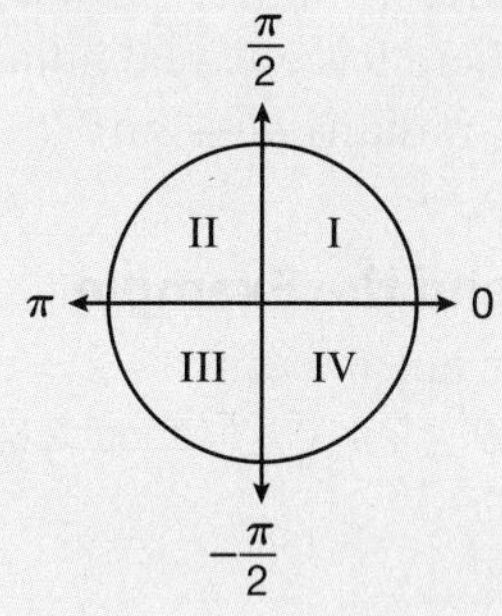

Example 2

Students evaluate inverse trigonometric functions.

Additional Example 2

Find each inverse trigonometric function value that exists. Give answers in radians and degrees.

a. $\text{Sin}^{-1}\frac{\sqrt{3}}{2}$ $\frac{\pi}{3}$, 60°

b. $\text{Cos}^{-1}\left(-\frac{1}{2}\right)$ $\frac{2\pi}{3}$, 120°

Extend the Example

Find each of the following values.

a. $\text{Cos}^{-1}(\sin 30°)$ $\frac{\pi}{3}$, 60°

b. $\text{Sin}(\text{Tan}^{-1}1)$ $\frac{\sqrt{2}}{2}$

ALTERNATE METHOD FOR EXAMPLE 2

Have students graph $y = \text{Tan}^{-1}x$ and use the trace function to find y when $x = -1$. -0.785398 Point out that this value is in radians. Have students multiply by $\frac{180}{\pi}$ to convert to degrees. $-45°$

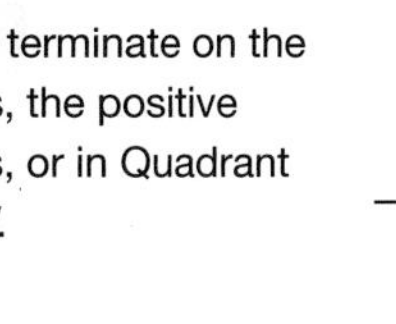

Example 3

Students use inverse trigonometric functions to solve equations.

Additional Example 3

a. Solve $2\cos\theta - 1 = 0$, for $0° \le \theta \le 360°$. 60°, 300°

b. Solve $3\tan\theta + 3 = 0$, for $0° \le \theta \le 360°$. 135°, 315°

c. Solve $\sqrt{3}\tan\theta + 3 = 0$, where θ is any real number of radians. $\frac{2\pi}{3} + \pi n$

Extend the Example

Solve $\tan^2\theta + \tan\theta - 2 = 0$, for $0 \le \theta \le 2\pi$. $\frac{\pi}{4}$, $\frac{5\pi}{4}$, about 2.03, about 5.18

Example 4

Students use a calculator to solve trigonometric equations.

Additional Example 4

Solve each equation to the nearest tenth. Use the given restrictions.

a. $8\sin\theta = 5$, for $0° \le \theta \le 90°$ 38.7°

b. $8\sin\theta = 5$, for $90° \le \theta \le 180°$ 141.3°

TEACHER TIP

Remind students that $\tan 45° = 1$ and tell them to use this to check their calculator settings. When they evaluate $\text{Tan}^{-1}\,1$, they should get 45. If they get 0.7854, the calculator is set to radians. Students can either change the setting to degrees or multiply radian answers by $\frac{180}{\pi}$ to convert to degrees.

Caution

The inverse cosine key on a calculator will only give the solution in the domain of the inverse cosine function.

$\text{Cos}^{-1}\frac{\sqrt{3}}{2} = 30°$

Example 3 Solving Trigonometric Equations

a. Solve $2\cos\theta = \sqrt{3}$, for $0° \le \theta \le 360°$.

SOLUTION

$2\cos\theta = \sqrt{3}$ — $\cos\theta$ is unknown.

$\frac{2\cos\theta}{2} = \frac{\sqrt{3}}{2}$ — Divide each side by 2 to isolate $\cos\theta$.

$\cos\theta = \frac{\sqrt{3}}{2}$

$\theta = 30°$ or $330°$ — Use the unit circle.

The solutions are 30° and 330°.

b. Solve $5\sin\theta = 5$, for $0° \le \theta \le 360°$.

SOLUTION

$5\sin\theta = 5$ — $\sin\theta$ is unknown.

$\sin\theta = 1$ — Divide each side by 5.

$\theta = 90°$ — Use the unit circle.

The solution is 90°.

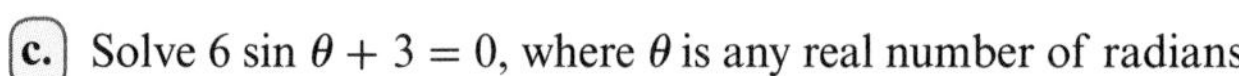

c. Solve $6\sin\theta + 3 = 0$, where θ is any real number of radians.

SOLUTION

$6\sin\theta + 3 = 0$ — $\sin\theta$ is unknown.

$6\sin\theta = -3$ — Subtract 3 from each side.

$\sin\theta = -\frac{1}{2}$ — Divide each side by 6.

$\theta = \frac{7\pi}{6}$ or $\frac{11\pi}{6}$ or any coterminal angle

The solutions are $\frac{7\pi}{6} + 2\pi n$ and $\frac{11\pi}{6} + 2\pi n$, where n is an integer.

Caution

If the answer on your calculator screen is 0.927295218 when you enter $\cos^{-1}(0.6)$, your calculator is set to radian mode instead of degree mode.

Example 4 Solving Trigonometric Equations Using a Calculator

Solve each equation to the nearest tenth. Use the given restrictions.

a. $10\,\text{Cos}\,\theta = 6$, for $0° \le \theta \le 180°$

SOLUTION

$10\,\text{Cos}\,\theta = 6$ — $\text{Cos}\,\theta$ is unknown.

$\text{Cos}\,\theta = 0.6$ — Divide each side by 10.

$\theta = \text{Cos}^{-1}(0.6)$ — Use the inverse cosine key on your calculator.

$\theta \approx 53.1°$

The solution is 53.1°.

INCLUSION

Use the "rule of quarters" to review the sine function for special angles in quadrant I.

sin 0°	sin 30°	sin 45°	sin 60°	sin 90°
$\sqrt{\frac{0}{4}}$	$\sqrt{\frac{1}{4}}$	$\sqrt{\frac{2}{4}}$	$\sqrt{\frac{3}{4}}$	$\sqrt{\frac{4}{4}}$
0	$\frac{1}{2}$	$\frac{\sqrt{2}}{2}$	$\frac{\sqrt{3}}{2}$	1

Have students work in pairs to make the table at the right, sketching triangles as needed. Then help students extend the table to 360°.

deg	rad	sin	cos	tan
0°	0	0	1	0
30°	$\frac{\pi}{6}$	$\frac{1}{2}$	$\frac{\sqrt{3}}{2}$	$\frac{\sqrt{3}}{3}$
45°	$\frac{\pi}{4}$	$\frac{\sqrt{2}}{2}$	$\frac{\sqrt{2}}{2}$	1
60°	$\frac{\pi}{3}$	$\frac{\sqrt{3}}{2}$	$\frac{1}{2}$	$\sqrt{3}$
90°	$\frac{\pi}{2}$	1	0	---

b. $10 \cos \theta = 6$, for $270° < \theta < 360°$

SOLUTION

Because of the restrictions, the terminal side of θ is in Quadrant IV. Find the angle that terminates in Quadrant IV that has the same cosine value as 53.1°.

$\theta \approx 360° - 53.1°$

$\theta \approx 306.9°$

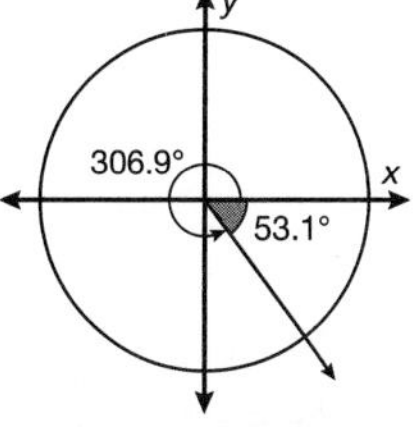

θ has a reference angle of 53.1°, and $270° < \theta < 360°$

Example 5 Application: Navigation

A pair of hikers plan to walk from a campground to a waterfall. The waterfall is 2.5 miles east and 0.5 mile north of the campground. To the nearest degree, in what direction should the hikers head?

Step 1: Draw a diagram.

The hikers' direction should be based on θ, the measure of an acute angle of a right triangle.

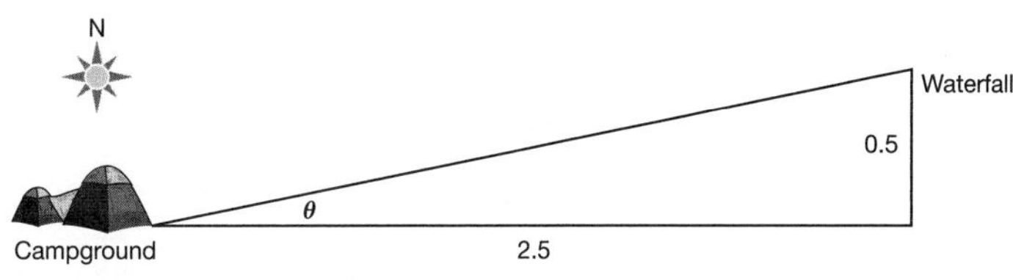

Step 2: Find the value of θ.

$\text{Tan } \theta = \frac{\text{opposite}}{\text{adjacent}}$ Use the tangent ratio.

$\text{Tan } \theta = \frac{0.5}{2.5} = 0.2$ Substitute 0.5 for opposite and 2.5 for adjacent. Then simplify.

$\theta = \text{Tan}^{-1} 0.2$

$\theta \approx 11°$

The hikers should head 11° north of east.

Lesson Practice

a. Describe all the values of $\cos^{-1}\frac{\sqrt{3}}{2}$. *(Ex 1)* — $\frac{\pi}{6} + 2\pi n$ and $\frac{11\pi}{6} + 2\pi n$, where n is an integer

b. Evaluate $\text{Cos}^{-1}\left(-\frac{\sqrt{3}}{2}\right)$ in both radians and degrees if it exists *(Ex 2)* — $\frac{5\pi}{6}$, or 150°

c. Evaluate $\text{Sin}^{-1}\left(-\frac{3}{2}\right)$ in both radians and degrees if it exists. *(Ex 2)* — undefined

d. Solve $2 \sin \theta = -1$, for $0° \leq \theta \leq 360°$. *(Ex 3)* — 210° and 330°

e. Solve $-\cos \theta = -1$, for $0° \leq \theta \leq 360°$. *(Ex 3)* — 0° and 360°

f. Solve $10 \cos \theta - 5 = 0$, where θ is any real number of radians. *(Ex 3)* — $\frac{\pi}{3} + 2\pi n$ and $\frac{5\pi}{3} + 2\pi n$, where n is an integer

Error Alert Remind students that they can check answers to problems such as Example 4b by making sure the cosine of 306.9° is about equal to 0.6.

Example 5

Students use inverse trigonometric functions to solve applications problems.

Extend the Example

Compass *bearing* is an angle measured in a clockwise direction from due north. On what compass bearing should the hikers head? 79°

Additional Example 5

A 20-foot ladder leans against the side of a barn. The top of the ladder is $16\frac{1}{2}$ feet above the ground. Find the angle the ladder makes with the ground to the nearest degree. 56°

Lesson Practice

Problems g–h

Scaffolding Ask: **"How can the answer to problem g be used to solve problem h? Why does this work?"** Sample: Subtract it from 180°. The sine of θ and $180° - \theta$ are the same.

Problem i

Error Alert An answer of 21° is not correct. This is a compass bearing as measured clockwise from due north. Draw a diagram to show students the difference.

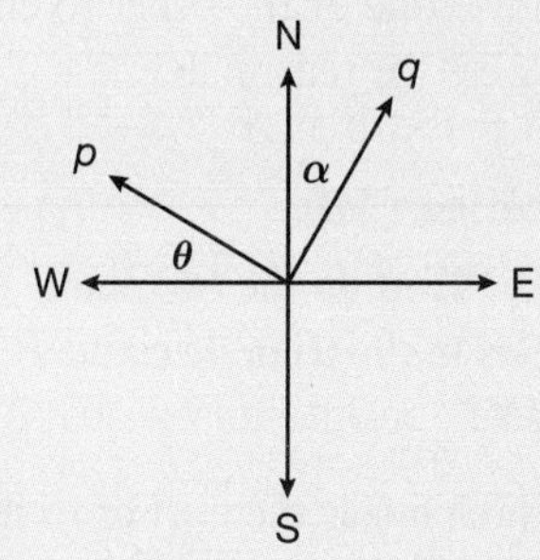

Heading p is 21° north of west.
Heading q is 21°.

ENGLISH LEARNERS

Remind students that arc lengths in circles can be measured in degrees. For example, a central angle of 45° cuts off an arc measuring 45°. Draw a sketch to show this.

Write the term **arcsine** on the board and explain this is another term for the inverse function of the sine. It is shortened to arcsin in the same way that sine is shortened to sin.

Both $\text{Sin}^{-1}x$ and arcsin x mean "the angle that has a sine equal to the number x." Since a central angle and a related arc have the same degree measure, students can think of arcsine x as "the arc that has a sine equal to the number x." (On a unit circle, the inverse sine in radians is not only an angle, it is the length of an arc.) Some students may find the notation arcsin easier to understand than Sin^{-1}.

g. Solve the equation to the nearest tenth. Use the given restrictions.
(Ex 4) $5 \sin \theta = 2$, for $-90° \leq \theta \leq 90°$ 23.6°

h. Solve the equation to the nearest tenth. Use the given restrictions.
(Ex 4) $5 \sin \theta = 2$, for $90° < \theta < 180°$ 156.4°

i. *(Ex 5)* A group of hikers plan to walk from a parking lot to an overlook. The overlook is 1.6 miles west and 0.6 mile north of the parking lot. To the nearest degree, in what direction should the hikers head?
21° north of west

Practice Distributed and Integrated

1. *(56)* Given $\theta = -1787°$, find the measure of the reference angle. 13°

Convert each measure from degrees to radians.

2. *(63)* 60° $\frac{\pi}{3}$ **3.** *(63)* 125° $\frac{25\pi}{36}$ **4.** *(63)* −240° $-\frac{4\pi}{3}$

5. *(51)* Use synthetic substitution to find $f(-3)$ for $f(x) = 7x^4 - 3x^3 + x^2 + 11$. 668

6. *(58)* Complete the square and factor the resulting perfect square trinomial: $x^2 + 6x$.
$x^2 + 6x + 9 = (x + 3)^2$

Simplify.

7. *(48)* $\dfrac{\frac{a}{b}}{\frac{a+b}{b}}$ $\frac{a}{a+b}$

8. *(48)* $\dfrac{\frac{s}{a+b} + \frac{x}{b}}{\frac{a}{s+x}}$ $\frac{(s+x)(bs+ax+bx)}{ab(a+b)}$

***9.** *(67)* **Error Analysis** A student incorrectly solved the equation $\sin\theta = -0.55$, for $90° \leq \theta \leq 270°$, as shown below. What error did the student make? Find the correct solution.

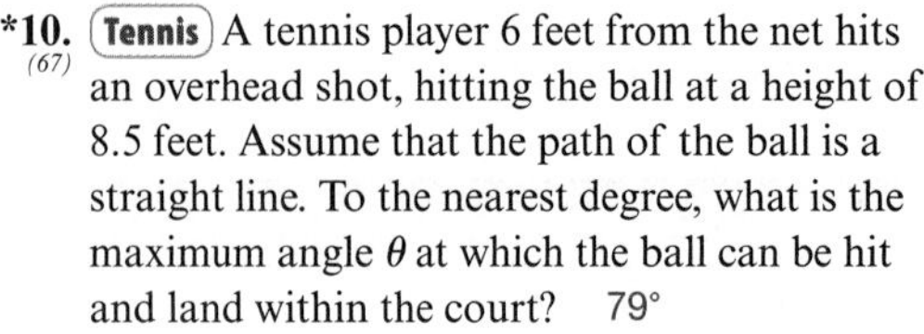

$$\sin \theta = -0.55$$
$$\sin^{-1}(-0.55) \approx -33.4°$$
$$\theta \approx 180° - 33.4°$$
$$\theta \approx 146.6°$$

9. The student subtracted 33.4° from 180°, obtaining an angle that terminates in Quadrant II and whose sine is positive. An angle with a negative sine value that satisfies $90° \leq \theta \leq 270°$ terminates in Quadrant III, so 33.4° must be added to 180° to obtain the correct answer, 213.4°.

***10.** *(67)* **Tennis** A tennis player 6 feet from the net hits an overhead shot, hitting the ball at a height of 8.5 feet. Assume that the path of the ball is a straight line. To the nearest degree, what is the maximum angle θ at which the ball can be hit and land within the court? 79°

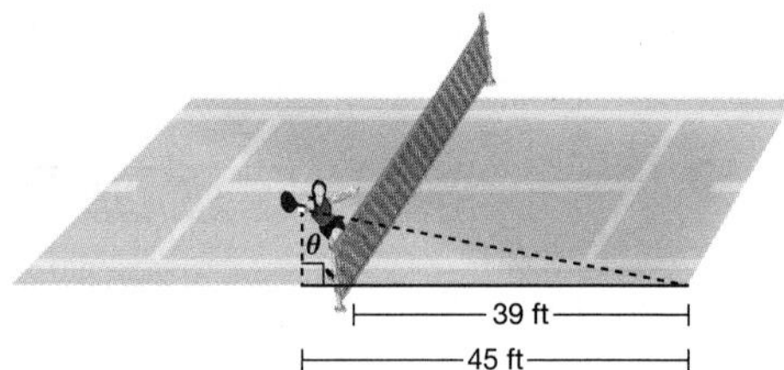

***11.** *(66)* **Graphing Calculator** **a.** Graph $y = x^4 + 2x^3 - 12x^2 + 14x - 5$ on a graphing calculator. What are the x-intercepts? −5 and 1

b. Find the multiplicity of each root of $x^4 + 2x^3 - 12x^2 + 14x - 5 = 0$ by factoring. −5 has a multiplicity of 1 and 1 has a multiplicity of 3.

Check for Understanding

The questions below help assess the concepts taught in this lesson.

"Sketch a graph to show that $y = \sin^{-1}x$ is a relation and not a function."

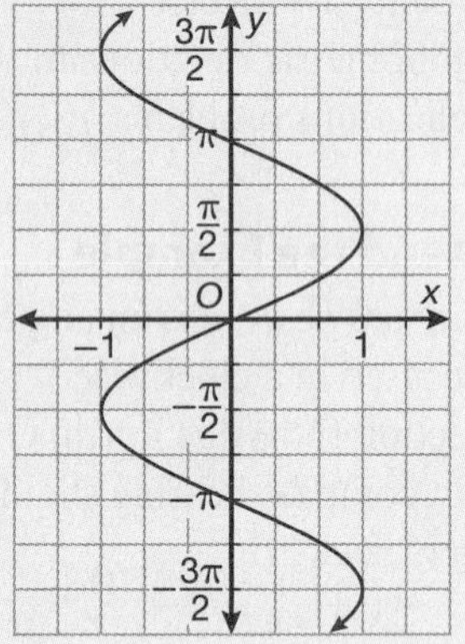

"What happens when you try to evaluate $\sin^{-1}1.5$ on a calculator? Why?" You get an error message. The function $y = \sin x$ has no values greater than $|1|$, so $\sin^{-1}1.5$ is not a real number. Note: Some calculators may give a complex number value for $\sin^{-1}1.5$.

3 Practice

Math Conversations

Discussions to strengthen understanding

Problems 2–4

Error Alert

Students may multiply by $\frac{180}{\pi}$ instead of $\frac{\pi}{180}$. Remind them that $\pi = 180°$, and $\frac{\pi}{2} = 90°$. They can use one or the other to check answers for reasonableness.

Problem 10

Ask: **"How do the two acute angles in the triangle compare to 45°?"** one greater, one less

"Which one is the answer to the problem?" angle greater than 45°

INCLUSION

Have students use a graphing calculator to graph $y = \cos x$ and $x = \cos y$. Model how to sketch both graphs on the same grid. Add the line for $y = x$. Have students use paper folding or a mirror to see that the graphs of $y = \cos x$ and $x = \cos y$ are reflections across the line with equation $y = x$. Discuss how this shows that the two equations represent inverse relations. **"Which equation represents a function?"** $y = \cos x$ **"Which does not?"** $x = \cos y$

12. Minimize $P = 4x + 6y$ for the constraints $\begin{array}{l} 0 \le x \le 4 \\ y \ge 1 \\ y \ge -x + 4 \end{array}$ (3, 1)
(54)

***13. Multiple Choice** Which is a solution of $5 + 2x^2 = -3x$? D
(65)

A 1 B $\frac{5}{2}$ C $\frac{3}{4} + \frac{\sqrt{31}}{4}$ D $-\frac{3}{4} - \frac{\sqrt{31}}{4}i$

***14. (Contact Lenses)** The contact lens prescription for Asia's left eye is stronger than the prescription for her right eye. If Asia accidentally mixed up her contact lenses, what is the probability that she will put the correct lens in either eye on the first try? Explain. 50%; Whichever lens she picks, she is equally likely to put it in the correct or the incorrect eye.
(Inv 5)

***15. Multi-Step** Complete parts a–d to determine the measure of the angle formed by the hands of a clock when the time is 3:24. Find all measures in radians.
(63)

a. Find x, the angle formed at 3:00. $\frac{\pi}{2}$

b. Find $(x + y + z)$, the angle through which the minute hand moves in 24 minutes. $\frac{4\pi}{5}$

c. Find y, the angle through which the hour hand moves in 24 minutes. $\frac{\pi}{15}$

d. Find z, the angle formed by the minute hand and hour hand when the time is 3:24. $\frac{7\pi}{30}$

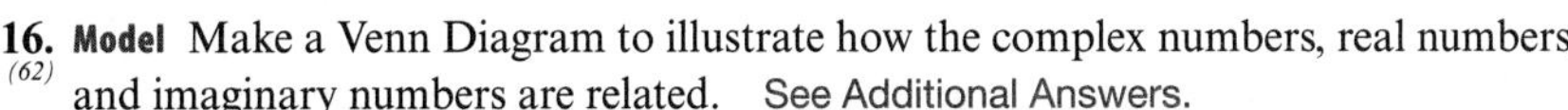

16. Model Make a Venn Diagram to illustrate how the complex numbers, real numbers, and imaginary numbers are related. See Additional Answers.
(62)

17. (Finance) The value of a stock over the past five years where x is the number of years is modeled by $x^3 - 2x^2 + 5x - 10$. Factor this expression. $(x - 2)(x^2 + 5)$
(61)

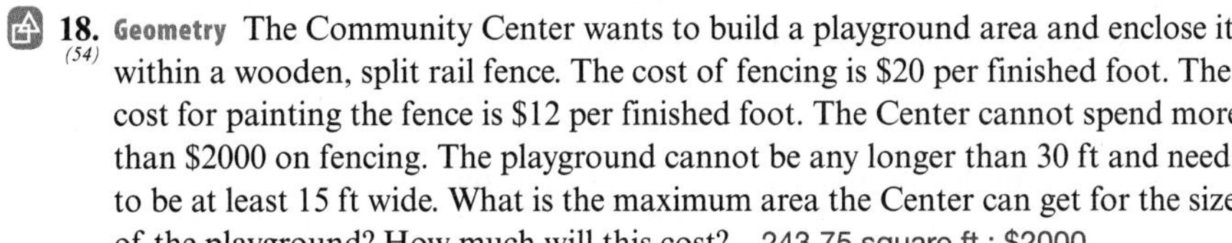

18. Geometry The Community Center wants to build a playground area and enclose it within a wooden, split rail fence. The cost of fencing is \$20 per finished foot. The cost for painting the fence is \$12 per finished foot. The Center cannot spend more than \$2000 on fencing. The playground cannot be any longer than 30 ft and needs to be at least 15 ft wide. What is the maximum area the Center can get for the size of the playground? How much will this cost? 243.75 square ft.; \$2000
(54)

19. Error Analysis A cup contains 15 pink beads, 24 purple beads, and 18 gold beads. Three beads are individually selected with replacement. The work below is used to find the probability that one of each color bead is selected in the order pink, purple, gold. Is the work correct? If not, explain the error and find the correct solution. If so, explain each step of the work. Yes
(60)

K = event of pink bead drawn

U = event of purple bead drawn

G = event of gold bead drawn

$P(K,U,G) = P(K) \cdot P(U) \cdot P(G)$

$= \frac{5}{19} \cdot \frac{8}{19} \cdot \frac{6}{19} \approx 0.035$

$P(K) = \frac{15}{57} = \frac{5}{19}$ $P(U) = \frac{24}{57} = \frac{8}{19}$ $P(G) = \frac{18}{57} = \frac{6}{19}$

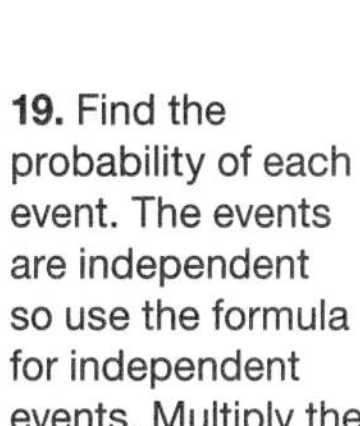

19. Find the probability of each event. The events are independent so use the formula for independent events. Multiply the three probabilities.

20. Multiple Choice Choose the letter that best represents $\sqrt[3]{\frac{216x^{12}}{4}}$ simplified. B
(59)

A $\frac{3x^4\sqrt[3]{4}}{2}$ B $3x^4\sqrt[3]{2}$ C $6x^4\sqrt[3]{4}$ D $\frac{3x^4\sqrt[3]{2}}{2}$

CHALLENGE

In the diagram at the right, the water level rises and falls according to the motion of the tides. The depth of the water varies with time t in hours according to $d = 40 + 60\cos\left[\frac{\pi}{6}(t - 2)\right]$. The time is midnight when $t = 0$. What is the earliest time in the day when the water level is just at the top of the 80-cm post? about 3:36 A.M. when $t = 3.61$

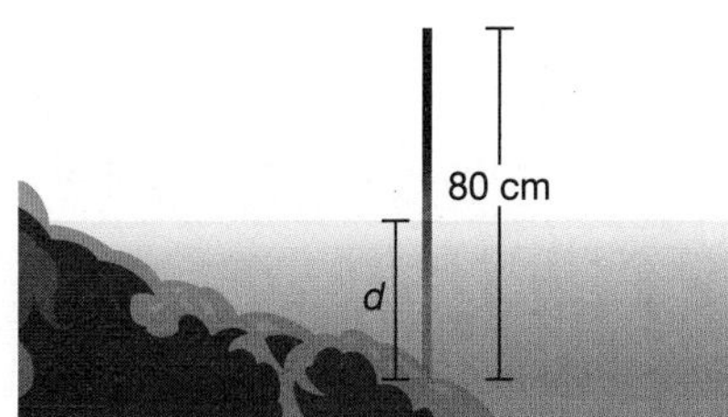

Problem 17

Extend the Problem

a. Graph the equation $y = x^3 - 2x^2 + 5x - 10$.

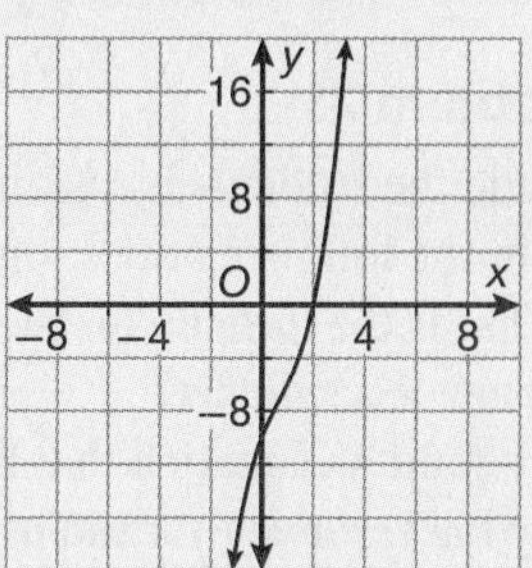

b. For what values of the domain does this model make sense? Why? $x \ge 2$; Sample: For $x < 2$, the values of the expression $x^3 - 2x^2 + 5x - 10$ are negative. Only positive values of the stock make sense in the problem context.

Problem 19

Extend the Problem

Find the probability of getting one of each color in the order pink, purple, gold if the beads are *not* replaced after each selection. Show the probability fractions you use.
$\frac{15}{57} \cdot \frac{24}{56} \cdot \frac{18}{55} \approx 0.037$

Problem 20

Error Alert

If students choose the wrong answer, review rationalizing the denominator of a cube root with this example.

$$\frac{1}{\sqrt[3]{4}} = \frac{1}{\sqrt[3]{2 \cdot 2}} \cdot \frac{\sqrt[3]{2}}{\sqrt[3]{2}} = \frac{\sqrt[3]{2}}{2}$$

Problem 23
Extend the Problem

Find k in $D(8, k)$ so that the measure of $m\angle DOB = 45°$. $k = 8$

Problem 25

Guide the students by asking them the following questions. **"What is the formula for the volume of a cylinder?"** $V = \pi r^2 h$ **"We want an equation that has only the variable r for radius. What can be substituted for h?"** Since $h = r + 5$, substitute $r + 5$ for h. **"What can be substituted for V?"** Substitute 450, the value given in the problem. **"Use 3.14 for π. What is the resulting polynomial?"** $450 = 3.14r^2(r + 5)$

Have students write the polynomial in standard form and graph the related equation. **"How does this show the answer to the problem?"** Sample: The value of the x-intercept is the radius.

Problem 30
Extend the Problem

Explain how to solve the problem by graphing. Sample: Graph the related equation $y = -16t^2 + 177$. The positive x-intercept is the solution to the problem. Use a trace function to approximate this value.

***21.** (66) **Analyze** When solving $x^3 + 7x^2 + 7x - 6 = 0$, why is it not necessary to use synthetic substitution after one of the roots is found?

22. (58) **Write** A ball is tossed with an initial velocity of 74 feet per second from the top of a building that is 50 feet tall. The height, h, of the ball in feet after t seconds can be approximated by the equation $h = -16t^2 + 74t + 50$. The ball will be 20 feet from the ground when $t = -0.375$ second and $t = 5$ seconds. Explain why you would not use the solution $t = -0.375$ second.

***23.** (67) **Coordinate Geometry** Find $m\angle AOB$ to the nearest tenth of a degree, using these points: $A(8, 3)$, $O(0, 0)$, and $B(8, 0)$. 20.6°

24. (55) **Verify** Explain why the probability of choosing first, second, and third place winners for a photo when randomly choosing from the top 10 athletes is $\frac{1}{{}_{10}C_3}$. See Additional Answers.

***25.** (66) **Storage** The volume of a can of dog food is 450 cubic inches. The height of the can is 5 inches greater than its radius. Write a polynomial in standard form, using 3.14 for π, that can be used to find the radius. (Round the constant to the nearest integer.) Then find the approximate radius by using a graphing calculator. $r^3 + 5r^2 - 143 = 0$, 4 centimeters

26. (56) **Generalize** Suppose θ is an angle in standard position and $Q(x, y)$ is a point on the terminal side of the angle. Explain how the signs (positive or negative) of $\sin\theta$, $\cos\theta$, and $\tan\theta$ depend on which quadrant Q lies in. See Additional Answers.

27. (60) **School** A teacher has 3 red crayons, 7 yellow crayons, 5 green crayons, and 2 blue crayons. A yellow crayon and then a blue crayon are chosen at random without replacement. Are these events dependent or mutually exclusive? Dependent

28. (57) The number of rabbits increases exponentially. At first there were 400. Three years later there were 1600. How many rabbits would there be after 10 years? 40,637 rabbits

29. (54) Maximize $P = 5x + 2y$ for the constraints $\begin{array}{l} y \geq 0 \\ x \geq 0 \\ y \leq -x + 10 \\ y \leq 2x + 1 \end{array}$ (10, 0)

***30.** (65) **Physical Science** The South Falls waterfalls in Silver Falls State Park in Oregon are 177 feet high. The equation $-16t^2 + 177 = 0$ gives the number of seconds it takes for a drop of water at the top of the falls to reach the pool of water below. Solve the equation by using the quadratic formula. Round to the nearest hundredth of a second. 3.33 seconds

21. The quotient is a factor of the polynomial. Because it is of degree two, it can be solved by using the quadratic formula.

22. Possible response: In this situation negative time represents the time before the ball was tossed and we are looking at after the ball was tossed.

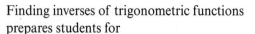

CHALLENGE

Write a compound sentence equivalent to each equation. Hint: Your first answer should have the form $x =$ ____ and $|y| \leq$ ____.

a. $y = \text{Sin}^{-1}x$ $x = \text{Sin}\, y$ and $|y| \leq \frac{\pi}{2}$

b. $y = \text{Cos}^{-1}x$ $x = \text{Cos}\, y$ and $0 \leq y \leq \pi$

c. $y = \text{Tan}^{-1}x$ $x = \text{Tan}\, y$ and $|y| < \frac{\pi}{2}$

LOOKING FORWARD

Finding inverses of trigonometric functions prepares students for

- **Lesson 71** Using the Law of Sines
- **Lesson 77** Using the Law of Cosines
- **Lesson 82** Graphing Sine and Cosine Functions
- **Lesson 86** Translating Sine and Cosine Functions
- **Lesson 90** Graphing the Tangent Function

LESSON 68

Finding Conditional Probability

Warm Up

1. **Vocabulary** If the occurrence of one event affects the probability of the second event, the two events are dependent. (55)

2. As a percent, what is the probability of getting heads on all three flips of a coin? 12.5% (55)

3. A bag contains 8 red marbles, 16 white marbles, and 4 black marbles. What is the probability of randomly selecting a white or black marble? $\frac{5}{7} \approx 71.4\%$ (55)

New Concepts

The probability of two independent events is the product of their individual probabilities. However, finding the probability of two dependent events requires finding a *conditional probability*. Recall that $P(B|A)$ is a conditional probability. It is read as "the probability of B given that A has occurred."

Dependent Events
If A and B are dependent events, then $P(A \text{ and } B) = P(A) \cdot P(B|A)$.

Example 1 Finding the Probability of Dependent Events

a. Suppose the two spinners shown are each spun once. Find the probability that the first spinner lands on 2 and the sum of the spinners is 6.

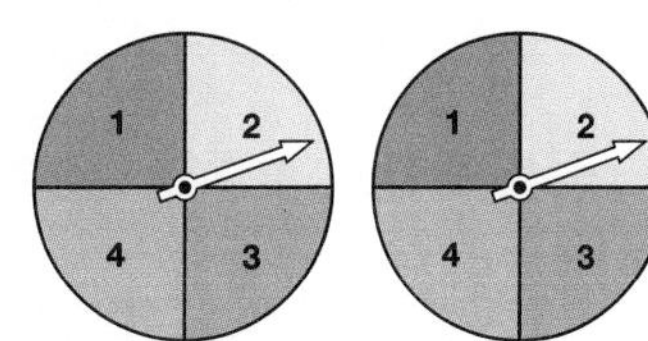

Math Reasoning

Analyze Name another way of finding the probability of the events in Example 1a.

Out of 16 favorable outcomes, only 1 has a 2 on the first spin and a sum of 6.

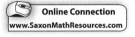

SOLUTION Assign event A to be the first spinner landing on 2 and event B to be the sum of the spinners is 6. Determine if the events are dependent. It helps to list all the outcomes in the sample space. The first numbers are from the first spinner, and the second numbers are from the second spinner. If event A *does not* occur, $P(B) = \frac{3}{16}$ because out of 16 possible outcomes, 3 have a sum of 6. These pairs are boxed. If event A *does* occur, $P(B) = \frac{1}{4}$ because out of 4 possible pairs only one has a sum of 6.

1, 1	2, 1	3, 1	4, 1
1, 2	2, 2	3, 2	[4, 2]
1, 3	2, 3	[3, 3]	4, 3
1, 4	[2, 4]	3, 4	4, 4

1, 1	2, 1	3, 1	4, 1
1, 2	2, 2	3, 2	4, 2
1, 3	2, 3	3, 3	4, 3
1, 4	[2, 4]	3, 4	4, 4

Since the occurrence of event A affects the probability of event B, the events are dependent.

$P(A \text{ and } B) = P(A) \cdot P(B|A) = \frac{1}{4} \cdot \frac{1}{4} = \frac{1}{16}$

Online Connection www.SaxonMathResources.com

LESSON 68

1 Warm Up

For problems 2 and 3, ask: **"Are the events dependent or independent?"** 2. independent 3. neither; this is a single event.

2 New Concepts

In this lesson, students learn to compute conditional probabilities.

Example 1

Students use a sample space to find the probability of two dependent events both occurring.

Additional Example 1

Slips of paper for five prizes numbered 1–5 are put in a bag. A contestant draws one number, then replaces it, and then the next contestant draws a number.

a. Find the probability that the first number is 3 and the sum of the numbers is greater than 5. $\frac{3}{25}$

b. Find the probability that the first number is odd and the product of the numbers is even. $\frac{6}{25}$

MATH BACKGROUND

The probability of an event given the occurrence of another event is called *conditional probability*. For events A and B, the conditional probability of A given B is written $P(A|B)$ and can be defined as:

$$P(A|B) = \frac{P(A \text{ and } B)}{P(B)}$$

For two dependent events,

$$P(A \text{ and } B) = P(A) \cdot P(B|A).$$

When events A and B are independent, the occurrence of one has no effect on the other. Then, $P(A \text{ and } B) = P(A)P(B)$, and

$$P(A|B) = P(A)$$
$$P(B|A) = P(B)$$

A useful relationship between $P(A|B)$ and $P(B|A)$ is given by Bayes' Theorem:

$$P(B|A) = P(A|B) \cdot \frac{P(B)}{P(A)}$$

LESSON RESOURCES

Student Edition Practice Workbook 68
Reteaching Master 68
Adaptations Master 68
Challenge and Enrichment Master C68

Error Alert Make sure students understand the sample space is a set of ordered pairs.

Extend the Example

Use Example 1, part a. Make a Venn diagram to show the sample spaces are not mutually exclusive.

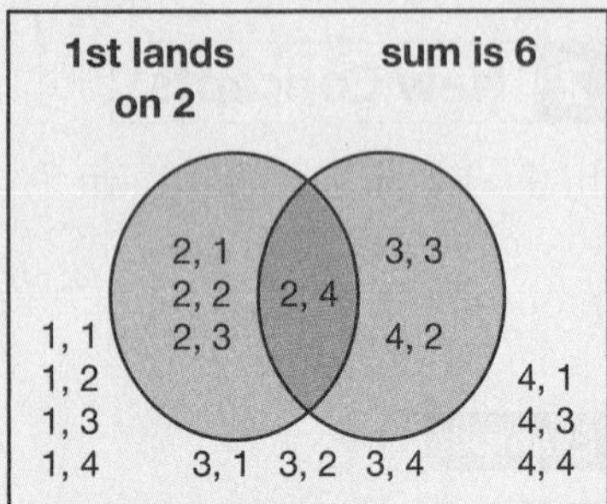

Example 2

Students use data given in a table to find conditional probabilities.

Additional Example 2

The table shows the number of raffle tickets sold over a three-day festival. One ticket will be drawn for the grand prize.

	Fri	Sat	Sun
Adult	245	482	167
Child	86	119	42
Senior	103	251	94

a. Find $P(\text{adult}|\text{Friday})$.

$\frac{245}{245 + 86 + 103} \approx 56.5\%$

b. Find $P(\text{Sunday}|\text{child or senior})$.

$\frac{42 + 94}{86 + 119 + 42 + 103 + 251 + 94}$

$\approx 19.6\%$

Extend the Example

Use the raffle ticket chart in Additional Example 2. Ten prizes will be awarded in all. What are the chances that two particular children from a particular family (or any particular pair of people) will win both prizes?

$\frac{1}{1589} \times \frac{1}{1588}$, or 1 in 2,523,332

b. Suppose the two spinners shown are each spun once. Find the probability that the first spinner lands on an odd number and the sum of the spinners is greater than 4.

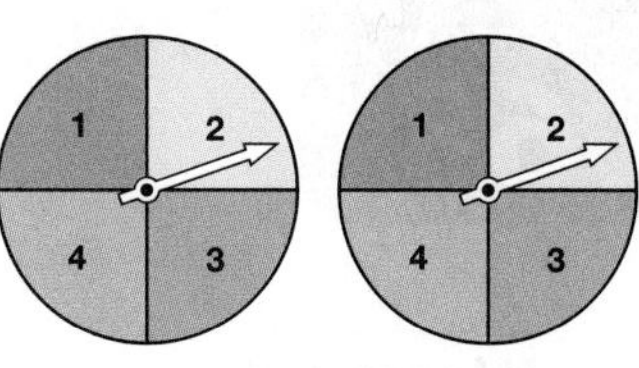

SOLUTION

Confirm that the events are dependent.

If event A *does not* occur, $P(B) = \frac{10}{16} = \frac{5}{8}$ because out of 16 possible outcomes, 10 have a sum greater than 4.

If event A *does* occur, $P(B) = \frac{4}{8} = \frac{1}{2}$ because out of 8 possible pairs (those in the first and third columns), 4 have a sum greater than 4.

1, 1	2, 1	3, 1	4, 1
1, 2	2, 2	3, 2	4, 2
1, 3	2, 3	3, 3	4, 3
1, 4	2, 4	3, 4	4, 4

1, 1	2, 1	3, 1	4, 1
1, 2	2, 2	3, 2	4, 2
1, 3	2, 3	3, 3	4, 3
1, 4	2, 4	3, 4	4, 4

Since the occurrence of event A affects the probability of event B, the events are dependent.

$P(A \text{ and } B) = P(A) \cdot P(B|A) = \frac{1}{2} \cdot \frac{1}{2} = \frac{1}{4}$

Example 2 Using a Table to Find Conditional Probability

The table shows the results of a survey that asked students to state the year and season of their birthday.

	1992	1993	1994
Winter	10	16	14
Spring	6	9	11
Summer	12	11	8
Fall	14	9	12

Hint

First circle or highlight the row(s) or column(s) with the given condition(s), that is, event *A*.

a. Find $P(\text{Winter}|1993)$.

SOLUTION $P(\text{Winter}|1993)$ is the probability of a birthday occurring in the winter, given that it occurred in 1993. Since the condition is that it must be in the year 1993, focus on the 1993 column.

$$\frac{\text{winter}}{\text{all seasons}} : \frac{16}{16 + 9 + 11 + 9} = \frac{16}{45} \approx 35.6\%$$

b. Find $P(1992|\text{Spring or Summer})$.

SOLUTION $P(1992|\text{Spring or Summer})$ is the probability of a birthday occurring in 1992, given that it occurred in the spring or summer. Since the condition is that it must be in the spring or summer, focus on those rows.

$$\frac{1992}{\text{spring or summer all years}} : \frac{6 + 12}{6 + 9 + 11 + 12 + 11 + 8} = \frac{18}{57} = \frac{6}{19} \approx 31.6\%$$

When items are selected and not replaced, the events are dependent. For each successive selection, the total number of outcomes, which are the values in the denominators, decreases by one.

484 Saxon Algebra 2

ALTERNATE METHOD FOR EXAMPLE 2: MANIPULATIVE USE

Materials: 2 clear glass jars labeled #1 and #2, 30 black marbles, 50 white marbles, turntable (optional)

Jar #1 has 10 black marbles and 30 white. Jar #2 has 20 of each. Choose one jar at random, and then draw one marble.

Demonstrate by having a volunteer spin the turntable, choose a jar, then draw a marble.

Now present the problem: If someone gets a white marble, what is the probability it came from jar #1?

	Jar #1	Jar #2	Total
Black	10	20	30
White	30	20	50
Total	40	40	80

Point to the row for white marbles. Write:

$P(A)$ = choosing jar #1
$P(B)$ = choosing white marble
$P(A|B)$ = 30 out of 50, or 0.6

Example 3 Using a Calculator to Find Conditional Probability

A raffle is being held at a school function. A container has the names of the 587 juniors and 618 seniors who are participating on slips of paper. Prizes are being given to the first, second, and third names pulled from the container. Once a student wins a prize, his or her name is not returned to the container. What is the probability that the first two prizes go to juniors and the third prize goes to a senior?

SOLUTION After the first junior wins, there is one less junior name in the container, which is also one less name overall. After the second junior wins, there is one less name overall again. There are $587 + 618 = 1205$ names in all.

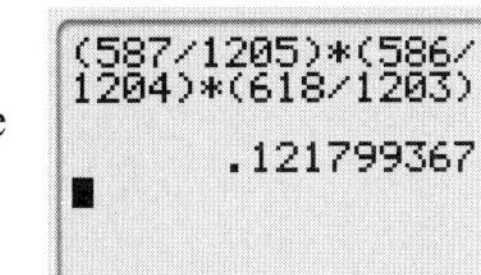

$$P(\text{junior, junior, senior}) = \frac{587}{1205} \cdot \frac{586}{1204} \cdot \frac{618}{1203} \approx 0.122$$

The probability is about 12.2%.

Math Reasoning

Analyze Calculate P(junior, senior, junior). How does it compare to Example 3?

P(junior, senior, junior) ≈ 0.122; it is the same.

Example 4 Application: Quality Control

At a mailing center, it was found that on Tuesday, 44 out of 662 envelopes were stamped upside down, on Wednesday, 16 out of 251 envelopes were stamped upside down, and on Thursday, 3 out of 598 envelopes were stamped upside down. Find the probability that an envelope was stamped on Wednesday given that it was stamped right-side up.

SOLUTION

1. **Understand** Make a table to organize the information. Subtract to find the number of envelopes stamped right-side up.

	Tues.	Wed.	Thurs.
Right-side Up	618	235	595
Upside Down	44	16	3

2. **Plan** The condition is that the envelope was stamped right-side up. Find the sum of the envelopes stamped right-side up; this will be the denominator.

3. **Solve** Use a calculator.

$$\frac{235}{618 + 235 + 595} = \frac{235}{1448} \approx 0.162$$

The probability is about 16.2%.

4. **Check** Use estimation to check for reasonableness. From the given information, about 1500 envelopes were stamped and about 250 of those were stamped on Wednesday. The majority of those stamped on Wednesday were stamped right-side up, and $\frac{250}{1500} = \frac{1}{6} = 16\frac{2}{3}\%$.

Math Reasoning

Estimate Estimate the probability that an envelope was stamped on Thursday given that it was stamped upside down.

about 5%

Example 3

Students find probabilities of dependent events.

Extend the Example

Prove that P(junior, junior, senior) = P(senior, junior, junior).

$$\frac{587 \cdot 586 \cdot 618}{1205 \cdot 1204 \cdot 1203} = \frac{618 \cdot 587 \cdot 586}{1205 \cdot 1204 \cdot 1203}$$

Additional Example 3

Three baseball caps are chosen at random and without replacement from a box that contains these colors: 6 tan, 8 gray, 9 black, and 12 blue. Find the probability that all three caps are gray. $\frac{8}{35} \cdot \frac{7}{34} \cdot \frac{6}{33} \approx 0.0086$

TEACHER TIP

Have students include columns and rows showing totals when they make charts such as the one in Example 4.

Example 4

Students solve a conditional probability problem by organizing data in a table.

Error Alert Emphasize that P(Wednesday|right-side up) is different from P(right-side up| Wednesday); i.e., $\frac{235}{1448} \neq \frac{235}{251}$.

Additional Example 4

It took Pleasant Puzzles 3 months to manufacture a new puzzle. In May, 976 out of 978 passed the quality control check. In June, 1,031 out of 1,035 passed. In July, 984 out of 987 passed. Find the probability that a defective puzzle was made in July. $\frac{1}{3}$

INCLUSION

Materials: large clear glass jar

For Example 3, emphasize that when the names are not replaced, the total outcomes decrease by 1 with each drawing. Illustrate with an easier example: With 10 names in a hat, your chances of being chosen are 1 in 10. On the second drawing, your chances are 1 in 9.

Model this example for students using a large glass jar and 10 slips of paper. Write 10 different names with a large marker on slips of paper or cards. Have a volunteer draw one card. Ask **"What is the chance of a student getting his or her name drawn?"** 1 out of 10 **"How many names are left in the jar?"** 9 **"How are the chances of getting picked different on the next draw?"** Sample: Now the chance is 1 out of 9. The chances increase.

Lesson Practice

Problem d

Error Alert Check that students find $P(10^{th}|\text{History})$ and not $P(\text{History}|10^{th})$.

$P(10^{th}|\text{History})$ $\frac{45}{45 + 19 + 26}$ $P(\text{History}|10^{th})$ $\frac{45}{34 + 45 + 52 + 9}$

Problems e and f

If students have trouble, have them solve easier problems first, such as using the numbers 7 men and 3 women for problem e.

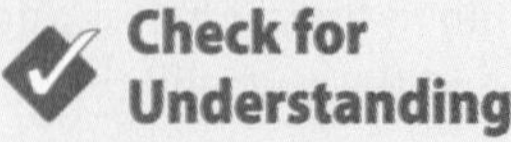

Check for Understanding

The questions below help assess the concepts taught in this lesson.

"What does it mean for two events to be dependent? Give an example." Sample: The probability of one is affected by whether or not the other occurs; drawing two names when the first is not replaced

"Two events aré independent. What is the conditional probability of event A, given that event B has occurred? Give an example." $P(A)$, the same as if B does not happen; Sample: getting heads when flipping a coin and spinning a four-color spinner

3 Practice

Math Conversations

Discussions to strengthen understanding

Problem 3

Error Alert

Remind students to check final answers for any common factors. For example, $(x - 5)(3x - 6)$ is not correct because $3x - 6$ can be factored into $3(x - 2)$.

Lesson Practice

Suppose the two spinners shown are each spun once. (Ex 1)

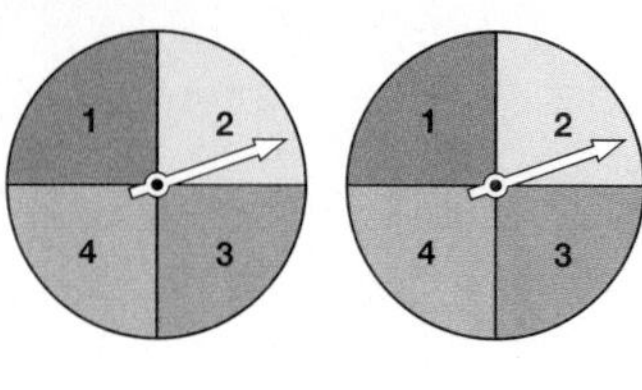

a. Find the probability that the first spinner lands on 4 and the product of the spinners is less than 10. $\frac{1}{8} = 12.5\%$

b. Find the probability that the first spinner lands on a number less than 4 and the sum of the numbers is less than 6. $\frac{9}{16} = 56.25\%$

The table shows the results of a survey that asked students from three grade levels to pick their favorite subject from those listed. (Ex 2)

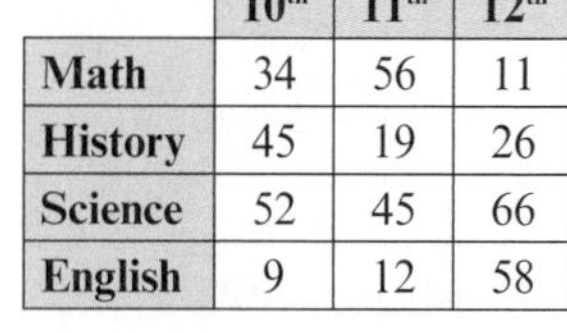

	10th	11th	12th
Math	34	56	11
History	45	19	26
Science	52	45	66
English	9	12	58

c. Find $P(\text{Math}|12)$. $\frac{11}{161} \approx 6.8\%$

d. Find $P(10\text{th}|\text{History})$. $\frac{1}{2} = 50\%$

e. (Ex 3) A raffle is being held at a mall. A box has the names of the 237 men and 318 women who are participating on slips of paper. Gift certificates are being given to the first five names pulled from the box. Once a person wins a certificate, his or her name is not returned to the box. What is the probability that the first three certificates go to men and the last two certificates go to women? About 2.6%

f. (Ex 4) At a factory, it was found that during the morning shift, 32 out of the 2666 boxes of nails that were filled had unacceptable weights, and during the evening shift, 11 out of the 1870 boxes of nails that were filled had unacceptable weights. Find the probability that a box was filled in the evening, given that its weight was found acceptable. About 41.4%

Practice Distributed and Integrated

1. (62) Solve $s^2 - 22 = -112$. Write the solutions in terms of i. $\pm 3i\sqrt{10}$

Factor completely.

2. (23) $-3pax + pax^2 + 2pa$ $pa(x - 2)(x - 1)$

3. (23) $30 + 3x^2 - 21x$ $3(x - 5)(x - 2)$

4. (58) **Multi-Step** Use $x^2 - 62x + 961 = 26$.

a. Explain why the left side of the equation is a perfect square trinomial. $961 = 31^2$ and $62 = 31 \cdot 2$

b. Factor $x^2 - 62x + 961$. $(x - 31)^2$

c. Solve the equation for x. $x = 31 \pm \sqrt{26}$

INCLUSION

Use Example 4 to help students interpret conditional probability statements. Write: $P(\text{Wednesday}|\text{right-side up})$.

Discuss different ways this can be described.

- Find the probability that an envelope was stamped on Wednesday given that it was right-side up.
- Find the probability that a right-side up envelope was stamped on Wednesday.
- If an envelope chosen at random is right-side up, what is the probability it was stamped on Wednesday?

Point out that the condition "right-side up" sometimes comes first in the problem statement; sometimes it comes second. Write: $P(\text{right-side up}|\text{Wednesday})$

Have students translate this into different verbal statements.

***5.** **Error Analysis** Find and correct the error a student made in determining the roots and their multiplicity in $x^3 - 4x^2 + 4x = 0$.
(66)

$$x^3 - 4x^2 + 4x = 0$$
$$x(x^2 - 4x + 4) = 0$$
$$x(x-2)(x-2) = 0$$

The only root is 2 and its multiplicity is 2.

5. The student did not take the factor of x into account. 0 is also a root, with a multiplicity of 1.

6. **Analyze** What does it mean for an event to have the first number in the odds in favor ratio greater than the second number? There are more favorable outcomes than unfavorable outcomes; the probability is greater than 50%.
(55)

7. **Geometry** Write an expanded expression for the volume of the cube shown. $8b^3 + 60b^2 + 150b + 125$ cm^3
(49)

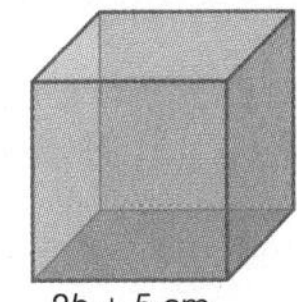

***8.** **Housing** The table shows estimated housing occupancy for three states for the year 2006.
(68)

Find the probability that a randomly selected house from one of these states is in Nevada. Then find the probability that a randomly selected house from one of these states is in Nevada given that it is vacant. Round each percent to the nearest tenth. 10.4%, 11.5%

	Occupied Houses	Vacant Houses
Mississippi	1,075,521	165,918
Nevada	936,828	128,439
New York	7,088,376	819,138

Simplify.

9. $-64^{-\frac{2}{3}}$ $-\frac{1}{16}$
(59)

10. $\dfrac{-3}{-9^{-\frac{3}{2}}}$ 81
(59)

11. $(-8)^{\frac{1}{3}}$ −2
(59)

12. Find the arc length of a sector with a radius of 4 in. and central angle $\theta = \frac{\pi}{6}$. $s =$ about 2.09 in.
(63)

***13.** **Probability** A bag contains 30 red marbles and 10 white marbles. If three marbles are randomly chosen without replacement, what is the probability of selecting all red or all white marbles? About 42.3%
(68)

14. **Surveying** A surveyor is standing on top of a hill that is 600 meters from a bridge. Her angle of elevation to the top of the bridge is 14° and her angle of depression to the bottom of the bridge is 26°. To the nearest tenth of a meter, what is the height of the bridge? 442.2 meters
(46)

***15.** **Generalize** Insert = or ≠ to make each statement true.
(68)

If A and B are independent events, then $P(B|A)$ ☐ $P(B)$. =

If A and B are dependent events, then $P(B|A)$ ☐ $P(B)$. ≠

16. **Statistics** How do probability and statistics compare and contrast?
(60)

16. Sample: Both can be used to make predictions, but probability uses all possibilities, whereas statistics uses observed data.

17. **Multiple Choice** Which angle does *not* have a reference angle of 30°? **B**
(56)
A −30° B 120° C 570° D −150°

Problem 5

Remind students that a *root* is any number that makes the equation true. Ask what happens when $x = 0$. Sample: The equation is true, so 0 is a root.

ENGLISH LEARNERS

Write the term conditional probability on the board and underline the word part **condition.** Discuss the everyday meaning of condition as "a restricting, limiting, or modifying circumstance." Use this example: You can go to the game if you do your homework. Have students identify the condition. Label the two parts of the statement as event A and event B.

Event A: You do your homework.
Event B: You can go to the game.

Relate this example to the notation $P(B|A)$, reading it as "the probability of event B, given that event A has occurred."

Problem 18

If students need a hint, draw a 30°-60°-90° right triangle on the board. Label the hypotenuse 2 and the shorter leg 1. Have students find the cosine of the 60° angle. 0.5

Problem 21

To help students get started, have a volunteer explain why $3\sqrt{18}$ equals $9\sqrt{2}$. Sample: $3\sqrt{18} = 3\sqrt{9 \cdot 2} = 3\sqrt{9} \cdot \sqrt{2} = 3 \cdot 3\sqrt{2} = 9\sqrt{2}$

Problem 24

Guide the students by asking them the following questions.

"How do you subtract a binomial?" Add its opposite.

"What is the opposite of the complex number $2 + 3i$?" $-2 - 3i$

Problem 25

Extend the Problem

a. Choice D describes the values of what inverse sine? $\sin^{-1}\frac{\sqrt{3}}{2}$

b. Which answer describes $\cos^{-1}\frac{1}{2}$? D

c. If $\sin^{-1}\frac{1}{2} = \theta$, what is $\tan\theta$? $\frac{\sqrt{3}}{3}$

Problem 29

Guide the students by asking them the following questions.

"How can a right triangle be used to model the problem?" Use the legs for the distances south and west. The hypotenuse is the distance the cars are apart.

"Show how the Pythagorean Theorem relates the distances." $(40t)^2 + [60(t - 1)]^2 = 300^2$

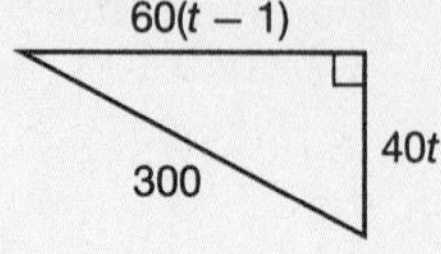

***18.** (67) **Estimate** Use what you know about the unit circle and special angles to estimate $\text{Cos}^{-1}(0.48)$ in degrees. Do not use a calculator. Explain your method. See Additional Answers.

19. (63) **Write** Describe how to determine cos 150° by using its reference angle.

19. Possible answer: The reference angle is 30°. $\cos 30° = \frac{\sqrt{3}}{2}$, 150° terminates in Quadrant II, and the cosine of any angle terminating in Quadrant II is negative, so $\cos 150° = -\frac{\sqrt{3}}{2}$.

Simplify.

20. (44) $3\sqrt{\frac{5}{2}} - 2\sqrt{\frac{2}{5}}$ $\frac{11\sqrt{10}}{10}$

21. (44) $3\sqrt{18} + 2\sqrt{50} - \sqrt{98}$ $12\sqrt{2}$

22. (Inv 5) Calculate the binomial probability $P(12, 200, 0.09)$ to the nearest hundredth of a percent using the formula $P(n, N, p) = \frac{N!}{n!(N-n)!}p^n(1-p)^{N-n}$. 3.44%

***23.** (54) **Graphing Calculator** Describe the feasible region for the set of inequalities $x \geq 0$, $x \leq 4$, $y \geq 0$, $2y + x \leq 25$. A bounded region: (0, 0), (0, 12.5), (4, 0), (4, 10.5)

24. (62) **Error Analysis** Find and correct the error a student made in subtracting complex numbers.

$$(7 - 4i) - (2 + 3i)$$
$$5 - i$$

See Additional Answers.

***25.** (67) **Multiple Choice** Which describes all the values of $\sin^{-1}\frac{1}{2}$ where $0 \leq \theta \leq 2\pi$? B

A $\frac{5\pi}{6}$ **B** $\frac{\pi}{6}$

C $\frac{2\pi}{3}$ **D** $\frac{\pi}{3}$

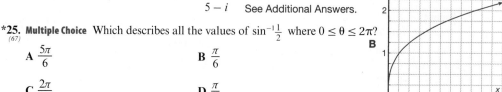

26. (59) **Estimate** Sketch a graph of the equation $y = \frac{\sqrt[3]{6\pi^2 x}}{2\pi}$, where y is the radius of a sphere and x is the volume of the sphere. Use the graph to estimate the volume of a sphere with a radius of 2 cm. Use the graph to estimate the radius of a sphere with a volume of 14 cm³. 34 cm³; about 1.5 cm

27. (61) **Volume** The volume of a California king size mattress is $12x^3 - 36x^2 - 432x - 384$ cubic inches. Factor the polynomial given that $x - 8$ is a factor. Then find the volume given that $x = 20$. $12(x - 8)(x + 1)(x + 4)$, 72,576 cubic inches

***28.** (64) **Plant Nutrition** The pH of a soil is given by the function $\text{pH} = -\log[\text{H}^+]$, where $[\text{H}^+]$ represents the concentration of hydrogen ions in moles per liter. Most plants require soil with a hydrogen ion concentration between 0.0001 and 0.00000001 moles per liter. What pH values correspond to these hydrogen ion concentration values? 4.0 and 8.0

***29.** (65) **Travel** A driver leaves a parking lot and heads due south at a rate of 40 miles per hour. An hour later, another driver leaves the same parking lot and heads due west at a rate of 60 miles per hour. Approximately how long will it take for the cars to be 300 miles apart? 4.8 hours

***30.** (68) **Multi-Step** Two bags each contain papers labeled with numbers 1 through 5. One paper is selected from each.

a. Explain why selecting a 5 from the first bag and the sum of the numbers is greater than 5 are dependent events.

b. Find the probability of both events.

30a. If a 5 is not first selected, the probability of a sum greater than 5 is $\frac{3}{5}$. If a 5 is first selected, the probability changes to 1.
b. The probability of both events is $\frac{1}{5}$.

CHALLENGE

If some letters and envelopes get all mixed up so that each letter is randomly inserted into an envelope, what is the probability that the first three of the letters end up in the correct envelopes? Sample: $\frac{1}{n} \cdot \frac{1}{n-1} \cdot \frac{1}{n-2}$, where n is the number of letters

LOOKING FORWARD

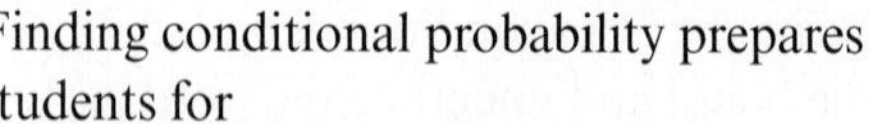

Finding conditional probability prepares students for

- **Lesson 73** Using Sampling
- **Lesson 80** Finding the Normal Distribution
- **Lesson 116** Finding Best Fit Models
- **Lesson 118** Recognizing Misleading Data

LESSON 69

Simplifying Complex Expressions

Warm Up

1. (62) **Vocabulary** A number that can be written in the form $a + bi$ where a and b are real numbers is a complex number.

2. (19) Multiply $(3x - 5)(4x + 2)$. $12x^2 - 14x - 10$

3. (40) Simplify $\frac{5}{\sqrt{5}}$. $\sqrt{5}$

4. (62) Add $(3 + 2i) + (6 - 8i)$. $9 - 6i$

New Concepts

Complex numbers $(a + bi)$ can be graphed on a complex plane, where the horizontal axis represents the real part, a, and the vertical axis represents the imaginary part, bi.

Math Language

The **imaginary axis** is sometimes referred to as the ***i*-axis.**

Example 1 Graphing Complex Numbers

Graph each number on the complex plane.

a. $3 + 4i$ **b.** $-2 - 3i$

c. $-4i$ **d.** 1

SOLUTION

a. Move 3 units to the right and 4 units up.

b. Move 2 units to the left and 3 units down.

c. Move 0 units right or left and 4 units down.

d. Move 1 unit to the right and 0 units up or down.

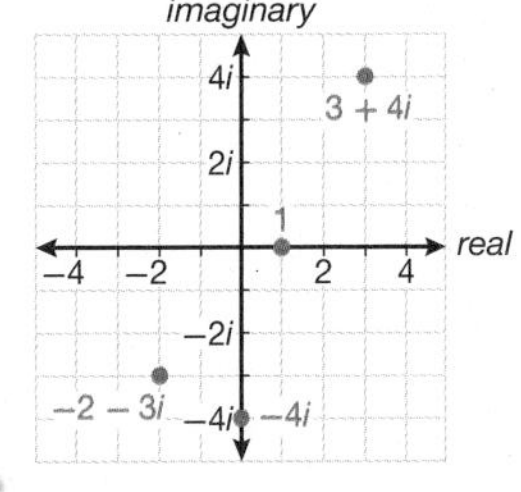

The **absolute value of a complex number** is its distance from the origin. Unless the point is on the x- or i-axis, the distance is the length of a line segment that forms the hypotenuse of a right triangle and can be found using the Pythagorean Theorem.

Absolute Value of a Complex Number

$$|a + bi| = \sqrt{a^2 + b^2}$$

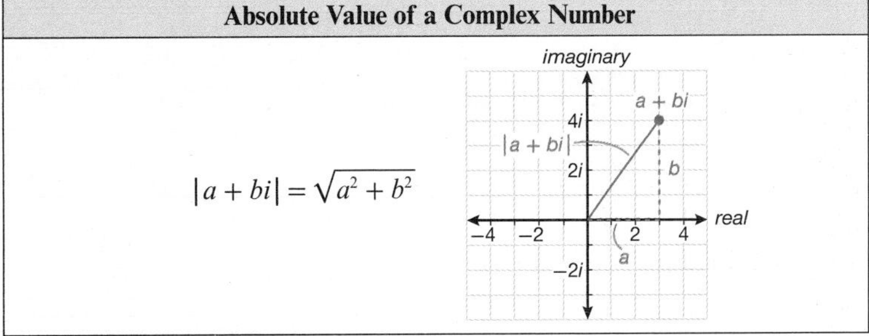

LESSON 69

1 Warm Up

For problem 1, remind students that a complex number is composed of an imaginary part and a real part.

2 New Concepts

In this lesson, students learn to graph, multiply, evaluate powers of, divide, and find the absolute value of complex numbers.

Example 1

Graphing numbers in the complex plane is similar to graphing ordered pairs on the x-y plane.

Additional Example 1

Graph each number on the complex plane.

a. $2 - 3i$ **b.** $-6 + i$

c. $0.5i$ **d.** 0

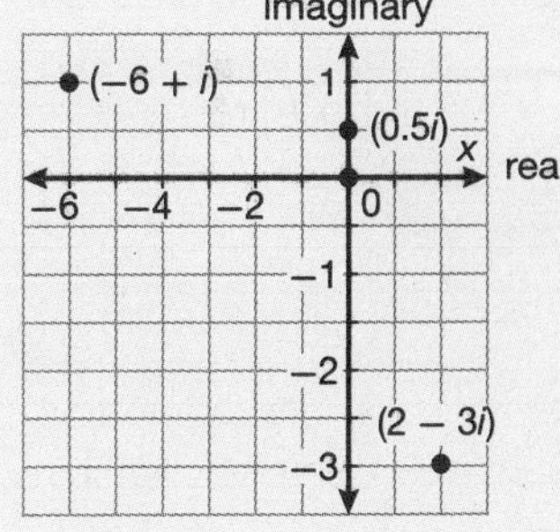

MATH BACKGROUND

Imaginary numbers were really conceived in the 1600s, even before negative numbers were well-understood! They were first introduced when scientists and mathematicians were solving polynomial equations. It wasn't until the 1800s that people understood that imaginary numbers actually represented physical quantities and they became an accepted branch of mathematics. As a note, the term imaginary was coined before then, and considered derogatory, since these numbers didn't represent, or mean, anything.

Today, imaginary numbers are used in analyzing electrical systems, particularly in the switch between time-based and frequency-based representations. They are fundamental in understanding quantum mechanics and fractals (particularly when graphing the famous Mandelbrot set).

LESSON RESOURCES

Student Edition Practice Workbook 69
Reteaching Masters 69
Adaptations Masters 69
Challenge and Enrichment Masters C69

Example 2

Reiterate to students that the absolute value of a complex number is the distance from (0, 0) on a graph.

Additional Example 2

Find the absolute value of each number.

a. $-5 - 2i$ $\sqrt{29}$

b. $5 + 2i$ $\sqrt{29}$

c. $8i$ 8

Example 3

Be sure that students understand that multiplying complex numbers is just like multiplying any other polynomials. The only difference is that powers of i, which will be covered in the next example, should be simplified.

Additional Example 3

Multiply. Write each answer in the form $a + bi$.

a. $2i(-2 - 2i)$ $4 - 4i$

b. $(1 + i)(-9 - 2i)$ $-7 - 11i$

Example 2 **Finding the Absolute Value of Complex Numbers**

Find the absolute value of each number.

a. $3 + 4i$

SOLUTION $|a + bi| = \sqrt{a^2 + b^2}$

$$|3 + 4i| = \sqrt{3^2 + 4^2}$$
$$= \sqrt{9 + 16} = \sqrt{25} = 5$$

b. $-2 - 3i$

SOLUTION $|a + bi| = \sqrt{a^2 + b^2}$

$$|-2 - 3i| = \sqrt{(-2)^2 + (-3)^2}$$
$$= \sqrt{4 + 9} = \sqrt{13}$$

c. $-5i$

SOLUTION $|a + bi| = \sqrt{a^2 + b^2}$

$$|-5i| = \sqrt{0^2 + (-5)^2}$$
$$= \sqrt{25} = 5$$

Math Reasoning

Verify Use the formula for the absolute value of a complex number to show that $|-1|$ is 1.

$$|-1 + 0i| = \sqrt{(-1)^2 + 0^2}$$
$$= \sqrt{1}$$
$$= 1$$

When multiplying complex numbers, remember that $i^2 = -1$.

Example 3 **Multiplying Complex Numbers**

Multiply. Write answers in the form $a + bi$.

a. $-4i(7 + 3i)$

SOLUTION

$-4i(7 + 3i)$	
$= -28i - 12i^2$	Distributive Property
$= -28i - 12(-1)$	$i^2 = -1$
$= -28i + 12$	Simplify.
$= 12 - 28i$	Write in standard form.

b. $(5 + 4i)(6 - 2i)$

SOLUTION

$(5 + 4i)(6 - 2i)$	
$= 30 - 10i + 24i - 8i^2$	Use the FOIL method.
$= 30 + 14i - 8i^2$	Simplify.
$= 30 + 14i - 8(-1)$	$i^2 = -1$
$= 30 + 14i + 8$	Simplify.
$= 38 + 14i$	Write in standard form.

INCLUSION

When simplifying, multiplying, and dividing complex numbers, students can mark the terms with different colored pencils to denote real terms, terms with an i, and terms with an i^2. This will help them to combine like terms.

Study the powers of i below.

Powers of i	
$i^1 = i$	$i^5 = i \cdot i^4 = i(1) = i$
$i^2 = -1$	$i^6 = i \cdot i^5 = i(i) = i^2 = -1$
$i^3 = i \cdot i^2 = i(-1) = -i$	$i^7 = i \cdot i^6 = i(-1) = -i$
$i^4 = i \cdot i^3 = i(-i) = -i^2 = -(-1) = 1$	$i^8 = i \cdot i^7 = i(-i) = -i^2 = -(-1) = 1$

Notice that the four simplified values of i, -1, $-i$, and 1 repeat such that $i = i^5$, $i^2 = i^6$, $i^3 = i^7$, and $i^4 = i^8$. Any power of i can be found by dividing the exponent of i by four and using the remainder.

When the remainder is ...	The expression is equivalent to ...
0	$i^4 = 1$
1	$i^1 = i$
2	$i^2 = -1$
3	$i^3 = -i$

Example 4 **Evaluating Powers of i**

Simplify each expression.

a. i^{30}

SOLUTION $30 \div 4 = 7$ R 2, so $i^{30} = i^2 = -1$.

b. $5i^{12}$

SOLUTION $12 \div 4 = 3$ R 0, so $i^{12} = i^4 = 1$.
$5i^{12} = 5(1) = 5$

c. $-2i^{13}$

SOLUTION $13 \div 4 = 3$ R 1, so $i^{13} = i^1 = i$.
$-2i^{13} = -2(i) = -2i$

Caution

A simplified expression does not have a radical in the denominator. Because $i = \sqrt{-1}$, an expression with i in the denominator is not simplified.

To eliminate a radical in a denominator, multiply both the numerator and denominator of the fraction by the conjugate of the denominator. The **complex conjugate** of $a + bi$ is $a - bi$.

Example 5 **Dividing Complex Numbers**

a. Divide 3 by $6 + i\sqrt{5}$. Write the answer in the form $a + bi$.

SOLUTION $\frac{3}{6 + i\sqrt{5}}$

$\frac{3}{6 + i\sqrt{5}}\left(\frac{6 - i\sqrt{5}}{6 - i\sqrt{5}}\right)$ Multiply the numerator and the denominator by the complex conjugate of the denominator.

$\frac{18 - 3i\sqrt{5}}{36 - 5i^2}$ Distribute and simplify.

$\frac{18 - 3i\sqrt{5}}{41} = \frac{18}{41} - \frac{3\sqrt{5}}{41}i$

Example 4

Students should be quickly able to recreate the table of powers of i. Also, they should note that $(-1)^n$ gives a repeating pattern of 1 and -1. The pattern resulting from i^n includes i, $-i$, -1, and 1.

Additional Example 4

Simplify each expression.

a. i^{27} $-i$

b. $3i^{333}$ $3i$

c. $-i^9$ $-i$

Example 5

Students should recognize that when they multiply a complex number by its complex conjugate, they will get a real number.

Error Alert Students are likely to drop an exponent or a negative sign when multiplying by the complex conjugate. One thing they can keep in mind is that the product of a complex number and its conjugate is a real number. If they don't get a real number on doing the multiplication, they should check for errors.

Additional Example 5

a. Divide 10 by $2 + i\sqrt{2}$. Write the answer in the form $a + bi$.
$\frac{10}{3} - \frac{5}{3}\sqrt{2}i$

b. Divide $6 + 21i$ by $3i$. Write the answer in the form $a + bi$.
$7 - 2i$

ENGLISH LEARNERS

Be sure that students know the difference between imaginary and complex numbers. Also, students need to know what the **conjugate** of a complex number is.

You may want students to use an index card and write the term with an example for each.

As with so many English words, conjugate can have many meanings. English learners may be learning to conjugate verbs, which bears no resemblance to the conjugate of a complex number.

Lesson Practice

Problem h

Error Alert Students may write $-40 - 72i$ because a positive times a negative is negative. Remind them to write down and evaluate i^2.

Check for Understanding

The question below helps assess the concepts taught in this lesson.

"Can the product of two complex numbers yield a real number? If so, when?" The product of a complex number with its conjugate is a real number.

3 Practice

Math Conversations

Discussions to strengthen understanding

Problem 5

"What operation will isolate $x^{\frac{1}{7}}$?" Raise each side of the equation to the 7th power.

Problem 6

"What operation will isolate $x^{\frac{2}{3}}$?" Raise each side of the equation to the $\left(\frac{3}{2}\right)$ power.

---

b. Divide $4 + i$ by $6i$. Write the answer in the form $a + bi$.

Math Reasoning

Analyze Why is $-6i$ the conjugate of $6i$?

$-6i = 0 - 6i$ and the conjugate is $0 + 6i = 6i$.

SOLUTION $\frac{4+i}{6i}$

$\frac{4+i}{6i}\left(\frac{-6i}{-6i}\right)$ Multiply the numerator and the denominator by the complex conjugate of the denominator.

$\frac{-24i - 6i^2}{-36i^2}$ Distribute.

$\frac{-24i - 6(-1)}{-36(-1)}$ Simplify.

$\frac{-24i + 6}{36} = -\frac{24}{36}i + \frac{6}{36} = -\frac{2}{3}i + \frac{1}{6} = \frac{1}{6} - \frac{2}{3}i$

Lesson Practice

a.–d.

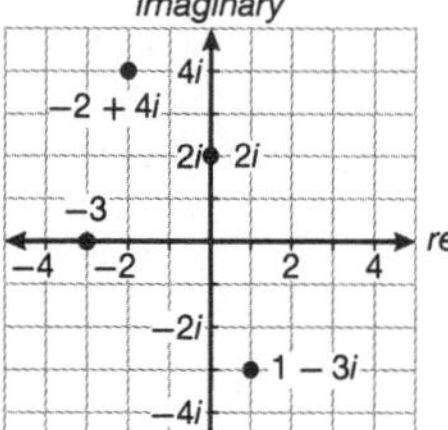

Graph each number on the complex plane.
(Ex 1)

a. $1 - 3i$ **b.** $-2 + 4i$ **c.** -3 **d.** $2i$

Find the absolute value of each number.
(Ex 2)

e. $7 - 2i$ $\sqrt{53}$ **f.** $-5 + i$ $\sqrt{26}$ **g.** $10i$ 10

Multiply. Write answers in the form $a + bi$.
(Ex 3)

h. $8i(-9 - 5i)$ $40 - 72i$ **i.** $(2 - 3i)(5 + 9i)$ $37 + 3i$

Simplify each expression.
(Ex 4)

j. i^{18} -1 **k.** $-3i^{11}$ $3i$ **l.** $\frac{1}{2}i^{21}$ $\frac{1}{2}i$

m. Divide $3 + 3i$ by $3i$. Write the answer in the form $a + bi$. $1 - i$
(Ex 5)

n. Divide -4 by $2 + i\sqrt{3}$. Write the answer in the form $a + bi$. $-\frac{8}{7} + \frac{4\sqrt{3}}{7}i$
(Ex 5)

Practice Distributed and Integrated

Solve for $f(x) = 0$ using the quadratic formula.

1. $f(x) = x^2 + 8x - 3$ $x = -4 \pm \sqrt{19}$
(65)

2. $f(x) = 3x^2 - 10x + 4$ $x = \frac{5 \pm \sqrt{13}}{3}$
(65)

3. **Probability** A bag holds 53 yellow marbles, 17 red marbles, and 30 green marbles. What is the probability of not choosing a red marble? $\frac{83}{100}$
(55)

4. A savings account earns interest at an annual rate of 3.8%, compounded quarterly. If the account begins with a principal amount of $2,700, what will its value be after 14 years? $4,584.77
(57)

Solve for x.

5. $x^{\frac{1}{7}} = 5$ 78,125
(59)

6. $x^{\frac{2}{3}} = 36$ 216
(59)

CHALLENGE

Write the simplest polynomial equation with roots i, $-i$, $1 + \sqrt{2}i$, and $1 - \sqrt{2}i$.
$x^4 - 2x^3 + 4x^2 - 2x + 3 = 0$

***7.** **Multiple Choice** In which quadrant of the complex plane is $5 - i$ located? D
(69)
A Quadrant I   B Quadrant II   C Quadrant III   D Quadrant IV

8. **Write** Explain how to use synthetic division to determine if $x + 6$ is a factor of $x^3 + 3x^2 - 28x - 60$ and then perform the division.
(61)

8. If $x + 6$ is a factor, then $P(-6) = 0$ because 0 means there is no remainder. The remainder is 0, so $x + 6$ is a factor.

$$\begin{array}{r|rrrr} -6 & 1 & 3 & -28 & -60 \\ & & -6 & 18 & 60 \\ \hline & 1 & -3 & -10 & 0 \end{array}$$

Simplify.

9. $\frac{1}{4}\sqrt{-256}$. $4i$
(62)

10. $\frac{1}{2}\sqrt{-2500}$. $25i$
(62)

11. Given $\theta = -920°$, find the measure of the reference angle. 20°
(56)

***12.** **Generalize** Show that the product of any two complex conjugates, $a + bi$ and $a - bi$, is a real number. The imaginary parts become eliminated.
(69)

$(a + bi)(a - bi)$
$a^2 - b^2i^2$
$a^2 - b^2(-1)$
$a^2 + b^2$

***13.** Evaluate the inverse trigonometric function $\text{Sin}^{-1}\left(-\frac{\sqrt{2}}{2}\right)$. Give your answer in both radians and degrees. $-\frac{\pi}{4}$; $-45°$
(67)

14. Why can't the matrix below be used as an encoding matrix for a cipher?
(Inv 4)

$$\begin{bmatrix} 5 & -2 & 3 \\ 0 & 0 & 7 \\ 0 & 0 & 13 \end{bmatrix}$$

Sample answer: The determinant of the matrix is 0, therefore the matrix doesn't have an inverse and would not be able to be decoded.

15. **Amusement Parks** You get on a ferris wheel ride, and the ferris wheel turns through 1370°. How much further must the wheel turn before you are at the bottom again?
(56)
70°

***16.** **Error Analysis** Find and correct the error a student made in finding $P(\text{AM}|\text{Male})$.
(68)

$$P(\text{AM}|\text{Male}) = \frac{16}{20} = \frac{4}{5} = 80\%$$

	Male	Female
AM	16	4
PM	8	12

16. The student found $P(\text{Male}|\text{AM})$. The condition is that the person must be male, and there are 24 males. Of those, 16 are in the AM. The probability is $\frac{16}{24} = \frac{2}{3} = 66\frac{2}{3}\%$.

***17.** **Graphing Calculator** **a.** Graph $y = x^3 + 6x^2 - 32$ on a graphing calculator. What are the x-intercepts? -4 and 2
(66)

b. Find the multiplicity of each root of $x^3 + 6x^2 - 32 = 0$ by factoring. -4 has a multiplicity of 2 and 2 has a multiplicity of 1.

***18.** **Formulate** Give a rule for finding $P(B|A)$. *Hint:* Consider the rule for $P(A \text{ and } B)$ for dependent events. $P(B|A) = \frac{P(A \text{ and } B)}{P(A)}$
(68)

19. **Multiple Choice** Which equation is equivalent to $10^x = 0.1$? C
(64)
A $\log_{0.1}10 = x$ B $\log_{0.1}x = 10$
C $\log_{10}0.1 = x$ D $\log_{10}x = 0.1$

Problem 8

Extend the Problem

Write the quadratic expression that results from dividing the original expression by $(x + 6)$.
$x^2 - 3x - 10$

Factor this expression.
$(x - 5)(x + 2)$

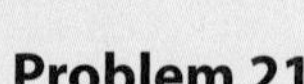

Problem 21

Remind students to work from the inside out when working with parentheses. Order of operations is very important.

Problem 25

Error Alert

Students are likely to calculate the distance traveled in a day instead of in an hour. They first need to realize that Earth rotates once in 24 hours and that the problem asks for the distance traveled in *one hour*.

Problem 29

Students will need to interpret the fact that they get two complex numbers when they solve the quadratic equation. In this problem, time is a real quantity, so the absence of a real value means that the event cannot happen.

20. (60) **Formulate** Write a formula for $P(A \text{ or } B \text{ or } C)$. Use the diagram to the right to help you. $P(A \text{ or } B \text{ or } C) = P(A) + P(B) + P(C) - P(A \text{ and } B) - P(B \text{ and } C) - P(A \text{ and } C) + P(A \text{ and } B \text{ and } C)$

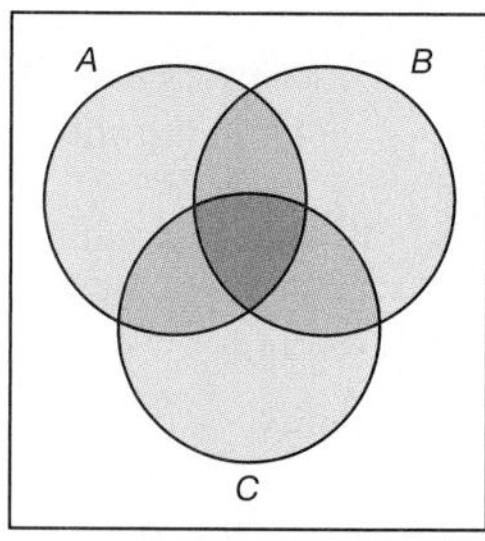

21. (67) **Multi-Step** Let $f(\theta) = \text{Sin}\,\theta$ and $g(\theta) = \text{Sin}^{-1}\theta$, where θ is in radians.

a. Evaluate $f\left(g\left(\frac{1}{2}\right)\right)$. Show your steps. $f\left(g\left(\frac{1}{2}\right)\right) = \text{Sin}\left(\text{Sin}^{-1}\left(\frac{1}{2}\right)\right) = \text{Sin}\left(\frac{\pi}{6}\right) = \frac{1}{2}$

b. Evaluate $g\left(f\left(\frac{\pi}{6}\right)\right)$. Show your steps. $g\left(f\left(\frac{\pi}{6}\right)\right) = \text{Sin}^{-1}\left(\text{Sin}\left(\frac{\pi}{6}\right)\right) = \text{Sin}^{-1}\left(\frac{1}{2}\right) = \frac{\pi}{6}$

c. Based on part a, what is the value of $f(g(x))$? Based on part b, what is the value of $g(f(x))$? x, x

22. (58) **Error Analysis** Examine the work below. Find and explain the error. Then find the correct solution.

$$x^2 - 44x + 484 = 121$$
$$(x - 22)^2 = 121$$
$$x - 22 = 11$$
$$x = 33$$

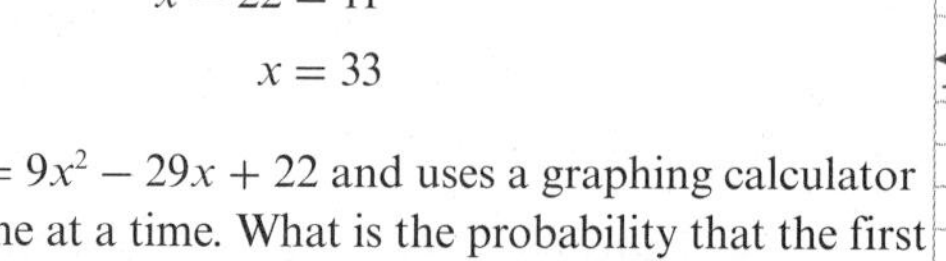

24. $-1 - i$;

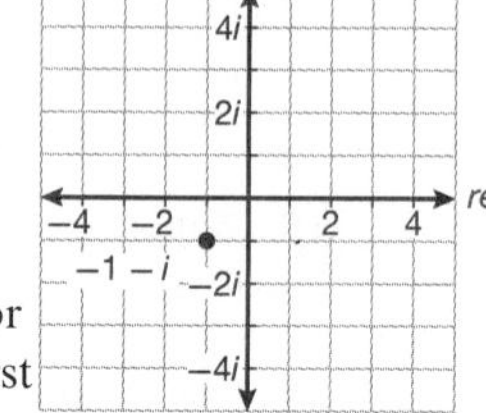

***23.** (65) **Probability** A student graphs $y = 9x^2 - 29x + 22$ and uses a graphing calculator to find the value of the zeros one at a time. What is the probability that the first zero the student finds is negative? Why? 0%, because both zeros are positive.

***24.** (69) **Multi-Step** Simplify $i^{22} + i^{15}$. Then graph the number on the complex plane.

22. The error is in the third line. By the square root property $x - 22 = 11$ and $x - 22 = -11$; $x = 11, 33$

25. (63) **Planet Rotation** Venus is only slightly smaller than Earth; its radius is approximately 3757 miles. But it rotates much more slowly; it takes 243 Earth days for Venus to make one complete rotation. If an object is fixed on Venus's equator, how far does it travel in 1 hour due to Venus's rotation? approximately 4.05 miles

26. (64) **Analyze** Describe the value(s) of b^x when $b = 1$ and when $b \neq 1$.

***27.** (69) Find the absolute value of $|3 - 4i|$. 5

***28.** (69) Find the absolute value of $|6 + 2i|$. $2\sqrt{10}$

29. (62) **Sports** A football player playing in a domed stadium kicks a football straight up into the air. The height of the football after t seconds can be modeled by $-16t^2 + 80t$. The dome has a height of about 288 feet. The solutions of $-16t^2 + 80t = 288$ give the number of seconds it will take for the football to reach the top of the dome. Solve the equation. Will the football reach the top of the dome? If so, when? $\frac{5}{2} \pm \frac{i}{2}\sqrt{47}$, The time is not a real number; the football will never reach the top of the dome.

26. Possible answer: If $b = 1$, then $b^x = 1$ for all values of x. If $b \neq 1$, then b^x has different values, and those values are determined by the values of x.

30. (59) **Geometry** Find the area of the triangle to the right. 2 cm²

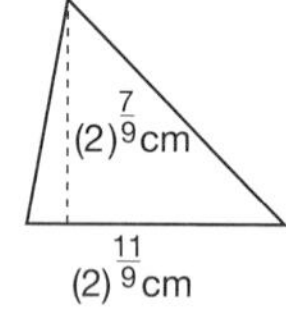

LOOKING FORWARD

Simplifying complex expressions prepares students for

- **Lesson 83** Writing Quadratic Equations from Roots
- **Lesson 85** Finding Polynomial Roots II

LESSON **70**

Solving Radical Equations

Warm Up

1. **Vocabulary** In the expression $\sqrt[3]{x}$, 3 is referred to as the index.
(40)
2. Simplify $\sqrt{64}$. 8
(40)
3. Simplify $\sqrt[3]{-125}$. −5
(40)
4. Solve $x^2 + 5x - 30 = 6$. −9, 4
(35)
5. Write $(x + 6)^{\frac{1}{2}}$ in radical form. $\sqrt{x+6}$
(40)

New Concepts

A **radical equation** is an equation that contains at least one radical whose radicand contains a variable.

Radical Equations	Not Radical Equations
$\sqrt{x+3} + 1 = 4$	$x - \sqrt{5} = 8$
$\sqrt[3]{2x} + 5 = \sqrt[3]{x-1}$	$\sqrt[4]{25} = x - 3$

Math Reasoning

Analyze Does cubing each side of $x = 5$ result in extraneous solutions? Explain.

No, $x^3 = 125$ has only one solution, 5.

To solve a radical equation, first isolate the radical on one side of the equation. Then raise both sides of the equation to the power of the index of the radical. This will clear the radical.

It is critical that the solutions of a radical equation be checked because some of the solutions obtained may be extraneous solutions. An extraneous solution is a solution of a derived equation that is not a solution of the original equation.

For example, the equation $x = 5$ has one solution, 5. But when both sides of the equation are squared, the resulting equation $x^2 = 25$ has two solutions, −5 and 5. The solution −5 is extraneous because it is not a solution of the original equation.

Example 1 Solving Equations Containing One Square Root

Solve each equation.

a. $\sqrt{x-5} = 14$

SOLUTION The radical is already isolated on the left side.

$\sqrt{x-5} = 14$

$\left(\sqrt{x-5}\right)^2 = 14^2$ Square both sides of the equation.

$x - 5 = 196$ Simplify.

$x = 201$ Add 5 to both sides.

Check $\sqrt{x-5} = 14$

$\sqrt{201-5} \stackrel{?}{=} 14$

$\sqrt{196} \stackrel{?}{=} 14$

$14 = 14$ ✓

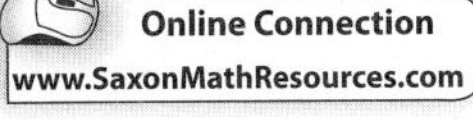

Online Connection
www.SaxonMathResources.com

LESSON 70

1 Warm Up

Problem 2 is a good introduction to radical equations. While $\sqrt{64}$ can be either ±8, when solving radical equations, we'll only be concerned with the positive, or principal, root. For problem 3, point out to students that there is only one answer, −5. $-5^3 = -125$ but $5^3 \neq -125$.

2 New Concepts

In this lesson, students learn to solve equations involving one or two radicals algebraically. They learn to check answers graphically. They also investigate extraneous solutions, how they arise, and how to recognize them.

Discuss the definition of **radical equation** and extraneous solutions.

Example 1

Students solve equations with one square root.

Additional Example 1

Solve each equation.

a. $\sqrt{x-25} = 2$ $x = 29$

b. $\sqrt{3x-17} - 2 = 6$ $x = 27$

MATH BACKGROUND

Students have learned that the square root of a positive number yields two answers, one positive and the other negative. When solving square root equations only the positive square root will be considered. The positive square root is called the **principal square root.** This ensures that solutions are real.

When students advance to working with radical *functions,* every x-value maps to only one y-value. This yields a restricted domain that accounts for only considering the positive square root.

A good way to show this to students is to have them graph $y = \sqrt{x}$ on their calculators. They will see that only the top half shows on the graph. No negative y-values are shown because their calculator is graphing the function based on real numbers, not just the equation. At the least, students need to know that we want only real answers, and we work only with the positive square root when solving radical equations.

LESSON RESOURCES

Student Edition Practice Workbook 70
Reteaching Masters 70
Adaptations Masters 70
Challenge and Enrichment Masters C70

Example 2

The only difference between solving problems like these and problems as in Example 1 is that both sides of the equation are cubed (instead of squared) to eliminate the radical sign. The principles are exactly the same.

Error Alert Students are likely to try to cube the problem before they add 6 to each side. If they do this, they will still have a variable under a radical sign. That is their clue that they didn't perform the equation solving steps in order.

Additional Example 2

Solve each equation.

a. $\sqrt[3]{2x-26}-4=0$ $x = 45$

b. $-3\sqrt[3]{x+13}=-9$ $x = 14$

b. $\sqrt{6x+7}+3=9$

SOLUTION First isolate the radical on the left.

$\sqrt{6x+7}+3=9$

$\sqrt{6x+7}=6$	Subtract 3 from both sides of the equation.
$(\sqrt{6x+7})^2=6^2$	Square both sides.
$6x+7=36$	Simplify.
$6x=29$	Subtract 7 from both sides.
$x=\frac{29}{6}$	Divide both sides by 6.

Check $\sqrt{6x+7}+3=9$

$\sqrt{6\left(\frac{29}{6}\right)+7}+3\stackrel{?}{=}9$

$\sqrt{36}+3\stackrel{?}{=}9$

$9=9$ ✓

Example 2 Solving Equations Containing One Cube Root

Solve each equation.

a. $\sqrt[3]{4x+4}-6=0$

SOLUTION First isolate the radical.

$\sqrt[3]{4x+4}-6=0$

$\sqrt[3]{4x+4}=6$	Add 6 to each side.
$(\sqrt[3]{4x+4})^3=6^3$	Cube both sides to clear the cube root.
$4x+4=216$	Simplify.
$4x=212$	Subtract 4 from each side.
$x=53$	Divide both sides by 4.

Check $\sqrt[3]{4x+4}-6=0$

$\sqrt[3]{4(53)+4}-6\stackrel{?}{=}0$

$\sqrt[3]{216}-6\stackrel{?}{=}0$

$6-6\stackrel{?}{=}0$

$0=0$ ✓

b. $-2\sqrt[3]{x-8}=14$

SOLUTION Isolate the radical by dividing.

$-2\sqrt[3]{x-8}=14$

$\sqrt[3]{x-8}=-7$	Divide both sides by −2.
$(\sqrt[3]{x-8})^3=(-7)^3$	Cube both sides.
$x-8=-343$	Simplify.
$x=-335$	Add 8 to each side.

Math Reasoning

Verify Check that −335 is a solution of $-2\sqrt[3]{x-8}=14$.

$-2\sqrt[3]{-335-8}$
$=-2\sqrt[3]{-335-8}$
$=-2(-7)$
$=14$

ENGLISH LEARNERS

Say the words radical and **radicand** as they sound very similar. Have students repeat each word. Define radicand as the expression under the radical sign.

Discuss the fact that in $\sqrt{x-7}$, $x-7$ is the radicand and $\sqrt{x-7}$ is the radical.

Have students indicate the radical and the radicand in the radical expression $\sqrt[3]{2x+17}-4$. Radical $\sqrt[3]{2x+17}$; radicand $2x+17$

Have students write their own radical expression and identify both the radicand and the radical and tell how they are related. The radicand is the expression under the radical sign while the radical is the expression and the radical sign.

Math Language

Indices is the plural of index.

Sometimes an equation has two radicals. If their indices are the same and each radical is on a different side of the equation, it is simplest to raise each side of the equation to the power of the index.

If the indices on the radicals differ, the solution can be estimated by using a graphing calculator. Graphing calculators are also very useful in checking solutions.

Example 3 Solving Equations Containing Two Radicals

Solve each equation. Check the solutions graphically.

a. $\sqrt{8x-15}=\sqrt{4x+5}$

SOLUTION $\sqrt{8x-15}=\sqrt{4x+5}$

$(\sqrt{8x-15})^2=(\sqrt{4x+5})^2$ Square both sides.

$8x-15=4x+5$ Simplify.

$4x=20$ Isolate x.

$x=5$

Check Graph $Y1=\sqrt{8x-15}$ and $Y2=\sqrt{4x+5}$. The intersection point is the solution. Use the **intersect** command located in the **Calculate** (2nd Trace) menu. The curves intersect at $x=5$.

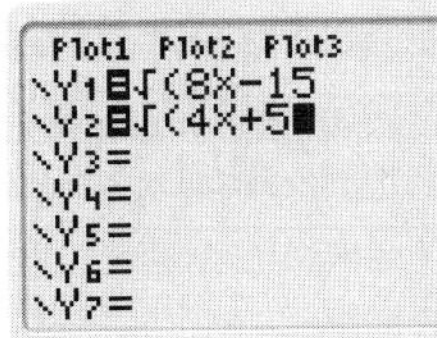

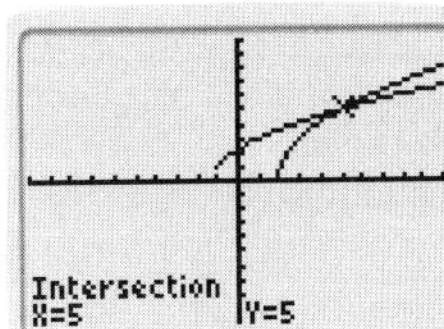

b. $\sqrt[3]{3x}=2\sqrt[3]{x-1}$

SOLUTION $\sqrt[3]{3x}=2\sqrt[3]{x-1}$

$(\sqrt[3]{3x})^3=(2\sqrt[3]{x-1})^3$ Cube both sides.

$3x=8(x-1)$ Simplify.

$3x=8x-8$ Distribute 8.

$-5x=-8$ Isolate x.

$x=\frac{8}{5}=1.6$

Graphing Calculator Tips

To type the cube root symbol, press **Math** and choose it from the items in the Math list.

Check Graph $Y1=\sqrt[3]{3x}$ and $Y2=2\sqrt[3]{x-1}$. The curves intersect at $x=1.6$.

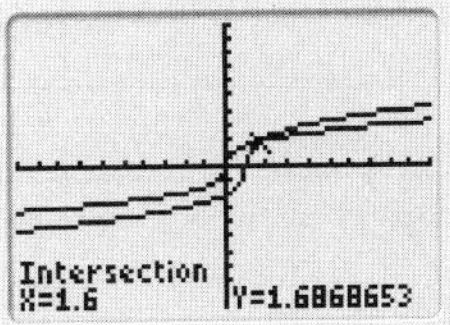

Example 3

To help students understand how to check their solutions graphically, remind them that the solution to two simultaneous equations is the intersection of the two curves on a graph. In these types of problems, the equation can be written as two simultaneous equations.

Then students can graph each side of the equation and find the intersection. The graphs represent all possible solutions of the right side of the equation and all possible solutions of the left side of the equation. The intersection of the two curves is the point that makes both statements true.

Additional Example 3

Solve each equation. Check the solutions graphically.

a. $\sqrt{3x-7}=\sqrt{2x+19}$ $x=26$

b. $\sqrt[3]{x}=\frac{1}{2}\sqrt[3]{4x+4}$ $x=1$

c. $\sqrt{2x+1}-\sqrt[3]{-10x}-3=0$ $x\approx 0.435$

INCLUSION

Help students make a check list of steps to use when solving radical equations. Have them write the steps on a note card or in their class notes. It may be more convenient to use the steps given below. Use the words in bold face as key word reminders.

1. **solate.** Isolate the radical, if possible. If there are two radicals, put one on each side of the equal sign.
2. **o er.** Raise both sides of the equation to a power that is equal to the index number.
3. **ol e.** Solve the resulting equation.
4. **C ec .** Check for extraneous solutions.

Example 4

For this example, it becomes critical that students realize we are only working with positive square roots. The negative root is generally not considered a viable solution.

Additional Example 4

Solve each equation.

a. $\sqrt{x} + 5 = 1$ There is no solution.

b. $x + 3 = \sqrt{6x + 13}$ $x = \pm 2$

c. $\sqrt{2x} - \sqrt[3]{-5x} - 6 = 0$

SOLUTION Move one of the radicals to the right side. Then use a graphing calculator.

$$\sqrt{2x} - \sqrt[3]{-5x} - 6 = 0$$

$$\sqrt{2x} - 6 = \sqrt[3]{-5x}$$ Add $\sqrt[3]{-5x}$ to each side.

Graph $Y1 = \sqrt{2x} - 6$ and $Y2 = \sqrt[3]{-5x}$. The curves intersect at $x \approx 4.83$.

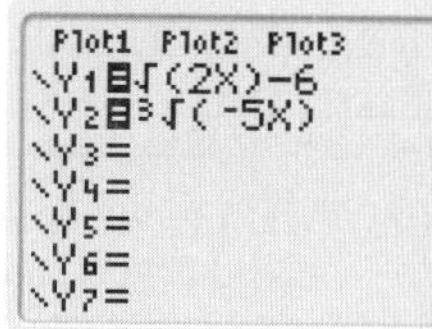

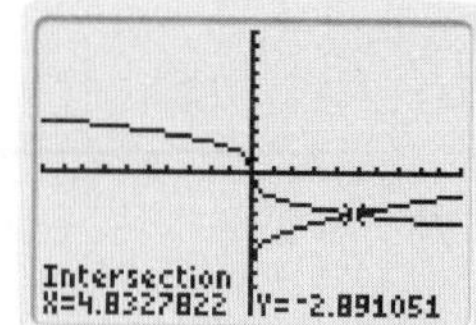

Math Reasoning

Analyze How can you see in the first step of 4a that the equation has no solutions?

The principal square root of a real number is never negative.

Example 4 Solving Equations with Extraneous Solutions

Solve each equation.

a. $\sqrt{x} - 4 = -8$

SOLUTION $\sqrt{x} - 4 = -8$

$\sqrt{x} = -4$ Add 4 to each side to isolate the radical.

$(\sqrt{x})^2 = (-4)^2$ Square both sides.

$x = 16$ Simplify.

Check $\sqrt{x} - 4 = -8$

$\sqrt{16} - 4 \stackrel{?}{=} -8$

$4 - 4 \stackrel{?}{=} -8$

$0 \neq -8$

The solution of 16 is extraneous. The equation has no solutions.

b. $x + 1 = \sqrt{2x + 10}$

SOLUTION $x + 1 = \sqrt{2x + 10}$ The radical is isolated on the right.

$(x + 1)^2 = \left(\sqrt{2x + 10}\right)^2$ Square both sides.

$x^2 + 2x + 1 = 2x + 10$ Simplify.

$x^2 - 9 = 0$ Solve the quadratic equation.

$x^2 = 9$

$x = \pm 3$

Check $x + 1 = \sqrt{2x + 10}$ $\qquad$ $x + 1 = \sqrt{2x + 10}$

$3 + 1 \stackrel{?}{=} \sqrt{2(3) + 10}$ $\qquad$ $-3 + 1 \stackrel{?}{=} \sqrt{2(-3) + 10}$

$4 \stackrel{?}{=} \sqrt{16}$ $\qquad$ $-2 \stackrel{?}{=} \sqrt{4}$

$4 = 4$ ✓ $\qquad$ $-2 \neq 2$

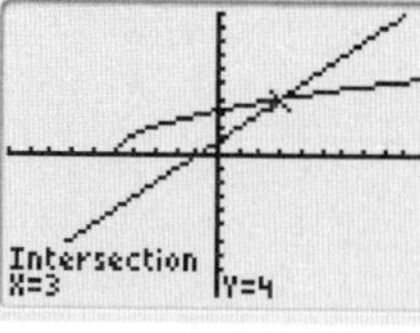

The solution of -3 is extraneous. The only solution is 3.

ALTERNATE METHOD FOR EXAMPLE 4

For Example 4, have students write the equations in standard form and substitute y for 0, then use their graphing calculators to find the solutions for x.

a. $\sqrt{x} + 5 = 1$ $\sqrt{x} + 4 = y$; There is no solution.

b. $x + 3 = \sqrt{6x + 13}$ $x + 3 - \sqrt{6x + 13} = y$; $x = \pm 2$

498 Saxon Algebra 2

Example 5 Application: Physics

The period of a pendulum, T, is the time it takes for the pendulum to make one back-and-forth swing, and is given by $T = 2\pi\sqrt{\frac{L}{9.8}}$, where L is the length of the pendulum in meters. Find the length of a pendulum whose period is 3 seconds.

SOLUTION Substitute 3 for T in the formula and solve for L.

$$3 = 2\pi\sqrt{\frac{L}{9.8}}$$

$$\frac{3}{2\pi} = \sqrt{\frac{L}{9.8}} \quad \text{Isolate the variable.}$$

$$\left(\frac{3}{2\pi}\right)^2 = \left(\sqrt{\frac{L}{9.8}}\right)^2 \quad \text{Square both sides.}$$

$$\frac{9}{4\pi^2} = \frac{L}{9.8} \quad \text{Simplify.}$$

$$9.8\left(\frac{9}{4\pi^2}\right) = L \quad \text{Isolate } L.$$

$$2.23 \approx L$$

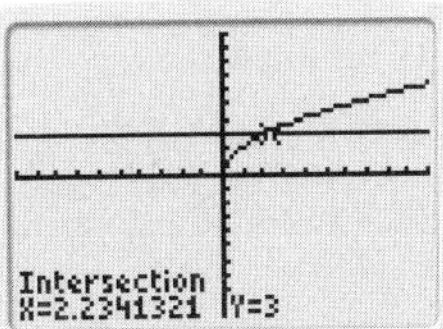

The length of the pendulum is about 2.23 meters.

Lesson Practice

Solve each equation.

a. (Ex 1) $\sqrt{2x+3} = 21$ 219

b. (Ex 1) $11 = \sqrt{x-7} - 2$ 176

c. (Ex 2) $\sqrt[3]{2x} + 1 = 0$ $-\frac{1}{2}$

d. (Ex 2) $4\sqrt[3]{3x-4} = 16$ $\frac{68}{3}$

e. (Ex 3) $\sqrt{9x} = \sqrt{5x+2}$ $\frac{1}{2}$

f. (Ex 3) $-\sqrt[3]{2x} = \sqrt[3]{4x+7}$ $-\frac{7}{6}$

g. (Ex 3) $\sqrt{3x} + \sqrt[3]{x-4} - 5 = 0$ ≈ 5.18

h. (Ex 4) $\sqrt{-1-4x} = \sqrt{x-11}$ no real solutions

i. (Ex 4) $x = \sqrt{6-5x}$ 1

j. (Ex 5) The period of a pendulum, T, is the time it takes for the pendulum to make one back-and-forth swing, and is given by $T = 2\pi\sqrt{\frac{L}{9.8}}$, where L is the length of the pendulum in meters. Find the length of a pendulum whose period is 5 seconds. About 6.21 meters

Practice Distributed and Integrated

Solve the equations. Write the solutions in the form $a + bi$.

1. (62) $3p^2 + 7 = -9p^2 + 4$ $\pm\frac{1}{2}i$

2. (62) $2x^2 + 31 = 9$ $\pm i\sqrt{11}$

***3.** (66) Find the roots and give the multiplicity of each root: $x^3 - 7x^2 + 11x - 5 = 0$ 3. $x = 1$ with multiplicity of 2; $x = 5$ with multiplicity of 1

4. (53) Let $f(x) = 3x + 1$ and $g(x) = x - 2$. Find the composite function $f(g(x))$. $f(g(x)) = 3x - 5$

CHALLENGE

Find the roots and give the multiplicity of each root: $x^6 - 2x^5 - 21x^4 + 20x^3 + 71x^2 - 114x + 45 = 0$ $x = 1$ with multiplicity of 3, $x = -3$ with multiplicity of 2, and $x = 5$ with multiplicity of 1.

Example 5

Students may have seen a large pendulum in a museum. Often, the length is so great that the pendulum takes up two stories. Increasing the length increases the time to complete one cycle.

As a visual, students can use pieces of string with weights tied on the end and just vary the length of the string by hand as they estimate how quickly the pendulum completes a cycle.

Additional Example 5

The period of a pendulum, T, is the time it takes for the pendulum to make one back-and-forth swing, and it is given by $T = 2\pi\sqrt{\frac{L}{9.8}}$, where L is the length of the pendulum in meters. Find the length of a pendulum whose period is 10 seconds. about 24.82 meters

Extend the Example

The pendulum that hung in the Smithsonian Museum in Washington, D.C. for many years (until 1998) made 10,800 full cycles in a day. Challenge students to determine the length of the pendulum. about 15.89 meters

Lesson Practice

Problem h

Scaffolding Students can square both sides of the equation, solve, and get an answer of 2. When substituted into the original equation, it yields $3i = 3i$, which is true. When students use their calculators to graph $y_1 = \sqrt{-1-4x}$, they get an error message since y_1 is imaginary for all $x > 0$ (our domain restriction), so there is no intersection, which means there is no real solution.

Check for Understanding

The question below helps assess the concepts taught in this lesson.

"Radical equations are often solved by graphing. Explain how this ties into using only the positive square root and eliminating extraneous solutions." The calculator automatically limits the domain. Extraneous roots are not shown.

3 Practice

Math Conversations

Discussions to strengthen understanding

Problem 5

"What is the problem asking?" Find the probability that a customer bought pizza OR used a credit card.

"Is there an 'overlap' in this probability problem?" Yes—some people bought pizza and used a credit card.

"What must you do as a result of the overlap?" Use subtraction so people are not counted twice.

Problem 16

"Write down the information about wages and write an equation that relates the wages for each person to the total amount the store can pay." The experienced worker earns \$20/hr and the inexperienced worker earns \$15/hr. $20x + 15y \leq 400$

"State the relationship between the two types of workers and the profits in words." The higher paid worker produces half again as much as the lower paid worker.

"Is there a point where it makes sense to hire the lower paid worker?" No

5. (60) Of the 220 people who came into the Italian deli on Friday, 104 bought pizza and 82 used a credit card. Half of the people who bought pizza used a credit card. What is the probability that a customer bought pizza or used a credit card? $\frac{67}{110}$ or about 0.61

Solve for x by completing the square.

6. (58) $x^2 = 9x - 7$ $\frac{9}{2} \pm \frac{\sqrt{53}}{2}$

7. (58) $-5x - 6 = -x^2$ 6, −1

***8.** (70) **Lighthouses** The number of miles m a person can see on a clear day is approximated by $m = 1.2116\sqrt{h}$, where h is the person's height in feet above sea level. If a person standing at the top of the Barnegat Lighthouse in New Jersey on a clear day can see a distance of 16 miles, what is the person's height above sea level? About 174 feet

9. (55) **Error Analysis** The odds in favor of an event are 9 to 2. To the nearest percent, what is the probability of the event? 82%

10. (61) **Multiple Choice** What is $P(-3)$ if $x + 3$ is a factor of $2x^3 + 2x^2 - 10x + 6$? **B**
A −3 B 0 C 3 D 6

11. (59) **Velocity of an Electron** The velocity at which an electron orbits the nucleus of an atom is known as the Fermi-Thomas velocity and can be found using the expression $\frac{Z^{\frac{2}{3}}}{137}c$, where Z is the number of protons in the nucleus and c is the speed of light. What is the Fermi-Thomas velocity for cobalt, which has 27 protons, in terms of c? Round to the nearest thousandths place. 0.066c

***12.** (70) **Write** What is an extraneous solution? When can it occur?

12. Possible answer: An extraneous solution is not a solution of the original equation, but a solution of an equation that was generated while solving the original equation; it can be formed when both sides of the equation are squared.

13. (63) **Estimate** Use what you know about the unit circle and special angles to estimate tan 43°. Do not use a calculator. Explain your method. Possible answer: tan 43° ≈ 1; 43° is close to 45°, and tan 45° = 1.

***14.** (69) **Graphing Calculator** With your calculator in **a + bi** mode, find the following.
a. $(64 - 82i)(26 + 31i)$ $4206 - 148i$ **b.** $-3.7i(2.25 + 4.5i)$ $16.65 - 8.325i$

15. (62) **Electrical Engineering** A circuit has a current of 5 amps, and a second circuit has a current of $(14 - 9i)$ amps. Find the sum of the currents. $19 - 9i$ amps

16. (54) **Temporary Employees** A department store is planning to hire up to 24 temporary employees for a tent sale. Experienced workers will be paid \$20 per hour and inexperienced workers will be paid \$15 per hour. The company can pay up to \$400 per hour for the temporary employees. Experienced workers produce 1.5 times more profit than inexperienced workers. How many of each type of worker should be hired to maximize the company's profits? 20 experienced workers

***17.** (69) **Multi-Step** The product of a number and its multiplicative inverse is 1.
a. State the multiplicative inverse of $2 + 3i$. $\frac{1}{2 + 3i}$
b. Simplify the multiplicative inverse. $\frac{2 - 3i}{13}$
c. Verify Show that your answer in part b is the multiplicative inverse by multiplying it by $2 + 3i$. $\frac{2-3i}{13} \cdot 2 + 3i = \frac{4 - 9i^2}{13} = \frac{4 + 9}{13} = \frac{13}{13} = 1$

CHALLENGE

Solve $\sqrt{x} = \sqrt[3]{x - 1}$ using a graphing calculator. Then, clear the radicands and create a polynomial equation. Graph that equation on the calculator and find the zero. Compare the two results. Explain. No answer for the first. The polynomial equation is $x^3 - x^2 + 2x - 1 = 0$. The graph has a zero at $x \approx 0.57$. If you substitute 0.57 for x in the original equation, you can see that it is an extraneous solution.

Factor each expression completely.

18. (61) $8c^3 + 343$ $(2c + 7)(4c^2 - 14c + 49)$ **19.** (61) $-5z^3 + 320$ $-5(z - 4)(z^2 + 4z + 16)$

20. (66) **Generalize** How does the Rational Root Theorem make factoring polynomials easier? What must be true about a polynomial before it used?

20. It reduces the number of roots that must be tested by using synthetic division. Before using it, the polynomial equation must be in standard form and all of the coefficients must be integers.

***21.** (67) **Wheelchair Accessibility** A contractor designed the wheelchair ramp shown in the diagram. The ramp must satisfy a building code that specifies 4.7° as the maximum angle of elevation, labeled θ in the diagram. Does the design satisfy the building code? Justify your answer. Yes; $\theta = \text{Sin}^{-1}\left(\frac{4}{50}\right) \approx 4.59°$, so the measure of the angle in the design is less than 4.7°.

θ 50 ft 4 ft

22. (50) Find an equation for the inverse of $y = 5x^3 - 20$. Determine whether each relation is a function. $y = \sqrt[3]{0.2x + 4}$; Yes, they are both functions.

23. (65) **Verify** A student used factoring to find that the solutions of $4x^2 - 11x - 20 = 0$ are -1.25 and 4. Show how to verify these solutions with the Quadratic Formula. Use $a = 4$, $b = -11$ and $c = -20$.

23. $\frac{-b \pm \sqrt{b^2 - 4ac}}{2a} = \frac{11 \pm \sqrt{121 - 4(4)(-20)}}{8} = \frac{11 \pm \sqrt{441}}{8} = \frac{11 \pm 21}{8} = 4 \text{ and } -\frac{5}{4} = -1.25$

24. (54) Maximize $P = 4.5x + 2.4y$ for the constraints $\begin{array}{l} y \geq 0 \\ x \geq 0 \\ y \geq x \\ y \leq -2x + 9 \end{array}$ (0, 9)

25. (64) **Error Analysis** A student converted the exponential equation $4^{-2} = \frac{1}{16}$ to logarithmic form by writing $\log_4(-2) = \frac{1}{16}$. What is the error? Write the correct logarithmic equation.

25. Possible answer: The student wrote $\frac{1}{16}$ as the logarithm, but $\frac{1}{16}$ is not the exponent in the exponential equation. Correct equation: $\log_4 \frac{1}{16} = -2$

26. (52) **Geometry** Each side of the regular hexagon shown is 7 cm. Find the length of the diagonal $\overline{AE}$. Round your answer to the nearest tenth. (The measure of one interior angle of an n-gon is $\frac{(n-2)180°}{n}$.) about 12.1 cm

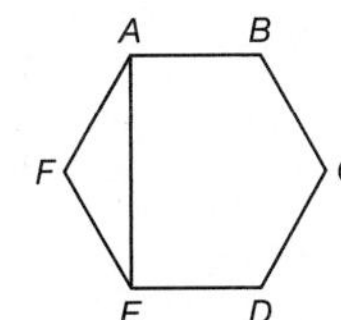

27. (60) **Write** Examine the formula for the probability of two inclusive events. Explain why $P(A \text{ and } B)$ is subtracted from the formula.

$$P(A \textbf{ or } B) = P(A) + P(B) - P(A \textbf{ and } B)$$

27. Because the events are inclusive, $P(A)$ includes the overlap of B and $P(B)$ includes the overlap of A so that the overlap is counted twice.

28. (53) **Multi-Step** A clothing store has a sale in which all the shirts are 20% off. On the last day of the sale, all shirts have an additional 25% off. Find a function describing how much a shirt with price p will cost on the last day. Solve the function. See Additional Answers.

***29.** (70) **Probability** A number cube is rolled twice. What is the probability that the number facing up on each roll shows a solution of $\sqrt{2x - 8} = x - 4$? $\frac{1}{9} \approx 11.1\%$

***30.** (68) **Multiple Choice** A bag of grapes contains 9 green grapes and 15 red grapes. If 4 grapes are chosen at random, without replacement, what is the approximate probability that the first two grapes are green and the last two grapes are red? **B**

A 4.6% **B** 5.9% **C** 7.1% **D** 13%

Problems 18 and 19

Extend the Problem

Use the factored expressions to find the zeros of the function. For problem 18, $c = -\frac{7}{2}$, $c = \frac{-7 \pm 7i\sqrt{3}}{4}$; For problem 19, $z = 4$, $z = -2 \pm 2i\sqrt{3}$.

Problem 24

Error Alert

For this problem, students may find the point of intersection of the lines $y = x$ and $y = -2x + 9$.

Remind students that the coordinates of each of the vertices must be substituted into the objective function to find the point that maximizes the function.

Problem 28

TEACHER TIP

Tell students to think of this problem in terms of composite functions.

LOOKING FORWARD

Solving radical equations prepares students for

- **Lesson 75** Graphing Radical Functions

INVESTIGATION

7

Materials

- Pencil, graph paper, and calculator

Discuss

Students will investigate how data is collected, displayed, and described.

Define bias, population, sample, median, mode, mean, variance, and standard deviation.

Problem 1

Tell students that poorly constructed survey questions will yield either inaccurate or unusable responses.

Problems 4 and 5

TEACHER TIP

The response frequencies are graphed directly onto the bar graph. When completing the circle graph, dividing student responses by the total number of responses for each category will give the percentage label for each sector. Multiplying that value by 360° will allow the sectors to be mathematically precise.

Data can also be displayed using stem-and-leaf plots and box-and-whisker plots.

Collecting Data

Exercise Suppose you want to find out what students at your school do for exercise, and then make a graph to display the results.

1. You construct this survey question: "What do you do for exercise?" Think about some possible responses. How many different responses do you think you would get if you asked 100 students? Answers will vary.
2. Is "dance" a response you thought of for question 1? Is "skateboarding" or "martial arts" a response you thought of? Answers will vary.
3. Is it possible that some students do more than one type of exercise? Yes

The answers to survey questions are data items, so collecting the answers is a form of collecting data. When constructing a survey question, it is often important to limit the number of possible responses so that you will be able to organize, display, analyze, and interpret the data you collect. Provide enough response choices so that there is a choice for everyone, and make sure the choices don't overlap. That is, construct them so that there is clearly only one response. In the table below, the question about exercise is rephrased and answer choices are supplied, along with numbers of responses.

Online Connection www.SaxonMathResources.com

Math Reasoning

Analyze Refer to the table. Which choice is needed so that everyone can choose at *least one* response? What word(s) in the question allows everyone to be able to choose *exactly one* response? other; best or main

"Which of the following best describes your main type of exercise?"

Response	Frequency
A. Competitive sports (team and individual)	24
B. Run, jog, or walk (not competitive)	16
C. Swim or bicycle (not competitive)	5
D. Strength training (weights and exercise equipment)	15
E. Other	20

A bar graph and a circle graph are both appropriate ways to display this data. Copy and complete the bar graph and circle graph below.

Hint

24 of 80 responses were *Competitive*. To get the central angle measure for the *Competitve* sector in the circle graph, multiply 360° by the appropriate decimal.

$\frac{24}{80} = 0.30$

$0.30 \times 360° = 108°$

4.

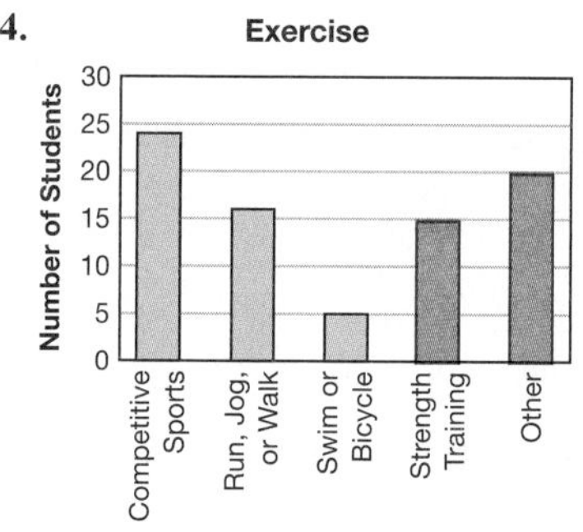

5.

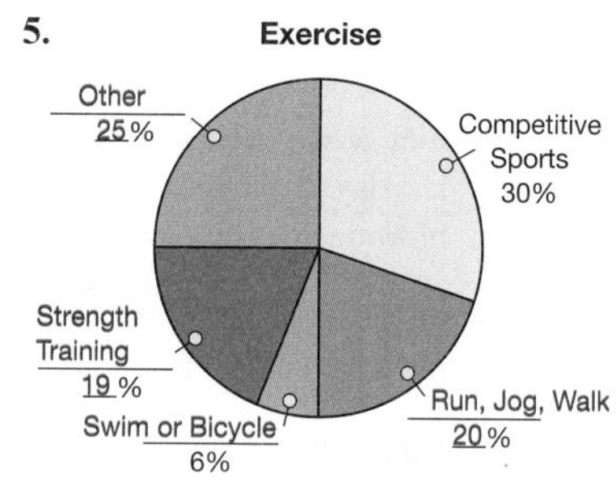

INVESTIGATION RESOURCES

Reteaching Master Investigation 7

MATH BACKGROUND

Statistics is defined as the science of collecting, organizing, and interpreting numerical data. This branch of mathematics was begun by John Graunt, who was born in London in 1620. He began the process of examining data by compiling mortality tables in an attempt to study the spread of bubonic plague.

A well-designed statistical experiment begins with a survey. If the survey questions are carefully constructed without bias, the results of the experiment will be meaningful. In a society, citizens continually analyze results of medical studies, political polls, and business data. How often do we as a society question the bias in these surveys?

6. Biased; Possible explanation: The phrase "with most high school students" could influence a student to agree. Possible rewrite: Do you think parents give high school students too little freedom to make their own decisions?

7. Biased; Possible explanation: The phrase "unfair policy" could influence a student to not support the policy. Possible rewrite: Do you support the policy of requiring community service as a high school requirement?

11. Self-selected, Biased; Possible explanation: The request for campaign contributions could result in a set of responses that is not a fair representation of the population.

14. Stratified, Probably biased; Possible explanation: It is not likely that there are approximately equal numbers of registered Democrats, Republicans, and Independents, so choosing 50 of each would probably be significantly out of proportion to their actual numbers.

Analyze and Write A survey question is *biased* if there is a reasonable chance that it could influence a response because of the way it is constructed. Determine whether each question below is biased. Explain your answer. If the question is biased, rewrite it so that it is not biased.

6. Do you agree with most high school students that parents give them too little freedom to make their own decisions?

7. Do you support the unfair policy of requiring community service as a high school requirement?

8. Do you think energy conservation should be a high priority for state and national elected officials? Not biased

9. Write a biased survey question. Then rewrite it to remove the bias. Answers will vary.

A *population* is a group being studied. Populations are often too large to survey, so a subset of the population called a *sample* is surveyed. If a sample is not a fair representation of the population, it is biased. If a sample is a fair representation of the population, it is unbiased. When properly chosen in an appropriate situation, any of the following can be an unbiased sample.

- *Random sample* – Each member of the population has an equal chance of being selected.
- *Systematic sample* – Members are chosen based on a rule.
- *Stratified sample* – The population is divided into non-overlapping subgroups, and members are chosen at random from the subgroups.
- *Self-selected sample* – Members volunteer to be in the sample.

Analyze and Write Identify the type of sample and determine whether it is biased. Explain your answer.

10. A manager asks every tenth customer who enters her store whether they like the recent remodeling of the store. Systematic; Not biased

11. A candidate mails a survey about an upcoming election along with a request for campaign contributions, enclosing a return envelope for responses.

12. For a survey about school policies, a student randomly chooses 25 students from each grade. (There are approximately 200 students in each grade.) Stratified; Not biased

13. There are 645 employees at a company. The president assigns the integers 1 through 645, one to each employee, and then randomly chooses 50 integers and surveys the corresponding employees. Random; Not biased

14. Every voter in a town is registered as a Democrat, a Republican, or an Independent. For a survey of registered voters, 50 are randomly chosen from each group.

15. **Multi-Step** Complete parts a–d. Check students' work.

    a. Construct a survey question with 4 or 5 response choices.

    b. Identify a population. Describe 3 or 4 possible samples of different types. Identify each type and state whether it is biased or unbiased.

Problems 6–9

Extend the Problem

Identify examples of bias in mail survey forms or newspaper or magazine articles. Choose one example of a biased question or statement. Explain why the question/statement is biased and then rewrite it to eliminate the bias.

TEACHER TIP

Give students examples of samples and the corresponding population.

Ex. Sample—junior class,

Population—all students attending the school

Ex. Sample—teenagers,

Population—all U.S. residents

Problems 10–14

Scaffolding

Questions to ask when determining the sample type

1. Do members volunteer? Yes; Self-selected
2. Is there a rule that determines selection? Yes; Systematic
3. Does each member have an equal chance of being selected? Yes; Random
4. Is the population divided into subgroups, and then does each member have an equal chance of being selected? Yes > Stratified

Problem 11

Error Alert Students may have difficulty identifying this as a self-selected sample. Even though the candidate mails the survey, the receiver volunteers to be part of the sample by returning the survey.

ENGLISH LEARNERS

Define **bias.** Say:

"A bias is when someone or something is unfairly liked or disliked. A biased sample attempts to influence someone unfairly."

Explain the meaning of bias by giving the following example: Instead of choosing the best player, Joe selected Jose for the baseball team even though Jose had never played baseball. Jose was Joe's best friend. Therefore, Joe's selection of Jose was biased in favor of Jose. Joe's choice was biased against the best baseball player.

TEACHER TIP

To reduce computations, use the calculator to compute the mean, median, variance, and standard deviation.

Problem 19

Error Alert When calculating the variance, do not forget about the frequency of data elements. Notice that each frequency is the coeffcient of each term.

Problem 20

TEACHER TIP

Since the standard deviation is the spread of data, it is the positive square root of the variance.

Investigation Practice

Math Conversations

Discussion to strengthen understanding

Problem a

Remember to calculate the measure of each central angle to draw an accurate circle graph.

Problems b and c

The phrase "Round to the nearest hour" limits the responses. It avoids overlapping responses and provides a choice for all survey members.

Math Reasoning

Analyze A bar graph and circle graph both show relative sizes of categories. Which type better shows how the size of each category compares to the whole?

Circle graph

c. Construct a frequency table. Show a reasonable distribution of responses.

d. Construct a bar graph and circle graph to show the data.

It is useful to describe some data sets with *measures of center* such as *mode, median,* and *mean,* and with *measures of spread* such as *variance* and *standard deviation.*

A teacher chose 2 students at random from each of the 10 sophomore homeroom classes in a school and asked "To the nearest half hour, what is the average number of hours per school night that you spend on homework?" The table below shows the data distribution.

Hours	0	0.5	1.0	1.5	2.0	2.5	3.0	3.5	4.0 or more
Frequency	0	1	4	5	5	3	1	1	0

Hint

To find the median, order the 20 data values from least to greatest, and then find the average of the 10th and 11th values.

Reading Math

The symbol for standard deviation is σ, the Greek lower case letter *sigma.*

16. Identify the population and the type of sample. Determine whether the sample is biased. Population: all sophomores in the school; Sample: stratified, not biased

17. Find the mode(s) and median. modes: 1.5, 2.0; median = 1.75

18. Supply the missing terms in the numerator, and then evaluate the expression to find the mean: $\bar{x} = \frac{1(0.5) + 4(1.0) + 5(1.5) + \ldots + 1(3.5)}{20}$. 5(2.0) + 3(2.5) + 1(3.0); 1.8

19. The formula for variance is $\sigma^2 = \frac{(x_1 - \bar{x})^2 + (x_2 - \bar{x})^2 + \ldots + 1(x_n - \bar{x})^2}{n}$, where $x_1, x_2, \ldots, x_n$ are the data values and $\bar{x}$ is the mean. Supply the missing terms in the numerator, and then evaluate the expression to find the variance: $\sigma^2 = \frac{1(0.5 - \bar{x})^2 + 4(1.0 - \bar{x})^2 + 5(1.5 - \bar{x})^2 + \ldots + 1(3.5 - \bar{x})^2}{20}$

19. $5(2.0 - \bar{x})^2 + 3(2.5 - \bar{x})^2 + 1(3.0 - \bar{x})^2$; 0.535

20. The standard deviation is the square root of the variance: $\sigma = \sqrt{\sigma^2}$. Find the standard deviation to the nearest thousandth. 0.731

Investigation Practice

a. Model Students were asked the survey question, "On average, how many hours per week do you email or use the Internet? Round to the nearest hour." The frequency table below shows the results. Construct a histogram and a circle graph to show the data. (A histogram is a bar graph in which adjacent bars touch.) See Additional Answers.

Response	0–2	3–5	6–8	9–11	12 or more
Frequency	4	12	22	7	5

b. Analyze Suppose the instruction "Round to the nearest hour" were not included in the survey question in part a. Why might it be difficult for a student to choose a response? Possible answer: There would be no way for a student to give a response such as 2.5 hours.

c. Analyze Suppose the response choices were 0–3, 3–6, 6–9, 9–12, and 12 or more. Why might it be difficult to interpret a histogram showing the results?

c. Possible answer: Students who emailed or used the Internet 3 hours per week could be represented in either the 0–3 bar or the 3–6 bar. A similar statement applies for 6, 9, and 12 hours.

504 Saxon Algebra 2

e. Biased; Possible explanation: The phrase "Knowing that teenagers tend to be irresponsible" could influence a student to answer no. Possible rewrite: Should people younger than 18 be allowed to drive without an adult in the vehicle?

g. Biased; Possible explanation: The first sentence could influence a student to believe that recent climate changes are part of a natural long-term climate cycle rather than global warming caused by humans, and therefore believe that global warming is not a serious problem. Possible rewrite: Do you believe that global warming is a serious problem?

h. Self-selected; Not biased

i. Systematic, Biased; Possible explanation: Residents that live within a half mile of the proposed site could be more likely to not approve than residents who live farther away. The council members want to know if town residents approve, so the sample should be a fair representation of all residents in the town.

Determine whether each question below is biased. Explain your answer. If the question is biased, rewrite it so that it is not biased.

d. How many people live in your household? Not biased

e. Knowing that teenagers tend to be irresponsible, should people younger than 18 be allowed to drive without an adult in the vehicle?

f. Knowing that the current sales tax rate is 5%, do you support a new rate of 6%, beginning next year? Not biased

g. There are some scientists who believe that recent climate changes are part of a natural long-term climate cycle rather than global warming caused by humans. Do you believe that global warming is a serious problem?

Identify the type of sample and determine whether it is biased. Explain your answer.

h. A utility company mails a survey to all its customers asking them to rate customer service, enclosing a return envelope for responses.

i. A developer wants to build a store. Town council members want to know if town residents approve. They survey all residents that live within a half mile of the proposed site.

j. A school principal selects 2 students at random from each class in the school to survey about students' study habits. Stratified; Not biased

k. The junior class president wants opinions on student parking rules. She uses a list of all 255 juniors, and assigns each junior a different integer from 1 through 255. She uses a random integer generator on a calculator until she gets 20 different integers from 1 through 255. She chooses the 20 corresponding students to survey. Random; Not biased

Six students were chosen at random from each grade in a high school and asked "At what age did you have your first job?" The table below shows the data distribution.

Age	13	14	15	16	17	18	19
Frequency	1	4	8	7	3	0	1

l. Identify the population and the type of sample. Determine whether the sample is biased. All students in the school; Stratified, not biased

m. Find the mode, median, and mean. mode = 15; median = 15; mean $\approx$ 15.46

n. Find the variance. $\sigma^2 \approx 1.582$

o. Find the standard deviation. $\sigma \approx 1.258$

p. Construct your own survey question. Identify the population and the type of sample. Determine whether the sample is biased. Find the mode(s), median, and mean. Find the variance and standard deviation. Check students' answers.

Problems d–g

Any question that contains an influential opinion rather than a statement of fact tends to be biased.

Problems l–o

Recall that the sample is a subset of the population.

To determine the mode, select the value(s) that has the greatest frequency. Add each value and divide by the number of values to find the mean. Order the values from least to greatest before determining the median. In this example, there are 24 values, so find the mean of the 12th and 13th values.

Problem p

Use the example on page 504 to help construct the survey question. When finished writing, ask yourself the following questions:

Does everyone have an answer choice?

Can everyone choose exactly one response?

Create the data so that the measures of center and spread can be found.

LOOKING FORWARD

Collecting, displaying, and describing data prepares students for

- **Lesson 80** Finding the Normal Distribution

Lesson Planner

Lesson	New Concepts
71	Using the Law of Sines
72	Using the Properties of Logarithms
Lab 11	*Graphing Calculator Lab:* Calculating Confidence Intervals
73	Using Sampling
74	Finding the Discriminant
75	Graphing Radical Functions
	Cumulative Test 14, Performance Task 14
76	Finding Polynomial Roots I
77	Using the Law of Cosines
78	Solving Quadratic Equations II
79	Understanding Piecewise Functions
Lab 12	*Graphing Calculator Lab:* Calculating Normal Distribution Areas and Z-Scores
80	Finding the Normal Distribution
	Cumulative Test 13, Performance Task 13
INV 8	Investigation: Finding the Area Under a Curve

Resources for Teaching

- Student Edition
- Teacher's Edition
- Student Edition eBook
- Teacher's Edition eBook
- Resources and Planner CD
- Solutions Manual
- Instructional Masters
- Technology Lab Masters
- Warm Up and Teaching Transparencies
- Instructional Presentations CD
- Online activities, tools, and homework help **www.SaxonMathResources.com**

Resources for Practice and Assessment

- Student Edition Practice Workbook
- Course Assessments
- Standardized Test Practice
- College Entrance Exam Practice
- Test and Practice Generator CD using ExamView™

Resources for Differentiated Instruction

- Reteaching Masters
- Challenge and Enrichment Masters
- Prerequisite Skills Intervention
- Adaptations for Saxon Algebra 2
- Multilingual Glossary
- English Learners Handbook
- TI Resources

Pacing Guide

Resources and Planner CD for lesson planning support

45-Minute Class

Day 1	Day 2	Day 3	Day 4	Day 5	Day 6
Lesson 71	Lesson 72	Lesson 73 Lab 11	Lesson 74	Lesson 75	Cumulative Test 14
Day 7	**Day 8**	**Day 9**	**Day 10**	**Day 11**	**Day 12**
Lesson 76	Lesson 77	Lesson 78	Lesson 79	Lesson 80 Lab 12	Cumulative Test 15
Day 13					
Investigation 8					

Block: 90-Minute Class

Day 1	Day 2	Day 3	Day 4	Day 5	Day 6
Lesson 71 Lesson 72	Lab 11 Lesson 73 Lesson 74	Lesson 75 Cumulative Test 14	Lesson 76 Lesson 77	Lesson 78 Lesson 79 Lab 12	Lesson 80 Cumulative Test 15
Day 7					
Investigation 8 Lesson 81					

** For suggestions on how to implement Saxon Math in a block schedule, see the Pacing section at the beginning of the Teacher's Edition.*

Differentiated Instruction

Below Level		Advanced Learners	
Warm Up	SE pp. 506, 512, 521, 528, 534, 540, 546, 552, 558, 565	Challenge	TE pp. 511, 517, 526, 531, 538, 545, 551, 557, 561, 569
Skills Bank	SE pp. 862–885	Extend the Example	TE pp. 507, 514, 524, 532, 541, 542, 553, 554, 568
Reteaching Masters	Lessons 71–80, Investigation 8	Extend the Problem	TE pp. 510, 518, 527, 535, 538, 543, 544 545, 550, 551, 555, 556, 557, 571
Warm Up Transparencies	Lessons 71–80	Challenge and Enrichment Masters	Challenge: C71–C80 Enrichment: E78, E79
Prerequisite Skills Intervention	Lessons 81, 82		
English Learners		**Special Needs**	
EL Tips	TE pp. 507, 513, 522, 529, 535, 543, 549, 554, 559, 566	Inclusion Tips	TE pp. 509, 515, 516, 524, 525, 530, 536, 544, 547, 550, 555, 559, 568, 573
Multilingual Glossary	Booklet and Online	Adaptations for Saxon Algebra 2	Lessons 71–80, Cumulative Tests 14, 15
English Learners Handbook			
For All Learners			
Exploration	SE pp. 513	Alternate Method	TE pp. 510, 518, 523, 532, 542, 553, 560, 567
Caution	SE pp. 559	Online Tools	
Hints	SE pp. 508, 512, 513, 516, 528, 547, 548, 553, 554		
Error Alert	TE pp. 508, 509, 511, 515, 518, 519, 525, 526, 530, 533, 537, 538, 539, 540, 543, 544, 547, 549, 550, 552, 555, 556, 559, 562, 568, 570, 573		

SE = Student Edition; TE = Teacher's Edition

Math Vocabulary

Lesson	New Vocabulary		Maintained	EL Tip in TE
71	Law of Sines		acute angle right triangle	opposite
72	change of base formula		base inverse exponent	conjecture
73	bias capture-recapture method cluster sample convenience sampling population probability sampling sample size	sampling simple random sample stratified sample systematic sample voluntary response sampling	proportion	stratified
74	discriminant		complex number root solution	root of an equation
75	cube root function radical function	square root function	inverse	radical
76	polynomial roots		factor zeros of a function	coefficient constant term factor
77	Heron's Formula Law of Cosines		cosine	regulations
78			quadratic formula	polynomial equation polynomial function
79	piecewise function	step function	vertical line test	step function
80	bell curve normal distribution	standard deviation z-score	mean	normal
INV 8			area interval	partition

SECTION OVERVIEW 8

Math Highlights

Enduring Understandings – The "Big Picture"

After completing Section 8, students will understand:

- How to apply the Laws of Sines and Cosines.
- How to solve for the zeros of polynomial functions.
- How to graph piecewise and radical functions.
- How to convert a given data value into from a standard normal distribution into a z-score.
- How to use the properties of logarithms.

Essential Questions

- What is the difference between a population and a sample?
- How is the discriminant used when graphing a quadratic function?
- How is the square root function related to the quadratic function?
- How is a piecewise function evaluated for a value?

Math Content Strands

Linear Functions

- Lesson 79 Understanding Piecewise Functions

Exponential and Logarithmic Functions

- Lesson 72 Using the Properties of Logarithms

Polynomials and Polynomial Functions

- Lesson 76 Finding Polynomial Roots I

Probability and Statistics

- Lesson 73 Using Sampling
- Lesson 80 Finding the Normal Distribution
- Lab 11 Graphing Calculator: Calculating Confidence Intervals
- Lab 12 Graphing Calculator: Calculating Normal Distribution Areas and Z-Scores

Quadratic Functions

- Lesson 74 Finding the Discriminant
- Lesson 78 Solving Quadratic Equations II

Rational and Radical Functions

- Lesson 75 Graphing Radical Functions

Trigonometry

- Lesson 71 Using the Law of Sines
- Lesson 77 Using the Law of Cosines

Sequences, Series, and Logic

- Investigation 8 Finding the Area Under the Curve

Connections in Practice Problems

	Lessons
Coordinate Geometry	71, 72, 77
Data Analysis	74, 78
Geometry	71, 72, 73, 74, 75, 76, 77, 78, 79, 80
Probability	73, 75, 76, 77, 79, 80

Math Processes

Reasoning and Communication

	Lessons
• Analyze	71, 72, 73, 74, 76, 78, 79, 80
• Error analysis	71, 72, 73, 74, 75, 76, 77, 78, 79, 80
• Estimate	73, 74, 76, 80
• Formulate	71, 72, 73, 77, 79
• Generalize	71, 74, 77, 78, 79, 80
• Justify	74, 75, 77, 79
• Math reasoning	71, 73, 74, 77, 79, 80
• Model	76
• Multiple choice	71, 72, 73, 74, 75, 76, 77, 78, 79, 80
• Multi-step	71, 72, 73, 74, 75, 76, 77, 78, 79, 80
• Predict	75, 78
• Verify	72, 74, 76, 77, 79
• Write	71, 72, 73, 75, 78, 80
• Graphing Calculator	71, 72, 73, 74, 75, 76, 77, 78, 79, 80

Connections

In Examples: Architecture, Estimating an animal population, Geology, Marketing comparison, Orienteering, Postal service rates, Projectile motion, Rocketry, Surveying, Vertical motion

In Practice problems: Astronomy, Automobile tires, Aviation, Bay bridge, Biology, Business, Celebrating, Clock face, Comparison shopping, Delivery charges, Electrical engineering, Fencing, Flowers, Geography, Geology, Government, Gravity on the moon, Horses, Lighthouses, Marketing, Medicine, Navigation, Physical science, Physics, Population, Projectile motion, Quality control, Rock climbing, Safety regulations, Soccer, Sports, Storage, Tennis, Travel

Content Trace

Lesson	Warm Up: Prerequisite Skills	New Concepts	Where Practiced	Where Assessed	Looking Forward
71	Lessons 46, 67	Using the Law of Sines	Lessons 71, 72, 73, 74, 75, 76, 79, 80, 82, 83, 85, 86, 89, 90, 91, 94, 95, 98	Cumulative Tests 15, 18, 22	Lesson 77
72	Lessons 3, 64	Using the Properties of Logarithms	Lessons 72, 73, 74, 75, 76, 77, 78, 80, 81, 82, 83, 84, 85, 88, 90, 97, 101, 117	Cumulative Tests 15, 19, 21	Lessons 81, 87, 102, 110
73	Skills Bank, Lesson 7	Using Sampling	Lessons 73, 74, 75, 76, 77, 79, 80, 81, 82, 83, 84, 85, 86, 88, 89, 90, 91, 92, 93, 94, 95, 96, 97, 99, 102	Cumulative Tests 15, 19	Lessons 80, 116, 118
74	Lessons 27, 35, 62	Finding the Discriminant	Lessons 74, 75, 76, 77, 78, 79, 80, 81, 82, 83, 84, 85, 86, 87, 88, 89, 90, 92, 94, 96, 97	Cumulative Tests 15, 16, 23	Lesson 78, 83, 85, 89
75	Lessons 4, 11, 50	Graphing Radical Functions	Lessons 75, 76, 77, 79, 80, 81, 83, 84, 85, 86, 87, 88, 89, 91, 92, 93, 94, 96, 97, 99	Cumulative Tests 15, 18	Lessons 93, 109, 111
76	Lessons 23, 65	Finding Polynomial Roots I	Lessons 76, 77, 78, 80, 82, 83, 84, 85, 86, 88, 89, 91, 92, 93, 94, 95, 98	Cumulative Tests 16, 17, 21	Lessons 85, 95, 101, 106
77	Lessons 46, 67, 71	Using the Law of Cosines	Lessons 77, 78, 79, 80, 81, 82, 83, 84, 85, 86, 88, 89, 91, 92, 94, 95, 96, 97, 99, 101, 102, 104, 112	Cumulative Tests 16, 19	Lessons 82, 86, 90, 103
78	Lessons 35, 65	Solving Quadratic Equations II	Lessons 78, 79, 80, 81, 82, 83, 84, 85, 86, 87, 88, 89, 90, 91, 92, 93, 94, 96, 108	Cumulative Tests 16, 17, 20, 22	Lessons 83, 89
79	Lessons 4, 26, 27, 34	Understanding Piecewise Functions	Lessons 79, 80, 83, 84, 85, 86, 87, 88, 89, 91, 92, 93, 95, 97, 98, 99, 100, 101, 103, 104, 105, 109	Cumulative Tests 16, 19	Lessons 90, 103
80	Lessons 25, 55	Finding the Normal Distribution	Lessons 80, 81, 82, 84, 85, 86, 87, 88, 91, 92, 93, 94, 95, 96, 97, 99, 100, 101, 102, 104, 106, 111	Cumulative Tests 16, 19	Lessons 116, 118
INV 8	N/A	Investigation: Finding the Area Under a Curve	Lessons 106, 113	Cumulative Test 17	N/A

Ongoing Assessment

	Type	Feature	Intervention *
BEFORE instruction	Assess Prior Knowledge	• Diagnostic Test	• Prerequisite Skills Intervention
BEFORE the lesson	Formative	• Warm Up	• Skills Bank • Reteaching Masters
DURING the lesson	Formative	• Lesson Practice • Math Conversations with the Practice problems	• Additional Examples in TE • Test and Practice Generator (for additional practice sheets)
AFTER the lesson	Formative	• Check for Understanding (closure)	• Scaffolding Questions in TE
AFTER 5 lessons	Summative	After Lesson 75 • Cumulative Test 14 • Performance Task 14 After Lesson 80 • Cumulative Test 15 • Performance Task 15	• Reteaching Masters • Test and Practice Generator (for additional tests and practice)
AFTER 20 lessons	Summative	• Benchmark Tests	• Reteaching Masters • Test and Practice Generator (for additional tests and practice)

* for students not showing progress during the formative stages or scoring below 80% on the summative assessments

Evidence of Learning – What Students Should Know

Because the Saxon philosophy is to provide students with sufficient time to learn and practice each concept, a lesson's topic will not be tested until at least five lessons after the topic is introduced.

On the Cumulative Tests that are given during this section of ten lessons, students should be able to demonstrate the following competencies:

- Apply the rules of exponents.
- Perform operations with matrices.
- Find the determinant of a matrix.
- Solve linear equations and graph their related function.
- Identify functions and use function notation.
- Recognize and solve problems involving direct variation.
- Factor polynomial expressions.

Test and Practice Generator CD using ExamView™

The Test and Practice Generator is an easy-to-use benchmark and assessment tool that creates unlimited practice and tests in multiple formats and allows you to customize questions or create new ones. A variety of reports are available to track student progress toward mastery of the standards throughout the year.

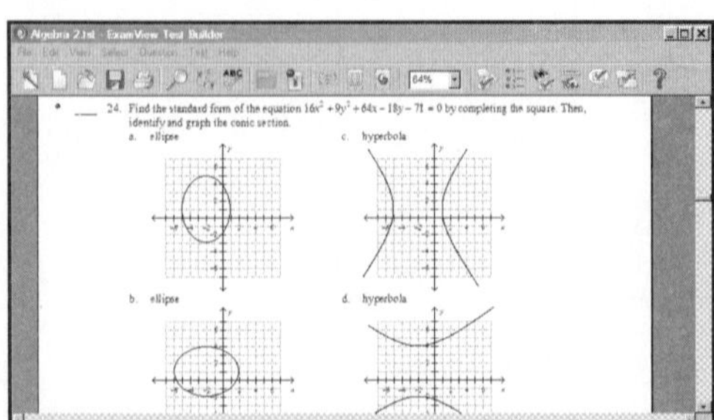

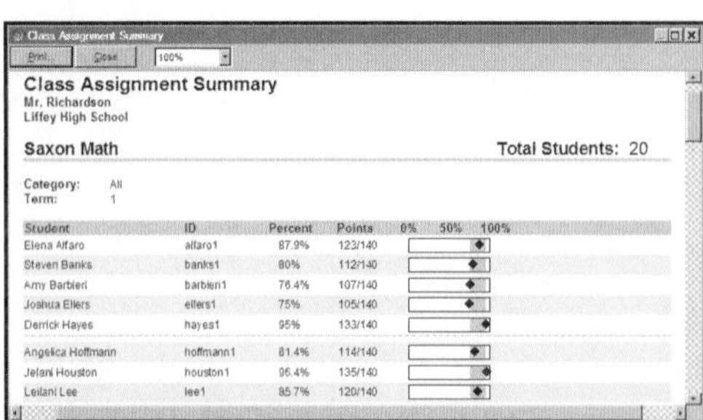

Assessment Resources

Resources for Diagnosing and Assessing

- **Student Edition**
  - Warm Up
  - Lesson Practice
- **Teacher's Edition**
  - Math Conversations with the Practice problems
  - Check for Understanding (closure)
- **Course Assessments**
  - Diagnostic Test
  - Cumulative Tests
  - Performance Tasks
  - Benchmark Tests

Resources for Test Prep

- **Student Edition**
  - Multiple-choice practice problems
  - Multiple-step and writing problems
  - Daily cumulative practice
- **Standardized Test Practice**
- **College Entrance Exam Practice**
- **Test and Practice Generator CD using Exam View™**

Resources for Intervention

- **Student Edition**
  - Skills Bank
- **Teacher's Edition**
  - Additional Examples
  - Scaffolding questions
- **Prerequisite Skills Intervention**
  - Worksheets
- **Reteaching Masters**
  - Lesson instruction and practice sheets
- **Test and Practice Generator CD using ExamView™**
  - Lesson practice problems
  - Additional tests

Cumulative Tests

The assessments in Saxon Math are frequent and consistently placed after every five lessons to offer a regular method of ongoing testing. These cumulative assessments check mastery of concepts from previous lessons.

Performance Tasks

The Performance Tasks can be used in conjunction with the Cumulative Tests and are scored using a rubric.

After Lesson 75

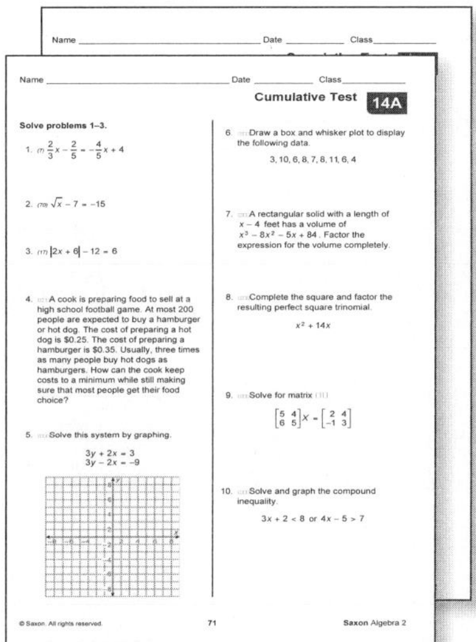

Name ________ Date ________ Class ________

Cumulative Test 14A

Solve problems 1–3.

1. (7) $\frac{2}{3}x - \frac{2}{5} = -\frac{4}{5}x + 4$
2. (70) $\sqrt{x} - 7 = -15$
3. (17) $|2x + 6| - 12 = 6$
4. A cook is preparing food to sell at a high school football game. At most 200 people are expected to buy a hamburger or hot dog. The cost of preparing a hot dog is $0.25. The cost of preparing a hamburger is $0.35. Usually, three times as many people buy hot dogs as hamburgers. How can the cook keep costs to a minimum while still making sure that most people get their food choice?
5. Solve this system by graphing.
   $3y + 2x = 3$
   $3y - 2x = -9$
6. Draw a box and whisker plot to display the following data.
   3, 10, 6, 8, 7, 8, 11, 6, 4
7. A rectangular solid with a length of $x - 4$ feet has a volume of $x^3 - 8x^2 - 5x + 84$. Factor the expression for the volume completely.
8. Complete the square and factor the resulting perfect square trinomial.
   $x^2 + 14x$
9. Solve for matrix
   $\begin{bmatrix} 5 & 4 \\ 6 & 5 \end{bmatrix} X = \begin{bmatrix} 2 & 4 \\ -1 & 3 \end{bmatrix}$
10. Solve and graph the compound inequality.
    $3x + 2 < 8$ or $4x - 5 > 7$

© Saxon. All rights reserved. 71 Saxon Algebra 2

After Lesson 80

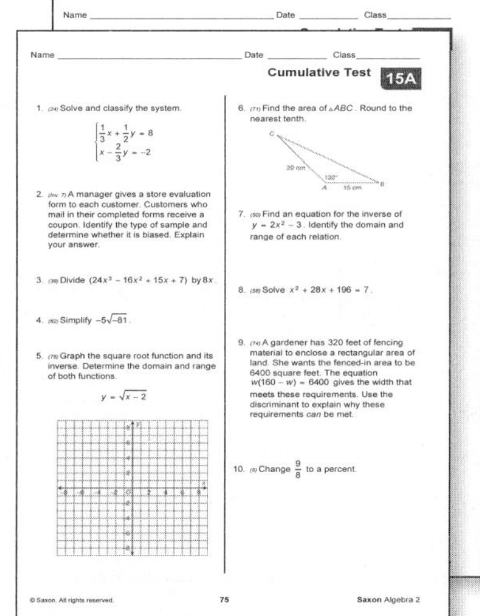

Name ________ Date ________ Class ________

Cumulative Test 15A

1. (24) Solve and classify the system.
   $\begin{cases} \frac{1}{3}x + \frac{1}{2}y = 8 \\ x - \frac{2}{3}y = -2 \end{cases}$
2. (Inv. 7) A manager gives a store evaluation form to each customer. Customers who mail in their completed forms receive a coupon. Identify the type of sample and determine whether it is biased. Explain your answer.
3. (38) Divide $(24x^3 - 16x^2 + 15x + 7)$ by $8x$.
4. (62) Simplify $-5\sqrt{-81}$.
5. (78) Graph the square root function and its inverse. Determine the domain and range of both functions.
   $y = \sqrt{x - 2}$
6. (71) Find the area of $\triangle ABC$. Round to the nearest tenth.
7. (50) Find an equation for the inverse of $y = 2x^2 - 3$. Identify the domain and range of each relation.
8. (58) Solve $x^2 + 28x + 196 = 7$.
9. (74) A gardener has 320 feet of fencing material to enclose a rectangular area of land. She wants the fenced-in area to be 6400 square feet. The equation $w(160 - w) = 6400$ gives the width that meets these requirements. Use the discriminant to explain why these requirements *can* be met.
10. (6) Change $\frac{9}{8}$ to a percent.

© Saxon. All rights reserved. 75 Saxon Algebra 2

For use with Performance Tasks

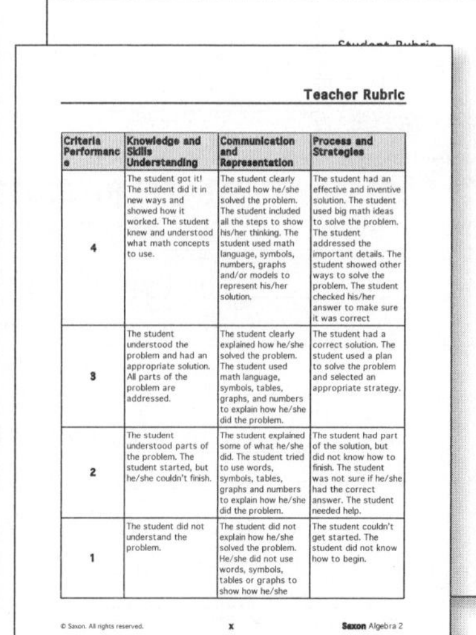

Teacher Rubric

Criteria Performance	Knowledge and Skills Understanding	Communication and Representation	Process and Strategies
4	The student got it! The student did it in new ways and showed how it worked. The student knew and understood what math concepts to use.	The student clearly detailed how he/she solved the problem. The student included all the steps to show his/her thinking. The student used math language, symbols, numbers, graphs and/or models to represent his/her solution.	The student had an effective and inventive solution. The student used big math ideas to solve the problem. The student addressed the important details. The student showed other ways to solve the problem. The student checked his/her answer to make sure it was correct
3	The student understood the problem and had an appropriate solution. All parts of the problem are addressed.	The student clearly explained how he/she solved the problem. The student used math language, symbols, tables, graphs, and numbers to explain how he/she did the problem.	The student had a correct solution. The student used a plan to solve the problem and selected an appropriate strategy.
2	The student understood parts of the problem. The student started, but he/she couldn't finish.	The student explained some of what he/she did. The student tried to use words, symbols, tables, graphs and numbers to explain how he/she did the problem.	The student had part of the solution, but did not know how to finish. The student was not sure if he/she had the correct answer. The student needed help.
1	The student did not understand the problem.	The student did not explain how he/she solved the problem. He/she did not use words, symbols, tables or graphs to show how he/she	The student couldn't get started. The student did not know how to begin.

© Saxon. All rights reserved. x Saxon Algebra 2

SECTION OVERVIEW 8

LESSON 71

1 Warm Up

Remind students that for an acute angle θ in a right triangle, $\sin\theta = \frac{\text{opposite side}}{\text{hypotenuse}}$.

2 New Concepts

In this lesson, students find the area of a triangle with unknown height. They use the Law of Sines to find the unknown side or angle of a triangle.

Discuss how to find the area of a triangle when the lengths of any two sides and their included angle are given. Explain what is meant by included angle.

Example 1

Point out that the lengths of the two sides are 24 inches and 55 inches, and their included angle is $\angle B$, which measures 115°.

Additional Example 1

Find the area of $\triangle ABC$. Round to the nearest tenth.

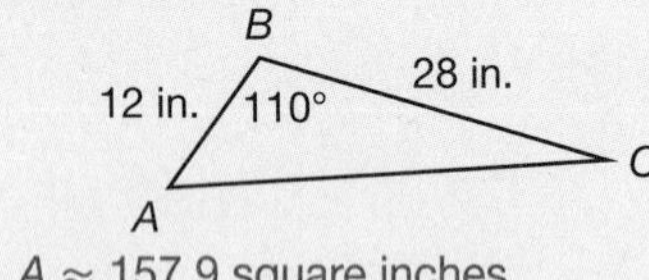

$A \approx 157.9$ square inches

LESSON 71

Using the Law of Sines

Warm Up

1. **Vocabulary** Given an acute angle of a right triangle, the ratio of the opposite side and the hypotenuse is the ___sine___ (*sine/cosine*) of the angle. (46)

2. Find the value of the sine of $\angle A$. $\frac{7}{25} = 0.28$ (46)

3. Estimate $m\angle x$ if $\sin x \approx 0.438$. about 26° (67)

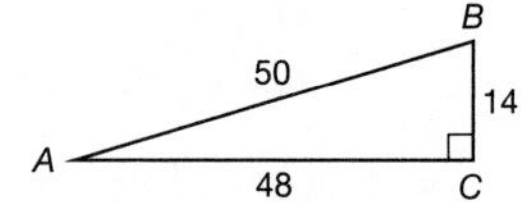

New Concepts

In $\triangle ABC$ at right, $\sin A = \frac{h}{c}$. To solve this equation for h, multiply both sides by c: $c \sin A = h$.

The area of $\triangle ABC$ is given by $\frac{1}{2}bh$. By substitution, it can be written as $\frac{1}{2}b(c \sin A)$. This means that the area of a triangle can be found when the height is not known, but the lengths of any two sides and their included angle are known.

Math Language

The **included angle** between two sides is the angle formed by the intersection of those sides.

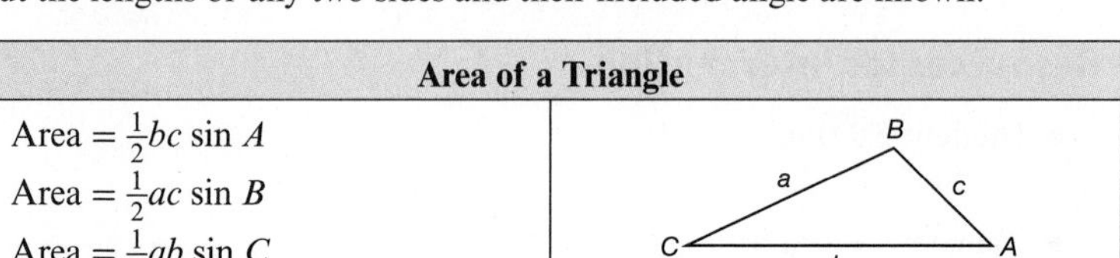

Area of a Triangle	
$\text{Area} = \frac{1}{2}bc \sin A$ $\text{Area} = \frac{1}{2}ac \sin B$ $\text{Area} = \frac{1}{2}ab \sin C$	(triangle with vertices B, C, A and sides a, b, c)

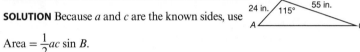

Example 1 **Finding the Area of a Triangle with Unknown Height**

Find the area of $\triangle ABC$. Round to the nearest tenth.

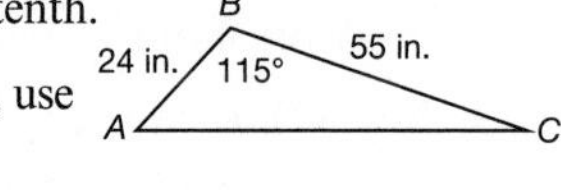

SOLUTION Because a and c are the known sides, use

$\text{Area} = \frac{1}{2}ac \sin B$.

$\text{Area} = \frac{1}{2}(55)(24) \sin 115°$ Substitute known values.

$\text{Area} \approx 598.1631394$ Simplify the right side.

The area of the triangle is about 598.2 square inches.

Based on which measurements are known, any of the three formulas can be used to find the area of a given triangle, so $\frac{1}{2}bc \sin A = \frac{1}{2}ac \sin B = \frac{1}{2}ab \sin C$. Simplifying these equations results in the **Law of Sines.**

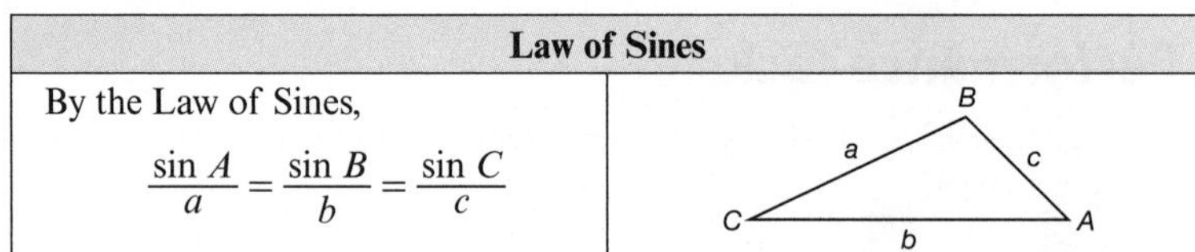

Law of Sines	
By the Law of Sines, $\frac{\sin A}{a} = \frac{\sin B}{b} = \frac{\sin C}{c}$	(triangle with vertices B, C, A and sides a, b, c)

Online Connection www.SaxonMathResources.com

LESSON RESOURCES

Student Edition Practice Workbook 71
Reteaching Master 71
Adaptations Master 71
Challenge and Enrichment Master C71

MATH BACKGROUND

The Law of Sines is one method of finding missing angles and side measures of a non-right triangle.

The other method used to solve a triangle is the Law of Cosines which is covered in Lesson 77. This law is used to find the measure of an angle when the measures of all three sides of a triangle are given, and to find the length of the third side of a triangle when two sides and their included angle are given.

For any triangle, ABC, the Law of Cosines states

$a^2 = b^2 + c^2 - 2bc \cos A$
$b^2 = a^2 + c^2 - 2ac \cos B$
$c^2 = a^2 + b^2 - 2ab \cos C$

By the Law of Sines, any of the following equations are true: $\frac{\sin A}{a} = \frac{\sin B}{b}$, $\frac{\sin B}{b} = \frac{\sin C}{c}$, and $\frac{\sin A}{a} = \frac{\sin C}{c}$. These equations can be used to find a missing angle or side measure in a triangle.

The Law of Sines can be used when ...

- the measures of two angles and any side of a triangle are known (angle-angle-side (AAS) or angle-side-angle (ASA))
- the measures of two sides and an angle opposite one of those sides is known (side-side-angle (SSA)).

Sometimes, a problem asks for a triangle to be solved. This means to find all the missing angle and side measures.

Example 2 Finding the Unknown Side of a Triangle

a. Find b. Round to the nearest tenth.

SOLUTION Use $\frac{\sin A}{a} = \frac{\sin B}{b}$ because all but one of the terms in this equation are known.

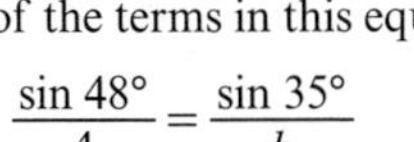

$\frac{\sin 48°}{4} = \frac{\sin 35°}{b}$ Substitute known values.

$b \sin 48° = 4 \sin 35°$ Cross multiply.

$b = \frac{4 \sin 35°}{\sin 48°}$ Divide both sides by sin 48°.

$b \approx 3.1$ Use a calculator to simplify.

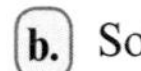

b. Solve $\triangle MNP$.

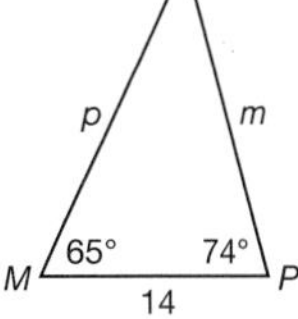

SOLUTION Find $m\angle N$ by subtracting the sum of $m\angle M$ and $m\angle P$ from 180°. $m\angle N = 180° - (65° + 74°) = 41°$.

Use $\frac{\sin M}{m} = \frac{\sin N}{n}$ to find m.

$\frac{\sin 65°}{m} = \frac{\sin 41°}{14}$

$m \sin 41° = 14 \sin 65°$

$m = \frac{14 \sin 65°}{\sin 41°}$

$m \approx 19.3$

Use $\frac{\sin P}{p} = \frac{\sin N}{n}$ to find p.

$\frac{\sin 74°}{p} = \frac{\sin 41°}{14}$

$p \sin 41° = 14 \sin 74°$

$p = \frac{14 \sin 74°}{\sin 41°}$

$p \approx 20.5$

When the given information consists of two sides and a nonincluded angle (SSA), it may be possible that the information describes two different triangles.

Possible Triangles

Given a, c, and $m\angle A$ in $\triangle ABC$, if $h < a < c$, then there are two possible triangles where:

- $h = c \sin A$
- the sum of the measures of $\angle C$ in each triangle is 180°.

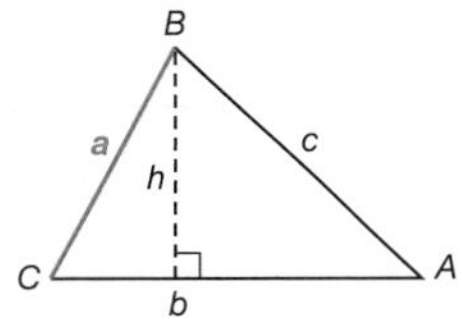

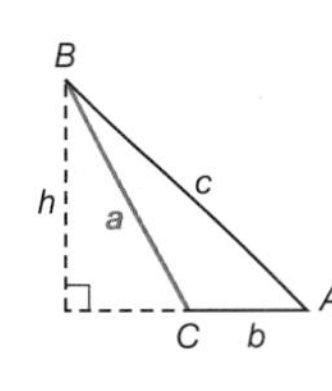

Math Reasoning

Analyze Why is it not possible to use a sine, cosine, or tangent ratio to find a missing side length in Example 2A?

The triangle is not a right triangle.

Math Reasoning

Generalize Without using variables, state what must be true for there to be two triangles given SSA.

The length of the side opposite the given angle must be greater than the height but less than the length of the other given side.

Example 2

Extend Example 2a

Have students find the measure of $\angle C$ and the area of $\triangle ABC$ to the nearest tenth. $m\angle C = 97°$; Area ≈ 6.2

Additional Example 2

a. Find b. Round to the nearest tenth.

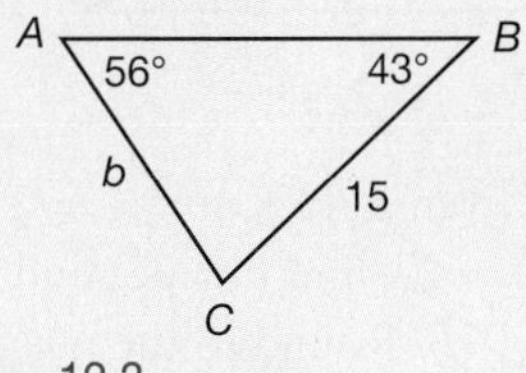

$b \approx 12.3$

b. Solve $\triangle MNP$.

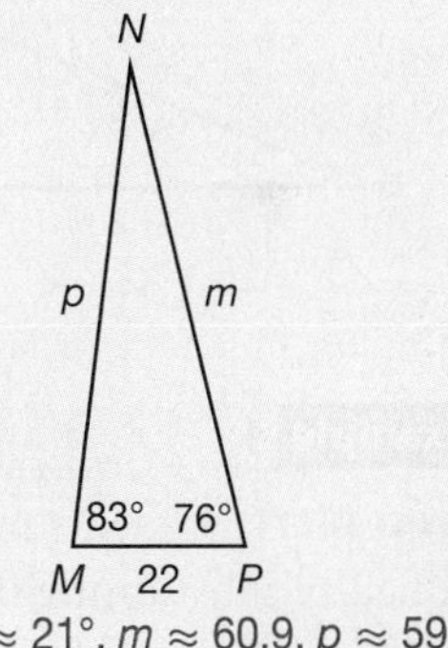

$m\angle N \approx 21°$, $m \approx 60.9$, $p \approx 59.6$

ENGLISH LEARNERS

To help students understand the meaning of **opposite**, define opposite as being directly across from each other.

Discuss examples of other things that are opposites, such as opposite interior angles, opposite sides of the table, opposite sides of the road, and so forth.

Have students identify the opposite side of each angle in example 2.

Connect the meaning of opposite with the side opposite the given angle for the Law of Sines. Tell students that the Law of Sines uses sides and angles that are opposite or across from one another.

Example 3

Remind students to use $\sin^{-1}x$ to find the measure of the angle.

Additional Example 3

a. Find $m\angle B$. Round to the nearest tenth.

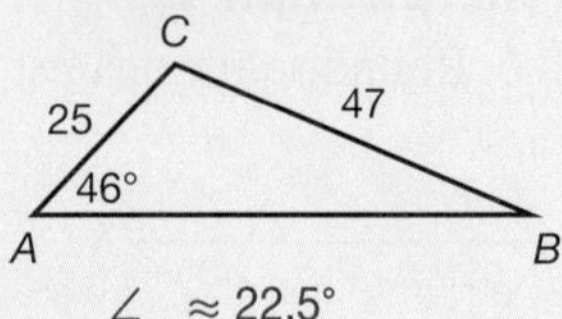

$\angle \approx 22.5°$

b. Given $\triangle ABC$, $m\angle A = 21°$, $a = 27$, and $b = 32$, find $m\angle B$. Round to the nearest tenth.

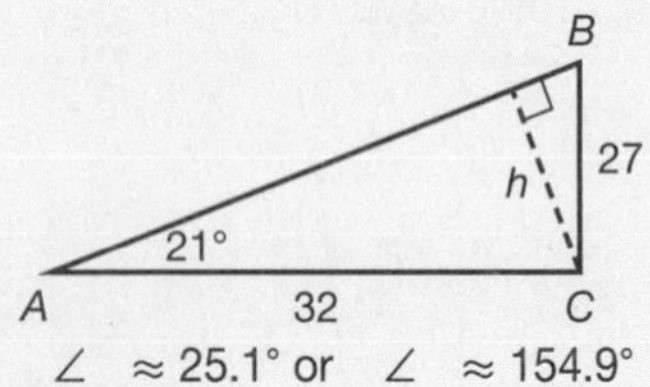

$\angle \approx 25.1°$ or $\angle \approx 154.9°$

Example 4

Error Alert Students may have difficulty substituting the correct values for the variables in the Law of Sines. Have students first identify the values given for $\angle A$ and c. Remind students that they can find the measure of $\angle C$ by subtracting the sum of the measures of $\angle A$ and $\angle B$ from 180°.

When using the Law of Sines if the side opposite the given angle is less than the other given side, the sides must be compared to the height to determine the number of possible triangles.

Hint

Unless otherwise stated, do not assume that diagrams are drawn to scale.

Example 3 Finding the Unknown Angle of a Triangle

a. Find $m\angle B$. Round to the nearest tenth.

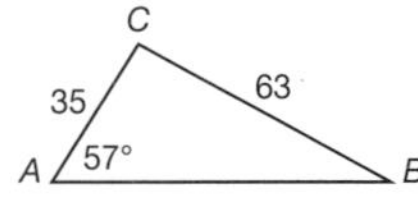

SOLUTION Since $63 > 35$, there is only one triangle with these measures.

Use $\frac{\sin A}{a} = \frac{\sin B}{b}$.

$\frac{\sin 57°}{63} = \frac{\sin B}{35}$ Substitute the known values.

$63 \sin B = 35 \sin 57°$ Cross multiply.

$\sin B = \frac{35 \sin 57°}{63}$ Divide both sides by 63.

$m\angle B \approx 27.8°$ Use $\text{Sin}^{-1}x$.

b. Given $\triangle ABC$, $m\angle A = 14°$, $a = 20$, and $b = 25$, find $m\angle B$. Round to the nearest tenth.

Hint

A triangle has three heights. Use the height from the vertex of the included angle of the given sides when comparing a, b, and h.

SOLUTION Sketch the triangle.

The side opposite the given angle is less than the other given side. Find h: $h = 25\sin 14° \approx 6$.

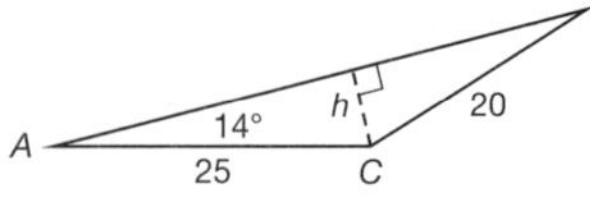

Because $6 < 20 < 25$, there are two possible triangles.

Use $\frac{\sin A}{a} = \frac{\sin B}{b}$.

$\frac{\sin 14°}{20} = \frac{\sin B}{25}$ Substitute the known values.

$20 \sin B = 25 \sin 14°$ Cross multiply.

$\sin B = \frac{25 \sin 14°}{20}$ Divide both sides by 20.

$m\angle B \approx 17.6°$ Use $\text{Sin}^{-1}x$.

Subtract from 180° to find the other possible value of $m\angle B$: $180° - 17.6° = 162.4°$. So $m\angle B \approx 17.6°$ or $\approx 162.4°$.

The process of determining a location or distance of an object by sighting it from two fixed points a known distance apart is called triangulation. Triangulation can be used to solve many real word problems.

Example 4 Application: Surveying

A surveyor stands on the east end of a bridge and finds that the angle formed by the bridge and the line of sight with a lighthouse is 32°. The surveyor then walks to the west end and finds the angle formed by the bridge and lighthouse to be 55°. Estimate the distance from the bridge to the lighthouse, given that the bridge has a length of 80 yards.

508 **Saxon** *Algebra 2*

SOLUTION Draw a diagram of the situation. The distance from the bridge to the lighthouse is a height of the triangle.

Use the Law of Sines to find a. Then find h.

Find $m\angle C$ by subtracting from 180°. Then use $\frac{\sin A}{a} = \frac{\sin C}{c}$.

$$\frac{\sin 55°}{a} = \frac{\sin 93°}{80} \rightarrow a \sin 93° = 80 \sin 55° \rightarrow a = \frac{80 \sin 55°}{\sin 93°} \approx 65.62$$

$$\sin 32° = \frac{h}{65.62} \rightarrow h = 65.62 \sin 32° \approx 34.8$$

The distance is about 34.8 yards.

Check Use the tangent ratio on the two right triangles:

$$\tan 32° = \frac{34.8}{x} \rightarrow x \approx 56, \tan 55° = \frac{34.8}{y} \rightarrow y \approx 24, \text{ and } 56 + 24 = 80.$$

Lesson Practice

a. Find the area of $\triangle ABC$. Round to the nearest tenth. *(Ex 1)* 431.9 m²

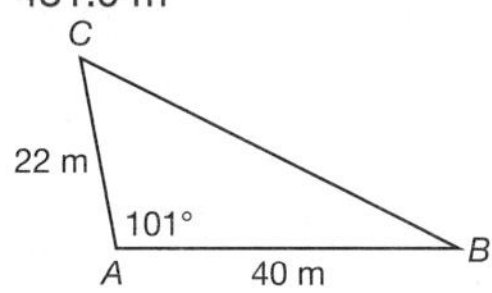

b. Find a. Round to the nearest tenth. *(Ex 2)* 14.7

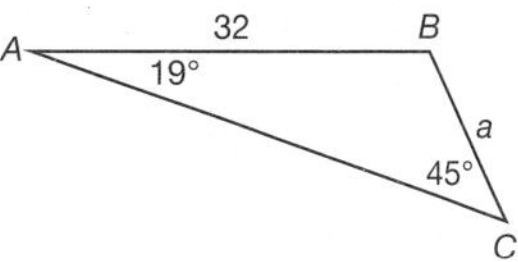

c. Solve $\triangle RST$. *(Ex 2)* $m\angle R = 100°$, $s \approx 5.4$, $t \approx 6.3$

d. Find $m\angle A$. Round to the nearest tenth. *(Ex 3)* 21.6°

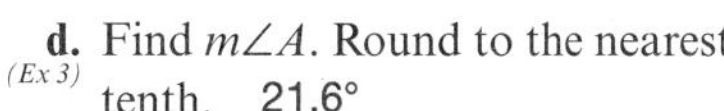

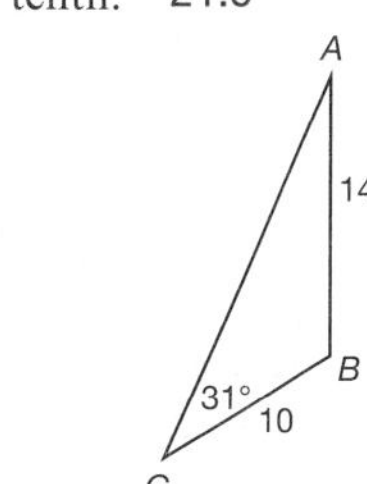

e. Given $\triangle ABC$, $m\angle A = 63°$, $a = 38$, and $c = 40$, find $m\angle C$. Round to the nearest tenth. *(Ex 3)* $m\angle C \approx 69.7°$ or $\approx 110.3°$

f. A surveyor stands on the south end of a roof and finds that the angle formed by the roof and the line of sight with a flagpole is 38°. The surveyor then walks to the north end of the roof and finds the angle formed by the roof and flagpole to be 64°. Estimate the distance from the roof to the flagpole, given that the roof has a length of 225 feet. *(Ex 4)* About 127.3 feet

INCLUSION

To simplify the process of finding the solution to Example 4, have students use construction paper of two colors to model the problem.

After students find the length of a, have students cut out two triangles and label the sides and angles. Then have them find the length of h using the larger of the two triangles. Then place the two triangles together to form the original triangle.

Additional Example 4

A surveyor stands on the east end of a pier and finds that the angle formed by the pier and the line of sight with a lighthouse is 42°. The surveyor then walks to the west end and finds the angle formed by the pier and lighthouse to be 68°. Estimate the distance from the pier to the lighthouse, given that the pier has a length of 90 yards.
$d \approx 59.4$ yards

Lesson Practice

Problem b

Error Alert Students may incorrectly use the Law of Sines. Make sure they use $\frac{\sin A}{a} = \frac{\sin C}{c}$, then solve for a, where $a = \frac{32 \sin 19°}{\sin 45°}$.

Check for Understanding

The questions below help assess the concepts taught in this lesson.

1. **"Explain how to find the area of a triangle with sides of 18 m and 32 m that include an angle of 124°."** Substitute the known values into the area formula: $\frac{1}{2}(18)(32)\sin 124°$. Then simplify. The area is 238.8 square meters.
2. **"How do you find b, given $m\angle A = 32°$, $m\angle B = 56°$, and $BC = 5$?"** Use the Law of Sines and substitute the given values.
$\frac{\sin 32}{5} = \frac{\sin 56}{b}$
$b = \frac{5 \sin 56}{\sin 32} \approx 7.8$

3 Practice

Math Conversations

Discussions to strengthen understanding

Problem 4

Students should recognize that $4x - 8 = 4(x-2)$. Divide $4x^5 - 129$ first by $x-2$, then by 4.

Problem 6

Guide students by asking the following questions.

"How do you write the inverse of $y = -3x$?" $x = -3y$

"What is the equation in terms of y?" $y = -\frac{1}{3}x$

"What are the domain and range of $y = -\frac{1}{3}x$?" any real number

Problem 12

Extend the Problem

Have students find the other trigonometric functions for θ.

$\tan\theta = \frac{6\sqrt{2}}{7}$, $\cot\theta = \frac{7\sqrt{2}}{12}$,
$\sec\theta = \frac{11}{7}$, $\csc\theta = \frac{11\sqrt{2}}{12}$

TEACHER TIP

For problem 14, have students write the Law of Sines and then work the problem only from the diagram. Have them compare their answer to the one the student made. Students should then be able to find the error, based on their own work.

Practice Distributed and Integrated

Solve.

1. (66) $3x(x^2 + 7x - 25) = 0$ $x = -9.603, 0, 2.603$

2. (66) $4x(2x^2 + 9x - 45) = 0$ $x = -7.5, 0, 3$

Use synthetic division to divide.

3. (51) $5x^3 - 10x^2 + 20x - 15$ by $x - 1$ $5x^2 - 5x + 15$

4. (51) $4x^5 - 129$ by $4x - 8$ $x^4 + 2x^3 + 4x^2 + 8x + 16 - \frac{1}{x-2}$

5. (58) **Write** The square root property states: If $x^2 = a$, then $x = \pm\sqrt{a}$. Explain why x must be positive or negative. Whether x is negative or positive x^2 is always positive. If x is unknown then there is no way to know for sure if it is the positive x or the negative x.

6. (50) Find an equation for the inverse of $y = -3x$. Identify the domain and range of the inverse function. $y = -\frac{1}{3}x$; domain: x is any real number; range: y is any real number

7. (61) **Coordinate Geometry** Because $x - a$ is a factor of $P(x)$ when $P(a) = 0$, a is an x-intercept of the graph of $P(x)$. Which of the following ordered pairs must be on the graph of $P(x) = x^3 - 7x^2 + 36$? $(-2, 0)(3, 0)(6, 0)$

$(-6, 0)$ $(-4, 0)$ $(-2, 0)$ $(1, 0)$ $(3, 0)$ $(6, 0)$

8. (54) **Flowers** Jay is planting a maximum of 40 bulbs of lilies and tulips in her garden. She wants more tulips, x, than lilies, y. Write a system of inequalities and find the maximum number of lily bulbs Jay can plant. $x \geq 0$, $y \geq 0$, $x + y \leq 40$, $x > y$; 19 lily bulbs

9. (59) **Multiple Choice** Choose the letter that best represents $\sqrt[4]{625x^{28}}$ simplified. A

A $5x^7$ **B** $25x^{14}$ **C** $25x^7$ **D** $5x^{14}$

***10.** (71) **Geography** On a map, line segments connecting three southeast Texas cities form a triangle as shown to the right. To the nearest mile, what is the distance from Mathis to Cuero? 78 miles

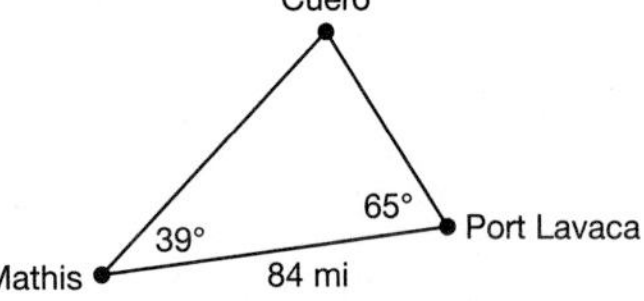

11. (65) **Write** Why must you write a quadratic equation in standard form before using the Quadratic Formula?

11. The formula works when the terms are all on the same side of the equation. Using a coefficient of a term that is on the wrong side of the equation will give a value that has the wrong sign, and ultimately lead to incorrect solutions. Writing the terms in decreasing order makes it less likely to choose the wrong coefficient.

12. (52) Angle θ is an acute angle of a right triangle and $\cos\theta = \frac{7}{11}$. Find the sine of angle θ. $\sin\theta = \frac{6\sqrt{2}}{11}$

13. (66) **Analyze** $3 - 6\sqrt{2}$ is a root of a polynomial equation. What must be another root of the equation? Why? $3 + 6\sqrt{2}$ because of the Irrational Root Theorem.

***14.** (71) **Error Analysis** Explain and correct the error a student made in finding the value of x. The 49° angle is not opposite the side labeled x. The second fraction should be $\frac{\sin 68°}{x}$ and $x \approx 16.6$.

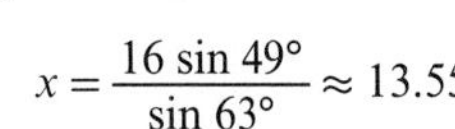

$$\frac{\sin 63°}{16} = \frac{\sin 49°}{x}$$

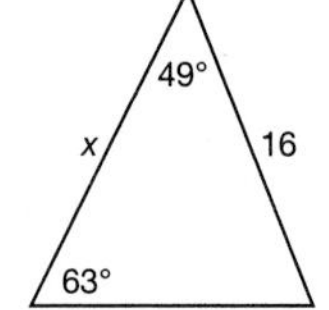

$$x = \frac{16 \sin 49°}{\sin 63°} \approx 13.55$$

ALTERNATE METHOD FOR PROBLEMS 3 AND 4

After students have worked the problems using synthetic division, have them rework the problems using long division. Both methods should yield the same result.

*15. (Quality Control) In a factory, a sample of items is checked during all three work shifts. During the first shift, 2 out of 11 items were found defective. During the second shift, 0 out of 13 items were found defective. During the third shift, 4 out of 20 items were found defective. What is the probability that an item was checked during the first shift, given that is was not defective? $\frac{9}{38} \approx 23.7\%$
(68)

*16. **Graphing Calculator** Estimate the solution of $\sqrt{3x+1} - 4 + \sqrt[3]{x} = 0$ to the nearest hundredth. ≈ 2.12
(70)

17. **Formulate** The half-life of Thorium-229 is 7340 years. Formulate an exponential function representing the amount of a grams of Thorium-229 remaining after t years. Use the function to find how much of a 200 gram sample of Thorium-229 will be left after 10,000 years. $y = a\left(\frac{1}{2}\right)^{\frac{t}{7340}}$; about 78 g
(57)

*18. **Error Analysis** To find the tangent of 300°, a student used its reference angle as follows: $\tan 60° = \sqrt{3}$, therefore $\tan 300° = \sqrt{3}$. What is the error? Find the correct value of tan 300°. The student did not adjust the sign. The terminal side of 300° is in Quadrant IV, where tangent values are negative. $\tan 300° = -\sqrt{3}$
(63)

19. Let $f(x) = 5x^2$ and $g(x) = -4x$. Find the composite function $f(g(x))$.
(53)

19. $f(-4x) = 5(-4x)^2$
$= 5(16x^2)$
$= 80x^2$

20. **Geometry** Find the area of the shaded region of the regular hexagon. $5\sqrt{3} \approx 8.66 \text{ cm}^2$
(52)

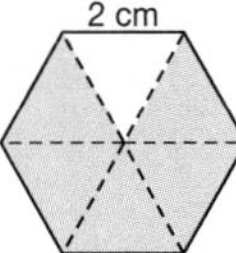

21. Maximize $P = 2x + y$ for the constraints $x \geq 0$, $y \geq 0$, $x + y \leq 6$ (6, 0)
(54)

*22. **Analyze** Explain why $x - \sqrt{5} = 2x$ is not a radical equation. A radical equation has a variable as a radicand. In this equation, the radicand is the constant 5.
(70)

23. Use long division to divide $-x^4 - 7x^3 + 6x^2 - 1$ by $x - 3$. $-x^3 - 10x^2 - 24x - 72 - \frac{217}{x-3}$
(38)

*24. **Multi-Step** Simplify $\frac{4 - 8i + 2 + i}{7 + 3i + 2i}$. Write the answer in the form $a + bi$. $\frac{7}{74} - \frac{79}{74}i$
(69)

25. **Multi-Step** A dietician asked 26 high school students how often they eat breakfast. The students eat breakfast a mean of 2.5 days per week and there is a standard deviation of 1.36.
(Inv 7)

a. If Stephanie eats breakfast 5 days per week, how many standard deviations above the mean is she? 1.84

b. If Darryl eats breakfast 1 day per week, how many standard deviations below the mean is he? 1.1

c. Who is closest to the sample mean? Darryl

26. (Bay Bridge) A sailor in a boat beneath the San Francisco Bay Bridge shoots a flare straight up. The height of the flare after t seconds is modeled by $-16t^2 + 96t$. The bridge is 220 feet above the water and the sailor is 12 feet above the water. The solutions of $-16t^2 + 96t = 208$ give the number of seconds it will take for the flare to reach the bridge. Will the flare reach the bridge? If so, when? $3 \pm 2i$, The time is not a real number; the flare will never reach the bottom of the bridge.
(62)

*27. **Multiple Choice** What is the area of $\triangle ABC$ if $a = 7$ in., $b = 9$ in., and $m\angle C = 23°$? A
(71)
A about 12.3 in² **B** about 24.6 in² **C** about 29 in² **D** about 49.2 in²

Simplify.

*28. $\frac{2 + 5i}{i}$ $5 - 2i$
(69)

*29. i^7 $-i$
(69)

30. $49^{\frac{5}{12}} \cdot 49^{\frac{1}{12}}$ 7
(59)

Problem 18

Before students begin the problem, review the sine and cosine values in each quadrant.

Problem 19

Error Alert

Students may square only x instead of $-4x$. Have them write $-4x$ in parentheses and then do the substitution.

Problem 24

TEACHER TIP

Have students simplify the denominator and numerator first. Then multiply the numerator and denominator by the conjugate $7 - 5i$.

Problem 27

Remind students to use $\frac{1}{2}ab \sin C$ to find the area of the triangle.

Problem 29

Have students rewrite i^7 in terms of even powers.

$i^7 = i^2 \cdot i^2 \cdot i^2 \cdot i$

Remind students that $i^2 = -1$.

Problem 30

Remind students to add the exponents and then to reduce the fraction.

CHALLENGE

Find the perimeter and area of an isosceles triangle given the base angles measure 53°30' and the non-congruent side measures 50 inches. Round to the nearest tenth.
The congruent sides are about 42 inches. The perimeter of the triangle is about 134 inches. The area of the triangle is about 844 square inches.

LOOKING FORWARD

Using the Law of Sines prepares students for

- **Lesson 77** Using the Law of Cosines

LESSON 72

1 Warm Up

Remind students to add the exponents in problem 3.

2 New Concepts

In this lesson, students simplify exponential and logarithmic expressions, evaluate a logarithm by changing the base, approximate logarithms, and apply the Power Property of Logarithms.

Review the definition of *logarithm.* Explain that $b^x = a$ is equivalent to $\log_b a = x$.

LESSON RESOURCES

Student Edition Practice Workbook 72
Reteaching Master 72
Adaptations Master 72
Challenge and Enrichment Master C72

LESSON 72

Using the Properties of Logarithms

Warm Up

1. **Vocabulary** In the expression $\log_5 20$, the number 5 is the ___base___.
(64)

2. Evaluate $(2^3)^3$. 512
(3)

3. Simplify $2^x \cdot 2^{(x+y)}$. $2^{(2x+y)}$
(3)

New Concepts

Since a logarithm is the exponent applied to a base to obtain a given value, $b^x = a$ is equivalent to $\log_b a = x$.

The definition of a logarithm can be used to find the inverse of an exponential function.

$y = b^x$	The exponential function with base b
$x = b^y$	Interchange the variables to find the inverse.
$y = \log_b x$	Write $x = b^y$ in its logarithmic form.

Inverse functions

The graphs of inverse functions are reflective images of each other with respect to line $y = x$. The parent function $y = b^x$ for $b > 1$ is shown below, along with its inverse function $y = \log_b x$.

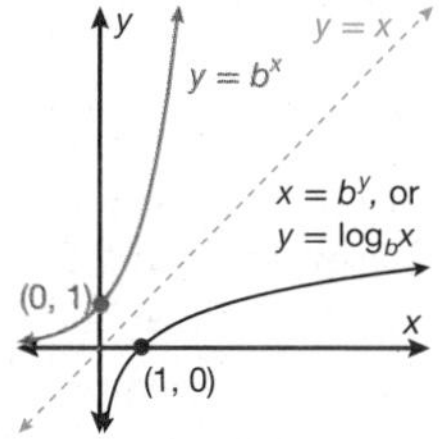

The value of b determines the exact shape of the graphs. The function graphs for $b = 2$ are shown below.

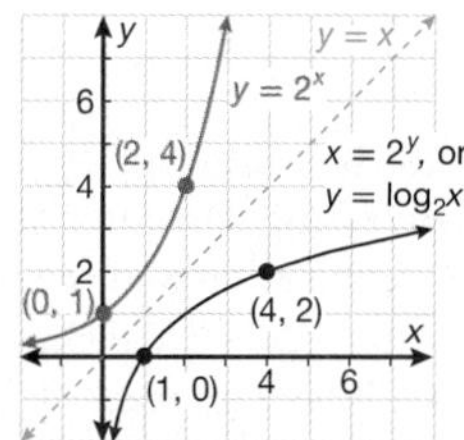

The definition of logarithm can also be used to obtain the following rules.

Inverse Properties of Logarithms
$b^{\log_b x} = x$ and $\log_b b^x = x$

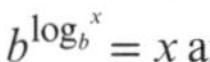

Online Connection
www.SaxonMathResources.com

These rules can be used to simplify exponential or logarithmic expressions.

MATH BACKGROUND

Common logarithms use base 10. Natural logarithms (ln) use base e. The letter e, like π, is an irrational number. Leonhard Euler proved that the limit of $\left(1 + \frac{1}{n}\right)^n$ approaches 2.7182.... This number is called e after Euler.

Like common logarithms, natural logarithms are used to solve application problems. One such problem is compound interest. Some banks compound interest continuously. To find the investment at time t, use the continuous compound formula, $A = Pe^{rt}$.

Example 1 Simplifying Exponential and Logarithmic Expressions

a. Simplify $\log_5 5^{2c+3}$.

SOLUTION

$\log_5 5^{2c+3} = 2c + 3$ Inverse Property of Logarithms

b. Simplify $2^{\log_2 p}$.

SOLUTION

$2^{\log_2 p} = p$ Inverse Property of Logarithms

Most calculators calculate logarithms only in base 10 or base *e*. One way a logarithm with a base other than 10 or *e* can be evaluated is by applying the **change of base formula.**

Change of Base Formula
For $a > 0$ and $a \neq 1$ and any base b such that $b > 0$ and $b \neq 1$, $\log_b x = \frac{\log_a x}{\log_a b}$.

Example 2 Evaluating a Logarithm by Changing the Base

Evaluate $\log_4 8$.

Hint

You can also evaluate $\log_4 8$ by changing to base e. $\log_4 8 = \frac{\ln 8}{\ln 4} = 1.5$

SOLUTION

Method 1: Change to base 10.

$\log_4 8 = \frac{\log 8}{\log 4}$

$\approx \frac{0.903}{0.602}$ Use a calculator.

$= 1.5$ Divide.

Method 2: Change to base 2, because both 4 and 8 are powers of 2.

$\log_4 8 = \frac{\log_2 8}{\log_2 4} = \frac{3}{2}$

$= 1.5$

Exploration Discovering the Properties of Logarithms

The logarithm $\log_2 32$ can be written as $\log_2 (4 \cdot 8)$.

1. Evaluate $\log_2 4$ and $\log_2 8$. 2, 3
2. What is the sum of $\log_2 4$ and $\log_2 8$? 5
3. Since $\log_2 32$ can be written as $\log_2 2^5$ by the inverse Property of Logarithms, $\log_2 2^5 =$ 5.
4. Compare the value of $\log_2 32$ and $\log_2 4 + \log_2 8$. The values are equal.
5. **Generalize** If $\log_2 32 = \log_2 (4 \cdot 8) = \log_2 4 + \log_2 8$, then a make a conjecture about $\log_b (mn)$. $\log_b (mn) = \log_b m + \log_b n$.
6. **Generalize** Use the process shaped by Problems 1–5 to make a conjecture about $\log_b \left(\frac{m}{n}\right)$. Use the statement $\log_2 4 = \log_2 \frac{64}{16} = \log_2 64 - \log_2 16$ as a model. $\log_b \left(\frac{m}{n}\right) = \log_b m - \log_b n$

Example 1

Students use an extension of the definition of a logarithm.

Additional Example 1

a. Simplify $3^{\log_3 (x+1)}$. $x + 1$

b. Simplify $\log_2 2^{3a+b}$. $3a + b$

Example 2

Use the Hint to show students how to evaluate $\log_4 8$ by changing to base *e*.

Additional Example 2

Evaluate $\log_{81} 27$. 0.75

TEACHER TIP

When evaluating logarithms by changing the base, students may tend to use the graphing calculator when the solution can be calculated mentally. Help them to recognize problems in which mental math is possible. If the base and the number can be expressed as a power of the same base, then the logarithm can be evaluated using mental math. Point out that method 2 of Example 2 uses the fact that $8 = 2^3$ and $4 = 2^2$, so the logarithm can easily be calculated.

Exploration

Students make conjectures about the Product and Quotient Properties of Logarithms.

ENGLISH LEARNERS

To help students understand the meaning of **conjecture,** define it as an opinion formed without sufficient evidence or proof.

Discuss examples of conjectures that students may have made in science class before doing an experiment. Explain that the conjecture might have been a guess.

Have students explain the conjectures they made in steps 5 and 6 of the Exploration.

Connect the meaning of conjecture with steps 5 and 6. Supply other examples, and have students look at their conjecture to see if it satisfies the sample problems.

Example 3

Extend the Example

Have students check the answer in part a by using the change of base formula, base e or 10, and a graphing calculator.

Additional Example 3

a. Approximate the value of $\log_2 80$. Use $\log_2 5 \approx 2.322$.
$\log_2 80 \approx 6.322$

b. Approximate the value of $\log 2400$. Use $\log 24 \approx 1.3802$.
$\log 2400 \approx 3.3802$

Product Property of Logarithms
For any positive numbers m, n, and b $(b \neq 1)$, $\log_b mn = \log_b m + \log_b n$

To prove the Product Property of Logarithms, let $b^x = m$ and $b^y = n$. Then $\log_b m = x$ and $\log_b n = y$.

$b^x b^y = mn$

$b^{x+y} = mn$ Product of Powers Property

$\log_b b^{x+y} = \log_b mn$ Take the logarithm of each side.

$x + y = \log_b mn$ Inverse Property of Logarithms

$\log_b m + \log_b n = \log_b mn$ Substitute $\log_b m$ for x and $\log_b n$ for y.

Example 3 **Approximating the Logarithm of a Product**

a. Approximate the value of $\log_3 63$. Use $\log_3 7 \approx 1.7712$.

SOLUTION

$\log_3 63 = \log_3 (7 \cdot 3^2)$ Factor 63 so that one of the factors is a power of 3.

$= \log_3 7 + \log_3 3^2$ Product Property of Logarithms

$= \log_3 7 + 2$ Inverse Property of Logarithms

$\approx 1.7712 + 2$ Substitute 1.7712 for $\log_3 7$.

≈ 3.7712 Add.

Hint

The solutions in Example 3 can be checked by approximating $3^{3.7712}$ and $10^{1.7782}$ with a calculator.

b. Approximate the value of $\log 60$. Use $\log 6 \approx 0.7782$.

SOLUTION

$\log 60 = \log (6 \cdot 10)$ Factor 60 so that one of the factors is a power of 10.

$= \log 6 + \log 10$ Product Property of Logarithms

$= 0.7782 + \log 10$ Substitute 0.7782 for log 6

$\approx 0.7782 + 1$ Inverse Property of Logarithms

≈ 1.7782 Add.

Quotient Property of Logarithms
For any positive numbers m, n, and b $(b \neq 1)$, $\log_b \frac{m}{n} = \log_b m - \log_b n$

To prove the Quotient Property of Logarithms, let $b^x = m$ and $b^y = n$. Then $\log_b m = x$ and $\log_b n = y$.

$\frac{b^x}{b^y} = \left(\frac{m}{n}\right)$

$b^{x-y} = \frac{m}{n}$ Quotient of Powers Poperty

$\log_b b^{x-y} = \log_b \left(\frac{m}{n}\right)$ Take the logarithm of each side.

$x - y = \log_b \left(\frac{m}{n}\right)$ Inverse Property of Logarithms

$\log_b m - \log_b n = \log_b \left(\frac{m}{n}\right)$ Substitute $\log_b m$ for x and $\log_b n$ for y.

Example 4 Approximating the Logarithm of a Quotient

a. Approximate the value of $\log_4 6$. Use $\log_4 48 \approx 2.7925$ and $\log_4 8 = 1.5$.

SOLUTION

$\log_4 6 = \log_4 \frac{48}{8}$	Express 6 as a quotient.
$= \log_4 48 - \log_4 8$	Quotient Property of Logarithms
$\approx 2.7925 - 1.5$	Substitute the given values.
≈ 1.2925	Subtract.

Hint

The solution in Example 4b can be checked by approximating $e^{2.9014}$ with a calculator.

b. Approximate the value of $\ln \frac{e^4}{3}$. Use $\ln 3 \approx 1.0986$.

SOLUTION

$\ln \frac{e^4}{3} = \ln e^4 - \ln 3$	Quotient Property of Logarithms
$\approx 4 - \ln 3$	Inverse Property of Logarithms
$\approx 4 - 1.0986$	Substitute 1.0986 for ln 3
≈ 2.9014	Subtract.

Power Property of Logarithms
For any real number p and positive numbers a and b ($b \neq 1$), $\log_b a^p = p\log_b a$

Example 5 Applying the Power Property of Logarithms

a. Simplify $\log_3 81^2$.

SOLUTION

$\log_3 81^2 = 2 \log_3 81$	Power Property of Logarithms
$= 2 \cdot 4$	$\log_3 81 = 4$ because $3^4 = 81$.
$= 8$	Multiply.

b. Write $\ln \left(\frac{5e}{x}\right)^2$ as a sum or difference of terms.

SOLUTION

$\ln \left(\frac{5e}{x}\right)^2 = 2 \ln \frac{5e}{x}$	Power Property of Logarithms
$= 2(\ln 5e - \ln x)$	Quotient Property of Logarithms
$= 2(\ln 5 + \ln e - \ln x)$	Product Property of Logarithms
$= 2(\ln 5 + 1 - \ln x)$	Inverse Property of Logarithms
$= 2 \ln 5 + 2 - 2 \ln x$	Distribute the 2.

Example 4

Error Alert Students may add the given values as they did with the logarithm of a product. Review the Quotient Property of Logarithms.

Additional Example 4

a. Approximate the value of $\log_3 25$. Use $\log_3 125 \approx 4.3949$ and $\log_3 5 \approx 1.4650$. $\log_3 25 \approx 2.9299$

b. Approximate the value of $\ln \frac{e^6}{4}$. Use $\ln 4 \approx 1.3863$. $\ln \frac{e^6}{4} \approx 4.6137$

Example 5

Remind students that $\log_b a^p = p \log_b a$.

Additional Example 5

a. Simplify $\log_4 64^3$. 9

b. Write $\ln \left(\frac{4e}{y}\right)^x$ as a sum or difference of terms. $x \ln 4 + x - x \ln y$

INCLUSION

When using the Product Property of Logarithms, remind students to find a factor that has the same base as the logarithmic expression. The prime factorization of the number can sometimes be helpful in finding that base. In Example 3a, $63 = 7 \cdot 9 = 7 \cdot 3 \cdot 3$. The base in the logarithmic expression is 3, and the prime factorization shows that the number can be expressed as $7 \cdot 3^2$.

Example 6

Guide students through each step in the example. Review properties of logarithms if necessary.

Additional Example 6

The Richter magnitude M of an earthquake is expressed by $M = \frac{2}{3}\log\left(\frac{E}{10^{11.8}}\right)$, where E is the energy released in ergs. In 1906 an earthquake of magnitude 8.3 struck San Francisco. Find the energy released by that earthquake. $E \approx 1.78 \times 10^{24}$ ergs

Lesson Practice

Problem h

Scaffolding Before students evaluate $\log_5 125$, they should apply the Power Property of Logarithms.

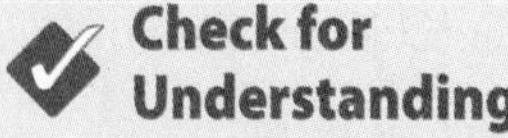

Check for Understanding

The questions below help assess the concepts taught in this lesson.

1. **"Explain how to evaluate $\log_8 16$ by changing to base 2."** Write $\log_8 16$ as $\frac{\log_2 16}{\log_2 8}$. Evaluate the numerator and the denominator. $\log_2 16 = 4$ and $\log_2 8 = 3$. So $\log_8 16 = \frac{4}{3}$.
2. **"How do you simplify $\log_4 64^5$?"** Use the Power Property of Logarithms to get $5\log_4 64$. Evaluate $\log_4 64$, which is 3, because $4^3 = 64$. Then multiply: $5 \times 3 = 15$.

Example 6 **Application: Geology**

The Richter magnitude M of an earthquake is expressed by $M = \frac{2}{3}\log\left(\frac{E}{10^{11.8}}\right)$, where E is the energy released in ergs. In 1989 an earthquake of magnitude 7.1 struck San Francisco. Find the energy released by that earthquake.

SOLUTION

$7.1 = \frac{2}{3}\log\left(\frac{E}{10^{11.8}}\right)$	Substitute 7.1 for M.
$\frac{3}{2}(7.1) = \log\left(\frac{E}{10^{11.8}}\right)$	Multiply both sides by $\frac{3}{2}$.
$10.65 = \log E - \log 10^{11.8}$	Quotient Property of Logarithms
$10.65 = \log E - 11.8$	Inverse Property of Logarithms
$22.45 = \log E$	Add 11.8 to both sides.
$10^{22.45} = E$	Write the logarithmic equation in exponential form.
$E \approx 2.82 \times 10^{22}$	Use a calculator to evaluate.

The energy released was approximately 2.82×10^{22} ergs.

Hint

The display 2.818382931E22 means $2.818382931 \times 10^{22}$, which is approximately 2.82×10^{22}.

Lesson Practice

a. (Ex 1) Simplify $10^{\log(3a-1)}$. $3a - 1$

b. (Ex 1) Simplify $\ln e^{x+1}$. $x + 1$

c. (Ex 2) Evaluate $\log_{32} 64$. 1.2

d. (Ex 3) Approximate the value of $\log_2 40$. Use $\log_2 5 \approx 2.3219$. 5.3219

e. (Ex 3) Approximate the value of log 1900. Use $\log 19 \approx 1.2788$. 3.2788

f. (Ex 4) Approximate the value of $\log_5 4$. Use $\log_5 60 \approx 2.5440$ and $\log_5 15 \approx 1.6826$. 0.8614

g. (Ex 4) Approximate the value of $\log \frac{11}{10{,}000}$. Use $\log 11 \approx 1.0414$. −2.9586

h. (Ex 5) Simplify $\log_5 125^4$. 12

i. (Ex 5) Rewrite $\ln\left(\frac{x+2}{2e^2}\right)$ as a sum or difference of terms. $\ln(x + 2) - \ln 2 - 2$

j. (Ex 6) The Richter magnitude M of an earthquake is expressed by $M = \frac{2}{3}\log\left(\frac{E}{10^{11.8}}\right)$, where E is the energy released in ergs. In 2007 an earthquake of magnitude 6.6 occurred near the west coast of Japan. Find the energy released by that earthquake. approximately 5.01×10^{21} ergs

Practice Distributed and Integrated

1. (41) Find the distance between (6,0) and (−3, −3). $3\sqrt{10}$

2. (26) Find the equation of the line that has a slope of $\frac{2}{5}$ and passes through (3, −5) in slope-intercept form. $y = \frac{2}{5}x - \frac{31}{5}$

INCLUSION

Have students use a spreadsheet program instead of a calculator. A spreadsheet program such as Excel can evaluate a logarithmic expression, given the base and the number.

Simplify.

3. (40) $4\sqrt{3} \cdot 5\sqrt{2} \cdot 6\sqrt{12}$ $720\sqrt{2}$

4. (40) $4\sqrt{63} - 3\sqrt{28}$ $6\sqrt{7}$

***5.** (72) **Write** Explain why $\log_2 2^x = x$. Possible answer: Exponential and logarithmic operations are inverse operations.

6. (67) **Tennis** A tennis player 8 feet from the net hits an overhead shot, hitting the ball at a height of 8 feet. Assume that the path of the ball is a straight line. To the nearest degree, what is the maximum angle θ at which the ball can be hit and land within the court? 80°

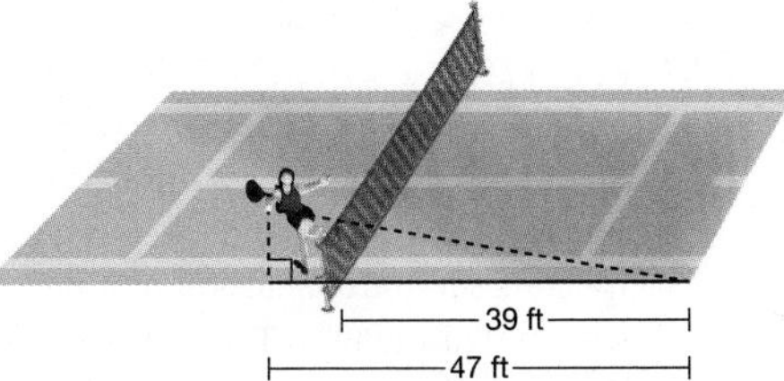

7. (57) **Formulate** Formulate an expression for the amount Imani will have in her bank account at the end of ten years if she invests a principal of $2500 at an annual interest rate of 6.4%, compounded quarterly. $2500(1.016)^{40}$

8. (69) Find the absolute value of $|3 + i|$. $\sqrt{10}$

9. (54) Describe the feasible region for the set of inequalities $0 \le x \le 15$, $y \ge 0$, $3y + 4x \le 75$. Region bounded by: (0, 0), (0, 25), (15, 0), (15, 5)

***10.** (71) Solve $\triangle DEF$ given that $m\angle D = 65°$, $m\angle E = 47°$, and $d = 102$. $m\angle F = 68°$, $e = 82.3$, $f = 104.3$

11. (63) **Multiple Choice** If an angle in standard position has a measure of $\frac{3\pi}{4}$ radians, in what point does its terminal side intersect the unit circle centered at the origin? A

A $\left(-\frac{\sqrt{2}}{2}, \frac{\sqrt{2}}{2}\right)$ **B** $\left(-\frac{\sqrt{2}}{2}, -\frac{\sqrt{2}}{2}\right)$ **C** $\left(-\frac{1}{2}, \frac{\sqrt{3}}{2}\right)$ **D** $\left(-\frac{1}{2}, -\frac{\sqrt{3}}{2}\right)$

12. (65) **Travel** A driver leaves a gas station and heads due north at a rate of 50 miles per hour. Two hours later, a truck driver leaves the same gas station and heads due east at a rate of 40 miles per hour. Approximately how long will it take for the vehicles to be 450 miles apart? 7.7 hours

***13.** (72) **Multi-Step** Suppose that the population of a certain town increases at the rate of 6% per year and that the current population is 2210.

a. Write an exponential function that gives the population as a function of x, the number of elapsed years. $y = 2210(1.06)^x$

b. Write a logarithmic function that gives the number of elapsed years as a function of x, the population. $y = \log_{1.06} \frac{x}{2210}$

c. To the nearest tenth, how many years will it take for the population to exceed 3000? 5.2 years

***14.** (68) **Analyze** Explain why the probability of events that involve selection of items without replacement involve conditional probabilities.

14. The probability of selecting the second item given the condition that the first item was selected is different from what it would be if the first item were never selected. Because there is one fewer item to choose from, the denominator is one less that what it would be otherwise.

***15.** (72) **Multiple Choice** Which is equal to $5^{\log_5 x}$? B

A 1 **B** x **C** $5x$ **D** 5^x

3 Practice

Math Conversations

Discussions to strengthen understanding

Problem 7

Guide students by asking the following questions.

"What are you finding?" the amount after 10 years

"What is the formula for compound interest?" $A = P\left(1 + \frac{r}{n}\right)^{nt}$

"What is the principal?" $2500

"The interest is compounded how many times a year?" 4

"What is the interest in decimal form?" 0.064

"You want to know the amount after how many years?" 10

"Substitute the values into the formula. What equation do you get?" $A = 2500\left(1 + \frac{0.064}{4}\right)^{4 \cdot 10}$

Problem 8

"The absolute value of $a + bi$ is equal to its distance from the origin. How do you write that distance?" $\sqrt{a^2 + b^2}$

"What are the values of a and b?" $a = 3$ and $b = 1$

"What value is the radicand?" 10

"What is the final answer?" $\sqrt{10}$

CHALLENGE

Solve for x.

$\log_b x = 5\log_b 2 - 2\log_b 4$
$\log_b x = \log_b 2^5 - \log_b 4^2$
$\log_b x = \log_b 32 - \log_b 16$
$\log_b x = \log_b \frac{32}{16}$
$\log_b x = \log_b 2$
$x = 2$

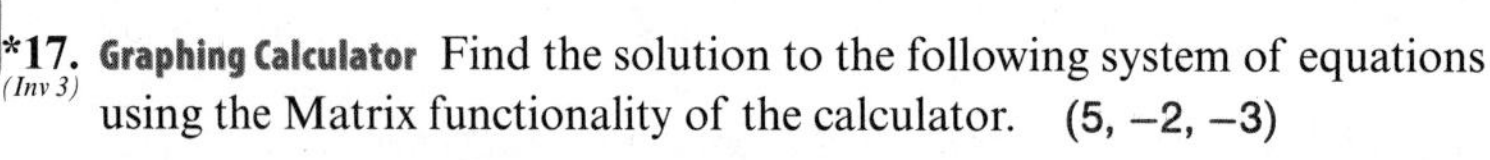

Problem 19
Extend the Problem
Have students find the approximate perimeter of the triangle. The missing sides lengths are about 13 units and 7 units; $P \approx 35$ units.

Problems 20 and 21
Remind students to add or subtract the real terms and then add or subtract the imaginary terms.

Problem 23
Error Alert
Students may forget to multiply the terms by the reciprocal of the determinant or have the incorrect terms in the matrix. Remind students that the inverse of a 2×2 matrix is defined as $\frac{1}{ad-bc}\begin{vmatrix} d & -b \\ -c & a \end{vmatrix}$.

Problem 26
Remind students that in a complex plane, the horizontal axis is the set of real numbers and the vertical axis is the imaginary axis.

16. (63) **Clock Face** The minute hand of a certain clock is 20 inches long. How far does the tip of the minute hand travel in 45 minutes, to the nearest inch? 94 inches

***17.** (Inv 3) **Graphing Calculator** Find the solution to the following system of equations using the Matrix functionality of the calculator. (5, −2, −3)

$$-2x + y + 4z = -24$$
$$-5x + 7y - z = -36$$
$$8x - 3y + z = 43$$

18. (52) **Error Analysis** Kyle carefully measures two sides of a triangle and finds that the longest side has a length of 2 inches, and the second longest side has a length of $\sqrt{3}$ inches. He comes to the conclusion that the shorter leg must have length 1. What is wrong with his reasoning? This is a valid conclusion only if you know that the triangle is a right triangle.

***19.** (71) **Verify** Show that the value of x can be found by either using the sine ratio or the Law of Sines. See Additional Answers.

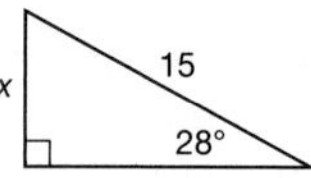

Add or subtract. Write the answer in the form $a + bi$.

20. (62) $(6 - 3i) + (5 + 4i)$ $11 + i$

21. (62) $(8 + 20i) - (-8 + 12i)$ $16 + 8i$

***22.** (71) **Coordinate Geometry** Explain how to use the Law of Sines to find the area of a triangle whose vertices are at (−4, 0), (6, 0), and (0, 6). Then find the area. See Additional Answers.

23. (32) Find the inverse of $\begin{bmatrix} 16 & 8 \\ 2 & 0 \end{bmatrix}$. $\begin{bmatrix} 0 & .5 \\ .125 & -1 \end{bmatrix}$

24. (62) **Analyze** Explain how to add a real number to a complex number. Provide an example.

24. Add the real parts and add the imaginary parts. The imaginary part for the real number is 0i. Sample:
$3 + (5 + 6i)$
$(3 + 0i) + (5 + 6i)$
$8 + 6i$

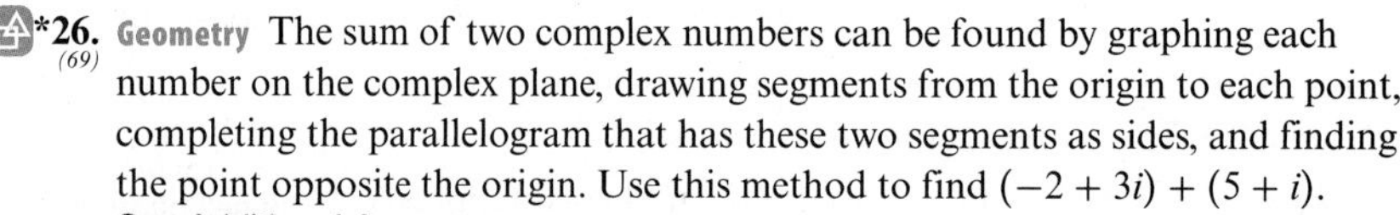

***25.** (70) **Lighthouses** The number of miles m a person can see on a clear day is approximated by $m = 1.2\sqrt{h}$, where h is the person's height above sea level. Suppose a person standing at the top of the Little Sable Point Lighthouse in Michigan on a clear day can see a distance of 12.4 miles. To the nearest foot, what is the person's height above sea level? About 107 feet

***26.** (69) **Geometry** The sum of two complex numbers can be found by graphing each number on the complex plane, drawing segments from the origin to each point, completing the parallelogram that has these two segments as sides, and finding the point opposite the origin. Use this method to find $(-2 + 3i) + (5 + i)$. See Additional Answers.

27. (Inv 6) **Error Analysis** Isaiah added 196 to both sides of the equation $x^2 + 16x + 60 = 0$ so he could make the perfect square. What error did he make? Isaiah squared 16 instead of dividing 16 by 2 and then squaring 8.

28. (Inv 7) Write a biased survey question. Then rewrite it to remove the bias. Answers will vary.

Solve by substitution.

29. (21) $2y - x = 6$, $y - 2x = -3$ (4, 5)

30. (21) $3x + 2y = 12$, $8x - 2y = 10$ (2, 3)

ALTERNATE METHOD FOR PROBLEMS 29 AND 30

Have students work the problems again using the elimination method. For problem 29, students can multiply the top or bottom equation by −2. For problem 30, students can eliminate y immediately and get $11x = 22$, or $x = 2$.

LOOKING FORWARD

Using the properties of logarithms prepares students for

- **Lesson 81** Using Natural Logarithms
- **Lesson 87** Evaluating Logarithmic Expressions
- **Lesson 102** Solving Logarithmic Equations and Inequalities
- **Lesson 110** Graphing Logarithmic Functions

LAB
11

Calculating Confidence Intervals

Graphing Calculator Lab (*Use with Lesson 73, 80, 118*)

A graphing calculator can be used to find confidence intervals.

Calculating the Confidence Interval Estimate of a Population Proportion

1. Calculate the confidence interval using the **"A: PropZInt"** feature.
   a. From the home screen, press the STAT button. Then press ▶ twice to reach the **TESTS** menu.

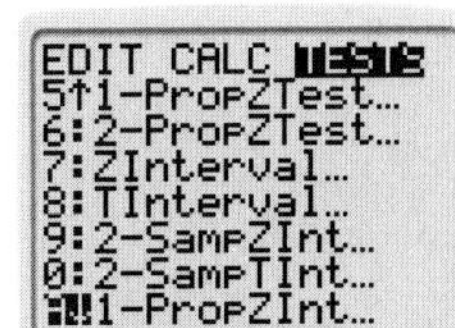

   b. Press ▼ to [**A: 1-PropZInt...**] and press ENTER. The 1-PropZInt-screen will appear so that the statistic values can be entered.

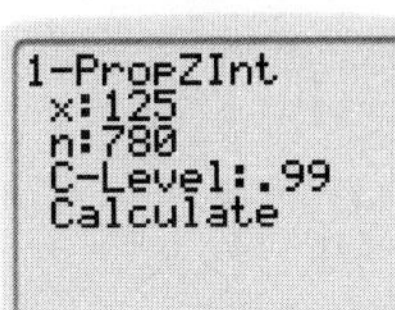

   c. Press 1 2 5 to enter x (successes). Then press ENTER.
   d. Press 7 8 0 to enter n (sample size). Then press ENTER.
   e. Press . 9 9 to enter the C-Level (confidence level). Then press ENTER to move to the **Calculate** option.
   f. Press ENTER to calculate the confidence interval. The values that appear inside the parentheses form the confidence interval.

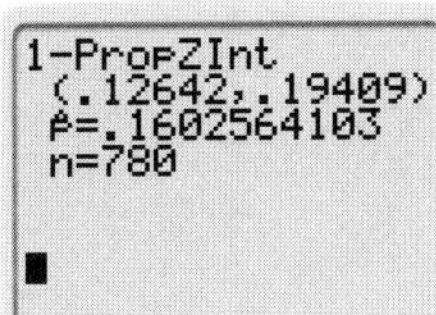

Hint

If the number of successes x is not given, then use the formula $x = n\hat{p}$ to calculate x.

Calculating the Confidence Interval Estimate of a Population Mean

2. Calculate the confidence interval when the standard deviation is known.
   a. To access this feature, follow step **1a.** Press ▼ to select [**7:ZInterval...**] and press ENTER.

ZInterval
Inpt:Data Stats
σ:2.78
x̄:7.8
n:788
C-Level:.99
Calculate

   b. First, select the type of input. Press ▶ to highlight **Stats** and press ENTER. Then press ▼ to enter the first statistic value.
   c. Enter the σ (population standard deviation). Press 2 . 7 8, and press ▼ to move to the next item.
   d. Continue to enter the other values. Enter $\overline{X}$(sample mean) as 7.8, n (sample size) as 788, and C-Level (confidence level) as .99.
   e. Move the cursor to the **Calculate** option. Press ENTER to calculate the confidence interval. The values that appear inside the parentheses form the confidence interval.

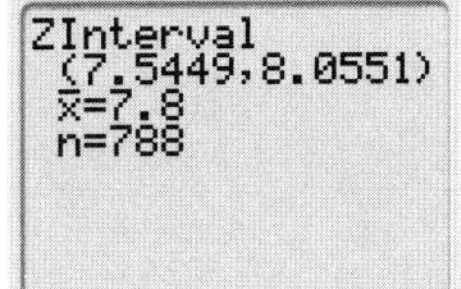

LAB
11

Materials

- graphing calculator

Discuss

In this lab, students will calculate confidence intervals using three statistical functions.

TEACHER TIP

A confidence interval involves estimating a value with an indication of how accurate the estimate is. The two parts of a confidence interval are the interval and the confidence level expressed as a percent.

Calculating the Confidence Interval Estimate of a Population Proportion

The meaning of the confidence interval can be described in this way. In repeated samples, the true population proportion lies in the interval 0.126 and 0.194, 99% of the time.

Discuss the calculator functions.

1-PropZInt computes a confidence interval for an unknown proportion of successes. The number of successes and sample size are given. **ZInterval** also computes a confidence interval but does so for a population where the population mean is unknown and population standard deviation and sample mean are given.

Calculating the Confidence Interval Estimate of a Population Mean

TEACHER TIP

To choose the appropriate test, students must know the difference between the population standard deviation, σ, and the sample standard deviation, Sx.

Problem 3

To calculate a confidence interval using **TInterval,** input the sample mean, sample standard deviation, and the sample size. The population mean and population standard deviation are not known.

3 Practice

Problem a

Use **1-PropZInt** since the sample size and number of successes are given.

Problem b

Use **ZInterval** since the population standard deviation, sample mean, and sample size are given.

Problem c

Use **TInterval** since the population standard deviation is unknown.

Graphing Calculator Tip

For these examples, the statistics values are given, so **Stats** is the type of input. When statistics values need to be calculated from stored data, choose the option **Data** as the type of input.

3. Calculate the confidence interval when the standard deviation is unknown.

a. To access this feature, follow step **1a.** Press to select **[8: TInterval...]** and press ENTER.

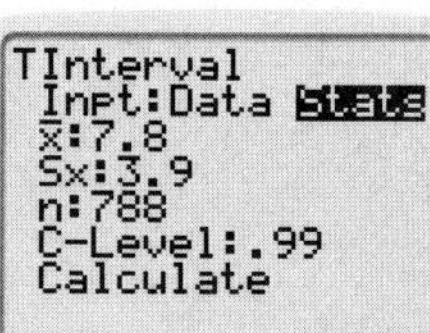

b. Select the type of input. Press to highlight Stats and press ENTER.

c. Use to move to the next entry. Enter $\overline{X}$(sample mean) as 7.8, Sx (standard deviation) as 3.9, n (sample size) as 788, and C-Level (confidence level) as .99.

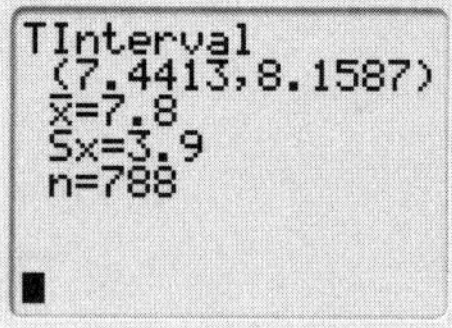

d. Move the cursor to the **CALCULATE** option and press ENTER to calculate the confidence interval. The values that appear inside the parentheses form the confidence interval.

Lab Practice

a. Find the 97% confidence interval estimate of a population proportion p when $x = 450$ and $n = 3655$. (0.11132, 0.13491)

b. Find the 95% confidence interval estimate of a population mean μ when $\sigma = 5744$, $\overline{X} = 38{,}576$, and $n = 43$. (36,859, 40,293)

c. Find the 95% confidence interval estimate of a population mean μ when $\overline{X} = 510$, $Sx = 115$, and $n = 33$. (469.22, 550.78)

520 Saxon Algebra 2

LESSON 73

Using Sampling

Warm Up

1. **Vocabulary** Two ratios set equal to each other form a proportion.
(SB)

2. Solve for b: $\frac{24}{b} = \frac{33}{66}$. $b = 48$
(7)

3. Find the value of n given $n = \frac{pq}{s}$, $p = 16$, $q = 32$, and $s = 8$. $n = 64$
(7)

New Concepts

A **population** is a group of individuals about which information is desired. When the population is large enough to make it difficult to examine every individual in it, such as the population of all American citizens, information from a sample of the population is obtained instead.

A **sample** is part of a population. The **sample size** is the number of individuals in a sample. When the sample is representative of the population studied, results from analyzing the sample can be extended to the entire population.

Example 1 Identifying the Population and Sample

Describe the individuals in the population and in the sample.

Math Reasoning

Analyze In Example 1b, why is it wrong to say that the population is every citizen in Jefferson County?

Not every citizen is registered to vote.

a. A newspaper reporter surveyed 5 women from a high school basketball team to determine how they feel about the men's team getting new uniforms when they did not get new uniforms.

SOLUTION The population is all the women on that school's female basketball team. The sample is the 5 women that spoke to the reporter.

b. Every registered voter in Jefferson County received a questionnaire in the mail to be filled out and returned two weeks later.

SOLUTION The population is every registered voter in Jefferson County, and the sample is those individuals who chose to fill out and return the survey on time.

The process of choosing the sample to be examined is called **sampling.** Valid sampling is very important. If the sample does not represent the population, the results of any analyses done on the sample are useless. A representative sample will have the same characteristics as the population. For example if the population is about 30% female, a representative sample would also be about 30% female.

Online Connection
www.SaxonMathResources.com

In **probability sampling,** every individual in the population has a known probability of being selected and this probability is greater than 0.

MATH BACKGROUND

The simplest method of probability sampling—simple random sampling—has both advantages and drawbacks. The main advantage of this method is that it avoids bias. As long as the sample size is not too small, the results will be representative of the population. Understanding the results of a simple random sample is straightforward. A disadvantage is that the method may not provide a correct representation of the population if the population size is small or if the population does not have similar characteristics throughout. For example, if the population is students in a school, and the sample contains mostly girls, the results will not apply to the entire population. This problem can be avoided by using an adequately large sample size or by using one of the other methods of probability sampling.

LESSON 73

1 Warm Up

Use problem 2 of the Warm Up to practice solving proportions.

2 New Concepts

In this lesson, students learn to identify populations and different types of sampling.

Example 1

Students identify a population and a sample.

Additional Example 1

Describe the individuals in the population and in the sample.

a. Richard asked three of his friends what they thought about the new movie at the theater. Population: Richard's friends; Sample: the three friends he asked

b. A restaurant gave an evaluation form to every customer who ate at the restaurant on Saturday. The form asked customers to evaluate the restaurant that day and mail in the form. Population: every customer who ate at the restaurant on Saturday; Sample: customers who mailed in the form

LESSON RESOURCES

Student Edition Practice Workbook 73
Reteaching Master 73
Adaptations Master 73
Challenge and Enrichment Master C73

Example 2

Students identify a probability sample and determine the type of probability sample described.

Additional Example 2

Tell if the sampling method performed was a probability sample. If not, explain why not. If so, state the type of probability sample.

a. A candidate wants to know which issues are the biggest concerns to people living in the city. She stands outside an apartment building and talks with many of the people who enter or leave on Saturday.
Not a probability sample; not all people in the city had a chance of being asked about the issues.

b. The name of every guest at a party is written on a card. The cards are placed in a bag, and two cards are randomly drawn from the bag. The guests whose names are on the cards win a door prize.
The sample is a simple random sample; every guest has the same chance of winning a prize.

Math Reasoning

Analyze Why is a stratified sample not a simple random sample?

Every possible group of n individuals does not have the same chance of being selected.

Probability Samples

Type	Definition	Example
Simple Random Sample (SRS)	Every member of the population has an equal chance of being chosen.	The names of all students in a class are put in a hat and five names are chosen at random.
Stratified Sample	The population is divided into mutually exclusive groups which have similar characteristics and a SRS is done on each group.	The class is divided into boys and girls and three names are chosen at random from each group.
Systematic Sample	A member of the group is chosen at a regular interval.	The names are listed at random and every eighth name is selected.
Cluster Sample	The population is divided into groups called clusters and the clusters are randomly chosen.	A survey may be given to a randomly selected homeroom.

Example 2 Identifying a Probability Sample

Tell if the sampling method performed was a probability sample. If not, explain why not. If so, state the type of probability sample.

(a.) A student wants to know what the senior class thinks about the suggested prom theme. He surveys every other senior who steps onto his bus.

SOLUTION The sample is not a probability sample because seniors who take another bus, are absent, or walk, bike, or drive to school have no chance of being selected for the survey.

(b.) A teacher assigns every student in her class a number from 1 to 40 and uses a calculator to choose random integers from 1 to 40. The students corresponding to the first 5 numbers generated are designated to be group leaders.

SOLUTION The sample is a simple random sample because every student has the same chance of being chosen and every possible group of 5 students has the same chance of being chosen.

An SRS can be made by using either the random number generator on a calculator, or by using a table of random digits. A table of random digits is shown below.

62010	60482	89824	08705	57913	46815	76221
30402	04710	12255	15279	31264	24680	38689
04633	61396	93751	98362	59553	62398	66607
63157	48257	29223	66773	89022	43069	91349
53787	35824	84823	86792	74771	91784	23826

To make an SRS by using the table, first assign each individual in the population a number. All individuals should have the same number of digits in their number. If choosing a sample of 10 individuals, assign 2-digit numbers: 01, 02, 03...10. If choosing a sample of 100 individuals, assign 3-digit numbers: 001, 002, 003...100. Then start at any row in the table and read the numbers straight across.

ENGLISH LEARNERS

Write the words strata and **stratified** on the board. Have students listen as you say the words. Then have students say the words themselves.

Explain that strata means layers, and stratified means formed into layers. Demonstrate by drawing layers on the board.

Have students apply the words to describe things they have seen, such as layers of rock exposed on the sides of mountains or layers of a cake.

Help students connect the definitions of strata and stratified to the definition of stratified sampling. The groups of a population are like layers of things which have characteristics in common.

Example 3 Choosing an SRS by using a Table of Random Digits

Twenty four names are numbered and listed below. Five must be randomly chosen for a sample. Use the Random Number Table and the instructions for using the table to determine the five names that will be picked for the sample.

01 Ann	02 Luke	03 Cassie	04 Finn	05 Jared	06 Tanela
07 Jude	08 Gunner	09 Drew	10 Halle	11 Colby	12 Anton
13 Aaron	14 Kenya	15 Ensa	16 Jarvis	17 Ming	18 Buhay
19 Alice	20 Steven	21 Pia	22 Niko	23 Leah	24 Ben

Random Number Table

046336 139693 751983 625955 362398 666071 858190 305192 911319
263157 482572 922366 773890 224306 991349 331116 368248 864530

Instructions Look at each consecutive 2-digit number. Ignore those numbers that are not one of the labeled numbers (01 through 24). Ignore numbers that repeat. Pick up on the second row wherever the first row leaves off, as if the table were written as one long continuous string of numbers.

SOLUTION Stop once five numbers from 01 through 24 have been identified. These numbers are shown in bold.

046336 **13**9693 75**19**83 625955 36**23**98 666071 858190 305192 911319
263157 482572 922366 773890 **22**4306 991349 331116 368248 864530

Make sure to look at the consecutive two-digit numbers. In the first group the numbers are 04, 63 and 36. Note: 46 is not a valid number.

The numbers 04, 13, 19, 23, and 22 correspond to Finn, Aaron, Alice, Leah, and Niko.

Not all sampling methods actually performed are a probability sample.

In **convenience sampling,** the surveyor simply selects whoever is convenient for them to select. For example, this may be those individuals who happen to walk by. It is not a probability sample, because people in the population who do not walk by the surveyor have no chance of being chosen.

In **voluntary response sampling,** the individuals in the sample choose themselves. For example, a population may receive a questionnaire in the mail. The sample consists of only those people who choose to return it. Note that controversial questions tend to be answered mostly by those people who have very strong opinions about that issue.

Math Language

Voluntary response sampling is also known as **self-selected sampling.**

Both convenience and voluntary response sampling can lead to **bias.** A sampling method is biased if it favors certain outcomes. The sample is then not representative of the population, and the results of surveying the individuals in the sample do not truly reflect that of the population.

Bias can result not only from poor sampling, but from poorly worded questions as well. Questions that are confusing or that lead the reader towards a certain side are biased.

Example 3

The example demonstrates how to choose a simple random sample by using a table of random digits.

TEACHER TIP

Suggest that students check their work by identifying the chosen numbers from the table twice.

Additional Example 3

Ten names already numbered are listed below. Three must be randomly chosen for a sample. What three names will be picked for the sample if numbers are chosen from the random number table shown on the student page?

25 Terrence	26 Justin
27 Jennifer	28 Sandra
29 Brad	30 Julio
31 Austin	32 Cory
33 Frank	34 Zoe

Julio, Justin, Austin

ALTERNATE METHOD FOR EXAMPLE 3

Have students solve the problem by using random numbers generated by a graphing calculator. Students will notice that the answers of everyone in the class are different, and these are different from the answers in the example. Stress that obtaining different solutions every time is one of the benefits of using a simple random sample.

Example 4

The example demonstrates types of bias in survey questions.

Extend the Example

Have students reword the survey question to eliminate the bias. Sample: Do you think that the school colors should be changed from the green and black we currently have to gold and purple?

Additional Example 4

a. A survey asks students, "Do you agree that the recent unfair decision that students should be banned from making important calls with cell phones on bus trips should be reversed?" Explain the bias in the question. The question leads students to say yes by saying the decision is unfair and saying the calls are important.

b. The junior class is voting on the band to have at a school dance. The vote will be held after school on Thursday. Explain the bias in the voting method. The vote is biased because students who are unable to stay after school Thursday will not get to vote.

Example 5

The example uses the capture-recapture method to estimate an animal population.

Additional Example 5

Researchers capture and mark 30 squirrels in a park. The next week, researchers capture 40 squirrels and 18 of them are marked from the previous month. Estimate the squirrel population in the park. About 67 squirrels

Example 4 Identifying Bias

a. A survey asks students, "Do you agree that the school colors should be changed from the drab green and black we currently have to a vibrant gold and purple that will signify strength and determination?" Explain the bias in the question.

SOLUTION The question is biased because it leads students to say *yes* by using positive adjectives for only one set of the colors. It is also biased because it only gives one side of the situation. It does not discuss possible problems or issues that could arise with switching colors.

Math Reasoning

Formulate Write a question for Example 4a that will lead the students to say *no*.

Possible answer: "Do you agree that the school colors should be changed, even though it would destroy our heritage, ignore our traditions, and be a huge waste of money?"

b. An article in a magazine asks readers to go online and answer a question related to the article. Explain the bias in the sampling method.

SOLUTION The sample is biased against those readers without internet access because they will not be able to answer the question. It is also biased against those readers that did not read the article. Therefore, the sample will have a greater percentage of people interested in that topic and that have internet access than that of the population.

Sampling can be used to estimate the size of a population. A common method used to estimate animal populations is called the **capture-recapture method.**

In the simplest of the capture-recapture techniques, a researcher visits an area and marks, or tags, every animal they capture. They later return to the same area, after enough time has passed that the marked animals should completely mingle with any unmarked animals. Another group of this animal population is captured. The researcher uses the following proportion to then estimate the population of the animal in the area.

$$\frac{\text{number of marked animals on 2nd visit}}{\text{number of all animals captured on 2nd visit}} = \frac{\text{number of animals originally marked}}{\text{total population of animals in area}}$$

Example 5 Application: Estimating an Animal Population

A researcher visits a pond and captures and marks 20 fish. On a return visit the next day, the researcher captures 32 fish, and 12 of them are marked from the previous day. Estimate the fish population in the pond.

Math Reasoning

Find the confidence interval estimate of the population proportion p when $x = 12$ and $n = 32$.

(0.20726, 0.54274)

SOLUTION Write and solve the capture-recapture proportion.

$$\frac{12}{32} = \frac{20}{n}$$

$$12n = 640$$

$$n \approx 53$$

There are about 53 fish in the pond.

INCLUSION

Have students use colored markers to model the capture-recapture method for animal populations. Give a pair of students a box with 50 markers in it. Then, have them draw out and mark 15 of the markers modeling the capture. Next, have the student return the markers to the box and mix them thoroughly. Have another student randomly draw 20 markers from the box modeling the recapture. Have students count the colored markers and set up a proportion to estimate the population in the box.

Lesson Practice

Describe the individuals in the population and in the sample.

a. Population: all parents and guardians of students in that school; Sample: the parents and guardians the principal actually spoke to

b. Population: all customers who shop at the store; Sample: the customers who answer the survey

a. (Ex 1) A principal of a middle school talked to and questioned parents and guardians of the students about a new dress code.

b. (Ex 1) Receipts from a certain grocery store ask customers to go online to complete a survey about their shopping experience.

Tell if the sampling method performed was a probability sample. If not, explain why not. If so, state the type of probability sample.

c. (Ex 2) The school secretary takes the list of names of students who are absent that day, randomly chooses a starting point, selects every 10th student, and calls their parent or guardian to ask if they know that the student was absent. Yes, systematic sample

d. (Ex 2) A coach wants to know about how many students are interested in joining the track team. He asks students on both the male and female soccer teams if they, or anyone they know, would like to run on the track team. No, students not on the soccer team did not have a chance of being asked.

e. (Ex 3) Twenty four names already numbered are listed below. Five must be randomly chosen for a sample. What five names will be picked for the sample if numbers are chosen from the random number table shown below? Cassie, Drew, Aaron, Steven, and Jarvis

11 Ann	12 Luke	13 Cassie	14 Finn	15 Jared	16 Tanela
17 Jude	18 Gunner	19 Drew	20 Halle	21 Colby	22 Anton
23 Aaron	24 Kenya	25 Ensa	26 Jarvis	27 Ming	28 Buhay
29 Alice	30 Steven	31 Pia	32 Niko	33 Leah	34 Ben

046336 139693 751983 625955 362398 666071 858190 305192 911319
263157 482572 922366 773890 224306 991349 331116 368248 864530

f. The question is written in a confusing manner; students may think the question is saying something that it is not.

g. Viewers who do not have cell phones will not be represented in the sample at all. Viewers who feel strongly about the issue may text their response several times.

f. (Ex 4) A survey asks students, "Do you disagree that the president of the school should not be allowed to run for re-election?" Explain the bias in the question.

g. (Ex 4) A TV show asks viewers to answer a question by texting their response on their cell phone. Explain the bias in the sampling method.

h. (Ex 5) A researcher visits a park and captures and tags 43 chipmunks. On a return visit two days later, the researcher captures 50 chipmunks, and 38 of them are tagged from the previous visit. Estimate the number of chipmunks in the park. About 57 chipmunks

Practice Distributed and Integrated

Write the logarithmic equation in exponential form.

1. (64) $\log_{10} 10{,}000{,}000 = 7$ $10^7 = 10{,}000{,}000$ **2.** (64) $\log_6 216 = 3$ $6^3 = 216$

3. (52) **Explain** Explain why all 45° –45° –90° triangles are similar. See Additional Answers.

INCLUSION

Have students draw several 45°-45°-90° triangles on a coordinate grid, each having a different size. Then have them write proportions of the sides to demonstrate how corresponding sides are proportional for all of the triangles.

Lesson Practice

Problem d

Error Alert Students may confuse the population and sample and assume the problem describes a probability sample because everyone in the sample was questioned. Remind them to consider which group the surveyor was interested in.

Problem f

Scaffolding When determining bias, caution students to look for double negatives which reverse the meaning of the sentence or question. In this survey, the two negatives are, "disagree" and "should not be allowed."

Check for Understanding

The questions below help assess the concepts taught in this lesson.

1. **What is a sentence that describes the relationship between a population and a sample?** Possible answer: A sample is a part of a population.
2. **How are stratified sampling and cluster sampling alike and different?** Both divide the population into groups, but the cluster samples are randomly chosen while the stratified groups are based on similar characteristics.

3 Practice

Math Conversations

Discussions to strengthen understanding

Problem 3

"What is the mathematical definition of *similar*?" corresponding angles are congruent; corresponding sides are proportional

Problem 9

Error Alert

Students may not divide the equation by the coefficient of the quadratic term. Remind students that the coefficient of the quadratic term must be +1, before completing the square.

*4. (71) State the case applicable to the given measurements (AAS, ASA, or SSA). Then decide whether the measurements determine one triangle, two triangles, or no triangle. A = 40°; C = 75°; c = 20 AAS; one triangle

Solve for the roots of the polynomial:

5. (66) $6x(x^2 + x - 20) = 0$ $x = -5, 0, 4$

6. (66) $2x(x^2 + 9x - 52) = 0$ $x = -13, 0, 4$

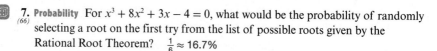

7. (66) **Probability** For $x^3 + 8x^2 + 3x - 4 = 0$, what would be the probability of randomly selecting a root on the first try from the list of possible roots given by the Rational Root Theorem? $\frac{1}{6} \approx 16.7\%$

Solve for x by completing the square:

8. (58) $-x^2 + 6x = -12$ $3 \pm \sqrt{21}$

9. (58) $-4 = -x^2 - 3x$ 1, −4

*10. (73) **Business** The owner of a frozen food company wants to know how many people would agree to pay slightly more for products sold in recycled packages than non-recycled packages. She hires a surveyor to stand in the aisles of randomly selected grocery stores which sell the company's product to survey buyers of frozen food products. Define the population and sample in this situation. What groups of people would not be represented in the sample and why?

10. Population: all customers of the grocery stores that sell this company's product; Sample: those customers that were surveyed

Possible answer: people that shop for food online and have it delivered

11. (53) **Multi-Step** Let $f(x) = x - 6$ and $g(x) = 3x$.

a. Find the composition functions $(f \circ g)(x)$ and $(g \circ f)(x)$. $(f \circ g)(x) = 3x - 6$; $(g \circ f)(x) = 3x - 18$

b. Evaluate the composite functions $(f \circ g)(x)$ and $(g \circ f)(x)$ for $x = -1$. $(f \circ g)(-1) = -9$; $(g \circ f)(-1) = -21$

*12. (64) **Write** Explain why there is no value of x that makes the equation $\log_1 10 = x$ true. Possible answer: 1^x does not equal 10 for any value of x.

Convert each measure from radians to degrees.

13. (63) $\frac{6\pi}{4} = 270°$

14. (63) $\frac{2\pi}{3} = 120°$

*15. (67) **Navigation** A camper plans to canoe to an island. The island is 1500 meters south and 950 meters west of her starting point. To the nearest degree, in what direction should she head? 32° west of south

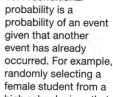

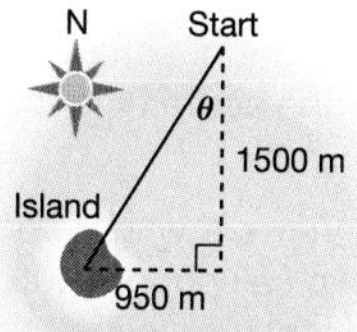

*16. (73) **Multi-Step** Explain why the question below is biased. Then rewrite the question without bias. "Do you not agree that junk food should not be sold in school vending machines?" See Additional Answers.

17. (65) **Multiple Choice** Which is a solution of $3x^2 - 7x - 2 = 0$? C

A $\frac{1}{3}$ B 2 C $\frac{7 + \sqrt{73}}{6}$ D $\frac{7}{6} - \frac{\sqrt{73}}{6}i$

18. (68) **Write** What is a conditional probability? Give an example.

18. A conditional probability is a probability of an event given that another event has already occurred. For example, randomly selecting a female student from a high school, given that the student is in the 11th grade.

*19. (73) **Estimate** A researcher using the stratified sampling method has chosen a sample of 12 female athletes and 17 female non-athletes from a population of 305 female students. About how many students in the population are athletes? About 126 students

CHALLENGE

Have students write an example of probability sampling, convenience sample, and voluntary response sample. Then, have students write an example of each type of probability sampling: simple random sampling, stratified sampling, systematic sampling, and cluster sampling.
See student work.

20. (59) **Error Analysis** Is the work below correct? If not, find and explain the error, and give the correct solution.

$$x^{\frac{1}{7}} = 2$$
$$\left(x^{\frac{1}{7}}\right)^{\frac{7}{1}} = 2$$
$$x^{1} = 2$$
$$x = 2$$

No; The error is in the second line. When dealing with equations, whatever is done to one side of the equation, the exact same thing must be done to the other side of the equation.; 128

21. (67) Solve to the nearest tenth using the given restrictions: $\tan\theta = 2.42$, for $180° \leq \theta \leq 360°$ 247.5°

***22.** (72) **Geology** The Richter magnitude M of an earthquake is expressed by $M = \frac{2}{3}\log\left(\frac{E}{10^{11.8}}\right)$, where E is the energy released in ergs. An earthquake near Peru in 2007 had a magnitude of 8.0. Find the energy released by that earthquake. approximately $10^{23.8}$, or 6.31×10^{23} ergs

23. (58) **Multi-Step** Use $x^2 + 30x + 225 = 13$.

a. Explain why the equation is a perfect square. $225 = 15^2$ and $30 = 15 \cdot 2$

b. Factor $x^2 + 30x + 225$. $(x + 15)^2$

c. Solve the equation for x. $x = -15 \pm \sqrt{13}$

***24.** (72) **Error Analysis** To rewrite $\ln 4e^3$ without an exponent, a student wrote $\ln 4e^3 = \ln 4 \cdot \ln e^3 = (\ln 4)(3) = 3 \ln 4$.

What is the error? Rewrite $\ln 4e^3$ without an exponent correctly.

25. (57) **Population** The population of the state of Florida in various years is shown below.

Year	1900	1950	1990	2005
Population (thousands)	529	2771	12,937	17,789

Write an exponential model that approximates this data. What population is predicted by this model for the year 2010? Sample: $P(t) = 529e^{0.0331t}$, where t is the number of years since 1900; 21,171,000

***26.** (71) **Graphing Calculator** Find the area of $\triangle BCD$ given $c = 3.62$, $b = 1.45$, and $m\angle D = 33.25°$. Round to the nearest hundredth. 1.44 sq un.

27. (55) **Geometry** Find the probability that a point chosen randomly inside the figure is in the shaded region. 50%

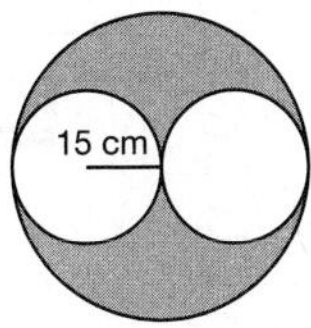

***28.** (70) **Multiple Choice** Solve $x = \sqrt{-14x - 45}$. A

A no solutions **B** −9 **C** −5 **D** −9 and −5

29. (69) **Analyze** How is graphing in the complex plane similar to, and different from, graphing in the xy- coordinate plane?

30. (36) Write the equation of a line in slope intercept form that is parallel to $y = -\frac{3}{2}x + 4$ and passes through (1, 5). $y = -\frac{3}{2}x + \frac{13}{2}$

24. Possible answer: The student applied the Product Property of Logarithms incorrectly. Correct expression: $\ln 4e^3 = \ln 4 + \ln e^3 = \ln 4 + 3$

29. Possible answer: It is similar because first you move to the right or left, and then you move up or down. It is different because both axes in the xy-plane represent real numbers but the vertical axis in the complex plane represents imaginary numbers.

Problem 20

Extend the Problem

"How could the equation in the first line be written as a logarithm?" $\log_x 2 = \frac{1}{7}$

Problem 27

Guide the students by asking them the following questions.

"What is the area of each small unshaded circle?" $\pi(15)^2$

"What is the total area of the unshaded part?" $2\pi(15)^2$

"What is the total area of the shaded and unshaded parts?" $\pi(30)^2$

Problem 28

Extend the Problem

"Why does the problem have no solutions?" When the equation is evaluated for $x = -5$ and $x = -9$, a positive radicand results. However, the radical equals x, which is −5 or −9, respectively. This is not possible. The radical sign indicates that the positive, or principal square root, is required.

LOOKING FORWARD

Using sampling prepares students for

- **Lesson 80** Finding the Normal Distribution
- **Lesson 116** Finding Best Fit Models
- **Lesson 118** Recognizing Misleading Data

LESSON

74

1 Warm Up

Use problems 2 and 3 in the Warm Up to review solving equations with the quadratic formula and graphing a polynomial to determine the roots of an equation.

2 New Concepts

In this lesson, students learn to analyze the discriminant of a polynomial to determine the types of roots in the equation.

Discuss the definitions of the quadratic formula, a discriminant, and a complex root.

Example 1

Students will use the discriminant of each quadratic equation to determine the type of roots in each equation.

Additional Example 1

Use the discriminant to describe the roots of each equation.

a. $27x^2 + 3 = 18x$
$b^2 - 4ac = (-18)^2 - 4(27)(3) = 324 - 324 = 0$; The equation has one real root.

b. $3x^2 + 11x - 8 = 0$
$b^2 - 4ac = (11)^2 - 4(3)(-8) = 121 + 96 = 217$; The equation has two real roots.

LESSON RESOURCES

Student Edition Practice Workbook 74
Reteaching Master 74
Adaptations Master 74
Challenge and Enrichment Master C74

LESSON 74

Finding the Discriminant

Warm Up

1. Vocabulary Where the graph of a function intersects the x-axis is where the roots or solutions of the related equation are found. (35)

2. Solve using the quadratic formula $2x^2 - 4x + 25 = 0$. (62)

$1 + \frac{1}{2}i\sqrt{46}$, $1 - \frac{1}{2}i\sqrt{46}$

3. Graph $y = 3x^2 + 4 - 24x$ to determine how many roots the equation $0 = 3x^2 + 4 - 24x$ has. 2 roots (35)

4. Write $f(x) = (x - 4)^2 + 3$ in standard form. $f(x) = x^2 - 8x + 19$ (27)

New Concepts

The quadratic formula, $x = \frac{-b \pm \sqrt{b^2 - 4ac}}{2a}$, gives the solutions of any quadratic equation. The radicand in the formula, $b^2 - 4ac$, is called the **discriminant.** The discriminant can be used to tell if the equation has zero, one, or two solutions.

Math Language

A **solution** of an equation can also be called a **root** of the equation.

Analyzing the Discriminant

For $ax^2 + bx + c = 0$, $(a \neq 0)$ and related function $y = ax^2 + bx + c$		
$b^2 - 4ac > 0$	$b^2 - 4ac = 0$	$b^2 - 4ac < 0$
Equation: 2 real roots Function: 2 x-intercepts	Equation: 1 real root with multiplicity of 2 Function: 1 x-intercept	Equation: 0 real roots 2 complex roots Function: 0 x-intercepts

Example 1 Describing the Roots of a Quadratic Equation

Use the discriminant to describe the roots of each equation.

a. $4x^2 + 25 = 20x$

SOLUTION Write the equation in standard form: $4x^2 - 20x + 25 = 0$.

$b^2 - 4ac = (-20)^2 - 4(4)(25) = 400 - 400 = 0$

Because the discriminant is 0, the equation has one real root.

b. $2x^2 + 7x - 99 = 0$

SOLUTION $b^2 - 4ac = (7)^2 - 4(2)(-99) = 49 + 792 = 841$

Because the discriminant is positive, the equation has 2 real roots.

Online Connection
www.SaxonMathResources.com

MATH BACKGROUND

A quadratic equation with real coefficients can have either one or two distinct real roots, or two distinct complex roots. In this case, the discriminant determines the number and nature of the roots. There are three cases: If the discriminant is positive, there are two distinct roots, both of which are real numbers. If the discriminant is zero, there is exactly one distinct root, and that root is a real number. If the discriminant is negative, there are no real roots.

Point out to students that the discriminant allows them to discriminate, or distinguish between, the types of roots that a quadratic equation may have.

Students may find it helpful to know that if the discriminant is equal to zero, then the related quadratic equation can be solved by factoring.

c. $3x^2 + 6x + 5 = 0$

SOLUTION $b^2 - 4ac = (6)^2 - 4(3)(5) = 36 - 60 = -24$

Because the discriminant is negative, the equation has 2 complex roots.

Example 2 Using a Positive Discriminant

A player standing on a 10-foot hill kicks a ball straight up at a velocity of 55 feet per second. He hopes it goes above the roof of a nearby building which is 50 feet above the ground. The function that gives the height of the ball after x seconds is given by $y = -16x^2 + 55x + 10$. Use the discriminant to explain why the ball *will* reach the desired height.

SOLUTION Substitute 50 for y and write the equation in standard form.

$50 = -16x^2 + 55x + 10 \longrightarrow 0 = -16x^2 + 55x - 40$

Find the discriminant:

$b^2 - 4ac = (55)^2 - 4(-16)(-40) = 3025 - 2560 = 465$

Since the discriminant is positive, there are two real solutions, indicating that the ball has a height of 50 feet twice. The solutions give the number of seconds at which the height is 50 feet.

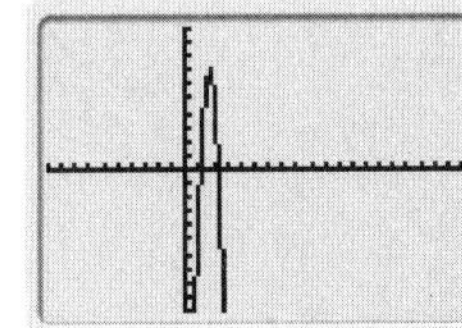

Math Reasoning

Analyze In Example 2, how do you know the ball's maximum height will be greater than 50 feet?

If 50 ft was the maximum height, there would be only one solution.

Example 3 Using a Zero Discriminant

A homeowner has 120 feet of fencing material to enclose a rectangular dog pen. She wants the dog to have 900 square feet of space inside the pen. The equation $w(60 - w) = 900$ gives the width of a pen that meets these requirements. Use the discriminant to explain why these requirements *can* be met.

SOLUTION Write the equation as a quadratic in standard form.

$w(60 - w) = 900 \longrightarrow 60w - w^2 = 900 \longrightarrow -w^2 + 60w - 900 = 0$

Find the discriminant:

$b^2 - 4ac = (60)^2 - 4(-1)(-900) = 3600 - 3600 = 0$

Since the discriminant is 0, there is one real solution, indicating that there exists one width which meets the requirements. The solution gives this width.

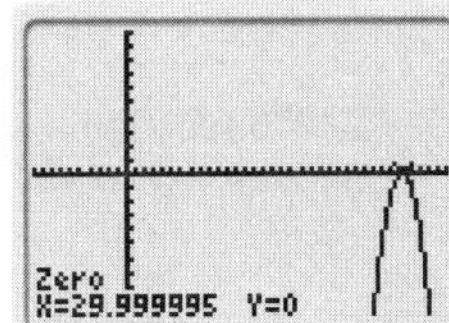

c. $2x^2 + 6x = -5$
$b^2 - 4ac = (6)^2 - 4(2)(5) = 36 - 40 = -4$; The equation has two complex roots.

Example 2

Students will use the positive discriminant and apply it to a real world example.

Additional Example 2

A miniature rocket is launched from the ground with a goal to go over a bar 25 feet high. Use the discriminant to determine if the rocket will go over the bar. The total height of the rocket is described by the function $y = -8x^2 + 30x + 12$.

Substitute 25 for y and solve the discriminant.

$25 = -8x^2 + 30x + 12$
$0 = -8x^2 + 30x - 13$
$b^2 - 4ac = (30)^2 - 4(-8)(-13)$
$= 900 - 416 = 484$

The discriminant is positive indicating there are two times the ball will reach 25 feet, therefore the rocket will travel over the bar.

Example 3

Students will use a zero discriminant and apply it to a real world example.

Additional Example 3

A coin is tossed and its height is described by the equation $y = -18x^2 + 24x$. Will the coin be 8 feet high more than once?

$8 = -18x^2 + 24x$
$0 = -18x^2 + 24x - 8$
$b^2 - 4ac = (24)^2 - 4(-18)(-8) = 576 - 576 = 0$

The discriminant shows only one solution will be found, so there is only one time the coin will reach 8 feet.

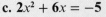

ENGLISH LEARNERS

Define the **root of an equation** as the zero of the function. It is the x value when y is equal to zero.

Discuss how finding a discriminant can be an easier method to evaluating problems instead of finding exact solutions of x in certain quadratic equations.

Apply the discriminant to a quadratic equation and show how the discriminant can show the number of solutions there will be without even using the entire quadratic formula.

Look at the three graphs on page 528. Locate the zeros of each function, and discuss how they relate to the roots of the equation.

Example 4

Students will use the negative discriminant and apply it to a real world example.

Additional Example 4

Using Additional Example 3, show why the coin will not reach 9 feet high. A negative discriminant shows that there are no real solutions at a height of 9 feet.

Example 5

Students will find the discriminant to determine values for specific problems.

Additional Example 5

In the rocketry example, if the rocket is launched from the ground at an initial velocity of 75 feet per second, what would the maximum height be? The rocket equation is $y = -16x^2 + 75x$.

The maximum height would be when the discriminant is equal to zero.

$b^2 - 4ac = 0$

$(75)^2 - 4(-16)c = 0$

$\frac{(75)^2}{4(-16)} = c$

$c = -87.89$

$y = -16x^2 + 75x - 87.89$

$87.89 = -16x^2 + 75x$

$h_{max} = 87.89$ ft

Lesson Practice

Problem c

Error Alert Students may calculate the discriminant incorrectly by forgetting that the c value is negative. To avoid negative errors, remind students to put the equation in standard form before calculating the discriminant.

Math Reasoning

Analyze In Example 4, why is the length equal to $25 - w$ given that the width is w?

The perimeter is 50. The sum of the two lengths is $50 - 2w$, so one length is half as much, $25 - w$.

Example 4 Using a Negative Discriminant

A frame maker has 50 inches of framing material with which to make a picture frame. He wants to frame a picture that has an area of 160 square inches. The equation $w(25 - w) = 160$ gives the width of the frame that meets these requirements. Use the discriminant to explain why these requirements can *not* be met.

SOLUTION Write the equation as a quadratic in standard form.

$w(25 - w) = 160 \longrightarrow 25w - w^2 = 160 \longrightarrow -w^2 + 25w - 160 = 0$

Find the discriminant: $b^2 - 4ac = (25)^2 - 4(-1)(-160) = 625 - 640 = -15$

Since the discriminant is negative, there are no real solutions. The frame maker cannot make a frame for this picture with only 50 inches of framing material.

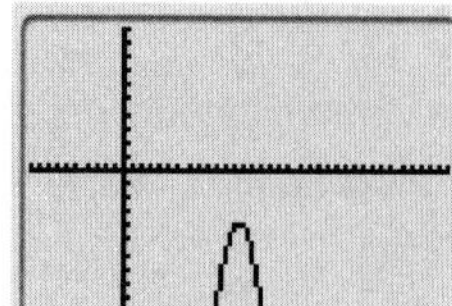

Example 5 Application: Rocketry

Two scientists are firing rockets. The first scientist is setting his off at ground level at an initial velocity of 75 feet per second. The second scientist is setting hers off from a deck 25 feet above the ground at a velocity of 70 feet per second. Will either of the rockets reach a height of 100 feet above the ground? If so, which one?

SOLUTION The function for the height, in feet, of an object shot straight up at an initial velocity of v and height h is $y = -16x^2 + vx + h$.

Write an equation for each scientist's rocket.

1st scientist: $100 = -16x^2 + 75x \longrightarrow 0 = -16x^2 + 75x - 100$

2nd scientist: $100 = -16x^2 + 70x + 25 \longrightarrow 0 = -16x^2 + 70x - 75$

Find the discriminant of each equation.

1st scientist: $b^2 - 4ac \longrightarrow (75)^2 - 4(-16)(-100) = 5625 - 6400 = -775$

2nd scientist: $b^2 - 4ac \longrightarrow (70)^2 - 4(-16)(-75) = 4900 - 4800 = 100$

The discriminant for the equation for the second scientist is positive, so the second equation has two real solutions. Her rocket will reach 100 feet. The rocket of the first scientist will not reach 100 feet because the equation has no real solutions.

Math Reasoning

Analyze How long after setting it off does the second scientist's rocket reach its maximum height? What is this height?

2.1875 seconds, about 101.56 feet

Lesson Practice

Use the discriminant to describe the roots of each equation.
(Ex 1)

a. $16 + x^2 = 8x$ 1 real root

b. $2x^2 + 12x + 23 = 0$ 2 complex roots

c. $3x^2 - x = 14$ 2 real roots

INCLUSION

For students that struggle identifying which discriminant form gives which specific root, help them make their own table which identifies the different forms of the discriminant and each type of solution it may give.

Also, you may have them use a calculator or graphing program to graph the parabola after finding the discriminant. Students can compare the number of x-intercepts of their graphs to the number of solutions they found using the discriminant.

d. The discriminant is 192. Since it is positive, the equation $-16x^2 + 40x = 22$ has 2 real solutions which are the times the ball is at these heights.

e. The discriminant is 0. Since it is 0, the equation $w(140 - w) = 4900$ has 1 solution which is the width.

f. The discriminant is -13.75. Since it is negative, the equation $w(17.5 - w) = 80$ has no real solutions, so there is no width that can be used with only 35 inches of framing material.

d. (Ex 2) A tennis player hits a tennis ball straight up at a velocity of 40 feet per second. The ceiling in the gym she is in has a height of 22 feet. The function that gives the height of the ball after x seconds is given by $y = -16x^2 + 40x$. Use the discriminant to explain why the ball *will* hit the ceiling above her.

e. (Ex 3) A farmer has 280 feet of fencing material to enclose a rectangular area for his pigs and chickens. He wants the fenced-in area to be 4900 square feet. The equation $w(140 - w) = 4900$ gives the width that meets these requirements. Use the discriminant to explain why these requirements *can* be met.

f. (Ex 4) A frame maker has 35 inches of framing material with which to make a picture frame. He wants to frame a picture that has an area of 80 square inches. The equation $w(17.5 - w) = 80$ gives the width of the frame that meets these requirements. Use the discriminant to determine why these requirements can *not* be met.

g. (Ex 5) Two technicians are setting off fireworks. The first technician is setting his off at ground level at an initial velocity of 140 feet per second. The second technician is setting his off from a deck 15 feet above the ground at a velocity of 120 feet per second. Will either of the fireworks reach a height of 275 feet above the ground? If so, which one? Yes, the firework set off by the first technician will reach a height 275 feet above the ground.

Practice Distributed and Integrated

Use synthetic division to divide.

1. (61) $x^4 - 2$ by $x + 1$ $\quad x^3 - x^2 + x - 1 - \frac{1}{x+1}$ **2.** (61) $x^3 - 2$ by $x - 5$ $\quad x^2 + 5x + 25 + \frac{123}{x-5}$

***3.** (57) **Graphing Calculator** Use a graphing calculator to investigate the behavior of the following 4 functions for the domain $x \geq 0$: $y = e^x$, $y = x$, $y = x^2$, and $y = x^3$. Write a short paragraph comparing the growth rate of these four functions as the value of x increases.

3. Sample: For x between 0 and 1, the function $y = e^x$ is greatest, followed by $y = x$, $y = x^2$, and $y = x^3$ in that order. The 3 polynomial functions meet at (1, 1), and then for $x > 1$, they reverse position; $y = x^3$ grows faster than $y = x^2$, which grows faster than $y = x$. The graph of $y = e^x$ is always greater than $y = x$ and $y = x^2$ for positive x. $y = x^3$ grows faster than $y = e^x$, but eventually, at about $x = 4.5$ and beyond, $y = e^x$ has the greatest rate of growth.

***4.** (74) **Rock Climbing** A rock climber at the bottom of the King and Queen Seat outcropping in Rocks State Park in Maryland shoots a flare from a flare gun. The height of the flare, in meters, can be modeled by $y = -5x^2 + 32x + 1$, where x is number of seconds after the flare is set off. Use the discriminant to explain if the flare will reach the height of the outcropping, given that the outcropping has a height of 58 meters. No; discriminant $= -116$, no solutions

5. (66) **Storage** The volume of a cylindrical bucket is 1696 cubic inches. The height of the bucket is 9 inches greater than its radius. Write a polynomial in standard form, without π, that can be used to find the radius (Round the constant to the nearest integer.) $r^3 + 9r^2 - 540 = 0$

6. (56) Given $\theta = 400°$, find a positive and negative coterminal angle.
Sample: 40°, −320°

Problem d

Scaffolding Substitute the height of the ball for y in the height function. Collect all terms on one side of the equation and evaluate the discriminant. The discriminant shows two positive roots meaning it would travel higher than 22 feet if it did not hit the ceiling.

Check for Understanding

The questions below help assess the concepts taught in this lesson.

"What does a discriminant help determine?" Sample: The discriminant can tell how many solutions the equation will have and what type of roots they will be.

"How are roots of a polynomial found graphically?" Sample: The roots are located at the value where the graph intersects the x-axis.

3 Practice

Math Conversations

Discussions to strengthen understanding

Problem 6

Coterminal angles are found by adding or subtracting a full circle (360°) to the angle given. This may continue until positive and negative coterminal angles are found.

CHALLENGE

If in a quadratic equation $a = 3c$ and $b = 20$, what is the value of a and c if the discriminant is 0?

$a = 3c; \quad b = 20$

$b^2 - 4ac = 0$

$(20)^2 - 4(3c)(c) = 0$

$400 - 12c^2 = 0$

$12c^2 = 400$

$c^2 = \frac{100}{3}$

$c \approx \pm 5.77$

$a \approx \pm 17.32$

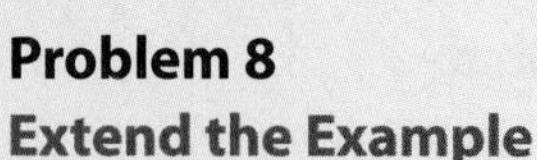

Problem 8

Extend the Example

What is the probability that the student will choose an eraser first and then a binder?

$P_{total} = P_{eraser} \times P_{binder}$

$P_{total} = \frac{13}{40} \times \frac{2}{39} = \frac{26}{1560}$

$\approx 0.017 = 1.7\%$

Problem 18

Guide the students by asking them the following question.

"How are complex numbers combined?" Complex numbers should be combined by adding only the like terms from each component.

7. (61) **Multiple Choice** Which is *not* a factor of $x^3 + 9x^2 + 2x - 48$? **A**

A $x - 4$ **B** $x - 2$ **C** $x + 3$ **D** $x + 8$

8. (68) A prize box contains 5 stickers, 13 smiley erasers, 20 pencils, and 2 binders. Find the probability that the student randomly chooses 2 prizes, a sticker first and then a pencil. 6.4%

9. (57) The number of mice increased exponentially. At first there were 85 mice. Twelve years later there were 1700 mice. How many mice would there be at the end of 130 years? 1.10×10^{16} mice

***10.** (74) **Analyze** How does the discriminant of a quadratic equation indicate if the real solutions are rational or irrational? The solutions are rational if the discriminant is a perfect square, otherwise the solutions are irrational.

11. (69) **Multiply** $2(3i)$. Write the result in the form $a + bi$. $0 + 6i$

12. (63) **Automobiles Tires** The diameter of a certain automobile tire, mounted on the wheel, is 25 inches. How far does the automobile go when the tire rotates 10 times? Give your answer to the nearest foot. 65 feet

Solve.

13. (70) $\sqrt{9x} + 11 = 14$ 1

14. (70) $-4\sqrt{x} - 6 = -20$ $12\frac{1}{4}$

15. (65) **Analyze** When using a graphing calculator to solve a quadratic equation, for what type of solutions can exact answers be found?

15. Exact answers can only be found when the solutions are rational. If the solutions are irrational, they can only be estimated. They cannot be found at all if they are nonreal solutions.

16. (69) **Electrical Engineering** The flow of a current, I, the resistance to the flow, Z, and the voltage, E, are related by $E = I(Z)$. Find the resistance of a circuit (in ohms) if the voltage is $265 - 135i$ volts and the current is $26 - 30i$ amps. $\frac{2735}{394} + \frac{555}{197}i$ ohms

***17.** (71) **Geometry** Find the perimeter of $\triangle XYZ$ given $m\angle X = 40°$, $m\angle Z = 70°$, and $y = 33$ cm. About 88.6 cm

18. (62) **Error Analysis** Which student incorrectly added the complex numbers? Explain the error.

Student A	Student B
$(6 + 2i) + (-3 - 9i)$ $8i - 12i$ $-4i$	$(6 + 2i) + (-3 - 9i)$ $3 - 7i$

18. Student A made the error. The real parts of complex numbers are not added to the imaginary parts. The real parts are added to the real parts and the imaginary parts are added to the imaginary parts.

***19.** (73) **Government** Suppose a politician must visit 5 counties in Maine. His human resource personnel form a simple random sample by listing each county and numbering it as shown below. If they use the line of random digits shown below, which 5 counties will the politician visit? Somerset, Lincoln, Knox, Androscoggin, Penobscot

50: Androscoggin	51: Aroostook	52: Cumberland	53: Franklin
54: Hancock	55: Kennebec	56: Knox	57: Lincoln
58: Oxford	59: Penobscot	60: Piscataquis	61: Sagadahoc
62: Somerset	63: Waldo	64: Washington	65: York

62010	60482	89824	08705	57913	46815	76221	25650	89337	53603	73597

ALTERNATE METHOD FOR PROBLEM 11

First write each term to be multiplied in $a + bi$ form. Then multiply using the foil method. After multiplication, add like terms keeping the real and imaginary terms separate.

$(2 + 0i)(0 + 3i) = 0 + 6i + 0 + 0 = 0 + 6i$

*20. **Multiple Choice** Which sampling method would introduce the greatest possible (73) amount of bias? C

A systematic sampling B stratified sampling

C convenience sampling D simple random sampling

21. Katie rolls a 1–6 number cube twice. What is the probability she will roll an odd (60) number and then an even number? $\frac{1}{4}$

*22. **Justify** Explain why $3^{\log_3 2x} = 2x$. Possible answer: Exponential and logarithmic (72) operations are inverse operations.

Factor each expression completely.

23. (61) $3y^5 - 48y^3$ $3y^3(y - 4)(y + 4)$

24. (61) $x^3 + x^2 + x + 1$ $(x + 1)(x^2 + 1)$

*25. **Multi-Step** (74) a. Write $16x^2 = 25$ in standard form. $16x^2 - 25 = 0$

b. Find the discriminant of the equation in part a. 1600

c. Use the discriminant to describe the solutions of the equation in part a. 2 real solutions

d. **Verify** Solve the equation in part a. 1.25, −1.25

26. **Estimate** The hypotenuse of a 45° –45° –90° triangle is between 120 and 130 cm (52) long. Estimate the length of each leg. 85–92 cm

*27. **Generalize** Raise both sides of the equation $x = 4$ to the second, third, fourth, and (70) fifth powers. Solve each equation. In which cases are there extraneous solutions? In general, when could raising both sides by the same power generate extraneous solutions?

27. There are extraneous solutions when both sides are raised to the second and fourth powers. Raising both sides to an even power could generate extraneous solutions.

28. **Multi-Step** Let $f(\theta) = \text{Tan}\ \theta$ and $g(\theta) = \text{Tan}^{-1}\ \theta$, where θ is in radians. (67)

a. Evaluate $f(g(1))$ and $g\left(f\left(\frac{\pi}{4}\right)\right)$. Show your steps.

b. Based on part a, what is the value of $f(g(x))$? x

28a. $f(g(1)) = \text{Tan}(\text{Tan}^{-1}(1)) = \text{Tan}\left(\frac{\pi}{4}\right) = 1$; $g\left(f\left(\frac{\pi}{4}\right)\right) = \text{Tan}^{-1}\left(\text{Tan}\left(\frac{\pi}{4}\right)\right) = \text{Tan}^{-1}(1) = \frac{\pi}{4}$

c. Rename $g(\theta)$ as $f^{-1}(\theta)$. What property of inverse functions is illustrated in part a? $f(f^{-1}(x)) = f^{-1}(f(x)) = x$

29. **Data Analysis** Use the double-bar chart to estimate the conditional (68) probabilities.

a. $P(\text{boy} \mid \text{10th grade})$ About 45%

b. $P(\text{10th grade} \mid \text{boy})$ About 33%

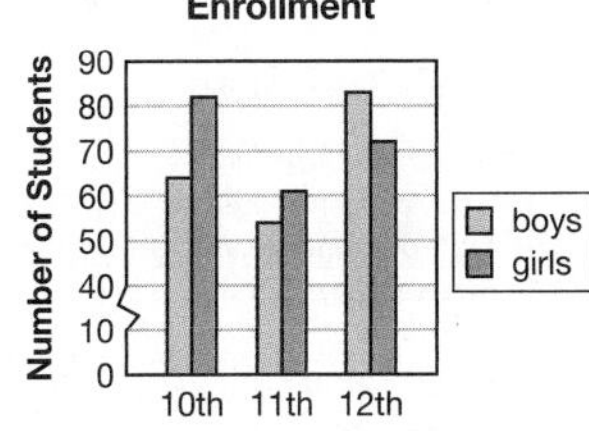

30. **Error Analysis** What error did the student make in factoring the difference of cubes? (61)

$$c^6 - 216$$
$$(c^2 - 6)(c^4 - 6c^2 + 36)$$

In the second factor, the sign of the second term is the opposite of the sign between the terms in the first factor.

Problem 21

Error Alert

Students may want to combine the two rolls into one probability with twelve total options, but remind the students that if you want one result AND a second result, the two probabilities must be multiplied together to get the total probability.

Problem 26

Compute the lengths of the legs of the triangle by using trigonometric functions. Use a hypotenuse of 120 cm and 130 cm. Remember, the legs of the triangle will be equal in length.

LOOKING FORWARD

Using factoring prepares students for

- **Lesson 78** Solving Quadratic Equations II
- **Lesson 83** Writing Quadratic Equations from Roots
- **Lesson 85** Finding Polynomial Roots II
- **Lesson 89** Solving Quadratic Inequalities

LESSON 75

1 Warm Up

Use the Warm Up to review the prerequisite skills for this lesson.

2 New Concepts

In this lesson, students learn to graph radical functions.

Example 1

Students graph and compare a square root function and its inverse.

Additional Example 1a

a. Graph the square root function and its inverse. Determine the domain and range of both functions.
$y = \sqrt{x - 2}$

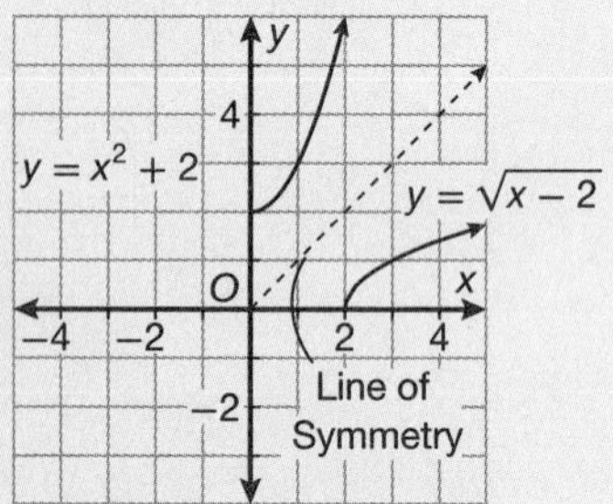

The domain of the quadratic function is $x \geq 0$. The range is $y \geq 2$. For the radical function, the domain $x \geq 2$ and the range is all real numbers greater than or equal to zero.

LESSON 75 Graphing Radical Functions

Warm Up

1. **Vocabulary** The expression $\sqrt{x}$ is the inverse of the expression x^2. (50)
2. True or false. The expression $5x^2$ is a monomial of degree two. True (11)
3. What is the domain of $y = 3x^2 + 2 - 3$? All real numbers (4)

New Concepts

A **radical function** is written in one of two forms, with a radical or with a fractional exponent.

Radical Version	Fractional Exponent Version
$f(x) = \sqrt[n]{g(x)}$	$f(x) = (g(x))^{\frac{1}{n}}$

In each case, n is an integer and $g(x)$ is a function. In the case of the radical version, the n is also referred to as the index. A radical function is the inverse of a power function.

Math Language

A **square root function** is a function whose rule contains a variable under a square root sign.

Example 1 The Square Root Function

a. Graph the square root function and its inverse. Determine the domain and range of both functions.

$y = \sqrt{x - 1}$

SOLUTION

Step 1: To find the inverse, interchange y and x and solve for y:

$x = \sqrt{y - 1}$

$x^2 = y - 1$

$y = x^2 + 1$

Since the range of the original function is $y \geq 0$, the domain of the inverse function is $x \geq 0$.

Math Reasoning

Generalize What does a comparison of the x-y table of a function and its inverse show?

The x- and y- values are interchanged.

Step 2: Graph the square root function and the quadratic, its inverse, using x-y tables and the domains of each function:

$y = \sqrt{x - 1}$

x	y
1	0
2	1
5	2

$y = x^2 + 1$

x	y
0	1
1	2
2	5

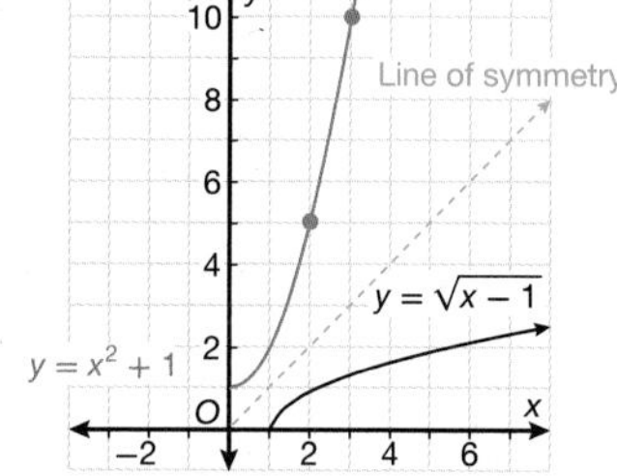

The domain of the inverse, $y = x^2 + 1$, is $x \geq 0$ and the range is $y \geq 1$. For the radical function, $y = \sqrt{x - 1}$, the domain is $x \geq 1$ and the range is all real numbers greater than zero.

LESSON RESOURCES

Student Edition Practice Workbook 75
Reteaching Master 75
Adaptations Master 75
Challenge and Enrichment Master C75

MATH BACKGROUND

Remind students that the square root of a negative number is not a real number. For example, $\sqrt{-16}$ does not have a real number solution. However, the solution can be written as $\pm 4i$, where i is an imaginary number. Recall that i^2 is equal to -1. So the answer can be written as $\sqrt{-1} \cdot \sqrt{16} = \pm i4 = \pm 4i$.

However, in this lesson, only real numbers are considered. Therefore, radicals that contain negative numbers are not covered in this lesson. The domain and range of the functions will only be real numbers.

Math Reasoning

Write Consider a radical function $f(x) = \sqrt[n]{g(x)}$, where n is an even number. What restrictions are there to the domain of this function?

The domain is restricted to values such that $g(x) \geq 0$.

b. Graph the square root function and its inverse.

$y = (2x - 3)^{\frac{1}{2}} + 4$

SOLUTION

Step 1: To find the inverse, interchange y and x and solve for y:

$$x = (2y - 3)^{\frac{1}{2}} + 4$$
$$x - 4 = (2y - 3)^{\frac{1}{2}}$$
$$(x - 4)^2 = 2y - 3$$
$$y = \frac{(x - 4)^2 + 3}{2} \quad \text{Remember } x \geq 4.$$

Step 2: Graph the square root function and the quadratic, its inverse:

$y = (2x - 3)^{\frac{1}{2}} + 4$

x	y
1.5	4
2	5
6	3

$y = \frac{(x - 4)^2 + 3}{2}$

x	y
4	1.5
5	2
3	6

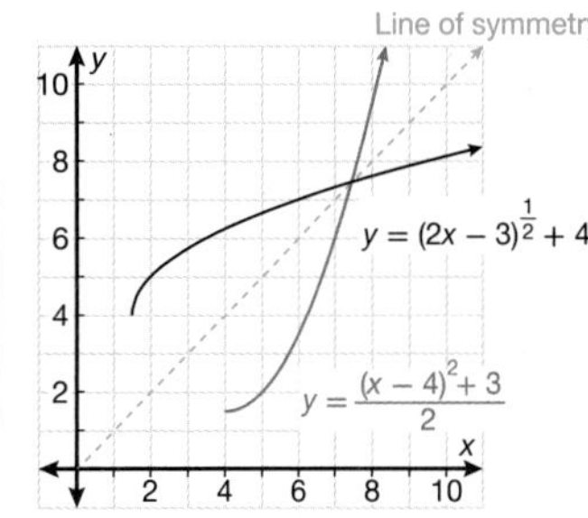

Math Language

A **cube root function** is the function $f(x) = \sqrt[3]{x}$.

Example 2 The Cube Root Function

a. Graph the cube root function and its inverse.

$y = \sqrt[3]{x + 1}$

SOLUTION

Step 1: To find the inverse, interchange y and x and solve for y:

$$x = \sqrt[3]{y + 1}$$
$$x^3 = y + 1$$
$$y = x^3 - 1$$

Step 2: Graph the cube root function and the cubic, its inverse:

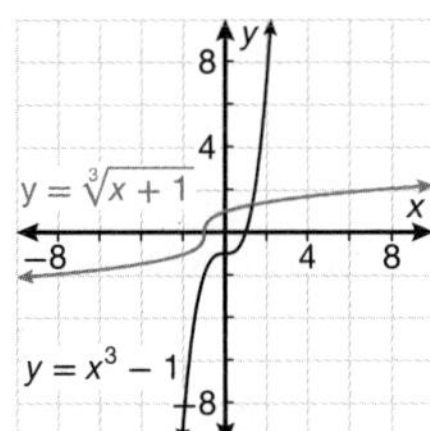

Additional Example 1b

b. Graph the square root function and its inverse.

$y = (x - 3)^{\frac{1}{2}} + 4$

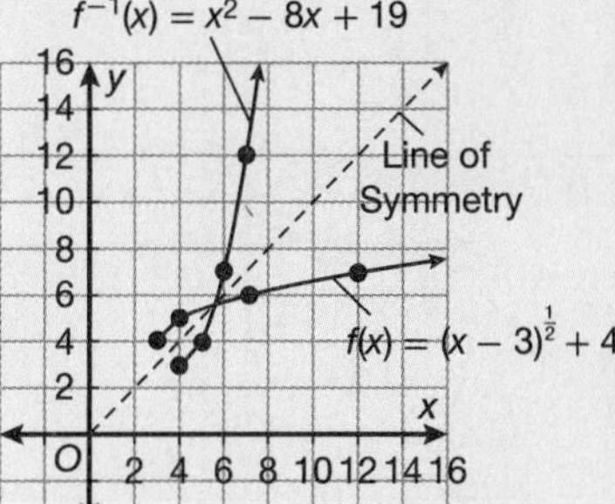

Extend Example 1b

Have students find the domain and range of both functions.

The domain of the quadratic $x \geq 4$. The range is $y \geq \frac{3}{2}$. For the radical function, the domain is $x \geq \frac{3}{2}$. The range is $y \geq 4$.

Example 2

These examples show students how to graph a cubic root function and its inverse.

Additional Example 2

a. Graph the cubic root function and its inverse.

$y = \sqrt[3]{x + 2}$

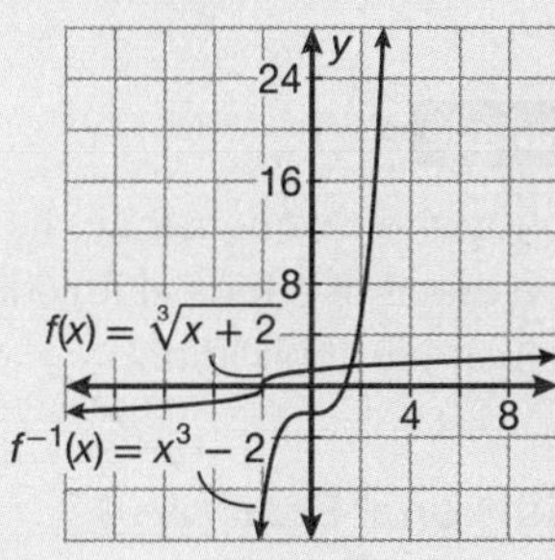

ENGLISH LEARNERS

For this lesson, explain the meaning of the word **radical**. Say:

"The term radical is derived from the Latin word radicalis which means 'root'."

In math, a radical function uses a root sign to indicate the solution of the function is a number multiplied by itself a number of times. For example, the radical function $\sqrt{4}$ has the roots of ± 2, which means $+2$ or -2 multiplied by itself equals 4.

The term radical is also used in chemistry to refer to a group of atoms that are bonded together and react as a single unit in chemical reactions.

Connect the meaning of the term radical to its Latin origin as you explain how to graph radical functions in Examples 1 and 2.

Additional Example 2

b. Graph the cube root function and its inverse.

$y = (3x + 1)^{\frac{1}{3}} + 2$

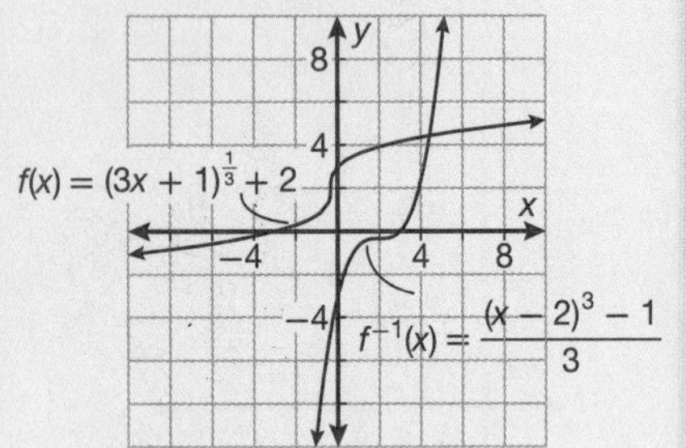

Example 3

Remind students to close off parentheses when entering the function into a graphing calculator.

Additional Example 3

Graph the radical function. Determine the domain and range.

$f(x) = \sqrt{x+2} + \sqrt[3]{x+1}$

The domain of the function is $x \geq -2$ and the range is $f(x) \geq -1$.

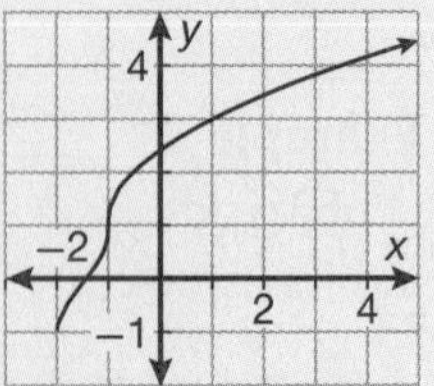

Example 4

This example demonstrates how to use a graph of a radical function in a real-life application.

Additional Example 4

A construction crew is building a highway ramp to connect a service road to an interstate. The equation $y = \frac{\sqrt{2^2 + (x-1)^2}}{2}$ is for a 1:10 scale model. Graph the function and find the height of the ramp at $x = 1$ and $x = 10$.

Height at $x = 1$ is 10;
Height at $x = 10$ is 46.

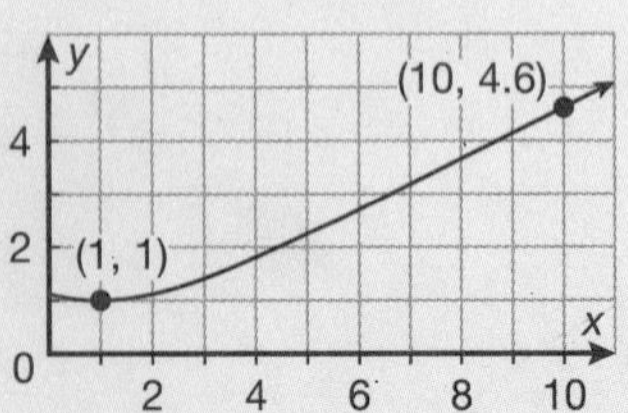

Math Reasoning

Write Consider a radical function $f(x) = \sqrt[n]{g(x)}$, where n is an odd number. What restrictions are there to the domain of this function?

There are no restrictions to the domain.

b. Graph the cube root function and its inverse.

$y = (2x + 3)^{\frac{1}{3}} - 4$

SOLUTION

Step 1: To find the inverse, interchange y and x and solve for y:

$$x = (2y + 3)^{\frac{1}{3}} - 4$$

$$(x + 4)^3 = 2y + 3$$

$$y = \frac{(x+4)^3 - 3}{2}$$

Step 2: Graph the cube root function and the cubic, its inverse:

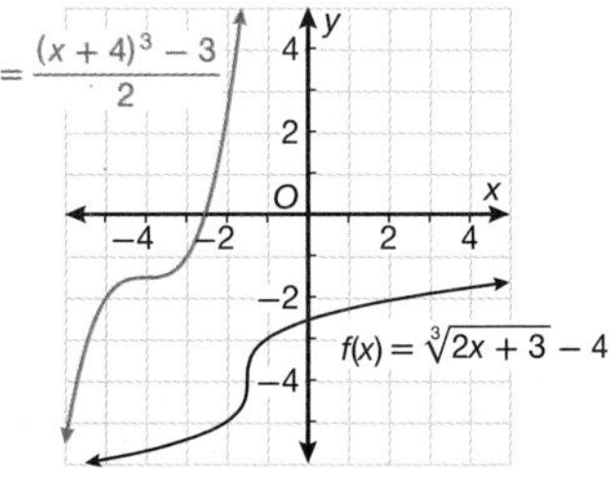

Example 3 Radical Functions with Different Indexes

Graph the radical function using a graphing calculator. Determine the domain and range.

$f(x) = \sqrt{x+1} + \sqrt[3]{x+2}$

SOLUTION The domain of the function is $x \geq -1$ and the range is $f(x) \geq 1$.

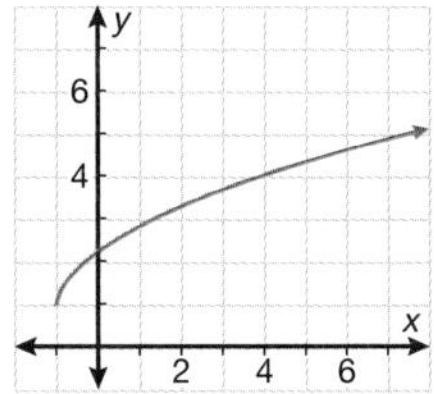

Math Reasoning

Analyze Explain why $f(x)$ does not accept x values less then -1.

Values less than -1 result in complex roots for the $\sqrt{x+1}$ term.

Example 4 Application: Architecture

An architect is constructing a building with a roof in the shape of a hyperbola. The equation shown below is for a 1:10 scale model. Graph the function and find the height of the building at $x = 1$ and $x = 15$.

$$y = \frac{\sqrt{5^2 + (x-5)^2}}{3}$$

SOLUTION

Height at 1 = 21.3

Height at 15 = 37.3

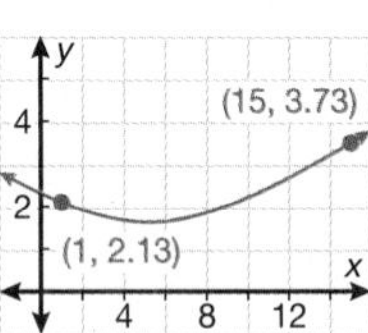

INCLUSION

Graphing radical functions and their inverses can be challenging whether it is done by hand or by using a graphing calculator. Encourage students to draw in the line $y = x$ before graphing the functions. Remind them that the graphs should be reflections of each other over this line. Once the radical function has been graphed, reflecting selected points over the line can help them determine the domain (and range) of its inverse.

Lesson Practice

a. Graph the square root function and its inverse. Determine the domain and range of both functions. $y = \sqrt{3x - 2}$ See Additional Answers.
(Ex 1)

b. Graph the square root function and its inverse. Determine the domain and range of both functions. $y = (4x + 9)^{\frac{1}{2}}$ See Additional Answers.
(Ex 1)

c. Graph the cube root function and its inverse. $y = \sqrt[3]{4x + 3}$ See Additional Answers.
(Ex 2)

d. Graph the cube root function and its inverse. $y = (5x - 4)^{\frac{1}{3}} + 7$ See Additional Answers.
(Ex 2)

e. Graph the radical function. Determine the domain and range.
(Ex 3)

$$f(x) = \sqrt{3x - 1} + \sqrt[3]{4x + 9}$$ See Additional Answers.

f. Graph the radical function and find where it intersects $y = 3$.
(Ex 4)

$$y = \frac{\sqrt{6^2 + (x - 7)^2}}{4}$$ See Additional Answers.

Practice Distributed and Integrated

***1.** Find the area of $\triangle ABC$ with the given side lengths and included angle. $b = 11$, $c = 7$, $m\angle A = 120°$ About 33.3
(71)

2. Find the roots and give the multiplicity of each root: $2x^3 - 4x^2 + 2x = 0$ $x = 0$ with multiplicity of 1; $x = 1$ with multiplicity of 2
(66)

3. (**Medicine**) If a patient ingests medicine containing a grams of a drug, the amount left in the patient's bloodstream after t hours is given by the equation $y = ae^{-0.119t}$. After how much time will exactly one-third of the drug still be circulating in the bloodstream? About 9.2 hours
(57)

***4.** **Multi-Step** **a.** Find the radical function that is the inverse of $y = (x - 3)(x^2 + 3x + 9)$.
(75)
b. Identify its domain and range. $y = \sqrt[3]{x + 27}$; domain and range: all real numbers

5. **Error Analysis** Which student made an error in finding $|4 + 11i|$? Describe the error.
(69)

Student A	Student B
$\sqrt{4^2 + 11^2}$	$\sqrt{4^2 - 11^2}$
$\sqrt{16 + 121}$	$\sqrt{16 - 121}$
$\sqrt{137}$	$\sqrt{-105} = i\sqrt{105}$

5. Student B made the error. The radicand is the sum of the squares, not the difference of the squares.

***6.** (**Celebrating**) On the Fourth of July, a technician on Bedloe's Island is planning to shoot confetti straight up behind the Statue of Liberty. The function $y = -4.9x^2 + 45x + 1$ gives the height of a piece of confetti, in meters, after x seconds. The statue has a height of 93 meters. Use the discriminant to explain if a piece of confetti will reach the top of the statue. Yes, discriminant = 221.8, two real solutions
(74)

7. (**Sports**) In basketball, the basket through which the ball is thrown consists of a metal hoop that has a 9-inch radius. Use the formula $r = \sqrt{\frac{A}{\pi}}$ to find the area of the hoop. About 254.5 square inches
(70)

Lesson Practice

Problem a

Scaffolding Remind students to exchange the positions of x and y in the function and solve for y to find the inverse function. Because you cannot graph a negative number inside a square root, the domain is $x \geq \frac{2}{3}$. The range is all real numbers greater than or equal to zero.

Problem f

Error Alert If students are using a graphing calculator to graph the function, remind them to use multiple sets of parentheses when entering the equation.

Check for Understanding

The questions below help assess the concepts taught in this lesson.

"In what two forms are radical functions written?" with a radical or with a fractional exponent

"How can you find the domain of x for a radical function with an even index?" Set the expression under the radical sign ≥ 0 and solve for x.

3 Practice

Math Conversations

Discussions to strengthen understanding

Problem 2

Guide students by asking them the following questions.

"How do you solve the equation?"

$$2x(x^2 - 2x + 1) = 0$$
$$2x(x - 1)(x - 1) = 0$$
$$2x = 0; x = 0$$
$$x - 1 = 0; x = 1$$

"What is the multiplicity of $x = 0$?" 1

"What is the multiplicity of $x = 1$?" 2

8. (67) **Multiple Choice** What is the solution set of the equation $2 \cos \theta + \sqrt{2} = 0$, for $0° \leq \theta \leq 360°$? D

A $\{30°, 330°\}$ B $\{45°, 135°\}$ C $\{30°, 150°\}$ D $\{135°, 225°\}$

***9.** (75) **Predict** Consider the radical function $f(x) = (g(x))^{\frac{1}{n}}$. Suppose that the graph of $f(x)$ is a straight line for increasing values of x. What can you conclude about $g(x)$? It is a monomial of degree n or a constant function.

10. (63) **Write** Describe how to determine tan 240° by using its reference angle.

10. Possible answer: The reference angle is 60°. $\tan 60° = \sqrt{3}$, 240° terminates in Quadrant III, and the tangent of any angle terminating in Quadrant III is positive, so $\tan 240° = \sqrt{3}$.

***11.** (68) **Probability** In a factory, a sample of items produced is checked during all three work shifts. The table shows the results of these checks for one day. What is the probability that an item was checked during the third shift given that it was found to be defective? About 69.2%

	1st Shift	2nd Shift	3rd Shift
Defective	3	5	18
Not Defective	119	109	132

12. (52) **Multi-Step** **a.** Given the triangle, find the lengths of side x and y.

b. Draw a perpendicular line to the hypotenuse from vertex A, calling the new point of intersection D. Find the length of AD and DC. $AD = 4\sqrt{3}$; $DC = 4$

12a. $x = 16$, $y = 8\sqrt{3}$

12b. 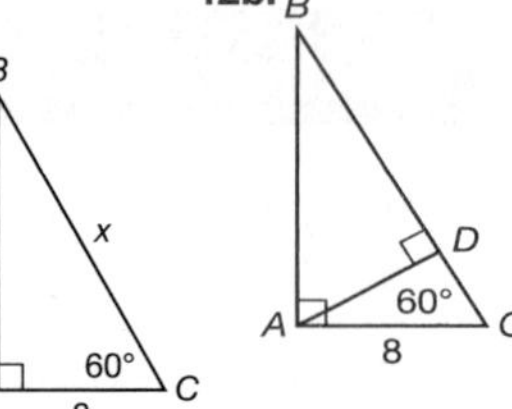

***13.** (71) **Write** What is meant by *triangulation*?

13. Possible answer: Triangulation is the process of finding a certain distance when the angles formed from the imaginary line connecting two fixed points a known distance apart and the lines from the fixed points to the object are known.

14. (61) **Geometry** The volume of a right prism is the product of the area of its base and its height. The height of a right prism with a volume of $6x^3 + 69x^2 + 3x - 330$ cubic units is $x + 11$ units. Find a polynomial expression for the area of the base. $6x^2 + 3x - 30$

15. (62) Write each expression in terms of i, and then subtract: $(-1 + \sqrt{-9}) - (-1 - \sqrt{-64})$. $11i$

16. (65) **Physics** The number of seconds it takes for a rocket fired from a deck 10 feet off the ground at a velocity of 50 feet per second to return to the ground is given by $-16t^2 + 50t + 10 = 0$. Solve the equation. Round to the nearest hundredth. 3.31 seconds

Determine whether the linear binomial is a factor of the polynomial.

17. (61) $P(x) = x^3 - 10x^2 + 19x + 30$; $x - 6$ yes

18. (61) $P(x) = 3x^3 - 2x^2 - 61x - 20$; $x - 4$ no

19. (66) **Write** Tell what is meant by the *multiplicity* of a root.

19. For root r, the multiplicity of r is the number of times the factor $x - r$ occurs when the polynomial in the polynomial equation, when written in standard form, is completely factored.

Write the logarithmic equations in exponential form.

20. (64) $\log_{10} 100{,}000 = 5$ $10^5 = 100{,}000$

21. (64) $\log_4 1024 = 5$ $4^5 = 1024$

Problem 12

Point out to students that triangle ABC is a 30°-60°-90° triangle. Remind them that the sides are in the ratio of $1 : \sqrt{3} : 2$. Also, when the perpendicular line AD is drawn, two new 30°-60°-90° triangles are formed—$\triangle ADC$ and $\triangle BAD$.

Extend the Problem

Have students find the area of triangle ABC. $A \approx 55.4$ square units

Problem 16

Error Alert

Students can use the quadratic formula to solve for t. They will get two possible solutions, but remind them to look at the solutions to see if all of the solutions are possible. There is actually only one possible solution although the quadratic formula gives two solutions.
$t = -0.189$ seconds and
$t = 3.31$ seconds.

A negative time is not possible.

CHALLENGE

Challenge students to use synthetic division and factoring to determine the x-intercepts.
$x = 5$
$x = 6$
$x = -1$

*22. **Error Analysis** Two students are finding the inverse of $y = \sqrt[4]{x^2 + 4}$ but get different results. Which student made the mistake? Student B incorrectly takes the fourth root of x instead of raising it to the fourth power.
(75)

Student A	Student B
$x = \sqrt[4]{y^2 + 4}$	$x = \sqrt[4]{y^2 + 4}$
$x^4 = y^2 + 4$	$x^{\frac{1}{4}} = y^2 + 4$
$y = \sqrt{x^4 - 4}$	$y = \sqrt{x^{\frac{1}{4}} - 4}$

23. Find all the possible values of $\sin^{-1}\left(\frac{1}{2}\right)$. $\frac{\pi}{6} + 2\pi n$; $\frac{5\pi}{6} + 2\pi n$, where n is an integer
(67)

24. A calculator is programmed to generate random integers from 1 to 100 inclusive when the enter button is pressed. If the enter button is pressed twice, what is the probability of getting a multiple of 10 and a number greater than 60? $\frac{1}{25}$
(55)

*25. **Multiple Choice** The discriminant of a quadratic equation is -2. Which describes the solutions of the equation? **D**
(74)
A 1 real solution **B** 1 complex solution **C** 2 real solutions **D** 2 complex solutions

Solve.

26. $\log_6 \frac{5}{8}$ -0.263
(72)

27. $\log_6 40$ 2.059
(72)

28. **Multiple Choice** What are the solutions of $x^2 + 8x = -25$? **C**
(62)
A $\pm 3i$ **B** $\pm 5i$ **C** $-4 \pm 3i$ **D** $4 \pm 5i$

*29. **Graphing Calculator** To generate single digit random numbers on a calculator, press MATH and select **[randInt(]** from the PRB menu and type 0, 9 in parentheses. Then press enter.
(73)

a. Form a simple random sample of 3 individuals from the 10 listed below.

0: Greg	1: Pam	2: Tyler	3: Lakisha	4: Jon
5: Larry	6: Mark	7: Tammy	8: Li	9: Diane

See student work.

b. Under what circumstances would you have to press enter more than 3 times? The same number is generated more than once.

*30. **Justify** Explain why $\ln e^{2x-1} = 2x - 1$. Possible answer: Exponential and logarithmic operations are inverse operations.
(72)

Example 28

Error Alert

Students can use the quadratic formula to solve for x. Remind them that the equation must be in standard form before they use the quadratic formula or the signs will be incorrect, which will give an incorrect solution.

LOOKING FORWARD 

Graphing radical functions prepares students for

- **Lesson 93** Solving Exponential Equations and Inequalities
- **Lesson 109** Making Graphs and Using Equations of Hyperbolas
- **Lesson 111** Transforming Polynomial Functions

LESSON 76

1 Warm Up

For problem 3, remind students to be careful using negative signs.

2 New Concepts

Students use factoring and graphing to find or approximate roots of polynomials.

Example 1

Students use the Zero Product Property to find the roots of a factored polynomial function.

Additional Example 1

Find the roots of the polynomial function.

$0 = -x(x+4)\left(x - \frac{1}{2}\right)$ $0, -4, \frac{1}{2}$

Example 2

Students find the zeros of polynomial functions that do not have constant terms.

Error Alert Students often forget to include 0 in their solution sets.

Additional Example 2

Find the zeros of the polynomial function.

a. $f(x) = 6x^3 + 21x^2 + 18x$
$0, -2, -\frac{3}{2}$

LESSON 76

Finding Polynomial Roots I

Warm Up

1. **Vocabulary** In the expression $2x(x + 3)$, the term outside the parentheses is called a monomial ___factor___. (23)
2. Factor the expression $2x^2 - 12x$. $2x(x - 6)$ (23)
3. Solve using the quadratic formula. $5x^2 - 12x + 13 = 0$ $x \approx 1.2 + 1.077i$, $1.2 - 1.077i$ (65)

New Concepts

Polynomial roots are the solutions of a polynomial equation. These roots are the zeros of the related polynomial function which are the x-intercepts of the graph of the function.

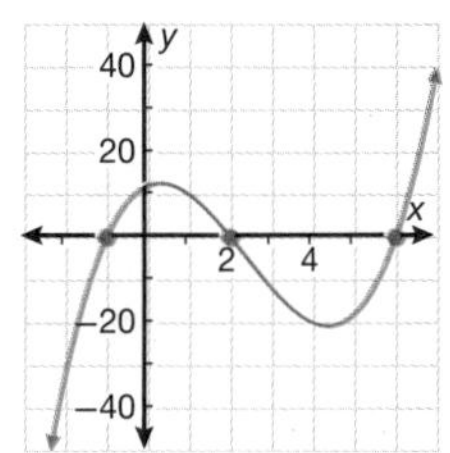

Example 1 Finding the Roots of a Factored Polynomial

Find the roots of the polynomial function.

$0 = 2x(x - 5)(2x - 3)$

SOLUTION Since the polynomial is already factored and cannot be factored further, set each factor equal to zero.

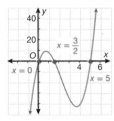

$2x = 0$	$x - 5 = 0$	$2x - 3 = 0$
$x = 0$	$x = 5$	$x = \frac{3}{2}$

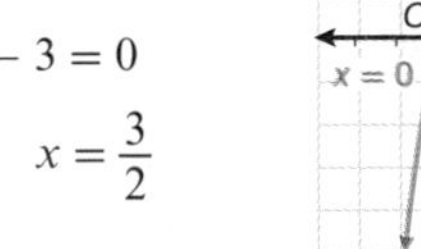

The roots are 0, 5 and $\frac{3}{2}$.

Math Reasoning

Verify If a polynomial function $f(x)$ has a zero $x = 0$, then explain why the polynomial has no constant term.

For a polynomial function to have $x = 0$ as a zero, then x can be factored so that $f(x) = x \cdot g(x)$.

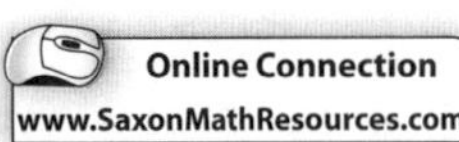

Online Connection
www.SaxonMathResources.com

Example 2 Finding Monomial Factors to Determine Zeros

a. Find the zeros of the polynomial function.

$f(x) = 6x^3 + 10x^2 + 4x$

SOLUTION

Step 1: When there are no constant terms, there is a linear factor.

$6x^3 + 10x^2 + 4x = 0 \rightarrow 2x(3x^2 + 5x + 2) = 0 \rightarrow 2x = 0 \rightarrow x = 0$

Step 2: Now factor the quadratic using the quadratic formula.

$$x = \frac{-5 \pm \sqrt{5^2 - 4(3)(2)}}{(2)(3)} = \frac{-5 \pm \sqrt{25 - 24}}{6} = \frac{-5 \pm 1}{6}$$

The zeros are 0, -1, and $-\frac{2}{3}$.

LESSON RESOURCES

Student Edition Practice Workbook 76
Reteaching Master 76
Adaptations Master 76
Challenge and Enrichment Master C76

MATH BACKGROUND

Finding exact solutions for one-variable linear and quadratic equations is a straightforward matter. In the former case, solve for the unknown using inverse operations; in the latter, use factoring or the quadratic formula.

The situation is very different once the degree of a polynomial equation is greater than 2. Although there are formulas in terms of radicals for the roots of cubic and quartic equations, they are lengthy and tedious.

In general, equations of degree five and higher cannot be solved using only operations, factoring, and extraction of roots. There are exceptions; for example, if one rational root can be found for a 5th degree equation, it can be reduced to degree 4 and then solved. Attempting to factor a higher-degree polynomial is thus a good first strategy.

These remarks refer to obtaining *exact* solutions. Approximate real solutions can easily be obtained by graphing.

b. Find the real zeros of $f(x) = x^4 - 3x^3 + 2x^2 - 6x$.

SOLUTION

Step 1: Identify the monomial factor: $x(x^3 - 3x^2 + 2x - 6) = 0$.

Step 2: Graph the cubic factor to identify additional roots.

Step 3: Divide the cubic factor by $(x - 3)$ to find the quadratic factor.

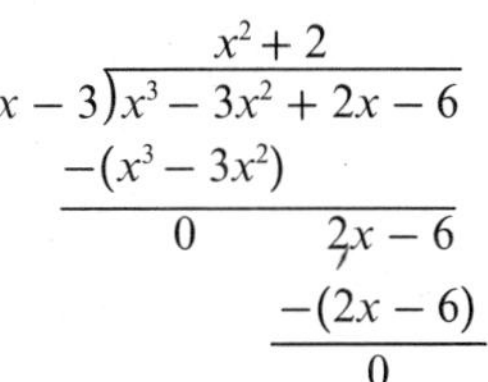

$$\begin{array}{r} x^2 + 2 \\ x - 3\overline{)x^3 - 3x^2 + 2x - 6} \\ -(x^3 - 3x^2) \\ \hline 0 \quad 2x - 6 \\ -(2x - 6) \\ \hline 0 \end{array}$$

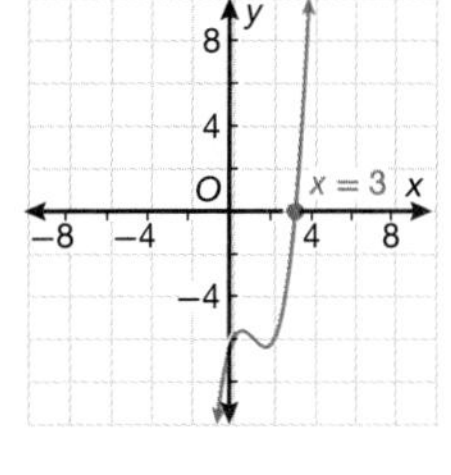

So, $x^4 - 3x^3 + 2x^2 - 6x = x(x - 3)(x^2 + 2)$. The real zeros are $x = 0$ and $x = 3$.

Math Reasoning

Analyze If the function $f(x)$ has a binomial factor of degree 2, does this factor always provide a real zero of the polynomial function?

Not always. For example, $(x^2 + 1)$ has no real zeros.

Example 3 Finding Binomial Factors to Determine Roots

a. Find the real roots of $0 = (x + 3)(x^2 + 4) - (x + 3)(4x + 1)$.

SOLUTION

Step 1: Look for binomial factors to simplify the expression.

$(x + 3)(x^2 + 4) - (x + 3)(4x + 1) = 0$

$(x + 3)(x^2 - 4x + 3) = 0$

Step 2: Factor the quadratic expression to find the remaining roots.

$(x + 3)(x - 3)(x - 1) = 0$

The real roots are $x = -3$, $x = 3$, and $x = 1$.

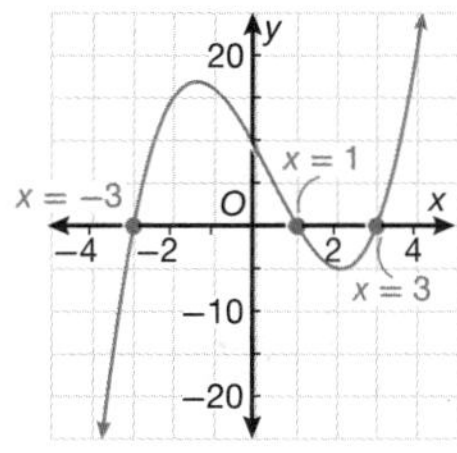

b. Find the real roots of the polynomial equation.

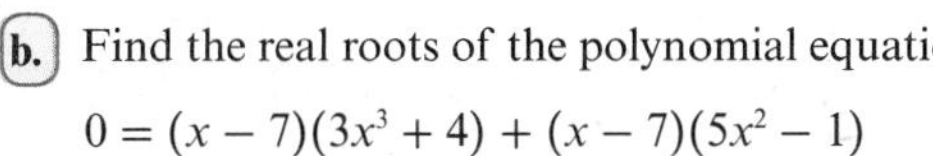

$0 = (x - 7)(3x^3 + 4) + (x - 7)(5x^2 - 1)$

SOLUTION

Step 1: Look for binomial factors to simplify the expression.

$(x - 7)(3x^3 + 4) + (x - 7)(5x^2 - 1) = 0$

$(x - 7)(3x^3 + 5x^2 + 3) = 0$

Step 2: Graph the cubic factor to identify additional roots.

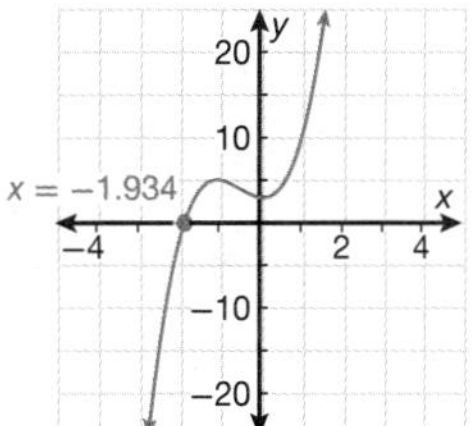

So, $f(x) = (x - 7)(3x^3 + 4) + (x - 7)(5x^2 - 1)$ has two real roots, $x = -1.934$ and $x = 7$.

b. Find the real zeros of $f(x) = 2x^4 - 14x^3 + 26x^2 - 30x$ 10 15

Example 3

Students find the real roots of polynomial equations with binomial factors.

Additional Example 3

a. Find the roots of $0 = (x - 2)(x^2 + 2) - (x - 2)(4x + 7)$ −1 12 5

b. Find the roots of the polynomial equation. $0 = (x + 4)(2x^3 - 7) + (x + 4)(5 - 3x)$ 1 −4 11.4 59

Extend the Example

Find all three roots of the equation $0 = x^3 + 5x^2 + 4x + 20$. Hint: Use the factor by grouping method. −5 12*i* 1−2*i*

Example 4

Students solve a polynomial equation.

Additional Example 4

Solve $2x^4 = 8x^3 - x^2 - 13x$. Approximate solutions to two decimal places. 0, −1.08, 1.87, 3.22

Example 5

Students use a polynomial equation to solve an application problem.

Additional Example 5

An object is thrown from a height of 15 ft at an initial speed of 12 ft/sec. How long does it take the object to hit the ground? Use the equation $h = -16t^2 + v_0t + h_0$. approximately 1.41 seconds

Example 4 Solving Polynomial Equations

Solve the following equation.

$5x^4 = 5x^3 - 8x^2 - 2x$

SOLUTION

Step 1: In this equation there is a monomial equal to a trinomial. Place all the terms on the same side of the equation and factor the linear term.

$x(-5x^3 + 5x^2 - 8x - 2) = 0$

Step 2: Graph the cubic factor to identify additional roots.

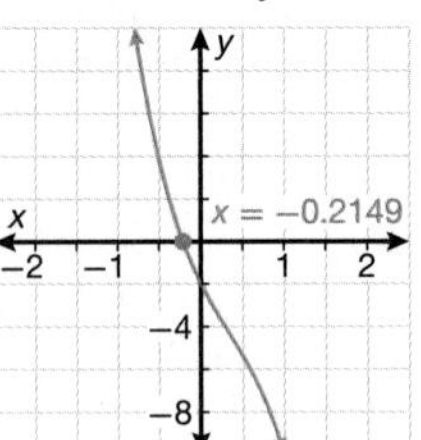

So, $x(-5x^3 + 5x^2 - 8x - 2) = 0$ has two real roots, $x = 0$ and $x \approx -0.2149$.

Reading Math

The use of the subscript 0 is commonly used in physics to denote the initial instance of time, height, velocity, etc.

Example 5 Application: Projectile Motion

The equation below can be used to find the distance from the ground at time t for a ball thrown from a height h_o at an initial speed of v_o. Suppose a ball is thrown with an initial speed of $v_o = 5$ from a height $h_o = 25$. How long will it take the ball to hit the ground?

$h = -4.9t^2 + v_ot + h_o$

SOLUTION

Finding the time means solving the following equation.

$0 = -4.9t^2 + 5t + 25$

This equation can be solved using the quadratic formula.

$$t = \frac{-5 \pm \sqrt{5^2 - 4(-4.9)(25)}}{2(-4.9)}$$

$$= \frac{-5 \pm \sqrt{515}}{-9.8}$$

$t \approx -1.80547$ or 2.82588

Ignoring the negative root, the time it will take for the ball to hit the ground is approximately 2.83 seconds.

ALTERNATE METHOD FOR EXAMPLE 4

Write $5x^4 = 5x^3 - 8x^2 - 2x$ on the board and have students change it to standard form. They will get two different answers:

$-5x^4 + 5x^3 - 8x^2 - 2x = 0$
$5x^4 - 5x^3 + 8x^2 + 2x = 0$

Point out that these polynomial equations have the same solutions. Then write the two related polynomial functions.

$f(x) = -5x^4 + 5x^3 - 8x^2 - 2x$
$f(x) = 5x^4 - 5x^3 + 8x^2 + 2x$

Have students graph both functions using a graphing calculator. Ask: **"Do these two functions have the same graph? If not, how are the graphs different?"** No. One is a bowl shape opening downwards; the other opens upwards. **"Do the two functions have the same zeros? How can you find the real zeros from the graphs?"** Yes. Find the x-intercepts of either graph. Have students use the calculator to find the real zeros. 0, −0.214925

Lesson Practice

Find the roots or zeros.

a. $x = 0, \frac{7}{2}, -9$
c. $x = 0, -0.2933, 1.5155$
d. $x = -4, 5.7417, -1.7417$

a. (Ex 1) $0 = 4x(2x - 7)(x + 9)$

b. (Ex 2) $f(x) = 7x^3 - 8x^2 + 3x$ $x = 0$

c. (Ex 2) $f(x) = -9x^3 + 11x^2 + 4x$

d. (Ex 3) $0 = (x + 4)(x^2 - 9) - (x + 4)(4x + 1)$

e. (Ex 3) $0 = (x - 12)(4x^2 + 3) - (x - 12)(7x - 2)$ $x = 12$

f. (Ex 4) Solve the following equation. $6x^3 = 4x^4 + 3x^2 - 7x$ $x = 0, 1.6757$

g. (Ex 5) Suppose a ball is thrown with an initial speed of $v_o = 18$ from a height $h_o = 35$. To the nearest hundredth of a second, how long will it take the ball to hit the ground? Use the projectile motion equation below.

$$h = -4.9t^2 + v_ot + h_o$$ approximately 5.08 seconds

Practice Distributed and Integrated

***1.** (76) Let $f(x) = x^2 - 4$ and $g(x) = x + 1$. Find the roots of $f(g(x))$. $x = -3$ and 1

2. (50) Find an equation for the inverse of $y = -2x^5 - 10$. $y = \sqrt[5]{-0.5x - 5}$

***3.** (75) The volume of an ice cube has decreased from x^3 to $\frac{x^3}{3} - 9$, while still maintaining its cubic shape. What is the new length of each side of the cube? $\sqrt[3]{\frac{x^3}{3} - 9}$

4. (63) Find the sine, cosine, and tangent of 270°. $\sin(270°) = -1$, $\cos(270°) = 0$, $\tan(270°)$ is undefined.

5. (50) Find an equation for the inverse of $y = 4x^2 + 12$. $y = \pm\sqrt{0.25x - 3}$

***6.** (76) **Multiple Choice** Which of the following is not a factor of $x^3 - 6x^2 + 11x - 6$? A

A $(x - 4)$ B $(x - 3)$ C $(x - 2)$ D $(x - 1)$

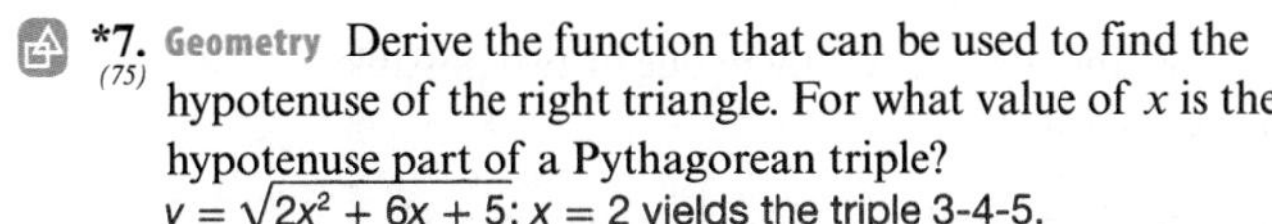

***7.** (75) **Geometry** Derive the function that can be used to find the hypotenuse of the right triangle. For what value of x is the hypotenuse part of a Pythagorean triple?
$y = \sqrt{2x^2 + 6x + 5}$; $x = 2$ yields the triple 3-4-5.

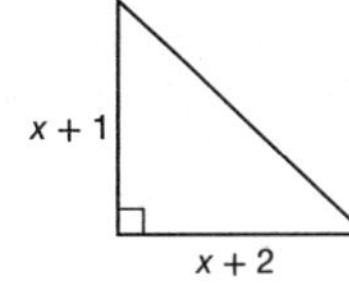

***8.** (75) **Physics** The equation for finding the period of a pendulum is the radical function $T = 2\pi\sqrt{\frac{L}{9.8}}$. The period is the amount of time it takes for the pendulum to complete one back-and-forth sweep. How much longer does a pendulum need to be to double the period? 4 times as long

9. (57) **Biology** In the absence of predators and diseases, and with enough food, a population of brown rats can increase by 6300% per year. Suppose you start with an initial population of three breeding pairs of rats. Write an exponential function to model the population size after t years. $y = 6 \cdot 63^t$

Lesson Practice

Problem f

Scaffolding Review the steps needed to solve this problem: Write the polynomial in standard form. Factor out the common factor x. One real root is 0. Graph the cubic to approximate the second real root.

Problem g

Error Alert Remind students to discard the negative root as it does not make sense in the problem context. Discuss the distinction between solving the *equation* and solving the *problem*.

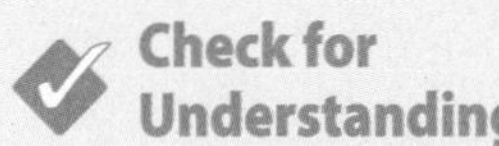

Check for Understanding

The questions below help assess the concepts taught in this lesson.

"Use the polynomial equation $x^2 + 2x - 15 = 0$ to explain the difference between factors and roots." Sample: The factors of the polynomial are $(x + 5)$ and $(x - 3)$. The roots of the equation are −5 and 3.

3 Practice

Math Conversations

Discussions to strengthen understanding

Problem 2

Error Alert

Remind students to solve for y after interchanging the x and y variables.

ENGLISH LEARNERS

Write these terms and examples on the board:

polynomials	$x^3 + 3x^2 - 4x - 12$	$(x^2 - 4)(x + 3)$
polynomial equations	$x^3 + 3x^2 - 4x - 12 = 0$	$(x^2 - 4)(x + 3) = 0$
polynomial functions	$y = x^3 + 3x^2 - 4x - 12$	$y = (x^2 - 4)(x + 3)$
	$f(x) = x^3 + 3x^2 - 4x - 12$	$f(x) = (x^2 - 4)(x + 3)$

Use the examples to review the terms **coefficient, constant term,** and **factor.**

Problem 11

Error Alert

Students who answer **D** are using -72 to find p. Remind students that p is a factor of the constant term of the related polynomial.

Problem 15

Have students sketch the triangle. Point out that the problem gives two sides and a nonincluded angle.

Extend the Problem

Solve $\triangle PQR$. $m\angle R \approx 29.45°$, $m\angle Q \approx 115.55°$, $q \approx 33.03$

10. (73) **Sports** A reporter went to a baseball game and asked fans who passed through the front gate at the end of the game if they thought the town could use a larger, more improved stadium. 98% of those surveyed answered *yes*. The reporter wrote in the paper that "98% of the city's population wants a new stadium." Discuss the problems with this situation. See Additional Answers.

11. (66) **Multiple Choice** Which is a possible rational root of $2x^3 + x^2 - 72x = 36$? B
A 7 **B** 9 **C** 10 **D** 72

12. (72) **Multi-Step** Two measures of sound are loudness and intensity. They are related by the function $L(I) = 10\log\frac{I}{I_0}$, where $L(I)$ is loudness in decibels, I is intensity in watts per square meter, and $I_0 \approx 10^{-12}$ watt per square meter, the intensity of a barely audible sound.
   a. The loudness of conversational speech is about 60 decibels. Find the intensity of a sound with a loudness of 60 decibels. Write your answer without an exponent. 0.000001 watt per square meter
   b. The threshold of discomfort to the human ear is about 120 decibels. Find the intensity of a sound with a loudness of 120 decibels. 1 watt per square meter
   c. When the loudness doubles from 60 dB to 120 dB, by what factor is the intensity multiplied? 1,000,000

13. (68) **Horses** A paddock contains 5 thoroughbreds, 6 quarter horses, 8 mustangs, and 2 ponies. Find the probability that the first random choice is a thoroughbred and the second random choice is a quarter horse (chosen without replacement) for the upcoming horse show. about 7.14%

*14. (76) **Multi-Step** Suppose that $f(x) = (x - 5)(x^2 - 12) + (x - 5)(-3x - x)$.
   a. Find the zeros of the function. $x = 5, x = 6, x = -2$
   b. Based on the solution in part **a**, how many x-intercepts does the graph of the $f(x)$ have? 3
   c. Simplify $f(x)$ and determine its degree. $x^3 - 9x^2 + 8x + 60$; 3

15. (71) **Analyze** In $\triangle PQR$, $m\angle P = 35°$, $r = 18$, and $p = 21$. Are there one or two possible triangles that can have these measures? Explain.

15. One triangle, because the side opposite the given angle is longer than the other given side.

16. (61) The volume of a rectangular solid with a length of $x - 8$ feet has a volume of $x^3 - 2x^2 - 40x - 64$ cubic feet. Factor the expression for the volume completely. $(x - 8)(x + 2)(x + 4)$

*17. (74) **Graphing Calculator** Graph $y = -3.25x^2 - 0.3x + 7.5$ to determine if $-3.25x^2 - 0.3x + 7.5 = 0$ has one, two, or zero real solutions. two real solutions

18. (70) **Error Analysis** Explain the error the student made below.

$$x - 2 = \sqrt{3x}$$
$$(x - 2)^2 = (\sqrt{3x})^2$$
$$x^2 - 4 = 3x$$
$$x^2 - 3x - 4 = 0$$
$$(x - 4)(x + 1) = 0$$
$$x = 4 \quad \text{or} \quad x = -1$$

18. The student did not properly square the binomial on the left side. $(x-2)^2 = x^2 - 4x + 4$

INCLUSION

Discuss why a polynomial function with no constant term always has 0 as a root. Say: **"Write an example of a polynomial with no constant term."** Sample: $x^2 + 2x$ **"Now write the related equation by setting your polynomial equal to 0."** $x^2 + 2x = 0$ **"Why is zero one solution of this equation?"** Substituting 0 for x makes the equation true.

Repeat with other polynomials such as $5x^4 - 2x^3 + 17x^2 - 9x$. Point out that, as long as there is no constant term, the related polynomial equation will always have 0 as a solution.

Extend the discussion to relate equations and functions using an example such as $x^2 + 2x = 0$ and $f(x) = x^2 + 2x$. Explain that 0 is a solution of the equation and a zero of the function.

544 Saxon Algebra 2

19. **Projectile Motion** The Leaning Tower of Pisa in Italy measures 180.4 feet from the
(58) ground on the lower side of the tower. If an object is thrown into the air, with an initial velocity of 96 feet per second, from the top of the lower side, the height, h, of the object in feet after t seconds can be described by the equation: $h = -16t^2 + 96t + 180.4$. Find the time at which the object will reach the ground. Round your answer to the tenths place. 7.5 seconds

20. **Estimate** Use properties of the unit circle and special angles to estimate
(67) $\cos^{-1}(0.48)$ in degrees. Do not use a calculator. Explain your method. See Additional Answers.

21. **Error Analysis** Find and correct the error a student made in solving $6x^2 + 5 - x = 0$.
(65)

$$x = \frac{-b \pm \sqrt{b^2 - 4ac}}{2a}$$
$$= \frac{-5 \pm \sqrt{25 - 4(6)(-1)}}{12}$$
$$= \frac{-5 \pm \sqrt{49}}{12}$$
$$= \frac{-5 \pm 7}{12} = \frac{1}{6} \text{ and } -1$$

The student did not rewrite the equation in standard form to see that $b = -1$ and not 5. The correct answer is $\frac{1}{12} \pm \frac{\sqrt{119}}{12}i$.

22. A tree casts a shadow as shown in the picture. What is
(52) the height of the tree? about 15 ft

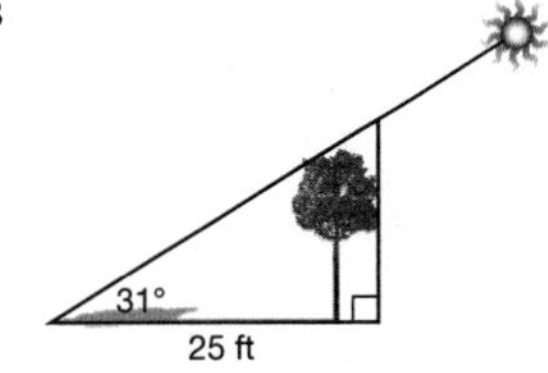

23. **Verify** Show why $2i\sqrt{2}$ is a square root of -8. $(2i\sqrt{2})^2 = 4(i^2)2 = 8i^2 = 8(-1) = -8$
(69)

24. A patient is injected with medication. $C(t) = Ae^{-0.42t}$ gives the amount of the
(57) medication in the bloodstream after t hours. If the initial dose is 300 mg, after how many hours will it be 70 mg? 3.46 hours

*25. **Analyze** Suppose that polynomial function $f(x)$ has n zeros and polynomial
(76) function $g(x)$ has m zeros. What must be true for $f(x) \cdot g(x)$ to have $n + m$ zeros? The zeros of $f(x)$ and $g(x)$ must be unique.

26. Mark rolled a 1–6 number cube four times. What is the probability of Mark
(60) rolling an odd number each time? $\frac{1}{16}$

*27. Find the roots of the polynomial function $3x(2x - 9)(x + 5)$. $x = -5, 0, \frac{9}{2}$
(76)

28. **Probability** A photo documentary includes 36 slides in a portfolio. If the teacher
(55) randomly chooses 5 slides from the portfolio, what is the probability that the teacher picks either the first five slides or the last five slides? $\frac{1}{188{,}496} \approx 0.000005$

Find the discriminant of the quadratic equation and give the number and type of solutions of the equation.

29. $x^2 - 8x + 16 = 0$ 0; one real solution
(74)

30. $s^2 + 7s + 11 = 0$ 5; two real solutions
(74)

Problem 20

If students need help getting started, have them draw a 30°-60°-90° right triangle and find the cosine of 60°. 0.5

Problem 22

Write $25\tan\left(31 \cdot \frac{\pi}{180}\right)$ on the board and ask students to explain why it gives the solution to the problem. Sample: It gives the solution when the calculator is set in radian mode. The tangent of 31° equals the height of the tree divided by 25, so 25 times tan 31° is the solution.

Problems 29–30
Extend the Problems

Describe the graphs of the related functions. The graph of $y = x^2 - 8x + 16$ will touch the x-axis in just one point. The graph of $y = s^2 + 7s + 11$ will intersect the x-axis in two points.

CHALLENGE

One root of the following equation is $5 - i$. Find the other roots. $5 + i, 2 + i, 2 - i$

$$x^4 - 14x^3 + 71x^2 - 154x + 130 = 0$$

Hint: Imaginary roots occur in conjugate pairs. Write the factors of the related polynomial. Find their product, then divide it into the polynomial to find the other quadratic factor. $x^2 - 4x + 5$

LOOKING FORWARD

Finding polynomial roots prepares students for

- **Lesson 85** Finding Polynomial Roots II
- **Lesson 95** Factoring Higher-Order Polynomials
- **Lesson 101** Making Graphs of Polynomial Functions
- **Lesson 106** Using the Fundamental Theorem of Algebra

LESSON 77

1 Warm Up

Use problem 1 to remind students that the sine, cosine, and tangent ratios can be used to find missing or unknown sides in *right* triangles.

2 New Concepts

In Lesson 71, students used the Law of Sines to solve problems with oblique triangles. In this lesson, they learn the Law of Cosines and Heron's formula.

Example 1

Students use the Law of Cosines to find the length of a missing side in a triangle and then solve for the measures of the angles using the Law of Sines..

Additional Example 1

Solve $\triangle DEF$. $e \approx 40.2$, $m\angle D \approx 44.7°$, $m\angle F \approx 32.3°$

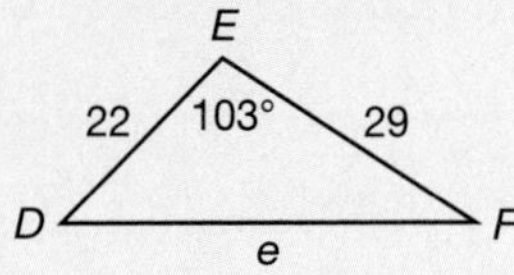

LESSON RESOURCES

Student Edition Practice Workbook 77
Reteaching Master 77
Adaptations Masters 77
Challenge and Enrichment Master C77

LESSON 77

Using the Law of Cosines

Warm Up

1. **Vocabulary** For an acute angle in a right triangle, the ratio of the adjacent side to the hypotenuse is the cosine of the angle. (46)

2. Find the value of x to the nearest tenth. 3.5 (46)

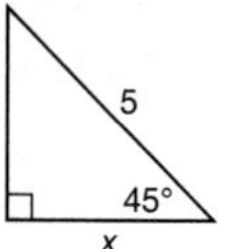

3. Estimate $m\angle A$ if $\cos A \approx 0.454$. 63° (67)

4. Find b in $\triangle ABC$ given $m\angle A = 95°$, $m\angle B = 20°$, and $c = 14$. $b \approx 5.28$ (71)

New Concepts

For a triangle that is not a right triangle, the Law of Sines can sometimes be used to find a missing measure. It can be used when given two angle measures and a side length or two side lengths and a nonincluded angle measure.

The **Law of Cosines** can be used other times, specifically when

- the measures of two sides and the included angle are known (side-angle-side (SAS)).
- the measures of all three sides of a triangle are known (side-side-side (SSS)).

To derive the Law of Cosines, let h be the altitude and $AD = x$ in $\triangle ABC$ shown at right.

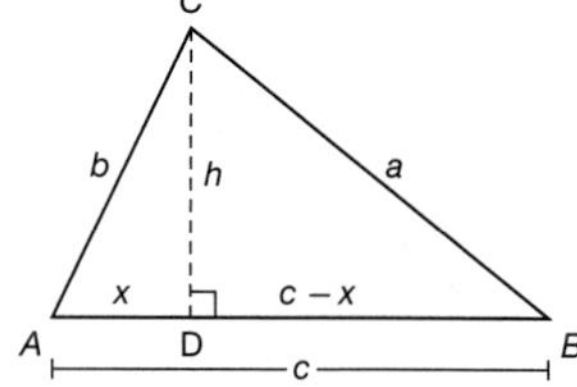

Then $DB = c - x$.

In $\triangle ABC$, $b^2 = x^2 + h^2$ and $\cos A = \frac{x}{b}$ or $x = b\cos A$.

Write an equation that relates the side lengths of $\triangle DCB$.

$a^2 = (c - x)^2 + h^2$	Pythagorean Theorem
$= c^2 - 2cx + x^2 + h^2$	Square the binomial.
$= c^2 - 2cx + b^2$	Substitute b^2 for $x^2 + h^2$.
$= c^2 - 2cb\cos A + b^2$	Substitute $b\cos A$ for x.
$= b^2 + c^2 - 2cb\cos A$	Commutative Property of Addition
$= b^2 + c^2 - 2bc\cos A$	Commutative Property of Multiplication

Math Reasoning

Generalize State all the patterns you see in the Law of Cosines.

The squared variables on the right are not on the left; the variables after 2 are the same as those squared on the right, the angle after cos is opposite the side squared on the left side. The operation signs are the same in all three forms.

Law of Cosines

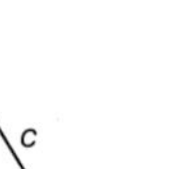

By the Law of Cosines,

$a^2 = b^2 + c^2 - 2bc \cos A$

$b^2 = a^2 + c^2 - 2ac \cos B$

$c^2 = a^2 + b^2 - 2ab \cos C$

MATH BACKGROUND

The Law of Cosines relates the sides of a triangle to the cosine of one of the angles. The length of one side can be computed from the other two sides and the angle between them. Or, an angle can be computed from the lengths of the three sides. The Law of Cosines is a generalization of the Pythagorean Theorem, which holds only in right triangles. For acute triangles, the cosine is positive; for obtuse triangles, it is negative.

The Law of Cosines has many applications. For example, it is equivalent to the formula for finding the dot product of two vectors, $\vec{b} \cdot \vec{c} = ||\vec{b}||\,||\vec{c}||\cos A$.

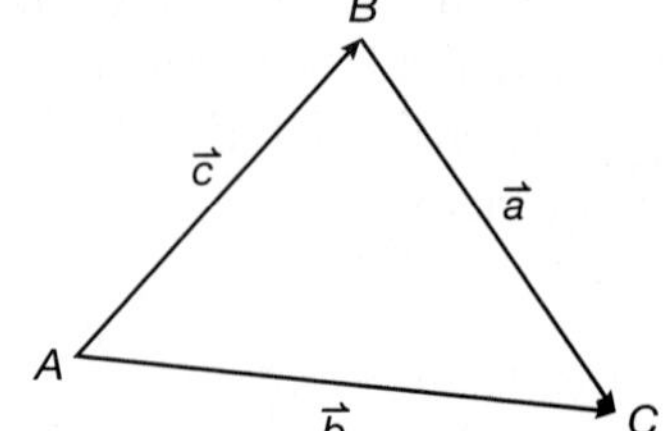

Example 1 Finding the Unknown Side of a Triangle

Solve $\triangle RST$.

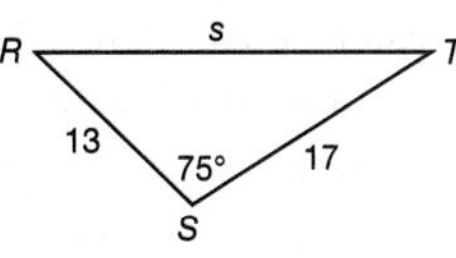

SOLUTION Find s by using $s^2 = r^2 + t^2 - 2rt\cos S$.

$s^2 = 17^2 + 13^2 - 2(17)(13)\cos 75°$	Substitute known values.
$s^2 \approx 343.6$	Simplify the right side.
$s \approx 18.5$	Take the positive square root.

Find one of the remaining angle measures by using the Law of Sines.

Use $\frac{\sin S}{s} = \frac{\sin R}{r}$ to find $m\angle R$.

$$\frac{\sin 75°}{18.5} = \frac{\sin R}{17}$$

$$18.5\sin R = 17\sin 75°$$

$$\sin R = \frac{17\sin 75°}{18.5} \approx 0.8876$$

$$m\angle R \approx 63°$$

Hint

Check solutions for reasonableness by remembering that the longest side is opposite the largest angle.

Find the measure of the third angle by subtracting: $180° - (75° + 63°) = 42°$.

$s \approx 18.5$, $m\angle R \approx 63°$, $m\angle T \approx 42°$

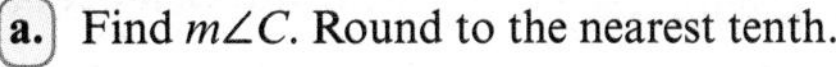

Example 2 Finding the Unknown Angle of a Triangle

a. Find $m\angle C$. Round to the nearest tenth.

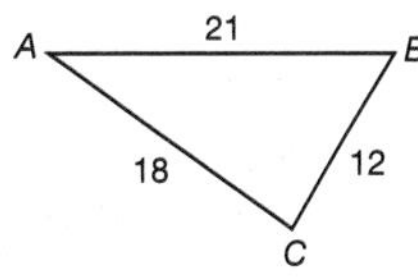

SOLUTION Use $c^2 = a^2 + b^2 - 2ab\cos C$.

$21^2 = 12^2 + 18^2 - 2(12)(18)\cos C$	Substitute the known values.
$441 = 468 - 432\cos C$	Simplify.
$0.0625 = \cos C$	Solve for cos C.
$86° \approx m\angle C$	Use $\text{Cos}^{-1}x$.

b. In $\triangle DEF$, $d = 60$, $e = 48$, and $f = 14$, find $m\angle D$. Round to the nearest tenth.

SOLUTION Use $d^2 = e^2 + f^2 - 2ef\cos D$.

$60^2 = 48^2 + 14^2 - 2(48)(14)\cos D$	Substitute the known values.
$3600 = 2500 - 1344\cos D$	Simplify.
$-0.8185 \approx \cos D$	Solve for cos D.
$145° \approx m\angle D$	Use $\text{Cos}^{-1}x$.

Example 2

Students use the Law of Cosines to find the measure of an unknown angle in an obtuse triangle. Point out that in each example the lengths of three sides of the triangle are given.

Error Alert Students may try to subtract 432 from 468 in Example 2a and 1344 from 2500 in Example 2b. Replace $\cos C$ and $\cos D$ with x to show that they are not like terms and cannot be subtracted.

Additional Example 2

a. Find $m\angle Q$. Round to the nearest tenth. 111.3°

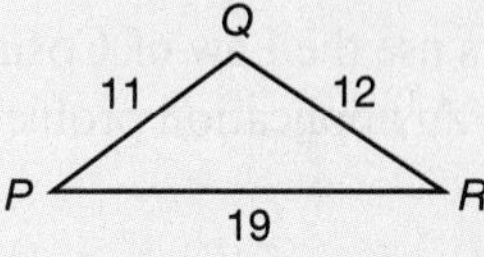

b. Given $\triangle XYZ$, $x = 4$, $y = 6$, and $z = 7$, find $m\angle X$. Round to the nearest tenth. 34.8°

INCLUSION

Draw an acute triangle ABC on the board. As you label the sides a, b, and c, emphasize that the letter of the angle and side opposite match; for example, side a is opposite angle A. Circle the letter a and explain that both the Law of Sines and the Law of Cosines can be used to find the length of side a. Write the first two ratios of the Law of Sines on the board and show students how to solve for a. Contrast the three measures needed to use each law.

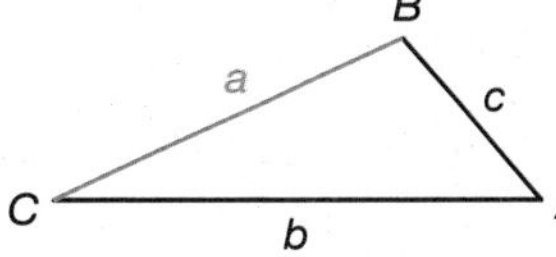

Law of Sines: $a = b \times \frac{\sin A}{\sin B}$

Law of Cosines: $a = \sqrt{b^2 + c^2 - 2bc\cos A}$

Example 3

Heron's formula can be derived from the Law of Cosines. Explain that the quantity s in the formula is the *semi-perimeter* of the triangle. It is calculated by finding the perimeter and then dividing by 2.

Additional Example 3

Find the area of the triangle. Round to the nearest tenth. 41.5 square units

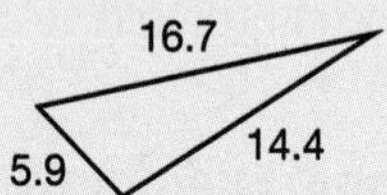

Example 4

Students use the Law of Cosines to solve an application problem.

Additional Example 4

Two groups of hikers leave camp heading in different directions at the same time. One group averages 3 mi/h; the other averages 4.5 mi/h. After three hours, the groups are 12 miles apart. Assuming they walked in a straight path, what is the measure of the angle between the two compass headings of the groups? Explain your steps. 60.6°; Sample: Use a triangle with sides of 9, 13.5, and 12 miles. Find the measure of the angle opposite the 12-mile side.

The area of a triangle can be determined when the three sides of the triangle are the only measures given using **Heron's Formula.** The Law of Cosines can be used to prove Heron's Formula. This proof is left for more advanced mathematics courses.

Heron's Formula	
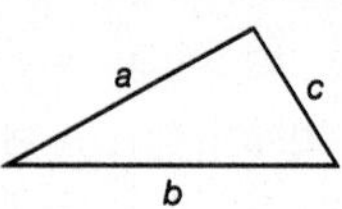	$A = \sqrt{s(s-a)(s-b)(s-c)}$, where $s = \frac{1}{2}(a+b+c)$.

Math Reasoning

Justify Why does it not matter which values are substituted for a, b, and c?

Sample: The difference of s and each side length is found and all three will be multiplied.

Example 3 Using Heron's Formula to Find the Area of a Triangle

Find the area of the triangle. Round to the nearest tenth.

SOLUTION First find s.

$$s = \frac{1}{2}(a+b+c)$$

$$s = \frac{1}{2}(9+11+18) = 19$$

Then use $A = \sqrt{s(s-a)(s-b)(s-c)}$.

$$A = \sqrt{19(19-9)(19-11)(19-18)}$$

$$A = \sqrt{19(10)(8)(1)}$$

$$A = \sqrt{19(10)(8)(1)} = \sqrt{1520} \approx 39$$

The area of the triangle is about 39 square units.

Example 4 Application: Orienteering

Hiker A leaves camp and hikes in a straight path for 3 miles at an angle 30° west of north. Hiker B leaves the same camp and hikes in a fairly straight path for 8 miles at an angle 80° east of north. If Hiker A stays where he is and Hiker B uses her GPS device to walk straight towards him, estimate the time it will take Hiker B to reach Hiker A if Hiker B's average hiking rate is 2.75 miles per hour.

SOLUTION

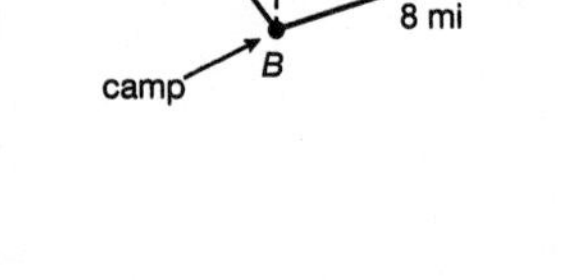

Draw a diagram of the situation.

Use the Law of Cosines to find b.

Then use $t = \frac{d}{r}$ to find the time.

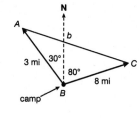

Use $b^2 = a^2 + c^2 - 2ac\cos B$.

$$b^2 = 8^2 + 3^2 - 2(8)(3)\cos 110°$$

$$b^2 \approx 89.42$$

$$b \approx 9.5$$

The distance is about 9.5 miles. Divide the distance by the rate to find the time: $t \approx \frac{9.5}{2.75} \approx 3.5$. It will take Hiker B about 3 hours 30 minutes to reach Hiker A.

548 Saxon Algebra 2

Lesson Practice

a. Find c. Round to the nearest tenth. (Ex 1)

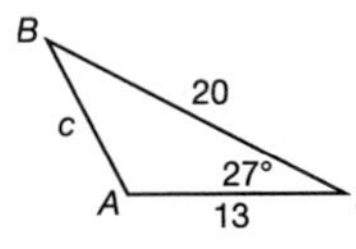

10.3

b. Solve $\triangle DEF$. (Ex 1)

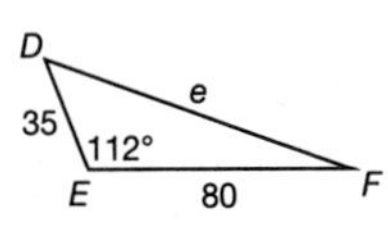

$e \approx 98.6$, $m\angle D = 49°$, $m\angle F = 19°$

c. Find $m\angle C$. Round to the nearest tenth. (Ex 2) 23.2°

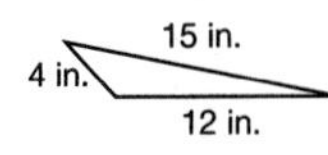

d. Given $\triangle FGH$, $f = 9.2$, $g = 5$, and $h = 10.1$, find $m\angle G$. Round to the nearest tenth. (Ex 2) $m\angle G \approx 29.6°$

e. Find the area of the triangle. Round to the nearest tenth. (Ex 3) About 17.7 sq. in.

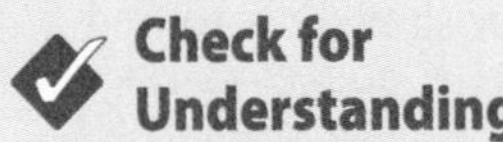

f. A boat leaves a dock and travels in a straight path for 22 miles at an angle 75° west of north. Another boat leaves the same dock and travels in a straight path for 40 miles at an angle 60° east of north. If the second boat puts down her anchor and the first boat travels directly towards the second, estimate the time it will take the first boat to reach the second boat if the first boat travels at a constant rate of 14 miles per hour. (Ex 4) About 4.1 hrs

Practice Distributed and Integrated

*1. (17) **Safety Regulations** A company's safety regulations require the wire rope used to suspend a 100-ton load to have a thickness that is within $\frac{3}{8}$ inch of $1\frac{3}{4}$ inches. Write and solve an absolute value equation to find the minimum safe thickness of rope. $\left|x - 1\frac{3}{4}\right| = \frac{3}{8}$; $1\frac{3}{8}$ inches

Write the exponential equations in logarithmic form.

2. (64) $3^7 = 2187$ $\log_3 2187 = 7$

3. (64) $12^2 = 144$ $\log_{12} 144 = 2$

*4. (74) Find the discriminant of the quadratic equation $7r^2 - 5 = 2r + 9r^2$. Give the number and type of solutions of the equation. −36; two imaginary solutions

Combine into one logarithm.

5. (72) $6 \ln x + 4 \ln y$ $\ln x^6y^4$

6. (72) $\ln 40 + 2\ln\frac{1}{2} + \ln x$ $\ln 10x$

*7. (77) **Generalize** A student said that every time the Law of Cosines is used to find an angle measure, both sides of the equation will be divided by a negative number. Is the student correct or incorrect? Explain. See Additional Answers.

ENGLISH LEARNERS

For problem 1, explain the meaning of the word **regulations.** Say:

"Regulations are rules that are followed to ensure safety or order. For example, sports teams must follow regulations so that the players are less likely to be injured and so that the game is played fairly."

Have students name other ways that regulations are used. Sample: Regulations are used in schools and to control traffic.

Lesson Practice

Problem b

Scaffolding Ask: **"What do you need to find?"** side e and angles D and F **"Why can't you use the Law of Sines?"** Two angles and a side or two sides and an angle opposite one of those sides must be known. **"What should you find first?"** side e **"How will you find it?"** Use the Law of Cosines.

Problem e

Remind students to start by finding the semi-perimeter. $s = 15.5$ in.

Check for Understanding

The questions below help assess the concepts taught in this lesson.

1. **"What happens to the Law of Cosines if one of the angles in the triangle is a right angle?"** If $m\angle C = 90°$, then $\cos C = 0$ and $c^2 = a^2 + b^2 - 2ab \cos C$ becomes $c^2 = a^2 + b^2$, the Pythagorean Theorem.

2. **"Explain how to decide whether to use Heron's formula or an area formula with a sine."** Sample: Use Heron's Formula when three sides are given. Use an area formula with a sine when given two sides and an included angle.

3 Practice

Math Conversations

Discussions to strengthen understanding

Problem 4

Error Alert

Check that students remember to first write the quadratic polynomial in standard form. If necessary, remind them that the discriminant is $b^2 - 4ac$, the quantity under the square root sign in the quadratic formula.

Problem 9

Error Alert

If students choose the wrong answer, have them try again after solving the easier problem

$\sqrt[4]{\sqrt[3]{a}} : \sqrt[4]{\sqrt[3]{a}} = \sqrt[4]{a^{\frac{1}{3}}}$

$= \left(a^{\frac{1}{3}}\right)^{\frac{1}{4}} = a^{\frac{1}{12}}.$

Problem 11

Guide the students by asking them the following questions.

"The first step is to find the lengths of the sides of the triangle. How can you do that?" Use the Distance Formula. Have a volunteer show how to find the length of one of the sides.

Sample: $\sqrt{(-7-1)^2 + (-5-7)^2}$ ≈ 14.4

Problem 13

Error Alert

Students may not simplify completely. Remind them that $i^2 = -1$ when simplifying their product.

Problem 15

Guide the students by asking them the following question.

"What are you given to solve the problem?" slope and one point

"What form of the equation of the line will you begin with?" the point-slope form, $y - y_1 = m(x - x_1)$

Problem 19

Suggest that students use x to stand for each side of the square base. Have them make a sketch of the prism to see that the volume can be found using the equation $V = x \cdot x \cdot (x+8)$.

Extend the Problem

Graph the related function $y = x^3 + 8x^2 - 325$. How does this show the solution to the problem? Sample: The x-intercept is 5, so 5 is the value of x that makes y equal 0. So, 5 is a root of the related polynomial equation and the length of each side of the square base.

---

8. (52) Find the exact values of x and y. $x = 8\sqrt{3}, y = 16$

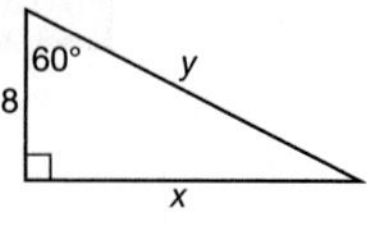

***9.** (75) **Multiple Choice** Which of the following is equivalent to $y = \sqrt[4]{\sqrt[3]{x^3 + 2x^2 + 4}}$? A

A $y = (x^3 + 2x^2 + 4)^{\frac{1}{12}}$ B $y = (x^3 + 2x^2 + 4)^{\frac{3}{4}}$

C $y = (x^3 + 2x^2 + 4)^{\frac{4}{3}}$ D $y = (x^3 + 2x^2 + 4)^{12}$

***10.** (68) **Graphing Calculator** A school is made up of 334 freshmen and 229 sophomores. Four students are chosen at random for a newspaper interview. Use a calculator to find the probability that all four students are freshmen. About 12.3%

***11.** (77) **Coordinate Geometry** Explain how to use Heron's formula to find the area of a triangle whose vertices are at $(-7, -5)$, $(1, 7)$, and $(2, -1)$. Then find the area.

12. (73) **Formulate** Write a formula that estimates an animal population N, when M are marked on the first visit, and m of the n captured on the second visit are marked. $N = \frac{nM}{m}$

13. (62) **Error Analysis** Describe and correct the error in simplifying the expression.

$$(1 + 2i)(4 - i) = 4 - i + 8i - 2i^2 = 2i^2 + 7i + 4$$

***14.** (Inv 4) A message is put into matrix A and encoded using cipher matrix C. Will the same encoded message result from AC as CA? Why? No, because matrix multiplication is not commutative.

15. (26) Find the equation of the line in slope-intercept form that passes through $(5, -3)$ and has a slope of $\frac{2}{9}$. $y = \frac{2}{9}x - \frac{37}{9}$

16. (69) **Multiple Choice** Which expression is *not* equivalent to 1? A

A i^{18} B i^{24} C i^{32} D i^{56}

***17.** (77) A triangle has side lengths of 14 feet, 15 feet, and 21 feet. Use Heron's formula to find the area of the triangle. 104.9 ft²

18. (56) P is a point on the terminal side of θ in standard position. Find the exact value of the six trigonometric functions for θ where $P(-5, 5)$.

19. (66) **Multi-Step** A rectangular prism with a square base has a height that is 8 inches longer than the length of one side of the base. Its volume is 325 cubic inches.

a. Write a polynomial equation in standard form that can be used to find the length of one side of the base. $x^3 + 8x^2 - 325 = 0$

b. List the possible rational roots. $\pm 1, \pm 5, \pm 13, \pm 25\ \pm 65, \pm 325$

c. Find the length of one side of the base. 5 inches

11. Use the distance formula three times to find the lengths of the sides of the triangle. Area ≈ 38

13. $i^2 = -1$, so $-2i^2 = 2$; $4 - i + 8i - 2i^2 = 6 + 7i$

18. $\sin\theta = \frac{\sqrt{2}}{2}$; $\cos\theta = -\frac{\sqrt{2}}{2}$; $\tan\theta = -1$; $\csc\theta = \sqrt{2}$; $\sec\theta = -\sqrt{2}$; $\cot\theta = -1$

INCLUSION

Review the terms acute, obtuse, and right to classify angles by size. Draw three triangles on the board—right, acute, and obtuse. Explain that acute and obtuse triangles are called oblique, a term for any triangle that does not have a right angle.

Start a two-column chart to compare properties and useful theorems about the two types of triangles. Have students suggest trigonometric and area relationships for the chart.

Right Triangle	Oblique Triangle
one 90° angle	no 90° angles
sine ratio	Law of Sines
cosine ratio	Law of Cosines
tangent ratio	Heron's formula
Pythagorean Theorem	$A = \frac{1}{2}bc \sin A$
$a^2 + b^2 = c^2$	$A = \frac{1}{2}ac \sin B$
$A = \frac{1}{2}\text{base} \cdot \text{height}$	$A = \frac{1}{2}ab \sin C$

***20.** **Error Analysis** A student is solving for the roots of $y = (x^2 - 3)(x^2 + 2) - (x^2 - 3)(6x + 5)$, what mistake did he make?
(76)

$$(x^2 - 3)(x^2 + 2) - (x^2 - 3)(6x + 5) = (x^2 - 3)(x^2 + 6x + 7)$$

Use the quadratic formula,

$$x = \frac{-6 \pm \sqrt{6^2 - 4(1)(7)}}{2(1)} = \frac{6 \pm \sqrt{36 - 28}}{2} = 3 \pm \sqrt{2}$$

There are a total of four roots of $f(x)$: $x = \pm\sqrt{3}$ and $3 \pm \sqrt{2}$

20. The student forgot to distribute the negative sign through (6x + 5).

21. Solve using the quadratic formula. Write the solution as complex numbers in standard form. $f(x) = x^2 + 4$ $x = \pm 2i$
(65)

***22.** **Generalize** Suppose that the polynomial functions $f(x)$ and $g(x)$ are each a sum of square terms. Give an example where $f(x) \cdot g(x) = 0$ has exactly two complex solutions. Sample: $f(x) = g(x) = x^2 + 9$
(76)

23. **Verify** Explain how to check that $x = 7$ is a solution of $\sqrt{6 + x} - \sqrt{2x - 1} = 0$ by using a graphing calculator.
(70)

23. Graph $y = \sqrt{6 + x}$ and $y = \sqrt{2x - 1}$ and find their point of intersection. The x-coordinate of the intersection point is the solution. It is 7 for these graphs.

***24.** **Geology** The Richter magnitude M of an earthquake is expressed by $M = \frac{2}{3}\log\left(\frac{E}{10^{11.8}}\right)$, where E is the energy released in ergs. The 1906 San Francisco earthquake, with a magnitude between 7.7 and 8.3, was the worst earthquake disaster in U.S. history. Describe the amount of energy released by that earthquake. approximate values: between $10^{23.35}$, or 2.24×10^{23} ergs and $10^{24.25}$, or 1.78×10^{24} ergs
(72)

25. **Geometry** What is the measure of the base angle θ of the isosceles trapezoid, to the nearest tenth of a degree? 66.4°
(67)

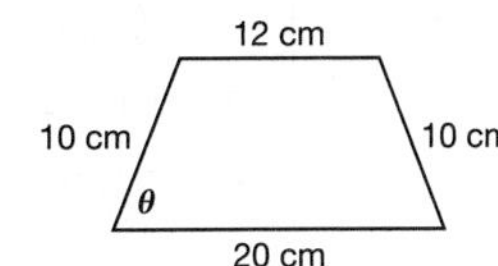

26. **Sports** The area of a tennis court being used for the Special Olympics has an area that can be represented by $x^2 - 24x - 432 + 18x$ square feet. Factor this polynomial by grouping. $(x + 18)(x - 24)$
(61)

27. There are 20 orange marbles and 13 green marbles in a sack. An orange marble is randomly selected and replaced. Then a green marble is randomly selected. Are these events dependent or mutually exclusive? Mutually exclusive (independent)
(60)

28. **Generalize** What will be the value of the discriminant of an equation if the vertex of the related function is located in Quadrant II and the parabola opens upward? Why?
(74)

28. The value will be negative because the parabola never crosses the x-axis, meaning that the function has no x-intercepts and the related equation has no solutions.

29. **Probability** A farmer has four sheepdogs and three beagles. If he randomly chooses a dog to accompany him on a walk, what is the probability of him taking a walk with a sheepdog? $\frac{4}{7}$
(59)

30. Solve: $2x + 5 = x^2$ $1 \pm \sqrt{6}$
(58)

Problem 25

If students need help getting started, put this figure on the board.

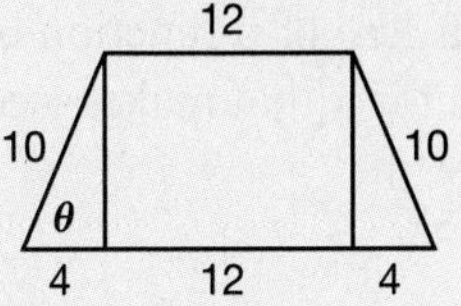

Ask which trigonometric ratio can be used to find θ.
cosine, $\cos\theta = \frac{4}{10}$

Problem 27

Extend the Problem

You reach into the bag and grab three marbles. What is the probability that they are all green? Show your work.
$\frac{13}{33} \cdot \frac{12}{32} \cdot \frac{11}{31} \approx 5.2\%$

CHALLENGE

A parallelogram with sides of 40 cm and 70 cm has a 36° acute angle.

a. What is the measure of each obtuse angle? 144°

b. Find the lengths of the diagonals to the nearest tenth of a centimeter. 44.4 cm, 105.0 cm

LOOKING FORWARD

Using the law of cosines prepares students for

- **Lesson 82** Graphing Sine and Cosine Functions
- **Lesson 86** Translating Sine and Cosine Functions
- **Lesson 90** Graphing the Tangent Function
- **Lesson 103** Graphing Reciprocal Trigonometric Functions

LESSON 78

1 Warm Up

For problem 3, remind students that a *zero* of a function is a value for x that makes y equal 0.

2 New Concepts

In previous lessons, students have learned to solve polynomial equations by factoring, completing the square, and using the quadratic formula. This lesson extends the factoring techniques to special third and fourth degree equations.

Remind students that the *sum* of two squares can't be factored over the real numbers.

Example 1

Students use the difference of two squares to solve quadratic equations.

Additional Example 1

a. Solve $121a^2 - 64 = 0$. $\frac{8}{11}, -\frac{8}{11}$

b. Solve $400y^2 = 36$. $0.3, -0.3$

Error Alert Encourage students to always factor out common constant factors; for example, $400y^2 = 36$ can be simplified to $100y^2 = 9$. Students may make fewer errors with the simpler equivalent equations.

LESSON RESOURCES

Student Edition Practice Workbook 78
Reteaching Master 78
Adaptations Master 78
Challenge and Enrichment Master C78

LESSON 78

Solving Quadratic Equations II

Warm Up

1. (65) **Vocabulary** The expression $\frac{-b \pm \sqrt{b^2 - 4ac}}{2a}$ is the quadratic formula.

2. (65) Solve $5x^2 - 3x + 5 = 0$. $\frac{3 \pm i\sqrt{91}}{10} \approx 0.3 \pm 0.9539i$

3. (35) Find the zero(s) of $y = x^2 + 8x + 16$ graphically. -4

New Concepts

Some quadratic equations can be solved by factoring the *difference of two squares* and then applying the Zero Product Property, which states that if a product is zero, then at least one of its factors is zero.

Difference of Two Squares
$a^2 - b^2 = (a + b)(a - b)$

Math Language

To solve an equation means to find its solutions, or roots.

Example 1 Solving Quadratic Equations

a. Solve $9x^2 - 25 = 0$.

SOLUTION $9x^2 - 25 = 0$

$(3x)^2 - (5)^2 = 0$ Write the left side as $a^2 - b^2$.

$(3x + 5)(3x - 5) = 0$ Factor the difference of squares.

$3x + 5 = 0$ or $3x - 5 = 0$ Zero Product Property

$3x = -5$ $\quad 3x = 5$

$x = -\frac{5}{3}$ or $x = \frac{5}{3}$ Solve each equation.

The roots are $-\frac{5}{3}$ and $\frac{5}{3}$.

Check Substitute each value into the original equation.

$$9x^2 - 25 = 0 \qquad 9x^2 - 25 = 0$$

$$9\left(-\frac{5}{3}\right)^2 - 25 \stackrel{?}{=} 0 \qquad 9\left(\frac{5}{3}\right)^2 - 25 \stackrel{?}{=} 0$$

$$9\left(\frac{25}{9}\right) - 25 \stackrel{?}{=} 0 \qquad 9\left(\frac{25}{9}\right) - 25 \stackrel{?}{=} 0$$

$$25 - 25 \stackrel{?}{=} 0 \qquad 25 - 25 \stackrel{?}{=} 0$$

$$0 = 0 \checkmark \qquad 0 = 0 \checkmark$$

MATH BACKGROUND

The Fundamental Theorem of Algebra states that every polynomial equation with a degree greater than one has at least one complex root. In fact, if the equation has positive degree n, it will have exactly n roots. If the coefficients are real numbers, imaginary roots—if any—will occur in conjugate pairs. If $a + bi$ is a root, so is $a - bi$.

An even more useful theorem is the Factor Theorem. Over the set of complex numbers, $x - r$ is a factor of a polynomial $P(x)$ if and only if r is a root of $P(x) = 0$. If $P(x)$ can be factored, then $P(x) = 0$ can be solved.

Except in special cases such as the difference of squares in this lesson, polynomial equations of degree greater than 2 can be difficult to solve. Approximate solutions can be obtained by graphing.

b. Solve $7x^2 = 63$.

SOLUTION $7x^2 = 63$

$7x^2 - 63 = 0$ Subtract 63 from both sides.

$7(x^2 - 9) = 0$ Factor: The GCF is 7.

$7(x + 3)(x - 3) = 0$ Factor the difference of squares.

$x + 3 = 0$ or $x - 3 = 0$ Zero Product Property

$x = -3$ or $x = 3$ Solve each equation.

The roots are –3 and 3.

Example 2 Solving a Cubic Equation with a Quadratic Factor

Solve $10x^3 - 10x = 0$.

SOLUTION

$10x^3 - 10x = 0$ Factor: The GCF is 10x.

$10x(x^2 - 1) = 0$ Factor the difference of squares.

$10x(x + 1)(x - 1) = 0$ Zero Product Property

$10x = 0$ or $x + 1 = 0$ or $x - 1 = 0$ Solve each equation.

$x = 0$ or $x = -1$ or $x = 1$

The roots are 0, −1, and 1.

Hint

The Zero Product Property applies to any number of factors. If $abc = 0$, then $a = 0$ or $b = 0$ or $c = 0$.

Check Substitute each value into the original equation.

$10x^3 - 10x = 0$	$10x^3 - 10x = 0$	$10x^3 - 10x = 0$
$10(0)^3 - 10(0) \stackrel{?}{=} 0$	$10(-1)^3 - 10(-1) \stackrel{?}{=} 0$	$10(1)^3 - 10(1) \stackrel{?}{=} 0$
$10(0) - 0 \stackrel{?}{=} 0$	$10(-1) + 10 \stackrel{?}{=} 0$	$10(1) - 10 \stackrel{?}{=} 0$
$0 - 0 \stackrel{?}{=} 0$	$-10 + 10 \stackrel{?}{=} 0$	$10 - 10 \stackrel{?}{=} 0$
$0 = 0$ ✓	$0 = 0$ ✓	$0 = 0$ ✓

Example 3 Solving a Quartic Equation

a. Solve $x^4 - 16 = 0$.

SOLUTION $x^4 - 16 = 0$

$(x^2)^2 - (4)^2 = 0$ Write the left side as $a^2 - b^2$.

$(x^2 + 4)(x^2 - 4) = 0$ Factor the difference of squares.

$(x^2 + 4)(x + 2)(x - 2) = 0$ Factor the difference of squares again.

$x^2 + 4 = 0$ or $x + 2 = 0$ or $x - 2 = 0$ Zero Product Property

$x^2 = -4$

$x = \pm\sqrt{-4}$

$x = \pm 2i$ or $x = -2$ or $x = 2$ Solve each equation.

The complex roots are $2i$ and $-2i$.

The real roots are −2 and 2.

TEACHER TIP

Emphasize the importance of setting the polynomial equal to 0. Neither the Factor Theorem nor the Zero Product Property can be applied unless the polynomial equation is in the form $P(x) = 0$.

Example 2

Students solve a cubic equation that has a quadratic factor that is a difference of two squares.

Additional Example 2

Solve $4x^3 = 49x$. 0, 3.5, −3.5

Extend the Example

Have students predict the shape of the graph of the related function, $y = 10x^3 - 10x$, and then graph it to check their predictions.

Example 3

Students solve a quartic equation that is a difference of two squares, then verify the real roots by graphing the related function.

Additional Example 3

a. Solve $x^4 = 625$. 5, −5, $5i$, $-5i$

b. Verify the real roots of $x^4 = 625$ graphically. The x-intercepts of the related function $f(x) = x^4 - 625$ are −5 and 5.

ALTERNATE METHOD FOR EXAMPLE 1

Write the general form of a difference of squares polynomial equation $a^2x^2 - b^2 = 0$. Ask:

"Why is this the difference of two squares?" First term is square of ax; second term is square of b.

Have students solve the equation for x.
$x = \pm\sqrt{\frac{b^2}{a^2}} = \pm\frac{|b|}{|a|}$

"Why are there two solutions to this equation?" A positive real number has two square roots, one positive and one negative.

Show students how to use this strategy to solve the polynomial equation $9x^2 - 25 = 0$.

$$9x^2 - 25 = 0$$
$$3^2x^2 - 5^2 = 0$$
$$3^2x^2 = 5^2$$
$$x^2 = \frac{5^2}{3^2}$$
$$x = \pm\frac{5}{3}$$

The solutions of $9x^2 - 25 = 0$ are $\frac{5}{3}$ and $-\frac{5}{3}$.

Example 4

Students solve a quadratic equation that is the difference of two perfect square trinomials.

Additional Example 4

Solve $(25x^2 - 20x + 4) - (16x^2 + 8x + 1) = 0$. $\frac{1}{9}, 3$

Example 5

Students use the difference of squares to solve a quadratic applications problem. Point out using the difference of squares makes sense because 4.9 and 40 are both one-tenth of the perfect squares 49 and 400.

Extend the Example

How long does it take for the object to hit the ground if it is dropped from 19.6 m? 2 seconds

Additional Example 5

A piece of cardboard is 8 in. longer than it is wide. An open rectangular box is made by cutting out a 2-in. square from each corner and turning up the flaps. If the volume of the box is 168 in³, find the dimensions of the original piece of cardboard. 10 in., 18 in.

b. Verify the real roots of $x^4 - 16 = 0$ graphically.

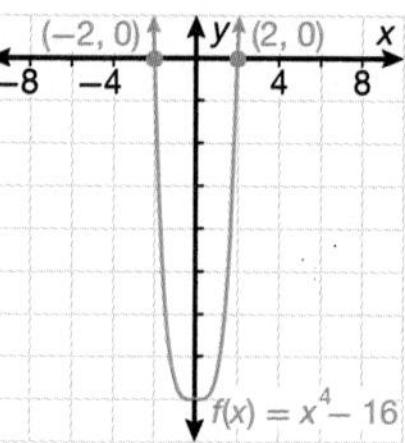

SOLUTION Graph the related function $f(x) = x^4 - 16$. The x-intercepts are -2 and 2. They are the real roots of the equation $x^4 - 16 = 0$.

Example 4 Solving a Quadratic Equation Using Perfect Squares

Solve $(9x^2 - 12x + 4) - (x^2 + 10x + 25) = 0$.

SOLUTION

$(9x^2 - 12x + 4) - (x^2 + 10x + 25) = 0$ The trinomials are perfect squares.

$(3x - 2)^2 - (x + 5)^2 = 0$ Write each trinomial as the square of a binomial. Then factor the difference of squares.

$[(3x - 2) + (x + 5)][(3x - 2) - (x + 5)] = 0$

$[4x + 3][2x - 7] = 0$ Simplify inside the brackets.

$4x + 3 = 0$ or $2x - 7 = 0$ Zero Product Property

$x = -\frac{3}{4}$ or $x = \frac{7}{2}$ Solve each equation.

The roots are $-\frac{3}{4}$ and $\frac{7}{2}$.

Example 5 Application: Vertical Motion

The height of a free-falling object (neglecting air resistance) is given by the function $h(t) = -4.9t^2 + v_0t + h_0$, where h_0 is the initial height in meters, v_0 is the initial velocity in meters per second, and $h(t)$ is the height in meters at time t seconds. How long does it take for an object to hit the ground after it is dropped from a height of 40 meters?

Hint

If an object is dropped, its initial velocity is zero. If projected down, its initial velocity is negative. If projected up, its initial velocity is positive.

SOLUTION

Understand When the object hits the ground, $h(t) = 0$.

Plan Write and solve an equation that is related to the height function.

Solve $h(t) = -4.9t^2 + v_0t + h_0$ Write the height function.

$0 = -4.9t^2 + 0t + 40$ Substitute the known values.

$0 = -4.9t^2 + 40$ Simplify.

$0 = 4.9t^2 - 40$ Multiply by −1 to get a positive leading coefficient.

$0 = 49t^2 - 400$ Multiply by 10 to get the difference of two squares.

Math Reasoning

Write Explain why only one side of the equation $0 = -4.9t^2 + 40$ changes when you multiply both sides by −1.

Multiplying 0 by any number results in 0.

ENGLISH LEARNERS

Write these terms on the board:

polynomial equation

polynomial function

Start with $(x - 2)(x + 2)$. Have students write the expression as a polynomial in standard form by multiplying the binomial factors together. $x^2 - 4$

Ask what values for x make the polynomial equal 0. 2, −2

Next, write the **polynomial equation** $(x - 2)(x + 2) = 0$. Show that it is equivalent to $x^2 - 4 = 0$. The values 2 and −2 are solutions. They are also called roots.

Explain that the following are all ways to show a **polynomial function**.

$y = (x - 2)(x + 2)$ $f(x) = (x - 2)(x + 2)$

$y = x^2 - 4$ $f(x) = x^2 - 4$

The values 2 and −2 are zeros of this function. They are the values for x that make the function equal 0.

$$0 = (7t + 20)(7t - 20)$$ Factor the difference of squares.

$$7t + 20 = 0 \text{ or } 7t - 20 = 0$$ Apply the Zero Product Property.

$$t = -\frac{20}{7} \text{ or } t = \frac{20}{7}$$ Solve each equation. Use the positive solution.

It takes the object $\frac{20}{7} \approx 2.86$ seconds to hit the ground.

Check $-4.9\left(\frac{20}{7}\right)^2 + 40 = 0$, so the height is 0 when $t = \frac{20}{7}$.

Lesson Practice

Solve.

a. (Ex 1) $100x^2 - 1 = 0$ $-\frac{1}{10}$ and $\frac{1}{10}$ **b.** (Ex 1) $6x^2 = 150$ -5 and 5

c. (Ex 2) $18x^3 - 32x = 0$ $-\frac{4}{3}$ and $\frac{4}{3}$ and 0 **d.** (Ex 3) $16x^4 - 1 = 0$ $-\frac{1}{2}i, \frac{1}{2}i, -\frac{1}{2}, \frac{1}{2}$

e. 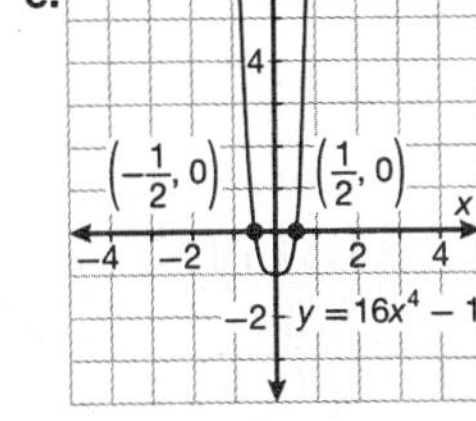

e. (Ex 3) Verify the real roots of $16x^4 - 1 = 0$ graphically.

f. (Ex 4) Solve $(x^2 + 16x + 64) - (36x^2 - 12x + 1) = 0$. -1 and $\frac{9}{5}$

g. (Ex 5) The height of a free-falling object (neglecting air resistance) is given by the function $h(t) = -4.9t^2 + v_0t + h_0$, where h_0 is the initial height in meters, v_0 is the initial velocity in meters per second, and $h(t)$ is the height in meters at time t seconds. How long does it take for an object to hit the ground after it is dropped from a height of 62.5 meters? $\frac{25}{7} \approx 3.57$ seconds

Practice Distributed and Integrated

***1.** (77) In $\triangle LMN$, $MN = 13$, $LN = 3$, and the $m\angle N = 36°$. Find LM. about 10.7

2. (56) Given $\theta = -164°$, find a positive and negative coterminal angle. Possible answer: 196°, – 524°

Solve.

3. (66) $4x(2x^2 + 9x - 45) = 0$ $x = -7.5, 0, 3$

4. (66) $2x(x^2 - 4x + 6) = 0$ $x = 0, 2 \pm i\sqrt{2}$

***5.** (78) $2x^2 + 9x + 4 = 0$ $x = -0.5, -4$

***6.** (78) $3x^3 - 12x = 0$ $x = -2, 0, 2$

7. (52) **Multiple Choice** In the diagram, triangle ABC is dilated to get triangle LMN. What is the scale factor? **C**

A $\sqrt{5}$ **B** $2\sqrt{5}$ **C** 7 **D** 14

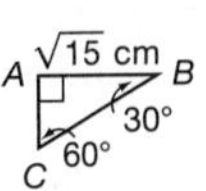

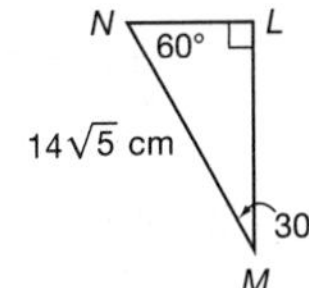

8. (65) **Multi-Step a.** Write the equation $\frac{3}{4}x^2 + \frac{3}{8}x + 1 = 0$ without fractions. $6x^2 + 3x + 8 = 0$

b. Find the roots of the equation. $-\frac{1}{4} + \frac{\sqrt{183}}{12}i, -\frac{1}{4} - \frac{\sqrt{183}}{12}i$

***9.** (78) **Analyze** Describe how to solve the equation $2.5x^2 - 0.4 = 0$ by factoring the difference of two squares. Possible answer: Multiply both sides by 10 to get $25x^2 - 4 = 0$, then factor and solve.

INCLUSION

Review the Zero Product Property starting with the equation $8x = 0$. **"What number makes this equation true?"** $x = 0$ Replace the x with y to get $xy = 0$. **"The solution to this equation is a set of ordered pairs. We can show them on a graph."** Graph the lines for $y = \frac{0}{x}$ and $x = \frac{0}{y}$. **"Either x or y must equal zero to make $xy = 0$ true. What are the solutions to $xy = 0$?"** $x = 0$, $y = 0$, or both equal zero

Continue the discussion using examples that increase gradually in difficulty; for example:

$x(y - 2) = 0$ $x = 0$ or $y = 2$
$x(y + 2) = 0$ $x = 0$ or $y = -2$
$(x - 1)(y + 2) = 0$ $x = 1$ or $y = -2$
$(x - 2)(y + 2) = 0$ $x = 2$ or $y = -2$
$(x - 2)(x + 2) = 0$ $x = 2$ or $x = -2$

Point out that the left side of the final equation equals the difference of two squares. If necessary, have students do the multiplication.

Lesson Practice

Problem b

Students should begin by setting the polynomial equal to 0.

Problem f

Scaffolding Ask students to explain how they know the two expressions are perfect squares.

Check for Understanding

The questions below help assess the concepts taught in this lesson.

"How can you apply the Zero Product Property to the equation $(2x - 3)(2x + 3) = 0$?" $2x + 3 = 0$ or $2x - 3 = 0$

"Is the equation equivalent to $4x^2 - 9 = 0$? Explain." Yes; Equivalent equations have the same solution set.

3 Practice

Math Conversations

Discussions to strengthen understanding

Problem 4

Extend the Problem

Use the discriminant to explain why this equation has only one real root. The discriminant $4^2 - 4 \cdot 1 \cdot 6$ is negative.

Problem 7

Guide the students by asking them the following questions.

"Does the diagram show corresponding sides?" No. There is one hypotenuse and one leg. **"How can you find side NL?"** Take half of the hypotenuse.

"How can you find side ML?" Use the Pythagorean Theorem or multilpy NL by $\sqrt{3}$.

Problem 10

Error Alert

If students choose the wrong answer, point out how far apart the answer choices are. Have them sketch the triangle and use any reasonable number, say 20 m, as a height. The area with base 48 m is 480 m², which eliminates choices A, C, and D.

Problem 20

Extend the Problem

If you are 5 ft. 3 in. tall and want to see for 10 miles, how far above sea level do you need to stand? Give your answer in feet and inches to the nearest inch.
62 ft 10 in.

*10. (77) **Multiple Choice** What is the area of $\triangle ABC$ if $a = 34$ m, $b = 25$ m, and $c = 48$ m? **B**
A about 54 m² B about 404 m² C about 6147 m² D about 163,529 m²

*11. (54) **Graphing Calculator** Describe the feasible region for the inequalities. $0 \le x \le 20$, $y \ge 10$, $6y + 8x \ge 105$. Unbounded region with vertices: (5.625, 10), (0, 17.5), (20, 10)

12. (57) **Error Analysis** To graph the function $y = 3^x + 2$, Eric started out by graphing $y = 3^x$ (the dashed curve). He then translated it 2 units to the right. Explain Eric's error, and write an equation for the function he graphed.
He translated 2 units right instead of 2 units up. So, he graphed $y = 3^{x-2}$

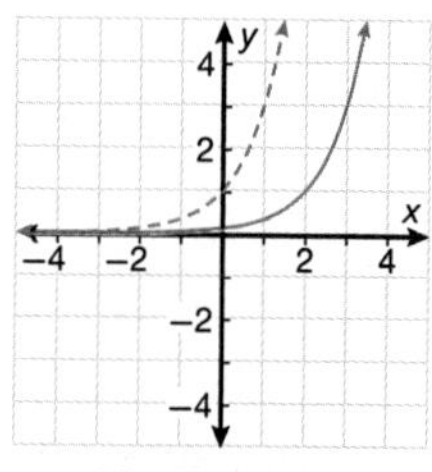

13. (59) **Multi-Step** Use $\left(5^{\frac{1}{2}} \cdot 5^{\frac{2}{7}}\right)^{\frac{2}{11}}$

a. Which property of rational exponents should be applied first to simplify the expression? Explain.

b. Which property of rational exponents should be applied next? Power of a Power Property

c. Simplify the expression. $\sqrt[7]{5}$

13a. Product of Powers Property; By the order of operations you must first perform operations within any grouping symbols.

14. (60) **Data Analysis** The following table summarizes data obtained by the U.S. Census Bureau on computers in households. If one of the surveyed members of the household is randomly selected, find the probability that the member of the household is male or has a computer. Round to the ten thousandths place. 0.8002

Gender of Household Member

Computer	Male	Female
Yes	39,475	30,461
No	20,583	22,607

Use synthetic division to divide.

15. (51) $4x^2 + 7x + 10$ by $x + 2$ $4x - 1 + \frac{12}{x + 2}$

16. (51) $2x^2 - 6x - 12$ by $x - 5$ $2x + 4 + \frac{8}{x - 5}$

17. (28) Identify any excluded values for $\frac{2x - 10}{10 - 2x}$. Then simplify the expression. 5; −1

18. (62) **Analyze** Classify the number $a + bi$ when both a and b are equal to 0. Explain.
The number is 0 + 0, which is 0, a real number.

19. (67) **Write** Describe how to use the sine function to define the inverse sine function.

19. Sample: Define the inverse sine function as $\text{Sin}^{-1} a = \theta$, where $\sin \theta = a$.

20. (70) **Physical Science** The number of miles m a person can see on a clear day is approximated by $m = 1.2116\sqrt{h}$, where h is the person's height above sea level. Suppose a person standing on a pier can see for 6 miles. To the nearest tenth of a foot, what is their height above sea level? About 24.5 feet

21. (69) **Predict** If every complex number with an absolute value of $\sqrt{58}$ is graphed, what geometric figure is formed and why? A circle, because every point is the same distance from a given point, the origin.

 **22.** **Geometry** The angle measures of five different triangles are given below.
(68)

30°, 60°, 90° 45°, 45°, 90° 60°, 60°, 60° 20°, 20°, 140° 50°, 60°, 70°

a. If three triangles are chosen at random, without replacement, what is the probability that the first two triangles are right triangles and the last triangle is obtuse? $\frac{1}{30} \approx 3.3\%$

b. If three triangles are chosen at random, without replacement, what is the probability that all three are right triangles? 0%

c. If three triangles are chosen at random, without replacement, what is the probability that all three are isosceles triangles? $\frac{1}{10} = 10\%$

23. **Error Analysis** Alex and Robert each tried to simplify the expression $\frac{4+\sqrt{3}}{5-\sqrt{3}}$. Who is correct? Explain your reasoning.
(44)

Robert

$$\frac{4+\sqrt{3}}{5-\sqrt{3}} = \frac{4+\sqrt{3}}{5-\sqrt{3}} \cdot \frac{4-\sqrt{3}}{4-\sqrt{3}} = \frac{4^2-(\sqrt{3})^2}{20-5\sqrt{3}-4\sqrt{3}+3} = \frac{13}{23-9\sqrt{3}}$$

Alex

$$\frac{4+\sqrt{3}}{5-\sqrt{3}} = \frac{4+\sqrt{3}}{5-\sqrt{3}} \cdot \frac{5+\sqrt{3}}{5+\sqrt{3}} = \frac{4(5)+4\sqrt{3}+5\sqrt{3}+(\sqrt{3})(\sqrt{3})}{5^2-(\sqrt{3})^2} = \frac{23+9\sqrt{3}}{22}$$

23. Alex is correct. To simplify, you must multiply both numerator and denominator by the conjugate of the denominator. Robert multiplied by the conjugate of the numerator instead.

***24.** **Gravity on the Moon** The height of a free-falling object on the moon (neglecting air resistance) is given by the function $h(t) = -0.8t^2 + v_0t + h_0$, where h_0 is the initial height in meters, v_0 is the initial velocity in meters per second, and $h(t)$ is the height in meters at time t seconds. How long does it take for an object to hit the surface of the moon after it is dropped from a height of 20 meters? (Hint: Multiply both sides of the quadratic equation by the number that makes the coefficient of the quadratic term a perfect square.) 5 seconds
(78)

***25.** A triangle has side lengths of 12 feet, 16 feet, and 18 feet. Use Heron's formula to find the area of the triangle. about 94.1 ft^2
(77)

26. Maximize $P = 2x + 5y$ for the constraints $x \geq 0$, $y \geq 0$, $y \leq 1.5x + 1$, $y \leq -x + 6$. (2, 4)
(54)

***27.** **Generalize** Suppose that polynomial functions $f(x)$ and $g(x)$ are each a difference of square terms. What can you say about the roots of $f(x) \cdot g(x)$?
(76)
Assuming that $f(x) \neq g(x)$, then there are at least four roots to the polynomial function.

***28.** **Fencing** A homeowner has 90 feet of fencing material to enclose a rectangular dog pen. He wants the dog to have 600 square feet of space inside the pen. The equation $w(20 - w) = 600$ gives the width of a pen that meets these requirements. Use the discriminant to explain whether or not these requirements can be met.
(74)

$w(20 - w) = 600 \rightarrow 20w - w^2 = 600 \rightarrow -w^2 + 20w - 600 = 0$
$b^2 - 4ac = (20)^2 - 4(-1)(-600) = 400 - 2400 = -2000$
The requirements cannot be met; since the discriminant is negative, the roots will be imaginary.

Use the change of base formula to evaluate the logarithm.

29. $\log_7 19$ about 1.513
(72)

30. $\log_6 \frac{24}{5}$ about 0.875
(72)

Problem 23

Remind students that to simplify the expression they must rationalize the denominator.
Ask: **"How can you tell that Robert's answer is incorrect?"**
The denominator is not a rational number. Point out that students should still check the steps in Alex's answer—just in case *both* answers are wrong.

Problem 25

You may need to write Heron's formula on the board.

$$A = \sqrt{s(s-a)(s-b)(s-c)}$$

where s is half the perimeter of the triangle.

Problem 28

Extend the Problem

What is the area of the largest rectangular dog pen that can be made with 90 ft of fence if the owner uses the side of the garage as one side of the pen? 1012.5 ft^2

 **CHALLENGE**

Explain how this diagram shows the difference of two squares.

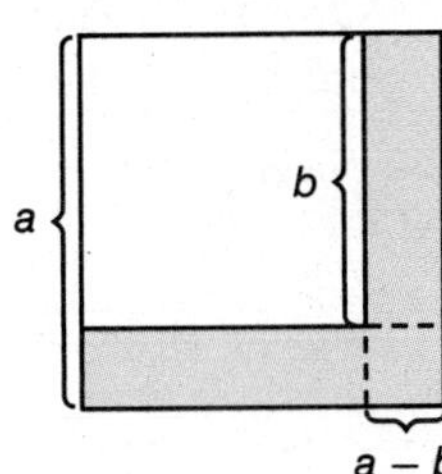

Area of entire square is a^2; white square is b^2. Difference is area of gray regions. It is $2 \cdot b(a - b) + (a - b)^2$, which equals $a^2 - b^2$.

LOOKING FORWARD 

Solving quadratic equations prepares students for

- **Lesson 83** Writing Quadratic Equations from Roots
- **Lesson 89** Solving Quadratic Inequalities

LESSON 79

1 Warm Up

For problem 3, allow students to use a graphing calculator.

2 New Concepts

Students graph, evaluate, and write rules for piecewise functions.

Example 1

Students graph piecewise functions.

Additional Example 1

The table shows the prices for a ski lift. Graph the piecewise function showing the ski lift price for someone x years of age.

Ski Area Ticket Prices	
Age	**Price**
12 and under	$39
between 12 and 60	$79
60 and over	$69

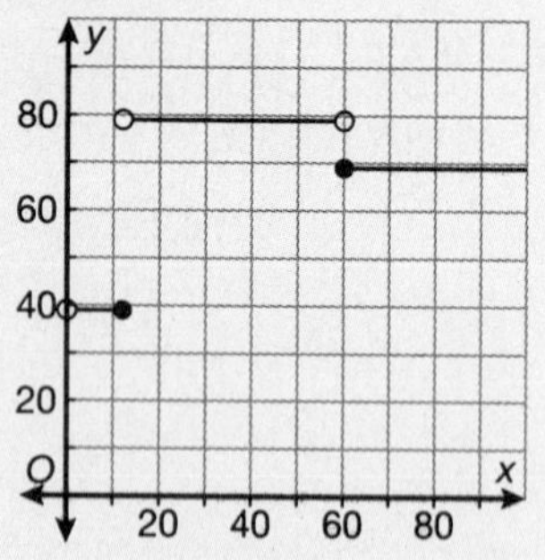

LESSON RESOURCES

Student Edition Practice Workbook 79
Reteaching Master 79
Adaptations Master 79
Challenge and Enrichment Master C79

LESSON 79

Understanding Piecewise Functions

Warm Up

1. **Vocabulary** According to the vertical line test, a function can have only one point that intersects any vertical line. (4)

2. What are the domain and range for $y = -3x + 2$? (34)

2. Domain and range: all real numbers.

3. For what values of the domain is $f(x) > 0$? $-3 < x < -1$ (27)

$f(x) = -(x + 2)^2 + 1$

4. Write the equation of the line with slope 3 that passes through the point (50, 200) in slope intercept form. $y = 3x + 50$ (26)

New Concepts

A **piecewise function** is a function comprised of at least two functions. Each function defines a different part of the function's domain.

Example 1 Graphing a Piecewise Function

The information in the table shows the admission prices to a local museum. Graph the piecewise function showing the museum admission cost for someone x years of age.

Museum Admission Prices	
Age	**Price**
under 12	$5
12–50	$12
over 50	$10

SOLUTION The domain of the function is divided into three different intervals:

Under age 12: $x < 12$

Ages 12 to 50: $12 \leq x \leq 50$

Over age 50: $x > 50$

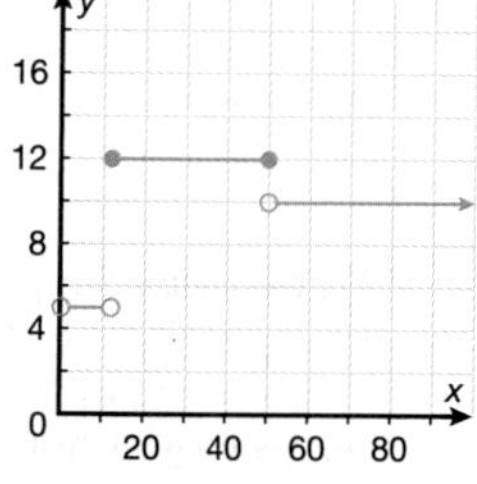

For the interval $x < 12$, the range is 5. For the interval $12 \leq x \leq 50$, the range is 12. For the interval $x > 50$, the range is 10. The graph of the function is a step function.

Math Language

The **step function** gets its name from its graph which sometimes resembles steps on a staircase.

A **step function** is a piecewise function that is constant for each interval in its domain. The graph of the museum admission prices is a step function. Notice that the step function passes the vertical line test. Piecewise functions have all the attributes of a function.

To evaluate a function for a given value of x, find the domain interval to which x belongs. Then find the corresponding range value.

558 Saxon Algebra 2

MATH BACKGROUND

Piecewise functions are found in many real world situations. Several functions with different domains are used to describe the situation depending on the constraints of the input values. Shipping businesses, services that charge by increments of time, and vendors that sell items in bulk are all examples of situations where the cost function is generated by multiple functions.

Example 2 Evaluating a Piecewise Function

Evaluate the piecewise function for $x = 0$ and $x = 5$.

$$f(x) = \begin{cases} 12, & \text{if } x < 0 \\ -5, & \text{if } 0 \le x < 5 \\ 2, & \text{if } x \ge 5 \end{cases}$$

SOLUTION When $x = 0, f(x) = -5$, so $f(0) = -5$.

When $x = 5, f(x) = 2$, so $f(5) = 2$.

Example 3 Writing a Piecewise Function

Write a piecewise function rule for the graph.

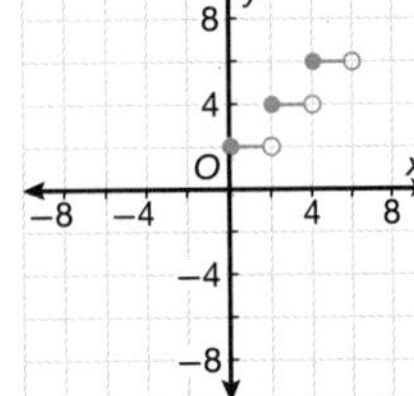

SOLUTION The function is a step function comprised of three linear pieces that are represented by line segments on the graph. For $0 \le x < 2$, the graph is the line segment $y = 2$. For $2 \le x < 4$, the graph is the line segment $y = 4$. For $4 \le x < 6$, the graph is the line segment $y = 6$. The function rule is:

$$f(x) = \begin{cases} 2, & \text{if } 0 \le x < 2 \\ 4, & \text{if } 2 \le x < 4 \\ 6, & \text{if } 4 \le x < 6 \end{cases}$$

Reading Math

Open circles are used when the symbols < or > are in the domain. Closed circles are used for ≤ and ≥.

Example 4 Graphing a Piecewise Function

Graph the function $f(x) = \begin{cases} 2x + 1, & \text{if } x < -1 \\ -3x, & \text{if } -1 \le x < 2. \\ x^2 - 10, & \text{if } x \ge 2 \end{cases}$

SOLUTION The function is comprised of two linear pieces and a quadratic piece. Use a table of values to graph each piece of the function.

x	$f(x) = 2x + 1$	$f(x) = -3x$	$f(x) = x^2 - 10$
−2	−3		
−1	−1	3	
0		0	
2		−6	−6
3			−1
4			6
5			15

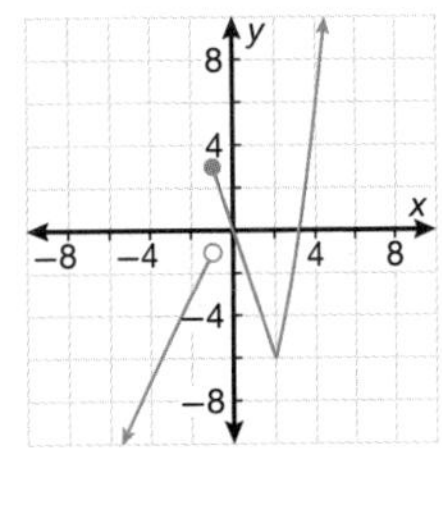

Plot the points (−2, −3) and (−1, −1) and draw a ray whose endpoint is (−1, −1). Plot the points (−1, 3), (0, 0), and (2, −6) and draw a line segment with endpoints (−1, 3) and (2, −6). Plot the points (2, −6), (3, −1), (4, 6), and (5, 15) and draw a curve connecting the points. Draw an open circle at (−1, −1) and a closed circle at (−1, 3). No circle is needed at (2, −6) because the function is continuous at that point.

Caution

Do not choose x-values which are not included in the domain of the function.

Example 2

Error Alert Students may evaluate the wrong 'piece' of the function for the x-value. Have the students circle the correct piece before evaluating.

Additional Example 2

Evaluate the piecewise function for $x = -2$ and $x = 3$.

$$f(x) = \begin{cases} -2, & \text{if } x < -2 \\ 0, & \text{if } -2 \le x \le 2 \\ 2, & \text{if } x > 2 \end{cases}$$

$f(-2) = 0$ and $f(3) = 2$.

Example 3

Tell students that they should have as many equations as there are 'pieces' to the function.

Additional Example 3

Write a piecewise function rule for the graph shown.

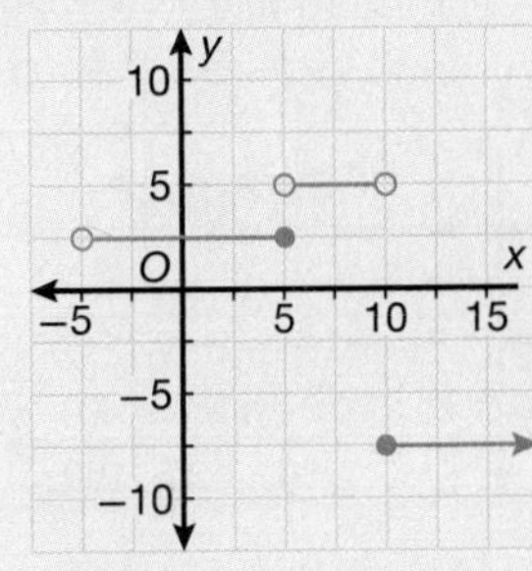

$$f(x) = \begin{cases} 2.5, & \text{if } -5 < x \le 5 \\ 5, & \text{if } 5 < x < 10 \\ -7.5, & \text{if } x \ge 10 \end{cases}$$

Example 4

Remind students that each equation only occurs for certain x-values.

Additional Example 4

Graph the function

$$f(x) = \begin{cases} x, & \text{if } x \le 0 \\ x^2, & \text{if } 0 < x < 3. \\ 3x, & \text{if } x \ge 3 \end{cases}$$

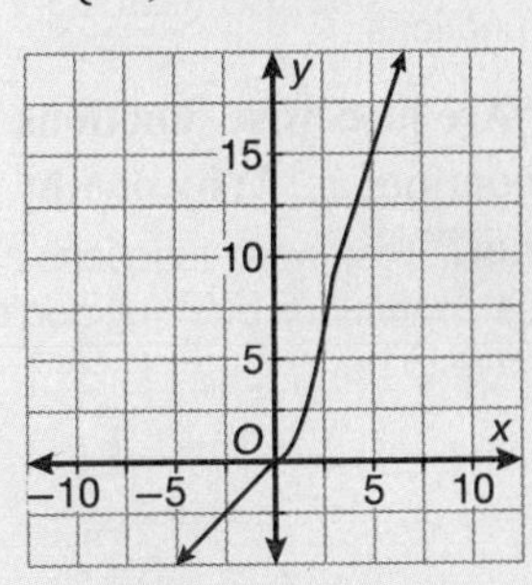

ENGLISH LEARNERS

Use a drawing of steps or stairs when defining **step functions** for students.

Explain that these functions are constant (like the top of a step) for each interval in their domains.

Have students write the equation for each "piece" of a step function above the correct section of its graph. This will allow students to connect the steps of the equation to its graph.

INCLUSION

Students can use their graphing calculators in this section. If necessary, they can graph each piece of the piecewise function for all x, and then use the part of each piece for which the domain is defined.

Example 5

Situations with changing rates are often piecewise functions.

Additional Example 5

The shipping rates for a catalog store for up to $200 of merchandise are shown in the table. Write and graph a piecewise function for the shipping cost of a purchase with a cost of x dollars.

Shipping Rates for Purchases	
Purchase Price	**Shipping Rate**
$25 and under	$3.95
$25.01 to $50	$5.95
$50.01 to $100	$7.95
$100.01 to $150	$9.95
$150.01 to $200	$11.95

$$f(x) = \begin{cases} 3.95, & \text{if } 0 < x \le 25 \\ 5.95, & \text{if } 25.01 \le x \le 50 \\ 7.95, & \text{if } 50.01 \le x \le 100 \\ 9.95, & \text{if } 100.01 \le x \le 150 \\ 11.95, & \text{if } 150.01 \le x \le 200 \end{cases}$$

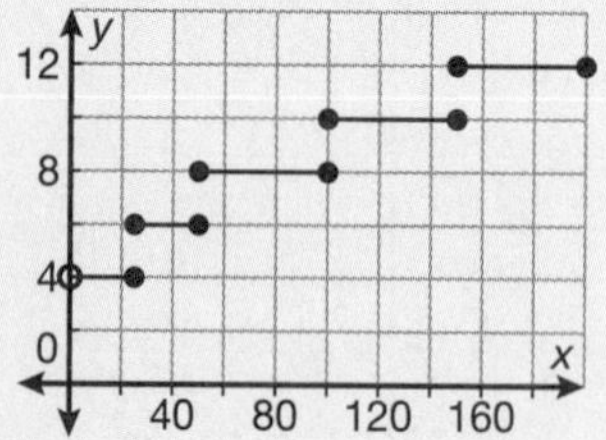

Lesson Practice

Problem c

Scaffolding As students determine the rule for each section, they should write the domain restrictions immediately to avoid confusion.

Check for Understanding

The questions below help assess the concepts taught in this lesson.

1. **"What comprises a piecewise function?"** two or more functions
2. **"Are piecewise functions continuous? Why or why not?"** Piecewise functions can be continuous but they don't have to be.

Example 5 Application: Postal Service Rates

The United States Postal Service insurance rates for up to $500 of coverage are shown in the table. Write and graph a piecewise function for the cost of x dollars of insurance coverage.

USPS Insurance Rates for Domestic Mail	
Fee	**Insurance Coverage**
$1.65	up to $50
$2.05	$50.01 to $100
$2.45	$100.01 to $200
$4.60	$200.01 to $300
$5.50	$300.01 to $400
$6.40	$400.01 to $500

SOLUTION The information in the table represents a step function. The function rule is:

$$f(x) = \begin{cases} 1.65, & \text{if } x \le 50 \\ 2.05, & \text{if } 50 < x \le 100 \\ 2.45, & \text{if } 100 < x \le 200 \\ 4.60, & \text{if } 200 < x \le 300 \\ 5.50, & \text{if } 300 < x \le 400 \\ 6.40, & \text{if } 400 < x \le 500 \end{cases}$$

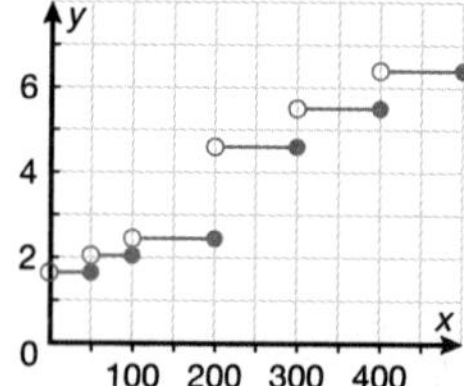

Lesson Practice

a. (Ex 1) The information in the table shows the admission prices to an amusement park. Graph the piecewise function showing the admission cost for someone x years of age. See Additional Answers.

Amusement Park Admission Prices	
Age	**Price**
6 and under	$10
7–18	$20
over 18	$25

b. (Ex 2) Evaluate $f(x) = \begin{cases} 5x - 2, & \text{if } x < -3 \\ 2x + 2, & \text{if } -3 \le x < 10 \\ x^2 + 4, & \text{if } x \ge 10 \end{cases}$ for $x = -3$ and $x = 10$. $f(-3) = -4$; $f(10) = 104$

c. (Ex 3) Write a piecewise function rule for the graph. $f(x) = \begin{cases} -1, & \text{if } x < 0 \\ 4, & \text{if } x \ge 0 \end{cases}$

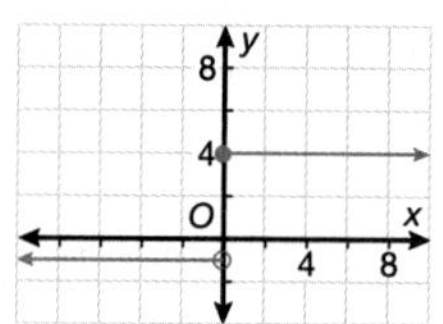

d. (Ex 4) Graph the piecewise function $f(x) = \begin{cases} x + 1, & \text{if } x \le 1 \\ 1, & \text{if } 1 < x < 2 \\ 4, & \text{if } x \ge 2 \end{cases}$ See Additional Answers.

e. (Ex 5) A plumber charges $50 per hour for the first 3 hours and $25 per hour after that. Write and graph a piecewise function for the cost of x hours of service. See Additional Answers.

ALTERNATE METHOD FOR LESSON PRACTICE b

Solutions to inequalities can often be found by graphing. In this case, the last piece of the function will have a large value for y for the given domain value. This third piece can be graphed on a graphing calculator. Use the function tool on the calculator to find the y-value for $x = 10$.

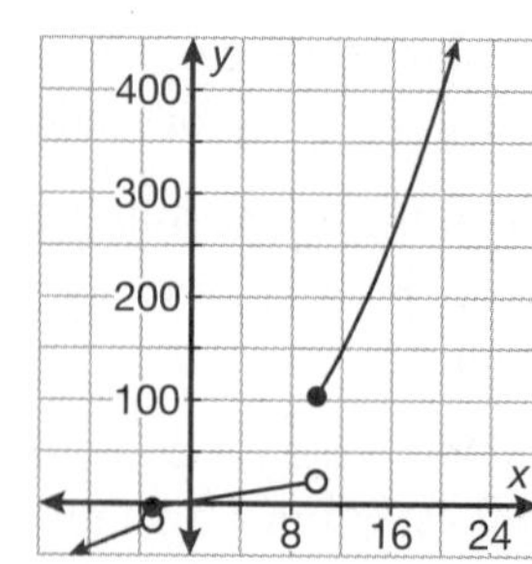

Students can graph the piecewise function, then test the values of $f(x)$ for the given values of x.

Practice Distributed and Integrated

1. (55) **Probability** A bag contains 3 white marbles and 7 purple marbles. What is the probability of picking a white marble, keeping it out of the bag, and then picking a purple marble? $\frac{21}{90} \approx .23$

Solve.

2. (70) $\sqrt[3]{x} - 10 = -3$ 343

3. (70) $\sqrt[3]{x-3} + 2 = 4$ 11

***4.** (77) **Generalize** What information must be known to be able to use the Law of Cosines to find a missing measure in a triangle? Either the lengths of all three sides or the lengths of two sides and the included angle

Solve.

***5.** (78) $x^4 - 81 = 0$ $x = \pm 3i, -3, 3$

***6.** (78) $12x = 9x^2 + 4$ $x = \frac{2}{3}$

***7.** (78) $8x^3 - 392x = 0$ $x = -7, 0, 7$

8. (46) **Multi-Step** **a.** A box in the shape of a rectangular prism has a 4 ft × 4 ft square base, and a volume of $64\sqrt{6}$ cubic feet. Find the height of the box. $4\sqrt{6}$ ft

b. Find the length of the longest stick that can fit inside the box. $8\sqrt{2}$ ft

c. When this stick is placed inside the box, what is the measure of the angle it forms with the vertical face of the box? 30°

9. (Inv 5) **Verify** Suppose you are conducting an experiment consisting of rolling a number cube 40 times to find the probability of rolling a 2 seven times. Is this a binomial experiment? State why or why not.

9. Yes, there are 40 trials and only 2 possible outcomes, 2 or not a 2. Each trial is independent of the next and the probability of success is the same from trial to trial.

10. (53) **Multi-Step** Let $f(x) = 2x$ and $g(x) = x^2$. See Additional Answers.

a. Find the composition functions $(f \circ g)(x)$ and $(g \circ f)(x)$.

b. Evaluate the composite functions $(f \circ g)(x)$ and $(g \circ f)(x)$ for $x = 2$.

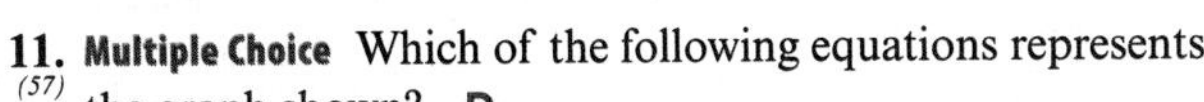

11. (57) **Multiple Choice** Which of the following equations represents the graph shown? D

A $y = -3^x + 2$

B $y = -3^{x+1} + 2$

C $y = \left(\frac{1}{3}\right)^{x+1} - 2$

D $y = -\left(\frac{1}{3}\right)^{x-1} + 2$

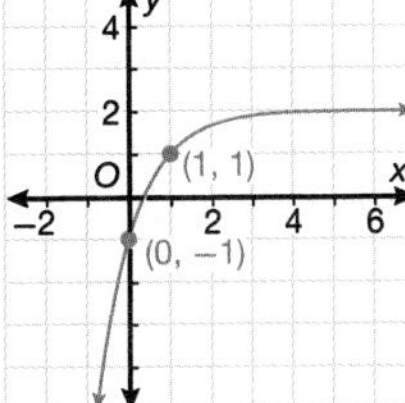

12. (59) Simplify the expression $2^{\frac{1}{3}} \cdot 4^{\frac{1}{6}} \cdot 8^{\frac{1}{9}}$. 2

13. (60) **Soccer** Of the 65 students going on the soccer trip, 43 are players and 12 are left-handed. Only 5 of the left-handed players are soccer players. What is the probability that one of the students on the trip is a soccer player or is left-handed? $\frac{10}{13}$

14. (52) Find the unknown lengths of the triangle shown. leg: $2\sqrt{3}$, hypotenuse: $4\sqrt{3}$

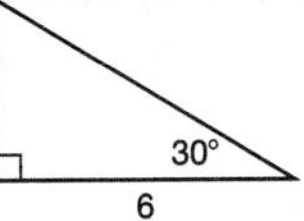

3 Practice

Math Conversations

Discussions to strengthen understanding

Problem 3

Guide the students by asking them the following questions.

"How will you isolate the radical?" Subtract 2 from each side.

"How will you eliminate the radical?" Cube both sides of the equation.

"How will you isolate x?" Add 3 to both sides.

CHALLENGE

Write a piecewise function for federal income taxes in the U.S. based on the information for a single individual as shown in the table:

If taxable income is over--	But not over--	The tax is:
$0	$7,550	10% of the amount over $0
$7,550	$30,650	$755 plus 15% of the amount over $7,550
$30,650	$74,200	$4,220.00 plus 25% of the amount over $30,650
$74,200	$154,800	$15,107.50 plus 28% of the amount over $74,200
$154,800	$336,550	$37,675.50 plus 33% of the amount over $154,800
$336,550	no limit	$97,653.00 plus 35% of the amount over $336,550

$$f(x) = \begin{cases} 0.1x, \text{ if } 0 < x \le 7550 \\ 0.15x - 377.5, \text{ if } 7550 < x \le 30,650 \\ 0.25x - 3442.50, \text{ if } 30,650 < x \le 74,200 \\ 0.28x - 5668.50, \text{ if } 74,200 < x \le 154,800 \\ 0.33x - 13,408.50, \text{ if } 154,800 < x \le 336,550 \\ 0.35x - 20,139.50, \text{ if } 336,550 < x \end{cases}$$

Problem 20

Discuss the differences between continuous functions and discontinuous functions.

Problem 22

Error Alert

Students may multiply all the items by $5 and add to $25. Remind them to subtract 10 from the total number of items before multiplying by the additional charge of $5, then add to $25 for the total cost.

15. (20) Given $f(x) = 3x - 5$ and $g(x) = x + 4$, find $(fg)(x)$. $3x^2 + 7x - 20$

***16.** (65) **Graphing Calculator** Solve $2x^2 + x - 4 = 0$ by using a graphing calculator. $-1.686, 1.186$

17. (63) **Error Analysis** Describe and correct the student's error in finding the area of a sector with a radius of 6 centimeters and a central angle of 40°. See Additional Answers.

$$A = \frac{1}{2}(6)^2(40) = 720 \text{ cm}^2$$

18. (73) **Analyze** How is using a table of random digits to form a sample of 20 individuals different from using it to form a sample of 150 individuals?

18. For the first sample, 2-digit numbers are found in the table. For the second sample, 3-digit numbers are found.

19. (69) **Probability** For i^a, if a is randomly chosen from the numbers 20 through 30 inclusive, what is the probability that the value of the expression is 1 or –1? $\frac{6}{11} \approx 54.5\%$

***20.** (79) **Justify** Explain why $f(x) = \begin{cases} x + 1, & \text{if } x < -2 \\ 3, & \text{if } -2 \leq x < 8 \\ 15, & \text{if } x \geq 8 \end{cases}$ is not a step function.

20. A step function is a piecewise function that is constant for each interval. This function is not constant for the interval $x < -2$.

21. (66) **Marketing** The logo for a new math product includes the graph of the polynomial $3x^3 + 5x^2 - 6x - 8 = 0$. What coordinates will the project manager give the art production team to be sure the curve crosses the x-axis at the correct locations? $(-1, 0), (-2, 0)$, and $\left(\frac{4}{3}, 0\right)$

***22.** (79) **Delivery Charges** A garden center delivers up to 10 items for a $25 delivery charge. There is an additional charge of $5 per item for each additional item delivered. Write a piecewise function for the cost having x items delivered. See Additional Answers.

23. (67) **Analyze** Describe how the range of the inverse sine function and the range of the inverse tangent function are different. Explain why they are different.

23. The range of the inverse sine function includes $-\frac{\pi}{2}$ and $\frac{\pi}{2}$, and the range of the inverse tangent function does not include these two values. Sample: Sine values exist for $-\frac{\pi}{2}$ and $\frac{\pi}{2}$, but tangent values do not exist for these two values.

Use the discriminant to find all values for which the equation has (a) two real solutions, (b) one real solution, and (c) two imaginary solutions.

***24.** (74) $x^2 - 4x - c = 0$ $c > -4, c = -4, c < -4$

***25.** (74) $-4x^2 - 10x + c = 0$ $c > -6.25, c = -6.25, c < -6.25$

26. (68) **Multiple Choice** A coin purse contains 6 dimes, 2 nickels, and 10 pennies. When selecting three coins, one at a time, without replacement, what is the approximate probability of randomly selecting 3 pennies? **B**

A 12.3% **B** 14.7% **C** 20.4% **D** 29.4%

27. (71) **Formulate** Show how to derive the Law of Sines from the three expressions for the area of a triangle: $\frac{1}{2}bc \sin A = \frac{1}{2}ac \sin B = \frac{1}{2}ab \sin C$. See Additional Answers.

28. (32) Find A^{-1} for $A = \begin{bmatrix} 1 & -1 \\ 4 & -6 \end{bmatrix}$. $\begin{bmatrix} 3 & -\frac{1}{2} \\ 2 & -\frac{1}{2} \end{bmatrix}$

29. (75) **Aviation** As an airplane is taking off from a runway, the force of lift on the plane can be calculated using the equation shown below. The plane begins to fly when the force of lift is equal to the weight of the plane. Find the radical function that can be used to find the minimum speed for flight.

Lift $= kv^2$, for constant k and velocity v $v = \sqrt{\frac{\text{Weight of the plane}}{k}}$

***30.** (79) Evaluate the piecewise function for $x = -3$ and $x = 4$.

$$f(x) = \begin{cases} 3x - 1 & \text{if } x < 0 \\ 2x^2 & \text{if } 0 \leq x < 4 \\ 1 - x & \text{if } 4 \leq x \end{cases}$$ $-10, -3$

LOOKING FORWARD 

Solving piecewise functions prepares students for

- **Lesson 90** Graphing the Tangent Function
- **Lesson 103** Graphing Reciprocal Trigonometric Functions

LAB 12

Calculating Normal Distribution Areas and Z-Scores

Graphing Calculator Lab (*Use with Lesson 80*)

A graphing calculator can be used to find the area under the normal curve given the bounds, mean, and standard deviation. Use a normal distribution with a mean of 26 and a standard deviation of 3 to find the probability of a value between 26 and 30.

Calculating the Area under the Normal Curve

```
DISTR DRAW
1:normalpdf(
2:normalcdf(
3:invNorm(
4:tpdf(
5:tcdf(
6:X²pdf(
7↓X²cdf(
```

1. Calculate an area under the normal curve with upper and lower bounds.
   a. Press 2nd VARS to open the **DISTR** menu.
   b. Press ▼ to select [**2: normalcdf (**] and press ENTER.
   c. To calculate the area, the data needs to be entered in this order: (lower, upper, mean, standard deviation). To do this press: 2
   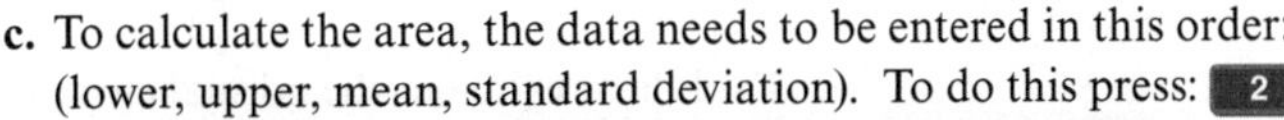
   d. Now press ENTER to calculate the area.

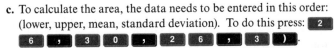

```
normalcdf(26,30,
26,3)
          .4087887176
```

2. To calculate an area under the curve to the left of an upper bound use [**2: normalcdf (**]. Enter –999999 as a lower bound, 30 as the upper bound, 26 as the mean, and 3 as the standard deviation. Refer to step **1c**.

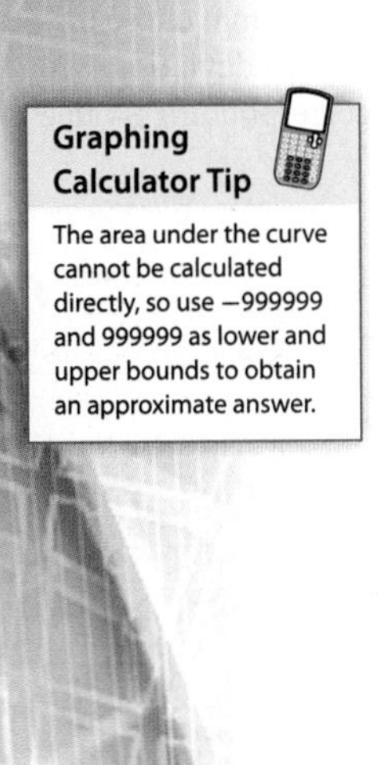

Graphing Calculator Tip

The area under the curve cannot be calculated directly, so use –999999 and 999999 as lower and upper bounds to obtain an approximate answer.

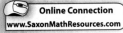

```
normalcdf(-99999
9,30,26,3)
          .9087887181
normalcdf(26,999
999,26,3)
          .4999999995
```

3. To calculate an area under the curve to the right of an lower bound use [**2: normalcdf (**]. Enter 26 as a lower bound, 999999 as the upper bound, 26 as the mean, and 3 as the standard deviation. Refer to step **1c**.

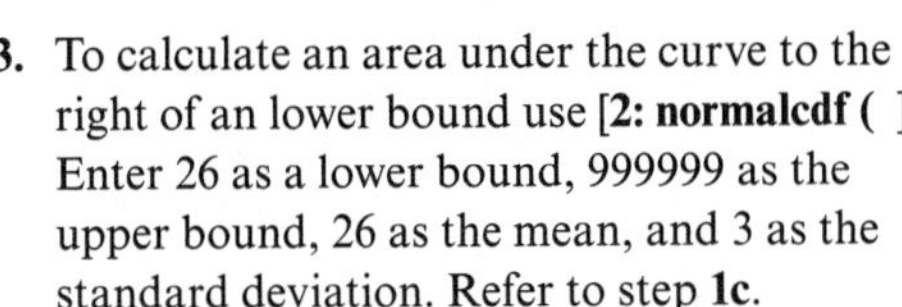

4. Graphing the area under the normal curve
   a. Adjust the viewing window to Xmin=15, Xmax=40, Xscl=1, Ymin=–0.1, Ymax=0.2, Yscl=0.05, and Xres=1.
   b. From the home screen, press 2nd VARS to open the **DISTR** menu.
   c. Press ▶ to select the **DRAW** menu.
   d. Press ENTER to select [**1: ShadeNorm** ( ].
   e. In this order, enter (lower, upper, mean, standard deviation). Refer to step **1c**.
   f. Now press ENTER to generate the graph.

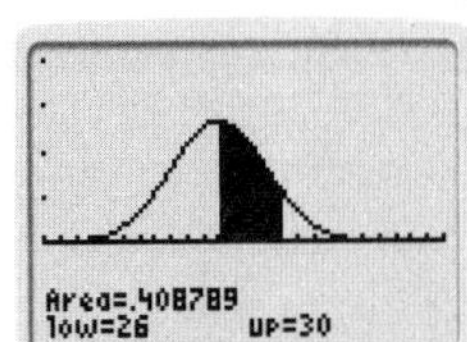

Online Connection
www.SaxonMathResources.com

LAB 12

Materials

- graphing calculator

Discuss

In this lab, students will calculate the area under the normal curve and z-scores using distribution functions.

Define normal curve, standard deviation, and z-score.

TEACHER TIP

A normal distribution is described by a normal curve that is symmetric, single-peaked and bell-shaped. The standard deviation controls the spread of the curve. The greater the standard deviation, the greater the spread of the curve.

Calculating the Area Under the Normal Curve

Discuss the calculator functions.

DISTR stands for distribution. **normalcdf(** calculates the cumulative normal distribution probability between the lower and upper bound for a given mean and standard deviation. **ShadeNorm(** draws the normal density function defined by the mean and standard deviation. The area between the lower and upper bound is shaded.

TEACHER TIP

After graphing, instruct students to clear their drawing by using the **1:ClrDraw** command found in the **DRAW** menu.

TEACHER TIP

Discuss *z*-score. If x is an observation from a distribution that has a mean μ and standard deviation σ, the standardized value of x is $z = \frac{x - \mu}{\sigma}$. Therefore, *z*-scores are standardized values that can be expressed using a common scale.

Calculating a *z*-Score Given a Corresponding Area

To calculate the *z*-score, **invNorm(** can be used. This command computes the inverse cumulative normal distribution function for an area under the normal distribution curve. The area for step 2 is approximately 0.4088. Since the given value, 30, is greater than the mean of 26, to find the total area left of the given value, add 0.5, the area from the mean to the upper or lower bound, to the area: 0.5 + 0.4088 = 0.9088.

Additional Problem

The heights of women are approximately normally distributed with a mean of 65" and a standard deviation of 2.4". What proportion of all women are between 65" and 68" tall. In addition, calculate the *z*-score.

Normalcdf(65,68,65,2.4) = 0.39435 Given value = 68; 68 > 65 so 0.5 + 0.39435 = 0.89435 **invNorm**(0.89435,0,1) = 1.249 Students can also check their z-score answer by using $z = \frac{x - \mu}{\sigma} = \frac{68 - 65}{2.4} \approx 1.25$.

3 Practice

TEACHER TIP

Use **normalcdf** (lower, upper, mean,standard deviation).

Calculating a Z-Score Given a Corresponding Area

5. Since the area entered into [**3: invNorm (**] is interpreted as area left of a given upper bound, use the area calculated in step **2.**
   a. From the home screen, press 2nd VARS to open the **DISTR** menu.
   b. Press ▼ to select [**3: invNorm (**] and press ENTER.
   c. To calculate a z-score, the following data needs to be entered within the parenthesis: total area left of the given upper bound value, mean, and the standard deviation. To do this enter:

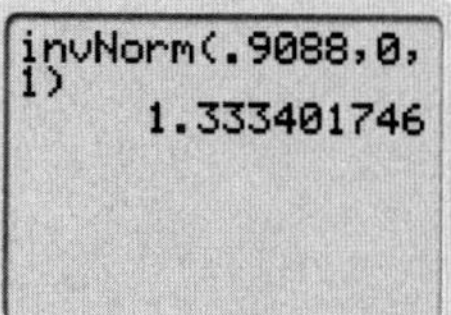

   d. Now press ENTER to calculate the z-score.

Graphing Calculator

When calculating the z-score using the **invNorm** function, the default value for mean is 0 and the default value for standard deviation is 1.

Lab Practice

a. Find the area under the normal curve for values between 115 and 130, given the mean is 130 and the standard deviation is 50. 0.1179

b. Use the graphing calculator to graph area under the normal curve for values up to 180, given the mean is 130 and the standard deviation is 50. Use –9999 as the lower bound. Then find the corresponding z-value for this area. 0.9998

Sample:

Area=.841345 low=-9999 up=180

Finding the Normal Distribution

LESSON 80

Warm Up

1. **Vocabulary** For a set of data, the mean [mean/median/mode] is the average of the data. (25)

2. True or False: The probability of an event must be a number between 0 and 1. True (55)

3. True or False: The standard deviation of {1, 3, 5, 7, 10} is less than the standard deviation of {3, 4, 5, 6, 7}. False (25)

4. Find the mean and median of 1, 2, 87. 30, 2 (25)

1 Warm Up

For problem 3, students should analyze the sets to determine which set of data has the greatest spread.

New Concepts

The table and histogram below show the frequencies of the sum of two number cubes, each numbered 1–6, after 1000 rolls.

Sum	Frequency
2	29
3	49
4	97
5	126
6	128
7	155
8	128
9	114
10	90
11	61
12	23

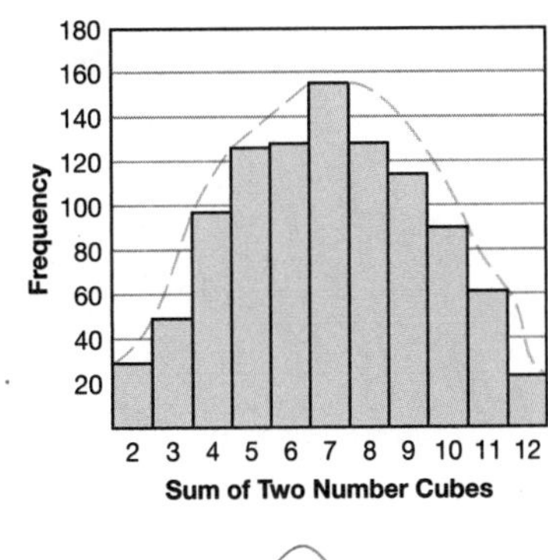

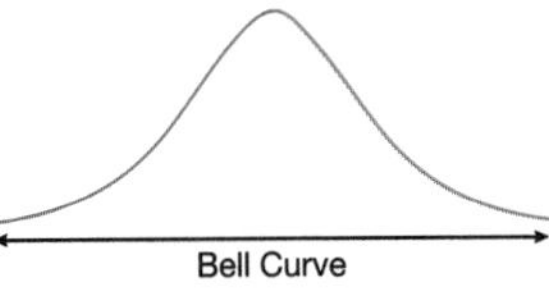

Math Language

A **bell curve** can be called a normal curve. It always has one peak. The width and height depend on the standard deviation of the data. The **standard deviation** σ is a measure of the spread of the data from the mean.

The curve in this histogram, which is formed by drawing a line through the tops of the histogram bars, is referred to as a **bell curve.** Data that is bell shaped has a **normal distribution,** which means that the data is symmetric about the mean. The curve is symmetric about the mean because the mean, median, and mode are equal. Data that is approximately normally distributed can be modeled by the bell curve.

The mean μ and standard deviation σ determine the location, spread, and the height of the bell curve. As the curve widens, more data values are farther from the mean than closer to the mean.

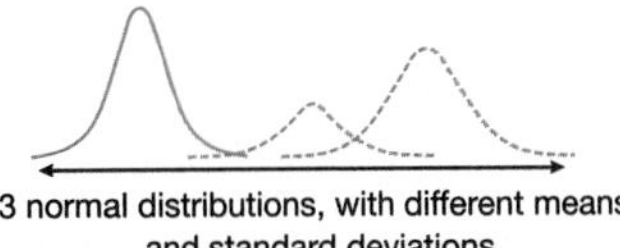
3 normal distributions, with different means and standard deviations

2 New Concepts

Students learn about the normal distribution and how the mean and standard deviation relate to the normal distribution.

Discuss the definitions of bell curve, normal distribution, standard normal distribution, and z-score.

MATH BACKGROUND

The mathematical expression for the normal distribution was formulated by Abraham de Moivre in the early 1700s, primarily as a result of working with games of chance. In addition to describing results of games of chance, the normal distribution also effectively represents experimental error analysis and models for natural phenomena. It is an important model for behavioral sciences, often used to describe psychological data.

The normal distribution is described mathematically by:

$y = \frac{1}{\sigma\sqrt{2\pi}} e^{\left[\frac{-(x-\mu)^2}{2\sigma^2}\right]}$ where μ is the mean of the data and σ is the standard deviation.

Synonyms include 'the bell-shaped curve' and 'Gaussian distribution.'

LESSON RESOURCES

Student Edition Practice Workbook 80
Reteaching Master 80
Adaptations Master 80
Challenge and Enrichment Master C80

Example 1

Remind students that they are looking for multiples of the standard deviation and using the 68-95-99.7 rule.

Additional Example 1

A set of measurements of laser beam power is normally distributed with a mean of 28.2 GW (gigawatts) and a standard deviation of 0.7 GW.

a. What percent of the laser shots have a power between 26.8 and 29.6 GW? 95%

b. What percent of the shots have a power between 27.5 and 28.9 GW? 68%

c. What percent of the shots have a power between 28.9 and 29.6 GW? 13.5%

TEACHER TIP

Collecting actual data (students' heights is a good example) plotting that data to see the curve, calculating the mean and standard deviation, and describing the data will help students understand and visualize the concept.

Since the area under the curve contains 100% of the data, the bell curve can be used to interpret values and draw conclusion. The 68-95-99.7 rule states that for any normal distribution the following properties apply:

- About 68% of the data lie within 1 standard deviation of the mean.
- About 95% of the data lie within 2 standard deviations of the mean.
- About 99.7% of the data lie with 3 standard deviations of the mean.

Math Language

The Greek letter μ is read "mu" and the Greek letter σ is read "sigma".

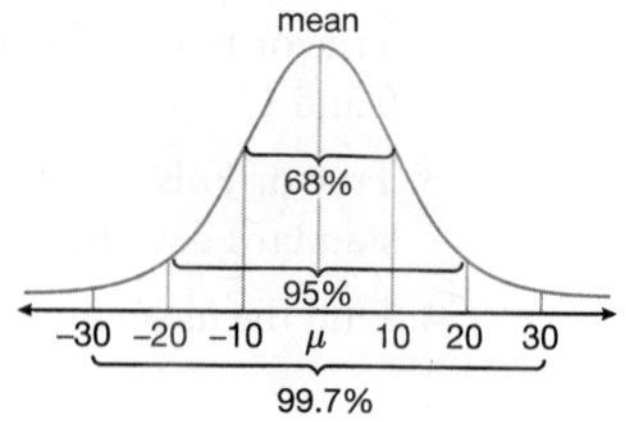

The sign of σ tells whether the number of standard deviations is above or below the mean.

Example 1 **Using the Mean and Standard Deviation of a Normal Distribution**

A set of test scores are normally distributed with a mean of 75 and a standard deviation of 4.

(a.) What percent of the scores are between 67 and 83?

SOLUTION Find how many deviations 67 and 83 are away from the mean. $75 - 67 = 8$, $83 - 75 = 8$, and $8 \div 4 = 2$. The scores are two standard deviations away from the mean, so about 95% of the scores are between 67 and 83.

(b.) What percent of the scores are between 75 and 79?

SOLUTION 68% of the scores are between 71 and 79. Because the data is distributed symmetrically about the mean, about half of 68%, or 34%, of the scores are between 75 and 79.

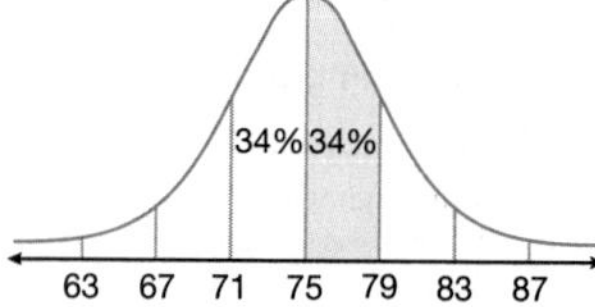

Math Reasoning

Analyze What percent of the scores are less than 83?

Since 50% of the scores are below the mean and 47.5% of the scores are between the mean and 83, 97.5% of the scores are less than 83.

(c.) What percent of the scores are between 79 and 83?

SOLUTION 95% of the scores are between 67 and 83. That means half, or 47.5%, is above the mean. Since 34% of the scores are between 75 and 79, then only 47.5% − 34%, or 13.5%, of the scores are between 79 and 83.

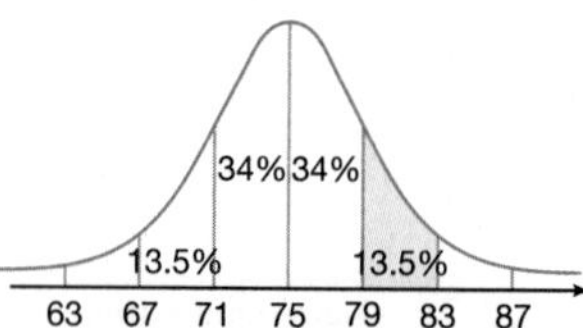

ENGLISH LEARNERS

For this lesson, define the word **normal**.

"The word normal means to be like a regular type or pattern. For example, the normal shape of a dinner plate is round."

Discuss that it is normal for cars to have four wheels and bikes to have two wheels. Have students think of other uses of the word normal.

A normal distribution can be standardized, which is helpful in identifying how far a data value is from the mean.

Standard Normal Distribution

A standard normal distribution is a normal distribution that has a mean of 0 and a standard deviation of 1.

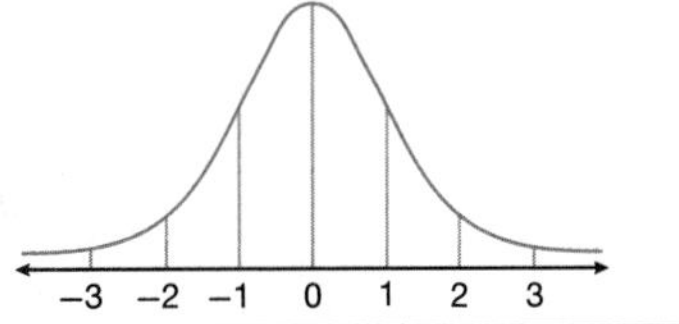

The value of a data point on the standard normal distribution is a *z*-**score.** It is a standardized value and its absolute value is equal to the number of standard deviations it is away from the mean. The sign tells if it is above or below the mean. A *z*-score of −2.5 is 2.5 standard deviations *below* the mean. A *z*-score of 1.8 is 1.8 standard deviations *above* the mean.

Standardizing different normal distributions onto a common scale allows for them to be compared using *z*-scores. To convert any given data value taken from a normal distribution to a *z*-score, subtract the mean from the data value and divide by the standard deviation.

***z*-score**

Given that *x* is a data value of a normally distributed set of data, the

$$z\text{-score} = \frac{x - \text{mean}}{\text{standard deviation}}.$$

Example 2 Finding *z*-Scores

The weights of cans produced in a factory have a mean of 6.5 ounces and a standard deviation 0.25 ounces.

a. A randomly selected can weighs 6.9 ounces. How many standard deviations is this above the mean?

SOLUTION Find the *z*-score, the standardized weight.

$$z\text{-score} = \frac{6.9 - 6.5}{0.25} = \frac{0.4}{0.25} = 1.6$$

The standardized weight is 1.6; the can is 1.6 standard deviations above the mean.

b. A randomly selected can weighs 6.4 ounces. How many standard deviations is this below the mean?

SOLUTION Find the *z*-score, the standardized weight.

$$z\text{-score} = \frac{6.4 - 6.5}{0.25} = \frac{-0.1}{0.25} = -0.4$$

The standardized weight is −0.4; the can is 0.4 standard deviations below the mean.

If the absolute value of a *z*-score for a data value is extremely large, then the data value may be an outlier.

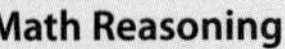

Math Reasoning

Estimate What is the actual weight of a can if its standardized weight is −2.82? Round the answer to the nearest tenth.

about 5.8 ounces

Example 2

Remind students that the *z*-score can be either positive or negative.

Additional Example 2

The weights of cereal boxes have an average of 23.0 oz and a standard deviation of 0.3 oz.

a. A randomly selected box has a weight of 22.6 oz. How many standard deviations is this below the mean? about 1.33

b. A randomly selected box weighs 23.1 oz. How many standard deviations is this above the mean? about 0.33

ALTERNATE METHOD FOR EXAMPLE 2

Instead of using the equation for *z*-scores, students can start with the mean, and count up (or down) by standard deviations. The mean weight of a can is 6.5 ounces. In part a, the randomly selected can weighs 6.9 ounces. Starting with 6.5, count to 6.75 (one standard deviation). That leaves a 'remainder' of 0.15 which is 0.6 standard deviations $\frac{0.15}{0.25} = 0.6$. So the randomly selected can has a weight of 1.6 standard deviations above the mean.

Example 3 Application: Making Comparisons

Student A received a score of 63 on a test where the scores are normally distributed with a mean of 50 and a standard deviation of 8. Student B received a score of 32 on a test where the scores are normally distributed with a mean of 28 and a standard deviation of 1.8. Which student scored better compared to the rest of their class?

SOLUTION

1. **Understand** Two normal distributions are being compared.
2. **Plan** Standardize each score. The student with the greater standardized score did better.
3. **Solve**

Student A

$$z\text{-score} = \frac{63 - 50}{8} = \frac{13}{8} = 1.625$$

Student B

$$z\text{-score} = \frac{32 - 28}{1.8} = \frac{4}{1.8} \approx 2.22$$

Student B has the greater standardized score and did better compared to the rest of their class than did Student A.

4. **Check** On Student A's test, a score of 66 is two standard deviations above the mean and on Student B's test, 31.6 is two standard deviations above the mean. Student A's score of 63 is *within* two standard deviations, and Student B's score of 32 is *above* two standard deviations.

Hint

Student A's score was 1.625 standard deviations above the mean. Student B's score was 2.22 standard deviations above the mean.

Lesson Practice

A set of test scores are normally distributed with a mean of 300 and a standard deviation of 18.

a. (Ex 1) Between what two scores do 99.7% of the data fall? 246 and 354

b. (Ex 1) What percent of the scores are between 264 and 300? 47.5%

c. (Ex 1) What percent of the scores are between 282 and 336? 81.5%

d. (Ex 1) What percent of the scores are greater than 318? 16%

The weights of hammers produced in a factory have a mean of 12.2 ounces and a standard deviation 0.08 ounces.

e. (Ex 2) A randomly selected hammer weighs 12 ounces. How many standard deviations is this below the mean? 2.5 standard deviations below

f. (Ex 2) A randomly selected hammer weighs 12.3 ounces. How many standard deviations is this above the mean? 1.25 standard deviations above

g. (Ex 3) Student A received a score of 445 on a test where the scores are normally distributed with a mean of 450 and a standard deviation of 12. Student B received a score of 170 on a test where the scores are normally distributed with a mean of 175 and a standard deviation of 15. Which student scored better compared to the rest of their class? Student B

Example 3

Error Alert Students may look only at the difference (score—mean) in scores, and not compare the differences to the standard deviations and conclude that Student A outperformed the class much more than Student B. Remind them that the difference of the scores must be divided by the standard deviation to determine how far the data value is from the mean, which is measured in standard deviations.

Extend the Example

What can you conclude about a test score if the standardized score is equal to 0? The test score is equal to the mean.

Additional Example 3

A person is offered a job in Bismarck, ND for $34,500 and one in Anchorage, AK for $51,500. The mean income in Bismarck is about $32,000 with a standard deviation of $4,500. The mean income in Anchorage is about $48,000 with a standard deviation of $7,000. Where will the person earn more compared to other workers? ND; The job in ND pays about 0.56 standard deviations above mean. The job in AK pays about 0.5 standard deviations above mean.

Lesson Practice

Problem e

Scaffolding Students should use the definition of z-scores. Since the standard deviation is so small (0.08), they might be surprised at how many standard deviations 12 oz is away from the mean.

Problem g

Error Alert Since both scores are below the mean, the student with the smaller z-score did better on the test.

 INCLUSION

Sketches of bell-shaped curves with information clearly labeled (the mean and the number of standard deviations) will help all students visualize different normal distributions. Shading the sketches with different colors, representing the number of standard deviations, is helpful.

Practice Distributed and Integrated

1. (50) Find an equation for the inverse of $y = x^2 - 7$. Determine whether each relation is a function. $y = \pm\sqrt{x + 7}$; the inverse is not a function

***2.** (80) A set of results are normally distributed with a mean of 88 and a standard deviation of 4. Find the percent of results between 80 and 96. 95%

3. (60) Given a deck of cards, what is the probability of randomly drawing two ace cards without replacing the first card? $\frac{1}{221}$

4. (57) The number of lemmings grew exponentially. At first there were 400,000. Three weeks later there were 1,200,000. How many would there be after 8 weeks? 7,488,302 lemmings

***5.** (80) A set of scores have a mean of 43 and a standard deviation of 2. Find the z-score for an outcome of 37. −3

6. (52) **(Astronomy)** The binary star system 12 Bootis consists of two stars with nearly equal mass, and therefore a nearly equal gravitational pull. The distance between the two stars changes slightly over time, but is on average about 18.7 million kilometers. Suppose a spaceship crew wants to position their spaceship at a point equidistant from both stars, and so that the gravitational pulls were perpendicular to each other. How far from each star would the spaceship have to be? About 13.2 million km

7. (56) P is a point on the terminal side of θ in standard position. Find the exact value of the six trigonometric functions for θ where $P(2, 9)$.

7. $\sin\theta = \frac{9\sqrt{85}}{85}$; $\sec\theta = \frac{\sqrt{85}}{2}$; $\cos\theta = \frac{2\sqrt{85}}{85}$; $\csc\theta = \frac{\sqrt{85}}{9}$; $\tan\theta = \frac{9}{2}$; $\cot\theta = \frac{2}{9}$

8. (62) **Analyze** What are the values of a and b in the imaginary unit i? $a = 0$ and $b = 1$

9. (59) Simplify $\frac{13^{\frac{1}{3}} \cdot 13^{\frac{1}{4}}}{13^{\frac{1}{12}} \cdot 13^{\frac{1}{2}}}$. $\left[\frac{13^{\frac{7}{12}}}{13^{\frac{7}{12}}}\right] = 13^0 = 1$

10. (63) **Multiple Choice** What is the radian measure of a 90° angle? C

A $-\frac{\pi}{2}$ radian **B** −1 radian **C** $\frac{\pi}{2}$ radian **D** 1 radian

11. (70) **(Biology)** The formula $SA = \sqrt{\frac{mk}{36}}$ approximates the surface area SA in square meters of a human being with a height of m meters and a mass of k kilograms. Approximate the mass of a person who has a surface area of 1.64 square meters and a height of 1.7 meters. About 57 kg

12. (64) **Multi-Step** **a.** Write the equation $y = \log_3 \frac{1}{9}$ in exponential form. What value of y makes both equations true? $3^y = \frac{1}{9}$; $y = -2$

b. Complete the table of values for the function $y = \log_3 x$.

x	$\frac{1}{9}$	$\frac{1}{3}$	1	3	9
$y = \log_3 x$	−2	−1	0	1	2

c. Plot the points and sketch the graph of the function.

12c.

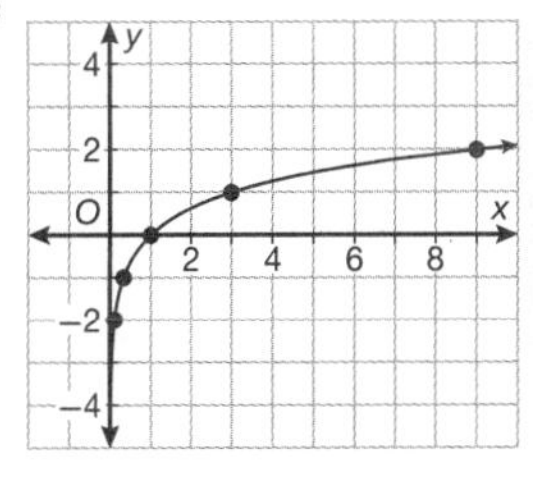

CHALLENGE

Using the information from Additional Example 1, what percent of the shots have a power over 30.3 GW? 0.15%

Check for Understanding

The questions below help assess the concepts taught in this lesson.

"Explain what a set of data with a standard deviation of zero would look like. Will this data set form a normal distribution?" A standard deviation of zero means that all the data points are the same. That is not a normal distribution.

"What is the meaning of standard deviation?" Sample: Standard deviation is a measure of the distance that a data value varies from the mean of the data values in a set.

3 Practice

Math Conversations

Discussions to strengthen understanding

Problem 4

"Write the general form for an exponential equation." $y = ab^x$

"What variable does 400,000 represent in the equation?" It is a, the initial amount.

"What other variable are known?" Three weeks later ($x = 3$), there were 1.2 million ($y = 1{,}200{,}000$). Now you can solve for b.

"Write the exponential equation for this situation." $y = 400{,}000 \cdot (\sqrt[3]{3})^x$

Problem 7

Draw and label a picture to help solve this problem.

Problem 13

Error Alert

Students may think they can't solve this problem since there are 'two' unknowns (both legs). Remind them that they can write two equations, one using the perimeter and one using the Pythagorean Theorem.

Problem 14

Students can also factor out the GCF of 16 to get a difference of two squares, $(x^2)^2$ and 1^2.

Problem 19

Error Alert

If students answer $\frac{1}{6}$, they did not realize that the probability was a conditional probability.

13. (65) **Geometry** The length of the hypotenuse of a right triangle is 75 inches. Find the lengths of the legs given that the perimeter is 168 inches. 21 inches and 72 inches

***14.** (78) **Write** Explain why the equation $16x^4 - 16 = 0$ can be solved by factoring the difference of two squares. Sample: $16x^4 - 16$ is the difference of two squares; it can be written as $(4x^2)^2 - (4)^2$.

15. (66) **Error Analysis** Find and correct the error a student made in determining the possible rational roots of $2x^3 + 7x^2 - 5x - 4 = 0$.

$$\frac{\pm1, \pm2}{\pm1, \pm2, \pm4} = \pm1, \pm\frac{1}{2}, \pm\frac{1}{4}, \pm2$$

15. The student used $\frac{q}{p}$ instead of $\frac{p}{q}$: $\frac{\pm1, \pm2, \pm4}{\pm1, \pm2} = \pm1, \pm\frac{1}{2}, \pm2, \pm4$.

16. (67) **Navigation** "Lines" of longitude are actually circles that get closer together as you travel north or south from the equator. The formula for the approximate length l of a 1° arc of longitude in miles is $l \approx 69.033 \cos \theta$, where θ is the latitude in degrees at some point on the 1° arc of longitude.

a. At what latitude, to the nearest degree, is the length of a 1° arc of longitude approximately 53.6 miles? 39°

b. The latitude at the equator is 0° and the latitude at the Arctic Circle is about 66°N. To the nearest mile, how much longer is the length of a 1° arc of longitude at the equator than at the Arctic Circle? 41 miles

17. (73) **Error Analysis** A student said that a cluster sample is a type of simple random sample because every cluster has an equal chance of being chosen. Explain the error in the student's thinking.

17. The probability of every possible group of n individuals is not the same. For instance, the probability of selecting a group that consists of half the people in one cluster and half the people in another cluster is 0.

18. (68) A box of colored pencils only holds primary colors. It has 5 red, 8 yellow, and 3 blue. Find the probability that a student will randomly grab 2 yellow pencils without replacement. 23.33%

19. (74) **Probability** Given that the discriminant is nonnegative and chosen randomly from the following list, find the probability that the equation it was derived from has exactly one real solution. 25%

$$7, 0, -1, 4, -3, 5$$

20. (69) **Electrical Engineering** The flow of a current, I, the resistance to the flow, Z, and the voltage, E, are related by $E = I(Z)$. Find the voltage of a circuit if the current is $40 - 36i$ amps and the resistance is $8 + 3i$ ohms. $428 - 168i$ volts

21. (71) **Geography** On a map, line segments connecting three southwest Virginia cities form a triangle as shown below. To the nearest tenth of a mile, what is the distance from Danville to South Boston if 1 inch = 13.5 miles? 27.4 miles

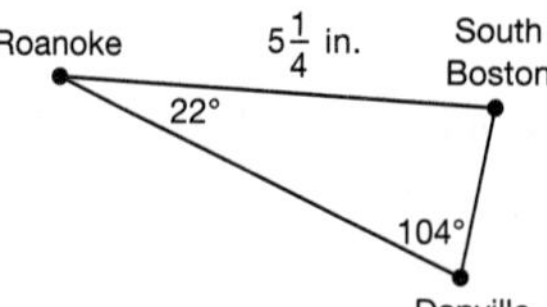

570 Saxon Algebra 2

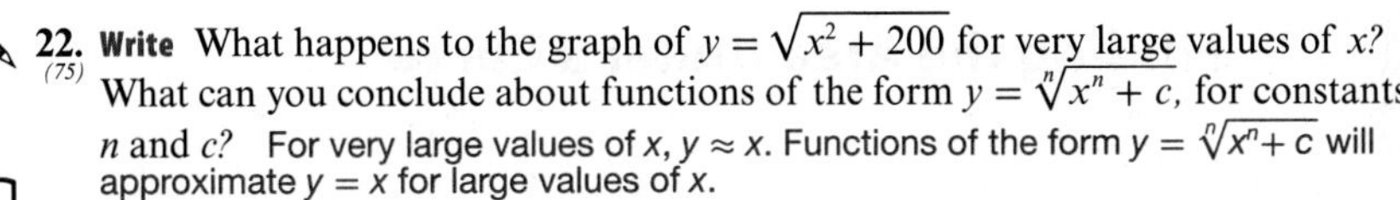

22. (75) **Write** What happens to the graph of $y = \sqrt{x^2 + 200}$ for very large values of x? What can you conclude about functions of the form $y = \sqrt[n]{x^n + c}$, for constants n and c? For very large values of x, $y \approx x$. Functions of the form $y = \sqrt[n]{x^n + c}$ will approximate $y = x$ for large values of x.

***23.** (76) **Graphing Calculator** Use a graphing calculator to test this hypothesis: If a cubic function has two roots, one of the roots must have a multiplicity of 2. Students should conclude this is true.

***24.** (80) **Multiple Choice** Which z-score is closest to the mean of a standardized normal distribution? **B**

A -2.36 **B** -0.45 **C** 0.78 **D** 2.9

25. (72) **Analyze** What pair of inverse functions contain the ordered pairs $(1.5, 3^{1.5})$ and $(3^{1.5}, 1.5)$? $y = 3^x$ and $y = \log_3 x$

***26.** (80) **Generalize** Write <, =, or >.

When standardizing a data value selected from a normally distributed set of data,

z ◯ 0 when the mean is greater than the data value. <

z ◯ 0 when the mean is less than the data value. >

***27.** (77) **Estimate** In $\triangle PQR$, $p = 7.8935$, $q = 3.456$, and $r = \sqrt{37}$. Estimate the area of the triangle. Accept estimates between 8 and 10 square units.

***28.** (79) **Comparison Shopping** At a party shop, balloons cost \$2 each if you buy fewer than 12, \$1.75 each if you buy between 12 and 24, inclusive, and \$1.50 each if you buy more than 24. Write a piecewise function for the cost of buying x balloons.

28. $f(x) = \begin{cases} 2x & \text{if } 0 < x < 12 \\ 1.75x & \text{if } 12 \le x \le 24 \\ 1.50x & \text{if } x > 24 \end{cases}$

Evaluate each piecewise function for $x = \frac{1}{2}$ and $x = -10$.

***29.** (79) $f(x) = \begin{cases} 7, & \text{if } x < 0 \\ x^2, & \text{if } 0 \le x < 10 \\ -x^2, & \text{if } x \ge 10 \end{cases}$ $f(\frac{1}{2}) = \frac{1}{4}$; $f(-10) = 7$

***30.** (79) $f(x) = \begin{cases} \frac{1}{2}, & \text{if } x < 1 \\ x - 4, & \text{if } 1 \le x < 10 \\ -x - 9, & \text{if } x \ge 10 \end{cases}$ $f(\frac{1}{2}) = \frac{1}{2}$; $f(-10) = \frac{1}{2}$

Problem 27

Extend the Problem

Estimate the perimeter of $\triangle PQR$.
17.43 units

LOOKING FORWARD 

Finding the normal distribution prepares students for

- **Lesson 116** Finding Best Fit Models
- **Lesson 118** Recognizing Misleading Data

INVESTIGATION

8

Finding the Area Under a Curve

Finding the area under a curve requires using calculus. But you can estimate the area under a curve with a good deal of accuracy without using calculus. Suppose you want to find the area under the curve shown below from $0 \le x \le 4$.

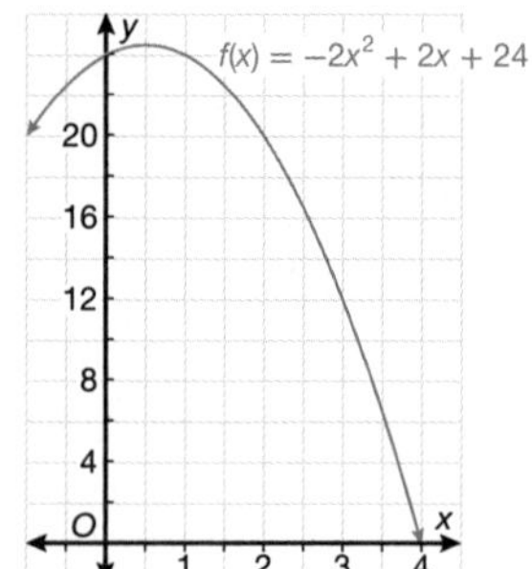

1. To begin the process of estimating the area, we will partition the region from $0 \le x \le 4$ into four rectangular regions, as shown. What is the width of each rectangular region? 1 unit

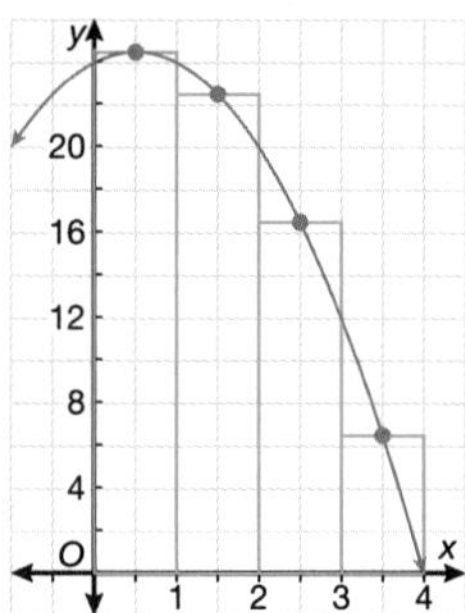

2. The height of each rectangle is the value of $f(x)$ at the points indicated on the graph. Use a calculator to find the height of each rectangle for the points shown. (Height is calculated at the value of x, the midpoint of a given interval. For example, if the first interval is from 0 to 1, then x starts at 0.5 continuing with increments of 1. Likewise, if the first interval is from 0 to 0.5, then x starts at 0.25 and continues with increments of 0.5.)

x	$f(x) = -2x^2 + 2x + 24$
0.5	24.5
1.5	22.5
2.5	16.5
3.5	6.5

INVESTIGATION

8

Materials

- Pencil, graph paper, and calculator

Discuss

Students will estimate the area under a curve using rectangular partitions.

Problem 1

At this point, choosing the number of rectangles and their width should be done for the convenience of the student. Note that all the curves illustrated are continuous.

Problem 2

Plot the points first. Remember that these are midpoints of the width of each rectangle. Mark off the width of each rectangle and then sketch the rectangles.

Problem 4

Since there are now 8 rectangular regions, the first interval is from 0 to 0.5 and x begins at 0.25 continuing with increments of 0.5.

INVESTIGATION RESOURCES

Reteaching Master Investigation 8

MATH BACKGROUND

This investigation gives students a good introduction to integral Calculus. Determining the area under a curve using equal partitions gives only an estimate. In more advanced work, the area bounded by the curve and the y-axis can be estimated using horizontal rectangles. Also, unequal intervals can be used. In future endeavors, students will learn that determining the area under a curve will lead to the definition of a definite integral in Calculus.

ENGLISH LEARNERS

For step 1, explain the meaning of the word **partition.** Say,

"To partition means to divide something into parts. The room was partitioned into two parts."

Have students name objects or regions that can be partitioned. Then have them partition the region in step 1 into eight rectangular regions.

3. Find and add the areas of the rectangular regions to estimate the total area under the curve from $0 \le x \le 4$. 70 square units

4. Now calculate the table with x values at increments of 0.5 with a total of 8 rectangular regions. Find and add the areas of the rectangular regions to estimate the total area under the curve from $0 \le x \le 4$. 69.5 square units

5. The exact area of the curve from $0 \le x \le 4$ is $69\frac{1}{3}$. Compare your estimate to the actual value. The estimated answer is greater than the actual area.

6. Is there a way of improving the accuracy of the estimated area using the rectangle technique? Explain. Yes. Sample answer: If the widths of the rectangles are smaller, then the estimated area will be more accurate.

You can use a summation formula to find the estimated area under a curve. The graph of the function shown is partitioned into eight rectangles.

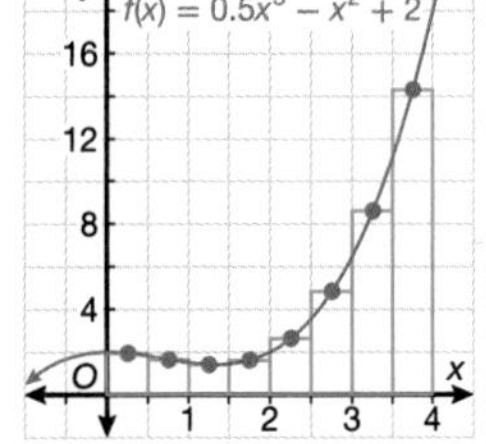

The summation formula for finding the estimated area is

$$\text{Total Area} = 0.5\left(\sum_{i=1}^{8} f(x_i)\right)$$

7. Each term in the series is multiplied by 0.5. What is the significance of this term? It represents the width of the rectangle.

8. Extend and complete the table to $i = 8$ to find each term in the series. See Additional Answers.

i	x_i	$f(x_i) = 0.5x^3 - x^2 + 2$
1	0.25	≈ 1.95
2	0.75	≈ 1.65
3	1.25	≈ 1.41
4	1.75	≈ 1.62

9. Calculate the estimated area. 18.5 square units

Investigation Practice

a. Estimate the area under the curve $y = -x^2 + 5x + 7$ from $0 \le x \le 5$. Use five partitions. 56.25 square units

Estimate the area under the curve $y = -x^3 + 11x^2 + 7x + 1$ from $0 \le x \le 10$.

b. Write the summation formula to find the estimated area with ten partitions. Total Area = $\left(\sum_{i=1}^{10} f(x)\right)$

c. Use a table to calculate each term in the series to find the estimated area. 1530 square units

Problem 4

To emphasize that this process computes an estimate of the area, instruct students to shade the rectangles. Compare the shaded parts of the rectangle that are not under the curve with the non-shaded parts under the curve. As the number of rectangles increase, the widths of the rectangles become smaller which means that the rectangles fit the curve better. This accounts for the more accurate estimate.

TEACHER TIP

The summation formula represents the sum of 8 terms beginning with $f(x_1)$ and ending with $f(x_8)$.

Error Alert

The 0.5 term in the summation series has nothing to do with the 0.5 coefficient of the x^3 term in the function.

Problem 9

Extend the Problem

Give the starting value of x and the increment to find the area under the curve using a total of 16 rectangles.

The first interval is from 0 to 0.25 and x begins at 0.125 continuing with increments of 0.25.

Investigation Practice

Math Conversations

Discussions to strengthen understanding

Problem a

Remember that 5 partitions mean 5 rectangles. The first interval is from 0 to 1 and x begins at 0.5 continuing with increments of 1.

Problem b

Use the summation formula in Problem 6 as a model. In the table, i should range from 1 to 10.

INCLUSION

Students will be familiar with finding the area of a rectangle. Explain that finding the area under a curve is the process of adding the areas of many rectangles together. Label the length and width on each rectangle and write the math work horizontally if needed. Area under the curve = Area of 1st rectangle + Area of 2nd rectangle + Area of 3rd rectangle +…

Expand the summation formula

$0.5\left(\sum_{i=1}^{8} f(x_i)\right) = 0.5(f(x_1) + f(x_2) + f(x_3) + f(x_4) + f(x_5) + f(x_6) + f(x_7) + f(x_8)) =$ width(1st length + 2nd length + … + 8th length).

Lesson Planner

Lesson	New Concepts
81	Using Natural Logarithms
82	Graphing the Sine and Cosine Functions
83	Writing Quadratic Equations from Roots
84	Solving Rational Equations
85	Finding Polynomial Roots II
	Cumulative Test 16, Performance Task 16
86	Translating Sine and Cosine Functions
87	Evaluating Logarithmic Expressions
88	Solving Abstract Equations
89	Solving Quadratic Inequalities
90	Graphing the Tangent Function
	Cumulative Test 17, Performance Task 17
INV 9	Understanding Step Functions

Resources for Teaching

- Student Edition
- Teacher's Edition
- Student Edition eBook
- Teacher's Edition eBook
- Resources and Planner CD
- Solutions Manual
- Instructional Masters
- Technology Lab Masters
- Warm Up and Teaching Transparencies
- Instructional Presentations CD
- Online activities, tools, and homework help **www.SaxonMathResources.com**

Resources for Practice and Assessment

- Student Edition Practice Workbook
- Course Assessments
- Standardized Test Practice
- College Entrance Exam Practice
- Test and Practice Generator CD using ExamView™

Resources for Differentiated Instruction

- Reteaching Masters
- Challenge and Enrichment Masters
- Prerequisite Skills Intervention
- Adaptations for Saxon Algebra 2
- Multilingual Glossary
- English Learners Handbook
- TI Resources

Pacing Guide

Resources and Planner CD for lesson planning support

45-Minute Class

Day 1	Day 2	Day 3	Day 4	Day 5	Day 6
Lesson 81	Lesson 82	Lesson 83	Lesson 84	Lesson 85	Cumulative Test 16
Day 7	**Day 8**	**Day 9**	**Day 10**	**Day 11**	**Day 12**
Lesson 86	Lesson 87	Lesson 88	Lesson 89	Lesson 90	Cumulative Test 17
Day 13					
Investigation 9					

Block: 90-Minute Class

Day 1	Day 2	Day 3	Day 4	Day 5	Day 6
Investigation 8 Lesson 81	Lesson 82 Lesson 83	Lesson 84 Lesson 85	Cumulative Test 16 Lesson 86	Lesson 87 Lesson 88	Lesson 89 Lesson 90
Day 7					
Cumulative Test 17 Investigation 9					

** For suggestions on how to implement Saxon Math in a block schedule, see the Pacing section at the beginning of the Teacher's Edition.*

Differentiated Instruction

Below Level		Advanced Learners	
Warm Up	SE pp. 574, 580, 586, 592, 598, 606, 612, 617, 623, 630	Challenge	TE pp. 579, 584, 591, 597, 604, 610, 615, 621, 626, 629, 634
Skills Bank	SE pp. 862–885	Extend the Example	TE pp. 576, 598, 613, 618, 631, 636
Reteaching Masters	Lessons 81–90, Investigation 9	Extend the Problem	TE pp. 579, 595, 597, 610, 615, 616, 621, 628, 633
Warm Up Transparencies	Lessons 81–90	Challenge and Enrichment Masters	Challenge: C81–C90 Enrichment: E81
English Learners		**Special Needs**	
EL Tips	TE pp. 576, 581, 587, 593, 601, 609, 614, 620, 624, 628, 633, 636	Inclusion Tips	TE pp. 575, 582, 588, 596, 599, 608, 614, 619, 627, 631, 632
Multilingual Glossary	Booklet and Online	Adaptations for Saxon Algebra 2	Lessons 81–90; Cumulative Tests 16, 17
English Learners Handbook			
For All Learners			
Caution	SE pp. 601, 612, 631	Alternate Method	TE pp. 577, 589, 595, 600, 602, 607, 613, 618, 625
Hints	SE pp. 575, 576, 582, 587, 588, 594, 606, 607, 618, 619, 625, 630, 632	Online Tools	
Error Alert	TE pp. 575, 577, 578, 585, 587, 588, 589, 595, 597, 602, 603, 609, 611, 612, 613, 615, 618, 621, 624, 625, 627, 628, 633, 636		

SE = Student Edition; TE = Teacher's Edition

Math Vocabulary

Lesson	New Vocabulary		Maintained	EL Tip in TE
81	natural logarithm		base	decay
82	amplitude cycle of a periodic function period of a periodic function	periodic function	continuous discontinuous	period
83			FOIL	treat
84	rational equation	rational function	rational	rational
85	Rational Root Theorem		Difference of squares	cubic quadratic quartic
86	phase shift		periodic function	constructive destructive
87			change of base formula natural logarithm	cool
88	abstract equation		least common denominator	formula
89	quadratic inequality in one variable quadratic inequality in two variables		boundary line	compound critical
90			periodic function	tangent
INV 9	greatest integer function		step function	parking lot

Math Highlights

Enduring Understandings – The "Big Picture"

After completing Section 9, students will understand:

- How to use natural logarithms.
- How to graph sine, cosine and tangent functions.
- How to solve rational and abstract equations, quadratic inequalities, and step functions.

Essential Questions

- Which trigonometric functions are continuous?
- What is the formula for changing a logarithmic base?

Math Content Strands

Linear Equations and Functions

• Investigation 9	Understanding Step Functions

Polynomials

• Lesson 85	Finding Polynomial Roots II

Rational and Radical Functions

• Lesson 84	Solving Rational Equations
• Lesson 88	Solving Abstract Equations

Quadratic Functions

• Lesson 83	Writing Quadratic Equations from Roots
• Lesson 89	Solving Quadratic Inequalities

Trigonometry

• Lesson 82	Graphing the Sine and Cosine Functions
• Lesson 86	Translating Sine and Cosine Functions
• Lesson 90	Graphing the Tangent Function

Exponential and Logarithmic Functions

• Lesson 81	Using Natural Logarithms
• Lesson 87	Evaluating Logarithmic Expressions

Connections in Practice Problems

	Lessons
Coordinate Geometry	84, 90
Data Analysis	86, 89
Geometry	81, 82, 83, 84, 85, 86, 87, 88, 89, 90
Probability	81, 82, 83, 85, 87, 88
Statistics	88

Math Processes

Reasoning and Communication

	Lessons
• Analyze	81, 82, 83, 84, 85, 86, 87, 88, 89, 90, Inv. 9
• Error analysis	81, 82, 83, 84, 85, 86, 87, 88, 89, 90
• Estimate	83, 85, 88
• Formulate	82, 84, 85, 89, Inv. 9
• Generalize	82, 83, 84, 86, 87, 90, Inv. 9
• Justify	87, 89, 90, Inv. 9
• Math reasoning	83, 84, 89, Inv. 9
• Model	81, 82, 86, 87
• Multiple choice	81, 82, 83, 84, 85, 86, 87, 88, 89, 90
• Multi-step	81, 82, 83, 84, 85, 86, 87, 88, 89, 90
• Verify	81, 82, 85, 86, 89, 90
• Write	81, 82, 83, 85, 86, 87, 88, 89, 90
• Graphing Calculator	81, 82, 83, 84, 85, 86, 87, 88, 89, 90, Inv. 9

Connections

In Examples: Aquarium; Arches; Business; Cell phone rates; Constructive and destructive interference; Distance, rate, and time; Lasers; Medicine; Newton's law of cooling; Parking lot; Radio signals; Roller coaster design

In Practice problems: Aquarium, Bacteria, Chemistry, Cliff height, Construction, Delivery charges, Diameter, Earthquakes, Economics, Electrical engineering, Farming, Fractals, Geography, Geology, Government, Gravity on the moon, Housing, Jewelry, Jewelry making, National parks, Navigation, Paleontology, Pendulum, Physics, Postal rates, Radio, Radioisotopes, Ranching, Running, Soccer, Sound, Students, Surveying, Vertical motion and gravity

Content Trace

Lesson	Warm Up: Prerequisite Skills	New Concepts	Where Practiced	Where Assessed	Looking Forward
81	Lessons 64, 72	Using Natural Logarithms	Lessons 82, 83, 84, 85, 86, 87, 88, 89, 90, 91, 92, 93, 94, 95, 96, 99	Cumulative Tests 17, 20	Lessons 87, 102, 110
82	Lessons 4, 46	Graphing the Sine and Cosine Functions	Lessons 83, 84, 85, 86, 87, 88, 89, 90, 92, 93, 94, 96, 97, 98, 100, 101, 102, 104, 107, 108, 112	Cumulative Tests 17, 18	Lessons 86, 90, 103
83	Lessons 19, 23	Writing Quadratic Equations from Roots	Lessons 84, 85, 86, 87, 88, 89, 90, 91, 92, 93, 94, 95, 96, 98, 99, 100, 101, 102, 103, 105, 113	Cumulative Tests 17, 19, 22	Lessons 88, 89, 101, 111
84	Lessons 23, 28, 37	Solving Rational Equations	Lessons 85, 86, 87, 88, 89, 90, 91, 92, 93, 95, 96, 97, 98, 99, 100, 101, 102, 103, 105, 108, 109, 110	Cumulative Tests 17, 19, 22	Lessons 94, 100, 107
85	Lessons 65, 78	Finding Polynomial Roots II	Lessons 86, 87, 88, 89, 90, 91, 92, 93, 96, 97, 98, 101, 102, 103, 105, 106, 107, 109, 110, 111	Cumulative Tests 17, 18	Lessons 95, 101, 106, 111
86	Lesson 82	Translating Sine and Cosine Functions	Lessons 87, 88, 89, 90, 92, 96, 97, 98, 102, 105, 109, 110	Cumulative Tests 18, 23	Lessons 90, 119
87	Lessons 72, 81	Evaluating Logarithmic Expressions	Lessons 88, 89, 90, 92, 93, 94, 95, 96, 97, 98, 99, 100, 101, 104, 105, 106, 107, 112, 115, 119	Cumulative Tests 18, 19, 21	Lessons 93, 102
88	Lessons 7, 23, 37, 40, 51	Solving Abstract Equations	Lessons 89, 90, 91, 93, 94, 96, 97, 98, 102, 103, 104, 105, 108, 109, 112, 113, 114, 117	Cumulative Tests 18, 22	Lessons 91, 93, 98
89	Lessons 39, 65	Solving Quadratic Inequalities	Lessons 90, 92, 93, 94, 96, 97, 98, 99, 100, 101, 103, 107, 108, 110, 111, 113, 115, 118	Cumulative Test 19	Lesson 94
90	Lessons 82, 86	Graphing the Tangent Function	Lessons 91, 93, 94, 95, 96, 98, 100, 101, 103, 104, 105, 110, 111, 113, 114, 117, 118	Cumulative Tests 18, 19	Lessons 96, 103, 119
INV 9	N/A	Understanding Step Functions	Lessons 107, 109	Cumulative Test 19	N/A

SECTION OVERVIEW 9

Ongoing Assessment

	Type	Feature	Intervention *
BEFORE instruction	Assess Prior Knowledge	• Diagnostic Test	• Prerequisite Skills Intervention
BEFORE the lesson	Formative	• Warm Up	• Skills Bank • Reteaching Masters
DURING the lesson	Formative	• Lesson Practice • Math Conversations with the Practice problems	• Additional Examples in TE • Test and Practice Generator (for additional practice sheets)
AFTER the lesson	Formative	• Check for Understanding (closure)	• Scaffolding Questions in TE
AFTER 5 lessons	Summative	After Lesson 85 • Cumulative Test 16 • Performance Task 16 After Lesson 90 • Cumulative Test 17 • Performance Task 17	• Reteaching Masters • Test and Practice Generator (for additional tests and practice)
AFTER 20 lessons	Summative	• Benchmark Tests	• Reteaching Masters • Test and Practice Generator (for additional tests and practice)

* for students not showing progress during the formative stages or scoring below 80% on the summative assessments

Evidence of Learning – What Students Should Know

Because the Saxon philosophy is to provide students with sufficient time to learn and practice each concept, a lesson's topic will not be tested until at least five lessons after the topic is introduced.

On the Cumulative Tests that are given during this section of ten lessons, students should be able to demonstrate the following competencies:

- Use the Law of Cosines.
- Solve piecewise functions.
- Find the normal distribution.
- Write quadratic equations from roots.

Test and Practice Generator CD using ExamView™

The Test and Practice Generator is an easy-to-use benchmark and assessment tool that creates unlimited practice and tests in multiple formats and allows you to customize questions or create new ones. A variety of reports are available to track student progress toward mastery of the standards throughout the year.

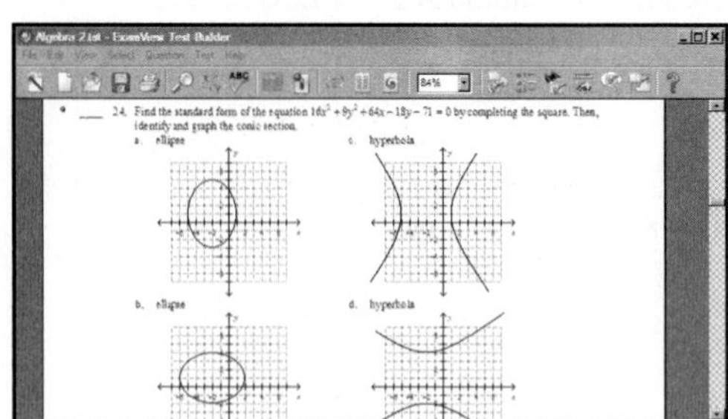

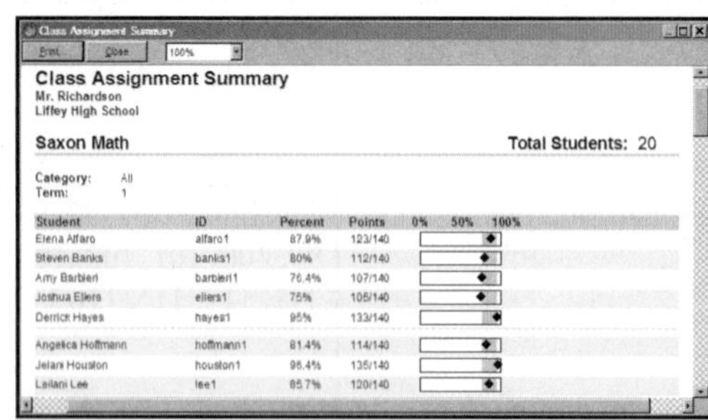

Assessment Resources

Resources for Diagnosing and Assessing

- **Student Edition**
  - Warm Up
  - Lesson Practice
- **Teacher's Edition**
  - Math Conversations with the Practice problems
  - Check for Understanding (closure)
- **Course Assessments**
  - Diagnostic Test
  - Cumulative Tests
  - Performance Tasks
  - Benchmark Tests

Resources for Test Prep

- **Student Edition**
  - Multiple-choice practice problems
  - Multiple-step and writing problems
  - Daily cumulative practice
- **Standardized Test Practice**
- **College Entrance Exam Practice**
- **Test and Practice Generator CD using ExamView™**

Resources for Intervention

- **Student Edition**
  - Skills Bank
- **Teacher's Edition**
  - Additional Examples
  - Scaffolding questions
- **Prerequisite Skills Intervention**
  - Worksheets
- **Reteaching Masters**
  - Lesson instruction and practice sheets
- **Test and Practice Generator CD using ExamView™**
  - Lesson practice problems
  - Additional tests

Cumulative Tests

The assessments in Saxon Math are frequent and consistently placed after every five lessons to offer a regular method of ongoing testing. These cumulative assessments check mastery of concepts from previous lessons.

Performance Tasks

The Performance Tasks can be used in conjunction with the Cumulative Tests and are scored using a rubric.

After Lesson 85

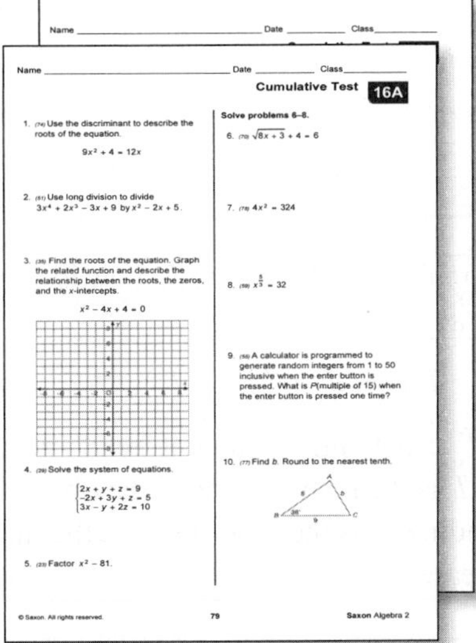

Name ______ Date ______ Class ______

Cumulative Test 16A

1. (74) Use the discriminant to describe the roots of the equation.
$9x^2 + 4 = 12x$

2. (51) Use long division to divide $3x^4 + 2x^3 - 3x + 9$ by $x^2 - 2x + 5$.

3. (35) Find the roots of the equation. Graph the related function and describe the relationship between the roots, the zeros, and the x-intercepts.
$x^2 - 4x + 4 = 0$

4. (29) Solve the system of equations.
$\begin{cases} 2x + y + z = 9 \\ -2x + 3y + z = 5 \\ 3x - y + 2z = 10 \end{cases}$

5. (23) Factor $x^2 - 81$.

Solve problems 6–8.

6. (70) $\sqrt{8x+3} + 4 = 6$

7. (78) $4x^2 = 324$

8. (59) $x^{\frac{5}{3}} = 32$

9. (55) A calculator is programmed to generate random integers from 1 to 50 inclusive when the enter button is pressed. What is P(multiple of 15) when the enter button is pressed one time?

10. (77) Find b. Round to the nearest tenth.

© Saxon. All rights reserved. 79 Saxon Algebra 2

After Lesson 90

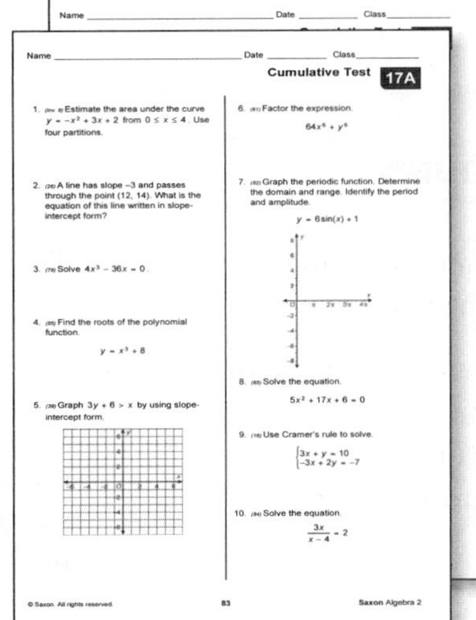

Name ______ Date ______ Class ______

Cumulative Test 17A

1. (Inv. 8) Estimate the area under the curve $y = -x^2 + 3x + 2$ from $0 \le x \le 4$. Use four partitions.

2. (26) A line has slope −3 and passes through the point (12, 14). What is the equation of this line written in slope-intercept form?

3. (76) Solve $4x^3 - 36x = 0$.

4. (85) Find the roots of the polynomial function.
$y = x^3 + 8$

5. (39) Graph $3y + 6 > x$ by using slope-intercept form.

6. (81) Factor the expression.
$64x^6 + y^6$

7. (82) Graph the periodic function. Determine the domain and range. Identify the period and amplitude.
$y = 6\sin(x) + 1$

8. (65) Solve the equation.
$5x^2 + 17x + 6 = 0$

9. (16) Use Cramer's rule to solve.
$\begin{cases} 3x + y = 10 \\ -3x + 2y = -7 \end{cases}$

10. (84) Solve the equation.
$\frac{3x}{x-4} = 2$

© Saxon. All rights reserved. 83 Saxon Algebra 2

For use with Performance Tasks

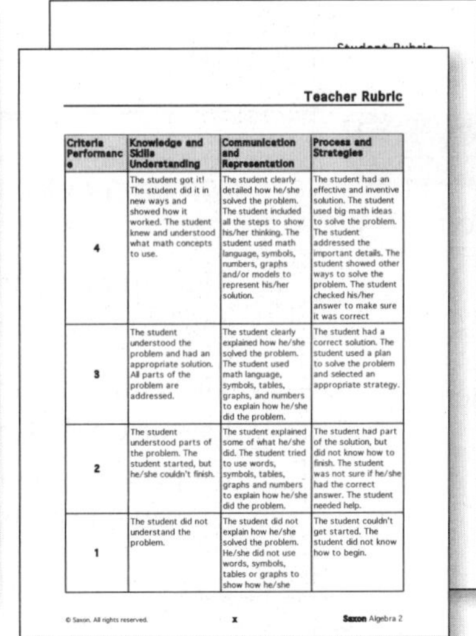

Teacher Rubric

Criteria Performance	Knowledge and Skills Understanding	Communication and Representation	Process and Strategies
4	The student got it! The student did it in new ways and showed how it worked. The student knew and understood what math concepts to use.	The student clearly detailed how he/she solved the problem. The student included all the steps to show his/her thinking. The student used math language, symbols, numbers, graphs and/or models to represent his/her solution.	The student had an effective and inventive solution. The student used big math ideas to solve the problem. The student addressed the important details. The student showed other ways to solve the problem. The student checked his/her answer to make sure it was correct
3	The student understood the problem and had an appropriate solution. All parts of the problem are addressed.	The student clearly explained how he/she solved the problem. The student used math language, symbols, tables, graphs, and numbers to explain how he/she did the problem.	The student had a correct solution. The student used a plan to solve the problem and selected an appropriate strategy.
2	The student understood parts of the problem. The student started, but he/she couldn't finish.	The student explained some of what he/she did. The student tried to use words, symbols, tables, graphs and numbers to explain how he/she did the problem.	The student had part of the solution, but did not know how to finish. The student was not sure if he/she had the correct answer. The student needed help.
1	The student did not understand the problem.	The student did not explain how he/she solved the problem. He/she did not use words, symbols, tables or graphs to show how he/she	The student couldn't get started. The student did not know how to begin.

© Saxon. All rights reserved. x Saxon Algebra 2

LESSON 81

1 Warm Up

Review the Product and Quotient Properties of Logarithms for Problems 2 and 3.

2 New Concepts

In this lesson, students simplify exponential and logarithmic expressions and apply properties of natural logarithms.

Discuss the meaning of **natural logarithm** and its notation. Tell students that e is an irrational number like π, and it is approximately equal to 2.718.

Example 1

Discuss how to simplify logarithmic expressions.

Additional Example 1

a. Simplify $e^{\ln 2x}$. $2x$

b. Simplify $\ln e^{2d^2+d}$. $2d^2 + d$

LESSON 81

Using Natural Logarithms

Warm Up

1. (64) **Vocabulary** In the expression $\log 20$, the ___base___ is 10.

2. (72) Write $\log xy$ as a sum or difference of terms. $\log x + \log y$

3. (72) Write $\log \frac{x}{y}$ as a sum or difference of terms. $\log x - \log y$

4. (64) **Multiple Choice** Which is $9^2 = 81$ in logarithmic form? C

A $\log_2 9 = 81$ B $\log_2 81 = 9$

C $\log_9 81 = 2$ D $\log_{81} 9 = 2$

New Concepts

Since a logarithm is the exponent applied to a base to obtain a given value, $b^x = a$ is equivalent to $\log_b a = x$.

Reading Math

$\log_{10} a$ is denoted $\log a$. $\log_e a$ is denoted $\ln a$, and is read "natural log of a."

When the base is e, the logarithm is called the **natural logarithm,** denoted ln, and the equations above are written as follows.

$$e^x = a \Leftrightarrow \ln a = x$$

The Inverse Properties of Logarithms were previously used to simplify logarithmic expressions. In this lesson the Inverse Property of Logarithms will be used to simplify logarithmic expressions where the base is the constant e.

Inverse Properties of Logarithms
$e^{\ln x} = x$ and $\ln e^x = x$, where $x > 0$

Example 1 Simplifying Exponential and Logarithmic Expressions

Hint

The Inverse Properties of Exponents and Logarithms involving base e are special cases.

a. Simplify $e^{\ln p}$.

SOLUTION

$e^{\ln p} = p$ Inverse Properties of Logarithms

b. Simplify $\ln e^{3c^2+1}$.

SOLUTION

$\ln e^{3c^2+1} = 3c^2 + 1$ Inverse Properties of Logarithms

Properties of logarithms are the same for base e.

Properties of Natural Logarithms		
Product Property	$\ln ab = \ln a + \ln b$	for any positive numbers a and b.
Quotient Property	$\ln \frac{a}{b} = \ln a - \ln b$	for any positive numbers a and b.
Power Property	$\ln a^p = p \ln a$	for any positive number a and real number p.

LESSON RESOURCES

Student Editions Practice Workbook 81
Reteaching Master 81
Adaptations Master 81
Challenge and Enrichment Master C81

MATH BACKGROUND

The natural logarithm can be applied to applications other than decay.

The natural logarithm is used in Newton's Law of Cooling, which is used to model the temperature change of an object with the temperature in its surroundings.

The formula used for Newton's Law is defined as

$$T(t) = T_s + (T_0 - T_s)e^{-kt}$$

where T_0 is the initial temperature of the object, T_s is the temperature of the object's surroundings, t is the time, and k is the rate of decrease.

The exponential function with base e and the natural logarithmic function are inverse functions, as shown below.

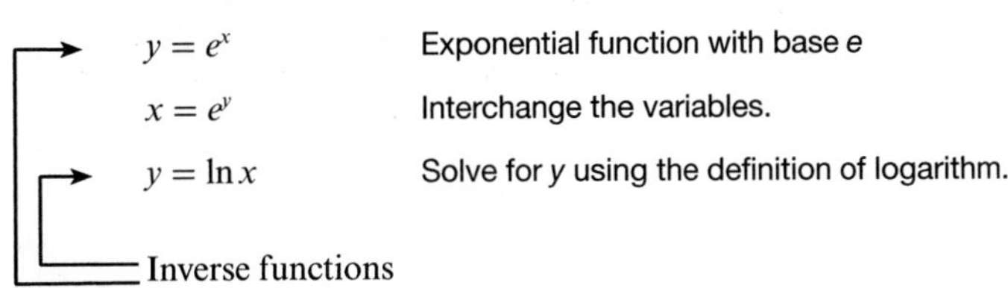

$y = e^x$ Exponential function with base e
$x = e^y$ Interchange the variables.
$y = \ln x$ Solve for y using the definition of logarithm.
Inverse functions

Example 2 Applying Properties of Natural Logarithms

Rewrite each expression as a sum or difference of terms if possible. Then simplify.

a. $\ln 6e$

SOLUTION

$\ln 6e = \ln 6 + \ln e$	Product Property
$= \ln 6 + 1$	$\ln e = 1$ because $e^1 = e$.

b. $\ln \frac{3e}{x}$

SOLUTION

$\ln \frac{3e}{x} = \ln 3e - \ln x$	Quotient Property
$= \ln 3 + \ln e - \ln x$	Product Property
$= \ln 3 + 1 - \ln x$	$\ln e = 1$ because $e^1 = e$.
$= \ln 3 - \ln x + 1$	

c. $\ln e^{5x^2}$

SOLUTION

$\ln e^{5x^2} = 5x^2 \ln e$	Power Property
$= 5x^2 \cdot 1$	$\ln e = 1$ because $e^1 = e$.
$= 5x^2$	

d. $\ln\left(\frac{2x^3}{e^4}\right)^2$

SOLUTION

$\ln\left(\frac{2x^3}{e^4}\right)^2 = 2\ln\left(\frac{2x^3}{e^4}\right)$	Power Property
$= 2(\ln 2x^3 - \ln e^4)$	Quotient Property
$= 2(\ln 2 + \ln x^3 - \ln e^4)$	Product Property
$= 2(\ln 2 + 3\ln x - 4)$	Power Property, $\ln e^a = a$
$= 2\ln 2 + 6\ln x - 8$	Distribute the 2.

Example 2

Error Alert Students may forget to simplify $\ln e$ as 1. Remind them $\ln e = 1$ because $e^1 = e$.

Additional Example 2

Rewrite each expression as a sum or difference of terms if possible. Then simplify.

a. $\ln 10e$ $\ln 10 + 1$

b. $\ln \frac{5e}{y}$ $\ln 5 - \ln y + 1$

c. $3\ln e^{6x^2}$ $18x^2$

d. $\ln\left(\frac{4c^3}{e^2}\right)^4$ $4\ln 4 + 12\ln c - 8$

INCLUSION

Have students highlight the numbers for a and b with different color markers. In Example 2a, students would highlight 6 with a yellow marker and e with a pink marker throughout.

Example 3

Extend the Example

Have students work in pairs to find the half-life of an element of their choice. Have them calculate how long it would take 1.0 gram of that element to decay to 0.1 gram.

Additional Example 3

Radium is an alkaline earth metal and extremely radioactive. Its isotope Ra-226 has a half-life of 1,602 years and decays into radon gas. How long will it take for 1.0 gram of Ra-226 to decay to 0.2 gram?
about 3,716.95 years

Lesson Practice

Problem c

Error Alert Students may confuse the properties and treat the 4 like an exponent to get $4\ln e$ or 4. Point out to students that to simplify $\ln 4e$ they need to use the Product Property since $4e$ is a product.

Recall the exponential growth function $A = Pe^{rt}$ that is used to model the amount in an account where interest is compounded continuously. This function can be written in a general way to represent other growth and decay situations.

Natural Base Functions
$N(t) = N_0e^{kt}$ is a natural base exponential growth function and $N(t) = N_0e^{-kt}$ is a natural base exponential decay function, where $N_0 = N(0)$ is the original amount ($t = 0$) and $k > 0$ is a constant.

In order to solve a related exponential equation, where there is a variable in the exponent, the logarithm of both sides of the equation must be taken.

Example 3 Application: Medicine

Thallium is a radioactive substance that can be injected into the blood as part of a health test for the heart. It is then tracked through the bloodstream by a special camera. Thallium has a half-life of 73.1 hours. How long will it take for 1 gram of thallium to decay to 0.1 gram?

SOLUTION

Step 1: Find the constant k for thallium.

$N(t) = N_0e^{-kt}$	Write the natural decay function.
$0.5 = 1e^{-k(73.1)}$	Substitute 0.5 for $N(t)$, 1 for N_0, and 73.1 for t.
$\ln 0.5 = \ln e^{-k(73.1)}$	Take the natural logarithm of both sides.
$\ln 0.5 = -73.1k$	Inverse Properties of Logarithms.
$k = \frac{\ln 0.5}{-73.1} \approx 0.00948$	

> **Hint**
> Substitute 0.5 for $N(t)$ and 73.1 for t because 50% of the initial amount remains after 73.1 hours. Substitute 1 for N_0 because 100% is the initial amount.

Step 2: Write the decay function and solve for t.

$N(t) = N_0e^{-0.00948t}$	Substitute 0.00948 for k.
$0.1 = 1e^{-0.00948t}$	Substitute 1 gram for the initial amount and 0.1 gram for the amount at time t.
$\ln 0.1 = \ln e^{-0.00948t}$	Take the natural logarithm of both sides.
$\ln 0.1 = -0.00948t$	Inverse Properties of Logarithms
$t = \frac{\ln 0.1}{-0.00948} \approx 242.9$	

> **Hint**
> By taking the natural logarithm of both sides of the equation, the inverse property of exponents and logarithms can be used to eliminate e.

It will take about 242.9 hours for 1 gram of thallium to decay to 0.1 gram.

Lesson Practice

a. Simplify $e^{\ln(3d-1)}$. $3d - 1$
(Ex 1)

b. Simplify $\ln e^{u^3+u}$. $u^3 + u$
(Ex 1)

c. Rewrite $\ln 4e$ as a sum or difference of terms if possible. Then simplify.
(Ex 2) $\ln 4 + 1$

d. Rewrite $\ln\frac{2x}{e}$ as a sum or difference of terms if possible. Then simplify.
(Ex 2) $\ln 2 + \ln x - 1$

ENGLISH LEARNERS

To help students understand the meaning of **decay**, define decay as to decrease in size, quantity, activity, or force.

Discuss other meanings of decay: to fall into ruin, to decline in health or strength, to undergo decomposition. Tell students synonyms for decay: decomposition, crumble, decline, decompose, and disintegrate.

Have students identify things that have or may decay, such as bones, teeth, food, old buildings, and so on.

Connect the meaning of decay to decay of an element. Decay of an element is a spontaneous disintegration. Have students explain how decay is used in Example 3.

e. Rewrite $\ln 8e^{-x^3}$ as a sum or difference of terms if possible. Then simplify. $\ln 8 - x^3$
(Ex 2)

f. Rewrite $\ln\left(\frac{5e^2}{v^3}\right)^3$ as a sum or difference of terms if possible. Then simplify. $3\ln 5 - 9\ln v + 6$
(Ex 2)

g. Determine how long it will take for 200 mg of chromium-49, which has a half-life of about 42.3 minutes, to decay to 5 mg.
(Ex 3)
about 225 minutes

Practice Distributed and Integrated

1. Find an equation for the inverse of $y = x^2 + 3$. Determine whether each relation is a function. $y = \pm\sqrt{x-3}$; the given relation is a function, the inverse is not a function
(50)

***2.** Weights have a mean of 35 lbs and a standard deviation of 0.5 lbs. Find the z-score for a weight of 36.8 lbs. 3.6
(80)

Determine the domain and range.

3. $y = -4\sqrt{x+2}$
(75)
domain: $x \geq -2$, range: $y \leq 0$

4. $y = \frac{1}{2}\sqrt{x}$
(75)
domain: $x \geq 0$; range: $y \geq 0$

***5.** Rewrite $\ln 14e$ as a sum or difference of terms if possible. Then simplify. $\ln 14 + 1$
(81)

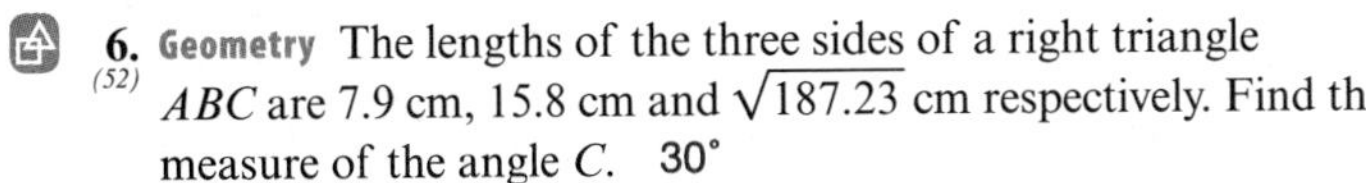

6. Geometry The lengths of the three sides of a right triangle ABC are 7.9 cm, 15.8 cm and $\sqrt{187.23}$ cm respectively. Find the measure of the angle C. 30°
(52)

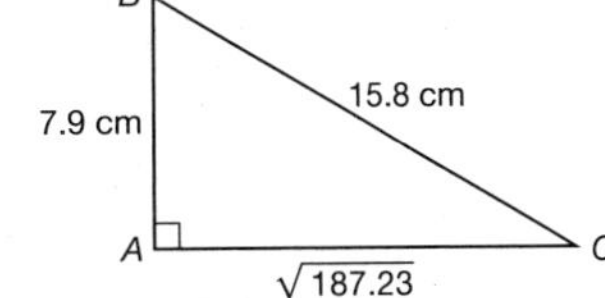

7. Write Explain why $e^{\ln x} = x$. Sample: Exponential and logarithmic operations are inverse operations.
(72)

8. Let $p(u) = 2u + 5$ with domain {1, 3, 5, 7} and $r(u) = u - 3$ with domain {6, 8}. What are the domain and range of $p(r(u))$? domain: {6, 8}; range: {11, 15}
(53)

9. Verify Show by synthetic division that $x + 9$ is a factor of $6x^3 + 51x^2 - 27x$.
(61)

9.

−9	6	51	−27
		−54	27
	6	−3	0

; The binomial is a factor because the remainder is 0.

10. Fractals Some fractals are produced using the formula $Z_{n+1} = (Z_n)^2 + c$. Find Z_2 if $Z_1 = 0.3 + 0.8i$ and $Z_2 = (Z_1)^2 + 0.5$. $-0.05 + 0.48i$
(69)

11. Error Analysis A box contains 16 red balls numbered 1–16, 10 green balls numbered 27–36, and 14 yellow balls numbered 47–60. A ball is randomly selected from the box. The work below is used to find the probability that the ball selected is yellow or a one-digit number. Explain why the work is incorrect.
(60)

Y = event of yellow ball selected D = event of one-digit number selected

$P(Y) = \frac{14}{40} = \frac{7}{20}$ $P(D) = \frac{9}{60} = \frac{3}{20}$

$P(Y \text{ or } D) = P(Y) \cdot P(D) = \frac{7}{20} \cdot \frac{3}{20} = 0.0525$

11. Although the numbers go up to 60 there are only 40 balls so $P(D)$ is incorrect. Also, the probabilities would be added, not multiplied.

12. Multi-Step A 5 inch by 7 inch photo is framed and the total area of the photo and the frame is 50 square inches.
(65)

a. Write a quadratic expression in standard form to represent the situation. $4x^2 + 24x - 15 = 0$

b. Find the width of the frame to the nearest hundredth of an inch. 0.57 inch

Check for Understanding

The questions below help assess the concepts taught in this lesson.

1. "How do you simplify $\ln e^{x^2+3}$?" Sample: Use the Power Property to get $(x^2 + 3)\ln e$. By definition, $\ln e = 1$. So, $\ln e^{x^2+3} = x^2 + 3$.

2. "How do you write $\ln \frac{6e}{2x}$ as a sum or difference of terms?" Use the Quotient Property to get $\ln 6e - \ln 2x$. Use the Product Property twice to get $\ln 6 + \ln e - (\ln 2 + \ln x)$. Then simplify the expression: $\ln 6 - \ln 2 - \ln x + 1$.

3 Practice

Math Conversations

Discussions to strengthen understanding

Problem 1

Guide the students by asking them the following questions.

"What kind of graph is $y = x^2 + 3$?" a parabola

"Is this relation a function?" Yes, $y = x^2 + 3$ is a function.

"How do you find the inverse of $y = x^2 + 3$?" Substitute x for y and y for x. Then solve for y.

Problem 5

"What property do you use to simplify $\ln 14e$?" Product Property

"What is $\ln e$?" 1

ALTERNATE METHOD FOR PROBLEM 9

Have students show by factoring that $x + 9$ is a factor of $6x^3 + 51x^2 - 27x$.

$3x(2x^2 + 17x - 9)$

$3x(2x - 1)(x + 9)$

Problem 17

Remind students to divide both sides by 2 before solving for x.

Problem 19

Error Alert

Students may add 7 to both sides of the equation instead of subtracting 7. Review the steps for solving an equation by having students isolate the term $\sqrt{3x}$ and then solve the equation.

Problem 21

TEACHER TIP

Have students rewrite the equation in the form $ax^2 + bx + c = 0$. Then find the discriminant by substituting the values for a, b, and c into the expression $b^2 - 4ac$. Remind students that if the result is 0, then the equation has one real solution.

Solve by completing the square.

13. (78) $2d^2 = 8 + 10d$ $\quad d = \frac{5}{2} \pm \frac{\sqrt{41}}{2}$

14. (78) $-3x^2 + 18x = -30$ $\quad x = 3 \pm \sqrt{19}$

15. (68) **Housing** The table shows estimated housing occupancy for three states for the year 2006. Find the probability that a randomly selected house from one of these states is vacant given that the house is in Idaho. Write the probability as a percent rounded to the nearest hundredth. 10.91%

	Occupied Houses	Vacant Houses
Idaho	548,555	67,148
Florida	7,106,042	1,425,818
Illinois	4,724,252	475,491

16. (23) **Running** The expression representing a runner's speed is $120x^2 - 60x - 240$ feet per minute. Find the expression for the runner's speed in feet per second.
$2x^2 - x - 4$ ft/s

***17.** (78) **Multiple Choice** What are the roots of the equation $2x^2 = 50$? **C**
A 0 and 50 **B** 0 and 25 **C** 5 and −5 **D** 25 and −25

18. (73) **Multi-Step** Explain why the question below leads the reader to vote *no*. Then rewrite the question in a way that leads the reader to vote *yes*.

"A new shopping mall will bring more traffic to our already congested streets, increasing the noise and pollution levels and the time it takes to drive anywhere. Do you want a new shopping mall in our area?"

18. Sample: The question only tells the negative side of a new shopping mall. "A new shopping mall will give our jobless people jobs and bring more money to our community. Do you want a new shopping mall in our area?"

19. (70) **Multiple Choice** Solve $\sqrt{3x} + 7 = 9$. **B**
A $\frac{3}{4}$ **B** $\frac{4}{3}$ **C** $\frac{16}{3}$ **D** $\frac{256}{3}$

***20.** (81) **Analyze** What pair of inverse functions contain the ordered pairs $\left(e^{\frac{1}{2}}, \frac{1}{2}\right)$ and $\left(\frac{1}{2}, e^{\frac{1}{2}}\right)$?
$y = \ln x$ and $y = e^x$

21. (74) **Ranching** A rancher has 380 feet of fencing material to enclose a rectangular area for her llamas. She wants the fenced-in area to be 9025 square feet. The equation $w(190 - w) = 9025$ gives the width of a rectangle that meets these requirements. Use the discriminant to explain if the rancher has enough material to build a fence that meets these requirements. Yes, discriminant = 0, one real solution

***22.** (81) **Paleontology** Carbon 14 is an isotope that is used to determine ages of fossils. It has a half-life of about 5730 years, which means that 50% of an initial amount will decay in 5730 years. To the nearest year, how long will it take for 51% of an initial amount to decay? (Use the natural decay function $N(t) = N_0e^{-kt}$.) 5897 years

23. (67) **Write** Explain why the inverses of the trigonometric functions are not functions.
Sample: There are many angles that have any given trigonometric function value.

***24.** (81) Given $N(t) = 0.3$, $N_0 = 1$, $k = 0.0974$, write the decay function and solve for t.
$0.3 = e^{-0.0974t}$, $t = 12.36$

25. (76) **Construction** Concrete is going to be poured into a container in the shape of a rectangular prism. The container is constructed from the form shown. If the volume of concrete is 300, what are the actual dimensions of the container to the nearest hundredth? $1 \times 12.25 \times 24.5$

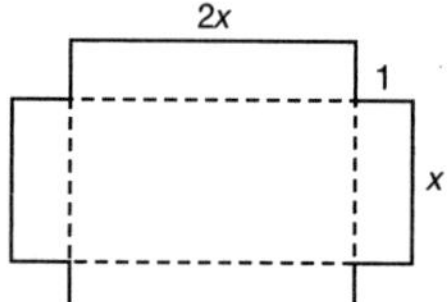

***26.** (81) **Probability** An experiment consists of choosing a random integer from the integers 1 through 10 inclusive. Five trials are conducted. What is the probability that an integer greater than 2 is chosen on every trial?
$0.8^5 = 0.32768 = 32.768\%$

578 Saxon Algebra 2

***27.** (77) **Graphing Calculator** Find c in $\triangle BCD$ given $b = 34.729$, $d = 21.65$, and $m\angle C = 125.37°$. Round to the nearest thousandth. $c = 50.451$

***28.** (80) **Model** The heights of a group of children are normally distributed with a mean of 42 inches and a standard deviation of 2.2 inches. Draw a bell curve and label 3 standard deviations above and below the mean.

29. (67) Evaluate the inverse trigonometric function $\text{Cos}^{-1}\left(\frac{\sqrt{3}}{2}\right)$. Give you answer in both radians and degrees. $\frac{\pi}{6}$; 30°

***30.** (80) A set of results are normally distributed with a mean of 26 and a standard deviation of 2. Find the percent of results > 22. 97.5%

28.

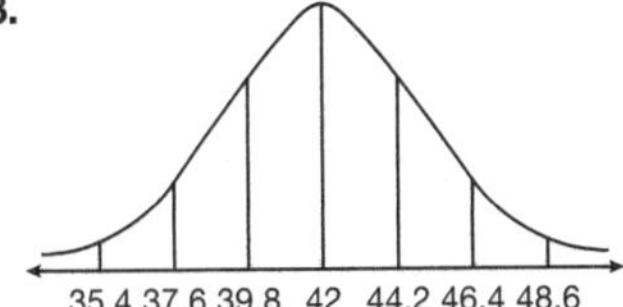

Problem 24

TEACHER TIP

For problem 24, have students note that k is already given. Have them follow Step 2 in Example 3. If necessary, supply students with the decay function, and guide them on how solve for t.

Problem 27

Extend the Problem

Have students find the area of $\triangle BCD$. Round to the nearest thousandth.

$A = \frac{1}{2}(34.729)(21.65)\sin 125.37$

$A \approx 306.554$

CHALLENGE

Carbon-14 has a half-life of about 5,700 years. How long will it take 100 grams of carbon-14 to decay to 25 grams?

about 11,000 years

LOOKING FORWARD

Using natural logarithms prepares students for

- **Lesson 87** Evaluating Logarithmic Expressions
- **Lesson 102** Solving Logarithmic Equations and Inequalities
- **Lesson 110** Graphing Logarithmic Functions

LESSON 82

1 Warm Up

Before students begin Problems 2 and 3, supply them with functions and have them graph $f(x - 1)$ and $f(x) + 1$ for those functions.

2 New Concepts

Discuss period of a periodic function, sine function, cosine function and amplitude. Explain how to determine the period and amplitude. Explain how to graph sine and cosine functions.

LESSON RESOURCES

Student Edition Practice Workbook 82
Reteaching Master 82
Adaptations Master 82
Challenge and Enrichment Master C82

LESSON 82

Graphing the Sine and Cosine Functions

Warm Up

1. (4) **Vocabulary** For a given function $f(x)$, the function $f(x) + 1$ is a ________ of the original function. transformation

2. (4) True or False. For a given function $f(x)$, the function $f(x - 1)$ is a vertical shift of the original function. false

3. (4) True or False. For a given function $f(x)$, the function $f(x) + 1$ is a vertical shift of the original function. true

4. (46) **Multiple Choice** Which is the same as $\sin \frac{\pi}{6}$? **B**
   A 0 **B** 0.5 **C** 1 **D** $\frac{\sqrt{2}}{2}$

New Concepts

A **periodic function** is a function that repeats exactly in regular intervals, called periods. A **cycle of a periodic function** is the shortest repeating part of a periodic graph or function. The **period of a periodic function** is the length of a cycle measured in units of the independent variable.

A sine function is an example of a periodic function. The sine function $y = \sin x$ can be graphed by matching the measure x of an angle in standard position with the y-coordinate of the intersection point of the terminal side of the angle and the unit circle.

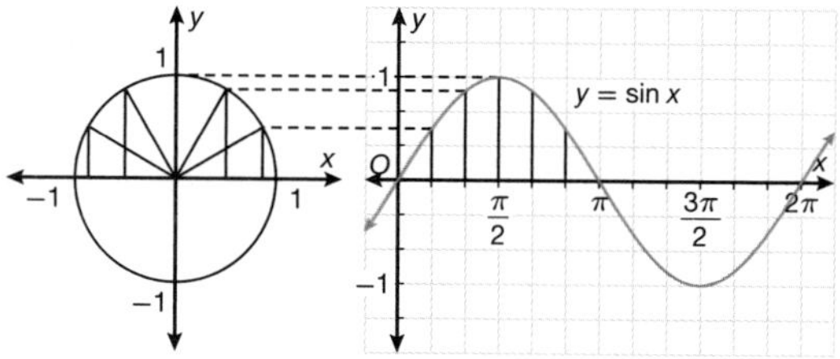

The cosine function is graphed in a similar manner with the measure x of an angle in standard position matching with the x-coordinate of the intersection point of the terminal side of the angle and the unit circle.

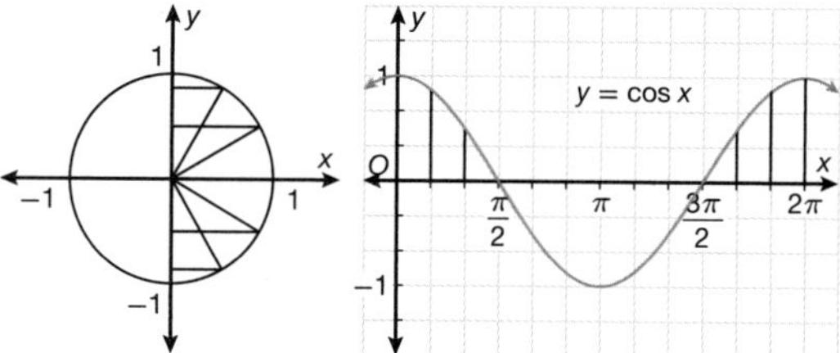

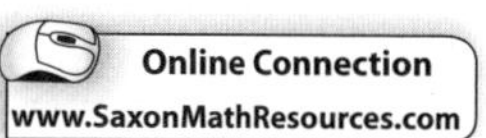

Looking at the graphs you can see that one cycle of each function is completed in 2π radians; so the period of the sine and cosine function is 2π.

MATH BACKGROUND

The sine and cosine functions are the first of the six trigonometric functions students will graph. While the sine and cosine graphs are *continuous,* the graphs of the other four functions, tangent, cotangent, secant, and cosecant, are *discontinuous.* The graphs have breaks where the function is not defined.

The **amplitude** of a period function is half the distance between the maximum and minimum values of the range. The amplitude is always positive. For the sine and cosine functions, the maximum value of the range is 1 and the minimum value of the range is -1, with a distance of 2 between. So, the amplitude is $\frac{2}{2} = 1$.

Example 1 Finding the Amplitude and Period Graphically

a. Use the graph of $y = 3 \sin 4x$ to find the amplitude and period of the function.

SOLUTION

The range has a maximum value of 3 and a minimum value of 3 with a distance of 6 between them.

The amplitude is $\frac{6}{2} = \mathbf{3}$.

There are 4 cycles graphed in 2π. The period is the length of 1 cycle.

The period is $\frac{2\pi}{4} = \boldsymbol{\frac{\pi}{2}}$.

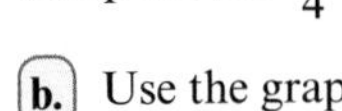

b. Use the graph of $y = -2 \sin 3x$ to find the amplitude and period of the function.

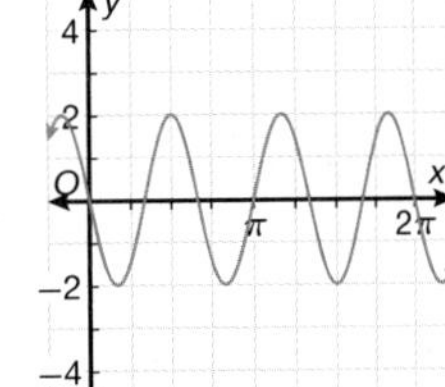

SOLUTION

The range has a maximum value of 2 and a minimum value of 2 with a distance of 4 between them.

The amplitude is $\frac{4}{2} = \mathbf{2}$.

There are 3 cycles graphed in 2π. The period is the length of 1 cycle.

The period is $\boldsymbol{\frac{2\pi}{3}}$.

Math Reasoning

Generalize How is the number of cycles related to the coefficient of x in the equation?

The number of cycles is equal to the coefficient of x.

Math Reasoning

Generalize How is the amplitude related to the coefficient of the trig function?

How does a negative value of the coefficient of the trig function affect the graph?

The amplitude is equal to the absolute value of the coefficient of the trig function.; The negative value reflects the graph over the x-axis.

Properties of Sine and Cosine Graphs
For the graphs of $y = a \sin bx$ or $y = a \cos bx$ where x is in radians and $a \neq 0$ • the amplitude is $\lvert a \rvert$. • the number of cycles in the interval from 0 to 2π is b. • the period is $\frac{2\pi}{b}$.

To graph a sine or cosine function, locate five points equally spaced through one cycle. These points will be the zeros, the maximums, and the minimums. For the sine function if $a > 0$, the pattern of these points is zero-max-zero-min-zero and if $a < 0$, the pattern of these points is zero-min-zero-max-zero. For the cosine function if $a > 0$, the pattern of these points is max-zero-min-zero-max and if $a < 0$, the pattern of these points is min-zero-max-zero-min.

Additional Example 1

a. Use the graph of $y = 10 \sin 2x$ to find the amplitude and period of the function. Amplitude: 10; Period: π

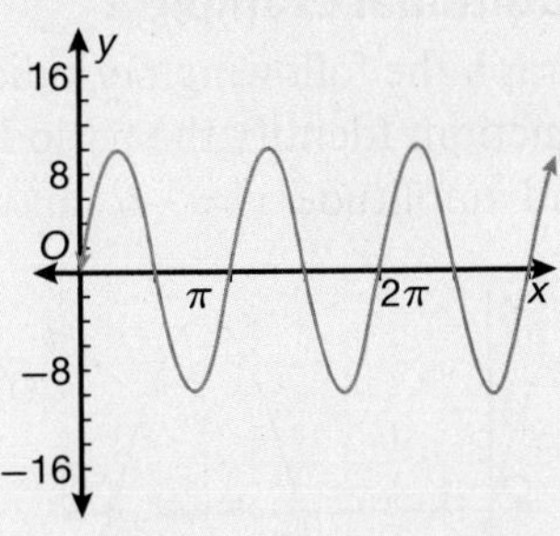

b. Use the graph of $y = -3\sin\frac{1}{2}x$ to find the amplitude and period of the function Amplitude: 3; Period: 4π

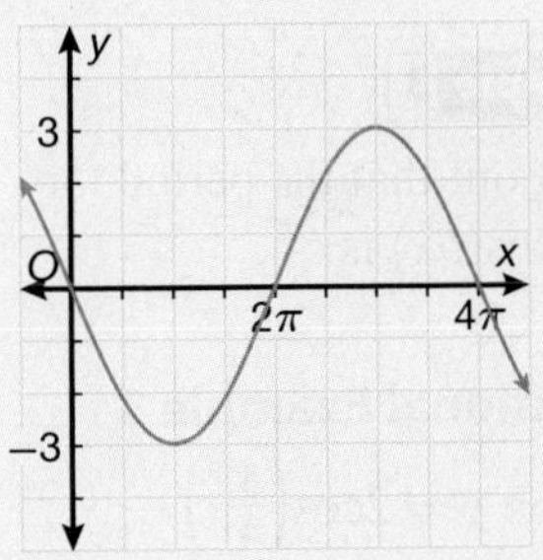

ENGLISH LEARNERS

To help students understand the meaning of the word **period,** define period as a completion of a cycle.

Discuss other examples of period, such as a period or era in history, period as a division of time for a class, and so on.

Have students identify the period in Example 3.

Connect the meaning of period with the period of a function. In their own words, have students define the period of a function.

Example 2

Point out that the period for $y = \sin(bx)$ is $\frac{2\pi}{b}$

Additional Example 2

Graph the following periodic function. Identify the period and amplitude. $y = -6\sin(x)$

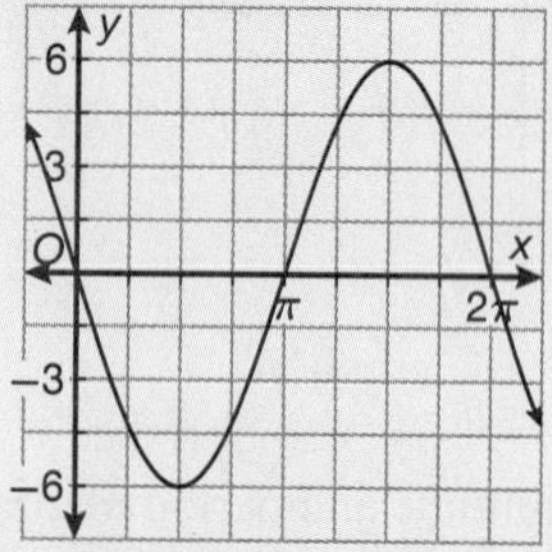

Period: 2π; Amplitude: 6

Example 3

Point out that the period for $y = \cos(bx)$ is $\frac{2\pi}{b}$.

Additional Example 3

Graph $y = 2\cos\left(\frac{3}{4}x\right)$

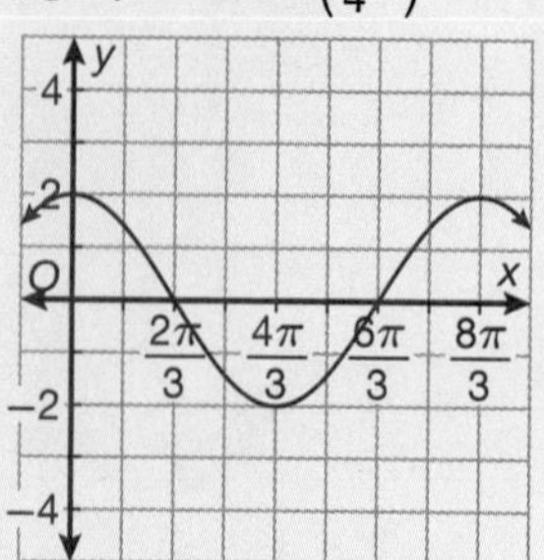

Example 4

Additional Example 4

Two radio signals of the same period are shown on the graph.

a. Write an equation for Signal W in terms of the sine function. $y = 5\sin 1x$

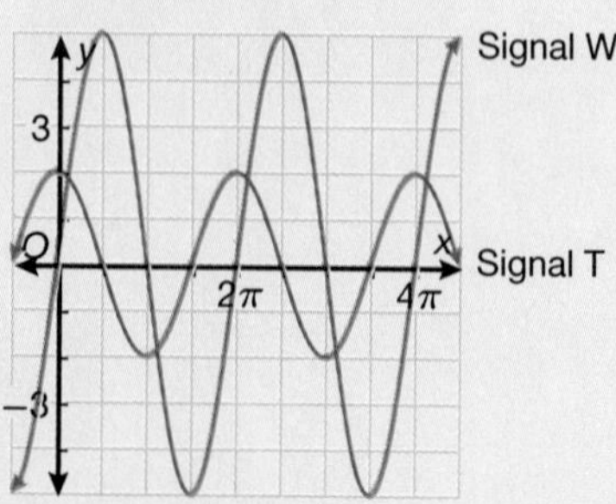

Math Reasoning

Formulate What is the period for $y = \sin(ax)$?

Period $= \frac{2\pi}{a}$

Example 2 Graphing $y = a\sin(bx)$

Graph $y = 3\sin\frac{1}{2}x$.

SOLUTION

Step 1: Find the amplitude $a = 3$. $|a| = 3$, so the amplitude is 3.

Step 2: Find the period of the function.

$\frac{2\pi}{b} = \frac{2\pi}{\frac{1}{2}} = 4\pi$, so the period is 4π.

Step 3: Divide the period into fourths.

$\frac{1}{4}(4\pi) = \pi$, $\frac{2}{4}(4\pi) = 2\pi$, $\frac{3}{4}(4\pi) = 3\pi$

Step 4: Since $a > 0$, plot the pattern zero-max-zero-min-zero using the values of the amplitude and the period.

Example 3 Graphing $y = a\cos(bx)$

Graph $y = 4\cos 2x$.

SOLUTION

Step 1: Find the amplitude $a = 4$. $|a| = 4$, so the amplitude is 4.

Step 2: Find the period of the function.
$b = 2$, so there are 2 cycles in 2π. $\frac{2\pi}{b} = \frac{2\pi}{2} = \pi$, so the period is π.

Step 3: Divide the period into fourths.

$\frac{1}{4}(\pi) = \frac{\pi}{4}$, $\frac{2}{4}(\pi) = \frac{\pi}{2}$, $\frac{3}{4}(\pi) = \frac{3\pi}{4}$.

Step 4: Since $a > 0$, plot the pattern max-zero-min-zero-max using the values of the amplitude and the period.

Example 4 Application: Radio Signals

Two radio signals of the same period are shown on the graph. Write an equation for Signal W in terms of the sine function.

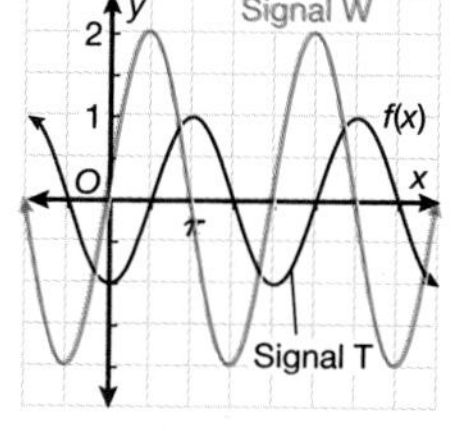

SOLUTION

To write an equation, first find a and b. Find the amplitude, a, by dividing the distance between the maximum range value and the minimum range value by 2.

$|a| = \frac{4}{2} = 2$ Since the sine pattern is zero-max-zero-min-zero, the value of a is positive.

INCLUSION

These steps may be helpful to students when graphing functions of the form $y = a\sin bx$ and $y = a\cos bx$.

Step 1: Determine the amplitude.

Step 2: Find the period.

Step 3: Divide the period into fourths.

Step 4: Use a to determine the pattern.

Step 5: Plot the five critical points and connect them with a smooth curve.

Have students copy these steps and keep them for future reference.

Find b by determining the length of the period from the graph and using the relationship between the period and b.

$$\text{period} = \frac{2\pi}{b}$$

$$2\pi = \frac{2\pi}{b}$$

$$b = 1$$

The equation is $y = 2 \sin 1x$ or $y = 2 \sin x$.

Lesson Practice

Use the graph of each function to determine the amplitude and the period.

a. $y = -2 \sin 4x$ (Ex 1)
Amplitude: 2; Period: $\frac{\pi}{2}$

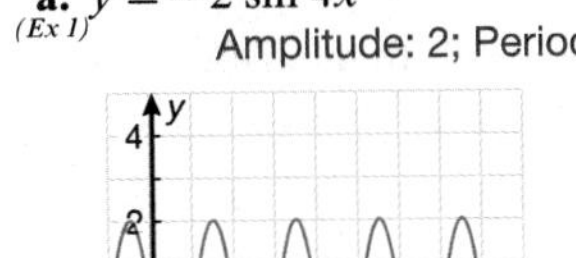

b. $y = 5 \cos \frac{1}{2}x$ (Ex 1) Amplitude: 5; Period: 4π

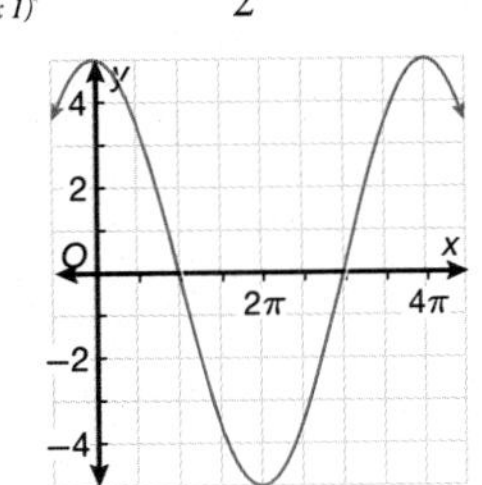

Graph each function.

c. $y = 4 \sin 2x$ (Ex 2)

d. $y = -3 \sin \frac{1}{4}x$ (Ex 2)

e. $y = 3 \cos 2x$ (Ex 3)

f. $y = -3 \cos \frac{1}{4}x$ (Ex 3)

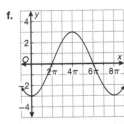

g. (Ex 4) Write an equation for Signal T in terms of the cosine function. $y = 2 \cos x$

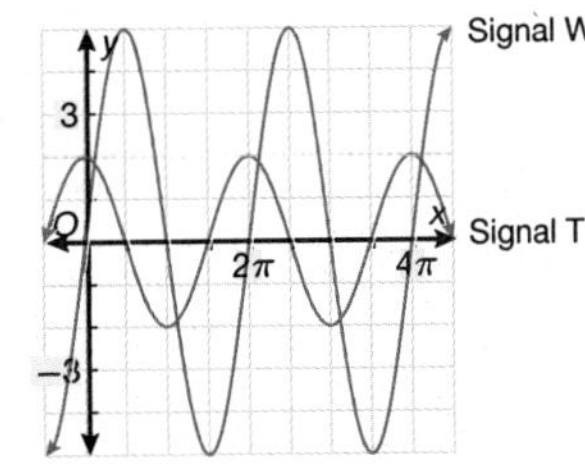

c.

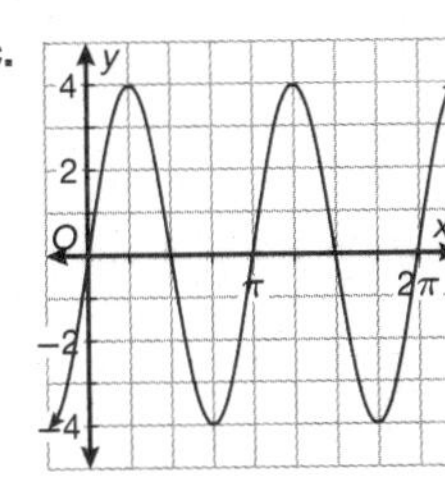

d.

e.

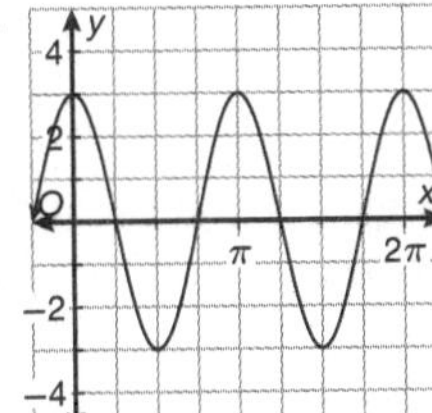

f.

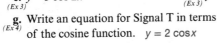

Practice Distributed and Integrated

1. (76) Which of the following is not a factor of $x^3 - 15x^2 + 74x - 120$? **D**
A $(x - 6)$ **B** $(x - 5)$ **C** $(x - 4)$ **D** $(x - 3)$

2. (57) **Bacteria** A colony of bacteria begins with a population of 28, and after 45 minutes the population is 572. How long will it take the colony to grow to 1,200 bacteria?
About 56 minutes

***3.** (82) Given $h(x) = -2\sin(x)$, identify the amplitude and period. Graph the function.
Amplitude = 2, Period = 2π

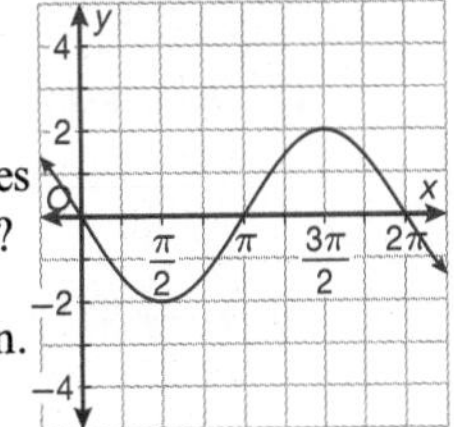

Lesson Practice

Problem b

Scaffolding Have the students determine the period by writing the complex fraction $\frac{2\pi}{\frac{1}{2}}$ as a division problem. Remind them to divide by fractions, you multiply by the reciprocal.

Check for Understanding

The questions below help assess the concepts taught in this lesson.

"How do you find the period for the graph of $y = \sin(bx)$?" The period equals $\frac{2\pi}{b}$. Substitute the value of b into the expression and simplify.

"How do you find the amplitude for the graph of $y = -2\cos(3x)$?"
The amplitude is the absolute value of a which is 2.

3 Practice

Math Conversations

Discussions to strengthen understanding

Problem 9

"What parts of the triangle are given?" two sides and an included angle

"What formula do you use?"
$A = \frac{1}{2}bc \sin A$

"Substitute the values into the formula. What is the area of $\triangle ABC$ to the nearest tenth?"
$A \approx 42.2$

Problem 13

TEACHER TIP

Before students begin the problem, have them explain the difference between $\frac{1}{\cos\theta}$ and $\text{Cos}^{-1}\theta$. If necessary, give students the equation $\cos\theta = \frac{1}{2}$ to help them with their explanation.

Problem 14

Have students set the expression to 0. Be sure students factor out $2x$ first to $2x(6x^2 + 2x - 1)$ before using the quadratic formula.

*4. **Graphing Calculator** Solve $x^2 + 2x + 1 = 0$ by using a graphing calculator. (65)
-1

5. Find the roots and give the multiplicity of each root: $x^3 + 2x^2 - 3x = 0$. (76)
$x = -3$ with multiplicity of 1, $x = 0$ with multiplicity of 1, $x = 1$ with multiplicity of 1.

6. Find the exact values of x and y in an isosceles right triangle with a hypotenuse 21 units long and legs x and y. (52) $x = \frac{21\sqrt{2}}{2}, y = \frac{21\sqrt{2}}{2}$

*7. Write $\ln\left(\frac{4x^2}{e^3}\right)^3$ as a sum or difference of terms if possible. Then simplify. (81)
$3\ln 4 + 6\ln x - 9$

Find the area of $\triangle ABC$ with the given side lengths and included angle.

8. $B = 124°, a = 9, c = 11$ (71) about 41.0

9. $A = 68°$ and $b = 13, c = 7$ (71) about 42.2

10. **Geometry** The volume of a pyramid is given by the formula $V = \frac{1}{3}Bh$, where B is the area of the base and h is the height of the pyramid. A pyramid with a square base has a volume of 108 cubic units. (66)

a. Write a polynomial equation in standard form that can be used to find the length of one side of the base if the height is 3 units longer than the base.
$x^3 + 3x^2 - 324 = 0$

b. Solve the polynomial equation to find the length of one side. (Hint: The length is less than 10 units.) 6 units

*11. In a study of 748 subjects, the mean height was 168.8 centimeters and the standard deviation was 8.9 centimeters. Assuming the distribution is normal, what is the range of heights that the middle 68% of the subjects fell into? (80) 159.9 cm to 177.7 cm

12. **Aquarium** The recommended range for the pH of aquarium water for most fish is from 6 to 8. Use the formula $\text{pH} = -\log[\text{H}^+]$, and write the equivalent range for $[\text{H}^+]$, the concentration of hydrogen ions in moles per liter. Write your answer without exponents. (72) 0.00000001 to 0.000001 mole per liter

13. **Error Analysis** A student incorrectly solved the equation $\cos\theta = 0.8$, for $0 \le \theta \le \pi$, as shown. $\cos\theta = 0.8 \rightarrow \theta = \text{Cos}^{-1}(0.8) \rightarrow \theta = \frac{1}{\cos(0.8)} \rightarrow \theta \approx 1.44$. What is the error? Find the correct solution. (67) The student interpreted $\text{Cos}^{-1}(0.8)$ as a reciprocal instead of as an inverse trigonometric function value. $\theta \approx 0.64$ radian

Find the roots of the polynomial function.

14. $f(x) = 12x^3 + 4x^2 - 2x$ (76) $x = 0, \frac{-1 \pm \sqrt{7}}{6}$

15. $f(x) = (x - 2)(x^2 + 6) - (x - 2)(7x + 4)$ (76) $x = 2, \frac{7 \pm \sqrt{41}}{2}$

16. **Probability** A used car lot contains 16 red cars, 14 gold cars, 9 black cars, and 6 blue cars. A customer needs 5 cars for their new company. Find the probability that they will randomly choose 5 gold cars. (68) 0.16%

*17. Graph $y = 2\cos 3x$. (82) See Additional Answers.

18. **Multiple Choice** Choose the answer that best represents the probability of flipping two coins five times and always showing tails. (60) C

A 0.5 **B** 0.0005 **C** 0.001 **D** 0.01

19. **Verify** Show that the product of two imaginary numbers (bi and ci) can be either positive or negative. (69) Possible answer: If $b = 2$ and $c = 3$, then $bi(ci) = 2i(3i) = 6i^2 = 6(-1) = -6$. If $b = -2$ and $c = 3$, then $bi(ci) = -2i(3i) = -6i^2 = -6(-1) = 6$.

584 Saxon Algebra 2

CHALLENGE

A sine functions has a period of 3. Its maximum value is 7 and its minimum value is -1. Without using a calculator, find the equation of this sine function. (Hint: The graph of the function described represents a vertical shift of a function with the same period, but a maximum and minimum value of 4 and -4, respectively.)

$y = 4\sin\left(\frac{2}{3}\pi x\right) + 3$

20. **Generalize** Suppose a researcher captures and tags n animals, goes back, captures
(73) $n - 1$ animals, and finds that all of the $n - 1$ animals are tagged. What is the estimated animal population? The population is about n animals.

Multiply. Write the result in the form $a + bi$.

21. $2(3i)$ $0 + 6i$
(69)

22. $-4(5i)$ $0-20i$
(69)

*23. **Write** Explain why $e^{\ln(x-3)} = x - 3$. Possible answer: Exponential and logarithmic
(81) operations are inverse operations

24. **Surveying** A surveyor stands on the south end of a roof and finds that the angle
(71) formed by the roof and the line of sight with a flagpole is 33°. The surveyor then walks to the north end of the roof and finds the angle formed by the roof and the flagpole to be 61°. Estimate the distance from the roof to the flagpole, given that the roof has a length of 50 feet. about 23.88 ft

25. **Vertical Motion** The height of a free-falling object (neglecting air resistance) is
(78) given by the function $h(t) = -16t^2 + v_0t + h_0$, where h_0 is the initial height in feet, v_0 is the initial velocity in feet per second, and $h(t)$ is the height in feet at time t seconds. How long does it take for an object to hit the ground after it is dropped from a height of 49 feet? 1.75 seconds

26. **Multi-Step** a. Write $5x - 3x^2 = 10$ in standard form. $-3x^2 + 5x - 10 = 0$
(74)
b. Find the discriminant of the equation in part a. -95
c. Use the discriminant to describe the solutions of the equation in part a. 2 complex solutions

27. **Pendulum** The period of a pendulum, T, is the time it takes for
(70) the pendulum to make one back-and-forth swing, and is given by $T = 2\pi\sqrt{\frac{L}{9.8}}$, where L is the length of the pendulum in meters. Find the length of a pendulum whose period is 4 seconds. $L \approx 3.97$ meters

*28. How many cycles of the function $y = 3\cos(2x)$ are in the interval 0 to 2π. 2
(82)

29. **Write** Without writing a formula, explain how to find the area of a triangle given
(77) its three side lengths.

*30. **Radioisotopes** Thallium, a radioisotope used to track blood flow, has a half-life of
(81) about 73.1 hours. How long will it take for 1 mg of thallium to decay to 0.7 mg? Use the natural decay function $N(t) = N_0e^{-kt}$.
about 37.6 hours

29. Possible answer: First add the side lengths and divide the sum by two. Then find the difference between this value, s, and each of the three sides. Next, find the product of these three differences and the value of s. Last, take the square root of this product.

Problem 26

Remind students of the three cases for the discriminant.

(1) If the discriminant is greater than 0, there are two real roots.

(2) If the discriminant is equal to 0, there is one real root.

(3) If the discriminant is greater than 0, there are two complex roots.

Problem 27

Error Alert

Students may forget to square both sides of the equation. Remind students what they do to one side of the equation they must do to the other.

LOOKING FORWARD

Graphing the sine and cosine functions prepares students for

- **Lesson 86** Translating Sine and Cosine Functions
- **Lesson 90** Graphing the Tangent Function
- **Lesson 103** Graphing Reciprocal Trigonometric Functions

LESSON 83

1 Warm Up

Use problems 2 and 3 in the Warm Up to review factoring a quadratic expression and multiplying terms to get a polynomial.

2 New Concepts

In this lesson, students derive quadratic equations from given roots. They will see that there are an infinite number of quadratic equations that have the given roots.

Example 1

In order to derive the equations, students use the converse of the Zero Product Property when the roots are real.

Additional Example 1

a. Write a quadratic equation whose roots are −4 and 7. $x^2 - 3x - 28 = 0$

b. Write three equations whose roots are 5 and 2. Sample:
$x^2 - 7x + 10 = 0$
$2x^2 - 14x + 20 = 0$
$3x^2 - 21x + 30 = 0$

LESSON RESOURCES

Student Edition Practice Workbook 83
Reteaching Master 83
Adaptations Master 83
Challenge and Enrichment Master C83

LESSON 83

Writing Quadratic Equations from Roots

Warm Up

1. (19) **Vocabulary** To multiply two binomials use the FOIL method.

2. (23) Factor the quadratic expression $x^2 - 7x + 12$. $(x - 3)(x - 4)$

3. (19) Multiply the binomials $(2x + 4)(x - 5)$. $2x^2 - 6x - 20$

New Concepts

Recall that the Zero Product Property states that if $ab = 0$, then $a = 0$ or $b = 0$. The converse of the Zero Product Property is also true.

Math Language

The **converse** of an if-then statement exchanges the words that follow *if* with the words that follow *then.*

Converse of the Zero Product Property
If $a = 0$ or $b = 0$, then $ab = 0$.

Use the converse to write a quadratic function when given the roots of the function.

Example 1 Deriving Quadratic Equations with Two Roots

a. Write a quadratic equation whose roots are −3 and 5.

SOLUTION Work backwards from solving a quadratic equation.

$x = -3$ or $x = 5$	Write the roots as solutions of two equations.
$x + 3 = 0$ or $x - 5 = 0$	Make the right side of each equation 0.
$(x + 3)(x - 5) = 0$	Converse of the Zero Product Property
$x^2 - 2x - 15 = 0$	Multiply the binomials.

The equation $x^2 - 2x - 15 = 0$ has roots of −3 and 5.

Check: The zeros of $y = x^2 - 2x - 15$ occur at −3 and 5.

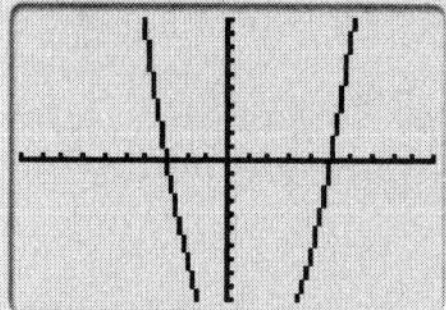

b. Write three quadratic equations whose roots are −4 and −1.

SOLUTION Write the roots as solutions of two equations: $x = -4$ or $x = -1$, and make one side equal to 0: $x + 4 = 0$ or $x + 1 = 0$. Use the Converse of the Zero Product Property to find the basic equation. Add a constant factor to find other quadratic equations with the same roots.

$(x + 4)(x + 1) = 0$	$2(x + 4)(x + 1) = 0$	$3(x + 4)(x + 1) = 0$
$x^2 + 5x + 4 = 0$	$2x^2 + 10x + 8 = 0$	$3x^2 + 15x + 12 = 0$

Graph $y = x^2 + 5x + 4$, $y = 2x^2 + 10x + 8$, and $y = 3x^2 + 15x + 12$. They have the same zeros.

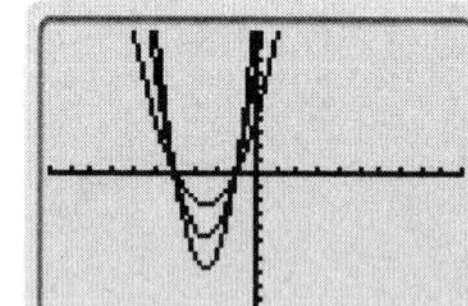

Online Connection
www.SaxonMathResources.com

MATH BACKGROUND

A quadratic equation is a second-order polynomial equation with a single variable. Because it is a second-order polynomial equation, the Fundamental Theorem of Algebra guarantees that it has two solutions. These solutions may be both real and both complex.

The roots can be determined by solving for the discriminant of the equation. Quadratic equations can be used to model parabolic equations as well as other functions in real world examples.

Every quadratic equation has two roots. However, when the roots are identical, it is more common to say that the equation has one root.

Example 2 Deriving Quadratic Equations with One Root

a. Write a quadratic equation whose root is 6.

SOLUTION Treat the single root of 6 as two identical roots of 6.

$x = 6$ or $x = 6$	Write the roots as solutions of two equations.
$x - 6 = 0$ or $x - 6 = 0$	Make the right side of each equation 0.
$(x - 6)(x - 6) = 0$	Converse of the Zero Product Property
$x^2 - 12x + 36 = 0$	Multiply the binomials.

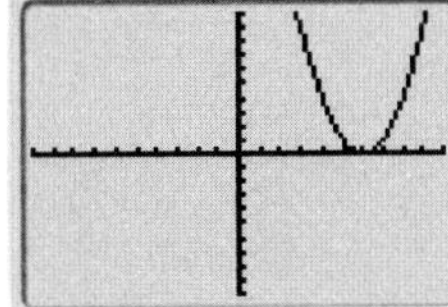

The equation $x^2 - 12x + 36 = 0$ has one real root of 6.

Check The zero of $y = x^2 - 12x + 36$ occurs at 6.

b. Write three quadratic equations so that the root of each is -2.

SOLUTION Treat the single root as two roots and write them as solutions of two equations: $x = -2$ or $x = -2$. Make one side equal to 0: $x + 2 = 0$ or $x + 2 = 0$. Use the Converse of the Zero Product Property to find the basic equation. Add a constant factor to find other quadratic equations with the same roots.

Hint

The constant factor can be positive or negative. It can be a whole number or a fraction.

$(x + 2)(x + 2) = 0$	$-(x + 2)(x + 2) = -1(0)$	$-3(x + 2)(x + 2) = -3(0)$
$x^2 + 4x + 4 = 0$	$-x^2 - 4x - 4 = 0$	$-3x^2 - 12x - 12 = 0$

Graph $y = x^2 + 4x + 4$, $y = -x^2 - 4x - 4$, and $y = -3x^2 - 12x - 12$. They have the same zero.

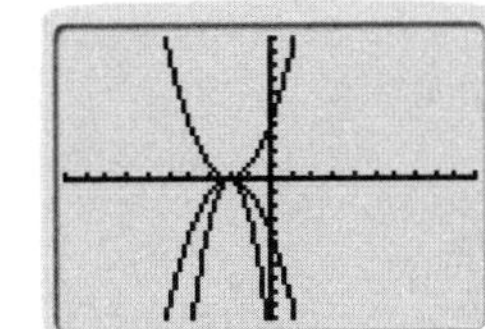

Example 3 Deriving Quadratic Equations with Complex Roots

a. Write a quadratic equation whose roots are $3 + 2i$ and $3 - 2i$.

SOLUTION Write the roots as a solution to one equation.

$x = 3 \pm 2i$	Use $\pm$ symbol.
$x - 3 = \pm 2i$	Isolate the imaginary term.
$x - 3 = \pm\sqrt{-4}$	Write the imaginary term as a square root.
$(x - 3)^2 = -4$	Square both sides.
$x^2 - 6x + 9 = -4$	Expand the binomial.
$x^2 - 6x + 13 = 0$	Add 4 to each side.

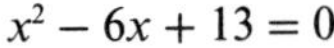

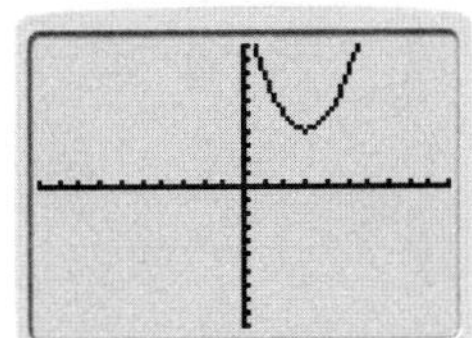

The function $y = x^2 - 6x + 13$ has no real zeros.

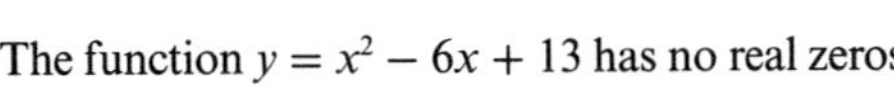

Example 2

When the discriminant of a quadratic equation is zero, the equation has one double root.

Additional Example 2

a. Write a quadratic equation whose root is 8.
$x^2 - 16x + 64 = 0$

b. Write three quadratic equations so that the root of each is -4.
$x^2 + 8x + 16 = 0$
$2x^2 + 16x + 32 = 0$
$3x^2 + 24x + 48 = 0$

Example 3

Students will work backwards to write a quadratic equation when given complex roots.

Additional Example 3

a. Write a quadratic equation whose roots are $6 + 4i$ and $6 - 4i$. $x^2 - 12x + 52 = 0$

Error Alert

Watch for students who forget the middle term when expanding the binomial.

ENGLISH LEARNERS

For Example 2b, explain one of the meanings of the word treat. Say:

"To treat something a certain way means to consider or use it in a specific way. The students treated the coins as game pieces in the checker game to replace the missing pieces."

Have students list ways to treat objects so that they can be reused or recycled. Sample: Plastic grocery bags can be treated as trash bags.

b. Write three equations whose roots are $9i$ and $-9i$.
$x^2 + 81 = 0$
$-x^2 - 81 = 0$
$2x^2 + 162 = 0$

Example 4

Students will derive a quadratic equation as it applies to a real world example.

Additional Example 4

A train tunnel has a parabolic shape. It is 35 feet high and 60 feet wide. Derive a quadratic equation to approximate the curve.
$y \approx -0.039x^2 + 2.34x - 0.1$

Error Alert Be sure to have students distribute the negative sign to each component when multiplying a negative with a polynomial. Errors may also occur when combining like terms to form a final equation.

b. Write three quadratic equations whose roots are $3i$ and $-3i$.

SOLUTION Write the roots as a solution to one equation.

$x = \pm 3i$	Use $\pm$ symbol.
$x = \pm\sqrt{-9}$	Write the imaginary term as a square root.
$x^2 = -9$	Square both sides.
$x^2 + 9 = 0$	Add 9 to each side.

Multiply each side by a non-zero constant.

$$x^2 + 9 = 0$$
$$2(x^2 + 9) = 2(0) \rightarrow 2x^2 + 18 = 0$$
$$-1(x^2 + 9) = -1(0) \rightarrow -x^2 - 9 = 0$$

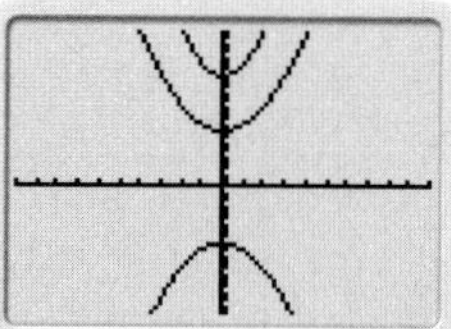

The graphs of $y = x^2 + 9$, $y = 2x^2 + 18$, and $y = -x^2 - 9$ are shown. None cross the x-axis.

Math Reasoning

Analyze What characteristic is common to the graphs of the equations whose roots are $3i$ and $-3i$?

The parabolas have the same line of symmetry ($x = 0$).

Example 4 **Application: Arches**

The bases of an arch are 70 feet apart. The arch has a height of 40 feet. Write a quadratic function to approximate the arch.

SOLUTION

1. **Understand** An arch is parabolic. A parabola's function can be determined when given the vertex and the coordinates of another point.

2. **Plan** Set the x-intercepts at (0, 0) and (70, 0) to represent the bases. The x-coordinate of the vertex is halfway between them at 35. The y-coordinate is the height 40. The vertex is located at (35, 40).

3. **Solve** Use the vertex form of a quadratic function: $y = a(x - h)^2 + k$. Substitute 35 for h and 40 for k. Substitute the x- and y-coordinates of either x-intercept for x and y. Then solve for a.

$$0 = a(0 - 35)^2 + 40$$
$$-40 = a(1225)$$
$$\frac{-40}{1225} = a$$
$$\frac{-8}{245} = a$$

Write the function:

$$y = \frac{-8}{245}(x - 35)^2 + 40$$

Expand the binomial and distribute to write the quadratic in standard form.

$$y = \frac{-8}{245}x^2 + \frac{16}{7}x$$

4. **Check** Graph the function on a graphing calculator.

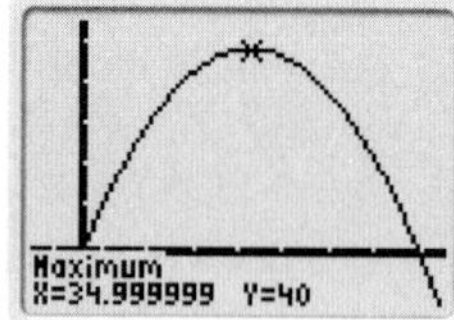

Caution

The y-intercept, -0.425, is not 0 because of rounding.

INCLUSION

For students having trouble understanding the process of deriving the quadratic equation, have them compare the steps to the sequence of solving for the roots of a quadratic equation.

Allow them write each step out. Then, have them compare those steps to the steps needed to work backward to derive the equation. This should help them see they are working backwards to derive a quadratic equation.

a. Possible answer: $x^2 + 4x - 21 = 0$

b. Possible answers: $x^2 - 5x + 6 = 0$, $2x^2 - 10x + 12 = 0$, and $3x^2 - 15x + 18 = 0$

c. Possible answer: $x^2 + 10x + 25 = 0$

d. Possible answers: $x^2 - 8x + 16 = 0$, $\frac{1}{2}x^2 - 4x + 8 = 0$, and $-x^2 + 8x - 16 = 0$

e. Possible answer: $x^2 - 2x + 17 = 0$

f. Possible answers: $x^2 + 49 = 0$, $\frac{1}{7}x^2 + 7 = 0$, and $-x^2 - 49 = 0$

Lesson Practice

a. (Ex 1) Write a quadratic equation whose roots are -7 and 3.

b. (Ex 1) Write three quadratic equations whose roots are 2 and 3.

c. (Ex 2) Write a quadratic equation whose root is -5.

d. (Ex 2) Write three quadratic equations so that the root of each is 4.

e. (Ex 3) Write a quadratic equation whose roots are $1 + 4i$ and $1 - 4i$.

f. (Ex 3) Write three quadratic equations whose roots are $7i$ and $-7i$.

g. (Ex 4) The bases of an arch are 50 feet apart. The arch has a height of 30 feet. Write a quadratic function to approximate the arch. $y = -0.048x^2 + 2.4x$

Practice Distributed and Integrated

Simplify each expression.

1. (59) $(8 \cdot 216)^{\frac{1}{3}}$ 12

2. (59) $\dfrac{6^{\frac{14}{9}}}{6^{\frac{6}{9}}}$ $\sqrt[9]{6^8} \approx 4.92$

3. (68) A box of crayons has 3 purples, 5 reds, 8 greens, and 2 oranges. Find the probability that a student will randomly choose 1 purple, 2 red, and 1 green crayon in that order without replacement. 0.65%

Factor each expression completely.

4. (61) $32z^5 - 2z$ $2z(2z - 1)(2z + 1)(4z^2 + 1)$

5. (61) $a^5b^2 - a^2b^4 + 2a^4b - 2ab^3 + a^3 - b^2$ $(a^3 - b^2)(ab + 1)^2$

***6.** (60) **Multi-Step** A doctor organized data about her patients' ages and genders in the chart below.

a. Are the events male client under 36 or male client over 75 mutually exclusive or inclusive? Explain why. Mutually exclusive; Any given male client cannot be both younger than 36 and older than 75.

b. Find the probability that a patient is male under 36 or male over 75. Round to the hundredths place. 0.23

c. Use the probability found in part b to find the probability that three clients, selected randomly with replacement, are male under 36 or male over 75. Round to the hundredths place. 0.01

Gender of Client

Age	Male	Female
18–35	39	41
36–55	45	52
56–75	54	40
76+	47	56

7. (53) Let $f(x) = 2x + 5$ and $g(x) = 3x$. Evaluate the composition $(f \circ g)(4)$ using two different methods. See Additional Answers.

8. (65) **Generalize** The Quadratic Formula can be written as $x = -\frac{b}{2a} \pm \frac{\sqrt{b^2 - 4ac}}{2a}$. How does this form show the symmetry of a parabola? See Additional Answers.

9. (72) **Multiple Choice** Which is equal to $\log_{20} 20^{a-b}$? A

A $a - b$ **B** $20(a - b)$ **C** $\frac{a}{b}$ **D** $\frac{20^a}{20^b}$

***10.** (66) **Graphing Calculator** Solve $2x^3 + 4x^2 - 39x - 45 = 0$ by using a graphing calculator. $-5, \frac{3 + 3\sqrt{3}}{2}, \frac{3 - 3\sqrt{3}}{2}$

ALTERNATE METHOD FOR PROBLEM 1

A second way to solve this problem is to distribute the exponent to each number and then multiply the numbers together.

$(8 \cdot 216)^{\frac{1}{3}}$

$= 8^{\frac{1}{3}} \cdot 216^{\frac{1}{3}}$

$= 2 \cdot 6$

$= 12$

Lesson Practice

Problem c

Error Alert Students may automatically write $(x - 5)(x - 5)$. Stress that writing the first step, $x = -5$, will help them to remember to add 5 to both sides of the equation, giving $(x + 5)(x + 5) = 0$.

Problem g

Scaffolding Start by finding the x-intercepts and the coordinates of the vertex.

For simplicity, always use the origin as the left base of the arch.

Check for Understanding

The questions below help assess the concepts taught in this lesson.

1. **"What are the steps to deriving a quadratic equation from given roots?"** Sample: Write the roots as solutions of two equations. Make one side of each equation equal to 0. Use the converse of the Zero-Product Property. Multiply the binomials to form the quadratic equation.

2. **"How do you form a quadratic equation with only one root?"** Sample: The one root is used for both zeros of the equation. The same steps would be taken to derive the quadratic equation, but the root given would be used as both roots.

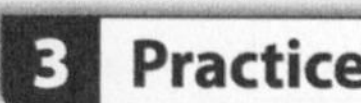

3 Practice

Math Conversations

Discussions to strengthen understanding

Problem 12

Set the vertices for each point of the arch. Vertices should be set for each x-intercept and for the vertex of the arch. Use the vertex form of the quadratic equation in order to correctly derive a function for the arch.

Problem 14

Multiply the current times the resistance to solve for the voltage. Remember that i equals $\sqrt{-1}$ and the FOIL method can be used to multiply the binomials.

Problem 20

Note that the relationship between the velocity and the radius of the earth is a squared relationship.

11. (75) **Analyze** Suppose that $f(x) = \sqrt[m]{g(x)} + \sqrt[n]{h(x)}$. If mn is an odd number, what can you conclude about the domain and range of $f(x)$? Why? If mn is odd, then m and n are each odd. This means that the domain and range are all real numbers.

***12.** (83) **National Parks** The Landscape Arch, in Arches National Park, is the longest natural stone arch in the world. Its length is about 290 feet and its height is about 78 feet. Write a quadratic function to approximate the arch. Sample: $y \approx -0.0037x^2 + 1.073x$

13. (67) **Estimate** Use what you know about the unit circle and special angles to estimate $\text{Sin}^{-1}(0.02)$ in degrees. Do not use a calculator. Explain your method.

13. Possible estimate: $\text{Sin}^{-1}(0.02) \approx 1°$; Possible explanation: 0.02 is close to 0 and $\text{Sin}^{-1} 0 = 0°$. $\text{Sin}^{-1}(0.02)$ is the measure of an angle that terminates in Quadrant I, so the angle measure must be positive.

14. (69) **Electrical Engineering** The flow of a current, I, the resistance to the flow, Z, and the voltage, E, are related by $E = I(Z)$. Find the voltage if the current is $24 - 28i$ amps and the resistance is $5 + i$ ohms. $148 - 116i$ volts

15. (78) **Write** Explain why the equation $x^4 - 625 = 0$ can be solved by factoring the difference of two squares. Possible answer: $x^4 - 625$ is the difference of two squares; it can be written as $(x^2)^2 - (5^2)^2$.

16. (70) **Geometry** The formula $d = \sqrt{l^2 + w^2 + h^2}$ gives the length of a diagonal d of a $l \times w \times h$ rectangular prism. Prism A has a width of 3 inches, a length of 7 inches, and a diagonal whose length is about 9.1 inches. Prism B has a width of 2 inches, a length of 8 inches, and a diagonal whose length is about 10.2 inches. Which prism has the greater height and by how much? Prism B by about 1 inch

17. (71) **Analyze** When can you find the area of a triangle without knowing the height of the triangle? When you know the lengths of two sides and the measure of the included angle, or when you know the lengths of the three sides.

18. (73) **Government** Suppose a politician must visit 4 states on the East Coast. His human resource personnel form a simple random sample by listing each state on the East Coast and numbering it as shown below. If they use the line of random digits shown below, which 4 states will the politician visit? New York, Georgia, Rhode Island, and New Hampshire

10: ME	11: NH	12: MA	13: RI	14: CT	15: NY	16: NJ
17: DE	18: MD	19: VA	20: NC	21: SC	22: GA	23: FL

63157	48257	29223	66713	89022	43069	91349	33111	63682	48864	53097

19. (74) **Multi-Step** **a.** Write $-18x^2 - 84x = 98$ in standard form. $-18x^2 - 84x - 98 = 0$

b. Factor the left side of the equation in part a. $-2(9x^2 + 42x + 49) = 0$

c. Find and use the discriminant to describe the solutions of the equation in part A. 0, 1 real solution

20. (76) **Physics** A satellite in orbit accelerates according to the equation below, for orbital speed v and distance from the Earth's center r. Two satellites are in orbit, one at a speed of v and the other at a speed of $5v$. How far from Earth's center is the faster satellite compared to the slower one if they both have the same acceleration?

$$\text{acceleration} = \frac{v^2}{r}$$ 25r

CHALLENGE

Write an equation that has the roots 3, 4, and 5.

$x = 3$ $\quad x = 4$ $\quad x = 5$

$x - 3 = 0$ $\quad x - 4 = 0$ $\quad x - 5 = 0$

$(x - 3)(x - 4)(x - 5) = 0$

$(x^2 - 7x + 12)(x - 5) = 0$

$x^3 - 12x^2 + 47x - 60 = 0$

21. **Error Analysis** Explain and correct the error a student made in finding $m\angle C$.
(77)

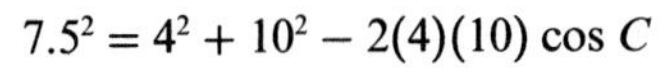

$7.5^2 = 4^2 + 10^2 - 2(4)(10) \cos C$

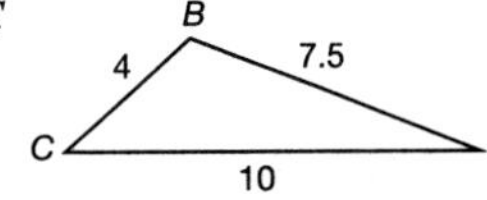

$56.25 = 116 - 80 \cos C$

$56.25 = 36 \cos C$

$1.5625 = \cos C$

Error

80 cannot be subtracted from 116. 116 should be subtracted from each side, and then both sides should be divided by -80. $m\angle C \approx 41.7°$

*22. **Multiple Choice** Which equation is a quadratic equation with a single root of 7? C
(83)
A $x(x + 7) = 0$ **B** $x^2 - 7 = 0$ **C** $(x - 7)(x - 7) = 0$ **D** $(x + 7)(x + 7) = 0$

*23. **Error Analysis** Two students are finding the period of $y = 4\sin\left(\frac{1}{\pi}x\right)$ but get different results. Which student made the mistake?
(82)

Student B incorrectly recalls that $\sin(x)$ has period π.

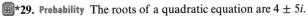

Student A	Student B
The period is where $y = 0$	The period is where $y = 0$
$\frac{1}{\pi}x = 2\pi$	$\frac{1}{\pi}x = \pi$
$x = 2\pi^2 \leftarrow$ Period	$x = \pi^2 \leftarrow$ Period

24. Find the area of ΔABC with the given side lengths and included angle. $a = 19$, $c = 8$, $B = 75°$ about 73.4
(71)

*25. **Economics** The formula for continuously compounded interest is $A = Pe^{rt}$, where A is the total amount, P is the principal, r is the annual interest rate, and t is the time in years. To the nearest hundredth of a percent, what annual interest rate would be necessary for the value of an investment to double in 10 years if the interest is compounded continuously? 6.93%
(81)

Evaluate each piecewise function for $x = 0$ and $x = 2$.

26. $f(x) = \begin{cases} 5, \text{ if } x < 0 \\ x + 2, \text{ if } 0 \le x \le 8 \\ 2x^2 + 1, \text{ if } x > 8 \end{cases}$ $f(0) = 2$; $f(2) = 4$
(79)

27. $f(x) = \begin{cases} 9, \text{ if } x < -1 \\ 12, \text{ if } -1 \le x \le 0 \\ 20, \text{ if } x > 0 \end{cases}$ $f(0) = 12$; $f(2) = 20$
(79)

*28. **Multiple Choice** Which of the following has a period of π? D
(82)
A $y = \sin(2\pi x)$ **B** $y = \sin(\pi x)$ **C** $y = \sin(x)$ **D** $y = \sin(2x)$

*29. **Probability** The roots of a quadratic equation are $4 \pm 5i$.
(83)
a. What is the probability that the related function crosses the x-axis? 0%

b. What is the probability that the related function has a minimum or maximum at $x = 4$? 100%

*30. Write a quadratic equation whose roots are 6 and -2. $x^2 - 4x - 12$
(83)

Problem 24

Use $\frac{1}{2}ac \sin B$ to find the area.

LOOKING FORWARD

Writing quadratic equations from roots prepares students for

- **Lesson 88** Solving Abstract Equations
- **Lesson 89** Solving Quadratic Inequalities
- **Lesson 101** Making Graphs of Polynomial Functions
- **Lesson 111** Transforming Polynomial Functions

LESSON 84

1 Warm Up

Problem 4

Remind students that the LCD must include all the factors of both denominators.

2 New Concepts

In this lesson, students learn to solve rational equations.

Discuss the definitions of **rational function** and **rational equation.**

Example 1

These examples demonstrate how to solve rational equations by cross multiplying.

Additional Example 1

Solve each equation.

a. $\frac{4}{x+3} = \frac{6}{x-2}$ $x = -13$

b. $\frac{8}{x-6} = \frac{1}{x+6}$ $x = -\frac{54}{7}$

LESSON 84

Solving Rational Equations

Warm Up

1. **Vocabulary** The quotient of two polynomials is a ___rational___ (*rational/radical*) expression. (28)

2. Find the LCM of $4x^2$ and $6x^3y$. $12x^3y$ (37)

3. Add $\frac{5}{3x+6} + \frac{x}{x+2}$. $\frac{5+3x}{3(x+2)}$ (37)

4. **Multiple Choice** Which is the LCD of $\frac{3x^2}{x^2-8x+16}$ and $\frac{2}{5x^2-15x-20}$? **D** (37)

   A $6x^2$ **B** $(x-4)(x+1)$

   C $5(x-4)(x+1)$ **D** $5(x-4)^2(x+1)$

5. Simplify $\frac{x^2+4x-12}{6x-12}$. $\frac{x+6}{6}$ (23)

New Concepts

A **rational function** is a function whose rule is a rational expression.

An equation that contains at least one rational expression is a **rational equation.** It is important to notice that rational equations sometimes have extraneous solutions. Since dividing by 0 is undefined in mathematics, any solution that yields a fraction with a denominator of 0 when it is substituted into the original equation is extraneous.

There are several methods that can be used to solve rational equations. Cross-multiplying can be used when the rational equation is expressed as a proportion.

Example 1 Solving Rational Equations with Cross Multiplication

Solve each equation.

(a.) $\frac{30}{x^2-25} = \frac{3}{x-5}$

SOLUTION Cross multiply to solve for x.

$\frac{30}{x^2-25} = \frac{3}{(x-5)}$

$30(x-5) = 3(x^2-25)$	Cross multiply.
$30x - 150 = 3x^2 - 75$	Distribute.
$0 = 3x^2 - 30x + 75$	Addition Property of Equality.
$0 = 3(x^2 - 10x + 25)$	Factor.
$0 = 3(x-5)(x-5)$	Factor.
$x = 5$	Solve for x.

Now substitute $x = 5$ back into the equation to check for an extraneous solution.

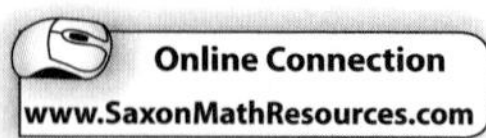

LESSON RESOURCES

Student Edition Practice Workbook 84
Reteaching Master 84
Adaptations Master 84
Challenge and Enrichment Master C84

MATH BACKGROUND

Many of the problems in this lesson require students to clear the fractions as part of the solution process.

Remind students that to clear a fraction, you multiply both sides of the equation by the numbers or expressions in all of the denominators. For example, to clear the fraction in the following equation $\frac{4x}{x-3} = \frac{15}{x-2}$, you must multiply both sides of the equation by $(x-3)$ and $(x-2)$. This process clears the fraction and results in the following equation, $4x(x-2) = 15(x-3)$. This process creates an equivalent equation that is easier to solve.

$$\frac{30}{x^2 - 25} = \frac{3}{x - 5}$$
$$\frac{30}{5^2 - 25} = \frac{3}{5 - 5}$$
$$\frac{30}{0} = \frac{3}{0}$$

Each side of this equation is undefined, so the solution $x = 5$ is extraneous and the equation has no solution.

b. $\frac{9}{5 - x} = \frac{x}{x - 5}$

SOLUTION

$$\frac{9}{5 - x} = \frac{x}{x - 5}$$

$9x - 45 = 5x - x^2$	Cross multiply, and distribute.
$0 = -x^2 - 4x + 45$	Addition Property of Equality
$0 = (-x + 5)(x + 9)$	Factor.
$x = 5$ or -9	Solve.

Check each solution.

$$\frac{9}{(5 - 5)} = \frac{5}{(5 - 5)} \qquad \frac{9}{5 - (-9)} = \frac{-9}{(-9) - 5}$$
$$\frac{9}{5} = \frac{5}{0} \qquad \frac{9}{14} = \frac{9}{14}$$

The solution $x = 5$ is extraneous because it makes the denominators of the original equation equal to zero. Since -9 makes the equation true, the only solution to this rational equation is $x = -9$.

When a rational equation contains one fraction, the equation can first be simplified by multiplying both sides of the equation by the fraction's denominator.

Example 2 Solving Rational Equations by Multiplication

Solve each equation.

a. $\frac{4x}{x - 9} = 15$

SOLUTION Multiply both sides of the equation by the fraction's denominator.

$$\frac{10x}{x - 9} = 15$$

$10x = 15x - 135$	Multiply both sides by $(x - 9)$.
$-5x = -135$	Addition Property of Equality
$x = 27$	Solve.

Substitute the solution into the original equation to check for an extraneous answer. Since 27 makes the original equation true, the solution is $x = 27$.

Example 2

These examples show students how to solve rational equations by eliminating fractions.

Additional Example 2

Solve each equation.

a. $\frac{-8}{x} + 5 = x - 4$

$x = 1$ and 8

b. $\frac{2}{x - 1} = 4$

$x = 1.5$

TEACHER TIP

Remind students that the quadratic formula is $x = \frac{-b \pm \sqrt{b^2 - 4ac}}{2a}$. This equation can be used to solve for x if the equation is in the form $ax^2 + bx + c = 0$ and $a \neq 0$.

ENGLISH LEARNERS

For this lesson, explain the meaning of the word **rational**. Say:

"The term rational is derived from the Latin word rationalis which means ratio."

In an earlier lesson, you learned that a rational number is a real number that can be written as a ratio of *a*/*b*, where *a* and *b* are integers, and *b* is not equal to zero.

The term rational also means "having reason or understandable." You might have heard someone being referred to as a rational person. The person is a reasonable person.

Example 3

This example demonstrates how to solve rational equations using an LCD.

Additional Example 3

Solve for x.

$$\frac{-8}{x} + \frac{5}{4x^2 + 8x} = x - 4$$

$x = -\frac{5}{3}$

Hint

Instead of finding a least common denominator, you can also multiply by each factor of each denominator in the problem one-by-one.

b. $\frac{8}{x} + 2 = 2$

SOLUTION

Multiply both sides of the equation by the fraction's denominator.

$$\frac{8}{x} + 2 = x$$

$$x(\frac{8}{x} + 2) = x(x)$$

$$8 + 2x = x^2$$

$$0 = x^2 - 2x - 8$$

$$0 = (x - 4)(x + 2)$$

$$x = 4 \text{ or } x = -2$$

Substitute both solutions into the original equation to check for extraneous answers. Since 4 and –2 both make the original equation true the solutions are $x = 4$ and $x = -2$.

When the rational equation has the sum or difference of two rational expressions, the equation can first be simplified by multiplying both sides of the equation by the least common denominator.

Example 3 Solving Rational Equations with a Common Denominator

Solve for x.

$$\frac{x + 5}{x + 3} + \frac{28}{x^2 + 8x + 15} = 4$$

SOLUTION

Factor the polynomial and find a common denominator. In this problem, the common denominator is $(x + 3)(x + 5)$.

$$\frac{x + 5}{x + 3} + \frac{28}{x^2 + 8x + 15} = 4$$

$$\frac{x + 5}{x + 3} + \frac{28}{(x + 3)(x + 5)} = 4$$

Now multiply both sides of the equation by this common denominator.

$$(x + 3)(x + 5)\left(\frac{x + 5}{x + 3} + \frac{28}{(x + 3)(x + 5)}\right) = 4(x + 3)(x + 5)$$

$$(x + 5)^2 + 28 = 4(x^2 + 8x + 15)$$

$$x^2 + 10x + 25 + 28 = 4x^2 + 32x + 60)$$

$$0 = 3x^2 + 22x + 7$$

Use the quadratic formula to solve this equation.

$$x = \frac{-22 \pm \sqrt{22^2 - 4(3)(7)}}{6} = -\frac{1}{3} \text{ and } -7.$$

Check for extraneous solutions. Since $-\frac{1}{3}$ and -7 both make the original equation true, the solution is $x = -\frac{1}{3}$ or $x = -7$.

Example 4 Application: Distance, Rate, and Time

An athlete runs 12 kilometers on Saturday and bikes 30 kilometers on Sunday. The total time spent working out was 4 hours. Find the time spent working out each day if the rate of travel on Sunday was twice what it was on Saturday.

SOLUTION Because $d = rt$, $r = \frac{d}{t}$. Write an expression for the rate of travel on each day. If t = time on Saturday, then $4 - t$ = time on Sunday.

The rate on Sunday was twice what it was on Saturday.

$$\frac{30}{4-t} = 2\left(\frac{12}{t}\right)$$

$$t(\cancel{4-t})\left(\frac{30}{\cancel{4-t}}\right) = t(4-t)\left(\frac{24}{t}\right)$$

$$30t = 96 - 24t$$

$$54t = 96$$

$$t = 1.\overline{7}$$

The time was about 1.8 hours on Saturday and $4 - 1.8 = 2.2$ hours on Sunday.

Math Reasoning

Analyze Show the same answer is found when t is the time on Sunday and $4 - t$ is the time on Saturday.

t is about 2.2. Subtract from 4 to get Saturday's time.

Lesson Practice

Solve each equation.

a. (Ex 1) $\frac{2x-2}{3x} = \frac{5}{2}$ $x = \frac{-4}{11}$

b. (Ex 1) $\frac{30}{x} = \frac{x+4}{2}$ $x = 6$ and -10

c. (Ex 2) $\frac{3x}{x+3} = -1$ $x = -\frac{3}{4}$

d. (Ex 2) $5 - \frac{4}{x} = x$ $x = 1$ and $x = 4$

e. (Ex 3) $\frac{8x}{x-1} - \frac{x+33}{x^2+2x-3} = 9$ $x = 2$ and $x = 3$

f. (Ex 3) $\frac{3x}{x^2-1} = \frac{4}{x}$ $x = -2$ and $x = 2$

g. (Ex 4) A biker biked 18 miles on pavement and 6 miles on dirt. The total biking time was 5 hours. Find the time spent biking on each surface if the rate of biking on the dirt was three-fourths of what it was biking on the pavement. About 1.54 hours on dirt and about 3.46 hours on pavement

ALTERNATE METHOD FOR LESSON PRACTICE C

This equation is a proportion, so it can also be solved by cross multiplying.

$$3x = -(x+3)$$

$$3x = -x - 3$$

$$4x = -3$$

$$x = -\frac{3}{4}$$

Example 4

This example demonstrates how to solve a rational equation in a real-life application.

Additional Example 4

An athlete bikes 32 kilometers and then walks 5 kilometers. The total time spent exercising was 3.5 hours. If the biking rate was 2.5 times the walking rate, determine the time spent on each type of exercise. Round the answer to the nearest tenth of an hour. The time spent walking was about 1.0 hour. The time spent biking was about 2.5 hours.

Extend the Problem

Have students check their solution by graphing.

Lesson Practice

Problem C

Error Alert Students may divide carelessly and answer $-\frac{4}{3}$ instead of $-\frac{3}{4}$.

Check for Understanding

The questions below help assess the concepts taught in this lesson.

"Why is clearing a fraction important when solving a rational equation?" Clearing a fraction makes the equation easier to solve.

"Why is it important to check your calculated solutions to see if they are possible solutions?" Some calculated solutions produce a zero in the denominator, which is a restricted value and not a possible solution.

3 Practice

Math Conversations

Discussions to strengthen understanding

Problem 8

Encourage students to make a sketch showing the relationships among the three cities before they attempt to solve the problem.

Problem 15

Guide the students by asking them the following questions.

"What do each of the variables represent?" The diameter of the rope is d. The weight lifted is w.

"The diameter of the rope is given for the two scenarios. What are the new equations?"

$2.5 = \frac{\sqrt{15w}}{\pi}$ and $3 = \frac{\sqrt{15w}}{\pi}$

"How can you use the equations to answer the question?" Solve each for w and subtract the results.

Practice Distributed and Integrated

1. (56) Given $\theta = 504°$, find the measure of the reference angle. 36°

Find all the possible values.

2. (67) $\cos^{-1}\left(\frac{1}{2}\right)$ $\frac{\pi}{3} + 2\pi n$; $\frac{5\pi}{3} + 2\pi n$, where n is an integer

3. (67) $\tan^{-1}(1)$ $\frac{\pi}{4} + 2\pi n$; $\frac{5\pi}{4} + 2\pi n$, where n is an integer

4. (64) **Coordinate Geometry** The graph of the logarithmic function $y = \log_3 x$ is shown. Estimate the shaded area. Possible answer: 10 square units

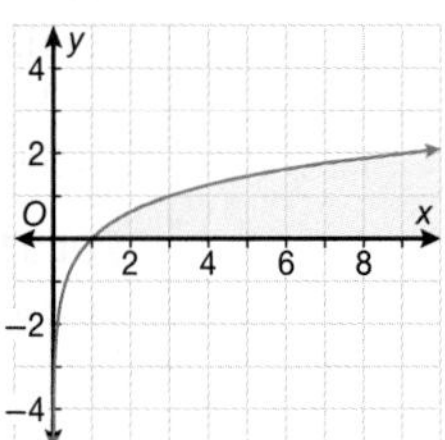

5. (74) Use the discriminant to find all values of c for which $x^2 - x + c = 0$ has (a) two real solutions, (b) one real solution, and (c) two complex solutions.
$c < 0.25$, $c = 0.25$, $c > 0.25$

6. (58) Complete the square and factor the resulting perfect square trinomial: $x^2 - 24x$. $x^2 - 24x + 144 = (x - 12)^2$

7. (80) **Analyze** The z-score of an unknown data value is −1.4. Find the data value given that the mean of the data is 60 and the standard deviation is 12. 43.2

8. (77) **Geography** A map of southwest Illinois shows that Waterloo is 34 miles from Chester and 44 miles from Pinckneyville. Pinckneyville is 27 miles from Chester. Find the number of square miles enclosed in the triangle formed by the lines connecting these three cities. Round to the nearest square mile. 459 mi²

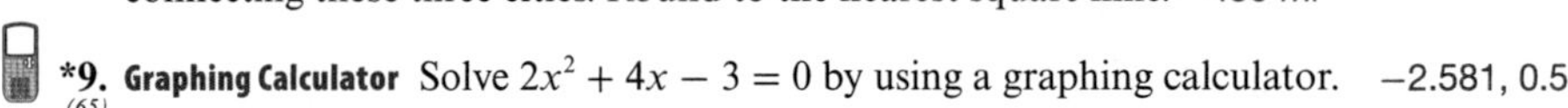

***9.** (65) **Graphing Calculator** Solve $2x^2 + 4x - 3 = 0$ by using a graphing calculator. −2.581, 0.581

***10.** (81) **Multiple Choice** Which is equal to $e^{\ln 4x^2}$? D

A $8x$ **B** $\ln 8x$ **C** $2 \ln 4x$ **D** $4x^2$

11. (68) **Housing** The table shows estimated housing occupancy for three states for the year 2006. Find the probability that a randomly selected house from one of these states is in Texas given that it is occupied. Write the probability as a percent rounded to the nearest hundredth. 68.56%

	Occupied Houses	Vacant Houses
Virginia	2,905,071	325,750
Texas	8,109,388	1,115,532
Utah	814,028	87,294

12. (78) **Analyze** Describe how to solve the equation $\frac{1}{2}x^2 - 2 = 0$ by factoring the difference of two squares. Sample: Multiply both sides by 2 to get $x^2 - 4 = 0$, then factor and solve.

13. (69) **Error Analysis** Which student made an error in finding $|2 - i|$? Describe the error.

Student A: $\sqrt{2^2 + 0^2} \rightarrow \sqrt{4} \rightarrow 2$ Student B: $\sqrt{2^2 + (-1)^2} \rightarrow \sqrt{4 + 1} \rightarrow \sqrt{5}$

13. Student A made the error. The value of b is −1, not 0.

***14.** (83) Write a quadratic equation whose root is 7. $x^2 - 14x + 49 = 0$

INCLUSION

Entering rational expressions into a graphing calculator can be confusing. Tell students to write the expressions with parentheses on paper before entering them into the calculator.

15. (Diameter) The formula $d = \frac{\sqrt{15w}}{\pi}$ gives the diameter in inches of the rope needed to lift w tons. How much more weight can be lifted with a rope of diameter 3 inches than with a rope of diameter 2.5 inches? About 1.81 tons more
(70)

16. (Sound) Two measures of sound are loudness and intensity. They are related by the function $L(I) = 10\log\frac{I}{I_0}$, where $L(I)$ is loudness in decibels, I is intensity in watts per square meter, and $I_0 \approx 10^{-12}$ watt per square meter, the intensity of a barely audible sound. The sound intensity near a speaker is 0.01 watt per square meter. What is the loudness in decibels? 100 decibels
(72)

*17. **Multi-Step** Write a quadratic equation with roots of $5 + 3i$ and $5 - 3i$ so that the parabola of the related function opens up. Then write one so that the parabola opens down and is wider than the one that opens up. Possible answers: $x^2 - 10x + 34 = 0$ and $-\frac{1}{2}x^2 + 5x - 17 = 0$
(83)

18. **Multiple Choice** Which type of sampling is *not* a type of probability sampling? B
(73)
A simple random sampling **B** voluntary response sampling
C cluster sampling **D** systematic sampling

Solve.

*19. $2 + \frac{1}{x} = 4$ $x = \frac{1}{2}$ (84)

*20. $\frac{2}{x+2} + \frac{8}{x-2} = \frac{14}{x^2-4}$ $x = \frac{1}{5}$ (84)

*21. $\frac{-6}{x-3} = 1$ $x = -3$ (84)

22. **Generalize** What will be the value of the discriminant of an equation if the vertex of the related function is located in Quadrant III and the parabola opens upward? Why?
(74)

*23. Write a quadratic equation whose roots are 6 and −1. $x^2 - 5x - 6 = 0$
(83)

24. (Students) Of the 70 students going on the soccer trip, 58 are players and 8 are left-handed. Six of the left-handed students are soccer players. What is the probability that one of the students on the trip is a soccer player or is left-handed?
(60)

24. About 0.86

25. **Analyze** The graph of a radical function $f(x) = \sqrt[n]{g(x)}$ is shown. What can you conclude about n? Because the domain has a lower limit, n is an even number.
(75)

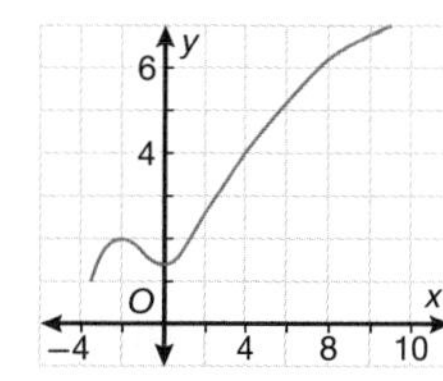

*26. **Formulate** Suppose that $f(x) = \sin(ax)$ and $g(x) = \sin(bx)$. If $f(x)$ completes four periods when $g(x)$ completes one, what is the relationship between a and b? $4b = a$
(82)

27. **Geometry** The volume of a rectangular prism is $3x^3 + 5x^2 - 12x$. What are the dimensions of the rectangular prism? $(x) \times (x + 3) \times (3x - 4)$
(76)

28. **Multi-Step** At a florist shop, roses cost \$3.50 each if you buy fewer than 12, \$3.00 each if you buy between 12 and 24, and \$2.50 each if you buy more than 24. Write a piecewise function for the cost per rose when buying x roses. Then, graph the function. See Additional Answers.
(79)

22. The value will be positive because the parabola crosses the x-axis twice, meaning that the function has two x-intercepts and the related equation has two solutions.

29. In $\triangle RST$, $ST = 8.9$, $RT = 12.2$, and the $m\angle T = 78°$. Find $m\angle S$. 61.9°
(77)

*30. **Error Analysis** A student said that the equation $\frac{3}{x^2 + 7x + 10} + \frac{1}{x^2 + 10x + 25} = 24$ can be solved by multiplying both sides of the equation by $(x + 2)(x + 5)$. Why is this not true? See Additional Answers.
(84)

Example 27

Guide the students by asking them the following questions.

"What is the formula for finding the volume of a rectangular prism?" length × width × height

"What is the first step in factoring this expression?" Factor out the GCF of x.

Example 29

Error Alert

Remind students that the law of cosines must be used if the given information is of the form SAS.

Problem 30

Extend the Problem

Factor the denominators and determine what solutions for x are excluded values. The excluded values are −5 and −2.

CHALLENGE

Graph the equation in Problem 30, $\frac{3}{x^2 + 7x + 10} + \frac{1}{x^2 + 10x + 25} = 24$ and determine if the excluded values that you found above are reflected in the graph.

The excluded values, $x = -5$ and $x = -2$, are reflected in the graph. The graph approaches these values, but does not pass through them.

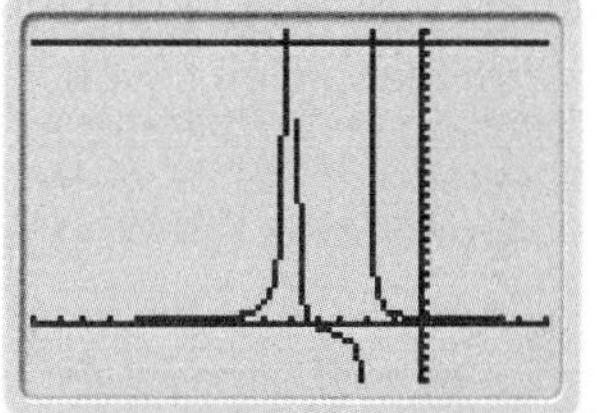

LOOKING FORWARD

Solving rational equations prepares students for

- **Lesson 94** Solving Rational Inequalities
- **Lesson 100** Graphing Rational Functions I
- **Lesson 107** Graphing Rational Functions II

Lesson 84 597

LESSON 85

1 Warm Up

Use the Warm Up to review methods for factoring polynomials.

2 New Concepts

In this lesson, students learn to look for certain patterns when factoring cubic binomials. They use the Rational Root Theorem to identify possible roots of polynomial equations.

Example 1

Students find the factors of a cubic binomial by identifying the binomial as either the sum of cubes or the difference of cubes.

Extend the Example

What would be the solution to Example 1a if the binomial were the sum of the cubes? $x = -3$

What would be the solution to Example 1b if the binomial were the difference of the cubes? $x = 4$

Additional Example 1

Find the real roots of the polynomial function.

a. $y = x^3 - 125$ $x = 5$

b. $y = x^3 + 216$ $x = -6$

LESSON RESOURCES

Student Edition Practice Workbook 85
Reteaching Master 85
Adaptations Master 85
Challenge and Enrichment Master C85

LESSON 85

Finding Polynomial Roots II

Warm Up

1. (78) **Vocabulary** The expression $x^2 - 4$ is a _______ and has factors $(x + 2)$ and $(x - 2)$. difference of squares

2. (78) Factor the expression $16x^4 - 81$. $(4x^2 + 9)(2x - 3)(2x + 3)$

3. (65) Solve using the quadratic formula. $3x^2 - 29x - 84 = 0$ $x = -\frac{7}{3}, 12$

New Concepts

Cubic polynomials that are either the sum or difference of cubes can be factored as follows,

$$x^3 + a^3 = (x + a)(x^2 - ax + a^2)$$
$$x^3 - a^3 = (x - a)(x^2 + ax + a^2)$$

Look for such patterns when you need to factor a cubic binomial.

Example 1 Using the Sums and Differences of Cubes

a. Find the real roots of the polynomial function.

$y = x^3 - 27$

SOLUTION

Since $27 = 3^3$, this is a difference of cubes.

$y = x^3 - 27 = (x - 3)(x^2 + 3x + 9)$

To see if the quadratic term has real roots, find the discriminant.

$3^2 - 4(1)(9) = -27 \rightarrow$ complex roots

The polynomial function $y = x^3 - 27$ has one real root: $x = 3$.

b. Find the real roots of the polynomial function.

$y = x^3 + 64$

SOLUTION

Since $64 = 4^3$, this is a sum of cubes.

$y = x^3 + 64 = (x + 4)(x^2 - 4x + 16)$

To see if the quadratic term has real roots, find the discriminant.

$(-4)^2 - 4(1)(16) = -48 \rightarrow$ complex roots

The polynomial function $y = x^3 + 64$ has one real root: $x = -4$.

Math Reasoning

Verify Show that if a polynomial is a sum or difference of cubes, there is only one real root.

In either case, the discriminant of the quadratic is negative.
$(-a)^2 - 4(1)(a^2)$
$= -3a^2$
$a^2 - 4(1)(a^2)$
$= -3a^2$
So, the first factored binomial is the only real root.

Some non-cubic functions can still follow the patterns of the sums and differences of cubes. Look for polynomials $f(x)$ and $g(x)$ that are of the form,

$$f(x) = g^3(x) + a^3 = (g(x) + a)(g^2(x) - ag(x) + a^2)$$
$$f(x) = g^3(x) - a^3 = (g(x) - a)(g^2(x) + ag(x) + a^2)$$

Online Connection
www.SaxonMathResources.com

MATH BACKGROUND

One of the key tools in solving polynomial equations is synthetic division. Synthetic division gives the coefficients of the resulting polynomial that are also the coefficients of the quotient with a divisor whose linear factor contains the root used in the synthetic division. The degree of the quotient is one less than the degree of the dividend. This quotient, together with the remainder, is called the depressed equation.

The advantage of using the most recent depressed equation to solve polynomial equations is that ultimately the divisions will lead to a quadratic equation that can be solved by factoring or using the quadratic formula. Once a root has been found, the most recent depressed equation should be used to test another possible rational root.

Example 2 Using Cubic Sums and Difference Patterns

a. Find the real roots of the polynomial equation.

$$x^6 - 64 = 0$$

Math Reasoning

Verify Show that if $x^6 - 64$ is factored as a difference of squares, the results are the same as factoring it as a difference of cubes.

$(x^3)^2 - 8^2$
$= (x^3 - 8)(x^3 + 8)$
$= (x^3 - 2^3)(x^3 + 2^3)$
The roots are ± 2.

SOLUTION

Note that $x^6 = (x^2)^3$ and $64 = 4^3$. Therefore the polynomial can be rewritten as a difference of cubes.

$$f(x) = (x^2)^3 - 4^3 = (x^2 - 4)((x^2)^2 + 4(x^2) + 16)$$
$$= (x^2 - 4)(x^4 + 4x^2 + 16)$$

The factor $(x^2 - 4)$ is a difference of squares with real roots $x = \pm 2$. Graph the quartic factor to see if it intersects the x-axis.

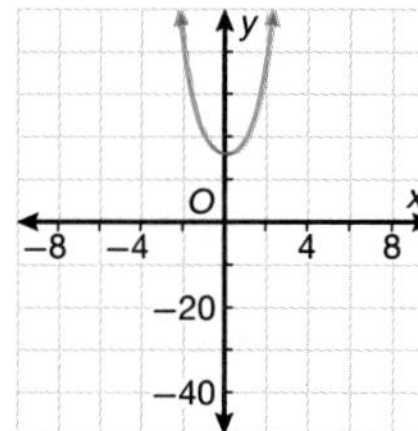

The polynomial function $f(x) = x^6 - 64$ has two real roots: $x = 2$ and $x = -2$.

b. Find the real roots of the polynomial equation.

$$x^9 + 27 = 0$$

SOLUTION

Note that $x^9 = (x^3)^3$ and $27 = 3^3$. Therefore the polynomial can be rewritten as a sum of cubes.

$$f(x) = (x^3)^9 + 3^3 = (x^3 + 3)((x^3)^2 - 3(x^3) + 9)$$
$$= (x^3 + 3)(x^6 - 3x^3 + 9)$$

The factor $(x^3 + 3)$ is itself a sum of cubes and can be further factored.

$$f(x) = (x + \sqrt[3]{3})(x^2 - \sqrt[3]{3}x + \sqrt[3]{9})(x^6 - 3x^3 + 9)$$

Graphs of the two polynomial factors show there are no other roots.

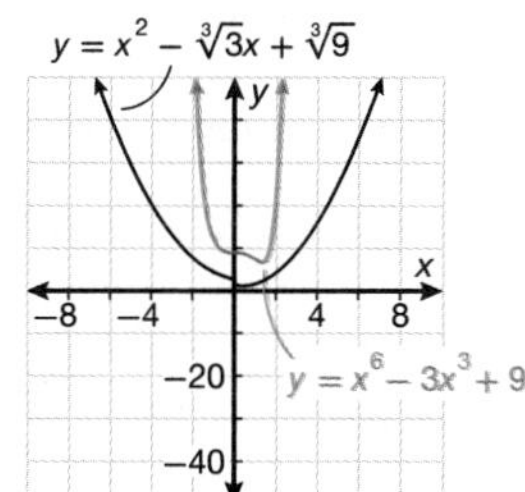

The real root is $x = -\sqrt[3]{3}$.

Example 2

Students identify and apply cubic sums and difference patterns when finding the roots of a polynomial function.

Additional Example 2

Find the real roots of the polynomial function.

a. $f(x) = x^6 - 729$ $x = \pm 3$

b. $f(x) = x^9 + 64$ $x = \sqrt[3]{-4}$

TEACHER TIP

Draw students' attention to the sentence in the solution to Example **2b** that states $(x^3 + 3)$ is a sum of cubes. Students may not recognize this as a sum of cubes because they are thinking only about integers. Point out the method of cubing a cube root.

INCLUSION

Remind students that finding a polynomial's roots means to find where the function crosses the x-axis. A visual way to help students understand what they are doing is to have them use a graphing calculator and graph each function to check their solutions.

Example 3

Students solve a cubic equation by graphing the equation and identifying the point where the curve crosses the x-axis.

Additional Example 3

Find the real roots of the cubic equation. $4x^3 - 5x^2 + 3x - 4 = 0$.
$x \approx 1.2763$

Example 4

Students use the Rational Root Theorem to identify possible roots for a polynomial equation.

Additional Example 4*a*

a. Find the rational roots for the following polynomial equation.
$x^3 + 4x^2 + x - 6 = 0$
$x = -3, -2$, and 1

Graphing Calculator Tip

For help in finding the zeros of graphs, see Graphing Calculator Lab 3 on page 84.

Example 3 Solving Cubic Equations

Find the real roots of $3x^3 - 7x^2 + 4x - 12 = 0$.

SOLUTION To find the real roots of the equation, graph the polynomial function

$$y = 3x^3 - 7x^2 + 4x - 12$$

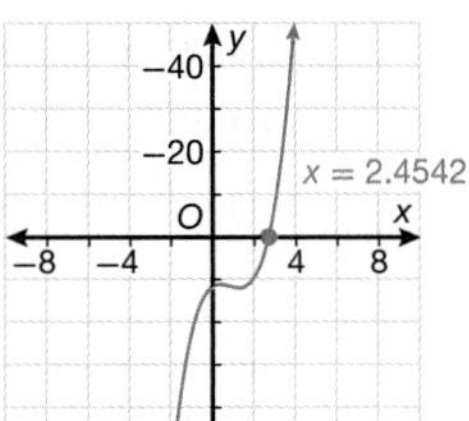

The real root is approximately 2.4542.

Rational Root Theorem
If a polynomial equation has rational roots, then use the **Rational Root Theorem** to find these roots. To do so, follow these steps. **1.** Write the polynomial in this form, where the term with the highest power, a_nx^n, is the leading term and the constant term, a_0, is the last term. $a_nx^n + a_{n-1}x^{n-1} + \ldots + a_0$ **2.** Find all the factors of a_n and a_0. **3.** Let q be one of the factors of a_n and p be one of the factors of a_0. List all possible rational numbers $\frac{p}{q}$. **4.** Test if $\left(x - \frac{p}{q}\right)$ is a factor of the polynomial using synthetic division. If a polynomial has a rational root, then it will be one of the $\frac{p}{q}$ terms.

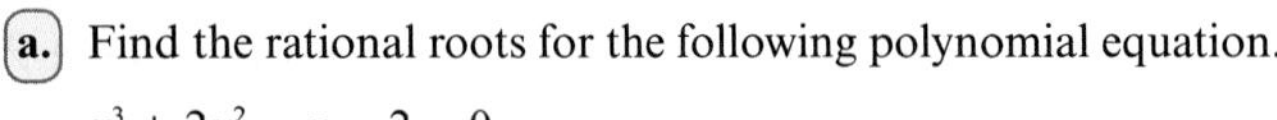

Example 4 Using the Rational Root Theorem

a. Find the rational roots for the following polynomial equation.

$$x^3 + 2x^2 - x - 2 = 0$$

SOLUTION

Use the Rational Root Theorem to find any roots that are rational roots. The terms that need to be factored are 1 and −2. The possible values of p are $\pm1, \pm2$ and for q are ±1. So, $\frac{p}{q} = \{2, -2, 1, -1\}$. Use synthetic division to test roots.

$$\begin{array}{r|rrrr} 2 & 1 & 2 & -1 & -2 \\ & & 2 & 8 & 14 \\ \hline & 1 & 4 & 7 & 12 \end{array} \;\text{✗} \qquad \begin{array}{r|rrrr} -2 & 1 & 2 & -1 & -2 \\ & & -2 & 0 & 2 \\ \hline & 1 & 0 & -1 & 0 \end{array} \;\checkmark$$

$x^3 + 2x^2 - x - 2 = (x + 2)(x^2 - 1) = (x + 2)(x - 1)(x + 1)$

All the real roots are rational: $x = -2, 1$, and -1.

ALTERNATE METHOD FOR EXAMPLE 4a

After students have solved additional Example **4a** using the Rational Root Theorem, have them solve the problem by graphing the function on a graphing calculator and identifying the zeros.

b. Find the real roots for the following polynomial equation.

$$x^4 - x^3 - 8x + 8 = 0$$

SOLUTION

Step 1: Use the Rational Root Theorem.

Factors of 1: ±1 ← Values of q Factors of 8: $\pm1, \pm2, \pm4, \pm8$ ← Values of p

$$\frac{p}{q} = \{\pm1, \pm2, \pm4, \pm8\}$$

Find the first root that yields a factor:

$$\begin{array}{r|rrrrr} 1 & 1 & -1 & 0 & -8 & 8 \\ & & 1 & 0 & 0 & -8 \\ \hline & 1 & 0 & 0 & -8 & 0 \end{array} \checkmark$$

$$x^4 - x^3 - 8x + 8 = (x - 1)(x^3 - 8)$$

Step 2: Use the Rational Root Theorem to find additional roots, or use a polynomial pattern. $(x^3 - 8)$ is a difference of cubes.

$(x - 1)(x - 2)(x^2 + 2x + 4)$

The discriminant of the quadratic term is negative yielding complex roots. The only real roots are $x = 1$ and $x = 2$.

c. Find the real roots for the following polynomial equation.

$$2x^4 - 9x^3 + 2x^2 + 9x - 4 = 0$$

SOLUTION

Step 1: Use the Rational Root Theorem.

Factors of 2: $\pm1, \pm2$ ← Values of q Factors of 4: $\pm1, \pm2, \pm4$ ← Values of p

$$\frac{p}{q} = \left\{\pm\frac{1}{2}, \pm1, \pm2, \pm4\right\}$$

Find the first rational number that yields a factor:

$$\begin{array}{r|rrrrr} \frac{1}{2} & 2 & -9 & 2 & 9 & -4 \\ & & 1 & -4 & -1 & 4 \\ \hline & 2 & -8 & -2 & 8 & 0 \end{array} \checkmark$$

$$2x^4 - 9x^3 + 2x^2 + 9x - 4 = \left(x - \frac{1}{2}\right)(2x^3 - 8x^2 - 2x + 8)$$
$$= (2x - 1)(x^3 - 4x^2 - x + 4)$$

Step 2: Use the Rational Root Theorem on the cubic term.

$$\frac{p}{q} = \{\pm1, \pm2, \pm4\}$$

$$\begin{array}{r|rrrr} 1 & 1 & -4 & -1 & 4 \\ & & 1 & -3 & -4 \\ \hline & 1 & -3 & -4 & 0 \end{array} \checkmark$$

$(2x - 1)(x - 1)(x^2 - 3x - 4)$

Caution

Remember that rational roots can be positive or negative.

Additional Example 4b and c

Find the real roots for the following polynomial equations.

b. $f = x^4 - 2x^3 - 27x + 54 = 0$
$x = 2, 3$

c. $f = 2x^4 - 7x^3 + x^2 + 7x - 3 = 0$
$x = -1, \frac{1}{2}, 1, 3$

TEACHER TIP

Be sure students understand that often the roots of a polynomial can be found using different methods. They should use the method that seems easiest for each problem.

 **ENGLISH LEARNERS**

Discuss the terms **quadratic, cubic,** and **quartic.** Help students pronounce and define each of the words. Students should understand that the terms refer to the highest-power term in a polynomial.

Discuss the difference between quadratic and quartic. The words look similar but have different meanings.

Write the three terms on the board, and have students write an example of a polynomial for each. For example, $x^2 + x + 4$ is quadratic, $5x^3 + 2x^2 + 9$ is cubic, and $x^4 + 1$ is quartic.

Help students connect the terms to familiar items. Relate cubic to a cube, and relate quartic to a quarter.

Example 5

Students find the roots of a polynomial function applied to a roller coaster design.

Additional Example 5

A portion of a roller coaster is modeled by the polynomial function $y = -0.2x^3 + 3x^2 - 9.6x + 8.8.$

Graph the function for positive values only and find the positive roots. $x = 2, 11$

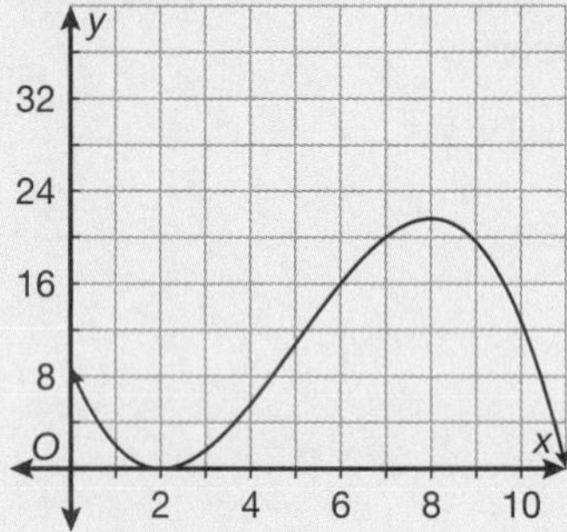

Lesson Practice

Problem e

Error Alert Students may think a problem has no solution if they are unable to easily factor the polynomial or apply a pattern they have learned. Remind them that graphing a polynomial is another method.

Step 3: Use the Quadratic Formula.

$$x = \frac{3 \pm \sqrt{(-3)^2 - 4(1)(-4)}}{2} = \frac{3 \pm 5}{2} = 4 \text{ and } -1$$

The real roots are $x = \frac{1}{2}, 1, -1,$ and 4.

Example 5 Application: Roller Coaster Design

A portion of a roller coaster is modeled by the polynomial function $y = -0.4x^3 + 4.8x^2 - 8.4x + 4$. Graph the function for positive values only and find the positive roots.

SOLUTION

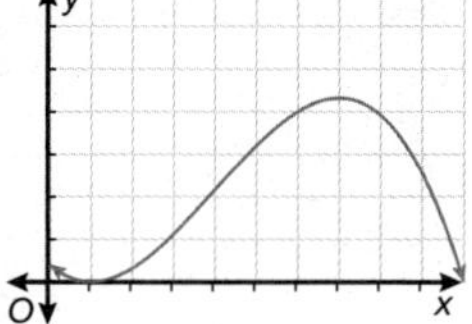

Step 1: You can use the Rational Root Theorem even when the terms are decimals by multiplying by powers of 10.

$$-0.4x^3 + 4.8x^2 - 8.4x + 4 = 0$$
$$-4x^3 + 48x^2 - 84x + 40 = 0$$
$$-x^3 + 12x^2 - 21x + 10 = 0$$

Factors of -1: ± 1 ← Values of q

Factors of 10: $\pm 1, \pm 2, \pm 5, \pm 10$ ← Values of p

$\frac{p}{q} = \{\pm 1, \pm 2, \pm 5, \pm 10\}$

Find the first rational number that yields a factor:

1	−1	12	−21	10	
		−1	11	−10	✓
	−1	11	−10	0	

$$-x^3 + 12x^2 - 21x + 10 = (x - 1)(-x^2 + 11x - 10)$$

Step 2: Use the Quadratic Formula.

$$x = \frac{-11 \pm \sqrt{11^2 - 4(-1)(-10)}}{2(-1)} = \frac{-11 \pm \sqrt{81}}{-2}$$

$$= \frac{11 \pm 9}{2} = 10 \text{ and } 1$$

The roots are $x = 10$ and 1.

Lesson Practice

a. Find the roots of $x^3 - 8 = 0$. $x = 2$
(Ex 1)

b. Find the roots of $x^3 + 125 = 0$. $x = -5$
(Ex 1)

c. Find the roots of $x^9 - 512 = 0$. $x = 2$
(Ex 2)

d. Find the roots of $x^6 - 729 = 0$. $x = 3$ and $x = -3$
(Ex 2)

e. Find the roots of the cubic equation $5x^3 + 2x - 1 = 0$. $x = 0.3717$
(Ex 3)

ALTERNATE METHOD FOR EXAMPLE 5

Remind students that after they identify one root of a polynomial, they can use different methods for finding other roots. In this case, point out that they might be able to easily identify the roots of the quadratic term simply by inspection.

602 Saxon Algebra 2

f. Find the rational roots for $4x^3 - 4x^2 + 9x - 9 = 0$. $x = 1$
(Ex 4)

g. Find the rational roots for $x^4 - 2x^3 - 27x + 54 = 0$. $x = 2$ and 3
(Ex 4)

h. Find the rational roots for $4x^3 + 4x^2 - 29x + 21 = 0$. $x = 1.5, -3.5, 1$
(Ex 4)

i. Find the rational roots for $0.05x^3 - 1.3x^2 + 9.6x - 14.4 = 0$. $x = 2$ and 12
(Ex 5)

Practice Distributed and Integrated

Find the roots of the given equations.

1. $y = 6x^2 + 7x - 1$ (76) $x = 0.1287$ and -1.2953

2. $y = x^4 - 27x$ (76) $x = 0$ and 3

*3. Which of the following is not a root of $f(x) = 3x^3 - 19x^2 + 22x + 24$? **B** (85)

A $-\frac{2}{3}$ B $\frac{2}{3}$ C 3 D 4

Determine whether each of the following are step functions.

4. $f(x) = \begin{cases} 12, \text{ if } x < 1 \\ x + 12, \text{ if } x \geq 1 \end{cases}$ (79)
Not a step function

5. $f(x) = \begin{cases} 0, \text{ if } x < 0 \\ 5, \text{ if } x \geq 0 \end{cases}$ (79) Step function

6. **Geometry** $\overline{AB}$ is tangent to the circle at point A and $\overline{BC}$ is tangent to the circle at point C. What is the length of $\widehat{AC}$? Give the answer in exact form and to the nearest tenth of a centimeter. $\frac{20\pi\sqrt{3}}{9}$ cm ≈ 12.1 cm (63)

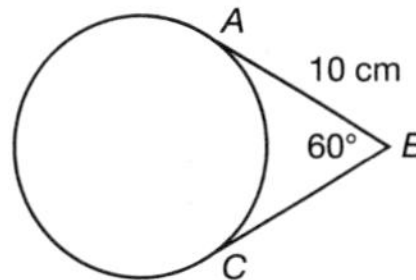

7. **Gravity on the Moon** The height of a free-falling object on the moon (neglecting air resistance) is given by the function $h(t) = -0.8t^2 + v_0t + h_0$, where h_0 is the initial height in meters, v_0 is the initial velocity in meters per second, and $h(t)$ is the height in meters at time t seconds. How long does it take for an object to hit the surface of the moon after it is dropped from a height of 125 meters? (Hint: Multiply both sides of a quadratic equation by a number so that the coefficient of the quadratic term is a perfect square.) 12.5 seconds (78)

8. The student did not use the total of the females in the denominator. The probability is $\frac{4}{16} = \frac{1}{4} = 25\%$.

8. **Error Analysis** Find and correct the error a student made in finding $P(\text{AM}|\text{Female})$. (68)

$$P(\text{AM}|\text{Female}) = \frac{4}{12} = \frac{1}{3} = 33\frac{1}{3}\%$$

	Male	Female
AM	16	4
PM	8	12

9. **Pendulum** The period of a pendulum, T, is the time it takes for the pendulum to make one back-and-forth swing, and is given by $T = 2\pi\sqrt{\frac{L}{9.8}}$, where L is the length of the pendulum in meters. Find the length of a pendulum whose period is 1.5 seconds. $L \approx .56$ meters (70)

10. Ty tosses a quarter three times. What is the probability that the quarter will land on tails all three times? $\frac{1}{8}$ (55)

*11. **Write** How is deriving a quadratic equation from two complex roots different from deriving a quadratic equation from two real roots? See Additional Answers. (83)

Problem i

Scaffolding Remind students that the Rational Root Theorem is a useful method for identifying roots when other methods seem too difficult. Problems that involve decimals may not be as difficult as they first appear.

Check for Understanding

The questions below help assess the concepts taught in this lesson.

"How can synthetic division reveal whether the possible roots found with the Rational Root Theorem are actually roots?" A root used with synthetic division will have no remainder.

"Which method of solving cubic equations do you feel is most difficult? Explain." Sample: Using the Rational Root Theorem followed by synthetic division is most difficult because it has many steps.

3 Practice

Math Conversations

Discussions to strengthen understanding

Problem 2

Guide students by asking the following question.

"Is it possible to use a pattern to solve this problem? Explain." Yes; first factor out one x, which identifies 0 as a factor. Then, use the difference of cubes pattern.

Problem 10

Error Alert

Students may think that because the coin could land on either of two sides each time, the probability is $\frac{1}{2}$. Remind students that the probability is multiplied each time the coin is tossed.

Problem 12

Guide students by asking the following questions.

"Will you use the Law of Sines or the Law of Cosines to solve this problem?" Law of Sines

"Why?" The given information is of the form ASA.

Problem 14

This problem provides an opportunity to review scientific notation with students and operations using scientific notation.

Problem 15

Have students use the equation editor to enter Y_1 and Y_2. Let $Y_1 = \frac{x^4}{2} + \frac{1}{x^2+1}$ and $Y_2 = x + 3$. Next have them use ZOOM 6 to set the window. Tell them that the solution(s) will be the x-coordinates of the intersection points of the two graphs. So, by using 2ND CALC 5, the students can find the solutions −1.28 and 1.73.

12. (71) **Navigation** Two ships 320 yards apart spot the same lighthouse, as shown in the diagram. How much farther is ship B from the lighthouse than ship A? About 95.5 yards

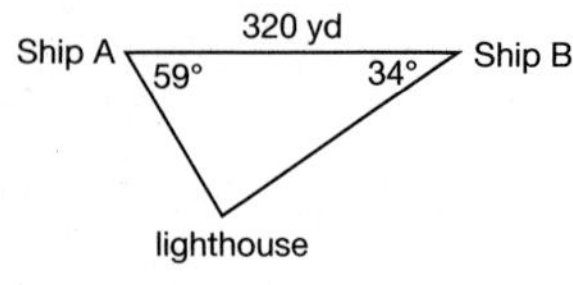

13. (78) **Error Analysis** A student solved the equation $2x^3 - 72x = 0$ as shown below. What is the error?

$2x^3 - 72x = 0 \rightarrow 2x(x^2 - 36) = 0 \rightarrow 2x(x+6)(x-6) = 0 \rightarrow x = -6$ or $x = 6$

The student omitted 0 as one of the solutions.

14. (72) **Geology** The Richter magnitude M of an earthquake is expressed by $M = \frac{2}{3}\log\left(\frac{E}{10^{11.8}}\right)$, where E is the energy released in ergs. The earthquake of greatest magnitude, 9.5, occurred in 1960 in the Pacific, near the coast of Chile. Find the energy released by that earthquake. approximately $10^{26.05}$, or 1.12×10^{26} ergs

***15.** (84) **Graphing Calculator** Use a graphing calculator to estimate the solution(s) of $\frac{x^4}{2} + \frac{1}{x^2+1} = x + 3$. About −1.28 and 1.73

16. (73) **Write** Explain what is meant by voluntary response sampling and why it is not a form of probability sampling. See Additional Answers.

17. (80) **Multi-Step** The scores on a test are normally distributed with a mean of 86 and a standard deviation of 3.

a. What percent of the scores are between 83 and 89? 68%

b. Tell how you can use the answer in part a to find the percent of scores that are either less than 83 or greater than 89. Then find the percent. Subtract from 100%, 32%

c. Tell how you can use the answer in part b to find the percent of scores that are less than 83. Then find the percent. Divide by 2, 16%

Find the restricted values for the rational equations.

***18.** (84) $\frac{1}{5} - \frac{1}{x+5} = \frac{4}{3x^2}$ $x = -5, 0$

***19.** (84) $\frac{x}{3} + \frac{x+3}{x-1} = \frac{4}{x-1}$ $x = 1$

20. (74) **Estimate** Estimate the discriminant of $43.876x^2 + \frac{4}{5}x - 4.128 = 0$. Accept answers between 700 and 800.

***21.** (85) Let $f(x) = x^3 - 27$ and $g(x) = x + 2$. Find the roots of $f(g(x))$. $x = 1$

22. (75) **Physics** The equation $h = -4.9t^2 + v_o t + h_o$ can be used to find the distance from the ground at time t for a ball thrown from a height h_o at an initial speed of v_o. Use the technique of completing the square to derive the function that can be used to calculate t. Sample: $t = \frac{v_o}{9.8} \pm \sqrt{\frac{h_o - h}{4.9} + \left(\frac{v_o}{9.8}\right)^2}$

23. (52) Let $f(x) = 3x$, $g(x) = x - 5$, and $h(x) = x^2 - 2$. Find the composite function $f(g(h(x)))$. See Additional Answers.

24. (77) **Analyze** In $\triangle ABC$, $m\angle A = 63°$, $b = 15$, and $c = 8$. To find a, which should be used, the Law of Sines or the Law of Cosines. Why?

24. The Law of Cosines, because two sides and the included angle are known. There would not be enough information to make an equation for the Law of Sines.

CHALLENGE

Find the roots of the following polynomial functions.

a. $f(x) = x^5 - 64x^3 + 2x^2 - 128$ $x = \pm 8, \sqrt[3]{-2}$

b. $f(x) = x^7 + 5x^4 - 4x^3 - 20$ $x = \pm\sqrt{2}, \sqrt[3]{-5}$

*25. **Probability** A machine on an assembly line makes an acceptable product 90% of the time. (81)

a. Ten samples are chosen at random. What is the probability that all 10 samples are acceptable? $0.9^{10} \approx 0.35$, or 35%

b. At what number of samples is the probability 10% or less? Let n represent the number of samples. Write an equation and use natural logarithms to solve it.

25b. 22 or more samples

*26. **Write** A radio station asks for listeners to call in and vote for their favorite high school football team. Identify the type of sample and determine whether it is biased. Explain your answer. self-selected; biased; The population is unfairly represented because only those listening to the station know of the survey. (Inv 7)

27. **Multiple Choice** Which is the graph of the function $f(x) = \begin{cases} -x, \text{ if } x < 0 \\ 3, \text{ if } x \geq 0 \end{cases}$? **D** (79)

A
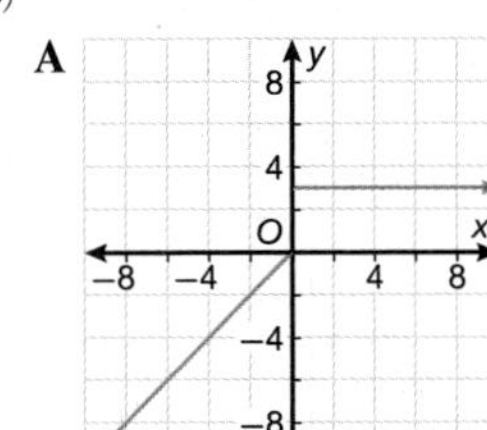

B
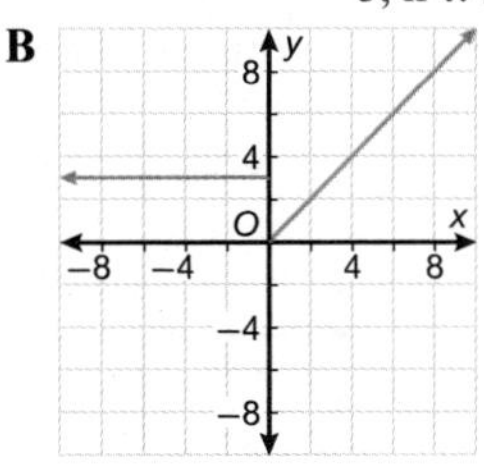

C
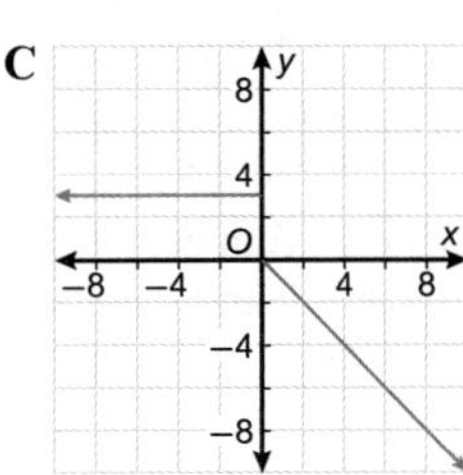

D
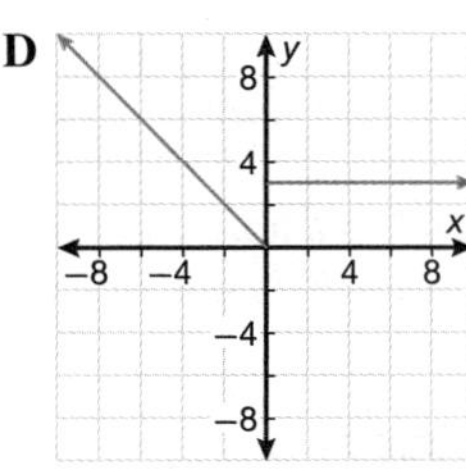

Identify all the real roots.

*28. $x^3 - 729 = 0$ $x = 9$ (85)

*29. $x^4 - 13x^3 + 55x^2 - 81x + 18 = 0$ $x = 2 \pm \sqrt{3}, 3, 6$ (85)

*30. Graph $y = -2\sin\left(\frac{1}{4}x\right)$ (82)

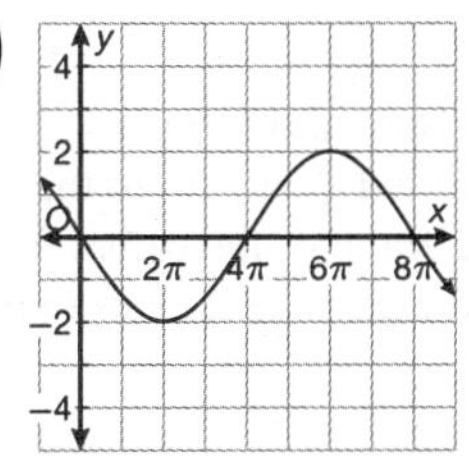

Problem 28

"What should you do when you see a problem of the form $x^3 \pm a$?" Check if the term a is a perfect cube.

"What can you do if the term a is a perfect cube?" Use the sum or difference of cubes as a solution pattern.

"What can you do if the term a is not a perfect cube?" Use the sum or difference of cubes solution pattern by writing a as $\sqrt[3]{a^3}$.

LOOKING FORWARD

Finding polynomial roots prepares students for

- **Lesson 95** Factoring Higher-Order Polynomials
- **Lesson 101** Making Graphs of Polynomial Functions
- **Lesson 106** Using the Fundamental Theorem of Algebra
- **Lesson 111** Tranforming Polynomial Functions

LESSON 86

1 Warm Up

Discuss the definitions of period and amplitude.

2 New Concepts

Students graph transformations of the sine and cosine functions.

Example 1

Additional Example 1

Describe the phase shift of each function and graph it.

a. $y = \sin(x - \pi)$ π units right

b. $y = \cos\left(x + \frac{\pi}{2}\right)$ $\frac{\pi}{2}$ units left

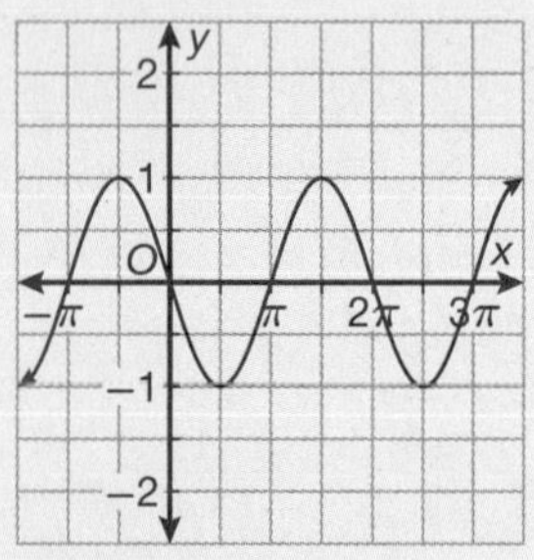

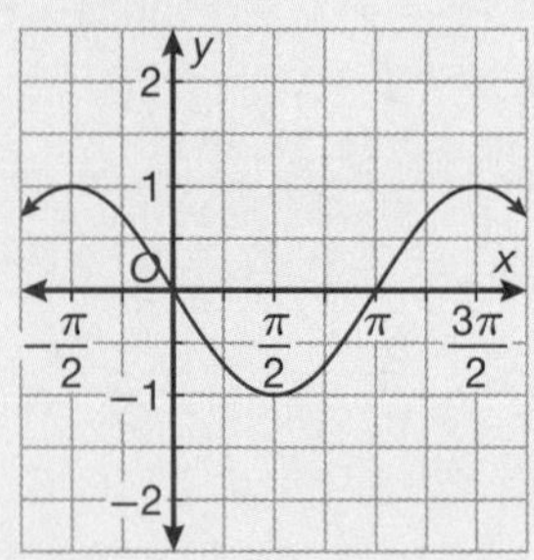

LESSON 86

Translating Sine and Cosine Functions

Warm Up

1. (82) **Vocabulary** The function $y = \sin(x)$ is an example of a periodic function.

2. (82) What is the amplitude of $y = 5\sin(x)$? 5

3. (82) What is the period of $y = \cos(2x)$? π

New Concepts

Periodic functions can be translated horizontally and vertically with the same methods used for other functions like the quadratic function in Lesson 30.

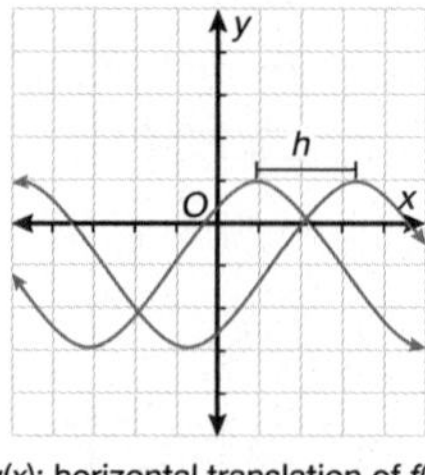

g(x): horizontal translation of f(x)
g(x) = f(x − h)

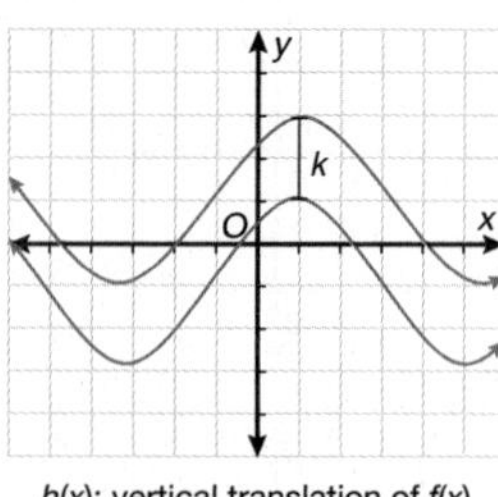

h(x): vertical translation of f(x)
h(x) = f(x) + k

A **phase shift** is a horizontal translation of a periodic function. A periodic function $f(x - h)$ is shifted h units to the right if $h > 0$ and h units to the left if $h < 0$.

Hint

The parent functions $y = \cos(x)$ and $y = \sin(x)$ have periods of 2π.

Math Reasoning

Verify Create a table of values comparing $\cos(x)$ and $\sin\left(x + \frac{\pi}{2}\right)$ to verify that sine and cosine are phase shifted by $\frac{\pi}{2}$.

Check students' work.

Example 1 Graphing Phase Shifts

Describe the phase shift of each function and then graph it.

a. $y = \sin\left(x - \frac{\pi}{2}\right)$

SOLUTION

Write the function in standard form. $h = \frac{\pi}{2}$ and $h > 0$; the graph is shifted $\frac{\pi}{a}$ radians to the right. To graph begin with the graph of the parent function $y = \sin x$ and shift the graph $\frac{\pi}{2}$ radians to the right.

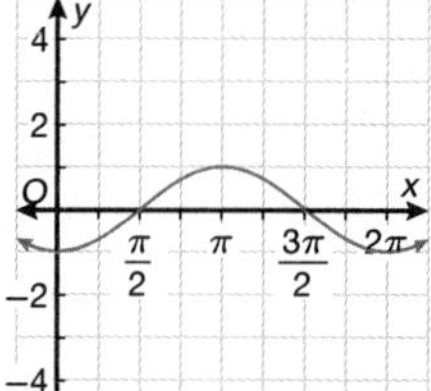

b. $y = \cos(x + \pi)$

SOLUTION

Write the function in standard form first.

$y = \cos(x - (-\pi))$

$h = -\pi$ and $h < 0$; the graph is shifted π units to the left. To graph begin with the graph of the parent function $y = \cos x$ and shift the graph π radians to the left.

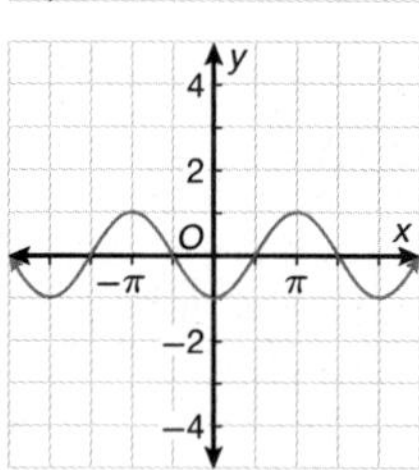

Online Connection
www.SaxonMathResources.com

LESSON RESOURCES

Student Edition Practice Workbook 86
Reteaching Master 86
Adaptations Master 86
Challenge and Enrichment Master C86

MATH BACKGROUND

Once students become familiar with the graph of the cosine function, they will see that the graph is identical to the graph of the sine function under a translation of $\frac{\pi}{2}$ units to the left or right.

In fact, the cosine function is a derivative of the sine function, originally called *co*-sine because the cosine of an angle is equivalent to the *sine* of the angle's complement.

Because of this relationship, the sine and cosine functions share some of the same properties. For example, the period of each function is 2π, the amplitude is 1, the domain is all real numbers, and the range is $-1 \le y \le 1$.

In the function $f(x) + k$, the value of k determines the vertical shift of the graph. If $k > 0$, the graph is shifted up k units from $f(x)$ and if $k < 0$, the graph is shifted down k units from $f(x)$.

Example 2 Graphing Vertical Shifts

Describe the vertical shift of each function and then graph it.

a. $y = \sin x + 2$

SOLUTION

$k = 2$ and $k > 0$; the graph is shifted 2 units up. To graph, begin with the graph of the parent function $y = \sin x$ and shift the graph up 2 units.

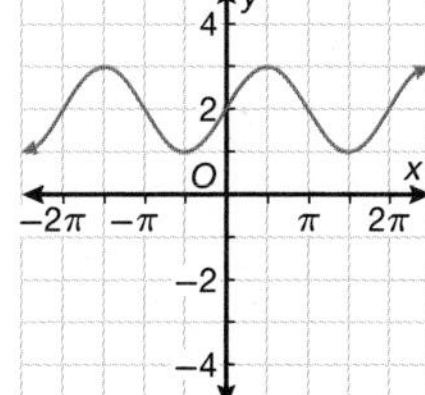

b. $y = \cos x - 1$

SOLUTION

Write the function in standard form first.

$y = \cos x + (-1)$.

$k = -1$ and $k < 0$; the graph is shifted 1 unit down. To graph, begin with the graph of the parent function $y = \cos x$ and shift the graph 1 unit down.

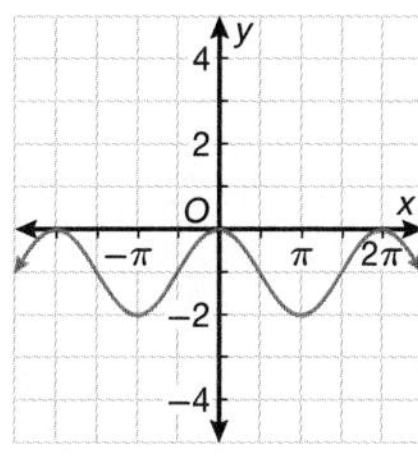

A translation can also be formed by combining a vertical shift and a horizontal shift.

Example 3 Graphing a Combination of Shifts

Describe the shifts of the function and then graph it.

$y = \sin(x + \pi) + 2$

SOLUTION

Write the function in standard form first.

$y = \sin\left(x - (-\pi)\right) + 2$

$h = -\pi$ and $h < 0$; the graph is shifted π radians to the left. $k = 2$ and $k > 0$; the graph is shifted 2 units up. To graph, begin with the graph of the parent function $y = \sin x$ and shift the graph π radians to the left and 2 units up.

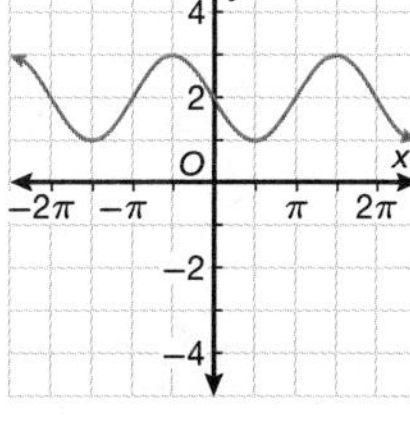

To graph a more complicated translated function, a simpler member of the sine or cosine functions can be used.

Example 2

Additional Example 2

Describe the vertical shift of each function and graph it.

a. $y = \sin x - 3$ 3 units down

b. $y = \cos x + 1$ 1 unit up

a.

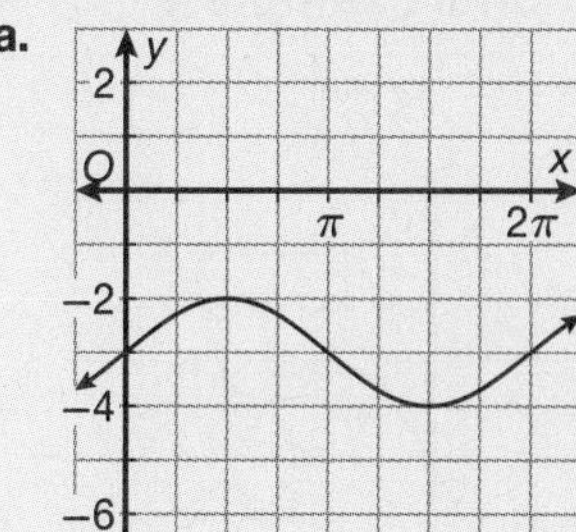

b.

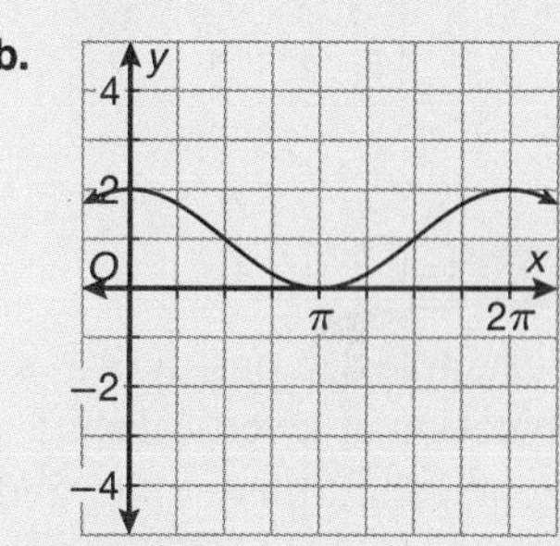

Example 3

This example demonstrates a combination of a vertical shift and a horizontal shift.

Additional Example 3

Describe the shifts of the function and graph it.

$y = \sin\left(x + \frac{\pi}{2}\right) - 1$ $\frac{\pi}{2}$ units left and 1 unit down

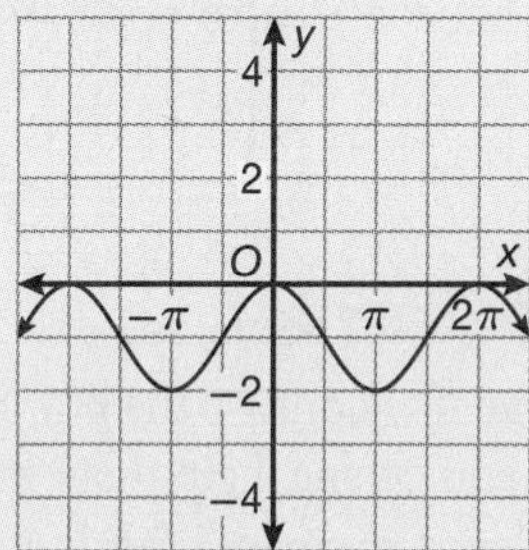

ALTERNATE METHOD

For Examples 1 and 2, show students how to use a table of values to find points on the graphs of various transformed cosine functions. Have them make a table of values for the parent function, then use those values to find ordered pairs on the transformed functions.

Sine and Cosine Functions in Standard Form	
$y = a\sin b(x - h) + k$	$y = a\cos b(x - h) + k$
The measure of angle x is in radians. $\lvert a\rvert$ = amplitude, the vertical stretch or shrink of the graph of the function, $\frac{2\pi}{b}$ = period, where $b > 0$, h = horizontal or phase shift, and k = vertical shift.	

The sine and cosine functions in standard form can be graphed using transformations of the functions $y = a\sin bx$ and $y = a\cos bx$.

Example 4 Graphing $y = a\cos(b(x - h)) + k$

Graph $y = 3\cos(2(x - \pi)) + 1$

SOLUTION

Begin by graphing the simpler function $y = 3\cos 2x$ involving only amplitude and period changes.

The amplitude is the $|a| = |3| = 3$ and the period is $\frac{2\pi}{b} = \frac{2\pi}{2} = \pi$.

Since the amplitude is positive the pattern to graph is max-zero-min-zero-max.

$h = \pi$ and $h > 0$; so the graph is shifted π radians to the right.

$k = 1$ and $k > 0$; so the graph is shifted 1 units up.

Shift the graph of $y = 3\sin 2x$ π radians to the right and 1 units up.

Example 5 Graphing $y = a\sin(b(x + h)) - k$

Graph $y = -2\sin\left(\frac{1}{2}(x + \pi)\right) - 1$

SOLUTION

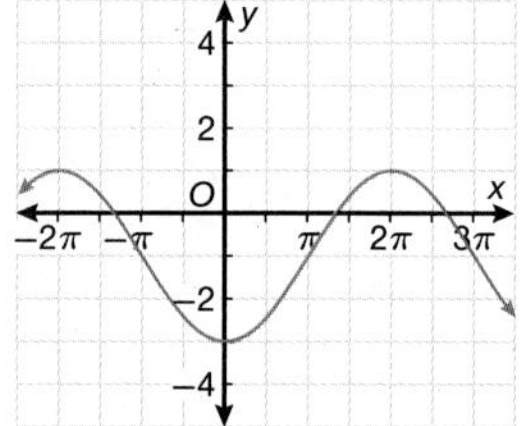

Begin by graphing the simpler function $y = -2\sin\frac{1}{2}x$ involving only amplitude and period changes.

The amplitude is the $|a| = |-2| = 2$ and the period is $\frac{2\pi}{b} = \frac{2\pi}{\frac{1}{2}} = 4\pi$.

Since the amplitude is negative, the pattern to graph is zero-min-zero-max-zero.

Write in standard form to determine h and k.

$$y = -2\sin\left(\frac{1}{2}(x - (-\pi))\right) + (-1)$$

$h = -\pi$ and $h < 0$; so the graph is shifted π radians to the left.

$k = -1$ and $k < 0$; so the graph is shifted 1 unit down.

Shift the graph of $y = -2\sin\frac{1}{2}x$ π radians to the left and 1 unit down.

Example 4

This example demonstrates a combination of a vertical shift, horizontal shift, phase shift, and an amplitude change of a cosine function.

Additional Example 4

Graph $y = 2\cos\left(x - \frac{\pi}{2}\right) + 2$.

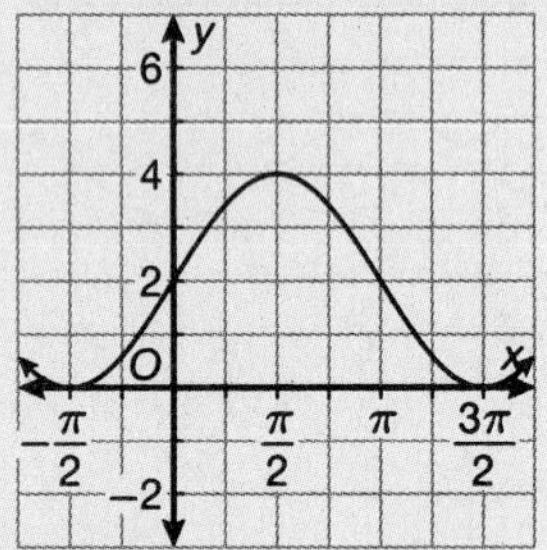

Example 5

This example demonstrates a combination of a vertical shift, horizontal shift, phase shift, and an amplitude change of a sine function.

Additional Example 5

Graph $y = -1\sin(2(x + \pi)) - 3$.

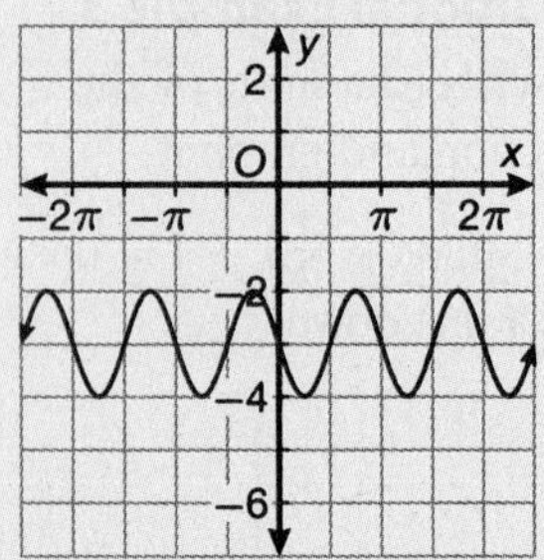

TEACHER TIP

If students confuse the graphs of sine and cosine, help them find the "starting point" for drawing each graph by relating the graph to the unit circle. At 0 radians, the terminal side intersects at (1, 0). So $\sin(0) = 0$ and $\cos(0) = 1$. The graph of $y = \sin x$ contains (0, 0). The graph of $y = \cos x$ contains (0, 1).

INCLUSION

Students may have difficulty seeing the shifts in the graphs. If so, graph the function and its parent function on the chalkboard. Use masking tape for the axes and different color chalk for each function. Help students choose an appropriate interval (such as $\frac{\pi}{4}$, $\frac{\pi}{3}$, $\frac{\pi}{2}$, or π) for marking off the x-axis to graph the five critical points of the function.

Lesson Practice

Describe the phase shift of each function and then graph it.
(Ex 1)

a. $y = \sin(x - \pi)$ right π units
See Additional Answers.

b. $y = \cos(x + 2\pi)$ left 2π units
See Additional Answers.

Describe the vertical shift of each function and then graph it.
(Ex 2)

c. $y = \sin x - 3$ 3 units down
See Additional Answers.

d. $y = \cos x + 2$ 2 units up
See Additional Answers.

e. Describe the shifts of the function $y = \sin(x + \pi) - 2$ and then graph it. left π units and 2 units down; See Additional Answers.
(Ex 3)

Graph each function.

f. $y = 2\cos(4(x - \pi)) + 3$
(Ex 4) See Additional Answers.

g. $y = -1\sin(2(x + \pi)) - 3$
(Ex 5) See Additional Answers.

Practice Distributed and Integrated

1. Given a deck of cards, what is the probability of randomly drawing a face card, and then a number card without replacement of the first card? (The ace is not a face or number card) $\frac{36}{221}$
(60)

Solve.

2. $\sqrt[3]{8x^3 - 1} = 2x - 1$ $0, \frac{1}{2}$
(70)

3. $\sqrt[3]{12x - 5} - \sqrt[3]{8x + 15} = 0$ 5
(70)

4. Find the roots and give the multiplicity of each root: $x^3 + 12x^2 + 36x = 0$
(66) $x = -6$ with multiplicity of 2, $x = 0$ with multiplicity of 1

***5.** Determine the period of the function $y = 3\cos\left(\frac{\pi}{2}x\right)$. period = 4
(8)

6. **Jewelry** A jeweler is about to finish his sales for the year. He has 8 diamonds, 6 tanzanite stones, 9 opal stones, and 3 sapphires. A customer comes in needing three stones for a ring setting. Find the probability that the customer will choose 2 tanzanite stones and 1 sapphire. 3.46%
(67)

7. Find the range and standard deviation for the following set of data;
(25)

{35, 67, 21, 16, 24, 51, 18, 32}. 51, 16.7

***8.** Consider the function $f(x) = 3\cos(2x)$. Determine the period and amplitude of the function. Period: π; Amplitude 3
(86)

***9.** **Multiple Choice** Which triangle cannot be solved by using the Law of Sines? **D**
(71)

A
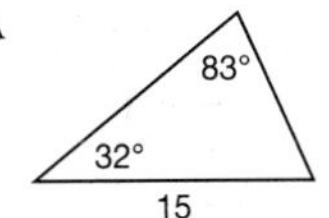

B
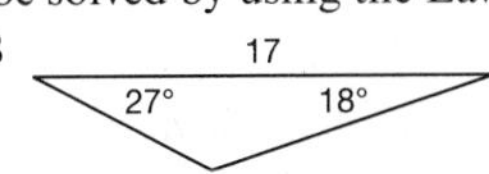

C
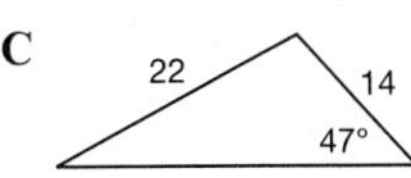

D
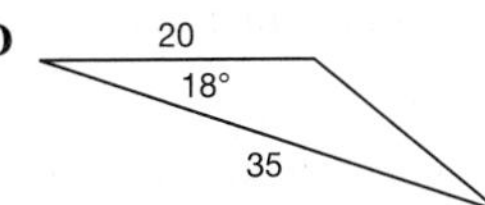

ENGLISH LEARNERS

For problem 6, explain the meaning of the word **jeweler.** If possible, show students jewelry, such as a ring, bracelet, or watch.

"A jeweler is a person who makes or repairs jewelry."

Discuss that a jeweler may also sell precious stones, watches, and often silverware and china, as well as jewelry.

Lesson Practice

Problem f

Scaffolding Have students first graph the function $y = 2\cos 4x$, then have them shift the graph π units right and 3 units up.

Check for Understanding

The questions below help assess the concepts taught in this lesson.

1. **"Explain how to graph one period of the parent function $y = \cos x$."** Label the x-axis from 0 to 2π by intervals of $\frac{\pi}{2}$. Label the y-axis from -1 to 1. Plot the points $(0, 1)$, $\left(\frac{\pi}{2}, 0\right)$ $(\pi, -1)$, $\left(\frac{3\pi}{2}, 0\right)$, and $(2\pi, 1)$ and connect with a smooth curve.

2. **"Explain how each variable a, b, c, and d transforms the graph of $y = \cos x$ into the graph of $y = a\cos(bx + c) + d$."** a changes the amplitude from 1 to a. b changes the period from 2π into $\frac{2\pi}{b}$. c causes a phase shift to the left (+) or right (−), and d translates the graph up (+) or down (−).

3 Practice

Math Conversations

Discussions to strengthen understanding

Problem 5

Remind students that they can find the period by dividing 2π by $\frac{\pi}{2}$. To divide, they should multiply by the reciprocal of $\frac{\pi}{2}$.

Problem 9

Have students state the Law of Sines and explain what each variable means before determining to which triangle the Law can be applied.

Problem 11

Error Alert

When using Heron's formula, students might use 12.7 for s. Remind students that s is the semi-perimeter, not the length of one side.

Problem 17

Suggest that students solve the equation using a graphing calculator.

Problem 18

Remind students to clear the denominators by multiplying each term on each side of the equation by the least common multiple of 7.5, z, and 6.

Problem 19

Extend the Problem

"How much of a 300-gram sample of the material will remain after 258 years?" 6.15 grams

"If the original weight of a sample is estimated to have been 20 grams and the current weight is 8 grams, what is the age of the sample?" 60.81 years

10. (80) **Generalize** Given a data value that is to be standardized and the mean of the data set, how can you tell if the z-score will be positive or negative without performing any calculations. It will be positive if it is greater than the mean and negative if it is less than the mean.

11. (77) An equilateral triangle has a side length of 12.7 centimeters. Find the area of the triangle by using Heron's formula. About 69.8 square centimeters

***12.** (86) Which of the following has a vertical shift of 2 up? **A**

A $y = \cos(2x) + 2$ **B** $y = \cos(2\pi x) - 2$

C $y = 2\cos(x)$ **D** $y = \cos\left(\frac{x}{2}\right)$

13. (74) **Geometry** The perimeter of a rectangle is 52 units.

a. Write an expression for the length if the width is represented by w. $26 - w$

b. Write a quadratic equation in standard form to show that the product of the length and width is 169 square units. $-w^2 + 26w - 169 = 0$

c. Find the discriminant of the equation. Explain what it means in terms of the rectangle. 0; it means there is one solution to the equation and one width that gives an area of 169 square units and a perimeter of 52 units.

***14.** (85) **Graphing Calculator** Use a graphing calculator to test this hypothesis: If a cubic function has only one rational root, then the other roots are complex. Students should conclude this is false. The remaining roots can be irrational.

15. (75) Determine the domain and range of the function $f(x) = \sqrt{x-4} + 3$ and its inverse. The domain of $f(x)$ is $x \geq 4$ and the range is $y \geq 3$. The domain of $f^{-1}(x)$ is $x \geq 3$ and the range is $y \geq 4$.

16. (58) Complete the square and factor the resulting perfect square trinomial: $x^2 + 30x$. $x^2 + 30x + 225 = (x + 15)^2$

***17.** (76) **Physics** Acceleration due to gravity is different on different planets. The equation below can be used to find the distance from the ground at time t for a ball thrown from a height h_o at an initial speed of v_o. Use the table to determine how long it will take a ball thrown with an initial speed of 20 at a height of 35 to hit the ground on Mars. 12.14 seconds

$$h = -\frac{1}{2}at^2 + v_o t + h_o$$

Planet	Acceleration (a)
Mercury	3.59
Venus	8.87
Mars	3.77
Jupiter	25.95
Saturn	11.08
Uranus	10.67
Neptune	14.07

18. (84) **Data Analysis** The harmonic mean x of y and z is given by the formula $\frac{2}{x} = \frac{1}{y} + \frac{1}{z}$. Find z when $x = 7.5$ and $y = 6$. $z = 10$

19. (81) A radioactive material has a half life of 46 hours. Find the decay constant. $k = 0.015$

20. (78) **Multi-Step** Complete parts a-b to help graph the quadratic function $y = \frac{1}{4}x^2 - \frac{9}{4}$.

a. Find the points in which the graph intersects the x-axis. $(-3, 0)$ and $(3, 0)$

b. Find the vertex. $\left(0, -\frac{9}{4}\right)$

c. Graph the function. See Additional Answers.

CHALLENGE

Have students use various values for a, b, c, and d to create several graphs of the function $y = a\cos(bx + c) + d$ on graph paper. They should record the equation of each graph on a separate sheet of paper. Then, have them trade graph papers and study their partner's graphs to try to determine the equation of the graph.

21. **Error Analysis** Jake graphed the piecewise function (79)

$f(x) = \begin{cases} x, \text{ if } x < 0 \\ 3, \text{ if } x \geq 0 \end{cases}$ incorrectly. Explain Jake's error.

Jake graphed $f(x) = -x$ for $x < 0$ instead of $f(x) = x$.

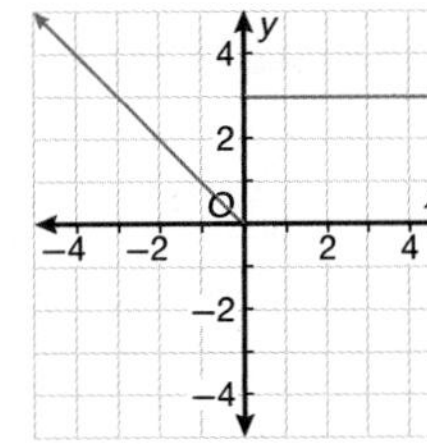

22. **Multi-Step** Suppose that the population of a certain species decreases at the rate of 5% per year and that the current population of that species in a certain habitat is 150. (57)

a. Write an exponential function that gives the population as a function of x, the number of elapsed years. (Hint: $0 < b < 1$). See Additional Answers.

b. Write a logarithmic function that gives the number of elapsed years as a function of x, the population. See Additional Answers.

c. To the nearest tenth, how many years will it take for the population to drop below 100? about 7.9 years

***23.** **(Physics)** Two wheels spin in opposite directions. The larger wheel completes a cycle in 4 seconds and the smaller wheel completes a cycle in 9 seconds. The two squares attached to the wheels are facing each other at time $t = 0$. How many seconds elapse before they are back in sync? 36 seconds (86)

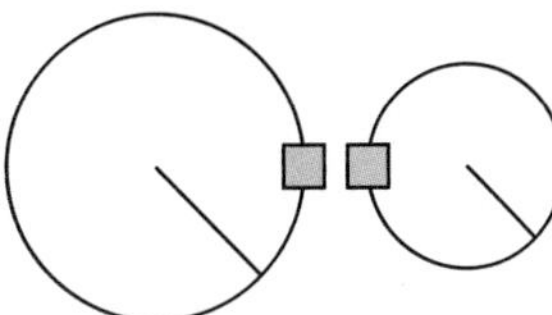

24. P is a point on the terminal side of θ in standard position. Find the exact value of the six trigonometric functions for θ where $P(-2, -1)$. See Additional Answers. (56)

25. **Write** What is the converse of the Zero-Product Property? What can it be used for? (83)

25. The converse of the Zero-Product Property states that if $a = 0$ or $b = 0$ then the product $ab = 0$. It can be used to write a quadratic equation given its two roots.

26. **(Government)** Suppose a politician must visit 6 counties in Massachusetts. Her human resource personnel form a simple random sample by listing each county and numbering it as shown below. If they use the line of random digits shown below, which 6 counties will the politician visit? Barnstable, Franklin, Dukes, Hampshire, Essex, Suffolk (73)

01: Barnstable	02: Berkshire	03: Bristol	04: Dukes	05: Essex
06: Franklin	07: Hampden	08: Hampshire	09: Middlesex	10: Nantucket
11: Norfolk	12: Plymouth	13: Suffolk	14: Worcester	

62010	60482	89824	08705	57913	46815	76221	25650	89337	53603	73597

27. **Analyze** Why is the amplitude of $\sin(\sin(x))$ 0.84 and not 1? The interior term $\sin(x)$ has a range of –1 to 1, the maximum value of $\sin(\sin(x))$ is $\sin\left(\sin\left(\frac{\pi}{2}\right)\right) = \sin(1) = 0.84$. (82)

Identify all the real roots:

***28.** $x^3 - 216$ $x = 6$ (85)

***29.** $x^9 + 125 = 0$ $x = -\sqrt[3]{5}$ (85)

30. Find the distance between the points $(2, -1)$ and $(5, 4)$. $\sqrt{34}$ (41)

Problem 22

Guide students by asking the following questions:

"What is the annual rate of decrease?" 5%

"What percent remains at the end of each year?" 95%

"What is the original amount?" 150

Problem 24

Remind students that the terminal side is one side of a triangle. The other two legs are the x-axis and a vertical segment.

Problem 25

Guide students by asking the following questions:

"What does the Zero Product Property state?" The Zero Product Property states that if the product of two expressions is 0, then one or both of the expressions must be equal to zero.

"What is the converse of the Zero Product Property?" The converse of the Zero Product Property states that if one or both factors is zero, then the product must be zero.

Problem 27

Error Alert

Students might think that the amplitude is 1 because the coefficient on sine is 1. Remind students that the amplitude of the sine function is a when $y = a\sin x$. The function in this problem does not take that form. Its greatest value occurs at $\sin(1) = 0.84$.

LOOKING FORWARD

Graphing the cosine function prepares students for:

- **Lesson 90** Graphing the Tangent Function
- **Lesson 119** Solving Trigonometric Equations

LESSON 87

1 Warm Up

Remind students that every logarithm has a base. A natural logarithm has base e, while a common logarithm has base 10.

2 New Concepts

Most of the problems in this lesson can be solved using more than one series of steps. Encourage students to share alternate solutions with the class.

Example 1

In this example, properties of logarithms are used to manipulate expressions into forms that facilitate finding an answer.

Additional Example 1

a. Use the properties of logarithms to evaluate $\log_3(27r)^4$ when $r = 243$. 32

b. Use the properties of logarithms to evaluate $\ln(12e)^3$. 10.45

Error Alert Students might write $\log(mn) = \log(m) \cdot \log(n)$. Remind them to study the properties carefully and refer to them as needed.

LESSON RESOURCES

Student Edition Practice Workbook 87
Reteaching Master 87
Adaptations Master 87
Challenge and Enrichment Master C87

LESSON 87 Evaluating Logarithmic Expressions

Warm Up

1. **Vocabulary** The type of logarithm that has e as the base is the natural logarithm. (81)

2. Simplify $\ln(exy)$. $1 + \ln(x) + \ln(y)$ (81)

3. Simplify $\ln\left(\frac{x}{ey}\right)$. $\ln(x) - 1 - \ln(y)$ (81)

4. Express as a common logarithm $\log_7(100)$. $\frac{\log(100)}{\log(7)} = \frac{2}{\log(7)}$ (72)

New Concepts

Properties of logarithms can be used to evaluate expressions. Recall the log rules:

$$\log_b(mn) = \log_b(m) + \log_b(n)$$
$$\log_b(m^n) = n\log_b(m)$$

Caution

When the exponent becomes a multiplier, it must be distributed to all terms in the log expression.

Example 1 Evaluating Expressions of the Form $\log_a(bc)^d$

a. Use the properties of logarithms to evaluate $\log_4(16x)^3$ when $x = 256$.

SOLUTION

Step 1: Use the second rule to write the expression as $3 \cdot \log_4(16x)$.

Step 2: Apply the first rule:

$3 \cdot (\log_4 16 + \log_4 x)$. Since $\log_4 16 = 2$, then

$3 \cdot (\log_4 16 + \log_4 x) = 3 \cdot (2 + \log_4 x)$ or $6 + 3\log_4 x$.

Step 3: Evaluate when $x = 256$,

$6 + 3\log_4 256 = 6 + 3 \cdot 4 = 6 + 12 = 18$.

b. Use the properties of logarithms to evaluate $\ln(7e)^2$.

SOLUTION

Step 1: Use the second rule to write the expression as:

$\ln(7e)^2 = 2 \cdot \ln(7e)$.

Step 2: Use the first rule to expand.

$2 \cdot \ln(7e) = 2(\ln 7 + \ln e)$

Step 3: Evaluate.

$2(\ln 7 + \ln e) \approx 2(1.95 + 1) = 2(2.95) = 5.9$

Sometimes when evaluating and solving logarithmic equations, the change of base formula is utilized. Recall $\log_b x = \frac{\log_a x}{\log_a b}$, where a is the new base.

MATH BACKGROUND

Inverse operations are operations that have the effect of "undoing" each other. Students are familiar with several inverse operations: addition and subtraction, multiplication and division, squaring and taking the square root.

Logarithms and exponentials are inverse operations. In the same way that subtraction "undoes" addition, taking a logarithm "undoes" raising a quantity to an exponent. So, if $9 = 3^2$, then $\log_3 9 = 2$.

This inverse relationship is useful in solving exponential equations, where the variable appears in the exponent. Taking the log of each side brings the variable out of the exponent so that other inverse operations can be employed to isolate it.

The inverse relationship is also helpful in solving equations like $\ln(x - 4) = 3$, where the variable appears in the logarithm. If $\ln(x - 4) = 3$, then $e^3 = x - 4$.

Example 2 Using the Change of Base Formula

a. Use the change of base formula to convert $\log_{100}(10x)^2$ to base 10. Then evaluate when $x = 1000$.

SOLUTION

$\log_{100}(10x)^2 = 2 \cdot \log_{100}(10x)$

$2 \cdot \log_{100}(10x) = 2\left(\frac{\log 10x}{\log 100}\right)$ Use the change of base formula.

$2\left(\frac{\log 10x}{\log 100}\right) = 2\left(\frac{\log 10 + \log x}{\log 100}\right)$

$= 2\left(\frac{\log 10 + \log 1000}{\log 100}\right)$ Evaluate for $x = 1000$.

$= 2\left(\frac{1+3}{2}\right) = 4$

b. Use the change of base formula to convert $\log_4(2x)^3$ to base e. Then evaluate when $x = 6$.

SOLUTION

$\log_4(2x)^3 = 3 \cdot \log_4(2x)$

$3 \cdot \log_4(2x) = 3\left(\frac{\ln 2x}{\ln 4}\right)$ Use the change of base formula.

$3\left(\frac{\ln 2x}{\ln 4}\right) = 3\left(\frac{\ln 2 + \ln x}{\ln 4}\right)$ Use the log rules.

$= 3\left(\frac{\ln 2 + \ln 6}{\ln 4}\right)$ Evaluate for $x = 6$.

$\approx 3\left(\frac{0.6931 + 1.7918}{1.3863}\right) \approx 5.3774$

Hint

The change of base formula can also be used with the natural log function.

Example 3 Solving Logarithmic Equations Using the Change of Base Formula

Solve $1000^{9x} = 100$ for x.

SOLUTION

$1000^{9x} = 100$

$\log_{1000} 100 = 9x$ Simplify using log rules.

$\left(\frac{\log 100}{\log 1000}\right) = 9x$ Use the change of base formula.

$\frac{2}{3} = 9x$ Simplify and solve for x.

$x = \frac{2}{27}$

ALTERNATE METHOD

Solve Example 3 using common bases:

Solve $1000^{9x} = 100$ for x.

$(10^3)^{9x} = 10^2$

$10^{27x} = 10^2$

$27x = 2$

$x = \frac{2}{27}$

Example 2

Since the numbers in the expression are powers of 10, changing the logarithm from base 100 to base 10 allows the expression to be easily simplified.

Additional Example 2

a. Use the change of base formula to convert $\log_{100}(1000x)^3$ to base 10. Then evaluate when $x = 10$. $3\left(\frac{\log 1000 + \log x}{\log 100}\right)$; 6

b. Use the change of base formula to convert $\log_9(3x)^5$ to base e. Then evaluate when $x = 4$. $5\left(\frac{\ln 3 + \ln x}{\ln 9}\right)$; 5.6546

Error Alert When using the change of base formula, students sometimes write $\log_b x = \log_a \frac{x}{b}$ instead of $\log_b x = \frac{\log_a x}{\log_a b}$. Have them be sure that the change of base formula results in the quotient of logarithms, not the logarithm of a quotient.

Example 3

This example shows how the change of base formula can be utilized in solving an exponential equation.

Extend the Example

"How can you check your solution?" Substitute $\frac{2}{27}$ for x and make sure the equation is true:

$1000^{9x} = 100$

$1000^{9\left(\frac{2}{27}\right)} \stackrel{?}{=} 100$

$1000^{\frac{2}{3}} \stackrel{?}{=} 100$

$(10^3)^{\frac{2}{3}} \stackrel{?}{=} 10^2$

$10^2 = 10^2$

Additional Example 3

Solve $32^{4x} = 8$ for x. $\frac{3}{20}$

Example 4

In a future course, students will use a differential equation to determine the values of the constants k and C. Here, the values are given.

Additional Example 4

A cup of tea is brewed at 95°C and served in a room with temperature 20°C. If $C = 4.3175$ and $k = -0.0690$, how long will it take the tea to cool to 65°C? 7.4 min

TEACHER TIP

Help students remember the meaning of each variable in the formula $T = e^{kt+C} + R$: T is for temperature, k and C are for cooling constants, t is for time, and R is for "room" (ambient) temperature.

Lesson Practice

Problem b

Scaffolding Have students break the problem down into steps. Call on different students to complete and explain each step.

Problem f

Be sure students understand they should use $10^{7.1} \times I_0$ for I.

Check for Understanding

The questions below help assess the concepts taught in this lesson.

1. **"Explain how to use the change of base formula. When is it useful?"** Change $\log_b x$ into $\frac{\log_a x}{\log_a b}$. It is useful when $\log_a x$ and/or $\log_a b$ are easy to evaluate.

2. **"How can you solve an exponential equation?"** Use a logarithm to "undo" an exponent, which brings the variable out of the exponent. Then, evaluate logarithms using a calculator, and use standard inverse operations to solve.

Example 4 **Application: Newton's Law of Cooling**

Newton's Law of Cooling states that the rate at which an object cools is related to the difference in temperature between the object and its environment. The formula $T = e^{kt+C} + R$ can be used to determine the desired temperature of the object, T, the cooling time in minutes, t, or the temperature of the environment of the object, R. Solve the formula for t and then determine the amount of time needed to cool a cup of water from 80°C to 55°C in a room temperature of 25°C. Use $k = -0.200064$ and $C = 4.0073$.

SOLUTION

$$T = e^{kt+C} + R$$

$$e^{kt+C} = T - R$$

$$\ln(T - R) = kt + C$$

$$kt = \ln(T - R) - C$$

$$t = \frac{\ln(T - R) - C}{k}$$

$$t = \frac{\ln(55 - 25) - 4.0073}{-0.200064}$$

$$t \approx 3.03$$

The water would take approximately 3.03 minutes to cool.

Lesson Practice

a. Use the properties of logarithms to evaluate $\log_6(36x)^2$ when $x = 216$. 10
(Ex 1)

b. Use the properties of logarithms to evaluate $\ln(10e)^3$. 9.908
(Ex 1)

c. Use the change of base formula to convert $\log_7(5x)^3$ to base 10. Then evaluate when $x = 5$. 4.9625
(Ex 2)

d. Use the change of base formula to convert $\log_8(11x)^2$ to base e. Then evaluate when $x = 10$. 4.5209
(Ex 2)

e. Solve $5^{3x} = 20$ for x. 0.6205
(Ex 3)

f. The magnitude of an earthquake can be found on the Richter scale using the equation $R = \log\frac{I}{I_o}$ where I represents intensity and I_o represents the intensity of a zero-level earthquake. The 1989 California earthquake's intensity was $10^{7.1}$ times I_o. Evaluate to find R, the magnitude on the Richter scale.
(Ex 4)

f. $R = \log\frac{I}{I_o} = \log\frac{10^{7.1} I_o}{I_o} = \log 10^{7.1} = 7.1$ on the Richter scale

Practice Distributed and Integrated

1. A cabinet contains 12 blue cups, 12 red cups, and 20 green cups. What is the probability that a green cup and a blue cup are chosen at random in that order with replacement? $\frac{15}{121}$
(60)

INCLUSION

If students have difficulty following the solution to the problem in Example 4, walk them through the steps one by one, writing explanations for each step, for example, *subtract R from both sides; divide both sides by k*, etc. Remind them that even with logarithms, the fundamental idea for solving equations is the same: an operation must be done to both sides in order to maintain the equality of the expressions on each side.

ENGLISH LEARNER

For Example 4, explain the meaning of the word cool. Say:

"To cool means to lower or reduce the temperature of something. If a cup of tea is too hot to drink, then wait until it cools down."

Have students list ways to cool a hot cup of soup. Sample: put ice in the soup; let it stand by itself at room temperature

Simplify.

2. (69) $\frac{8 + 2i}{1 + 3i}$ $\frac{7}{5} - \frac{11}{5}i$

3. (69) $i^{22} + i^{15}$ $-1 - i$

4. (53) Let $f(x) = x^2 + 1$ and $g(x) = 7 - x$. What are the domain and range of $(f \circ g)(x)$? D: all real numbers; R: all real numbers greater than or equal to 1

5. (75) Which of the following is equivalent to $y = \left(\sqrt{x^2 + 3x + 2}\right)^{\frac{1}{3}}$? C

A $y = \sqrt[3]{x^2 + 3x + 2}$ **B** $y = \sqrt{\sqrt[3]{x^2 + 3x + 2}}$

C $y = \sqrt[3]{\sqrt{x^2 + 3x + 2}}$ **D** $y = \sqrt[3]{(x + 2)(x + 1)}$

6. (59) **Multi-Step** Use $\frac{13^{\frac{2}{3}} \cdot 13^{\frac{1}{4}}}{13^{\frac{1}{12}} \cdot 13^{\frac{1}{2}}}$.

a. Which property of rational exponents should be applied first to simplify the expression, explain?

6a. Product of Powers Property; By the order of operations you must first perform operations within any grouping symbols.

b. Which property of rational exponents should be applied next? Quotient of Powers Property

c. Simplify the expression. $13^{\frac{1}{3}}$

***7.** (86) **Model** Graph $y = 2\cos(2x) - 3$ See Additional Answers.

Find the sine, cosine, and tangent of the given angle.

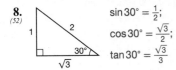

8. (52)

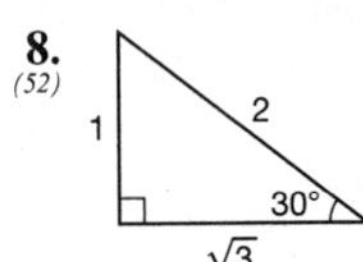

$\sin 30° = \frac{1}{2}$; $\cos 30° = \frac{\sqrt{3}}{2}$; $\tan 30° = \frac{\sqrt{3}}{3}$

9. (52)

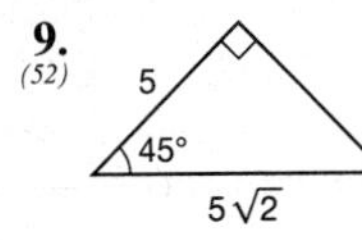

$\sin 45° = \frac{\sqrt{2}}{2}$; $\cos 45° = \frac{\sqrt{2}}{2}$; $\tan 45° = 1$

10. (83) **Multiple Choice** Which equation does *not* have the exact same roots as the others? D

A $(x + 1)(x - 7) = 0$ **B** $2(x + 1)(x - 7) = 0$

C $4(x + 1)3(x - 7) = 0$ **D** $x(x + 1)(x - 7) = 0$

11. (68) **(Radio)** A radio station needs 4 different songs to complete the song set for the end of their show. They can pick from 16 eighties hits, 20 nineties hits, and 18 current top hits. Find the probability that the DJ will select 2 current hits and 2 eighties hits in that order for his show. 0.97%

***12.** (87) **(Earthquakes)** Solve $R = \log\frac{I}{I_o}$ for I and then determine the intensity of an earthquake with a magnitude, R, of 7. Your answer should be in terms of I_o.

12. $I = I_o 10^R$; $I = I_o 10^7 = 10{,}000{,}000 I_o$; The intensity is 10,000,000 times the intensity of a zero-level earthquake.

13. (78) **Probability** The right triangle is inscribed in the circle. Suppose a point is chosen at random inside the circle. What is the probability that the chosen point is inside the triangle? $\frac{1}{\pi} \approx 0.318$

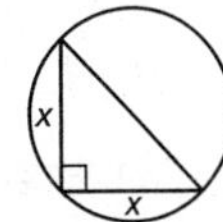

***14.** (87) **Justify** The solution of $100^{2x} = 1000$ is $x = \frac{3}{4}$.

$100^{2x} = 1000$; $\log_{100} 1000 = 2x$; $x = \frac{1}{2}\left(\frac{\log 1000}{\log 100}\right) = \frac{1}{2}\left(\frac{3}{2}\right) = \frac{3}{4}$

3 Practice

Math Conversations

Discussions to strengthen understanding

Problem 12

Error Alert

People often think that an earthquake measuring 7 on the Richter scale is 7 times the intensity of one with magnitude 1. Be sure they understand that it is actually 10^7 times as great.

Problem 14

Extend the Problem

Have students solve the problem in as many different ways as they can, sharing their solutions with the class. They can use common logarithms, natural logarithms, equal bases, or other methods.

CHALLENGE

Have students prepare a proof of the change of base formula and present an explanation of the proof to the class:

Prove: $\log_b x = \frac{\log_a x}{\log_a b}$ or $\log_a b \cdot \log_b x = \log_a x$

Let $\log_a b = u$; then $a^u = b$.
Let $\log_b x = v$; then $b^v = x$.
Let $\log_a x = w$; then $a^w = x$.

By the Transitive Property, $x = x$, so $b^v = a^w$.
By Substitution, $(a^u)^v = a^w$.
Since $a^{uv} = a^w$, $uv = w$.
Substitute back, $\log_a b \cdot \log_b x = \log_a x$ and $\log_b x = \frac{\log_a x}{\log_a b}$.

Problem 15

Warn students to pay attention to their choice of inequality symbols. The key phrase "up to" indicates that the symbol $\leq$ (not $<$) should be used.

Problem 18

"In a normal distribution, 99.7% of the data falls within how many standard deviations of the mean?" 3

Problem 20

Remind students that the equation must be written in the form $ax^2 + bx + c = 0$ before they can find values for *a, b,* and *c* and find the discriminant.

Problem 21

Extend the Problem

"Use the change of base formula and a calculator to evaluate the expression when x is 100." 10.89

Problem 24

Guide students with the following questions:

"What is the surface area of a sphere with radius 20 inches?" 1600π square inches

"What is the surface area of a sphere with radius 15 inches?" 900π square inches

"What is the difference?" 700π square inches

Problem 25

Guide students with the following questions:

"What is the period of the cosine wave?" 2

"How do you use the period to find the value of b?" The period is $2 = \frac{2\pi}{b}$, so b is π.

15. (79) **Postal Rates** The rates for first-class mail (retail letters and cards) are shown in the table. Write a piecewise function that represents the cost of mailing a first-class letter. See Additional Answers.

Fee	Weight
\$0.41	up to 1 ounce
\$0.58	greater than 1 ounce and up to 2 ounces
\$0.75	greater than 2 ounces and up to 3 ounces
\$0.92	greater than 3 ounces and up to 3.5 ounces

16. (81) **Error Analysis** To rewrite $\ln\frac{5e}{x^2}$, a student wrote $\ln\frac{5e}{x^2} = \frac{\ln 5e}{\ln x^2} = \frac{\ln 5 + \ln e}{2\ln x} = \frac{\ln 5 + 1}{2\ln x}$. What is the error? Rewrite $\ln\frac{5e}{x^2}$ as a sum or difference of terms correctly.

16. Sample: The student applied the Quotient Property of Logarithms incorrectly. Correct expression: $\ln 5 - 2\ln x + 1$

***17.** (85) **Generalize** Suppose there are two cubic functions: $f(x) = x^3 - a^3$ and $g(x) = x^3 - b^3$. If $f(x) \cdot g(x)$ crosses the x-axis at only one point, what can you conclude about a and b? They are equal.

***18.** (80) **Graphing Calculator** The weights of bridge tokens are normally distributed with a weight of 4.85 g and a standard deviation of 0.068 g. Find the range of weights for the middle 99.7% of bridge tokens. 4.646 g and 5.054 g

19. (36) Find the equation of the line perpendicular to the graph of $y = 2x - 4$ that crosses $(2, -8)$. $y = -\frac{1}{2}x - 7$

20. (74) **Farming** A farmer has 820 feet of fencing material to enclose a rectangular grazing area for his livestock. He wants the area to be at least 50,000 square feet. The equation $w(410 - w) = 50{,}000$ gives the width of a rectangle that meets these requirements. Use the discriminant to explain if the farmer has enough material to build a fence that meets these requirements. No, discriminant = −31,900, no real solutions

***21.** (87) **Error Analysis** A student rewrote the expression $\log_7(2x)^4$ as $4\log_7 2 + \log_7 x$.

a. Describe the student's error. The student did not distribute the multiplier 4 to both terms.

b. Rewrite the original expression. $4\log_7 2 + 4\log_7 x$

Simplify.

22. (81) $\ln e^{7x}$ $7x$

23. (81) $\ln e^{x+4}$ $x + 4$

24. (70) **Geometry** The formula $r = \sqrt{\frac{S}{4\pi}}$ gives the radius of a sphere with a surface area S. How much greater is the surface area of a sphere with a radius of 20 inches than a radius of 15 inches? Give your answer in terms of π. 700π square inches greater

***25.** (86) **Physics** Every two seconds a radio beacon emits a signal. If the magnitude of the signal is 10, write the periodic function that models the signal using the form $y = a\cos(bx)$. $y = 10\cos(\pi x)$

***26.** (84) **Analyze** What are the steps to solving a rational equation algebraically? See Additional Answers.

Solve for x.

***27.** (87) $1000^{6x} = 10$ $x = \frac{1}{18}$

***28.** $100^{3x} = 10$ $x = \frac{1}{6}$

29. (81) **Write** Explain why $\ln e^{x^2+3} = x^2 + 3$. Sample: Exponential and logarithmic operations are inverse operations.

30. (82) Given $g(x) = 4\sin(3x)$, identify the period. $\frac{2\pi}{3}$

LOOKING FORWARD

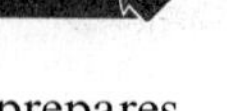

Evaluating logarithmic expressions prepares students for:

- **Lesson 93** Solving Exponential Equations and Inequalities
- **Lesson 102** Solving Logarithmic Equations and Inequalities

LESSON 88 Solving Abstract Equations

Warm Up

1. **Vocabulary** For the fractions $\frac{1}{r}$ and $\frac{3}{2s}$, the ________ is $2rs$. least common denominator
(37)

2. Solve for x. $2x + 3 = x - 17$ -20
(7)

3. Solve for x by factoring. $4x^2 - 35x - 50 = 0$ $-\frac{5}{4}$ and 10
(23)

4. **Multiple Choice** Which of these is a factor of $3x^4 - 6x^3 + 6x^2 + 3x - 30$? **C**
(51)

A $x - 6$
B $x + 6$
C $3x - 6$
D $3x + 6$

5. Simplify the expression $\sqrt[4]{x^8} \cdot \sqrt[3]{x^4}$. $x^3\sqrt[3]{x}$
(40)

New Concepts

An **abstract equation**, also called a literal equation, has two or more variables. Formulas are literal equations. It is often useful to solve a literal equation for one of its variables.

Math Language

The word **literal** is derived from the Latin word *littera*, which means *letter*.

Example 1 Solving an Abstract Linear Equation

A formula that relates Fahrenheit temperature and Celsius temperature is $F = \frac{9}{5}C + 32$. Solve the formula for C.

SOLUTION

$$F = \frac{9}{5}C + 32$$

$$F - 32 = \frac{9}{5}C \qquad \text{Subtract 32 from both sides.}$$

$$\frac{5}{9}(F - 32) = \frac{5}{9} \cdot \frac{9}{5}C \qquad \text{Multiply both sides by } \tfrac{5}{9}\text{, the reciprocal of } \tfrac{9}{5}.$$

$$\frac{5}{9}(F - 32) = C$$

Example 2 Solving Abstract Polynomial Equations

a. The formula for the surface area S of a right circular cylinder is $S = 2\pi r^2 + 2\pi rh$. Solve the formula for h.

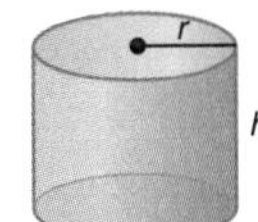

SOLUTION

$$S = 2\pi r^2 + 2\pi rh$$

$$S - 2\pi r^2 = 2\pi rh \qquad \text{Subtract } 2\pi r^2 \text{ from both sides.}$$

$$\frac{S - 2\pi r^2}{2\pi r} = h \qquad \text{Divide both sides by } 2\pi r.$$

MATH BACKGROUND

By this point, students are familiar with solving equations. To solve an equation, means to find the value(s) of the variable(s) that make the equation true.

Solving an abstract equation is different. To solve an abstract equation for a variable x means to perform operations that create an equivalent equation in which x is isolated (alone, with no coefficient) on one side and does not appear at all on the other side.

A formula gives the value of a desired variable (output) when the values of one or more other variables (input) are known. Often, it is useful to be able to manipulate formulas in order to change the output variable.

Show students some formulas and discuss the inputs and outputs. For example, in $A = lw$, length and width are inputs and area is output. We use this form of the formula when we know length and width and need to find area. The form $w = A \div l$ would be useful when area and length are known and width is unknown.

LESSON 88

1 Warm Up

In Problem 2, remind students that to solve for x means to isolate x on one side of the equation.

2 New Concepts

Students use inverse operations and the quadratic formula to isolate a given variable in a formula.

Example 1

Explain that one form of the equation has °C as input and °F as output, while the other has °F as input and °C as output.

Additional Example 1

A formula relating the length and width of a rectangle to its perimeter is $P = 2l + 2w$. Solve the formula for l. $l = \frac{P - 2w}{2}$

Example 2

Point out that the answer for Example **2a** could be written $\frac{S}{2\pi r} - r = h$

Additional Example 2a

a. The formula for the surface area of a square pyramid is $S = s^2 + 2sl$. Solve the formula for l. $l = \frac{S - s^2}{2s}$

LESSON RESOURCES

Student Edition Practice Workbook 88
Reteaching Master 88
Adaptations Master 88
Challenge and Enrichment Master C88

Additional Example 2b

b. The formula for the surface area of a square pyramid is $A = s^2 + 2sl$. Solve the formula for s. $s = \frac{-2l \pm \sqrt{4l^2 + 4A}}{2} = -l \pm \sqrt{l^2 + A}$

Extend the Example

An object is thrown with initial velocity 2.5 meters per second from a height of 20 meters. The acceleration due to gravity is −9.8 m/sec. Have students find how much time has elapsed when the object is 10 meters off the ground. 1.70627 sec

TEACHER TIP

Before solving a literal equation using the quadratic formula, have students take a moment to write and label the values of a, b, and c. Encourage them to work slowly and neatly when using the quadratic formula.

Example 3

Error Alert Students might become confused when trying to keep the variables R, R_1, and R_2 straight. Suggest that they copy the formula onto a separate sheet and replace R_1 and R_2 with A and B, respectively. When they have solved for A, they can return to the original variable names.

Additional Example 3

The formula $\frac{d_1}{r_1} + \frac{d_2}{r_2} = t$ gives the total time for a trip in which the first leg of length d_1 is traveled at rate r_1 and the second leg of length d_2 is traveled at rate r_2. Solve the formula for r_1. $r_1 = \frac{d_1 r_2}{tr_2 - d_2}$

Hint

In the equation, g is the acceleration due to gravity, v_0 is the initial velocity, and h_0 is the initial height.

b. The height h of a free-falling object (neglecting air resistance) is given by the equation $h = \frac{1}{2}gt^2 + v_0t + h_0$. Solve the equation for t.

SOLUTION

Use the quadratic formula $x = \frac{-b \pm \sqrt{b^2 - 4ac}}{2a}$ to solve for t.

$$h = \frac{1}{2}gt^2 + v_0t + h_0$$

$$0 = \frac{1}{2}gt^2 + v_0t + h_0 - h$$ Write the equation in the form $0 = ax^2 + bx + c$.

$$0 = \frac{1}{2}gt^2 + v_0t + h_0 - h$$ Identify coefficients in the quadratic equation.

$$t = \frac{-v_0 \pm \sqrt{v_0^2 - 4\left(\frac{1}{2}g\right)(h_0 - h)}}{2\left(\frac{1}{2}g\right)}$$ Substitute $a = \frac{1}{2}g$, $b = v_0$, and $c = h - h_0$.

$$t = \frac{-v_0 \pm \sqrt{v_0^2 - 2g(h_0 - h)}}{g}$$ Simplify.

$$t = \frac{-v_0 \pm \sqrt{v_0^2 - 2gh_0 + 2gh}}{g}$$ Distribute $-2g$.

Example 3 Solving Abstract Rational Equations

The total resistance R is given by the formula $R = \frac{1}{\frac{1}{R_1} + \frac{1}{R_2}}$. Solve the formula for R_1.

SOLUTION To simplify a complex fraction, multiply the numerator and denominator of the complex fraction by the LCD of the fractions of the numerator and denominator.

$$R = \frac{1}{\frac{1}{R_1} + \frac{1}{R_2}}$$

$$R = \frac{1}{\frac{1}{R_1} + \frac{1}{R_2}} \cdot \frac{R_1R_2}{R_1R_2}$$ Since R_1R_2 is the least common denominator of $\frac{1}{R_1}$ and $\frac{1}{R_2}$, multiply by $\frac{R_1R_2}{R_1R_2}$ to simplify the complex fraction.

$$R = \frac{R_1R_2}{\frac{R_1R_2}{R_1} + \frac{R_1R_2}{R_2}}$$ Distribute.

$$R = \frac{R_1R_2}{R_2 + R_1}$$ Simplify.

$$R(R_2 + R_1) = R_1R_2$$ Multiply both sides by the new LCD, $R_2 + R_1$.

$$RR_2 + RR_1 = R_1R_2$$ Distribute R.

$$RR_2 = R_1R_2 - RR_1$$ Collect all R_1 terms on one side.

$$RR_2 = R_1(R_2 - R)$$ Factor out R_1.

$$\frac{RR_2}{R_2 - R} = R_1$$ Divide both sides by $R_2 - R$.

618 *Saxon Algebra 2*

ALTERNATE METHOD FOR EXAMPLE 2

Students might prefer to add the fractions in the denominator first:

$$R = \frac{1}{\frac{1}{R_1} + \frac{1}{R_2}}$$

$$R = \frac{1}{\frac{R_2 + R_1}{R_1R_2}}$$

$$R = \frac{R_1R_2}{R_2 + R_1}$$

Example 4 Solving an Abstract Radical Equation

A formula for the lateral surface area L of a right circular cone is $L = \pi r\sqrt{r^2 + h^2}$. Solve the formula for h.

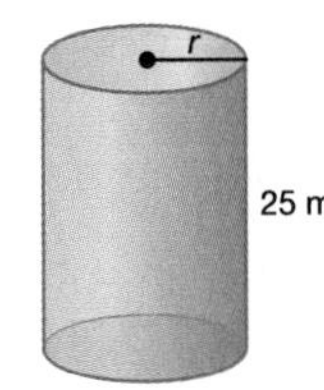

Math Reasoning

Write Squaring both sides of an equation can introduce an extraneous solution if negative numbers are involved. Explain why that does not apply in this case.

The variables, in this case, represent distances, which are always positive numbers.

SOLUTION

$$L = \pi r\sqrt{r^2 + h^2}$$

$$\frac{L}{\pi r} = \sqrt{r^2 + h^2}$$ Divide both sides by πr.

$$\frac{L^2}{\pi^2 r^2} = r^2 + h^2$$ Square both sides.

$$\frac{L^2}{\pi^2 r^2} - r^2 = h^2$$ Subtract r^2 from both sides.

$$\sqrt{\frac{L^2}{\pi^2 r^2} - r^2} = h$$ Take the square root of both sides.

Example 5 Application: An Aquarium

The AquaDom in Berlin, Germany is a cylindrical aquarium with an elevator tube inside. It is the largest acrylic glass cylinder in the world, with a height of 25 meters and a volume of approximately 2400 cubic meters (including the elevator tube). What is the approximate radius of the AquaDom?

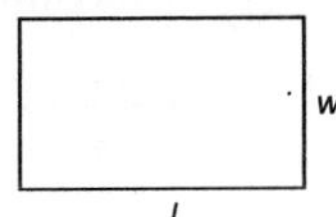

SOLUTION

Solve the formula for the volume of a cylinder for r.

$$V = \pi r^2 h$$ Write the formula for the volume of a cylinder.

$$\frac{V}{\pi h} = r^2$$ Divide both sides by πh.

$$\sqrt{\frac{V}{\pi h}} = r$$ Take the square root of both sides.

$$\sqrt{\frac{2400}{\pi \cdot 25}} = r$$ Substitute the known values for V and h.

$$r \approx 5.5$$ Use a calculator to find the approximate value of r.

The approximate radius of the AquaDom is 5.5 meters.

Hint

An approximation for the irrational number π is 3.14, but the π key on a calculator gives a better approximation.

Check Substitute 5.5 for r and 25 for h in the volume formula.

$V = \pi r^2 h \approx 3.14(5.5)^2(25) \approx 2375$, which is close to 2400. So the answer is reasonable.

Lesson Practice

a. (Ex 1) The formula for the perimeter of a rectangle is $P = 2l + 2w$. Solve the formula for w. $w = \frac{P - 2l}{2}$

w
l

Example 4

Remind students to completely isolate the radical expression before raising both sides to a power.

Additional Example 4

Heron's formula for the area of a triangle with semi-perimeter s is $A = \sqrt{s(s-a)(s-b)(s-c)}$. Solve the formula for b.

$b = s - \frac{A^2}{s(s-a)(s-c)}$

Example 5

Students might want to substitute the values of V and h into the volume formula before solving for r. This is a valid technique, but make sure they can solve the literal equation for r as well.

Additional Example 5

The Eartha model in Yarmouth, Maine is the largest rotating and revolving globe in the world, with a volume of approximately 37,423 cubic feet. What is the approximate radius of Eartha?

20.75 feet

INCLUSION

Students might have trouble making the connection between solving equations in one variable and solving abstract equations. Show an equation like $6(2x - 3) = 7^2 - 7$ and ask students to solve it. Most likely, they will first simplify, then isolate the variable. Next, show them how they could solve the equation for x without doing any simplification beforehand. Relate this method to solving an abstract equation.

Method 1:	Method 2:
$6(2x - 3) = 7^2 - 7$	$6(2x - 3) = 7^2 - 7$
$12x - 18 = 7^2 - 7$	$2x - 3 = \frac{7^2 - 7}{6}$
$12x - 18 = 49 - 7$	$2x = \frac{7^2 - 7}{6} + 3$
$12x - 18 = 42$	$x = \frac{\frac{7^2 - 7}{6} + 3}{2}$
$12x = 60$	
$x = 5$	$x = 5$

Lesson Practice

Problem c

Scaffolding First, have students write the equation in the form $0 = ar^2 + br + c$. Then, ask them to identify the values of a, b, and c. Finally, have them solve using the quadratic formula.

Check for Understanding

The questions below help assess the concepts taught in this lesson.

1. **"Explain how to solve a literal equation for a given variable."** Treat all other variables like constants. Perform inverse operations to isolate the variable on one side so that it does not appear at all on the other side.

2. **"When is the quadratic formula used to solve a literal equation?"** When the equation can be written in the form $0 = ax^2 + bx + c$, where x is the variable you're solving for.

3 Practice

Math Conversations

Discussions to strengthen understanding

Problem 3

"According to the Rational Root Theorem, what are the possible rational roots?" $\pm1, \pm2, \pm3, \pm5, \pm6, \pm10, \pm15, \pm30$

"Start testing roots. What is one root that yields a factor?" -1

"How can you use –1 to find the other rational roots?" Use synthetic division to divide by -1, then see if the resulting quadratic expression can be factored.

b. (Ex 2) The formula for the area of a circular ring is $A = \pi R^2 - \pi r^2$. Solve the formula for R. $R = \sqrt{\frac{A + \pi r^2}{\pi}}$

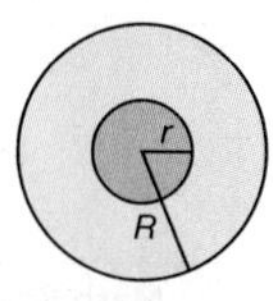

c. (Ex 2) A formula for the total surface area S of a right circular cone is $S = \pi r^2 + \pi rl$. Solve the formula for r. (Hint: All quantities are positive.) $r = \frac{-\pi l + \sqrt{\pi^2 l^2 + 4\pi S}}{2\pi}$

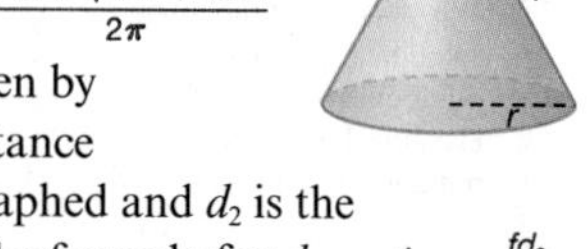

d. (Ex 3) The focal length f for a camera lens is given by the formula $f = \frac{d_1 d_2}{d_1 - d_2}$, where d_1 is the distance from the lens to the object being photographed and d_2 is the distance from the lens to the film. Solve the formula for d_1. $d_1 = \frac{fd_2}{f - d_2}$

e. (Ex 4) The length d of a diagonal of a rectangular prism is $d = \sqrt{l^2 + w^2 + h^2}$. Solve the equation for h. $h = \sqrt{d^2 - l^2 - w^2}$

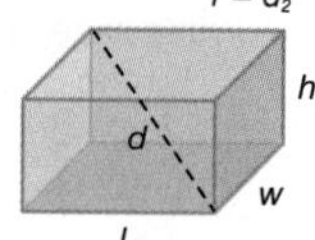

f. (Ex 5) Earth is nearly spherical with an approximate surface area of 197,000,000 square miles. The surface area S of a sphere is $S = 4\pi r^2$. Solve the formula for r and then use your result to find the approximate radius of Earth. $r = \sqrt{\frac{S}{4\pi}}$; 3960 miles

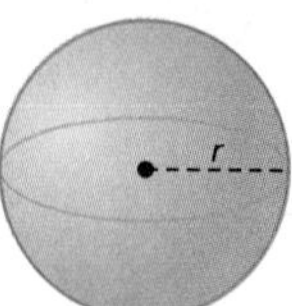

Practice Distributed and Integrated

Write the exponential equation in logarithmic form.

1. (63) $5^3 = 125$ $\log_5 125 = 3$

2. (63) $20^3 = 8000$ $\log_{20} 8000 = 3$

Identify all the real roots.

3. (85) $x^3 + 8x^2 - 23x - 30 = 0$ $x = -10, -1, 3$

4. (85) $6x^3 + 12x^2 - 18x = 0$ $x = -3, 0, 1$

Write the expression as a complex number in standard form.

5. (62) $(1 - 9i)(1 - 4i)(4 - 3i)$ $-179 + 53i$

6. (62) $(3 + 2i) + (5 - i) + 6i$ $8 + 7i$

7. (81) **Analyze** What pair of inverse functions contain the ordered pairs $(3, e^3)$ and $(e^3, 3)$? $y = e^x$ and $y = \ln x$

8. (72) **Chemistry** Hydrochloric acid is classified as a strong acid, with a pH of 1. The pH of a solution is given by the formula $\text{pH} = -\log [H^+]$, where $[H^+]$ represents the concentration of hydrogen ions in moles per liter. What is the hydrogen ion concentration in hydrochloric acid? 0.1 mole per liter

***9.** (87) **Multiple Choice** The expression $\log_2(8x)^2$ when $x = 16$ is equivalent to: C

A 7 B 12 C 14 D 16

ENGLISH LEARNERS

Explain the meaning of the word **formula.** Say:

"A formula is an equation. It shows how one quantity depends on one or more other quantities."

Connect the definition to the formula $d = \sqrt{l^2 + w^2 + h^2}$. Show how the value of d depends on the values of l, w, and h.

Discuss everyday uses of the word formula. For example, infant formula is manufactured using precise amounts of many ingredients. The final product depends on the amounts used and the way in which they are combined.

Have students identify a formula in the lesson and explain in their own words the relationship between the quantities.

10. **Probability** A researcher visits a pond and captures and tags 75 fish. On a return visit, the researcher captures 130 fish, and 68 of them are found to be tagged. What is the probability that a randomly chosen fish in the pond was marked on the first day? About 52.3%
(73)

***11.** **Write** Explain why $A = \frac{1}{2}h(b_1 + b_2)$ and $h = \frac{2A}{b_1 + b_2}$ describe the same relationship among the variables A, h, b_1, and b_2. Sample: If you solve $A = \frac{1}{2}h(b_1 + b_2)$ for h, the result is $h = \frac{2A}{b_1 + b_2}$.
(88)

12. **Write** How can finding the discriminant of a quadratic equation help you decide which method you will use to solve the equation? See Additional Answers.
(74)

Solve each formula for the indicated variable.

***13.** Given $S = 2\pi r^2 + 2\pi rh$, solve for r. $r = \frac{-\pi h \pm \sqrt{\pi(\pi h^2 + 2s)}}{2\pi}$
(88)

***14.** Given $\frac{5}{9}(F - 32) = C$, solve for F. $F = \frac{9}{5}C + 32$
(88)

15. **Physics** According to Einstein's theory of relativity, as an object moves faster, it appears shorter in length to a stationary observer. The equation below shows the relationship between the original length of the object and the new length, where v is the speed of the object and c is the speed of light. Suppose the ratio of the original length to the new length is 2:1. How fast is the object going as a factor of c? $\frac{c}{2}\sqrt{3}$
(75)

$$\text{New length} = (\text{Original length})\sqrt{1 - \frac{v^2}{c^2}}$$

16. **Multiple Choice** Solve $\frac{2}{3x + 15} + \frac{1}{3} + \frac{x}{x + 5} = \frac{4}{9}$. A
(84)

A -0.125 B 1 C -6.625 D no solution

17. **Geometry** An isosceles triangle with base angles of 45° and base measuring $x + 1$ has the same area as a square with sides x. What integer value of x is a solution to this problem? $x = 1$
(76)

***18.** **Multi-Step** a. Use the change of base formula to convert $\log_2(6x)^2$ to base e. $2\frac{\ln 6x}{\ln 2}$
(87)

b. Evaluate when $x = 1$. 5.17

19. **Error Analysis** Explain and correct the error a student made in using Heron's formula to find the area of a triangle with side lengths of 3, 10, and 11.
(77)

$$A = \sqrt{24(21)(14)(13)} \approx 302.9 \text{ sq. units}$$

19. The student used the wrong value for s. s is half the perimeter, or 12. The area is about 14.7 square units.

Identify the period and amplitude.

***20.** $y = \frac{1}{2}\cos(2x)$ $a = \frac{1}{2}, p = \pi$
(82)

***21.** $y = \frac{2}{3}\cos 4x$ $a = \frac{2}{3}, p = \frac{\pi}{2}$
(82)

22. **Estimate** Without using a calculator, estimate the root(s) of the equation $x^2 - 62 = 0$ to the nearest integer(s). Explain your answer by discussing x-intercepts. See Additional Answers.
(78)

***23.** Use the change of base formula to solve $\log_6 \frac{24}{5}$. $\log_6 \frac{24}{5} \approx 0.875$
(87)

24. **Delivery Charges** An appliance store delivers up to 4 items for a \$50 delivery charge. There is an additional charge of \$15 per item for each additional item delivered. Write a piecewise function for the cost having x items delivered. $f(x) = \begin{cases} 50, \text{ if } 0 < x \le 4 \\ 50 + 15(x - 4), \text{ if } x > 4 \end{cases}$
(79)

CHALLENGE

A formula that gives the height h above sea level in terms of air temperature (t), atmospheric pressure (p) and atmospheric pressure at sea level (c) is $h = (30t + 8000)\ln\left(\frac{c}{p}\right)$. Solve the formula for p. $p = \frac{c}{e^{\left(\frac{h}{30t+8000}\right)}}$

Problem 12

Before students begin writing, ask them, **"The discriminant can be positive, negative, or zero. What does each case tell you about the solution(s)?"** When the discriminant is negative, there are complex roots. When it is zero, there is one rational root. When it is positive, there are two roots. A perfect square under the radical gives two rational roots; any other positive number under the radical gives two irrational roots.

Problem 17

Guide students by asking the following questions:

"What kind of triangle does the problem describe?" 45°-45°-90°

"What is the length of the hypotenuse of the 45°-45°-90° isosceles triangle." $x + 1$

"What is the length of each leg?" $\frac{x+1}{\sqrt{2}}$

"What is the triangle's area?" $\frac{1}{2} \cdot \frac{x+1}{\sqrt{2}} \cdot \frac{x+1}{\sqrt{2}}$ or $\frac{x^2 + 2x + 1}{4}$

"What equation can be used to solve the problem?" $\frac{x^2 + 2x + 1}{4} = x^2$

Problem 23

Error Alert

Some calculators will return the wrong answer if students fail to close parentheses when entering a logarithm. For example, to enter the expression ln24 – ln5, they must enter ln(24) – ln(5).

Problem 24

Extend the Problem

"What is the domain of the piecewise function?" natural numbers

"What is the range?" $y = 50 + 15x$, where x is a whole number.

Problem 26

Before solving, ask students, **"How many standard deviations from the mean are scores of 70 and 130?"** 70 is 2 standard deviations below; 130 is 2 standard deviations above.

"In a normal distribution, what percent of the data lie within 2 standard deviations of the mean?" 95%

Problem 28

Remind students that if a is a root of the quadratic equation $f(x) = 0$, then $(x - a)$ is a factor of $f(x)$.

Problem 30

Tell students that $\overline{x}$ is read "x-bar" and represents the mean. The Greek letter σ is read "sigma" and represents the standard deviation.

***25.** (86) Describe the phase shift of the function $y = 2\sin\left(x - \frac{\pi}{2}\right) + 7$

25. shifted right $\frac{\pi}{2}$ radians

26. (80) **Multi-Step** IQ test scores are often adjusted to have a mean of 100 and a standard deviation of 15.

a. What percent of people have an IQ between 70 and 130? 95%

b. Suppose a person scores 150 on an IQ test. How many standard deviations is their score above the mean? About 3.3

27. (82) **Radio** A radio signal generates the following data. Use the data to model the periodic function. $y = \sin(5x)$

x	0	$\frac{\pi}{4}$	$\frac{2\pi}{5}$	$\frac{\pi}{2}$
y	0	-0.707	0	1

***28.** (83) **Graphing Calculator** Write a quadratic equation with roots of -2.58 and 1.002. Check your work by graphing the related function and finding the zeros. Sample: $x^2 + 1.578x - 2.58516 = 0$

29. (70) **Error Analysis** Describe and correct the error in solving the equation.

$$(x + 7)^{\frac{1}{2}} = 5$$
$$[(x + 7)^{\frac{1}{2}}]^2 = 5$$
$$x + 7 = 5$$
$$x = -2$$

Both sides must be raised to the power 2. $\left[(x + 7)^{\frac{1}{2}}\right]^2 = 5^2$; $x + 7 = 25$; $x = 18$

***30.** (88) **Statistics** In a normal distribution a z-score is the number of standard deviations a particular data value lies above or below the mean. In a normal distribution with mean $\overline{x}$ and standard deviation σ, the z-score of a data value x is given by $z = \frac{x - \overline{x}}{\sigma}$.

a. Solve the formula for x. $x = z\sigma + \overline{x}$

b. A data value in a certain normal distribution is 2 standard deviations below the mean of 76. The standard deviation is 5.5. What is the data value? 65

LOOKING FORWARD

Solving abstract equations prepares students for:

- **Lesson 91** Making Graphs and Solving Equations of Circles
- **Lesson 93** Solving Exponential Equations and Inequalities
- **Lesson 98** Making Graphs and Using Equations of Ellipses

LESSON 89 Solving Quadratic Inequalities

Warm Up

1. **Vocabulary** The ________ of the graph of an inequality is dashed for > and < and solid for ≥ and ≤. (39) boundary line

2. Is (0, 5) a solution of $y < 2x + 5$? (39) no

3. Solve $24x^2 - 14x = 3$. (65) $-\frac{1}{6}$ and $\frac{3}{4}$

New Concepts

A **quadratic inequality in two variables** is an inequality that can be written in the standard form of $y < ax^2 + bx + c$, where $a \neq 0$, and < can be replaced with >, ≤, or ≥.

Graphing Quadratic Inequalities

The graph of a quadratic inequality divides the plane into a region that contains the solutions and a region that does not contain the solutions. In a quadratic inequality, the boundary is a parabola. The curve is dashed if it does not contain solutions (< or >) and solid if it does contain solutions (≤ or ≥).

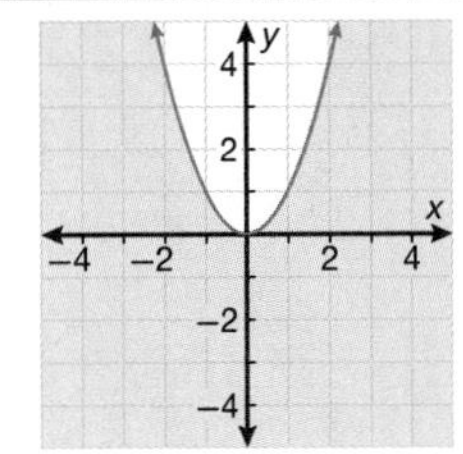

Example 1 Graphing Quadratic Inequalities

Graph $y > -2x^2 + 12x - 16$.

SOLUTION Graph $y = -2x^2 + 12x - 16$ with a dashed line and then shade above the parabola.

Step 1: Find the x-coordinate of the vertex point: $\frac{-b}{2a} = \frac{-12}{2(-2)} = 3$.
Find the y-coordinate of the vertex point: $y = -2(3)^2 + 12(3) - 16 = 2$.
Plot the vertex (3, 2).

Step 2: Plot the y-intercept $(0, c)$: $(0, -16)$.

Step 3: Find the x-intercepts:

$0 = -2x^2 + 12x - 16$

$0 = -2(x^2 - 6x + 8)$

$0 = -2(x - 2)(x - 4)$

The x-intercepts are 2 and 4.

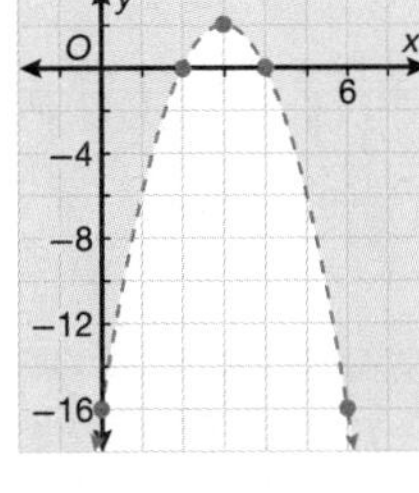

Step 4: Shade above the parabola because in standard form, the symbol is >.

Check the test point (0, 0): $y \overset{?}{>} -2x^2 + 12x - 16$

$0 > -16$ **True**

Math Reasoning

Justify How do you know (6, −16) is a point on the parabola?

By using (0, −16) and the fact that $x = 3$ is the line of symmetry.

Online Connection
www.SaxonMathResources.com

LESSON 89

1 Warm Up

Problem 3

Students should begin by writing the equation in standard form.

2 New Concepts

In this lesson, students learn to solve quadratic inequalities and systems of quadratic inequalities graphically and algebraically.

Example 1

Graphing a quadratic inequality is similar to graphing a linear inequality. Now, the boundary is a curve rather than a line.

Additional Example 1

Graph $y \leq 4x^2 - 2x - 6$.

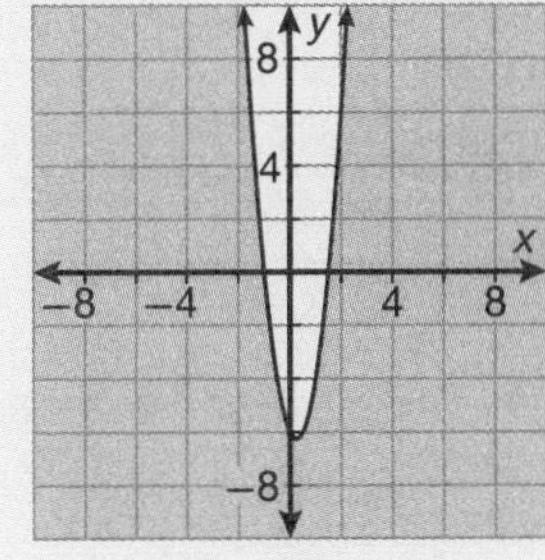

MATH BACKGROUND

Inequalities are used to demonstrate circumstances where more than one solution to a problem exists. The boundaries and regions formed by systems of inequalities help us find ranges for which we will have a desired result.

One example for the use of inequalities can be found by examining makers of candy. Many times, the melting point of the various ingredients will determine the range of temperatures for which the desired consistency will be achieved.

Another example for the use of inequalities can be found in business. By using certain parameters, business owners can have a visual representation of the circumstances where they will have profits or losses. The parameters can be the cost of production of x number of items versus the profit after the sale of y items.

LESSON RESOURCES

Student Edition Practice Workbook 89
Reteaching Master 89
Adaptations Master 89
Challenge and Enrichment Master C89

Example 2

This example uses a graphing calculator to solve quadratic inequalities in one variable. This example introduces students to the concept of critical points.

Error Alert Watch for students who choose the wrong region as the solution. Stress that the inequality symbol tells them to look at where the curve is either above or below the line.

Additional Example 2

Solve each inequality with a graphing calculator.

a. $x^2 + 8x + 16 < 4$
$-6 < x < -2$

b. $x^2 - 7x + 14 \geq 4$
$x \leq 2$ or $x \geq 5$

A **quadratic inequality in one variable,** $ax^2 + bx + c < d$, where $a \neq 0$, is an inequality that can be formed by replacing y with d and $<$ with $\leq$, $>$, or $\geq$. It can be solved either graphically or algebraically.

Example 2 Solving Quadratic Inequalities with a Graphing Calculator

Solve each inequality with a graphing calculator.

a. $x^2 - 3x - 7 \leq 3$

SOLUTION Graph $Y1 = x^2 - 3x - 7$ and $Y2 = 3$. The solutions are those x-values for which the parabola is at or below the line $y = 3$. To find these x-values, find the points of intersection.

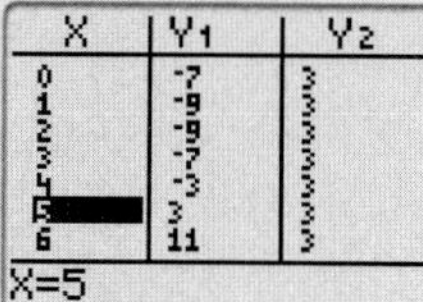

The graph of $Y1 = x^2 - 3x - 7$ equals 3 when $x = -2$ and $x = 5$. The graph is below $y = 3$ for all the x-values between -2 and 5. The solution set can be written as $-2 \leq x \leq 5$.

Use the Table function as a check. Look for where $Y1 \leq Y2$.

X	Y1	Y2
-3	11	3
-2	3	3
-1	-3	3
0	-7	3
1	-9	3
2	-9	3
3	-7	3

X=-2

X	Y1	Y2
0	-7	3
1	-9	3
2	-9	3
3	-7	3
4	-3	3
5	3	3
6	11	3

X=5

b. $x^2 + 10x + 22 > 6$

SOLUTION Graph $Y1 = x^2 + 10x + 22$ and $Y2 = 6$. The solutions are those x-values for which the parabola is above the line. Find the points of intersection.

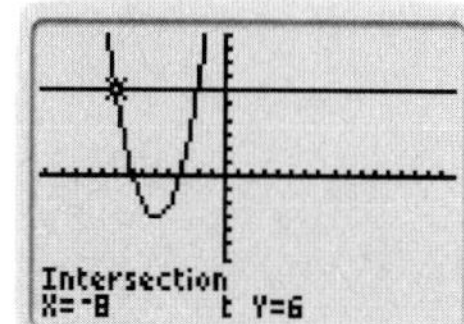

The graph of $Y1 = x^2 + 10x + 22$ equals 6 when $x = -8$ and $x = -2$. The graph is above $y = 6$ for all the x-values less than -8 or greater than -2. The solution set can be written as $x < -8$ or $x > -2$.

Use the Table function as a check. Look for where $Y1 > Y2$.

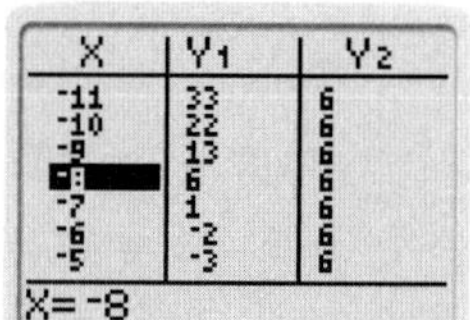

X	Y1	Y2
-11	33	6
-10	22	6
-9	13	6
-8	6	6
-7	1	6
-6	-2	6
-5	-3	6

X=-8

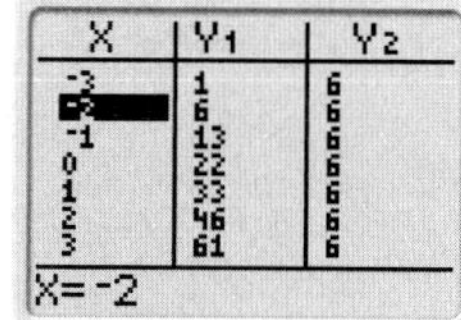

X	Y1	Y2
-3	1	6
-2	6	6
-1	13	6
0	22	6
1	33	6
2	46	6
3	61	6

X=-2

The solutions in Example 2 can be graphed on a number line. Notice that in both cases, there are two values called *critical points* or *critical values*, which separate the number line into three regions which either contain or do not contain solutions.

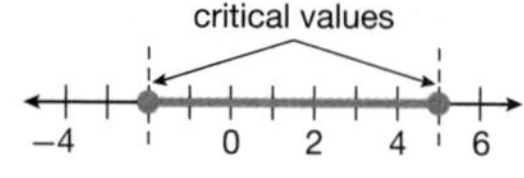

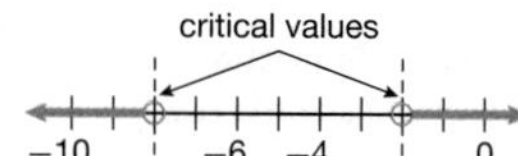

Math Reasoning

Analyze Give an example of a quadratic inequality with one critical point.

Possible answer: $x^2 > 0$.

ENGLISH LEARNERS

The word **critical** has many different meanings. Ask students to use the word critical in a sentence to help them understand the different uses of the word. Some possible examples include:

The patient was in critical condition.

It is critical that the package gets shipped today.

John was critical of the movie.

The meaning of the word critical in the context of critical points or critical values in mathematics is where or when some quality, property, or phenomenon suffers a definite change.

Example 3 Solving Quadratic Inequalities Algebraically

a. Solve $x^2 + x > 20$ algebraically.

SOLUTION Write the related equation in standard form and solve for x to find the critical values.

$$x^2 + x = 20$$
$$x^2 + x - 20 = 0$$
$$(x - 4)(x + 5) = 0$$

The critical values are 4 and −5. They separate the number line into the three regions, $x < -5$, $-5 < x < 4$, and $x > 4$. Test a point in each region to see if that region does or does not contain solutions.

Interval	Test Value	Is the test value a solution?
$x < -5$	−6	$(-6)^2 + -6 \overset{?}{>} 20$ $30 > 20$ Yes
$-5 < x < 4$	0	$(0)^2 + 0 \overset{?}{>} 20$ $0 > 20$ No
$x > 4$	5	$(5)^2 + 5 \overset{?}{>} 20$ $30 > 20$ Yes

The two "outer regions" are solutions.

The solution is $x < -5$ or $x > 4$.

Hint

Remember that *and* statements are intersections and *or* statements are unions.

b. Solve $x^2 - 3x - 18 \le 0$ algebraically.

SOLUTION Write the related equation and solve for x to find the critical values.

$$x^2 - 3x - 18 = 0$$
$$(x + 3)(x - 6) = 0$$

The critical values are −3 and 6. They separate the number line into the three regions, $x \le -3$, $-3 \le x \le 6$, and $x \ge 6$. Test a point in each region to see if that region does or does not contain solutions.

Interval	Test Value	Is the test value a solution?
$x \le -3$	−4	$(-4)^2 - 3(-4) - 18 \overset{?}{\le} 0$ $10 \le 0$ No
$-3 \le x \le 6$	0	$(0)^2 - 3(0) - 18 \overset{?}{\le} 0$ $-18 \le 0$ Yes
$x \ge 6$	7	$(7)^2 - 3(7) - 18 \overset{?}{\le} 0$ $10 \le 0$ No

The "inner region" contains the solutions.

The solution is $-3 \le x \le 6$.

Example 3

Remind students to set the equation equal to zero before finding the critical values.

Error Alert Watch for students who include the critical values in the solution to a strict inequality.

Additional Example 3

a. Solve $x^2 + 4x < 21$ algebraically. $-7 < x < 3$

b. Solve $x^2 + 8x + 15 \ge 0$ algebraically. $x \le -5$ or $x \ge -3$

ALTERNATE METHOD FOR EXAMPLE 3

Have students use a graphing calculator to solve and check the answers to Examples 3*a* and 3*b*.

Example 4

Point out that any point can be tested algebraically to determine if it is a solution. Have students test points in each of the different regions.

Additional Example 4

Solve $\begin{matrix} y < x^2 + 4x + 3 \\ y > x - 2 \end{matrix}$ by graphing. Name one point that is a solution and one point that is not.

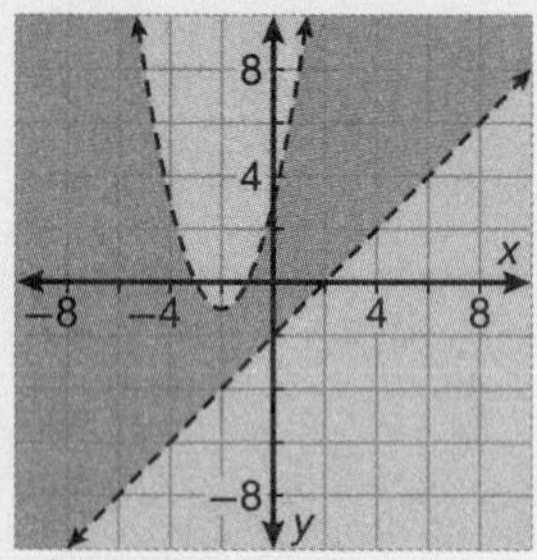

(0, 0) is a solution and (8, 1) is not.

Example 5

Remind students that the model is not linear. There are two critical points for the quadratic model.

Additional Example 5

The cost of manufacturing a product is modeled by $y = -10x^2 + 600x - 1300$, where x is the number of items produced. To make a profit, the cost of manufacturing the product must be less than \$5000. How many items can the company produce and still make a profit? $x \leq 13$ or $x \geq 47$

As with a system of linear inequalities, the solution of a system that includes quadratic inequalities is contained in the overlapping region.

Math Reasoning

Verify Show algebraically that (1, 2) is a solution.

$2 \geq 1^2 + 2(1) - 1$
$2 \geq 2$
$2 < 2(1) + 3$
$2 < 5$

Example 4 Solving Systems that Include Quadratic Inequalities

Solve $\begin{matrix} y \geq x^2 + 2x - 1 \\ y < 2x + 3 \end{matrix}$ by graphing. Name one point that is a solution and one that is not.

SOLUTION Graph each inequality on the same coordinate plane.

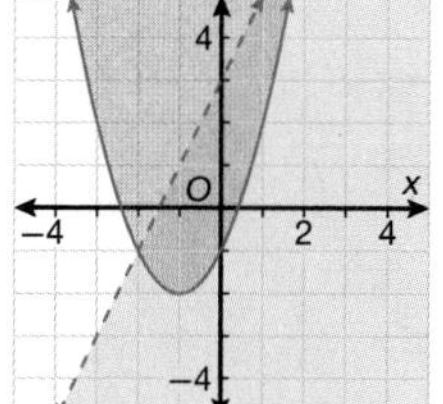

The solutions are contained in the overlapping region.

(0, 0) is a solution.

(−3, 1) is not a solution.

Example 5 Application: Business

The profit per trip, in dollars, for an adventure company offering tours is modeled by $y = -14x^2 + 650x - 2200$, where x is the number of people on the tour. Trips are cancelled if a minimum of \$1000 cannot be made in profit. How many people must be on a trip for the company to earn \$1000 or more?

SOLUTION

1. **Understand** The answer is the solution of $-14x^2 + 650x - 2200 \geq 1000$.

2. **Plan** Graph $Y1 = -14x^2 + 650x - 2200$ and $Y2 = 1000$. Find the x-values for which the first graph has greater y-values than the second.

3. **Solve** Round the x-values to whole numbers because they represent numbers of people. Think: If about 5.6 is the solution, there must be greater than 5 people. If 40.8 is a solution, there must be less than 41 people.

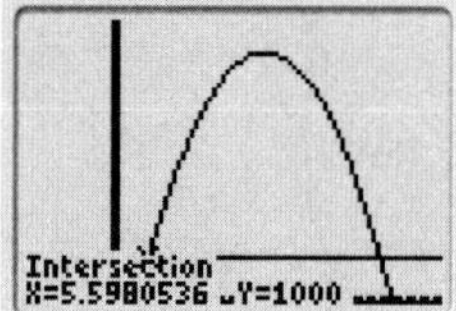

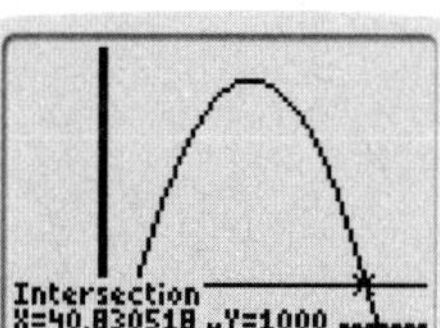

There must be between 6 and 40 people inclusivey.

4. **Check** Use the Table function to see the actual amounts of profit earned for each number of people.

X	Y1	Y2
2	−956	1000
3	−376	1000
4	176	1000
5	700	1000
6	1196	1000
7	1664	1000
8	2104	1000

X=6

X	Y1	Y2
35	3400	1000
36	3056	1000
37	2684	1000
38	2284	1000
39	1856	1000
40	1400	1000
41	916	1000

X=40

CHALLENGE

Solve $\begin{matrix} y > x^2 + 4x + 3 \\ y \leq -x^2 + 9 \end{matrix}$ by graphing.

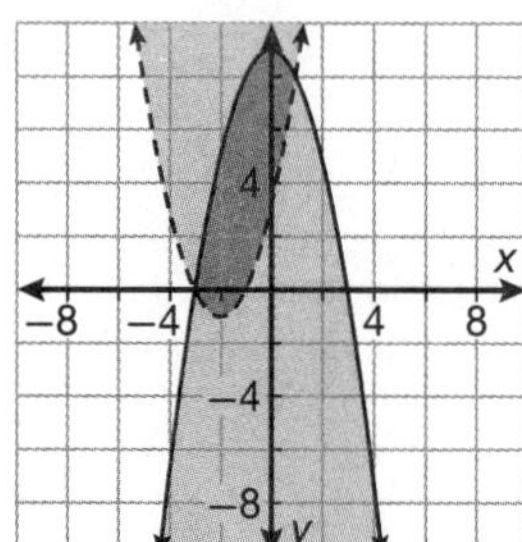

Lesson Practice

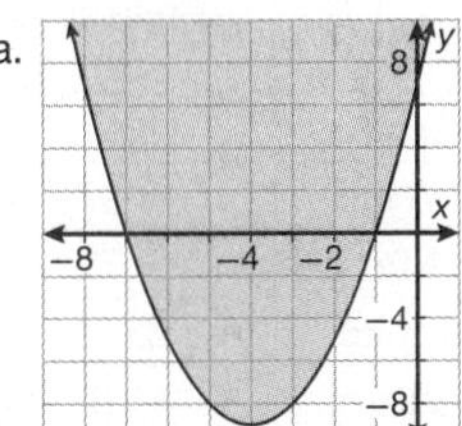
a.

a. Graph $y \geq x^2 + 8x + 7$.
(Ex 1)

Solve each inequality with a graphing calculator.

b. $-x^2 + 2x + 11 < -4$ $x < -3$ or $x > 5$
(Ex 2)

c. $14 \geq x^2 - 8x + 26$ $2 \leq x \leq 6$
(Ex 2)

d. Solve $x^2 + 8x < 9$ algebraically. $-9 < x < 1$
(Ex 3)

e. Solve $2x^2 - 9x - 1 \geq 4$ algebraically. $x \leq -\frac{1}{2}$ or $x \geq 5$
(Ex 3)

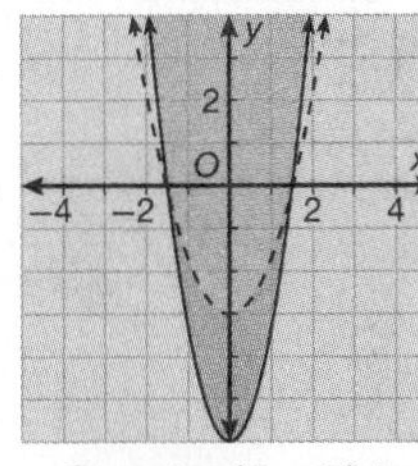
f.

Sample: (0, −5) is a solution, (3, 0) is not.

f. Solve $\begin{matrix} y < x^2 - 3 \\ y \geq 2x^2 - 6 \end{matrix}$ by graphing. Name one point that is a solution and one that is not.
(Ex 4)

g. The profit per trip, in dollars, for an adventure company offering tours is modeled by $y = -16x^2 + 720x - 1950$, where x is the number of people on the tour. How many people must be on a trip for the company to earn at least \$3000 in profit? Between 9 and 36 people inclusive
(Ex 4)

Practice Distributed and Integrated

1. Evaluate the inverse trigonometric function $\text{Tan}^{-1}(\sqrt{3})$. Give your answer in both radians and degrees. $\frac{\pi}{3}$; 60°
(67)

Solve algebraically.

*2. $3x^2 - 13x > 10$ $x < -\frac{2}{3}$ or $x > 5$
(89)

*3. $5x^2 - 6x - 2 < 0$ $-0.3 < x < 1.5$
(89)

4. Find the arc length and area of a sector with the given radius r and central angle θ. $r = 12$ ft, $\theta = 150°$ s = about 31.4 ft, area = about 188 ft^2
(63)

5. A prize box contains 5 stickers, 13 erasers, 20 pencils and 2 highlighters. Find the probability that a student randomly chooses a sticker and a pencil when choosing 2 prizes. 12.82%
(68)

6. **Error Analysis** Explain and correct the error a student made in writing a quadratic equation with a root of 9. $\begin{matrix} x = 9 \\ x - 9 = 0 \end{matrix}$ There are two identical roots of 9. $(x - 9)(x - 9) = 0$; $x^2 - 18x + 81 = 0$
(83)

7. **Write** Explain how to write a piecewise function rule from a graph. Determine the domain for each piece and then use the graph to write the function for each domain.
(79)

8. **Multiple Choice** A quadratic equation has 1 real solution. Which could be the discriminant of the equation? C
(74)

A −6 B −4 C 0 D 4

*9. **Formulate** Consider the function $f(x) = \cos(x - \theta)$. For what value of θ is the graph of $f(x)$ the same as the graph of $y = \sin(x)$? $\theta = \frac{\pi}{2}$
(86)

10. Graph the cube root function and its inverse. $y = -2\sqrt[3]{x + 5} + 5$
(75)

10.

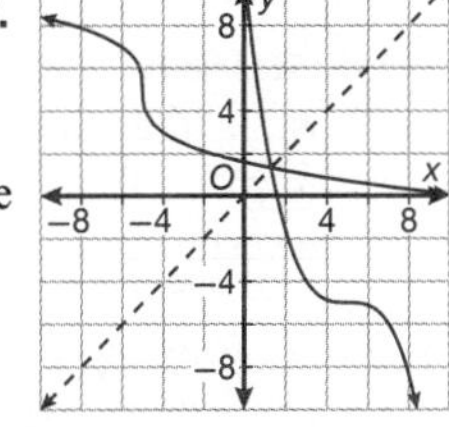

*11. **Justify** Explain why the solution of $x^2 - 4x + 7 > -5$ is the set of all real numbers. Sample: The graph of $y = x^2 - 4x + 7$ is always above the graph of $y = -5$.
(89)

INCLUSION

Provide pre-printed number lines for students to use to solve quadratic inequalities. Have students factor the related equation to find the critical values. Next have them plot the critical values on a pre-printed number line using either a closed or open circle as appropriate. As a check, encourage students to substitute each critical point into the original inequality to see if the point is a solution of the inequality.

Have students then choose one point from each region created on the number line by the critical points and substitute each point into the original inequality. If the inequality is true for a selected point, tell students to shade the entire region from which that point was chosen. Remind them that any point in that region will satisfy the inequality.

Lesson Practice

Problem b

Scaffolding Have students first divide through by −1. Remind them to change the inequality to >.

Problem f

Error Alert Students might name a point such as (0, 0) as a solution. Show algebraically that it only satisfies one, not both, inequalities.

Check for Understanding

The questions below help assess the concepts taught in this lesson.

"Explain how to graph a quadratic inequality in two variables." Sample: Graph the parabola. Shade the region defined by the inequality and test a point in the shaded region to check.

"Explain how to solve a system of inequalities that includes a quadratic inequality." Sample: Graph each inequality on the same coordinate plane. The solutions are contained in the overlapping region.

3 Practice

Math Conversations

Discussions to strengthen understanding

Problem 1

"What does it mean to find the inverse trigonometric function $\text{Tan}^{-1}(\sqrt{3})$?" You are finding the angle whose tangent is $\sqrt{3}$.

Problem 15

Error Alert

Watch for students who simply add and subtract 3 from the mean and choose answer C.

Problem 16

Extend the Problem

"Classify the triangle according to the lengths of its sides and the measures of its angles." obtuse scalene

Problem 18

Extend the Problem

If Worker A can paint a room in x hours and Worker B can paint a room in x hours, how long will it take the workers to paint the room together? $0.5x$ hours

12. (76) **Physics** Acceleration due to gravity is different on different planets. The equation below can be used to find the distance from the ground at time t for a ball thrown from a height h_o at an initial speed of v_o. Use the table to determine how long it will take a ball thrown with an initial speed of 35 at a height of 100 to hit the ground on Mercury. 22.03 seconds

$$h = -\frac{1}{2}at^2 + v_o t + h_o$$

Planet	Acceleration (a)
Mercury	3.59
Venus	8.87
Mars	3.77
Jupiter	25.95
Saturn	11.08
Uranus	10.67
Neptune	14.07

*13. (88) **Analyze** Solve the equation $A = \pi r^2$ for r. Determine whether the solutions represent possible values for the radius of a circle. Explain.

13. Solutions: $r = \sqrt{\frac{A}{\pi}}$ and $-\sqrt{\frac{A}{\pi}}$; If A is the area of a circle, then only the solution $r = \sqrt{\frac{A}{\pi}}$ represents a possible value for the radius because it is positive; the other solution is negative.

14. (77) **Geometry** Three sides of a triangle measure 46 inches, 22 inches, and 50 inches. Classify the triangle by its side and angle measures. acute scalene

15. (80) **Multiple Choice** The weights of a group of children are normally distributed with a mean of 68 pounds and a standard deviation of 3 pounds. What is the range of the middle 95% of the weights? **B**
A 59 lbs to 77 lbs **B** 62 lbs to 74 lbs **C** 65 lbs to 71 lbs **D** 68 lbs to 77 lbs

16. (71) Solve $\triangle MAP$ given that $m\angle A = 12°$, $m\angle P = 93°$, and $m = 16$. $m\angle M = 75°$, $p \approx 16.5$, $a \approx 3.4$

17. (82) **Physics** Two springs have two different weights attached at the ends. The movement of each weight is modeled by the periodic functions shown, where t is the time in seconds. How often will the weights be at the top of their movement at the same time? every 2 seconds

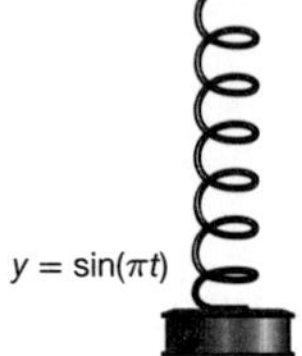

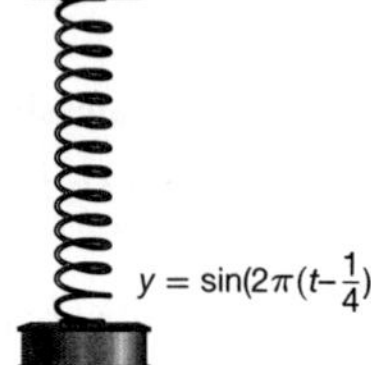

18. (84) **Multi-Step** Worker A can paint a room in 3 hours and Worker B can paint the same size room in 4 hours.
   a. If it takes x hours to complete a job, the work rate is $\frac{1}{x}$ because $\frac{1}{x}$ of the job can be completed in one hour. Write a work rate for each worker. Worker A: $\frac{1}{3}$, Worker B: $\frac{1}{4}$
   b. Workers A and B worked together and painted a room (same size as above) in h hours. Write expressions to show the amount of work done by each worker. 18b. Worker A: $\frac{1}{3}h$, Worker B: $\frac{1}{4}h$
   c. Add the expressions in part b together and set them equal to 1 to represent one room. Solve the equation for h. How long did it take the workers to paint the room working together? About 1.7 hours

19. (81) **Economics** The formula for continuously compounded interest is $A = Pe^{rt}$, where A is the total amount, P is the principal, r is the annual interest rate, and t is the time in years. To the nearest tenth, how many years would it take for the value of an investment to double at an annual interest rate of 6%, compounded continuously? 11.6 years

20. (57) A savings account earns interest at an annual rate of 4.5%, compounded continuously. If the account begins with a principal amount of $3000, what will its value be after 5 years? $3756.97

ENGLISH LEARNERS

Students may have difficulty with the term compound. In the English language, the term **compound** can mean "to intensify" or "to put together."

Define compound interest as the interest which includes, or puts together, the principal amount as well as the interest charged for the previous period.

Explain that the amount of interest paid in a previous period then becomes part of the principal amount, so you can calculate each year individually, or use the formula to find the total interest.

21. Error Analysis Two students are solving for the roots of $y = x^{12} - 1$ but get different results. Which student made the mistake? Student B incorrectly writes the binomial factor as $(x - 1)$ instead of $(x^4 - 1)$.
(85)

Student A	Student B
$x^{12} - 1 = (x^4)^3 - 1$ $= (x^4 - 1)((x^4)^2 + x^4 + 1)$ $= (x^2 + 1)(x^2 - 1)(x^8 + x^4 + 1)$ $= (x + 1)(x - 1)(x^2 + 1)(x^8 + x^4 + 1)$ The roots of $y = x^{12} - 1$ are ± 1.	$x^{12} - 1 = (x^4)^3 - 1$ $= (x - 1)((x^4)^2 + x^4 + 1)$ $= (x - 1)(x^8 + x^4 + 1)$ The root of $y = x^{12} - 1$ is 1.

***22. Data Analysis** The Ehrenberg relation $\log(w) = 0.8h + 0.4 \pm 0.04$ shows the relationship between height h and weight w in young children ages 5 through 13. Complete the table for the range of weight values.
(87)

h (m)	0.91	0.93	0.96	0.99	1.01
w (kg)	12.2–14.7	12.7–15.3	13.4–16.1	14.2–17.1	14.7–17.7

23. Write Tell if the sampling method performed was a probability sample. If not, explain why not. If so, state the type of probability sample.
(73)

A person running for local office asks drivers in a local gas/convenience station if they agree with the new gas tax being proposed. He asks every other driver who pulls into the station.

23. Sample: The sample is not a probability sample because he does not talk to the consumers who walk in to the station, nor does he question people on bikes, motorcycles, or ones using only the convenience station.

Solve.

***24.** $5 - \sqrt{x + 7} = 3$ $\quad -3$
(88)

***25.** $\sqrt{x + 2} = 2 - \sqrt{x}$ $\quad \frac{1}{4}$
(88)

***26. Graphing Calculator** Use a graphing calculator to estimate the solutions of $-23.4 < x^2 + 7.56x - 40$. Round to the nearest hundredth. $x < -9.34$ or $x > 1.78$
(89)

27. Vertical Motion and Gravity The height of a free-falling object (neglecting air resistance) is given by the function $h(t) = -4.9t^2 + v_0t + h_0$, where h_0 is the initial height in meters, v_0 is the initial velocity in meters per second, and $h(t)$ is the height in meters at time t seconds. How long does it take for an object to hit the ground after it is dropped from a height of 44.1 meters? 3 seconds
(78)

***28. Cliff Height** The Cliffs of Moher at Hag's Head offer one of the most spectacular views on the Atlantic coast of Ireland. If a boat is 90 meters from the base of the cliff, then it is 150 meters from an observer at the top of the cliff. Solve the equation $a^2 + b^2 = c^2$ for b. Then find the height of the cliff. $b = \sqrt{c^2 - a^2}$; 120 meters
(88)

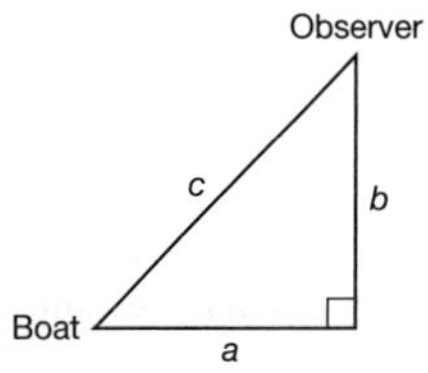

29. Solve $\triangle ABC$ given that $m\angle C = 114°$, $a = 8$, and $b = 6$. $m\angle A = 38°$, $m\angle B = 28°$, $c = 11.8$
(77)

30. Rewrite $\ln\left(\frac{e^5}{x^7}\right)^4$ as a sum or difference of terms if possible. Then simplify.
(81)
$4(\ln e^5 - \ln x^7) \rightarrow 20 - 28 \ln x$

Problem 22

Guide the students by asking them the following questions.

"How do you solve the equation for *w*?" exponentiate each side of the equation

"How many values of *w* will there be for each value of *h*?" two

Problem 25

Guide the students by asking them the following questions.

"How do you solve an equation with radicals on both sides of the equal sign?" square both sides of the equation

"If there is still a radical on one side of the equation, what do you need to do to solve the equation?" Isolate the square root, and square both sides of the equation again.

CHALLENGE

The area of a circle is $(36 - x)^2\pi$ square units. What are the possible values of x for which this area is possible? $x < 36$

LOOKING FORWARD

Solving quadratic inequalities prepares students for:

- **Lesson 94** Solving Rational Inequalities

LESSON 90

1 Warm Up

Review the meaning of a periodic function with students.

2 New Concepts

In this lesson, students learn to graph the tangent function.

Example 1

Discuss with students why the function $y = 5\tan(x)$ is undefined at the same values for which the parent function is undefined.

Additional Example 1

$y = \frac{1}{2}\tan(x)$ is undefined.

Graph $y = 2\tan(x)$

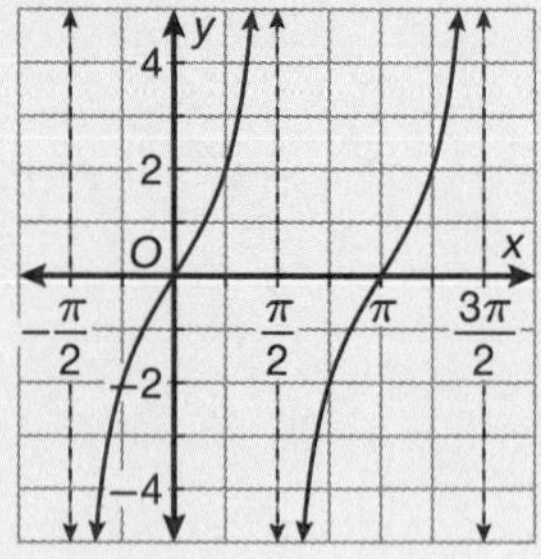

LESSON RESOURCES

Student Edition Practice Workbook 90
Reteaching Master 90
Adaptations Master 90
Challenge and Enrichment Master C90

LESSON 90 Graphing the Tangent Function

Warm Up

1. **Vocabulary** The function $y = \cos(x)$ is a trigonometric function that is periodic. (86)

2. What is the period of $y = 5\cos(3x)$? $\frac{2\pi}{3}$ (86)

3. What is the period of $y = \sin(4x)$? $\frac{\pi}{2}$ (82)

New Concepts

A tangent function is an example of a periodic function. It is based on the trigonometric ratio, $\tan(x) = \frac{\sin(x)}{\cos(x)}$. Therefore when $\cos(x) = 0$, the tangent is undefined. These values are excluded from the domain and represented on the graph by asymptotes. The tangent has no maximum or minimum values so the amplitude is undefined.

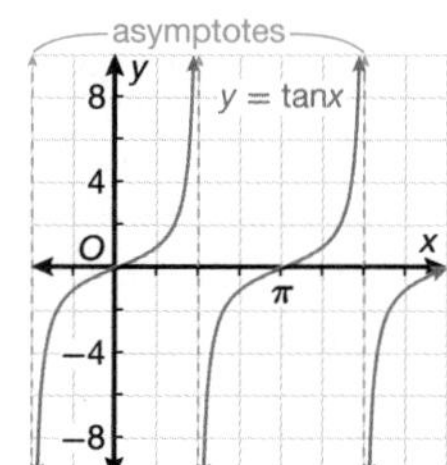

Domain: $\{x | x \neq \frac{\pi}{2} + \pi n$ where n is an integer.$\}$

Range: $\{y | -\infty < y < \infty\}$

Period: π

Amplitude: undefined

Properties of Tangent Functions
If $y = a \tan bx$, with $b > 0$ • $\frac{\pi}{b}$ is the period of the function • One cycle occurs in the interval from $-\frac{\pi}{2b}$ to $\frac{\pi}{2b}$ • Vertical asymptotes occur at each end of the cycle

To graph one cycle of a tangent function, use the asymptotes and three points. These five elements are equally spaced through one cycle. To find the x-coordinates of these points, divide the interval into fourths. The y-coordinates of the three points are $(-a)$, 0, and (a). The pattern of these points is asymptote-$(-a)$-zero-(a).

Math Reasoning

Verify Create a table of values to show that the period of $y = \tan(x)$ is π.

Check students' work.

Example 1 **Graphing $y = a \cdot \tan(x)$**

Graph $y = 5\tan(x)$.

SOLUTION The graph is a vertical stretch of the parent function.

Find the period of the function.

$$\frac{\pi}{b} = \frac{\pi}{1} = \pi$$

Find the interval of one cycle to locate asymptotes.

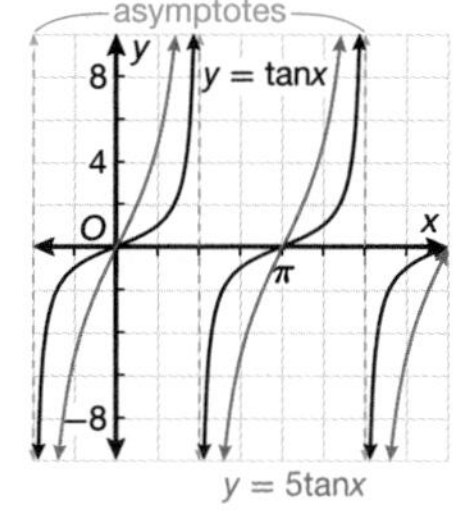

MATH BACKGROUND

Trigonometric functions have many applications. The first uses of trigonometric functions were created for astronomy and geography over 2000 years ago.

The use of trigonometric functions has extended to physics, chemistry, and engineering, among other things.

Trigonometry is used because it provides an understanding of space.

$-\frac{\pi}{2b} = -\frac{\pi}{2(1)} = -\frac{\pi}{2}$ $\quad \frac{\pi}{2b} = \frac{\pi}{2(1)} = \frac{\pi}{2}$

The asymptotes are $x = -\frac{\pi}{2}$ and $x = \frac{\pi}{2}$.

Determine the three points to use by dividing the interval into fourths to find the x-coordinates. The y-coordinates of the three points are $(-a)$, 0, and (a).

$\left(-\frac{\pi}{4}, -5\right), (0, 0), \left(\frac{\pi}{4}, 5\right)$

Use the pattern $(-a)$-zero-(a). Repeat the cycle.

A tangent function can be also be translated vertically. In the function $y = a \tan(bx) + d$, the value of d determines the shift. If $d > 0$, the graph shifts up and if $d < 0$, the graph shifts down. Similar to graphing translations of the sine and cosine functions, a simpler member of the tangent function family can be used.

Hint

Recall that $f(x) + k$ is a vertical shift of $f(x)$.

Example 2 Graphing $y = a \cdot \tan(x) + d$

Graph the function $y = \frac{1}{2}\tan(x) + 5$. Determine its period.

SOLUTION

asymptotes

$y = \tan x$

$y = \frac{1}{2}\tan x + 5$

Use $y = \frac{1}{2}\tan(x)$ as the parent function.

Find the period of the function.

$$\frac{\pi}{1} = \frac{\pi}{1} = \pi$$

Find the interval of one cycle to locate asymptotes.

$-\frac{\pi}{2b} = -\frac{\pi}{2(1)} = -\frac{\pi}{2}$ $\quad \frac{\pi}{2b} = \frac{\pi}{2(1)} = \frac{\pi}{2}$

The asymptotes are $x = -\frac{\pi}{2}$ and $x = \frac{\pi}{2}$.

Determine the three points to use by dividing the interval into fourths. Since $d > 0$ and the graph is shifted up 5, add 5 to the value of the y-coordinates.

$\left(-\frac{\pi}{4}, -\frac{1}{2} + 5\right), (0, 0 + 5), \left(\frac{\pi}{4}, \frac{1}{2} + 5\right)$

The three points to graph are $\left(-\frac{\pi}{4}, \frac{9}{2}\right), (0, 5), \left(\frac{\pi}{4}, \frac{11}{2}\right)$

Use the pattern $(-a)$-zero-(a). Repeat the cycle.

Hint

Be sure to use $\frac{\pi}{b}$ to find the period of a tangent function.

Example 3 Graphing $y = a \cdot \tan(bx) - d$

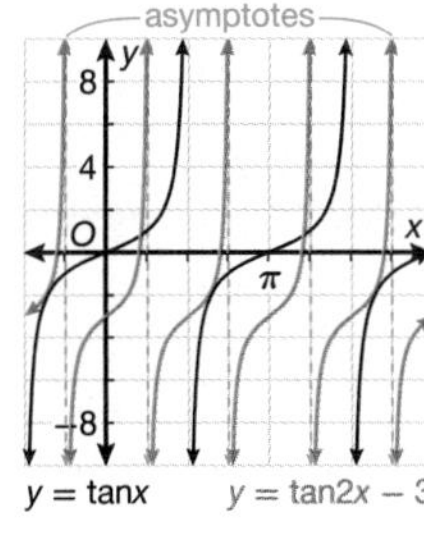

Graph $y = \tan(2x) - 3$. Identify its period and undefined values.

SOLUTION

Use $y = \tan(2x)$ as the parent function.

Find the period of the function.

$$\frac{\pi}{2} = \frac{\pi}{2}$$

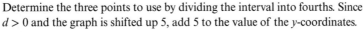

Example 2

Additional Example 2

Graph the function $y = 4\tan(x) + 2$.

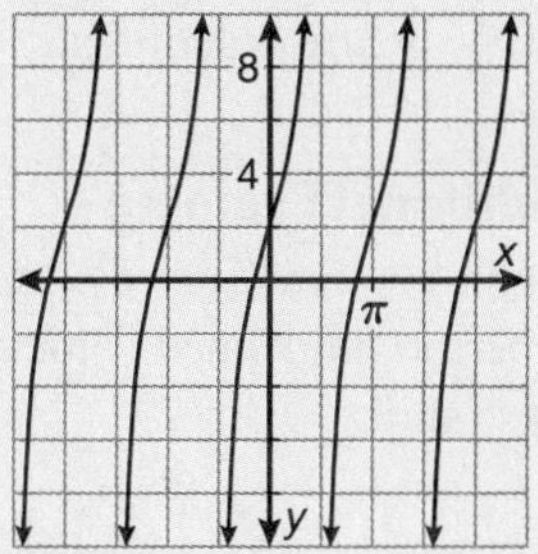

Example 3

Functions of the form $y = a\tan(bx) + c$ have a period of $\frac{\pi}{|b|}$ and are undefined where $\cos(bx) = 0$. The asymptotes are found at $x = \frac{\pi}{2|b|} + n\frac{\pi}{|b|}$, for integer values of n.

Extend the Example

Write another tangent function that has the same period as $y = \tan(4x)$. Sample: $y = 2\tan(4x)$

Additional Example 3

Graph $y = \tan(4x) - 4$. Identify its period and undefined values. period: $\frac{\pi}{3}$ asymptotes: $x = \frac{\pi}{6} + n\frac{\pi}{3}$

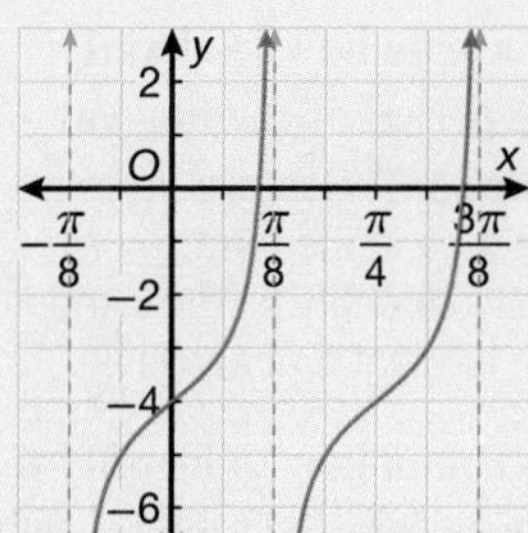

INCLUSION

Have students draw the asymptotes for Example 3 to help them understand that the function is undefined at those values of x.

Example 4

When a function of the form $y = \tan(bx - c)$ is written as $y = \tan\left(b\left(x - \frac{c}{b}\right)\right)$, the phase shift $\frac{c}{b}$, is easily identified.

Additional Example 4

Graph $y = \tan(2x - 5)$. Identify its period, undefined values, and phase shift.

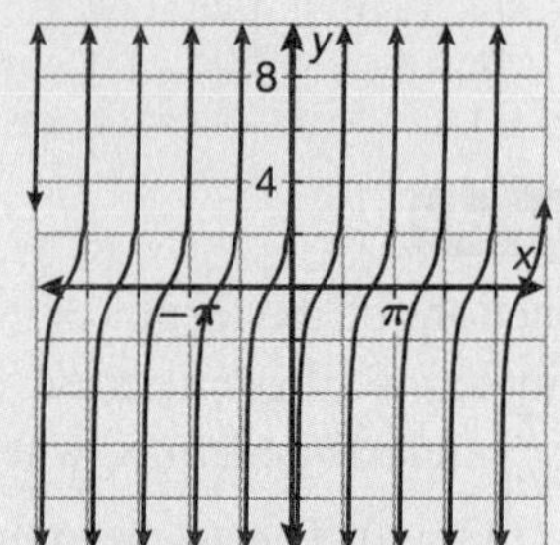

Period: $\frac{\pi}{2}$ Undefined values: $\frac{5}{2} + \frac{\pi}{4} + n\frac{\pi}{2}$ Phase shift: $\frac{5}{2}$

Lesson Practice

Problem a

Remind students that the function is undefined at the asymptotes, where $x = \frac{\pi}{2|b|} + n\frac{\pi}{|b|}$.

Check for Understanding

The questions below help assess the concepts taught in this lesson.

1. **"Explain how to identify the period of the tangent function."** Sample: Write the function in the form $y = a\tan(bx) + c$ to identify b. The period of the tangent function is $\frac{\pi}{|b|}$.
2. **"Explain how to identify the values for which the tangent function is undefined."** Sample: Write the function in the form $y = a\tan(bx) + c$ to identify b. The values for which the function is undefined are located at $x = \frac{\pi}{2|b|} + n\frac{\pi}{|b|}$, where n is an integer.

Find the interval of one cycle to locate asymptotes.

$$-\frac{\pi}{2b} = -\frac{\pi}{2(2)} = -\frac{\pi}{4} \qquad \frac{\pi}{2b} = \frac{\pi}{2(2)} = \frac{\pi}{4}$$

The asymptotes are $x = -\frac{\pi}{4}$ and $x = \frac{\pi}{4}$.

Determine the three points to use by dividing the interval into fourths. Since $d < 0$, the graph is shifted down, add -5 to the value of $(-a)$ and (a).

$$\left(-\frac{\pi}{8}, -1 + (-5)\right), (0, 0 + (-5)), \left(\frac{\pi}{8}, 1 + (-5)\right)$$

The three points to graph are $\left(-\frac{\pi}{8}, -6\right)$, $(0, -5)$ $\left(\frac{\pi}{8}, 4\right)$

Use the pattern $(-a)$-zero-(a). Repeat the cycle.

Hint

The undefined values of the parent tangent function are $x = \frac{\pi}{2} + \pi n$.

Example 4 Graphing $y = a\tan(b(x - c)) + d$

Graph $y = \tan\left(x - \frac{\pi}{2}\right)$. Identify its period, undefined values, and phase shift.

SOLUTION

The graph is a horizontal shift or phase shift of $\frac{\pi}{2}$.

Period: $\frac{\pi}{1} = \pi$

Phase shift: $\frac{\pi}{2}$

Undefined values: $\frac{\pi}{2} + \frac{\pi}{2} + \pi n = \pi n$

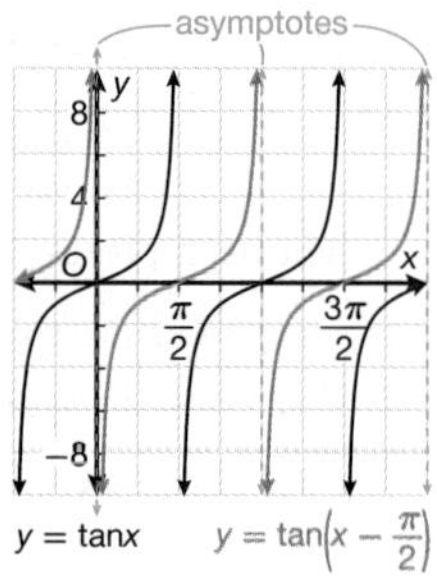

Lesson Practice

a. Graph $y = 10\tan(x)$. (Ex 1)

a.

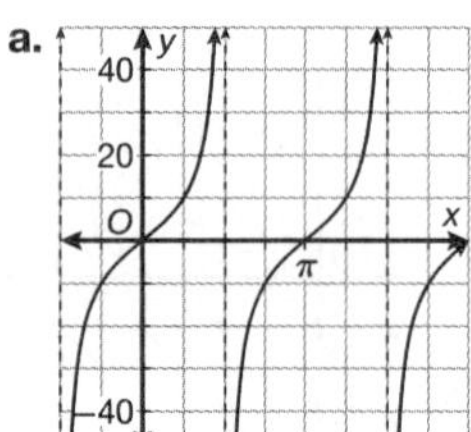

b. Graph the function $y = 8\tan(x) + 4$. Determine its period. (Ex 2) See Additional Answers.

c. Graph $y = \tan(6x)$ and compare its period to that of the parent function. Identify values where the function is undefined. (Ex 3) See Additional Answers.

d. Graph $y = \tan\left(\frac{1}{4}x\right)$ and compare its period to that of the parent function. Identify values where the function is undefined. (Ex 3) See Additional Answers.

e. Graph $y = \tan(7x) + 5$. Identify its period and undefined values. (Ex 3) See Additional Answers.

f. Graph $y = 2\tan\left(x - \frac{\pi}{3}\right)$. Identify its period, undefined values, and phase shift. (Ex 4) See Additional Answers.

INCLUSION

Students may have difficulty seeing the shifts in the graphs. If so, graph the function and its parent function on the floor. Use masking tape for the axes and asymptotes and different color string for each function.

Practice Distributed and Integrated

1. (71) **Geography** On a map, line segments connecting three southeast Texas cities form a triangle as shown. About how many square miles are within the triangle? About 270 mi²

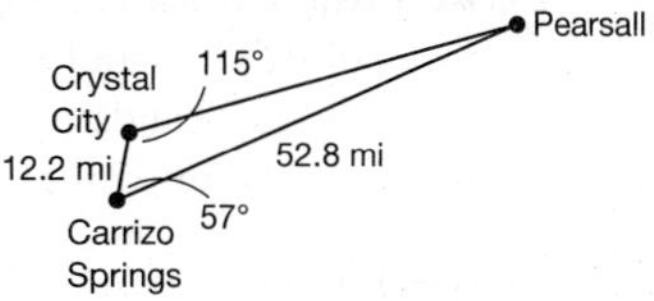

2. (85) **Construction** The sheet of metal shown is rolled into a cylinder along the longer side. The area of the sheet is 6 square units. Find the radius of the cylinder. $\frac{15}{2\pi}$

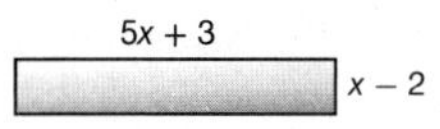

***3.** (90) **Jewelry Making** A jeweler is changing the angle of a facet for a diamond ring from θ to φ. The vertical distances change as shown in the diagram, while the value of w remains constant. Derive the function that the jeweler can use to find values of θ when the other values are known. $\theta = \tan^{-1}\left(\tan(\varphi)\frac{h_2}{h_1}\right)$

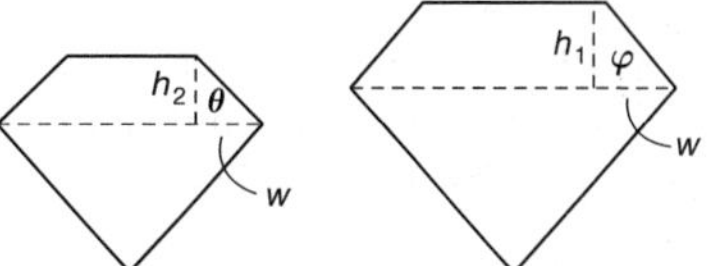

4. (55) A bin has 3 apples and 5 oranges. What is the probability of selecting two apples chosen at random without replacement? $\frac{3}{28}$

Write each expression as a radical.

5. (59) $13^{\frac{3}{11}}$ $\sqrt[11]{13^3}$

6. (59) $22^{\frac{5}{9}}$ $\sqrt[9]{22^5}$

7. (61) **Geometry** The volume of a rectangular solid with a length of $x + 10$ feet has a volume of $x^3 + 18x^2 + 95x + 150$ cubic feet. Factor the expression for the volume completely. $(x + 10)(x + 3)(x + 5)$

8. (66) Solve for the roots of the polynomial: $7x(x^2 + 4x - 12) = 0$. $x = -6, 0, 2$

9. (72) **Geology** The Richter magnitude M of an earthquake is expressed by $M = \frac{2}{3}\log\left(\frac{E}{10^{11.8}}\right)$, where E is the energy released in ergs. In 2007 an earthquake of magnitude 8.0 occurred near the coast of Central Peru. Find the energy released by that earthquake. Approximately 6.31×10^{23} ergs

10. (73) **Error Analysis** A student said that a systematic sampling method is biased because the first individual on the list will always be chosen. Explain the error in the student's thinking. The first name on the list is not always the starting point. The starting point should be chosen randomly.

11. (74) **Soccer** A player standing on a 15-foot hill kicks a ball straight up at a velocity of 45 feet per second. She wants it to go above the roof of a nearby shed which is about 40 feet above the ground. The function that gives the height of the ball after x seconds is given by $y = -16x^2 + 45x + 15$. Use the discriminant to explain whether the ball will/will not reach the desired height. The ball will reach the desired height because the discriminant is positive and has two real solutions.

12. (73) **Analyze** Why is systematic sampling a probability sample but not a simple random sample? Every individual has a known chance, greater than 0, of being selected, but not every group of n individuals has an equal chance of being selected. For instance, two consecutive individuals will not be in the same sample.

3 Practice

Math Conversations

Discussions to strengthen understanding

Problem 1

"What is the problem asking you to find?" the area of the triangle whose vertices lie at each city

"What formula is used?" $A = \frac{1}{2}bc \sin A$

Problem 4

Extend the Problem

"Is the probability the same if the first item picked is replaced?" no

"What is the probability of choosing two apples with replacement?" $\frac{9}{64}$

Problems 5 and 6

Error Alert

Watch for students who use the numerator as the index instead of the denominator.

Problem 7

"What is the first step in solving the problem?" Divide the polynomial by $x + 10$ using long division or synthetic division.

Problem 12

"What is a systematic sampling?" a sample where every nth element is selected from the population.

ENGLISH LEARNERS

The word **tangent** has several different meanings in the English language.

Geometrically, a line tangent to a circle intersects the circle in exactly one point.

Tangent can also mean an abrupt change of course as in a digression from the main topic.

Discuss the different meanings of the word tangent with students and tell them that the context in which the word is used will define its meaning.

Problem 13

"How many roots does the polynomial have?" four

"What is the first step in solving the problem?" factor out a 2 on the left side of the equation

"What special product is $x^4 - 256$?" the difference of two squares

Problem 18

"What are the roots of the quadratic equation $x^2 - 9 = 0$?" 3 and −3

"What are the roots of the quadratic equation $2x^2 - 18 = 0$?" 3 and −3

"How do the graphs of $y = x^2 - 9$ and $2x^2 - 18$ differ?" The vertex of the graph of $y = x^2 - 9$ is at the point (0, −9). The vertex of the graph of $y = 2x^2 - 18$ is at (0, −18).

"What are the x-intercepts of each function?" Both functions intersect the x-axis at (−3, 0) and (3, 0).

Problem 20

"What is an odd function?" a function where $f(-x) = -f(x)$

"What is an even function?" a function where $f(-x) = f(x)$

"Which of the other five trigonometric functions are odd?" sine, cosecant, and cotangent

Solve.

13. (78) $2x^4 - 512 = 0$ $x = \pm 4i, -4, 4$

14. (78) $3x^2 + 4x - 4 = 0$ $x = -2, \frac{2}{3}$

15. (80) **Multi-Step** The ages of a certain group of people are normally distributed with a mean of 42 years and a standard deviation of 6.5 years. What percent of the ages are between 29 and 55? How you can use that answer to find the percent of ages that are between 42 and 55? Find that percent. 95%; Divide by 2, 47.5%

16. (81) **Justify** Explain why $x = e^y$ and $y = \ln x$ are equivalent equations. See Additional Answers.

17. (86) Using $f(x) = \sin(x)$ as a guide, find the phase shift in $h(x) = \sin\left(x + \frac{\pi}{4}\right)$. Phase shift = $\frac{\pi}{4}$ to the left

18. (83) **Generalize** Given a quadratic equation, how can you write another quadratic equation with the same roots? Multiply both sides of the equation by a non-zero constant.

19. (84) Gene can paint a room in 8 hours and Chandra and Gene working together can paint the room in 5 hours. How long would it take Chandra to paint the room by herself? $13\frac{1}{3}$ hours

***20.** (90) **Analyze** Is $y = \tan(\theta)$ an odd or an even function? Explain. An odd function because $\tan(-x) = -\tan(x)$.

***21.** (90) **Coordinate Geometry** Write the version of the slope formula that can be used to find the tangent function. $\tan(\theta) = \frac{y_2 - y_1}{x_2 - x_1}$

***22.** (89) **Write** Describe how to solve a quadratic inequality algebraically. See Additional Answers.

***23.** (88) **Multiple Choice** Solve $A = \frac{1}{2}bh$ for b. Which equation shows the correct solution? A

A $b = \frac{2A}{h}$ **B** $b = \frac{A}{2h}$ **C** $b = A - \frac{1}{2}h$ **D** $b = \frac{1}{2}Ah$

***24.** (87) Use the change of base formula to convert $\log_2(x)^3$ to base e. Then evaluate when $x = 1$. $3\frac{\ln x}{\ln 2}$; 0

***25.** (85) **Graphing Calculator** A portion of a roller coaster is modeled by the polynomial function $y = 0.000013x^4 - 0.00255x^3 + 0.13505x^2 - 0.51x + 0.5$. Use a graphing calculator to find the roots of the polynomial. no roots

Solve using a table.

***26.** (89) $x^2 - 2x \geq 8$ $x \leq -2$ or $x \geq 4$

***27.** (89) $x^2 - 15x + 50 < 0$ $5 < x < 10$

***28.** (86) Find the period of $y = \cos\left(\frac{1}{\sqrt{5} - 1}x\right)$. $2\pi(\sqrt{5} - 1)$

29. (82) Given $q(x) = -\sin\left(\frac{\pi}{2}x\right)$, identify the amplitude and period. Amplitude = 1, Period = 4

30. (83) Write a quadratic equation whose roots are $8 \pm 5i$. $x^2 - 16x + 89 = 0$

CHALLENGE

Write the equation of the function shown in the graph.

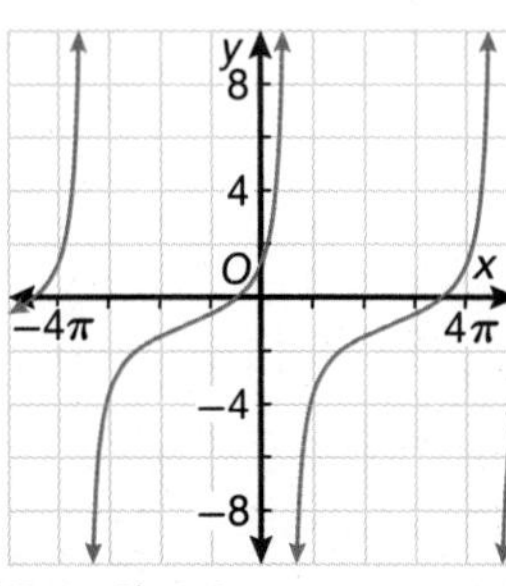

$y = \tan(0.25x - 2) - 1$

LOOKING FORWARD

Graphing the tangent function prepares students for:

- **Lesson 96** Using Polar Coordinates
- **Lesson 103** Graphing Reciprocal Trigonometric Functions
- **Lesson 119** Solving Trigonometric Equations

INVESTIGATION 9

Understanding Step Functions

Cell Phone Rates A cell phone company charges customers for each phone call that they make. A call costs \$0.50 for a connection fee plus \$0.10 for each minute of the call. The company rounds the time of the call down to the nearest whole minute.

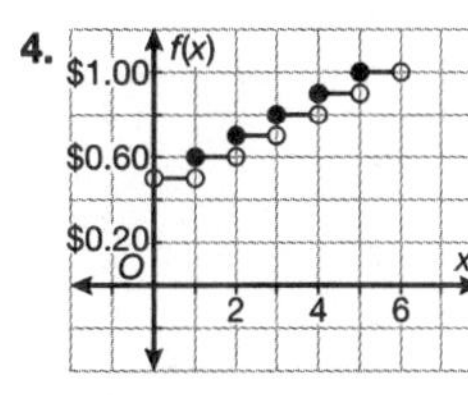

1. Find the cost of each phone call:
   a. a 5-minute call \$1.00
   b. a $5\frac{1}{4}$-minute call \$1.00
   c. a $\frac{1}{4}$-minute call \$0.50
2. **Justify** If a phone call lasts for 30 seconds, would the customer be charged for the phone call? Explain. Yes; although 30 seconds is rounded down to 0 minutes, there is still a connection fee.
3. **Analyze** Consider the costs of a 5-minute and a $5\frac{1}{4}$-minute phone call. Would a phone call that lasted $5\frac{1}{4}$ minutes cost more than a 5-minute call? Explain. No; $5\frac{1}{4}$ rounded down to the nearest whole number is 5 minutes.
4. **Generalize** Complete the table below. Then graph the function as a piecewise function.

x	$f(x)$
$0 < x < 1$	\$0.50
$1 \leq x < 2$	\$0.60
$2 \leq x < 3$	\$0.70
$3 \leq x < 4$	\$0.80
$4 \leq x < 5$	\$0.90
$5 \leq x < 6$	\$1.00

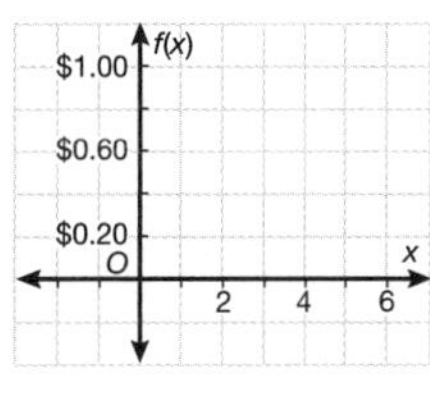

Graphing Calculator

For help with graphing systems, see the graphing calculator keystrokes on page 19.

Math Reasoning

Generalize What type of function do the values in the table represent? step

A step function is a piecewise function that is constant over each interval in its domain. Step functions consist of line segments, rays, or both that resemble steps of a staircase.

One type of step function is the greatest integer function. The following are ways in which the simplest greatest integer function can be written:

$$f(x) = [x] \qquad f(x) = [\![x]\!] \qquad f(x) = \lfloor x \rfloor$$

The cell phone rate problem is represented by a greatest integer function because it rounds the number of minutes down to the nearest integer. The **greatest integer function**, $f(x) = [x]$, is a function where the output, $f(x)$, is the greatest integer that is either less than or equal to the input, x.

Online Connection
www.SaxonMathResources.com

INVESTIGATION 9

Materials

- Pencil, graph paper, and calculator

Discuss

Students will complete tables, graphs, and applications of step functions. Two special step functions will be examined. Define step function, greatest integer function, and least integer function.

Problem 4

Examine the values of $f(x)$ in the chart. The step of this function, or the difference in $f(x)$ values, is 0.10.

TEACHER TIP

Remind students that closed points on the graph mean that the point is included ($\leq$). Open points indicate that the value is not included ($<$). Point out that this graph consists of disconnected segments of equal length.

MATH BACKGROUND

The step function is a piecewise constant function with a finite number of pieces. This function is discontinuous and is constant over a given interval. The function values change from interval to interval. The step function is sometimes called the postage stamp function because the process of assigning letter weights to postage amounts is an example of a step function.

INVESTIGATION RESOURCES

Reteaching Master
Investigation 9

Problem 5

Students should use their knowledge of linear functions to complete 5a. Have students write the equation in the form $y = mx + b$.

Have students modify the greatest integer function to complete 5c. Remind them to consider the connection fee.

TEACHER TIP

Compare and contrast the table and graph of the least integer function with that of the greatest integer function.

Problem 6

Extend the Problem

Change the function to $f(x) = 8\lceil x \rceil$. What is the charge per hour of parking? What part of the table would change? The charge is $8.00 per hour. The values of $f(x)$ would change to 8, 16, 24, 32, 40, and 48.

Error Alert Students sometimes graph step functions as continuous functions. Each piece of the table should be graphed separately. This function can be considered as six small functions graphed on the same axes.

5. Suppose the company uses the exact number of minutes, x, to calculate the total cost of a phone call.

   a. **Multiple Representations** Write a linear function to represent the cost, $f(x)$, of a phone call. $f(x) = 0.10x + 0.50$

   b. **Discuss** How can the equation be changed to represent the cost of a phone call when the company rounds the length of time down to the nearest minute? Replace the variable, x, with $[x]$.

   c. Write the equation to represent the cost, $f(x)$, of a phone call when the company rounds the length of time, x, down to the nearest minute. $f(x) = 0.10[x] + 0.50$

   d. **Graphing Calculator** Use a graphing calculator to graph the equation in part **c.**

5d.

Another type of step function is the least integer function. The least integer function rounds any number up to the nearest integer. The simplest form of this equation looks like:

$$f(x) = \lceil x \rceil.$$

The least integer function is a function where the output, $f(x)$, is the least integer that is either greater than or equal to the input, x. Use this definition in the following problem.

Calculator Tip

To graph greatest integer functions, click on the **MATH** key and select the **NUM** menu. Then, select **5: int(**.

Parking Lot Customers are charged by the hour to park in a lot. The length of time that a car is parked is rounded up to the nearest hour. The function for the cost for parking is $f(x) = 6\lceil x \rceil$ where x is the time in hours and $f(x)$ is the cost of parking in dollars.

6. Complete the table by filling in the intervals of time, x, and the cost, $f(x)$.

   a. Draw a graph to represent the information in the table.

   b. Use the graph. What is the cost of parking in the lot for 2 hours? 1.5 hours? less than 1 hour? $12, $12, $6

   c. Use the table. What is the charge per hour of parking? $6

6a.

x	$f(x)$
$0 < x \leq 1$	$6
$1 < x \leq 2$	$12
$2 < x \leq 3$	$18
$3 < x \leq 4$	$24
$4 < x \leq 5$	$30
$5 < x \leq 6$	$36

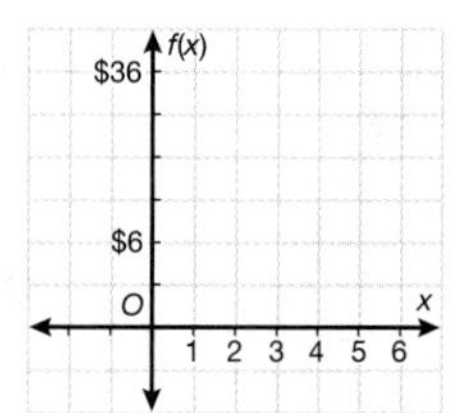

INCLUSION

Explain the difference between the greatest integer function and the least integer function. Discuss the following example.

Given $x = 3.7$, using the greatest integer function, $f(x) = \lfloor x \rfloor = \lfloor 3.7 \rfloor = 3$.

Using the least integer function, $f(x) = \lceil x \rceil = \lceil 3.7 \rceil = 4$.

Write key words on the board.

Greatest integer function—round down ↓

Least integer function—round up ↑

Students may have difficulty with rounding down when using the greatest integer function and rounding up when using the least integer function. Review the definitions of both functions.

Investigation Practice

A grocery store charges \$0.03 per ounce for bananas. The store weighs the fruit on a produce scale, and then rounds the weight of the produce up to the nearest ounce.

a. $f(x) = 0.03\lceil x \rceil$

c. least integer function; the number of ounces is rounded up to the nearest ounce.

a. Write a function to represent the total cost for x ounces of bananas.

b. What is the domain for this function? domain: $x > 0$

c. Which step function is this? Explain.

d. Complete the table for the following step function. Use the information from your table to graph the function.

d.

x	$f(x)$
$0 < x \leq 1$	0.03
$1 < x \leq 2$	0.06
$2 < x \leq 3$	0.09
$3 < x \leq 4$	0.12
$4 < x \leq 5$	0.15
$5 < x \leq 6$	0.18

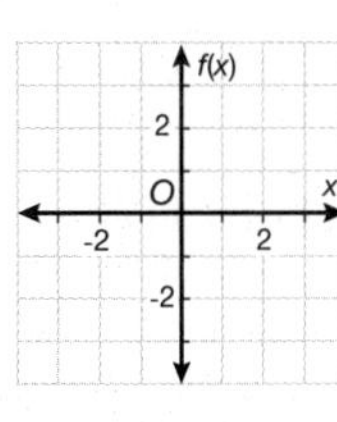

Formulate Below is a graph of a step function. $f(x) = 2\lceil x \rceil$

e. Complete the table, and then write a function that represents the graph.

f. What type of step function is represented by the graph? least integer function

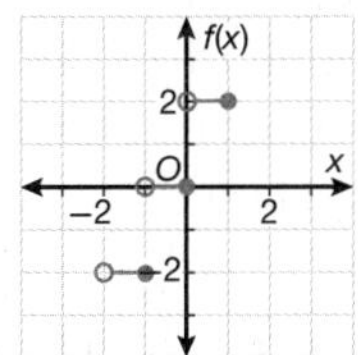

x	$f(x)$
$-2 < x \leq -1$	-2
$-1 < x \leq 0$	0
$0 < x \leq 1$	2

ENGLISH LEARNER

For Problem 6, explain the meaning of the term **parking lot.** Say:

"A parking lot is a place where a car can be left for a period of time. You can leave your car in the parking lot while you shop inside the store."

Ask students to name places where they would have to pay for leaving a car in a parking lot. Sample: downtown, airport, amusement park

Investigation Practice

Math Conversations

Discussions to strengthen understanding

Problems a–c

Scaffolding

1. **"Is this an example of a greatest integer or least integer function? Why?"** Least integer function; The cost of the produce is rounded up to the nearest ounce.
2. **"What is the coefficient of the step function?"** 0.03
3. **"What do the x-values represent in this problem?"** weight in ounces
4. **"Look at the $f(x)$ values to determine the step of this function."** The step is 0.03.

Problem d

Use integer values for $f(x)$ when completing the table.

Problems e and f

"How does the graph indicate that values are rounded up?" The right endpoint of each segment is closed.

Lesson Planner

Lesson	New Concepts
Lab 13	*Graphing Calculator Lab:* Graphing in Parametric Mode
91	Making Graphs and Solving Equations of Circles
92	Finding Arithmetic Sequences
93	Solving Exponential Equations and Inequalities
94	Solving Rational Inequalities
95	Factoring Higher-Order Polynomials
	Cumulative Test 18, Performance Task 18
96	Using Polar Coordinates
97	Finding Geometric Sequences
98	Making Graphs and Using Equations of Ellipses
99	Using Vectors
100	Graphing Rational Functions I
	Cumulative Test 19, Performance Task 19
INV 10	Graphing Polar Models

Resources for Teaching

- Student Edition
- Teacher's Edition
- Student Edition eBook
- Teacher's Edition eBook
- Resources and Planner CD
- Solutions Manual
- Instructional Masters
- Technology Lab Masters
- Warm Up and Teaching Transparencies
- Instructional Presentations CD
- Online activities, tools, and homework help **www.SaxonMathResources.com**

Resources for Practice and Assessment
Factorilng Higher Order Polynimials

- Student Edition Practice Workbook
- Course Assessments
- Standardized Test Practice
- College Entrance Exam Practice
- Test and Practice Generator CD using ExamView™

Resources for Differentiated Instruction

- Reteaching Masters
- Challenge and Enrichment Masters
- Prerequisite Skills Intervention
- Adaptations for Saxon Algebra 2
- Multilingual Glossary
- English Learners Handbook
- TI Resources

Pacing Guide

Resources and Planner CD for lesson planning support

45-Minute Class

Day 1	Day 2	Day 3	Day 4	Day 5	Day 6
Lesson 91	Lesson 92	Lesson 93	Lesson 94	Lesson 95	Cumulative Test 18
Day 7	**Day 8**	**Day 9**	**Day 10**	**Day 11**	**Day 12**
Lesson 96	Lesson 97	Lesson 98	Lesson 99	Lesson 100	Cumulative Test 19
Day 13					
Investigation 10					

Block: 90-Minute Class

Day 1	Day 2	Day 3	Day 4	Day 5	Day 6
Lesson 91 Lesson 92	Lesson 93 Lesson 94	Lesson 95 Cumulative Test 18	Lesson 96 Lesson 97	Lesson 98 Lesson 99	Lesson 100 Cumulative Test 19
Day 7					
Investigation 10 Lesson 101					

**For suggestions on how to implement Saxon Math in a block schedule, see the Pacing section at the beginning of the Teacher's Edition.*

Differentiated Instruction

Below Level		Advanced Learners	
Warm Up	SE pp. 640, 646, 652, 658, 665, 671, 678, 684, 690, 696	Challenge	TE pp. 644, 650, 656, 664, 670, 676, 681, 683, 688, 692, 695, 701
Skills Bank	SE pp. 862–885	Extend the Example	TE pp. 644, 647, 648, 654, 655, 661, 667, 672, 681, 691, 692
Reteaching Masters	Lessons 91–100, Investigation 10	Extend the Problem	TE pp. 657, 663, 669, 677, 682, 688, 695
Warm Up Transparencies	Lessons 91–100	Challenge and Enrichment Masters	Challenge: C91–C100 Enrichment: E91
Prerequisite Skills Intervention	Skill 44		
English Learners		**Special Needs**	
EL Tips	TE pp. 641, 647, 659, 668, 672, 682, 685, 694, 699, 704	Inclusion Tips	TE pp. 642, 649, 660, 662, 667, 673, 674, 675, 680, 687, 693, 698, 700
Multilingual Glossary	Booklet and Online	Adaptations for Saxon Algebra 2	Lessons 91–100; Cumulative Tests 18, 19
English Learners Handbook			
For All Learners			
Exploration	SE pp. 646	Alternate Method	TE pp. 654, 661, 663, 666, 669, 679, 691, 697
Caution	SE pp. 654	Online Tools	
Hints	SE pp. 641, 642, 643, 652, 660, 672, 678, 684, 703		
Error Alert	TE pp. 641, 643, 644, 647, 648, 649, 654, 656, 662, 664, 666, 669, 674, 677, 679, 680, 681, 682, 685, 689, 691, 692, 693, 695, 698, 701, 703		

SE = Student Edition; TE = Teacher's Edition

Math Vocabulary

Lesson	New Vocabulary		Maintained	EL Tip in TE
91	conic section		radius	resemble
92	arithmetic sequence common difference explicit formula finite sequence	infinite sequence sequence term of a sequence	domain	sequence
93			base decreasing function increasing function	
94	rational inequality		least common denominator	interval
95	Factor Theorem	Remainder Theorem	factor	population
96	polar equation		sine	customary
97	common ratio	geometric sequence	term of a sequence	cruise
98	co-vertices of an ellipse eccentricity ellipse foci of an ellipse	major axis minor axis polar coordinate vertex of an ellipse	circle	eccentric
99	dot product vector	vector addition vector subtraction	real part	ray
100			asymptote polynomial	asymptote
INV 10			polar equation	cardioid rose curve

SECTION OVERVIEW 10

Math Highlights

Enduring Understandings – The "Big Picture"

After completing Section 10, students will understand:

- How to make graphs and how to solve equations of circles and ellipses.
- How to use polar coordinates and how to graph polar models.
- How to use the remainder and factor theorems.
- How to graph rational functions.

Essential Questions

- How do I use vectors?
- How do I solve exponential equations and inequalities?
- How do I solve rational inequalities?

Math Content Strands

Matrices

• Lesson 99	Using Vectors

Polynomials and Polynomial Functions

• Lesson 95	Factoring Higher-Order Polynomials

Rational and Radical Functions

• Lesson 94	Solving Rational Inequalities
• Lesson 100	Graphing Rational Functions I

Trigonometry

• Lesson 96	Using Polar Coordinates
• Investigation 10	Graphing Polar Models

Exponential and Logarithmic Functions

• Lesson 93	Solving Exponential Equations and Inequalities

Conic Sections

• Lab 13	Graphing Calculator: Graphing in Parametric Mode
• Lesson 91	Making Graphs and Solving Equations of Circles
• Lesson 98	Making Graphs and Using Equations of Ellipses

Sequences, Series, and Logic

• Lesson 92	Finding Arithmetic Sequences
• Lesson 97	Finding Geometric Sequences

Connections in Practice Problems

	Lessons
Coordinate Geometry	92, 97, 99
Data Analysis	94, 100
Geometry	91, 92, 93, 94, 95, 96, 97, 98, 99, 100
Probability	91, 93, 94, 98, 99
Statistics	96

Math Processes

Reasoning and Communication

	Lessons
• Analyze	91, 92, 93, 94, 95, 96, 97, 98, 99, 100
• Error analysis	91, 92, 93, 94, 95, 96, 97, 98, 99, 100
• Estimate	93, 95, 97
• Formulate	91, 92, 94, 96, 97
• Generalize	91, 93, 95, 96, 98, 99, 100, Inv. 10
• Justify	91, 92, 94, 95, 96, 97, 98, 100
• Math reasoning	91, 92, 94, 97
• Model	97, 98
• Multiple choice	91, 92, 93, 94, 95, 96, 97, 98, 99, 100
• Multi-step	91, 92, 93, 94, 95, 96, 97, 98, 99, 100
• Predict	95
• Verify	91, 92, 93, 96, 97, 99, 100
• Write	91, 92, 96, 97, 98, 99, 100
• Graphing Calculator	91, 92, 93, 94, 95, 96, 97, 98, 99, 100, Inv. 10

Connections

In Examples: Astronomy, Braking distance, Cell phone tower, Compound interest, Cost per person, Electricity, Navigation, Planetary orbits, Salary

In Practice problems: Acoustics, Basketball, Boating, Business, Cell phone tower, Chemistry, City planning, College admissions, Delivery charges, Depreciation, Drafting, the Ehrenberg relation, Engines, Fast food, Geography, Government, Gravity, Home maintenance, Juggling, Medicine, National highways, National parks, Optics, Packaging, Parking, Phone service, Physics, Population, Prom, Research, Savings, Science, Seismology, Simple interest, Sound intensity, Sports, Surveying, Tourist attractions, Travel

Content Trace

Lesson	Warm Up: Prerequisite Skills	New Concepts	Where Practiced	Where Assessed	Looking Forward
91	Lessons 41, 63	Making Graphs and Solving Equations of Circles	Lessons 91, 92, 93, 94, 95, 96, 97, 99, 100, 102, 103, 105, 106, 107, 108, 109, 110, 115, 116	Cumulative Tests 19, 20	Lessons 96, 109, 114
92	Skills Bank, Lessons 4, 7	Finding Arithmetic Sequences	Lessons 92, 93, 94, 95, 96, 97, 99, 103, 104, 105, 107, 108, 110, 111, 114, 116, 117	Cumulative Tests 19, 20, 21	Lessons 97, 105, 113
93	Lessons 3, 47	Solving Exponential Equations and Inequalities	Lessons 93, 94, 96, 97, 101, 102, 103, 105, 107, 109, 110, 111, 113, 114, 115, 119	Cumulative Tests 19, 20	Lessons 102, 110
94	Lessons 84, 89	Solving Rational Inequalities	Lessons 94, 95, 96, 98, 100, 103, 104, 105, 106, 107, 108, 112, 113, 116, 117	Cumulative Tests 19, 20	Lesson 102
95	Lessons 35, 51	Factoring Higher-Order Polynomials	Lessons 95, 96, 98, 100, 101, 103, 104, 105, 107, 111, 112, 117	Cumulative Tests 19, 20	Lessons 101, 106
96	Lesson 46	Using Polar Coordinates	Lessons 96, 97, 98, 99, 100, 101, 102, 103, 104, 106, 107, 109, 111, 112, 115	Cumulative Tests 20, 21	Investigation 10
97	Lessons 2, 92	Finding Geometric Sequences	Lessons 97, 98, 101, 102, 103, 104, 106, 107, 109, 111, 112, 113, 114, 115, 119	Cumulative Tests 20, 21	Lessons 105, 113
98	Lessons 2, 91	Making Graphs and Using Equations of Ellipses	Lessons 98, 99, 101, 102, 103, 104, 106, 111, 112, 114, 117	Cumulative Tests 20, 21	Lessons 109, 114
99	Lessons 9, 41, 62	Using Vectors	Lessons 99, 100, 101, 102, 103, 104, 106, 107, 108, 111, 112, 113, 118	Cumulative Tests 20, 21	Lesson 104
100	Lessons 23, 28	Graphing Rational Functions I	Lessons 100, 101, 102, 103, 104, 106, 107, 109, 111, 112, 114, 116, 119	Cumulative Tests 20, 21	Lessons 101, 107, 111, 117
INV 10	N/A	Graphing Polar Models	Lessons 115, 117	Cumulative Test 21	N/A

Ongoing Assessment

	Type	Feature	Intervention *
BEFORE instruction	Assess Prior Knowledge	• Diagnostic Test	• Prerequisite Skills Intervention
BEFORE the lesson	Formative	• Warm Up	• Skills Bank • Reteaching Masters
DURING the lesson	Formative	• Lesson Practice • Math Conversations with the Practice problems	• Additional Examples in TE • Test and Practice Generator (for additional practice sheets)
AFTER the lesson	Formative	• Check for Understanding (closure)	• Scaffolding Questions in TE
AFTER 5 lessons	Summative	After Lesson 95 • Cumulative Test 18 • Performance Task 18 After Lesson 100 • Cumulative Test 19 • Performance Task 19	• Reteaching Masters • Test and Practice Generator (for additional tests and practice)
AFTER 20 lessons	Summative	• Benchmark Tests	• Reteaching Masters • Test and Practice Generator (for additional tests and practice)

* for students not showing progress during the formative stages or scoring below 80% on the summative assessments

Evidence of Learning – What Students Should Know

Because the Saxon philosophy is to provide students with sufficient time to learn and practice each concept, a lesson's topic will not be tested until at least five lessons after the topic is introduced.

On the Cumulative Tests that are given during this section of ten lessons, students should be able to demonstrate the following competencies:

- Solve rational inequalities and quadratic inequalities.
- Find arithmetic sequences.
- Evaluate logarithmic expressions.
- Make graphs and solve equations of circles.

Test and Practice Generator CD using ExamView™

The Test and Practice Generator is an easy-to-use benchmark and assessment tool that creates unlimited practice and tests in multiple formats and allows you to customize questions or create new ones. A variety of reports are available to track student progress toward mastery of the standards throughout the year.

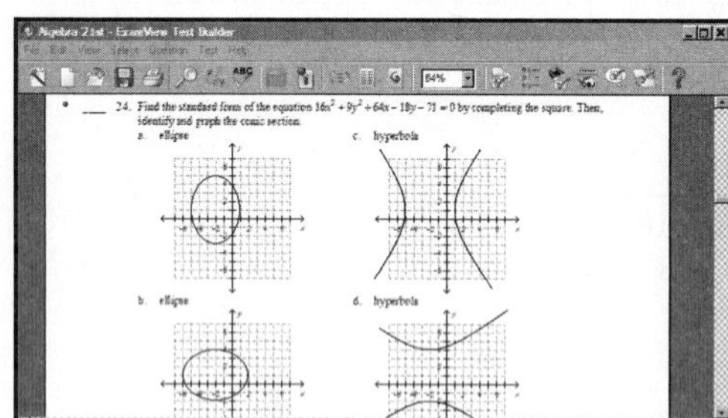

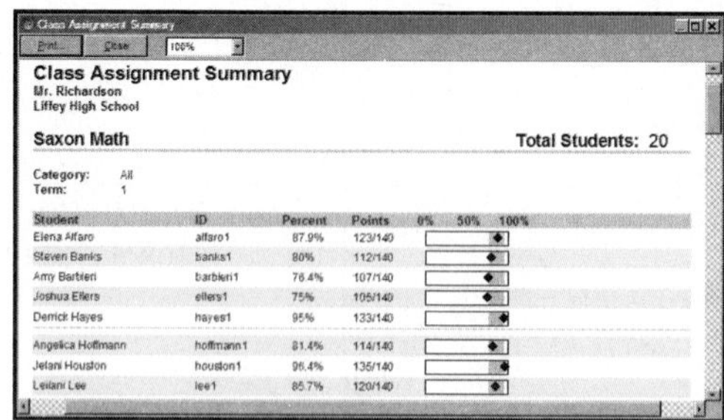

Assessment Resources

Resources for Diagnosing and Assessing

- **Student Edition**
  - Warm Up
  - Lesson Practice
- **Teacher's Edition**
  - Math Conversations with the Practice problems
  - Check for Understanding (closure)
- **Course Assessments**
  - Diagnostic Test
  - Cumulative Tests
  - Performance Tasks
  - Benchmark Tests

Resources for Test Prep

- **Student Edition**
  - Multiple-choice practice problems
  - Multiple-step and writing problems
  - Daily cumulative practice
- **Standardized Test Practice**
- **College Entrance Exam Practice**
- **Test and Practice Generator CD using ExamView™**

Resources for Intervention

- **Student Edition**
  - Skills Bank
- **Teacher's Edition**
  - Additional Examples
  - Scaffolding questions
- **Prerequisite Skills Intervention**
  - Worksheets
- **Reteaching Masters**
  - Lesson instruction and practice sheets
- **Test and Practice Generator CD using ExamView™**
  - Lesson practice problems
  - Additional tests

Cumulative Tests

The assessments in Saxon Math are frequent and consistently placed after every five lessons to offer a regular method of ongoing testing. These cumulative assessments check mastery of concepts from previous lessons.

Performance Tasks

The Performance Tasks can be used in conjunction with the Cumulative Tests and are scored using a rubric.

After Lesson 95

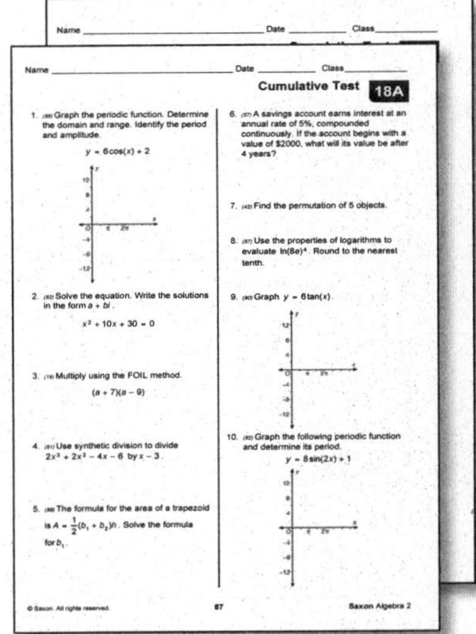

Name ______ Date ______ Class ______

Cumulative Test 18A

1. (86) Graph the periodic function. Determine the domain and range. Identify the period and amplitude.
   $y = 6\cos(x) + 2$
2. (82) Solve the equation. Write the solutions in the form $a + bi$.
   $x^2 + 10x + 30 = 0$
3. (19) Multiply using the FOIL method.
   $(a + 7)(a - 9)$
4. (81) Use synthetic division to divide $2x^3 + 2x^2 - 4x - 6$ by $x - 3$.
5. (86) The formula for the area of a trapezoid is $A = \frac{1}{2}(b_1 + b_2)h$. Solve the formula for b_1.
6. (57) A savings account earns interest at an annual rate of 5%, compounded continuously. If the account begins with a value of $2000, what will its value be after 4 years?
7. (42) Find the permutation of 5 objects.
8. (87) Use the properties of logarithms to evaluate $\ln(8e)^4$. Round to the nearest tenth.
9. (90) Graph $y = 6\tan(x)$.
10. (82) Graph the following periodic function and determine its period.
    $y = 8\sin(2x) + 1$

© Saxon. All rights reserved. 87 Saxon Algebra 2

After Lesson 100

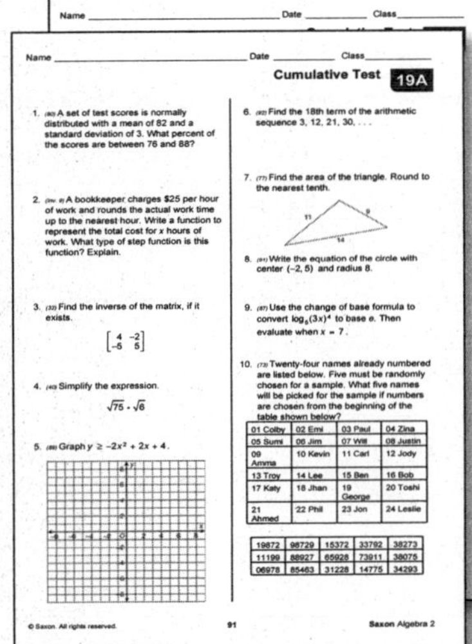

Name ______ Date ______ Class ______

Cumulative Test 19A

1. (80) A set of test scores is normally distributed with a mean of 82 and a standard deviation of 3. What percent of the scores are between 76 and 88?
2. (Inv. 8) A bookkeeper charges $25 per hour of work and rounds the actual work time up to the nearest hour. Write a function to represent the total cost for x hours of work. What type of step function is this function? Explain.
3. (32) Find the inverse of the matrix, if it exists.
   $\begin{bmatrix} 4 & -2 \\ -5 & 5 \end{bmatrix}$
4. (40) Simplify the expression.
   $\sqrt{75} \cdot \sqrt{6}$
5. (89) Graph $y \geq -2x^2 + 2x + 4$.
6. (92) Find the 18th term of the arithmetic sequence 3, 12, 21, 30, . . .
7. (77) Find the area of the triangle. Round to the nearest tenth.
8. (91) Write the equation of the circle with center $(-2, 5)$ and radius 8.
9. (87) Use the change of base formula to convert $\log_6(3x)^4$ to base e. Then evaluate when $x = 7$.
10. (73) Twenty-four names already numbered are listed below. Five must be randomly chosen for a sample. What five names will be picked for the sample if numbers are chosen from the beginning of the table shown below?

01 Colby	02 Emi	03 Paul	04 Zina
05 Sumi	06 Jim	07 Will	08 Justin
09 Amma	10 Kevin	11 Carl	12 Jody
13 Troy	14 Lee	15 Ben	16 Bob
17 Katy	18 Jhan	19 George	20 Toshi
21 Ahmed	22 Phil	23 Jon	24 Leslie

19872	98729	15372	33792	38273
11199	88927	65928	73911	38075
06978	85463	31228	14775	34293

© Saxon. All rights reserved. 91 Saxon Algebra 2

For use with Performance Tasks

Teacher Rubric

Criteria Performance	Knowledge and Skills Understanding	Communication and Representation	Process and Strategies
4	The student got it! The student did it in new ways and showed how it worked. The student knew and understood what math concepts to use.	The student clearly detailed how he/she solved the problem. The student included all the steps to show his/her thinking. The student used math language, symbols, numbers, graphs and/or models to represent his/her solution.	The student had an effective and inventive solution. The student used big math ideas to solve the problem. The student addressed the important details. The student showed other ways to solve the problem. The student checked his/her answer to make sure it was correct
3	The student understood the problem and had an appropriate solution. All parts of the problem are addressed.	The student clearly explained how he/she solved the problem. The student used math language, symbols, tables, graphs, and numbers to explain how he/she did the problem.	The student had a correct solution. The student used a plan to solve the problem and selected an appropriate strategy.
2	The student understood parts of the problem. The student started, but he/she couldn't finish.	The student explained some of what he/she did. The student tried to use words, symbols, tables, graphs and numbers to explain how he/she did the problem.	The student had part of the solution, but did not know how to finish. The student was not sure if he/she had the correct answer. The student needed help.
1	The student did not understand the problem.	The student did not explain how he/she solved the problem. He/she did not use words, symbols, tables or graphs to show how he/she	The student couldn't get started. The student did not know how to begin.

© Saxon. All rights reserved. x Saxon Algebra 2

SECTION OVERVIEW 10

LAB

13

Materials

- graphing calculator

Discuss

In this lab, students will graph conic sections through two different methods using the graphing calculator.

TEACHER TIP

Either method of graphing a conic section in this Lab may require changing the given equation. For graphing circles, solve the given equation for y. When graphing an equation that describes a conic section other than a circle, change the equation into polar form.

LAB

13

Graphing a Circle and a Polar Equation

Graphing Calculator Lab (*Use with Lessons 91, 96*)

Graphing Calculator

Refer to Calculator Lab 1 on page 19 for graphing a function.

Graphing a Circle in Function Mode

1. Enter the equation of the circle $(x-3)^2+(y-5)^2=21$ as the two functions, $y=\pm\sqrt{21-(x-3)^2}+5$.

a. Press Y= to access the Y= equation editor screen.

b. Type $\sqrt{21-(x-3)^2}+5$ into Y_1 and $-\sqrt{21-(x-3)^2}+5$ into Y_2

c. Press GRAPH to graph the functions.

d. Use the ZOOM or WINDOW button to adjust the window. The graph will have a more circular shape using ZOOM 5 rather than ZOOM 6.

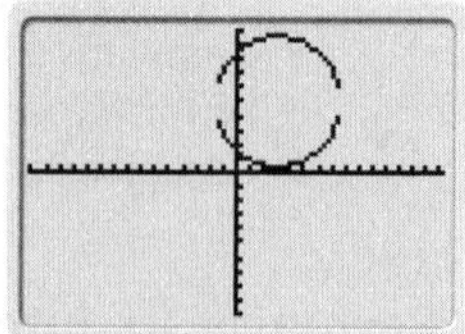

Graphing a Polar Equation

2. Change the mode of the calculator to polar mode.

a. Press MODE. Press ▼ two times to highlight **RADIAN,** and then press enter.

b. Press ▼ to **FUNC,** and then ▶ two times to highlight **POL,** and then press ENTER.

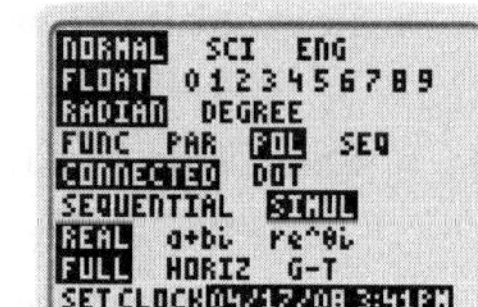

c. Press ▼ two more times to **SEQUENTIAL,** press ▶ to highlight **SIMUL,** and then press ENTER.

d. To exit the **MODE** menu, press 2nd MODE.

3. Enter the equation of the circle $(x-3)^2+(y-5)^2=34$ as the polar equation $r=6\cos\theta-10\sin\theta$.

a. Press Y= to access the r_1 = equation editor screen.

b. Type in $6\cos\theta-10\sin\theta$ into r_1 by pressing 6 COS X,T,θ,n) −

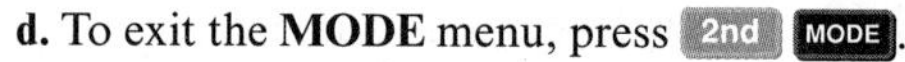

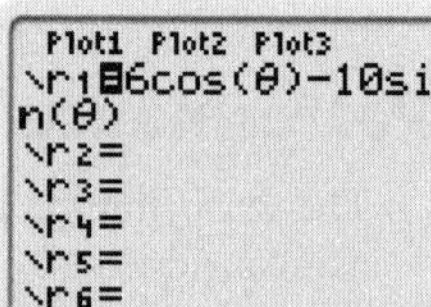

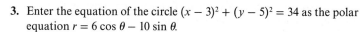

Online Connection
www.SaxonMathResources.com

638 Saxon Algebra 2

Graphing Calculator

When graphing an equation in **DEGREE** mode, set the θmin value to 0, the θmax value to 360, and the θstep to 1 to graph the entire equation with points at every degree.

4. Adjust the viewing window to polar values.

   a. Press WINDOW and type in the following values:

$\theta\text{min} = 0$	$\text{Xmin} = -16$	$\text{Ymin} = -15$
$\theta\text{max} = 2\pi$	$\text{Xmax} = 21$	$\text{Ymax} = 10$
$\theta\text{step} = \pi/16$	$\text{Xscl} = 1$	$\text{Yscl} = 1$

   A similar result may be obtained by pressing ZOOM 5.

   b. The θmin and θmax values determine the minimum and maximum input for the equation. The θstep value determines the increments of the input.

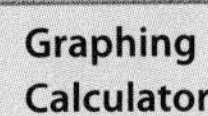

Graphing Calculator

The points on the graph are formed by the θstep values. Then, the points are connected with lines. For curved graphs choose small θstep values so that a smoother curve is produced.

5. Press GRAPH to graph the equation.

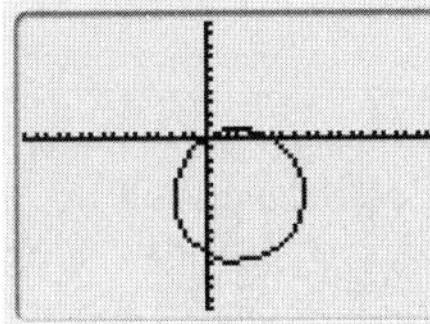

Lab Practice

a. Graph the equation of the circle $(x + 2)^2 + (y - 7)^2 = 14$ in function mode.

b. Graph the equation of the limacon $r = 1 + 3 \cos \theta$ using the given viewing window.

$\theta\text{min} = 0$	$\text{Xmin} = -2$	$\text{Ymin} = -3$
$\theta\text{max} = 2\pi$	$\text{Xmax} = 5$	$\text{Ymax} = 3$
$\theta\text{step} = \pi/16$	$\text{Xscl} = 1$	$\text{Yscl} = 1$

a.

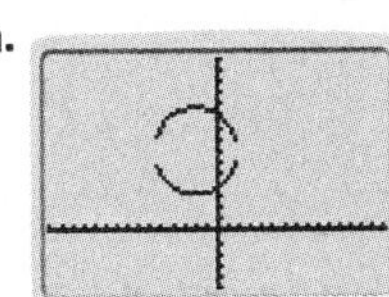

$-10 \le x \le 5;\ -2 \le y \le 14$

b.

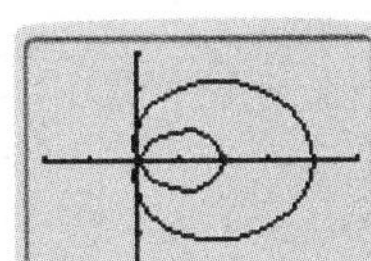

Practice Problem

Problem a

Scaffolding Have students change the equation so that it is written as two semicircle functions by solving the equation for y. Remind them to type each equation the Y= equation editor screen. When the two semicircles are graph they should form a circle.

LESSON 91

1 Warm Up

Use problems 2 and 3 in the Warm Up to review finding the distance between two points and to recall the rules for using the unit circle.

2 New Concepts

In this lesson, students learn the equation of a circle and how to graph a circle on the coordinate plane.

The circle is the first of four conic sections they will be studying.

Example 1

Students will graph a circle centered at the origin.

Additional Example 1

a. Sketch the graph of $x^2 + y^2 = 9$.

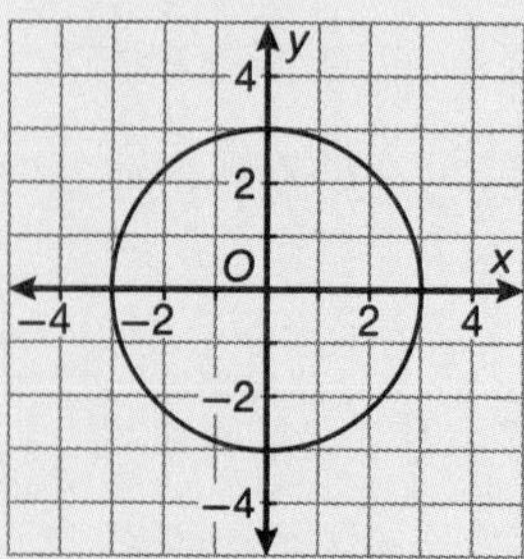

LESSON 91

Making Graphs and Solving Equations of Circles

Warm Up

1. (63) **Vocabulary** The radius of a circle is the distance from the center of the circle to any point on the circle.

2. (41) Find the length of the segment with endpoints at (3, 5) and (−10, 7). **2.** $\sqrt{173}$ units

3. (63) True or False: The unit circle passes through the point (1, 1). false

New Concepts

A **conic section** is a plane figure formed by the intersection of a double right cone and a plane. The circle is one of the four possible conic sections.

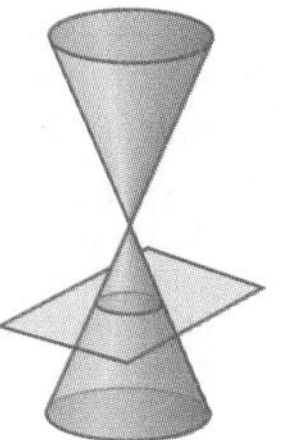

Math Language

A circle is formed by the intersection of right cone and a plane that is parallel to the base of the cone, except where the intersection is at the vertex of the cone.

A circle is not a function because it does not pass the vertical line test. If the center of the circle is located at (0, 0), then, using the Distance Formula, the radius of the circle is given by $r = \sqrt{(x - 0)^2 + (y - 0)^2}$. Simplifying the radicand and squaring both sides gives $r^2 = x^2 + y^2$.

The equation of a circle with center (0, 0) and radius r is

$$x^2 + y^2 = r^2.$$

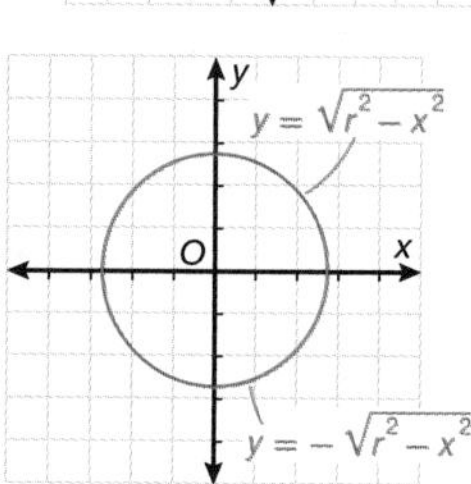

Math Reasoning

Justify A parabola is a conic section. How can a parabola be formed from a plane and a double-right cone?

One part of the cone is sliced by the plane at an angle.

The equation of a circle must be transformed into two functions in order to graph it on a graphing calculator in function mode. Isolate y and then enter the positive and negative square roots into the equation editor as two functions. The graphs of the two functions are semicircles that, together, form a circle.

$$x^2 + y^2 = r^2$$
$$y^2 = r^2 - x^2$$
$$y = \pm\sqrt{r^2 - x^2}$$

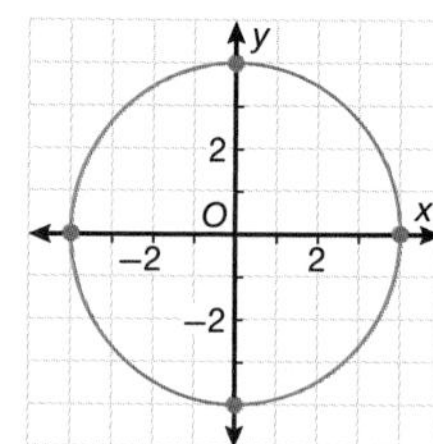

Example 1 Graphing Circles Centered at the Origin

a. Sketch the graph of $x^2 + y^2 = 16$.

SOLUTION 16 equals the value of the radius squared, so the radius is 4 units.

Step 1: Plot the center at (0, 0).

Step 2: Since the radius is 4, plot the points 4 units above, below, left, and right of the center.

Step 3: Sketch a circle that passes through the four points.

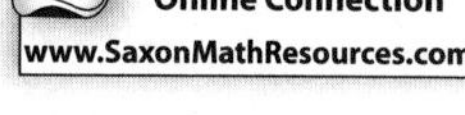

LESSON RESOURCES

Student Edition Practice Workbook 91
Reteaching Master 91
Adaptations Master 91
Challenge and Enrichment Master C91

MATH BACKGROUND

A circle is a set of points on a plane that all have the same distance from a common center. The distance between the center and any point on the circle is the radius of the circle. The center of the circle can be called the origin or the vertex of the circle.

The equation of the circle can be found by solving for the distance between the center and any point on the circle. The equation of the circle is then defined as $(x - h)^2 + (y - k)^2 = r^2$, where (h, k) is the center and r is the radius.

Graphing Calculator 

To keep the circle from looking distorted, press **ZOOM** and choose **ZSquare.**

b. Graph $x^2 + y^2 = 10$ on a graphing calculator.

SOLUTION Solve for y. Graph each of two resulting functions.

$$x^2 + y^2 = 10$$
$$y^2 = 10 - x^2$$
$$y = \pm\sqrt{10 - x^2}$$

```
Plot1 Plot2 Plot3
\Y1■√(10-X²)
\Y2■-√(10-X²)
\Y3=
\Y4=
\Y5=
\Y6=
\Y7=
```

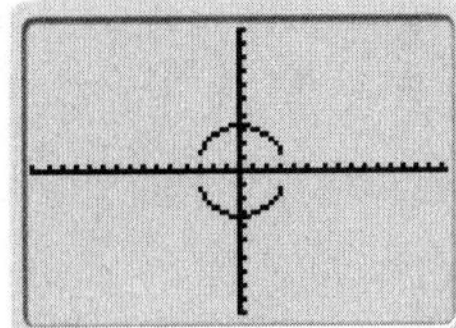

The center of the circle shown at right is located at (h, k).

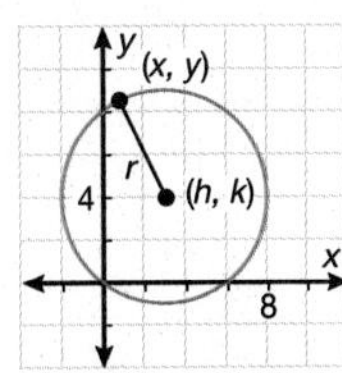

Using the Distance Formula, the radius of the circle is given by $r = \sqrt{(x - h)^2 + (y - k)^2}$. Squaring both sides gives $r^2 = (x - h)^2 + (y - k)^2$.

Standard Form of an Equation of a Circle
The equation of a circle with center (h, k) and radius r is $(x - h)^2 + (y - k)^2 = r^2$.

In order to graph a circle, the center and the radius of the circle must be determined.

Example 2 Graphing Circles Not Centered at the Origin

Hint

Be careful choosing the values of h and k, as the formula involves subtraction. Think:

$(x + 2)^2 = (x - (-2))^2$.

a. Sketch the graph of $(x + 2)^2 + (y - 1)^2 = 9$.

SOLUTION The radius is $\sqrt{9}$, or 3.

Step 1: Plot the center at $(-2, 1)$.

Step 2: Since the radius is 3, plot the points 3 units above, below, left, and right of the center.

Step 3: Sketch a circle that passes through these four points.

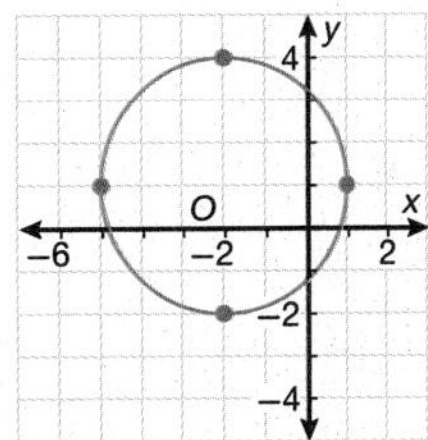

b. Graph $(x - 7)^2 + (y + 3)^2 = 15$ on a graphing calculator.

SOLUTION Solve for y. Graph each of the two resulting functions.

$$(y + 3)^2 = 15 - (x - 7)^2$$
$$y + 3 = \pm\sqrt{15 - (x - 7)^2}$$
$$y = \pm\sqrt{15 - (x - 7)^2} - 3$$

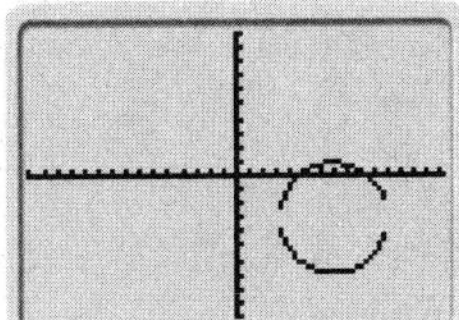

b. Graph $x^2 + y^2 = 20$ on a graphing calculator.

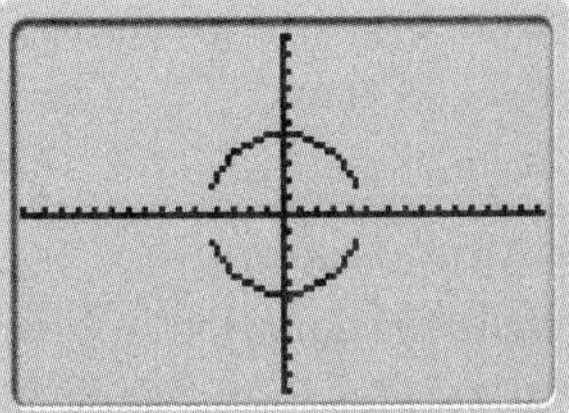

Example 2

Students will sketch graphs of circles that are not centered on the origin.

Additional Example 2

a. Sketch the graph of $(x + 4)^2 + (y - 3)^2 = 16$.

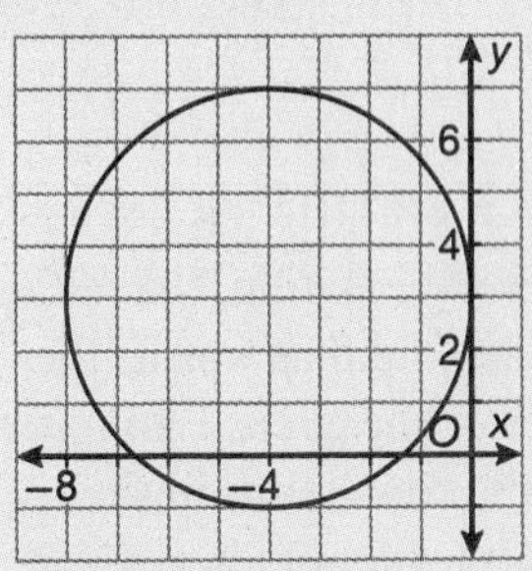

b. Graph $(x - 11)^2 + (y + 8)^2 = 11$ using a graphing calculator.

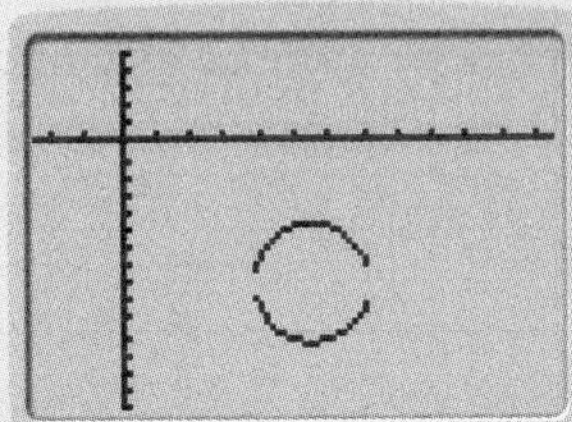

Error Alert When entering expressions for the semi-circles into the equation editor, students may enter the entire rule under the radicand. It may be easier for students to use the Commutative Property of Addition and write the number that is not under the radical symbol first.

Example 3

Students will determine the equation of a circle from the constraints given.

Additional Example 3

a. Write the equation of a circle with center $(-4, 5)$ and radius 5. $(x + 4)^2 + (y - 5)^2 = 25$

b. Write the equation of the circle with center $(3, -2)$ that contains the point $(-4, 2)$. $(x - 3)^2 + (y + 2)^2 = 65$

c. Write the equation of the circle that has a diameter whose endpoints are located at $(7, 5)$ and $(3, 3)$. $(x - 5)^2 + (y - 4)^2 = 5$

TEACHER TIP

For every equation, the radius must be found as well as the center of the circle. Emphasize that the constraints in the problem will not always give these requirements directly. They will have to be solved for using different methods such as the midpoint or distance formula.

Sometimes the center and the radius of a circle are not explicitly given, so it is necessary to use the Distance and/or Midpoint Formula to determine these unknown parts.

For a segment whose endpoints are at (x_1, y_1) and (x_2, y_2),

Distance Formula	Midpoint Formula
$d = \sqrt{(x_2 - x_1)^2 + (y_2 - y_1)^2}$	$M = \left(\frac{x_1 + x_2}{2}, \frac{y_1 + y_2}{2}\right)$

Example 3 Writing the Equation of a Circle

a. Write the equation of the circle with center $(-3, -1)$ and radius 7.

SOLUTION Substitute $h = -3$, $k = -1$, and $r = 7$ into $(x - h)^2 + (y - k)^2 = r^2$.

$$(x - (-3))^2 + (y - (-1))^2 = 7^2$$
$$(x + 3)^2 + (y + 1)^2 = 49$$

b. Write the equation of the circle with center $(-2, 4)$ that contains the point $(5, 2)$.

SOLUTION Find the length of the radius by using the Distance Formula.

$$r = \sqrt{(5 - (-2))^2 + (2 - 4)^2}$$
$$= \sqrt{7^2 + (-2)^2}$$
$$= \sqrt{53}$$

Substitute $h = -2$, $k = 4$, and $r = \sqrt{53}$ into $(x - h)^2 + (y - k)^2 = r^2$.

$$(x - (-2))^2 + (y - 4)^2 = \left(\sqrt{53}\right)^2$$
$$(x + 2)^2 + (y - 4)^2 = 53$$

c. Write the equation of the circle that has a diameter whose endpoints are located at $(3, 1)$ and $(6, 3)$.

SOLUTION The center of the circle is midway between the endpoints of a diameter. Use the Midpoint Formula.

$$M = \left(\frac{x_1 + x_2}{2}, \frac{y_1 + y_2}{2}\right) = \left(\frac{3 + 6}{2}, \frac{1 + 3}{2}\right) = (4.5, 2)$$

Find the distance between the center and either of the points on the circle.

$$r = \sqrt{(3 - 4.5)^2 + (1 - 2)^2}$$
$$= \sqrt{3.25}$$

Substitute $h = 4.5$, $k = 2$, and $r = \sqrt{3.25}$ into $(x - h)^2 + (y - k)^2 = r^2$.

$$(x - 4.5)^2 + (y - 2)^2 = \left(\sqrt{3.25}\right)^2$$
$$(x - 4.5)^2 + (y - 2)^2 = 3.25$$

Hint

The radius will always be greater than 0. A radius less than or equal to 0 indicates an error.

INCLUSION

Have the students draw all the given points on a graph. Next, have them solve for necessary constraints, which are the center and the radius of the circle. Once the radius and center have been found, have them substitute the solved values into the equation. Solving graphically, may help ease the transition for learners.

Example 4 Application: Astronomy

The orbit of Earth around the Sun resembles a circle. Given that Earth travels about 584.3 million miles in one orbit, write an equation for the circle that models Earth's orbit around the Sun.

Hint

$C = \pi d$ can also be written as $C = 2\pi r$.

SOLUTION The distance Earth travels in one orbit is the circumference of the circle, and $C = \pi d$. Let the Sun be at (0, 0) on the coordinate plane, where a unit represents one million miles. Find the diameter and divide by 2 to find the radius.

$$C = \pi d$$

$584.3 \approx \pi d$ Substitute 584.3 for C.

$185.988 \approx d$ Divide both sides by π.

Divide the diameter by 2 to find the radius: $r \approx 92.994 \approx 93$.
Write the equation of the circle. Substitute $r = 93$ in $x^2 + y^2 = r^2$.

$x^2 + y^2 = 93^2 \rightarrow x^2 + y^2 = 8649$

The equation $x^2 + y^2 = 8649$ models Earth's orbit around the Sun, where the Sun is located at (0, 0).

Lesson Practice

a. (Ex 1) Sketch the graph of $x^2 + y^2 = 36$. See Additional Answers.

b. (Ex 1) Graph $x^2 + y^2 = 25$ on a graphing calculator. See Additional Answers.

c. (Ex 2) Sketch the graph of $(x - 5)^2 + (y - 3)^2 = 4$. See Additional Answers.

d. (Ex 2) Graph $(x + 8)^2 + (y - 1)^2 = 22$ on a graphing calculator. See Additional Answers.

e. (Ex 3) Write the equation of the circle with center (6, −7) and radius 9.

e. $(x - 6)^2 + (y + 7)^2 = 81$

f. (Ex 3) Write the equation of the circle with center (7, −4) that contains the point (8, 1). $(x - 7)^2 + (y + 4)^2 = 26$

g. (Ex 3) Write the equation of the circle that has a diameter whose endpoints are located at (−2, 3) and (4, 9). $(x - 1)^2 + (y - 6)^2 = 18$

h. (Ex 4) The orbit of Venus around the Sun resembles a circle. Given that Venus travels about 421 million miles in one orbit, write an equation for the circle that models Venus's orbit around the Sun. $x^2 + y^2 = 4489$, where the Sun is located at (0, 0)

Practice Distributed and Integrated

1. (70) **Geometry** The radius of a sphere is given by $r = \sqrt[3]{\frac{3V}{4\pi}}$, where V is the volume of the sphere. Approximate the volume of a sphere with a radius of 4.5 centimeters. about 381.7 cm^3

***2.** (91) **Multi-Step** The map of a town is placed on a coordinate grid. A radio station's transmitter is located at (0, 2), and the signal can be picked up by anyone within 95 miles of the transmitter. Write the equation of the circle that represents the broadcast area for the station's signal. Show how to use the equation to prove that a person located at (94, 6) can pick up the signal. See Additional Answers.

ENGLISH LEARNERS

For Example 4, explain the meaning of the word **resemble.** Say:

"To resemble means to look similar to something. For the play, the students painted trees on a large piece of cloth to resemble a forest."

Have students list other props they could use in a play to resemble real objects. Sample: aluminum foil crown to resemble silver crown

Example 4

Students will use the equation of a circle and apply it to a real world application.

Extend the Example

If the sun's position shifted from the origin to 20 million miles in the positive x direction and 30 million miles in the positive y direction, what would be Earth's now orbit equation?
$(x - 20)^2 + (y - 30)^2 = 8649$

Additional Example 4

Similarly to Earth's orbit, the moon travels 29,516 km around Earth every month. Derive an equation for the orbit of the moon assuming it is circular.
$x^2 + y^2 = 22{,}071{,}204$

Lesson Practice

Problem d

Error Alert Students may use 22 rather than $\sqrt{22}$ for the radius. Remind students to take the square root of the entire expression.

Problem g

Scaffolding Begin by finding the midpoint of this diameter, which is the center. Next, find the distance of the radius using the distance formula between the center and one of the points given. Substitute the center and radius values found into the circle equation.

Check for Understanding

The questions below help assess the concepts taught in this lesson.

"What two constraints must be found in order to write the equation for a circle?"
Sample: The center of the circle and the radius must be found.

"How can you graph a circle using a graphing calculator?"
Sample: Solve for y and enter each semicircle function into the graphing calculator.

3 Practice

Math Conversations

Discussions to strengthen understanding

Problem 3

To complete the square, divide the middle term by two and square the value. This will give the number that is needed to be added to both sides of the equation. Remind students to account for the constant term of 2.

Problem 10

Extend the Example

"To shift the graph to the left in the x direction, what must h be?"
negative

"To shift the graph up in the y direction what must k be?"
positive

Problem 13

Error Alert

Students may add incorrectly if they do not find a common denominator before adding. Have the students find a common denominator with a new corresponding numerator then add the numerators together.

3. (58) Given that $x^2 - 5x + 2 = 0$, what needs to be added to both sides of the equation to get a perfect square on the left side? $\frac{17}{4}$

4. (71) Solve $\triangle ABC$. $A \approx 37.6°, B \approx 38.4°, a \approx 15.7$

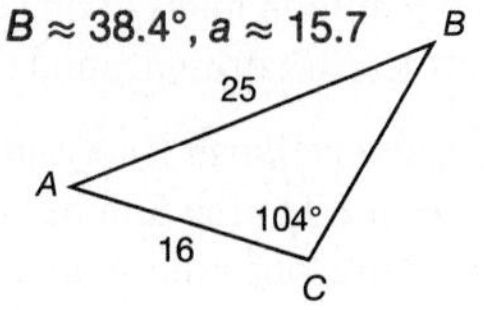

5. (63) A spiral staircase has 15 steps. Each step is a sector with a radius of 42 inches and a central angle of $\frac{\pi}{8}$. What is the length of the arc formed by the outer edge of a step? about 16.5 in.

***6.** (90) **Error Analysis** Two students are finding the period of $y = \tan\left(\frac{3}{5}x\right)$ but get different results. Which student made the mistake?

Student A	Student B
Period $= \frac{2\pi}{b} = \frac{2\pi}{\frac{3}{5}} = \frac{10\pi}{3}$	Period $= \frac{\pi}{b} = \frac{\pi}{\frac{3}{5}} = \frac{5\pi}{3}$

6. Student A uses the incorrect formula for finding the period of a tangent function.

7. (78) **Multi-Step** For each value of the leading coefficient a, write the quadratic function in the form $y = ax^2 + c$ that has zeros -2 and 2. (Hint: The value of c can be positive or negative.)

a. $a = 1$ $y = x^2 - 4$ **b.** $a = \frac{1}{2}$ $y = \frac{1}{2}x^2 - 2$ **c.** $a = -1$ $y = -x^2 + 4$

d. Graph the functions on the same coordinate system. See Additional Answers.

e. How many quadratic functions exist that have two given zeros? an infinite number

8. (55) A random number generator will output integers from 1 to 100. What is P(multiple of 5) with the generation of the first number? 0.2

9. (63) Find the arc length of a sector with a radius of 8 inches and a central angle of 110°. about 15.4 in.

***10.** (91) **Generalize** What must be true about the values of h and k for a circle whose center is located in Quadrant II? h must be negative and k must be positive.

11. (75) Explain why $f(x) = \sqrt{3x} + 5$ is a radical function. Sample: The function rule is a radical expression that contains a variable in the radicand.

***12.** (91) The endpoints of a diameter are located at $(-2, -1)$ and $(4, -1)$. Write an equation for this circle. $(x - 1)^2 + (y + 1)^2 = 9$

13. (84) **Optics** The focal length of a lens, f, the distance from the lens to the object, o, and the distance from the lens to the image, i, are related by the formula $\frac{1}{f} = \frac{1}{o} + \frac{1}{i}$. Find f if o is 12 inches and i is 8 inches. 4.8 inches

14. (83) **Analyze** How is deriving a quadratic equation from two identical roots different from deriving a quadratic equation from two unique roots?

14. Sample: In standard form, one side of the equation derived from the identical roots is a perfect square trinomial.

CHALLENGE

Rearrange the equation of the circle below so that the center and radius can be identified. Then identify them.

$$x - \sqrt{23 - \left(y - \sqrt{10}\right)^2} = \sqrt{3}$$

$$\left(x - \sqrt{3}\right)^2 + \left(y - \sqrt{10}\right)^2 = 23$$

The center is $\left(\sqrt{3}, \sqrt{10}\right)$.

$r = \sqrt{23}$

644 Saxon Algebra 2

15. (73) **Sports** A sports columnist wants to survey college basketball coaches about whether they think women's basketball nets should be raised to the same measure as in men's basketball. The writer mails out surveys to all the coaches and uses only the surveys that are returned. Identify the type of sample described. Since the coaches can choose whether or not to respond, the sample is a self-selected sample.

***16.** (83) Write a quadratic equation whose roots are $7 + 3i$ and $7 - 3i$. $x^2 - 14x + 58 = 0$

Find the roots of the polynomial function.

17. (76) $f(x) = 15x^3 + 3x^2 - 6x$
$x = 0, \frac{-1 \pm \sqrt{41}}{10}$

18. (76) $f(x) = (x + 1)(4x^2 + 4) - (x + 1)(2x - 3)$
$x = -1$

***19.** (90) **Verify** Let $f(x) = \cos(x)$ and $g(x) = \tan(x)$. Compare the graph of $f(x)\,g(x)$ and $h(x) = \sin(x)$. The graph of $f(x)\,g(x)$ is identical to the graph of $h(x)$, but it is not defined at $(2n + 1)\frac{\pi}{2}$, for integer values of n.

***20.** (90) Identify the period and undefined values of $y = \tan(12x) + 3$. period: $\frac{\pi}{12}$; undefined values: $\frac{\pi}{24} + n\frac{\pi}{12}$

21. (71) **Surveying** A surveyor stands on the east end of a boardwalk and finds that the angle formed by the boardwalk and the line of sight with a lighthouse is 76°. The surveyor then walks to the west end and finds the angle formed by the boardwalk and lighthouse to be 60°. Estimate the closest distance from the boardwalk to the lighthouse, given that the boardwalk has a length of 2700 feet. about 3266 feet

***22.** (91) **Graphing Calculator** Graph $(x - 1)^2 + (y + 9)^2 = 7$ on a graphing calculator. Use the Trace feature to find the y-intercepts. (0, −6.55051) and (0, −11.44949)

23. (77) **Geography** A map of southeast Illinois shows that Flora is 44.4 miles from Carmi and 42.6 miles from Mt. Carmel. Mt. Carmel is 34.4 miles from Carmi. Find the number of square miles enclosed in the triangle that is formed when lines connecting these three cities are drawn. Round to the nearest square mile.
686 mi^2

24. (80) **College Admissions** In 2005, the mean score on the ACT reading test was 21.3 with a standard deviation of 6. The mean score on the mathematics test was 20.7 with a standard deviation of 5. Assume both distributions are normally distributed. Who would you say performed better: a student who got a score of 27 on the reading test or a student who got a score of 24 on the math test? Why?

24. the student who took the reading test; The reading score is 0.95 standard deviations above the mean, while the math score is only 0.66 deviations above the mean.

25. (79) Evaluate the piecewise function $f(x) = \begin{cases} 8, & \text{if } x \le 0 \\ 3x - 1, & \text{if } x > 0 \end{cases}$ for $x = -0.4$, $x = 0$, and $x = 6$. $f(x) = 8, 8, 17$

26. (81) **Multiple Choice** Which is equal to $\ln e^{x^2}$? **B**
A $2x$ **B** x^2 **C** $2 \ln x$ **D** $\ln 2e^x$

***27.** (85) **Formulate** Find the roots of $(x^3)^3 - a^3$. The polynomial has one root: $x = \sqrt[3]{a}$.

28. (78) **Probability** The right triangle is inscribed in the circle. Suppose a point is chosen at random inside the circle. What is the probability that the chosen point is NOT inside the triangle? $1 - \frac{1}{\pi} \approx 0.682$

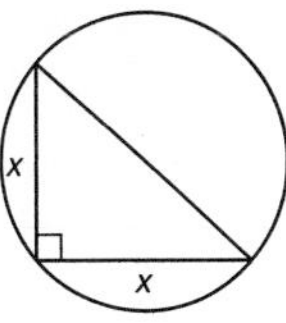

***29.** (88) **Write** Explain why $F = \frac{9}{5}C + 32$ and $C = \frac{5}{9}(F - 32)$ describe the same relationship between F and C. Sample: If you solve $F = \frac{9}{5}C + 32$ for C, the result is $C = \frac{5}{9}(F - 32)$.

30. (56) P is a point on the terminal side of θ in standard position. Find the exact value of the six trigonometric functions for θ where $P(-8, -8)$. See Additional Answers.

Problem 17

Set the polynomial equal to zero, then solve for x. Factor out common terms. Then, solve by completing the square, factoring into two terms, or using the quadratic formula. Since the leading term of the polynomial is an x^3 term, then there should be three roots.

Problem 22

Remember, circles cannot be graphed as written in most graphing calculators. The variable y must be solved for first. This should give two answers; a positive and negative square root function. Plug both of these equations into the graphing calculator to form the circle. Then use the Trace function to solve for the y-intercepts.

LOOKING FORWARD

Making graphs and solving equations of circles prepares students for

- **Lesson 96** Using Polar Coordinates
- **Lesson 109** Making Graphs and Using Equations of Hyperbolas
- **Lesson 114** Identifying Conic Sections

LESSON 92

1 Warm Up

Review function terminology.

A function $y = f(x)$ has ordered pairs (x, y).	
Domain	Range
Input	Output
x	y

2 New Concepts

In this lesson, students learn that an arithmetic sequence is formed by *adding* the same number (the common *difference d*) to any term to get the next term. They learn to use the explicit formula for an arithmetic sequence: $a_n = a_1 + (n - 1)d$.

Example 1

Students find the next three terms of an arithmetic sequence.

Additional Example 1

Find the common difference of the arithmetic sequence and use it to find the next three terms.

50, 38, 26, 14, ... 2, −10, −22

LESSON 92 Finding Arithmetic Sequences

Warm Up

1. **Vocabulary** In a function, the ___domain___ (*domain*|*range*) is made up of the input values. (4)

2. Solve $18 = 6 + 2(n - 1)$. $n = 7$ (7)

3. True or False: The answer to a subtraction problem is called the difference. (SB) true

New Concepts

Exploration **Exploring Sequences**

In a DVD club, a member receives 8 DVDs the first month and 3 DVDs every month thereafter.

Step 1: Complete the table.

Month	1	2	3	4	5
Total Number of DVDs	8	11	14	17	20

Step 2: Describe a pattern in the total number of DVDs. 3 more than the previous month

Step 3: Find the total number of DVDs for months 6, 7, and 8. 23, 26, 29

Step 4: Graph the data. What type of function models the data? Why? What is the domain of the function? See Additional Answers.

A **sequence** is an ordered list of numbers. Each number in the sequence is a **term.** A sequence can be **finite** {2, 4, 6, 8}, or **infinite** {5, 15, 45, 135, ...}.

Sequences can be written as functions, where the domain is the set of natural numbers and the range is the set of terms. It is common to use the function name of a for a sequence with the term number, or domain, written as a subscript. Therefore a_1 is the first term of a sequence, a_2 is the second term, and a_n is the nth term.

Math Reasoning

Justify Show that {5, 15, 45, 135, ...} is not an arithmetic sequence.

The differences are 10, 30, and 90, which are not the same.

If the differences between the consecutive terms in a sequence are the same, then the sequence is an **arithmetic sequence.** The finite sequence {2, 4, 6, 8} is arithmetic because the difference between any two consecutive terms is 2.

The difference of 2 is called the common difference. The **common difference** of any arithmetic sequence is found by subtracting any term from its successive term. It can be used to extend an infinite sequence.

Example 1 Identifying and Using the Common Difference

Find the common difference of the arithmetic sequence and use it to find the next three terms.

−14, −9, −4, 1, ...

SOLUTION Subtract a term from the term that follows it: $1 - (-4) = 5$.

Find the next three terms by adding 5: $1 + 5 = 6$, $6 + 5 = 11$, and $11 + 5 = 16$.

The next three terms are 6, 11, and 16.

LESSON RESOURCES

Student Edition Practice Workbook 92
Reteaching Master 92
Adaptations Master 92
Challenge and Enrichment Masters C92, E92
Technology Lab Master 92

MATH BACKGROUND

A sequence can be thought of as a function, where in each ordered pair, the second element is a term of the sequence, and the first element is the ordinal position of the term. For example, the sequence {2, 4, 6, 8} in ordered pair notation is {(1, 2), (2, 4), (3, 6), (4, 8)}. The domain of an infinite sequence is the entire set of natural numbers, and the domain of a finite sequence is a subset of the natural numbers.

Below are some different, but equivalent, explicit formulas for an arithmetic sequence.

$a_n = a_1 + (n - 1)d$; a_1 is the first term, a_n is the nth term, and $n \geq 1$.

$a_n = a_0 + nd$; a_0 is the first term, a_{n-1} is the nth term, and $n \geq 0$.

$a_n = a_m + (n - m)d$; a_m is any term, $n \geq 0$, and $m \geq 0$.

Math Language

To find the nth term using a *recursive formula*, the previous term must be known. The recursive formula is $a_n = a_{n-1} + d$.

An **explicit formula** defines the *n*th term of a sequence in terms of *n*, meaning that the *n*th term can be found without knowing the previous term.

For the arithmetic sequence {10, 14, 18, 22, 26, ...},

$a_1 = 10 + \mathbf{0}(4)$, $a_2 = 10 + \mathbf{1}(4)$, $a_3 = 10 + \mathbf{2}(4)$, $a_4 = 10 + \mathbf{3}(4)$, $a_5 = 10 + \mathbf{4}(4), \ldots a_n = 10 + (n-1)4$.

Arithmetic Sequence
The *n*th term of an arithmetic sequence is given by $a_n = a_1 + (n-1)d$.

Example 2 Finding the *n*th Term of an Arithmetic Sequence

(a.) Find the 15th term of the arithmetic sequence 4, 15, 26, 37, ...

SOLUTION Find d: $37 - 26 = 11$. Then use the formula $a_n = a_1 + (n-1)d$.

$a_{15} = 4 + (15-1)11$ — Substitute 15 for n, 4 for a_1, and 11 for d.

$a_{15} = 158$ — Simplify.

(b.) Find the 18th term of the arithmetic sequence 11, 5, −1, −7, ...

SOLUTION Find d: $5 - 11 = -6$. Then use the formula $a_n = a_1 + (n-1)d$.

$a_{18} = 11 + (18-1)(-6)$ — Substitute 18 for n, 11 for a_1, and −6 for d.

$a_{18} = -91$ — Simplify.

The formula $a_n = a_m + (n-m)d$ can be used to find any term when given any two terms of the sequence.

Example 3 Finding the *n*th Term Given Any Two Terms

(a.) Find a_1 of an arithmetic sequence given that $a_7 = 34$ and $a_{16} = 61$.

SOLUTION In the formula $a_n = a_m + (n-m)d$, replace m with 7 and n with 16.

$a_{16} = a_7 + (16-7)d$

$61 = 34 + (16-7)d$ — Substitute a_{16} with 61 and a_7 with 34.

$61 = 34 + 9d$ — Solve for d.

$27 = 9d$

$3 = d$

Now find a_1. Use the formula $a_n = a_1 + (n-1)d$ and either of the known terms.

$61 = a_1 + (16-1)3$ — Substitute 61 for a_n and 16 for n.

$61 = a_1 + 45$ — Solve for a_1.

$16 = a_1$

The first term of the sequence is 16.

Check by using a_1 to find the 7th term: $a_7 = 16 + (7-1)3 = 16 + 18 = 34$.

Example 2

Students use the explicit formula $a_n = a_1 + (n-1)d$ to find a specified term, given the first few terms in an arithmetic sequence.

Extend the Example

Have students use the recursive formula $a_n = a_{n-1} + d$ to find the 16th term in Example 2a. 169

Additional Example 2

a. Find the 12th term of the arithmetic sequence 8, 17, 26, 35, ... 107

b. Find the 20th term of the arithmetic sequence 51, 45, 39, 33, ... −63

Error Alert When finding the common difference, students might subtract in the wrong order. Remind them to write the two consecutive terms in the reverse of the listed order.

Example 3

Students are given two non-consecutive terms in an arithmetic sequence, and use them to find a specified term in the sequence.

Additional Example 3

a. Find a_1 of an arithmetic sequence given that $a_9 = 22$ and $a_{20} = 66$. −10

ENGLISH LEARNERS

Discuss these everyday meanings of **sequence**:

- the following of one thing after another
- an ordered collection of things

Explain that a sequence in mathematics is an ordered list of numbers in which the same rule determines what number follows any number in the list.

Ask students to connect the everyday meanings of sequence to the mathematical meaning of sequence. For example, a password that is used to access an account can be considered a sequence because the order of the characters in the password is important.

b. Find a_{13} of an arithmetic sequence given that $a_7 = -243$ and $a_{24} = -345$. −279

Error Alert When modifying the formula $a_n = a_1 + (n - 1)d$, remind students that when they replace a_1 with a known term, they must replace the subscript with the index of that known term.

Example 4

Students use an arithmetic sequence to solve a problem about regular salary increases.

Extend the Example

Have students find the year in which the employee's salary is $57,540. 21st year

Additional Example 4

Suppose you deposit the same amount each month in a bank account that does not earn interest. At the end of the sixth month, there is $566 in the account. At the end of the twentieth month, there is $1056 in the account. How much was in the account at the end of the first month? $391

Math Reasoning

Analyze How can you tell that the common difference will be a positive number before doing any calculations?

The 12th term is greater than the 5th term.

b. Find a_8 of an arithmetic sequence given that $a_5 = -180$ and $a_{12} = -138$.

SOLUTION In the formula $a_n = a_m + (n - m)d$, replace m with 5 and replace n with 12.

$a_{12} = a_5 + (12 - 5)d$

$-138 = -180 + (12 - 5)d$ Substitute a_{12} with −138 and a_5 with −180.

$-138 = -180 + 7d$ Solve for d.

$42 = 7d$

$6 = d$

Now find a_8. Use $a_n = a_m + (n - m)d$, replacing m with 8, 6 for d, and using one of the given terms.

$a_{12} = a_8 + (12 - 8)(6)$ Use $n = 12$.

$-138 = a_8 + (12 - 8)(6)$ Substitute a_{12} with −138.

$-138 = a_8 + 24$ Solve for a_8.

$-162 = a_8$

The eighth term of the sequence is −162.

Since the eighth and twelfth terms are not too far from the fifth term, the answer could be checked by adding the common difference of 6.

a_5	a_6	a_7	$\mathbf{a_8}$	a_9	a_{10}	a_{11}	$\mathbf{a_{12}}$
−180	−174	−168	**−162**	−156	−150	−144	**−138**

Example 4 Application: Salary

Richard's salary is structured so that after the first year, he receives an annual raise of a set amount. What was his starting salary if his salary in his fourth year was $41,135 and his salary in his fourteenth year was $50,785?

SOLUTION

Substitute the given information into the formula $a_n = a_m + (n - m)d$. Replace a_m with a_4, or 41,135, m with 4, a_n with a_{14}, or 50,785, and n with 14.

$50{,}785 = 41{,}135 + (14 - 4)d$

$50{,}785 = 41{,}135 + 10d$

$9650 = 10d$

$965 = d$

Find a_1.

$50{,}785 = a_1 + (14 - 1)965$

$50{,}785 = a_1 + 12{,}545$

$38{,}240 = a_1$

Richard's starting salary was $38,240.

Check Use a_1 to find the 4th term: $a_4 = 38{,}240 + (4 - 1)965 = 41{,}135$.

Math Reasoning

Formulate Study what is being done to find d and formulate a way to find it without writing an equation.

Subtract the term values and divide by the difference of the positions of the terms.

648 Saxon Algebra 2

Lesson Practice

a. Find the common difference of the arithmetic sequence $9\frac{1}{2}$, $10\frac{1}{4}$, 11, $11\frac{3}{4}$, ... Then, find the next three terms. (Ex 1) $d = \frac{3}{4}$; $12\frac{1}{2}$, $13\frac{1}{4}$, 14

b. Find the 44th term of the arithmetic sequence −121, −112, −103, −94, ... (Ex 2) 266

c. Find the 33rd term of the arithmetic sequence 0.56, 0.38, 0.2, 0.02, ... (Ex 2) −5.2

d. Find a_1 of an arithmetic sequence given that $a_3 = 33$ and $a_7 = 63$. (Ex 3) 18

e. Find a_3 of an arithmetic sequence given that $a_7 = 75$ and $a_{12} = -125$. (Ex 3) 235

f. Beverly's salary is structured so that after the first year, she receives an annual raise of a set amount. What was her starting salary if her salary in her sixth year was $31,975 and her salary in her thirteenth year was $36,420? (Ex 4) $28,800

Practice Distributed and Integrated

*1. **Formulate** Give an example of a sequence that is formed by adding numbers in a pattern but is not arithmetic. (92) Sample: 1, 2, 4, 7, 11, 16

2. **Home Maintenance** A homeowner can rake and bag the leaves in his yard in 5 hours. If he works with his children, the job can be done in 3 hours. How long would it take for just the children to rake and bag the leaves in the yard? (84) 7.5 hours

*3. **Multiple Choice** What is the 40th term of the arithmetic sequence whose first term is 13 and whose second term is 15.5? (92) C

A 97.5 B 100 C 110.5 D 123.5

4. **Multi-Step** Find the radical function that is the inverse of $y = x^2 - 6x + 9$. Identify its domain and range. (75) $y = \sqrt{x} + 3$; domain: $x \geq 0$, range: $y \geq 3$

5. Evaluate the inverse trigonometric function $\cos^{-1}(-1)$. Give your answer in both radians and degrees. (67) π; 180°

6. **Write** Describe the characteristics of a data set that is normally distributed. (80)

6. Sample: When graphed, the data is single-peaked, bell-shaped, and symmetric about the mean. 68% of the data is within one standard deviation of the mean, 95% of the data is within two standard deviations of the mean, and 99.7% of the data is within three standard deviations of the mean.

*7. **Coordinate Geometry** If $A(5, 2)$ and $B(-4, -3)$ are the endpoints of a diameter of a circle, what is the equation of the circle? (91) $(x - 0.5)^2 + (y + 0.5)^2 = 26.5$

*8. Write the equation for a circle centered at (2, −9) with a radius of 3. (91) $(x - 2)^2 + (y + 9)^2 = 9$

9. **Geometry** A geometry teacher has a database with 400 problems about triangles. Can she choose a sample of questions by using a stratified sampling method where the strata are *right triangles, isosceles triangles,* and *scalene triangles*? Why or why not? (73) No. The strata are not mutually exclusive. A triangle can be both right and isosceles or both right and scalene.

INCLUSION

To help students remember the correct order of subtraction for finding a common difference, write several terms of an arithmetic sequence on index cards, one term on each card. Then have students use their hands to choose two consecutive terms and reverse their order.

Lesson Practice

Problem b

Error Alert Students might think that d should be negative because the terms are negative. Show that the terms are increasing: $-121 + 9 = -112$.

Check for Understanding

The questions below help assess the concepts taught in this lesson.

"How are terms in an arithmetic sequence related?" Sample: The difference between two consecutive terms is the same as the difference between any two other consecutive terms.

"What does each variable represent in the formula $a_n = a_1 + (n - 1)d$?" Sample: a_n represents the nth term in an arithmetic sequence, a_1 represents the 1st term, n represents the position of the nth term, and d represents the common difference.

3 Practice

Math Conversations

Discussions to strengthen understanding

Problem 5

Guide students by asking them the following questions.

"How do you read the inverse trigonometric function given in the problem?" inverse cosine of negative one

"Identify the degree measures of several angles in standard position whose cosine is −1." Sample: 180°, −180°, 540°

"What is the only angle in the range of the inverse cosine function whose cosine is −1?" π; 180°

Problems 16 and 17

Remind students that the zero(s) of the polynomial $f(x)$, the root(s) of the equation $f(x) = 0$, and the x-intercept(s) of the graph of $f(x)$ are all different names for the same number(s).

Problem 19

Discuss why $a_6 = 359$. Begin by asking what term number is represented after one hour of driving.

10. (76) **Physics** A satellite in orbit accelerates according to the equation acceleration $= \frac{v^2}{r}$, for orbital speed v and distance from Earth's center r. Two satellites are in orbit, one at a distance of r and the other at a distance of $2r$. How fast should the outer satellite travel to have the same acceleration as the inner satellite? speed of outer satellite $= \sqrt{2}$ (speed of inner satellite)

11. (69) Multiply $(3 + i)(1 - 4i)$. Write the result in the form $a + bi$. $7 - 11i$

12. (77) **Multiple Choice** Which triangle cannot be solved by using the Law of Cosines? C

A
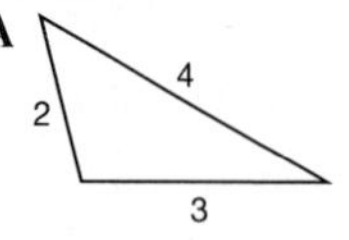

B
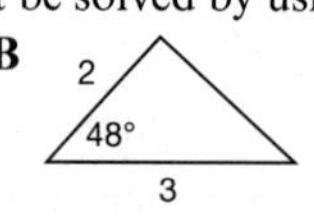

C
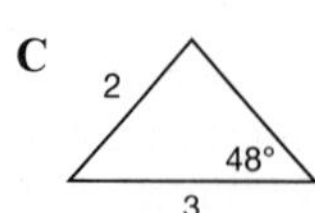

D
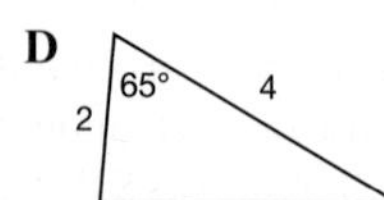

13. (81) **Multi-Step** Technetium-99m, a radioisotope used to image the skeleton and the heart muscle, has a half-life of about 6 hours.

a. How long will it take for 1 mg of technetium-99m to decay to 0.2 mg? (Use the natural decay function $N(t) = N_0 e^{-kt}$.) about 13.93 hours

b. On a calculator, graph the function $y_1 = 1 \cdot e^{-kx}$, using the value of k you found in part **a.** Also graph the functions $y_2 = 0.5$ and $y_3 = 0.2$. (suggested window values: x [−1, 20] and y [−0.1, 1.1]) See Additional Answers.

c. Describe what is represented by the relationships among the graphs of y_1, y_2, and y_3. See Additional Answers.

14. (79) **Delivery Charges** A furniture store delivers up to 4 items for a \$75 delivery charge. There is an additional charge of \$25 per item for each additional item delivered. Write a piecewise function for the cost of having x items delivered. $f(x) = \begin{cases} 75 & x \le 4 \\ 75 + 25(x - 4) & x > 4 \end{cases}$

***15.** (92) Find the 17th term of the arithmetic sequence 4, 21, 38, … 276

Find the roots of the polynomials.

16. (58) $y = 4x^2 + 5x - 1$ $x \approx 0.1754$ and -1.4254

17. (76) $y = x^4 - 16$ $x = 2$ and -2

18. (85) **Geometry** A rectangular prism has a volume of $3x^3 - 8x^2 + 3x + 2$. Find the linear dimensions. $(3x + 1)$, $(x - 1)$, and $(x - 2)$

***19.** (92) **Travel** A driver on the Pennsylvania turnpike turned on the cruise control at milepost 30, Warrendale, and kept it on until milepost 359, the Delaware River Bridge, exactly 5 hours later. Show how to use an arithmetic sequence to find the speed at which the car traveled during those 5 hours. $a_6 = a_1 + (6 - 1)(d)$; $359 = 30 + 5d$; $329 = 5d$; $65.8 = d$; The speed was 65.8 miles per hour.

***20.** (86) **Graphing Calculator** Graph $y = 5\cos 2(x - 3\pi)$ using a graphing calculator. Determine its period and phase shift. $p = \pi$, shift $= 3\pi$

***21.** (87) **Verify** Show that $\log_5 (125x)^2$ equals 8 when $x = 5$. $\log_5 (125x)^2 = 2(\log_5 125 + \log_5 5) = 2(3 + 1) = 8$

22. (57) A principal amount of \$1,500 earns interest at an annual rate of 2.7%, compounded monthly. What will its value be after 7 years? \$1,811.68

CHALLENGE

Find the sum of all the terms in each sequence. (Hint: For each sequence, form pairs that have the same sum.)

a. 2, 4, 6, 8, …, 20
5 × 22 = 110

b. 2, 4, 6, 8, …, 100
25 × 102 = 2550

c. 2, 4, 6, 8, …, 1000
250 × 1002 = 250,500

*23. **Write** When solving a quadratic inequality, what is meant by the *critical values*?
(89)

24. Solve $6t^2 + 5 = 2t^2 + 1$. Write the solution in terms of i. $\pm i$
(62)

25. **Analyze** Which equations have the same solutions as $x^2 - 8x + 7 = 0$?
(83)

$-x^2 + 8x - 7 = 0$ $\quad -x^2 + 8x + 7 = 0$ $\quad -2x^2 + 8x - 7 = 0$

$2x^2 - 8x + 14 = 0$ $\quad 2x^2 - 16x + 14 = 0$

$-x^2 + 8x - 7 = 0$; $2x^2 - 16x + 14 = 0$

Write the exponential equation in logarithmic form or vice versa.

26. $11^4 = 14{,}641$ $\quad \log_{11} 14{,}641 = 4$
(64)

27. $\log_9 729 = 3$ $\quad 9^3 = 729$
(64)

*28. **Basketball** A drafter is creating the plans for a sport and fitness center, which includes an official-size basketball court. On her grid, the units represent feet. The center of the basketball court's center circle is located at $(-14, -1)$, and another point on the center circle is located at $(-14, 2)$. Write an equation for this circle. $(x + 14)^2 + (y + 1)^2 = 9$
(91)

29. **Error Analysis** A student found that the discriminant of a quadratic equation was 0 and therefore the number of solutions of the equation was also 0. Correct the student's reasoning.
(74)

30. Solve by completing the square: $4x^2 = -12x + 4$. $\quad x = -\frac{3}{2} \pm \frac{\sqrt{13}}{2}$
(78)

23. Sample: The critical values are the values that separate a number line into regions that contain solutions and regions that do not contain solutions. They are the intersection points of the graph on the left side of the inequality and the graph on the right side of the inequality.

29. A discriminant of 0 means that nothing is added or subtracted from $-b$. It is just divided by $-2a$. This result is therefore the one real solution of the equation.

Problem 28

Ask students how they can find the radius without using the distance formula.

Subtract the y-coordinates because the x-coordinates are the same.

LOOKING FORWARD

Finding arithmetic sequences prepares students for

- **Lesson 97** Finding Geometric Sequences
- **Lesson 105** Finding Arithmetic Series
- **Lesson 113** Using Geometric Series

LESSON 93

1 Warm Up

Use problems 2 and 3 to review exponential expressions.

2 New Concepts

In this lesson, students learn to solve application problems by solving exponential equations and inequalities.

Example 1

Additional Example 1

a. Solve for x: $5^{x-2} = 125$ $x = 5$

b. Solve for x: $4^x = 32^{x-2}$ $x = 4$

c. Solve for x: $3^{x+1} = \frac{1}{27}$ $x = -4$

LESSON RESOURCES

Student Edition Practice Workbook 93
Reteaching Master 93
Adaptations Master 93
Challenge and Enrichment Master C93

LESSON 93

Solving Exponential Equations and Inequalities

Warm Up

1. (3) **Vocabulary** In the expression $(1.005)^x$, the ___base___ is 1.005.
2. (47) What is the base in the expression $240(1.022)^x$? 1.022
3. (47) What is the base in the expression $50(1 + 0.04)^x$? $1 + 0.04$

New Concepts

Exponential equations cannot always be solved using the same properties that are used to solve linear equations. One property that can be used to solve simple exponential equations is the Property of Equality.

Math Language

An equation that contains one or more exponential expressions is an exponential equation.

Property of Equality for Exponential Functions
If a is any positive number other than 1 and $a^x = a^y$, then $x = y$.

To apply the property of equality, each side of the equation must be written with the same base, a. If they are not written in the same base, they must be written as a power of the same base.

Hint

Review Lesson 3 to read about the rules of exponents that are necessary to solve exponential equations like these.

Example 1 Using the Property of Equality

a. Solve for x: $2^x = 16$

SOLUTION

Write 16 as an exponent with a base of 2.

$16 = 2^4$

Therefore, $2^x = 2^4$.

By the Property of Equality, $x = 4$.

b. Solve for c: $9^{c+2} = 27^2$

SOLUTION

Both sides of the equation can be written with a base of 3.

$9^{c+2} = (3^2)^{c+2} = 3^{2c+4}$

$27^2 = (3^3)^2 = 3^6$

By the Property of Equality, $2c + 4 = 6$, so $c = 1$.

c. Solve for t: $2^t = \frac{1}{16}$

SOLUTION

It may seem like the right side of this equation cannot be written as a power of 2, but recall that it is in fact a negative power of 2.

$\frac{1}{16} = 2^{-4}$

By the Property of Equality, $t = -4$.

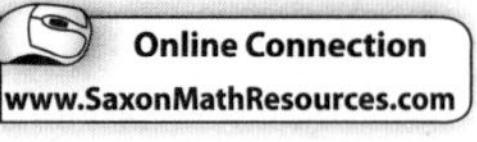
Online Connection
www.SaxonMathResources.com

MATH BACKGROUND

Students learn two methods that can be used to solve differential equations in this lesson. The first method is to rewrite base of an exponent as a common power so that both sides of the equation can be compared directly. This approach can usually be done without a calculator and is often faster.

The second approach is to take the logarithm or natural logarithm of both sides of an equation. This approach usually requires a calculator but can be used to solve a broader range of problems. It is very important to master this method, as it is used extensively in several areas of higher mathematics.

Another way to solve an exponential function is to apply the Power Property of Logarithms. Recall from Lesson 72 that the Power Property of Logarithms says that $\log a^p = p \log a$.

To apply the Power Property, take the logarithm of both sides of an exponential equation and simplify the result.

Example 2 Solving by Taking the Logarithm of Each Side

Hint

Don't forget the product and quotient rules of logarithms, which may also be useful in simplifying exponential equations as you solve them.

a. Solve for x: $200 = 1.05^x$

SOLUTION

$200 = 1.05^x$	
$\log 200 = \log 1.05^x$	Take the logarithm of both sides.
$\log 200 = x \log 1.05$	Apply the Power Property.
$x = \frac{\log 200}{\log 1.05}$	Divide by log 1.05.
$x \approx 108.59$	Evaluate.

b. Solve for y: $7^{2y+1} = 4^{-y}$

SOLUTION

$4^{-y} = 7^{2y+1}$	
$\log 4^{-y} = \log 7^{2y+1}$	Take the logarithm of both sides.
$-y \log 4 = (2y + 1)\log 7$	Apply the Power Property.
$-y \log 4 = 2y \log 7 + \log 7$	Distribute.
$-y \log 4 - 2y \log 7 = \log 7$	Subtract $2y$ log 7 from each side.
$y(-\log 4 - 2 \log 7) = \log 7$	Factor.
$y = \frac{\log 7}{(-\log 4 - 2 \log 7)}$	Division Property of Equality.
$y \approx -0.37$	Evaluate.

If e is used in an exponential equation, solve the equation by taking the natural log of both sides. Recall the inverse property of logarithms: $\ln e^x = x$.

Example 3 Solving Exponential Equations with *e*

a. Solve for x: $5 = 6e^x$

SOLUTION

$6e^x = 5$	
$\ln 6e^x = \ln 5$	Take the logarithm of both sides.
$\ln 6 + \ln e^x = \ln 5$	Apply the Product Property.
$\ln 6 + x = \ln 5$	Apply the Inverse Property.
$x \approx -0.18$	Subtract and evaluate.

Example 2

In this example, students solve exponential equations by taking a logarithm of both sides of the equation.

Additional Example 2

a. Solve for r: $5^r = 8(5)^{2r}$ $r \approx 1.29$

b. Solve for m: $2^{2m-1} = 3^{m+2}$
$m \approx 10.05$

Example 3

In this example, students apply the Inverse Property of Logarithms to solve equations that include e.

Additional Example 2

Solve for x: $3e^x = 12e^{2x}$
$x \approx -1.39$

Example 4

Students use logarithms to solve exponential inequalities.

Extend the Example

For Example 3a, have students enter the function $y = 2^{n-1}$ into a graphing calculator and use the TABLE feature to find that 1.34E8 is the approximate function value for $n = 28$. Elicit that $1.34E8 = 1.34 \times 10^8$, which represents 134,000,000 cents, or \$1,340,000.

Additional Example 4

a. Suppose a web site receives 1 hit on the first day, 3 hits on the second day, and so on, receiving triple the number of hits on each new day. What is the first day on which the web site will receive more than 10 million hits? day 16

b. An appliance dealer wants to sell an oven to clear out her inventory. She marks down the price 5% at the beginning of every day. The regular price of the oven is \$329.99. She marks down the price the first time on day 1. On what day will the price first be below \$100? day 24

Error Alert There are several ways that students are likely to get an incorrect value for the expression log(50) – log(199.50) ÷ log(0.90) Here is one possible *incorrect* expression: log(50) – log(199.50) ÷ log(0.90)

Here is an example of a *correct* expression:
(log (50) – log (199.50)) ÷ log (0.90).

Example 4 Solving Exponential Inequalities

a. Suppose you receive a gift of 1 cent on the first day, 2 cents on the second day, and so on, receiving double the amount on each new day. What is the first day on which you will receive more than \$1 million?

SOLUTION \$1 million = \$1,000,000 = 100,000,000 cents = 10^8 cents

On day 1 you receive 2^0 cents, on day 2 you receive 2^1 cents, and so on, receiving 2^{n-1} cents on day n.

$2^{n-1} > 10^8$	Write an inequality.
$\log 2^{n-1} > \log 10^8$	Take the logarithm of both sides.
$\log 2^{n-1} > 8$	Simplify.
$(n-1)\log 2 > 8$	Apply the Power Property of Logarithms.
$n - 1 > \frac{8}{\log 2}$	Divide both sides by log 2.
$n > \frac{8}{\log 2} + 1 \approx 27.6$	Use a calculator to approximate.

The first day on which you will receive more than \$1 million is day 28.

Check Day 27: 2^{26} cents = 67,108,864 cents = \$671,088.64

Day 28: 2^{27} cents = 134,217,728 cents = \$1,342,177.28

b. A merchant is having trouble selling a jacket and decides to mark down the price 10% at the beginning of every day. The regular price of the jacket is \$199.50. He marks the price down for the first time on day 1. On what day will the price first be below \$50?

SOLUTION The price on day n is $199.50(1 - 0.10)^n$, or $199.50(0.90)^n$.

$199.50(0.90)^n < 50$	Write an inequality.
$\log [199.50(0.90)^n] < \log 50$	Take the common logarithm of both sides.
$\log 199.50 + \log (0.90)^n < \log 50$	Apply the Product Property of Logarithms.
$\log (0.90)^n < \log 50 - \log 199.50$	Subtract log 199.50 from both sides.
$n \log (0.90) < \log 50 - \log 199.50$	Apply the Power Property of Logarithms.
$n > \frac{\log 50 - \log 199.50}{\log 0.90}$	Divide both sides by log 0.90 and reverse the inequality symbol.
$n > 13.13$	Use a calculator to approximate.

The price will first be below \$50 on day 14.

Caution

Know the sign of a logarithm if you divide both sides of an inequality by that logarithm. log m is negative if $0 < m < 1$. log m is positive if $m > 1$.

ALTERNATE METHOD FOR EX. 4

In each problem in Example 4, an equation could be solved instead of an inequality, and an appropriate analysis of the context would lead to the correct answer. For instance, in Example 4a, the solution to $2^{n-1} = 10^8$ is $n = \frac{8}{\log 2} + 1 \approx 27.6$. In the context of the problem, the day number must be 28.

ALTERNATE METHOD FOR EX. 4b

$$199.50(0.90)^n < 50$$

$$(0.90)^n < \frac{50}{199.50}$$

$$\log(0.90)^n < \log \frac{50}{199.50}$$

$$n\log(0.90) < \log \frac{50}{199.50}$$

$$n > \frac{\log \frac{50}{199.50}}{\log (0.90)} \approx 13.13$$

Example 5 Application: Compound Interest

How long will it take an investment to double in value at 9% interest compounded quarterly (4 times per year)?

SOLUTION $A = P\left(1 + \frac{r}{n}\right)^{nt}$ Write the compound interest formula.

$2P = P\left(1 + \frac{0.09}{4}\right)^{4t}$ Substitute 2*P* for *A* because *P* will double. Substitute 0.09 for *r* and 4 for *n*.

$2 = (1.0225)^{4t}$ Divide both sides by *P* and simplify.

$\log 2 = \log (1.0225)^{4t}$ Take the common logarithm of both sides.

$\log 2 = 4t \log (1.0225)$ Apply the Power Property of Logarithms.

$\frac{\log 2}{4 \log (1.0225)} = t$ Divide both sides by 4 log 1.0225.

$t \approx 7.79$ years Use a calculator to approximate.

The interest is compounded quarterly, so the compounding will likely occur when t has these values: 7, 7.25, 7.50, 7.75, and 8. The value of the investment will not have doubled when $t = 7.75$, but it will have more than doubled when $t = 8$.

Check When $t = 7.75$: $A = P\left(1 + \frac{0.09}{4}\right)^{(4)(7.75)} = P(1.0225)^{31} \approx 1.993P$

When $t = 8$: $A = P\left(1 + \frac{0.09}{4}\right)^{(4)(8)} = P(1.0225)^{32} \approx 2.038P$

Graphing Calculator Tip 

The expression log (2) ÷ 4 log (1.0225) is NOT correct for solving Example 4 because it equals $\left(\frac{\log 2}{4}\right)$ (log 1.0225). A correct expression is log (2) ÷ (4 log (1.0225)).

Lesson Practice

Solve for the variable in each equation.

a. $49^{2y} = 343^{2y+3}$ $y = -4.5$ (Ex 1)

b. $3^r = 9^5$ $r = 10$ (Ex 1)

c. $25^t = \frac{1}{25}$ $t = -1$ (Ex 1)

d. $45 = 2.3^{2x}$ $x \approx 2.29$ (Ex 2)

e. $3e^{2c+1} = 432$ $c \approx 1.98$ (Ex 3)

f. (Ex 4) Stock in a certain company was purchased on December 31, 2007, for $1.50 per share. Suppose the price of a share doubles every year. What is the first year in which the price of a share will be greater than $90? 2013

g. (Ex 4) The regular price of a rug is $325. The price is marked down 6% at the beginning of each week, beginning with week 1. In what week will the price first be below $200? week 8

h. (Ex 5) How long will it take an investment to increase 50% in value at 4.8% interest compounded monthly (12 times per year)? 8.46 years, or about 8 years and 6 months

ENGLISH LEARNERS

Explain the meaning of the word **quarterly**. Say:

"If something happens quarterly, it happens four times a year. The root of the word comes from quarter, meaning one-fourth of something."

Quarterly is often used to talk about interest and other financial events. Have students brainstorm to come up with some more words that are used to describe the periodic compounding of interest and define them. Examples include annually, monthly, and bi-annually.

Example 5

Students substitute values into the general compound interest formula and solve the resulting equation to find how long it takes a certain investment to double in value.

Extend the Example

Have students find how many years it takes an investment to double in value at 9% interest compounded monthly, daily, and continuously. Have them obtain answers with 4 decimal places for comparison purposes.
monthly: 7.7305 years
daily: 7.7026 years
continuously: 7.7016 years

Additional Example 5

How long will it take an investment to increase 50% in value at 6% interest compounded monthly? approximately 6.77 years

Lesson Practice

Problem e

Scaffolding Remind students that there are two possible ways they could solve this problem. Once they take the natural log of both sides, they may see immediately that $\ln e^{2c+1} = 2c + 1$. For students who do not make the connection, encourage them to expand the expression using the rules of exponents. Once they have done so and found that this will also simplify to $2c + 1$, go back and remind them that $\ln e^x = x$.

Check for Understanding

The questions below help assess the concepts taught in this lesson.

"If an exponential equation has a constant on one side, how can you solve the equation by graphing?" Sample: Graph a function for the constant, graph a function for the expression on the other side, and then find the point of intersection.

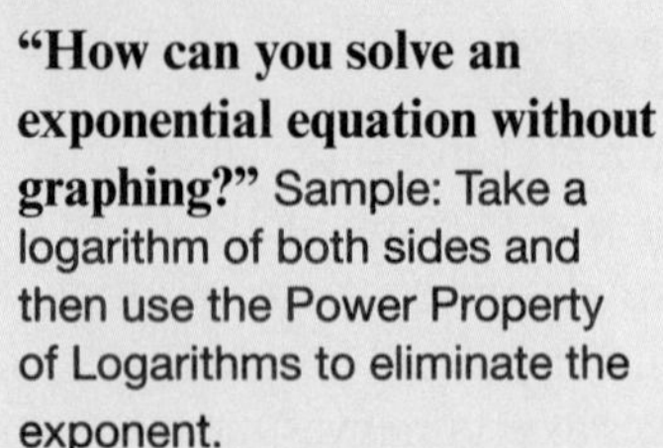

"How can you solve an exponential equation without graphing?" Sample: Take a logarithm of both sides and then use the Power Property of Logarithms to eliminate the exponent.

3 Practice

Math Conversations

Discussions to strengthen understanding

Problem 2

Error Alert

Students sometimes try to divide out *log* as shown below.

$$1.4 = 1.06^x$$

$$\log 1.4 = \log 1.06^x$$

$$\log 1.4 = x \log 1.06$$

$$\frac{\not{\log} 1.4}{\not{\log} 1.06} = x$$

$$\frac{1.4}{1.06} = x$$

Remind them that log does not represent a number; it is the name of a function.

Another error is to incorrectly apply the Quotient Property of Logarithms:

$$\frac{\log 1.4}{\log 1.06} = x$$

$$\log 1.4 - \log 1.06 = x$$

Remind students of the correct property:

$\log \frac{m}{n} = \log m - \log n.$

Problem 3

Guide students by asking them the following questions.

"What value will you substitute for h_0, and why?" 14.4, because the initial height is the height from which the object is dropped

"What value will you substitute for $h(t)$, and why?" 0, because the height is 0 when the object hits the ground

"What value will you substitute for v_0, and why?" 0, because the object is dropped, and therefore there is no initial velocity

Practice Distributed and Integrated

1. (73) **Fast Food** At a fast food restaurant, each take-out order has a ticket in the bottom of the bag asking customers to call an 800 number to register for a prize drawing. Describe the individuals in the population and in the sample. population: all the customers who order take-out; sample: the ones who call the number

***2.** (93) **Multiple Choice** Which equation is equivalent to $1.4 = 1.06^x$? D

A $x = 1.4 - 1.06$ **B** $x = \log 1.4 - \log 1.06$ **C** $x = \frac{1.4}{1.06}$ **D** $x = \frac{\log 1.4}{\log 1.06}$

3. (78) **Gravity** The height of a free-falling object (neglecting air resistance) is given by the function $h(t) = -4.9t^2 + v_0t + h_0$, where h_0 is the initial height in meters, v_0 is the initial velocity in meters per second, and $h(t)$ is the height in meters at time t seconds. How long does it take for an object to hit the ground after it is dropped from a height of 14.4 meters? $\frac{12}{7} \approx 1.71$ seconds

***4.** (92) **Verify** The first term of an arithmetic sequence is 19 and the common difference is 9. Show that the 13th term is 127. $a_{13} = 19 + (12)(9) = 19 + 108 = 127$

***5.** (92) **Geometry** A cube has 6 sides. When two cubes are joined together, the figure has 10 sides. When three cubes are joined together, to form a row, there are 14 sides. Show how to use an arithmetic sequence to find the number of sides in a row of 20 cubes joined together. $a_{20} = 6 + (20 - 1)(4)$; $a_{20} = 82$

Determine the domain and range for each of the following.

6. (75) $y = -3\sqrt[3]{x}$ domain and range: all real numbers

7. (75) $y = (x + 1)^{\frac{1}{2}} + 8$ domain: $x \geq -1$, range: $y \geq 8$

***8.** (92) Find the common difference and use it to find the next three terms. 4, 6.5, 9, ... 11.5, 14, 16.5

***9.** (91) **Science** Vredefort is an impact crater located in South Africa. Given that its circumference is about 942.5 kilometers, write an equation for the circle that represents the rim of the crater, assuming the center is located at the origin of a coordinate plane. $x^2 + y^2 = 22{,}500$

***10.** (93) Solve for x: $4^{3x-6} = 32^{x+4}$ $x = 32$

11. (84) **Generalize** Describe two ways to find the solution(s) of $\frac{3}{3x+9} + \frac{2}{3} = x - 1$ on a graphing calculator. See Additional Answers.

***12.** (90) **Graphing Calculator** Graph $y = \tan(2x + 3)$ on your graphing calculator. Identify its period, undefined values, and phase shift. period: $\frac{\pi}{2}$; undefined values: $\frac{\pi}{4} - \frac{3}{2} + n\frac{\pi}{2}$; phase shift: $\frac{3}{2}$

***13.** (89) **Tourist Attractions** The world's largest pair of cowboy boots are located outside of a mall in San Antonio, Texas. The boots are 40 feet tall. Suppose a painter at the top of a boot drops a paintbrush. The height of the brush, in feet, after x seconds, is modeled by $y = -16x^2 + 40$. Write and solve a quadratic inequality that can be solved to find the time span for which the brush is above a second painter located 20 feet beneath the first painter. Round to the nearest hundredth of a second. $-16x^2 + 40 > 20$, between 0 and 1.12 seconds after the drop

***14.** (93) **Depreciation** A truck is purchased for \$18,500 on January 2, 2007. Its value decreases 16% each year. In what year will its value first be less than \$2,000? 2020

CHALLENGE

Solve $e^{2x} - 5e^x + 6 = 0$.

(Hint: $e^{2x} = (e^x)^2$)

$x = \ln 2 \approx 0.693$, $x = \ln 3 \approx 1.099$

15. **Multi-Step** The formula for the area of a sector of a circle is $A = \frac{\theta r^2}{2}$, where θ is the central angle measure in radians and r is the radius.
(88)

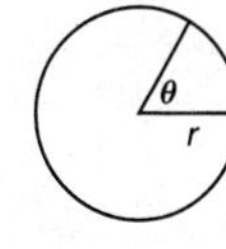

a. A landscape architect wants to create a flower bed in the shape of a sector of a circular ring, as shown by the shaded region. Write a formula for the area S of a sector of a circular ring. $S = \frac{\theta R^2 - \theta r^2}{2}$

b. Solve the formula you wrote in part **a** for θ. $\theta = \frac{2S}{R^2 - r^2}$

c. The landscape architect wants the area S of the flower bed to be 200 square feet, with $R = 25$ feet and $r = 10$ feet. Determine the necessary angle measure θ and then convert it to the nearest degree. 0.76 radian ≈ 44°

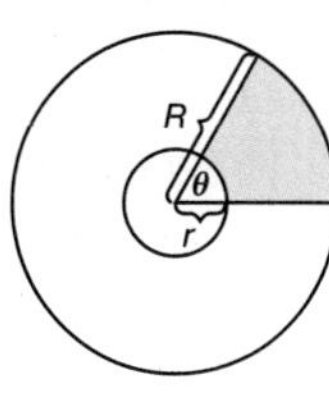

16. **Error Analysis** A student rewrote the expression $\log_8 (3x)$ as $\frac{\ln 8}{\ln 3 + \ln x}$.
(87)

a. Describe the student's error. The student switched the numerator and denominator in the change of base formula.

b. Rewrite the original expression correctly. $\frac{\ln 3 + \ln x}{\ln 8}$

17. **Analyze** Consider the polynomial function $f(x) = ax^2 + bx + c$. Suppose that the polynomial is divisible by $\left(x - \frac{c}{a}\right)$. Use synthetic division to show that $a + b + c = 0$.
(85)
See Additional Answers.

18. Which of the following has a period of 2π? **C**
(82)

A $y = \sin(2\pi x)$ **B** $y = \sin(\pi x)$ **C** $y = \sin(x)$ **D** $y = \sin\left(\frac{x}{2}\right)$

*19. **Estimate** Thallium has a half-life of 73.1 hours. Estimate how long it will take for 1 gram of thallium to decay to 0.26 gram. Explain your method.
(93)

19. Sample: 145 hours; It would take 2 x 73.1 = 146.2 hours for 1 gram to decay to 0.25 gram, so it would take slightly less than 146.2 hours for 1 gram to decay to 0.26 gram.

Solve to the nearest tenth using the given restrictions.

20. $\sin \theta = 0.95$, for $-90° \le \theta \le 90°$ 71.8°
(67)

21. $\cos \theta = -0.181$, for $180° \le \theta \le 360°$ 259.6°
(67)

Determine the domain and range of each function.

22. $f(x) = \begin{cases} 0, & \text{if } x < 0 \\ 3, & \text{if } x \ge 0 \end{cases}$
(79)
domain: all real numbers; range: {0, 3}

23. $f(x) = \begin{cases} x, & \text{if } 0 < x < 10 \\ 10, & \text{if } x \ge 10 \end{cases}$
(79)
domain: $x > 0$; range: $0 < x \le 10$

Solve the following equations.

24. $3x^4 = 12x^3 - 9x^2 + 6x$ $x = 0, 3.27$
(76)

25. $x^3 = 2x^4 - 5x^2 + 4x$ $x = 0, 1, \frac{-1 \pm \sqrt{33}}{4}$
(76)

26. **Generalize** Given that a, b, c, and d are real numbers, explain why $(x - a)(x - b) = 0$ and $(cx - ca)(dx - db) = 0$ have the same roots. What are the roots?
(83)

26. The left side of $(cx - ca)(dx - db) = 0$ can be factored and the equation written as $c(x - a)d(x - b) = 0$ and $cd(x - a)(x - b) = 0$, where cd is a real number not equal to zero. Using the Zero Product Property, both equations have roots of a and b.

27. Given $N(t) = 0.6$, $N_o = 1$, $k = 0.6372$, write the decay function and solve for t.
(81)
$0.6 = e^{-0.6372t}$, $t = 0.802$

28. Write a quadratic equation whose roots are −5 and 4. $x^2 + x - 20 = 0$
(83)

29. **Error Analysis** A student says that the roots of the equation $x^4 - 81 = 0$ are −3 and 3. What complex roots were left out? $-3i$ and $3i$.
(78)

30. **Probability** The area under a normal curve is the probability that a randomly selected data value from that data set falls within that interval. Suppose the weights of cereal boxes have a mean of 15.5 ounces with a standard deviation of 0.4 ounces. What is the probability that a randomly selected box of cereal weighs less than 14.7 ounces? 0.025 or 2.5%
(80)

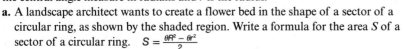

Problem 19

Ask these questions to give students a hint:

"How long will it take for 1 gram of thallium to decay to 0.5 gram?" 73.1 hours

"What is half of 0.5?" 0.25

Problems 22 and 23

Extend the Problem

Determine the domain and range of the function.

$f(x) = \begin{cases} x^2 + 1, & \text{if } x > 0 \\ |x| + 1, & \text{if } x \le 0 \end{cases}$

domain: all real numbers; range: $\{y \mid y \ge 1\}$

LOOKING FORWARD

Solving exponential equations and inequalities prepares students for

- **Lesson 102** Solving Logarithmic Equations and Inequalities
- **Lesson 110** Graphing Logarithmic Functions

LESSON 94

1 Warm Up

Before students begin problem 2, have them solve the equation algebraically.

2 New Concepts

In this lesson, students solve rational inequalities using the LCD, using sign tables, and using a calculator. They also solve rational inequalities by finding the values of test points.

Point out the steps of solving rational inequalities. If necessary, review how to solve rational equations algebraically.

Example 1

Discuss both cases to consider: $x + 2 > 0$ or $x + 2 < 0$.

Additional Example 1

Solve $\frac{5}{x+3} < 7$ by using the LCD. $x < -3$ or $x > -\frac{16}{7}$

LESSON RESOURCES

Student Edition Practice Workbook 94
Reteaching Master 94
Adaptations Master 94
Challenge and Enrichment Master C94

LESSON 94 Solving Rational Inequalities

Warm Up

1. **Vocabulary** To clear the fractions in a rational equation, multiply both sides of the equation by the ________. least common denominator
(84)

2. Solve $\frac{2x}{x+5} = 14$ by using a graphing calculator. $x = -5.833333$
(84)

3. Solve $x^2 + 10x < -16$ algebraically. $-8 < x < -2$
(89)

New Concepts

A **rational inequality** is an inequality that contains at least one rational expression. They can be solved algebraically or graphically. When a rational inequality is solved by using the LCD, the LCD could be positive or negative.

Math Reasoning

Analyze What is the restricted value of the inequality in Example 1?

-2

Example 1 Solving Rational Inequalities Using the LCD

Solve $\frac{6}{x+2} < 8$ by using the LCD.

SOLUTION Case 1: The LCD is positive.

Step 1: The LCD is $x + 2$. Since it is positive, $x + 2 > 0$, so $x > -2$.

Step 2: Multiply both sides of the inequality by $x + 2$.

$$(x+2)\frac{6}{x+2} < 8(x+2)$$

$6 < 8x + 16$ Simplify.

$-10 < 8x$ Solve for x.

$x > -1.25$

The solution must satisfy both $x > -2$ from Step 1 and $x > -1.25$ from Step 2, therefore, $x > -1.25$.

Case 2: The LCD is negative.

Step 1: The LCD is $x + 2$. Since it is negative, $x + 2 < 0$, so $x < -2$.

Step 2: Multiply both sides of the inequality by $x + 2$.

$(x+2)\frac{6}{x+2} > 8(x+2)$ Reverse the inequality sign.

$6 > 8x + 16$ Simplify.

$-10 > 8x$ Solve for x.

$x < -1.25$

The solution must satisfy both $x < -2$ from Step 1 and $x < -1.25$ from Step 2, therefore, $x < -2$.

Combine the solutions from both cases: $x < -2$ or $x > -1.25$.

Math Reasoning

Justify Why did the direction of the sign change in Case 2?

Both sides of an inequality are multiplied by a negative number.

Online Connection
www.SaxonMathResources.com

MATH BACKGROUND

Solving rational inequalities combines knowledge of solving rational equations and solving inequalities. Polynomials can be in the numerator or denominator of a rational inequality, and thus, factoring skills are also involved.

As with solving quadratic inequalities, rational inequalities can be solved by finding critical values, or boundary points, and testing a point in each interval they form. Recall that one side must be equal to 0 to find the critical values.

Example 2 Solving Rational Inequalities by Finding the Values of Test Points

Solve $\frac{x+4}{x^2+x-6} \leq 0$ by finding the values of test points.

SOLUTION The right side is already 0. Find the boundary points.

Factor. Find the values that make either the numerator or denominator 0.

$$\frac{x+4}{(x-2)(x+3)} \leq 0$$

The numerator is 0 when $x = -4$. The denominator is zero when $x = 2$ or $x = -3$.

The boundary points are -4, -3, and 2. This gives four intervals to test. Use < or > for the asymptotes of 2 and -3. These values are restricted because they make the fraction undefined.

Interval	Test Value	Is the test value a solution?
$x \leq -4$	-5	$\frac{-5+4}{(-5)^2+(-5)-6} \stackrel{?}{\leq} 0$ $-\frac{1}{14} \leq 0$ Yes
$-4 \leq x < -3$	-3.5	$\frac{-3.5+4}{(-3.5)^2+(-3.5)-6} \stackrel{?}{\leq} 0$ $\frac{2}{11} \leq 0$ No
$-3 < x < 2$	0	$\frac{0+4}{0^2+0-6} \stackrel{?}{\leq} 0$ $-\frac{2}{3} \leq 0$ Yes
$x > 2$	5	$\frac{5+4}{(5)^2+(5)-6} \stackrel{?}{\leq} 0$ $\frac{9}{24} \leq 0$ No

The value of x is a solution when $x \leq -4$ or $-3 < x < 2$.

Math Reasoning

Analyze Why is $\leq$ instead of < used in $x \leq 4$?

When $x = 4$, the fraction is equal to 0, which makes the inequality true.

Finding the actual value of a test point can become cumbersome. Notice that all that is really required from the test point is its sign. The intervals that contain solutions to the inequality have a negative sign because negative values are less than 0.

The sign of the rational expression can be determined by finding the sign of the numerator and denominator, or by finding the sign of each factor.

Example 2

The boundary points are the points that make the related equation equal to zero or undefined.

Additional Example 2

Solve $\frac{x-8}{x^2+x-12} \leq 0$ by finding the values of test points. $x < -4$ or $3 < x \leq 8$

TEACHER TIP

After finding the boundary points, have students list the points in order from least to greatest and then form intervals.

ENGLISH LEARNERS

To help students understand the meaning of **interval** for this lesson, define interval as the set of all real numbers between two endpoints.

Discuss other examples of intervals, such as a time interval: length of time, and musical interval: the difference of pitch between two notes.

Have students draw the intervals in Example 2 on a number line. Point out the boundary points.

Connect the meaning of interval by pointing out the intervals in the table. Explain that the intervals provide a set of real numbers for test points.

Example 3

Using a sign table is more efficient than finding actual values of test points.

Additional Example 3

a. Solve $\frac{x+3}{x-5} > 0$ by finding the sign of the numerator and denominator of the rational expression. $x < -3$ or $x > 5$

b. Solve $\frac{(x+4)}{(x-3)(x+2)(x+1)} \geq 0$ by finding the sign of each factor of the rational expression. $x \leq -4$ or $-2 < x < -1$ or $x > 3$

Example 3 Solving Rational Inequalities Using Sign Tables

a. Solve $\frac{x-6}{x+2} > 0$ by finding the sign of the numerator and denominator of the rational expression.

SOLUTION The right side is already 0. Find the boundary points.

The numerator is 0 when $x = 6$. The denominator is zero when $x = -2$.

The boundary points are -2 and 6. This gives three intervals to test.

They are listed in the top row with a test value below them.

For each interval, find the signs of the numerator and denominator. Find the sign of the value of the rational expression for that interval by analyzing the signs of the numerator and denominator.

Hint

The quotient is negative when the signs are different and positive when the signs are the same.

	$x < -2$	$-2 < x < 6$	$x > 6$
Test value for x	-3	0	9
Numerator: $x - 6$	$-$	$-$	$+$
Denominator: $x + 2$	$-$	$+$	$+$
Value of rational expression	$+$	$-$	$+$

The value of x is a solution when $x < -2$ or $x > 6$.

b. Solve $\frac{(x-5)}{(x+1)(x-4)(x-7)} \geq 0$ by finding the sign of each factor of the rational expression.

SOLUTION The right side is already 0. Find the boundary points.

The numerator is 0 when $x = 5$. The denominator is zero when $x = -1$, $x = 4$, or $x = 7$.

The boundary points are -1, 4, 5, and 7. This gives five intervals to test. Use < or > for the undefined values (asymptotes) of -1, 4, and 7.

Find the product of the "signs" of the factors to find the sign of the expression.

	$x < -1$	$-1 < x < 4$	$4 < x \leq 5$	$5 \leq x < 7$	$x > 7$
Test value for x	-2	0	4.5	6	10
$x - 5$	$-$	$-$	$-$	$+$	$+$
$x + 1$	$-$	$+$	$+$	$+$	$+$
$x - 4$	$-$	$-$	$+$	$+$	$+$
$x - 7$	$-$	$-$	$-$	$-$	$+$
Value of rational expression	$+$	$-$	$+$	$-$	$+$

The value of x is a solution when $x < -1$ or $4 < x \leq 5$ or $x > 7$.

INCLUSION

Have students use a spreadsheet for the sign tables. Enter the intervals and rational expressions. Students enter + or $-$ in the appropriate cell.

Example 4 Solving Rational Inequalities by Using a Graphing Calculator

Solve $\frac{x}{x-5} \leq 4$ by using a graphing calculator.

SOLUTION Graph $Y1 = \frac{x}{x-5}$ and $Y2 = 4$.

Look for where the first graph intersects or is below the line. The entire left part of the rational expression is below the line. This occurs for all x-values to the left of the asymptote of $x = 5$, so one part of the solution is $x < 5$.

```
Plot1 Plot2 Plot3
\Y1=X/(X-5)
\Y2=4
\Y3=
\Y4=
\Y5=
\Y6=
\Y7=
```

Use the intersect command to find where the right part of the graph is below the line. The intersection is at $x = 6.\overline{6}$, so the second part of the solution is $x \geq 6.\overline{6}$.

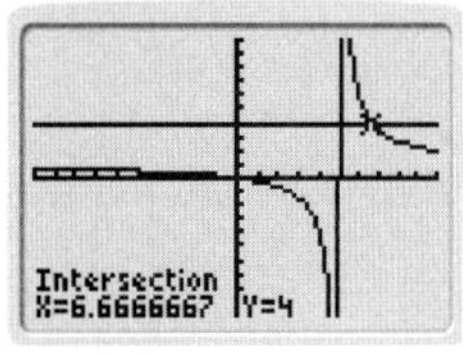

The solution of the inequality is $x < 5$ or $x \geq 6.\overline{6}$.

Check the solutions by viewing the table.

X	Y1	Y2
4.7	-15.67	4
4.8	-24	4
4.9	-49	4
5	ERROR	4
5.1	51	4
5.2	26	4
5.3	17.667	4

X=4.9

X	Y1	Y2
6.3	4.8462	4
6.4	4.5714	4
6.5	4.3333	4
6.6	4.125	4
6.7	3.9412	4
6.8	3.7778	4
6.9	3.6316	4

X=6.7

Graphing Calculator Tip

Press 2nd Window (Tblset) to change the increments at which the x-values increase in the table.

Example 5 Application: Cost per Person

A group of students are sharing the cost of a \$50 gift for their teacher. Write and solve an inequality to show the numbers of students whose participation would bring the cost per student to less than \$4.25.

SOLUTION

1. Understand The cost per student is $\frac{50}{x}$ where x is the number of students.

2. Plan Solve $\frac{50}{x} < 4.25$.

3. Solve Graph $Y1 = \frac{50}{x}$ and $Y2 = 4.25$.

Find the point of intersection. The first graph is below the line for all x-values greater than the x-value of the point of intersection. Since x represents numbers of people, round up to 12 people. Since the number of people must be positive, disregard the negative solutions.

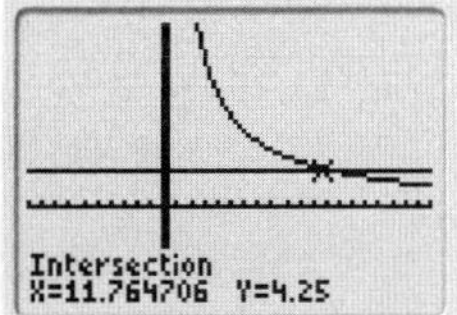

Twelve or more students must participate to have a per person cost of less than \$4.25.

4. Check Look at the values in the table.

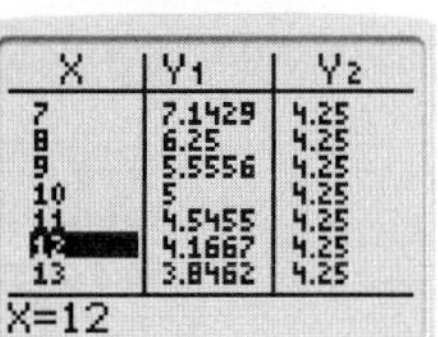

X	Y1	Y2
7	7.1429	4.25
8	6.25	4.25
9	5.5556	4.25
10	5	4.25
11	4.5455	4.25
12	4.1667	4.25
13	3.8462	4.25

X=12

Example 4

Encourage students to make their own table of values to check the solution.

Additional Example 4

Solve $\frac{x}{x+8} \geq -1$ by using a graphing calculator. $x < -8$ or $x \geq -4$

Example 5

Extend the Example

Use the table to find how many students are needed to bring the cost per student to less than \$3 per student. 17

Additional Example 5

A group of students are sharing the cost of a \$60 gift for their teacher. Write and solve an inequality to show the number of students whose participation would bring the cost per students to less than \$3.50. $\frac{60}{x} < 3.5$; 18 or more students must participate to have a per person cost of less than \$3.50.

ALTERNATE METHOD FOR EXAMPLE 5

Have students solve the inequality algebraically. Discuss why the case of $x < 0$ is not needed.

$$\frac{50}{x} < 4.25$$

$$(x)\frac{50}{x} < 4.25(x)$$

$$50 < 4.25x$$

$$\frac{50}{4.25} < x$$

$$x > \frac{50}{4.25} \approx 11.76$$

Since the number of people must be positive the case of $x < 0$ is not needed.

Lesson Practice

Problem a

Error Alert Students may forget to consider two cases. Have them make two columns to write each case in a column.

Check for Understanding

The questions below help assess the concepts taught in this lesson.

"What are different ways to solve a rational inequality?"
A rational inequality can be solved using the LCD, using test points, using sign tables, and using a graphing calculator.

"How do you solve $\frac{x-3}{x+1} > 0$?"
Find the boundary points, which are 3 and −1. Test the three intervals, $x < -1$, $-1 < x < 3$, and $x > 3$, using a sign table. The solution is $x < -1$ or $x > 3$.

3 Practice

Math Conversations

Discussions to strengthen understanding

Problem 1

Guide the students by asking them the following questions.

"What is the quadratic formula?"
$x = \frac{-b \pm \sqrt{b^2 - 4ac}}{2a}$

"Substitute the values for *a*, *b*, and *c* into the formula. What expression do you get?"
$x = \frac{-2 \pm \sqrt{-12}}{2}$

"What is $\sqrt{-12}$ simplified?" $2i\sqrt{3}$

"Simplify the expression. What is your final answer?" $-1 \pm i\sqrt{3}$

Lesson Practice

a. (Ex 1) Solve $\frac{7}{x+4} \le 3$ by using the LCD. $x < -4$ or $x \ge -\frac{5}{3}$

b. (Ex 2) Solve $\frac{x-8}{x^2+7x+10} \ge 0$ by finding the values of test points. $-5 < x < -2$ or $x \ge 8$

c. (Ex 3) Solve $\frac{x+1}{x-4} < 0$ by finding the sign of the numerator and denominator of the rational expression. $-1 < x < 4$

d. (Ex 3) Solve $\frac{(x+8)}{(x-2)(x-5)(x+1)} > 0$ by finding the sign of each factor of the rational expression. $x < -8$ or $-1 < x < 2$ or $x > 5$

e. (Ex 4) Solve $\frac{x}{x+6} \ge -2$ by using a graphing calculator. $x < -6$ or $x \ge -4$

f. (Ex 5) A group of students are sharing the cost of a $75 gift for their teacher. Write and solve an inequality to show the number of students whose participation would bring the cost per student to less than or equal to $6.25. $\frac{75}{x} \le 6.25$, 12 or more students

Practice Distributed and Integrated

Solve using the quadratic formula. Write the solution as complex numbers in standard form.

1. (65) $f(x) = x^2 + 2x + 4$ $x = -1 \pm i\sqrt{3}$

2. (65) $f(x) = x^2 - x + 12$ $x = \frac{1 \pm i\sqrt{47}}{2}$

3. (88) Given $P = 2l + 2w$, find l. $l = \frac{P - 2w}{2}$

***4.** (94) **Multi-Step** **a.** Factor both the numerator and denominator of $\frac{x^2 - 3x - 18}{x^2 - 16} \le 0$. $\frac{(x-6)(x+3)}{(x-4)(x+4)} \le 0$

b. Determine the intervals created by the critical values. $x < -4$, $-4 < x \le -3$, $-3 \le x < 4$, $4 < x \le 6$, $x \ge 6$

c. The intervals for which test values are negative contain the solutions. What is the solution? $-4 < x \le -3$ or $4 < x \le 6$

5. (80) The average height of giant sunflowers is 6 feet tall and the standard deviation is 3 inches. Find the z-score for a giant sunflower that is 5 feet 6 inches tall. $z = -2$

6. (78) **Multiple Choice** What are the roots of the equation $(4x^2 - 4x + 1) - (16x^2 - 24x + 9) = 0$? **B**

A $\frac{2}{3}$ and -2 **B** $\frac{2}{3}$ and 1 **C** $\frac{1}{2}$ and $-\frac{3}{4}$ **D** $\frac{1}{2}$ and $\frac{3}{4}$

***7.** (94) **Government** Suppose the citizens of counties in the state of Texas had the option to donate an equal amount of money toward a one million dollar donation to be given to a charity. Write and solve an inequality to show the number of counties whose citizen participation would bring the cost per county to less than $6500. There are 254 counties in Texas. $\frac{1{,}000{,}000}{x} < 6500$, $154 \le x \le 254$

8. (80) **Error Analysis** A student said if a number cube is rolled and the results are recorded in a histogram, a smooth curve drawn through the tops of the histogram would resemble a bell curve. Explain the error in the student's thinking.

8. The probability of rolling each number is the same. The bars on the histogram would be about the same height, and not bell-shaped.

INCLUSION

Have students use different color markers, pencils, or pens to write + and − in the tables.

*9. **Justify** Explain why there are four intervals when solving $\frac{(x+2)}{(x-3)(x+1)}$ by using test
(94) points. See Additional Answers.

10. **Geometry** The perimeter of an isosceles triangle is 200 inches. The base has a length
(77) of 92 inches. Find the measure of the vertex angle. about 116.8°

*11. **Analyze** If \$500 is invested at 4% compounded monthly, then at the end of t years
(93) the investment will have the value A, where A is given by the expression $500\left(1 + \frac{0.04}{12}\right)^{12t}$. What expression gives the value A if the compounding is daily instead of monthly? $500\left(1 + \frac{0.04}{365}\right)^{365t}$

12. What is the side length c in $\triangle ABC$ if $A = 32°$, $C = 67°$, and $b = 31$ ft? 28.9 ft
(71)

*13. **Error Analysis** While attempting to solve an inequality, a student performed the step
(93) shown below.

$$n \log(0.5) < \log 2 - \log 20$$
$$n < \frac{\log 2 - \log 20}{\log 0.5}$$

What is the error? What is the correct step?

Sample: log(0.5) is negative, so the inequality symbol should be reversed. Correct step: $n\log(0.5) < \log 2 - \log 20$; $n > \frac{\log 2 - \log 20}{\log 0.5}$

14. An object is thrown upward from a height of 15 feet at an initial velocity of 35 feet
(74) per second. How long will it take the object to hit the ground? about 2.6 seconds

15. **Business** The profit earned from selling tickets to a certain event is modeled by
(89) $y = -1.25x^2 + 66x - 720$. If the cost per ticket will be a whole number amount, what range of ticket prices will earn a profit of at least \$100? from \$20 to \$32 inclusive

*16. A school's enrollment increases 6.5% a year and is currently 1100. How long will it
(93) take to reach 1500 students? 4.93 years

17. **Probability** A student has a spinner with four equal sections labeled 2, 4, 6, and 8.
(68) If he spins the spinner twice, find the probability that the first spin lands on 6 and the sum of the results is less than or equal to 10. $\frac{1}{8}$ or 12.5%

*18. **Multiple Choice** Which of the following has a period of 2π? D
(90)
A $y = \tan(2x)$ **B** $y = \tan(2\pi x)$ **C** $y = 2\tan(x)$ **D** $y = \tan\left(\frac{x}{2}\right)$

*19. **Graphing Calculator** With the Table set to increase by 1, enter $15 + (x - 1)(-4)$ for
(92) Y1 to represent an arithmetic sequence whose first term is 15 and whose common difference is −4. Use the table to find the 6th and 15th terms. −5 and −41

20. **Formulate** Write a quadratic equation with roots of −1 and 5 so that the parabola
(83) of the related function opens up. Then write one so that the parabola opens down.
Possible answers: $x^2 - 4x - 5 = 0$ and $-x^2 + 4x + 5 = 0$

*21. **Analyze** When finding the nth term of an arithmetic sequence, when will the value
(92) added to the first term be positive and when will it be negative?

21. It will be positive when the common difference is positive and negative when the common difference is negative.

22. Given $k(x) = 3\sin(x)$, identify the amplitude and period. amplitude = 3,
(82) period $= 2\pi$

Problem 11

Remind students that if interest is compounded daily, then $n = 365$.

Problem 12
Extend the Problem

Have students find the area of $\triangle ABC$. area ≈ 237 ft²

Problem 13
TEACHER TIP

Have students simplify the expression with a calculator. Students will see that log 0.5 is negative, and that the inequality symbol should have been reversed.

ALTERNATE METHOD FOR PROBLEM 22

Have students graph the function and determine the amplitude and period by looking at the graph.

Problem 23

Error Alert

Students may square 28 and use that value in the equation for a circle instead of finding *r*, then squaring that value. Review the equation for a circle. Point out r^2 in the equation.

Problem 25

Error Alert

Students may have difficulty working with subscripts. Have students substitute *x* for d_1 and *y* for d_2.

Problem 30

Have students factor out 2*x* first. Then use the Quadratic Formula to solve for *x*.

***23.** (91) **Drafting** A computer-aided drafting technician is drawing a bicycle wheel such that the center is located at (6, 2) on the coordinate grid. Each unit on the grid represents one inch. What is the equation of the wheel given that it has a diameter of 28 inches? $(x - 6)^2 + (y - 2)^2 = 196$

24. (73) **Data Analysis** Twelve names already numbered are listed below. Three must be randomly chosen for a sample. What three names will be picked if numbers are chosen from the string of random numbers below?

15 Ann	16 Luke	17 Cassie	18 Finn	19 Jared	20 Tanela
21 Jude	22 Gunner	23 Drew	24 Halle	25 Colby	26 Anton

60201 60482 89824 08705 17913 46815 76221 25650 89337 53603 73597 04633

Tanela, Luke, Cassie

25. (88) Given $f = \frac{1}{\frac{1}{d_1} + \frac{1}{d_2}}$, find d_2. $d_2 = \frac{fd_1}{d_1 - f}$

26. (75) **Physics** The equation for finding the period of a pendulum is a radical function given by $T = 2\pi\sqrt{\frac{L}{9.8}}$. The period is the amount of time it takes for the pendulum to complete a back-and-forth sweep. How much shorter does a pendulum need to be to have half the period? $\frac{L}{4}$

27. (81) **Chemistry** Uranium-238 is a naturally abundant isotope because of its long half-life. Its half-life is about 4.5 billion years. About how long would it take for just 1% of an initial amount to decay? (Use the natural decay function $N(t) = N_0e^{-kt}$.)
about 65,000,000 years

28. (87) Using the change of base formula, solve for *y* when $x = 2$ and $x = 4$ given that $y = \frac{\log x}{\log 2}$. (2, 1), (4, 2)

Find the zeros of the polynomial function.

29. (76) $f(x) = 4x(7x - 3)(6x + 1)$ $x = -\frac{1}{6}, 0, \frac{3}{7}$

30. (76) $f(x) = 16x^3 - 24x^2 + 6x$ $x = 0, \frac{3 \pm \sqrt{3}}{4}$

CHALLENGE

Solve $\frac{x + 5}{2x^3 - x^2 - 43x + 60} \leq 0$ without using a calculator. $\frac{3}{2} < x < 4$

LOOKING FORWARD

Solving rational inequalities prepares students for

- **Lesson 102** Solving Logarithmic Equations and Inequalities

LESSON 95

Factoring Higher-Order Polynomials

Warm Up

1. **Vocabulary** If $f(x) = ax^2 + bx + c$ is divisible by $(x - d)$, then $(x - d)$ is a ___factor___ of $f(x)$. (35)

2. Use synthetic division to test if $6x^3 - 5x^2 - 34x + 40$ is divisible by $(x - 2)$. (51)

2. The polynomial is divisible by $(x - 2)$.

3. Use synthetic division to test if $20x^3 - 53x^2 - 122x + 56$ is divisible by $(x - 2)$. (51) The polynomial is not divisible by $(x - 2)$.

New Concepts

A constant a is a root of polynomial $P(x)$ if $P(a) = 0$.

You can use the Reminder Theorem and the Factor Theorem to test for roots of a polynomial.

Remainder Theorem
The **Remainder Theorem** states:
If the polynomial function $P(x)$ is divided by $x - a$, then the remainder r is $P(a)$.

Factor Theorem
The **Factor Theorem** states:
For any polynomial $P(x)$,$(x - a)$ is a factor of $P(x)$ if and only if $P(a) = 0$.

Math Reasoning

Generalize Suppose a polynomial $P(x)$ has no real roots. What does the Factor Theorem state about such a polynomial?

There is no value a such that $P(a) = 0$.

Use the Factor Theorem to test if a value is a root of a polynomial.

Example 1 Using the Factor Theorem to Test for Roots

a. Determine if $x = 5$ is a root of $P(x)$.

$$P(x) = 2x^6 - 43x^5 + 75x^4 + 1765x^3 - 857x^2 - 22{,}542x - 30{,}240$$

SOLUTION

Use synthetic division to test if $P(5) = 0$. Divide $P(x)$ by $(x - 5)$.

5	2	−43	75	1765	−857	−22,542	− 30,240
		10	−165	−450	6,575	28,590	30,240
	2	−33	−90	1,315	5,718	6,048	0

Since $P(5) = 0$, 5 is a root of the polynomial.

LESSON 95

1 Warm Up

Problems 2 and 3

Review the process of synthetic division with students.

2 New Concepts

In this lesson, students use synthetic division to divide polynomials. Students will also use the Remainder Theorem and the Factor Theorem to test for roots of polynomials.

Example 1

Error Alert Errors can occur in calculations. Have students recheck their work.

Additional Example 1

a. Determine if $x = 3$ is a root of $P(x)$.

$P(x) = 2x^6 - 49x^5 + 1254x^4 + 1445x^3 - 20{,}585x^2 + 32{,}635x - 42{,}780$ Since $P(3) = r(3) = 0$, 3 is a root of $P(x)$.

MATH BACKGROUND

Synthetic division is an abbreviated form of long division. When a divisor is in the form $x - k$, then synthetic division can be used. Students were first introduced to synthetic division to divide polynomials. The Remainder Theorem and using synthetic division to evaluate polynomials was also introduced at that time.

The process of synthetic division is as follows: To divide polynomial $P(x)$ by $x - k$, begin by writing k and the coefficients of $P(x)$ on the first line. Bring down the first coefficient of the quotient, a. Multiply a by k. Write the product under b, the second coefficient. Add b and ka. The result, $b + ka$, is the second coefficient. Continue the pattern.

LESSON RESOURCES

Student Edition Practice Workbook 95
Reteaching Master 95
Adaptations Master 95
Challenge and Enrichment Master C95

b. Determine if $x = -5$ is a root of $P(x)$.

$P(x) = 7x^8 - 43x^7 + 186x^6 - 432x^5 - 564x^4 + 1432x^3 - 1821x^2 + 1852x + 1808$

Since $P(-5) = r(-5) \neq 0$, -5 is not a root of $P(x)$.

Example 2

Students will use the Rational Root Theorem and repeated synthetic division to determine the roots of a polynomial.

Error Alert Students may not check the possible root 1 a second time. Remind students that roots can have a multiplicity greater than 1.

Additional Example 2

Find all the rational roots of $P(x) = x^5 + 5x^4 - 20x^2 - 16x$.

The roots are **−4, −2, −1, 2,** and **0.**

b. Determine if $x = -7$ is a root of $P(x)$.

$P(x) = 9x^8 - 101x^7 + 195x^6 + 622x^5 - 621x^4 - 1565x^3 - 1947x^2 + 2772x + 2940$

SOLUTION

Use synthetic division to test if $r(-7) = 0$. Divide $P(x)$ by $(x + 7)$.

−7	9	−101	195	622	−621	−1565	−1947	2772	2940
		−63	1148	−9401	61,453	−425,824	2,991,723	−20,928,432	146,479,620
	9	−164	1343	−8779	60,832	−427,389	2,989,776	−20,925,660	146,482,560

Since $P(-7) = r(-7) \neq 0$, -7 is not a root of the polynomial.

Example 2 Finding Roots of $P(x)$

Find all the rational roots of $P(x) = x^5 + 4x^4 - 10x^2 - x + 6$.

SOLUTION

By the Rational Root Theorem, the possible rational roots are ±1, ±2, ±3, ±6.

Use synthetic division to test the roots.

1	1	4	0	−10	−1	6
		1	5	5	−5	−6
	1	5	5	−5	−6	0

Since $P(1) = 0$, 1 is a root of the polynomial.

$P(x) = (x - 1)(x^4 + 5x^3 + 5x^2 - 5x - 6)$.

By the Rational Root Theorem, the possible rational roots of the quartic quotient are ±1, ±2, ±3, ±6. Use synthetic division to test the roots.

1	1	5	5	−5	−6
		1	6	11	6
	1	6	11	6	0

Since $P(1) = 0$, 1 is a root of the polynomial with multiplicity 2.

$P(x) = (x - 1)(x - 1)(x^3 + 6x^2 + 11x + 6)$.

By the Rational Root Theorem, the possible rational roots of the cubic quotient are ±1, ±2, ±3, ±6. Use synthetic division to test the roots.

1	1	6	11	6
		1	7	18
	1	7	18	24

−1	1	6	11	6
		−1	−5	−6
	1	5	6	0

Since $P(-1) = 0$, -1 is a root of the polynomial.

$P(x) = (x - 1)(x - 1)(x + 1)(x^2 + 5x + 6)$

The last quotient is a quadratic that can be factored.

$P(x) = (x - 1)(x - 1)(x + 1)(x + 2)(x + 3)$

The roots are **1**, **−1**, **−2**, and **−3**. The root 1 has a multiplicity 2.

ALTERNATE METHOD FOR EXAMPLE 2

Have students enter $P(x)$ in the Y= Editor on a graphing calculator.

Use the table feature to check which possible roots make $P(x) = 0$.

Math Reasoning

Analyze Suppose that a polynomial $P(x)$ has two real roots a and b. Could $P(x)$ be of degree 3?

No, because then $P(x)$ would be of the form $P(x) = (x - a)(x - b)(x - c)$, which implies a third real root.

Example 3 Application: Braking Distance

When a car needs to be brought to an immediate stop, it takes time for someone to step on the brake and time for the car to come to a complete stop. During these times, the car is still moving. The stopping distance is how far the car travels during this time frame. A reasonable mathematical model for the stopping distance d, in feet, based on the car's speed s, in miles per hour, is shown below. Use the Remainder Theorem to evaluate $d(20)$, $d(30)$, and $d(55)$.

$d(s) = 0.05s^2 + 2.2s$

SOLUTION Use synthetic division.

20	0.05	2.2	0
		1	64
	0.05	3.2	64

30	0.05	2.2	0
		1.5	111
	0.05	3.7	111

55	0.05	2.2	0
		2.75	272.25
	0.05	4.95	272.25

The stopping distances are $d(20) = 64$ ft, $d(30) = 111$ ft $d(55) = 272.25$ ft.

Lesson Practice

Determine if $x = 7$ is a root of $P(x)$.
(Ex 1)

a. $P(x) = 2x^6 - 43x^5 + 75x^4 + 1765x^3 - 857x^2 - 22{,}542x - 30{,}240$

a. It is not a root.

b. $P(x) = 9x^8 - 101x^7 + 195x^6 + 622x^5 - 621x^4 - 1565x^3 - 1947x^2 + 2772x + 2940$ It is a root.

c. (Ex 2) Find all the rational roots of $P(x) = x^3 + 4x^2 + 1x - 6$. −3, −2, 1

d. (Ex 3) The height of an object thrown at 40 feet per second can be modeled by $h(t) = -16t^2 + 40t$ where h is the height in feet and t is time in seconds. Use the remainder theorem to find the height of the object after 2 seconds. 16 feet

INCLUSION

To help students align numbers while they are doing synthetic division in Example 3, have them use a computer to make a table. Have students enter numbers in the appropriate cells.

Example 3

Extend the Example

Have students use the substitution method to check their answers.

Additional Example 3

When a car needs to be brought to an immediate stop, it takes time for someone to step on the brake and time for the car to come to a complete stop. During these times, the car is still moving, and the stopping distance is how far the car travels during this time frame. A reasonable mathematical model for the stopping distance, d, in feet, based on the car's speed, s, in miles per hour, is $d(s) = 0.05s^2 + 2.2s$. Use the Remainder Theorem to evaluate $d(15)$, $d(40)$, and $d(60)$. The stopping distances are $d(15) = 44.25$ ft; $d(40) = 168$ ft; $d(60) = 312$ ft

Lesson Practice

Problems a and b

Scaffolding Have students use the substitution method to check their answers.

Check for Understanding

The questions below help assess the concepts taught in this lesson.

"How do you determine if a number, x, is a root of $P(x)$?" Use synthetic division to test if $r(x) = 0$. If $P(x) = r(x) = 0$, then the number x is a root of $P(x)$.

"How do you use the Remainder Theorem to evaluate $d(10) = 0.05s^2 + 2.2s$?" The Remainder Theorem says $P(a) = r(a)$. Use synthetic division. So, $d(10) = 27$.

3 Practice

Math Conversations

Discussions to strengthen understanding

Problem 6

Guide the students by asking them the following questions.

"What is the Proportion Property of a direct variation?" $\frac{y_1}{x_1} = \frac{y_2}{x_2}$

"Which variable do you want to solve for?" x_2

"What number do you substitute for y_1?" 8 **"for x_1?"** 3 **"for y_2?"** 12

"What proportion do you get?" $\frac{8}{3} = \frac{12}{x_2}$

"Solve for x_2. How many cups of sugar are used with 12 cups of flour?" 4.5 cups

Problem 10

"What is the Power Property of natural logarithms?" $\ln a^p = p \ln a$

"What expression do you get after using the Power Property?" $x \cdot 2 \ln e$

"What is $\ln e$ equal to?" 1

"What is your final answer?" $2x$

Practice Distributed and Integrated

Solve.

1. $x - \frac{6}{x} = 1$ $x = 3, -2$ (84)
2. $\frac{x^2 + x - 6}{x + 1} = 0$ $x = -3, 2$ (84)
3. $\frac{7x}{3x + 2} = 2$ $x = 4$ (84)

4. (57) Does the graph of $y = b^x + k$, through the points $(3, -3)$ and $(5, 0)$, model exponential growth or decay? growth

*5. (94) Solve $\frac{1}{x^3} \geq 5$. Round to the nearest thousandth. $0 < x \leq 0.585$

6. (8) In a certain recipe, the amount of sugar is directly proportional to the amount of flour. If 3 cups of sugar are used with 8 cups of flour, how many cups of sugar are used with 12 cups of flour? 4.5 cups

*7. (95) **Error Analysis** Two students were evaluating $P(-4)$ for the polynomial $P(x)$, but they got different results. Which student made the mistake?

$$P(x) = x^6 + 4x^5 - x^4 - 6x^3 - 8x^2 + 2x + 8$$

Student A

$$\begin{array}{r|rrrrrrr} -4 & 1 & 4 & -1 & -6 & -8 & 2 & 8 \\ & & -4 & 0 & 4 & 8 & 0 & -8 \\ \hline & 1 & 0 & -1 & -2 & 0 & 2 & 0 \end{array}$$

$P(-4) = 0$

Student B

$$\begin{array}{r|rrrrrrr} 4 & 1 & 4 & -1 & -6 & -8 & 2 & 8 \\ & & 4 & 32 & 124 & 472 & 1856 & 7432 \\ \hline & 1 & 8 & 31 & 118 & 464 & 1858 & 7440 \end{array}$$

$P(-4) = 7440$

7. Student B incorrectly used 4 instead of −4 in the synthetic division.

*8. (94) **Analyze** When solving $\frac{(x-4)(x+6)}{(x+2)(x-3)} \geq 0$, which intervals will use strict inequalities (< or >) and why?

8. The middle three intervals, $-6 \leq x < -2$, $-2 < x < 3$, and $3 < x \leq 4$, because they contain the asymptotes of −2 and 3. These values make the inequality undefined.

*9. (93) **Multi-Step** As of the 2000 U.S. census, Nevada had the fastest growing population of all the states, and Connecticut had nearly the slowest (47th out of 50). The table below is based on U.S. census statistics.

	Nevada	Connecticut
Population in 2000 (to nearest thousand)	1,998,000	3,406,000
Average annual increase (1990–2000)	5.21%	0.36%

a. Write a function ($y_1 = ab^t$), where y_1 represents Nevada's population t years after 2000. $y_1 = 1{,}998{,}000(1.0521)^t$

b. Write a function ($y_2 = ab^t$), where y_2 represents Connecticut's population t years after 2000. $y_2 = 3{,}406{,}000(1.0036)^t$

c. Write and solve an equation to predict the year in which Nevada's population will overtake Connecticut's population.

9c. $y_1 = y_2$; $1{,}998{,}000(1.0521)^t = 3{,}406{,}000(1.0036)^t$; $\log 1{,}998{,}000 + \log (1.0521)^t = \log 3{,}406{,}000 + \log (1.0036)^t$; $\log 1{,}998{,}000 + t\log (1.0521) = \log 3{,}406{,}000 + t\log (1.0036)$; $\log 1{,}998{,}000 - \log 3{,}406{,}000 = t\log 1.0036 - t\log 1.0521$; $\log 1{,}998{,}000 - \log 3{,}406{,}000 = t(\log 1.0036 - \log 1.0521)$; $\frac{\log 1{,}998{,}000 - \log 3{,}406{,}000}{\log 1.0036 - \log 1.0521} = t$; $11.30 \approx t$; Predicted year: 2011 or 2012 (The month of the census is not given.)

Simplify each of the following.

10. (81) $2 \ln e^x$ $2x$

11. (81) $x \cdot \ln e^3$ $3x$

ENGLISH LEARNERS

To help students understand the meaning of **population,** define population as the number of people or animals that occupy an area or a region.

Discuss population as it is used in statistics: an entire group from which samples can be drawn. Present examples of populations that students may have read about in other math classes, such as asking women about childcare.

Have students identify the population discussed in problems 9 and 12 (people of Nevada, elephants in the preserve).

Connect the meaning of population to the populations discussed in problems 9 and 12. Point out that both problems show a number of people or animals that occupy an area (Nevada) or a region (the preserve).

12. **Estimate** A researcher visits a wildlife preserve and marks endangered African elephants. He marks 6 elephants and releases them. On a return visit several months later, he comes across 16 elephants, and 4 of them are marked from the previous visit. Estimate the elephant population in the preserve. There are about 24 elephants in the preserve.
(73)

13. **Surveying** A surveyor finds that the lengths between three stakes on the ground are 125 feet, 182 feet, and 211 feet. He connects the stakes with string, forming a triangle. To the nearest tenth, what is the measure of the largest angle in this triangle? 84.7°
(77)

14. Determine the domain and range of the function $f(x) = \begin{cases} -x, & \text{if } x < 0 \\ 4, & \text{if } 0 \leq x < 10. \\ 18, & \text{if } x \geq 10 \end{cases}$
(79) Domain: all real numbers; Range: all positive real numbers

15. **Research** In a study of 413 men, the mean height was 174.1 centimeters and the standard deviation was 7 centimeters. Assuming that the distribution is normal, approximate the z-score of a man whose height is 182 centimeters. about 1.13
(80)

16. A set of values has a mean of 13 and a standard deviation of 0.625. Find the z-score of a value of 10.25. −4.4
(80)

17. **Justify** Formulate a conjecture (statement) about the degree of a polynomial that is a sum or difference of polynomials compared to the degree of the polynomials that are added or subtracted to get that sum or difference. Give examples to justify your conjecture. (Hint: Name the polynomials P_1, P_2, P_3, etc. to make it easy to refer to them.)
(11)

17. A polynomial that is the result of adding or subtracting polynomials can have any degree less than or equal to the polynomial with the greatest degree. Possible examples: $P_1 = 5x^3 + x$ has degree 3, $P_2 = -x^2 - x + 1$ has degree 2, and $P_3 = -5x^3 - x - 2$ has degree 3. The degree of $P_1 + P_2$ is 3 and the degree of $P_1 + P_3$ is 0.

18. **Geometry** The area of a rectangular field is 100 square meters. The field is 15 meters longer than it is wide. Find the length and width of the field. The field is 5 meters wide and 20 meters long.
(23)

***19.** **Multiple Choice** Which of the following polynomials has $P(5) = 0$? D
(95)

A $P(x) = 48x^6 + 212x^5 - 1098x^4 - 5298x^3 + 1174x^2 + 22{,}350x + 18{,}900$

B $P(x) = 48x^6 + 644x^5 + 2754x^4 + 2154x^3 - 12{,}974x^2 - 30{,}750x - 18{,}900$

C $P(x) = 48x^6 + 868x^5 + 6282x^4 + 23{,}238x^3 + 46{,}274x^2 + 46{,}950x + 18{,}900$

D $P(x) = 48x^6 - 268x^5 - 818x^4 + 4282x^3 + 6254x^2 - 14{,}790x - 18{,}900$

20. **Multiple Choice** Identify which property or properties of real numbers are being demonstrated. D
(1)

$$(2 \cdot 9) \cdot 5 = (2 \cdot 5) \cdot 9$$

A Commutative Property of Multiplication

B Associative Property of Multiplication

C Distributive Property

D Both **A** and **B**

***21.** Write a possible polynomial $P(x)$ that fits the parameters $P(0) = 0$, $P(2) = 20$, and $P(-4) = 0$. Sample: $P(x) = \frac{5}{3}x^2 + \frac{20}{3}x$
(95)

***22.** Use the properties of logarithms to expand the expression $\ln (8x)^3 + \ln e\left(\frac{2x}{3}\right)$.
(87) $3 \ln 8 + 4 \ln x + 1 + \ln 2 - \ln 3$

Problem 14

Have students read $-x$ as the opposite of x. The opposite of a negative number is a positive number.

Problem 18
Extend the Problem

Have students find the perimeter of the rectangular field. 50 meters

Problem 20

Remind students the Commutative Property of Multiplication is $a \cdot b = b \cdot a$ and the Associative Property of Multiplication is $(a \cdot b) \cdot c = a \cdot (b \cdot c)$.

Problem 22
Error Alert

Students may not use the Product Property or Quotient Property correctly. Provide students with examples so that they can look at the examples as they work the problem.

ALTERNATE METHOD FOR PROBLEM 18

Have students make a list of the factors whose product is 100.

Then have students choose the pair where one factor is 15 more than the other.

Problem 26

Remind students that they cannot assume angle A is a right angle.

Problem 27

Remind students that the equation for a circle with its center at (h, k) and radius r is $(x - h)^2 + (y - k)^2 = r^2$.

Problem 28

Students can also think of 18 months as 20 months – 2 months. Use the Distributive Property: 125(20) – 125(2). Multiply: 2500 – 250. Subtract: 2250. The amount saved will be $2250.

23. (13) **Predict** The table below shows the sales in dollars, y, made by a gift shop x years after it opened.

Years	2	5	8
Sales	$30,000	$75,000	$120,000

a. Plot the data on a coordinate grid and draw a line that fits the data. See student work.

b. Use the line to predict the total sales 15 years after the shop opened. approximately $225,000

23a. Sample:

Sales in Thousands ($): 0, 20, 40, 60, 80, 100, 120, 140; Years Since Opening: 2, 4, 6, 8

24. (76) **Error Analysis** A student performs the following steps while finding the roots of $y = (x^2 - 7)(3x^2 + 4) - (x^2 - 7)(8x - 3)$. What is his mistake?

$$(x^2 - 7)(3x^2 + 4) - (x^2 - 7)(8x - 3) = (x^2 - 7)(3x^2 - 8x + 1)$$

24. The student incorrectly distributes the negative sign to the constant term.

***25.** (92) **Travel** A driver on the Pennsylvania turnpike turned on the cruise control at milepost 30, Warrendale, and kept it on until milepost 242, Harrisburg West, exactly 4 hours later. Show how to use an arithmetic sequence to find the speed at which the car traveled during those 4 hours. $a_5 = a_1 + (5 - 1)(d)$; $242 = 30 + 4d$; $212 = 4d$; $53 = d$; The speed was 53 miles per hour.

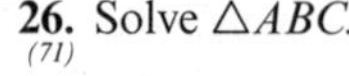

26. (71) Solve $\triangle ABC$. $A \approx 99.5°$, $C \approx 24.5°$, $a \approx 16.7$

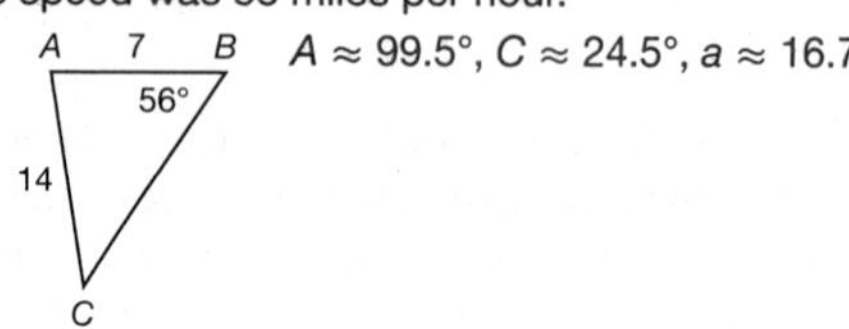

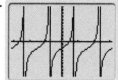

***27.** (91) Write the equation for the circle centered at (3, 8) with a radius of 4. $(x - 3)^2 + (y - 8)^2 = 16$

28. (1) John saves $125 each month. Use the Distributive Property to mentally calculate the amount of money that he will save in 18 months.

***29.** (90) **Graphing Calculator** Use a graphing calculator to graph the function $y = 3\tan(2x - 2\pi) - 4$. Identify its period, undefined values, and phase shift.

***30.** (83) Write a quadratic equation whose root is -3. Sample: $-x^2 - 6x - 9 = 0$

28. Sample: Think of 18 months as 10 months + 8 months. Write an expression for the savings in 18 months: 125(10 + 8). Use the Distributive Property: 125(10) + 125(8). Multiply: 1250 + 1000. Add: 2250. The amount saved will be $2250.

29. 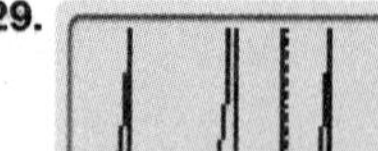 ; period: $\frac{\pi}{2}$ undefined values: $\frac{\pi}{4} + \pi + n\frac{\pi}{2}$; phase shift: π.

CHALLENGE

Determine if the polynomial $P(x)$ has a zero remainder when divided by $(x - 2)$. Determine $Q(x)$.

$P(x) = x^{10} - 34x^9 + 106x^8 - 130x^7 + 214x^6 - 747x^5 + 1814x^4 - 2362x^3 + 2735x^2 - 4298x + 3624$

$P(x)$ has a remainder of 0.

$Q(x) = x^9 - 32x^8 + 42x^7 - 46x^6 + 122x^5 - 503x^4 + 808x^3 - 746x^2 + 1243x - 1812$

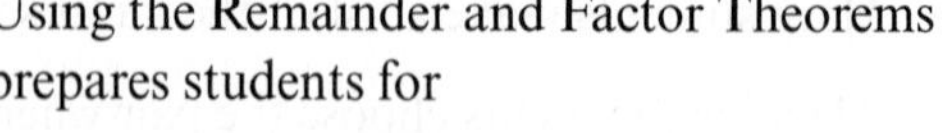

LOOKING FORWARD

Using the Remainder and Factor Theorems prepares students for

- **Lesson 101** Making Graphs of Polynomial Functions
- **Lesson 106** Using the Fundamental Theorem of Algebra

670 Saxon Algebra 2

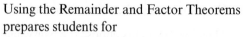

LESSON 96 Using Polar Coordinates

Warm Up

1. **Vocabulary** The trigonometric ratio $\frac{\text{opposite side}}{\text{hypotenuse}}$ is called the sine ratio. (46)

2. $\cos \pi =$ -1 (46)

3. $\sin \pi =$ 0 (46)

New Concepts

A polar coordinate system in a plane is formed by a fixed point *O*, called the pole (or origin), and a ray, called the polar axis, whose endpoint is *O*. Each point in the plane can be assigned polar coordinates as follows.

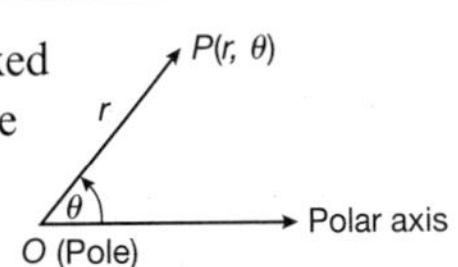

Polar Coordinates
Every point *P* in the polar coordinate system has an ordered pair of **polar coordinates** (r, θ), where • *r* is the directed distance from *O* to *P*, and • θ is the directed angle measure counterclockwise from the polar axis to $\overline{OP}$.

The point $P(2, \frac{7\pi}{6})$ lies 2 units from the pole on the terminal side of the angles $\frac{7\pi}{6}$. In a rectangular coordinate system, every point has exactly one ordered pair (x, y). But in a polar coordinate system, every point has an infinite number of ordered pairs. The point *P* shown at the right has coordinates $\left(2, \frac{7\pi}{6}\right)$. But the angle with measure $\frac{7\pi}{6} + 2\pi = \frac{19\pi}{6}$ also has terminal ray $\overrightarrow{OP}$, so point *P* also has coordinates $\left(2, \frac{19\pi}{6}\right)$.

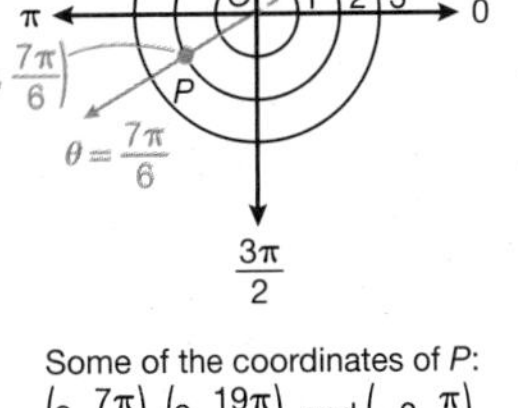

Some of the coordinates of *P*: $\left(2, \frac{7\pi}{6}\right)$, $\left(2, \frac{19\pi}{6}\right)$, and $\left(-2, \frac{\pi}{6}\right)$

And because *r* is a *directed* distance, point *P* also has coordinates $\left(-2, \frac{\pi}{6}\right)$. To understand this, notice that point *Q* has coordinates $\left(2, \frac{\pi}{6}\right)$; the point with coordinates $\left(-2, \frac{\pi}{6}\right)$ is point *P*, which is 2 units from the pole, on the ray *opposite* $\overrightarrow{OQ}$.

> **Math Language**
>
> A **rectangular coordinate system** is also called a **Cartesian coordinate system.**

In general, the point (r, θ) can be represented as $(r, \theta \pm 2n\pi)$ or $(-r, \theta \pm (2n + 1)\pi)$, where *n* is any integer.

To relate the Cartesian and Polar coordinate systems, let the pole system coincide with the origin of a Cartesian (rectangular) coordinate system and let the polar axis coincide with the positive *x*-axis. Then $\cos \theta = \frac{x}{r}$, $\sin \theta = \frac{y}{r}$, and $\tan \theta = \frac{y}{x}$.

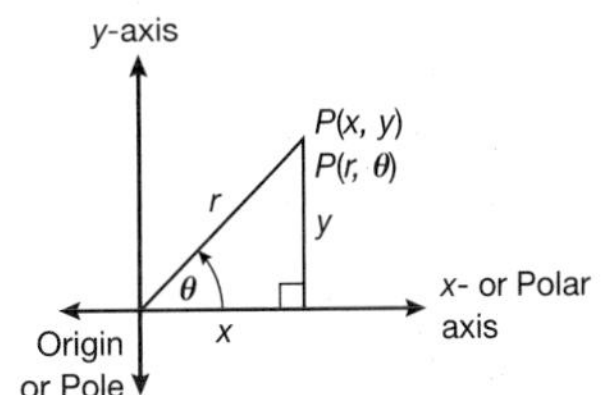

> **Online Connection**
> www.SaxonMathResources.com

LESSON 96

1 Warm Up

Have students also review the trigonometric ratios for cosine and tangent.

2 New Concepts

In this lesson, students learn to convert polar coordinates to Cartesian coordinates and vice versa. Students will also graph polar equations by hand and on a graphing calculator.

Discuss the definition of polar coordinate system, pole, polar axis, and polar coordinates. Explain that polar coordinates represent a point on a two-dimensional plane.

TEACHER TIP

Explain to students that Cartesian refers to anything by Rene Descartes. Because Descartes is credited with first using the rectangular coordinate system, it is also referred to as a Cartesian coordinate system.

MATH BACKGROUND

Students have been working with the Cartesian coordinate system in which a point is described by two coordinates. The coordinates indicate the horizontal and vertical direction taken to plot the point. There are many other coordinate systems in use in mathematics. The polar coordinate system in this lesson is useful when a point is best described by its distance from the origin.

The cylindrical coordinate system and the spherical coordinate system are two other types of polar coordinate systems that are three dimensional. The cylindrical coordinate system represents a point in space by an angle, a distance from the origin, and the height. The spherical coordinate system represents a point in space with two angles and the distance from the origin.

LESSON RESOURCES

Student Edition Practice Workbook 96
Reteaching Master 96
Adaptations Master 96
Challenge and Enrichment Master C 96

Example 1

Point out that Cartesian coordinates are of the form (x, y).

Additional Example 1

a. Convert $\left(3, \frac{3\pi}{2}\right)$ to Cartesian coordinates. $(0, -3)$

b. Convert $\left(4, \frac{5\pi}{4}\right)$ to Cartesian coordinates. $(-2\sqrt{2}, -2\sqrt{2})$

Example 2

Students are shown that a point in a polar coordinate system has an infinite number of ordered pairs.

Extend the Example

Find two additional polar representations for $(-3, -3)$.
$\left(3\sqrt{2}, \frac{13\pi}{4}\right)$, $\left(3\sqrt{2}, \frac{-3\pi}{4}\right)$

Additional Example 2

a. Convert $(2, -2)$ to polar coordinates. $\left(2\sqrt{2}, \frac{7\pi}{4}\right)$

TEACHER TIP

Be sure students understand that in Example 2, we know θ terminates in quadrant III because the x- and y-values are both negative.

To convert coordinates, use the following equations.

Converting Coordinates	
Polar to Cartesian $x = r\cos\theta$ $y = r\sin\theta$	**Cartesian to Polar** $\tan\theta = \frac{y}{x}$ $r^2 = x^2 + y^2$

Example 1 Converting Polar Coordinates to Cartesian Coordinates

a. Convert $\left(2, \frac{\pi}{2}\right)$ to Cartesian coordinates.

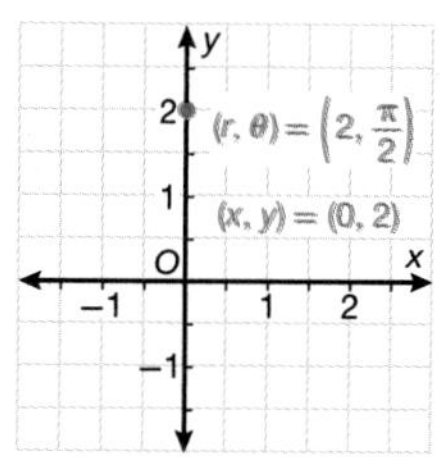

SOLUTION

$$x = r\cos\theta = 2\cos\frac{\pi}{2} = 2(0) = 0$$

$$y = r\sin\theta = 2\sin\frac{\pi}{2} = 2(1) = 2$$

The Cartesian coordinates are $(0, 2)$.

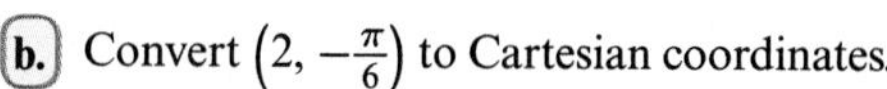

b. Convert $\left(2, -\frac{\pi}{6}\right)$ to Cartesian coordinates.

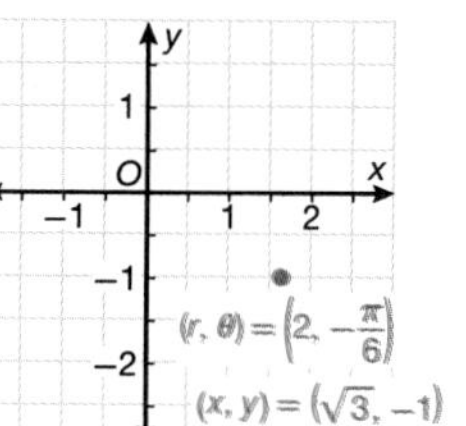

SOLUTION

$-\frac{\pi}{6}$ is equivalent to $-30°$.

$$x = r\cos\theta = 2\cos\left(-\frac{\pi}{6}\right) = 2\left(\frac{\sqrt{3}}{2}\right) = \sqrt{3}$$

$$y = r\sin\theta = 2\sin\left(-\frac{\pi}{6}\right) = 2\left(-\frac{1}{2}\right) = -1$$

The Cartesian coordinates are $(\sqrt{3}, -1)$.

Example 2 Converting Cartesian Coordinates to Polar Coordinates

a. Convert $(-3, -3)$ to polar coordinates.

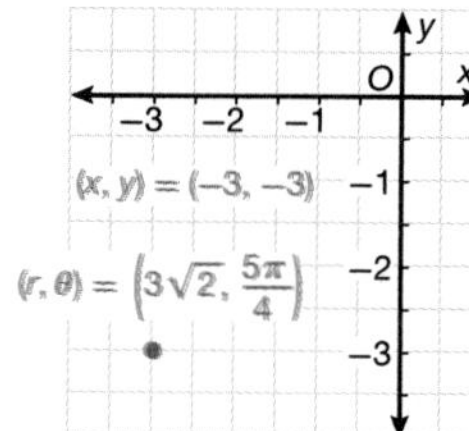

SOLUTION

$\tan\theta = \frac{y}{x} = \frac{-3}{-3} = 1$

Since $(-3, -3)$ lies in quadrant III, θ terminates in quadrant III. Therefore, one value of θ is $\frac{5\pi}{4}$.

$r^2 = x^2 + y^2 = (-3)^2 + (-3)^2 = 18$

$r = \sqrt{18} = 3\sqrt{2}$

One ordered pair of polar coordinates is $\left(3\sqrt{2}, \frac{5\pi}{4}\right)$.

Hint

$\text{Tan}^{-1}\,1 = \frac{\pi}{4}$, and θ terminates in quadrant III, so one value of θ is $\frac{\pi}{4} + \pi = \frac{5\pi}{4}$.

ENGLISH LEARNERS

Explain the meaning of the word **customary**. Say:

"Customary describes the usual way that something is practiced. For example, it is customary to shake hands when meeting a new friend."

Have students name a customary practice.
Sample: opening the door for someone else

672 *Saxon Algebra 2*

b. Convert (0, −1) to polar coordinates.

SOLUTION

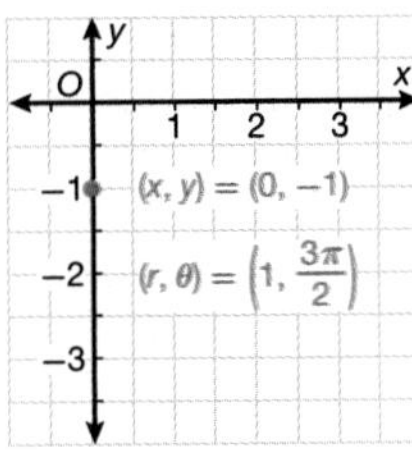

$\tan\theta = \frac{y}{x} = \frac{-1}{0}$, which is undefined. Since θ terminates on the negative y-axis, one value of θ is $\frac{3\pi}{2}$.

$r^2 = x^2 + y^2 = (0)^2 + (-1)^2 = 1$

$r = 1$

One ordered pair of polar coordinates is $\left(1, \frac{3\pi}{2}\right)$.

A **polar equation** is an equation for a curve with coordinates r and θ. There are two basic polar equations $r = k$ and $\theta = \alpha$, where k is a positive constant and α is a constant. The graph of $r = k$ forms a circle and the graph of $\theta = \alpha$ forms a line through the origin. These graphs can be identified by converting these types of basic polar equations into the Cartesian coordinate system.

Example 3 Graphing Polar Equations

a. Graph $r = 2$.

SOLUTION

A circle with all points 2 units from the pole.

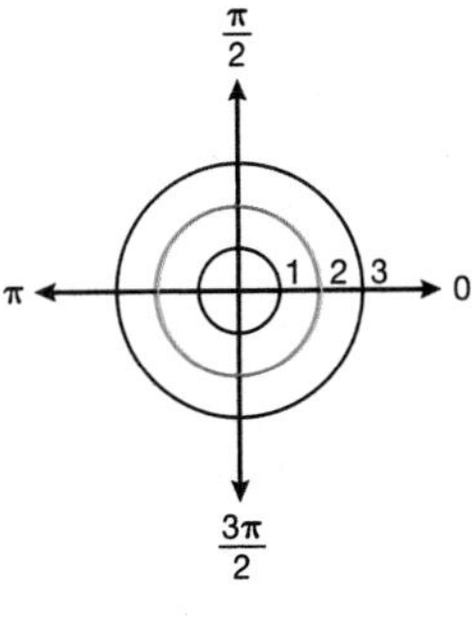

Check Convert to a Cartesian equation.

$r = 2$

$r^2 = 4$ Square both sides.

$x^2 + y^2 = 4$ $r^2 = x^2 + y^2$

This is the Cartesian equation of the same circle.

b. Graph $\theta = \frac{\pi}{6}$.

SOLUTION

The graph consists of all points on the line that makes an angle of $\frac{\pi}{6}$ radian with the positive x-axis.

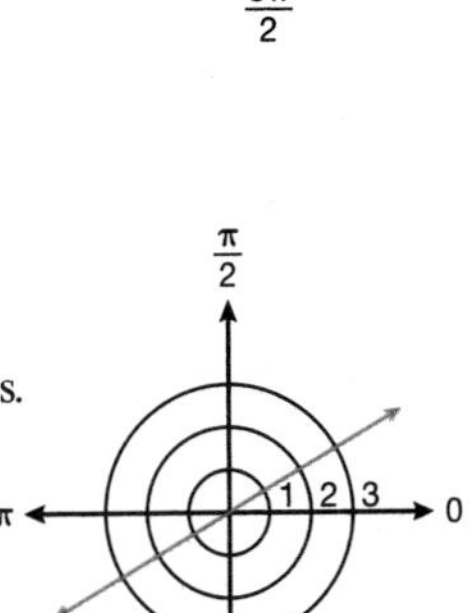

Check Convert to a Cartesian equation.

$\tan\theta = \frac{y}{x}$ Definition of $\tan\theta$.

$\tan\frac{\pi}{6} = \frac{y}{x}$ Substitute $\theta = \frac{\pi}{6}$.

$\frac{\sqrt{3}}{3} = \frac{y}{x}$ Evaluate $\tan\frac{\pi}{6}$.

$y = \frac{\sqrt{3}}{3}x$ Solve for y.

Math Reasoning

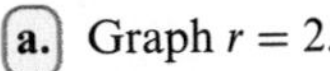

Analyze If a is a positive constant, describe the graphs of polar equations of the following forms.

$r = a$ and $\theta = a$

$r = a$ is a circle around the pole with a radius of a. $\theta = a$ is a line through the pole with an angle of a radians.

INCLUSION

Have students trace a rectangular grid directly over a polar grid so they can visualize how the points relate. Show students that the point (0, 1) in rectangular coordinates is the same as $\left(1, \frac{\pi}{2}\right)$ in polar coordinates.

Additional Example 2

b. Convert $(-1, 0)$ to polar coordinates. $(1, \pi)$

Example 3

Students will graph only the simplest form of a polar equation.

Additional Example 3

a. Graph $r = 3$.

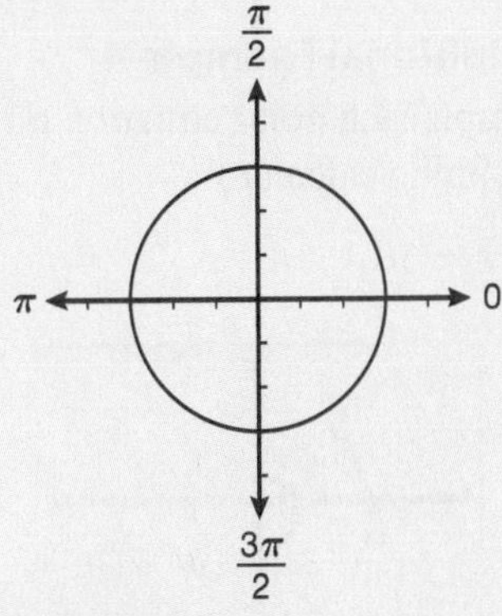

b. Graph $\theta = \frac{\pi}{4}$.

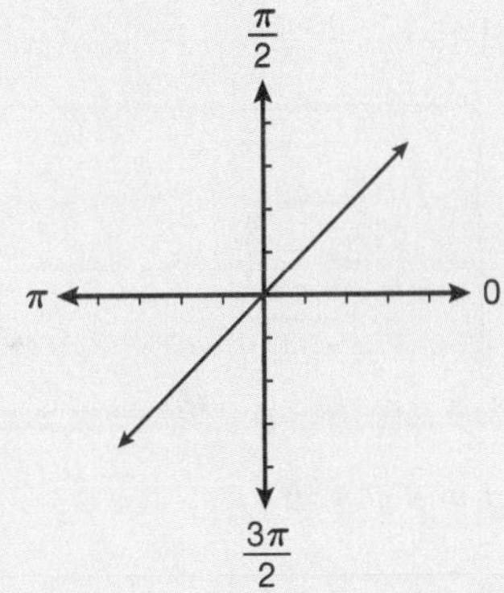

Example 4

Students explore more complicated graphs using a graphing calculator.

Error Alert Students often forget to put the calculator in both radian mode and polar mode. Remind students to visualize a point or two on the graph to be sure the graphing calculator represents the correct graph.

Additional Example 4

Graph each polar equation on a graphing calculator.

a. $r = 3\theta$

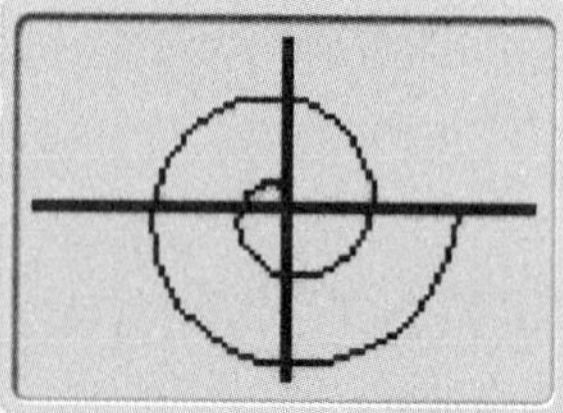

b. $r = 1 - \cos\theta$

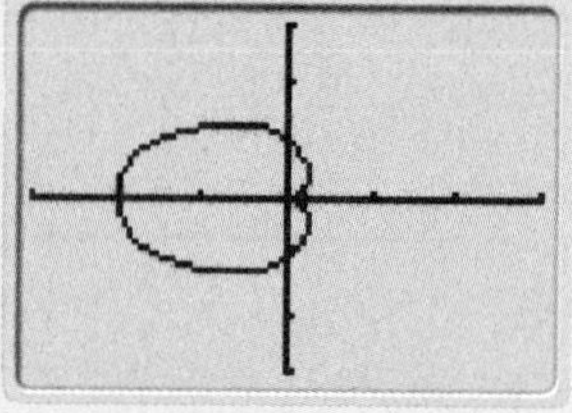

c. $r = 4\cos 3\theta$

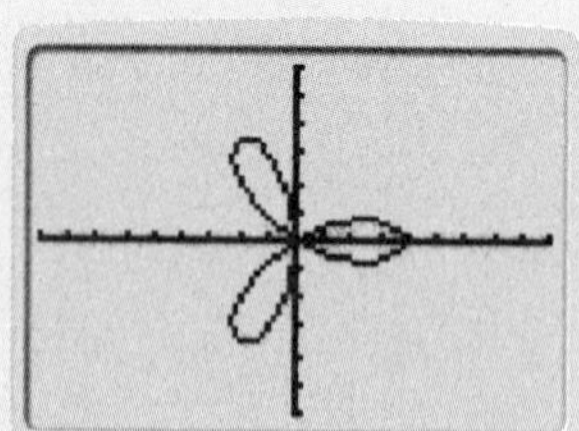

To graph a polar equation that has two variables, make a table and plot points. Below is a table of values that could be used to begin the graph of the polar equation $r = 2\theta$.

θ	0	$\frac{\pi}{6}$	$\frac{\pi}{3}$	$\frac{\pi}{2}$
$r(\theta) = 2\theta$	0	$\frac{\pi}{3} \approx 1.05$	$\frac{2\pi}{3} \approx 2.09$	$\pi \approx 3.14$

Graphing polar equations by plotting points is often a long process. The equation in the table above is graphed by calculator in Example 4a.

Graphing Calculator Tip

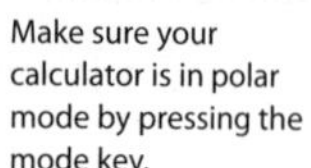

Make sure your calculator is in polar mode by pressing the mode key.

Math Language

The graphs in Example 4 have these names:
a. Archimedean spiral
b. cardioid
c. rose

Example 4 Graphing Polar Equations on a Graphing Calculator

Graph each polar equation on a graphing calculator.

a. $r = 2\theta$

SOLUTION

Use the window indicated below.

$\theta\text{min} = 0$ $\quad X\text{min} = -36$

$\theta\text{max} = 4\pi$ $\quad X\text{max} = 36$

$\theta\text{step} = \frac{\pi}{24}$ $\quad Y\text{min} = -24$

$Y\text{max} = 24$

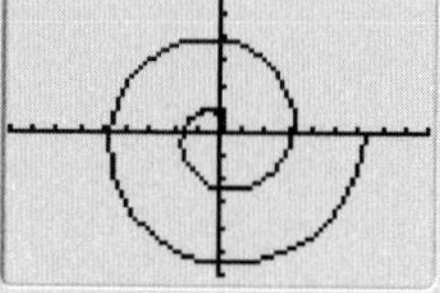

b. $r = 1 - \sin\theta$

SOLUTION

Use the window indicated below.

$\theta\text{min} = 0$ $\quad X\text{min} = -3$

$\theta\text{max} = 2\pi$ $\quad X\text{max} = 3$

$\theta\text{step} = \frac{\pi}{24}$ $\quad Y\text{min} = -3$

$Y\text{max} = 1$

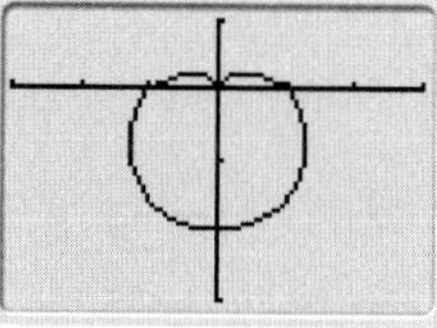

c. $r = 5\cos 2\theta$

SOLUTION

Use the window indicated below.

$\theta\text{min} = 0$ $\quad X\text{min} = -9$

$\theta\text{max} = 2\pi$ $\quad X\text{max} = 9$

$\theta\text{step} = \frac{\pi}{24}$ $\quad Y\text{min} = -6$

$Y\text{max} = 6$

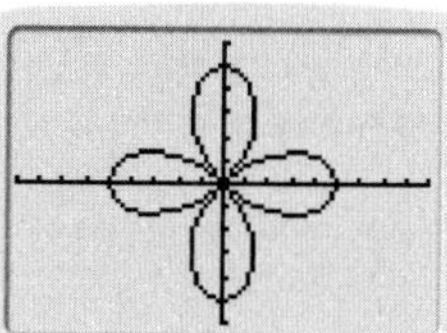

INCLUSION

Have students practice conversion on a unit circle so they see that the rectangular coordinates convert as shown in the table.

Rectangular (x, y)	Polar (r, θ)
(1, 0)	(1, 0)
(0, 1)	$\left(1, \frac{\pi}{2}\right)$
(−1, 0)	$(1, \pi)$
(0, −1)	$\left(1, \frac{3\pi}{2}\right)$

Example 5 Application: Cell Phone Tower

A planned cell phone tower will service an area with a 5-mile radius. It is to be located 3 miles east and 4 miles north of a highway intersection. Write and graph a polar equation to show the boundary of the region that will be serviced. Place the highway intersection at the pole.

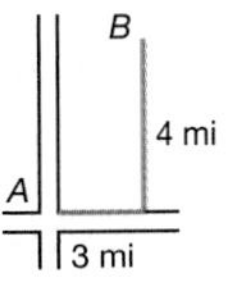

SOLUTION

The boundary is a circle with radius 5 and center (3, 4) on a Cartesian coordinate system, so the Cartesian equation is $(x-3)^2+(y-4)^2=5^2$.

$(x-3)^2+(y-4)^2=25$

$x^2-6x+9+y^2-8y+16=25$ Expand the binomials.

$x^2+y^2-6x-8y=0$ Simplify.

$r^2-6r\cos\theta-8r\sin\theta=0$ $x^2+y^2=r^2$, $x=r\cos\theta$, and $y=r\sin\theta$.

$r(r-6\cos\theta-8\sin\theta)=0$ Factor.

$r-6\cos\theta-8\sin\theta=0$ $r\neq 0$, so $r-6\cos\theta-8\sin\theta=0$.

$r=6\cos\theta+8\sin\theta$ Add $6\cos\theta+8\sin\theta$ to both sides.

The polar equation is $r=6\cos\theta+8\sin\theta$. Graph the polar equation on a calculator.

Use the window indicated below.

$\theta\text{min}=0$ $X\text{min}=-3$

$\theta\text{max}=2\pi$ $X\text{max}=15$

$\theta\text{step}=\frac{\pi}{24}$ $Y\text{min}=-2$ $Y\text{max}=10$

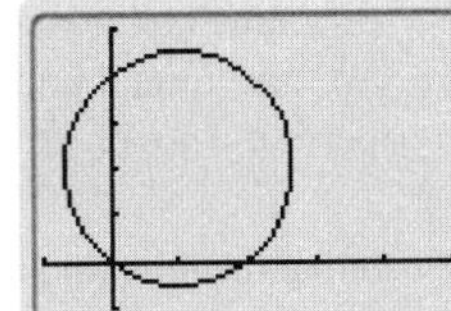

Lesson Practice

a. Convert $(3, \pi)$ to Cartesian coordinates. $(-3, 0)$
(Ex 1)

b. Convert $\left(1, \frac{2\pi}{3}\right)$ to Cartesian coordinates. $\left(-\frac{1}{2}, \frac{\sqrt{3}}{2}\right)$
(Ex 1)

c. Convert $(2\sqrt{3}, -2)$ to polar coordinates. Sample: $\left(4, \frac{11\pi}{6}\right)$
(Ex 2)

d. Convert $(-4, 0)$ to polar coordinates. Sample: $(4, \pi)$
(Ex 2)

e. Graph $r = 3$. See Additional Answers.
(Ex 3)

f. Graph $\theta = \frac{3\pi}{4}$. See Additional Answers.
(Ex 3)

g. Graph $r = \theta$ on a graphing calculator. See Additional Answers.
(Ex 4)

h. Graph $r = 1 + \cos\theta$ on a graphing calculator. See Additional Answers.
(Ex 4)

i. Graph $r = 4\sin 3\theta$ on a graphing calculator. See Additional Answers.
(Ex 4)

j. A planned cell phone tower will service an area with a 2-mile radius. It is to be located 2 miles north of an office building. Write and graph a polar equation to show the boundary of the region that will be serviced. Place the location of the building at the pole. $r = 4\sin\theta$; See Additional Answers.
(Ex 5)

INCLUSION

Tell students to graph the polar coordinates $(3, \pi)$ directly on a rectangular grid to help them see how the conversion formula works with Lesson Practice problem a. Tell students to start at (3, 0) on the x-axis, then visualize where they will end if the line must rotate 180°. Show students that they will be on the x-axis. So the rectangular coordinates would be $(-3, 0)$.

Example 5

Students will write a polar equation to represent a real-life situation.

Additional Example 5

A planned cell phone tower will service an area with a 13-mile radius. It is to be located 12 miles north and 5 miles east of a highway intersection. Write and graph a polar equation to show the boundary of the region that will be served. Place the highway intersection at the pole.
$r = 10\cos\theta + 24\sin\theta$

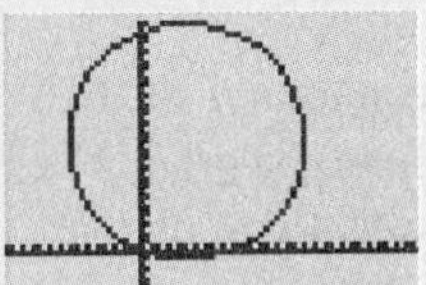

Lesson Practice

Problem f

Scaffolding Before graphing, have students think of all points on a line that will make an angle of $\frac{3\pi}{4}$ with the positive x-axis.

Check for Understanding

The questions below help assess the concepts taught in this lesson.

"What will a graph of $r = a$ look like? Explain how to graph this equation." The graph $r = a$ is a circle; Draw a circle with a radius of a at the pole.

"How do you convert a Cartesian equation of a circle into an equivalent polar equation?" Substitute $r\cos\theta$ for x, $r\sin\theta$ for y, and r^2 for $x^2 + y^2$.

3 Practice

Math Conversations

Discussions to strengthen understanding

Problem 2

Have students sketch a map on a grid to help them visualize the cities.

Problem 11

Guide the students by asking them the following questions.

"What is the formula for a falling object in feet per second?"
$h(t) = -16t^2 + v_0t + h_0$

"What is the equation if the ball starts 4 feet above the ground and has an initial velocity of 40 feet per second?"
$h(t) = -16t^2 + 40t + 4$

"Rewrite the equation if the ball ends at a height of 3 feet."
$3 = -16t^2 + 40t + 4$

"Explain how to solve the problem."
Solve for t using the quadratic equation.

Practice Distributed and Integrated

1. (87) **Multi-Step** **a.** Use the change of base formula to convert $\log_{1000}(10x)^2$ to base 10. $2\frac{\log 10x}{\log 1000}$
b. Evaluate when $x = 100$. 2

2. (52) **Geography** The city of Madera, California, is 95 miles due southeast of Stockton, which is 95 miles due southwest of South Lake Tahoe. How far would you have to fly from Madera to South Lake Tahoe, and in what direction? about 134 miles due north

***3.** (96) Convert $\left(-3, \frac{\pi}{2}\right)$ to Cartesian coordinates. (0, −3)

4. (73) A taxicab company that wants to know if customers are satisfied has each driver survey three customers during the day. Is the sample biased? Explain. The sample is biased because the drivers can choose to survey only customers that were satisfied.

***5.** (95) **Justify** Suppose that for polynomials $P_1(x)$ and $P_2(x)$, there are constants a and b such that $P_1(a) = P_2(b) = 0$. Is it correct to conclude that b is a root of $P_1(x)$ and a is a root of $P_2(x)$? Explain.

5. No; Just because a is a root of $P_1(x)$, it doesn't follow that a is also a root of $P_2(x)$. The same goes for b and $P_1(x)$.

Solve and graph the following compound inequalities.

6. (10) $3t > 18$ or $t - 3 < 0$ $t < 3$ or $t > 6$ See Additional Answers.

7. (10) $-(h - 2) > 7$ or $-8 \geq -2h$ See Additional Answers.

8. (1) **Statistics** The table shows the number of home runs hit by a softball player over a three-year period. Use properties of real numbers to mentally calculate the average annual home runs that she hit during this period. about 13

	Year 1	Year 2	Year 3
Home runs	8	15	17

Determine the domain and range.

9. (75) $y = \frac{3}{4}x^{\frac{1}{3}} - 1$ domain and range: all real numbers

10. (75) $f(x) = \sqrt{x + 2} + \sqrt[3]{x - 1}$ domain: $x \geq -2$, range $f(x) \geq \sqrt[3]{-3}$

11. (74) **Juggling** A juggler tosses a ball into the air. The ball leaves the juggler's hand 4 feet above the ground and has an initial velocity of 40 feet per second. The juggler catches the ball when it falls back to a height of 3 feet. How long is the ball in the air? The ball is in the air 2.5 seconds.

12. (77) In $\triangle LMN$, $LM = 14$, $MN = 8$, and $m\angle M = 84°$. Find LN. 15.4

13. (88) **Simple Interest** The simple interest formula is $A = P + Prt$, where P is the principal, or original amount invested, r is the annual simple interest rate, and A is the value of the investment at the end of t years. Solve the formula for t. Then determine how many years it will take for an investment to double in value at a 5% annual simple interest rate. $t = \frac{A-P}{Pr}$; 20 years

14. (82) **Geometry** Derive the function that can be used to find the area of an isosceles triangle with base a and congruent sides measuring b. Each base angle measures θ. Express in simplified form. $y = \frac{1}{2}ab\sin(\theta)$

CHALLENGE

The equation $r = a + b\cos\theta$ is called a limacon. The graph of $r = 1 + 2\cos\theta$ looks like this:

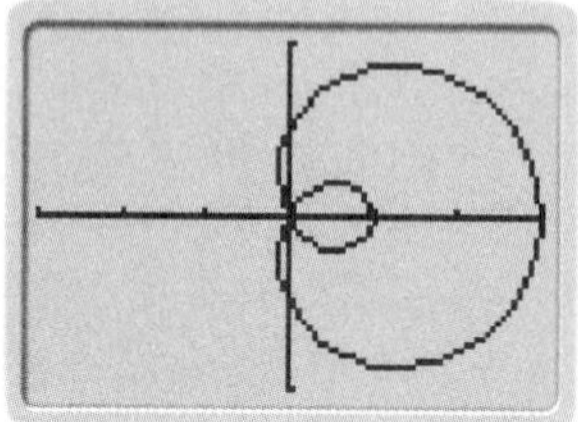

Substitute positive values for a and b in the equation. What is true of a and b when the limacon has an inner loop? What is true of a and b when the limacon has no inner loop? If $a < b$, the limacon has an inner loop. If $a > b$, the limacon has no loop.

*15. **Multiple Choice** Which equation represents a circle centered at (–5, 4) with a radius (91) of 3? D

A $(x - 5)^2 + (y + 4)^2 = 3$
B $(x - 5)^2 + (y + 4)^2 = 9$
C $(x + 5)^2 + (y - 4)^2 = 3$
D $(x + 5)^2 + (y - 4)^2 = 9$

16. **National Parks** The Surprise Arch, in Arches National Park, has a span of about (83) 60 feet and a height of about 50 feet. Write a quadratic function to approximate the arch. $y \approx -0.056x^2 + 3.33x$

*17. Find the roots of $y = x^9 - x^7 - 8x^6 - 16x^5 + 8x^4 + 16x^3 + 128x^2 - 128$. $x = \pm 2, \pm 1$ (95)

18. **Formulate** Solve $\frac{1}{a} + \frac{1}{b} = \frac{1}{c}$ for c. $c = \frac{ab}{a+b}$ (84)

19. Find the roots of $f(x) = 0.15x^3 - 2.85x^2 + 14.85x - 12.15$ using the Rational (85) Root Theorem. $x = 1$ and 9

*20. **Graphing Calculator** Use a graphing calculator to graph $y = \cos(7x)$ and compare its (86) period to that of the parent function. The period of the parent function is 2π and the period of $y = \cos(7x)$ is $\frac{2\pi}{7}$.

21. **Multiple Choice** Which is not a solution of $\begin{matrix} y \le -x^2 + 4x + 8 \\ y < -3x + 1 \end{matrix}$? D (89)

A (0, 0)
B (0, –3)
C (1, –6)
D (2, –2)

22. Let $f(x) = \tan(5x + 5)$ and $g(x) = 3x + 5$. Find the period of $f(g(x))$. $\frac{\pi}{15}$ (90)

*23. A kayaker paddles with the current for 7 miles, turns around, and paddles against (84) the current for 7 miles. The average paddling rate is 3 miles per hour. Write an inequality to represent the speed of the current if the total time is less than 7 hours. $\frac{42}{(3+c)(3-c)} < 7$

24. **Error Analysis** To rewrite $\ln(ex)^3$, a student wrote (81) $\ln(ex)^3 = \ln(3 \cdot (ex)) = \ln 3 + \ln(ex) = \ln 3 + \ln e + \ln x = \ln 3 + \ln x + 1$. What is the error? Rewrite $\ln(ex)^3$ as a sum or difference of terms correctly.

24. Sample: The student applied the Power Property of Logarithms incorrectly. Correct expression: $3 + 3 \ln x$

*25. **Write** Explain why every point in a polar coordinate system has more than one (96) set of polar coordinates. Sample: Any point with coordinates (r, θ) also has coordinates $(-r, \theta + \pi)$.

*26. **Savings** During week 1, a customer opened a bank account with \$450. Each week (92) thereafter, the customer deposits \$50. How much will the customer have in the account after the deposit is made during week 52? \$3000

27. **Error Analysis** A student says that the roots of the equation $4x^3 - 36x = 0$ are –3 (78) and 0. What is the error? The student omitted 3 as one of the solutions.

28. **Verify** Use FOIL to verify the difference of two squares formula $a^2 - b^2 = (a + b)$ (23) $(a - b)$. $(a + b)(a - b) = a(a) - a(b) + b(a) - b(b) = a^2 - ab + ab - b^2 = a^2 - b^2$

29. **Analyze** How are z-scores of –0.5 and 0.5 alike? How are they different? (80)

29. They are similar in that they are both the same distance away from the mean. They are different in that –0.5 is below the mean and 0.5 is above the mean.

*30. **Cell Phone Tower** A planned cell phone tower will service an area with a 6 mile (96) radius. It is to be located 6 miles west of a small town. Write a polar equation of the boundary of the region that will be serviced. Place the location of the town at the pole. Graph the equation on a calculator. See Additional Answers.

LOOKING FORWARD

Polar equations prepare students for

- **Investigation 10** Graphing Polar Models

Problem 18

Tell students to add $\frac{1}{a} + \frac{1}{b}$ and write as a single fraction, then cross multiply and solve for c.

Problem 19

Error Alert

Students might forget that the Rational Root Theorem can be used with decimals by multiplying the terms by a power of 10. Remind students to multiply the terms in problem 19 by 100 to eliminate decimals.

Problem 20

Extend the Problem

Have students find the amplitude, domain, and range of $y = \cos(7x)$.
Amplitude is 1, domain is all real numbers, and range is $-1 \le y \le 1$.

TEACHER TIP

In problem 21, tell students that when the answer choices include coordinates of 0, the values can be substituted quickly.

LESSON 97

1 Warm Up

For problem 2, remind students of the definition of an arithmetic sequence: a list of numbers in which the difference between adjacent terms is a constant.

2 New Concepts

In this lesson, students learn to find the common ratio and the nth term in a geometric sequence.

Example 1

Students find the common ratio and three more terms.

Additional Example 1

Find the common ratio of each geometric sequence and use it to find the next three terms.

a. $25, -5, 1, -0.2, \ldots$ $r = -0.2$; $0.04, -0.008, 0.0016$

b. $10, 10\sqrt{3}, 30, 30\sqrt{3}, \ldots$ $r = \sqrt{3}$; $90, 90\sqrt{3}, 270$

TEACHER TIP

Discuss the meaning of *consecutive terms* using the simple examples $2, 4, 6, 8, \ldots$ and $2, 4, 8, 16, 32, \ldots$. Have students describe the two sequences. Sample: arithmetic, add 2; geometric, doubling or constant 2

LESSON RESOURCES

Student Edition Practice Workbook 97
Reteaching Master 97
Adaptations Master 97
Challenge and Enrichment Masters C97, E97

LESSON 97 Finding Geometric Sequences

Warm Up

1. (92) **Vocabulary** Each number in a sequence is called a ___term___.
2. (92) True or False: The sequence {2, 4, 8, 16} is arithmetic. false
3. (2) Simplify $5(-3)^4$. 405

New Concepts

The sequence {3, 6, 12, 24, 48} is not arithmetic because the differences between consecutive terms are not the same. However, the ratio of any two consecutive terms is the same.

$$\frac{48}{24} = 2, \frac{24}{12} = 2, \frac{12}{6} = 2, \frac{6}{3} = 2$$

This makes the sequence geometric. In a **geometric sequence,** the ratio of successive terms is a constant other than 1. This constant is called the **common ratio.** It is found by dividing a term by its previous term and can be used to extend an infinite sequence.

Example 1 Identifying and Using the Common Ratio

Find the common ratio of each geometric sequence and use it to find the next three terms.

a. $6, 3, \frac{3}{2}, \frac{3}{4}, \ldots$

SOLUTION Divide a term by a previous term: $3 \div 6 = \frac{1}{2}$.

Find the next three terms by multiplying by $\frac{1}{2}$:
$\frac{3}{4} \cdot \frac{1}{2} = \frac{3}{8}, \frac{3}{8} \cdot \frac{1}{2} = \frac{3}{16}$, and $\frac{3}{16} \cdot \frac{1}{2} = \frac{3}{32}$.

The next three terms are $\frac{3}{8}, \frac{3}{16}$, and $\frac{3}{32}$.

b. $-4, 8, -16, 32, \ldots$

SOLUTION Divide a term by a previous term: $32 \div -16 = -2$.

Find the next three terms by multiplying by -2:
$32 \cdot -2 = -64$, $-64 \cdot -2 = 128$, and $128 \cdot -2 = -256$.

The next three terms are -64, 128, and -256.

Hint

For $a \neq 0$, $a^0 = 1$.

An explicit formula can be determined to find the nth term of a geometric sequence.

For the geometric sequence {2, 6, 18, 54, 162, ...},
$a_1 = 2(3)^0$, $a_2 = 2(3)^1$, $a_3 = 2(3)^2$, $a_4 = 2(3)^3$, $a_5 = 2(3)^4$.

MATH BACKGROUND

In a geometric sequence, also called a geometric progression, each term equals the product of the previous term and a fixed non-zero number called the common ratio. By convention, the ratio is designated r, the terms a, and the term numbers n. Thus, $a_{n+1} = a_n r$.

A useful equation relates the nth term to the first term and the common ratio: $a_n = a_1 r^{n-1}$.

The value of the common ratio r determines the behavior of the sequence. If $r > 0$, all terms have the same sign as the first term. If $r < 0$, the sequence alternates from positive to negative.

Geometric means are terms inserted between any two nonconsecutive terms. The geometric mean is also the nth root of the product of all the members of a data set with n members.

Math Reasoning

Formulate What is a recursive formula for a geometric sequence?

$a_n = a_{n-1}r$

Geometric Sequences
The nth term of a geometric sequence is given by $$a_n = a_1r^{n-1},$$ where r is the common ratio.

Example 2 Finding the nth Term of a Geometric Sequence

a. Find the tenth term of the geometric sequence 3, 12, 48, 192, ...

SOLUTION Find r: $12 \div 3 = 4$. Then use the formula $a_n = a_1r^{n-1}$.

$a_{10} = 3(4)^{10-1}$ Substitute 10 for n, 3 for a_1, and 4 for r.

$a_{10} = 3(262{,}144)$ Simplify.

$a_{10} = 786{,}432$

b. Find the 8th term of the geometric sequence 810, −270, 90, −30, ...

SOLUTION Find r: $-30 \div 90 = -\frac{1}{3}$. Then use the formula $a_n = a_1r^{n-1}$.

$a_8 = 810\left(-\frac{1}{3}\right)^{8-1}$ Substitute 8 for n, 810 for a_1, and $-\frac{1}{3}$ for r.

$a_8 = 810\left(-\frac{1}{2187}\right)$ Simplify.

$a_8 = -\frac{810}{2187} = -\frac{10}{27}$

The formula $a_n = a_mr^{n-m}$ can be used to find a term when given either a term and the common ratio or any two terms of the sequence.

Example 3 Finding the nth Term Given a Term and r

The fifth term of a geometric sequence is 567. The common ratio is 3. Find the ninth term.

SOLUTION In the formula $a_n = a_mr^{n-m}$, replace both instances of m with 5, replace n with 9, and replace r with 3.

$a_9 = a_5r^{9-5}$

$a_9 = 567(3)^4$

$a_9 = 567(81)$

$a_9 = 45{,}927$

When r must first be found, there may be two cases, depending on whether an even root or an odd root must be taken. This could lead to two possible values for the nth term.

TEACHER TIP

For problems that involve geometric sequences, have students begin by recording the given values for the variables n, a, and r.

Example 2

Students use the formula $a_n = a_1r^{n-1}$ to find the nth term of a geometric sequence given the first four terms.

Error Alert If students forget the minus sign in a problem such as part b, point out that the terms alternate between positive and negative. Ask: **"Are the even terms positive or negative?"** negative

"What can you tell about the sign of the term from the value of n in a_n?" In this sequence, if n is odd, a term is positive. If n is even, it is negative.

Additional Example 2

a. Find the 11th term of the geometric sequence 64, 32, 16, 8, ... 0.0625 or $\frac{1}{16}$

b. Find the 15th term in the sequence 5, −10, 20, . . . 81,920

Example 3

Students find the nth term of a geometric sequence given the common ratio and one of the other terms.

Additional Example 3

The fourth term of a geometric sequence is 80. The common ratio is 0.2. Find the tenth term. 0.00512

ALTERNATE METHOD FOR EXAMPLE 1

Explain that in a geometric sequence with first term a_1 and common ratio r, the next terms of the sequence are given by this equation.

$$a_{n+1} = a_n \cdot r, \text{ where } n = 1, 2, 3, \ldots$$

Write this sequence on the board: 6, 3, 1.5, 0.75, ... Have students identify a_1 and a_2. $a_1 = 6$, $a_2 = 3$

Ask: **"How can you confirm this is a geometric sequence?"** Sample: Check that each of the three ratios between adjacent terms equals the same number. Have students use the formula $a_{n+1} = a_n \cdot r$ to find the common ratio r. $r = 0.5$ Then have them find the next three terms, writing their answers in decimal form. 0.375, 0.1875, 0.09375

Example 4

Students find the nth term of a geometric sequence given any two terms.

Additional Example 4

a. Find a_1 of a geometric sequence given that $a_5 = 0.25$ and $a_8 = -31.25$. 0.0004

b. Find a_7 of a geometric sequence given that $a_2 = 600$ and $a_4 = 1350$. 4556.25 or −4556.25

Error Alert Students might assume that even with two cases, there is only one answer. Use the table at the bottom of the page to show that there are sometimes two possible answers for a given term.

TEACHER TIP

An equiangular spiral forms a lovely model for a geometric sequence. The radii are in geometric progression if the angles increase uniformly. If the radii are equally spaced, then the segments of the spiral are a geometric progression.

Example 4 Finding the *n*th Term Given Any Two Terms

a. Find a_1 of a geometric sequence given that $a_4 = 32$ and $a_9 = 1024$.

SOLUTION In the formula $a_n = a_m r^{n-m}$, replace m with 4 and replace n with 9.

$a_9 = a_4 r^{9-4}$

$1024 = 32r^5$ Substitute a_9 with 1024 and a_4 with 32.

$32 = r^5$ Solve for r.

$2 = r$ Take the fifth root of each side.

Now find a_1. Use either of the known terms.

$32 = a_1(2)^{4-1}$ Substitute 32 for a_n and 4 for n.

$32 = a_1(8)$ Solve for a_1.

$4 = a_1$

The first term of the sequence is 4.

Check

Check by using a_1 to find the ninth term: $a_9 = 4(2)^8 = 4(256) = 1024$.

b. Find a_7 of a geometric sequence given that $a_3 = -36$ and $a_5 = -324$.

SOLUTION In the formula $a_n = a_m r^{n-m}$, replace m with 3 and replace n with 5.

$a_5 = a_3 r^{5-3}$

$-324 = -36r^2$ Substitute a_5 with −324 and a_3 with −36.

$9 = r^2$ Solve for r.

$\pm 3 = r$ Take the square root of each side.

Now find a_7. Consider both $r = 3$ and $r = -3$.

Case 1: $r = 3$	Case 2: $r = -3$
$a_7 = a_3(3)^{7-3}$	$a_7 = a_3(-3)^{7-3}$
$a_7 = -36(3)^4$	$a_7 = -36(-3)^4$
$a_7 = -36(81)$	$a_7 = -36(81)$
$a_7 = -2916$	$a_7 = -2916$

In this example, both possible values of r give the same value for a_7. The seventh term of the sequence is −2916.

Math Reasoning

Verify Use the formula to show that a_4 has two possible values.

$a_4 = -36(3)^1 = -108$ or $a_4 = -36(-3)^1 = 108$

Check

	a_3	a_4	a_5	a_6	a_7
$r = 3$	−36	−108	−324	−972	−2916
$r = -3$	−36	108	−324	972	−2916

INCLUSION

Use Example 2, part a, to help students become comfortable with the subscripts and superscripts in $a_n = a_1 r^{n-1}$. Begin this chart on the board:

Term Number	n	1	2	3	4
Term Value	a_n	3	12	48	192

Have students use the chart to identify a_1, a_2, and so on. $a_1 = 3$, $a_2 = 12$, $a_3 = 48$, $a_4 = 192$

Use questions such as the following in the discussion: **"What happens to $a_n = a_1 r^{n-1}$ when n equals 1?"** $a_n = a_1$ **"How can you use $a_n = a_1 r^{n-1}$ to find the common ratio r?"** Sample: Substitute the first term and any other term. The term number of the latter equals n. Solve for r.

Example 5 Application: Salary

An employee's salary is structured so that he earns \$43,400 in the first year with a 3.5% raise each year thereafter. How much can the employee expect to earn in his fifteenth year?

Math Reasoning

Justify Why is r equal to 1.035?

3.5% = 0.035, and since it must be added to the previous term, add 100%, or 1, to it: 1 + 0.035 = 1.035.

SOLUTION The salaries each year form a geometric sequence where $r = 1.035$. Substitute 15 for n, 43,400 for a_1, and 1.035 for r in $a_n = a_1r^{n-1}$.

$$a_{15} = 43{,}400(1.035)^{15-1}$$

$$a_{15} = 70{,}251.34 \quad \text{Round to the hundredths place.}$$

The employee's salary in the fifteenth year will be \$70,251.34.

Check Use a graphing calculator.

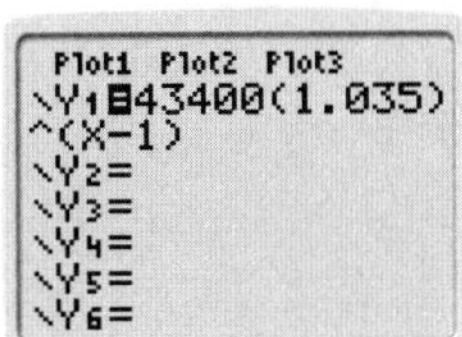

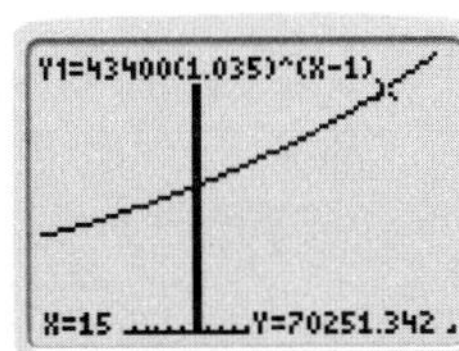

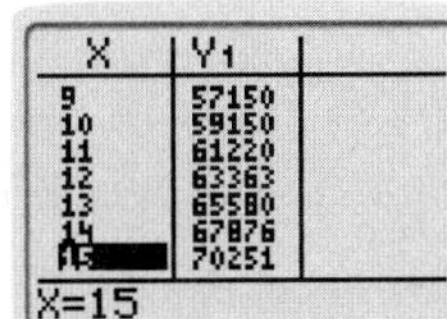

Lesson Practice

Find the common ratio of each geometric sequence and use it to find the next three terms.

a. 2, 0.2, 0.02, 0.002, ... (Ex 1)

b. $-200, -40, -8, -\frac{8}{5}...$ (Ex 1)

a. $r = 0.1$; 0.0002, 0.00002, 0.000002

b. $r = \frac{1}{5}$; $-\frac{8}{25}, -\frac{8}{125}, -\frac{8}{625}$

c. Find the ninth term of the geometric sequence −1, 5, −25, 125, ... (Ex 2) −390,625

d. Find the eleventh term of the geometric sequence 16, 4, 1, $\frac{1}{4}$, ... (Ex 2) $\frac{1}{65{,}536}$

e. The fourth term of a geometric sequence is $1\frac{1}{4}$. The common ratio is $-\frac{1}{2}$. Find the eighth term. (Ex 3) $\frac{5}{64}$

f. Find a_1 of a geometric sequence given that $a_3 = 128$ and $a_6 = 8192$. (Ex 4) 8

g. Find a_9 of a geometric sequence given that $a_4 = 24$ and $a_6 = 96$. (Ex 4) 768 or −768

h. An employee's salary is structured so that he earns \$35,890 in the first year with a 4.25% raise each year thereafter. How much can the employee expect to earn in his tenth year? (Ex 5) \$52,198.50

Practice Distributed and Integrated

*1. Given $V = \pi r^2h$, find h. (88) $h = \frac{V}{\pi r^2}$

2. **Write** A survey asks students, "Who would you vote for in the next school election, the relatively unknown sophomore Eileen Johnson, or the popular Zack Jennings?" Explain the bias in the question. (73)

2. The question is biased because it leads students to vote for the more popular candidate. The survey shouldn't focus on popularity, but should focus on each candidate's qualifications.

Simplify the following expressions.

3. $8^{\log_8 x}$ (72) x

4. $\log_3 81^x$ (72) $4x$

Example 5

Students use $a_n = a_1r^{n-1}$ to solve an application problem.

Additional Example 5

If the beginning salary is \$52,500 and the annual raise is 2.7%, what will the person's salary be after 5 years? \$58,403.80

Extend the Example

If the employee starts at \$40,000 and is making \$68,000 after 15 years, what was the annual salary increase? Round to the nearest tenth of a percent. 3.9%

Lesson Practice

Problem d

Scaffolding Ask: **"What will you find first to solve this problem?"** the common ratio

"How will you find it?" Divide second term by first.

Problem g

Error Alert Students may find only the positive root. Remind students that the equation has two roots, 2 and −2.

Check for Understanding

The questions below help assess the concepts taught in this lesson.

"What is the difference between an arithmetic and geometric sequence?" Sample: In the former, each term equals the sum of a constant and the previous term. In the latter, each term equals the product of a constant and the previous term.

"How many ratios do you need to check to prove that a finite sequence is geometric?" Samples: Every pair of adjacent terms. If there are n terms, you must check $n - 1$ ratios.

"When will the signs of the terms alternate?" When r is negative

CHALLENGE

Use this diagram.

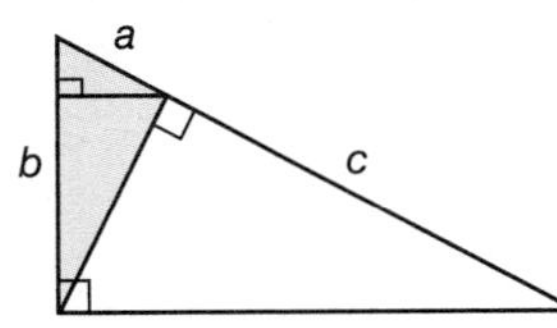

a. How is the shaded triangle related to the entire large triangle, the one made up of both the shaded and white regions? They are similar.

b. How does the diagram show that $\frac{b}{a} = \frac{a+c}{b}$? Sample: Ratio of hypotenuse to shorter leg is same in both triangles.

c. If $\frac{b}{a}$ represents the common ratio, write the geometric sequence represented by the right triangle diagram. $a, b, (a + c)$

3 Practice

Math Conversations

Discussions to strengthen understanding

Problem 6

Have students begin by explaining why the polynomial is *not* a perfect square. 36 is not the square of half of 18.

Error Alert If students try to subtract $6x$ from the polynomial, point out that action will produce a negative radical term on the right side of the equation.

Problems 8–9

Extend the Problem

Find AD and DA.
$\begin{bmatrix} -50 & -6 \\ -35 & -11 \end{bmatrix}$, $\begin{bmatrix} -68 & 16 \\ -51 & 7 \end{bmatrix}$

Problem 11

Guide the students by asking them the following question.

"Why do both students start with $b^2 - 4ac$?" That is the discriminant in the quadratic formula. If necessary, review what the discriminant tells about the nature of the solutions in a quadratic equation.

Problem 14

If students need a hint, ask:
"What angle is formed by the diagonal of a square?" 45°
"How do you write that angle in radians?" $\frac{\pi}{4}$

---

*5. (97) **Multi-Step** The value of a car in its first year was $18,900. Each year thereafter, the value was 85% of what it was the previous year. The values each year form a geometric sequence.

a. Write a formula to find the value of the car in the nth year. $a_n = 18{,}900(0.85)^{n-1}$

b. Find the value of the car in year 6. $8,386.03

6. (Inv 6) What number can be added to both sides of the equation $x^2 + 18x + 36 = 0$ to make it a perfect square? 45

7. (70) **Analyze** How can you tell that $4 + \sqrt{x} = 1$ will have no solutions? When 4 is subtracted from both sides, the square root equals a negative number.

Find each of the following matrix operations for $A = \begin{bmatrix} -6 & 2 \\ -1 & -3 \end{bmatrix}$ and $D = \begin{bmatrix} 11 & 2 \\ 8 & 3 \end{bmatrix}$.

8. (5) Find $A + D$. $\begin{bmatrix} 5 & 4 \\ 7 & 0 \end{bmatrix}$

9. (5) Find $D - 3A$. $\begin{bmatrix} 29 & -4 \\ 11 & 12 \end{bmatrix}$

*10. (97) Find the fifteenth term of the geometric sequence 2, 6, 18, ... 9,565,938

11. (74) **Error Analysis** Which student made an error in determining the number of solutions of $-3x^2 + 6x = 4$? What was the error?

Student A:	$b^2 - 4ac$	**Student B:**	$b^2 - 4ac$
	$6^2 - 4(-3)(4)$		$6^2 - 4(-3)(-4)$
	$36 + 48$		$36 - 48$
	84		-12
	2 real solutions		2 complex solutions

11. Student A used the wrong value for c. When the equation is written in standard form, it becomes $-3x^2 + 6x - 4 = 0$, so $c = -4$.

*12. (96) **Estimate** Write approximate polar coordinates for the point with Cartesian coordinates (6, 6.2). Explain your method.

12. Sample: $\left(6\sqrt{2}, \frac{\pi}{4}\right)$; The point with Cartesian coordinates (6, 6.2) is close to the point with Cartesian coordinates (6, 6), which has $\left(6\sqrt{2}, \frac{\pi}{4}\right)$ as polar coordinates.

13. (62) **Geometry** A student is told to draw a rectangle so that the perimeter is 48 units and the area is 150 square units. The equation $24x - x^2 = 150$ gives the values of x that meet these criteria where x is the length of the rectangle. Solve the equation. Describe your findings. $12 \pm i\sqrt{6}$; The rectangle does not exist because there is no real number for the length, x.

*14. (96) **City Planning** A park lawn is a square. A diagonal sidewalk is planned, shown as $\overline{AB}$ in the diagram. Using point A as the pole and $\overrightarrow{AC}$ as the polar axis, write a polar equation of the line that contains $\overline{AB}$. Sample: $\theta = \frac{\pi}{4}$

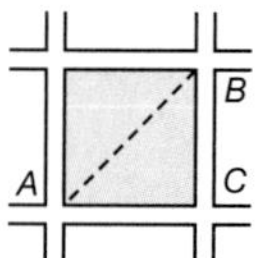

15. (22) **Coordinate Geometry** Graph {(2, 4), (5, 6), (–1, 0), (7, 10)}. Determine if this relation is a function. Determine if the graph is continuous, discontinuous, and/or discrete. See Additional Answers.

16. (75) **Model** Graph the square root function and its inverse. $y = \frac{1}{3}\sqrt{x} - 4$ See Additional Answers.

17. (84) **National Highways** In Texas, the speed limit on state highways at night is 5 miles per hour less than what it is during the day. A driver drove 350 miles during the day and 195 miles at night, with the cruise control set to the appropriate speed limit. The total driving time was 8 hours. Write and solve a rational equation to find the speed limit during the day. $\frac{350}{r} + \frac{195}{r-5} = 8$; 70 mph

ENGLISH LEARNERS

For Problem 17, explain the meaning of the word **cruise.** Say:

"To cruise means to drive at a constant speed. The cruise control on a car automatically keeps the car at a constant speed."

Ask students why cruise control is useful. Sample: It helps keep the driver's eyes on the road instead of on the speedometer, which makes driving safer.

682 Saxon Algebra 2

***18. Multiple Choice** The second term of a geometric sequence is 16 and the fourth term is 1. What is the common ratio? **D**
(97)

A $\frac{1}{16}$ B $\pm\frac{1}{16}$ C $\frac{1}{4}$ D $\pm\frac{1}{4}$

19. Analyze Consider the polynomial function $f(x) = ax^4 + bx^3 + cx^2 + dx + e$. Suppose that the polynomial is divisible by $(x - 1)$. Use synthetic division to show that $a + b + c + d + e = 0$. See Additional Answers.
(85)

20. Physics Two wheels spin in the same direction. The larger wheel completes a cycle in 3 seconds and the smaller wheel completes a cycle in 5 seconds. The two squares attached to the wheels are facing each other at time $t = 0$. How many seconds elapse before they are back in sync? 15 seconds
(86)

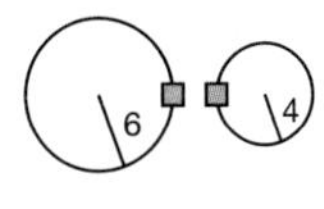

21. Find the common difference of the arithmetic sequence −62, −67, −72, −77, ... −5
(92)

***22. Graphing Calculator** Graph $\begin{matrix} 4y + 12 > x^2 \\ -\frac{1}{2}x \geq y \\ y \geq -2 \end{matrix}$ on your graphing calculator. Name two points in the solution set. Sample: (0, 0) and (1, −2)
(89)

23. Multiple Choice Which of the following has a period of 7π? **B**
(82)

A $y = \cos(7x)$ B $y = \cos\left(\frac{2}{7}x\right)$ C $y = \cos(3.5x)$ D $y = \cos\left(\frac{x}{7}\right)$

24. Given $g(x) = 0.5\sin(2x)$, identify the amplitude and period.
(82) amplitude = 0.5, period = π

25. A set of values has a mean of 15 and a standard deviation of 1.5. Find the percent of values above 18. 2.5%
(80)

26. Evaluate the piecewise function $f(x) = \begin{cases} 9 - 5x, \text{ if } x < -0.1 \\ 2, \quad \text{if } -0.1 \leq x \leq 2 \\ x^3 - x, \text{ if } 2 < x \leq 6 \\ 3 - x^2, \text{ if } x > 6 \end{cases}$ for $x = -0.4$, $x = 0$, and $x = 6$. 11, 2, 210
(79)

***27. Medicine** Cobalt-60 is an isotope that is used in radiation therapy for cancer patients. It has a half-life of about 5.3 years. How long will it take for 1 gram of cobalt-60 to decay to 0.9 gram? (Use the natural decay function $N(t) = N_0e^{-kt}$.) approximately 0.8 year
(93)

28. Boating A boat leaves a dock and travels in a straight path for 6 miles at an angle 15° north of east. Another boat leaves the same dock and travels in a straight path for 11 miles at an angle 65° south of east. If the second boat puts down an anchor and the first boat travels directly toward the second, estimate the time it will take the first boat to reach the second boat if the first boat travels at a constant rate of 8 miles per hour. about 1.4 hours, or 1 hour and 24 minutes
(77)

***29.** The endpoints of a diameter of a circle are located at (−10, −2) and (2, −2). Write an equation for this circle. $(x + 4)^2 + (y + 2)^2 = 36$
(91)

30. Convert $\log_6 (5x)^4$ to base e. Then evaluate when $x = 3$. $\frac{4\ln(5) + 4\ln(x)}{\ln 6}$; $x \approx 6.05$
(87)

Problem 29

You may need to review the midpoint formula.

A segment with endpoints at (x_1, y_1) and (x_2, y_2) has a midpoint with these coordinates.

$$\left(\frac{x_1 + x_2}{2}, \frac{y_1 + y_2}{2}\right)$$

CHALLENGE

Geometric means are the terms between any two nonconsecutive terms of a geometric sequence.

a. Insert two geometric means between 4 and 500. 20, 100

b. Insert three geometric means between 512 and 2. 128, 32, 8

LOOKING FORWARD

Finding geometric sequences prepares students for

- **Lesson 105** Finding Arithmetic Series
- **Lesson 113** Using Geometric Series

LESSON

98

1 Warm Up

For Problem 2, remind students that subtracting a number from x translates the circle horizontally. Subtracting a number from y translates the circle vertically.

2 New Concepts

This lesson introduces students to a second conic section, the **ellipse**.

LESSON 98

Making Graphs and Using Equations of Ellipses

Warm Up

1. (91) **Vocabulary** The graph of $x^2 + y^2 = r^2$ is a circle.
2. (91) What figure does the equation $(x - 1)^2 + (y - 1)^2 = 5^2$ form? 2. a circle of radius 5 centered at (1, 1)
3. (91) Where does $x^2 + y^2 = 7^2$ touch the x-axis? (7, 0) and (−7, 0)
4. (2) If $c^2 = a^2 - b^2$, which of these is the value of c if $a = 13$ and $b = 5$? A
   A $c = \pm 12$ **B** $c = \pm\sqrt{194}$
   C $c = \pm 144$ **D** $c = \pm 194$
5. (2) If $c^2 = a^2 - b^2$, find c if $a = 4$ and $b = 3$. $c = \pm\sqrt{7}$

New Concepts

An **ellipse** is the set of all points P in a plane such that the sum of the distance from P to two fixed points F_1 and F_2 is constant. The two fixed points, F_1 and F_2, are called the **foci**. An ellipse has two axes. The **major axis** is the longer axis of the ellipse and passes through the foci. The endpoints of the major axis are the **vertices** of the ellipse. The **minor axis** is the shorter axis of the ellipse. and its endpoints are the **co-vertices**. The major and minor axes are perpendicular and their point of intersection is the center of the ellipse.

Math Reasoning

Model Take a length of string and thumbtack both ends to a sheet of paper so that the string is not taut. Take a pencil and use the string as a guide to drawing an ellipse. What role do the thumbtacks play?

They are equivalent to the foci.

$$\frac{x^2}{a^2} + \frac{y^2}{b^2} = 1.$$

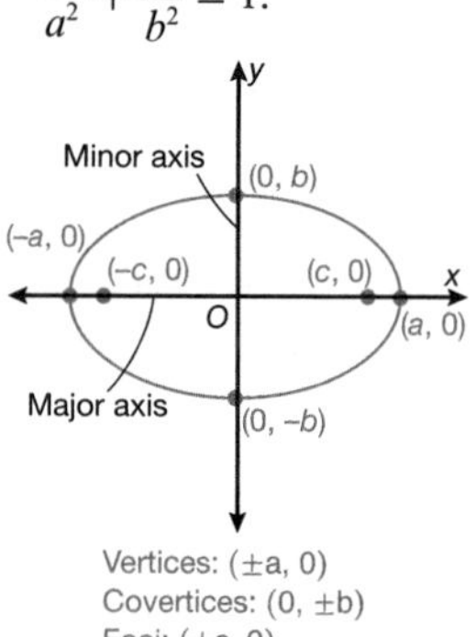

Vertices: (±a, 0)
Covertices: (0, ±b)
Foci: (±c, 0)

$$\frac{x^2}{b^2} + \frac{y^2}{a^2} = 1.$$

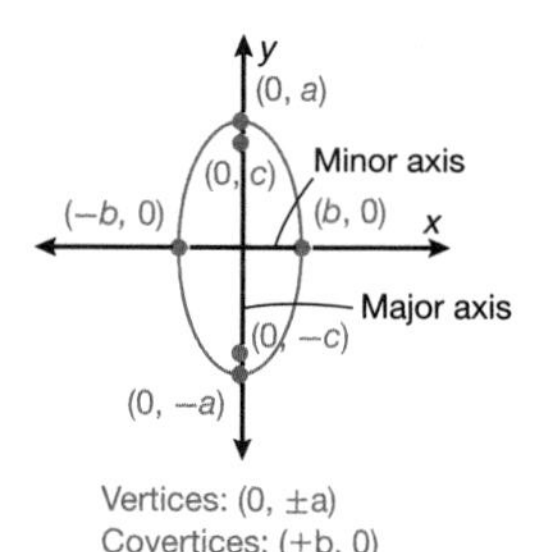

Vertices: (0, ±a)
Covertices: (±b, 0)
Foci: (0, ±c)

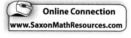

Standard Form of the Equation of an Ellipse: Center at (0, 0)

Major Axis Horizontal	Major Axis Vertical
$\frac{x^2}{a^2} + \frac{y^2}{b^2} = 1$	$\frac{y^2}{a^2} + \frac{x^2}{b^2} = 1$
Vertices: $(a, 0), (-a, 0)$	Vertices: $(0, a), (0, -a)$
Foci: $(c, 0), (-c, 0)$	Foci: $(0, c), (0, -c)$
Co-vertices: $(0, b), (0, -b)$	Co-vertices: $(b, 0), (-b, 0)$

Online Connection
www.SaxonMathResources.com

LESSON RESOURCES

Student Edition Practice Workbook 98
Reteaching Master 98
Adaptations Master 98
Challenge and Enrichment Master C98
Technology Lab Master 98

MATH BACKGROUND

Circles and ellipses have important similarities. Unlike the other conic sections, they are closed figures.

An ellipse can be thought of as a "stretched-out circle." Because the equation of a circle can be written in the form $\frac{x^2}{r^2} + \frac{y^2}{r^2} = 1$, the circle can be thought of as a "perfect" ellipse; the denominators being equal make the lengths of the major and minor axes equal. When the denominators are unequal, the figure is stretched in one direction.

A circle has eccentricity 0 because $\sqrt{1 - \frac{r^2}{r^2}} = 0$. The major and minor axes of a circle are perpendicular diameters; since $c = \sqrt{r^2 - r^2} = 0$, the foci in a circle are located 0 units from the center. So, a circle is an ellipse in which the two foci lie at the same point.

Example 1 Writing an Equation of an Ellipse

Write an equation in standard form for the ellipse with center (0, 0).

SOLUTION

Step 1: Choose the appropriate standard form.

$\frac{x^2}{a^2} + \frac{y^2}{b^2} = 1$ The horizontal axis is longer.

Step 2: Identify the values of a and b.

$a = 4$ The vertex (4,0) gives the value of a.

$b = 2$ The co-vertex (0,2) gives the value of b.

Step 3: Write the equation.

$\frac{x^2}{4^2} + \frac{y^2}{2^2} = 1$ Substitute the values of a and b into the equation.

The equation of the ellipse is $\mathbf{\frac{x^2}{4^2} + \frac{y^2}{2^2} = 1}$.

Hint

a always corresponds to the major (longer) axis of the ellipse.

There is an important relationship among a, b, and c: $c^2 = a^2 - b^2$. This relationship can be used to find the foci of an ellipse.

The eccentricity, e, of an ellipse is a measure of its curvature. Eccentricity is defined as $\frac{c}{a}$, where c is the distance from the center to a focus and a is the distance from the center to a vertex.

Example 2 Graphing an Ellipse Centered at the Origin

Graph the following equation. Find the vertices, co-vertices and the foci. Calculate the eccentricity e.

$25x^2 + 9y^2 = 225$

SOLUTION

Step 1: Write the equation in standard form by dividing both sides by the constant term.

$\frac{x^2}{9} + \frac{y^2}{25} = 1$ $\frac{y^2}{5^2} + \frac{x^2}{3^2} = 1$

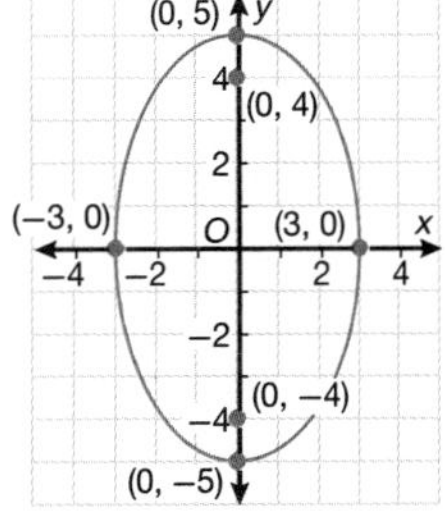

Step 2: Find the values of a, b, and c.

From the equation, $a = 5$ and $b = 3$.

Use the equation $c^2 = a^2 - b^2$ to find c.

$c^2 = 5^2 - 3^2$

$c = 4$

The vertices are **(0, ±5)**, the co-vertices are **(±3, 0)**, and the foci are **(0, ±4)**.

The eccentricity is $\frac{c}{a} = \mathbf{\frac{4}{5}}$.

Example 1

Using the graph of an ellipse, students write the equation of an ellipse centered at the origin.

Additional Example 1

Write an equation in standard form for the ellipse with center (0, 0).

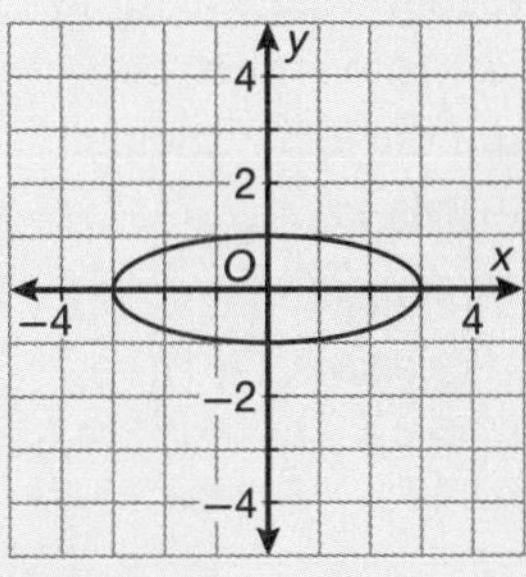

$\frac{x^2}{3^2} + y^2 = 1$

Example 2

The eccentricity of an ellipse is a measure of how much it deviates from circular. A circle has an eccentricity of 0. An ellipse has an eccentricity between 0 and 1.

Additional Example 2

Graph the following equation. Find the vertices, co-vertices and the foci. Calculate the eccentricity e.

$100x^2 + 36y^2 = 3600$

vertices: (0, ±10); co-vertices: (±6, 0); foci: (0, ±8); $e = \frac{c}{a} = \frac{4}{5}$

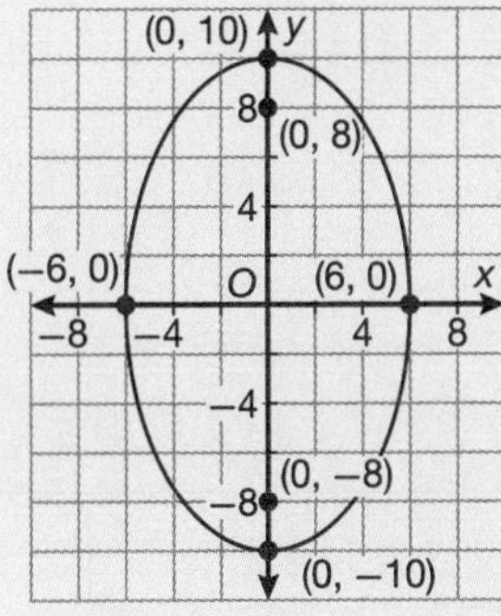

ENGLISH LEARNERS

Tell students that the word eccentric has meaning in everyday use as well as in mathematics. Say:

"To be eccentric means to be out of the ordinary."

For example, a person might have eccentric taste in clothes or a hobby he pursues to an unusual degree.

Discuss how an ellipse is related to a circle. Show students that an ellipse is an "odd" circle, so it has eccentricity.

Show students a series of ellipses with increasing eccentricity, explaining that the further an ellipse is from circular, the greater its eccentricity. Have them select two ellipses and state which has greater eccentricity, saying, "This ellipse has greater eccentricity than this ellipse."

Example 3

Error Alert Students might think that subtracting from x and y translates the graph left and down. Review standard form of an ellipse, pointing out the minus sign.

Additional Example 3

Graph the following equation. Find the center, vertices, co-vertices and the foci. Calculate the eccentricity e.

$9(x - 3)^2 + 16(y - 1)^2 = 144$

center: (3, 1); vertices: (7, 1)(−1, 1); co-vertices: (3, 4)(3, −2); foci: $(3 + \sqrt{7}, 1)$, $(3 - \sqrt{7}, 1)$; $e = \frac{\sqrt{7}}{4}$

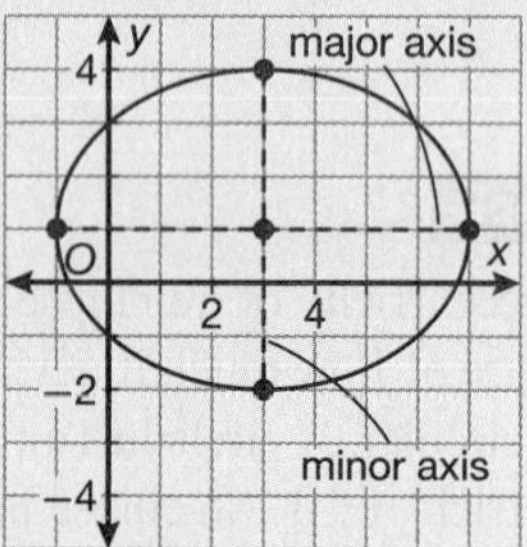

Ellipses can be translated so that the center is not the origin.

Standard Form of the Equation of an Ellipse: Center at (h, k)	
Major Axis Horizontal	Major Axis Vertical
$\frac{(x-h)^2}{a^2} + \frac{(y-k)^2}{b^2} = 1$	$\frac{(y-k)^2}{a^2} + \frac{(x-h)^2}{b^2} = 1$
Vertices: $(h + a, k)$, $(h - a, k)$	Vertices: $(h, k + a)$, $(h, k - a)$
Foci: $(h + c, k)$, $(h - c, k)$	Foci: $(h, k + c)$, $(h, k - c)$
Co-vertices: $(h, k + b)$, $(h, k - b)$	Co-vertices: $(h + b, k)$, $(h - b, k)$

Math Reasoning

Analyze Why is the equation of an ellipse not a function?

The graph does not pass the vertical line test.

Example 3 Graphing Ellipses Not Centered at the Origin

Graph the following equation. Find the center, vertices, co-vertices and the foci. Calculate the eccentricity e.

$$9(x - 2)^2 + 64(y - 5)^2 = 576$$

SOLUTION

Step 1: Write the equation in standard form by dividing both sides by the constant term.

$$\frac{(x-2)^2}{64} + \frac{(y-5)^2}{9} = 1 \qquad \frac{(x-2)^2}{8^2} + \frac{(y-5)^2}{3^2} = 1$$

Step 2: Find the values of a, b, c, h, and k.

The graph has a horizontal axis so, from the equation, $a = 8$, $b = 3$, $h = 2$, and $k = 5$.

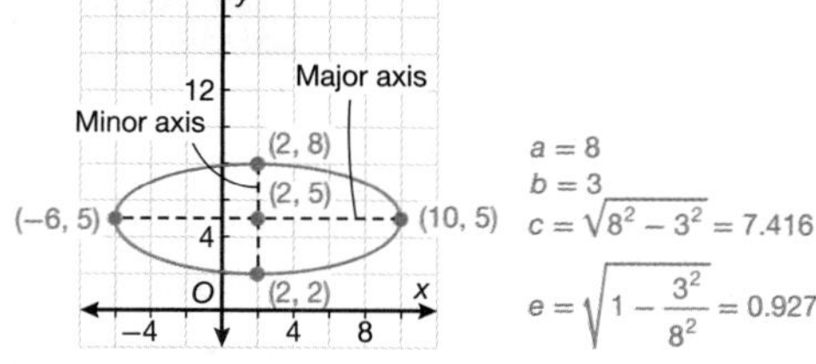

Use the equation $c^2 = a^2 - b^2$ to find c.

$c^2 = 8^2 - 3^2$

$c = \sqrt{55} \approx 7.416$

The eccentricity is $\frac{c}{a} = \frac{\sqrt{55}}{8} \approx \mathbf{0.927}$.

Step 3: Find the translated center, vertices, co-vertices, and foci.

Center: **(2, 5)**

Vertices: $(2 + 8, 5), (2 - 8, 5) \longrightarrow$ **(10, 5), (−6, 5)**

Foci: $\mathbf{(2 + \sqrt{55}, 5), (2 - \sqrt{55}, 5)}$

Co-vertices: $(2, 5 + 3), (2, 5 - 3) \longrightarrow$ **(2, 8), (2, − 2)**

The geometric definition of an **ellipse** is the locus of points such that the sum of distances from any point on the ellipse to the foci is constant.

$$r_1 + r_2 = 2a$$

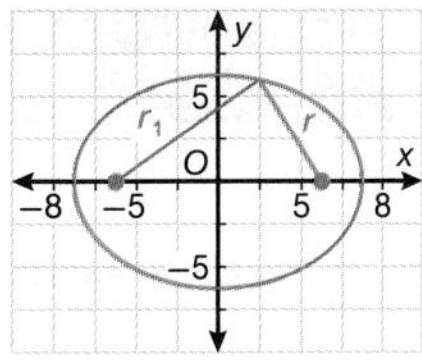

Example 4 Application: Planetary Orbits

All the planets have elliptical orbits, but each has a different eccentricity. The table lists each planet's orbital eccentricity. Write the equation of an ellipse centered at the origin that can be used as a model of Earth's orbit.

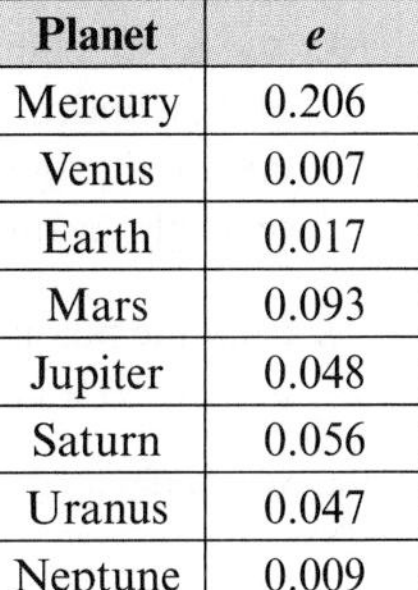

Planet	e
Mercury	0.206
Venus	0.007
Earth	0.017
Mars	0.093
Jupiter	0.048
Saturn	0.056
Uranus	0.047
Neptune	0.009

SOLUTION Use the eccentricity to find the relationship between a and b.

$$e = 0.017 = \sqrt{1 - \frac{b^2}{a^2}}$$

$$0.0003 = 1 - \frac{b^2}{a^2}$$

$$\frac{b^2}{a^2} = 0.9997$$

$$b = 0.9998a$$

A scale model of Earth's orbit maintains this relationship between a and b. So, let $a = 1$ to get this equation and graph.

$$\frac{x^2}{1^2} + \frac{y^2}{0.9998^2} = 1$$

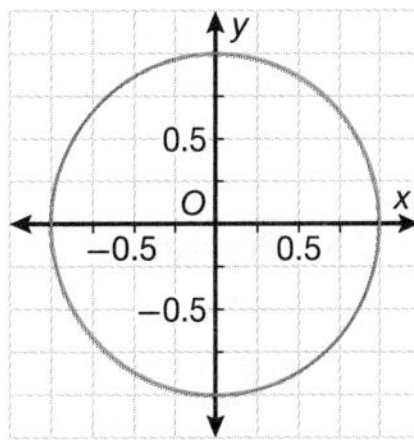

Math Reasoning

Analyze Why does the Earth's orbit look more circular than oval?

The eccentricity is close to zero.

Lesson Practice

a. (Ex 1) Write an equation in standard form for the ellipse with center (0, 0). $\frac{x^2}{5^2} + \frac{y^2}{2^2} = 1$

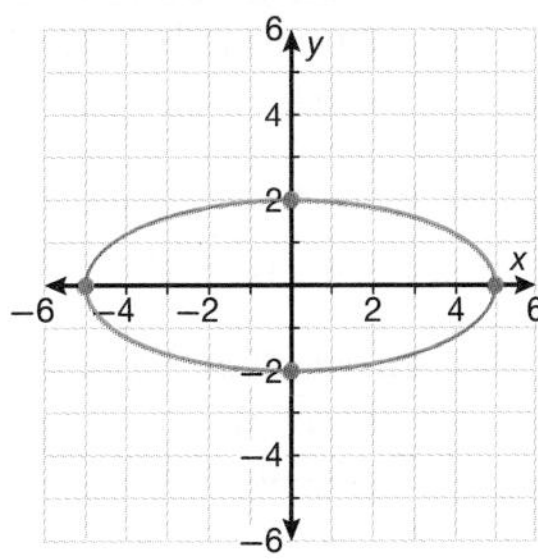

Graph the following equations. Find the center, vertices, co-vertices and the foci. Calculate the eccentricity *e*.

b. (Ex 2) $16x^2 + 36y^2 = 576$ See Additional Answers.

c. (Ex 3) $9(x - 2)^2 + 64(y - 5)^2 = 576$

d. (Ex 4) Write the equation of an ellipse centered at the origin that can be used as a model of Mars's orbits. $\frac{x^2}{1^2} + \frac{y^2}{0.9957^2} = 1$

INCLUSION

Help kinesthetic and visual learners get a feel for circles and ellipses by providing these activities.

Model a cone with a carrot (cut a flat "base" for the carrot). Then, model a conic section by slicing the carrot parallel to its base. Show students how the cut surface of the carrot is a circle.

Using another carrot "cone," slice at an angle, and show students that the cut surface is an ellipse. Continue making cuts at different angles to model different eccentricities.

The definitions of circle and ellipse can be modeled using thumbtacks and a loop of string. For a circle, tack one end of the string down and loop the other end around a pencil. Pull the string taut and draw the circle. For an ellipse, tack both ends of the string down slightly apart from each other. Use the pencil to push the middle of the string out until taut, and draw the ellipse.

Example 4

Point out that the equation of Earth's orbit is very close to being the equation of a circle since the denominators are nearly equal. So, Earth's orbit is nearly circular; thus, its eccentricity is close to zero.

Additional Example 4

Write the equation of an ellipse centered at the origin that can be used as a model of Mercury's orbit. $\frac{x^2}{1^2} + \frac{y^2}{0.9786^2} = 1$

Lesson Practice

Problem c

Scaffolding First, have students graph the center (2, 5). Then, have them identify the lengths of the major and minor axes and count to graph their endpoints. Encourage them to sketch the ellipse carefully, paying attention to its symmetry and curvature.

Check for Understanding

The questions below help assess the concepts taught in this lesson.

"What does the equation of an ellipse tell you about its graph?" The numerators tell you where the center will be. The denominators tell you which direction the major axis lies in, and the lengths of the major and minor axes.

"How is an ellipse like a circle? How is it different?" Each figure is a locus of points that meets a distance criterion. A circle is the set of points a constant distance from a point (the center). An ellipse is the set of points for which the sum of the distances to two fixed points (the foci) is constant.

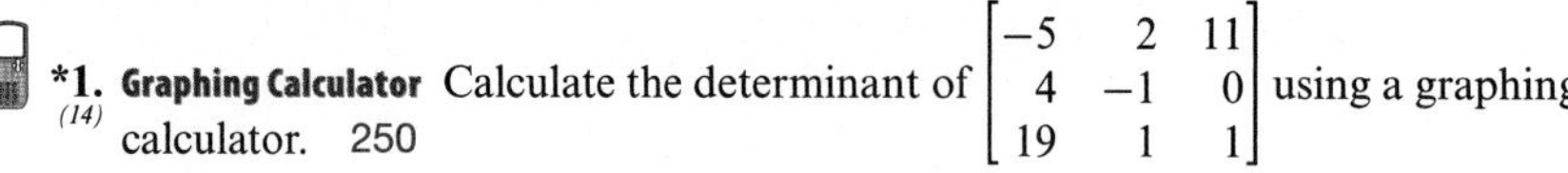

Practice Distributed and Integrated

*1. **Graphing Calculator** Calculate the determinant of $\begin{bmatrix} -5 & 2 & 11 \\ 4 & -1 & 0 \\ 19 & 1 & 1 \end{bmatrix}$ using a graphing calculator. 250
(14)

*2. **Generalize** How many ellipses have an eccentricity of 0.5 and cross the minor axis at (0, 2)? There are an infinite number, one for every possible orientation of an ellipse that also crosses that point.
(98)

*3. **(Optics)** An elliptical mirror is modeled by the equation $\frac{x^2}{15^2} + \frac{y^2}{10^2} = 1$. The property of an elliptical mirror is that if you shine a beam of light from a focal point to the mirror, the light is reflected toward the other focal point. What is the length of the two light beams? 30
(98)

4. Find the missing side lengths and angle measures of $\triangle ABC$. $A = 73°$; $a = 18$; $b = 11$ $B \approx 35.8°$, $C \approx 71.2°$, $c \approx 17.8$
(71)

*5. Write the equation of the ellipse given by $2x^2 + 3y^2 = 6$ in standard form. $\frac{x^2}{(\sqrt{3})^2} + \frac{y^2}{(\sqrt{2})^2} = 1$
(98)

6. **(Packaging)** The manager of a company that sells pasta is looking into a new container shape of a rectangular prism whose base is square and whose height is 5 inches greater than the length of one side of the base. If the volume is 28 cubic inches, what is the length of one side of the base? What is the height?
2 inches; 7 inches
(66)

7. **Geometry** A rectangle has length $4c$ and width d. Another rectangle has length 16 and width $(2 + 5c)$. Write a simplified expression of their combined area.
$4cd + 80c + 32$
(2)

*8. **(Population)** The estimated population of the District of Columbia from 2005 to 2006 decreased by about 0.089%. Assuming that the percent of decrease stays the same, the populations each year form a geometric sequence. Show how to use the formula for the nth term of a geometric sequence to find the population of DC in 2012 given that the estimated population in 2005 was 582,049. (Hint: Call 2005 year 1.)
$a_8 = a_1(r)^{n-1}$; $a_8 = 582{,}049(0.99911)^7$; $a_8 = 578{,}433$
(97)

9. **(The Ehrenberg Relation)** The Ehrenberg relation $\log(w) = 0.8h + 0.4 \pm 0.04$ shows the relationship between height h and weight w in young children ages 5 through 13. Solve for h and determine the height, in meters, of a child who weighs 40 kilograms.
(87)

9. $h = \frac{\log(w) - 0.4 \pm 0.04}{0.8}$; The child is between 1.45 m and 1.55 m tall.

10. **Write** Explain how to graph $3x + 5y = -35$ using slope and intercept. Be sure to show each step. See Additional Answers.
(13)

*11. **Error Analysis** Explain and correct the error a student made in finding the common ratio of the geometric sequence 270, 90, 30, 10, …
The student divided in the wrong order: $r = \frac{10}{30} = \frac{1}{3}$. $r = \frac{30}{10} = 3$
(97)

12. Given $h(x) = 6\sin(8x - 9)$, identify the amplitude and period. amplitude = 6, period = $\frac{\pi}{4}$
(82)

13. Find the roots of the polynomial function.
$f(x) = (x + 8)(3x^2 - 6) - (x + 8)(11x - 4)$ $x = -8, \frac{11 \pm \sqrt{145}}{6}$
(76)

*14. **Justify** Suppose that for polynomials $P_1(x)$ and $P_2(x)$ there are constants a and b such that $P_1(a) \neq 0$ and $P_2(b) \neq 0$. Is it correct to conclude that b is *not* a root of $P_1(x)$ and a is *not* a root of $P_2(x)$? Explain.
(95)

14. No; Just because a is not a root of $P_1(x)$, it doesn't follow that a is also not a root of $P_2(x)$. The same goes for b and $P_1(x)$.

688 *Saxon* Algebra 2

3 Practice

Math Conversations

Discussions to strengthen understanding

Problem 3

Suggest that students find the sum of the distances from (0, 10) to each focus. Have them sketch the needed line segments and use the Pythagorean Theorem to find their lengths.

Problem 9

Be sure students understand that the relation they write gives a range of heights for a given weight. They should treat the relation as two separate equations: $h = \frac{\log w - 0.4 + 0.04}{0.8}$ and $h = \frac{\log w - 0.4 - 0.04}{0.8}$.

Problem 11

Extend the Problem

After correcting the common ratio, have students find an expression for the 9th term in the sequence. $\frac{270}{3^8}$

CHALLENGE

Challenge students to use the definition of an ellipse to write the equation of an ellipse for which the sum of the distances from any point on the ellipse to the foci is 10 and the foci are at (−4, 0) and (4, 0).
$\frac{x^2}{25} + \frac{y^2}{9} = 1$

15. **Acoustics** A guitar string is strummed twice, which creates two waves along (86) the string. The first wave is reflected back and meets the second wave. If the waves are modeled by the equations below, what happens when the waves meet? (Hint: When one wave's crest coincides with another wave's trough, they tend to cancel each other out. This called destructive interference.)

$y = \cos\left(x - \frac{\pi}{2}\right)$ $\quad$ $y = \cos\left(x + \frac{\pi}{2}\right)$ They destructively interfere so that $y = 0$.

16. **Error Analysis** A student attempted to solve the formula $V = \frac{1}{3}\pi r^3$ for r and wrote (88) $r = \sqrt[3]{\frac{V}{3\pi}}$. What is the error? Solve the formula for r correctly. Sample: The student divided by 3 instead of multiplying by 3. Correct answer: $r = \sqrt[3]{\frac{3V}{\pi}}$

Simplify.

17. (3) $\dfrac{(x^{-2}yp)^{-3}(x^0yp)^2}{(2x^2)^{-2}}$ $\quad \left(\frac{4x^{10}}{yp}\right)$

18. (3) $-\dfrac{3x^2y}{xx} + \dfrac{2x^{-2}x^4}{y^{-1}x^2} - \dfrac{5xy^2}{xy}$ $\quad -6y$

19. **Multi-Step** A rectangular window has dimensions of 9 feet by 12 feet. The homeowner (89) wants to increase the window size by lengthening two sides by the same amount as shown. The area of the window is to remain less than 300 square feet.

a. Write an inequality to find the range of the amounts that can be added to the two sides. $x^2 + 21x + 108 < 300$

b. Solve the inequality. between 0 feet and about 6.9 feet

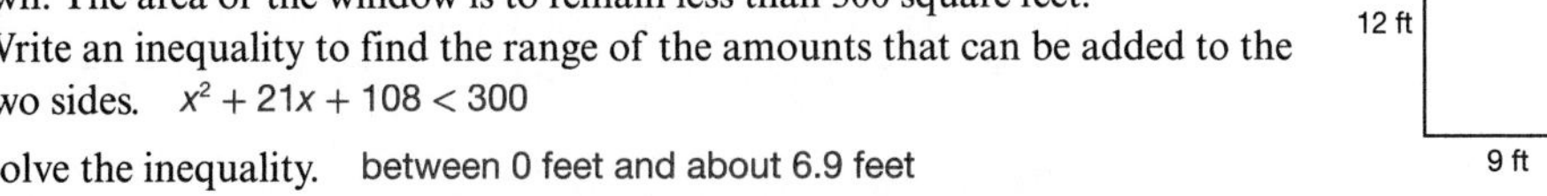

x ft
12 ft
9 ft
x ft

20. **Model** For what values of θ is $y = \dfrac{\sin(x)}{\cos(x - \theta)}$ the equivalent of $y = \tan(\theta)$? (90) for $\theta = 2\pi n$ for integer values of n

Evaluate each piecewise function for $x = 3$ and $x = 0$.

21. (79) $f(x) = \begin{cases} x^2 - 5, & \text{if } x \le 0 \\ x^2, & \text{if } 0 < x < 3 \end{cases}$

$f(3)$ is undefined; $f(0) = -5$

22. (79) $f(x) = \begin{cases} \frac{1}{2}, & \text{if } x < 1 \\ x, & \text{if } 1 \le x < 10 \\ -x, & \text{if } x \ge 10 \end{cases}$

$f(3) = 3$; $f(0) = \frac{1}{2}$

23. Write a quadratic equation whose roots are $5i$ and $-5i$. $x^2 + 25 = 0$ (83)

Identify all the real roots.

24. (85) $x^3 + 10x^2 + 17x = 28$ $\quad x = -7, -4, 1$

25. (85) $x^3 - 343 = 0$ $\quad x = 7$

*26. **Multiple Choice** When solving $\dfrac{x^2 + 5x - 6}{x^2 - 12x + 32} > 0$ by using a sign table, for how many (94) intervals will a test point need to be chosen? C

A 3 **B** 4 **C** 5 **D** 6

Simplify.

27. (48) $\dfrac{\frac{1}{2} - \frac{4}{15}}{\frac{5}{6} + \frac{1}{9}}$ $\quad \frac{21}{85}$

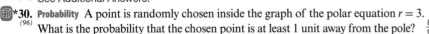

28. (48) $\dfrac{\frac{1}{x+1} - \frac{1}{x-1}}{\frac{x}{x^2 - 1}}$ $\quad -\frac{2}{x}$

29. **Write** How and why is the LCD used to solve a rational equation? (84) See Additional Answers.

*30. **Probability** A point is randomly chosen inside the graph of the polar equation $r = 3$. (96) What is the probability that the chosen point is at least 1 unit away from the pole? $\frac{8}{9}$

LOOKING FORWARD

Making graphs and solving equations of ellipses prepares students for

- **Lesson 109** Making Graphs and Using Equations of Hyperbolas
- **Lesson 114** Identifying Conic Sections

Problem 15

Have students graph each function and observe that for every x, $y_1 = -y_2$. So, the sum of the y-coordinates for every x is 0.

Problem 19

Error Alert

Students might give $-27.86 < x < 6.89$ as the solution set. Remind students to use common sense to narrow down the solution set to a realistic range given the constraints of the problem.

Problem 20

Guide students with the following questions:

"What trigonometric identity relates sine, cosine, and tangent?" $\tan x = \frac{\sin x}{\cos x}$

"When is $\cos x = \cos(x - \theta)$?" when θ shifts the cosine function one or more complete phases to the right or left

"What expression shows repeated shifts of the cosine function by a measure of 2π?" $\cos(x - 2n\pi)$, where n is any integer

Problem 30

Guide students with the following questions:

"What does the graph of $r = 3$ look like?" a circle centered at the pole with radius 3

"What is the area of the circle?" 9π square units

"What is the area that is *not* at least 1 unit from the pole?" It is bounded by $r = 1$, and has area π square units.

"What is the area that *is* at least 1 unit from the pole?" $9\pi - \pi$, or 8π square units

LESSON 99

1 Warm Up

For problem 2, ask students to describe the type of matrix that *can* be multiplied by a 2 × 3 matrix. any matrix with 3 rows

2 New Concepts

In this lesson, students relate vectors to Cartesian and complex coordinate systems. They find sums, differences, and dot products.

Example 1

Students represent vectors in various ways and find the orientation angle of a vector from the coordinates of its terminal point.

Additional Example 1

Graph vector $\vec{z}$ whose endpoints are at the origin and the point with given coordinates on the Cartesian and complex planes. Express the Cartesian version as a coordinate matrix and the complex version as a complex number. Find the orientation of the vector.

a. (8, 2) Check students' graphs; $\vec{z} = \begin{bmatrix} 8 \\ 2 \end{bmatrix}$; $\vec{z} = 8 + 2i$; $\theta \approx 14.04°$

b. (−4, −7) Check students' graphs; $\vec{z} = \begin{bmatrix} -4 \\ -7 \end{bmatrix}$; $\vec{z} = -4 - 7i$; $\theta \approx 240.26°$

LESSON RESOURCES

Student Edition Practice Workbook 99
Reteaching Masters 99
Notetaking Masters 99
Adaptations Masters 99
Challenge and Enrichment Master C99

LESSON 99 Using Vectors

Warm Up

1. **Vocabulary** For the complex number $a + bi$, the a term is known as the real part. *(62)*

2. True or False: A 2 × 3 matrix can be multiplied by another 2 × 3 matrix. false *(9)*

3. What is the distance between the points (3, 7) and (−2, 3)? about 6.4 *(41)*

New Concepts

A **vector** is a quantity that has magnitude, orientation, and direction.

There are several ways of expressing vector quantities, including complex numbers and matrices. Vectors can be graphed on Cartesian coordinate systems as well as complex coordinate systems.

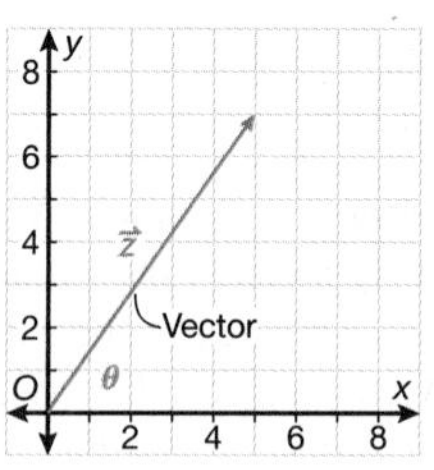

For vector $\vec{z}$:
$|\vec{z}| \rightarrow$ magnitude
$\theta \rightarrow$ orientation

Example 1 Graphing Vectors

a. Graph vector $\vec{z}$ whose endpoints are the origin and (5, 7) on the Cartesian and complex planes. Express the Cartesian version as a coordinate matrix and the complex version as a complex number. Find the orientation of the vector.

SOLUTION

Cartesian Coordinate System | **Complex Coordinate System**

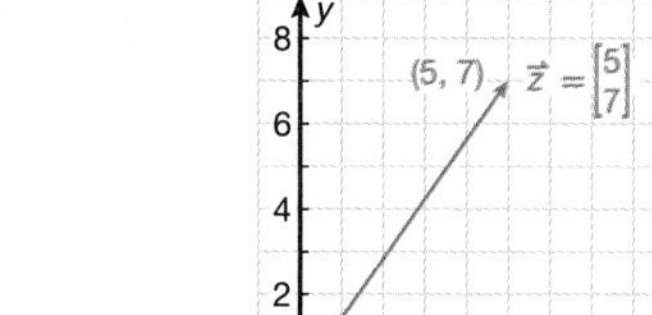

> **Math Reasoning**
>
> **Verify** How do you know that the angle of orientation is 54.46°?
>
> $\arctan\left(\frac{7}{5}\right) = 54.46°$

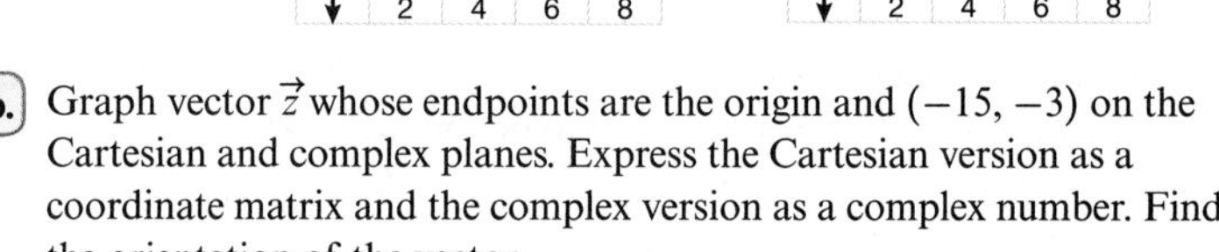

b. Graph vector $\vec{z}$ whose endpoints are the origin and (−15, −3) on the Cartesian and complex planes. Express the Cartesian version as a coordinate matrix and the complex version as a complex number. Find the orientation of the vector.

SOLUTION

Cartesian Coordinate System | **Complex Coordinate System**

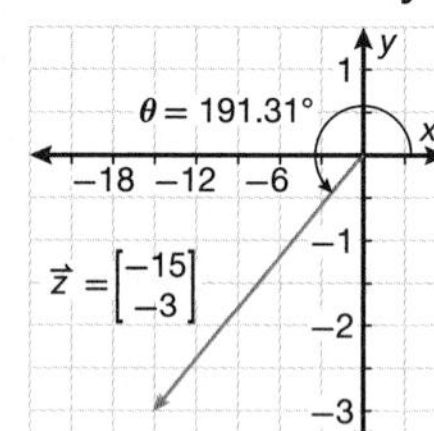

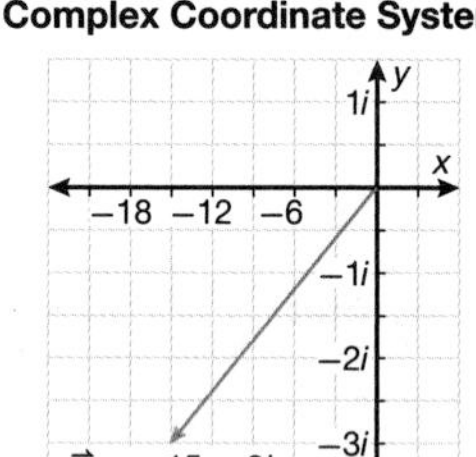

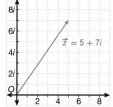

> **Math Reasoning**
>
> **Verify** How do you know that the angle of orientation is 191.31°?
>
> $\theta = 180° + \arctan\frac{-3}{-15} = 191.31°$

MATH BACKGROUND

The directed line segments known as vectors can represent a number of different concepts: complex numbers, translations of two-dimensional space, forces, velocity—anything with both magnitude and direction. In contrast, quantities such as temperature, length, and mass have only magnitude and no direction. When discussing vectors, quantities with only magnitude are called scalars.

Vectors can be described by the number of their coordinates. A two-vector has two coordinates and can be shown in two-dimensional space, a three-vector has three coordinates, and an n-vector has n coordinates.

Vectors can be added, subtracted, and multiplied by scalars. There is more than one kind of vector multiplication. These include the dot product, the cross product, and the tensor direct product.

Hint

When adding terms in matrices, the terms are added according to their positions. Vector addition and subtraction is similar to matrix addition and subtraction.

Vectors can be added and subtracted.

Vector Addition	Vector Subtraction
$\begin{bmatrix} x_1 \\ y_1 \end{bmatrix} + \begin{bmatrix} x_2 \\ y_2 \end{bmatrix} = \begin{bmatrix} x_1 + x_2 \\ y_1 + y_2 \end{bmatrix}$	$\begin{bmatrix} x_1 \\ y_1 \end{bmatrix} - \begin{bmatrix} x_2 \\ y_2 \end{bmatrix} = \begin{bmatrix} x_1 - x_2 \\ y_1 - y_2 \end{bmatrix}$
$(a + bi) + (c + di) = (a + c) + (b + d)i$	$(a + bi) - (c + di) = (a - c) + (b - d)i$
Vector Addition 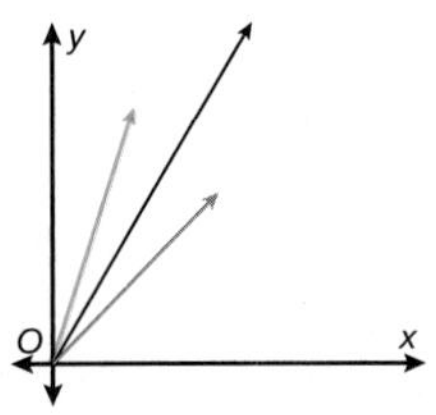	Vector Subtraction 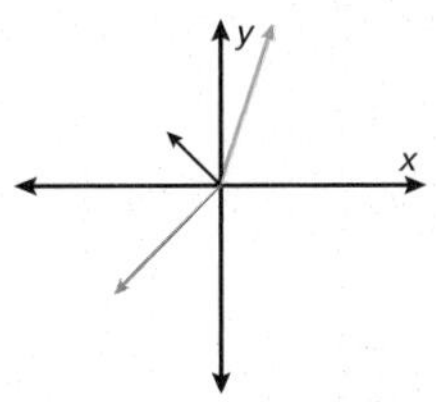

Example 2 **Adding and Subtracting Vectors**

a. Find the vector sum $\vec{A} + \vec{B}$ using matrix and complex addition.

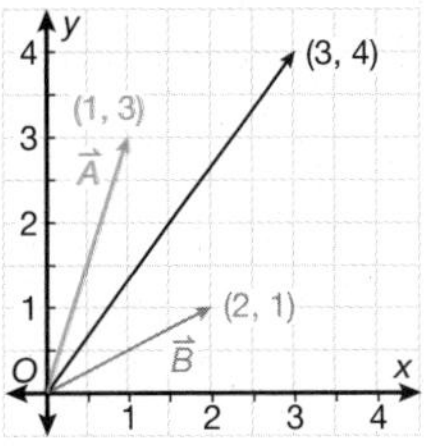

SOLUTION

$\begin{bmatrix} 1 \\ 3 \end{bmatrix} + \begin{bmatrix} 2 \\ 1 \end{bmatrix} = \begin{bmatrix} 3 \\ 4 \end{bmatrix}$ $\quad (1 + 3i) + (2 + i) = 3 + 4i$

b. Find the vector difference $\vec{A} - \vec{B}$ using matrix and complex subtraction.

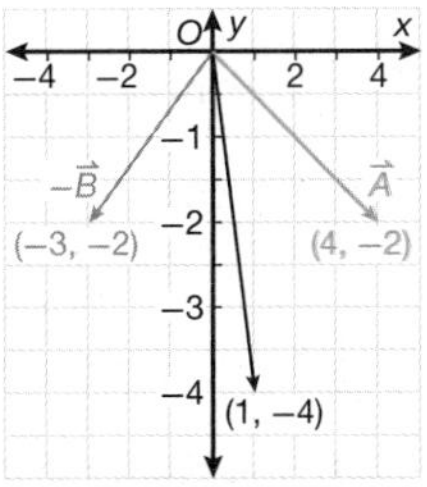

SOLUTION

$\begin{bmatrix} 4 \\ -2 \end{bmatrix} - \begin{bmatrix} 3 \\ 2 \end{bmatrix} = \begin{bmatrix} 1 \\ -4 \end{bmatrix}$ $\quad (4 - 2i) - (3 + 2i) = 1 - 4i$

Online Connection
www.SaxonMathResources.com

Vectors can be multiplied by a process known as finding the **dot product.** The dot product is a scalar quantity, not a vector.

Error Alert If students get 60.26° for Additional Example 1b, point out that both coordinates of the terminal point of the vector are negative. So, the angle measure must be between 180° and 270°.

Example 2

Students add and subtract vectors using two methods: matrices and complex number computation.

Additional Example 2

Use matrix and complex number computation to find the vector sum $\vec{A} + \vec{B}$ and the vector difference $\vec{A} - \vec{C}$.

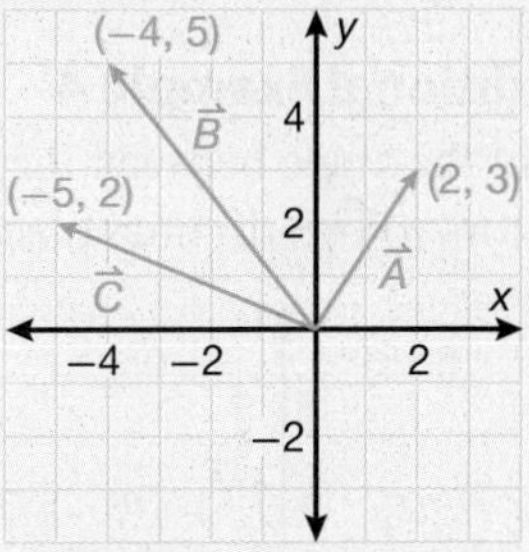

a. vector sum $\vec{A} + \vec{B}$ $\begin{bmatrix} -2 \\ 8 \end{bmatrix}$, $-2 + 8i$

b. vector difference $\vec{A} - \vec{C}$ $\begin{bmatrix} 7 \\ 1 \end{bmatrix}$, $7 + i$

Extend the Example

A zero vector starts and stops at the origin. Show that this zero vector is an identity element for vector addition. Sample: The sum of any vector and a zero vector is the original vector. Using matrix notation, $\begin{bmatrix} p \\ q \end{bmatrix} + \begin{bmatrix} 0 \\ 0 \end{bmatrix} = \begin{bmatrix} p \\ q \end{bmatrix}$.

TEACHER TIP

Have students identify the terminal point of the vector in the first illustration. Discuss using the inverse tangent function to find the measure of the angle the vector makes with the origin.

ALTERNATE METHOD FOR EXAMPLE 2

Introduce the unit vectors $\vec{i}$ and $\vec{j}$. The first has the direction of the positive x-axis; the second, the positive y-axis. Then point out that any vector can be expressed in terms of the unit vectors $\vec{i}$ and $\vec{j}$. An alternate method of vector addition and subtraction involves resolving the two vectors into their x and y components.

If the vectors $\vec{A}$ and $\vec{B}$, in terms of their x and y components, are $\vec{A} = x_1\vec{i} + y_1\vec{j}$ and $\vec{B} = x_2\vec{i} + y_2\vec{j}$, then

$\vec{A} + \vec{B} = (x_1 + x_2)\vec{i} + (y_1 + y_2)\vec{j}$, and

$\vec{A} - \vec{B} = (x_1 - x_2)\vec{i} + (y_1 - y_2)\vec{j}$.

Have students apply these definitions by adding and subtracting vectors from the origin to (3, −2) and (1, 5). sum: $4\vec{i} + 3\vec{j}$; difference: $2\vec{i} - 7\vec{j}$

Example 3

Students compute the dot product of two vectors.

Additional Example 3

Find the dot product $\vec{A} \cdot \vec{B}$. 39

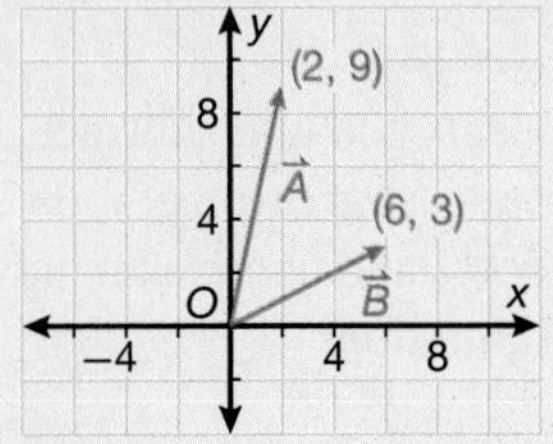

Example 4

Students compute the angle between the two vectors.

Additional Example 4

Find the angle between the vectors to two decimal places.

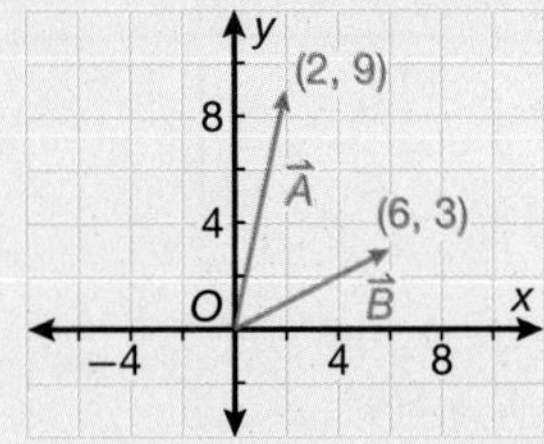

50.91°

Error Alert When students use the dot product formula, remind them to double check the placement of the coordinates of the two ordered pairs.

Extend the Example

Two nonzero vectors are perpendicular if and only if their dot product equals 0. Use this fact to find a vector perpendicular to the one with terminal point (6, 3). any vector with terminal point on the line $y = -2x$

The dot product can be found by using the coordinate vectors.

$$[x_1 y_1] \times \begin{bmatrix} x_2 \\ y_2 \end{bmatrix} = x_1x_2 + y_1y_2$$

Example 3 The Dot Product of Two Vectors

Find the dot product $\vec{A} \cdot \vec{B}$.

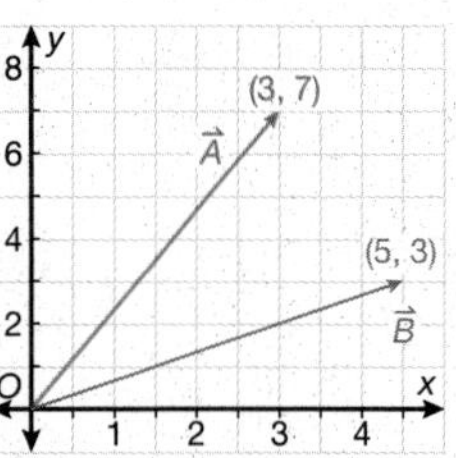

SOLUTION

$$[3 \quad 7] \times \begin{bmatrix} 5 \\ 3 \end{bmatrix} = 15 + 21 = 36$$

The magnitude of a vector, represented by $|\vec{A}|$, in standard position can be determined by using the distance formula with the endpoints of the vector, the origin (0, 0) and (x_1, y_1).

$$|\vec{A}| = \sqrt{(x_1 - 0)^2 + (y_1 - 0)^2} = \sqrt{(x_1)^2 + (y_1)^2}$$

The angle between two nonzero vectors can be found using the dot product of the two vectors and the magnitude of each vector.

$$\cos\theta = \frac{x_1x_2 + y_1y_2}{\sqrt{(x_1)^2 + (y_1)^2}\sqrt{(x_2)^2 + (y_2)^2}}$$

$$\theta = \arccos\frac{x_1x_2 + y_1y_2}{\sqrt{(x_1)^2 + (y_1)^2}\sqrt{(x_2)^2 + (y_2)^2}}$$

Example 4 Finding the Angle between Two Vectors

Find the angle between the vectors $\vec{A}$ and $\vec{B}$.

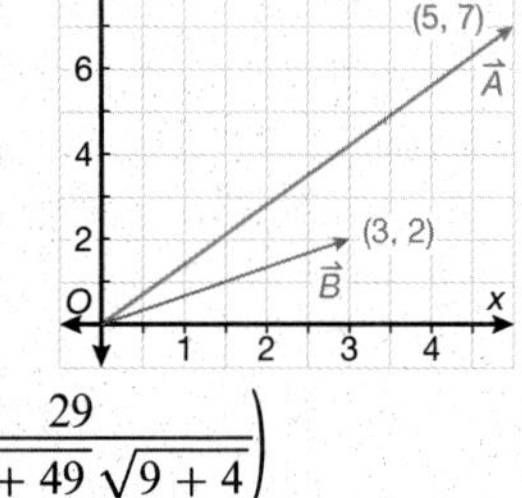

SOLUTION

Use the coordinates to find the angle.

$$\theta = \arccos\left(\frac{x_1x_2 + y_1y_2}{\sqrt{x_1{}^2 + y_1{}^2}\sqrt{x_2{}^2 + y_2{}^2}}\right)$$

$$\theta = \arccos\left(\frac{5 \cdot 3 + 7 \cdot 2}{\sqrt{5^2 + 7^2}\sqrt{3^2 + 2^2}}\right) = \arccos\left(\frac{29}{\sqrt{25 + 49}\sqrt{9 + 4}}\right)$$

$$= \arccos(0.935) = 20.77°$$

If you know the magnitude and orientation of a vector, you can derive the horizontal and vertical components by using the properties of a right triangle.

$$\cos\theta = \frac{x}{|\vec{A}|} \qquad x = |\vec{A}|\cos\theta$$

$$\sin\theta = \frac{y}{|\vec{A}|} \qquad y = |\vec{A}|\sin\theta$$

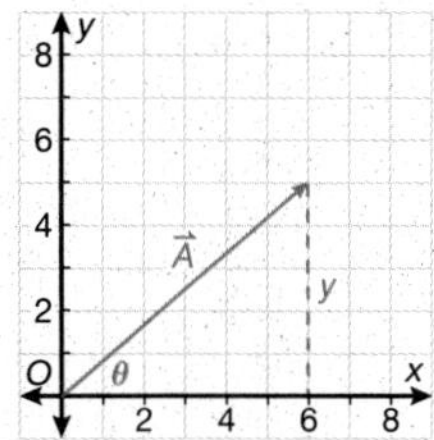

692 Saxon Algebra 2

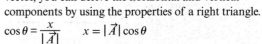

Example 5 Application: Navigation

An airplane traveling north at 500 mph hits a 60 mph headwind blowing 30° south of due west. What is the actual speed and direction of the plane?

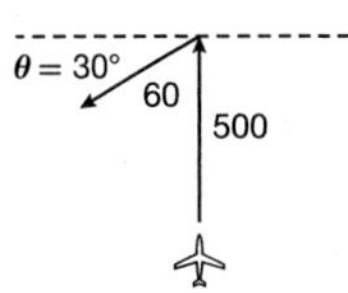

SOLUTION

Step 1: Find the horizontal and vertical components.

$$\begin{bmatrix} 0 \\ 500 \end{bmatrix} + \begin{bmatrix} -60\cos(30°) \\ -60\sin(30°) \end{bmatrix} = \begin{bmatrix} -51.96 \\ 470 \end{bmatrix}$$

Step 2: Find the magnitude and direction.

Magnitude **Direction**

$\sqrt{(-51.96)^2 + 470^2} = 472.86$ $\theta = \arccos\left(\frac{-51.96}{472.86}\right) = 96.31°$ NNW

The plane is heading 96.31° NNW at 472.86 mph.

Lesson Practice

a. (Ex 1) Express a vector whose endpoint is at (10, 5) as a coordinate matrix and a complex number. $\begin{bmatrix} 10 \\ 5 \end{bmatrix}$; $10 + 5i$

b. (Ex 1) Express a vector whose endpoint is at (−12, −36) as a coordinate matrix and a complex number. $\begin{bmatrix} -12 \\ -36 \end{bmatrix}$; $-12 - 36i$

c. (Ex 2) Add the vectors $\begin{bmatrix} 5 \\ 4 \end{bmatrix}$ and $\begin{bmatrix} -6 \\ 4 \end{bmatrix}$. $\begin{bmatrix} -1 \\ 8 \end{bmatrix}$

d. (Ex 2) Subtract the vectors $\begin{bmatrix} -10 \\ 7 \end{bmatrix}$ and $\begin{bmatrix} -3 \\ 9 \end{bmatrix}$. $\begin{bmatrix} -7 \\ -2 \end{bmatrix}$

e. (Ex 3) Find the dot product between the vectors $\begin{bmatrix} -10 \\ 7 \end{bmatrix}$ and $\begin{bmatrix} -3 \\ 9 \end{bmatrix}$. 93

f. (Ex 4) Find the angle between the vectors $\begin{bmatrix} -8 \\ 12 \end{bmatrix}$ and $\begin{bmatrix} 9 \\ -12 \end{bmatrix}$. 176.82°

g. (Ex 5) An airplane traveling north at 600 mph hits a 30 mph headwind blowing east at a 40° angle south of due east. What is the actual speed and direction of the plane? 580.26 mph; 87.73° NNE

Practice Distributed and Integrated

1. (70) **Error Analysis** Explain the error a student made below.
$5 + \sqrt{x} = 3 \rightarrow \sqrt{x} = -2 \rightarrow (\sqrt{x})^2 = (-2)^2 \rightarrow x = 4$ The solution is 4.

1. Sample: The student did not check the answer in the original equation. 4 is an extraneous solution because it does not make the original equation true. The equation has no solutions.

***2.** (98) **Generalize** How many ellipses have an eccentricity of 0? Explain. None. A figure with an eccentricity of zero is a circle.

3. (81) **Write** Explain why $\ln e^{x^2+3} = x^2 + 3$. Sample: Exponential and logarithmic operations are inverse operations.

4. (8) **(Engines)** Two-stroke engines require a premix of gas and oil. The amount of gas used varies directly with the amount of oil used. In some two-stroke engines, 5 gal of gas requires 20 oz of oil.

INCLUSION

Explain that two vectors with the same magnitude and direction are equal. Illustrate with several examples. Point out that any vector can be translated to one that starts at the origin. So, students can think of a vector as just the ordered pair at its "pointy" end.

Present this simplified definition of vector addition: For every pair of vectors (a, b) and (c, d), the sum is $(a + c, b + d)$.

Use the vectors (5, 2) and (2, 6) to show how to use the parallelogram rule for addition.

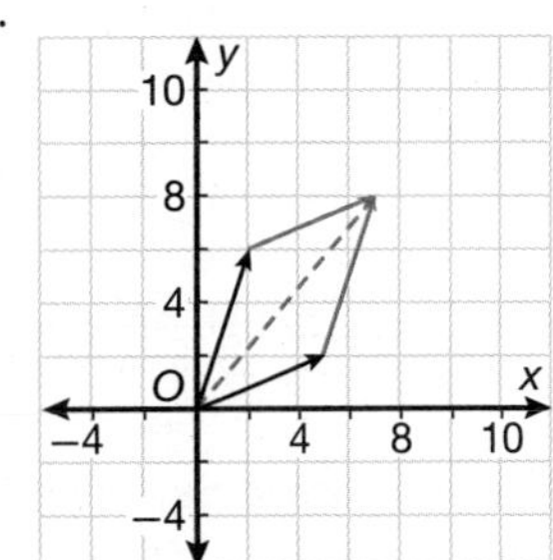

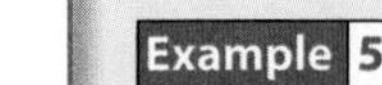

Example 5

Students apply vector concepts to solve an applications problem.

Additional Example 5

A plane heads on a bearing of 120° with an airspeed of 190 mph. The wind is blowing south at 15 mph. Find the actual speed and direction of the plane.
177 mph, 122.3° NNW

Lesson Practice

Problem e

Error Alert Check that students multiply coordinates in the correct order, computing $(-10 \cdot -3) + (7 \cdot 9)$ rather than $(-10 \cdot 9) + (7 \cdot -3)$. Tell them to add the product of the "tops" to the product of the "bottoms."

Check for Understanding

The questions below help assess the concepts taught in this lesson.

"If you are given the initial and terminal points of a vector, how can you find its direction?" Sample: Graph the vector and draw a right triangle. Use the inverse tangent function to find the angle the vector makes with the *x*-axis.

"When are two vectors equal?" when they have the same magnitude and the same direction

"Why is it useful for physicists to represent forces and velocities as vectors?" Sample: They are quantities with magnitude and direction. Vector addition can be used to find resultant forces and velocities.

3 Practice

Math Conversations

Discussions to strengthen understanding

Problem 2

Have students sketch an ellipse through $(0, \pm 2)$ and $(\pm a, 0)$. Point out the minor axis is vertical, so a must be greater than 2. The eccentricity equals $\frac{\sqrt{a^2 - 2^2}}{a}$.

Problem 8

Review the purpose of finding the z-score for a set of data. It indicates how many standard deviations a data point is from the mean and can be used to compare observations from different distributions.

Problem 10

Remind students that a quintic polynomial has a degree of 5.

a. Write the proportion that can be used to find how many ounces of oil to use with 9 gal of gas. $\frac{5}{9} = \frac{20}{x}$

b. Solve the proportion in part **a.** $x = 36$ oz

c. Check the answer from part **b** with the proportion from part **a.**

4c. $\frac{5}{9} = \frac{20}{36} \Rightarrow 5(36) = 9(20) \Rightarrow 180 = 180$

5. (11) **Geometry** Write a polynomial in standard form that represents the total area formed by the rectangle and trapezoid. (Hint: The formula for the area of a trapezoid is $A = \frac{1}{2}(b_1 + b_2)h$. $\frac{3}{2}x^2 + \frac{25}{2}x$

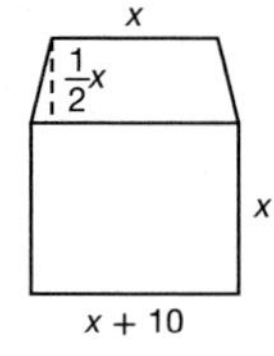

6. (68) **Probability** A student has a spinner with four equal sections labeled 2, 4, 6, and 8. If the student spins the spinner two times, find the probability that the first spin lands on a 4 and the sum of the results is greater than or equal to 10. 12.5%

7. (79) Evaluate the piecewise function $f(x) = \begin{cases} x - x^2, & \text{if } x \leq 1 \\ 12, & \text{if } 1 < x \leq 2 \\ -6, & \text{if } 2 < x < 4 \\ -x - 8, & \text{if } x \geq 4 \end{cases}$ for $x = -0.4$, $x = 0$, and $x = 6$. −0.56, 0, −14

8. (80) **Error Analysis** Explain and correct the error a student made in finding the z-score for a data value of 15, taken from a normally distributed set of data, where the mean is 20 and the standard deviation is 4.

$$z = \frac{20 - 15}{4} = \frac{5}{4} = 1.25$$

8. In the numerator, the mean should be subtracted from the data value, not the other way around. $z = \frac{15 - 20}{4} = -\frac{5}{4} = -1.25$

9. (77) In $\triangle RST$, $ST = 17$, $RT = 20$, and $m\angle T = 38°$. Find $m\angle S$. 84.3°

10. (11) **Write** If two quintic polynomials are added, what are all the possible types of the resulting polynomial (classified by degree)? quintic, quartic, cubic, quadratic, linear, and constant

11. (75) The graph of $y = \sqrt[4]{x + 1} + \sqrt[3]{x + 1}$ is shown to the right. Use the axis of symmetry to draw the inverse function. See Additional Answers.

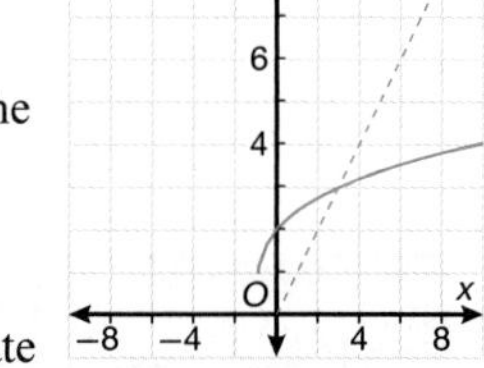

12. (91) **Seismology** To locate the epicenter of an earthquake, a seismologist graphs the circles created from three seismographs in different locations and finds their point of intersection.

a. The equations below were created from the readings of three seismographs where each unit represents one mile. Sketch the circles on the same coordinate plane.

$$(x + 4)^2 + (y - 4)^2 = 25$$
$$(x - 1)^2 + (y + 3)^2 = 49$$
$$(x - 5)^2 + (y - 4)^2 = 16$$

12a.

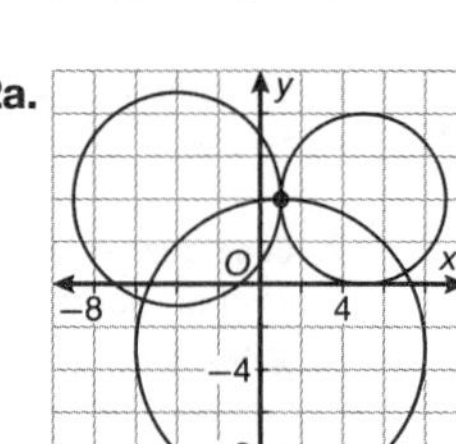

b. Estimate the location of the epicenter. (1, 4)

13. (73) **Prom** A member of the prom committee polls 40 random seniors from the senior class meeting to ask about possible locations for the prom. Describe the individuals in the population and in the sample. Population: all seniors in the class meeting; Sample: the 40 polled seniors

ENGLISH LEARNERS

Discuss the geometric definition of a ray. Draw an example on the board. Point out that it has a beginning point, but no ending point. The point at the beginning of a ray is called the endpoint.

Next draw a line segment and point to the two endpoints. Change one of these to an arrow.

Say: **"I've now turned the line segment into a directed line segment. It has a beginning and an end. This is also called a vector."** Emphasize the difference between a vector and a ray. The latter is infinite in length.

Show a vector drawn on a coordinate grid. Discuss the initial (beginning) point and the terminal (ending) point. When a vector starts at the origin, (0, 0), the ordered pair at its end describes the vector. From the ordered pair, students can find the length (magnitude) of the vector and its direction (angle with the x-axis.)

14. **National Parks** Kolob Arch in Zion National Park is one of the longest arches in the world with a span of about 288 feet and a height of about 105 feet. Write a quadratic function to approximate the arch. $y \approx -0.005x^2 + 1.458x$
(83)

15. **Sound Intensity** The loudness of a given sound is represented by $d = 10\log \frac{I}{I_o}$ where d is decibels, I is intensity of the sound, and I_o is the intensity of a sound that can just be heard by humans. Determine the decibel level of a sound with an intensity of $(2.3 \times 10^9)I_o$. The decibel level is 93.62.
(87)

16. Use cross multiplying to show that $\frac{3}{x+5} = \frac{2}{x+5}$ has no solution.
(84)

16. $3x + 15 = 2x + 10$; $x = -5$ is not a solution because it makes both rational expressions undefined.

17. **Write** An English teacher needs to pick 5 students to present book reports to the class. The teacher writes the names of all students in the class on pieces of paper, puts the pieces in a hat, and chooses 5 names without looking. Determine what type of sample is used and whether it is biased or unbiased. Explain your answer.
(73)

17. The sample is random and unbiased. Each student has an equal chance of being selected.

***18.** **Analyze** Can a quadratic inequality have no critical values? Explain.
(89)

18. Yes, if the inequality has no solutions, or if the solution is all real numbers, then the graphs of the left and right sides of the inequality will not intersect.

***19.** **Coordinate Geometry** The points (1, −5), (2, −11), (3, −17), (4, −23), and (5, −29) represent the first five terms of an arithmetic sequence. What is the common difference? What is the y-coordinate when the x-coordinate is 12? −6; −71
(92)

***20.** **Graphing Calculator** Use a graphing calculator to find the inverse of the matrix, if it exists. $H = \begin{bmatrix} 2 & 1 & 3 \\ 1 & 1 & 2 \\ 1 & 4 & 6 \end{bmatrix}$ $\begin{bmatrix} -2 & 6 & -1 \\ -4 & 9 & -1 \\ 3 & -7 & 1 \end{bmatrix}$
(32)

***21.** Find the dot product between the vectors $\begin{bmatrix} 6 \\ 8 \end{bmatrix}$ and $\begin{bmatrix} 2 \\ 7 \end{bmatrix}$. 68
(99)

***22.** **Multiple Choice** Which are polar coordinates for the point with Cartesian coordinates $(-3, -3\sqrt{3})$? D
(96)

A $\left(3, \frac{7\pi}{6}\right)$ **B** $\left(3, \frac{4\pi}{3}\right)$ **C** $\left(6, \frac{7\pi}{6}\right)$ **D** $\left(6, \frac{4\pi}{3}\right)$

***23.** Write an equation in standard form for the ellipse with center (0, 0), vertex (6, 0), and covertex (0, −5). $\frac{x^2}{36} + \frac{y^2}{25} = 1$
(98)

Solve.

24. $3\frac{2}{5}x - 4\frac{1}{10}x = 2\frac{1}{4}$ $x = -\frac{45}{14}$
(2)

25. $0.02(p - 2) = 0.03(2p - 6)$ $p = 3.5$
(2)

***26.** Use the Rational Root Theorem to find the roots of $y = 2x^3 - 3x^2 - 8x + 12$. $x = 2, -2, 1.5$
(85)

Add.

27. $3xy^2m + \frac{4}{x}$ $\frac{3x^2y^2m + 4}{x}$
(37)

28. $\frac{5x^2}{pm} - 4 + \frac{c}{p^2m}$ $\frac{5x^2p - 4p^2m + c}{p^2m}$
(37)

***29.** **Multi-Step** Find the magnitude of vectors $\begin{bmatrix} -3 \\ 7 \end{bmatrix}$ and $\begin{bmatrix} 3 \\ 7 \end{bmatrix}$. Calculate the angle between the two vectors. Then calculate the dot product. Magnitude of A and B: 7.62; $\theta = 46.4°$; dot product: 40
(99)

30. Find the distance between (−3, 7) and (4, −2). $\sqrt{130}$
(41)

Problem 16

Error Alert

If students solve $3x + 15 = 2x + 10$ and say that −5 is a solution, remind them they must always check answers in the *original* equation. Ask what number must be excluded from the domain and why. −5; It makes the denominators equal 0.

Problem 19

Write the sequence −5, −11, −17, −23, −29 on the board and have students compare it to the ordered pairs in the problem.

Ask: **"What is shown by the first coordinates in the ordered pairs?"** the term numbers

"How can you use the formula $a_n = a_1 + (n - 1)d$ to find the 12th term?" Use −5 as the first term, a_1. The common difference d is −6. Let $n = 12$ and solve for a_{12}.

Problem 26

Extend the Problem

a. Is $f(x) = 2x^3 - 3x^2 - 8x + 12$ the only cubic polynomial function with the roots 2, −2, and −1.5? No, there are an infinite number.

b. Write a general equation for a function with these three roots. Sample: $f(x) = k(x^3 - 1.5x^2 - 4x + 6)$

CHALLENGE

In a three-dimensional coordinate system, a vector can be represented by an ordered triple. Show that the vectors $\vec{A} = (3, 4, -8)$ and $\vec{B} = (4, -7, -2)$ are perpendicular. Hint: Find the dot product of the vectors. Sample: $\vec{A} \cdot \vec{B} = (3 \cdot 4) + (4 \cdot -7) + (-8 \cdot -2) = 0$, so $\cos\theta = 0$ and $\theta = 90°$.

LOOKING FORWARD

Using vectors prepares students for

- **Lesson 104** Finding Transformations

LESSON 100

1 Warm Up

For problem 3, remind students that the denominator cannot be equal to zero.

2 New Concepts

Students learn about graphing polynomial functions, with a focus on finding asymptotes and points of discontinuity.

Example 1

Students find the values of x which would make the denominator zero to identify discontinuities.

Additional Example 1

Find any points of discontinuity for each rational function.

a. $y = \dfrac{x+8}{x^2 - 2x - 3}$ $x = -3$, $x = 1$

b. $y = \dfrac{(x+8)(2x+5)}{(2x+5)}$ none

LESSON 100 Graphing Rational Functions I

Warm Up

1. **Vocabulary** In order for $\frac{1}{g(x)}$ to be a rational expression, $g(x)$ must be a polynomial not equal to zero. (28)

2. Write $\dfrac{4x^2 - 11x - 20}{3x^2 + 21x - 54}$ in factored form. (23) $\dfrac{(4x+5)(x-4)}{3(x-2)(x+9)}$

3. What values of x are not allowed for this expression? $\dfrac{1}{7x^2 + 3x - 4}$ (23)

3. $x = \frac{4}{7}$ and $x = -1$

New Concepts

A rational function is of the form

$f(x) = \dfrac{g(x)}{h(x)}$ for polynomials $g(x)$ and $h(x)$. The domain of $f(x)$ is all real numbers except those for which $h(x) = 0$.

A real number a that makes the denominator of a rational function equal to zero is not in the domain of the function. The graph of the function is discontinuous at $x = a$.

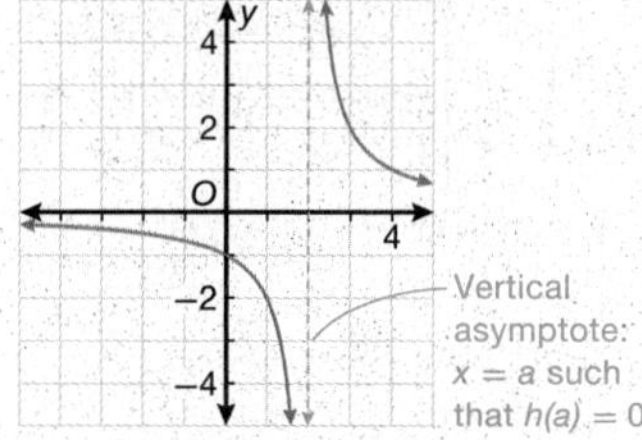

Example 1 Finding Points of Discontinuity

Find any points of discontinuity for each rational function.

a. $y = \dfrac{x+1}{x^2 + 5x + 6}$

SOLUTION

The function is undefined when the denominator equals zero. Set the denominator equal to zero and solve.

$$x^2 + 5x + 6 = 0$$
$$(x+2)(x+3) = 0$$
$$(x+2) = 0 \qquad (x+3) = 0$$
$$x = -2 \qquad x = -3$$

The points of discontinuity are **−2** and **−3**.

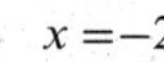

Online Connection
www.SaxonMathResources.com

LESSON RESOURCES

Student Edition Practice Workbook 100
Reteaching Master 100
Adaptations Master 100
Challenge and Enrichment Masters C100

MATH BACKGROUND

Polynomial functions are well-suited for modeling data. Their behavior near $x = 0$ makes them good choices for modeling data with multiple maxima and minima, such as swings in the stock market. As x increases, polynomials act like power functions. Polynomial functions can model electrical circuit behavior, as well as the path of light as it passes through optical components.

As students study calculus and ordinary differential equations, they will learn to approximate complicated functions using polynomials. Scientists often 'guess' the power of a polynomial for approximating data by examining the shape of the data. Obviously, linear data calls for a first-order equation. Second-order equations are parabolas, and so on.

(b.) $y = \frac{x+5}{x^2+6}$

SOLUTION

The function is undefined when the denominator equals zero. Set the denominator equal to zero and solve.

$$x^2+6=0$$
$$x^2=-6$$
$$x=\pm\sqrt{-6}=\pm i\sqrt{6}$$

Since $i\sqrt{6}$ is not a real number, there is no point of discontinuity.

A vertical asymptote or a hole in the graph occurs at a point of discontinuity. If there are no common factors in the numerator and denominator, there are vertical asymptotes at the points of discontinuity. If there are common factors in the numerator and denominator, there are either holes or vertical asymptotes at the points of discontinuity.

Example 2 Finding Vertical Asymptotes and Holes

In each rational function, describe the vertical asymptotes and holes for the graph.

(a.) $y = \frac{(x+1)}{(x+4)(x-2)}$

SOLUTION

The points of discontinuity are −4 and 2 and since these are no common factors of the numerator and denominator, $x = -4$ and $x = 2$ are vertical asymptotes.

Hint

When the factors in the numerator and denominator are the same and thus cancel, a hole will occur at the x-value that causes the factor to equal zero.

(b.) $y = \frac{(x+5)(x+6)}{(x+6)(x+5)(x+6)}$

SOLUTION

Since there are common factors in the numerator and denominator, the graph of this rational function is the same as $y = \frac{1}{x+6}$, except it has a hole at $x = -5$. The vertical asymptote is at $x = -6$.

The graph of a rational function has at most one horizontal asymptote. If the degree of the denominator is greater than the degree of the numerator the graph has a horizontal asymptote at $y = 0$. If the degree of the numerator is greater than the degree of the denominator, then the graph has no horizontal asymptote. If the degrees of the numerator and denominator are equal, then the graph has a horizontal asymptote at $y = \frac{a}{b}$, where a is the coefficient of the term with the highest degree in the numerator and b is the coefficient of the term with the highest degree in the denominator.

Example 2

Remind students to look for factors that are the same in the numerator and the denominator.

Additional Example 2

In each rational function, describe the vertical asymptotes and holes for the graph.

a. $y = \frac{(x+3)}{(x+5)(x-2)}$ vertical asymptotes: $x = -5$, $x = 2$

b. $y = \frac{(x-4)(x+7)}{(x+7)(x-4)(x+7)}$ vertical asymptote: $x = -7$, hole: $x = 4$

ALTERNATE METHOD FOR EXAMPLE 2

Use a graphing calculator to find the vertical asymptotes for the function. Then substitute those x-values into the denominator to see that they really force the denominator to zero.

Example 3

Additional Example 3

Find the horizontal asymptotes of each rational function.

a. $y = \dfrac{8x^2 + 3}{2x^2 - 7}$ $x = 4$

b. $y = \dfrac{3x^2 + 2x - 8}{x - 8}$ none

Example 4

Error Alert Students may list all zeros of the denominator as vertical asymptotes, when, in fact, some are discontinuities, but not asymptotes.

a. Graph $y = \frac{7}{7 - x}$. Identify any vertical asymptotes.
asymptote as $x = -7$

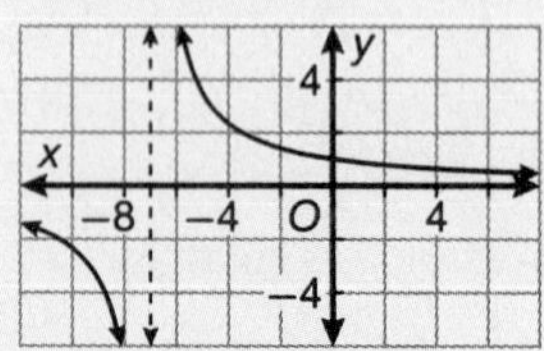

b. $y = \dfrac{x^2 + 8x + 7}{x^3 - 49x}$. Vertical asymptotes are at $x = 0$ and $x = 7$. There is a hole at $x = -7$.

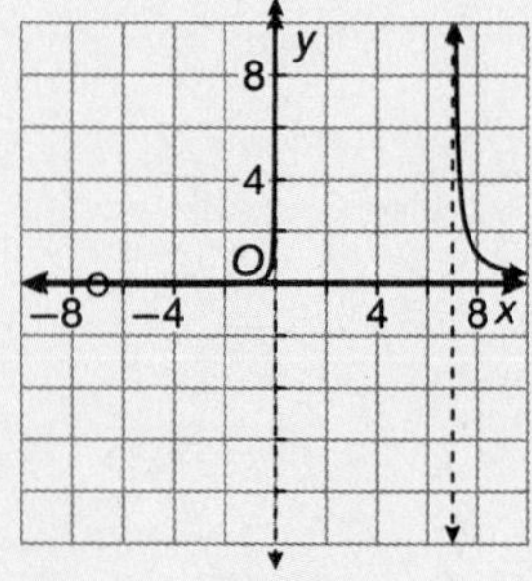

Example 3 **Finding Horizontal Asymptotes**

Find the horizontal asymptotes of each rational function.

a. $y = \dfrac{3x^2 + 2}{x^2 - 5}$

SOLUTION

Since the degree of the numerator and denominator are equal, the equation of the vertical asymptotes is $\mathbf{y = \frac{3}{1} = 3}$.

b. $y = \dfrac{2x^2 + 3x + 7}{x - 5}$

SOLUTION

Since the degree of the numerator is greater than the degree of the denominator, there is no horizontal asymptote.

Example 4 **Graphing Using Asymptotes**

Graph the following function. Identify any asymptotes.

a. $y = \dfrac{2}{x - 1}$

SOLUTION

Determine any points of discontinuity.

$x - 1 = 0$

$x = 1$

There is a point of discontinuity at $x = 1$. Since the numerator and denominator have no common factors, $x = 1$ is a vertical asymptote.

Vertical asymptote: $x = 1$

Since the degree of the denominator is greater than the degree of the numerator, the graph has a horizontal asymptote at $y = 0$.

Calculate the values of y for values of x near the asymptotes. Plot these points and sketch the graph.

> **Math Reasoning**
>
> **Verify** Show that as x gets infinitely large, there is a horizontal asymptote at $y = 0$.

As x, gets infinitely large the denominator of $\frac{2}{x-1}$ gets infinitely large and the fraction approaches 0.

b. $y = \dfrac{x^2 + 2x - 8}{x^3 - 4x}$

SOLUTION

$$y = \frac{x^2 + 2x - 8}{x^3 - 4x} = \frac{(x-2)(x+4)}{x(x^2 - 4)} = \frac{(x-2)(x+4)}{x(x+2)(x-2)}$$

$$= \frac{(x+4)}{x(x+2)}$$

A common factor divides out of both the numerator and denominator, leaving vertical asymptotes $x = 0$ and $x = -2$. However, $x = 2$, while not an asymptote, is still not part of the function and is graphed as a "hole."

> **Math Reasoning**
>
> **Generalize** Identify the holes and vertical asymptotes for rational functions of the form $y = \frac{x-a}{x^2 - a^2}$.

$y = \dfrac{x - a}{(x - a)(x + a)}$; There is a hole at $x = a$ and an vertical asymptote at $x = -a$.

INCLUSION

Polynomial functions are very visual, and can be graphed on a graphing calculator. Students can use the calculator to help them find the asymptotes and discontinuities. Once they know the asymptotes and discontinuities, they can re-create the rational polynomial function this way:

$$y = \frac{\textit{discontinuity} \times \textit{factor}}{\textit{discontinuity} \times \textit{asymptote} \times \textit{asymptote}}.$$

The order of the numerator lets students know how many factors they still need to find. Once all of the factors have been found, students can multiply out the numerator and denominator to check with the original polynomial function.

The x-intercepts of a rational function occur when the value of the function is zero for any value in the domain. The x-intercept is -4.

Calculate the values of y for values of x near the asymptotes. Plot these points and the x-intercepts. Sketch the graph.

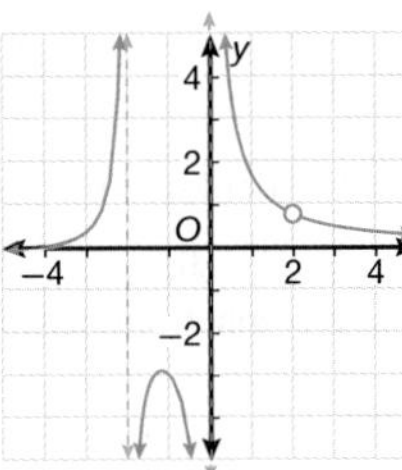

Lesson Practice

Find any points of discontinuity for each rational function. *(Ex 1)*

a. $y = \dfrac{x + 2}{x^2 - 4x - 5}$ $x = -1, x = 5$ **b.** $y = \dfrac{(2x + 7)(x + 3)}{(x + 3)}$ $x = -3$

In each rational function, describe the vertical asymptotes and holes for the graph. *(Ex 2)*

c. $y = \dfrac{(x + 7)}{(x + 3)(x - 5)}$ **d.** $y = \dfrac{(x + 5)(x + 6)}{(x + 6)(x + 5)(x + 6)}$

vertical asymptotes: $x = -3$ and $x = 5$ vertical asymptotes: $x = -6$; hole: $x = -5$

Find the horizontal asymptotes of each rational function. *(Ex 3)*

e. $y = \dfrac{6x^2 + 3}{2x^2 + 4}$ $y = 3$

f. $y = \dfrac{2x^2 + 3x + 7}{x - 5}$ none

Graph the following functions. Identify any asymptotes or holes. *(Ex 4)*

g. $y = \dfrac{4}{x - 2}$

h. $y = \dfrac{2}{x^3 - x}$

Graph the following functions. Identify any asymptotes, holes, and x-intercepts. *(Ex 4)*

i. $y = \dfrac{x^2 - 2x - 15}{x^2 + 5x + 6}$

j. $y = \dfrac{x^2 - 2x - 15}{x^3 - 9x}$

g.

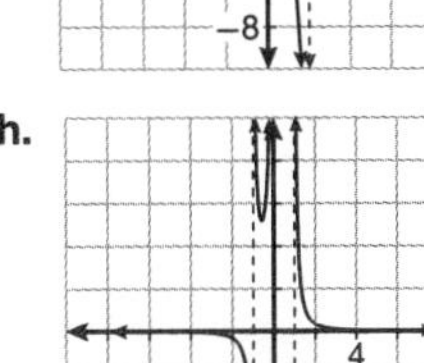

h.

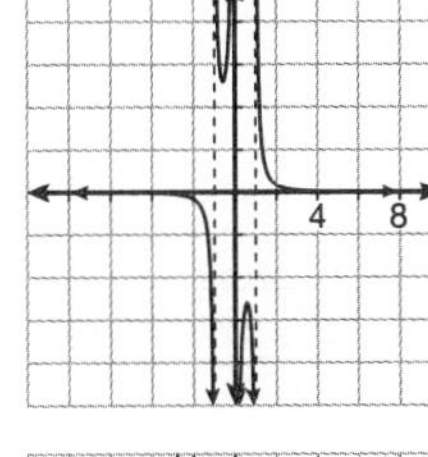

i.

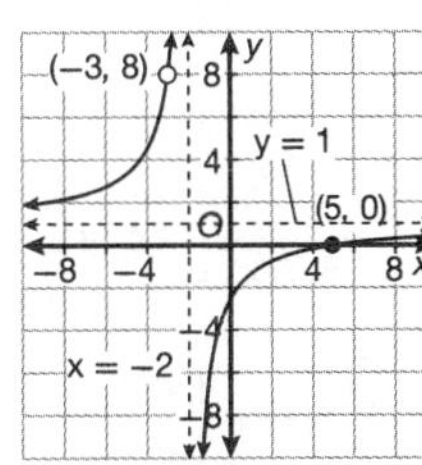

j.

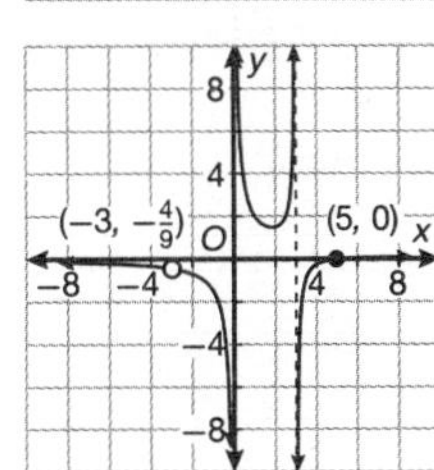

Lesson Practice

Problem d

Scaffolding Remind students that a zero in the denominator does not necessarily denote an asymptote. It might be a discontinuity instead.

Check for Understanding

The questions below help assess the concepts taught in this lesson.

"How do graphs of polynomial functions resemble graphs of piecewise functions?" Polynomial functions are often not continuous for all x. In that way, they appear piecewise, making different shapes on different sides of the asymptotes. Intervals can be written to show the values of the domain for each piece; however, the function rule is the same for all the different pieces.

"When is an excluded value of the function a hole rather than an asymptote?" when the related factor is also in the numerator

ENGLISH LEARNERS

Define **asymptote** as a line that a graph approaches as the variable becomes very large or small. Have students give an example of a rational function and identify its asymptotes.

Finally, differentiate between an asymptote and a discontinuity using examples in the lesson.

Lesson 100 699

3 Practice

Math Conversations

Discussions to strengthen understanding.

Problem 8

Guide the students by asking them the following questions.

"How many pieces are there?" 2

"How many equations will there be?" 2

"What is the domain of the piece on the left?" $x < 0$

"What is the equation of the piece on the left?" $y = 9$

"What is the domain of the piece on the right?" $x \geq 5$

"What is the equation of the piece on the right?" $y = -4$

Problem 9

"What is the domain of the piece on the left?" $x < 0$

"What type of equation will represent the piece on the left?" linear

"What is the domain of the piece on the right?" $x \geq 0$

"What type of equation will represent the piece on the right?" quadratic

Problem 10

Have students explain why A is *not* the answer.

"The denominator is 0 at $x = 7$ for A. Why isn't the answer A?" The numerator is also 0 at $x = 7$, therefore it is a discontinuity and not an asymptote.

Practice Distributed and Integrated

Solve.

1. (84) $x = 4 + \frac{5}{x}$ $\quad x = 5, -1$

2. (84) $-x^2 - 2x - 1 > 2$ no solution

***3.** (99) **Error Analysis** Two students calculated the angle between vectors $\vec{A} = \begin{bmatrix} 12 \\ 9 \end{bmatrix}$ and $\vec{B} = \begin{bmatrix} 17 \\ 8 \end{bmatrix}$ but their results were different. Which student made the mistake?
Student B mistakenly transposed the x and y terms in the numerator.

Student A	Student B
$\theta = \arccos\left(\frac{(12 \cdot 17) + (9 \cdot 8)}{\sqrt{12^2 + 9^2}\sqrt{17^2 + 8^2}}\right)$	$\theta = \arccos\left(\frac{(12 \cdot 9) + (17 \cdot 8)}{\sqrt{12^2 + 9^2}\sqrt{17^2 + 8^2}}\right)$
$= 11.67°$	$= 30.03°$

4. (36) Find the equation of the line parallel to $y = 7x + 6$ that crosses (6, 10). $\quad y = 7x - 32$

***5.** (96) **Phone Service** A planned cell phone tower will service an area with a 13-mile radius. It is to be located 5 miles east and 12 miles south of a radio tower. Write a polar equation of the boundary of the region that will be serviced. Place the location of the radio tower at the pole. Graph the equation on a calculator.
See Additional Answers.

6. (56) **Multi-Step** The formula $\theta = \frac{180°(n-2)}{n}$ gives the measure of each interior angle of an n-sided regular polygon.

a. Use the formula to find the measure of an interior angle of a regular decagon. $\quad 144°$

b. Find the reference angle for the interior angle. $\quad 36°$

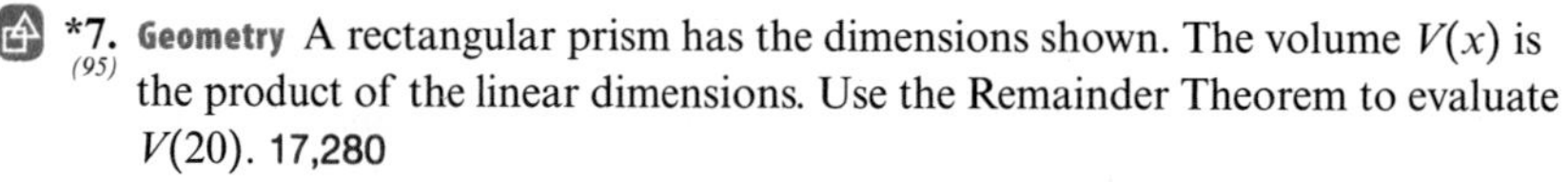

***7.** (95) **Geometry** A rectangular prism has the dimensions shown. The volume $V(x)$ is the product of the linear dimensions. Use the Remainder Theorem to evaluate $V(20)$. 17,280

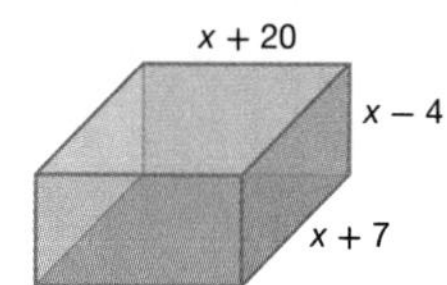

Write a piecewise function rule for each graph.

8. (79)

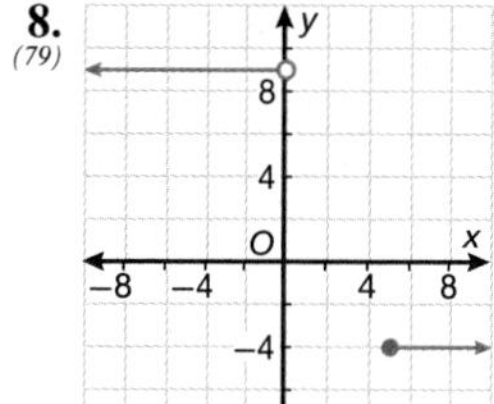

9. (79)

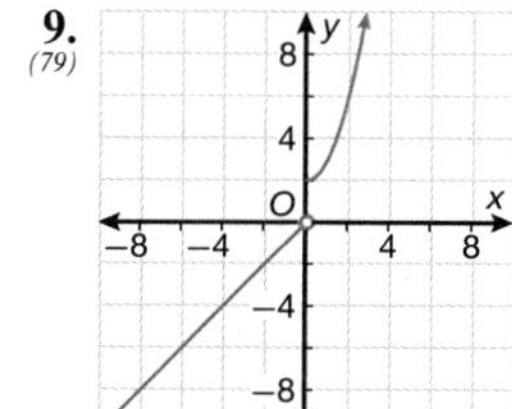

8. $f(x) = \begin{cases} 9, \text{ if } x < 0 \\ -4, \text{ if } x \geq 5 \end{cases}$

9. $f(x) = \begin{cases} x, \text{ if } x < 0 \\ x^2 + 2, \text{ if } x \geq 0 \end{cases}$

***10.** (100) **Multiple Choice** Which of the following rational functions includes a vertical asymptote at $x = 7$? **D**

A $y = \frac{x - 7}{x^2 - 49}$ $\qquad$ **B** $y = \frac{x - 7}{x^2 + 12x + 35}$

C $y = \frac{x^2 - 16}{x^2 + 11x + 28}$ $\qquad$ **D** $y = \frac{x^2 - 16}{x^2 - 11x + 28}$

INCLUSION

Giving students the polynomial function, already in factored form, will allow them to graph the function by hand. They can show the asymptotes and discontinuity on the graph using colored pencils. These visual cues will give them an idea of x-values to choose for completing a chart of values. Graphing by hand will help students see the trends of polynomial functions, and how much the value of the function can change for relatively small changes in x.

700 Saxon Algebra 2

11. **Analyze** Use the table of values for $y = \log_2 x^2$ to answer the questions.
(87)

x	−4	−3	−2	−1	0	1	2	3	4
y	4	3.17	2	0	–	0	2	3.17	4

a. As the negative x values increase to 0, what happens to the y values? The y values decrease to 0.

b. As the positive x values increase, what happens to the y values? The y values increase.

12. **Justify** Can the difference of two polynomials have a greater degree than the sum of the same two polynomials? Justify your answer with an example.
(11)

12. Yes; Possible example: Let $P_1 = 3x^2 - x - 2$ and $P_2 = -3x^2 - x - 2$. Then $P_1 + P_2 = -2x - 4$ and $P_1 - P_2 = 6x^2$.

*13. **Graphing Calculator** Use a graphing calculator to evaluate $y = 2x + 3$ for the given domain: −2, −1, 0, 1, 2. Identify the range of the function and classify the function.
(22)
range: −1, 1, 3, 5, 7; discrete

14. **Parking** An airport parking garage costs $38 per day for the first week. After that, the cost decreases to $35 per day. Write a piecewise function for the cost of parking x days. See Additional Answers.
(79)

15. **Analyze** Suppose that for polynomials $P_1(x)$ and $P_2(x)$ there is a constant a such that $P_1(a) = P_2(a) = 0$. What can you conclude about the graphs of $P_1(x)$ and $P_2(x)$?
(95)
They intersect at $x = a$.

16. **Research** In a study of 413 men and 335 women, the mean height of men was 174.1 centimeters with a standard deviation of 7 centimeters. The mean height of women was 162.3 centimeters with a standard deviation of 6.2 centimeters. Assume both distributions are normal. Compare the actual height of a man with a z-score of 2 to the actual height of a woman whose z-score is 2. man: 188.1 cm; woman: 174.7 cm
(80)

17. **Data Analysis** The number of days it takes to complete a year for different planets is shown in the table. Let Earth's yearly motion be modeled by $y = \sin(0.017x)$. How would you model Jupiter's motion? Hint: The days in a year corresponds to the period of the function. Jupiter: $y = \sin(0.0015x)$
(82)

Planet	Mercury	Venus	Earth	Mars	Jupiter	Saturn	Uranus	Neptune
Days in a Year	88.03	224.63	365.25	686.67	4331.87	10,760.27	30,681.00	60,193.20

*18. **Error Analysis** Which student made an error in determining intervals to check for solutions and nonsolutions of $\frac{x-2}{(x+7)(x-5)} \geq 0$? What is the error?
(94)

Student A	Student B
$x \leq -7$	$x < -7$
$-7 \leq x \leq 2$	$-7 < x \leq 2$
$2 \leq x \leq 5$	$2 \leq x < 5$
$x \geq 5$	$x > 5$

18. Student A made the error. The critical values obtained from the denominator should have < or > because when "or equal to" is included, the denominator becomes undefined.

19. **Analyze** Identify which property of real numbers is being demonstrated by $(4 \cdot 6) \cdot 5 = 4 \cdot (6 \cdot 5) = 4 \cdot 30 = 120$. Explain why this property might be helpful in solving this problem without a calculator. Associative Property of Multiplication; $(6 \cdot 5)$ is a multiple of 10, so it is easier to multiply $4 \cdot 30$ than $24 \cdot 5$.
(1)

Problem 17

Error Alert

Students may try to use the actual number of days of Jupiter's revolution instead of the ratio of Jupiter's revolution to Earth's revolution. Help them see they need to use the ratio by substituting in for x after the equation is written.

CHALLENGE

In a parallel circuit, the total resistance, R_T, is found using the equation below. Suppose that a parallel circuit has two resistors of magnitude R and $R + 1$. Solve for R_T. Identify any asymptotes or holes.

$$\frac{1}{R_T} = \frac{1}{R_1} + \frac{1}{R_2} + \frac{1}{R_3} \cdots$$

$R_T = \frac{R(R+1)}{2R+1}$, vertical asymptote at $R = -\frac{1}{2}$

Problem 22

Remind students that the periodic function used to represent this type of motion is $y = A\cos \omega t$, where A is the amplitude of the motion and ω is the angular frequency. Angular frequency is related to frequency by $\omega = 2\pi f$ and frequency and the period are inversely related.

20. (89) **Multi-Step** The perimeter of a rectangular garden will be 100 feet. Write an inequality to find the widths that will give an area of at least 450 square feet. Solve the inequality and round to the nearest tenth. $-x^2 + 50x \geq 450$, between 11.8 feet and 38.2 feet

21. (90) For what values of θ is $y = \frac{\sin(x)}{\cos(x - \theta)}$ no longer a periodic function? $\theta = (2n + 1)\frac{\pi}{2}$, for integer values of n

22. (82) **Physics** Every millisecond a radio beacon emits a signal. If the magnitude of the signal is 100, write the periodic function that models the signal using the form $y = a\cos(bx)$. $y = 100\cos(2000\pi x)$

Simplify.

23. (40) $2\sqrt{3}\left(5\sqrt{3} - 2\sqrt{6}\right)$ $30 - 12\sqrt{2}$

24. (40) $2\sqrt{3} \cdot 3\sqrt{6} \cdot 5\sqrt{12}$ $180\sqrt{6}$

25. (91) **Write** A student wants to graph a circle whose equation is $(x - 5)^2 + (y - 5)^2 = 2$ on a graphing calculator. How would you explain to the student how this can be done?

25. Sample: The goal is to isolate the y-variable, so first subtract $(x - 5)^2$ from both sides of the equation. To undo the square on the left, take the square root of both sides, remembering both the positive and negative root on the right. Isolate y by adding 5 to each side. Graph both functions.

26. (100) **Physics** In a parallel circuit, the total resistance, R_T, is found using $\frac{1}{R_T} = \frac{1}{R_1} + \frac{1}{R_2} + \frac{1}{R_3} \ldots$. Suppose that a parallel circuit has two resistors of magnitude R and $2R + 1$. Solve for R_T. $R_T = \frac{R(2R + 1)}{3R + 1}$

Divide.

27. (38) $x^4 + 5x^3 - 6x^2$ by $(x - 1)$ $x^3 + 6x^2$

28. (38) $x^4 - 20x^3 + 123x^2 - 216x$ by $(x - 3)$ $x^3 - 17x^2 + 72x$

29. (99) Add vectors $\begin{bmatrix}10\\6\end{bmatrix}$ and $\begin{bmatrix}4\\5\end{bmatrix}$. $\begin{bmatrix}14\\11\end{bmatrix}$

***30.** (99) Subtract vectors $\begin{bmatrix}10\\4\end{bmatrix}$ and $\begin{bmatrix}3\\14\end{bmatrix}$. $\begin{bmatrix}7\\-10\end{bmatrix}$

LOOKING FORWARD 

Graphing rational functions prepares students for

- **Lesson 101** Making Graphs of Polynomial Functions
- **Lesson 107** Graphing Rational Functions II
- **Lesson 111** Transforming Polynomial Functions
- **Lesson 117** Solving Systems of Nonlinear Equations

INVESTIGATION 10

Graphing Polar Models

An equation in polar coordinates uses the variables r and θ.

Polar Equations for Circles

A circle can be graphed using the polar equations:

$r = a \sin \theta$ $\qquad$ $r = a \cos \theta$

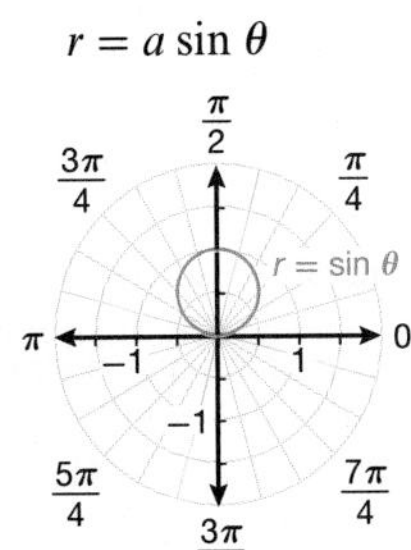

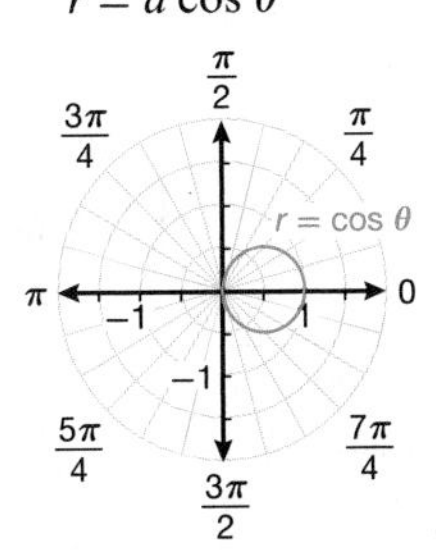

1. How do the graphs of $r = \sin \theta$ and $r = \cos \theta$ compare to the unit circle?
2. Graph $r = \sin \theta$ and then graph $r = a \sin \theta$ for three values of a where $0 < a < 1$. How did the value of a change the graph from the parent graph?
3. Graph $r = \cos \theta$ and then graph $r = a \cos \theta$ for three values of a where $a > 1$. How did the value of a change the graph from the parent graph?

Graphing Calculator

To graph polar equations with your graphing calculator, press the MODE key and select the POL option. Once in this mode, pressing the Y= key allows you to input an equation in $r = f(\theta)$ mode.

Polar Equations for Spirals

One of the simplest polar equations that uses the variable θ is $r = \theta$. Its graph is a spiral.

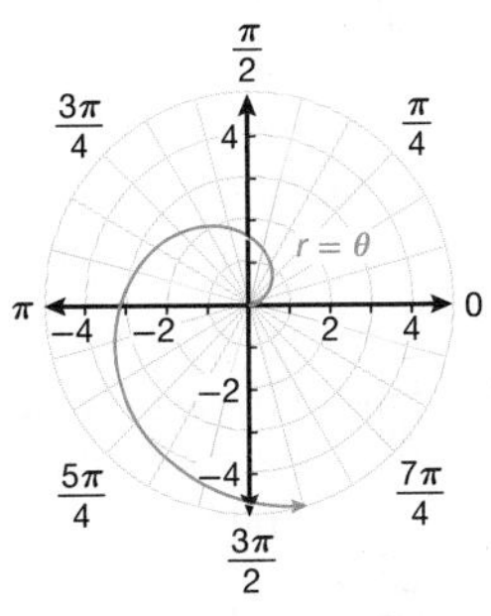

4. Make a table of values for $r = \theta$ on a graphing calculator. How does the value of r change compared to changes in θ? The value of r increases as θ increases.
5. Graph $r = \theta$ and then graph $r = c\theta$ for three values of c where $0 < c < 1$. How did the value of c change the graph from the parent graph? The curvature of the spiral increased.
6. Graph $r = \theta$ and then graph $r = c\theta$ for three values of c where $c > 1$. How did the value of a change the graph from the parent graph? The curvature of the spiral decreased.

MATH BACKGROUND

The polar coordinate system is created by fixing a point called the pole and drawing a fixed horizontal ray extending to the right from the pole. The fixed ray is called the polar axis. The remaining axes of note in the polar system are the $\frac{\pi}{2}$-axis, π-axis, and the $\frac{3\pi}{2}$-axis. A point is plotted by drawing a radius vector or ray from the pole to any point in the system. The number associated with the absolute value of the radius vector is r and θ is the measure of the angle between the polar axis and the radius vector.

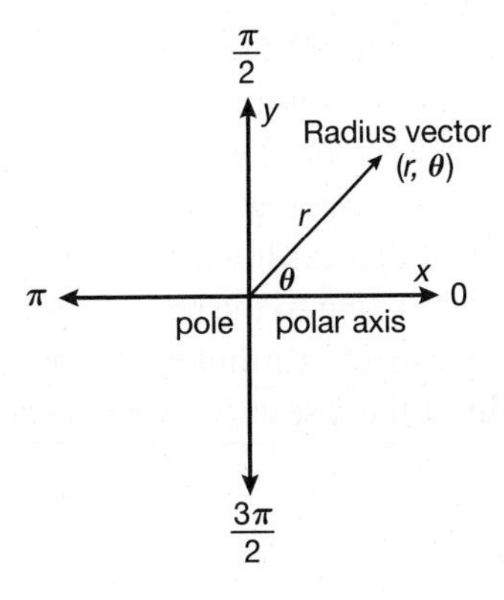

INVESTIGATION 10

Materials

- Pencil, polar graph paper, and graphing calculator

Discuss

Students will examine and graph polar equations. Equations of polar graphs including conic sections will be written and graphed on the graphing calculator. Define polar form of an equation, eccentricity, focus, and conic sections.

TEACHER TIP

The Cartesian equation $y = 1$ is a line while the polar equation $r = 1$ is a circle. The equation $r = \pm\sqrt{x^2 + y^2}$ is used to convert polar equations to Cartesian equations. So, $r = 1$ is equivalent to $1 = x^2 + y^2$ in rectangular form.

Error Alert Students may not obtain a complete graph when graphing polar equations. If this problem occurs, reset θmax. The default value is 2π. Use multiples of π such as 3π, 4π, etc.

1. The graph of $r = \sin \theta$ is the unit circle translated up the length of the radius. The graph of $r = \cos \theta$ is the unit circle translated right the length of the radius.

2. The circles are smaller than the parent circle and translated to the right. As a decreased the size of the circle decreased.

3. The circles are larger than the parent circle and translated up. As a increased the size of the circle increased.

Problems 12–13

The value of a controls the size of the circle. The radius equals $\frac{a}{2}$. When graphing a rose curve, $|a|$ determines the length of the petal.

TEACHER TIP

To extend the Investigation, challenge students to research and graph additional polar graphs. A few examples are given.

The spiral of Archimedes
$r = k\theta$
The hyperbolic spiral
$r\theta = k$
The limacon
$r = a \pm b\cos\theta$ or $r = a \pm b\sin\theta$
The lemniscate
$r^2 = a^2\sin 2\theta$ or $r^2 = a^2\cos 2\theta$

Graphing Calculator

The graph on the right shows values of θ ranging from 0 to 2π. With a graphing calculator, you can set θ to higher values. Press on the WINDOW key and set θmax to a greater multiple of π.

For linear equations of the form $r = a\theta + b$, the graph is also a spiral.

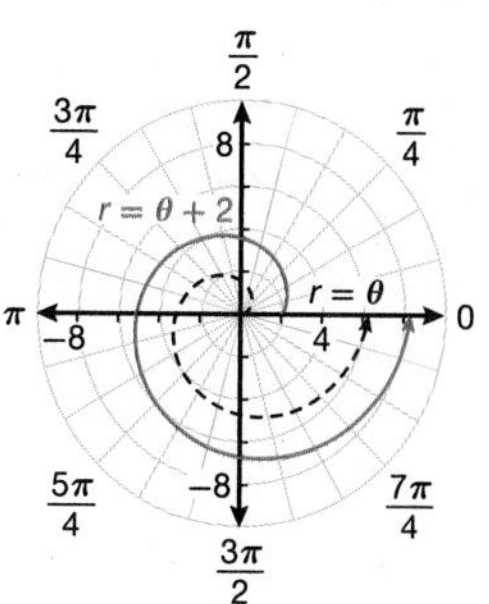

7. **Graphing Calculator** Describe the role of a and b in the graph of $r = a\theta + b$. The coefficient a determines the curvature of the spiral and b is the translation of the graph along the horizontal axis.

Math-Reasoning

Verify Use a graphing calculator to show that the general form of the of the equation, $r = a(\sin(\theta) + 1)$, always yields the graph of a cardioid.

See students' work.

A more general form of the equation $r = \theta$ is $r = a\sin(b\theta) + c$. Below are some of the interesting graphs that result from different values of a, b, and c. The graph of $r = \sin(\theta) + 1$ is a heart-shaped curve known as a cardioid. The graph of $r = 3\sin(2\theta)$ is called a rose curve.

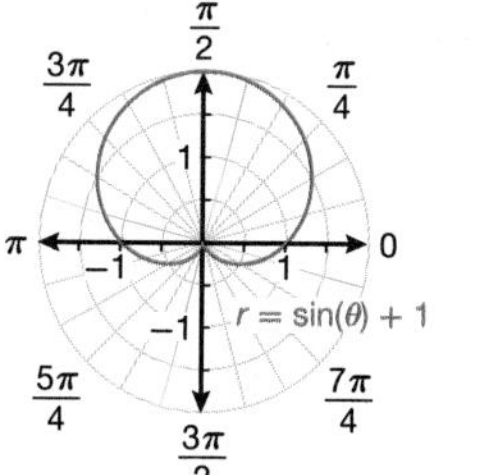

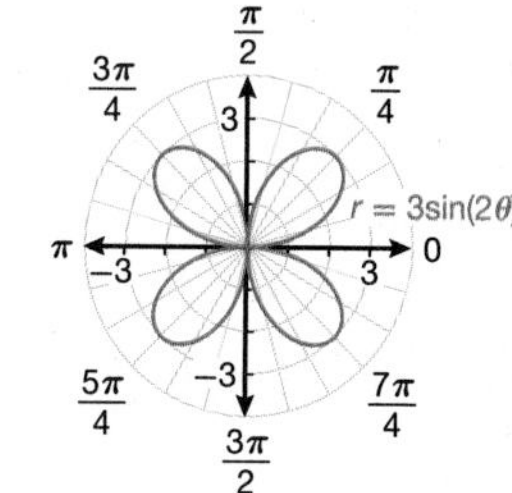

8. The number of petals is twice the value of b.

8. Graph 3 rose curves given by the general equation $y = \sin(b\theta)$ where b is an even integer. How does the number of petals relate to the value of b?

9. Graph 3 rose curves given by the general equation $y = \sin(b\theta)$ where b is an odd integer and not equal to 1. How does the number of petals relate to the value of b? The number of petals equals the value of b.

10. What would be the value of b in the equation of a rose curve with 20 petals? $b = 10$

11. 19 petals

11. How many petals are in a rose curve given by the equation $y = \sin(19\theta)$?

12. Graph the rose curve $y = a\sin(2\theta)$ where $a = 1$. Graph 3 more rose curves by choosing the value of a to be greater than 1. How did the graph change? The length of the petals increases.

13. Graph the rose curve $y = a\sin(2\theta)$ where $a = 1$. Graph 3 more rose curves by choosing the value $0 < a < 1$. How did the graph change? The length of the petals decreases.

The Polar Equations for Conic Sections

The general form of the polar equation for conic sections is shown below. By varying the value of the constant e, the graph will be a circle, ellipse, parabola, or hyperbola.

$$r = \frac{l}{1 + e\sin(\theta)}$$

ENGLISH LEARNERS

Draw a **cardioid** and a **rose curve** on the board. Have students comment on what the shapes resemble. Lead students to connect the heart-shaped graph with the cardioid. Explain that cardio- is found in a number of words relating to the heart–cardiovascular, cardiac arrest, cardiologist. Have students connect the rose curve with the flower shaped graph.

Caution

The variable e used in polar equations determines the eccentricity of the conic section. It is not the constant e, which equals approximately 2.718.

Graphing Calculator The variable e is the eccentricity, or a measure of the curvature of a conic section. For each of the following graphs, let the value of l remain constant, while varying the value of e.

14. Choose a value for l and let $e = 0$. What kind of conic section is this graph? a circle

15. Choose a value for l. Choose values of e from the range $0 < e < 1$. What kind of conic section is this graph? an ellipse

16. Choose a value for l and let $e = 1$. What kind of conic section is this graph? a parabola

The variable l represents the vertical distance from the conic section's focus or center and the curve itself.

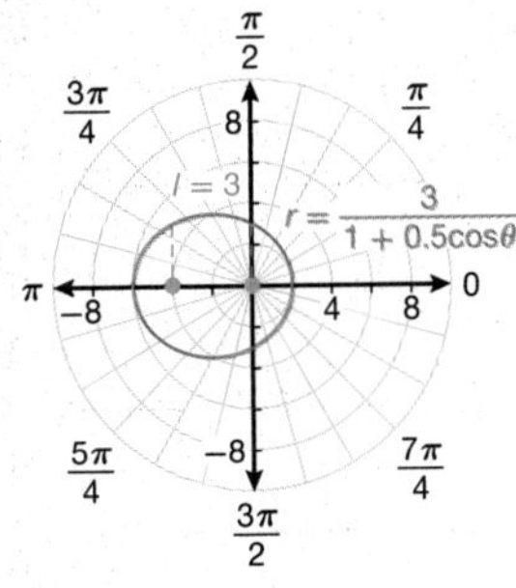

17. In the case of a circle, what does the value of l represent? the radius of the circle

Graphing Calculator Write and graph the equation of a conic section based on the requirements below.

18. A parabola with $l = 3$ See Additional Answers.

19. A circle of radius 7 See Additional Answers.

20. An ellipse with $l = 10$ See Additional Answers.

Investigation Practice

a. Give a parameter change for the circle equation $r = 2 \sin \theta$ that will increase the size of the circle. Sample: $r = 3 \sin \theta$

b. Describe the change of the graph $r = 3\theta$ from the parent function $r = \theta$. The curvature of the spiral decreased.

c. Write an equation for a rose curve with 16 petals. $y = \sin(8\theta)$

d. Write an equation for a rose curve with 9 petals. $y = \sin(9\theta)$

e. Write an equation for a rose curve that has the same number of petals but lengthened in the equation $y = 2 \sin(3\theta)$. Sample: $y = 4 \sin(3\theta)$

f. What kind of conic section is given by the equation $r = \frac{2}{1 + 0.5 \sin(\theta)}$? ellipse

g. What kind of conic section is given by the equation $r = \frac{4}{1 + 1 \sin(\theta)}$? parabola

Problems 14–16

As each value of eccentricity changes the conic section changes. Adjust your window to create complete graphs.

Investigation Practice

Math Conversations

Discussions to strengthen understanding

Problems f and g

Remind students that e determines the eccentricity, and therefore, determines the type of conic section that the equation models.

Lesson Planner

Lesson	New Concepts
101	Making Graphs of Polynomial Functions
102	Solving Logarithmic Equations and Inequalities
103	Graphing Reciprocal Trigonometric Functions
104	Finding Transformations
105	Finding Arithmetic Series
	Cumulative Test 20, Performance Task 20
106	Using the Fundamental Theorem of Algebra
107	Graphing Rational Functions II
108	Using Fundamental Trigonometric Identities
109	Making Graphs and Using Equations of Hyperbolas
110	Graphing Logarithmic Functions
	Cumulative Test 21, Performance Task 21
INV 11	Using De Moivre's Theorem

Resources for Teaching

- Student Edition
- Teacher's Edition
- Student Edition eBook
- Teacher's Edition eBook
- Resources and Planner CD
- Solutions Manual
- Instructional Masters
- Technology Lab Masters
- Warm Up and Teaching Transparencies
- Instructional Presentations CD
- Online activities, tools, and homework help **www.SaxonMathResources.com**

Resources for Practice and Assessment

- Student Edition Practice Workbook
- Course Assessments
- Standardized Test Practice
- College Entrance Exam Practice
- Test and Practice Generator CD using ExamView™

Resources for Differentiated Instruction

- Reteaching Masters
- Challenge and Enrichment Masters
- Prerequisite Skills Intervention
- Adaptations for Saxon Algebra 2
- Multilingual Glossary
- English Learners Handbook
- TI Resources

Pacing Guide

Resources and Planner CD for lesson planning support

45-Minute Class

Day 1	Day 2	Day 3	Day 4	Day 5	Day 6
Lesson 101	Lesson 102	Lesson 103	Lesson 104	Lesson 105	Cumulative Test 20
Day 7	**Day 8**	**Day 9**	**Day 10**	**Day 11**	**Day 12**
Lesson 106	Lesson 107	Lesson 108	Lesson 109	Lesson 110	Cumulative Test 21
Day 13					
Investigation 11					

Block: 90-Minute Class

Day 1	Day 2	Day 3	Day 4	Day 5	Day 6
Investigation 10 Lesson 101	Lesson 102 Lesson 103	Lesson 104 Lesson 105	Cumulative Test 20 Lesson 106	Lesson 107 Lesson 108	Lesson 109 Lesson 110
Day 7					
Cumulative Test 21 Investigation 11					

**For suggestions on how to implement Saxon Math in a block schedule, see the Pacing section at the beginning of the Teacher's Edition.*

Differentiated Instruction

Below Level		Advanced Learners	
Warm Up	SE pp. 706, 714, 719, 725, 732, 738, 745, 752, 757, 764	Challenge	TE pp. 713, 718, 723, 730, 736, 743, 748, 756, 760, 767, 778
Skills Bank	SE pp. 862–885	Extend the Example	TE pp. 715, 726, 732, 733, 741, 772
Reteaching Masters	Lessons 101–110, Investigation 11	Extend the Problem	TE pp. 724, 737, 743, 745, 749, 756, 761, 768, 769
Warm Up Transparencies	Lessons 101–110	Challenge and Enrichment Masters	Challenge: C101–C110 Enrichment: E101, E102
English Learners		**Special Needs**	
EL Tips	TE pp. 710, 716, 720, 726, 735, 740, 746, 753, 758, 761, 766, 772	Inclusion Tips	TE pp. 707, 708, 715, 722, 727, 734, 742, 747, 749, 754, 758, 761, 765, 771
Multilingual Glossary	Booklet and Online	Adaptations for Saxon Algebra 2	Lessons 101–110 Cumulative Tests 20, 21
English Learners Handbook			
For All Learners			
Exploration	SE pp. 738	Alternate Method	TE pp. 711, 712, 715, 721, 728, 733, 739, 741, 755, 759
Caution	SE pp. 709, 715, 721, 728, 733	Online Tools	
Hints	SE pp. 706, 707, 708, 714, 719, 720, 721, 726, 727, 738, 739, 753, 765, 770, 772		
Error Alert	TE pp. 710, 711, 715, 716, 717, 718, 721, 729, 730, 731, 735, 736, 739, 741, 742, 744, 751, 755, 758, 759, 762, 763, 767, 771		

SE = Student Edition; TE = Teacher's Edition

Math Vocabulary

Lesson	New Vocabulary		Maintained	EL Tip in TE	
101	end behavior local maximum local minimum	turning point	coefficient	flap	
102	logarithmic equation	logarithmic inequality	base	In log	logarithm logarithmic
103			period reciprocal	reciprocal	
104			transformations	horizontal vertical	
105	arithmetic series partial sum	series sigma notation summation notation	arithmetic sequence common difference	sequence series	
106	Fundamental Theorem of Algebra		complex numbers conjugate pairs multiplicity	complex real	
107	slant asymptotes		rational functions polynomial long division	slant	
108	trigonometric identity		tangent	identity	
109	branch of a hyperbola foci hyperbola	hyperbolic geometry vertex of a hyperbola	completing the square	maintain	
110	logarithmic function natural logarithmic function		exponential function	decibel	
INV 11			complex number	interchangeable	

SECTION OVERVIEW 11

Math Highlights

Enduring Understandings – The "Big Picture"

After completing Section 11, students will understand:

- How to graph polynomial, rational, logarithmic, and reciprocal trigonometric functions.
- How to solve logarithmic equations and inequalities.
- How to recognize and apply transformations of graphs.
- How to find the sum of an arithmetic series.
- How to apply the Fundamental Theorem of Algebra and De Moivre's Theorem.
- How to use trigonometric identities.
- How to graph hyperbolas and use hyperbolic geometry.

Essential Questions

- In the set of complex numbers an n degree polynomial function has how many zeros?
- What is the end behavior of the graph of a polynomial function of an odd degree?
- What transformation is produced when a constant is added to a parent function?
- How are hyperbolas related to circles, ellipses, and parabolas?

Math Content Strands

Conic Sections

• Lesson 109	Making Graphs and Using Equations of Hyperbolas

Exponential and Logarithmic Functions

• Lesson 102	Solving Logarithmic Equations and Inequalities
• Lesson 110	Graphing Logarithmic Functions

Matrices

• Lesson 104	Finding Transformations

Polynomials and Polynomial Functions

• Lesson 101	Making Graphs of Polynomial Functions
• Lesson 106	Using the Fundamental Theorem of Algebra

Rational and Radical Functions

• Lesson 107	Graphing Rational Functions II

Sequences, Series, and Logic

• Lesson 105	Finding Arithmetic Series

Trigonometry

• Lesson 103	Graphing Reciprocal Trigonometric Functions
• Lesson 108	Using Fundamental Trigonometric Identities
• Investigation 11	Using De Moivre's Theorem

Connections in Practice Problems

	Lessons
Algebra	110
Coordinate Geometry	105, 108
Data Analysis	104, 109
Geometry	101, 102, 103, 104, 105, 106, 107, 108, 109, 110
Probability	102, 107
Statistics	106

Math Processes

Reasoning and Communication

	Lessons
• Analyze	101, 102, 103, 104, 105, 106, 107, 108, 109, 110
• Error analysis	101, 102, 103, 104, 105, 106, 107, 108, 109, 110
• Estimate	105, 107
• Formulate	103, 104, 106, 107, 108, 109
• Generalize	101, 102, 106, 107, 108, 109, 110
• Justify	102, 103, 105, 106
• Math reasoning	101, 102, 103, 105, 106, 107, 108, 109, 110
• Model	103, 104, 110
• Multiple choice	101, 102, 103, 104, 105, 106, 107, 108, 109, 110
• Multi-step	101, 102, 103, 104, 105, 106, 107, 108, 109, 110
• Predict	101
• Verify	105, 106, 107, 108, 109, 110
• Write	101, 102, 103, 104, 105, 106, 107, 108, 109
• Graphing Calculator	101, 102, 103, 104, 105, 106, 107, 108, 109, 110

Connections

In Examples: Airplane landings, Consumer finance, Exercise, Farming, Graphical analysis, Hyperbolic geometry, IQ formula, Population growth, Sheet metal fabrication, Sound

In Practice problems: Athletic field, Business, Cafeteria, Chemistry, Commodities, Construction, Consumer finance, Finance, Football, Furniture design, Geography, Government, Ice cream, Jet stream, Jewelry making, Landscape design, Lockbox, Medicine, Motor vehicle ownership, National highways, National monuments, National parks, Optics, Physics, Population, Population growth, Radioactive decay, Retirement funds, Salaries, Simple interest, Soccer, Sound, Space science, Surveying, Tourist attractions, Town government, Union membership

Content Trace

Lesson	Warm Up: Prerequisite Skills	New Concepts	Where Practiced	Where Assessed	Looking Forward
101	Lessons 11, 19, 66	Making Graphs of Polynomial Functions	Lessons 102, 103, 104, 105, 106, 108, 109, 110, 114, 116, 117, 118	Cumulative Tests 21, 22	Lesson 104
102	Lessons 72, 81, 87	Solving Logarithmic Equations and Inequalities	Lessons 103, 104, 105, 106, 108, 109, 110, 111, 112, 113, 114, 117, 119	Cumulative Tests 21, 22	Lesson 110
103	Lessons 46, 86, 90	Graphing Reciprocal Trigonometric Functions	Lessons 104, 106, 108, 114	Cumulative Tests 21, 22	Lessons 108, 119
104	Lessons 17, 33, 75	Finding Transformations	Lessons 105, 106, 107, 108, 112, 114, 115, 116, 117, 119	Cumulative Tests 21, 23	Lesson 110
105	Lesson 92	Finding Arithmetic Series	Lessons 106, 107, 109, 112, 113, 114, 116, 117, 118, 119	Cumulative Tests 21, 22	Lesson 113
106	Lessons 61, 66	Using the Fundamental Theorem of Algebra	Lessons 107, 108, 109, 110, 112, 114, 115, 116, 117, 118, 119	Cumulative Tests 22, 23	Lesson 111
107	Lessons 38, 100	Graphing Rational Functions II	Lessons 108, 109, 110, 113, 115, 116, 118, 119	Cumulative Tests 22, 23	Lessons 109, 110, 113
108	Lesson 46	Using Fundamental Trigonometric Identities	Lessons 109, 110, 114, 115, 118	Cumulative Tests 22, 23	Lessons 112, 115, 119
109	Lessons 26, 58	Making Graphs and Using Equations of Hyperbolas	Lessons 110, 111, 112, 114, 115, 116, 117	Cumulative Tests 22, 23	Lesson 114
110	Lesson 72	Graphing Logarithmic Functions	Lessons 111, 115, 117, 118, 119	Cumulative Tests 22, 23	Lesson 116
INV 11	N/A	Using De Moivre's Theorem	Lessons 111, 119	Cumulative Test 23	N/A

Ongoing Assessment

	Type	Feature	Intervention *
BEFORE instruction	Assess Prior Knowledge	• Diagnostic Test	• Prerequisite Skills Intervention
BEFORE the lesson	Formative	• Warm Up	• Skills Bank • Reteaching Masters
DURING the lesson	Formative	• Lesson Practice • Math Conversations with the Practice problems	• Additional Examples in TE • Test and Practice Generator (for additional practice sheets)
AFTER the lesson	Formative	• Check for Understanding (closure)	• Scaffolding Questions in TE
AFTER 5 lessons	Summative	After Lesson 105 • Cumulative Test 20 • Performance Task 20 After Lesson 110 • Cumulative Test 21 • Performance Task 21	• Reteaching Masters • Test and Practice Generator (for additional tests and practice)
AFTER 20 lessons	Summative	• Benchmark Tests	• Reteaching Masters • Test and Practice Generator (for additional tests and practice)

* for students not showing progress during the formative stages or scoring below 80% on the summative assessments

Evidence of Learning – What Students Should Know

Because the Saxon philosophy is to provide students with sufficient time to learn and practice each concept, a lesson's topic will not be tested until at least five lessons after the topic is introduced.

On the Cumulative Tests that are given during this section of ten lessons, students should be able to demonstrate the following competencies:

- Find the nth term given any two terms; find the nth term of an arithmetic sequence.
- Solve increasing exponential equations.
- Find the dot product of two vectors.
- Convert Cartesian coordinates to polar coordinates.
- Graph ellipses not centered at the Origin.

Test and Practice Generator CD using ExamView™

The Test and Practice Generator is an easy-to-use benchmark and assessment tool that creates unlimited practice and tests in multiple formats and allows you to customize questions or create new ones. A variety of reports are available to track student progress toward mastery of the standards throughout the year.

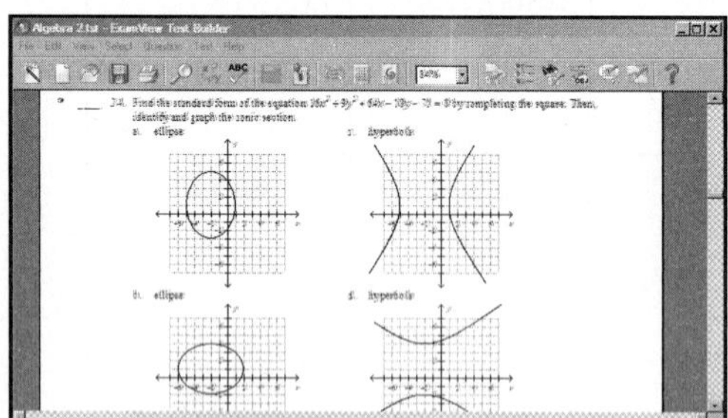

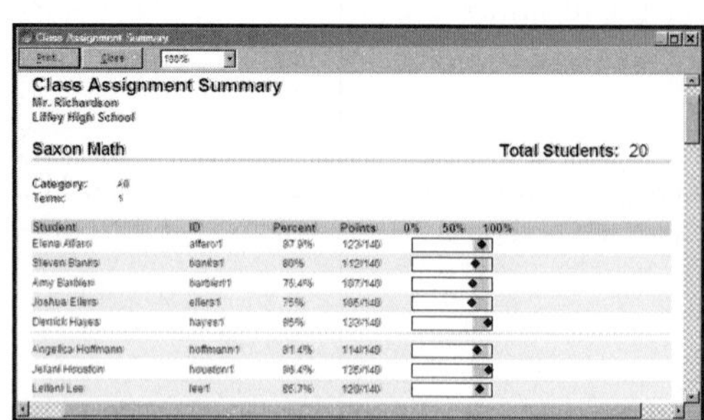

Assessment Resources

Resources for Diagnosing and Assessing

- **Student Edition**
  - Warm Up
  - Lesson Practice
- **Teacher's Edition**
  - Math Conversations with the Practice problems
  - Check for Understanding (closure)
- **Course Assessments**
  - Diagnostic Test
  - Cumulative Tests
  - Performance Tasks
  - Benchmark Tests

Resources for Test Prep

- **Student Edition**
  - Multiple-choice practice problems
  - Multiple-step and writing problems
  - Daily cumulative practice
- **Standardized Test Practice**
- **College Entrance Exam Practice**
- **Test and Practice Generator CD using ExamView™**

Resources for Intervention

- **Student Edition**
  - Skills Bank
- **Teacher's Edition**
  - Additional Examples
  - Scaffolding questions
- **Prerequisite Skills Intervention**
  - Worksheets
- **Reteaching Masters**
  - Lesson instruction and practice sheets
- **Test and Practice Generator CD using ExamView™**
  - Lesson practice problems
  - Additional tests

Cumulative Tests

The assessments in Saxon Math are frequent and consistently placed after every five lessons to offer a regular method of ongoing testing. These cumulative assessments check mastery of concepts from previous lessons.

Performance Tasks

The Performance Tasks can be used in conjunction with the Cumulative Tests and are scored using a rubric.

After Lesson 105

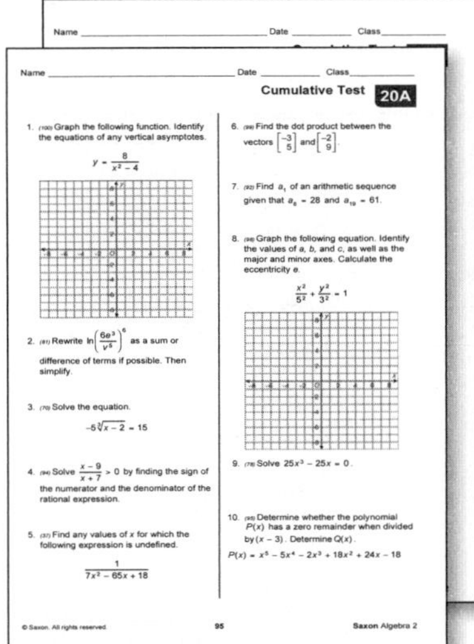

Name ______________ Date ________ Class ________

Cumulative Test **20A**

1. Graph the following function. Identify the equations of any vertical asymptotes.
$$y = \frac{8}{x^2 - 4}$$
2. Rewrite $\ln\left(\frac{6e^3}{v^5}\right)^6$ as a sum or difference of terms if possible. Then simplify.
3. Solve the equation.
$$-5\sqrt[3]{x-2} = 15$$
4. Solve $\frac{x-9}{x+7} > 0$ by finding the sign of the numerator and the denominator of the rational expression.
5. Find any values of x for which the following expression is undefined.
$$\frac{1}{7x^2 - 65x + 18}$$
6. Find the dot product between the vectors $\begin{bmatrix}-3\\5\end{bmatrix}$ and $\begin{bmatrix}-2\\9\end{bmatrix}$.
7. Find a_1 of an arithmetic sequence given that $a_8 = 28$ and $a_{19} = 61$.
8. Graph the following equation. Identify the values of a, b, and c, as well as the major and minor axes. Calculate the eccentricity e.
$$\frac{x^2}{5^2} + \frac{y^2}{3^2} = 1$$
9. Solve $25x^3 - 25x = 0$.
10. Determine whether the polynomial $P(x)$ has a zero remainder when divided by $(x - 3)$. Determine $Q(x)$.
$$P(x) = x^5 - 5x^4 - 2x^3 + 18x^2 + 24x - 18$$

© Saxon. All rights reserved. 95 Saxon Algebra 2

After Lesson 110

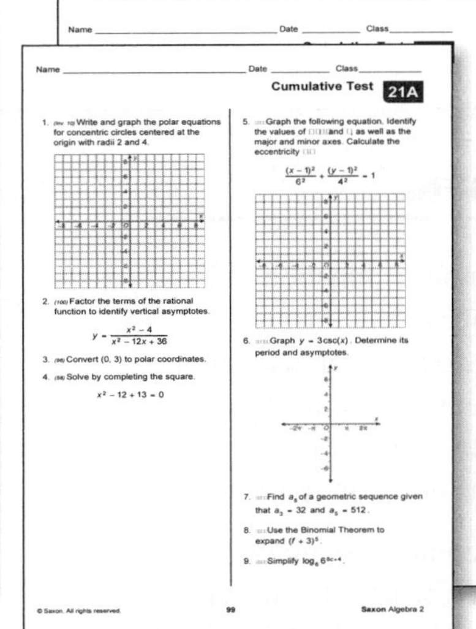

Name ______________ Date ________ Class ________

Cumulative Test **21A**

1. Write and graph the polar equations for concentric circles centered at the origin with radii 2 and 4.
2. Factor the terms of the rational function to identify vertical asymptotes.
$$y = \frac{x^2 - 4}{x^2 - 12x + 36}$$
3. Convert (0, 3) to polar coordinates.
4. Solve by completing the square.
$$x^2 - 12 + 13 = 0$$
5. Graph the following equation. Identify the values of [illegible] and [illegible] as well as the major and minor axes. Calculate the eccentricity [illegible].
$$\frac{(x-1)^2}{6^2} + \frac{(y-1)^2}{4^2} = 1$$
6. Graph $y = 3\csc(x)$. Determine its period and asymptotes.
7. Find a_8 of a geometric sequence given that $a_3 = 32$ and $a_5 = 512$.
8. Use the Binomial Theorem to expand $(f + 3)^5$.
9. Simplify $\log_6 6^{8c+4}$.

© Saxon. All rights reserved. 99 Saxon Algebra 2

For use with Performance Tasks

Teacher Rubric

Criteria Performance	Knowledge and Skills Understanding	Communication and Representation	Process and Strategies
4	The student got it! The student did it in new ways and showed how it worked. The student knew and understood what math concepts to use.	The student clearly detailed how he/she solved the problem. The student included all the steps to show his/her thinking. The student used math language, symbols, numbers, graphs and/or models to represent his/her solution.	The student had an effective and inventive solution. The student used big math ideas to solve the problem. The student addressed the important details. The student showed other ways to solve the problem. The student checked his/her answer to make sure it was correct
3	The student understood the problem and had an appropriate solution. All parts of the problem are addressed.	The student clearly explained how he/she solved the problem. The student used math language, symbols, tables, graphs, and numbers to explain how he/she did the problem.	The student had a correct solution. The student used a plan to solve the problem and selected an appropriate strategy.
2	The student understood parts of the problem. The student started, but he/she couldn't finish.	The student explained some of what he/she did. The student tried to use words, symbols, tables, graphs and numbers to explain how he/she did the problem.	The student had part of the solution, but did not know how to finish. The student was not sure if he/she had the correct answer. The student needed help.
1	The student did not understand the problem.	The student did not explain how he/she solved the problem. He/she did not use words, symbols, tables or graphs to show how he/she	The student couldn't get started. The student did not know how to begin.

© Saxon. All rights reserved. x Saxon Algebra 2

LESSON 101

1 Warm Up

In Problem 3, students can begin by factoring out the GCF, x.

2 New Concepts

In this lesson, students learn to classify different types of graphs based on their degree.

Discuss the definitions of end behavior, odd degree, and even degree. In order to analyze the graphs of a polynomial function, the degree and end behavior must be classified.

TEACHER TIP

Let students use nonformal words for end behavior before using the mathematical words and notation. For example, "on the left, the function goes down," can be upgraded to "as x decreases, y decreases," which can be upgraded to "as x approaches negative infinity, the function values approach negative infinity."

LESSON 101 Making Graphs of Polynomial Functions

Warm Up

1. **Vocabulary** For the polynomial $2x^3 - x + 5$, the leading coefficient is 2. (11)
2. If $f(x) = 2x^3 - x + 5$, then $f(-2) =$ -9. (11)
3. Find the real zeros of $g(x) = x^3 + 3x^2 + 2x$ by factoring. $-2, -1, 0$ (66)
4. Simplify $x - 2(3x - 1)$. $-5x + 2$ (19)
5. Multiply $3y^2(-3y)$. $-9y^3$ (19)

New Concepts

Polynomial functions are classified by their degree. Some characteristics of graphs of polynomial functions are shown below.

Hint

Below is the graph of $f(x) = x^4$, the parent quartic function.

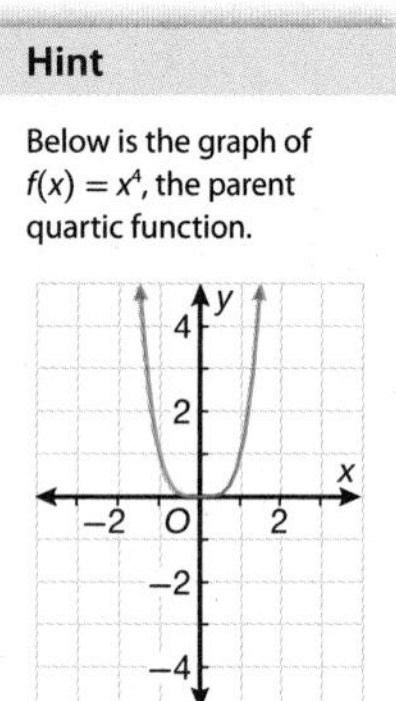

Graphs of Polynomial Functions		
Linear function Degree 1	Quadratic function Degree 2	Cubic function Degree 3
Quartic function Degree 4	Quintic function Degree 5	
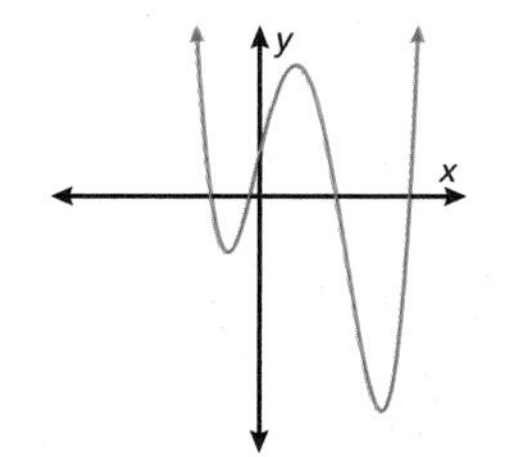	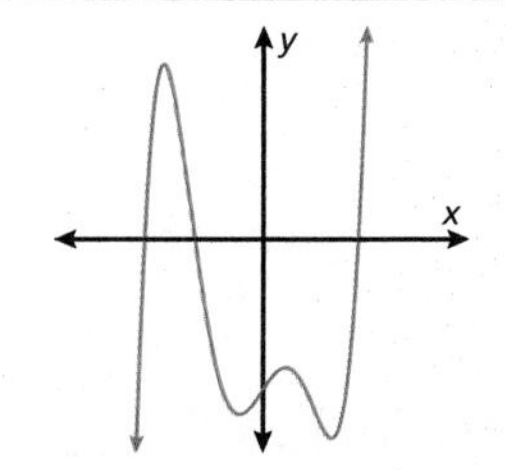	
All linear function graphs are lines. All quadratic function graphs are parabolas. The shapes of cubic, quartic, and quintic function graphs have more variety than shown above.		

End behavior is a description of the y-values of a function as x approaches positive infinity ($x \to +\infty$) or negative infinity ($x \to -\infty$). End behavior of a polynomial function is determined by its degree and leading coefficient. Knowing about end behavior is helpful when graphing a polynomial function.

LESSON RESOURCES

Student Edition Practice Workbook 101
Reteaching Master 101
Adaptations Master 101
Challenge and Enrichment Masters C101, E101

MATH BACKGROUND

The graph of a polynomial function can be used in many applications. It is used when the position, velocity, or acceleration of an object needs to be determined. A polynomial graph can correctly characterize the movements of the object in space.

In addition, the maximum and minimum parts of the graph can be used to answer specific questions to solve application problems.

Hint

Notice that if the polynomial has an even degree: both ends head upward ($a > 0$) or downward ($a < 0$). If the polynomial has an odd degree: the ends head in opposite directions, one upward and the other downward, with the direction determined by whether $a > 0$ or $a < 0$.

Polynomial End Behavior

$P(x)$ has ...	Odd Degree	Even Degree
Leading coefficient $a > 0$	As $x \to -\infty$, $P(x) \to -\infty$. As $x \to +\infty$, $P(x) \to +\infty$.	As $x \to -\infty$, $P(x) \to +\infty$. As $x \to +\infty$, $P(x) \to +\infty$.
Leading coefficient $a < 0$	As $x \to -\infty$, $P(x) \to +\infty$. As $x \to +\infty$, $P(x) \to -\infty$.	As $x \to -\infty$, $P(x) \to -\infty$. As $x \to +\infty$, $P(x) \to -\infty$.

Example 1 Determining End Behavior of Polynomial Functions

Identify the leading coefficient and degree, and describe the end behavior.

a. $P(x) = 2x^3 + 3x^2 - 4x + 1$

SOLUTION

The leading coefficient is 2, which is positive.

The degree is 3, which is odd.

As $x \to +\infty$, $P(x) \to +\infty$, and as $x \to -\infty$, $P(x) \to -\infty$.

b. $R(x) = x^2 - x^6 - 5x$

SOLUTION

Rewrite the function in standard form: $R(x) = -x^6 + x^2 - 5x$.

The leading coefficient is -1, which is negative.

The degree is 6, which is even.

As $x \to -\infty$, $P(x) \to -\infty$, and as $x \to +\infty$, $P(x) \to -\infty$.

Hint

Both the leading coefficient and the degree of the polynomial are contained in the term of the greatest degree. When determining end behavior, you can ignore all other terms.

Example 1

Given a polynomial function, students describe the graph's end behavior.

Additional Example 1

Identify the leading coefficient and degree, and describe the end behavior.

a. $F(x) = x^2 + 3x^4 - 5x^7 + 7$

The leading coefficient is -5, which is negative. The degree is 7, which is odd.

As $x \to +\infty$, $P(x) \to -\infty$.

As $x \to -\infty$, $P(x) \to +\infty$.

b. $G(x) = 3x^6 + 11x^5 + 4x^4$

The leading coefficient is 3, which is positive. The degree is 6, which is even.

As $x \to +\infty$, $P(x) \to +\infty$.

As $x \to -\infty$, $P(x) \to +\infty$.

INCLUSION

Define the end behavior as how the graph reacts as x takes on large positive and large negative values. Start by showing how the graph reacts when x is equal to 10, then 100, then 1000 and so on and show how this can be extrapolated to infinity. Allow students to use a calculator, recording the results in a table of values, to show the effect of large positive or negative x-values on the y-values, or end behavior.

Connect the degree of the polynomial to the shape of the graph. Make sure the students understand that only the largest exponent will determine the general shape of the graph.

Apply a polynomial function to the velocity of a car versus time. Note that the maximum and minimum parts of the graph will show at what times the car was moving the fastest and the slowest.

Example 2

Students describe a function based on its graph.

Additional Example 2

Determine whether the function graphed has an odd or even degree and a positive or negative leading coefficient.

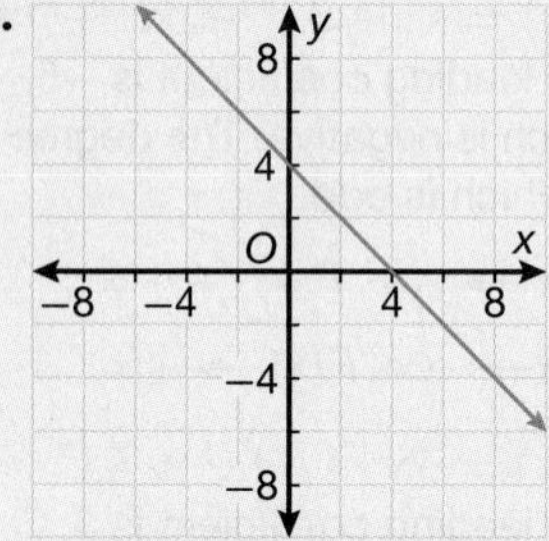

$P(x)$ is of odd degree with a negative leading coefficient.

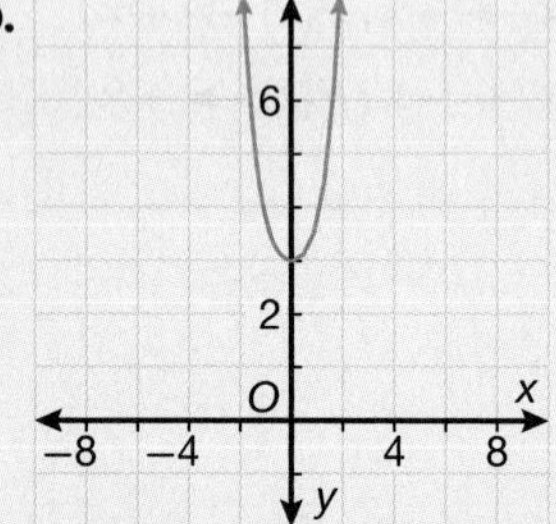

$P(x)$ is of even degree with a positive leading coefficient.

Example 3

Students can use what they know about end behavior when graphing a polynomial function.

Additional Example 3

Graph the function.

$f(x) = -7x^4 - 4x^3 + 2x^2 + 9$

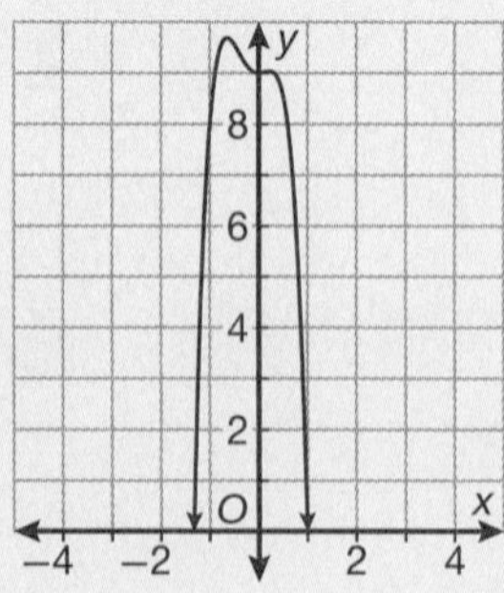

Example 2 Using Graphs to Analyze Polynomial Functions

Determine whether the function graphed has an odd or even degree and a positive or negative leading coefficient.

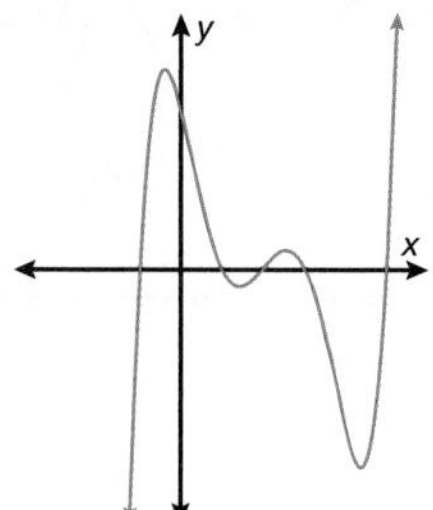

b.

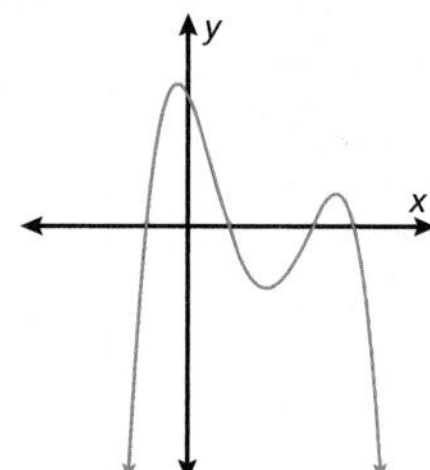

SOLUTION

a. As $x \rightarrow -\infty$, $P(x) \rightarrow -\infty$, and as $x \rightarrow +\infty$, $P(x) \rightarrow +\infty$.

$P(x)$ is of odd degree with a positive leading coefficient.

SOLUTION

b. As $x \rightarrow -\infty$, $P(x) \rightarrow -\infty$, and as $x \rightarrow +\infty$, $P(x) \rightarrow -\infty$.

$P(x)$ is of even degree with a negative leading coefficient.

Use the following steps to graph a polynomial function.

Steps for Graphing a Polynominal Function
1. Identify the real zeros of the function.
2. Make a table of ordered pairs. Include the x-intercept(s), x-values that lie between the x-intercepts, and the y-intercept.
3. Plot the points from your table.
4. Determine the end behavior.
5. Sketch the graph.

Example 3 Graphing a Polynomial Function

Graph the function.

$f(x) = x^3 + 2x^2 - 5x - 6$

SOLUTION

Step 1: To identify the real zeros, begin by identifying the possible rational roots of the equation $1x^3 + 2x^2 - 5x - 6 = 0$. Use the Rational Root Theorem. Since $p = -6$ and $q = 1$, the possible rational roots are ±1, ±2, ±3, and ± 6.

Next, test possible rational roots until a zero is identified.

Test $x = 1$.

1	1	2	−5	−6
		1	3	−2
	1	3	−2	−8

Test $x = -1$.

−1	1	2	−5	−6
		−1	−1	6
	1	1	−6	0

$x = -1$ is a zero, and $f(x) = (x + 1)(x^2 + x - 6)$.

Factor to identify the other zeros. $f(x) = (x + 1)(x + 3)(x - 2)$

The real zeros are -1, -3, and 2. These are the x-intercepts.

Hint

The zeros of $f(x)$, the roots of $y = 0$, and the x-intercepts of the graph of $f(x)$ are all different names for the same numbers.

INCLUSION

For students struggling with graphing, it may be beneficial to have them create a larger table in order to plot more points before sketching. Plotting more points will help the students see the nature of the graph and how the curve progresses as x becomes larger or smaller.

The number of points used in the table can be increased until the student feels comfortable sketching the graph.

Caution

Do not assume that (1, −8) is lower than all other nearby points. See the graph below.

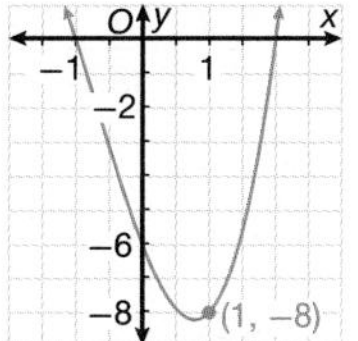

If more exact values for the turning points are required, beyond what a sketch can provide, a graphing calculator can be used.

Step 2: Make a table of ordered pairs. Include the x-intercepts, x-values that lie between x-intercepts, and the y-intercept.

x	−3	−2	−1	0	1	2
y	0	4	0	−6	−8	0

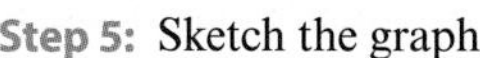

The x-intercepts are −3, −1, and 2. The y-intercept is −6.

Step 3: Plot the points from the table.

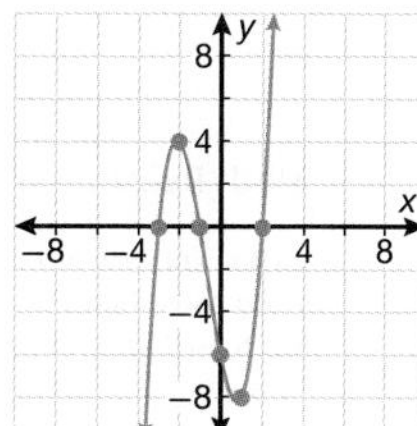

Step 4: Determine the end behavior. The degree is odd and the leading coefficient is positive, so as $x \rightarrow -\infty$, $P(x) \rightarrow -\infty$, and as $x \rightarrow +\infty$, $P(x) \rightarrow +\infty$.

Step 5: Sketch the graph.

A **turning point** is where a graph changes from increasing to decreasing or from decreasing to increasing values of y. The function value at a turning point is either a *local maximum* or *local minimum*.

Local Maxima and Minima
For a function $f(x)$, $f(a)$ is a **local maximum** if there is an interval around a such that $f(x) < f(a)$ for every x-value in the interval except a.
For a function $f(x)$, $f(a)$ is a **local minimum** if there is an interval around a such that $f(x) > f(a)$ for every x-value in the interval except a.

A polynomial function of degree n has at most n x-intercepts and at most $n - 1$ turning points. If the function has exactly n distinct real zeros, then it has exactly n x-intercepts and exactly $n - 1$ turning points. You can use a graphing calculator to find local maxima and minima. In some cases, they will be approximate values.

Reading Math

Maxima is the plural form of maximum. **Minima** is the plural form of *minimum*.

Example 4 Determining Local Maxima and Minima with a Calculator

Graph $g(x) = 2x^3 + x^2 - 6x + 5$ on a calculator, and then determine the local maxima and local minima.

SOLUTION

Step 1: Graph.

The graph appears to have one local minimum and one local maximum.

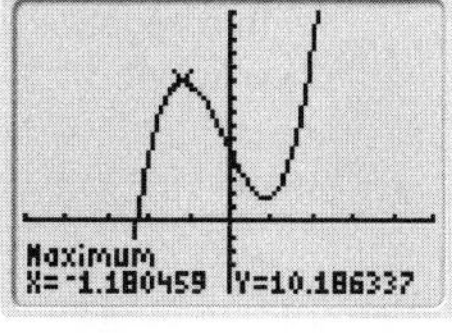

Step 2: Determine the local maximum.

Press 2nd TRACE (CALC) to access the **CALC** menu. Choose **4:maximum**.

The local maximum is approximately 10.1863.

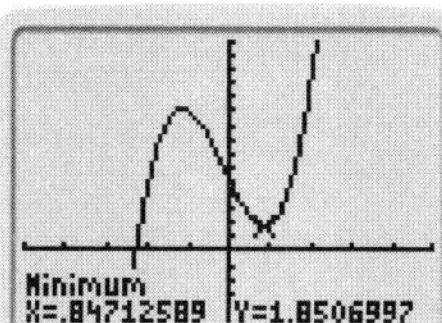

Step 3: Determine the local minimum.

Press 2nd TRACE (CALC) to access the **CALC** menu. Choose **3:minimum**.

The local minimum is approximately 1.8507.

Example 4

Students will determine the local maxima and local minima points of a function using their calculators.

Additional Example 4

Graph $g(x) = 8x^5 + 7x^2 - 4x + 3$ on a calculator, and then determine the local maxima and local minima.

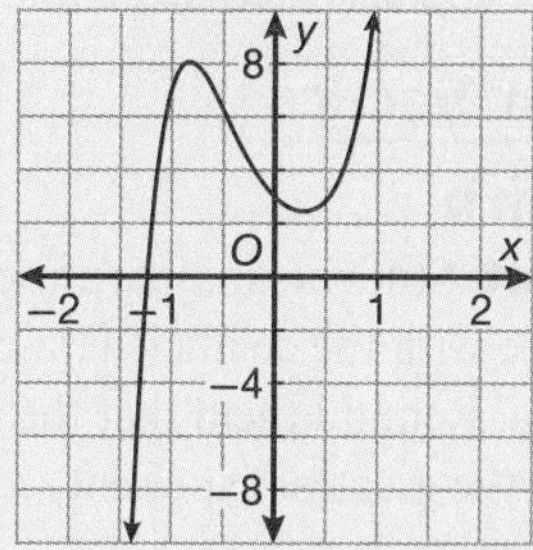

local maximum: approximately 8.07
local minimum: approximately 2.44

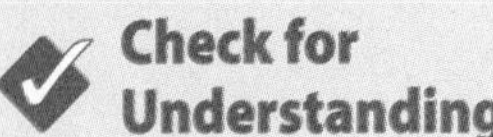

Example 5

Students will use their knowledge of functions and graphs to solve an application problem.

Additional Example 5

A rectangular box was designed with a length of $(10 - x)$ ft, a height of x ft, and a width of $(10 - 2x)$ ft. What is the maximum volume that the box can have? approximately 96.23 ft³

Lesson Practice

Problem b

Error Alert Students may confuse the degree with the coefficient and vice versa. Remind them that the degree is the greatest exponent.

Problem e

Scaffolding Before beginning, have students state the expected end behavior.

Check for Understanding

The questions below help assess the concepts taught in this lesson.

"What do the leading coefficient and the degree of the polynomial function tell us about its graph?" Sample: The leading coefficient and degree tell us about the end behavior (y-values) of the graph as x goes towards negative and positive infinity.

"What are major points that need to be graphed for a function to be sketched?" Sample: x-intercepts, y-intercept, zeros, points between x-intercepts

Example 5 Application: Sheet Metal Fabrication

A sheet metal mechanic plans to construct an open box from a 12 ft by 15 ft rectangular sheet of metal by cutting squares from the corners and folding up the flaps. Find the maximum possible volume of the box.

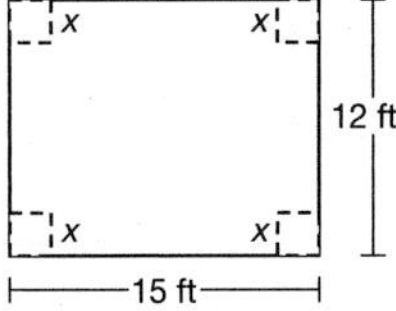

SOLUTION

Write a function to represent volume.

$V(x) = x(15 - 2x)(12 - 2x)$

Graph the function. Note that values of x greater than 6 or less than 0 do not make sense for this problem.

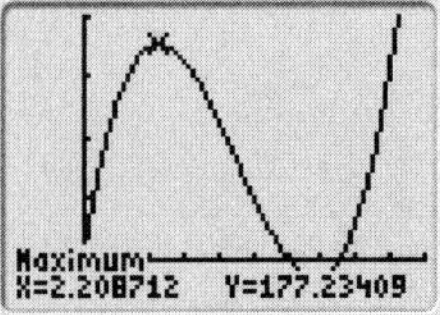

The graph has a local maximum of approximately 177.2 when $x \approx 2.21$. So, the maximum possible volume is approximately 177.2 ft³.

> **Math Reasoning**
>
> **Write** Explain why values of x greater than 6 or less than 0 do not make sense for this problem.
>
> These values would make the dimensions of the box negative.

Lesson Practice

a. (Ex 1) Identify the leading coefficient and degree, and describe the end behavior of $f(x) = x^4 + 6x - 8$.

a. The leading coefficient is 1. The degree is 4. As $x \to -\infty$, $f(x) \to +\infty$, and as $x \to +\infty$, $f(x) \to +\infty$.

b. (Ex 1) Identify the leading coefficient and degree, and describe the end behavior of $g(x) = -2x^5 + 3x^4 - x$.

b. The leading coefficient is −2. The degree is 5. As $x \to -\infty$, $g(x) \to +\infty$, and as $x \to +\infty$, $g(x) \to -\infty$.

c. (Ex 2) The function $f(x)$ is graphed. Determine whether $f(x)$ has an odd or even degree and a positive or negative leading coefficient. $f(x)$ is of odd degree with a negative leading coefficient.

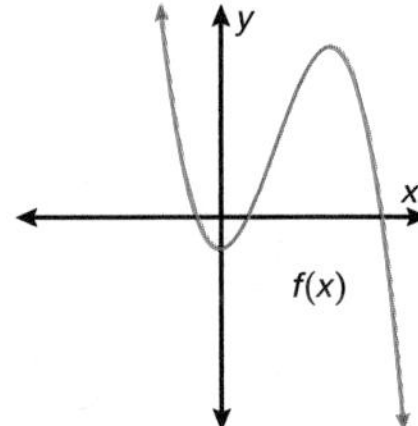

d. (Ex 2) The function $g(x)$ is graphed. Determine whether $g(x)$ has an odd or even degree and a positive or negative leading coefficient.

d. $g(x)$ is of odd degree with a negative leading coefficient.

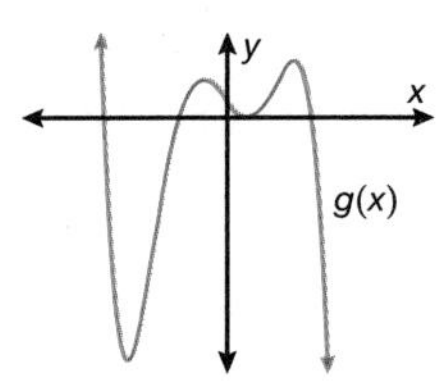

e. (Ex 3) Graph the function $f(x) = x^3 - 2x^2 - 5x + 6$. See Additional Answers.

f. (Ex 4) Graph $g(x) = x^4 - 4x^3 + 3x + 8$ on a calculator, and then determine the local maxima and local minima. See Additional Answers.

g. (Ex 5) An open box is to be made from an 8 ft by 10 ft rectangular sheet of metal by cutting squares from the corners and folding up the flaps. Find the maximum possible volume of the box. approximately 52.5 ft³

ENGLISH LEARNERS

For Example 5, explain the meaning of the word **flap**. Say,

"A flap is a thin, flat piece or part that is connected to an object. The flaps on a box are folded over the top to close the box."

Have students cut out square corners from a sheet of construction paper to show how the flaps can be folded to make an open box.

Ask, **"What is the effect of cutting larger square corners?"** The result of cutting larger squares is a deeper box.

Practice Distributed and Integrated

1. Determine whether the matrices are inverses.
(32)

$$A = \begin{bmatrix} 2 & 7 \\ -1 & -2 \end{bmatrix} \text{ and } L = \begin{bmatrix} -\frac{2}{3} & -\frac{7}{3} \\ \frac{1}{3} & \frac{2}{3} \end{bmatrix}$$ yes

*2. **Furniture Design** A table top is to consist of a rectangular region with a semicircle on each end. The perimeter is to be 200 inches. Find the maximum possible area of the rectangular region. approximately 1592 square inches
(101)

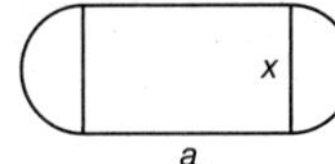

*3. **Graphing Calculator** Use a graphing calculator to determine how long it will take an investment of \$1000 to grow to \$1800 at 6% interest compounded monthly. approximately 9.82 years
(93)

4. **Error Analysis** Explain and correct the error a student made in solving $x^2 + 4x > 12$ algebraically. See Additional Answers.
(89)

$$x^2 + 4x - 12 > 0$$
$$(x - 2)(x + 6) > 0$$

critical values: 2, −6
solutions: $-6 < x < 2$

5. Find the roots of $f(x) = 0.1x^3 - 1.4x^2 + 6.0x - 7.2$ using the Rational Root Theorem. $x = 2$ and $x = 6$
(85)

*6. The product of two variables is a constant. Show that this describes a rational function. $xy = k$, where k is a constant. This means that $y = \frac{k}{x}$, which is a rational function.
(100)

Factor.

7. $6x^3 - 12x^2 - 18x + 6$ $6(x^3 - 2x^2 - 3x + 1)$
(23)

8. $x^2 - 64$ $(x + 8)(x - 8)$
(23)

*9. **Physics** Work is defined as the dot product of the force, $\vec{F}$, on an object and the displacement, $\vec{d}$. If $\theta = 45°$, $|\vec{F}| = 25$, and $|\vec{d}| = 10$, how much work is exerted on the wooden block? 176.78
(99)

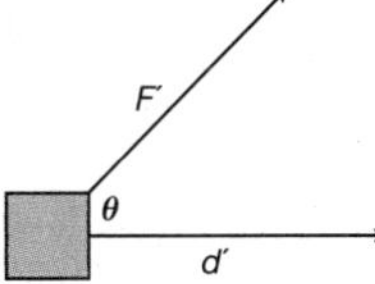

10. Solve for x, y, and z: $\begin{bmatrix} 1 & x^2 \\ y + 4 & \frac{y}{2} \end{bmatrix} = \begin{bmatrix} z + 2 & 25 \\ 16 & x + 1 \end{bmatrix}$. $x = 5, y = 12, z = -1$
(5)

ALTERNATE METHOD FOR PROBLEM 5

The zeros can be found by graphing the function and determining where on the graph the function crosses the x-axis.

From the graph, it can be seen that the zeros for this function are at $x = 2$ and $x = 6$.

3 Practice

Math Conversations

Discussions to strengthen understanding

Problem 10

Remind students that since the matrices are equal, they can create an equation that sets elements of the left matrix equal to corresponding elements of the right matrix. (Example: $1 = z + 2$) Once this is done, solve for the unknown variables.

Problem 11

Error Alert

Students may incorrectly solve the problem by substituting the value in the wrong function equation. Be sure the students know the bounds for each function so that they can solve the function within the given constraints.

Problem 14

Guide the students by asking them the following questions.

"What is the formula for deriving an equation for an arch?"
$y = a(x - h)^2 + k$

"What are the values of *h* and *k*?"
By setting one x-intercept to (0, 0), the values of h and k will denote the vertex, which is located halfway along the span of the arch, at the maximum height of the arch. Vertex = (32.5, 45)

11. (79) Evaluate the piecewise function $f(x) = \begin{cases} -12 \text{ if } x < 1 \\ 7x \text{ if } 1 \leq x \leq 4 \\ 2x - x^2 \text{ if } 4 < x \end{cases}$ for $x = -3$ and $x = 4$.
−12, 28

12. (33) Ice Cream A store has 31 flavors of ice cream. They also have a choice of chocolate or rainbow sprinkles and chocolate or caramel syrup. Assume a child picks one flavor ice cream, one type of sprinkle, and one type of syrup. How many different desserts could the child make? 124

***13.** (97) **Predict** Without using a formula, how can you find the 100th term of the geometric sequence, 3, −3, 3, −3, ...? The 100th term is −3 because the common ratio is −1, making every even-numbered term −3.

14. (83) National Parks The Black Arch, in Arches National Park, has a span of about 65 feet and a height of about 45 feet. Write a quadratic function to approximate the arch. $y \approx -0.04(x - 32.5)^2 + 45$

15. (80) A set of data is normally distributed with a mean of 34 and a standard deviation of 2.7. Find the percent of data that is less than 25.9. 0.15%

16. (77) **Geometry** A triangle has side lengths of 14 meters, 19 meters, and 21 meters. Use Heron's formula to find the area of the triangle. 129.8 m²

***17.** (96) **Multi-Step** Complete parts a–d to graph a polar equation and analyze the graph.

a. Graph the polar equation $r = \frac{\cos\theta}{\sin^2\theta}$ on a calculator, using these window settings: $\theta \min = 0$, $\theta \max = \pi$, $\theta \text{step} = \frac{\pi}{24}$, $X \min = -1$, $X \max = 11$, $Y \min = -4$, $Y \max = 4$. See Additional Answers.

b. What shape does the graph appear to be? Sample: Parabola

c. Convert the polar equation to a Cartesian equation. (Hint: Multiply both sides by $\sin^2\theta$, then multiply both sides by r, and then substitute x for $r\cos\theta$ and y for $r\sin\theta$.) $y^2 = x$

d. The equation obtained in part c is the inverse of what function? $y = x^2$

18. (9) Football The first table below shows the scoring plays made in three games by the Philadelphia Eagles. The second table shows the point value of each play. Use matrix multiplication to find out in which game the team scored the most points.

$\begin{bmatrix} 3 & 2 & 3 \\ 2 & 3 & 2 \\ 3 & 1 & 3 \end{bmatrix}\begin{bmatrix} 6 \\ 3 \\ 1 \end{bmatrix} = \begin{bmatrix} 27 \\ 23 \\ 24 \end{bmatrix}$; The most points were scored in game #9.

Plays Made

Game	Touchdown	Field Goal	Extra Point
#9	3	2	3
#15	2	3	2
#16	3	1	3

Point Value

Touchdown	6
Field Goal	3
Extra Point	1

19. (72) Expand the expression $\log 3x^4$. $\log 3 + 4 \log x$

ALTERNATE METHOD FOR PROBLEM 18

Instead of matrix multiplication, this problem can be solved by setting up a system of equations to solve for the total points of each game.

$a(6) + b(3) + c(1) = total$

Game #9

$3(6) + 2(3) + 3(1) = 27$

Game #15

$2(6) + 3(3) + 2(1) = 23$

Game #16

$3(6) + 1(3) + 3(1) = 24$

Clearly, Game #9 has the highest point total.

20. Multiple Choice Based on the data set below, what is the relationship between x and y? C
(12)

x	1	2	3	4
y	4	2	$1\frac{1}{3}$	1

A Joint Variation
B Direct Variation
C Inverse Variation
D None of the above

21. Multiple Choice Which of the following points is not on the ellipse $\frac{x^2}{4^2} + \frac{y^2}{7^2} = 1$? A
(98)

A $(-7, 0)$ B $(4, 0)$ C $(0, -7)$ D $(-4, 0)$

22. Error Analysis Two students are finding the period of $y = 5\sin\left(\frac{1}{\sqrt{2}+1}x\right)$ but get different results. Which student made the mistake? Student A incorrectly divides $\sqrt{2} + 1$.
(82)

Student A	Student B
The period is $\frac{2\pi}{b}$. Period $= \frac{2\pi}{\sqrt{2}+1}$	The period is $\frac{2\pi}{b}$. Period $= 2\pi(\sqrt{2}+1)$

23. Analyze How can a rational equation with all linear polynomials form a quadratic equation after the fractions are cleared? Give a simple example. See Additional Answers.
(84)

24. Write Explain the steps used to apply the change of base formula. See Additional Answers.
(87)

25. Generalize Find the period and phase shift of $y = a\tan(bx + c)$. Period: $\frac{\pi}{b}$; phase shift: $-\frac{c}{b}$
(90)

***26.** Let $f(x) = x - 1$ and $g(x) = x^2 - 1$. Find the vertical asymptotes and holes for $\frac{f(x)}{f(g(x))}$. Vertical asymptotes at $x = \pm\sqrt{2}$
(100)

Use $P(x) = x^3 - 10x^2 + 19x + 30$.

***27.** Determine if $x - 6$ is a factor of $P(x)$. yes
(95)

***28.** Factor $P(x)$. $(x - 6)(x - 5)(x + 1)$
(95)

29. Determine if (1, 1) is a solution of the inequality $y < -5x + 3$. no
(39)

***30. Analyze** Which function has end behavior that is different from the end behavior of the others? Explain. See Additional Answers.
(101)

$f(x) = 4x^3 - x^2 - 2x$ $g(x) = x^7 - 1$ $h(x) = -3x^3 - 3x^4 + x^5$ $k(x) = -5x^3 + x^2 + x$

Problem 21

Have students substitute the ordered pair into the ellipse equation. The points will not be on the ellipse if the equation does not equal 1.

Problem 26

Remind students that vertical asymptotes can be found when the denominator of $f(g(x))$ is equal to zero. Set the denominator equal to zero and solve for x.

Problem 30

Guide the students by asking them the following questions.

"What aspects of the polynomial are used to determine end behavior?"
Leading coefficient and degree

"Which term do you look at to determine the leading coefficient?"
Look at the coefficient of the term with the highest exponent.

CHALLENGE

Graph:
$f(x) = -7x^6 + 5x^4 - 2x^3 + 4x^2 - 3x + 8$

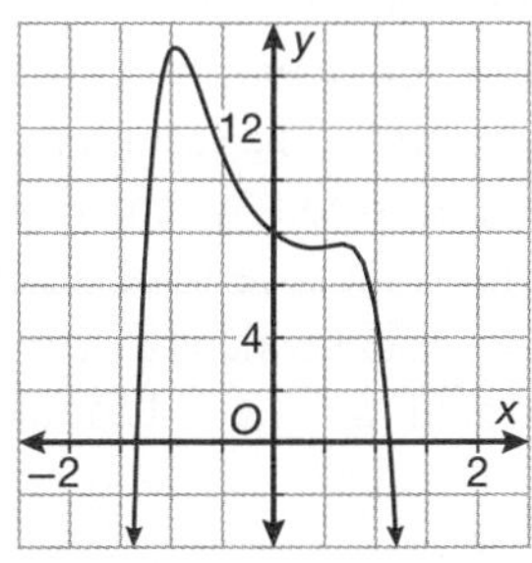

LOOKING FORWARD

Making graphs of polynomial functions prepares students for

- **Lesson 104** Finding Transformations

LESSON 102

1 Warm Up

Use the Warm Up to review properties of logarithms.

2 New Concepts

In this lesson, students apply properties of logarithms to solve logarithmic equations and inequalities.

Example 1

Students use properties of logarithms and exponents to solve logarithmic equations. Review and practice these properties as needed.

Additional Example 1

a. Solve $\log_7(x-4)=2$. $x=53$

b. Solve $\log_8 x^3=4$. $x=16$

TEACHER TIP

Logarithms can sometimes seem like a mystery: students may have difficulty understanding their purpose or their meaning. Use the solutions to example 1 to remind students that logarithms are another way of expressing exponents.

LESSON 102 Solving Logarithmic Equations and Inequalities

Warm Up

1. **Vocabulary** In the expression ln t, the ___base___ is e. (81)
2. What is the value of $\log_3 9$? 2 (87)
3. True or False: $\log m+\log(m+4)=\log[m(m+4)]$ true (72)
4. True or False: $\log a-\log(a-6)=\log[a-(a-6)]$ false (72)
5. Write $\log_x x=1$ in exponential form. $x^1=x$ (72)

New Concepts

A **logarithmic equation** is an equation with a logarithmic expression that contains a variable. A **logarithmic inequality** is an inequality with a logarithmic expression that contains a variable. You can use the following properties of logarithms to solve logarithmic equations and inequalities.

If $\log_b x=\log_b y$, then $x=y$.	Definition of logarithm
$b^{\log_b x}=x$ and $\log_b b^x=x$.	Inverse Properties of Logarithms and Exponents
$\log_b mn=\log_b m+\log_b n$	Product Property of Logarithms
$\log_b \frac{m}{n}=\log_b m-\log_b n$	Quotient Property of Logarithms
$\log_b a^p=p\log_b a$	Power Property of Logarithms

Hint

In the properties, the values of b, m, n, and a must be positive, and $b\neq 1$.

Example 1 Solving Logarithmic Equations

a. Solve $\log_5(x+2)=3$.

SOLUTION

$\log_5(x+2)=3$	
$5^{\log_5(x+2)}=5^3$	Use 5 as the base for both sides.
$x+2=125$	Use an inverse property of logarithms and exponents.
$x=123$	Subtract 2 from both sides.

Hint

Using the definition of logarithm, Example 1a can also be solved by expressing the logarithm in exponential form:

$5^3=x+2$

b. Solve $\log_8 x^3=2$.

SOLUTION

$\log_8 x^3=2$	
$3\log_8 x=2$	Power Property of Logarithms
$\log_8 x=\frac{2}{3}$	Divide both sides by 3 to isolate $\log_8 x$.
$x=8^{\frac{2}{3}}$	Definition of a logarithm
$x=(2^3)^{\frac{2}{3}}$	Write 8 as 2^3.
$x=2^2$, or 4	Power of a Power Property

Online Connection www.SaxonMathResources.com

LESSON RESOURCES

Student Edition Practice Workbook 102
Reteaching Master 102
Adaptations Master 102
Challenge and Enrichment Masters C102, E102

MATH BACKGROUND

There are two methods for solving logarithmic equations. In the first method, apply the rules of logarithms until the equation has the general form $\log_b n=\log_b m$. Use $n=m$ to find the solution. In the second method, apply the rules of logarithms until the equation has the general form $\log_b x=y$. Use the exponential equation $b^y=x$ to find the solution.

You can only take a logarithm of a positive number, and the base cannot equal 1. Graphing a logarithm shows the reason for the first requirement, because the graph is always positive. The second requirement can be understood by remembering that a logarithm is the inverse of an exponential: $\log_b x=y$ is equivalent to $x=b^y$. The value $b=1$ would mean $x=1$ for all y-values.

c. Solve $\log x + \log(x - 1) = \log 6$.

SOLUTION

$\log x + \log(x - 1) = \log 6$	
$\log[x(x - 1)] = \log 6$	Product Property of Logarithms
$x(x - 1) = 6$	If $\log_b x = \log_b y$, then $x = y$.
$x^2 - x - 6 = 0$	Multiply, and then subtract 6 from both sides.
$x = 3$ or $x = -2$	Solve the equation.

> **Caution**
>
> Check calculated solutions to verify that they are solutions of the original equation.

Check Check both solutions in the original equation.

$\log x + \log(x - 1) = \log 6$

$\log 3 + \log(3 - 1) \stackrel{?}{=} \log 6$

$\log 3 + \log 2 \stackrel{?}{=} \log 6$

$\log(3 \cdot 2) \stackrel{?}{=} \log 6$

$\log 6 = \log 6$ ✓

$\log x + \log(x - 1) = \log 6$

$\log(-2) + \log(-2 - 1) \stackrel{?}{=} \log 6$ ✗

$\log(-2)$ is undefined.

The only solution is $x = 3$.

To solve a logarithmic inequality, the following logarithmic property will be used.

If $\log_b x < \log_b y$, then $b^{\log_b x} < b^{\log_b y}$ and $x < y$.

Example 2 Solving a Logarithmic Inequality

Solve $\log 12x - \log 4 < \log 25$.

SOLUTION

$\log 12x - \log 4 < \log 25$	
$\log\left(\frac{12x}{4}\right) < \log 25$	Quotient Property of Logarithms
$\log 3x < \log 25$	Simplify.
$3x < 25$	If $\log_b x < \log_b y$, then $x < y$.
$x < \frac{25}{3}$	Divide both sides by 3.

Example 3 Using a Graph and Table to Solve

Use a graph and table on a graphing calculator to solve $\log x - \log 5 = \log 17$.

SOLUTION Enter $\log x - \log 5$ as **Y1** and $\log 17$ as **Y2.**

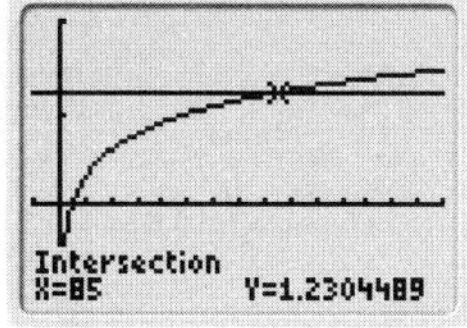

Find the x-value of the point of intersection of the graphs.

X	Y1	Y2
70	1.1461	1.2304
75	1.1761	1.2304
80	1.2041	1.2304
85	1.2304	1.2304
90	1.2553	1.2304
95	1.2788	1.2304
100	1.301	1.2304

X=85

Find the x-value for which Y1 = Y2.

The solution is $x = 85$.

Additional Example 1

c. Solve $\log x + \log(x + 2) = \log 8$. $x = 2$

Error Alert A common mistake when solving logarithmic equations is to add logarithms instead of multiplying, and to subtract logarithms instead of dividing.

Example 2

Students apply properties of logarithms to solve a logarithmic inequality.

Additional Example 2

Solve $\log 18x - \log 9 < \log 7$. $x < \frac{7}{2}$

Example 3

Students solve a logarithmic equation using a graphing calculator.

Extend the Example

Have students verify the graphical solution to the equation by solving the equation algebraically.

Additional Example 3

Use a graph and table on a graphing calculator to solve $\log x - \log 9 = \log 12$. $x = 108$

ALTERNATE METHOD FOR EXAMPLE 3

Some students may be able to easily solve certain logarithmic equations mentally by applying the properties of logarithms. In the equation in example 3, students may notice that $\frac{x}{5} = 17$, so $x = 85$.

INCLUSION

Students who have difficulty with abstract procedures may benefit from having an index card with the logarithmic properties written on it. As students work through a problem, have them refer to the card and identify the property that applies to each step of the problem.

Example 4

Students use a logarithmic equation to model population growth.

Additional Example 4

Based on U.S. Census statistics, the population of Indiana for the years 1950–1990 can be modeled by the equation $y = 1530 + 1055 \ln t$, where $10 \leq t \leq 50$, $t = 10$ represents 1950, and y is the population in thousands. Use the model to approximate the year in which the population of Indiana reached 5,000,000. 1967

Lesson Practice

Problem b

Error Alert Students may think that they have to find 125^4 to solve the problem. Remind them to look for shortcuts to avoid cumbersome calculations, that is $125^4 = (5^3)^4 = (5^4)^3$.

Problem f

Scaffolding Remind students that the answer is not t, but the starting year (1950) added to $t-10$.

Check for Understanding

The questions below help assess the concepts taught in this lesson.

"What is the goal when solving logarithmic equations?" Apply the definition and properties of logarithms until you can eliminate logarithms and solve for the variable.

"How is solving a logarithmic equation related to solving an exponential equation?" After you apply properties of logarithms, you may have formed an equation that can be transformed to and solved as an exponential equation.

Example 4 Application: Population Growth

Based on U.S. Census statistics, the population of Connecticut for the years 1950–1990 can be modeled by the equation

$$y = 147 + 812 \ln t,$$

where $10 \leq t \leq 50$, $t = 10$ represents 1950, and y is the population in thousands. Use the model to approximate the year in which the population of Connecticut reached 3,000,000.

SOLUTION

$147 + 812 \ln t = y$	Write the model.
$147 + 812 \ln t = 3000$	Since y is in thousands, substitute 3000 for y.
$812 \ln t = 2853$	Subtract 147 from both sides.
$\ln t = \frac{2853}{812}$	Divide both sides by 812.
$\ln t \approx 3.513$	Use a calculator to approximate.
$e^{\ln t} \approx e^{3.513}$	Use e as the base on both sides.
$t \approx e^{3.513}$	Use an inverse property of logarithms and exponents.
$t \approx 34$	Use a calculator to approximate.

Since $t = 10$ represents 1950, then $t \approx 34$ represents $1950 + 24 = 1974$.

Using the model, the population of Connecticut reached 3,000,000 in approximately 1974.

Math Reasoning

Write Note that $e^{3.513} \approx 33.5$. Explain why 1973 is another reasonable answer for Example 4.

Sample: When $t = 33.5$, the population is 3,000,000, which means this occurred during the middle of year 1973.

Lesson Practice

a. (Ex 1) Solve $\log_3(x - 1) = 2$. $x = 10$

b. (Ex 1) Solve $\log_{125} x^3 = 4$. $x = 625$

c. (Ex 1) Solve $\log x + \log(x + 9) = 1$. $x = 1$

d. (Ex 2) Solve $\log 45x - \log 3 \geq 1$. $x \geq \frac{2}{3}$

e. (Ex 3) Use a graph and table on a graphing calculator to solve $\log x - \log 2 = \log 75$. See Additional Answers.

f. (Ex 4) Based on U.S. Census statistics, the population of Ohio for the years 1950–1990 can be modeled by the equation $y = 3875 + 1876 \ln t$, where $10 \leq t \leq 50$, $t = 10$ represents 1950, and y is the population in thousands. Use the model to approximate the year in which the population of Ohio reached 10,000,000. 1966

Practice Distributed and Integrated

1. (80) A set of scores have a mean of 74 and a standard deviation of 5. Find the percent of scores between 69 and 84. 81.5%

Find the roots of each equation.

2. (85) $y = 4x^2 + 5x - 1$ $x \approx 0.1754$ and -1.4254

3. (85) Find the roots of $y = x^4 - 16$. $x = 2$ and -2

ENGLISH LEARNERS

Draw students' attention to the different forms of the word logarithm found in this lesson. Have students say the words logarithm, logarithmic, log, and ln (natural logarithm).

Discuss the meaning of each term and how it is used. Point out that logarithm is a noun; logarithmic is an adjective, which tells about a noun; and log and ln are shortened versions of the terms. Make sure students understand the difference between log and ln.

Provide students with sentences where either logarithm or logarithmic should be used. Ask them to decide which term is appropriate.

Have students identify each term when it is used in the lesson. Ask them why each is used in the particular case.

716 Saxon Algebra 2

***4.** (102) **Union Membership** Beginning in the 1930s, labor union membership in the U.S. grew dramatically. During the years 1935–1955, labor union membership in the U.S. can be modeled by the equation $y = -4.4 + 12.6\ln t$, where $5 \le t \le 25$, $t = 5$ represents 1935, and y is the percent of the U.S. labor force that were union members. Use the model to approximate the year in which union membership in the U.S. reached 30%. 1945

***5.** (101) **Analyze** A cubic polynomial function $f(x)$ has exactly three real zeros; they are 1, 3, and 4. It has a relative maximum at an x-value between 3 and 4. Describe the end behavior of $f(x)$. As $x \to -\infty$, $f(x) \to +\infty$, and as $x \to +\infty$, $f(x) \to -\infty$.

6. (84) **National Highways** In Rhode Island, the speed limit outside a business or residential district is twice the speed limit inside a business or residential district. A driver drove 12.5 miles inside business and residential districts and 75 miles outside of business and residential districts for a total driving time of 2 hours. Suppose the driver kept a constant speed at the posted speed limits. Write and solve a rational equation to find the speed limit inside a business or residential district. $\frac{12.5}{r} + \frac{75}{2r} = 2$, 25 mph

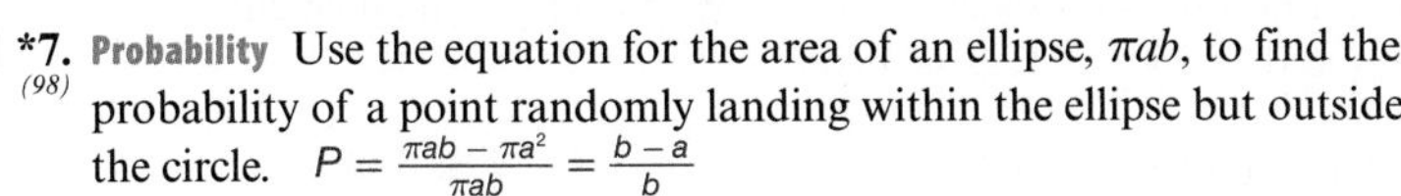

***7.** (98) **Probability** Use the equation for the area of an ellipse, πab, to find the probability of a point randomly landing within the ellipse but outside the circle. $P = \frac{\pi ab - \pi a^2}{\pi ab} = \frac{b-a}{b}$

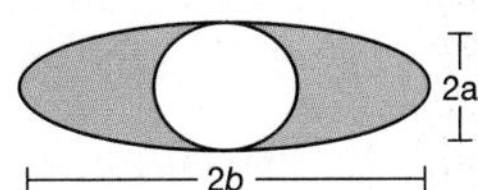

8. (96) **Construction** The diagram represents a plan for a deck in the shape of an isosceles trapezoid. Write polar coordinates for points A, B, C, and D. Use point A as the pole and $\overrightarrow{AD}$ as the polar axis. Sample: $A(0,0)$, $B(\sqrt{160}, \tan^{-1} 3)$ $\approx (12.65, 1.25)$, $C(\sqrt{340}, \tan^{-1}\frac{12}{14})$ $\approx (18.44, 0.71)$, $D(18, 0)$

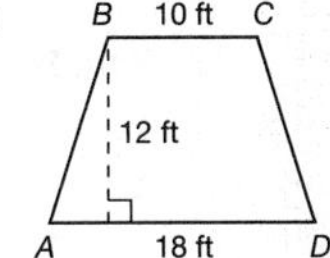

***9.** (99) **Generalize** For two nonzero vectors $\vec{A}$ and $\vec{B}$, what must be true for $\vec{A} + \vec{B} = 0$? The vectors must have the same magnitude and opposite orientations.

10. (32) Find the inverse of the matrix $T = \begin{bmatrix} -6 & -2 \\ 11 & -3 \end{bmatrix}$, if it exists. $\begin{bmatrix} -\frac{3}{40} & \frac{1}{20} \\ -\frac{11}{40} & -\frac{3}{20} \end{bmatrix}$

***11.** (100) **Geometry** Write the rational function that shows the ratio of the surface area to the volume for a right circular cylinder. Identify any asymptotes. $f(r, h) = \frac{2h + 2r}{hr}$; asymptotes at $h = 0$ and $r = 0$

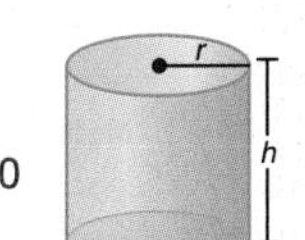

12. (77) **Geography** On a map of southwest Illinois, line segments connect Jerseyville, Carlinville, and Litchfield. The angle formed at Jerseyville measures 18°. The distance from Jerseyville to Carlinville is 28 miles and the distance from Jerseyville to Litchfield is 37 miles. To the nearest tenth of a mile, what is the distance from Carlinville to Litchfield? 13.5 miles

13. (88) **Analyze** The formula for the surface area of a sphere is $S = 4\pi r^2$. The formula for the volume of a sphere is $V = \frac{4}{3}\pi r^3$. Solve each equation for r. Explain why the first equation has a solution that cannot represent a possible value for the radius. Then tell why this is not true of the second equation. See Additional Answers.

14. (93) **Write** Explain why the equations $4^x = 100$ and $x \log 4 = 2$ are equivalent. See Additional Answers.

15. (73) **Town Government** A town council wants to know if residents support having an off-leash area for dogs in the town park. Eighty dog owners are surveyed at the park. Describe the individuals in the population and in the sample.

15. The population is all residents in the town; the sample is the 80 dog owners surveyed.

3 Practice

Math Conversations

Discussions to strengthen understanding

Problem 4

Error Alert

Remind students not to change 30% to a decimal, since y is the percent of the U.S. labor force that were union members.

Problem 6

Error Alert

Students may think that they need to multiply the distances by the speed rather than divide by the speed.

Guide them by asking the following questions.

"What is the relationship between speed, time, and distance?" Distance equals speed times time.

"What is the general form of the equation, in words?" The time for the trip inside the business districts plus the time for the trip outside the business district equals the total time.

Problem 11

Error Alert

Students might say there is a hole at h. Have them write the numerator as $2(h + r)$ to show why the h's cannot be divided out.

Problem 18

Error Alert

Students will get an error message using the method in part b if their window does not extend to at least 14 units on the right.

Problem 27

Error Alert

Students may not add the two missing zero coefficients. Remind students to make sure to fill in missing terms with zero-coefficient terms.

*16. (102) **Multiple Choice** What is the solution to $\log 5x + \log 2 = 4$? A

A $x = 1000$ B $x = 1428.6$ C $x = 1999.6$ D $x = 9990$

*17. (102) Solve $\log_4(4x + 7) = \log_4 11x$. 1

*18. (97) **Graphing Calculator** The first term of a geometric sequence is 9 and the common ratio is $\frac{2}{3}$.

a. Explain how to use the Table function to find the value of the 14th term. See Additional Answers.

b. Explain how to use the Graph function to find the value of the 14th term. See Additional Answers.

c. Rounded to the nearest ten-thousandth, what is the value of the 14th term? $y \approx 0.0462$

19. (82) Given $g(x) = 3 \sin \frac{1}{2}(x)$, identify the amplitude and period. Amplitude = 3, Period = 4π

20. (85) **Physics** A spaceship is coming in for a landing on Mars. The equation $h = -1.885t^2 + v_ot + h_o$ can be used to find the distance h from the ground at time t based on an initial height h_o and an initial speed of v_o. To the nearest hundredth of a second, how long it will take the ship to land from an initial height of 2000 and an initial speed of 200? 115.3 seconds

*21. (101) **Error Analysis** A student identified the degree of $P(x) = 2x^3 + 3x^2 - x^4$ as 3. What is the error? The student chose the degree of the first term, not the term with the greatest degree. The degree is 4.

22. (91) **Multi-Step** The map of a town is placed on a coordinate grid. The center of a small earthquake is located at $(-1, -3)$ and can be felt up to 12 miles away.

a. Write the equation of the circle that represents the border of the affected area. $(x + 1)^2 + (y + 3)^2 = 144$

b. **Justify** Show how to use the equation in part a to prove that people in a building located at $(11, -2)$ did not feel the earthquake. Sample: change the equation to the inequality $(x + 1)^2 + (y + 3)^2 \leq 144$ and substitute $(11, -2)$ for x and y: $(11 + 1)^2 + (-2 + 3)^2 \overset{?}{\leq} 144$; $144 + 1 \overset{?}{\leq} 144$; $145 \leq 144$ False; Since the inequality is false, the building was not in the affected area.

23. (9) **Multi-Step** Use $A = \begin{bmatrix} 10 & 1 \\ 4 & 10 \end{bmatrix}$ and $B = \begin{bmatrix} 11 & 4 \\ 16 & 11 \end{bmatrix}$.

a. Find AB. $\begin{bmatrix} 126 & 51 \\ 204 & 126 \end{bmatrix}$ b. Find BA. $\begin{bmatrix} 126 & 51 \\ 204 & 126 \end{bmatrix}$ c. Is AB = BA? c. Yes; $\begin{bmatrix} 126 & 51 \\ 204 & 126 \end{bmatrix} = \begin{bmatrix} 126 & 51 \\ 204 & 126 \end{bmatrix}$

24. (83) Write a quadratic equation whose roots are $6 \pm 2i$. $x^2 - 12x + 40 = 0$

*25. (100) Factor the terms of the rational function $y = \frac{x^2 + 3x - 4}{x - 2}$ to identify vertical asymptotes. Asymptote at $x = 2$

*26. (98) Write an equation in standard form for the ellipse with center $(0, 0)$, $a = 4$ and $b = 6$. $\frac{x^2}{16} + \frac{y^2}{36} = 1$ or $\frac{x^2}{36} + \frac{y^2}{16} = 1$

Divide using synthetic division.

27. (51) $x^3 - 6$ by $x - 2$ $x^2 + 2x + 4 + \frac{2}{x - 2}$

28. (51) $x^3 + 3x^2 + 7x + 5$ by $x + 1$ $x^2 + 2x + 5$

29. (41) Find the distance between $(-2, 5)$ and $(3, 4)$. $\sqrt{26}$

30. (5) Solve $4\begin{bmatrix} 2 & 1 \\ -6 & 3.5 \end{bmatrix} - 3\begin{bmatrix} 0 & 0.4 \\ 8 & -2 \end{bmatrix}$. $\begin{bmatrix} 8 & 2.8 \\ -48 & 20 \end{bmatrix}$

CHALLENGE

Use properties of logarithms to solve the equations.

a. $(\log x)^2 + \log x^2 - 15 = 0$ $x = 0.00001$ and $x = 1000$

b. $(\log x)^2 + \log x^5 - 14 = 0$ $x = 0.0000001$ and $x = 100$

LOOKING FORWARD

Solving logarithmic equations and inequalities prepares students for

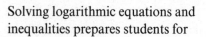

- **Lesson 110** Graphing Logarithmic Functions

Graphing Reciprocal Trigonometric Functions

Warm Up

1. Vocabulary The function $y = \cot(x)$ is an example of a reciprocal trigonometric function. (46)

2. What is the period of the function of $y = 3\tan(x)$? π (90)

3. What are the asymptotes of the function $y = \tan(2x) + 2$? $x = \frac{\pi}{4} + \frac{\pi}{2}n$ (90)

4. Graph the function $y = 3\cos(x)$. See Additional Answers. (86)

New Concepts

The cosecant function is the reciprocal of the sine function. Since $\csc(x) = \frac{1}{\sin(x)}$, cosecant is undefined when $\sin(x) = 0$. The graph of cosecant has vertical asymptotes at the locations where it is undefined. Cosecant has the same period as sine. Cosecant has no absolute maxima or minima, so it has no amplitude. The graph of $y = a \cdot \csc(bx)$, where $a \neq 0$, has a period of $\frac{2\pi}{|b|}$ and asymptotes located at $x = \frac{\pi n}{|b|}$.

Hint

$\sin(x) = 0$ when $x = \pi n$, where n is an integer.

Example 1 Graphing the Cosecant Function

a. Graph $y = \csc(x)$. Determine its period and asymptotes.

SOLUTION Graph $y = \sin x$. Vertical asymptotes of $y = \csc(x)$ occur where $\sin(x) = 0$ which are the x-intercepts. Find the reciprocals of the y-values on the sine curve to sketch $y = \csc(x)$.

x	$\sin(x)$	$\csc(x)$
0	0	undefined
$\frac{\pi}{4}$	0.707	1.414
$\frac{\pi}{2}$	1	1

$y = \csc(x)$ has a period of 2π. The asymptotes occur at $x = \pi n$, where n is an integer.

b. Graph $y = \csc(2x)$. Determine its period and asymptotes.

SOLUTION $y = \csc(2x)$ has a period of $\frac{2\pi}{|2|} = \pi$. The asymptotes occur at $x = \frac{\pi}{|2|}n = \frac{\pi}{2}n$, where n is an integer.

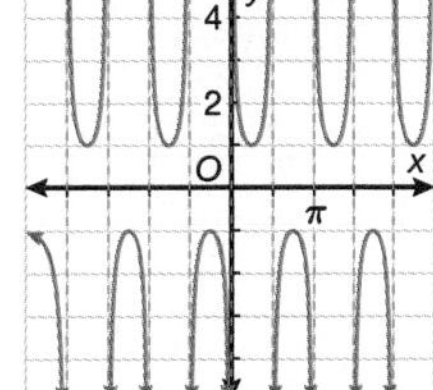

Online Connection
www.SaxonMathResources.com

MATH BACKGROUND

When given a choice, most people would prefer to multiply rather than divide when solving mathematical equations by hand. Before calculators and computers, this was especially true for engineers, physicists, and others who used advanced mathematics in their daily life. Reciprocal trigonometric functions were used in the past to avoid division. For example, rather than divide by the cosine to several significant digits, an engineer would prefer to multiply by the secant.

Thus the secant, cosecant and cotangent were commonly used. Although now the use of computers has made division as easily achievable as multiplication, the reciprocal trigonometric functions are still used in formulas for engineering, mathematics, and physics.

LESSON 103

1 Warm Up

Remind students that a reciprocal is a multiplicative inverse.

2 New Concepts

Students graph the cosecant, secant, and cotangent functions.

Example 1

Students graph and describe the cosecant function.

Additional Example 1

a. Graph $y = \csc(3x)$. Determine its period and asymptote. period $\frac{2\pi}{3}$, asymptotes at $x = \frac{\pi}{3}n$, where n is an integer

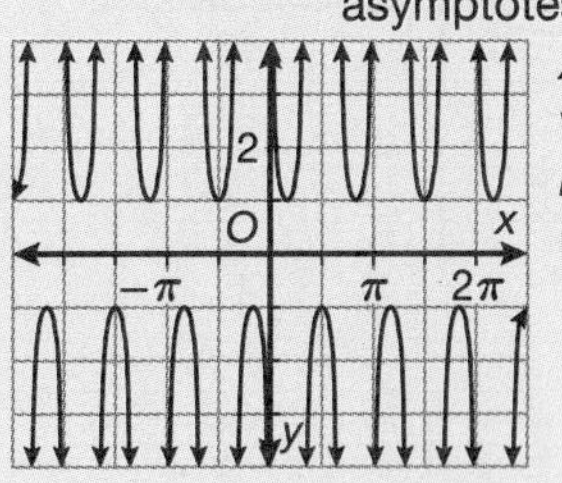

b. Graph $y = 2\csc(x)$. Determine its period and asymptote. period 2π, asymptotes at $x = \pi n$, where n is an integer

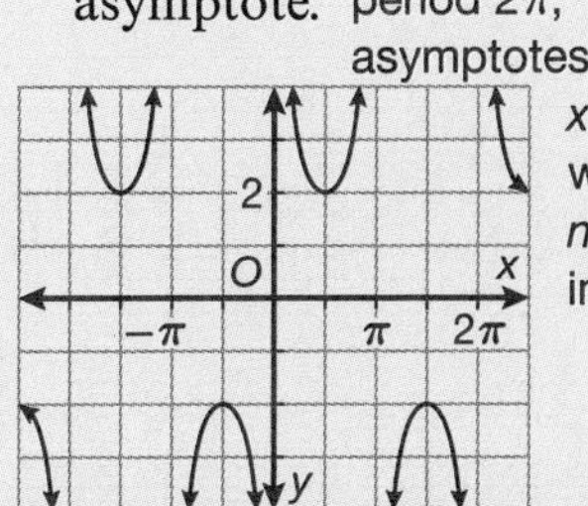

LESSON RESOURCES

Student Edition Practice Workbook 103
Reteaching Master 103
Adaptations Master 103
Challenge and Enrichment Masters C103

Example 2

Students graph the secant function.

Additional Example 2

a. Graph $y = \sec(2x)$. Determine its period and asymptotes. period is π, asymptotes at $x = \frac{\pi}{4} + \frac{\pi}{2}n$, where n is an integer

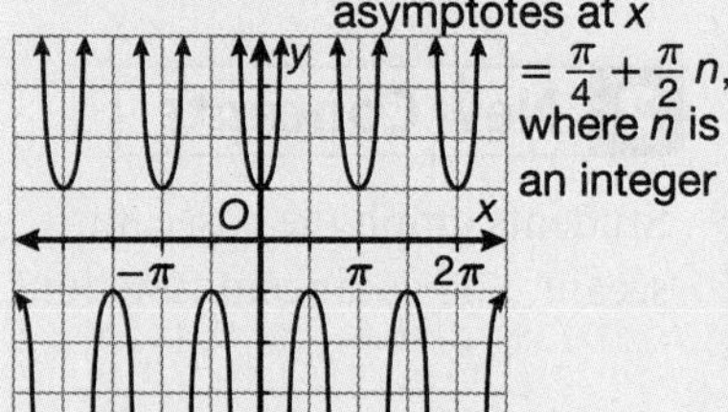

b. Graph $y = 2\sec\left(\frac{x}{2}\right)$. Determine its period and asymptotes. period is 4π, asymptotes at $x = \pi + 2\pi n$, where n is an integer

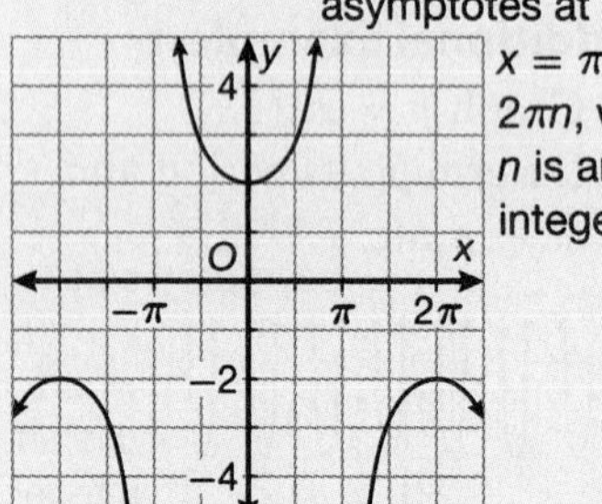

Hint

$\cos(x) = 0$ when $x = \frac{\pi}{2} + \pi n$, where n is an integer.

The secant function is the reciprocal of the cosine function. Since $\sec(x) = \frac{1}{\cos(x)}$, secant is undefined when $\cos(x) = 0$. The graph of secant has vertical asymptotes at the locations where it is undefined. Secant has the same period as cosine. Secant has no absolute maxima or minima, so it has no amplitude. The graph of $y = a \cdot \sec(bx)$, where $a \neq 0$, has a period of $\frac{2\pi}{|b|}$ and asymptotes located at $x = \frac{\pi}{2|b|} + \frac{\pi}{|b|}n$.

Example 2 Graphing the Secant Function

a. Graph $y = \sec(x)$. Determine its period and asymptotes.

SOLUTION Graph $y = \cos x$. Vertical asymptotes of $y = \sec(x)$ occur where $\cos(x) = 0$ which are the x-intercepts. Find the reciprocals of the y-values on the cosine curve to sketch $y = \sec(x)$.

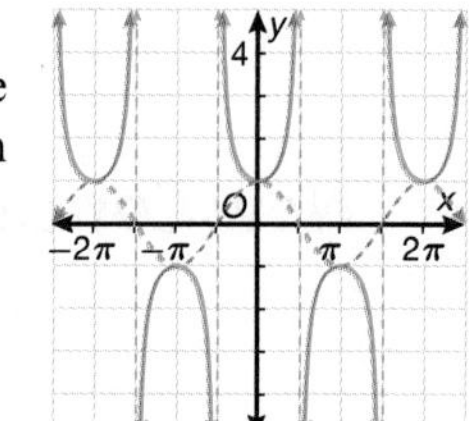

x	$\cos(x)$	$\sec(x)$
0	1	1
$\frac{\pi}{4}$	0.707	1.414
$\frac{\pi}{2}$	0	undefined
$\frac{3\pi}{4}$	−0.707	−1.414
π	1	1

$y = \sec(x)$ has a period of 2π. The asymptotes occur at $x = \frac{\pi}{2} + \pi n$, where n is an integer.

b. Graph $y = \sec\left(\frac{x}{2}\right)$. Determine its period and asymptotes.

SOLUTION $y = \sec\left(\frac{x}{2}\right)$ has a period of $\frac{2\pi}{\left|\frac{1}{2}\right|} = 4\pi$.

The asymptotes occur at $x = \frac{\pi}{2\left|\frac{1}{2}\right|} + \frac{\pi}{\left|\frac{1}{2}\right|}n =$ $\pi + 2\pi n$, where n is an integer.

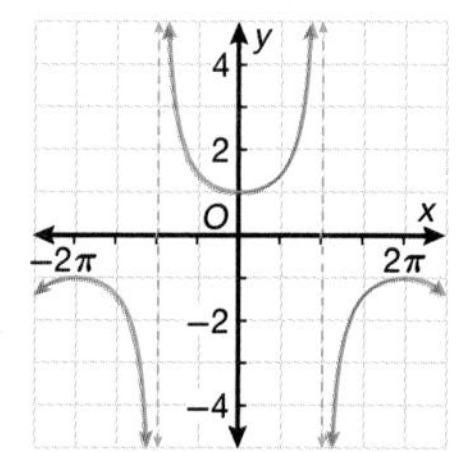

Hint

$\tan(x) = 0$ when $x = \pi n$, where n is an integer.

The cotangent function is the reciprocal of the tangent function. Since $\cot(x) = \frac{1}{\tan(x)}$, cotangent is undefined when $\tan(x) = 0$. The graph of cotangent has vertical asymptotes at the locations where it is undefined. Cotangent has the same period as tangent. Cotangent has no absolute maxima or minima, so it has no amplitude. The graph of $y = a \cdot \cot(bx)$, where $a \neq 0$, has a period of $\frac{\pi}{|b|}$ and asymptotes located at $x = \frac{\pi n}{|b|}$.

ENGLISH LEARNERS

Explain the meaning of the word **reciprocal.** Say:

"To reciprocate means to go back and forth. In mathematics, reciprocal means the multiplicative inverse."

Show students a fraction and its reciprocal. Show additional examples if needed. Say:

"$\frac{2}{3}$ is the reciprocal of $\frac{3}{2}$."

Next explain the reciprocal of the trigonometric functions. Explain that special names have been given to these reciprocals. Say:

"$\frac{1}{\sin x}$ is the reciprocal of $\sin x$. This reciprocal is called cosecant. So $\csc x = \frac{1}{\sin x}$."

Continue with the explanation for secant and cotangent.

Example 3 Graphing the Cotangent Function

Graph $y = \cot(x)$. Determine its period and asymptotes.

SOLUTION Graph $y = \tan x$. Vertical asymptotes for $y = \cot x$ occur where $\tan(x) = 0$ which are the x-intercepts. $y = \cot x$ has x-intercepts where $y = \tan x$ has vertical asymptotes.

$y = \cot(x)$ has a period of π. The asymptotes occur at $x = \pi n$, where n is an integer.

$y = \tan x$

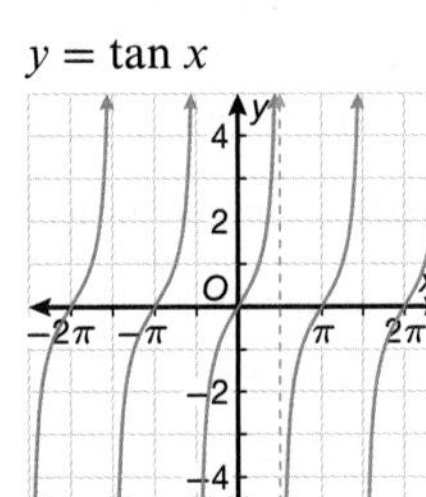

$y = \cot(x)$

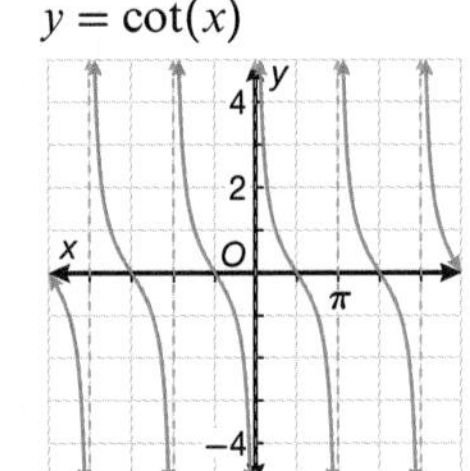

Math Reasoning

Analyze Explain why $y = \tan x$ has asymptotes where $\cos x = 0$.

Sample: Since $\tan x = \frac{\sin x}{\cos x}$, $\tan x$ is undefined where the denominator equals 0.

Example 4 Using a Graphing Calculator to Graph a Reciprocal Trigonometric Function

Use a graphing calculator to graph $y = \sec(x)$.

SOLUTION

There are no specific keys or menu items on the graphing calculator for the secant, cosecant, or cotangent functions. In order to graph them on the graphing calculator, use:

$$\csc(x) = \frac{1}{\sin(x)} \qquad \sec(x) = \frac{1}{\cos(x)} \qquad \cot(x) = \frac{1}{\tan(x)}$$

Caution

$\frac{1}{\cos(x)} \neq \cos^{-1}(x)$

Step 1: On the calculator, press the **MODE** button and set the **RADIAN** mode.

Step 2: Enter the equation $Y = \frac{1}{\cos}(X)$.

Step 3: Press the **ZOOM** button and select 7 ↓**ZTrig**

The graph of $y = \sec(x)$ is displayed.

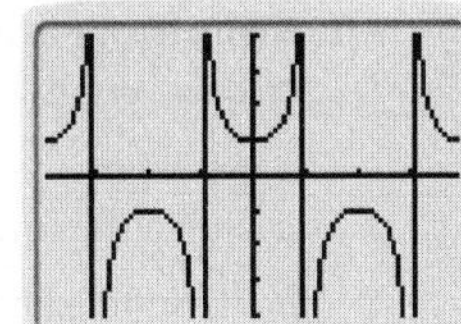

Example 3

Students graph the cotangent function.

Additional Example 3

Graph $y = 2\cot(x)$. Determine its period and asymptotes.

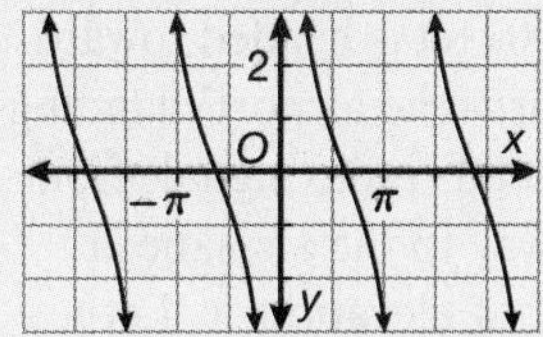

period is π; asymptotes occur at $x = \pi n$, where n is an integer.

Example 4

Students will use a graphing calculator to graph reciprocal functions.

Additional Example 4

Use a graphing calculator to graph $y = \csc(x)$.

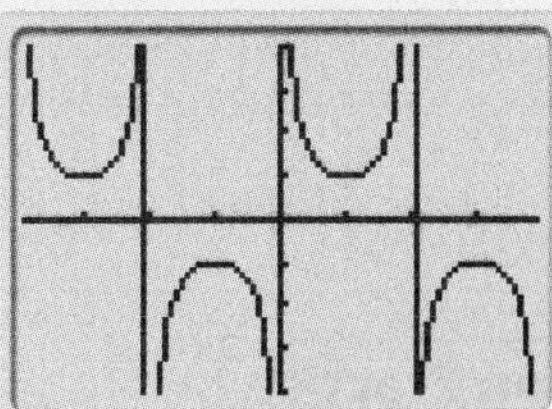

Error Alert Students are often confused between the words inverse and reciprocal. Finding the inverse refers to "undoing" an operation. For example, finding a square root is the inverse of squaring a number.

ALTERNATE METHOD FOR EXAMPLE 4

Students may also use the x^{-1} key on the calculator to graph the functions. To graph $y = \sec(x)$:

Step 1: On the calculator, press the **MODE** button and set the **RADIAN** mode.

Step 2: Enter the equation $Y = \cos(X)^{-1}$. *(Be sure students understand that $\cos(x)^{-1}$ is a reciprocal and $\cos^{-1}(x)$ is an inverse. Students must use the reciprocal.)*

Step 3: Press the **ZOOM** button and select 7↓**Trig.**

The graph of $y = \sec(x)$ is displayed as shown in Example 4.

Example 5

Students use a reciprocal trig function to represent a real life situation.

Additional Example 5

An airplane flying at an altitude of 20,000 feet is headed toward an airport. The airport's landing system sends radar signals from the runway to the airplane at an angle of elevation, x. Let y be the horizontal distance from the runway to a point directly below the airplane. Write y as a function of x and sketch the graph of the function over the interval 0 to π.

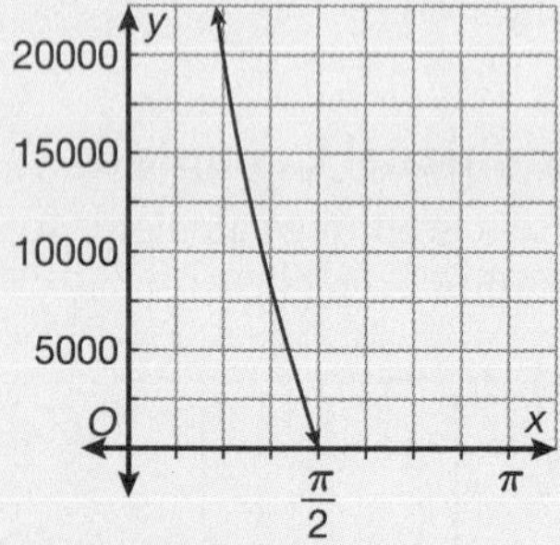

$y = 20{,}000 \cot(x)$

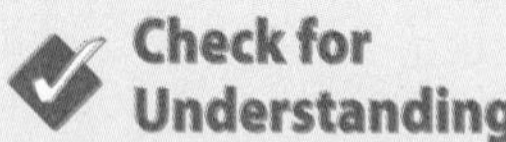

Problems a–f

Scaffolding Tell students to first find the period and asymptotes of the functions. Then have them use this information to draw an appropriate scale for the graph. Last, have students graph the functions.

Check for Understanding

The question below helps assess the concepts taught in this lesson.

"Explain how the period and asymptotes of $y = a\csc(bx)$, $y = a\sec(bx)$, and $y = a\cot(bx)$ can be compared." The cosecant and secant functions have the same period, which is $\frac{2\pi}{|b|}$. The cosecant and the cotangent have the same asymptotes, which are $\frac{\pi n}{|b|}$, where n is an integer.

Example 5 **Application: Airplane Landings**

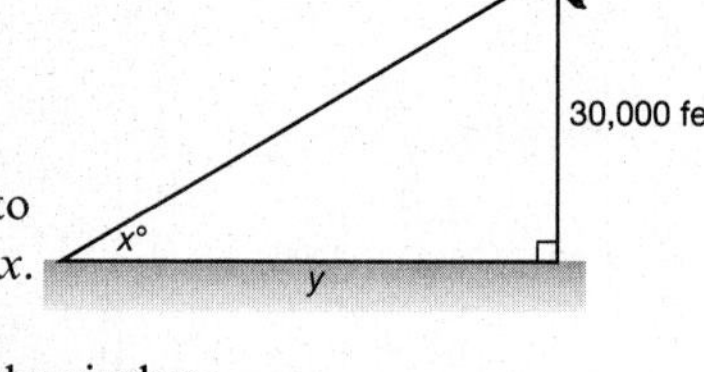

An airplane flying at an altitude of 30,000 feet is headed toward an airport. The airport's landing system sends radar signals from the runway to the airplane at an angle of elevation, x. Let y be the horizontal distance from the runway to a point directly below the airplane. Write y as a function of x and sketch the graph of the function over the interval 0 to π.

SOLUTION Use the cotangent function:

$$\cot(x) = \frac{\text{adjacent}}{\text{opposite}} = \frac{y}{30{,}000}$$

$$30{,}000 \cot(x) = y$$

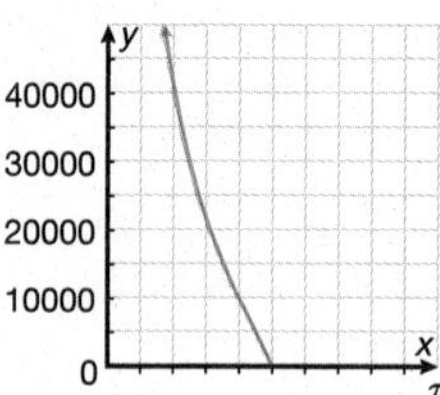

Lesson Practice

a–f. See Additional Answers.

a. Graph $y = 2\csc(x)$. Determine its period and asymptotes. (Ex 1)

b. Graph $y = \csc\left(\frac{1}{2}\right)x$. Determine its period and asymptotes. (Ex 1)

c. Graph $3\sec(x)$. Determine its period and asymptotes. (Ex 2)

d. Graph $\sec(2x)$. Determine its period and asymptotes. (Ex 2)

e. Graph $4\cot(x)$. Determine its period and asymptotes. (Ex 3)

f. Graph $\frac{1}{4}\cot(2x)$. Determine its period and asymptotes. (Ex 3)

g. Use a graphing calculator to graph $y = \frac{4}{5}\csc(x)$. See Additional Answers. (Ex 4)

h. An airplane is flying at an altitude of 22,000 feet. Signals are sent to the airplane from the runway at an angle of elevation, x. Let y be the distance from the runway to a point directly below the airplane. Write y as a function of x and sketch the graph of the function over the interval 0 to π. See Additional Answers. (Ex 5)

Practice Distributed and Integrated

*1. **Graphing Calculator** Use a graphing calculator to graph $y = 3\sec(2x)$ from 0 to 2π. (103) See Additional Answers.

2. **Multi-Step** A drinking glass is to be in the shape of a frustum of a right circular cone. The formula for the volume of a frustum of a right circular cone is $V = \frac{\pi(r^2 + rR + R^2)h}{3}$. (88)

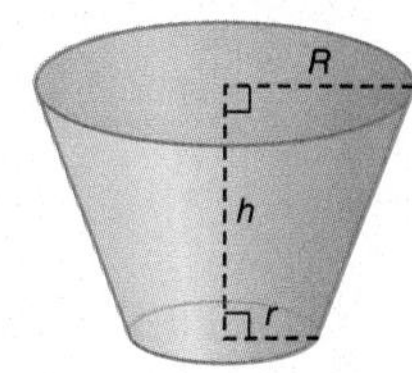

a. Solve the formula for h. $h = \frac{3V}{\pi(r^2 + rR + R^2)}$

b. If $R = 5$ centimeters and $r = 4$ centimeters, what is the minimum height necessary, to the nearest tenth of a centimeter, so that the glass will hold at least 500 cubic centimeters? 7.9 cm

INCLUSION

Have students create a chart to help them remember how to find the period and asymptotes of reciprocal functions. Point out that the period is found in the same way for cosecant and secant functions and the asymptotes are found in the same way for cosecant and cotangent functions.

	Period	Asymptotes
csc	$\frac{2\pi}{\lvert b\rvert}$	$\frac{\pi n}{\lvert b\rvert}$, where n is an integer
sec	$\frac{2\pi}{\lvert b\rvert}$	$\frac{\pi}{2\lvert b\rvert} + \frac{\pi n}{\lvert b\rvert}$, where n is an integer
cot	$\frac{\pi}{\lvert b\rvert}$	$\frac{\pi n}{\lvert b\rvert}$, where n is an integer

***3.** (101) **Landscape Design** A landscape architect has 96 feet of landscape timber to enclose a garden, using an existing wall for one side as shown. The area of the garden can be modeled by $A(x) = 96x - 3x^2$, where x is in feet. Find the maximum area of the garden. 768 ft²

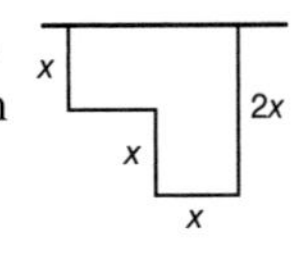

4. (96) **Multiple Choice** What are the Cartesian coordinates for the point with polar coordinates $(5, -\frac{\pi}{4})$? C

A $(5\sqrt{2}, -5\sqrt{2})$ B $(-5\sqrt{2}, 5\sqrt{2})$ C $\left(\frac{5\sqrt{2}}{2}, -\frac{5\sqrt{2}}{2}\right)$ D $\left(-\frac{5\sqrt{2}}{2}, \frac{5\sqrt{2}}{2}\right)$

***5.** (97) **Population** The estimated population of Illinois from 2005 to 2006 increased by about 0.52%. Assuming that the percent of increase stays the same, the populations each year form a geometric sequence. Show how to use the formula for the nth term of a geometric sequence to find the population of Illinois in 2010 given that the estimated population in 2005 was 12,765,427. $a_6 = a_1 (r)^{n-1}$; $a_6 = 12{,}765{,}427\ (1.0052)^5$; $a_6 = 13{,}100{,}798$

6. (33) How many 4-digit pass codes can be made using the numbers 1–5, if numbers may be repeated? 625 possible pass codes

7. (89) **Business** The profit earned from selling tickets to a certain event is modeled by $y = -1.5x^2 + 80x - 600$. If the cost per ticket will be a whole number amount, what range of ticket prices will earn a profit? What range of ticket values will earn a profit of at least \$200? from \$10 to \$44 inclusive; from \$14 to \$40 inclusive

8. (21) Solve the system by substitution. $\begin{array}{l} 2x + 5y = 7 \\ x + 4y = 2 \end{array}$ The solution is (6, −1).

9. (99) **Geometry** For any two vectors expressed as complex numbers, find the dot product from the components of the complex numbers. For $\vec{A} = a + bi$ and $\vec{B} = c + di$, $\vec{A} \cdot \vec{B} = ac + bd$.

10. (92) **Justify** When the ordered pairs (n, a_n) for the sequence {3, 7, 11, 15, 19} are graphed, the points form a straight line. Show algebraically why the slope is equal to the common difference.

10. Sample: The common difference is 19 − 15 = 4. Using the formula, $a_n = a_1 + (n - 1)d$, the function is $a_n = 3 + (n - 1)(4)$, which simplifies to $a_n = 3 + 4n - 4$ or $a_n = 4n - 1$. Using x and y, this is the same as $y = 4x - 1$, where 4 is the slope.

***11.** (100) **Model** The graph of a rational function has vertical asymptotes at $x = 7$ and -3 and holes at $x = -2$ and 0. Write an equation of a function that can be used to model these data points. Sample: $y = \frac{x(x + 2)}{(x + 2)x(x - 7)(x + 3)}$

12. (84) **Multiple Choice** To solve the equation, what should both sides of $\frac{1}{x^2 - 4} + \frac{3}{4x + 8} = \frac{6}{x}$ be multiplied by? C

A $(x + 2)(x - 2)$ B $4(x + 2)(x - 2)$

C $4x(x + 2)(x - 2)$ D $4x(x + 2)^2$

13. (11) **Formulate** Give an example of two trinomials whose sum has 6 terms. See Additional Answers.

14. (25) Find the range and standard deviation of the data set 10, 12, 7, 11, 20, 7, 8, 6, 9. range: 14; standard deviation: 4

***15.** (98) **Formulate** The eccentricity of an ellipse centered at the origin is 0.92. The graph of the ellipse crosses the minor axis at (0, 2). Write the equation of the ellipse. $\frac{x^2}{5.1^2} + \frac{y^2}{2^2} \approx 1$

3 Practice

Math Conversations

Discussions to strengthen understanding

Problem 4

Point out that a θ value of $-\frac{\pi}{4}$ indicates an angle at 315°. This angle is in quadrant IV where the x-coordinate is positive and the y-coordinate is negative. Therefore, choices B and D can be eliminated.

Problem 14

Guide the students by asking them the following questions.

"What is the range?" Range is the maximum value minus the minimum value.

"What is the range for this set of data?" 20 − 6 = 14

"What are the steps for finding standard deviation?" First find the mean. Then subtract the mean from each data value and square the difference. Sum these squares and divide by the number of values. Take the square root to find standard deviation.

"What is the mean?" 10

"What is the sum of the squared differences?" 144

"What is the sum of the squared differences divided by n?" 16

"What is the standard deviation?" 4

CHALLENGE

Use your graphing calculator to graph $y = \sin(x)$ and $y = \csc(x)$ in the same window. Then explain how the asymptotes of $y = \csc(x)$ are related to the graph of $y = \sin(x)$.

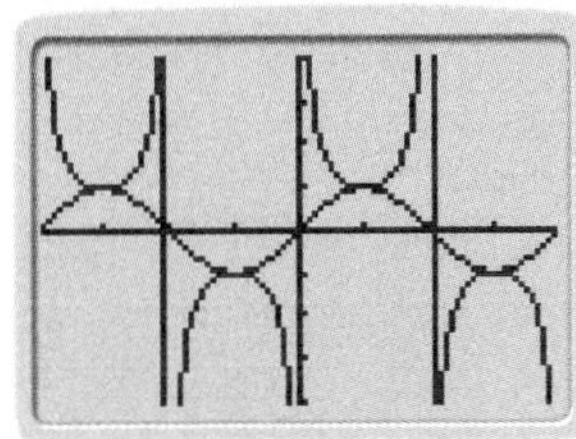

The asymptotes of $y = \csc(x)$ occur whenever $\sin(x) = 0$. From the graph shown for $y = \sin(x)$, this occurs at -2π, $-\pi$, 0, π, and 2π. So the asymptotes of $y = \csc(x)$ will also be at -2π, $-\pi$, 0, π, and 2π.

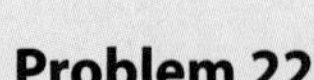

Problem 22

Remind students that $N(t)$ is the amount remaining, N_0 is the initial amount at $t = 0$, and t is the time in the units given in the problem.

Problem 24

Extend the Problem

What is the correct solution for $\log x + 5 = 4$? $x = \frac{1}{10}$

Problem 28

Error Alert

When reading the phrase "up to 6 items" students will often forget to include exactly 6 items in the piecewise function. Encourage students to check that the price of exactly 6 items is included in the function and fits the information given.

Problem 29

Remind students to solve for 0 on one side of the inequality before simplifying.

16. (83) **National Monuments** The height and span of the arch legs of the St. Louis Gateway Arch are both 630 feet. Write a quadratic function to approximate the arch. $y \approx -0.0063x^2 + 4x$

Identify all the real roots.

17. (85) $x^9 + 1331 = 0$ $x = -\sqrt[3]{11}$

18. (85) $x^3 + 10x^2 + 17x = 28$ $x = -7, -4, 1$

19. (90) **Physics** Derive an equation that an air traffic controller can use to find the angle an airplane makes with the horizon, given the plane's altitude h and its horizontal distance from the airport d. $\theta = \tan^{-1}\left(\frac{h}{d}\right)$

20. (95) Evaluate the polynomial $P(x)$ for $x = 4$. $P(x) = 2x^3 - 3x^2 + x - 5$ $P(4) = r(4) = 79$

***21.** (103) Find the period and asymptotes for $y = 3 \cot \frac{2}{3}x$. Period $= \frac{3\pi}{2}$; asymptotes $= \frac{3\pi}{2}n$, where n is an integer

22. (93) **Multi-Step** Iron-62 has a half-life of 68 seconds.

a. Use the natural decay function $N(t) = N_0e^{-kt}$ to find the decay constant k for iron-62. See Additional Answers.

b. Write the natural decay function for iron-62 and solve for t to find how long it would take 10 grams to decay to 7 grams. See Additional Answers.

23. (91) **Error Analysis** Explain and correct the error a student made in graphing $x^2 + y^2 = 4$. The student used the square of the radius as the radius. The radius is the square root of 4, or 2. See Additional Answers.

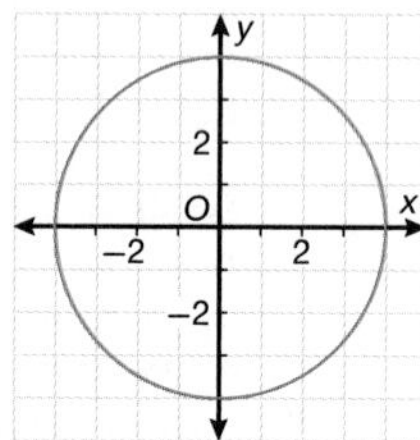

***24.** (102) **Error Analysis** A student solved $\log x + 5 = 4$ incorrectly, obtaining 9,995 as the solution. What error did the student likely make? Sample: The student solved $\log(x + 5) = 4$.

***25.** (102) **Write** Can a logarithmic equation have a negative number as a solution? Justify your answer. Give an example, if possible. Yes; Possible justification: $\log x^2 = 2$ has solutions 10 and −10.

Simplify the expression.

26. (40) $\frac{48}{\sqrt{3}}$ $16\sqrt{3}$

27. (40) $\sqrt{108} + \sqrt{12} + \sqrt{112}$ $8\sqrt{3} + 4\sqrt{7}$

28. (79) Write a piecewise function for a hardware store that will deliver up to 6 items for a \$35 delivery charge. There is a \$7 charge for each additional item. $y = \begin{cases} 35 \text{ if } x \le 6 \\ 7(x - 6) + 35 \text{ if } x > 6 \end{cases}$

***29.** (94) Solve $\frac{x^2 - 3x + 2}{x - 3} < x$ by finding the values of test points. $x < 3$

***30.** (103) A traffic helicopter is flying at an altitude of 8,000 feet. The driver spots an accident at angle of depression, x. Let y be the distance from the accident to a point directly below the helicopter. Write y as a function of x. $\cot x = \frac{\text{adjacent}}{\text{opposite}} = \frac{y}{8{,}000}$; $y = 8000 \cot x$

724 *Saxon* Algebra 2

LOOKING FORWARD

Graphing reciprocal trigonometric functions prepares students for

- **Lesson 108** Using Fundamental Trigonometric Identities
- **Lesson 119** Solving Trigonometric Equations

LESSON 104

Finding Transformations

Warm Up

1. **Vocabulary** ________ can be used to change the graph of one function into the graph of a different function. (17) Transformations

2. Write the equation that will shift $f(x) = |x|$ to the left 2 units. (17) $g(x) = |x + 2|$

3. Which quadrant(s) is $f(x) = \sqrt{x} + 20$ graphed in? (75) Quadrant I

New Concepts

A graph can be altered to form new equations by shifting the graph vertically or horizontally, reflecting the graph about the x- and y-axis, and stretching or compressing the graph.

Math Language

The function $f(x) = \sqrt{x}$ is called the **Square Root Parent Function.** A **parent function** is a basic function to which transformations are applied to create a family of functions.

The table below summarizes the transformations.

Transformation	Equation	Change in the Graph
Vertical Shifts	$y = f(x) + a$	If $a > 0$, then the graph of f shifts up by a units. If $a < 0$, then the graph of f shifts down by a units.
Horizontal Shifts	$y = f(x - a)$	If $a < 0$, then the graph of f shifts to the left a units. If $a > 0$, then the graph of f shifts to the right a units.
Reflections	$y = -f(x)$	Reflects the graph of f about the x-axis.
	$y = f(-x)$	Reflects the graph of f about the y-axis.
Vertical Stretch/ Compression	$y = af(x)$	If $a > 1$, the graph of f vertically stretches. If $0 < a < 1$, the graph of f vertically compresses.

Example 1 Transforming the Square Root Function

(a.) Use the graph of $f(x) = \sqrt{x}$ to sketch the graph of $g(x) = \sqrt{x} - 7$.

SOLUTION Compare the equation $g(x)$ to that of $f(x)$. The equation for $g(x)$ subtracts 7 from each value of $f(x)$.

$y = g(x) = \sqrt{x} - 7 = f(x) - 7$

The graph of $g(x)$ will have the same shape as $f(x)$ only it will be shifted down 7 units.

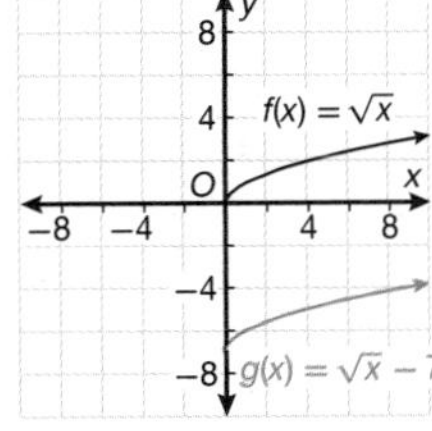

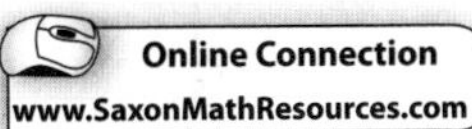

MATH BACKGROUND

The parent function in a family of functions, has the simplest algebraic rule in that family. Each operation performed on the rule of a parent function corresponds to a transformation of its graph. Transformations of a parent function graph yield graphs that are all in the same family. The table on this page applies to all functions, not just square root functions. For example, if $f(x) = x^3$, then the graph of $y = f(x) + 2 = x^3 + 2$ can be obtained by shifting the graph of $f(x)$ up 2 units.

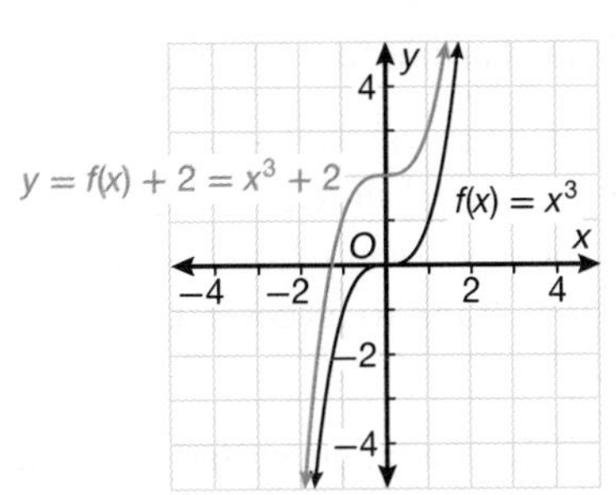

LESSON 104

1 Warm Up

For Problem 2, remind students of the standard form $y = a|x - h| + k$.

2 New Concepts

In this lesson, students learn to sketch graphs of functions by applying transformations to the parent function $f(x) = \sqrt{x}$ and $f(x) = b^x$.

Example 1

Remind students that the square root function has a limited domain and range.

Additional Example 1

a. Use the graph of $f(x) = \sqrt{x}$ to sketch the graph of $g(x) = \sqrt{x} + 3$.

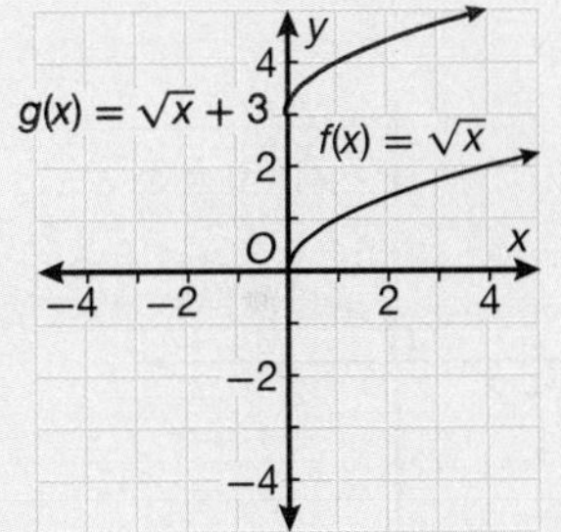

LESSON RESOURCES

Student Edition Practice Workbook 104
Reteaching Master 104
Adaptations Master 104
Challenge and Enrichment Master C93

Additional Example 1

b. Use the graph of $f(x) = \sqrt{x}$ to sketch the graph of $h(x) = \sqrt{x - 2}$.

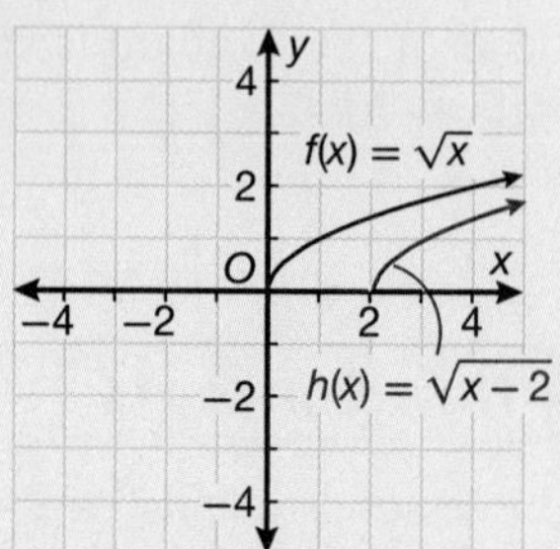

c. Use the graph of $f(x) = \sqrt{x}$ to sketch the graph of $j(x) = \sqrt{(-x)}$.

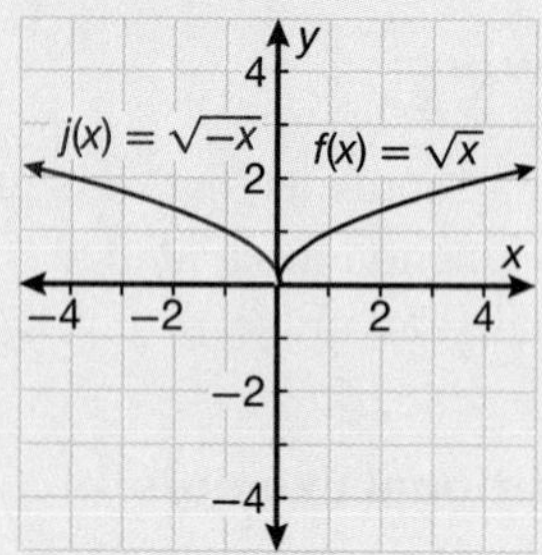

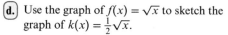

d. Use the graph of $f(x) = \sqrt{x}$ to sketch the graph of $k(x) = 3\sqrt{x}$.

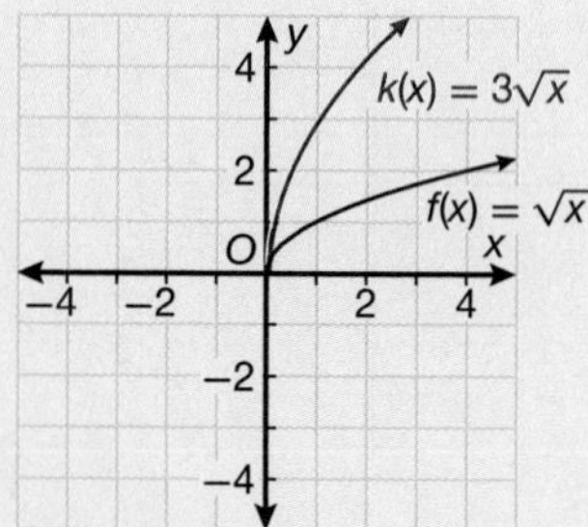

Extend the Example

If the graph of $f(x)$ is transformed, the result is called the image. If (a, b) is a point on the graph of $f(x) = \sqrt{x}$, describe the image of (a, b) on the graph of $f(x) = \sqrt{x + 3}$. $(a - 3, b)$

b. Use the graph of $f(x) = \sqrt{x}$ to sketch the graph of $h(x) = \sqrt{x + 9}$.

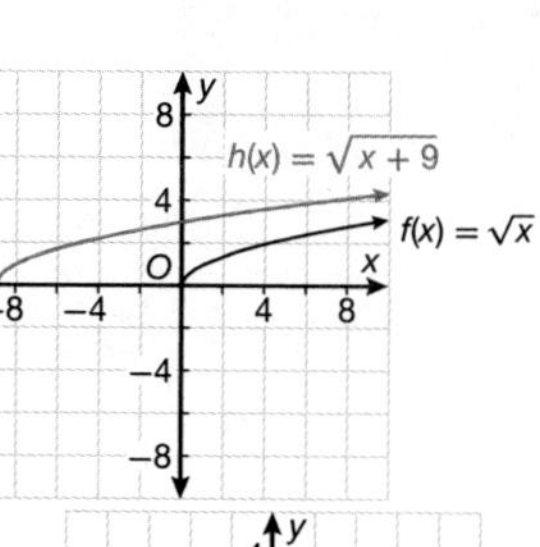

SOLUTION Compare the equation $h(x)$ to that of $f(x)$.

$y = h(x) = \sqrt{x + 9} = f(x - (-9))$

The graph of $h(x)$ will have the same shape as $f(x)$ only it will be shifted to the left 9 units.

c. Use the graph of $f(x) = \sqrt{x}$ to sketch the graph of $j(x) = -\sqrt{x}$.

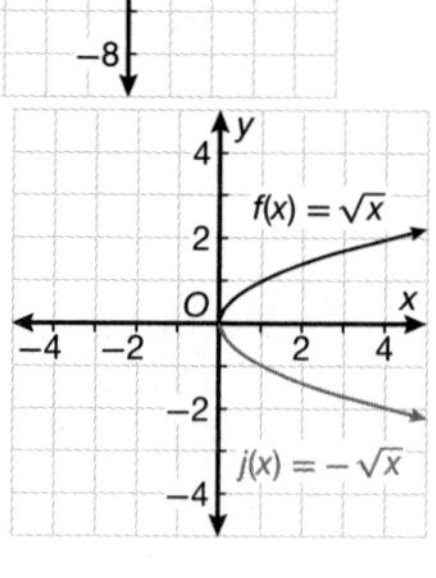

SOLUTION Compare the equation $j(x)$ to that of $f(x)$. The equation for $j(x)$ is the opposite of each value of $f(x)$.

$y = j(x) = -\sqrt{x} = -f(x)$

The graph of $j(x)$ is a reflection about the x-axis of $f(x)$.

Hint

To find the coordinates of a graph that is being vertically stretched or compressed, multiply each y-coordinate of the parent function by the constant a.

d. Use the graph of $f(x) = \sqrt{x}$ to sketch the graph of $k(x) = \frac{1}{2}\sqrt{x}$.

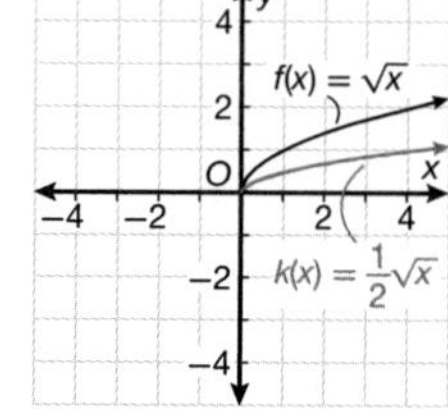

SOLUTION Compare the equation $k(x)$ to that of $f(x)$. The equation for $k(x)$ multiplies each value of $f(x)$ by $\frac{1}{2}$.

$y = k(x) = \frac{1}{2}\sqrt{x} = \frac{1}{2}f(x)$

By vertically compressing $f(x)$, $k(x)$ is obtained.

A function with multiple transformations can be graphed by implementing the transformations in the following order: horizontal shifts, then vertical stretching or compressing, then reflections, and then vertical shifts.

Example 2 Finding Multiple Transformations of the Square Root Function

Use the graph of $f(x) = \sqrt{x}$ to sketch the graph of $g(x) = -\sqrt{x - 4} + 8$.

SOLUTION

Step 1

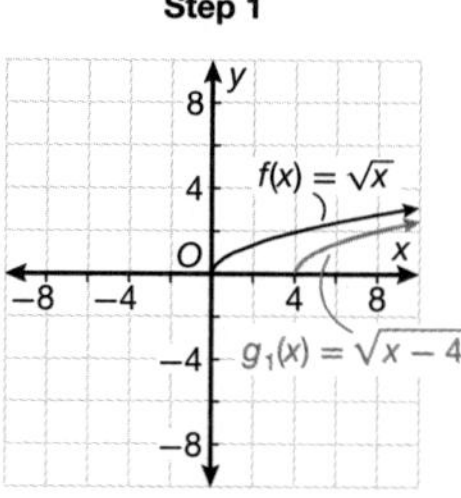

Step 1: Horizontal Shifts; The graph of $f(x)$ shifts to the right 4 units.

Step 2: Vertical Stretching or Compressing; Since $f(x)$ is not multiplied by a constant, there is no vertical stretching or compressing.

ENGLISH LEARNERS

Explain the meanings of **vertical** and **horizontal**. Say:

"Vertical means up or down."

On the board, show a graph and its image after a vertical shift. Show by pointing that you move vertically from a point on the original graph to its corresponding image point.

Say: **"Horizontal means left or right."**

Demonstrate the meaning of a horizontal shift in a similar way.

Step 3: Reflections: Since $f(x)$ is replaced by $-f(x)$, this reflects the equation about the x-axis.

Step 3

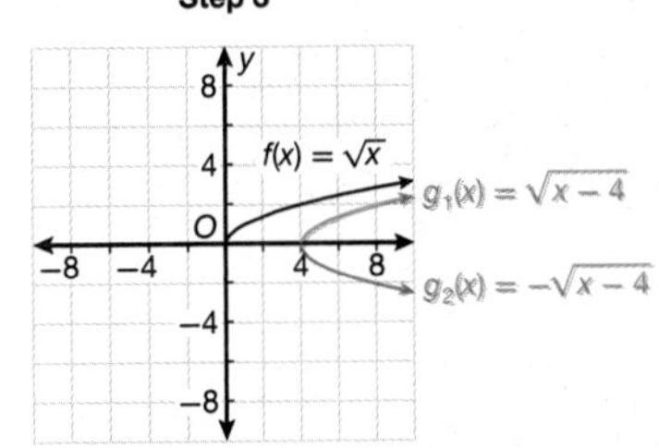

Step 4: Vertical Shifts: Since 8 is being added to $f(x)$, this will shift up the graph 8 units. See the graph at right.

Step 4

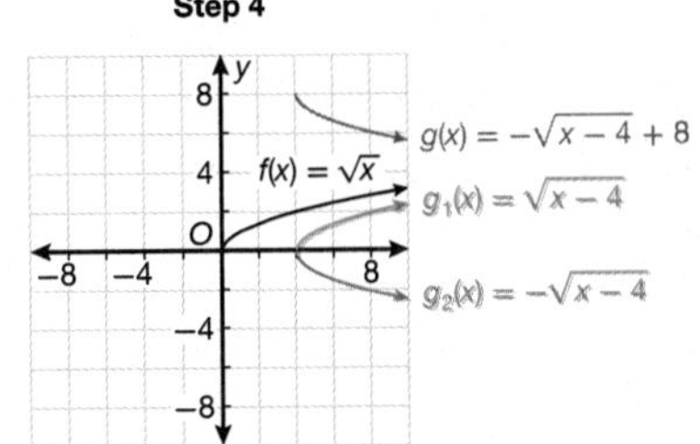

Hint

Exponential parent functions are of the form $f(x) = b^x$.

Transformations can also be performed on exponential functions to obtain new graphs. Horizontal and vertical translations can be used to shift the graph up, down, left, and right.

The table below summarizes transformations of exponential functions.

Transformation	Equation	Change in the Graph
Vertical Translations	$y = b^x + a$	If $a > 0$, raises the graph of f by a units. If $a < 0$, lowers the graph of f by a units.
Horizontal Translations	$y = b^{x-a}$	If $a < 0$, shifts the graph of f to the left a units. If $a > 0$, shifts the graph of f to the right a units.
Reflections	$y = -b^x$	Reflects the graph of f about the x-axis.
	$y = b^{-x}$	Reflects the graph of f about the y-axis.
Vertical Stretching/ Compressing	$y = ab^x$	If $a > 1$, vertically stretches the graph of f. If $0 < a < 1$, vertically compresses the graph of f.

Example 3 Translating an Exponential Function

a. Use the graph of $f(x) = 3^x$ to sketch the graph of $g(x) = 3^x + 5$.

SOLUTION Compare the equation $g(x)$ to that of $f(x)$. The equation for $g(x)$ adds 5 to each value of $f(x)$.

$y = g(x) = 3^x + 5 = f(x) + 5$

The graph of $g(x)$ will have the same shape as $f(x)$ only it will be shifted up 5 units.

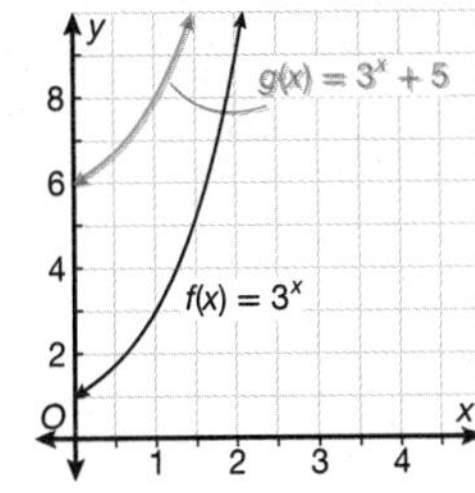

Example 2

This example shows how to apply several transformations. For convenience of language, the process is described as applying multiple transformations to a function. In fact, only one transformation is applied to the original function, then the next transformation is applied to the resulting function, and so on.

Additional Example 2

Use the graph of $f(x) = \sqrt{x}$ to sketch the graph of $g(x) = -\sqrt{x+3} - 5$.

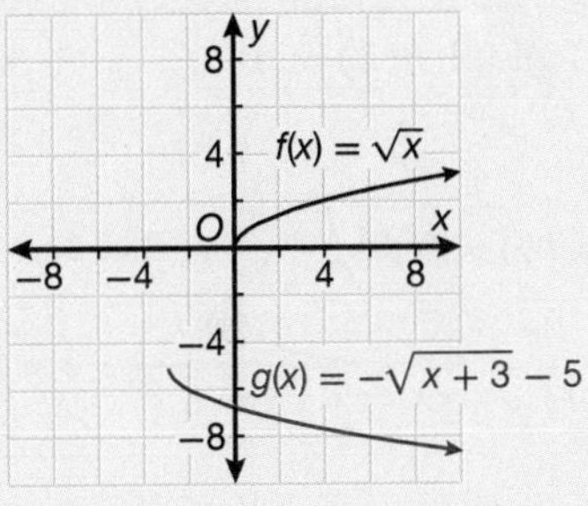

TEACHER TIP

Have students draw all their graphs on graph paper. You may wish to make copies of graphs that already have the parent function graphed on it. This will help students maintain the correct shape in their transformed graphs.

INCLUSION

Seeing and comparing graphs are fundamental requirements in this lesson. To accommodate different learning styles, use frequent verbal descriptions as you compare graphs visually. Emphasize key words such as *vertical, horizontal, shift, reflect, y-axis, x-axis, stretch,* and *compress.*

Example 3

This example shows a vertical and horizontal shift of an exponential function.

Additional Example 3

a. Use the graph of $f(x) = 3^x$ to sketch the graph of $g(x) = 3^x - 2$.

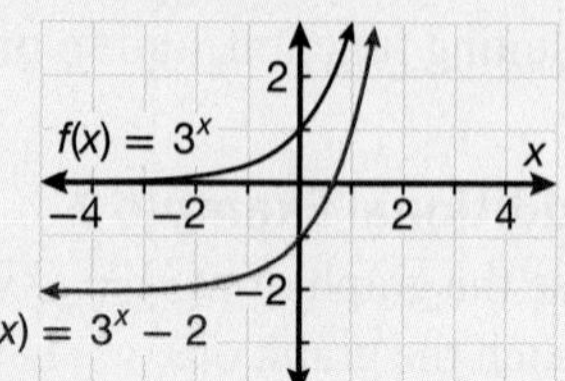

b. Use the graph of $f(x) = 3^x$ to graph $h(x) = 3^{x+3}$.

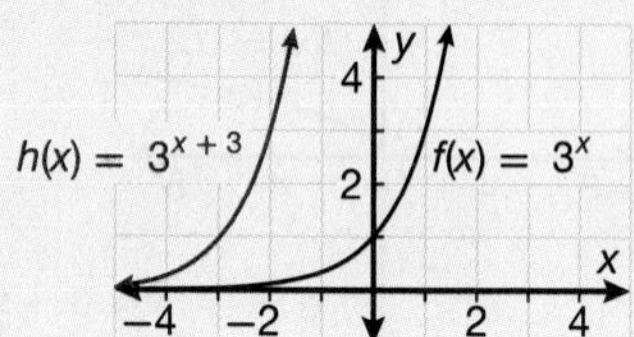

Example 4

This example shows reflections of an exponential function.

Additional Example 4

a. Use the graph of $f(x) = 2^x$ to sketch the graph of $g(x) = -2^x$.

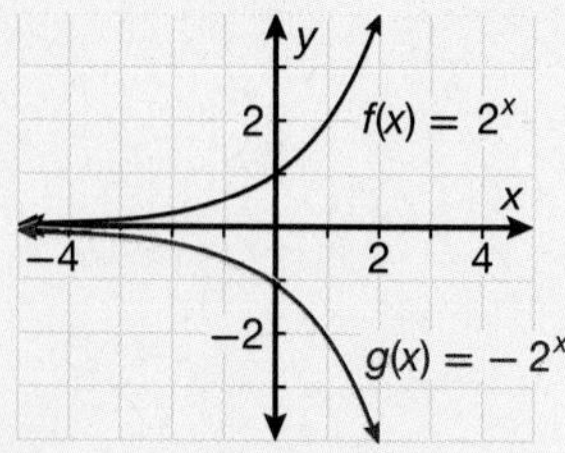

b. Use the graph of $f(x) = 2^x$ to sketch the graph of $h(x) = 2^{-x}$.

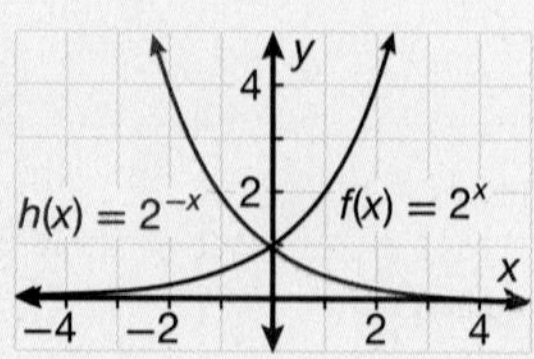

b. Use the graph of $f(x) = 3^x$ to sketch the graph of $h(x) = 3^{x-5}$.

SOLUTION Compare the equation $h(x)$ to that of $f(x)$.

$y = h(x) = 3^{x-5} = f(x - 5)$

The graph of $h(x)$ will have the same shape as $f(x)$ only it will be shifted to the right 5 units.

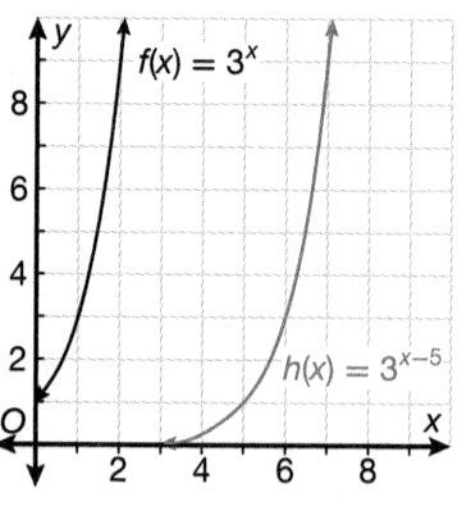

Example 4 Reflecting Exponential Functions

Math Reasoning

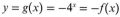

Write Explain the difference between the change in a function that is reflected about the *x*-axis and about the *y*-axis.

If a new function is formed by replacing *x* with –*x*, then it is a reflection about the *y*-axis. If a new function is formed by replacing *f*(*x*) with –*f*(*x*), then it is a reflection about the *x*-axis.

a. Use the graph of $f(x) = 4^x$ to sketch the graph of $g(x) = -4^x$.

SOLUTION Compare the equation $g(x)$ to that of $f(x)$. The equation for $g(x)$ is the opposite of $f(x)$.

$y = g(x) = -4^x = -f(x)$

The graph of $g(x)$ is a reflection about the x-axis of $f(x)$.

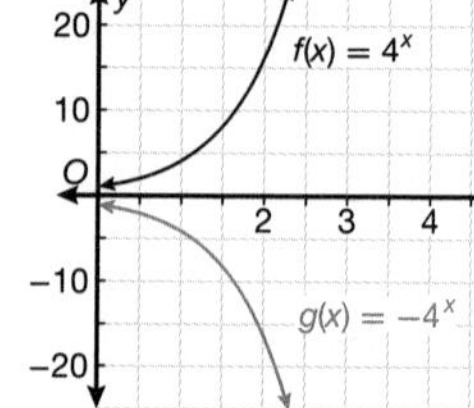

b. Use the graph of $f(x) = 4^x$ to sketch the graph of $h(x) = 4^{-x}$.

SOLUTION Compare the equation $h(x)$ to that of $f(x)$. The equation for $h(x)$ is the opposite at each value of x.

$y = h(x) = 4^{-x} = f(-x)$

The graph of $h(x)$ is a reflection about the y-axis of $f(x)$.

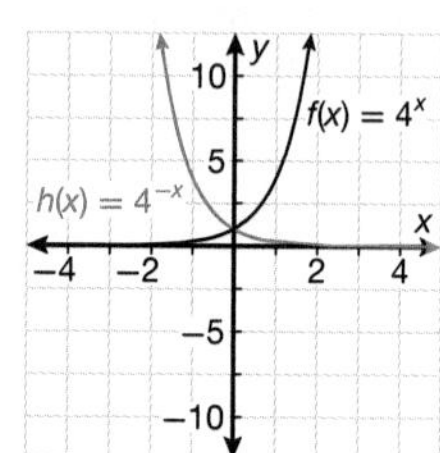

Example 5 Application: IQ Formula

The function $n(x) = 2\sqrt{x} - 9$ is used by psychologists to determine the number of nonsense syllables, $n(x)$, a person with an IQ of x can repeat. Use the graph of $f(x) = \sqrt{x}$ to sketch the graph of $n(x) = 2\sqrt{x} - 9$. Then use the graph of $n(x) = 2\sqrt{x} - 9$ to estimate the number of nonsense syllables a person with an IQ of 121 can repeat.

SOLUTION

To find the graph of $n(x)$, implement transformations to the graph of $f(x)$. The function $n(x)$ involves multiple transformations.

Implement the transformations in the correct order.

Step 1: Horizontal Shifts: none

Step 2: Vertical Stretching or Compressing:
$f(x)$ is being multiplied by 2, so the graph is vertically stretched by a factor 2.

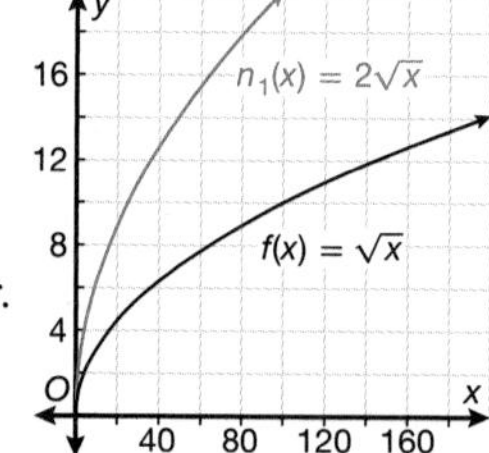

ALTERNATE METHOD FOR EXAMPLE 4b

Use a table to graph $h(x)$.

x	−2	−1	0	1	2
4^x	0.0625	0.25	1	4	16
4^{-x}	16	4	1	0.25	0.0625

Step 3: Reflections: none

Step 4: Vertical Shifts: 9 is being subtracted from $f(x)$. This will lower the graph 9 units.

Now use the graph to approximate the value of $n(x)$ when $x = 121$.

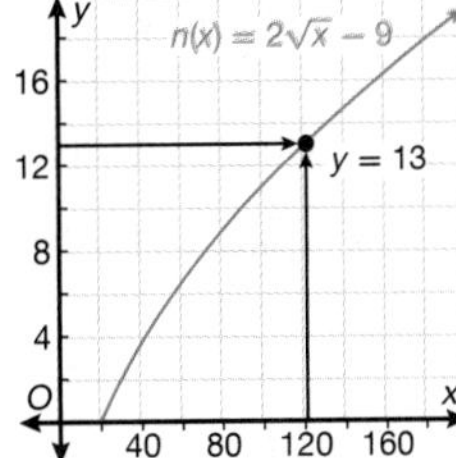

Substitute for the value of x in the function $n(x)$. See if this value is close to the value found.

$n(121) = 2\sqrt{121} - 9 = 2(11) - 9 = 22 - 9 = 13$

A person with an IQ of 121 can repeat 13 nonsense syllables.

Lesson Practice

Use the graph of $f(x) = \sqrt{x}$ to sketch each of the following.

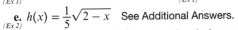

a. $h(x) = \sqrt{x} + 10$ (Ex 1)

b. $h(x) = \sqrt{x - 1}$ (Ex 1)

c. $h(x) = -\sqrt{x}$ (Ex 1)

d. $h(x) = 4\sqrt{x}$ (Ex 1) See Additional Answers.

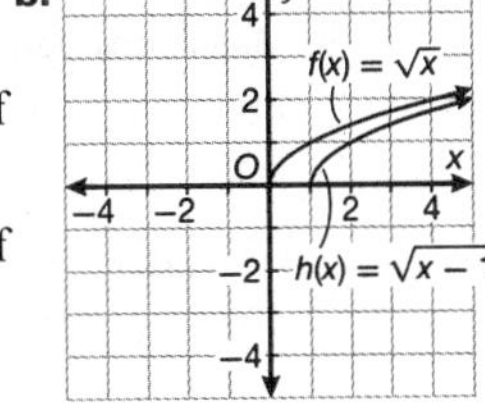

e. $h(x) = \frac{1}{5}\sqrt{2 - x}$ (Ex 2) See Additional Answers.

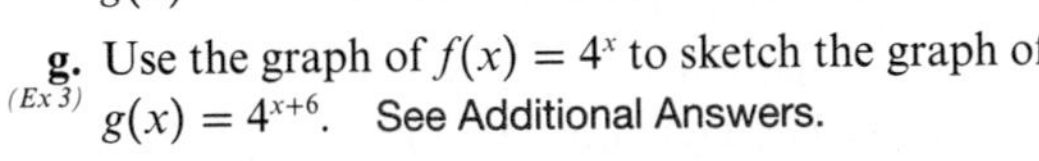

f. (Ex 3) Use the graph of $f(x) = 5^x$ to sketch the graph of $g(x) = 5^x - 4$. See Additional Answers.

g. (Ex 3) Use the graph of $f(x) = 4^x$ to sketch the graph of $g(x) = 4^{x+6}$. See Additional Answers.

h. (Ex 4) Use the graph of $f(x) = 10^x$ to sketch the graph of $g(x) = -10^x$. See Additional Answers.

i. (Ex 4) Use the graph of $f(x) = 7^x$ to sketch the graph of $g(x) = 7^{-x}$. See Additional Answers.

j. (Ex 5) The time T, in seconds, for the period of a simple pendulum can be estimated by the equation $T(x) = 2.009\sqrt{x}$, where x is the length, in meters, of the pendulum. Use the graph of $f(x) = \sqrt{x}$ to sketch the graph of $T(x) = 2.009\sqrt{x}$. Use the graph of $T(x)$ to estimate the length of a pendulum whose period is 4 seconds. about 3.96 m, See Additional Answers.

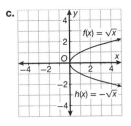

Practice Distributed and Integrated

1. (94) **Multiple Choice** When solving $\frac{x^2 + 5x - 6}{x^2 - 12x + 32}$ by using a sign table, for how many intervals will a test point need to be chosen? **C**

A 3 **B** 4 **C** 5 **D** 6

2. (77) A triangle has side lengths of 7.5 meters, 11 meters, and 13 meters. Use Heron's formula to find the area of the triangle. 41.2 m²

***3.** (103) Graph $y = 4\cot\left(\frac{1}{2}x\right)$. Determine its period and asymptotes. See Additional Answers.

Example 5

Transformations are applied to a real-world function.

Additional Example 5

A rancher has 3 square miles of grazing land. He wants to add a square-shaped lot to increase the amount of grazing land. The function $g(x) = \sqrt{x - 3}$ represents the length, in miles, of the side of the added square-shaped lot that will result in a total of x square miles of grazing land. Use the graph of $f(x) = \sqrt{x}$ to graph $g(x) = \sqrt{x - 3}$. Then use the graph of $g(x) = \sqrt{x - 3}$ to estimate the length of the side of the square-shaped lot that will result in a total of 8 square miles of grazing land.
approximately 2.25 miles

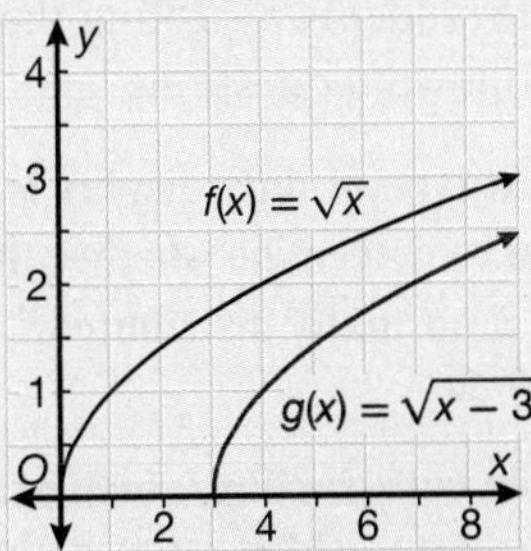

Lesson Practice

Problem a

Error Alert Students might translate to the left instead of up. Point out that the "+10" is not part of the radicand.

Check for Understanding

The questions below help assess the concepts taught in this lesson.

"How can you determine whether to shift a graph vertically or horizontally?" Sample: If a number is added to $f(x)$, then shift vertically. If a number is added to x, then shift horizontally.

"How can you determine which axis to reflect a graph over?" Sample: To obtain the graph of $-f(x)$, reflect the graph of $f(x)$ over the x-axis. To obtain the graph of $f(-x)$, reflect the graph of $f(x)$ over the y-axis.

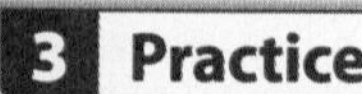

3 Practice

Math Conversations

Discussions to strengthen understanding

Problem 6

Error Alert

Students might obtain the correct answers and incorrectly conclude that those answers are true facts. Remind them that the given function is only a *model* for the situation described. Without knowing actual data values, there is no way to determine how closely the model fits the data. The *actual* lowest monthly NASDAQ Composite during 2002 was different than the answer to Problem 6.

Problem 11

Guide students by asking them the following questions.

"What type of data display is useful to determine whether the data is normally distributed?" histogram

"When constructing a histogram for the data, which set of numbers should be placed on the horizontal axis?" number of sides in polygon

*4. (90) **Graphing Calculator** Use a graphing calculator to graph $y = \tan(x + 6)$. Identify the period and undefined values of the function. Period: π
Asymptotes: $\frac{\pi}{2} - 6 + \pi n$, where n is an integer

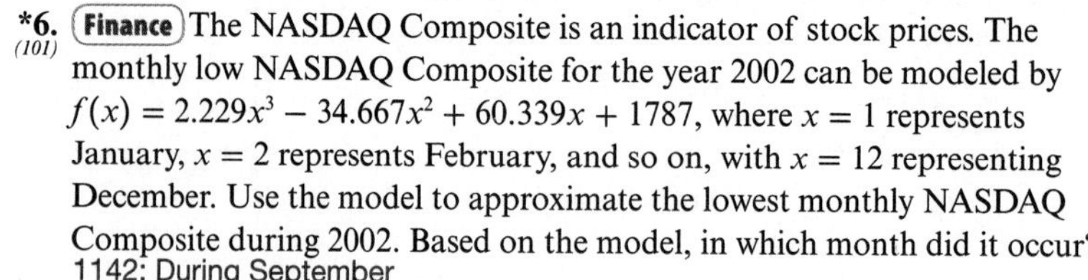

*5. (104) **Error Analysis** In the coordinate plane shown, functions $f(x) = \sqrt{x}$ and $g(x) = 3\sqrt{x - 5} - 5$ are graphed. Is the graph of g correct? If not, find and explain the error and sketch the correct graph of g. See Additional Answers.

*6. (101) **Finance** The NASDAQ Composite is an indicator of stock prices. The monthly low NASDAQ Composite for the year 2002 can be modeled by $f(x) = 2.229x^3 - 34.667x^2 + 60.339x + 1787$, where $x = 1$ represents January, $x = 2$ represents February, and so on, with $x = 12$ representing December. Use the model to approximate the lowest monthly NASDAQ Composite during 2002. Based on the model, in which month did it occur?
1142; During September

7. (95) **Analyze** Suppose that for polynomial $P(x)$, $P(a) = 0$ for constant a. What can you conclude about the graph of rational function $f(x) = \frac{1}{P(x)}$? There is a vertical asymptote at $x = a$.

8. (96) **Error Analysis** A student incorrectly converted the polar coordinates $(-1, \pi)$ to the Cartesian coordinates $(-1, 0)$. What is the error? Find the correct Cartesian coordinates. Sample: The point with polar coordinates $(-1, \pi)$ is on the positive x-axis in the Cartesian coordinate system. Correct answer: $(1, 0)$

9. (87) **Radioactive Decay** A radioactive substance decays based on $d = d_0e^{-0.0063t}$. The time, in days, is represented by t, and d_0 represents the initial amount of the radioactive substance. Solve for t. $t = -\frac{1}{0.0063}\left(\ln\frac{d}{d_0}\right)$

10. (97) **Chemistry** The half-life of Barium-131 is 12 days. The amounts of Barium-131 after every half-life (every 12th day) form a geometric sequence. What is the common ratio of this sequence? $\frac{1}{2}$

11. (80) **Geometry** The students in a geometry class each chose a polygon that has between 3 and 12 sides and wrote a paragraph about its side and angle measures. The table shows how many students chose each type of polygon. Tell if the data is normally distributed. Explain your answer. No, the histogram is not bell-shaped, it is double-peaked.

Number of Sides in Polygon	3	4	5	6	7	8	9	10	11	12
Number of Students Who Chose Polygon	2	5	7	6	2	5	6	8	4	1

12. (98) **Formulate** The eccentricity of an ellipse centered at $(-3, 5)$ is 0.9682. The graph of the ellipse crosses the major axis at $(-3, 21)$. Write the equation of the ellipse. $\frac{(x-(-3))^2}{4^2} + \frac{(y-5)^2}{16^2} = 1$

13. (28) Identify any excluded values for the expression $\frac{12m^7}{3m^9}$, then simplify. $m \neq 0, \frac{4}{m^2}$

*14. (99) **Multiple Choice** In what quadrant is the vector $22 + (-33)i$? D
A I **B** II **C** III **D** IV

15. (34) **Formulate** Rewrite the following equation in slope-intercept form: $6x - 8y = 24$. $y = \frac{3}{4}x - 3$

*16. (100) **Model** The graph of a rational function has vertical asymptotes at $x = 0, -1$, and 3 and a hole at $x = 5$. Write an equation of a function that can be used to model these data points. Sample: $y = \frac{(x-5)}{(x-5)x(x+1)(x-3)} = \frac{x-5}{x^4 - 7x^3 + 7x^2 + 15x}$

CHALLENGE

Describe step-by-step how to transform the graph of $f(x) = \sqrt{x}$ to obtain the graph of $g(x) = 4\sqrt{-x + 3}$. For each step, write the new function to be graphed and the transformation that yields that graph.

Sample: Graph $g_1(x) = \sqrt{-x}$ by reflecting the graph of $f(x) = \sqrt{x}$ about the y-axis. Then graph $g_2(x) = \sqrt{-(x-3)}$ by shifting the graph of g_1 to the right 3 units. Then graph $g_3(x) = 4\sqrt{-x+3}$ by stretching the graph of g_2 vertically by a factor of 4.

17. **Data Analysis** The rates for media mail are shown in the table. Write a piecewise function that represents the cost of mailing a first-class letter. (79)
See Additional Answers.

Fee	Weight
\$1.30	up to 1 ounce
\$1.64	greater than 1 ounce and up to 2 ounces
\$1.98	greater than 2 ounces and up to 3 ounces

*18. **Error Analysis** Describe and correct the error in finding $\csc\theta$, given that θ is an acute angle of a right triangle and $\cos\theta = \frac{7}{11}$. (103)

$$\csc\theta = \frac{1}{\cos\theta} = \frac{11}{7}$$

18. Cosecant is not the reciprocal of cosine, it is the reciprocal of sine; $\sin\theta = \frac{6\sqrt{2}}{11}$, $\csc\theta = \frac{1}{\sin\theta} = \frac{11}{6\sqrt{2}} = \frac{11\sqrt{2}}{12}$

19. **Salaries** An employee's salary is structured so that after the first year, the employee receives an annual raise of a set amount. What was the employee's starting salary if the salary in the eighth year was \$42,710 and the salary in the 17th year was \$50,135? (92) \$36,935

*20. **Multi-Step** The Richter magnitude M of an earthquake is expressed by $M = \frac{2}{3}\log\left(\frac{E}{10^{11.8}}\right)$, where E is the energy released in ergs. (102)

a. Find the energy released by an earthquake of magnitude 6. $10^{20.8}$, or approximately 6.3096×10^{20} ergs

b. Find the energy released by an earthquake of magnitude 7. $10^{22.3}$, or approximately 1.9953×10^{22} ergs

c. By what factor is the energy multiplied when the magnitude is increased by 1? $10^{1.5}$, or approximately 31.6

21. **Simple Interest** The simple interest formula is $A = P + Prt$, where P is the principal, or original amount invested, r is the annual simple interest rate, and A is the value of the investment at the end of t years. Solve the formula for P. Then determine the amount P that must be invested at 5% annual simple interest to have a value of \$10,000 at the end of 2 years. (88) $P = \frac{A}{1+rt}$; \$9,090.91

22. Darryl lives 2 miles from the mall and Taylor lives 8 miles from the same mall. Write an inequality to determine how far Darryl and Taylor live from each other. (10) $6 \le x \le 10$

*23. **Write** Explain in complete sentences what must be done to an equation to vertically shift a graph down. (104) To vertically shift a graph down, you must subtract a value from each y-coordinate of the graph.

Use matrices $B = \begin{bmatrix} 3\frac{1}{2} & -\frac{1}{2} & -\frac{1}{4} \end{bmatrix}$ **and** $C = \begin{bmatrix} 2\frac{1}{2} & \frac{1}{2} & -3 \end{bmatrix}$.

24. Find $-C$. (5) $\begin{bmatrix} -2\frac{1}{2} & -\frac{1}{2} & 3 \end{bmatrix}$

25. Find $\frac{1}{2}C + 4B$. (5) $\begin{bmatrix} 15\frac{1}{4} & -1\frac{3}{4} & -2\frac{1}{2} \end{bmatrix}$

26. Divide, and identify all values of x that make the expression $\frac{x^2+6x+9}{x^2-9} \div (x-7)$ undefined. (31) $\frac{x+3}{(x-3)(x-7)}$; $x \ne -3, 3, 7$

Solve and classify each of the following systems.

27. (24) $4x - 3y = 10$, $8x - 6y = 20$ — infinite solutions; consistent and dependent

28. (24) $7x + 2y = 11$, $-2x + 3y = 29$ — $(-1, 9)$, consistent and independent

29. Using $\sin(x)$ as a guide, find the phase shift in $g(x) = 2\sin 3(x - 8) + 5$. (82) Phase shift is 8 units to the right

*30. Find the period and asymptotes of $y = -\sec 4x$. (103) Period $= \frac{\pi}{2}$; asymptotes $= \frac{\pi}{8} + \frac{\pi}{2}n$, where n is an integer

Problem 17

Error Alert

Students may not include 1 ounce as a domain value for the first function of the piecewise function. You may need to explain to students that if a measure goes "up to" a certain number, it includes that number.

Problem 18

"How can you find the measure of the opposite side?" Use the Pythagorean Theorem.

LOOKING FORWARD 

Finding transformations prepares students for

- **Lesson 110** Graphing Logarithmic Functions

LESSON **105**

1 Warm Up

Problem 2

Have students determine the common difference before finding the next three terms.

2 New Concepts

An indicated sum of the terms of a sequence is called a series. In this lesson, students learn about arithmetic series, which are indicated sums of terms of arithmetic sequences. The indicated sum of the first n terms of a sequence is a series, also called the nth partial sum of the sequence.

Example 1

The rule, or explicit formula, for the terms in Example 1a is $a_k = 2k$. The rule in Example 1b is $a_k = 10 - k$.

Extend the Example

Let S_n represent the nth partial sum of the infinite arithmetic sequence 2, 4, 6, 8,.... Find S_8. 72

Additional Example 1

a. Find the sum of $\sum_{k=1}^{5} 3k$. 45

LESSON **105**

Finding Arithmetic Series

Warm Up

1. **Vocabulary** In an arithmetic sequence, the ________ is the difference between successive terms. common difference (92)

2. Find the next three terms of the arithmetic sequence −2, −5, −8, −11, ... (92)

3. Find the 14th term of the arithmetic sequence 11, 18, 25, 32, ... 102 (92)

2. −14, −17, −20

New Concepts

Recall that a sequence is an ordered list of numbers, or terms. Some sequences are arithmetic, with common differences, and some are geometric, with common ratios.

A **series** is the indicated sum of the terms of a sequence. An **arithmetic series** is the sum of the terms of an arithmetic sequence. It can be finite or infinite.

Arithmetic Sequence	Arithmetic Series
4, 9, 14, 19	4 + 9 + 14 + 19
8, 5, 2, −1, ...	8 + 5 + 2 + (−1) + ...

Math Language

The *indicated sum* is the expression that shows each addend. The *sum* is the actual result of adding the terms.

The sum, S, of a finite sequence is the sum of its terms. An infinite series does not have a sum, but it does have partial sums. A partial sum is the sum of the first n terms, indicated by S_n. For $8 + 5 + 2 + (-1) + \ldots$, S_4 is the sum of the first four terms, so $S_4 = 14$.

A shorthand way of writing a series is to use **summation notation**, sometimes called **sigma notation**, because it uses the Greek letter sigma, Σ.

Summation Notation

For the series $\sum_{k=1}^{n} a_k = a_1 + a_2 + a_3 + \ldots + a_n$, the integer k is called the index, 1 is the lower limit of summation, and n is the upper limit of summation.

Example 1 Finding the Sum of an Arithmetic Series Given in Summation Notation

a. Find the sum of $\sum_{k=1}^{6} 2k$.

SOLUTION Write the indicated sum by replacing k with the given limits of summation. Then add the terms of the series.

$$\sum_{k=1}^{6} 2k = 2(1) + 2(2) + 2(3) + 2(4) + 2(5) + 2(6)$$
$$= 2 + 4 + 6 + 8 + 10 + 12$$
$$= 42$$

LESSON RESOURCES

Student Edition Practice Workbook 105
Reteaching Master 105
Adaptations Master 105
Challenge and Enrichment Master C105

MATH BACKGROUND

A series is an indicated sum, so the phrase *sum of the series* can be confusing. (Taken literally, it means *sum of the indicated sum.*) *Sum of the series* is the traditional phrase for *value of the series*. So, for example, 3 + 6 + 9 + 12 is a series because it is an indicated sum. The sum of the series, or its value, is 30.

A finite series can be represented by $\sum_{k=1}^{n} a_k$, where k is called the index of summation, 1 is the lower limit of summation, and n is the upper limit of summation. An infinite series can be represented by $\sum_{k=1}^{\infty} a_k$.

The word series is both singular (*a series*) and plural (*several series*). If an infinite series has a real number value, then it is *convergent*. However, no infinite arithmetic series is convergent.

b. Find the sum of $\sum_{k=3}^{7} 10 - k$.

SOLUTION

$$\sum_{k=3}^{7} 10 - k = (10 - 3) + (10 - 4) + (10 - 5) + (10 - 6) + (10 - 7)$$
$$= 7 + 6 + 5 + 4 + 3$$
$$= 25$$

Caution

The lower limit of summation is often 1, but it does not have to be.

Example 2 Writing an Arithmetic Series in Summation Notation

Write each arithmetic series in summation notation.

a. $5 + 10 + 15 + 20$

SOLUTION *Think:* The terms increase by 5. Each is a multiple of 5, so the rule is $5k$.

$\sum 5k$ Write the rule.

$\sum_{k=1}^{4} 5k$ Determine the limits of summation.

b. $14 + 11 + 8 + 5 + 2 + (-1)$

SOLUTION *Think:* The terms decrease by 3, so $3k$ is part of the rule. The first term is 14, so $3k$ must be 0 for the first term.

$\sum 14 - 3k$ Write the rule.

$\sum_{k=0}^{5} 14 - 3k$ Determine the limits of summation.

A formula for the sum of an arithmetic series can be found by writing an arithmetic series forwards and backwards and then adding the series.

Hint

Notice that the vertical addends are the first and last term, then the second and next to the last term, and so on.

Consider the series $3 + 7 + 11 + 15 + 19 + 23 + 27$.

$$S_7 = 3 + 7 + 11 + 15 + 19 + 23 + 27$$
$$S_7 = 27 + 23 + 19 + 15 + 11 + 7 + 3$$
$$2S_7 = 30 + 30 + 30 + 30 + 30 + 30 + 30$$
$$2S_7 = 7(30)$$
$$S_7 = \frac{7(30)}{2}$$

Notice that $7 = n$ and $30 = a_1 + a_n$. Then, $S_n = \frac{n(a_1 + a_n)}{2} = \frac{n}{2}(a_1 + a_2)$.

Sum of a Finite Arithmetic Series
The sum of the first n terms of an arithmetic series, S_n, is $\frac{n}{2}(a_1 + a_2)$.

A **partial sum** is the sum S_n of a specified number of terms, n, of an infinite series.

Additional Example 1

b. Find the sum of $\sum_{k=5}^{10} 2 - k$. -33

Extend the Example

Let S_n represent the nth partial sum of the infinite arithmetic sequence 9, 6, 3, 0,.... Find S_7. 0

Example 2

The example shows how to write summation notation for a series. There are two basic steps. First find a rule, and then find the limits of summation (values of k so that the rule yields the correct terms a_k).

Additional Example 2

Write each arithmetic series in summation notation.

a. $8 + 16 + 24 + 32 + 40$ $\sum_{k=1}^{5} 8k$

b. $20 + 14 + 8 + 2 + (-4)$ $\sum_{k=0}^{4} 20 - 6k$

ALTERNATE METHOD FOR EXAMPLE 2b

There is more than one summation notation for any series. If it is desirable to use $3k$ as part of the rule and $k = 1$ for the first term, then ask: From what number do I need to subtract 3(1) to obtain 14? That number is 17, so the rule $17 - 3k$ can be used. Therefore, a different summation notation for the series

$14 + 11 + 8 + 5 + 2 + (-1)$ is $\sum_{k=1}^{6} 17 - 3k$.

Example 3

To find the partial sum S_n, students must know the value of the first and nth term of the series.

Additional Example 3

a. Find the partial sum S_{20} for the infinite arithmetic series $5 + 12 + 19 + 26 + ...$ 1430

b. Evaluate the series $\sum_{k=1}^{17}(5k - 4)$. 697

Example 4

Fitness programs that involve a constant increase in time or distance can be represented by a series.

Additional Example 4

A manager of a new clothing store sets a goal of selling \$120,000 worth of clothes in the first month, and to increase sales by \$15,000 each month for the next 7 months. Find the total sales for the first 8 months that will be required if the goal is to be met. \$1,380,000

Example 3 Finding the Sum of the First *n* Terms of a Series

a. Find the partial sum S_{12} for the infinite arithmetic series $6 + 14 + 22 + 30 + ...$

SOLUTION The formula for the sum requires a_1, which is given, and a_{12}, which can be found once the common difference, d, is known.

$d = 30 - 22 = 8$ Subtract to find d.

$a_{12} = 6 + (12 - 1)(8)$ $a_n = a_1 + (n - 1)d$

$a_{12} = 94$ Simplify.

Now use $S_n = \frac{n}{2}(a_1 + a_2)$.

$S_{12} = \frac{12}{2}(6 + 94)$ Substitute 12 for n, 6 for a_1, and 94 for a_{12}.

$S_{12} = 600$ Simplify.

b. Evaluate the series $\sum_{k=1}^{20}(3 + 2k)$.

SOLUTION Substitute 1 and 20 for k to find a_1 and a_{20}.

$a_1 = 3 + 2(1) = 5$

$a_{20} = 3 + 2(20) = 43$

Now use $S_n = \frac{n}{2}(a_1 + a_2)$.

$S_{20} = \frac{20}{2}(5 + 43)$ Substitute 20 for n, 5 for a_1, and 43 for a_{20}.

$S_{20} = 480$ Simplify.

Check by using a graphing calculator.

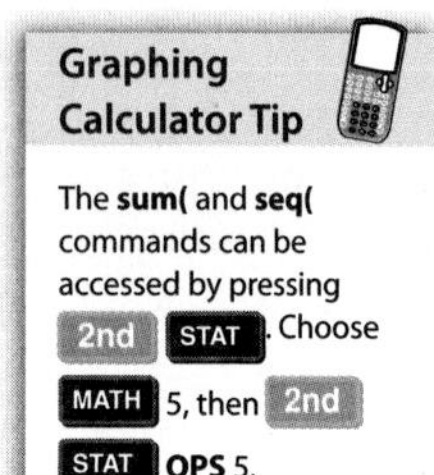

Graphing Calculator Tip
The sum(and seq(commands can be accessed by pressing 2nd STAT. Choose MATH 5, then 2nd STAT OPS 5.

Example 4 Application: Exercise

An athlete is on a 10-day running plan. On the plan, the athlete is to run 3 miles on the first day, and on each day thereafter, run 0.5 mile longer than the previous day. How many total miles will the athlete have run while on the plan?

SOLUTION

1. **Understand** The miles ran each day form a finite arithmetic sequence. The sum of the miles form an arithmetic series.

2. **Plan** Find a_{10} so that S_{10} can be calculated.

INCLUSION

Have students work in small groups. Write a finite arithmetic sequence on the chalkboard. Then each group works together to write the associated series, summation notation for the series, and the sum (value) of the series. An example is shown below.Leader: 9, 15, 21, 27, 33

Group: $9 + 15 + 21 + 27 + 33$

$$\sum_{k=0}^{4}(9 + 6k) = 105$$

Math Reasoning

Justify In the Check, why do the limits of summation of $3 + 0.5x$ go from 0 to 9?

It begins with 0 so that the first term is 3, and ends in 9 because there are 10 terms.

3. Solve Use $a_n = a_1 + (n - 1)d$ to find a_{10}.

$$a_{10} = 3 + (10 - 1)(0.5)$$
$$a_{10} = 7.5$$

Use $S_n = n\left(\frac{a_1 + a_n}{2}\right)$ to find S_{10}.

$$S_{10} = 10\left(\frac{3 + 7.5}{2}\right)$$
$$S_{10} = 52.5$$

The athlete will have run a total of 52.5 miles on the plan.

4. Check Use a graphing calculator.

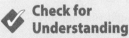

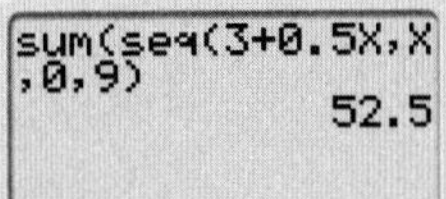

Lesson Practice

a. (Ex 1) Find the sum of $\sum_{k=1}^{10} k$. 55

b. (Ex 1) Find the sum of $\sum_{k=1}^{4} 5 + 2k$. 40

Write each arithmetic series in summation notation.

c. (Ex 2) $8 + 16 + 24 + 32 + 40 + 48$ $\sum_{k=1}^{6} 8k$

d. (Ex 2) $25 + 28 + 31 + 34$ $\sum_{k=0}^{3} 25 + 3k$

e. (Ex 3) Find S_{18} for the arithmetic series $5 + (-5) + (-15) + (-25) + \ldots$ -1440

f. (Ex 3) Evaluate the series $\sum_{k=1}^{33} 6k$. 3366

g. (Ex 4) An athlete is on a 7-day bicycling plan. On the plan, the athlete is to bike 6 miles on the first day, and on each day thereafter, bike 1.5 miles longer than the previous day. How many total miles will the athlete have biked while on the plan? 73.5 miles

Practice Distributed and Integrated

***1.** (95) Let $f(x) = x^4$ and $g(x) = x^2 - 5x + 6$. Find $P(3)$ for $P(x) = f(g(x))$. $P(3) = 0$

***2.** (105) **Verify** The first and second terms of an arithmetic sequence are 48 and 30 respectively. Show that the sum of the first 16 terms is -1392. See Additional Answers.

***3.** (104) **Multiple Choice** The graph is a translation of the graph of $f(x) = \sqrt{x}$. Choose the letter of the equation that best represents the graph. D

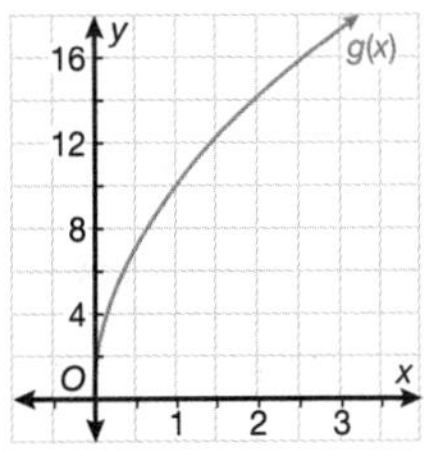

A $g(x) = \sqrt{x + 10}$ **B** $g(x) = \frac{1}{10}\sqrt{x}$

C $g(x) = \sqrt{x} + 10$ **D** $g(x) = 10\sqrt{x}$

ENGLISH LEARNERS

Explain the meanings of sequence and series. Emphasize that a sequence is a list and a series is a sum.

Say: **"A sequence is an ordered list of numbers, called terms. A series is a sum of terms."**

Write on the board, reading the words:

2, 4, 6, 8 sequence

2 + 4 + 6 + 8 series

Ask students for the sum (value) of the series. 20

Lesson Practice

Problem e

Error Alert Students might look at the first two terms and conclude that $d = 0$. Have them look at other terms to see that this cannot be true.

Problem f

Scaffolding Students must first substitute 1 and 33 for k to find the first and last terms.

Check for Understanding

The questions below help assess the concepts taught in this lesson.

1. **"Explain what a series is and how it is related to a sequence."** Sample: A series is an indicated sum of the terms of a sequence.
2. **"How is summation notation useful?"** Sample: It allows you to represent a series without writing all the terms.
3. **"Describe in words how to find the sum of the first *n* terms of a finite arithmetic series."** Sample: Add the first and last terms and then multiply that result by the quotient of *n* and 2.

3 Practice

Math Conversations

Discussions to strengthen understanding

Problem 1

Guide students by asking them the following questions.

"How do you indicate $P(3)$, using the letters f and g?" $f(g(3))$

"To evaluate $f(g(3))$, what should be evaluated first?" $g(3)$

Problem 6

Error Alert

Given a fixed perimeter, the rectangle with maximum area is a square. Students might incorrectly infer that the rectangle with the maximum possible area in this problem is a square. Point out that there is no condition placed on the perimeter of the rectangle.

Problem 12

"What should you multiply both sides of the equation by to eliminate the denominator?" $(r + w)(r - w)$

"How can you isolate d on the right side?" Factor out d and then divide.

***4.** (104) **Retirement Funds** A Teachers Retirement System paid out an interest rate of 4% compounded annually from 1920 to 1955. The function $A(x) = P \cdot 1.04^x$ can be used to calculate the amount in the account, $A(x)$, after x years with the original amount placed in the account, P. Use the function $f(x) = 1.04^x$ to sketch a graph of the equation $A(x) = P \cdot 1.04^x$ if the original amount in the account is $1,000. See Additional Answers.

5. (83) Write a quadratic equation whose root is 7. $x^2 - 14x + 49 = 0$

***6.** (101) **Coordinate Geometry** A rectangle has a side on the x-axis, a side on the y-axis, and a vertex in Quadrant I on the graph of $y = -\frac{1}{4}x^2 + 6$. Find the maximum possible area of the rectangle and the corresponding vertex (x, y). Maximum area ≈ 11.31 square units; $x \approx 2.83$, $y = 4$

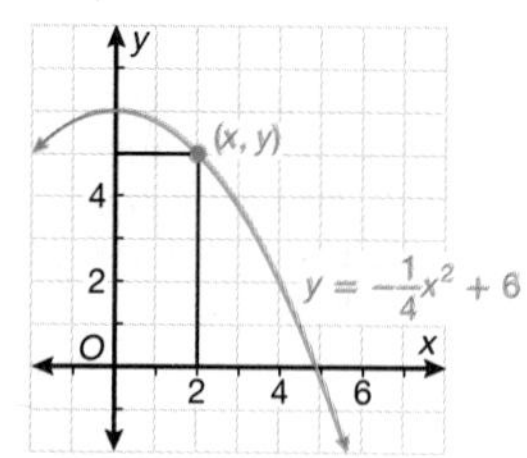

7. (10) **Geometry** A triangle has a base of 10 cm and a height of x cm. Write and solve an inequality for all the values of x that will result in a triangle with an area of at least 95 cm. $\frac{1}{2}bh \geq 95$; $\frac{1}{2}(10)x \geq 95$; $5x \geq 95$; $x \geq 19$

8. (69) Graph each of the complex numbers on the same coordinate plane. See Additional Answers.

a. $2i$ **b.** $-4i$ **c.** $3 + i$

9. (92) Find the 4th term of an arithmetic sequence if the first term is 6.2 and the 19th term is 33.2. 10.7

10. (9) **Cafeteria** C.J., Lyle, and Avery had lunch together. C.J. bought 1 drink, 3 sandwiches, and 3 snacks. Lyle bought 2 drinks, 1 sandwich, and 4 snacks. Avery bought 2 drinks, 2 sandwiches, and 5 snacks. The cost of a drink is $1.00, a sandwich is $3.50, and a snack is $1.50. Use matrices to determine how much each person spent and who spent the most money. See Additional Answers.

11. (32) Use an inverse matrix to solve the linear system given by $\begin{aligned} -3x + y - 8z &= 18 \\ x - 2y + z &= 11 \\ 2x - 2y + 5z &= -17 \end{aligned}$.
$x = 46.4$, $y = 8.4$, $z = -18.6$

12. (88) **Jet Stream** The jet stream is a wind pattern. Between London and New York the jet stream generally blows west to east, sometimes at hundreds of miles per hour. The total time t (in hours) of a round-trip flight is modeled by the equation $t = \frac{d}{r - w} + \frac{d}{r + w}$, where r is the average speed of the plane in miles per hour, w is the average speed of the jet stream in miles per hour, and d is the one-way distance in miles.

a. Solve the equation for d. $d = \frac{t(r - w)(r + w)}{2r}$

b. If the average speed of a plane is 500 miles per hour and the average speed of the jet stream is 100 miles per hour, then it would take 14.4 hours for a round-trip flight from London to New York. Find the distance from London to New York. 3456 miles

***13.** (105) **Graphing Calculator** Use the **sum(seq(** commands to find the sum of $\sum_{k=1}^{100} 4.25k$.
21,462.5

CHALLENGE

You are writing a 5-year business plan for a retail store. The sales goal for the first year is $400,000. The sales goal for all 5 years is $3,000,000. Assuming a constant annual increase in sales, what annual increase is necessary for this business plan? Show how to find your answer. $100,000 increase each year

$$S_n = n\left(\frac{a_1 + a_n}{2}\right)$$
$$3{,}000{,}000 = 5\left(\frac{400{,}000 + a_5}{2}\right)$$
$$800{,}000 = a_5$$
$$a_n = a_1 + (n - 1)d$$
$$800{,}000 = 400{,}000 + (5 - 1)d$$
$$100{,}000 = d$$

*14. Evaluate the series $\sum_{k=1}^{10}(8 - 3k)$. -85
(105)

15. **Error Analysis** Explain and correct the error made in the steps shown below. See Additional Answers.
(84)

$$\frac{2}{3x+6} + 4 = \frac{1}{2} \rightarrow {}^{2}\cancel{6}\cancel{(x+2)}\left(\frac{2}{\cancel{3}\cancel{(x+2)}} + 4\right) = {}^{3}\cancel{6}(x+2)\left(\frac{1}{\cancel{2}}\right) \rightarrow 4 + 8 = 3x + 6$$

*16. **Government** Suppose counties in the state of California had the option to donate an equal amount of money towards a \$500,000 donation to be given to a charity. Write and solve an inequality to show the number of counties whose participation would bring the cost per county to less than \$14,000. There are 58 counties in California.
(94)
$\frac{500{,}000}{x} < 14{,}000$, between 36 and 58 counties

17. **Multiple Choice** Which of the following is not a root of $f(x) = 8x^3 - 18x^2 + 3x + 2$? A
(85)

A -3 B $-\frac{1}{4}$ C $\frac{1}{2}$ D 2

18. **Multi-Step** Use the properties of logarithms to rewrite the expression $\log_3(9x)^5$. Evaluate the expression when $x = 81$. $10 + 5\log_3 x$; $10 + 5\log_3 81 = 30$
(87)

19. **Surveying** Derive an equation that a surveyor can use to find the height (h) of a mountain given the angle of elevation (θ) and the distance from the mountain (d).
(90)
$h = d\tan\theta$

20. Solve the system $\begin{aligned} 3x - y &= 2 \\ 6x + 3y &= 14 \end{aligned}$ by substitution. The solution is $\left(\frac{4}{3}, 2\right)$.
(21)

21. **Analyze** Is a circle a function? Why or why not? Sample: No, there are several x-values that are paired to two different y-values.
(91)

*22. **Write** Explain why the inequalities $2(3)^x < 310$ and $\log 2 + x \log 3 < \log 310$ are equivalent. See Additional Answers.
(93)

23. Solve the compound inequality $4 < 3x + 1 \leq 10$ by writing and solving two inequalities. Show the steps you followed to reach your answers.
(10)
See Additional Answers.

24. A line has slope 5 and crosses the y-axis at $(0, 3)$. What is the equation of the line written in slope-intercept form? $y = 5x + 3$
(26)

25. **Write** Explain how to simplify this problem: 12.65 in. + 30.1 in. + 15.843 in.
(18)

25. First add the numbers together, which is 58.593. Then you have to round to one decimal place because of significant digits, which is 58.6 in.

26. Determine if $(7, 19)$ is a solution of the inequality $y > 4x + 8$. No
(39)

Evaluate each piecewise function for $x = -2$ and $x = 0$.

27. $f(x) = \begin{cases} 7x, & \text{if } x < -2 \\ 0, & \text{if } x \geq -2 \end{cases}$
(79)
$f(-2) = 0$; $f(0) = 0$

28. $f(x) = \begin{cases} 15, & \text{if } x \leq -2 \\ -x^2, & \text{if } -2 < x \leq 0 \\ 2 + x, & \text{if } x > 0 \end{cases}$
(79)
$f(-2) = 15$; $f(0) = 0$

*29. **Estimate** Estimate the solution to $1 + \log x = 3.998$. Explain your method.
(102)
Sample: $x \approx 1000$; The solution to $1 + \log x = 4$ is $x = 1000$.

30. Convert $\log_8 (9x)^2$ to base 10. Then evaluate when $x = 4$. $2\left(\frac{\log(9x)}{\log 8}\right)$; $x \approx 3.45$
(87)

Problem 21

Extend the Problem

Write an equation of the circle with radius 3 and center $(0, 0)$. Then write two functions y_1 and y_2 whose graphs together form that circle.

$x^2 + y^2 = 9$; $y_1 = \sqrt{9 - x^2}$; $y_2 = -\sqrt{9 - x^2}$

Problem 24

Extend the Problem

Write the equation in standard form. $-5x + y = 3$

LOOKING FORWARD 

Finding arithmetic series prepares students for

- **Lesson 113** Using Geometric Series

Lesson 105 737

LESSON 106

1 Warm Up

Remind students to use the coefficient of the leading term and the constant when finding possible rational roots.

2 New Concepts

In this lesson, students learn the **Fundamental Theorem of Algebra**.

Remind students that the degree of an equation is the largest degree of all the terms.

LESSON 106

Using the Fundamental Theorem of Algebra

Warm Up

1. **Vocabulary** The multiplicity of a root r is the number of times $x - r$ appears as a factor. (66)

2. Use synthetic division to determine if $x + 1$ is a factor of $P(x) = 15x^3 + 22x^2 + 5x - 2$. If so, give the remaining quadratic factor. (61) 2. Yes, $15x^2 + 7x - 2$

3. Use the Rational Root Theorem to identify the possible rational roots of $x^3 - 2x^2 - 9x + 18 = 0$ (66) $\pm1, \pm2, \pm3, \pm6, \pm9, \pm18$

4. Identify all the real roots of $4x^5 - 8x^4 - 32x^3 = 0$. (66) 0, −2, 4

New Concepts

Making Conjectures About Roots of Polynomial Functions

Complete the table. Include multiplicities in the last column.

$P(x)$	Factored Form of $P(x)$	Roots of $P(x) = 0$	Number of Roots
$x^2 - 16$	$(x + 4)(x - 4)$	−4, 4	2
$x^3 - 5x^2 + 8x - 4$	$(x - 1)(x - 2)^2$	1, 2	3
$x^5 - x^4 - 2x^3$	$x^3(x + 1)(x - 2)$	−1, 0, 2	5
$x^4 - 9x^2$	$x^2(x + 3)(x - 3)$	−3, 0, 3	4
$x^5 - 3x^4 - 10x^3$	$x^3(x - 5)(x + 2)$	−2, 0, 5	5

Look for a pattern in the table. Make a conjecture about the number of roots and $P(x)$. Based on your conjecture, what would you say about the roots of $x^{10} - 5x^7 + 12x = 0$? The degree of the polynomial is the number of roots. There would be ten roots.

Hint

Remember that the set of complex numbers includes the real and the imaginary numbers.

The degree of every function in the exploration is the same as the number of roots of the related equation. This is true for all polynomials and is described in the following theorem.

Fundamental Theorem of Algebra
The **Fundamental Theorem of Algebra** states that every polynomial function of degree $n \geq 1$ has at least one zero in the set of complex numbers. A corollary of the theorem is that, including multiplicities, a polynomial function of degree $n \geq 1$ has exactly n zeros.

Online Connection
www.SaxonMathResources.com

In other words, a function of degree n has n zeros, so a polynomial equation of degree n has n roots. These roots may be real or complex.

LESSON RESOURCES

Student Edition Practice Workbook 106
Reteaching Master 106
Adaptations Master 106
Challenge and Enrichment Master C106

MATH BACKGROUND

Previously, students have learned to find real and/or complex roots of polynomials as well as state the multiplicity of a root. The Fundamental Theorem of Algebra combines these pieces of information. This theorem shows that the system of complex numbers is sufficient to provide solutions to any polynomial written with complex numbers. Carl Friedrich Gauss is credited with the first proof of the Fundamental Theorem of Algebra.

Point out to students that the theorem does not provide a way to find the roots, it simply proves the roots exist. In fact, Evariste Galois has proved that there will never be a general formula for solving polynomials of degree 5 or higher.

A quadratic function always has two zeros, so a quadratic equation always has two roots: either two distinct real roots, one real root with multiplicity of 2, or two complex roots.

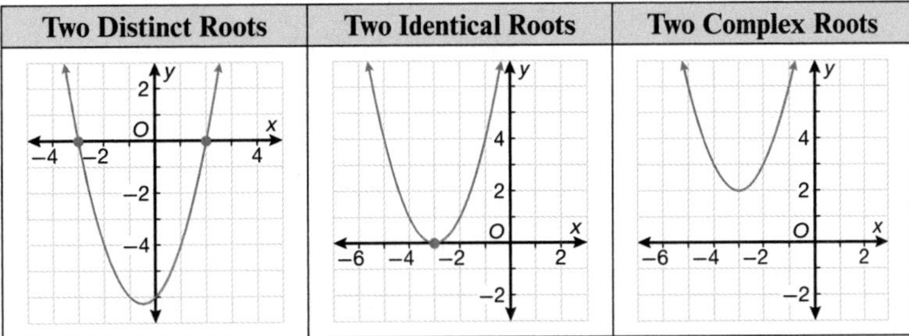

Two Distinct Roots
Two Identical Roots
Two Complex Roots

A cubic function also has three possible cases. These are: three distinct roots, three real roots, one of which has a multiplicity of 2, one root of multiplicity 3, or one real root and two complex roots.

Example 1 Finding Roots of Cubic Equations

a. Solve $x^3 + 12x^2 + 44x + 48 = 0$ by finding all the roots.

SOLUTION Identify possible roots by using the Rational Root Theorem: $\pm48, \pm24, \pm16, \pm12, \pm8, \pm6, \pm4, \pm3, \pm2, \pm1$. Test roots by using synthetic division.

$$\begin{array}{r|rrrr} -6 & 1 & 12 & 44 & 48 \\ & & -6 & -36 & -48 \\ \hline & 1 & 6 & 8 & 0 \end{array} \quad (x + 6) \text{ is a factor.}$$

The equation can be written as $(x + 6)(x^2 + 6x + 8) = 0$.

Factor the quadratic, and the equation is $(x + 6)(x + 2)(x + 4) = 0$, making the solutions -6, -2, and -4.

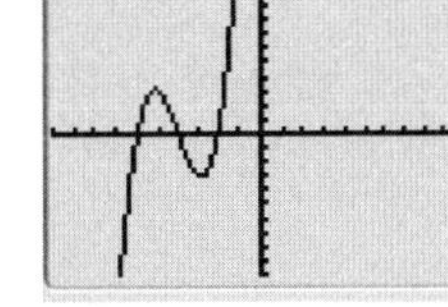

The graph of $y = x^3 + 12x^2 + 44x + 48$ has three real roots.

b. Solve $x^3 - 4x^2 + 4x = 0$ by finding all the roots.

SOLUTION Possible roots are $\pm4, \pm2, \pm1$.

$$\begin{array}{r|rrr} 2 & 1 & -4 & 4 \\ & & 2 & -4 \\ \hline & 1 & -2 & 0 \end{array} \quad (x - 2) \text{ is a factor.}$$

The equation can be written as $(x - 2)(x^2 - 2x) = 0$. The quadratic has a GCF of x, so the equation can be written as $(x - 2)(x)(x - 2) = 0$, or $x(x - 2)^2 = 0$. The solutions are 0 and 2.

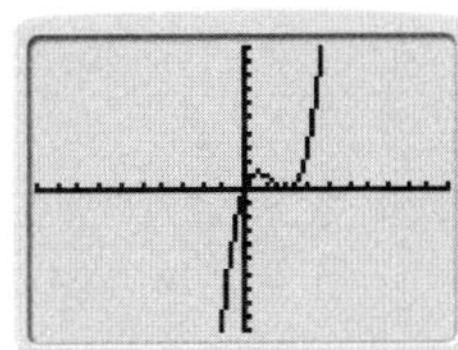

The graph of $y = x^3 - 4x^2 + 4x$ has three real roots, one of which has a multiplicity of 2.

Hint

Start with the smaller possible roots, so that the calculations are easier.

Example 1

Every cubic function has three roots.

Additional Example 1

a. Solve $x^3 + x^2 - 22x - 40 = 0$ by finding all the roots.
The solutions are -4, -2, and 5.

b. Solve $x^3 - 8x^2 + 16x = 0$ by finding all the roots.
The solutions are 0 and 4.

Error Alert Students might use synthetic division to test several roots without using the remaining quadratic. Remind students that if a factor is found, they can use synthetic division to test the roots of the new smaller polynomial factor.

TEACHER TIP

Tell students to use whatever factoring method they choose to factor in the quickest possible way. For example, students can take out the common factor of x in the equation $x^3 - 4x^2 + 4x = 0$ in Example 1b to yield $x(x^2 - 4x + 4) = 0$. Point out that the quadratic can be factored as $(x - 2)^2$.

ALTERNATE METHOD FOR EXAMPLE 1

Have students test smaller factors by substituting the possible factor into the equation. Afterward, explain that since substitution is a time-consuming process, it is best used to check answers after using the Rational Root Theorem.

$(1)^3 + 12(1)^2 + 44(1) + 48 \neq 0$

$(-1)^3 + 12(-1)^2 + 44(-1) + 48 \neq 0$

$(2)^3 + 12(2)^2 + 44(2) + 48 \neq 0$

$(-2)^3 + 12(-2)^2 + 44(-2) + 48 = 0$

When the factor is found, use synthetic division to find the remaining factors.

Additional Example 1

c. Solve $x^3 - 5x^2 - 7x + 51 = 0$ by finding all the roots. The solutions are -3, $4 + i$, and $4 - i$.

Example 2

A graphing calculator can be used to identify rational roots. This can be a huge time saver.

Additional Example 2

a. Solve $2x^4 + 7x^3 + 23x^2 + 112x - 144 = 0$ by finding all the roots. $1, -4.5, 4i, -4i$

TEACHER TIP

Remind students that if they find a root, the remaining possible roots can be tested on the unfactored polynomial. In general, tell students to use the integer first to find the unfactored polynomial before using the rational number. This might reduce calculations with the decimal.

c. Solve $x^3 - 9x^2 + 25x - 25 = 0$ by finding all the roots.

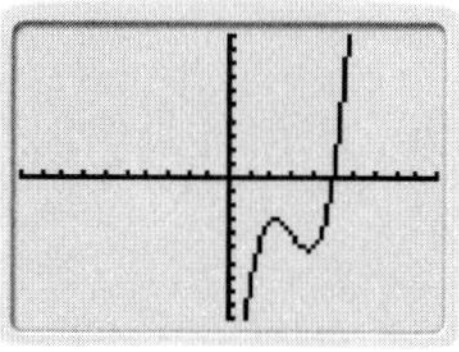

SOLUTION Possible roots are $\pm 25, \pm 5, \pm 1$.

$$\begin{array}{r|rrrr} 5 & 1 & -9 & 25 & -25 \\ & & 5 & -20 & 25 \\ \hline & 1 & -4 & 5 & 0 \end{array} \quad (x - 5) \text{ is a factor.}$$

The equation can be written as $(x - 5)(x^2 - 4x + 5) = 0$.

The quadratic cannot be factored; use the Quadratic Formula.

$$x = \frac{4 \pm \sqrt{16 - 4(1)(5)}}{2} = \frac{4 \pm \sqrt{-4}}{2} = \frac{4 \pm 2i}{2} = 2 \pm i$$

The solutions are 5, $2 + i$, and $2 - i$. The graph of $y = x^3 - 9x^2 + 25x - 25$ illustrates one real root and two complex roots.

Math Reasoning

Justify Why must a cubic equation have at least one real root?

Because the two ends of the graph of a cubic function head in opposite directions, the graph must eventually intersect the x-axis in at least once.

To find roots of equations whose polynomial is of a degree greater than three, it helps to use a graphing calculator to first identify the rational roots. Then use algebra to find any complex roots and/or the exact values of the irrational roots, since a graphing calculator only approximates irrational roots.

Example 2 Finding Roots of Polynomials with Degree > 3

a. Solve $2x^4 - 3x^3 + 4x^2 - 27x - 126 = 0$ by finding all the roots.

SOLUTION A graphing calculator shows that -2 and 3.5 are roots.

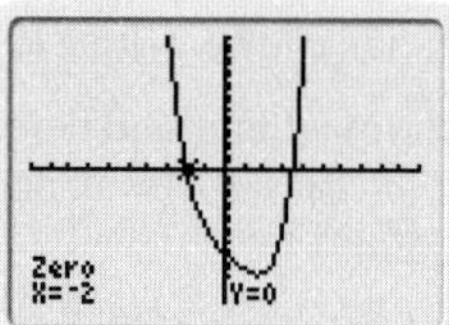

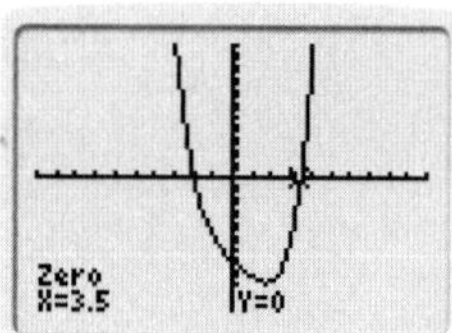

Use synthetic division to find the remaining unfactored polynomial.

$$\begin{array}{r|rrrrr} -2 & 2 & -3 & 4 & -27 & -126 \\ & & -4 & 14 & -36 & 126 \\ \hline & 2 & -7 & 18 & -63 & 0 \end{array} \qquad \begin{array}{r|rrrr} 3.5 & 2 & -7 & 18 & -63 \\ & & 7 & 0 & 63 \\ \hline & 2 & 0 & 18 & 0 \end{array}$$

The equation can be written as $(x + 2)(x - 3.5)(2x^2 + 18) = 0$ or $2(x + 2)(x - 3.5)(x^2 + 9) = 0$. Solve $x^2 + 9 = 0$ to find the complex factors.

$$x^2 + 9 = 0$$
$$x^2 = -9$$
$$x = \pm\sqrt{-9} = \pm 3i$$

The four solutions are -2, 3.5, $3i$ and $-3i$.

ENGLISH LEARNERS

The words real and complex are used to describe the Fundamental Theorem of Algebra. Explain the meanings of **real** and **complex**. Say:

"An object is said to be real if it occurs in fact or actuality. An object is said to be complex if it is complicated. In math, a real root means the root occurs where the graph crosses the x-axis. A complex root occurs on an 'imaginary' axis."

Write the following roots on the board:

$4, -5, \frac{2}{3}, \pm 4i, 1 \pm \sqrt{3}$

Have students identify which would be considered real roots and which would be considered complex roots.

b. Solve $x^5 - x^4 - 14x^3 - 26x^2 - 19x - 5 = 0$ by finding all the roots.

SOLUTION A graphing calculator shows that −1 and 5 are roots.

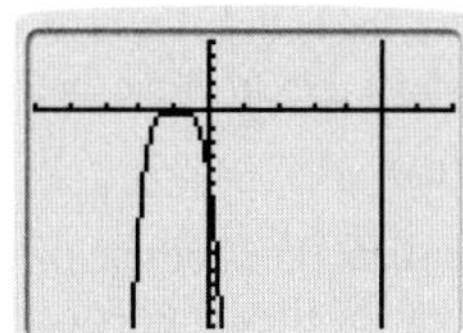

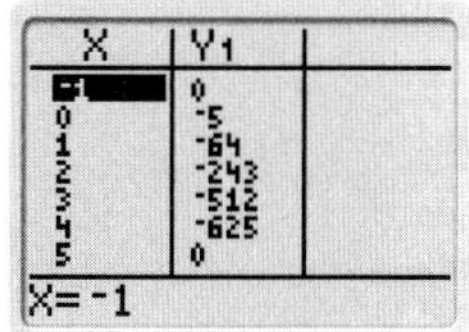

Use synthetic division to find the remaining unfactored polynomial.

$$\begin{array}{r|rrrrrr} 5 & 1 & -1 & -14 & -26 & -19 & -5 \\ & & 5 & 20 & 30 & 20 & 5 \\ \hline & 1 & 4 & 6 & 4 & 1 & 0 \end{array} \qquad \begin{array}{r|rrrrr} -1 & 1 & 4 & 6 & 4 & 1 \\ & & -1 & -3 & -3 & -1 \\ \hline & 1 & 3 & 3 & 1 & 0 \end{array}$$

By the Rational Root Theorem, the equation $x^3 + 3x^2 + 3x + 1 = 0$ has possible roots of −1 or 1. Continue to use synthetic division to check if −1 is a multiple root.

$$\begin{array}{r|rrrr} -1 & 1 & 3 & 3 & 1 \\ & & -1 & -2 & -1 \\ \hline & 1 & 2 & 1 & 0 \end{array} \qquad \begin{array}{r|rrr} -1 & 1 & 2 & 1 \\ & & -1 & -1 \\ \hline & 1 & 1 & 0 \end{array}$$

$x^5 - x^4 - 14x^3 - 26x^2 - 19x - 5 = 0$

$(x + 1)(x + 1)(x + 1)(x + 1)(x + 5) = 0$

The root of −1 has a multiplicity of 4, and the root of 5 has a multiplicity of 1.

The solutions are −1 and 5.

Math Reasoning

Verify Show by factoring that $x^2 + 2x + 1 = 0$ has a double root of −1.

$x^2 + 2x + 1 = 0$
$(x + 1)(x + 1) = 0$
$x + 1 = 0$ or $x + 1 = 0$
$x = -1$ or $x = -1$

Notice in the graph of $y = x^5 - x^4 - 14x^3 - 26x^2 - 19x - 5$ above, the graph touches but does not cross the root of −1, while it crosses at the root of 5. A graph will always touch but not cross when the root has an even-numbered multiplicity and cross at an odd-numbered multiplicity.

Remember, just as irrational roots come in conjugate pairs, $a \pm b\sqrt{c}$, complex roots always come in conjugate pairs, $a \pm bi$.

Example 3 Using Conjugates to Write a Polynomial Function

Write the lowest degreed polynomial function with zeros $5 + i$ and $1 + \sqrt{3}$.

SOLUTION Because both irrational and complex roots come in pairs, there are four roots: $5 + i, 5 - i, 1 + \sqrt{3}, 1 - \sqrt{3}$. Begin by writing the function as the product of the factors. Then multiply carefully.

$P(x) = (x - (5 + i))(x - (5 - i))\left(x - (1 + \sqrt{3})\right)\left(x - (1 - \sqrt{3})\right)$

$P(x) = ((x - 5 - i)(x - 5 + i))\left((x - 1 - \sqrt{3})(x - 1 + \sqrt{3})\right)$

$P(x) = (x^2 - 5x + ix - 5x + 25 - 5i - ix + 5i - i^2) \cdot$
$(x^2 - x + x\sqrt{3} - x + 1 - \sqrt{3} - x\sqrt{3} + \sqrt{3} - 3)$

$P(x) = (x^2 - 10x + 26)(x^2 - 2x - 2) = x^4 - 12x^3 + 44x^2 - 32x - 52$

Example 2

Extend the Example

Tell students to show how to check answers in problem **2b** by using the roots to find factors that when multiplied will result in the original polynomial.

$(x - 5)(x + 1)^4$
$= (x - 5)(x + 1)^2(x + 1)^2$
$= (x - 5)(x^2 + 2x + 1)(x^2 + 2x + 1)$
$= (x - 5)(x^4 + 4x^3 + 6x^2 + 4x + 1)$
$= x^5 - x^4 - 14x^3 - 26x^2 - 19x - 5$

Additional Example 2

b. Solve $x^5 + 2x^4 - 39x^3 + 16x^2 + 260x - 336 = 0$ by finding all the roots.
2, 2, −3, 4, −7

Example 3

Remind students to pay close attention to distributing signs when multiplying factors.

Additional Example 3

Write the simplest polynomial function with zeros $2 + i$ and $1 + \sqrt{5}$.
$P(x) = x^4 - 6x^3 + 9x^2 + 6x - 20$

Error Alert Most errors are made when students do not multiply carefully. After reading through Example 3, tell students to close their textbooks and write a polynomial function using the zeros given: $5 + i$ and $1 + \sqrt{3}$. Then have students check their work against the example shown to determine if they are multiplying correctly.

ALTERNATE METHOD FOR EXAMPLE 3

Students may also multiply by using the difference of squares. This method will be shown on the first two terms. Have the student use the method on the second two terms.

$(x - (5 + i))(x - (5 - i))$		$\left(x - (1 + \sqrt{3})\right)\left(x - (1 - \sqrt{3})\right)$
$= ((x - 5) - i)((x - 5) + i)$	*regroup*	$= \left((x - 1) - \sqrt{3}\right)\left((x - 1) + \sqrt{3}\right)$
$= (x - 5)^2 - i^2$	*multiply*	$= (x - 1)^2 - (\sqrt{3})^2$
$= x^2 - 10x + 25 + 1$	*simplify*	$= x^2 - 2x + 1 - 3$
$= x^2 - 10x + 26$		$= x^2 - 2x - 2$

Example 4

Students will solve a real-life problem by finding roots for a polynomial of degree 3.

Additional Example 4

A grain silo is shaped like a cylinder with a hemisphere on top. The height of the cylindrical part is 30 feet. The radius of the hemisphere is x feet. The volume of the entire silo is 9000π cubic feet. Find the radius of the silo. 15 feet

Lesson Practice

Problem e

Error Alert Students may forget to use a zero coefficient for the x term when using synthetic division.

Check for Understanding

The questions below help assess the concepts taught in this lesson.

1. **"Name the methods you can use to find the roots of a polynomial equation."** Roots can be found by using the graphing calculator, synthetic division, factoring, and/or the quadratic formula. The Rational Root Theorem can also be used to give a list of the possible roots.

2. **"How can you write a polynomial function when given one irrational and/or one complex root?"** Use the fact that both types of roots come in conjugate pairs. Multiply factors of the form (x–root) together.

Example 4 **Application: Farming**

A grain silo is shaped like a cylinder with a hemisphere on top. The height of the cylindrical part is 25 feet. The radius of the hemisphere is x feet. The volume of the entire silo is 4752π cubic feet. Find the radius of the silo.

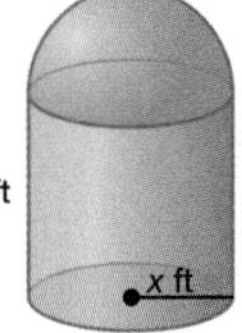

Math Reasoning

Analyze How is the volume of a hemisphere derived from the volume of a sphere?

The volume of a sphere is $\frac{4}{3}\pi r^3$, and a hemisphere is half the entire volume, so the volume of a hemisphere is $\frac{1}{2} \cdot \frac{4}{3}\pi r^3 = \frac{2}{3}\pi r^3$.

SOLUTION

1. **Understand** The volume of the hemisphere plus the volume of the cylinder equals the volume of the entire silo.

2. **Plan** $V_{\text{hemisphere}} = \frac{2}{3}\pi r^3$ and $V_{\text{cylinder}} = \pi r^2 h$.

3. **Solve** Substitute x for r and 25 for h.

$$\frac{2}{3}\pi x^3 + \pi x^2(25) = 4752\pi$$ Add the volumes.

$$\frac{2}{3}\pi x^3 + 25\pi x^2 - 4752\pi = 0$$ Write in standard from.

$$\frac{2}{3}x^3 + 25x^2 - 4752 = 0$$ Divide both sides by π.

Use a graphing calculator.

It appears that 12 is a root.

Use synthetic division to check.

$$\begin{array}{r|rrrr} 12 & \frac{2}{3} & 25 & 0 & -4752 \\ & & 8 & 396 & 4752 \\ \hline & \frac{2}{3} & 33 & 396 & 0 \end{array}$$

Because the polynomial is cubic, there must be two other roots. Use the quadratic formula: $x = \frac{-33 \pm \sqrt{33^2 - 4\left(\frac{2}{3}\right)(396)}}{\frac{4}{3}} = \frac{-33 \pm \sqrt{33}}{\frac{4}{3}} \approx -20.4$ and -29.1.

The radius must be positive, so the radius is 12 feet.

4. **Check** Substitute 12 for r: $V = \frac{2}{3}\pi(12)^3 + \pi(12)^2(25) = 4752\pi$.

Lesson Practice

Solve the following equations by finding all the roots.

a. $x^3 + x^2 - 17x + 15 = 0$ (Ex 1) a. –5, 1, and 3

b. $x^3 - 2x^2 - 4x + 8 = 0$ (Ex 1) –2 and 2

c. $x^3 - 7x^2 + 9x + 17 = 0$ (Ex 1) c. –1, $4 + i$, $4 - i$

d. $x^4 - 8x^3 + 13x^2 + 16x - 30 = 0$ (Ex 2) d. 3, 5, $-\sqrt{2}$, $\sqrt{2}$

e. $x^5 - 5x^4 - 5x^3 + 45x^2 - 108 = 0$ (Ex 2) –2 and 3

f. Write the simplest polynomial function with zeros $2 - 3i$ and $\sqrt{7}$. (Ex 3) $P(x) = x^4 - 4x^3 + 6x^2 + 28x - 91$

g. A grain silo is shaped like a cylinder with a cone on top. The height of the cylindrical part is 20 feet. The radius and height of the cone is x feet. The volume of the entire silo is 1863π cubic feet. Find the radius of the silo. (Ex 4) 9 feet

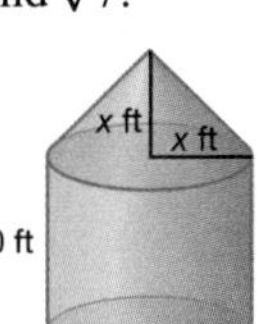

INCLUSION

When multiplying trinomials in Example 3, remind students that they can line up like terms to help make simplifying easier. For example,

$$(x^2 - 4x + 5)(x^2 - 2x - 4)$$

$$\begin{array}{rrrrr} x^4 & -2x^3 & -4x^2 & & \\ & -4x^3 & +8x^2 & +16x & \\ & & +5x^2 & -10x & -20 \\ \hline x^4 & -6x^3 & +9x^2 & +6x & -20 \end{array}$$

Practice Distributed and Integrated

*1. (Medicine) A vitamin is shaped like a cylinder with congruent hemispheres on either end. If the volume of the vitamin is 22.5π cubic millimeters, and the height of the cylindrical part is 8 millimeters, what is the radius of the vitamin? 1.5 mm
(106)

*2. (Population Growth) Based on U.S. Census statistics, the population of Maryland for the years 1950–1990 can be modeled by the equation $y = -1202 + 1495\ln t$, where $10 \leq t \leq 50$, $t = 10$ represents 1950, and y is the population in thousands. Use the model to approximate the year in which the population of Maryland reached 3,000,000. 1957
(102)

3. **Generalize** How is solving a quadratic inequality similar to and different from solving a rational inequality? See Additional Answers.
(94)

*4. **Analyze** Explain the difference between S_9 and a_9 for an arithmetic series. S_9 is the sum of the first 9 terms and a_9 is the value of the 9th term.
(105)

*5. **Error Analysis** Explain and correct the error a student made in writing the arithmetic series {9 + 13 + 17 + 21 + 25} in summation notation.
(105)

$$\sum_{k=1}^{5} 9 + 4k$$

6. **Multiple Choice** Using the change of base formula, $\log_{12} 5$ is equivalent to: B
(87)

A $\frac{\log 12}{\log 5}$ B $\frac{\log 5}{\log 12}$ C $\frac{\log_5 10}{\log_{12} 10}$ D $\frac{\ln 12}{\ln 5}$

7. Graph $y = \frac{2}{3}\csc(x)$. Determine its period and asymptotes.
(103) See Additional Answers.

8. Use the Binomial Theorem to expand $(x + 3y)^3$ $x^3 + 9x^2y + 27xy^2 + 27y^3$
(49)

*9. (Retirement Funds) A teachers' retirement program paid out an interest rate of 3% compounded annually from 1955 to 1963. The function $A(x) = P \cdot 1.03^x$ can be used to calculate the amount in the account, $A(x)$, after x years with the original amount placed in the account, P. Use the function $f(x) = 1.03^x$ to sketch a graph of the equation $A(x) = P \cdot 1.03^x$ if the original amount in the account is $10,000. See Additional Answers.
(104)

10. The endpoints of a diameter of a circle are located at (−8, 4) and (2, 4). Write an equation for this circle. $(x + 3)^2 + (y - 4)^2 = 25$
(91)

*11. **Analyze** A polynomial function $f(x)$ of degree 4 has exactly four real zeros; they are −1, 2, 3, and 6. It also has a negative y-intercept. Describe the end behavior of $f(x)$. As $x \to -\infty$, $f(x) \to +\infty$, and as $x \to +\infty$, $f(x) \to +\infty$.
(101)

 12. **Geometry** For the equation to calculate eccentricity, $e = \sqrt{1 - \frac{b^2}{a^2}}$, what is the value of e as a approaches infinity? For this limiting value, is the figure still an ellipse? e approaches 1; no
(98)

13. **Multiple Choice** What is the 11th term of a geometric sequence that starts −4, 4, ...? B
(97)

A −4,194,304 B −4 C 4 D 4,194,304

14. Convert $f(x) = (x - 3)^2 + 6$ into standard form. $y = x^2 - 6x + 15$
(27)

5. The student used the wrong values for k. As is, the first term is 13, not 9, so the domain should go from 0 to 4. $\sum_{k=0}^{4} 9 + 4k$

CHALLENGE

Write the simplest polynomial function with zeros $3 + i$, $1 + \sqrt{2}$, and 4. Name all the roots. The simplest polynomial is $x^5 - 12x^4 + 53x^3 - 98x^2 + 46x + 40$. The roots are $3 + i$, $3 - i$, $1 + \sqrt{2}$, $1 - \sqrt{2}$, and 4.

3 Practice

Math Conversations

Discussions to strengthen understanding

Problem 8

Remind students that Pascal's Triangle can be used to expand the expression. Because the expression is to the 3rd power, tell students to use ${}_3C_0$, ${}_3C_1$, ${}_3C_2$, and ${}_3C_3$ as the coefficients.

Extend the Problem

Have students show that their answer is correct by evaluating both forms of the expression for $x = 2$ and $y = -1$. Sample: For $x = 2$ and $y = -1$: $(x + 3y)^3 = -1$ and $x^3 + 9x^2y + 27xy^2 + 27y^3 = -1$

Problem 10

Guide the students by asking them the following questions.

"What is true about the diameter of a circle?" It goes through the center of the circle.

"What is the midpoint of the diameter?" (−3, 4)

"How can you find the radius?" Use the distance formula to find the distance between the midpoint and one of the endpoints of the diameter.

"What is the radius of the circle?" 5

"What is the equation of the circle?" $(x + 3)^2 + (y - 4)^2 = 25$

Problem 22

Error Alert

Students might have difficulty remembering the meaning of polar coordinates. Remind students the first coordinate indicates the length and the second coordinate indicates the angle. Tell students to use geometric principles to determine the length of $\overline{AC}$.

Problem 25

Error Alert

Students may treat this as a permutations problem, finding a permutation of 26 items taken 3 at a time. Explain that this will include all arrangements of each group of 3 students. For example, groups with students A, B, and C will be counted as 6 distinct groups: ABC, ACB, BCA, BAC, CAB, and CBA. The same three students are in each group. Explain that order does not matter in the situation described in the problem, so it is solved using a combination of 26 students taken 3 at a time.

Problem 26

Point out that the range 46 to 54 is found by 50 ± 4. This indicates data within one standard deviation of the mean.

Simplify the expression.

15. (87) $\log_6 36^x$ $2x$

16. (87) $\log_5 125^x$ $3x$

***17.** (100) **Multi-Step** Let $f(x) = x^2 - 9$ and $g(x) = x + 4$. Find $\frac{f(x)}{f(g(x))}$ and then determine the vertical asymptotes and holes for it. See Additional Answers.

***18.** (30) **Graphing Calculator** Graph $f(x) = -x^2 + 2$ using a graphing calculator. Compare with the graph of x^2, and explain how the graph is shifted. See Additional Answers.

19. (85) **Physics** A spaceship is coming in for a landing on Jupiter. The equation $h = -12.95t^2 + v_0t + h_0$ can be used to find the distance h from the ground at time t based on an initial height h_0 and an initial speed of v_0. To the nearest hundredth of a second, how long it will take the ship to land from a height of 2000 and an initial speed of 200? 22.35 seconds

Simplify.

20. (48) $\frac{6}{x} + \frac{2x}{x+2}$ $\frac{2x^2 + 6x + 12}{x^2 + 2x}$

21. (48) $\frac{\frac{1}{x+5}}{\frac{x}{2}}$ $\frac{2}{x^2 + 5x}$

22. (96) **Athletic Field** The diagram represents a soccer field. Write polar coordinates for points A, B, C, and D. Use point A as the pole and $\overrightarrow{AD}$ as the polar axis. Sample: $A(0, 0)$, $B\left(60, \frac{\pi}{2}\right)$, $C\left(\sqrt{13{,}600}, \tan^{-1} 0.6\right) \approx (116.62, 0.54)$, $D(100,0)$

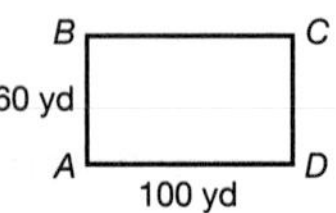

23. (42) Find the number of permutations of 9 objects taken 6 at a time. 60,480

24. (Inv 8) Estimate the area under the curve $y = -x^2 + 5x + 5$ from $0 \le x \le 5$. Use 5 partitions. 46.25

25. (33) A teacher needs 3 volunteers to go to the cafeteria to get ice for the next chemistry lab. With a class of 26 students, how many different ways can the teacher choose the volunteers for the task? 2600

26. (80) **Statistics** A set of results are normally distributed with a mean of 50 and a standard deviation of 4. Find the percent of results between 46 and 54. 68%

***27.** (106) **Multi-Step** Consider the polynomial equation $x^3 + x = 0$.

a. How many roots must it have and why? 3, because the polynomial is a cubic.

b. Factor the polynomial. Name a real root. $x(x^2 + 1) = 0$, 0 is a real root.

c. Find the remaining two roots. $\pm i$

d. Graph the polynomial on a graphing calculator and tell how the graph supports your answer. See Additional Answers.

28. (91) **Write** Explain how to write the equation of a circle given the endpoints of a diameter of the circle. See Additional Answers.

***29.** (106) Write the simplest polynomial function given the following roots: $-\frac{3}{4}$, 6, -1
$P(x) = x^3 - \frac{17}{4}x^2 - \frac{39}{4}x - \frac{9}{2}$

30. (99) **Formulate** For two nonzero vectors $\vec{A}$ and $\vec{B}$ what must be true for $\vec{A} \cdot \vec{B} = 0$?
$\theta = 90°$

LOOKING FORWARD

Using the Fundamental Theorem of Algebra prepares students for

- **Lesson 111** Transforming Polynomial Functions

LESSON 107

Graphing Rational Functions II

Warm Up

1. synthetic division

1. **Vocabulary** To determine that $\frac{2x^2 + 12x - 15}{x - 3} = 2x + 18 + \frac{39}{x - 3}$ use ________. (38)
2. Simplify $\frac{x^2 - 6x + 9}{x^2 - 9}$. $\frac{(x-3)}{(x+3)}$ (38)
3. What are the vertical asymptotes of $f(x) = \frac{2x - 1}{3x^2 - 28x + 32}$? $x = \frac{4}{3}$ and $x = 8$ (100)

New Concepts

A graph of a rational function $f(x) = \frac{g(x)}{h(x)}$, for polynomials $g(x)$ and $h(x) \neq 0$, can exhibit three types of asymptotes. Each type of asymptote has a characteristic equation.

Math Language

A **slant asymptote** is a linear asymptote that is neither horizontal nor vertical, and can be called an oblique asymptote.

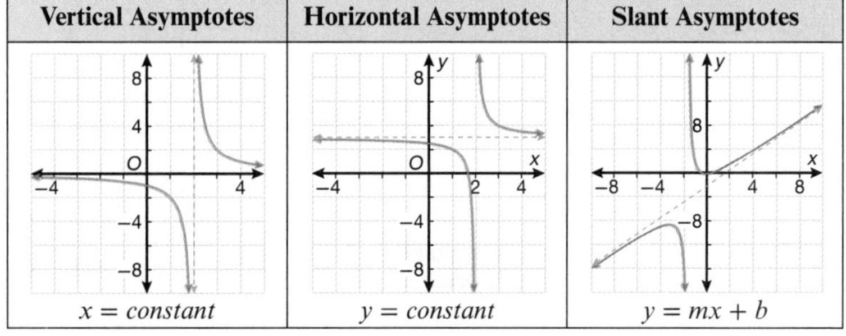

Vertical Asymptotes	Horizontal Asymptotes	Slant Asymptotes
$x = constant$	$y = constant$	$y = mx + b$

The equations for slant asymptotes are linear equations with a defined, nonzero slope that are derived from the rational function itself.

Math Reasoning

Analyze Suppose a rational function $g(x)$ has a vertical asymptote at $x = a$, such that $f(a)$ is not defined. If this same function has a slant asmptote $y = mx + b$, why is $y(a)$ defined?

Since y is an asymptote for $g(x)$, y is not the same function as $g(x)$. Therefore, y will not have the same domain restriction as $g(x)$.

Example 1 Finding the Equation of a Slant Asymptote

Find the equation of the slant asymptote for the following rational function.

$$f(x) = \frac{2x^2 - 11x + 5}{x - 4}$$

SOLUTION

Step 1: Graph the equation to verify that there is a slant asymptote.

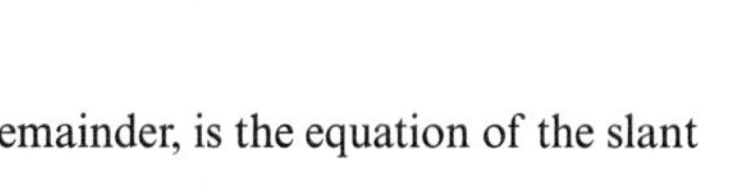

Step 2: Divide the numerator by the denominator using polynomial division.

$$\begin{array}{r} 2x - 3 \\ (x-4)\overline{)2x^2 - 11x + 5} \\ -(2x^2 - 8x) \\ 0 - 3x + 5 \\ -(-3x + 12) \\ 0 - 7 \end{array}$$

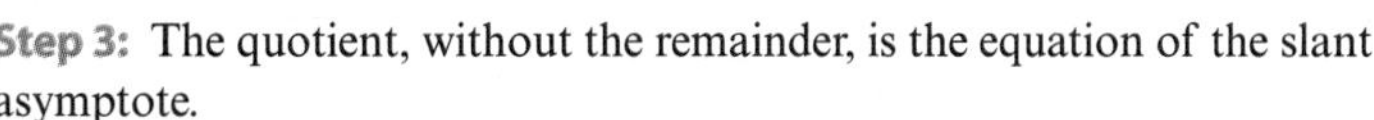

Step 3: The quotient, without the remainder, is the equation of the slant asymptote.

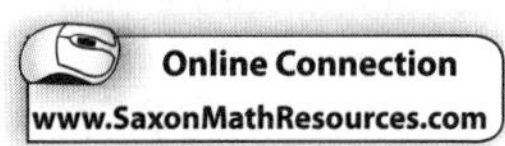

Online Connection
www.SaxonMathResources.com

LESSON 107

1 Warm Up

Remind students that vertical asymptotes occur when the denominator equals 0.

2 New Concepts

In this lesson, students continue to learn to graph rational functions.

Discuss the definition of **slant asymptotes**. Remind students that a vertical asymptote occurs where the function is undefined. A horizontal asymptote indicates where the graph will go as $x \to \pm\infty$.

Example 1

Students will find a slant asymptote by using polynomial division.

Additional Example 1

Find the equation of the slant asymptote for the following rational function.

$f(x) = \frac{x^2 + 10x + 3}{x + 2}$

$y = x + 8$

TEACHER TIP

Tell students that the rational function can have either a horizontal *or* a slant asymptote, but not both.

LESSON RESOURCES

Student Edition Practice Workbook 107
Reteaching Master 107
Adaptations Master 107
Challenge and Enrichment Master C107
Technology Lab Master 107

MATH BACKGROUND

In Lesson 100, students learned about vertical asymptotes, horizontal asymptotes, and holes when graphing rational expressions. In this lesson, students are introduced to the case where the degree of the numerator is one greater than the degree of the denominator. In this case, the rational function will have a slant asymptote.

In this example, students find the equation of a slant asymptote for quadratic and cubic polynomials.

TEACHER TIP

Remind students to use the quotient, without the remainder, as the slant asymptote as shown in Example 1.

Also, tell students that slant asymptotes are also referred to as oblique asymptotes.

Additional Example 2

Find the equation of the slant asymptote for the following rational function.

$f(x) = \dfrac{x^3 + 2x - 4}{x^2 - 1}$

Slant asymptote is at $y = x$.

TEACHER TIP

Remind students that a graph can never cross a vertical asymptote because the function is undefined at that point. However, the horizontal and slant asymptotes describe the end behavior of the function. Therefore, the graph may cross the horizontal and slant asymptotes

Math Reasoning

Verify Explain why functions of the form $y = \frac{ax^3 + bx^2 + cx + d}{ax + b}$ for nonzero values of a, b, c, and d, do not have slant asymptotes.

The degree of the numerator is 2 greater than the degree of the denominator; therefore, the quotient will not be linear.

A slant asymptote will occur when the degree of the numerator is one greater than the degree of the denominator.

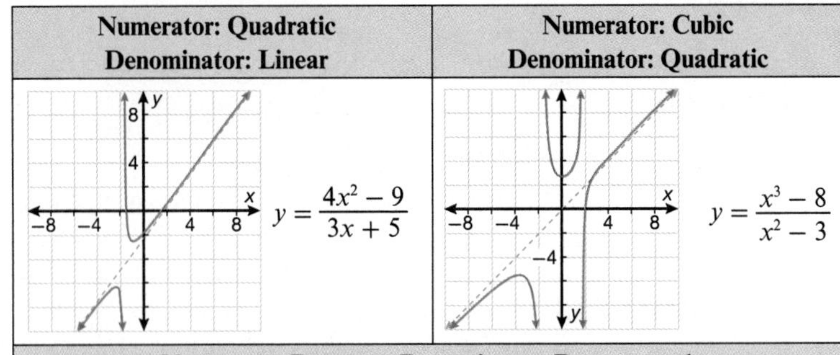

Numerator: Quadratic
Denominator: Linear
$y = \frac{4x^2 - 9}{3x + 5}$
Numerator: Cubic
Denominator: Quadratic
$y = \frac{x^3 - 8}{x^2 - 3}$

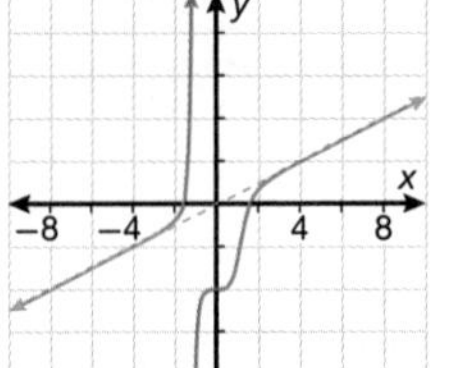

Example 2 Slant Asymptotes with Quadratic and Cubic Terms

Find the equation of the slant asymptote for the following rational function.

$$f(x) = \frac{x^3 - x^2 - 7x + 10}{-2x^2 + 10x - 5}$$

SOLUTION

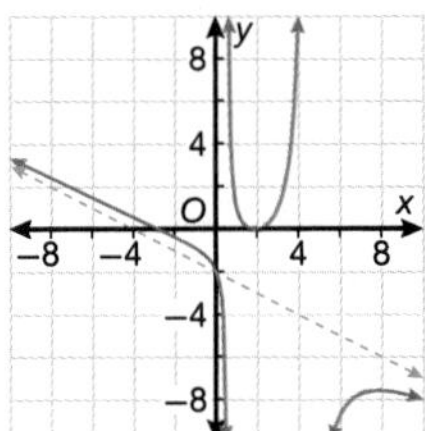

Step 1: Graph the equation to verify that there is a slant asymptote. Or, verify that the degree of the numerator is one greater than the degree of the denominator. Since the numerator is a cubic and the denominator is a quadratic, the numerator is one greater than the denominator.

Step 2: Divide the numerator by the denominator using polynomial division.

$$\begin{array}{r} -0.5x - 2 \\ (-2x^2 + 10x - 5)\overline{)x^3 - x^2 - 7x + 10} \\ \underline{-(x^3 - 5x^2 + 2.5x)} \\ 0 + 4x^2 - 9.5x + 10 \\ \underline{-(4x^2 - 20x + 10)} \\ 0 \quad + 10.5x \end{array}$$

$$f(x) = \frac{x^3 - x^2 - 7x + 10}{-2x^2 + 10x - 5} = (-0.5x - 2) + \frac{10.5x}{-2x^2 + 10x - 5}$$

Step 3: The quotient, without the remainder, is the equation of the slant asymptote.

$$f(x) = -0.5x - 2$$

ENGLISH LEARNERS

Review meanings of horizontal and vertical with students. Say:

"A horizontal line is flat and parallel to the ground. A vertical line goes straight up and down and is perpendicular to the ground."

Draw examples of each line on the board. Write the description next to each line.

Introduce the word **slant.** Say:

"A slant line is a line that is neither horizontal or vertical."

Draw an example of a slant line on the board.

Next draw several lines on the board and have students identify them as horizontal, vertical, or slant lines.

When graphing the rational functions in the lesson, connect the meaning to each type asymptote by referring to the examples on the board.

To graph a rational function, first find all asymptotes, holes, and intercepts. Calculate the values of y for values of x near the asymptotes. Then plot the points and sketch the graph.

Example 3 **Graphing a Rational Function**

Graph $f(x) = \dfrac{x^4 - 256}{x^3 + x^2 - 14x - 24}$.

SOLUTION **Step 1:** Determine if there is a horizontal or slant asymptote. Since the degree of the numerator is one more than the degree of the denominator, there is no horizontal asymptote, but there is a slant asymptote.

Divide to find the slant asymptote.

$$\frac{x^4 - 256}{x^3 + x^2 - 14x - 24} = (x - 1) + \frac{(15x^2 + 10x - 280)}{(x^3 + x^2 - 14x - 24)}$$

The slant asymptote is $y = x - 1$.

Math Reasoning

Analyze Consider rational function

$f(x) = \frac{g(x)}{h(x)}$

If $f(a)$ is undefined for $x = a$, what needs to be true for there to be a vertical asymptote at $x = a$?

$(x - a)$ is not a factor of $g(x)$.

Step 2: Factor the numerator and denominator to find vertical asymptotes and holes.

Numerator

$$x^4 - 256 = (x^2 - 16)(x^2 + 16) = (x - 4)(x + 4)(x^2 + 16)$$

Denominator

Use the Rational Root Theorem to factor $x^3 + x^2 - 14x - 24$.

Possible Rational Roots:

$\pm1, \pm2, \pm1, \pm2, \pm3, \pm4, \pm6, \pm8, \pm24$

Find the first root that yields a factor through synthetic division:

1	1	1	−14	−24
		1	2	−12
	1	2	−12	−36 ✗

−1	1	1	−14	−24
		−1	0	14
	1	0	−14	10 ✗

−2	1	1	−14	−24
		−2	2	24
	1	−1	−12	0 ✓

$$f(x) = \frac{(x - 4)(x + 4)(x^2 + 16)}{(x + 2)(x^2 - x - 12)} = \frac{(x - 4)(x + 4)(x^2 + 16)}{(x + 2)(x - 4)(x + 3)}$$

There are vertical asymptotes at $x = -2$ and $x = -3$.

There is a hole at $x = 4$.

Step 3: Find the x- and y-intercepts.

The x-intercept occurs at $x = -4$, since $f(-4) = 0$. The y-intercept occurs at $x = 10\frac{2}{3}$, since $f(0) = \dfrac{(0)^4 - 256}{(0)^3 + (0)^2 - (0)x - 24} = 10\frac{2}{3}$.

Step 4: Graph the asymptotes, holes, and intercepts. Calculate the values of y for values of x near the asymptotes. Then plot the points and sketch the graph.

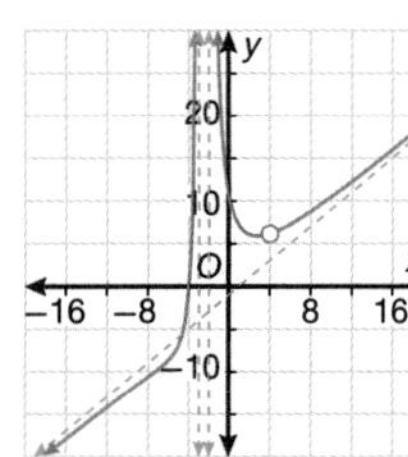

Example 3

Students find vertical, horizontal, or slant asymptotes as well as holes, if they exist.

Additional Example 3

Graph

$$f(x) = \frac{x^4 + 2x^3 - 5x^2 - 6x}{x^3 + 2x^2 - x - 2}$$

Hole at $x = -1$, vertical asymptotes at $x = 1$ and $x = -2$, slant asymptote at $y = x$.

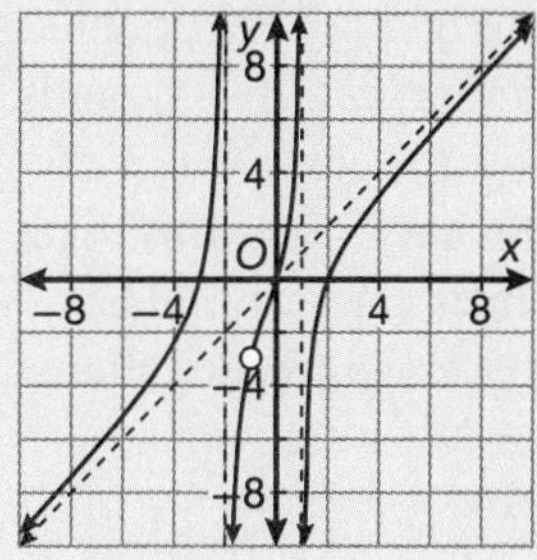

TEACHER TIP

Tell students how to use the degree of the numerator and denominator to find the horizontal asymptote.

- If denominator degree > numerator degree, horizontal asymptote at $y = 0$.
- If denominator degree = numerator degree, find horizontal asymptote by dividing leading coefficients.
- If denominator degree < numerator degree, there are no horizontal asymptotes.

INCLUSION

When finding the slant asymptote for a rational function, have students graph the asymptote on their graphing calculator to help them check. Let students use the graphing calculator to graph each rational function in the lesson so they are aware of the calculator limitations in viewing.

Example 4

Students will use a rational function to answer a real-world problem about cost savings.

Additional Example 4

As the weight in a car increases, its miles per gallon (mpg) decreases. A reasonable model for this behavior is shown in the rational function below. Use the function to identify the mpg for cars weighing 1100 pounds and cars weighing 2000 pounds. Determine the cost savings of the lighter car if the car is used 20,000 miles per year and gas costs on average \$3 per gallon.

$$f(x) = \frac{7500}{0.1x - 25}$$

about \$720

Lesson Practice

Problem c

Scaffolding Remind students that if there is a slant asymptote, there will be no horizontal asymptote and vice versa.

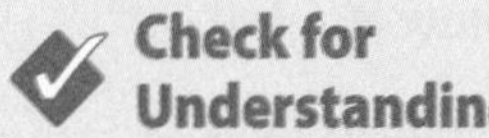

Check for Understanding

The questions below help assess the concepts taught in this lesson.

"Explain how to find a slant asymptote if it exists in a rational function." A slant asymptote is found by dividing the denominator into the numerator using polynomial division. The quotient without the remainder is the equation of the slant asymptote.

"How can you tell if a rational function has a slant asymptote?" The degree of the denominator is one less than the degree of the numerator.

Example 4 **Application: Consumer Finance**

As the weight of a car increases, its miles per gallon (mpg) decreases. A reasonable model for this behavior is shown in the rational function below, where x is the weight of the car, in pounds. Use the function to identify the mpg for cars weighing 1750 pounds and cars weighing 2140 pounds. Determine the cost savings if the car is used 20,000 miles per year and gas costs on average \$3 per gallon.

$$f(x) = \frac{7500}{0.1x - 25}$$

SOLUTION

Step 1: Graph the function. Set the WINDOW as shown below.

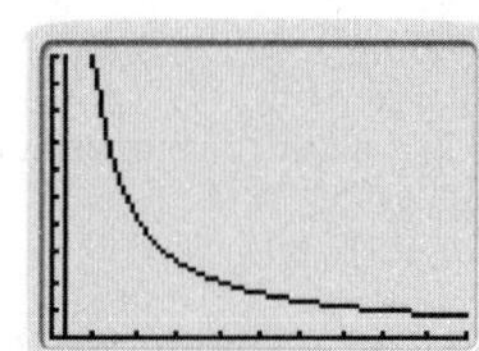

$x_{min} = 0$

$x_{max} = 10{,}000$

$y_{min} = 0$

$y_{max} = 100$

Step 2: Use the TRACE feature to find the mpg. For a car weighing 1750 pounds, the mpg is 50. For a car weighing 2140 pounds, the mpg is approximately 40.

Math Reasoning

Verify Use the equation $f(x) = \frac{7500}{0.1x - 25}$ to verify the values you found for Step 2.

$f(1750) = \frac{7500}{0.1(1750) - 25}$
$= 50$

$f(2140) = \frac{7500}{0.1(2140) - 25}$
≈ 40

Step 3: Determine the number of gallons of fuel needed per year for each weight of car using the formula:

$$\text{Gallons of fuel} = \frac{\text{Miles traveled}}{\text{Miles per gallon}}$$

40 mpg vehicle	50 mpg vehicle
$\frac{20{,}000}{40} = 500$	$\frac{20{,}000}{50} = 400$

Step 4: Determine the cost savings.

$$(500 - 400)\$3 = \$300$$

Lesson Practice

a. (Ex 1) Find the equation of the slant asymptote for the following rational function: $f(x) = \frac{3x^2 + 12x - 5}{x - 7}$. $y = 3(x + 11)$

b. (Ex 2) Find the equation of the slant asymptote for the following rational function: $f(x) = \frac{-15x^3 - 2x^2 - 9x + 17}{x^2 - 5}$. $y = -(15x + 2)$

c. (Ex 3) Graph $f(x) = \frac{x^8 - 1}{x^7 - x^4 - 16x^3 + 16}$.

c. Vertical asymptotes: $x = -2, 2$
Hole: $x = 1$
Slant asymptote: $y = x$

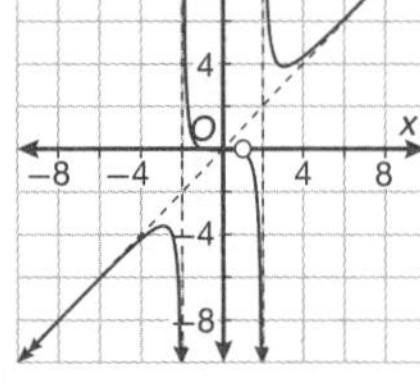

d. (Ex 4) Use the rational function $f(x) = \frac{7500}{0.1x - 25}$ to determine the mpg for cars weighing 1313 pounds and 1484 pounds. about 70.6 and 60.8 mpg

CHALLENGE

Have students write a possible rational function with a vertical asymptote at 1, a hole at 2, and a slant asymptote at $y = x + 1$.

Sample answer: $f(x) = \frac{x^3 - 2x^2 - 4x + 8}{x^2 - 3x + 2}$

Practice Distributed and Integrated

1. Multiply and then evaluate for $t = 2$, $k = 5$: $\frac{4t^3k^7}{8t} \cdot \frac{3k^3}{6t^4k^9}$. $\frac{k}{4t^2}$; $\frac{5}{16}$
(31)

***2.** Find S_{30} for $101 + 95 + 89 + 83 + \ldots$ 420
(105)

3. Estimate Write approximate Cartesian coordinates for the point with polar coordinates $\left(2, \frac{1}{2}\right)$. Explain your method.
(96)

***4. Multiple Choice** Which of the following rational functions has a slant asymptote of $y = 2x - 4$? D
(107)

A $y = \frac{2x^2 + 1}{2x + 1}$ **B** $y = \frac{x^3 - 8}{0.5x^2 + x + 5}$

C $y = \frac{(2x - 4)^2}{x + 8}$ **D** $y = \frac{2x^2 - 1}{x + 2}$

5. 1 in 6 cars sold on a lot are silver. Today, 4 cars were sold. What is the probability that 2 of the cars sold were silver? about 0.12
(49)

3. Sample: $(\sqrt{3}, 1)$; The point with polar coordinates $\left(2, \frac{1}{2}\right)$ is close to the point with polar coordinates $\left(2, \frac{\pi}{6}\right)$, which has Cartesian coordinates $(\sqrt{3}, 1)$.

***6.** If the 1st term of a geometric sequence is 5 and the common ratio is -4, what is the 6th term? -5120
(97)

***7. Graphing Calculator** Graph $y = 6^x$ and $y = \left(\frac{1}{6}\right)^x$ on a graphing calculator and describe the graphs. They are reflections of each other over the y-axis.
(47)

7.

8. Error Analysis A student said that the finite sequence {5, 10, 20, 35, 55, 80} is arithmetic because it is formed by adding numbers in a pattern. Explain and correct the student's reasoning. In an arithmetic sequence, the numbers added to the previous number must be constant.
(92)

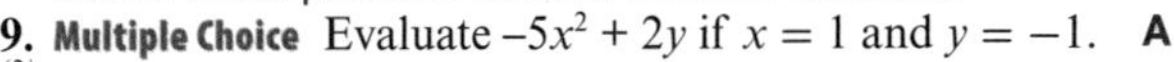

9. Multiple Choice Evaluate $-5x^2 + 2y$ if $x = 1$ and $y = -1$. A
(2)

A -7 **B** -3 **C** 3 **D** 7

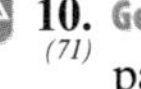

10. Geometry Derive the function that can be used to find the area of the parallelogram. Express in simplified form. $y = ab\sin(\theta)$
(71)

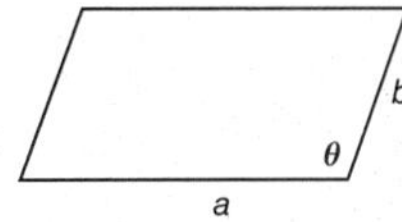

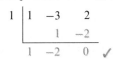

Divide.

11. $5x^4 - 2x^3 - 7x^2 - 39$ by $2x$
(38) $2.5x^3 - x^2 - 3.5x - \frac{39}{2x}$

12. $3x^2 - 11x - 26$ by $(x - 5)$ $3x + 4 - \frac{6}{x - 5}$
(38)

13. Error Analysis A student solves for the roots of $y = x^3 - 3x + 2$; what was his mistake?
(85) The student incorrectly leaves out a squared term in the synthetic division.

Factors of 1: ± 1 ← Values of q Factors of 2: ± 1, 2 ← Values of p $\frac{p}{q} = \{\pm1, 2\}$

1	1	−3	2
		1	−2
	1	−2	0 ✓

$y = (x - 1)(x^2 - 2)$ The roots of $y = x^3 - 3x + 2$ are $x = 1$ and $\pm\sqrt{2}$.

14. Error Analysis A student said that a polynomial equation with roots of 4 and $6 + i$ will have exactly four roots because each has a conjugate pair, -4 and $6 - i$. Explain the error in the student's thinking. Real roots do not come in conjugate pairs, so -4 is not necessarily a root.
(106)

INCLUSION

Let students work in pairs to answer questions about graphing rational functions. Have one student focus on finding vertical asymptotes and holes while the other finds the horizontal or slant asymptote, if either exists. Tell students they must explain their conclusions to their partner. Then have students graph the rational function together to test their results. Tell students to switch roles for the next question so that each has experience with the different types of asymptotes.

3 Practice

Math Conversations

Discussions to strengthen understanding

Problem 6

Remind students the formula for a geometric sequence is $a_n = a_1r^{n-1}$ where a_1 is the first term and r is the common ratio.

Problem 7

Remind students to use parentheses around the $\frac{1}{6}$ when entering the equations in a graphing calculator.

Problem 13

Extend the Problem

What are the roots of $y = x^3 - 3x + 2$? 1 and -2

Problem 14

Extend the Problem

Write the simplest polynomial function with zeros 4 and $6 + i$. $f(x) = x^3 - 16x^2 + 85x - 148$

Problem 16

Guide the students by asking them the following questions.

"What is the equation of a circle?" $(x - h)^2 + (y - k)^2 = r^2$

"What does (h, k) represent?" (h, k) is the center point of the circle.

"What does r represent?" r is the radius of the circle.

"What are the center points of the graphs?" Both are (0, 7).

"What is the radius of each circle?" $\sqrt{20}$ and $\sqrt{24}$

Problem 22

Guide the students by asking them the following questions.

"What is the rational function for the car getting 20 miles per gallon?" $y = \frac{20{,}000 + 6750x}{x}$

"What is the rational function for the car getting 40 miles per gallon?" $y = \frac{40{,}000 + 3375x}{x}$

"How can you find when the 40 mpg car is a better deal?" Graph both equations and find where the graph of the 40-mpg car is below the graph of the 20-mpg car.

15. (Inv 9) **Multi-Step** To join the local gym, there is a \$60 initial sign-up fee and an additional monthly fee. If you join the gym for 6 months, it is \$50 per month. If you join the gym for 1 year, the monthly fee is \$45 per month. There is a \$5 monthly discount for each year added to your membership, up to 5 years.

a. If you join the gym for 6 months, and then sign up for an additional year, what will be the total cost? \$900

b. What will the total cost be if you later add an additional 6 months? \$1200

c. If you join the gym for 2 years, what will be the total cost? \$1080

d. How much money will you save by joining the gym for 2 years initially? \$120

16. (91) **Analyze** How is the graph of $x^2 + (y - 7)^2 = 20$ similar to, and different from, the graph of $x^2 + (y - 7)^2 = 24$? They are similar in that they have the same center point: (0, 7). They are different because their radii are different: $\sqrt{20}$ and $\sqrt{24}$.

***17.** (100) **Generalize** Show that rational functions of the form $f(x) = \frac{1}{x^2n}$, for positive integers n, are even functions. For even functions $f(-x) = f(x)$. For this function, $f(-x) = \frac{1}{(-x)^2n} = \frac{1}{(-1)^2(x)^2n} = \frac{1}{x^2n} = f(x)$.

18. (94) **Write** Describe two ways to use a sign table to solve rational inequalities. When should each be used? See Additional Answers.

19. (95) **Space Science** If you throw a ball in the air, the height (h) it travels is based on the acceleration due to gravity (g), the initial height (h_o) the object is thrown from, its initial speed (v_o), and the time (t) that the object is in the air. The table shows different values of g for different planets. Use the Remainder Theorem to compare $h(10)$ for Earth and Saturn, assuming that $h_o = 100$ and $v_o = 100$. Account for any differences. $h_{Earth}(10) = 609.5$; $h_{Saturn}(10) = 546$; the forces of gravity on Earth and Saturn are close in value.

$$h(t) = -\frac{1}{2}gt^2 + v_ot + h_o$$

Planet	Gravity, g(m/s²)
Mercury	3.59
Venus	8.87
Earth	9.81
Mars	3.77
Jupiter	25.95
Saturn	11.08
Uranus	10.67
Neptune	14.07

20. (87) **Commodities** P represents the selling price, in dollars, of a commodity and x represents the demand, in number sold per day. This relationship is indicated by the equation $p = p_0e^{-ax}$. Solve the equation for x. $x = -\frac{1}{a}\ln\left(\frac{p}{p_o}\right)$

21. (93) **Population Growth** The population of Japan grew at an average annual rate of approximately 0.26% from 1990 to 2000, and the population in 2000 was 127,000,000 (rounded to the nearest million). If the population continues to increase at the same rate, in what year will it reach 150,000,000? 2064 or 2065 (The month of the census is not given.)

***22.** (107) **Consumer Finance** You want to compare the cost of buying a more expensive car that has a higher miles per gallon (mpg) rating to a less expensive car with low mpg. Use the data in the table to generate two rational functions. Assume that the number of miles traveled is 30,000 and the cost of fuel is \$4.50 per gallon. Use the graph of both functions to determine the number of years it takes for the car with 40 mpg to be a better deal than the car with 20 mpg. See Additional Answers.

MPG	Car Price
20	\$20,000
40	\$40,000

$$\text{Yearly cost} = \frac{\text{Price} + \frac{\text{Miles traveled}}{\text{MPG}} \times \text{Cost of Fuel per Gallon} \times \text{Number of Years}}{\text{Number of Years}}$$

750 Saxon Algebra 2

23. (99) **Multi-Step** Find the magnitude of vectors $\begin{bmatrix}3\\6\end{bmatrix}$ and $\begin{bmatrix}2\\-5\end{bmatrix}$. Calculate the dot product and then calculate the angle between the two vectors. Magnitude of A: 6.71; magnitude of B: 5.39; $\theta = 131.64°$; dot product: −24

***24.** (104) **Probability** The probability that a single coin tossed in the air will not land tails up until the nth toss can be found using the equation $P(n) = 0.5(0.5)^{n-1}$, where $P(x)$ is the probability and n is the number of times the coin is tossed. Use the graph of $f(n) = 0.5^n$ to sketch a graph of $P(n)$. Use the graph of $P(n)$ to estimate the probability that the coin will not land tails up until the third toss. See Additional Answers.

***25.** (107) **Formulate** Write a possible rational function that fits these parameters: Vertical asymptotes $x = \pm 1$; slant asymptote $y = 3x + 1$. Sample: $y = \frac{3x^3 + x^2}{x^2 - 1}$

Find the zeros of the quadratic function.

26. (35) $f(x) = x^2 + 21x - 46$ $x = -23, 2$

27. (35) $f(x) = x^2 + \frac{5}{12}x - \frac{1}{6}$ $x = -\frac{2}{3}, \frac{1}{4}$

Simplify.

28. (44) $\frac{1}{5 + \sqrt{6}} =$ $\frac{5 - \sqrt{6}}{19}$

29. (44) $\frac{3 + \sqrt{7}}{2 - \sqrt{10}} =$ $\frac{\sqrt{70} + 3\sqrt{10} + 2\sqrt{7} + 6}{-6}$

30. (89) **Tourist Attractions** The world's tallest thermometer is located in Baker, California, with a height of 134 feet. Suppose a maintenance worker at the top drops a nail. The height of the nail, in feet, after x seconds, is modeled by $y = -16x^2 + 134$. Write and solve a quadratic inequality that can be solved to find the time span for which the nail remains at least 50 feet above the ground. Round to the nearest hundredth of a second. $-16x^2 + 134 \geq 50$, between 0 and 2.29 seconds after the drop

Problem 25

Error Alert

Students might believe a vertical asymptote exists when in fact it is a hole. Be sure students check to see if the factor in the denominator can be divided with a factor in the numerator before stating the vertical asymptotes.

LOOKING FORWARD 

Graphing rational functions prepares students for

- **Lesson 109** Making Graphs and Using Equations of Hyperbolas
- **Lesson 110** Graphing Logarithmic Functions
- **Lesson 113** Using Geometric Series

LESSON 108

1 Warm Up

In problems 2 and 3, remind students of the mnemonic device SOH-CAH-TOA.

2 New Concepts

The Pythagorean equation $x^2 + y^2 = 1$, based on the unit circle, is used to derive trigonometric identities.

Example 1

The identity $\sin^2\theta + \cos^2\theta = 1$ is demonstrated for 30° and $\frac{\pi}{4}$.

Additional Example 1

a. Show that $\sin^2\theta + \cos^2\theta = 1$ for $\theta = 60°$.

$$\sin^2 60° + \cos^2 60° = \left(\frac{\sqrt{3}}{2}\right)^2 + \left(\frac{1}{2}\right)^2$$
$$= \frac{3}{4} + \frac{1}{4} = 1$$

b. A ship is headed in the direction shown in the diagram. Show that for this angle, $\sin^2\theta + \cos^2\theta = 1$.

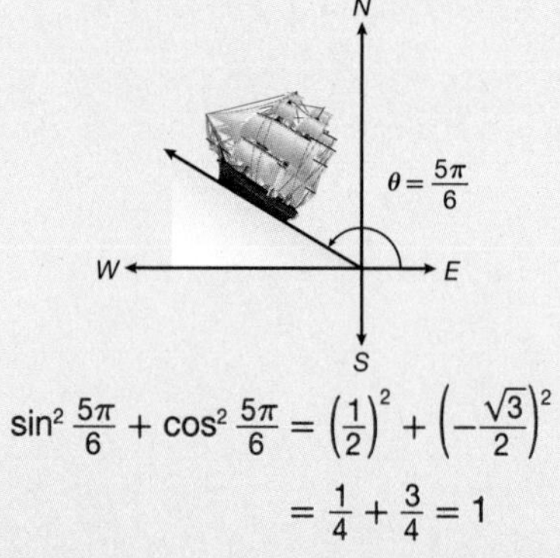

$$\sin^2\frac{5\pi}{6} + \cos^2\frac{5\pi}{6} = \left(\frac{1}{2}\right)^2 + \left(-\frac{\sqrt{3}}{2}\right)^2$$
$$= \frac{1}{4} + \frac{3}{4} = 1$$

LESSON RESOURCES

Student Edition Practice Workbook 108
Reteaching Master 108
Adaptations Master 108
Challenge and Enrichment Master C108
Technology Lab Master 108

LESSON 108 Using Fundamental Trigonometric Identities

Warm Up

1. **Vocabulary** The ratio $\frac{\sin(x)}{\cos(x)}$ is the tangent ratio. (46)

2. True or false. For a right triangle the ratio $\frac{\text{adjacent side}}{\text{hypotenuse}}$ is the sine ratio. false (46)

3. True or false. For a right triangle the ratio $\frac{\text{opposite side}}{\text{hypotenuse}}$ is the cosine ratio. false (46)

New Concepts

A **trigonometric identity** is a trigonometric equation that is true for all values of the variable for which the statement is defined. The trigonometric ratios derived from the unit circle give rise to trigonometric identities based on those ratios.

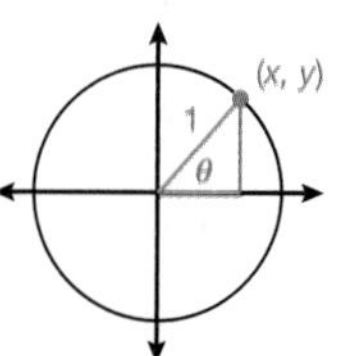

By the Pythagorean Theorem, for any point (x, y) on the unit circle $y^2 + x^2 = 1$.

Since $\cos(\theta) = \frac{x}{1} = x$ and $\sin(\theta) = \frac{y}{1} = y$, substituting these terms into the equation of the unit circle yields the first trigonometric identity,

$$\sin^2(\theta) + \cos^2(\theta) = 1$$

Math Reasoning

Verify Show that this trigonometric identity is true even for a circle whose radius is not equal to 1.

$y^2 + x^2 = 2^2$
$(2\sin(\theta))^2 + (2\cos(\theta))^2 = 4$
$4\sin^2(\theta) + 4\cos^2(\theta) = 4$
$\sin^2(\theta) + \cos^2(\theta) = 1$

Example 1 **Using the Trigonometric Identity $\cos^2(\theta) + \sin^2(\theta) = 1$**

a. Show that $\sin^2(\theta) + \cos^2(\theta) = 1$ for $\theta = 30°$.

SOLUTION

$$\sin^2(30°) + \cos^2(30°) = \left(\frac{1}{2}\right)^2 + \left(\frac{\sqrt{3}}{2}\right)^2$$
$$= \frac{1}{4} + \frac{3}{4}$$
$$= 1$$

Tip

For help evaluating trigonometric functions use the unit circle in Lesson 63.

b. A 12-foot ladder is tipped against a building at angle $\theta = \frac{\pi}{4}$, as shown. Show that for this angle $\sin^2(\theta) + \cos^2(\theta) = 1$.

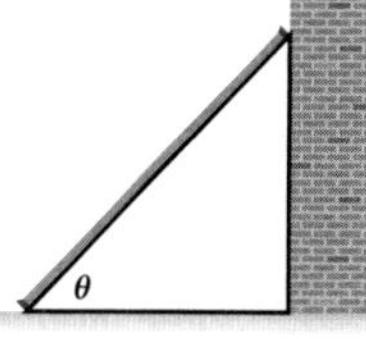

SOLUTION

$$\sin^2\left(\frac{\pi}{4}\right) + \cos^2\left(\frac{\pi}{4}\right) = \left(\frac{\sqrt{2}}{2}\right)^2 + \left(\frac{\sqrt{2}}{2}\right)^2$$
$$= \frac{2}{4} + \frac{2}{4}$$
$$= 1$$

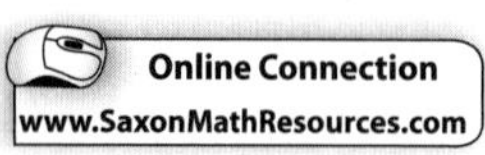

MATH BACKGROUND

An identity is an equation that is true for all values of the variable(s) for which all expressions in the equation are defined. Some examples follow.

$2x = 8 - x + 3x - 8$	identity
$\frac{x^2 - 25}{x - 5} + y = x + 5 + y$	identity
$3x = x + 8$	not an identity (true only for $x = 4$)

This lesson uses the Pythagorean identities. Some other categories are listed below. (Only the first identity in each category is listed.)

Reciprocal Identity	$\sin\theta = \frac{1}{\csc\theta}$
Quotient Identity	$\tan\theta = \frac{\sin\theta}{\cos\theta}$
Cofunction Identity	$\sin\left(\frac{\pi}{2} - \theta\right) = \cos\theta$
Even/Odd Identity	$\sin(-\theta) = -\sin\theta$

Take the trigonometric identity $\sin^2(\theta) + \cos^2(\theta) = 1$ and divide both sides by $\cos^2(\theta)$ to get another trigonometric identity.

$$\frac{\sin^2(\theta)}{\cos^2(\theta)} + \frac{\cos^2(\theta)}{\cos^2(\theta)} = \frac{1}{\cos^2(\theta)}$$

$$\tan^2(\theta) + 1 = \sec^2(\theta)$$

Hint

Recall that $\frac{\sin(\theta)}{\cos(\theta)} = \tan(\theta)$ and $\frac{1}{\cos(\theta)} = \sec(\theta)$.

Example 2 Using the Trigonometric Identity $\tan^2(\theta) + 1 = \sec^2(\theta)$

a. Using the information in the diagram, show that $\tan^2(\theta) + 1 = \sec^2(\theta)$ for $\theta = 45°$.

SOLUTION

$$\tan^2(45°) + 1 = (1)^2 + 1 = 2$$

$$\sec^2(45°) = \frac{1}{\cos^2(45°)} = \frac{1}{\left(\frac{1}{\sqrt{2}}\right)^2} = 2$$

Therefore $\tan^2\theta + 1 = \sec^2\theta$ for $\theta = 45°$.

b. Show that $\tan^2\left(\frac{\pi}{3}\right) + 1 = \sec^2\left(\frac{\pi}{3}\right)$.

SOLUTION

$$\tan^2\left(\frac{\pi}{3}\right) + 1 = \left(\sqrt{(3)}\right)^2 + 1 = 3 + 1 = 4$$

$$\sec^2\left(\frac{\pi}{3}\right) = \frac{1}{\cos^2\frac{\pi}{3}} = \frac{1}{\left(\frac{1}{2}\right)^2} = 4$$

Therefore $\tan^2(\theta) + 1 = \sec^2(\theta)$ for $\theta = \frac{\pi}{3}$.

Take the trigonometric identity $\sin^2\theta + \cos^2\theta = 1$ and divide both sides by $\sin^2(\theta)$.

$$1 + \frac{\cos^2(\theta)}{\sin^2(\theta)} = \frac{1}{\sin^2(\theta)}$$

$$1 + \cot^2(\theta) = \csc^2(\theta)$$

Example 3 Using the Trigonometric Identity $1 + \cot^2(\theta) = \csc^2(\theta)$

a. Show that $1 + \cot^2(\theta) = \csc^2(\theta)$ for 135°.

SOLUTION

$$1 + \cot^2(135°) = 1 + \frac{1}{\tan^2(135°)} = 1 + \frac{1}{(-1)^2} = 2$$

$$\csc^2(135°) = 1 + \frac{1}{\sin^2(135°)} = \frac{1}{\left(\frac{1}{\sqrt{2}}\right)^2} = 2$$

Example 2

The identity $1 + \tan^2\theta = \sec^2\theta$ is demonstrated for 45° and $\frac{\pi}{3}$.

Additional Example 2

a. Show that $\tan^2\theta + 1 = \sec^2\theta$ for the angle in the diagram.

$\theta = 150°$

$$\tan^2 150° + 1 = \left(\frac{-1}{\sqrt{3}}\right)^2 + 1 = \frac{4}{3}$$

$$\sec^2 150° = \frac{1}{(\cos 150°)^2} = \frac{1}{\left(-\frac{\sqrt{3}}{2}\right)^2} = \frac{4}{3}$$

b. Show that $\tan^2\frac{5\pi}{4} + 1 = \sec^2\frac{5\pi}{4}$.

$$\tan^2\frac{5\pi}{4} + 1 = 1 + 1 = 2$$

$$\sec^2\frac{5\pi}{4} = \frac{1}{\cos^2\frac{5\pi}{4}} = \frac{1}{\left(\frac{-\sqrt{2}}{2}\right)^2} = \frac{1}{\frac{2}{4}} = 2$$

TEACHER TIP

Explain that $\sin^2\theta$ represents $(\sin\theta)^2$, and that a similar shorthand is used for squares of other trigonometric expressions.

Example 3

The identity $1 + \cot^2\theta = \csc^2\theta$ is demonstrated for 135° and $\frac{2\pi}{3}$.

Additional Example 3

a. Show that $1 + \cot^2\theta = \csc^2\theta$ for $\theta = 90°$.

$$1 + \cot^2 90° = 1 + (0)^2 = 1$$

$$\csc^2(90°) = \frac{1}{\sin^2(90°)} = \frac{1}{(1)^2} = 1$$

ENGLISH LEARNERS

Discuss the meaning of identity. Say:

"The identity of a person is a set of characteristics that make them different from other people. The identity of a person is a way in which that person is known or recognized."

Name some important people who are known for playing a certain sport. Have students name ways in which these people are identified.

Explain in mathematics, the identity equations are equations that demonstrate characteristics between trigonometric functions.

b. Show that $1 + \cot^2\frac{17\pi}{6} = \csc^2\frac{17\pi}{6}$.

$1 + \cot^2\frac{17\pi}{6} = 1 + (-\sqrt{3})^2 =$

$1 + 3 = 4$

$\csc^2\frac{17\pi}{6} = \frac{1}{\sin^2\frac{17\pi}{6}} = \frac{1}{\left(\frac{1}{2}\right)^2} = \frac{1}{\frac{1}{4}} = 4$

Example 4

The identity $\sin^2\theta + \cos^2\theta = 1$ is verified by referring to the graphs of $y_1 = \cos^2 x$ and $y_2 = \sin^2 x$ on the same coordinate system.

Additional Example 4

Describe how to use graphs to verify that $\tan^2\theta + 1 = \sec^2\theta$. Then use a graphing calculator to verify the identity. Sample: Graph $y_1 = 1 + \tan^2\theta$ and $y_2 = \sec^2\theta$ on the same coordinate system and verify that the graphs coincide.

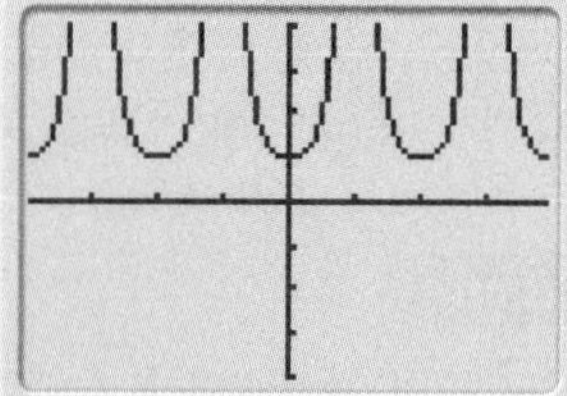

Check for Understanding

The questions below help assess the concepts taught in this lesson.

"Why is $\sin^2\theta + \cos^2\theta = 1$ called an identity?" Sample: All values of θ make it true.

"Name a value of θ that does not make the equation $\tan^2\theta + 1 = \sec^2\theta$ true. Explain why the equation is an identity." Sample: 90°; It is an identity because all values of θ for which $\tan\theta$ and $\sec\theta$ are defined make the equation true.

"Describe how to demonstrate the identity $1 + \cot^2\theta = \csc^2\theta$ for $\theta = 45°$." Sample: Show that $1 + \cot^2 45°$ has the same value as $\csc^2 45°$.

b. Show that $1 + \cot^2\left(\frac{2\pi}{3}\right) = \csc^2\left(\frac{2\pi}{3}\right)$.

SOLUTION

$$1 + \cot^2\left(\frac{2\pi}{3}\right) = 1 + \left(\frac{1}{-\sqrt{3}}\right)^2 = 1 + \frac{1}{3} = 1\frac{1}{3}$$

$$\csc^2\left(\frac{2\pi}{3}\right) = \left(\frac{2}{\sqrt{3}}\right)^2 = \frac{4}{3} = 1\frac{1}{3}$$

Example 4 Application: Graphical Analysis

Show graphically that the following trigonometric identity is true.

$$\sin^2(\theta) + \cos^2(\theta) = 1$$

SOLUTION

Graph $y_1 = \cos^2(x)$ and $y_2 = \sin^2(x)$ on the same coordinate system.

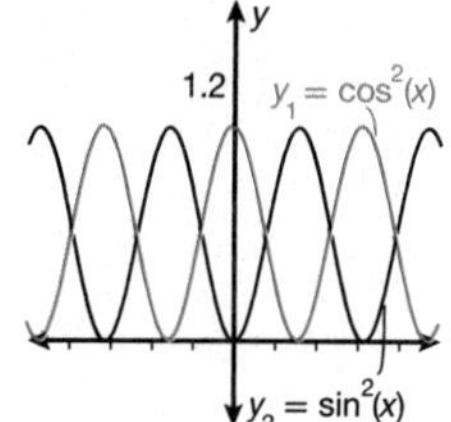

Each graph has an amplitude of 0.5 and is symmetric about the line $y = 0.5$. Therefore, at any given point on the graph, y_1 and y_2 are the same distance from $y = 0.5$.

For $y_1 > y_2$,

$$y_1 - 0.5 = 0.5 - y_2$$
$$\cos^2(x) - 0.5 = 0.5 - \sin^2(x)$$
$$\cos^2(x) + \sin^2(x) = 0.5 + 0.5$$
$$\cos^2(x) + \sin^2(x) = 1$$

For $y_2 < y_1$,

$$0.5 - y_1 = y_2 - 0.5$$
$$0.5 - \cos^2(x) = \sin^2(x) - 0.5$$
$$\cos^2(x) + \sin^2(x) = 0.5 + 0.5$$
$$\cos^2(x) + \sin^2(x) = 1$$

Lesson Practice

a. Show that $\sin^2(\theta) + \cos^2(\theta) = 1$ for $\theta = 60°$. $\left(\frac{\sqrt{3}}{2}\right)^2 + \left(\frac{1}{2}\right)^2 = \frac{3}{4} + \frac{1}{4} = 1$
(Ex 1)

b. Show that $\sin^2(\theta) + \cos^2(\theta) = 1$ for $\theta = \pi$. $(0)^2 + (-1)^2 = 1$
(Ex 1)

c. Show that $\tan^2(\theta) + 1 = \sec^2(\theta)$, for $\theta = 98.5°$. See Additional Answers.
(Ex 2)

d. Show that $\tan^2(\theta) + 1 = \sec^2(\theta)$, for $\theta = \frac{5\pi}{4}$. See Additional Answers.
(Ex 2)

e. Show that $1 + \cot^2(\theta) = \csc^2(\theta)$, for $\theta = 212°$. See Additional Answers.
(Ex 3)

f. Show that $1 + \cot^2(\theta) = \csc^2(\theta)$, for $\theta = \frac{\pi}{6}$. See Additional Answers.
(Ex 3)

g. Explain why $1 + \cot^2(\theta) = \csc^2(\theta)$. (Hint: graph $y_1 = \cot^2(\theta)$ and $y_2 = \csc^2(\theta)$. y_2 is y_1 shifted up one unit. Therefore $\csc^2\theta = \cot^2\theta + 1$. See Additional Answers.
(Ex 4)

Practice Distributed and Integrated

Write the exponential equations in logarithmic form.

1. $6^5 = 7776$ $\log_6 7776 = 5$
(64)

2. $x^3 = 6859$ $\log_x 6859 = 3$
(64)

INCLUSION

Encourage students to write squares of trigonometric function values in both ways as shown below.

$$\sin^2\theta = (\sin\theta)^2$$
$$\sin^2 30° = (\sin 30°)^2$$

*3. Let $f(x) = \sin(x)$ and $g(x) = (x - 1)(x + 1)$. Find $g(f(x)) + 1$. $\sin^2(x)$
(108)

4. Construction A construction team has 230 feet of fencing material for which to fence in a rectangular play area. They were told that the play area should be at least 3000 square feet. Find the range of possible widths they could use. From 40 feet to 75 feet inclusive
(89)

*5. **Write** Explain in complete sentences what must be done to an equation to vertically stretch the graph. To vertically stretch a graph you must multiply each y-coordinate of the graph by a value greater than one.
(104)

6. Lockbox A homeowner is choosing a combination to the lockbox for the house. Four digits (1–9) can be chosen. How many combinations can be made if a digit cannot be repeated? 3024
(33)

*7. **Generalize** Use the trig ratios $\cos(\theta) = \frac{x}{r}$ and $\sin(\theta) = \frac{y}{r}$ to show that $\frac{1}{1 - \frac{1}{1 + \tan^2(\theta)}} = \csc^2(\theta)$. See Additional Answers.
(108)

8. **Analyze** A quadratic trinomial in standard form is added to another quadratic trinomial in standard form and the result is written in standard form. The leading coefficients of the two trinomials are opposites. What are all the possible types of the resulting polynomial (classified by degree)? linear and constant
(11)

9. **Multiple Choice** Solve $S = B + \frac{1}{2}pl$ for l. Which equation shows the correct solution? D
(88)

A $l = \frac{1}{2}(S - B)p$ B $l = S - B - \frac{1}{2}p$ C $l = \frac{2S - B}{p}$ D $l = \frac{2S - 2B}{p}$

10. Write a function that has zeros -6, -2, and 1. $f(x) = x^3 + 7x^2 + 4x - 12$
(35)

*11. **Formulate** Write a possible rational function that fits these parameters: Vertical asymptotes $x = \pm 2$; slant asymptote $y = -2x + 3$. Sample answer: $y = \frac{-2x^3 + 3x^2}{x^2 - 4}$
(107)

12. Use the Binomial Theorem to expand $(2x + y)^2$. $4x^2 + 4xy + y^2$
(49)

13. **Multiple Choice** Which ordered pair contains a local maximum of $g(x) = 2x^3 - 3x^2 - 12x$? A
(101)

A $(-1, 7)$ B $(0, 0)$ C $(4, 32)$ D $(5, 115)$

14. **Analyze** Is the sequence $\{5, 5, 5, 5\}$ an arithmetic sequence? Why or why not?
(92) Yes, the differences between consecutive terms are constant: 0

15. Use synthetic substitution to find $f(4)$ for $f(x) = 3x^4 + 6x^2 - x - 22$. 838
(51)

16. Soccer A drafter is creating the plans for a sport and fitness center, which includes an official size soccer field. On her grid, the units represent yards and the endpoints of a diameter of the center circle are located at $(23, -4)$ and $(29, -4)$. Write an equation for this circle. $(x - 26)^2 + (y + 4)^2 = 9$
(91)

*17. Find the real zeros of $y = x^5 - 4x^3 - x^2 + 4$. $x = \pm 2, 1$
(107)

18. Solve $\frac{x + 3}{x - 6} > 0$ by finding the sign of the numerator and denominator. $x < -3$ or $x > 6$
(94)

ALTERNATE METHOD FOR EXAMPLE 4

Have the students graph $y = \sin^2\theta + \cos^2\theta$ and $y = 1$ on the same coordinate system and verify that the graphs coincide.

3 Practice

Problem 10

Error Alert

Students sometimes use the wrong sign when they write a factor of a polynomial. For the zero -6, they might write $x - 6$, which is incorrect. Remind them that the factor $x - c$ corresponds to the zero c of a function, so $x - (-6) = x + 6$ corresponds to the zero -6.

Problem 25

Extend the Problem

Suppose $m\angle ABC = 100°$. Find the length of $\overline{AC}$ to the nearest hundredth. 34.31 units

*19. **Multi-Step** A polynomial equation has roots of 6 and $7i$.
(106)

a. What is the minimum degree of the polynomial? Name the other roots if there are any. 3; $-7i$

b. What is the simplest polynomial equation with these roots? $x^3 - 6x^2 + 49x - 294 = 0$

c. Give another polynomial equation with these roots. Possible answer: $2x^3 - 12x^2 + 98x - 588 = 0$

20. **Coordinate Geometry** Use a table of values to graph $f(x) = |x - 4| + 2$.
(17)

21. Given $a^2 + b^2 = c^2$. Solve for b. $b = \sqrt{c^2 - a^2}$
(88)

22. **Physics** Two springs have two different weights attached at the ends. The movement of each weight is modeled by the periodic functions shown, where t is the time in seconds. How often will both weights be at their lowest point at the same time. Roughly every $\frac{\pi}{2}$ seconds.
(82)

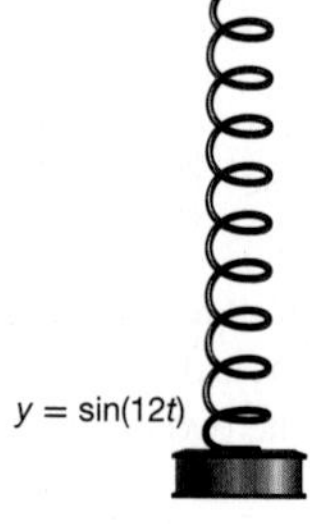
$y = \sin(12t)$

$y = \sin(28t)$

23. **Error Analysis** Two students are subtracting two vectors written as complex numbers but they get different results. Which student made the mistake?
(99)

Student A incorrectly distributes the minus sign to the terms of the second complex number.

Student A	Student B
$(3 + 4i) - (-5 + 3i)$ $= (3 - 5) + (4 - 3)i$ $= -2 + i$	$(3 + 4i) - (-5 + 3i)$ $= (3 + 5) + (4 - 3)i$ $= 8 + i$

*24. **Sound** Two measures of sound are loudness and intensity. They are related by the function $L(I) = 10 \log \frac{I}{I_0}$, where $L(I)$ is loudness in decibels, I is intensity in watts per square meter, and $I_0 \approx 10^{-12}$ watt per square meter, the intensity of a barely audible sound. The loudness of a quiet library is about 40 decibels. Find the intensity that corresponds to a loudness of 40 decibels. 10^{-8}, or 0.00000001 watt per square meter
(102)

20. (graph)

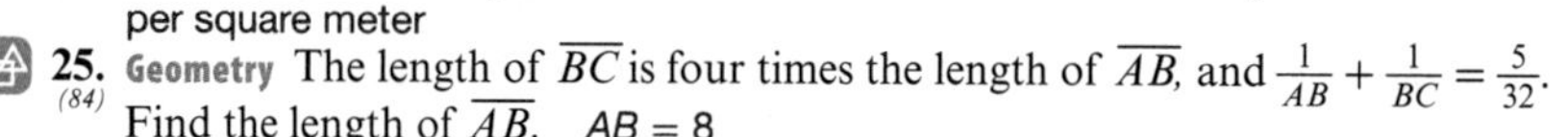

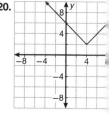

25. **Geometry** The length of $\overline{BC}$ is four times the length of $\overline{AB}$, and $\frac{1}{AB} + \frac{1}{BC} = \frac{5}{32}$. Find the length of $\overline{AB}$. $AB = 8$
(84)

*26. **Error Analysis** A student is simplifying the expression below using trigonometric identities. What mistake did the student make? Student incorrectly converts $\csc^2(x)$.
(108)

$$\frac{1 - \cos^2(x)}{1 - \frac{1}{1 + \cot^2(x)}} = \frac{\sin^2(x)}{1 - \frac{1}{\csc^2(x)}} = \frac{\sin^2(x)}{1 - \cos^2(x)} = \frac{\sin^2(x)}{\sin^2(x)} = 1$$

Solve.

27. $63x^3 - 7x = 0$ $x = -\frac{1}{3}, 0, \frac{1}{3}$
(78)

28. $4x^3 + 6x^2 - 40x = 0$ $x = -4, 0, \frac{5}{2}$
(78)

29. A line passes through points $(-2, 4)$ and $(0, 5)$. Write the equation of the line in slope-intercept form. $y = \frac{1}{2}x + 5$
(26)

*30. **Graphing Calculator** Graph $y = 2\sec(x)$ on your graphing calculator. Determine its period and asymptotes.
(103)

30. $y = 2\sec(x)$ has a period of 2π. The asymptotes occur at $x = \frac{\pi}{2} + \pi n$, where n is an integer.

CHALLENGE

Use one or more fundamental trigonometric identities to simplify

$\sec^2\theta\,(1 - \sin^2\theta)$. Show your steps.

Sample:

$\sec^2\theta\,(1 - \sin^2\theta)$

$= (1 + \tan^2\theta)(\cos^2\theta)$

$= \cos^2\theta + \cos^2\theta\tan^2\theta$

$= \cos^2\theta + \cos^2\theta\,\frac{\sin^2\theta}{\cos^2\theta}$

$= \cos^2\theta + \sin^2\theta$

$= 1$

LOOKING FORWARD

Using fundamental trigonometric identities prepares students for

- **Lesson 112** Using Sum and Difference Identities
- **Lesson 115** Finding Double-Angle and Half-Angle Identities
- **Lesson 119** Solving Trigonometric Equations

LESSON 109

Making Graphs and Using Equations of Hyperbolas

Warm Up

1. (58) **Vocabulary** To convert the equation $x^2 + 10x + 3 = 0$ to $(x + 5)^2 = 22$ involves using the technique of ________. completing the square

2. (26) What is the equation of the line with slope 3 that passes through $(2, -25)$? 2. $y = 3x - 31$

3. (58) Solve by completing the square: $2x^2 - 4x + 10 = 0$. $(x - 1)^2 + 4 = 0$; $x = 1 \pm 2i$

New Concepts

A **hyperbola** is the set of points P in a plane such that the difference of the distances from P to two fixed points F_1 and F_2, called the **foci,** is a constant. The standard form of the equation of an hyperbola depends on the orientation of the hyperbola. The **transverse axis** is the segment that lies on the line containing the foci and has endpoints on a hyperbola. The endpoints are the **vertices** of a hyperbola.

Horizontal Orientation	Vertical Orientation
$\frac{x^2}{a^2} - \frac{y^2}{b^2} = 1$	$\frac{y^2}{a^2} - \frac{x^2}{b^2} = 1$
$y = -\frac{b}{a}x$, $y = \frac{b}{a}x$, $(0, b)$, $(-c, 0)$, $(c, 0)$, $(-a, 0)$, $(a, 0)$, $(0, -b)$, x, y	$(0, a)$, $(0, c)$, $y = -\frac{a}{b}x$, $y = \frac{a}{b}x$, $(-b, 0)$, $(b, 0)$, $(0, -c)$, $(0, -a)$, x, y
$c = \sqrt{a^2 + b^2}$, Eccentricity: $e = \sqrt{1 + \frac{b^2}{a^2}} = \frac{c}{a}$	
Foci: $(-c, 0)$ and $(c, 0)$ Vertices: $(-a, 0)$ and $(a, 0)$ Asymptotes: $y = \pm\frac{b}{a}x$	Foci: $(0, -c)$ and $(0, c)$ Vertices: $(0, a)$ and $(0, -a)$ Asymptotes: $y = \pm\frac{a}{b}x$

Math Reasoning

Verify Show that $\sqrt{1 + \frac{b^2}{a^2}} = \frac{c}{a}$.

$\sqrt{1 + \frac{b^2}{a^2}} = \sqrt{\frac{a^2}{a^2} + \frac{b^2}{a^2}}$

$= \sqrt{\frac{a^2 + b^2}{a^2}} = \frac{\sqrt{a^2 + b^2}}{\sqrt{a^2}}$

$= \frac{\sqrt{a^2 + b^2}}{a} = \frac{c}{a}$

Math Reasoning

Analyze Why are the values of c and e not dependent on the orientation of the hyperbola?

The formulas for calculating these values use the value of a and b regardless of whether they are horizontal or vertical.

Example 1 Graphs of Hyperbolas Centered at the Origin

a. Graph $\frac{x^2}{5^2} - \frac{y^2}{4^2} = 1$. Identify the values of a, b, and c, as well as the orientation of the graph. Determine the eccentricity e and the asymptotes.

SOLUTION Horizontal orientation

$a = 5$; $b = 4$

$c = \sqrt{5^2 + 4^2} \approx 6.4031$, $e = \sqrt{1 + \frac{4^2}{5^2}} \approx 1.2806$

Asymptotes: $y = \pm\frac{4}{5}x$

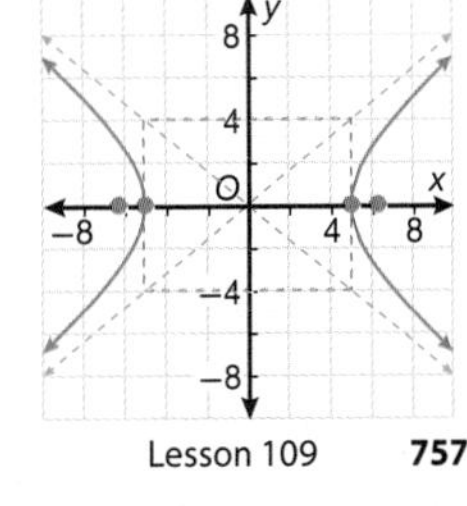

LESSON 109

1 Warm Up

Problem 3

Remind students they need to add $\left(\frac{b}{2}\right)^2$ to both sides of the equation to complete the square.

2 New Concepts

Example 1

These examples show students how to graph hyperbolas centered at the origin and to identify a, b, c, the eccentricity, and the asymptotes.

Additional Example 1

Graph the following equations. Identify the values of a, b, and c, as well as the orientation of the graph. Determine the eccentricity e and the asymptotes.

a. $\frac{x^2}{3^2} - \frac{y^2}{1^2} = 1$

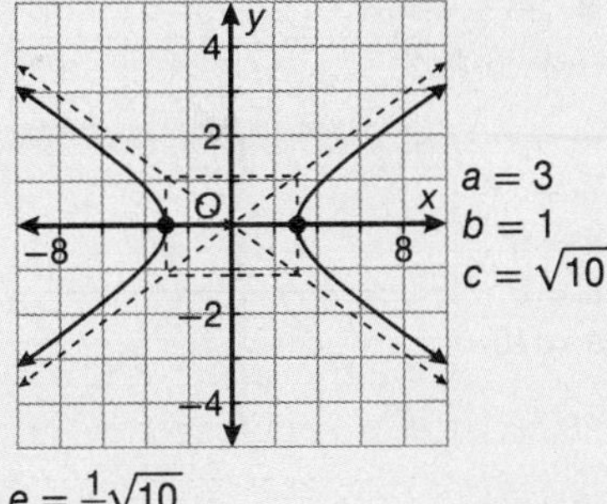

$a = 3$
$b = 1$
$c = \sqrt{10}$

$e = \frac{1}{3}\sqrt{10}$
asymptotes: $y = \pm\frac{1}{3}$

LESSON RESOURCES

Student Edition Practice Workbook 109
Reteaching Master 109
Adaptations Master 109
Challenge and Enrichment Master C109

MATH BACKGROUND

Students have graphed parabolas, circles, and ellipses earlier in the course. Compare the equation of a hyperbola with the equations of the other conic sections.

Circle: $(x - h)^2 + (y - k)^2 = r^2$

Parabola: $x - h = \frac{1}{4p}(y - k)^2$ or

$y - k = \frac{1}{4p}(x - h)^2$

Ellipse: $\frac{(x - h)^2}{a^2} + \frac{(y - k)^2}{b^2} = 1$ or

$\frac{(x - h)^2}{b^2} + \frac{(y - k)^2}{a^2} = 1$

Hyperbola: $\frac{(x - h)^2}{a^2} - \frac{(y - k)^2}{b^2} = 1$ or

$\frac{(y - k)^2}{a^2} - \frac{(x - h)^2}{b^2} = 1$

b. $\frac{y^2}{7^2} - \frac{x^2}{5^2} = 1$

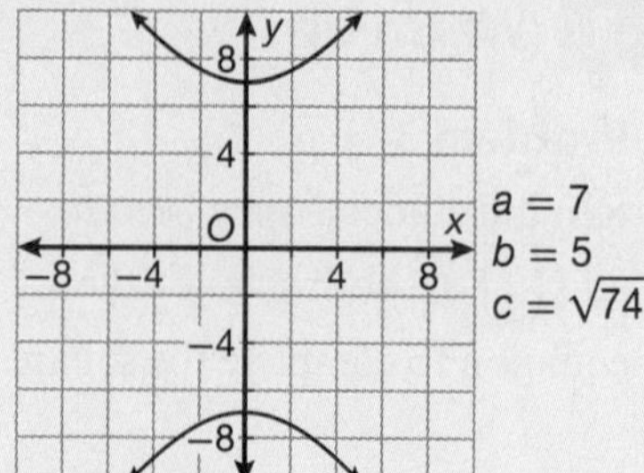

$a = 7$
$b = 5$
$c = \sqrt{74}$

$e = \frac{1}{7}\sqrt{74}$

asymptotes: $y = \pm\frac{7}{5}x$

Example 2

These examples show students how to graph hyperbolas not centered at the origin.

Error Alert Watch for students who use $(-h, -k)$ when finding the equations of the asymptotes.

Additional Example 2

Graph the following equations. Identify the values of a, b, and c, as well as the orientation of the graph. Determine the eccentricity and the asymptotes.

a. $\frac{(x-2)^2}{8^2} - \frac{(y-1)^2}{6^2} = 1$

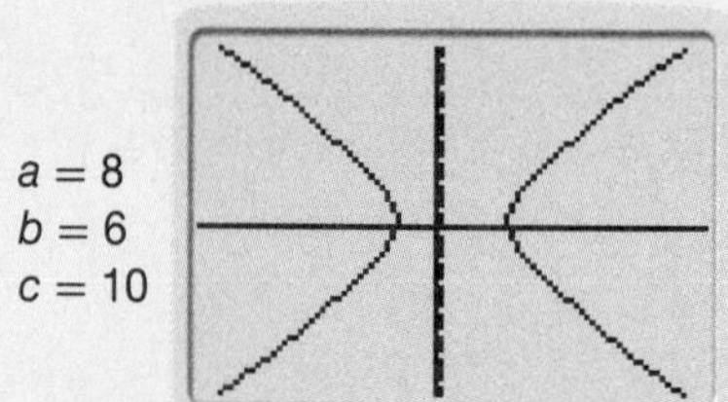

$a = 8$
$b = 6$
$c = 10$

$e = \frac{5}{4}$

asymptotes: $y = \frac{3}{4}x - \frac{1}{2}$, $y = -\frac{3}{4}x + \frac{5}{2}$

b. Graph $\frac{y^2}{8^2} - \frac{x^2}{6^2} = 1$. Identify the values of a, b, and c, as well as the orientation of the graph. Determine the eccentricity e and the asymptotes.

SOLUTION Vertical orientation

$a = 8$

$b = 6$

$c = \sqrt{8^2 + 6^2} = 10$

$e = \sqrt{1 + \frac{6^2}{8^2}} = 1.25$

Asymptotes: $y = \pm\frac{4}{3}x$

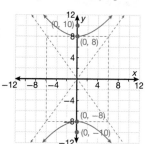

A hyperbola does not need to be centered at the origin.

Math Language

One of the two symmetrical parts of the hyperbola is called a **branch.** A hyperbola has two branches.

Horizontal Orientation	Vertical Orientation
$\frac{(x-h)^2}{a^2} - \frac{(y-k)^2}{b^2} = 1$	$\frac{(y-k)^2}{a^2} - \frac{(x-h)^2}{b^2} = 1$
$(h-a, k)$, $(h+a, k)$, (h, k), $(h-c, k)$, $(h+c, k)$	$(h, k+c)$, $(h, k+a)$, (h, k), $(h, k-a)$, $(h, k-c)$

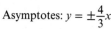

Example 2 **Graphs of Hyperbolas Not Centered at the Origin**

Graph each equation. Identify the values of a, b, and c, as well as the orientation of the graph. Determine the eccentricity and the asymptotes.

a. $\frac{(x-3)^2}{5^2} - \frac{(y-5)^2}{4^2} = 1$

SOLUTION Horizontal orientation

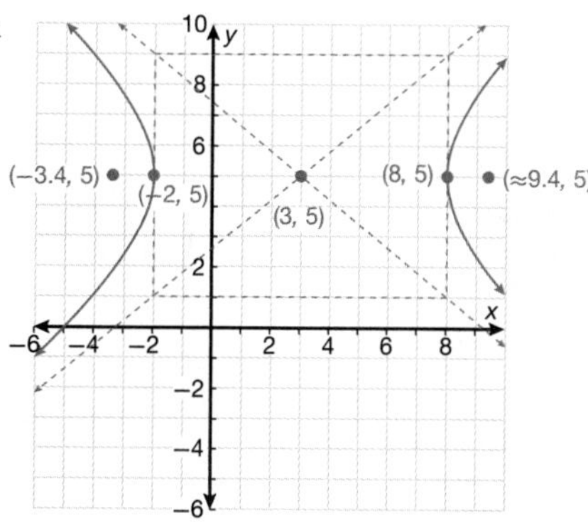

$a = 5 \quad b = 4$

$c = \sqrt{5^2 + 4^2} \approx 6.4031$

$e = \sqrt{1 + \frac{4^2}{5^2}} \approx 1.2806$

Finding the equations of the asymptotes requires using the slope formula, since the hyperbola is not centered at the origin.

Step 1: Calculate the slope.

$m = \pm\frac{b}{a} = \pm\frac{4}{5}$

758 *Saxon Algebra 2*

INCLUSION

This lesson contains many unfamiliar words with difficult pronunciations. Reinforce the definitions and pronunciations of each word by using the diagram.

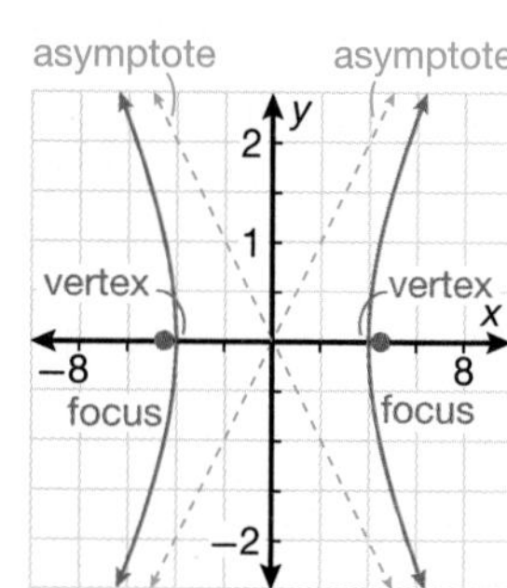

Step 2: Use the slope formula for each asymptote. Use (h, k).

$$m = \frac{y - y_1}{x - x_1} \qquad m = \frac{y - y_1}{x - x_1}$$

$$\frac{4}{5} = \frac{y-5}{x-3} \qquad -\frac{4}{5} = \frac{y-5}{x-3}$$

$$4x - 12 = 5y - 25 \qquad -4x + 12 = 5y - 25$$

$$y = \frac{4}{5}x + \frac{13}{5} \qquad y = -\frac{4}{5}x + \frac{37}{5}$$

b. $\dfrac{(y-4)^2}{6^2} - \dfrac{(x-7)^2}{3^2} = 1$

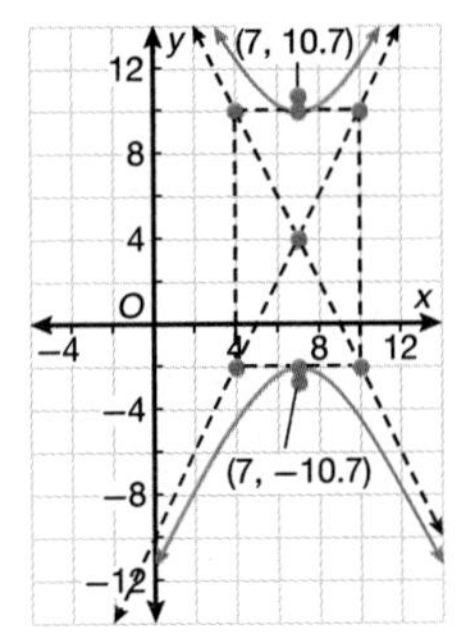

SOLUTION Vertical orientation

$a = 6 \qquad b = 3$

$c = \sqrt{6^2 + 3^2} \approx 6.7082$

$e = \sqrt{1 + \frac{3^2}{6^2}} \approx 1.1180$

Asymptotes: $y = 2x - 10 \quad y = -2x + 18$

When the equation of a hyperbola is in standard form, it is easier to graph.

Example 3 Deriving the Equation of a Hyperbola in Standard Form

Change $54y - 9y^2 + 4x^2 - 32x - 53 = 0$ to the equation of a hyperbola in standard form.

SOLUTION **Step 1:** Organize the terms into x- and y-terms.

$$(4x^2 - 32x) - (9y^2 - 54y) - 53 = 0$$

$$4(x^2 - 8x) - 9(y^2 - 6y) - 53 = 0$$

Step 2: Complete the square for the x- and y-terms in the parentheses. Be sure to subtract the values that are added to complete the square. See the highlighted numbers.

$$4(x^2 - 8x + 16) - 9(y^2 - 6y + 9) - 53 - 64 + 81 = 0$$

$$4(x-4)^2 - 9(y-3)^2 - 36 = 0$$

Step 3:

$4(x-4)^2 - 9(y-3)^2 = 36$ — Put the constant term on the right side of the equation.

$\dfrac{4(x-4)^2}{36} - \dfrac{9(y-3)^2}{36} = 1$ — Divide both sides by that number to get 1 on the right.

$\dfrac{(x-4)^2}{9} - \dfrac{(y-3)^2}{4} = 1$

$\dfrac{(x-4)^2}{3^2} - \dfrac{(y-3)^2}{2^2} = 1$ — Express the denominators as squares.

ALTERNATE METHOD FOR EXAMPLE 3

Students can move the constant term to the right side of the equation in Step 1. Then add to the right side as the squares are completed on the left.

$$4(x^2 - 8x) - 9(y^2 - 6y) = 53$$

$$4(x^2 - 8x + 16) - 9(y^2 - 6y + 9) = 53 + 64 - 81$$

$$4(x-4)^2 - 9(y-3)^2 = 36$$

b. $\dfrac{(y-3)^2}{9^2} - \dfrac{(x-5)^2}{2^2} = 1$

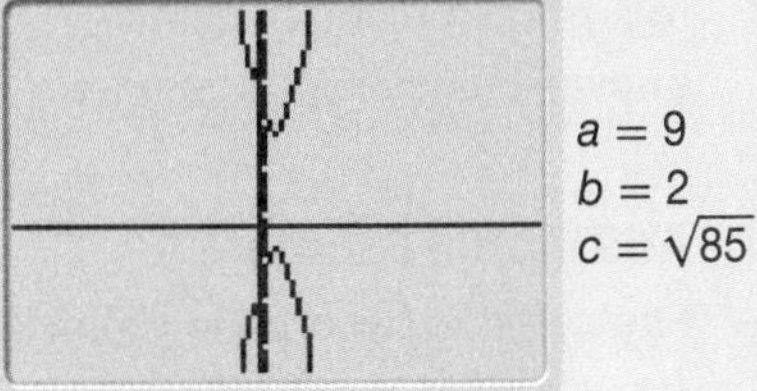

$a = 9$
$b = 2$
$c = \sqrt{85}$

$e = \frac{1}{9}\sqrt{85}$

asymptotes: $y = \frac{9}{2}x - \frac{39}{2}$,
$y = -\frac{9}{2}x + \frac{51}{2}$

Example 3

This example shows students how to use completing the square to write the equation of a hyperbola in standard form.

Additional Example 3

Take the following equation and change it to the equation of a hyperbola in standard form.

$64y - 16y^2 + 4x^2 - 32x - 64 = 0$

$\dfrac{(x-4)^2}{4^2} - \dfrac{(y-2)^2}{2^2} = 1$

Error Alert In example 3, ensure that students do not subtract 16 and 9 instead of subtracting $(4 \cdot 16)$ and $(-9 \cdot 9)$ when they are completing the square.

Example 4

This example introduces students to a branch of mathematics known as hyperbolic geometry.

Additional Example 4

Show that in hyperbolic geometry, $1 + \sin h^2(x) = \cos h^2(x)$.

$1 + \sin h^2(x) = 1 + \left(\frac{e^x - e^{-x}}{2}\right)^2$

$= 1 + \frac{(e^x - e^{-x})^2}{4}$

$= \frac{4}{4} + \frac{e^{2x} - 2e^x e^{-x} + e^{-2x}}{4}$

$= \frac{4 + e^{2x} - 2 + e^{-2x}}{4}$

$= \frac{e^{2x} + 2 + e^{-2x}}{4}$

$= \frac{(e^x + e^{-x})^2}{2^2}$

$= \left(\frac{e^x + e^{-x}}{2}\right)^2$

$= \cos h^2(x)$

$\cos h^2(x) - \sin h^2(x) = 1$

$\cos h^2(x) - \sin h^2(x) + \sin h^2(x)$

$= 1 + \sin h^2(x)$

$\cos h^2(x) = 1 + \sin h^2(x)$

Lesson Practice

Problems a–d

Scaffolding Have students first determine if the orientation is horizontal or vertical.

Check for Understanding

The questions below help assess the concepts taught in this lesson.

"Explain how to use the equation of a hyperbola of the form $\frac{x^2}{a^2} - \frac{y^2}{b^2} = 1$ to identify the foci and vertices." Sample: The hyperbola is centered at the origin, so the vertices are located at $(-a, 0)$ and $(a, 0)$. The foci are located at $(-c, 0)$ and $(c, 0)$, where $c = \sqrt{a^2 + b^2}$.

"Explain why the eccentricity and the value of c are not affected by where the hyperbola is centered." Sample: The values of h and k determine whether the hyperbola is centered at the origin or not. These values are not used to determine the eccentricity and c.

The properties of hyperbolas give rise to what is known as hyperbolic geometry. **Hyperbolic geometry** has its own set of trigonometric identities, as shown below.

Hyperbolic Geometry

For any point (x, y) on the unit hyperbola,

$$x^2 - y^2 = 1$$

$$\cos h(x) = \frac{e^x + e^{-x}}{2}$$

$$\sin h(x) = \frac{e^x - e^{-x}}{2}$$

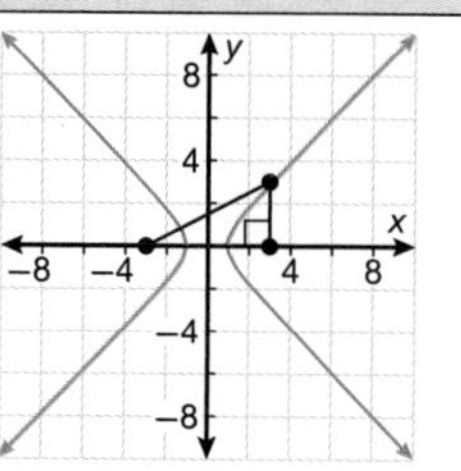

The function $\cos h(x)$ is known as the hyperbolic cosine, and $\sin h(x)$ is known as the hyperbolic sine.

Example 4 **Application: Hyperbolic Geometry**

Show that in hyperbolic geometry,

$\cos h^2(x) - \sin h^2(x) = 1$

SOLUTION Using the definitions of the hyperbolic trigonometric functions,

$$\cos h^2(x) - \sin h^2(x) = \left(\frac{e^x + e^{-x}}{2}\right)^2 - \left(\frac{e^x - e^{-x}}{2}\right)^2$$

$$= \frac{1}{4}(e^{2x} + 2e^x e^{-x} + e^{-2x} - e^{2x} + 2e^x e^{-x} - e^{-2x})$$

$$= \frac{1}{4}(2 + 2) = 1$$

Lesson Practice

Graph each equation. Identify the values of *a*, *b*, and *c*, as well as the orientation of the graph. Determine the eccentricity *e* and the asymptotes.

a.–e. See Additional Answers.

a. (Ex 1) $\frac{x^2}{6^2} - \frac{y^2}{4^2} = 1$

b. (Ex 1) $\frac{y^2}{7^2} - \frac{x^2}{5^2} = 1$

c. (Ex 2) $\frac{(x-5)^2}{7^2} - \frac{(y-4)^2}{5^2} = 1$

d. (Ex 2) $\frac{(y-8)^2}{9^2} - \frac{(x-5)^2}{6^2} = 1$

e. (Ex 3) Take the following equation and change it to the equation of a hyperbola in standard form. $54y - 9y^2 + 4x^2 - 32x - 161 = 0$

f. (Ex 4) What is $\sin h^2(x) - \cos h^2(x)$? -1

CHALLENGE

Find the equation of the hyperbola with vertices at $(0, 3)$ and $(0, -3)$ and asymptotes of $y = \pm\frac{1}{2}x$.

$\frac{y^2}{3^2} - \frac{x^2}{6^2} = 1$

Practice Distributed and Integrated

Simplify.

1. (48) $\frac{x+4}{x^2-x-12}+\frac{2x}{x+3}$ $\frac{2x^2-7x+4}{x^2-x-12}$

2. (48) $\dfrac{\frac{x-1}{x+5}}{\frac{x+6}{x-3}}$ $\frac{x^2-4x+3}{x^2+11x+30}$

Convert from Cartesian to polar coordinates.

3. (96) $(-5, -5)$ $\left(5\sqrt{2}, \frac{5\pi}{4}\right)$

4. (96) $(0, -4)$ $\left(4, \frac{3\pi}{2}\right)$

*5. (109) **Formulate** A hyperbola has asymptotes with equations $y = \pm x$. The graph of the hyperbola crosses the x-axis at $(5, 0)$. Write the equation of the hyperbola.

5. $\frac{x^2}{5^2} - \frac{y^2}{5^2} = 1$

6. (32) Determine whether the matrices are inverses. $M \cdot N = I$ and $N \cdot M = I$ so M and N are inverses.

$M = \begin{bmatrix} 10 & -3 \\ 3 & -1 \end{bmatrix}$ $N = \begin{bmatrix} 1 & -3 \\ 3 & -10 \end{bmatrix}$

7. (Inv 9) **Data Analysis** The general sizing chart for infant/toddler shoe sizes is shown to the right. Lana is buying shoes for her 9-month-old brother. What shoe size(s) can she buy? Does this table form a function? Explain.

Age (in months)	Size
$3 \le x \le 6$	2
$6 \le x \le 9$	3
$9 \le x \le 12$	4

7. Possible answer: Lana can buy a size 4 or a size 3. The table does not form a function because there is more than one size for the same age. Therefore the graph will not pass the vertical line test.

8. (101) **Analyze** Explain why the leading coefficient and degree of the highest-degree term of a polynomial function are the only characteristics that determine end behavior.

8. Possible answer: As $x \to \pm\infty$, the absolute value of the highest-degree term becomes much greater than the absolute value of the sum of all the other terms, and the difference between the absolute value of the highest-degree term and the absolute value of the sum of all the other terms increases.

9. (93) **Error Analysis** To evaluate $\frac{\log 2}{12 \log 1.05}$ with a calculator, a student entered $\log(2) \div 12\log(1.05)$. What is the error? What is a correct expression to enter on a calculator? $\log(2) \div 12\log(1.05) = \left(\frac{\log 2}{12}\right)(\log 1.05)$. Possible correct expression: $\log(2) \div (12\log(1.05))$

*10. (109) **Space Science** A satellite is following a hyperbolic path, and there are two monitoring stations located at the foci of the hyperbola. What data can be used to ensure that the satellite is maintaining its hyperbolic trajectory? The difference in distance from the satellite to the foci should be a constant.

11. (96) **Analyze** Point P has polar coordinates (r, θ). Describe all the polar coordinates of point P that have r as the first coordinate. Possible answer: $(r, \theta \pm 2n\pi)$, where n is any integer

Solve.

12. (5) $\frac{1}{4}\begin{bmatrix} 2 & 4 \\ 6 & 8 \end{bmatrix} + \begin{bmatrix} -2 & 1 \\ -\frac{1}{2} & 5 \end{bmatrix}$ $\begin{bmatrix} -1\frac{1}{2} & 2 \\ 1 & 7 \end{bmatrix}$

13. (84) $\frac{x^2-x-12}{x-2} = 0$ $x = -3, 4$

*14. (108) **Graphing Calculator** Graph $y_1 = \cot^2(x)$ and $y_2 = \csc^2(x)$. Use the information in the graphs to prove the trigonometric identity $1 + \cot^2(x) = \csc^2(x)$. at any given point $y_1 = \cot^2(x)$ is exactly 1 unit below $y_2 = \csc^2(x)$

15. (85) **Construction** The sheet of metal shown is rolled into a cylinder along the longer side. The area of the sheet is 22 square units. Find the radius of the cylinder. $\frac{11}{2\pi}$

3x + 2

x − 1

3 Practice

Math Conversations

Discussions to strengthen understanding

Problem 2

"What is the first step in solving the problem?" Rewrite the problem as a multiplication problem by multiplying the numerator by the reciprocal of the denominator.

Problem 6

"What is true about two matrices that are inverses?" Their product is the identity matrix.

Problem 12

"Which operation is performed first?" The scalar multiplication

"Can the two resulting matrices be added? Why?" Yes, they have the same dimensions.

Problem 15

Extend the Problem

"Find the volume of the cylinder." $\frac{121}{2\pi}$

ENGLISH LEARNERS

For Problem 10, explain the meaning of the word **maintain.** Say:

"To maintain means to continue. It is helpful to maintain a binder with a daily planner as a reminder when the homework is due."

Have students name some responsibilities they maintain throughout the year. Sample: change the oil on the car, practice tennis daily

Problem 18

"How do you know the formula is not solved for P?" P is on both sides of the equation.

Problem 21

Error Alert

Watch for students who choose A because the circles have the same center. Remind students that concentric circles have radii of different lengths.

16. (36) Find the equation of the line perpendicular to the graph of $y = 19$ that passes through the point $(6, -5)$. $x = 6$

17. (79) Evaluate the piecewise function $f(x) = \begin{cases} 2 - x \text{ if } x \leq 5 \\ -x^2 \text{ if } 5 < x < 8 \\ 6 \text{ if } 8 \leq x \end{cases}$ for $x = -8$ and $x = 5$. 10, −3

18. (88) **Error Analysis** A student solved the formula $A = P + Prt$ for P as shown below. What is the error? Solve the formula for P correctly. See Additional Answers.

$$A = P + Prt$$
$$A - P = Prt$$
$$A - \frac{P}{rt} = P$$

***19.** (108) **Multiple Choice** Which expression is equivalent to $\frac{1}{1 + \tan^2(\theta)}$? D

A $\tan^2(\theta)$ **B** $\csc^2(\theta)$ **C** $\sin^2(\theta)$ **D** $\cos^2(\theta)$

20. (46) **Geometry** A wall casts a shadow depending on the angle of the sun. Derive the equation that can be used to find the length of the shadow, L. $L = \frac{h}{\tan(\theta)}$

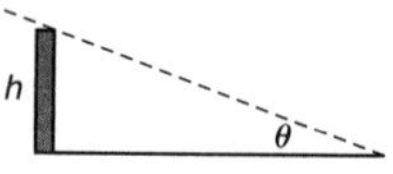

21. (91) **Multiple Choice** Concentric circles have the same center but different radii. Which pair of equations represents a pair of concentric circles? B

A $(x - 1)^2 + (y + 2)^2 = 6$ and $(x - 1)^2 + (y + 2)^2 = 6$

B $(x - 1)^2 + (y + 2)^2 = 6$ and $(x - 1)^2 + (y + 2)^2 = 8$

C $(x - 1)^2 + (y + 2)^2 = 6$ and $(x - 2)^2 + (y + 1)^2 = 6$

D $(x - 1)^2 + (y + 2)^2 = 6$ and $(x - 2)^2 + (y + 8)^2 = 12$

***22.** (102) **Population Growth** Based on U.S. Census statistics, the population of New Jersey for the years 1950–1990 can be modeled by the equation $y = 628 + 1842 \ln t$, where $10 \leq t \leq 50$, $t = 10$ represents 1950, and y is the population in thousands. Use the model to approximate the year in which the population of New Jersey reached 7,000,000. 1971 or 1972

23. (93) **Multi-Step** The table below is based on census statistics from India and China.

	China	India
Population in 2000 (to nearest million)	1,267,000,000	1,005,000,000
Average annual increase (1990–2000)	1.04%	1.83%

a. Write a function of the form $y_1 = ab^t$, where y_1 represents China's population t years after 2000. $y_1 = 1{,}267{,}000{,}000(1.0104)^t$

b. Write a function of the form $y_2 = ab^t$, where y_2 represents India's population t years after 2000. $y_2 = 1{,}005{,}000{,}000(1.0183)^t$

c. Write and solve an equation to predict the year in which India's population will overtake China's population. See Additional Answers.

***24.** (107) **Physics** If you throw a ball in the air, the vertical distance d that it travels over time t is found using the equation $d(t) = -4.9t^2 + v_0t + d_0$. The term v_o is the initial speed that the object is thrown, and d_o is the initial height the object is thrown from. The rational function $y = \frac{d(t)}{t}$ is the average speed the object has traveled. Find the slant asymptotes of this equation for the function that has $v_o = 65$ and $d_o = 25$.
$y = -4.9t + 65$

***25.** (97) **Write** How is a geometric sequence similar to an arithmetic sequence? See Additional Answers.

26. (100) **Generalize** An odd function is a function with a graph that is symmetric with respect to the origin. A function is odd if and only if $f(-x) = -f(x)$. Show that rational functions of the form $f(x) = \frac{1}{x(2n+1)}$, for positive integers n, are odd functions. See Additional Answers.

***27.** (105) **Physics** The number of feet an object falls during each second after it is dropped is given by the sequence 16, 48, 80, 112, ... It takes between 8 and 9 seconds for an object that falls off the top of the John Hancock Center in Chicago to hit the ground. Show how to use an arithmetic series to estimate the height of the John Hancock Center. See Additional Answers.

28. (28) Identify any excluded values and then simplify the expression $\frac{4x+28}{x^2-49}$. $x = -7, 7, \frac{4}{x-7}$

***29.** (106) Determine where the graph of $y = (x+4)(x+4)(x+4)(x-2)(x-6)(x-6)$ passes through the x-axis and where it just touches the x-axis. It passes through at $(-4, 0)$ and $(2, 0)$ and touches the x-axis at $(6, 0)$.

***30.** (109) The distance between the two foci of a hyperbola is 10. The slopes of the asymptotes are $\pm\frac{3}{4}$. Write one possible equation for such a hyperbola.
Sample answer: $\frac{x^2}{4^2} - \frac{y^2}{3^2} = 1$

Problem 26

"What is an odd function?" A function where $f(-x) = -f(x)$

"How can you determine if the function is odd?" Find $f(-x)$ and see if it is equal to $-\frac{1}{x(2n+1)}$.

Problem 28

Error Alert

Students might simplify before finding excluded values.

LOOKING FORWARD 

Making graphs and solving equations of hyperbolas prepares students for:

- **Lesson 114** Identifying Conic Sections

LESSON

110

1 Warm Up

Use the Warm Up to review the prerequisite skills for this lesson.

2 New Concepts

Students graph and transform logarithmic functions.

Example 1

Students see how the values of a, b, and c change the graph.

Additional Example 1

Make a table using the given values to graph the function and its inverse. Describe the domain and range of the function.

$f(x) = \left(\frac{1}{2}\right)^x$; $x = -2, -1, 0, 1,$ and 2

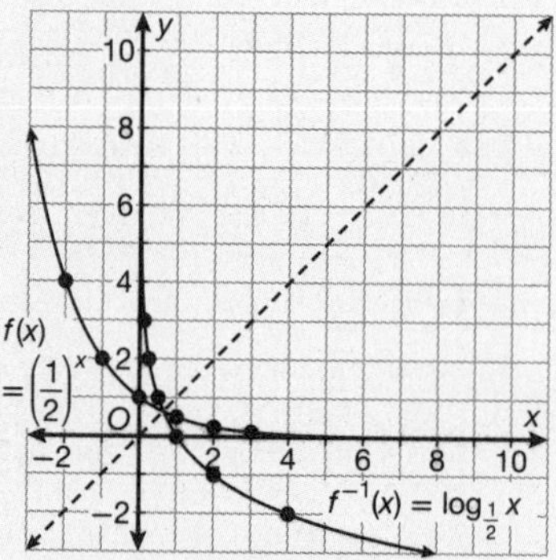

Domain of $f(x) = \left(\frac{1}{2}\right)^x$: all real numbers, Range: $f(x) > 0$; Domain of $f^{-1}(x) = \log_{\frac{1}{2}} x$ is $x > 0$, Range: $f^{-1}(x)$ all real numbers

LESSON RESOURCES

Student Edition Practice Workbook 110
Reteaching Master 110
Adaptations Master 110
Challenge and Enrichment Master C110

LESSON 110

Graphing Logarithmic Functions

Warm Up

1. **Vocabulary** A log base e is known as a ________. natural logarithm
(72)

2. Write $\log \frac{(x^2 - 1)}{x - 3}$ as the sum and difference of logs. $\log(x - 1) + \log(x + 1) - \log(x - 3)$
(72)

3. Rewrite $\log_6(78)$ as a natural logarithm. $\frac{\ln(78)}{\ln(6)}$
(72)

New Concepts

A **logarithmic function** is the inverse of an exponential function. The graph of the logarithmic function has a similar shape to the graph of the corresponding exponential function. The graphs are reflected across the graph of $y = x$.

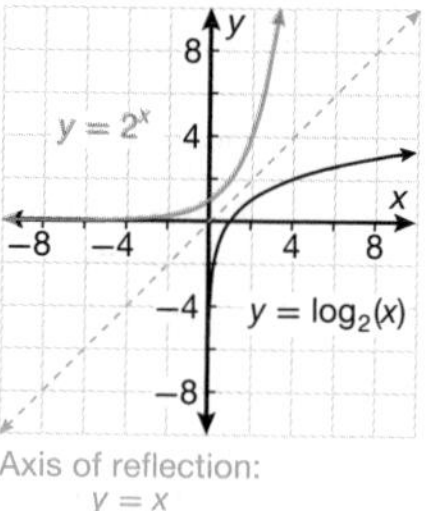

Axis of reflection: $y = x$

Recall that when a graph is reflected across the line $y = x$, the domain and range of each function are switched. So if the point (0, 1) is on the graph of $f(x)$, then (1, 0) is on the graph of $f^{-1}(x)$.

Sample: Using a table of values, graph the inverse of the logarithm function–its related exponential function. Then reverse the ordered pairs and graph the logarithmic function.

Math Reasoning

Generalize Explain how to graph a logarithmic function with a base other than 10 or e.

Hint

Recall that a change in the constant term of a function represents a vertical shift.

Example 1 Graphing Functions of the Form $f(x) = \log_b x$

Make a table using the given values to graph the function and its inverse. Describe the domain and range of the function.

$f(x) = 2^x$; $x = -2, -1, 0, 1,$ and 2

SOLUTION

x	−2	−1	0	1	2
$f(x) = 2^x$	$\frac{1}{4}$	$\frac{1}{2}$	1	2	4

Graph the line $y = x$. Reverse the ordered pairs to graph the inverse function $f^{-1}(x) = \log_2 x$.

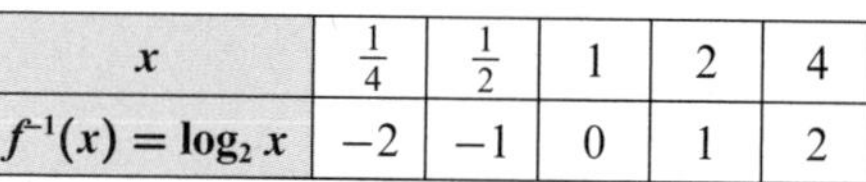

x	$\frac{1}{4}$	$\frac{1}{2}$	1	2	4
$f^{-1}(x) = \log_2 x$	−2	−1	0	1	2

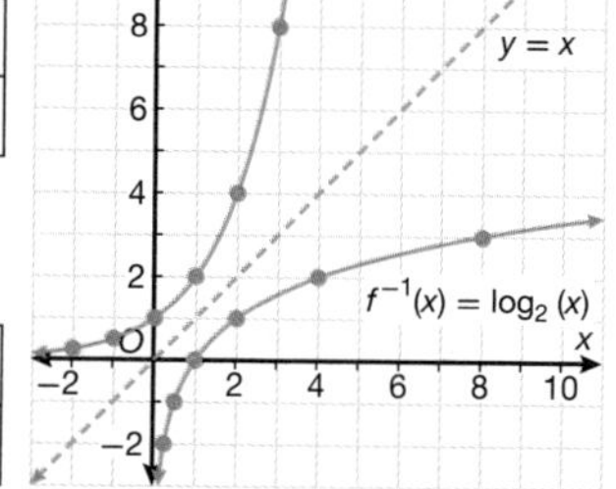

The domain of $f(x) = 2^x$ is all real numbers. The range is $f(x) > 0$. So, the domain of the inverse function $f^{-1}(x) = \log_2 x$ is $x > 0$, and the range $f^{-1}(x)$ is all real numbers.

When graphing a logarithmic function, make a note of four key constants: the coefficient a of the function, the base b of the logarithm, the coefficient c of the x-term, and the constant term.

$$f(x) = a\log_b(cx) + k$$

Recall that e is the natural base, which is equal to approximately 2.7182818…. The **natural logarithmic function** is the function $f(x) = \ln x$, which is the inverse of the natural exponential function $f(x) = e^x$. The domain of $f(x) = \ln x$ is $x > 0$ and the range is all real numbers.

MATH BACKGROUND

In previous lessons, students have graphed exponential functions and used the properties of logarithms to evaluate expressions. Since $y = 2^x$ and $y = \log_2(x)$ are inverse functions, the graph of $y = \log_2(x)$ is a reflection of the graph of $y = 2^x$ along the axis of reflection $y = x$.

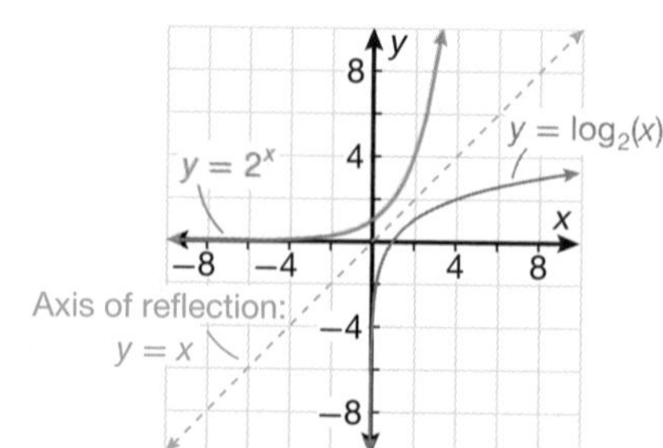

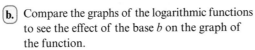

Example 2 Graphing Functions of the Form $f(x) = a\log_b(cx)$

a. Compare the graphs of the two logarithmic functions to see the effect of the variable a on the graph of the function.

$$y = \log_3(x) \text{ and } y = 2\log_3(x)$$

SOLUTION

From the graphs, note that the larger the value of the coefficient a, the faster the height of the graph increases.

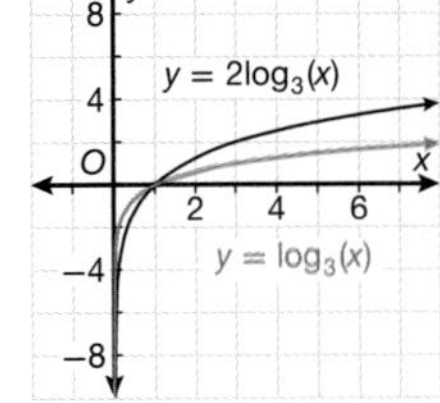

b. Compare the graphs of the logarithmic functions to see the effect of the base b on the graph of the function.

$$y = \ln(x) \qquad y = \log(x)$$

SOLUTION

From the graphs, note that the larger the value of the base, the slower the height of the graph increases.

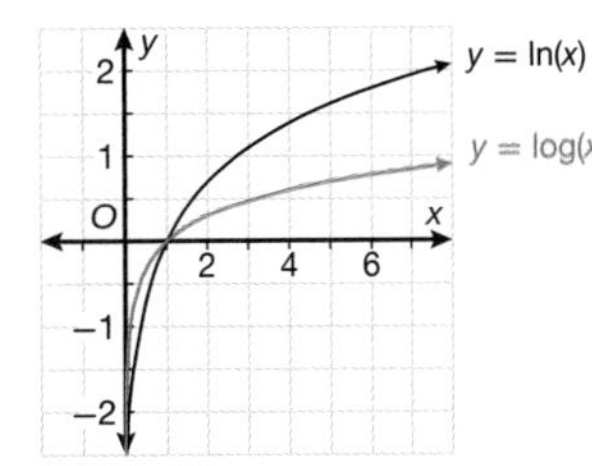

c. Compare the graphs of the logarithmic functions to see the effect of the coefficient c on the graph of the function.

$$y = \ln(x) \quad y = \ln(5x) \quad y = \ln(10x)$$

SOLUTION

From the graphs, note that the larger the value of the coefficient, the faster the height of the graph increases.

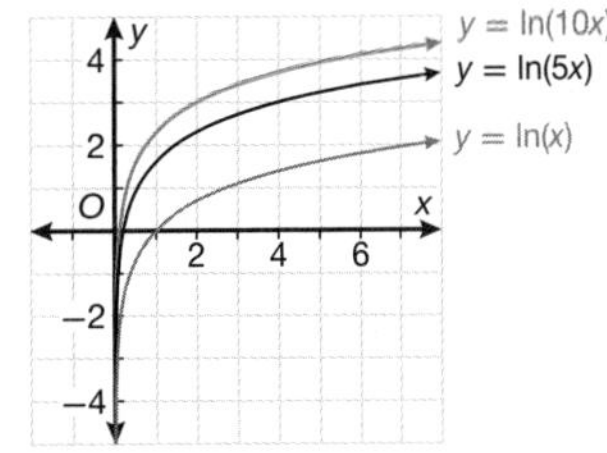

When a logarithmic function is a composite function, look for ways of simplifying the function using the laws of logarithms.

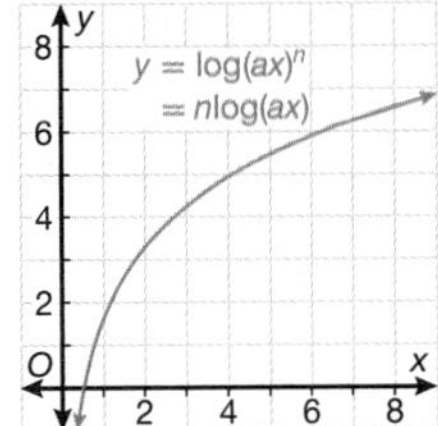

Math Reasoning

Verify Why do the graphs intersect at $x = 1$? What can you conclude about all logarithmic functions?

It represents a number raised to the zero power, which is always 1. This means that $a\log_b(1) = 0$.

Math Reasoning

Analyze Suppose that for two logarithmic functions $f(x)$ and $g(x)$,

$$|f(x_1)| > |g(x_1)|$$

for $x_1 > 1$. What can you conclude about the bases of $f(x)$ and $g(x)$?

$g(x)$ has a higher base than $f(x)$.

Math Reasoning

Analyze For logarithmic functions of the form $f(x) = \log(ax)^n$, which values of n allow for input values of $x < 0$?

values of n that are even numbers

Online Connection
www.SaxonMathResources.com

INCLUSION

Remind students of the definition of an inverse function. Reinforce that $y = b^x$ and $y = \log_b(x)$ are inverse functions, and use the graph of $y = b^x$ to show students how to graph the function $y = \log_b(x)$. Graph logarithmic functions and their inverses on the board. Have students match the correct equation with the correct graph.

Allow students to use a graphing calculator to help graph and check their work.

Additional Example 2

a. Compare the graphs of the two logarithmic functions to see the effect of the variable a on the graph of the function.

$$y = \log_5(x) \text{ and } y = 4\log_5(x)$$

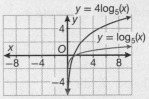

The graph of the equation with coefficient $a = 4$ grows faster than the graph of the equation with coefficient $a = 1$.

b. Compare the graphs of the two logarithmic functions to see the effect of the base b on the graph of the function.

$$y = \log_2 x \text{ and } y = \log x$$

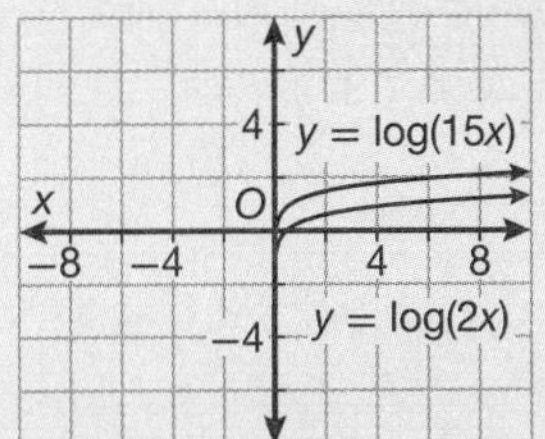

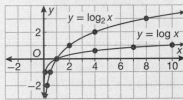

The graph of the equation with base $b = 2$ grows slower than the graph of the equation with base $b = 1$.

c. Compare the graphs of the two logarithmic functions to see the effect of the coefficient c on the graph of the function.

$$y = \log(2x) \text{ and } y = \log(15x)$$

The graph of the equation with coefficient $c = 15$ grows faster than the graph of the equation with coefficient $c = 2$.

Example 3

This example presents an application of logarithms. The decibel system for measuring sound is a logarithmic system.

Additional Example 3

How much louder is the sound of street traffic than the sound of a whisper? Street Traffic: 70 dB Whisper: 20 dB

$10^5 = 100{,}000$ times louder

Lesson Practice

Problems a–e

Scaffolding Allow students to use graphing calculators to help graph or check their graphs.

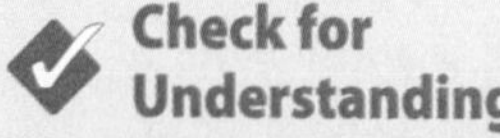

Check for Understanding

The question below helps assess the concepts taught in this lesson.

"Explain how the graph of the function $y = b^x$ is related to the function $y = \log_b(x)$."

Sample: The functions are inverses. Their graphs are reflections of each other across the line $y = x$.

Example 3 Application: Sound

Sound is measured in the decibel system, a logarithmic system using the equation $\text{db} = 10\log\left(\frac{I}{I_0}\right)$, where $I_0 = 1 \times 10^{-12}$. The sound of a jet is 140 dB and the sound of a vacuum cleaner is 80 dB. Find how much more intense the sound of a jet taking off is than the sound of a vacuum cleaner.

SOLUTION The difference between two sound levels, db_1 and db_2, results in

$$\text{db}_2 - \text{db}_1 = 10\log\left(\frac{I_2}{I_0}\right) - 10\log\left(\frac{I_1}{I_0}\right) = 10\log\left(\frac{I_2}{I_1}\right).$$

Solve this equation for the db levels of 140 and 80.

$$\text{db}_2 - \text{db}_1 = 10\log\left(\frac{I_2}{I_1}\right)$$

$$140 - 80 = 10\log\left(\frac{I_2}{I_1}\right)$$

$$60 = 10\log\left(\frac{I_2}{I_1}\right)$$

$$6 = \log\left(\frac{I_2}{I_1}\right)$$

$$10^6 = \frac{I_2}{I_1}$$

$$I_2 = 10^6 I_1$$

The intensity of sound of a jet is a million times louder than a vacuum cleaner.

Lesson Practice

a. (Ex 1) Make a table using the given values to graph the function and its inverse. Describe the domain and range of the function. See Additional Answers.

$$f(x) = 3^x;\ x = -2, -1, 0, 1, \text{ and } 2$$

b. (Ex 2) Compare the graphs of the two logarithmic functions to see the effect of the variable a on the graph of the function.

$$y = 12\log(x) \text{ and } y = -12\log(x)$$

b. The graphs are mirror images of each other.

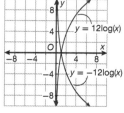

c. (Ex 2) Compare the graphs of the two logarithmic functions to see the effect of the base b on the graph of the function. See Additional Answers.

$$y = 5\ln(x) \qquad y = 5\log(x)$$

d. (Ex 2) Compare the graphs of the three logarithmic functions to see the effect of the coefficient c on the graph of the function. See Additional Answers.

$$y = \ln(-x) \qquad y = \ln(-5x) \qquad y = \ln(-10x)$$

e. (Ex 3) The sound of a whisper is 20 dB and the threshold of hearing is 0 dB. How much louder is a whisper than the threshold of hearing?

100 times louder

ENGLISH LEARNERS

For Example 3, explain the meaning of the word decibel.

"Decibel is a measure of loudness."

Explain that decibel is a unit for expressing the relative intensity of sounds on a scale from 0 to about 130. Zero is the least perceptible sound and 130 is the average level at which pain is felt due to the intensity of sound.

Practice Distributed and Integrated

***1.** (85) Use the Rational Root Theorem to find the roots of
$y = 12x^{11} - 23x^{10} + 10x^9 - 12x^8 + 23x^7 - 10x^6 - 12x^5 + 23x^4 - 10x^3 + 12x^2 - 23x + 10$. $x = -1, \frac{5}{4}, \frac{2}{3}, 1$

2. (92) **Multiple Choice** The first term of an arithmetic sequence is −12 and the fifteenth term is −54. What is the common difference? **B**
A −4.4 B −3 C 3 D 4.4

Write the polynomials in standard form.

3. (27) $16x = 2 - x^2 + y$ $y = x^2 + 16x - 2$

4. (27) $-9 + 13x = 4x^2 - y$ $y = 4x^2 - 13x + 9$

5. (37) For what values of x is the denominator of the expression $\frac{3}{x^2 + x - 30}$ zero? $x = 5$, $x = -6$

6. (106) **Multi-Step** A shipping crate has dimensions of x, $x - 1$, and $x - 2$.
a. What is the simplest polynomial function that represents the volume of the crate? $y = x^3 - 3x^2 + 2x$
b. Describe the possible zeros of the function. Three zeros, at least one is real
c. What are the dimensions of the crate if the volume is 120 cubic units? 4 by 5 by 6

***7.** (110) **Analyze** A chemical process goes at a logarithmic pace to create a chemical by-product. How long will it take to go from 1 unit of by-product to 2 units? Express your answer as a function of the base of the logarithm. The time it takes is $b^2 - b$, where b is the base of the logarithm.

8. (14) **Analyze** Find the determinant of the multiplicative identity matrix $\begin{bmatrix} 1 & 0 \\ 0 & 1 \end{bmatrix}$. 1

***9.** (84) **Optics** The focal length of a lens, f, the distance from the lens to the object, o, and the distance from the lens to the image, i, are related by the formula $\frac{1}{f} = \frac{1}{o} + \frac{1}{i}$. Find i if f is 4 cm and o is 48 cm. $4.\overline{36}$ cm

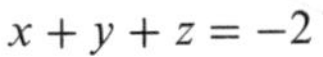

***10.** (32) **Graphing Calculator** Solve the system using a graphing calculator.
$$x + y + z = -2$$
$$3x + 3y + z = -18$$
$$4x + 2y + z = -20$$
$x = -5, y = -3, z = 6$

11. (42) Find the number of outfits possible using 2 of 4 shirts and 2 of 3 pants. There are 18 possible outfits.

***12.** (102) **Motor Vehicle Ownership** The number of motor vehicles owned in U.S. households during the years 1970–2000 can be modeled by the equation $y = -82{,}110 + 70{,}059 \ln t$, $10 \le t \le 40$, where $t = 10$ represents 1970, and y is the number of motor vehicles owned in households, in thousands. Use the model to approximate the year in which the number of motor vehicles owned in U.S. households reached 100 million. 1973

***13.** (109) **Generalize** A hyperbola has the form $ax^2 + by^2 + cx + dy + e = 0$. Complete the square for the x-term. $a(x + \frac{c}{2a})^2$

14. (53) Let $f(x) = 12\log(4x)$ and $g(x) = \frac{1}{\sqrt{x}}$. Find the x-intercept for $f(g(x))$. $x = 16$

15. (91) **Analyze** How can the equation of a circle located at the origin be derived from the equation of a circle located at any point?

15. The equation of a circle located at any point is $(x - h)^2 + (y - k)^2 = r^2$, where h and k are coordinates of the center. If the center is at the origin, then $h = k = 0$ and the formula can be simplified: $(x - 0)^2 + (y - 0)^2 = r^2$, $x^2 + y^2 = r^2$.

CHALLENGE

Graph the logarithmic functions.

$y = \log(3x)$ $y = \log(3x) + 1$ $y = \log(3x) + 3$

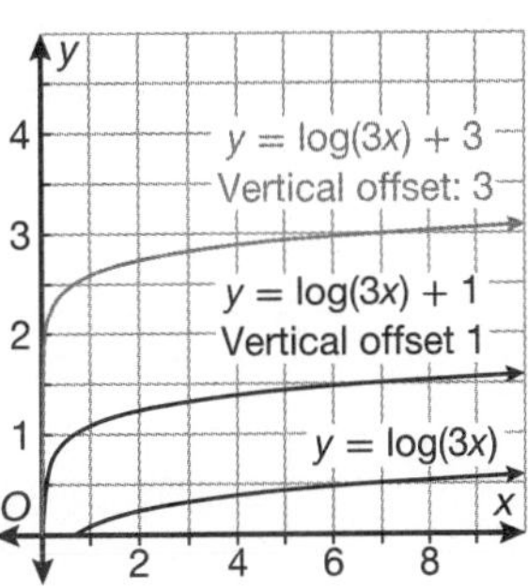

3 Practice

Math Conversations

Discussions to strengthen understanding

Problem 1

"What does the Rational Root Theorem state?" Every rational root of a polynomial has the form $\frac{p}{q}$, where p is a factor of a_0 and q is a factor of a_n.

"What is the degree of the polynomial?" 11

"How many roots does the polynomial have?" 11

"How many *rational* roots does the polynomial have?" 4

Problem 2

"Will the common difference be a positive number or a negative number?" Negative

"How do you know?" The numbers in the sequence are decreasing in value.

Problem 3

"What does it mean for a polynomial to be in standard form?" A polynomial is in standard form if its terms are written in descending order by exponents.

Problem 8

Error Alert

Students who answer −1 have used $cd - ab$ to find the determinant.

Problem 15

"What is the standard form for the equation of a circle with center at (h, k)?"
$(x - h)^2 + (y - k)^2 = r^2$

Problem 19

"What should the y-coordinate be?" –5

Extend the Problem

Have students find the correct equations for the asymptotes. $y = \frac{7}{9}x - \frac{50}{3}$ and $y = -\frac{7}{9}x + \frac{20}{3}$

Problem 24

"What is the formula for the volume of a square pyramid?" $V = \frac{1}{3}Bh$, where B is the area of the base.

"How do you find the dimensions of the base when you know the height and the volume?" Solve the formula for B.

16. (93) A club's membership increases 4% each year. There are 800 members. How long until it reaches 1000? 5.69 years

Divide using synthetic division.

17. (51) $x^4 - 1$ by $x + 1$ $x^3 - x^2 + x - 1$

18. (51) $x^3 - 7$ by $x - 5$ $x^2 + 5x + 25 + \frac{118}{x-5}$

***19.** (109) **Error Analysis** A student is finding the equations of the asymptotes for the hyperbola with following equation: $\frac{(x-15)^2}{9^2} - \frac{(y+5)^2}{7^2} = 1$. What is her mistake? **19.** She used the wrong y-coordinate.

Calculate the slopes: $m = \pm\frac{7}{9}$

Use the slope formula:

$\frac{7}{9} = \frac{y-5}{x-15}$ $y = \frac{7}{9}x - \frac{20}{3}$ | $-\frac{7}{9} = \frac{y-5}{x-15}$ $y = -\frac{7}{9}x - \frac{50}{3}$

Use the triangle to solve problems 20 and 21.

20. (46) Find the cosecant of $\angle A$. $\frac{17}{6.4} \approx 2.66$

21. (46) Find the secant of $\angle A$. $\frac{17}{15.8} \approx 1.08$

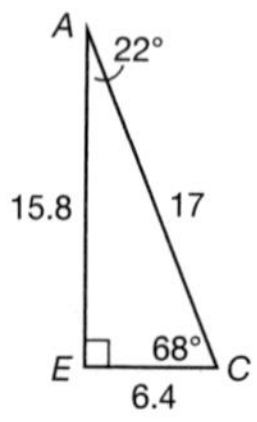

22. (89) **Multiple Choice** What are the solutions of $x^2 + 4x < 5$? A

A $-5 < x < 1$ **B** $-1 < x < 5$ **C** $x < -5$ or $x > 1$ **D** $x < -1$ or $x > 5$

***23.** (108) **Model** Do the trigonometric identities hold true even if each function is phase shifted by angle θ? Provide examples to support your claim. Answers will vary, but students should conclude that the trig identities are true.

24. (85) **Geometry** A pyramid with a square base has a height of $3x$ and a volume of $x^3 + 4x^2 + 4x$. Find the dimensions of the square base. $(x + 2)$ by $(x + 2)$

***25.** (107) **Algebra** The sum of the first n consecutive integers can be found by using the function $f(n) = \frac{1}{2}n(n + 1)$. The sum of the first n consecutive odd integers can be found by using the function $f(n) = n^2$. Write the rational function that is the ratio of the sum of the first n consecutive integers to the sum of the first n consecutive odd integers. Graph the function to find the horizontal asymptote. Explain the significance of the asymptote.

25. $f(n) = \frac{1}{2} + \frac{1}{2n}$; horizontal asymptote: $y = \frac{1}{2}$; as the number of integers increases, the ratio approaches $\frac{1}{2}$.

26. (86) **Error Analysis** Two students are finding the period of $y = \cos\left(\frac{2}{3}x\right)$ but get different results. Which student made the mistake? Student B incorrectly divides by $\frac{2}{3}$.

Student A	Student B
Period $= \frac{2\pi}{b} = \frac{2\pi}{\frac{2}{3}} = \frac{6\pi}{2} = 3\pi$	Period $= \frac{2\pi}{b} = \frac{2\pi}{\frac{2}{3}} = \frac{4\pi}{3}$

27. (90) **Jewelry Making** A jeweler is changing the angle of a facet for a diamond ring from θ to φ. The vertical distances change as shown in the diagram, while the width remains constant. Derive the function that the jeweler can use to find values of θ when the other values are known. $\theta = \tan^{-1}\left(\tan(\varphi)\frac{h_2}{h_1}\right)$

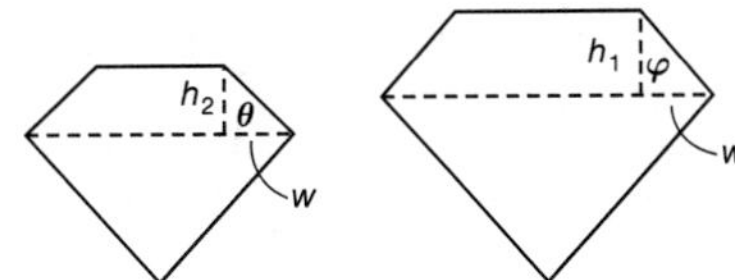

28. (101) **Finance** The Dow Jones Industrial Average (DJIA) is an indicator of stock prices. The quarterly high DJIA for 1999–2003 can be modeled by $f(x) = 0.195x^4 - 5.035x^3 + 6.205x^2 + 338.331x + 10219$, where $x = 1$ represents the first quarter (January–March 1999), $x = 2$ represents the second quarter (April–June 1999), and so on, with $x = 20$ representing the last quarter (October–December 2003). Use the model to approximate the highest quarterly Dow Jones Industrial Average during 1999–2003. Based on the model, in which quarter did it occur? 11,645.81; quarter #6 (April–June 2000)

Solve by factoring.

29. (35) $0 = x^2 + 4x - 21$ $x = -7$ or 3

30. (35) $x^2 - 16 = 0$ $x = -4$ or 4

Problems 29 and 30

Extend the Problem

Have students sketch the graph of both functions using the roots.

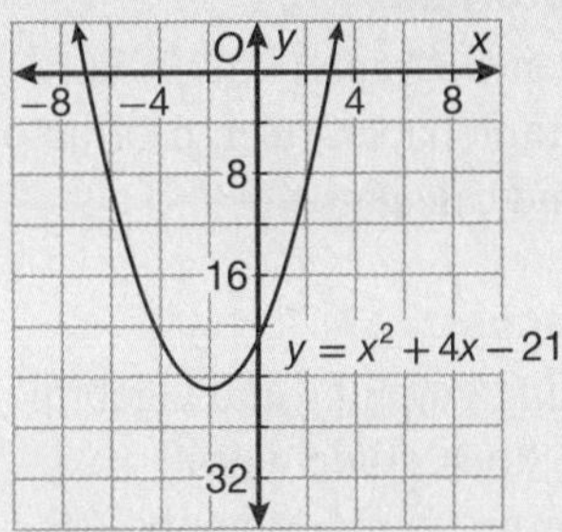

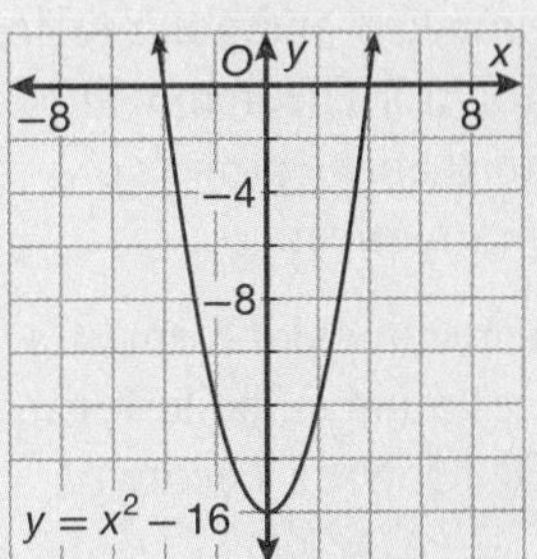

LOOKING FORWARD

Graphing logarithmic functions prepares students for:

- **Lesson 116** Finding Best Fit Models

INVESTIGATION

11

Materials

- Pencil, graph paper, polar graph paper, ruler, protractor, and calculator

Discuss

Using graphing and algebraic methods, students will convert complex numbers to trigonometric and polar forms. De Moivre's Theorem will be used to evaluate powers of complex numbers.

Define rectangular form of a complex number, polar form, and De Moivre's Theorem.

Problem 1

Instruct students to identify a and b before graphing each complex number. a is graphed on the real axis and b is graphed on the imaginary axis.

TEACHER TIP

Instruct students to identify the quadrant in which each point lies. This process will become significant later in the investigation.

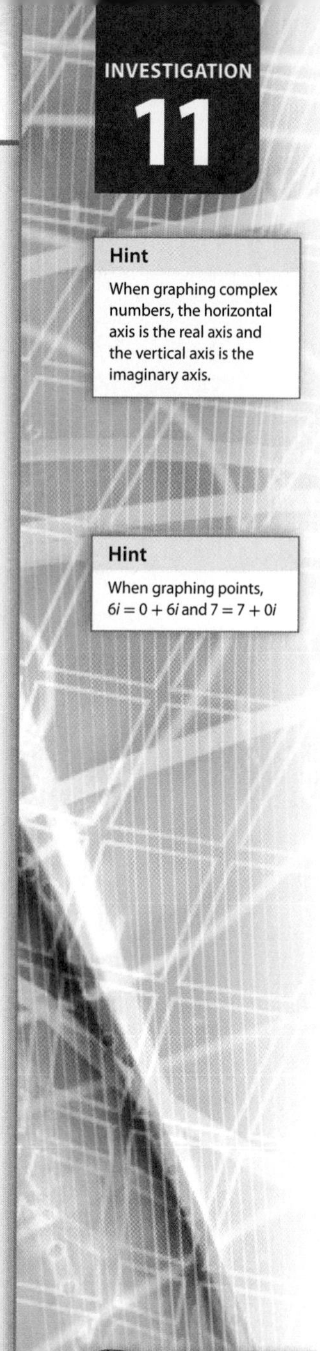

INVESTIGATION

11

Using De Moivre's Theorem

Hint

When graphing complex numbers, the horizontal axis is the real axis and the vertical axis is the imaginary axis.

All complex numbers can be graphed on a complex plane. A complex number of the form $a + bi$ can be graphed with a as the x-coordinate and b as the y-coordinate. This is called the rectangular form of a complex number.

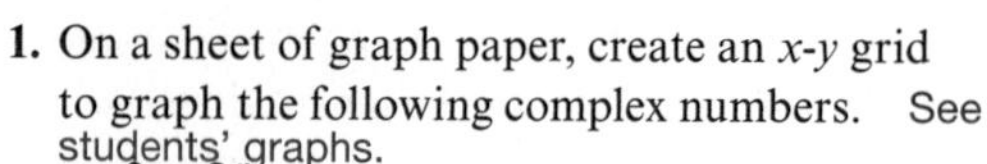

1. On a sheet of graph paper, create an x-y grid to graph the following complex numbers. See students' graphs.
   a. $3 + 2i$
   b. $-10 + 5i$
   c. $6i$
   d. $-10i$
   e. 7
   f. -9

Hint

When graphing points, $6i = 0 + 6i$ and $7 = 7 + 0i$

Refer again to the point on the imaginary plane represented by $4 + 3i$. If a segment is drawn from the origin to this point, and a segment is also drawn from the point straight down to the real axis, a right triangle is formed.

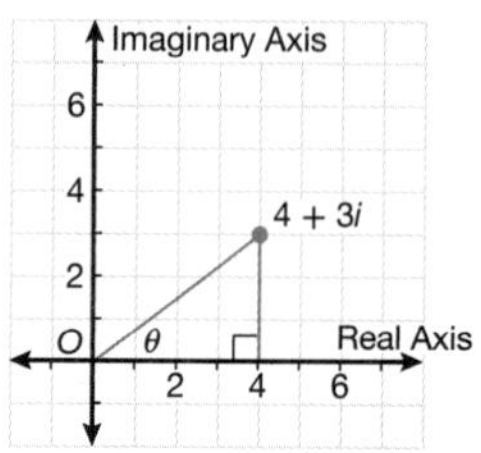

The measure of the angle between the real axis and the hypotenuse of this right triangle is θ. That is, θ is the angle with the positive x-axis as its initial side and the hypotenuse of the right triangle as its terminal side. Using the graph of the complex number to find the corresponding coordinate on the standard coordinate grid, the trigonometric ratios, and a graphing calculator, the measure of θ can be determined.

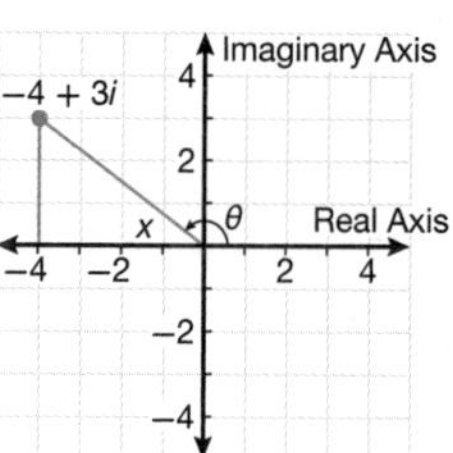

For example, the graph of $-4 + 3i$ corresponds to the graph of $(-4, 3)$. The length of the side adjacent to angle x is 4 units and the length of the side opposite angle x is 3 units. So, $\tan x = \frac{3}{4}$. Using a graphing calculator and $\tan^{-1}\left(\frac{3}{4}\right) = x$, $x \approx 36.87°$. Subtract 36.87° from 90° to find the complement of angle x (53.13°). Last, to find the approximate value of θ, add: $53.13° + 90° = 143.13°$. Angle $\theta \approx 143.13°$. (Notice that the same result can be found by subtracting the measure of angle x from 180°. That is, $180° - 53.13° = 143.13°$.)

Online Connection
www.SaxonMathResources.com

INVESTIGATION RESOURCES

Reteaching Master
Investigation 11

MATH BACKGROUND

De Moivre's Theorem, named after the French mathematician Abraham De Moivre, calculates any power of a complex number. It can also be used to determine the roots of a complex number.

The rectangular and polar forms of a complex number are different representations of equivalent points. The representation that is used depends upon the application involved.

2. Find the measure of θ when each complex numbers is graphed on the complex plane.

   a. $4 + 4i$ $\theta = 45°$
   b. $-7 + 14i$ $\theta \approx 116.57°$
   c. $3 + (-9i)$ $\theta \approx 288.43°$
   d. $-2 + 8i$ $\theta \approx 104.03°$
   e. $2 - 5i$ $\theta \approx 291.80°$
   f. $-4 + i$ $\theta \approx 165.96°$

Caution

To calculate θ based on the values of a and b, use $\tan^{-1}\left(\frac{b}{a}\right)$. Also, keep track of the quadrant in which the complex number is found.

3. For each of the complex numbers in problem 2, complete the table and calculate the hypotenuse r of corresponding right triangle.

a	b	$r = \sqrt{a^2 + b^2}$
4	4	5.66
−7	14	15.65
3	−9	9.49
−2	8	8.25
2	−5	5.39
−4	1	4.12

Another way of writing and graphing complex numbers is to use polar coordinates. Recall that polar coordinates take two arguments: the magnitude of a segment and the counterclockwise angle from the x-axis to that segment.

Polar form for complex numbers works in the same way. In the graph shown here, the right triangle and θ can be used to express the real and imaginary parts of the complex number z, where $z = a + bi$, with trigonometric ratios.

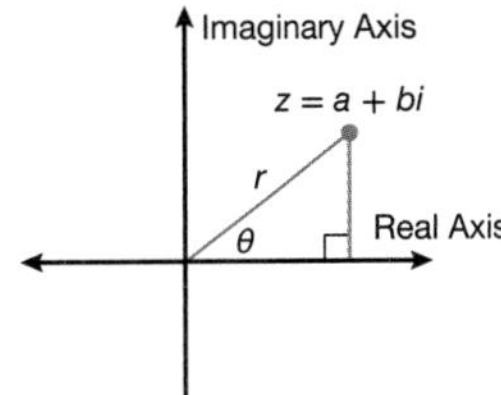

Let r be the length of the hypotenuse. Then the real part of this coordinate, a, can be found using the equation:

$$\cos\theta = \frac{a}{r}$$

$$a = r\cos\theta$$

And the imaginary part is:

$$\sin\theta = \frac{b}{r}$$

$$b = r\sin\theta$$

So $z = a + bi$ in polar form is $z = r\cos\theta + i(r\sin\theta)$. To convert from rectangular coordinates to polar coordinates, find the value of r using the Pythagorean Theorem and the value of θ as shown above, then substitute these values into the polar form of the equation $z = r\cos\theta + i(r\sin\theta)$.

INCLUSION

Discuss and explain the conversion process. In this lesson, two forms are examined. Converting a complex number to polar form is similar to translating Spanish to English. Formulas and rules must be followed to produce equivalent statements. Write the following conversion formula on the board and suggest that students place it on an index card for quick reference if they are having trouble converting from one form to the other.

$$a + bi = \sqrt{a^2 + b^2}\,\cos\left(\tan^{-1}\frac{b}{a}\right) + i\sqrt{a^2 + b^2}\,\sin\left(\tan^{-1}\frac{b}{a}\right)$$

This formula looks complex, but it integrates the Pythagorean Theorem and an inverse trigonometric ratio into the polar form to express the conversion.

Problem 5

Remind students that the value of θ depends on the quadrant that the point is located in. Write the following chart if necessary.

Quadrant 1: $0° < \theta < 90°$

Quadrant 2: $90° < \theta < 180°$

Quadrant 3: $180° < \theta < 270°$

Quadrant 4: $270° < \theta < 360°$

Problem 7

For convenience use $0° < \theta < 360°$. To determine θ, examine the quadrant in which the point lies and use the inverse tangent formula.

TEACHER TIP

In this investigation, De Moivre's Theorem is used as a time saver. It is easier to use De Moivre's Theorem than the stated summation formula or binomial expansion.

4. Convert the following complex numbers in rectangular form to polar form.

a. $z = 4 - 2i$ $\quad z = 4.47\cos(333.43)° + i4.47\sin(333.43)°$

b. $z = -1 - i$ $\quad z = \sqrt{2}\cos(225°) + i\sqrt{2}\sin(225°)$

c. $z = 3 + 4i$ $\quad z = 5\cos(53.13°) + i5\sin(53.13°)$

To convert from polar form to rectangular form, simplify the polar form by evaluating the trigonometric ratios. For example:

$$\sqrt{2}\cos(45°) + i\sqrt{2}\sin(45°)$$
$$= \sqrt{2}\left(\frac{\sqrt{2}}{2}\right) + i\sqrt{2}\left(\frac{\sqrt{2}}{2}\right)$$
$$= 1 + i$$

5. Convert the complex numbers in polar form to rectangular form.

a. $7\cos(45°) + i7\sin(45°)$ $\quad \frac{7\sqrt{2}}{2} + \frac{7\sqrt{2}}{2}i$

b. $10\cos(90°) + i10\sin(90°)$ $\quad 10i$

c. $5\cos(120°) + i5\sin(120°)$ $\quad -2.5 + \frac{5\sqrt{3}}{2}i$

d. $17\cos(200°) + i17\sin(200°)$ $\quad -15.97 - 5.81i$

Graphing Calculator Tip

Make sure the calculator is set to degree mode. Incorrect values will result if the radian mode is used.

6. For each of the complex numbers in question 5, complete the table for values a, b, r, and θ.

r	θ	a	b
7	45°	4.95	4.95
10	90°	0	10
5	120°	−2.5	4.33
17	200°	−15.97	−5.81

7. For each of the complex numbers written in $a + bi$ form, convert to polar form. (Hint: The magnitude of z, $|z|$ is equal to r.)

$a + bi$	r	θ	Polar Form
$4 + 6i$	7.2	56.31°	$7.2\cos(56.31°) + i7.2\sin(56.31°)$
$7 + 7i$	9.90	45°	$9.90\cos(45°) + i9.90\sin(45°)$
$-3 + 4i$	5	126.87°	$5\cos(126.87°) + i5\sin(126.87°)$
15	15	0°	$15\cos(0°) + i15\sin(0°)$
$28i$	28	90°	$28\cos(90°) + i28\sin(90°)$

While the rectangular and polar forms of a complex number are interchangeable, complex numbers of the form $(a + bi)^n$, for any integer n, are much easier to calculate in polar form. The reason for this is De Moivre's Theorem, which states,

$$(r\cos(\theta) + ir\sin(\theta))^n = r^n\cos(n\theta) + ir^n\sin(n\theta)$$

ENGLISH LEARNERS

Explain the meaning of the word **interchangeable.** Say,

"Interchangeable means to be able to be changed or replaced with something else. Usually items that are interchangeable have similar sizes, shapes, or quantities."

Ask, **"If two cars have interchangeable parts, then what could be true about the cars?"** Sample: they may be the same model

According to De Moivre's Theorem, a complex number in trigonometric form, when raised to any integer power, remains a binomial and is therefore much easier to calculate. Compare the De Moivre form to the binomial expansion of the $a + bi$ form:

$$(a + bi)^2 = (a^2 - b^2) + i2ab$$
$$(a + bi)^3 = (a^3 - 3ab^2) + i(-b^3 + 3a^2b)$$
$$(a + bi)^4 = (a^4 + b^4 - 6a^2b^2) + i4(a^3b - ab^3)$$
$$(a + bi)^n = \sum_{k=0}^{n} \frac{n!}{k!\,(n-k)!} a^{n-k}b^k$$

8. Use De Moivre's Theorem to write each of the expressions below in the standard form $a + bi$.

Hint

Make sure that $n\theta < 360°$. If necessary, subtract multiples of 360°.

a. $[7\cos(20°) + i7\sin(20°)]^3$. $171.5 + 297.05i$
b. $[3\cos(45°) + i3\sin(45°)]^2$. $9i$
c. $[2\cos(120°) + i2\sin(120°)]^4$. $-8 + 13.86i$
d. $[\cos(210°) + i\sin(210°)]^3$. $-i$
e. $[4\cos(180°) + i4\sin(180°)]^2$. 16
f. $[2\cos(30°) + i2\sin(30°)]^6$. -64

9. Use De Moivre's Theorem to evaluate the following complex numbers. Express the results in polar form.

a. $(3 + 4i)^3$ $125\cos(159.39°) + i125\sin(159.39°)$
b. $(10 - 10i)^4$ $40{,}000\cos(180°) + i40{,}000\sin(180°)$
c. $(5 + 12i)^6$ $13^6\cos(44.28°) + i13^6\sin(44.28°)$
d. $(-4 + 0i)^8$ $4^8\cos(0°) + i4^8\sin(0°)$
e. $(0 + 7i)^{12}$ $7^{12}\cos(0°) + i7^{12}\sin(0°)$

Investigation Practice

a. For each of the complex numbers written in rectangular form, convert to polar form.

$a + bi$	r	θ	Polar Form
$5 + (-5i)$	7.07	315°	$7.07\cos(315°) + i7.07\sin(315°)$
$-7 + 10i$	12.21	124.99°	$12.21\cos(124.99°) + i12.21\sin(124.99°)$
$0 + 18i$	18.00	90°	$18\cos(90°) + i18\sin(90°)$
$25 + 0i$	25.00	0°	$25\cos(0°) + i25\sin(0°)$
$-9 + (-3i)$	9.49	198.43°	$9.49\cos(198.43°) + i9.49\sin(198.43°)$

Use De Moivre's Theorem to evaluate the following complex numbers. Express the results in polar form.

b. $(2 + 7i)^4$ $2809\cos(296.22°) + i2809\sin(296.22°)$
c. $(1 - 13i)^7$ $64{,}057{,}682.83\cos(120.79°) + i64{,}057{,}682.83\sin(120.79°)$
d. $(6 + 8i)^8$ $10^8\cos(65.04°) + i10^8\cos(65.04°)$
e. $(-9 + 0i)^{12}$ $9^{12}\cos(0°) + i9^{12}\sin(0°)$
f. $(0 + 19i)^{15}$ $19^{15}\cos(270°) + i19^{15}\sin(270°)$

TEACHER TIP

Calculate r and θ. Then substitute into De Moivre's Theorem. Do not forget to multiply θ by n.

Investigation Practice

Math Conversations

Discussions to strengthen understanding

Problem a

Have students refer to the conversion table on page 772. Be careful when calculating θ.

Problem b

Have students calculate r and θ, and then substitute into De Moivre's Theorem. For large powers of r, leave the expression in exponential form.

Lesson Planner

Lesson	New Concepts
111	Transforming Polynomial Functions
112	Using Sum and Difference Identities
113	Using Geometric Series
114	Identifying Conic Sections
115	Finding Double-Angle and Half-Angle Identities
	Cumulative Test 22, Performance Task 22
LAB 14	Determining Regression Models
116	Finding Best Fit Models
117	Solving Systems of Nonlinear Equations
118	Recognizing Misleading Data
119	Solving Trigonometric Equations
	Cumulative Test 23, Performance Task 23
INV 12	Investigation: Using Mathematical Induction

Resources for Teaching

- Student Edition
- Teacher's Edition
- Student Edition eBook
- Teacher's Edition eBook
- Resources and Planner CD
- Solutions Manual
- Instructional Masters
- Technology Lab Masters
- Warm Up and Teaching Transparencies
- Instructional Presentations CD
- Online activities, tools, and homework help **www.SaxonMathResources.com**

Resources for Practice and Assessment

- Student Edition Practice Workbook
- Course Assessments
- Standardized Test Practice
- College Entrance Exam Practice
- Test and Practice Generator CD using ExamView™

Resources for Differentiated Instruction

- Reteaching Masters
- Challenge and Enrichment Masters
- Prerequisite Skills Intervention
- Adaptations for Saxon Algebra 2
- Multilingual Glossary
- English Learners Handbook
- TI Resources

Pacing Guide

Resources and Planner CD for lesson planning support

45-Minute Class

Day 1	Day 2	Day 3	Day 4	Day 5	Day 6
Lesson 111	Lesson 112	Lesson 113	Lesson 114	Lesson 115	Cumulative Test 22
Day 7	**Day 8**	**Day 9**	**Day 10**	**Day 11**	**Day 12**
Lesson 116	Lesson 117	Lesson 118	Lesson 119	Cumulative Test 23	Investigation 12

Block: 90-Minute Class

Day 1	Day 2	Day 3	Day 4	Day 5	Day 6
Lesson 111 Lesson 112	Lesson 113 Lesson 114	Lesson 115 Cumulative Test 22	Lesson 116 Lesson 117	Lesson 118 Lesson 119	Cumulative Test 23 Investigation 12

** For suggestions on how to implement Saxon Math in a block schedule, see the Pacing section at the beginning of the Teacher's Edition.*

Differentiated Instruction

Below Level		Advanced Learners	
Warm Up	SE pp. 774, 780, 786, 793, 798, 804, 811, 819, 825	Challenge	TE pp. 778, 785, 791, 797, 802, 808, 815, 822, 830
Skills Bank	SE pp. 862–885	Extend the Example	TE pp. 776, 789, 798, 799, 809, 819, 825
Reteaching Masters	Lessons 111–119, Investigation 12	Extend the Problem	TE pp. 777, 779, 791, 803, 810, 823, 827, 830
Warm Up Transparencies	Lessons 111–119	Challenge and Enrichment	Challenge: C111–C119 Enrichment: E114, E117
Prerequisite Skills Intervention	Skill 85, 86		
English Learners		**Special Needs**	
EL Tips	TE pp. 775, 783, 788, 795, 800, 805, 807, 814, 820, 829, 832	Inclusion Tips	TE pp. 776, 782, 787, 794, 801, 818, 821, 826, 832
Multilingual Glossary	Booklet and Online	Adaptations for Saxon Algebra 2	Lessons 111–119; Cumulative Test 23
English Learners Handbook			
For All Learners			
Exploration	SE pp. 788	Alternate Method	TE pp. 777, 784, 791, 796, 799
Caution	SE pp. 776, 793, 795, 800, 808	Online Tools	
Hints	SE pp. 774, 775, 776, 780, 781, 786, 788, 793, 798, 799, 800, 819, 821, 826, 827, 832, 834		
Error Alert	TE pp. 775, 777, 778, 782, 790, 792, 794, 800, 803, 805, 807, 809, 811, 814, 816, 818, 823, 824, 826, 829		

SE = Student Edition; TE = Teacher's Edition

Math Vocabulary

Lesson	New Vocabulary		Maintained	EL Tip in TE
111			translation	translate
112	rotation matrix		cosine	spring
113	converge diverge	geometric series infinite geometric series limit	common ratio	converge diverge
114	general form of a conic section		circle conic section	expand
115			identity radian	quadrant
116	exponential regression logarithmic regression	quadratic model quadratic regression	correlation	space
117	nonlinear system of equations		parabola	nonlinear
118			probability	misleading
119			identity	cons pros
INV 12	mathematical induction			consecutive

SECTION OVERVIEW 12

Math Highlights

Enduring Understandings – The "Big Picture"

After completing Section 12, students will understand:

- How to find best fit models.
- How to use geometric series.
- How to find half angle and double angle identities.
- How to solve systems of nonlinear equations.
- Sum and difference identities.
- How to solve trigonometric functions.

Essential Questions

- How can I recognize misleading data?
- How do I graph polynomial functions?
- What are conic sections and how can I identify them?

Math Content Strands

Conic Sections

• Lesson 114	Identifying Conic Sections
• Lesson 117	Solving Systems of Nonlinear Equations

Polynomials and Polynomial Functions

• Lesson 111	Transforming Polynomial Functions

Probability and Statistics

• Lab 14	Determining Regression Models
• Lesson 116	Finding Best Fit Models
• Lesson 118	Recognizing Misleading Data

Sequences, Series, and Logic

• Lesson 113	Using Geometric Series
• Investigation 12	Using Mathematical Induction

Trigonometry

• Lesson 112	Using Sum and Difference Identities
• Lesson 115	Finding Double-Angle and Half-Angle Identities
• Lesson 119	Solving Trigonometric Equations

Connections in Practice Problems

	Lessons
Algebra	115
Coordinate Geometry	114, 115, 116, 117, 118
Data Analysis	112, 119
Geometry	111, 112, 113, 114, 115, 116, 118, 119
Probability	111, 113, 117, 118

Math Processes

Reasoning and Communication

	Lessons
• Analyze	111, 112, 113, 114, 115, 116, 117, 118, 119
• Error analysis	111, 112, 113, 114, 115, 116, 117, 118, 119
• Estimate	113, 114
• Formulate	112, 116, 117, 119
• Generalize	112, 115, 117
• Justify	111, 115, 117, 118
• Math reasoning	112, 113, 116, 117, 118
• Model	113, 115, 117, 119
• Multiple choice	111, 112, 114, 115, 116, 117, 118, 119
• Multi-step	111, 112, 113, 114, 115, 116, 117, 118, 119
• Predict	111, 116
• Verify	113, 117, Inv. 12
• Write	111, 112, 113, 114, 116, 118, 119
• Graphing Calculator	111, 112, 113, 114, 115, 116, 117, 118, 119

Connections

In Examples: Event planning, a Height function, Migratory populations, Population, Racing, Salaries, Sports

In Practice problems: Automobiles, Baseball attendance, Baseball salaries, Business, Carousel, Construction, Editors, Entertainment, Exercise, Farming, Finance, Forestry, Furniture, International landmarks, Manufacturing, Money, Navigation, Optics, Organizing, Physics, Population, Population growth, Postage, Probability, Recreation, Retirement funds, Salaries, Savings, Savings accounts, Soccer, Solar eclipses, Temperature, Theater, Travel, Unions

Content Trace

Lesson	Warm Up: Prerequisite Skills	New Concepts	Where Practiced	Where Assessed	Looking Forward
111	Lesson 20	Transforming Polynomial Functions	Lessons 111, 112, 113, 114, 116, 117, 118	Cumulative Test 23	Saxon Precalculus
112	Lesson 46	Using Sum and Difference Identities	Lessons 112, 113, 114, 116, 118	Cumulative Test 23	Lesson 119
113	Lesson 97	Using Geometric Series	Lessons 113, 114, 116, 118, 119	Cumulative Test 23	Saxon Precalculus
114	Lessons 19, 74, 91	Identifying Conic Sections	Lessons 114, 115, 116, 118, 119	Cumulative Test 23	Lesson 117
115	Lessons 63, 112	Finding Double-Angle and Half-Angle Identities	Lessons 115, 116, 117, 118, 119	Cumulative Test 23	Lesson 119
116	Lessons 21, 45, 47, 55, 97	Finding Best Fit Models	Lessons 116, 117, 118, 119	N/A	Lessons in other Saxon High School Math programs
117	Lessons 109, 114	Solving Systems of Nonlinear Equations	Lessons 117, 118, 119	N/A	Lessons in other Saxon High School Math programs
118	Lesson 73	Recognizing Misleading Data	Lessons 118, 119	N/A	Lessons in other Saxon High School Math programs
119	Lessons 23, 28, 108	Solving Trigonometric Equations	Lesson 119	N/A	Lessons in other Saxon High School Math programs
INV 12	N/A	Investigation: Using Mathematical Induction	N/A	N/A	N/A

Ongoing Assessment

	Type	Feature	Intervention *
BEFORE instruction	Assess Prior Knowledge	• Diagnostic Test	• Prerequisite Skills Intervention
BEFORE the lesson	Formative	• Warm Up	• Skills Bank • Reteaching Masters
DURING the lesson	Formative	• Lesson Practice • Math Conversations with the Practice problems	• Additional Examples in TE • Test and Practice Generator (for additional practice sheets)
AFTER the lesson	Formative	• Check for Understanding (closure)	• Scaffolding Questions in TE
AFTER 5 lessons	Summative	After Lesson 115 • Cumulative Test 22 • Performance Task 22 After Lesson 119 • Cumulative Test 23 • Performance Task 23	• Reteaching Masters • Test and Practice Generator (for additional tests and practice)
AFTER 20 lessons	Summative	• Benchmark Tests	• Reteaching Masters • Test and Practice Generator (for additional tests and practice)

* for students not showing progress during the formative stages or scoring below 80% on the summative assessments

Evidence of Learning – What Students Should Know

Because the Saxon philosophy is to provide students with sufficient time to learn and practice each concept, a lesson's topic will not be tested until at least five lessons after the topic is introduced.

On the Cumulative Tests that are given during this section of ten lessons, students should be able to demonstrate the following competencies:

- Understand trigonometric functions and their reciprocals.
- Find the sum of a geometric series.
- Graph hyperbolas centered at the Origin.
- Solve quadratic equations.
- Evaluate expressions with sum and difference identities.
- Find roots of cubic equations.
- Solve a system of equations by substitution.

Test and Practice Generator CD using ExamView™

The Test and Practice Generator is an easy-to-use benchmark and assessment tool that creates unlimited practice and tests in multiple formats and allows you to customize questions or create new ones. A variety of reports are available to track student progress toward mastery of the standards throughout the year.

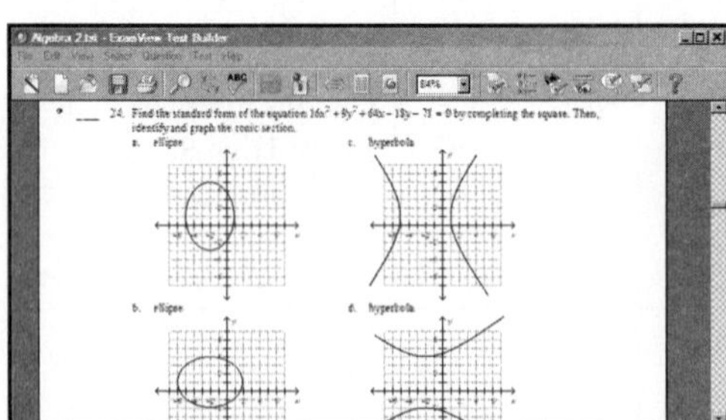

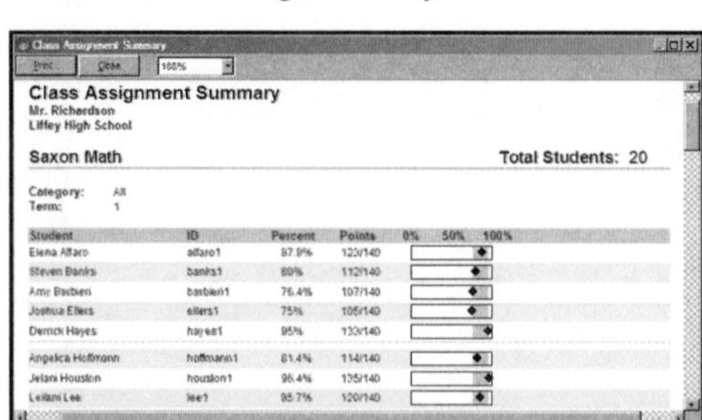

Assessment Resources

Resources for Diagnosing and Assessing

- **Student Edition**
  - Warm Up
  - Lesson Practice
- **Teacher's Edition**
  - Math Conversations with the Practice problems
  - Check for Understanding (closure)
- **Course Assessments**
  - Diagnostic Test
  - Cumulative Tests
  - Performance Tasks
  - Benchmark Tests

Resources for Test Prep

- **Student Edition**
  - Multiple-choice practice problems
  - Multiple-step and writing problems
  - Daily cumulative practice
- **Standardized Test Practice**
- **College Entrance Exam Practice**
- **Test and Practice Generator CD using ExamView™**

Resources for Intervention

- **Student Edition**
  - Skills Bank
- **Teacher's Edition**
  - Additional Examples
  - Scaffolding questions
- **Prerequisite Skills Intervention**
  - Worksheets
- **Reteaching Masters**
  - Lesson instruction and practice sheets
- **Test and Practice Generator CD using ExamView™**
  - Lesson practice problems
  - Additional tests

Cumulative Tests

The assessments in Saxon Math are frequent and consistently placed after every five lessons to offer a regular method of ongoing testing. These cumulative assessments check mastery of concepts from previous lessons.

Performance Tasks

The Performance Tasks can be used in conjunction with the Cumulative Tests and are scored using a rubric.

After Lesson 115

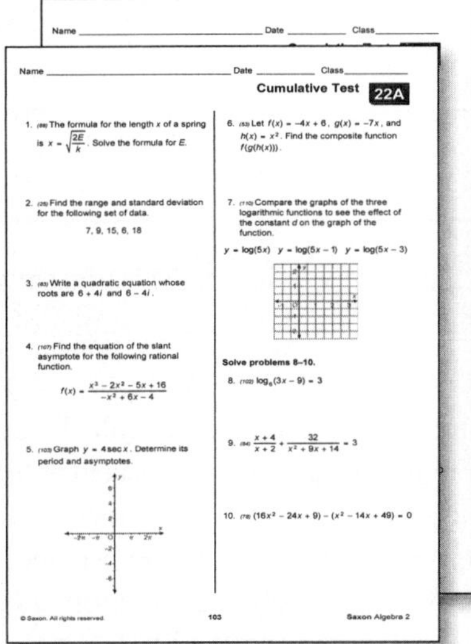

Name ______________ Date ________ Class ________

Cumulative Test 22A

1. The formula for the length x of a spring is $x = \sqrt{\frac{2E}{k}}$. Solve the formula for E.

2. Find the range and standard deviation for the following set of data.
   7, 9, 15, 6, 18

3. Write a quadratic equation whose roots are $6 + 4i$ and $6 - 4i$.

4. Find the equation of the slant asymptote for the following rational function.
   $f(x) = \frac{x^3 - 2x^2 - 5x + 16}{-x^2 + 6x - 4}$

5. Graph $y = 4\sec x$. Determine its period and asymptotes.

6. Let $f(x) = -4x + 6$, $g(x) = -7x$, and $h(x) = x^2$. Find the composite function $f(g(h(x)))$.

7. Compare the graphs of the three logarithmic functions to see the effect of the constant d on the graph of the function.
   $y = \log(5x)$ $y = \log(5x - 1)$ $y = \log(5x - 3)$

Solve problems 8–10.

8. $\log_6(3x - 9) = 3$

9. $\frac{x+4}{x+2} + \frac{32}{x^2 + 9x + 14} = 3$

10. $(16x^2 - 24x + 9) - (x^2 - 14x + 49) = 0$

© Saxon. All rights reserved. 103 Saxon Algebra 2

After Lesson 119

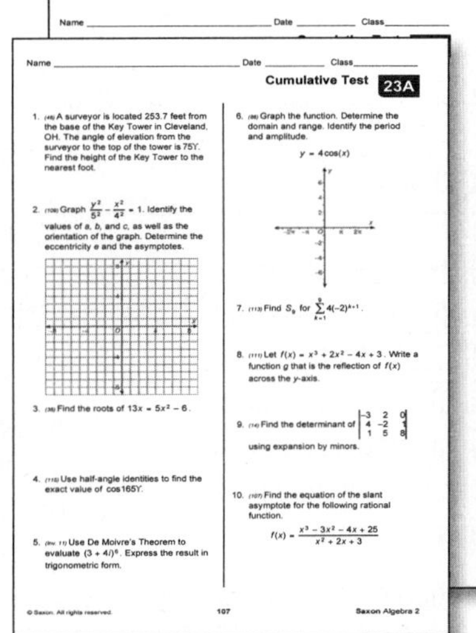

Name ______________ Date ________ Class ________

Cumulative Test 23A

1. A surveyor is located 253.7 feet from the base of the Key Tower in Cleveland, OH. The angle of elevation from the surveyor to the top of the tower is 75Y. Find the height of the Key Tower to the nearest foot.

2. Graph $\frac{y^2}{5^2} - \frac{x^2}{4^2} = 1$. Identify the values of a, b, and c, as well as the orientation of the graph. Determine the eccentricity e and the asymptotes.

3. Find the roots of $13x = 5x^2 - 6$.

4. Use half-angle identities to find the exact value of cos 165Y.

5. Use De Moivre's Theorem to evaluate $(3 + 4i)^6$. Express the result in trigonometric form.

6. Graph the function. Determine the domain and range. Identify the period and amplitude.
   $y = 4\cos(x)$

7. Find S_9 for $\sum_{k=1}^{9} 4(-2)^{k+1}$.

8. Let $f(x) = x^3 + 2x^2 - 4x + 3$. Write a function g that is the reflection of $f(x)$ across the y-axis.

9. Find the determinant of $\begin{vmatrix} -3 & 2 & 0 \\ 4 & -2 & 1 \\ 1 & 5 & 8 \end{vmatrix}$ using expansion by minors.

10. Find the equation of the slant asymptote for the following rational function.
    $f(x) = \frac{x^3 - 3x^2 - 4x + 25}{x^2 + 2x + 3}$

© Saxon. All rights reserved. 107 Saxon Algebra 2

For use with Performance Tasks

Teacher Rubric

Criteria Performance	Knowledge and Skills Understanding	Communication and Representation	Process and Strategies
4	The student got it! The student did it in new ways and showed how it worked. The student knew and understood what math concepts to use.	The student clearly detailed how he/she solved the problem. The student included all the steps to show his/her thinking. The student used math language, symbols, numbers, graphs and/or models to represent his/her solution.	The student had an effective and inventive solution. The student used big math ideas to solve the problem. The student addressed the important details. The student showed other ways to solve the problem. The student checked his/her answer to make sure it was correct
3	The student understood the problem and had an appropriate solution. All parts of the problem are addressed.	The student clearly explained how he/she solved the problem. The student used math language, symbols, tables, graphs, and numbers to explain how he/she did the problem.	The student had a correct solution. The student used a plan to solve the problem and selected an appropriate strategy.
2	The student understood parts of the problem. The student started, but he/she couldn't finish.	The student explained some of what he/she did. The student tried to use words, symbols, tables, graphs and numbers to explain how he/she did the problem.	The student had part of the solution, but did not know how to finish. The student was not sure if he/she had the correct answer. The student needed help.
1	The student did not understand the problem.	The student did not explain how he/she solved the problem. He/she did not use words, symbols, tables or graphs to show how he/she	The student couldn't get started. The student did not know how to begin.

© Saxon. All rights reserved. x Saxon Algebra 2

LESSON 111

1 Warm Up

A translation can be vertical or horizontal.

2 New Concepts

Students transform polynomial functions.

Example 1

Students translate polynomial functions.

Additional Example 1

For $f(x) = x^3 + 4$, write the rule for each function and sketch its graph.

a. $g(x) = f(x) + 9$ $g(x) = x^3 + 13$

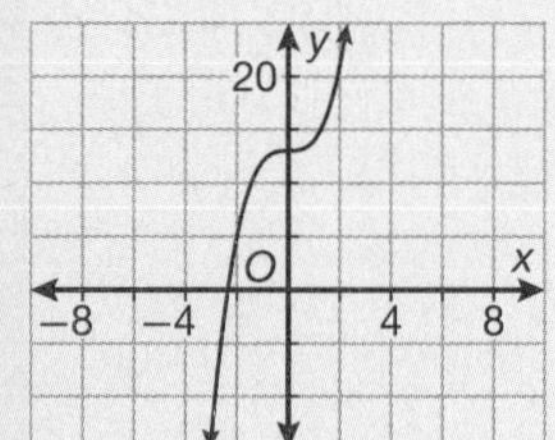

b. $g(x) = f(x - 3)$
$g(x) = (x - 3)^3 + 4$

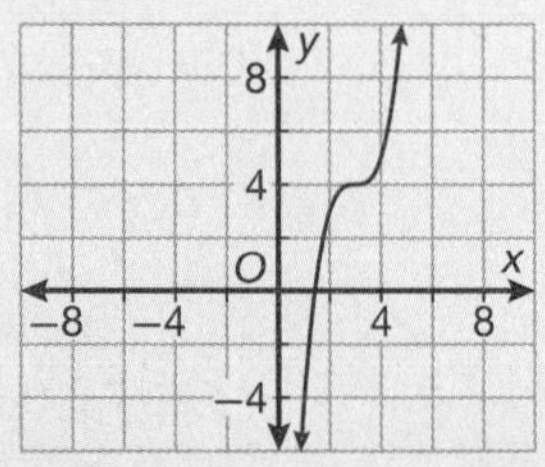

LESSON 111 Transforming Polynomial Functions

Warm Up

1. (20) **Vocabulary** A shift transformation is a translation.
2. (20) If $f(x) = 5x^2 - x + 1$, then $f(x) + 3 =$ $5x^2 - x + 4$.
3. (20) If $f(x) = x - 6$, then $2 \cdot f(x) =$ $2x - 12$.

New Concepts

You can perform the same transformations on all polynomial functions that you performed on quadratic and linear functions.

Transformations of $f(x)$		
Transformation	**$f(x)$ notation**	**Examples for $f(x) = x^3$**
Vertical translation	$f(x) + k$	$g(x) = x^3 + 2$ 2 units up $g(x) = x^3 - 5$ 5 units down
Horizontal translation	$f(x - h)$	$g(x) = (x - 1)^3$ 1 unit right $g(x) = (x + 3)^3$ 3 units left
Vertical stretch/ compression	$af(x)$	$g(x) = 4x^3$ stretch by a factor of 4 $g(x) = \frac{1}{3}x^3$ compress by a factor of $\frac{1}{3}$
Horizontal stretch/ compression	$f\left(\frac{1}{b}x\right)$	$g(x) = \left(\frac{1}{5}x\right)^3$ stretch by a factor of 5 $g(x) = (2x)^3$ compress by a factor of $\frac{1}{2}$
Reflection	$-f(x)$ $f(-x)$	$g(x) = -x^3$ across x-axis $g(x) = (-x)^3$ across y-axis

Hint

You can use a calculator to check your graph.

Example 1 Translating a Polynomial Function

For $f(x) = x^3 + 2$, write the rule for each function and sketch its graph.

a. $g(x) = f(x) + 3$

SOLUTION

$g(x) = (x^3 + 2) + 3 = x^3 + 5$

Translate the graph of $f(x)$ 3 units up.

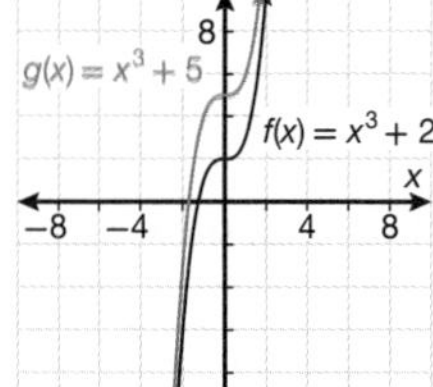

b. $g(x) = f(x - 4)$

SOLUTION

$g(x) = (x - 4)^3 + 2$

Translate the graph of $f(x)$ 4 units to the right.

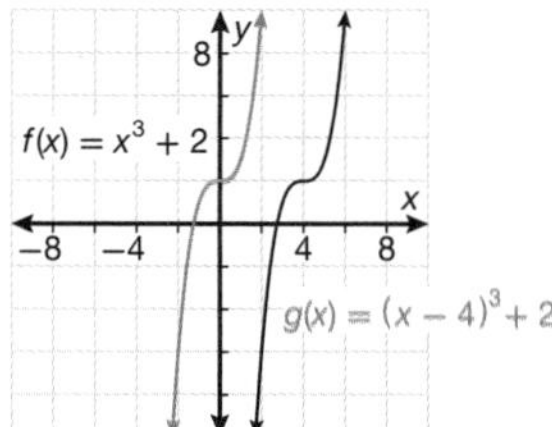

Online Connection
www.SaxonMathResources.com

LESSON RESOURCES

Student Edition Practice Workbook 111
Reteaching Master 111
Adaptations Master 111
Challenge and Enrichment Master C111
Technology Lab Master 111

MATH BACKGROUND

The transformations here are like those applied to geometric figures. A vertical or horizontal translation of a figure may be called a slide. The figure's orientation does not change. A translation can also be considered equivalent to a change in the origin of the coordinate system.

Figures may be stretched or compressed by using a scale factor. A familiar example is a scale factor on maps, such as 1 cm = 5 km.

A stretch or compression may also be called a dilation. Similar figures are examples of stretches or compressions.

Reflecting a figure is sometimes called a flip. When a figure or function is reflected across the x-axis, each point (x, y) becomes $(x, -y)$. Across the y-axis, (x, y) becomes $(-x, y)$. A glide reflection is a combination of a reflection and a translation.

Example 2 Reflecting a Polynomial Function

Let $f(x) = x^3 - 8x^2 + 4x - 10$. Write a function g that performs each transformation.

a. Reflect $f(x)$ across the x-axis.

> **Hint**
>
> To write the rule for $-f(x)$, change every sign of $f(x)$.

SOLUTION

$g(x) = -f(x)$

$g(x) = -(x^3 - 8x^2 + 4x - 10)$

$g(x) = -x^3 + 8x^2 - 4x + 10$

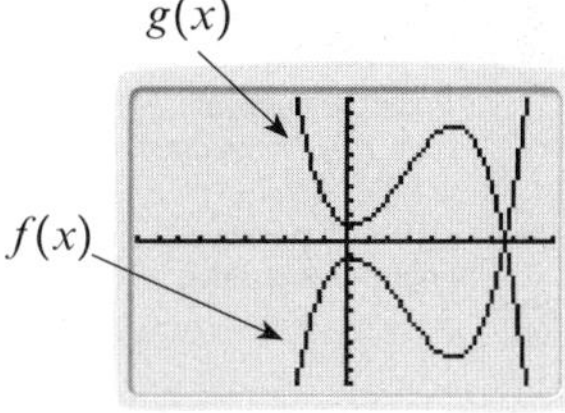

Check Graph both functions. The graph of $g(x)$ is a reflection of $f(x)$ across the x-axis.

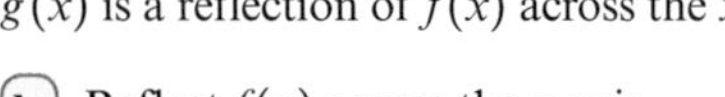

b. Reflect $f(x)$ across the y-axis.

SOLUTION

$g(x) = f(-x)$

$g(x) = (-x)^3 - 8(-x)^2 + 4(-x) - 10$

$g(x) = -x^3 - 8x^2 - 4x - 10$

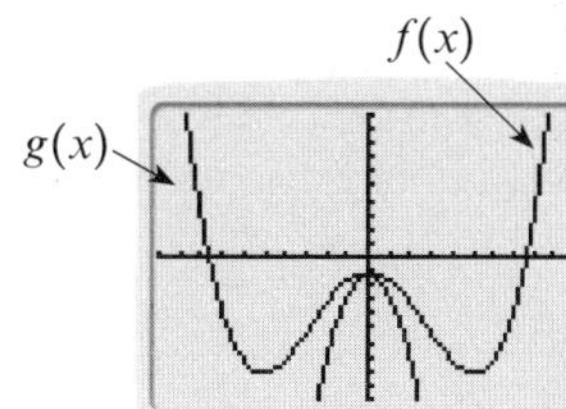

Check Graph both functions. The graph of $g(x)$ is a reflection of $f(x)$ across the y-axis.

Example 3 Compressing and Stretching a Polynomial Function

Let $f(x) = x^4 - 5x^2 + 4$. Graph f and g on the same coordinate plane. Describe g as a transformation of f.

a. $g(x) = 2f(x)$

SOLUTION

$g(x) = 2f(x)$

$g(x) = 2(x^4 - 5x^2 + 4)$

$g(x) = 2x^4 - 10x^2 + 8$

$g(x)$ is a vertical stretch of $f(x)$.

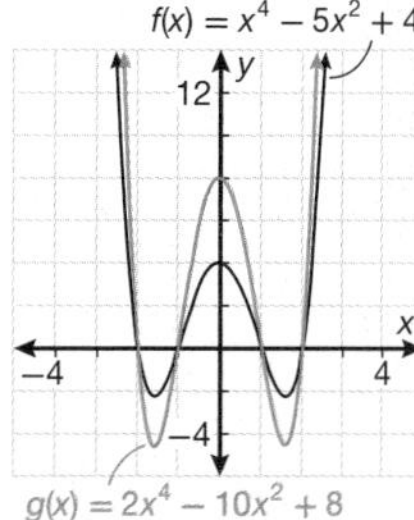

b. $g(x) = f(3x)$

SOLUTION

$g(x) = f(3x)$

$g(x) = (3x)^4 - 5(3x)^2 + 4$

$g(x) = 81x^4 - 45x^2 + 4$

$g(x)$ is a horizontal compression of $f(x)$.

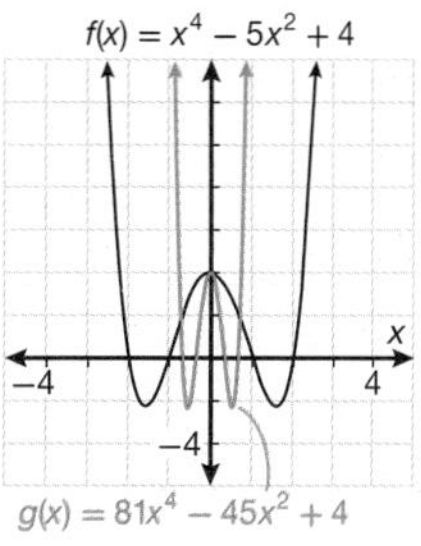

ENGLISH LEARNERS

Students may be familiar with the definition of **translate** which means to change a word from one language to another. Explain that in mathematics, translate means moving the graph of a function from one location on the coordinate grid to another. Explain that a translation is a change in something.

"What is being changed in the translation of a word or phrase?" language

"What is being changed in the translation of a function on a coordinate system?" its location

Graph a line on a coordinate system. Ask students to translate the word *line* into a different language. Then ask them to translate the line on the coordinate grid by drawing it in a different location.

Point out places in the lesson where the words *translate* and *translation* are used. Have students define the word in context.

Example 2

In this example, students reflect a polynomial function across the x-axis and the y-axis.

Error Alert Students may confuse $f(-x)$ with $-f(x)$ and simply change every sign of $f(x)$. Draw their attention to the solution of Example **2b.** Point out that some signs do not change. To avoid errors, they should place the $-x$ in parentheses in the function, and then determine if the sign of each variable or constant should change.

Additional Example 2

Let $f(x) = x^3 - 6x^2 + 3x - 5$. Write a function g that performs each transformation.

a. Reflect $f(x)$ across the x-axis. $g(x) = -x^3 + 6x^2 - 3x + 5$

b. Reflect $f(x)$ across the y-axis. $g(x) = -x^3 - 6x^2 - 3x - 5$

Example 3

Students transform a function by compressing or stretching it.

Additional Example 3

Let $f(x) = x^4 - 3x^2 + 7$. Graph f and g on the same coordinate plane. Describe g as a transformation of f.

a. $g(x) = 5f(x)$ $g(x)$ is a vertical stretch of $f(x)$.

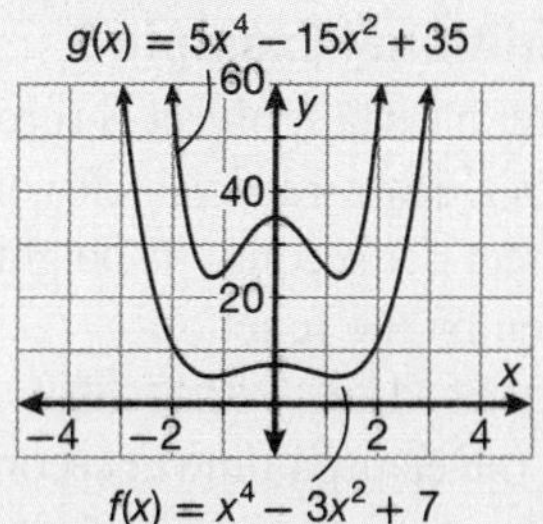

b. $g(x) = f(4x)$ $g(x)$ is a horizontal compression of $f(x)$.

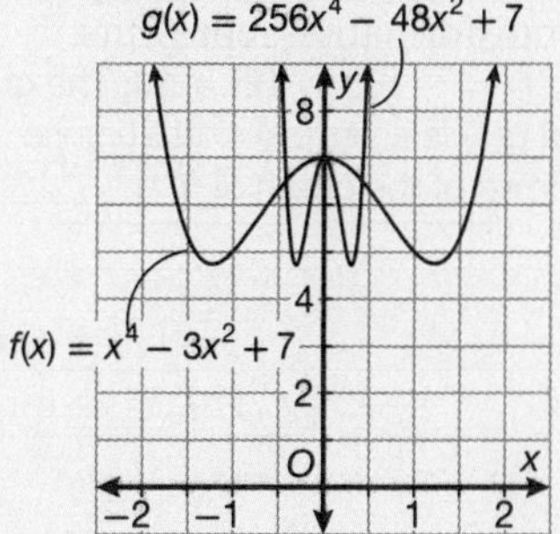

Lesson 111 775

Example 4

Students write functions that are combinations of transformations.

Additional Example 4

Write a function that transforms $f(x) = 4x^3 + 3$ in each of the following ways. Support your solution by using a graphing calculator.

a. Stretch vertically by a factor of 3, and shift 6 units right.
$g(x) = 12(x - 6)^3 + 9$

b. Reflect across the x-axis and shift 7 units up.
$g(x) = -4x^3 + 4$

Extend the Example

Point out that the order in which a transformation occurs is sometimes important. Use Example **4b** as an example. Have students determine what $h(x)$ would be if they first shifted the function $f(x)$ up 18 units and then reflected it across the x-axis.

$h(x) = -(f(x) + k)$
$= -(2x^3 + 5 + 18)$
$= -2x^3 - 23$

Example 5

Students use transformations of functions to describe motion.

Additional Example 5

After a certain object is thrown with a downward velocity of 12 feet per second, its height is given by the function $h(t) = -16t^2 - 12t + 30$, where t is the elapsed time in seconds and air resistance is neglected. Let $g(t) = h(t) - 20$. Write the rule for g, and explain what the transformation represents.
$g(t) = -16t^2 - 12t + 10$; The graph of $g(t)$ is a vertical shift 20 units down of the graph of $h(t)$.

Example 4 Combining Transformations

Write a function that transforms $f(x) = 2x^3 + 5$ in each of the following ways. Support your solution by using a graphing calculator.

a. Stretch vertically by a factor of 4, and shift 5 units left.

SOLUTION

Hint

To get the graph of $f(x - h)$, shift the graph of $f(x)$:
- left if h is negative.
- right if h is positive.

A vertical stretch is represented by $af(x)$, and a horizontal shift is represented by $f(x - h)$. Combining the two transformations gives $g(x) = af(x - h)$. Substitute 4 for a and -5 for h.

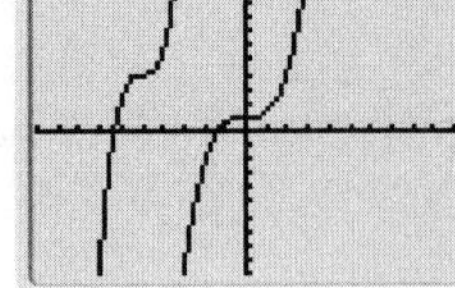

$g(x) = 4f(x - (-5))$

$g(x) = 4f(x + 5)$

$g(x) = 4(2(x + 5)^3 + 5)$

$g(x) = 8(x + 5)^3 + 20$

b. Reflect across the x-axis and shift 18 units up.

SOLUTION

A reflection across the x-axis is represented by $-f(x)$, and a vertical shift is represented by $f(x) + k$. Combining the two transformations gives $h(x) = -f(x) + k$.

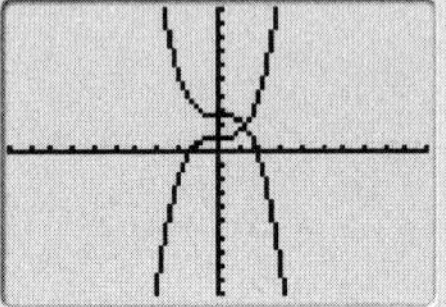

Substitute 18 for k.

$h(x) = -f(x) + 18$

$h(x) = -(2x^3 + 5) + 18$

$h(x) = -2x^3 + 13$

Example 5 Application: A Height Function

After a certain object is thrown with an upward velocity of 40 feet per second, its height is given by the function $h(t) = -16t^2 + 40t + 10$, where t is the elapsed time in seconds and air resistance is neglected. Let $g(t) = h(t) + 5$. Write the rule for g, and explain what the transformation represents.

SOLUTION

Caution

The graph of $h(t) = -16t^2 + 40t + 10$ does not represent the path of the object; it only represents the height.

$g(t) = h(t) + 5$

$g(t) = -16t^2 + 40t + 10 + 5$

$g(t) = -16t^2 + 40t + 15$

The rule is $g(t) = -16t^2 + 40t + 15$. The graph of $g(t)$ is a vertical shift 5 units up of the graph of $h(t)$. If the height of object H is given by $h(t)$ and the height of object G is given by $g(t)$, then object G is 5 feet higher than object H at all times that both objects are in the air.

INCLUSION

Help students develop a kinesthetic understanding of translations by providing them with several cardboard cutouts resembling functions on a graph, such as an elongated S to resemble a cubic function or a wide U to resemble a square function. Draw a large coordinate system on the board and have students move their "functions" to demonstrate different transformations.

776 *Saxon Algebra 2*

Lesson Practice

a. Given $f(x) = x^3 - 1$, write the rule for $g(x) = f(x) + 5$. Sketch the graphs of f and g. See Additional Answers.
(Ex 1)

b. Given $f(x) = x^3 - 1$, write the rule for $g(x) = f(x + 3)$. Sketch the graphs of f and g. See Additional Answers.
(Ex 1)

c. Let $f(x) = x^3 + x^2 - 6x - 1$. Write a function g that is the reflection of $f(x)$ across the x-axis. $g(x) = -x^3 - x^2 + 6x + 1$
(Ex 2)

d. Let $f(x) = x^3 + x^2 - 6x - 1$. Write a function g that is the reflection of $f(x)$ across the y-axis. $g(x) = -x^3 + x^2 + 6x - 1$
(Ex 2)

e.–g. See Additional Answers.

e. Let $f(x) = 16x^4 - 24x^2 + 4$ and $g(x) = \frac{1}{4}f(x)$. Graph f and g on the same coordinate plane. Describe g as a transformation of f.
(Ex 3)

f. Let $f(x) = 16x^4 - 24x^2 + 4$ and $g(x) = f\left(\frac{1}{2}x\right)$. Graph f and g on the same coordinate plane. Describe g as a transformation of f.
(Ex 3)

g. Write a function g that transforms $f(x) = 8x^3 - 2$ as follows: Compress vertically by a factor of $\frac{1}{2}$, and move the x-intercept 3 units right. Support your solution by using a graphing calculator.
(Ex 4)

h. Write a function h that transforms $f(x) = 8x^3 - 2$ as follows: Reflect across the x-axis, and move the x-intercept 4 units left. Support your solution by using a graphing calculator. See Additional Answers.
(Ex 4)

i. After a certain object is thrown with a downward velocity of 15 feet per second, its height is given by the function $h(t) = -16t^2 - 15t + 200$, where t is the elapsed time in seconds and air resistance is neglected. Let $g(t) = h(t) - 40$. Write the rule for g, and explain what the transformation represents.
(Ex 5)

i. $g(t) = -16t^2 - 15t + 160$; The graph of $g(t)$ is a vertical shift 40 units down of the graph of $h(t)$. If the height of object H is given by $h(t)$ and the height of object G is given by $g(t)$, then object G is 40 feet lower than object H at all times that both objects are in the air.

Practice Distributed and Integrated

1. A line has slope -4 and passes through (6, 8). What is the equation of the line written in slope intercept form? $y = -4x + 32$
(26)

***2.** Baseball Attendance The *cumulative* attendance at home baseball games for the years 1996–2005 can be modeled by $f(x) = 1.922x^4 - 36.769x^3 + 132.212x^2 + 3558.615x - 11$, where x is the number of years since 1995 and $f(x)$ is in thousands. (Cumulative means the statistic for each year is the sum of that year's attendance and all the previous years' attendances.) Describe the transformation $g(x) = f(x - 1)$ by writing the rule for $g(x)$ and explaining the change in the context of the problem. See Additional Answers.
(111)

***3.** Use matrix multiplication to show that the dot product of two vectors that are perpendicular to each other is zero. $\begin{bmatrix} a \\ 0 \end{bmatrix} \cdot [0 \quad b] = a \cdot 0 + 0 \cdot b = 0$
(99)

ALTERNATE METHOD FOR EXAMPLE 4b

Have students sketch the graphs on the board using one color for $f(x)$ and a second color for $h(x)$. Have them use a third color to draw a point on $f(x)$ and the analogous point on $h(x)$. Repeat with several other points on the graphs to emphasize the type of translation.

Lesson Practice

Problem b

Error Alert Students may think that they have to expand $(x + 3)^3 - 1$ in order to graph a problem like this. Point out that as long as they can recognize the type of transformation and they know the original function, they can graph the transformed function.

Problem f

Scaffolding Ask students how the transformation would change if it were $g(x) = f(2x)$ instead of $f\left(\frac{1}{2}x\right)$. The function would be a compression rather than a stretch.

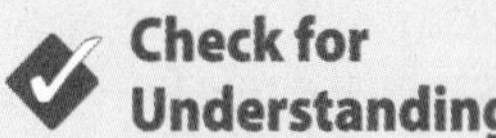

Check for Understanding

The questions below help assess the concepts taught in this lesson.

"How does a transformation affect the shape of a function?" The shape of the curve doesn't change for translations and reflections. Stretches and compressions, however, change the shape of the function.

"Why does $g(x) = f(-x)$ reflect across the y-axis?" The y values do not change, and the x values change only in sign.

3 Practice

Math Conversations

Discussions to strengthen understanding

Problem 1

Extend the Problem

"What is the general form of the slope-intercept equation?" $y = mx + b$

"What equation can you use if you know the slope and a point?" $(y - y_1) = m(x - x_1)$

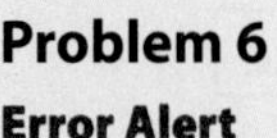

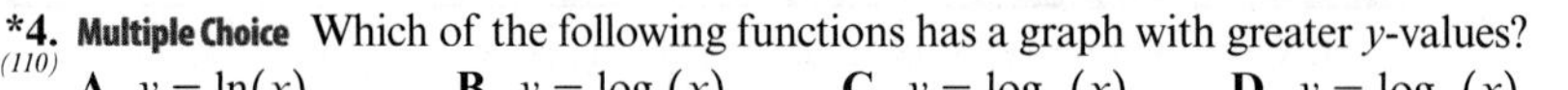

Problem 6

Error Alert

Remind students that an open circle on a line graph means the number is not included. Encourage them to consider whether each inequality sign includes an equality mark.

Problem 10

Guide students by asking the following questions.

"What is the difference in the number of rows between row 3 and row 14?" 11

"What is the difference in number between 13 seats and 24 seats?" 11

"What must be the rule for the arithmetic sequence?" +1

***4.** (110) **Multiple Choice** Which of the following functions has a graph with greater y-values? **B**

A $y = \ln(x)$ B $y = \log_2(x)$ C $y = \log_{20}(x)$ D $y = \log_{15}(x)$

***5.** (Inv 11) Given the complex number $8 + 24i$ written in $a + bi$ form, convert it to the trigonometric and polar forms. $25.3\cos(71.6°) + i25.3\sin(71.6°)$, $(25.3, 71.6°)$

6. (10) Solve and graph the compound inequality $-8 < 4(x + 1)$ and $12 > 4x$. See Additional Answers.

7. (89) **Error Analysis** Explain the error or errors a student made in graphing $x^2 + 1 > y$. The student shaded the wrong region because (0, 0) is a solution. The student should have also used a dashed line.

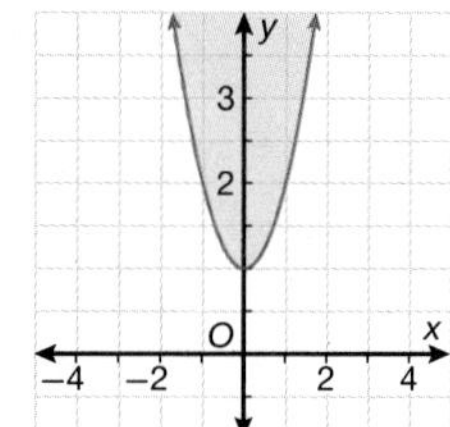

8. (90) **Multiple Choice** Which of the following has a period of $\frac{1}{5}\pi$? **C**

A $y = 5\tan(x)$ B $y = \tan(x - 5)$ C $y = \tan(5x)$ D $y = \tan\left(\frac{x}{5}\right)$

***9.** (109) **Geometry** In hyperbolic geometry, $\tanh(x) = \frac{\sinh(x)}{\cosh(x)}$. Show that $1 - \tanh^2(x) = \frac{1}{\cosh^2(x)}$. See Additional Answers.

10. (92) **Theater** The number of seats in the first 14 rows of the center orchestra aisle of the Marquis Theater in New York City form an arithmetic sequence. The third row has 13 seats and the last row has 24 seats. Find the number of seats in the 7th row. 17 seats

11. (50) **Temperature** The formula $C = \frac{5}{9}(F - 32)$ relates Celsius temperature C and Fahrenheit temperature F. Solve the formula for F. Then write and solve a new equation to find the number that represents the same temperature on both scales. (Hint: Substitute x for both C and F.) $F = \frac{9}{5}C + 32$; $\frac{9}{5}x + 32 = \frac{5}{9}(x - 32)$; $x = -40$; $-40°F$ and $-40°C$ represent the same temperature.

12. (93) **Analyze** Cobalt-58ml has a half-life of 9.04 hours. Calculate mentally how long it would take for 4 grams of cobalt-58ml to decay to 1 gram. Explain your method.

12. Sample: 18.08 hours; It would take 9.04 hours for 4 grams to decay to 2 grams, and then another 9.04 hours for 2 grams to decay to 1 gram.

13. (95) **Construction** Use the Remainder Theorem to determine the volume of the box if $x = 3$. 6721 cubic units

(Box dimensions: $15x + 2$, $4x - 1$, $3x + 4$)

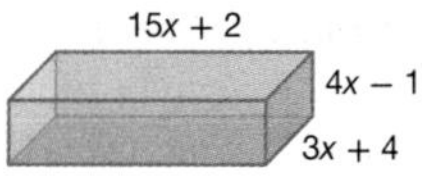

14. (29) How many solutions does the system of equations have, and what type of solution is it? No solutions, inconsistent

$$x + 5y - 2z = 1$$
$$-x - 2y + z = 6$$
$$-2x - 7y + 3z = 7$$

15. (97) **Write** Describe how to find the nth term of a geometric sequence, given the first and second terms.

15. Divide the second term by the first term to find the common ratio. Raise the common ratio to the power of $n - 1$, and multiply the result by the first term.

***16.** (110) **Predict** Which function has the greater x-intercept, $f(x) = \log_b(x)$ or $g(x) = \log_b(\log_b(x))$? What can you conclude about the function with the greater x-intercept. $\log_b(\log_b(x))$ has the greater x-intercept because it increases at a slower rate than $\log_b(x)$.

CHALLENGE

Suppose $f(x) = x^2$. Show that $g(x) = x^2 - 4x + 8$ is a vertical translation of 4 units up and a horizontal translation of 2 units right.

$$g(x) = x^2 - 4x + 8$$
$$= (x^2 - 4x + 4) + 4$$
$$= (x - 2)^2 + 4$$

Suppose $f(x) = x^3$. Show that $h(x) = x^3 + 6x^2 + 12x + 3$ is a vertical translation of 5 units down and a horizontal translation of 2 units left.

$$h(x) = x^3 + 6x^2 + 12x + 3$$
$$= (x^3 + 6x^2 + 12x + 8) - 5$$
$$= (x^2 + 4x + 4)(x + 2) - 5$$
$$= (x + 2)^2(x + 2) - 5$$
$$= (x + 2)^3 - 5$$

17. **Multi-Step** Complete parts a–c to graph a polar equation and analyze the graph.
(96)

a. Convert the Cartesian equation $y = x^2$ to a polar equation by using $x = r\cos\theta$ and $y = r\sin\theta$. (Hint: Factor and then eliminate the case $r = 0$.) $r = \frac{\sin\theta}{\cos^2\theta}$

b. Graph the polar equation on a calculator, using these window settings: $\theta\text{min} = 0$, $\theta\text{max} = \frac{\pi}{2}$, $\theta\text{step} = \frac{\pi}{24}$, $X\text{min} = -6$, $X\text{max} = 6$, $Y\text{min} = -1$, $Y\text{max} = 7$. Do you get the same graph as the graph of $y = x^2$? Explain why or why not. See Additional Answers.

c. If $\theta\text{min} = 0$ is used as a window setting, what is the least value of θmax needed to get the same graph as the graph of $y = x^2$? Explain. Sample: $\theta\text{max} = \pi$; This value allows points in Quadrant II.

*18. Write the equation $5x^2 + 2y^2 = 10$ as an ellipse in standard form. $\frac{x^2}{(\sqrt{2})^2} + \frac{y^2}{(\sqrt{5})^2} = 1$
(98)

*19. **Graphing Calculator** Graph the function $y = \frac{x^2 - 7x - 60}{x + 3}$ on a graphing calculator. Identify any vertical asymptote(s). See Additional Answers.
(100)

20. **Analyze** Without graphing, determine the point in which the graphs of $y = \log x$ and $y = 3\log x$ intersect. Explain your reasoning. (1, 0); Possible explanation: The solution to $\log x = 3\log x$ is $x = 1$, and $\log 1 = 0$, so the point of intersection is (1, 0).
(102)

21. Determine whether the linear binomial $x + 3$ is a factor of the polynomial $P(x) = x^3 + 19x^2 + 79x - 35$. No
(61)

*22. **Justify** Give an example of a polynomial function of degree 3 or higher whose reflection across the x-axis is the same as its reflection across the y-axis. Justify your answer. Sample: $f(x) = x^3 - x$; $f(-x) = -f(x) = -x^3 + x$
(111)

23. Write a quadratic function that has zeros 18 and 3. $f(x) = x^2 - 21x + 54$
(35)

24. Let $f(x) = x^3 - 125$ and $g(x) = 2x - 1$. Find the roots of $f(g(x))$. $x = 3$
(85)

Find the roots of the equations.

25. $0 = 3x^3 + 2x^2 + 1$ $x = -1$
(90)

26. $0 = 5x^4 + 2x^3 + x^2$ $x = 0$
(90)

Solve the equations.

*27. $\log(12x - 11) = \log(3x + 13)$ $\frac{8}{3}$
(102)

*28. $\log_2(x - 4) = 6$ 68
(102)

29. Scores from a test have a mean of 87 and a standard deviation of 4.3. A randomly selected test has a score of 82.5. Find the z-score for this test. −1.05
(80)

30. **Probability** Five folded pieces of paper are in a hat. Three are to be chosen at random. Is it a dependent or independent event if the papers are not returned to the hat once they are chosen? Dependent
(33)

LOOKING FORWARD

Transforming polynomial functions will be further developed in other Saxon Secondary Mathematics courses.

Problem 18

Extend the Problem

Find the eccentricity. about 0.775

Problem 21

"What method can you use to determine whether the linear binomial is a factor?" Sample answer: synthetic division

"How can you tell from synthetic division whether the linear binomial is a factor?" If there is no remainder, the linear binomial is a factor.

Problem 23

Prompt students to recall what must be true in order for a number a to be a zero of a polynomial. The polynomial must have a factor of the form $x - a$.

Problem 28

Students can begin by rewriting the logarithmic expression as an exponential expression.

LESSON

112

1 Warm Up

Use Problems 2 and 3 in the Warm Up to review trigonometric function values in special triangles.

2 New Concepts

Students use sum and difference identities to help simplify functions and to solve for exact values of trigonometric functions.

Example 1

Students will use sum and difference formulas to evaluate expressions.

Additional Example 1

a. Find the exact value of sin 15°.

$$\sin 15° = \sin(45° - 30°)$$
$$= \sin 45° \cos 30° - \cos 45° \sin 30°$$
$$= \frac{\sqrt{2}}{2} \cdot \frac{\sqrt{3}}{2} - \frac{\sqrt{2}}{2} \cdot \frac{1}{2}$$
$$= \frac{\sqrt{6}}{4} - \frac{\sqrt{2}}{4} = \frac{\sqrt{6}-\sqrt{2}}{4}$$

b. Find the exact value of $\sin\left(\frac{5\pi}{12}\right)$.

$$\sin\left(\frac{5\pi}{12}\right) = \sin\left(\frac{\pi}{6} + \frac{\pi}{4}\right)$$
$$= \sin\left(\frac{\pi}{6}\right)\cos\left(\frac{\pi}{4}\right) + \cos\left(\frac{\pi}{6}\right)\sin\left(\frac{\pi}{4}\right)$$
$$= \frac{1}{2} \cdot \frac{\sqrt{2}}{2} + \frac{\sqrt{3}}{2}\frac{\sqrt{2}}{2}$$
$$= \frac{\sqrt{2}+\sqrt{6}}{2}$$

LESSON RESOURCES

Student Edition Practice Workbook 112
Reteaching Master 112
Adaptations Master 112
Challenge and Enrichment Master C112

LESSON 112

Using Sum and Difference Identities

Warm Up

1. **Vocabulary** The ratio $\frac{x}{r}$ is the cosine ratio. (46)

2. $\sin 30° =$ $\frac{1}{2}$ (52)

3. $\tan 45° =$ 1 (52)

New Concepts

A trigonometric identity is a trigonometric equation that is true for all values of the variables for which every expression in the equation is defined.

Sum and Difference Identities are used to simplify and evaluate expressions.

Sum and Difference Identities	
Sum Identities	**Difference Identities**
$\sin(A+B) = \sin A \cos B + \cos A \sin B$	$\sin(A-B) = \sin A \cos B - \cos A \sin B$
$\cos(A+B) = \cos A \cos B - \sin A \sin B$	$\cos(A-B) = \cos A \cos B + \sin A \sin B$
$\tan(A+B) = \frac{\tan A + \tan B}{1 - \tan A \tan B}$	$\tan(A-B) = \frac{\tan A - \tan B}{1 + \tan A \tan B}$

Example 1 Evaluating Expressions with Sum and Difference Identities

a. Find the exact value of cos 75°.

SOLUTION Write 75° as 30° + 45° so that known trigonometric function values of 30° and 45° can be used.

$\cos 75° = \cos(30° + 45°)$ — Write 75° as 30° + 45°.

$= \cos 30° \cos 45° - \sin 30° \sin 45°$ — Apply the $\cos(A+B)$ identity.

$= \frac{\sqrt{3}}{2} \cdot \frac{\sqrt{2}}{2} - \frac{1}{2} \cdot \frac{\sqrt{2}}{2}$ — Evaluate.

$= \frac{\sqrt{6}}{4} - \frac{\sqrt{2}}{4} = \frac{\sqrt{6}-\sqrt{2}}{4}$ — Simplify.

b. Find the exact value of $\sin\left(-\frac{\pi}{12}\right)$.

SOLUTION

$\sin\left(-\frac{\pi}{12}\right) = \sin\left(\frac{\pi}{4} - \frac{\pi}{3}\right)$ — Write $\sin\left(-\frac{\pi}{12}\right)$ as $\sin\left(\frac{\pi}{4} - \frac{\pi}{3}\right)$.

$= \sin\frac{\pi}{4}\cos\frac{\pi}{3} - \cos\frac{\pi}{4}\sin\frac{\pi}{3}$ — Apply the $\sin(A-B)$ identity.

$= \frac{\sqrt{2}}{2} \cdot \frac{1}{2} - \frac{\sqrt{2}}{2} \cdot \frac{\sqrt{3}}{2}$ — Evaluate.

$= \frac{\sqrt{2}}{4} - \frac{\sqrt{6}}{4} = \frac{\sqrt{2}-\sqrt{6}}{4}$ — Simplify.

Hint

In Example 1b, there is more than one expression that can be substituted for $-\frac{\pi}{12}$. For example, $-\frac{\pi}{12} = \frac{\pi}{4} - \frac{\pi}{3}$ and $-\frac{\pi}{12} = \frac{\pi}{6} - \frac{\pi}{4}$.

Online Connection
www.SaxonMathResources.com

MATH BACKGROUND

The sum and difference identities are important because they are used to show how the different values of sine and cosine are related to each other at specific angles. They are very useful in proofs that show the exact value of specific trigonometric functions.

Sum and difference identities can also be used to evaluate angles that would not normally be solved for by hand. By separating the angle into two angles whose exact values are known, sum and difference identities can be used to evaluate the function.

Example 2 Using the Pythagorean Theorem with Sum and Difference Identities

Evaluate $\tan(A - B)$ if $\sin A = \frac{3}{5}$, $90° < A < 270°$, $\cos B = -\frac{15}{17}$, and $180° < B < 360°$.

SOLUTION

Step 1: Find $\tan A$ and $\tan B$.

$90° < A < 270°$ and $\sin A$ is positive, so A is in Quadrant II.

$$\sin A = \frac{3}{5} = \frac{y}{r}$$

$180° < B < 360°$ and $\cos B$ is negative, so B is in Quadrant III.

$$\cos B = \frac{-15}{17} = \frac{x}{r}$$

$$x^2 + y^2 = r^2$$
$$x^2 + 3^2 = 5^2$$
$$x = -\sqrt{25 - 9} = -4$$
$$\tan A = \frac{y}{x} = \frac{3}{-4} = -\frac{3}{4}$$

$$x^2 + y^2 = r^2$$
$$(-15)^2 + y^2 = 17^2$$
$$y = -\sqrt{289 - 225} = -8$$
$$\tan B = \frac{y}{x} = \frac{-8}{-15} = \frac{8}{15}$$

Step 2: Use the difference identity to find $\tan(A - B)$.

$$\tan(A - B) = \frac{\tan A - \tan B}{1 + \tan A \tan B}$$

$$= \frac{-\frac{3}{4} - \frac{8}{15}}{1 + \left(-\frac{3}{4}\right)\left(\frac{8}{15}\right)} = -\frac{77}{36}$$

Substitute $-\frac{3}{4}$ for $\tan A$ and $\frac{8}{15}$ for $\tan B$. Then simplify.

The sum identities for sine and cosine can be used to derive a matrix for rotating a point in a plane. To rotate a point $P(x, y)$ through an angle θ, you can use the **rotation matrix** $\begin{bmatrix} \cos\theta & -\sin\theta \\ \sin\theta & \cos\theta \end{bmatrix}$.

Using a Rotation Matrix
Let $P(x, y)$ be any point in a plane. Let $P'(x', y')$ be the image of P after a rotation of θ degrees counterclockwise about the origin. Then $\begin{bmatrix} \cos\theta & -\sin\theta \\ \sin\theta & \cos\theta \end{bmatrix}\begin{bmatrix} x \\ y \end{bmatrix} = \begin{bmatrix} x' \\ y' \end{bmatrix}$.

Math Reasoning

Write Explain why x is negative in the diagram for angle A.

Sample: Because x-values in Quadrant II are always negative

Hint

Use an inverse trigonometric function and a calculator to verify that $A \approx 143.13°$. Then find the measures of B and $(A - B)$ to check the value of $\tan(A - B)$.

Example 2

Students will use the sum and difference identities along with the Pythagorean Theorem to evaluate functions.

Additional Example 2

Evaluate $\tan(A + B)$ if $\sin A$ is $\frac{4}{5}$, $0° < A < 90°$, $\cos B$ is $\frac{5}{13}$, and $180° < B < 360°$.

$\tan A = \frac{4}{3}$ and $\tan B = -\frac{12}{5}$

$$\tan(A + B) = \frac{\tan A + \tan B}{1 - \tan A \tan B}$$

$$= \frac{\frac{4}{3} - \frac{12}{5}}{1 - \frac{4}{3} \cdot -\frac{12}{5}} = \frac{-16}{63}$$

TEACHER TIP

In order to accurately use the identities, it is essential that the students learn the trigonometric values of certain right triangles so they can be easily solved for in fraction form and used throughout the rest of the problem.

Lesson 112 781

Example 3

Students will apply their knowledge of sums and differences as well as trigonometry to solve a rotational matrix.

Additional Example 3

Find the coordinates of the points in the image after a 60-degree rotation counterclockwise about the origin.

$$R_{60^\circ} = \begin{bmatrix} \cos 60^\circ & -\sin 60^\circ \\ \sin 60^\circ & \cos 60^\circ \end{bmatrix}$$

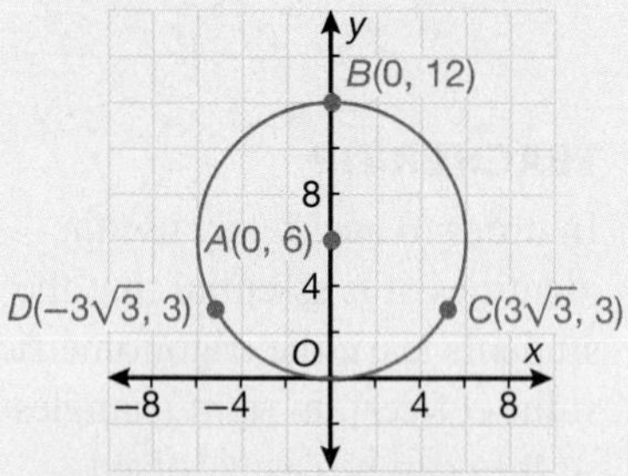

$A'(-3\sqrt{3}, 3)$ $B'(-6\sqrt{3}, 6)$
$C'(0, 6)$ $D'(-3\sqrt{3}, -3)$

Lesson Practice

Problem b

Error Alert Students may reduce the fractions incorrectly during the problem while trying to combine radicals in the numerator or in the denominator. To avoid this, be sure that students are aware that radicals cannot be added or subtracted from each other unless the radicands are the same.

Problem d

Scaffolding Evaluate which quadrant each value will be in before solving the problem. Using the sum and difference identities, it is clear that $\cos A$, $\cos B$, and $\sin B$ must be solved for using the given $\sin A$ and $\tan B$. This can be used to solve for $\cos(A + B)$.

Example 3 **Using a Rotation Matrix**

Find the coordinates of the images of the points in the figure after a 60° rotation counterclockwise about the origin.

SOLUTION

Step 1: Write a rotation matrix and a matrix of the coordinates of the points in the figure.

$$R_{60^\circ} = \begin{bmatrix} \cos 60^\circ & -\sin 60^\circ \\ \sin 60^\circ & \cos 60^\circ \end{bmatrix} \quad \text{Rotation matrix}$$

$$S = \begin{bmatrix} 0 & 0 & \sqrt{3} & -\sqrt{3} \\ 2 & 4 & 1 & 1 \end{bmatrix} \quad \text{Matrix of point coordinates}$$

Step 2: Find the matrix product.

$$R_{60^\circ} \times S = \begin{bmatrix} \cos 60^\circ & -\sin 60^\circ \\ \sin 60^\circ & \cos 60^\circ \end{bmatrix}\begin{bmatrix} 0 & 0 & \sqrt{3} & -\sqrt{3} \\ 2 & 4 & 1 & 1 \end{bmatrix}$$

$$= \begin{bmatrix} -\sqrt{3} & -2\sqrt{3} & 0 & -\sqrt{3} \\ 1 & 2 & 2 & -1 \end{bmatrix}$$

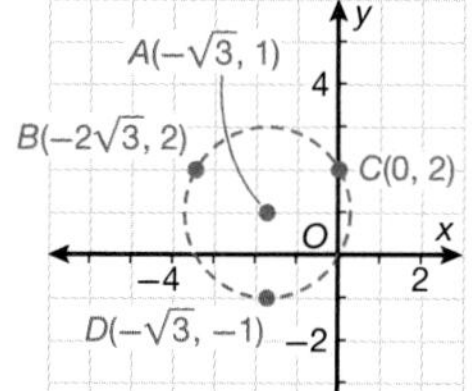

The image points after a 60° rotation counterclockwise about the origin are $A'(-\sqrt{3}, 1)$, $B'(-2\sqrt{3}, 2)$, $C'(0, 2)$, and $D'(-\sqrt{3}, -1)$.

Lesson Practice

a. (Ex 1) Find the exact value of $\tan 105^\circ$. $\frac{\sqrt{3}+1}{1-\sqrt{3}}$ or $-2-\sqrt{3}$

b. (Ex 1) Find the exact value of $\cos\left(\frac{11\pi}{12}\right)$. $\frac{-\sqrt{2}-\sqrt{6}}{4}$

c. (Ex 2) Evaluate $\cos(A + B)$ if $\sin A = \frac{24}{25}$, $-90^\circ < A < 90^\circ$, $\tan B = -1$, and $-90^\circ < B < 90^\circ$. $\frac{31\sqrt{2}}{50}$

d. (Ex 3) Find the coordinates of the images of the points in the figure after a 45° rotation counterclockwise about the origin. $A'\left(\frac{\sqrt{2}}{2}, \frac{\sqrt{2}}{2}\right)$ $B'(-\sqrt{2}, -\sqrt{2})$ $C'\left(\frac{\sqrt{2}-3\sqrt{6}}{2}, \frac{\sqrt{2}+3\sqrt{6}}{2}\right)$

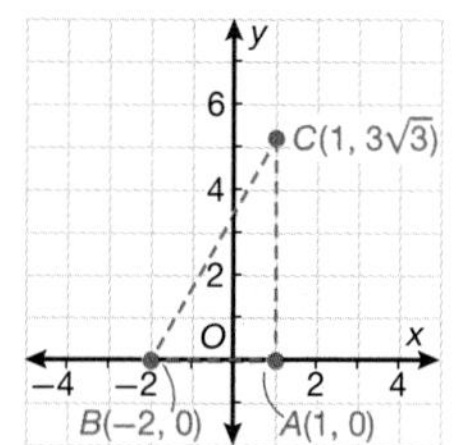

INCLUSION

For students unable to break down an angle into two easier solvable angles by the sum and difference formula, first have them solve the problem in their calculator for the whole angle.

Next have them apply the formula and show them that the result is equal. This will help them to understand that the identities although in a different form are equal.

Furthermore, show that if the angles can be broken down into angles involving special right triangles, then an exact value for the function can be found.

Practice Distributed and Integrated

Write the expression in simplest form.

1. $\frac{3}{\sqrt[4]{144}}$ (40) $\frac{\sqrt{3}}{2}$

2. $\frac{\sqrt[3]{9}}{\sqrt[5]{27}}$ (40) $\sqrt[15]{3}$

3. (82) **Data Analysis** The number of days it takes to complete a year for different planets is shown in the table. Let Earth's yearly motion be modeled by $y = \sin(0.017x)$. How would you model Venus' motion? Venus: $y = \sin(0.028x)$

Planet	Days in a Year
Mercury	88.03
Venus	224.63
Earth	365.25
Mars	686.67
Jupiter	4331.87
Saturn	10760.27
Uranus	30681.00
Neptune	60193.20

4. (18) Convert 30 hours into seconds. 108,000 seconds

***5.** (112) Find the exact value of sin 75°. $\frac{\sqrt{2}+\sqrt{6}}{4}$

***6.** (106) **Graphing Calculator** Graph $y = x^7 - 3x^4 - 2$ and describe the solutions of $x^7 - 3x^4 - 2 = 0$. Round real solutions to the nearest thousandth if needed. There is a real solution of about 1.503 with an odd multiplicity. The remaining solutions are not real.

7. (11) **Geometry** Write a polynomial in standard form that represents the shaded area formed by the two rectangles. $2x^2 - 3x + 15$

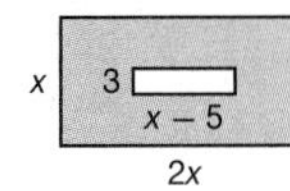

8. (95) **Multiple Choice** Which of the following polynomials has $P(3) = 533{,}386$? **A**

A $P(x) = x^{12} + 3x^6 + 5x^2 - 100x + 13$

B $P(x) = x^{14} + 3x^7 + 5x^2 - 100x + 13$

C $P(x) = x^{11} + 3x^5 + 5x^2 - 100x + 13$

D $P(x) = x^9 + 3x^5 + 5x^4 - 100x + 13$

***9.** (109) **Formulate** A hyperbola with vertical orientation has asymptotes with equations $y = \frac{4}{3}x - \frac{11}{3}$ and $y = -\frac{4}{3}x + \frac{29}{3}$. Write the equation of the hyperbola. $\frac{(y-3)^2}{4^2} - \frac{(x-5)^2}{3^2} = 1$

10. (94) **Error Analysis** Find the error(s) in the sign chart for $\frac{x+4}{(x-5)(x-1)} < 0$. What is the solution of the inequality?

	$x < -4$	$-4 < x < 1$	$1 < x < 5$	$x > 5$
	−5	0	3	8
$x + 4$	−	+	+	+
$x - 5$	−	−	−	+
$x - 1$	+	−	+	+
Value of expression	+	−	−	+

10. In $x < -4$, $(-5 - 1)$ is negative and the value of the expression is negative. In $-4 < x < 1$, the value of the expression is positive. The solution is $x < -4$ or $1 < x < 5$.

ENGLISH LEARNERS

Explain the meaning of the word **counterclockwise**, in Example 4.

Say, **"To move clockwise means to rotate in a similar way to the hands of a clock."**

Have students draw a labeled analog clock on a piece a plain paper. Have them draw an arc starting from the 12 to the 3. Have them draw an arrow at the end of the arc pointing toward the 3. Explain that the arc describes a clockwise direction.

Say, **"To move counterclockwise means to rotate in the opposite direction of the hands of a clock."**

Have them form an arc starting from the 12 to the 7. Have them draw an arrow at the end of the arc pointing toward the 7. Explain that the arc describes a counterclockwise direction.

Check for Understanding

The questions below help assess the concepts taught in this lesson.

"When are sum and difference identities mainly used?" Sample: when it is necessary to solve for an angle that can be broken down into two easily solved angles such as 30, 45, or 60 degrees.

"When using sum and difference identities, what must be taken into consideration?" Sample: The correct quadrant must be used based on the information given as well as knowledge of exact values of trigonometric functions of special right triangles.

3 Practice

Math Conversations

Discussion to strengthen understanding.

Problem 1

"What steps do you need to take to solve this problem?" First, simplify each radical. Next, multiply to remove the radical from the denominator. Finally, reduce any values if necessary.

Problem 8

Although students could substitute $x = 3$ into each equation to find which function is equal to the value desired, it may be quicker to use synthetic division and look for a remainder of 533,386.

Problem 10

After finding the error in the first column ($x < -4$), students should be able to see that there must be another error because the values of each expression (last row) should alternate.

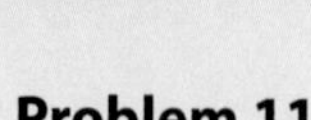

Problem 11

Remind students that the square must be complete on both the y terms and the x terms, and moving the constant term to the other side of the equation may help avoid confusion while completing the square.

Problem 13

Suggest that students substitute the given values into the given expression to check their work.

Problem 15

Point out that $(x + 4)$ is the simplified form of the expression $(x - (-4))$, so the graph of $g(x) = (x + 4)^3 + 1$ is shifted 4 units to the left of the graph of $f(x) = x^3 + 1$.

11. (98) **Analyze** Describe a method for converting a polynomial of the form $ax^2 + by^2 + cx + dy + e = 0$ to an ellipse in standard form, assuming the graph is an ellipse. Use this method with the polynomial $x^2 + 9y^2 - 10x - 18y + 7 = 0$.

11. Complete the square for each quadratic term, then divide by the constant term to get the equation of an ellipse in standard form; $\frac{(x-5)^2}{(\sqrt{27})^2} + \frac{(y-1)^2}{(\sqrt{3})^2} = 1$

***12.** (111) **Multi-Step** $f(x) = x^3 - 6x^2 + 4$ has turning points at (0, 4) and (4, −28). Identify the turning points of each function and justify your answers. See Additional Answers.

a. $\frac{1}{4}f(x)$ **b.** $f\left(\frac{1}{4}x\right)$ **c.** $f\left(x - \frac{1}{4}\right)$

13. (31) Multiply, then evaluate for $a = 2$, $b = 3$. $\frac{6a^2b}{4ab} \cdot \frac{3ab^3}{5a^2b^2}$ $\frac{9b}{10}; \frac{27}{10}$

14. (99) **Navigation** An airplane travels 225 mph 30° south of due west for two hours. The pilot makes an adjustment so that the plane then flies for another three hours at 268 mph 20° north of due west. What is the distance and direction of the plane from its original position? 1231.8 miles due west

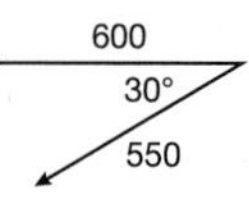

***15.** (111) **Error Analysis** To graph $g(x) = (x + 4)^3 + 1$, a student shifted the graph of $f(x) = x^3 + 1$ right 4 units. What is the error? The graph of $f(x) = x^3 + 1$ should be shifted left 4 units.

16. (100) **Generalize** Show that for rational functions $y = \frac{1}{x} + n$, with constant n, the horizontal asymptote is $y = n$. Sample: n is the vertical displacement of the function. For large values of x, the function approaches n.

17. (102) **Unions** From the 1930s on, labor union membership in the U.S. grew dramatically. During the years 1935–1955, labor union membership in the U.S. can be modeled by the equation $y = -4.4 + 12.6 \ln t$, where $5 \le t \le 25$, $t = 5$ represents 1935, and y is the percent of the U.S. labor force that were union members. Use the model to approximate the year in which union membership in the U.S. reached 30%. 1945 or 1946

***18.** (104) **Savings Accounts** A share certificate pays 5% interest, compounded yearly. The function $A(x) = P \cdot 1.05^x$ can be used to calculate the amount in the account, $A(x)$, after x years with the original amount, placed in the account, P. Use the function $f(x) = 1.05^x$ to sketch a graph of the equation $A(x) = P \cdot 1.05^x$ if the original amount in the account is $50,000. See Additional Answers.

19. (96) **Analyze** P has polar coordinates (r, θ). Write polar coordinates for P that have a different 1st coordinate. Sample: $(-r, \theta + \pi)$

***20.** (112) **Multiple Choice** Given that $\tan A = \frac{1}{2}$ and $\tan B = \frac{1}{4}$, what is the value of $\tan(A + B)$? D

A $\frac{2}{9}$ **B** $\frac{2}{7}$ **C** $\frac{2}{3}$ **D** $\frac{6}{7}$

ALTERNATE METHOD FOR PROBLEM 13

Instead of multiplying the two fractions immediately, and then substituting the values of the variables, it is simpler to first reduce the fractions to lowest terms, and then evaluate the function.

$$\frac{6a^2b}{4ab} \cdot \frac{3ab^3}{5a^2b^2} = \frac{6a}{4} \cdot \frac{3b}{5a} = \frac{3a}{2} \cdot \frac{3b}{5a} = \frac{9b}{10} = \frac{9(3)}{10} = \frac{27}{10}$$

By reducing first, the fraction can be solved easily after the exponents have been reduced.

*21. (106) **Farming** A grain silo is shaped like a cylinder with a hemisphere on top. The height of the cylindrical part is 28 feet. The radius of the hemisphere is x feet. The volume of the entire silo is 8550π cubic feet. Find the radius of the silo. 15 feet

22. (37) Find any values of x for which the following expression is undefined: $\frac{1}{x^3 + 4x^2 - 21x}$. $x = -7, 0, 3$

*23. (112) **Write** What is the value of $\cos\frac{2\pi}{5}\cos\frac{3\pi}{5} - \sin\frac{2\pi}{5}\sin\frac{3\pi}{5}$? Explain how to answer without a calculator. See Additional Answers.

*24. (105) **Organizing** A homeowner organized wooden planks in his backyard into 12 rows where each row has 2 more planks than the row above it. How many planks are there if the bottom row has 32 planks? See Additional Answers.

25. (88) Given $d = \sqrt{l^2 + w^2 + h^2}$, find l. $l = \pm\sqrt{d^2 - w^2 - h^2}$

26. (77) In $\triangle LMN$, $LM = 24$, $MN = 29$, and $m\angle M = 65°$. Find LN. 28.8

27. (35) Write a cubic function that has zeros 0, 16, and −9. $f(x) = x^3 - 7x^2 - 144x$

28. (97) **Salaries** An employee's salary is structured so that he earns $25,925 in the first year and a 2.75% raise each year thereafter. How much can the employee expect to earn in his 10th year? $33,094.46

29. (32) Solve the system. $\begin{aligned} y + z + w &= 6 \\ -y + 3z - w &= 2 \\ 2y - z + w &= 5 \end{aligned}$ $y = 3$, $z = 2$, $w = 1$

30. (87) Evaluate $\log_{10}(15x)^2$ when $x = 1$. $x \approx 2.352$

Problem 21

Guide the students by asking them the following questions.

"What is the formula for the volume of the cylinder, the hemisphere, and the entire silo?"

$V_{cylinder} = \pi r^2 h$

$V_{hemisphere} = \frac{2\pi r^3}{3}$

$V_{silo} = V_{cylinder} + V_{hemisphere}$

"What is the equation for the radius in terms of the other variables in the problem?" Convert the formula into a polynomial in terms of r.

$\frac{2}{3}\pi r^3 + \pi r^2 h - V_{silo} = 0$

"How can you solve for the radius?" The radius can be solved by finding the roots of the third degree polynomial.

CHALLENGE

Find the exact value of $\tan(A + B) + \sin(A + B)$ if $A + B = 75°$.

$\tan(A + B) + \sin(A + B)$
$= \tan(30° + 45°) + \sin(30° + 45°)$
$= 4.696$

LOOKING FORWARD

Using sum and difference identities prepares students for

- **Lesson 119** Solving Trigonometric Equations

LESSON

113

1 Warm Up

Have students find the common ratio in problem 2.

2 New Concepts

In this lesson, students find the sum of a finite geometric series, determine if a series is convergent or divergent, and find the sum of a convergent infinite geometric series.

Discuss the terms series, arithmetic series, and geometric series. Explain the formula for the sum of a finite geometric series. Point out that a_1 is the first term, S_n is the sum of the first n terms, and r is the common ratio of the series.

LESSON

113 Using Geometric Series

Warm Up

1. **Vocabulary** In a geometric sequence, the ________ is found by dividing a term by the previous term. (97) common ratio

2. Find the next three terms of the geometric sequence $-2, 10, -50, 250, \ldots$ (97)

2. −1250, 6250, −31,250

3. Find the 9th term of the geometric sequence $\frac{2}{3}, \frac{1}{6}, \frac{1}{24}, \ldots$ (97) $\frac{1}{98,304}$

New Concepts

Recall that a series is the indicated sum of the terms of a sequence. In an arithmetic series, the terms are those of an arithmetic sequence. In a **geometric series,** the terms are those of a geometric sequence.

Arithmetic Series	Geometric Series
$4 + 9 + 14 + 19$	$4 + 8 + 16 + 32$
$8 + 5 + 2 + (-1) + \ldots$	$1 + (-3) + 9 + (-27) + \ldots$

A formula for the sum of a finite geometric series can be found by multiplying the partial sum of a geometric series by the common ratio, and then subtracting.

Consider the series $S_n = ar^0 + ar^1 + ar^2 + ar^3 + ar^4 + \ldots + ar^n$ where a is the first term of the series and r is the common ratio.

Multiply the entire series by r, using rules of exponents to simplify, and then subtract the result from the original series. Notice that all but two terms will cancel out.

$$S_n = ar^0 + ar^1 + ar^2 + ar^3 + ar^4 + \ldots + ar^{n-1}$$
$$-\ rS_n = ar^1 + ar^2 + ar^3 + ar^4 + \ldots + ar^{n-1} + ar^n$$
$$S_n - rS_n = ar^0 - ar^n$$
$$(1 - r)S_n = ar^0 - ar^n$$

Hint

Remember, the nth term of a geometric series, a_n, equals $a_1(r)^{n-1}$, for example $a_7 = a_1r^6$.

Solving for S_n yields a formula to find the sum of n terms of any finite geometric series.

$$S_n = \frac{ar^0 - ar^n}{1 - r} = a\left(\frac{1 - r^n}{1 - r}\right).$$

Sum of a Finite Geometric Series
The sum of the first n terms of a geometric series, S_n, is $a_1\left(\frac{1 - r^n}{1 - r}\right)$.

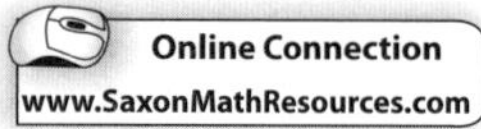
Online Connection
www.SaxonMathResources.com

Note that the formula gives a partial sum if the series is infinite. It gives the actual sum if the series is finite with n terms.

LESSON RESOURCES

Student Edition Practice Workbook 113
Reteaching Master 113
Adaptations Master 113
Challenge and Enrichment Masters C113
Technology Lab Master 113

MATH BACKGROUND

A *series* is the indicated sum of the terms of a sequence. A *geometric series* is the indicated sum of the terms of a *geometric sequence*.

A geometric sequence has consecutive terms that are compared by dividing to find a common ratio of the numbers. The ratio of the consecutive terms is a constant. This constant is called the *common ratio*.

The formula for the nth term of any geometric sequence is $a_n = a_1r^{n-1}$.

An *arithmetic series* is the indicated sum of the terms of the arithmetic sequence. The formula for finding a partial sum S_n of an arithmetic series is $S_n = \frac{n[2a_1 + (n-1)d]}{2}$.

Example 1 Finding the Sum of a Geometric Series

a. Find S_9 for the geometric series $1 + 4 + 16 + 64 + \ldots$

SOLUTION The formula for the sum requires a_1, which is 1, n, which is 9, and r which can be found by dividing: $64 \div 16 = 4$.

Now use $S_n = a_1\left(\frac{1 - r^n}{1 - r}\right)$.

$$S_9 = 1\left(\frac{1 - 4^9}{1 - 4}\right) \quad \text{Substitute.}$$

$$S_9 = 1\left(\frac{1 - 262{,}144}{-3}\right) \quad \text{Simplify.}$$

$$S_9 = 1(87{,}381) = 87{,}381$$

Check by using a graphing calculator.

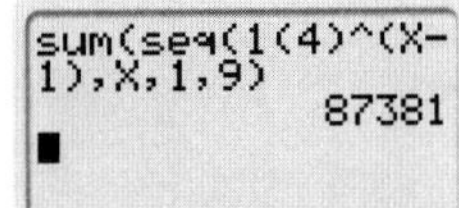

Hint

Notice that the equation is in the form $a_n = a_1(r)^{n-1}$, so $a_1 = 3$

b. Find S_{11} for the sequence $a_k = 3(-2)^{k-1}$.

SOLUTION Substitute 1 for k to find a_1.

$a_1 = 3(-2)^{1-1} = 3$

$n = 11$ and r is -2.

Now use $S_n = a_1\left(\frac{1 - r^n}{1 - r}\right)$.

$$S_{11} = 3\left(\frac{1 - (-2)^{11}}{1 - (-2)}\right) \quad \text{Substitute.}$$

$$S_{11} = 3\left(\frac{1 - (-2048)}{3}\right) \quad \text{Simplify.}$$

$$S_{11} = 3\left(\frac{2049}{3}\right) = 2049$$

Graphing Calculator Tip

Be sure to enclose -2 in parentheses when raising it to the 11th power.

Check by using a graphing calculator.

View the individual terms in the TABLE.

```
Plot1 Plot2 Plot3
\Y1=3*(-2)^(X-1)
\Y2=
\Y3=
\Y4=
\Y5=
\Y6=
```

X	Y1
1	3
2	-6
3	12
4	-24
5	48
6	-96
7	192

X=1

Example 1

Students find the nth term for a geometric series.

Additional Example 1

a. Find S_8 for the geometric series $1 + 5 + 25 + 125 + \ldots$. 97,656

b. Find S_9 for the sequence $15(-3)^{k-1}$. 73,815

TEACHER TIP

In part a, ensure that students understand why $a_1 = 1$, $n = 9$, and $r = 4$ before substituting the values into the formula.

INCLUSION

Have students use a spreadsheet program to find S_n. Set up cells for a_1, r, n, $1 - r^n$, $1 - r$, and $a_1\left(\frac{1 - r^n}{1 - r}\right)$.

Students enter values for a_1, r, and n. The spreadsheet can then simplify and find the answer to the expression.

Lesson 113 787

Exploration

TEACHER TIP

Summarize the exploration by telling students that the sum of an infinite geometric series is the ratio of the first term and the difference between 1 and the common ratio.

Discuss infinite geometric series, limit, convergent series, and divergent series. Point out that if $0 < |r| < 1$, then the series converges; and if $|r| > 1$, then the series diverges.

Exploration **Exploring an Infinite Geometric Series**

Materials needed: graph paper, graphing calculator

Step 1: Copy the chart. Then draw a 16 by 16 unit square on graph paper. Enter the perimeter in the chart.

Square	Perimeter	Cumulative Sum of Perimeters
16 by 16	64	64
8 by 8	32	96
4 by 4	16	112
2 by 2	8	120
1 by 1	4	124
0.5 by 0.5	2	126

> **Hint**
>
> In the first row of the chart, the cumulative sum of the perimeters is the same as the perimeter.

Step 2: Starting at one corner of this square, draw a new square with sides that are half as long as the first. Find the perimeter of this square. Continue making new squares with sides as half as long as the previous square and finding their perimeters. Complete the chart.

Step 3: Write a geometric series for the first n terms of the series in summation notation. Then use a graphing calculator to find the first 10, 15, and 25 terms of the series. $\sum_{k=1}^{n} 64\left(\frac{1}{2}\right)^{k-1}$, 127.875, $\approx$127.9960938, $\approx$127.9999962

Step 4: Evaluate $\frac{64}{1-\frac{1}{2}}$. How is this value related to the answers in Step 3?

128, the sums in Step 3 get closer and closer to this value

An **infinite geometric series** has infinitely many terms, and as the exploration above indicates, the partial sums of some infinite geometric series can get closer and closer to a fixed number. The fixed number is called the **limit**, and is considered the sum of the infinite series.

An infinite series only has a sum when the absolute value of the common ratio is between 0 and 1. These series are said to **converge.**

An infinite series does not have a sum when the absolute value of the common ratio is greater than 1. These series are said to **diverge.**

Convergent Series	Divergent Series
$20 + 10 + 5 + 2.5 + 1.25 + 0.625 + \ldots$	$20 + 40 + 80 + 160 + 320 + 640 + \ldots$
$r = \frac{1}{2}$	$r = 2$
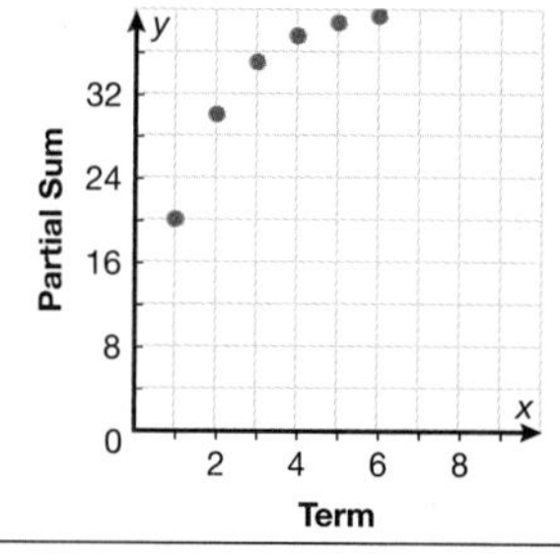	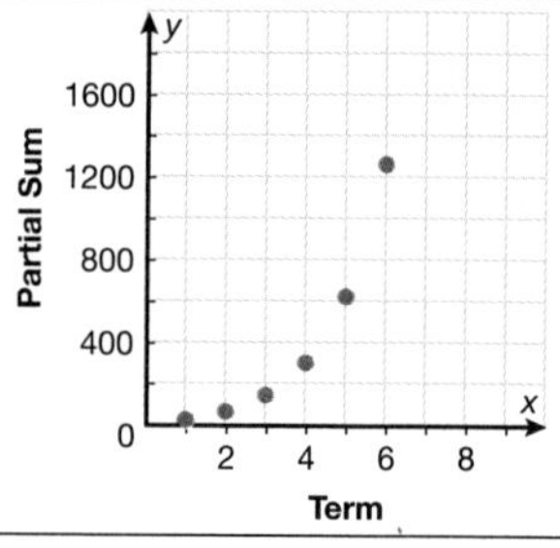

ENGLISH LEARNERS

To help students understand the meaning of convergent series and divergent series, define **converge** as a verb meaning to move toward one point; and define **diverge** as a verb meaning to move away.

Have the students list examples of things that may converge or diverge, such as converging and diverging roads.

Then, have students describe the two graphs they see at the bottom of the student page.

Encourage them to use the terms converge and diverge.

Connect the meaning of converge and diverge to convergent series and divergent series. Have students describe a convergent series and a divergent series by pointing out the differences between the two graphs.

Example 2 Determining if a Series is Convergent or Divergent

Determine if the geometric series converges or diverges.

a. $\frac{6}{5} + \frac{4}{5} + \frac{8}{15} + \frac{16}{45} + \ldots$

SOLUTION Find r and compare it to 1: $r = \frac{16}{45} \div \frac{8}{15} = \frac{\overset{2}{\cancel{16}}}{\underset{3}{\cancel{45}}} \cdot \frac{\overset{1}{\cancel{15}}}{\underset{1}{\cancel{8}}} = \frac{2}{3}$.

Because $\left|\frac{2}{3}\right| < 1$, the series converges and has a sum.

b. $3 + (-9) + 27 + (-81) + \ldots$

SOLUTION Find r and compare it to 1: $r = \frac{-9}{3} = -3$.

Because $|-3| > 1$, the series diverges and does not have a sum.

Math Reasoning

Analyze Use the formula for the sum of a finite geometric series to verify the sum formula for the infinite geometric with $< |r| < 1$.

As the value of the exponent of r increases, the fraction decreases to very small values, so the numerator approaches 1.

$a_1\left(\frac{1}{1-r}\right) = \frac{a_1}{1-r}$

As the ratio in Step 4 of the Exploration on the previous page implies, the sum of an infinite geometric series, if there is one, is the ratio of the first term and the difference between 1 and the common ratio.

Sum of an Infinite Geometric Series
The sum of an infinite geometric series, S, is $\frac{a_1}{1-r}$, where r is the common ratio and $0 < \lvert r \rvert < 1$.

Example 3 Finding the Sum of an Infinite Geometric Series

Find the sum of the geometric series $16 + (-4) + 1 + \left(-\frac{1}{4}\right) + \ldots$

SOLUTION Find r: $r = \frac{-4}{16} = -\frac{1}{4}$.

Now use $S = \frac{a_1}{1-r}$.

$S = \frac{16}{1 - \left(-\frac{1}{4}\right)}$ Substitute 16 for a_1 and $-\frac{1}{4}$ for r.

$S = 12\frac{4}{5}$ Simplify.

Check by using a graphing calculator. Graph the equation given by substituting into the formula for the sum of a finite geometric series, $y = 16\left(\frac{1-(-0.25)^x}{1-(-0.25)}\right)$. Then look at the table for this graph. As x increases, y approaches 12.8.

Graphing Calculator Tip

The calculator rounds; the sums are numbers close to 12.8, but not actually 12.8.

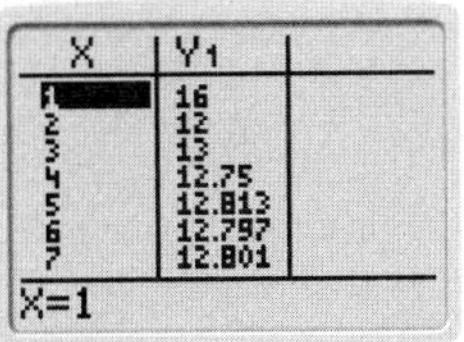

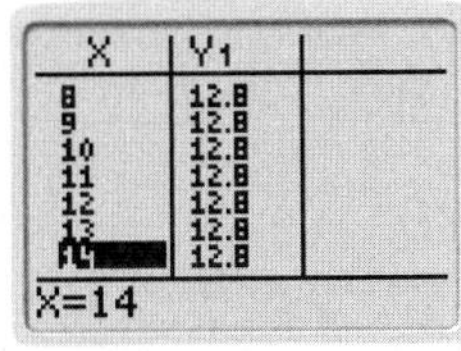

Example 2

Students determine whether a series is convergent or divergent.

Additional Example 2

Determine if the geometric series converges or diverges.

a. $\frac{2}{3} + \frac{1}{2} + \frac{3}{8} + \frac{9}{32} + \ldots$

Because $\left|\frac{3}{4}\right|$ is between 0 and 1, the series converges and has a sum.

b. $2 + (-4) + 8 + (-16) + \ldots$

Because $|-2| > 1$, the series diverges and does not have a sum.

Example 3

Students find the sum of an infinite geometric series.

Additional Example 3

Find the sum of the geometric series $600 + (-120) + 24 - \left(\frac{24}{5}\right) + \ldots$. 500

Extend the Example

Have students use their calculators to estimate S by summing up the terms given. Then have them use the formula. Have students compare estimates to the value they found using the formula.

Example 4

Students use geometric series to solve real-world problems.

Error Alert Students may substitute 0.035 for r. Remind students that they need to add the raise amount to the original salary amount, that is add 1 to 0.035.

Additional Example 4

An employee earns $32,000 in the first year with a 3.1% raise each year thereafter. How much can she expect to earn in total after 10 years? $368,538.08

Lesson Practice

Problem c

Error Alert Students might assume the series converges just because the common ratio is a fraction. Point out that the absolute value of the fraction is greater than one.

Check for Understanding

The questions below help assess the concepts taught in this lesson.

"How do you know if an infinite geometric series converges or diverges?" Find the value of r. If $0 < |r| < 1$, then the series converges. If $|r| > 1$, then the series diverges.

"For a geometric series, what is meant by a limit?" the number that the partial sums of a convergent series gets close to, as n increases

Example 4 Application: Salaries

An employee's salary is structured so that he earns $43,400 in the first year and a 3.5% raise each year thereafter. How much can the employee expect to earn in total after 15 years with this company?

SOLUTION

Math Reasoning

Analyze If the series were infinite, would it converge or diverge? Why?

It would diverge because 1.035 > 1.

1. **Understand** The indicated sum of the yearly salaries form a finite geometric series with $r = 1.035$.

2. **Plan** Use $S_n = a_1\left(\frac{1 - r^n}{1 - r}\right)$.

3. **Solve** $S_{15} = 43{,}400\left(\frac{1 - (1.035)^{15}}{1 - 1.035}\right) \approx 837{,}432.55$

The employee can expect to earn $837,432.55 over the course of 15 years.

4. **Check** Use a graphing calculator.

Lesson Practice

a. Find S_{10} for the geometric series $6 + (-12) + 24 + (-48) + \ldots$ −2046
(Ex 1)

b. Find S_9 for the sequence $a_k = 400\frac{1}{4}^{k-1}$. $S_9 \approx 533.33$
(Ex 1)

Determine if the geometric series converges or diverges.
(Ex 2)

c. $15 + (-25) + \frac{125}{3} + \left(-\frac{625}{9}\right) + \ldots$ diverges

d. $90 + 30 + 10 + \frac{10}{3} + \ldots$ converges

e. Find the sum of the geometric series $700 + 140 + 28 + \left(\frac{28}{5}\right) + \ldots$ 875
(Ex 3)

f. An employee's salary is structured so that he earns $27,700 in the first year and a 2.85% raise each year thereafter. How much can the employee expect to earn in total after 20 years with this company? $733,056.22
(Ex 4)

Practice Distributed and Integrated

*1. **Verify** Show numerically that a convergent geometric series has a sum of 125 if the first term is 25 and the common ratio is $\frac{4}{5}$. $S = \frac{25}{1 - \frac{4}{5}} = \frac{25}{\frac{1}{5}} = 25 \times \frac{5}{1} = 125$
(113)

2. Identify any excluded values, then simplify the expression $\frac{x^2 + 4x - 12}{x^2 + 6x}$. $x = -6, 0, \frac{x - 2}{x}$
(28)

790 Saxon Algebra 2

***3.** (111) **Baseball Attendance** The season attendance at Baltimore Orioles home games for the years 1996-2005 can be modeled by $f(x) = 7.300x^3 - 116.411x^2 + 363.122x + 3400$, where x is the number of years since 1995 and $f(x)$ is in thousands. Describe the transformation $g(x) = f(x) + 100$ by writing the rule for $g(x)$ and explaining the change in the context of the problem.

3. $g(x) = 7.300x^3 - 116.411x^2 + 363.122x + 3500$; Sample: The function $g(x)$ models what would have been the season attendance if 100,000 more people had attended games each year.

4. (48) Simplify: $\dfrac{\frac{x}{x+2}}{2x + \frac{x}{5}}$. $\frac{5}{11x + 22}$

5. (37) Add: $\dfrac{5}{2x^8} + \dfrac{7}{2x^8}$. $\frac{6}{x^8}$

6. (31) Simplify: $\dfrac{x(y^3 + 6)}{4x + 8} \cdot \dfrac{x+2}{x^2y^2} \div \dfrac{y}{x}$. $\frac{y^3 + 6}{4y^3}$

***7.** (112) **Travel** The London Eye is a Ferris wheel with an approximate diameter of 440 feet, making one full rotation in 30 minutes. The diagram represents the London Eye centered on a coordinate grid. From this view, the Ferris wheel rotates counterclockwise. To the nearest tenth, what will be the coordinates of point P in one minute? Assume a constant rate. Show how you arrived at your answer. See Additional Answers.

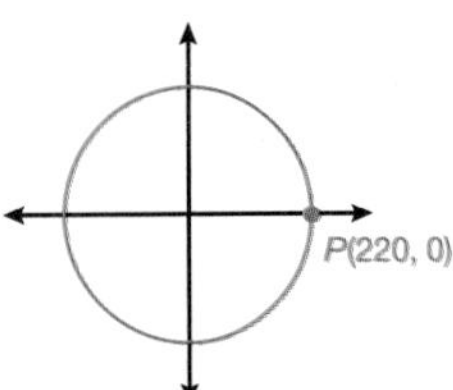

8. (88) Given $A = \frac{1}{2}(b_1 + b_2)h$, find b_1. $b_1 = \frac{2A}{h} - b_2$

***9.** (112) **Error Analysis** Given that $\sin A = \frac{4}{5}$ and $90° < A < 270°$, a student found $\cos A$ as shown at the right. What is the error? What is the correct value of $\cos A$?

$$x^2 + y^2 = r^2$$
$$x^2 + 4^2 = 5^2$$
$$x = \sqrt{25 - 16} = 3$$
$$\cos A = \frac{x}{r} = \frac{3}{5}$$

9. Sample: The error is leaving off the ± sign after taking the square root of both sides of the equation. Because $90° < A < 270°$, A terminates in Quadrant II. Therefore, $x = -3$; Correct answer: $\cos A = -\frac{3}{5}$.

10. (12) **Geometry** Write the equation for the area of a triangle as a joint variation. $\frac{A}{bh} = \frac{1}{2}$

11. (83) **Write** Write a quadratic equation whose roots are 4 and 1. $x^2 - 5x + 4 = 0$

12. (89) **Model** Sketch a system of inequalities, which includes at least one quadratic inequality, such that the system has no solutions. See Additional Answers.

Find the mean, median, and mode for the following sets of data.

13. (25) 18, 20, 14, 15, 20, 17, 16
mean: 17.1; median: 17; mode: 20

14. (25) 21, 23, 22, 25, 28, 31, 28
mean: 25.4; median: 25; mode: 28

***15.** (30) **Graphing Calculator** Graph the function $y = -2x^2 - 6x + 3$ using your graphing calculator. Determine the vertex and axis of symmetry. Vertex: $\left(-1\frac{1}{2}, 7\frac{1}{2}\right)$; Axis of symmetry: $x = -1\frac{1}{2}$

16. (37) Find the LCM. $\dfrac{1}{2x^2 - 3x - 2} - \dfrac{1}{x^2 - 4}$ $(2x + 1)(x - 2)(x + 2)$

***17.** (102) **Estimate** Estimate the solution to $\log_2 25x = \log_2 151$. Explain your method.
Sample: $x \approx 6$; Since the logarithm on each side has the same base, set $25x = 151$ and solve for x.

***18.** (107) **Multi-Step** Let $f(x) = x^2 - 1$ and $g(x) = x^2 - 1$.

a. Find $\dfrac{x^5}{f(g(x))}$. $\frac{x^3}{x^2 - 2}$

b. Find all asymptotes and holes for $\dfrac{x^5}{f(g(x))}$. Slant asymptote: $y = x$; vertical asymptotes: $x = \pm\sqrt{2}$; hole: $x = 0$

19. (Inv 8) Estimate the area under the curve $y = \frac{1}{2}x^2 + 4x + 1$ from $0 \le x \le 4$. Use 4 partitions. 46.5

3 Practice

Math Conversations

Discussions to strengthen understanding

Problem 4

Suggest students begin by adding the terms in the denominator by rewriting $2x$ as $\frac{10x}{5}$.

Problem 8

"What do you do to remove $\frac{1}{2}$ from the right side of the equation?" Multiply both sides of the equation by 2.

"What equation do you now have?" $2A = (b_1 + b_2)h$

"What variable do you move next?" h

"How do you move h?" Multiply both sides of the equation by $\frac{1}{h}$.

"What equation do you now have?" $\frac{2A}{h} = (b_1 + b_2)$

"How do you move b_2?" Subtract b_2 from both sides of the equation.

Problem 17

Have students determine the actual answer for problem 17 and compare it to their estimate.

Problem 19

Students will need to set their table increments to 0.5 and find the y-values for 0.5, 1.5, 2.5, and 3.5.

CHALLENGE

A seagull is a km from the water. During each minute, the seagull travels $\frac{3}{5}$ as far as it did the previous minute. How far does the seagull travel during the first three minutes of its descent?
$\frac{49}{25}a$ or $1.96a$

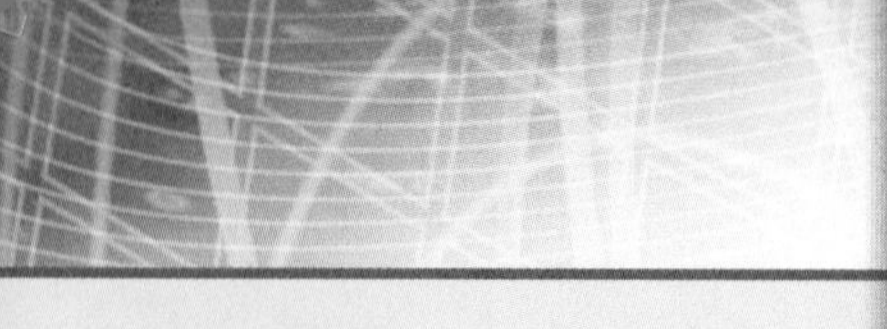

Problem 22

Error Alert

Students may not see that this problem is an arithmetic series, not a geometric series. Have students identify the common difference. Remind students that if they are adding a constant to each term, then they are finding the sum of an arithmetic series.

Problem 25

Remind students $y = \tan x$ has a period of π. Have them set $2x = \pi$ and solve for x.

Problem 26

Extend the Problem

Have students solve the equation for t.

$$0.25 = e^{-0.04332t}$$
$$\ln 0.25 = -0.04332t$$
$$t = \frac{\ln 0.25}{-0.04322} \approx 32$$

Problem 28

Have students eliminate answers which are obviously incorrect.

"Explain why choices A and C can be eliminated immediately." Because $r > 1$ for both series, the series for choices A and C diverge.

"This leaves choices B and D. Which is the answer?" B

"Explain your reasoning." For choice D, although $r = -5$, $|r| = 5$ and therefore that series diverges. By process of elimination, choice B is the correct answer.

*20. (113) **Multi-Step** A job-seeker has offers from two companies. Job A offers a first-year salary of \$31,225 with a 1.85% raise every year thereafter. Job B offers a first-year salary of \$28,995 with a 2.25% raise each year thereafter. With which job will he make more money all together after 15 years? What is the difference? Job A, \$23,594.73

21. (49) Use the Binomial Theorem to expand $(n + 2m)^4$. $16m^4 + 32m^3n + 24m^2n^2 + 8mn^3 + n^4$

*22. (105) **Exercise** An athlete is on a 12-day jogging plan. On the plan, the athlete is to jog 3 miles on the first day, and on each day thereafter, jog 0.75 miles longer than the previous day. How many total miles will the athlete have jogged while on the plan? 85.5 miles

23. (21) Solve the system $\begin{matrix} 10x - 2y = 16 \\ 5x + 3y = -12 \end{matrix}$ by substitution. The solution is $\left(\frac{3}{5}, -5\right)$.

*24. (113) **Salaries** A salary is structured so that the employee earns a 1.5% raise each year after the first year. How much did the employee earn in the first year if his total after 10 years was \$393,967.18? \$36,810

25. (90) Determine the period of $y = 3\tan(2x) + 6$. $\frac{\pi}{2}$

26. (93) **Multiple Choice** A substance has a half-life of 16 years. Which equation can be solved to find the approximate number of years t that it will take for 2 grams of the substance to decay to 0.5 gram? C

A $2 = e^{-0.5t}$ **B** $2 - 0.5 = e^{-16t}$

C $0.25 = e^{-0.04332t}$ **D** $0.5 = e^{-0.04332t}$

27. (94) **Probability** **a.** Write a simplified rational expression to represent the probability of a randomly selected point in the larger circle also being in the smaller circle. $\frac{x^2}{x^2 + 4x + 4}$

b. Write and solve a rational inequality to represent the values of x for which the probability is less than or equal to 0.25.

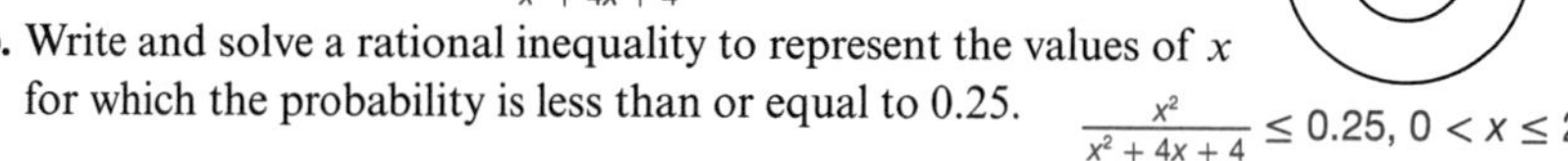

$\frac{x^2}{x^2 + 4x + 4} \le 0.25$, $0 < x \le 2$

*28. (113) **Multiple Choice** Which series converges? B

A $2 + 4 + 8 + 16 + \ldots$ **B** $16 + 8 + 4 + 2 + \ldots$

C $3 + 15 + 75 + 375 + \ldots$ **D** $3 + (-15) + 75 + (-375) + \ldots$

29. (97) **Analyze** When finding the nth term of a geometric sequence, given any two terms, what must be true about the given terms in order for there to be two possible values for the common ratio? Why?

29. The difference of the term numbers must be an even number because then the exponent is even and an even root must be taken on each side of the equation.

30. (99) **Analyze** Describe geometrically what the matrix equation below shows.

$$\begin{bmatrix} |\vec{A}|\cos(60) \\ |\vec{A}|\sin(60) \end{bmatrix} + \begin{bmatrix} |\vec{B}|\cos(30) \\ |\vec{B}|\sin(30) \end{bmatrix} = \begin{bmatrix} |\vec{A}|\cos(60) + |\vec{B}|\cos(30) \\ |\vec{A}|\sin(60) + |\vec{B}|\sin(30) \end{bmatrix}$$

Vector A, which is at a 60° angle, is added to vector B, which is at a 30° angle.

792 Saxon Algebra 2

ALTERNATE METHOD FOR PROBLEM 23

Have students rework the problem using the elimination method. Students can multiply the bottom equation by -2 to eliminate x.

$$\begin{aligned} 10x - 2y &= 16 \\ -10x - 6y &= 24 \\ \hline -8y &= 40 \\ y &= -5 \end{aligned}$$

Students then substitute -5 into one of the original equations to find the value of x.

LOOKING FORWARD

Geometric series will be further developed in other Saxon Secondary Mathematics courses.

LESSON 114 Identifying Conic Sections

Warm Up

1. **Vocabulary** A <u>circle</u> is the set of all points in a plane that are equidistant from a fixed point. (91)

2. Multiply $(x - 8)^2$. $x^2 - 16x + 64$ (19)

3. Find the discriminant of $x^2 + 5x - 12 = 0$. 73 (74)

New Concepts

Standard Forms for Conic Sections with Center (h, k)		
Circle	$(x - h)^2 + (y - k)^2 = r^2$	
	Horizontal Axis	Vertical Axis
Ellipse	$\frac{(x-h)^2}{a^2} + \frac{(y-k)^2}{b^2} = 1; a > b$	$\frac{(x-h)^2}{b^2} + \frac{(y-k)^2}{a^2} = 1; a > b$
Hyperbola	$\frac{(x-h)^2}{a^2} - \frac{(y-k)^2}{b^2} = 1$	$\frac{(y-k)^2}{a^2} - \frac{(x-h)^2}{b^2} = 1$
Parabola	$x - h = \frac{1}{\pm 4p}(y - k)^2$	$y - k = \frac{1}{\pm 4p}(x - h)^2$

Example 1 Identifying Conic Sections in Standard Form

Identify the conic section for each standard form equation.

a. $\frac{(x-3)^2}{36} + \frac{(y+3)^2}{16} = 1$

SOLUTION $\frac{(x-3)^2}{36} + \frac{(y+3)^2}{16} = 1$ can be written as $\frac{(x-3)^2}{6^2} + \frac{[y-(-3)]^2}{4^2} = 1$.
The equation is an ellipse with a horizontal major axis.

Hint

A parabola has only one squared term in its equation.

b. $x - 7 = \frac{1}{16}(y - 1)^2$

SOLUTION $x - 7 = \frac{1}{16}(y - 1)^2$ can be written as $x - 7 = \frac{1}{4(4)}(y - 1)^2$.
The equation is a parabola with a horizontal axis of symmetry.

The equation for any conic section can be written in the general form $Ax^2 + Bxy + Cy^2 + Dx + Ey + F = 0$. The coefficients A, B, and C can be used to identify conic sections.

Caution

A circle has both $B = 0$ and $A = C$.

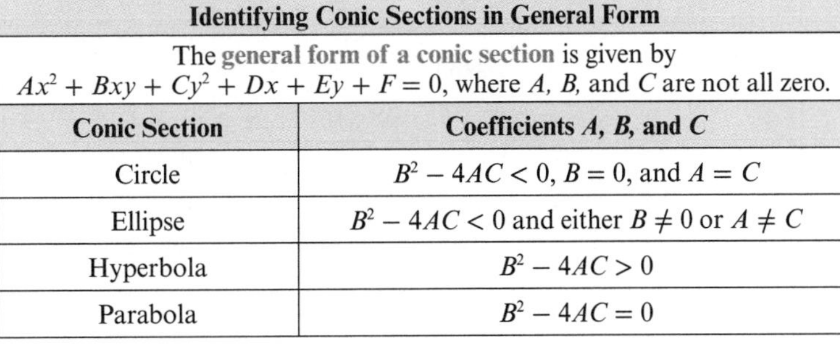

Identifying Conic Sections in General Form	
The **general form of a conic section** is given by $Ax^2 + Bxy + Cy^2 + Dx + Ey + F = 0$, where A, B, and C are not all zero.	
Conic Section	**Coefficients A, B, and C**
Circle	$B^2 - 4AC < 0$, $B = 0$, and $A = C$
Ellipse	$B^2 - 4AC < 0$ and either $B \neq 0$ or $A \neq C$
Hyperbola	$B^2 - 4AC > 0$
Parabola	$B^2 - 4AC = 0$

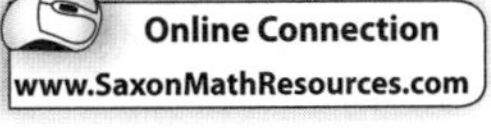

MATH BACKGROUND

Students have a great deal of experience with the standard form of the four conic sections, parabola, circle, ellipse, hyperbola.

In Lesson 27, students connected the parabola with the quadratic function and found the standard form through manipulating the vertex form.

In Lesson 91, students graphed the circle given the radius and center of the circle. The standard form was used for graphing.

In Lesson 98, students graphed ellipses centered at the origin and not centered at the origin. Given the radius and center, students wrote the equation for a circle in standard form in Lesson 91.

In Lesson 109, students graphed hyperbolas centered at the origin and not centered at the origin. Students derived the equation of a hyperbola in standard form.

LESSON 114

1 Warm Up

For problem 3, remind students that the discriminant to a quadratic equation is $b^2 - 4ac$.

2 New Concepts

In this lesson, students identify conic sections in standard and general form, and find the general form for a conic section.

Example 1

Students identify conic sections in standard form.

TEACHER TIP

For part a, remind students that the value of a is always larger than the value of b for an ellipse.

Additional Example 1

Identify the conic section for each standard form equation.

a. $\frac{(x-4)^2}{49} - \frac{(y+5)^2}{64} = 1$
The equation is a hyperbola with a horizontal major axis.

b. $y - 3 = \frac{1}{20}(x - 2)^2$
The equation is a parabola with a vertical axis of symmetry.

LESSON RESOURCES

Student Edition Practice Workbook 114
Reteaching Master 114
Adaptation Masters 114
Challenge and Enrichment Masters C114, E114

Example 2

Students identify conic sections in general form.

Error Alert Students may place terms in the incorrect order or may not notice that a term with coefficient A, B, or C is missing. Have students write $Ax^2 + Bxy + Cy^2 + Dx + Ey + F = 0$ on the top line. Underneath, have students write the terms given in the problem.

Additional Example 2

Identify the conic section for each general form equation.

a. $x^2 + y^2 + 6x - 10y + 22 = 0$
The conic section is a circle.

b. $y^2 - 8y + 3x + 31 = 0$
The conic section is a parabola.

Example 3

Students find the general form of an equation.

Additional Example 3

Write each equation in general form.

a. $y - 3 = \frac{1}{8}(x - 5)^2$
$x^2 - 10x - 8y + 49 = 0$

b. $\frac{(x + 3)^2}{16} - \frac{(y - 4)^2}{24} = 1$
$3x^2 - 2y^2 + 18x + 16y - 53 = 0$

Example 2 Identifying Conic Sections in General Form

Identify the conic section for each general form equation.

a. $4x^2 + 9y^2 - 16x - 108y + 304 = 0$

SOLUTION

Step 1: Identify the values of A, B, and C.

$$A = 4, B = 0, \text{ and } C = 9.$$

Step 2: Find $B^2 - 4AC$.

$$0^2 - 4(4)(9) = -144$$

$B^2 - 4AC < 0$, so the conic section is either a circle or an ellipse.
Since $A \neq C$, the conic section is an ellipse.

Math Language

$B^2 - 4AC > 0$ is called the **discriminant** of the equation $Ax^2 + Bxy + Cy^2 + Dx + Ey + F = 0$.

b. $x^2 - 3x + 2y + 5 = 0$

SOLUTION

Step 1: Identify the values of A, B, and C.

$$A = 1, B = 0, \text{ and } C = 0.$$

Step 2: Find $B^2 - 4AC$.

$$0^2 - 4(1)(0) = 0$$

$B^2 - 4AC = 0$, so the conic section is a parabola.

If you know the equation of a conic section in standard form, you can write the equation in general form by expanding the binomials.

Example 3 Finding the General Form for a Conic Section

Write each equation in general form.

a. $y + 2 = \frac{1}{16}(x + 6)^2$

SOLUTION

$$y + 2 = \frac{1}{16}(x^2 + 12x + 36)$$ Expand the binomial.

$$16y + 32 = x^2 + 12x + 36$$ Multiply both sides by 16.

$$x^2 + 12x - 16y + 4 = 0$$ Write in general form.

b. $\frac{(y - 4)^2}{25} - \frac{(x + 2)^2}{20} = 1$

SOLUTION

$$\frac{(y^2 - 8y + 16)}{25} - \frac{(x^2 + 4x + 4)}{20} = 1$$ Expand the binomials.

$$4(y^2 - 8y + 16) - 5(x^2 + 4x + 4) = 100$$ Multiply both sides by 100.

$$4y^2 - 32y + 64 - 5x^2 - 20x - 20 = 100$$ Simplify.

$$-5x^2 + 4y^2 - 20x - 32y - 56 = 0$$ Write in general form.

INCLUSION

Have students use a yellow marker to highlight the coefficients for A, B, and C.

Example 4 **Application: Racing**

An oval stockcar race track can be modeled by the equation $x^2 + 4y^2 + 2x - 16y - 19 = 0$. Write the equation in standard form.

SOLUTION The track is an oval, so the equation represents an ellipse. Use the method of completing the square to write the equation in standard form.

$x^2 + 2x + \_\_ + 4y^2 - 16y + \_\_ = 19$ — Rearrange terms.

$x^2 + 2x + \_\_ + 4(y^2 - 4y + \_\_) = 19$ — Factor 4 from the y^2 and y terms.

Caution

The coefficients of the x^2 and y^2 terms must be 1 to use the completing the square method.

Complete each square:

$$x^2 + 2x + \left(\frac{2}{2}\right)^2 + 4\left[y^2 - 4y + \left(\frac{-4}{2}\right)^2\right] = 19 + \left(\frac{2}{2}\right)^2 + 4\left(\frac{-4}{2}\right)^2$$

$(x + 1)^2 + 4(y - 2)^2 = 36$ — Factor and simplify.

$\frac{(x + 1)^2}{36} + \frac{(y - 2)^2}{9} = 1$ — Divide each side by 36.

Check The equation is of the form of an ellipse: $\frac{(x - h)^2}{a^2} + \frac{(y - k)^2}{b^2} = 1$.

Lesson Practice

Identify the conic section for each standard form equation.
(Ex 1)

a. $x^2 + y^2 = 225$ circle

b. $\frac{(x - 4)^2}{25} + \frac{y^2}{49} = 1$ ellipse

Identify the conic section for each general form equation.
(Ex 2)

c. $5x^2 - 4y^2 - 40x - 16y - 36 = 0$ hyperbola

d. $3x^2 - 24x - y + 50 = 0$ parabola

Write each equation in general form.

e. (Ex 3) $x - 2 = \frac{1}{4}(y + 3)^2$ $y^2 - 4x + 6y + 17 = 0$

f. (Ex 3) $(x - 5)^2 + (y + 8)^2 = 64$ $x^2 + y^2 - 10x + 16y + 25 = 0$

g. (Ex 4) The path of a circular Ferris wheel can be modeled by the equation $x^2 + y^2 - 30x - 30y - 175 = 0$. Write the equation in standard form. $(x - 15)^2 + (y - 15)^2 = 625$

Practice Distributed and Integrated

1. (32) Solve for matrix X. $\begin{bmatrix} 1 & 5 \\ 0 & -2 \end{bmatrix} X = \begin{bmatrix} 3 & -1 & 0 \\ 6 & 8 & 4 \end{bmatrix}$ $X = \begin{bmatrix} 18 & 19 & 10 \\ -3 & -4 & -2 \end{bmatrix}$

2. (90) Identify the values for which $y = \frac{1}{2}\tan(2x)$ is undefined. $\frac{\pi}{4} + n\frac{\pi}{2}$

Simplify each expression.

3. (40) $\sqrt[3]{-125}$ -5

4. (40) $\sqrt[3]{12} \cdot \sqrt[3]{18}$ 6

ENGLISH LEARNERS

To help students understand the expression "expand the binomial," define **expand** as a verb to open up or to increase in number.

Discuss other meanings and examples of expand, such as to increase in size or volume or to expand on a theme by writing more details. Have students give assorted examples of expansion.

Then, have students expand the binomials in Example **3b** by using the FOIL method or the Distributive Property.

Connect the definition to the phrase "expand the binomial." Have students explain how they expanded the binomial in Example **3b**.

Example 4

Additional Example 4

An oval stockcar race track can be modeled by the equation $x^2 + 4y^2 - 6x + 32y + 57 = 0$. Write the equation in standard form. $\frac{(x - 3)^2}{16} + \frac{(y + 4)^2}{4} = 1$

Lesson Practice

Problem a

Scaffolding Have students identify the center (h, k), which is $(0, 0)$. Elicit response from students that 225 is the radius squared of a circle.

Check for Understanding

The questions below help assess the concepts taught in this lesson.

"How do you identify a conic section whose equation is given in general form?" Identify the values of and . Find the discriminant, $^2 - 4$ of the equation. Then compare $^2 - 4$ to 0. If the determinant is less than zero, determine if = .

"How do you write $y - 3 = \frac{1}{24}(x + 5)^2$ in general form?" First, expand the binomial. Then multiply both sides by 24. Last, write in general form. The general form is $x^2 + 10x - 24y + 97 = 0$.

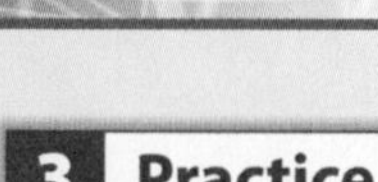

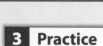

3 Practice

Math Conversations

Discussions to strengthen understanding

Problem 10

"The equation represents a carousel's path. The equation represents which conic section?" a circle

"Rearrange the terms. What equation do you get?" $x^2 - 10x + y^2 - 10y = 575$

"Complete the square. What numbers do you add to both sides? What is the equation?" 25 and 25; $x^2 - 10x + 25 + y^2 - 10y + 25 = 575 + 25 + 25$

"Simplify the equation. What is the equation in standard form?" $(x - 5)^2 + (y - 5)^2 = 625$

*5. (111) **Baseball Salaries** The total payroll of a baseball team for the years 1996–2005 can be modeled by $f(x) = 0.048x^3 + 0.605x^2 + 5.649x + 45$, where x is the number of years since 1995 and $f(x)$ is in millions of dollars. Describe the transformation $g(x) = f(x) - 20$ by writing the rule for $g(x)$ and explaining the change in the context of the problem.

5. $g(x) = 0.048x^3 + 0.605x^2 + 5.649x + 25$; Possible explanation: The function $g(x)$ models a team payroll that was $20,000,000 less each year than that of the given team.

6. (26) **Multi-Step** A line passed through points $(-2, 4)$ and $(0, 5)$. Write the equation of the line in slope-intercept form. Then, determine the x and y-intercepts. $y = \frac{1}{2}x + 5$; x-intercept: $(-10, 0)$ and y-intercept: $(0, 5)$

7. (104) **Write** Explain what must be done to an equation to horizontally shift the graph to the right. Change $f(x)$ to $f(x + a)$ where a is negative.

8. (100) **Physics** A satellite in circular orbit moving at speed v has an acceleration a of $\frac{v^2}{r}$, where r is the radius of the circular orbit. Write and graph the family of functions for calculating the acceleration for $v = 1, 2, 3, 4$, and 5. At what radius does the acceleration range from $a = 0.5$ to 12.5? See Additional Answers.

*9. (114) **Write** An equation of a conic section written in general form has $B^2 - 4AC < 0$. Explain why you need more information to identify the conic section.

9. The graph could be a circle or an ellipse. If $B = 0$ and $A = C$, the conic section is a circle. If either $B \neq 0$ or $A \neq C$ then the conic section is an ellipse.

*10. (114) **Carousel** A carousel's path can be modeled by the equation $x^2 + y^2 - 10x - 10y - 575 = 0$. Write the equation in standard form. $(x - 5)^2 + (y - 5)^2 = 625$

Evaluate.

11. (105) $\sum_{k=1}^{20}(0.75k - 5)$ 57.5

12. (105) $\sum_{k=2}^{7}(8 + 5k)$ 183

*13. (103) **Graphing Calculator** Graph $y = 6\cot(x)$ on a calculator. Determine its period and asymptotes. $y = 6\cot(x)$ has a period of π. The asymptotes occur at $x = \pi n$, where n is an integer.

14. (102) **Analyze** For what values of x is the equation $\log x^2 = 2\log x$ true? Explain why the equations $\log x^2 = 2$ and $2\log x = 2$ are not equivalent.

14. $\log x^2 = 2\log x$ is true for all $x > 0$. Possible explanation: The solutions to $\log x^2 = 2$ are 10 and -10, but the only solution to $2\log x = 2$ is 10.

15. (97) **Coordinate Geometry** The points $(1, -5)$, $(2, -10)$, $(3, -20)$, and $(4, -40)$ represent the first four terms of a geometric sequence. What is the common ratio? What is the y-coordinate when the x-coordinate is 6? 2, -160

*16. (114) **Multiple Choice** Which is the standard form of the equation $x^2 - 4x - 8y - 84 = 0$? B

A $(x - 2)^2 = 8(y + 11)$

B $\frac{1}{8}(x - 2)^2 = y + 11$

C $8(x - 2)^2 = y + 11$

D $(x - 2)^2 = \frac{1}{8}(y + 11)$

17. (29) Solve the system of equations: $\begin{matrix} 4x - 8y + 2z = 10 \\ -3x + y - 2z = 6 \\ -2x + 4y - z = 8 \end{matrix}$. no solution

18. (106) **Business** The profits in thousands of dollars for a business over x years can be approximated by $f(x) = x^4 - 37x^3 + 406x^2 - 1068x - 1512$. The company broke even in the 18th year of business. What other years did they break even? The 6th and 14th years

ALTERNATE METHOD FOR PROBLEM 15

Have students graph the points $(1, -5)$, $(2, -10)$, $(3, -20)$, and $(4, -40)$ on a coordinate grid. Have students extend the graph. From the graph, have students write the ordered pair when $x = 6$.

19. **Multi-Step** Silver-101 has a half-life of 11.1 minutes.
(93)
a. Use the natural decay function $N(t) = N_0e^{-kt}$ to find the decay constant k for silver-101.
b. Write the natural decay function for silver-101 and solve for t to find how long it would take 5 grams to decay to 1 gram.

19a. $N(t) = N_0e^{-kt}$
$0.5 = 1e^{-k(11.1)}$
$\ln 0.5 = \ln e^{-k(11.1)}$
$\ln 0.5 = -11.1k$
$k = \frac{\ln 0.5}{-11.1} \approx 0.06245$

20. **Write** Explain why a polynomial function that has exactly n distinct real zeros must have exactly $n - 1$ turning points. See Additional Answers.
(101)

19b. $N(t) = N_0e^{-0.06245t}$
$1 = 5e^{-0.06245t}$
$0.2 = e^{-0.06245t}$
$\ln 0.2 = \ln e^{-0.06245t}$
$\ln 0.2 = -0.06245t$
$t = \frac{\ln 0.2}{-0.06245}$
≈ 25.8 minutes

21. Let $f(x) = \frac{1}{x^2 - 1}$ and $g(x) = \csc(x)$. Find $f(g(x)) + 1$. $\sec^2(x)$
(108)

***22.** Find a_1 of an arithmetic sequence such that $a_9 = 60$ and $a_{13} = 8$. 164
(92)

***23.** **International Landmarks** The first level of the Eiffel Tower is about 57 meters above the ground. Suppose a ball is dropped from this level and rebounds 30% of its previous height after each bounce.
(113)
a. Use summation notation to write an infinite geometric series to represent the total distance the ball travels after it initially hits the ground. Keep in mind the ball travels both down and up on each bounce. $\sum_{k=1}^{n} 2(17.1)(0.3)^{k-1}$
b. Find the sum of the series from part a. Round to the nearest tenth.
48.9 meters

24. The foci of a hyperbola are $(\pm 13, 0)$. The equations of the asymptotes are $y = \frac{5}{12}x - \frac{20}{3}$ and $y = -\frac{5}{12}x - \frac{10}{3}$. Write the equation of the hyperbola.
(109)
$\frac{(x-4)^2}{12^2} - \frac{(y+5)^2}{5^2} = 1$

25. **Geometry** The area of a circle is given by $A = \pi r^2$. Solve the formula for r. If the ratio of areas of two circles is 2:1, what is the ratio of the radii? $r = \sqrt{\frac{A}{\pi}}$; $\sqrt{2} : 1$
(88)

***26.** **Error Analysis** Explain and correct the error a student made finding the sum of the infinite geometric series $5 + \frac{15}{2} + \frac{45}{4} + \ldots$.
(113)
Student's work: $S = \frac{5}{1 - \frac{3}{2}} = \frac{5}{-\frac{1}{2}} = -10$

26. The series diverges because the absolute value of the common ratio is greater than 1. The series does not have a sum.

27. **Multiple Choice** Which series is not an arithmetic series? C
(105)

A $\sum_{k=1}^{5} 16k$ **B** $\sum_{k=1}^{5} 16k + 2$ **C** $\sum_{k=1}^{5} 16^k$ **D** $\sum_{k=1}^{5} \frac{1}{16}k$

28. 1 in 3 people that enter a post office wears glasses. At noon, 4 people enter. What is the probability that 2 of the 4 people are wearing glasses? 0.30
(49)

29. **Error Analysis** A student writes the equation $16x^2 + 9y^2 = 144$ in standard form. What is his mistake? The student incorrectly simplifies the rational terms.
(98)

$$16x^2 + 9y^2 = 144 \longrightarrow \frac{16}{144}x^2 + \frac{9}{144}y^2 = 1 \longrightarrow \frac{x^2}{16} + \frac{y^2}{9} = 1 \longrightarrow \frac{x^2}{4^2} + \frac{y^2}{3^2} = 1$$

***30.** **Estimate** Without using a calculator, estimate the coordinates of the image point that results when the point (1, 1) is rotated 47° counterclockwise about the origin. Explain your reasoning. See Additional Answers.
(112)

Problem 22

TEACHER TIP

Students can find the common difference by subtracting: $8 - 60 = -52$, and then dividing: $-\frac{52}{4} = -13$.

Problem 26

Before students begin the problem, review under what conditions an infinite geometric series converges ($0 < |r| < 1$) and when it diverges ($|r| > 1$). Remind students that if the series diverges, it does not have a sum.

Problem 29

Have students simplify the equation and write it in standard form before looking at the work. Then have them compare their work to the work shown in the problem.

CHALLENGE

Write the equation in standard form.

$841x^2 + 1225y^2 + 408{,}726x + 404{,}250y + 81{,}980{,}609 = 0$

$\frac{(x+243)^2}{1225} + \frac{(y+165)^2}{841} = 1$

LOOKING FORWARD

Identifying conic sections prepares students for

- **Lesson 117** Solving Systems of Nonlinear Equations

LESSON 115

1 Warm Up

Use the Warm Up to review trigonometric properties for this lesson.

2 New Concepts

In the lesson, students learn how to use the double angle and half angle identities to evaluate expressions, prove other identities, and solve an application problem.

Example 1

A value is given for $\sin\theta$, and students learn how to find the values of $\sin 2\theta$ and $\cos 2\theta$.

Extend the Example

Use inverse trigonometric functions and a graphing calculator to find approximate values of θ and 2θ. $\theta \approx 19.47°$, $2\theta \approx 38.94°$

Additional Example 1

Find $\sin 2\theta$ and $\cos 2\theta$ if $\cos\theta = \frac{2}{5}$ and $0° < \theta < 90°$.

$\sin 2\theta = \frac{4\sqrt{21}}{25}$, $\cos 2\theta = -\frac{17}{25}$

LESSON RESOURCES

Student Edition Practice Workbook 115
Reteaching Master 115
Adaptations Master 115
Challenge and Enrichment Master C115

LESSON 115

Finding Double-Angle and Half-Angle Identities

Warm Up

1. **Vocabulary** A ___radian___ is a unit of measure based on arc length. (63)

2. State the sign of sine, cosine, and tangent for each quadrant. (63)

3. What is the exact value of sin 105°? (112) $\frac{\sqrt{6}+\sqrt{2}}{4}$

2. Q1: sin +, cos +, tan +
Q2: sin +, cos −, tan −
Q3: sin −, cos −, tan +
Q4: sin −, cos +, tan −

New Concepts

The double-angle identities and half-angle identities are special cases of the sum and difference identities.

Double-Angle Identities		
$\sin 2\theta = 2\sin\theta\cos\theta$	$\cos 2\theta = \cos^2\theta - \sin^2\theta$ $\cos 2\theta = 2\cos^2\theta - 1$ $\cos 2\theta = 1 - 2\sin^2\theta$	$\tan 2\theta = \frac{2\tan\theta}{1-\tan^2\theta}$

Example 1 Evaluate Expressions with Double-Angle Identities

Find $\sin 2\theta$ and $\cos 2\theta$ if $\sin\theta = \frac{1}{3}$ and $0° < \theta < 90°$.

SOLUTION

Hint

Use $\sin^2\theta + \cos^2\theta = 1$ to find the value of $\cos\theta$.

Step 1: The identity for $\sin 2\theta$ requires $\cos\theta$. Find $\cos\theta$.

$\cos\theta = \sqrt{1-\sin^2\theta}$ Pythagorean Identity

$= \sqrt{1-\left(\frac{1}{3}\right)^2}$ Substitute $\frac{1}{3}$ for $\sin\theta$.

$= \sqrt{\frac{8}{9}}$ Simplify.

$= \frac{2\sqrt{2}}{3}$

Step 2: Find $\sin 2\theta$.

$\sin 2\theta = 2\sin\theta\cos\theta$ Apply identity for $\sin 2\theta$.

$= 2\left(\frac{1}{3}\right)\left(\frac{2\sqrt{2}}{3}\right)$ Substitute $\frac{2\sqrt{2}}{3}$ for $\cos\theta$ and $\frac{1}{3}$ for $\sin\theta$.

$= \frac{4\sqrt{2}}{9}$ Simplify.

Step 3: Find $\cos 2\theta$.

$\cos 2\theta = 1 - 2\sin^2\theta$ Select an identity for $\cos 2\theta$.

$= 1 - 2\left(\frac{1}{3}\right)^2$ Substitute for $\sin\theta$.

$= \frac{7}{9}$ Simplify.

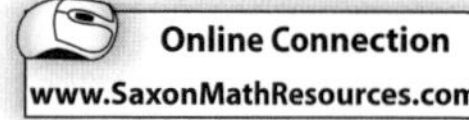
Online Connection
www.SaxonMathResources.com

MATH BACKGROUND

The double-angle identities can be derived by using sum identities and a Pythagorean identity. The method is shown below.

$$\cos 2\theta = \cos(\theta+\theta)$$
$$= \cos\theta\cos\theta - \sin\theta\sin\theta$$
$$= \cos^2\theta - \sin^2\theta$$

$$\cos 2\theta = \cos^2\theta - \sin^2\theta$$
$$= (1-\sin^2\theta) - \sin^2\theta$$
$$= 1 - 2\sin^2\theta$$

A derivation of a half-angle identity is shown.

$\cos 2A = 1 - 2\sin^2 A$ Let $2A = \theta$;

$\cos\theta = 1 - 2\sin^2\frac{\theta}{2}$ then $A = \frac{\theta}{2}$.

$$2\sin^2\frac{\theta}{2} = 1 - \cos\theta$$

$$\sin^2\frac{\theta}{2} = \frac{1-\cos\theta}{2}$$

$$\sin\frac{\theta}{2} = \pm\sqrt{\frac{1-\cos\theta}{2}}$$

Double-angle identities can be used to prove trigonometric identities.

Example 2 Prove Identities with Double-Angle Identities

Prove each identity.

a. $\tan\theta(\cos 2\theta + 1) = \sin 2\theta$

SOLUTION

$\tan\theta(\cos 2\theta + 1) = \tan\theta((2\cos^2\theta - 1) + 1)$	Substitute $\cos 2\theta = 2\cos^2\theta - 1$.
$= \tan\theta(2\cos^2\theta)$	Simplify.
$= \frac{\sin\theta}{\cos\theta}(2\cos^2\theta)$	Substitute $\tan\theta = \frac{\sin\theta}{\cos\theta}$.
$= 2\sin\theta(\cos\theta)$	Simplify.
$= \sin 2\theta$	Substitute double angle identity $\sin 2\theta = 2\sin\theta(\cos\theta)$.

Hint

To prove an identity, modified only one side until it matches the other side.

b. $\cos 2\theta + 2\sin^2\theta = 1$

SOLUTION

$\cos 2\theta + 2\sin^2\theta = (2\cos^2\theta - 1) + 2\sin^2\theta$	Substitute $\cos 2\theta = 2\cos^2\theta - 1$.
$= 2(\cos^2\theta + \sin^2\theta) - 1$	Regroup.
$= 2(1) - 1$	Simplify.
$= 1$	

Half-angle identities can be used to calculate values that are not usually known.

Half-Angle Identities

$$\sin\frac{\theta}{2} = \pm\sqrt{\frac{1-\cos\theta}{2}} \qquad \cos\frac{\theta}{2} = \pm\sqrt{\frac{1+\cos\theta}{2}} \qquad \tan\frac{\theta}{2} = \pm\sqrt{\frac{1-\cos\theta}{1+\cos\theta}}$$

Choose + or − depending on the location of $\frac{\theta}{2}$.

Example 3 Evaluate Expressions with Half-Angle Identities

Use half-angle identities to find the exact value of each trigonometric expression.

a. sin 105°

SOLUTION Select the identity to use and choose + or − depending on the location of $\frac{\theta}{2}$. sin 105° is located in QII, so $\sin\frac{210}{2} = \sqrt{\frac{1-\cos 210°}{2}}$.

The cosine of 210° is $-\frac{\sqrt{3}}{2}$. Substitute and solve.

$$\sqrt{\frac{1-\left(\frac{-\sqrt{3}}{2}\right)}{2}} = \sqrt{\frac{1}{2}+\frac{\sqrt{3}}{4}} = \frac{\sqrt{2+\sqrt{3}}}{2}$$

ALTERNATE METHOD FOR EXAMPLE 2a

You can prove an identity by beginning with one expression and writing a series of equal expressions, ending with the other expression. The reason for each step must be obvious.

$$\tan\theta(\cos 2\theta + 1) = \tan\theta(2\cos^2\theta - 1 + 1)$$
$$= \tan\theta(2\cos^2\theta)$$
$$= \frac{\sin\theta}{\cos\theta}(2\cos^2\theta)$$
$$= 2\sin\theta\cos\theta$$
$$= \sin 2\theta$$

Example 2

Two identities are proved, using the identities for $\sin 2\theta$ and $\cos 2\theta$.

Additional Example 2

Prove each identity.

a. $\tan\theta\sin 2\theta = 2\sin^2\theta$

$\tan\theta\sin 2\theta \stackrel{?}{=} 2\sin^2\theta$

$\tan\theta(2\sin\theta\cos\theta) \stackrel{?}{=} 2\sin^2\theta$

$\frac{\sin\theta}{\cos\theta}(2\sin\theta\cos\theta) \stackrel{?}{=} 2\sin^2\theta$

$2\sin^2\theta \stackrel{\checkmark}{=} 2\sin^2\theta$

b. $\tan 2\theta(1+\tan\theta) = \frac{2\tan\theta}{1-\tan\theta}$

$\tan 2\theta(1+\tan\theta) \stackrel{?}{=} \frac{2\tan\theta}{1-\tan\theta}$

$\frac{2\tan\theta}{1-\tan^2\theta}(1+\tan\theta) \stackrel{?}{=} \frac{2\tan\theta}{1-\tan\theta}$

$\frac{2\tan\theta(1+\tan\theta)}{(1-\tan\theta)(1+\tan\theta)} \stackrel{?}{=} \frac{2\tan\theta}{1-\tan\theta}$

$\frac{2\tan\theta}{1-\tan\theta} \stackrel{\checkmark}{=} \frac{2\tan\theta}{1-\tan\theta}$

Example 3

The half-angle identities are used to find trigonometric function values.

Extend the Example

After students have completed Example **3a**, have them use a graphing calculator to find approximate values of sin 105° and $\sqrt{\frac{1}{2}+\frac{\sqrt{3}}{4}}$. 0.9659

Additional Example 3

a. Use a half-angle identity to find the exact value of sin 67.5°. $\frac{\sqrt{2+\sqrt{2}}}{2}$

TEACHER TIP

Emphasize the importance of identifying the quadrant in which an angle terminates. Ask students to complete the table for $\theta = 100°$.

	Sign if $\theta = 100°$		
	sinθ	**cosθ**	**tanθ**
θ	+	−	−
$\frac{\theta}{2}$	+	+	+
2θ	−	−	+

Additional Example 3

b. Use a half-angle identity to find the exact value of $\cos \frac{13\pi}{12}$. $-\frac{\sqrt{2+\sqrt{3}}}{2}$

Example 4

A value is given for $\sin\theta$, and θ is placed in an interval of values so that the quadrant in which θ terminates can be determined. Students learn how to use the given information to find the values of $\sin\frac{\theta}{2}$, $\cos\frac{\theta}{2}$, and $\tan\frac{\theta}{2}$.

Additional Example 4

Find $\sin\frac{\theta}{2}$, $\cos\frac{\theta}{2}$, and $\tan\frac{\theta}{2}$ if $\cos\theta = -\frac{5}{13}$ and $180° < \theta < 270°$. $\sin\frac{\theta}{2} = \frac{3\sqrt{13}}{13}$, $\cos\frac{\theta}{2} = -\frac{2\sqrt{13}}{13}$, $\tan\frac{\theta}{2} = -\frac{3}{2}$

Error Alert Students often make sign errors when applying double-and half-angle identities. Encourage them to make sketches for reference as they decide whether answers are reasonable. The sketch below is helpful for Example 4.

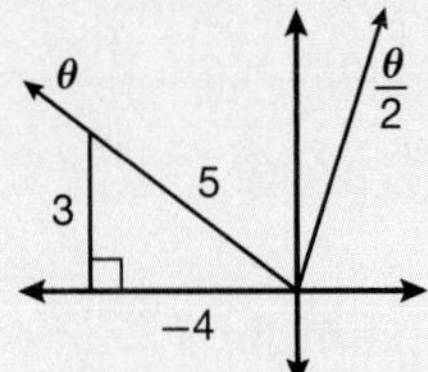

b. $\cos \frac{5\pi}{8}$

Caution

Remember cosine is negative in the second quadrant.

SOLUTION Select the identity to use and choose + or − depending on the location of $\frac{\theta}{2}$. The cosine of $\frac{5\pi}{8}$ is negative, as it is located in QII, so

$$\cos\frac{5\pi}{8}\cos\left(\frac{1}{2}\right)\left(\frac{5\pi}{4}\right) = -\sqrt{\frac{1+\cos\frac{5\pi}{4}}{2}}.$$

The value of $\cos\frac{5\pi}{4} = -\frac{\sqrt{2}}{2}$.

Substitute and solve. $\cos\frac{5\pi}{8} = -\sqrt{\frac{1+\cos\frac{5\pi}{4}}{2}} = -\sqrt{\frac{1+\frac{-\sqrt{2}}{2}}{2}}$

$$= -\sqrt{\frac{1}{2}+\frac{-\sqrt{2}}{4}} = \frac{-\sqrt{2-\sqrt{2}}}{2}$$

Example 4 **Using the Pythagorean Theorem with Half-Angle Identities**

Find $\sin\frac{\theta}{2}$, $\cos\frac{\theta}{2}$, and $\tan\frac{\theta}{2}$ if $\sin\theta = \frac{3}{5}$ and $90° < \theta < 180°$.

SOLUTION

Step 1: Use the Pythagorean Identity, $\sin^2\theta + \cos^2\theta = 1$, to find $\cos\theta$. Since $90° < \theta < 180°$, $\cos\theta$ is negative.

$\left(\frac{3}{5}\right)^2 + \cos^2\theta = 1 \qquad \cos^2\theta = \frac{16}{25} \qquad \cos\theta = -\frac{4}{5}$

Step 2: Evaluate $\sin\frac{\theta}{2}$. $\sin\frac{\theta}{2}$ is positive since $45° < \frac{\theta}{2} < 90°$.

Hint

Multiply $90° < \theta < 180°$ by $\frac{1}{2}$. Then choose the correct sign of the identity for $\sin\frac{\theta}{2}$ and $\cos\frac{\theta}{2}$.

$\sin\frac{\theta}{2} = +\sqrt{\frac{1-\cos\theta}{2}} = \sin\frac{\theta}{2} = \sqrt{\frac{1-\left(-\frac{4}{5}\right)}{2}}$ Substitute $\cos\theta = -\frac{4}{5}$.

$= \sqrt{\left(\frac{9}{5}\right)\left(\frac{1}{2}\right)} = \sqrt{\frac{9}{10}} = \frac{3\sqrt{10}}{10}$ Simplify.

Step 3: Evaluate $\cos\frac{\theta}{2}$. $\cos\frac{\theta}{2}$ is positive since $45° < \theta < 90°$.

$\cos\frac{\theta}{2} = +\sqrt{\frac{1+\cos\theta}{2}} = \cos\frac{\theta}{2} = \sqrt{\frac{1+\left(-\frac{4}{5}\right)}{2}}$ Substitute $\cos\theta = -\frac{4}{5}$.

$= \sqrt{\left(\frac{1}{5}\right)\left(\frac{1}{2}\right)} = \sqrt{\frac{1}{10}} = \frac{\sqrt{10}}{10}$ Simplify.

Step 4: Evaluate $\tan\frac{\theta}{2}$. Substitute $\cos\theta = -\frac{4}{5}$ to solve.

$\tan\frac{\theta}{2} = \sqrt{\frac{1-\cos\theta}{1+\cos\theta}} = \sqrt{\frac{1-\left(-\frac{4}{5}\right)}{1+\left(-\frac{4}{5}\right)}} = \sqrt{9} = 3$ Simplify.

ENGLISH LEARNERS

Review the meaning of **quadrant.** Say:

"The prefix *quad* means *four*. The coordinate system is divided into four quadrants."

Write on the board and pronounce these words: quadrant, quadrilateral, and quadruple. Sketch a coordinate system on the board, numbering the quadrants 1–4.

Example 5 Application: Sports

The horizontal distance x traveled by an object launched from ground level with an initial speed v and angle θ is given by $x = \frac{1}{32}v^2 \sin 2\theta$. What horizontal distance will a football travel if it is kicked from ground level with an initial speed of 80 feet per second at an angle of 30°? Round your answer to the nearest hundredth.

SOLUTION

$$x = \frac{1}{32}v^2 \sin 2\theta$$

$= \frac{1}{32}(80)^2 \sin 2(30°)$ Substitute given values.

$= (200)(2(\sin 30)(\cos 30))$ Use $\sin 2\theta = 2\sin\theta\cos\theta$.

$= 400\left(\frac{1}{2}\right)\left(\frac{\sqrt{3}}{2}\right)$ Substitute values and simplify.

$= 100\sqrt{3} \approx 173.21$ feet

a. $\sin 2\theta = \frac{4\sqrt{6}}{25}$; $\cos 2\theta = \frac{23}{25}$

b. $\cos 2\theta = 1 - \sin 2\theta \tan\theta$

$= 1 - 2\sin\theta\cos\theta\tan\theta$

$= 1 - 2\sin\theta\cos\theta\frac{\sin\theta}{\cos\theta}$

$= 1 - 2\sin^2\theta$

$\cos 2\theta = \cos 2\theta$

c. $\cot\theta = \frac{\sin 2\theta}{1 - \cos 2\theta}$

$= \frac{2\sin\theta\cos\theta}{1 - (1 - 2\sin^2\theta)}$

$= \frac{2\sin\theta\cos\theta}{2\sin^2\theta}$

$= \frac{\cos\theta}{\sin\theta} = \cot\theta$

f. $\sin\frac{\theta}{2} = \frac{2\sqrt{2}}{3}$, $\cos\frac{\theta}{2} = -\frac{1}{3}$, $\tan\frac{\theta}{2} = -2\sqrt{2}$

Lesson Practice

a. Find $\sin 2\theta$ and $\cos 2\theta$ if $\sin\theta = \frac{1}{5}$ and $0° < \theta < 90°$.
(Ex 1)

b. Prove the identity $\cos 2\theta = 1 - \sin 2\theta\tan\theta$ using double-angle identities.
(Ex 2)

c. Prove the identity $\cot\theta = \frac{\sin 2\theta}{1 - \cos 2\theta}$ using double-angle identities.
(Ex 2)

d. Use half-angle identities to find the exact value of $\cos 75°$. $\frac{\sqrt{2 - \sqrt{3}}}{2}$
(Ex 3)

e. Use half-angle identities to find the exact value of $\tan\frac{\pi}{12}$. $2 - \sqrt{3}$
(Ex 3)

f. Find $\sin\frac{\theta}{2}$, $\cos\frac{\theta}{2}$, and $\tan\frac{\theta}{2}$ if $\cos\theta = -\frac{7}{9}$ and $180° < \theta < 270°$.
(Ex 4)

g. The horizontal distance x traveled by a football kicked from ground level with an initial speed v and angle θ is given by $x = \frac{1}{32}v^2 \sin 2\theta$. What horizontal distance will a football travel if it is kicked from ground level with an initial speed of 100 feet per second at an angle of 45°? 312.5 feet
(Ex 5)

Practice Distributed and Integrated

1. **Analyze** In the rational function $f(x) = \frac{g(x)}{h(x)}$, if polynomial $g(x)$ is of degree $3m + 1$, what must the degree of $h(x)$ be for $f(x)$ to have a slant asymptote? $3m$
(107)

Factor completely.

2. $x^2 - 9x - 10$ $(x - 10)(x + 1)$
(23)

3. $4ax + ax^2 - 5a$ $a(x + 5)(x - 1)$
(23)

4. **Model** Write and graph the polar equation of a rose with 5 petals, each of length 4. $4\sin(5\theta)$ or $-4\sin(5\theta)$
(Inv 10)

4.

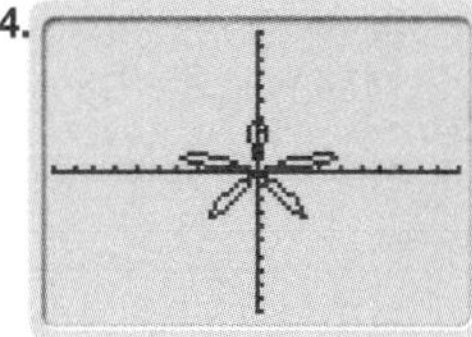

Example 5

This example shows how to use the double angle identity for $\sin 2\theta$ to solve an application problem.

Additional Example 5

A golf ball is hit from the ground with an initial speed of 200 feet per second at an angle of 22.5°. What horizontal distance will the ball travel? (Neglect air resistance.) $625\sqrt{2}$ feet

Lesson Practice

Problem f

Scaffolding Remind students to divide all three terms of the compound inequality $180° < \theta < 270°$ by 2 to identify the quadrant in which $\frac{\theta}{2}$ terminates.

Check for Understanding

The questions below help assess the concepts taught in this lesson.

"If $\sin\theta = \frac{1}{5}$ and $90° < \theta < 180°$, how could you find $\sin 2\theta$ and $\cos 2\theta$?" Sample: First find $\cos\theta$, determining the correct sign by the quadrant in which θ terminates. Then use the double angle identity for $\sin 2\theta$ and any of the double angle identities for $\cos 2\theta$.

"Why do the half-angle identities have the plus or minus symbol?" Sample: The square root symbol indicates a nonnegative number, but $\sin\frac{\theta}{2}$, $\cos\frac{\theta}{2}$, and $\tan\frac{\theta}{2}$ can be negative.

INCLUSION

Place this diagram on a bulletin board. Have students copy it and use it for reference.

Quadrant II		Quadrant I	
$\sin\theta$	+	$\sin\theta$	+
$\cos\theta$	−	$\cos\theta$	+
$\tan\theta$	−	$\tan\theta$	+
Quadrant III		**Quadrant IV**	
$\sin\theta$	−	$\sin\theta$	−
$\cos\theta$	−	$\cos\theta$	+
$\tan\theta$	+	$\tan\theta$	−

3 Practice

Math Conversations

Discussions to strengthen understanding

Problem 10

Guide students by asking them the following questions.

"What variables can be in a polar equation? r and θ

"What does each variable represent? r represents a directed distance from the pole and θ represents an angle.

"What does it mean if r is the only variable that appears in the equation? All points in the plane that satisfy the value of r are on the graph.

***5.** (115) **Soccer** The horizontal distance x traveled by an object kicked from ground level with an initial speed v and angle θ is given by $x = \frac{1}{32}v^2 \sin 2\theta$. A soccer player would like to determine the maximum distance her ball will travel depending on the angle of the ball leaving the ground. She knows she can kick with an initial velocity of 80 feet per second.

a. Find the distance traveled for an angle of 30°, 45°, 70°, and 90°. about 173.2 ft, 200 ft, 128.6 ft, and 0 ft

b. Which angle maximizes the distance? Use the value of $\sin 2\theta$ to explain. See Additional Answers.

***6.** (108) **Coordinate Geometry** Graph $y_1 = 1 + \sec^2(x)\sin^2(x)$ and $y_2 = \tan^2(x)$. Use the information in the graphs to prove the following: $\sec^2(x)\sin^2(x) = \tan^2(x)$.
At any given point, $1 + \sec^2(x)\sin^2(x) - \tan^2(x) = 1$. Therefore, $\sec^2(x)\sin^2(x) = \tan^2(x)$.

7. (55) Gisella spins a spinner with equal-sized sections numbered 1–6. In one spin, what is the likelihood that the spinner will stop on an even number? $\frac{1}{2}$

Write the exponential equation in logarithmic form.

8. (64) $16^4 = 65536$ $\log_{16} 65536 = 4$

9. (64) $3^{14} = 4782969$ $\log_3 4782969 = 14$

10. (96) **Geometry** Describe the geometric figure represented by the polar equation $r = 4$.
circle with radius 4 and center at the pole of a polar coordinate system

***11.** (114) **Recreation** A bungee jumper's path can be modeled by the equation $x^2 - 10x - 12y - 95 = 0$.

a. What conic section models the situation? parabola

b. Write the equation in standard form. $\frac{1}{12}(x - 5)^2 = (y + 10)$

Divide using long division.

12. (38) $4x^4 + 5x - 4$ by $x^2 - 3x + 2$ **12.** $4x^2 + 12x + 28 + \frac{65x - 60}{x^2 - 3x + 2}$

13. (38) $x^3 - 2$ by $x - 5$ $x^2 + 5x + 25 + \frac{123}{x - 5}$

14. (97) **Error Analysis** Explain and correct the error a student made in finding the 8th term of the geometric sequence 2, −10, 50, −250, ...

$$a_8 = 2(-5)^8$$
$$a_8 = 2(390{,}625) = 781{,}250$$

The exponent in the formula is one less than the value of n: $a_8 = 2(-5)^{8-1} = 2(-5)^7 = -156,250$.

***15.** (115) **Justify** Use half-angle identities to find the exact value of cos 112.5°. Show your work. $-\frac{\sqrt{2 - \sqrt{2}}}{2}$

16. (32) Use an inverse matrix to solve the linear system. $\begin{aligned} 4x - y &= 10 \\ -7x - 2y &= -25 \end{aligned}$ $x = 3, y = 2$

17. (106) **Multiple Choice** A polynomial equation has roots of $1 + 2i$, 0, and $3i$. What is the minimum degree of the polynomial? C

A 3   **B** 4   **C** 5   **D** 6

***18.** (109) Which of the following are the equations for the asymptotes of $\frac{(x-9)^2}{12^2} - \frac{(y-13)^2}{7^2} = 1$? B

A $y = \frac{12}{7}x - \frac{17}{7}$; $y = -\frac{12}{7}x + \frac{199}{7}$

B $y = \frac{7}{12}x + \frac{31}{4}$; $y = -\frac{7}{12}x + \frac{73}{4}$

C $y = \frac{12}{7}x + \frac{17}{7}$; $y = -\frac{12}{7}x - \frac{199}{7}$

D $y = \frac{7}{12}x - \frac{31}{4}$; $y = -\frac{7}{12}x - \frac{73}{4}$

802 Saxon Algebra 2

CHALLENGE

Derive an identity for $\tan\frac{\theta}{2}$ that does not contain a square root expression. (Hint: Multiply the radicand by $\frac{1 - \cos\theta}{1 - \cos\theta}$.)

$$\tan\frac{\theta}{2} = \pm\sqrt{\frac{1 - \cos\theta}{1 + \cos\theta}}$$
$$= \pm\sqrt{\frac{1 - \cos\theta}{1 + \cos\theta} \cdot \frac{1 - \cos\theta}{1 - \cos\theta}}$$
$$= \pm\sqrt{\frac{(1 - \cos\theta)^2}{1 - \cos^2\theta}}$$
$$= \pm\sqrt{\frac{(1 - \cos\theta)^2}{\sin^2\theta}}$$
$$= \pm\frac{\sqrt{(1 - \cos\theta)^2}}{\sqrt{\sin^2\theta}}$$
$$= \pm\frac{1 - \cos\theta}{\sin\theta}$$

*19. **Analyze** Without dividing, how can you tell if the common ratio of a geometric sequence is positive or negative? If the signs of consecutive terms alternate, the common ratio is negative.
(97)

20. Convert $\log_8 (32x)^4$ to base e. Then evaluate when $x = 5$. $4\frac{\ln(32x)}{\ln 8} \approx 9.76$
(87)

21. Solve $4x^2 + 8x - 21 \geq 0$ algebraically. $x \leq -3.5$ or $x \geq 1.5$.
(89)

22. **Retirement Funds** A retirement system paid out an interest rate of 2.25% compounded annually from 1963 to 1965. The function $A(x) = P \cdot 1.0225^x$ can be used to calculate the amount in the account, $A(x)$, after x years with the original amount placed in the account, P. Use the function $f(x) = 1.0225^x$ to sketch a graph of the equation $A(x) = P \cdot 1.0225^x$ if the original amount in the account is \$15,000. See Additional Answers.
(104)

23. **Population Growth** Based on census statistics, the population of the United States grew at an average annual rate of approximately 1.24% from 1990 to 2000, and the population in 2000 was 281,000,000 (rounded to the nearest million). If the population continues to increase at the same rate, in what year will it reach 400,000,000? 2028 or 2029 (The month of the census is not given.)
(93)

*24. **Multi-Step** **a.** Identify the conic section for the equation $x^2 + (y - 2)^2 = 36$. circle
(114)
b. Write an equivalent equation in general form. $x^2 + y^2 - 4y - 32 = 0$

*25. **Graphing Calculator** Use a graphing calculator to solve the system of equations.
(29)

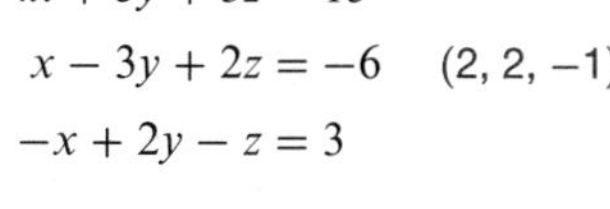

$$4x + 5y + 3z = 15$$
$$x - 3y + 2z = -6 \quad (2, 2, -1)$$
$$-x + 2y - z = 3$$

26. **Algebra** Using the information in the figure below show algebraically that $1 + \cot^2(\theta) = \csc^2(\theta)$.
(108)

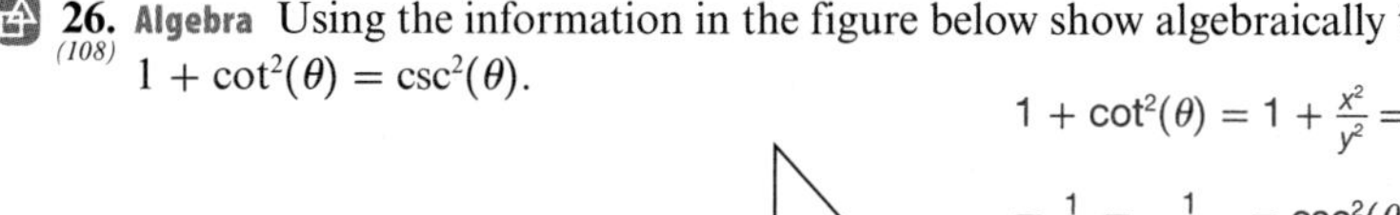

$1 + \cot^2(\theta) = 1 + \frac{x^2}{y^2} = \frac{(x^2 + y^2)}{y^2} = \frac{c^2}{y^2}$

$= \frac{1}{\frac{y^2}{c^2}} = \frac{1}{\sin^2(\theta)} = \csc^2(\theta)$.

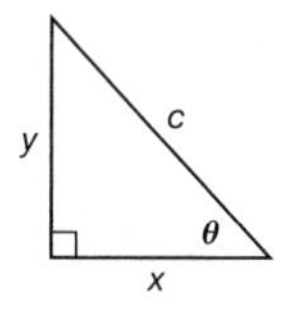

27. **Error Analysis** Explain and correct the error a student made in graphing $(x - 2)^2 + (y + 9)^2 = 25$.
(91)
See Additional Answers.

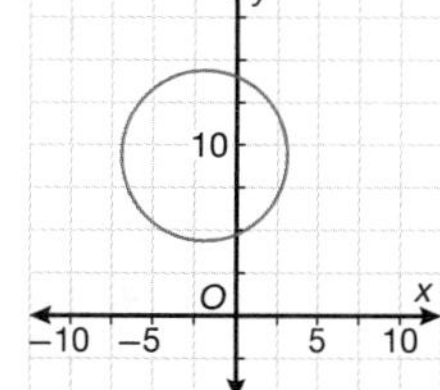

28. **Editors** A publishing company needs 4 editors for the next big assignment. How many ways can the editors be chosen from a pool of 13 editors? 715
(33)

*29. **Generalize** The function $y = a\log_b(cx)$ has an x-intercept at $x = \frac{1}{c}$. What is the x-intercept for $y = a\log_b(cx - d)$? $x = \frac{1 + d}{c}$.
(110)

30. Identify the domain, range, and asymptote(s) of $y = \left(\frac{7}{11}\right)^x + 3$. Domain = all real numbers, Range = all positive integers above 3, asymptote is the line $y = 3$
(47)

Problem 20

Error Alert

Students sometimes apply the Quotient Property of Logarithms incorrectly, as shown below.

$$\log_8(32x)^4 = 4\log_8(32x)$$
$$= 4\frac{\ln(32x)}{\ln 8}$$
$$= 4(\ln 32x - \ln 8) \quad \text{X}$$

One correct set of steps is shown below.

$$\log_8(32x)^4 = 4\log_8(32x)$$
$$= 4\frac{\ln(32x)}{\ln 8}$$
$$= 4\frac{\ln(32 \cdot 5)}{\ln 8}$$
$$= 4\frac{\ln 160}{\ln 8}$$
$$\approx 9.7626$$

Problem 21

Extend the Problem

Have students graph the function $y = 4x^2 + 8x - 21$ on a graphing calculator, and then use the CALCULATE/zero feature to verify their algebraic solution.

LOOKING FORWARD

Finding double-angle and half-angle identities prepares students for

- **Lesson 119** Solving Trigonometric Equations

LAB

14

Materials

- graphing calculator

Discuss

Students will find the coefficient of determination R^2 and different regression models for a given set of data.

TEACHER TIP

Remind students to find several different regression models and compare the R^2 to find the best-fit model.

LAB

14

Determining Regression Models

Graphing Calculator Lab (*Use with Lesson 116*)

Graphing Calculator

Refer to Calculator Lab 5 for clearing and entering data into list.

Graphing Calculator

Refer to Calculator Lab 5 for turning on the plot feature.

Calculate a Regression Model

1. Enter the values from the table into L1 and L2.

Table 1	
L_1	L_2
6	2
5	3
1	3
4	4
9	9
7	5
11	5

2. Turn on the diagnostics feature. Press [2nd] [0] to open the **CATALOG** menu. Scroll down to **DiagnosticsOn** and press [ENTER] twice. Turn on plot feature.

3. Calculate a regression model and transfer the equation to the "y = screen".

   a. Press [STAT], and then [▶] over to CALC.

   ```
   QuadReg L1,L2,Y1
   ```

   b. Press [▼] to access the desired model: **[5:QuadReg], [6:CubicReg],** or **[7:QuartReg]**. For this example, chose **[5:QuadReg]** feature and press [ENTER].

   c. When **QuadReg** appears on your main screen, press [2nd] [1] [,] to type in L1 and [2nd] [2] [,] to type in L2. Press [VARS] [▶] to access the Y-VARS menu. Press [ENTER] to select **[1: Function]**. Press [ENTER] to select **[1: Y1]**.

   d. Once back on the main screen, press [ENTER] to calculate the Quadratic Regression. R^2, or r^2, value will be displayed along with the other statistic values.

   ```
   QuadReg
    y=ax²+bx+c
    a=.0176928269
    b=.1947276797
    c=2.400824244
    R²=.3505985468
   ```

4. Graph the equation and the scatter plot.

   a. Make sure **Plot1** is customized and highlighted in the **Y**= menu so that data points appear in the graph with the regression line.

   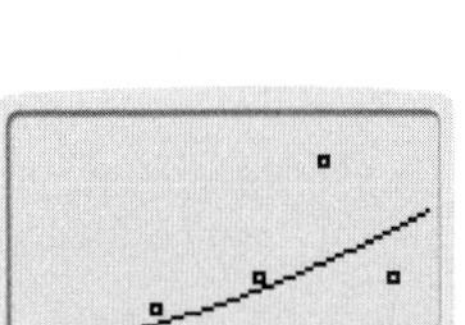

   b. Press [ZOOM] [9] to select **[9: ZoomStat]** which graphs the regression line and the data points.

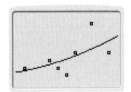

Online Connection
www.SaxonMathResources.com

804 *Saxon* *Algebra 2*

Lab Practice

1. 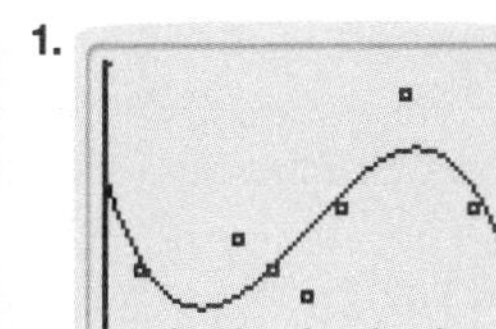

1. Using the data in L1 and L2 from Table 1, find the equation of the regression line and calculate R^2 value using a cubic regression. Plot the regression line along with the data points. $R^2 = 0.577$; $y = -0.042x^3 + 0.770x^2 - 3.383x + 5.999$
2. Using the data in L1 and L2 from Table 2, find the equation of the regression line and calculate R^2 value using a natural logarithmic regression. $R^2 = 0.969$; $y = 0.212 + 0.917\ln(x)$

Table 2	
L_1	L_2
5	1.7
2.7	1.2
32	3.6
17	2.9
12	2.3
25	2.9
47	3.8

Problems 1 and 2

Error Alert

Students who do not receive the R^2 value on the output screen may not have the diagnostic feature turned on. Remind them that this is an essential step.

Additional Problem 2

For the same set of data, find the R^2 value using the linear regression model and compare the R^2 value for the natural logarithmic model. Determine which is the best-fit model. Explain your answer. The natural logarithmic function models the data better because the absolute value of its coefficient of determination, $|R^2|$, is closer to 1.

Lab 14 805

LESSON 116

1 Warm Up

Problem 4

Have students solve the first equation for b, and then substitute into the second equation.

2 New Concepts

In this lesson, students learn about best fit models which are curves. They will be able to fit data with quadratic, polynomial, exponential, and logarithmic models.

Example 1

In this example, data is fit to a quadratic model.

Additional Example 1

Write a quadratic function that models the data shown in the table.

Year	1	2	3	4	5	6
Pop.	4	12	27	48	75	107

$y \approx 3x^2 - 0.29x + 1$

TEACHER TIP

Review the steps for using a graphing calculator to find the correlation coefficient and to graph the line of best fit. Remind students that lines of best fit are estimates.

LESSON RESOURCES

Student Edition Practice Workbook 116
Reteaching Master 116
Adaptations Master 116
Challenge and Enrichment Master C116
Technology Lab Master 116

LESSON 116 Finding Best Fit Models

Warm Up

1. (45) **Vocabulary** The correlation coefficient, r, tells how well a line fits a set of points and ranges from -1 to 1.

2. (97) Find the constant ratio in the geometric sequence $\left\{\frac{5}{6}, \frac{5}{8}, \frac{15}{32}, \frac{45}{128}\right\}$. $\frac{3}{4}$

3. (47) Which function is shown in the graph? **A**

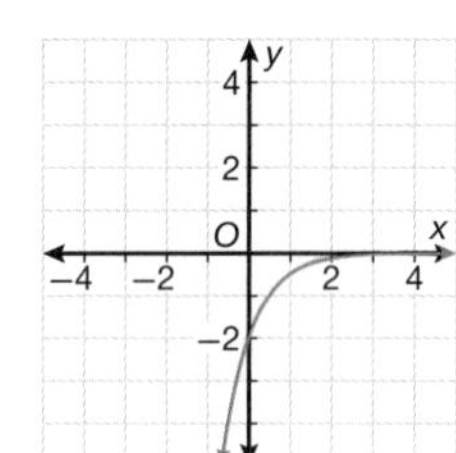

A $y = -2\left(\frac{1}{4}\right)^x$

B $y = -2(4)^x$

C $y = -4\left(\frac{1}{2}\right)^x$

D $y = 4\left(\frac{1}{2}\right)^x$

4. (21) Solve the system of equations.

$3a + b = -5$
$2a - 6b = 30$ $\quad a = 0, b = -5$

New Concepts

Recall that regression is the process of identifying a relationship between variables. In a linear regression, a line of best fit was used to describe and predict points in a scatter plot.

Best fit models are not always lines; they can also be curves. When a quadratic function best fits the points, the model is said to be a **quadratic model** and the regression is said to be a **quadratic regression.**

Math Language

Quadratic regression is a statistical method used to fit a quadratic model to a given set of data.

In a quadratic function, when the x-values are equally spaced, the y-values have constant nonzero second differences.

x-values	−2	−1	0	1	2
y-values	8	2	0	2	8

First differences: −6 −2 2 6
Second differences: 4 4 4

Example 1 Fitting Data with a Quadratic Model

Write a quadratic function that models the data shown in the table.

Year	1	2	3	4	5	6
Population	3	10	23	42	66	94

SOLUTION The second differences are almost constant.

Online Connection www.SaxonMathResources.com

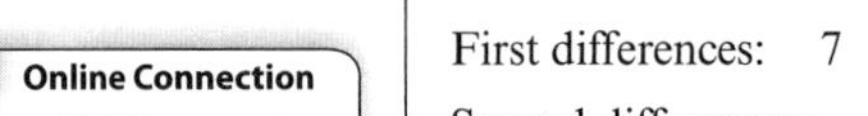

First differences: 7 13 19 24 28

Second differences: 6 6 5 4

MATH BACKGROUND

In lesson 45, students learned how to find the line of best fit. Students created scatterplots and wrote the equation for the line of best fit based on the scatterplot.

In this lesson, quadratic, cubic, quartic, exponential, and logarithmic models are examined. Common differences and ratios between the y-values are used to determine which type of function best models the data. Quadratic functions have second differences which are equal. Cubic functions have third differences which are constant. Quartic functions have fourth differences which are constant. Exponential functions have a constant ratio.

The QuadReg, CubicReg, QuartReg, ExpReg, and LnReg utilities on a graphing calculator help to fit data with the different models as well.

Math Language

The R^2 value is called the **coefficient of determination.** The closer it is to 1, the better it fits the data.

Graphing Calculator 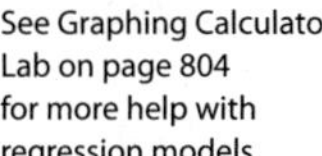

See Graphing Calculator Lab on page 804 for more help with regression models.

Enter the data into a graphing calculator and choose **QuadReg** for a quadratic regression from the STAT CALC menu. A quadratic model of the data is $y \approx 2.66x^2 - 0.28x + 0.3$. Graph the function and the data to see how well the model fits.

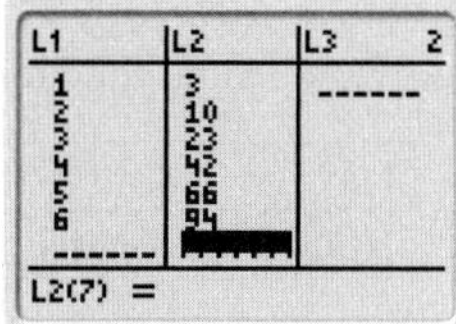

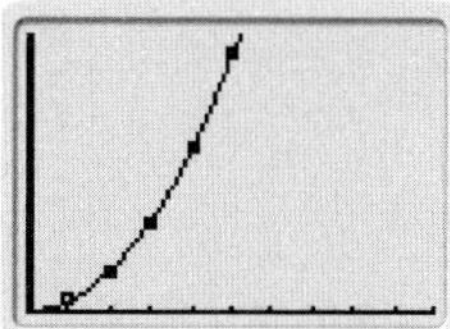

Some data are best modeled by polynomial models where the polynomial has a degree greater than two. To determine which polynomial model to use, either graph the given data, or look at the differences in the y-values, when given equally spaced x-values.

Model	Differences in y-value
Linear model	Constant first differences
Quadratic model	Constant second differences
Cubic model	Constant third differences
Quartic model	Constant fourth differences

Example 2 Fitting Data with a Polynomial Model

Write a cubic function that models the data shown in the table.

Year	1	2	3	4	5	6
Stock value	\$4	\$6	\$10	\$17	\$29	\$47

SOLUTION Notice that the third differences are almost constant.

First differences: 2 4 7 12 18

Second differences: 2 3 5 6

Third differences: 1 2 1

```
CubicReg
 y=ax³+bx²+cx+d
 a=.2407407407
 b=-.5277777778
 c=1.945767196
 d=2.333333333
 R²=.9999883529
```

Enter the data into a graphing calculator and choose **CubicReg** for a cubic regression from the STAT CALC menu. A cubic model is $y \approx 0.24x^3 - 0.53x^2 + 1.95x + 2.33$. The R^2 value and the graph show that the function models the data well.

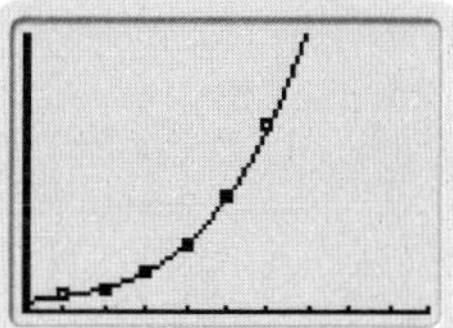

Math Reasoning

Predict Use the model to predict the stock value in Year 7.

\$72.67

Example 2

In this example, data is fit to a polynomial model.

Error Alert Remind students that the values in a table display only part of a graph of a function. Encourage students to look at common differences in addition to graphing the data.

Additional Example 2

Write a cubic function that models the data shown in the table.

Year	1	2	3	4	5	6
Value	\$6	\$10	\$16	\$26	\$42	\$67

$y \approx 0.38x^3 - 1.40x^2 + 5.65x + 1.33$

ENGLISH LEARNERS

Explain the meaning of the word space. Say,

"To space means to arrange things in a way that places a region or an interval of time or region between things. Handwriting that has equally spaced letters looks more organized."

Draw an example of a number line that has unevenly spaced intervals. Have students redraw the number line with equally spaced intervals.

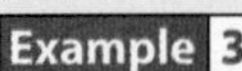

Example 3

In this example, data is fit to an exponential model.

Additional Example 3

Write an exponential function that models the data shown in the table.

Month	1	2	3	4	5	6
Balance	\$10	\$21	\$42	\$84	\$170	\$340

$y \approx 5.05(2.02)^x$

Example 4

In this example, data is fit to a logarithmic model.

Additional Example 4

Write a logarithmic function that models the data shown in the table.

Mins.	1	2	3	4	5	6
MPH	12	18	23	27	30	31

$y \approx 11.32 + 11.1\ln(x)$

Data that does not have constant differences may have constant or near constant ratios. For these, use an **exponential regression** to find an exponential model.

Example 3 Fitting Data with an Exponential Model

Write an exponential function that models the data shown in the table.

Day	1	2	3	4	5	6
Number of e-mails	14	28	49	98	196	343

SOLUTION The ratios between consecutive y-values are 2, 1.75, 2, 2, and 1.75. Since they all either 2 or near 2, an exponential regression is appropriate.

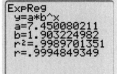

Enter the data into a graphing calculator and choose **ExpReg** to get an exponential function in the form $y = ab^x$. An exponential model of the data is $y \approx 7.45(1.9)^x$.

To enter any regression equation directly into Y1, press VARS, choose Statistics, and choose RegEQ from the EQ menu.

ExpReg
y=a*b^x
a=7.450080211
b=1.903224982
r²=.9989701351
r=.9994849349

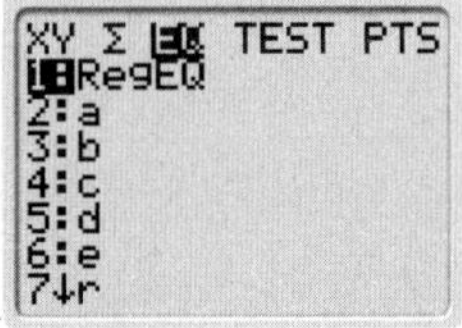

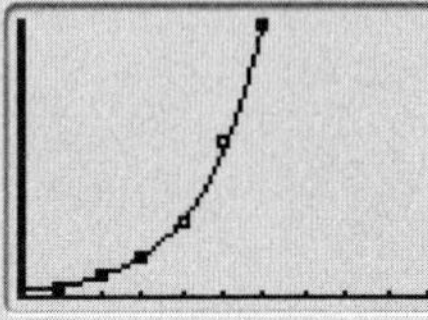

The R^2 value and the graph show that the function models the data well.

Some data are best modeled by a logarithmic function. For this data set use a **logarithmic regression** to find a logarithmic model.

Example 4 Fitting Data with a Logarithmic Model

Write a logarithmic function that models the data shown in the table.

Number of minutes	1	2	3	4	5	6
Miles per hour	24	32	39	43	47	49

SOLUTION Notice that the y-values continue to increase, but the amounts of increase become less and less as the number of minutes increase.

Enter the data into a graphing calculator and choose **LnReg** to get a natural logarithmic function in the form $y = a + b\ln(x)$. A logarithmic model of the data is $y \approx 23.27 + 14.34\ln(x)$.

Caution

Be sure to choose **LnReg** and not **LinReg** from the Calc menu.

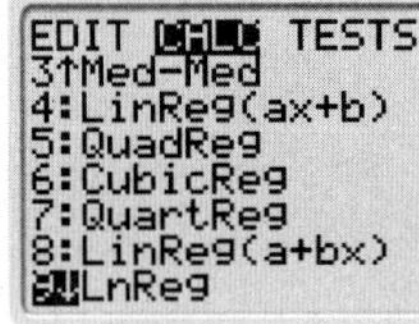

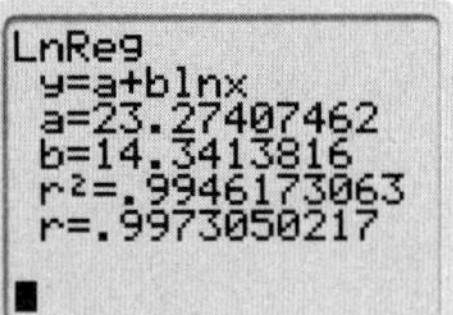

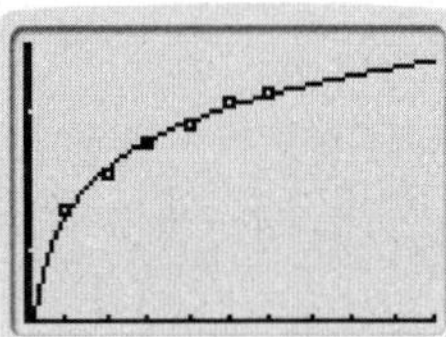

The R^2 value and the graph show that the function models the data well.

CHALLENGE

Use an exponential model for the data in the table. When will the number of bacteria reach 10,000?

Minutes	0	1	2	3	4	5
Number of Bacteria	180	230	305	395	500	610

$y \approx 182.29(1.28)^x$

The population will reach 10,000 after 16 minutes.

Example 5 Application: Population

The population for a certain town for given years is shown in the table.

Year	1991	1992	1995	2000	2006	2007
Population	4680	4824	5716	6205	8944	8991

Find the model that best fits the data. Then use the model to estimate the population of the town in 2002.

SOLUTION

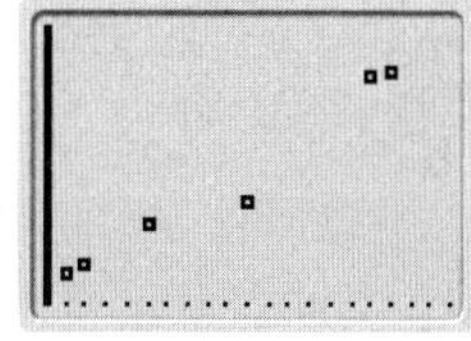

1. **Understand** The x-values are not equally spaced. Use a graphing calculator to help decide which types of regressions to try. For simplicity, the x-values can be the number of years after the year 1990.

2. **Plan** The data points are somewhat close to forming a line, although a nonlinear model may better fit the data. Compare the R^2 values for different types of regression models to find which fit is best.

3. **Solve** The R^2 values are as follows, linear: ≈ 0.9604, quadratic: ≈ 0.9818, cubic: ≈ 0.9868, quartic: 0.9941, exponential: ≈ 0.9764, logarithmic: ≈ 0.8039.

   The quartic model is the best fit. The function is $y \approx -0.474x^4 + 17.73x^3 - 205.718x^2 + 1014.48x + 3717.54$.

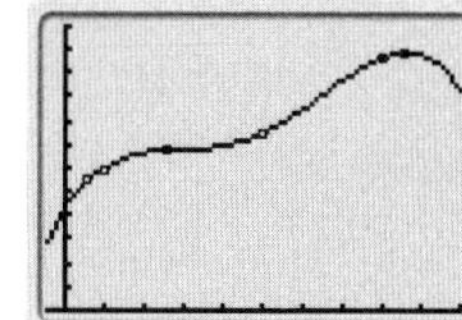

Find the value of the function when $x = 12$. This can be done by graphing the equation, choosing **value** from the Calc menu, and typing 12 for X =. This model estimates the population in 2002 to be about 7081.

4. **Check** Compare the answer with the numbers in the table to check for reasonableness. 2002 is between 2000 and 2006 and 7081 is between 6205 and 8944, so the answer is reasonable.

Math Reasoning

Analyze Would you use the quartic model to predict the population for the year 2012? Explain.

No, the population has been increasing and the quartic model will give a lower population in the future.

Lesson Practice

a. Write a quadratic function that models the data shown in the table. *(Ex 1)*

Temperature (°C)	−5	−4	−3	−2	−1	0
Number of Campers	8	12	15	19	19	20

b. Write a quartic function that models the data shown in the table. *(Ex 2)*

Week	10	20	30	40	50	60
Value of Stock	\$42	\$25	\$9	\$12	\$27	\$41

c. Write an exponential function that models the data shown in the table. *(Ex 3)*

Minutes	1	2	3	4	5	6
Number of Bacteria	115	168	250	371	547	808

a. $y \approx -0.482x^2 + 0.018x + 19.96$

b. $y \approx -0.0000646x^4 + 0.0088x^3 - 0.35x^2 + 3.62x + 32.83$

c. $y \approx 77.41(1.478)^x$

Example 5

This example presents a population application which fits a quartic model.

Extend the Example

Which model would be the worst fit for the data? logarithmic

Additional Example 5

The population for a certain town for given years is shown in the table.

Year	1998	2000	2001	2004	2006
Pop (mill)	0.75	1.22	1.3	1.5	1.61

Find the model that best fits the data. Then use the model to estimate the population of the town in 2002.

Sample: $y \approx -0.00098x^4 + 0.05x^3 - 0.96x^2 + 8.11x - 24.50$; 1.36 million

Lesson Practice

Problems a–d

Scaffolding Have students first identify the common differences or ratios for each data set. Then have students graph the data to ensure that the suggested model is correct.

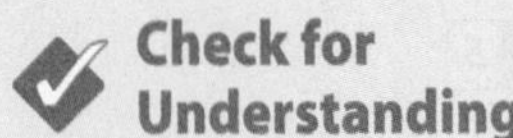

Check for Understanding

The questions below help assess the concepts taught in this lesson.

"Explain how to use common differences among the y-values to identify a polynomial model." Sample: Linear models have constant first differences. Quadratic models have constant second differences. Cubic models have constant third differences. Quartic models have constant fourth differences. In general, nth models have constant nth differences.

"Explain how the data for a cubic model differs from the data for an exponential model." Sample: The y-values for a cubic model have third differences that are equal. The y-values for an exponential model have constant ratios.

3 Practice

Math Conversations

Discussions to strengthen understanding

Problem 3

Extend the Problem

"Determine the number of outcomes if you choose an even number greater than 25 from the numbers 1 through 50." 13

"Determine the number of outcomes if you choose an odd number greater than 25 from the numbers 1 through 50." 12

"How can you use this information to find the number of outcomes if you choose an even or an odd number greater than 25 between 1 and 50?" add the values; $12 + 13 = 25$

d. $y \approx -30.94 + 41.5\ln(x)$

d. (Ex 4) Write a logarithmic function that models the data shown in the table.

Years since 1990	3	6	9	12	15	18
Animal population	15	43	60	72	82	89

e. quartic model; Sample: $y \approx -0.0000822x^4 + 0.0039x^3 - 0.067x^2 + 0.51x - 0.175$, about 1,340,000

e. (Ex 5) The population for a certain town for given years is shown in the table.

Year	1993	1997	1999	2001	2005	2007
Population (millions)	0.85	1.25	1.28	1.31	1.39	1.42

Find the model that best fits the data. Use the year 1990 as the initial time. Then use the model to estimate the population of the town in 2003.

Practice Distributed and Integrated

***1.** (116) **Multi-Step** Write a cubic function to model the data in the table. Then estimate the value of y when x is 3. How does the estimate change when a quartic function is used instead? $y \approx -1.993x^3 - 0.063x^2 - 0.967x + 1.54$, about -55.7, it decreases to -59.6

x	-10	-5	0	5	10
y	1996	263	-12	-245	-2010

***2.** (113) **International Landmarks** The Santa Justa Elevator (Elevador de Santa Justa) in Lisbon, Portugal is 45 meters tall. Suppose a ball is dropped from the top of the elevator and rebounds 25% of its previous height after each bounce.

a. Use summation notation to write an infinite geometric series to represent the total distance the ball travels after it initially hits the ground. Keep in mind that the ball travels both down and up on each bounce. $\sum_{k=1}^{n} 2(11.25)(0.25)^{k-1}$

b. Find the sum of the series from part a. 30 meters

c. Find the total distance the ball travels by adding the distance traveled before the ball initially hit the ground. 75 meters

3. (33) Determine the number of outcomes if you choose an even number or an odd number greater than 25 between the numbers 1 through 50. 25 outcomes

4. (107) Find the roots of $y = x^9 - 8x^6 - x^3 + 8$. $x = \pm 1, 2$

***5.** (116) **Population** The table shows the approximate populations of the United States for certain decades.

Year	1930	1940	1960	1980	1990	2000
Population (millions)	1.23	1.32	1.79	2.27	2.49	2.81

a. List the following types of regressions in order from those of best fit to worst fit for the data: linear, quadratic, cubic, quartic, logarithmic, and exponential.

b. Use the first model listed for the answer in part a to estimate the population of the United States in 1950. about 1.54 million

5a. quartic, cubic, quadratic, exponential, linear, logarithmic

Simplify the expressions.
(40)

6. $\sqrt{15} \cdot \sqrt{5}$ $5\sqrt{3}$

7. $\sqrt{175} - \sqrt{63} + \sqrt{20}$ $2\sqrt{7} + 2\sqrt{5}$

8. The last term of a finite arithmetic sequence is 33 and the common difference is −9. Find the 5th term of the sequence given that there are 21 terms in all. 177
(92)

*9. **Error Analysis** A student claims that $\cot\theta\cos\theta - \sin\theta = \cos 2\theta \csc\theta$ is NOT an identity based on the work shown below. What is the student's error?
(115)

$$\cot\theta\cos\theta - \sin\theta \stackrel{?}{=} \cos 2\theta \csc\theta$$
$$\stackrel{?}{=} \cos^2\theta - \sin^2\theta\left(\frac{1}{\sin\theta}\right)$$
$$\stackrel{?}{=} \cos^2\theta - \sin\theta$$
See Additional Answers.

10. Divide and then evaluate for $x = 7$: $\frac{x+9}{3x} \div \frac{3x+27}{x}$. $\frac{x(x+9)}{9x(x+9)}$; $\frac{1}{9}$
(31)

*11. **Coordinate Geometry** Find the coordinates of the images of points A, B, and C after a 25° rotation counterclockwise about the origin. Round answers to the nearest hundredth. Show how you arrived at your answers.
(112)
See Additional Answers.

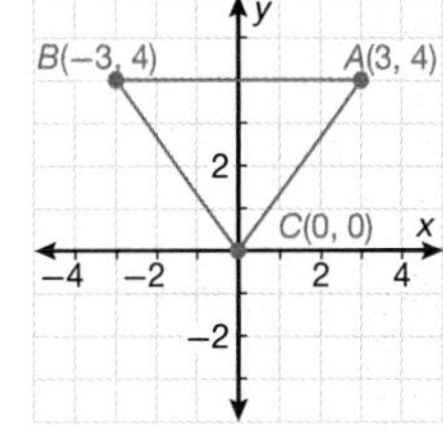

Determine if the given points are solutions of the inequalities.

12. $(3, -3)$; $y \le \frac{2}{3}x - 5$ Yes
(39)

13. $(-2, -6)$; $y < 9x - 3$ No
(39)

*14. **Analyze** Choosing from translations, stretches, compressions, and reflections, which transformation(s) can result in a polynomial function which has a different description of end behavior than that of the original polynomial function? Justify your answer. See Additional Answers.
(111)

15. **Optics** A diagram of a hyperbolic mirror is shown. The property of a hyperbolic mirror is that if you shine a beam of light from the mirror, the light is reflected toward the focal point. For this mirror, where should you place a view lens to see the converging light? At (5, 0)
(109)

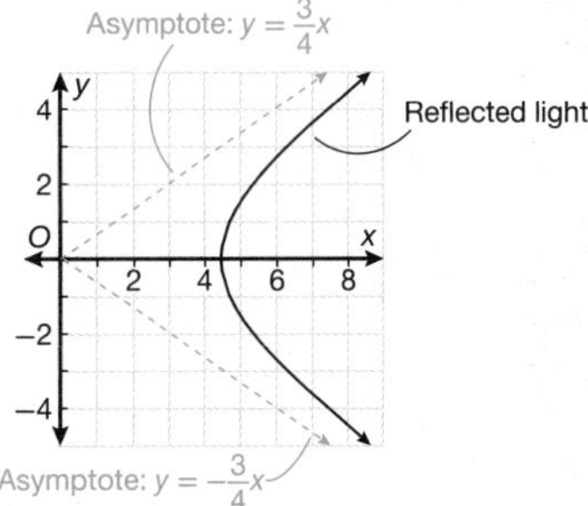

*16. **Write** Tell why the graph of the equation $4x^2 + 4xy + y^2 - 12x + 8y + 36 = 0$ is not a parabola. The equation contains two squared terms. The equation of a parabola has only one squared term.
(114)

Find the roots of the equations.

17. $y = 12x^5 - 49x^4 + 49x^3 - 96x^2 + 392x - 392$ $x = 2, \frac{7}{3}, \frac{7}{4}$
(106)

18. $y = x^{14} - x^{12} - x^{11} + x^9 - x^5 + x^3 + x^2 - 1$ $x = 1$
(106)

Problem 7

Error Alert

Watch for students who add the radicands and answer $\sqrt{175 - 63 + 20} = \sqrt{132}$. If necessary tell them to begin by writing each radicand as a product of factors.

Problem 8

Students may not realize that they are given that the 21st term is 33.

Problem 10

Guide students by asking them the following question.

"How do you divide two rational expressions?" Multiply the first expression by the reciprocal of the second.

Problem 15

Students can find the values of a and b from the slope of the line which is the asymptote. For a hyperbola, $c = \sqrt{(a^2 + b^2)}$.

Problem 20

Guide students by asking them the following questions.

"What do you need to know about a circle to write its equation?" its center and radius

"How do you find the radius of a circle if you know its circumference?" Solve the equation $C = 2\pi r$ for r.

Problem 24

Guide students by asking them the following question.

"How do you find $\sin\frac{\theta}{2}$ if you know $\cos\theta$?" Use the half-angle formula $\sin\frac{\theta}{2} = \pm\sqrt{\frac{1-\cos\theta}{2}}$

Problem 27

Guide students by asking them the following questions.

"How do you find the inverse of a function?" Interchange x and y and solve for y.

"Is the inverse of a function always a function?" No

19. (100) **Multiple Choice** Which of the following rational functions includes a hole at $x = -5$? C

A $y = \frac{x^2 - 25}{x^2 - 12x + 35}$ B $y = \frac{x^2 - 25}{x^2 - 14x + 48}$

C $y = \frac{x^2 - 25}{x^2 - x - 30}$ D $y = \frac{x^2 - 25}{x^2 + x - 30}$

20. (91) **Geometry** Write the equation of a circle if its center is located at $(5, -1)$ and its circumference is 20π units. $(x - 5)^2 + (y + 1)^2 = 100$

21. (101) **Error Analysis** A student described the end behavior of $f(x) = -x^2 + 2x^3 + x^4$ as shown below. What error did the student likely make? Describe the end behavior correctly. See Additional Answers.

As $x \to +\infty, f(x) \to -\infty$, and as $x \to -\infty, f(x) \to -\infty$.

***22.** (116) **Graphing Calculator** Perform a quadratic regression for the data in the table. Give the R^2 value. Use the function to predict the y-value when x is 6.
$y \approx -0.117x^2 + 1.79x - 6.8$, about 0.9942, about −0.282

x	1.5	2.6	3.5	4.5	8
y	−4.3	−3.05	−2.11	−0.95	0

23. (106) **Forestry** The volume of a giant sequoia, in cubic feet, can be approximated by the function $y = 0.485x^3 - 362x^2 + 89{,}889x - 7{,}379{,}874$, where x is the height of the tree, between 220 feet and 280 feet inclusive. What are the possible heights of a tree whose volume is 45,000 cubic feet? Hint: Set the Window of your graphing calculator to the range of heights for which the function is given. Sample: about 228 feet, 253 feet, and 265 feet

***24.** (115) **Multiple Choice** Which of the following is the exact value of $\sin\frac{\theta}{2}$ if $\cos\theta = -\frac{1}{4}$ and $90° < \theta < 180°$. B

A $-\frac{\sqrt{10}}{4}$ B $\frac{\sqrt{10}}{4}$ C $-\frac{\sqrt{6}}{4}$ D $\frac{\sqrt{6}}{4}$

25. (94) **Money** The members of a bowling team are sharing the cost of a $125 gift for their team leader. Write and solve an inequality to show the numbers of members whose participation would bring the cost per member to less than $7.50. $\frac{125}{x} < 7.5$, 17 or more members

26. (104) **Write** Explain in complete sentences what must be done to an equation to vertically compress the graph. To vertically compress a graph, you must multiply each y-coordinate of the graph by a value between zero and one.

27. (50) Find an equation for the inverse of $y = 4x^2 + 24$. $y = \frac{1}{2}\sqrt{x - 24}$

Factor completely. (61)

28. $x^3 + 7x^2 + 7x - 15$
$(x + 5)(x + 3)(x - 1)$

29. $x^4 + 3x^3 - 25x^2 + 9x - 84$
$(x + 7)(x - 4)(x^2 + 3)$

***30.** (105) **Formulate** Substitute the formula for the nth term of an arithmetic sequence into the formula for the sum of the first n terms of an arithmetic series. In what situation could this new formula be used? $S_n = n\left(\frac{2a_1 + (n-1)d}{2}\right)$, It can be used to find the sum of the first n terms, given the number of terms, the first term, and the common ratio. It is not necessary to know the value of the nth term.

LOOKING FORWARD 

Finding best fit models will be further developed in other Saxon Secondary Math courses.

LESSON 117

Solving Systems of Nonlinear Equations

Warm Up

1. (114) **Vocabulary** Of the four conic sections, only a parabola has only one squared term when written in standard form.

2. (114) True or False: $9x^2 + 25y^2 = 900$ is the equation of a hyperbola. False

3. (109) Sketch the graph of $25x^2 - 9y^2 = 225$. See Additional Answers.

New Concepts

When at least one equation in a system of equations is nonlinear, the system is a **nonlinear system of equations.** As with a system of linear equations, the solution set is the point, or points, where the graphs of the equations intersect. These coordinates are the values that make all the equations in the system true.

When one or both of the equations are equations of conic sections, there can 0, 1, 2, 3, or 4 points of intersection. Possible intersections between a parabola and a circle are shown to the right.

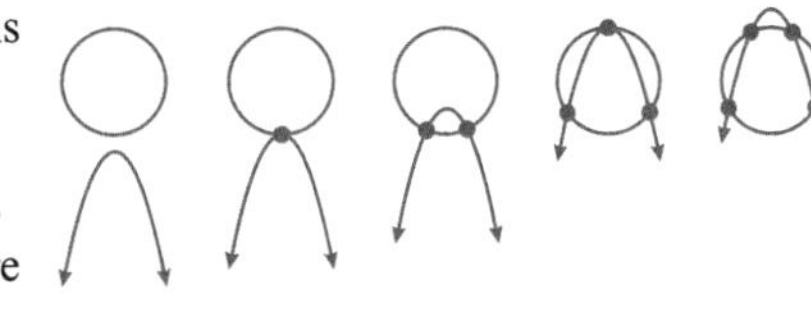

Math Reasoning

Model Sketch another way a circle and a parabola can have no points of intersection.

Sample:

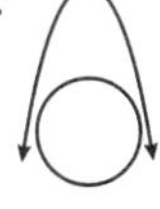

Methods for solving nonlinear systems are the same as for linear systems: by substitution, by elimination, and by graphing.

Example 1 Solving a Nonlinear System by Substitution

Solve $\begin{matrix} x^2 + y^2 = 13 \\ x + y - 5 = 0 \end{matrix}$ by using the substitution method.

SOLUTION The solution is the intersection point(s) of a circle and a line. There could be 0, 1, or 2 solutions.

Step 1: Solve the second equation for either x or y: $x = 5 - y$.

Step 2: Substitute $5 - y$ for x in the first equation and solve for y.

$$x^2 + y^2 = 13$$
$$(5 - y)^2 + y^2 = 13$$
$$25 - 10y + y^2 + y^2 = 13$$
$$12 - 10y + 2y^2 = 0$$
$$2y^2 - 10y + 12 = 0$$
$$2(y^2 - 5y + 6) = 0$$
$$2(y - 2)(y - 3) = 0$$
$$y = 2 \text{ or } y = 3$$

Step 3: Substitute both 2 and 3 for y and solve for x.

When $y = 2$: $x + y - 5 = 0$
$$x + 2 - 5 = 0$$
$$x - 3 = 0$$
$$x = 3$$

When $y = 3$: $x + y - 5 = 0$
$$x + 3 - 5 = 0$$
$$x - 2 = 0$$
$$x = 2$$

Step 4: Write the solutions: (2, 3) and (3, 2).

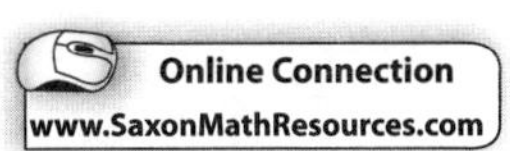
Online Connection
www.SaxonMathResources.com

LESSON 117

1 Warm Up

In Problem 3, have students write the equation in standard form first, and then sketch the graph.

2 New Concepts

In this lesson, students learn to solve nonlinear systems of equations.

Example 1

In this example, students are shown how to solve a nonlinear system using the substitution method.

Additional Example 1

Solve $\begin{matrix} y = x - 3 \\ x^2 + y^2 = 17 \end{matrix}$ by using the substitution method.
(4, 1) and (−1, −4)

MATH BACKGROUND

Students have solved systems of linear equations using substitution, elimination, and graphing. When one of the equations in a system is nonlinear, the system is considered nonlinear.

Some examples of nonlinear systems with just one nonlinear equation include a line and a conic section. These systems can have zero, one, or two solutions.

Some examples of nonlinear systems with two nonlinear, or conic, equations are two circles, two ellipses, or a circle and a hyperbola. These systems can have zero, one, two, three, or four solutions.

LESSON RESOURCES

Student Edition Practice Workbook 117
Reteaching Master117
Adaptations Master 117
Challenge and Enrichment Masters C117, E117

Example 2

In this example, students are shown how to solve a nonlinear system using the elimination method.

Error Alert Watch for students who use only the positive square root when taking the square root of both sides of an equation.

Additional Example 2

Solve $\begin{matrix} 9x^2 + 4y^2 = 64 \\ 16x^2 - 4y^2 = 36 \end{matrix}$ by using the elimination method. $(2, \sqrt{7})$, $(-2, \sqrt{7})$, $(2, -\sqrt{7})$, $(-2, -\sqrt{7})$

Example 3

In this example, students are shown how to solve a nonlinear system by graphing each equation in the system.

Additional Example 3

Solve $\begin{matrix} -2x + y = -8 \\ y = x^2 - x - 6 \end{matrix}$ by using the graphing method.
(2, −4) and (1, −6)

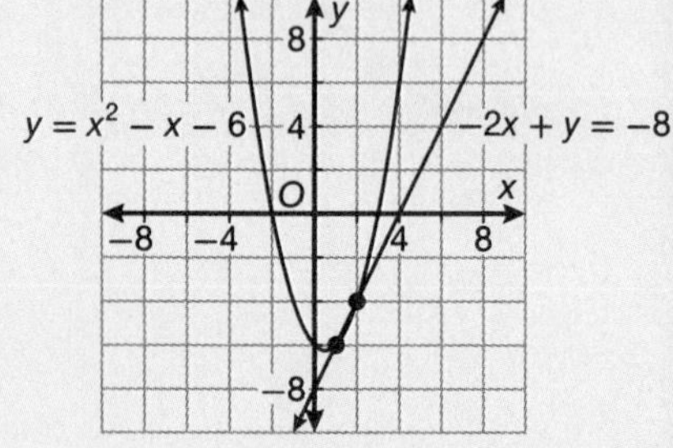

Example 2 **Solving a Nonlinear System by Elimination**

Solve $\begin{matrix} x^2 - y^2 = 7 \\ x^2 + y^2 = 25 \end{matrix}$ by using the elimination method.

SOLUTION The solution is the intersection point(s) of a hyperbola and a circle. There could be up to 4 solutions.

Step 1: Eliminate either x^2 or y^2. Since the y^2-terms are already opposites, it makes sense to eliminate those.

$x^2 - y^2 = 7$ $+x^2 + y^2 = 25$	Align the equations.
$2x^2 = 32$	Add the equations vertically.
$x^2 = 16$	Divide both sides by 2.
$x = \pm 4$	Take the square root of each side.

Step 2: Substitute both −4 and 4 for x and solve for y.

When $x = -4$: $x^2 + y^2 = 25$	When $x = 4$: $x^2 + y^2 = 25$
$(-4)^2 + y^2 = 25$	$(4)^2 + y^2 = 25$
$16 + y^2 = 25$	$16 + y^2 = 25$
$y^2 = 9$	$y^2 = 9$
$y = \pm 3$	$y = \pm 3$

Step 3: Write the solutions: $(-4, -3)$, $(-4, 3)$, $(4, -3)$, $(4, 3)$.

The graphs of the equations support four solutions.

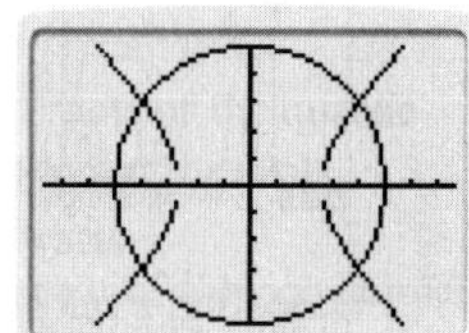

Example 3 **Solving a Nonlinear System by Graphing**

Solve $\begin{matrix} 5y = 3x \\ xy = 15 \end{matrix}$ by using the graphing method.

SOLUTION Graph each equation and find the points of intersection.

Rewrite the first equation as $y = \frac{3}{5}x$.

Plot the point with the y-intercept, (0, 0), and move up 3, right 5 to plot anther point.

Rewrite the second equation as $y = \frac{15}{x}$.

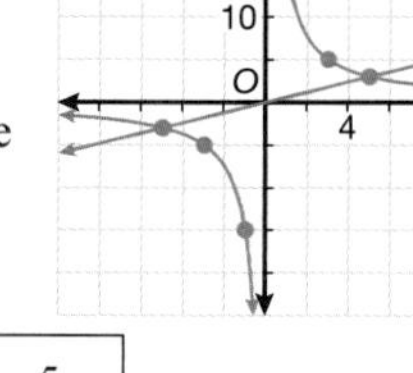

x	−5	−3	−1	1	3	5
$y = \frac{15}{x}$	−3	−5	−15	15	5	3

The graphs intersect at $(-5, -3)$ and $(5, 3)$.

Math Reasoning

Justify How does $B^2 - 4AC$ show that the graph of the second equation will be a hyperbola?

$B = 1, A = C = 0$, so $B^2 - 4AC = 1$ and $1 > 0$.

ENGLISH LEARNERS

Explain to students that the word **nonlinear** means not linear or not a line. Write and graph a linear system of equations on the board. Then, write and graph a nonlinear system of equations which includes one line on the board.

"A linear system of equations has only linear equations in the system. A nonlinear system of equations has at least one nonlinear equation in the system."

Point to the corresponding systems as you describe them. Put different examples of linear and nonlinear systems on the board and have the students differentiate between the two systems.

Example 4 Solving a System by Using a Graphing Calculator

Solve $\begin{matrix} x^2 + y^2 = 25 \\ x^2 + 2y^2 = 34 \end{matrix}$ by using a graphing calculator.

SOLUTION Solve each equation for y.

$$\begin{aligned} x^2 + y^2 &= 25 \\ y^2 &= 25 - x^2 \\ y &= \pm\sqrt{25 - x^2} \end{aligned} \qquad \begin{aligned} x^2 + 2y^2 &= 34 \\ 2y^2 &= 34 - x^2 \\ y^2 &= \frac{34 - x^2}{2} \\ y &= \pm\sqrt{\frac{34 - x^2}{2}} \end{aligned}$$

```
Plot1 Plot2 Plot3
\Y1■√(25-X²
\Y2■-√(25-X²
\Y3■√((34-X²)/2)
\Y4■-√((34-X²)/2
)■
\Y5=
```

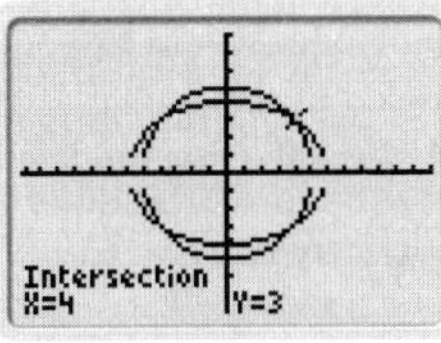

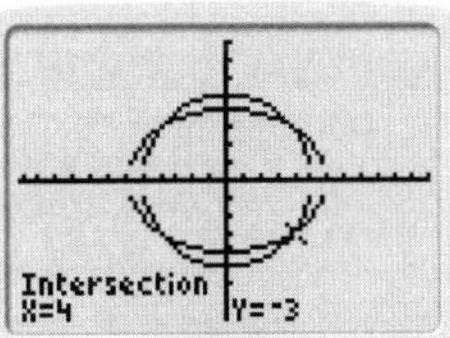

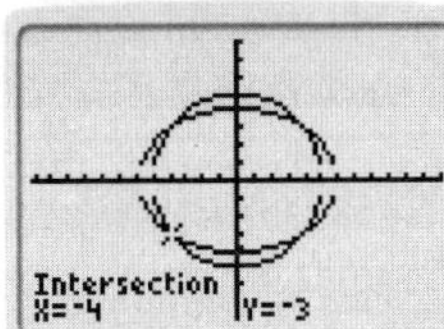

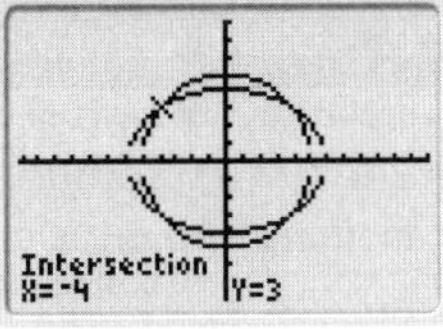

The solutions are (4, 3), (4, −3), (−4, −3), and (−4, 3).

Graphing Calculator

Watch the equation at the top of the screen to see which graph the cursor is on. Use the arrow keys to move among the graphs.

Example 5 Application: Event Planning

A planner is designing a rollerblading and bicycling exhibit. She laid a coordinate grid over the available space. She would like the rollerblading arena to be in the area enclosed by $2x^2 + 3y^2 = 50$ and the biking paths along the curves modeled by $y^2 - x^2 = 25$. Will the biking paths intersect the arena? If so, where?

SOLUTION Solve for y.

$$\begin{aligned} 2x^2 + 3y^2 &= 50 \\ + \;\; -x^2 + y^2 &= 25 \end{aligned} \longrightarrow \begin{aligned} 2x^2 + 3y^2 &= 50 \\ + \;\; -2x^2 + 2y^2 &= 50 \\ \hline 5y^2 &= 100 \\ y^2 &= 20 \\ y &= \pm\sqrt{20} \end{aligned}$$

Solve for x.

$$\begin{aligned} y^2 - x^2 &= 25 \\ (\sqrt{20})^2 - x^2 &= 25 \\ 20 - x^2 &= 25 \\ -x^2 &= 5 \\ x^2 &= -5 \end{aligned} \qquad \begin{aligned} y^2 - x^2 &= 25 \\ (-\sqrt{20})^2 - x^2 &= 25 \\ 20 - x^2 &= 25 \\ -x^2 &= 5 \\ x^2 &= -5 \end{aligned}$$

For both, the values of x are not real, so the system has no solutions. The bike paths will not intersect the arena.

Example 4

In this example, students are shown how to solve a nonlinear system using a graphing calculator.

Additional Example 4

Solve $\begin{matrix} y = (x + 1)^2 \\ xy = -2 \end{matrix}$ by using a graphing calculator. (−2, 1)

Example 5

In this example, students are shown how to use a nonlinear system to solve a real-world problem about event planning.

Additional Example 5

Two event planners are responsible for the design of an auto racing exhibit. They have each laid a coordinate grid over the available space. One planner would like the racers to make laps around the curve modeled by $4x^2 + 9y^2 = 100$ and the other would like to hold a drag race along the line $x + y = 7$. As is, will the path of the auto racers making laps and the drag racers ever cross? No, the system has no solution.

CHALLENGE

Solve $\begin{matrix} \frac{x^2}{16} - \frac{y^2}{36} = 1 \\ -\frac{3}{2}x + y = 0 \end{matrix}$ by using the graphing method.

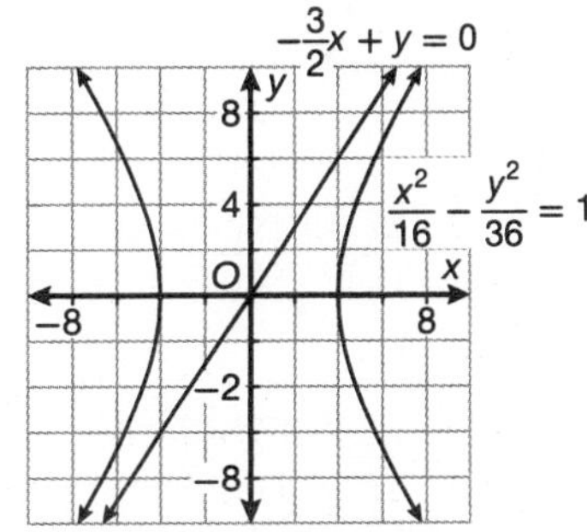

The system has no solution. $-\frac{3}{2}x + y = 0$ is an asymptote of the hyperbola.

Lesson Practice

Problems a–d

Scaffolding Have students identify the graph of each equation in the systems and determine the possible number of solutions to the system.

Problem b

Error Alert Students may solve the system correctly, but then write the solutions incorrectly by inadvertently reversing the x- and y-coordinates. Remind them to check that the x- and y-coordinates are in the correct order.

Check for Understanding

The questions below help assess the concepts taught in this lesson.

"Explain how to solve a nonlinear system of equations." Sample: You use the same methods as were used to solve a system of linear equations: substitution, elimination, graphing, and a graphing calculator.

"Suppose a system contains the equations of an ellipse and a parabola. Discuss the possible solutions to the system." Sample: The ellipse and the parabola may not intersect, or they may intersect at one, two, three, or four points.

Lesson Practice

a. (Ex 1) Solve $\begin{matrix} x^2 - y^2 = 48 \\ x = 7y \end{matrix}$ by using the substitution method. (7, 1) and (−7, −1)

b. (Ex 2) Solve $\begin{matrix} x^2 + y^2 = 16 \\ x^2 - 2y^2 = 1 \end{matrix}$ by using the elimination method. $(\sqrt{11}, \sqrt{5}), (\sqrt{11}, -\sqrt{5}), (-\sqrt{11}, \sqrt{5}), (-\sqrt{11}, -\sqrt{5})$

c. (Ex 3) Solve $\begin{matrix} y + 2 = 2x \\ xy = 24 \end{matrix}$ by using the graphing method. (−3, −8), (4, 6)

d. (Ex 4) Solve $\begin{matrix} y^2 - x^2 = 36 \\ 2x + y = -1.5 \end{matrix}$ by using a graphing calculator. (−4.5, 7.5), (2.5, −6.5)

e. (Ex 5) Two event planners are responsible for the design of a boating exhibit. They have each laid a coordinate grid over the lake that will be used. One planner would like boaters to be able to make laps around the curve modeled by $9x^2 + 16y^2 = 144$ and the other would like to hold a speedboat race along the line modeled by $3x + 4y = 12$. As is, will the path of the speedboaters intersect the path of the boaters making laps? If so, where? Yes, at (0, 3) and (4, 0)

Practice Distributed and Integrated

***1.** (109) **Generalize** For a hyperbola of the form $ax^2 + by^2 + cx + dy + e = 0$, what must be true about a and b if the orientation of the hyperbola is vertical. $a < 0$ and $b > 0$

2. (88) Given $A = \frac{1}{2}d_1d_2$ find d_1. $d_1 = \frac{2A}{d_2}$

3. (47) **Savings** \$2,000 is deposited into a savings account. How much money will be in the account in 30 years if there is an 8% interest rate compounded quarterly? \$21,530.33

***4.** (111) **Multiple Choice** The graph of $g(x)$ is the graph of $f(x) = 3x^4 - 4$ shifted 2 units left. Which is the correct rule for $g(x)$? A

A $g(x) = 3(x + 2)^4 - 4$ **B** $g(x) = 3(x - 2)^4 - 4$

C $g(x) = 3x^4 - 2$ **D** $g(x) = 3x^4 - 6$

5. (106) **Probability** A function is randomly selected from the list below and graphed.

$P(x) = x^3 + 2x^2 - 13x + 10$, $Q(x) = x^3 - 2x^2 + x$, $R(x) = 3x^3 + 48x$, $S(x) = 2x^3 - 32x$, $T(x) = x^3 - 7x^2 + 4x - 28$

What is the probability that the graph has exactly one x-intercept? What are the odds in favor? 40%; 2 to 3

Simplify the logarithms.

6. (72) $\log_7 5^3$ $3\log_7 5$

7. (72) $\log_5 42 - \log_5 7$ $\log_5 6$

***8.** (116) **Justify** Tell why it is incorrect to call the R^2 value the *correlation coefficient.* 8. The correlation coefficient is r and it only measures the strength of a linear regression. R^2 values measure the strength of nonlinear regressions.

9. (95) Determine if $P(x) = 3x^3 - 4x^2 - 28x - 16$ has a zero remainder when divided by $x + 2$. Determine $Q(x)$. $x + 2$ is a factor of $P(x)$. $Q(x) = 3x^2 - 10x - 8$

816 *Saxon* Algebra 2

*10. **Graphing Calculator** Graph $y = -x^2 + 3$ on your calculator. Classify the function as discrete or continuous and identify the range. Continuous, $y \leq 3$
(22)

11. Find a_6 of an arithmetic sequence given that $a_3 = 55$ and $a_{20} = 140$. 70
(92)

*12. **Recreation** A boy's remote-controlled airplane is making loops in a park and the path can be modeled by $4x^2 + y^2 = 25$. A girl's remote-controlled plane is making a straight line that can be modeled by $2x + y = 7$. Is there any chance that the two planes will collide? If so, where? Yes, at (1.5, 4) or (2, 3)
(117)

13. **Analyze** Explain why you must consider two cases when solving a rational inequality by using the LCD. If the LCD includes a variable, then the value of that variable is unknown. It could be positive or negative.
(94)

14. **Physics** As an airplane comes in for a landing, the pilot wants to maintain a constant angle relative to the ground. If the pilot wants to maintain an angle between 30 and 40 degrees, define the bounds on x for the tangent function $y = \tan x$ in radians that monitor the plane's orientation. $0.5236 \leq x \leq 0.6981$
(63)

15. **Coordinate Geometry** For the sequence {2, 4, 6, 8, 10}, graph the ordered pairs (n, a_n) and (n, S_n). How do the graphs compare? See Additional Answers.
(105)

16. **Multiple Choice** Which of the following points is not on the ellipse $\frac{x^2}{2^2} + \frac{y^2}{5^2} = 1$? C
(98)
A (0, 5) B (2, 0) C (5, 0) D (−2, 0)

17. **Multi-Step** A manufacturer wants to design an open box with a square base and a total surface area of 200 square inches. a–c. See Additional Answers.
(101)
a. Write an equation that relates x, h, and 200. Solve it for h.
b. Write a function $V(x)$ for the volume of the box.
c. Graph $V(x)$ on a graphing calculator. Find the maximum possible volume of the box and the corresponding dimensions.

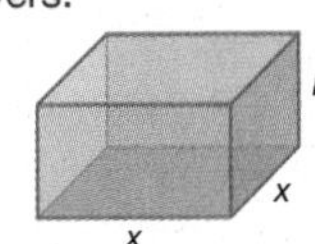

*18. **Analyze** What is the maximum number of intersection points that a circle and a line can have? 2 points
(117)

19. **Formulate** In the coordinate plane, functions f and g are graphed. If g is a translation of $f = \sqrt{x}$, find an equation for g. $g(x) = \sqrt{-x - 3.5}$
(104)

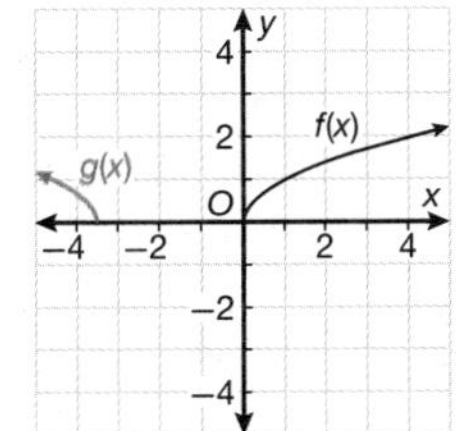

*20. **Multi-Step** Consider the system $\begin{array}{l} x^2 - y^2 = 15 \\ 9x^2 + 16y^2 = 160 \end{array}$.
(117)
a. What figures do the graphs of each equation make? hyperbola and ellipse
b. At most, how many solutions could there be? 4
c. Solve the system by elimination. (4, 1), (4, −1), (−4, 1), (−4, −1)
d. **Verify** If you were to verify your solutions by using a graphing calculator, what would be the equations you would enter? See Additional Answers.

3 Practice

Math Conversations

Discussions to strengthen understanding

Problem 10

"What does it mean for a function to be continuous?" The graph of the function has no breaks in it.

"What is the graph of $y = -x^2 + 3$?" a parabola

Problem 12

"What types of equations are modeled in this problem?" A conic equation and a linear equation

"What conic section is modeled by $4x^2 + y^2 = 25$?" An ellipse

"If given the choice between solving by elimination or by substitution, which would you choose and why?" Sample: Substitution, because the variables do not have the same degree so addition will not eliminate a term.

Problem 15

"What do n, a_n, and S_n represent?" n is the term, a_n is value of the nth term, and S_n is the sum of the first n terms.

Problem 17

For part b, remind students that $V = lwh$. Their answer to part a will allow x to be the only variable in the function.

Problem 20

Error Alert

Ensure that students do not mistake $x^2 - y^2 = 15$ for the equation of a circle.

Problem 23

Students should use the LinReg feature on their graphing calculators.

Problem 24

Error Alert

Students who answer 2506.29 have their calculators in Radian, rather than Degree, mode.

Problem 30

"Is the sequence arithmetic or geometric?" arithmetic

"What is the common difference?" 7

21. (36) Find the equation of the line that passes through the point (1, 7) and is perpendicular to the line $y = -\frac{1}{2}x + 4$. $y = 2x + 5$

22. (Inv 10) Describe the graph of a conic section whose eccentricity is 2 and vertical distance from its focus or center is 2 and write the general equation in polar form. $r = \frac{2}{1 + 2\sin(\theta)}$; hyperbola

23. (45) Use the data in the table to write the equation for the line of best fit. $y = 4.2x - 2$

Level	2	3	4	5	6
Cars Sold	8	10	13	18	25

***24.** (115) (**Entertainment**) The horizontal distance x traveled by an object launched from ground level with an initial speed v and angle θ is given by $x = \frac{1}{32}v^2 \sin 2\theta$. A firework with a shell size of 36 inches has an initial velocity of 481 feet per second. What horizontal distance will a firework travel if it is launched from ground level at an angle of 85°? about 1255.48 feet

Solve.

25. (102) $\log_5 625$ 4

26. (102) $\log_5 (5x + 9) = \log_5 6x$ 9

27. (110) **Error Analysis** Two students are simplifying the logarithmic function below, but they get different results. Which student made the mistake? Student A factored incorrectly.

$$y = \log(9x^2 + 30x + 25)$$

Student A	Student B
$y = \log(9x^2 + 30x + 25)$ $= \log((3x + 5)(3x + 6))$ $= \log(3x + 5) + \log(3x + 6)$	$y = \log(9x^2 + 30x + 25)$ $= \log(9x^2 + 2 \cdot 3 \cdot 5x + 5^2)$ $= \log(3x + 5)^2$ $= 2\log(3x + 5)$

28. (101) Describe the end behavior of the graph of the polynomial function $f(x) = -2x^3 + 7x - 4$. $f(x) \longrightarrow +\infty$ as $x \longrightarrow -\infty$ and $f(x) \longrightarrow -\infty$ as $x \longrightarrow +\infty$

***29.** (116) (**Finance**) The table shows stock values of a certain stock for 5 different days.

Day	3	6	8	14	16
Value of Stock	\$38	\$21	\$15	\$34	\$52

Use a sketch of the scatter plot to determine if a quartic or logarithmic model would better fit the data. Then write the function of the chosen regression model. quartic, $y \approx -0.002x^4 + 0.083x^3 - 0.484x^2 - 5.74x + 57.5$

***30.** (105) Find S_{18} for 2, 9, 16, 23, 30, … 1107

INCLUSION

To help determine the end behavior, allow students to use a graphing calculator to graph the function.

LOOKING FORWARD 

Solving systems of nonlinear equations will be further developed in other Saxon Secondary Math courses.

LESSON 118

Recognizing Misleading Data

Warm Up

1. **Vocabulary** In probability sampling, every individual has a known probability, greater than 0, of being selected. (73)

2. True or False: In simple random sampling, every person and every possible group has an equal chance of being chosen. (73) True

3. A reporter wants to know what teens think of a proposed curfew and asks every 10th teen leaving a convenience store if they believe the curfew is best for all the citizens of the county. Identify the sample and the population. (73)

3. sample: every teen interviewed, population: every teen in the county

New Concepts

Statistical claims are not always accurate. These inaccuracies can come from poor sampling methods, poorly worded questions, distorted data displays, and the misuse of data.

Recall that a biased sample is one that is not representative of its population. Someone making a claim about a population based on a biased sample may or may not know that their sample is biased. Biased samples can be the result of using a sample that is not a probability sample, such as a volunteer or convenience sample.

Hint

In a **probability sample,** every member of the population has a known, nonzero, chance of being selected.

Inaccurate data may also be the result of using a sample that is too small. A simple random sample that chooses only 5 people from a population of 10,000 is likely to be biased.

Example 1 Identifying Misleading Data through Sampling Methods

A reporter for a school newspaper asks students to go to the school website and report which school sport is their favorite so that she can write a story featuring the history and popularity of that particular sport. Why are the results likely to be misleading?

SOLUTION Although every student may have the opportunity to use a school computer, it is a voluntary response sample and therefore likely to be biased, with the reported sport being more popular than what it actually is. In addition, students may be more likely to choose a sport that is in-season. Therefore, baseball may be most popular if the poll is conducted in the spring, or football if the poll is conducted in the fall. Also, students may pick the sport with the most successful team, regardless of whether that sport is their favorite.

A representative sample of a large enough size does not guarantee that the data collected from that sample will be accurate. The question can be worded in a way that leads people towards a certain response.

Measurement data, such as for height or weight, is most accurate when the surveyor takes the measurement. This is because people tend to round numerical answers to the nearest 5 or 10. People may also lie about personal characteristics; this factor cannot be controlled except by measuring on the spot.

Online Connection www.SaxonMathResources.com

LESSON 118

1 Warm Up

Ask students if the time of day could bias the sample in problem 3.

2 New Concepts

Students learn to recognize misleading data.

Example 1

Voluntary response samples are usually biased, yet they are often used because they require less effort to plan and collect.

Extend the Example

Discuss ways to make the sample less biased. Sample: Randomly choose a sample by having every 5th student who enters the school identify his or her favorite sport.

Additional Example 1

A reporter wants to know what people think of a new road tax levied on trucks. She asks every 10th trucker who pulls into a roadside truck stop. Why are the results likely to be misleading? Sample: The sample is likely to be biased because she interviewed only people directly affected by the tax.

MATH BACKGROUND

In lesson 73, students learned the different methods of sampling: probability sampling, simple random sampling, stratified sampling, systematic sampling, cluster sampling, convenience sampling, and voluntary response sampling.

Some of these methods are biased and can lead to a list of problems. The data may represent only a small percentage of the people it is perceived to represent. If the questions are worded incorrectly, the survey may be misinterpreted by either the people being surveyed, or by the population reading the results.

Statistical claims are misleading when they present results that lead the observer to a false conclusion. Although no method is completely accurate, it is extremely important for a survey to be as unbiased as possible to correctly convey the data.

LESSON RESOURCES

Student Edition Practice Workbook 118
Reteaching Master 118
Adaptations Master 118
Challenge and Enrichment Master C118

Example 2

Closed multiple-choice questions are biased unless they include every possible answer.

Additional Example 2

The owner of an ice cream shop gives the following survey question to each of his customers.

What is your favorite flavor of ice cream?

a. *vanilla* **c.** *strawberry*

b. *chocolate* **d.** *chocolate chip*

How can the results of this survey be misleading?
Sample: Customers are given only four choices, which are the most popular flavors. This forces those who answer the survey to choose one of the four, which may not be their favorite flavor, just their favorite among the four choices.

Example 3

In this example students learn how graphs can be misleading. Reinforce the importance of reading the title of a graph and examining the values on each axis.

Additional Example 3

Explain how the graph could be misleading.

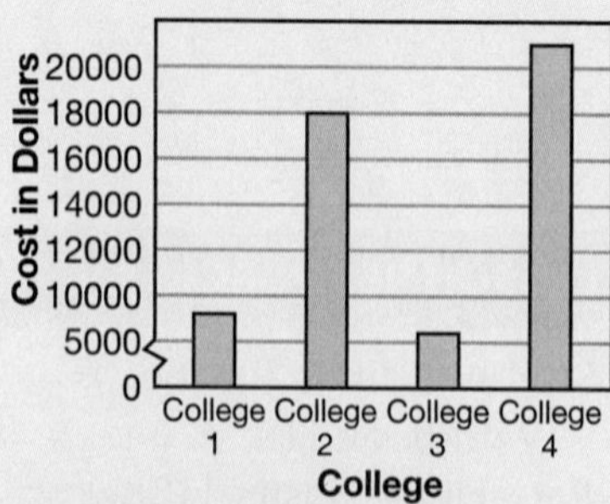

Sample: Because the vertical axis does not begin at zero and because the increment changes, the differences in the heights of the bars is misleading. Without looking at the scale, you might assume that College 2 is 4 times as expensive as College 1, when the actual costs are \$8,000 and \$18,000.

Math Language

A **closed question** has a limited number of answers such as: yes/no, true/false, or a multiple-choice option.

Survey questions which are multiple-choice are biased when they do not give every possible answer as a choice, leaving people to either skip the question or choose an answer that does not reflect their true feelings.

Example 2 Identifying Misleading Data through Questioning

The manager of an apartment complex posts the following survey in every tenant's mailbox.

Next month, maintenance workers must enter homes for an annual inspection. You must be home during the inspection. We value your time and would like your input on making the inspection schedule. Which is most convenient for you?

a. *Weekdays, before noon*

b. *Weekdays, between noon and 5 pm*

c. *Weekdays, between 5 pm and 9 pm*

How can the results of this survey be misleading?

SOLUTION A tenant who works during the day and goes to school at night cannot easily be home during the week, so their most convenient time is on the weekend, but this is not given as an option. Therefore, they may not respond to the survey, or they may unhappily answer one of the given options. This could give management the impression that their tenants are okay with being home during the week, which may not be the case. Leaving the question open for tenants to write in a time frame would give the most accurate results.

Accurate data can be made to appear misleading by the way it is displayed. For example, a bar graph that does not begin at zero can make small differences between categories appear greater than they are.

When art is used instead of bars in a bar graph, the size of the art may make the data appear misleading because the reader will be drawn to the area of the figure, and not necessarily the actual numbers to which the pictures extend. For example, suppose one category has a value twice as much as another. Only the height of the bar or figure used should be doubled, but if the width is doubled as well, it will give the misleading impression that the value is four times as large as the other.

Example 3 Identifying Misleading Data through Data Displays

Explain how the graph could be misleading.

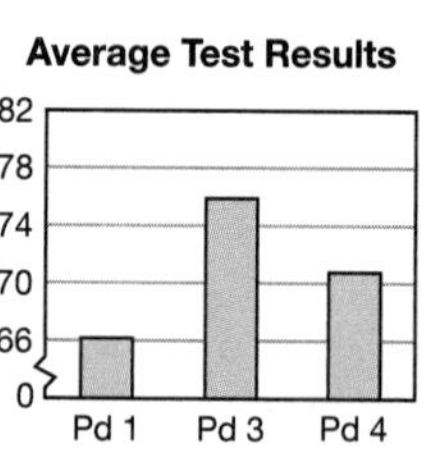

SOLUTION Because the vertical axis does not begin at 0, the difference in the heights of the bars is misleading. Without looking at the numbers, it would appear that the average score for Period 4 is twice that of Period 1 and that the average score for Period 3 is greater than three times that of Period 1. In actuality, the difference between the greatest and lowest score is only 10 points.

ENGLISH LEARNERS

Discuss the meaning of the word misleading.

"Misleading means to lead in a wrong direction either by mistake or on purpose."

Ask 3 or 4 students what their favorite color is and then make a misleading statement about it. For example, if 2 people say they like the color red, ask, **"If I say 2 out of 4 people like the color red, is that misleading?"**
Sample: Yes, because you *only* asked 4 people.

"How can I change the statement so that it is not misleading?" Sample: 2 of the 4 people I asked preferred the color red.

Give other examples of misleading data and have students change them so that they are no longer misleading.

An outlier is a value much lower or higher than the numbers in the rest of the data set. A value less than $Q_1 - 1.5(\text{IQR})$ or greater than $Q_3 + 1.5(\text{IQR})$ is considered to be an outlier. Recall that an outlier can greatly affect the mean of a data set. When a data set includes an outlier, reporting the median will be less misleading than reporting the mean. An alternative is to report the mean without the outlier, but this should be noted, especially if the sample size is small. Likewise, reporting the range of a data set that includes an outlier could be misleading as well.

A common misuse of statistics is to assume that correlation is causation. A correlation between two sets of data means that there is a relationship between the data sets. For example, student athletes may have a higher grade point average than the rest of the student body. This does not mean that one can report that playing sports causes students to do better in school. There could be any number of reasons, or combinations of reasons, for the correlation.

Example 4 Identifying Misleading Uses of Data

The prices of the houses sold in one week in a certain county are \$162,000, \$185,000, \$159,000, \$205,000, and \$2,000,000. A statement in the newspaper reads, *"Average home prices last week in the county were over half a million dollars."* Why is the statement misleading? What would be a better statement?

SOLUTION The statement is misleading because only one of the homes sold for an amount greater than a half million dollars. It would be less misleading to report the statistic as the median. Another option is to report that the average sale price of 4 out of the 5 homes sold last week was \$177,750.

Lesson Practice

a. (Ex 1) A sales person for a new lotion gave samples of the lotion to four dermatologists and asked them if they would recommend it to their patients. Three of the dermatologists said they would. The sales person wrote a brochure stating that 3 out of 4 dermatologists recommend the lotion. Why is the claim misleading?

b. (Ex 2) A student wants to know the average height difference between boys and girls in the eleventh grade. In 11th-grade homerooms, the student walks up and down the rows, asking other students to state their height, in inches. How can the results of this survey be misleading?

c. (Ex 3) Explain how the graph could be misleading.

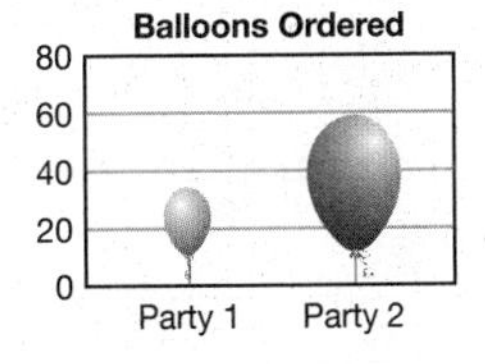

d. (Ex 4) A study showed that individuals who visit a dentist twice a year tend to make more money than individuals who visit less than twice a year. Can it be concluded that visiting a dentist causes a person to make more money? Explain.
No, correlation is not causation. It could be that individuals that make more money can afford to visit a dentist more often.

a. The sample size of 4 dermatologists is too small to be trusted as accurate.

b. Students will tend to round their heights. Also, because they are still growing, they may not know their current height, and either give their height from their last check up, or just guess it. Last, since the answer is being given orally, in front of their peers, they may lie and say they are taller than they are.

c. Because the second balloon is twice as wide as well as twice as high as the first, a reader just looking at the size of the balloons may think there were four times as many balloons ordered for the second party than the first, when it was really about twice as many.

INCLUSION

To help students better understand why some sampling methods lead to misleading data, have students work in groups to identify better ways of sampling in Examples 1 and 2.

Example 4

This example shows how an outlier in the data can be used to create a misleading statement.

Additional Example 4

The salaries of eight attorneys in a law firm are \$80,000, \$70,000, \$75,000, \$85,000, and \$700,000. A recruiter for the law firm told a prospective employee that *"The average salary for attorneys at the firm is over \$200,000."* Why is the statement misleading? What questions could the prospective employee ask to better understand the statement?
Sample: The statement is misleading because only one of the salaries is \$200,000 or greater. The prospective employee could ask for the median salary.

Lesson Practice

Problem c

Scaffolding Have students use a table to write down the statistics shown in the graph. This will remove the impact of the difference in the size of the balloons.

Check for Understanding

The questions below help assess the concepts taught in this lesson.

"What are closed questions and why do they lead to misleading statistics?" Sample: A closed question is a question with a limited number of answers. They lead to misleading statistics because people may skip the question or choose an answer that is not accurate.

"Explain why an outlier may lead to misleading statistics." Sample: An outlier may cause the mean of a data set to be skewed in one direction. Most of the data values may not be close to the average when there is an outlier.

3 Practice

Math Conversations

Discussions to strengthen understanding

Problem 1

"Why is an arithmetic series used to find the total and not a geometric series?" The difference of consecutive terms is constant.

Problems 2 and 3

"How many zeros does each function have?" four

Problem 7

"How do you determine whether or not a point is a solution to the inequality?" Substitute −6 for x and 10 for y. If the statement is true, the point is a solution.

Practice Distributed and Integrated

1. (105) **Savings** A teen deposits money into a savings account. The first week she deposits \$20. Each week thereafter, she deposits \$10 more than the previous week. Show how to use an arithmetic series to find the total amount of money in the account after 16 weeks. See Additional Answers.

Find the zeros of the functions.

2. (85) $y = 36x^4 - 27x^3 - 13x^2 + 3x + 1$ $x = 1, \pm\frac{1}{3}, -\frac{1}{4}$

3. (85) $y = 80x^4 - 64x^3 - 21x^2 + 4x + 1$ $x = 1, \pm\frac{1}{4}, -\frac{1}{5}$

***4.** (118) **Automobiles** Explain why the graph is misleading. Who might have made the graph and why? See Additional Answers.

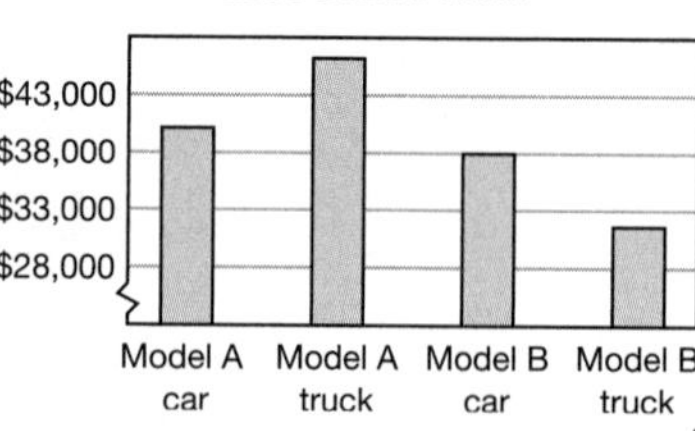

5. (115) **Multi-Step** If $\tan\theta = \frac{5}{12}$ and $0° < \theta < 90°$.

a. What is $\cos\theta$? $\frac{12}{13}$

b. What is the exact value of $\sin\frac{\theta}{2}$? $\frac{\sqrt{26}}{26}$

6. (89) **Geometry** The perimeter of a rectangle is 82 feet. Write and solve an inequality to find the width, rounded to the nearest tenth, for which the rectangle has an area less than 250 square feet. $41w - w^2 < 250$, $0 < w < 7.5$ or $33.5 < w < 41$

7. (39) Determine if $(-6, 10)$ is a solution of the inequality $y > \frac{4}{3}x + 11$. Yes

8. (107) **Analyze** The graph of the rational function $f(x) = \frac{g(x)}{h(x)}$ has holes at $x = \pm c$, for constant c. Define a new polynomial using $j(x)$ that is equivalent to $h(x)$ and takes the values of c into account. $h(x) = j(x)(x^2 - c^2)$

***9.** (116) **Probability** Suppose for the data set {(1, 4), (4, 10), (6, 11), (10, 12), (12, 13)} that one of the following regression models is randomly chosen to predict a value: linear, quadratic, cubic, quartic, exponential, and logarithmic. What is the probability that the R^2 value for the chosen model is less than 0.95? $\frac{1}{3} \approx 33.3\%$

10. (106) **Analyze** Can a sixth-degree polynomial function have exactly six irrational roots? Why or why not? Yes, irrational roots come in pairs, so there would be three conjugate pairs of irrational roots.

11. (115) **Write** Find $\sin 2\theta$ and $\cos 2\theta$ if $\cos\theta = -\frac{1}{4}$ and $90° < \theta < 180°$. Did you need to find the value of $\sin\theta$ to find these values? Explain.

***12.** (116) **Postage** The cost of a US first class stamp for given years are shown in the table.

Year	1895	1914	1947	1966	1973	1980	1982	1991	2001	2006	2007
Cost, in cents	2	2	3	5	8	15	20	29	34	39	41

a. Find an exponential function to model the data. Use the number of years before or after 1900 for x. Use the model to predict the cost of a stamp in 2025. $y \approx 1.3(1.03)^x$, \$0.52

b. Predict the cost of a stamp in 2025 when a quartic model is used instead. \$0.51

c. Justify Which price do you think is more reliable? Why? See Additional Answers.

11. $\sin 2\theta = -\frac{\sqrt{15}}{8}$; $\cos 2\theta = -\frac{7}{8}$ I did not need to find $\sin\theta$ because once $\cos 2\theta$ was found you could solve for $\sin\theta$ in the $\cos 2\theta$ identity and then substitute it and solve for $\sin 2\theta$ in the $\cos 2\theta$ identity.

12c. Possible answer: \$0.51 because the R^2 value for the quartic value is greater than for the exponential model, although predicting beyond the given domain is not very trustworthy to begin with.

822 Saxon Algebra 2

CHALLENGE

A study showed that people who eat two or more oranges a day have fewer colds than people who do not. Can it be concluded that eating oranges prevents colds? Explain.

No. Correlation is not causation. Oranges contain vitamin C which may be a factor in preventing colds, but consuming two oranges a day does not guarantee you will never get a cold.

13. Error Analysis Find and correct the error a student made in stating that the graph of
(114)
the equation $\frac{(x-4)^2}{25} + \frac{(y-1)^2}{8} = 1$ is a hyperbola. The student did not consider the sign between the two terms. The sign is +, so the graph is an ellipse.

***14. Multiple Choice** A data set has an outlier. Which statement is false? **B**
(118)

A Reporting the mean is likely to be misleading.

B Reporting the median is likely to be misleading.

C Reporting the range is likely to be misleading.

D Reporting either the mean or range is likely to be misleading.

15. Write What is a limit and when does a geometric series have a limit?
(113)

16. Identify the leading coefficient, degree, and describe the end behavior
(101)
of $f(x) = x^4 - x^3 - 4x^2 + 4$. The leading coefficient is 1. The degree is 4. as $x \to -\infty$ $f(x) \to +\infty$ and as $x \to +\infty$, $f(x) \to +\infty$

***17. Multiple Choice** Which could not have three points of intersection? **A**
(117)

A circle and line | **B** hyperbola and circle

C circle and ellipse | **D** two parabolas

15. A limit is the number that the partial sums of a geometric series approaches. It is considered the sum of an infinite geometric series when the absolute value of the common ratio of the series is less than one.

18. **Furniture** The diagram represents a table top in the shape
(112)
of a regular hexagon centered on a coordinate grid. To the nearest hundredth, what are the coordinates of point P'? Show how you arrived at your answer. (Hint: Use a rotation matrix.)

$$(-1.50, -2.60); \begin{bmatrix} \cos 60° & -\sin 60° \\ \sin 60° & \cos 60° \end{bmatrix} \begin{bmatrix} -3 \\ 0 \end{bmatrix} =$$

$$\begin{bmatrix} -3\cos 60° \\ -3\sin 60° \end{bmatrix} \approx \begin{bmatrix} -1.50 \\ -2.60 \end{bmatrix}$$

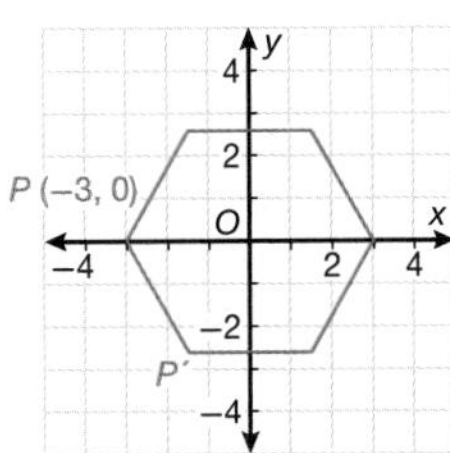

20b. $g(x) = \frac{3\pi}{2}x^3$; Possible explanation: When the height of the water is doubled, the volume is multiplied by 8.

***19. Justify** A pollster suggests the following question to be on a ballot. 'Do you support
(118)
a new traffic light on First Street and Walnut Street which engineers claim will reduce accidents by up to 65%?' Another pollster says that this question is biased and must be changed. Explain why this pollster is correct in saying the question is biased. The question leads people to say yes by giving a safety claim, a positive impact of the new light. No mention of possible negative impacts is given.

***20. Multi-Step** This conical container has a radius of 6 feet and a height of 8 feet.
(111)

a. Write a function $V(x)$ that gives the volume of water in the container when the height of the water is x feet. $V(x) = \frac{3}{16}\pi x^3$

b. Describe the transformation $g(x) = V(2x)$ by writing the rule for $g(x)$ and explaining the change in the context of the problem.

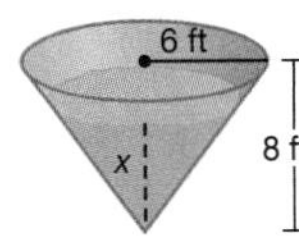

Divide using synthetic division.

21. $x^4 - 11x^3 + 14x^2 + 80x$ by $x + 2$
(51)
$x^3 - 13x^2 + 40x$

22. $x^3 - 57x + 56$ by $x - 1$ $x^2 + x - 56$
(51)

23. Solve the equation by finding all the roots: $x^4 - 2x^3 - 14x^2 - 2x - 15 = 0$.
(106)
$x = i, -i, -3, 5$

24. Let $f(x) = \tan(x)$ and $g(x) = 3x - 2$. Find the period of $f(g(x))$. $\frac{\pi}{3}$
(90)

***25. Graphing Calculator** Graph the function $y = -4x^2 + 8x + 2$. Determine the vertex
(30)
and axis of symmetry. Vertex: (1, 6); Axis of symmetry: $x = 1$

Problem 14

Extend the Problem

Explain why the median is a better indicator of the average when there is an outlier in the data. The median is the value in the middle of the ordered data set. It is positional. The value of an extreme data point does not affect the median.

Problem 17

Error Alert

If students choose D, have them see what happens when one parabola opens vertically and the other horizontally. This configuration allows for up to 3 or 4 intersection points.

Lesson 118 823

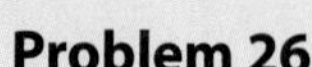

Problem 26

Extend the Problem

"What is the graph of the equation $x = y + 2$?" a line

"What is the graph of the equation $x^2 - y^2 = 16$?" a hyperbola

"How many possible points of intersection are there?" two

Problem 29

Error Alert

Watch for students who include the 4 of diamonds twice and answer 17.

***26.** (117) **Error Analysis** Explain and correct the error(s) a student made in solving the system $\begin{matrix} x = y + 2 \\ x^2 - y^2 = 16 \end{matrix}$.

$(y + 2)^2 - y^2 = 16$	$x = y + 2$
$y^2 + 4y + 4 - y^2 = 16$	$x = 3 + 2$
$4y + 4 = 16$	$x = 5$
$y = 3$	The solution is (3, 5).

26. The student wrote the coordinates in the wrong order. The solution is (5, 3).

***27.** (85) Use the Rational Root Theorem to find the roots of $y = 2x^7 - x^6 - 15x^5 + 18x^4 - 2x^3 + x^2 + 15x - 18$. $x = -3, -1, 1, 1.5, 2$

28. (108) **Coordinate Geometry** The graphs of $y_1 = \tan^2(x)$ and $y_2 = \sec^2(x)$ are shown at right. The graph of y_1 has a y-intercept of 0, and the graph of y_2 has a y-intercept of 1. Use the graphs to prove the trigonometric identity, $1 + \tan^2(x) = \sec^2(x)$. At any point x, $\sec^2(x) - \tan^2(x) = 1$ coincides with $1 + \tan^2(x) = \sec^2(x)$.

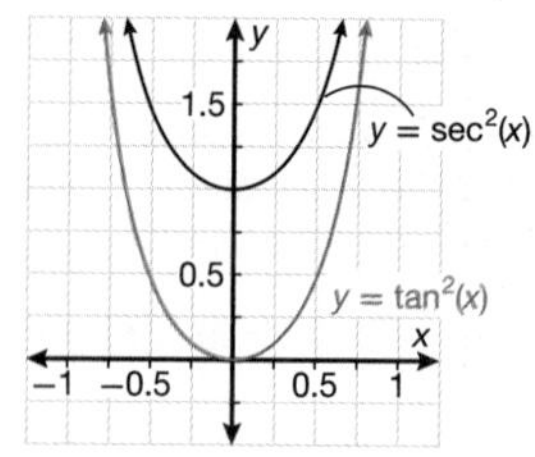

29. (33) A card is drawn at random from a standard deck. How many outcomes are in the event of drawing a diamond or a 4? 13 diamonds + three 4's (excluding the 4 of diamonds) = 16 possible outcomes.

30. (42) Evaluate $4! \cdot 6!$ 17,280

LOOKING FORWARD

Recognizing misleading data will be further developed in other Saxon Secondary Math courses.

LESSON 119

Solving Trigonometric Equations

Warm Up

1. (28) **Vocabulary** An identity is an equation that is true for all values of the variable.

2. (23) What is the only positive solution of $x^2 - 9 = 8x$? 9

3. (108) Complete the trigonometric identity $\sin^2 x + \cos^2 x =$ 1.

4. (108) What is the reciprocal trigonometric identity for $\sin\theta$? $\frac{1}{\csc\theta}$

New Concepts

When solving trigonometric equations, use the same methods for solving algebraic equations and apply the inverse trigonometric functions.

Graphing Calculator

Check your answers by graphing $y = 4\cos\theta - 1$ and $y = 3\cos\theta$ on the same screen over the interval $0° \leq x \leq 360°$, then find any points of intersection.

The graphs intersect at $\theta = 0$, 360°.

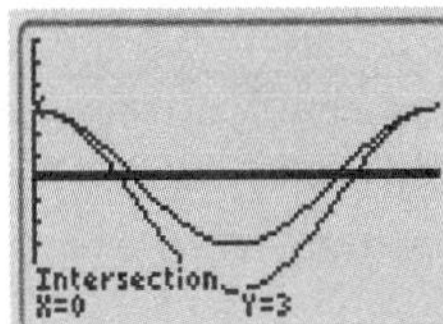

Example 1 Solving Trigonometric Equations with Infinitely Many Solutions Algebraically

Find all the solutions of $4\cos\theta - 1 = 3\cos\theta$.

SOLUTION

Solve for θ such that $0° \leq \theta \leq 360°$ over the principal values of the cosine.

$4\cos\theta - 1 = 3\cos\theta$ Subtract $3\cos\theta$ from both sides.

$\cos\theta - 1 = 0$ Add 1 to both sides.

$\cos\theta = 1$ Apply the inverse cosine.

$\theta = \cos^{-1}(1)$, 360° $\theta = 0°$ when $0° \leq \theta \leq 360°$

$\theta = 0° + 360°n$ when n is any integer

Example 2 Solving Trigonometric Equations in Quadratic Form

Find the exact solutions for each equation.

a. $2\sin^2 x - 2\sin x = 1 - 3\sin x$ for $0° \leq x \leq 360°$

SOLUTION

$2\sin^2 x - 2\sin x = 1 - 3\sin x$ Subtract 1 from both sides. Add $3\sin x$ to both sides.

$2\sin^2 x + \sin x - 1 = 0$ Factor by comparing to $2z^2 + z - 1 = 0$ where $z = \sin x$.

$(2\sin x - 1)(\sin x + 1) = 0$ Apply the Zero Product Property. Apply the inverse sine to each equation.

$2\sin x - 1 = 0$ or $\sin x + 1 = 0$

$\sin x = \frac{1}{2}$ $\sin x = -1$

$x = 30°, 150°$ $x = 270°$

$2\sin^2 x - 2\sin x = 1 - 3\sin x$ when $x = 30°$, 150° and 270°

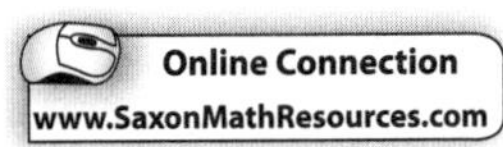
Online Connection www.SaxonMathResources.com

MATH BACKGROUND

To solve a trigonometric equation algebraically, it is helpful to first treat the trigonometric function as a variable. After isolating the trigonometric function, solve for the actual variable.

Some trigonometric equations have no solution. A simple example is $2\sin\theta = 6$. Isolating the trigonometric function yields $\sin\theta = 3$, which has no solution because the greatest possible sine value is 1.

If an equation does have a solution, and there is no domain specified, then the equation has an infinite number of solutions because the trigonometric functions are periodic. For example, two solutions of the equation $2\sin\theta = 1$ are $\theta = \frac{\pi}{6}$ and $\theta = \frac{5\pi}{6}$. If no domain is specified, then the domain is unrestricted, and the solutions are given by $\frac{\pi}{6} + 2n\pi$, $\frac{5\pi}{6} + 2n\pi$, where n is any integer.

LESSON 119

1 Warm Up

Use the Warm Up to review the trigonometric identities for this lesson.

2 New Concepts

In this lesson, trigonometric equations are solved algebraically and graphically.

Example 1

Students learn how to solve trigonometric equations with infinite solutions by using algebra.

Extend the Example

Ask students to describe all the solutions in radian measure. $\theta = 0 + 2\pi n$, where n is any integer.

Additional Example 1

Find all the solutions of $\sin\theta + 2 = 2\sin\theta + 3$. $\theta = -90° + 360°n$, where n is any integer.

Example 2

In this example, two equations in quadratic form are solved, one by factoring and the other by the quadratic formula.

Additional Example 2

a. Find the exact solutions for $3\tan^2 x - \tan x = 2\tan^2 x - 2\tan x$, where $0° \leq x < 360°$. 0°, 135°, 180°, 315°

LESSON RESOURCES

Student Edition Practice Workbook 119
Reteaching Master 119
Adaptations Master 119
Challenge and Enrichment Master C119

Additional Example 2

b. Find the exact solutions for $12\cos^2 z - 1 = -5\cos z$, where $0 \le z < \pi$. Approximate each solution to the nearest hundredth.

$z = \text{Cos}^{-1}\left(\frac{-5+\sqrt{73}}{24}\right) \approx$

1.42 radians

$z = \text{Cos}^{-1}\left(\frac{-5-\sqrt{73}}{24}\right) \approx$

2.17 radians

Error Alert In Example 2b, students might solve the quadratic equation for tan z and then stop, writing the results as the solutions. Remind them to apply the inverse tangent function to those results to obtain the solutions.

Example 3

A trigonometric identity and factoring are used to solve an equation in quadratic form.

Additional Example 3

Use a trigonometric identity to find the exact solutions for $\cos 2\theta = 3\sin\theta + 2$, where $0 \le \theta < 2\pi$. $\frac{7\pi}{6}, \frac{3\pi}{2}, \frac{11\pi}{6}$

b. $\tan^2 z - 3\tan z = 5$ for $-\frac{\pi}{2} < z < \frac{\pi}{2}$

SOLUTION Use the Quadratic Formula.

$\tan^2 z - 3\tan z = 5$ — Subtract 5 from both sides.

$\tan^2 z - 3\tan z - 5 = 0$ — Substitute 1 for *a*, −3 for *b*, and −5 for *c*, into the Quadratic Formula and Simplify.

$$\tan z = \frac{-(-3) \pm \sqrt{(-3)^2 - 4(1)(-5)}}{2(1)}$$

$$\tan z = \frac{3 \pm \sqrt{29}}{2}$$

Apply the inverse tangent to each equation. Use a calculator.

$$z = \text{Tan}^{-1}\left(\frac{3+\sqrt{29}}{2}\right)$$

$$\approx 1.34 \text{ radians or } z = \text{Tan}^{-1}\left(\frac{3-\sqrt{29}}{2}\right) \approx -0.87 \text{ radians}$$

$\tan^2 z - 3\tan z = 5$ when $z = 1.34$ and -0.87 radians

Hint

Note that the range of the sine and cosine functions is −1 to 1, but the range of the tangent function is all real numbers. So, the domain of the inverse tangent function includes numbers less than −1 and greater than 1.

When solving equations involving more than one function, trigonometric identities often can be used to write the equation with only one trigonometric function.

Example 3 Solving Trigonometric Equations with Trigonometric Identities

Use trigonometric identities to find the exact solutions.

$2\sin^2\theta + 2 = 3 - \cos\theta$ for $0 \le \theta < 2\pi$.

SOLUTION

$$2\sin^2\theta + 2 = 3 - \cos\theta$$

$2(1 - \cos^2\theta) + 2 = 3 - \cos\theta$ — Use the trig identity $\sin^2\theta + \cos^2\theta = 1$ to replace $\sin^2\theta$

$-2\cos^2\theta + \cos\theta + 1 = 0$ — Distribute and collect terms on the left side.

$2\cos^2\theta - \cos\theta - 1 = 0$ — Divide both sides by −1.

$(2\cos\theta + 1)(\cos\theta - 1) = 0.$ — Factor terms.

$2\cos\theta + 1 = 0$ or $\cos\theta - 1 = 0$ — Apply Zero Product Property.

$\cos\theta = -\frac{1}{2}$ or $\cos\theta = 1$ — Solve for θ, when $0 \le \theta < 2\pi$

$$\theta = \frac{2\pi}{3} \text{ or } \frac{4\pi}{3} \text{ or } \theta = 0$$

Hint

Your goal is to have only one trigonometric function in the resulting equation.

INCLUSION

Show these labels for Example 3.

$\sin^2\theta + \cos^2\theta = 1$ ← Identity

$\sin^2\theta = 1 - \cos^2\theta$

$2\sin^2\theta + 2 = 3 - \cos\theta$ ← Equation

$2(\sin^2\theta) + 2 = 3 - \cos\theta$

↑ Expression ($\sin^2\theta$)

$2(1 - \cos^2\theta) + 2 = 3 - \cos\theta$

↑ Expression ($1 - \cos^2\theta$)

Example 4 Solving Trigonometric Equations Using a Graphing Calculator

Graphing Calculator Tip

When entering equations, Theta (θ) will display on most calculators only if the calculator is in polar mode. Do NOT use polar mode. Instead, simply note that the variable is x.

Find all the solutions of $3\tan\theta - 3 = \tan\theta - 1$ for $-\frac{\pi}{2} < \theta < \frac{\pi}{2}$ using a graphing calculator.

SOLUTION

Graph $y = 3\tan\theta - 3$ and $y = \tan\theta - 1$ in the same viewing window for $-\frac{\pi}{2} < \theta < \frac{\pi}{2}$.

Find the intersection of the two graphs using the calc menu on your calculator.

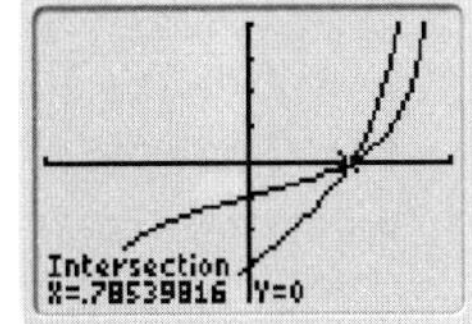

Between $-\frac{\pi}{2}$ and $\frac{\pi}{2}$ the graphs only intersect at $\theta \approx 0.7854$. Therefore the only solution to $3\tan\theta - 3 = \tan\theta - 1$ for $-\frac{\pi}{2} \le \theta < \frac{\pi}{2}$ is $\theta \approx 0.7854$.

Example 5 Application: Migratory Populations

The number of goldfinches in a coastal county of New England varies cyclically over the course of the year as the birds migrate. The approximate number of goldfinches in the county can be modeled by $P(t) = 250\cos\left(\frac{\pi}{6}(t + 6)\right) + 250$, where P is the number of birds and t is number of months. In which month does the population first reach 375 birds?

SOLUTION

1. **Understand** The number of birds during each month can be found by substituting the approximate value (1–12) for t.

2. **Plan** To find the month or months in which the population reaches 375 birds, you need to substitute 375 for $P(t)$ and solve for t.

3. **Solve**

$$250\cos\left(\frac{\pi}{6}(t + 6)\right) + 250 = 375$$ Substitute 375 for $P(t)$.

$$250\cos\left(\frac{\pi}{6}(t + 6)\right) = 125$$ Subtract 250 from both sides.

$$\cos\left(\frac{\pi}{6}(t + 6)\right) = \frac{1}{2}$$ Divide each side by 250.

$$\frac{\pi}{6}(t + 6) = \cos^{-1}\left(\frac{1}{2}\right)$$ Apply the inverse cosine.

$$\cos^{-1}\left(\frac{1}{2}\right) = \frac{\pi}{3}\left(\text{or } \frac{5\pi}{3}, \frac{7\pi}{3}, \frac{11\pi}{3}, \ldots\right)$$

$$\frac{\pi}{6}(t + 6) = \frac{\pi}{3} \Rightarrow t = -4$$ Test $\frac{\pi}{3}$. not a solution because $1 \le t \le 12$.

$$\frac{\pi}{6}(t + 6) = \frac{5\pi}{3} \Rightarrow t = 4$$ Test $\frac{5\pi}{3}$. $t = 4$ is the solution

The population first reaches 375 birds in April.

Hint

$\cos\theta = \frac{1}{2}$ for $\theta = \frac{\pi}{3}, \frac{5\pi}{3}, \frac{7\pi}{3}, \frac{11\pi}{3} \ldots$ therefore $\cos^{-1}\left(\frac{1}{2}\right) = \frac{\pi}{3}$ and also $\frac{5\pi}{3}, \frac{7\pi}{3}, \frac{11\pi}{3} \ldots$

Example 4

The CALCULATE/intersect feature on a graphing calculator is used to solve an equation.

Additional Example 4

Find all the solutions of $3\tan\theta = 2\cos\theta$ using a graphing calculator. $\frac{\pi}{6} + 2n\pi$, $\frac{5\pi}{6} + 2n\pi$, where n is any integer.

Example 5

This example shows how to solve a problem about bird migration.

Extend the Problem

Does the population of birds reach 375 another time after the month of April? If so, when? Yes, August.

Additional Example 5

The monthly sales of a certain product at a retail store is modeled by $f(x) = 20\sin\frac{\pi(x - 5)}{6} + 50$, where $x = 1$ represents January, $x = 2$ represents February, and so on, with $x = 12$ representing December. In what month do the sales first reach 60? June

Lesson Practice

Problem c

Scaffolding First solve the quadratic equation for $\tan z$ using the quadratic formula. Then solve for z using the inverse tangent function.

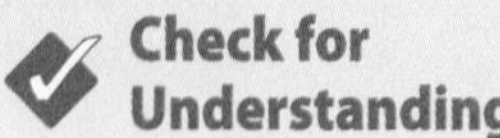

Check for Understanding

The questions below help assess the concepts taught in this lesson.

"Describe how to solve a trigonometric equation that contains a single trigonometric function." Isolate the trigonometric function and then apply the corresponding inverse trigonometric function to solve for the variable.

"Describe how to solve a trigonometric equation that contains more than one trigonometric function." Use one or more trigonometric identities to find an equivalent equation that contains a single trigonometric function; then solve.

"Describe how to solve a trigonometric equation in quadratic form." Use factoring or the quadratic formula to solve for the trigonometric expression. Then use an inverse trigonometric function to solve for the variable.

3 Practice

Math Conversations

Discussions to strengthen understanding

Problem 4

Guide students with the following suggestions and questions.

"For part b, what technique is needed to write the equation in standard form?" Completing the square

"Write an equivalent equation that is suitable for completing the square, including spaces for missing terms."

$x^2 - 8x + \quad + y^2 - 40y + \quad = 209$

4. **Check** Check your answer using a graphing calculator.

Graph: $250 \cos\left(\frac{\pi}{6}(t + 6)\right) + 250 = 375$

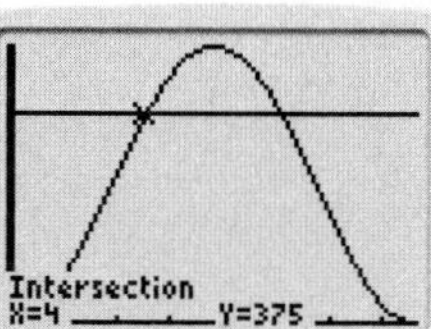

Lesson Practice

a. Find all the solutions of $8 \sin \theta + 1 = 4 \sin \theta - 1$ algebraically. (Ex 1)

$8\sin\theta + 1 = 4\sin\theta - 1 \Rightarrow 4\sin\theta = -2 \Rightarrow \sin\theta = -\frac{1}{2} \Rightarrow \theta = \frac{7\pi}{6} + 2\pi n, \frac{11\pi}{6} + 2\pi n$

b. Solve $4\cos^2 x = 4\cos x - 1$ for $0° \le x < 360°$. (Ex 2)

$4\cos^2 x = 4\cos x - 1 \Rightarrow 4\cos^2 x - 4\cos x + 1 = 0 \Rightarrow (2\cos x - 1)(2\cos x - 1) = 0 \Rightarrow \cos x = \frac{1}{2} \Rightarrow x = \cos^{-1}\left(\frac{1}{2}\right) \Rightarrow x = 60°, 300°$

c. Solve $3 \tan^2 z - \tan z - 3 = 0$ for $-\frac{\pi}{2} < z < \frac{\pi}{2}$. See Additional Answers. (Ex 2)

d. Use trigonometric identities to solve $1 - \cos^2 \theta + 3 \sin \theta = \sin \theta - 1$ for $0° \le \theta < 360°$. See Additional Answers. (Ex 3)

e. Find all the solutions of $\sin \theta - \frac{1}{2} = 2 \sin \theta + \frac{1}{2}$ for $0 \le \theta \le 2\pi$ using a graphing calculator. See Additional Answers. (Ex 4)

f. As in Example 5, in which month of the year does the bird population first reach 125 birds? February (Ex 5)

Practice Distributed and Integrated

1. **Analyze** A polynomial equation has a root of $2 + 3i$ and this root has a multiplicity of 2. What is the least degree that the polynomial can be? Why? (106)
The least degree is 4 because each of those roots has a conjugate pair.

*2. **Write** Describe the difference between an equation and an identity. (119)

2. Sample: An equation need not be true for any values of the variable, but an identity must be true for all values of the variable

3. If a private school's enrollment is 600 students and it increases 5% each year, how long will it take to get 800 students? about 6 years (93)

4. **Multi-Step** The boundary of the set of possible points for the epicenter of an earthquake recorded at an observation station can be represented by the equation $x^2 + y^2 - 8x - 40y - 209 = 0$. (114)
   a. What conic section represents the situation? Circle
   b. Write the equation in standard form. $(x - 4)^2 + (y - 20)^2 = 625$

5. Find the number of combinations of 16 objects taken 12 at a time. 1820 (42)

*6. **Graphing Calculator** Solve $\begin{aligned} 25x^2 + 4.3y^2 &= 89 \\ x^2 + y^2 &= 9.8 \end{aligned}$. Round to the nearest hundredth. (117)
(1.50, 2.75), (−1.50, 2.75), (1.50, −2.75), (−1.50, −2.75)

*7. **Solar Eclipses** For a solar eclipse to be possible, the moon must be near the line between the earth and the sun within 3 days of a new moon. Suppose the cycle of the moon can be modeled by $M(t) = \cos\left(\frac{\pi}{14}t\right)$, where t is the number of days from now. The minimum value of $M(t)$ represents a new moon. How many days from now is the next new moon? When $P(t) = 2\sin^2\left(\frac{\pi}{14}t\right) + \cos\left(\frac{\pi}{14}t\right) - \frac{1}{2}$ equals $M(t)$, the moon is on the line between earth and the sun. Is a solar eclipse possible before the next new moon? Why or why not? Explain. (119)

7. New moon: $\cos\left(\frac{\pi}{14}t\right) = -1 \Rightarrow \frac{\pi}{14}t = \cos^{-1}(-1) = \pi \Rightarrow t = 14$. So, the next new moon will occur 14 days from now. Solar eclipse: Yes, a solar eclipse is possible because the moon will be on the line between the earth and the sun after $11\frac{2}{3}$ days (so, within 3 days of the new moon on day 14).

828 *Saxon Algebra 2*

*8. **Write** When surveying, what are the pros and cons of open questions and closed (118) questions? See Additional Answers.

9. Find the common ratio of the geometric sequence and use it to find the next three (97) terms. 14, 2, $\frac{2}{7}$... $\frac{1}{7}$; $\frac{2}{49}$, $\frac{2}{343}$, $\frac{2}{2401}$

*10. **Data Analysis** What could be misleading about the graph (118) shown? The perspective makes the heights misleading. It looks like the lowest population occurred in year 3 but it was actually lowest in year 1.

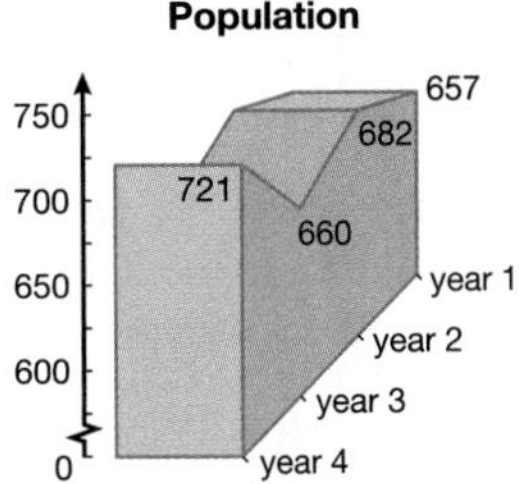

11. Use De Moivre's Theorem to evaluate the complex number $(6 - 7i)^3$ to express the (Inv 11) result in trigonometric form. $783.7\cos(211.8°) + i783.7\sin(211.8°)$

*12. **Model** Sketch diagrams to show how two parabolas can intersect in 0, 1, 2, 3, or (117) 4 points. See Additional Answers.

*13. **Multiple Choice** For what values $0 \le \theta < 2\pi$ does $\sin 2\theta = \sin\theta$? C (119)

A $\theta = \frac{1}{2}$ **B** $\theta = 0, \frac{1}{2}$ **C** $\theta = 0, \frac{\pi}{3}, \pi, \frac{5\pi}{3}$ **D** $\theta = \frac{\pi}{3}, \frac{5\pi}{3}$

14. **Population** The year when the world population reached each billion mark is (116) shown in the table.

Population (billions)	1	2	3	4	5	6
Year	1800	1927	1960	1974	1987	1999

Find a logarithmic function to model the data and use it to predict when the world population will reach 8 billion. $y \approx 1824.4 + 106.48\ln(x)$, 2045

15. **Finance** The monthly rent for an apartment is \$850 the first year. Every year (113) thereafter, the rent increases by 2%. Write a geometric series in summation notation to represent the total rent paid after 10 years. Then find the sum. $\sum_{k=1}^{10} 850(1.02)^{k-1}$, \$9,307.26

*16. **Multiple Choice** Which data set is best modeled by an exponential function? B (116)

A {(1, −16), (2, −12), (3, −8), (4, −4), (5, 0)}

B {(1, −16), (2, −8), (3, −4), (4, −2), (5, −1)}

C {(1, −16), (2, 0), (3, 16), (4, 32), (5, 48)}

D {(1, −16), (2, −64), (3, −144), (4, −256), (5, −400)}

17. **Manufacturing** The horizontal distance x traveled by a golf ball struck from (115) ground level with an initial speed v and angle θ is given by $x = \frac{1}{32}v^2\sin 2\theta$. The rule determined by the United States Golf Association states that the initial velocity of a golf ball cannot exceed 255 feet per second when tested under specified conditions. If a ball is manufactured with the highest allowed initial velocity, use the equation to determine the horizontal distance of the ball if it is hit at an angle of 45°. 2032.03 feet

Problem 13

Error Alert

If students divide both sides of the equation by $\sin\theta$, they will eliminate $\sin\theta$ and possibly "lose" the solution $\theta = 0$.

Incorrect method:

$$\sin 2\theta = \sin\theta$$
$$2\sin\theta\cos\theta = \sin\theta$$
$$\frac{2\sin\theta\cos\theta}{\sin\theta} = \frac{\sin\theta}{\sin\theta}$$
$$2\cos\theta = 1$$

Correct method:

$$\sin 2\theta = \sin\theta$$
$$2\sin\theta\cos\theta = \sin\theta$$
$$2\sin\theta\cos\theta - \sin\theta = 0$$
$$\sin\theta(2\cos\theta - 1) = 0$$
$$\sin\theta = 0 \text{ or } 2\cos\theta - 1 = 0$$
$$\sin\theta = 0 \text{ or } \cos\theta = \frac{1}{2}$$
$$\left\{0, \frac{\pi}{3}, \pi, \frac{5\pi}{3}\right\}$$

Problem 16

In each choice, the x-values increase by a constant amount. Therefore, students can focus on changes in the y-values.

ENGLISH LEARNERS

For Problem 8, explain the meaning of the phrase **pros** and **cons**. Say,

"Pros and cons are associated with an idea, method, task, situation, etc. The pros are the advantages. The cons are the disadvantages."

Have students name a pro and a con of using a backpack. Sample: A pro is the ability to carry items easier; A con is the time it takes to fill it.

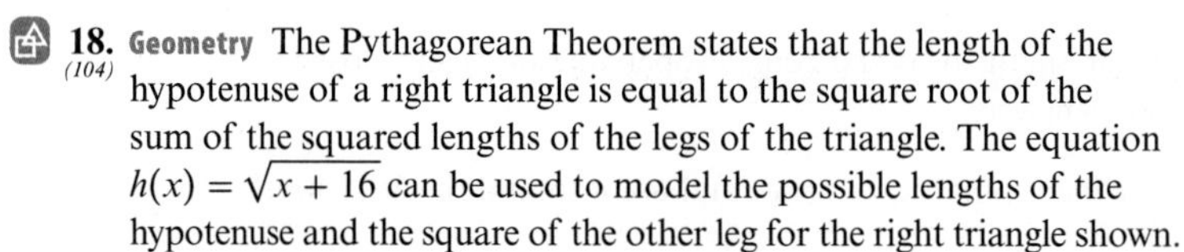

Problem 26

Extend the Problem

Have students write the given expression and its simplest form without using radical symbols. $5(48)^{\frac{1}{3}} - 750^{\frac{1}{3}} = 5(6)^{\frac{1}{3}}$

Problem 29

TEACHER TIP

Have students discuss alternative ways to collect the sample data and determine which method will exhibit unbiased data.

18. (104) **Geometry** The Pythagorean Theorem states that the length of the hypotenuse of a right triangle is equal to the square root of the sum of the squared lengths of the legs of the triangle. The equation $h(x) = \sqrt{x + 16}$ can be used to model the possible lengths of the hypotenuse and the square of the other leg for the right triangle shown. Use $f(x) = \sqrt{x}$ to find the graph of $h(x) = \sqrt{x + 16}$. Then use the graph of $h(x)$ to find two possibilities for the lengths of the other leg and the hypotenuse. See Additional Answers.

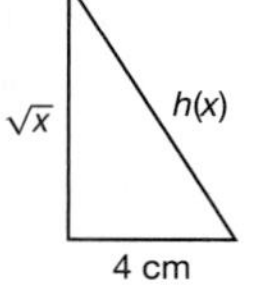

19. (107) **Formulate** The graph of a rational function includes the asymptote shown to the right. Write an equation that fits these parameters. Sample: $y = \frac{x^2 + 2x - 1}{x - 1}$

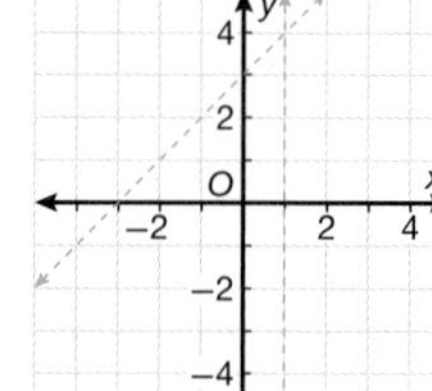

20. (110) **Multi-Step** Let $f(x) = 12\log(4x)$ and $g(x) = \frac{x + 2}{(x^4 - 1)}$. Find the x-intercepts of $f(g(x))$. $x = -1.3698, 2.0347$

21. (87) **Temperature** Using Newton's Law of Cooling $T = e^{(kt+C)} + R$, determine the amount of time needed to cool a cup of water (80ºC) to 50ºC in a room temperature of 30ºC. Use $k = -0.200064$ and $C = 4.0073$. $t \approx 5.06$ minutes

22. (102) **Error Analysis** A student solved $\log 2x + \log 4 = 3$ as shown. What is the error? What is the correct solution? $\log 2x + \log 4 \neq \log(2x + 4)$; Correct solution: 125

$$\log 2x + \log 4 = 3 \rightarrow \log(2x + 4) = 3 \rightarrow 2x + 4 = 1000 \rightarrow x = 498$$

23. (105) The common difference in an arithmetic series is 8 and the first term is −160. Find the sum of the first 40 terms. −160

Find the roots of the equations.

24. (100) $y = 6x^4 - 4x^3 - 8x^2 + 4x + 2$ $x = \pm 1, -\frac{1}{3}$

25. (100) $y = 15x^4 - 16x^3 - 56x^2 + 64x - 16$ $x = \pm 2, \frac{2}{5}, \frac{2}{3}$

Write the expression in simplest form.

26. (40) $5\sqrt[3]{48} - \sqrt[3]{750}$ $5\sqrt[3]{6}$

27. (40) $\frac{\sqrt[4]{36} \cdot \sqrt[4]{9}}{\sqrt[4]{4}}$ 3

***28.** (119) **Multi-Step** Consider the equation $3\tan^2 z + 2\tan z - 1 = 0$.

a. What values of $-90° \leq z \leq 90°$ satisfy the equation? $z = 18.43°$ and $-45°$

b. For how many of the values of z that satisfy the equation does $\sin z = \cos z$? none

***29.** (118) **Error Analysis** A student with a part-time job at a movie theater uses ticket stubs he found on the floor to collect data about the types of movies people watch on different days. He says that he takes a simple random sample of the stubs he finds, so his sample cannot be biased. Find the error in the student's reasoning.

29. The stubs he finds on the floor to begin with are not a random sample, they are a convenience sample because the stubs are those that are convenient to use. People who attend certain types of movies may be more likely to toss their stubs on the floor, rather than tossing them in the trash can, or taking them home.

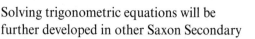

30. (45) The data in the table is represented by an exponential function. Use the data to solve for the correlation coefficient, r. 0.9999

Time (in years)	1	2	3	4	5
Bunnies	30	100	335	1100	3650

CHALLENGE

Solve $5\cos^2 x = 4 - 5\cos x$, where $0 \leq x < \pi$, and explain your method.

The only solution is

$x = \text{Cos}^{-1}\left(\frac{-5 + \sqrt{105}}{10}\right) \approx 1.02$ radians. The other result from the quadratic formula is

$\cos x = \left(\frac{-5 - \sqrt{105}}{10}\right) \cdot \left(\frac{-5 - \sqrt{105}}{10}\right) \approx -1.52$, so

$\text{Cos}^{-1}\left(\frac{-5 - \sqrt{105}}{10}\right)$ does not exist.

LOOKING FORWARD

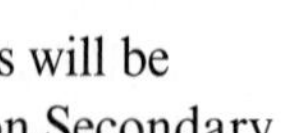

Solving trigonometric equations will be further developed in other Saxon Secondary Math courses.

INVESTIGATION

12

Using Mathematical Induction

A mathematical proof is true for all values that relate to the proof. This is what makes a mathematical proof a powerful tool. One type of mathematical proof is **mathematical induction**.

In an arithmetic sequence the value of each term a_k can be calculated based on its position k in the sequence. For the sequence of consecutive integers the formula for each term is $a_k = k$. The sum of consecutive integers 1 to n can be calculated using this formula,

$$\sum_{k=1}^{n} k = \frac{n(n+1)}{2}.$$

1. Show that this formula works for $n = 10, 20,$ and 30. Check students' work.
2. Why is the formula a better way of calculating the result? As n gets larger in value, the number of calculations is still the same.

While you can show that this formula works for *any* value of n, a mathematical proof needs to show that this formula works for *every* value of n. Proof by mathematical induction is a three-step process.

Step 1: Show that the base case is true.

3. **Verify** Show that the base case $n = 1$ is true. Check students' work.

Step 2: Assume the case is true for an arbitrary number of terms, represented by m.

4. Rewrite the formula using m instead of n. $\sum_{k=1}^{m} k = \frac{m(m+1)}{2}$

Step 3: Show that the formula is true for $m + 1$.

5. Add the next term a_{m+1} to the formula from question 4 and simplify the expression. See Additional Answers.
6. **Verify** Show that the new expression from question 5 is the result of the summation formula for $m + 1$. See Additional Answers.
7. When all three steps are true, then the mathematical proof is complete through the process of induction. Is $\sum_{k=1}^{n} k = \frac{n(n+1)}{2}$ true? Yes

Suppose that you want to generate the formula for adding consecutive even numbers. For example, the sum of consecutive even integers is shown for the first six even numbers:

$$0 = 0$$
$$0 + 2 = 2$$
$$0 + 2 + 4 = 6$$
$$0 + 2 + 4 + 6 = 12$$
$$0 + 2 + 4 + 6 + 8 = 20$$
$$0 + 2 + 4 + 6 + 8 + 10 = 30$$

Online Connection
www.SaxonMathResources.com

INVESTIGATION

12

Materials

Pencil and paper

Discuss

Students will prove statements using the three step process of mathematical induction.

Define **mathematical induction.**

TEACHER TIP

Verify that students are writing all three steps. The proof is not complete until all steps are written.

Students sometimes have difficulty with step 3. To show that the formula is true for the next integer or $m + 1$:

1. Add the formula for m terms to the next term of $m + 1$ to get $\frac{m(m+1)}{2} + (m + 1)$.
2. Generate the formula for $m + 1$.
$$\sum_{k=1}^{m+1} k = \frac{(m+1)((m+1)+1)}{2}$$
3. The goal is to show algebraically that $\frac{(m+1)((m+1)+1)}{2} = \frac{m(m+1)}{2} + (m + 1)$.

MATH BACKGROUND

Mathematical induction is an example of deductive reasoning. Euclid first used induction in an informal way, but the steps we use today were developed in the 1500's. Mathematical induction consists of three rigid steps. The process is begun by showing a formula is true for a given value, usually 0 or 1. The inductive steps involve assuming that the formula is true for an integer, m, and then showing that it is true for the next integer, $m + 1$. If the formula is valid for the next integer, then by repetition it will also be true for the next integer and the next integer, etc. In this way, the statement is proven true for all values. Mathematical induction is a good tool for proving the validity of a formula that is thought to be true.

INVESTIGATION RESOURCES

Reteaching Master Investigation 12

8. Write a formula that can be used to generate even numbers only for any integer value of k. $a_k = 2k$

9. Write the summation expression that uses Σ and the expression from question 8 that can be used to find the sum of consecutive even integers. $\sum_{k=1}^{n} 2k$

10. Find the general form that does not use Σ that can be used to find the sum of n consecutive even integers for any value of n. $n(n + 1)$

The sum of consecutive even integers from 0 to n can be calculated using this formula,

$$\sum_{k=1}^{n} 2k = n(n + 1).$$

Hint

For Problem 12c, substitute $m + 1$ in the original formula $\sum_{k=0}^{n} 2k$.

11. Show that this formula works for $n = 10$, 20, and 30. Check students' work.

12. To show that this formula works for every value of n, use mathematical induction.

   a. Show that this formula works for the base case of $n = 1$. Check students' work.
   b. Assume that the formula works for value m, and rewrite the formula. $m(m + 1)$
   c. Show that the formula still works for $m + 1$. See Additional Answers.

Investigation Practice

Suppose that you want to generate the formula for adding the set of consecutive odd integers from 1 to n.

c. $\sum_{k=1}^{n} (2k - 1)$

a. Generate the first five sums of this series. Check students' work.
b. Write a formula that can be used to generate odd numbers only for any value of k. $a_k = 2k - 1$
c. Write the summation expression that uses Σ and the expression from problem **b** that can be used to find the sum of consecutive odd integers.
d. Find the general form that does not use Σ that can be used to find the sum of n consecutive odd integers for any value of n. n^2

Use mathematical induction to prove the formula from problem **a**.

e. Show that this formula works for the base case of $n = 1$. Check students' work.
f. Assume that the formula works for value m, and rewrite the formula. m^2
g. Show that the formula still works for $m + 1$. See Additional Answers.

TEACHER TIP

Note that $n(n + 1)$ and the summation formula represents a sum. The summation formula can be expressed as a series.

Investigation Practice

Math Conversations

Discussions to strengthen understanding

Problem a

Point out to students that the sums are perfect squares. The formula should generate consecutive perfect squares.

Problem g

Show students that $(m + 1)^2 = m^2 + [2(m + 1) - 1]$

INCLUSION

Discuss and explain the process of mathematical induction. Compare the process to a set of dominoes set up in a row. If the first domino falls, the next one will fall, etc. Convey to the students that a mathematical induction proof proves a statement true for one value, and then the next one, etc. Therefore the statement is true for every value.

ENGLISH LEARNERS

Explain the meaning of the word **consecutive.** Say,

"If the numbers in a set of numbers are consecutive, then each number follows one after another. The numbers 4, 5, and 6 are consecutive."

Have students name situations where events occur consecutively. Sample: class periods, public transportation bus departures

i. Incorrect formula,; The correct formula is $\frac{5n(n+1)}{2}$.

Use mathematical induction to prove or disprove the following formulas. For formulas that are incorrect, determine if there is a correct formula.

h. The sum of consecutive multiples of 3 The formula is true.

$$\sum_{k=1}^{n} 3k = \frac{3n(n+1)}{2}.$$

i. The sum of consecutive multiples of 5:

$$\sum_{k=1}^{n} 5k = \frac{n(n+1)}{5}.$$

j. Generate the formula for finding the sum of the consecutive numbers that are divisible by both 3 and 5. Use mathematical induction to prove the formula. $\sum_{k=1}^{n} 15k = \frac{15n(n+1)}{2}$; Sample: The LCM of 3 and 5 is 15. To find the formula for the sum of consecutive numbers divisible by 3 and 5, find the formula for the sum of consecutive numbers divisible by 15: $\sum_{k=1}^{n} 15k = \frac{15n(n+1)}{2}$.

Problem i

Remind students to start with the base case. If the statement fails the first step, the statement is incorrect.

Problem j

If a number is divisible by 3 and 5, it is also divisible by 15.

Investigation 12 833

APPENDIX LESSON 1

Changes in Measure

New Concepts

Use the formulas for area, surface area, and volume to determine how changes in measure affect other measures.

Example 1 Determining How Changes in Measure Affect Area

a. The length of a rectangle is doubled. What is the change in the area of the rectangle?

SOLUTION

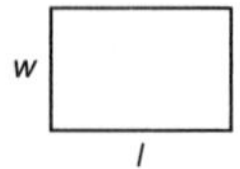

The area of the rectangle before the length is doubled is $A = lw$.

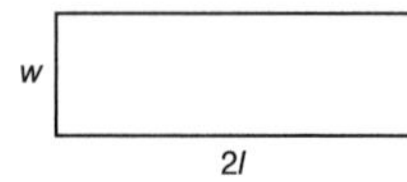

The area of the rectangle after the length is doubled is $A = (2l)w$. Using the Associative Property of Multiplication, you can express the area as:

$$A = 2(lw)$$

When the length of a rectangle is doubled, the area of the rectangle is also doubled.

Hint

Remember, the Associative Property of Multiplication states that for any real numbers, a, b, and c:

$a(bc) = (ab)c$

b. The length and width of a rectangle are each doubled. What is the change in the area of the rectangle?

SOLUTION The area of the rectangle before the length and width are doubled is $A = lw$. The area of the rectangle after the length and width are doubled is $A = (2l)(2w)$. Using the Commutative and Associative Properties of Multiplication, the area can be expressed as:

$$A = 4(lw)$$

When the length and width of a rectangle are doubled, the area of the rectangle is four times the original area.

Predict

What do you think the change in area will be if the length and width are tripled?

The new area will be nine times the original.

834 Saxon Algebra 2

Example 2 Determining How Changes in Measure Affect Surface Area and Volume

a. The length of the side of a cube is halved. What is the change in the surface area and volume of the cube?

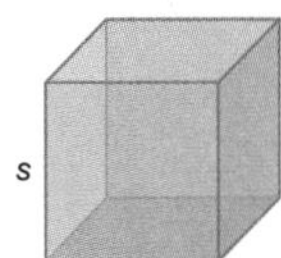

SOLUTION

$\frac{1}{2}s$

The surface area of the cube before the side is halved is $SA = 6s^2$.
The volume of the cube before the side is halved is $V = s^3$.

Surface Area	Volume
The surface area of the cube after the side is halved is: $SA = 6\left(\frac{1}{2}s\right)^2 = 6\left(\frac{1}{4}s^2\right) = \frac{1}{4}(6s^2)$ When the side of a cube is halved, the surface area is $\left(\frac{1}{2}\right)^2$ or $\frac{1}{4}$ of the original surface area.	The volume of the cube after the side is halved is: $V = \left(\frac{1}{2}s\right)^3 = \left(\frac{1}{8}s^3\right) = \frac{1}{8}(s^3)$ When the side of a cube is halved, the volume is $\left(\frac{1}{2}\right)^3$ or $\frac{1}{8}$ of the original volume.

b. The height of a cylinder is tripled. What is the change in the volume of the cylinder?

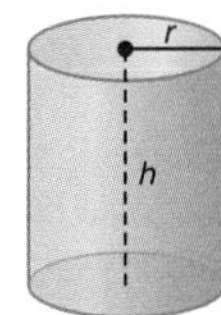

Generalize

If the height of a cylinder is multiplied by any positive real number, how does the volume of the cylinder change?

The volume is multiplied by the same number.

SOLUTION

The volume of the cylinder before the height is tripled is $V = \pi r^2 h$.

The volume of the cylinder after the height is tripled is:

$$V = \pi r^2(3h) = 3(\pi r^2 h).$$

When the height of a cylinder is tripled, the volume is tripled.

APPENDIX LESSONS

Appendix Lesson 1 835

c. The diameter of a sphere is doubled. What is the change in the surface area of the sphere?

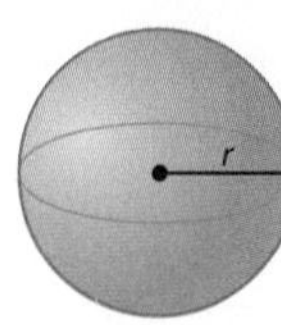

SOLUTION

The surface area of the sphere before the diameter is doubled is $SA = 4\pi r^2$.

When the diameter of a sphere is doubled, the radius is also doubled.

The surface area of the sphere after the diameter is doubled is:

$$4\pi(2r)^2 = 4\pi(4r^2) = 16\pi r^2 = 4(4\pi r^2)$$

When the diameter of a sphere is doubled, the surface area is quadrupled, or 4 times the original surface area.

d. If each dimension of a rectangular prism is halved, what will be the change in the volume of the prism?

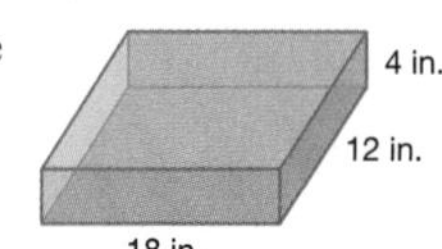

SOLUTION

The volume of the rectangular prism before the changes in measure is $V = (18)(12)(4) = 864$ cubic inches.

The volume of the rectangular prism after the changes in measure is $V = \left(\frac{18}{2}\right)\left(\frac{12}{2}\right)\left(\frac{4}{2}\right) = (9)(6)(2) = 108$ cubic inches.

The new volume is $\left(\frac{1}{2}\right)^3$ or $\frac{1}{8}$ the original volume.

Example 3 Application: Sports

The diameter of a softball is about 1.5 times the diameter of a baseball. What is the relationship between the volumes of the balls?

SOLUTION Softballs and baseballs are spheres. The formula for the volume of a sphere is $V = \frac{4}{3}\pi r^3$. If the diameter of a softball is 1.5 times the diameter of a baseball, then the radius of the softball is also 1.5 times the radius of the baseball.

Let r represent the radius of the baseball and $1.5r$ represent the radius of the softball. Then the volume of the softball is:

$$V = \frac{4}{3}\pi(1.5r)^3 = \frac{4}{3}\pi(3.375r^3) = 3.375\left(\frac{4}{3}\pi r^3\right)$$

The volume of the softball is $(1.5)^3$ or 3.375 times the volume of the baseball.

Generalize

If the diameter of one sphere is x times the diameter of another sphere, then the radius of the first is also x times the radius of the second.

836 Saxon Algebra 2

Lesson Practice

a. (Ex 1) The height of a triangle is doubled. What is the change in the area of the triangle? The area is doubled.

b. (Ex 1) The bases and height of a trapezoid are tripled. What is the change in the area of the trapezoid? The new area is nine times the original area.

c. (Ex 2) The length of each side of a cube is divided by 5. What is the change in the surface area and volume of the cube?

d. (Ex 2) The height of a cone is quadrupled. What is the change in the volume of the cone? The volume is quadrupled.

e. (Ex 2) The radius of a sphere is tripled. What is the change in the volume of the sphere? The new volume is 27 times the volume of the original sphere.

f. (Ex 2) A rectangular prism is 12 feet long, 8.2 feet wide, and 4 feet high. The length and height are halved. What is the change in the volume of the prism? The volume is one-fourth the original volume.

g. (Ex 3) The diameter of one circular pool is twice the diameter of a second circular pool. The height of both pools is 4 feet. What is the relationship between the volumes of the pools? The volume of the larger pool is four times the volume of the smaller pool.

c. The surface area is $\frac{1}{25}$ the original surface area. The volume is $\frac{1}{125}$ the original volume.

APPENDIX LESSONS

Appendix Lesson 1 837

APPENDIX LESSON 2

Computer Spreadsheets

New Concepts

An **electronic spreadsheet** is used to organize and manipulate data. Formulas and functions can be used to perform arithmetic and logical operations on the data in a spreadsheet.

Spreadsheets contain rows and columns of information, just as tables and matrices do. Rows are labeled with numbers and columns are labeled with letters. The intersection of a row and a column is called a **cell.** Each cell has a unique label known as the **cell address.** For example, the cell in the first row and first column of the spreadsheet has the address A1. The cell in the fifth row and third column has the address C5. To enter data in a cell, click on the cell and type in the data.

Connect

Remember, array elements are named using their row and column. Spreadsheet elements, called cells, are also named using their row and column.

Example 1 Creating a Computer Spreadsheet

For two consecutive years, a cyclist recorded the number of miles he rode during training each month. His recorded information is shown below. Store the information in a computer spreadsheet.

Handwritten Record of Miles Biked

	Miles Biked	
Month	Year 1	Year 2
Jan	200	230
Feb	150	220
Mar	324	325
Apr	278	256
May	200	155
Jun	199	178
Jul	125	188
Aug	145	130
Sep	180	167
Oct	178	224
Nov	230	231
Dec	120	101

SOLUTION

Enter the data into a spreadsheet. If a mistake is made while entering the data, retype the data by moving out of the cell and then back into it, or edit the data in the formula bar.

H16 ▾ fx

	A	B	C	D	E
1		Year 1	Year 2	Difference	
2	Jan	200	230		
3	Feb	150	220		
4	Mar	324	325		
5	Apr	278	256		
6	May	200	155		
7	Jun	199	178		
8	Jul	125	188		
9	Aug	145	130		
10	Sep	180	167		
11	Oct	178	224		
12	Nov	230	231		
13	Dec	120	101		
14					

Formulas and functions are used to manipulate data in the spreadsheet. A formula is like an expression. It can be used to perform arithmetic operations on the data in the spreadsheet.

838 Saxon Algebra 2

APPENDIX LESSONS

Example 2 Using a Formula in a Spreadsheet

Using the spreadsheet created in Example 1, find the difference between the distances the cyclist biked each month from year 1 to year 2.

SOLUTION Create a formula to calculate the difference. To subtract the number of miles in January of year 1 from the number of miles in January of year 2, type the formula =C2−B2 in cell D2.

D2 =C2-B2

	A	B	C	D	E
1		Year 1	Year 2	Difference	
2	Jan	200	230	30	
3	Feb	150	220		
4	Mar	324	325		
5	Apr	278	256		
6	May	200	155		
7	Jun	199	178		
8	Jul	125	188		
9	Aug	145	130		
10	Sep	180	167		
11	Oct	178	224		
12	Nov	230	231		
13	Dec	120	101		
14					

Now copy the formula in cell D2 to the remaining cells. The spreadsheet will automatically adjust the formula to use the data in the corresponding row.

I13

	A	B	C	D	E
1		Year 1	Year 2	Difference	
2	Jan	200	230	30	
3	Feb	150	220	70	
4	Mar	324	325	1	
5	Apr	278	256	-22	
6	May	200	155	-45	
7	Jun	199	178	-21	
8	Jul	125	188	63	
9	Aug	145	130	-15	
10	Sep	180	167	-13	
11	Oct	178	224	46	
12	Nov	230	231	1	
13	Dec	120	101	-19	
14					

Example 3 Using a Function in a Spreadsheet

a. Using the spreadsheet from Example 2, find the total number of miles the cyclist biked in year 1 and the total he biked in year 2.

SOLUTION Use a function to find the totals. A function is a program that performs a specific, commonly used task. To find the totals for each year, use the SUM() function. Type =SUM(B2:B13) in cell B15.

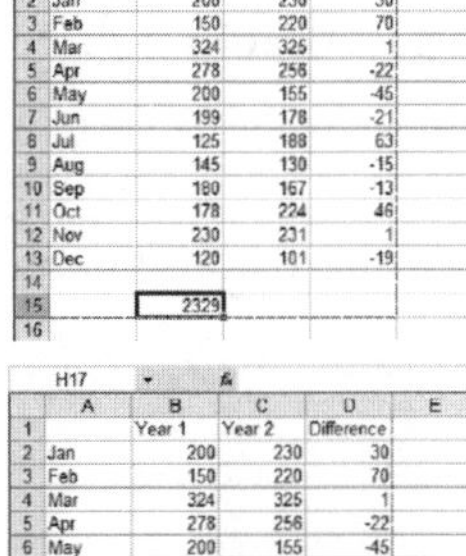
B15 =SUM(B2:B13)

	A	B	C	D	E
1		Year 1	Year 2	Difference	
2	Jan	200	230	30	
3	Feb	150	220	70	
4	Mar	324	325	1	
5	Apr	278	256	-22	
6	May	200	155	-45	
7	Jun	199	178	-21	
8	Jul	125	188	63	
9	Aug	145	130	-15	
10	Sep	180	167	-13	
11	Oct	178	224	46	
12	Nov	230	231	1	
13	Dec	120	101	-19	
14					
15		2329			
16					

Analyze

What formula could also be used to find the sum of cells B2 through B13?

=B2+B3+B4+B5 +B6+ B7+B8+B9 +B10+B11+B12 +B13

Copy the formula in cell B15 to cell C15, and the spreadsheet will automatically adjust the function to use the data in the corresponding column.

H17

	A	B	C	D	E
1		Year 1	Year 2	Difference	
2	Jan	200	230	30	
3	Feb	150	220	70	
4	Mar	324	325	1	
5	Apr	278	256	-22	
6	May	200	155	-45	
7	Jun	199	178	-21	
8	Jul	125	188	63	
9	Aug	145	130	-15	
10	Sep	180	167	-13	
11	Oct	178	224	46	
12	Nov	230	231	1	
13	Dec	120	101	-19	
14					
15		2329	2405		
16					

b. Find the sum of the difference column.

SOLUTION Copy the formula in cell B15 to cell D15.

D15 =SUM(D2:D13)

	A	B	C	D	E
1		Year 1	Year 2	Difference	
2	Jan	200	230	30	
3	Feb	150	220	70	
4	Mar	324	325	1	
5	Apr	278	256	-22	
6	May	200	155	-45	
7	Jun	199	178	-21	
8	Jul	125	188	63	
9	Aug	145	130	-15	
10	Sep	180	167	-13	
11	Oct	178	224	46	
12	Nov	230	231	1	
13	Dec	120	101	-19	
14					
15		2329	2405	76	
16					

Analyze

What formula could also be used to find the sum of the difference column?

Possible answer: =C15–B15

Appendix Lesson 2 839

Example 4 Using a Spreadsheet to Answer Questions About Data

Use the spreadsheet created in Example 3 to answer each question.

a. During which months in year 2 did the cyclist bike a greater number of miles than he did in the corresponding months in year 1?

SOLUTION Look in the difference column and find the months whose numbers are positive.

M7

	A	B	C	D	E
1		Year 1	Year 2	Difference	
2	Jan	200	230	30	
3	Feb	150	220	70	
4	Mar	324	325	1	
5	Apr	278	256	-22	
6	May	200	155	-45	
7	Jun	199	178	-21	
8	Jul	125	188	63	
9	Aug	145	130	-15	
10	Sep	180	167	-13	
11	Oct	178	224	46	
12	Nov	230	231	1	
13	Dec	120	101	-19	
14					
15		2329	2405	76	
16					

The cyclist biked a greater number of miles during the months of January, February, March, July, October, and November in year 2 than in year 1.

b. How many more miles did the cyclist bike in year 2 than in year 1?

SOLUTION Look in the sum of the difference column.

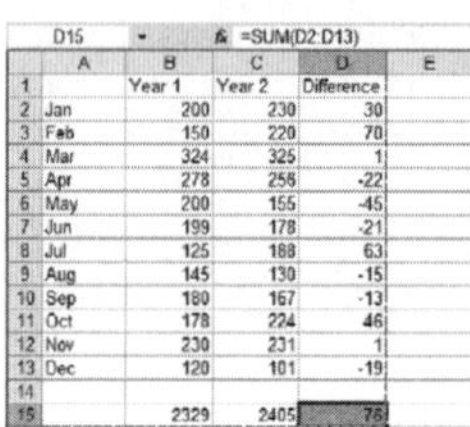

D15 =SUM(D2:D13)

	A	B	C	D	E
1		Year 1	Year 2	Difference	
2	Jan	200	230	30	
3	Feb	150	220	70	
4	Mar	324	325	1	
5	Apr	278	256	-22	
6	May	200	155	-45	
7	Jun	199	178	-21	
8	Jul	125	188	63	
9	Aug	145	130	-15	
10	Sep	180	167	-13	
11	Oct	178	224	46	
12	Nov	230	231	1	
13	Dec	120	101	-19	
14					
15		2329	2405	76	
16					

The cyclist biked 76 more miles in year 2 than in year 1.

Example 5 Application: Graphs

Using the spreadsheet from Example 3, create a bar graph to display the data for year 1.

SOLUTION Select the data from cell A2 through B13.

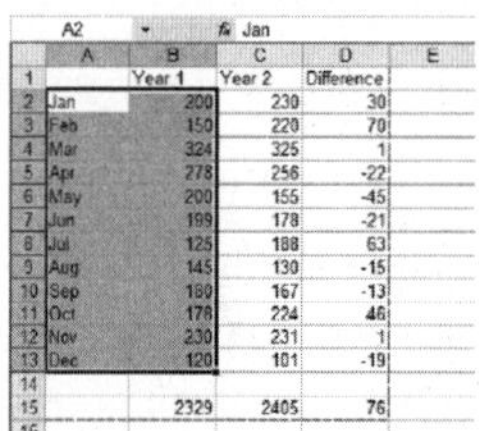

A2 Jan

	A	B	C	D	E
1		Year 1	Year 2	Difference	
2	Jan	200	230	30	
3	Feb	150	220	70	
4	Mar	324	325	1	
5	Apr	278	256	-22	
6	May	200	155	-45	
7	Jun	199	178	-21	
8	Jul	125	188	63	
9	Aug	145	130	-15	
10	Sep	180	167	-13	
11	Oct	178	224	46	
12	Nov	230	231	1	
13	Dec	120	101	-19	
14					
15		2329	2405	76	
16					

Select the Chart Wizard button from the toolbar and choose Column as the chart type and Clustered Column as the chart subtype. Click the Finish button.

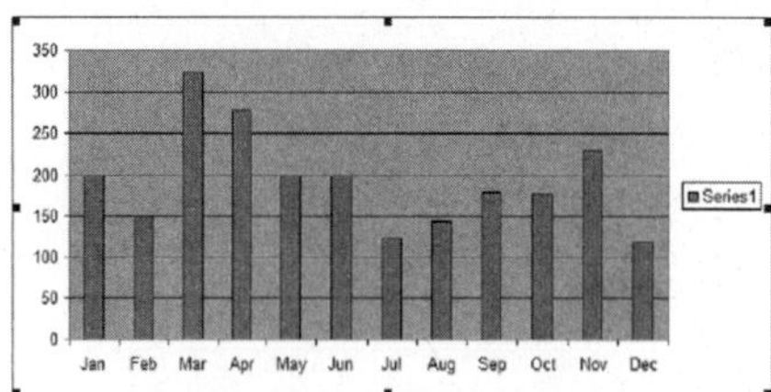

840 Saxon Algebra 2

Lesson Practice

a. The 2007 ticket prices for a major league franchise are shown. The prices of each kind of ticket will be increased by 5% for the 2008 season. Create a spreadsheet showing the 2007 and 2008 ticket prices.
(Ex 1 and 3)

Table of Ticket Prices

	Ticket Prices 2007
Terrace Box	$30
Upper Reserved	$10
Upper Box	$20
Club Box	$55
Field Box	$40
Lower Box	$40

A11

	A	B	C	D
1		2007	2008	
2	Terrace Box	30	31.5	
3	Upper Reserved	10	10.5	
4	Upper Box	20	21	
5	Club Box	55	57.75	
6	Field Box	40	42	
7	Lower Box	40	42	
8				

b. Add a column to the spreadsheet to display the amount of increase in the cost of ticket prices from 2007 to 2008.
(Ex 2)

b. A13

	A	B	C	D	E
1		2007	2008	Amount of Increase	
2	Terrace Box	30	31.5	1.5	
3	Upper Reserved	10	10.5	0.5	
4	Upper Box	20	21	1	
5	Club Box	55	57.75	2.75	
6	Field Box	40	42	2	
7	Lower Box	40	42	2	
8					

c. How much would it cost to purchase two terrace box seat tickets in 2008? **$63**
(Ex 4)

d. Create a double bar graph to display the ticket information for both years.
(Ex 5)

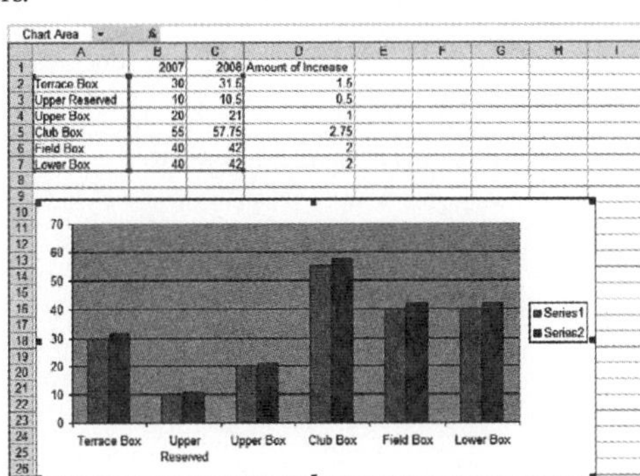
Chart Area

	A	B	C	D
1		2007	2008	Amount of Increase
2	Terrace Box	30	31.5	1.5
3	Upper Reserved	10	10.5	0.5
4	Upper Box	20	21	1
5	Club Box	55	57.75	2.75
6	Field Box	40	42	2
7	Lower Box	40	42	2

APPENDIX LESSONS

Appendix Lesson 2 841

APPENDIX LESSON 3

Precision and Accuracy

New Concepts

The *accuracy* of a measurement refers to how close it is to the actual or accepted value.

Precision can refer to any of the following:

- how tightly together a set of measurements is clustered
- how close a single measurement is to the mean of a set
- the interval of values implied by the last significant digit in a number

Relative error is a measure of accuracy.

$$\text{Relative error} = \frac{|\text{Measured value} - \text{Accepted value}|}{\text{Accepted value}}$$

Relative deviation is a measure of precision.

$$\text{Relative deviation} = \frac{|\text{Measured value} - \text{Mean value of the set}|}{\text{Mean value of the set}}$$

Example 1 Finding a Measure of Accuracy

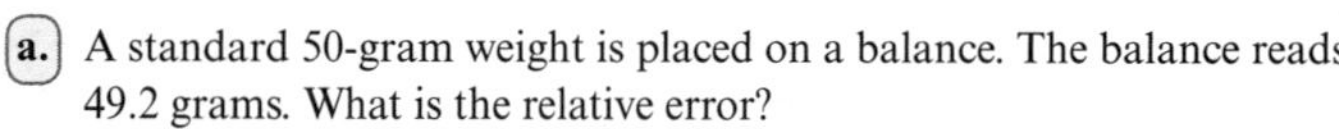

a. A standard 50-gram weight is placed on a balance. The balance reads 49.2 grams. What is the relative error?

SOLUTION

$$\text{Relative error} = \frac{|49.2 - 50|}{50}$$

$$= \frac{0.8}{50}$$ The absolute error is 0.8 gram.

$$= 0.016, \text{ or } 1.6\%$$

b. A standard 2000-gram weight is placed on a balance. The balance reads 2006 grams. What is the relative error?

SOLUTION

$$\text{Relative error} = \frac{|2006 - 2000|}{2000}$$

$$= \frac{6}{2000}$$ The absolute error is 6 grams.

$$= 0.003, \text{ or } 0.3\%$$

The following points in Example 1 are worth noting:

- The absolute error is greater in part b, but the relative error is greater in part a.
- A gram is a measure of mass, not weight. But in this context the distinction is not important.

842 Saxon Algebra 2

- The actual weight of a "standard 50-gram weight" might not be 50 grams. (It might be closer to 50.001 grams.) This illustrates why accuracy refers to an actual or *accepted* value.

The simplest method of gauging the precision of a set of measurements is to compare the ranges. The range is the difference between the greatest and least values in the set.

APPENDIX LESSONS

Example 2 Comparing Precision in Sets of Data

All the measurements below are in grams. Using range, which set shows a greater degree of precision?

Set A: 14.3, 14.0, 14.3, 14.5

Set B: 22.9, 22.9, 23.2, 22.8

SOLUTION

The range of set A is $14.5 - 14.0 = 0.5$.

The range of set B is $23.2 - 22.8 = 0.4$.

Set B shows a greater degree of precision.

Example 3 Finding a Measure of Precision

Eight different balances are used to weigh the same object. The results, in grams, are listed below.

19.8 19.9 19.9 20.0 20.1 20.3 20.3 20.3

Then a student weighs the same object, obtaining 19.9 grams. What is the relative deviation associated with the student's result?

SOLUTION

$$\text{Mean value} = \frac{19.8 + 19.9 + 19.9 + 20.0 + 20.1 + 20.3 + 20.3 + 20.3}{8}$$

$$= 20.075$$

$$\text{Relative deviation} = \frac{|19.9 - 20.075|}{20.075}$$

$$= \frac{0.175}{20.075}$$ The absolute deviation is 0.175 gram.

$$\approx 0.009, \text{ or } 0.9\%$$

The last *significant digit* in a decimal number is the rightmost digit. When a quantity is measured, the last significant digit in the reported measurement implies (indicates) the degree of precision. For example, a reported length of 16 cm implies that the measured length is closer to 16 cm than to either 15 cm or 17 cm. But a reported length of 16.0 cm implies that the measured length is closer to 16.0 cm than to either 15.9 cm or 16.1 cm.

APPENDIX LESSONS

Appendix Lesson 3 843

Example 4 Finding an Implied Interval of Values

For each reported measurement, state the implied interval of values that contains the measured value x.

a. Reported length 16 cm

SOLUTION

The last significant digit is 6, which is in the ones place.

$16 - 0.5 = 15.5$, $16 + 0.5 = 16.5$ Subtract and add half of 1.

$15.5 \text{ cm} \leq x < 16.5 \text{ cm}$ State the implied interval of values that contains the measured value x.

To understand why the inequality symbols $\leq$ and $<$ are used, note that when 15.5 is rounded to the nearest whole number, the result is 16, and when 16.5 is rounded to the nearest whole number, the result is 17.

b. Reported weight 3.24 kg

SOLUTION

The last significant digit is 4, which is in the hundredths place.

$3.24 - 0.005 = 3.235$, $3.24 + 0.005 = 3.245$ Subtract and add half of 0.01.

$3.235 \text{ kg} \leq x < 3.245 \text{ kg}$ State the implied interval of values that contains the measured value x.

Example 5 Determining if a Measurement is Within Tolerance Limits

Use the stated tolerance limits for each manufactured product to determine if the given measurement is acceptable.

a. The length of a bolt is required to be 3.2 cm $\pm$ 2%. Is 3.1 cm acceptable?

SOLUTION

$0.02 \times 3.2 = 0.064$ Find 2% of 3.2.

$3.136 \leq x \leq 3.264$ State the interval of values that are acceptable.

$3.136 \leq 3.1 \leq 3.264$ is not true, so 3.1 cm is not acceptable.

b. The diameter of a pipe is required to be $\frac{3}{4}$ in. $\pm\frac{1}{32}$ in. Is $\frac{49}{64}$ in. acceptable?

SOLUTION

$\frac{3}{4} - \frac{1}{32} = \frac{48}{64} - \frac{2}{64} = \frac{46}{64}$ and $\frac{3}{4} + \frac{1}{32} = \frac{48}{64} + \frac{2}{64} = \frac{50}{64}$.

$\frac{46}{64} \leq x \leq \frac{50}{64}$ State the interval of values that are acceptable.

$\frac{46}{64} \leq \frac{49}{64} \leq \frac{50}{64}$ is true, so $\frac{49}{64}$ in. is acceptable.

844 *Saxon Algebra 2*

APPENDIX LESSONS

Example 6 Use Accuracy and Precision to Compare Measurements

Suppose the actual length of an object is known to be 1.39 m, and these three different measurements are reported for the object: 1.33 m, 1.37 m, and 1.4 m. Compare the reported measurements, discussing accuracy and precision.

SOLUTION

The implied interval of values for each measurement is shown in the diagram.

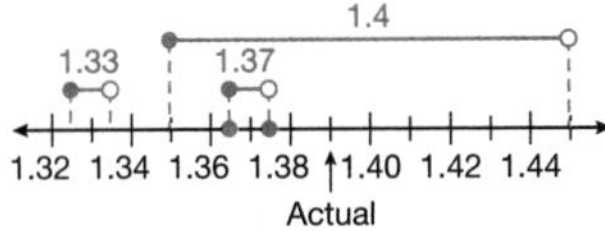

Accuracy: The most accurate is 1.37 because its interval is closest to 1.39. To compare 1.33 and 1.4, choose the endpoint of each corresponding interval that is farthest from 1.39, and then compare those endpoints. Comparing 1.325 and 1.45, you can see that 1.45 is closer to 1.39. So, 1.4 is the next most accurate. The least accurate is 1.33.

Precision: 1.33 and 1.37 are equally precise because the last significant digit for each number is in the same place. The least precise is 1.4.

Lesson Practice

a. *(Ex 1)* A standard 200-gram weight is placed on a balance. The balance reads 201.2 grams. What is the relative error? 0.6%

b. *(Ex 1)* A timer is set for 3 minutes. It rings after 2 minutes 58 seconds has elapsed. What is the relative error? approximately 1.1%

c. *(Ex 2)* Two groups measure the temperature of a liquid 5 times, with the results shown below. Using range, which group has greater precision?

Group A: 85.6°C, 85.4°C, 85.0°C, 86.2°C, 86.2°C
Group B: 86.0°C, 86.4°C, 85.0°C, 86.2°C, 85.8°C Group A

d. *(Ex 3)* Some researchers weigh a fossil. The mean weight is 10.1 grams. What is the relative deviation associated with a measured weight of 10.0 grams? approximately 1%

e. *(Ex 4)* For a reported measurement of 124 g, what is the implied interval of values that contains the measured value x? $123.5 \text{ g} \le x < 124.5 \text{ g}$

f. *(Ex 4)* For a reported measurement of 124.0 g, what is the implied interval of values that contains the measured value x? $123.95 \text{ g} \le x < 124.05 \text{ g}$

g. *(Ex 5)* A serving of cereal is required to be 56 g ± 5%. Is 58 g acceptable? yes

h. *(Ex 5)* The thickness of a sheet of plastic is required to be $\frac{5}{8}$ in. $\pm \frac{1}{64}$ in. Is $\frac{39}{64}$ in. acceptable? yes

i. *(Ex 6)* Suppose the actual weight of an object is known to be 35.2 g, and these measured weights are reported for the object: 35 g, 34.8 g, and 35.5 g. Compare the reported measurements, discussing accuracy and precision.
Most accurate: 35.5 g; Next most accurate: 34.8 g; Least accurate: 35 g;
Equally precise: 34.8 g and 35.5 g; Least precise: 35 g

Appendix Lesson 3 845

APPENDIX LESSON 4

Predictions

New Concepts

A *prediction* is a statement about something that is not known. Two methods of making predictions are extrapolation and interpolation.

- *Extrapolation* is the process of obtaining a value that corresponds to a value that is outside of the known data set.
- *Interpolation* is the process of obtaining a value that corresponds to a value that is between known values in the data set.

A simple way to extrapolate and interpolate is to use proportions.

Example 1 Using Proportions to Extrapolate and Interpolate

The table shows data that relates heating cost to average temperature.

Average temperature (°F)	40	44	50	57
Monthly heating bill ($)	126	102	86	71

a. Extrapolate to predict the monthly heating bill for a month with an average temperature of 60°F.

SOLUTION

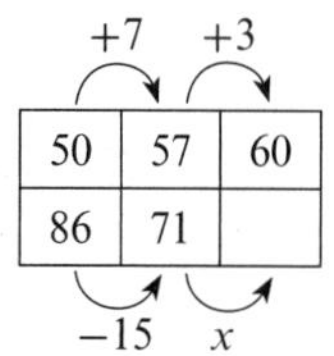

Use the differences +7 and −15 from the last interval in which both values are known. Use the differences +3 and x for the next interval.

$\frac{7}{-15} = \frac{3}{x}$ Write and solve a proportion.

$x \approx -6.43$

$71 - 6.43 = 64.57$ Use the value of x to compute the predicted value.

The predicted monthly heating bill is $64.57.

b. Interpolate to predict the monthly heating bill for a month with an average temperature of 46°F.

846 Saxon Algebra 2

SOLUTION

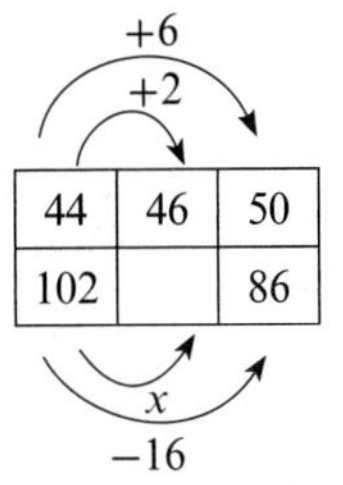

Use the differences +6 and −16 from the interval with known endpoints that contains the unknown value. Use the differences +2 and x that correspond to the unknown value.

$$\frac{6}{-16} = \frac{2}{x}$$ Write and solve a proportion.

$$x \approx -5.33$$

$102 - 5.33 = 96.67$ Use the value of x to compute the predicted value.

The predicted monthly heating bill is \$96.67.

Using a proportion to extrapolate or interpolate is appropriate for a data set that is linear or nearly linear. It is usually better to use a linear regression model because it consideres all of the data, not just certain intervals. *Regression* is a process of finding an equation that models a set of data.

Example 2 Using a Linear Regression Model to Predict

The table shows data that relates gas mileage and engine size for several cars. Predict the mileage for a car with an engine size of 3.5 liters.

Engine size (liters)	1.8	2.3	3.0	2.3	3.0	2.5	2.0	1.8
Mileage (mi/gal)	37	26	22	30	20	25	34	32

SOLUTION Enter the engine sizes into list **L1** and the mileages into list **L2** on a graphing calculator. Press STAT, then choose **CALC,** and then **4: LinReg** to obtain a linear regression model. The linear regression model, or equation of the line of best fit, is $y \approx -11.74x + 55.70$, where x represents engine size in liters and y represents mileage in miles per gallon.

The correlation coefficient is $r \approx -0.94$. Make a scatter plot of the data and graph the equation.

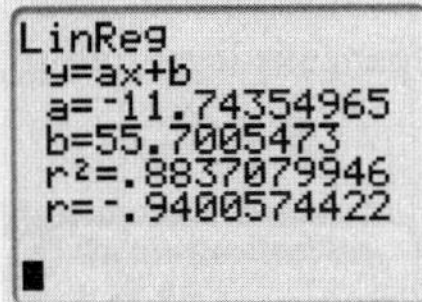

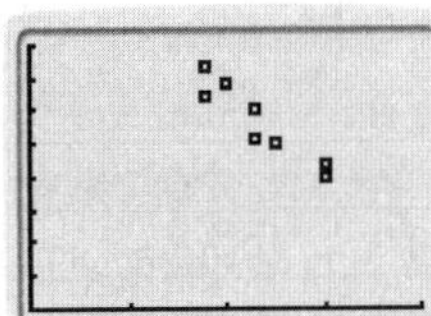

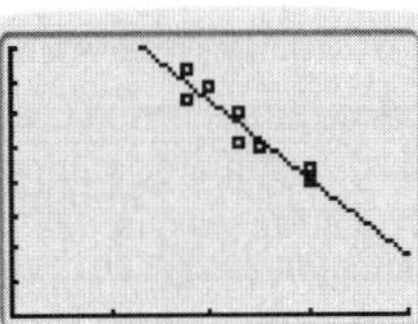

$y \approx -11.74x + 55.70$ Substitute 3.5 for x in the equation.

$y \approx -11.74(3.5) + 55.70$

$y \approx 14.61$

The predicted mileage for a car with an engine size of 3.5 liters is approximately 14.6 miles per gallon.

APPENDIX LESSONS

Appendix Lesson 4 847

You can obtain different regression models for any data set. Some of the regression models available on a graphing calculator are linear, quadratic, cubic, quartic, natural logarithmic, and exponential. After entering data into lists, press STAT, then choose **CALC,** and then scroll down. Choose different models and compare the values of the coefficients of determination, denoted by either r^2 or R^2.

Example 3 Choosing a Regression Model to Predict

The table shows the opening value of a stock index on the first day of trading in various years. Use a regression model to estimate the value on the first day of trading in 2004. State whether extrapolation or interpolation was used.

Year	Price (\$)	Year	Price (\$)
1996	616	2001	1320
1997	741	2002	1148
1998	970	2005	1212
1999	1229	2006	1248
2000	1469	2007	1418

SOLUTION

Let x represent the number of years since 1995. So $x = 1$ represents 1996, $x = 2$ represents 1997, and so on, with $x = 12$ representing 2007. Enter the x-values into list **L1** and the prices into **L2.** Obtain the following regression models and verify the values of the coefficients of determination, r^2 and R^2.

Linear $r^2 \approx 0.48$ Quadratic $R^2 \approx 0.74$ Cubic $R^2 \approx 0.87$

Quartic $R^2 \approx 0.90$ Natural logarithmic $r^2 \approx 0.70$ Exponential $r^2 \approx 0.50$

The quartic model seems to be the most appropriate choice because R^2 is closest to 1.

Press Y=, and then enter the quartic function model.

Use the TABLE feature to find the function value for $x = 9$, which represents 2004.

Graph the function. Make a scatter plot of the data.

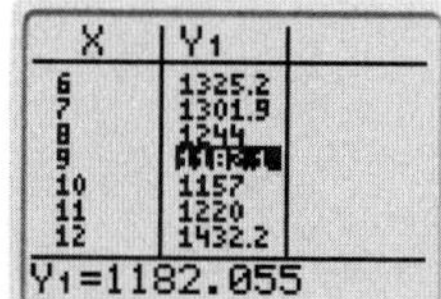

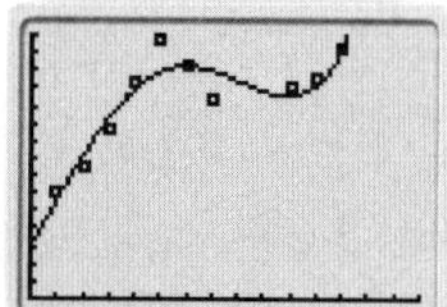

Using a quartic model, the estimated value on the first day of trading in 2004 is \$1182. Interpolation was used because the estimated value corresponds to 2004, which is between known values in the data set.

848 *Saxon Algebra 2*

Lesson Practice

a. (Ex 1) The table shows rug prices. Extrapolate to predict the price of a rug with an area of 180 ft^2. Interpolate to predict the price of a rug with an area of 35 ft^2. $630.43; $135.67

Area of Rug (ft^2)	24	54	80	108
Price ($)	99	199	309	399

b. (Ex 2) The table shows data that relates number of gallons of gasoline used and several driving distances. Write the best-fit linear regression model for the data. Use the model to predict the number of miles that will be driven if 4 gallons are used. State whether extrapolation or interpolation was used. $y \approx 38.55x - 27.79$; approximately 126.4 miles; interpolation

Gallons used	3.8	1.2	2.1	6.7	2.3	2.5	5.9
Miles driven	120	27	50	236	56	66	195

c. (Ex 3) The table shows the student enrollment on the opening day at a school for several years. Using $x = 1$ for 1998, write the best regression model for the data. Use the model to predict the enrollment on opening day of 2009. State whether extrapolation or interpolation was used.
$y \approx -0.539x^4 + 14.460x^3 - 134.835x^2 + 477.646x + 622$; 748; extrapolation

Year	Students	Year	Students
1998	990	2002	1076
1999	1108	2005	1030
2000	1220	2006	986
2001	1184	2007	986

Appendix Lesson 4 849

APPENDIX LESSON 5

Scale Factor

New Concepts

A **dilation** is a transformation that changes the size of a figure by enlarging or reducing the figure. The figure is dilated about a fixed point called the **center of dilation.** The figure before the dilation is called the **pre-image** and the dilated figure is called the **image.** The **scale factor** of a dilation is the ratio of a side length of the image to the corresponding side length of the pre-image. If the scale factor is between 0 and 1, the dilation is a reduction. If the scale factor is greater than 1, the dilation is an enlargement.

Math Language

A **transformation** changes the size or position of a figure. Other common transformations include translations, rotations, and reflections.

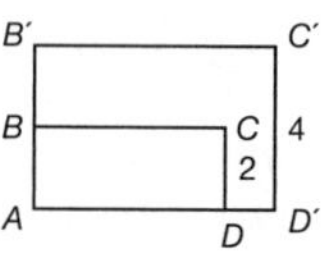

$A'B'C'D'$ is an enlargement of $ABCD$. The center of dilation is point A and the scale factor is the ratio $\frac{4}{2} = 2$.

You can perform dilations on the coordinate plane. When the origin is the center of dilation, multiply the scale factor, t by the coordinates of the pre-image to find the coordinates of the image.

Example 1 Drawing a Dilation with a Scale Factor Greater than 1

a. Draw a dilation of square $ABCD$ whose center of dilation is (0, 0). Use a scale factor of 4.

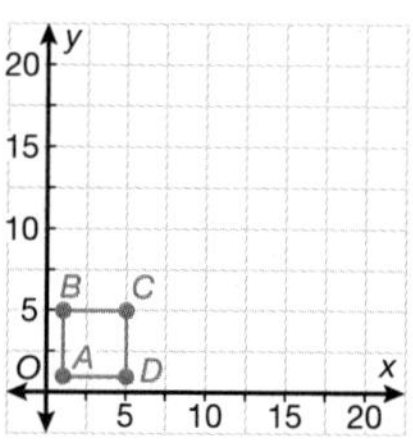

SOLUTION Multiply the coordinates of each vertex by the scale factor, 4. Then draw the image.

$A(1, 1)$ maps to $A'(4 \cdot 1, 4 \cdot 1) = A'(4, 4)$

$B(1, 5)$ maps to $B'(4 \cdot 1, 4 \cdot 5) = B'(4, 20)$

$C(5, 5)$ maps to $C'(4 \cdot 5, 4 \cdot 5) = C'(20, 20)$

$D(5, 1)$ maps to $D'(4 \cdot 5, 4 \cdot 1) = D'(20, 4)$

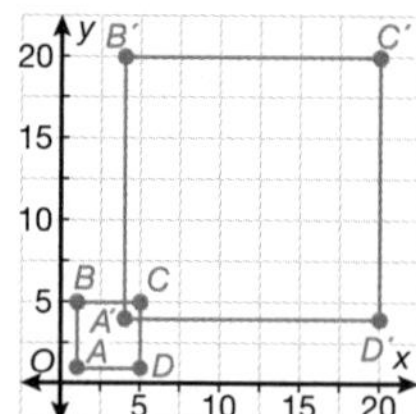

850 Saxon Algebra 2

b. Draw a dilation of triangle ABC whose center of dilation is $(0, 0)$. Use a scale factor of $\frac{3}{2}$.

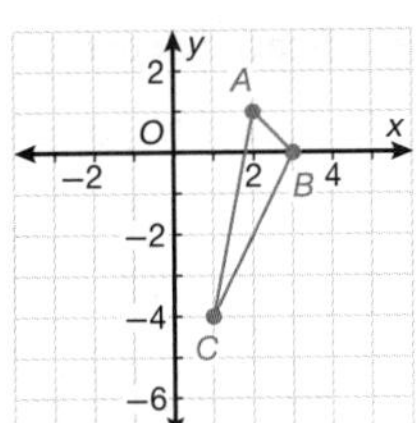

Hint

Use the scale factor to first determine if a dilation is a reduction or an enlargement.

SOLUTION Multiply the coordinates of each vertex by the scale factor, $\frac{3}{2}$. Then draw the image.

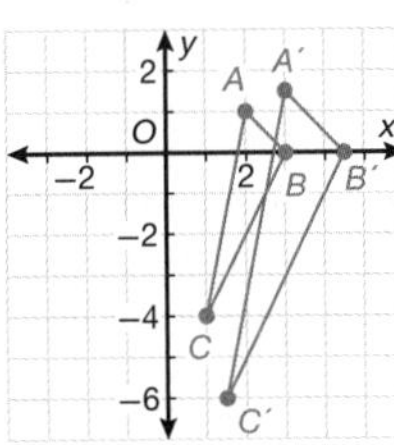

$A(2, 1)$ maps to $A'\left(\frac{3}{2} \cdot 2, \frac{3}{2} \cdot 1\right) = A'\left(3, \frac{3}{2}\right)$

$B(3, 0)$ maps to $B'\left(\frac{3}{2} \cdot 3, \frac{3}{2} \cdot 0\right) = B'\left(\frac{9}{2}, 0\right)$

$C(1, -4)$ maps to $C'\left(\frac{3}{2} \cdot 1, \frac{3}{2} \cdot (-4)\right) = C'\left(\frac{3}{2}, -6\right)$

Example 2 Drawing a Dilation with a Scale Factor Between 0 and 1

Draw a dilation of rectangle $ABCD$ whose center of dilation is $(0, 0)$. Use a scale factor of $\frac{1}{2}$.

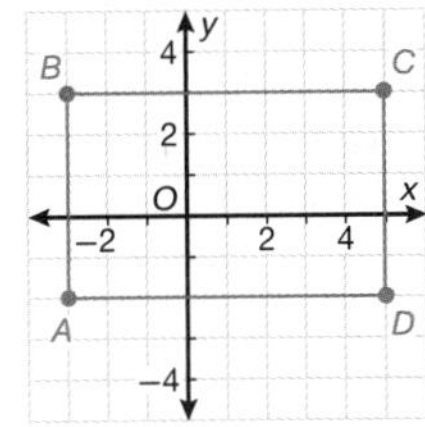

SOLUTION Multiply the coordinates of each vertex by the scale factor, $\frac{1}{2}$. Then draw the image.

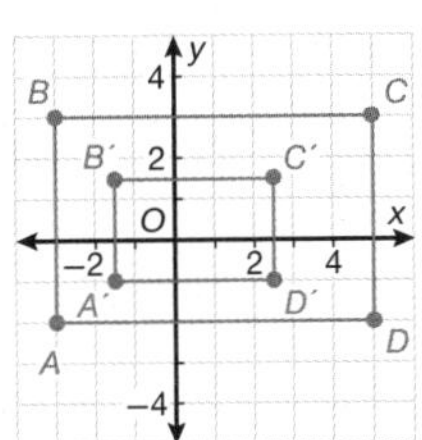

$A(-3, -2)$ maps to $A'\left(\frac{1}{2} \cdot -3, \frac{1}{2} \cdot -2\right) = A'\left(-\frac{3}{2}, -1\right)$

$B(-3, 3)$ maps to $B'\left(\frac{1}{2} \cdot -3, \frac{1}{2} \cdot 3\right) = B'\left(-\frac{3}{2}, \frac{3}{2}\right)$

$C(5, 3)$ maps to $C'\left(\frac{1}{2} \cdot 5, \frac{1}{2} \cdot 3\right) = C'\left(\frac{5}{2}, \frac{3}{2}\right)$

$D(5, -2)$ maps to $D'\left(\frac{1}{2} \cdot 5, \frac{1}{2} \cdot -2\right) = D'\left(\frac{5}{2}, -1\right)$

APPENDIX LESSONS

Appendix Lesson 5 851

Example 3 Finding a Scale Factor

Trapezoid $H'I'J'K'$ is a dilation of trapezoid $HIJK$. Find the scale factor.

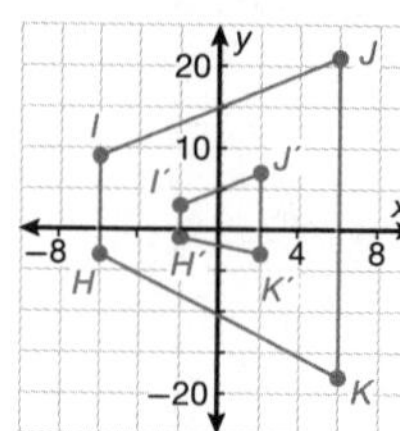

SOLUTION The dilation is a reduction so the scale factor is between 0 and 1. The length of $\overline{H'I'}$ is 4 and the length of its corresponding side on the pre-image $\overline{HI}$ is 12. The scale factor is $\frac{4}{12} = \frac{1}{3}$.

A dilation is a similarity transformation. The pre-image and image of a dilation are similar figures.

Two figures are similar if and only if the ratios of the lengths of their corresponding sides are equal and the corresponding angles are equal.

Caution

Translations, reflections, and rotations preserve the size of the pre-image. Dilations do not.

Example 4 Finding Coordinates of Vertices of Similar Triangles

Find the coordinates of the vertices of a triangle which is similar to triangle DEF where the ratios of the lengths of the corresponding sides of the triangles are $\frac{5}{2}$. Draw the similar triangle on the coordinate plane.

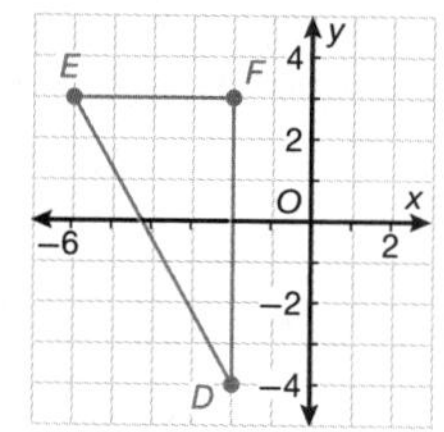

SOLUTION Find the dilation of triangle DEF using a scale factor of $\frac{5}{2}$.

$D(-2, -4)$ maps to $D'\left(\frac{5}{2} \cdot (-2), \frac{5}{2} \cdot (-4)\right) = D'(-5, -10)$

$E(-6, 3)$ maps to $E'\left(\frac{5}{2} \cdot (-6), \frac{5}{2} \cdot 3\right) = E'\left(-15, \frac{15}{2}\right)$

$F(-2, 3)$ maps to $F'\left(\frac{5}{2} \cdot (-2), \frac{5}{2} \cdot 3\right) = F'\left(-5, \frac{15}{2}\right)$

The coordinates of the triangle similar to triangle DEF are $D'(-5, -10)$, $E'\left(-15, \frac{15}{2}\right)$, and $F'\left(-5, \frac{15}{2}\right)$

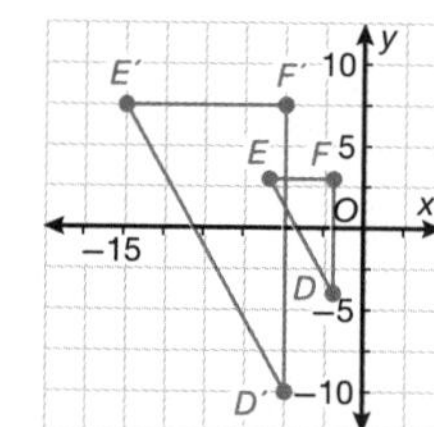

852 Saxon Algebra 2

Example 5 Application: Copy Machines

You want to reduce a photograph that is 8 inches by 8 inches to fit on the page of a newspaper. The photograph on the newspaper needs to be 6 inches by 6 inches. What scale factor should be used to reduce the photograph? What percentage should be used when reducing the photograph on the copy machine?

SOLUTION You are reducing a square photograph. The scale factor for the reduction is the ratio of a side length of the image to the corresponding side length of the pre-image or $\frac{6}{8}$.

To find the percentage used, write the ratio as a percent.

$\frac{6}{8} = 75\%$

You need to make a copy that is 75% of the original size.

Generalize

When making an enlargement on a copy machine, the percentage used will always be greater than what percent? 100%

Lesson Practice

a. Draw a dilation of a triangle with vertices $X(0, 1)$, $Y(-3, 5)$, and $Z(2, 3)$ whose center of dilation is $(0, 0)$. Use a scale factor of 1.2.
(Ex 1)

b. Draw a dilation of a square with vertices $A(-4, 0)$, $B(0, 4)$, $C(4, 0)$, and $D(0, -4)$ whose center of dilation is $(0, 0)$. Use a scale factor of $\frac{1}{4}$
(Ex 2)

c. Parallelogram $Q'R'S'T'$ is a dilation of $QRST$. Find the scale factor. 3
(Ex 3)

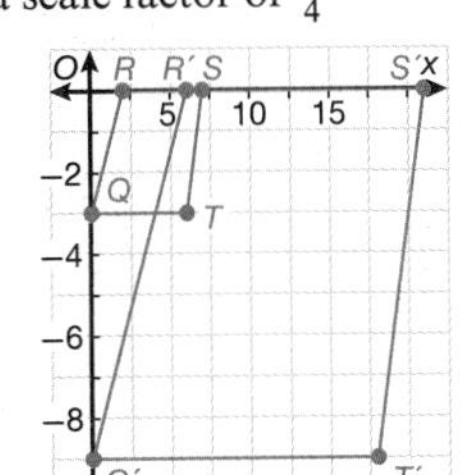

d. Find the coordinates of the vertices of a triangle that is similar to triangle RST where the ratios of the lengths of the corresponding sides of the triangles are $\frac{1}{2}$. (0.5, −1), (2, 1.5), and (3.5, −1)
(Ex 4)

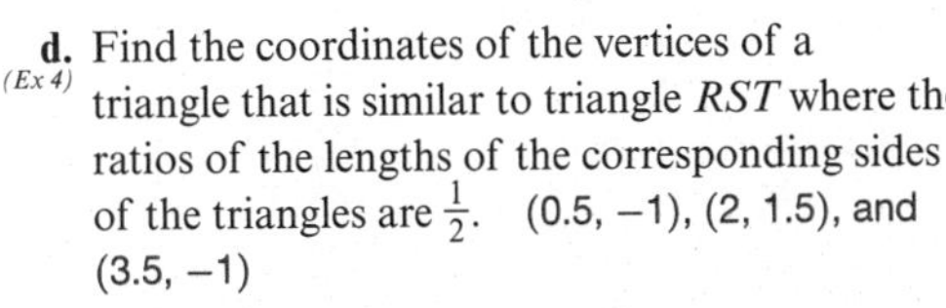

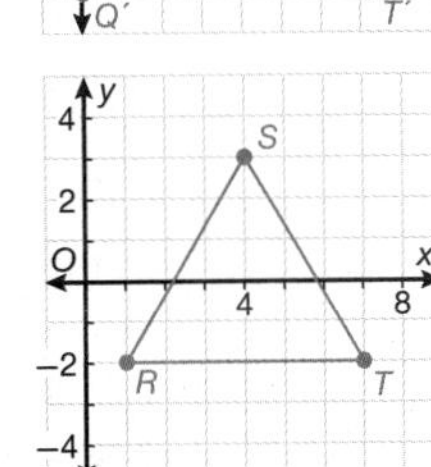

e. You want to enlarge a photograph that is 3 inches by 5 inches to fit on the title page of a yearbook. The photograph in the yearbook needs to be 7.5 inches by 12.5 inches. What scale factor should be used to enlarge the photograph? 2.5
(Ex 5)

What percentage should be used when enlarging the photograph on the copy machine? 250%

a.

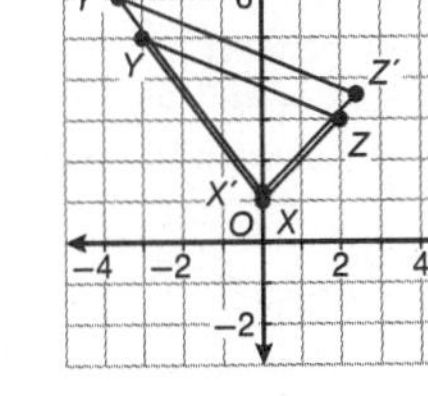

b.

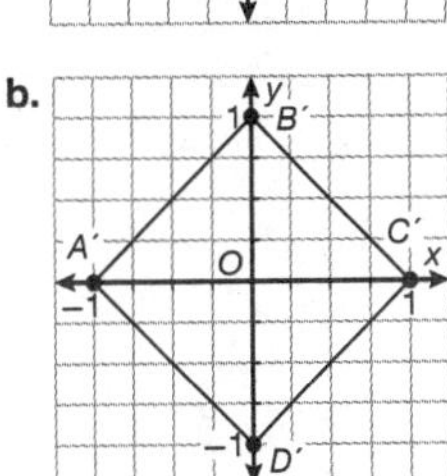

APPENDIX LESSONS

APPENDIX LESSONS

Appendix Lesson 5 853

APPENDIX LESSON 6

Regions and Solids

New Concepts

Polygons are closed figures made up of line segments called sides. **Polyhedra** are **solids** made up of polygons, where each polygon is called a **face** and the sides of the faces are called **edges.**

A polygon is a two-dimensional figure and a polyhedron is a three-dimensional figure.

Polygons	Polyhedra

Example 1 Identifying Polygons and Polyhedra

Tell if each figure is a polygon, a polyhedron, or neither.

a.

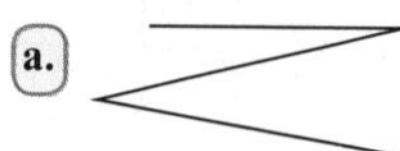

SOLUTION The figure is two-dimensional and made up of segments, but the figure is not closed. It is neither a polygon nor a polyhedron.

b.

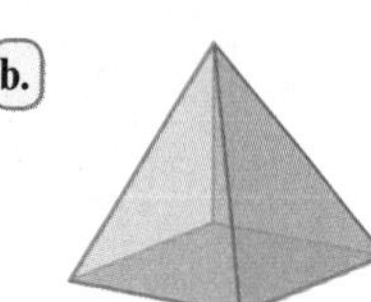

SOLUTION The figure is a three-dimensional solid made up of polygons. The figure is a polyhedron.

c.

SOLUTION The figure is a closed two-dimensional figure and all the sides are segments. The figure is a polygon.

d.

SOLUTION The figure is a three-dimensional solid, but the faces are not polygons. It is neither a polygon nor a polyhedron.

854 Saxon Algebra 2

Example 2 Identifying Faces and Edges

Give the number of faces and edges of each polyhedron. Identify the polygons that make up the faces.

a.

SOLUTION There are 6 faces and 12 edges. Every face is a square.

b.

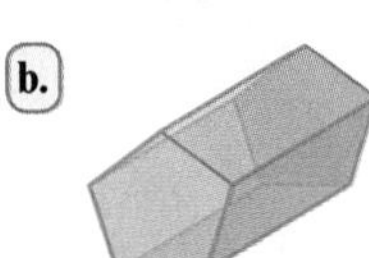

SOLUTION There are 7 faces and 15 edges. Two of the faces are pentagons and five of the faces are rectangles.

A **net** is a pattern that, when folded, forms a solid. The solid may or may not be a polyhedron. One possible net for a cube is shown to the right.

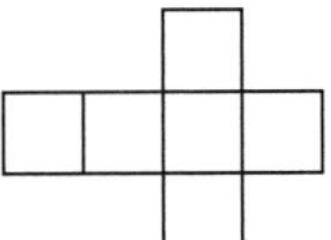

Example 3 Identifying Solids from Nets

Draw the solid from its net.

a.

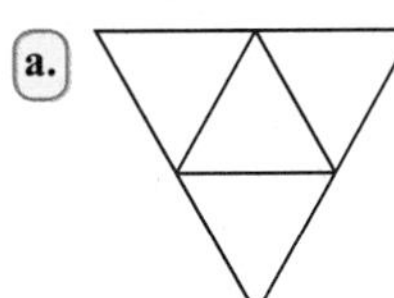

SOLUTION The middle triangle is the base, or bottom, of the figure. Fold the remaining faces up and the figure is a pyramid.

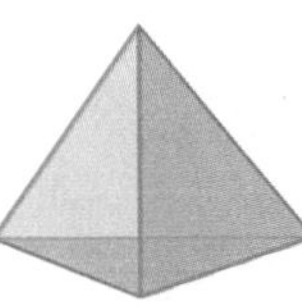

b.

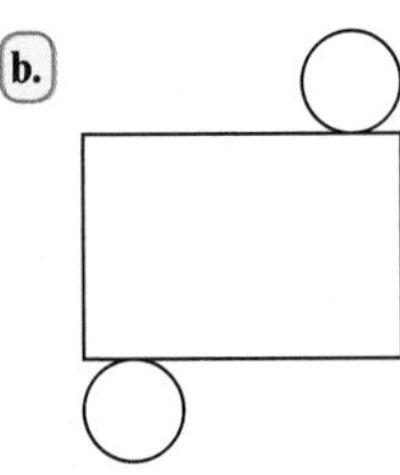

SOLUTION Bend the rectangle to join the left and right sides together. Fold the circles to form the top and bottom of a cylinder.

APPENDIX LESSONS

Appendix Lesson 6 855

Example 4 Drawing Nets for Solids

Draw a net for the solid.

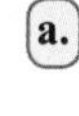

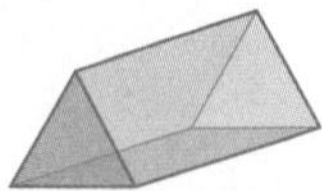

SOLUTION The solid is a polyhedron made up of three congruent rectangles and two congruent triangles.

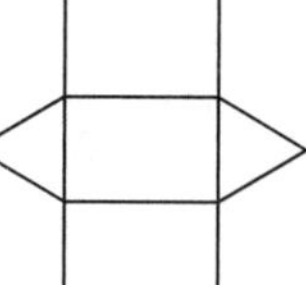

SOLUTION The solid is a rectangular prism. There are three pairs of congruent rectangles (top and bottom, front and back, left and right).

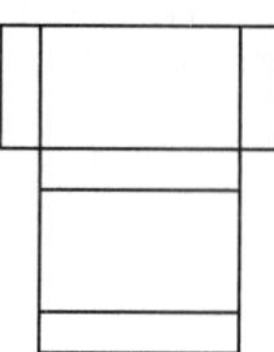

The surface area of a polyhedron is the sum of the areas of its faces.

Example 5 Finding Surface Area by Using a Net

Find the surface area of the square pyramid shown by the net.

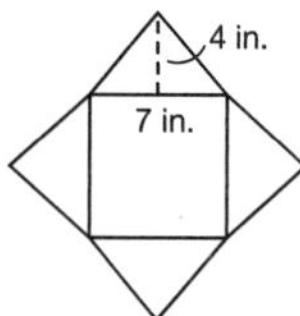

SOLUTION

Area of the square base: $s^2 = 7^2 = 49$

Area of each triangular face: $\frac{1}{2}bh = \frac{1}{2}(7)(4) = 14$

Sum of areas: $49 + 4(14) = 105$

The surface area is 105 square inches.

856 *Saxon* Algebra 2

APPENDIX LESSONS

Lesson Practice

Tell if each figure is a polygon, a polyhedron, or neither.

a. *(Ex 1)*

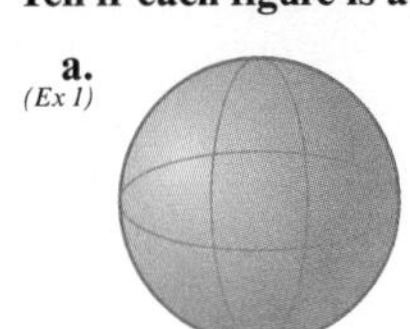

Neither

b. *(Ex 1)*

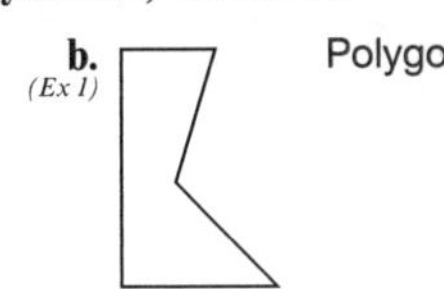

Polygon

c. *(Ex 1)*

Neither

d. *(Ex 1)*

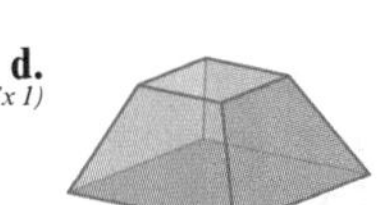

Polyhedron

Give the number of faces and edges of each polyhedron. Identify the polygons that make up the faces.

e. *(Ex 2)*

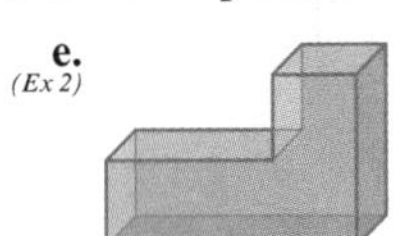

8 faces (2 hexagons, 6 rectangles), 18 edges

f. *(Ex 2)*

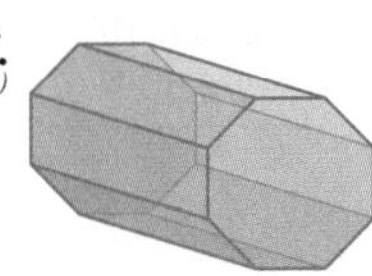

10 faces (2 octagons, 8 rectangles), 24 edges

Draw the solid from its net.

g. *(Ex 3)*

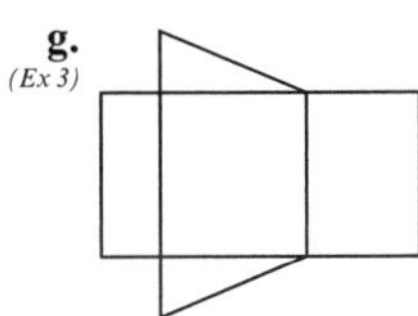

h. *(Ex 3)*

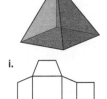

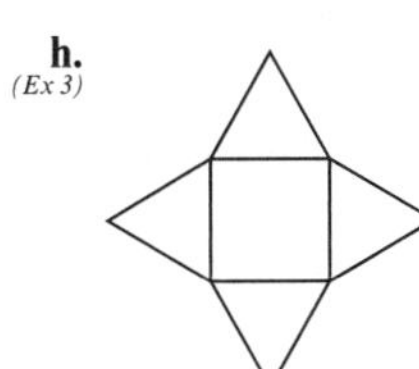

Draw a net for the solid.

i. *(Ex 4)*

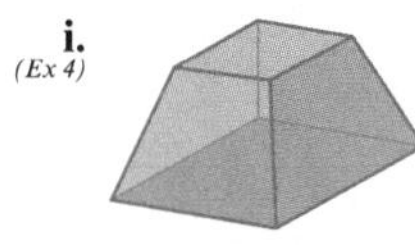

j. *(Ex 4)*

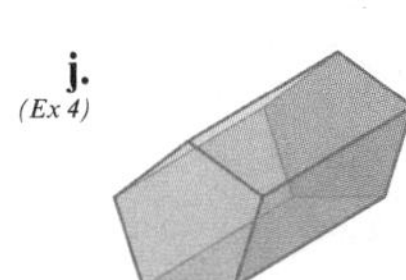

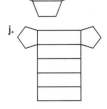

k. *(Ex 5)* Find the surface area of the rectangular prism shown by the net.

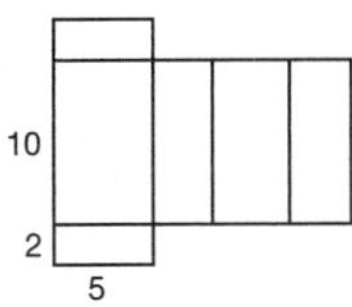

160 square units

g.

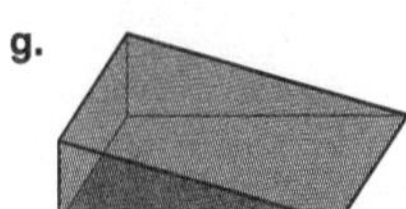

h.

i.

j.

APPENDIX LESSONS

APPENDIX LESSON 7

Apply Scientific Notation

New Concepts

Scientific notation is a way of expressing very small or very large numbers in a shorthand way by using powers of 10. Numbers are written as a product, where the first factor is a decimal greater than or equal to 1 but less than 10. The second factor is a power of 10, and the exponent on the power is an integer.

Standard Notation	Scientific Notation
12,850,000,000	1.285×10^{10}
30,000,000,000,000,000	3×10^{16}
0.000000000098	9.8×10^{-11}
0.00000005002	5.002×10^{-8}

Notice that for numbers greater than 1, the exponent is positive, and for numbers between 0 and 1, the exponent is negative.

To convert from standard to scientific notation, move the decimal point after the first nonzero digit. Then count the number of places the decimal point moved. This number will be used in writing the exponent on the power of 10. The exponent is positive if the original number is greater than 1, and negative if the original number is between 0 and 1.

To convert from scientific to standard notation, move the decimal point the number of places indicated by the exponent on the power of 10. If the exponent is positive, move the decimal point to the right; if it is negative, move the decimal point to the left.

Example 1 Converting Between Standard Notation and Scientific Notation

a. Write 0.000000000239 in scientific notation.

SOLUTION Place the decimal point after the first nonzero digit to form the first factor: 2.39. Count the number of places from this place to the current decimal point: 10. Because the count was to the left, the exponent is negative: -10. The answer is 2.39×10^{-10}.

b. Write 7,300,000 in scientific notation.

SOLUTION Place the decimal point after the first nonzero digit to form the first factor: 7.3. Count the number of places from this place to the current decimal point: 6. Because the count was to the right, the exponent is positive: 6. The answer is 7.3×10^{6}.

858 Saxon Algebra 2

APPENDIX LESSONS

c. Write 1.043×10^{15} in standard notation.

SOLUTION Move the decimal point 15 places to the right, adding zeros as placeholders: 1,043,000,000,000,000.

d. Write 7×10^{-11} in standard notation.

SOLUTION Move the decimal point 11 places to the left, adding zeros as placeholders. Remember that the 7 = 7.0, so the number is 0.00000000007.

Both scientific and graphing calculators allow the user to enter numbers in scientific notation and to see results in scientific notation.

On a scientific calculator, look for the SCI mode. In this mode, the power of 10 may be displayed as an exponent to the right of the first factor.

On a graphing calculator, press the Mode key to view and change modes. The options Normal, Scientific (Sci), and Engineering (Eng) are in the first row.

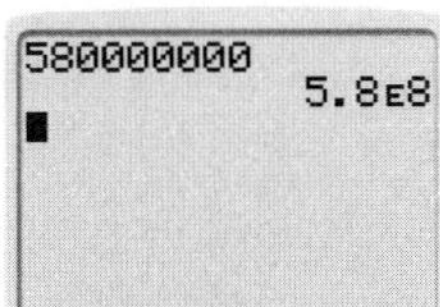

In Sci mode, when a number is entered in standard notation and the Enter key is pressed, the number is returned in scientific notation.

The E represents the "×10" part of the scientific notation expression.

A number can be entered in scientific notation, in any mode. Use the EE key to represent the "×10" part of the expression. This is above the comma key. Notice that although EE is pressed, only E appears on the screen. Scientific notation can also be entered on a calculator by using the exponent key.

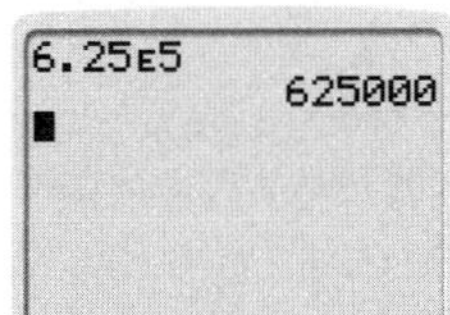

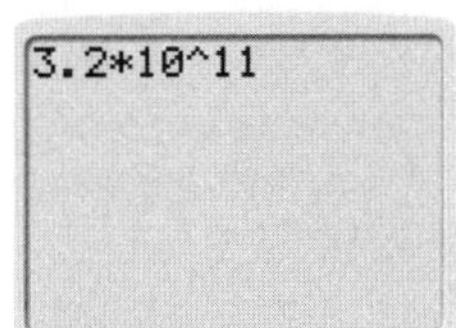

On a scientific calculator, look for an EE or EXP key to use. Otherwise, refer to the owner's manual.

Example 2 Expressing Scientific Notation on a Graphing Calculator

a. What number, in standard notation, is displayed on the screen?

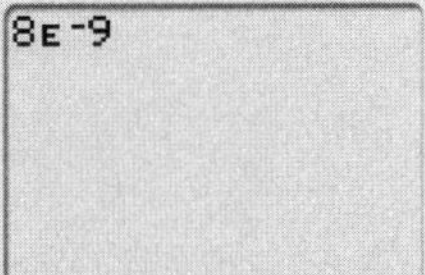

SOLUTION The number is 8×10^{-9}, which is equivalent to 0.000000008.

Appendix Lesson 7 859

b. Write both the expression entered, and the answer, in standard notation.

SOLUTION The expression entered was $(5.02 \times 10^{12}) - (1.3 \times 10^{9})$, or 5,020,000,000,000 − 1,300,000,000. The solution is 5.0187×10^{12}, which is 5,018,700,000,000.

Scientific notation is so named because of its role in the sciences.

Example 3 Application: Science

a. A mole is a standard unit in chemistry, defined to be 6.022×10^{23} molecules of a substance. How many molecules are in 14.5 moles of a given substance?

SOLUTION Multiply the number of molecules in a mole by the number of moles.

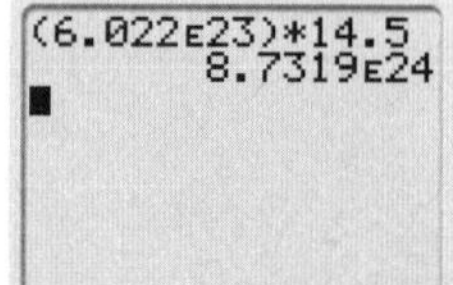

There are 8.7319×10^{24} molecules in the substance.

b. Pluto has a mass of about 1.3×10^{22} kilograms. Jupiter has a mass of about 1.899×10^{27} kilograms. About how many times greater is the mass of Jupiter than the mass of Pluto?

SOLUTION Divide the mass of Jupiter by the mass of Pluto.

The mass of Jupiter is about 146,000, or 1.46×10^{5}, times that of Pluto.

c. About twenty-nine percent, or 1.48×10^{8} square kilometers, of the earth's surface is covered in water. Approximate the total surface area of the earth. Write the answer in both scientific and standard notation.

SOLUTION

1. **Understand** Think of the situation as a percent problem, where the part is given and the whole is what is being asked for.

2. **Plan** Write a percent sentence and convert it to an equation.

1.48×10^{8} is 29% of the earth's surface.

$$1.48 \times 10^{8} = 0.29x$$

860 Saxon Algebra 2

APPENDIX LESSONS

3. Solve Solve for x.

$$1.48 \times 10^8 = 0.29x$$

$$\frac{1.48 \times 10^8}{0.29} = \frac{0.29x}{0.29}$$ Divide both sides by 0.29.

```
(1.48E8)/0.29
      510344827.6
```

$510344827.6 = x$ Use a calculator.

The surface area of the earth is about 510,000,000, or 5.1×10^8 square kilometers.

4. Check Find 29% of 510,000,000. It is 147,900,000 square kilometers, a number very close to that given for the amount of the earth's surface covered by water.

d. On average, an atom is about 10^{-8} centimeters in size. About how many meters long would 2.7×10^{14} atoms be, if placed in a row side by side?

SOLUTION Multiply the average size of an atom by the number of atoms. This gives the length in centimeters. To convert to meters, divide by 100.

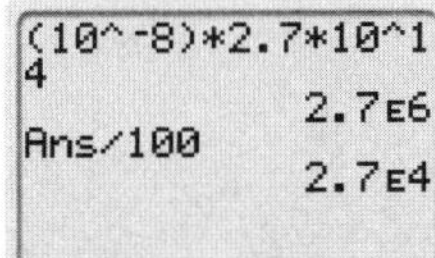

The row would be 27,000 meters long.

Lesson Practice

a. Write 0.00000004 in scientific notation. 4×10^{-8}
(Ex 1)

b. Write 354,000,000,000,000 in scientific notation. 3.54×10^{14}
(Ex 1)

c. Write 9.9×10^{-5} in standard notation. 0.000099
(Ex 1)

d. Write 6.02×10^9 in standard notation. 6,020,000,000
(Ex 1)

e. What number, in standard notation, is displayed on the screen?
(Ex 2) 1,040,000,000,000

```
1.04E12
```

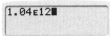

f. Write both the expression entered, and the answer, in standard notation.
(Ex 2) 0.0000325 + 0.00414; 0.0041725

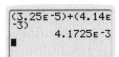

```
(3.25E-5)+(4.14E
-3)
         4.1725E-3
```

g. A mole is defined to be 6.022×10^{23} molecules of a substance. How many molecules are in 8.15 moles of a given substance? 4.90793×10^{24}
(Ex 3)

h. Earth has a mass of about 5.974×10^{24} kilograms. Neptune has a mass of about 1.024×10^{26} kilograms. About how many times greater is the mass of Neptune than the mass of Earth? about 17 times
(Ex 3)

i. The diameter of Venus is about 1.2×10^4 kilometers, which is about 95% the diameter of Earth. Approximate the diameter of Earth. Write the answer in both scientific and standard notation. 1.26×10^4; 12,600 km
(Ex 3)

j. On average, an atom is about 10^{-10} meters in size. About how many kilometers long would 5×10^{10} atoms be, if placed in a row side by side? 0.005 km
(Ex 3)

Appendix Lesson 7 861

Skills Bank

Estimation

Skills Bank Lesson 1

An **estimate** can be used to determine whether an answer is reasonable.

One way to estimate is to round some or all of the numbers to their greatest non-zero place value, then do the operation.

Example 1 Estimating by Rounding to the Greatest Non-Zero Place Value

Find a good estimate.

a. 48,304 + 2,349

SOLUTION

$48{,}304 + 2{,}349 \approx 50{,}000 + 2{,}000$
$= 52{,}000$

A good estimate is **about 52,000.**

b. 628 × 4,791

SOLUTION

$628 \times 4{,}791 \approx 600 \times 5{,}000$
$= 3{,}000{,}000$

A good estimate is **about 3,000,000.**

Another way to estimate is to round the numbers to nearby numbers that make the operation easy to do. These numbers are called compatible numbers.

Example 2 Estimating Using Compatible Numbers

Find a good estimate.

a. 478 + 619

SOLUTION

Rounding each number to the nearest 25 makes it easy to add.

$478 + 619 \approx 475 + 625 = 400 + 600$
$+ 100 = 1{,}100$

A good estimate is **about 1,100.**

b. 3827 ÷ 595

SOLUTION

Round to numbers that are easy to divide and will leave no remainder.

$3827 \div 595 \approx 3600 \div 600$
$= 6$

A good estimate is **about 6.**

Skills Bank Practice

Estimate. Possible estimates are given. Accept reasonable estimates.

a. 38×82 3,200
b. $8{,}320 - 94$ 8,220
c. $0.078 \div 2$ 0.04
d. $0.042 + 0.78$ 0.84
e. $618 \cdot 68$ 42,000
f. $3958 \div 492$ 8
g. $906 + 378$ 1,278
h. 439×87 36,000
i. 4023×50 200,000
j. $9387 - 1959$ 7,387
k. $8{,}374 + 3{,}305 + 91$ 11,800
l. $948 - 298$ 648
m. $402 \div 95$ 4
n. $6{,}306 \div 928$ 7
o. $38 \times 5{,}820$ 240,000
p. $4{,}503 - 581$ 4,000
q. 298×682 210,000
r. $4.982 - 0.593$ 4.382

862 Saxon Algebra 2

Mental Math

Skills Bank Lesson 2

Use these mental math strategies to help you add, subtract, multiply, and divide.

Compensation: When adding or subtracting, change one number, then make up for it later.

Example 1 Using Compensation to Add

Add: 47 + 28

SOLUTION

47 + 28	Change 47 to 50 by adding 3.
50 + 28 = 78	Add.
78 − 3 = 75	Subtract 3 from the sum.

Equal Additions: When subtracting, move each number up or down the number line by the same amount.

Example 2 Using Equal Additions to Subtract

Subtract: 91 − 25

SOLUTION

Add 5 to each number.

91 − 25 = 96 − 30 = 66

Real Number Properties: Use the Associative, Commutative, and/or Distributive Properties.

Example 3 Using Real Number Properties with Mental Math

a. Commutative and Associative Properties:
$6 \times 9 \times 5 = (6 \times 5) \times 9 = 30 \times 9 = 270$

b. Distributive Property:
$4 \times 27 = (4 \times 20) + (4 \times 7) = 80 + 28 = 108$

c. Associative Property:
$(15 + 17) + 13 = 15 + (17 + 13) = 15 + 30 = 45$

Skills Bank Practice

Use mental math to evaluate.

a. 42 + 19 + 8 69 **b.** 8 × 71 568 **c.** 63 − 28 35 **d.** 75 + 17 92

e. 6 × 12 × 5 360 **f.** 514 − 298 216 **g.** 3.2 + 2.5 + 4.5 10.2 **h.** 4 × 241 964

i. 7 × 81 567 **j.** 45 + 92 137 **k.** 138 − 29 109 **l.** 32 + 78 110

m. 949 + 111 1,060 **n.** 7 × 26 182 **o.** 14 + 91 + 6 111 **p.** 2 × 18 × 5 180

q. 482 − 197 285 **r.** 4 × 3 × 15 180 **s.** 77 + 48 125 **t.** 2 × 7 × 25 × 2 700

u. 57 + 245 302 **v.** 8 × 32 256 **w.** 92 − 47 45 **x.** 14 × 7 98

SKILLS BANK

Skills Bank 863

Exponents

Skills Bank Lesson 3

A **power** is an expression that shows repeated multiplication. In a power, an **exponent** shows how many times a **base** is used as a factor, as shown below:

$$\text{Base} \longrightarrow a^2 \longleftarrow \text{Exponent}$$
$$= a \cdot a$$

Example 1

Simplify.

3^4

SOLUTION

$3^4 = 3 \cdot 3 \cdot 3 \cdot 3 = 81$

You can use the following rules to simplify expressions with exponents.

$$a^0 = 1 \qquad a^1 = a \qquad -a^n = -(a^n)$$

When n is even, $(-a)^n = a^n$.

Using the Rules of Exponents

Example 2

Simplify.

5^0

SOLUTION

$5^0 = 1$

Example 3

Simplify.

-4^2

SOLUTION

$-4^2 = -(4^2)$

$= -(4 \cdot 4) = -16$

Example 4

Simplify.

$(-3)^3$

SOLUTION

$(-3)^3 = (-3) \cdot (-3)^2$

$= (-3) \cdot 3^2 = (-3) \cdot 3 \cdot 3$

$= (-3) \cdot 9 = -27$

Skills Bank Practice

Simplify each expression.

a. 3^2 9 **b.** 9^0 1 **c.** 17^1 17 **d.** 5^4 625

e. -1^5 −1 **f.** 0^8 0 **g.** $(-4)^3$ −64 **h.** -8^1 −8

i. $(-2)^6$ 64 **j.** -5^0 −1 **k.** $(3x)^2$ $9x^2$ **l.** $(-3)^3 + 4^2$ −11

m. $(-3)^3 - (-3)^2$ −36 **n.** $(-x)^4 + (2x)^2$ $x^4 + 4x^2$ **o.** $-7^0 + (-2)^2$ 3

p. $(-9)^1 + (-9)^0$ −8 **q.** $7^3 + (-7)^3$ 0 **r.** $7 - 8^1$ −1

Expand each expression.

s. 11^3 $11 \cdot 11 \cdot 11$ **t.** -6^7 $-(6 \cdot 6 \cdot 6 \cdot 6 \cdot 6 \cdot 6 \cdot 6)$

u. $(-13)^5$ $(-13) \cdot (-13) \cdot (-13) \cdot (-13) \cdot (-13)$ **v.** $-(-2)^3$ $-((-2) \cdot (-2) \cdot (-2))$

w. 4^8 $4 \cdot 4 \cdot 4 \cdot 4 \cdot 4 \cdot 4 \cdot 4 \cdot 4$ **x.** $(-5)^2$ $(-5) \cdot (-5)$

864 Saxon Algebra 2

Operations with Decimals

Skills Bank Lesson 4

Operations with Decimals	
To **add** or **subtract**:	Align decimal points. Bring the decimal point directly down into the answer.
To **multiply**:	Multiply as with whole numbers. The number of decimal places in the product is the same as the total number of decimal places in the factors.
To **divide**:	Multiply dividend and divisor by the power of 10 that makes the divisor a whole number. Divide as with whole numbers, placing the decimal point in the quotient directly above the decimal point in the dividend.

Example 1 **Adding Decimals**

Add: $3.25 + 6.1$

SOLUTION

$$\begin{array}{r} 3.25 \\ +\ 6.1 \\ \hline 9.35 \end{array}$$

Example 2 **Subtracting Decimals**

Subtract: $4.083 - 2.96$

SOLUTION

$$\begin{array}{r} \overset{3}{\cancel{4}}.\overset{10}{\cancel{0}}83 \\ -\ 2.96 \\ \hline 1.123 \end{array}$$

Example 3 **Multiplying Decimals**

Multiply: 6.23×0.8

SOLUTION

$6.23 \leftarrow$ 2 decimal places

$\times\ 0.8 \leftarrow$ 1 decimal place

$4.984 \leftarrow$ 3 decimal places

Example 4 **Dividing Decimals**

Divide: $0.1922 \div 0.62$

SOLUTION

$0.62\overline{)0.1922} \longrightarrow$

$(0.62 \times 100)\overline{)(0.1922 \times 100)}$

$$\begin{array}{r} 0.31 \\ 62\overline{)19.22} \\ -186 \\ \hline 62 \\ -62 \\ \hline 0 \end{array}$$

Skills Bank Practice

Simplify.

a. $4.6 + 3.92$ 8.52 **b.** $(2.5)(1.5)$ 3.75 **c.** $2.4 \div 0.08$ 30 **d.** $3.05 - 1.6$ 1.45

e. 4.9×2.27 11.123 **f.** $3.6 + 4.12$ 7.72 **g.** $0.105 - 0.06$ 0.045 **h.** $0.054 \div 0.36$ 0.15

i. 0.2×3.8 0.76 **j.** $2.4 + 8.03$ 10.43 **k.** $60 \div 0.04$ 1,500 **l.** 5.25×8 42

m. $0.98 + 0.35$ 1.33 **n.** $4.074 \div 1.4$ 2.91 **o.** 3.6×0.4 1.44 **p.** $6.52 - 2.74$ 3.78

q. $4.872 - 0.084$ 4.788 **r.** 32.4×18.9 612.36 **s.** $2.334 \div 0.04$ 58.35 **t.** $3.1 + 4.82$ 7.92

SKILLS BANK

Skills Bank 865

Compare and Order Rational Numbers

Skills Bank Lesson 5

To compare and order rational numbers, convert them to the same form (fraction, decimal, percent). Graph each number on a number line.

Example 1 **Compare $\frac{2}{5}$ and 0.7.**

Step 1: Rewrite the fraction as a decimal to solve:

$\frac{2}{5} = 2 \div 5 = 0.4$

Step 2: Graph each of the numbers on a number line

Step 3: Compare using <, >, or =.

Since 0.4 is further on the left of the number line than 0.7, $0.4 < 0.7$ which means $\frac{2}{5} < 0.7$

Example 2 **Write 0.5, −2, $\frac{4}{5}$, and 10% in order from least to greatest.**

Order the numbers from least to greatest using a number line.

−2 10% $\frac{4}{5}$

−2 −1 0 0.5 1 2

In order from least to greatest, the numbers are **−2, 10%, 0.5, $\frac{4}{5}$.**

Skills Bank Practice

Compare using <, >, or =.

a. $\frac{1}{2}$ [>] 0.3 **b.** 0.65 [=] $\frac{13}{20}$ **c.** −3 [<] $-\frac{45}{20}$ **d.** $\frac{2}{5}$ [>] 25%

e. 17.5% [=] $\frac{7}{40}$ **f.** $\frac{6}{5}$ [<] 1.5 **g.** $\frac{3}{4}$ [>] $\frac{5}{8}$ **h.** 1 [=] 100%

i. $-\frac{15}{7}$ [<] −2 **j.** 1.27 [<] $\frac{37}{13}$ **k.** $\frac{23}{40}$ [=] 0.575 **l.** 0.87 [>] 75%

m. $\frac{2}{17}$ [<] 17% **n.** 23% [>] $\frac{5}{28}$ **o.** $-\frac{14}{23}$ [<] −0.45 **p.** 0.034 [<] 34%

Write in order from least to greatest.

q. 0.6, 1.4, 30%, $\frac{15}{21}$ 30%, 0.6, $\frac{15}{21}$, 1.4

r. −5, $-\frac{27}{7}$, −0.01, −0.45 −5, $-\frac{27}{7}$, −0.45, −0.01

s. 0.7, 40%, $\frac{3}{5}$, $\frac{1}{8}$ $\frac{1}{8}$, 40%, $\frac{3}{5}$, 0.7

t. 0.56, 0.65, 55%, $\frac{2}{3}$ 55%, 0.56, 0.65, $\frac{2}{3}$

u. 1.7, 50%, $\frac{46}{90}$, 0.05 0.05, 50%, $\frac{46}{90}$, 1.7

v. −1.5, $-\frac{63}{20}$, $-\frac{57}{40}$, −2.3 $-\frac{63}{20}$, −2.3, −1.5, $-\frac{57}{40}$

866 Saxon Algebra 2

Operations with Fractions

Skills Bank Lesson 6

A **fraction** names part of a whole.

Operations with Fractions	
To **add** or **subtract**:	Write equivalent fractions with a common denominator. Add or subtract the numerators. The denominator of the sum or difference is the same as the common denominator.
To **multiply**:	The numerator of the product is the product of the numerators. The denominator of the product is the product of the denominators.
To **divide**:	To divide by a fraction, multiply by its reciprocal.

Example 1 Adding Fractions

Add: $\frac{1}{2} + \frac{4}{5}$

SOLUTION

$\frac{1}{2} + \frac{4}{5} = \frac{5}{10} + \frac{8}{10} = \frac{13}{10} = 1\frac{3}{10}$

Example 2 Subtracting Fractions

Subtract: $\frac{3}{8} - \frac{1}{6}$

SOLUTION

$\frac{3}{8} - \frac{1}{6} = \frac{9}{24} - \frac{4}{24} = \frac{5}{24}$

Example 3 Multiplying Fractions

Multiply: $\frac{2}{5} \times \frac{3}{8}$

SOLUTION

$\frac{2}{5} \times \frac{3}{8} = \frac{2 \times 3}{5 \times 8} = \frac{6}{40} = \frac{3}{20}$

Example 4 Dividing Fractions

Divide: $\frac{3}{7} \div \frac{4}{5}$

SOLUTION

$\frac{3}{7} \div \frac{4}{5} = \frac{3}{7} \times \frac{5}{4} = \frac{3 \times 5}{7 \times 4} = \frac{15}{28}$

SKILLS BANK

Skills Bank Practice

Simplify. Write the answer in lowest terms.

a. $\frac{2}{5} + \frac{1}{10}$ $\frac{1}{2}$

b. $\frac{3}{8} - \frac{1}{5}$ $\frac{7}{40}$

c. $\frac{1}{6} \cdot \frac{4}{5}$ $\frac{2}{15}$

d. $\frac{5}{6} \div \frac{1}{8}$ $6\frac{2}{3}$

e. $\frac{7}{9} - \frac{3}{5}$ $\frac{8}{45}$

f. $\frac{11}{12} \times \frac{3}{55}$ $\frac{1}{20}$

g. $\frac{7}{15} + \frac{2}{3}$ $1\frac{2}{15}$

h. $\frac{12}{17} \div \frac{3}{8}$ $1\frac{15}{17}$

i. $\frac{7}{8} \times \frac{1}{3}$ $\frac{7}{24}$

j. $6 \div \frac{3}{4}$ 8

k. $\frac{5}{8} + \frac{4}{5}$ $1\frac{17}{40}$

l. $6\frac{1}{8} - 2\frac{5}{6}$ $3\frac{7}{24}$

m. $1\frac{2}{3} \times 6\frac{1}{8}$ $10\frac{5}{24}$

n. $7\frac{3}{8} \div 6$ $1\frac{11}{48}$

o. $10 - 3\frac{7}{12}$ $6\frac{5}{12}$

p. $5\frac{1}{4} + 8\frac{7}{8}$ $14\frac{1}{8}$

q. $\frac{8}{19} - \frac{7}{38} + \frac{3}{19}$ $\frac{15}{38}$

r. $\frac{14}{26} \cdot \frac{13}{49} \cdot \frac{7}{10}$ $\frac{1}{10}$

s. $2\frac{2}{5} + 9\frac{1}{5} - 7\frac{3}{5}$ 4

SKILLS BANK

Skills Bank 867

Negative Numbers and Operations with Integers

Skills Bank Lesson 7

A **negative number** is less than zero. The **absolute value** of a number is its distance from zero. **Opposite** numbers lie the same distance from zero, but in different directions.

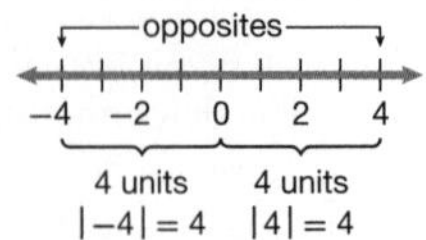

To add numbers with the same sign, add their absolute values. The sign of the sum is the same as the sign of the addends.

Examples: $4 + 9 = 13$

$-8 + -2 = -10$

To add numbers with different signs, subtract their absolute values. The sign of the sum is the same as the sign of the number with greater absolute value.

Examples: $4 + (-7) = -3$

$-9 + 4 = -5$

To subtract a number, add its opposite.

Examples: $6 - 9 = 6 + (-9) = -3$

$7 - (-6) = 7 + (+6) = 13$

$-5 - 8 = -5 + (-8) = -13$

To multiply two numbers, multiply their absolute values. The product of two numbers with the same sign is positive. The product of two numbers with different signs is negative.

Examples: $-8 \times -3 = 24$

$9 \times -2 = -18$

To divide two numbers, divide their absolute values. The quotient of two numbers with the same sign is positive. The quotient of two numbers with different signs is negative.

Examples: $-40 \div -5 = 8$

$10 \div -2 = -5$

Skills Bank Practice

Simplify.

a. $5 + 12$ 17 **b.** $48 \div -6$ −8 **c.** $7(-5)$ −35 **d.** $1.6 \cdot -2$ −3.2

e. $32 \div 4$ 8 **f.** $4.3 + (-8.1)$ −3.8 **g.** $4 - 9$ −5 **h.** $(-2) \cdot (-9)$ 18

i. $-42 + -12$ −54 **j.** -12×4 −48 **k.** $-540 \div -0.9$ 600 **l.** $100 - (-4)$ 104

m. -10×-14 140 **n.** $-81 \div 9$ −9 **o.** $-6 + 13$ 7 **p.** $16 - (-3)$ 19

Ratios, Proportions, Percents

Skills Bank Lesson 8

A **ratio** is a comparison of two numbers by division. A **proportion** shows that two ratios are equal. In a proportion, **cross-products** are equal. For example, $\frac{2}{3} = \frac{4}{6}$ and the cross-products, $2 \cdot 6 = 3 \cdot 4 = 12$.

Example 1 **Solving a Proportion**

Solve for x. $\frac{8}{13} = \frac{x}{117}$

SOLUTION Cross-multiply to find the cross-products. Then, solve for x.

$$\frac{8}{13} = \frac{x}{117}$$

$$(13)x = (8)(117)$$

$$13x = 936$$

$$x = 72$$

A **percent** is a ratio that compares a number to 100.

Example 2 **Solving Problems with Percents**

a. What percent of 112 is 44.8?

SOLUTION Write and solve a proportion:

$$\frac{44.8}{112} = \frac{x}{100}$$

$$112x = 4480$$

$$x = 40$$

44.8 is 40% of 112.

b. What is 80% of 60

SOLUTION Write and solve a proportion:

$$\frac{x}{60} = \frac{80}{100}$$

$$100x = 4800$$

$$48 = x$$

48 is 80% of 60.

Skills Bank Practice

a. Write a proportion to find 5% of 10. $\frac{x}{10} = \frac{5}{100}$

b. Solve for x. $\frac{19}{x} = \frac{57}{12}$ 4

c. What is 11% of 14? 1.54

d. What percent of 80 is 3? 3.75%

e. Find the cross-product to determine if the proportion is true or false. $\frac{7}{9} = \frac{84}{108}$ 756 = 756; True

f. What percent of 300 is 81? 27%

g. What is 25% of 88? 22

h. Solve for x. $\frac{23}{x} = \frac{46}{50}$ 25

SKILLS BANK

SKILLS BANK

Skills Bank 869

Time, Rate, Distance

Skills Bank Lesson 9

When an object moves in a straight path with constant speed, the distance (d) it travels is the product of the rate (r) and the time traveled (t). Use the formula $\boldsymbol{d = rt}$ to solve problems.

Example 1 **Using $d = rt$**

A cyclist travels 16.5 miles in 1.5 hours. What is her average rate of speed?

SOLUTION

$$d = rt$$

$$16.5 = r \cdot 1.5$$

$$\frac{16.5}{1.5} = r$$

$$11 = r$$

The cyclist's average rate of speed is 11 miles per hour.

Example 2 **Using $d = rt$ to Solve Problems**

Two trains leave a station traveling in opposite directions. The slower train travels 10 mph slower than the faster train. If the trains are 325 miles apart after 2.5 hours, what is the speed of each train?

SOLUTION

	r	t	d
Faster Train	r	2.5	$2.5r$
Slower Train	$r - 10$	2.5	$2.5(r - 10)$

Use a table to organize the information.

Write an equation: $2.5r + 2.5(r - 10) = 325$

$$2.5r + 2.5r - 25 = 325$$

$$5r - 25 = 325$$

$$5r = 350$$

$$r = 70$$

The faster train's rate is 70 mph. The slower train's rate is 70 − 10, or 60 mph.

Skills Bank Practice

a. Find d when $r = 7$ mph and $t = 6$ hours. 42 mi

b. Find t when $r = 3.5$ mph and $d = 34.3$ miles. 9.8 h

c. Mark drove 312 miles to the beach. The trip took 6.25 hours. What was Mark's average rate of speed? Round to the nearest whole number. 50 miles per hour

d. Two runners leave a gym at 10:00 AM and run in opposite directions. One runs at 6 mph and the other runs at 5 mph. How far apart will the runners be at 10:30 AM? 5.5 miles

e. A runner training for a marathon leaves home running at 9 mph. At a certain point, he turns around and runs along the same route back home at 6 mph. If the entire run lasts 2.5 hours, how far has the runner run altogether? 18 miles

870 *Saxon Algebra 2*

Coordinate Plane/Ordered Pairs

Skills Bank Lesson 10

The **coordinate plane** is formed by the x-axis and the y-axis. Their point of intersection is called the **origin.** Each location on the coordinate plane can be described using an **ordered pair,** which describes its location relative to the origin.

An ordered pair is written in the form (x, y), where x is the point's **x-coordinate** and y is its **y-coordinate.**

For the point $(-4, 2)$, the coordinates indicate that the point is located 4 units to the left of the origin, and 2 units up from the origin.

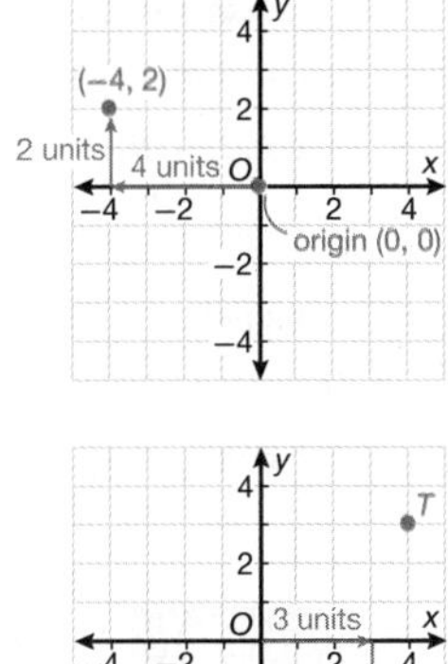

Example: Graph the point $N(3, -2)$.

- Start at the origin.
- Move 3 units to the right because the x-coordinate is $+3$.
- Move 2 units down because the y-coordinate is -2.
- Draw a point and label it N.

Example: Give the coordinates of T

- Start at the origin.
- Count to the right 4 units. The x-coordinate is 4.
- Count up 3 units. The y-coordinate is 3.
- The coordinates of T are $(4, 3)$.

SKILLS BANK

Skills Bank Practice

Graph each point on the coordinate plane like point $P(-5, 8)$ shown.

a. $A(2, 0)$
b. $B(-3, 1)$
c. $C(2, -4)$
d. $D(0, 2)$
e. $E(5, 7)$
f. $F(6, -1)$
g. $G(-3, -2)$
h. $H(8, 6)$
i. $I(2, 7)$
j. $J(-5, -6)$
k. $K(5, -2)$
l. $L(-6, -2)$
m. $M(4, 1)$
n. $N(-6, 0)$
o. $O(1, 4)$

Name the coordinates of each point.

p. P (−4, 2)
q. Q (0, −4)
r. R (2, 3)
s. S (6, −7)
t. T (−7, −1)
u. U (2, 6)
v. V (4, 0)
w. W (−3, −5)
x. X (−5, 8)

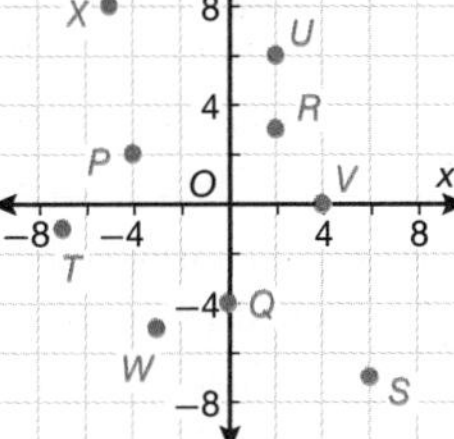

SKILLS BANK

Skills Bank 871

Plane Figures and Coordinate Geometry

Skills Bank Lesson 11

Graph a plane figure on the coordinate plane by plotting and labeling its vertices.

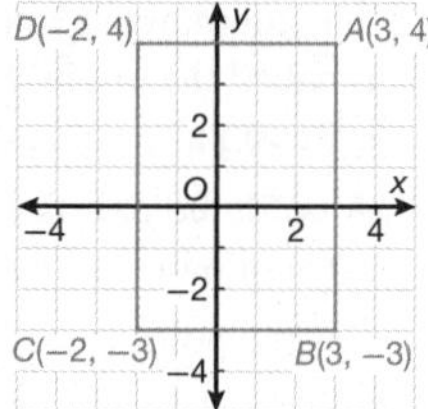

Example 1 **Identifying a Figure Using its Vertices**

Describe polygon $ABCD$ with $A(3, 4)$, $B(3, -3)$, $C(-2, -3)$, and $D(-2, 4)$.

SOLUTION

Graph each point, then connect the vertices. Polygon $ABCD$ is a rectangle.

The **midpoint** of a line segment with endpoints (x_1, y_1) and (x_2, y_2) is located at $\left(\frac{x_1 + x_2}{2}, \frac{y_1 + y_2}{2}\right)$.

The **distance**, d, between points (x_1, y_1) and (x_2, y_2) is given by

$$d = \sqrt{(x_2 - x_1)^2 + (y_2 - y_1)^2}$$

Example 2 **Classifying a Triangle**

Given $A(7, 1)$, $B(3, -4)$, and $C(-1, 1)$, classify ΔABC as scalene, isosceles, or equilateral.

SOLUTION

Use the distance formula to find the length of each side.

$$AB = \sqrt{(3 - 7)^2 + (-4 - 1)^2} = \sqrt{(-4)^2 + (-5)^2} = \sqrt{16 + 25} = \sqrt{41}$$

$$BC = \sqrt{(-1 - 3)^2 + (1 - (-4))^2} = \sqrt{(-4)^2 + (5)^2} = \sqrt{16 + 25} = \sqrt{41}$$

$$AC = \sqrt{(-1 - 7)^2 + (1 - 1)^2} = \sqrt{(-8)^2 + (0)^2} = \sqrt{64 + 0} = \sqrt{64} = 8$$

The triangle has two congruent sides. So, ΔABC is isosceles.

Skills Bank Practice

For a and b, graph the polygon with the given vertices. Describe the polygon.

a. $(-4, 3)$, $(4, -5)$, and $(4, 3)$ right isosceles triangle

b. $(-4, -2)$, $(2, 2)$, $(5, 0)$, $(-1, -4)$ parallelogram

c. A square has vertices at $(-2, -2)$, $(1, 1)$ and $(4, -2)$. Name the coordinates of its fourth vertex. $(1, -5)$

d. A segment has endpoints at $(0, -4)$ and $(3, -7)$. Find the coordinates of the midpoint. Find the length of the segment. $(1.5, -5.5)$; $\sqrt{18}$ or $3\sqrt{2}$

e. Given $A(4, 2)$, $B(0, 9)$, and $C(-4, 2)$, classify ΔABC as scalene, isosceles, or equilateral. isosceles

f. A quadrilateral has vertices at $(-1, 1)$, $(2, 6)$, $(5, 1)$, and $(2, -4)$. Show that the quadrilateral is a rhombus. The length of each side is $\sqrt{34}$, so the quadrilateral is a rhombus.

g. A circle has diameter with endpoints $(-8, 1)$ and $(-3, 13)$. Find the center of the circle. Find the area of the circle. center: $(-5.5, 7)$; area: $\frac{169\pi}{4}$

h. Given $R(4, 3)$, $S(0, 9)$, and $T(-4, 2)$, find the length of the segment with one endpoint at T and the other at the midpoint of $\overline{RS}$. $\sqrt{52}$

872 Saxon Algebra 2

Parallel Lines and Transversals

Skills Bank Lesson 12

When a **transversal** intersects parallel lines, certain pairs of angles are congruent.

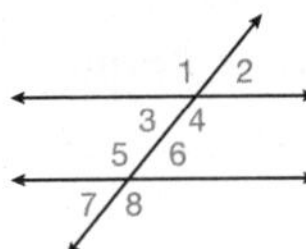

Corresponding angles lie in the same position relative to the parallel lines and the transversal. For example, $\angle 5 \cong \angle 1$.

Corresponding angles have the same measure. For example, $m\angle 5 = m\angle 1$.

Alternate interior angles lie between the parallel lines and on opposite sides of the transversal. For example, $\angle 3 \cong \angle 6$.

Alternate interior angles have the same measure. For example, $m\angle 3 = m\angle 6$.

Alternate exterior angles lie outside the parallel lines and on opposite sides of the transversal. For example, $\angle 1 \cong \angle 8$.

Alternate interior angles have the same measure. For example, $m\angle 1 = m\angle 8$.

SKILLS BANK

Example 1 Identifying Angle Relationships

Use the diagram above to idenitfy the relationship between the given angles.

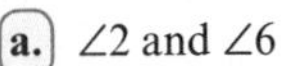

a. $\angle 2$ and $\angle 6$

SOLUTION

The angles lie to the right of the transversal, above the lines.

$\angle 2$ and $\angle 6$ are corresponding angles.

b. $\angle 7$ and $\angle 2$

SOLUTION

The angles lie outside the parallel lines, on opposite sides of the transversal.

$\angle 7$ and $\angle 2$ are alternate exterior angles.

c. $\angle 5$ and $\angle 4$

SOLUTION

The angles lie inside the parallel lines, on opposite sides of the transversal.

$\angle 7$ and $\angle 2$ are alternate interior angles.

Skills Bank Practice

Use the diagram at right. Lines *a* and *b* are parallel.

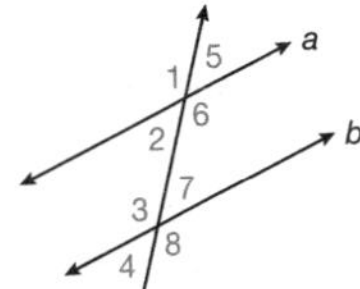

a. $m\angle 2 = m\angle$ ______ because they are corresponding angles. 4

b. $m\angle 8 = m\angle$ ______ because they are alternate exterior angles. 1

c. $m\angle 3 = m\angle$ ______ because they are alternate interior angles. 6

d. $m\angle 4 = m\angle 5$ because they are ______ angles alternate exterior

e. $m\angle 2 = m\angle 7$ because they are ______ angles alternate interior

f. $m\angle 5 = m\angle 7$ because they are ______ angles corresponding

g. If $m\angle 3 = 135°$, find the measure of each numbered angle.
$m\angle 3 = m\angle 8 = m\angle 1 = m\angle 6 = 135°$; $m\angle 2 = m\angle 4 = m\angle 5 = m\angle 7 = 45°$

SKILLS BANK

Skills Bank 873

Angle Measurement

Skills Bank Lesson 13

Angles are measured in degrees (°). Use a **protractor** to find the measure of an angle.

Example **Using a Protractor to Measure an Angle**

Use a protractor to find the measure of $\angle ABC$.

SOLUTION

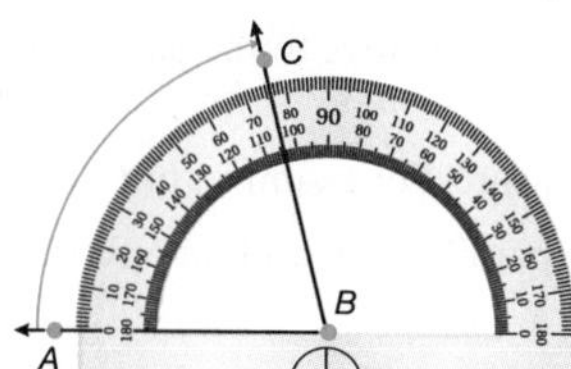

The measure of $\angle ABC$ is 76°. $m\angle ABC = 76°$.

Skills Bank Practice

Use a protractor to measure each angle.

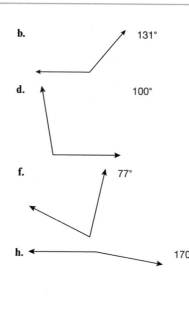

a. 45°

b. 131°

c. 80°

d. 100°

e. 72°

f. 77°

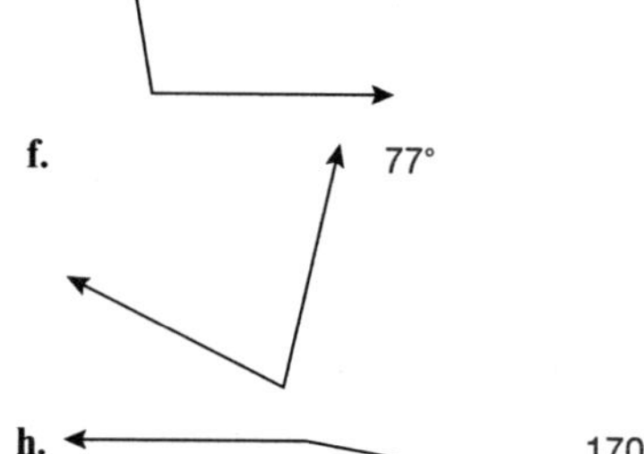

g. 55°

h. 170°

i. 33°

874 *Saxon Algebra 2*

Angle Relationships

Skills Bank Lesson 14

Two angles are **complementary** if the sum of their measures is 90°.

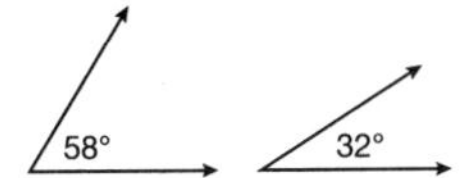

Since 58° + 32° = 90°, these angles are complementary.

Two angles are **supplementary** if the sum of their measures is 180°.

Since 60° + 120° = 180°, these angles are supplementary.

Vertical angles are formed when two lines intersect. They share a vertex. Vertical angles are congruent (they have the same measure).

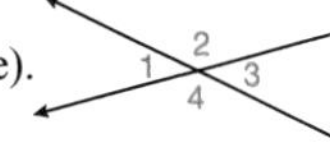

$\angle 1$ and $\angle 3$ are vertical angles. $m\angle 1 = m\angle 3$

$\angle 2$ and $\angle 4$ are vertical angles. $m\angle 1 = m\angle 4$

Adjacent angles share a vertex and a side, and do not overlap.

$\angle PTS$ and $\angle RTS$ are adjacent angles. They share vertex T and side $\overrightarrow{TS}$.

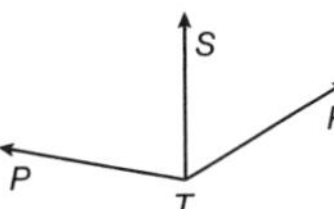

SKILLS BANK

Skills Bank Practice

Find the measure of an angle that is complementary to the angle with the given measure.

a. 30° 60° **b.** 88° 2° **c.** 17° 73° **d.** 47° 43°

Find the measure of an angle that is supplementary to the angle with the given measure.

e. 19° 161° **f.** 122° 58° **g.** 163° 17° **h.** 81° 99°

Complete.

i. $\angle SMK$ and $\angle$____ are vertical angles. $\angle TMR$

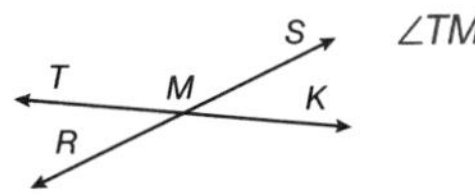

j. $\angle$____ and $\angle$____ are adjacent. $\angle AMB$; $\angle BMZ$

Solve for *x*.

k. $\angle RMS$ and $\angle SMD$ are supplementary. $x = 16$

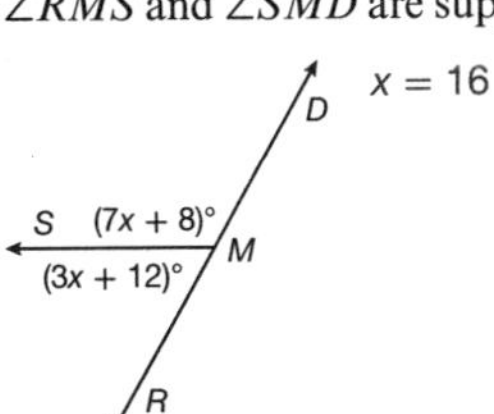

l. $x = 35$

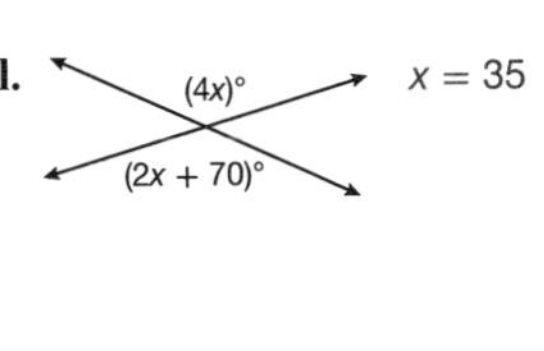

SKILLS BANK

Skills Bank 875

Properties of Polygons

Skills Bank Lesson 15

A **polygon** is a closed plane figure that is made up of line segments called **sides.** Each side intersects exactly two others, at its endpoints. These endpoints are the **vertices** of the polygon. In an **equilateral** polygon, all sides are congruent. In an **equiangular** polygon, all interior angles are congruent. In a **regular** polygon, all sides are congruent and all interior angles are congruent.

Polygon	Number of Sides
Triangle	3
Quadrilateral	4
Pentagon	5
Hexagon	6
Heptagon	7
Octagon	8
Nonagon	9
Decagon	10
Hendecagon	11
Dodecagon	12
n-gon	n

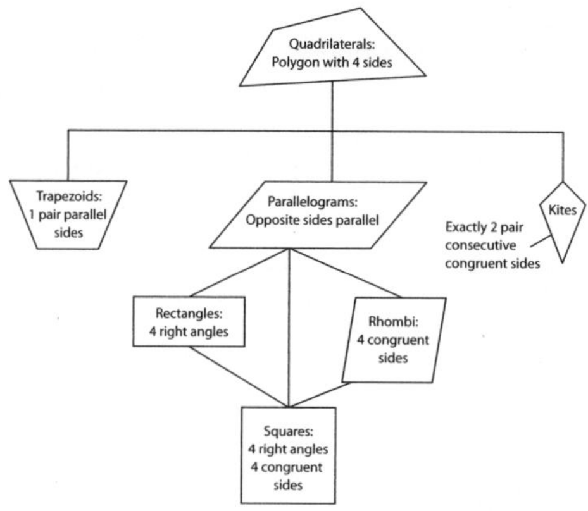

The sum of the measures of each interior angle in an n-sided convex polygon is $180°(n - 2)$.

Example 1 Finding the Measure of Each Interior Angle of a Polygon

Find the measure of each interior angle of a regular hexagon.

SOLUTION

A hexagon has 6 sides, so $n = 6$. The sum of the angle measures is $180°(6 - 2)$, or $720°$. Each interior angle in a regular hexagon is congruent. So, each interior angle measures $720° \div 6$, or $120°$.

Skills Bank Practice

For a–d, give all the names that apply to each figure.

a. 

b. 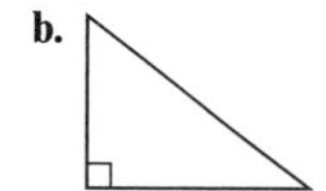

c. **d.** 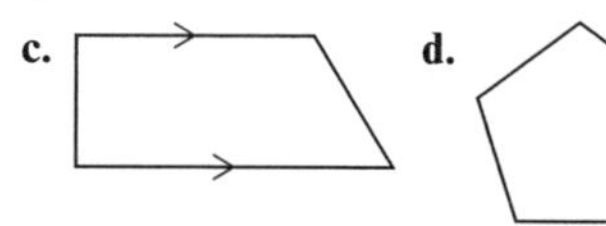

a. polygon, quadrilateral, parallelogram, rhombus

b. polygon, triangle, right triangle, scalene triangle

c. polygon, quadrilateral, trapezoid

d. polygon, pentagon

e. What is the sum of the interior angle measures in a pentagon? 540°

f. An octagon has angles measuring 100°, 135°, 130°, 145°, 115°, and 105°. What is the measure of each of the other two angles if they have the same measure? 175°

g. What is the measure of each interior angle in a regular decagon? 144°

876 *Saxon* Algebra 2

Geometric Formulas

Skills Bank Lesson 16

Use these formulas for area (A) and volume (V) using base area (B), perimeter (P), radius (r), length (l), width (w), and height (h). (Note: in the surface area of a regular pyramid P is the perimeter of the base, and l is the slant height of the pyramid.)

	Rectangular Prism	Cylinder	Sphere	Regular Pyramid
Volume	Bh	$\pi r^2 h$	$\frac{4}{3}\pi r^3$	$\frac{1}{3}Bh$
Surface Area	$2lw + 2wh + 2lh$	$2\pi r(r + h)$	$4\pi r^2$	$B + \frac{1}{2}Pl$

Example 1 Using a Volume Formula

Find the volume of a rectangular prism that has a length of 6 cm, width of 3 cm, and a height of 5 cm.

SOLUTION

$V = 6 \cdot 3 \cdot 5$

$= 90 \text{ cm}^3$

Example 2 Using a Surface Area Formula

Find the surface area of a rectangular prism that has a length of 14 cm, a height of 10 cm, and a base with an area of 168 cm².

SOLUTION

$SA = 2 \cdot 14 \cdot \frac{168}{14} + 2 \cdot \frac{168}{14} \cdot 10 + 2 \cdot 14 \cdot 10$

$= 336 + 240 + 280$

$= 856 \text{ cm}^3$

SKILLS BANK

Skills Bank Practice

Find each measure. Round to the nearest hundredth.

a. Find the volume of a cylinder with a circumference of 14 m and a height of 7 m. 109.18 m³

b. Find the radius of a sphere with a volume of 113.1 in³. 3 in.

c. Find the surface area of a regular pyramid with a slant height of 23 cm and a square base that has a length of 15 cm. 915 cm²

d. Find the surface area. 263.9 cm²

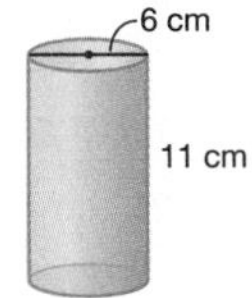

e. Find the volume. 42.41 m³

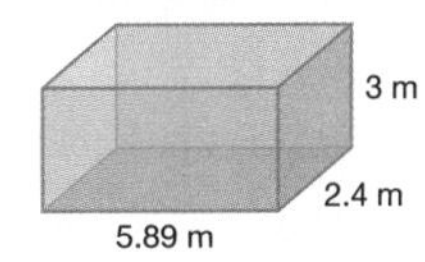

f. Find the height of a regular pyramid with a base area of 12 in.² and a volume of 32 in.³. 8 in.

g. Find the volume of a regular pyramid with an octagonal base that has an area of 27 ft² and a height of 7 ft. 63 ft³

h. Find the radius of a cylinder with a height of 8 cm and a surface area of 96π cm². 4 cm

i. Find the volume of a cylinder with radius and height of 9 cm and a sphere with a radius of 9 cm. Which is larger? By how much?

i. volume of cylinder: 729π cm³ volume of sphere: 972π cm³; The sphere's volume is $\frac{4}{3}$ of the cylinder's volume.

SKILLS BANK

Skills Bank 877

Area of Polygons, Circles, and Composite Figures

Skills Bank Lesson 17

Use formulas to find areas of figures. For a figure that is made up of one or more other shapes (a **composite** figure), break the figure down into basic shapes, then find the area of each one. Use the table of area formulas for some common polygons, to find the area of the composite figures.

Parallelogram	Circle	Trapezoid	Rectangle	Triangle
h, b	r	b_1, h, b_2	w, l	h, b
$A = bh$	$A = \pi r^2$	$A = \frac{1}{2}(b_1 + b_2)h$	$A = lw$	$A = \frac{1}{2}bh$

Example 1 Finding the Area of a Figure

Find the area of each figure.

SOLUTION

$A = \frac{1}{2}(b_1 + b_2)h$

$= \frac{1}{2}(18 + 24)10$

$= 210 \text{ cm}^2$

18 cm
10 cm
24 cm

SOLUTION

$A = lw + \frac{1}{2}\pi r^2$

$\approx 22 \cdot 10 + \frac{1}{2} \cdot 3.14 \cdot 11^2$

$\approx 220 + 189.97$

$\approx 409.97 \text{ in}^2$

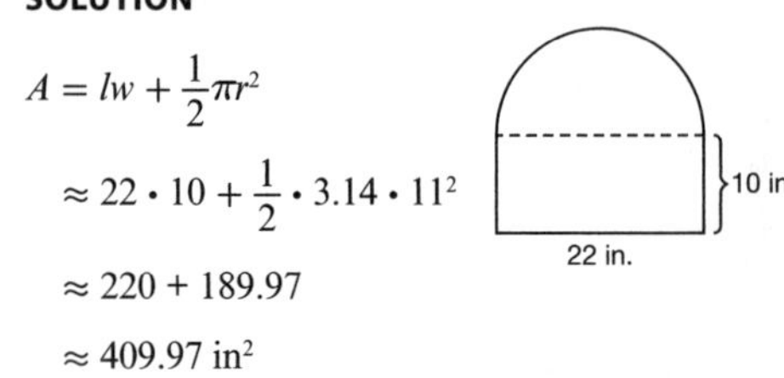

Skills Bank Practice

Find the area of each figure. (Use 3.14 for π.)

a. 84 m²

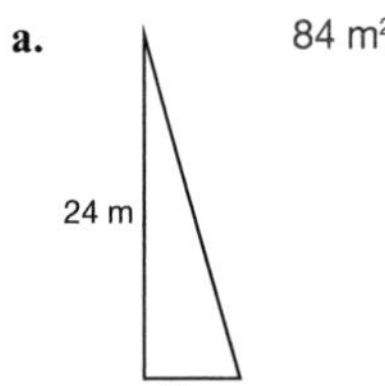

b.

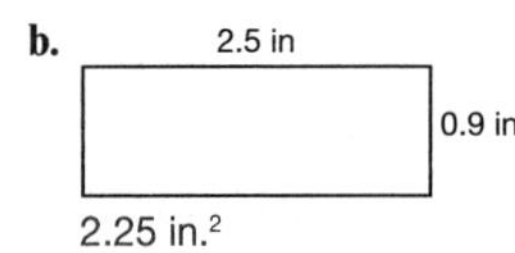

2.25 in.²

c.

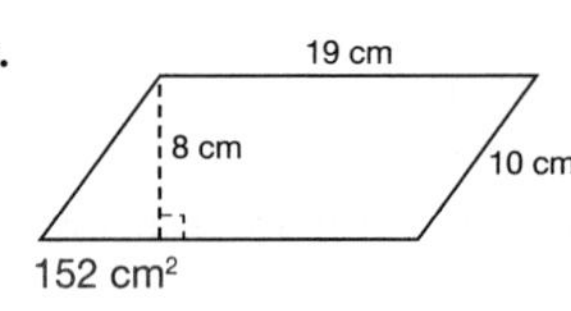

152 cm²

d. 28 ft²

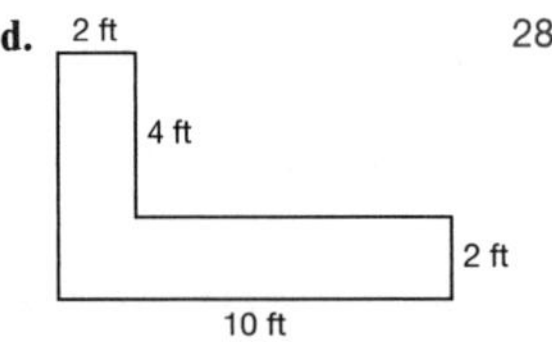

e. 212 cm²

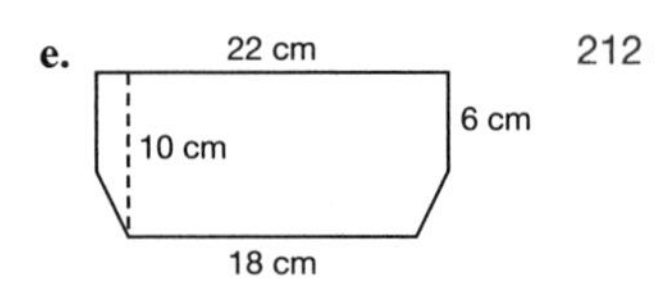

f. 1,827.84 mm²

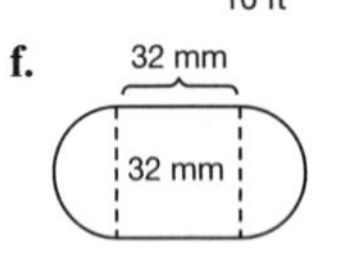

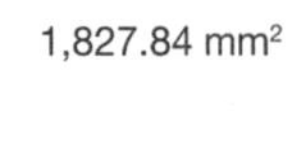

g. 50 in.²

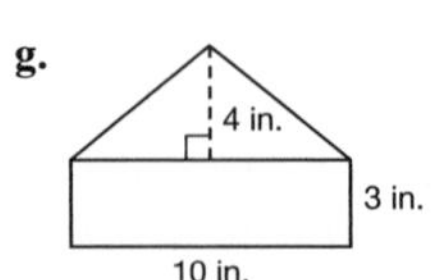

878 Saxon Algebra 2

Angle Relationships in Circles and Polygons

Skills Bank Lesson 18

A **regular** polygon has congruent interior angles and congruent sides. The measure of each interior angle of a regular polygon with n sides is $\left(\frac{n-2}{n}\right) \cdot 180$.

These formulas apply to a circle of radius R circumscribed and a circle of radius r inscribed in a regular n-gon.

$$s = 2R\sin\left(\frac{180°}{n}\right) \qquad r = R\cos\left(\frac{180°}{n}\right)$$

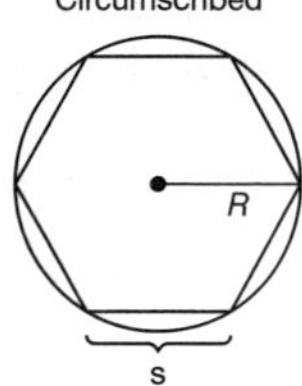

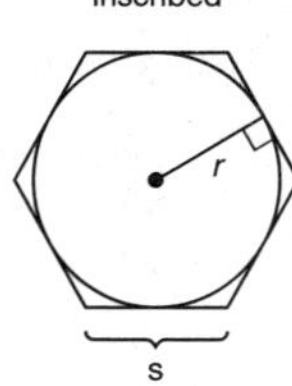

Example 1 **Finding Side Length Using Circumscribed Circles**

A circle with radius 4 cm is circumscribed around a regular pentagon. Find the length of each side of the pentagon. Round to the nearest hundredth.

SOLUTION $s = 2R\sin\left(\frac{180°}{n}\right) = 2 \cdot 4 \cdot \sin\left(\frac{180°}{5}\right) = 8 \cdot \sin(36°) \approx 4.70$ cm

4 cm

Example 2 **Finding Side Length Using Inscribed Circles**

A circle with radius 6 inches is inscribed in a regular octagon. Find the length of each side of the octagon. Round to the nearest hundredth.

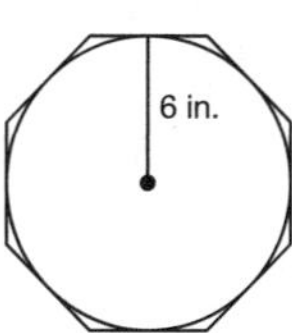

SOLUTION

Step 1: Find the value of R.

$6 = R\cos\left(\frac{180°}{8}\right)$

$R = \dfrac{6}{\cos\left(\frac{180°}{8}\right)}$

$R \approx 6.49$

Step 2: Find the value of s.

$s = 2R\sin\left(\frac{180°}{n}\right)$

$s = 2 \cdot 6.49 \cdot \sin\left(\frac{180°}{8}\right)$

$s = 12.98 \cdot \sin(22.5°)$

$s \approx 4.97$ in.

The length of each side of the octagon is approximately 4.97 inches.

Skills Bank Practice

Find the measure of each interior angle of the given regular polygon. Round to the nearest hundreth.

a. A circle with radius 7 m is inscribed in a regular hexagon. Find the length of each side of the hexagon. 8.08 m

b. A circle with radius 10 ft is circumscribed around a regular triangle. Find the radius of the circle that can be inscribed in the same regular triangle. 5 ft

c. A circle with radius 5 cm is inscribed in a square. Find the length of each side of the square. 10 cm

d. A circle with radius 30 inches is circumscribed around a regular decagon. Find the radius of the circle that can be inscribed in the same regular decagon. 28.53 in.

e. A circle is inscribed in a regular heptagon with side length 4 meters. Find the length of the radius of the circle. 4.15 m

SKILLS BANK

Skills Bank 879

Views of Solid Figures

Skills Bank Lesson 19

An **isometric** drawing is a way of drawing a three dimensional figure using isometric dot paper, which has equally spaced dots in a repeating triangular pattern.

Example 1 **Drawing an Isometric View of a Figure**

Draw an isometric view of the figure shown.

SOLUTION

An **orthographic view** is a two-dimensional view of a three-dimensional figure, taken from a position directly in front of, above, or to the side of the figure.

Example 2 **Finding the Orthographic View of a Figure**

Show top, front, and side views of the figure.

SOLUTION

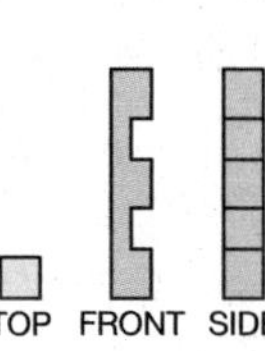

Skills Bank Practice

Draw the isometric view of each figure in the dot grids provided.

a.

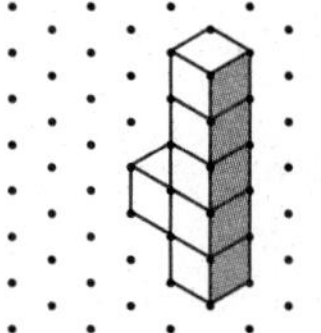

b.

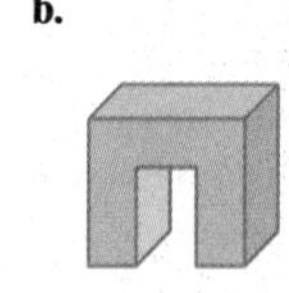

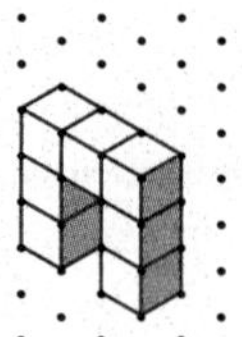

Draw the top, front, and side orthographic views of each figure.

c.

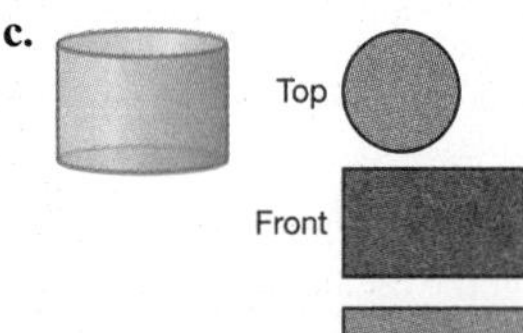

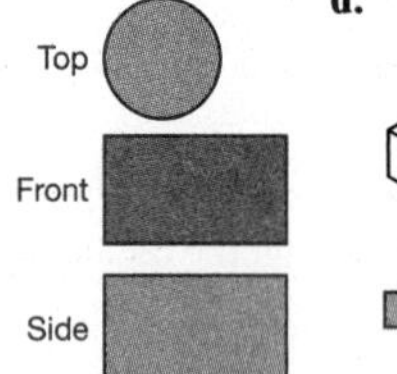

d.

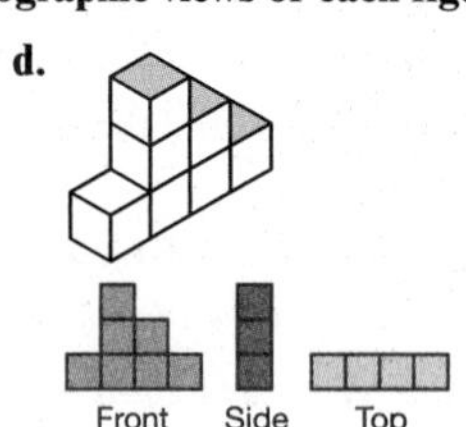

e.

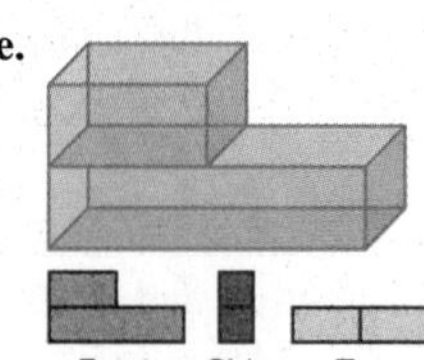

880 *Saxon Algebra 2*

Geometric Patterns and Tessellations

Skills Bank Lesson 20

Patterns of figures can often be described numerically.

Example 1 Finding the Next Stage of a Geometric Pattern

The first four stages of a pattern are shown. Write a sequence for the number of dots in each stage. Explain the pattern and find the next term.

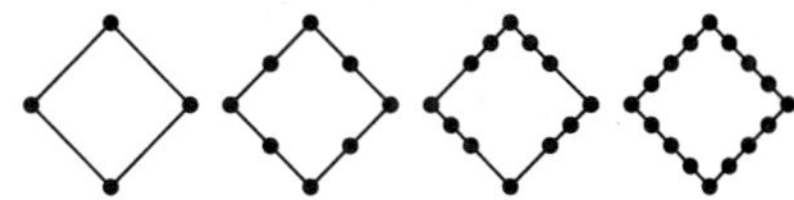

SOLUTION A table can help you see a pattern in the sequence of numbers: In each stage, the number of dots increases by 4. There will be 20 dots in the 5th stage.

Stage	1	2	3	4
Dots	4	8	12	16

A **tessellation** is a repeating pattern of plane shapes that completely covers an area without any gaps or overlaps. One simple example of a tessellation is square tiles completely covering a floor. No tiles overlap, and there are no gaps between tiles.

Example 2 Finding a Numeric Pattern in a Tessellation

In a tessellation of squares, squares are added to create the stages that are numbered inside the squares. How many squares will be added to create the 3rd stage?

2	2	2
2	1	2
2	2	2

SOLUTION

Add squares around the outside of the figure.

You will use 16 squares.

3	3	3	3	3
3	2	2	2	3
3	2	1	2	3
3	2	2	2	3
3	3	3	3	3

Skills Bank Practice

Find and describe the pattern in the described sequence. Give the next number in the sequence.

a. The number of non-overlapping triangles in each stage. 1, 4, 7, 10; add 3; 13

b. The number of dots in each stage. 4, 6, 8, 10, 12; add 2; 14

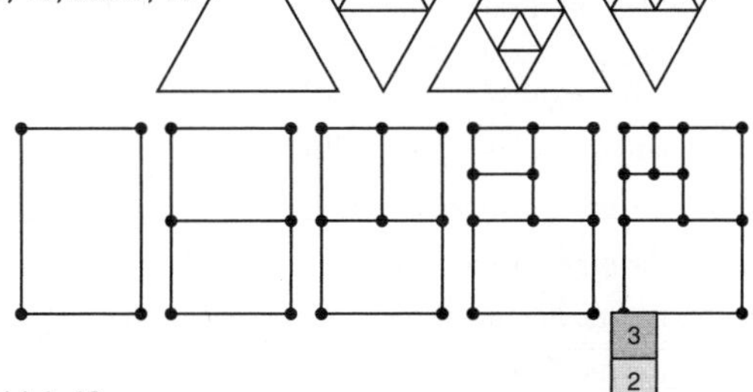

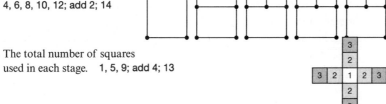

c. The total number of squares used in each stage. 1, 5, 9; add 4; 13

		3		
		2		
3	2	1	2	3
		2		
		3		

SKILLS BANK

SKILLS BANK

Skills Bank 881

Stem-and-Leaf Plots

Skills Bank Lesson 21

A **stem-and-leaf plot** is a way to arrange the numbers in a data set according to place value.

Example 1 Making a Stem-and-Leaf Plot

Make a stem-and-leaf plot of the data.

18, 22, 15, 22, 31, 35, 27, 19, 29, 9, 25, 20, 58, 12, 56, 25, 15, 23

SOLUTION

Write the data in order from least to greatest:

9, 12, 15, 15, 18, 19, 20, 22, 22, 23, 25, 25, 27, 29, 31, 35, 56, 58

In the stem-and-leaf plot, the tens place digit of each number is a stem.

The ones digit of each number is a leaf.

Stems	Leaves
0	9
1	2, 5, 5, 8, 9
2	0, 2, 2, 3, 5, 5, 7, 9
3	1, 5
4	
5	6, 8

Skills Bank Practice

For a and b, make a stem-and-leaf plot for the set of data.

a. Number of Minutes Students Practiced Piano

9, 12, 15, 15, 18, 19, 20, 22, 22, 23, 25, 25, 27, 29, 31, 35, 56, 58

a.

Stems	Leaves
0	9
1	2, 5, 5, 8, 9
2	0, 2, 2, 3, 5, 5, 7, 9
3	1, 5
4	
5	6, 8

b. Chapter 1 Test Scores

70, 83, 88, 90, 68, 82, 99, 79, 79, 81, 100, 90, 86, 90, 70, 79, 90, 92, 94,75, 62, 73, 83, 96, 64, 98

b.

Stems	Leaves
6	2, 4, 8
7	0, 0, 3, 5, 9, 9, 9
8	1, 2, 3, 3, 6, 8
9	0, 0, 0, 0, 2, 4, 6, 8, 9
10	0

c. The stem-and-leaf plot shows the number of boxes of popcorn sold at basketball games last season. Use the stem-and-leaf plot to answer the questions.

Stem	Leaves
8	3, 5, 5, 8, 9
9	0, 3, 6
10	0, 2, 8, 4, 6, 6, 6
11	3, 6
12	0, 1

i. For how many games was data collected? 19

ii. What was the least number of boxes sold? 83

iii. What was the greatest number of boxes sold? 121

iv. What was the median number of boxes sold? 102

v. What was the mode number of boxes sold? 106

882 Saxon Algebra 2

Statistical Graphs

Skills Bank Lesson 22

You can display data using a **statistical graph.**

Use a **bar graph** to compare amounts. Use a **circle graph** to compare parts of a whole.

Example 1 Making a Bar Graph and Circle Graph

Make a bar graph and circle graph for the data.

Sophomore Class Foreign Languages

French	Latin	Spanish	German
68	39	105	38

SOLUTION

Place the languages along the horizontal axis and numbers along the vertical axis. Label each axis and give the graph a title.

Sophomore Foreign Languages

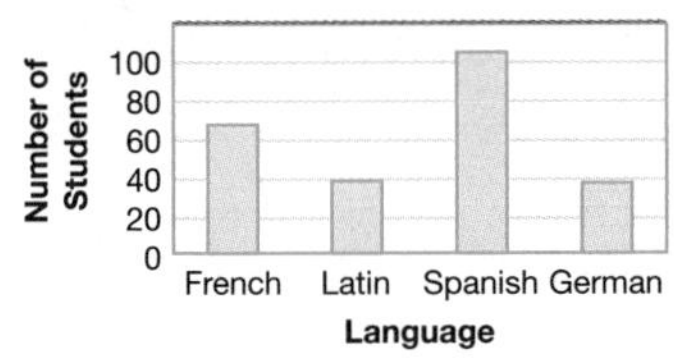

Find the percent of the total for each language. Multiply the percent by 360° to find the measure of the central angle for each language.

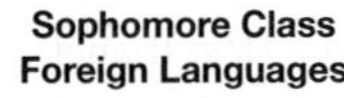

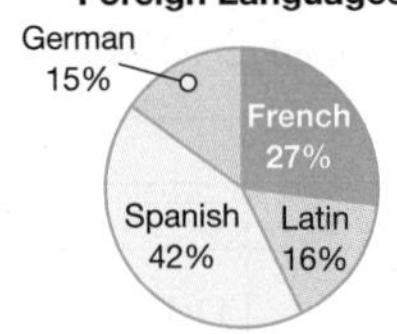

Skills Bank Practice

a. Draw a circle graph of the data.

School Population by Grade			
9th	10th	11th	12th
254	233	261	203

b. Draw a bar graph of the data.

Number of Songs Downloaded						
Mon	Tue	Wed	Thu	Fri	Sat	Sun
28	32	25	16	30	18	32

a. School Population by Grade

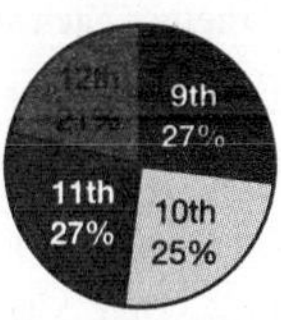

b. Number of Songs Downloaded

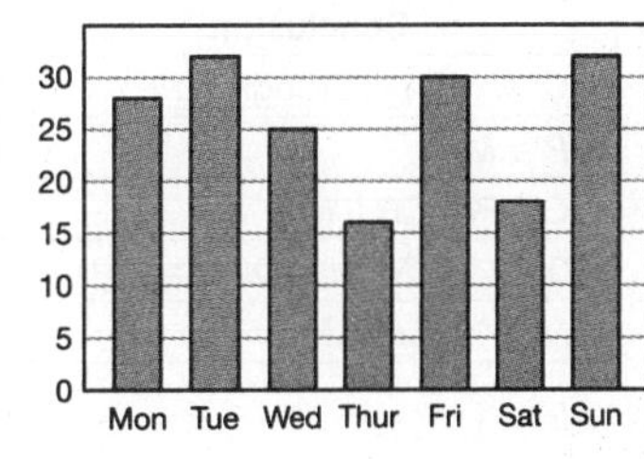

SKILLS BANK

SKILLS BANK

Skills Bank 883

Proofs

Skills Bank Lesson 23

A **proof** is a logical argument that shows a conclusion to be true or false. In a mathematical proof, each step must be justified by a property, theorem, definition, or other accepted rule.

Example 1 Proving Expressions Equal

Prove that $(x + 1)^2 - 9 = (x + 4)(x - 2)$

SOLUTION Simplify each side and determine whether the expressions are equivalent.

$(x + 1)^2 - 9 \stackrel{?}{=} (x + 4)(x - 2)$	Given
$x^2 + 2x + 1 - 9 \stackrel{?}{=} x^2 - 2x + 4x - 8$	Distributive Property
$x^2 + 2x - 8 = x^2 + 2x - 8$ ✓	Add.

The sides are equal. So, $(x + 1)^2 - 9 = (x + 4)(x - 2)$.

Example 2 Proofs in Geometry

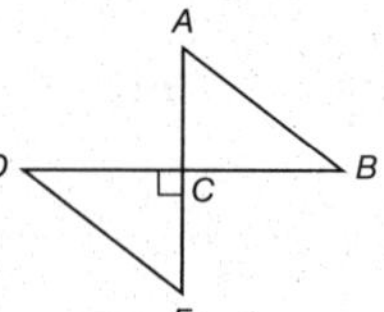

Prove that ΔABC is a right triangle.

SOLUTION Make justified conclusions.

Conclusion	Justification
$\angle DCF$ is a right angle.	Given
$\angle DCF$ and $\angle ACB$ are vertical angles.	Definition of vertical angles
$\angle ACB$ is a right angle	Vertical angles are congruent.
ΔABC is a right triangle.	Definition of a right triangle.

Skills Bank Practice

Prove whether each statement is true or false. **a.** false; $x^2 + 10x + 25 \neq x^2 + 25$

a. $(x + 5)^2 = x^2 + 25$

b. $x(x - 3) + 5x - 9 = (x + 1)^2 - 10$ true

c. $(x + 3)(x + 2)(x + 1) = x^3 + 6x^2 + 11x + 6$ true

d. $(x + 7)(x - 4) = (x + 2)(x + 1)$ false; $-28 \neq 2$

e. Prove that $\Delta MQP \cong \Delta PNM$

Given: $MQPN$ is a parallelogram

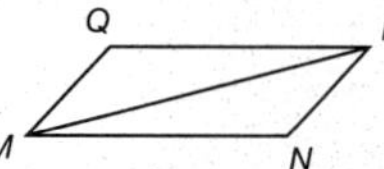

Conclusion	Justification
$MQPN$ is a parallelogram.	Given
$MP \cong MP$	Reflexive Property
$MQ \parallel PN$; $QP \parallel MN$	Definition of Parallelogram
$\angle QMP \cong \angle MPN$; $\angle QPM \cong \angle PMN$	Alternate Interior Angles are Congruent
$\Delta MQP \cong \Delta PNM$	Angle-Side-Angle Congruence Theorem

884 Saxon Algebra 2

Venn Diagrams

Skills Bank Lesson 24

A **Venn Diagram** shows relationships among the elements of two or more sets.

Example Making a Venn Diagram

Make a Venn Diagram using the positive integers from 1 to 20.

A: the set of even numbers

B: the set of factors of 12

C: the set of factors of 20.

SOLUTION

Draw three overlapping circles.

Label one circle for each set.

Place the elements in the appropriate region of the diagram.

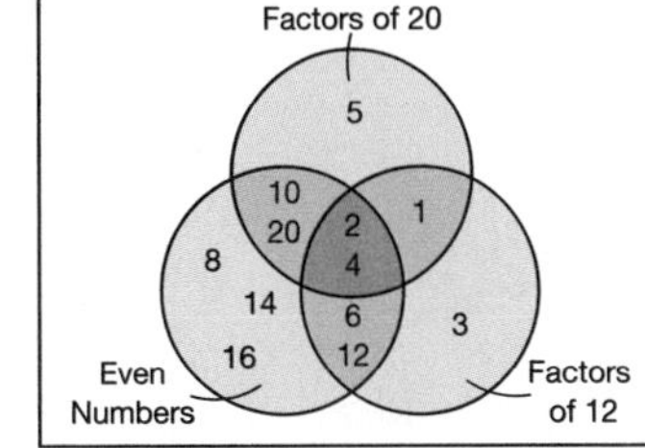

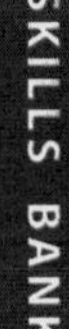

Skills Bank Practice

Draw a Venn Diagram of the sets.

a. A: factors of 40
B: factors of 15

b. A: positive integers less than 21
B: factors of 10
C: the first 5 multiples of 2

c. A: the primary colors
B: the colors in the American Flag

d. A: weekdays (business days)
B: weekend days

Draw a Venn Diagram to represent the situations described.

e. There are 12 students in a Math class and 13 students in a Science class. Five of the students are in both the Math and the Science class.

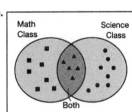

a.

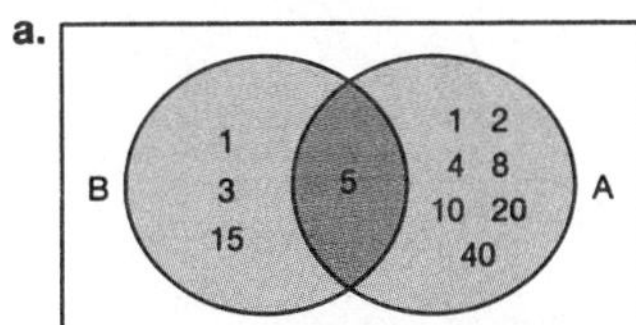

b.

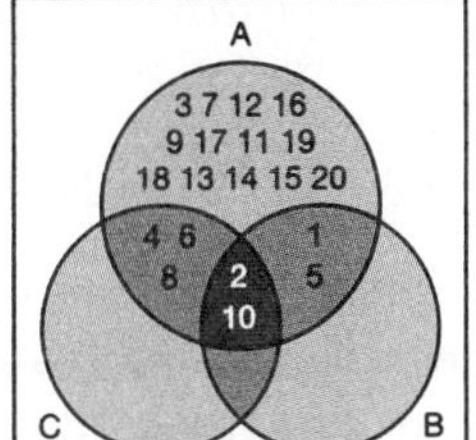

c.

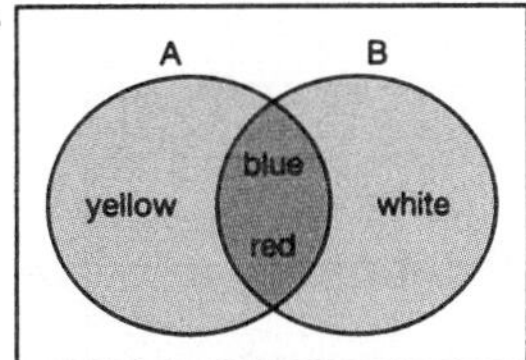

d.

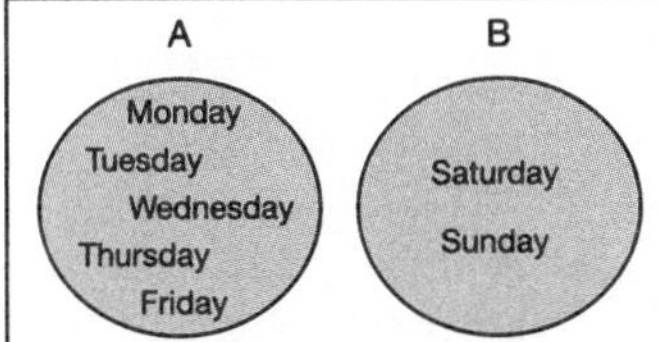

e.

Math Class

Science Class

Both

SKILLS BANK

Skills Bank 885

Properties and Formulas

Properties

Addition and Subtraction Properties for Inequalities
(10)

For real numbers a, b, and c, if $a < b$, then $a + c < b + c$ and $a - c < b - c$.

The relationship also holds true for $>$, $\leq$, and $\geq$.

Addition Property of Equality
(7)

If $a = b$, then $a + c = b + c$.

Arithmetic Sequence
(92)

The nth term of an arithmetic sequence is given by $a_n = a_1 + (n - 1)d$.

Associative Property of Addition
(1)

Let a, b, and c be real numbers, then $(a + b) + c = a + (b + c)$.

Associative Property of Multiplication
(1)

Let a, b, and c be real numbers, then $(ab)c = a(bc)$.

Binomial Theorem
(49)

If n is a nonnegative integer, then

$$(a + b)^n = ({}_nC_0)a^nb^0 + ({}_nC_1)a^{n-1}b^1 + \ldots + ({}_nC_{n-1})a^1b^{n-1} + ({}_nC_n)a^0b^n = \sum_{r=0}^{n}({}_nC_r)a^{n-r}b^r$$

where ${}_nC_r = \frac{n!}{r!(n - r)!}$.

Cartesian to Polar
(96)

$\tan\theta = \frac{y}{x}$

$r^2 = x^2 + y^2$

Change of Base Formula
(72)

For $a > 0$ and $a \neq 1$ and any base b such that $b > 0$, and $b \neq 1$, $\log_b x = \frac{\log_a x}{\log_a b}$.

Closure Property of Addition
(1)

If a and b are real numbers, then $a + b$ is a real number.

Closure Property of Multiplication
(1)

If a and b are real numbers, then ab is a real number.

Commutative Property of Addition
(1)

Let a and b be real numbers, then $a + b = b + a$.

Commutative Property of Multiplication
(1)

Let a and b be real numbers, then $ab = ba$.

Converse of Pythagorean Theorem
(41)

If the sum of the squares of the lengths of the two shorter sides of a triangle equals the square of the length of the longest side, then the triangle is a right triangle.

Cramer's Rule
(16)

The solutions of the linear system $\begin{cases} ax + by = e \\ cx + dy = f \end{cases}$ are $x = \frac{\begin{vmatrix} e & b \\ f & d \end{vmatrix}}{D}$ and $y = \frac{\begin{vmatrix} a & e \\ c & f \end{vmatrix}}{D}$, where D is the determinant of the coefficient matrix.

Difference of Squares
(78)

$$a^2 - b^2 = (a + b)(a - b)$$

Difference of Two Cubes
(61)

$$a^3 - b^3 = (a - b)(a^2 + ab + b^2)$$

886 Saxon Algebra 2

Discriminant
(74)

The discriminant of a quadratic equation $ax^2 + bx + c = 0$, is $b^2 - 4ac$.

If $b^2 - 4ac > 0$, there are two real solutions.

If $b^2 - 4ac = 0$, there is one real solution.

If $b^2 - 4ac < 0$, there are no real solutions.

Distance Formula
(41)

The distance d between any two points with coordinates (x_1, y_1) and (x_2, y_2) is $d = \sqrt{(x_2 - x_1)^2 + (y_2 - y_1)^2}$.

Distributive Property
(1)

Let a, b, and c be real numbers, $a(b + c) = ab + ac$.

Division Property of Equality
(7)

If $a = b$ and $c \neq 0$, then $a \div c = b \div c$.

Dot product
(99)

$A \cdot B = |A||B| \cos \theta$

Factor Theorem
(61)

For polynomial $P(x)$, $(x - a)$ is a factor of $P(x)$ if and only if $P(a) = 0$.

Fundamental Theorem of Algebra
(106)

Every polynomial function of degree $n \geq 1$ has at least one zero in the set of complex numbers.

Geometric Sequence
(97)

The nth term of a geometric sequence is given by $a_n = a_1 r^{n-1}$, where r is the common ratio.

Heron's Formula
(77)

$A = \sqrt{s(s - a)(s - b)(s - c)}$, where $s = \frac{1}{2}(a + b + c)$.

Identity Property of Addition
(1)

$$a + 0 = a,\ 0 + a = a$$

Identity Property of Multiplication
(1)

$$a \cdot 1 = a,\ 1 \cdot a = a$$

Inverse of a 2 × 2 Matrix
(32)

If $A = \begin{bmatrix} a & b \\ c & d \end{bmatrix}$ and $ad - cb \neq 0$, then the inverse of A is: $A^{-1} = \frac{1}{|A|}\begin{bmatrix} d & -b \\ -c & a \end{bmatrix} = \frac{1}{ad - cb}\begin{bmatrix} d & -b \\ -c & a \end{bmatrix}$.

Inverse Property of Addition
(1)

$a + (-a) = 0$

Inverse Property of Multiplication
(1)

$a \cdot \frac{1}{a} = 1, a \neq 0$

Irrational Root Theorem
(66)

If a polynomial $P(x)$ has rational coefficients, and $a + b\sqrt{c}$ is a root of $P(x) = 0$, where a and b are rational and $\sqrt{c}$ is irrational, then $a - b\sqrt{c}$ is also a root of $P(x) = 0$.

Law of Cosines
(77)

$a^2 = b^2 + c^2 - 2bc \cos A$

$b^2 = a^2 + c^2 - 2ac \cos B$

$c^2 = a^2 + b^2 - 2ab \cos C$

Law of Sines
(71)

For $\triangle ABC$ with side a opposite angle A, side b opposite angle B, and side c opposite angle C, $\frac{\sin A}{a} = \frac{\sin B}{b} = \frac{\sin C}{c}$.

Matrix Addition and Subtraction
(5)

For matrices $A = \begin{bmatrix} a_1 & a_2 \\ a_3 & a_4 \end{bmatrix}$ and $B = \begin{bmatrix} b_1 & b_2 \\ b_3 & b_4 \end{bmatrix}$,

$A + B = \begin{bmatrix} a_1 \pm b_1 & a_2 \pm b_2 \\ a_3 \pm b_3 & a_4 \pm b_4 \end{bmatrix}$.

PROPERTIES AND FORMULAS

PROPERTIES AND FORMULAS

Properties and Formulas 887

Matrix Determinant
(14)

For a square 2×2 matrix such as $\begin{bmatrix} a & b \\ c & d \end{bmatrix}$, the determinant equals $ad - cb$.

Matrix Multiplicative Identity
(9)

The product of any matrix A and the multiplicative identity matrix I is matrix A.

$AI = IA = A$

Midpoint Formula
(91)

For a segment whose endpoints are at (x_1, y_1) and (x_2, y_2), $M = \left(\frac{x_1 + x_2}{2}, \frac{y_1 + y_2}{2}\right)$.

Multiplication and Division Properties for Inequalities
(10)

For real numbers a, b, and c,

If $c < 0$ and $a < b$, then $ac > bc$ and $\frac{a}{c} > \frac{b}{c}$.

If $c > 0$ and $a < b$, then $ac < bc$ and $\frac{a}{c} < \frac{b}{c}$.

Also holds true for $>$, $\leq$, and $\geq$.

Multiplication Property of Equality
(7)

If $a = b$ and $c \neq 0$, then $ac = bc$.

Negative Exponent Property
(3, 59)

If n is any real number and x is any real number that is not zero, $x^{-n} = \frac{1}{x^n}$.

Percent of Change
(6)

$$\text{percent of change} = \frac{\text{amount of increase or decrease}}{\text{original amount}}$$

Polar Coordinates to Cartesian
(96)

$x = r\cos\theta$

$y = r\sin\theta$

Power of a Power Property
(59)

For any nonzero real number a and rational numbers m and n, $(a^m)^n = a^{m \cdot n}$.

Power of a Product Property
(59)

For all nonzero real numbers a and b and rational number m, $(ab)^m = a^m \cdot b^m$.

Power of a Quotient Property
(59)

For all nonzero real numbers a and b and rational number m, $\left(\frac{a}{b}\right)^m = \frac{a^m}{b^m}$.

Power Property of Logarithms
(72)

For any real number p and positive numbers a and $b(b = 1)$, $\log_b a^p = p\log_b a$.

Power Property of Natural Logarithms
(81)

For any real number p and positive number a, $\ln a^p = p\ln a$.

Power Property for Exponents
(3)

If m, n, and x are real numbers, $(x^m)^n = x^{m \cdot n}$.

Product of Powers Property
(59)

For any nonzero real number a and rational numbers m and n, $a^m \cdot a^n = a^{m+n}$.

Product Property of Natural Logarithms
(81)

For any positive numbers a and b, $\ln ab = \ln a + \ln b$.

Product Property of Logarithms
(72)

For any positive numbers, m, n, and b $(b \neq 1)$, $\log_b mn = \log_b m + \log_b n$.

Product Property of *n*th Roots
(59)

For $a > 0$ and $b > 0$, $\sqrt[n]{ab} = \sqrt[n]{a} \cdot \sqrt[n]{b}$.

Product Property for Exponents
(3)

If m, n, and x are real numbers and $x \neq 0$, $x^m \cdot x^n = x^{m+n}$.

888 *Saxon* Algebra 2

Product Rule for Radicals
(40)

Given that a and b are real numbers and n is an integer greater than 1, $\sqrt[n]{ab} = \sqrt[n]{a} \cdot \sqrt[n]{b}$ and $\sqrt[n]{a} \cdot \sqrt[n]{b} = \sqrt[n]{ab}$.

Pythagorean Theorem
(41)

If a triangle is a right triangle, the sum of the squares of the lengths of the legs equals the square of the length of the hypotenuse.

Quotient of Powers Property
(28)

For $a \neq 0$, and integers m and n, $\frac{a^m}{a^n} = a^{m-n}$.

Quotient Property of Logarithms
(72)

For any positive numbers, m, n, and b $(b \neq 1)$, $\log_b \frac{m}{n} = \log_b m - \log_b n$.

Quotient Property of Natural Logarithms
(81)

For any positive numbers a and b, $\ln \frac{a}{b} = \ln a - \ln b$.

Quotient Property of *n*th Roots
(59)

For $a > 0$ and $b > 0$, $\sqrt[n]{\frac{a}{b}} = \frac{\sqrt[n]{a}}{\sqrt[n]{b}}$.

Rational Exponents Property
(59)

For m and n integers and $n \neq 0$:

$$a^{\frac{1}{n}} = \sqrt[n]{a}$$

$$a^{\frac{m}{n}} = \left(\sqrt[n]{a}\right)^m = \sqrt[n]{a^m}$$

Rational Root Theorem
(66)

If a polynomial $P(x)$ has integer coefficients, then every rational root of $P(x) = 0$ can be written in the form $\frac{p}{q}$, where p is a factor of the constant term and q is a factor of the leading coefficient of $P(x)$.

Remainder Theorem
(51)

If a polynomial $f(x)$ is divided by $x - k$, the remainder is $r = f(k)$.

Remainder Theorem
(95)

For polynomials $P(x)$ and $(x - a)$, $P(x) = (x - a)Q(x) + r(x)$. The term $Q(x)$ is the quotient and the term $r(x)$ is the remainder. In particular, when $x = a$, $P(a) = r(a)$.

Scalar Multiplication
(5)

For matrix $A = \begin{bmatrix} a_1 & a_2 \\ a_3 & a_4 \end{bmatrix}$ and any real number k,

$$k \cdot A = k\begin{bmatrix} a_1 & a_2 \\ a_3 & a_4 \end{bmatrix} = \begin{bmatrix} ka_1 & ka_2 \\ ka_3 & ka_4 \end{bmatrix}.$$

Scientific Notation
(3)

A number written as the product of two factors in the form $a \times 10^n$, where $1 \leq a < 10$, and n is an integer.

Square Root Property
(58)

If $x^2 = a$, then $x = \pm\sqrt{a}$ for any $a > 0$.

Subtraction Property of Equality
(7)

If $a = b$, then $a - c = b - c$.

Sum of a Finite Geometric Series
(113)

The sum of the first n terms of a geometric series, S_n, is $a_1\left(\frac{1 - r^n}{1 - r}\right)$.

Sum of an Arithmetic Series
(105)

The sum of the first n terms of an arithmetic series, S_n, is $n\left(\frac{a_1 + a_n}{2}\right)$.

Sum of an Infinite Geometric Series
(113)

The sum of an infinite geometric series, S, is $\frac{a_1}{1 - r}$, where r is the common ratio and $0 < |r| < 1$.

Sum of Two Cubes
(61)

$$a^3 + b^3 = (a + b)(a^2 - ab + b^2)$$

PROPERTIES AND FORMULAS

Properties and Formulas 889

Transitive Property for Inequalities
(10)

For real numbers a, b, and c, If $a < b$ and $b < c$, then $a < c$.
Also holds true for $>$, $\leq$, and $\geq$.

Trigonometric Ratios
(46)

$$\text{cosecant of } \angle A = \frac{1}{\text{sine of } \angle A} = \frac{\text{length of hypotenuse}}{\text{length of leg opposite to } \angle A}$$

$$\text{secant of } \angle A = \frac{1}{\text{cosine of } \angle A} = \frac{\text{length of hypotenuse}}{\text{length of leg adjacent to } \angle A}$$

$$\text{cotangent of } \angle A = \frac{1}{\text{tangent of } \angle A} = \frac{\text{length of leg adjacent to } \angle A}{\text{length of leg opposite } \angle A}$$

Zero Exponent Property
(59)

For any nonzero real number a, $a^0 = 1$.

Zero Product Property
(23, 35)

Let a and b be real numbers. If $ab = 0$, then $a = 0$ or $b = 0$.

Formulas

Perimeter

Rectangle	$P = 2l + 2w$ or $P = 2(l + w)$
Square	$P = 4s$

Circumference

Circle	$C = \pi d$ or $C = 2\pi r$

Area

Rectangle	$A = lw$
Triangle	$A = \frac{1}{2}bh$
Trapezoid	$A = \frac{1}{2}(b_1 + b_2)h$
Circle	$A = \pi r^2$

Surface Area

Cube	$S = 6s^2$
Cylinder	$S = 2\pi r^2 + 2\pi rh$
Cone	$S = \pi r^2 + \pi rl$

Volume

Where B is the area of the base of a solid figure,

Prism or cylinder	$V = Bh$
Pyramid or cone	$V = \frac{1}{3}Bh$

Linear Equations

Slope formula	$m = \frac{y_2 - y_1}{x_2 - x_1}$
Slope-intercept form	$y = mx + b$
Point-slope form	$y - y_1 = m(x - x_1)$
Standard form	$Ax + By = C$

Quadratic Equations

Standard form	$ax^2 + bx + c = 0$
Axis of symmetry	$x = -\frac{b}{2a}$
Discriminant	$b^2 - 4ac$
Quadratic formula	$x = \frac{-b \pm \sqrt{b^2 - 4ac}}{2a}$

890 *Saxon Algebra 2*

Sequences

nth term of an arithmetic sequence

$$a_n = a_1 + (n - 1)d$$

nth term of an geometric sequence

$$a_n = a_1 \cdot r^{n-1}$$

Trigonometric Ratios

$$\text{sine of } \angle A = \frac{\text{length of leg opposite } \angle A}{\text{length of hypotenuse}}$$

$$\text{cosine of } \angle A = \frac{\text{length of leg adjacent to } \angle A}{\text{length of hypotenuse}}$$

$$\text{tangent of } \angle A = \frac{\text{length of leg opposite } \angle A}{\text{length of leg adjacent to } \angle A}$$

Percents

$$\text{Percent of change} = \frac{\text{amount of increase or decrease}}{\text{original amount}}$$

Permutations and Combinations

$P(n, r)$ permutation of n objects taken r at a time

$$_nP_r = \frac{n!}{(n - r)!}$$

$C(n, r)$ combination of n objects taken r at a time

$$_nC_r = \frac{n!}{r!(n - r)!}$$

$n!$ $n! = n \cdot (n - 1) \cdot (n - 2) \cdot \ldots \cdot 1$

Probability

$$P(\text{event}) = \frac{\text{number of favorable outcomes}}{\text{total number of outcomes}}$$

$P(A)$ probability of event A

Probability of Complement

$$P(\text{not event}) = 1 - P(\text{event})$$

Probability of Independent events

$$P(A \text{ and } B) = P(A) \cdot P(B)$$

Probability of Dependent events

$$P(A \text{ and } B) = P(A) \cdot P(B \text{ after } A)$$

Probability of Mutually Exclusive Events

$$P(A \text{ or } B) = P(A) + P(B)$$

Probability of Inclusive Events

$$P(A \text{ or } B) = P(A) + P(B) - P(A \text{ and } B)$$

Additional Formulas

Direct variation $y = kx$

Inverse variation $y = \frac{k}{x}; x \neq 0$

Distance formula $d = \sqrt{(x_2 - x_1)^2 + (y_2 - y_1)^2}$

Distance traveled $d = rt$

Exponential decay $y = kb^x; k > 0, 0 < b < 1$

Exponential growth $y = kb^x; k > 0, b > 1$

Midpoint of a segment $M = \left(\frac{x_1 + x_2}{2}, \frac{y_1 + y_2}{2}\right)$

Symbols

Comparison Symbols

$<$	less than
$>$	greater than
$\leq$	less than or equal to
$\geq$	greater than or equal to
$\neq$	not equal to
$\approx$	approximately equal to

PROPERTIES AND FORMULAS

Properties and Formulas 891

Geometry

$\cong$	is congruent to
$\sim$	is similar to
$^\circ$	degree(s)
$\angle ABC$	angle ABC
$m\angle ABC$	the measure of angle ABC
$\triangle ABC$	triangle ABC
$\overleftrightarrow{AB}$	line AB
$\overline{AB}$	segment AB
$\overrightarrow{AB}$	ray AB
AB	length of $\overline{AB}$
∟	right angle
$\perp$	is perpendicular to
$\parallel$	is parallel to

Real Numbers

$\mathbb{R}$	the set of real numbers
$\mathbb{Q}$	the set of rational numbers
$\mathbb{Z}$	the set of integers
$\mathbb{W}$	the set of whole numbers
$\mathbb{N}$	the set of natural numbers

Additional Symbols

$\pm$	plus or minus
$a \cdot b$, ab, or $a(b)$	a times b
$\|-5\|$	the absolute value of -5
%	percent
π	pi, $\pi \approx 3.14$, or $\pi \approx \frac{22}{7}$
$f(x)$	function notation: f of x
a^n	a to nth power
a_n	nth term of a sequence
(x, y)	ordered pair
$x{:}y$	ratio of x to y, or $\frac{x}{y}$
{ }	set braces
$\sqrt{x}$	nonnegative square root of x

Table of Metric Measures

Length

1 kilometer (km) = 1000 meters (m)

1 meter = 100 centimeters (cm)

1 centimeter = 10 millimeters (mm)

Capacity and Volume

1 liter (L) = 1000 milliliters (mL)

Mass

1 kilogram (kg) = 1000 grams (g)

1 gram = 1000 milligrams (mg)

Table of Customary Measures

Length

1 mile (mi) = 5280 feet (ft)

1 mile = 1760 yards (yd)

1 yard = 3 feet

1 yard = 36 inches (in.)

1 foot = 12 inches

892 Saxon Algebra 2

Capacity and Volume

1 gallon (gal) = 4 quarts (qt)

1 quart = 2 pints (pt)

1 pint = 2 cups (c)

1 cup = 8 fluid ounces (fl oz)

Weight

1 ton = 2000 pounds (lb)

1 pound = 16 ounces (oz)

Customary and Metric Measures

1 inch = 2.54 centimeters

1 yard ≈ 0.9 meters

1 mile ≈ 1.6 kilometers

Time

1 year = 365 days

1 year = 12 months

1 month ≈ 4 weeks

1 year = 52 weeks

1 week = 7 days

1 day = 24 hours

1 hour (hr) = 60 minutes (min)

1 minute = 60 seconds (s)

PROPERTIES AND FORMULAS

Properties and Formulas 893

English/Spanish Glossary

English	Example	Spanish
A		
absolute value of a complex number (69) The absolute value of $a + bi$ is the distance from the origin to the point (a, b) in the complex plane and is denoted $\lvert a + bi \rvert = \sqrt{a^2 + b^2}$.	$\lvert 2 + 3i \rvert = \sqrt{2^2 + 3^2} = \sqrt{13}$	**valor absoluto de un número complejo** (69) El valor absoluto de $a + bi$ es la distancia desde el origen hasta el punto (a, b) en el plano complejo y se expresa $\lvert a + bi \rvert = \sqrt{a^2 + b^2}$.
absolute value of a real number (17) The absolute value of x is the distance from zero to x on a number line, denoted $\lvert x \rvert$. $\lvert x \rvert = \begin{cases} x & \text{if } x \geq 0 \\ -x & \text{if } x < 0 \end{cases}$	$\lvert 3 \rvert = 3$ $\lvert -3 \rvert = 3$	**valor absoluto de un número real** (17) El valor absoluto de x es la distancia desde cero hasta x en una recta numérica y se expresa $\lvert x \rvert$. $\lvert x \rvert = \begin{cases} x & \text{si } x \geq 0 \\ -x & \text{si } x < 0 \end{cases}$
absolute value function (17) A function whose rule contains absolute-value expressions.	$f(x) = \lvert x \rvert$	**función de valor absoluto** (17) Función cuya regla contiene expresiones de valor absoluto.
abstract equation (88) An equation with two or more variables; also called a literal equation.	$V = \frac{1}{3}bh$	**ecuación abstracta** (88) Una ecuación con dos o más variables; también llamada una ecuación literal.
accuracy (18) An indication of how close a measurement corresponds to the actual value being measured.	For an object with a length of 2.35 cm, a measurement of 2.37 cm is more accurate than a measurement of 2.31.	**exactitud** (18) Un indicador de qué tan cercana está una medida con respecto al valor real medido.

English	Example	Spanish
A		
addition counting principle (33) If one outcome can occur in n_1 ways and a second outcome can occur in n_2 ways, then there are $n_1 + n_2$ total outcomes. For k different categories of outcomes, the total number of outcomes is $n_1 + n_2 + \ldots + n_k$.	There are 6 total outcomes in the event *flip a coin or spin the spinner.* 2 outcomes 4 outcomes	**principio de conteo** (33) Si un resultado puede ocurrir en n_1 maneras y un segundo resultado puede ocurrir en n_2 maneras, entonces hay un total de $n_1 + n_2$ de resultados. Para k diferentes categorías de resultados, el número total de resultados es $n_1 + n_2 + \ldots + n_k$.
additive inverse of a matrix (5) A matrix where each entry is the opposite of each entry in another matrix. Two matrices are additive inverses if their sum is the zero matrix.	$\begin{bmatrix} 1 & -2 \\ 0 & 4 \end{bmatrix}$ and $\begin{bmatrix} -1 & 2 \\ 0 & -4 \end{bmatrix}$ are additive inverses.	**inverso aditivo de una matriz** (5) Matriz en la cual cada entrada es el opuesto de cada entrada en otra matriz. Dos matrices son inversos aditivos si su suma es la matriz cero.
address (5) The location of an entry in a matrix, given by the row and column in which the entry appears. In matrix A, the address of the entry in row i and column j is a_{ij}.	In the matrix $A = \begin{bmatrix} 2 & 3 \\ 4 & 1 \end{bmatrix}$, the address of the entry 2 is a_{11}, the address of the entry 3 is a_{12}.	**dirección** (5) Ubicación de una entrada en una matriz, indicada por la fila y la columna en las que aparece la entrada. En la matriz A, la dirección de la entrada de la fila i y la columna j es a_{ij}.
algebraic expression (2) An expression that contains at least one variable.	$2x + 3y$	**expresión algebraica** (2) Expresión que contiene por lo menos una variable.
amplitude (82) The amplitude of a periodic function is half the difference of the maximum and minimum values (always positive).	maximum: 3 minimum: −3 amplitude $= \frac{1}{2}[3 - (-3)] = 3$	**amplitud** (82) La amplitud (siempre positiva) de una función periódica es la mitad de la diferencia entre los valores máximo y mínimo.
angle of rotation (56) An angle formed by a rotating ray, called the terminal side, and a stationary reference ray, called the initial side.	Terminal side 135° 45° Initial side	**ángulo de rotación** (56) Ángulo formado por un rayo en rotación, denominado lado terminal, y un rayo de referencia estático, denominado lado inicial.

English	Example	Spanish
A		
arc (63) An unbroken part of a circle consisting of two points on the circle, called the endpoints, and all the points on the circle between them.	R S	**arco** (63) Parte continua de un círculo formada por dos puntos del círculo denominados extremos y todos los puntos del círculo comprendidos entre éstos.
arc length (63) The distance along an arc measured in linear units.	10 ft, D, 90°, C $m\widehat{CD} = 5\pi$ ft	**longitud de arco** (63) Distancia a lo largo de un arco medida en unidades lineales.
arithmetic sequence (92) A sequence whose successive terms differ by the same nonzero number d, called the *common difference*.	4, 7, 10, 13, 16, ... +3 +3 +3 +3 $d = 3$	**sucesión aritmética** (92) Sucesión cuyos términos sucesivos difieren en el mismo número distinto de cero d, denominado *diferencia común*.
arithmetic series (105) The indicated sum of the terms of an arithmetic sequence.	$4 + 7 + 10 + 13 + 16 + \ldots$	**serie aritmética** (105) Suma indicada de los términos de una sucesión aritmética.
asymptote (47) A line that a graph approaches as the value of a variable becomes extremely large or small.	Asymptote	**asíntota** (47) Línea recta a la cual se aproxima una gráfica a medida que el valor de una variable se hace sumamente grande o pequeño.
axis of symmetry (27) A line that divides a plane figure or a graph into two congruent reflected halves.	Axis of symmetry	**eje de simetría** (27) Línea que divide una figura plana o una gráfica en dos mitades reflejadas congruentes.
B		
base of a power (SB 3) The number in a power that is used as a factor.	$3^4 = 3 \cdot 3 \cdot 3 \cdot 3 = 81$ base	**base de una potencia** (SB 3) Número de una potencia que se utiliza como factor.

English	Example	Spanish
B		
base of an exponential function (maintained) The value of b in a function of the form $f(x) = ab^x$, where a and b are real numbers with $a \neq 0$, $b > 0$, and $b \neq 1$.	$f(x) = 5(2)^x$ base	**base de una función exponencial** (repaso) Valor de b en una función del tipo $f(x) = ab^x$, donde a y b son números reales con $a \neq 0$, $b > 0$, y $b \neq 1$.
bell curve (80) A single-peaked symmetric curve formed by drawing a line through the tops of the bars of a histogram, representing the normal distribution of a data set.	11 14 17 20 23 26 29	**curva de bell** (80) Una curva simétrica con sólo una cresta que se forma dibujando una línea a través de las partes superiores de las barras de un histograma que representa la distribución normal de un conjunto de datos.
bias (73) Systematic error that creates a sample that is not representative of its population, favoring some groups more than others.	A sample by which a surveyor questions every person on a certain street corner is biased against those that do not walk that route.	**sesgo** (73) Error sitemático que crea una muestra que no es representativa de su población, favoreciendo a algunos grupos más que a otros.
binomial (11) A polynomial with two terms.	$x + y$ $2a^2 + 3$ $4m^3n^2 + 6mn^4$	**binomio** (11) Polinomio con dos términos.
binomial experiment (49) A probability experiment consists of n identical and independent trials whose outcomes are either successes or failures, with a constant probability of success p and a constant probability of failure q, where $q = 1 - p$ or $p + q = 1$.	A multiple-choice quiz has 10 questions with 4 answer choices. The number of trials is 10. If each question is answered randomly, the probability of success for each trial is $\frac{1}{4} = 0.25$ and the probability of failure is $\frac{3}{4} = 0.75$.	**experimento binomial** (49) Experimento de probabilidades que comprende n pruebas idénticas e independientes cuyos resultados son éxitos o fracasos, con una probabilidad constante de éxito p y una probabilidad constante de fracaso q, donde $q = 1 - p$ ó $p + q = 1$.

B

English	Example	Spanish
binomial probability (49) In a binomial experiment, the probability of r successes out of n trials is $P(r) = {}_nC_r \cdot p^r q^{n-r}$.	In the binomial experiment earlier, the probability of randomly guessing 6 problems correctly is $P = {}_{10}C_6(0.25)^6(0.75)^4 \approx 0.016$.	**probabilidad binomial** (49) En un experimento binomial, la probabilidad de r éxitos de un total de n intentos es $P(r) = {}_nC_r \cdot p^r q^{n-r}$.
Binomial Theorem (49) For any positive integer n, $(x + y)^n = {}_nC_0x^ny^0 + {}_nC_1x^{n-1}y^1 + {}_nC_2x^{n-2}y^2 + \cdots + {}_nC_{n-1}x^1y^{n-1} + {}_nC_nx^0y^n$	$(x + 2)^4 = {}_4C_0x^42^0 + {}_4C_1x^32^1 + {}_4C_2x^22^2 + {}_4C_1x^12^3 + {}_4C_4x^02^4 = x^4 + 8x^3 + 24x^2 + 32x + 16$	**Teorema de los binomios** (49) Dado un entero positivo n, $(x + y)^n = {}_nC_0x^ny^0 + {}_nC_1x^{n-1}y^1 + {}_nC_2x^{n-2}y^2 + \cdots + {}_nC_{n-1}x^1y^{n-1} + {}_nC_nx^0y^n$
boundary line (39) A line that divides a coordinate plane into two half-planes.	Boundary Line	**línea de límite** (39) Línea que divide un plano coordenado en dos semiplanos.
box-and-whisker plot (25) A method of showing how data is distributed by using the median, quartiles, and minimum and maximum values; also called a *box plot*.	Minimum, First quartile, Median, Third quartile, Maximum	**gráfica de mediana y rango** (25) Método para demostrar la distribución de datos utilizando la mediana, los cuartiles y los valores mínimos y máximos; también llamado *gráfica de caja*.
branch of a hyperbola (109) One of the two symmetrical parts of the hyperbola.	Branch	**rama de una hipérbola** (109) Una de las dos partes simétricas de la hipérbola.

C

English	Example	Spanish
capture-recapture method (73) A sampling method used to estimate the size of a population. It requires two separate visits, where subjects are captured during both visits.	Visit 1: capture and mark 30 animals Visit 2: capture 50 animals, 20 are marked There are about n animals in the population, where $\frac{20}{30} = \frac{50}{n}$, so $n = 75$.	**método de captura-recaptura** (73) Un método de muestreo utilizado para estimar el tamaño de una población. Requiere de dos visitas separadas donde los sujetos son capturados durante ambas visitas.

C

English	Example	Spanish
change of base formula (72) For $a > 0$ and $a \neq 1$ and any base b such that $b > 0$ and $b \neq 1$, $\log_b x = \frac{\log_a x}{\log_a b}$.	$\log_4 8 = \frac{\log_2 8}{\log_2 4}$	**fórmula para cambiar de base** (72) Para $a > 0$ y $a \neq 1$ y cualquier base b tal que $b > 0$ y $b \neq 1$, $\log_b x = \frac{\log_a x}{\log_a b}$.
circle (91) The set of points in a plane that are a fixed distance from a given point called the center of the circle.	O	**círculo** (91) Conjunto de puntos en un plano que se encuentran a una distancia fija de un punto determinado denominado centro del círculo.
closure (maintained) A set of numbers is said to be closed, or to have closure, under a given operation if the result of the operation on any two numbers in the set is also in the set.	The natural numbers are closed under addition because the sum of two natural numbers is always a natural number.	**cerradura** (repaso) Se dice que un conjunto de números es cerrado, o tiene cerradura, respecto de una operación determinada, si el resultado de la operación entre dos números cualesquiera del conjunto también está en el conjunto.
cluster sampling (Inv 7) Sampling in which the population is first divided into groups, called clusters, and then a number of clusters are randomly selected.	Blocks of houses are randomly selected from all the blocks in a given neighborhood. Every house in a chosen block belongs in the sample.	**muestreo por cúmulos** (Inv 7) Muestreo en el cual la población primero se divide en grupos, llamados cúmulos, y después un número de cúmulos son seleccionados al azar.
coefficient (maintained) A number multiplied by a variable.	In the expression $2x + 3y$, 2 is the coefficient of x and 3 is the coefficient of y.	**coeficiente** (repaso) Número multiplicado por una variable.
coefficient matrix (16) The matrix of the coefficients of the variables in a linear system of equations.	System of equations: $2x + 3y = 11$, $5x - 4y = 16$ Coefficient matrix: $\begin{bmatrix} 2 & 3 \\ 5 & -4 \end{bmatrix}$	**matriz de coeficientes** (16) Matriz de los coeficientes de las variables en un sistema lineal de ecuaciones.

GLOSARIO

C

English	Example	Spanish
coefficient of determination (116) The number R^2, with $0 \leq R^2 \leq 1$, that shows the fraction of the data that are close to the curve of best fit and, thus, how well the curve fits the data.	QuadReg y=ax²+bx+c a=1.013528963 b=7.485785061 c=73.78780488 R²=.9852723622	**coeficiente de determinación** (116) El número R^2, con $0 \leq R^2 \leq 1$, que muestra la fracción de los datos cercanos a la línea de mejor ajuste y, por lo tanto, cuánto se ajusta la línea de mejor ajuste a los datos.
combination (42) A selection of a group of objects in which order is *not* important. The number of combinations of r objects chosen from a group of n objects is denoted ${}_nC_r$.	For 4 objects A, B, C, and D, there are ${}_4C_2 = 6$ different combinations of 2 objects: AB, AC, AD, BC, BD, CD.	**combinación** (42) Selección de un grupo de objetos en la cual el orden *no* es importante. El número de combinaciones de r objetos elegidos de un grupo de n objetos se expresa así: ${}_nC_r$.
common difference (92) In an arithmetic sequence, the nonzero constant difference of any term and the previous term.	In the arithmetic sequence 3, 5, 7, 9, 11, ..., the common difference is 2.	**diferencia común** (92) En una sucesión aritmética, diferencia constante distinta de cero entre cualquier término y el término anterior.
common logarithm (64) A logarithm whose base is 10, denoted $\log_{10}$ or just log.	$\log 100 = \log_{10}100 = 2$, since $10^2 = 100$.	**logaritmo común** (64) Logaritmo de base 10, que se expresa $\log_{10}$ o simplemente log.
common ratio (97) In a geometric sequence, the constant ratio of any term and the previous term.	In the geometric sequence 32, 16, 18, 4, 2 ..., the common ratio is $\frac{1}{2}$.	**razón común** (97) En una sucesión geométrica, la razón constante r entre cualquier término y el término anterior.
completing the square (58) A process used to form a perfect-square trinomial. To complete the square of $x^2 + bx$, add $\left(\frac{b}{2}\right)^2$.	$x^2 + 6x + \blacksquare$ Add $\left(\frac{6}{2}\right)^2 = 9$. $x^2 + 6x + 9$ $(x + 3)^2$ is a perfect square.	**completar el cuadrado** (58) Proceso utilizado para formar un trinomio cuadrado perfecto. Para completar el cuadrado de $x^2 + bx$, hay que sumar $\left(\frac{b}{2}\right)^2$.

C

English	Example	Spanish
complex conjugate (69) The complex conjugate of any complex number $a + bi$, denoted $\overline{a + bi}$, is $a - bi$.	$\overline{4 + 3i} = 4 - 3i$ $\overline{4 - 3i} = 4 + 3i$	**conjugado complejo** (69) El conjugado complejo de cualquier número complejo $a + bi$, expresado como $\overline{a + bi}$, es $a - bi$.
complex fraction (48) A fraction that contains one or more fractions in the numerator, the denominator, or both.	$\frac{\frac{1}{2}}{1 + \frac{2}{3}}$	**fracción compleja** (48) Fracción que contiene una o más fracciones en el numerador, en el denominador, o en ambos.
complex number (62) Any number that can be written as $a + bi$, where a and b are real numbers and $i = \sqrt{-1}$.	$4 + 2i$ $5 + 0i = 5$ $0 - 7i = -7i$	**número complejo** (62) Todo número que se puede expresar como $a + bi$, donde a y b son números reales e $i = \sqrt{-1}$.
complex plane (69) A set of coordinate axes in which the horizontal axis is the real axis and the vertical axis is the imaginary axis; used to graph complex numbers.	Imaginary axis Real axis	**plano complejo** (69) Conjunto de ejes coordenado en el cual el eje horizontal es el eje real y el eje vertical es el eje imaginario; se utiliza para representar gráficamente números complejos.
composite figure (SB 17) A plane figure made up of triangles, rectangles, trapezoids, circles, and other simple shapes, or a three-dimensional figure made up of prisms, cones, pyramids, cylinders, and other simple three-dimensional figures.	18 in. 12 in.	**figura compuesta** (SB 17) Figura plana compuesta por triángulos, rectángulos, trapecios, círculos y otras formas simples, o figura tridimensional compuesta por prismas, conos, pirámides, cilindros y otras figuras tridimensionales simples.
composite function (53) A function of the form $(f \cdot g)(x)$, or $f(g(x))$, where the input for function f is the output of function g.	If $f(x) = x + 2$ and $g(x) = x^2$, then $f(g(x)) = x^2 + 2$.	**función compuesta** (53) Una función de la forma $(f \cdot g)(x)$, o $f(g(x))$, donde la entrada para la función f es la salida de la función g.

GLOSSARY/ GLOSARIO

C

English	Example	Spanish
composition of functions (53) The composition of functions f and g, written as $(f \circ g)(x)$ and defined as $f(g(x))$ uses the output of $g(x)$ as the input for $f(x)$.	If $f(x) = x^2$ and $g(x) = x + 1$, the composite function $(f \circ g)(x) = (x + 1)^2$.	**composición de funciones** (53) La composición de las funciones f y g, expresada como $(f \circ g)(x)$ y definida como $f(g(x))$ utiliza la salida de $g(x)$ como la entrada para $f(x)$.
compound event (60) An event made up of two or more simple events.	In the experiment of tossing a coin and rolling a number cube, the event of the coin landing heads and the number cube landing on 3.	**suceso compuesto** (60) Suceso formado por dos o más sucesos simples.
compression (30) A transformation that pushes the points of a graph horizontally toward the y-axis or vertically toward the x-axis.		**compresión** (30) Transformación que desplaza los puntos de una gráfica horizontalmente hacia el eje y o verticalmente hacia el eje x.
conditional probability (55) The probability of event B, given that event A has already occurred or is certain to occur, denoted $P(B \mid A)$; used to find probability of dependent events.		**probabilidad condicional** (55) Probabilidad del suceso B, dado que el suceso A ya ha ocurrido o es seguro que ocurrirá, expresada como $P(B \mid A)$; se utiliza para calcular la probabilidad de sucesos dependientes.
conic section (91) A plane figure formed by the intersection of a double right cone and a plane. Examples include circles, ellipses, hyperbolas, and parabolas.	Circle Ellipse Parabola Hyperbola	**sección cónica** (91) Figura plana formada por la intersección de un cono regular doble y un plano. Algunos ejemplos son círculos, elipses, hipérbolas y parábolas.
conjugates (44) Binomials of the form $a + b$ and $a - b$. The terms are the same; the signs before b are opposites.	$3 + \sqrt{2}$ and $3 - \sqrt{2}$ are radical conjugates.	**conjugados** (44) Binomios de la forma $a + b$ y $a - b$. Los términos son los mismos; los signos antes de b son opuestos.

C

English	Example	Spanish
conjunction (Inv 1) A compound statement that uses the word *and*.	3 is less than 5 AND greater than 0.	**conjunción** (Inv 1) Enunciado compuesto que contiene la palabra *y*.
consistent system (15) A system of equations or inequalities that has at least one solution.	$\begin{cases} x + y = 6 \\ x - y = 4 \end{cases}$ solution: (5, 1)	**sistema consistente** (15) Sistema de ecuaciones o desigualdades que tiene por lo menos una solución.
constant of variation (8) The constant k in direct, inverse, joint, and combined variation equations.	$y = 5x$ constant of variation	**constante de variación** (8) La constante k en ecuaciones de variación directa, inversa, conjunta y combinada.
constant term (2) A term in a function or expression that does not contain variables.	$f(x) = 3x + 5$ Constant term	**término constante** (2) Término de una función o expresión que no contiene variables.
constraint (54) One of the inequalities that define the feasible region in a linear-programming problem.	**Constraints:** $x > 0$, $y > 0$, $x + y \le 8$, $3x + 5y \le 30$ **Feasible region**	**restricción** (54) Una de las desigualdades que definen la región factible en un problema de programación lineal.
continuous function (22) A function whose graph is an unbroken line or curve with no gaps or breaks.		**función continua** (22) Función cuya gráfica es una línea recta o curva continua, sin espacios ni interrupciones.
convenience sampling (73) Creating a sample by using who or what is most convenient or available.	A student surveys the same people she talks to everyday: her own friends, family, and teachers.	**muestrear convenientemente** (73) Crear una muestra utilizando a personas o cosas que sean las más convenientes y que estén disponibles.

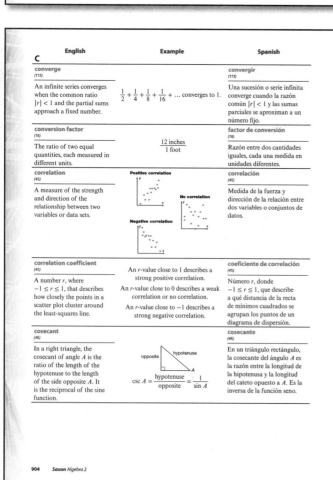

GLOSSARY/ GLOSARIO

C

English	Example	Spanish
converge (113) An infinite series converges when the common ratio $\lvert r \rvert < 1$ and the partial sums approach a fixed number.	$\frac{1}{2} + \frac{1}{4} + \frac{1}{8} + \frac{1}{16} + \ldots$ converges to 1.	**convergir** (113) Una sucesión o serie infinita converge cuando la razón común $\lvert r \rvert < 1$ y las sumas parciales se aproximan a un número fijo.
conversion factor (18) The ratio of two equal quantities, each measured in different units.	$\frac{12 \text{ inches}}{1 \text{ foot}}$	**factor de conversión** (18) Razón entre dos cantidades iguales, cada una medida en unidades diferentes.
correlation (45) A measure of the strength and direction of the relationship between two variables or data sets.	Positive correlation No correlation Negative correlation	**correlación** (45) Medida de la fuerza y dirección de la relación entre dos variables o conjuntos de datos.
correlation coefficient (45) A number r, where $-1 \le r \le 1$, that describes how closely the points in a scatter plot cluster around the least-squares line.	An r-value close to 1 describes a strong positive correlation. An r-value close to 0 describes a weak correlation or no correlation. An r-value close to -1 describes a strong negative correlation.	**coeficiente de correlación** (45) Número r, donde $-1 \le r \le 1$, que describe a qué distancia de la recta de mínimos cuadrados se agrupan los puntos de un diagrama de dispersión.
cosecant (46) In a right triangle, the cosecant of angle A is the ratio of the length of the hypotenuse to the length of the side opposite A. It is the reciprocal of the sine function.	$\csc A = \frac{\text{hypotenuse}}{\text{opposite}} = \frac{1}{\sin A}$	**cosecante** (46) En un triángulo rectángulo, la cosecante del ángulo A es la razón entre la longitud de la hipotenusa y la longitud del cateto opuesto a A. Es la inversa de la función seno.

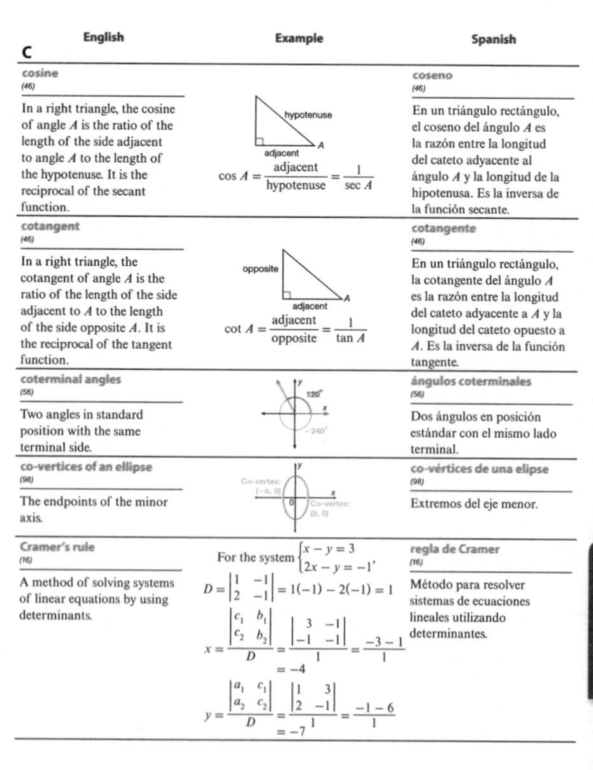

C

English	Example	Spanish
cosine (46) In a right triangle, the cosine of angle A is the ratio of the length of the side adjacent to angle A to the length of the hypotenuse. It is the reciprocal of the secant function.	$\cos A = \frac{\text{adjacent}}{\text{hypotenuse}} = \frac{1}{\sec A}$	**coseno** (46) En un triángulo rectángulo, el coseno del ángulo A es la razón entre la longitud del cateto adyacente al ángulo A y la longitud de la hipotenusa. Es la inversa de la función secante.
cotangent (46) In a right triangle, the cotangent of angle A is the ratio of the length of the side adjacent to A to the length of the side opposite A. It is the reciprocal of the tangent function.	$\cot A = \frac{\text{adjacent}}{\text{opposite}} = \frac{1}{\tan A}$	**cotangente** (46) En un triángulo rectángulo, la cotangente del ángulo A es la razón entre la longitud del cateto adyacente a A y la longitud del cateto opuesto a A. Es la inversa de la función tangente.
coterminal angles (56) Two angles in standard position with the same terminal side.	120°, −240°	**ángulos coterminales** (56) Dos ángulos en posición estándar con el mismo lado terminal.
co-vertices of an ellipse (98) The endpoints of the minor axis.	Co-vertex: $(-b, 0)$; Co-vertex: $(b, 0)$	**co-vértices de una elipse** (98) Extremos del eje menor.
Cramer's rule (16) A method of solving systems of linear equations by using determinants.	For the system $\begin{cases} x - y = 3 \\ 2x - y = -1 \end{cases}$, $D = \begin{vmatrix} 1 & -1 \\ 2 & -1 \end{vmatrix} = 1(-1) - 2(-1) = 1$ $x = \frac{\begin{vmatrix} c_1 & b_1 \\ c_2 & b_2 \end{vmatrix}}{D} = \frac{\begin{vmatrix} 3 & -1 \\ -1 & -1 \end{vmatrix}}{1} = \frac{-3 - 1}{1} = -4$ $y = \frac{\begin{vmatrix} a_1 & c_1 \\ a_2 & c_2 \end{vmatrix}}{D} = \frac{\begin{vmatrix} 1 & 3 \\ 2 & -1 \end{vmatrix}}{1} = \frac{-1 - 6}{1} = -7$	**regla de Cramer** (16) Método para resolver sistemas de ecuaciones lineales utilizando determinantes.

GLOSSARY/ GLOSARIO

C

English	Example	Spanish
cross products (SB 8) In the statement $\frac{a}{b} = \frac{c}{d}$, bc and ad are the cross products.	$\frac{1}{2} = \frac{3}{6}$ Cross products: $2 \cdot 3 = 6$ *and* $1 \cdot 6 = 6$	**productos cruzados** (SB 8) En el enunciado $\frac{a}{b} = \frac{c}{d}$, bc y ad son los productos cruzados.
cube root function (75) The function $f(x) = \sqrt[3]{x}$.	$f(x) = \sqrt[3]{x}$	**función de raíz cúbica** (75) La función $f(x) = \sqrt[3]{x}$.
cubic function (101) A polynomial function of degree 3.	$f(x) = x^3$	**función cúbica** (101) Función polinomial de grado 3.
cycle of a periodic function (82) The shortest repeating part of a periodic graph or function.	Cycle	**ciclo de una función periódica** (82) La parte repetida más corta de una gráfica o función periódica.

D

English	Example	Spanish
decreasing function (57) A function whose output value decreases as its input value increases.		**función decreciente** (57) Una función cuyo valor de salida decrece conforme su valor de entrada aumenta.
degree of a monomial (11) The sum of the exponents of the variables in the monomial.	$4x^2y^5z^3$ Degree: $2 + 5 + 3 = 10$; 5 Degree: $0\ (5 = 5x^0)$	**grado de un monomio** (11) Suma de los exponentes de las variables del monomio.
degree of a polynomial (11) The degree of the term of the polynomial with the greatest degree.	$3x^2y^2 + 4xy^5 - 12x^3y^2$ Degree 6; Degree 4, Degree 6, Degree 5	**grado de un polinomio** (11) Grado del término del polinomio con el grado máximo.
dependent events (33) Events for which the occurrence or nonoccurrence of one event affects the probability of the other event.	From a bag containing 3 red marbles and 2 blue marbles, drawing a red marble, and then drawing a blue marble without replacing the first marble.	**sucesos dependientes** (33) Dos sucesos son dependientes si el hecho de que uno de ellos se cumpla o no afecta la probabilidad del otro.

D

English	Example	Spanish
dependent system (15) A system of equations that has infinitely many solutions.	$\begin{cases} x + y = 3 \\ 2x + 2y = 6 \end{cases}$	**sistema dependiente** (15) Sistema de ecuaciones que tiene infinitamente muchas soluciones.
dependent variable (4) The output of a function; a variable whose value depends on the value of the input, or independent variable.	$y = 2x + 1$ dependent variable.	**variable dependiente** (4) Salida de una función; variable cuyo valor depende del valor de la entrada, o variable independiente.
determinant (14) A real number associated with a square matrix. The determinant of $A = \begin{bmatrix} a & b \\ c & d \end{bmatrix}$ is $\lvert A \rvert = ad - bc$.	$\begin{vmatrix} 2 & -1 \\ 3 & 4 \end{vmatrix} = 2(4) - (-1)(3) = 11$	**determinante** (14) Número real asociado con una matriz cuadrada. La determinante de $A = \begin{bmatrix} a & b \\ c & d \end{bmatrix}$ es $\lvert A \rvert = ad - bc$.
difference of two squares (23) A polynomial of the form $a^2 - b^2$, which may be written as the product $(a + b)(a - b)$.	$x^2 - 4 = (x + 2)(x - 2)$	**diferencia de dos cuadrados** (23) Polinomio del tipo $a^2 - b^2$, que se puede expresar como el producto $(a + b)(a - b)$.
dimensions of a matrix (5) A matrix with m rows and n columns has dimensions $m \times n$, read "m by n."	$\begin{bmatrix} -3 & 2 & 1 & -1 \\ 4 & 0 & -5 & 2 \end{bmatrix}$ Dimensions 2×4	**dimensiones de una matriz** (5) Una matriz con m filas y n columnas tiene dimensiones $m \times n$, expresadas "m por n".
direct variation (8) A linear relationship between two variables, x and y, that can be written in the form $y = kx$, where k is a nonzero constant.	$y = 2x$	**variación directa** (8) Relación lineal entre dos variables, x e y, que puede expresarse en la forma $y = kx$, donde k es una constante distinta de cero.
discontinuous function (22) A function whose graph has one or more jumps, breaks, or holes.		**función discontinua** (22) Función cuya gráfica tiene uno o más saltos, interrupciones u hoyos.

D

English	Example	Spanish
discriminant (74) The discriminant of the quadratic equation $ax^2 + bx + c = 0$ is $b^2 - 4ac$.	The discriminant of $2x^2 - 5x - 3$ is $(-5)^2 - 4(2)(-3) = 25 + 24 = 49$.	**discriminante** (74) El discriminante de la ecuación cuadrática $ax^2 + bx + c = 0$ es $b^2 - 4ac$.
disjoint events (60) Events that have no outcomes in common.	When rolling a number cube, rolling an even number and rolling a 3 are disjoint events.	**sucesos excluyentes** (60) Sucesos que no tienen resultados posibles en común.
disjunction (Inv 1) A compound statement that uses the word *or*.	John will walk to work OR he will stay home.	**disyunción** (Inv 1) Enunciado compuesto que contiene la palabra *o*.
distance formula (41) In a coordinate plane, the distance from (x_1, y_1) to (x_2, y_2) is $d = \sqrt{(x_2 - x_1)^2 + (y_2 - y_1)^2}$.	The distance from (2, 1) to (6, 4) is $d = \sqrt{(6-2)^2 + (4-1)^2} = \sqrt{4^2 + 3^2} = \sqrt{16 + 9} = 5$.	**fórmula de distancia** (41) En un plano coordenado, la distancia desde (x_1, y_1) hasta (x_2, y_2) es $d = \sqrt{(x_2 - x_1)^2 + (y_2 - y_1)^2}$.
diverge (113) An infinite series diverges when the common ratio $\lvert r \rvert \geq 1$ and the partial sums do not approach a fixed number.	$1 + 2 + 4 + 8 + 16 + \ldots$ diverges.	**divergir** (113) Una serie infinita diverge cuando la razón común $\lvert r \rvert \geq 1$ y las sumas parciales no se aproximan a un número fijo.
domain (4) The set of all possible input values of a relation or function.	The domain of the function $f(x) = \sqrt{x}$ is $\{x \mid x \geq 0\}$.	**dominio** (4) Conjunto de todos los posibles valores de entrada de una función o relación.
dot product (99) The sum of the products of the x- and y-coordinates of the endpoints of two vectors that begin at the origin.	$A = (3, 7)$ and $B = (-2, -5)$; $A \cdot B = (3)(-2) + (7)(-5) = -6 - 35 = -41$	**producto punto** (99) La suma de los prductos de las coordenadas x e y de los extremos de dos vectores que comienzan en el origen.
double roots (35) Two identical roots, or solutions, of an equation.	$x^2 - 4x + 4 = 0$ has a double root of 2. $x^2 - 4x + 4 = 0$; $(x - 2)(x - 2) = 0$; $x - 2 = 0$ or $x - 2 = 0$; $x = 2$ or $x = 2$	**raíces dobles** (35) Dos raíces idénticas, o soluciones, de una ecuación.

E

English	Example	Spanish
eccentricity (98) A number that denotes how close or how far an ellipse is from being a circle. The eccentricity of a circle is 0. The eccentricity of an ellipse is greater than 0 and less than 1.	The eccentricity of the ellipse on the left is greater than that of the ellipse on the right.	**excentricidad** (98) Un número que denota qué tan cerca o tan lejos está una elipse de ser un círculo. La excentricidad de una elipse es mayor que 0 y es menor que 1.
elimination method (24) A method used to solve systems of equations in which one variable is eliminated by adding or subtracting two equations of the system.		**méthodo de eliminación** (24) Método utilizado para resolver sistemas de ecuaciones por el cual se elimina una variable sumando o restando dos ecuaciones del sistema.
ellipse (98) The set of all points P in a plane such that the sum of the distances from P to two fixed points F_1 and F_2, called the foci, is constant.	Foci	**elipse** (98) Conjunto de todos los puntos P de un plano tal que la suma de las distancias desde P hasta los puntos fijos F_1 y F_2, denominados focos, es constante.
element (5) Each value in a matrix; also called an entry.	3 is the element in the first row and second column of $A = \begin{bmatrix} 2 & 3 \\ 0 & 1 \end{bmatrix}$, denoted a_{12}.	**elemento** (5) Cada valor de una matriz; también denominado entrada.
end behavior (101) The trends in the y-values of a function as the x-values approach positive and negative infinity.	End behavior: $f(x) \to \infty$ as $x \to \infty$; $f(x) \to -\infty$ as $x \to -\infty$	**comportamiento extremo** (101) Tendencia de los valores de y de una función a medida que los valores de x se aproximan al infinito positivo y negativo.
equally likely outcomes (55) Outcomes are equally likely if they have the same probability of occurring. If an experiment has n equally likely outcomes, then the probability of each outcome is $\frac{1}{n}$.	If a coin is tossed, and heads and tails are equally likely, then $P(\text{heads}) = P(\text{tails}) = \frac{1}{2}$.	**resultados igualmente probables** (55) Los resultados son igualmente probables si tienen la misma probabilidad de ocurrir. Si un experimento tiene n resultados igualmente probables, entonces la probabilidad de cada resultado es $\frac{1}{n}$.

GLOSSARY/ GLOSARIO

English	Example	Spanish
E		
equation (7) A mathematical statement that two expressions are equivalent.	$x + 4 = 7$ $2 + 3 = 6 - 1$ $(x - 1)^2 + (y + 2)^2 = 4$	**ecuación** (7) Enunciado matemático que indica que dos expresiones son equivalentes.
evaluate (2) To find the value of an algebraic expression by substituting a number for each variable and simplifying by using the order of operations.	Evaluate $2x + 7$ for $x = 3$. $2x + 7$ $2(3) + 7$ $6 + 7$ 13	**evaluar** (2) Calcular el valor de una expresión algebraica sustituyendo cada variable por un número y simplificando mediante el orden de las operaciones.
event (33) An outcome or set of outcomes in a probability experiment.	In the experiment of rolling a number cube, the event "an odd number" consists of the outcomes 1, 3, and 5.	**suceso** (33) Resultado o conjunto de resultados en un experimento de probabilidad.
expected value (maintained) The weighted average of the numerical outcomes of a probability experiment.	The table shows the probability of getting a given score by guessing on a three-question quiz. Score: 0, 1, 2, 3 Probability: 0.42, 0.42, 0.14, 0.02 The expected value is a score of $0(0.42) + 1(0.42) + 2(0.14) + 3(0.02) = 0.76$.	**valor esperado** (repaso) Promedio ponderado de los resultados numéricos de un experimento de probabilidad.
experiment (33) An operation, process, or activity in which outcomes can be used to estimate probability.	Tossing a coin 10 times and noting the number of heads.	**experimento** (33) Una operación, proceso o actividad cuyo resultado se puede usar para estimar la probabilidad.
experimental probability (55) The ratio of the number of times an event occurs to the number of trials, or times, that an activity is performed.	Kendra made 6 of 10 free throws. The experimental probability that she will make her next free throw is $P(\text{free throw}) = \frac{\text{number made}}{\text{number attempted}} = \frac{6}{10}$.	**probabilidad experimental** (55) Razón entre la cantidad de veces que ocurre un suceso y la cantidad de pruebas, o veces, que se realiza una actividad.
explicit formula (92) A formula that defines the nth term a_n, or general term, of a sequence as a function of n.	Sequence: 4, 7, 10, 13, 16, 19, ... Explicit formula: $a_n = 1 + 3n$	**fórmula explícita** (92) Fórmula que define el enésimo término a_n, o término general, de una sucesión como una función de n.

English	Example	Spanish
E		
exponent (3) The number that indicates how many times the base in a power is used as a factor.	$3^4 = 3 \cdot 3 \cdot 3 \cdot 3 = 81$ exponent	**exponente** (3) Número que indica la cantidad de veces que la base de una potencia se utiliza como factor.
exponential decay (57) An exponential function of the form $f(x) = ab^x$ in which $a > 0$ and $0 < b < 1$. If r is the rate of decay, then the function can be written $y = a(1 - r)^t$, where a is the initial amount and t is the time.	$y = 3\left(\frac{1}{2}\right)^x$	**decremento exponencial** (57) Función exponencial del tipo $f(x) = ab^x$ en la cual $0 < b < 1$. Si r es la tasa decremental, entonces la función se puede expresar como $y = a(1 - r)^t$, donde a es la cantidad inicial y t es el tiempo.
exponential equation (93) An equation that contains one or more exponential expressions.	$2^{x+1} = 8$	**ecuación exponencial** (93) Ecuación que contiene una o más expresiones exponenciales.
exponential function (47) A function of the form $f(x) = ab^x$, where a and b are real numbers with $a \neq 0$, $b > 0$, and $b \neq 1$.	$f(x) = 2^x$	**función exponencial** (47) Función del tipo $f(x) = ab^x$, donde a y b son números reales con $a \neq 0$, $b > 0$ y $b \neq 1$.
exponential growth (57) An exponential function of the form $f(x) = ab^x$ in which $a > 0$ and $b > 1$. If r is the rate of growth, then the function can be written $y = a(1 + r)^t$, where a is the initial amount and t is the time.	$f(x) = 2^x$	**crecimiento exponencial** (57) Función exponencial del tipo $f(x) = ab^x$ en la que $b > 1$. Si r es la tasa de crecimiento, entonces la función se puede expresar como $y = a(1 + r)^t$, donde a es la cantidad inicial y t es el tiempo.
exponential regression (116) A statistical method used to fit an exponential model to a given data set.	ExpReg	**regresión exponencial** (116) Método estadístico utilizado para ajustar un modelo exponencial a un conjunto de datos determinado.

GLOSSARY/ GLOSARIO

English	Example	Spanish
E		
extraneous solution (17) A solution of a derived equation that is not a solution of the original equation.	To solve $\sqrt{x} = -2$, square both sides; $x = 4$. Check $\sqrt{4} = -2$ is false; so 4 is an extraneous solution.	**solución extraña** (17) Solución de una ecuación derivada que no es una solución de la ecuación original.
F		
Factor Theorem (95) For any polynomial $P(x)$, $(x - a)$ is a factor of $P(x)$ if and only if $P(a) = 0$.	$(x - 1)$ is a factor of $P(x) = x^2 - 1$ because $P(1) = 1^2 - 1 = 0$.	**Teorema del factor** (95) Dado el polinomio $P(x)$, $(x - a)$ es un factor de $P(x)$ si y sólo si $P(a) = 0$.
factorial (42) If n is a positive integer, then n factorial, written $n!$, is $n \cdot (n-1) \cdot (n-2) \cdot \ldots \cdot 2 \cdot 1$. The factorial of 0 is defined to be 1.	$7! = 7 \cdot 6 \cdot 5 \cdot 4 \cdot 3 \cdot 2 \cdot 1 = 5040$ $0! = 1$	**factorial** (42) Si n es un entero positivo, entonces el factorial de n, expresado como $n!$, es $n \cdot (n-1) \cdot (n-2) \cdot \ldots \cdot 2 \cdot 1$. Por definición, el factorial de 0 es 1.
factoring (23) The process of writing a number or algebraic expression as a product.	$x^2 - 4x - 21 = (x - 7)(x + 3)$	**factoreo** (23) Proceso por el que se expresa un número o expresión algebraica como un producto.
favorable outcome (55) The occurrence of one of several possible outcomes of a specified event or probability experiment.	In the experiment of rolling an odd number on a number cube, the favorable outcomes are 1, 3, and 5.	**resultado favorable** (55) Cuando se produce uno de varios resultados posibles de un suceso específico o experimento de probabilidades.
feasible region (54) The set of points that satisfy the constraints in a linear-programming problem.	Constraints: $x > 0$ $y > 0$ $x + y \leq 8$ $3x + 5y \leq 30$ Feasible region	**región factible** (54) Conjunto de puntos que cumplen con las restricciones de un problema de programación lineal.

English	Example	Spanish
F		
finite sequence (92) A sequence with a finite number of terms.	1, 2, 3, 4, 5	**sucesión finita** (92) Sucesión con un número finito de términos.
first differences (maintained) The differences between y-values of a function for evenly spaced x-values.	x: 0, 1, 2, 3 y: 3, 7, 11, 15 first differences +4 +4 +4	**primeras diferencias** (repaso) Diferencias entre los valores de y de una función para valores de x espaciados uniformemente.
first quartile (25) The median of the lower half of a data set, denoted Q_1. Also called *lower quartile*.	Lower half: 18, 23, 28, | Upper half: 49, 36, 42 First quartile	**primer cuartil** (25) Mediana de la mitad inferior de un conjunto de datos, expresada como Q_1. También se llama *cuartil inferior*.
focus (pl. foci) of a hyperbola (109) One of two fixed points F_1 and F_2 that are used to define a hyperbola. For every point P on the hyperbola, $PF_1 - PF_2$ is constant.	Focus: $(-c, 0)$ Focus: $(c, 0)$	**foco de una hipérbola** (109) Uno de los dos puntos fijos F_1 y F_2 utilizados para definir una hipérbola, Para cada punto P de la hipérbola, $PF_1 - PF_2$ es constante.
focus (pl. foci) of an ellipse (98) One of two fixed points F_1 and F_2 that are used to define an ellipse. For every point P on the ellipse, $PF_1 + PF_2$ is constant.	Focus: $(0, c)$ Focus: $(0, -c)$	**foco de una elipse** (98) Uno de los dos puntos fijos F_1 y F_2 utilizados para definir una elipse. Para cada punto P de la elipse, $PF_1 + PF_2$ es constante.
function (4) A relation in which every input is paired with exactly one output.	6, 5, 2, 1 → −4, −1, 0	**función** (4) Una relación en la que cada entrada corresponde exactamente a una salida.
function notation (4) If x is the independent variable and y is the dependent variable, then the function notation for y is $f(x)$, read "f of x," where f names the function.	equation: $y = 2x$ function notation: $f(x) = 2x$	**notación de función** (4) Si x es la variable independiente e y es la variable dependiente, entonces la notación de función para y es $f(x)$, que se lee "f de x", donde f nombra la función.

GLOSSARY/ GLOSARIO

English	Example	Spanish
F		
Fundamental Counting Principle (33)		**Principio fundamental de conteo** (33)
For n items, if there are m_1 ways to choose a first item, m_2 ways to choose a second item after the first item has been chosen, and so on, then there are $m_1 \cdot m_2 \cdot \ldots \cdot m_n$ ways to choose n items.	If there are 4 colors of shirts, 3 colors of pants, and 2 colors of shoes, then there are $4 \cdot 3 \cdot 2 = 24$ possible outfits.	Dados n elementos, si existen m_1 formas de elegir un primer elemento, m_2 formas de elegir un segundo elemento después de haber elegido el primero, y así sucesivamente, entonces existen $m_1 \cdot m_2 \cdot \ldots \cdot m_n$ formas de elegir n elementos.
Fundamental Theorem of Algebra (106)		**Teorema fundamental del álgebra** (106)
Every polynomial function of degree $n \geq 1$ has at least one zero, where a zero may be a complex number.	$y = x^3 - x^2 - 5x + 9$ has at least one zero.	Cada función polinomial de grado $n \geq 1$ tiene por lo menos un cero, donde un cero puede ser un número complejo.
G		
general form of a conic section (114)	A circle with a vertex at (1, 2) and radius 3 has the general form $x^2 + y^2 - 2x - 4y - 4 = 0$.	**forma general de una sección cónica** (114)
$Ax^2 + Bxy + Cy^2 + Dx + Ey + F = 0$, where A and B are not both 0.		$Ax^2 + Bxy + Cy^2 + Dx + Ey + F = 0$, donde A y B no son los dos 0.
geometric probability (55)		**probabilidad geométrica** (55)
A form of theoretical probability determined by a ratio of geometric measures such as lengths, areas, or volumes.	The probability of the pointer landing on red is $\frac{5}{24}$.	Método para calcular probabilidades basado en una medida geométrica como la longitud, el área o el volumen.
geometric sequence (97)		**sucesión geométrica** (97)
A sequence in which the ratio of successive terms is a constant r, called the common ratio, where $r \neq 0$ and $r \neq 1$.	1, 2, 4, 8, 16, … ($\cdot 2$ $\cdot 2$ $\cdot 2$ $\cdot 2$) $r = 2$	Sucesión en la que la razón de los términos sucesivos es una constante r, denominada razón común, donde $r \neq 0$ y $r \neq 1$.
geometric series (113)		**serie geométrica** (113)
The indicated sum of the terms of a geometric sequence.	$1 + 2 + 4 + 8 + 16 + \ldots$	Suma indicada de los términos de una sucesión geométrica.

English	Example	Spanish
G		
greatest common factor (GCF) (maintained)	The GCF of $4x^3y$ and $6x^2y$ is $2x^2y$. The GCF of 27 and 45 is 9.	**máximo común divisor (MCD)** (repaso)
The product of the greatest integer and the greatest power of each variable that divides evenly into each term.		Producto del entero mayor y la potencia mayor de cada variable que divide exactamente cada término.
greatest integer function (Inv 9)		**función de entero mayor** (Inv 9)
A function denoted by $f(x) = [x]$ or $f(x) = \lfloor x \rfloor$ in which the number x is rounded down to the greatest integer that is less than or equal to x.	$\lfloor 4.98 \rfloor = 4$ $\lfloor -2.1 \rfloor = -3$	Función expresada como $f(x) = [x]$ ó $f(x) = \lfloor x \rfloor$ en la cual el número x se redondea hacia abajo hasta el entero mayor que sea menor que o igual a x.
greatest common monomial factor (23)		**máximo monomio común** (23)
A monomial that divides evenly into every term of a polynomial; its coefficient is the greatest common factor of the coefficients in the polynomial; its variables must occur in every term of the polynomial, the highest degree of each of its variables being the lowest degree of that variable in the polynomial.	The greatest monomial factor of $12x^3y^2 - 18x^4y + 6x^2y^2 + 6x^2yz$ is $6x^2y$.	Un monomio que divide sin residuo a cada término de un polinomio; su coeficiente es el máximo factor común de los coeficientes en el polinomio; sus variables deben de estar presentes en cada término del polinomio, el grado más alto de cada una de sus variables debe ser el grado más bajo de esa variable en el polinomio.
growth factor (57)	$12{,}000(1 + 0.14)^t$ (growth factor)	**factor de crecimiento** (57)
The base $1 + r$ in an exponential expression.		La base $1 + r$ en una expresión exponencial.
H		
half-life (57)		**vida media** (57)
The half-life of a substance is the time it takes for one-half of the substance to decay.	Carbon-14 has a half-life of 5730 years, so 5 g of an initial amount of 10 g will remain after 5730 years.	La vida media de una sustancia es el tiempo que tarda la mitad de la sustancia en desintegrarse y transformarse en otra sustancia.

English	Example	Spanish
H		
half-plane (39)		**semiplano** (39)
The part of the coordinate plane on one side of a line, which may include the line.		Parte del plano coordenado de un lado de una línea, que puede incluir la línea.
Heron's Formula (77)		**fórmula de Herón** (77)
A triangle with side lengths a, b, and c has area $A = \sqrt{s(s-a)(s-b)(s-c)}$, where s is one-half the perimeter, or $s = \frac{1}{2}(a + b + c)$.	$s = \frac{1}{2}(3 + 6 + 7) = 8$ $A = \sqrt{8(8-3)(8-6)(8-7)}$ $= \sqrt{80} = 4\sqrt{5}$ square units	Un triángulo con longitudes de lado a, b y c tiene un área $= \sqrt{s(s-a)(s-b)(s-c)}$, donde s es la mitad del perímetro ó $s = \frac{1}{2}(a + b + c)$.
horizontal asymptote (47)	asymptote	**azíntota horizontal** (47)
A horizontal line that a graphed function approaches.		Una línea horizontal a la que se aproxima la gráfica de una función.
horizontal line (34)	$y = 3$	**recta horizontal** (34)
A line described by the equation $y = b$, where b is the y-intercept.		Línea descrita por la ecuación $y = b$, donde b es la intersección con el eje y.
hyperbola (109)	Focus: $(-c, 0)$ Focus: $(c, 0)$	**hipérbola** (109)
The set of all points P in a plane such that the difference of the distances from P to two fixed points F_1 and F_2, called the foci, is a constant $d = \lvert PF_1 - PF_2 \rvert$.		Conjunto de todos los puntos P en un plano tal que la diferencia de las distancias de P a dos puntos fijos F_1 y F_2, llamados focos, es una constante $d = \lvert PF_1 - PF_2 \rvert$.
hyperbolic geometry (109)		**geometría hiperbólica** (109)
A non-Euclidean geometry; in this geometry, through a point not on a line there are at least two lines parallel to the given line.		Una geometría no-Euclideana; en esta geometría, a través de un punto que no está en una línea, hay por lo menos dos líneas paralelas a dicha línea.
hypotenuse (41)	hypotenuse	**hipotenusa** (41)
The side opposite the right angle in a right triangle.		Lado opuesto al ángulo recto de un triángulo rectángulo.

English	Example	Spanish
I		
imaginary axis (69)	Imaginary axis; Real axis	**eje imaginario** (69)
The vertical axis in the complex plane, it graphically represents the purely imaginary part of complex numbers.		Eje vertical de un plano complejo. Representa gráficamente la parte puramente imaginaria de los números complejos.
imaginary number (62)		**número imaginario** (62)
The square root of a negative number, written in the form bi, where b is a real number and i is the imaginary unit, $\sqrt{-1}$. Also called a *pure imaginary number*.	$\sqrt{-16} = \sqrt{16} \cdot \sqrt{-1} = 4i$	Raíz cuadrada de un número negativo, expresado como bi, donde b es un número real e i es la unidad imaginaria, $\sqrt{-1}$. También se denomina *número imaginario puro*.
imaginary part of a complex number (62)		**parte imaginaria de un número complejo** (62)
For a complex number of the form $a + bi$, the real number b is called the imaginary part, represented graphically as b units on the imaginary axis of a complex plane.	$5 + 6i$ (real part, imaginary part)	Dado un número complejo del tipo $a + bi$, el número real b se denomina parte imaginaria y se representa gráficamente como b unidades en el eje imaginario de un plano complejo.
imaginary unit (62)	$\sqrt{-1} = i$	**unidad imaginaria** (62)
The unit in the imaginary number system, $\sqrt{-1}$.		Unidad del sistema de números imaginarios, $\sqrt{-1}$.
inclusive events (60)	In the experiment of rolling a number cube, rolling an even number and rolling a number less than 3 are inclusive events because the outcome 2 is both even and less than 3.	**sucesos inclusivos** (60)
Events that have one or more outcomes in common.		Sucesos que tienen uno o más resultados en común.
inconsistent system (15)		**sistema inconsistente** (15)
A system of equations or inequalities that has no solution.	$\begin{cases} y = 2.5x + 5 \\ y = 2.5x - 5 \end{cases}$ is inconsistent.	Sistema de ecuaciones o desigualdades que no tiene solución.

GLOSSARY/ GLOSARIO

I

English	Example	Spanish
increasing function (57) A function whose output value increases as its input value increases.		**función creciente** (57) Una función cuyo valor de salida aumenta conforme su valor de entrada aumenta.
independent events (33) Events for which the occurrence or non-occurrence of one event does not affect the probability of the other event.	From a bag containing 3 red marbles and 2 blue marbles, drawing a red marble, replacing it, and then drawing a blue marble.	**sucesos independientes** (33) Dos sucesos son independientes si el hecho de que se produzca o no uno de ellos no afecta la probabilidad del otro suceso.
independent system (15) A system of equations that has exactly one solution.	$\begin{cases} y = -x + 4 \\ y = x + 2 \end{cases}$ Solution: (1, 3)	**sistema independiente** (15) Sistema de ecuaciones que tiene exactamente una solución.
independent variable (4) The input of a function; a variable whose value determines the value of the output, or dependent variable.	$y = 2x + 1$ independent variable	**variable independiente** (4) Entrada de una función; variable cuyo valor determina el valor de la salida, o variable dependiente.
index (40) In the radical $\sqrt[n]{x}$, which represents the *n*th root of *x*, *n* is the index. In the radical $\sqrt{x}$, the index is understood to be 2.	The radical $\sqrt[3]{8}$ has an index of 3.	**índice** (40) En el radical $\sqrt[n]{x}$, que representa la enésima raíz de *x*, *n* es el índice. En el radical $\sqrt{x}$, se da por sentado que el índice es 2.
inequality (10) A statement that compares two expressions by using one of the following symbols: $<, >, \leq, \geq$, or $\neq$.	$x \geq -2$	**desigualdad** (10) Enunciado que compara dos expresiones utilizando uno de los siguientes símbolos: $<, >, \leq, \geq$, ó $\neq$.
infinite geometric series (113) A geometric series with infinitely many terms.	$\frac{1}{10} + \frac{1}{100} + \frac{1}{1000} + \frac{1}{10{,}000} + \ldots$	**serie geométrica infinita** (113) Serie geométrica con una cantidad infinita de términos.

I

English	Example	Spanish
infinite sequence (92) A sequence with infinitely many terms.	1, 3, 5, 7, 9, 11, …	**sucesión infinita** (92) Sucesión con un número infinito de términos.
initial side (56) The ray that lies on the positive *x*-axis when an angle is drawn in standard position.	Terminal side, 45°, 135°, Initial side	**lado inicial** (56) El rayo que se encuentra en el eje positivo *x* cuando se traza un ángulo en la posición estándar.
integer (1) A member of the set of whole numbers and their opposites.	… −3, −2, −1, 0, 1, 2, 3 …	**entero** (1) Miembro del conjunto de números cabales y sus opuestos.
intercepts (13) On a coordinate plane, the points where a graph intersects the axes.	*x*-intercept, *y*-intercept	**intersecciones** (13) En un plano coordenado, los puntos donde una gráfica interseca a los ejes.
intersect (15) When two or more lines, or segments, cross or meet; meeting point is called point of intersection.	The lines intersect at (−3, −2).	**intersecar** (15) Cuando dos o más rectas o segmentos de rectas se cruzan; el punto donde se cruzan es llamado punto de intersección.
inverse cosine function (67) If the domain of the cosine function is restricted to $[0, \pi]$, then the function $\cos\theta = a$ has an inverse function $\text{Cos}^{-1} a = \theta$, also called *arccosine*.	$\text{Cos}^{-1}\frac{1}{2} = \frac{\pi}{3}$	**función coseno inverso** (67) Si el dominio de la función coseno se restringe a $[0, \pi]$, entonces la función $\cos\theta = a$ tiene una función inversa $\text{Cos}^{-1} a = \theta$, también llamada *arco coseno*.

GLOSSARY/GLOSARIO

I

English	Example	Spanish
inverse function (50) The function that results from exchanging the input and output values of a one-to-one function. The inverse of $f(x)$ is denoted $f^{-1}(x)$.	$f(x) = x^3$, $y = x$, $f^{-1}(x) = \sqrt[3]{x}$	**función inversa** (50) Función que resulta de intercambiar los valores de entrada y salida de una función uno a uno. La función inversa de $f(x)$ se expresa $f^{-1}(x)$.
inverse matrix (32) A square matrix such that the product of it and another matrix forms an identity matrix.	The inverse matrix of $\begin{bmatrix} 5 & 2 \\ 8 & 4 \end{bmatrix}$ is $\begin{bmatrix} 1 & -\frac{1}{2} \\ -2 & 1\frac{1}{4} \end{bmatrix}$ because $\begin{bmatrix} 5 & 2 \\ 8 & 4 \end{bmatrix} \cdot \begin{bmatrix} 1 & -\frac{1}{2} \\ -2 & 1\frac{1}{4} \end{bmatrix} = \begin{bmatrix} 1 & 0 \\ 0 & 1 \end{bmatrix}$.	**matriz inversa** (32) Una matriz cuadrada tal que el producto de ella por otra matriz resulta en la matriz identidad.
inverse relation (50) The inverse of the relation consisting of all ordered pairs (x, y) is the set of all ordered pairs (y, x). The graph of an inverse relation is the reflection of the graph of the relation across the line $y = x$.		**relación inversa** (50) La inversa de la relación que consta de todos los pares ordenados (x, y) es el conjunto de todos los pares ordenados (y, x). La gráfica de una relación inversa es el reflejo de la gráfica de la relación sobre la línea $y = x$.
inverse sine function (67) If the domain of the sine function is restricted to $\left[-\frac{\pi}{2}, \frac{\pi}{2}\right]$, then the function $\sin\theta = a$ has an inverse function, $\text{Sin}^{-1} a = \theta$, also called *arcsine*.	$\text{Sin}^{-1}\frac{\sqrt{3}}{2} = \frac{\pi}{3}$	**función seno inverso** (67) Si el dominio de la función seno se restringe a $\left[-\frac{\pi}{2}, \frac{\pi}{2}\right]$, entonces la función $\sin\theta = a$ tiene una función inversa, $\text{Sin}^{-1} a = \theta$, también llamada *arco seno*.
inverse tangent function (67) If the domain of the tangent function is restricted to $\left(-\frac{\pi}{2}, \frac{\pi}{2}\right)$, then the function $\tan\theta = a$ has an inverse function, $\text{Tan}^{-1} a = \theta$, also called *arctangent*.	$\text{Tan}^{-1}\sqrt{3} = \frac{\pi}{3}$	**función tangente inversa** (67) Si el dominio de la función tangente se restringe a $\left(-\frac{\pi}{2}, \frac{\pi}{2}\right)$, entonces la función $\tan\theta = a$ tiene una función inversa, $\text{Tan}^{-1} a = \theta$, también llamada *arco tangente*.

I

English	Example	Spanish
inverse variation (12) A relationship between two variables, *x* and *y*, that can be written in the form $y = \frac{k}{x}$, where *k* is a nonzero constant and $x \neq 0$.	$y = \frac{24}{x}$	**variación inversa** (12) Relación entre dos variables, *x* e *y*, que puede expresarse en la forma $y = \frac{k}{x}$, donde *k* es una constante distinta de cero y $x \neq 0$.
irrational number (1) A real number that cannot be expressed as the ratio of two integers.	$\sqrt{2}, \pi, e$	**número irracional** (1) Número real que no se puede expresar como una razón de enteros.
iteration (maintained) The repetitive application of the same rule.	First iteration Second iteration Third iteration	**iteración** (repaso) Aplicación repetitiva de la misma regla.

J

English	Example	Spanish
joint variation (12) A relationship among three variables that can be written in the form $y = kxz$, where *k* is a nonzero constant.	$y = 3xz$	**variación conjunta** (12) Relación entre tres variables que se puede expresar de la forma $y = kxz$, donde *k* es una constante distinta de cero.

L

English	Example	Spanish
Law of Cosines (77) For $\triangle ABC$ with side lengths *a*, *b*, and *c*, $a^2 = b^2 + c^2 - 2bc\cos A$ $b^2 = a^2 + c^2 - 2ac\cos B$ $c^2 = a^2 + b^2 - 2ab\cos C$.	$b^2 = 7^2 + 5^2 - 2(7)(5)\cos 100°$ $b^2 \approx 86.2$ $b \approx 9.3$	**Ley de cosenos** (77) Dado $\triangle ABC$ con longitudes de lado *a*, *b* y *c*, $a^2 = b^2 + c^2 - 2bc\cos A$ $b^2 = a^2 + c^2 - 2ac\cos B$ $c^2 = a^2 + b^2 - 2ab\cos C$.
Law of Sines (71) For $\triangle ABC$ with side lengths *a*, *b*, and *c*, $\frac{\sin A}{a} = \frac{\sin B}{b} = \frac{\sin C}{c}$.	$\frac{\sin 49°}{r} = \frac{\sin 40°}{20}$ $r = \frac{20 \sin 49°}{\sin 40°} \approx 23.5$	**Ley de senos** (71) Dado $\triangle ABC$ con longitudes de lado *a*, *b* y *c*, $\frac{\sin A}{a} = \frac{\sin B}{b} = \frac{\sin C}{c}$.

GLOSSARY/GLOSARIO

English	Example	Spanish
L		
leading coefficient (11) — The coefficient of the first term of a polynomial in standard form.	$3x^2 + 7x - 2$ Leading coefficient	**coeficiente principal** (11) — Coeficiente del primer término de un polinomio en forma estándar.
least common denominator (LCD) (maintained) — The least common multiple of two or more given denominators.	The LCD of $\frac{3}{4}$ and $\frac{5}{6}$ is 12.	**mínimo común denominador (mcd)** (repaso) — Mínimo común múltiplo de dos o más denominadores dados.
least common multiple (LCM) (maintained) — The smallest positive integer (or polynomial) that is a multiple of two numbers (or polynomials.)	The LCM of 10 and 18 is 90. The LCM of $2x^2$ *and* $5x^3$ *is* $10x^3$.	**mínimo común múltiplo (mcm)** (repaso) — El número (o polinomio) positivo más pequeño que es un múltiplo de dos números (o polinomios).
leg of a right triangle (41) — One of the two sides of the right triangle that form the right angle.	leg, leg	**cateto de un triángulo rectángulo** (41) — Uno de los dos lados de un triángulo rectángulo que forman el ángulo recto.
likelihood (55) — a measure of the chance of something happening.	The likelihood of snow in Miami in June is very low.	**posibilidad** (55) — Una medida de la probabilidad de que algo ocurra.
like radical terms (40) — Radical terms having the same radicand and index.	$3\sqrt{2x}$ and $\sqrt{2x}$ Like radicals; $\sqrt{3x}$ and $\sqrt{2x}$ Unlike radicals	**radicales semejantes** (40) — Términos radicales que tienen el mismo radicando e índice.
like terms (2) — Terms with the same variables raised to the same exponents.	$3a^3b^2$ and $7a^3b^2$ Like terms; $4xy^2$ and $6x^2y$ Unlike terms	**términos semejantes** (2) — Términos con las mismas variables elevadas a los mismos exponentes.
limit (113) — A number (or infinity) that the terms of an infinite sequence or series approach as the term number increases.	The series $\frac{1}{2} + \frac{1}{4} + \frac{1}{8} + \frac{1}{16} + \ldots$ has a limit of 1.	**límite** (113) — Número (o infinito) al que se aproximan los términos de una sucesión o serie infinita a medida que aumenta el número de términos.

English	Example	Spanish
L		
line of best fit (45) — The line that comes closest to all of the points in a data set.		**línea de mejor ajuste** (45) — Línea que más se acerca a todos los puntos de un conjunto de datos.
linear equation in one variable (maintained) — An equation that can be written in the form $ax = b$, where a and b are constants and $a \neq 0$.	$x + 1 = 7$	**ecuación lineal en una variable** (repaso) — Ecuación que puede expresarse en la forma $ax = b$, donde a y b son constantes y $a \neq 0$.
linear function (34) — A function that can be written in the form $f(x) = mx + b$, where x is the independent variable and m and b are real numbers. Its graph is a line.	$y = \frac{1}{2}x - 2$	**función lineal** (34) — Función que puede expresarse en la forma $f(x) = mx + b$, donde x es la variable independiente y m y b son números reales. Su gráfica es una línea.
linear inequality in two variables (39) — An inequality that can be written in one of the following forms: $y < mx + b$, $y > mx + b$, $y \le mx + b$, $y \ge mx + b$, or $y \neq mx + b$, where m and b are real numbers.	$2x + 3y \le 6$ $y > \frac{1}{2}x - 7$	**desigualdad lineal en dos variables** (39) — Desiqualdad que puede expresarse de una de las siguientes formas: $y < mx + b$, $y > mx + b$, $y \le mx + b$, $y \ge mx + b$, o $y \neq mx + b$, donde m y b son números reales.
linear programming (54) — A method of finding a maximum or minimum value of a linear function, called the *objective function*, that satisfies a given set of conditions, called *constraints*.	Constraints: $x \ge 0$, $40x + 60y \le 1440$, $y \ge \frac{1}{3}x$, $y \le 16$. Feasible Region: (0, 16), (0, 0), (12, 16), (24, 8). For the given constraints, the objective function $P = 18x + 25y$ is maximized at (24, 8).	**programación lineal** (54) — Método para calcular un valor máximo o mínimo de una función lineal, denominada *función objetiva*, que cumple con una serie dada de condiciones, denominadas *restricciones*.
linear regression (45) — A statistical method used to fit a linear model to a given data set.	LinReg y=ax+b a=2.753883892 b=71.97383483 r²=.9825297615 r=.9912263927	**regresión lineal** (45) — Método estadístico utilizado para ajustar un modelo lineal a un conjunto de datos determinado.

GLOSSARY/ GLOSARIO

English	Example	Spanish
L		
linear system (15) — A system of equations containing only linear equations.	$\begin{cases} y = 2x + 1 \\ x + y = 8 \end{cases}$	**sistema lineal** (15) — Sistema de ecuaciones que contiene sólo ecuaciones lineales.
local maximum (101) — For a function f, $f(a)$ is a local maximum if there is an interval around a such that $f(x) < f(a)$ for every x-value in the interval except a.	Local maximum	**máximo local** (101) — Dada una función f, $f(a)$ es el máximo local si hay un intervalo en a tal que $f(x) < f(a)$ para cada valor de x en el intervalo excepto a.
local minimum (101) — For a function f, $f(a)$ is a local minimum if there is an interval around a such that $f(x) > f(a)$ for every x-value in the interval except a.	Local minimum	**mínimo local** (101) — Dada una función f, $f(a)$ es el mínimo local si hay un intervalo en a tal que $f(x) > f(a)$ para cada valor de x en el intervalo excepto a.
logarithm (64) — The exponent that a specified base must be raised to in order to get a certain value.	$\log_2 8 = 3$, because 3 is the power that 2 is raised to in order to get 8; or $2^3 = 8$.	**logaritmo** (64) — Exponente al cual debe elevarse una base determinada a fin de obtener cierto valor.
logarithmic equation (102) — An equation that contains a logarithm of a variable.	$\log x + 3 = 7$	**ecuación logarítmica** (102) — Ecuación que contiene un logaritmo de una variable.
logarithmic function (110) — A function of the form $f(x) = \log_b x$, where $b \neq 1$ and $b > 0$, which is the inverse of the exponential function $f(x) = b^x$.	$f(x) = \log_4 x$	**función logarítmica** (110) — Función del tipo $f(x) = \log_b x$, donde $b \neq 1$ y $b > 0$, que es la inversa de la función exponencial $f(x) = b^x$.
logarithmic inequality (102) — An inequality that contains a logarithm of a variable.	$\log x - \log 2 \le \log 75$	**desigualdad logarítmica** (102) — Una desigualdad que contiene un logaritmo de una variable.
logarithmic regression (116) — A statistical method used to fit a logarithmic model to a given data set.	LnReg	**regresión logarítmica** (116) — Método estadístico utilizado para ajustar un modelo logarítmico a un conjunto de datos determinado.

English	Example	Spanish
M		
main diagonal (of a matrix) (9) — The diagonal from the upper left corner to the lower right corner of a matrix.	$\begin{bmatrix} 3 & 1 & 2 \\ 5 & 0 & 1 \\ 2 & 7 & 6 \end{bmatrix}$	**diagonal principal (de una matriz)** (9) — Diagonal que se extiende desde la esquina superior izquierda hasta la esquina inferior derecha de una matriz.
major axis (98) — The longer axis of an ellipse. The foci of the ellipse are located on the major axis, and its endpoints are the *vertices of the ellipse*.	Vertex: (0, a); Major axis; Vertex: (0, −a)	**eje mayor** (98) — El eje más largo de una elipse. Los focos de la elipse se encuentran sobre el eje mayor y sus extremos son los *vértices de la elipse*.
mathematical induction (Inv 12) — A type of mathematical proof. To prove that a statement is true for all natural numbers n, first show that the statement is true for $n = 1$; then assume it is true for some number k and prove that it is true for $k + 1$. It follows that the statement is true for all values of n.		**inducción matemática** (Inv 12) — Tipo de demostración matemática. Para demostrar que un enunciado se cumple para todos los números naturales n, primero se demuestra que el enunciado se cumple para $n = 1$; luego se supone que se cumple para un número k y se demuestra que se cumple para $k + 1$. Por lo tanto, el enunciado se cumplirá para todos los valores de n.
matrix (5) — A rectangular array of numbers.	$\begin{bmatrix} 1 & 0 & 3 \\ -2 & 2 & -5 \\ 7 & -6 & 3 \end{bmatrix}$	**matriz** (5) — Arreglo rectangular de números.
matrix addition (5) — Adding each element in one matrix to the element that is in the same location in a second matrix.	$\begin{bmatrix} 1 & 0 \\ 7 & 4 \end{bmatrix} + \begin{bmatrix} -5 & 9 \\ 6 & 3 \end{bmatrix} = \begin{bmatrix} -4 & 9 \\ 13 & 7 \end{bmatrix}$	**adición de matrices** (5) — Sumar cada elemento en una matriz al elemento que está en el mismo lugar en una segunda matriz.
matrix equation (5) — An equation of the form $AX = B$, where A is the coefficient matrix, X is the variable matrix, and B is the constant matrix of a system of equations.	$\begin{bmatrix} 3 & 7 \\ 9 & 1 \end{bmatrix} + X = \begin{bmatrix} 5 & 9 \\ 2 & -6 \end{bmatrix}$	**ecuación matricial** (5) — Ecuación del tipo $AX = B$, donde A es la matriz de coeficientes, X es la matriz de variables y B es la matriz de constantes de un sistema de ecuaciones.

GLOSSARY/ GLOSARIO

M

English	Example	Spanish
matrix of constants (32) A matrix consisting of the constants used in a system of equations.	For $\begin{cases} 2x+4y=8 \\ 3x-y=-2 \end{cases}$, it is $\begin{bmatrix} 8 \\ -2 \end{bmatrix}$.	**matriz de constantes** (32) Una matriz que consiste en de las constantes utilizadas en un sistema de ecuaciones.
matrix of variables (32) A matrix consisting of the variables used in a system of equations.	For $\begin{cases} 2x+4y+z=8 \\ 3x-y-7z=-2 \\ x+6y-2z=1 \end{cases}$, it is $\begin{bmatrix} x \\ y \\ z \end{bmatrix}$.	**matriz de variables** (32) Una matriz que consiste en las variables utilizadas en un sistema de ecuaciones.
matrix subtraction (maintained) Subtracting each element in one matrix from the element that is in the same location in a second matrix.	$\begin{bmatrix} 1 & 0 \\ 7 & 4 \end{bmatrix} - \begin{bmatrix} -5 & 9 \\ 6 & 3 \end{bmatrix} = \begin{bmatrix} 6 & -9 \\ 1 & 1 \end{bmatrix}$	**resta de matrices** (repaso) Restar cada elemento en una matriz del elemento que está en el mismo lugar en una segunda matriz.
maximum value of a function (30) The y-value of the highest point on the graph of the function.	Maximum value	**máximo de una función** (30) Valor de y del punto más alto en la gráfica de la función.
mean (25) The sum of all the values in a data set divided by the number of data values; also called the *average*.	Data set: 4, 6, 7, 8, 10 Mean: $\frac{4+6+7+8+10}{5} = \frac{35}{5} = 7$	**media** (25) Suma de todos los valores de un conjunto de datos dividido entre el número de valores de datos; también llamada *promedio*.
measure of central tendency (25) A measure that describes the center of a data set.	the mean, median, or mode	**medida de tendencia dominante** (25) Medida que describe el centro de un conjunto de datos.
measure of dispersion (25) A statistic that indicates how spread out, or dispersed, the data values are; common measures are range and standard deviation.	For data set: 5, 8, 12, 14, 16 range = 11, standard deviation ≈ 4.47 For data set: 1, 9, 41, 60, 95 range = 94, standard deviation ≈ 38.41	**medida de dispersión** (25) Una estadística que indica que tan alejados o tan dispersados están los valores de datos; medidas comunes son rango y desviación estándar.

M

English	Example	Spanish
measure of variation (maintained) A measure that describes the spread of a data set.	the range, variance, standard deviation, or interquartile range	**medida de variación** (repaso) Medida que describe la dispersión de un conjunto de datos.
median (25) For an ordered data set with an odd number of values, the median is the middle value. For an ordered data set with an even number of values, the median is the average of the two middle values.	8, 9, (9), 12, 15 Median: 9; 4, 6, (7, 10), 10, 12 Median: $\frac{7+10}{2}$ = 8.5	**mediana de un conjunto de datos** (25) Dado un conjunto de datos ordenados con un número impar de valores, la mediana es el valor del medio. Dado un conjunto de datos ordenados con un número par de valores, la mediana es el promedio de los dos valores del medio.
minimum value of a function (30) The y-value of the lowest point on the graph of the function.	Minimum value	**mínimo de una función** (30) Valor y del punto más bajo en la gráfica de la función.
minor (14) The minor of an element in a matrix is the determinant of the terms that remain when the row and column for that element are deleted.	For $\begin{bmatrix} 2 & -1 & 6 \\ 5 & 7 & 4 \\ 1 & 0 & 3 \end{bmatrix}$, the minor of 2 is $\begin{vmatrix} 7 & 4 \\ 0 & 3 \end{vmatrix}$.	**menor** (14) El menor de un elemento en una matriz es el determinante de los términos que quedan cuando la fila y la columa para ese elemento son eliminadas.
minor axis (98) The shorter axis of an ellipse. Its endpoints are the co-vertices of the ellipse.	Co-vertex: (−b, 0); Co-vertex: (b, 0); Minor axis	**eje menor** (98) El eje más corto de una elipse. Sus extremos son los co-vértices de la elipse.
mode (25) The value or values that occur most frequently in a data set; if all values occur with the same frequency, the data set is said to have no mode.	Data set: 3, 6, (8, 8), 10 Mode: 8; Data set: 2, (5, 5, 7, 7) Modes: 5 and 7; Data set: 2, 3, 6, 9, 11 No mode	**moda** (25) El valor o los valores que se presentan con mayor frecuencia en un conjunto de datos. Si todos los valores se presentan con la misma frecuencia, se dice que el conjunto de datos no tiene moda.

GLOSSARY/ GLOSARIO

M

English	Example	Spanish
monomial (11) A number or a product of numbers and variables with whole-number exponents, or a polynomial with one term.	$8x$, 9, $3x^2y^4$	**monomio** (11) Número o producto de números y variables con exponentes de números cabales, o polinomio con un término.
monomial factor (23) A common factor of a polynomial that is a number, variable, or product of numbers and variables.	$14x^2 + 20x^3$ has a monomial factor of $2x^2$.	**factor monomial** (23) Un factor común de un polinomio que es un número, variable, o producto de números y variables.
multiple root (maintained) A root r is a multiple root when the factor $(x-r)$ appears in the equation more than once.	3 is a multiple root of $P(x) = (x-3)^2$.	**raíz múltiple** (repaso) Una raíz r es una raíz múltiple cuando el factor $(x-r)$ aparece en la ecuación más de una vez.
multiplicative identity matrix (9) A square matrix with 1 in every entry of the main diagonal and 0 in every other entry.	$\begin{bmatrix} 1 & 0 \\ 0 & 1 \end{bmatrix}$, $\begin{bmatrix} 1 & 0 & 0 \\ 0 & 1 & 0 \\ 0 & 0 & 1 \end{bmatrix}$	**matriz de identidad multiplicativa** (9) Una matriz cuadrada que contiene 1 en cada entrada de la diagonal principal y 0 en las demás entradas.
multiplicative inverse of a square matrix (32) The multiplicative inverse of square matrix A, if it exists, is notated A^{-1}, where the product of A and A^{-1} is the identity matrix.	The multiplicative inverse of $A = \begin{bmatrix} -2 & 5 \\ 1 & -3 \end{bmatrix}$ is $A^{-1} = \begin{bmatrix} -3 & -5 \\ -1 & -2 \end{bmatrix}$, because $AA^{-1} = A^{-1}A = \begin{bmatrix} 1 & 0 \\ 0 & 1 \end{bmatrix}$.	**inverso multiplicativo de una matriz cuadrada** (32) El inverso multiplicativo de una matriz cuadrada A, si existe, se escribe A^{-1}, donde el producto de A y A^{-1} es la matriz de identidad.
multiplicity (66) If a polynomial $P(x)$ has a multiple root at r, the multiplicity of r is the number of times $(x-r)$ appears as a factor in $P(x)$.	For $P(x) = (x-3)^2$, the root 3 has a multiplicity of 2.	**multiplicidad** (66) Si un polinomio $P(x)$ tiene una raíz múltiple en r, la multiplicidad de r es la cantidad de veces que $(x-r)$ aparece como factor en $P(x)$.

M

English	Example	Spanish
mutually exclusive events (33) Two events are mutually exclusive if they cannot both occur in the same trial of an experiment.	In the experiment of rolling a number cube, rolling a 3 and rolling an even number are mutually exclusive events.	**sucesos mutuamente excluyentes** (33) Dos sucesos son mutuamente excluyentes si ambos no pueden ocurrir en la misma prueba de un experimento.

N

English	Example	Spanish
natural logarithm (81) A logarithm with base e, written as ln.	$\ln 5 = \log_e 5 \approx 1.6$	**logaritmo natural** (81) Logaritmo con base e, que se escribe ln.
natural logarithmic function (110) The function $f(x) = \ln x$, which is the inverse of the natural exponential function $f(x) = e^x$. Domain is $\{x \mid x > 0\}$; range is all real numbers.		**función logarítmica natural** (110) Función $f(x) = \ln x$, que es la inversa de la función exponencial natural $f(x) = e^x$. El dominio es $\{x \mid x > 0\}$; el rango es todos los números reales.
negative exponent (3) A base raised to a negative exponent is equal to the reciprocal of that base raised to the opposite exponent: $b^{-n} = \frac{1}{b^n}$.	$5^{-3} = \frac{1}{5^3} = \frac{1}{125}$	**exponente negativo** (3) Una base elevada a un exponente negativo es igual al recíproco de dicha base elevado al exponente opuesto: $b^{-n} = \frac{1}{b^n}$.
net (maintained) A diagram of the faces of a three-dimensional figure arranged in such a way that the diagram can be folded to form the three-dimensional figure.	10 m; 6 m; 10 m; 6 m	**plantilla** (repaso) Diagrama de las caras y superficies de una figura tridimensional que se puede plegar para formar la figura tridimensional.
nonlinear system of equations (117) A system in which at least one of the equations is not linear.	$y = 2x^2$ $y = -3x^2 + 5$	**sistema no lineal de ecuaciones** (117) Sistema en el cual por lo menos una de las ecuaciones no es lineal.

GLOSSARY/ GLOSARIO

English	Example	Spanish
N		
no slope (maintained) The slope of a vertical line; the run equals 0.	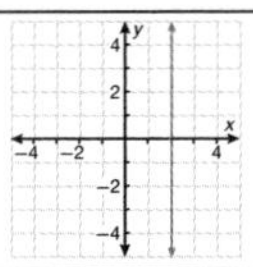	**sin pendiente** (repaso) La pendiente de una línea vertical; la distancia horizontal es igual a 0.
normal distribution (80) A distribution of data that is bell-shaped and symmetric about the mean.	mean: 20, standard deviation: 3 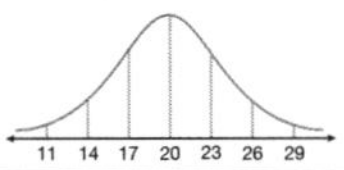 11 14 17 20 23 26 29	**distribución normal** (80) Una distribución de datos que tiene la forma de una campana y que es simétrica con respecto a la media.
nth root (59) The *n*th root of a number *a*, written as $\sqrt[n]{a}$ or $a^{\frac{1}{n}}$, is a number that is equal to *a* when it is raised to the *n*th power.	$\sqrt[5]{32} = 2$, because $2^5 = 32$.	**enésima raíz** (59) La enésima raíz de un número *a*, que se escribe como $\sqrt[n]{a}$ o $a^{\frac{1}{n}}$, es un número igual a *a* cuando se eleva a la enésima potencia.
O		
objective function (54) The function to be maximized or minimized in a linear programming problem.	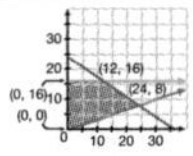 The objective function $P = 18x + 25y$ is maximized at (24, 8).	**función objetiva** (54) Función que se debe maximizar o minimizar en un problema de programación lineal.
obtuse angle (maintained) An angle that measures greater than 90° and less than 180°.		**ángulo obtuso** (repaso) Ángulo que mide más de 90° y menos de 180°.
opposite (SB 7) The opposite of a number *a*, denoted $-a$, is the number that is the same distance from zero as *a*, on the opposite side of the number line. The sum of opposites is 0.	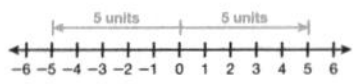 5 units 5 units 5 and −5 are opposites.	**opuesto** (SB 7) El opuesto de un número *a*, expresado $-a$, es el número que se encuentra a la misma distancia de cero que *a*, del lado opuesto de la recta numérica. La suma de los opuestos es 0.

English	Example	Spanish
O		
order of operations (maintained) A process for evaluating expressions: First, perform operations in parentheses or other grouping symbols. Second, evaluate powers and roots. Third, perform all multiplication and division from left to right. Fourth, perform all addition and subtraction from left to right.	$2 + 3^2 - (7 + 5) \div 4 \cdot 3$ $2 + 3^2 - 12 \div 4 \cdot 3$ Add inside parentheses. $2 + 9 - 12 \div 4 \cdot 3$ Evaluate the power. $2 + 9 - 3 \cdot 3$ Divide. $2 + 9 - 9$ Multiply. $11 - 9$ Add. 2 Subtract.	**orden de las operaciones** (repaso) Proceso para evaluar las expresiones: Primero, realizar las operaciones entre paréntesis u otros símbolos de agrupación. Segundo, evaluar las potencias y las raíces. Tercero, realizar todas las multiplicaciones y divisiones de izquierda a derecha. Cuarto, realizar todas las sumas y restas de izquierda a derecha.
ordered triple (29) A set of three numbers that can be used to locate a point (*x*, *y*, *z*) in a three-dimensional coordinate system.	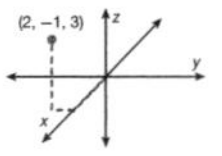 (2, −1, 3)	**tripleta ordenada** (29) Conjunto de tres números que se pueden utilizar para ubicar un punto (*x*, *y*, *z*) en un sistema de coordenadas tridimensional.
origin (SB 10) The intersection of the *x*- and *y*-axes in a coordinate plane. The coordinates of the origin are (0, 0).	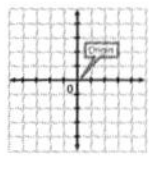	**origen** (SB 10) Intersección de los ejes *x* e *y* en un plano coordenado. Las coordenadas del origen son (0, 0).
outcome (33) A possible result of a probability experiment.	In the experiment of rolling a number cube, the possible outcomes are 1, 2, 3, 4, 5, and 6.	**resultado** (33) Resultado posible en un experimento de probabilidades.
outlier (25) A data value that is far removed from the rest of the data. A value less than $Q_1 - 1.5(\text{IQR})$ or greater than $Q_3 + 1.5(\text{IQR})$ is considered to be an outlier.	 Most of data Mean Outlier	**valor extremo** (25) Valor de datos que está muy alejado del resto de los datos. Un valor menor que $Q_1 - 1.5(\text{IQR})$ o mayor que $Q_3 + 1.5(\text{IQR})$ se considera un valor extremo.

GLOSSARY/ GLOSARIO

English	Example	Spanish
O		
overlapping events (60) Events that have at least one outcome in common.	When rolling a number cube, rolling an even number and rolling a 2 are overlapping events.	**sucesos coincidentes** (60) Sucesos que tienen por lo menos un resultado posible en común.
P		
parabola (27) The shape of the graph of a quadratic function. All parabolas have a symmetric *u*-shape.	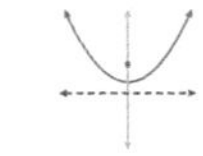	**parábola** (27) Forma de la gráfica de una función cuadrática. Todas las parábolas tienen una forma de *u* simétrica.
parameter (Inv 2) One of the constants in a function or equation that may be changed. Also the third variable in a set of parametric equations.	$y = (x - h)^2 + k$ parameters	**parámetro** (Inv 2) Una de las constantes en una función o ecuación que se puede cambiar. También es la tercera variable en un conjunto de ecuaciones paramétricas.
parametric equations (Inv 2) A pair of equations that define the *x*- and *y*-coordinates of a point in terms of a third variable called a parameter.	$x(t) = t + 1$ $y(t) = -2t$	**ecuaciones paramétricas** (Inv 2) Par de ecuaciones que definen las coordenadas *x* e *y* de un punto en función de una tercera variable denominada parámetro.
parent function (17) The simplest function with the defining characteristics of the family. Functions in the same family are transformations of their parent function.	$f(x) = x^2$ is the parent function for $g(x) = x^2 + 4$ and $h(x) = 5(x + 2)^2 - 3$.	**función madre** (17) La función más básica con las características de la familia. Las funciones de la misma familia son transformaciones de su función madre.
partial sum (105) Indicated by $S_n = \sum_{i=1}^{n} a_i$, the sum of a specified number of terms *n* of a sequence whose total number of terms is greater than *n*.	For the sequence $a_n = n^2$, the fourth partial sum of the infinite series $\sum_{k=1}^{\infty} k^2$ is $\sum_{k=1}^{4} k^2 = 1^2 + 2^2 + 3^2 + 4^2 = 30$.	**suma parcial** (105) Expresada por $S_n = \sum_{i=1}^{n} a_i$, la suma de un número específico *n* de términos de una sucesión cuyo número total de términos es mayor que *n*.

English	Example	Spanish
P		
Pascal's triangle (42) A triangular arrangement of numbers in which every row starts and ends with 1 and each other number is the sum of the two numbers above it.	1 1 1 1 2 1 1 3 3 1 1 4 6 4 1	**triángulo de Pascal** (42) Arreglo triangular de números en el cual cada fila comienza y termina con 1 y cada uno de los demás números es la suma de los dos números que están encima de él.
percent of change (6) An increase or decrease given as a percent of the original amount. Percent increase describes an amount that has grown. Percent decrease describes an amount that has been reduced.		**porcentaje de cambio** (6) Incremento o disminución dada como un porcentaje de la cantidad original. El porcentaje de incremento describe una cantidad que ha aumentado. El porcentaje de disminución describe una cantidad que se ha reducido.
perfect square (maintained) A number whose positive square root is a whole number.	36 is a perfect square because $\sqrt{36} = 6$.	**cuadrado perfecto** (repaso) Número cuya raíz cuadrada positiva es un número cabal.
perfect-square trinomial (23) A trinomial whose factored form is the square of a binomial. A perfect-square trinomial has the form $a^2 - 2ab + b^2 = (a - b)^2$ or $a^2 + 2ab + b^2 = (a + b)^2$.	$x^2 + 6x + 9$ is a perfect-square trinomial, because $x^2 + 6x + 9 = (x + 3)^2$.	**trinomio cuadrado perfecto** (23) Trinomio cuya forma factorizada es el cuadrado de un binomio. Un trinomio cuadrado perfecto tiene la forma $a^2 - 2ab + b^2 = (a - b)^2$ ó $a^2 + 2ab + b^2 = (a + b)^2$.
period of a periodic function (82) The length of a cycle measured in units of the independent variable (usually time in seconds).	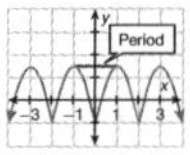 Period	**periodo de una función periódica** (82) Longitud de un ciclo medido en unidades de la variable independiente (generalmente el tiempo en segundos).
periodic function (82) A function that repeats exactly in regular intervals, called *periods*.	sin(*x*), cos(*x*), and tan(*x*) are all periodic functions.	**función periódica** (82) Función que se repite exactamente a intervalos regulares denominados *períodos*.

GLOSSARY/ GLOSARIO

GLOSSARY/ GLOSARIO

P

English	Example	Spanish
permutation (42) An arrangement of a group of objects in which order is important. The number of permutations of r objects from a group of n objects is denoted $_nP_r$.	For 4 objects A, B, C, and D, there are $_4P_2 = 12$ different permutations of 2 objects: AB, AC, AD, BC, BD, CD, BA, CA, DA, CB, DB, and DC.	**permutación** (42) Arreglo de un grupo de objetos en el cual el orden es importante. El número de permutaciones de r objetos de un grupo de n objetos se expresa $_nP_r$.
phase shift (86) A horizontal translation of a periodic function.	g is a phase shift of $f \frac{\pi}{2}$ units left.	**cambio de fase** (86) Traslación horizontal de una función periódica.
piecewise function (79) A function that is a combination of one or more functions.	$f(x) = \begin{cases} -4 & \text{if } x \le 0 \\ x+1 & \text{if } x > 0 \end{cases}$	**función a trozos** (79) Función que es una combinación de una o más funciones.
point of discontinuity (22) A point on a graph that is not connected; appears as a hole in the graph.		**punto de discontinuidad** (22) Un punto en una gráfica que no está conectado; aparece como un agujero en la gráfica.
point-slope form (26) The point-slope form of a linear equation is $y - y_1 = m(x - x_1)$, where m is the slope and (x_1, y_1) is a point on the line.	The equation of the line through $(2, 1)$ with slope 3 is $y - 1 = 3(x - 2)$.	**forma de punto y pendiente** (26) La forma de punto y pendiente de una ecuación lineal es $y - y_1 = m(x - x_1)$, donde m es la pendiente y (x_1, y_1) es un punto en la línea.

P

English	Example	Spanish
polar coordinate (96) An ordered pair (r, θ) where r is the directed distance from O to P and θ is the directed angle measure counterclockwise from the polar axis to $\overline{OP}$.		**coordenada polar** (96) Un par ordenado (r, θ) donde r es la distancia dirigida desdo O hasta P y θ es la medida del ángulo dirigido en el sentido contrario al de las manecillas de reloj, desde el eje polar hasta $\overline{OP}$.
polar equation (96) An equation involving r and θ, where r determines the radius from the origin and [theta] indicates the angle formed with the positive x-axis.	$r(\theta) = 6 \sin \theta$	**ecuación polar** (96) Una ecuación que involucra r y θ, donde r determina el radio desde el origen y [theta] indica el ángulo formado con el eje x positivo.
polynomial (11) A monomial or a sum or difference of monomials.	$2x^2 + 3x - 7$	**polinomio** (11) Monomio o suma o diferencia de monomios.
polynomial factor (76) A factor of a polynomial that is a polynomial.	$x - 2$ and $x + 5$ are binomial factors of $x^2 + 3x - 10$ because $x^2 + 3x - 10 = (x - 2)(x + 5)$.	**factor polinomial** (76) Un factor de un polinomio que es un polinomio.
polynomial function (11) A function whose rule is a polynomial.	$f(x) = x^3 - 8x^2 + 19x - 12$	**función polinomial** (11) Función cuya regla es un polinomio.
polynomial roots (76) The solutions of a polynomial equation; the zeros of the related polynomial function.	$x^3 - 13x - 12 = 0$ $(x + 1)(x + 3)(x - 4) = 0$ $x = -1$ or $x = -3$ or $x = 4$ The roots of $x^3 - 13x - 12 = 0$ are -1, -3, and 4.	**raíces polinomiales** (76) Las soluciones de una ecuación polinomial; los ceros de la función polinomial relacionada.
population (73) A group of individuals about which information is desired.	A mayor wanting to know how many people will vote for him will survey citizens registered to vote in his city; the population is every citizen in his city that is registered to vote.	**población** (73) Un grupo de individuos de los cuales se desea información.

GLOSSARY/ GLOSARIO

P

English	Example	Spanish
power (SB 3) An expression written with a base and an exponent or the value of such an expression.	$2^3 = 8$, so 8 is the third power of 2.	**potencia** (SB 3) Expresión escrita con una base y un exponente o el valor de dicha expresión.
precision (18) The number of significant digits in a measurement.	A measurement of 4.3 cm is more precise than a measure of 4 cm.	**precisión** (18) El número de dígitos significativos en una medición.
prime polynomial (23) A polynomial that cannot be factored	$x + 5$ $x^2 - x + 14$	**polinomio primo** (23) Un polinomio que no puede ser factorizado.
principal root (40) The positive root of a number, indicated by the radical sign.	$\sqrt{36} = 6$	**raíz principal** (40) Raíz cuadrada positiva de un número, expresada por el signo de radical.
probability (55) A number from 0 to 1 (or 0% to 100%) that is the measure of how likely an event is to occur.	A bag contains 3 red marbles and 4 blue marbles. The probability of choosing a red marble is $\frac{3}{7}$.	**probabilidad** (55) Número entre 0 y 1 (o entre 0% y 100%) que describe cuán probable es que ocurra un suceso.
probability distribution for an experiment (maintained) The function that pairs each outcome with its probability.	A number cube is rolled 10 times. The results are shown in the table. Outcome: 1, 2, 3, 4, 5, 6 Probability: $\frac{1}{10}$, $\frac{1}{5}$, $\frac{1}{5}$, 0, $\frac{3}{10}$, $\frac{1}{5}$	**distribución de probabilidad para un experimento** (repaso) Función que asigna a cada resultado su probabilidad.
probability experiment (55) An occurrence whose outcome is uncertain.	**Probability Experiments** spinning a spinner, flipping a coin, choosing a name from a hat without looking	**experimento de probabilidad** (55) Un suceso cuyo resultado no está definido.
probability sampling (73) Sampling in which every individual in the population has a known probability of being selected and this probability is greater than 0.	Choosing names from a hat: knowing the number of names in the hat results in knowing the probability of each name being selected.	**muestreo de probabilidad** (73) Muestreo en el cual cada individuo en la población tiene una probabilidad conocida de ser seleccionado y esta probabilidad es mayor que 0.

P

English	Example	Spanish
proportion (SB 8) A statement that two ratios are equal; $\frac{a}{b} = \frac{c}{d}$.	$\frac{2}{3} = \frac{4}{6}$	**proporción** (SB 8) Enunciado que establece que dos razones son iguales; $\frac{a}{b} = \frac{c}{d}$.

Q

English	Example	Spanish
quadratic equation (27) An equation that can be written in the form $ax^2 + bx + c = 0$, where a, b, and c are real numbers and $a \neq 0$.	$x^2 + 3x - 4 = 0$ $x^2 - 9 = 0$	**ecuación cuadrática** (27) Ecuación que se puede expresar como $ax^2 + bx + c = 0$, donde a, b y c son números reales y $a \neq 0$.
quadratic formula (Inv 6) The formula $x = \frac{-b \pm \sqrt{b^2 - 4ac}}{2a}$, which gives solutions, or roots, of equations in the form $ax^2 + bx + c = 0$, where $a \neq 0$.	The solutions of $2x^2 - 5x - 3 = 0$ are given by $x = \frac{-(-5) \pm \sqrt{(-5)^2 - 4(2)(-3)}}{2(2)}$ $= \frac{5 \pm \sqrt{25 + 24}}{4} = \frac{5 \pm 7}{4}$; $x = 3$ or $x = -\frac{1}{2}$.	**fórmula cuadrática** (Inv 6) La fórmula $x = \frac{-b \pm \sqrt{b^2 - 4ac}}{2a}$, que da soluciones, o raíces, para las ecuaciones del tipo $ax^2 + bx + c = 0$, donde $a \neq 0$.
quadratic function (27) A function that can be written in the form $f(x) = ax^2 + bx + c$, where a, b, and c are real numbers and $a \neq 0$, or in the form $f(x) = a(x - h)^2 + k$, where a, h, and k are real numbers and $a \neq 0$.	$f(x) = x^2 - 6x + 8$	**función cuadrática** (27) Función que se puede expresar como $f(x) = ax^2 + bx + c$, donde a, b y c son números reales y $a \neq 0$, o como $f(x) = a(x - h)^2 + k$, donde a, h y k son números reales y $a \neq 0$.
quadratic inequality in one variable (89) An inequality that can be written in the form $ax^2 + bx = c < d$, where a, b, c, and d are real numbers and $a \neq 0$. The symbol $<$ can be replaced with $>$, $\le$, or $\ge$.	$x^2 + 8x + 24 > 10$	**desigualdad cuadrática de una variable** (89) Una desigualdad que puede ser escrita en la forma $ax^2 + bx + c < d$, donde a, b, c, y d son números reales y $a \neq 0$. El símbolo $<$ puede ser reemplazdo por $>$, $\le$, o $\ge$

GLOSSARY/ GLOSARIO

English	Example	Spanish
Q		
quadratic inequality in two variables *(89)* An inequality that can be written in one of the following forms: $y < ax^2 + bx + c$, $y > ax^2 + bx + c$, $y \leq ax^2 + bx + c$, $y \geq ax^2 + bx + c$, or $y \neq ax^2 + bx + c$, where a, b, and c are real numbers and $a \neq 0$.	$y > -x^2 - 2x + 3$	**desigualdad cuadrática en dos variables** *(89)* Desigualdad que puede expresarse de una de las siguientes formas: $y < ax^2 + bx + c$, $y > ax^2 + bx + c$, $y \leq ax^2 + bx + c$, $y \geq ax^2 + bx + c$, o $y \neq ax^2 + bx + c$, donde a, b y c son números reales y $a \neq 0$.
quadratic model *(116)* A quadratic function used to represent a set of data.	x: 4, 6, 8, 10; $f(x)$: 27, 52, 89, 130 A quadratic model for the data is $f(x) = x^2 + 3.3x - 2.6$.	**modelo cuadrático** *(116)* Función cuadrática que se utiliza para representar un conjunto de datos.
quadratic regression *(116)* A statistical method used to fit a quadratic model to a given data set.	QuadReg y=ax²+bx+c a=.3972484911 b=-3.120086049 c=11.93757771 R²=.9964146101	**regresión cuadrática** *(116)* Método estadístico utilizado para ajustar un modelo cuadrático a un conjunto de datos determinado.
quartic function *(11)* A polynomial function of degree 4.	$f(x) = x^4 + 2x^3 - x^2 - 1$	**función de cuarto grado** *(11)* Una función polinomial de cuarta potencia.
R		
radian *(63)* A unit of angle measure based on arc length. In a circle of radius r, if a central angle has a measure of 1 radian, then the length of the intercepted arc is r units.	$\theta \approx 1$ radian 2π radians $= 360°$ 1 radian $\approx 57°$	**radián** *(63)* Unidad de medida de un ángulo basada en la longitud del arco. En un círculo de radio r, si un ángulo central mide 1 radián, entonces la longitud del arco abarcado es r unidades. 2π radianes $= 360°$ 1 radián $\approx 57°$

English	Example	Spanish
R		
radical *(40)* An indicated root of a quantity.	$\sqrt{36} = 6$, $\sqrt[3]{27} = 3$	**radical** *(40)* Raíz indicada de una cantidad.
radical equation *(70)* An equation that contains a variable within a radical.	$\sqrt{x + 3} + 4 = 7$	**ecuación radical** *(70)* Ecuación que contiene una variable dentro de un radical.
radical function *(75)* A function whose rule contains a variable within a radical.	(0, 0), (1, 1), (4, 2), (9, 3) $f(x) = \sqrt{x}$	**función radical** *(75)* Función cuya regla contiene una variable dentro de un radical.
radical symbol *(40)* The symbol $\sqrt{\ }$ used to denote a root. The symbol is used alone to indicate a square root or with an index, $\sqrt[n]{\ }$, to indicate the nth root.	$\sqrt{36} = 6$, $\sqrt[3]{27} = 3$	**símbolo de radical** *(40)* Símbolo $\sqrt{\ }$ que se utiliza para expresar una raíz. Puede utilizarse solo para indicar una raíz cuadrada, o con un índice, $\sqrt[n]{\ }$, para indicar la enésima raíz.
radicand *(40)* The expression under a radical sign.	$\sqrt{x + 3} - 2$ Radicand	**radicando** *(40)* Número o expresión debajo del signo de radical.
random *(55)* Occurring by chance.	A random number is a number chosen without using any system or pattern.	**aleatorio** *(55)* Algo que ocurre al azar.
random event *(55)* An event that occurs by chance.	Getting heads on the flip of a coin and rolling an even number on a number cube are random events.	**suceso aleatorio** *(55)* Un suceso que ocurre al azar.
random sample *(73)* A sample selected from a population so that each member of the population has an equal chance of being selected.	Mr. Hansen chose a random sample of the class by writing each student's name on a slip of paper, mixing up the slips, and drawing five slips without looking.	**muestra aleatoria** *(73)* Muestra seleccionada de una población tal que cada miembro de ésta tenga igual probabilidad de ser seleccionado.
range of a data set *(25)* The difference of the greatest and least values in the data set.	The data set {3, 3, 5, 7, 8, 10, 11, 11, 12} has a range of $12 - 3 = 9$.	**rango de un conjunto de datos** *(25)* La diferencia del mayor y menor valores en un conjunto de datos.

English	Example	Spanish
R		
range of a function or relation *(4)* The set of output values of a function or relation.	The range of $y = x^2$ is $\{y \mid y \geq 0\}$.	**rango de una función o relación** *(4)* Conjunto de los valores de salida de una función o relación.
rate *(maintained)* A ratio that compares two quantities measured in different units.	$\frac{55 \text{ miles}}{1 \text{ hour}} = 55$ mi/h	**tasa** *(repaso)* Razón que compara dos cantidades medidas en diferentes unidades.
ratio *(SB 8)* A comparison of two quantities by division.	$\frac{1}{2}$ or 1:2	**razón** *(SB 8)* Comparación de dos números mediante una división.
rational equation *(84)* An equation that contains one or more rational expressions.	$\frac{x + 2}{x^2 + 3x - 1} = 6$	**ecuación racional** *(84)* Ecuación que contiene una o más expresiones racionales.
rational exponent *(59)* An exponent that can be expressed as $\frac{m}{n}$ such that if m and n are integers, then $b^{\frac{m}{n}} = \sqrt[n]{b^m} = \left(\sqrt[n]{b}\right)^m$.	$4^{\frac{3}{2}} = \sqrt{4^3} = \sqrt{64} = 8$ $4^{\frac{3}{2}} = \left(\sqrt{4}\right)^3 = 2^3 = 8$	**exponente racional** *(59)* Exponente que se puede expresar como $\frac{m}{n}$ tal que, si m y n son números enteros, entonces $b^{\frac{m}{n}} = \sqrt[n]{b^m} = \left(\sqrt[n]{b}\right)^m$.
rational expression *(28)* An algebraic expression whose numerator and denominator are polynomials and whose denominator has a degree ≥ 1.	$\frac{x + 2}{x^2 + 3x - 1}$	**expresión racional** *(28)* Expresión algebraica cuyo numerador y denominador son polinomios y cuyo denominador tiene un grado ≥ 1.
rational function *(84)* A function whose rule can be written as a rational expression.	$f(x) = \frac{x + 2}{x^2 + 3x - 1}$	**función racional** *(84)* Función cuya regla se puede expresar como una expresión racional.
rational inequality *(94)* An inequality that contains one or more rational expressions.	$\frac{x + 2}{x^2 + 3x - 1} \geq 6$	**desigualdad racional** *(94)* Desigualdad que contiene una o más expresiones racionales.

English	Example	Spanish
R		
rationalizing the denominator *(40)* A method of rewriting a fraction by multiplying by another fraction that is equivalent to 1 in order to remove radical terms from the denominator.	$\frac{1}{\sqrt{2}}\left(\frac{\sqrt{2}}{\sqrt{2}}\right) = \frac{\sqrt{2}}{2}$	**racionalizar el denominador** *(40)* Método que consiste en escribir nuevamente una fracción multiplicándola por otra fracción equivalente a 1 a fin de eliminar los términos radicales del denominador.
rational number *(1)* A number that can be written in the form $\frac{a}{b}$, where a and b are integers and $b \neq 0$.	$3, 1.75, 0.\overline{3}, -\frac{2}{3}, 0$	**número racional** *(1)* Número que se puede expresar como $\frac{a}{b}$, donde a y b son números enteros y $b \neq 0$.
Rational Root Theorem *(85)* If a polynomial $P(x)$ has integer coefficients, then every rational root of $P(x) = 0$ can be written in the form $\frac{p}{q}$, where p is a factor of the constant term and q is a factor of the leading coefficient of $P(x)$.	For $3x^2 + 4x^2 - x + 6 = 0$, 6 is a possible rational root because $6 = \frac{6}{1}$ and 6 is a factor of 6 and 1 is a factor of 3.	**Teorema de la raíz racional** *(85)* Si un polonomio $P(x)$ tiene coeficientes enteros, entonces cada raíz racional de $P(x) = 0$ puede ser escrita en la forma $\frac{p}{q}$, donde p es un factor del término constante y q es un factor del primer coeficiente de $P(x)$.
real axis *(69)* The horizontal axis in the complex plane; it graphically represents the real part of complex numbers.	Imaginary axis Real axis	**eje real** *(69)* Eje horizontal de un plano complejo. Representa gráficamente la parte real de los números complejos.
real number *(1)* A rational or irrational number. Every point on the number line represents a real number.	$-5, 0, \frac{2}{3}, \sqrt{2}, 3.1, \pi$	**número real** *(1)* Número racional o irracional. Cada punto de la recta numérica representa un número real.
real part of a complex number *(62)* For a complex number of the form $a + bi$, a is the real part.	$5 + 6i$ Real part; Imaginary part	**parte real de un número complejo** *(62)* Dado un número complejo del tipo $a + bi$, a es la parte real.

English	Example	Spanish
R		
reciprocal (31) For a real number $a \neq 0$, the reciprocal of a is $\frac{1}{a}$. The product of reciprocals is 1.	$\frac{1}{2}$ is the reciprocal of 2. $\frac{5}{3}$ is the reciprocal of $\frac{3}{5}$.	**recíproco** (31) Dado el número real $a \neq 0$, el recíproco de a es $\frac{1}{a}$. El producto de los recíprocos es 1.
reference angle (56) For an angle in standard position, the reference angle is the positive acute angle formed by the terminal side of the angle and the x-axis.	45° is the reference angle of 135° in standard position.	**ángulo de referencia** (56) Dado un ángulo en posición estándar, el ángulo de referencia es el ángulo agudo positivo formado por el lado terminal del ángulo y el eje x.
reflection (27) A transformation that reflects, or "flips," a graph or figure across a line, called the line of reflection, such that each reflected point is the same distance from the line of reflection but is on the opposite side of the line.		**reflexión** (27) Transformación que refleja, o invierte, una gráfica o figura sobre una línea, llamada la línea de reflexión, de manera tal que cada punto reflejado esté a la misma distancia de la línea de reflexión pero que se encuentre en el lado opuesto de la línea.
regression (45) The statistical study of the relationship between variables.		**regresión** (45) Estudio estadístico de la relación entre variables.
relation (4) A set of ordered pairs.	$\{(0, 5), (0, 4), (2, 3), (4, 0)\}$	**relación** (4) Conjunto de pares ordenados.
Remainder Theorem (95) If the polynomial function $P(x)$ is divided by $x - a$, then the remainder r is $P(a)$.	$P(x) = x^4 - 5x^3 x - 2$ $P(x) \div (x - 3) = -P(3)$ 3⌋ 1 −5 −2 1 −2 3 −6 −24 −69 1 −2 −8 −23 [−71] → remainder $P(3) = -71$	**Teorema del residuo** (95) Si la función polinomial $P(x)$ es dividia entre $x - a$, entonces el residuo r es $P(a)$.
replacement set (maintained) A set of numbers that can be substituted for a variable.	The solution set of $y = x + 3$ for the replacement set $\{1, 2, 3\}$ is $\{4, 5, 6\}$.	**conjunto de reemplazo** (repaso) Conjunto de números que pueden sustituir una variable.

English	Example	Spanish
R		
right angle (maintained) An angle that measures 90°.		**ángulo recto** (repaso) Ángulo que mide 90°.
right triangle (41) A triangle with one right angle.		**triángulo rectángulo** (41) Triángulo con un ángulo recto.
root of an equation (35) Any value of the variable that makes the equation true.	The roots of $(x - 2)(x + 1) = 0$ are 2 and −1.	**raíz de una ecuación** (35) Cualquier valor de la variable que transforme la ecuación en verdadera.
rotation (56) A transformation that rotates or turns a figure about a point called the center of rotation.		**rotación** (56) Transformación que hace rotar o girar una figura sobre un punto llamado centro de rotación.
rotation matrix (112) A matrix used to rotate a figure about the origin.	Matrix $\begin{bmatrix} 0 & 1 \\ -1 & 0 \end{bmatrix}$ was used to rotate the figure 90° clockwise.	**matriz de rotación** (112) Matriz utilizada para rotar una figura sobre el origen.
S		
sample (73) Part of a population.	A student wants to know what the teachers at a school think about the new salary plan. He chooses eight teachers to talk to. These eight teachers make up a sample.	**muestra** (73) Parte de una población.
sample size (73) The number of individuals in a sample.	A student interviewed 10 of the athletes on the basketball team. The sample size is 10.	**tamaño de una muestra** (73) El número de individuos en una muestra.

English	Example	Spanish
S		
sample space (33) The set of all possible outcomes of a probability experiment.	In the experiment of rolling a number cube, the sample space is $\{1, 2, 3, 4, 5, 6\}$.	**espacio muestral** (33) Conjunto de todos los resultados posibles en un experimento de probabilidades.
sampling (73) The process of choosing a sample to represent a population.	To determine who to interview, a student obtained a class roster and chose every 15th name on the list.	**muestrear** (73) El proceso de escojer una muestra que representa a una población.
scalar (5) A number that is multiplied by a matrix.	$3\begin{bmatrix} 1 & -2 \\ 2 & 3 \end{bmatrix} = \begin{bmatrix} 3 & -6 \\ 6 & 9 \end{bmatrix}$ scalar	**escalar** (5) Número que se multiplica por una matriz.
scale factor (maintained) The multiplier used on each dimension to change one figure into a similar figure.		**factor de escala** (repaso) El multiplicador utilizado en cada dimensión para transformar una figura en una figura semejante.
scatter plot (maintained) A graph with points plotted to show a possible relationship between two sets of data.		**diagrama de dispersión** (repaso) Gráfica con puntos dispersos para demostrar una relación posible entre dos conjuntos de datos.
scientific notation (3) A method of writing very large or very small numbers, by using powers of 10, in the form $m \times 10^n$, where $1 \leq m < 10$ and n is an integer.	$1.256 \times 10^{13} = 12{,}560{,}000{,}000{,}000$ $7.5 \times 10^{-6} = 0.0000075$	**notación científica** (3) Método que consiste en escribir números muy grandes o muy pequeños utilizando potencias de 10 del tipo $m \times 10^n$, donde $1 \leq m < 10$ y n es un número entero.
secant of an angle (46) In a right triangle, the ratio of the length of the hypotenuse to the length of the side adjacent to angle A. It is the reciprocal of the cosine function.	$\sec A = \frac{\text{hypotenuse}}{\text{adjacent}} = \frac{1}{\cos A}$	**secante de un ángulo** (46) En un triángulo rectángulo, la razón entre la longitud de la hipotenusa y la longitud del cateto adyacente al ángulo A. Es la inversa de la función coseno.

English	Example	Spanish
S		
second differences (maintained) Differences between first differences of a function.	first differences +3 +5 +7 second differences +2 +2	**segundas diferencias** (repaso) Diferencias entre las primeras diferencias de una función.
sequence (92) A list of numbers that often form a pattern.	1, 2, 4, 8, 16, …	**sucesión** (92) Lista de números que generalmente forman un patrón.
series (105) The indicated sum of the terms of a sequence.	1 + 2 + 4 + 8 + 16 + …	**serie** (105) Suma indicada de los términos de una sucesión.
shift (30) A translation of a graph; the sliding of every point on the graph the same number of units in the same direction.		**desplazamiento** (30) Una traslación de una gráfica; el deslizamiento de cada punto en una gráfica en un número igual de unidades en la misma dirección.
Sierpinski triangle (maintained) A fractal formed from a triangle by removing triangles with vertices at the midpoints of the sides of each remaining triangle.		**triángulo de Sierpinski** (repaso) Fractal formado a partir de un triángulo al cual se le recortan triángulos cuyos vértices se encuentran en los puntos medios de los lados de cada triángulo restante.
sigma notation (105) A way of indicating the sum of a series; it uses the capital Greek letter, sigma.	$\sum_{k=1}^{5} 2k = 2(1) + 2(2) + 2(3) + 2(4) + 2(5) = 30$	**notación sigma** (105) Una manera de indicar la suma de una serie; utiliza la letra griega mayúscula sigma.
significant digits (18) Any digit that is measured or estimated; includes all nonzero digits, zeros between nonzero digits, and zeros to the right of both the decimal point and the last nonzero digit; zeros used for placeholders are not significant.	**605**: 3 significant digits 0.000**2380**: 4 significant digits **72**0: 2 significant digits	**dígitos significativos** (18) Cualquier dígito que es medido o estimado; incluye a todos los dígitos distintos de cero entre dígitos que no son cero y los ceros a la derecha del punto decimal y al último dígito que no es cero; los ceros que se usan para llenar lugares no son significativos.

English	Example	Spanish
S		
similar *(maintained)* Two figures are similar if they have the same shape but not necessarily the same size.		**semejantes** *(repaso)* Dos figuras son semejantes si tienen la misma forma pero no necesariamente el mismo tamaño.
simple random sample *(73)* A sample consisting of n individuals, where every individual has an equal chance of being chosen and every possible group of n individuals has an equal chance of being chosen.	A teacher assigns every student a unique number and chooses numbers from a random number table.	**muestra simple al azar** *(73)* Una muestra que consiste en n individuos, donde cada individuo tiene la misma posibilidad de ser escojido y cada grupo posible de n individuos tiene la misma oportunidad de ser escojido.
simplify *(maintained)* To perform all indicated operations.	$3(4) + 7$ $12 + 7$ 19	**simplificar** *(repaso)* Realizar todas las operaciones indicadas.
sine *(46)* In a right triangle, the ratio of the length of the side opposite $\angle A$ to the length of the hypotenuse.	opposite, hypotenuse, A $\sin A = \frac{\text{opposite}}{\text{hypotenuse}}$.	**seno** *(46)* En un triángulo rectángulo, razón entre la longitud del cateto opuesto a $\angle A$ y la longitud de la hipotenusa.
singular matrix *(32)* A matrix that does not have an inverse; its determinant is 0.	$A = \begin{bmatrix} 3 & 6 \\ 1 & 2 \end{bmatrix}$ is a singular matrix because $\det A = 3(2) - (1)(6) = 0$.	**matriz singular** *(32)* Una matriz que no tiene inversa; su determinante es cero.
slant asymptote *(107)* An asymptote that is neither horizontal nor vertical, can be called an oblique asymptote.		**asíntota inclinada** *(107)* Una asíntota que no es ni horizontal ni vertical; puede ser llamada una asíntota oblicua.

English	Example	Spanish
S		
slope *(13)* A measure of the steepness of a line. If (x_1, y_1) and (x_2, y_2) are any two points on the line, the slope of the line, known as m, is represented by the equation $m = \frac{y_2 - y_1}{x_2 - x_1}$.	(5, 6), rise, (1, 2), run $m = \frac{6-2}{5-1} = \frac{4}{4} = 1$	**pendiente** *(13)* Medida de la inclinación de una línea. Dados dos puntos (x_1, y_1) y (x_2, y_2) en una línea, la pendiente de la línea, denominada m, se representa por la ecuación $m = \frac{y_2 - y_1}{x_2 - x_1}$.
slope-intercept form *(13)* The slope-intercept form of a linear equation is $y = mx + b$, where m is the slope and b is the y-intercept.	$y = -2x + 4$ slope, y-intercept	**forma de pendiente-intersección** *(13)* La forma de pendiente-intersección de una ecuación lineal es $y = mx + b$, donde m es la pendiente y b es la intersección y.
solution of an equation *(7)* The value or set of values that makes an equation true.	The solution set of $x^2 = 9$ is $\{-3, 3\}$.	**solución de una ecuación** *(7)* Un valor o conjunto de valores que hacen verdadero un enunciado.
special right triangle *(52)* A 45°-45°-90° triangle or a 30°-60°-90° triangle.	60°, 2, 1, 30°, $\sqrt{3}$; 45°, $\sqrt{2}$, 1, 45°, 1	**triángulo rectángulo especial** *(52)* Triángulo de 45°-45°-90° ó triángulo de 30°-60°-90°.
square matrix *(9)* A matrix with the same number of rows as columns.	$\begin{bmatrix} 1 & 2 \\ 0 & -3 \end{bmatrix}, \begin{bmatrix} 1 & -3 & 1 \\ 2 & 0 & -2 \\ 0 & 1 & 3 \end{bmatrix}$	**matriz cuadrada** *(9)* Matriz con el mismo número de líneas y columnas.
square root *(40)* A number that is multiplied to itself to form a product is called a square root of that product.	-4 and 4 are square roots of 16 because $(-4)^2 = 16$ and $4^2 = 16$.	**raíz cuadrada** *(40)* El número que se multiplica por sí mismo para formar un producto se denomina la raíz cuadrada de ese producto.
square root function *(75)* A function whose rule contains a variable under a square root sign.	(0, 0), (1, 1), (4, 2), (9, 3) $f(x) = \sqrt{x}$	**función de raíz cuadrada** *(75)* Función cuya regla contiene una variable bajo un signo de raíz cuadrada.

English	Example	Spanish
S		
standard deviation *(25)* A measure of dispersion of a data set. The standard deviation σ is the square root of the variance.	Data set: $\{6, 7, 7, 9, 11\}$ Mean: $\frac{6+7+7+9+11}{5} = 8$ Variance: $\frac{1}{5}(4+1+1+1+9) = 3.2$ Standard deviation: $\sigma = \sqrt{3.2} \approx 1.8$	**desviación estándar** *(25)* Medida de dispersión de un conjunto de datos. La desviación estándar σ es la raíz cuadrada de la varianza.
standard form of a linear equation *(26)* $Ax + By = C$, where A, B, and C are real numbers.	$2x + 3y = 6$	**forma estándar de una ecuación lineal** *(26)* $Ax + By = C$, donde A, B y C son números reales.
standard form of a polynomial *(11)* A polynomial in one variable is written in standard form when the terms are in order from greatest degree to least degree.	$3x^3 - 5x^2 + 6x - 7$	**forma estándar de un polinomio** *(11)* Un polinomio de una variable se expresa en forma estándar cuando los términos se ordenan de mayor a menor grado.
standard form of a quadratic equation *(27)* $ax^2 + bx + c = 0$, where a, b, and c are real numbers and $a \neq 0$.	$2x^2 + 3x - 1 = 0$	**forma estándar de una ecuación cuadrática** *(27)* $ax^2 + bx + c = 0$, donde a, b y c son números reales y $a \neq 0$.
standard position *(56)* An angle in standard position has its vertex at the origin and its initial side on the positive x-axis.	236°	**posición estándar** *(56)* Ángulo cuyo vértice se encuentra en el origen y cuyo lado inicial se encuentra sobre el eje x.
statistics *(25)* The branch of mathematics that involves the collection, analysis, and comparison of sets of data.	A student was using statistics when she surveyed other students, made graphs of the data she collected, and calculated means and standard deviations of the data.	**estadística** *(25)* La rama de las matemáticas que involucra la recolección, análisis y comparación de conjuntos de datos.
step function *(79)* A piecewise function that is constant over each interval in its domain.		**función escalón** *(79)* Función a trozos que es constante en cada intervalo en su dominio.

English	Example	Spanish
S		
stratified sample *(73)* A sample chosen by dividing the population into mutually exclusive groups which have similar characteristics and performing a simple random sample on each subgroup.	Divide students into males and females and randomly choose students from each group.	**muestra estratificada** *(73)* Una muestra que se escoje dividiendo a la población en grupos mutuamente excluyentes, los cuales tienen características similares, y que se obtiene realizando un muestreo simple al azar de cada subgrupo.
stretch *(30)* A transformation that pulls the points of a graph horizontally away from the y-axis or vertically away from the x-axis.		**estiramiento** *(30)* Transformación que desplaza los puntos de una gráfica en forma horizontal alejándolos del eje y o en forma vertical alejándolos del eje x.
substitution method *(21)* A method used to solve systems of equations by solving an equation for one variable and substituting the resulting expression into the other equation(s).	$\begin{cases} 2x + 3y = -1 \\ x - 3y = 4 \end{cases}$ Solve for x. $x = 4 + 3y$ Substitute into the first equation and solve. $2(4 + 3y) + 3y = -1$ $y = -1$ Then solve for x. $x = 4 + 3(-1) = 1$	**méthodo de sustitución** *(21)* Método utilizado para resolver sistemas de ecuaciones resolviendo una ecuación para una variable y sustituyendo la expresión resultante en las demás ecuaciones.
summation notation *(105)* A method of notating the sum of a series using the Greek letter $\sum$ (capital *sigma*).	$\sum_{k=1}^{5} 3k = 3 + 6 + 9 + 12 + 15 = 45$	**notación de sumatoria** *(105)* Método de notación de la suma de una serie que utiliza la letra griega $\sum$ (*sigma* mayúscula).
synthetic division *(51)* A shorthand method of dividing by a linear binomial of the form $(x - a)$ by writing only the coefficients of the polynomials.	$(x^3 - 7x + 6) \div (x - 2)$ $\begin{array}{r\|rrrr} 2 & 1 & 0 & -7 & 6 \\ & & 2 & 4 & 6 \\ \hline & 1 & 2 & -3 & 0 \end{array}$ $(x^3 - 7x + 6) \div (x - 2)$ $= x^2 + 2x - 3$	**división sintética** *(51)* Método abreviado de división que consiste en dividir entre un binomio lineal del tipo $(x - a)$ escribiendo sólo los coeficientes de los polinomios.

GLOSSARY/ GLOSARIO

English	Example	Spanish
S		
synthetic substitution (51) The process of using synthetic division to evaluate a polynomial.	$P(x) = x^3 - 2x^2 + 4x + 3$ $5 \rfloor\ 1 \quad -2 \quad 4 \quad 3$ $5 \quad 15 \quad 95$ $1 \quad 3 \quad 19 \quad \boxed{98}$ $P(5) = 98$	**sustitución sintética** (51) El proceso de utilizar división sintética para evaluar un polinomio.
systematic sampling (73) A method of sampling where the individuals in the population are listed and every *n*th individual is chosen.	Call every 10th phone number from a list of phone numbers.	**muestreo sistemático** (73) Un método de muestreo donde se hace una lista de los individuos en la población y cada n_{avo} individuo es escojido.
system of equations (15) A set of two or more equations that have two or more variables.	$\begin{cases} 2x + 3y = -1 \\ x^2 = 4 \end{cases}$	**sistema de ecuaciones** (15) Conjunto de dos o más ecuaciones que contienen dos o más variables.
system of linear equations (15) *See* linear system.		**sistema de ecuaciones lineales** (15) *Ver* sistema lineal.
system of linear inequalities (43) A system of inequalities in two or more variables in which all of the inequalities are linear.	$\begin{cases} 2x + 3y \geq -1 \\ x - 3y < 4 \end{cases}$	**sistema de desigualdades lineales** (43) Sistema de desigualdades en dos o más variables en el que todas las desigualdades son lineales.
T		
tangent of an angle (46) In a right triangle, the ratio of the length of the leg opposite $\angle A$ to the length of the leg adjacent to $\angle A$.	opposite, adjacent, A $\tan A = \dfrac{\text{opposite}}{\text{adjacent}}$	**tangente de un ángulo** (46) En un triángulo rectángulo, razón entre la longitud del cateto opuesto a $\angle A$ y la longitud del cateto adyacente a $\angle A$.
term of an expression (2) The parts of the expression that are added or subtracted.	$3x^2 + 6x - 8$ Term Term Term	**término de una expresión** (2) Partes de la expresión que se suman o se restan.
term of a sequence (92) An element or number in the sequence.	5 is the third term in the sequence 1, 3, 5, 7, …	**término de una sucesión** (92) Elemento o número de una sucesión.

English	Example	Spanish
T		
terminal side (56) For an angle in standard position, the ray that is rotated relative to the positive *x*-axis.	Terminal side, 45°, 135°, Initial side, 0, x, y	**lado terminal** (56) Dado un ángulo en una posición estándar, el rayo que rota en relación con el eje positivo *x*.
theoretical probability (55) The ratio of the number of equally likely outcomes in an event to the total number of possible outcomes.	The theoretical probability of rolling an odd number on a number cube is $\frac{3}{6} = \frac{1}{2}$.	**probabilidad teórica** (55) Razón entre el número de resultados igualmente probables de un suceso y el número total de resultados posibles.
third quartile (25) The median of the upper half of a data set. Also called *upper quartile*.	Lower half Upper half (18, 23, 28,) (29, 36, 42) Third quartile	**tercer cuartil** (25) La mediana de la mitad superior de un conjunto de datos. También se llama *cuartil superior*.
three-dimensional coordinate system (Inv 3) A space that is divided into eight regions by an *x*-axis, a *y*-axis, and a *z*-axis. The locations, or coordinates, of points are given by ordered triples.	z, xy-plane, y, x, xz-plane, yz-plane	**sistema de coordenadas tridimensional** (Inv 3) Espacio dividido en ocho regiones por un eje *x*, un eje *y* y un eje *z*. Las ubicaciones, o coordenadas, de los puntos son dadas por tripletas ordenadas.
transformation (17) A change in the position, size, or shape of a figure or graph.		**transformación** (17) Cambio en la posición, tamaño o forma de una figura o gráfica.
transverse axis (109) The axis of symmetry of a hyperbola that contains the vertices and foci.	Focus: (−c, 0), Vertex: (−a, 0), y, Focus: (c, 0), Vertex: (a, 0), Transverse axis	**eje transversal** (109) Eje de simetría de una hipérbola que contiene los vértices y focos.
tree diagram (33) A branching diagram that shows all possible combinations or outcomes of an experiment.	A, BA, AB, CBA BCA BAC CAB ACB ABC	**diagrama de árbol** (33) Diagrama con ramificaciones que muestra todas las combinaciones o resultados posibles de un experimento.

GLOSSARY/ GLOSARIO

English	Example	Spanish
T		
trial (33) In probability, a single repetition or observation of an experiment.	In the experiment of rolling a number cube, each roll is one trial.	**prueba** (33) En repetición u observación de un experimento.
trigonometric function (46) A function whose rule is given by a trigonometric ratio.	$f(x) = \sin x$	**función trigonométrica** (46) Función cuya regla es dada por una razón trigonométrica.
trigonometric identity (108) A trigonometric equation that is true for all values of the variable for which the statement is defined.	$\tan\theta = \dfrac{\sin\theta}{\cos\theta}$	**identidad trigonométrica** (108) Una ecuación trigonométrica que es verdadera para todos los valores de la variable para la cual se define el enunciado.
trigonometric ratio (46) Ratio of the lengths of two sides of a right triangle.	A, B, C, a, b, c $\sin A = \frac{a}{c}$, $\cos A = \frac{b}{c}$, $\tan A = \frac{a}{b}$	**razón trigonométrica** (46) Razón entre dos lados de un triángulo rectángulo.
trigonometry (46) The study of the measurement of triangles and of trigonometric functions and their applications.		**trigonometría** (46) Estudio de la medición de los triángulos y de las funciones trigonométricas y sus aplicaciones.
trinomial (11) A polynomial with three terms.	$4x^2 + 3xy - 5y^2$	**trinomio** (11) Polinomio con tres términos.
turning point (101) A point on the graph of a function that corresponds to a local maximum (or minimum) where the graph changes from increasing to decreasing (or vice versa).	Turning point	**punto de inflexión** (101) Punto de la gráfica de una función que corresponde a un máximo (o mínimo) local donde la gráfica pasa de ser creciente a decreciente (o viceversa).

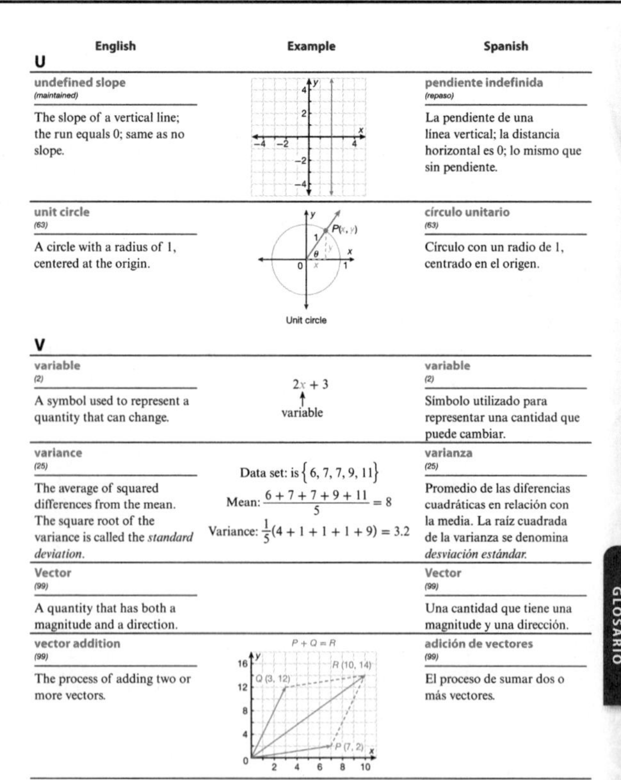

English	Example	Spanish
U		
undefined slope (maintained) The slope of a vertical line; the run equals 0; same as no slope.		**pendiente indefinida** (repaso) La pendiente de una línea vertical; la distancia horizontal es 0; lo mismo que sin pendiente.
unit circle (63) A circle with a radius of 1, centered at the origin.	P(x, y), θ, 1 Unit circle	**círculo unitario** (63) Círculo con un radio de 1, centrado en el origen.
V		
variable (2) A symbol used to represent a quantity that can change.	$2x + 3$ variable	**variable** (2) Símbolo utilizado para representar una cantidad que puede cambiar.
variance (25) The average of squared differences from the mean. The square root of the variance is called the *standard deviation*.	Data set: is $\{6, 7, 7, 9, 11\}$ Mean: $\frac{6+7+7+9+11}{5} = 8$ Variance: $\frac{1}{5}(4+1+1+1+9) = 3.2$	**varianza** (25) Promedio de las diferencias cuadráticas en relación con la media. La raíz cuadrada de la varianza se denomina *desviación estándar*.
Vector (99) A quantity that has both a magnitude and a direction.		**Vector** (99) Una cantidad que tiene una magnitud y una dirección.
vector addition (99) The process of adding two or more vectors.	P + Q = R, R (10, 14), Q (3, 12), P (7, 2)	**adición de vectores** (99) El proceso de sumar dos o más vectores.

GLOSSARY/ GLOSARIO

V

English	Example	Spanish
vector subtraction (99) The process of subtracting one vector from another vector; equivalent to adding the opposite of a vector.	$P - Q = P + (-Q) = R$	**resta de vectores** (99) El proceso de restar un vector de otro vector; equivalente a sumar el opuesto de un vector.
Venn diagram (SB 24) A diagram used to show relationships between sets.	Even and Prime Numbers	**diagrama de Venn** (SB 24) Diagrama utilizado para mostrar la relación entre conjuntos.
vertex form of a quadratic function (30) A quadratic function written in the form $f(x) = a(x - h)^2 + k$, where a, h, and k are constants and (h, k) is the vertex.	$f(x) = (x - 2)^2 + 2$	**forma en vértice de una función cuadrática** (30) Una función cuadrática expresada en la forma $f(x) = a(x - h)^2 + k$, donde a, h y k son constantes y (h, k) es el vértice.
vertex of a hyperbola (vertices) (109) The endpoints of the transverse axis of the hyperbola.		**vértice de una hipérbola (vértices)** (109) Extremos del eje transversal de la hipérbola.
vertex of an absolute-value graph (17) The point on the axis of symmetry of the graph.		**vértice de una gráfica de valor absoluto** (17) Punto en el eje de simetría de la gráfica.
vertex of an ellipse (vertices) (98) The endpoints of the major axis of the ellipse.		**vértice de una elipse (vértices)** (98) Extremos del eje mayor de la elipse.
vertex of a parabola (27) The highest or lowest point on the parabola.		**vértice de una parábola** (27) Punto más alto o más bajo de una parábola.

V

English	Example	Spanish
vertical line (maintained) A line whose equation is $x = a$, where a is the x-intercept. The slope of a vertical line is undefined.		**línea vertical** (repaso) Línea cuya ecuación es $x = a$, donde a es la intersección con el eje x. La pendiente de una línea vertical es indefinida.
vertical-line test (4) A test used to determine whether a relation is a function. If any vertical line crosses the graph of a relation more than once, the relation is not a function.	Function; Not a function	**prueba de la línea vertical** (4) Prueba utilizada para determinar si una relación es una función. Si una línea vertical corta la gráfica de una relación más de una vez, la relación no es una función.
voluntary response sampling (73) A sampling method in which the individuals in the sample choose themselves.	A news broadcast asks viewers to call in and answer *yes* or *no* to a poll question.	**muestreo de respuesta voluntaria** (73) Un método de muestreo en el cual los individuos en la muestra se escojen ellos mismos.

W

English	Example	Spanish
whole number (1) The set of natural numbers and zero.	$0, 1, 2, 3, 4, 5, \ldots$	**número cabal** (1) Conjunto de los números naturales y cero.

X

English	Example	Spanish
x-intercept (13) The x-coordinate(s) of the point(s) where a graph intersects the x-axis.		**intersección con el eje x** (13) Coordenada/s x de uno o más puntos donde una gráfica corta el eje x.

Y

English	Example	Spanish
y-intercept (13) The y-coordinate(s) of the point(s) where a graph intersects the y-axis.		**intersección con el eje y** (13) Coordenada/s y de uno o más puntos donde una gráfica corta el eje y.

Z

English	Example	Spanish
z score (80) The value of a data point on the standard normal distribution.	z score of 1.4: value is 1.4 standard deviations above the mean; z score of -2.3: value is 2.3 standard deviations below the mean	**puntaje z** (80) El valor de un punto de datos en la distribución normal estándar.

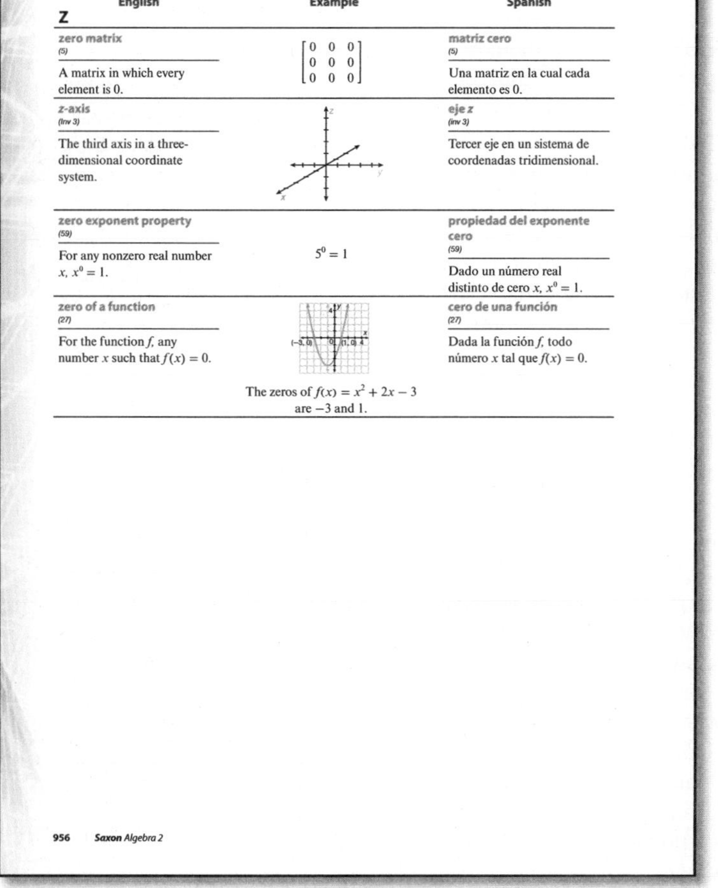

Z

English	Example	Spanish
zero matrix (5) A matrix in which every element is 0.	$\begin{bmatrix} 0 & 0 & 0 \\ 0 & 0 & 0 \\ 0 & 0 & 0 \end{bmatrix}$	**matriz cero** (5) Una matriz en la cual cada elemento es 0.
z-axis (Inv 3) The third axis in a three-dimensional coordinate system.		**eje z** (Inv 3) Tercer eje en un sistema de coordenadas tridimensional.
zero exponent property (59) For any nonzero real number x, $x^0 = 1$.	$5^0 = 1$	**propiedad del exponente cero** (59) Dado un número real distinto de cero x, $x^0 = 1$.
zero of a function (27) For the function f, any number x such that $f(x) = 0$.	The zeros of $f(x) = x^2 + 2x - 3$ are -3 and 1.	**cero de una función** (27) Dada la función f, todo número x tal que $f(x) = 0$.

Lesson 3

Practice

11. Let the circumference be C, the number of girls be g, and the average height be h. Then, $C = g \times h = 3 \times 10^7 \times 1.4 \times 10^{-3}$. The Commutative Property of Multiplication allows for these numbers to be multiplied in any order to give $C = 10^7 \times 10^{-3} \times 3 \times 1.4$. The exponents of 10 can be added mentally to give $C = 10^4 \times 3 \times 1.4$. Let $1.4 = 1 + 0.4$. Then, $3 \times 1.4 = 3(1 + 0.4) = 3 + 1.2 = 4.2$ by the Distributive Property and mental math. Therefore, $C = 10^4 \times 4.2 = 4.2 \times 10^4$ km by the Commutative Property of Multiplication.

12a. Think of \$18 as \$20 − \$2. Write an expression: $0.1(20 - 2)$. Use the distributive property: $0.1(20) - 0.1(2)$. Multiply: $2 - 0.2$. Subtract: 1.8. A 10% tip is \$1.80.

16. The first square has one side of length $5u - u = 4u$. So, the area of the first square $= (4u)(4u) = 16u^2$. The second square has one side of length $4u - 2u = 2u$. So, the area of the second square $= (2u)(2u) = 4u^2$. The combined area $= 16u^2 + 4u^2 = 20u^2$.

18. $3(-1) - 2(1) + (1)(-1)2 - 5(-1) + 4(1)(-1)2 + 6(1) = -3 - 2 + 1 + 5 + 4 + 6 =$
$11 - 2g + 4f + 5fg^2 =$
$-2(-1) + 4(1) + 5(1)(-1)^2 =$
$2 + 4 + 5 = 11$

20. Calculating a number to any exponent is the same as multiplying a number by itself the number of times indicated by the exponent. One multiplied by itself is always one, so one raised to the millionth power will still be one.

21. Student A should not have made the 2 negative when moving 2 to the −3 from the numerator to the denominator. Student B should not have added the exponents for $(2^2 + 2)$ in the denominator.

23. V = Surface Area • Depth $= 8.24 \times 10^{13} \cdot 3.93 \times 10^3 = 3.24 \times 10^{17}$ m^3. Two times the volume of the Atlantic Ocean is $2(3.24 \times 10^{17}) = 6.48 \times 10^{17}$ m^3. V = Surface Area • Depth $= 1.66 \times 10^{14}\ m^2 \times 3.93 \times 10^3\ m \approx 6.5 \times 10^{17}\ m^3$.

25. Length times width is an area of one side. Volume divided by this area gives the measurement of the other side, which is the height. First simplify the volume and area.
Volume: $\frac{x^3y^2x^{-2}}{y^{-3}x^2y} = \frac{y^4}{x}$
Area: $\frac{x^{-2}y^3x^{-1}}{y^{-4}x^{-2}y^2} = \frac{y^5}{x}$
height = volume ÷ area = volume × reciprocal of area $= \frac{y^4}{x} \cdot \frac{x}{y^5} = \frac{1}{y}$

29. Associative Property of Multiplication; 9 • 9 is generally memorized as equaling 81, but 27 • 3 is more difficult to multiply without a calculator.

Lesson 4

Practice

28. Sample; $(-36 + 36) + 17$ Associative Property of Addition

$0 + 17$	Additive Inverse
17	Identity Property of Addition

Lesson 5

Practice

16a. $2\pi R = 2\pi\begin{pmatrix} 3 & 3.5 \\ 4 & 4.5 \end{pmatrix}$

16b. No, to find the area of the circle every element of matrix R would have to be squared and there is no way to do that using an addition or scalar-multiplication matrix operation.

19. A graph represents the graph of a function if a single value of x results only in a single value of y. A vertical line is drawn at a single value of x. If the vertical line intercepts the graph more than once, it results in more than one y-value, and it is not a function. If the vertical line intercepts the graph only once, it results in a single y-value, and it is a function.

Lesson 9

Practice

21. Neither student is correct. Both sets are functions. The 9's that Britan references are an x-value and a y-value, not one value of x paired with two different values of y. The −1's that Sara references are one value of y paired with two different values of x, not one value of x paired with two different values of y.

24. $\begin{bmatrix} 2 & 3 & 4 \\ 1 & 6 & 6 \\ 3 & 3 & 3 \end{bmatrix}\begin{bmatrix} 2 \\ 3 \\ 0.5 \end{bmatrix} = \begin{bmatrix} 15 \\ 23 \\ 16.5 \end{bmatrix}$; Triangle 2 has the greatest perimeter.

Lesson 10

Practice

17a. You need 0.76 times the number of dollars you have to find the number of euros you have. So $e = 0.76d$. Then, $f = 1.22d$, so $e = \frac{0.76f}{1.22}$.

17b. $e = \frac{0.76(5)}{1.22} \approx 3$, which represents that on that day, 5 francs was equivalent to about 3 euros.

17c. From the given data, it took more francs than euros to equal a given amount. That is similar to the answer obtained in part b).

18b. The amount of change for each is the same, 10. This will be the numerator for both fractions; the first has a denominator of 50, the second a denominator of 60; With like numerators, the fraction with the lesser denominator is the greater fraction and greater percent.

Investigation 1

3. The cases where $p \rightarrow q$ is true yields this table. The fourth column shows the resulting values for $q \rightarrow p$. As a result, the converse of $p \rightarrow q$ is not always true.

p	q	$p \rightarrow q$	$q \rightarrow p$
T	T	T	T
F	T	T	F
F	F	T	T

4. The cases where $p \rightarrow q$ is true yields this table.

p	q	$p \rightarrow q$
T	T	T
F	T	T
F	F	T

Use it to generate this truth table. This shows that if $p \rightarrow q$, then $\neg q \rightarrow \neg p$ is also true.

$\neg q$	$\neg p$	$\neg q \rightarrow \neg p$
F	F	T
F	T	T
T	T	T

10b.

p	q	r	$(p \vee q) \rightarrow r$
T	T	T	T
T	T	F	F
T	F	T	T
T	F	F	F
F	T	T	T
F	F	T	T
F	T	F	F
F	F	F	T

Lesson 13

Practice

4.

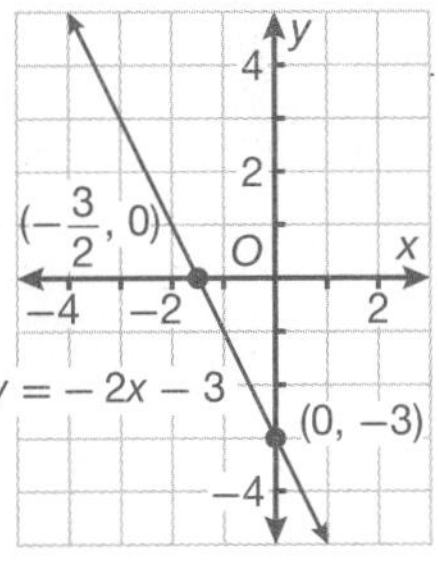

Lesson 15

Additional Example 1

a.

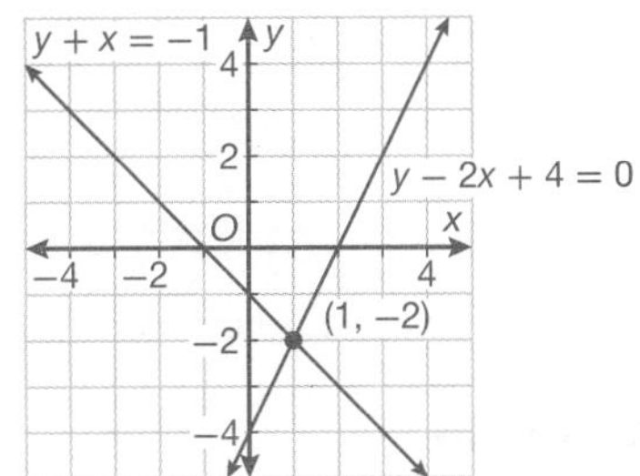

b.

$y - 2x + 4 = 0$	
x	y
–1	–6
0	–4
1	–2
2	0

$y + x = -1$	
x	y
–1	0
0	–1
1	–2
2	–3

Practice

10b.

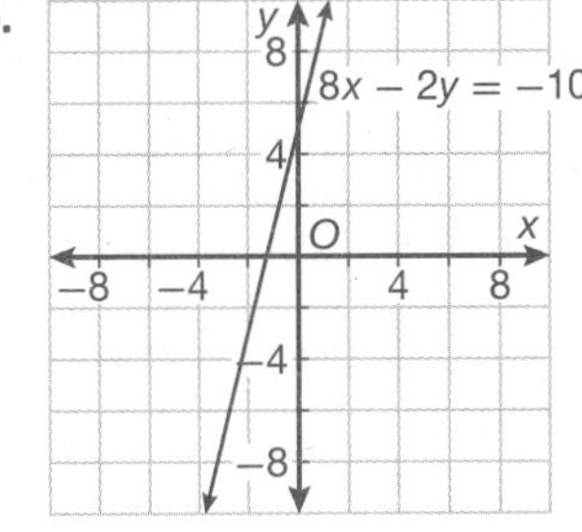

Lab 4

Practice

a.

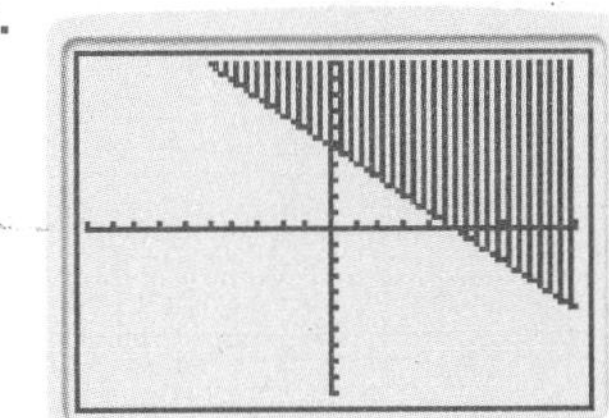

b.

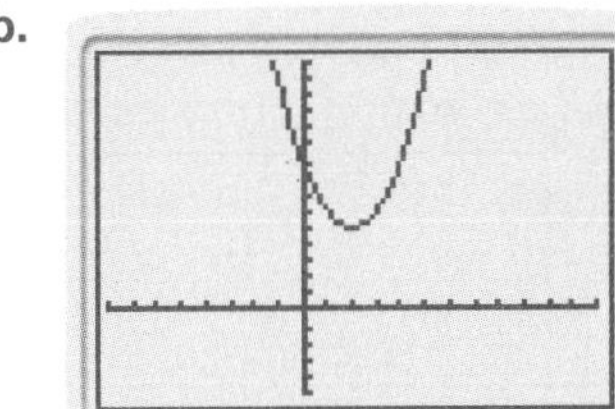

c.

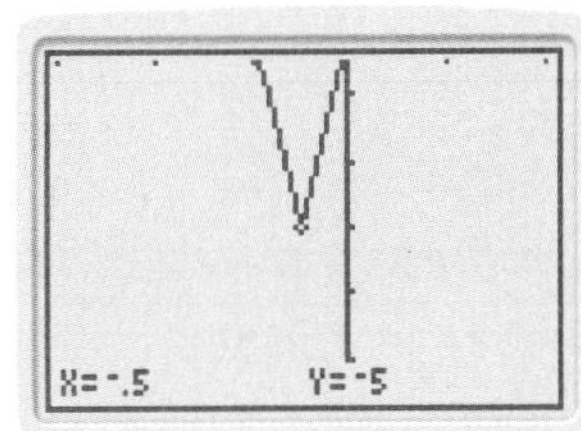

Lesson 17

Exploration.

a.

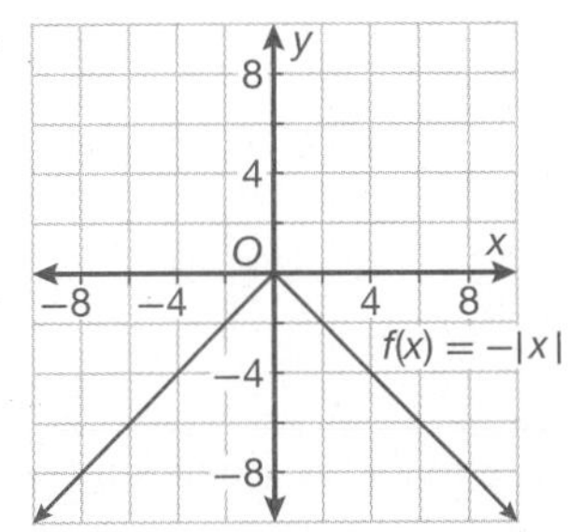

b.

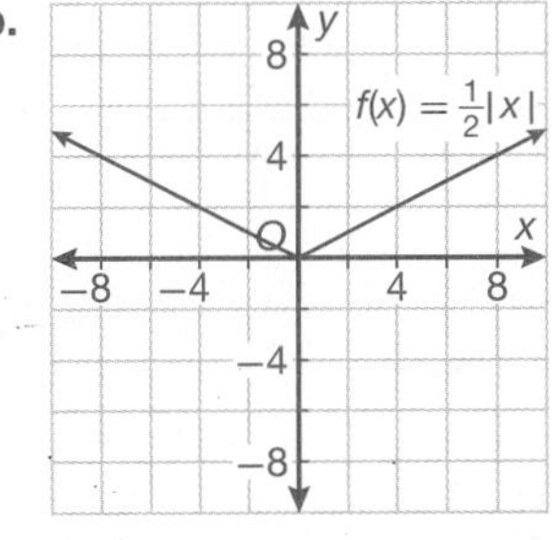

c.

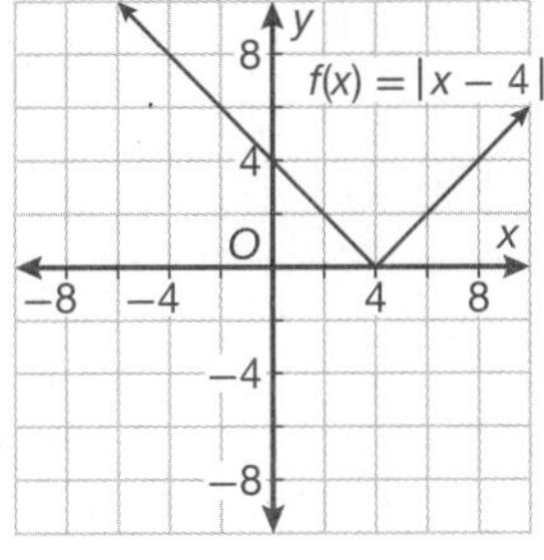

d.

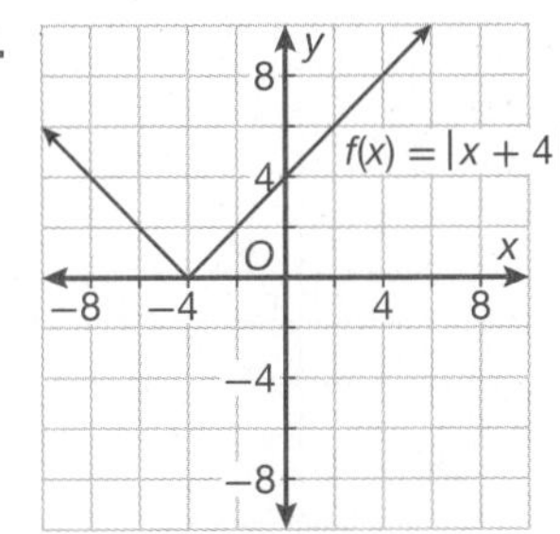

e.

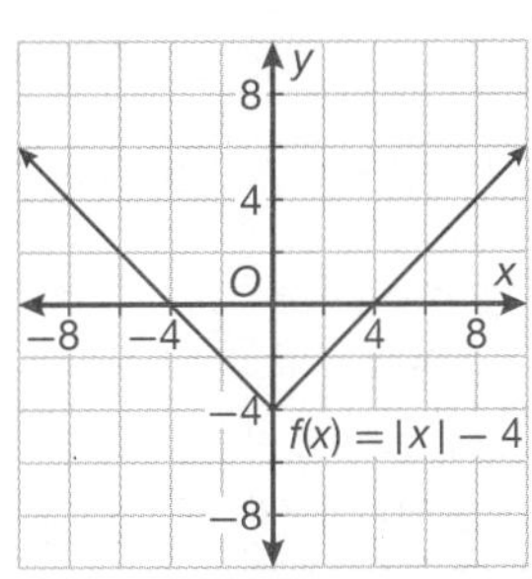

f.

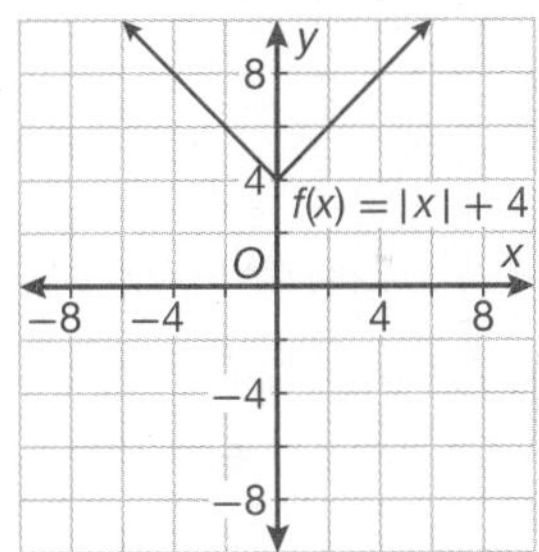

g. h moves the graph right if it is positive and left if it is negative; k moves the graph up if it is positive and down if it is negative.

h. The coefficient a causes the graph to open up or down and changes the shape by stretching or shrinking the graph.

Lesson Practice

a. $x = 4$ or $x = -10$

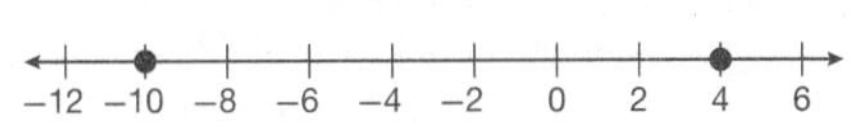

e. $-10 < x < 6$

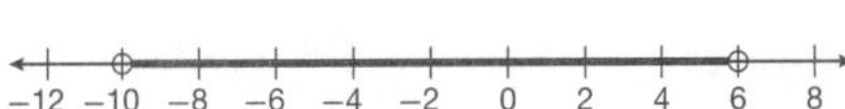

g. $x \geq 8$ or $x \leq 1$

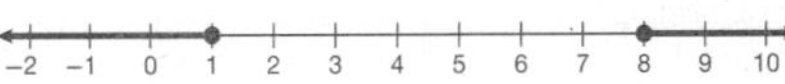

ADDITIONAL ANSWERS

13.

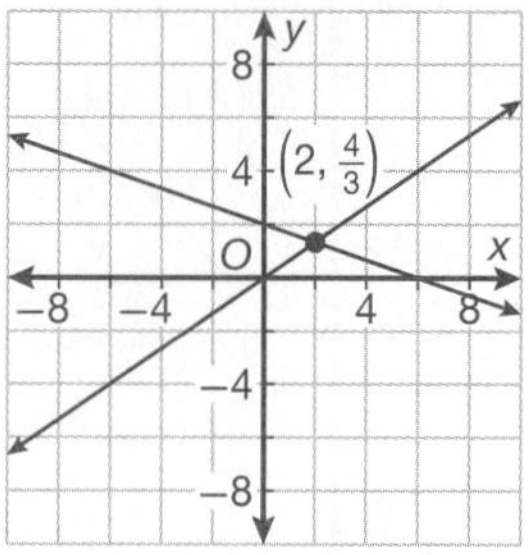

21a.

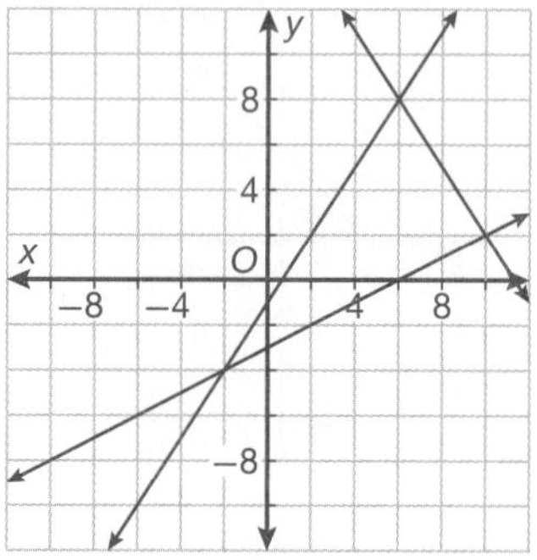

;

triangle

23.

x	−3	0	3	6	9
y	3	−2	−7	−12	−17

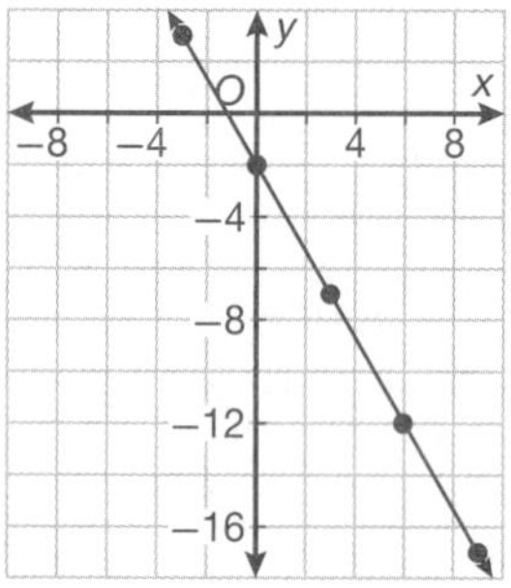

24.

x	0	2	4	6	8
y	5	4	3	2	1

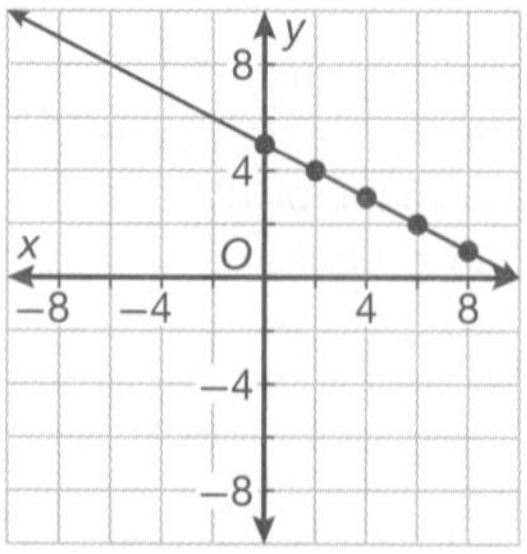

Lesson 20

Lesson Practice

e.

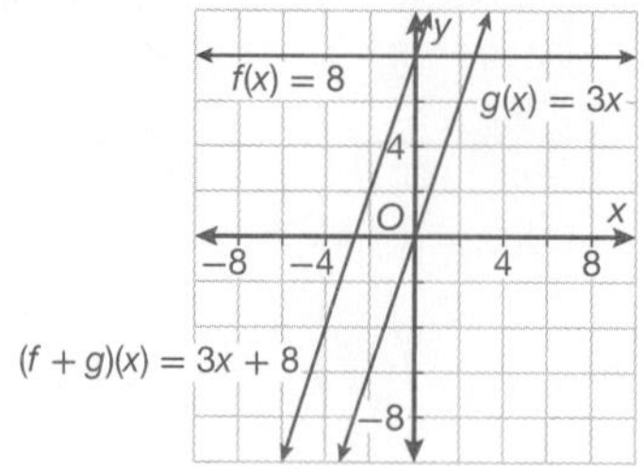

f.

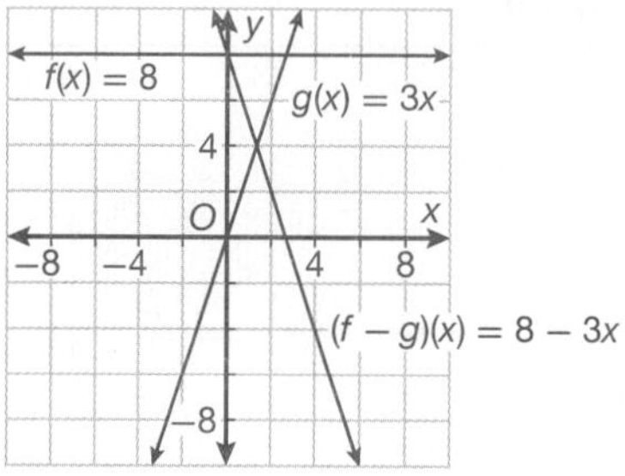

Practice

2a. $x = \dfrac{\begin{vmatrix} 5 & 1 \\ -4 & q \end{vmatrix}}{\begin{vmatrix} 1 & 1 \\ p & q \end{vmatrix}}, y = \dfrac{\begin{vmatrix} 1 & 5 \\ p & -4 \end{vmatrix}}{\begin{vmatrix} 1 & 1 \\ p & q \end{vmatrix}}$

2c.

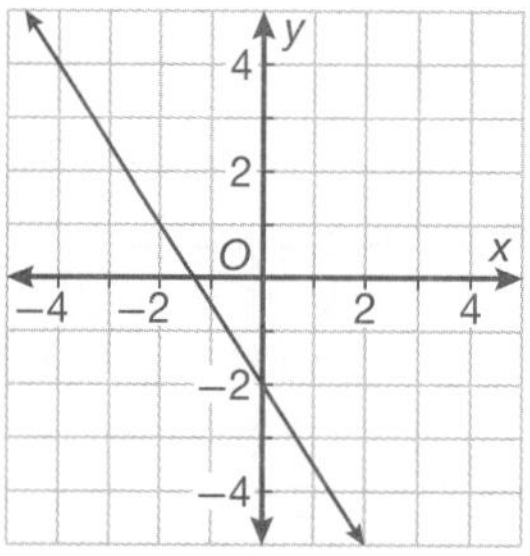

2d. Possible answer: (−2, 1) and $\begin{cases} x + y = 5 \\ -2x + y = -4 \end{cases}$.

2e.

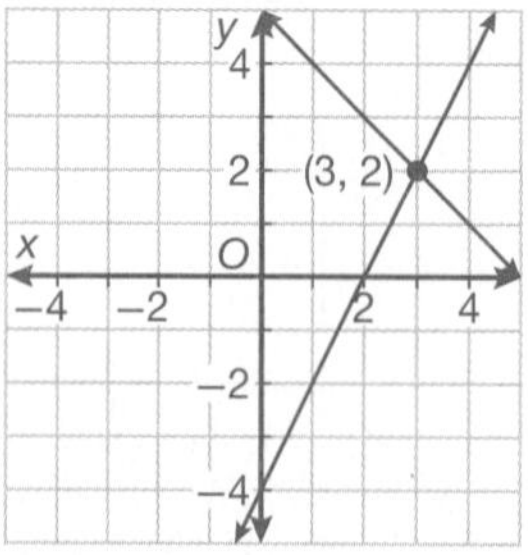

;

The intersection point is the same as the solution.

28. $x \le -2$ or $x \ge -\frac{2}{3}$;

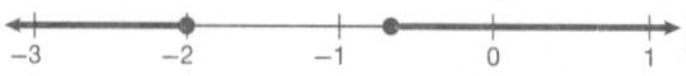

; yes

Investigation 2

3.

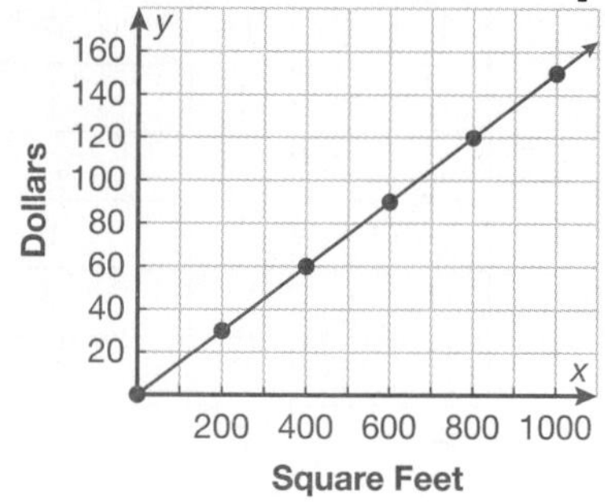

7.

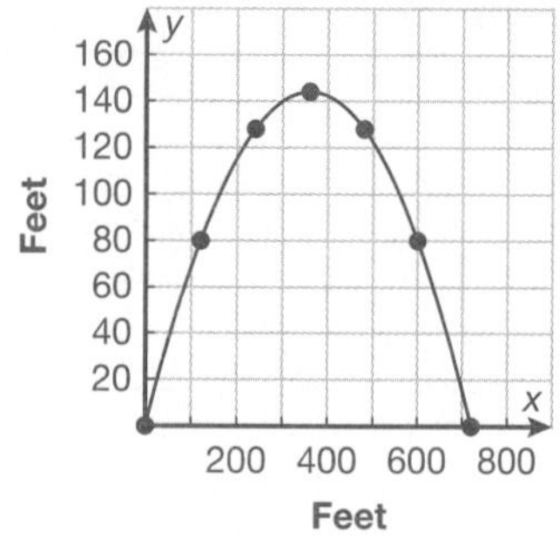

Investigation Practice

b.

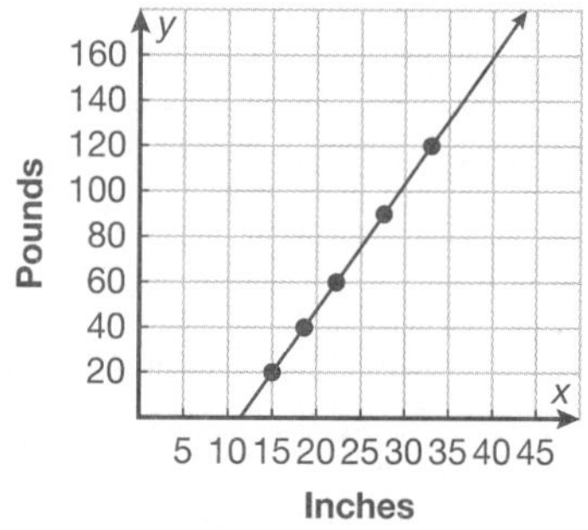

Lesson 23

Practice

23. Since matrix A is a 3×3 matrix and matrix B is a 3×2, the number of columns of A is the same as the number of rows of B. The product AB is defined.

$$\begin{bmatrix} 5 & 2 & 14 \\ 9 & 11 & 18 \\ 3 & 7 & 6 \end{bmatrix} \cdot \begin{bmatrix} 15 & 6 \\ 7 & 13 \\ 10 & 16 \end{bmatrix}$$

$$= \begin{bmatrix} 5 \cdot 15 + 2 \cdot 7 + 14 \cdot 10 & 5 \cdot 6 + 2 \cdot 13 + 14 \cdot 16 \\ 9 \cdot 15 + 11 \cdot 7 + 18 \cdot 10 & 9 \cdot 6 + 11 \cdot 13 + 18 \cdot 16 \\ 3 \cdot 15 + 7 \cdot 7 + 6 \cdot 10 & 3 \cdot 6 + 7 \cdot 13 + 6 \cdot 16 \end{bmatrix}$$

$$= \begin{bmatrix} 229 & 280 \\ 392 & 485 \\ 154 & 205 \end{bmatrix}$$

Multiply matrix A R1 by matrix B C1 and add the products to get entry R1C1 of the product matrix.

Multiply matrix *A* R1 by matrix *B* C2 and add the products to get entry R1C2 of the product matrix.

Multiply matrix *A* R2 by matrix *B* C1 and add the products to get entry R2C1 of the product matrix.

Multiply matrix *A* R2 by matrix *B* C2 and add the products to get entry R2C2 of the product matrix.

Multiply matrix *A* R3 by matrix *B* C1 and add the products to get entry R3C1 of the product matrix.

Multiply matrix *A* R3 by matrix *B* C2 and add the products to get entry R3C2 of the product matrix.

25a. 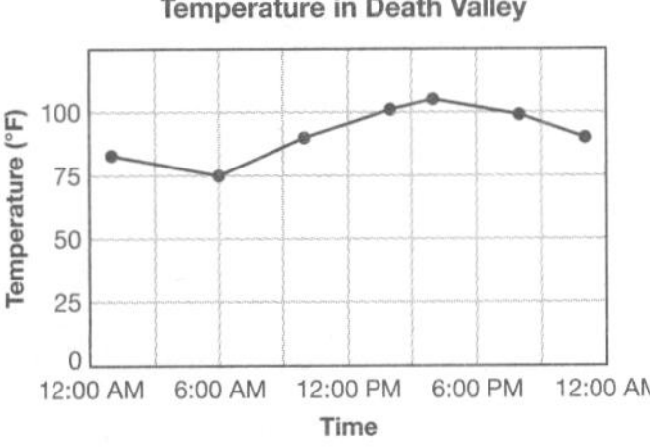

Lesson 24

Practice

19. Not necessarily; The value of a polynomial is not determined by degree alone; it also depends on the coefficients and the value(s) substituted for the variable(s). Possible examples: Let $P_1 = x^3$ and $P_2 = x^2$. Then for $x = 3$, the value of P_1 is 27 and the value of P_2 is 9. But for $x = -3$, the value of P_1 is -27 and the value of P_2 is 9.

Lesson 26

Practice

20. No; From the first line to the second line the negative sign in front of $2y$ was dropped.

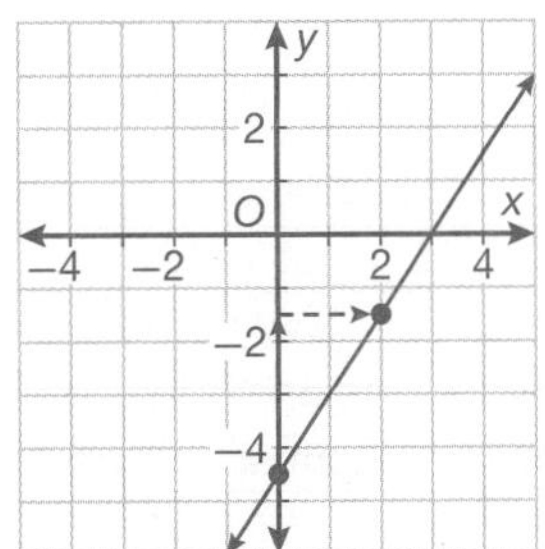

$3x - 2y = 9$

$-2y = -3x + 9$

$y = \frac{3}{2}x - 4\frac{1}{2}$

slope $= \frac{3}{2}$; y-intercept $= \left(0, -4\frac{1}{2}\right)$

24. They are similar in that for both types, both the x- and y-terms are eliminated, leaving a statement without variables that is either true or false. They are different in that the statement is true when there are infinitely many solutions and false when there are no solutions.

Lesson 28

Practice

24. 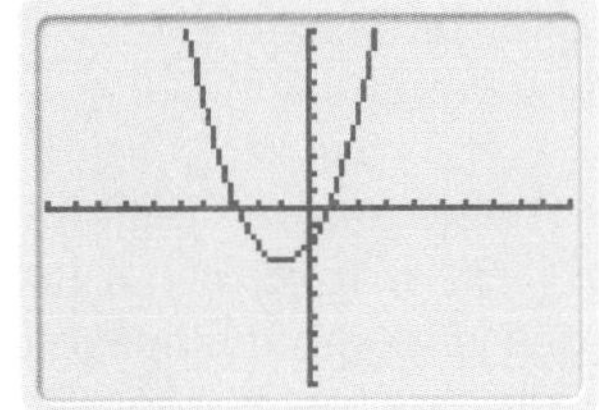 ;

parabola

Lesson 29

Practice

20. Possible answer: Factor $v^2 - 7v + 10$ to $(v - 5)(v - 2)$. Area is length times width, and the side length for the side along the x-axis is the difference between the x-values. So, let $v - 5 = x - (4 + v)$. Then, $x = 2v - 1$. So, a possible adjacent vertex is $(2v - 1, 0)$.

23a. $\begin{cases} 4n + 2r = 37.20 \\ 2n + 4r = 26.40 \end{cases}$

23b. Solving the first equation for r, $r = 18.60 - 2n$. Substituting into second equation, $2n + 4(18.60 - 2n) = 26.40$; $2n + 74.4 - 8n = 26.40$. Solving for n, $n = 8$, so the almonds cost \$8 per pound. Then, raisins cost \$2.60 per pound; $r = 18.60 - 2n = 18.60 - 2(8) = 2.6$. One pound of each should cost \$8 + \$2.60 = \$10.60.

24. First see if the x- or y-terms are opposites. If they are, add the two equations and solve for the variable that is not eliminated. Substitute into either original equation to solve for the other variable. If neither of the variable terms are opposites, multiply one or both equations by a constant so that either the x- or y-terms become opposites.

Lesson 30

Practice

12. The graph of $y = -5x^2 + 381$ is narrower than the parent function, is shifted vertically 381 units up, and opens downward. The graph of $y = -5x^2 + 442$ is also narrower than the parent function, is shifted vertically 442 units up, and also opens downward. The two graphs have the same width, open downward, and are vertical shifts of each other.

18. The Addition Property of Equality; because both sides of an equation are equivalent expressions, adding an equation to another is like adding equal expressions to both sides of the equation.

Lesson 32

Practice

19a. $\frac{2r + 2h}{rh}$ **19b.** $\frac{r + 2h}{rh}$

19c. The larger container is more economical because $\frac{r + 2h}{rh} < \frac{2r + 2h}{rh}$. ($r$ and h have only positive values.)

Lesson 33

Practice

10. Multiplication is commutative. Division is not commutative. Possible justification for multiplication: Multiplication of real numbers is commutative, and all rational expressions represent real numbers, so multiplication of rational expressions is commutative. Possible justification for division (a counterexample): $\frac{2x}{y} \div \frac{y}{x} = \frac{2x}{y} \cdot \frac{x}{y} = \frac{2x^2}{y^2}$, but $\frac{y}{x} \div \frac{2x}{y} = \frac{y}{x} \cdot \frac{y}{2x} = \frac{y^2}{2x^2}$

Lesson 34

Practice

f. 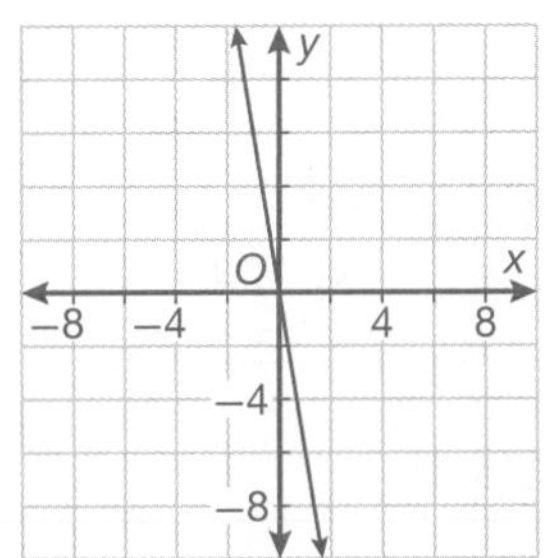

g. 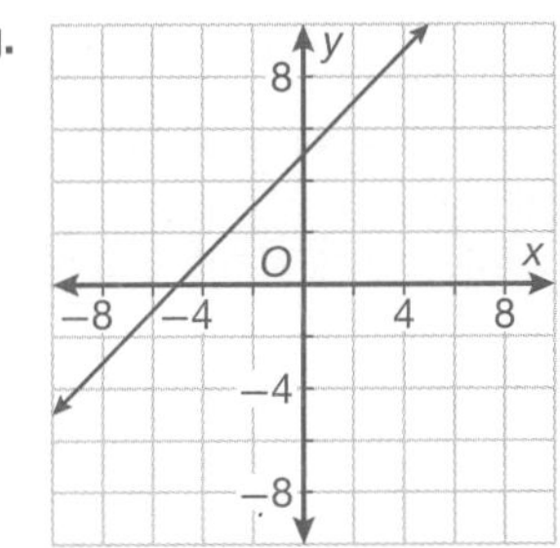

ADDITIONAL ANSWERS

h.

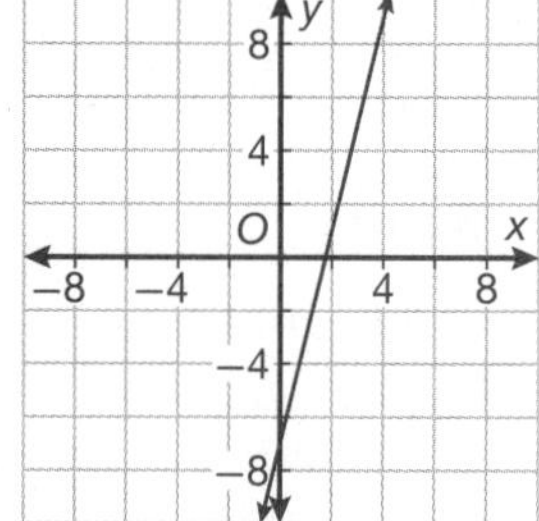

i.

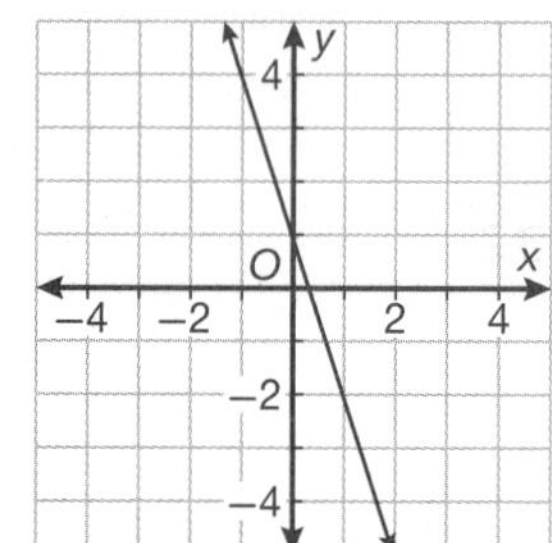

j.

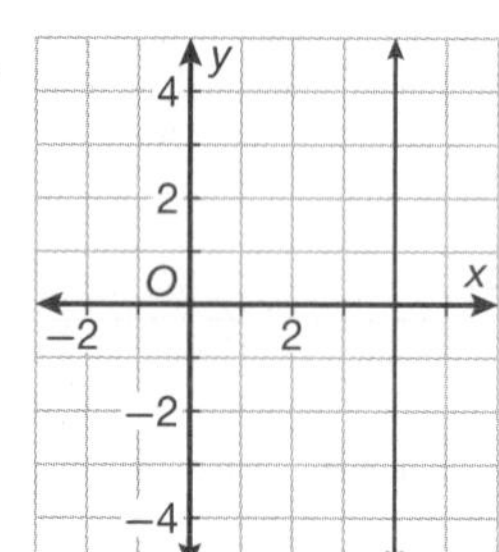

k.

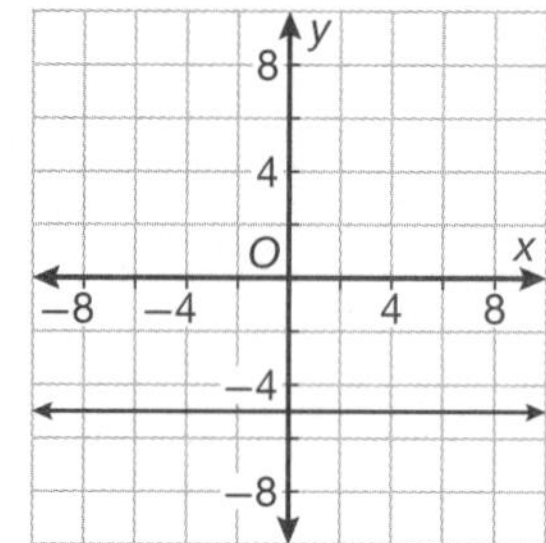

l.

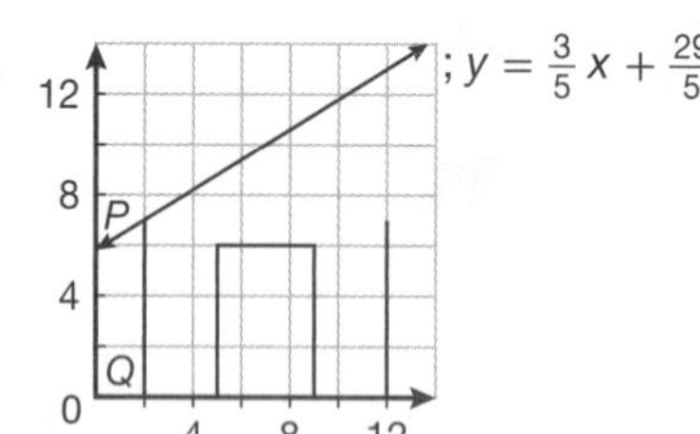

; $y = \frac{3}{5}x + \frac{29}{5}$

Lesson 35

Practice

e. −4 and 2 are the roots of the equation, the zeros of the related function $f(x) = x^2 + 2x - 8$, and the x-intercepts of the graph.

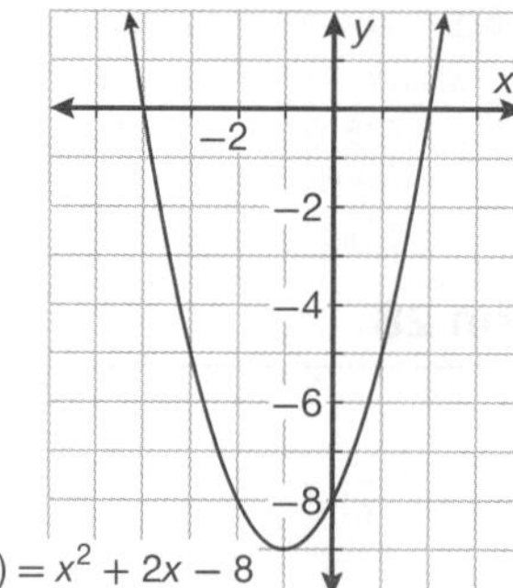

$f(x) = x^2 + 2x - 8$

16. Possible answer: Factor $a^2 - 8a + 16$ to $(a - 4)(a - 4)$. Area is length multiplied by width, and each side length is $a - 4$. The side length along the x-axis is the difference between the x values. So, $a - 4 = x - (a - 1)$. Then, $x = 2a - 5$. So, a possible adjacent vertex is $(2a - 5, 0)$.

Lesson 38

Practice

13. 1 and only 1; Possible explanation: The graph of a quadratic function is a parabola that opens either up or down and extends without end to the left and to the right. So for any quadratic function, the graph intersects the y-axis in at least one point. And, the graph intersects the y-axis in at most one point because no vertical line can intersect the graph of a function in more than one point.

Lesson 39

Lesson Practice

f.

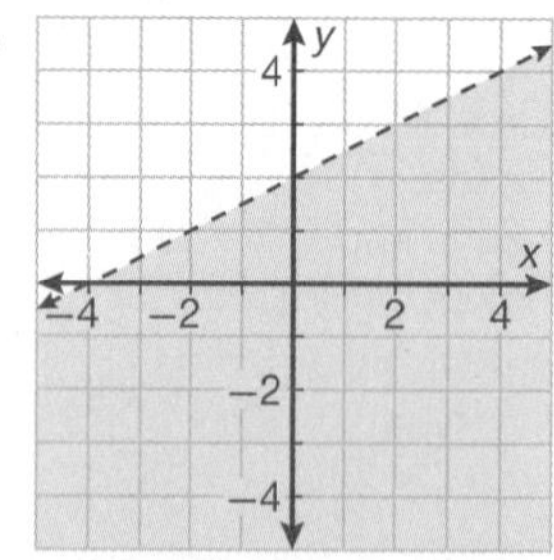

h.

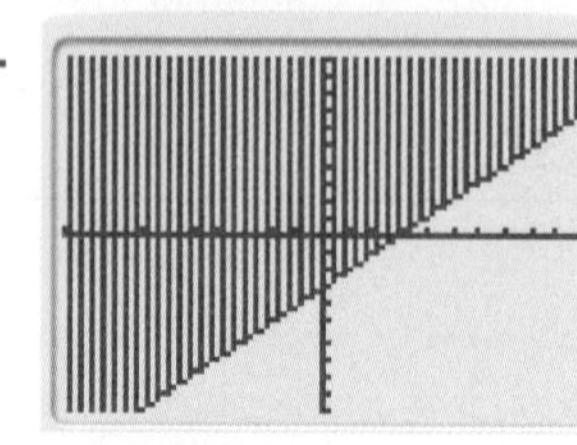

i.

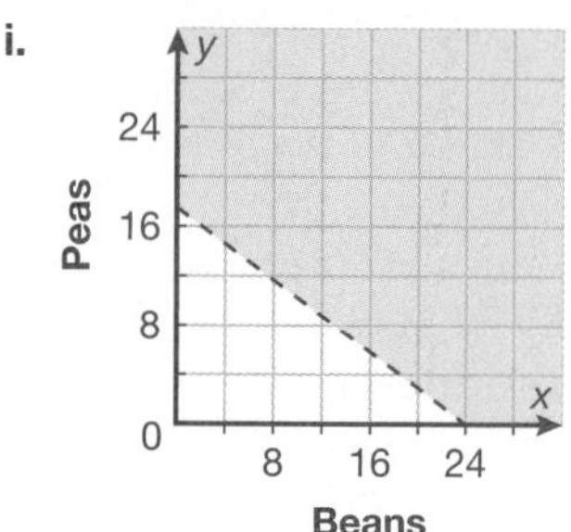

Practice

17. $x(x + 3) = 180$

$x = -15$ or $x = 12$ Choose the positive solution. $x = 12$ and $x + 3 = 15$. The maximum dimensions of a large envelope are 12 inches and 15 inches.

21.

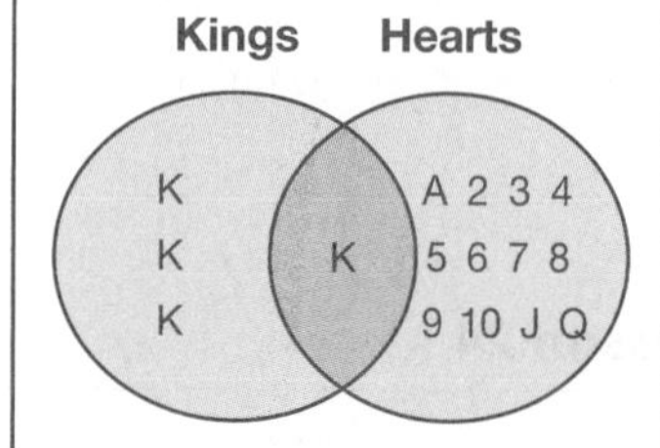

25. The equation for the path of the rocket is $y = a(x - h)^2 + k$. Substituting the values and solving:

$200 = a(5.00 - 3.75)^2 + 225$; $-25 = a(1.25)^2$; $-25 = 1.5625a$; $-16 = a$

Lesson 42

Practice

12. Eliminate x-terms:

$$\begin{cases} -2(2x + 3y) = -2(13) \\ 4x - 9y = -79 \end{cases}$$

$$\begin{aligned} -4x - 6y &= -26 \\ +4x - 9y &= -79 \\ \hline -15y &= -105 \\ y &= 7 \\ 2x + 3(7) &= 13 \\ 2x + 21 &= 13 \\ 2x &= -8 \\ x &= -4 \end{aligned}$$

Eliminate y-terms:

$$\begin{cases} 3(2x + 3y) = 3(13) \\ 4x - 9y = -79 \end{cases}$$

$$\begin{aligned} 6x + 9y &= 39 \\ +4x - 9y &= -79 \\ \hline 10x &= -40 \\ x &= -4 \\ 2(-4) + 3y &= 13 \\ -8 + 3y &= 13 \end{aligned}$$

$$3y = 21$$
$$y = 7$$

25.

Tomato	Tuna	Juice	Tomato, Tuna, Juice
		Milk	Tomato, Tuna, Milk
	Roast Beef	Juice	Tomato, Roast Beef, Juice
		Milk	Tomato, Roast Beef, Milk
	Ham	Juice	Tomato, Ham, Juice
		Milk	Tomato, Ham, Milk
Chicken	Tuna	Juice	Chicken Noodle, Tuna, Juice
		Milk	Chicken Noodle, Tuna, Milk
	Roast Beef	Juice	Chicken Noodle, Roast Beef, Juice
		Milk	Chicken Noodle, Roast Beef, Milk
	Ham	Juice	Chicken Noodle, Ham, Juice
		Milk	Chicken Noodle, Ham, Milk

30.

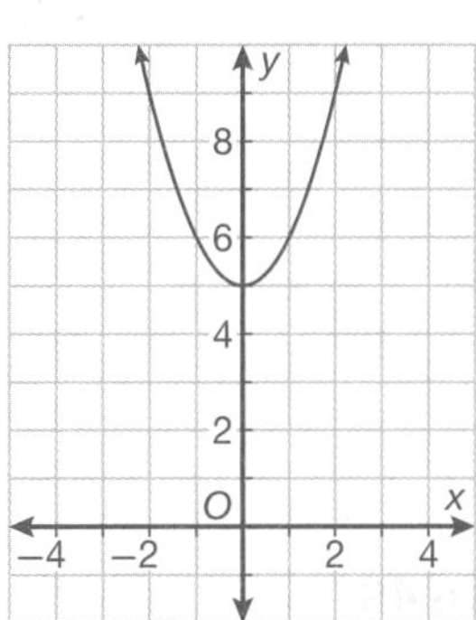

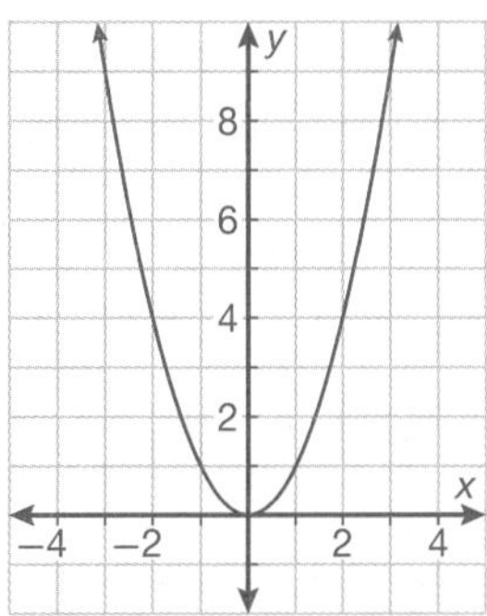

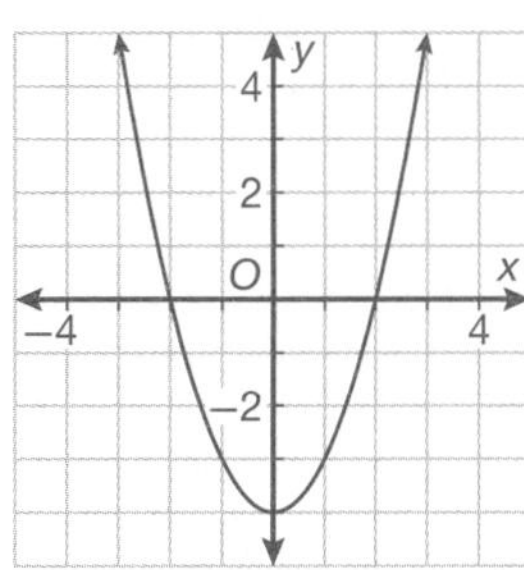

Lesson 43

Lesson Practice

e.

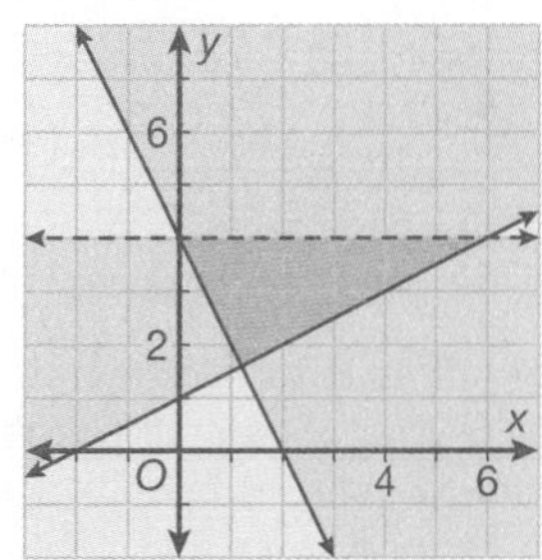

The solution set of the system consists of all points on the two lower sides of the triangle formed by the three boundary lines and all points inside the triangle.

Practice

8a.

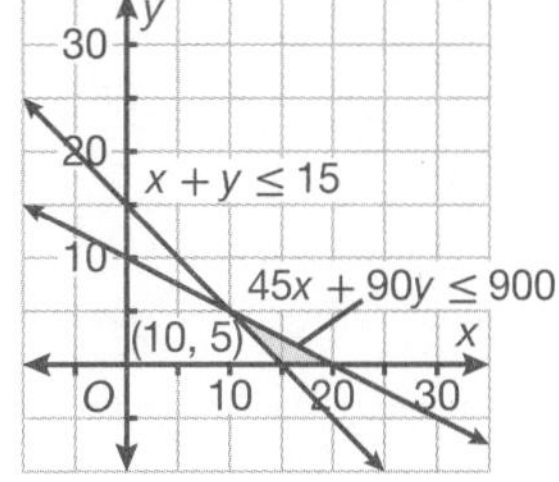

24.

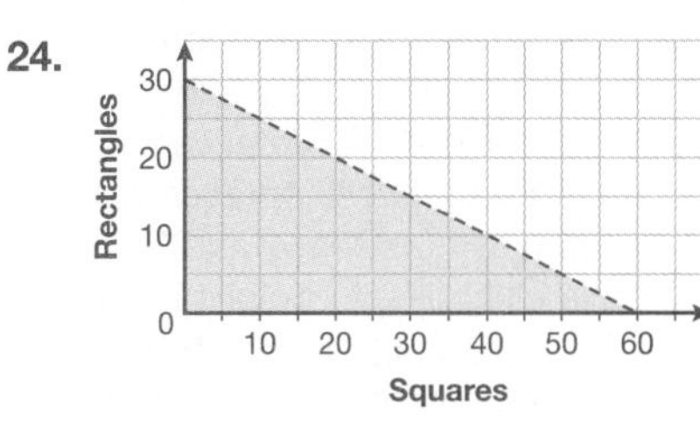

Lesson 44

Practice

6. The incorrect half-plane is shaded for $2x - y \leq 2$. Correct graph:

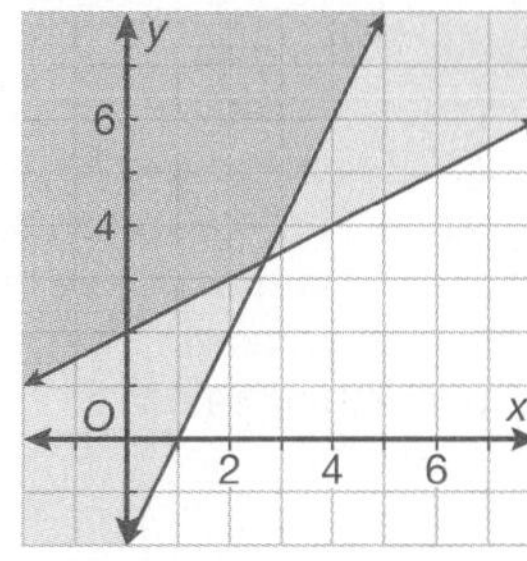

8. Sample: 10 items taken 4 at a time $C(10,4) = 210$ and 10 items taken 6 at a time $C(10,6) = 210$ are the same. Another way to think of this is that when you take 4 items from 10 you leave 6 items behind. The number of ways you can take 4 must be the same as the number of ways you can leave 6 items behind.

27. Sample: One way is to pick a point in either half-plane. If the point is a solution, then shade that half-plane; if the point is not a solution, then shade the other half-plane. Another way is to solve the inequality for y, getting $y > -\frac{1}{2}x + 3$. Because this has the form $y > mx + b$, shade above the boundary line.

29. If the order of the flavors is not important, for example if the frozen yogurt was in a dish, use combinations: $C(5,3) = 10$. If the order of the flavors is important, for example if the flavors were stacked in a cone, use permutations $P(5,3) = 60$.

Lesson 45

Practice

1a. and **1b.**

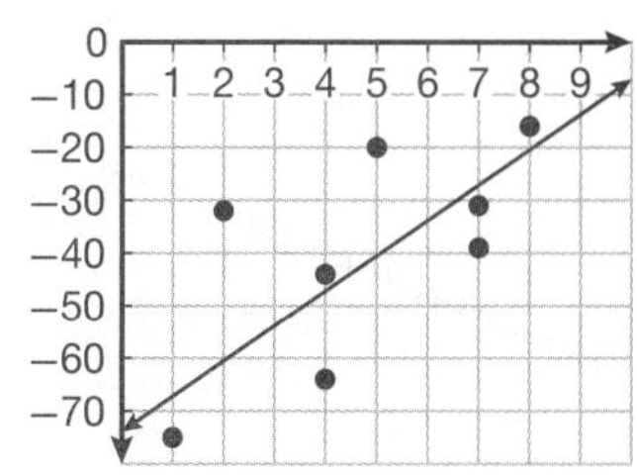

12.

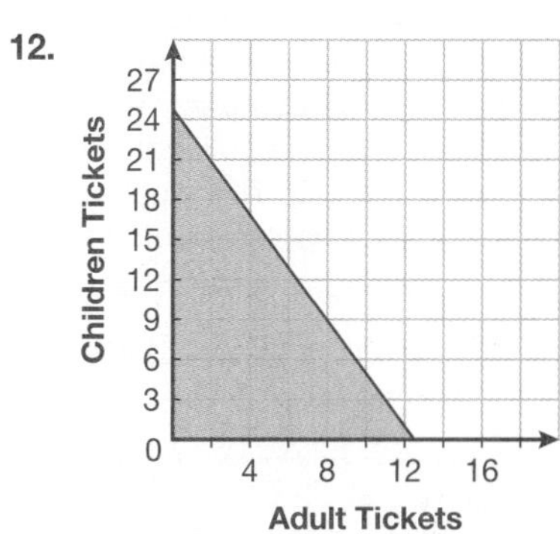

;

The point (6, 15) is not in the shaded region, so the tourists can not buy 6 adult tickets and 15 children's tickets.

22. $C - 0 = \frac{5}{9}(F - 32)$; Rate of change $= \frac{5}{9}$; Possible description: C increases 5 degrees for every 9-degree increase in F.

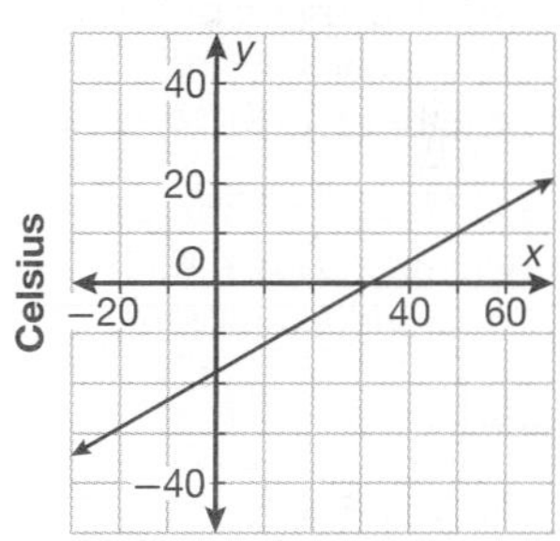

Lesson 47

Lesson Practice

b.

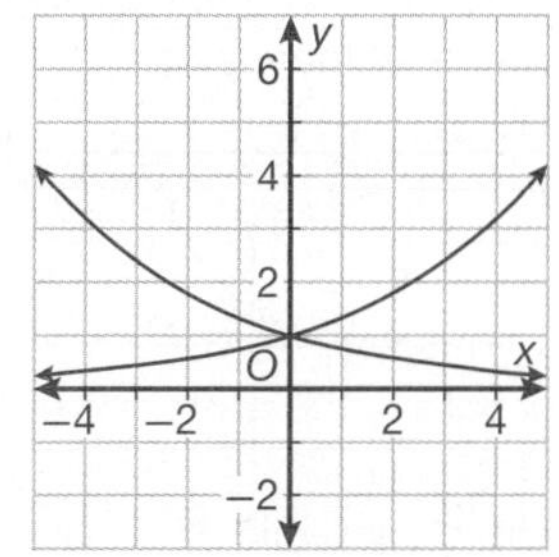

Because the functions have the form $y = b^x$ and the bases are reciprocals, the graphs are reflection images of each other over the y-axis.

ADDITIONAL ANSWERS

c.

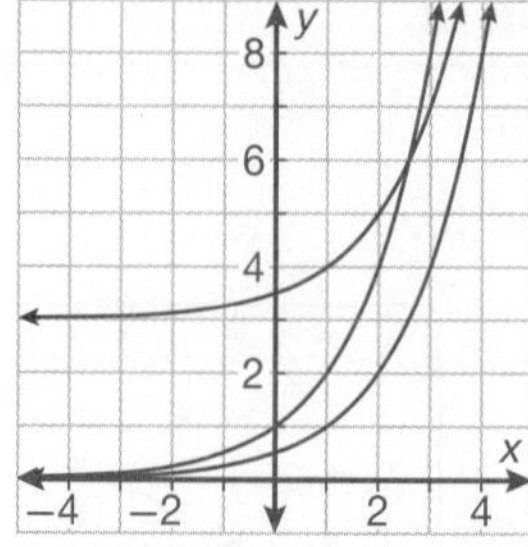

y_1 is the parent function of all exponential functions with base 2. The domain of all the functions is the set of all real numbers. The range of y_1 and y_2 is the set of all positive real numbers. The range of y_3 is the set of all real numbers greater than 3. The graph of y_2 is a vertical compression of the graph of y_1 by a factor of $\frac{1}{2}$. The graph of y_3 is a vertical shift 3 units up of the graph of y_2.

d.

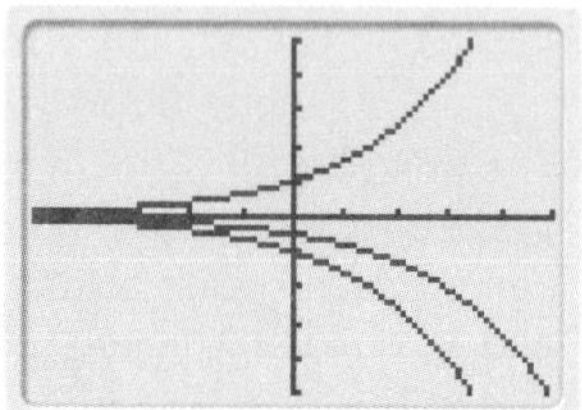

y_1 is the parent function of all exponential functions with base 1.6. The graph of y_2 is a reflection of the graph of y_1 over the x-axis. The graph of y_3 is a vertical compression of the graph of y_2 by a factor of $\frac{1}{2}$.

e. $1126.49 if compounded quarterly; $1127.16 if compounded monthly

Practice

1. $\frac{3x^2 + 21x + 36}{14x^3 + 25x^2 + 62x + 16}$

4. Graph y_1 is the parent function of all graphs with base 2.3. Graph y_2 is a vertical compression of y_1 by a factor of $\frac{1}{6}$. Graph y_3 is a reflection of y_2 over the x-axis.

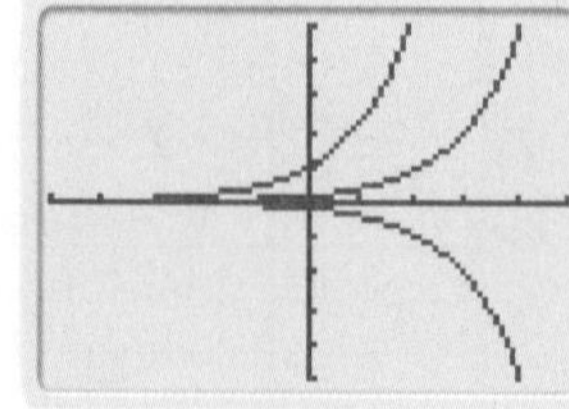

8a. $x + y \leq 20$
$10x + 15y \geq 240$

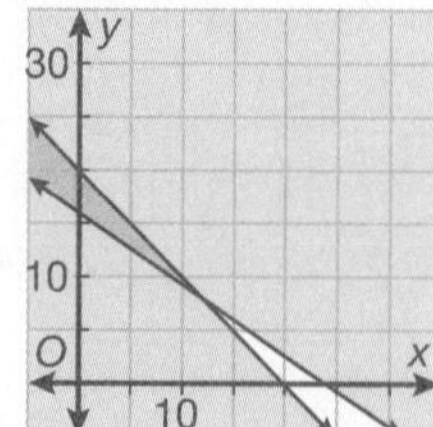

8c. (0, 20), (0, 16), (12, 8); Possible description: (0, 20) represents 0 hours in the library and 20 hours landscaping for total earnings of $300; (0, 16) represents 0 hours in the library and 16 hours landscaping for total earnings of $240; (12, 8) represents 12 hours in the library and 8 hours landscaping for total earnings of $240.

15. The product of an expression and its radical conjugate is a rational number. When multiplying a binomial with its conjugate, the first terms and the last terms are squares of the radical terms. This eliminates the radical from those terms. The inner multiplications will cancel each other as the sum of opposite terms is 0, so the multiplication results in a rational number with no radicals.

18.

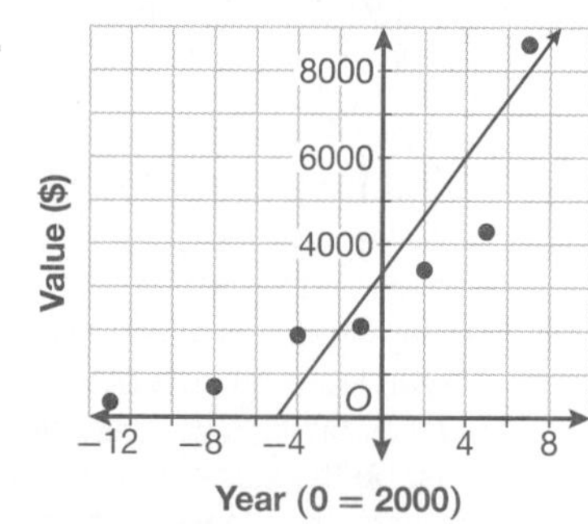

25. The lines form a triangle.

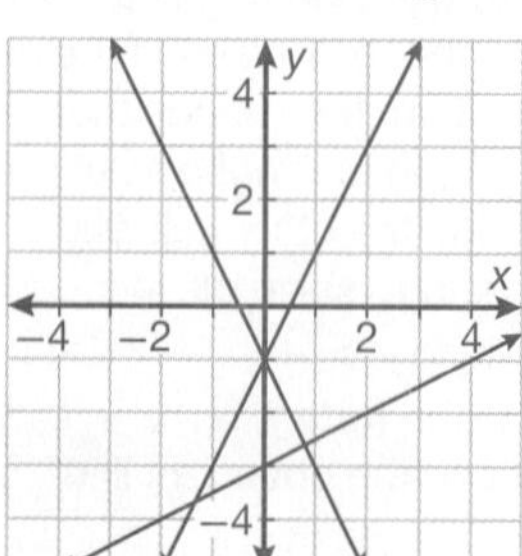

Lesson 48

Practice

13. The mean is noted instead of the median. 14 should be marked in the box instead of 13.2.

15a.

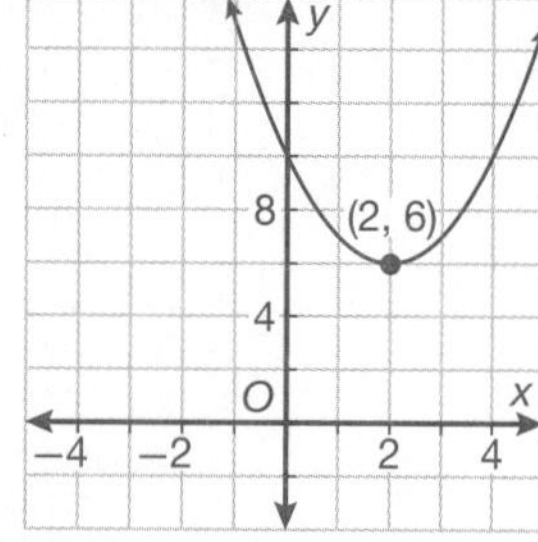

27. $2.5x + 5y \geq 2000$

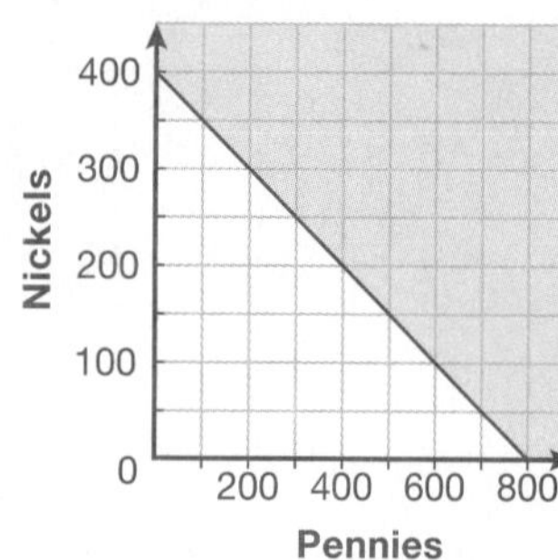

Lesson 49

Practice

11. Sample answer: The graph of the product function is the line $y = 2x + 6$, except for the points of discontinuity at the x-values 0 and 1.

13a–b.

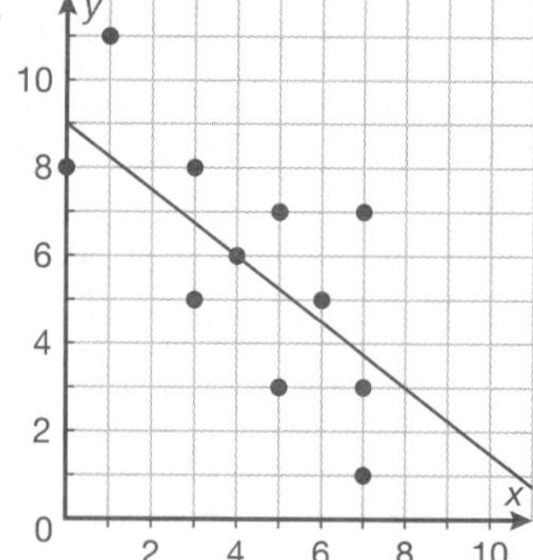

15a. $x + y \leq 24$
$27x + 45y \leq 720$

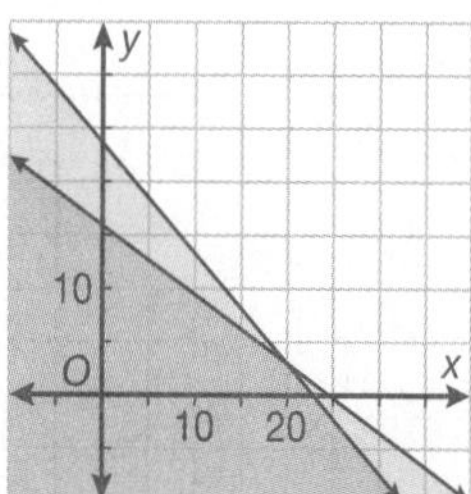

15b. The points in the graph of the system that represent all the possible combinations of outfield grandstand seats and right field box seats you can buy are all points with both coordinates nonnegative integers.

15c. (20, 4); Sample explanation: It represents 20 outfield grandstand seats and 4 right field box seats at a total cost of \$720, the maximum that can be spent.

22. The student multiplied by the wrong radical conjugate. The student multiplied by the radical conjugate of the numerator and the denominator rather than multiplying both the numerator and the denominator by the radical conjugate of the denominator.

The correct answer is: $\frac{2\sqrt{2}+6}{3\sqrt{2}+\sqrt{5}} \cdot$

$$\frac{3\sqrt{2}-\sqrt{5}}{3\sqrt{2}-\sqrt{5}} = \frac{12-2\sqrt{10}+18\sqrt{2}-6\sqrt{5}}{18-5}$$

$$= \frac{12-2\sqrt{10}+18\sqrt{2}-6\sqrt{5}}{13}$$

25.

$2x - 7 = -(7 - 2x)$ Given

$= -7 + 2x$ Distributive Property

$= 2x - 7$ Commutative Property of Addition

Lesson 50

Lesson Practice

d. The inverse is $y = \pm\sqrt{2x+8}$, which is not a function.

Relation	Domain	Range
$y = \frac{1}{2}x^2 - 4$	x is any real number.	$y \geq -4$
$y = \pm\sqrt{2x+8}$	$x \geq -4$	$y \geq 0$

e. Require that $x \geq 0$ in the function $y = \frac{1}{2}x^2 - 4$. Then, $f(x) = \frac{1}{2}x^2 - 4, x \geq 0$ and $f^{-1}(x) = \sqrt{2x+8}$.

Function	Domain	Range
$f(x) = \frac{1}{2}x^2 - 4,\ x \geq 0$	$x \geq 0$	$y \geq -4$
$f^{-1}(x) = \sqrt{2x+8}$	$x \geq -4$	$y \geq 0$

Practice

15.

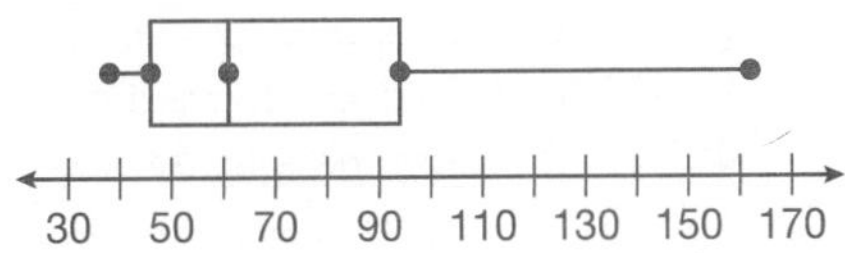

21. Possible answer: The boundary lines for the inequalities are parallel because they have the same slope, 3. All solutions of $y > 3x + 1$ are above its boundary line and all solutions of $y < 3x - 1$ are below its boundary line. Also, the boundary line for $y > 3x + 1$ is above the boundary line for $y < 3x - 1$ because it has the greater y-intercept. Therefore, there is no ordered pair that is a solution of both inequalities.

26. In the ratio, the numerator is a leg length and the denominator is the length of the hypotenuse. Since the hypotenuse is the greatest side of a right triangle, the numerator is never greater than the denominator, making it impossible for the fraction to have a value greater than or equal to 1.

28b. No solution; The second and third equations have coefficients that are multiples of each other but the constants are not multiples.

Lesson 51

Practice

25. Choose some values for x and solve for the corresponding value of y.

$y = \frac{3}{4}(-1) + 9 = 8.25$

$y = \frac{3}{4}(0) + 9 = 9$

$y = \frac{3}{4}(1) + 9 = 9.75$

Construct a table of the values.

x	-1	0	1
y	8.25	9	9.75

Plot each ordered pair on a coordinate grid.

29a. $x + y \leq 16$
$8x + 12y \geq 150$

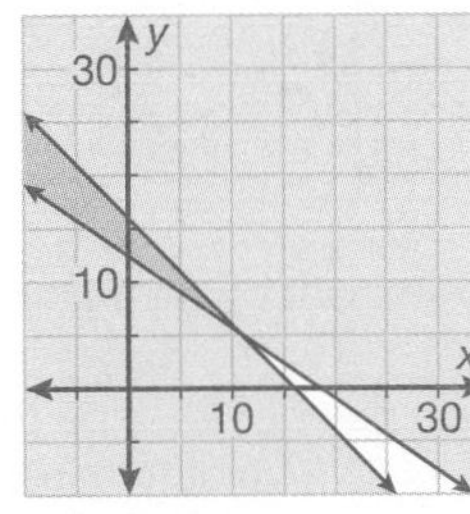

29b. Possible description: All meaningful solutions are the ordered pairs of the solution set on and inside the triangle whose left side is the segment from (0, 12.5) to (0, 16).

29c. (0, 16), (0, 12.5), (10.5, 5.5); Possible description: (0, 16) represents 0 hours for the recreation department and 16 hours at the candy store for total earnings of \$192; (0, 12.5) represents 0 hours for the recreation department and 12.5 hours at the candy store for total earnings of \$150; (10.5, 5.5) represents 10.5 hours for the recreation department and 5.5 hours at the candy store for total earnings of \$150.

30. $(a + b)^5 = a^5 + 5a^4b + 10a^3b^2 + 10a^2b^3 + 5ab^4 + b^5$; The terms that have the same coefficient have exponents that are reversed, as in $10a^3b^2$ and $10a^2b^3$.

Lesson 54

Practice

20. Because the y-intercept is 13, the point (0, 13) appears on the graph. Use this point and (1, 9) to solve for a.

$13 = a(0 - 1)^2 + 9$
$13 = a + 9$
$4 = a$

The equation in vertex form is $y = 4(x - 1)^2 + 9$. To write it in standard form, square the binomial and simplify:

$y = 4(x - 1)^2 + 9$
$y = 4(x^2 - 2x + 1) + 9$
$y = 4x^2 - 8x + 4 + 9$
$y = 4x^2 - 8x + 13$

Lesson 55

Practice

7. Possible answer: There are solutions in quadrant I, such as (1, 2). Every solution of the system has a positive x-coordinate because it must satisfy $x \geq 1$. And every solution of the system has a positive y-coordinate because it must satisfy $y > x$. Therefore, both coordinates of every solution of the system are positive, and every solution lies in quadrant I.

16. The domain for both functions is the set of all real numbers. The range of the function $y = 3^x$ is the set of real numbers greater than 0, or $\{y \mid y > 0\}$, and the range of $y = 3^x + 5$ is the set of real numbers greater than 5, or $\{y \mid y > 5\}$.

25. The trigonometric ratios associated with the inner angles are the same regardless of the lengths of the sides of the triangles. Since the ratios are the same and the angles are congruent, the corresponding sides of the triangles are proportional.

Lesson 56

Lesson Practice

c.

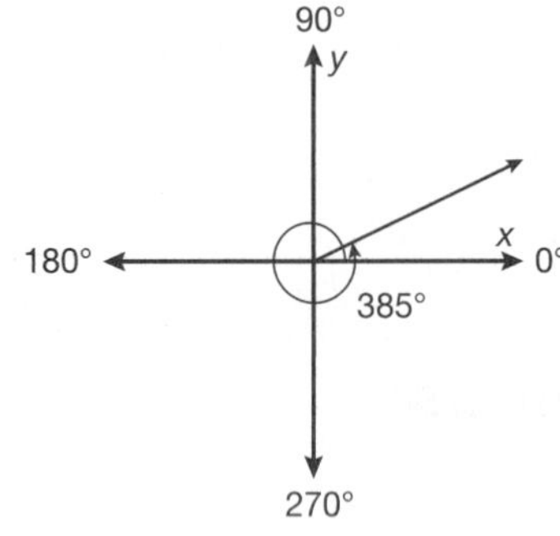

i. $\sin\theta = -\frac{8}{17}$, $\cos\theta = -\frac{15}{17}$,

$\tan\theta = \frac{8}{15}$, $\cot\theta = \frac{15}{8}$,

$\csc\theta = -\frac{17}{8}$, $\sec\theta = -\frac{17}{15}$

Practice

3. $\sin\theta = -\frac{24}{25}$, $\cos\theta = \frac{7}{25}$, $\tan\theta = -\frac{24}{7}$, $\csc\theta = -\frac{25}{24}$, $\sec\theta = \frac{25}{7}$, $\cot\theta = -\frac{7}{24}$

4. $\sin\theta = \frac{2}{3}$, $\cos\theta = -\frac{\sqrt{5}}{3}$, $\tan\theta = -\frac{2\sqrt{5}}{5}$, $\csc\theta = \frac{3}{2}$, $\sec\theta = -\frac{3\sqrt{5}}{5}$, $\cot\theta = -\frac{\sqrt{5}}{2}$

9.
$$(x)(x) = 196$$
$$x^2 - 196 = 0$$
$$(x + 14)(x - 14) = 0$$
$$x = -14 \text{ and } 14$$

The measurement cannot be −14 feet; hence the room's measurements are 14 feet by 14 feet.

19.

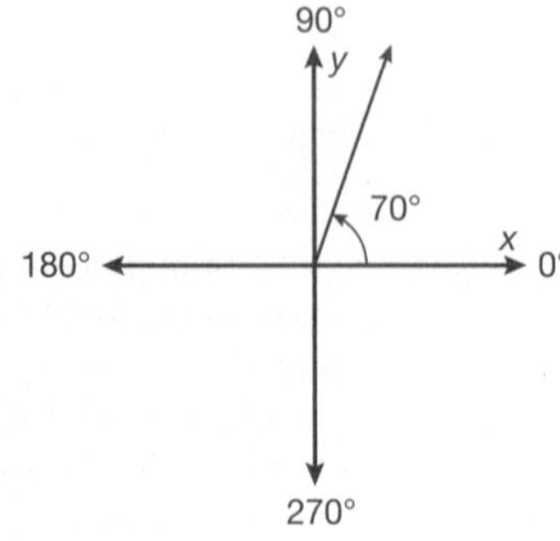

20.

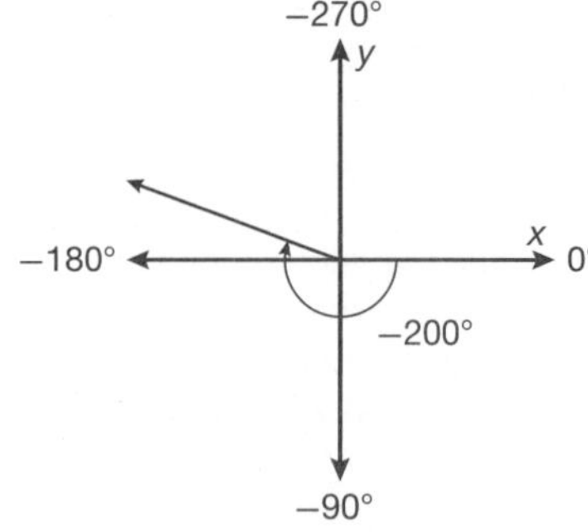

21.

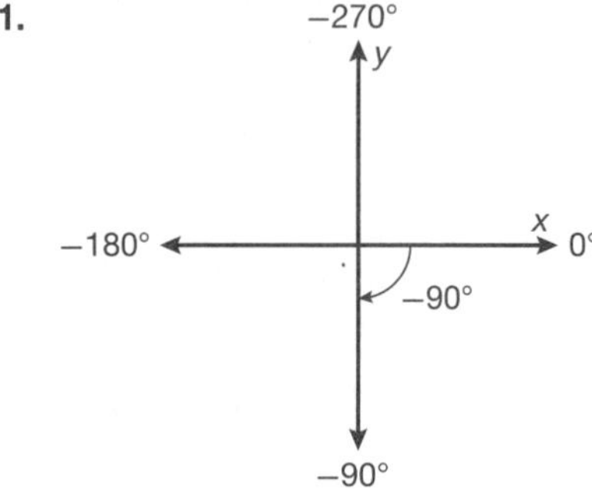

Lesson 57

Practice

15. One way is to graph the points with the intercepts of $2y - x = 6$: (0, 3) and (−6, 0). Connect the points with a dashed line. Choose the test point (0, 0). Because $0 < 6$ is true, the origin is in the region to be shaded, so shade below the line. The other way to graph the inequality is to first write the inequality in slope-intercept form: $y < \frac{1}{2} + 3$. Graph the point with the y-intercept (0, 3) and find a second point by moving up one and right two from there. Connect the points with a dashed line. Shade below the line because the symbol is less than.

24.

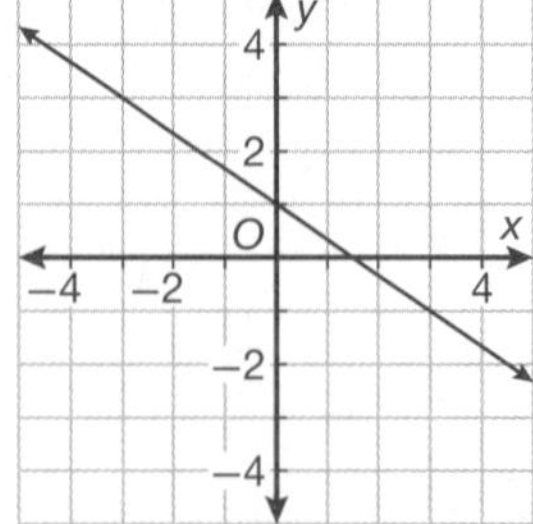

26. The determinant of the matrix is $3 - (-8) = 11$. The determinant of a single number must be the number itself. (The determinant is not the number's absolute value, as the determinant notation might indicate.)

28a. $y \geq x$
$7.5x + 15y \leq 300$

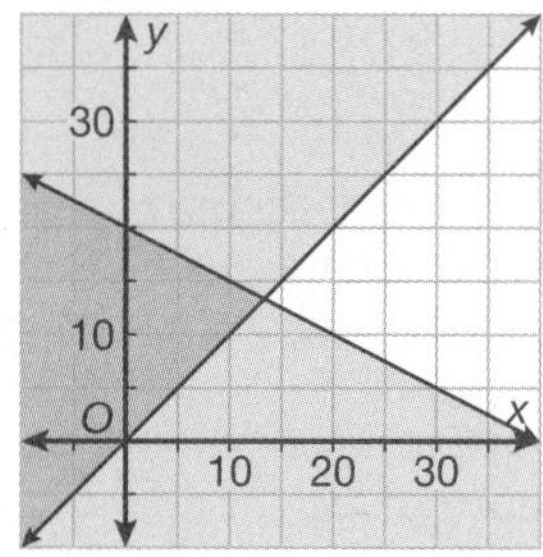

29. Sample answer: $I = 234e^{0.0933t}$, where t is the number of years since 1950; 63,153 billion dollars or $63,153,000,000,000

Lesson 59

Practice

14.

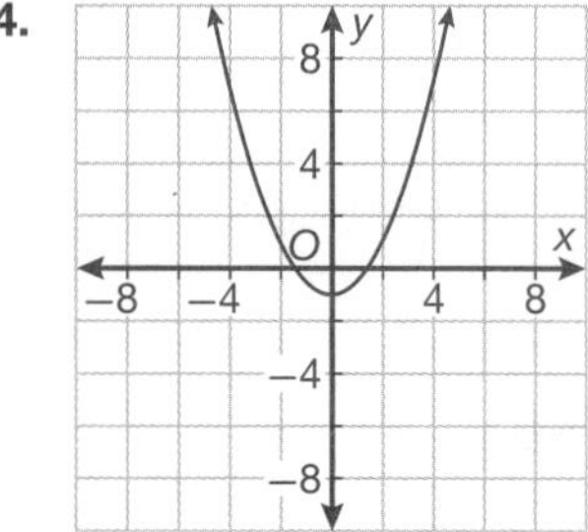

x	−4	−2	0	2	4
y	7	1	−1	1	7

15.

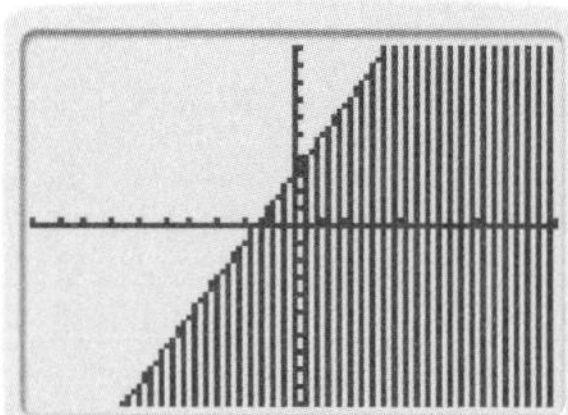

16. In order for $\sqrt[4]{-256}$ to have a real root there must be some value b such that $-256 = b^4$. If b is positive then $b^4 = b \cdot b \cdot b \cdot b$ is positive. If b is negative then $b^4 = -b \cdot -b \cdot -b \cdot -b = b^2 \cdot b^2$ is also positive. Therefore there is no way to achieve a negative value when raising a number to an even power.

26. The line joining the point and its x-coordinate makes an angle of 90° with the x-axis. So the triangle formed is a right triangle. The line $y = x$ makes an angle 45° with the x-axis. So the triangle formed is a 45°-45°-90° right triangle. All 45°-45°-90° triangles are similar.

27. A conditional probability is the probability of an event given that another event has already occurred. For example, suppose a bag has 5 red and 10 yellow chips. The probability of a yellow chip is $\frac{10}{15} = \frac{2}{3}$. But if a yellow chip was already picked, there are only 9 yellow chips and 14 chips in all, so the probability of selecting a yellow chip, given that one was already picked, is $\frac{9}{14}$.

Investigation 6

3a–c.

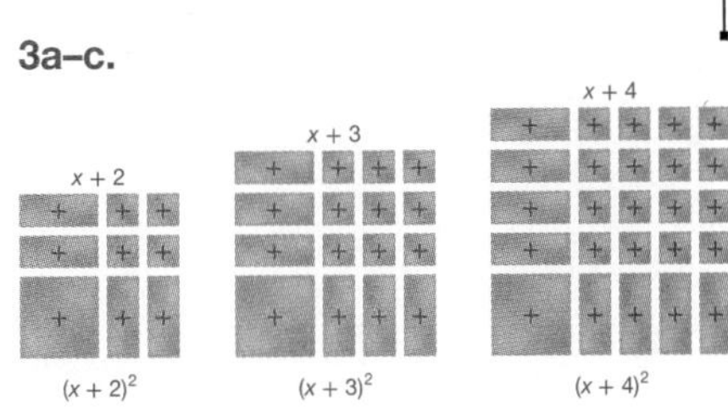

6a. For 6a, there should be a vertical line, one x^2 tile, 6 x-tiles, and one unit tile on the left and nothing on the right. The tiles should be arranged so there are three x-tiles on each of two adjacent sides of the squared tile, so it's obvious that eight unit tiles are missing.

Lesson 61

Practice

1.

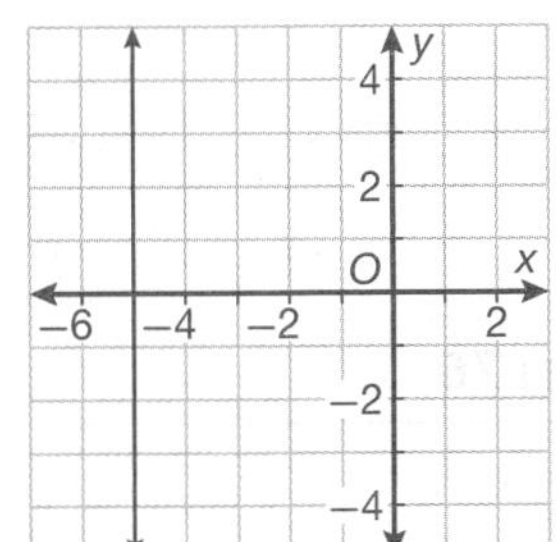

2.

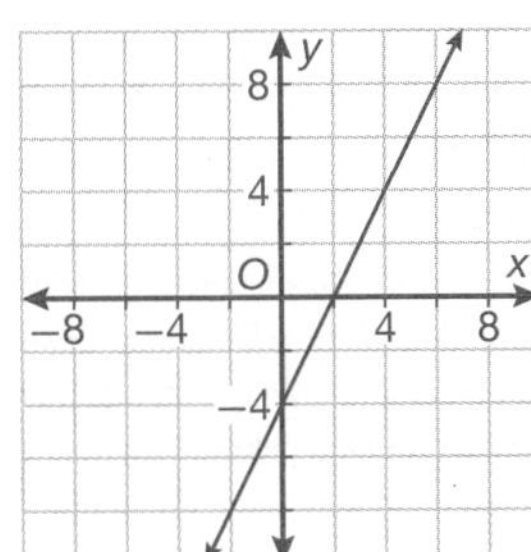

3.

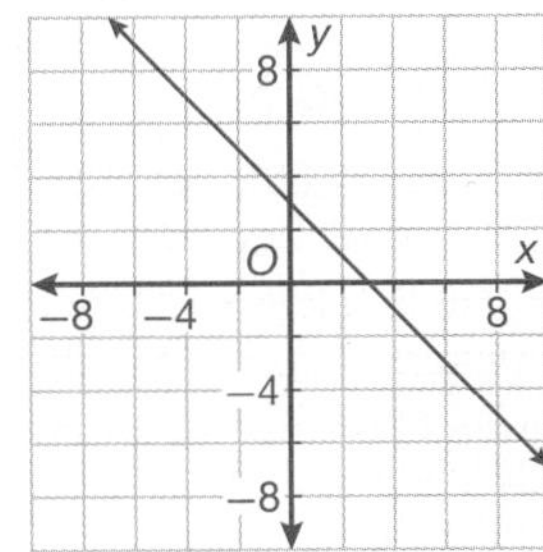

Lesson 63

Practice

21. When adding polynomials, only like terms can be combined. When adding and subtracting complex numbers, only like parts can be combined, where all real numbers are like and all the imaginary parts are like. Just as unlike terms cannot be combined, real parts cannot be combined with imaginary parts.

Lesson 64

Practice

29. The data sets that they represent are the same as far as how close the points are to forming a line: moderately close. However, the data set with a coefficient of −0.45 is a negative correlation, meaning the points fall from left to right, while the data set with a coefficient of 0.45 is a positive correlation, meaning the points rise from left to right.

Lesson 65

Practice

18c.

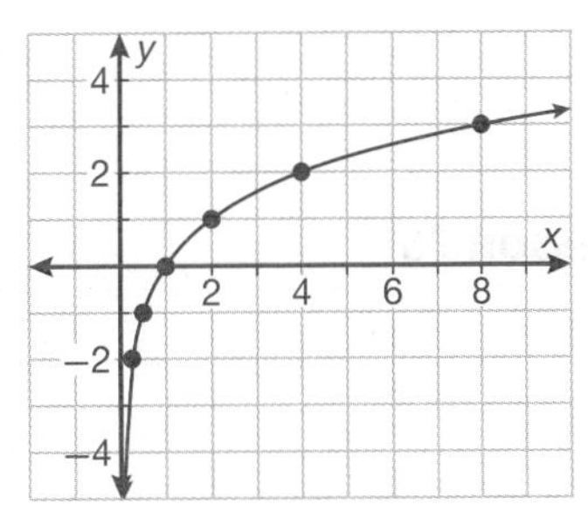

20.

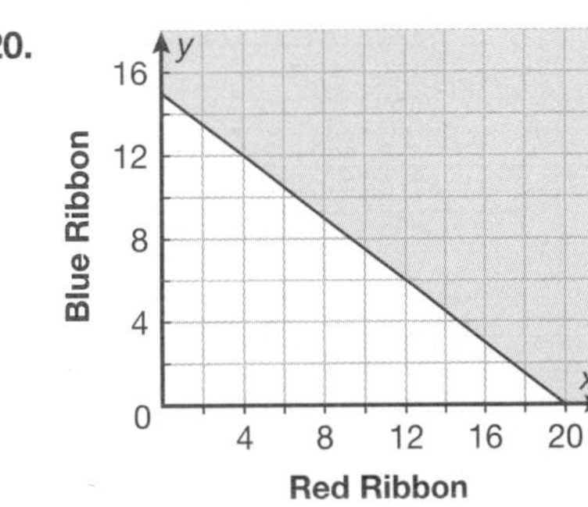

Lesson 66

Practice

24a. Inclusive; Some math books are paperbacks.

26. Group the terms so that there are the same number of terms in each group and so that each group has a common factor. Once the common factors are factored out, factor out the common polynomial factor, if there is one. Factor either of the two factors if needed.

29. Method 1

$g(-2) = 4(-2)^2 + 1$

$g(-2) = 17$

$f(17) = 8(17) - 6$

$(f \cdot g)(-2) = 130$

Method 2

$f(g(x)) = f(4x^2 + 1)$

$f(g(x)) = 8(4x^2 + 1) - 6$

$= 32x^2 + 2$

$(f \cdot g)(-2) = 32(-2)^2 + 2 = 130$

Lesson 67

Practice

16.

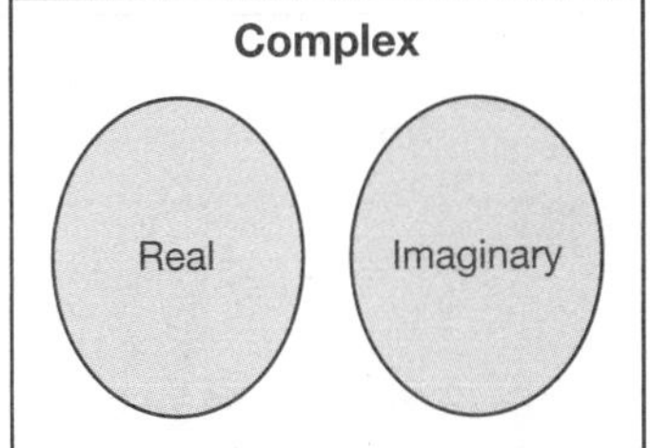

24. The denominator shows how many groups of three can be formed from a group of 10. The order in which the three are picked is irrelevant as long as it is those three. The numerator is 1 because there is only one group of three people that make up the top three.

26. x is positive in Quadrants I and IV and negative in II and III; y is positive in I and II and negative in III and IV; $r = \sqrt{x^2 + y^2}$ is always positive. So, $\sin\theta = \frac{y}{r}$ is positive in I and II, negative in III and IV; $\cos\theta = \frac{x}{r}$ is positive in I and IV, negative in II and III; $\tan\theta = \frac{y}{x}$ is positive in I and III, negative in II and IV.

Lesson 68

Practice

18. Possible estimate: $\text{Cos}^{-1}(0.48) \approx 61°$; Possible explanation: 0.48 is slightly less than 0.5 and $\text{Cos}^{-1}(0.5) = 60°$. $\text{Cos}^{-1}(0.48)$ should be slightly greater than $\text{Cos}^{-1}(0.5)$ because if two angles terminate in Quadrant I, the smaller angle has the greater x-coordinate and therefore has the greater cosine value.

ADDITIONAL ANSWERS

24. The student added the imaginary parts when they should have been subtracted.
The correct answer is $5 - 7i$.

Lesson 70

Practice

28. $s(p) = p - 0.2p$
$d(p) = p - 0.25p$
$d(s(p)) = d(p - 0.2p)$
$= p - 0.2p - 0.25(p - 0.2p)$
$= p - 0.2p - 0.25p + .050p$
$= p - 0.40p$
$= 0.60p$
The shirt will cost 0.60 times the normal price on the last day.

Investigation 7

a. **Internet and Email Use**

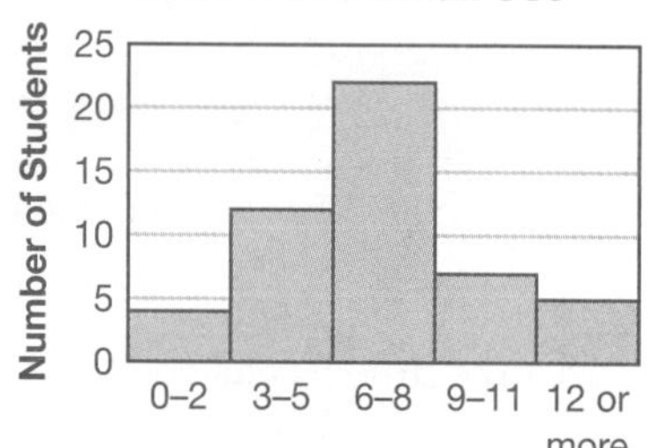

Number of Hours

Internet and Email Use

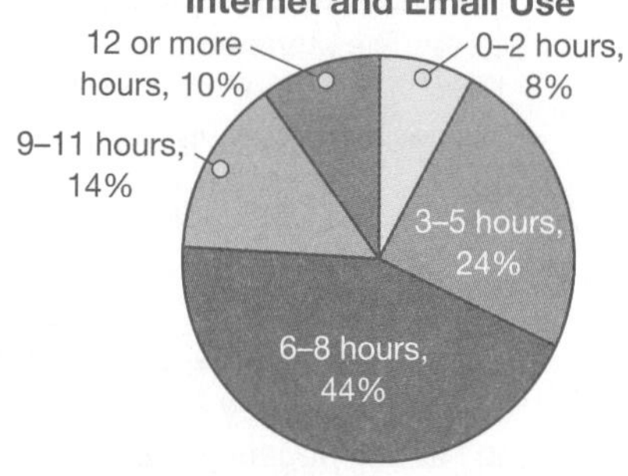

Lesson 72

Practice

19. $\frac{\sin 28^\circ}{x} = \frac{\sin 90^\circ}{15}$
$\sin 90^\circ x = 15 \sin 28^\circ$ and
$x = \frac{15 \sin 28^\circ}{\sin 90^\circ}$
$x \approx 7.042$
$\sin 28^\circ = \frac{\text{opp}}{\text{hyp}}$
$\sin 28^\circ = \frac{x}{15}$
$15 \sin 28^\circ = x$
$7.042 \approx x$

22. Possible answer: Find the distance between $(-4, 0)$ and $(6, 0)$ as 10 by counting or subtracting x-coordinates. Find the length of another side by using the distance formula. Find the angle formed by the x-axis and the segment from a point on the x-axis to $(0, 6)$ by using the y-axis and the inverse sine function. Two side lengths and the included angle are now known. Use the formula. The area is about 30 square units.

26. $3 + 4i$

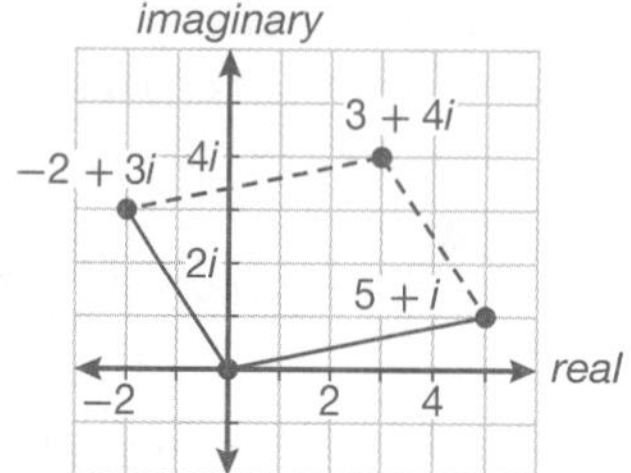

Lesson 73

Practice

3. The trigonometric ratios associated with the inner angles are the same regardless of the lengths of the sides of the triangles. Since the ratios are the same and the angles are congruent, the corresponding sides of the triangles are proportional.

16. Possible answer: The question is confusing because of the double negative. "Should junk food be sold in school vending machines?"

Lesson 75

Lesson Practice

a.

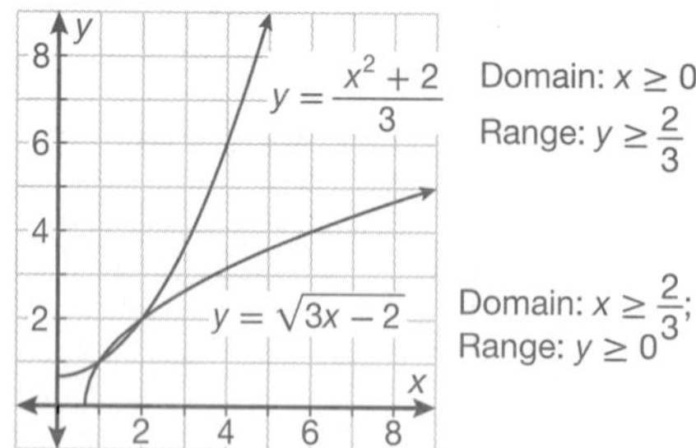

b.

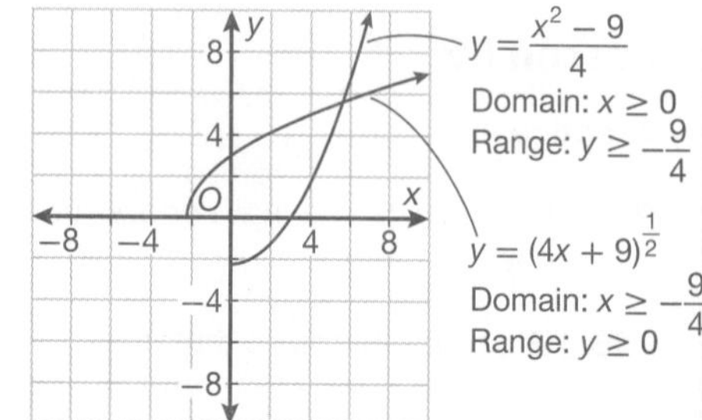

c.

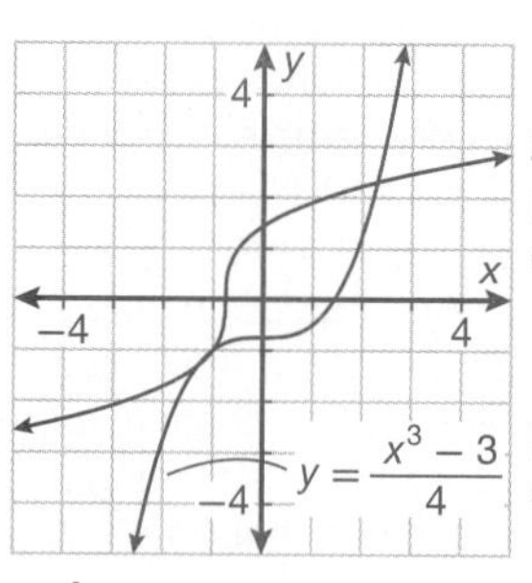

$y = \sqrt[3]{4x + 3}$
Domain and range: all real numbers

Domain and range: all real numbers

d.

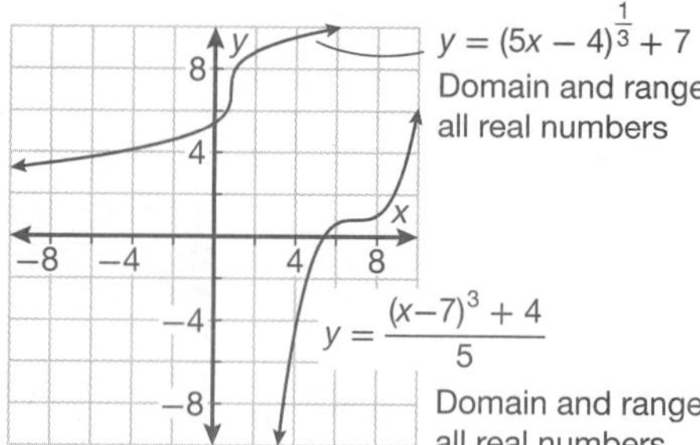

e.

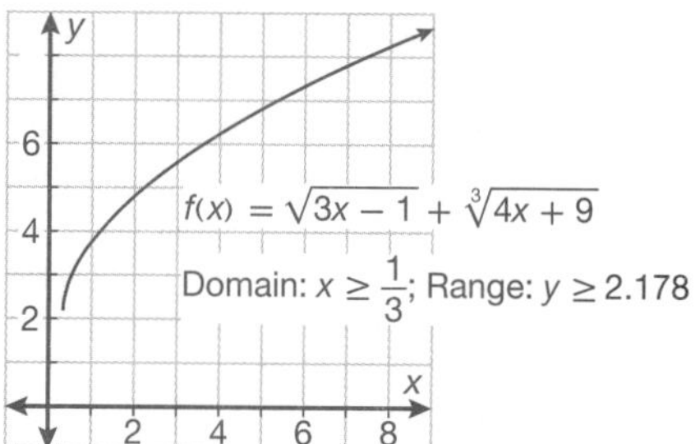

f.

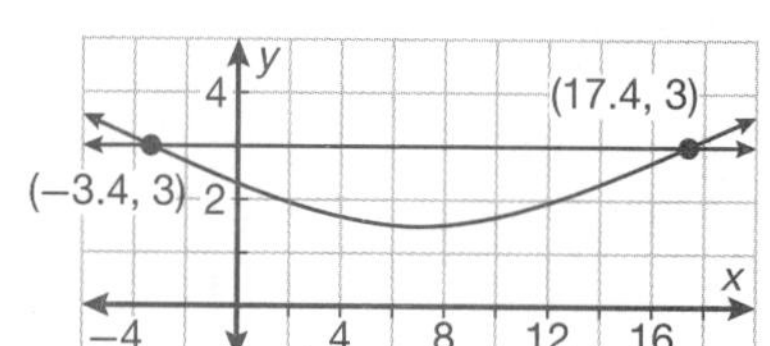

Lesson 76

Practice

10. Sample: There is bias in the sample because the reporter asked sports fans and not everybody in the city (the reported population) is a sports fan. The reporter also asked as the game was letting out and the front gate would be crowded. The question was leading because it only gave a pro of a new stadium and not any possible cons.

20. Sample: $\cos^{-1}(0.48) \approx 61^\circ$; Sample explanation: 0.48 is slightly less than 0.5 and $\cos^{-1}(0.5) = 60^\circ$. $\cos^{-1}(0.48)$ should be slightly greater than $\cos^{-1}(0.5)$ because if two angles terminate in Quadrant I, the smaller angle has the greater x-coordinate and therefore has the greater cosine value.

Lesson 77

Practice

7. Sample: The student is correct. To isolate the cosine of the missing angle measure, the sum of the squares is subtracted from each side. The minus sign which comes from the formula is now the sign of the remaining expression. Because the side lengths are always positive, there is no chance that this expression will ever have a positive sign in front of it. To isolate the cosine of the angle, divide both sides by this negative coefficient.

Lesson 79

Lesson Practice

a.

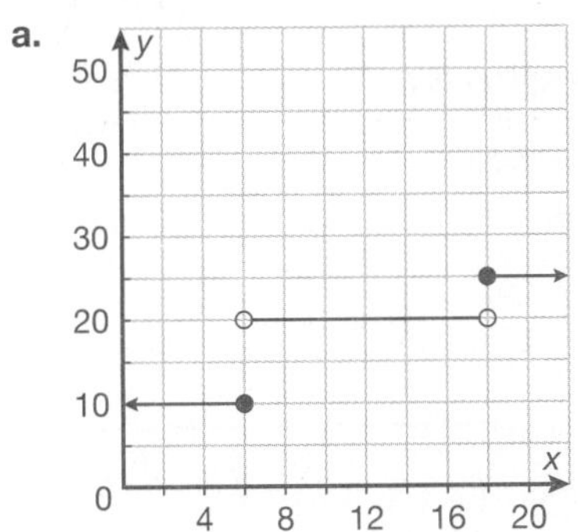

d.

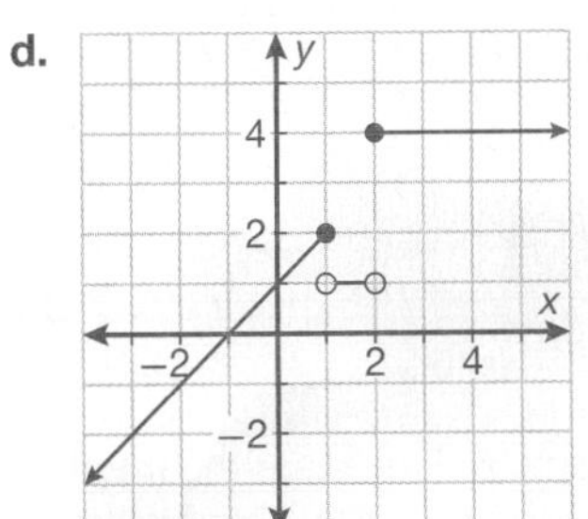

e. $f(x) = \begin{cases} 50x, & \text{if } 0 \leq x \leq 3 \\ 25x + 75, & \text{if } 3 < x \end{cases}$

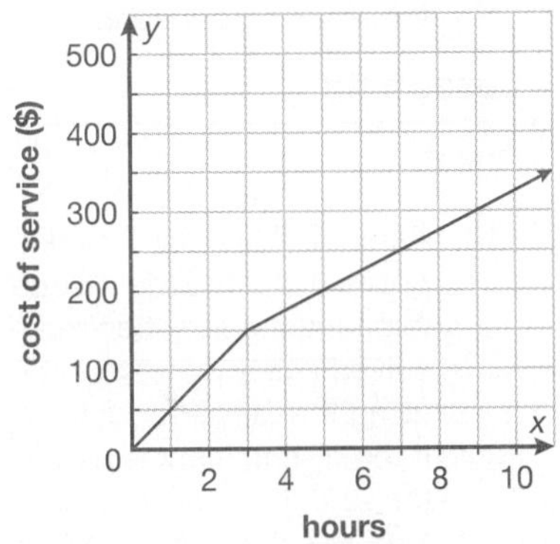

Practice

10a. $(f \cdot g)(x) = 2x^2$; $(g \cdot f)(x) = 4x^2$;

10b. $(f \cdot g)(2) = 8$; $(g \cdot f)(2) = 16$

17. The angle measure must be in radians before using the formula. $A = \frac{1}{2}(6)^2\left(\frac{2\pi}{9}\right) \approx 12.6 \text{ cm}^2$

22. $f(x) = \begin{cases} 25, & x \leq 10 \\ 25 + 5(x - 10), & x > 10 \end{cases}$

27. $\frac{1}{2}bc\sin A = \frac{1}{2}ac\sin B = \frac{1}{2}ab\sin C$

$2(\frac{1}{2}bc\sin A) = 2(\frac{1}{2}ac\sin B)$

$= 2(\frac{1}{2}ab\sin C)$

$\frac{bc\sin A}{abc} = \frac{ac\sin B}{abc} = \frac{ab\sin C}{abc}$

$\frac{\sin A}{a} = \frac{\sin B}{b} = \frac{\sin C}{c}$

Investigation 8

8.

i	x_i	$f(x_i) = 0.5x^3 - x^2 + 2$
5	2.25	≈ 2.63
6	2.75	≈ 4.84
7	3.25	≈ 8.60
8	3.75	≈ 14.30

Lesson 82

Lesson Practice

c.

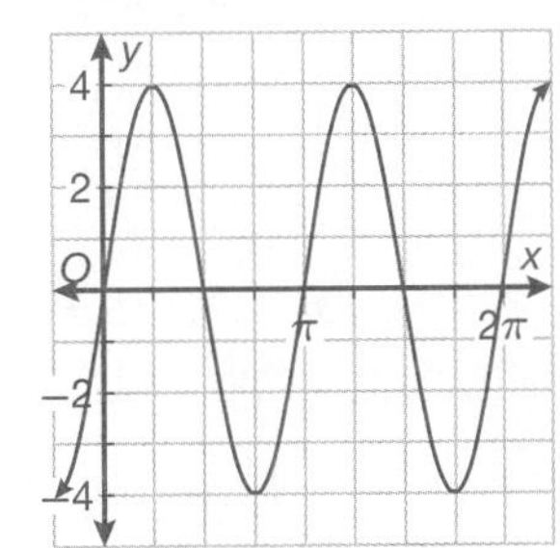

d.

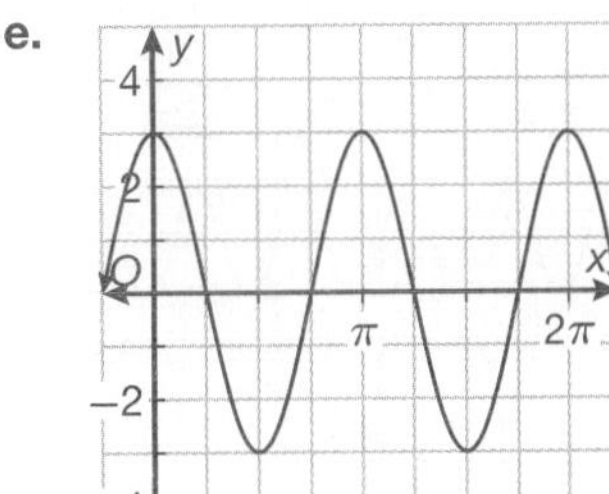

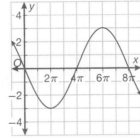

e.

f.

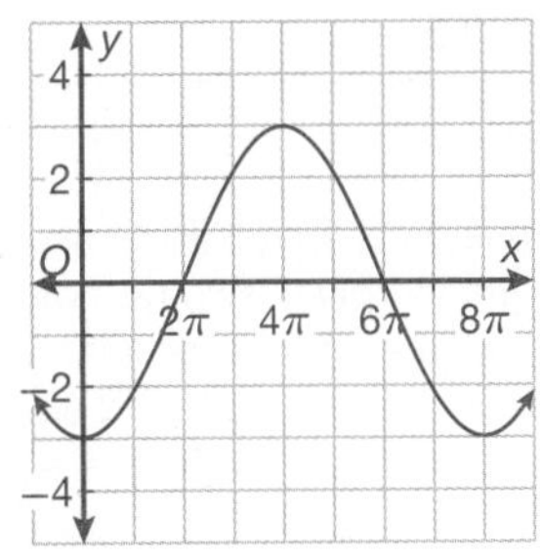

Period: $\frac{2\pi}{6} = \frac{\pi}{3}$

Lesson 83

Practice

7. Method 1

$g(4) = 3(4) = 12$

$f(x) = 2x + 5$

$f(x) = 2(12) + 5$

$(f \circ g)(4) = 29$

Method 2

$f(g(x)) = f(3x)$

$= 2(3x) + 5$

$= 6x + 5$

$(f \circ g)(4) = 6(4) + 5 = 29$

8. The equation $x = \frac{-b}{2a}$ is the axis of symmetry which passes through the vertex of the parabola whose x-coordinate is $\frac{-b}{2a}$. The expression $\pm \frac{\sqrt{b^2 - 4ac}}{2a}$ shows that the zeros are the same distance from the axis of symmetry.

Lesson 84

Practice

28. $f(x) = \begin{cases} 3.5x, \text{ if } x < 12 \\ 3x, \text{ if } 12 \leq x \leq 24. \\ 2.50x, \text{ if } x > 24 \end{cases}$

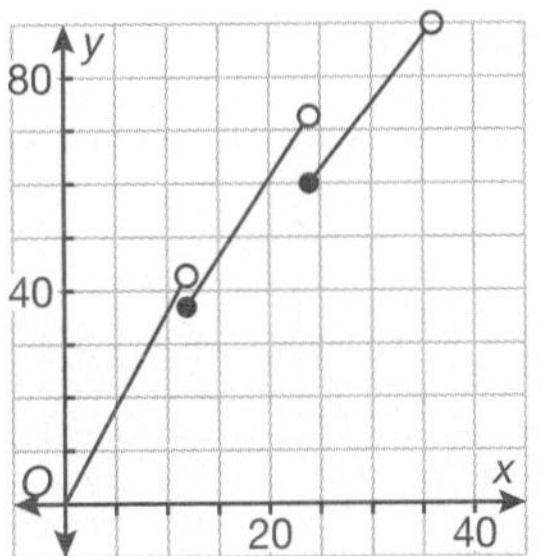

30. It would not clear the second fraction whose denominator is $(x + 5)(x + 5)$. The LCD is $(x + 2)(x + 5)(x + 5)$, so both sides of the equation should be multiplied by that.

ADDITIONAL ANSWERS

Lesson 85

Practice

11. Possible answer: To derive an equation given two complex roots, you write a single equation, isolate the imaginary part, and square both sides. To derive an equation from two real roots, you write two equations and use the converse of the Zero Product Property.

16. Sample: In voluntary response sampling, individuals choose whether or not they want to be part of the sample. Answering questionnaires and online surveys are ways in which people choose to be part of a sample. They do not qualify as probability samples because the probability of an individual being part of the sample is unknown.

23. $f(g(h(x))) = f(g(x^2 - 2))$
$= f((x^2 - 2) - 5)$
$= f(x^2 - 7)$
$= 3(x^2 - 7)$
$= 3x^2 - 21$

Lesson 86

Lesson Practice

a.

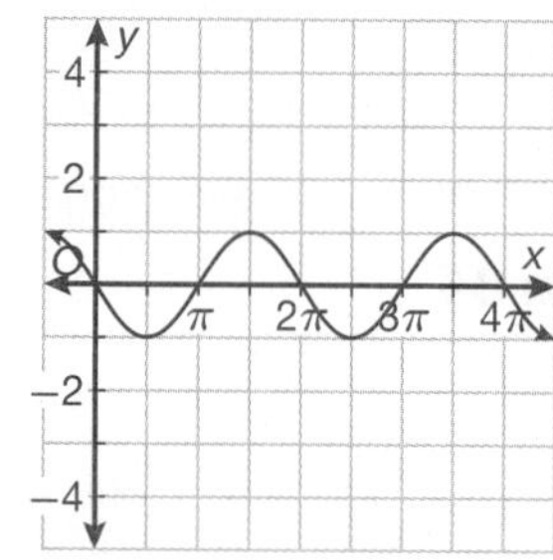

Domain: All real numbers
Range: $-1 \le y \le 1$
Amplitude: 1
Period: 2π

b.

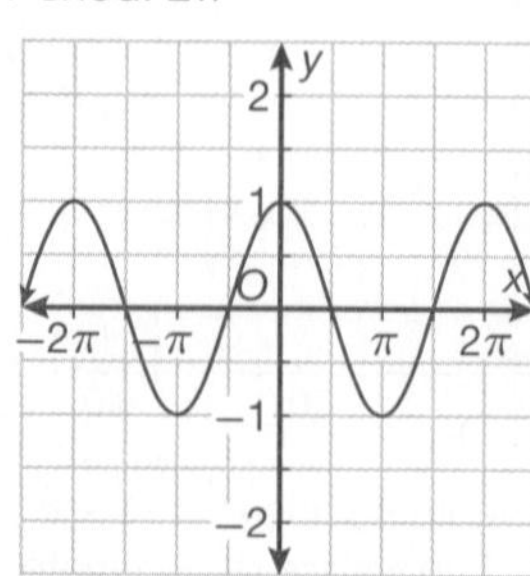

Domain: All real numbers
Range: $-1 \le y \le 1$
Amplitude: 1
Period: 2π

c.

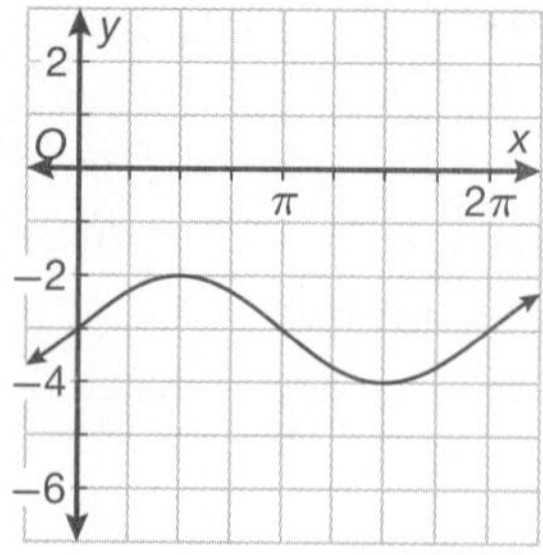

Vertical shift: 3 units down

d.

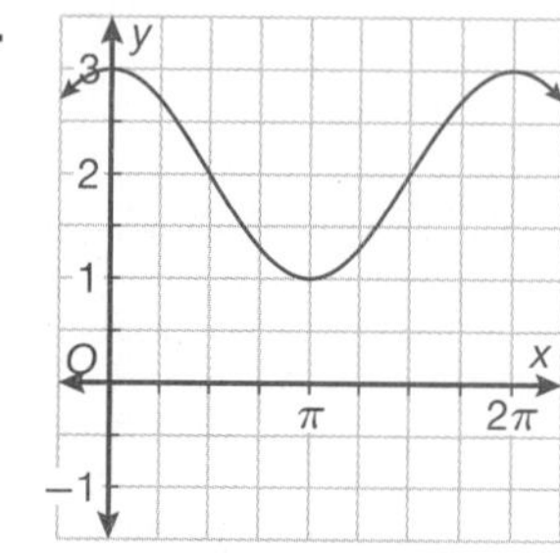

Vertical shift: 2 units up

e.

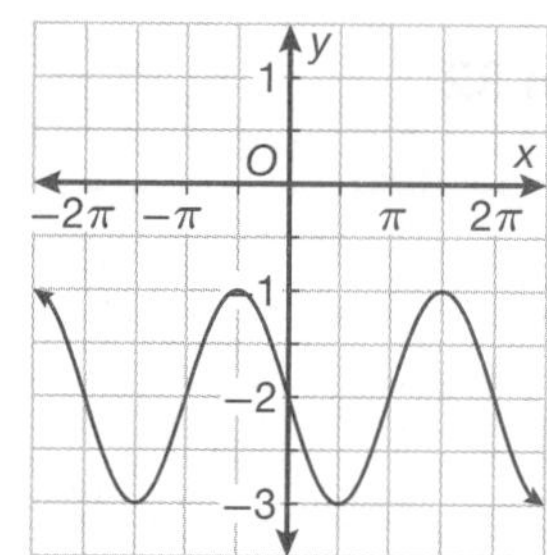

Shifts: right π units and 2 units down

f.

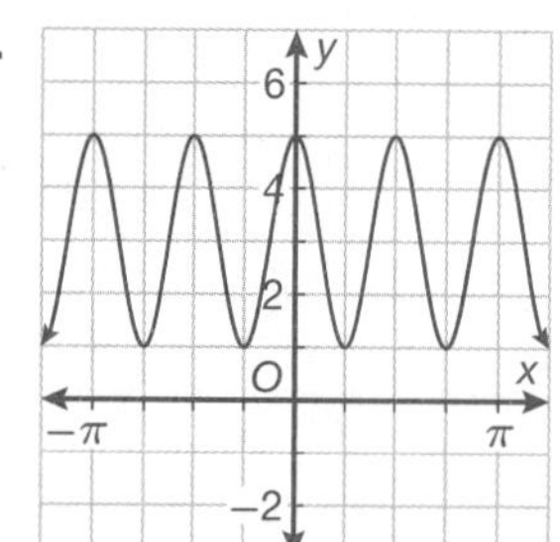

g.

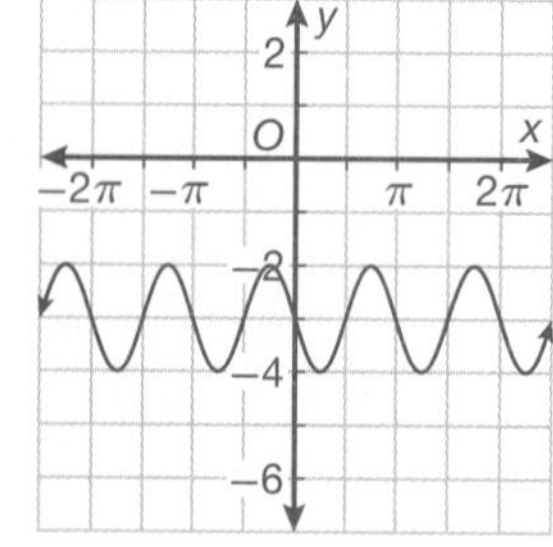

Practice

20c.

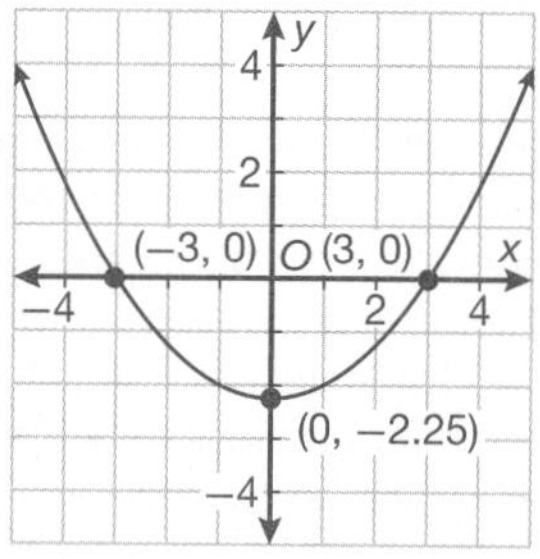

22a. $y = 150(0.95)^x$

22b. $y = \log_{0.95} \frac{x}{150}$

24. $\sin\theta = -\frac{\sqrt{5}}{5}$ $\quad \sec\theta = -\frac{\sqrt{5}}{2}$

$\cos\theta = -\frac{2\sqrt{5}}{5}$ $\quad \csc\theta = -\sqrt{5}$

$\tan\theta = \frac{1}{2}$ $\quad \cot\theta = 2$

Lesson 87

Practice

7.

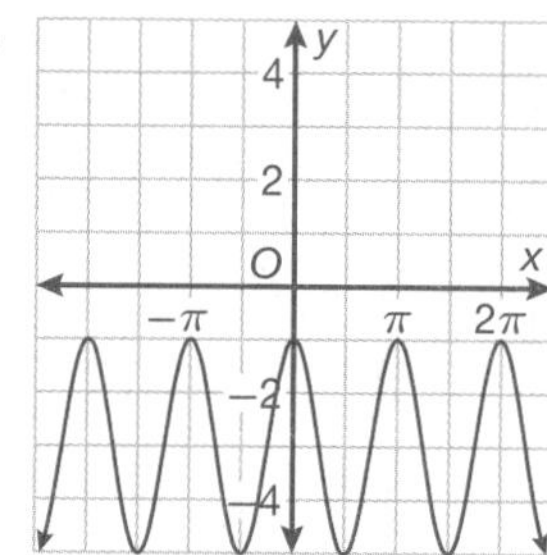

15.
$$f(x) = \begin{cases} 0.41, & x \le 1 \\ 0.58, & 1 < x \le 2 \\ 0.75, & 2 < x \le 3 \\ 0.92, & 3 < x \le 3.5 \end{cases}$$

26. Sample: First clear the fractions by finding the LCD. This may require factoring. Then multiply both sides of the equation by the LCD. This will eliminate the fractions. Solve the resulting equation.

Lesson 88

Practice

12. Sample: If the discriminant is positive and a perfect square, it means the equation may be solved easily by factoring and using the Zero Product Property. If the discriminant is negative, the solutions are complex, so it is best to solve using the Quadratic Formula.

22. −8 and 8; Sample: The positive x-intercept of $f(x) = x^2 - 62$ is between 7 (the positive x-intercept of $f(x) = x^2 - 49$) and 8 (the positive x-intercept of $f(x) = x^2 - 64$). It is closer to 8, so the nearest integer to the positive x-intercept of $f(x) = x^2 - 62$ is 8. By similar reasoning, the nearest integer to the negative x-intercept of $f(x) = x^2 - 62$ is -8.

Lesson 90

Lesson Practice

b. Period: π

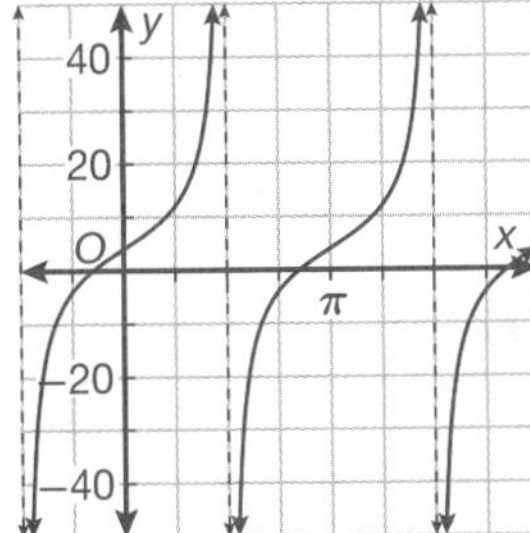

c. Period: $\frac{\pi}{6}$; Asymptotes: $x = \frac{\pi}{12} + n\frac{\pi}{6}$

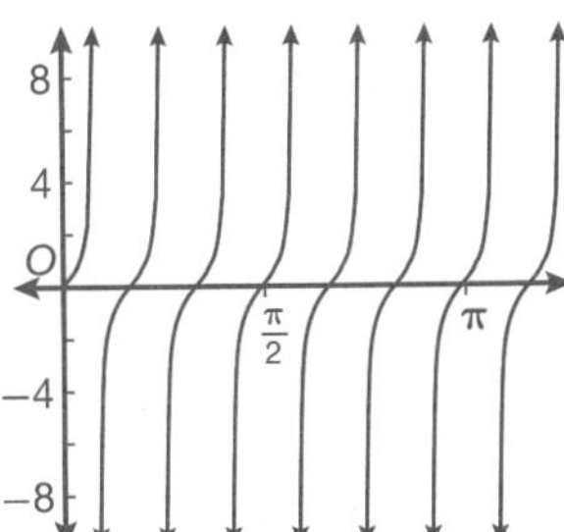

d. Period: 4π; Undefined values: $x = 2\pi + 4n\pi$;

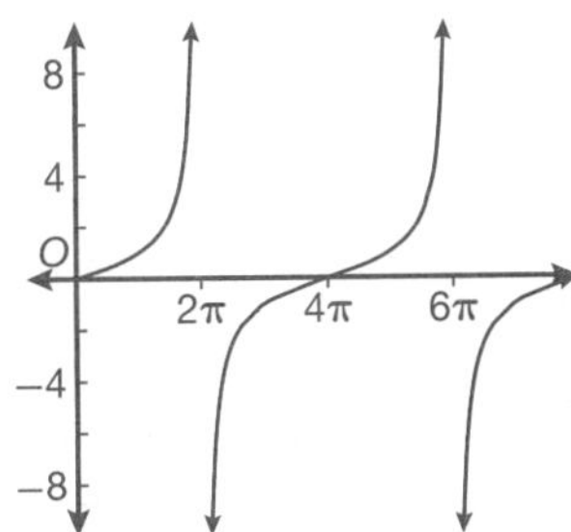

e. Period: $\frac{\pi}{7}$; Undefined values: $x = \frac{\pi}{14} + n\frac{\pi}{7}$;

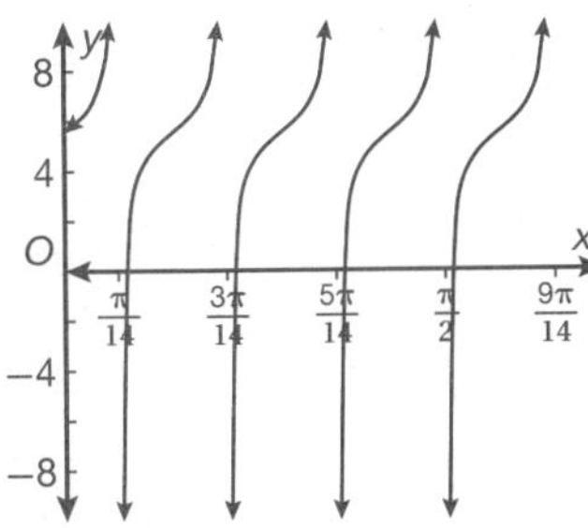

f. Period: π; Undefined values: $x = 5\frac{\pi}{6} + n\frac{\pi}{2}$; Phase shift: $\frac{\pi}{3}$

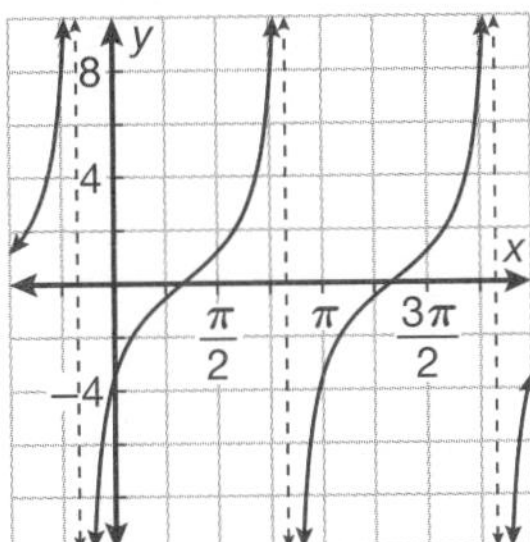

Practice

16. Sample: A logarithm is the exponent that is applied to a specific base to obtain a given value. In the equation $x = e^y$, y is the exponent that is applied to the base e to obtain the value x. Therefore, y is the logarithm of x, using base e. That is, y is the natural logarithm of x.

22. Possible answer: First write the related equation in standard form. Solve the equation to find the critical values. Test a point in each region formed by the critical values. Use the results to write the solution. The solution consists of the regions for which the test point satisfies the original inequality.

Lesson 91

Lesson Practice

a.

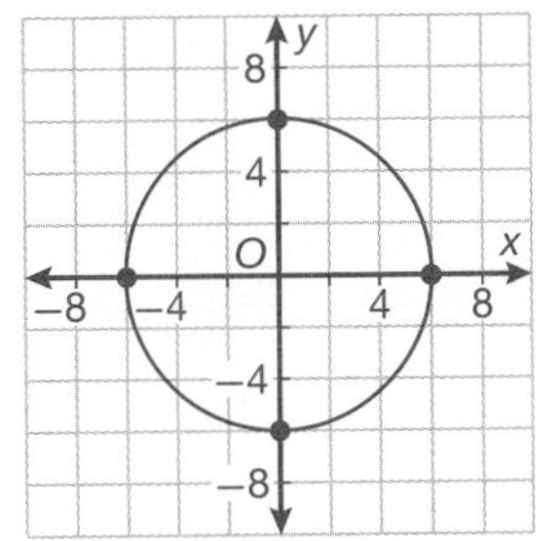

b.

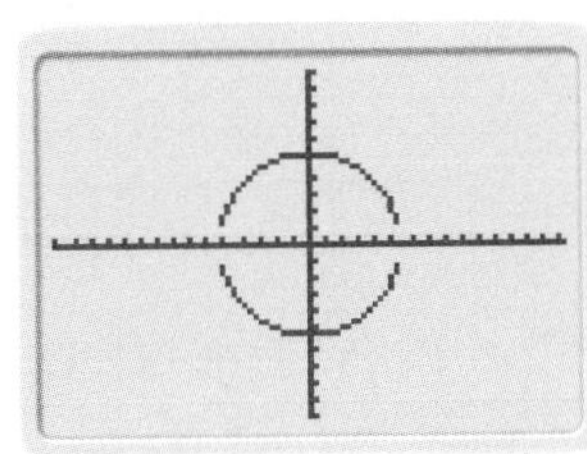

c.

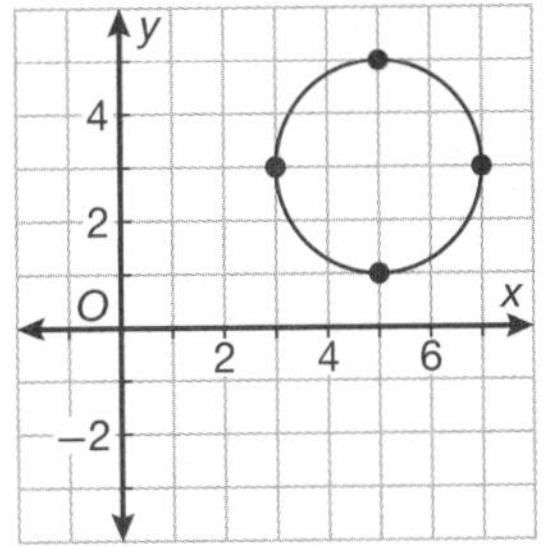

d.

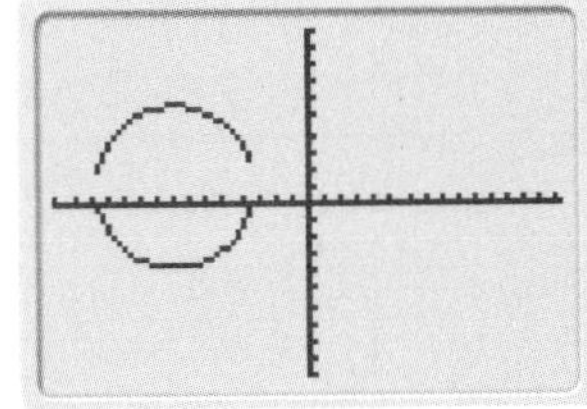

Practice

2. $x^2 + (y - 2)^2 = 9025$; Sample: change the equation to the inequality $x^2 + (y - 2)^2 \leq 9025$ and substitute (94, 6) for x and y: $94^2 + (6 - 2)^2 \overset{?}{\leq} 9025$; $8836 + 16 \overset{?}{\leq} 9025$; $8852 \leq 9025$. Since the inequality is true, the person can pick up the signal.

7d.

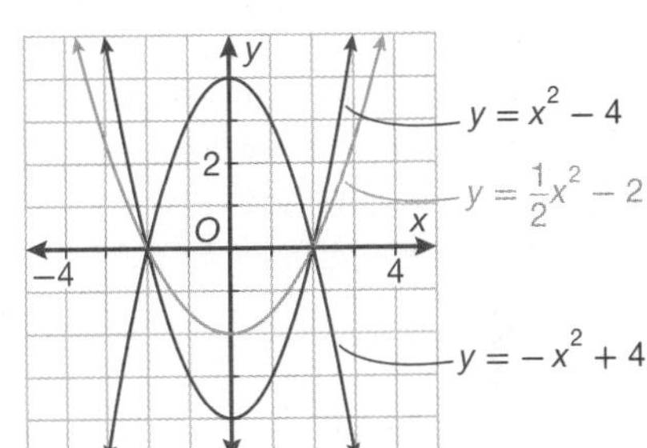

30. $\sin\theta = -\frac{\sqrt{2}}{2}$; $\sec\theta = -\sqrt{2}$; $\cos\theta = -\frac{\sqrt{2}}{2}$; $\csc\theta = -\sqrt{2}$; $\tan\theta = 1$; $\cot\theta = 1$

Lesson 92

Exploration

Step 4.

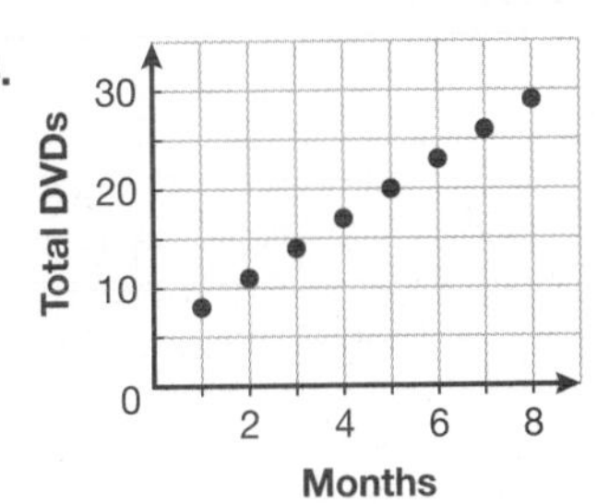

ADDITIONAL ANSWERS

The graph is a discrete function because you cannot have partial DVDs. The domain is the natural numbers.

Practice

13b.

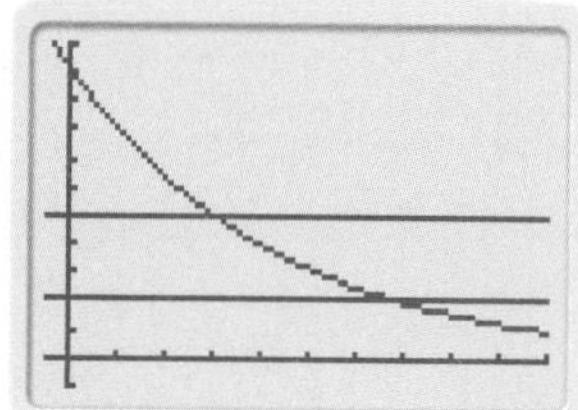

13c. Sample: The graph of y_1 intersects the graph of y_2 at approximately (6, 0.5), representing the fact that 50% of an initial amount remains after approximately 6 hours. The graph of y_1 intersects the graph of y_3 at approximately (13.93, 0.2), representing the fact that 20% of an initial amount remains after approximately 13.93 hours.

Lesson 93

Practice

11. One way is to enter the left side of the expression for Y1, enter the right side of the expression for Y2, and find the point(s) of intersection. The other way is to set the right side equal to 0 by subtracting $(x - 1)$ from both sides, entering the new left side for Y1 and finding the zeros.

17.

$\frac{c}{a}$	a	b	c
		c	$\frac{c}{a}(b + c)$
	a	$b + c$	0

If $(x - \frac{c}{a})$ is a factor:

$\frac{c}{a}(b + c) + c = 0;$

$bc + c^2 + ac = 0; b + c + a = 0$

Lesson 94

Practice

9. The critical values are the boundary points of each interval. These values occur at either a zero or an asymptote, so they occur where either the numerator or denominator is 0. In the given inequality, this happens three times, and three boundary points divide a number line into four intervals.

Lesson 96

Lesson Practice

e.

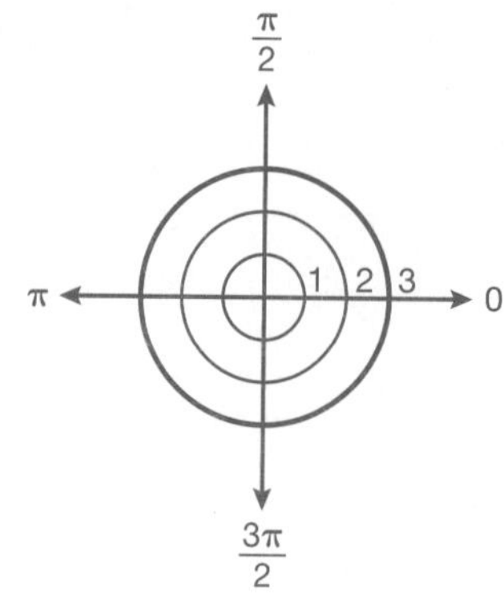

f.

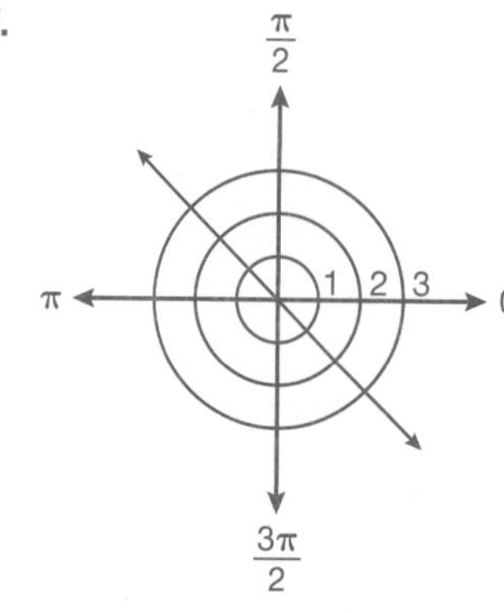

g.

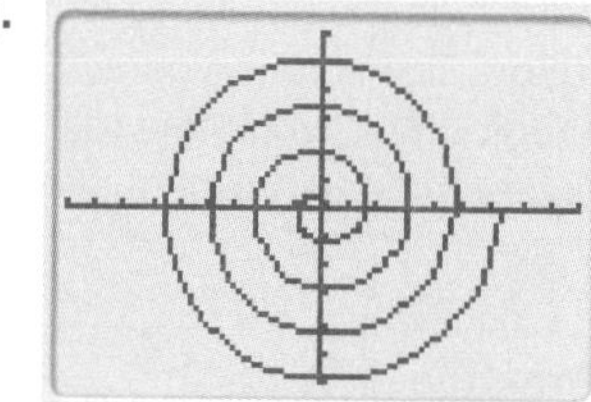

h.

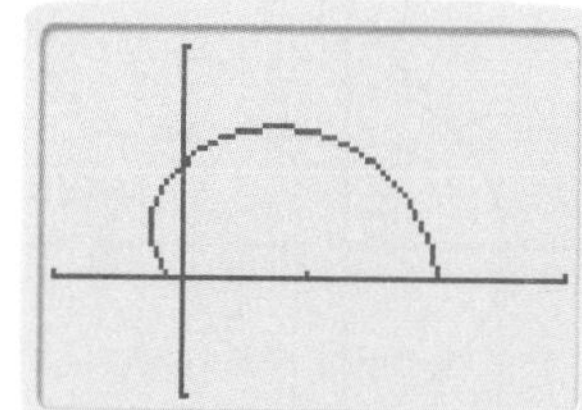

i.

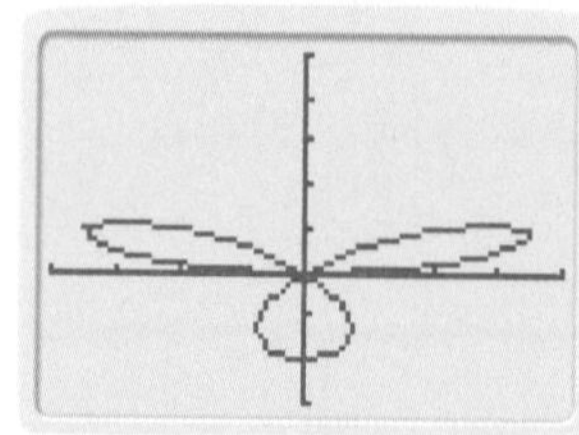

j. $r = 4\sin\theta$

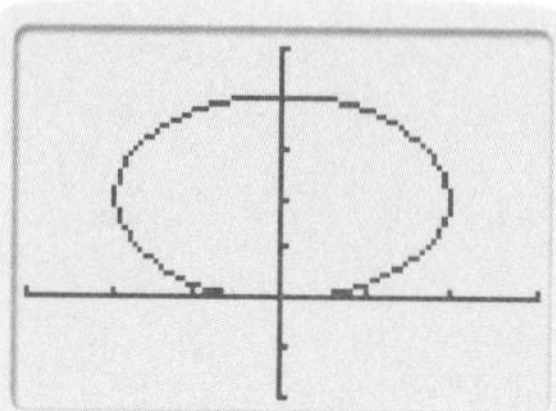

Practice

6. −8 −4 0 4 8

7. $h < -5$ or $h \geq 4$;

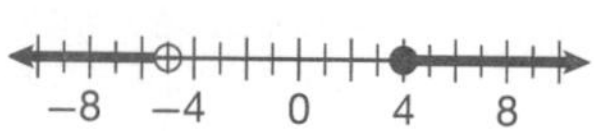

30. $r = -12\cos\theta$

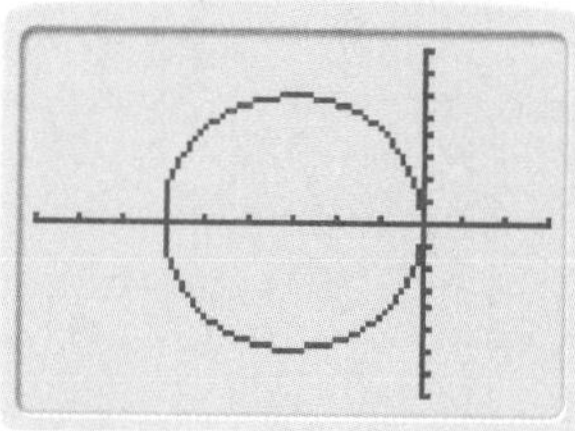

Lesson 97

Practice

15.

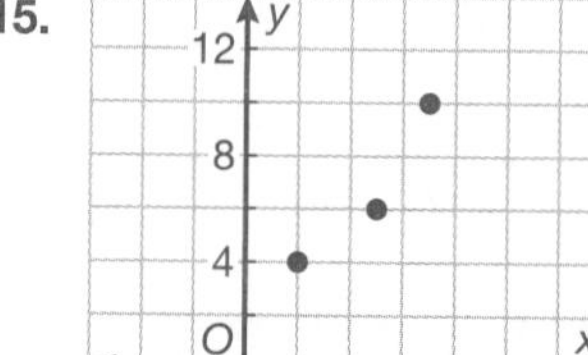

;

discrete, discontinuous function

16.

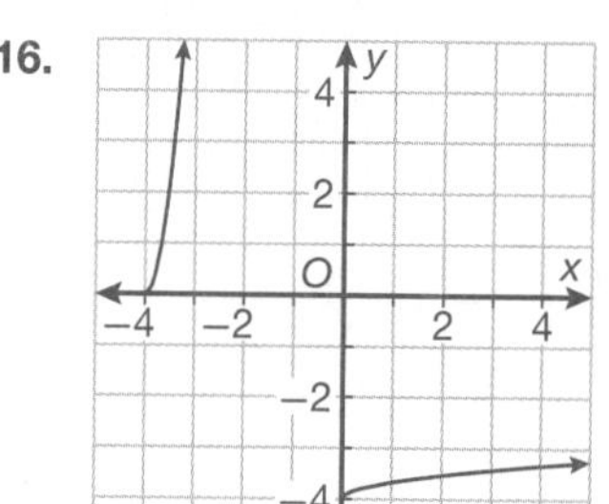

19. If $(x - 1)$ is a factor:

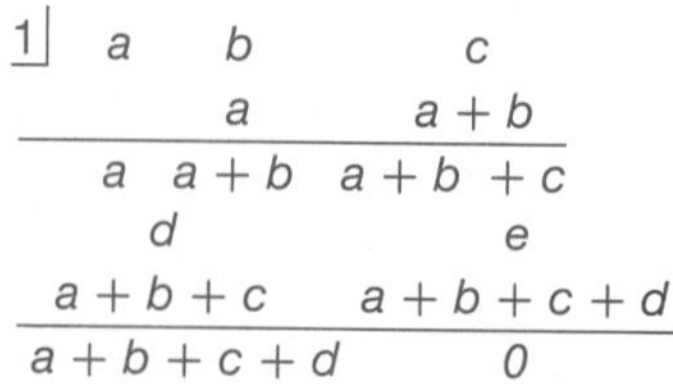

1	a	b	c
		a	$a + b$
	a	$a + b$	$a + b + c$

d	e
$a + b + c$	$a + b + c + d$
$a + b + c + d$	0

Because $(x-1)$ is a factor, synthetic division by 1 will yield a 0 remainder, therefore $a + b + c + d + e = 0$.

Lesson 98

Lesson Practice

b.

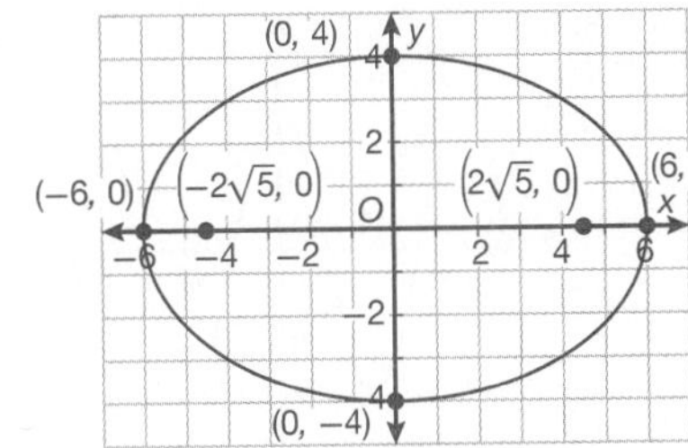

$a = 6$

$b = 4$

$c = 2\sqrt{5}$

$e = \frac{\sqrt{5}}{3}$

c.

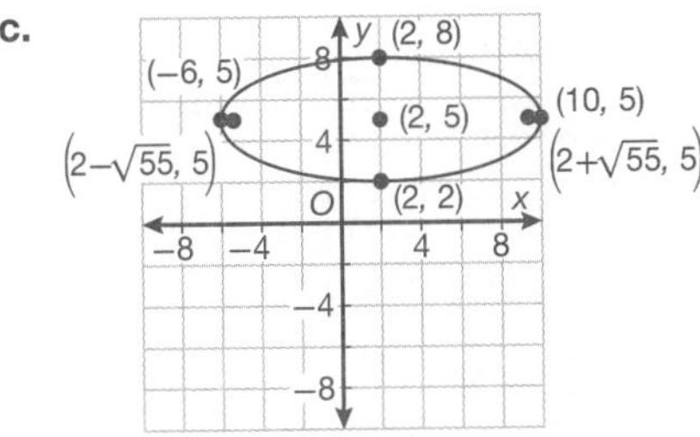

$a = 8$

$b = 3$

$c = \sqrt{55}$

$e = \frac{\sqrt{55}}{8}$

Practice

10. Rewrite the equation in slope-intercept form: $3x + 5y = -35 \rightarrow y = -\frac{3}{5}x - 7$. Pull the slope and y-intercept from the equation: slope $= -\frac{3}{5}$, y-intercept $= (0, -7)$. Plot the y-intercept $= (0, -7)$. Use the numerator of the slope to move up or down and the denominator to move left or right, to plot another point. Start at the intercept and move down 3 and right 5 to plot another point at $(5, -10)$. Draw a line that passes through both of the plotted points, with arrows on both ends of the line.

29. The LCD is the LCM of the denominators, so every denominator can be divided into it. Both sides of the equation are multiplied by the LCD, so every term is multiplied by the LCD. The denominator divides out with all or some of the factors in the LCD. Any remaining terms are multiplied by the numerator. What remains is an equation without fractions.

Lesson 99

Lesson Practice

11.

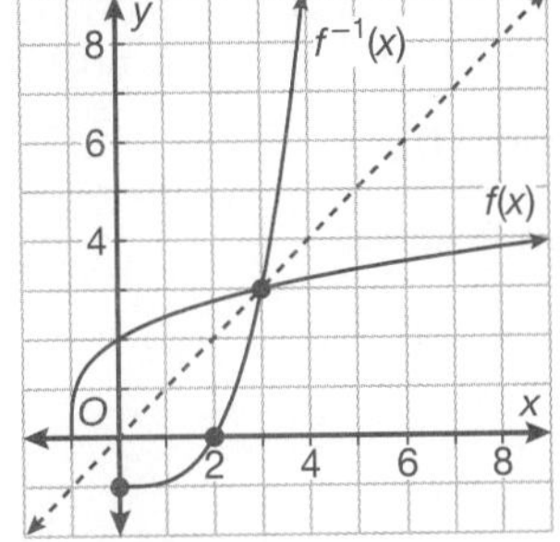

Lesson 100

Lesson Practice

g. Asymptote at $x = 2$;
Hole: none

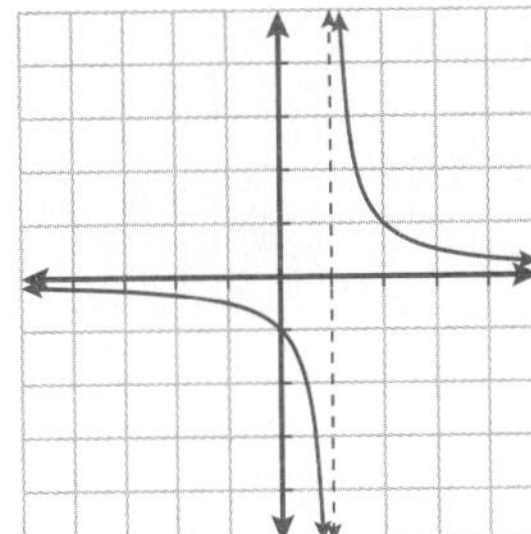

h. Asymptotes: $x = 0$; $x = 1$; $x = -1$; $y = 0$

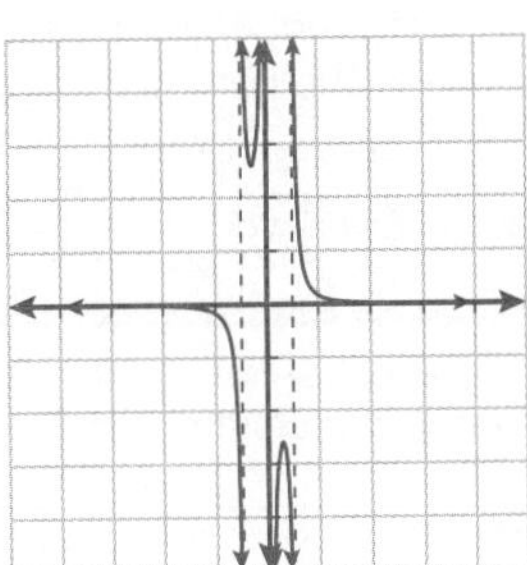

i. Hole: $(-3, 8)$
Vertical asymptote: $x = -2$
Horizontal asymptote: $y = 1$
x-intercept: $(5, 0)$

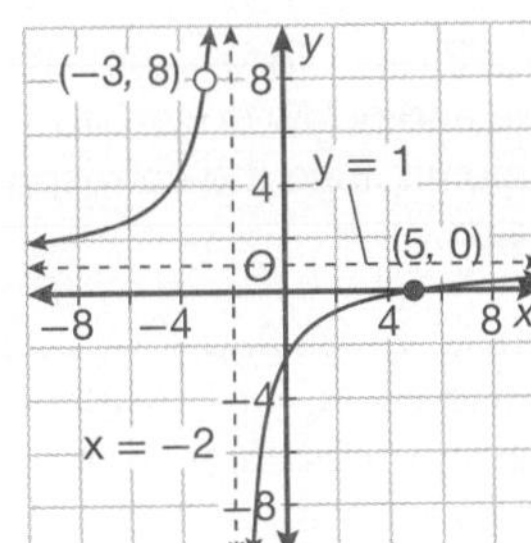

j. Hole: $\left(-3, -\frac{4}{9}\right)$
Vertical asymptotes: $x = 0, x = 3$
Horizontal asymptote: $y = 0$
x-intercept: $(5, 0)$

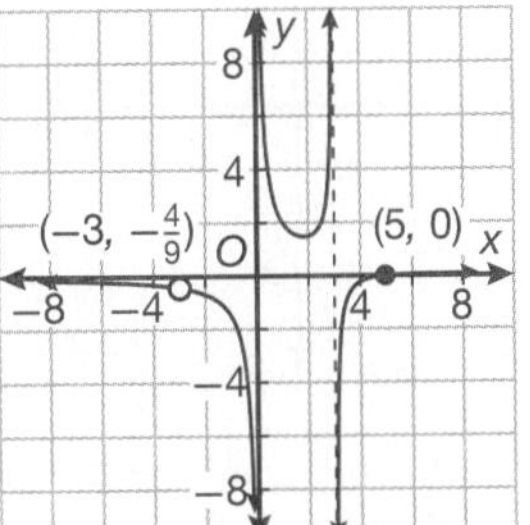

Practice

5. $r = 10\cos\theta - 24\sin\theta$;

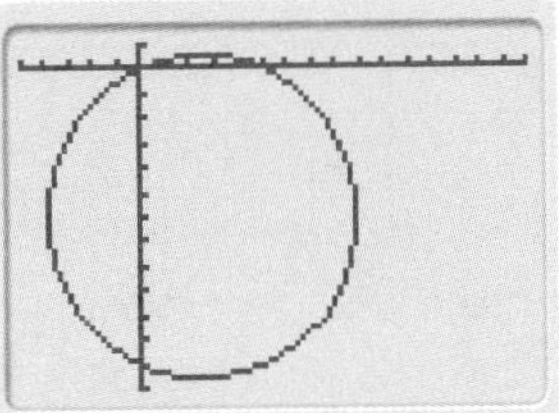

14. $\begin{cases} 38x, \text{ if } x \leq 7 \\ 35(x - 7) + 266, \text{ if } x > 7 \end{cases}$

Investigation 10

18. Sample: $r = \pm\frac{3}{1 + \sin(\theta)}$

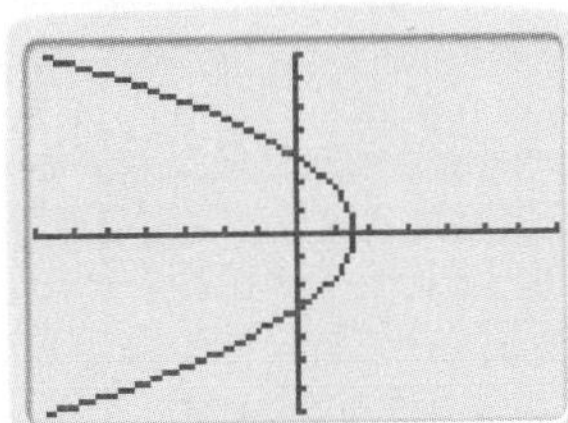

19. Sample: $r = \pm 7$ or $r = 14\sin(\theta)$

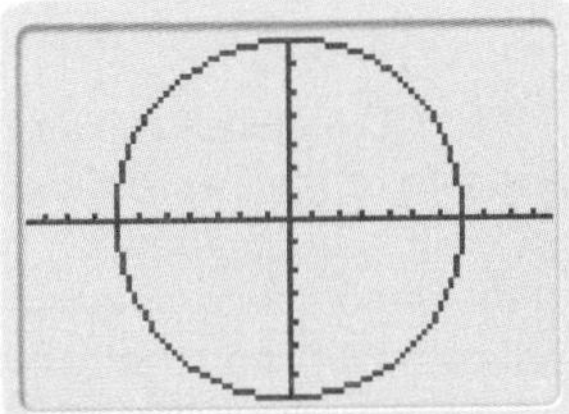

20. Sample: $r = \frac{10}{1 + 5\cos(\theta)}$

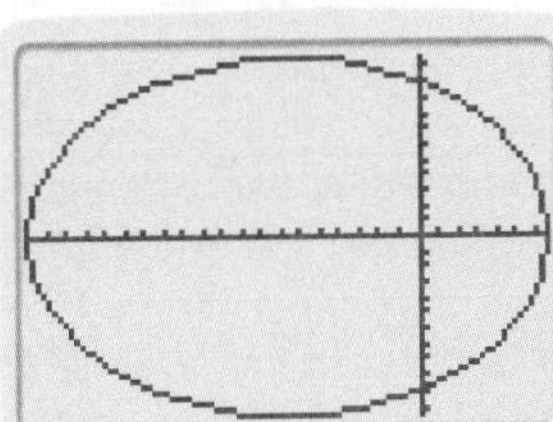

ADDITIONAL ANSWERS

Lesson 101

Lesson Practice

e.

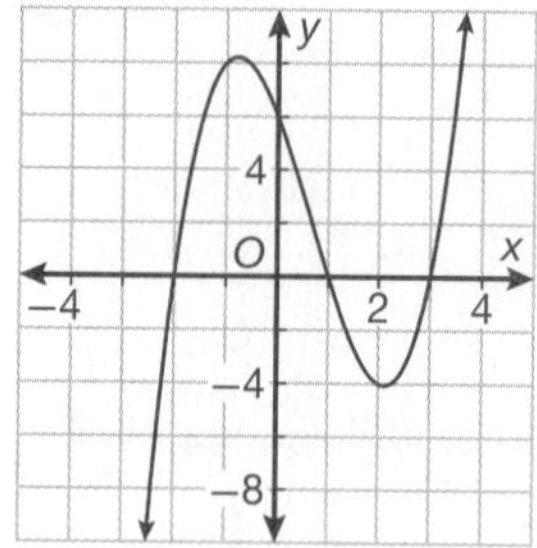

f. local minima: 7.054 and −10.13; local maximum: 9.076;

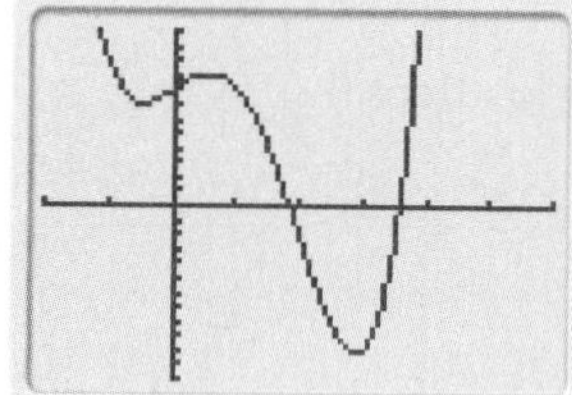

Practice

4. The student did not test the regions and chose the wrong region for the solutions. The test value of 0 gives $-12 > 0$ which is false, so the region between −6 and 2 does not contain the solutions. The test values of −7 and 3, however, lead to true statements, so the solutions are $x < -6$ or $x > 2$.

17a.

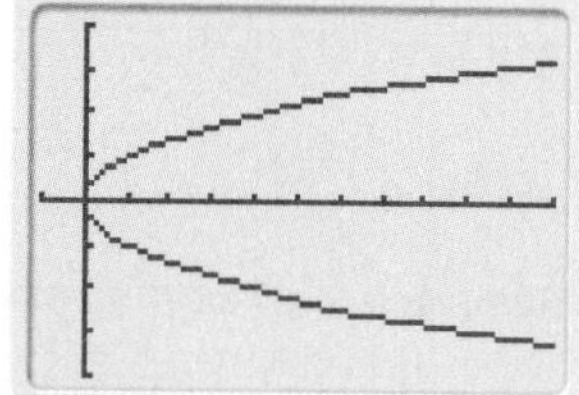

23. If the LCD includes the variable and one of the fractions has the variable in the numerator, but not in the denominator, the variables will be multiplied together when both sides are multiplied by the LCD because the variables will not divide out. For example, $\frac{5}{x} + \frac{x}{3} = 10$; $3x\left(\frac{5}{x}\right) + 3x\left(\frac{x}{3}\right) = 3x(10)$; $15 + x^2 = 30x$

24. Given $\log_b x$, use x as the new log argument in the numerator with the new base a: $\log_a x$. Use the b as the new log argument in the denominator with the new base a: $\log_a b$. This can be used in the same manner with natural log.

30. $k(x) = -5x^3 + x^2 + x$; Its highest-degree term has a negative coefficient, and the coefficient of the highest-degree term of each of the other functions is positive.

Lesson 102

Lesson Practice

e. $x = 150$;

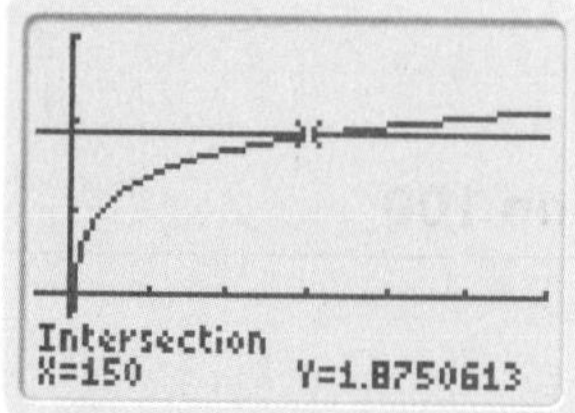

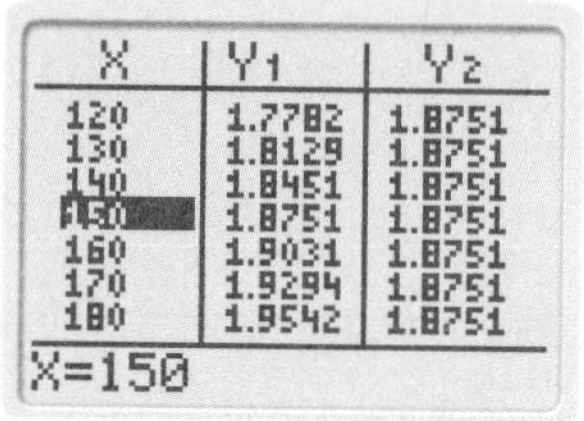

X	Y1	Y2
120	1.7782	1.8751
130	1.8129	1.8751
140	1.8451	1.8751
150	1.8751	1.8751
160	1.9031	1.8751
170	1.9294	1.8751
180	1.9542	1.8751

X=150

Practice

13. $S = 4\pi r^2$; $r = \pm\sqrt{\frac{S}{4\pi}}$; The solution for r when solving the surface area formula for r has two possible solutions, one positive, one negative. The negative solution cannot represent the value of the radius. $V = \frac{4}{3}\pi r^3$; $r = \sqrt[3]{\frac{3V}{4\pi}}$. The solution for r in the volume formula yields only a positive solution, so it is a possible solution for the radius.

14. Sample: To solve $4^x = 100$, you can take the log of both sides, obtaining the equivalent equation $\log 4^x = \log 100$. Then you can apply the Power Property of Logarithms and the fact that $\log 100 = 2$, obtaining the equivalent equation $x \log 4 = 2$.

18a. Enter $9\left(\frac{2}{3}\right)^{x-1}$ for Y1. Access the table and arrow down to 14 in the x-column. Find the corresponding y-value.

18b. Sample: Press 2nd TRACE and choose value. Type in 14 for the x-value. Press enter. The y-value is displayed.

Lesson 103

Warm Up

4.

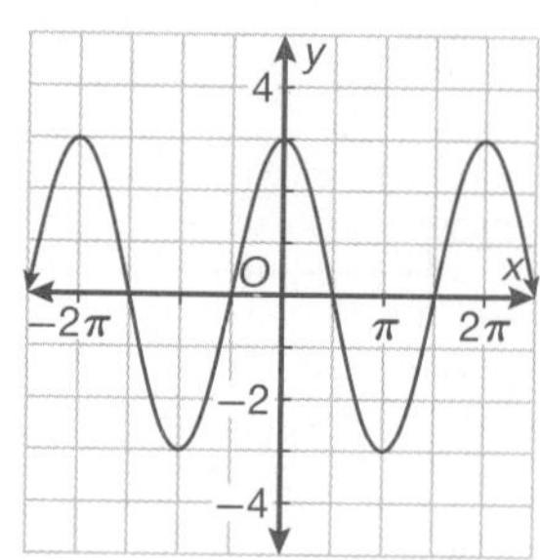

Lesson Practice

a.

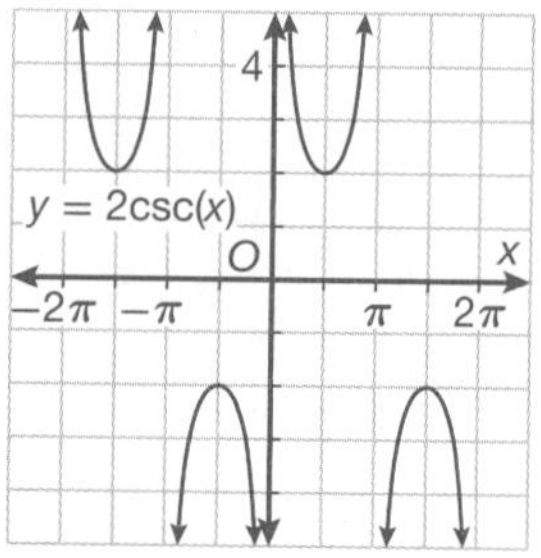

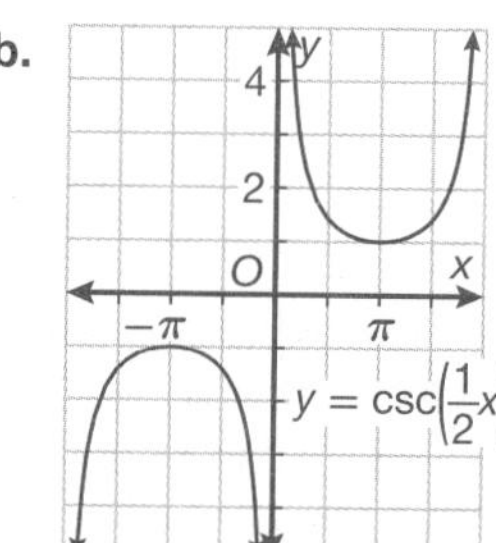

Period: 2π
asymptotes: $x = \pi n$, where n is an integer

b.

Period: 4π
asymptotes: $x = 2\pi n$, where n is an integer

c.

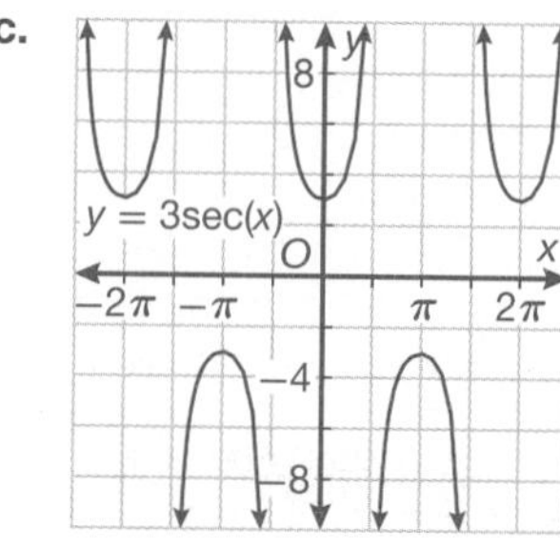

Period: 2π
asymptotes: $x = \frac{\pi}{2} + \pi n$, where n is an integer

d.

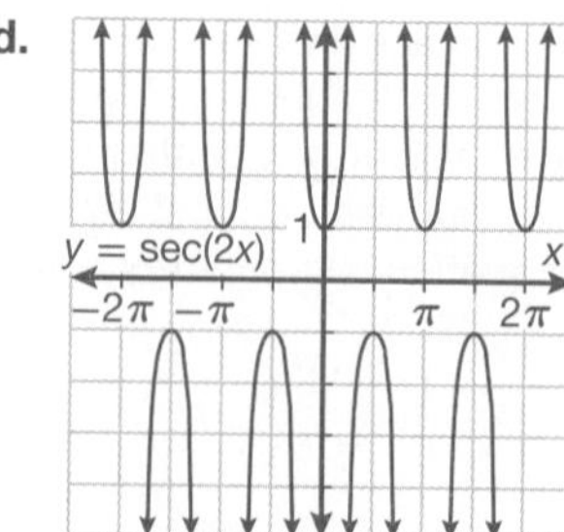

Period: π
asymptotes: $x = \frac{\pi}{4} + \frac{\pi}{2}n$, where n is an integer

e. $y = 4\cot(x)$

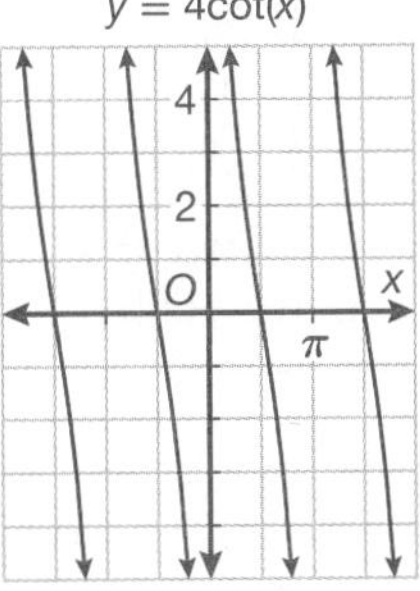

Period: π
asymptotes: $x = \pi n$, where n is an integer

f. $y = \frac{1}{4}\cot(2x)$

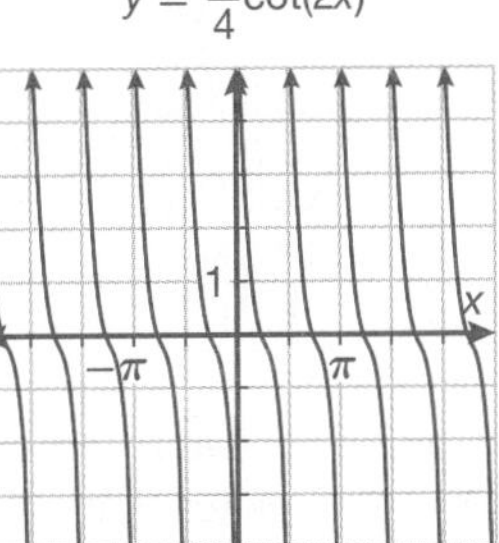

Period: $\frac{\pi}{2}$
asymptotes: $x = \frac{\pi n}{2}$, where n is an integer

g.

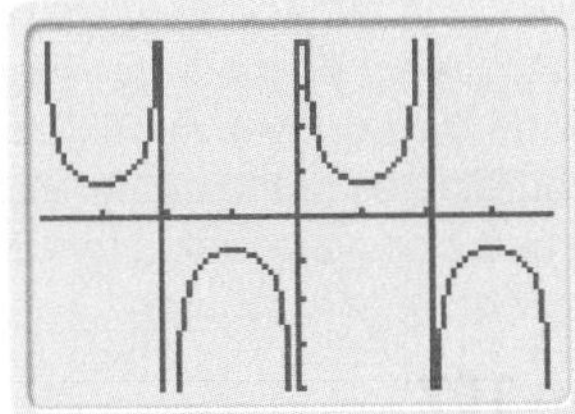

h.

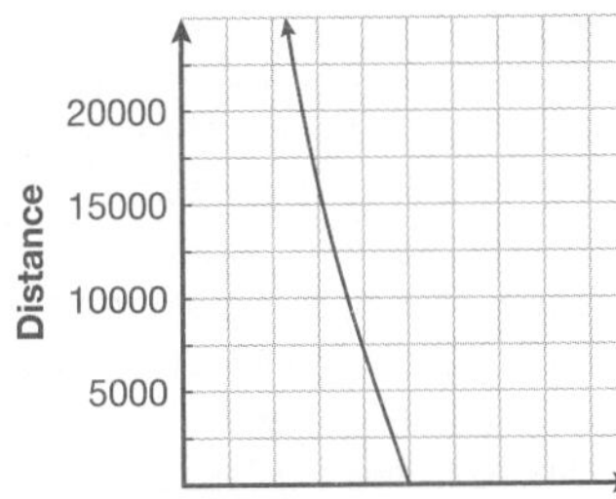

$y = 22{,}000\cot(x)$

Practice

1.

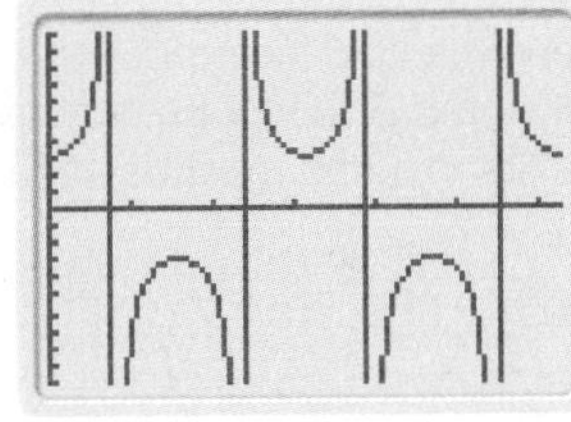

13. Sample: Let $p_1 = x^6 + x^5 + x^4$ and $p_2 = x^3 + x^2 + x$. Then $p_1 + p_2 = x^6 + x^5 + x^4 + x^3 + x^2 + x$.

22a. $N(t) = N_0e^{-kt}$; $0.5 = 1e^{-k(68)}$; $\ln 0.5 = \ln e^{-k(68)}$; $\ln 0.5 = 68k$; $k = \frac{\ln 0.5}{-68} \approx 0.01019$

22b. $N(t) = N_0e^{-0.01019t}$; $7 = 10e^{-0.01019t}$; $0.7 = e^{-0.01019t}$; $\ln 0.7 = \ln e^{-0.01019t}$; $\ln 0.7 = -0.01019t$; $t = \frac{\ln 0.7}{-0.01019} \approx 35$ seconds

23.

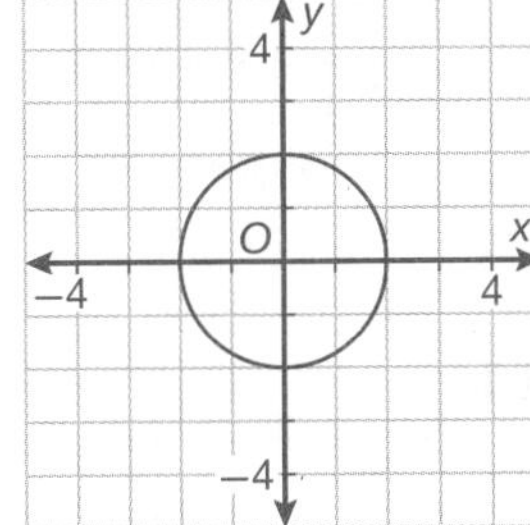

Lesson 104

Lesson Practice

d.

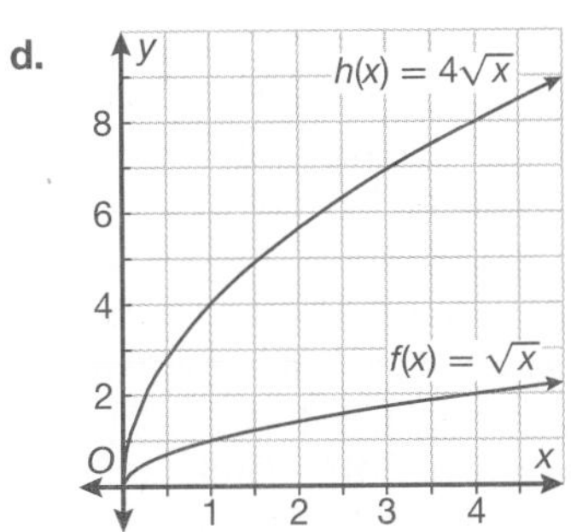

e.

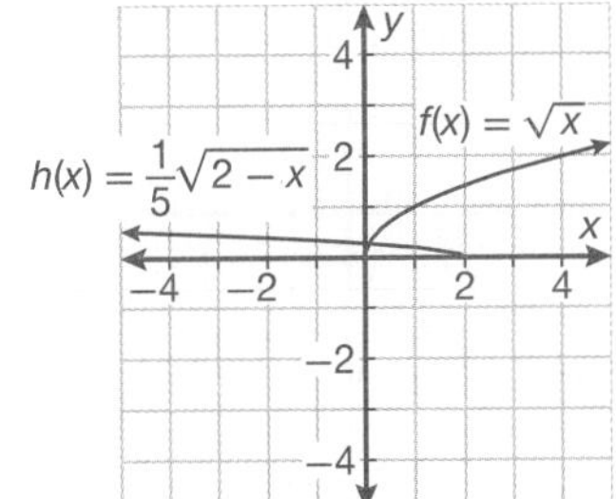

f.

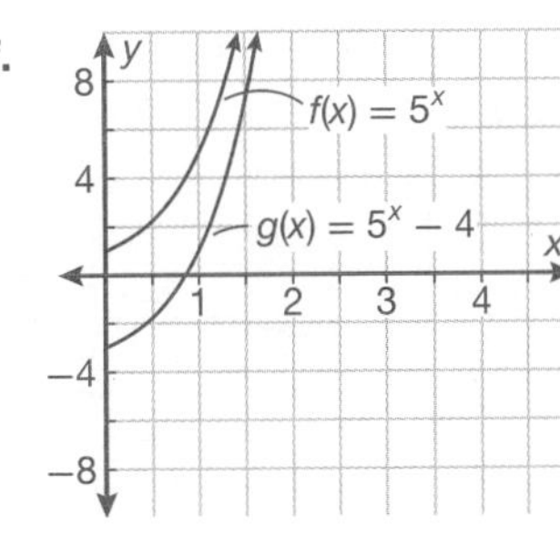

g.

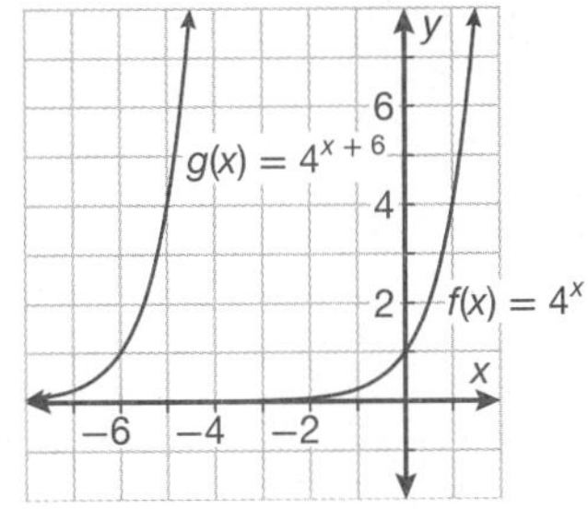

h.

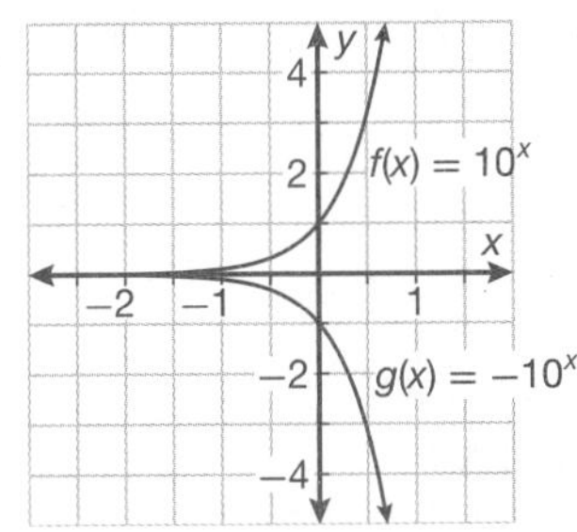

i.

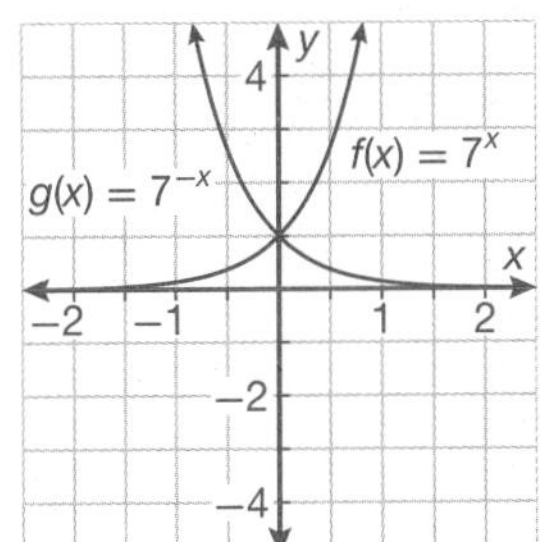

j.

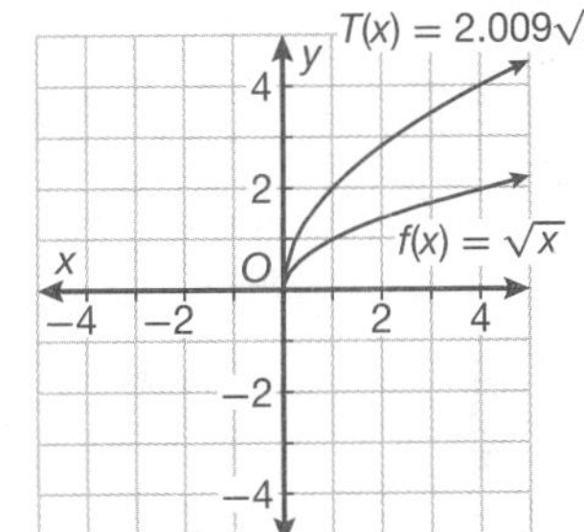

Practice

3. $y = 4\cot\frac{1}{2}x$ has a period of 2π. The asymptotes occur at $x = 2\pi n$, where n is an integer.

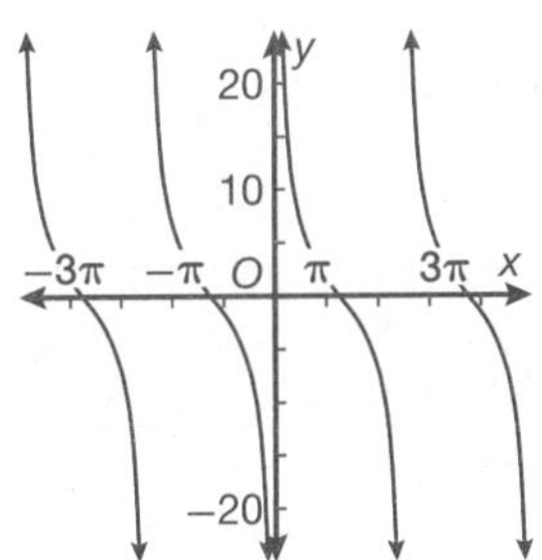

5. Sample: The graph was horizontally shifted to the left instead of the right.

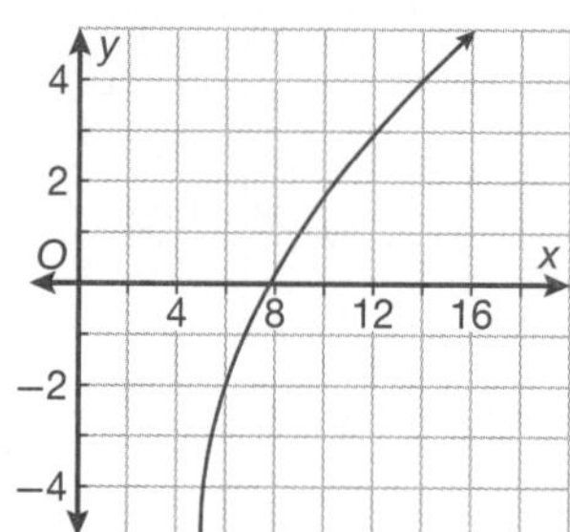

17. $f(x) = \begin{cases} 1.3, \text{ if } 0 < x \leq 1 \\ 1.64, \text{ if } 1 < x \leq 2 \\ 1.98, \text{ if } 2 < x \leq 3 \end{cases}$

Lesson 105

Practice

2. $a_{16} = 48 + (15)(-18) = -222;$

$$S_{16} = 16\left(\frac{48 + (-222)}{2}\right) = -1392$$

4.

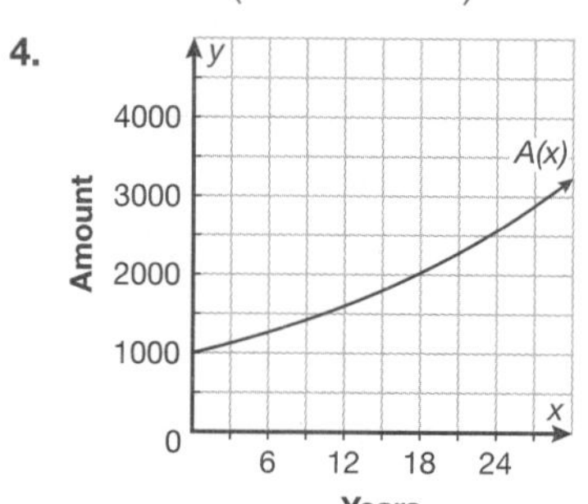

8.

10. $\begin{bmatrix} 1 & 3 & 3 \\ 2 & 1 & 4 \\ 2 & 2 & 5 \end{bmatrix} \cdot \begin{bmatrix} 1.00 \\ 3.50 \\ 1.50 \end{bmatrix}$

$$= \begin{bmatrix} 1 \cdot 1.00 + 3 \cdot 3.50 + 3 \cdot 1.50 \\ 2 \cdot 1.00 + 1 \cdot 3.50 + 4 \cdot 1.50 \\ 2 \cdot 1.00 + 2 \cdot 3.50 + 5 \cdot 1.50 \end{bmatrix}$$

$$= \begin{bmatrix} 16.00 \\ 11.50 \\ 16.50 \end{bmatrix} \quad \text{Avery}$$

15. The student did not multiply both terms on the left by the LCD.

$$6(x + 2)\left(\frac{2}{3(x + 2)}\right) + 6(x + 2)(4)$$

$$= 6(x + 2)\left(\frac{1}{2}\right)$$

$$4 + 24x + 48 = 3x + 6$$

$$52 + 24x = 3x + 6$$

$$21x = -46$$

$$x = -\frac{46}{21}$$

22. Sample: To solve $2(3)^x < 310$, you can take the log of both sides, obtaining the equivalent inequality $\log(2(3)^x) < \log 310$. Then you can apply the Product Property of Logarithms, obtaining the equivalent inequality $\log 2 + \log 3^x < \log 310$. Then you can apply the Power Property of Logarithms, obtaining the equivalent inequality $\log 2 + x \log 3 < \log 310$.

23. $4 < 3x + 1 \quad 3x + 1 \leq 10$
$3 < 3x \qquad 3x \leq 9$
$1 < x \qquad x \leq 3$

Lesson 106

Practice

3. Sample: Both can be solved by finding critical values and using test points to determine which intervals created by the critical values contain the solutions of the inequality. In a quadratic inequality, the greatest number of critical values is two and the greatest number of intervals is three. A rational inequality can have more than two critical values and three intervals.

7.

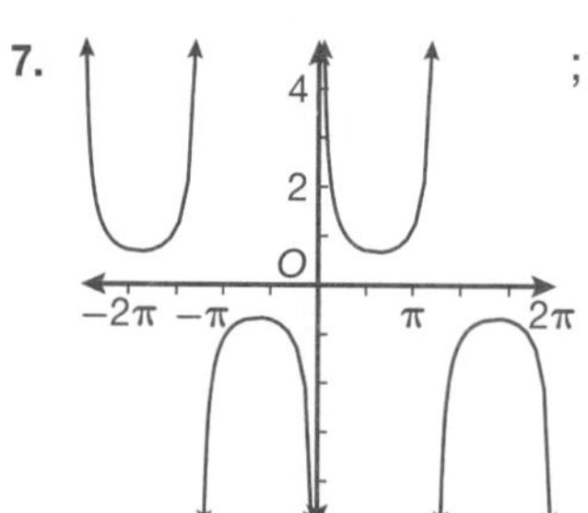

;

Period: 2π. The asymptotes occur at $x = \pi n$, where n is an integer.

9.

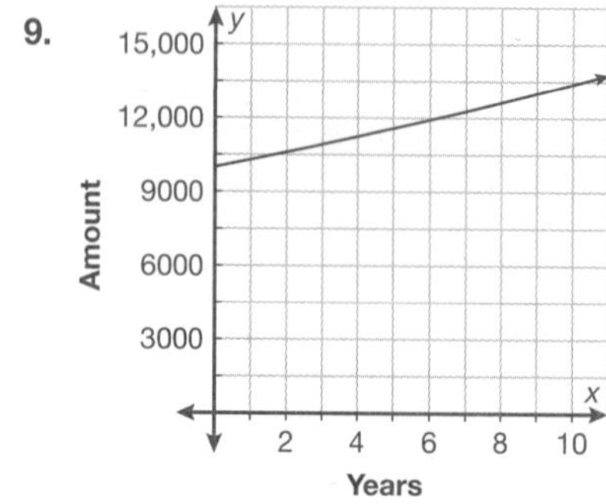

17. $\frac{x^2 - 9}{x^2 + 8x + 7}$ Vertical asymptotes at $x = -7$ and at $x = -1$

18. ;

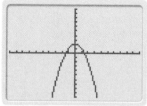

The vertex is shifted up 2 units and opens down. Both have the same axis of symmetry.

27d. The graph intersects the x-axis at 0, so it has a real root of degree 1 at (0, 0). There are no other x-intercepts, so the remaining two roots are not real.

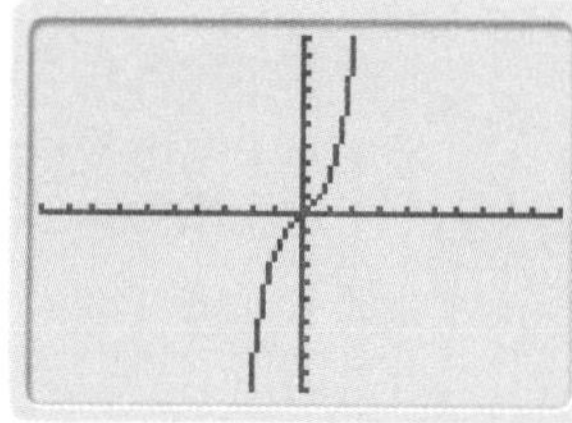

28. The midpoint of a diameter of a circle is the center of the circle, so first find the midpoint of a segment with those endpoints. The radius is the distance from this center point to any point on the circle, so use the distance formula to find the distance between the center point and either of the two points that are endpoints of the diameter. Write the equation substituting the coordinates of the center point for h and k and the radius for r in $(x - h)^2 + (y - k)^2 = r^2$.

Lesson 107

Practice

18. One way is to find the sign of the value of the numerator and denominator for a test point in each interval. If the signs are the same, the expression is positive in that interval, and if the signs are different, the expression is negative in that interval. Another way is to find the value of each factor in each interval and then determine the sign of the rational expression based on those signs. This method only works if the polynomials are, or can be, factored. If the polynomials cannot be factored, the first method must be used.

22.

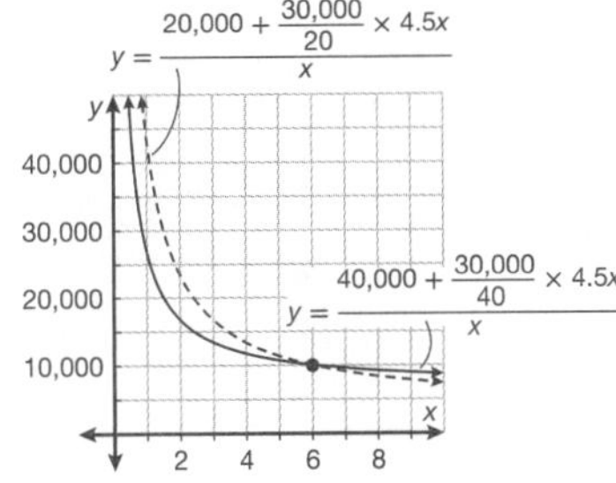

The 40 mpg car becomes a better deal after roughly 6 years.

24. 0.125;

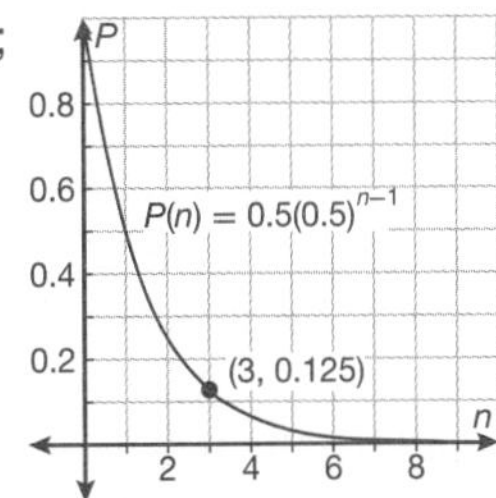

Lesson 108

Lesson Practice

c. $1 + \tan^2(98.5°) \approx 1 + 44.77157 = 45.77157$, $\sec^2(98.5°) = \frac{1}{\cos^2(98.5°)} \approx 45.77157$

d. $1 + \tan^2\left(\frac{5\pi}{4}\right) = 1 + (1)^2 = 2$, $\sec^2\left(\frac{5\pi}{4}\right) = (-\sqrt{2})^2 = 2$

e. $1 + \cot^2(212°) \approx 1 + 2.561 = 3.561$, $\csc^2(212°) \approx 3.561$

f. $\cot^2(\frac{\pi}{6}) + 1 = (\sqrt{3})^2 + 1 = 4$, $\csc^2(\frac{\pi}{6}) = (2)^2 = 4$

g.

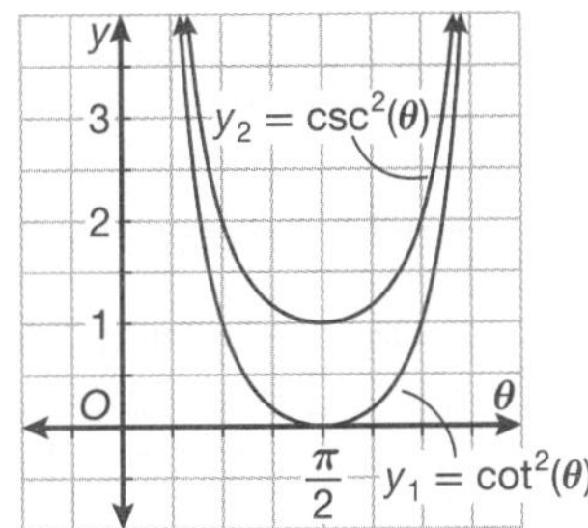

Practice

7. $\frac{1}{1 - \frac{1}{1 + \tan^2(\theta)}}$

$= \frac{1}{1 - \frac{1}{1 + \frac{y^2}{x^2}}} = \frac{1}{1 - \frac{1}{\frac{x^2 + y^2}{x^2}}} = \frac{1}{1 - \frac{x^2}{x^2 + y^2}}$

$= \frac{1}{\frac{x^2 + y^2 - x^2}{x^2 + y^2}}$

$= \frac{x^2 + y^2}{y^2} = \frac{r^2}{y^2} = \csc^2(\theta)$

Lesson 109

Lesson Practice

a. Horizontal orientation; $a = 6$; $b = 4$; $c \approx 7.211$; $e \approx 1.2019$; Asymptotes: $y = \pm\frac{2}{3}x$

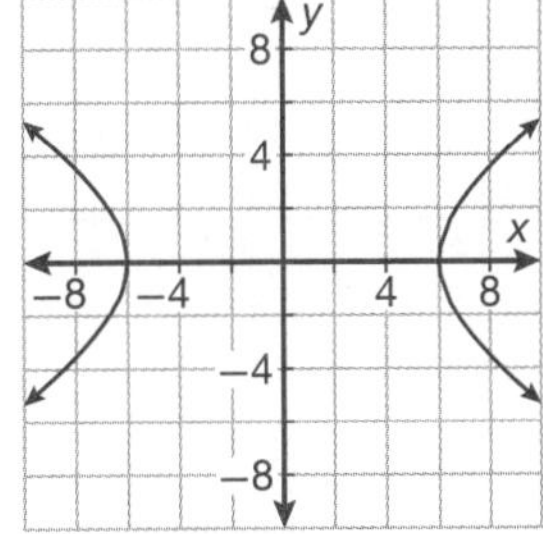

b. Vertical orientation; $a = 7$; $b = 5$; $c \approx 8.6023$; $e \approx 1.2289$; Asymptotes: $y = \pm\frac{7}{5}x$

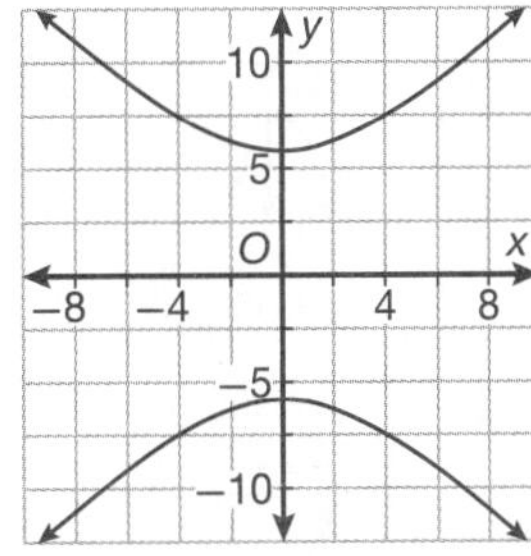

c. Horizontal orientation; $a = 7$; $b = 5$; $c \approx 8.6023$; $e \approx 1.2289$; Asymptotes: $y = \frac{5}{7}x + \frac{3}{7}$ and $y = -\frac{5}{7}x + \frac{53}{7}$

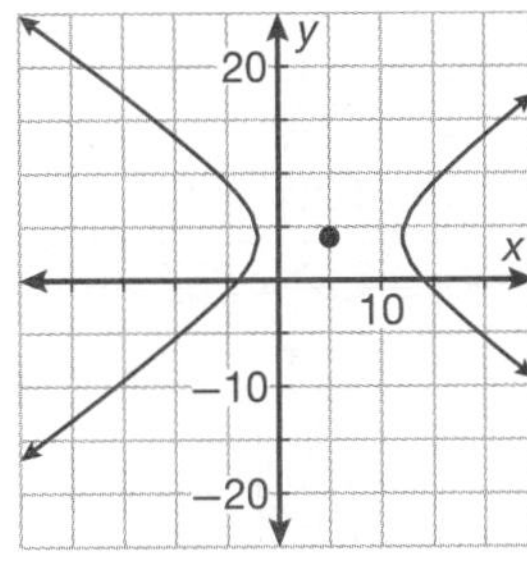

d. Vertical orientation; $a = 9$; $b = 6$; $c \approx 10.8167$; $e \approx 1.2019$; Asymptotes: $y = \frac{3}{2}x + \frac{1}{2}$ and $y = -\frac{3}{2}x + \frac{31}{2}$

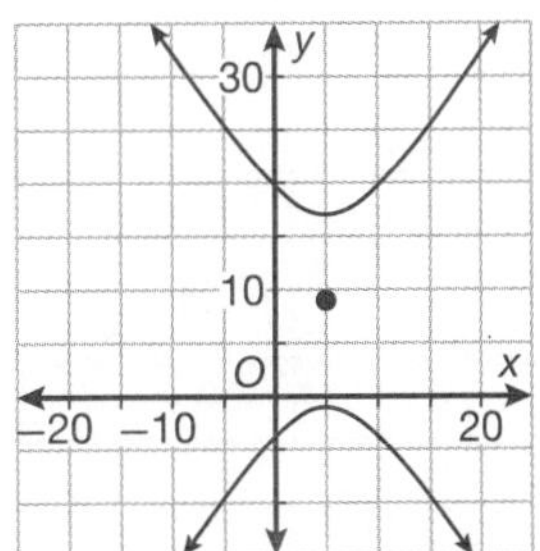

e. $\frac{(x-4)^2}{6^2} - \frac{(y-3)^2}{4^2} = 1$

Practice

18. Possible answer: The student's expression for P contains P. When an equation is solved for a variable correctly, the expression for the variable cannot contain that variable. Correct solution:

$A = P + Prt$

$A = P(1 + rt)$

$\frac{A}{1 + rt} = P$

23c. $1{,}267{,}000{,}000(1.0104)^t = 1{,}005{,}000{,}000(1.0183)^t$

$\log(1{,}267{,}000{,}000(1.0104)^t) = \log(1{,}005{,}000{,}000(1.0183)^t)$

$\log 1{,}267{,}000{,}000 + \log(1.0104)^t = \log 1{,}005{,}000{,}000 + \log(1.0183)^t$

$\log 1{,}267{,}000{,}000 + t\log 1.0104 = \log 1{,}005{,}000{,}000 + t\log 1.0183$

$\log 1{,}267{,}000{,}000 - \log 1{,}005{,}000{,}000 = t\log 1.0183 - t\log 1.0104$

$\log 1{,}267{,}000{,}000 - \log 1{,}005{,}000{,}000 = t(\log 1.0183 - \log 1.0104)$

$\frac{\log 1{,}267{,}000{,}000 - \log 1{,}005{,}000{,}000}{\log 1.0183 - \log 1.0104} = t$

$29.75 \approx t$

Predicted year: 2029 or 2030 (The month of the census is not given.)

25. Possible answer: Both a geometric sequence and an arithmetic sequence are an ordered list of numbers, where each term, except the first, is generated by performing an operation on the previous term. They are also similar in that the nth term of either can be found by using a formula given the first term and the common difference or common ratio.

26. For odd functions, $f(-x) = -f(x)$. For this function, $f(-x)$ $= \frac{1}{(-x)(2n+1)}$ $= -\frac{1}{x(2n+1)} = -f(x)$.

27. Find the sum of the first 8 and 9 terms of the series.

$a_8 = a_1 + (8 - 1)(d)$
$a_8 = 16 + (7)(32)$
$a_8 = 240$
$a_9 = a_1 + (9 - 1)(d)$
$a_9 = 16 + (8)(32)$
$a_9 = 272$
$S_8 = 8\left(\frac{16 + 240}{2}\right) = 1024$
$S_9 = 9\left(\frac{16 + 272}{2}\right) = 1296$

The height is between 1024 and 1296 feet.

Lesson 110

Lesson Practice

a.

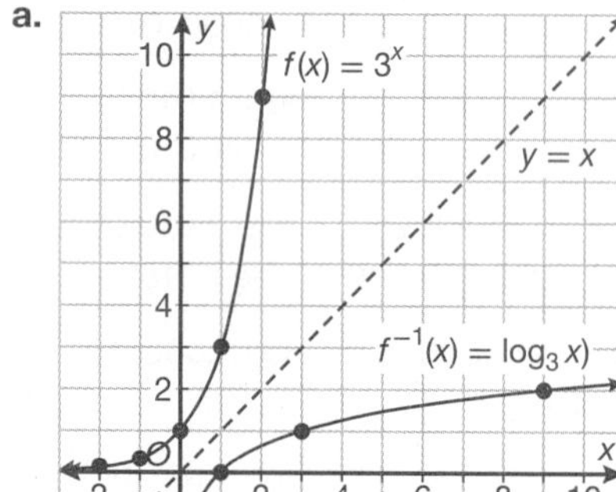

Domain of $f(x) = 3^x$: all real numbers, Range: $f(x) > 0$; Domain of $f^{-1}(x) = \log_3 x$ is $x > 0$, Range $f^{-1}(x)$ all real numbers.

c. The higher the base the shorter the graph.

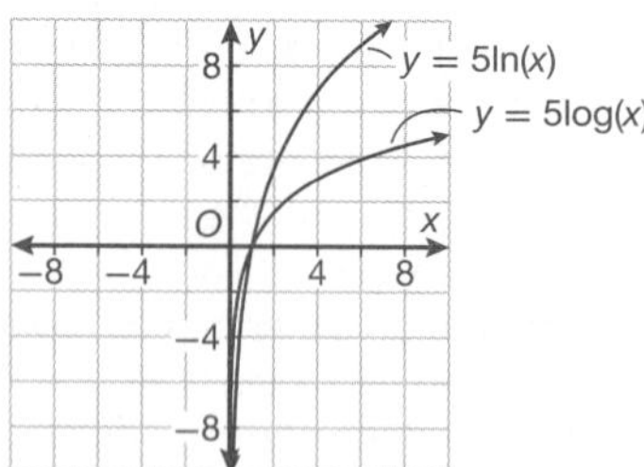

d. The higher the absolute value of c, the taller the graph.

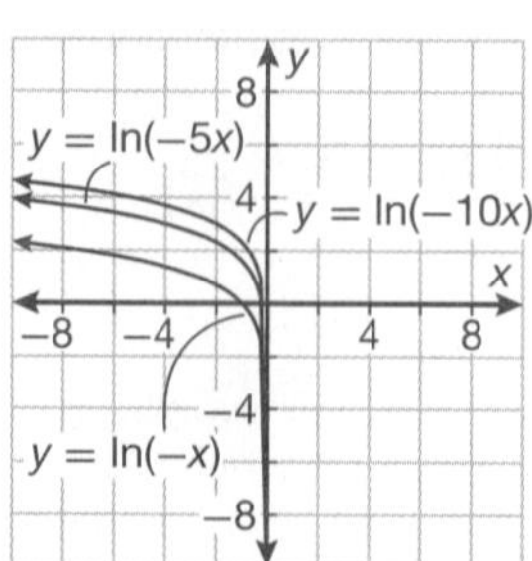

Lesson 111

Lesson Practice

a. $g(x) = x^3 + 4$

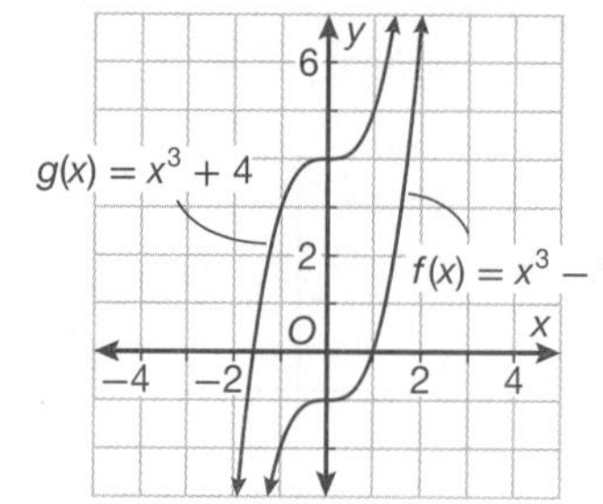

b. $g(x) = (x + 3)^3 - 1$

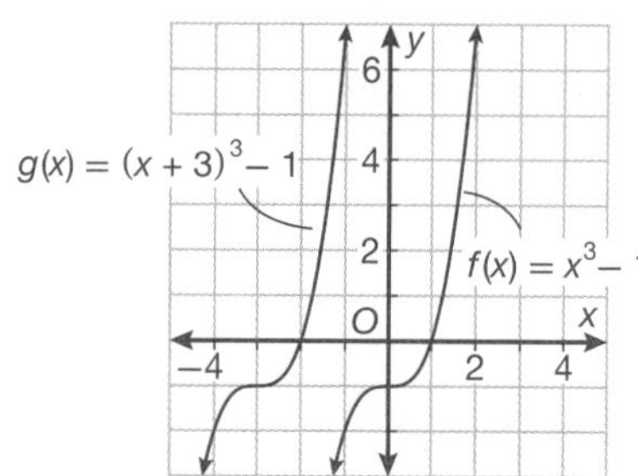

e. g is a vertical compresson of f;

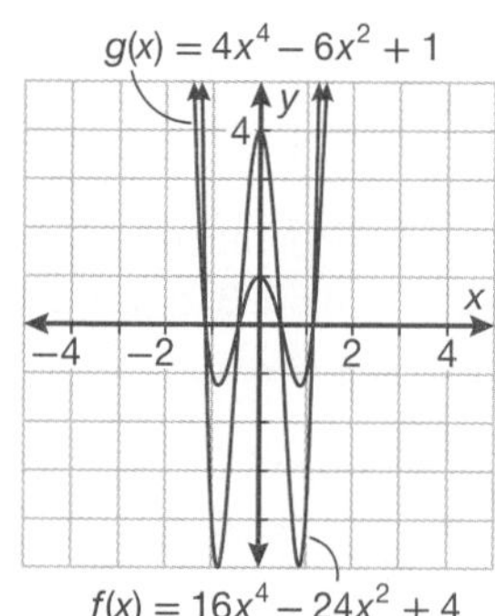

f. g is a horizontal stretch of f;

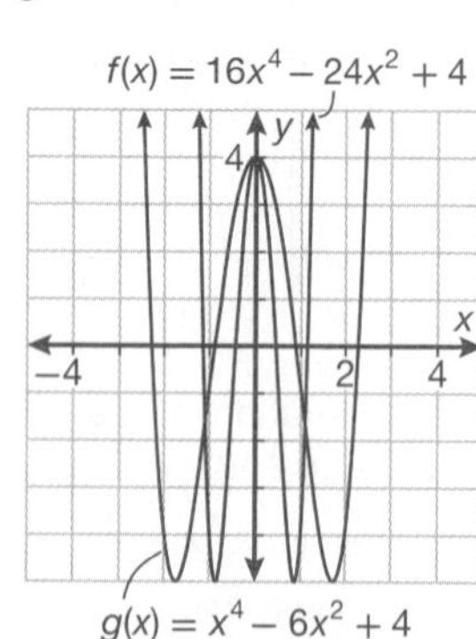

g. $g(x) = 4(x - 3)^3 - 1$

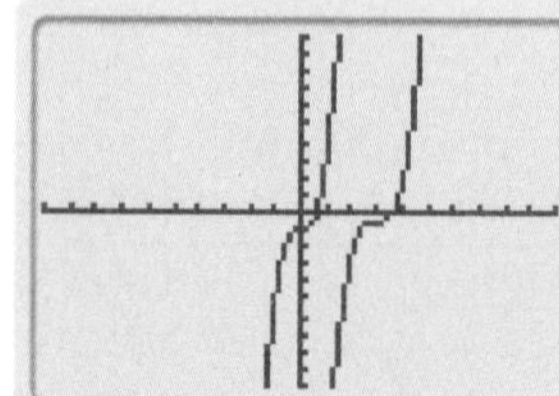

h. $h(x) = -8(x + 4)^3 + 2$

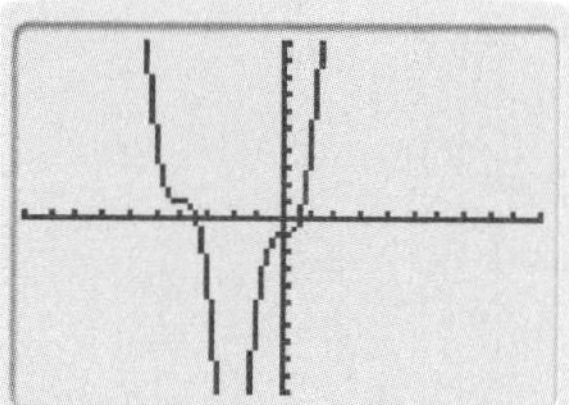

Practice

2. Sample: $g(x) = 1.922(x - 1)^4 - 36.769(x - 1)^3 + 132.212(x - 1)^2 + 3558.615(x - 1) - 11$; The function values of $g(x)$ are the same as those of $f(x)$, but they lag behind by one season. That is, $g(2) = f(1)$, $g(3) = f(2)$, and so on. If no fans had attended in 1996, then $g(x)$ would be the model for the years 1996–2005.

6. $-3 < x < 3$;

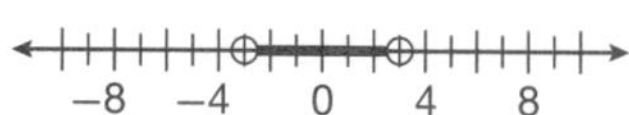

9. Sample: $1 - \tanh^2(x) \stackrel{?}{=} \frac{1}{\cosh^2(x)}$;

$1 - \frac{\sinh^2(x)}{\cosh^2(x)} \stackrel{?}{=} \frac{1}{\cosh^2(x)}$;

$\frac{\cosh^2(x)}{\cosh^2(x)} - \frac{\sinh^2(x)}{\cosh^2(x)} \stackrel{?}{=} \frac{1}{\cosh^2(x)}$;

$\frac{\cosh^2(x) - \sinh^2(x)}{\cosh^2(x)} \stackrel{?}{=} \frac{1}{\cosh^2(x)}$;

$\frac{1}{\cosh^2(x)} = \frac{1}{\cosh^2(x)}$ ✓

17b.

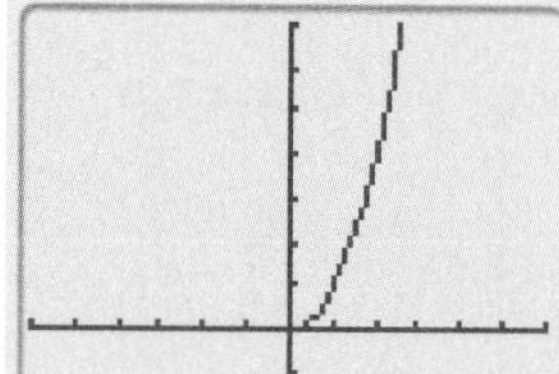

Sample: No; The graph of $y = x^2$ lies in Quadrants I and II (and one point is on the origin). When θmin $= 0$, θmax $= \frac{\pi}{2}$ are used as window settings, angles that terminate in Quadrant II are excluded. And, only positive values are obtained for $\sin\theta$ and $\cos^2\theta$. Therefore, only positive values are obtained for $r = \frac{\sin\theta}{\cos^2\theta}$. Therefore, it is not possible to obtain a point in Quadrant II

19.

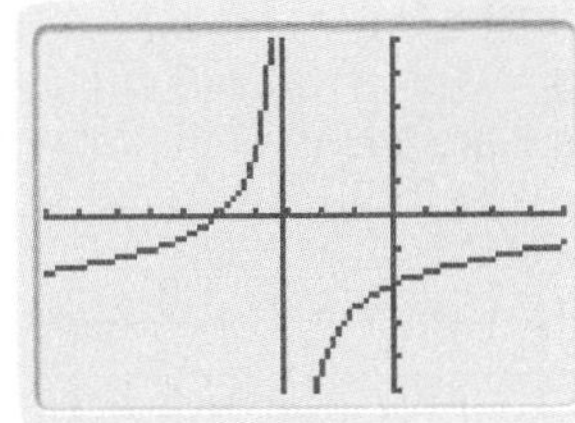

vertical asymptote: $x = -3$
Window: Xmin = -15, Xmax = 5, Xscl = 1, Ymin = -40, Ymax = 40, Yscl = 4, Xres = 1

Lesson 112

Practice

12a. $(0, 1)$ and $(4, -7)$; This is a vertical compression by a factor of $\frac{1}{4}$. Each point has the same x-coordinate and $\frac{1}{4}$ the y-coordinate as its corresponding point of $f(x)$.

12b. $(0, 4)$ and $(16, -28)$; This is a horizontal stretch by a factor of 4. Each point has 4 times the x-coordinate and the same y-coordinate as its corresponding point of $f(x)$.

12c. $\left(\frac{1}{4}, 4\right)$ and $\left(4\frac{1}{4}, -28\right)$; This is a horizontal translation $\frac{1}{4}$ unit to the right. Each point has an x-coordinate $\frac{1}{4}$ greater than that of its corresponding point of $f(x)$ and the same y-coordinate as that of its corresponding point of $f(x)$.

18.

$A(x) = 50000 \times 1.05^x$

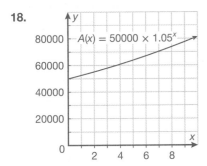

23. -1; Sample: By the cosine sum identity, $\cos\frac{2\pi}{5}\cos\frac{3\pi}{5} - \sin\frac{2\pi}{5}\sin\frac{3\pi}{5} = \cos\left(\frac{2\pi}{5} + \frac{3\pi}{5}\right) = \cos\pi = -1$.

24. Let $a_1 = 32$ and find a_{12}, the number of planks in the top row: $a_{12} = a_1 + (12 - 1)(d)$; $a_{12} = 32 + (11)(-2)$; $a_{12} = 10$. Then find the sum: $S_{12} = 12\left(\frac{32 + 10}{2}\right) = 252$.

Lesson 113

Practice

7. $(215.2, 45.7)$;

$$\begin{bmatrix}\cos 12^\circ & -\sin 12^\circ \\ \sin 12^\circ & \cos 12^\circ\end{bmatrix}\begin{bmatrix}220 \\ 0\end{bmatrix} = \begin{bmatrix}220\cos 12^\circ \\ 220\sin 12^\circ\end{bmatrix} \approx \begin{bmatrix}215.2 \\ 45.7\end{bmatrix}$$

12. Sample:

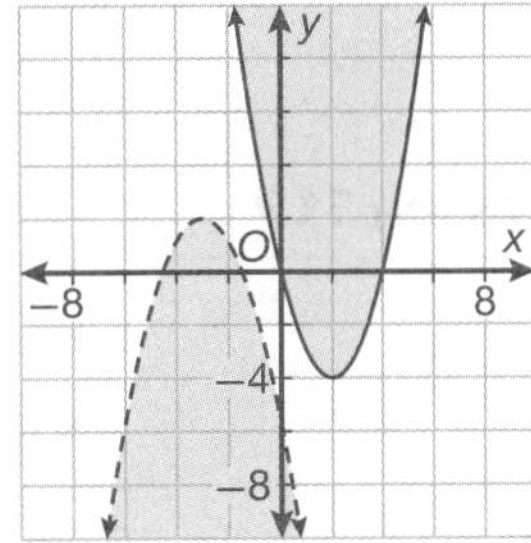

Lesson 114

Lesson Practice

8.

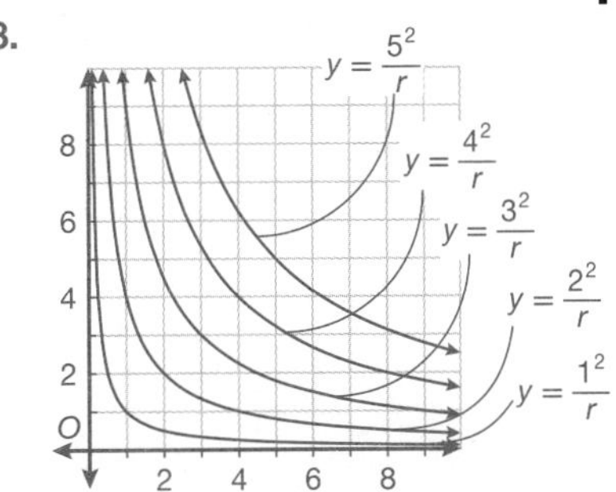

acceleration ranges from 0.5 to 12.5 at $r = 2$

20. Possible answer: A polynomial function that has exactly n distinct real zeros has exactly n x-intercepts. If there are n x-intercepts, then there are $n - 1$ intervals between consecutive x-intercepts. The graph is continuous and must either increase and then decrease or decrease and then increase in each of those intervals, so it must have exactly one turning point in each of those intervals.

30. Possible estimate: $(0, \sqrt{2})$; Possible explanation: $(0, \sqrt{2})$ is the image point that results when the point $(1, 1)$ is rotated 45° counterclockwise about the origin.

Lesson 115

Practice

5b. If $\sin 2\theta$ is a fractional value, it will decrease the distance. Because $\sin 2(45°) = 2\sin(45)(\cos(45)) = 1$, this is the only value that will not decrease the distance the ball will be kicked.

22.

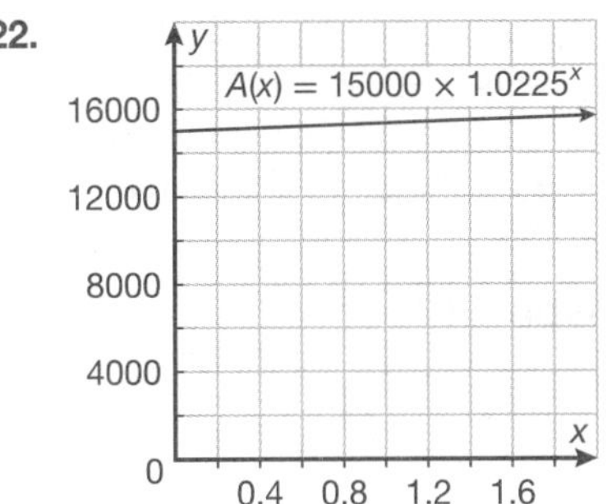

27. The student used the wrong coordinates for the center. Because the formula uses negative signs before h and k, $h = 2$, and $k = -9$. The center is $(2, -9)$.

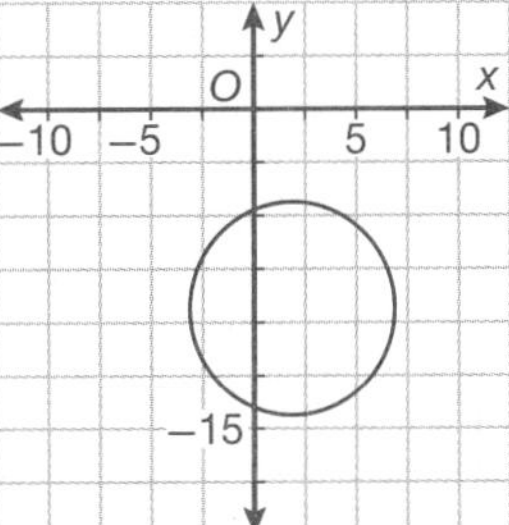

Lesson 116

Practice

9. The student forgot to distribute $\csc\theta$ to $\cos^2\theta - \sin^2\theta$. The correct answer would be:

$\cot\theta\cos\theta - \sin\theta \stackrel{?}{=} \cos 2\theta\csc\theta$;

$\cot\theta\cos\theta - \sin\theta \stackrel{?}{=} (\cos^2\theta - \sin^2\theta)\left(\frac{1}{\sin\theta}\right)$;

$\cot\theta\cos\theta - \sin\theta \stackrel{?}{=} \frac{\cos^2\theta}{\sin\theta} - \frac{\sin^2\theta}{\sin\theta}$;

$\cot\theta\cos\theta - \sin\theta \stackrel{?}{=} \frac{\cos\theta}{\sin\theta}(\cos\theta) - \sin\theta$;

$\cot\theta\cos\theta - \sin\theta \stackrel{?}{=} \cot\theta\cos\theta - \sin\theta$ ✓

11. $A'(1.03, 4.89)$; $B'(-4.41, 2.36)$; $C'(0,0)$;

$$\begin{bmatrix}\cos 25^\circ & -\sin 25^\circ \\ \sin 25^\circ & \cos 25^\circ\end{bmatrix}\begin{bmatrix}3 & -3 \\ 4 & 4\end{bmatrix} = \begin{bmatrix}3\cos 25^\circ - 4\sin 25^\circ & -3\cos 25^\circ - 4\sin 25^\circ \\ 3\sin 25^\circ + 4\cos 25^\circ & -3\sin 25^\circ + 4\cos 25^\circ\end{bmatrix} \approx \begin{bmatrix}1.03 & -4.41 \\ 4.89 & 2.36\end{bmatrix}$$

14. only reflections; Sample: End behavior is determined only by the sign of the coefficient and the degree of the highest-degree term. None of the transformations can change the degree, and only a reflection can change the sign of the coefficient.

21. Sample: The student probably identified the leading coefficient as -1. Correct description: As $x \longrightarrow +\infty$, $f(x) \longrightarrow +\infty$, and as $x \longrightarrow -\infty$, $f(x) \longrightarrow +\infty$.

Lesson 117

Warm Up

3.

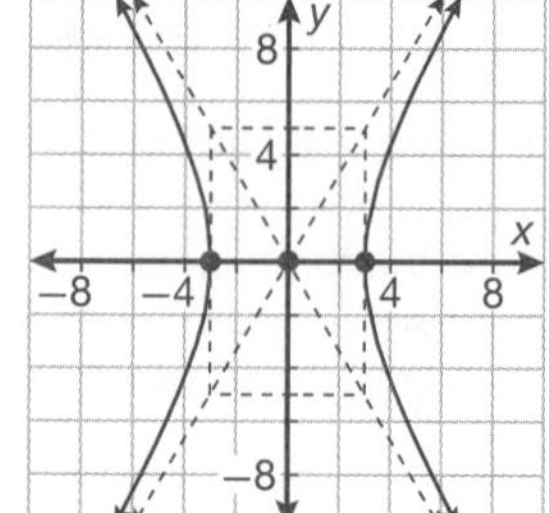

15. The terms form a line; the partial sums form a curve.

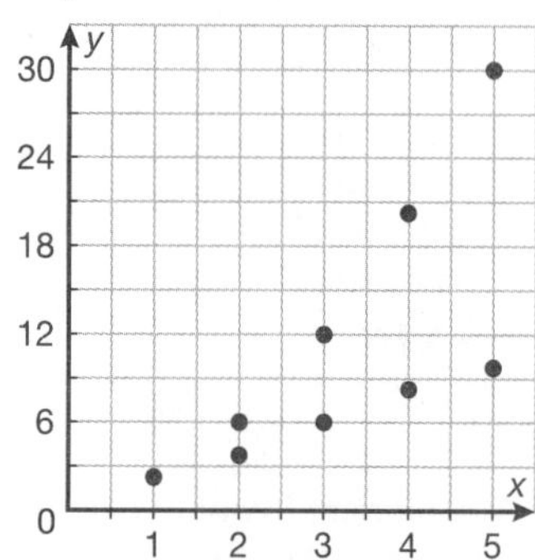

17a. $200 = x^2 + 4xh;\ h = \frac{200 - x^2}{4x}$

17b. $V(x) = 50x - \frac{x^3}{4}$

17c. Maximum volume $\approx 272.17\text{ in}^3$; $x \approx 8.16$ in.; $h \approx 4.08$ in.;

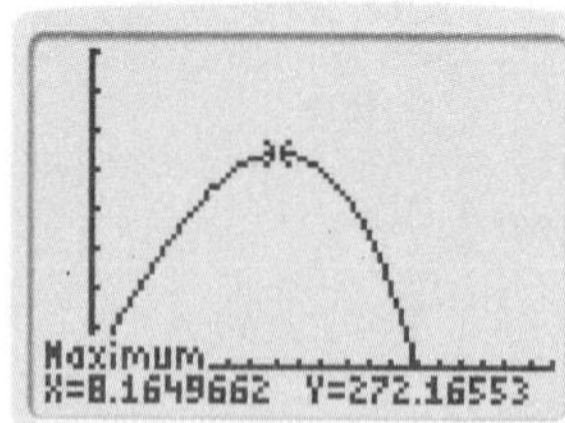

20d. $y = \sqrt{x^2 - 15},\ y = -\sqrt{x^2 - 15},$

$y = \sqrt{\frac{160 - 9x^2}{16}},\ y = -\sqrt{\frac{160 - 9x^2}{16}}$

Lesson 118

Practice

1. $a_{16} = a_1 + (16 - 1)(d)$
$a_{16} = 20 + (15)(10)$
$a_{16} = 170$
$S_{16} = 16\left(\frac{20 + 170}{2}\right) = 1520$

4. The graph is misleading because the values on the vertical axis start just below the lowest value, making the model A vehicles appear much more expensive than they actually are. A salesperson for model B might have made the graph to get customers from a neighboring model A dealership to buy his cars instead.

12c. Sample: \$0.51 because the R^2 value for the quartic value, 0.984, is greater than for the exponential model, 0.890, although predicting beyond the given domain is not very trustworthy to begin with.

Lesson 119

Lesson Practice

c. $3\tan^2 z - \tan z - 3 = 0 \Rightarrow \tan z$

$= \frac{-(-1) \pm \sqrt{(-1)^2 - 4(3)(-3)}}{2(3)}$

$= \frac{1 \pm \sqrt{37}}{6} \Rightarrow z = \text{Tan}^{-1}\left(\frac{1 \pm \sqrt{37}}{6}\right)$

$\Rightarrow z = 0.87, -0.70$

d. $\sin^2\theta + 3\sin\theta = \sin\theta - 1$
$\Rightarrow \sin^2\theta + 2\sin\theta + 1 = 0$
$\Rightarrow (\sin\theta + 1)(\sin\theta + 1) = 0$
$\Rightarrow \sin\theta = -1 \Rightarrow \theta = 270°$

e. $x \approxeq 4.712$

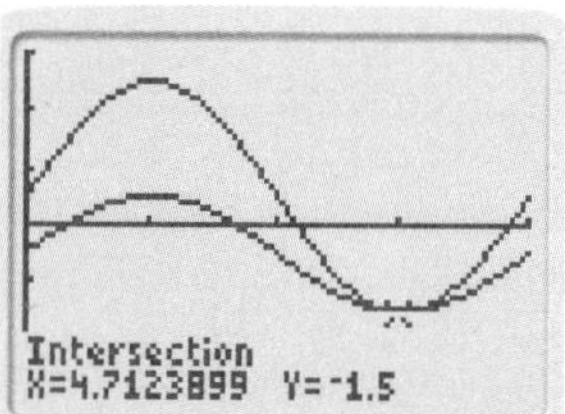

8. Sample: An open question allows for people to write in whatever they want without limiting their replies. It allows for answers that the surveyor may not have thought of. The con of an open question is that there may be too many replies to easily analyze. A closed question can make analyzing data easier, but it may exclude options that may be valid, forcing people to choose answers they don't want.

12.

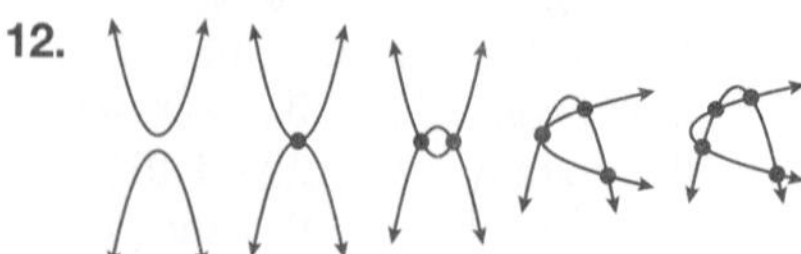

18. Sample: hyp. = 5 cm, leg = 3 cm; hyp. = 6 cm, leg = $2\sqrt{5}$ cm;

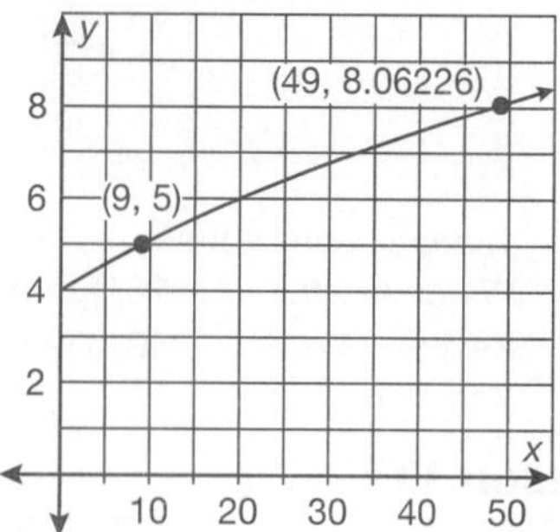

Investigation 12

5. $a_{m+1} = m + 1$

$\left(\sum_{k=1}^{m} k\right) + a_{m+1} = \frac{m(m+1)}{2} + (m + 1)$

$= \frac{m^2 + m}{2} + \frac{2m + 2}{2}$

$= \frac{m^2 + 3m + 2}{2}$

$= \frac{(m + 1)(m + 2)}{2}$

6. $\sum_{k=1}^{m+1} k = \frac{(m + 1)((m + 1) + 1)}{2}$

$= \frac{(m + 1)(m + 2)}{2}$

$\sum_{k=1}^{m+1} k = \left(\sum_{k=1}^{m} k\right) + a_{m+1}$

12c. $m(m + 1) + 2(m + 1)$
$= m^2 + m + 2m + 2$
$= m^2 + 3m + 2 = (m + 1)(m + 2)$
$= (m + 1)((m + 1) + 1)$, which maintains the form of the original expression.

Investigation Practice

g. $a_{m+1} = 2(m + 1) - 1 = 2m + 1$

$\sum_{k=1}^{m} 2k - 1 = m^2$, by assumption

$\sum_{k=1}^{m+1} 2k - 1 = \left(\sum_{k=1}^{m} 2k - 1\right) + a_{m+1}$

$= (m^2) + (2m + 1)$

$= (m + 1)^2$

Therefore, the formula works for all values of n.

A

B

C

D

E

N

O

P